ARCHBOLD

2008

AUSTRALIA
LBC Information Services
Sydney

CANADA and USA
Carswell
Toronto

HONG KONG
Sweet & Maxwell Asia

NEW ZEALAND
Brookers
Wellington

A CIP catalogue record for this book is available from the British Library

ISBN-13 978-184-70325-4

No natural forests were destroyed to make this product; only farmed
timber was used and replanted

© Sweet & Maxwell Limited
2008

ARCHBOLD

MAGISTRATES' COURTS CRIMINAL PRACTICE

2008

LONDON
SWEET & MAXWELL
2008

Published in 2007 by Sweet & Maxwell Limited of
100 Avenue Road,
London NW3 3PF
www.sweetandmaxwell.co.uk
Typeset by Sweet & Maxwell Ltd, 100 Avenue Road, London, NW3 3PF

Printed and bound in Great Britain by
William Clowes Ltd, Beccles, Suffolk

PREFACE

This is the fourth edition of this book which the authors and publishers believe is becoming recognised as a helpful and authoritative guide both for practitioners in the magistrates' court and for students of criminal procedure and practice. It is designed to complement the well-established *Archbold* which is regarded as the definitive guide to Crown Court proceedings.

This book remains a work in progress, both to reflect the fast and frequent legislative developments in the criminal justice system and also driven by the responses and needs of our readers. We continue to welcome suggestions and comments to enable us to improve the content and format. New editions are produced on an annual basis with a supplement six months later so that new legislation and case law can be regularly and swiftly incorporated.

There is reference in this edition to the 12-month custodial sentence and the allocation procedure both introduced by the *Criminal Justice Act* 2003. They are yet to be implemented but unlike the custody plus provisions it appears that the intention remains to extend sentencing powers in the magistrates' courts and to amend the mode of trial procedure. One of the difficulties of producing a guide of this type is the sometimes disjointed and sporadic nature of legislative change where statutory provisions are enacted but not implemented and new statutes amend several existing ones. This presents a challenge, not only in deciding what to include or omit but also in ensuring all relevant amendments are addressed. In this edition new legislation covered includes the *Domestic Violence, Crime and Victims Act* 2004; the *Animal Welfare Act* 2006; the *Fraud Act* 2006; the *Identity Cards Act* 2006; the *Racial and Religious Hatred Act* 2006; the *Road Safety Act* 2006; and the *Violent Crime Reduction Act* 2006.

In addition recently issued Sentencing Guidelines on Domestic Violence and Reduction for Guilty Pleas are covered. Relevant case law has been updated in all chapters but in particular in respect of bad character evidence in Chapter 10. The appendices have all been clarified and updated.

I would like to express my heart felt gratitude to and admiration of the hard working editorial team. William Carter, Jeremy Coleman, Louise Cowen, David Corker, Gaynor Houghton-Jones, Gillian Jones, Stephen Leake, Kevin McCormac and Stephen Shay have all met tight deadlines with speed and efficiency. It is a pleasure to work with such a dedicated and experienced team. I must also include the previous editor, Nicola Padfield, who did much to shape this publication and whose expert contributions have been greatly appreciated over the past three years.

I would also like to thank our colleagues at Sweet & Maxwell who are responsible for all aspects of the production and marketing of this book and would mention in particular Nicky Penn and Victoria Wilson who remain unflappable in times of crisis and whose good humour and support keep me on course when courage fails.

Barbara Barnes

July 2007

CONTENTS

Contents

CONTENTS

CONTENTS

CONTENTS

CONTENTS

ABBREVIATIONS

ASBO..Anti-Social Behaviour Order
CCSU..Council of Civil Service Unions
CDRO..Criminal Defence Representation Order
CJA..Criminal Justice Act
CJCSA..Criminal Justice and Court Services Act
CJPOA..Criminal Justice and Public Order Act
CLA..Criminal Law Act
CPIA..Criminal Procedure and Investigations Act
CPS..Crown Prosecution Service
CRO..Community Rehabilitation Order
CYPA..Children and Young Persons Act
DCW..Designated Case Worker
DTTO..Drug Treatment and Testing Order
FACT..Federation against Copyright Theft
ISSP..Intensive Supervision and Surveillance Program
JOPI..Joint Operational Instructions
MDO..Mentally Disordered Offenders
PACE..Police and Criminal Evidence Act 1984
PCC(S)A..Powers of Criminal Courts (Sentencing) Act
POCA..Protection of Children Act
PSR..Pre-sentence Report
RIPA..Regulation of Investigatory Powers Act
RTA..Road Traffic Act
SOA..Sexual Offences Act
SSR..Specific Sentence Report
YJCEA..Youth Justice and Criminal Evidence Act
YOT..Youth Offending Team

TABLE OF STATUTES

[Paragraph numbers in bold type denote where the text of the statute is printed.]

TABLE OF STATUTUTORY INSTRUMENTS

[Paragraph numbers in bold type denote where the text of the statutory instrument is printed]

TABLE OF CASES

TABLE OF CASES

TABLE OF CASES

Part I

Pre-Trial Issues

CHAPTER 1

CRIMINAL INVESTIGATIONS

I. INVESTIGATORY POWERS

A. INTRODUCTION

The law governing the police's powers in conducting criminal investigations is pri- **1–1** marily contained in the *Police and Criminal Evidence Act* 1984 as amended, and as supplemented by a series of Codes of Practice (see *post*, Annex A). The 1984 Act is not, however, a complete code of a police officer's powers or duties. Common law powers (such as the power to arrest for breach of the peace) remain. Further powers subsequently have been enacted, such as the *Police Act* 1997, ss.91–108 (authorisation of covert entry upon and interference with property or with wireless telegraphy by the police, Revenue and Customs officers, and others); the *Regulation of Investigatory Powers Act* 2000 (dealing with all forms of covert surveillance which do not involve covert entry upon or interference with property or wireless telegraphy); the *Criminal Justice and Police Act* 2001 (see *post*, §§ 1–67 *et seq.*); and, as from April 1, 2006, the *Serious Organised Crime and Police Act* 2005, ss.60–70 (prosecution powers to compel individuals to answer questions or produce relevant documents pursuant to disclosure notices).

B. POLICE AND CRIMINAL EVIDENCE ACT 1984 (PACE) AND CODES OF PRACTICE

(1) Legislative background

Police and Criminal Evidence Act 1984, s.66

Codes of practice

66.—(1) The Secretary of State shall issue codes of practice in connection with— **1–2**
    (a) the exercise by police officers of statutory powers—
        (i) to search a person without first arresting him;
        (ii) to search a vehicle without making an arrest;
    or
        (iii) to arrest a person;
    (b) the detention, treatment, questioning and identification of persons by police officers;

    (c) searches of premises by police officers; and

    (d) the seizure of property found by police officers on persons or premises.

    (2) Codes shall (in particular) include provision in connection with the exercise by police officers of powers under section 63B above.

[This section is printed as amended by the *Criminal Justice and Court Services Act* 2000, s.57(4); and the *Serious Organised Crime and Police Act* 2005, ss.110(3) and 174(2), and Sched. 17.]

1–3   Section 63B (*post*, § 18–76) allows the police to test a person in police detention for the presence of Class A drugs.

1–4   There are eight Codes of Practice. The full text is in Appendix A and also on the Police Home Office website at *http://www.homeoffice.gov.uk*. The Codes are:

    A. Code of Practice for the Exercise by; Police Officers of Statutory Powers to Stop and Search; Police Officers and Police Staff of Requirements to Record Public Encounters.

    B. Code of Practice for Searches of Premises by Police Officers and the Seizure of Property found by Police Officers on Persons or Premises.

    C. Code of Practice for Detention, Treatment and Questioning of Persons by Police Officers.

    D. Code of Practice for the Identification of Persons by Police Officers.

    E. Code of Practice on Tape Recording of Interviews with Suspects.

    F. Code of Practice on Visual Recording of Interviews with Suspects.

    G. Code of Practice for the Statutory Power of Arrest by Police Officers.

    H. Code of Practice for Detention, Treatment and Questioning of Persons under section 41 of and Schedule 8 to the *Terrorism Act* 2000.

1–5   The original Codes first came into force as follows: Codes A to D on January 1, 1986; Code E on July 29, 1988; and Code F on May 7, 2002. The latest revision of Codes B, and D to F, came into force on January 1, 2006, along with new Code G: *Police and Criminal Evidence Act 1984 (Codes of Practice) Order* 2005 (S.I. 2005 No. 3503). The latest revision of Code C, and new Code H, came into force on July 20, 2006: *Police and Criminal Evidence Act 1984 (Code of Practice C and Code of Practice H) Order* 2006 (S.I. 2006 No. 1938). The latest revision of Code A came into force on August 31, 2006: *Police and Criminal Evidence Act 1984 (Codes of Practice) (Revisions to Code A) Order* 2006 (S.I. 2006 No. 2165).

(2) Status of the Codes

1–6   The Codes are admissible in evidence and the court may take account of any relevant provision: *PACE Act* 1984, s.67(11), *post*, § 1–8.

    In *McCay* (1990) 91 Cr.App.R. 84, the Court of Appeal referred to Code D as having the full authority of Parliament, but the correctness of this decision has been doubted: [1990] Crim.L.R. 338 at 340. In *Quinn* [1995] 1 Cr.App.R. 480, Code D was referred to as a "statutory code". The status of the Codes is clear from sections 60, 66 and 67 of the *PACE Act* 1984: they are codes of practice designed to regulate the conduct of persons charged with the duty of investigating offences.

1–7   Annexes elaborate upon aspects of the Codes and must be observed. Notes for guidance advise upon the application of the Codes and Annexes but do not have the binding effect of the codes themselves although they are there to be followed.

    Copies of the Codes should be available at Police Stations for public consultation and for reference for police officers and detained persons.

(3) Application of the Codes

Police and Criminal Evidence Act 1984, s.67

Codes of Practice—supplementary

1–8   **67.**—(1–7D) [*Provisions for the issue and revision of codes of practice.*]

(8) [*Repealed.*]

(9) Persons other than police officers who are charged with the duty of investigating offences or charging offenders shall in the discharge of that duty have regard to any relevant provision of a code.

(9A) Persons on whom powers are conferred by—

(a) any designation under section 38 or 39 of the *Police Reform Act* 2002 (police powers for police authority employees); or

(b) any accreditation under section 41 of that Act (accreditation under community safety accreditation schemes),

shall have regard to any relevant provision of a code of practice to which this section applies in the exercise or performance of the powers and duties conferred or imposed on them by that designation or accreditation.

(10) A failure on the part—

(a) of a police officer to comply with any provision of a code; or

(b) of any person other than a police officer who is charged with the duty of investigating offences or charging offenders to have regard to any relevant provision of a code in the discharge of that duty, or

(c) of a person designated under section 38 or 39 or accredited under section 41 of the *Police Reform Act* 2002 to have regard to any relevant provision of a code in the exercise or performance of the powers and duties conferred or imposed on him by that designation or accreditation,

shall not of itself render him liable to any criminal or civil proceedings.

(11) In all criminal and civil proceedings any code shall be admissible in evidence; and if any provision of a code appears to the court or tribunal conducting the proceedings to be relevant to any question arising in the proceedings it shall be taken into account in determining that question.

(12), (13) [*Armed forces etc.*]

[This section is printed as amended, and repealed in part, by the *Armed Forces Act* 1996, s.5 and Sched. 1, Pt IV, para. 105; the *Police Act* 1996, s.103(3) and Sched. 9; the *Criminal Justice and Police Act* 2001, ss.76(2) and 77; the *Police Reform Act* 2002, s.107(1) and (2), Sched. 7, para. 9(6)-(8), and Sched. 8; the *Criminal Justice Act* 2003, ss.11(1) and 332, and Sched. 37, Pt 1; and as amended, as from a day to be appointed, by the *Armed Forces Act* 2006, s.378(1), and Sched. 16, para. 101 (substitution of subsections (12) and (13) for subsection (12)).]

The Codes of Practice apply to: **1–9**

(a) police officers (sections 60(1), 60A(1), 66(1) and 67(10) of the *PACE Act* 1984)— this includes police forces such as the British Transport Police; and

(b) persons "other than police officers who are charged with the duty of investigating offences or charging offenders" (s.67(9)).

As to category (b), the court will consider whether a duty exists either in common law, statute or contract. A store detective has been held to have a duty to investigate incidents (*Bayliss* (1993) 98 Cr.App.R. 235) but a headteacher has not (*DPP v. G, The Times*, November 24, 1997). An inspector of the RSPCA may be bound (*RSPCA v. Eager* [1995] Crim.L.R. 59) as was an officer of the Federation Against Copyright Theft (*Joy v. FACT* [1993] Crim.L.R. 588). Both officers of Revenue and Customs and officers of the Serious Fraud Office have been held to be bound by the Codes: *Okafor* (1994) 99 Cr.App.R. 97; *R. v. Director of SFO, ex p. Saunders* [1988] Crim.L.R. 837; and *Gill* [2004] 1 Cr.App.R. 20.

In the case of *Ristic* (2004) 148 S.J. 942, it was held that a prison support officer who assisted with searching visitors at a prison was not a person charged with a duty to investigate offences and so was not bound by the Codes of Practice. His evidence which consisted of unsolicited but overheard remarks was held not to be in breach of any code but could be challenged and excluded under section 78 of *PACE* 1984.

Where the Code refers to duties to be carried out by police officers at a police station it may be impractical for investigators who are not police officers to comply with those requirements. A Social Security investigator was held not to be in breach of the Code in failing to advise of the right to free legal advice on interview. This provision of the Code was held only to apply to investigators at the police station where the free Legal Aid representation scheme applied and a duty solicitor could be called: *R. (Social Security Secretary) v. South Central Division Magistrates*, *Daily Telegraph*, November 28, 2000, DC.

As to the exclusion of evidence obtained in breach of the Codes, see *post*, §§ 10–140 *et seq.*

C. STOP AND SEARCH

(1) Introduction

1–10   Section 1 of the *Police and Criminal Evidence Act* 1984 gives the police power to stop and search in England and Wales. Other statutory powers of stop and search also exist, *e.g. Firearms Act* 1968, s.47(3); *Misuse of Drugs Act* 1971, s.23(2), and *Terrorism Act* 2000, s.44. Under section 60 of the *Criminal Justice and Public Order Act* 1994, extended powers of search were introduced. Even where consent to a search is given, a statutory power of search must exist and the Code will still apply.

General

1–11   Code A sets out the principles governing the power of the police to stop and search persons and vehicles. Under section 117 of the *Police and Criminal Evidence Act* 1984, officers are permitted to use "reasonable force" if necessary in the exercise of this and other powers conferred under the Act.

(2) Reasonable grounds for suspecting

1–12   When exercising the power to stop and search persons or vehicles a constable must have reasonable grounds for suspecting that stolen or prohibited articles will be found. The existence of a reasonable suspicion is crucial to the existence of the power to stop and search.

"Reasonable suspicion" is not defined in the Act. Code A, paras 2.2 to 2.9, provide guidance on what amounts to a reasonable suspicion. There must be an objective basis for the suspicion based on facts, information or intelligence which are relevant to the likelihood of finding prohibited articles or stolen property: para. A:2.2. A reasonable suspicion cannot be based only on personal factors relevant to the suspect, (*e.g.* age, appearance or known record). There must also be reliable supporting intelligence or information or some specific behaviour by the person concerned giving rise to the suspicion. A reasonable suspicion cannot be based on generalisations or stereotypical images of certain groups or categories of people as more likely to be involved in criminal activity. See *post*, Appendix A.

The test as to whether reasonable grounds for the suspicion to justify an arrest existed is partly subjective, in that the arresting officer must have formed a genuine suspicion that the person being arrested was guilty of an offence, and partly objective, in that there had to be reasonable grounds for forming such a suspicion; such grounds could arise from information received from another (even if it subsequently proves to be false), provided that a reasonable man, having regard to all the circumstances, would regard them as reasonable grounds for suspicion; but a mere order from a superior officer to arrest a particular individual could not constitute reasonable grounds for such suspicion: *O'Hara v. Chief Constable of the Royal Ulster Constabulary* [1997] A.C. 286, HL.

See also *Siddiqui v. Swain* [1979] R.T.R. 454, 457, DC, in which "reasonable grounds to suspect" in the *Road Traffic Act* 1972, s.8(5) (now the *Road Traffic Act* 1988, s.7) were said to "import the further requirement that the constable in fact suspects"; *Parker v. Chief Constable of the Hampshire Constabulary*, unreported, June 25, 1999, CA (Civ. Div.), where it was held that an officer who had reasonable grounds to think it "possible" that one of two people in a car was someone he was entitled to arrest had been justified in arresting that person; and *Cumming v. Chief Constable of Northumbria Police, The Times*, January 2, 2004, CA (Civ. Div.) (there is nothing in principle to prevent (a) opportunity from amounting to reasonable grounds for suspicion, or (b) the police arresting more than one person even if the crime can only have been committed by one person).

As to having reasonable grounds for suspecting that an offence has been committed (see section 24(2), *post*, § 1–106), it is not necessary that an officer should have in mind specific statutory provisions, or that he should mentally identify specific offences with technicality or precision. He must, however, reasonably suspect the existence of facts amounting to an offence of a kind that he has in mind; unless he can do that, he cannot comply with his obligation under section 28(3) (*post*, § 1–114) to inform the suspect of the grounds of arrest: *Chapman v. DPP* (1988) 89 Cr.App.R. 190, DC; *Mossop v. DPP* [2003] 6 *Archbold News* 1, DC.

In *Kynaston v. DPP* (1987) 87 Cr.App.R. 200, DC, it was held that where the validity of an arrest is in issue, if the defence do not raise the question whether there were reasonable grounds for suspicion, it is open to the court, in appropriate circumstances, to infer that such grounds existed.

If the arresting officer knows at the time of arrest that there is no possibility of a charge being made, the arrest would be unlawful as he must have acted on an irrelevant consideration or for some improper motive: *Plange v. Chief Constable of South Humberside Police, The Times*, March 23, 1992, CA (Civ. Div.). *Plange* was referred to, without disapproval, in *Chalkley and Jeffries* [1998] 2 Cr.App.R. 79, CA, but the court seems to have thought that an arrest would be lawful if there were reasonable grounds to suspect the person arrested to be guilty of the offence for which he was told he was being arrested, even though the arresting officer knew that there was no intention to prosecute him for that offence, provided that the true reason for the arrest was to facilitate the investigation and prevention of more serious crime. This was *obiter*, as the officers who made the arrest knew nothing of their superiors' motives, and because, in any event, the validity of the arrest was irrelevant to the determination of the appeal.

(3) Power of constable to stop and search persons and vehicles

Police and Criminal Evidence Act 1984, s.1

Power of constable to stop and search persons, vehicles etc

1.—(1) A constable may exercise any power conferred by this section—   **1–13**

    (a) in any place to which at the time when he proposes to exercise the power the public or any section of the public has access, on payment or otherwise, as of right or by virtue of express or implied permission; or

    (b) in any other place to which people have ready access at the time when he proposes to exercise the power but which is not a dwelling.

(2) Subject to subsection (3) to (5) below, a constable—

    (a) may search—

        (i) any person or vehicle;

        (ii) anything which is in or on a vehicle,

    for stolen or prohibited articles, any article to which subsection (8A) below applies or any firework to which subsection (8B) below applies; and

    (b) may detain a person or vehicle for the purpose of such a search.

(3) This section does not give a constable power to search a person or vehicle or anything in or on a vehicle unless he has reasonable grounds for suspecting that he will find stolen or prohibited articles, any article to which subsection (8A) below applies or any firework to which subsection (8B) below applies.

(4) If a person is in a garden or yard occupied with and used for the purposes of a dwelling or on other land so occupied and used, a constable may not search him in the exercise of the power conferred by this section unless the constable has reasonable grounds for believing—

(a) that he does not reside in the dwelling; and

(b) that he is not in the place in question with the express or implied permission of a person who resides in the dwelling.

(5) If a vehicle is in a garden or yard occupied with and used for the purposes of a dwelling or on other land so occupied and used, a constable may not search the vehicle or anything in or on it in the exercise of the power conferred by this section unless he has reasonable grounds for believing—

(a) that the person in charge of the vehicle does not reside in the dwelling; and

(b) that the vehicle is not in the place in question with the express or implied permission of a person who resides in the dwelling.

1–14   (6) If in the course of such a search a constable discovers an article which he has reasonable grounds for suspecting to be a stolen or prohibited article, an article to which subsection (8A) below applies or a firework to which subsection 8B below applies he may seize it.

(7) An article is prohibited for the purposes of this Part of this Act if it is—

(a) an offensive weapon; or

(b) an article—

    (i)   made or adapted for use in the course of or in connection with an offence to which this sub-paragraph applies; or

    (ii)   intended by the person having it with him for such use by him or by some other person.

(8) The offences to which subsection (7)(b)(i) above applies are—

(a) burglary;

(b) theft;

(c) offences under section 12 of the *Theft Act* 1968 (taking motor vehicle or other conveyance without authority);

(d) fraud (contrary to section 1 of the *Fraud Act* 2006); and

(e) offences under section 1 of the *Criminal Damage Act* 1971 (destroying or damaging property).

(8A) This subsection applies to any article in relation to which a person has committed, or is committing or is going to commit an offence under section 139 of the *Criminal Justice Act* 1988.

(8B) This subsection applies to any firework which a person possesses in contravention of a prohibition imposed by fireworks regulations.

(8C) In this section—

(a) "firework" shall be constructed in accordance with the definition of "fireworks" in section 1(1) of the *Fireworks Act* 2003, and

(b) "fireworks regulations" has the same meaning as in that Act.

(9) In this Part of this Act "offensive weapon" means any article—

(a) made or adapted for use for causing injury to persons; or

(b) intended by the person having it with him for such use by him or by some other person.

[This section is printed as amended by the *Criminal Justice Act* 1988, s.140, Pt 1; the *Criminal Justice Act* 2003, ss.1 and 332 and Sched. 37; the *Serious Organised Crime and Police Act* 2005, s.115; and the *Fraud Act* 2006, s.14(1) and Sched. 1, para. 21.]

1–15   The term "constable" covers every police officer of whatever rank: *Lewis v. Cattle* [1938] 2 K.B. 454.

As to "reasonable grounds for suspecting", see *ante*, § 1–12.

Section 139 of the *Criminal Justice Act* 1988 refers to unlawful possession of a bladed article.

(4) Provisions relating to search under section 1

Police and Criminal Evidence Act 1984, s.2

Provisions relating to search under s.1 and other powers

1–16   **2.**—(1) A constable who detains a person or vehicle in the exercise—

> (a) of the power conferred by section 1 above; or
> (b) of any other power—
>> (i)   to search a person without first arresting him; or
>> (ii) to search a vehicle without making an arrest,
>> need not conduct a search if it appears to him subsequently—
>>> (i)   that no search is required; or
>>> (ii) that a search is impracticable.

(2) If a constable contemplates a search, other than a search of an unattended vehicle, in the exercise—

> (a) of the power conferred by section 1 above; or
> (b) of any other power, except the power conferred by section 6 below and the power conferred by section 27(2) of the *Aviation Security Act* 1982—
>> (i)   to search a person without first arresting him; or
>> (ii) to search a vehicle without making an arrest,
>> it shall be his duty, subject to subsection (4) below, to take reasonable steps before he commences the search to bring to the attention of the appropriate person—
>>> (i)   if the constable is not in uniform, documentary evidence that he is a constable; and
>>> (ii) whether he is in uniform or not, the matters specified in subsection (3) below;
>>> and the constable shall not commence the search until he has performed that duty.

1–17

(3) The matters referred to in subsection (2)(ii) above are—

> (a) the constable's name and the name of the police station to which he is attached;
> (b) the object of the proposed search;
> (c) the constable's grounds for proposing to make it; and
> (d) the effect of section 3(7) or (8) below, as may be appropriate.

(4) A constable need not bring the effect of section 3(7) or (8) below to the attention of the appropriate person if it appears to the constable that it will not be practicable to make the record in section 3(1) below.

(5) In this section "the appropriate person" means—

> (a) if the constable proposes to search a person, that person; and
> (b) if he proposes to search a vehicle, or anything in or on a vehicle, the person in charge of the vehicle.

(6) On completing a search of an unattended vehicle or anything in or on such a vehicle in the exercise of any such power as is mentioned in subsection (2) above a constable shall leave a notice—

> (a) stating that he has searched it;
> (b) giving the name of the police station to which he is attached;
> (c) stating that an application for compensation for any damage caused by the search may be made to that police station; and
> (d) stating the effect of section 3(8) below.

(7) The constable shall leave the notice inside the vehicle unless it is not reasonably practicable to do so without damaging the vehicle.

(8) The time for which a person or vehicle may be detained for the purposes of such a search is such time as is reasonably required to permit a search to be carried out either at the place where the person or vehicle was first detained or nearby.

(9) Neither the power conferred by section 1 above nor any other power to detain and search a person without first arresting him or to detain and search a vehicle without making an arrest is to be construed—

> (a) as authorising a constable to require a person to remove any of his clothing in public other than an outer coat, jacket or gloves; or
> (b) as authorising a constable not in uniform to stop a vehicle.

(10) This section and section 1 above apply to vessels, aircraft and hovercraft as they apply to vehicles.

Section 6 of the Act confers defined powers of stop and search on constables employed in undertakings related to railways, road and water transport and docks and harbours, **1–18** etc. Searches may be carried out on vehicles before they leave the goods areas of the relevant premises. The *Aviation Security Act* 1982 confers powers to stop and search persons and vehicles leaving a cargo area of an aerodrome.

Under the Code, a constable may stop and question a suspect and then has a discretion not to proceed with a search if it is unnecessary or impracticable. If the search is to proceed the officer has a duty to comply with the requirements of this section, providing the information specified. All these details must be recorded in writing and the person involved has a right to be given a copy of this record either in person or if the search was of an unattended vehicle, then the record must be left with the vehicle. Any failure to comply with the section means a constable is not acting in the execution of his duty and a search will not be lawful: *Osman v. DPP* (1999) 163 J.P. 725, DC. See also *R. (Bonner) v. DPP* [2005] A.C.D. 227 (56), QBD, where it was held that the requirements of section 2 and the Codes had to be strictly observed prior to an intended search even where the person apprehended knew that the search was being conducted by a police officer and there were fears for the safety of an officer.

(5) Duty to make records concerning searches

Police and Criminal Evidence Act 1984, s.3

Duty to make records concerning searches

1–19   **3.**—(1) Where a constable has carried out a search in the exercise of any such power as is mentioned in section 2(1) above, other than a search—

(a) under section 6 below; or

(b) under section 27(2) of the *Aviation Security Act* 1982,

he shall make a record of it in writing unless it is not practicable to do so.

(2) If—

(a) a constable is required by subsection (1) above to make a record of a search; but

(b) it is not practicable to make the record on the spot,

he shall make it as soon as practicable after the completion of the search.

(3) The record of a search of a person shall include a note of his name, if the constable knows it, but a constable may not detain a person to find out his name.

(4) If a constable does not know the name of a person whom he has searched, the record of the search shall include a note otherwise describing that person.

(5) The record of a search of a vehicle shall include a note describing the vehicle.

1–20   (6) The record of a search of a person or a vehicle—

(a) shall state—

(i)   the object of the search;

(ii) the grounds for making it;

(iii) the date and time when it was made;

(iv) the place where it was made;

(v)   whether anything, and if so what, was found;

(vi) whether any, and if so what, injury to a person or damage to property appears to the constable to have resulted from the search; and

(b) shall identify the constable making it.

(7) If a constable who conducted a search of a person made a record of it, the person who was searched shall be entitled to a copy of the record if he asks for one before the end of the period specified in subsection (9) below.

(8) If—

(a) the owner of a vehicle which has been searched or the person who was in charge of the vehicle at the time when it was searched asks for a copy of the record of the search before the end of the period specified in subsection (9) below; and

(b) the constable who conducted the search made a record of it,

the person who made the request shall be entitled to a copy.

(9) The period mentioned in subsections (7) and (8) above is the period of 12 months beginning with the date on which the search was made.

(10) The requirements imposed by this section with regard to records of searches of

vehicles shall apply also to records of searches of vessels, aircraft and hovercraft.

(6) Road checks

Police and Criminal Evidence Act 1984, s.4

Road checks

4.—(1) This section shall have effect in relation to the conduct of road checks by police offic- **1–21**
ers for the purpose of ascertaining whether a vehicle is carrying—

  (a) a person who has committed an offence other than a road traffic offence or a ve-
     hicle excise offence;
  (b) a person who is a witness to such an offence;
  (c) a person intending to commit such an offence; or
  (d) a person who is unlawfully at large.

(2) For the purposes of this section a road check consists of the exercise in a locality of
the power conferred by section 163 of the *Road Traffic Act* 1988 in such a way as to stop
during the period for which its exercise in that way in that locality continues all vehicles or
vehicles selected by any criterion.

(3) Subject to subsection (5) below, there may only be such a road check if a police officer of the rank of superintendent or above authorises it in writing.

(4) An officer may only authorise a road check under subsection (3) above—

  (a) for the purpose specified in subsection (1)(a) above, if he has reasonable
     grounds—
    (i) for believing that the offence is an indictable offence; and
    (ii) for suspecting that the person is, or is about to be, in the locality in which
         vehicles would be stopped if the road check were authorised;
  (b) for the purpose specified in subsection (1)(b) above, if he has reasonable grounds
     for believing that the offence is an indictable offence;
  (c) for the purpose specified in subsection (1)(c) above, if he has reasonable
     grounds—
    (i) for believing that the offence would be an indictable offence; and
    (ii) for suspecting that the person is, or is about to be, in the locality in which
         vehicles would be stopped if the road check were authorised;
  (d) for the purpose specified in subsection (1)(d) above, if he has reasonable grounds
     for suspecting that the person is, or is about to be, in that locality.

(5) An officer below the rank of superintendent may authorise such a road check if it **1–22**
appears to him that it is required as a matter of urgency for one of the purposes specified
in subsection (1) above.

(6) If an authorisation is given under subsection (5) above, it shall be the duty of the officer who gives it—

  (a) to make a written record of the time at which he gives it; and
  (b) to cause an officer of the rank of superintendent or above to be informed that it
     has been given.

(7) The duties imposed by subsection (6) above shall be performed as soon as it is
practicable to do so.

(8) An officer to whom a report is made under subsection (6) above may, in writing, authorise the road check to continue.

(9) If such an officer considers that the road check should not continue, he shall record
in writing—

  (a) the fact that it took place; and
  (b) the purpose for which it took place.

(10) An officer giving an authorisation under this section shall specify the locality in
which vehicles are to be stopped.

(11) An officer giving an authorisation under this section, other than an authorisation
under subsection (5) above—

  (a) shall specify a period, not exceeding seven days, during which the road check
     may continue; and
  (b) may direct that the road check—

      (i)   shall be continuous; or

      (ii) shall be conducted at specified times, during that period.

1–23   (12) If it appears to an officer of the rank of superintendent or above that a road check ought to continue beyond the period for which it has been authorised he may, from time to time, in writing specify a further period, not exceeding seven days, during which it may continue.

      (13) Every written authorisation shall specify—

      (a) the name of the officer giving it;

      (b) the purpose of the road check; and

      (c) the locality in which vehicles are to be stopped.

      (14) The duties to specify the purposes of a road check imposed by subsections (9) and (13) above include duties to specify any relevant indictable offence.

      (15) Where a vehicle is stopped in a road check, the person in charge of the vehicle at the time when it is stopped shall be entitled to obtain a written statement of the purpose of the road check if he applies for such a statement not later than the end of the period of twelve months from the day on which the vehicle was stopped.

      (16) Nothing in this section affects the exercise by police officers of any power to stop vehicles for purposes other than those specified in subsection (1) above.

[This section is printed as amended by the *Road Traffic (Consequential Provisions) Act* 1988, s.4, and Sched. 3, para. 27; and the *Serious Organised Crime and Police Act* 2005, s.111, and Sched. 7, para. 43.]

Road Traffic Act 1988, s.163

Power of police to stop vehicles

1–24   **163.**—(1) A person driving a mechanically propelled vehicle on a road must stop the vehicle on being required to do so by a constable in uniform or a traffic officer.

      (2) A person riding a cycle on a road must stop the cycle on being required to do so by a constable in uniform or a traffic officer.

      (3) If a person fails to comply with this section he is guilty of an offence.

      (4) [*Repealed.*]

[This section is printed as amended by the *Road Traffic Act* 1991, s.48, and Sched. 4, para. 67; the *Police Reform Act* 2002, s.49(1); the *Traffic Management Act* 2004, s.6(4); and, as repealed in part, by the *Serious Organised Crime and Police Act* 2005, ss.111 and 174(2), Sched. 7, para. 27(3), and Sched. 17, Pt 2.]

Section 4 extends the power to stop vehicles on the road to enable searches to be made. A constable in uniform has power under the *Road Traffic Act* 1988, s.163 to stop vehicles. Section 4 allows for the power under section 163 to be used for a specified time, not exceeding seven days, in a specified locality for the purposes of carrying out searches of vehicles under section 1. There is no requirement for a reasonable suspicion to attach to the individual vehicles that are stopped but *PACE* 1984, ss.1 and 2 must still be complied with as any search is carried out. The checks must be authorised by a senior officer unless it is a matter of urgency. The authorisation may only be given if the authorising officer has reasonable grounds for believing the matters listed in section 4(4).

(7) Power to stop and search in anticipation of violence

Criminal Justice and Public Order Act 1994, s.60

Powers to stop and search in anticipation of violence

1–25   **60.**—(1) If a police officer of or above the rank of inspector reasonably believes—

      (a) that incidents involving serious violence may take place in any locality in his police area, and that it is expedient to give an authorisation under this section to prevent their occurrence, or

      (b) that persons are carrying dangerous instruments or offensive weapons in any locality in his police area without good reason, he may give an authorisation that the powers conferred by this section are to be exercisable at any place within that locality for a specified period not exceeding 24 hours.

(2) [*Repealed.*]

(3) If it appears to an officer of or above the rank of superintendent that it is expedient to do so, having regard to offences which have, or are reasonably suspected to have, been committed in connection with any activity falling within the authorisation, he may direct that the authorisation shall continue in being for a further 24 hours.

(3A) If an inspector gives an authorisation under subsection (1) he must, as soon as it is practicable to do so, cause an officer of or above the rank of superintendent to be informed.

(4) This section confers on any constable in uniform power—

    (a) to stop any pedestrian and search him or anything carried by him for offensive weapons or dangerous instruments;

    (b) to stop any vehicle and search the vehicle, its driver and any passenger for offensive weapons or dangerous instruments.

(4A) [*Repealed.*]

(5) A constable may, in the exercise of the powers conferred by subsection (4) above, stop any person or vehicle and make any search he thinks fit whether or not he has any grounds for suspecting that the person or vehicle is carrying weapons or articles of that kind.

(6) If in the course of a search under this section a constable discovers a dangerous instrument or an article which he has reasonable grounds for suspecting to be an offensive weapon, he may seize it.

(7) This section applies (with the necessary modifications) to ships, aircraft and hovercraft as it applies to vehicles.

(8) A person who fails

    (a) to stop, or to stop a vehicle

    (b) [*Repealed.*]

when required to do so by a constable in the exercise of his powers under this section shall be liable on summary conviction to imprisonment for a term not exceeding *one month* [51 weeks] or to a fine not exceeding level 3 on the standard scale or both.

(9) Any authorisation under this section shall be in writing signed by the officer giving it and shall specify the grounds on which it is given and the locality in which and the period during which the powers conferred by this section are exercisable and a direction under subsection (3) above shall also be given in writing or, where that is not practicable, recorded in writing as soon as it is practicable to do so.

(9A) The preceding provisions of this section, so far as they relate to an authorisation by **1–26** a member of the British Transport Police Force (including one who for the time being has the same powers and privileges as a member of a police force for a police area), shall have effect as if the references to a locality in his police area were references to any locality in or in the vicinity of any policed premises, or to the whole or any part of any such premises.

(10) Where a vehicle is stopped by a constable under this section, the driver shall be entitled to obtain a written statement that the vehicle was stopped under the powers conferred by this section if he applies for such a statement not later than the end of the period of twelve months from the day on which the vehicle was stopped as respects a pedestrian who is stopped and searched under this section.

(10A) A person who is searched by a constable under this section shall be entitled to obtain a written statement that he was searched under the powers conferred by this section if he applies for such a statement not later than the end of the period of twelve months from the day on which he was searched.

(11) In this section—

    "British Transport Police Force" means the constables appointed under section 53 of the *British Transport Commission Act* 1949;

    "dangerous instruments" means instruments which have a blade or are sharply pointed;

    "offensive weapon" has the meaning given by section 1(9) of the *Police and Criminal Evidence Act* 1984 or [*Scotland*]; and "policed premises", in relation to England and Wales, has the meaning given by section 53(3) of the *British Transport Commission Act* 1949 and [*Scotland*].

    "vehicle" includes a caravan as defined in section 29(1) of the *Caravan Sites and Control of Development Act* 1960.

(11A) For the purposes of this section, a person carries a dangerous instrument or an offensive weapon if he has it in his possession.

(12) The powers conferred by this section are in addition to and not in derogation of, any power otherwise conferred.

[This section is printed as amended and repealed in part by the *Knives Act* 1997, s.8; the *Crime and Disorder Act* 1998, s.25; the *Anti-Terrorism, Crime and Security Act* 2001, ss.101 and 125, and Scheds 7 and 8; and, as from a day to be appointed, by the *Criminal Justice Act* 2003, s.280(2), and Sched. 26, para. 45(1) and (2) (substitution of words in square brackets for italicised words).]

1–27   This section allows for random stop and search powers to be exercised by any police constable in uniform in any locality where an authorisation has been given. This is a temporary extension of police powers available in the specific situations outlined. The Notes for Guidance state that the authorisation given under the section must have an objective basis such as intelligence or information about a history of violence at a particular location or an increase in crime involving weapons in the area. The authorising officer must determine the geographical area that constitutes a "locality". The power can be authorised for 24 hours and extended for a further 24 hours if the conditions of the section are met.

The power of search is limited to offensive weapons or dangerous instruments that have a blade or are sharply pointed. Unlike the power to stop and search in section 1 of *PACE Act* 1984, a constable in uniform may exercise the powers conferred under section 60(4) if he or she thinks fit, regardless of whether there are any grounds for suspecting that the person or vehicle is carrying offensive weapons or dangerous articles. If during the course of a search under this section a constable discovers a dangerous instrument or an article which he or she has reasonable grounds for suspecting to be an offensive weapon, it may be seized. Items seized may be retained in accordance with section 60A of the *Criminal Justice and Public Order Act* 1994 and regulations made by the Secretary of State. Section 2 of the 1984 Act applies with the requirements to explain and record the searches.

(8) Power to require removal of disguises

Criminal Justice and Public Order Act 1994, s.60AA

Powers to require removal of disguises

1–28   **60AA.**—(1) Where—
- (a) an authorisation under section 60 is for the time being in force in relation to any locality for any period, or
- (b) an authorisation under subsection (3) that the powers conferred by subsection (2) shall be exercisable at any place in a locality is in force for any period,

those powers shall be exercisable at any place in that locality at any time in that period.

(2) This subsection confers power on any constable in uniform—
- (a) to require any person to remove any item which the constable reasonably believes that person is wearing wholly or mainly for the purpose of concealing his identity;
- (b) to seize any item which the constable reasonably believes any person intends to wear wholly or mainly for that purpose.

(3) If a police officer of or above the rank of inspector reasonably believes—
- (a) that activities may take place in any locality in his police area that are likely (if they take place) to involve the commission of offences, and
- (b) that it is expedient, in order to prevent or control the activities, to give an authorisation under this subsection,

he may give an authorisation that the powers conferred by this section shall be exercisable at any place within that locality for a specified period not exceeding twenty-four hours.

(4) If it appears to an officer of or above the rank of superintendent that it is expedient to do so, having regard to offences which—
- (a) have been committed in connection with the activities in respect of which the authorisation was given, or

    (b) are reasonably suspected to have been so committed,
he may direct that the authorisation shall continue in force for a further twenty-four hours.

    (5) If an inspector gives an authorisation under subsection (3), he must, as soon as it is practicable to do so, cause an officer of or above the rank of superintendent to be informed.

    (6) Any authorisation under this section—

        (a) shall be in writing and signed by the officer giving it; and

        (b) shall specify—

            (i) the grounds on which it is given;

            (ii) the locality in which the powers conferred by this section are exercisable;

            (iii) the period during which those powers are exercisable;

and a direction under subsection (4) shall also be given in writing or, where that is not practicable, recorded in writing as soon as it is practicable to do so.

1–29   (7) A person who fails to remove an item worn by him when required to do so by a constable in the exercise of his power under this section shall be liable, on summary conviction, to imprisonment for a term not exceeding *one month* [51 weeks] or to a fine not exceeding level 3 on the standard scale or both.

    (8) The preceding provisions of this section, so far as they relate to an authorisation by a member of the British Transport Police Force (including one who for the time being has the same powers and privileges as a member of a police force for a police area), shall have effect as if references to a locality or to a locality in his police area were references to any locality in or in the vicinity of any policed premises, or to the whole or any part of any such premises.

    (9) In this section "British Transport Police Force" and "policed premises" has the same meaning as in section 60.

    (10) The powers conferred by this section are in addition to, and not in derogation of, any power otherwise conferred.

    (11) This section does not extend to Scotland.

[This section was inserted by the *Anti-terrorism, Crime and Security Act* 2001, s.94(1). It is printed as amended, as from a day to be appointed, by the *Criminal Justice Act* 2003, s.280(2), and Sched. 26, para. 45(1) and (3) (substitution of words in square brackets for italicised words).]

1–30   The authorisation itself must be properly documented but the exercise of this power has not been held to be a search so the requirements of section 2 of *PACE* 1984 do not apply: *DPP v. Avery* [2002] 1 Cr.App.R. 31, DC.

D. Entry, Search and Seizure

(1) Introduction

1–31   Part II of the *PACE Act* 1984 (*i.e.* sections 8 to 23) consolidates many, but not all, police powers of entry, search and seizure. It contains provisions relating to search warrants, privileged material (sections 8–16), and seizure (sections 19–22). Section 8 creates a general power to obtain a search warrant from a justice of the peace in the case of an indictable offence. Sections 15 (search warrants—safeguards), 16 (execution of warrants) and 19 (general power of seizure), relate to all powers of entry, including those not repealed by the 1984 Act. There are many statutes enabling a justice of the peace to issue a warrant authorising a constable to search for and seize certain items and to enter premises for the purpose of doing so: see the statutes listed *post*, § 1–84 (powers to which the *Criminal Justice and Police Act* 2001, s.50, applies). There are also statutory powers relating to search and seizure, not printed in this work, exercisable in the Crown Court: see the *PACE Act* 1984, s.9 and Sched. 1; the *Drug Trafficking Act* 1994, ss.55–59A; and the *Proceeds of Crime Act* 2002, ss.343–379.

1–32   Where an officer wishes to gain entry to premises for the purposes of a search and he believes consent is either unforthcoming or impracticable, application will be made to a magistrate or district judge for a search warrant. The warrant from the court will authorise the officer to enter and search named premises for specific items. Such applications will be made in writing generally in standard format and will be signed and substantiated on oath or affirmation. The application can be made to the magistrate or district judge in court, in the retiring room or, in urgent situations, out of hours to the magistrate or district judge at home. The requirements of section 8 of *PACE* 1984 must be fully complied with and the principles of the European Convention on Human Rights must be considered, particularly Article 8 which provides the right to respect for privacy and family life. The granting authority must be satisfied that the issue of a warrant is a proportional step and that the infringement of Article 8 rights is in accordance with the law and necessary in a democratic society in the interests of national security, public safety or the economic well-being of the country, for the prevention of disorder or crime, for the protection of health and morals or for the protection of the rights and freedom of others.

A search of premises has been held to be an interference with Article 8 rights (see *Funke v. France* (1993) 16 E.H.R.R. 297; *Chappell v. UK* (1990) 12 E.H.R.R. 1) and justification for the infringement is necessary. The prevention of crime or the protection of others would form the required qualification on the enjoyment of the right to privacy. Questions of proportionality must also be considered not only in the issue of the warrant but also the way in which it is to be executed. Magistrates may inquire into the nature of the premises and whether families and neighbours will be treated with respect and sensitivity within the remit of the warrant.

The powers of seizure under the *PACE Act* 1984 and many other statutes were considerably extended by the provisions of *Criminal Justice and Police Act* 2001, Pt 2. The intention was first to remedy the problem highlighted by the decision in *R. v. Chesterfield JJ., ex p. Bramley* [2000] Q.B. 576, DC (no entitlement to seize items for purpose of sifting through them later to see whether they fall within scope of warrant), and secondly, to give the police and others power to seize and retain material which could not itself be seized but which is inextricably linked with material which is liable to be seized. The second of these purposes is related to the difficulties encountered with modern technology and the increasing use of computers. For the text of Part 2, see *post,* §§ 1–67 *et seq.* Guidance in relation to the new powers is included in the Code of Practice for the Searching of Premises by Police Officers and the Seizure of Property found by Police Officers on Persons or Premises (Code B): see paras B:7.7 *et seq.* (Appendix A).

As to entry on or interference with property for the purpose of preventing or detecting serious crime under the *Police Act* 1997, see *post,* § 1–87. As to entry under a warrant to search for and seize documents required under a disclosure notice issued pursuant to the *Serious Organised Crime and Police Act* 2005, see *post,* §§ 1–89 *et seq.*

(2) Warrant to enter and search premises

Police and Criminal Evidence Act 1984, s.8

Power of justice of the peace to authorise entry and search of premises

1–33   **8.**—(1) If on an application made by a constable a justice of the peace is satisfied that there are reasonable grounds for believing—

(a) that an indictable offence has been committed; and

(b) that there is material on premises mentioned in subsection (1A) below which is likely to be of substantial value (whether by itself or together with other material) to the investigation of the offence; and

(c) that the material is likely to be relevant evidence; and

(d) that it does not consist of or include items subject to legal privilege, excluded material or special procedure material; and

(e) that any of the conditions specified in subsection (3) below applies in relation to each set of premises specified in the application,

he may issue a warrant authorising a constable to enter and search the premises.

(1A) The premises referred to in subsection (1)(b) above are—

(a) one or more sets of premises specified in the application (in which case the application is for a "specific premises warrant"); or

Part I

(b) any premises occupied or controlled by a person specified in the application, including such sets of premises as are so specified (in which case the application is for an "all premises warrant").

(1B) If the application is for an all premises warrant, the justice of the peace must also be satisfied—

(a) that because of the particulars of the offence referred to in paragraph (a) of subsection (1) above, there are reasonable grounds for believing that it is necessary to search premises occupied or controlled by the person in question which are not specified in the application in order to find the material referred to in paragraph (b) of that subsection; and

(b) that it is not reasonably practicable to specify in the application all the premises which he occupies or controls and which might need to be searched.

(1C) The warrant may authorise entry to and search of premises on more than one occasion if, on the application, the justice of the peace is satisfied that it is necessary to authorise multiple entries in order to achieve the purpose for which he issues the warrant.

(1D) If it authorises multiple entries, the number of entries authorised may be unlimited, or limited to a maximum.

(2) A constable may seize and retain anything for which a search has been authorised under subsection (1) above.

(3) The conditions mentioned in subsection (1)(e) above are—

(a) that it is not practicable to communicate with any person entitled to grant entry to the premises;

(b) that it is practicable to communicate with a person entitled to grant entry to the premises but it is not practicable to communicate with any person entitled to grant access to the evidence;

(c) that entry to the premises will not be granted unless a warrant is produced;

(d) that the purpose of a search may be frustrated or seriously prejudiced unless a constable arriving at the premises can secure immediate entry to them.

(4) In this Act "relevant evidence", in relation to an offence, means anything that would be admissible in evidence at a trial for the offence.

(5) The power to issue a warrant conferred by this section is in addition to any such power otherwise conferred.

(6) This section applies in relation to a relevant offence (as defined in section 28D(4) of the *Immigration Act* 1971) as it applies in relation to an indictable offence.

[This section is printed as amended by the *Immigration and Asylum Act* 1999, s.169(1), and Sched. 14, para. 80(1) and (2); and the *Serious Organised Crime and Police Act* 2005, ss.111, 113(1)-(4), and 114(1) and (2), and Sched. 7, para. 43(1) and (3).]

For "items subject to legal privilege", see section 10, *post*, § 1–37; for "excluded material", see sections 11 to 13, *post*, §§ 1–40 *et seq.*; and for "special procedure material", see section 14, *post*, § 1–43. As to the extension of Part II so as to have effect as if the references to indictable offences in section 8 included any conduct which is an offence under the law of a country or territory outside the United Kingdom and would constitute an indictable offence if it had occurred in any part of the United Kingdom, see section 16 of the *Crime (International Co-operation) Act* 2003 (as amended by the *Serious Organised Crime and Police Act* 2005, s.111, and Sched. 7, para. 51(1) and (2)).

This section confers on district judges and magistrates the power to authorise **1–34** constables to enter and search premises. The exercise of the power is also subject to the safeguards contained in section 15—see *post*, § 1–45.

The power under section 8 is "draconian"; before issuing a warrant, a magistrate must be satisfied, amongst other requirements set out in the section, that the material in question is not *prima facie* subject to legal privilege within section 10(1) or special procedure material as defined by section 14; and, if there is any doubt, the application should be refused, leaving the applicant to apply to a Crown Court judge under section 9 and Schedule 1 (Crown Court judge's power to make production order or issue warrant in relation to excluded material or special procedure material): *R. v. Guildhall Magistrates' Court, ex p. Primlaks Holdings Co (Panama) Inc* [1990] 1 Q.B. 261, CA.

Before a warrant to enter and search premises may be issued the district judge or magistrate before whom the information is laid must be satisfied that there are reasonable grounds for believing that the conditions set out in the section exist. This means they must:

a.) Identify the indictable offence.

b.) Check whether the warrant is for specific premises or for all premises. Check the details of all addresses or locations to be searched, which can include premises or vehicles. In the case of multi-occupancy premises such as hostels or offices care must be taken to clarify the parameters of the search. For an all premises warrant, check the details of the person named as being in occupation or control of the premises specified and also check that there is good reason why all the premises in his control or occupation cannot be specified in view of the nature of the offence alleged and the material sought.

c.) Check the number of entries required under the warrant and the reasons for requesting multiple entries either limited or not.

d.) Check the list and specification of the items being sought and confirm that they are likely to be of substantial value to the investigation.

e.) Check why these items would be relevant and admissible at the trial and confirm that the items being sought are not subject to legal privilege or in any other way confidential. (A search of business or office premises—especially a lawyer's office may give rise to immediate concerns under this provision).

f.) Inquiries should also be made about the nature of the premises and whether any vulnerable people such as children or the elderly may be affected by the execution of a warrant.

g.) Check whether a search warrant has been issued previously for the same premises and confirm the history of any earlier application.

1–35   The officer may be questioned on oath to ascertain this information and a record of any answers should be appended to the information.

It is not a condition precedent to granting a search warrant under section 8 that other methods of obtaining the material have been tried without success or have not been tried because they are bound to fail: *R. v. Billericay Justices, ex p. Frank Harris (Coaches)* [1991] Crim.L.R. 472.

1–36   If an item is seized as apparently falling within the scope of the warrant, but subsequently transpires to be subject to legal professional privilege, its seizure does not thereby become unlawful unless the officer had reasonable grounds to believe it to be subject to legal privilege at the time of seizure (see section 19(6) of the 1984 Act (*post*, § 1–56)): *ex p. Bramley, ante*, § 1–32. The court said that if an officer comes across material which may be privileged, he should try to reach agreement at the time of the search as to whether it is privileged but, if agreement is impossible, it would be wise to package any such items separately for later analysis: he is not bound to accept at face value a claim to privilege. As to packaging separately items falling within the search criteria, but which may be privileged, see also *R. v. Customs and Excise Commrs, ex p. Popely* [1999] S.T.C. 1016, DC. In both *ex p. Bramley* and *ex p. Popely*, the court dissented from the view expressed in *R. v. Southwark Crown Court, ex p. Gross* [1998] C.O.D. 445, DC, that the innocent seizure of privileged material is unlawful. As to the duty to return legally privileged material that has been seized, see section 54 of the *Criminal Justice and Police Act* 2001 (*post*, § 1–74). Note also that section 19(6) of the 1984 Act (*ante*) is disapplied in relation to the extended powers of seizure provided for in sections 50 and 51 of the 2001 Act (*post*, §§ 1–67 *et seq.*).

(3) Items subject to legal privilege, excluded material, special procedure material

Police and Criminal Evidence Act 1984, s.10

Meaning of "items subject to legal privilege"

1–37   10.—(1) Subject to subsection (2) below, in this Act "items subject to legal privilege" means—

(a) communications between a professional legal adviser and his client or any person representing his client made in connection with the giving of legal advice to the client;

(b) communications between a professional legal adviser and his client or any person representing his client or between such an adviser or his client or any such representative and any other person made in connection with or in contemplation of legal proceedings and for the purposes of such proceedings; and

(c) items enclosed with or referred to in such communications and made—

    (i) in connection with the giving of legal advice; or

    (ii) in connection with or in contemplation of legal proceedings and for the purposes of such proceedings, when they are in the possession of a person who is entitled to possession of them.

(2) Items held with the intention of furthering a criminal purpose are not items subject to legal privilege.

Records of a conveyancing transaction, including details of the financing, are not **1–38** privileged, but correspondence between the solicitor and his client about the conveyance could be privileged if the letters contained advice: *R. v. Inner London Crown Court, ex p. Baines and Baines* [1988] Q.B. 579. Attendance notes of a solicitor on his client were held not to be privileged, as they simply provided a record of time and did not amount to the giving of legal advice: *R. v. Crown Court at Manchester, ex p. Rogers* [1999] 2 Cr.App.R. 267. A completed application form for legal aid was held to be privileged as being made in contemplation of legal proceedings: *R. v. Crown Court at Snaresbrook, ex p. DPP* [1988] Q.B. 532.

Where a scientist carried out tests on a blood sample provided by the defence, it was held that the sample was an item made for the purposes of legal proceedings and so was covered by section 10: *R* [1995] 1 Cr.App.R. 183.

In *R. v. Central Criminal Court, ex p. Francis and Francis* [1989] A.C. 346, it was held that communications made between a lawyer and his client in the furtherance of a criminal purpose could not be protected by legal privilege (following the leading case at common law, *Cox and Railton* (1884) 14 Q.B.D. 153). Legal privilege could not extend to cover such advice irrespective of the innocence of the lawyer and section 10 was interpreted widely to remove that privilege no matter which party had the intention of furthering a criminal purpose. In this case the documents in dispute were to be used in the furtherance of money laundering by drug traffickers.

A court is entitled to look at an item to determine whether it is held with the intention of furthering a criminal purpose: *R. v. Governor of Pentonville Prison, ex p. Osman* (1988) 90 Cr.App.R. 281, DC. In relation to documents held by a solicitor acting for a defendant in pending criminal proceedings, a claim to legal professional privilege can be defeated where there is evidence of a specific agreement to pervert the course of justice, which is freestanding and independent, in the sense that it does not require any judgment to be reached in relation to the issues to be tried in the pending proceedings: *R. (Hallinan Blackburn Gittings & Nott (a firm)) v. Crown Court at Middlesex Guildhall* [2005] 1 W.L.R. 766, DC (applied in *Kuwait Airways Corp v. Iraqi Airways Co (No. 6)* [2005] 1 W.L.R. 2734, CA (Civ. Div.)).

Where legal privilege does not attach to documents, there could still be special proce- **1–39** dure material under section 14 if there exists an express or implied undertaking to hold them in confidence: *R. v. Guildhall Magistrates' Court, ex p. Primlaks Holdings Co (Panama) Inc* [1990] 1 Q.B. 261, CA.

Police and Criminal Evidence Act 1984, ss.11, 12

Meaning of "excluded material"

11.—(1) Subject to the following provisions of this section, in this Act "excluded material" **1–40** means—

(a) personal records which a person has acquired or created in the course of any trade, business, profession or other occupation or for the purposes of any paid or unpaid office and which he holds in confidence;

     (b) human tissue or tissue fluid which has been taken for the purposes of diagnosis or medical treatment and which a person holds in confidence;

     (c) journalistic material which a person holds in confidence and which consists—

        (i) of documents; or

        (ii) of records other than documents.

(2) A person holds material other than journalistic material in confidence for the purposes of this section if he holds it subject—

     (a) to an express or implied undertaking to hold it in confidence; or

     (b) to a restriction on disclosure or an obligation of secrecy contained in any enactment, including an enactment contained in an Act passed after this Act.

(3) A person holds journalistic material in confidence for the purposes of this section if—

     (a) he holds it subject to such an undertaking, restriction or obligation; and

     (b) it has been continuously held (by one or more persons) subject to such an undertaking, restriction or obligation since it was first acquired or created for the purposes of journalism.

Meaning of "personal records"

1–41   **12.** In this Part of this Act "personal records" means documentary and other records concerning an individual (whether living or dead) who can be identified from them and relating—

     (a) to his physical or mental health;

     (b) to spiritual counselling or assistance given or to be given to him; or

     (c) to counselling or assistance given or to be given to him, for the purposes of his personal welfare, by any voluntary organisation or by any individual who—

        (i) by reason of his office or occupation has responsibilities for his personal welfare; or

        (ii) by reason of an order of a court has responsibilities for his supervision.

Hospital records of admission to or discharge from hospital can fall under the definition of "personal records" because they relate to a person's physical or mental health: see *R. v. Cardiff Crown Court, ex p. Kellam, The Times*, May 3, 1993, DC.

Police and Criminal Evidence Act 1984, ss.13, 14

Meaning of "journalistic material"

1–42   **13.**—(1) Subject to subsection (2) below, in this Act "journalistic material" means material acquired or created for the purposes of journalism.

(2) Material is only journalistic material for the purposes of this Act if it is in the possession of a person who acquired or created it for the purposes of journalism.

(3) A person who receives material from someone who intends that the recipient shall use it for the purposes of journalism is to be taken to have acquired it for those purposes.

Meaning of "special procedure material"

1–43   **14.**—(1) In this Act "special procedure material" means—

     (a) material to which subsection (2) below applies; and

     (b) journalistic material, other than excluded material.

(2) Subject to the following provisions of this section, this subsection applies to material, other than items subject to legal privilege and excluded material, in the possession of a person who—

     (a) acquired or created it in the course of any trade, business, profession or other occupation or for the purpose of any paid or unpaid office; and

     (b) holds it subject—

        (i) to an express or implied undertaking to hold it in confidence; or

        (ii) to a restriction or obligation such as is mentioned in section 11(2)(b) above.

(3) Where material is acquired—

     (a) by an employee from his employer and in the course of his employment; or

     (b) by a company from an associated company,

it is only special procedure material if it was special procedure material immediately before the acquisition.

(4) Where material is created by an employee in the course of his employment, it is only special procedure material if it would have been special procedure material had his employer created it.

(5) Where material is created by a company on behalf of an associated company, it is only special procedure material if it would have been special procedure material had the associated company created it.

(6) A company is to be treated as another's associated company for the purposes of this section if it would be so treated under section 302 of the *Income and Corporation Taxes Act* 1970.

Frequent applications are made to search for and seize "special procedure material". **1–44** This includes records held by solicitors and accountants or banks and building societies and also films or photographs held by the media.

In *R. v. Leeds Magistrates' Court, ex p. Dumbleton* [1993] Crim.L.R. 866, DC, it was held that the protection of special procedure material could not attach to forged documents, as they could not have been acquired or created in the course of the profession of a solicitor. Furthermore, a dishonest solicitor could not be said to hold a forged document subject to an express or implied undertaking to hold it in confidence, there being no confidence in iniquity.

(4) Safeguards

Police and Criminal Evidence Act 1984, s.15

Search warrants—safeguards

15.—(1) This section and section 16 below have effect in relation to the issue to constables **1–45** under any enactment, including an enactment contained in an Act passed after this Act, of warrants to enter and search premises; and an entry on or search of premises under a warrant is unlawful unless it complies with this section and section 16 below.

(2) Where a constable applies for any such warrant, it shall be his duty—
    (a) to state—
        (i) the ground on which he makes the application;
        (ii) the enactment under which the warrant would be issued; and
        (iii) if the application is for a warrant authorising entry and search on more than one occasion, the ground on which he applies for such a warrant, and whether he seeks a warrant authorising an unlimited number of entries, or (if not) the maximum number of entries desired;
    (b) to specify the matters set out in subsection (2A) below; and
    (c) to identify, so far as is practicable, the articles or persons to be sought.

(2A) The matters which must be specified pursuant to subsection (2)(b) above are—
    (a) if the application relates to one or more sets of premises specified in the application, each set of premises which it is desired to enter and search;
    (b) if the application relates to any premises occupied or controlled by a person specified in the application-
        (i) as many sets of premises which it is desired to enter and search as it is reasonably practicable to specify;
        (ii) the person who is in occupation or control of those premises and any others which it is desired to enter and search;
        (iii) why it is necessary to search more premises than those specified under sub-paragraph (i); and
        (iv) why it is not reasonably practicable to specify all the premises which it is desired to enter and search.

(3) An application for such a warrant shall be made ex parte and supported by an information in writing.

(4) The constable shall answer on oath any question that the justice of the peace or judge hearing the application asks him.

(5) A warrant shall authorise an entry on one occasion only unless it specifies that it authorises multiple entries.

(5A) If it specifies that it authorises multiple entries, it must also specify whether the number of entries authorised is unlimited, or limited to a specified maximum.

(6) A warrant—

    (a) shall specify—

        (i) the name of the person who applies for it;

        (ii) the date on which it is issued;

        (iii) the enactment under which it is issued; and

        (iv) each set of premises to be searched, or (in the case of an all premises warrant) the person who is in occupation or control of premises to be searched, together with any premises under his occupation or control which can be specified and which are to be searched; and

    (b) shall identify, so far as is practicable, the articles or persons to be sought.

(7) Two copies shall be made of a warrant which specifies only one set of premises and does not authorise multiple entries; and as many copies as are reasonably required may be made of any other kind of warrant.

(8) The copies shall be clearly certified as copies.

[This section is printed as amended and repealed in part by the *Serious Organised Crime and Police Act* 2005, ss.113(1) and (5)-(8), 114(1) and (3)-(7), and 174(2), and Sched. 17; and the *Serious Organised Crime and Police Act 2005 (Amendment) Order* 2005 (S.I. 2005 No. 3496).]

Subject to modifications, section 15 of the 1984 Act has effect in relation to the issue of a warrant under sections 19(4) or 23(1) of the *Animal Welfare Act* 2006: *Animal Welfare Act* 2006, s.53 and Sched. 2.

1–46   In *Longman* (1988) 88 Cr.App.R. 148, CA, the court suggested that the word "it" in section 15(1) referred to the warrant rather than the entry or search; that Parliament's real intention had probably been that the warrant should comply with section 15 and the entry and search with section 16; but that the point would be left unresolved (see p. 153). However, in *R. v. Central Criminal Court, ex p. A.J.D. Holdings Ltd* [1992] Crim.L.R. 669, DC, the court refused to accept that *Longman* left it open to the court to hold that the invalidity of a warrant did not necessarily make a search unlawful.

A search warrant referring to items in general terms, (*e.g.* "bank accounts") did not contravene section 15(6)(b) where it was clear, reading the warrant as a whole, that the references related to the suspected offences identified in the supporting information: *R. (Paul da Costa & Co (a firm)) v. Thames Magistrates' Court* [2002] S.T.C. 267, DC.

In *R. v. Chief Constable of Lancashire, ex p. Parker* (1992) 97 Cr.App.R. 90, DC, the court observed that it is highly desirable for the copying and certification of copies under section 15(7) and (8) to be carried out by the issuing court, compliance with those provisions being the responsibility of the judge or magistrate who issues the warrant (although he can delegate the issuing process to court staff). The court held that copies of the warrant have to be clearly certified as such, and that it would be contrary to the legislature's purpose if a judge could authorise the police to replace the whole or part of the original warrant, for the purpose of its execution, by an uncertified photocopy which he has not seen. It was suggested *obiter* that, where a warrant consists of more than one page, something more than the judge's signature and the court stamp on one page would be desirable as a means of authenticating the whole: the judge might, for example, initial the other pages, and in the case of a three-page warrant the pages might be numbered 1/3, etc.

Both the information and the warrants must be signed and dated by the person granting the application. The time of the application will also be noted on the documents so that time limits can be observed. The information is lodged with the Court and the original warrant and copies are taken by the officer.

Sometimes requests are made for copies of informations as well as warrants. Such copies can be provided to other Courts or to legal representatives if the Court is satisfied of the reason why the information is required. There are issues about the protection of informants so disclosure of the information may not be automatic to the individual whose premises were searched.

(5) Execution of the warrant

Police and Criminal Evidence Act 1984, s.16

Execution of warrants.

16.—(1) A warrant to enter and search premises may be executed by any constable.   **1–47**

(2) Such a warrant may authorise persons to accompany any constable who is executing it.

(2A) A person so authorised has the same powers as the constable whom he accompanies in respect of—

(a) the execution of the warrant, and

(b) the seizure of anything to which the warrant relates.

(2B) But he may exercise those powers only in the company, and under the supervision, of a constable.

(3) Entry and search under a warrant must be within three months from the date of its issue.

(3A) If the warrant is an all premises warrant, no premises which are not specified in it may be entered or searched unless a police officer of at least the rank of inspector has in writing authorised them to be entered.

(3B) No premises may be entered or searched for the second or any subsequent time under a warrant which authorises multiple entries unless a police officer of at least the rank of inspector has in writing authorised that entry to those premises.

(4) Entry and search under a warrant must be at a reasonable hour unless it appears to the constable executing it that the purpose of a search may be frustrated on an entry at a reasonable hour.

(5) Where the occupier of premises which are to be entered and searched is present at the time when a constable seeks to execute a warrant to enter and search them, the constable—

(a) shall identify himself to the occupier and, if not in uniform, shall produce to him documentary evidence that he is a constable;

(b) shall produce the warrant to him; and

(c) shall supply him with a copy of it.

(6) Where—

(a) the occupier of such premises is not present at the time when a constable seeks to execute such a warrant; but

(b) some other person who appears to the constable to be in charge of the premises is present,

subsection (5) above shall have effect as if any reference to the occupier were a reference to that other person.

(7) If there is no person present who appears to the constable to be in charge of the premises, he shall leave a copy of the warrant in a prominent place on the premises.

(8) A search under a warrant may only be a search to the extent required for the   **1–48** purpose for which the warrant was issued.

(9) A constable executing a warrant shall make an endorsement on it stating—

(a) whether the articles or persons sought were found; and

(b) whether any articles were seized, other than articles which were sought,

and, unless the warrant is a warrant specifying one set of premises only, he shall do so separately in respect of each set of premises entered and searched, which he shall in each case state in the endorsement.

(10) A warrant shall be returned to the appropriate person mentioned in subsection (10A) below—

(a) when it has been executed; or

(b) in the case of a specific premises warrant which has not been executed, or an all premises warrant, or any warrant authorising multiple entries, upon the expiry of the period of three months referred to in subsection (3) above or sooner.

(10A) The appropriate person is—

(a) if the warrant was issued by a justice of the peace, the designated officer for the local justice area in which the justice was acting when he issued the warrant;

(b) if it was issued by a judge, the appropriate officer of the court from which he is-
        sued it.

(11) A warrant which is returned under subsection (10) above shall be retained for 12
months from its return—

(a) by the designated officer for the local justice area, if it was returned under
       paragraph (i) of that subsection; and

(b) by the appropriate officer, if it was returned under paragraph (ii).

(12) If during the period for which a warrant is to be retained the occupier of premises
to which it relates asks to inspect it, he shall be allowed to do so.

[This section is printed as amended by the *Access to Justice Act* 1999, s.90(1), and
Sched. 13, para. 126; the *Criminal Justice Act* 2003, s.2; the *Courts Act* 2003, s.109(1),
and Sched. 8, para. 281; the *Serious Organised Crime and Police Act* 2005, ss.113(1)
and (9), and 114(1) and (8); and the *Serious Organised Crime and Police Act 2005
(Amendment) Order* 2005 (S.I. 2005 No. 3496).]

Subject to modifications, section 16 of the 1984 Act has effect in relation to the issue
of a warrant under sections 19(4) or 23(1) of the *Animal Welfare Act* 2006: *Animal
Welfare Act* 2006, s.53 and Sched. 2.

1–49   Section 16 provides safeguards for the execution of warrants under section 8 as
amended. A search warrant is valid for three months. If it has not been executed during
that time it must be returned to the court issuing it. With respect to multiple entries and
entry to unspecified premises allowed on a warrant the written authorisation of a senior
officer is required before such a power may be exercised. This ensures that the execution of such warrants is subject to proper scrutiny and is properly recorded. The
outcome of all searches must be endorsed on the warrant separately in respect of each
of the sets of premises searched. The police may execute the warrant and there is power
for members of other agencies involved in the investigations leading to the issue of the
warrant to execute it and seize items under the supervision of the constable. Such authorised persons must observe the Codes of Practice. Officers of other agencies may be
authorised to accompany the police but the number should be restricted and those
persons must not exceed their authority: *R. v. Reading Justices, Chief Constable of
Avon and Somerset and Intervention Board for Agricultural Produce, ex p. South
West Meat Ltd* [1992] Crim.L.R. 672.

1–50   As soon as possible after entry and before search the officer should identify himself
and if not in uniform a warrant card should be produced for inspection. The original
search warrant itself should also be produced and be made available for inspection. The
procedure relating to the warrant must comply with both sections 15 and 16 or the
entry and search will be unlawful: *Longman* [1988] 1 W.L.R. 619, CA. The Administrative Court has considered the extent of officers' powers on the execution of search
warrants. In *DPP v. Meaden* [2004] Crim.L.R. 587, it was held that officers executing a
search warrant were not exceeding their duty when they restricted individuals to certain
rooms on the premises during the currency of the search.

The endorsed warrant will be returned to the Court and kept with the information
for at least 12 months.

(6) Entry to arrest

Police and Criminal Evidence Act 1984, s.17

Entry for purpose of arrest etc.

1–51   **17.**—(1) Subject to the following provisions of this section, and without, prejudice to any
other enactment, a constable may enter and search any premises for the purpose—

(a) of executing—

(i) a warrant of arrest issued in connection with or arising out of criminal
     proceedings; or

(ii) a warrant of commitment issued under section 76 of the *Magistrates' Courts
     Act* 1980;

(b) of arresting a person for an indictable offence;

(c) of arresting a person for an offence under—

    (i) section 1 (prohibition of uniforms in connection with political objects) of the *Public Order Act* 1936;

    (ii) any enactment contained in section 6 to 8 or 10 of the *Criminal Law Act* 1977 (offences relating to entering and remaining on property);

    (iii) section 4 of the *Public Order Act* 1986 (fear or provocation of violence);

    (iiia) section 4 (driving etc. when under influence of drink or drugs) or section 163 (failure to stop when required to do so by a constable in uniform) of the *Road Traffic Act* 1988;

    (iiib) section 27 of the *Transport and Works Act* 1992 (which relates to offences involving drink or drugs,

    (iv) section 76 of the *Criminal Justice and Public Order Act* 1994 (failure to comply with interim possession order);

    (v) any of sections 4, 5, 6(1) and (2), 7 and 8(1) and (2) of the *Animal Welfare Act* 2006 (offences relating to the prevention of harm to animals);

(ca) of arresting, in pursuance of section 32(1A) of the *Children and Young Persons Act* 1969, any child or young person who has been remanded or committed to local authority accommodation under section 23(1) of that Act;

(caa) of arresting a person for an offence to which section 61 of the *Animal Health Act* 1981 applies;

(cb) of recapturing any person who is, or is deemed for any purpose to be, unlawfully at large while liable to be detained—

    (i) in a prison, remand centre, young offender institution or secure training centre, or

    (ii) in pursuance of section 92 of the *Powers of Criminal Courts (Sentencing) Act* 2000 (dealing with children and young persons guilty of grave crimes), in any other place;

(d) of recapturing any person whatever who is unlawfully at large and whom he is pursuing; or

(e) of saving life or limb or preventing serious damage to property.

(2) Except for the purpose specified in paragraph (e) of subsection (1) above, the pow- **1–52** ers of entry and search conferred by this section—

(a) are only exercisable if the constable has reasonable grounds for believing that the person whom he is seeking is on the premises; and

(b) are limited, in relation to premises consisting of two or more separate dwellings, to powers to enter and search—

    (i) any parts of the premises which the occupiers of any dwelling comprised in the premises use in common with the occupiers of any other such dwelling; and

    (ii) any such dwelling in which the constable has reasonable grounds for believing that the person whom he is seeking may be.

(3) The powers of entry and search conferred by this section are only exercisable for the purposes specified in subsection (1)(c)(ii) or (iv) above by a constable in uniform.

(4) The power of search conferred by this section is only a power to search to the extent that is reasonably required for the purpose for which the power of entry is exercised.

(5) Subject to subsection (6) below, all the rules of common law under which a constable has power to enter premises without a warrant are hereby abolished.

(6) Nothing in subsection (5) above affects any power of entry to deal with or prevent a breach of the peace.

[This section is printed as amended by and repealed in part by the *Public Order Act* 1986, s.40(2), and Sched. 2, para. 7; the *Criminal Justice and Public Order Act* 1994, s.168(2), and Sched. 1, para. 53; the *Prisoners (Return to Custody) Act* 1995, s.2(1); the *Powers of Criminal Courts (Sentencing) Act* 2000, s.165(1), and Sched. 9, para. 95; the *Police Reform Act* 2002, s.49(2); the *Serious Organised Crime and Police Act* 2005, s.111, and Sched. 7, paras 43(1) and (4), and 58; and the *Animal Welfare Act* 2006, s.24.]

1–53   The power of entry pursuant to section 17(1)(b) is only available to an officer who has reasonable grounds for suspicion, but such grounds can be inferred: *Kynaston v. DPP* (1987) 87 Cr.App.R. 200, DC, *ante*, § 1–12.

A police officer exercising his power pursuant to section 17 to enter premises may use reasonable force, if necessary: the *PACE Act* 1984, s.117, *post*, § 1–119. He should, unless the circumstances make it impossible, impracticable or undesirable, give any occupant present the reason for his exercising that power of entry: *O'Loughlin v. Chief Constable of Essex* [1998] 1 W.L.R. 374, CA (Civ. Div.). If the real reason is to arrest a person inside (section 17(1)(b)), it is insufficient to tell the occupants that he wishes to "speak to" that person about the offence: *ibid*.

Where police officers are invited onto premises by an occupier or other person authorised to do so, who had been told by them the reason for their entry, they are lawfully on the premises, and they do not have to comply with section 17, which applies to entry and search in the absence of consent: *Riley v. DPP* (1989) 91 Cr.App.R. 14, DC; *Hobson v. Chief Constable of the Cheshire Constabulary* (2003) 168 J.P. 111, DC.

Section 17(1)(d) contemplates an act of pursuit, a chase, however short in time and distance, and does not cover a situation where the police form an intention to arrest and decide to put it into practice by resorting to the premises where they believe that the person sought might be found: *D'Souza v. DPP* (1992) 96 Cr.App.R. 278, HL.

For an example of justifiable entry under section 17(1)(e) (saving life or limb), see *Blench v. DPP* (2004) 69 J.C.L. 98, DC (police responding to emergency call to effect that man was trying to take baby from house).

Police and Criminal Evidence Act 1984, s.18

Entry and search after arrest

1–54   **18.**—(1) Subject to the following provisions of this section, a constable may enter and search any premises occupied or controlled by a person who is under arrest for an indictable offence, if he has reasonable grounds for suspecting that there is on the premises evidence, other than items subject to legal privilege, that relates—

    (a) to that offence; or

    (b) to some other indictable offence which is connected with or similar to that offence.

(2) A constable may seize and retain anything for which he may search under subsection (1) above.

(3) The power to search conferred by subsection (1) above is only a power to search to the extent that is reasonably required for the purpose of discovering such evidence.

(4) Subject to subsection (5) below, the powers conferred by this section may not be exercised unless an officer of the rank of inspector or above has authorised them in writing.

(5) A constable may conduct a search under subsection (1) above—

    (a) before the person is taken to a police station or released on bail under section 30A; and

    (b) without obtaining an authorisation under subsection (4) above,

if the condition in subsection (5A) is satisfied

(5A) The condition is that the presence of the person at a place (other than a police station) is necessary for the effective investigation of the offence.

(6) If a constable conducts a search by virtue of subsection (5) above, he shall inform an officer of the rank of inspector or above that he has made the search as soon as practicable after he has made it.

(7) An officer who—

    (a) authorises a search; or

    (b) is informed of a search under subsection (6) above, shall make a record in writing—

        (i) of the grounds for the search; and

        (ii) of the nature of the evidence that was sought.

(8) If the person who was in occupation or control of the premises at the time of the search is in police detention at the time the record is top be made, the officer shall make the record as part of his custody record.

[This section is printed as amended by the *Police Reform Act* 2002, s.107(1), and Sched. 7, para. 9(1); the *Criminal Justice Act* 2003, s.12, and Sched. 1, paras 1 and 2; and the *Serious Organised Crime and Police Act* 2005, s.111, and Sched. 7, para. 43(1) and(5).]

Section 18(1) is modified in relation to Revenue and Customs officers by the *Police*   **1–55** *and Criminal Evidence Act 1984 (Application to Customs and Excise) Order* 1985 (S.I. 1985 No. 1800) as amended. The effect of the modification is to replace "an indictable offence" with "any indictable offence which relates to an assigned matter, as defined in section 1 of the *Customs and Excise Management Act* 1979".

For the power to search premises where an arrest takes place, see section 32 of the Act, *post*, § 1–130.

The reasoning in *O'Loughlin v. Chief Constable of Essex, ante*, § 1–53, applies equally to section 18: *Linehan v. DPP* [2000] Crim.L.R. 861, DC (officers proposing to enter premises by force should have told the occupier their purpose, *i.e.* to search for the proceeds of a burglary for which the occupier's son had been arrested).

The word "anything" in section 18(2) entitles a constable to seize a vehicle and not just its parts or contents, even though the vehicle itself is "premises" for the purposes of the Act (s.23, *post*, 1–65): *Cowan v. Condon* [2000] 1 W.L.R. 254, CA (Civ. Div.).

Section 18(7) is directory only; non-compliance does not automatically invalidate the search: *Krohn v. DPP* [1997] C.O.D. 345, DC.

For a case where evidence obtained through a search was held to be properly admitted notwithstanding a breach of section 18(8), see *Wright* [1994] Crim.L.R. 55, CA.

Section 18 does not have the effect of abolishing common law rules as to entry and search after arrest, it being a well established principle that a rule of law is not extinguished by a statute unless the statute makes that clear by express provision or clear implication: *R. (Rottman) v. Commr of Police of the Metropolis* [2002] 2 A.C. 692, HL. At common law, a police officer who entered a house and arrested a suspect pursuant to a warrant of arrest had power to search the entire house and seize any articles which provided evidence against the suspect; that power applied to extradition crimes as well as domestic crimes; and it survived the 1984 Act: *ibid*.

In *R. (Hewitson) v. Chief Constable of the Dorset Police, The Times*, January 6, 2004, DC, the court refused to extend the police's common law power of search, as explained in *Rottman, ante*, to searching a flat in circumstances where (a) the suspect was arrested away from the flat and its curtilage, (b) the search was more than two hours after the arrest, and (c) the link between the suspect and the flat was tenuous, the flat belonging to a friend and the suspect being only an occasional visitor.

(7) General power of seizure

Police and Criminal Evidence Act 1984, s.19

General power of seizure etc.

19.—(1) The powers conferred by subsections (2), (3) and (4) below are exercisable by a con-   **1–56** stable who is lawfully on any premises.

(2) The constable may seize anything which is on the premises if he has reasonable grounds for believing—

(a) that it has been obtained in consequence of the commission of an offence; and

(b) that it is necessary to seize it in order to prevent it being concealed, lost, damaged, altered or destroyed.

(3) The constable may seize anything which is on the premises if he has reasonable grounds for believing—

(a) that it is evidence in relation to an offence which he is investigating or any other offence; and

(b) that it is necessary to seize it in order to prevent the evidence being concealed, lost, altered or destroyed.

(4) The constable may require any information which is stored in any electronic form

and is accessible from the premises to be produced in a form in which it can be taken away and in which it is visible and legible or [from which it can readily be produced in a visible and legible form] if he has reasonable grounds for believing—

    (a) that—

        (i) it is evidence in relation to an offence which he is investigating or any other offence; or

        (ii) it has been obtained in consequence of the commission of an offence; and

    (b) that it is necessary to do so in order to prevent it being concealed, lost, tampered with or destroyed.

(5) The powers conferred by this section are in addition to any power otherwise conferred.

(6) No power of seizure conferred on a constable under any enactment (including an enactment contained in an Act passed after this Act) is to be taken to authorise the seizure of an item which the constable exercising the power has reasonable grounds for believing to be subject to legal privilege.

[This section is printed as amended by the *Criminal Justice and Police Act* 2001, s.70, and Sched. 2, para. 13.]

1–57   For the disapplication of subsection (6) in relation to the powers of seizure under sections 50 and 51 of the *Criminal Justice and Police Act* 2001, see subsection (4) of those sections, *post*, §§ 1–68, 1–70.

Unlike section 17, *ante*, § 1–51, which by subsection (5) expressly abolished with one exception all the rules of common law under which a constable had power to enter premises, section 19(5) provides that the powers conferred by the section are in addition to any power otherwise conferred.

For the meaning of "anything" (s.19(2)), see *Cowan v. Condon, ante*, § 1–55.

Section 19 refers to "evidence" (s.19(3),(4)), as opposed to "relevant evidence", which is defined in section 8(4) (*ante*, § 1–33), in relation to an offence, as "anything that would be admissible in evidence at a trial for the offence".

The references to an "offence" in section 19(3) do not include foreign offences; in the absence of an express provision to the contrary, "offence" in a statute means a domestic offence: *R. (Rottman) v. Commr of Police of the Metropolis, ante*, § 1–55.

(8) Power to seize computerised information

Police and Criminal Evidence Act 1984, s.20

Extension of powers of seizure to computerised information

1–58   **20.**—(1) Every power of seizure which is conferred by an enactment to which this section applies on a constable who has entered premises in the exercise of a power conferred by an enactment shall be construed as including a power to require any information stored in any electronic form and accessible from the premises to be produced in a form in which it can be taken away and in which it is visible and legible or from which it can readily be produced in a visible and legible form.

    (2) This section applies—

        (a) to any enactment contained in an Act passed before this Act;

        (b) to sections 8 and 18 above;

        (c) to paragraph 13 of Schedule 1 to this Act; and

        (d) to any enactment contained in an Act passed after this Act.

[This section is printed as amended by the *Criminal Justice and Police Act* 2001, s.70, and Sched. 2, para. 13.]

(9) Access and copying

Police and Criminal Evidence Act 1984, s.21

Access and copying

1–59   **21.**—(1) A constable who seizes anything in the exercise of a power conferred by any enactment, including an enactment contained in an Act passed after this Act, shall, if so requested by a person showing himself—

    (a) to be the occupier of premises on which it was seized; or

    (b) to have had custody or control of it immediately before the seizure,

provide that person with a record of what he seized.

    (2) The officer shall provide the record within a reasonable time from the making of the request for it.

    (3) Subject to subsection (8) below, if a request for permission to be granted access to anything which—

    (a) has been seized by a constable; and

    (b) is retained by the police for the purpose of investigating an offence,

is made to the officer in charge of the investigation by a person who had custody or control of the thing immediately before it was so seized or by someone acting on behalf of such a person, the officer shall allow the person who made the request access to it under the supervision of a constable.

    (4) Subject to subsection (8) below, if a request for a photograph or copy of any such thing is made to the officer in charge of the investigation by a person who had custody or control of the thing immediately before it was so seized, or by someone acting on behalf of such a person, the officer shall—

    (a) allow the person who made the request access to it under the supervision of a constable for the purpose of photographing or copying it; or

    (b) photograph or copy it, or cause it to be photographed or copied.

    (5) A constable may also photograph or copy, or have photographed or copied, anything which he has power to seize, without a request being made under subsection (4) above.

    (6) Where anything is photographed or copied under subsection (4)(b) above, the photograph or copy shall be supplied to the person who made the request.

    (7) The photograph or copy shall be so supplied within a reasonable time from the making of the request.

    (8) There is no duty under this section to grant access to, or to supply a photograph or copy of, anything if the officer in charge of the investigation for the purposes of which it was seized has reasonable grounds for believing that to do so would prejudice—

    (a) that investigation;

    (b) the investigation of an offence other than the offence for the purposes of investigating which the thing was seized; or

    (c) any criminal proceedings which may be brought as a result of—

        (i) the investigation of which he is in charge; or

        (ii) any such investigation as is mentioned in paragraph (b) above.

    (9) The references to a constable in subsections (1), (2), (3)(a) and (5) include a person authorised under section 16(2) to accompany a constable executing a warrant.

[This section is printed as amended by the *Criminal Justice Act* 2003, s.12, and Sched. 1, paras 1 and 3.]

1–60   A refusal to grant access under section 21(8) should be challenged by way of judicial review: *Allen v. Chief Constable of Cheshire Constabulary, The Times*, July 16, 1988.

Where company documents have been seized the person who had control immediately before the seizure has right of access. This right is vested in the company and not the directors or former directors: *Re DPR Futures Ltd* [1989] 1 W.L.R. 778.

(10) Retention

Police and Criminal Evidence Act 1984, s.22

Retention

1–61   **22.**—(1) Subject to subsection (4) below, anything which has been seized by a constable or taken away by a constable following a requirement made by virtue of section 19 or 20 above may be retained so long as is necessary in all the circumstances.

    (2) Without prejudice to the generality of subsection (1) above—

    (a) anything seized for the purposes of a criminal investigation may be retained, except as provided by subsection (4) below—

    (i)   for use as evidence at a trial for an offence; or

    (ii)   for forensic examination or for investigation in connection with an offence; and

  (b)   anything may be retained in order to establish its lawful owner, where there are reasonable grounds for believing that it has been obtained in consequence of the commission of an offence.

(3) Nothing seized on the ground that it may be used—

  (a)   to cause physical injury to any person;

  (b)   to damage property;

  (c)   to interfere with evidence; or

  (d)   to assist in escape from police detention or lawful custody,

may be retained when the person from whom it was seized is no longer in police detention or the custody of a court or is in the custody of a court but has been released on bail.

(4) Nothing may be retained for either of the purposes mentioned in subsection (2)(a) above if a photograph or copy would be sufficient for that purpose.

(5) Nothing in this section affects any power of a court to make an order under section 1 of the *Police (Property) Act* 1897.

(6) This section also applies to anything retained by the police under section 28H(5) of the *Immigration Act* 1971.

(7) The reference in subsection (1) to anything seized by a constable includes anything seized by a person authorised under section 16(2) to accompany a constable executing a warrant.

[This section is printed as amended by the *Immigration and Asylum Act* 1999, s.169(1), and Sched. 14, para. 80(1) and (3); and the *Criminal Justice Act* 2003, s.12, and Sched. 1, paras 1 and 4.]

1–62   The police are not entitled to retain property where the seizure was not in compliance with sections 15 and 16 of the *Police and Criminal Evidence Act* 1984 and so was unlawful. This section only applies to property which is lawfully in the possession of the police: *R. v. Chief Constable of Lancashire, ex p. Parker* (1993) 97 Cr.App.R. 90.

     In *Settelen v. Metropolitan Police Commissioner, Daily Telegraph*, October 7, 2004, Ch.D., the court held that, where material was lawfully seized in a search during one investigation, the police could only retain the material pursuant to section 22 in relation to a subsequent unrelated investigation if it was "necessary" to do so.

1–63   The system for recovery of property retained by Customs officers was considered in *R. v. Southampton Justices, ex p. Newman* (1988) 88 Cr.App.R. 202. Documents had been seized from the defendant's home on his arrest by Customs officers. He applied to the court for an order under section 48 of the *Magistrates' Courts Act* 1980 for the return of this property. It was held that section 48 did not apply, because it referred to the return of property taken from the defendant's person and not from his home at the time of arrest. The Court conceded that this left the defendant with no direct remedy as, although the *Police and Criminal Evidence Act* 1984, ss.17 and 19, applied to Customs officers by virtue of the *PACE (Application to Customs and Excise) Order* 1985 (S.I. 1985 No. 1800), s.22(5) did not and neither did the *Police Property Act* 1897. It was suggested that the court has an inherent power to control the proceedings, so it might in these circumstances adjourn or refuse to proceed if it thought it in the interests of justice that the documents should be returned to the defendant to enable him to prepare his defence.

1–64   The provisions of section 48 of the *MCA* 1980, and the *Police Property Act* 1897, whereby application may be made to the magistrates court for the return of property in police possession to the owner or any person as the court thinks meet are preserved. See *post*, §§ 20–130 *et seq.*

(11) Meaning of "premises" etc.

Meaning of "premises" etc.

1–65   **23.** In this Act—

"premises" includes any place and, in particular, includes—

(a) any vehicle, vessel, aircraft or hovercraft;

(b) any offshore installation;

(ba) any renewable energy installation;

(c) any tent or movable structure; and

"offshore installation" has the meaning given to it by section 1 of the *Mineral Workings (Offshore Installations) Act* 1971;

"renewable energy installation" has the same meaning as in Chapter 2 of Part 2 of the *Energy Act* 2004.

[This section is printed as amended by the *Energy Act* 2004, s.103(2).]

(12) Additional powers of seizure from premises

The powers of seizure under the *PACE* 1984 were considerably extended under the **1–66** provisions of the *Criminal Justice and Police Act* 2001. See *ante*, § 1–32.

Criminal Justice and Police Act 2001, s.50

Additional powers of seizure from premises

50.—(1) Where—　　　　　　　　　　　　　　　　　　　　　　　　　　　　　**1–67**

(a) a person who is lawfully on any premises finds anything on those premises that he has reasonable grounds for believing may be or may contain something for which he is authorised to search on those premises,

(b) a power of seizure to which this section applies or the power conferred by subsection (2) would entitle him, if he found it, to seize whatever it is that he has grounds for believing that thing to be or to contain, and

(c) in all the circumstances, it is not reasonably practicable for it to be determined, on those premises—

(i) whether what he has found is something that he is entitled to seize, or

(ii) the extent to which what he has found contains something that he is entitled to seize,

that person's powers of seizure shall include power under this section to seize so much of what he has found as it is necessary to remove from the premises to enable that to be determined.

(2) Where—

(a) a person who is lawfully on any premises finds anything on those premises ("the seizable property") which he would be entitled to seize but for its being comprised in something else that he has (apart from this subsection) no power to seize,

(b) the power under which that person would have power to seize the seizable property is a power to which this section applies, and

(c) in all the circumstances it is not reasonably practicable for the seizable property to be separated, on those premises, from that in which it is comprised,

that person's powers of seizure shall include power under this section to seize both the seizable property and that from which it is not reasonably practicable to separate it.

(3) The factors to be taken into account in considering, for the purposes of this section, **1–68** whether or not it is reasonably practicable on particular premises for something to be determined, or for something to be separated from something else, shall be confined to the following—

(a) how long it would take to carry out the determination or separation on those premises;

(b) the number of persons that would be required to carry out that determination or separation on those premises within a reasonable period;

(c) whether the determination or separation would (or would if carried out on those premises) involve damage to property;

(d) the apparatus or equipment that it would be necessary or appropriate to use for the carrying out of the determination or separation; and

(e) in the case of separation, whether the separation—

(i) would be likely, or

§ 1–68   CRIMINAL INVESTIGATIONS   [CHAP. 1

    (ii) if carried out by the only means that are reasonably practicable on those premises, would be likely,

to prejudice the use of some or all of the separated seizable property for a purpose for which something seized under the power in question is capable of being used.

(4) Section 19(6) of the 1984 Act and Article 21(6) of the *Police and Criminal Evidence (Northern Ireland) Order* 1989 (S.I. 1989 No. 1341 (N.I. 12)) (powers of seizure not to include power to seize anything that a person has reasonable grounds for believing is legally privileged) shall not apply to the power of seizure conferred by subsection (2).

(5) This section applies to each of the powers of seizure specified in Part 1 of Schedule 1.

(6) Without prejudice to any power conferred by this section to take a copy of any document, nothing in this section, so far as it has effect by reference to the power to take copies of documents under section 28(2)(b) of the *Competition Act* 1998, shall be taken to confer any power to seize any document.

(13) Additional powers of seizure from the person

Criminal Justice and Police Act 2001, s.51

Additional powers of seizure from the person

1–69   **51.**—(1) Where—

  (a) a person carrying out a lawful search of any person finds something that he has reasonable grounds for believing may be or may contain something for which he is authorised to search,

  (b) a power of seizure to which this section applies or the power conferred by subsection (2) would entitle him, if he found it, to seize whatever it is that he has grounds for believing that thing to be or to contain, and

  (c) in all the circumstances it is not reasonably practicable for it to be determined, at the time and place of the search—

    (i) whether what he has found is something that he is entitled to seize, or

    (ii) the extent to which what he has found contains something that he is entitled to seize,

that person's powers of seizure shall include power under this section to seize so much of what he has found as it is necessary to remove from that place to enable that to be determined.

(2) Where—

  (a) a person carrying out a lawful search of any person finds something ("the seizable property") which he would be entitled to seize but for its being comprised in something else that he has (apart from this subsection) no power to seize,

  (b) the power under which that person would have power to seize the seizable property is a power to which this section applies, and

  (c) in all the circumstances it is not reasonably practicable for the seizable property to be separated, at the time and place of the search, from that in which it is comprised,

that person's powers of seizure shall include power under this section to seize both the seizable property and that from which it is not reasonably practicable to separate it.

1–70   (3) The factors to be taken into account in considering, for the purposes of this section, whether or not it is reasonably practicable, at the time and place of a search, for something to be determined, or for something to be separated from something else, shall be confined to the following—

  (a) how long it would take to carry out the determination or separation at that time and place;

  (b) the number of persons that would be required to carry out that determination or separation at that time and place within a reasonable period;

  (c) whether the determination or separation would (or would if carried out at that time and place) involve damage to property;

  (d) the apparatus or equipment that it would be necessary or appropriate to use for the carrying out of the determination or separation; and

30

(e) in the case of separation, whether the separation—

   (i) would be likely, or

   (ii) if carried out by the only means that are reasonably practicable at that time and place, would be likely,

to prejudice the use of some or all of the separated seizable property for a purpose for which something seized under the power in question is capable of being used.

(4) Section 19(6) of the 1984 Act and Article 21(6) of the *Police and Criminal Evidence (Northern Ireland) Order* 1989 (S.I. 1989 No. 1341 (N.I. 12)) (powers of seizure not to include power to seize anything a person has reasonable grounds for believing is legally privileged) shall not apply to the power of seizure conferred by subsection (2).

(5) This section applies to each of the powers of seizure specified in Part 2 of Schedule 1.

(14) Procedure for exercise of additional powers

Criminal Justice and Police Act 2001, s.52

Notice of exercise of power under s.50 or 51

52.—(1) Where a person exercises a power of seizure conferred by section 50, it shall (subject **1–71** to subsections (2) and (3)) be his duty, on doing so, to give to the occupier of the premises a written notice—

(a) specifying what has been seized in reliance on the powers conferred by that section;

(b) specifying the grounds on which those powers have been exercised;

(c) setting out the effect of subsections 59 to 61;

(d) specifying the name and address of the person to whom notice of an application under section 59(2) to the appropriate judicial authority in respect of any of the seized property must be given; and

(e) specifying the name and address of the person to whom an application may be made to be allowed to attend the initial examination required by any arrangements made for the purposes of section 53(2).

(2) Where it appears to the person exercising on any premises a power of seizure conferred by section 50—

(a) that the occupier of the premises is not present on the premises at the time of the exercise of the power, but

(b) that there is some other person present on the premises who is in charge of the premises,

subsection (1) of this section shall have effect as if it required the notice under that subsection to be given to that other person.

(3) Where it appears to the person exercising a power of seizure conferred by section 50 that there is no one present on the premises to whom he may give a notice for the purposes of complying with subsection (1) of this section, he shall, before leaving the premises, instead of complying with that subsection, attach a notice such as is mentioned in that subsection in a prominent place to the premises.

(4) Where a person exercises a power of seizure conferred by section 51 it shall be his **1–72** duty, on doing so, to give a written notice to the person from whom the seizure is made—

(a) specifying what has been seized in reliance on the powers conferred by that section;

(b) specifying the grounds on which those powers have been exercised;

(c) setting out the effect of subsections 59 to 61;

(d) specifying the name and address of the person to whom notice of any application under section 59(2) to the appropriate judicial authority in respect of any of the seized property must be given; and

(e) specifying the name and address of the person to whom an application may be made to be allowed to attend the initial examination required by any arrangements made for the purposes of section 53(2).

(5) The Secretary of State may by regulations made by statutory instrument, after consultation with the Scottish Ministers, provide that a person who exercises a power of

seizure conferred by section 50 shall be required to give a notice such as is mentioned in subsection (1) of this section to any person, or send it to any place, described in the regulations.

(6) Regulations under subsection (5) may make different provision for different cases.

(7) A statutory instrument containing regulations under subsection (5) shall be subject to annulment in pursuance of a resolution of either House of Parliament.

(15) Return or retention of seized property

Criminal Justice and Police Act 2001, ss.53–58

Examination and return of property seized under s.50 or 51

1–73   **53.**—(1) This section applies where anything has been seized under a power conferred by section 50 or 51.

(2) It shall be the duty of the person for the time being in possession of the seized property in consequence of the exercise of that power to secure that there are arrangements in force which (subject to section 61) ensure—

  (a) that an initial examination of the property is carried out as soon as reasonably practicable after the seizure;

  (b) that that examination is confined to whatever is necessary for determining how much of the property falls within subsection (3);

  (c) that anything which is found, on that examination, not to fall within subsection (3) is separated from the rest of the seized property and is returned as soon as reasonably practicable after the examination of all the seized property has been completed; and

  (d) that, until the initial examination of all the seized property has been completed and anything which does not fall within subsection (3) has been returned, the seized property is kept separate from anything seized under any other power.

(3) The seized property falls within this subsection to the extent only—

  (a) that it is property for which the person seizing it had power to search when he made the seizure but is not property the return of which is required by section 54;

  (b) that it is property the retention of which is authorised by section 56; or

  (c) that it is something which, in all the circumstances, it will not be reasonably practicable, following the examination, to separate from property falling within paragraph (a) or (b).

(4) In determining for the purposes of this section the earliest practicable time for the carrying out of an initial examination of the seized property, due regard shall be had to the desirability of allowing the person from whom it was seized, or a person with an interest in that property, an opportunity of being present or (if he chooses) of being represented at the examination.

(5) In this section, references to whether or not it is reasonably practicable to separate part of the seized property from the rest of it are references to whether or not it is reasonably practicable to do so without prejudicing the use of the rest of that property, or a part of it, for purposes for which (disregarding the part to be separated) the use of the whole or of a part of the rest of the property, if retained, would be lawful.

Obligation to return items subject to legal privilege

1–74   **54.**—(1) If, at any time after a seizure of anything has been made in exercise of a power of seizure to which this section applies—

  (a) it appears to the person for the time being having possession of the seized property in consequence of the seizure that the property—

    (i) is an item subject to legal privilege, or

    (ii) has such an item comprised in it,

    and

  (b) in a case where the item is comprised in something else which has been lawfully seized, it is not comprised in property falling within subsection (2),

it shall be the duty of that person to secure that the item is returned as soon as reasonably practicable after the seizure.

(2) Property in which an item subject to legal privilege is comprised falls within this subsection if—

(a) the whole or a part of the rest of the property is property falling within subsection (3) or property the retention of which is authorised by section 56; and

(b) in all the circumstances, it is not reasonably practicable for that item to be separated from the rest of that property (or, as the case may be, from that part of it) without prejudicing the use of the rest of that property, or that part of it, for purposes for which (disregarding that item) its use, if retained, would be lawful.

(3) Property falls within this subsection to the extent that it is property for which the person seizing it had power to search when he made the seizure, but is not property which is required to be returned under this section or section 55.

(4) This section applies—

(a) to the powers of seizure conferred by sections 50 and 51;

(b) to each of the powers of seizure specified in Parts 1 and 2 of Schedule 1; and

(c) to any power of seizure (not falling within paragraph (a) or (b)) conferred on a constable by or under any enactment, including an enactment passed after this Act.

Obligation to return excluded and special procedure material

55.—(1) If, at any time after a seizure of anything has been made in exercise of a power to which this section applies— **1–75**

(a) it appears to the person for the time being having possession of the seized property in consequence of the seizure that the property—

(i) is excluded material or special procedure material, or

(ii) has any excluded material or any special procedure material comprised in it,

(b) its retention is not authorised by section 56, and

(c) in a case where the material is comprised in something else which has been lawfully seized, it is not comprised in property falling within subsection (2) or (3),

it shall be the duty of that person to secure that the item is returned as soon as reasonably practicable after the seizure.

(2) Property in which any excluded material or special procedure material is comprised falls within this subsection if—

(a) the whole or a part of the rest of the property is property for which the person seizing it had power to search when he made the seizure but is not property the return of which is required by this section or section 54; and

(b) in all the circumstances, it is not reasonably practicable for that material to be separated from the rest of that property (or, as the case may be, from that part of it) without prejudicing the use of the rest of that property, or that part of it, for purposes for which (disregarding that material) its use, if retained, would be lawful.

(3) Property in which any excluded material or special procedure material is comprised falls within this subsection if—

(a) the whole or a part of the rest of the property is property the retention of which is authorised by section 56; and

(b) in all the circumstances, it is not reasonably practicable for that material to be separated from the rest of that property (or, as the case may be, from that part of it) without prejudicing the use of the rest of that property, or that part of it, for purposes for which (disregarding that material) its use, if retained, would be lawful.

(4) This section applies (subject to subsection (5)) to each of the powers of seizure specified in Part 3 of Schedule 1. **1–76**

(5) In its application to the powers of seizure conferred by—...

(b) section 56(5) of the *Drug Trafficking Act* 1994,

(c) [*Northern Ireland*], and

(d) section 352(4) of the *Proceeds of Crime Act* 2002,

this section shall have effect with the omission of every reference to special procedure material.

(6) In this section, except in its application to—

(a) the power of seizure conferred by section 8(2) of the 1984 Act,

(b) [*Northern Ireland*],

(c) each of the powers of seizure conferred by the provisions of paragraphs 1and 3 of Schedule 5 to the *Terrorism Act* 2000, and

(d) the power of seizure conferred by paragraphs 15 and 19 of Schedule 5 to that Act of 2000, so far only as the power in question is conferred by reference to paragraph 1 of that Schedule,

"special procedure material" means special procedure material consisting of documents or records other than documents.

[This section is printed as amended and repealed in part by the *Proceeds of Crime Act* 2002, ss.456 and 457, Sched. 11, para. 40(2), and Sched. 12.]

Property seized by constables etc.

1–77   **56.**—(1) The retention of—

(a) property seized on any premises by a constable who was lawfully on the premises,

(b) property seized on any premises by a relevant person who was on the premises accompanied by a constable, and

(c) property seized by a constable carrying out a lawful search of any person,

is authorised by this section if the property falls within subsection (2) or (3).

(2) Property falls within this subsection to the extent that there are reasonable grounds for believing—

(a) that it is property obtained in consequence of the commission of an offence; and

(b) that it is necessary for it to be retained in order to prevent its being concealed, lost, damaged, altered or destroyed.

(3) Property falls within this subsection to the extent that there are reasonable grounds for believing—

(a) that it is evidence in relation to any offence; and

(b) that it is necessary for it to be retained in order to prevent its being concealed, lost, altered or destroyed.

(4) Nothing in this section authorises the retention (except in pursuance of section 54(2)) of anything at any time when its return is required by section 54.

(4A) Subsection (1)(a) includes property seized on any premises—

(a) by a person authorised under section 16(2) of the 1984 Act to accompany a constable executing a warrant, or

(b) by a person accompanying a constable under section 2(6) of the *Criminal Justice Act* 1987 in the execution of a warrant under section 2(4) of that Act.

(5) In subsection (1)(b) the reference to a relevant person's being on any premises accompanied by a constable is a reference only to a person who was so on the premises under the authority of—

(a) a warrant under section 448 of the *Companies Act* 1985 authorising him to exercise together with a constable the powers conferred by subsection (3) of that section;

(b) [*Northern Ireland*];

(c)-(e) [*repealed by* Financial Services and Markets Act 2000 (Consequential Amendments and Repeals) *2001 (S.I. 2001 No. 3649), art. 364*].

[This section is printed as amended by the *Criminal Justice Act* 2003, s.12, and Sched. 1, para. 14.]

Retention of seized items

1–78   **57.**—(1) This section has effect in relation to the following provisions (which are about the retention of items which have been seized and are referred to in this section as "the relevant provisions")—

(a)-(r) [*see* post].

(2) The relevant provisions shall apply in relation to any property seized in exercise of a power conferred by section 50 or 51 as if the property had been seized under the power of seizure by reference to which the power under that section was exercised in relation to that property.

(3) Nothing in any of sections 53 to 56 authorises the retention of any property at any time when its retention would not (apart from the provisions of this Part) be authorised by the relevant provisions.

(4) Nothing in any of the relevant provisions authorises the retention of anything after an obligation to return it has arisen under this Part.

The provisions listed in subsection (1) (as amended) are: (a) the *PACE Act* 1984, s.22; (c) the *Taxes Management Act* 1970, s.20CC(3); (f) the *Companies Act* 1985, s.448(6); (g) the *Weights and Measures (Packaged Goods) Regulations* 2006 (S.I. 2006 No. 659), Sched. 7; (k) the *Human Fertilisation and Embryology Act* 1990, s.40(4); (l) the *Knives Act* 1997, s.5(4); (m) the *Data Protection Act* 1998, Sched. 9, para. 7(2); (n) the *Competition Act* 1998, s.28(7); (o) the *Financial Services and Markets Act* 2000, s.176(8); (p) the *Freedom of Information Act* 2000, Sched. 3, para. 7(2); (pa) the *Enterprise Act* 2002, s.227F; (q) the *Human Tissue Act* 2004, Sched. 5, para. 5(4); and (r) the *Animal Welfare Act* 2006, Sched. 7, para. 12(3). Paragraphs (b), (d) and (i) relate to Northern Ireland. Paragraphs (e), (h) and (j) were repealed by S.I. 2001 No. 3649 (*ante*, § 1–77), art. 364.

Person to whom seized property is to be returned

58.—(1) Where—   **1–79**
    (a) anything has been seized in exercise of any power of seizure, and
    (b) there is an obligation under this Part for the whole or any part of the seized property to be returned,
the obligation to return it shall (subject to the following provisions of this section) be an obligation to return it to the person from whom it was seized.

    (2) Where—
    (a) any person is obliged under this Part to return anything that has been seized to the person from whom it was seized, and
    (b) the person under that obligation is satisfied that some other person has a better right to that thing than the person from whom it was seized,
his duty to return it shall, instead, be a duty to return it to that other person or, as the case may be, to the person appearing to him to have the best right to the thing in question.

    (3) Where different persons claim to be entitled to the return of anything that is required to be returned under this Part, that thing may be retained for as long as is reasonably necessary for the determination in accordance with subsection (2) of the person to whom it must be returned.

    (4) References in this Part to the person from whom something has been seized, in relation to a case in which the power of seizure was exercisable by reason of that thing's having been found on any premises, are references to the occupier of the premises at the time of the seizure.

    (5) References in this section to the occupier of any premises at the time of a seizure, in relation to a case in which—
    (a) a notice in connection with the entry or search of the premises in question, or with the seizure, was given to a person appearing in the occupier's absence to be in charge of the premises, and
    (b) it is practicable, for the purpose of returning something that has been seized, to identify that person but not to identify the occupier of the premises,
are references to that person.

(16) Remedies and safeguards

Section 59 of the 2001 Act allows any person with a relevant interest in seized prop- **1–80** erty to make an application to the "appropriate judicial authority". By section 64, this means a Crown Court judge in England and Wales (or, in relation to specified statutes, the High Court). Where such an application is made, sections 60 and 61 provide for a duty to secure the seized property, and section 62 provides for inextricably linked property.

(17) Construction of Part 2 of the Criminal Justice and Police Act 2001

Criminal Justice and Police Act 2001, s.63

Copies

63.—(1) Subject to subsection (3)—   **1–81**

(a) in this Part, "seize" includes "take a copy of", and cognate expressions shall be construed accordingly;

(b) this Part shall apply as if any copy taken under any power to which any provision of this Part applies were the original of that of which it is a copy; and

(c) for the purposes of this Part, except sections 50 and 51, the powers mentioned in subsection (2) (which are powers to obtain hard copies etc. of information which is stored in electronic form) shall be treated as powers of seizure, and references to seizure and to seized property shall be construed accordingly.

(2) The powers mentioned in subsection (1)(c) are any powers which are conferred by—

(a)–(i) [*see* post].

(3) Subsection (1) does not apply to section 50(6) or 57.

The provisions listed in subsection (1) are: (a) the *PACE Act* 1984, ss.19(4) and 20; (c) the *Firearms Act* 1968, s.46(3); (d) the *Gaming Act* 1968, s.43(5)(aa); (e) the *Taxes Management Act* 1970, s.20C(3A); (f) the *Food Safety Act* 1990, s.32(6)(b); (h) the *Competition Act* 1998, s.28(2)(f); and (i) the *Nuclear Safeguards Act* 2000, s.8(2)(c). Paragraphs (b) and (g) relate to Northern Ireland.

For section 64 of the 2001 Act, see *ante*, § 1–80.

Criminal Justice and Police Act 2001, s.65

Meaning of "legal privilege"

1–82   **65.**—(1) Subject to the following provisions of this section, references in this Part to an item subject to legal privilege shall be construed—

(a) for the purposes of the application of this Part to England and Wales, in accordance with section 10 of the 1984 Act (meaning of "legal privilege");

(b) [*Scotland*];

(c) [*Northern Ireland.*]

(2) In relation to property which has been seized in exercise, or purported exercise, of—

(a) the power of seizure conferred by section 28(2) of the *Competition Act* 1998, or

(b) so much of any power of seizure conferred by section 50 as is exercisable by reference to that power,

references in this Part to an item subject to legal privilege shall be read as references to a privileged communication within the meaning of section 30 of that Act.

(3) [*Corresponds to subs. (2) with substitution of references to* Taxes Management Act *1970, s.20C and s.20C(4A).*]

(3A) In relation to property which has been seized in exercise, or purported exercise, of—

(a) the power of seizure conferred by section 352(4) of the *Proceeds of Crime Act* 2002, or

(b) so much of any power of seizure conferred by section 50 as is exercisable by reference to that power,

references in this Part to an item subject to legal privilege shall be read as references to privileged material within the meaning of section 354(2) of that Act.

(4) An item which is, or is comprised in, property which has been seized in exercise, or purported exercise, of the power of seizure conferred by section 448(3) of the *Companies Act* 1985 shall be taken for the purposes of this Part to be an item subject to legal privilege if, and only if, the seizure of that item was in contravention of section 452(2) of that Act (privileged information).

(5) [*Northern Ireland.*]

(6) [*Corresponds to subs. (4) with substitution of references to* Timeshare Act *1992, Sched. 2, para. 3(2) and para. 3(4).*]

(7) [*Corresponds to subs. (4) with substitution of references to* Data Protection Act *1998, Sched. 9, para. 1 and para. 9.*]

(8) [*Corresponds to subs. (4) with substitution of references to* Freedom of Information Act *2000, Sched. 3, para. 1 and para. 9.*]

(8A) [*Corresponds to subs. (4) with substitution of references to* Enterprise Act *2002, s.227C and s.227B(4).*]

(9) An item which is, or is comprised in, property which has been seized in exercise, or purported exercise, of so much of any power of seizure conferred by section 50 as is exercisable by reference to a power of seizure conferred by—

(a)-(f) [*the powers of seizure mentioned in subss. (4) to (8A) respectively*],

shall be taken for the purposes of this Part to be an item subject to legal privilege if, and only if, the item would have been taken for the purposes of this Part to be an item subject to legal privilege had it been seized under the power of seizure by reference to which the power conferred by section 50 was exercised.

[This section is printed as amended by the *Proceeds of Crime Act* 2002, s.456, and Sched. 11, para. 40(5); and the *Enterprise Act 2002 (Amendment) Regulations* 2006 (S.I. 2006 No. 3663).]

Criminal Justice and Police Act 2001, s.66

General interpretation of Part 2

66.—(1) In this Part—

1–83

"appropriate judicial authority" has the meaning given by section 64;

"documents" includes information recorded in any form;

"item subject to legal privilege" shall be construed in accordance with section 65;

"premises" includes any vehicle, stall or moveable structure (including an offshore installation) and any other place whatever, whether or not occupied as land;

"offshore installation" has the same meaning as in the *Mineral Workings (Offshore Installations) Act* 1971;

"return", in relation to seized property, shall be construed in accordance with section 58, and cognate expressions shall be construed accordingly;;

"seize", and cognate expressions, shall be construed in accordance with section 63(1) and subsection (5) below;;

"seized property", in relation to any exercise of a power of seizure, means (subject to subsection (5)) anything seized in exercise of that power; and

"vehicle" includes any vessel, aircraft or hovercraft.

(2) In this Part references, in relation to a time when seized property is in any person's possession in consequence of a seizure ("the relevant time"), to something for which the person making the seizure had power to search shall be construed—

(a) where the seizure was made on the occasion of a search carried out on the authority of a warrant, as including anything of the description of things the presence or suspected presence of which provided grounds for the issue of the warrant;

(b) where the property was seized in the course of a search on the occasion of which it would have been lawful for the person carrying out the search to seize anything which on that occasion was believed by him to be, or appeared to him to be, of a particular description, as including—

(i) anything which at the relevant time is believed by the person in possession of the seized property, or (as the case may be) appears to him, to be of that description; and

(ii) anything which is in fact of that description;

(c) where the property was seized in the course of a search on the occasion of which it would have been lawful for the person carrying out the search to seize anything which there were on that occasion reasonable grounds for believing was of a particular description, as including—

(i) anything which there are at the relevant time reasonable grounds for believing is of that description; and

(ii) anything which is in fact of that description;

(d) where the property was seized in the course of a search to which neither paragraph (b) nor paragraph (c) applies, as including anything which is of a description of things which, on the occasion of the search, it would have been lawful for the person carrying it out to seize otherwise than under section 50and 51; and

(e) where the property was seized on the occasion of a search authorised under section 82 of the *Terrorism Act* 2000 (seizure of items suspected to have been, or to be intended to be, used in commission of certain offences), as including anything—

      (i) which is or has been, or is or was intended to be, used in the commission of an offence such as is mentioned in subsection (3)(a) or (b) of that section; or

      (ii) which at the relevant time the person who is in possession of the seized property reasonably suspects is something falling within sub-paragraph (i).

(3) For the purpose of determining in accordance with subsection (2), in relation to any time, whether or to what extent property seized on the occasion of a search authorised under section 9 of the *Official Secrets Act* 1911 (seizure of evidence of offences under that Act having been or being about to be committed) is something for which the person making the seizure had power to search, subsection (1) of that section shall be construed—

    (a) as if the reference in that subsection to evidence of an offence under that Act being about to be committed were a reference to evidence of such an offence having been, at the time of the seizure, about to be committed; and

    (b) as if the reference in that subsection to reasonable ground for suspecting that such an offence is about to be committed were a reference to reasonable ground for suspecting that at the time of the seizure such an offence was about to be committed.

(4) References in subsection (2) to a search include references to any activities authorised by virtue of any of the following—

    (a)-(n) [*see* post].

(5) References in this Part to a power of seizure include references to each of the powers to take possession of items under—

    (b)-(i) [*see* post],

and references in this Part to seizure and to seized property shall be construed accordingly.

(6) In this Part, so far as it applies to England and Wales —

    (a) references to excluded material shall be construed in accordance with section 11 of the 1984 Act (meaning of "excluded material"); and

    (b) references to special procedure material shall be construed in accordance with section 14 of that Act (meaning of "special procedure material").

(7) [*Northern Ireland.*]

(8) References in this Part to any item or material being comprised in other property include references to its being mixed with that other property.

(9) [*Northern Ireland.*]

The provisions listed in subsection (4) (as amended) are: (a) the *Trade Descriptions Act* 1968, s.28(1); (b) the *Fair Trading Act* 1973, s.29(1); (c) the *Prices Act* 1974, Sched., para. 9; (d) the *Consumer Credit Act* 1974, s.162(1); (e) the *Estate Agents Act* 1979, s.11(1); (g) the *Weights and Measures Act* 1985, s.79, and the *Weights and Measures (Packaged Goods) Regulations* 2006 (S.I. 2006 No. 659), Sched. 7; (h) the *Consumer Protection Act* 1987, s.29; (j) the *Food Safety Act* 1990, s.35(2); (k) the *Property Misdescriptions Act* 1991, Sched., para. 3; (m) the *Timeshare Act* 1992, Sched. 2, para. 3; (ma) the *Enterprise Act* 2002, s.227C; (n) the *Human Tissue Act* 2004, Sched. 5, para. 2; (o) the *General Product Safety Regulations* 2005 (S.I. 2005 No. 1803), reg. 22; and (p) the *Animal Welfare Act* 2006, ss. 26(1), 27(1), 28(1) and 29(1). Paragraphs (f), (i) and (l) relate to Northern Ireland.

The provisions listed in subsection (5) are: (b) the *Companies Act* 1985, s.448(3); (f) the *Criminal Justice Act* 1987, s.2(5); (g) the *Human Fertilisation and Embryology Act* 1990, s.40(2); (h) the *Competition Act* 1998, s.28(2)(c); and (i) the *Financial Services and Markets Act* 2000, s.176(5). Paragraphs (a), (c) and (e) were repealed by S.I. 2001 No. 3649, art. 364 (*ante*, § 1–77). Paragraph (d) relates to Northern Ireland.

(18)　Powers of seizure under 2001 Act (Schedule 1)

Powers to which section 50 applies (list 1)

1–84   Schedule 1, Part 1, lists the powers of seizure conferred by the following enactments: (1) the *PACE Act* 1984, Pts II and III; (3) the *Official Secrets Act* 1911, s.9(1); (4) the *Children and Young Persons (Harmful Publications) Act* 1955, s.3(1); (5) the *Obscene Publications Act* 1959, s.3(1) and (2); (8) the *Firearms Act* 1968, s.46; (9) the *Trade*

Descriptions Act 1968, s.28(1)(c) and (d); (10) the *Theft Act* 1968, s.26(3); (13) the *Taxes Management Act* 1970, s.20C; (14) the *Misuse of Drugs Act* 1971, s.23(2) and (3); (15) the *Immigration Act 1971*, ss. 28D(3), 28E(5) and 28F(6); (16) the *Fair Trading Act* 1973, s.29(1)(c) and (d); (17) the *Biological Weapons Act* 1974, s.4(1)(b), (c) and (d); (18) the *Prices Act* 1974, Sched., para. 9(2); (19) the *Consumer Credit Act* 1974, s.162(1)(c) and (d); (21) the *Protection of Children Act* 1978, s.4(2); (23) the *Customs and Excise Management Act* 1979, s.118C(4); (24) the *Estate Agents Act* 1979, s.11(1)(c); (25) the *Indecent Displays (Control) Act* 1981, s.2(3); (26) the *Forgery and Counterfeiting Act* 1981, ss. 7(1) and 24(1); (27), (28), (29) the *Betting and Gaming Duties Act* 1981, Sched. 1, para. 16(2), Sched. 3, para. 17(2), and Sched. 4, para. 17(2); (34) the *Video Recordings Act* 1984, s.17(2); (35) the *Companies Act* 1985, s.448(3); (36) the *Weights and Measures Act* 1985, s.79(2)(b); (39) the *Protection of Military Remains Act* 1986, s.6(3); (41) the *Greater London Council (General Powers) Act* 1986, s.12; (44) the *Criminal Justice Act* 1987, s.2(5); (45) the *Consumer Protection Act* 1987, s.29(4), (5) and (6); (48) the *Copyright, Designs and Patents Act* 1988, ss. 109(4), 200(3A) and 297B(4); (50) the *Food Safety Act* 1990, s.32(6); (51) the *Computer Misuse Act* 1990, s.14(4); (52) the *Human Fertilisation and Embryology Act* 1990, s.40(2); (53) the *Property Misdescriptions Act* 1991, Sched., para. 3(3); (54) the *Dangerous Dogs Act* 1991, s.5(2); (56) the *Timeshare Act* 1992, Sched. 2, para. 3(2); (56A) the *Charities Act* 1993, s.31A(3); (57) the *Finance Act* 1994, Sched. 7, para. 4(3); (58) the *Value Added Tax Act* 1994, Sched. 11, para. 10(3); (58A) the *Trade Marks Act* 1994, s.92A(4); (59) the *Drug Trafficking Act* 1994, s.56(5); (60) the *Chemical Weapons Act* 1996, s.29(2)(c), (d) and (e); (61) the *Finance Act* 1996, Sched. 5, para. 5(2); (63) the *Knives Act* 1997, s.5(2); (64) the *Nuclear Explosions (Prohibitions and Inspections) Act* 1998, s.10(2)(c), (d) and (e); (65) the *Data Protection Act* 1998, Sched. 9, para. 1; (66) the *Landmines Act* 1998, s.18(3)(c), (d) and (e); (67) the *Competition Act* 1998, s.28(2); (68) the *Nuclear Safeguards Act* 2000, s.8(2); (69) the *Financial Services and Markets Act* 2000, s.176(5); (70) the *Terrorism Act* 2000, s.82(3); (71) *ibid.*, Sched. 5, paras 1, 3, 11, 15 and 19; (72) the *Finance Act* 2000, s.130(2); (73) the *Freedom of Information Act* 2000, Sched. 3, para. 1; (73A) the *Proceeds of Crime Act* 2002, s.352; (73A [*sic*]) the *International Criminal Court Act* 2001, Sched. 5, para. 9; (73B) the *Enterprise Act* 2002, s.194(2); (73BA) the *Enterprise Act* 2002, s.227C; (73C) the *Crime (International Co-operation) Act* 2003, ss.17 and 22; (73D) the *Extradition Act* 2003, ss.156(5), 160(5), 161(4), 162(6) and (7), and 164 (6) and (7); (73E) the *Human Tissue Act* 2004, s.56, and Sched. 6, para. 5(1) and(2); (73E [*sic*]) the *Licensing Act* 2003, s.90; (73F) the *Serious Organised Crime and Police Act* 2005, s.66; (73F [*sic*]) the *Gambling Act* 2005, s.317; (73G) the *General Product Safety Regulations* 2005 (S.I. 2005 No. 1803), reg. 22(4)-(6); (73G [*sic*]) the *Weights and Measures (Packaged Goods) Regulations* 2006 (S.I. 2006 No. 659), Sched. 5, para. 4; (73H) the *Terrorism Act* 2006, s.28; and (73I) the *Animal Welfare Act* 2006, Sched. 2 and para. 10(2)(j).

　　Paragraph 7 was repealed by the *Licensing Act* 2003, s.199, and Sched. 7. Paragraphs 6, 11 and 20 were repealed by the *Gambling Act* 2005, s.356, and Sched. 16, para. 18. Paragraphs 32, 40 and 43 were repealed by S.I. 2001 No. 3649, art. 364 (*ante*, § 1–77). Paragraph 37 was repealed by the *Weights and Measures (Packaged Goods) Regulations* 2006 (S.I. 2006 No. 659), reg. 1(2), and Sched. 1, Pt 2, paras (24) and (27)(b). Paragraph 47 was repealed by the *Proceeds of Crime Act* 2002, s.457 and Sched. 12. Paragraph 49 was repealed by the *Crime (International Co-operation) Act* 2003, s.91, and Sched. 6. Paragraph 56A was inserted by the *Charities Act* 2006, s.26(2). The first paragraph 73A was inserted by the *Proceeds of Crime Act* 2002, s.456, and Sched. 11, para. 40(6). Paragraph 73(B) (renumbered by a correction slip) was inserted by the *Enterprise Act* 2006, s.194(5). Paragraph 73(BA) was inserted by the *Enterprise Act 2002 (Amendment) Regulations* 2006 (S.I. 2006 No. 3363), regs. 24 and 28. Paragraph 48 was amended, and paragraph 58A and the second paragraph 73A were inserted, by the *Criminal Justice and Police Act 2001 (Powers of Seizure) Order* 2003 (S.I. 2003 No. 934). Paragraphs 73C and 73D were inserted by the *Crime (International Co-operation) Act* 2003, s.26(3), and the *Extradition Act* 2003, s.165(2), respectively.

Paragraph 73E was inserted by the *Human Tissue Act* 2004, s.56, and Sched. 6, para. 5(1) and (4). A second paragraph 73E (renumbered erroneously by the *Gambling Act* 2005, s.356, and Sched. 16, para. 18) was inserted by the *Licensing Act* 2003, s.198, and Sched. 6, paras 119 and 128(a). Paragraph 73F was inserted by the *Serious Organised Crime and Police Act 2005*, s.68. A second paragraph 73F was inserted by the *Gambling Act* 2005, s.356, and Sched. 16, para. 18. The first paragraph 73G was inserted by the *General Product Safety Regulations* 2005 (S.I. 2005 No. 1803), reg. 47(3). A second paragraph 73G was inserted by S.I. 2006 No. 659 (*ante*), reg. 1(2), and Sched. 1, Pt 2, paras (24) and (27)(c). Paragraph 73H was inserted by the *Terrorism Act* 2006, s.28(6)(a). Paragraph 73I was inserted by the *Animal Welfare Act* 2006, s.64, and Sched. 3, para. 14.

Paragraphs 2, 12, 22, 30, 31, 33, 38, 42, 46, 55 and 62 relate to Northern Ireland.

Powers to which section 51 applies (list 2)

1–85   Schedule 1, Part 2, lists the powers of seizure conferred by the following enactments: (74) the *PACE Act* 1984, Pt III; (76) as (8) in list 1; (77) as (14) in list 1; (78) the *Immigration Act* 1971, s.28G(7); (79) as (17) in list 1; (81) the *Criminal Justice and Public Order Act* 1994, s.139(10); (82) the *Terrorism Act* 2000, s.43(4); (83) as (71) in list 1; and (83A) the *Extradition Act* 2003, s.163(6) and (7) (inserted by s.165(3) of that Act). Paragraphs 75 and 80 relate to Northern Ireland.

Powers to which section 55 applies (list 3)

1–86   Schedule 1, Part 3, lists the powers of seizure conferred by the following enactments: (84) the *PACE Act* 1984, s.8(2); (86) as (3) in list 1; (87) as (4) in list 1; (88) as (5) in list (1); (91) as (8) in list 1; (92) as (10) in list 1; (95) the *Immigration Act* 1971, s.28D(3); (96) as (17) in list 1; (98) as (21) in list 1; (100) as (25) in list 1; (101) as (26) in list 1; (103) as (34) in list 1; (106) as (48) in list 1; (107) as (51) in list 1; (107A) as (58A) in list 1; (108) as (59) in list 1; (109) (i) the *Terrorism Act* 2000, Sched. 5, paras 1 and 3, and (ii) *ibid.*, paras 15 and 19, but so far only as the power in question is conferred by reference to para. 1 of that Schedule; (110) the *Proceeds of Crime Act* 2002, s.352(4); (111) the *Licensing Act* 2003, s.90; (112) the *Gambling Act* 2005, s.317; (113) the *Terrorism Act* 2006, s.28. Paragraphs 85, 94, 99, 102 and 104 relate to Northern Ireland.

Paragraphs 89, 93 and 97 were repealed by the *Gambling Act* 2005, s.356, and Sched. 16, para. 18. Paragraph 90 was repealed, and paragraph 111 (as renumbered by the *Gambling Act, ibid.*) inserted, by the *Licensing Act* 2003, ss.198 and 199, and Scheds 6, paras 119 and 128(b), and 7. Paragraph 105 was repealed, and paragraph 110 was added, by the *Proceeds of Crime Act* 2002, ss.456 and 457, and Scheds 11, para. 40(7), and 12. Paragraph 106 was amended, and paragraph 107A was inserted, by S.I. 2003 No. 934 (*ante*). Paragraph 112 was inserted by the *Gambling Act, ibid.* Paragraph 113 was inserted by the *Terrorism Act* 2006, s.28(6)(b).

(19) Interception of communications and surveillance

Police Act 1997, ss.91–108 and Regulation of Investigatory Powers Act 2000, ss.5–11

1–87   Part III of the *Police Act* 1997, ss.91–108, allows for authorisation of covert entry upon and interference with property or with wireless telegraphy by the police, Revenue and Customs and others. The Act in part attempts to meet the astonishment expressed by Lord Nolan in *R. v. Khan (Sultan)* [1997] A.C. 558 at 582, HL, at the lack of a statutory system regulating the use of surveillance devices by the police. Such a system has existed in this field in relation to the intelligence services since the *Security Services Act* 1989 and the *Intelligence Services Act* 1994. The powers contained in the Act are supplementary to existing police powers: section 93(7).

1–88   All forms of covert surveillance which do not involve covert entry upon or interference with property or wireless telegraphy came under the *Regulation of Investigatory*

Powers Act 2000. The Act is an attempt to put covert policing on a statutory footing and an implicit acceptance that a non-statutory basis for such activity would breach the *Human Rights Act* 1998: see *Hansard*, H.C., Vol. 345, col. 677, and the remarks of the Home Office Minister in the press notice accompanying the draft codes (Notice 291/ 2000). The Act distinguishes between directed (section 26(2)) and intrusive surveillance (section 26(3)–(5)). "Directed surveillance" is defined as covert surveillance that is undertaken in relation to a specific investigation or a specific operation which is likely to result in the obtaining of private information about a person. "Intrusive surveillance" is defined as covert surveillance carried out in relation to anything taking place on residential premises. The Act also provides for the use of "covert human intelligence sources". This is defined as a person who establishes or maintains a personal relationship with a person for the covert purpose of using the relationship to obtain information or provide access to information to another person or covertly disclosing information obtained by the use of such a relationship or as a consequence of the existence of such a relationship (section 26(8)); and it has been held to included an undercover police officer: *Hardy* [2003] 1 Cr.App.R. 30, CA. The protections for any suspect are greater in respect of intrusive surveillance than in respect of directed surveillance or the use of covert human intelligence sources.

All conduct defined in section 26 will be lawful provided it is carried out in relation to the authorisation to which it relates (section 27). The Act does not make a failure to obtain an authorisation a criminal offence, but the explanatory notes accompanying the Act (para. 180) recognise that such a failure may mean that the law enforcement agency had acted unlawfully under the *Human Rights Act* 1998, s.6. Such covert activity must be both necessary and proportionate (sections 28, 29 and 32) and the Act sets out specific criteria. The Act sets up a system of authorisations and supervision by a number of commissioners and tribunals. There are three Codes of Practice: the *Regulation of Investigatory Powers (Interception of Communications): Code of Practice) Order* 2002 (S.I. 2002 No. 1693); the *Regulation of Investigatory Powers (Covert Human Intelligence Sources: Code of Practice) Order* 2002 (S.I. 2002 No. 1932); and the *Regulation of Investigatory Powers (Covert Surveillance: Code of Practice) Order* 2002 (S.I. 2002 No. 1933). Full texts may be found on the website at www.homeoffice.gov.uk. S.I. 2002 No. 1933 covers not only activity under Part II of the 2000 Act, but also activity under Part III of the 1997 Act, replacing the Code of Practice issued under section 101. As to the importance of compliance with the Act and the Codes, see *Harmes and Crane* [2006] 7 *Archbold News* 1, CA.

Neither the 1997 Act nor the 2000 Act purports to deal with the question of the admissibility of evidence obtained under their provisions. Their relevance is confined to the fact that they provide a framework of law by which the legality of the actions of the police may be judged; where evidence has been unlawfully obtained, this is a matter to be taken into account by a court in deciding whether it is fair to admit it (*PACE Act* 1984, s.78, *post*, § 10–140). It is the effect on the fairness of the proceedings that is important, rather than the illegality of the police's conduct: Lord Nolan in *Khan*, *ante*, at p. 582. Fairness, however, is not to be confined to procedural fairness, and evidence may be excluded because it has been obtained by unfair means: per Lord Nicholls (paras 11 and 12) and Lord Scott (para. 122) in *Looseley* [2002] 1 Cr.App.R. 29, HL.

(20) Serious Organised Crime and Police Act 2005, ss. 60–70 (Chapter 1)

Disclosure notices—summary

Sections 60 to 70 of the 2005 Act are headed "Investigatory Powers of DPP, etc.". Section 60 provides for the DPP, the Director of Revenue and Customs Prosecutions, and the Lord Advocate to give "disclosure notices" in connection with the investigation of offences to which Chapter 1 of Part 2 applies. Each may delegate such powers. Section 61 lists the offences to which the powers apply. They are "lifestyle offences" under the *Proceeds of Crime Act* 2002, offences under the *Terrorism Act* 2000, ss.15 to 18, any

1–89

offence which is a qualifying offence (as to which see subs. (2)) under the *Customs and Excise Management Act* 1979, s.170, the *Value Added Tax Act* 1994, s.72, the *Theft Act* 1968, s.17, or any qualifying common law offence of cheating in relation to the public revenue, or an attempt or conspiracy to commit any such offence.

Section 62 provides for a disclosure notice (as to which, see section 62(3)) to be given to a person where it appears to the investigating authority that there are reasonable grounds for suspecting that an offence to which Chapter 1 applies has been committed, that any person has information which relates to a matter relevant to the investigation of that offence, and that there are reasonable grounds for believing that information which may be provided by that person in compliance with a disclosure notice is likely to be of substantial value (whether or not by itself) to that investigation. Section 63 contains provision as to the production of documents where a disclosure notice has been given. Section 64 contains restrictions on the requirement to produce information (privileged information, "excluded material" within the *PACE Act* 1984, information subject to obligation of confidence, etc.). Section 65 restricts the use of statements made in response to a requirement imposed under section 62 or 63. The statement may not be used against the maker in criminal proceedings, except in the specified circumstances. Sections 66 and 67 provide for enforcement. Section 66 sets out the procedure for the issue and execution of a warrant in order to seize documents subject to a disclosure notice. Section 67(1) makes it a summary offence for a person, without reasonable excuse, to fail to comply with a requirement imposed on him under section 62 or 63. Section 67(2) provides for an either way offence where a person, in purported compliance with any such requirement, knowingly or recklessly makes a statement that is false or misleading in a material particular. Section 67(3) creates a summary offence of wilfully obstructing any person in the exercise of any rights conferred by a warrant under section 66. Section 68 inserts a reference to the power of seizure under section 66 into Part 1 of Schedule 1 to the *Criminal Justice and Police Act* 2001 (*ante*, § 1–84). Section 69 prescribes the manner in which a disclosure notice may be given. Section 70 provides for the interpretation of Chapter 1.

Commencement

1–90 Sections 60 to 70 came into force on April 1, 2006: *Serious Organised Crime and Police Act 2005 (Commencement No. 1, Transitional and Transitory Provisions) Order* 2005 (S.I. 2005 No. 1521).

Legislation

Investigatory powers of DPP etc.
1–91   **60.**—(1) This Chapter confers powers on—
  (a) the Director of Public Prosecutions,
  (b) the Director of Revenue and Customs Prosecutions, and
  (c) [*Scotland*]
  (d) [*Northern Ireland*],
in relation to the giving of disclosure notices in connection with the investigation of offences to which this Chapter applies or in connection with a terrorist investigation.

(2) The Director of Public Prosecutions may, to such extent as he may determine, delegate the exercise of his powers under this Chapter to a Crown prosecutor.

(3) The Director of Revenue and Customs Prosecutions may, to such extent as he may determine, delegate the exercise of his powers under this Chapter to a Revenue and Customs Prosecutor.

(4) [*Scotland.*]

(4A) [*Northern Ireland.*]

(5) In this Chapter "the Investigating Authority" means —
  (a) the Director of Public Prosecutions,
  (b) the Director of Revenue and Customs Prosecutions, or
  (c) [*Scotland*]
  (d) [*Northern Ireland.*]

(6) But, in circumstances where the powers of any of those persons are exercisable by any other person by virtue of subsection (2), (3) (4) or (4A), references to "the Investigating Authority" accordingly include any such other person.

(7) In this Chapter "terrorist investigation" means an investigation of—

(a) the commission, preparation or instigation of acts of terrorism,

(b) any act or omission which appears to have been for the purposes of terrorism and which consists in or involves the commission, preparation or instigation of an offence, or

(c) the commission, preparation or instigation of an offence under the *Terrorism Act* 2000 or under Part 1 of the *Terrorism Act* 2006 other than an offence under section 1 or 2 of that Act.

[This section is printed as amended by the *Terrorism Act* 2006, s.33(1) and (2); and the *Northern Ireland (Miscellaneous Provisions) Act* 2006, s.26(2), and Sched. 3, paras 1 and 2.]

Offences to which this Chapter applies

61.—(1) This Chapter applies to the following offences— **1–92**

(a) any offence listed in Schedule 2 to the *Proceeds of Crime Act* 2002 (lifestyle offences: England and Wales);

(b) [*Scotland*];

(ba) [*Northern Ireland*];

(c) any offence under sections 15 to 18 of the *Terrorism Act* 2000 (offences relating to fund-raising, money laundering etc.);

(d) any offence under section 170 of the *Customs and Excise Management Act* 1979 (fraudulent evasion of duty) or section 72 of the *Value Added Tax Act* 1994 (offences relating to VAT) which is a qualifying offence;

(e) any offence under section 17 of the *Theft Act* 1968 or [*Northern Ireland*] (false accounting), or any offence at common law of cheating in relation to the public revenue, which is a qualifying offence;

(f) any offence under section 1 of the *Criminal Attempts Act* 1981 or [*Northern Ireland, Scotland*] of attempting to commit any offence in paragraph (c) or any offence in paragraph (d) or (e) which is a qualifying offence;

(g) any offence under section 1 of the Criminal Law Act 1977 or [*Northern Ireland, Scotland*] of conspiracy to commit any offence in paragraph (c) or any offence in paragraph (d) or (e) which is a qualifying offence;

(h) in England and Wales—

(i) any common law offence of bribery;

(ii) any offence under section 1 of the *Public Bodies Corrupt Practices Act* 1889 (corruption in office);

(iii) the first two offences under section 1 of the *Prevention of Corruption Act* 1906 (bribes obtained by or given to agents).

(2) For the purposes of subsection (1) an offence in paragraph (d) or (e) of that subsection is a qualifying offence if the Investigating Authority certifies that in his opinion—

(a) in the case of an offence in paragraph (d) or an offence of cheating the public revenue, the offence involved or would have involved a loss, or potential loss, to the public revenue of an amount not less than £5,000;

(b) in the case of an offence under section 17 of the *Theft Act* 1968 or [*Northern Ireland*], the offence involved or would have involved a loss or gain, or potential loss or gain, of an amount not less than £5,000.

(3) A document purporting to be a certificate under subsection (2) is to be received in evidence and treated as such a certificate unless the contrary is proved.

(4), (5) [*Provision for amendment of subss. (1) and (2) by order.*]

[This section is printed as amended by the *Serious Organised Crime and Police Act 2005 (Amendment of Section 61(1)) Order* 2006 (S.I. 2006 No. 1629); and by the *Northern Ireland (Miscellaneous Provisions) Act* 2006, s.26(2), and Sched. 3, paras 1 and 3.]

Disclosure notices

62.—(1) If it appears to the Investigating Authority— **1–93**

   (a) that there are reasonable grounds for suspecting that an offence to which this Chapter applies has been committed,

   (b) that any person has information (whether or not contained in a document) which relates to a matter relevant to the investigation of that offence, and

   (c) that there are reasonable grounds for believing that information which may be provided by that person in compliance with a disclosure notice is likely to be of substantial value (whether or not by itself) to that investigation,

he may give, or authorise an appropriate person to give, a disclosure notice to that person.

   (1A) If it appears to the Investigating Authority—

   (a) that any person has information (whether or not contained in a document) which relates to a matter relevant to a terrorist investigation, and

   (b) that there are reasonable grounds for believing that information which may be provided by that person in compliance with a disclosure notice is likely to be of substantial value (whether or not by itself) to that investigation

he may give, or authorise an appropriate person to give, a disclosure notice to that person.

   (2) In this Chapter "appropriate person" means—

   (a) a constable,

   (b) a member of the staff of SOCA who is for the time being designated under section 43, or

   (c) an officer of Revenue and Customs.

[*Saving in relation to Northern Ireland.*]

   (3) In this Chapter "disclosure notice" means a notice in writing requiring the person to whom it is given to do all or any of the following things in accordance with the specified requirements, namely—

   (a) answer questions with respect to any matter relevant to the investigation;

   (b) provide information with respect to any such matter as is specified in the notice;

   (c) produce such documents, or documents of such descriptions, relevant to the investigation as are specified in the notice.

   (4) In subsection (3) "the specified requirements" means such requirements specified in the disclosure notice as relate to—

   (a) the time at or by which,

   (b) the place at which, or

   (c) the manner in which,

the person to whom the notice is given is to do any of the things mentioned in paragraphs (a) to (c) of that subsection; and those requirements may include a requirement to do any of those things at once.

   (5) A disclosure notice must be signed or counter-signed by the Investigating Authority.

   (6) This section has effect subject to section 64 (restrictions on requiring information etc.).

[This section is printed as amended by the *Terrorism Act* 2006, s.33(3); and the *Northern Ireland (Miscellaneous Provisions) Act* 2006, s.26(2), and Sched. 3, paras 1 and 4.]

Production of documents

1–94   **63.**—(1) This section applies where a disclosure notice has been given under section 62.

   (2) An authorised person may—

   (a) take copies of or extracts from any documents produced in compliance with the notice, and

   (b) require the person producing them to provide an explanation of any of them.

   (3) Documents so produced may be retained for so long as the Investigating Authority considers that it is necessary to retain them (rather than copies of them) in connection with the investigation for the purposes of which the disclosure notice was given.

   (4) If the Investigating Authority has reasonable grounds for believing—

   (a) that any such documents may have to be produced for the purposes of any legal proceedings, and

   (b) that they might otherwise be unavailable for those purposes,

they may be retained until the proceedings are concluded.

   (5) If a person who is required by a disclosure notice to produce any documents does

not produce the documents in compliance with the notice, an authorised person may require that person to state, to the best of his knowledge and belief, where they are.

(6) In this section "authorised person" means any appropriate person who either—

(a) is the person by whom the notice was given, or

(b) is authorised by the Investigating Authority for the purposes of this section.

(7) This section has effect subject to section 64 (restrictions on requiring information etc.).

Restrictions on requiring information etc.

64.—(1) A person may not be required under section 62 or 63—   **1–95**

(a) to answer any privileged question,

(b) to provide any privileged information, or

(c) to produce any privileged document,

except that a lawyer may be required to provide the name and address of a client of his.

(2) A "privileged question" is a question which the person would be entitled to refuse to answer on grounds of legal professional privilege in proceedings in the High Court.

(3) "Privileged information" is information which the person would be entitled to refuse to provide on grounds of legal professional privilege in such proceedings.

(4) A "privileged document" is a document which the person would be entitled to re-fuse to produce on grounds of legal professional privilege in such proceedings.

(5) A person may not be required under section 62 to produce any excluded material (as defined by section 11 of the *Police and Criminal Evidence Act* 1984 or [*Northern Ireland*]).

(6), (7) [*Scotland.*]

(8) A person may not be required under section 62 or 63 to disclose any information or produce any document in respect of which he owes an obligation of confidence by virtue of carrying on any banking business, unless—

(a) the person to whom the obligation of confidence is owed consents to the disclosure or production, or

(b) the requirement is made by, or in accordance with a specific authorisation given by, the Investigating Authority.

(9) Subject to the preceding provisions, any requirement under section 62 or 63 has ef-fect despite any restriction on disclosure (however imposed).

[This section is printed as amended by the *Northern Ireland (Miscellaneous Provi-sions) Act* 2006, s.26(2), and Sched. 3, paras 1 and 5.]

Restrictions on use of statements

65.—(1) A statement made by a person in response to a requirement imposed under section   **1–96**
62 or 63 ("the relevant statement") may not be used in evidence against him in any criminal proceedings unless subsection (2) or (3) applies.

(2) This subsection applies where the person is being prosecuted—

(a) for an offence under section 67 of this Act, or

(b) for an offence under section 5 of the *Perjury Act* 1911 (false statements made on oath otherwise than in judicial proceedings or made otherwise than on oath), or

(c) for an offence under [*Scotland*] or at common law for an offence of attempting to pervert the course, or defeat the ends, of justice.

(3) This subsection applies where the person is being prosecuted for some other of-fence and—

(a) the person, when giving evidence in the proceedings, makes a statement incon-sistent with the relevant statement, and

(b) in the proceedings evidence relating to the relevant statement is adduced, or a question about it is asked, by or on behalf of the person.

Power to enter and seize documents

66.—(1) A justice of the peace may issue a warrant under this section if, on an information on   **1–97**
oath laid by the Investigating Authority, he is satisfied—

(a) that any of the conditions mentioned in subsection (2) is met in relation to any documents of a description specified in the information, and

(b) that the documents are on premises so specified.

(2) The conditions are—

(a) that a person has been required by a disclosure notice to produce the documents but has not done so;

(b) that it is not practicable to give a disclosure notice requiring their production;

(c) that giving such a notice might seriously prejudice the investigation of an offence to which this Chapter applies.

(3) A warrant under this section is a warrant authorising an appropriate person named in it—

(a) to enter and search the premises, using such force as is reasonably necessary;

(b) to take possession of any documents appearing to be documents of a description specified in the information, or to take any other steps which appear to be necessary for preserving, or preventing interference with, any such documents;

(c) in the case of any such documents consisting of information recorded otherwise than in legible form, to take possession of any computer disk or other electronic storage device which appears to contain the information in question, or to take any other steps which appear to be necessary for preserving, or preventing interference with, that information;

(d) to take copies of or extracts from any documents or information falling within paragraph (b) or (c);

(e) to require any person on the premises to provide an explanation of any such documents or information or to state where any such documents or information may be found;

(f) to require any such person to give the appropriate person such assistance as he may reasonably require for the taking of copies or extracts as mentioned in paragraph (d).

(4) A person executing a warrant under this section may take other persons with him, if it appears to him to be necessary to do so.

(5) A warrant under this section must, if so required, be produced for inspection by the owner or occupier of the premises or anyone acting on his behalf.

(6) If the premises are unoccupied or the occupier is temporarily absent, a person entering the premises under the authority of a warrant under this section must leave the premises as effectively secured against trespassers as he found them.

(7) Where possession of any document or device is taken under this section—

(a) the document may be retained for so long as the Investigating Authority considers that it is necessary to retain it (rather than a copy of it) in connection with the investigation for the purposes of which the warrant was sought, or

(b) the device may be retained for so long as he considers that it is necessary to retain it in connection with that investigation,

as the case may be.

(8) If the Investigating Authority has reasonable grounds for believing—

(a) that any such document or device may have to be produced for the purposes of any legal proceedings, and

(b) that it might otherwise be unavailable for those purposes,

it may be retained until the proceedings are concluded.

(9) Nothing in this section authorises a person to take possession of, or make copies of or take extracts from, any document or information which, by virtue of section 64, could not be required to be produced or disclosed under section 62 or 63.

(10), (11) [*Scotland, Northern Ireland.*]

[This section is printed as amended by the *Northern Ireland (Miscellaneous Provisions) Act* 2006, s.26(2), and Sched. 3, paras 1 and 7.]

Offences in connection with disclosure notices or search warrants

1–98   **67.**—(1) A person commits an offence if, without reasonable excuse, he fails to comply with any requirement imposed on him under section 62 or 63.

(2) A person commits an offence if, in purported compliance with any requirement imposed on him under section 62 or 63—

(a) he makes a statement which is false or misleading, and

(b) he either knows that it is false or misleading or is reckless as to whether it is false or misleading.

"False or misleading" means false or misleading in a material particular.

(3) A person commits an offence if he wilfully obstructs any person in the exercise of any rights conferred by a warrant under section 66.

(4) A person guilty of an offence under subsection (1) or (3) is liable on summary conviction—

(a) to imprisonment for a term not exceeding 51 weeks, or

(b) to a fine not exceeding level 5 on the standard scale,

or to both.

(5) A person guilty of an offence under subsection (2) is liable—

(a) on conviction on indictment, to imprisonment for a term not exceeding two years or to a fine, or to both;

(b) on summary conviction, to imprisonment for a term not exceeding 12 months or to a fine not exceeding the statutory maximum, or to both.

(6), (7) [*Scotland, Northern Ireland.*]

[This section is printed as amended by the *Northern Ireland (Miscellaneous Provisions) Act* 2006, s.26(2), and Sched. 3, paras 1 and 8.]

Procedure applicable to search warrants

68. [*Amends* Criminal Justice and Police Act *2001, Sched. 1, ante,* § 1–84.]   **1–99**

Manner in which disclosure notice may be given

69.—(1) This section provides for the manner in which a disclosure notice may be given   **1–100**
under section 62.

(2) The notice may be given to a person by—

(a) delivering it to him,

(b) leaving it at his proper address,

(c) sending it by post to him at that address.

(3) The notice may be given—

(a) in the case of a body corporate, to the secretary or clerk of that body;

(b) in the case of a partnership, to a partner or a person having the control or management of the partnership business;

(c) in the case of an unincorporated association (other than a partnership), to an officer of the association.

(4) For the purposes of this section and section 7 of the *Interpretation Act* 1978 (service of documents by post) in its application to this section, the proper address of a person is his usual or last-known address (whether residential or otherwise), except that—

(a) in the case of a body corporate or its secretary or clerk, it is the address of the registered office of that body or its principal office in the United Kingdom,

(b) in the case of a partnership, a partner or a person having the control or management of the partnership business, it is that of the principal office of the partnership in the United Kingdom, and

(c) in the case of an unincorporated association (other than a partnership) or an officer of the association, it is that of the principal office of the association in the United Kingdom

(5) This section does not apply to Scotland.

Interpretation of Chapter 1

70.—(1) In this Chapter   **1–101**

"act of terrorism" includes anything constituting an action taken for the purposes of terrorism, within the meaning of the *Terrorism Act* 2000 (see section 1(5) of that Act);

"appropriate person" has the meaning given by section 62(2);

"the Investigating Authority" is to be construed in accordance with section 60(5) and (6);

"disclosure notice" has the meaning given by section 62(3);

"document" includes information recorded otherwise than in legible form;

"terrorism" has the same meaning as in the *Terrorism Act* 2000 (see section 1(1) to (4) of that Act);

"terrorist investigation" has the meaning given by section 60(7).

(2) In relation to information recorded otherwise than in legible form, any reference in this Chapter to the production of documents is a reference to the production of a copy of the information in legible form.

[This section is printed as amended by the *Terrorism Act* 2006, s.33(4).]

E. Arrest and Detention

(1) Introduction

1–102   In general, an arrest is constituted by a physical seizure or touching of the arrested person's body, with a view to his detention: see, *e.g. Brosch* [1988] Crim.L.R. 743, CA. But there may also be an arrest by mere words: see, *e.g. Alderson v. Booth* [1969] 2 Q.B. 216; 53 Cr.App.R.301, DC (arrest is constituted when any form of words is used which is calculated to bring to the suspect's notice, and does so, that he is under compulsion, and he thereafter submits to that compulsion); and *Inwood* (1973) 57 Cr.App.R. 529, CA (no magic formula, only the obligation to make it plain to the suspect by what is said and done that he is no longer a free man; different procedures might be needed according to the person's age, ethnic origin, knowledge of English, intellectual qualities, physical or mental disabilities).

A constable may use reasonable force, if necessary, to effect an arrest: the *PACE Act* 1984, s.117, *post*, § 1–119.

An arrest is unlawful unless at the time of the arrest or as soon as practicable after the arrest the arrested person is informed that he is under arrest and of the ground of the arrest, regardless of whether the fact of arrest is obvious (*PACE Act* 1984, s.28 (*post*, § 1–114)). This is subject to an exception in the case of a person who escapes (section 28(5)).

1–103   Powers of arrest, whether by police or any other persons are governed by statute and common law. Any arrest has to have a legal basis or it may amount to a criminal offence or give rise to civil liability.

The main police powers of arrest are—

1. Arrest without a warrant under the *PACE Act* 1984, Pt III (ss.24-33), *post*, §§ 1–106 *et seq.*
2. Arrest without a warrant under other statutes, either specifically preserved by the 1984 Act (s.26(2) and Sched. 2, *post*, § 1–111), or enacted subsequently (*e.g.* the *Public Order Act* 1986, s.5(4)).
3. Arrest with a warrant issued by a magistrate or district judge—*Magistrates' Courts Act* 1980, s.1 (*post* § 4–76).
4. Arrest with or without a warrant under *Criminal Justice and Public Order Act* 1994, Pt X (Cross-border enforcement).
5. Common law power of arrest for breach of the peace.

Code G (*post*, Appendix A) applies to the police's powers of arrest under the 1984 Act, s.24, as substituted by the *Serious Organised Crime and Police Act* 2005.

Consequences of arrest

1–104   Where a private citizen makes a lawful arrest either at common law or under statute, he should take the arrested person before a justice of the peace or a police officer, not necessarily forthwith, but as soon as reasonably possible: *John Lewis & Co Ltd v. Tims* [1952] A.C. 676, HL.

As to the obligations of a constable when he arrests someone for an offence, or takes someone into custody after he has been arrested for an offence by a person other than a constable, at any place other than at a police station, see section 30 of the *PACE Act* 1984 (*post*, § 1–122).

A person who is at a police station under arrest must be further arrested where it appears that if he were released he would be liable to arrest for some other offence (*PACE Act* 1984, s.31, *post*, § 1–129).

Section 32 provides for the search of a person upon arrest and for entry and search of any premises in which he was when arrested or immediately before he was arrested (*post*, § 1–130).

For the conditions and duration of the detention of an arrested person, see the *PACE Act* 1984, Pt IV, ss.34-52. Sections 34 to 46 are found *post*, §§ 1–133 *et seq.* For bail after arrest, see section 47, *post*, § 5–100. For the questioning and treatment of persons in custody, see ss. 53-65, *post*, §§ 1–150 *et seq.*

(2) Reasonable grounds for suspecting

See *ante*, § 1–12.   **1–105**

(3) Arrest without warrant

Police and Criminal Evidence Act 1984, s.24

Arrest without warrant: constables

24.—(1) A constable may arrest without a warrant—   **1–106**
    (a) anyone who is about to commit an offence;
    (b) anyone who is in the act of committing an offence;
    (c) anyone whom he has reasonable grounds for suspecting to be about to commit an offence;
    (d) anyone whom he has reasonable grounds for suspecting to be committing an offence.

(2) If a constable has reasonable grounds for suspecting that an offence has been committed, he may arrest without a warrant anyone whom he has reasonable grounds to suspect of being guilty of it.

(3) If an offence has been committed, a constable may arrest without a warrant—
    (a) anyone who is guilty of the offence;
    (b) anyone whom he has reasonable grounds for suspecting to be guilty of it.

(4) But the power of summary arrest conferred by subsection (1), (2) or (3) is exercisable only if the constable has reasonable grounds for believing that for any of the reasons mentioned in subsection (5) it is necessary to arrest the person in question.

(5) The reasons are—
    (a) to enable the name of the person in question to be ascertained (in the case where the constable does not know, and cannot readily ascertain, the person's name, or has reasonable grounds for doubting whether a name given by the person as his name is his real name);
    (b) correspondingly as regards the person's address;
    (c) to prevent the person in question—
        (i) causing physical injury to himself or any other person;
        (ii) suffering physical injury;
        (iii) causing loss of or damage to property;
        (iv) committing an offence against public decency (subject to subsection (6)); or
        (v) causing an unlawful obstruction of the highway;
    (d) to protect a child or other vulnerable person from the person in question;
    (e) to allow the prompt and effective investigation of the offence or of the conduct of the person in question;
    (f) to prevent any prosecution for the offence from being hindered by the disappearance of the person in question.

(6) Subsection (5)(c)(iv) applies only where members of the public going about their normal business cannot reasonably be expected to avoid the person in question.

[This section was substituted by the *Serious Organised Crime and Police Act* 2005, s.110(1) and (4).]

Although the power of arrest exists for any offence it may be exercised only in the cir- **1–107**
cumstances listed and also only when the officer has reasonable grounds to believe that it is necessary to arrest a person. The reasons that give rise to necessity are listed exhaustively in section 24(5).

The arresting officer must consider whether immediate arrest is necessary within the criteria or whether a summons or fixed penalty notice may be more appropriate and practical. With respect to subsections (d) and (e) the circumstances of the suspect and the nature of the offence must be considered. See Code G—Appendix A.

1–108   As to "reasonable grounds for suspecting", see *ante*, § 1–12.

(4) Arrest without a warrant by other persons

Police and Criminal Evidence Act 1984, s.24A

Arrest without warrant: other persons

1–109   **24A.**—(1) A person other than a constable may arrest without a warrant—

    (a) anyone who is in the act of committing an indictable offence;

    (b) anyone whom he has reasonable grounds for suspecting to be committing an indictable offence.

(2) Where an indictable offence has been committed, a person other than a constable may arrest without a warrant—

    (a) anyone who is guilty of the offence;

    (b) anyone whom he has reasonable grounds for suspecting to be guilty of it.

(3) But the power of summary arrest conferred by subsection (1) or (2) is exercisable only if—

    (a) the person making the arrest has reasonable grounds for believing that for any of the reasons mentioned in subsection (4) it is necessary to arrest the person in question; and

    (b) it appears to the person making the arrest that it is not reasonably practicable for a constable to make it instead.

(4) The reasons are to prevent the person in question—

    (a) causing physical injury to himself or any other person;

    (b) suffering physical injury;

    (c) causing loss of or damage to property; or

    (d) making off before a constable can assume responsibility for him.

[(5) This section does not apply in relation to an offence under Part 3 or 3A of the *Public Order Act* 1986.]

[This section was inserted by the *Serious Organised Crime and Police Act* 2005, s.110(1) and (4). Subsection (5) is inserted, as from a day to be appointed, by the *Racial and Religious Hatred Act* 2006, s.2.]

As to "reasonable grounds for suspecting", see *ante*, § 1–12.

As from January 1, 2007 (*Electoral Administration Act 2006 (Commencement No. 2, Transitional and Savings Provisions) Order* 2006 (S.I. 2006 No. 3412)), section 71 of the *Electoral Administration Act* 2006 disapplies section 24A in relation to the arrest of a person inside a polling station who has committed or is suspected of committing an offence contrary to section 60 (personation) of the *Representation of the People Act* 1983.

1–110   Where the defendant was acquitted at trial of the substantive offence it was held to invalidate the arrest by a citizen under the predecessor of section 24A(2) because no arrestable (now indictable) offence had been committed: *Self* (1992) 95 Cr.App.R. 42; *Walters v. W.H. Smith & Son Ltd* [1914] 1. K.B. 595.

(5) Other statutory powers of arrest without warrant

Police and Criminal Evidence Act 1984, s.26, Sched. 2

Repeal of statutory powers of arrest without warrant or order

1–111   **26.**—(1) Subject to subsection (2) below, so much of any Act (including a local Act) passed before this Act as enables a constable—

    (a) to arrest a person for an offence without a warrant; or

(b) to arrest a person otherwise than for an offence without a warrant or an order of a court,

shall cease to have effect.

(2) Nothing in subsection (1) above affects the enactments specified in Schedule 2 to this Act.

SCHEDULE 2

PRESERVED POWERS OF ARREST

Section 2 of the *Emergency Powers Act* 1920. **1–112**

Section 49 of the *Prison Act* 1952.

Section 13 of the *Visiting Forces Act* 1952.

Sections 186 and 190B of the Army Act *1955*.

Sections 186 and 190B of the Air Force Act *1955*.

Sections 104 and 105 of the Naval Discipline Act *1957*.

Section 32 of the *Children and Young Persons Act* 1969.

Section 24(2) of the *Immigration Act* 1971 and paragraphs 17, 24 and 33 of Schedule 2 and paragraph 7 of Schedule 3 to that Act.

Section 7 of the *Bail Act* 1976.

Schedule 5 to the *Reserve Forces Act* 1980.

Sections 18, 35(10), 36(8), 38(7), 136(1) and 138 of the *Mental Health Act* 1983.

Section 5(5) of the *Repatriation of Prisoners Act* 1984.

[This Schedule is printed as amended, and repealed in part, by the *Representation of the People Act* 1985, s.25(1); the *Prevention of Terrorism (Temporary Provisions) Act* 1989, s.25(2) and Sched. 9, Pt I; the *Road Traffic (Consequential Provisions) Act* 1988, s.4 and Sched. 1; the *Children Act* 1989, s.108(5) and (7), Sched. 13 and Sched. 15; the *Serious Organised Crime and Police Act* 2005, ss. 111 and 174(2), Sched. 7, para. 24(1) and (4), and Sched. 17; and the *Electoral Administration Act* 2006, s.74(2), and Sched. 2. The entries in relation to the *Army Act*, the *Air Force Act* and the *Naval Discipline Act* are repealed as from a day to be appointed: *Armed Forces Act* 2006, s.378(2), and Sched. 17.]

(6) Arrest for failing to comply with fingerprinting requirement

Police and Criminal Evidence Act 1984, s.27

Fingerprinting of certain offenders

27.—(1) If a person— **1–113**

(a) has been convicted of a recordable offence;

(b) has not at any time been in police detention for the offence; and

(c) has not had his fingerprints taken—

(i) in the course of the investigation of the offence by the police; or

(ii) since the conviction,

any constable may at any time not later than one month after the date of the conviction require him to attend a police station in order that his fingerprints may be taken.

(1A) Where a person convicted of a recordable offence has already had his fingerprints taken as mentioned in paragraph (c) of subsection (1) above, that fact (together with any time when he has been in police detention for the offence) shall be disregarded for the purposes of that subsection if—

(a) the fingerprints taken on the previous occasion do not constitute a complete set of his fingerprints; or

(b) some or all of the fingerprints taken on the previous occasion are not of sufficient quality to allow satisfactory analysis, comparison or matching.

(1B) Subsections (1) and (1A) above apply—

(a) where a person has been given a caution in respect of a recordable offence which, at the time of the caution, he has admitted, or

(b) where a person has been warned or reprimanded under section 65 of the *Crime and Disorder Act* 1998 for a recordable offence, as they apply where a person has been convicted of an offence, and references in this section to a conviction shall be construed accordingly.

(2) A requirement under subsection (1) above—

(a) shall give the person a period of at least 7 days within which he must so attend; and

(b) may direct him to so attend at a specified time of day or between specified times of day.

(3) Any constable may arrest without warrant a person who has failed to comply with a requirement under subsection (1) above.

(4) The Secretary of State may by regulations make provision for recording in national police records convictions for such offences as are specified in the regulations.

(4A) [*Repealed by* Criminal Justice and Police Act *2001, s.137 and Sched. 7, Pt II.*]

(5) [*Making of regulations.*]

[Subsections (1A) and (1B) were inserted by the *Criminal Justice and Police Act* 2001, s.78(1).]

By section 118(1) of the 1984 Act, "recordable offence" means any offence under which regulations to section 27, *ante*, apply. The *National Police Records (Recordable Offences) Regulations* 2000 (S.I. 2000 No. 1139) (as amended by the *National Police Records (Recordable Offences) (Amendment) Regulations* 2003 (S.I. 2003 No. 2823)) were made under subsection (4). They provide that there may be recorded in national police records convictions for, or cautions, reprimands and warnings given in respect of, offences punishable with imprisonment or for an offence included in a list of over 40 non-imprisonable offences. The reference to offences punishable with imprisonment is to be construed without regard to any prohibition or restriction imposed by or under any enactment on the punishment of young offenders. The regulations also provide that where a person's convictions are recordable, there may also be recorded his convictions for any other offences in the same proceedings.

For the meaning of "police detention", see *post*, § 1–132 (summarising section 118(2) of the 1984 Act).

The actual taking of fingerprints is provided for by section 61, *post*, § 1–156.

(7) Information to be given on arrest

Police and Criminal Evidence Act 1984, s.28

Information to be given on arrest

1–114   **28.**—(1) Subject to subsection (5) below, where a person is arrested, otherwise than by being informed that he is under arrest, the arrest is not lawful unless the person arrested is informed that he is under arrest as soon as is practicable after his arrest.

(2) Where a person is arrested by a constable, subsection (1) above applies regardless of whether the fact of the arrest is obvious.

(3) Subject to subsection (5) below, no arrest is lawful unless the person arrested is informed of the ground for the arrest at the time of, or as soon as is practicable after, the arrest.

(4) Where a person is arrested by a constable, subsection (3) above applies regardless of whether the ground for the arrest is obvious.

(5) Nothing in this section is to be taken to require a person to be informed—

(a) that he is under arrest; or

(b) of the ground for the arrest,

if it was not reasonably practicable for him to be so informed by reason of his having escaped from arrest before the information could be given.

1–115   In *Taylor v. Chief Constable of Thames Valley Police* [2004] 1 W.L.R. 3155, CA (Civ. Div.), the court said that section 28(3) reflects the common law as laid down in *Christie v. Leachinsky* [1947] A.C. 573, HL, and explained that the underlying rationale is that a person is entitled to know why he is being arrested; one reason for that is that he should have the opportunity of explaining any misunderstanding, or of calling attention to others for whom he might have been mistaken. The court said that the modern approach to section 28(3) is to ask whether, having regard to all the circumstances, the person arrested was told in simple, non-technical language that he could understand, the essential legal and factual grounds for his arrest (*Fox, Campbell and Hartley v. U.K.* (1990) 13 E.H.R.R. 157, ECtHR, para. 40, considering Article 5(2) of the European Convention); in future wrongful arrest cases, it will be unnecessary and undesirable to consider authority besides *Fox, ante*; thus, upon making an arrest for violent disorder, it had been sufficient to refer to "violent disorder" with a reference to the time and place; there had been no need to specify the precise way in which the arrestee was said to be taking part in the disorder.

As to there being no intent to prosecute the suspect for the offence for which he is ar- **1–116** rested, see *ante*, § 1–12. As to the unfairness of arresting and questioning for a lesser offence, when in fact the investigation relates to a more serious offence arising out of the same incident, see *Kirk* [2000] 1 Cr.App.R. 400, CA.

In *Wheatley v. Lodge* [1971] 1 W.L.R. 29, DC, it was held that a police officer arresting a deaf person or somebody who could not speak English had to do what a reasonable person would do in the circumstances.

Where an arrest is unlawful, on the ground that the accused has not been told what **1–117** acts are alleged to have constituted the offence for which he was arrested, this unlawfulness ceases when he is informed of the details at the police station: *Kulynycz* [1971] 1 Q.B. 367; 55 Cr.App.R. 34, CA. Where the initial arrest is valid and at the time of the arrest it is impracticable, because of the accused's physical resistance to the arrest, to inform him of the reason for the arrest, the initial arrest does not become invalid retrospectively when the officer fails to state the ground of arrest at the police station: *DPP v. Hawkins* (1988) 88 Cr.App.R. 166, DC (applied in *Blench v. DPP* (2004) 69 J.C.L. 98, DC).

In *Dawes v. DPP* [1995] 1 Cr.App.R. 65, DC, the defendant was detained by the **1–118** automatic activation of the door locks inside a car specially adapted by the police as a trap. It was held on appeal that he was arrested the moment that he was trapped inside the car, and that at that point the police were obliged to inform him of his arrest and his grounds of arrest as soon as practicable. Once the police discharged this duty, the arrest was made lawful. On the facts, the police had fulfilled the duty, but the court recommended that in future the police fix such cars with a device which automatically tells the offender that he has been arrested and why.

On arrest there is also a duty to caution in accordance with Code C, para. 10 either immediately prior to arrest or on arrest. Paragraph 10.1 explains when the caution must be given if there are grounds to suspect an offence may have been committed. Questions may be put to establish identity or ownership of items or in furtherance of the conduct of a search but once there are grounds to suspect an offence the person must be cautioned before any further questions about his involvement in the offence are put.

The requirement of cautioning before questioning does not extend to the asking of routine questions designed to establish ownership of an item. In *Senior* (2004) 148 S.J. 300 it was held that it was not necessary to caution a suspect before asking questions about the ownership of a suitcase known to contain drugs. Such a question had no element of surprise or unfairness but once a person identified himself as the owner the caution should be given. Also a person who came to the airport to meet a passenger who was suspected of carrying drugs in their luggage did not need to be cautioned before being asked questions. Such preliminary questions were designed to determine whether there were any reasonable objective grounds to suspect any involvement in the drug smuggling. Once suspicions arise the caution is necessary: *Perpont (Hutil Percena)* [2004] EWCA Crim 2562. See also *Kemsley v. DPP* [2004] WL 229280 where it was held that questions put about who was driving a car at the scene of an accident were an attempt to elicit information and a caution was not necessary. Similarly in *Ridehalgh v. DPP* [2005] EWHC 1100, Admin, it was held that the existence of grounds to suspect an offence is a pre-condition to the necessity to give a caution before questioning. Where an officer had asked questions about whether a defendant had been drinking alcohol and whether he had driven it was open to the magistrates to find that such questions were posed before the officer had grounds to suspect an offence of drinking and driving and so the provisions of Code C requiring a caution did not apply at that stage.

The words of the caution are—

"You do not have to say anything. But it may harm your defence if you do not mention when questioned something which you later rely on in court. Anything you do say may be given in evidence."

Minor deviations are not a breach of the code as long as the sense of it is preserved.

(8) Use of force in making arrest

Police and Criminal Evidence Act 1984, s.117

Power of constable to use reasonable force

1–119   **117.** Where any provision of this Act—

(a) confers a power on a constable; and

(b) does not provide that the power may only be exercised with the consent of some person, other than a police officer,

the officer may use reasonable force, if necessary, in the exercise of the power.

(9) Voluntary attendance at police station

Police and Criminal Evidence Act 1984, s.29

Voluntary attendance at police station, etc.

1–120   **29.** Where for the purpose of assisting with an investigation a person attends voluntarily at a police station or at any other place where a constable is present or accompanies a constable to a police station or any such other place without having been arrested—

(a) he shall be entitled to leave at will unless he is placed under arrest;

(b) he shall be informed at once that he is under arrest if a decision is taken by a constable to prevent him from leaving at will.

(10) Arrest elsewhere than at police station

1–121   Section 4 of the *Criminal Justice Act* 2003 introduces a scheme of "street bail" which allows for police officers to arrest a person on the street or elsewhere and then to grant bail without the need to escort them to a police station. No conditions may be imposed on the bail and the person involved is under a duty to attend later at a police station. Written notice must be given before the person is released which records the offence for which he has been arrested and the grounds of arrest. Failure to answer to street bail may lead to arrest without warrant. Section 4 amends section 30 of the *Police and Criminal Evidence Act* 1984 and adds sections 30A–30D to cover the arrangements for "street bail".

As from April 1, 2007 (*Police and Justice Act 2006 (Commencement No. 2, Transitional and Savings Provisions) Order* 2007 (S.I. 2007 No. 709)), the *Police and Justice Act* 2006, s.10 and Sched. 6, inserts sections 30CA and 30CB (dealing respectively with variation of section 30A bail by police and the court) after section 30C.

As from June 29, 2007 (*Police and Justice Act 2006 (Commencement No. 3) Order* 2007 (S.I. 2007 No. 1614)), sections 24A (arrest for failure to comply with conditions attached to conditional caution) and 24B (application of *PACE* provisions) are inserted into the *Criminal Justice Act* 2003 by the *Police and Justice Act* 2006, s.18(1). Where a person is arrested under section 24A, section 24B(1) and (2) applies various provisions of the 1984 Act, with such modifications as are necessary, to the arrest. Sections 30 to 30D (including new sections 30CA and 30CB) of the 1984 Act are all such provisions.

Police and Criminal Evidence Act 1984, ss.30–30D

Arrest elsewhere than at police station

30.—(1) Subsection (1A) applies where a person is, at any place other than a police station— **1–122**

 (a) arrested by a constable for an offence,or

 (b) taken into custody by a constable after being arrested for an offence by a person other than a constable.

(1A) The person must be taken by a constable to a police station as soon as practicable after the arrest.

(1B) Subsection (1A) has effect subject to section 30A (release on bail) and subsection (7) (release without bail).

(2) Subject to subsections (3) and (5) below, the police station to which an arrested person is taken under subsection (1A) above shall be a designated police station.

(3) A constable to whom this subsection applies may take an arrested person to any police station unless it appears to the constable that it may be necessary to keep the arrested person in police detention for more than six hours.

(4) Subsection (3) above applies—

 (a) to a constable who is working in a locality covered by a police station which is not a designated police station; and

 (b) to a constable belonging to a body of constables maintained by an authority other than a police authority.

(5) Any constable may take an arrested person to any police station if—

 (a) either of the following conditions is satisfied—

  (i) the constable has arrested him without the assistance of any other constable and no other constable is available to assist him;

  (ii) the constable has taken him into custody from a person other than a constable without the assistance of any other constable and no other constable is available to assist him; and

 (b) it appears to the constable that he will be unable to take the arrested person to a designated police station without the arrested person injuring himself, the constable or some other person.

(6) If the first police station to which an arrested person is taken after his arrest is not a designated police station, he shall be taken to a designated police station not more than six hours after his arrival at the first police station unless he is released previously.

(7) A person arrested by a constable at any place other than a police station must be released without bail if the condition in subsection (7A) is satisfied.

(7A) The condition is that, at any time before the person arrested reaches a police station, a constable is satisfied that there are no grounds for keeping him under arrest or releasing him on bail under section 30A.

(8) A constable who releases a person under subsection (7) above shall record the fact that he has done so.

(9) The constable shall make the record as soon as is practicable after the release.

(10) Nothing in subsection (1A) or in section 30A prevents a constable delaying taking a person to a police station or releasing him on bail if the condition in subsection (10A) is satisfied.

(10A) The condition is that the presence of the person at a place (other than a police station) is necessary in order to carry out such investigations as it is reasonable to carry out immediately.

(11) Where there is any such delay the reasons for the delay must be recorded when the person first arrives at the police station or (as the case may be) is released on bail.

(12) Nothing in subsection (1A) above shall be taken to affect—

 (a) paragraphs 16(3) or 18(1) of Schedule 2 to the *Immigration Act* 1971;

 (b) section 34(1) of the *Criminal Justice Act* 1972; or

 (c) any provision of the *Terrorism Act* 2000.

(13) Nothing in subsection (10) above shall be taken to affect paragraph 18(3) of Schedule 2 to the *Immigration Act* 1971.

[This section is printed as amended by the *Prevention of Terrorism (Temporary Provisions) Act* 1989, s.25(1), and Sched. 8; the *Terrorism Act* 2000, s.125, and Sched. 15, para. 5(2); and the *Criminal Justice Act* 2003, s.4(1)-(6).]

In *Khan* [1993] Crim.L.R. 54, the Court of Appeal warned police and customs officers that, even if they were justified (by virtue of section 30(10)) in delaying taking a subject to a police station in order to carry out a search, they should not abuse the opportunity by asking a lengthy series of questions to circumvent the codes of practice and that, if they did, they risked having the answers excluded under section 78. The warning was not heeded in *Raphaie* [1996] Crim.L.R. 812, CA, where the police asked a series of questions during a search lasting one-and-three-quarter hours. It was held that in so behaving the officers abused the power given to them by section 30(10), particularly as most of the admissions attributed to the appellant during the search were not relevant to it.

Bail elsewhere than at police station

1–123   **30A.**—(1) A constable may release on bail a person who is arrested or taken into custody in the circumstances mentioned in section 30(1).

(2) A person may be released on bail under subsection (1) at any time before he arrives at a police station.

(3) A person released on bail under subsection (1) must be required to attend a police station.

(3A) Where a constable releases a person on bail under subsection (1)—

(a) no recognizance for the person's surrender to custody shall be taken from the person,

(b) no security for the person's surrender to custody shall be taken from the person or from anyone else on the person's behalf,

(c) the person shall not be required to provide a surety or sureties for his surrender to custody, and

(d) no requirement to reside in a bail hostel may be imposed as a condition of bail.

(3B) Subject to subsection (3A), where a constable releases a person on bail under subsection (1) the constable may impose, as conditions of the bail, such requirements as appear to the constable to be necessary—

(a) to secure that the person surrenders to custody,

(b) to secure that the person does not commit an offence while on bail,

(c) to secure that the person does not interfere with witnesses or otherwise obstruct the course of justice, whether in relation to himself or any other person, or

(d) for the person's own protection or, if the person is under the age of 17, for the person's own welfare or in the person's own interests.

(4) Where a person is released on bail under subsection (1), a requirement may be imposed on the person as a condition of bail only under the preceding provisions of this section.

(5) The police station which the person is required to attend may be any police station.

[Section 30A was inserted by the *Criminal Justice Act* 2003, s.4. It is printed as amended by the *Police and Justice Act* 2006, s.10(1), and Sched. 6, paras 1 and 2.]

Bail under section 30A: notices

1–124   **30B.**—(1) Where a constable grants bail to a person under section 30A, he must give that person a notice in writing before he is released.

(2) The notice must state—

(a) the offence for which he was arrested, and

(b) the ground on which he was arrested.

(3) The notice must inform him that he is required to attend a police station.

(4) It may also specify the police station which he is required to attend and the time when he is required to attend.

(4A) If the person is granted bail subject to conditions under section 30A(3B), the notice also—

(a) must specify the requirements imposed by those conditions,

(b) must explain the opportunities under sections 30CA(1) and 30CB(1) for variation of those conditions, and

(c) if it does not specify the police station at which the person is required to attend, must specify a police station at which the person may make a request under section 30CA(1)(b).

(5) If the notice does not include the information mentioned in subsection (4), the person must subsequently be given a further notice in writing which contains that information.

(6) The person may be required to attend a different police station from that specified in the notice under subsection (1) or (5) or to attend at a different time.

(7) He must be given notice in writing of any such change as is mentioned in subsection (6) but more than one such notice may be given to him.

[Section 30B was inserted by the *Criminal Justice Act* 2003, s.4. It is printed as amended by the *Police and Justice Act* 2006, s.10(1), and Sched. 6, paras 1 and 3.]

Bail under section 30A: supplemental

30C.—(1) A person who has been required to attend a police station is not required to do so **1–125** if he is given notice in writing that his attendance is no longer required.

(2) If a person is required to attend a police station which is not a designated police station he must be—

(a) released, or

(b) taken to a designated police station,

not more than six hours after his arrival.

(3) Nothing in the *Bail Act* 1976 applies in relation to bail under section 30A.

(4) Nothing in section 30A or 30B or in this section prevents the re-arrest without a warrant of a person released on bail under section 30A if new evidence justifying a further arrest has come to light since his release.

[Section 30C was inserted by the *Criminal Justice Act* 2003, s.4.]

Bail under section 30A: variation of conditions by police

30CA.—(1) Where a person released on bail under section 30A(1) is on bail subject to condi- **1–126** tions—

(a) a relevant officer at the police station at which the person is required to attend, or

(b) where no notice under section 30B specifying that police station has been given to the person, a relevant officer at the police station specified under section 30B(4A)(c), may, at the request of the person but subject to subsection (2), vary the conditions.

(2) On any subsequent request made in respect of the same grant of bail, subsection (1) confers power to vary the conditions of the bail only if the request is based on information that, in the case of the previous request or each previous request, was not available to the relevant officer considering that previous request when he was considering it.

(3) Where conditions of bail granted to a person under section 30A(1) are varied under subsection (1)—

(a) paragraphs (a) to (d) of section 30A(3A) apply,

(b) requirements imposed by the conditions as so varied must be requirements that appear to the relevant officer varying the conditions to be necessary for any of the purposes mentioned in paragraphs (a) to (d) of section 30A(3B), and

(c) the relevant officer who varies the conditions must give the person notice in writing of the variation.

(4) Power under subsection (1) to vary conditions is, subject to subsection (3)(a) and (b), power—

(a) to vary or rescind any of the conditions, and

(b) to impose further conditions.

(5) In this section "relevant officer", in relation to a designated police station, means a custody officer but, in relation to any other police station—

(a) means a constable, or a person designated as a staff custody officer under section 38 of the *Police Reform Act* 2002, who is not involved in the investigation of the offence for which the person making the request under subsection (1) was under arrest when granted bail under section 30A(1), if such a constable or officer is readily available, and

(b) if no such constable or officer is readily available—
    (i) means a constable other than the one who granted bail to the person, if such a constable is readily available, and
    (ii) if no such constable is readily available, means the constable who granted bail.]

[This section is inserted into the 1984 Act, as from April 1, 2007, by the *Police and Justice Act* 2006, s.10 and Sched. 6, paras 1 and 4.]

Section 30CA is subject to section 24B(3)(a) of the 2003 Act, which modifies section 30CA(5)(a) to substitute, for the reference to being involved in the investigation of the offence, the following:
"a reference to being involved—
    (i) in the investigation of the offence in respect of which the person was given the conditional caution, or
    (ii) in investigating whether the person has failed, without reasonable excuse, to comply with any of the conditions attached to the conditional caution;".]

Bail under section 30A: variation of conditions by court

1–127   **30CB.**—(1) Where a person released on bail under section 30A(1) is on bail subject to conditions, a magistrates' court may, on an application by or on behalf of the person, vary the conditions if—
    (a) the conditions have been varied under section 30CA(1) since being imposed under section 30A(3B),
    (b) a request for variation under section 30CA(1) of the conditions has been made and refused, or
    (c) a request for variation under section 30CA(1) of the conditions has been made and the period of 48 hours beginning with the day when the request was made has expired without the request having been withdrawn or the conditions having been varied in response to the request.
    (2) In proceedings on an application for a variation under subsection (1), a ground may not be relied upon unless—
    (a) in a case falling within subsection (1)(a), the ground was relied upon in the request in response to which the conditions were varied under section 30CA(1), or
    (b) in a case falling within paragraph (b) or (c) of subsection (1), the ground was relied upon in the request mentioned in that paragraph,
but this does not prevent the court, when deciding the application, from considering different grounds arising out of a change in circumstances that has occurred since the making of the application.
    (3) Where conditions of bail granted to a person under section 30A(1) are varied under subsection (1)—
    (a) paragraphs (a) to (d) of section 30A(3A) apply,
    (b) requirements imposed by the conditions as so varied must be requirements that appear to the court varying the conditions to be necessary for any of the purposes mentioned in paragraphs (a) to (d) of section 30A(3B), and
    (c) that bail shall not lapse but shall continue subject to the conditions as so varied.
    (4) [*Identical to s.30CA(4), ante,* § 1–126.]]

[This section is inserted into the 1984 Act, as from April 1, 2007, by the *Police and Justice Act* 2006, s.10 and Sched. 6, paras 1 and 4.]

Failure to answer to bail under section 30A

1–128   **30D.**—(1) A constable may arrest without a warrant a person who—
    (a) has been released on bail under section 30A subject to a requirement to attend a specified police station, but
    (b) fails to attend the police station at the specified time.
    (2) A person arrested under subsection (1) must be taken to a police station (which may be the specified police station or any other police station) as soon as practicable after the arrest.

[(2A) A person who has been released on bail under section 30A may be arrested without a warrant by a constable if the constable has reasonable grounds for suspecting that the person has broken any of the conditions of bail.

(2B) A person arrested under subsection (2A) must be taken to a police station (which may be the specified police station mentioned in subsection (1) or any other police station) as soon as practicable after the arrest.]

(3) In subsection (1), "specified" means specified in a notice under subsection (1) or (5) of section 30B or, if notice of change has been given under subsection (7) of that section, in that notice.

(4) For the purposes of—

(a) section 30 (subject to the obligations in subsections (2) and (2B)), and

(b) section 31,

an arrest under this section is to be treated as an arrest for an offence.

[Section 30D was inserted by the *Criminal Justice Act* 2003, s.4. It is printed as amended by the *Police and Justice Act* 2006, s.10(1), and Sched. 6, paras 1 and 5.]

(11) Arrest for further offence

Police and Criminal Evidence Act 1984, s.31

Arrest for further offence

31. Where—   **1–129**

(a) a person—

(i) has been arrested for an offence; and

(ii) is at a police station in consequence of that arrest; and

(b) it appears to a constable that, if he were released from that arrest, he would be liable to arrest for some other offence,

he shall be arrested for that other offence.

As from June 29, 2007, section 31 is another provision applied to arrest for failure to comply with conditions attached to a conditional caution: see *ante*, § 1–121.

The purpose of this section is to prevent the release and re-arrest of a suspect that would result in an artificial extension of the detention periods regulated by section 41 of the 1984 Act, *et seq*. There is no requirement that the further arrest should occur as soon as practicable, only that it must be done before expiry of the relevant detention period: *Samuel* [1988] Q.B. 615.

(12) Search following arrest

Police and Criminal Evidence Act 1984, s.32

Search upon arrest

32.—(1) A constable may search an arrested person, in any case where the person to be   **1–130** searched has been arrested at a place other than a police station, if the constable has reasonable grounds for believing that the arrested person may present a danger to himself or others.

(2) Subject to subsections (3) to (5) below, a constable shall also have power in any such case—

(a) to search the arrested person for anything—

(i) which he might use to assist him to escape from lawful custody; or

(ii) which might be evidence relating to an offence; and

(b) if the offence for which he has been arrested is an indictable offence, to enter and search any premises in which he was when arrested or immediately before he was arrested for evidence relating to the offence.

(3) The power to search conferred by subsection (2) above is only a power to search to the extent that is reasonably required for the purpose of discovering any such thing or any such evidence.

(4) The powers conferred by this section to search a person are not to be construed as authorising a constable to require a person to remove any of his clothing in public other than an outer coat, jacket or gloves but they do authorise a search of a person's mouth.

(5) A constable may not search a person in the exercise of the power conferred by subsection (2)(a) above unless he has reasonable grounds for believing that the person to be searched may have concealed on him anything for which a search is permitted under that paragraph.

(6) A constable may not search premises in the exercise of the power conferred by subsection (2)(b) above unless he has reasonable grounds for believing that there is evidence for which a search is permitted under that paragraph on the premises.

(7) In so far as the power of search conferred by subsection (2)(b) above relates to premises consisting of two or more separate dwellings, it is limited to a power to search—

(a) any dwelling in which the arrest took place or in which the person arrested was immediately before his arrest; and

(b) any parts of the premises which the occupier of any such dwelling uses in common with the occupiers of any other dwellings comprised in the premises.

(8) A constable searching a person in the exercise of the power conferred by subsection (1) above may seize and retain anything he finds, if he has reasonable grounds for believing that the person searched might use it to cause physical injury to himself or to any other person.

(9) A constable searching a person in the exercise of the power conferred by subsection (2)(a) above may seize and retain anything he finds, other than an item subject to legal privilege, if he has reasonable grounds for believing—

(a) that he might use it to assist him to escape from lawful custody; or

(b) that it is evidence of an offence or has been obtained in consequence of the commission of an offence.

(10) Nothing in this section shall be taken to affect the power conferred by section 43 of the *Terrorism Act* 2000.

[This section is printed as amended by the *Prevention of Terrorism (Temporary Provisions) Act* 1989, s.25(1), and Sched. 8; the *Criminal Justice and Public Order Act* 1994, s.59(2); the *Terrorism Act* 2000, s.125, and Sched. 15, para. 5(3); and the *Serious Organised Crime and Police Act* 2005, s.111, and Sched. 7, para. 43(1) and (6).]

1–131   In its application to an offence under section 31(1) of the *London Olympic Games and Paralympic Games Act* 2006 (selling an Olympic ticket in a public place or in the course of a business otherwise than in accordance with a written authorisation issued by the London Organising Committee), this section permits the searching of a vehicle which a constable reasonably thinks was used in connection with the offence: 2006 Act, s.31(7).

A search under section 32 must be made at the time of the arrest and not several hours later: *Badham* [1987] Crim.L.R. 202, Crown Court (H.H. Judge Compston). *Cf.* section 18, *ante*, § 1–54 .

A suspected burglar's car keys were not "evidence relating to an offence" under section 32(2)(a)(ii): *Churchill* [1989] Crim.L.R. 226, CA.

It is a question of fact where officers rely on section 32 to justify a search whether that was the genuine reason for the officers in making the entry: *R. v. Beckford (Junior)* (1991) 94 Cr.App.R. 43, CA. The issue as to the officers' motive may go to the weight to be attached to their evidence: *ibid.*

"Premises" includes "any vehicle": s.23, *ante*, § 1–65. As to the use of force, see section 117, *ante*, § 1–119.

As to the extent of the power of seizure where a constable is making a search of premises in exercise of the power conferred by subsection (2)(b), see section 19 of the Act, *ante*, § 1–56.

(13) Detention after arrest

1–132   The Act and Codes provide a framework regulating the detention of suspects in police custody. Reasons for detention must be given and the length of time that a person may be detained is limited and subject to review. Rights of the suspect are protected covering the conduct of searches and the taking of forensic samples. A custody officer is appointed at designated police stations with specific duties and responsibilities for detained persons. A person is in detention when he or she is arrested for an offence and taken to a police station or when he attends voluntarily at a police station and is then arrested: the *PACE Act*, s.118. The time for recording detention starts to run from arrival at the police station or from 24 hours after arrest, whichever is earlier: section 41. The timetable for review is as follows—

6 hours	First review by police
+ 9 hours	Second review by police
+ 9 hours	Further review by police
24 hours	Charge required UNLESS
+ 12 hours	Authorised by senior officer. Then charge required UNLESS
36 hours	Application to court for warrant of further detention
+ 36 hours	Further detention order by court
+ 36 hours	Extension of further detention ordered by court BUT
96 hours	Maximum length of detention allowed before charge.

Longer periods of detention may be authorised under counter–terrorism provisions: see the *Terrorism Act* 2000.

Police and Criminal Evidence Act 1984, s.34

Limitations on police detention

34.—(1) A person arrested for an offence shall not be kept in police detention except in accordance with the provisions of this Part of this Act.

1–133

(2) Subject to subsection (3) below, if at any time a custody officer—

    (a) becomes aware, in relation to any person in police detention, that the grounds for the detention of that person have ceased to apply; and

    (b) is not aware of any other grounds on which the continued detention of that person could be justified under the provisions of this Part of this Act,

it shall be the duty of the custody officer, subject to subsection (4) below, to order his immediate release from custody.

(3) No person in police detention shall be released except on the authority of a custody officer at the police station where his detention was authorised or, if it was authorised at more than one station, a custody officer at the station where it was last authorised.

(4) A person who appears to the custody officer to have been unlawfully at large when he was arrested is not to be released under subsection (2) above.

(5) A person whose release is ordered under subsection (2) above shall be released without bail unless it appears to the custody officer—

    (a) that there is need for further investigation of any matter in connection with which he was detained at any time during the period of his detention; or

    (b) that, in respect of any such matter, proceedings may be taken against him or he may be reprimanded or warned under section 65 of the *Crime and Disorder Act* 1998

and, if it so appears, he shall be released on bail.

(6) For the purposes of this Part of this Act a person arrested under section 6D of the *Road Traffic Act* 1988 or section 30(2) of the *Transport and Works Act* 1992 is arrested for an offence.

(7) For the purposes of this Part a person who—

    (a) attends a police station to answer to bail granted under section 30A,

    (b) returns to a police station to answer to bail granted under this part, or

    (c) is arrested under section 30D or section 46A,

is to be treated as arrested for an offence and that offence is the offence in connection with which he was granted bail.

[(8) Subsection (7) does not apply in relation to a person who is granted bail subject to the duty mentioned in section 47(3)(b) and who either—

(a) attends a police station to answer to such bail, or

(b) is arrested under section 46A for failing to do so,

(provision as to the treatment of such persons for the purposes of this Part being made by section 46ZA).]

[This section is printed as amended by the *Road Traffic (Consequential Provisions) Act* 1988, s.4 and Sched. 3, para. 27(2); the *Criminal Justice and Public Order Act* 1994, s.29(3); the *Criminal Justice and Court Services Act* 2000, s.56(2); the *Police Reform Act* 2002, s.53(1); the *Railways and Transport Safety Act* 2003, s.107, and Sched. 7, para. 12; the *Criminal Justice Act* 2003, s.12, and Sched. 1, paras 1 and 5; and, as from April 1, 2007, in the local justice area of Lambeth and Southwark (*Police and Justice Act 2006 (Commencement No. 2, Transitional and Savings Provisions) Order* 2007 (S.I. 2007 No. 709)), and as from a day to be appointed elsewhere, the *Police and Justice Act* 2006, s.46(1) and (2) (addition of subsection (8)).]

As from June 29, 2007, section 34 is another provision applied to arrest for failure to comply with conditions attached to a conditional caution: see *ante*, § 1–121.

1–134　　The reference to section 65 of the *Crime and Disorder Act* 1998 in subsection (5)(b) relates to the system of court diversion for children and young persons.

The *Road Traffic Act* 1988 gives an officer power to arrest without warrant anyone who has provided a positive breath test at the roadside or who has failed to provide a specimen but the officer has reasonable cause to suspect that the person has alcohol his body. Section 46A gives power for a constable to arrest without warrant any person who has failed to answer their police bail back to the police station. In these situations an offence may not have been committed but this section means the defendant may be treated as if it had.

For the meaning of "police detention", see *ante*, § 1–132 (summarising section 118(2) of the 1984 Act).

Police and Criminal Evidence Act 1984, ss.35–36

Designated police stations

1–135　　**35.**—(1) The chief officer of police for each police area shall designate the police stations in his area which, subject to sections 30(3) and (5), 30A(5) and 30D(2) above, are to be the stations in that area to be used for the purpose of detaining arrested persons.

(2) A chief officer's duty under subsection (1) above is to designate police stations appearing to him to provide enough accommodation for that purpose.

(2A) The Chief Constable of the British Transport Police Force may designate police stations which (in addition to those designated under subsection (1) above) may be used for the purpose of detaining arrested persons.

(3) Without prejudice to section 12 of the *Interpretation Act* 1978 (continuity of duties) a chief officer—

(a) may designate a station which was not previously designated; and

(b) may direct that a designation of a station previously made shall cease to operate.

(4) In this Act "designated police station" means a police station for the time being designated under this section.

[This section is printed as amended by the *Anti-terrorism, Crime and Security Act* 2001, s.101, and Sched. 7; and the *Criminal Justice Act* 2003, s.12, and Sched. 1, paras 1 and 6.]

Custody officers at police stations

1–136　　**36.**—(1) One or more custody officers shall be appointed for each designated police station.

(2) A custody officer for a police station designated under section 35(1) above shall be appointed—

(a) by the chief officer of police for the area in which the designated police station is situated; or

(b) by such other police officer as the chief officer of police for that area may direct.

(2A) A custody officer for a police station designated under section 35(2A) above shall be appointed—

(a) by the Chief Constable of the British Transport Police Force; or

(b) by such other member of that Force as that Chief Constable may direct.

(3) *No officer may be appointed a custody officer unless he is of at least the rank of sergeant.*

[(3) No person may be appointed a custody officer unless—

(a) he is a police officer of at least the rank of sergeant; or

(b) he is a staff custody officer.]

(4) An officer of any rank may perform the functions of a custody officer at a designated police station if a custody officer is not readily available to perform them.

(5) Subject to the following provisions of this section and to section 39(2) below, none of the functions of a custody officer in relation to a person shall be performed by an *officer* [individual] who at the time when the function falls to be performed is involved in the investigation of an offence for which that person is in police detention at that time.

(6) Nothing in subsection (5) above is to be taken to prevent a custody officer—

(a) performing any function assigned to custody officers—

(i)   by this Act; or

(ii) by a code of practice issued under this Act;

(b) carrying out the duty imposed on custody officers by section 39 below;

(c) doing anything in connection with the identification of a suspect; or

(d) doing anything under sections 7 and 8 of the *Road Traffic Act* 1988.

(7) Where an arrested person is taken to a police station which is not a designated police station, the functions in relation to him which at a designated police station would be the functions of a custody officer shall be performed—

(a) by an officer [or a staff custody officer] who is not involved in the investigation of an offence for which he is in police detention, if *such an officer* [such a person] is readily available; and

(b) if no *such officer* [such person] is readily available, by the officer who took him to the station or any other officer.

(7A) Subject to subsection (7B), subsection (7) applies where a person attends a police station which is not a designated station to answer to bail granted under section 30A as it applies where a person is taken to such a station.

(7B) Where subsection (7) applies because of subsection (7A), the reference in subsection (7)(b) to the officer who took him to the station is to be read as a reference to the officer who granted him bail.

(8) References to a custody officer in [section 34 above or in] the following provisions of this Act include references to an *officer* [a person] other than a custody officer who is performing the functions of a custody officer by virtue of subsection (4) or (7) above.

(9) Where by virtue of subsection (7) above an officer of a force maintained by a police authority who took an arrested person to a police station is to perform the functions of a custody officer in relation to him, the officer shall inform an officer who—

(a) is attached to a designated police station; and

(b) is of at least the rank of inspector,

that he is to do so.

(10) The duty imposed by subsection (9) above shall be performed as soon as it is practicable to perform it.

[(11) In this section, "staff custody officer" means a person who has been designated as such under section 38 of the *Police Reform Act* 2002.]

[This section is printed as amended by the *Road Traffic (Consequential Provisions) Act* 1988, s.4 and Sched. 3, para. 27(3); and the *Criminal Justice Act* 2003, s.12, and Sched. 1, paras 1 and 7; and as amended, as from a day to be appointed, by the *Serious Organised Crime and Police Act* 2005, s.121(1)–(6) (insertion of words in square brackets, omission of words in italics).]

As from June 29, 2007, section 36 is another provision applied to arrest for failure to comply with conditions attached to a conditional caution: see *ante*, § 1–105. This is subject to modifications specified in the *Criminal Justice Act* 2003, s.24B(3). The references in the 1984 Act, s.34(5) and (7), to being involved in the investigation of an offence for which the person is in police detention, are substituted by references to being involved in the investigation of the offence in respect of which the person was given the conditional caution, or in investigating whether the person has failed, without reasonable excuse, to comply with any of the conditions attached to the conditional caution.

1–137   Sections 7 and 8 of the *Road Traffic Act* 1988 give the power to a constable to require specimens of breath or blood for analysis in road traffic investigations. The custody officer may perform these functions.

The Chief Constable has a duty to appoint at least one custody officer (of at least the rank of sergeant) for each designated station, but there is no requirement to ensure that a custody officer will always be available at a designated station to perform the duties of the custody officer: *Vince v. Chief Constable of Dorset Police* [1993] 1 W.L.R. 415, CA (Civ. Div.).

The functions of the investigating officer and the custody officer are to be kept separate under subsection (5). This provision was not breached where the custody officer, who was acting in co-operation with the investigating officers, placed the defendants in a bugged cell. The bugging of the cell was held not to be an oppressive or unfair method of obtaining the relevant evidence: *Bailey and Smith* (1993) 97 Cr.App.R. 365.

For the duties of a custody officer in general, see the 1984 Act, ss.37, 37A–D, and 38, *post*, §§ 4–41*et seq.*

Police and Criminal Evidence Act 1984, s.39

Responsibilities in relation to persons detained

1–138   **39.**—(1) Subject to subsections (2) and (4) below, it shall be the duty of the custody officer at a police station to ensure—

     (a) that all persons in police detention at that station are treated in accordance with this Act and any code of practice issued under it and relating to the treatment of persons in police detention; and

     (b) that all matters relating to such persons which are required by this Act or by such codes of practice to be recorded are recorded in the custody records relating to such persons.

(2) If the custody officer, in accordance with any code of practice issued under this Act, transfers or permits the transfer of a person in police detention—

     (a) to the custody of a police officer investigating an offence for which that person is in police detention; or

     (b) to the custody of an officer who has charge of that person outside the police station,

the custody officer shall cease in relation to that person to be subject to the duty imposed on him by subsection (1)(a) above; and it shall be the duty of the officer to whom the transfer is made to ensure that he is treated in accordance with the provisions of this Act and of any such codes of practice as are mentioned in subsection (1) above.

(3) If the person detained is subsequently returned to the custody of the custody officer, it shall be the duty of the officer investigating the offence to report to the custody officer as to the manner in which this section and the codes of practice have been complied with while that person was in his custody.

(4) If an arrested juvenile is transferred to the care of a local authority in pursuance of arrangements made under section 38(6) above, the custody officer shall cease in relation to that person to be subject to the duty imposed on him by subsection (1) above.

(5) [*Repealed by* Children Act *1989, s.108(7) and Sched. 15.*]

(6) Where—

     (a) an officer of higher rank than the custody officer gives directions relating to a person in police detention; and

     (b) the directions are at variance—

         (i) with any decision made or action taken by the custody officer in the performance of a duty imposed on him under this Part of this Act; or

         (ii) with any decision or action which would but for the directions have been made or taken by him in the performance of such a duty,

the custody officer shall refer the matter at once to an officer of the rank of superintendent or above who is responsible for the police station for which the custody officer is acting as custody officer.

[(7) In subsection (6) above—
    "police employee" means a person employed under section 15 of the *Police Act* 1996 ;
    "staff custody officer" has the same meaning as in the *Police Reform Act* 2002.]

[This section is printed as amended by the *Children Act* 1989, s.108(5), and Sched.
13, para. 54; and, as from a day to be appointed, by the *Serious Organised Crime and
Police Act* 2005, s.121(1) and (7) (insertion of subs. (7)).]

As from June 29, 2007, section 39 is another provision applied to arrest for failure to
comply with conditions attached to a conditional caution: see *ante*, § 1–105. This is
subject to modifications specified in the *Criminal Justice Act* 2003, s.24B(3). The references in the 1984 Act, s.39(2) and (3), to an offence, are substituted by references to failure to comply with conditions attached to a conditional caution.

(14) Review of detention

Police and Criminal Evidence Act 1984, s.40

Review of police detention
   40.—(1) Reviews of the detention of each person in police detention in connection with the   **1–139**
investigation of an offence shall be carried out periodically in accordance with the following provisions of this section—
    (a) in the case of a person who has been arrested and charged, by the custody of-
        ficer; and
    (b) in the case of a person who has been arrested but not charged, by an officer of at
        least the rank of inspector who has not been directly involved in the investigation.
    (2) The officer to whom it falls to carry out a review is referred to in this section as a
"review officer".
    (3) Subject to subsection (4) below—
    (a) the first review shall be not later than six hours after the detention was first au-
        thorised;
    (b) the second review shall be not later than nine hours after the first;
    (c) subsequent reviews shall be at intervals of not more than nine hours.
    (4) A review may be postponed—
    (a) if, having regard to all the circumstances prevailing at the latest time for it speci-
        fied in subsection (3) above, it is not practicable to carry out the review at that
        time;
    (b) without prejudice to the generality of paragraph (a) above—
         (i) if at that time the person in detention is being questioned by a police of-
             ficer and the review officer is satisfied that an interruption of the question-
             ing for the purpose of carrying out the review would prejudice the
             investigation in connection with which he is being questioned; or
        (ii) if at that time no review officer is readily available.
    (5) If a review is postponed under subsection (4) above it shall be carried out as soon as
practicable after the latest time specified for it in subsection (3) above.
    (6) If a review is carried out after postponement under subsection (4) above, the fact
that it was so carried out shall not affect any requirement of this section as to the time at
which any subsequent review is to be carried out.
    (7) The review officer shall record the reasons for any postponement of a review in the
custody record.
    (8) Subject to subsection (9) below, where the person whose detention is under review
has not been charged before the time of the review, section 37(1) to (6) above shall have effect in relation to him, but with the modifications specified in subsection (8A).

    (8A) The modifications are—   **1–140**
    (a) the substitution of references to the person whose detention is under review for
        references to the person arrested;
    (b) the substitution of references to the review officer for references to the custody
        officer; and
    (c) in subsection (6), the insertion of the following paragraph after paragraph (a)—

'(aa) asleep;'.

(9) Where a person has been kept in police detention by virtue of section 37(9) or 37D(5) above, section 37(1) to (6) shall not have effect in relation to him but it shall be the duty of the review officer to determine whether he is yet in a fit state.

(10) Where the person whose detention is under review has been charged before the time of the review, section 38(1) to (6B) above shall have effect in relation to him, but with the modifications specified in subsection (10A).

(10A) The modifications are—

(a) the substitution of a reference to the person whose detention is under review for any reference to the person arrested or to the person charged; and

(b) in subsection (5), the insertion of the following paragraph after paragraph (a)—

'(aa) asleep;'.

(11) Where—

(a) an officer of higher rank than the review officer gives directions relating to a person in police detention; and

(b) the directions are at variance—

(i) with any decision made or action taken by the review officer in the performance of a duty imposed on him under this Part of this Act; or

(ii) with any decision or action which would but for the directions have been made or taken by him in the performance of such a duty.

the review officer shall refer the matter at once to an officer of the rank of superintendent or above who is responsible for the police station for which the review officer is acting as review officer in connection with the detention.

(12) Before determining whether to authorise a person's continued detention the review officer shall give—

(a) that person (unless he is asleep); or

(b) any solicitor representing him who is available at the time of the review,

an opportunity to make representations to him about the detention.

(13) Subject to subsection (14) below, the person whose detention is under review or his solicitor may make representations under subsection (12) above either orally or in writing.

(14) The review officer may refuse to hear oral representations from the person whose detention is under review if he considers that he is unfit to make such representations by reason of his condition or behaviour.

[This section is printed as amended by the *Police Reform Act* 2002, s.52; and the *Criminal Justice Act* 2003, s.28, and Sched. 2, para. 4.]

As from June 29, 2007, section 40 is another provision applied to arrest for failure to comply with conditions attached to a conditional caution: see *ante*, § 1–105. This is subject to modifications specified in the *Criminal Justice Act* 2003, s.24B(4), so as to omit subsections (8) and (8A), and to substitute in subsection (9), for the reference to "section 37(9) or 37D(5)", a reference to the second sentence of section 24A(5).

1–141   Amendments inserted in the 1984 Act by the *Criminal Justice and Police Act* 2001 provide for reviews to be carried out by telephone (section 40A) and video-conferencing (section 45).

Section 6 of the *Criminal Justice Act* 2003 substitutes section 40A to allow for a review to be carried out by means of a discussion, conducted by telephone, with one or more persons at the police station where the arrested person is held. This does not apply though if the review could be carried out using video-conferencing facilities. The section came into force on January 29, 2004, and is dependent on equipment being available and regulations authorising its use.

(15) Time limit

Police and Criminal Evidence Act 1984, ss.41–42

Limits on period of detention without charge

1–142   41.—(1) Subject to the following provisions of this section and to sections 42 and 43 below, a person shall not be kept in police detention for more than 24 hours without being charged.

Part I

(2) The time from which the period of detention of a person is to be calculated (in this Act referred to as "the relevant time")—

   (a) in the case of a person to whom this paragraph applies, shall be—

      (i) the time at which that person arrives at the relevant police station; or

      (ii) the time 24 hours after the time of that person's arrest,

     whichever is the earlier;

   (b) in the case of a person arrested outside England and Wales, shall be—

      (i) the time at which that person arrives at the first police station to which he is taken in the police area in England or Wales in which the offence for which he was arrested is being investigated; or

      (ii) the time 24 hours after the time of that person's entry into England and Wales,

     whichever is the earlier;

   (c) in the case of a person who—

      (i) attends voluntarily at a police station; or

      (ii) accompanies a constable to a police station without having been arrested,

     and is arrested at the police station, the time of his arrest;

   (ca) in the case of a person who attends a police station to answer to bail granted under section 30A, the time when he arrives at the police station.

   (d) in any other case, except where subsection (5) below applies, shall be the time at which the person arrested arrives at the first police station to which he is taken after his arrest.

(3) Subsection (2)(a) above applies to a person if—

   (a) his arrest is sought in one police area in England and Wales;

   (b) he is arrested in another police area; and

   (c) he is not questioned in the area in which he is arrested in order to obtain evidence in relation to an offence for which he is arrested;

and in sub-paragraph (i) of that paragraph "the relevant police station" means the first police station to which he is taken in the police area in which his arrest was sought.

(4) Subsection (2) above shall have effect in relation to a person arrested under section 31 above as if every reference in it to his arrest or his being arrested were a reference to his arrest or his being arrested for the offence for which he was originally arrested.

(5) If—   **1–143**

   (a) a person is in police detention in a police area in England and Wales ("the first area"); and

   (b) his arrest for an offence is sought in some other police area in England and Wales ("the second area"); and

   (c) he is taken to the second area for the purposes of investigating that offence, without being questioned in the first area in order to obtain evidence in relation to it,

the relevant time shall be—

      (i) the time 24 hours after he leaves the place where he is detained in the first area; or

      (ii) the time at which he arrives at the first police station to which he is taken in the second area,

   whichever is the earlier.

(6) When a person who is in police detention is removed to hospital because he is in need of medical treatment, any time during which he is being questioned in hospital or on the way there or back by a police officer for the purpose of obtaining evidence relating to an offence shall be included in any period which falls to be calculated for the purposes of this Part of this Act, but any other time while he is in hospital or on his way there or back shall not be so included.

(7) Subject to subsection (8) below, a person who at the expiry of 24 hours after the relevant time is in police detention and has not been charged shall be released at that time either on bail or without bail.

(8) Subsection (7) above does not apply to a person whose detention for more than 24 hours after the relevant time has been authorised or is otherwise permitted in accordance with sections 42 or 43 below.

(9) A person released under subsection (7) above shall not be re-arrested without a war-

rant for the offence for which he was previously arrested unless new evidence justifying a further arrest has come to light since his release but this subsection does not prevent an arrest under section 46A below.

[This section is printed as amended by the *Criminal Justice and Public Order Act* 1994, s.29; and the *Criminal Justice Act* 2003, s.12, and Sched. 1.]

Authorisation of continued detention

1–144   **42.**—(1) Where a police officer of the rank of superintendent or above who is responsible for the police station at which a person is detained has reasonable grounds for believing that—

(a) the detention of that person without charge is necessary to secure or preserve evidence relating to an offence for which he is under arrest or to obtain such evidence by questioning him;

(b) an offence for which he is under arrest is an indictable offence; and

(c) the investigation is being conducted diligently and expeditiously.

he may authorise the keeping of that person in police detention for a period expiring at or before 36 hours after the relevant time.

(2) Where an officer such as is mentioned in subsection (1) above has authorised the keeping of a person in police detention for a period expiring less than 36 hours after the relevant time, such an officer may authorise the keeping of that person in police detention for a further period expiring not more than 36 hours after that time if the conditions specified in subsection (1) above are still satisfied when he gives the authorisation.

(3) If it is proposed to transfer a person in police detention to another police area, the officer determining whether or not to authorise keeping him in detention under subsection (1) above shall have regard to the distance and the time the journey would take.

(4) No authorisation under subsection (1) above shall be given in respect of any person—

(a) more than 24 hours after the relevant time; or

(b) before the second review of his detention under section 40 above has been carried out.

(5) Where an officer authorises the keeping of a person in police detention under subsection (1) above, it shall be his duty—

(a) to inform that person of the grounds for his continued detention; and

(b) to record the grounds in that person's custody record.

(6) Before determining whether to authorise the keeping of a person in detention under subsection (1) or (2) above, an officer shall give—

(a) that person; or

(b) any solicitor representing him who is available at the time when it falls to the officer to determine whether to give the authorisation,

an opportunity to make representations to him about the detention.

(7) Subject to subsection (8) below, the person in detention or his solicitor may make representations under subsection (6) above either orally or in writing.

(8) The officer to whom it falls to determine whether to give the authorisation may refuse to hear oral representations from the person in detention if he considers that he is unfit to make such representations by reason of his condition or behaviour.

(9) Where—

(a) an officer authorises the keeping of a person in detention under subsection (1) above; and

(b) at the time of the authorisation he has not yet exercised a right conferred on him by section 56 or 58 below,

the officer—

(i) shall inform him of that right;

(ii) shall decide whether he should be permitted to exercise it;

(iii) shall record the decision in his custody record; and

(iv) if the decision is to refuse to permit the exercise of the right, shall also record the grounds for the decision in that record.

(10) Where an officer has authorised the keeping of a person who has not been charged in detention under subsection (1) or (2) above, he shall be released from detention, either on bail or without bail, not later than 36 hours after the relevant time, unless—

(a) he has been charged with an offence; or

(b) his continued detention is authorised or otherwise permitted in accordance with
   section 43 below.

(11) A person released under subsection (10) above shall not be re-arrested without a
warrant for the offence for which he was previously arrested unless new evidence justifying
a further arrest has come to light since his release but this subsection does not prevent an
arrest under section 46A below.

[This section is printed as amended by the *Criminal Justice Act* 2003, s.7; and the
Serious Organised Crime and Police Act 2005, s.111, and Sched. 7, para. 43(1) and
(7).]

These provisions permit detention without charge for 24 hours from arrest or arrival **1–145**
at the police station, whichever is earlier. Section 41 gives details as to how the time
should be computed. Section 42 permits a senior officer to authorise continued detention on the grounds given for a further 12 hours making a total of 36 hours detention
without charge. The authorisation to extend the detention must be given within the first
24-hour period but after the second review which must occur at the latest 15 hours after
the detention was first authorised. If authorisation is given then for a period of less than
the 12 hours allowed it may be further extended up to the maximum of 12 hours as
long as any authorisation is made during the currency of the extended period of detention: *Taylor (Leroy)* [1991] Crim.L.R. 541. After 36 hours the person must be released
from detention and at that stage he can either be bailed to return to the police station or
simply released. If he is not bailed or released he must be charged or application for
further detention in custody can be made to a Court under the 1984 Act, s.43.

Police and Criminal Evidence Act 1984, s.43

Warrants of further detention

43.—(1) Where, on an application on oath made by a constable and supported by an infor- **1–146**
mation, a magistrates' court is satisfied that there are reasonable grounds for believing that the
further detention of the person to whom the application relates is justified, it may issue a warrant of further detention authorising the keeping of that person in police detention.

(2) A court may not hear an application for a warrant of further detention unless the
person to whom the application relates—

(a) has been furnished with a copy of the information; and

(b) has been brought before the court for the hearing.

(3) The person to whom the application relates shall be entitled to be legally represented
at the hearing and, if he is not so represented but wishes to be so represented—

(a) the court shall adjourn the hearing to enable him to obtain representation; and

(b) he may be kept in police detention during the adjournment.

(4) A person's further detention is only justified for the purposes of this section or section 44 below if—

(a) his detention without charge is necessary to secure or preserve evidence relating
   to an offence for which he is under arrest or to obtain such evidence by questioning him;

(b) an offence for which he is under arrest is an indictable offence; and

(c) the investigation is being conducted diligently and expeditiously.

(5) Subject to subsection (7) below, an application for a warrant of further detention
may be made—

(a) at any time before the expiry of 36 hours after the relevant time; or

(b) in a case where—

   (i) it is not practicable for the magistrates' court to which the application will
      be made to sit at the expiry of 36 hours after the relevant time; but

   (ii) the court will sit during the 6 hours following the end of that period,
   at any time before the expiry of the said 6 hours.

(6) In a case to which subsection (5)(b) above applies—

(a) the person to whom the application relates may be kept in police detention until
   the application is heard; and

(b) the custody officer shall make a note in that person's custody record—

      (i) of the fact that he was kept in police detention for more than 36 hours after the relevant time; and

      (ii) of the reason why he was so kept.

(7) If—

    (a) an application for a warrant of further detention is made after the expiry of 36 hours after the relevant time; and

    (b) it appears to the magistrates' court that it would have been reasonable for the police to make it before the expiry of that period,

the court shall dismiss the application.

(8) Where on an application such as is mentioned in subsection (1) above a magistrates' court is not satisfied that there are reasonable grounds for believing that the further detention of the person to whom the application relates is justified, it shall be its duty—

    (a) to refuse the application; or

    (b) to adjourn the hearing of it until a time not later than 36 hours after the relevant time.

(9) The person to whom the application relates may be kept in police detention during the adjournment.

(10) A warrant of further detention shall—

    (a) state the time at which it is issued;

    (b) authorise the keeping in police detention of the person to whom it relates for the period stated in it.

(11) Subject to subsection (12) below, the period stated in a warrant of further detention shall be such period as the magistrates' court thinks fit, having regard to the evidence before it.

(12) The period shall not be longer than 36 hours.

(13) If it is proposed to transfer a person in police detention to a police area other than that in which he is detained when the application for a warrant of further detention is made, the court hearing the application shall have regard to the distance and the time the journey would take.

(14) Any information submitted in support of an application under this section shall state—

    (a) the nature of the offence for which the person to whom the application relates has been arrested;

    (b) the general nature of the evidence on which that person was arrested;

    (c) what inquiries relating to the offence have been made by the police and what further inquiries are proposed by them;

    (d) the reasons for believing the continued detention of that person to be necessary for the purposes of such further inquiries.

(15) Where an application under this section is refused, the person to whom the application relates shall forthwith be charged or, subject to subsection (16) below, released, either on bail or without bail.

(16) A person need not be released under subsection (15) above—

    (a) before the expiry of 24 hours after the relevant time; or

    (b) before the expiry of any longer period for which his continued detention is or has been authorised under section 42 above.

(17) Where an application under this section is refused, no further application shall be made under this section in respect of the person to whom the refusal relates, unless supported by evidence which has come to light since the refusal.

(18) Where a warrant of further detention is issued, the person to whom it relates shall be released from police detention, either on bail or without bail, upon or before the expiry of the warrant unless he is charged.

(19) A person released under subsection (18) above shall not be re-arrested without a warrant for the offence for which he was previously arrested unless new evidence justifying a further arrest has come to light since his release; but this subsection does not prevent an arrest under section 46A below.

[This section is printed as amended by the *Criminal Justice and Public Order Act* 1994, s.29; and the *Serious Organised Crime and Police Act* 2005, s.111, and Sched. 7, para. 43(1) and (8).]

The maximum length of time for detention authorised by the police is 36 hours. If **1–147** more time is required before a person can be charged application on a sworn information may be made to a court for a warrant of further detention. The application should be made within court sitting hours if at all possible but the period of detention of 36 hours may sometimes expire at a weekend or other time when a court is not sitting. The time limits should be closely monitored and if the application will need to be made out of court sitting hours the justices' clerk should be notified in advance as a bench must be convened and legal representation for the person detained must be provided. There is also a period of six hours grace if it is impracticable to convene a court within the 36 hours. The court must be satisfied that the grounds of section 43(4) are made out and further detention may be ordered for as long as the court thinks fit up to a maximum of 36 hours. Application may be made on a sworn information to the court to extend a warrant of further detention for up to another 36 hours. The longest period of detention in total must not exceed 96 hours from when it first started to run.

In *R. v. Slough JJ., ex p. Stirling* [1987] Crim.L.R. 576, DC, it was held that section 43(5)(b) was not limited to a situation in which the 36-hour period expired at a time when the magistrates were not sitting at all. Where a magistrates' court was already sitting, the justices had a discretion upon being notified of the intention of a constable to make an application either to hear the application straightaway or to wait, provided they did not do so for longer than six hours after the end of the 36-hour period. However, the requirements of section 43(7) were mandatory. Here, the information to support the application was drafted eight minutes before the expiry of the 36-hour period. The clerk advised the court that it was not practicable to hear the application at that time and the application was adjourned to a time beyond the 36-hour period although within the extra six hours. The Divisional Court held that the application should have been refused as it could not be said that it would have been unreasonable for the police to draft the information earlier so as to ensure that the application was heard by the court before the expiry of the 36-hour period.

Police and Criminal Evidence Act 1984, s.44

Extension of warrants of further detention

44.—(1) On an application on oath made by a constable and supported by an information a **1–148** magistrates' court may extend a warrant of further detention issued under section 43 above if it is satisfied that there are reasonable grounds for believing that the further detention of the person to whom the application relates is justified.

(2) Subject to subsection (3) below, the period for which a warrant of further detention may be extended shall be such period as the court thinks fit, having regard to the evidence before it.

(3) The period shall not—

　　(a) be longer than 36 hours; or

　　(b) end later than 96 hours after the relevant time.

(4) Where a warrant of further detention has been extended under subsection (1) above, or further extended under this subsection, for a period ending before 96 hours after the relevant time, on an application such as is mentioned in that subsection a magistrates' court may further extend the warrant if it is satisfied as there mentioned; and subsections (2) and (3) above apply to such further extensions as they apply to extensions under subsection (1) above.

(5) A warrant of further detention shall, if extended or further extended under this section, be endorsed with a note of the period of the extension.

(6) Subsections (2), (3) and (14) of section 43 above shall apply to an application made under this section as they apply to an application made under that section.

(7) Where an application under this section is refused, the person to whom the application relates shall forthwith be charged or, subject to subsection (8) below, released, either on bail or without bail.

(8) A person need not be released under subsection (7) above before the expiry of any period for which a warrant of further detention issued in relation to him has been extended or further extended on an earlier application made under this section.

Police and Criminal Evidence Act 1984, s.45

Detention before charge—supplementary

1–149　　45.—(1) In sections 43 and 44 of this Act "magistrates' court" means a court consisting of two or more justices of the peace sitting otherwise than in open court.

(2) Any reference in this Part of this Act to a period of time or a time of day is to be treated as approximate only.

F. QUESTIONING AND TREATMENT OF DETAINED PERSONS

(1) Search of detained persons

1–150　　The police have powers to search persons in detention and to seize and retain anything found on them. Such personal searches are not only undertaken to discover, identify and look for evidence but also to remove anything that may be used to cause harm to people or property or assist escape. During detention the police may take fingerprint evidence and also intimate and non-intimate samples for forensic purposes and to obtain a DNA profile. The conduct of searches is regulated by the *PACE Act* 1984 as amended and Code C.

Police and Criminal Evidence Act 1984, s.54

Searches of detained persons

1–151　　54.—(1) The custody officer at a police station shall ascertain everything which a person has with him when he is—

　(a) brought to the station after being arrested elsewhere or after being committed to custody by an order or sentence of a court; or

　(b) arrested at the station or detained there, as a person falling within section 34(7), under section 37 above [or as a person to whom section 46ZA(4) or (5) applies].

(2) The custody officer may record or cause to be recorded all or any of the things which he ascertains under subsection (1).

(2A) In the case of an arrested person, any such record may be made as part of his custody record.

(3) Subject to subsection (4) below, a custody officer may seize and retain any such thing or cause any such thing to be seized and retained.

(4) Clothes and personal effects may only be seized if the custody officer—

　(a) believes that the person from whom they are seized may use them—

　　(i) to cause physical injury to himself or any other person;

　　(ii) to damage property;

　　(iii) to interfere with evidence; or

　　(iv) to assist him to escape; or

　(b) has reasonable grounds for believing that they may be evidence relating to an offence.

(5) Where anything is seized, the person from whom it is seized shall be told the reason for the seizure unless he is—

　(a) violent or likely to become violent; or

　(b) incapable of understanding what is said to him.

(6) Subject to subsection (7) below, a person may be searched if the custody officer considers it necessary to enable him to carry out his duty under subsection (1) above and to the extent that the custody officer considers necessary for that purpose.

(6A) A person who is in custody at a police station or is in police detention otherwise than at a police station may at any time be searched in order to ascertain whether he has with him anything which he could use for any of the purposes specified in subsection (4)(a) above.

(6B) Subject to subsection (6C) below, a constable may seize and retain, or cause to be seized and retained, anything found on such a search.

(6C) A constable may only seize clothes and personal effects in the circumstances specified in subsection (4) above.

(7) An intimate search may not be conducted under this section.

(8) A search under this section shall be carried out by a constable.

(9) The constable carrying out a search shall be of the same sex as the person searched.

[This section is printed as amended, and repealed in part, by the *Criminal Justice Act* 1988, s.147; the *Criminal Justice and Public Order Act* 1994, s.168(2) and Sched. 10, para. 55; the *Criminal Justice Act* 2003, s.8; and, as from April 1, 2007, in the local justice area of Lambeth and Southwark (*Police and Justice Act 2006 (Commencement No. 2, Transitional and Savings Provisions) Order* 2007 (S.I. 2007 No. 709)), and as from a day to be appointed elsewhere, the *Police and Justice Act* 2006, s.46(1) and (2) (addition of words in square brackets in subsection (1)(b)).]

As from June 29, 2007, section 54 of the 1984 Act applies to a person falling within the *Criminal Justice Act* 2003, s.24A(3) (persons bailed after having been arrested for failure to comply with conditions of caution and then attending police station to answer to bail or having been arrested for failure to answer to bail), and who is detained under that section, as it applies to a person falling within section 34(7) of the 1984 Act, and who is detained under section 37 of that Act: *Criminal Justice Act* 2003, s.24B(6), as inserted by the *Police and Justice Act* 2006, s.18(1).

An intimate search is defined in section 65 as a physical examination of body orifices **1–152** other than the mouth. See also section 62, *post*, § 1–165.

(2) Searches and examination to ascertain identity

Police and Criminal Evidence Act 1984, s.54A

Searches and examination to ascertain identity
    54A.—(1) If an officer of at least the rank of inspector authorises it, a person who is detained **1–153** in a police station may be searched or examined, or both—
    (a) for the purpose of ascertaining whether he has any mark that would tend to identify him as a person involved in the commission of an offence; or
    (b) for the purpose of facilitating the ascertainment of his identity.
    (2) An officer may only give an authorisation under subsection (1) for the purpose mentioned in paragraph (a) of that subsection if—
    (a) the appropriate consent to a search or examination that would reveal whether the mark in question exists has been withheld; or
    (b) it is not practicable to obtain such consent.
    (3) An officer may only give an authorisation under subsection (1) in a case in which subsection (2) does not apply if—
    (a) the person in question has refused to identify himself; or
    (b) the officer has reasonable grounds for suspecting that that person is not who he claims to be.
    (4) An officer may give an authorisation under subsection (1) orally or in writing but, if he gives it orally, he shall confirm it in writing as soon as is practicable.
    (5) Any identifying mark found on a search or examination under this section may be photographed—
    (a) with the appropriate consent; or
    (b) if the appropriate consent is withheld or it is not practicable to obtain it, without it.
    (6) Where a search or examination may be carried out under this section, or a photograph may be taken under this section, the only persons entitled to carry out the search or examination, or to take the photograph, are constables.
    (7) A person may not under this section carry out a search or examination of a person of the opposite sex or take a photograph of any part of the body of a person of the opposite sex.
    (8) An intimate search may not be carried out under this section.
    (9) A photograph taken under this section—
    (a) may be used by, or disclosed to, any person for any purpose related to the prevention or detection of crime, the investigation of an offence or the conduct of a prosecution; and

(b) after being so used or disclosed, may be retained but may not be used or disclosed except for a purpose so related.

1–154   (10) In subsection (9)—

(a) the reference to crime includes a reference to any conduct which—

   (i) constitutes one or more criminal offences (whether under the law of a part of the United Kingdom or of a country or territory outside the United Kingdom); or

   (ii) is, or corresponds to, any conduct which, if it all took place in any one part of the United Kingdom, would constitute one or more criminal offences;

   and

(b) the references to an investigation and to a prosecution include references, respectively, to any investigation outside the United Kingdom of any crime or suspected crime and to a prosecution brought in respect of any crime in a country or territory outside the United Kingdom.

(11) In this section—

(a) references to ascertaining a person's identity include references to showing that he is not a particular person; and

(b) references to taking a photograph include references to using any process by means of which a visual image may be produced, and references to photographing a person shall be construed accordingly.

(12) In this section "mark" includes features and injuries; and a mark is an identifying mark for the purposes of this section if its existence in any person's case facilitates the ascertainment of his identity or his identification as a person involved in the commission of an offence.

(13) Nothing in this section applies to a person arrested under an extradition arrest power.

[This section was inserted by the *Anti-terrorism, Crime and Security Act* 2001, s.90(1). It is printed as amended by the *Police Reform Act* 2002, s.107(1), and Sched. 7, para. 9(2); and the *Extradition Act* 2003, s.169(2).]

1–155   The *Criminal Justice Act* 2003, s.24B(7) (inserted as from June 29, 2007 by the *Police and Justice Act* 2006, s.18(1)), applies section 54A of the 1984 Act to a person detained at a police station under section 24A of the 2003 Act (arrest for failure to comply with conditions of caution), with the following modifications:

(a) in subsections (1)(a) and (12), after "as a person involved in the commission of an offence" there are inserted the words "or as having failed to comply with any of the conditions attached to his conditional caution"; and

(b) in subsection (9)(a), after "the investigation of an offence" there are inserted the words ", the investigation of whether the person in question has failed to comply with any of the conditions attached to his conditional caution".

Appropriate consent is defined in section 65 as being the consent of the person to be searched if they are over 17 years of age; the consent of the person himself and that of his parent or guardian where the person to be searched is aged 14 to 16; and the consent of the parent or guardian of the person to be searched where the person is 13 years of age or less.

(3) Fingerprinting, DNA profiling and samples

Police and Criminal Evidence Act 1984, s.61

Finger-printing

1–156   **61.**—(1) Except as provided by this section no person's fingerprints may be taken without the appropriate consent.

(2) Consent to the taking of a person's fingerprints must be in writing if it is given at a time when he is at a police station.

(3) The fingerprints of a person detained at a police station may be taken without the appropriate consent if—

(a) he is detained in consequence of his arrest for a recordable offence; and

  (b) he has not had his fingerprints taken in the course of the investigation of the offence by the police.

  (3A) Where a person mentioned in paragraph (a) of subsection (3) or (4) has already had his fingerprints taken in the course of the investigation of the offence by the police that fact shall be disregarded for the purposes of that subsection if—

  (a) the fingerprints taken on the previous occasion do not constitute a complete set of his fingerprints; or

  (b) some or all of the fingerprints taken on the previous occasion are not of sufficient quality to allow satisfactory analysis, comparison or matching (whether in the case in question or generally).

  (4) The fingerprints of a person detained at a police station may be taken without the **1–157** appropriate consent if—

  (a) he has been charged with a recordable offence or informed that he will be reported for such an offence; and

  (b) he has not had his fingerprints taken in the course of the investigation of the offence by the police.

  (4A) The fingerprints of a person who has answered to bail at a court or police station may be taken without the appropriate consent at the court or station if—

  (a) the court, or

  (b) an officer of at least the rank of inspector,

authorises them to be taken.

  (4B) A court or officer may only give an authorisation under subsection (4A) if—

  (a) the person who has answered to bail has answered to it for a person whose fingerprints were taken on a previous occasion and there are reasonable grounds for believing that he is not the same person; or

  (b) the person who has answered to bail claims to be a different person from a person whose fingerprints were taken on a previous occasion.

  (5) An officer may give an authorisation under subsection (4A) above orally or in writing **1–158** but, if he gives it orally, he shall confirm it in writing as soon as is practicable.

  (6) Any person's fingerprints may be taken without the appropriate consent if—

  (a) he has been convicted of a recordable offence;

  (b) he has been given a caution in respect of a recordable offence which, at the time of the caution, he has admitted; or

  (c) he has been warned or reprimanded under section 65 of the *Crime and Disorder Act* 1998 for a recordable offence.

  [(6A) A constable may take a person's fingerprints without the appropriate consent if—

  (a) the constable reasonably suspects that the person is committing or attempting to commit an offence, or has committed or attempted to commit an offence; and

  (b) either of the two conditions mentioned in subsection (6B) is met.

  [(6B) The conditions are that—

  (a) the name of the person is unknown to, and cannot be readily ascertained by, the constable;

  (b) the constable has reasonable grounds for doubting whether a name furnished by the person as his name is his real name.

  [(6C) The taking of fingerprints by virtue of subsection (6A) does not count for any of the purposes of this Act as taking them in the course of the investigation of an offence by the police.]

  (7) In a case where by virtue of subsection (3), (4) *or (6)* [, (6) or (6A)] above a person's fingerprints are taken without the appropriate consent—

  (a) he shall be told the reason before his fingerprints are taken; and

  (b) the reason shall be recorded as soon as is practicable after the fingerprints are taken.

  (7A) If a person's fingerprints are taken at a police station, [or by virtue of subsection (6A) at a place other than a police station,] whether with or without the appropriate consent—

  (a) before the fingerprints are taken, an officer [(or, in a subsection (6A) case, the constable)] shall inform him that they may be the subject of a speculative search; and

  (b) the fact that the person has been informed of this possibility shall be recorded as soon as is practicable after the fingerprints have been taken.

(8) If he is detained at a police station when the fingerprints are taken, the reason for taking them and, in the case falling within subsection (7A) above, the fact referred to in paragraph (b) of that subsection shall be recorded on his custody record.

(8A) Where a person's fingerprints are taken electronically, they must be taken in such a manner, and using such devices, as the Secretary of State has approved for the purposes of electronic fingerprinting.

(8B) The power to take the fingerprints of a person detained at a police station without the appropriate consent shall be exercisable by any constable.

(9) Nothing in this section—

- (a) affects any power conferred by paragraph 18(2) of Schedule 2 to the *Immigration Act* 1971 [, section 141 of the *Immigration and Asylum Act* 1999 or regulations made under section 144 of that Act]; or
- (b) applies to a person arrested or detained under the terrorism provisions.

(10) Nothing in this section applies to a person arrested under an extradition arrest power.

[This section is printed as amended by the *Criminal Justice and Public Order Act* 1994, s.168(2) and Sched. 10, para. 56; the *Terrorism Act* 2000, s.125 and Sched. 15, para. 5(7); the *Anti-Terrorism, Crime and Security Act* 2001, s.90(2); the *Criminal Justice and Police Act*, s.78(2)-(7); the *Police Reform Act* 2002, s.107(1), and Sched. 7, para. 9(3); the *Extradition Act* 2003, s.169(3); and the *Criminal Justice Act* 2003, s.9; and, as from a day to be appointed, by the *Immigration and Asylum Act* 1999, s.169(1), and Sched. 14, para. 80(1) and(4) (insertion of words in square brackets in subs. (9)); and the *Serious Organised Crime and Police Act* 2005, s.117(1)-(4) (insertion of words in square brackets, omission of italicised words in remainder of section).]

1–159   Fingerprints are defined in section 65 as a record in any form and produced by any method, of the skin pattern and other physical characteristics or features of a person's fingers or either of his palms.

Appropriate consent is that of the person to be fingerprinted himself, or in the case of a youth aged 14–16 his consent and that of his parent or guardian, and in the case of a youth under the age of 14 the consent of his parent or guardian.

Fingerprints after conviction can be taken under section 27 of *PACE* 1984. See *ante*, § 1–113.

A person is detained at a police station, and so prints can be taken, when he is held there temporarily having been remanded in custody by the magistrates' court: *Seymour* [1995] 9 *Archbold News* 1, CA.

Police and Criminal Evidence Act 1984, s.61A

Impressions of footwear

1–160   **61A.**—(1) Except as provided by this section, no impression of a person's footwear may be taken without the appropriate consent.

(2) Consent to the taking of an impression of a person's footwear must be in writing if it is given at a time when he is at a police station.

(3) Where a person is detained at a police station, an impression of his footwear may be taken without the appropriate consent if—

- (a) he is detained in consequence of his arrest for a recordable offence, or has been charged with a recordable offence, or informed that he will be reported for a recordable offence; and
- (b) he has not had an impression taken of his footwear in the course of the investigation of the offence by the police.

(4) Where a person mentioned in paragraph (a) of subsection (3) above has already had an impression taken of his footwear in the course of the investigation of the offence by the police, that fact shall be disregarded for the purposes of that subsection if the impression of his footwear taken previously is—

- (a) incomplete; or
- (b) is not of sufficient quality to allow satisfactory analysis, comparison or matching (whether in the case in question or generally).

(5) If an impression of a person's footwear is taken at a police station, whether with or without the appropriate consent—

(a) before it is taken, an officer shall inform him that it may be the subject of a speculative search; and

(b) the fact that the person has been informed of this possibility shall be recorded as soon as is practicable after the impression has been taken, and if he is detained at a police station, the record shall be made on his custody record.

(6) In a case where, by virtue of subsection (3) above, an impression of a person's footwear is taken without the appropriate consent—

(a) he shall be told the reason before it is taken; and

(b) the reason shall be recorded on his custody record as soon as is practicable after the impression is taken.

(7) The power to take an impression of the footwear of a person detained at a police station without the appropriate consent shall be exercisable by any constable.

(8) Nothing in this section applies to any person—

(a) arrested or detained under the terrorism provisions;

(b) arrested under an extradition arrest power.

[This section was inserted by the *Serious Organised Crime and Police Act* 2005, s.118.]

Intimate searches and samples

Police and Criminal Evidence Act 1984, s.55

Intimate searches

55.—(1) Subject to the following provisions of this section, if an officer of at least the rank of inspector has reasonable grounds for believing— **1–161**

(a) that a person who has been arrested and is in police detention may have concealed on him anything which—

(i) he could use to cause physical injury to himself or others; and

(ii) he might so use while he is in police detention or in the custody of a court; or

(b) that such a person—

(i) may have a Class A drug concealed on him; and

(ii) was in possession of it with the appropriate criminal intent before his arrest,

he may authorise an intimate search of that person.

(2) An officer may not authorise an intimate search of a person for anything unless he has reasonable grounds for believing that it cannot be found without his being intimately searched.

(3) An officer may give an authorisation under subsection (1) above orally or in writing but, if he gives it orally, he shall confirm it in writing as soon as is practicable.

(3A) A drug offence search shall not be carried out unless the appropriate consent has been given in writing.

(3B) Where it is proposed that a drug offence search be carried out, an appropriate officer shall inform the person who is to be subject to it—

(a) of the giving of the authorisation for it; and

(b) of the grounds for giving the authorisation.

(4) An intimate search which is only a drug offence search shall be by way of examination by a suitably qualified person.

(5) Except as provided by subsection (4) above, an intimate search shall be by way of examination by a suitably qualified person unless an officer of at least the rank of inspector considers that this is not practicable.

(6) An intimate search which is not carried out as mentioned in subsection (5) above shall be carried out by a constable.

(7) A constable may not carry out an intimate search of a person of the opposite sex.

(8) No intimate search may be carried out except—

     (a) at a police station;

     (b) at a hospital;

     (c) at a registered medical practitioner's surgery; or

     (d) at some other place used for medical purposes.

(9) An intimate search which is only a drug offence search may not be carried out at a police station.

(10) If an intimate search of a person is carried out, the custody record relating to him shall state—

     (a) which parts of his body were searched; and

     (b) why they were searched.

(10A) If the intimate search is a drug offence search, the custody record relating to that person shall also state—

     (a) the authorisation by virtue of which the search was carried out;

     (b) the grounds for giving the authorisation; and

     (c) the fact that the appropriate consent was given.

1–162   (11) The information required to be recorded by subsections (10) and (10A) above shall be recorded as soon as practicable after the completion of the search.

(12) The custody officer at a police station may seize and retain anything which is found on an intimate search of a person, or cause any such thing to be seized and retained—

     (a) if he believes that the person from whom it is seized may use it—

        (i) to cause physical injury to himself or any other person;

        (ii) to damage property;

        (iii) to interfere with evidence; or

        (iv) to assist him to escape; or

     (b) if he has reasonable grounds for believing that it may be evidence relating to an offence.

(13) Where anything is seized under this section, the person from whom it is seized shall be told the reason for the seizure unless he is—

     (a) violent or likely to become violent; or

     (b) incapable of understanding what is said to him.

(13A) Where the appropriate consent to a drug offence search of any person was refused without good cause, in any proceedings against that person for an offence—

     (a) the court, in determining whether there is a case to answer;

     (b) a judge, in deciding whether to grant an application made by the accused under paragraph 2 of Schedule 3 to the *Crime and Disorder Act* 1998 (applications for dismissal); and

     (c) the court or jury, in determining whether that person is guilty of the offence charged,

may draw such inferences from the refusal as appear proper.

(14) Every annual report—

     (a) under section 22 of the *Police Act* 1996; or

     (b) made by the Commissioner of Police of the Metropolis,

shall contain information about searches under this section which have been carried out in the area to which the report relates during the period to which it relates.

(14A) Every annual report under section 57 of the *Police Act* 1997 (reports by Director General of the National Crime Squad) shall contain information about searches authorised under this section by members of the National Crime Squad during the period to which the report relates.

(15) The information about such searches shall include—

     (a) the total number of searches;

     (b) the number of searches conducted by way of examination by a suitably qualified person;

     (c) the number of searches not so conducted but conducted in the presence of such a person; and

     (d) the result of the searches carried out.

(16) The information shall also include, as separate items—

     (a) the total number of drug offence searches; and

     (b) the result of those searches.

(17) In this section—

"the appropriate criminal intent" means an intent to commit an offence under—

- (a) section 5(3) of the *Misuse of Drugs Act* 1971 (possession of controlled drug with intent to supply to another); or
- (b) section 68(2) of the *Customs and Excise Management Act* 1979 (exportation etc. with intent to evade a prohibition or restriction);

"appropriate officer" means—

- (a) a constable,
- (b) a person who is designated as a detention officer in pursuance of section 38 of the *Police Reform Act* 2002 if his designation applies paragraph 33D of Schedule 4 to that Act, or
- (c) a person who is designated as a staff custody officer in pursuance of section 38 of that Act if his designation applies paragraph 35C of Schedule 4 to that Act;

"Class A drug" has the meaning assigned to it by section 2(1)(b) of the *Misuse of Drugs Act* 1971;

"drug offence search" means an intimate search for a Class A drug which an officer has authorised by virtue of subsection (1)(b) above; and

"suitably qualified person" means —

- (a) a registered medical practitioner; or
- (b) a registered nurse.

[This section is printed as amended by the *Criminal Justice Act* 1988, Sched. 15, para. 99; the *Criminal Justice and Police Act* 2001, s.79; and the *Drugs Act* 2005, s.3.]

An intimate search is physical examination of body orifices other than the mouth: the **1–163** *PACE Act* 1984, s.65. The Code of Practice for the Detention, Treatment and Questioning of Persons, Code C; Annex A gives specific guidance on the conduct of intimate searches. Customs officers have power to conduct intimate searches under section 55(1)(a) only: S.I. 1985 No. 1800.

Police and Criminal Evidence Act 1984, s.55A

X-rays and ultrasound scans

55A.—(1) If an officer of at least the rank of inspector has reasonable grounds for believing **1–164** that a person who has been arrested for an offence and is in police detention—

- (a) may have swallowed a Class A drug, and
- (b) was in possession of it with the appropriate criminal intent before his arrest,

the officer may authorise that an x-ray is taken of the person or an ultrasound scan is carried out on the person (or both).

(2) An x-ray must not be taken of a person and an ultrasound scan must not be carried out on him unless the appropriate consent has been given in writing.

(3) If it is proposed that an x-ray is taken or an ultrasound scan is carried out, an appropriate officer must inform the person who is to be subject to it—

- (a) of the giving of the authorisation for it, and
- (b) of the grounds for giving the authorisation.

(4) An x-ray may be taken or an ultrasound scan carried out only by a suitably qualified person and only at—

- (a) a hospital,
- (b) a registered medical practitioner's surgery, or
- (c) some other place used for medical purposes.

(5) The custody record of the person must also state—

- (a) the authorisation by virtue of which the x-ray was taken or the ultrasound scan was carried out,
- (b) the grounds for giving the authorisation, and
- (c) the fact that the appropriate consent was given.

(6) The information required to be recorded by subsection (5) must be recorded as soon as practicable after the x-ray has been taken or ultrasound scan carried out (as the case may be).

(7) Every annual report-

(a) under section 22 of the *Police Act* 1996, or

(b) made by the Commissioner of Police of the Metropolis,

must contain information about x-rays which have been taken and ultrasound scans which have been carried out under this section in the area to which the report relates during the period to which it relates.

(8) The information about such x-rays and ultrasound scans must be presented separately and must include—

(a) the total number of x-rays;

(b) the total number of ultrasound scans;

(c) the results of the x-rays;

(d) the results of the ultrasound scans.

(9) If the appropriate consent to an x-ray or ultrasound scan of any person is refused without good cause, in any proceedings against that person for an offence—

(a) the court, in determining whether there is a case to answer,

(b) a judge, in deciding whether to grant an application made by the accused under paragraph 2 of Schedule 3 to the *Crime and Disorder Act* 1998 (applications for dismissal), and

(c) the court or jury, in determining whether that person is guilty of the offence charged,

may draw such inferences from the refusal as appear proper.

(10) In this section "the appropriate criminal intent", "appropriate officer", "Class A drug" and "suitably qualified person" have the same meanings as in section 55 above.

[This section was inserted by section 5 of the *Drugs Act* 2005.]

A person who has been arrested may be X-rayed or scanned to see if there are drugs in his body. It relates only to Class A drugs and the power is only available if there are reasonable grounds to believe that the person arrested was in possession of the drugs with the appropriate criminal intent. That intent is defined as being an intention to commit an offence of possessing controlled drugs with intent to supply or drug smuggling under the *Customs and Excise Management Act* 1979. Consent must be given in writing and the search must be conducted under the proper medical conditions and fully recorded. If consent is refused without good cause the court may draw an adverse inference from that refusal at trial.

Police and Criminal Evidence Act, s.62

Intimate samples

1–165

62.—(1) Subject to section 63B below an intimate sample may be taken from a person in police detention only—

(a) if a police officer of at least the rank of inspector authorises it to be taken; and

(b) if the appropriate consent is given.

(1A) An intimate sample may be taken from a person who is not in police detention but from whom, in the course of the investigation of an offence, two or more non-intimate samples suitable for the same means of analysis have been taken which have proved insufficient—

(a) if a police officer of at least the rank of inspector authorises it to be taken; and

(b) if the appropriate consent is given.

(2) An officer may only give an authorisation under subsection (1) or (1A) above if he has reasonable grounds—

(a) for suspecting the involvement of the person from whom the sample is to be taken in a recordable offence; and

(b) for believing that the sample will tend to confirm or disprove his involvement.

(3) An officer may give an authorisation under subsection (1) or (1A) above orally or in writing but, if he gives it orally, he shall confirm it in writing as soon as is practicable.

(4) The appropriate consent must be given in writing.

(5) Where—

(a) an authorisation has been given; and

(b) it is proposed that an intimate sample shall be taken in pursuance of the authorisation, an officer shall inform the person from whom the sample is to be taken—

    (i) of the giving of the authorisation; and

    (ii) of the grounds for giving it.

(6) The duty imposed by subsection (5)(ii) above includes a duty to state the nature of the offence in which it is suspected that the person from whom the sample is to be taken has been involved.

(7) If an intimate sample is taken from a person—

    (a) the authorisation by virtue of which it was taken;

    (b) the grounds for giving the authorisation; and

    (c) the fact that the appropriate consent was given,

shall be recorded as soon as is practicable after the sample is taken.

(7A) If an intimate sample is taken from a person at a police station—

    (a) before the sample is taken, an officer shall inform him that it may be the subject of a speculative search; and

    (b) the fact that the person has been informed of this possibility shall be recorded as soon as practicable after the sample has been taken.

(8) If an intimate sample is taken from a person detained at a police station, the matters required to be recorded by subsection (7) or (7A) above shall be recorded in his custody record.

(9) In the case of an intimate sample which is a dental impression, the sample may be taken from a person only by a registered dentist.

(9A) In the case of any other form of intimate sample, except in the case of a sample of urine, the sample may be taken from a person only by—

    (a) a registered medical practitioner; or

    (b) a registered health care professional.

(10) Where the appropriate consent to the taking of an intimate sample from a person **1–166** was refused without good cause, in any proceedings against that person for an offence—

    (a) the court, in determining—

        (i) *whether to commit that person for trial; or*

        (ii) whether there is a case to answer; and

    (aa) a judge, in deciding whether to grant an application made by the accused under—

        (i) *section 6 of the* Criminal Justice Act *1987 (application for dismissal of charge of serious fraud in respect of which notice of transfer has been given under section 4 of that Act); or*

        (ii) *paragraph 5 of Schedule 6 to the* Criminal Justice Act *1991 (application for dismissal of charge of violent or sexual offence involving child in respect of which notice of transfer has been given under section 53 of that Act; and* [paragraph 2 of Schedule 3 to the *Crime and Disorder Act* 1998 (applications for dismissal); and]

    (b) the court or jury, in determining whether that person is guilty of the offence charged,

may draw such inferences from the refusal as appear proper.

(11) Nothing in this section applies to the taking of a specimen for the purposes of any of the provisions of sections 4 to 11 of the *Road Traffic Act* 1988 or of sections 26 to 38 of the *Transport and Works Act* 1992.

(12) Nothing in this section applies to a person arrested or detained under the terrorism procedures; and subsection (1A) shall not apply where the non-intimate samples mentioned in that subsection were taken under paragraph 10 of Schedule 8 to the *Terrorism Act* 2000.

[This section is printed as amended and repealed in part by the *Road Traffic (Consequential Provisions) Act* 1988, s.4 and Sched. 3, para. 27(4); the *Criminal Justice and Public Order Act* 1994, ss.54(1)-(5) and 168(1)-(3), and Scheds 9, para. 24, 10, paras 57 and 62(4)(a) and 11; the *Terrorism Act* 2000, s.125 and Sched. 15, para. 5(8); the *Criminal Justice and Court Services Act* 2000, s.74 and Sched. 7, para. 78; the *Criminal Justice and Police Act* 2001, s.80(1); and the *Police Reform Act* 2002, ss.53(2) and 54(1). Sub-paras (i) and (ii) of subs. (10)(aa) are replaced by the words in square brackets that follow them by the *Criminal Justice Act* 2003, s.41, and Sched. 3, para. 56(1) and (2)(b). This amendment came into force on May 9, 2005 (*Criminal*

Justice Act 2003 (Commencement No. 9) Order 2005 (S.I. 2005 No. 1267)) in relation to cases sent for trial under sections 51 or 51A(3)(d) of the *Crime and Disorder Act* 1998. Otherwise, it comes into force on a day to be appointed. Subsections (10)(a)(i) is repealed as from a day to be appointed by the *Criminal Justice Act* 2003, ss.41 and 332, Sched. 3, para. 56(2)(a), and Sched. 37, Pt 4.]

Intimate samples

1–167 Intimate samples are defined in section 65 as a sample of blood, semen or any other tissue fluid, urine or pubic hair; a dental impression; a swab taken from a person's body orifice other than the mouth. For appropriate consent, see *ante*, § 1–165.

Authorisation does not have to be sought before consent, but if authorisation were granted first any subsequent consent given may be on a dubious basis: *Butt*, unreported, February 20, 1998, CA. An analysis of the result of intimate samples taken under the provisions of this section in the course of an investigation can be used in proceedings for a separate investigation into a different offence: *Kelt* (1993) 99 Cr.App.R. 372.

Other samples

Police and Criminal Evidence Act 1984, s.63

Other samples

1–168   **63.**—(1) Except as provided by this section, a non-intimate sample may not be taken from a person without the appropriate consent.

(2) Consent to the taking of a non-intimate sample must be given in writing.

(2A) A non-intimate sample may be taken from a person without the appropriate consent if two conditions are satisfied.

(2B) The first is that the person is in police detention in consequence of his arrest for a recordable offence.

(2C) The second is that—

(a) he has not had a non-intimate sample of the same type and from the same part of the body taken in the course of the investigation of the offence by the police, or

(b) he has had such a sample taken but it proved insufficient.

(3) A non-intimate sample may be taken from a person without the appropriate consent if—

(a) he is being held in custody by the police on the authority of a court; and

(b) an officer of at least the rank of inspector authorises it to be taken without the appropriate consent.

(3A) A non-intimate sample may be taken from a person (whether or not he is in police detention or held in custody by the police on the authority of a court) without the appropriate consent if—

(a) he has been charged with a recordable offence or informed that he will be reported for such an offence; and

(b) either he has not had a non-intimate sample taken from him in the course of the investigation of the offence by the police or he had a non-intimate sample taken from him but either it was not suitable for the same means of analysis or, though so suitable, the sample proved insufficient.

(3B) A non-intimate sample may be taken from a person without the appropriate consent if he has been convicted of a recordable offence.

(3C) A non-intimate sample may also be taken from a person without the appropriate consent if he is a person to whom section 2 of the *Criminal Evidence (Amendment) Act* 1997 applies (persons detained following acquittal on grounds of insanity or finding of unfitness to plead).

(4) An officer may only give an authorisation under subsection (3) above if he has reasonable grounds—

(a) for suspecting the involvement of the person from whom the sample is to be taken in a recordable offence; and

(b) for believing that the sample will tend to confirm or disprove his involvement.

(5) An officer may give an authorisation under subsection (3) above orally or in writing **1–169**
but, if he gives it orally, he shall confirm it in writing as soon as is practicable.

(5A) An officer shall not give an authorisation under subsection (3) above for the taking
from any person of a non-intimate sample consisting of a skin impression if—

(a) a skin impression of the same part of the body has already been taken from that
person in the course of the investigation of the offence; and

(b) the impression previously taken is not one that has proved insufficient.

(6) Where—

(a) an authorisation has been given; and

(b) it is proposed that a non-intimate sample shall be taken in pursuance of the authorisation,

an officer shall inform the person from whom the sample is to be taken—

(i)   of the giving of the authorisation; and

(ii) of the grounds for giving it.

(7) The duty imposed by subsection (6)(ii) above includes a duty to state the nature of
the offence in which it is suspected that the person from whom the sample is to be taken
has been involved.

(8) If a non-intimate sample is taken from a person by virtue of subsection (3) above—

(a) the authorisation by virtue of which it was taken; and

(b) the grounds for giving the authorisation,

shall be recorded as soon as is practicable after the sample is taken.

(8A) In a case where by virtue of subsection (2A), (3A), (3B) or (3C) above a sample is
taken from a person without the appropriate consent—

(a) he shall be told the reason before the sample is taken; and

(b) the reason shall be recorded as soon as practicable after the sample is taken.

(8B) If a non-intimate sample is taken from a person at a police station, whether with or
without the appropriate consent—

(a) before the sample is taken, an officer shall inform him that it may be the subject
of a speculative search; and

(b) the fact that the person has been informed of this possibility shall be recorded as
soon as practicable after the sample has been taken.

(9) If a non-intimate sample is taken from a person detained at a police station, the mat- **1–170**
ters required to be recorded by subsection (8) or (8A) or (8B) above shall be recorded in
his custody record.

(9ZA) The power to take a non-intimate sample from a person without the appropriate
consent shall be exercisable by any constable.

(9A) Subsection (3B) above shall not apply to any person convicted before 10th April
1995 unless he is a person to whom section 1 of the *Criminal Evidence (Amendment) Act*
1997 applies (persons imprisoned or detained by virtue of pre-existing conviction for sexual offence etc).

[(9A) Where a non-intimate sample consisting of a skin impression is taken electronically from a person, it must be taken only in such manner, and using such devices, as the
Secretary of State has approved for the purpose of the electronic taking of such an
impression.]

(10) Nothing in this section applies to a person arrested or detained under the terrorism provisions word substituted by *Criminal Justice and Police Act* 2001, Part 3 section
80(1).

(11) Nothing in this section applies to a person arrested under an extradition arrest
power.

[This section is printed as amended by the *Criminal Justice and Public Order Act*
1994, ss. 55(1)-(5) and 168(2), and Sched. 10, paras 58 and 62(4)(b); the *Criminal Evidence (Amendment) Act* 1997, ss.1(2) and 2(2); the *Terrorism Act* 2000, s.125 and
Sched. 15, para. 5(9); the *Criminal Justice and Police Act* 2001, s.80(1),(3); the *Police
Reform Act* 2002, s.107(1), and Sched. 7, para. 9(4); the *Extradition Act* 2003, s.169(4);
and the *Criminal Justice Act* 2003, s.10; and as amended, as from a day to be appointed, by the *Criminal Justice and Police Act* 2001, s.80(4) (insertion of second subs.
numbered (9A)).]

Non-intimate samples include saliva, skin impressions, mouth swabs, hair (other than pubic hair) and samples from under the nails: *PACE* 1984, s.65.

For "appropriate consent", see *ante*, § 1–165.

Supplementary provisions

Police and Criminal Evidence Act 1984, s.63A

Fingerprints and samples: supplementary provisions

1–171   **63A.**—(1) Where a person has been arrested on suspicion of being involved in a recordable offence or has been charged with such an offence or has been informed that he will be reported for such an offence, fingerprints, or impressions of footwear or samples or the information derived from samples taken under any power conferred by this Part of this Act from the person may be checked against—

     (a) other fingerprints, or impressions of footwear or samples to which the person seeking to check has access and which are held by or on behalf of any one or more relevant law-enforcement authorities or which are held in connection with or as a result of an investigation of an offence;

     (b) information derived from other samples if the information is contained in records to which the person seeking to check has access and which are held as mentioned in paragraph (a) above.

[(1ZA) Fingerprints taken by virtue of section 61(6A) above may be checked against other fingerprints to which the person seeking to check has access and which are held by or on behalf of any one or more relevant law-enforcement authorities or which are held in connection with or as a result of an investigation of an offence.]

(1A) In subsection (1) [and (1ZA)] above "relevant law-enforcement authority" means—

     (a) a police force;

     (b) the Serious Organised Crime Agency;

     (c) [*Repealed.*];

     (d) a public authority (not falling within paragraphs (a) to (c)) with functions in any part of the British Islands which consist of or include the investigation of crimes or the charging of offenders;

     (e) any person with functions in any country or territory outside the United Kingdom which—

         (i) correspond to those of a police force; or

         (ii) otherwise consist of or include the investigation of conduct contrary to the law of that country or territory, or the apprehension of persons guilty of such conduct;

     (f) any person with functions under any international agreement which consist of or include the investigation of conduct which is—

         (i) unlawful under the law of one or more places,

         (ii) prohibited by such an agreement, or

         (iii) contrary to international law, or the apprehension of persons guilty of such conduct.

(1B) The reference in subsection (1A) above to a police force is a reference to any of the following—

     (a) any police force maintained under section 2 of the *Police Act* 1996 (police forces in England and Wales outside London);

     (b) the metropolitan police force;

     (c) the City of London police force;

     (d) any police force maintained under or by virtue of section 1 of the *Police (Scotland) Act* 1967;

     (e) the Police Service of Northern Ireland;

     (f) the Police Service of Northern Ireland Reserve;

     (g) the Ministry of Defence Police;

     (h) the Royal Navy Police;

     (i) the Royal Military Police;

     (j) the Royal Air Force Police;

    (k) *the Royal Marines Police;*

    (l) the British Transport Police;

    (m) the States of Jersey Police Force;

    (n) the salaried police force of the Island of Guernsey;

    (o) the Isle of Man Constabulary.

(1C) Where—

    (a) fingerprints, impressions of footwear or samples have been taken from any person in connection with the investigation of an offence but otherwise than in circumstances to which subsection (1) above applies, and

    (b) that person has given his consent in writing to the use in a speculative search of the fingerprints or of the samples and of information derived from them,

the fingerprints or impressions of footwear or, as the case may be, those samples and that information may be checked against any of the fingerprints, impressions of footwear, samples or information mentioned in paragraph (a) or (b) of that subsection.

(1D) A consent given for the purposes of subsection (1C) above shall not be capable of being withdrawn.

(2) Where a sample of hair other than pubic hair is to be taken the sample may be taken either by cutting hairs or by plucking hairs with their roots so long as no more are plucked than the person taking the sample reasonably considers to be necessary for a sufficient sample.

(3) Where any power to take a sample is exercisable in relation to a person the sample may be taken in a prison or other institution to which the *Prison Act* 1952 applies.

(3A) Where—

    (a) the power to take a non-intimate sample under section 63(3B) above is exercisable in relation to any person who is detained under Part III of the *Mental Health Act* 1983 in pursuance of—

        (i) a hospital order or interim hospital order made following his conviction for the recordable offence in question, or

        (ii) a transfer direction given at a time when he was detained in pursuance of any sentence or order imposed following that conviction, or

    (b) the power to take a non-intimate sample under section 63(3C) above is exercisable in relation to any person,

the sample may be taken in the hospital in which he is detained under that Part of that Act.

Expressions used in this subsection and in the *Mental Health Act* 1983 have the same meaning as in that Act.

(3B) Where the power to take a non-intimate sample under section 63(3B) above is exercisable in relation to a person detained in pursuance of directions of the Secretary of State under section 92 of the *Powers of Criminal Courts (Sentencing) Act* 2000 the sample may be taken at the place where he is so detained.

(4) Any constable may, within the allowed period, require a person who is neither in police detention nor held in custody by the police on the authority of a court to attend a police station in order to have a sample taken where—

    (a) the person has been charged with a recordable offence or informed that he will be reported for such an offence and either he has not had a sample taken from him in the course of the investigation of the offence by the police or he has had a sample so taken from him but either it was not suitable for the same means of analysis or, though so suitable, the sample proved insufficient; or

    (b) the person has been convicted of a recordable offence and either he has not had a sample taken from him since the conviction or he has had a sample taken from him (before or after his conviction) but either it was not suitable for the same means of analysis or, though so suitable, the sample proved insufficient.

(5) The period allowed for requiring a person to attend a police station for the purpose specified in subsection (4) above is—

    (a) in the case of a person falling within paragraph (a), one month beginning with the date of the charge or of his being informed as mentioned in that paragraph or one month beginning with the date on which the appropriate officer is informed of the fact that the sample is not suitable for the same means of analysis or has proved insufficient, as the case may be;

    (b) in the case of a person falling within paragraph (b), one month beginning with

1–172

1–173

the date of the conviction or one month beginning with the date on which the appropriate officer is informed of the fact that the sample is not suitable for the same means of analysis or has proved insufficient, as the case may be.

(6) A requirement under subsection (4) above—

(a) shall give the person at least 7 days within which he must so attend; and

(b) may direct him to attend at a specified time of day or between specified times of day.

(7) Any constable may arrest without a warrant a person who has failed to comply with a requirement under subsection (4) above.

(8) In this section "the appropriate officer" is—

(a) in the case of a person falling within subsection (4)(a), the officer investigating the offence with which that person has been charged or as to which he was informed that he would be reported;

(b) in the case of a person falling within subsection (4)(b), the officer in charge of the police station from which the investigation of the offence of which he was convicted was conducted.

[This section was inserted by the *Criminal Justice and Public Order Act* 1994, s.56. It is printed as amended by the *Criminal Procedure and Investigations Act* 1996, s.64(1); the *Criminal Evidence (Amendment) Act* 1997, ss.3 and 4; the *Power of Criminal Courts (Sentencing) Act* 2000, s.165(1) and Sched. 9, para. 97; the *Criminal Justice and Police Act* 2001, s.81; the *Serious Organised Crime and Police Act* 2005, ss.59 and 118(1) and (3), and Sched. 4, paras 43 and 46; and the *Armed Forces Act* 2006, s.378(1) and (2), and Sched. 16, para. 100(a); and as amended, as from a day to be appointed, by the *Serious Organised Crime and Police Act* 2005, s.117(5) (insertion of subs.(1ZA) and reference thereto in subs.(1A)); and the *Armed Forces Act* 2006, s.378(1) and (2), Sched. 16, para. 100(b), and Sched. 17 (amendment of subs. (1B)).]

1–174   Detention under section 92 of the *Powers of Criminal Courts (Sentencing) Act* 2000 relates to offenders under the age of 18 convicted of murder or other serious offences who are ordered to be detained at her Majesty's pleasure or other specified period.

A recordable offence is one to which regulations in section 27 apply. See *ante*, § 1–113.

This section allows for the checking of fingerprints and samples through several databases as an aid to detection.

Testing for the presence of Class A drugs

1–175   Under sections 63B and 63C of the 1984 Act the police have power to take a sample from a detained person to test for Class A drugs. The Act has been amended by the *Criminal Justice Act* 2003 and the *Drugs Act* 2005, s.7, so that such tests can now be done when a person is either arrested or charged. The power is exercisable in respect of trigger offences (listed in Schedule 6 to the *Criminal Justice and Court Services Act* 2000) or when a senior police officer has reasonable grounds to suspect that the misuse of Class A drugs was a causal or contributory factor to the offence. Once a sample has been taken and proves positive the result can be used in court to inform bail and sentencing decisions. It may also give rise to the police requiring the defendant to attend for drug assessment and treatment. For full details of the statutory provisions refer to Ch.18, Offences Involving Drugs, §§ 18–71 *et seq.*

Destruction of fingerprints and samples

Police and Criminal Evidence Act 1984, s.64

Destruction of fingerprints and samples
1–176   64.—(1A) Where—

(a) fingerprints, impressions of footwear or samples are taken from a person in connection with the investigation of an offence, and

(b) subsection (3) below does not require them to be destroyed,
the fingerprints, impressions of footwear or samples may be retained after they have fulfilled the
purposes for which they were taken but shall not be used by any person except for purposes related to the prevention or detection of crime, the investigation of an offence *or the conduct of a
prosecution* [, the conduct of a prosecution or the identification of a deceased person or of the
person from whom a body part came].

(1B) In subsection (1A) above—

   (a) the reference to using a fingerprint or an impression of footwear includes a refer-
       ence to allowing any check to be made against it under section 63A(1) or (1C)[
       above and to disclosing it to any person;

   (b) the reference to using a sample includes a reference to allowing any check to be
       made under section 63A(1) or (1C) above against it or against information derived
       from it and to disclosing it or any such information to any person;

   (c) the reference to crime includes a reference to any conduct which—

       (i) constitutes one or more criminal offences (whether under the law of a part
            of the United Kingdom or of a country or territory outside the United
            Kingdom); or

       (ii) is, or corresponds to, any conduct which, if it all took place in any one part
            of the United Kingdom, would constitute one or more criminal offences;
       and

   (d) the references to an investigation and to a prosecution include references,
       respectively, to any investigation outside the United Kingdom of any crime or
       suspected crime and to a prosecution brought in respect of any crime in a country
       or territory outside the United Kingdom.

[(1BA) Fingerprints taken from a person by virtue of section 61(6A) above must be
destroyed as soon as they have fulfilled the purpose for which they were taken.]

(3) If—

   (a) fingerprints, impressions of footwear or samples are taken from a person in con-
       nection with the investigation of an offence; and

   (b) that person is not suspected of having committed the offence,
they must, except as provided in the following provisions of this section, be destroyed as soon as
they have fulfilled the purpose for which they were taken.

(3AA) Samples, fingerprints and impressions of footwear are not required to be **1–177**
destroyed under subsection (3) above if—

   (a) they were taken for the purposes of the investigation of an offence of which a
       person has been convicted; and

   (b) a sample, fingerprint, (or as the case may be) an impression of footwear was also
       taken from the convicted person for the purposes of that investigation.

(3AB) Subject to subsection (3AC) below, where a person is entitled under *subsection (3)*
[subsection (1BA) or (3)] above to the destruction of any fingerprint or sample taken from him
(or would be but for subsection (3AA) above, neither the fingerprint, nor the impression of
footwear, nor the sample, nor any information derived from the sample, shall be used—

   (a) in evidence against the person who is or would be entitled to the destruction of that
       fingerprint, impression of footwear or sample; or

   (b) for the purposes of the investigation of any offence;
and subsection (1B) above applies for the purposes of this subsection as it applies for the purposes
of subsection (1A) above.

(3AC) Where a person from whom a fingerprint, impression of footwear or sample has
been taken consents in writing to its retention—

   (a) that [fingerprint,] impression of footwear or sample need not be destroyed
       under subsection (3) above;

   (b) subsection (3AB) above shall not restrict the use that may be made of the
       fingerprint, impression of footwear or sample or, in the case of a sample, of any[
       information derived from it; and

   (c) that consent shall be treated as comprising a consent for the purposes of section
       63A(1C) above;
and a consent given for the purpose of this subsection shall not be capable of being
withdrawn.

[This subsection does not apply to fingerprints taken from a person by virtue of section 61(6A)
above.]

(3AD) For the purposes of subsection (3AC) above it shall be immaterial whether the consent is given at, before or after the time when the entitlement to the destruction of the fingerprint, impression of footwear or sample arises.

(4) [*Repealed by* Criminal Justice and Police Act *2001, s.137 , and Sched. 7, Pt II.*]

(5) If fingerprints or impressions of footwear are destroyed—

    (a) any copies of the fingerprints or impressions of footwear shall also be destroyed; and

    (b) any chief officer of police controlling access to computer data relating to the fingerprints or impressions of footwear shall make access to the data impossible, as soon as it is practicable to do so.

(6) A person who asks to be allowed to witness the destruction of his fingerprints or impressions of footwear or copies of them shall have a right to witness it.

(6A) If—

    (a) subsection (5)(b) above falls to be complied with; and

    (b) the person to whose fingerprints or impressions of footwear the data relate asks for a certificate that it has been complied with,

such a certificate shall be issued to him, not later than the end of the period of three months beginning with the day on which he asks for it, by the responsible chief officer of police or a person authorised by him or on his behalf for the purposes of this section.

(6B) In this section—

"the responsible chief officer of police" means the chief officer of police in whose police area the computer data were put on to the computer.

1–178   (7) Nothing in this section—

    (a) affects any power conferred by paragraph 18(2) of Schedule 2 to the *Immigration Act* 1971 or section 20 of the *Immigration and Asylum Act* 1999 (disclosure of police information to the Secretary of State for use for immigration purposes); or

    (b) applies to a person arrested or detained under the terrorism provisions.

[This section is printed as amended by the *Criminal Justice Act* 1988, s.148; the *Criminal Justice and Public Order Act* 1994, s.57; the *Police Act* 1996, s.103, and Sched. 7, para. 37; the *Criminal Justice and Police Act* 2001, s.82; and the *Serious Organised Crime and Police Act* 2005, s.118(1) and (4); and as amended, as from a day to be appointed, by the *Serious Organised Crime and Police Act* 2005, s.117(6)-(10).]

1–179   For "fingerprints", see *ante*, § 1–159; for "intimate sample", see *ante*, § 1–167; and for "non-intimate sample", see *ante*, § 1–170.

In *Att.-Gen.'s Reference (No. 3 of 1999)* [2001] 1 Cr.App.R. 34, CA, it was held that the combined effect of the previous version of section 64(1) and (3B) was to enact an absolute prohibition on the use of samples which should have been destroyed, or information derived therefrom, in any subsequent proceedings. In the House of Lords ([2001] 2 A.C. 1), it was held that such evidence was not inadmissible merely because of a breach of these provisions, but such a breach was a relevant factor for the judge to take into account in exercising his discretion to exclude such evidence. Section 64 has now been amended by the *Criminal Justice and Police Act* 2001, s.82, so that the only "prohibition" relates to a person who provides a sample but who is not suspected of an offence. Following the reasoning in *Att.-Gen.'s Reference (No. 3 of 1999)*, if the sample in respect of such a person is improperly retained, this will not lead to the automatic exclusion of evidence derived therefrom.

Section 64 applies to DNA profiles: *Nathaniel* [1995] 2 Cr.App.R. 565, CA. The use of DNA profiles from destroyed samples to form a database for use for statistical purposes does not breach section 64: *Willoughby* [1997] 1 *Archbold News* 2, CA.

Section 64(1A) is not incompatible with Article 8(1) of the European Convention on Human Rights; even if Article 8 is engaged, the interference is justified under Article 8(2): *R. (S.) v. Chief Constable of South Yorkshire Police*; *R. (Marper) v. Same* [2004] 1 W.L.R. 2196, HL. The restriction in subsection (1A) applies to fingerprints and samples taken from volunteers and victims, as well as from suspects: *Lambeth London Borough v. S., C., V. and J. (by his guardian)* [2007] 1 F.L.R. 152, Fam. D. (Ryder J.).

Photographing of suspects

Police and Criminal Evidence Act 1984, s.64A

Photographing of suspects etc

1–180

64A.—(1) A person who is detained at a police station may be photographed—

    (a) with the appropriate consent; or

    (b) if the appropriate consent is withheld or it is not practicable to obtain it, without it.

(1A) A person falling within subsection (1B) below may, on the occasion of the relevant event referred to in subsection (1B), be photographed elsewhere than at a police station—

    (a) with the appropriate consent; or

    (b) if the appropriate consent is withheld or it is not practicable to obtain it, without it.

(1B) A person falls within this subsection if he has been—

    (a) arrested by a constable for an offence;

    (b) taken into custody by a constable after being arrested for an offence by a person other than a constable;

    (c) made subject to a requirement to wait with a community support officer under paragraph 2(3) or (3B) of Schedule 4 to the *Police Reform Act* 2002 ("the 2002 Act");

    (d) given a penalty notice by a constable in uniform under Chapter 1 of Part 1 of the *Criminal Justice and Police Act* 2001, a penalty notice by a constable under section 444A of the *Education Act* 1996, or a fixed penalty notice by a constable in uniform under section 54 of the *Road Traffic Offenders Act* 1988;

    (e) given a notice in relation to a relevant fixed penalty offence (within the meaning of paragraph 1 of Schedule 4 to the 2002 Act) by a community support officer by virtue of a designation applying that paragraph to him; or

    (f) given a notice in relation to a relevant fixed penalty offence (within the meaning of paragraph 1 of Schedule 5 to the 2002 Act) by an accredited person by virtue of accreditation specifying that that paragraph applies to him.

(2) A person proposing to take a photograph of any person under this section—

    (a) may, for the purpose of doing so, require the removal of any item or substance worn on or over the whole or any part of the head or face of the person to be photographed; and

    (b) if the requirement is not complied with, may remove the item or substance himself.

(3) Where a photograph may be taken under this section, the only persons entitled to take the photograph are constables.

(4) A photograph taken under this section—

    (a) may be used by, or disclosed to, any person for any purpose related to the prevention or detection of crime, the investigation of an offence or the conduct of a prosecution or to the enforcement of a sentence; and

    (b) after being so used or disclosed, may be retained but may not be used or disclosed except for a purpose so related.

(5) In subsection (4)—

    (a) the reference to crime includes a reference to any conduct which—

        (i) constitutes one or more criminal offences (whether under the law of a part of the United Kingdom or of a country or territory outside the United Kingdom); or

        (ii) is, or corresponds to, any conduct which, if it all took place in any one part of the United Kingdom, would constitute one or more criminal offences; and

    (b) the references to an investigation and to a prosecution include references, respectively, to any investigation outside the United Kingdom of any crime or suspected crime and to a prosecution brought in respect of any crime in a country or territory outside the United Kingdom; and

    (c) "sentence" includes any order made by a court in England and Wales when dealing with an offender in respect of his offence.

(6) References in this section to taking a photograph include references to using any process by means of which a visual image may be produced; and references to photographing a person shall be construed accordingly.

(6A) In this section, a "photograph" includes a moving image, and corresponding expressions shall be construed accordingly.

(7) Nothing in this section applies to a person arrested under an extradition arrest power.

[This section was inserted by the *Anti-Terrorism, Crime and Security Act* 2001, s.92. It is printed as amended by the *Police Reform Act* 2002, s.107(1), and Sched. 7, para. 9(5); the *Extradition Act* 2003, s.169(5); and the *Serious Organised Crime and Police Act* 2005, s.116.]

For "appropriate consent", see *ante*, § 1–165.

(4) Tape recording of interviews

Police and Criminal Evidence Act 1984, s.60

Tape-recording of interviews

1–181   **60.**—(1) It shall be the duty of the Secretary of State—

    (a) to issue a code of practice in connection with the tape-recording of interviews of persons suspected of the commission of criminal offences which are held by police officers at police stations; and

    (b) to make an order requiring the tape-recording of interviews of persons suspected of the commission of criminal offences, or of such descriptions of criminal offences as may be specified in the order, which are so held, in accordance with the code as it has effect for the time being.

(2) An order under subsection (1) above shall be made by statutory instrument and shall be subject to annulment in pursuance of a resolution of either House of Parliament.

1–182   Code E is the relevant code for the Tape Recording of Interviews with Suspects. The relevant order by the Secretary of State has been made for all police areas and now all interviews of those suspected of the commission of indictable offences must be tape recorded at police stations. The only exemption is for terrorism offences.

In addition there is a Practice Direction ([2002] 1 W.L.R. 2870) about the tape recording of police interviews in relation to the preparation for proceedings in the Crown Court which may also assist for magistrates' court proceedings.

Equipment is available for tapes to be played in the magistrates' courts and either full or edited transcripts may be adduced as evidence by the interviewing officer.

(5) Visual recording of interviews

Police and Criminal Evidence Act 1984, s.60A

Visual recording of interviews

1–183   **60A.**—(1) The Secretary of State shall have power—

    (a) to issue a code of practice for the visual recording of interviews held by police officers at police stations; and

    (b) to make an order requiring the visual recording of interviews so held, and requiring the visual recording to be in accordance with the code for the time being in force under this section.

(2) A requirement imposed by an order under this section may be imposed in relation to such cases or police stations in such areas, or both, as may be specified or described in the order.

(3) An order under subsection (1) above shall be made by statutory instrument and shall be subject to annulment in pursuance of a resolution of either House of Parliament.

(4) In this section—

    (a) references to any interview are references to an interview of a person suspected of a criminal offence; and

(b) references to a visual recording include references to a visual recording in which an audio recording is comprised.

[This section was inserted by the *Criminal Justice and Police Act* 2001, s.76(1).]

Orders making visual recordings of interview mandatory in certain police areas were revoked in November 2003. Police officers retain a discretion to record interviews visually.

Code F is the Code of Practice covering the Visual Recording of Interviews with Suspects.

(6) Right to have someone informed when arrested

Police and Criminal Evidence Act 1984, s.56

Right to have someone informed when arrested

56.—(1) Where a person has been arrested and is being held in custody in a police station or **1–184** other premises, he shall be entitled, if he so requests, to have one friend or relative or other person who is known to him or who is likely to take an interest in his welfare told, as soon as is practicable except to the extent that delay is permitted by this section, that he has been arrested and is being detained there.

(2) Delay is only permitted—

(a) in the case of a person who is in police detention for an indictable offence; and

(b) if an officer of at least the rank of inspector authorises it.

(3) In any case the person in custody must be permitted to exercise the right conferred by subsection (1) above within 36 hours from the relevant time, as defined in section 41(2) above.

(4) An officer may give an authorisation under subsection (2) above orally or in writing but, if he gives it orally, he shall confirm it in writing as soon as is practicable.

(5) Subject to subsection (5A) below an officer may only authorise delay where he has reasonable grounds for believing that telling the named person of the arrest—

(a) will lead to interference with or harm to evidence connected with an indictable offence or interference with or physical injury to other persons; or

(b) will lead to the alerting of other persons suspected of having committed such an offence but not yet arrested for it; or

(c) will hinder the recovery of any property obtained as a result of such an offence.

(5A) An officer may also authorise delay where he has reasonable grounds for believing that—

(a) the person detained for an indictable offence has benefited from his criminal conduct, and

(b) the recovery of the value of the property constituting the benefit will be hindered by telling the named person of the arrest.

(5B) For the purposes of subsection (5A) above the question whether a person has benefited from his criminal conduct is to be decided in accordance with Part 2 of the *Proceeds of Crime Act* 2002.

(6) If a delay is authorised—

(a) the detained person shall be told the reason for it; and

(b) the reason shall be noted on his custody record.

(7) The duties imposed by subsection (6) above shall be performed as soon as is practicable.

(8) The rights conferred by this section on a person detained at a police station or other premises are exercisable whenever he is transferred from one place to another; and this section applies to each subsequent occasion on which they are exercisable as it applies to the first such occasion.

(9) There may be no further delay in permitting the exercise of the right conferred by subsection (1) above once the reason for authorising delay ceases to subsist.

(10) Nothing in this section applies to a person arrested or detained under the terrorism provisions.

[This section is printed as amended and repealed in part by the *Drug Trafficking*

Offences Act 1986, s.32; the *Criminal Justice Act* 1988, s.99(2); the *Terrorism Act* 2000, s.125, and Sched. 15, para. 5(5); the *Criminal Justice and Police Act* 2001, s.74; the *Proceeds of Crime Act* 2002, s.456, and Sched. 11, para. 14(2); and the *Serious Organised Crime and Police Act* 2005, s.111, and Sched. 7, para. 43(1) and (9).]

1–185   Code C deals with the right of a person detained at the police station not to be held incommunicado (para. C5) and Annex B deals with the delay in notifying arrest or allowing access to legal advice.

(7) Additional rights of children and young persons

Children and Young Persons Act 1933, s.34

1–186   **34.**—(1) *[Repealed by* Criminal Justice Act *1991, s.56.]*

(2) Where a child or young person is in police detention, such steps as are practicable shall be taken to ascertain the identity of a person responsible for his welfare.

(3) If it is practicable to ascertain the identity of a person responsible for the welfare of the child or young person, that person shall be informed, unless it is not practicable to do so—

     (a) that the child or young person has been arrested;

     (b) why he has been arrested; and

     (c) where he is being detained.

(4) Where information falls to be given under subsection (3) above, it shall be given as soon as it is practicable to do so.

(5) For the purposes of this section the persons who may be responsible for the welfare of a child or young person are—

     (a) his parent or guardian; or

     (b) any other person who has for the time being assumed responsibility for his welfare.

(6) If it is practicable to give a person responsible for the welfare of the child or young person the information required by subsection (3) above, that person shall be given it as soon as it is practicable to do so.

(7) If it appears that at the time of his arrest a supervision order, as defined in section 163 of the *Powers of Criminal Courts (Sentencing) Act* 2000 or Part IV of the *Children Act* 1989, is in force in respect of him, the person responsible for his supervision shall also be informed as described in subsection (3) above as soon as it is reasonably practicable to do so.

(7A) If it appears that at the time of his arrest the child or young person is being provided with accommodation by or on behalf of a local authority under section 20 of the *Children Act* 1989, the local authority shall also be informed as described in subsection (3) above as soon as it is reasonably practicable to do so.

(8) The reference to a parent or guardian in subsection (5) above is in the case of a child or young person in the care of a local authority, a reference to that authority.

(9) The rights conferred on a child or young person by subsections (2) to (8) above are in addition to his rights under section 56 of the *Police and Criminal Evidence Act* 1984.

(10) The reference in subsection (2) above to a child or young person who is in police detention includes a reference to a child or young person who has been detained under the terrorism provisions; and in subsection (3) above "arrest" includes such detention.

(11) In subsection (10) above "the terrorism provisions" has the meaning assigned to it by section 65 of the *Police and Criminal Evidence Act* 1984.

[Subsection (2) to (11) were substituted by the *PACE Act* 1984, s.57. They are printed as subsequently amended and repealed in part by the *Children Act* 1989, s.108(5) and (7), and Scheds 13, para. 6(2) and (3), and 15; and the *Powers of Criminal Courts (Sentencing) Act* 2000, s.165(1), and Sched. 9, para. 1.]

(8) Right of access to a solicitor

Police and Criminal Evidence Act 1984, s.58

Access to legal advice

1–187   **58.**—(1) A person arrested and held in custody in a police station or other premises shall be entitled, if he so requests, to consult a solicitor privately at any time.

(2) Subject to subsection (3) below, a request under subsection (1) above and the time at which it was made shall be recorded in the custody record.

(3) Such a request need not be recorded in the custody record of a person who makes it at a time while he is at a court after being charged with an offence.

(4) If a person makes such a request, he must be permitted to consult a solicitor as soon as is practicable except to the extent that delay is permitted by this section.

(5) In any case he must be permitted to consult a solicitor within 36 hours from the relevant time, as defined in section 41(2) above.

(6) Delay in compliance with a request is only permitted—

    (a) in the case of a person who is in police detention for an indictable offence; and

    (b) if an officer of at least the rank of superintendent authorises it.

(7) An officer may give an authorisation under subsection (6) above orally or in writing but, if he gives it orally, he shall confirm it in writing as soon as is practicable.

(8) Subject to subsection (8A) below an officer may only authorise delay where he has reasonable grounds for believing that the exercise of the right conferred by subsection (1) above at the time when the person detained desires to exercise it—

    (a) will lead to interference with or harm to evidence connected with an indictable offence or interference with or physical injury to other persons; or

    (b) will lead to the alerting of other persons suspected of having committed such an offence but not yet arrested for it; or

    (c) will hinder the recovery of any property obtained as a result of such an offence.

(8A) An officer may also authorise delay where he has reasonable grounds for believing that—

    (a) the person detained for the indictable offence has benefited from his criminal conduct, and

    (b) the recovery of the value of the property constituting the benefit will be hindered by the exercise of the right conferred by subsection (1) above.

(8B) For the purposes of subsection (8A) above the question whether a person has benefited from his criminal conduct is to be decided in accordance with Part 2 of the *Proceeds of Crime Act* 2002.

(9) If delay is authorised—

    (a) the detained person shall be told the reason for it; and

    (b) the reason shall be noted on his custody record.

(10) The duties imposed by subsection (9) above shall be performed as soon as is practicable.

(11) There may be no further delay in permitting the exercise of the right conferred by subsection (1) above once the reason for authorising delay ceases to subsist.

(12) Nothing in this section applies to a person arrested or detained under the terrorism provisions.

[This section is printed as amended by the *Drug Trafficking Offences Act* 1986, s.32; the *Criminal Justice Act* 1988, s.99(3); the *Terrorism Act* 2000, s.125, and Sched. 15, para. 5(6); the *Proceeds of Crime Act* 2002, s.456, and Sched. 11, para. 14(3); and the *Serious Organised Crime and Police Act* 2005, s.111, and Sched. 7, para. 43(1) and (9).]

Right of access to a solicitor

Section 58 grants a person arrested and "held in custody in a police station or other **1–188** premises" the right to consult a solicitor "if he so requests". Section 23 (*ante*, § 1–65) defines "premises" as including "any place" and specifies a number of examples such as vehicles. In *Kerawalla* [1991] Crim.L.R. 451, CA, it was held that "held in custody" is narrower than "in custody", so that a person arrested and detained may be in custody but not yet "held in custody" for the purposes of section 58 until his custody has been authorised, as by a custody officer who satisfies himself that continued detention is authorised. Cf. *Sanusi* [1992] Crim.L.R. 43, CA (Customs officers' area at airport tantamount to a police station).

As to the duty to inform a person under arrest at a police station of his right to consult privately with a solicitor and that free independent legal advice is available, see

Code C:3.1 and 6.1; and as to the duty to remind a person being interviewed at a police station or other authorised place of detention of these rights, see Code C:11.2. As to the duty to take an arrestee to a police station as soon as practicable after arrest, see section 30 (*ante*, § 1–122).

The right of access to a solicitor under section 58(1) does not extend to a person on remand in custody at a magistrates' court, but there is a right of access at common law to be permitted to consult a solicitor as soon as reasonably practicable: *R. v. Chief Constable of South Wales, ex p. Merrick* [1994] 1 W.L.R. 663, DC.

A person, not under arrest, who is interviewed under caution by a trading standards officer other than at a police station, has no entitlement to non-means tested free legal advice: *R. (Beale) v. South East Wiltshire Magistrates' Court*, 167 J.P. 41, DC.

Denial of access

1–189   In *Samuel* [1988] Q.B. 615, 87 Cr.App.R. 232, CA, the right of access to legal advice was described as "one of the most important and fundamental rights of a citizen" (at pp. 630, 245). Where it was sought to justify denial of the right of access to a solicitor on "reasonable grounds", that could not be done except by reference to specific circumstances including evidence about the person detained or the actual solicitor involved. The word "will" in section 58(8) is deliberately restrictive implying, in conjunction with "belief", a belief that it would very probably happen. Such a belief would have to relate to an individual solicitor rather than solicitors generally or, in most instances, a duty solicitor (see also, on this point, *Silcott, Braithwaite and Raghip, The Times*, December 9, 1991, CA). Cases where solicitors were inadvertently used to pass on coded messages would be rare (although the court in *Alladice* (1988) 87 Cr.App.R. 380, CA, seemed to think otherwise).

A chief constable is not entitled to make a blanket order banning a probationary solicitor's representative from attending the police station to advise persons in custody. He could, however, under Code C:6.12A and 6.13, advise his officers that a particular representative was likely to hinder an investigation and the appropriate officer in a particular case could then decide whether he should be excluded: *R. (Thompson) v. Chief Constable of Northumbria Police* [2001] 1 W.L.R. 1342, CA.

Consequences of breach of section 58

1–190   Where there is a breach of section 58, a decision about admissibility will be governed by sections 76 and 78 of the 1984 *Act*: *Alladice, ante*. For cases where it was held on appeal that interviews in breach of section 58 should have been excluded under section 76, see *McGovern* (1990) 92 Cr.App.R. 228, CA (defendant aged 19, six months' pregnant, of limited intelligence), and *Chung* (1990) 92 Cr.App.R. 314, CA; and, under section 78, see *Samuel, ante, Absolam* (1988) 88 Cr.App.R. 332, CA; *Parris* (1988) 89 Cr.App.R. 68, CA; *Walsh* (1990) 91 Cr.App.R. 161, CA; and *Beycan* [1990] Crim.L.R. 185, CA. For cases where breaches of section 58 did not prevent the interviews' admissibility, see *Alladice, ante*, and *Dunford* (1991) 91 Cr.App.R. 150, CA.

Section 58 and drink driving cases

1–191   In *DPP v. Billington* (1988) 87 Cr.App.R. 68, DC, it was held:

(a) that there was nothing in section 58 or Code C which required the police to delay the taking of a specimen of breath, blood or urine for analysis under the *Road Traffic Act* 1988, s.7; and

(b) that failure to accord the defendant the right of consulting a solicitor as soon as practicable under section 58 did not thereby furnish the defendant with a reasonable excuse for failing to provide a specimen for analysis.

Billington was applied in *DPP v. Skinner; DPP v. Cornell* [1990] R.T.R. 254, DC, which was itself followed in *DPP v. Whalley* [1991] R.T.R. 161, DC: the effect of these decisions is that an arrested person cannot justify failure to supply a specimen on the ground that he is reading the codes of practice. This also applies to specimens taken under section 8 of the 1988 Act: *DPP v. Ward* [1999] R.T.R. 11, DC. See also *DPP v. Varley*, 163 J.P. 443, DC.

Whilst the public interest requires that the breath test procedure cannot be delayed to any significant extent, if there happens to be a solicitor in the charge room whom the detainee wishes to consult "for a couple of minutes" before deciding whether or not to provide specimens of breath he must be allowed to do so; similarly, if the detainee asks at that stage to speak to his solicitor or to the duty solicitor on the telephone for a couple of minutes and the solicitor is immediately available, he should be allowed to do so. If the detainee does no more than indicate a general desire to have legal advice, this is not a reason to delay the procedure: *Kennedy v. DPP* [2004] R.T.R. 6, DC; followed in *Kirkup v. DPP* [2004] Crim.L.R. 230, DC (where it was observed that a duty solicitor will not necessarily be immediately available or respond promptly), *Whitley v. DPP* [2004] Crim.L.R. 585, DC (what is practicable should be considered from the point of view of those at the police station at the time, rather than in hindsight), *Myles v. DPP* [2005] R.T.R. 1, DC (Commonwealth cases of limited assistance) and *Causey v. DPP*, 169 J.P. 331, DC (where the authorities are summarised).

Compatibility with the European Convention on Human Rights
Article 6(3) of the ECHR normally requires that an accused be allowed the benefit of **1–192** legal advice in the initial stages of interrogation. The right of private consultation may be limited for good cause: *Murray v. U.K.*, 22 E.H.R.R. 29, ECtHR. If an accused's right to an effective exercise of his defence rights has been infringed, it is not necessary to prove that the restriction had a prejudicial effect on the course of the trial: *Brennan v. U.K.* (2002) 34 E.H.R.R. 18, ECtHR.

In the context of legislation which permits adverse inferences to be drawn from silence, the right of access to legal advice is of "paramount importance": *Murray v. U.K.*, *ante*, at 67. Delaying access to legal advice in such cases, whatever the justification, is incompatible with the right to a fair trial guaranteed by Article 6(1) of the Convention and the right of access to legal advice under Article 6(3)(c): *ibid.*; and reiterated in a number of subsequent European Court of Human Rights cases: see *Condron v. U.K.* (2001) 31 E.H.R.R. 1; *Magee v. U.K.* (2001) 31 E.H.R.R. 35; *Averill v. U.K.* (2001) 31 E.H.R.R. 36. See also *Aspinall* [1999] 2 Cr.App.R. 115 at 121-122, CA; and Code C:10, and Annex C.

CONSTITUTION AND JURISDICTION

I. INTRODUCTION

The magistrates' court is a creature of statute and although the office of justice of the **2–1** peace dates back to the 14th century, the powers of the present day magistrate are based on more recent Acts of Parliament. The relevant statutes are the *Magistrates' Courts Act* 1980, which essentially outlines the jurisdiction and powers of the court and the *Courts Act* 2003, which provides for the appointment of magistrates, justices' clerks and district judges and the administration of the court. Parts 1–3 of the Act cover the court system, justices of the peace and the magistrates' courts specifically and came into force on April 1, 2005.

Magistrates' Courts Act 1980, s.148

"Magistrates' court"

   148.—(1) In this Act the expression "magistrates' court" means any justice or justices of the **2–2** peace acting under any enactment or by virtue of his or their commission or under the common law.

   (2) Except where the contrary is expressed, anything authorised or required by this Act to be done by, to or before the magistrates' court by, to or before which any other thing was done, or is to be done, may be done by, to or before any magistrates' court acting in the same local justice area as that court.

A magistrates' court has no jurisdiction unless it is specifically conferred by statute. It **2–3** is an inferior court and has no inherent jurisdiction. It is not a court of record so transcripts are not taken. The legal adviser may take a manual note of proceedings but this is not a verbatim record. The final record of all decisions and adjudications is the court register, which is generally computer generated and stored. Decisions of the magistrates' courts are subject to appeal to the Crown Court on fact and by way of case stated or judicial review to the High Court on cases of law or mixed fact and law. See Ch.11.

A magistrates' court normally comprises of a district judge or magistrates. A district judge sits alone and magistrates sit in benches of not less than two or more than three magistrates: *Magistrates' Courts Act* 1980, s.121; *Justices of the Peace (Size and Chairmanship of Bench) Rules* 2005 (S.I. 2005 No. 553). Normally there are three magistrates and objection may be taken to less than that number particularly when trials are to be heard. The problem with a bench of only two is the potential for disagreement. Some exceptions apply where magistrates may sit alone to conduct committals or to adjourn cases and also to give directions in early administrative hearings: *Magistrates' Courts Act* 1980, ss.4, 10; *Crime and Disorder Act* 1998, ss.49 and 50.

II. JUDGES OF THE MAGISTRATES' COURTS

(1) General

2–4   The jurisdiction of the magistrates' courts may be exercised by magistrates or District Judges (Magistrates' Courts) sitting in court with the justices' clerk or a qualified legal adviser.

Magistrates, otherwise known as justices of the peace or lay justices, are part-time unpaid volunteers and district judges are lawyers appointed to a full-time salaried post.

(2) Justices of the Peace

Courts Act 2003, ss.9–11

Meaning of "lay justice"

2–5   **9.** In this Act "lay justice" means a justice of the peace who is not a District Judge (Magistrates' Courts).

Appointment of lay justices etc.

2–6   **10.**—(1) Lay justices are to be appointed for England and Wales by the Lord Chancellor by instrument on behalf and in the name of Her Majesty.

(2) The Lord Chancellor—

    (a) must assign each lay justice to one or more local justice areas, and

    (b) may change an assignment so as to assign the lay justice to a different local justice area or to different local justice areas.

(3) Every lay justice is, by virtue of his office, capable of acting as such in any local justice area (whether or not he is assigned to it); but he may do so only in accordance with arrangements made by or on behalf of the Lord Chancellor.

(4) Rules may make provision about the training courses to be completed before a person may exercise functions as a lay justice in any proceedings or class of proceedings specified in the rules.

(5) Subsection (3) is subject to section 12 (the supplemental list).

(6) The functions conferred on the Lord Chief Justice by subsections (2) and (3) may be exercised only after consulting the Lord Chancellor.

(7) The Lord Chief Justice may nominate a judicial office holder (as defined in section 109(4) of the *Constitutional Reform Act* 2005) to exercise his functions under subsection (2) or (3).

Resignation and removal of lay justices

2–7   **11.**—(1) A lay justice may resign his office at any time.

(2) The Lord Chancellor may remove a lay justice from his office by an instrument on behalf and in the name of Her Majesty—

    (a) on the ground of incapacity or misbehaviour,

    (b) on the ground of a persistent failure to meet such standards of competence as are prescribed by a direction given by the Lord Chancellor with the concurrence of the Lord Chief Justice, or

    (c) if he is satisfied that the lay justice is declining or neglecting to take a proper part in the exercise of his functions as a justice of the peace.

Justices of the peace, also referred to as magistrates, do not receive a salary for their **2–8** work but they may claim expenses for travel, subsistence and financial loss: *Courts Act* 2003, s.15. No legal qualification is needed but conversely, there is no bar to barristers or solicitors holding office as a magistrate. Rules may make provision for the training, appraisal and development of lay justices, both at induction stage and for taking the chair in court: *Courts Act* 2003, s.19.

Magistrates are addressed in court through the Chairman as "Sir" or "Madam" and collectively as "Your Worships".

(3) District Judges (Magistrates' Courts)

Courts Act 2003, ss.22, 23, 25 and 26

Appointment etc.

22.—(1) Her Majesty may, on the recommendation of the Lord Chancellor, appoint a person **2–9** who has a 7 year general qualification to be a District Judge (Magistrates' Courts).

(2) A District Judge (Magistrates' Courts) must, before acting as such, take the oath of allegiance and judicial oath in accordance with the *Promissory Oaths Act* 1868 and the *Promissory Oaths Act* 1871.

(3) The Lord Chancellor may pay to a District Judge (Magistrates' Courts) such allowances as he may determine.

(4) Any such allowances are in addition to the salary charged on and paid out of the Consolidated Fund under section 9 of the *Administration of Justice Act* 1973.

(5) The Lord Chancellor may, with the concurrence of the Lord Chief Justice, remove a District Judge (Magistrates' Courts) from office on the ground of incapacity or misbehaviour.

Senior District Judge (Chief Magistrate)

23. The Lord Chancellor—   **2–10**

(a) may designate one of the District Judges (Magistrates' Courts) to be Senior District Judge (Chief Magistrate), and

(b) if he does so, may designate another of them to be the deputy of the Senior District Judge (Chief Magistrate).

District Judges (Magistrates' Courts) as justices of the peace

25.—(1) A District Judge (Magistrates' Courts) is by virtue of his office a justice of the peace **2–11** for England and Wales.

(2) It is the duty of a District Judge (Magistrates' Courts) to act as a justice of the peace in any local justice area in accordance with arrangements made by or on behalf of the Lord Chancellor.

(3) The Lord Chief Justice may nominate a judicial office holder (as defined in section 109(4) of the *Constitutional Reform Act* 2005) to exercise his functions under subsection (2).

District Judges (Magistrates' Courts) able to act alone

26.—(1) Nothing in the 1980 Act—   **2–12**

(a) requiring a magistrates' court to be composed of two or more justices, or

(b) limiting the powers of a magistrates' court when composed of a single justice,

applies to a District Judge (Magistrates' Courts).

(2) A District Judge (Magistrates' Courts) may—

(a) do any act, and

(b) exercise alone any jurisdiction,

which can be done or exercised by two justices, apart from granting or transferring a licence.

(3) Any enactment making provision ancillary to the jurisdiction exercisable by two justices of the peace also applies to the jurisdiction of a District Judge (Magistrates' Courts), unless the provision relates to granting or transferring a licence.

(4) This section does not apply to the hearing or determination of family proceedings (as defined by section 65 of the 1980 Act).

(5) "The 1980 Act" means the *Magistrates' Courts Act* 1980.

District Judges (Magistrates' Courts) are professional, salaried members of the **2–13** judiciary. Until 1997 they were called stipendiary magistrates and were appointed to particular commission areas generally within large metropolitan areas such as London, Manchester and Leeds. The *Justices of the Peace Act* 1997, s.10A changed the description of the judicial office to District Judge (Magistrates' Courts) and established a national bench led by the Senior District Judge (Chief Magistrate). The district judge will be assigned to a local justice area but may be directed by the Department for Constitutional Affairs through the Senior District Judge to sit at any court in England and Wales as required: *Courts Act* 2003, s.25.

2–14　　Unlike magistrates, a district judge will always sit alone in all criminal proceedings: *Courts Act* 2003, s.26. In order to develop the flexibility of judicial resources, section 65 of the *Courts Act* 2003 amends section 8 of the *Supreme Court Act* 1981 to allow District Judges (Magistrates' Courts) to exercise the jurisdiction of the Crown Court. Other functions are also conferred by Schedule 4 to the *Courts Act*. Section 65 came into force on April 1, 2005, under the *Courts Act 2003 (Commencement No.10) Order* 2005 (S.I. 2005 No. 910). Exercise of this jurisdiction will depend on any future allocation of work that may be made by the Lord Chancellor.

The Judicial Studies Board is responsible for training district judges and delivers induction and continuing training. Certain district judges are designated by the Lord Chancellor or the senior district judge to deal with particular types of specialist work such as youth court cases, extradition and applications for warrants of further detention under the *Terrorism Act* 2000.

A district judge is addressed as "Sir" or "Madam".

(4) Justices' clerks

2–15　　The justices' clerk and legal advisers give advice on law, practice and procedure to the justices of the peace.

Courts Act 2003, ss.27, 28, 29

Justices' clerks and assistant clerks

2–16　　27.—(1) A justices' clerk is a person who is—

　　(a) appointed by the Lord Chancellor under section 2(1), and

　　(b) designated by the Lord Chancellor as a justices' clerk.

(2) A person may be designated as a justices' clerk only if he—

　　(a) has a 5 year magistrates' court qualification,

　　(b) is a barrister or solicitor who has served for not less than 5 years as an assistant to a justices' clerk, or

　　(c) has previously been a justices' clerk.

(3) The Lord Chancellor—

　　(a) must assign each justices' clerk to one or more local justice areas, and

　　(b) subject to subsection (4), may change an assignment so as to assign the justices' clerk to a different local justice area or to different local justice areas.

(4) Before changing an assignment of a justices' clerk so that he is no longer assigned to a local justice area, the Lord Chancellor must consult—

　　(a) the chairman of the lay justices assigned to that area, or

　　(b) if it is not possible or not practicable to consult the chairman, the deputy chairman or such of the lay justices assigned to or acting in the area as appear to the Lord Chancellor appropriate.

(5) An assistant to a justices' clerk is a person who is—

　　(a) appointed by the Lord Chancellor under section 2(1) or provided under a contract made by virtue of section 2(4), and

　　(b) designated by the Lord Chancellor as an assistant to a justices' clerk.

(6) The Lord Chancellor may by regulations provide that, subject to such exceptions as may be prescribed by the regulations, a person may be designated as an assistant to a justices' clerk only if he—

　　(a) has a 5 year magistrates' court qualification, or

(b) has such qualifications as may be prescribed by, or approved by the Lord Chancellor in accordance with, the regulations.

(6A) The Lord Chief Justice may nominate a judicial office holder (as defined in section 109(4) of the *Constitutional Reform Act* 2005) to exercise his functions under this section.

(7) In this Part "assistant clerk" is short for "assistant to a justices' clerk".

Functions

28.—(1) Rules may make provision enabling things authorised to be done by, to or before a **2–17** single justice of the peace to be done instead by, to or before a justices' clerk.

(2) Rules may also make provision enabling things authorised to be done by, to or before a justices' clerk (whether by virtue of subsection (1) or otherwise) to be done instead by, to or before an assistant clerk.

(3) An enactment or rule of law which—

(a) regulates the exercise of any jurisdiction or powers of justices of the peace, or

(b) relates to things done in the exercise or purported exercise of any such jurisdiction or powers,

applies in relation to the exercise or purported exercise of any such jurisdiction or powers by a justices' clerk by virtue of subsection (1) as if he were a justice of the peace.

(4) The functions of a justices' clerk include giving advice to any or all of the justices of the peace to whom he is clerk about matters of law (including procedure and practice) on questions arising in connection with the discharge of their functions, including questions arising when the clerk is not personally attending on them.

(5) The powers of a justices' clerk include, at any time when he thinks he should do so, bringing to the attention of any or all of the justices of the peace to whom he is clerk any point of law (including procedure and practice) that is or may be involved in any question so arising.

(6) For the purposes of subsections (4) and (5) the functions of justices of the peace do not include functions as a judge of the Crown Court.

(7) Subsections (4) and (5) do not limit—

(a) the powers and duties of a justices' clerk, or

(b) the matters on which justices of the peace may obtain assistance from their clerk.

(8) In this section "rules" means rules made by the Lord Chancellor with the concurrence of the Lord Chief Justice.

(9) Before making any rules for the purposes of this section the Lord Chancellor must consult—

(a) the Criminal Procedure Rule Committee,

(b) the Family Procedure Rule Committee, and

(c) the Magistrates' Courts Rule Committee.

(10) The Lord Chief Justice may nominate a judicial office holder (as defined in section 109(4) of the *Constitutional Reform Act* 2005) to exercise his functions under this section.

Independence

29.—(1) A justices' clerk exercising—   **2–18**

(a) a function exercisable by one or more justices of the peace,

(b) a function specified in section 28(4) or (5) (advice on matters of law, including procedure and practice), or

(c) a function as a member of the Criminal Procedure Rule Committee or the Family Procedure Rule Committee,

is not subject to the direction of the Lord Chancellor or any other person.

(2) An assistant clerk who is exercising any such function is not subject to the direction of any person other than a justices' clerk.

The role of the justices' clerk is to advise the magistrates on law, practice and **2–19** procedure. These areas often overlap so advice is required on issues of mixed fact and law. The justices' clerk manages a team of legal advisers to whom powers are delegated to give legal advice to magistrates both in and out of court. Most legal advisers are solicitors or barristers and others hold recognised Court Clerk qualifications. The magistrate is not obliged to accept the advice and it is the bench, not the legal adviser, who is the ultimate decision-maker on questions of law and fact. However, it is accepted practice that they should do so, see *Jones v. Nicks* [1977] R.T.R. 72 when the bench acted against the advice of the legal adviser and accepted that the adverse effect on employment was a special reason not to endorse a driving licence. On appeal, it was held that the legal adviser had correctly explained the law to them and their decision against this advice was a nullity. Any magistrate will ignore legal advice at their peril for if a decision is made unsupported by the advice of the legal adviser, they could be held liable for errors affecting the liberty of the subject, *etc.* The *Consolidated Criminal Practice Direction* gives detailed explanation of the role of the legal adviser including the method in which advice should be tendered (see Appendix F–68).

Legal advisers are required under the *Consolidated Criminal Practice Direction* to advise on questions of law (including Human Rights), questions of mixed law and fact, matters of practice and procedure, other issues relevant to the matter before the court and structured decision making. The legal adviser will also assist the court in drawing up and recording the reasons for decisions. At all times the legal adviser must exercise care not to trespass on the judicial responsibility of the bench by usurping its functions.

2–20   The legal adviser's role is to advise on these matters only and they must not appear to be trying to influence the magistrate's factual decisions: *Stafford Justices, ex p. Ross* [1962] 1 W.L.R. 456. In this case the clerk to the justices was seen to pass a note to the magistrates which contained an argument on the facts pointing to the guilt of the accused. The conviction was quashed on appeal as it was held that the clerk was attempting to influence the decision of the magistrates on matters of fact.

The legal adviser has a duty to ensure that every case is conducted fairly and that responsibility may incorporate assisting unrepresented defendants, taking notes of the evidence as a reminder and also asking questions of witnesses and parties to clarify evidence or issues in the case.

The legal adviser should not retire with the magistrates as a matter of course when they consider their verdict. If once the magistrates leave court, the legal adviser becomes aware that there is a point of law upon which they might require assistance then an approach may be made to the magistrates in the retiring room, see *Uxbridge Justices, ex p. Smith* (1985) 149 J.P. 620, where counsel for the defence referred to a passage in a legal text book as support for his submission. The bench retired and the legal adviser took the opportunity of reading the passage in full and then informed counsel that she was going to see the magistrates in the retiring room to advise them of her view on the law. On appeal the court held that in the absence of any indication or suspicion that the legal adviser had taken part in deciding questions of fact or the verdict, she was just carrying out her responsibility to advise the bench on the law. In *Consett Justices, ex p. Postal Bingo Ltd* [1967] 2 Q.B. 9, the interventions of the justices' clerk were even more marked but nevertheless on appeal the court held that he was acting in accordance with his duties to advise the bench. The case involved a complex matter of mixed law and fact. The justices' clerk went out with the magistrates to the retiring room together with his assistant and stayed there for over two hours of deliberations. The High Court held that the bench were entitled to his advice on "entangled questions of law and fact" and that his presence on their retirement did not invalidate the decision. In *R. v. Eccles Justices, ex p. Fitzpatrick* (1989) 89 Cr.App.R. 324, the clerk initially refused to allow the defendant to apply to the magistrates to change his plea and then went out to join the bench in the retiring room for about 25 minutes without being requested to do so. After a guilty plea was entered the clerk left court again with the bench and stayed in the retiring room with them for 30 minutes. The magistrates' decision to commit the defendant to the Crown Court for sentence was quashed on appeal. It was held that the clerk should not retire with the magistrates unless clearly requested to do so. In the absence of any dispute on the law, the magistrates did not need the advice of their clerk and his querying the motives behind a request to have the plea put again was improper. There was a reasonable suspicion of interference by the clerk which made the process unsafe.

2–21   The law has moved on since these cases and it is doubtful that such a wide interpretation would now be given to the advisory role of the justices' clerk. The *Human Rights*

Act 1998 has had an impact on the transparency of communications between magistrates and legal advisers as expressed in the *Consolidated Criminal Practice Directions* (see Appendix F). The courts will be expected to limit and explain all consultations that take place out of court so that justice is seen to be done and Article 6 of the ECHR is observed.

Legal advice should be given in open court. Where advice is given in the retiring room without having been previously canvassed in open court it will be given on a provisional basis only to the magistrates. The substance of the advice should be repeated in open court allowing the parties to make representations and then the advice will be stated in open court with amendments as required.

In *R. (Murchison) v. Southend Magistrates' Court* [2006] WL 63683; ([2006] EWHC 569) it was held that legal advisers should only attend on magistrates in the retiring room when called upon to do so. Previous convictions of the defendant should only be referred to after the verdict has been delivered in open court. Where the record had been made available by the legal adviser to the justices prior to the announcement of verdict this was inappropriate practice but in the circumstances of the case it was decided that the conviction was not unsafe.

Where the defendant is unrepresented the legal adviser is under a duty to assist both the defendant and the court. This will consist of explaining procedures to the defendant and where evidence is given in a trial, identifying the points in issue and ensuring appropriate questions are put to witnesses and assisting the defendant to give evidence if they so wish so that opportunity is provided to put the defence case fully: *R. v. Chichester Justices, ex p. DPP* (1993) 157 J.P. 1049.

Under the *Justices' Clerks Rules* 2005, r.2, justices' clerks may perform tasks which are authorised to be done by, to or before a single magistrate. The powers are specified in the Schedule to the Rules and include the issue of summonses, allowing agreed adjournments, granting criminal defence representation orders and the giving of directions in trials. The justices' clerk may delegate these powers to the legal advisers. In practice this means that the legal adviser will often deal with cases whilst the Bench retire to consider other matters. The justices' clerk may also sit alone to conduct early administrative hearings where the powers allow for pleas to be taken; remands on agreed bail and directions relating to trials to be given: *Crime and Disorder Act* 1998, s.50.

III. CONSTITUTION OF THE MAGISTRATES' COURTS

Magistrates' Courts Act 1980, s.121

Constitution and place of sitting of court

121.—(1) A magistrates' court shall not try an information summarily or hear a complaint **2–22** except when composed of at least 2 justices unless the trial or hearing is one that by virtue of any enactment may take place before a single justice.

(2) A magistrates' court shall not hold an inquiry into the means of an offender for the purposes of section 82 above or determine under that section at a hearing at which the offender is not present whether to issue a warrant of commitment except when composed of at least 2 justices.

(3) [...]

(4) Subject to the provisions of any enactment to the contrary, a magistrates' court must sit in open court if it is

    (a) trying summarily an information for an indictable offence,

    (b) trying an information for a summary offence

    (c) imposing imprisonment

    (d) hearing a complaint

    (e) holding an inquiry into the means of an offender for the purposes of section 82.

(5) A magistrates' court composed of a single justice, shall not impose imprisonment for a period exceeding 14 days or order a person to pay more than £1.

(6) Subject to the provisions of subsection (7) below, the justices composing the court before which any proceedings take place shall be present during the whole of the proceedings; but if during the course of the proceedings any justice absents himself, he shall cease to act further therein and, if the remaining justices are enough to satisfy the requirements of the preceding provisions of this section, the proceedings may continue before a court composed of those justices.

(7) Where the trial of an information is adjourned after the accused has been convicted and before he is sentenced or otherwise dealt with, the court which sentences or deals with him need not be composed of the same justices as that which convicted him; but, where among the justices composing the court which sentences or deals with an offender there are any who were not sitting when he was convicted, the court which sentences or deals with the offender shall before doing so make such inquiry into the facts and circumstances of the case as will enable the justices who were not sitting when the offender was convicted to be fully acquainted with those facts and circumstances.

(8) This section shall have effect subject to the provisions of this Act relating to [family proceedings].

[This section is reprinted as amended by the *Children Act* 1989, Sched. 11, para. 8(c) and the *Courts Act* 2003, Sched. 8, para. 237.]

2–23   The minimum number of magistrates to hear a trial is two and it cannot be more than three: *Justices of the Peace (Size and Chairmanship of Bench) Rules* 2005.

IV. IMPARTIALITY OF MAGISTRATES

A. GENERAL

2–24   A magistrate is disqualified from sitting or adjudicating on a case if:
   (a) a statutory disqualification applies;
   (b) he would be a judge in his own cause;
   (c) there is evidence of actual bias; or
   (d) there is evidence of apparent bias.

Where a defendant demonstrates partiality or prejudice on the part of a judge there are irresistible grounds for objecting to the trial of the case by that judge.

Article 6 of ECHR guarantees a right to a fair and public hearing by "an independent and impartial tribunal". This includes the concept of subjective and objective impartiality. The subjective test is on the basis of the personal conviction of the particular judge and the objective test is ascertaining whether the judge offers guarantees sufficient to rule out any legitimate doubt as to the judge's impartiality: *Hauschildt v. Denmark* (1990) 12 E.H.R.R. 266.

If a magistrate is disqualified, he should declare an interest and withdraw from court. It is possible for the interest to be declared and the parties to waive any objection on the basis of bias.

B. STATUTORY DISQUALIFICATION

Courts Act 2003, s.41

Disqualification of lay justices who are members of local authorities
2–25   **41.**—(1) A lay justice who is a member of a local authority may not act as a member of the Crown Court or a magistrates' court in proceedings brought by or against, or by way of an appeal from a decision of—
   (a) that local authority,
   (b) a committee or officer of that local authority, or
   (c) if that local authority is operating executive arrangements (within the meaning of Part 2 of the *Local Government Act* 2000)—
       (i) the executive of that local authority (within the meaning of that Part), or

(ii) any person acting on behalf of that executive.

(2) A lay justice who is a member of the Common Council of the City of London may not act as a member of the Crown Court or a magistrates' court in proceedings brought by or against, or by way of an appeal from a decision of—

(a) the Corporation of the City,

(b) the Common Council, or

(c) a committee or officer of the Corporation or the Common Council.

(3) A joint committee, joint board, joint authority or other combined body—

(a) of which a local authority, the Corporation or the Common Council is a member, or

(b) on which the local authority, the Corporation or the Council is represented,

is to be regarded for the purposes of this section as a committee of the local authority, Corporation or Common Council.

(4) Any reference in this section to an officer of—

(a) a local authority,

(b) the Corporation, or

(c) the Common Council,

is to a person employed or appointed by, or by a committee of, the local authority, Corporation or Common Council in the capacity in which he is employed or appointed to act.

(5) No act is invalidated merely because of the disqualification under this section of the person by whom it is done.

(6) "Local authority" means–

    (a) a local authority within the meaning of the *Local Government Act* 1972,

    (b) a local authority constituted under section 2 of the *Local Government etc. (Scotland) Act* 1994,

    (c) a police authority established under section 3 of the *Police Act* 1996, the Metropolitan Police Authority or the Serious Organised Crime Agency,

    (d) the London Fire and Emergency Planning Authority,

    (e) a joint authority established under Part 4 of the *Local Government Act* 1985,

    (f) a National Park Authority,

    (g) the Broads Authority, or

    (h) a housing action trust established under Part 3 of the *Housing Act* 1988.

A "local authority" means a London borough council, a district council, a county **2–26** council, a parish council or a community council: *Local Government Act* 1972, s.270.

A magistrate who is a local councillor should not sit in court when the local authority is bringing a prosecution. He should declare an interest and withdraw from court. The case can continue with two magistrates sitting.

C. PARTY TO A CASE

It is one of the most fundamental principles of justice that a person cannot be a judge **2–27** in his own cause: *Dimes v. Proprietors of Grand Junction Canal* (1852) 3 H.L. Cas. 759.

Once it is shown that a magistrate is a party to a case or has an interest in the subject matter of the case he is disqualified without the need for any investigation into any actual bias. A direct pecuniary interest or proprietary interest in the outcome of a case acts as an automatic disqualification and an assumption of bias: *R. v. Bow Street Magistrates, ex p. Pinochet Ugarte (No. 2)* [1999] 1 All E.R. 577.

D. ACTUAL BIAS

It is rare that actual bias is shown, but where it is the magistrate must disqualify **2–28** himself: *Gough* [1993] 1 A.C. 646.

E. APPARENT BIAS

A judge is not disqualified from trying a case because he expresses a personal view **2–29** before the start of a case which touches upon issues of law and practice which then arise in the case: *Browne, The Times*, August 23, 1997.

In *Incal v. Turkey* (2000) 29 E.H.R.R. 449, the European Court of Human Rights summarised the convention jurisprudence. It held that in order to establish whether a tribunal is independent, regard must be had to the manner of appointment of its members and their terms of office, the existence of safeguards against outside pressure and the question whether it presents an appearance of impartiality. There are two tests as to the condition of impartiality: the first consists of trying to determine the personal conviction of a particular judge in a given case (the subjective approach) and the second in ascertaining whether the judge offered guarantees sufficient to exclude any legitimate doubt in this respect (the objective approach). Appearances may be important but what is at stake is the confidence which the courts in a democratic society must inspire in the public and with regard to the criminal courts, in the defendant. In deciding whether there is a legitimate reason to fear that a particular court lacks independence or impartiality, the perspective of the defendant is important, what is decisive however is whether his doubts as to the impartiality of the tribunal are objectively justified.

The law was reviewed in detail in *Gough* [1993] 1 A.C. 646 which concerned a claim of apparent bias by a juror who was the neighbour of the defendant's brother. The court went on to consider the authorities on apparent bias and sought to identify the test to be applied. In the case of magistrates it was said that the court should consider if there was a real danger of bias on the part of the magistrate in the sense that he might unfairly regard with favour or disfavour the case of a party before him. The test of bias is whether there is a real risk that the defendant might have been denied a fair trial.

2–30   In *R. v. Bow Street Magistrate, ex p. Pinochet Ugarte (No. 2)* [1999] 1 All E.R. 577; [1999] 2 W.L.R. 272, HL, a member of the tribunal dealing with the applicant's case was connected to a charity called Amnesty International, which had intervened in the case. It was held on appeal that it is an automatic disqualification if a judge acts in his own cause. The court was reluctant to extend the ambit of automatic disqualification to cover the present case but it was a fundamental principle that justice should not only be done, but be seen to be done. The judge's connection with a party to the case disqualified him from hearing the case.

There are many ways in which apparent bias might be claimed and it will depend on the circumstances of each case whether there is a risk that requires disqualification.

A remark by a magistrate that it was not the practice of the court to describe police officers as liars was held to amount to apparent bias as it demonstrated a strong reaction in favour of the police witnesses: *R. v. Highgate Justices, ex p. Riley* [1996] R.T.R. 150. The fact that solicitors representing a party in proceedings also advised the judge about personal matters did not mean that he would necessarily be biased in their favour and did not require him to disqualify himself after the connection had been disclosed: *Taylor v. Lawrence* [2002] 2 All E.R. 353.

Where the judge described an agreed basis of plea as "fatuous" and then reserved the *Newton* hearing to himself it was held that despite the robust language it was clear that the hearing was conducted with scrupulous fairness and a complaint of bias was not upheld (*George* [2006] Crim. L.R. 164, CA). Present or past professional connections between the judge and any lawyer appearing before him was held not of itself to give rise to bias or an appearance of bias. In such circumstances a party may waive his right to object but only if fully aware of all the circumstances and the consequences of the choices open to him (*Smith v. Kvaerner Cementation Foundations Ltd & the Bar Council* [2006] 150 S.J. 401). Where judicial bias is apparent then disqualification of the judge is automatic. Inconvenience, cost and delay are not matters to be taken into account; (*AWG Group Ltd (formerly Anglian Water Plc) v. Morrison* [2006] WL 63654). In the case of *Russell* [2006] EWCA Crim 470 the defendant escaped from the dock and attacked the judge during the summing up. The judge retired and discussed security arrangements with the officer in the case who had given evidence and then returned to continue the trial. An application to discharge the jury was refused. An appeal was lodged on the basis that the trial was unfair as the judge would have been biased having been attacked and having spoken in private to a prosecution witness and that the decision of the jury might have been affected as a result. On appeal it was held that any criticism of the judge was unfounded. The summing up was fair and balanced and no observer could conclude that for the judge to continue with the trial was unfair, particularly as the defendant had disrupted the trial by his own actions and could not thus demand a re-trial. The conviction was upheld. It is no doubt reassuring for those holding judicial office to know that being subjected to an unprovoked physical attack cannot entitle a defendant to choose the tribunal.

The magistrates must also be seen to be giving their clear and undivided attention to **2–31** the proceedings. Apparently falling asleep, dealing with other paperwork or reading other documents during a trial have all resulted in convictions being quashed as unsafe; *R. v. Weston-Super-Mare Justices, ex p. Taylor* [1981] Crim.L.R. 179; *R. v. Marylebone Stipendiary Magistrate, ex p. Perry* [1992] Crim.L.R. 514; and *R. v. South Worcestershire Justices, ex p. Daniels* [1997] 161 J.P. 121.

The test for apparent bias for a magistrate also applies to justices' clerks because they are part of the judicial process in the magistrates' courts: *Gough* (*ante*).

V. RIGHTS OF AUDIENCE AND COURT DRESS

Defendants in person, barristers and solicitors with rights conferred by the *Courts* **2–32** *and Legal Services Act* 1990 may address the court.

Magistrates' Courts Act 1980, s.122

Appearance by counsel or solicitor

122.—(1) A party to any proceedings before a magistrates' court may be represented by a **2–33** legal representative.

(2) Subject to subsection (3) below, an absent party so represented shall be deemed not to be absent.

(3) Appearance of a party by a legal representative shall not satisfy any provision of any enactment or any condition of a recognizance expressly requiring his presence.

Barristers and solicitors regularly appear in the magistrates' courts to represent **2–34** defendants. A defendant may not be in court, either because he is ill or has been removed for misconduct or he may simply choose not to attend. It is possible for the proceedings to continue with the lawyer acting in the interests of the absent defendant. Lawyers will also represent bodies corporate and enter pleas on their behalf without the need for company officers to be present.

In certain instances, statute requires that the defendant be present in court. Where a defendant has been released on bail to appear before the court, it is not sufficient for his legal representative to attend at court; bail must be answered in person as there is a duty to surrender to the custody of the court: *Bail Act* 1976, s.3. Bail may only be enlarged in absence if there is a reasonable cause for the failure to surrender. There are further specific provisions which require the defendant's presence even when represented, *e.g.* plea before venue should be dealt with in the presence of the accused unless he is removed from court because of his disorderly conduct: *Magistrates' Courts Act* 1980, s.17B; committal for trial to the Crown Court: *Magistrates' Courts Act* 1980, s.6(2) which requires the court to commit the accused for trial and the *Criminal Procedure Rules* 2005, r.10.2 which require the charge on which the defendant is to be committed to be read to him as part of the process. Under section 51 of the *Crime and Disorder Act* 1998, a person may only be sent for trial when he "appears" or is "brought before the court". Community penalties may be imposed only in the defendant's presence because of the legal requirement on the court to explain to the offender in ordinary language the effect of the order and the consequences of breach (see *Powers of Criminal Courts (Sentencing) Act* 2000). Similarly there is a legal requirement to explain to an offender the reasons why the court is imposing a custodial sentence: *Powers of Criminal Courts (Sentencing) Act* 2000, s.79.

Rights of audience are conferred by sections 27 and 28 of the *Courts and Legal Services Act* 1990. Duly qualified barristers and solicitors have a right of audience under these provisions. The court may also grant an individual right of audience to specified persons for specific proceedings under section 27(2)(c) of the Act. This discretion extends to any person in any proceedings: *R. v. Southwark Crown Court, ex p. Tawfick, The Times*, December 1, 1994.

Professional Codes of Conduct dictate the dress code for courts. Although wigs and gowns are not worn in the magistrates' court, a smart standard of dress is expected of all professionals appearing before the court.

VI. ADMINISTRATION OF THE MAGISTRATES' COURTS

2–35   The *Courts Act* 2003 makes provision about the courts and their procedure and practice. It unifies the Supreme Court, county courts and magistrates' courts into one court system, called Her Majesty's Court Service (HMCS) and the Lord Chancellor has a duty to maintain the new court system. In April 2007 an announcement was made by the Government that the Home Office would be split into two new departments for security and justice. The Home Office will retain responsibility for the police, crime reduction, immigration and asylum and would take on a greater role for security and counter-terrorism. A new Ministry of Justice will take over the present Department for Constitutional Affairs and the National Offender Management Service. It will have responsibility for criminal law, sentencing, prisons and probation.

VII. GENERAL JURISDICTION

(1) Legislation

Courts Act 2003 s.1

The general duty

2–36   **1.**—(1) The Lord Chancellor is under a duty to ensure that there is an efficient and effective system to support the carrying on of the business of—

(a) the Supreme Court,

(b) county courts, and

(c) magistrates' courts,

and that appropriate services are provided for those courts.

(2) In this Part—

(a) "the Supreme Court" includes the district probate registries, and

(b) "magistrates' court" includes a committee of justices.

(3) In this Part references to the Lord Chancellor's general duty in relation to the courts are to his duty under this section.

(4) The Lord Chancellor must, within 18 months of the coming into force of this section, and afterwards annually, prepare and lay before both Houses of Parliament a report as to the way in which he has discharged his general duty in relation to the courts.

2–37   The Lord Chancellor in order to discharge his duty has power to appoint officers and staff under section 2 of the *Courts Act* 2003 and he also has power to provide accommodation for court houses and offices: *Courts Act* 2003, s.3. Courts Boards are established under section 5 of the Act and their function is to scrutinise the arrangements made by the Lord Chancellor and to make recommendations on how his duty should be discharged.

2–38   The *Courts Act* 2003 creates a national commission area for the whole of England and Wales. This is divided into local justice areas which have the same boundaries as the previous petty sessions areas. See the *Local Justice Areas Order* 2005 (S.I. 2005 No. 554), which came into force on April 1, 2005.

(2) The commission of the peace and local justice areas

Courts Act 2003, ss.7, 8

The commission of the peace for England and Wales

7. There shall be a commission of the peace for England and Wales—   **2–39**
  (a) issued under the Great Seal, and
  (b) addressed generally, and not by name, to all such persons as may from time to time hold office as justices of the peace for England and Wales.

Local justice areas

8.—(1) England and Wales is to be divided into areas to be known as local justice areas.   **2–40**

(2) The areas are to be those specified by an order made by the Lord Chancellor.

(3) Each local justice area established by order under subsection (2) is to be known by such name as is specified in the order (but subject to subsection (4)).

(4) The Lord Chancellor may make orders altering local justice areas.

(5) "Altering", in relation to a local justice area, includes (as well as changing its boundaries)–
  (a) combining it with one or more other local justice areas,
  (b) dividing it between two or more other local justice areas, and
  (c) changing its name.

(6) Before making an order under subsection (4) in relation to a local justice area the Lord Chancellor must consult—
  (a) the justices of the peace assigned to the local justice area,
  (b) any courts board whose area includes the local justice area or a part of the local justice area, and
  (c) unless the alteration consists only of a change of name, any local authorities whose area includes the local justice area or a part of the local justice area.

(7) "Local authority" means–
  (a) any council of a county, a county borough, a London borough or a council of a district,
  (b) the Common Council of the City of London, or
  (c) a police authority established under section 3 of the *Police Act* 1996 or the Metropolitan Police Authority.

(8) The Lord Chief Justice may nominate a judicial office holder (as defined in section 109(4) of the *Constitutional Reform Act* 2005) to exercise his functions under this section.

Lay justices on appointment are assigned to a local justice area where they will sit to **2–41** dispense justice. District Judges (Magistrates' Courts) have a national jurisdiction and may be directed to sit anywhere in England and Wales but they will also be assigned to sit usually in one or more local justice areas.

(3) Jurisdiction for offences

Magistrates' Courts Act 1980, s.2

Jurisdiction to deal with charges

2.—(1) A magistrates' court for a commission area shall have jurisdiction to try all summary **2–42** offences committed within the commission area.

(2) Where a person charged with a summary offence appears or is brought before a magistrates' court in answer to a summons issued under paragraph (b) of section 1(2) above, or under a warrant issued under that paragraph, the court shall have jurisdiction to try the offence.

(3) A magistrates' court for a commission area shall have jurisdiction as examining justices over any offence committed by a person who appears or is brought before the court, whether or not the offence was committed within the commission area.

(4) Subject to sections 18 to 22 below and any other enactment (wherever contained) relating to the mode of trial of offences triable either way, a magistrates' court shall have jurisdiction to try summarily an offence triable either way in any case in which under subsection (3) above it would have jurisdiction as examining justices.

(5) A magistrates' court shall, in the exercise of its powers under section 24 below, have jurisdiction to try summarily an indictable offence in any case in which under subsection (3) above it would have jurisdiction as examining justices.

(6) A magistrates' court for any area by which a person is tried for an offence shall have jurisdiction to try him for any summary offence for which he could be tried by a magistrates' court for any other area.

(7) Nothing in this section shall affect any jurisdiction over offences conferred on a magistrates' court by any enactment not contained in this Act.

2–43   Once a defendant has been brought before a court in a local justice area under the relevant legal process the magistrates have power to deal with the case.

(4) Places, date and time of sittings of courts

Courts Act 2003, s.30

Places, dates and times of sittings

2–44   **30.**—(1) The Lord Chancellor may give directions as to the places in England and Wales at which magistrates' courts may sit.

(2) In exercising his powers under subsection (1), the Lord Chancellor shall have regard to the need to ensure that court-houses are accessible to persons resident in each local justice area.

(3) The Lord Chancellor may, with the concurrence of the Lord Chief Justice, give directions as to the distribution and transfer of the general business of magistrates' courts between the places specified in directions under subsection (1).

(4) Directions under subsection (3) may, in particular, contain provision that, where a person is charged with an offence and is being required to appear before a magistrates' court, the place where he is required to appear is one of the places described in subsection (5).

(5) The places are—

(a) a place in the local justice area in which the offence is alleged to have been committed;

(b) a place in the local justice area in which the person charged with the offence resides;

(c) a place in the local justice area in which the witnesses, or the majority of the witnesses, reside;

(d) a place where other cases raising similar issues are being dealt with.

(6) "The general business of magistrates' courts" does not include family proceedings (as defined in section 65 of the 1980 Act).

(7) The Lord Chancellor may give directions as to the days on which and times at which magistrates' courts may sit.

(8) Subject to any directions under subsection (7), the business of magistrates' courts may be conducted on any day and at any time.

(9) The Lord Chief Justice may nominate a judicial office holder (as defined in section 109(4) of the *Constitutional Reform Act* 2005) to exercise his functions under subsection (1) or (7).

2–45   In the national commission area all summary offences can be heard at any magistrates' court in England and Wales as can either way or indictable offences. The Lord Chancellor may make directions to ensure that the business of the courts is run efficiently. He may direct where magistrates' courts may sit and also how cases should be distributed amongst the courts in different areas. The directions recognise that the convenience of the defendant and the witnesses may dictate where a case should be heard which need not necessarily be in the court local to where the offence is alleged to have been committed.

VIII. TERRITORIAL JURISDICTION

A. INTRODUCTION

2–46   Generally, the courts are not concerned with conduct which occurs overseas: *Cox v. Army Council* [1963] A.C. 48.

Criminal offences may have a foreign element and in such cases the court will investigate the parliamentary intention in defining offences when deciding on any geographical limitation. In the absence of clear words to the contrary parliament is presumed not to have intended to make conduct occurring outside the territorial jurisdiction of the Crown a criminal offence triable in an English court: *Air India v. Wiggins* (1980) 71 Cr.App.R. 213. In the case of blackmail where the letter making the demand was posted in England the offence was held to be triable in England although the letter was directed to the intended victim abroad: *Treacy v. DPP* [1971] A.C. 537, HL.

Certain offences may be prosecuted in this country even where the offence was committed abroad, *e.g.* murder abroad by a British subject: *Offences against the Person Act* 1861, s.9; and terrorist acts committed in certain foreign countries: *Suppression of Terrorism Act* 1978, s.4.

There is provision for offenders to be extradited to England and Wales from foreign **2–47** countries for offences committed here and similarly offenders may be extradited out of this jurisdiction if they are found in England and Wales and are subject to trial abroad. See Ch.3. The complexities of international crime were recognised by the *Criminal Justice Act* 1993, which extends and clarifies the jurisdiction of the criminal courts in the UK in relation to crimes with a foreign element.

B. EMBASSIES AND CONSULATES

The building occupied by a foreign embassy or consulate and the land upon which it **2–48** stands remain the territory of the United Kingdom but diplomatic and consular premises are inviolable. The consent of the head of the mission is required before the local investigating authorities may gain entry. This can present problems in the magistrates' court when diplomatic representatives or their staff commit criminal offences. Vehicles bearing diplomatic plates can incur parking tickets or other road traffic violations. Before these offences can be successfully prosecuted there must be effective service of a summons or enforcement notice at the diplomatic premises. In such cases the prosecution may choose not to proceed. For more serious offences warrants of entry or arrest can only be executed with official consent from the Embassy authorities.

C. SHIPS

English courts have jurisdiction in respect of offences committed on board United **2–49** Kingdom ships if the defendant is a British citizen and is charged with having committed the offence on board any United Kingdom ship on the high seas, or in any foreign port or harbour, or on board any foreign ship to which he does not belong: *Merchant Shipping Act* 1995, s.281(a). If the defendant is not a British citizen English courts have jurisdiction if he is charged with having committed an offence on board any United Kingdom ship on the high seas: *Merchant Shipping Act* 1995, s.281(b). Section 3(A) of the *Magistrates' Courts Act* 1980 makes it clear that sections 280, 281 and 282 of the *Merchant Shipping Act* 1995 apply generally to offences under the law of England and Wales and not simply to specific offences under the Act.

D. AIRCRAFT

Offences committed on aeroplanes are covered by specific statutes (see Ch.20— **2–50** Aeroplanes and Airports) and the court has jurisdiction over any offences committed in the aircraft whilst it is in flight over the United Kingdom. Under section 92 of the *Civil Aviation Act* 1982, any act or omission taking place on board an aeroplane while on flight elsewhere than in or over the United Kingdom, if it constitutes an offence if committed on land, will be an offence in the air. Foreign aircraft are not affected by this Act unless the next landing of the aircraft is in the UK and where the vessel is registered elsewhere than the UK that the offence would constitute a criminal offence in the country of registration. The consent of the DPP is needed to prosecute offences committed on aircraft when not over UK airspace: section 92(2).

IX. SOVEREIGN AND DIPLOMATIC IMMUNITY

2–51   Diplomatic agents enjoy immunity from the criminal jurisdiction of the state of residence: *Diplomatic Privileges Act* 1964, Sched. 1, Art.31.

Members of diplomatic, administrative and technical staff of a mission and members of their families forming part of their household and domestic service staff are exempt from criminal proceedings: *Diplomatic Privileges Act* 1964, Sched. 1, Art.37. Private servants of members of the mission rather than servants of the mission itself enjoy no such immunity. Members of the families of diplomatic staff and members of the technical and administrative staff and their families who are British nationals or permanent residents do not enjoy immunity from criminal jurisdiction.

Where the question as to whether a defendant is entitled to diplomatic immunity under the *Diplomatic Privileges Act* 1964 arises, a certificate issued by or under the authority of the Secretary of State is conclusive evidence: *Diplomatic Privileges Act* 1964, s.4. In *R. v. Secretary of State for Foreign and Commonwealth Affairs, ex p. Trawnik, The Times,* April 18, 1985, the court held in a case of state immunity that a minister's certificate could not be challenged by way of judicial review except on the ground that it was a nullity or was issued beyond the scope of the minister's statutory power.

2–52   Diplomatic privilege cannot be pleaded successfully unless the Foreign and Commonwealth Office has been notified of the entry of the individual into the United Kingdom in accordance with the Vienna Convention on Diplomatic Relations, Article 10 even though Article 10 is not reproduced in the Schedule to the *Diplomatic Privileges Act* 1964: *R. v. Lambeth J.J., ex p. Yusufu* [1985] Crim.L.R. 510.

It is possible for the immunity to be waived. Waiver must be made by or on behalf of the representative of the country concerned and cannot be made by the defendant. Until such a waiver is made the proceedings are without jurisdiction and are void: *Madan* [1961] Crim.L.R. 253.

X. CHILDREN AND YOUNG PERSONS

2–53   Under section 68 of the *Criminal Justice Act* 1991 the magistrates' courts have jurisdiction in respect of summary and indictable offences only where the offender is aged 18 years and over. Offenders under the age of 18 years are dealt with by the youth court.

The magistrates' court has power to deal with young people under the age of 18 in restricted circumstances.

a)   If a person aged 17 or under appears alone before a magistrates' court, unless there is an adult co-defendant, the case must be adjourned to a youth court (*Children and Young Persons Act* 1933, s.46). The defendant may be remanded either on bail, in custody if aged 17 or to local authority accommodation if younger. A young person aged 15 or 16 can also be remanded to secure accommodation. Youth courts rarely sit on Saturdays or Bank Holidays so the youth will be produced at the adult court and will be remanded under this section to the next convenient youth court.

b)   If a young person aged under 18 is jointly charged with an adult the magistrates' court (as opposed to the youth court) may deal with him: *Children and Young Persons Act* 1933, s.46. If the adult elects or is committed for jury trial at the Crown Court, the magistrates may commit the young person for trial at the Crown Court if it is in the interests of justice to do so: *Magistrates' Courts Act* 1980, s.24. If the adult consents to summary trial and pleads not guilty then the magistrates can direct that the young person be tried jointly with the adult. The court also has discretion to sever the co-defendants if it is in the interests of justice and may remit the young person to a youth court for trial: *Magistrates' Courts Act* 1980, s.29. Factors to consider are the age and plea of the young person and the advisability of duplication of trials.

c) The magistrates' court must remit a young person who is convicted of a joint charge with an adult to the youth court for sentence unless satisfied it would be undesirable to do so. The appropriate youth court will be the court acting for the same area as the adult court or the youth court that has jurisdiction for the area where the young person resides: *Powers of Criminal Courts (Sentencing) Act* 2000, s.8(1) and (2). The circumstances in which a magistrates' court may find it undesirable to remit the young person are set out in section 8 of the Act. Instead of remittal the court may make a referral order if the case falls within the relevant conditions. The magistrates' court has power to sentence a young person on conviction in a joint matter with an adult if the court is of the opinion that the case is one which can properly be dealt with by means of an absolute or conditional discharge, a fine not exceeding £250 in the case of a young person aged 10–13 inclusive or £1,000 for a young person aged 14–17, or an order for the offender's parent or guardian to enter into a recognisance to take proper care of him and exercise proper control over him: *Powers of Criminal Courts (Sentencing) Act* 2000, s.8(6)–(8).

A co-defendant who is a young person may become an adult during the process of **2–54** the case. If he was 17 at the time of commission of the offence but reaches 18 before the first court appearance the adult court has jurisdiction and may hear the case. His young age should be taken into account on sentencing. If he appears as a youth co-defendant and reaches the age of 18 by the date of conviction, then he should be treated by the adult court as if he were still a young person with the restrictions on sentencing powers applying.

In *Ghafoor* [2002] Crim.L.R. 739, the defendant was 17 at the time of commission of an offence of rioting but was 18 by the time he was convicted. On appeal his sentence of four and a half years detention in a Young Offenders Institution was reduced to 18 months on the basis that taking his age into account at the time of the offence, this period of detention was equal to the length of any detention and training order that could properly have been imposed in the youth court. The relevant age for determining sentencing powers was the age at the time of the offence.

CHAPTER 3

EXTRADITION

I. INTRODUCTION

Extradition is the handing over by one country of a person who is alleged to have **3–1** committed a crime or who has been convicted of a criminal offence to another country, which has jurisdiction to deal with the crime.

Throughout the centuries it has been traditional for states to grant asylum to fugitives **3–2** from other countries. It also became established that countries would not give asylum to those who had committed crimes unless it was considered that those crimes were political in nature. A state may extend the cloak of its own immunity over state officials but it cannot be a blanket immunity as some activities cannot in international law be legal: *R. v. Bow Street Metropolitan Stipendiary Magistrate, ex p. Pinochet Ugarte (No. 3)* [2000] 1 A.C. 147. When determining whether a claim should succeed against a state official, the court should consider and balance at one and the same time all relevant factors: *Jones v. Ministry of the Interior of the Kingdom of Saudi Arabia (Secretary of State for Constitutional Affairs as intervenors)*: *Mitchell v. Al-Dali, The Times,* November 1, 2004.

Treaties between countries exist to facilitate the return of those who have committed or are alleged to have committed serious offences. The United Kingdom seeks extradition from elsewhere while other countries seek extradition from this country.

Bow Street Magistrates' Court in Central London, being the office of the senior district judge (chief magistrate) and those other district judges designated to hear extradition proceedings, was traditionally the centre for outward extradition in England and Wales. Upon its closure in July 2006 extradition proceedings are heard at the City of Westminster Court.

This chapter is concerned with magistrates' courts proceedings for outward extradi- **3–3** tion only. The proceedings are now covered by the *Extradition Act* 2003. All statutory references are to that Act.

There will be a number of cases already in the system that will follow the previous legislation but these will soon be completed and any new application will be made under this Act. Some case law arising from earlier legislation has been included as it may still give guidance in certain circumstances.

The Act categorises the United Kingdom's extradition partners into two. The Secre- **3–4** tary of State for the Home Office designates countries into each category. These categories may change. A country may migrate from category two to category one. No country may be designated under Part 1 where the death penalty would be available if the person were found guilty: section 1(3). There may also be special arrangements with modifications of the Act where a treaty is not in existence but there are memoranda of understanding, *e.g.* Rwanda: section 194.

3–5 The difference in procedure between the two categories is that the Secretary of State for the Home Office still has a role to play so far as category 2 countries are concerned whereas the Act introduces a fast track procedure in Part 1 initially for EU Member States and Gibraltar without the need for any intervention by the Secretary of State at any stage. A check will need to be made to ascertain which countries have been designated to which category at any particular time. In addition the designation of category two countries may give special terms, *e.g.* the USA does not have to provide *prima facie* evidence. This was decided not to be unlawful or irrational: *R. (Ian Norris) v. Secretary of State for the Home Department* [2006] 3 All E.R. 1011.

A request may be withdrawn and the person discharged. The 2003 Act is throwing up a number of problems with regard to Part 1: *Germany v. Kleinschmidt* [2005] EWHC 1373; [2005] 3 All E.R. 759 and interpretation must be approached on the twin assumptions that Parliament did not intend the provisions of Part 1 to be inconsistent with any Framework Decisions adopted by the European Council: *Office of the King's Prosecutor (Brussels) v. Armas* [2005] UKHL 67; [2006] 1 All E.R. 647. There is now a system of free movement of judicial decisions in criminal matters and practical solutions to legislative problems true to the spirit and the requirements of Framework Decisions, while properly safeguarding the liberty of the individual.

II. JURISDICTION

3–6 Extradition proceedings are dealt with by district judges who have been designated by the Lord Chancellor for that purpose: sections 67 and 137. Jurisdiction lies with the designated judge as opposed to the area or courthouse. The judge will normally sit at Bow Street Magistrates' Court but can sit elsewhere. A magistrate may deal with an application for a provisional warrant but arrangements are in place at Bow Street for such applications to be made there both in and out of normal court hours.

III. ARREST

3–7 The subject of an extradition request will normally be arrested on a warrant. The type of warrant will differ according to which part of the Act applies to the requesting state. The warrant may be a Part 1 warrant (European Arrest Warrant), or a Part 2 Provisional or certified warrant. Part 3 warrants refer to incoming extradition and are not dealt with here.

(1) Part 1 warrant

3–8 This has commonly been called the European Arrest Warrant. The provisions are contained in section 2 of the Act.

Extradition Act 2003, s.2

Part 1 warrant and certificate

3–9 **2.**—(1) This section applies if the designated authority receives a Part 1 warrant in respect of a person.

(2) A Part 1 warrant is an arrest warrant which is issued by a judicial authority of a category 1 territory and which contains—

    (a) the statement referred to in subsection (3) and the information referred to in subsection (4), or

    (b) the statement referred to in subsection (5) and the information referred to in subsection (6).

(3) The statement is one that—

    (a) the person in respect of whom the Part 1 warrant is issued is accused in the category 1 territory of the commission of an offence specified in the warrant, and

Part I

(b) the Part 1 warrant is issued with a view to his arrest and extradition to the category 1 territory for the purpose of being prosecuted for the offence.

(4) The information is—

(a) particulars of the person's identity;

(b) particulars of any other warrant issued in the category 1 territory for the person's arrest in respect of the offence;

(c) particulars of the circumstances in which the person is alleged to have committed the offence, including the conduct alleged to constitute the offence, the time and place at which he is alleged to have committed the offence and any provision of the law of the category 1 territory under which the conduct is alleged to constitute an offence;

(d) particulars of the sentence which may be imposed under the law of the category 1 territory in respect of the offence if the person is convicted of it.

(5) The statement is one that—

(a) the person in respect of whom the Part 1 warrant is issued is alleged to be unlawfully at large after conviction of an offence specified in the warrant by a court in the category 1 territory, and

(b) the Part 1 warrant is issued with a view to his arrest and extradition to the category 1 territory for the purpose of being sentenced for the offence or of serving a sentence of imprisonment or another form of detention imposed in respect of the offence.

(6) The information is—

(a) particulars of the person's identity;

(b) particulars of the conviction;

(c) particulars of any other warrant issued in the category 1 territory for the person's arrest in respect of the offence;

(d) particulars of the sentence which may be imposed under the law of the category 1 territory in respect of the offence, if the person has not been sentenced for the offence;

(e) particulars of the sentence which has been imposed under the law of the category 1 territory in respect of the offence, if the person has been sentenced for the offence.

(7) The designated authority may issue a certificate under this section if it believes that the authority which issued the Part 1 warrant has the function of issuing arrest warrants in the category 1 territory.

(8) A certificate under this section must certify that the authority which issued the Part 1 warrant has the function of issuing arrest warrants in the category 1 territory.

(9) The designated authority is the authority designated for the purposes of this Part by order made by the Secretary of State.

(10) An order made under subsection (9) may—

(a) designate more than one authority;

(b) designate different authorities for different parts of the United Kingdom.

A warrant is issued in the requesting State and sent to the UK for execution. It must **3–10** have been issued by a judicial authority and will state whether the person to be arrested is to be prosecuted or has been convicted. It will give details of identity, particulars of the offence, how it was committed or the fact of a conviction, the possible or actual sentence together with details of any other outstanding warrants. In a case involving multiple offences in which an aggregate sentence was imposed, section 2(6)(e) does not require Part 1 requesting states to segregate the separate components of the aggregate sentence in respect of each individual offence: *Trepac v. Slovakia*, unreported, November 22, 2006. Where a warrant fails to identify the provision of law under which the person's conduct is alleged to constitute an offence, it does not conform to the requirements of section 2 and is invalid: *Hunt v. Belgium* [2006] EWHC 165; [2006] 2 All E.R. 735; *Hall v. Germany* [2006] EWHC 462.

Section 2(4)(c) requires particulars of the circumstances in which the person was alleged to have committed the offence, including the conduct alleged to constitute the offence. Charges must not be vague, *e.g.* in English terms "obtaining by deception" would not suffice: *Von der Pahlen v. Austria* [2006] EWHC 1672. There is no need to get tied up in particular words. A description "misappropriation" is sufficient to satisfy particulars of conduct alleged as it is clearly theft and therefore there is no lack of specificity: *Sidlauskaite v. Prosecutor General's Office of the Republic of Lithuania* [2006] All E.R. (D) 276. It is not necessary for a warrant to state that the individual is "unlawfully at large" if it can be inferred from the warrant as a whole: *Kuprevicius v. Lithuania* [2006] EWHC 1518.

The case of *R. (Pillar) v. Bow Street Magistrates' Court* [2006] EWHC 1886 did not decide whether a warrant which did not comply with section 2(4) could be supplanted by additional information in certain circumstances but if there were to be supplemental material then that material would have to come from the requesting judicial authority.

If the warrant is not valid there is no jurisdiction to order extradition: *Boudhiba v. Spain* [2006] 3 All E.R. 574. It is not necessary or appropriate to subject a warrant to the requirements of specificity accorded to particulars of, or sometimes required of, a count in an indictment or an allegation in a civil pleading in this country: *Fofana v. Thubin* [2006] EWHC 744. The warrant itself can amount to a certificate required under section 64(2)(b) and (c): *Dabas v. High Court of Justice in Madrid, Spain* [2007] UKHL 6; *The Times*, March 5, 2007. Lord Bingham said that Part 1 of the Act had to be read in the context of the Framework Decision which intended to simplify and expedite procedures and which was binding on the UK. That Framework made no mention of a certificate but set out the requirements for a warrant. The warrant in this case complied with these requirements and a decision that a separate certificate was required would re-introduce an element of technicality which the Framework Decision intended to banish and would frustrate the intention that a warrant in common form should be uniformly acceptable in all member states.

It is not for the court to consider the merits of any proposed prosecution but there must be clarity in relation to the stage which proceedings have reached in the foreign jurisdiction: *Vey v. Public Prosecutor of Montlucon* [2006] EWHC 760. In this case the issue was whether the person was merely wanted for questioning or whether an accusation had been made.

The designated authority for England and Wales is the National Criminal Intelligence Service. That authority will certify whether the judicial authority has the function of issuing arrest warrants in the requesting country. The warrant must include particulars of the conduct which will be capable of constituting an extradition offence: *Palar v. Court of First Instance of Brussels* [2005] EWHC 915. The designation by European Member States of a body as a judicial authority is determinative of that body being a judicial authority for the purposes of section 2: *Enander v. Governor of HM Prison Brixton* [2005] EWHC 3036; [2006] 1 C.M.L.R. 37.

The transitional provisions provide that an Article 95 alert is to be treated as a Part 1 warrant: section 212.

3–11 Where a person is unlawfully at large from serving a sentence in a country other than the convicting country under special arrangements for the transfer of prisoners a warrant may be issued by either the convicting country or the country where he is serving the sentence: section 63.

Once the certificate has been issued by the designated authority a police or customs officer may execute the foreign warrant against a member of the public and, may do so, even if the warrant is not in his possession. There are also provisions for service personnel to be arrested by service policemen: section 3.

In cases of urgency a person may be arrested without warrant. This is called a provisional arrest and may take place where an officer has reasonable grounds for believing that a Part 1 warrant has been or will be issued: section 5.

Extradition Act 2003, s.5(1)–(2)

Provisional arrest

3–12 **5.**—(1) A constable, a customs officer or a service policeman may arrest a person without a warrant if he has reasonable grounds for believing—

Part I

(a) that a Part 1 warrant has been or will be issued in respect of the person by an authority of a category 1 territory, and

(b) that the authority has the function of issuing arrest warrants in the category 1 territory.

(2) A constable or a customs officer may arrest a person under subsection (1) in any part of the United Kingdom.

(2) Part 2 warrant

A warrant may be a provisional or certified warrant.   **3–13**

A certified warrant will be considered where a certificate has been sent from the Secretary of State to a designated district judge. The certificate will be issued where a category two country requests the extradition of someone either alleged to have committed an offence or who has been convicted of an offence and provides valid supporting documentation through the diplomatic channels to the Secretary of State. It is a matter for the Secretary of State whether the documents sent to him as the formal requisition comply with requirements: *R. v. Governor of Brixton Prison, ex p. Cuoghi, The Times*, May 12, 1998.

Extradition Act 2003, s.70

Extradition request and certificate

70.—(1) The Secretary of State must issue a certificate under this section if he receives a valid   **3–14** request for the extradition to a category 2 territory of a person who is in the United Kingdom.

(2) But subsection (1) does not apply if the Secretary of State decides under section 126 that the request is not to be proceeded with.

(3) A request for a person's extradition is valid if—

(a) it contains the statement referred to in subsection (4), and

(b) it is made in the approved way.

(4) The statement is one that the person—

(a) is accused in the category 2 territory of the commission of an offence specified in the request, or

(b) is alleged to be unlawfully at large after conviction by a court in the category 2 territory of an offence specified in the request.

(5) A request for extradition to a category 2 territory which is a British overseas territory is made in the approved way if it is made by or on behalf of the person administering the territory.

(6) A request for extradition to a category 2 territory which is the Hong Kong Special Administrative Region of the People's Republic of China is made in the approved way if it is made by or on behalf of the government of the Region.

(7) A request for extradition to any other category 2 territory is made in the approved way if it is made—

(a) by an authority of the territory which the Secretary of State believes has the function of making requests for extradition in that territory, or

(b) by a person recognised by the Secretary of State as a diplomatic or consular representative of the territory.

(8) A certificate under this section must certify that the request is made in the approved way.

(9) If a certificate is issued under this section the Secretary of State must send these documents to the appropriate judge—

(a) the request;

(b) the certificate;

(c) a copy of any relevant Order in Council.

The Secretary of State may choose not to issue a certificate if there are competing   **3–15** claims. He may defer the claim: section 126.

Upon receipt of the relevant documentation a designated judge may issue a warrant of arrest with or without bail: section 71.

It is important that a state requesting extradition fairly and properly describes the conduct alleged: *R. (Castillo) v. Spain* [2004] EWHC 1676; [2005] 1 W.L.R. 1043. The Secretary of State can infer from the whole of the documentation sent by the requesting state whether the person is an accused or convicted person: *Akaroglu v. Romania* [2007] EWHC 367, Admin. The facts must be clear and courts should be reluctant to fill a gap: *R. (Bleta) v. Secretary of State for the Home Department* [2004] EWHC 2034; [2005] 1 All E.R. 810. It has been held, under the old law, that the Secretary of State could issue a further authority to proceed to clarify the first: *Fernandes, Fernandes, Trevasso v. Governor of Brixton Prison, The Commonwealth of the Bahamas* [2004] EWHC 2207.

Extradition Act 2003, s.71(1)–(7)

Arrest warrant following extradition request

3–16   **71.**—(1) This section applies if the Secretary of State sends documents to the appropriate judge under section 70.

(2) The judge may issue a warrant for the arrest of the person whose extradition is requested if the judge has reasonable grounds for believing that—

     (a) the offence in respect of which extradition is requested is an extradition offence, and

     (b) there is evidence falling within subsection (3).

(3) The evidence is—

     (a) evidence that would justify the issue of a warrant for the arrest of a person accused of the offence within the judge's jurisdiction, if the person whose extradition is requested is accused of the commission of the offence;

     (b) evidence that would justify the issue of a warrant for the arrest of a person unlawfully at large after conviction of the offence within the judge's jurisdiction, if the person whose extradition is requested is alleged to be unlawfully at large after conviction of the offence.

(4) But if the category 2 territory to which extradition is requested is designated for the purposes of this section by order made by the Secretary of State, subsections (2) and (3) have effect as if "evidence" read "information".

(5) A warrant issued under this section may—

     (a) be executed by any person to whom it is directed or by any constable or customs officer;

     (b) be executed even if neither the warrant nor a copy of it is in the possession of the person executing it at the time of the arrest.

(6) If a warrant issued under this section in respect of a person is directed to a service policeman, it may be executed in any place where the service policeman would have power to arrest the person under the appropriate service law if the person had committed an offence under that law.

(7) In any other case, a warrant issued under this section may be executed in any part of the United Kingdom.

3–17   The designated district judge must be satisfied that the offence is an extradition offence and that a warrant for similar circumstances in the UK would be justified. The warrant may be executed even if it is not in the possession of the arresting officer.

It is not necessary for a warrant to slavishly follow the language of the statute but it has to make clear in some way that the person concerned is unlawfully at large. It is not the issue of a warrant which sets the process of extradition in train but the issue of a warrant which complies with the prescribed conditions: *Pinto v. Governor of Brixton Prison* [2004] EWHC 2986. In that case the person was described as not having, on the term (of a precarious prolonged exit) presented himself at the State Prison.

A provisional warrant may be issued under section 73 as a preliminary step at a time when no formal request for extradition has been made.

Extradition Act 2003, s.73(1)–(7)

Provisional warrant

3–18   **73.**—(1) This section applies if a justice of the peace is satisfied on information in writing and on oath that a person within subsection (2)—

(a) is or is believed to be in the United Kingdom, or

(b) is or is believed to be on his way to the United Kingdom.

(2) A person is within this subsection if—

(a) he is accused in a category 2 territory of the commission of an offence, or

(b) he is alleged to be unlawfully at large after conviction of an offence by a court in a category 2 territory.

(3) The justice may issue a warrant for the arrest of the person (a provisional warrant) if he has reasonable grounds for believing that—

(a) the offence of which the person is accused or has been convicted is an extradition offence, and

(b) there is written evidence falling within subsection (4).

(4) The evidence is—

(a) evidence that would justify the issue of a warrant for the arrest of a person accused of the offence within the justice's jurisdiction, if the person in respect of whom the warrant is sought is accused of the commission of the offence;

(b) evidence that would justify the issue of a warrant for the arrest of a person unlawfully at large after conviction of the offence within the justice's jurisdiction, if the person in respect of whom the warrant is sought is alleged to be unlawfully at large after conviction of the offence.

(5) But if the category 2 territory is designated for the purposes of this section by order made by the Secretary of State, subsections (3) and (4) have effect as if "evidence" read "information".

(6) A provisional warrant may—

(a) be executed by any person to whom it is directed or by any constable or customs officer;

(b) be executed even if neither the warrant nor a copy of it is in the possession of the person executing it at the time of the arrest.

(7) If a warrant issued under this section in respect of a person is directed to a service policeman, it may be executed in any place where the service policeman would have power to arrest the person under the appropriate service law if the person had committed an offence under that law.

It is quite common for this type of warrant to be sought where it is deemed urgent. **3–19** Many people wanted for extradition crimes are found to be in transit or about to leave the country or are on their way to this country and there is no time for a formal request under section 70. Information is often received from Interpol through police channels pending receipt of a formal extradition request and supporting documentation. The information should state that extradition will be sought and give sufficient facts about the person, the offence and the possible penalty.

Although an application may be made to a magistrate, applications are generally dealt with at Bow Street Magistrates' Court by a designated judge. The police will make contact with the justices' clerk or one of the legal advisers who will check the information for any defects and either draft a warrant for the judge's consideration or check a warrant which has already been prepared by the police. The practice of the legal adviser checking the process was approved in *R. v. Governor of Pentonville Prison, ex p. Osman (No.3)* [1990] 1 All E.R. 999.

The judge must be satisfied on the written information that the allegation would amount to an extradition offence and that a warrant is justified. In *R. v. Evans, ex p. Pinochet Ugarte, The Times*, November 3, 1998, a second provisional warrant was issued on the same information when the first warrant, having been issued in a very tight timescale, was found to be defective. That practice was upheld although Lord Bingham C.J. stated that it was unusual and generally undesirable.

The case of *R. v. Bow Street Magistrates' Court, ex p. Allison, The Times*, June 5, **3–20** 1997 defined an urgent case as one that is urgent at the time of the issue of the warrant, regardless of the cause of the urgency. In that case the person, who had been in custody awaiting extradition to the USA for other offences, was likely to be released very soon and was liable to abscond.

If a person is on his way, the judge should be satisfied that he has actually boarded a flight to this country and that there are no stops en route where he might get off.

The warrant may be executed even if it is not in the possession of the arresting officer. Premises may be entered and searched to facilitate an arrest. Upon arrest the person and the premises where the person was found or had recently been at, may be searched for evidence relating to the offence or the identity of the person: sections 161, 162 and 163.

3–21 After arrest the police also have powers under Part 4 of the Act in relation to entry and search of premises, seizure of material, the taking of photographs, fingerprints and other samples: sections 164–168. Codes of Practice are in existence.

The warrant may be issued with or without bail. Where the police bail the person, a police officer will liaise with the court to take account of the court lists and statutory time limits. The Secretary of State will be informed because where the person is arrested on a provisional warrant the court will need the Secretary of State's order before it can proceed. It should be noted that the judge must receive the certificate and supporting documentation within 45 days from the date of arrest (or any longer period agreed with a particular state) otherwise the person may be discharged.

IV. REPRESENTATION

3–22 The requesting state will in most cases be represented by the Crown Prosecution Service, which acts as an agent. Many of its powers, being peculiar to the law of England and Wales, *e.g.* discontinuance, do not apply in extradition matters. The requesting state may alternatively instruct a firm of solicitors.

The person arrested may instruct solicitors and may apply for a legal representation order. In *R. v. Bow Street Magistrates' Court, ex p. Shayler* [1999] 1 All E.R. 98 (albeit a potential inward extradition) the refusal of legal aid at the stage that a warrant had been issued but not executed was upheld.

V. PROCEDURE

A. FIRST APPEARANCE BEFORE THE COURT

3–23 Once a person is arrested he must be brought before a designated judge as soon as practicable except in the case where a person has been provisionally arrested under section 5 when he must be brought before the judge within 48 hours: sections 4, 6 and 72.

Habeas corpus is available to challenge a decision not to bring the arrested person before the court as soon as practicable: *Nikonovs v. Governor of Brixton Prison* [2005] EWHC 2405; [2006] 1 All E.R. 927. Here the person arrested had erroneously been taken before the court on a Monday instead of the previous Saturday due to a mistake of fact in believing a court was not sitting on that day.

In each case a copy of the warrant must be given to the person arrested as soon as practicable after arrest. Failure to do so may result in the person's discharge.

The prosecutor will prepare "charges" in the form of offences known to the law of England and Wales but they have no formal status. They are there to assist the judge: *R. v. Bow Street Magistrates' Court, ex p. Kline*, unreported, June 30, 1999.

3–24 The judge will want to establish identity and whether the person will consent to extradition. If consent is not forthcoming the judge must fix the date of the extradition hearing and timetable the rest of the proceedings. He may remand the person in custody or bail: sections 8, 71. The presumption of bail applies: section 198.

Identity

3–25 The question of identity must be established on a balance of probabilities: sections 7, 78. It is to be determined at the initial hearing. If resolved in the affirmative, the extradition follows. The 2003 Act does not contemplate that there could be a second chance to raise identity at a later hearing: *Nur v. Van Der Valk* [2005] EWHC 1874. It is doubtful whether a judge has the jurisdiction to review the finding of identity previously made at an earlier hearing; the appropriate route is judicial review: *Hilali v Central Court of Criminal Proceedings, Madrid* [2006] 4 All E.R. 435.

The defendant may admit that he is the person concerned. If identification is in dispute, however, evidence must be brought before the court. Photographic or video evidence may be submitted: *Bradshar, Re*, unreported, February 28, 1984; *R. v. Governor of Pentonville Prison, ex p. Rodriguez, The Times*, November 29, 1984, DC; *R. v. Governor of Pentonville Prison, ex p. Voets* [1986] 2 All E.R. 630.

A passport linking the fugitive to the papers was approved in *Khan, Re*, unreported, **3–26** June 30, 1995. Evidence of what was said at the time of arrest has also been approved: *R. v. Governor of Pentonville Prison, ex p. Boettlicher*, unreported, April 28, 1993. In that case the fugitive had given his name, address and date of birth as contained in the papers and had remarked that the alleged assault was against his girlfriend.

In *Osawe v. Government of HM Prison Brixton* [2003] EWHC 2140, fingerprints and photographs overruled the fact that the person's name was different from that on the papers. In *Artan Brahja v. 1) the Governor of HM Prison Brixton 2) the Government of Italy* [2003] EWHC 509 Admin, it was held, where details on the person's driving licence were different, that minor discrepancies were not sufficient to raise doubts over identity.

If there is insufficient evidence to show that the person is the one to whom the warrant refers he must be discharged.

An unusual name, date of birth, abode and passport number even if the latter is found in papers relating to a co-defendant is sufficient evidence for identification: *Savvas v. Govt. of Italy* [2004] EWHC 1233.

Consent to extradition

The court must inform the person of his right to consent to extradition and the fact **3–27** that consent will be irrevocable: sections 7 and 45 for Part 1 cases and sections 127 and 128 for Part 2 cases. They are in similar terms.

If the person wishes to consent there is no reason why the judge cannot proceed to order extradition or in Part 2 cases forward the case to the Secretary of State for his decision. The person must either be legally represented or has been offered legal aid but has refused or failed to apply or it has been refused or withdrawn. The consent must be recorded in writing. This is intended to provide a speedy process and protection is afforded through legal advice.

Where consent is not forthcoming, the judge will set the hearing date. In Part 1 proceedings the time limit set in section 8 is 21 days from the date of arrest but there is provision for a later date to be fixed if it is in the interests of justice. Subsequently the hearing may be adjourned further. The judge is expected to manage the progress of the case to ensure there is no undue delay. The person will either be remanded in custody or on bail.

So far as Part 2 proceedings are concerned the judge will proceed to timetable the **3–28** case in accordance with the statutory time limits. Where the arrest is under a certified warrant the hearing date must not be later than two months from the date that the person first appears before the court although this period may be extended if the interests of justice so require: section 75. Where the arrest is under a provisional warrant, a hearing must be fixed within two months from the date that the certificate from the Secretary of State is due to be received by the court.

B. The Extradition Hearing

(1) Extradition proceedings

Extradition proceedings are classified as a type of summary proceeding. They are **3–29** criminal proceedings for the purposes of legal representation under the *Access to*

Justice Act 1999. The general right to bail under the *Bail Act* 1976 applies. Statutory time limits must be complied with and extensions granted only in exceptional circumstances. Abuse of process can be considered in extradition proceedings but the rules of disclosure do not apply as they form part of an adversarial process which differs from extradition proceedings in which the court must satisfy itself that the requirements for making an order are satisfied. If a judge fears an abuse of process he should call for the necessary information or evidence for determining that issue and where fairness requires that material to be disclosed and the requesting authority or state will not agree, a judge should hold that fair process is impossible and discharge the person. An abuse of process argument may be a delaying tactic and a judge should be alert to that: *R. (United States of America) v. Bow Street Magistrates' Court* and *R. (Central Examining Court, Madrid) v. Bow Street Magistrates' Court* [2006] EWHC 2256; (2006) 156 N.L.J. 1440.

A diplomatic note is, in international law, regarding as binding on the issuing state. Diplomatic notes issued by the United States government guaranteeing that on extradition to the United States alleged terrorists will not be put on trial before a military commission nor designated as enemy combatants can be relied upon, in the absence of strong contrary evidence, as providing a sufficient guarantee that, if extradited, their human rights will be protected: *Ahmad v. Government of the United States of America* [2006] EWHC 2927; [2007] H.R.L.R. 8.

Extradition Act 2003, ss.9(1), (4), (5); 77(1), (4), (5)

Judge's powers at extradition hearing

3–30   **9. & 77.**—(1) In England and Wales, at the extradition hearing the appropriate judge has the same powers (as nearly as may be) as a magistrates' court would have if the proceedings were the summary trial of an information against the person in respect of whom the Part I warrant was issued.

(4) If the judge adjourns the extradition hearing he must remand the person in custody or on bail.

(5) If the judge remands the person in custody he may later grant bail.

3–31   The extradition hearing will be conducted as if it were a summary trial but no plea is taken as the person is not being tried in this country. The advocate for the requesting country will open the case and deal with preliminary matters. He will then introduce his evidence which will normally be in statement form and will be read. Any oral evidence will be taken in the form of a deposition. If identity or consent has not been determined before, the judge will deal with those matters at that stage. The judge may call for further information from the country seeking extradition pursuant to Article 15 of the European Council Framework Decision of June 13, 2002 on the European arrest warrant and the surrender procedures between Member States (2002/584/JHA; OJ/2002/L190).

There is power to adjourn: *Raffile v. United States of America* [2004] EWHC 2913; [2005] 1 All E.R. 889. In *Handa v. High Instance Court of Paris* [2004] EWHC 3116, it was stated that it is irrational to refuse to adjourn proceedings in circumstances where there is no statutory power enabling a serving prisoner to be released earlier than he should be in order that he could be extradited and where there is no reasonable cause for delay and no reasons not to adjourn.

3–32   In Part 2 cases the judge must ensure he has:
— the certificate from the Secretary of State;
— particulars of the person whose extradition is requested;
— particulars of the offence specified in the offence; and
— an arrest warrant issued in the requesting state or a certificate of conviction from the requesting state and details of the sentence, if any.

He must satisfy himself that the documents have been served upon the person: section 78.

The Secretary of State may extend the time in which the judge ought to receive the papers: *R. (Brown, formerly Bajinya) v. Belmarsh Prison Governor, The Times*, May 15, 2007.

Extradition Act 2003, s.78

Initial stages of extradition hearing

78.—(1) This section applies if a person alleged to be the person whose extradition is **3–33** requested appears or is brought before the appropriate judge for the extradition hearing.

(2) The judge must decide whether the documents sent to him by the Secretary of State consist of (or include)—

(a) the documents referred to in section 70(9);

(b) particulars of the person whose extradition is requested;

(c) particulars of the offence specified in the request;

(d) in the case of a person accused of an offence, a warrant for his arrest issued in the category 2 territory;

(e) in the case of a person alleged to be unlawfully at large after conviction of an offence, a certificate issued in the category 2 territory of the conviction and (if he has been sentenced) of the sentence.

(3) If the judge decides the question in subsection (2) in the negative he must order the person's discharge.

(4) If the judge decides that question in the affirmative he must decide whether—

(a) the person appearing or brought before him is the person whose extradition is requested;

(b) the offence specified in the request is an extradition offence;

(c) copies of the documents sent to the judge by the Secretary of State have been served on the person.

(5) The judge must decide the question in subsection (4)(a) on a balance of probabilities.

(6) If the judge decides any of the questions in subsection (4) in the negative he must order the person's discharge.

(7) If the judge decides those questions in the affirmative he must proceed under section 79.

(8) The reference in subsection (2)(d) to a warrant for a person's arrest includes a reference to a judicial document authorising his arrest.

The judge must decide whether the offence is an extradition offence and whether ex- **3–34** tradition is barred within the terms of the Act but he is not concerned with proof of the facts or possibilities of other relevant factors as those are matters for trial. It is sufficient that the conduct described in the request amounts to an offence in English law: *Kadre v. France* [2005] EWHC 1712; [2006] A.C.D. 26.

The need for a court to have sight of the warrant under section 8(2)(d) is in order to ensure that there are proceedings abroad but there is no requirement that every offence alleged is included in the warrant: *Hashmi v. United States of America* [2007] EWHC 564, Admin.

Service of documents under section 78(4) is mandatory but there is nothing in the statute to say that the documents must be served before the commencement of the extradition hearing. Neither does the Act expressly state by whom or by when service is to be effected. Normally service should be effected before the commencement of the hearing but in appropriate circumstances the court may adjourn the hearing under section 77(4) to enable service to be effected and in practice, it will be the CPS which will have to undertake service: *Germany v. Kleinschmidt, ante.*

(2) Extradition offence

The Act differentiates between those convicted of offences and sentenced and those **3–35** who are merely accused of committing offences.

Offenders who have been sentenced

Part 1 cases are dealt with under section 65.   **3–36**

Extradition Act 2003, s.65

Extradition offences: person sentenced for offence

3–37   **65.**—(1) This section applies in relation to conduct of a person if—

(a) he is alleged to be unlawfully at large after conviction by a court in a category 1 territory of an offence constituted by the conduct, and

(b) he has been sentenced for the offence.

(2) The conduct constitutes an extradition offence in relation to the category 1 territory if these conditions are satisfied—

(a) the conduct occurs in the category 1 territory and no part of it occurs in the United Kingdom;

(b) a certificate issued by an appropriate authority of the category 1 territory shows that the conduct falls within the European framework list;

(c) the certificate shows that a sentence of imprisonment or another form of detention for a term of 12 months or a greater punishment has been imposed in the category 1 territory in respect of the conduct.

(3) The conduct also constitutes an extradition offence in relation to the category 1 territory if these conditions are satisfied—

(a) the conduct occurs in the category 1 territory;

(b) the conduct would constitute an offence under the law of the relevant part of the United Kingdom if it occurred in that part of the United Kingdom;

(c) a sentence of imprisonment or another form of detention for a term of 4 months or a greater punishment has been imposed in the category 1 territory in respect of the conduct.

(4) The conduct also constitutes an extradition offence in relation to the category 1 territory if these conditions are satisfied—

(a) the conduct occurs outside the category 1 territory;

(b) a sentence of imprisonment or another form of detention for a term of 4 months or a greater punishment has been imposed in the category 1 territory in respect of the conduct;

(c) in corresponding circumstances equivalent conduct would constitute an extra-territorial offence under the law of the relevant part of the United Kingdom punishable with imprisonment or another form of detention for a term of 12 months or a greater punishment.

(5) The conduct also constitutes an extradition offence in relation to the category 1 territory if these conditions are satisfied—

(a) the conduct occurs outside the category 1 territory and no part of it occurs in the United Kingdom;

(b) the conduct would constitute an offence under the law of the relevant part of the United Kingdom punishable with imprisonment or another form of detention for a term of 12 months or a greater punishment if it occurred in that part of the United Kingdom;

(c) a sentence of imprisonment or another form of detention for a term of 4 months or a greater punishment has been imposed in the category 1 territory in respect of the conduct.

(6) The conduct also constitutes an extradition offence in relation to the category 1 territory if these conditions are satisfied—

(a) the conduct occurs outside the category 1 territory and no part of it occurs in the United Kingdom;

(b) a sentence of imprisonment or another form of detention for a term of 4 months or a greater punishment has been imposed in the category 1 territory in respect of the conduct;

(c) the conduct constitutes or if committed in the United Kingdom would constitute an offence mentioned in subsection (7).

(7) The offences are—

(a) an offence under section 51 or 58 of the *International Criminal Court Act* 2001 (genocide, crimes against humanity and war crimes);

(b) an offence under section 52 or 59 of that Act (conduct ancillary to genocide etc committed outside the jurisdiction);

(c) an ancillary offence, as defined in section 55 or 62 of that Act, in relation to an offence falling within paragraph (a) or (b);

(d) an offence under section 1 of the *International Criminal Court (Scotland) Act
2001* (genocide, crimes against humanity and war crimes);

(e) an offence under section 2 of that Act (conduct ancillary to genocide etc committed outside the jurisdiction);

(f) an ancillary offence, as defined in section 7 of that Act, in relation to an offence
falling within paragraph (d) or (e).

(8) For the purposes of subsections (3)(b), (4)(c) and (5)(b)—

(a) if the conduct relates to a tax or duty, it is immaterial that the law of the relevant
part of the United Kingdom does not impose the same kind of tax or duty or
does not contain rules of the same kind as those of the law of the category 1 territory;

(b) if the conduct relates to customs or exchange, it is immaterial that the law of the
relevant part of the United Kingdom does not contain rules of the same kind as
those of the law of the category 1 territory.

(9) This section applies for the purposes of this Part.

The definition of an extradition offence where a person has been sentenced depends **3–38**
upon whether the conduct has occurred within or outside the territory of the requesting
state.

Where the conduct has occurred in the territory of the requesting state, it is an extradition offence if it is certified as conduct within the European Framework list and he has
been sentenced to a minimum of 12 months' imprisonment or detention or it is an offence also within the UK and a sentence of four months' or more imprisonment or
detention has been imposed.

Where the conduct has occurred outside the territory of the requesting state, it is an
extradition offence if a minimum four-month sentence of imprisonment or detention
has been imposed and the conduct amounts to an extra-territorial offence in the UK
punishable with a minimum of 12 months or the conduct amounts to an offence punishable with a minimum of 12 months in UK and a minimum of four months has been
imposed in the requesting state or a minimum sentence of four months has been
imposed in the requesting state and the offence is one of genocide, crimes of humanity
or war crimes or an ancillary offence. A European arrest warrant can be validly executed for the surrender of a fugitive whose criminal conduct took place partly in the
state issuing the warrant and partly in the UK. Conduct in section 65 means the conduct
complained of or relied on in the warrant, but section 65(3) does not require that all
conduct takes place in the category 1 territory. It is enough that some of the conduct
takes place in that territory: *R. (Okandeji) v. Bow Street Magistrates' Court* [2005]
EWHC 2925; [2006] 1 W.L.R. 674.

A court may also order extradition in repatriation cases under section 63 where a
person is at large when he should be serving a sentence under the repatriation arrangements and outside the territory where he was originally convicted. The phrase "unlawfully at large" in section 63(2)(a) is not limited to what, in vernacular terms, is "over the
wall", *i.e.* an escape from prison. If the draftsman had intended to mean "escape" he
would have used that word. The words "in which he was serving a sentence" seem to
qualify territory rather than prison: *Chalitovas v. Lithuania* [2006] EWHC 1978.

Part 2 cases are dealt with under section 138. **3–39**

Extradition Act 2003, s.138

Extradition offences: person sentenced for offence

138.—(1) This section applies in relation to conduct of a person if— **3–40**

(a) he is alleged to be unlawfully at large after conviction by a court in a category 2
territory of an offence constituted by the conduct, and

(b) he has been sentenced for the offence.

(2) The conduct constitutes an extradition offence in relation to the category 2 territory
if these conditions are satisfied—

    (a) the conduct occurs in the category 2 territory;

    (b) the conduct would constitute an offence under the law of the relevant part of the United Kingdom punishable with imprisonment or another form of detention for a term of 12 months or a greater punishment if it occurred in that part of the United Kingdom;

    (c) a sentence of imprisonment or another form of detention for a term of 4 months or a greater punishment has been imposed in the category 2 territory in respect of the conduct.

(3) The conduct also constitutes an extradition offence in relation to the category 2 territory if these conditions are satisfied—

    (a) the conduct occurs outside the category 2 territory;

    (b) a sentence of imprisonment or another form of detention for a term of 4 months or a greater punishment has been imposed in the category 2 territory in respect of the conduct;

    (c) in corresponding circumstances equivalent conduct would constitute an extra-territorial offence under the law of the relevant part of the United Kingdom punishable with imprisonment or another form of detention for a term of 12 months or a greater punishment.

(4) The conduct also constitutes an extradition offence in relation to the category 2 territory if these conditions are satisfied—

    (a) the conduct occurs outside the category 2 territory and no part of it occurs in the United Kingdom;

    (b) the conduct would constitute an offence under the law of the relevant part of the United Kingdom punishable with imprisonment or another form of detention for a term of 12 months or a greater punishment if it occurred in that part of the United Kingdom;

    (c) a sentence of imprisonment or another form of detention for a term of 4 months or a greater punishment has been imposed in the category 2 territory in respect of the conduct.

(5) The conduct also constitutes an extradition offence in relation to the category 2 territory if these conditions are satisfied—

    (a) the conduct occurs outside the category 2 territory and no part of it occurs in the United Kingdom;

    (b) a sentence of imprisonment or another form of detention for a term of 4 months or a greater punishment has been imposed in the category 2 territory in respect of the conduct;

    (c) the conduct constitutes or if committed in the United Kingdom would constitute an offence mentioned in subsection (6).

(6) The offences are—

    (a) an offence under section 51 or 58 of the *International Criminal Court Act* 2001 (genocide, crimes against humanity and war crimes);

    (b) an offence under section 52 or 59 of that Act (conduct ancillary to genocide etc committed outside the jurisdiction);

    (c) an ancillary offence, as defined in section 55 or 62 of that Act, in relation to an offence falling within paragraph (a) or (b);

    (d) an offence under section 1 of the *International Criminal Court (Scotland) Act* 2001(genocide, crimes against humanity and war crimes);

    (e) an offence under section 2 of that Act (conduct ancillary to genocide etc committed outside the jurisdiction);

    (f) an ancillary offence, as defined in section 7 of that Act, in relation to an offence falling within paragraph (d) or (e).

(7) If the conduct constitutes an offence under the military law of the category 2 territory but does not constitute an offence under the general criminal law of the relevant part of the United Kingdom it does not constitute an extradition offence; and subsections (1) to (6) have effect subject to this.

(8) The relevant part of the United Kingdom is the part of the United Kingdom in which—

    (a) the extradition hearing took place, if the question of whether conduct constitutes an extradition offence is to be decided by the Secretary of State;

    (b) proceedings in which it is necessary to decide that question are taking place, in any other case.

  (9) Subsections (1) to (7) apply for the purposes of this Part.

Here conduct will amount to an extradition offence if it: **3–41**

1) occurs in the requesting state, the conduct would constitute an offence in England and Wales punishable with a minimum of 12 months' imprisonment or detention and a minimum of four months' imprisonment or detention has been imposed;

2) occurs outside the requesting state and a minimum of four months' imprisonment or detention has been imposed in the requesting state and the conduct would constitute an extra territorial offence under the law of England and Wales punishable with a minimum of 12 months' imprisonment or detention;

3) occurs outside the requesting state and no part of it has occurred within the UK and it would constitute an offence in England and Wales punishable with a minimum of 12 months' imprisonment or detention and a minimum sentence of four months' imprisonment or detention has been imposed in the requesting state;

4) occurs outside the requesting state and no part occurs within the UK, a minimum of four months' imprisonment or detention has been imposed in the requesting state and the conduct if committed in the UK would constitute an offence of genocide, crimes against humanity and war crimes or ancillary offences.

A certificate of conviction, the indictment and a transcript of the proceedings can establish the conviction: *Re Parkyn-Jackson (Bruce)* [1989] C.O.D. 188.

Those accused of crimes or unlawfully at large after conviction but before sentence

Part 1 cases are dealt with under section 64.   **3–42**

Extradition Act 2003, s.64

Extradition offences: person not sentenced for offence

  64.—(1) This section applies in relation to conduct of a person if—   **3–43**

    (a) he is accused in a category 1 territory of the commission of an offence constituted by the conduct, or

    (b) he is alleged to be unlawfully at large after conviction by a court in a category 1 territory of an offence constituted by the conduct and he has not been sentenced for the offence.

  (2) The conduct constitutes an extradition offence in relation to the category 1 territory if these conditions are satisfied—

    (a) the conduct occurs in the category 1 territory and no part of it occurs in the United Kingdom;

    (b) a certificate issued by an appropriate authority of the category 1 territory shows that the conduct falls within the European framework list;

    (c) the certificate shows that the conduct is punishable under the law of the category 1 territory with imprisonment or another form of detention for a term of 3 years or a greater punishment.

  (3) The conduct also constitutes an extradition offence in relation to the category 1 territory if these conditions are satisfied—

    (a) the conduct occurs in the category 1 territory;

    (b) the conduct would constitute an offence under the law of the relevant part of the United Kingdom if it occurred in that part of the United Kingdom;

    (c) the conduct is punishable under the law of the category 1 territory with imprisonment or another form of detention for a term of 12 months or a greater punishment (however it is described in that law).

  (4) The conduct also constitutes an extradition offence in relation to the category 1 territory if these conditions are satisfied—

    (a) the conduct occurs outside the category 1 territory;

    (b) the conduct is punishable under the law of the category 1 territory with imprisonment or another form of detention for a term of 12 months or a greater punishment (however it is described in that law);

    (c) in corresponding circumstances equivalent conduct would constitute an extraterritorial offence under the law of the relevant part of the United Kingdom punishable with imprisonment or another form of detention for a term of 12 months or a greater punishment.

(5) The conduct also constitutes an extradition offence in relation to the category 1 territory if these conditions are satisfied—

    (a) the conduct occurs outside the category 1 territory and no part of it occurs in the United Kingdom;

    (b) the conduct would constitute an offence under the law of the relevant part of the United Kingdom punishable with imprisonment or another form of detention for a term of 12 months or a greater punishment if it occurred in that part of the United Kingdom;

    (c) the conduct is so punishable under the law of the category 1 territory (however it is described in that law).

(6) The conduct also constitutes an extradition offence in relation to the category 1 territory if these conditions are satisfied—

    (a) the conduct occurs outside the category 1 territory and no part of it occurs in the United Kingdom;

    (b) the conduct is punishable under the law of the category 1 territory with imprisonment or another form of detention for a term of 12 months or a greater punishment (however it is described in that law);

    (c) the conduct constitutes or if committed in the United Kingdom would constitute an offence mentioned in subsection (7).

(7) The offences are—

    (a) an offence under section 51 or 58 of the *International Criminal Court Act* 2001 (genocide, crimes against humanity and war crimes);

    (b) an offence under section 52 or 59 of that Act (conduct ancillary to genocide etc committed outside the jurisdiction);

    (c) an ancillary offence, as defined in section 55 or 62 of that Act, in relation to an offence falling within paragraph (a) or (b);

    (d) an offence under section 1 of the *International Criminal Court (Scotland) Act* 2001 (genocide, crimes against humanity and war crimes);

    (e) an offence under section 2 of that Act (conduct ancillary to genocide etc committed outside the jurisdiction);

    (f) an ancillary offence, as defined in section 7 of that Act, in relation to an offence falling within paragraph (d) or (e).

(8) For the purposes of subsections (3)(b), (4)(c) and (5)(b)—

    (a) if the conduct relates to a tax or duty, it is immaterial that the law of the relevant part of the United Kingdom does not impose the same kind of tax or duty or does not contain rules of the same kind as those of the law of the category 1 territory;

    (b) if the conduct relates to customs or exchange, it is immaterial that the law of the relevant part of the United Kingdom does not contain rules of the same kind as those of the law of the category 1 territory.

(9) This section applies for the purposes of this Part.

3–44   For conduct to amount to an extradition offence it must either:

    1) occur in the requesting state with no part occurring within the UK and is punishable with a minimum of three years' imprisonment or detention; or

    2) occur in the requesting state and is punishable by a minimum of 12 months' imprisonment or detention and would constitute an offence in the UK if committed there; or

    3) occur outside the requesting state and is punishable with a minimum of 12 months' imprisonment or detention and would be an extra territorial offence under UK law punishable with a minimum of 12 months' imprisonment or detention; or

  4) occur outside the requesting state with no part of it occurring within the UK and would be an offence in the UK punishable with a minimum of 12 months' imprisonment or detention and is similarly punishable in the requesting state; or

  5) occur outside the requesting state with no part of it occurring within the UK and is punishable with a minimum of 12 months' imprisonment or detention and would also be an offence of genocide, war crimes or crimes against humanity or ancillary crimes if committed in the UK.

Section 64(3) does not preclude the extradition of a person who is alleged to have **3–45** committed a crime in a category 1 territory simply because some of his criminal conduct might have allegedly occurred within the United Kingdom: *Convery v. High Court of Rotterdam* [2005] EWHC 566.

Extradition offences are often transnational offences. In order to constitute an extradition offence not all the conduct constituting the offence has to occur in one territory. The word "also" in sections (3) to (6) does not of itself indicate that each subsection is exclusive of every other subsection. Subsections (2) to (6) form a list and conduct constitutes an extradition offence if any of them apply: *King's Prosecutor; Brussels v. Armas* [2005] 2 All E.R. 181.

Section 64(3)(c) is satisfied when actions which had taken place in UK have been **3–46** intentionally felt in another country so could be said to have occurred in that other country as well as the UK: *Hosseini v. France* [2006] EWHC 1333. The case of *Derevianko v. Lithuania* [2005] EWHC 1212 heard under the previous legislation, has held that an offence punishable by imprisonment for a term of "up to one year" incorporates a term of imprisonment for one year.

Part 2 cases are dealt with under section 137.

Extradition Act 2003, s.137

Extradition offences: person not sentenced for offence

137.—(1) This section applies in relation to conduct of a person if—   **3–47**

  (a) he is accused in a category 2 territory of the commission of an offence constituted by the conduct, or

  (b) he is alleged to be unlawfully at large after conviction by a court in a category 2 territory of an offence constituted by the conduct and he has not been sentenced for the offence.

 (2) The conduct constitutes an extradition offence in relation to the category 2 territory if these conditions are satisfied—

  (a) the conduct occurs in the category 2 territory;

  (b) the conduct would constitute an offence under the law of the relevant part of the United Kingdom punishable with imprisonment or another form of detention for a term of 12 months or a greater punishment if it occurred in that part of the United Kingdom;

  (c) the conduct is so punishable under the law of the category 2 territory (however it is described in that law).

 (3) The conduct also constitutes an extradition offence in relation to the category 2 territory if these conditions are satisfied—

  (a) the conduct occurs outside the category 2 territory;

  (b) the conduct is punishable under the law of the category 2 territory with imprisonment or another form of detention for a term of 12 months or a greater punishment (however it is described in that law);

  (c) in corresponding circumstances equivalent conduct would constitute an extraterritorial offence under the law of the relevant part of the United Kingdom punishable with imprisonment or another form of detention for a term of 12 months or a greater punishment.

 (4) The conduct also constitutes an extradition offence in relation to the category 2 territory if these conditions are satisfied—

  (a) the conduct occurs outside the category 2 territory and no part of it occurs in the United Kingdom;

(b) the conduct would constitute an offence under the law of the relevant part of the United Kingdom punishable with imprisonment or another form of detention for a term of 12 months or a greater punishment if it occurred in that part of the United Kingdom;

(c) the conduct is so punishable under the law of the category 2 territory (however it is described in that law).

(5) The conduct also constitutes an extradition offence in relation to the category 2 territory if these conditions are satisfied—

(a) the conduct occurs outside the category 2 territory and no part of it occurs in the United Kingdom;

(b) the conduct is punishable under the law of the category 2 territory with imprisonment for a term of 12 months or another form of detention or a greater punishment (however it is described in that law);

(c) the conduct constitutes or if committed in the United Kingdom would constitute an offence mentioned in subsection (6).

(6) The offences are—

(a) an offence under section 51 or 58 of the *International Criminal Court Act* 2001 (genocide, crimes against humanity and war crimes);

(b) an offence under section 52 or 59 of that Act (conduct ancillary to genocide etc committed outside the jurisdiction);

(c) an ancillary offence, as defined in section 55 or 62 of that Act, in relation to an offence falling within paragraph (a) or (b);

(d) an offence under section 1 of the *International Criminal Court (Scotland) Act* 2001 (genocide, crimes against humanity and war crimes);

(e) an offence under section 2 of that Act (conduct ancillary to genocide etc committed outside the jurisdiction);

(f) an ancillary offence, as defined in section 7 of that Act, in relation to an offence falling within paragraph (d) or (e).

(7) If the conduct constitutes an offence under the military law of the category 2 territory but does not constitute an offence under the general criminal law of the relevant part of the United Kingdom it does not constitute an extradition offence; and subsections (1) to (6) have effect subject to this.

(8) The relevant part of the United Kingdom is the part of the United Kingdom in which—

(a) the extradition hearing took place, if the question of whether conduct constitutes an extradition offence is to be decided by the Secretary of State;

(b) proceedings in which it is necessary to decide that question are taking place, in any other case.

(9) Subsections (1) to (7) apply for the purposes of this Part.

3–48   Conduct constitutes an extradition offence if it:

1) occurs in the category 2 state and is punishable there with a minimum of 12 months' imprisonment or detention and it also constitutes an offence in the UK similarly punishable;

2) occurs outside the category 2 state, is punishable with a minimum of 12 months' imprisonment or detention and would also be an extra-territorial offence in the UK similarly punishable;

3) occurs outside the category 2 state and no part of it occurred in the UK, is punishable with a minimum of 12 months' imprisonment or detention and is an offence in the UK similarly punishable;

4) occurs outside the category 2 state and no part occurred in the UK, is punishable with a minimum of 12 months' imprisonment or detention and the offence if committed in the UK would be one of genocide, crimes against humanity or war crimes or ancillary crimes.

3–49   The correct approach is to look at the essentials of the conduct relied on and consider whether if it had occurred in England it would have constituted an English offence. A district judge is not tied to considering the peculiarities of a requesting country's institutions, officials and procedures: *Norris v. United States of America* [2007] EWHC 71.

Although a judge has an implied jurisdiction to hold that the prosecutor is abusing the process of the court, no finding of abuse can be justified in a case where the category 2 territory, in this case the USA, does not have to prove that there is a case to answer, on the grounds that the prosecutor has refused or failed to disclose evidential material beyond what is contained in the extradition request: *R. (Bermingham) v. Director of the Serious Fraud Office*; *Bermingham v. United States of America* [2006] EWHC 200; [2006] 3 All E.R. 239.

It is not an extradition offence if it is an offence under the military law of the category 2 state but is not an offence under UK law. Extraterritoriality under section 137(2)(a) was discussed in *The Government of the United States of America v. Bentley* [2005] EWCH 1078. It was said that it is the court's duty, at least if the point is taken, to determine whether the conduct is punishable under the law of the category 2 territory. This may be done by means of a duly authenticated document under section 203(3).

(3) Restrictions or bars to extradition ss.11–25, 79, 95, 96

Extradition will not be ordered where any of the following bars are found to apply: **3–50**
— Double jeopardy;
— Extraneous considerations;
— Passage of time;
— Age (Part 1 only);
— Hostage-taking considerations;
— Speciality (Part 1 only);
— The person's earlier extradition to the UK from another country (Part 1 only).

Double jeopardy: ss.12, 80

No-one should be extradited if he would be entitled to claim double jeopardy. The **3–51** rule of double jeopardy covers both an acquittal or conviction of a criminal offence and the situation where following a trial for any offence founded on the same or substantially the same facts where the court would stay the prosecution as an abuse of process unless it could show that there are special circumstances why another trial should take place: *Connelly* [1964] A.C. 1254; *Humphries* [1977] A.C.T. 1; *Beedie* [1998] Q.B. 356; *Z* [2000] 2 A.C. 483. Where there is such significant overlap between an extradition offence specified in the warrant and facts relied on in an indictment charged in the UK, the extradition proceedings should be stayed: *Fofana, ante*. An acquittal of a co-accused is not a matter which the court should take into account: *Rottman v. Governor of HM Prison Brixton* [2003] EWHC 496. Extradition is not barred on the ground of double jeopardy by reason of the fact that a person has faced proceedings in relation to three, being convicted on one occasion, out of very many overt acts contained in an indictment for conspiracy. The conspiracy alleged in the case of *John v. Government of the United States of America* [2006] All E.R. (D) 357 was, in its duration, scale and reach of a wholly different order to the conduct which led to the person's conviction.

It must be noted that the *Criminal Justice Act* 2003 provides for the possibility of a **3–52** retrial on indictment in certain circumstances where there is new and compelling evidence and it is in the interests of justice that the crime is reinvestigated.

Under previous law it has been held that if a person has been discharged in previous extradition proceedings he can face further extradition proceedings on the same charges again: *Rees v. Secretary of State for the Home Department* [1986] 2 All E.R. 321.

Extraneous considerations: ss.13, 81

If it appears that a person will be prosecuted, prejudiced in his trial, punished or **3–53** detained on the grounds of race, religion, nationality, gender, sexual orientation or political opinion the judge will refuse extradition.

Passage of time: ss.14, 82

Where a lengthy period of time has elapsed between the commission of the offence **3–54** or being unlawfully at large and the extradition the court is entitled to consider whether it would be unjust or oppressive to extradite. Time is measured from the date of the commission of offence until the hearing of the application (in this case it was an application for habeas corpus); "unjust" is directed primarily to the risk of prejudice to the accused and the conduct of the trial itself whereas "oppressive" is directed to hardship to the accused from changes in his circumstances during the passage of time: *Steblins v. Latvia* [2006] EWHC 1272.

The issue is whether the person is able to have a fair trial after the particular period of time has elapsed: *Kakis v. Republic of Cyprus* (1978) 1 W.L.R. 779, HL. In *Woodcock v. New Zealand* [2003] EWHC Admin 2668, it was stated that the test to be applied was, having regard to the passage of time, whether it would be unjust to return the person for trial, not whether it would be unjust to try the accused. In carrying out that exercise the court had to have regard to whatever safeguards might exist in the domestic law of the requesting state to ensure that the accused would not be subjected to an unjust trial there. The domestic court would have a clearer picture of what evidence was available and the issues likely to arise and would be in a better position to decide whether a fair trial was possible. This was applied in *Beresford v. Australia* [2005] EWHC 2175, which was concerned with the delay in a complaint of sexual abuse. In that case it was confirmed that the domestic court is the court best suited to determining the issue of delay in the proceedings.

Rose L.J. said "where the passage of time is due to dilatory conduct on behalf of the requesting government, it tells in favour of the fugitive. Delay, on the part of the [person to be extradited] cannot, save in the most exceptional circumstances, count towards making his return unjust or oppressive". Where a warrant has been issued over six years ago there is a very real risk that the person would be prejudiced in the conduct of his defence by the passage of time and if the case turns on identification evidence, there is likely to be a much greater risk after that period of time of a wrong conviction. It is not for the person to show there was no good reason for the delay in issuing the warrant; the effect of section 11(3) taken with section 14 is that, if it appears to a court that it would be unjust or oppressive to extradite by reason of the passage of time, extradition is barred. There is no discretion: *Kociukow v. District Court of Bialystok III Penal Division (A Polish Judicial Authority)* [2006] EWHC 56; [2006] 2 All E.R. 451; see also *De Sousa v. Portugal* [2006] EWHC 455 and *Lisowski v. Regional Court of Bialystock, Poland* [2006] All E.R. (D) 377. Where a person has brought delay on himself, *i.e.* by a failure to reside, as required, at a certain address he cannot complain of it: *Zigmund v. Slovakia* [2005] EWHC 2507. Delay can include the proper investigation of the alleged offence(s); the court can also consider the fact that government officials and others were led to believe that there was no evidence: *Government of the Russian Federation v. Akhmed Zakaev*, unreported, November 2003. In *Sapstead v. Governor of Belmarsh Prison* [2004] EWHC 2352 a seven-year delay was held not to be unjust; see also *Carlyle-Clark v. Secretary of State for the Home Department* [2004] EWHC 2858; *Holmes v. Portugal* [2004] EWHC 2875 and *Owalabi v Court Number Four at the High Court of Justice in Spain* [2005] EWHC 2849, Admin.

A delay of up to ten years between the alleged extraditable offence's occurrence and the extradition proceedings being commenced in the UK was said to be unjust; there was no apparent explanation for the delay: *Senkus v. Lithuania* [2007] EWHC 345, Admin. Five years' delay which had been explained by the US authorities did not constitute an unjustified or disproportionate interference with Article 8; there was nothing exceptional about the personal, domestic and family circumstances of the person and nothing exceptional in the likely sentence: *McKinnon v. USA* [2007] EWHC 762, Admin.

Age: s.15

3–55   A person under the age of criminal responsibility had the offence occurred within England and Wales will not be extradited. Youths will be brought before designated judges on extradition matters and will not be taken to a youth court.

Hostage-taking considerations: ss.16, 83

Where communication between the person and the appropriate consular authorities **3–56** would not be possible and the conduct constitutes an offence or an attempt to commit an offence under section 1 of the *Taking of Hostages Act* 1982 extradition is barred.

Speciality: ss.17, 95

The rule of speciality limits the offences for which the person may be tried in the **3–57** country requesting extradition. In Part 1 extradition is barred unless arrangements have been made with the country concerned. Extradition is limited to those offences upon which a person has been extradited, those which are disclosed from the same facts, those to which consent has been given by a judge and those which are not punishable by imprisonment or detention. If the offence does not fall within the exceptions he must be given an opportunity to leave the country within 45 days from the date of his arrival. It does not apply if the person has consented to extradition or has waived his rights. A certificate issued by the Secretary of State is conclusive proof that there are arrangements between the UK and the other country.

In *Sutej v. Governor of Holloway Prison* [2005] EWHC 465, it was said that where a person had previously been discharged from extradition to Switzerland on particular criminal charges, the fact that the authorities indicated that a ruling would be made on those criminal charges, upon her return to Switzerland in respect of other related criminal charges did not mean that the extradition on related charges breached the principle of speciality protection. Where there is a large number of offences it is a matter for the local court to decide which charges to pursue. Courts or the Secretary of State can only consider whether there is a law in place to respect the speciality rule or whether there is cogent evidence that the speciality rule would not be followed: *Arain v. Germany, The Times*, March 24, 2006; [2006] EWHC 1702.

It is only in exceptional circumstances that, considering Article 8 ECHR, it will be disproportionate to extradite an individual. The individual would have to show in respect of each offence why it was disproportionate. In *Arain* it was held that it was impossible to see how extradition for conduct disclosing a large number of offences could be proportionate but then became disproportionate because a district judge had held that part of the conduct alleged did not amount to an offence in the UK. The application of speciality in US courts is affected by the view of the sending state. If a superseding indictment alleges offences not covered by the terms of the Act, the US authorities will not prosecute. Where the consent of the Secretary of State is required under section 95(4)(c) for prosecutions falling outside the scope of sections 95(4)(a), (b) and (d), that consent is not to be inferred but must be expressly given otherwise any subsequent trial will breach the speciality rule: *Welsh v. Secretary of State for the Home Department* [2006] EWHC 156; [2006] 3 All E.R. 204.

Earlier extradition to United Kingdom from another country: s.18

A person cannot be extradited where the consent of the first country is necessary **3–58** before he is extradited to another country and that consent has not been given: section 96.

In Part 2 cases, it is for the Secretary of State to decide the issue of speciality as well as other matters which might render extradition inappropriate.

(4) Other considerations

Convictions in absence: ss.20, 86

A person who has been convicted in his absence is protected by the terms of the Act. **3–59** In Part 1 cases the judge must decide whether the person absented himself from the trial deliberately. This is essentially a question of fact. If he decides in the affirmative then he must decide whether the extradition would be compatible with the *Human Rights Act* 1998, s.21. If the extradition is not compatible then the person must be discharged. In the case of *Falanga v. Italy* [2007] EWHC 268, DC it was said *obiter* that the court had difficulty with the proposition that section 21 only applied to prospective breaches of human rights and it did not enable a court to refuse extradition on the basis of reference to a past trial that was not in compliance with Article 6 ECHR.

If the judge decides that the person had not deliberately absented himself he must go on to decide whether the person would be entitled to a retrial or an appeal which would be heard as a retrial and that the person would be entitled to defend himself and to examine witnesses in person or through legal assistance of his own choosing and for that legal assistance to be free if he could not pay. If the person is not so entitled he must be discharged. In *Montpellier v. Wade* [2006] EWHC 1909, DC the person was held not to have absented himself from an appeal as he had been advised by the authorities that there would be no consequences of his failure to attend.

In Part 2 cases it is for the judge to decide whether the person was convicted in his absence and if so, whether he deliberately absented himself from his trial: section 85. The applicable standard of proof for a determination under section 85(3) is the criminal standard: *Mitoi v. Romania* [2006] EWHC 1977, DC. "His trial" contemplates a specific event and not the entire legal process: *Albania v. Bleta* [2005] EWHC 475; [2005] 3 All E.R. 351. If the judge decides the person has deliberately absented himself he must then proceed under section 87—see *post*. If not, then he decides whether the person has a right to a retrial or a review amounting to a retrial where the person has the right to defend himself and with free legal representation where he has not the means to pay as well as the right to examine and call witnesses. If he is so entitled then the judge goes on to decide whether, on the evidence supplied to him, a case to answer has been made out as if it were a summary trial against the person in this country: section 86. In *Lodhi v. 1) Governor of HM Prison Brixton 2) Government of the United Arab Emirates* [2001] EWCA Admin 178, it was stated that a person whose extradition was sought should be treated as a person accused rather than *autrefois convict* where he had been convicted in his absence but where the conviction would be set aside on his return. Under the former legislation it was stated in *Re Togyer* [2003] EWHC 1418, Admin, that it is not wrong to order the extradition of a person convicted in his absence where he had chosen not to take part in those proceedings and where, despite the low monetary value of the offence, his criminal record meant that the offence could not be treated as trivial. It is not for a court to examine the sufficiency of evidence leading to a conviction in the requesting State and come to a conclusion about the safety of the conviction: *Mariotti v. Italy* [2005] EWHC 2745, *The Times*, January 13, 2006. Where there is evidence that a trial in absence breached Article 6 ECHR because a person had not been afforded an adequate opportunity to challenge evidence adduced at the trial, a court is entitled to examine that evidence and reach a decision that the trial was not ECHR compliant and refuse jurisdiction: *Migliorelli v. Italy (No. 3)* [2006] EWHC 243, Admin. Where an individual who is sought for extradition has been absent from a sentencing appeal conducted in the sentencing state, which appeal results in an extension of his term of imprisonment, that absence does not render the sentencing appeal a conviction in the individual's absence as it was neither a trial nor a conviction but an appeal by way of review of the trial at which the individual had been convicted in his presence: *Virciglio v. Graz High Court of Austria* [2006] EWHC 3197, DC.

3–60   An accusation must be made in good faith: *Ingrid Sutej v. (1) Governor of HM Prison Holloway (2) Government of Switzerland* [2003] EWHC 1940, Admin; *Gulay Asliturk v. Government of Turkey* [2002] EWHC 2326. See *post*, § 3–70.

Domestic charges: ss.22, 88

3–61   Domestic charges take precedence and the extradition proceedings must be adjourned until their conclusion.

Persons serving sentences: ss.23, 89

Where a person for whom an extradition warrant has been issued is found to be **3–62**
serving a sentence in the UK, the extradition hearing may be adjourned until the
sentence has been served. On an application for an adjournment a judge was said to
have been irrational not to have considered that it was appropriate to determine the
matters under sections 11 and 21 where the person would not be released from prison
for at least three years and when any act of extradition would not occur until then: *R.
(Slator) v. Bow Street Magistrates' Court* [2006] EWHC 2628, DC.

Competing claims: ss.24, 90

Other claims may be deferred.   **3–63**

Physical or mental condition: ss.24, 90

Medical evidence may be introduced to show that it would be unjust or oppressive to **3–64**
extradite the person on the grounds of his physical or mental condition whereupon the
judge may order his discharge. In *R. (Warren) v. Secretary of State for the Home
Department* [2003] EWHC 1177, it was stated that the question of mental fitness to
stand trial as opposed to be extradited was a matter for the requesting state. The presence of a risk to a person's physical condition by the physical act of extradition does not
mean that extradition cannot be effected provided that proper assessment of the risk
posed is undertaken prior to extradition: *McCaughey v. (1) USA (2) Secretary of
State for the Home Department* LTL 20/01/06; *Niziol v. Poland*, unreported, April 18,
2007.

Human rights: s.87

There is a positive duty to consider whether the person's extradition would be com- **3–65**
patible with ECHR but it is neither necessary nor right to examine what a requesting
state does in practice provided that the Convention is unequivocally incorporated into
the state's body of laws and that the terms of the Convention would prevail if any
conflict arose between it and the state's laws: *Da An Chen v. Romania* [2006] EWHC
1752, DC. As French law fully incorporates ECHR, there is no risk that a person will not
receive a fair trial if extradited to France for alleged offences in relation to terrorism: *R.
(Mustapha Labsi) v. Secretary of State for the Home Department* [2005] EWHC
2931, Admin.

Extradition of itself invades Article 8 ECHR, the right to family life, and it, therefore
has to be shown that the extradition is in accordance with law and is proportionate:
Launder v. UK [1997] App 27279/95. Appellants who seek to rely upon Article 8 have
to be able to demonstrate a real risk of a flagrant breach of their Convention rights
upon extradition: *Colda v. Romania* [2006] EWHC 1150. It is only in exceptional circumstances that the extradition of a person to face trial on serious charges would be
held to be an unjustified or disproportionate interference with the right to family life:
Government of the United States of America v. Bentley, ante.

Substantial grounds must exist for finding that there would be a violation of human
rights: *Mamatkulov v. Turkey* (2005) 41 E.H.R.R. 25. It also said that Article 6 may be
violated if possible irregularities in the trial process were likely to constitute a flagrant
denial of justice. The test for substantial grounds is not on a balance of probabilities but
whether there is a real risk of the violation occurring: *Miklis v. Lithuania* [2006] 4 All
E.R. 808. The test for an Article 2 breach is one of "almost certainty": *Osman v. UK*
(1998) 29 E.H.R.R. 245; *Soering v. UK* (1989) 11 E.H.R.R. 439. A trial of a British
national is not unfair if the entire proceedings are not translated into English: *Daniels
v. Governor of Holloway Prison* [2005] EWHC 148, DC. From the moment of conviction when considering Article 5, the relevant part is Article 5(1)(a) rather than 5(1)(c)

and Article 5(3). It is, therefore, just and appropriate to extradite in those circumstances even where a defendant is not allowed to apply for bail on his return: *Ceausescu v. (1) Secretary of State for the Home Office (2) Romania* [2007] EWHC 1423, Admin. A life sentence without the possibility of parole or remission is not by its very nature necessarily and always a violation of ECHR: *R. (Ralston Wellington) v. Secretary of State for the Home Department* [2007] EWHC 1109, Admin. The use of evidence from an anonymous witness does not deprive a person of a fair trial: *R. (Al-Fawwaz) v. Governor of Brixton Prison* [2001] 1 W.LR. 1234. Evidence obtained through torture is inadmissible: *A v. Secretary of State for the Home Department* [2006] 1 All E.R. 575 .

Asylum claim: ss.39, 40, 121

3–66   Where the person makes an application for asylum during the course of the proceedings there is no need for the proceedings, to be adjourned but the person cannot be extradited until the asylum claim is finally determined.

VI. EVIDENCE

3–67   The evidence brought before the judge under Part 1 will be that sufficient under the terms of the Act for the judge to make an extradition order. The court will also hear representations. In *Re Evans* [1994] 1 W.L.R. 1006, under the former legislation, it was held that a person who was the subject of extradition proceedings could not call evidence to show that the conduct alleged did not amount to an extradition offence because it was not criminal in Sweden. It was held in *Sirvelis v. Governor of Brixton Prison* [2005] EWHC 2611 that a court is entitled to look carefully at the evidence given by an individual opposing extradition in order to form a view as to whether the evidence produced by the requesting state lacks any real credibility.

The evidence necessary for an extradition order under Part 2 for most of the category 2 countries will be that which is sufficient for a case to be answered: *Re Nielsen* [1984] 2 All E.R. 81, HL; *The Government of the United States of America v. McCaffery* [1984] 1 W.L.R. 867, HL; *R. v. Parekh* [1988] Crim.L.R. 832. There is no obligation on the requesting state to provide evidence from complainants or police officers involved: *Stepp v. USA* [2006] EWHC 1033. In considering an application a judge must distinguish between what might be material that was relevant and admissible at a trial in the requesting state and what was material that was relevant and admissible in extradition proceedings in the UK: *R. (Kaupitis) v. Prosecutor General's Office (Lithuania)* [2006] EWHC 2185. The essentials of extradition are to be decided on the criminal standard of proof: *The Government of the United States of America v. Bentley, ante*, although identity is to be determined under section 78(5) on a balance of possibilities. It is not for the court to weigh the evidence of the witnesses: *Hashmi v. United States of America, ante*.

It is necessary to determine firstly whether the conduct alleged to constitute the criminal offence charged occurs in the category 2 territory and then secondly whether any of the conduct was within that territory. The offender's evidence may be heard: *Re Gross* [1998] 3 All E.R. 624.

In these circumstances the test in *R. v. Galbraith*—see Part 3, *post*—will be used. That was commended by the House of Lords in *Alves v. DPP* [1992] 4 All E.R. 787. The UK government has agreed to dispense with the *prima facie* rule for certain countries, *e.g.* USA. Designation orders will need to be checked.

3–68   The court may receive properly authenticated evidence in the form of statements or affidavits received from the requesting state. It can also receive statements made in this country as well as hear evidence on oath or affirmation. Formal admissions may also be made.

Extradition Act 2003, ss.202, 205(1)–(2)

Receivable documents

3–69   **202.**—(1) A Part 1 warrant may be received in evidence in proceedings under this Act.

(2) Any other document issued in a category 1 territory may be received in evidence in proceedings under this Act if it is duly authenticated.

(3) A document issued in a category 2 territory may be received in evidence in proceedings under this Act if it is duly authenticated.

(4) A document issued in a category 1 or category 2 territory is duly authenticated if (and only if) one of these applies—

(a) it purports to be signed by a judge, magistrate or other judicial authority of the territory;

(b) it purports to be authenticated by the oath or affirmation of a witness.

(5) Subsections (2) and (3) do not prevent a document that is not duly authenticated from being received in evidence in proceedings under this Act.

Written statements and admissions

205.—(1) The provisions mentioned in subsection (2) apply in relation to proceedings under **3–70** this Act as they apply in relation to proceedings for an offence.

(2) The provisions are—

(a) section 9 of the *Criminal Justice Act* 1967 (proof by written statement in criminal proceedings);

(b) section 10 of the *Criminal Justice Act* 1967 (proof by formal admission in criminal proceedings);

Extradition proceedings are not a trial on the merits, however most of the rules **3–71** governing admissibility of evidence in England and Wales will apply.

Those termed rules of law, *e.g.* hearsay, will apply whereas those termed rules of practice, *e.g.* refreshing memory, will not: *R. v. Governor of Gloucester Prison, ex p. Miller* [1979] 2 All E.R. 1103. A summary of a witness's evidence can be given as hearsay evidence by another person: section 84(4): *India v. Rajarathinam*, unreported, November 6, 2006. Where exceptionally oral evidence has been introduced a district judge may refuse cross-examination where it would not be procedurally correct or not allowed in English law: *Fernandes, Fernandes, Travasso v. Governor of Brixton prison, The Commonwealth of the Bahamas, ante*.

The meaning of "accused person" was considered in *Re Ismail* [1999] A.C. 320. The House of Lords stated that it is more than mere suspicion that an individual has committed an offence and courts ought to adopt a purposive interpretation.

"It is necessary for our courts to adopt a cosmopolitan approach to the question whether as a matter of substance rather than form the requirement of there being an 'accused' person is satisfied. . .the Divisional court in this case posed the right test by addressing the broad question whether the competent authorities in the foreign jurisdiction had taken a step which can fairly be described as the commencement of a prosecution. But in the light of the diversity of cases which may come before the courts it is right to emphasise that ultimately the question whether a person is 'accused' …will require an intense focus on the particular facts of each case".

Where a person has not been convicted the provisions covering documentary evi- **3–72** dence are found in section 84.

Extradition Act 2003, s.84(1)–(7)

Case where person has not been convicted

84.—(1) If the judge is required to proceed under this section he must decide whether there **3–73** is evidence which would be sufficient to make a case requiring an answer by the person if the proceedings were the summary trial of an information against him.

(2) In deciding the question in subsection (1) the judge may treat a statement made by a person in a document as admissible evidence of a fact if—

(a) the statement is made by the person to a police officer or another person charged with the duty of investigating offences or charging offenders, and

(b) direct oral evidence by the person of the fact would be admissible.

(3) In deciding whether to treat a statement made by a person in a document as admissible evidence of a fact, the judge must in particular have regard—

(a) to the nature and source of the document;

(b) to whether or not, having regard to the nature and source of the document and to any other circumstances that appear to the judge to be relevant, it is likely that the document is authentic;

(c) to the extent to which the statement appears to supply evidence which would not be readily available if the statement were not treated as being admissible evidence of the fact;

(d) to the relevance of the evidence that the statement appears to supply to any issue likely to have to be determined by the judge in deciding the question in subsection (1);

(e) to any risk that the admission or exclusion of the statement will result in unfairness to the person whose extradition is sought, having regard in particular to whether it is likely to be possible to controvert the statement if the person making it does not attend to give oral evidence in the proceedings.

(4) A summary in a document of a statement made by a person must be treated as a statement made by the person in the document for the purposes of subsection (2).

(5) If the judge decides the question in subsection (1) in the negative he must order the person's discharge.

(6) If the judge decides that question in the affirmative he must proceed under section 87.

(7) If the judge is required to proceed under this section and the category 2 territory to which extradition is requested is designated for the purposes of this section by order made by the Secretary of State—

(a) the judge must not decide under subsection (1), and

(b) he must proceed under section 87.

3–74 Where the person has been convicted in his absence the evidential requirements are found in section 86.

Extradition Act 2003, s.86(1)–(7)

Conviction in person's absence

3–75   **86.**—(1) If the judge is required to proceed under this section he must decide whether there is evidence which would be sufficient to make a case requiring an answer by the person if the proceedings were the summary trial of an information against him.

(2) In deciding the question in subsection (1) the judge may treat a statement made by a person in a document as admissible evidence of a fact if—

(a) the statement is made by the person to a police officer or another person charged with the duty of investigating offences or charging offenders, and

(b) direct oral evidence by the person of the fact would be admissible.

(3) In deciding whether to treat a statement made by a person in a document as admissible evidence of a fact, the judge must in particular have regard—

(a) to the nature and source of the document;

(b) to whether or not, having regard to the nature and source of the document and to any other circumstances that appear to the judge to be relevant, it is likely that the document is authentic;

(c) to the extent to which the statement appears to supply evidence which would not be readily available if the statement were not treated as being admissible evidence of the fact;

(d) to the relevance of the evidence that the statement appears to supply to any issue likely to have to be determined by the judge in deciding the question in subsection (1);

(e) to any risk that the admission or exclusion of the statement will result in unfairness to the person whose extradition is sought, having regard in particular to whether it is likely to be possible to controvert the statement if the person making it does not attend to give oral evidence in the proceedings.

(4) A summary in a document of a statement made by a person must be treated as a statement made by the person in the document for the purposes of subsection (2).

(5) If the judge decides the question in subsection (1) in the negative he must order the person's discharge.

(6) If the judge decides that question in the affirmative he must proceed under section 87.

(7) If the judge is required to proceed under this section and the category 2 territory to which extradition is requested is designated for the purposes of this section by order made by the Secretary of State—

    (a) the judge must not decide under subsection (1), and

    (b) he must proceed under section 87.

In *Ginova v. Government of the Czech Republic* [2003] EWHC 2187, it was said **3–76** that the burden of proof on the requesting state to show that a person was unlawfully at large was proof beyond reasonable doubt. It is for a person to displace the presumption that the court document from the requesting state recording the hearing accurately reflects what happened: *Prenga v. Albania* [2006] EWHC 1616.

Where authentication of documents is required it is not necessary for each and every statement on oath to be certificated: *Oskar v. Government of Australia* [1988] A.C. 366. It is sufficient to have a certificate which sufficiently identifies all the statements which it certifies. In that case the statements were all tied together.

In *Lodhi, ante*, it was said that statements in English made by a non-English speaker had to be accompanied by a signature to a document written in his own language coupled with an attested translation of his signed affidavit into English.

It has been held that an affidavit is a document containing evidence whereas a deposition is a document recording evidence and both are admissible: *Fernandez v. Government of Singapore* [1971] 2 All E.R. 691.

In *Orechovsky v. Government of Slovakia* [2003] EWHC 2758, it was held that the **3–77** court could consider articles drawn from the internet concerning human rights abuse in the requesting state. The court was not restricted to hearing evidence in the strict sense.

There is no right of access to unused material: *R. v. Governor of Pentonville Prison, ex p. Lee* [1993] 3 All E.R. 504. This was approved in *Lodhi v. Governor of HM Prison Brixton* [2001] EHWC Admin 178. In *Kashamu* [2002] Q.B. 887, the extradition order was quashed on the grounds that the extradition proceedings were unfair as aresult of the non-disclosure of crucial evidence. The position of disclosure is unresolved but the court must ensure that the proceedings are fair: Article 6, ECHR.

The *Police and Criminal Evidence Act* 1984 does not strictly apply to extradition proceedings as a person has not been arrested for an offence. Case law has, however, confirmed that section 78 of that Act does apply: *R. v. Governor of Pentonville Prison, ex p. Walters* [1987] Crim.L.R. 577; *R. v. Governor of Pentonville Prison, ex p. Chinoy* [1992] 1 All E.R. 317; *R. v. Governor of Brixton Prison, ex p. Levin* [1997] 3 W.L.R. 117. In the latter case Lord Hoffman stated that extradition proceedings were criminal proceedings but of a very special kind. He confirmed that section 78 applied. He said:

> "The question is, therefore, whether the admission of the evidence would have such an adverse effect on the fairness of the decision to... extradite the accused for trial, even if the trial is a fair one... It would undermine the effectiveness of international treaty obligations if the courts were to superimpose discretions based on local notions of fairness upon the ordinary rules of admissibility. I do not wish to exclude the possibility that the discretion may be used in extradition proceedings founded upon evidence which, although technically admissible, has been obtained in a way which outrages civilised values. But such cases are also likely to be very rare."

In *R. (Saifi) v. Governor of Brixton Prison* [2001] 1 W.L.R. 1134, Rose L.J., in **3–78** rejecting a burden of proof test for section 78, stated that:

> "Under section 78 any circumstance which can reasonably have a bearing on fairness should be considered. The weight to be attached to an individual circumstance may increase or decrease because of the presence of other related or unrelated circumstances. The preponderance of all the circumstances may show that the admission of the evidence would have such an adverse effect on fairness as to require its exclusion."

Evidence of identity is admissible—see *ante*, § 3–25. In the case of *Anthony*, June 27,

1995, it was stated that when there is an issue as to whether the person brought before the magistrate is the person requested by the foreign state, that is a question which is fundamental to the jurisdiction of the magistrate.

The burden of proof is in accordance with the person being accused of a summary offence. The judge will weigh up the evidence but will not weigh the evidence: *R. v. Governor of Pentonville Prison, ex p. Osman* [1989] 3 All E.R. 701,

> "... it was the magistrate's duty to consider the evidence as a whole, and to reject any evidence which he considered worthless. In that sense was his duty to weigh up the evidence. But it was not his duty to weigh the evidence. He was neither entitled nor obliged to determine the amount of weight to be attached to any evidence, or to compare one witness with another. That would be for the jury at the trial. It follows that the magistrate was not concerned with the inconsistencies or contradictions in...evidence, unless they were such as to justify rejecting or eliminating his evidence altogether ... As a working guide, we could not do better than adopt the language of the magistrate ... substituting 'consider' for 'weigh'."

VII. THE DECISION

3–79   In Part 1 cases, the judge will make an extradition order or will discharge the person. If there is no appeal the extradition will then take place within ten days unless a later date is agreed: sections 35, 46. In Part 2 cases the judge will either commit the person in custody or on bail to await the Secretary of State's decision on extradition or will discharge him.

In *R. v. Bow Street Magistrates' Court, ex p. Allison, The Times*, June 2, 1998, it was held that there is no legal duty to give reasons but stated that in matters of such importance, in almost every case the judge should explain briefly the reasons for his conclusions. It is the practice at Bow Street to give reasons for the decision either immediately at the close of the proceedings in court, or, if the case has been a complicated or lengthy one, at an adjourned hearing. Normally the reasons are reduced to writing and supplied to the parties. In the *Pinochet* case they were also supplied to the press.

If a person has been ordered to be extradited under Part 1 and he is serving a sentence in this country, the judge may make the order subject to a condition that extradition is not to take place unless he has received an undertaking on behalf of the requesting state that the person will be returned to the UK to serve the remainder of his sentence on the conclusion either of the proceedings or the sentence to be served there: sections 37, 52 and 186. There is no provision in the Act for the removal of persons serving domestic sentences and this undermines sections 37 and 186: *Handa v. High Instance Court of Paris*; *R. (Handa) v Bow Street Magistrates' Court, ante*.

3–80   Where a person has been discharged and an appeal is pending then he will be remanded in custody or on bail pending the conclusion of the appeal: section 30.

VIII. CHALLENGING THE DECISION

3–81   An appeal may be made by the requesting state against discharge and by the person concerned against the order for extradition.

In Part 1 cases the appeal is to the High Court on a question of law and fact: section 26. The High Court may allow or dismiss the appeal: section 27. In Part 2 cases no appeal from a committal order by the judge shall lie until the Secretary of State has made his decision: section 103. An appeal will lie from the High Court to the House of Lords: section 32 and in certain instances the House may remit the case back to the district judge.

In exceptional circumstances, *habeas corpus* is available to an individual who has exhausted the statutory appeals system as an additional remedy: *Hilali v. Spain* [2007] EWHC 939, Admin. In this case it had been discovered that the prosecution would not be able to rely on the evidence of telephone intercepts and, therefore, the basis of the extradition order was undermined to such an extent that the person's return and continued detention prior to return was unlawful.

Extradition Act 2003, ss.26, 27

Appeal against extradition order

26.—(1) If the appropriate judge orders a person's extradition under this Part, the person **3–82** may appeal to the High Court against the order.

(2) But subsection (1) does not apply if the order is made under section 46 or 48.

(3) An appeal under this section may be brought on a question of law or fact.

(4) Notice of an appeal under this section must be given in accordance with rules of court before the end of the permitted period, which is 7 days starting with the day on which the order is made.

Court's powers on appeal under s.26

27.—(1) On an appeal under section 26 the High Court may—   **3–83**
    (a) allow the appeal;
    (b) dismiss the appeal.

(2) The court may allow the appeal only if the conditions in subsection (3) or the conditions in subsection (4) are satisfied.

(3) The conditions are that—
    (a) the appropriate judge ought to have decided a question before him at the extradition hearing differently;
    (b) if he had decided the question in the way he ought to have done, he would have been required to order the person's discharge.

(4) The conditions are that—
    (a) an issue is raised that was not raised at the extradition hearing or evidence is available that was not available at the extradition hearing;
    (b) the issue or evidence would have resulted in the appropriate judge deciding a question before him at the extradition hearing differently;
    (c) if he had decided the question in that way, he would have been required to order the person's discharge.

(5) If the court allows the appeal it must—
    (a) order the person's discharge;
    (b) quash the order for his extradition.

The High Court may allow the appeal only if it believes that the judge should have **3–84** decided a question before him differently and that difference would have led to the person's discharge. Its powers are to dismiss the application or to quash the extradition order and discharge the person.

Extradition Act 2003, s.28

Appeal against discharge at extradition hearing

28.—(1) If the judge orders a person's discharge at the extradition hearing the authority **3–85** which issued the Part 1 warrant may appeal to the High Court against the relevant decision.

(2) But subsection (1) does not apply if the order for the person's discharge was under section 41.

(3) The relevant decision is the decision which resulted in the order for the person's discharge.

(4) An appeal under this section may be brought on a question of law or fact.

(5) Notice of an appeal under this section must be given in accordance with rules of court before the end of the permitted period, which is 7 days starting with the day on which the order for the person's discharge is made.

The requesting state may appeal against discharge within seven days on a question of **3–86** law or fact. On appeal the High Court may allow the appeal if the judge ought to have decided a question differently and that would not have led to the person's discharge or a new issue has been raised or new evidence is available and that if heard by the judge would not have led to the person's discharge. There is no power to extend the time limit for serving the notice of appeal and a court's general powers of management found in CPR r.3.1(2)(a) apply only to compliance with rules, practice directions and court orders and not statutory provisions. Even where a notice cannot be filed because of a court's electrical blackout or closure compliance will fail: *Lithuania v. Barcys* [2007] EWHC 615, Admin.

Extradition Act 2003, s.29

Court's powers on appeal under s.28

3–87   **29.**—(1) On an appeal under section 28 the High Court may—

(a) allow the appeal;

(b) dismiss the appeal.

(2) The court may allow the appeal only if the conditions in subsection (3) or the conditions in subsection (4) are satisfied.

(3) The conditions are that—

(a) the judge ought to have decided the relevant question differently;

(b) if he had decided the question in the way he ought to have done, he would not have been required to order the person's discharge.

(4) The conditions are that—

(a) an issue is raised that was not raised at the extradition hearing or evidence is available that was not available at the extradition hearing;

(b) the issue or evidence would have resulted in the judge deciding the relevant question differently;

(c) if he had decided the question in that way, he would not have been required to order the person's discharge.

(5) If the court allows the appeal it must—

(a) quash the order discharging the person;

(b) remit the case to the judge;

(c) direct him to proceed as he would have been required to do if he had decided the relevant question differently at the extradition hearing.

(6) A question is the relevant question if the judge's decision on it resulted in the order for the person's discharge.

3–88   The specific procedure for Part 2 cases is contained in the following provisions.

Extradition Act 2003, ss.103–106

Appeal where case sent to Secretary of State

3–89   **103.**—(1) If the judge sends a case to the Secretary of State under this Part for his decision whether a person is to be extradited, the person may appeal to the High Court against the relevant decision.

(2) But subsection (1) does not apply if the person consented to his extradition under section 127 before his case was sent to the Secretary of State.

(3) The relevant decision is the decision that resulted in the case being sent to the Secretary of State.

(4) An appeal under this section may be brought on a question of law or fact.

(5) If an appeal is brought under this section before the Secretary of State has decided whether the person is to be extradited the appeal must not be heard until after the Secretary of State has made his decision.

(6) If the Secretary of State orders the person's discharge the appeal must not be proceeded with.

(7) No appeal may be brought under this section if the Secretary of State has ordered the person's discharge.

(8) If notice of an appeal under section 110 against the decision which resulted in the order for the person's discharge is given in accordance with subsection (5) of that section—

(a) subsections (6) and (7) do not apply;

(b) no appeal may be brought under this section if the High Court has made its decision on the appeal.

(9) Notice of an appeal under this section must be given in accordance with rules of court before the end of the permitted period, which is 14 days starting with the day on which the Secretary of State informs the person under section 100(1) or (4) of the order he

has made in respect of the person.

Court's powers on appeal under s.103

104.—(1) On an appeal under section 103 the High Court may—   **3–90**

(a) allow the appeal;

(b) direct the judge to decide again a question (or questions) which he decided at the extradition hearing;

(c) dismiss the appeal.

(2) The court may allow the appeal only if the conditions in subsection (3) or the conditions in subsection (4) are satisfied.

(3) The conditions are that—

(a) the judge ought to have decided a question before him at the extradition hearing differently;

(b) if he had decided the question in the way he ought to have done, he would have been required to order the person's discharge.

(4) The conditions are that—

(a) an issue is raised that was not raised at the extradition hearing or evidence is available that was not available at the extradition hearing;

(b) the issue or evidence would have resulted in the judge deciding a question before him at the extradition hearing differently;

(c) if he had decided the question in that way, he would have been required to order the person's discharge.

(5) If the court allows the appeal it must—

(a) order the person's discharge;

(b) quash the order for his extradition.

(6) If the judge comes to a different decision on any question that is the subject of a direction under subsection (1)(b) he must order the person's discharge.

(7) If the judge comes to the same decision as he did at the extradition hearing on the question that is (or all the questions that are) the subject of a direction under subsection (1)(b) the appeal must be taken to have been dismissed by a decision of the High Court.

Where a remitted question has been decided adversely to an appellant, the effect of section 104(7) is that the original appeal is taken to have been dismissed by the High Court. This is to avoid successive and repeated applications. That decision is not subject to judicial review and the only route of appeal is to the House of Lords. Remission can only be of a question which was originally decided at the extradition hearing. If a district judge goes beyond that question he acts beyond his powers under the section and judicial review is available: *Chen v. Romania* [2007] EWHC 520, Admin.

Appeal against discharge at extradition hearing

105.—(1) If at the extradition hearing the judge orders a person's discharge, an appeal to   **3–91**
the High Court may be brought on behalf of the category 2 territory against the relevant decision.

(2) But subsection (1) does not apply if the order for the person's discharge was under section 122.

(3) The relevant decision is the decision which resulted in the order for the person's discharge.

(4) An appeal under this section may be brought on a question of law or fact.

(5) Notice of an appeal under this section must be given in accordance with rules of court before the end of the permitted period, which is 14 days starting with the day on which the order for the person's discharge is made.

Court's powers on appeal under section 105

106.—(1) On an appeal under section 105 the High Court may—   **3–92**

(a) allow the appeal;

(b) direct the judge to decide the relevant question again;

(c) dismiss the appeal.

(2) A question is the relevant question if the judge's decision on it resulted in the order for the person's discharge.

(3) The court may allow the appeal only if the conditions in subsection (4) or the conditions in subsection (5) are satisfied.

(4) The conditions are that—

    (a) the judge ought to have decided the relevant question differently;

    (b) if he had decided the question in the way he ought to have done, he would not have been required to order the person's discharge.

(5) The conditions are that—

    (a) an issue is raised that was not raised at the extradition hearing or evidence is available that was not available at the extradition hearing;

    (b) the issue or evidence would have resulted in the judge deciding the relevant question differently;

    (c) if he had decided the question in that way, he would not have been required to order the person's discharge.

(6) If the court allows the appeal it must—

    (a) quash the order discharging the person;

    (b) remit the case to the judge;

    (c) direct him to proceed as he would have been required to do if he had decided the relevant question differently at the extradition hearing.

(7) If the court makes a direction under subsection (1)(b) and the judge decides the relevant question differently he must proceed as he would have been required to do if he had decided that question differently at the extradition hearing.

(8) If the court makes a direction under subsection (1)(b) and the judge does not decide the relevant question differently the appeal must be taken to have been dismissed by a decision of the High Court.

Where the High Court remits a question to the district judge for reconsideration on further evidence but the district judge comes to the same conclusion as at the original extradition hearing, the second decision of the district judge is deemed by statute to be a decision of the High Court as there is no purpose in the district judge's sending the case to the Secretary of State again under section 87(3): *R. (Okandeji) v. Bow Street Magistrates' Court, ante.*

IX. COSTS

3–93   Where extradition has been ordered costs may be awarded under section 60 for category 1 cases and section 133 for category 2.

Extradition Act 2003, ss.60(2), (4); 133(2), (4)

Costs where extradition ordered

3–94   **60. & 133.**—(2) … the appropriate judge may make such order as he considers just and reasonable with regard to the costs to be paid by the person.

(4) An order for costs under this section—

    (a) must specify their amount;

    (b) may name the person to whom they are to be paid.

3–95   Where extradition is ordered, the person may be ordered to pay a specific sum of costs which is considered just and reasonable. Where the person has been discharged or taken to be discharged, costs may be ordered under section 61 for category 1 cases and section 134 for category 2.

Extradition Act 2003, ss.61(2), (5)–(8);134(2), (5)–(8)

3–96   **61. & 134.**—(2) … an order under subsection (5) in favour of the person may be made by—

    (a) the appropriate judge, if the order for the person's discharge is made by him;

(5) An order under this subsection in favour of a person is an order for a payment of the appropriate amount to be made to the person out of money provided by Parliament.

(6) The appropriate amount is such amount as the judge or court making the order under subsection (5) considers reasonably sufficient to compensate the person in whose fa-

vour the order is made for any expenses properly incurred by him in the proceedings under this Part.

(7) But if the judge or court making an order under subsection (5) is of the opinion that there are circumstances which make it inappropriate that the person in whose favour the order is made should recover the full amount mentioned in subsection (6), the judge or court must—

(a) assess what amount would in his or its opinion be just and reasonable;

(b) specify that amount in the order as the appropriate amount.

(8) Unless subsection (7) applies, the appropriate amount—

(a) must be specified in the order, if the court considers it appropriate for it to be so specified and the person in whose favour the order is made agrees the amount;

(b) must be determined in accordance with regulations made by the Lord Chancellor for the purposes of this section, in any other case.

Here there are three options: **3–97**

1) where the judge considers that a person should not receive all his costs he should specify the amount of costs ordered;

2) where the judge considers that the person should receive all his costs he may specify the sum where the sum is agreed by the person; or

3) where the judge considers that the person should receive all his costs he may order that they may be taxed by the determining officer: section 62.

X. POST EXTRADITION

Under Part 1 where the extradition order has been made with consent, then, if a **3–98** request is made by the requesting state for extradition on another offence, the judge will hold a hearing to determine whether the offence is an extradition offence and whether he would order extradition if he had proceeded in the normal way: section 55. In Part 2 cases that is a matter for the Secretary of State.

Chapter 4

COMMENCEMENT OF PROCEEDINGS

I. PROSECUTION OF OFFENCES

A. General

A prosecution consists of the institution and pursuance of legal proceedings against **4–1** named persons or bodies. When a decision is made to prosecute a criminal case it will generally be started in the magistrates' court. Cases may be commenced in a variety of ways and by a number of different people, including private individuals, corporations and representatives of statutory organisations such as the police.

The Crown Prosecution Service on behalf of the police prosecutes the majority of **4–2** cases in the magistrates' courts. Prosecutions may also be brought by other prosecuting authorities such the Serious Fraud Office and the Revenue and Customs Prosecution Office. Government departments and local authorities are also empowered by specific statutes to institute and carry on prosecutions of certain offences.

The named individual who commences the prosecuting process may be described as the prosecutor, even if little or no role is taken by them personally in the subsequent court proceedings. Where the prosecution begins with the accused being charged at the police station, a police officer will commence the prosecution by signing the charge sheet. Where the prosecution begins with the laying of an information before a magistrate, the person who laid the information commences the prosecution. The prosecution may then be taken over from the individual prosecutor by the relevant prosecuting body which in the case of police officers will be the Crown Prosecution Service. A private individual either acting alone or on behalf of a body corporate may also prosecute a case through the criminal courts by applying to the court for a summons to commence the proceedings.

Anyone who appears in the magistrates' court to commence or carry on a prosecu- **4–3** tion will either be a private individual or a corporation both of whom may instruct a legal representative at their own expense or they will be an individual employed by a public authority which is publicly funded with statutory powers to conduct prosecutions. Public authorities may also instruct lawyers as agents to conduct prosecutions.

B. INSTITUTION AND CONDUCT OF PROCEEDINGS

(1) The Crown Prosecution Service

Prosecution of Offences Act 1985, s.1(1), (3), (6)–(7)

The Crown Prosecution Service

4–4   **1.**—(1) There shall be a prosecuting service for England and Wales (to be known as the "Crown Prosecution Service") consisting of—

     (a) the Director of Public Prosecutions, who shall be head of the Service;

     (b) the Chief Crown Prosecutors, designated under subsection (4) below, each of whom shall be the member of the Service responsible to the Director for supervising the operation of the Service in his area; and

     (c) the other staff appointed by the Director under this section.

(3) The Director may designate any member of the Service who has a general qualification (within the meaning of section 71 of the *Courts and Legal Services Act* 1990) for the purposes of this subsection, and any person so designated shall be known as a Crown Prosecutor.

(6) Without prejudice to any functions which may have been assigned to him in his capacity as a member of the Service, every Crown Prosecutor shall have all the powers of the Director as to the institution and conduct of proceedings but shall exercise those powers under the direction of the Director.

(7) Where any enactment (whenever passed)—

     (a) prevents any step from being taken without the consent of the Director or without his consent or the consent of another; or

     (b) requires any step to be taken by or in relation to the Director;

any consent given by or, as the case may be, step taken by or in relation to, a Crown Prosecutor shall be treated, for the purposes of that enactment, as given by or, as the case may be, taken by or in relation to the Director.

[This section is printed as amended by the *Courts and Legal Services Act* 1990, Sched. 10.]

4–5   The *Prosecution of Offences Act* 1985 established the Crown Prosecution Service (CPS) in England and Wales. The Director of Public Prosecutions is the head of the service and the prosecutor who conducts the case will either be a lawyer employed directly by the CPS or an appointed and approved solicitor or barrister who will act as agent. Such agents are subject to instructions from the CPS throughout the progress of the case including when matters arise in court. The CPS also employs designated caseworkers who are not legally qualified but who have limited rights of audience under section 7A of the *Prosecution of Offences Act* 1985. They deal with criminal proceedings other than trials and act as prosecutor in early first hearing cases when pleas of guilty are anticipated.

Prosecution of Offences Act 1985, ss.3 and 15(2)–(5)

Functions of the Director

4–6   **3.**—(1) The Director shall discharge his functions under this or any other enactment under the superintendence of the Attorney General.

(2) It shall be the duty of the Director, subject to any provisions contained in the *Criminal Justice Act* 1987—

     (a) to take over the conduct of all criminal proceedings, other than specified proceedings, instituted on behalf of a police force (whether by a member of that force or by any other person);

     (aa) to take over the conduct of any criminal proceedings instituted by an immigration officer (as defined for the purposes of the *Immigration Act* 1971) acting in his capacity as such an officer;

     (b) to institute and have the conduct of criminal proceedings in any case where it appears to him that—

         (i) the importance or difficulty of the case makes it appropriate that proceedings should be instituted by him; or

   (ii) it is otherwise appropriate for proceedings to be instituted by him;

 (ba) to institute and have the conduct of any criminal proceedings in any case where the proceedings relate to the subject-matter of a report a copy of which has been sent to him under paragraph 23 or 24 of Schedule 3 to the *Police Reform Act* 2002 (reports on investigations into conduct of persons serving with the police);

  (c) to take over the conduct of all binding over proceedings instituted on behalf of a police force (whether by a member of that force or by any other person);

  (d) to take over the conduct of all proceedings begun by summons issued under section 3 of the *Obscene Publications Act* 1959 (forfeiture of obscene articles);

  (e) to give, to such extent as he considers appropriate, advice to police forces on all matters relating to criminal offences;

 (ea) to have the conduct of any extradition proceedings;

 (eb) to give, to such extent as he considers appropriate, and to such persons as he considers appropriate, advice on any matters relating to extradition proceedings or proposed extradition proceedings;

 (ec) to give, to such extent as he considers appropriate, advice to immigration officers on matters relating to criminal offences;

  (f) to appear for the prosecution, when directed by the court to do so, on any appeal under—

   (i) section 1 of the *Administration of Justice Act* 1960 (appeal from the High Court in criminal cases);

   (ii) Part I or Part II of the *Criminal Appeal Act* 1968 (appeals from the Crown Court to the criminal division of the Court of Appeal and thence to the *House of Lords* [Supreme Court]); or

   (iii) section 108 of the *Magistrates' Courts Act* 1980 (right of appeal to Crown Court) as it applies, by virtue of subsection (5) of section 12 of the *Contempt of Court Act* 1981, to orders made under section 12 (contempt of magistrates' courts);

 (fa) to have the conduct of applications for orders under section 1C of the *Crime and Disorder Act* 1998 (orders made on conviction of certain offences) [, section 6 of the *Violent Crime Reduction Act* 2006 (orders on conviction in criminal proceedings)] and section 14A of the *Football Spectators Act* 1989 (banning orders made on conviction of certain offences);

 (faa) where it appears to him appropriate to do so, to have the conduct of applications made by him for orders under section 14B of the *Football Spectators Act* 1989 (banning orders made on complaint);

 (fb) where it appears to him appropriate to do so, to have the conduct of applications under section 1CA(3) of the *Crime and Disorder Act* 1998 for the variation or discharge of orders made under section 1C of that Act;

 (fc) where it appears to him appropriate to do so, to appear on any application under section 1CA of that Act made by a person subject to an order under section 1C of that Act for the variation or discharge of the order.

 [(fd) where it appears to him appropriate to do so, to have the conduct of applications under section 8(1)(b) of the *Violent Crime Reduction Act* 2006 for the variation or discharge of orders made under section 6 of that Act;

 (fe) where it appears to him appropriate to do so, to appear on any application under section 8(1)(a) of that Act by a person subject to an order under section 6 of that Act for the variation or discharge of the order.]

  (g) to discharge such other functions as may from time to time be assigned to him by the Attorney-General in pursuance of this paragraph.

(2A) Subsection (2)(ea) above does not require the Director to have the conduct of any extradition proceedings in respect of a person if he has received a request not to do so and—

  (a) in a case where the proceedings are under Part 1 of the *Extradition Act* 2003, the request is made by the authority which issued the Part 1 warrant in respect of the person;

  (b) in a case where the proceedings are under Part 2 of that Act, the request is made on behalf of the territory to which the person's extradition has been requested.

(3) In this section—

 "the court" means—

(a) in the case of an appeal to or from the criminal division of the Court of Appeal, that division;

(b) in the case of an appeal from a Divisional Court of the Queen's Bench Division, the Divisional Court; and

(c) in the case of an appeal against an order of a magistrates' court, the Crown Court;

"police force" means any police force maintained by a police authority under the *Police Act* 1996 and any other body of constables for the time being specified by order made by the Secretary of State for the purposes of this section; and

"specified proceedings" means proceedings which fall within any category for the time being specified by order made by the Attorney-General for the purposes of this section.

(4) The power to make orders under subsection (3) above shall be exercisable by statutory instrument subject to annulment in pursuance of a resolution of either House of Parliament.

[This section is printed as amended by the *Criminal Justice Act* 1987, Sched. 2, the *Police Act* 1996, Sched. 7, the *Police Act* 1997, Sched. 9, the *Immigration and Asylum Act* 1999, s.164, the *Police Reform Act* 2002, Sched. 7, the *Extradition Act* 2003, s.190, the *Anti social Behaviour Act* 2003, s.86 and Sched. 3, the *Asylum and Immigration (Treatment of Claimants, etc.) Act* 2004, s.7, and the *Serious Organised Crime and Police Act* 2005, s.140(5) and Scheds 4 and 17. The words in square brackets in s.3(2)(fa), (fd) and (fe) are to be inserted by the *Violent Crime Reduction Act* 2006, ss.7 and 8 and Sched. 3, as from a day to be appointed. Further, as from a day to be appointed, the words in italics in s.3(2)(f)(ii) are to be repealed and replaced by those in square brackets: *Constitutional Reform Act* 2005, Sched. 9.]

Interpretation of Part I

4–7   **15.**—(2) For the purposes of this Part, proceedings in relation to an offence are instituted—

(a) where a justice of the peace issues a summons under section 1 of the *Magistrates' Courts Act* 1980, when the information for the offence is laid before him;

(b) where a justice of the peace issues a warrant for the arrest of any person under that section, when the information for the offence is laid before him;

[(ba) where a public prosecutor issues a written charge and requisition for the offence, when the written charge and requisition are issued;]

(c) where a person is charged with the offence after being taken into custody without a warrant, when he is informed of the particulars of the charge;

(d) where a bill of indictment is preferred under section 2 of the *Administration of Justice (Miscellaneous Provisions) Act* 1933 in a case falling within paragraph (b) of subsection (2) of that section, when the bill of indictment is preferred before the court;

and where the application of this subsection would result in there being more than one time for the institution of the proceedings, they shall be taken to have been instituted at the earliest of those times.

(3) For the purposes of this Part, references to the conduct of any proceedings include references to the proceedings being discontinued and to the taking of any steps (including the bringing of appeals and making of representations in respect of applications for bail) which may be taken in relation to them.

(4) For the purposes of sections 3(2)(b), 5, 6 and 7(1) of this Act, binding over proceedings shall be taken to be criminal proceedings.

(5) For the purposes of section 5 of this Act, proceedings begun by summons issued under section 3 of the *Obscene Publications Act* 1959 (forfeiture of obscene articles) shall be taken to be criminal proceedings.

[The words in square brackets in s.15(2)(ba) are to be inserted by the *Criminal Justice Act* 2003, Sched. 36, as from a day to be appointed.]

4–8   The Director of Public Prosecutions is in charge of the CPS and he is accountable to the Attorney General who is a Law Officer of government and titular head of the English Bar. The appointment to Attorney General is political and the incumbent will usually be a member of the House of Commons. One of the responsibilities of the office is to prosecute in important criminal cases. The Solicitor-General is another Law Officer who is the subordinate of the Attorney General and in effect acts as his deputy.

The effect of section 3(2)(a) and (3) of the Act is to require the DPP to take over all **4–9** the prosecution of certain offences instituted by police forces maintained under the *Police Act* 1996 or otherwise specified in an order made by the Secretary of State. Police forces maintained under the 1996 Act are listed in Schedule 2 to that Act; and various other forces have been specified by the Secretary of State in the *Prosecution of Offences Act 1985 (Specified Police Forces) Order* 1985 (S.I. 1985 No. 1956).

The DPP has no duty to take over proceedings instituted by police forces for offences **4–10** which have been specified in an order made by the Attorney General. The *Prosecution of Offences Act 1985 (Specified Proceedings) Order* 1999 (S.I. 1999 No. 904) is an order made for that purpose, and it specifies proceedings for the following offences:

1) Fixed penalty offences within the meaning of section 51(1) of the *Road Traffic Offenders Act* 1988.
2) Offences under section 29(1) of the *Vehicle Excise and Registration Act* 1994.
3) Offences under sections 17(2), 18(3), 24(3), 26(1) and (2), 29, 31(1), 42(b), 47(1), 87(2), 143, 164(6) and (9), 165(3) and (6), 168 and 172(3) of the *Road Traffic Act* 1988.
4) All offences under the *Road Traffic Regulation Act* 1984, other than those under sections 35A(2), 43(5) and (12), 47(3), 52(1), 108(3), 115(1) and (2), 116(1) and 129(3) or those mentioned in paragraph 1, *ante*.
5) Offences in connection with contravention of the *Royal and Other Open Spaces Regulations* 1997, regs 3(9)(a) (involving a pedal cycle) and 3(9)(b) and 4(27) and, (28) and (30).

The offences cease to be "specified proceedings" once a summons has been served unless the necessary documents to enable the case to be dealt with on a written plea of guilty are also served on the offender with the summons. Proceedings also cease to be specified once the court starts to receive evidence but information provided to the court where a written plea of guilty has been entered is not treated as evidence for these purposes.

In practice this means that the court may deal with "specified proceedings" where written pleas are received to the listed offences in the absence of the CPS. The court will be assisted by the presence of a representative of the relevant police force.

Section 38 of the *Serious Organised Crime and Police Act* 2005 makes special provision for the prosecution of offences investigated by the Serious Organised Crime Agency. Under section 5 of the 2005 Act, SOCA has the power to institute criminal proceedings in England and Wales. It is not a police force, however, for the purposes of section 3(2) of the 1985 Act; and the DPP is accordingly under no duty under that section to take over proceedings instituted by it. Under section 38 of the 2005 Act, the DPP is empowered to institute and conduct proceedings arising out of a criminal investigation by SOCA in respect of a "non-designated" offence, and required to take over the conduct of criminal proceedings instituted by SOCA in respect of such an offence. The section confers corresponding powers and duties on the Director of the Revenue and Customs Prosecution Office in relation to "designated" offences.

Prosecution of Offences Act 1985, s.5

Conduct of prosecutions on behalf of the Service

5.—(1) The Director may at any time appoint a person who has a general qualification **4–11** (within the meaning of section 71 of the *Courts and Legal Services Act* 1990) to institute or take over the conduct of such criminal proceedings or extradition proceedings as the Director may assign to him.

(2) Any person conducting proceedings assigned to him under this section shall have all the powers of a Crown Prosecutor but shall exercise those powers subject to any instructions given to him by a Crown Prosecutor.

[This section is printed as amended by the *Courts and Legal Services Act* 1990, Sched. 10, and the *Extradition Act* 2003, s.190.]

4–12   This section allows agents to act for the CPS. The agent must be a barrister or solicitor from a list approved by the CPS. Individual cases will then be sent to the agent or they may be instructed to deal with all cases listed in the Court on any particular day. The agent will only act in the case in accordance with instructions from the CPS.

(2) Prosecution of offences by parties other than the CPS

(a) *General*

Prosecution of Offences Act 1985, ss.6 and 7(4)

Prosecutions instituted and conducted otherwise than by the Service

4–13   **6.**—(1) Subject to subsection (2) below, nothing in this Part shall preclude any person from instituting any criminal proceedings or conducting any criminal proceedings to which the Director's duty to take over the conduct of proceedings does not apply.

(2) Where criminal proceedings are instituted in circumstances in which the Director is not under a duty to take over their conduct, he may nevertheless do so at any stage.

Delivery of recognizances, etc., to Director

4–14   **7.**—(4) It shall be the duty of the designated officer for every magistrates' court to send to the Director, in accordance with the regulations, a copy of the information and of any depositions and other documents relating to any case in which—

(a) a prosecution for an offence before the magistrates' court is withdrawn or is not proceeded with within a reasonable time;

(b) the Director does not have the conduct of the proceedings; and

(c) there is some ground for suspecting that there is no satisfactory reason for the withdrawal or failure to proceed.

[This section is printed as amended by the *Courts Act* 2003, Sched. 8. There are no regulations supplemental to the section, following the revocation of the previously existing regulations by of the *Prosecution of Offences (Revocation) Regulations* 1997 (S.I. 1997 No. 739).]

Section 6(1) expressly preserves the rights of a private citizens and public authorities other than the CPS and the police to institute and conduct criminal prosecutions.

(b) *Other public prosecuting authorities*

Serious Fraud Office

4–15   Section 1 of the *Criminal Justice Act* 1987 establishes the Serious Fraud Office; makes provision for the appointment of the Director of the SFO, who is to discharge his functions under the superintendence of the Attorney General; confers a power on the director to investigate any suspected offence which appears to him on reasonable grounds to involve serious or complex fraud; and confers powers on the director to institute and have the conduct of any criminal proceedings which appear to him to relate to such fraud, and take over the conduct of any such proceedings at any stage. In *R. (Bermingham) v. Director of the Serious Fraud Office* [2006] 3 All E.R. 239, DC, it was held that the director was not obliged to exercise his investigatory powers in cases of transnational fraud with a view to pre-empting the potential trial venue in favour of this jurisdiction, simply because the rights of the prospective defendant under the European Convention on Human Rights might be violated if the trial were to take place in the potential foreign jurisdiction.

Revenue and Customs Prosecution Office

4–16   Section 34 *et seq.* of the *Commissioners for Revenue and Customs Act* 2005 make provision relating to the prosecution of Revenue and Customs offences. Section 34 establishes the office of Director of Revenue and Customs Prosecutions and provides that the Director and his staff are together to be referred to as the Revenue and Customs Prosecutions Office. Section 35 confers a power on the director to institute and conduct criminal proceedings relating to a criminal investigation by the Revenue and Customs (*i.e.* the Commissioners of Revenue and Customs, Revenue and Customs officers, and persons acting on their behalf); and requires him to take over the conduct of criminal proceedings instituted by the Revenue and Customs.

Local authorities

Section 222 of the *Local Government Act* 1972 provides that, where a local authority **4–17** considers it expedient for the promotion or protection of the interests of the inhabitants of its area, it may prosecute any legal proceedings. In *Monks v. Northamptonshire DC*, 166 J.P. 592, QBD, it was held that a local authority could, under section 222, institute proceedings in its own name, rather than in the name of a particular official. Local authorities are also empowered to commence and conduct prosecutions under a number of other enactments. *Inter alia*, section 4 of the *Road Traffic Offenders Act* 1988 specifies a number of road traffic offences in respect of which proceedings may be instituted by a local authority. In *Middlesbrough BC v. Safeer* [2002] 1 Cr.App.R. 23, DC, it was held that section 4 of the 1988 Act did not have the effect of precluding a local authority from instituting proceedings for a road traffic offence not specified in that section under section 222 of the 1972 Act.

Other public authorities

Various other specific enactments confer specific powers on different public authori- **4–18** ties to institute and conduct criminal proceedings.

(c) *Private prosecutions*

The right of the private citizen to institute and conduct a criminal prosecution is a **4–19** historical right originating in the earliest days of the legal process. It has been described as a "useful constitutional safeguard against capricious, corrupt or biased failure or refusal of those authorities to prosecute offenders against the criminal law": *per* Lord Diplock in *Gouriet v. Union of Post Office Workers* [1978] A.C. 435, HL. Despite the existence of the right, it is subject to a number of procedural constraints. The DPP will not be acting *ultra vires* if he exercises the power under section 6(2) to take over the conduct of proceedings instituted by a private prosecutor and then discontinues them under section 23 (*post*, § 7–131) or otherwise withraws or offers no evidence: see, *mutatis mutandis*, *Turner v. DPP*, 68 Cr.App.R. 70, DC; and *Raymond v. Att.-Gen.* [1982] Q.B. 839, DC.

As to whether it will be an abuse of process to bring a private prosecution against a person who has already received a police caution, see *Hayter v. L.* [1998] 1 W.L.R. 854, DC, and *Jones v. Whalley* [2007] A.C. 63, HL (*post*, § 8–97).

In *R. v. Belmarsh Magistrates' Court, ex p. Watts* [1999] 2 Cr.App.R. 188, DC, it was said that a private prosecutor was still a prosecutor, and hence subject to the same obligations as a minister of justice as are the public prosecuting authorities. However, in *Ewing v. Davis*, unreported, July 2, 2007, Q.B.D. (Mitting J.) ([2007] EWHC 1730 (Admin.)) it was held that the right to institute a private prosecution is not constrained by a requirement that the prosecution must be in the public interest and not conducted merely in order to pursue an individual grievance (*cf.* the criteria for the institution of a public prosecution, *post* §§ 4–22 *et seq.*). In so concluding, his Lordship observed that statutory provisions entitling the state to interfere with a private prosecution were to be found in the powers of the DPP to take over and discontinue a prosecution (*ibid.*), and the power of the Attorney-General to restrict vexatious prosecutions by seeking a criminal proceedings order from the High Court under the *Supreme Court Act* 1981, s.42.

Additional constraints on the right to institute a private prosecution to which his Lordship did not refer lie in the power of the Attorney-General to terminate proceedings by entering a *nolle prosequi*; and the possibility that the institution or carrying on of a prosecution is prohibited without the consent of the Attorney-General or the DPP (as to which, see *post*, §§ 4–30 *et seq.*). Furthermore, there is also the possibility that a summons will not issue upon the laying of an information (as to which, see *post*, §§ 4–75 *et seq.*). This latter factor will assume greater significance as a constraint on the right to institute a private prosecution when the written charging and requisitioning procedure is brought into force in full (as to which see *post*, §§ 4–54 *et seq.*), since the same constraint will no longer apply to the institution of public prosecutions.

(d) *Responsibility for conduct of prosecutions where multiple proceedings instituted*

4–20   With many bodies authorised under statute to conduct prosecutions, and the possibility that a private prosecutor might also institute proceedings, there are occasions when issues may arise over who should take responsibility for a prosecution.

Where a person other than a police officer arrests a suspect and takes him to the police station to be charged by a custody officer, it does not follow from the fact the suspect is charged by the custody officer that the proceedings are "instituted on behalf of a police force" within section 3(2)(a) of the *Prosecution of Offences Act* 1985 so that the DPP is bound to take over conduct of the proceedings; the right to prosecute was not surrendered by the person who effected the arrest simply because the police formally charged the suspect; a prosecution could only be said to have been instituted on behalf of a police force if a police force had investigated the matter, arrested the suspect and brought him to custody: *R. v. Stafford Magistrates' Court, ex p. Commissioners of Customs and Excise* [1991] 2 Q.B. 339, DC; and *R. (Hunt) v. Criminal Cases Review Commission* [2001] Q.B. 1108, DC.

4–21   In *R. v. Tower Bridge Metropolitan Stipendiary Magistrate, ex p. Chaudhry* [1994] Q.B. 340, DC, the Court considered the propriety of a private individual applying to take out a prosecution when proceedings had already been instituted by the CPS. The defendant was summoned by the CPS for an offence of driving without due care following an incident which resulted in a fatal accident. The mother of the motor cyclist who was killed applied to the magistrates, court for a summons against the defendant for causing death by dangerous driving. The court refused to issue the summons. On appeal the Divisional Court held that the magistrate was right to have regard to all relevant circumstances, including the fact that the CPS had already taken out a prosecution, when considering whether to issue a summons. In the absence of special circumstances, such as apparent bad faith on the part of the prosecutor, the Court said that magistrates should be slow to issue a private summons when the defendant was already subject to informations laid by the Crown.

In *R. (Charlson) v. Guildford Magistrates' Court* [2007] R.T.R. 1, QBD, Silber J. explained that what had been said in *ex p. Chaudhry* applied to the special situation where the public prosecuting authorities have already brought a prosecution in respect of the same matter and that prosecution was still pending. Where, however, the public prosecuting authority had previously commenced a prosecution in respect of the matter but had subsequently discontinued it, since a private prosecution does not need to satisfy the evidential or public interest tests applicable to a public prosecution, it was quite proper for magistrates to issue a summons for a private prosecution without requiring special circumstances. In deciding whether to issue a summons for a private prosecution in this latter situation, the magistrates should ascertain, (a) whether the allegation is an offence known to law and, if so, whether the ingredients of the offence are *prima facie* present, (b) whether any time-limit for prosecution operates as a bar to the issue of the summons, (c) whether the court has jurisdiction, (d) whether the informant has the necessary authority to prosecute, and (e) any other relevant facts.

(3) Decision to prosecute

Prosecution of Offences Act 1985, s.10

Guidelines for Crown Prosecutors

10.—(1) The Director shall issue a Code for Crown Prosecutors giving guidance on general **4–22** principles to be applied by them—

  (a) in determining, in any case—

    (i) whether proceedings for an offence should be instituted or, where proceedings have been instituted, whether they should be discontinued; or

    (ii) what charges should be preferred; and

  (b) in considering, in any case, representations to be made by them to any magistrates' court about the mode of trial suitable for that case.

(2) The Director may from time to time make alterations in the Code.

(3) The provisions of the Code shall be set out in the Director's report under section 9 of this Act for the year in which the Code is issued; and any alteration in the Code shall be set out in his report under that section for the year in which the alteration is made.

The most recent version of the Code was published in 2004 and is included at Appendix E. The Code is designed to ensure that fair and consistent decisions on public **4–23** prosecutions are made. The Code is published so that the principles applied by the CPS in exercising its functions are known to everyone involved in the criminal justice system whether professionals or members of the public. The duty of the CPS is expressed as being to ensure that "the right person is prosecuted for the right offence" and that all relevant facts are given to the court. The CPS also has a duty to review each case on a continuing basis to test the progress of the case against the Code.

The Code sets out two stages in the decision to institute a public prosecution: the **4–24** evidential test and the public interest test.

The evidential test must be satisfied for every case and then the public interest test will be considered. If the evidential test is not met then the prosecution will not proceed, no matter how serious the charge may be. If the evidential test is passed the case must still be tested against the public interest criteria.

The evidential test

The public prosecutor must be satisfied that there is sufficient evidence to provide a **4–25** "realistic prospect of conviction". This is an objective test based on whether a jury or bench, properly directed, is more likely than not to convict on the charge. The public prosecutor must decide whether the evidence is admissible and reliable. By asking these questions the strength of the prosecution case can be assessed.

The public interest test

This test recognises the fact that there exists no rule of law that requires suspected **4–26** criminal offences to be prosecuted automatically. Even if there is enough evidence to justify a prosecution the public interest in pursuing a prosecution must be considered. The Code lists some of the common factors which weigh both in favour of and against public prosecution. Factors in favour are aggravating circumstances of offences including the fact that conviction might lead to a significant sentence; that violence or a weapon was used during the offence; that the offence was likely to be repeated by the offender as a pattern of offences or that the offence is prevalent. Factors against a public prosecution include the fact that a nominal penalty is likely to be imposed; that the prosecution is likely to have a deleterious effect on the victim's physical or mental health or that the defendant is elderly at the time of the offence or was suffering from mental or physical ill health. At all times the serious nature of the offence will be borne in mind. These lists of factors are not exhaustive and the balancing exercise must be carefully performed by the public prosecutor.

4–27   In addition the Code provides that public prosecutors must take into account the views of the victims and the consequences to them of deciding not to prosecute.

In cases involving youths, the public prosecutor must consider the welfare of the youth when deciding whether to prosecute. The gravity of the offence will be relevant and whether a reprimand or final warning has previously been received by the youth.

In the case of adults, a public prosecutor may decide that a police caution would provide a suitable alternative to prosecution and the case may be referred back to the police who administer cautions when offences are admitted.

The Code also gives guidance on the selection of charges, mode of trial and the acceptance of guilty pleas (which may be accepted if the court will still be able to impose a sentence that matches the seriousness of the offence and should not be accepted solely for purposes of convenience) and re-starting prosecutions.

Judicial review of decisions to prosecute or not to prosecute

4–28   The decision as to whether a public prosecution should be instituted or continued involves an exercise of discretion. Although the scope of the discretion is broad, decisions not to institute a public prosecution, or to discontinue a prosecution, are susceptible to judicial review despite the possibility that an aggrieved person might institute a private prosecution: *R. v. Commissioner of Police of the Metropolis, ex p. Blackburn* [1968] 2 Q.B. 118, DC; *R. v. General Council of the Bar, ex p. Percival* [1991] 1 Q.B. 212, DC; *R. v. DPP, ex p. C.* [1995] 1 Cr.App.R. 136, DC. The power of review will be sparingly exercised in such cases, however, although the standard is not set too high: *R. v. DPP, ex p. Manning* [2001] Q.B. 330, DC. Grounds for ordering reconsideration of a decision not to prosecute may exist if it has been demonstrated, on an objective appraisal of the case, that a serious point or serious points supporting a prosecution have not been considered, or that, in a significant area, a conclusion as to what evidence is available to support a prosecution is irrational; but the points must have such force that it would be seriously arguable that the decision would otherwise be different had they been considered properly: *R. (Dennis) v. DPP* [2007] 2 *Archbold News* 3, DC. For a Commonwealth perspective on whether a public prosecutor who exercises the discretion to prosecute in favour of not bringing a prosecution may be guilty of an offence of doing an act tending or intended to pervert the course of justice, see *mutatis mutandis Beaudry v. R.*, 216 C.C.C. (3d) 353, Supreme Court of Canada.

In principle, decisions to institute or continue a prosecution are also susceptible to judicial review, provided that the decision had been made regardless of, or clearly contrary to, a settled policy which had been formulated in the public interest, such as a policy of cautioning juveniles: *R. v. Chief Constable of the Kent County Constabulary, ex p. L. (a minor)* [1993] 1 All ER 756, DC (*cf. R. (S.) v. DPP*, unreported, June 28, 2006, DC); *R. v. Inland Revenue Commissioners, ex p. Mead* [1993] 1 All ER 772, DC. However, a decision to prosecute for an offence would not be unlawful if it was outwith a policy that no one was to be prosecuted for a particular offence in the absence of certain aggravating circumstances; in such a case, it would be the policy itself that was unlawful: *R. (Mondelly) v. Commissoner of Police for the Metropolis*, 171 J.P. 121, DC (but *cf. R. v. Adaway*, 168 J.P.645, CA). The threshold which must be crossed before the power of review will be exercised is higher than in cases where a decision not to prosecute is challenged, and the remedy will generally not be available unless there was dishonesty or mala fides on the part of the prosecutor, or an exceptional circumstance: *R. v. DPP., ex p. Kebilene* [2000] 2 A.C. 326, HL. This is because the complaint will be capable of being dealt with in the trial process (such as by an application for a stay of the proceedings as an abuse of process): *Sharma v. Brown-Antoine* [2007] 1 W.L.R. 780, PC.

(4) Powers and duties of the prosecution

4–29   The Prosecutor has the duty of prosecuting the case at court, taking it through the preliminary stages of pre-trial hearings to calling evidence at trial and assisting with information at time of sentence. Full consideration of the duties are covered in the relevant sections, see Chs 8 and 10.

(5) Cases in which consent to prosecute is required

Prosecution of Offences Act 1985, s.25

Consents to prosecutions etc.

25.—(1) This section applies to any enactment which prohibits the institution or carrying on   **4–30**
of proceedings for any offence except—

    (a) with the consent (however expressed) of a Law Officer of the Crown or the Director; or

    (b) where the proceedings are instituted or carried on by or on behalf of a Law Officer of the Crown or the Director;

and so applies whether or not there are other exceptions to the prohibition (and in particular whether or not the consent is an alternative to the consent of any other authority or person).

(2) An enactment to which this section applies—

    (a) shall not prevent the arrest without warrant, or the issue or execution of a warrant for the arrest, of a person for any offence, or the remand in custody or on bail of a person charged with any offence; and

    (b) shall be subject to any enactment concerning the apprehension or detention of children or young persons.

(3) In this section "enactment" includes any provision having effect under or by virtue of any Act; and this section applies to enactments whenever passed or made.

DPP's consent

Following a decision to prosecute, some charges may require consent to be obtained   **4–31**
for the prosecution to be pursued.

The most common offences requiring DPP consent are shown below.

    Child abduction and kidnapping (*Child Abduction Act* 1984);

    Conspiracy (*Criminal Law Act* 1977, s.4);

    Health and safety at work (*Health and Safety at Work etc. Act* 1974, s.38—consent of the DPP or an inspector of the Environment Agency);

    Some sexual offences (*Sexual Offences Act* 1956, s.8);

    Theft or damage to property belonging to a husband or wife by a spouse (*Theft Act* 1968, s.30).

Attorney General's consent

The most common offences requiring the Attorney General's consent are shown   **4–32**
below.

    Conspiracy (*Criminal Law Act* 1977, s.4, where the substantive offence requires consent from the Attorney-General to prosecute);

    Contempt of court (*Contempt of Court Act* 1981, s.7—contempt in publications);

    Corruption of public servants (*Public Bodies Corrupt Practices Act* 1889, s.4);

    Customs proceedings (*Customs and Excise Management Act* 1979, s.147 where offences are tried summarily and were instituted initially in the name of the Attorney General);

    Explosive offences (*Explosive Substances Act* 1883, s.7);

    Highways offences (*Highways Act* 1980, s.312—the Attorney General must consent to any prosecution covered in this section other than one taken out by a person aggrieved or a highway authority or council having an interest in the enforcement of the Act);

Hi-jacking (*Aviation Security Act* 1982, s.8);

Public Health Offences (*Public Health Act* 1936, s.298 and *Public Health (Control Of Diseases) Act* 1984, s.64—consent needed for prosecutions other than by a party aggrieved or a council or body whose function it is to enforce the Act);

Trespassing on foreign missions (*Criminal Law Act* 1977, s.9).

Customs offences

4–33   Proceedings under the customs and excise Acts may only be instituted by or with the consent of the Director of Revenue and Customs Prosecutions, or by order of, or with the consent of, the Commissioners for Her Majesty's Revenue and Customs; and are commenced in the name of an officer (*Customs and Excise Management Act* 1979, s.145) but note such consent is not required where any person has been arrested for an offence for which he is liable to arrest by customs officers or police under this act and the Court may proceed to deal with the case although not instituted by order of the Commissioners, section 145(6) of the *Customs and Excise Management Act* 1979. This allows Courts to deal with such offences as being knowingly concerned in the fraudulent evasion of the prohibition on the importation of controlled drugs or conspiracy to commit that offence without the need for consent. Any customs officer authorised for that purpose may conduct proceedings in the magistrates' court, *Customs and Excise Management Act* 1979, s.155.

Evidence of consent

Prosecution of Offences Act 1985, s.26

Consents to be admissible in evidence

4–34   **26.** Any document purporting to be the consent of a Law Officer of the Crown, the Director or a Crown Prosecutor for, or to—

   (a) the institution of any criminal proceedings; or

   (b) the institution of criminal proceedings in any particular form;

and to be signed by a Law Officer of the Crown, the Director or, as the case may be, a Crown Prosecutor shall be admissible as *prima facie* evidence without further proof.

4–35   The consent will need to be produced in court following the first appearance but it is not required for the preliminary actions of arrest and charge. Where consent to prosecute is required by statute that consent must be given or the case will be a nullity.

Most cases requiring consent are serious in nature so will usually not give rise to summonses being issued but where authority to prosecute is required, the person before whom an information is laid should be satisfied that such authority has been obtained before issuing the summons.

The relevant consent to prosecute is proved by the production of a document that meets the requirements of section 26. At the hearing it will be presumed that authority was given and the prosecutor need not take any further steps unless the defence objects. Such an objection should be made before the close of the prosecution case. In the case of *Price v. Humphries* [1958] 2 Q.B. 353, DC, the court held that proof of consent was a formal matter and the prosecution was to be allowed to re-open it's case to produce the consent when late objection to the failure to produce it was taken by the defence.

If the defence requests proof of compliance with section 26 the prosecution must produce evidence that they have satisfied the statutory requirements as to consent. If such evidence is not forthcoming the justices are entitled to hold that there is no case to answer: *Anderton v. Frost* [1984] R.T.R. 106, DC, where computer generated informations named the Chief Constable as the informant the court held that the CPS had to prove in each case that the Chief Constable himself either laid the information or else had given written authority in each individual case to the officers concerned.

The court has to decide what evidence it would wish to hear to be able to determine **4–36** whether the consent was properly given and certified. It would appear difficult to challenge the validity of a certficate without challenging the *"bona fides"* of the officer or process concerned.

The purpose of a requirement for the consent of the Director of Public Prosecutions **4–37** or the Attorney General is to remove the right of private prosecution which would otherwise exist: *R. (Islamic Human Rights Commission) v. Civil Aviation Authority* [2007] A.C.D. 5, QBD. The traditional view was that where consent to prosecute is required and that consent is not given at all the proceedings will be a nullity: *R. v. Angel*, 52 Cr.App.R. 280, CA, and *R. v. Pearce*, 72 Cr.App.R. 295, CA. However, it may be that *Angel* and *Pearce* no longer represent the law following the change in the approach to procedural irregularities effected by *R. v. Soneji* [2006] 1 A.C. 340, HL, and *R. v. Ashton*; *R. v. Draz*; *R. v. O'Reilly* [2006] 2 Cr.App.R. 15, CA. This new approach was applied in *R. v. D.* [2007] Crim.L.R. 240, Crown Court at Lewes, where H.J.J. Richard Brown held that instituting a public prosecution against a person without the consent of the Director for an offence in respect of which such consent was required, and then obtaining consent subsequently, was properly to be described as a procedural failure which did not automatically render the court devoid of jurisdiction to try the offence. It is submitted that this decision is probably correct under the new approach as explained in *Soneji*, since the purpose of a requirement for consent of the Director (*ante*) will not be defeated in the case of a prosecution conducted by a crown prosecutor. Indeed, recourse to *Soneji* and *Ashton* may be unnecessary. In *R. v. Jackson* [1997] Crim.L.R. 293, CA, it was held that since section 1(7) of the *Prosecution of Offences Act* 1985 (*ante*, § 4–4) provides that any consent given by a crown prosecutor is to be treated as given by the Director, there need not be an express written consent where the proceedings are instituted by a crown prosecutor who establishes that he considered the consent requirement when making the decision to prosecute. As to cases where a prosecution is commenced by the charging of a suspect, although it may be arguable that the prosecution is technically instituted by the police officer who laid the charge, charging in many offences (and most, if not all, offences which require the consent of the DPP) now follows advice from a crown prosecutor (see *post*, §§ 4–38 *et seq.*) and it may be that the *Jackson* approach will be applicable where the crown prosecutor considered the consent requirement at that stage. For the avoidance of doubt, it must nonetheless remain the case that any proceedings will continue to be a nullity where they have been instituted by a private prosecutor without consent or where they have been instituted by a crown prosecutor or the Director institutes proceedings in a case where the consent of the Attorney is required.

II. CHARGING OF OFFENCES AT THE POLICE STATION

A. GENERAL

In criminal proceedings, a person suspected of committing an offence may attend **4–38** voluntarily at a police station or he may be arrested and taken to a police station. Once arrested, suspects may be detained for investigations to be carried out to determine if there is sufficient evidence to bring a charge. Those charged with an offence are either then bailed from the police station to attend at court or are brought to court in custody. The charge sheet which accompanies them gives information about the defendant, including his name, address, date of birth and ethnic origin together with details of the offence, the time of charge and release and any bail conditions.

The process of charging offences and the powers and duties of police officers to **4–39** charge offenders are found in the *Police and Criminal Evidence Act* 1984. Under section 66 of this Act, codes of practice have been drawn up which set out procedures to be followed during investigations.

Paragraphs 16.1 *et seq.* of the Code of Practice for the Detention, Treatment and Questioning of Persons by Police Officers ("Code C") make provision in connection with the charging of suspects at the police station: see Appendix A–88 *et seq.*

Once a custody officer has charged a suspect the prosecution commences. The Director of Public Prosecutions will take over the proceedings from the police unless that responsibility is assigned to another person (*q.v. Prosecution of Offences Act* 1985, s.6 (*ante*, § 4–13)).

4–40   Where a person other than a police officer investigated the matter, arrested the suspect and brought him to the police station to be charged by a custody officer, the fact the custody officer is a police officer does not require the DPP to take over conduct of the proceedings; the prosecution is instituted in such circumstances by the person who brought the suspect to the police station: see *ante*, § 4–20.

B. The Charging Process

(1) Duties of the custody officer before charge

Police and Criminal Evidence Act 1984, ss.37–37D

Duties of custody officer before charge

4–41   **37.**—(1) Where—

    (a) a person is arrested for an offence—

       (i) without a warrant; or

       (ii) under a warrant not endorsed for bail,

       the custody officer at each police station where he is detained after his arrest shall determine whether he has before him sufficient evidence to charge that person with the offence for which he was arrested and may detain him at the police station for such period as is necessary to enable him to do so.

    (2) If the custody officer determines that he does not have such evidence before him, the person arrested shall be released either on bail or without bail, unless the custody officer has reasonable grounds for believing that his detention without being charged is necessary to secure or preserve evidence relating to an offence for which he is under arrest or to obtain such evidence by questioning him.

    (3) If the custody officer has reasonable grounds for so believing, he may authorise the person arrested to be kept in police detention.

    (4) Where a custody officer authorises a person who has not been charged to be kept in police detention, he shall, as soon as is practicable, make a written record of the grounds for the detention.

    (5) Subject to subsection (6) below, the written record shall be made in the presence of the person arrested who shall at that time be informed by the custody officer of the grounds for his detention.

    (6) Subsection (5) above shall not apply where the person arrested is, at the time when the written record is made—

    (a) incapable of understanding what is said to him;

    (b) violent or likely to become violent; or

    (c) in urgent need of medical attention.

    (7) Subject to section 41(7) below, if the custody officer determines that he has before him sufficient evidence to charge the person arrested with the offence for which he was arrested, the person arrested—

    (a) shall be—

       (i) released without charge and on bail, or

       (ii) kept in police detention,

       for the purpose of enabling the Director of Public Prosecutions to make a decision under section 37B below,

    (b) shall be released without charge and on bail but not for that purpose,.

    (c) shall be released without charge and without bail, or

    (d) shall be charged.

    (7A) The decision as to how a person is to be dealt with under subsection (7) above shall be that of the custody officer.

    (7B) Where a person is dealt with under subsection (7)(a) above, it shall be the duty of the custody officer to inform him that he is being released, or (as the case may be) detained, to enable the Director of Public Prosecutions to make a decision under section 37B below.

(8) Where—

   (a) a person is released under subsection (7)(b) or (c) above; and

   (b) at the time of his release a decision whether he should be prosecuted for the offence for which he was arrested has not been taken,

it shall be the duty of the custody officer so to inform him.

(8A) Subsection (8B) applies if the offence for which the person is arrested is one in relation to which a sample could be taken under section 63B below and the custody officer—

   (a) is required in pursuance of subsection (2) above to release the person arrested and decides to release him on bail, or

   (b) decides in pursuance of subsection (7)(a) or (b) above to release the person without charge and on bail.

(8B) The detention of the person may be continued to enable a sample to be taken under section 63B, but this subsection does not permit a person to be detained for a period of more than 24 hours after the relevant time.

(9) If the person arrested is not in a fit state to be dealt with under subsection (7) above, he may be kept in police detention until he is.

(10) The duty imposed on the custody officer under subsection (1) above shall be carried out by him as soon as practicable after the person arrested arrives at the police station or, in the case of a person arrested at the police station, as soon as practicable after the arrest.

(15) In this Part of this Act—

   "arrested juvenile" means a person arrested with or without a warrant who appears to be under the age of 17;

   "endorsed for bail" means endorsed with a direction for bail in accordance with section 117(2) of the *Magistrates' Courts Act* 1980.

[This section is printed as amended by the *Children Act* 1989, Sched. 15, the *Criminal Justice Act* 1991, s.72 and Sched. 13, the *Criminal Justice and Public Order Act* 1994, s.29(1) and Sched. 11, the *Criminal Justice Act* 2003, Sched. 2, the *Drugs Act* 2005, Sched. 1, and the *Police and Justice Act* 2006, s.11, and Sched. 14.]

Guidance

37A.—(1) The Director of Public Prosecutions may issue guidance—   **4–42**

   (a) for the purpose of enabling custody officers to decide how persons should be dealt with under section 37(7) above or 37C(2) or 37CA(2) below, and

   (b) as to the information to be sent to the Director of Public Prosecutions under section 37B(1) below.

(2) The Director of Public Prosecutions may from time to time revise guidance issued under this section.

(3) Custody officers are to have regard to guidance under this section in deciding how persons should be dealt with under section 37(7) above or 37C(2) or 37CA(2) below.

(4) A report under section 9 of the *Prosecution of Offences Act* 1985 (report by DPP to Attorney General) must set out the provisions of any guidance issued, and any revisions to guidance made, in the year to which the report relates.

(5) The Director of Public Prosecutions must publish in such manner as he thinks fit—

   (a) any guidance issued under this section, and

   (b) any revisions made to such guidance.

(6) Guidance under this section may make different provision for different cases, circumstances or areas.

Consultation with the Director of Public Prosecutions

37B.—(1) Where a person is dealt with under section 37(7)(a) above, an officer involved in **4–43** the investigation of the offence shall, as soon as is practicable, send to the Director of Public Prosecutions such information as may be specified in guidance under section 37A above.

(2) The Director of Public Prosecutions shall decide whether there is sufficient evidence to charge the person with an offence.

(3) If he decides that there is sufficient evidence to charge the person with an offence, he shall decide—

   (a) whether or not the person should be charged and, if so, the offence with which he should be charged, and

(b) whether or not the person should be given a caution and, if so, the offence in respect of which he should be given a caution.

(4) The Director of Public Prosecutions shall give notice of his decision to an officer involved in the investigation of the offence.

(4A) Notice under subsection (4) above shall be in writing, but in the case of a person kept in police detention under section 37(7)(a) above it may be given orally in the first instance and confirmed in writing subsequently.

(5) If his decision is—

(a) that there is not sufficient evidence to charge the person with an offence, or

(b) that there is sufficient evidence to charge the person with an offence but that the person should not be charged with an offence or given a caution in respect of an offence,

a custody officer shall give the person notice in writing that he is not to be prosecuted.

(6) If the decision of the Director of Public Prosecutions is that the person should be charged with an offence, or given a caution in respect of an offence, the person shall be charged or cautioned accordingly.

(7) But if his decision is that the person should be given a caution in respect of the offence and it proves not to be possible to give the person such a caution, he shall instead be charged with the offence.

[(8) For the purposes of this section, a person is to be charged with an offence either—

(a) when he is in police detention at a police station (whether because he has returned to answer bail, because he is detained under section 37(7)(a) above or for some other reason), or

(b) in accordance with section 29 of the *Criminal Justice Act* 2003.]

(9) In this section "caution" includes—

(a) a conditional caution within the meaning of Part 3 of the *Criminal Justice Act* 2003, and

(b) a warning or reprimand under section 65 of the *Crime and Disorder Act* 1998.

Breach of bail following release under section 37(7)(a)

4–44   **37C.**—(1) This section applies where—

(a) a person released on bail under section 37(7)(a) above or subsection (2)(b) below is arrested under section 46A below in respect of that bail, and

(b) at the time of his detention following that arrest at the police station mentioned in section 46A(2) below, notice under section 37B(4) above has not been given.

(2) The person arrested—

(a) shall be charged, or

(b) shall be released without charge, either on bail or without bail.

(3) The decision as to how a person is to be dealt with under subsection (2) above shall be that of a custody officer.

(4) A person released on bail under subsection (2)(b) above shall be released on bail subject to the same conditions (if any) which applied immediately before his arrest.

Breach of bail following release under section 37(7)(b)

4–45   **37CA.**—(1) This section applies where a person released on bail under section 37(7)(b) above or subsection (2)(b) below—

(a) is arrested under section 46A below in respect of that bail,

(b) is being detained following that arrest at the police station mentioned in section 46A(2) below.

(2) The person arrested—

(a) shall be charged, or

(b) shall be released without charge, either on bail or without bail.

(3) The decision as to how a person is to be dealt with under subsection (2) above shall be that of a custody officer.

(4) A person released on bail under subsection (2)(b) above shall be released on bail subject to the same conditions (if any) which applied immediately before his arrest.

Release on bail under section 37: further provision

4–46   **37D.**—(1) Where a person is released on bail under section 37(7), 37C(2)(b) or 37CA(2)(b) above, a custody officer may subsequently appoint a different time, or an additional time, at which the person is to attend at the police station to answer bail.

(2) The custody officer shall give the person notice in writing of the exercise of the power under subsection (1).

(3) The exercise of the power under subsection (1) shall not affect the conditions (if any) to which bail is subject.

(4) Where a person released on bail under section 37(7)(a) or 37C(2)(b) above returns to a police station to answer bail or is otherwise in police detention at a police station, he may be kept in police detention to enable him to be dealt with in accordance with section 37B or 37C above or to enable the power under subsection (1) above to be exercised.

(4A) Where a person released on bail under section 37(7)(b) or 37CA(2)(b) above returns to a police station to answer bail or is otherwise in police detention at a police station, he may be kept in police detention to enable him to be dealt with in accordance with section 37CA above or to enable the power under subsection (1) above to be exercised.

(5) If the person mentioned in subsection (4) or (4A) above is not in a fit state to enable him to be dealt with as mentioned in that subsection or to enable the power under subsection (1) above to be exercised, he may be kept in police detention until he is.

(6) Where a person is kept in police detention by virtue of subsection (4), (4A) or (5) above, section 37(1) to (3) and (7) above (and section 40(8) below so far as it relates to section 37(1) to (3)) shall not apply to the offence in connection with which he was released on bail under section 37(7), 37C(2)(b) or 37CA(2)(b) above.

[Sections 37A, 37B, 37C and 37D were inserted by the *Criminal Justice Act* 2003, Sched. 2. They are printed as amended by the *Police and Justice Act* 2006, s.11 and Scheds 6 and 14. Section 37B(8) (set out in square brackets) is to be brought into force as from a day to be appointed. Section 37CA was inserted by the *Police and Justice Act* 2006, Sched. 6.]

The purpose behind the amendments made to the charging regime in *PACE* 1984 **4–47** by the *Criminal Justice Act* 2003 was to involve the Crown Prosecution Service at an earlier stage of a prosecution. Under section 37(7)(a), a custody officer may detain or release a person on bail in order to consult with the DPP as to whether that person should be charged. Sections 37A and 37B which have been inserted into *PACE* 1984 provide for the DPP to issue guidance on the exercise of the power to bail pending consultation and also allow for the DPP to consider the sufficiency of the evidence and advise on any charge or caution, including a conditional caution.

Such guidance has been issued by the DPP and it is crucial to the operation of the charging regime. In particular, the guidance provides that in most cases a Crown Prosecutor will be responsible for the decision to charge and the specifying or drafting of the charges. Schedule 3 to the *Commissioners for Revenue and Customs Act* 2005 applies sections 37 to 37B of the 1984 Act to persons arrested following a criminal investigation by the Revenue and Customs, as if references to the Director of Public Prosecutions were references to the Director of Revenue and Customs Prosecutions.

The custody officer is not obliged to investigate the lawfulness of the arrest before charging a suspect: *DPP v. L* [1999] Crim.L.R. 752, DC; and see *Al-Fayed v. Metropolitan Police Commissioner* [2005] 1 *Archbold News* 2, CA.

The periods of detention are specified in the Act. Even if there is not sufficient evidence to charge, detention may be ordered to protect evidence or elicit evidence by further questioning. Once the decision is made that there is sufficient evidence the suspect must be charged or released without charge, although he can at this stage be bailed to return to the police station at a later date whilst inquiries are still ongoing.

The custody officer has power to grant unconditional or conditional bail under sec- **4–48** tion 47 of *PACE* 1984 when exercising his power to release suspects under section 38. The provisions of the *Bail Act* 1976 apply, see Ch.5. The officer may impose similar conditions of bail as the court except those requiring residence in a bail hostel, co-operation with report writers or attendance at lawyers interviews. The officer may also entertain applications to vary bail conditions made by him. Section 41(7) limits the time of detention without charge to 24 hours initially. The suspect, if not charged must then

Part I

be released on bail or he may be released from detention with no direction about bail and therefore no legal duty to return to the police station. The period of detention may also be extended. When a person fails to answer police bail he may be arrested without a warrant: *PACE* 1984, ss.37C, 37D and 46A.

(2) Duties of custody officer after charge

Police and Criminal Evidence Act 1984, s.38

Duties of custody officer after charge

4–49   **38.**—(1) Where a person arrested for an offence otherwise than under a warrant endorsed for bail is charged with an offence, the custody officer shall, subject to section 25 of the *Criminal Justice and Public Order Act* 1994, order his release from police detention, either on bail or without bail, unless—

> (a) if the person arrested is not an arrested juvenile—
>> (i)   his name or address cannot be ascertained or the custody officer has reasonable grounds for doubting whether a name or address furnished by him as his name or address is his real name or address;
>> (ii) the custody officer has reasonable grounds for believing that the person arrested will fail to appear in court to answer to bail;
>> (iii) in the case of a person arrested for an imprisonable offence, the custody officer has reasonable grounds for believing that the detention of the person arrested is necessary to prevent him from committing an offence;
>> (iiia) in a case where a sample may be taken from the person under section 63B below, the custody officer has reasonable grounds for believing that the detention of the person is necessary to enable the sample to be taken from him;
>> (iv) in the case of a person arrested for an offence which is not an imprisonable offence, the custody officer has reasonable grounds for believing that the detention of the person arrested is necessary to prevent him from causing physical injury to any other person or from causing loss of or damage to property;
>> (v)   the custody officer has reasonable grounds for believing that the detention of the person arrested is necessary to prevent him from interfering with the administration of justice or with the investigation of offences or of a particular offence; or
>> (vi) the custody officer has reasonable grounds for believing that the detention of the person arrested is necessary for his own protection;
> (b) if he is an arrested juvenile—
>> (i)   any of the requirements of paragraph (a) above is satisfied (but, in the case of paragraph (a)(iiia) above, only if the arrested juvenile has attained the minimum age); or
>> (ii) the custody officer has reasonable grounds for believing that he ought to be detained in his own interests.

(2) If the release of a person arrested is not required by subsection (1) above, the custody officer may authorise him to be kept in police detention but may not authorise a person to be kept in police detention by virtue of subsection (1)(a)(iiia) after the end of the period of six hours beginning when he was charged with the offence.

(2A) The custody officer, in taking the decisions required by subsection (1)(a) and (b) above (except (a)(i) and (vi) and (b)(ii)), shall have regard to the same considerations as those which a court is required to have regard to in taking the corresponding decisions under paragraph 2(1) of Part I of Schedule 1 to the *Bail Act* 1976 (disregarding paragraph 2(2) of that Part).

(3) Where a custody officer authorises a person who has been charged to be kept in police detention, he shall, as soon as practicable, make a written record of the grounds for the detention.

(4) Subject to subsection (5) below, the written record shall be made in the presence of the person charged who shall at that time be informed by the custody officer of the grounds for his detention.

(5) Subsection (4) above shall not apply where the person charged is, at the time when the written record is made—

(a) incapable of understanding what is said to him;

(b) violent or likely to become violent; or

(c) in urgent need of medical attention.

(6) Where a custody officer authorises an arrested juvenile to be kept in police detention under subsection (1) above, the custody officer shall, unless he certifies—

(a) that, by reason of such circumstances as are specified in the certificate, it is impracticable for him to do so; or

(b) in the case of an arrested juvenile who has attained the age of 12 years, that no secure accommodation is available and that keeping him in other local authority accommodation would not be adequate to protect the public from serious harm from him,

secure that the arrested juvenile is moved to local authority accommodation.

(6A) In this section—

'local authority accommodation' means accommodation provided by or on behalf of a local authority (within the meaning of the *Children Act* 1989);

'minimum age' means the age specified in section 63B(3)(b) below.

'secure accommodation' means accommodation provided for the purpose of restricting liberty;

'sexual offence' means an offence specified in Part 2 of Schedule 15 to the *Criminal Justice Act* 2003;

'violent offence' means murder or an offence specified in Part 1 of that Schedule.

and any reference, in relation to an arrested juvenile charged with a violent or sexual offence, to protecting the public from serious harm from him shall be construed as a reference to protecting members of the public from death or serious personal injury, whether physical or psychological, occasioned by further such offences committed by him.

(6B) Where an arrested juvenile is moved to local authority accommodation under subsection (6) above, it shall be lawful for any person acting on behalf of the authority to detain him.

(7) A certificate made under subsection (6) above in respect of an arrested juvenile shall be produced to the court before which he is first brought thereafter.

(7A) In this section "imprisonable offence" has the same meaning as in Schedule 1 to the *Bail Act* 1976.

(8) In this Part of this Act "local authority" has the same meaning as in the *Children Act* 1989.

[This section is printed as amended by the *Children Act* 1989, Sched. 13, the *Criminal Justice Act* 1991, s.59, the *Criminal Justice and Public Order Act* 1994, ss.24 and 28 and Sched. 10, the *Criminal Justice and Court Services Act* 2000, s.57, the *Powers of Criminal Courts (Sentencing) Act* 2000, Sched. 9, the *Criminal Justice Act* 2003, s.5 and Scheds 32 and 36, and the *Drugs Act* 2005, Sched. 1.]

Once a suspect is charged the custody sergeant will decide whether to detain him in **4–50** custody to appear at court or to release him on bail with or without conditions for appearance at court at a later date. The custody sergeant is bound by the provisions of the *Bail Act* 1976, see Ch.5.

The custody officer may order detention for six hours if any of the conditions in section 38(1) are met. This now includes the power to detain to conduct a drugs test under section 63B of *PACE* 1984.

Section 25 of the *Criminal Justice and Public Order Act* 1994 applies in cases of murder, attempted murder, manslaughter, rape and attempted rape, if the defendant has previously been convicted of any such offence or culpable homicide and in the case of culpable homicide. On its face, the section appears to provide that bail should only be granted if there are exceptional circumstances to justify it. However, in *R. (O.) v. Crown Court at Harrow* [2007] 1 A.C. 249, HL, it was held that the subsection merely served as a reminder of the risks normally posed by defendants to whom it applied; it had no substantive effect upon the way in which bail applications should be determined under the *Bail Act* 1976.

Section 63B of *PACE* 1984 gives power for samples to be taken from a person in po-   **4–51** lice detention for the purpose of ascertaining whether the person has a Class A drug in his body. A period of six hours is deemed sufficient time to arrange for the sample to be taken.

Young persons may also be detained but the police have an over-riding duty to transfer young persons aged between 10 and 17 to local authority accommodation. In *R. (M.) v. Gateshead Metropolitan Borough Council* [2006] Q.B. 650, CA, it was held that where a local authority received a request from the police under subsection (6) to receive a juvenile whom a custody officer had authorised under subsection (1) to be kept in police detention, the authority was under a duty, pursuant to section 21(2) of the *Children Act* 1989, to provide accommodation in response to such request, regardless of whether or not the juvenile was within in its area at the time of the request; however, there was no absolute duty to provide secure accommodation where such accommodation was requested, merely a duty to provide accommodation.

Pursuant to paragraph 16 of Code C of the Codes of Practice, when a person is charged with an offence at a police station he must be cautioned and given written notice of the charge, which shows the particulars of the offence stated in simple language and the precise offence in law with which he is charged.

(3) Detention after charge

Police and Criminal Evidence Act 1984, s.46

Detention after charge

4–52　　46.—(1) Where a person—

    (a) is charged with an offence; and

    (b) after being charged—

        (i) is kept in police detention; or

        (ii) is detained by a local authority in pursuance of arrangements made under section 38(6) above,

    he shall be brought before a magistrates' court in accordance with the provisions of this section.

(2) If he is to be brought before a magistrates' court in the local justice area in which the police station at which he was charged is situated, he shall be brought before such a court as soon as is practicable and in any event not later than the first sitting after he is charged with the offence.

(3) If no magistrates' court in that area is due to sit either on the day on which he is charged or on the next day, the custody officer for the police station at which he was charged shall inform the designated officer for the area that there is a person in the area to whom subsection (2) above applies.

(4) If the person charged is to be brought before a magistrates' court in a local justice area other than that in which the police station at which he was charged is situated, he shall be removed to that area as soon as is practicable and brought before such a court as soon as is practicable after his arrival in the area and in any event not later than the first sitting of a magistrates' court in that area after his arrival in the area.

(5) If no magistrates' court in that area is due to sit either on the day on which he arrives in the area or on the next day—

    (a) he shall be taken to a police station in the area; and

    (b) the custody officer at that station shall inform the designated officer for the area that there is a person in the area to whom subsection (4) applies.

(6) Subject to subsection (8) below, where the designated officer for a local justice area has been informed—

    (a) under subsection (3) above that there is a person in the area to whom subsection (2) above applies; or

    (b) under subsection (5) above that there is a person in the area to whom subsection (4) above applies,

the designated officer shall arrange for a magistrates' court to sit not later than the day next following the relevant day.

(7) In this section "the relevant day"—

    (a) in relation to a person who is to be brought before a magistrates' court in the local justice area in which the police station at which he was charged is situated, means the day on which he was charged; and

    (b) in relation to a person who is to be brought before a magistrates' court for any other local justice area, means the day on which he arrives in the area.

    (8) Where the day next following the relevant day is Christmas Day, Good Friday or a Sunday, the duty of the designated officer under subsection (6) above is a duty to arrange for a magistrates' court to sit not later than the first day after the relevant day which is not one of those days.

    (9) Nothing in this section requires a person who is in hospital to be brought before a court if he is not well enough.

[This section is printed as amended by the *Courts Act* 2003, Sched. 8.]

The police have a duty under this section to produce a defendant from custody to **4–53** court as soon as practicable after charge. Most magistrates' courts are open from Monday to Friday so defendants can be produced either on the day of charge or the following day. Many courts are also open on Saturdays and Bank Holidays and on those days may deal with work for other courts in their area that are not open. It is not lawful for a policy to be promoted by a body responsible for running the magistrates court to restrict the convening of courts to weekdays only: *R. v. Avon Magistrates' Courts Committee, ex p. Broome* [1988] 1 W.L.R. 1246, DC.

Under the *Courts Act* 2003, s.30, the Lord Chancellor may give directions as to the days and times when a magistrates' court may sit and they may be directed to sit on any day at any time. See Ch.2.

III. WRITTEN CHARGING AND REQUISITIONING

General

As from a day to be appointed, the institution of all public prosecutions will be **4–54** governed by a new procedure. This will replace the laying of informations (other than by charging at the police station) and issue of summonses with a process under which the public prosecutor may issue a "written charge" which charges the person with an offence. The written charge must be accompanied by the issue of a "requisition" which requires the person to appear before a magistrates' court to answer the written charge. The new procedure is not in force generally, but is being piloted on a limited basis in a number of magistrates' courts sitting at specified locations: see § 4–56A, *post*. When the new procedure is brought into force in full, public prosecutors will no longer have the power to lay an information for the purpose of obtaining the issue of a summons. However, the power of a public prosecutor to lay an information in order to obtain an arrest warrant is retained. The new procedure does not apply to criminal proceedings instituted by private prosecutors, which will continue to be instituted by the laying of an information and the issue of a summons.

Criminal Justice Act 2003, ss.29 and 30

New method of instituting proceedings

    [**29.**—(1) A public prosecutor may institute criminal proceedings against a person by issuing a **4–55** document (a "written charge") which charges the person with an offence.

    (2) Where a public prosecutor issues a written charge, it must at the same time issue a document (a "requisition") which requires the person to appear before a magistrates' court to answer the written charge.

    (3) The written charge and requisition must be served on the person concerned, and a copy of both must be served on the court named in the requisition.

    (4) In consequence of subsections (1) to (3), a public prosecutor is not to have the power to lay an information for the purpose of obtaining the issue of a summons under section 1 of the *Magistrates' Courts Act* 1980.

 (5) In this section "public prosecutor" means—

  (a) a police force or a person authorised by a police force to institute criminal proceedings,

  (b) the Director of the Serious Fraud Office or a person authorised by him to institute criminal proceedings,

  (c) the Director of Public Prosecutions or a person authorised by him to institute criminal proceedings,

  (ca) the Director of Revenue and Customs Prosecutions or a person authorised by him to institute criminal proceedings,

  (cb) the Director General of the Serious Organised Crime Agency or a person authorised by him to institute criminal proceedings,

  (d) the Attorney General or a person authorised by him to institute criminal proceedings,

  (e) a Secretary of State or a person authorised by a Secretary of State to institute criminal proceedings,

  (f) the Commissioners for Her Majesty's Revenue and Customs or a person authorised by them to institute criminal proceedings,

  (g) [...], or

  (h) a person specified in an order made by the Secretary of State for the purposes of this section or a person authorised by such a person to institute criminal proceedings.

 (6) In subsection (5) "police force" has the meaning given by section 3(3) of the *Prosecution of Offences Act* 1985.]

[This section is printed as amended by the *Serious Organised Crime and Police Act* 2005, Sched. 4, and the *Commissioners for Revenue and Customs Act* 2005, s.50 and Sched. 4. It is not in force generally, but subsections (1) to (3), (5) and (6) have been brought into force for the purposes of a pilot scheme in a number of magistrates' courts sitting at specified locations: see § 4–56A, *post*.]

Further provision about new method

4–56   **[30.**—(1), (2) (power to make *Criminal Procedure Rules*)

 (3) (repealed)

 (4) Nothing in section 29 affects—

  (a) the power of a public prosecutor to lay an information for the purpose of obtaining the issue of a warrant under section 1 of the *Magistrates' Courts Act* 1980,

  (b) the power of a person who is not a public prosecutor to lay an information for the purpose of obtaining the issue of a summons or warrant under section 1 of that Act, or

  (c) any power to charge a person with an offence whilst he is in custody.

 (5) Except where the context otherwise requires, in any enactment contained in an Act passed before this Act—

  (a) any reference (however expressed) which is or includes a reference to an information within the meaning of section 1 of the *Magistrates' Courts Act* 1980 (or to the laying of such an information) is to be read as including a reference to a written charge (or to the issue of a written charge),

  (b) any reference (however expressed) which is or includes a reference to a summons under section 1 of the *Magistrates' Courts Act* 1980 (or to a justice of the peace issuing such a summons) is to be read as including a reference to a requisition (or to a public prosecutor issuing a requisition).

 (6) Subsection (5) does not apply to section 1 of the *Magistrates' Courts Act* 1980.

 (7) The reference in subsection (5) to an enactment contained in an Act passed before this Act includes a reference to an enactment contained in that Act as a result of an amendment to that Act made by this Act or by any other Act passed in the same Session as this Act.

 (8) In this section "public prosecutor", "requisition" and "written charge" have the same meaning as in section 29].

[This section is printed as amended by the *Courts Act 2003 (Consequential Amend-*

ments) Order 2004 (S.I. 2004 No. 2035). It is not in force generally, but it has been brought into force for the purposes of a pilot scheme in a number of specified magistrates' courts: see § 4–56A, *post.*]

Piloting of new procedure in magistrates' courts sitting at specified locations

As from July 25, 2007, the *Criminal Justice Act 2003 (Commencement No.16) Or-* **4–56a** *der* 2007 (S.I. 2007 No. 1999) brought sections 29(1) to (3), (5), (6) and 30 into force for the purposes of a pilot scheme. The provisions have effect only for the purposes of:

(a) criminal proceedings instituted by a public prosecutor within the meaning of section 29(5)(a) (*i.e.* a police force, or a person authorised by a police force to institute criminal proceedings), in a magistrates' court sitting at: Barking Magistrates' Court, Bexley Magistrates' Court, Brentford Magistrates' Court, Bromley Magistrates' Court, Coalville Magistrates' Court, Croydon Magistrates' Court, Harrow Magistrates' Court, Hendon Magistrates' Court, Knowsley Magistrates' Court, Loughborough Magistrates' Court, Melton Magistrates' Court, Oakham Magistrates' Court, Redbridge Magistrates' Court, Richmond Magistrates' Court, St Helens Magistrates' Court, Waltham Forest Magistrates' Court, City of Westminster Magistrates' Court, and Wimbledon Magistrates' Court; and

(b) criminal proceedings instituted by a public prosecutor within the meaning of section 29(5)(e) of the 2003 Act (*i.e.* a person authorised by a Secretary of State to institute criminal proceedings), who is authorised for the purposes of section 49 of the *Vehicle Excise and Registration Act* 1994 (authorised persons), in a magistrates' court sitting in Portsmouth Magistrates' Court.

It is to be noted that section 29(4) has not been brought into force as part of the pilot scheme; and it follows that the public prosecutors to whom the pilot scheme applies are not prohibited from instituting proceedings by the laying of an information to obtain the issue of a summons.

Form and content of written charge and requisition

Part 7 of the *Criminal Procedure Rules* (Appendix G–33 *et seq.*) has been amended **4–57** so that the rules applicable to informations and summonses also apply to written charges and requisitions. Accordingly, as to the form and content of written charges, see *post*, §§ 4–61 *et seq.*

IV. LAYING OF INFORMATION TO OBTAIN ISSUE OF SUMMONS

A. INTRODUCTION

Until the commencement of the written charging and requisitioning procedure **4–58** under sections 29 and 30 of the *Criminal Justice Act* 2003, public and private prosecutors may institute prosecutions by laying an information in order to obtain a summons requiring the person to appear before the court. Once the new provisions are brought into force, only private prosecutors will be able to use this procedure to institute proceedings. An information may also be laid to obtain a warrant for the arrest of the person: see *post*, §§ 4–89 *et seq.* This latter power will remain exercisable by both public and private prosecutors when the written charging and requisitioning procedure is brought into force.

B. INFORMATIONS

(1) General

An information is the statement by which a person authorised to issue a summons or **4–59** warrant is informed of an allegation of an offence: *Hughes* (1879) J.P. 556, CCR. The information will usually be made in writing (although it may also be made orally) by the informant and it will detail the nature of the alleged offence and the circumstances giving rise to it.

(2) Laying the information

4–60   The laying of an information is an administrative act performed by the prosecutor and it may be done by the prosecutor in person or by his counsel or solicitor or other person authorised in that behalf. The information is laid when it is received at the office of clerk to the justices in the relevant area: *R. v. Manchester Stipendiary Magistrate, ex p. Hill* [1983] 1 AC 328, HL.

An information may not be laid by an unincorporated association such as a police force because the definition of "person" in the *Interpretation Act* 1978 as "a body of persons whether corporate or unincorporated" was not intended to apply to the laying of informations: *Rubin v. DPP* [1990] 2 Q.B. 80, DC. In that case an information purported to have been laid by the Thames Valley Police. Watkins L.J. rejected the argument that "the police" could be regarded as the prosecutor. He said:

> "When the police bring a prosecution it has to be commenced by an information which has been laid by a member of the force; that is to say, by that member who reported the offence and the person accused of committing it or by the chief constable himself of some other member of the force authorised by him to lay an information."

In this particular case, the information was held not to be invalid because the identity of the informant was easily discovered and the defendant had not been misled.

In *Ealing Justices ex p. Dixon*, [1990] 2 Q.B. 91, DC, Woolf L.J. observed that it was preferable for an individual to lay an information even when the prosecutor was essentially an organisation such as the Federation Against Copyright Theft.

(3) Form and content of the information

(a) *General*

4–61   An information or complaint must comply with the requirements of rules 7.1–7.3 of the *Criminal Procedure Rules* 2005 (Appendix G–33, *et seq.*). It need not be in writing or on oath unless specifically required to be so by statute. The court should be informed of the precise nature of the offence alleged, including details of the date and place of the offence, the activity which is alleged to amount to an offence and the provision of statute (or common law) which makes the conduct an offence.

(b) *Rule against duplicity*

4–62   See *Criminal Procedure Rules* 2005, r.7.3 in Appendix G. Simply stated, the rule against duplicity prohibits the court from proceeding to the trial of an information which charges more than one offence: r.7.3(1). Although the rule is easily stated, in practice it is more difficult to determine what constitutes one offence.

4–63   An information alleging that a person did "unlawfully assault and batter" another would be bad for duplicity, because assault and battery are separate and distinct offences: *DPP v. Taylor* [1992] 1 Q.B. 645, DC. However, an information will not be bad for duplicity if it alleges one activity even if that activity involves more than one act: *Ware v Fox; Fox v. Dingley* [1967] 1 W.L.R. 379, DC; *Jemmison v. Priddle* [1972] 1 Q.B. 489, DC. This approach was approved and explained by Lord Morris of Borth-y-Gest in *DPP v. Merriman* [1973] A.C. 584, HL, in the following *dictum*:

> "If A attacks B and, in doing so, stabs B five times with a knife, has A committed one offence or five? If A in the dwelling-house of B steals ten different chattels, some perhaps from one rooms and some perhaps from others, has he committed one offence or several? ... In my view, such questions when they are asked are best answered by applying a common sense ap-

proach and by deciding what is fair in the circumstances. No precise formula can usefully be laid down, but . . . it will often be legitimate to bring a single charge in respect of what might be called one activity even though that activity may involve more than one act."

Thus no duplicity arose where a defendant had been convicted on two charges of theft and the evidence in relation to each charge revealed that he had stolen a number of separate items from different departments in a store (*R. v. Wilson*, 69 Cr.App.R. 83, CA); where a defendant was convicted on an information alleging the killing of two deer seconds apart (*Jemmison v. Priddle, ante*); where the defendant was charged in a single information with driving without due care and attention in relation to two separately observed incidents occurring two miles apart (*Horrix v. Mallam*, 148 J.P. 30, DC); and where an information charged the unlawful felling of a number of trees even though the felling had taken place over a number of days and there was a possibility of the existence of different defences in relation to different trees (*Cullen v. Jardine* [1985] Crim.L.R. 668, DC). However, in *Amos v. DPP* [1988] R.T.R. 198, DC, it was observed that "a bus driver who curses at a passenger with a cigarette in his mouth and refuses to divulge his destination at the same time is not involved in one activity but in three separate activities of cursing, smoking and refusing to divulge"; and that such conduct could not be charged in a single information. The court said that the rule against duplicity was designed to counter a true risk that there may be confusion in the presenting and meeting of charges which are mixed up and uncertain. To similar effect, the court in *Ministry of Agriculture, Fisheries & Food v. Nunn Corn (1987) Ltd* [1990] Crim.L.R. 268, DC, described the decision in *Cullen v. Jardine, ante*, as the "high water mark" of what does not amount to duplicity, and emphasised that the rule was one of elementary fairness and that its purpose was to enable the defendant to know the case he had to meet, such as when making submissions of no case to answer or pleas in mitigation.

An extension of the concept of a single activity is the principle that an information **4–64** will not be duplicitous if it discloses a "continuous offence". The following *dictum* of Lord Diplock in *DPP v. Merriman, ante*, has been relied on in support of the principle:

"Where a number of acts of a similar nature committed by one or more defendants were connected with one another, in the time and place of their commission or by their common purpose, in such a way that they could fairly be regarded as forming part of the same transaction or criminal enterprise, it was the practice, as early as the eighteenth century, to charge them in a single count of an indictment."

The principle was applied in *DPP v. McCabe*, 157 J.P. 443, DC, where it was held to have been appropriate to charge one offence of theft of 76 library books that were found together in the defendant's home and which must have taken from one or more of 32 different branches of a library owned by the same local authority. In *DPP v. Barton*, 165 J.P. 779, DC, the court, making express reference to the concept of acts forming part of the same criminal enterprise, held that 94 identical thefts of small sums of money committed by an employee from her place of work over a period of a year could be properly be charged in a single information alleging theft of the total amount between the start and finish dates. Each of the individual thefts were identified in a schedule, which particularised every date on which money was stolen and the amount involved. Whilst each line of the schedule could itself have given rise to a separate information, the court held that the charge in a single information was not duplicitous because the defendant did not have different defences in relation to different thefts and because it would have been "oppressive" to have 94 separate informations. The *Barton* approach was expressly approved by Lord Woolf C.J. in *R. v. Tovey ; R. v. Smith* [2005] 2 Cr.App.R.(S.) 100, CA, subject to the caveat that it should not be stretched further to cases where the evidence for the prosecution and the defence raises different issues in relation to the different acts alleged.

A further and related aspect of the concept of a single activity is the "general defi- **4–65** ciency" principle where a closely linked series of offences may be charged together in a single information because no particulars of the individual offences could be given: *R.*

v. Cain and others [1983] Crim.L.R. 802, CA. The rationale underlying cases of this type is that a charge alleging a general deficiency should be permitted because it was otherwise impossible to identify the individual offences. Thus in *R. v. Tomlin* [1954] 2 Q.B. 274, CCA, where a stock take at a shop revealed a cash deficiency since the previous stock-taking, a single count in an indictment alleging embezzlement of the aggregate amount on a day between the two stock takings was held to be maintainable.

4–66   Particular care is required where offences are expressed in statute as disjunctive activities. Informations in such cases must be drafted carefully to identify the precise offence alleged to have been committed. In *Mallon v. Allon* [1964] 1 Q.B. 385, DC, the manager of a licenced betting office had been convicted on an information which alleged that he had unlawfully admitted a person under the age of 18 and allowed him to remain contrary to section 5 of, and paragraph 2 of Schedule 2 to the *Betting and Gaming Act* 1960; the information was held to be duplicitous because section 5 of the Act created a single offence of contravening a rule in the schedule, yet the information alleged that two offences had been committed by the two separate activities of admitting and allowing to remain. The care required in relation to such offences will be all the more necessary where the penalty depends on the nature in which the offence was committed.

4–67   The rule against duplicity does not apply where two offences are set out in a single document: r.7.3(2); and a single document may contain a preamble containing particulars common to a number of otherwise separate allegations: *Shah v. Swallow* [1984] 1 W.L.R. 886, HL.

If it appears to the court at any stage in a trial that the information is duplicitous the court must ask the prosecutor to elect which offence he wished the court to proceed on. Where an election is made, the other offence must be struck out of the information and the court must then proceed to try the information afresh (possibly after adjournment if unfair prejudice has been occasioned to the defendant). Failure by the prosecutor to make the election will result in the information being dismissed: *Fox v. Dingley*; *Ware v. Fox* [1967] 1 W.L.R. 379, DC.

(c) *Statement of offence*

4–68   See *Criminal Procedure Rules* 2005, r.7.2 in Appendix G–23.

4–69   Under Article 6(3) of the European Convention on Human Rights every person charged with an offence has the right to be informed promptly, in a language that he understands, and in detail, of the nature and cause of the accusation. The purpose of this right is to provide the accused with the information needed to prepare a defence. Thus the information required must be more specific than the grounds of arrest required under Article 5(2) of the Convention.

The information must give sufficient particulars of the offence being charged which includes details of the legislative provisions, *i.e.* the Act, Schedule, regulations or rules which create the offence; reasonable information about the nature of the charge and elements of the offence alleged to have been committed and clear information about the place and date of the alleged offence: *Atterton v. Brown* [1945] K.B. 122, DC; *Stephenson v. Johnson* [1954] 1 W.L.R. 375, DC; *R. v. Abergavenny J, ex p. Barratt* [1994] R.T.R. 98, DC.

In *Dacre Son & Hartley Ltd v. North Yorkshire Trading Standards*, 169 J.P. 59, DC, it was held that when a challenge was made to the adequacy of particulars or a defect in the information, the critical issue was whether the defendant was prejudiced by the way in which the information was worded. The court said in this instance, the defendant was clear the case was against him because advanced information had been served and no prejudice was caused. If, however, critical aspects of the prosecution case that should have been revealed in the information in advance of the trial only become clear for the first time during the trial, then the position might well be different. The detail required in an information is both offence and fact dependent; a decision as to the adequacy of the particulars will therefore depend on the precise nature of the offence charged and the factual allegations upon which the charge depends. This approach was confirmed in the case of *Nash v. Birmingham Crown Court*, 169 J.P. 157, DC, where it was held that a defendant was entitled to know from the details of a summons what specific act or omission he was charged with. Here the summons alleged causing suffering to animals without specifying the conduct that amounted to the cruelty. Simply alleging causing suffering was held not to provide sufficient information. However, it was also held that since further information was given in time to the defendant this cured the defect.

A magistrate may not reconsider an application which has already been rejected by a fellow magistrate if there has been no material change to the substance of the information: *R. v. Worthing JJ, ex p. Norvell* [1981] 1 W.L.R. 413, DC.

(d) *Joint offenders*

An information may charge two or more defendants with having jointly committed **4–70** an offence: *R. v. Lipscombe, ex p. Biggins* (1862) 26 J.P. 244.

(4) Time-limit for laying the information

Magistrates' Courts Act 1980, s.127

Limitation of time

127.—(1) Except as otherwise expressly provided by any enactment and subject to subsection **4–71** (2) below, a magistrates' court shall not try an information or hear a complaint unless the information was laid, or the complaint made, within 6 months from the time when the offence was committed, or the matter of complaint arose.

(2) Nothing in—

    (a) subsection (1) above; or

    (b) subject to subsection (4) below, any other enactment (however framed or worded) which, as regards any offence to which it applies, would but for this section impose a time-limit on the power of a magistrates' court to try an information summarily or impose a limitation on the time for taking summary proceedings,

shall apply in relation to any indictable offence.

(3) Without prejudice to the generality of paragraph (b) of subsection (2) above, that paragraph includes enactments which impose a time-limit that applies only in certain circumstances (for example, where the proceedings are not instituted by or with the consent of the Director of Public Prosecutions or some other specified authority).

(4) Where, as regards any indictable offence, there is imposed by any enactment (however framed or worked, and whether falling within subsection (2) (b) above or not) a limitation on the time for taking proceedings on indictment for that offence no summary proceedings for that offence shall be taken after the latest time for taking proceedings on indictment.

A statutory time limit applies to the initiation of summary offences which ensures **4–72** prompt prosecution action and discourages delay.

Informations or complaints relating to summary only matters must be laid within six **4–73** months of the offence alleged. Other statutes may expressly provide for different time limits. When calculating computation of time general principles apply which are usually considered in civil rather than criminal case law.

The purpose of the time limit is to ensure that summary offences are charged and tried as soon as reasonably practicable after their commission. This principle was confirmed and elaborated upon in the case of *R. v. Scunthorpe Justices, ex p. McPhee and Gallagher*, 162 J.P. 635, DC.

When time is computed the day of the offence is excluded: *Stewart v. Chapman* [1951] 2 K.B. 792, DC. For periods calculated in months, the period ends at midnight on the day in the subsequent month that bears the same number as the day of the earlier month or the preceding number if no such number appears in the subsequent month: *Dodds v. Walker* [1981] 1 W.L.R. 1027, HL.

For an offence taking place continuously or intermittently over a period of time, the period runs from each day on which the offence is committed. There is no jurisdiction to hear an information in respect of offences alleged to have been committed more than six months prior to the date of the information: *R. v. Chertsey Justices, ex p. Franks* [1961] 2 Q.B. 152, DC.

Where a statute expressly provides for a different time-limit prohibiting the institution of a prosecution after the expiry of a specified period "from its discovery by the prosecutor", the relevant discovery is one which gives rise to a reasonable belief that an offence has been committed: *Tesco Stores Ltd v. London Borough of Harrow*, 167 J.P. 657, DC. This approach was approved in *R. v. Gale*, 169 J.P. 166, CA, where the accused had been placed under observation after information had been received that he was operating an unlicenced slaughterhouse, and several days later his premises were entered and slaughtered animals were discovered. It was held that the date of the "discovery" of the offence was date when the premises had been entered, since before that date there was evidence giving rise to suspicion but not knowledge of the "material facts which would found the offence".

If it is unclear whether an information has been laid within the requisite time the defendant is entitled to the benefit of the doubt: *Lloyd v. Young* [1963] Crim.L.R. 703, DC. It is important that the summons should clearly show the date when the information was laid so there is no doubt that the time limit was observed.

In *Atkinson v. DPP* [2005] 1 W.L.R. 96, DC, the court said that where magistrates were in doubt of the date when an information was laid jurisduction should not be accepted. In this case the information was dated a few days before the expiry of the time limit but the summons itself was issued some days after the limit. On the basis that the information could have been amended by the police whilst it was in the system awaiting being considered and a summons being issued it was held that the court could not be satisfied that the time limits had been compiled with.

There is not power to re-open a case following a mistaken ruling on the expiration of time limits. The *Verderers of the New Forest v. Young* [2005] A.C.D. 22, DC.

4–74   Delay in the laying of an information, although strictly within the time limits, is a factor which may be taken into account by the magistrate in deciding whether to issue a summons. A magistrate is entitled to inquire into the reasons for the delay in laying an information even when the statutory time limit has not been breached: *R. v. Clerk to the Medway JJ, ex p. Department of Health and Social Security* [1986] Crim.L.R. 686, DC; *Wei Hai Restaurant Ltd v. Kingston upon Hull City Council*, 166 J.P. 185, DC.

In the *Scunthorpe Justices* case (see *ante*) the defendant was charged with robbery. He tendered pleas to common assault and theft which the CPS were willing to accept. The court refused to allow the charge to be amended on the basis that the six month time-limit in respect of the assault charge had expired. On appeal the court recognised that the purpose of the time limit was to expedite the trial of summary matters but the court held that a charge could be amended to include a summary matter even if the limit had run out provided the new offence arose out of the same misdoing as the original charge and it was in the interests of justice to amend: *R. v. Scunthorpe Justices, ex p. McPhee and Gallagher* 162 J.P. 635, DC. However, in *Sainsbury's Supermarkets Ltd and J. Sainsbury plc v. Plymouth Magistrates' Court*, 170 J.P. 690, DC, it was held that where an offence had been committed by a subsidiary company, the information could not be amended outside the time-limit so as to charge the parent company with the offence; the effect would otherwise to be to prefer a charge against a new defendant outside the time limit since the two companies were distinct legal entities.

In *Manchester Stipendiary Magistrate ex p. Hill* [1983] 1 A.C. 328, the House of Lords considered in detail the process of laying informations before the magistrates. It was held that the information was laid and time stopped running on the offence when the information was received at the office of the justices' clerk. The receipt of the information was a "ministerial" act that can be performed by any member of staff and the information did not need to have been considered personally by the justices' clerk at that stage. In *Rockall v. Department for Environment, Food and Rural Affairs*, *The Times*, May 11, 2007, DC, it was held that where proceedings were instituted by the laying of an information sent by fax, the point at which the information was properly to be regarded as laid was the point at which the fax was retrievable, whether or not in fact retrieved. Whether the fax was retrievable was a matter to be established by inference or otherwise; and in the absence of any contrary evidence, fax headers and transmission sheets were capable of establishing the necessary facts.

C. ISSUING AND SERVICE OF SUMMONSES

(1) General

Upon the laying of an information a district judge or magistrate or other authorised **4–75** person may issue a summons requiring the person named in the information to appear before the court. A district judge or magistrate in addition has power to issue a warrant of arrest to bring the person named in the information before a magistrates' court: as to which, see §§ 4–89 *et seq.*

Magistrates' Courts Act 1980, s.1

Issue of summons to accused or warrant for his arrest

1.—(1) On an information being laid before a justice of the peace that a person has, or is **4–76** suspected of having committed an offence, the justice may issue—

    (a) a summons directed to that person requiring him to appear before a magistrates' court to answer the information, or

    (b) a warrant to arrest that person and bring him before a magistrates' court.

(2) [*Repealed by the* Courts Act *2003*].

(3) No warrant shall be issued under this section unless the information is in writing.

(4) No warrant shall be issued under this section for the arrest of any person who has attained the age of 18 unless—

    (a) the offence to which the warrant relates is an indictable offence or is punishable with imprisonment,or

    (b) the person's address is not sufficiently established for a summons to be served on him.

(5) [*Repealed by the* Courts Act *2003*].

(6) Where the offence charged is an indictable offence, a warrant under this section may be issued at any time notwithstanding that a summons has previously been issued.

(7) A justice of the peace may issue a summons or warrant under this section upon an information being laid before him notwithstanding any enactment requiring the information to be laid before two or more justices.

(8) [*Repealed by the* Courts Act *2003*].

[This section is printed as amended by the *Criminal Justice Act* 1991, Sched. 8, the *Courts Act* 2003, s.43 and Sched. 10, and the *Criminal Justice Act* 2003, Sched. 36. As from a day to be appointed, the *Criminal Justice Act* 2003, Sched. 36, will make further amendments to sub-sections (3) and (6) and will insert new subsections (6A) and (7A), the effect being to make provision in connection with written charges and requisitions.]

Once an information has been laid, the decision as to whether a summons or warrant **4–77** of arrest should issue under the section is a judicial function to be exercised by a district judge or magistrate. Under the *Justices' Clerks Rules* 2005 (S.I. 2005 No. 545) this function may be exercised by a justices' clerk or an assistant clerk who has been specifically authorised by the justices' clerk for that purpose. In *Gateshead Justices, ex p. Tesco Stores Ltd* [1981] Q.B. 470, DC, the applicant's summary convictions were quashed because the informations had been processed by assistants in the clerk's office who issued the summonses without referring them to a justice or a justices' clerk. The granting of summonses is more than a rubber-stamping exercise. The person considering the issue of the summons must be authorised to do so and must scrutinise the information to satisfy themselves that the requirements are met and that a summons may properly be granted.

(2) Form and content of summons

4–78   See *Criminal Procedure Rules* 2005, r.7.7 in Appendix G–39.

A summons must be signed by the person issuing it whether that is a district judge, magistrate, justices' clerk or authorised assistant. Alternatively the summons may be marked with the name of the person who granted it either in the form of a rubber stamp or electronic signature. The summons must state the time and place at which the person named in the summons is to appear.

There remains a discretion to issue the summons even if the information discloses an offence at law and is laid within the time-limits. The person considering the information must apply his mind to the contents and make a judicial decision whether to issue the summons. Application may be refused if it is vexatious or oppressive.

In *R. (DPP) v. Taylor* [2005] A.C.D. 23, QBD, the CPS advised the defendant that he would not be prosecuted for careless driving after a fatal road traffic accident. Following representations made to them by the victim's family, the CPS subsequently applied for a summons. It was held that the magistrates' refusal to issue a summons in those circumstances was a lawful exercise of their discretion and that the interests of justice test had been properly applied. But in the case of *R. (Mayor and Burgess of London Borough of Newham) v. Stratford Magistrates' Court*, 168 J.P. 658, QBD, the local authority applied for several summonses under both the *Trade Descriptions Act* 1968 and for offences of obtaining cash by deception under the *Theft Act* 1968. The informations were queried by the magistrates who were of the view that to issue summonses under both statutes would be duplicitous and the criminality of the defendant could be adequately reflected in fewer summonses. On appeal it was held that the magistrates had exceeded their discretion. The general principle was that the magistrates ought to issue summonses pursuant to informations, which, *prima facie*, were properly laid, unless there were compelling reasons not to do so, most obviously if an abuse of process or impropriety was involved; if where informations were properly laid, everything else was in order, and there was no abuse of process or impropriety involved, it was not the function of the magistrates' court at that stage to decide how the matter could thereafter be most fairly tried or dealt with.

4–79   The proposed defendant has no right to be heard when a summons is applied for but the court has a discretion to allow him to attend: *R. v. West London JJ, ex p. Klahn* [1979] 1 W.L.R. 933, DC. The person considering the issuing of a summons is entitled to make inquiries beyond the information, but is not under any duty to do so: *R. v. Clerk to the Bradford JJ, ex p. Sykes*, 163 J.P. 224, DC.

The decision whether to issue a summons is subject to judicial review by the Administrative Court: *R. v. Horseferry Road JJ, ex p. Independent Broadcasting Authority* [1987] Q.B. 54, DC. The High Court may quash a summons where it was issued in abuse of the process of the court and the allegations made were vexatious and oppressive: *R. v. Bury JJ, ex p. Anderton* [1987] Crim.L.R. 638, DC. Likewise, the reviewing court may compel the issue of a summons unreasonably refused.

(3) Effect of defective summons

Magistrates' Courts Act 1980, s.123

Defect in process

4–80   **123.**—(1) No objection shall be allowed to any information or complaint, or to any summons or warrant to procure the presence of the defendant, for any defect in it in substance or in form, or for any variance between it and the evidence adduced on behalf of the prosecutor or complainant at the hearing of the information or complaint.

(2) If it appears to a magistrates' court that any variance between a summons or warrant and the evidence adduced on behalf of the prosecutor or complainant is such that the

defendant has been misled by the variance, the court shall, on the application of the defendant, adjourn the hearing.

An irregularity or illegality in the mode of bringing a defendant before the court, if **4–81** not objected to at the hearing, does not invalidate the conviction: *Gray v. Customs Commissioners*, 48 J.P. 343, DC.

Although no objection is allowed to any information or complaint, or to any summons or warrant, for any defect in its substance or form, if the magistrate considers that any variance between a summons or warrant and the evidence adduced on behalf of the prosecutor or complainant is such that the defendant has been misled by that variance, the court must on the application of the defendant, adjourn the hearing. The effect of section 123(2) is that a summons can be amended: *Meek v. Powell* [1952] 1 K.B. 164, DC.

The amendment of an information by a magistrates' court is subject to judicial review and is liable to be quashed: *R. v. Greater Manchester JJ, ex p. Aldi GmbH & Co KG*, 159 J.P. 717, DC; *Marco (Croydon) Ltd v. Metropolitan Police* [1984] R.T.R. 24, DC.

A summons may be amended even if by the time the case comes before the court and the application to amend is made, the six months' time limit for laying an information in section 127 of the *Magistrates' Courts Act* 1980 has expired: *R v. Newcastle JJ, ex p. Bryce* [1976] R.T.R. 325, DC; *R. v. Sandwell J, ex p. West Midlands Passenger Transport Board* [1979] Crim.L.R. 56, DC.

The Divisional Court in *R. v. Scunthorpe JJ, ex p. McPhee*, 162 J.P. 635, DC, **4–82** enunciated the principles. The defendant was charged with robbery and it was held that the CPS could amend the charges to common assault and theft despite the fact that the six-month time limit in respect of the assault charge had expired. The Court held that the proper test was whether the new offences arose from the same or substantially the same facts and if they did, then the charges could be amended, having regard to the interests of justice and in particular the defendant's interest and the purpose of the time limit. See also *R. v. Blackburn JJ, ex p. Holmes*, 164 J.P. 163, DC; *R. v. Thames Magistrates' Court, ex p. Stevens*, 164 J.P. 233, DC; *R. (DPP) v. Everest*, 169 J.P. 345, QBD; and *cf. Sainsbury's Supermarkets Ltd and J. Sainsbury plc v. Plymouth Magistrates' Court*, 170 J.P. 690, DC.

The power of the magistrates to allow an application to amend and information was considered in *R. (James) v. DPP*, 168 J.P. 596, QBD. The defendant was charged with supplying a Class B drug contrary to section 4(1) of the *Misuse of Drugs Act* 1971. At the close of the defence case, a submission was made that the evidence did not make out the offence of supplying but only amounted to an attempt to supply. The prosecution then made application under section 123(1) to amend the information to charge the offence of attempting to supply a drug contrary to the *Criminal Attempts Act* 1981. The defendant objected to any amendment on the grounds that it was a major change with a different offence charged under a different statute. The magistrates allowed the amendment. On appeal by the defendant, the court held that the magistrates were acting within their powers under section 123 to amend the information. The wording of the section was very wide and there is no authority indicating the existence of any restriction on an amendment that resulted in a different offence under a different act of parliament being substituted. The main issue was to consider whether any injustice or prejudice would be caused to the defendant by such an amendment. In this case the defendant had suffered no prejudice. This case asserts the wide scope of section 123 and indicates that in the magistrates' court as in the Crown Court there is an extensive discretion to amend an information. It would appear to allow for the prosecution to see what offence is made out in the evidence and then apply to amend the charge to fit it with the only proviso being that the defendant must not be prejudiced thereby and would be entitled to an adjournment to address the changes if that is required in the interests of justice.

The power to amend and adjourn under section 123(2) is available until the case is ended and the magistrates are *"functus officio"*, so it is possible for a case to be adjourned after conviction and the charge amended before sentence: see *Allan v. Wiseman* [1975] Crim.L.R. 37, DC, where the defendant's name was amended on the charge after conviction but before the case was ended.

(4) Service of summons in the UK

4–83   See *Criminal Procedure Rules* 2005, Pt 4, in Appendix G–14 *et seq.* As from April 6, 2007, the *Criminal Procedure (Amendment) Rules* 2007 (S.I. 2007 No. 699) radically restated the rules contained in the part as to the service of documents. In particular, see rule 4.7. A summons or requisition may only be served on an individual by: (a) handing it to him in person; or (b) leaving it at, or sending it to by first class post, an address (i) where it is reasonably believed that the individual will receive it, or (ii) which is the office of the individual's legal representative. Modified versions of the same requirements apply to the service of summonses or requisitions on corporations.

4–84   If a person voluntarily attends the court, that attendance cures any want of process or any irregularity in service: *Hughes* (1879) L.R. 4 Q.B.D. 614, CCR. However where a person attends before a magistrate to draw attention to the irregularity and then withdraws from the case such conduct does not amount to an appearance so as to waive irregularity in service: *Pearks, Gunston & Tee Ltd v. Richardson* [1902] 1 K.B. 91, DC. Where the person appears before the magistrates' court he should be informed of the irregularity or omission and of the right to object because without that knowledge there can be no waiver: *R. v. Essex Justices, ex p. Perkins* [1927] 2 K.B. 475, DC.

(5) Service of summons overseas

Crime (International Co-operation) Act 2003, ss.3, 4 and 51(3)

General requirements for service of process
4–85   **3.**—(1) This section applies to any process issued or made for the purposes of criminal proceedings by a court in England and Wales or Northern Ireland.

(2) The process may be issued or made in spite of the fact that the person on whom it is to be served is outside the United Kingdom.

(3) Where the process is to be served outside the United Kingdom and the person at whose request it is issued or made believes that the person on whom it is to be served does not understand English, he must—

     (a) inform the court of that fact, and

     (b) provide the court with a copy of the process, or of so much of it as is material, translated into an appropriate language.

(4) Process served outside the United Kingdom requiring a person to appear as a party or attend as a witness—

     (a) must not include notice of a penalty,

     (b) must be accompanied by a notice giving any information required to be given by rules of court.

(5) If process requiring a person to appear as a party or attend as a witness is served outside the United Kingdom, no obligation to comply with the process under the law of the part of the United Kingdom in which the process is issued or made is imposed by virtue of the service.

(6) Accordingly, failure to comply with the process does not constitute contempt of court and is not a ground for issuing a warrant to secure the attendance of the person in question.

(7) But the process may subsequently be served on the person in question in the United Kingdom (with the usual consequences for non-compliance).

Service of process otherwise than by post
4–86   **4.**—(1) Process to which section 3 applies may, instead of being served by post, be served on a person outside the United Kingdom in accordance with arrangements made by the Secretary of State.

(2) But where the person is in a participating country, the process may be served in accordance with those arrangements only if one of the following conditions is met.

(3) The conditions are—
- (a) that the correct address of the person is unknown,
- (b) that it has not been possible to serve the process by post,
- (c) that there are good reasons for thinking that service by post will not be effective or is inappropriate.

General interpretation

51.—(3) In this Part, "process", in relation to England and Wales and Northern Ireland, **4–87** means any summons or order issued or made by a court and includes—
- (a) any other document issued or made by a court for service on parties or witnesses,
- (b) any document issued by a prosecuting authority outside the United Kingdom for the purposes of criminal proceedings.

See *Criminal Procedure Rules* 2005, r.32.1 (Appendix G–182), for the form and **4–88** content of the notice which, under section 3(4)(b), must accompany process served outside the United Kingdom requiring a person to appear as a party or attend as a witness. In particular, the notice must state that the person required by the process to appear as a party or attend as a witness can obtain information about his rights in connection therewith from the prosecuting authority which requested the process to be served (or in the case of a private prosecution, the court by which the process is served); and give particulars about that authority: r.32.1(2), (3). The particulars which must be given are the name and contact details of the prosecuting authority (or court) and the name and contact details of a person who can provide information about the rights of the person concerned: r.32.1(4). The justices' clerk must send, together with any process served outside the United Kingdom, any translation which is provided under section 3(3)(b) of the Act, any translation of the information required to be given by this rule which is provided to him: r.32.1(5).

V. WARRANTS OF ARREST AND STATUTORY DECLARATIONS

A. GENERAL

A warrant is the authority for the arrest of a person in certain defined circumstances, **4–89** issued either at the start of proceedings, or to secure attendance as they progress.

B. ISSUE OF WARRANT ON INFORMATION BEING LAID

Introduction

Summonses are generally issued for minor offences, which are summary only and **4–90** not imprisonable (*e.g.* most road traffic offences) where the name and address of the defendant are known. A summons may be issued for more serious offences, *e.g.* criminal damage or assault but usually only if the name of the defendant is known and he has a fixed address. If the information discloses more serious offences which are imprisonable and there are doubts over the whereabouts of the defendant or the likelihood of his answering a summons, a warrant may issue.

Magistrates' Courts Act 1980, s.1

See *ante*, § 4–60 for the wording of the section. Section 31 of the *Criminal Justice* **4–91** *Act* 2003 removed the requirement for the written information to be substantiated on oath.

This section gives the Court the power to ensure the attendance at court of a defendant to answer to charges disclosed in an information. A warrant issued under section 1 is referred to as a "first instance" warrant as it is the first step taken to bring a defendant to court who has not otherwise appeared to answer the charge. Applications for warrants under section 1 are made by individual police officers. The information will be in writing on a standard form and has to be signed by the officer. The information will outline the details of the offence and give the name and address (where known) of the person to be arrested. The information will be checked by court staff to ensure that the offence is indictable or punishable with imprisonment and if it is not the warrant will only issue if the address of the defendant is not known. The application will be dealt with either in court or in the retiring rooms as they are *ex parte* applications. In cases of urgency it may also be possible for application to be made out of hours to a district judge or magistrate at home.

The court will consider whether the warrant should be backed for bail or not but as a warrant will be issued in preference to a summons this would indicate that bail may not be appropriate: *Magistrates' Courts Act* 1980, s.117.

C. ISSUE OF WARRANT TO SECURE ATTENDANCE OF ACCUSED

Magistrates' Courts Act 1980, s.13

Non-appearance of accused: issue of warrant

4–92   **13.**—(1) Subject to the provisions of this section, where the court, instead of proceeding in the absence of the accused, adjourns or further adjourns the trial, the court may, issue a warrant for his arrest.

(2) Where a summons has been issued, the court shall not issue a warrant under this section unless the condition in subsection (2A) below or that in subsection (2B) below is fulfilled.

(2A) The condition in this subsection is that it is proved to the satisfaction of the court, on oath or in such other manner as may be prescribed, that the summons was served on the accused within what appears to the court to be a reasonable time before the trial or adjourned trial.

(2B) The condition in this subsection is that—

(a) the adjournment now being made is a second or subsequent adjournment of the trial.

(b) the accused was present on the last (or only) occasion when the trial was adjourned, and

(c) on that occasion the court determined the time for the hearing at which the adjournment is now being made.

(3) A warrant for the arrest of any person who has attained the age of 18 shall not be issued under this section unless—

(a) the offence to which the warrant relates is punishable with imprisonment, or

(b) the court, having convicted the accused, proposes to impose a disqualification on him.

(3A) A warrant for the arrest of any person who has not attained the age of 18 shall not be issued under this section unless—

(a) the offence to which the warrant relates is punishable in the case of a person who has attained the age of 18, with imprisonment, or

(b) the court, having convicted the accused, proposes to impose a disqualification on him.

(4) This section shall not apply to an adjournment on the occasion of the accused's conviction in his absence under subsection (5) of section 12 above or to an adjournment required by subsection (9) of that section.

(5) Where the court adjourns the trial—

(a) after having, either on that or on a previous occasion, received any evidence or convicted the accused without hearing evidence on his pleading guilty under section 9(3) above; or

(b) after having on a previous occasion convicted the accused without hearing evidence on his pleading guilty under 12(5) above,

the court shall not issue a warrant under this section unless it thinks it undesirable, by reason of the gravity of the offence, to continue the trial in the absence of the accused.

[This section is printed as amended by the *Criminal Procedure and Investigations Act* 1996, s.48, the *Magistrates' Courts (Procedure) Act* 1998, s.3, and the *Criminal Justice Act* 2003, s.31 and Sched. 37.]

The requirement for the information to be substantiated on oath is removed. The **4–93** new requirement is substituted that the offence is punishable with imprisonment for a person who has attained the age of 18.

This section gives power for the court to issue a warrant during the proceedings if the defendant fails to attend at court. It is most commonly used in road traffic matters. In such cases the court will first ensure that the summons has been properly served and that the defendant has had reasonable time to attend at court. If so satisfied the court may then proceed with the case in the absence of the defendant. If the case is proved the court may wish to disqualify the defendant from driving. If the court does not wish to disqualify and sentence him in absence the case may be adjourned and a notice sent to the defendant requiring him to attend. If he fails to attend after the adjournment notice is sent a warrant may be issued under this section. A warrant may also issue after a written plea of guilty has been received and the court wishes to impose a disqualification in the defendant's presence.

The court will need to consider whether a section 13 warrant should be backed for bail and will take into account the defendants attendance record and the gravity of the offence: *Magistrates' Courts Act* 1980, s.117.

D. STATUTORY DECLARATIONS

The court may not always issue a warrant for the arrest of a defendant who fails to **4–94** attend court. There is a discretion for the court to proceed with the case in the absence of the defendant under section 11 of the *Magistrates' Courts Act* 1980. The Act provides a safeguard for the absent defendant by allowing for proceedings commenced by way of summons to be invalidated when the defendant makes and serves a statutory declaration to the effect that he did not attend court because he was unaware of the court hearing date.

Magistrates' Courts Act 1980, s.14

Proceedings invalid where accused did not know of them

14.—(1) Where a summons has been issued under section 1 above and a magistrates' court **4–95** has begun to try the information to which the summons relates, then, if—

   (a) the accused, at any time during or after the trial, makes a statutory declaration that he did not know of the summons or the proceedings until a date specified in the declaration, being a date after the court has begun to try the information; and

   (b) within 21 days of that date the declaration is served on the designated officer for the court,

without prejudice to the validity of the information, the summons and all subsequent proceedings shall be void.

(2) For the purposes of subsection (1) above a statutory declaration shall be deemed to be duly served on the designated officer if it is delivered to him, or left at his office, or is sent in a registered letter or by the recorded delivery service addressed to him at his office.

(3) If on the application of the accused it appears to a magistrates' court (which for this purpose may be composed of a single justice) that it was not reasonable to expect the accused to serve such a statutory declaration as is mentioned in subsection (1) above within the period allowed by that subsection, the court may accept service of such a declaration by the accused after that period has expired; and a statutory declaration accepted under this subsection shall be deemed to have been served as required by that subsection.

(4) Where any proceedings have become void by virtue of subsection (1) above, the information shall not be tried again by any of the same justices.

[This section is printed as amended by the *Courts Act* 2003, Sched. 8.]

In proceedings in the magistrates' court, particularly those commenced by way of **4–96** summons, the prosecution may present the case in the absence of the defendant if the court is satisfied that the summons has been properly served.

Many cases are dealt with in this way, *e.g.* road traffic cases, but caution must be exercised and the seriousness of the offence will be taken into account. See also the guidelines in *Jones* at § 7–23. The prosecution evidence is heard, which usually consists of statements from prosecution witnesses which have been served under section 9 of the *Criminal Justice Act* 1967 and the court will go on to acquit or convict the defendant. If convicted, an adjournment notice may be sent to the defendant requiring his presence for sentencing and if he fails to answer to the notice a warrant may be issued for his arrest. The court may also proceed to sentence in absence.

The first a defendant may know about the proceedings is when an adjournment notice or notice of fine is received or a warrant is executed. It is then open to the defendant to make a statutory declaration under this section that he knew nothing of the proceedings and if that declaration is served on the court then the proceedings are invalidated. The additional requirement is that the declaration should be served on the court within 21 days of the date when the proceedings first came to the notice of the defendant but the court does have a discretion to accept service outside of the 21-day limit if it is not reasonable to expect the defendant to serve the declaration within that time.

Defendants will often make such declarations at court but it is possible for them to be made before a solicitor, etc. It is not necessary for the declaration to be made before the court where the proceedings took place but this will often be the case.

4–97   The effect of accepting service of the declaration is that the summons and all proceedings based on it will be void but the information is not affected: *Singh v. DPP* [1999] R.T.R. 424, DC. The Court will expunge the conviction and penalty from the records. The Prosecution has the right to re-institute proceedings using the original information and if present in court at the time when the statutory declaration is made and served, application may be made by the prosecution to re-issue the summons immediately and serve it personally on the defendant. Proceedings will then start again but must be tried before a fresh bench.

A defendant who knowingly and wilfully makes a false statement relating to his knowledge of the proceedings under this section may be prosecuted for perjury under section 5 of the *Perjury Act* 1911 and the applicant will be given a warning to this effect when the declaration is made.

I. INTRODUCTION

Cases in the magistrates' court are not always concluded at the first hearing. The **5–1** *Magistrates' Courts Act* 1980 confers powers of adjournment in several different circumstances and also gives the court power on adjournment to remand the accused either in custody or on bail during the period of any adjournment: section 128 of the *Magistrates' Courts Act* 1980.

Any decision to remand a person in criminal proceedings must be made in accordance with the provisions of the *Bail Act* 1976. The Act has been extensively amended by the *Magistrates' Courts Act* 1980, the *Criminal Justice Acts* of 1988 and 1991, the *Criminal Justice and Public Order Act* 1994 and the *Crime and Disorder Act* 1998. It is also amended by the *Criminal Justice Act* 2003, ss.13–21. Section 13, parts of section 15, sections 16, 17, 19, 20 and 21 came into force in April 2004. Section 18 came into force on April 4, 2005. Sections 14 and 15 came into force partially on January 1, 2007.

Under the *Bail Act* 1976 there is a general presumption that bail will be granted: **5–2** section 4(1). Bail can only be withheld if the exceptions to bail, listed in Schedule 1 to the Act, apply. When the court finds the exceptions to apply they must explain their reasons. The question of bail must be considered every time that an accused person appears before the court: section 4(2). When the accused appears in answer to bail or is brought before the court in custody and the case is to be adjourned, the court will invite the prosecution to make representations on bail. The prosecution may object to bail and explain the reasons why (Schedule 1 exceptions) or propose conditional or unconditional bail. The defence may then make an application for bail, arguing that either the exceptions are not made out or that the objections can be addressed by the imposition of conditions. The court has an inquisitorial role in bail proceedings and may ask questions of both parties to ensure that it has the required information to enable a proper decision on bail to be made. Also, notwithstanding any agreement reached by the prosecution and defence, it is the decision of the court whether bail should be granted and with what conditions.

The presumption of bail has been affected by the *Criminal Justice and Public Order Act* 1994 which requires that in respect of some specified serious offences, bail shall only be granted if there are exceptional circumstances to justify it.

The *Bail Act* 1976 must be applied so as to be compatible with Article 5 of the European Convention on Human Rights which secures the right to liberty. No person shall be deprived of their liberty save in specified circumstances and in accordance with a procedure prescribed by law. Article 5(1)(c) allows for detention in order to bring a person before a competent legal authority on reasonable suspicion of having committed a crime.

5–3   In relation to bail decisions, the European Court has said domestic courts must, "examine all the facts arguing for and against the existence of a genuine requirement of public interest justifying…a departure from the rule of respect for individual liberty and set them out in their decisions on applications for release": *Wemhoff v. Germany* [1979] 1 E.H.R.R. 55.

Case law also requires that the court must consider if there are "relevant and sufficient reasons" to justify detention and these reasons must be given: *Letellier v. France* [1992] 14 E.H.R.R. 83. This was held to require the exercise of a judicial discretion in reaching bail decisions which cannot be restricted by law: *CC v. UK* (1999) E.H.R.L.R. 210.

II. COURT BAIL

A. Gᴇɴᴇʀᴀʟ Rɪɢʜᴛ ᴛᴏ Bᴀɪʟ

Bail Act 1976, s.1

Meaning of "bail in criminal proceedings"
5–4   **1.**—(1) In this Act "bail in criminal proceedings" means—

         (a) bail grantable in or in connection with proceedings for an offence to a person who is accused or convicted of the offence, or

         (b) bail grantable in connection with an offence to a person who is under arrest for the offence or for whose arrest for the offence a warrant (endorsed for bail) is being issued.

(2) In this Act "bail" means bail grantable under the law (including common law) for the time being in force.

(3) Except as provided by section 13(3) of this Act, this section does not apply to bail in or in connection with proceedings outside England and Wales.

(4) Repealed.

(5) This section applies—

         (a) Whether the offence was committed in England or Wales or elsewhere, and

         (b) whether it is an offence under the law of England and Wales, or of any other country or territory.

(6) Bail in criminal proceedings shall be granted (and in particular shall be granted unconditionally or conditionally) in accordance with this Act.

[This section is reprinted as amended by the *Criminal Justice and Public Order Act* 1994, Sched. 11, para. 2.]

Bail Act 1976, s.2

Other definitions
5–5   **2.**—(1) In this Act, unless the context otherwise requires, "conviction" includes—

Part I

        (a) a finding of guilt,

        (b) a finding that a person is not guilty by reason of insanity,

        (c) a finding under section 11(1) of the *Powers of Criminal Courts (Sentencing) Act* 2000 (remand for medical examination) that the person in question did the act or made the omission charged, and

        (d) a conviction of an offence for which an order is made discharging the offender absolutely or conditionally,

        and "convicted" shall be construed accordingly.

  (2) In this Act, unless the context otherwise requires—

"bail hostel" means premises for the accommodation of persons remanded on bail,

"child" means a person under the age of fourteen,

"court" includes a judge of a court, or a justice of the peace and, in the case of a specified court, includes a judge or (as the case may be) justice having powers to act in connection with proceedings before that court,

"Courts-Martial Appeal rules" means rules made under section 49 of the *Courts-Martial (Appeals) Act* 1968,

"offence" includes an alleged offence,

"probation hostel" means premises for the accommodation of persons who may be required to reside there by a community order under section 177 of the *Criminal Justice Act* 2003,

"proceedings against a fugitive offender" means proceedings under the *Extradition Act* 1989 or section 2(1) or 4(3) of the *Backing of Warrants (Republic of Ireland) Act* 1965,

"surrender to custody" means, in relation to a person released on bail, surrendering himself into the custody of the court or of the constable (according to the requirements of the grant of bail) at the time and place for the time being appointed for him to do so,

"vary", in relation to bail, means imposing further conditions after bail is granted, or varying or rescinding conditions,

"young person" means a person who has attained the age of fourteen and is under the age of seventeen.

  (3) Where an enactment (whenever passed) which relates to bail in criminal proceedings refers to the person bailed appearing before a court it is to be construed unless the context otherwise requires as referring to his surrendering himself into the custody of the court.

  (4) Any reference in this Act to any other enactment is a reference thereto as amended, and includes a reference thereto as extended or applied, by or under any other enactment, including this Act.

[This section is reprinted as amended by the *Powers of Criminal Courts (Sentencing) Act* 2000, Sched. 9, para. (3)(b) and the *Courts Act* 2003, Sched. 10 which came into force on April 1, 2005 and the *Criminal Justice Act* 2003, Sched. 32 which came into force on April 4, 2005.]

  The definition of the term "surrender to custody" has been considered in case law. **5–6** Attendance by a defendant at court and "overtly subjecting himself to the court's directions" by appearance at an arraignment in the Crown Court was held to be a surrender to custody sufficient to relieve a surety of his obligations: *R. v. Central Criminal Court, ex p. Guney* [1995] 2 All E.R. 577 (Bingham L.J. dissenting). Reporting to a court official in accordance with published instructions was held to be a surrender to custody for the purposes of section 2(2) so that no offence was committed under section 6 of failing to surrender but departure from court later in the morning and without waiting for the case to be called on did engage the powers of section 7 and a warrant for arrest could be issued. Once a defendant has surrendered he is under an implied obligation not to leave the court without consent and court officials would be wise to make it clear that a person who reports to them must not leave the court without being given permission to do so: *DPP v. Richards* [1988] Q.B. 701. The question of whether a person has surrendered to custody depends on the facts of the case and not the precise nature of the constraints placed upon them. The fact that there are no security officers or gaolers present in court to restrain the defendant physically does not mean that a defendant cannot surrender to custody. A defendant who left the court after being sentenced to imprisonment rather than wait for the security officers to arrive was held to be unlawfully at large. The argument that he had never surrendered to custody because there was no person there to whose direct control he could submit and so he could not be at large was dismissed by the court on appeal: *Rumble (Jonathan Mark)* [2003] EWCA Crim 770.

Simply arriving at court at the time and place directed is not sufficient. There must be some statement or conduct signifying an indication of acceptance of the court's control: *Reader* (1987) 84 Cr.App.R. 294

Bail Act 1976, s.3

General provisions

5-7   **3.**—(1) A person granted bail in criminal proceedings shall be under a duty to surrender to custody, and that duty is enforceable in accordance with section 6 of this Act.

(2) No recognizance for his surrender to custody shall be taken from him.

(3) Except as provided by this section—

    (a) no security for his surrender to custody shall be taken from him,

    (b) he shall not be required to provide a surety or sureties for his surrender to custody, and

    (c) no other requirement shall be imposed on him as a condition of bail.

(4) He may be required, before release on bail, to provide a surety or sureties to secure his surrender to custody.

(5) He may be required, before release on bail, to give security for his surrender to custody.

The security may be given by him or on his behalf.

(6) He may be required to comply, before release on bail or later, with such requirements as appear to the court to be necessary

    (a) to secure that he surrenders to custody,

    (b) to secure that he does not commit an offence while on bail,

    (c) to secure that he does not interfere with witnesses or otherwise obstruct the course of justice whether in relation to himself or any other person,

    (ca) for his own protection or, if he is a child or young person, for his own welfare or in his own interests,

    (d) to secure that he makes himself available for the purpose of enabling inquiries or a report to be made to assist the court in dealing with him for the offence.

    (e) to secure that before the time appointed for him to surrender to custody, he attends an interview with an authorised advocate or authorised litigator, as defined by section 119(1) of the *Courts and Legal Services Act* 1990;

and, in any Act, "the normal powers to impose conditions of bail" means the powers to impose conditions under paragraph (a), (b), (c) or (ca) above.

(6ZAA) Subject to section 3AA below, if he is a child or young person he may be required to comply with requirements imposed for the purpose of securing the electronic monitoring of his compliance with any other requirement imposed on him as a condition of bail.

(6ZA) Where he is required under subsection (6) above to reside in a bail hostel or probation hostel, he may also be required to comply with the rules of the hostel.

(6A) In the case of a person accused of murder the court granting bail shall, unless it considers that satisfactory reports on his mental condition have already been obtained, impose as conditions of bail—

    (a) a requirement that the accused shall undergo examination by two medical practitioners, for the purpose of enabling such reports to be prepared; and

    (b) a requirement that he shall for that purpose attend such an institution or place as the court directs and comply with any other directions which may be given to him for that purpose by either of those practitioners.

(6B) Of the medical practitioners referred to in subsection (6A) above at least one shall be practitioner approved for the purposes of section 12 of the *Mental Health Act* 1983.

[(6C) Subsection (6D) below applies where—

(a) the court has been notified by the Secretary of State that arrangements for conducting a relevant assessment or, as the case may be, providing relevant follow-up have been made for the petty sessions area in which it appears to the court that the person referred to in subsection (6D) would reside if granted bail; and

(b) the notice has not been withdrawn.

(6D) In the case of a person ("P")—

(a) in relation to whom paragraphs (a) to (c) of paragraph 6B(1) of Part 1 of Schedule 1 to this Act apply;

(b) who, after analysis of the sample referred to in paragraph (b) of that paragraph, has been offered a relevant assessment or, if a relevant assessment has been carried out, has had relevant follow-up proposed to him; and

(c) who has agreed to undergo the relevant assessment or, as the case may be, to participate in the relevant follow-up,

the court, if it grants bail, shall impose as a condition of bail that P both undergo the relevant assessment and participate in any relevant follow-up proposed to him or, if a relevant assessment has been carried out, that P participate in the relevant follow-up.

(6E) In subsections (6C) and *(6D)* above—

(a) "relevant assessment" means an assessment conducted by a suitably qualified person of whether P is dependent upon or has a propensity to misuse any specified Class A drugs;

(b) "relevant follow-up" means, in a case where the person who conducted the relevant assessment believes P to have such a dependency or propensity, such further assessment, and such assistance or treatment (or both) in connection with the dependency or propensity, as the person who conducted the relevant assessment (or conducts any later assessment) considers to be appropriate in P's case,

and in paragraph (a) above "Class A drug" and "misuse" have the same meaning as in the *Misuse of Drugs Act* 1971, and "specified" (in relation to a Class A drug) has the same meaning as in Part 3 of the *Criminal Justice and Court Services Act* 2000.

(6F) In subsection (6E)(a) above, "suitably qualified person" means a person who has such qualifications or experience as are from time to time specified by the Secretary of State for the purposes of this subsection.

(7) If a parent or guardian of a child or young person consents to be surety for the child or young person for the purposes of this subsection, the parent or guardian may be required to secure that the child or young person complies with any requirement imposed on him by virtue of subsection (6)[, (6ZAA)] or (6A) above, but—

(a) no requirement shall be imposed on the parent or the guardian of a young person by virtue of this subsection where it appears that the young person will attain the age of seventeen before the time to be appointed for him to surrender to custody; and

(b) the parent or guardian shall not be required to secure compliance with any requirement to which his consent does not extend and shall not, in respect of those requirements to which his consent does extend, be bound in a sum greater than £50.

(8) Where a court has granted bail in criminal proceedings that court or, where that court has committed a person on bail to the Crown Court for trial or to be sentenced or otherwise dealt with, that court or the Crown Court may on application—

(a) by or on behalf of the person to whom bail was granted, or

(b) by the prosecutor or a constable,

vary the conditions of bail or impose conditions in respect of bail which has been granted unconditionally.

(8A) Where a notice of transfer is given under a relevant transfer provision, subsection (8) above shall have effect in relation to a person in relation to whose case the notice is given as if he has been committed on bail on the Crown Court for trial.

(8B) Subsection (8) above applies where a court has sent a person on bail to the Crown Court for trial under section 51 of the *Crime and Disorder Act* 1998 as it applies where a court has committed a person on bail to the Crown Court for trial.

(9) This section is subject to subsection (3) of section 11 of the *Powers of Criminal Courts (Sentencing) Act* 2000 (conditions of bail on remand for medical examination).

(10) This section is subject, in its application to bail granted by a constable, to section 3A of this Act.

(10) In subsection (8A) above "relevant transfer provision" means—

(a) section 4 of the *Criminal Justice Act* 1987, or

(b) section 53 of the *Criminal Justice Act* 1991.

[This section is reprinted as amended by the *Criminal Justice and Police Act* 2001, s.131(3) and by the *Criminal Justice Act* 2003, ss.13 and 19 which came into force in April 2004.]

5–8   For the definition of failing to surrender, see *ante*, § 5–6. Section 6 provides for the offence of failing to surrender to custody. Under section 3 pre or post-release requirements or conditions may be attached to bail.

Securities and sureties are pre-release conditions. A security is a sum of money or other valuable that the person bailed must deposit with the court before he can be released on bail. The asset will be returned when the case is completed but will be forfeited if the defendant fails to answer his bail: *Bail Act* 1976, s.5. It is easier for a court to accept cash or some other asset that is realisable and not affected by rights of third parties. A security may be deposited by the defendant or someone else on his behalf. Where a defendant deposited the title deeds to his house the court was not obliged to notify his mother who had a registered charge on the property but the security could only extend to the amount of the son's beneficial interest in the house: *R. (Stevens) v. Truro Magistrates' Court* [2002] 1 W.L.R. 144.

A surety is provided by someone other than the defendant. The surety enters into an undertaking that if the defendant fails to surrender to custody the surety will then forfeit the amount of money in which he has stood as surety and if the money cannot be paid the surety may be committed to prison in default: *Bail Act* 1976, s.8; *Magistrates' Courts Act* 1980, s.120. A surety may be taken in court or elsewhere, *e.g.* at a police station. The surety may agree to stand as surety until the next appointed court date or it may be made to be continuous to a certain event, *e.g.* committal to the Crown Court or first appearance at the Crown Court. A continuous surety is not obliged to attend at court in all the interim hearings for his surety to be taken again provided that the date to which he has agreed to stand as surety is clear.

Where the defendant is a child or young person and a parent or guardian stands as surety, the court may require the parent or guardian to ensure that the child or young person complies with any condition imposed: *Bail Act* 1976, s.3(7), *ante*. A condition under section 3(7) can only be imposed with the parent or guardian's consent and the surety may not exceed £50.

5–9   In all cases where bail is granted, whether the offence involved is imprisonable or non-imprisonable, the power to impose conditions under section 3 applies. Bail can only be withheld and a person remanded in custody on the grounds set out in the *Bail Act* 1976 (Scheds 1 and 2) which differ in relation to imprisonable and non-imprisonable offences. Refusal to consent to a condition of bail is not an exception to the right to bail in either case so a defendant cannot be remanded in custody for that reason: *R. v. Bournemouth Justices, ex p. Cross, Griffen and Pamment*, (1989) 89 Cr.App.R. 90.

Sections 3(3)(c) and (6) restrict the conditions that may be imposed where bail is granted.

When considering the imposition of conditions the court does not have to be satisfied that there are substantial grounds for believing that the instances listed in section 3(6) would occur. It is sufficient if the court "perceived a real and not fanciful risk" that the defendant may not surrender to custody, or may commit offences or interfere with witnesses or obstruct justice or not attend for reports or interviews. Conditions may then be necessary to address the risk. The test is more rigorous when the defendant is being refused bail and deprived of his liberty: *R. v. Mansfield Justices, ex p. Sharkey* [1985] 1 Q.B. 613.

5–10   Section 3A of the *Bail Act* 1976 relates to the granting of bail by the custody officer at a police station and gives the power to impose conditions on police bail. Conditions can only be imposed by the police where they appear necessary in order to prevent a failure to surrender, or the commission of further offences or the interference with witnesses or the obstruction of justice. Police bail cannot include a requirement to reside at a bail hostel or electronic monitoring.

Section 3AA of the *Bail Act* 1976 covers the electronic monitoring of compliance with bail conditions. Electronic monitoring or tagging is available for children and young persons. There is no specific statutory provision for the electronic tagging of adults to be a condition of bail. In a circular issued by Her Majesty's Court Service (HMCS) on September 5, 2005 (BI/241/24/09/05) it was indicated that resources are now available for the electronic tagging of adults on bail. Under section 3(6) the court has a power to impose such requirements as appear to be necessary. A condition of curfew monitored electronically may be necessary to address fears of failure to surrender, commission of offences or interference with witnesses. Particularly where otherwise a defendant would be remanded into custody the circular suggests that the imposition of a condition of curfew with tagging should be considered. The hours of the curfew are at the court's discretion but they must be proportionate. In addition a condition of residence is essential as the monitoring equipment needs to be installed at a fixed address.

This section was amended by the *Criminal Justice Act* 2003, s.19 which provides for further powers in relation to drug users. The court will be able to withold bail from defendants unless they consent to undergo assessments for drugs and participate in follow-up treatment during the period of the remand. The amendments came into force in April 2004 but are dependent on appropriate facilities being available.

Bail may be refused to an offender aged 18 or over who is charged with an imprisonable offence if the following conditions are fulfilled:

a) A drug test taken under section 63B of *PACE* 1984 or section 161 of the *Criminal Justice Act* 2003 shows the presence in his body of a specified Class A drug.

b) Either the offence is one under section 5(2) or (3) of the *Misuse of Drugs Act* 1971 (possession or possession with intent to supply) and relates to a specified Class A drug OR the court is satisfied there are substantial grounds for believing that misuse of a specified Class A drug caused or contributed to the offence or the offence was motivated by drug misuse.

c) The offender has refused to undergo assessment and/or follow up treatment offered consequent to the drug tests.

All assessments are carried out by qualified and trained personnel. The Class A drugs are specified by order by the Secretary of State for the Home Office and listed in Schedule 2, Part 1 of the *Misuse of Drugs Act* 1971.

Where the defendant agrees to the assessment and follow up treatment the court may grant bail but a condition must be imposed that the assessment and treatment be undertaken.

Bail Act 1976, s.4

General right to bail of accused persons and others

4.—(1) A person to whom this section applies shall be granted bail except as provided in **5–11** Schedule 1 to this Act.

(2) This section applies to a person who is accused of an offence when—

(a) he appears or is brought before a magistrates' court or the Crown Court in the course of or in connection with proceedings for the offence, or

(b) he applies to a court for bail or for a variation of the conditions of bail in connection with the proceedings.

This subsection does not apply as respects proceedings on or after a person's conviction of the offence or proceedings against a fugitive offender for the offence.

(3) This section also applies to a person who, having been convicted of an offence, appears or is brought before a magistrates' court or the Crown Court to be dealt with under–

(a) Part 2 of Schedule 3 to the *Powers of Criminal Courts (Sentencing) Act* 2000 (breach of certain youth community orders); or

(b) Part 2 of Schedule 8 to the *Criminal Justice Act* 2003 (breach of requirement of community order).

(4) This section also applies to a person who has been convicted of an offence and whose case is adjourned by the court for the purpose of enabling inquiries or a report to be made to assist the court in dealing with him for the offence.

(5) Schedule 1 to this Act also has effect as respects conditions of bail for a person to whom this section applies.

(6) In Schedule 1 to this Act "the defendant" means a person to whom this section applies and any reference to a defendant whose case is adjourned for inquiries or a report is a reference to a person to whom this section applies by virtue of subsection (4) above.

(7) This section is subject to section 41 of the *Magistrates' Courts Act* 1980 (restriction of bail by magistrates' court in cases of treason).

(8) This section is subject to section 25 of the *Criminal Justice and Public Order Act* 1994 (exclusion of bail in cases of homicide and rape).

(9) In taking any decisions required by Part I or II of Schedule 1 to this Act, the considerations to which the court is to have regard include, so far as relevant, any misuse of controlled drugs by the defendant ("controlled drugs" and "misuse" having the same meanings as in the *Misuse of Drugs Act* 1971).

[This section is reprinted as amended by the *Criminal Justice and Court Services Act* 2000, s.58 and the *Criminal Justice Act* 2003, Sched. 32 which came into force on April 4, 2005.]

5–12   Section 4 of the *Bail Act* 1976 creates a general right to bail for persons charged with an offence. A court must grant bail to any person accused of an offence or brought before a court for breach of a requirement of probation or community service order, if none of the exceptions specified in Schedule 1 applies. Where the defendant has previously been remanded in custody by the court, consideration must be given to whether bail should be granted on each occasion that the defendant is brought before the court regardless of whether the defendant makes an application: *Bail Act* 1976, Sched. 1, Pt IIA. This ensures that there is the periodic review of detention as required under Article 5 ECHR.

Section 4(1) does not apply once a person has been convicted of an offence. An appellant seeking bail pending the outcome of an appeal has no right to bail under this section. Section 4(1) does not apply to offenders who have been committed to the Crown Court for sentencing following conviction in the magistrates' court. In these situations a magistrate has the power to grant bail but the decision is entirely at the discretion of the court and there is no initial presumption either way. The *Bail Act* 1976 applies to offenders brought before the court in respect of any breach of a requirement of community penalties under the *Criminal Justice Act* 1991, Sched. 2, Pt 2. A convicted person has the right to bail if the case is adjourned for the purpose of obtaining reports but under paragraph 7, Schedule 1, Part I of the *Bail Act* 1976 there is an additional exception to the right to bail; the defendant need not be granted bail where it appears to the court that it would be impracticable to complete inquiries or make a report without keeping the defendant in custody.

Where a drugs test is carried out by the police under section 63B *PACE* 1984, the result of the test is relevant to a bail decision under section 4(9). The misuse of drugs may give rise to a fear of commission of further offences to feed the drug habit or failure to attend if affected by taking drugs.

Criminal Justice and Public Order Act 1994, s.25

No bail for defendants charged with or convicted of homicide or rape after previous conviction of such offences.

5–13   **25.**——(1) A person who in any proceedings has been charged with or convicted of an offence to which this section applies in circumstances to which it applies shall be granted bail in those proceedings only if the court or, as the case may be, the constable considering the grant of bail is satisfied that there are exceptional circumstances which justify it.

(2) This section applies, subject to subsection (3) below, to the following offences, that is to say—

(a) murder;

   (b) attempted murder;
   (c) manslaughter;
   (d) rape under the law of Scotland or Northern Ireland;
   (e) an offence under section 1 of the *Sexual Offences Act* 1956 (rape);
   (f) an offence under section 1 of the *Sexual Offences Act* 2003 (rape);
   (g) an offence under section 2 of that Act (assault by penetration);
   (h) an offence under section 4 of that Act (causing a person to engage in sexual activity without consent), where the activity caused involved penetration within subsection (4)(a) to (d) of that section;
   (i) an offence under section 5 of that Act (rape of a child under 13);
   (j) an offence under section 6 of that Act (assault of a child under 13 by penetration);
   (k) an offence under section 8 of that Act (causing or inciting a child under 13 to engage in sexual activity), where an activity involving penetration within subsection (3)(a) to (d) of that section was caused;
   (l) an offence under section 30 of that Act (sexual activity with a person with a mental disorder impeding choice), where the touching involved penetration within subsection (3)(a) to (d) of that section;
   (m) an offence under section 31 of that Act (causing or inciting a person, with a mental disorder impeding choice, to engage in sexual activity), where an activity involving penetration within subsection (3)(a) to (d) of that section was caused;
   (n) an attempt to commit an offence within any of paragraphs (d) to (m).

   (3) This section applies to a person charged with or convicted of any such offence only if he has been previously convicted by or before a court in any part of the United Kingdom of any such offence or of culpable homicide and, in the case of a previous conviction of manslaughter or of culpable homicide, if he was then sentenced to imprisonment or, if he was then a child or young person, to long-term detention under any of the relevant enactments.

   (4) This section applies whether or not an appeal is pending against conviction or sentence.

   (5) In this section—
   "conviction" includes—
   (a) a finding that a person is not guilty by reason of insanity;
   (b) a finding under section 4A(3) of the *Criminal Procedure (Insanity) Act* 1964 (cases of unfitness to plead) that a person did the act or made the omission charged against him; and
   (c) a conviction of an offence for which an order is made discharging the offender absolutely or conditionally;
   and "convicted" shall be construed accordingly; and
   "the relevant enactments" means—
   (a) as respects England and Wales, section 91 of the *Powers of Criminal Courts (Sentencing) Act* 2000;
   (b) as respects Scotland, sections 205(1) to (3) and 208 of the *Criminal Procedure (Scotland) Act* 1995;
   (c) as respects Northern Ireland, section 73(2) of the Children and Young Persons Act (Northern Ireland) 1968.

   (6) This section does not apply in relation to proceedings instituted before its commencement.

   [This section is printed as amended by the *Criminal Justice Act* 2003, Sched. 32.]

   Section 25 of the *Criminal Justice and Public Order Act* 1994 removes the presumption of bail in the case of persons who have been charged with or convicted of murder, attempted murder, manslaughter, rape or attempted rape and who have previously been convicted of any such offences as described in subsection (3). Then bail shall only be granted if the court or constable is satisfied that there are exceptional circumstances which justify it.   **5–14**

   In *Ilijokov v. Bulgaria* [2001] 7 *Archbold News* 1, the European Court of Human Rights held that a provision making pre-trial custody the rule for defendants charged with offences of a specified level of seriousness, except where there was not even a theo-   **5–15** retical possibility of absconding, commission of further offences or interference with witnesses violated Article 5(3) of the Convention, because it is for the state to satisfy the court that there are relevant and sufficient reasons for withholding bail. The "exceptional circumstances" referred to in section 25 of the *Criminal Justice and Public Order Act* 1994 preserve a sufficient discretion to ensure that Article 5 is not violated.

Bail Act 1976, s.5

Supplementary provisions about decisions on bail

5–16   **5.**—(1) Subject to subsection (2) below, where—

     (a) a court or constable grants bail in criminal proceedings, or

     (b) a court withholds bail in criminal proceedings from a person to whom section 4 of this act applies, or

     (c) a court, officer of a court or constable appoints a time or place or appoints a different time or place for a person granted bail in criminal proceedings to surrender to custody, or

     (d) a court or constable varies any conditions of bail or imposes conditions in respect of bail in criminal proceedings,

that court, officer or constable shall make a record of the decision in the prescribed manner and containing the prescribed particulars and, if requested to do so by the person in relation to whom the decision was taken, shall cause him to be given a copy of the record of the decision as soon as practicable after the record is made.

(2) Where bail in criminal proceedings is granted by endorsing a warrant of arrest for bail the constable who releases on bail the person arrested shall make the record required by subsection (1) above instead of the judge or justice who issued the warrant.

(2A) Where a magistrates' court or the Crown Court grants bail in criminal proceedings to a person to whom section 4 of this Act applies after hearing representations from the prosecutor in favour of withholding bail, then the court shall give reasons for granting bail.

(2B) A court which is by virtue of subsection (2A) above required to give reasons for its decision shall include a note of those reasons in the record of its decision and, if requested to do so by the prosecutor, shall cause the prosecutor to be given a copy of the record of the decision as soon as practicable after the record is made.

(3) Where a magistrates' court or the Crown Court—

     (a) withholds bail in criminal proceedings, or

     (b) imposes conditions in granting bail in criminal proceedings, or

     (c) varies any conditions of bail or imposes conditions in respect of bail in criminal proceedings,

and does so in relation to a person to whom section 4 of this Act applies, then the court shall, with a view to enabling him to consider making an application in the matter to another court, give reasons for withholding bail or for imposing or varying the conditions.

(4) A court which is by virtue of subsection (3) above required to give reasons for its decision shall include a note of those reasons in the record of its decision and shall (except in a case where, by virtue of subsection (5) below, this need not be done) give a copy of that note to the person in relation to whom the decision was taken.

(5) The Crown Court need not give a copy of the note of the reasons for its decision to the person in relation to whom the decision was taken where that person is represented by counsel or a solicitor unless his counsel or solicitor requests the court to do so.

(6) Where a magistrates' court withholds bail in criminal proceedings from a person who is not represented by counsel or a solicitor, the court shall—

     (a) if it is committing him for trial to the Crown Court or if it issues a certificate under subsection (6A) below, inform him that he may apply to the High Court or to the Crown Court to be granted bail;

     (b) in any other case, inform him that he may apply to the High Court for that purpose.

(6A) Where in criminal proceedings—

     (a) a magistrates' court remands a person in custody under section 11 of the *Powers of Criminal Courts (Sentencing) Act* 2000 (remand for medical examination) or any of the following provisions of the *Magistrates' Courts Act* 1980—

         (i) section 5 (adjournment of inquiry into offence);

(ii)   section 10 (adjournment of trial); or
(iii) section 18 (initial procedure on information against adult for offence triable either way),
after hearing full argument on an application for bail from him; and

(b) either—

(i)   it has not previously heard such argument on an application for bail from him in those proceedings; or
(ii) it has previously heard full argument from him on such an application but it is satisfied that there has been a change in his circumstances or that new considerations have been placed before it,

it shall be the duty of the court to issue a certificate in the prescribed form that they heard full argument on his application for bail before they refused the application.

(6B) Where the court issues a certificate under subsection (6A) above in a case to which paragraph (b)(ii) of that subsection applies, it shall state in the certificate the nature of the change of circumstances or the new considerations which caused it to hear a further fully argued bail application.

(6C) Where a court issues a certificate under subsection (6A) above it shall cause the person to whom it refuses bail to be given a copy of the certificate.

(7) Where a person has given security in pursuance of section 3(5) above and a court is satisfied that he failed to surrender to custody then, unless it appears that he had reasonable cause for his failure, the court may order the forfeiture of the security.

(8) If a court orders the forfeiture of a security under subsection (7) above, the court may declare that the forfeiture extends to such amount less than the full value of the security as it thinks fit to order.

(8A) An order under subsection (7) above shall, unless previously revoked, have effect at the end of twenty-one days beginning with the day on which it is made.

(8B) A court which has ordered the forfeiture of a security under subsection (7) above may, if satisfied on an application made by or on behalf of the person who gave it that he did after all have reasonable cause for his failure to surrender to custody, by order remit the forfeiture or declare that it extends to such amount less than the full value of the security as it thinks fit to order.

(8C) An application under subsection (8B) above may be made before or after the order for forfeiture has taken effect, but shall not be entertained unless the court is satisfied that the prosecution was given reasonable notice of the applicant's intention to make it.

(9) A security which has been ordered to be forfeited by a court under subsection (7) above shall, to the extent of the forfeiture—

(a) if it consists of money, be accounted for and paid in the same manner as a fine imposed by that court would be;
(b) if it does not consist of money, be enforced by such magistrates' court as may be specified in the order.

(9A) Where an order is made under subsection (8B) above after the order for forfeiture of the security in question has taken effect, any money which would have fallen to be repaid or paid over to the person who gave the security if the order under subsection (8B) had been made before the order for forfeiture took effect shall be repaid or paid over to him.

(10) In this section "prescribed" means, in relation to the decision of a court or an officer of a court, prescribed by Civil Procedure Rules, Courts-Martial Appeal Rules or Criminal Procedure Rules as the case requires or, in relation to a decision of a constable, prescribed by direction of the Secretary of State.

(11) This section is subject, in its application to bail granted by a constable, to section 5A of this Act.

[This section is reprinted as amended by the *Criminal Justice and Police Act* 2001, s.129(1) and the *Courts Act* 2003, Sched. 8 which came into force on April 1, 2003.]

5–17 Under this section the court will provide a written bail notice to the defendant. It includes details of exceptions found and reasons given for the decision and standard requirements of conditional bail to be deleted or amended as appropriate. There is also a duty on the court under section 5(2A) to give written reasons in cases where bail is granted after the prosecution has objected to bail. The provision of reasons enables the parties affected to consider fully the basis of an appeal.

At the first hearing at which the defendant is a person to whom section 4 applies, the court shall grant the defendant bail unless one of the exceptions under Part I or II of Schedule 1 applies. If the prosecution make representations against the grant of bail the defendant may support the application for bail with any argument in fact or law. The court must consider the question of bail regardless of whether the defendant makes an application for bail and must record reasons if the remand is to be in custody.

If bail is refused at the first hearing, the court is still bound to consider the question of bail at each subsequent hearing. An application for further remand in the absence of the defendant and with his consent under section 128(3A) of the *Magistrates' Courts Act* 1980 is not a hearing for this purpose. Section 4 does not apply in such a case because the defendant does not appear, is not brought before the court and makes no application for bail: *R. v. Dover and East Kent Justices, ex p. Dean* [1992] Crim.L.R. 33, DC.

5–18 After the first hearing at which the defendant is denied bail the defendant may support one more application for bail with any argument in fact or law, whether or not the argument has been raised previously. The purpose of the legislation is to provide for any argument being advanced on two occasions as of right, and at the second hearing the court is obliged to consider the matter *de novo*.

This is not always the effect of the legislation. Sometimes when a defendant faces a serious charge and is brought to court in custody there may be any number of reasons why a bail application is not made on the first appearance. When the defendant next appears before the court, an application for bail may be made and any argument raised as of right. If bail is withheld once more at the second hearing the defendant has no right to raise the same arguments again at later hearings, in effect depriving the defendant of the intended right to have two attempts at contesting the objections to bail made by the prosecution. If no application is made at the first hearing after that at which the court decided not to grant the defendant bail, the *Bail Act* 1976, para. 2 of Pt IIA, Sched. 1 does not apply so as to confer a right to make an application at subsequent hearings based on the same arguments of fact and law. The defendant always has the right to make an application for bail but whether the court is bound to entertain the application is a different question. There must be some material change of circumstance to warrant repeated applications: *R. v. Dover and East Kent Justices, ex p. Dean (ante).* Part IIA, paragraph 3 provides that where a person has been remanded in custody then at subsequent hearings the court need not hear arguments as to fact or law which it has heard previously. This implies that it has a discretion to do so. On that basis the court should not hear arguments as to fact or law which it has heard previously unless there has been such a change of circumstances as might justify a different decision. To do so would be to act in an appellate capacity which would be inappropriate: *R. v. Slough Justices, ex p. Duncan,* (1982) 75 Cr.App.R. 384, DC.

Where the court decides that a defendant should be remanded in custody because it has not been practicable to obtain sufficient information to consider a bail application, this does not amount to a decision to refuse bail within the meaning of paragraph 1 of Part IIA: *R. v. Calder Justices, ex p. Kennedy* [1992] Crim.L.R. 496.

5–19 The passage of time may require a court to hear further bail applications to ensure that the defendant's rights under Article 5 are reviewed regularly: *Neumeister v. Austria (No. 1)* (1979–80) 1 E.H.R.R. 91.

Under section 5(6A) a certificate that a full bail argument has taken place must be issued when the court remands a defendant in custody following the first full bail application. Such a certificate must also be issued if a further full bail application is allowed because of a change in circumstances or the identification of new considerations and the defendant is again remanded in custody. The certificate can be provided immediately and is often incorporated in the printed bail notice given to the defendant. The purpose of the certificate is to form the basis of an appeal against the bail decision to the Crown Court and to confirm that all avenues of argument in the magistrates' court have been exhausted.

A security can be imposed as a condition of bail: section 3. Section 5 provides for the procedure to be followed if the defendant fails to answer his bail. The order of forfeiture only takes effect after 21 days and in the meantime the court may serve a notice of forfeiture on the person who deposited the security whether that be the defendant or someone else on his behalf so they may make representations.

B. Bail Following Adjournment

Magistrates' Courts Act 1980, ss.5; 6(3), (4)

Adjournment of inquiry

5.—(1) A magistrates' court may, before beginning to inquire into an offence as examining **5–20** justices, or at any time during the inquiry, adjourn the hearing, and if it does so shall remand the accused.

(2) The court shall when adjourning fix the time and place at which the hearing is to be resumed; and the time fixed shall be that at which the accused is required to appear or be brought before the court in pursuance of the remand [or would be required to be brought before the court but for section 128(3A) below].

Discharge or committal for trial

6.—(3) Subject to section 4 of the *Bail Act* 1976 and section 41 below, the court may commit **5–21** a person for trial—

(a) in custody, that is to say, by committing him to custody there to be safety kept until delivered in due course of law, or

(b) on bail in accordance with the *Bail Act* 1976, that is to say, by directing him to appear before the Crown Court for trial;

and where his release on bail is conditional on his providing one or more surety or sureties and, in accordance with section 8(3) of the *Bail Act* 1976, the court fixes the amount in which the surety is to be bound with a view to his entering into his recognizance subsequently in accordance with subsections (4) and (5) or (6) of that section the court shall in the meantime commit the accused to custody in accordance with paragraph (a) of this subsection.

(4) Where the court has committed a person to custody in accordance with paragraph (a) of subsection (3) above, then, if that person is in custody for no other cause, the court may, at any time before his first appearance before the Crown Court, grant him bail in accordance with the *Bail Act* 1976 subject to a duty to appear before the Crown Court for trial.

Crime and Disorder Act 1998, s.52

Provisions supplementing section 51

52.—(1) Subject to section 4 of the *Bail Act* 1976, section 41 of the 1980 Act, regulations **5–22** under section 22 of the 1985 Act and section 25 of the 1994 Act, the court may send a person for trial under section 51 above—

(a) in custody, that is to say, by committing him to custody there to be safely kept until delivered in due course of law; or

(b) on bail in accordance with the *Bail Act* 1976, that is to say, by directing him to appear before the Crown Court for trial.

(2) Where—

(a) the person's release on bail under subsection (1)(b) above is conditional on his providing one or more sureties; and

(b) in accordance with subsection (3) of section 8 of the *Bail Act* 1976, the court fixes the amount in which a surety is to be bound with a view to his entering into his recognisance subsequently in accordance with subsections (4) and (5) or (6) of that section, the court shall in the meantime make an order such as is mentioned in subsection (1)(a) above.

(3) The court shall treat as an indictable offence for the purposes of section 51 above an offence which is mentioned in the first column of Schedule 2 to the 1980 Act (offences for which the value involved is relevant to the mode of trial) unless it is clear to the court, having regard to any representations made by the prosecutor or the accused, that the value involved does not exceed the relevant sum.

(4) In subsection (3) above "the value involved" and "the relevant sum" have the same meanings as in section 22 of the 1980 Act (certain offences triable either way to be tried summarily if value involved is small).

(5) A magistrates' court may adjourn any proceedings under section 51 above, and if it does so shall remand the accused.

(6) Schedule 3 to this Act (which makes further provision in relation to persons sent to the Crown Court for trial under section 51 above) shall have effect.

5–23   Where a magistrates' court commits a person for trial in the Crown Court on bail the bail ceases when the defendant surrenders to the Crown Court. If the Crown Court releases the defendant on bail, it must consider the suitability of any conditions afresh: *R. v. Kent Crown Court, ex p. Jodka* (1997) 161 J.P. 638, DC.

5–24   Committal for trial is not necessarily a new circumstance which entitles the defendant to make a new bail application. In *R. v. Slough Justices, ex p. Duncan* [1981] Q.B. 451 it was stated that new arguments in favour of bail may be advanced upon committal for trial because the strength of the prosecution case at the committal hearing may be better assessed.

5–25   If after committal for trial but before arraignment at the Crown Court there is an application to vary the conditions of bail, the magistrates' court has concurrent jurisdiction with the Crown Court to hear and determine the application: *R. v. Lincoln Magistrates' Court, ex p. Mawer* (1996) 160 J.P. 219.

The magistrates' court also has power to commit a defendant to the Crown Court for sentence under the *Powers of Criminal Courts (Sentencing) Act* 2000, ss.3 and 6 (see Part IV on Sentencing). The court has power to commit either on bail or in custody. Upon committal for sentence the usual practice should be to commit the defendant in custody only if he has been in custody prior to the committal hearing: *Rafferty* [1999] 1 Cr.App.R. 235, CA. In the judgment Thomas J. said—

> "In the usual case where a person who has been on bail pleads guilty at the plea before venue, the usual practice should be to continue bail, even if it is anticipated that a custodial sentence will be imposed by the Crown Court,unless there are good reasons for remanding the defendant in custody".

The encouragement to a defendant to plead guilty at the earliest opportunity is not then affected by a fear of being remanded into custody.

Magistrates' Courts Act 1980, ss.10; 17C; 18(4), (5)

Adjournment of trial

5–26   **10.**—(1) A magistrates' court may at any time, whether before or after beginning to try an information, adjourn the trial, and may do so, notwithstanding anything in this Act, when composed of a single justice.

(2) The court may when adjourning either fix the time and place at which the trial is to be resumed, or, unless it remands the accused, leave the time and place to be determined later by the court; but the trial shall not be resumed at that time and place unless the court is satisfied that the parties have had adequate notice thereof.

(3) A magistrates' court may, for the purpose of enabling inquiries to be made or of determining the most suitable method of dealing with the case, exercise its power to adjourn after convicting the accused and before sentencing him or otherwise dealing with him; but, if it does so, the adjournment shall not be for more than 4 weeks at a time unless the court remands the accused in custody and, where it so remands him, the adjournment shall not be for more than 3 weeks at a time.

(3A) A youth court shall not be required to adjourn any proceedings for an offence at any stage by reason only of the fact—

(a) that the court commits the accused for trial for another offence; or

(b) that the accused is charged with another offence.

(4) On adjourning the trial of an information the court may remand the accused and, where the accused has attained the age of 18 years, shall do so if the offence is triable either way and—

(a) on the occasion on which the accused first appeared, or was brought, before the court to answer to the information he was in custody or, having been released on bail, surrendered to the custody of the court; or

(b) the accused has been remanded at any time in the course of proceedings on the information;

and, where the court remands the accused, the time fixed for the resumption of the trial shall be that at which he is required to appear or be brought before the court in pursuance of the remand or would be required to be brought before the court but for section 128(3A) below.

Intention as to plea adjournment

17C. A magistrates' court proceeding under section 17A or 17B above may adjourn the proceedings at any time, and on doing so on any occasion when the accused is present may remand the accused, and shall remand him if—   **5–27**

   (a) on the occasion on which he first appeared, or was brought, before the court to answer to the information he was in custody or, having been released on bail, surrendered to the custody of the court; or

   (b) he has been remanded at any time in the course of proceedings on the information;

and where the court remands the accused, the time fixed for the resumption of proceedings shall be that at which he is required to appear or be brought before the court in pursuance of the remand or would be required to be brought before the court but for section 128(3A) below.

Initial procedure on information against adult for offence triable either way

18.—(4) A magistrates' court proceeding under sections 19 to 23 below may adjourn the proceedings at any time, and on doing so on any occasion when the accused is present may remand the accused, and shall remand him if—   **5–28**

   (a) on the occasion on which he first appeared, or was brought, before the court to answer to the information he was in custody or, having been released on bail, surrendered to the custody of the court; or

   (b) he has been remanded at any time in the course of proceedings on the information;

and where the court remands the accused, the time fixed for the resumption of the proceedings shall be that at which he is required to appear or be brought before the court in pursuance of the remand or would be required to be brought before the court but for section 128(3A) below.

(5) The functions of a magistrates' court under sections 19 to 23 below may be discharged by a single justice, but the foregoing provision shall not be taken to authorise the summary trial of an information by a magistrates' court composed of less than two justices.

C. Bail Pending an Appeal

Magistrates' Courts Act 1980, s.113

Bail on appeal or case stated

113.—(1) Where a person has given notice of appeal to the Crown Court against the decision of a magistrates' court or has applied to a magistrates' court to state a case for the opinion of the High Court, then, if he is in custody, the magistrates' court may, subject to section 25 of the *Criminal Justice and Public Order Act* 1994 grant him bail.   **5–29**

(2) If a person is granted bail under subsection (1) above, the time and place at which he is to appear (except in the event of the determination in respect of which the case is stated being reversed by the High Court) shall be—

   (a) if he has given notice of appeal, the Crown Court at the time appointed for the hearing of the appeal;

   (b) if he has applied for the statement of a case, the magistrates' court at such time within 10 days after the judgment of the High Court has been given as may be specified by the magistrates' court;

and any recognizance that may be taken from him or from any surety for him shall be conditioned accordingly.

(3) Subsection (1) above shall not apply where the accused has been committed to the Crown Court for sentence under section 3 of the *Powers of Criminal Courts (Sentencing) Act* 2000.

(4) Section 37(6) of the *Criminal Justice Act* 1948 (which relates to the currency of a sentence while a person is released on bail by the High Court) shall apply to a person released on bail by a magistrates' court under this section pending the hearing of a case stated as it applies to a person released on bail by the High Court under section 22 of the *Criminal Justice Act* 1967.

5–30　　The court may be reluctant to grant the appellant bail pending appeal where a custodial sentence has been imposed following conviction. Bail would only be appropriate in the most exceptional circumstances, *e.g.* if there was a strong likelihood of success of an appeal or that a sentence would have been served by the time the appeal would be heard: *Watton* (1979) 68 Cr.App.R. 293.

D. BAIL ON ARREST

Magistrates' Courts Act 1980, s.43

Bail on arrest

5–31　　**43.**—(1) Where a person has been granted bail under Part IV of the *Police and Criminal Evidence Act* 1984 subject to a duty to appear before a magistrates' court, the court before which he is to appear may appoint a later time as the time at which he is to appear and may enlarge the recognizances of any sureties for him at that time.

(2) The recognizance of any surety for any person granted bail subject to a duty to attend at a police station may be enforced as if it were conditioned for his appearance before a magistrates' court acting in the local justice area in which the police station named in the recognizance is situated.

E. BAIL WHERE APPEARANCE BEFORE CROWN COURT CONTEMPLATED

Magistrates' Courts Act 1980, s.43A

Functions of magistrates' court where a person in custody is brought before it with a view to his appearance before the Crown Court

5–32　　**43A.**—(1) Where a person in custody in pursuance of a warrant issued by the Crown Court with a view to his appearance before the Crown Court is brought before a magistrates' court in pursuance of section 81(5) of the *Supreme Court Act* 1981—

　　(a) the magistrates' court shall commit him in custody or release him on bail until he can be brought or appear before the Crown Court at the time and place appointed by the Crown Court;

　　(b) if the warrant is endorsed for bail, but the person in custody is unable to satisfy the conditions endorsed, the magistrates' court may vary those conditions, if satisfied that it is proper to do so.

(2) A magistrates' court shall have jurisdiction under subsection (1) whether or not the offence was committed, or the arrest was made, within the court's area.

5–33　　A person arrested on a Crown Court or "Bench" warrant may be brought before a magistrates' court usually on a Saturday or other day when the Crown Court is closed. The case may be adjourned to the next convenient date at the Crown Court with the defendant remanded on bail or in custody.

III. PRINCIPLES FOR GRANTING/DENYING BAIL

(1) Statutory grounds for refusal

5–34　　Section 4 of the *Bail Act* 1976 is subject to the First Schedule to the Act, which sets out the reasons why a defendant need not be granted bail. Part 1 applies to imprisonable offences, and Part II to non-imprisonable offences.

Bail Act 1976, Sched. 1

SCHEDULE 1

PERSONS ENTITLED TO BAIL: SUPPLEMENTARY PROVISIONS

PART I

Defendants Accused or Convicted of Imprisonable Offences

Defendants to whom Part I applies

1. The following provisions of this Part of this Schedule apply to the defendant if—   **5–35**
   (a) the offence or one of the offences of which he is accused or convicted in the proceedings is punishable with imprisonment, or
   (b) his extradition is sought in respect of an offence.

Exceptions to right to bail

2.—(1) The defendant need not be granted bail if the court is satisfied that there are substantial grounds for believing that the defendant, if released on bail (whether subject to conditions or not) would—
   (a) fail to surrender to custody, or
   (b) commit an offence while on bail, or
   (c) interfere with witnesses or otherwise obstruct the course of justice, whether in relation to himself or any other person.

(2) Where the defendant falls within one or more of paragraphs 2A, 6 and 6B of this Part of this Schedule, this paragraph shall not apply unless—
   (a) where the defendant falls within paragraph 2A, the court is satisfied as mentioned in sub-paragraph (1) of that paragraph;
   (b) where the defendant falls within paragraph 6, the court is satisfied as mentioned in sub-paragraph (1) of that paragraph;
   (c) where the defendant falls within paragraph 6B, the court is satisfied as mentioned in paragraph 6A of this Part of this Schedule or paragraph 6A does not apply by virtue of paragraph 6C of this Part of this Schedule.

2A.—(1) The defendant need not be granted bail if—
   (a) the offence is an indictable offence or an offence triable either way; and
   (b) it appears to the court that he was on bail in criminal proceedings on the date of the offence.

[2A.—(1) If the defendant falls within this paragraph he may not be granted bail unless the court is satisfied that there is no significant risk of his committing an offence while on bail (whether subject to conditions or not).

(2) The defendant falls within this paragraph if—
   (a) he is aged 18 or over, and
   (b) it appears to the court that he was on bail in criminal proceedings on the date of the offence.]

2B. The defendant need not be granted bail in connection with extradition proceedings if—
   (a) the conduct constituting the offence would, if carried out by the defendant in England and Wales, constitute an indictable offence or an offence triable either way; and
   (b) it appears to the court that the defendant was on bail on the date of the offence.

3. The defendant need not be granted bail if the court is satisfied that the defendant should be kept in custody for his own protection or, if he is a child or young person, for his own welfare.

4. The defendant need not be granted bail if he is in custody in pursuance of the sentence of a court or of any authority acting under any of the Services Acts.

5. The defendant need not be granted bail where the court is satisfied that it has not been practicable to obtain sufficient information for the purpose of taking the decisions required by this Part of this Schedule for want of time since the institution of the proceedings against him.

6. The defendant need not be granted bail if, having been released on bail in or in con-

nection with the proceedings for the offence or the extradition proceedings, he has been arrested in pursuance of section 7 of this Act.

[6.—(1) If the defendant falls within this paragraph, he may not be granted bail unless the court is satisfied that there is no significant risk that, if released on bail (whether subject to conditions or not), he would fail to surrender to custody.

(2) Subject to sub-paragraph (3) below, the defendant falls within this paragraph if–

    (a) he is aged 18 or over, and

    (b) it appears to the court that, having been released on bail in or in connection with the proceedings for the offence, he failed to surrender to custody.

(3) Where it appears to the court that the defendant had reasonable cause for his failure to surrender to custody, he does not fall within this paragraph unless it also appears to the court that he failed to surrender to custody at the appointed place as soon as reasonably practicable after the appointed time.

(4) For the purposes of sub-paragraph (3) above, a failure to give to the defendant a copy of the record of the decision to grant him bail shall not constitute a reasonable cause for his failure to surrender to custody.]

Exception applicable to drug users in certain areas

6A. Subject to paragraph 6C below, a defendant who falls within paragraph 6B below may not be granted bail unless the court is satisfied that there is no significant risk of his committing an offence while on bail (whether subject to conditions or not).

6B.—(1) A defendant falls within this paragraph if—

    (a) he is aged 18 or over;

    (b) a sample taken—

        (i) under section 63B of the Police and Criminal Evidence Act 1984 (testing for presence of Class A drugs) in connection with the offence; or

        (ii) under section 161 of the Criminal Justice Act 2003 (drug testing after conviction of an offence but before sentence),

  has revealed the presence in his body of a specified Class A drug;

    (c) either the offence is one under section 5(2) or (3) of the Misuse of Drugs Act 1971 and relates to a specified Class A drug, or the court is satisfied that there are substantial grounds for believing—

        (i) that misuse by him of any specified Class A drug caused or contributed to the offence; or

        (ii) (even if it did not) that the offence was motivated wholly or partly by his intended misuse of such a drug; and

    (d) the condition set out in sub-paragraph (2) below is satisfied or (if the court is considering on a second or subsequent occasion whether or not to grant bail) has been, and continues to be, satisfied.

(2) The condition referred to is that after the taking and analysis of the sample—

    (a) a relevant assessment has been offered to the defendant but he does not agree to undergo it; or

    (b) he has undergone a relevant assessment, and relevant follow-up has been proposed to him, but he does not agree to participate in it.

(3) In this paragraph and paragraph 6C below—

    (a) "Class A drug" and "misuse" have the same meaning as in the Misuse of Drugs Act 1971;

    (b) "relevant assessment" and "relevant follow-up" have the meaning given by section 3(6E) of this Act;

    (c) "specified" (in relation to a Class A drug) has the same meaning as in Part 3 of the Criminal Justice and Court Services Act 2000.

6C. Paragraph 6A above does not apply unless—

    (a) the court has been notified by the Secretary of State that arrangements for conducting a relevant assessment or, as the case may be, providing relevant follow-up have been made for the local justice area in which it appears to the court that the defendant would reside if granted bail; and

    (b) the notice has not been withdrawn.

Exception applicable only to defendant whose case is adjourned for inquiries or a report

7. Where his case is adjourned for inquiries or a report, the defendant need not be

granted bail if it appears to the court that it would be impracticable to complete the inquiries or make the report without keeping the defendant in custody.

Restrictions of conditions of bail

8.—(1) Subject to *sub-paragraph (3)* below, where the defendant is granted bail, no conditions shall be imposed under subsections (4) to (7) (except subsections (6)(d) or (e)) of section 3 of this Act unless it appears to the court that it is necessary to do so—

(a) for the purpose of preventing the occurrence of any of the events mentioned in paragraph 2(1) of this Part of this Schedule or

(b) for the defendant's own protection or, if he is a child or young person, for his own welfare or in his own interests

(1A) No condition shall be imposed under section 3(6)(d) of this Act unless it appears to be necessary to do so for the purpose of enabling inquiries or a report to be made.

(2) *Sub-paragraphs (1) and (1A)* above also apply on any application to the court to vary the conditions of bail or to impose conditions in respect of bail which has been granted unconditionally.

(3) The restriction imposed by *sub-paragraph (1A)* above shall not apply to the conditions required to be imposed under section 3(6A) of this Act or operate to override the direction in section 11(3) of the *Powers of Criminal Courts (Sentencing) Act* 2000 to a magistrates' court to impose conditions of bail under section 3(6)(d) of this Act of the description specified in the said section 11(3) in the circumstances so specified.

Decisions under paragraph 2

9. In taking the decisions required by paragraph 2(1), or in deciding whether it is satisfied as mentioned in paragraph 2A(1), *6(1)* or *6A.* of this Part of this Schedule, the court shall have regard to such of the following considerations as appear to it to be relevant, that is to say—

(a) the nature and seriousness of the offence or default (and the probable method of dealing with the defendant for it),

(b) the character, antecedents, associations and community ties of the defendant,

(c) the defendant's record as respects the fulfilment of his obligations under previous grants of bail in criminal proceedings,

(d) except in the case of a defendant whose case is adjourned for inquiries or a report, the strength of the evidence of his having committed the offence or having defaulted,

as well as to any others which appear to be relevant.

[9AA.—(1) This paragraph applies if—

(a) the defendant is under the age of 18, and

(b) it appears to the court that he was on bail in criminal proceedings on the date of the offence.

(2) In deciding for the purposes of paragraph 2(1) of this Part of this Schedule whether it is satisfied that there are substantial grounds for believing that the defendant, if released on bail (whether subject to conditions or not), would commit an offence while on bail, the court shall give particular weight to the fact that the defendant was on bail in criminal proceedings on the date of the offence.

9AB.—(1) Subject to sub-paragraph (2) below, this paragraph applies if—

(a) the defendant is under the age of 18, and

(b) it appears to the court that, having been released on bail in or in connection with the proceedings for the offence, he failed to surrender to custody.

(2) Where it appears to the court that the defendant had reasonable cause for his failure to surrender to custody, this paragraph does not apply unless it also appears to the court that he failed to surrender to custody at the appointed place as soon as reasonably practicable after the appointed time.

(3) In deciding for the purposes of paragraph 2(1) of this Part of this Schedule whether it is satisfied that there are substantial grounds for believing that the defendant, if released on bail (whether subject to conditions or not), would fail to surrender to custody the court shall give particular weight to—

(a) where the defendant did not have reasonable cause for his failure to surrender to custody, the fact that he failed to surrender to custody, or

(b) where he did have reasonable cause for his failure to surrender to custody, the fact that he failed to surrender to custody at the appointed place as soon as reasonably practicable after the appointed time.

(4) For the purposes of this paragraph, a failure to give to the defendant a copy of the record of the decision to grant him bail shall not constitute a reasonable cause for his failure to surrender to custody.]

9B. Where the court is considering exercising the power conferred by section 128A of the *Magistrates' Courts Act* 1980 (power to remand in custody for more than 8 clear days), it shall have regard to the total length of time which the accused would spend in custody if it were to exercise the power.

PART II

DEFENDANTS ACCUSED OR CONVICTED OF NON-IMPRISONABLE OFFENCES

Defendants to whom Part II applies

5–36   1. Where the offence or every offence of which the defendant is accused or convicted in the proceedings is one which is not punishable with imprisonment the following provisions of this Part of this Schedule apply.

Exceptions to right to bail

2. The defendant need not be granted bail if—
    (a) it appears to the court that, having been previously granted bail in criminal proceedings, he has failed to surrender to custody in accordance with his obligations under the grant of bail; and
    (b) the court believes, in view of that failure, that the defendant, if released on bail (whether subject to conditions or not) would fail to surrender to custody.

3. The defendant need not be granted bail if the court is satisfied that the defendant should be kept in custody for his own protection or, if he is a child or young person, for his own welfare.

4. The defendant need not be granted bail if he is in custody in pursuance of the sentence of a court or of any authority acting under any of the Services Acts.

5. The defendant need not be granted bail if—
    (a) having been released on bail in or in connection with the proceedings for the offence, he has been arrested in pursuance of section 7 of this Act, and
    (b) the court is satisfied that there are substantial grounds for believing that the defendant, if released on bail (whether subject to conditions or not) would fail to surrender to custody, commit an offence on bail or interfere with witnesses or otherwise obstruct the court of justice whether in relation to himself or any other person).

PART IIA

DECISIONS WHERE BAIL REFUSED ON PREVIOUS HEARING

5–37   1. If the court decides not to grant the defendant bail, it is the court's duty to consider, at each subsequent hearing while the defendant is a person to whom section 4 above applies and remains in custody, whether he ought to be granted bail.

2. At the first hearing after that at which the court decided not to grant the defendant bail he may support an application for bail with any argument as to fact or law that he desires (whether or not he has advanced that argument previously).

3. At subsequent hearings the court need not hear arguments as to fact or law which its has heard previously.

[This Schedule is printed as amended by the *Criminal Justice Act* 2003, ss.13, 20 and ss.14 and 15 which came into force (partially) on January 1, 2007: *Criminal Justice Act 2003 (Commencement No. 14 and Transitional Provision) Order* 2006 (S.I. 2006 No. 3217). The paragraphs printed in square brackets are the new provisions which apply only to offences carrying life imprisonment.]

Considerations on the granting of bail

5–38   Bail need not be granted if there are substantial grounds for believing that the defendant would fail to surrender to custody, commit an offence whilst on bail or interfere with witnesses or otherwise obstruct the course of justice. The test for withholding bail is more rigorous than the test for imposing conditions on bail. The court need not be satisfied that the consequences in paragraph 2(a)–(c) would actually occur if bail were to be granted. It has to be satisfied that there are substantial grounds for believing that they would occur. However, it is not enough for the court to have a subjective belief that there is a risk of one or more of the events in paragraph 2 occurring: *Mansfield Justices, ex p. Sharkey* [1985] Q.B. 613.

Consideration has been given in European case law to the reasons why a person may be refused bail and be deprived of his liberty. Substantial grounds for believing a person may fail to surrender to custody are sufficient grounds but the court has said that there must be "a whole set of circumstances .....which give reason to suppose that the consequences and hazards of flight will seem to him to be a lesser evil than continued imprisonment": *Stogmuller v. Austria* (1969) 1 E.H.R.R. 155. It has also been indicated that the aspects of the individual case must be taken into account which include,"the character of the person involved, his morals, his home, his occupation, his assets, his family ties and all kinds of links with the country in which he is being prosecuted.": *Neumeister v. Austria* (1968) 1 E.H.R.R. 91.

The severity of the potential sentence alone cannot of itself justify the refusal of bail. **5–39** There have to exist other grounds that give rise to the belief that the accused may abscond: *Letellier v. France* (1992) 14 E.H.R.R. 83; *W v. Switzerland* (1993) 17 E.H.R.R. 60; *Mansur v. Turkey* 20 E.H.R.R. 535. In *R. (Thompson) v. Central Criminal Court* [2005] EWHC 2345 it was held that a defendant charged with a serious offence and liable to a severe penalty may be considered likely to abscond if granted bail. If conditions cannot safely eliminate such a risk the court may refuse bail but the decision must be based on all relevant factors specific to the individual and the case and clear and explicit reasons for refusal of bail must be given by the court. See also *Hurnam v. State of Mauritius* [2006] 1 W.L.R. 857.

In relation to the commission of further offences it has been held that this may amount to "good and sufficient reason" and detention may be justified to prevent crime: *Matznetter v. Austria* (1969) 1 E.H.R.R. 198. Detention may also be justified for the preservation of public order where in offences of particular gravity there are substantial grounds to believe that public disorder may result from the accused's release: *Letellier v. France*.

Schedule 1 to the *Bail Act* is printed here as amended by section 14 and 15(1) and (2) of the *Criminal Justice Act* 2003 which were brought into force partially on January 1, 2007 by the *Criminal Justice Act 2003 (Commencement No. 14 and Transitional Provision) Order* 2006 (S.I. 2006 No. 3217). At this stage the statutory instrument makes it clear that the amendments only apply to offences which carry life imprisonment. The amendments are printed in square brackets. The existing wording of the Schedule still applies to all other offences.

The test has been changed where the court considers bail for a person charged with a relevant offence who has committed an offence whilst on bail or who has failed to surrender to bail during the proceedings. Where the defendant is 18 years or over and it appears to the court that he committed the offence whilst on bail then bail may not be granted unless the court is satisfied that there is no significant risk of his committing an offence if granted bail. Similarly, for a defendant aged 18 or over, where it appears that he was released on bail for the offence and failed to surrender to custody during the proceedings then bail may not be granted unless the court is satisfied that there is no significant risk of his failing to surrender to custody again if released on bail. If the court finds there was a reasonable cause for the failure to surrender then these provisions only apply if it appears to the court that the defendant failed to surrender to custody as soon as reasonably practicable after the appointed time. Failure to be provided with a copy of the bail record sheet cannot be a reasonable cause for failing to surrender at the appointed time.

Slightly different and less stringent provisions apply to youths. For defendants under the age of 18 the court must give "particular weight" to the fact that a defendant was on bail at the time when it appears to the court that he committed the offence in order to determine whether there are substantial grounds to believe that the defendant would commit offences if released on bail. Where a defendant aged under 18 has failed to surrender to bail previously then also "particular weight" must be given to that fact in determining whether there are substantial grounds to believe that he would fail to surrender in future if granted bail.

These amendments come into force on January 1, 2007 but only apply to offences carrying life imprisonment. In respect of section 14 which relates to offences committed on bail it applies only to offences committed on or after that date. For section 15 which covers failure to answer bail it applies where there has been a failure to surrender to bail in the proceedings on or after January 1, 2007. The provisions apply only to court bail and not to bail granted by the police.

These amendments provide a further refinement to the application of the *Bail Act* and are designed to ensure that compliance with ECHR is beyond dispute. Under the provisions of paragraph 2A of Schedule 1 which continue to apply to indictable or either way offences that do not attract a sentence of life imprisonment, bail need not be granted if it appears to the court that the defendant was on bail in criminal proceedings on the date of the offence. There is no qualification to that discretion. By the amendments of section 14 the presumption of bail is affected so that the defendant may not be granted bail if he was on bail at the date of the offence unless the court is satisfied there is no significant risk of further offences whilst on bail. The terminology "significant risk" differs from the substantial grounds referred to in paragraph 2(1) of the Schedule and appears to be a higher test. The "significant risk" test also applies in cases where the defendant appears to have failed to answer his bail in the proceedings and the amendments of section 15 also affect the presumption of bail so that the defendant may not be granted bail where he has failed to answer bail in the proceedings before. With respect to youths the test is not quite so high as "particular weight" is to be given to these aspects of the situation in order to determine whether there are substantial grounds for believing the defendant would commit offences or fail to answer his bail. The determination of significant risk does not apply to youths but the fact of offences being committed on bail in the past and a history of failing to answer bail in the proceedings would apparently contribute heavily to finding substantial grounds to believe that this would happen again in future if bail were granted.

As to the fear of interference with witnesses or the obstruction of justice, the court has indicated that a generalised risk that this might occur is not sufficient. A specific risk must be identifiable and supported by evidence: *Clooth v. Belgium* (1991) 14 E.H.R.R. 717. The risk may involve the interference with witnesses, warning suspects or destroying evidence: *Wemhoff v. Germany* (1979) 1 E.H.R.R. 55.

5–40   The court must have regard to the four considerations of paragraph 9, Schedule 1 as well as others that appear relevant. The desirability of a medical examination of a defendant charged with murder was held to be a relevant consideration which may amount to an exception to bail: *Vernege* [1982] 1 All E.R. 403.

The prosecution, when making representations about bail must ensure that relevant reasons are brought to the attention of the court. Previous convictions are relevant and where the accused has a criminal record, a copy may be handed to the court, but as far as possible detailed oral reference to it should be avoided: *Dyson* 29 Cr.App.R. 104. Sight of the record disqualifies the court from hearing any subsequent trial as the *Magistrates' Courts Act* 1980 provides that a magistrate shall not participate in trying the issue of a defendant's guilt on the summary trial of an information if in the course of the same proceedings, for the purpose of deciding whether the defendant should have bail, he or she has been informed of any previous convictions: *Magistrates' Courts Act* 1980, s.42. This section will be repealed by the *Criminal Justice Act* 2003, s.41 and Sched. 3.

IV. CONDITIONS OF BAIL

(1) Bail Act 1976, Sched. 1, para. 8

Paragraph 8 gives the power to impose conditions on bail. Section 3 of the *Bail Act* **5–41**
1976 sets out the types of conditions which may be attached to the grant of bail in criminal proceedings. When bail is granted to a person to whom section 4 applies, no condition may be attached unless it is considered necessary for the purpose of preventing
absconding, the commission of an offence on bail or interference with witnesses or the
obstruction of justice, or for the purpose of obtaining medical or other reports.

Pre-release

1. To provide a security or sureties (see *post*, for details). The imposition of sureties **5–42**
   and securities has been considered by the European Court which held that the
   figure set must take account of the means of the accused who deposits a security
   or the third person if standing as a surety. The relationship between the accused
   and the surety should also be considered: *Wemhoff v. Germany (ante)*; *Neumeister v. Austria, (ante)*.
2. To surrender a passport to the police. The surrender of a passport or other
   travel documents and indeed driving documents was held by the European
   Court to be proportional: *Stogmuller v. Austria, (ante)*. It is not appropriate
   for such documents to be surrendered to the magistrates' court as there is no
   procedure for the retention or disposal of such items.

Post-release

1. A condition of residence to live and sleep each night at a fixed, approved address. **5–43**
   This may stipulate residence at a bail or other type of hostel. The court should
   be assured that the address is suitable and in the case of hostels, a place should
   formally be confirmed by the appropriate authorities. It is also usual for a further condition to be attached when directing residence at a hostel that the rules
   and regulations of the hostel must be observed. The European Court has approved the proportionality of a condition of residence: *Schmid v. Austria*
   [1985] 44 D.R. 195. The National Offender Management Service has introduced
   a bail accommodation support service which has been contracted out to private
   suppliers. As from June 2007 the contractors may provide accommodation in
   cases where bail may be refused mainly because of the lack of a suitable address.
   Accommodation will be in houses and flats within the community and the person
   bailed will have to keep appointments with the support service on a weekly basis
   when help will be given to find permanent accommodation, etc. The service is
   aimed at low risk offenders. Availability of the support service will be indicated
   to the court through a bail information report from prison or probation.
2. A curfew may be imposed ordering the defendant to stay indoors at a specified
   address during specified hours. The court also has power under section 3(6) to
   require under a "doorstep" condition that the person bailed present himself at
   the doorstep of the premises during the hours of curfew if a police officer so
   demands. An electronic tag to monitor a curfew may also be ordered. Whether
   any such condition is necessary to protect the public, (*i.e.* proportional) is a
   question of fact for each case. *R. (CPS) v. Chorley Justices* [2002] EWHC
   2162.
3. The accused may be directed to report to a police station in person on specific
   days and at specific times. His attendance will be noted. It is advisable to check
   that the police station is at a convenient location for the accused and that it is
   open at the relevant times.
4. A condition of non-contact may be made in relation to specific persons who
   should be named. This condition is common in charges involving violence

where the alleged victim may be named but it may also relate to other witnesses or co-defendants. Direct and indirect contact which may be prohibited includes the use of mobile phones and texting either by the accused or someone else on his behalf.

5. The accused may be prohibited from going to certain specified areas. This could cover a specific address where an offence was said to have occurred or where the alleged victim lives. It could also cover a wider area, such as a shopping centre or the London Tube system where the offence is one that is habitually committed in those places. The area prohibited must be clearly identified and measurements are sometimes used, (*e.g.* not to go within 100 metres of …) and exceptions can be made to the exclusion by permitting appearances at court or solicitors if located within the prohibited area. If a defendant is excluded from his place of residence the condition may be expressed to allow one visit accompanied by a police officer to collect personal effects.

6. The accused may be required to attend at all appointments and to co-operate with all directions given for the preparation of reports.

5–44 The court and the police should ensure that the defendant is able to comply with any condition they intend to impose under section 3(6) and that such conditions are clearly expressed, proportional and enforceable. The list above is far from exhaustive and the court and police have a wide discretion to devise and impose such conditions as appear necessary. Any conditions must be designed to address the real risks of failing to surrender, committing further offences, obstructing justice or interfering with witnesses or failing to attend for interviews. The European Court has said that equal care must be taken in fixing appropriate bail conditions as in deciding on continued detention: *Iwanczuk v. Poland* (2004) 38 E.H.R.R. 8.

In deciding on conditions the court is entitled to use its knowledge of local events and conditions. In *R. v. Mansfield Justices, ex p. Sharkey* [1985] Q.B. 613, Lord Lane said at 625 that:

> "The question the justices should ask themselves is a simple one; 'Is this condition necessary for the prevention of the commission of an offence when on bail?' They are not obliged to have substantial grounds. It is enough if they perceive a real and not a fanciful risk of the offence being committed. Thus, section 3(6) and paragraph 8 give the court a wide discretion to inquire whether the condition is necessary."

5–45 The defendants were arrested on suspicion of public order offences allegedly committed during the miners' strike of 1984–85. The court was entitled to impose conditions of bail not to picket except in respect of their own pits. The court was not obliged to have substantial grounds for believing that a repetition of the defendant's conduct would occur. That perception could be based on knowledge of what was happening in the pits in the area.

5–46 Conditions on bail may be imposed in respect of offences which are not punishable by imprisonment. In *R. v. Bournemouth Magistrates' Court, ex p. Cross* [1989] Crim.L.R. 207, the defendant was in the habit of protesting at fox hunt meets. He was bailed in respect of a public order offence arising from such a protest on the condition that he did not attend another hunt meeting before his next court appearance. The Divisional Court held that the condition had been validly imposed as the magistrates had considered that it was necessary to prevent the commission of further offences.

(2) Sureties

5–47 A person who stands surety enters into a recognisance to pay a fixed sum of money if the defendant fails to attend court.

Bail Act 1976, s.8

Bail with sureties

5–48 **8.**—(1) This section applies where a person is granted bail in criminal proceedings on condition that he provides one or more surety or sureties for the purpose of securing that he surrenders to custody.

(2) In considering the suitability for that purpose of a proposed surety, regard may be had (amongst other things) to—

    (a) the surety's financial resources;

    (b) his character and any previous convictions of his; and

    (c) his proximity (whether in point of kinship, place of residence or otherwise) to the person for whom he is to be surety.

(3) Where a court grants a person bail in criminal proceedings on such a condition but is unable to release him because no surety or no suitable surety is available, the court shall fix the amount in which the surety is to be bound and subsections (4) and (5) below, or in a case where the proposed surety resides in Scotland subsection (6) below, shall apply for the purpose of enabling the recognizance of the surety to be entered into subsequently.

(4) Where this subsection applies the recognizance of the surety may be entered into before such of the following persons or descriptions of persons as the court may by order specify or, if it makes no such order, before any of the following persons, that is to say—

    (a) where the decision is taken by a magistrates' court, before a justice of the peace, a justices' clerk or a police officer who either is of the rank of inspector or above or is in charge of a police station or, if Criminal Procedure Rules so provide, by a person of such other description as is specified in the rules;

    (b) where the decision is taken by the Crown Court, before any of the persons specified in paragraph (a) above or, if Criminal Procedure Rules so provide, by a person of such other description as is specified in the rules;

    (c) where the decision is taken by the High Court or the Court of Appeal, before any of the persons specified in paragraph (a) above or, if Civil Procedure Rules or Criminal Procedure Rules so provide, by a person of such other description as is specified in the rules;

    (d) where the decision is taken by the Courts-Martial Appeal Court, before any of the persons specified in paragraph (a) above or, if Courts-Martial Appeal rules so provide, by a person of such other description as is specified in the rules;

and Civil Procedure Rules, Criminal Procedure Rules or Courts-Martial Appeal rules may also prescribe the manner in which a recognizance which is to be entered into before such a person is to be entered into and the persons by whom and the manner in which the recognizance may be enforced.

(5) Where a surety seeks to enter into his recognizance before any person in accordance with subsection (4) above but that person declines to take his recognizance because he is not satisfied of the surety's suitability, the surety may apply to—

    (a) the court which fixed the amount of the recognizance in which the surety was to be bound, or

    (b) a magistrates' court,

for that court to take his recognizance and that court shall, if satisfied of his suitability, take his recognizance.

(6) Where this subsection applies, the court, if satisfied of the suitability of the proposed surety, may direct that arrangements be made for the recognizance of the surety to be entered into in Scotland before any constable, within the meaning of the *Police (Scotland) Act* 1967, having charge at any police office or station in like manner as the recognizance would be entered into in England or Wales.

(7) Where, in pursuance of subsection (4) or (6) above, a recognizance is entered into otherwise than before the court that fixed the amount of the recognizance, the same consequences shall follow as if it had been entered into before that court.

[This section is printed as amended by the *Courts Act* 2003, Scheds 8 and 10.]

The obligation of a surety extends only to securing the defendant's attendance at **5–49** court. A surety is not responsible for preventing any other defaults while the defendant is on bail. A surety should only be required where there is a risk that the defendant will fail to surrender to custody.

A surety may be taken in court by the magistrates or out of court by a legal adviser or other person to whom the justices' clerk has delegated the power. A surety may also be taken at a police station by a police officer of the rank of inspector or above or by a prison governor if the accused is in prison: *Magistrates' Courts Rules* 1981, r.86. The procedure adopted will depend on the gravity of the charge and the amount of surety fixed by the court. The person taking the surety will investigate the matters listed in section 8(2) and production of bank statements, savings accounts and payslips may be required as evidence of financial resources. The nature of the relationship between the surety and the defendant must also be inquired into so the court may be satisfied of the extent of the influence the surety holds over the defendant. The nature of the responsibility that is being assumed must also be explained to the surety. The surety has a personal duty to ensure that the defendant surrenders to custody at the time and place specified. If the defendant fails to surrender the amount of the recognisance fixed or some of it may be ordered to be paid. If the money is not paid immediately or within a time set, the surety can be committed to prison in default of payment.

The defendant's representative has a particular responsibility to ensure that a surety would be able to meet his or her financial obligations before being tendered to the court: *R. v. Birmingham Crown Court, ex p. Rashid Ali* [1999] Crim.L.R. 504.

Bail Act 1976, s.9

Offence of agreeing to indemnify sureties in criminal proceedings

5–50   **9.**—(1) If a person agrees with another to indemnify that other against any liability which that other may incur as a surety to secure the surrender to custody of a person accused or convicted of or under arrest for an offence, he and that other person shall be guilty of an offence.

(2) An offence under subsection (1) above is committed whether the agreement is made before or after the person to be indemnified becomes a surety and whether or not he becomes a surety and whether the agreement contemplates compensation in money or in money's worth.

(3) Where a magistrates' court convicts a person of an offence under subsection (1) above the court may, if it thinks—

    (a) that the circumstances of the offence are such that greater punishment should be inflicted for that offence than the court has power to inflict, or

    (b) in a case where it sends that person for trial to the Crown Court for another offence, that it would be appropriate for him to be dealt with for the offence under subsection (1) above by the court before which he is tried for the other offence,

commit him in custody or on bail to the Crown Court for sentence.

(4) A person guilty of an offence under subsection (1) above shall be liable—

    (a) on summary conviction, to imprisonment for a term not exceeding 3 months or to a fine not exceeding £400 or to both; or

    (b) on conviction on indictment or if sentenced by the Crown Court on committal for sentence under subsection (3) above, to imprisonment for a term not exceeding 12 months or to a fine or to both.

(5) No proceedings for an offence under subsection (1) above shall be instituted except by or with the consent of the Director of Public Prosecutions.

Magistrates' Courts Act 1980, s.119

Postponement of taking recognizance

5–51   **119.**—(1) Where a magistrates' court has power to take any recognizance, the court may, instead of taking it, fix the amount in which the principal and his sureties, if any, are to be bound; and thereafter the recognizance may be taken by any such person as may be prescribed.

(2) Where, in pursuance of this section, a recognizance is entered into otherwise than before the court that fixed the amount of it, the same consequences shall follow as if it had been entered into before that court; and references in this or any other Act to the court before which a recognizance was entered into shall be construed accordingly.

(3) Nothing in this section shall enable a magistrates' court to alter the amount of a recognizance fixed by the High Court or the Crown Court.

5–52   *Criminal Procedure Rules* 2005, r.19.5 in Appendix G–79 explain the requirements to be complied with before a person subject to a surety may be released.

(3) Security

5–53   A person granted bail may be required to give security for his or her surrender to custody: *Bail Act* 1976, s.3(5). In *R. v. Truro Magistrates' Court, ex p. Stevens* [2002] 1 W.L.R. 144, DC, the court held that although Parliament had not limited the type of security which might be given under section 3(5) what was envisaged was the lodging of some asset, in cash or in kind, which could be readily forfeited on the defendant's non-appearance. However, the security could be given in less simple form if the justice of the case demanded it and it could be readily forfeited in the event of non-appearance without disputes with third parties. While it was permissible for a third party to make an asset available as security for the defendant, where a court failed to make clear the extent to which a third party's interest in registered land belonging to the defendant was the subject of the security, the security was to be interpreted as extending only to the defendant's beneficial interest.

Criminal Procedure Rules 2005, r.19.4 in Appendix G–78 enables the court to give **5–54** directions as to how a requirement of bail such as a surety shall be complied with.

(4) Application to vary conditions of bail

Under section 3(8)(a) of the *Bail Act* 1976 where bail has been granted subject to **5–55** conditions, the magistrates' court may, on application by the person granted bail or the prosecutor or constable vary the conditions of bail or impose conditions in respect of the bail already granted. Notice of the application must be given so that both the defendant and the prosecution can make representations. The defendant is not bound to appear and simple variations can be made in the absence of the defendant. The court is under no duty to notify a surety of any application to vary bail conditions particularly when the surety is expressed to be continuous as the surety should keep himself informed of the bail position. Any ignorance of the variation may be taken into account when the court considers forfeiting the surety: *R. v. Wells Street Magistrates' Court, ex p. Albanese* [1982] Q.B. 333. When the defendant has been committed to the Crown Court from the magistrates' court on bail then once he has surrendered to the Crown Court, that court is seised of all bail matters and any application to vary must be made to the Crown Court: *R. v. Lincoln Magistrates' Court, ex p. Mawer* (1996) 160 J.P. 219.

V. APPEAL AND RECONSIDERATION

A. GENERAL

The defence and the prosecution have the right to challenge bail decisions made by **5–56** both the police and the court.

A defendant detained by the police must be produced at a court as soon as is practicable after charge and then application for bail may be made to the court. If a defendant is remanded in custody by the court he has a right of appeal and may apply for bail to the Crown Court.

When the police impose conditions on bail the defendant may appeal to the magistrates' court for the conditions to be removed or varied. Where conditions are imposed by the magistrates' court, application may be made to the court to vary them or an appeal against certain conditions may be made to the Crown Court.

The prosecution may appeal to the Crown Court against a decision to grant bail where it was opposed. If fresh information comes to light the prosecution may also apply to the magistrates' court for a decision to grant bail to be reconsidered.

B. APPEAL TO MAGISTRATES' COURT IN RESPECT OF POLICE BAIL

Magistrates' Courts Act 1980, s.43B

Power to grant bail where police bail has been granted
   43B.—(1) Where a custody officer—   **5–57**
   (a) grants bail to any person under Part IV of the *Police and Criminal Evidence Act* 1984 in criminal proceedings and imposes conditions, or

(b) varies, in relation to any person, conditions of bail in criminal proceedings under section 3(8) of the *Bail Act* 1976

a magistrates' court may, on application by or on behalf of that person, grant bail or vary the conditions.

(2) On an application under subsection (1) the court, if it grants bail and imposes conditions or if it varies the conditions, may impose more onerous conditions.

(3) On determining an application under subsection (1) the court shall remand the applicant, in custody or on bail in accordance with the determination, and, where the court withholds bail or grants bail the grant of bail made by the custody officer shall lapse.

(4) In this section "bail in criminal proceedings" and "vary" have the same meanings as they have in the *Bail Act* 1976.

5–58   *Criminal Procedure Rules* 2005, r.19.1 in Appendix G–75.

5–59   Section 43B effectively allows for an appeal to the magistrates' court against a decision of a police officer to grant or vary conditional bail. A person aggrieved by any requirements imposed by the custody officer may apply to the court but the court then has the power to impose more onerous conditions or to remand the applicant in custody as well as to accede to the requested variation. The decision of the court overrides the decision of the officer. The procedure is set down in rule 19.1 which requires the application to be heard within 72 hours with the prosecution and sureties being given notice of the date and time of hearing.

C. Appeal to the High Court

5–60   The *Criminal Justice Act* 2003, s.17 abolished the High Court's jurisdiction in respect of magistrates' court bail where it duplicates that of the Crown Court (as of April 5, 2004).

D. Application to the Crown Court by Defendant

Supreme Court Act 1981, s.81(1)(g); (1J)

Bail

5–61   **81.**—(1) The Crown Court may, subject to section 25 of the *Criminal Justice and Public Order Act* 1994, grant bail to any person—

(g) who has been remanded in custody by a magistrates' court on adjourning a case under section 11 of the *Powers of Criminal Courts (Sentencing) Act* 2000 (remand for medical examination) or—

(i)   section 5 (adjournment of inquiry into offence);
(ii) section 10 (adjournment of trial); or
(iii) section 18 (initial procedure on information against adult for offence triable either way);

and the time during which a person is released on bail under any provision of this subsection shall not count as part of any term of imprisonment or detention under his sentence.

(1J) The Crown Court may only grant bail to a person under subsection (1)(g) if the magistrates' court which remanded him in custody has certified under section 5(6A)of the *Bail Act* 1976 that it heard full argument on his application for bail before it refused the application.

[This section is reprinted omitting paras (1)(a)–(f), (1A)–(1I), (2)–(7).]

5–62   The defendant has a right to apply to the Crown Court for bail, when remanded in custody, and against conditions imposed on bail.

Criminal Justice Act 2003, s.16

Appeal to Crown Court

5–63   **16.**—(1) This section applies where a magistrates' court grants bail to a person ("the person concerned") on adjourning a case under—

   (a) section 10 of the *Magistrates' Courts Act* 1980 (adjournment of trial),

   (b) section 17C of that Act (intention as to plea: adjournment),

   (c) section 18 of that Act (initial procedure on information against adult for offence triable either way),

   (d) section 24C of that Act (intention as to plea by child or young person: adjournment),

   (e) section 52(5) of the *Crime and Disorder Act* 1998 (adjournment of proceedings under section 51 etc), or

   (f) section 11 of the *Powers of Criminal Courts (Sentencing) Act* 2000 (remand for medical examination).

  (2) Subject to the following provisions of this section, the person concerned may appeal to the Crown Court against any condition of bail falling within subsection (3).

  (3) A condition of bail falls within this subsection if it is a requirement—

   (a) that the person concerned resides away from a particular place or area,

   (b) that the person concerned resides at a particular place other than a bail hostel,

   (c) for the provision of a surety or sureties or the giving of a security,

   (d) that the person concerned remains indoors between certain hours,

   (e) imposed under section 3(6ZAA) of the 1976 Act (requirements with respect to electronic monitoring), or

   (f) the person concerned makes no contact with another person.

  (4) An appeal under this section may not be brought unless subsection (5) or (6) applies.

  (5) This subsection applies if an application to the magistrates' court under section 3(8)(a) of the 1976 Act (application by or on behalf of person granted bail) was made and determined before the appeal was brought.

  (6) This subsection applies if an application to the magistrates' court—

   (a) under section 3(8)(b) of the 1976 Act (application by constable or prosecutor), or

   (b) under section 5B(1) of that Act (application by prosecutor),

was made and determined before the appeal was brought.

  (7) On an appeal under this section the Crown Court may vary the conditions of bail.

  (8) Where the Crown Court determines an appeal under this section, the person concerned may not bring any further appeal under this section in respect of the conditions of bail unless an application or a further application to the magistrates' court under section 3(8)(a) of the 1976 Act is made and determined after the appeal.

This provision which came into force in April 2004 gives a power to appeal to the **5–64** Crown Court against certain conditions of bail relating to residence away from a particular place or area or residence other than at a bail hostel; the provision of a surety or security; a curfew; electronic tagging or non-contact. Such an appeal can only be made where application to vary has already been made to the magistrates' court.

For full certificates of bail see section 5, *ante*.

E. APPEAL TO THE CROWN COURT BY PROSECUTION

Bail (Amendment) Act 1993, s.1

Prosecution right of appeal

  1.—(1) Where a magistrates' court grants bail to a person who is charged with or convicted of **5–65** an offence punishable by imprisonment, the prosecution may appeal to a judge of the Crown Court against the granting of bail.

  (2) Subsection (1) above applies only where the prosecution is conducted—

   (a) by or on behalf of the Director of Public Prosecutions; or

   (b) by a person who falls within such class or description of person as may be prescribed for the purposes of this section by order made by the Secretary of State.

  (3) Such an appeal may be made only if—

   (a) the prosecution made representations that bail should not be granted; and

   (b) the representations were made before it was granted.

  (4) In the event of the prosecution wishing to exercise the right of appeal set out in

subsection (1) above, oral notice of appeal shall be given to the magistrates' court at the conclusion of the proceedings in which such bail has been granted and before the release from custody of the person concerned.

(5) Written notice of appeal shall thereafter be served on the magistrates' court and the person concerned within two hours of the conclusion of such proceedings.

(6) Upon receipt from the prosecution of oral notice of appeal from its decision to grant bail the magistrates' court shall remand in custody the person concerned, until the appeal is determined or otherwise disposed of.

(7) Where the prosecution fails, within the period of two hours mentioned in subsection (5) above, to serve one or both of the notices required by that subsection, the appeal shall be deemed to have been disposed of.

(8) The hearing of an appeal under subsection (1) above against a decision of the magistrates' court to grant bail shall be commenced within forty-eight hours, excluding weekends and any public holiday (that is to say, Christmas Day, Good Friday or a bank holiday), from the date on which oral notice of appeal is given.

(9) At the hearing of any appeal by the prosecution under this section, such appeal shall be by way of re-hearing, and the judge hearing any such appeal may remand the person concerned in custody or may grant bail subject to such conditions (if any) as he thinks fit.

(10) In relation to a child or young person (within the meaning of the *Children and Young Persons Act* 1969)—

  (a) the reference in subsection (1) above to an offence punishable by imprisonment is to be read as a reference to an offence which would be so punishable in the case of an adult; and

  (b) the reference in subsection (6) above to remand in custody is to be read subject to the provisions of section 23 of the Act of 1969 (remands to local authority accommodation).

(11) The power to make an order under subsection (2) above shall be exercisable by statutory instrument and any instrument shall be subject to annulment in pursuance of a resolution of either House of Parliament.

[This section is printed as amended by the *Criminal Justice Act* 2003, s.18 which came into force on April 4, 2005.]

5–66   See *Criminal Procedure Rules* 2005, r.19.16 in Appendix G–90.

5–67   The prescribed prosecutors under section 1(2)(b) are the Serious Fraud Office, the Trade and Industry Department, HM Customs and Revenue, Secretary of State for Social Security and the Post Office: *Bail (Amendment) Act 1993 (Prescription of Prosecuting Authorities) Order* 1994 (S.I. 1994 No. 1438).

The prosecution has the right in the specified cases to appeal against a grant of bail when bail was originally opposed. The requirement that the offence carries a minimum sentence of five years imprisonment was removed by the *Criminal Justice Act* 2003, section 18 which requires only that the offence be imprisonable. Under section 5(2A), the court has a duty to provide written reasons when bail is granted after the prosecution has objected to bail which assists in the formulation of any subsequent appeal by the prosecution.

5–68   The requirement that oral notice of appeal be given to the magistrates' court "at the conclusion of the proceedings" was satisfied where notice was given five minutes after the case had been dealt with when the legal adviser was still at court although the magistrates had left the building: *R. v. Isleworth Crown Court, ex p. Clark* [1998] 1 Cr.App.R. 257. The hearing must be commenced within 48 hours of the end of the day on which oral notice of appeal is given: *R. v. Middlesex Guildhall Crown Court, ex p. Okoli* [2000] 1 Cr.App.R. 1.

5–69   Where a defendant who had been granted bail challenged the service of the written notice of appeal because it was not served within two hours of the oral notice he claimed that the appeal should be deemed disposed of under section 1(7). The court held, dismissing the appeal, that the prosecutor had used all due diligence to try and serve the notice and the failure to do so was due to circumstances beyond his control. The notice was served only three minutes late and as oral notice had been given the appellant was not prejudiced by this delay: *R. (Jeffrey) v. Warwick Crown Court* [2002] EWHC 2469; [2003] Crim. L.R. 190.

F. Reconsideration

Bail Act 1976, s.5B

Reconsideration of decisions granting bail

5B.—(1) Where a magistrates' court has granted bail in criminal proceedings in connection **5–70** with an offence, or proceedings for an offence, to which this section applies or a constable has granted bail in criminal proceedings in connection with proceedings for such an offence, that court or the appropriate court in relation to the constable may, on application by the prosecutor for the decision to be reconsidered,—

    (a) vary the conditions of bail,

    (b) impose conditions in respect of bail which has been granted unconditionally, or

    (c) withhold bail.

(2) The offences to which this section applies are offences triable on indictment and offences triable either way.

(3) No application for the reconsideration of a decision under this section shall be made unless it is based on information which was not available to the court or constable when the decision was taken.

(4) Whether or not the person to whom the application relates appears before it, the magistrates' court shall take the decision in accordance with section 4(1) (and Schedule 1) of this Act.

(5) Where the decision of the court on a reconsideration under this section is to withhold bail from the person to whom it was originally granted the court shall—

    (a) if that person is before the court, remand him in custody, and

    (b) if that person is not before the court, order him to surrender himself forthwith into the custody of the court.

(6) Where a person surrenders himself into the custody of the court in compliance with an order under subsection (5) above, the court shall remand him in custody.

(7) A person who has been ordered to surrender to custody under subsection (5) above may be arrested without warrant by a constable if he fails without reasonable cause to surrender to custody in accordance with the order.

(8) A person arrested in pursuance of subsection (7) above shall be brought as soon as practicable, and in any event within 24 hours after his arrest, before a justice of the peace and the justice shall remand him in custody.

In reckoning for the purposes of this subsection any period of 24 hours, no account shall be taken of Christmas Day, Good Friday or any Sunday.

(8A) Where the court, on a reconsideration under this section, refuses to withhold bail from a relevant person after hearing representations from the prosecutor in favour of withholding bail, then the court shall give reasons for refusing to withhold bail.

(8B) In subsection (8A) above, "relevant person" means a person to whom section 4(1) (and Schedule 1) of this Act is applicable in accordance with subsection (4) above.

(8C) A court which is by virtue of subsection (8A) above required to give reasons for its decision shall include a note of those reasons in any record of its decision and, if requested to do so by the prosecutor, shall cause the prosecutor to be given a copy of any such record as soon as practicable after the record is made.

(9) Criminal Procedure rules shall include provision—

    (a) requiring notice of an application under this section and of the grounds for it to be given to the person affected, including notice of the powers available to the court under it;

    (b) for securing that any representations made by the person affected (whether in writing or orally) are considered by the court before making its decision; and

    (c) designating the court which is the appropriate court in relation to the decision of any constable to grant bail.

[This section is reprinted as amended by the *Criminal Justice and Police Act* 2001, s.129(3) and the *Courts Act* 2003, Scheds 8 and 10 which came into force on April 4, 2005.]

See *Criminal Procedure Rules* 2005, r.19.2 in Appendix G–76.   **5–71**

The prosecutor may apply to the magistrates' court to for bail to be reconsidered **5–72** when new information comes to light affecting the original bail decision made either by the police or the court. This right does not apply to summary only offences.

It is envisaged that the defendant may be enjoying bail and the prosecutor discovers information not available earlier on the basis of which concerns arise about bail. The application must be heard within 72 hours, with notice being sent to the person affected, the prosecution and any surety. The case can then be dealt with before the scheduled adjourned date.

The court may decide a reconsideration application regardless of whether the accused appears before the court. When the court decides to withhold bail, the defendant may be arrested without a warrant and remanded in custody.

A magistrate is entitled to refuse bail notwithstanding that at the previous hearing unconditional bail had been granted. Where there had been no subsequent changes in the circumstances, but the court requested and obtained further information from the prosecutor at the second hearing which was not sought at the previous hearing the court's decision to refuse bail was upheld: *R. v. Tower Bridge Magistrates' Court, ex p. Gilbert* (1988) 152 J.P. 307.

VI. ABSCONDING AND BREACH OF BAIL CONDITIONS

A. Offence of Absconding while on Bail

Bail Act 1976, s.6

Offence of absconding by person released on bail

5–73   **6.**—(1) If a person who has been released on bail in criminal proceedings fails without reasonable cause to surrender to custody he shall be guilty of an offence.

(2) If a person who—

    (a) has been released on bail in criminal proceedings, and

    (b) having reasonable cause therefor, has failed to surrender to custody,

fails to surrender to custody at the appointed place as soon after the appointed time as is reasonably practicable he shall be guilty of an offence.

(3) It shall be for the accused to prove that he had reasonable cause for his failure to surrender to custody.

(4) A failure to give to a person granted bail in criminal proceedings a copy of the record of the decision shall not constitute a reasonable cause for that person's failure to surrender to custody.

(5) An offence under subsection (1) or (2) above shall be punishable either on summary conviction or as if it were a criminal contempt of court.

(6) Where a magistrates' court convicts a person of an offence under subsection (1) or (2) above the court may, if it thinks—

    (a) that the circumstances of the offence are such that greater punishment should be inflicted for that offence than the court has power to inflict, or

    (b) in a case where it commits that person for trial to the Crown Court for another offence, that it would be appropriate for him to be dealt with for the offence under subsection (1) or (2) above by the court before which he is tried for the other offence,

commit him in custody or on bail to the Crown Court for sentence.

(7) A person who is convicted summarily of an offence under subsection (1) or (2) above and is not committed to the Crown Court for sentence shall be liable to imprisonment for a term not exceeding 3 months or to a fine not exceeding level 5 on the standard scale or to both and a person who is so committed for sentence or is dealt with as for such a contempt shall be liable to imprisonment for a term not exceeding 12 months or to a fine or to both.

(8) In any proceedings for an offence under subsection (1) or (2) above a document purporting to be a copy of the part of the prescribed record which relates to the time and place appointed for the person specified in the record to surrender to custody and to be duly certified to be a true copy of that part of the record shall be evidence of the time and place appointed for that person to surrender to custody.

(9) For the purposes of subsection (8) above—

    (a) "the prescribed record" means the record of the decision of the court, officer or constable made in pursuance of section 5(1) of this Act;

    (b) the copy of the prescribed record is duly certified if it is certified by the appropriate officer of the court or, as the case may be, by the constable who took the decision or a constable designated for the purpose by the officer in charge of the police station from which the person to whom the record relates was released;

    (c) "the appropriate officer" of the court is—

        (i) in the case of a magistrates' court, the designated officer for the Court;

[(10) Section 127 of the *Magistrates' Courts Act* 1980 shall not apply in relation to an offence under subsection (1) or (2) above.

(11) Where a person has been released on bail in criminal proceedings and that bail was granted by a constable, a magistrates' court shall not try that person for an offence under subsection (1) or (2) above in relation to that bail (the "relevant offence") unless either or both of subsection (12) and (13) below applies.

(12) This subsection applies if an information is laid for the relevant offence within 6 months from the time of the commission of the offence.

(13) This subsection applies if an information is laid for the relevant offence no later than 3 months from the time of the occurrence of the first of the events mentioned in subsection (14) below to occur after the commission of the relevant offence.

(14) Those events are—

    (a) the person surrenders to custody at the appointed place;

    (b) the person is arrested, or attends at a police station, in connection with the relevant offence or the offence for which he was granted bail;

    (c) the person appears or is brought before a court in connection with the relevant offence or the offence for which he was granted bail.]

[This section is reprinted as amended by the *Access to Justice Act* 1999, Sched. 13, para. 89. This section was amended by the *Criminal Justice Act* 2003, s.15(3) which took effect in April 2004 and the *Courts Act* 2003, Sched. 8 which came into force on April 1, 2005.]

Under section 3(1) of the *Bail Act* 1976, a person granted bail in criminal proceedings is under a duty to surrender to custody. That duty is enforceable under section 6 of the Act. If a person released on bail fails without reasonable cause to surrender to custody he is guilty of an offence under section 6. Although "surrender to custody" means surrender "at the time and place for the time being appointed for him to do so" the *de minimis* rule should be applied if a defendant is only marginally late. Being seven minutes late was held not to constitute an offence under section 6: *R. v. Gateshead Justices, ex p. Usher* [1981] Crim.L.R. 491, DC.   **5–74**

The obligation of a person on bail is to comply with the directions of the court. Once a person has reported as instructed to the appropriate court official he has surrendered to custody and is under an implied obligation not to leave without consent. If the defendant leaves he is liable to be arrested under section 7(2) although no offence under section 6 may have been committed: *DPP v. Richards* [1988] Q.B. 701.

What amounts to "a reasonable cause" is a matter of fact in each case. A mistake about the date due to an administrative blunder by solicitors did not provide a reasonable excuse but was relevant for mitigation: *Laidlaw v. Atkinson, The Times*, August 2, 1986. Whether a mistake by a solicitor, such as giving the defendant the wrong date, amounts to a reasonable excuse is a question of fact to be decided in all the circumstances of the particular case: *R. v. Liverpool City J.J., ex p. Santos, The Times*, January 23, 1997, DC.

There are two offences under the section: **5–75**

    1) It is an offence to fail to surrender without reasonable cause; and

    2) It is an offence to fail to surrender as soon as is reasonably practicable after having had reasonable cause for failing to surrender initially.

The second limb of the section covers the situation of a defendant who may be too ill to attend as originally expected and so has reasonable cause for not coming to court but then fails to contact the court or surrender himself as soon as he has recovered.

The burden of proving the reasonable cause rests with the defendant to the civil standard of balance of probabilities: *Carr Briant* [1943] K.B. 607.

The court will deal with an absconder as a summary offence. There is no power to commit a bail offence to the Crown Court for trial because it is not an either way offence. The power to commit to the Crown Court only applies after conviction. In *Schiavo v. Anderton* [1987] Q.B. 20, DC, the defendant was granted bail in the magistrates' court pending summary trial but failed to answer bail. When he was brought before the court two years later on a warrant, he pleaded guilty to absconding and was committed to the Crown Court for sentence. In the Crown Court he argued that the magistrates' court had had no jurisdiction to try the matter, since no information had been laid within six months of the offences. The Divisional Court held that no information need be laid; the court heard the proceedings of its own motion and that the matter could be tried only by the court which granted bail.

The *Consolidated Criminal Practice Directions* gives detailed directions on bail and the failure to surrender, see Appendix F–15.

When a defendant fails to answer his bail, in the absence of any explanation the court will issue a warrant under section 7. When the warrant has been executed and the defendant appears before the court, it will be considered whether an offence under section 6 should be put. If the defendant is on police bail and failed to surrender to custody at his first court appearance the prosecutor will decide whether to initiate proceedings. An information must be laid within six months' of the offence or three months of the surrender to custody, arrest, or court appearance. Where the defendant fails to answer court bail, the court may initiate proceedings by its own motion at any time and the six month time-limit does not apply. The court will be invited to take proceedings by the prosecutor, if proceedings are considered appropriate: see also *Murphy v. DPP* [1990] 2 All E.R. 390; *R. v. Teeside Magistrates' Court, ex p. Bujnowski* [1997] Crim.L.R. 51.

5–76   Whether or not a warrant of arrest has been issued or executed, the question of proceedings regarding a possible failure to surrender will be dealt with by the Crown Prosecution Service whose discretion to invite the court to proceed is unfettered: *France v. Dewsbury Magistrates' Court* (1987) 152 J.P. 301. The court must give the defendant an opportunity to explain his failure to surrender and also to make submissions before sentence: *Davis (Seaton Roy)* (1989) 8 Cr.App.R. 64, CA; *Woods* (1986) 11 Cr.App.R. 551, CA. The fact that a defendant has been acquitted of the principal offence does not affect his criminality in relation to any offence under the *Bail Act* 1976: *Clarke* [2000] 1 Cr.App.R. 173.

The court also has the power to commit the defendant to the Crown Court for sentence on a bail offence if they consider their powers of sentencing to be insufficient or if the defendant has other related matters which are being committed for trial.

B. LIABILITY TO ARREST

Bail Act 1976, s.7

Liability to arrest for absconding or breaking conditions of bail

5–77   7.—(1) If a person who has been released on bail in criminal proceedings and is under a duty to surrender into the custody of a court fails to surrender to custody at the time appointed for him to do so the court may issue a warrant for his arrest.

(2) If a person who has been released on bail in criminal proceedings absents himself from the court at any time after he has surrendered into the custody of the court and before the court is ready to begin or to resume the hearing of the proceedings, the court may issue a warrant for his arrest; but no warrant shall be issued under this subsection where that person is absent in accordance with leave given to him by or on behalf of the court.

(3) A person who has been released on bail in criminal proceedings and is under a duty to surrender into the custody of a court may be arrested without warrant by a constable—

    (a) if the constable has reasonable grounds for believing that that person is not likely to surrender to custody;

(b) if the constable has reasonable grounds for believing that that person is likely to break any of the conditions of his bail or has reasonable grounds for suspecting that that person has broken any of those conditions; or

(c) in a case where that person was released on bail with one or more surety or sureties, if a surety notifies a constable in writing that that person is unlikely to surrender to custody and that for that reason the surety wishes to be relieved of his obligations as a surety.

(4) a person arrested in pursuance of subsection (3) above—

(a) shall, except where he was arrested within 24 hours of the time appointed for him to surrender to custody, be brought as soon as practicable and in any event within 24 hours after his arrest before a justice of the peace; and

(b) in the said excepted case shall be brought before the court at which he was to have surrendered to custody.

[In reckoning for the purposes of this subsection any period of 24 hours, no account shall be taken of Christmas Day, Good Friday or any Sunday.]

(5) A justice of the peace before whom a person is brought under subsection (4) above may, subject to subsection (6) below, if of the opinion that that person—

(a) is not likely to surrender to custody, or

(b) has broken or is likely to break any condition of his bail,

remand him in custody or commit him to custody, as the case may require, or alternatively, grant him bail subject to the same or to different conditions, but if not of that opinion shall grant him bail subject to the same conditions (if any) as were originally imposed.

(6) Where the person so brought before the justice is a child or young person and the justice does not grant him bail, subsection (5) above shall have effect subject to the provisions of section 23 of the *Children and Young Persons Act* 1969 (remands to the care of local authorities).

[This section is reprinted as amended by the *Criminal Law Act* 1977, Sched. 12 and the *Courts Act* 2003, Sched. 10 which came into force on April 1, 2005.]

See *Criminal Procedure Rules* 2005, r.19.12 in Appendix G–76.   **5–78**

Where the accused fails to surrender to custody in answer to his or her bail, the court may issue a warrant of arrest. Alternatively the court may adjourn and enlarge the defendant's bail under section 129 of the *Magistrates' Courts Act* 1980 but only if it is satisfied that there is a good reason for the defendant's non-attendance or attendance has been excused by the court.

Where a suspect is bailed from a police station pursuant to section 37(2) of the *Police and Criminal Evidence Act* 1984 and fails to attend the police station on a prescribed subsequent date he may be arrested without warrant: *Police and Criminal Evidence Act* 1984, s.46A.

A defendant may also be arrested by an officer without a warrant under section 7(3), **5–79** *ante*. The usual reason for arrest is a breach of a bail condition. The arrested person may be brought either before the court to which he should have surrendered or before the court sitting in the area in which he was arrested. The choice of court may be dictated by the time limit which requires the arrested person to be produced at court within 24 hours of his arrest. Where an arrested person is not brought before a court within 24 hours he has an absolute right to be released from custody. Bringing the defendant within the precincts or to the cells of a magistrates' court is not sufficient for this purpose; the defendant must actually appear before the magistrates: *R. v. Governor of Glen Parva Young Offenders Institution, ex p. G (a minor)* [1998] 2 Cr.App.R. 349. Once the defendant has been brought before the court, the hearing can then be adjourned to later in the day to be dealt with by a different bench: *R. (Hussain) v. Derby Magistrates' Court* [2001] 1 W.L.R. 2454.

When a person arrested under section 7 is brought before the magistrates' court he must be dealt with according to section 7(5). The magistrate has no power to commit the defendant to the Crown Court for a decision on the breach to be made there even when the original bail was granted by the Crown Court: *R. v. Teeside Magistrates' Court, ex p. Ellison* (2001) 165 J.P. 355, DC.

In *R. v. Liverpool City Justices, ex p. DPP* (1993) 95 Cr.App.R. 222, DC, detailed consideration was given to the operation of section 7.

5–80   — The section contemplates the constable who has arrested the person bailed bringing him before the court and stating the grounds for believing that the defendant has broken or is likely to break a condition of his bail; this may well involve the giving of "hearsay" evidence.

— Even where the defendant disputes the ground on which he was arrested, there is no necessity for the giving of evidence on oath or providing an opportunity to the person arrested, or his lawyer to cross-examine, or give evidence himself. Nevertheless the court must give the defendant an opportunity to respond to what the constable alleges.

5–81   — The court has no power to adjourn the proceedings, but must consider on the material before it whether it is able to form one of the opinions set out in section 7(5) and if it does so, go on to decide whether to remand the defendant in custody or on bail on the same or more stringent conditions.

— If the court feels unable to form one of the opinions set out in section 7(5) it must order the person concerned to be released on bail on the same terms as were originally imposed.

— Proceedings under section 7(5) do not preclude the defendant who has been remanded in custody from making an application for bail to the magistrates' court, Crown Court or to a judge as appropriate. The presumption in favour of granting bail under section 4 of the Act will be subject not only to the exceptions to the right to bail in Part 1, paragraph 2 of Schedule 1 to the Act but also to the exception in paragraph 6 of that Schedule.

5–82   Where a person is arrested pursuant to section 7(3) the procedure contained in section 7(5) does not involve the determination of a criminal charge within the meaning of Article 6(1) of the European Convention on Human Rights.

In *R. v. Havering Magistrates' Court, ex p. DPP* [2001] 1 W.L.R. 805, the DPP applied for judicial review of a decision of justices that proceedings brought against the defendant under the *Bail Act* 1976, s.7(5) should be withdrawn. The justices had found that oral evidence was necessary to show that the defendant had acted in breach of the conditions. The issue before the court related to the compatibility of the procedures under section 7(5) and Schedule 1, Part I, paragraph 6 of the Act with the right to a fair trial and the right to liberty and security guaranteed under the *Human Rights Act* 1998, Sched. 1, Pt I, Arts 6 and 5 respectively. The court held that since section 7 made provision for a means of achieving the purposes for which bail conditions were imposed, liability for detention under section 7 derived from the charge that a defendant faced as a means of securing those purposes and did not equate to the facing of a criminal charge. It followed that Article 6 did not have any direct relevance. The procedures would not breach Article 5 provided that the court evaluated the material presented in the context of the consequences to a defendant and, in particular, took account of the fact that where hearsay evidence was relied on, it had not been subject to cross-examination. A defendant should be given a fair opportunity to comment on the material upon which the proceedings were based. The court is not limited under Article 5 to only considering evidence that was admissible in the strict sense. The facts upon which the decision was based did not need to be proved to the criminal standard of proof. See also *R. v. Wirral Borough Magistrates' Court, ex p. McKeown* [2001] 2 Cr.App.R. 2, DC.

In *R. v. West London Magistrates' Court, ex p. Vickers* [2004] Crim.L.R. 63, the defendant sought judicial review of the magistrates' decision to remand him in custody following a finding that he had broken conditions of his bail. He argued that the magistrates had been wrong to hold that reasonable excuse was not a defence to an allegation of breaking a bail condition. He submitted that the words "without reasonable cause" should be read into the *Bail Act* 1976, s.7(5) otherwise the provision would be incompatible with the *Human Rights Act* 1998, Sched. 1 Pt I, Art.5. The application was refused on the basis that when magistrates were considering whether there had been a breach of a condition of bail under section 7(5), they had a duty to act fairly and give the bailed person the opportunity of responding to the allegation. However, they did not have to consider whether the defendant had a reasonable excuse for breaking the relevant condition. When, having satisfied themselves that a breach of condition had occurred, the magistrates were considering whether to admit the bailed person to bail again or remand him in custody, they should take into account the reasons for the breach, at which point issues relating to reasonable excuse might arise. Provided that the magistrates followed the procedure set out in *R. v. Havering Magistrates' Court, ex p. DPP* there would be no breach of Article 5.

C. Consequences for Sureties

Magistrates' Courts Act 1980, s.120

Forfeiture of recognizance

120.—(1) This section applies where—   **5–83**

    (a) a recognizance to keep the peace or to be of good behaviour has been entered into before a magistrates' court; or

    (b) any recognizance is conditioned for the appearance of a person before a magistrates' court, or for his doing any other thing connected with a proceeding before a magistrates' court.

(1A) If, in the case of a recognizance which is conditioned for the appearance of an accused before a magistrates' court, the accused fails to appear in accordance with the condition, the court shall—

    (a) declare the recognizance to be forfeited;

    (b) issue a summons directed to each person bound by the recognizance as surety, requiring him to appear before the court on a date specified in the summons to show cause why he should not be adjudged to pay the sum in which he is bound; and on that date the court may proceed in the absence of any surety if it is satisfied that he has been served with the summons.

(2) If, in any other case falling within subsection (1) above, the recognizance appears to the magistrates' court to be forfeited, the court may—

    (a) declare the recognizance to be forfeited; and

    (b) adjudge each person bound by it, whether as principal or surety, to pay the sum in which he is bound; but in a case falling within subsection (1)(a) above, the court shall not declare the recognizance to be forfeited except by order made on complaint.

(3) The court which declares the recognizance to be forfeited may, instead of adjudging any person to pay the whole sum in which he is bound, adjudge him to pay part only of the sum or remit the sum.

(4) Payment of any sum adjudged to be paid under this section, including any costs awarded against the defendant, may be enforced, and any such sum shall be applied, as if it were a fine and as if the adjudication were a summary conviction of an offence not punishable with imprisonment and so much of section 85(1) above as empowers a court to remit fines shall not apply to the sum but so much thereof as relates to remission after a term of imprisonment has been imposed shall so apply; but at any time before the issue of a warrant of commitment to enforce payment of the sum, or before the sale of goods under a warrant of distress to satisfy the sum, the court may remit the whole or any part of the sum either absolutely or on such conditions as the court thinks just.

(5) A recognizance such as is mentioned in this section shall not be enforced otherwise than in accordance with this section, and accordingly shall not be transmitted to the Crown Court nor shall its forfeiture be certified to that Court.

Where a defendant who is on conditional bail with a condition of a surety fails to appear the court must declare the recognisance (the amount of money fixed) forfeit and then issue a summons to the surety requiring appearance before the court to show "just cause" as to why the sum required should not be paid. The court may order that the recognisance be paid in full, or a lesser amount may be ordered reflecting the circumstances of the case. It is also open to the court to remit the recognisance in full and order that nothing be paid. If the recognisance cannot be paid the surety can be given time to pay and a period of imprisonment may be fixed in default of payment.   **5–84**

The power to declare a recognisance to be forfeited is strictly dependant on there being a breach of the condition of the recognisance; a mere breach of a condition of bail by the defendant provides no basis for declaring the recognisance to be forfeited: *R. v. Bow Street Magistrates' Court, ex p. Hart* [2002] 1 W.L.R. 1242, DC.

The burden of persuading the court that a recognisance should not be paid is upon the surety. The court must hear such evidence and argument as the surety wishes to put forward. The onus on the surety of showing that the full amount should not be lost is a heavy one: *R. v. Uxbridge Justices, ex p. Heward-Mills* [1983] 1 W.L.R. 56. An application to forfeit a surety is a civil proceeding and the standard of proof is the ordinary civil standard on the balance of probabilities: *R. v. Marlow Justices, ex p. O'Sullivan* [1984] Q.B. 381, DC.

Lack of culpability on the part of the surety is not, of itself, a ground for holding that the recognisance should not be paid: *R. v. Crown Court at Warwick, ex p. Smalley* (1987) 84 Cr.App.R. 51. In *R. v. Maidstone Crown Court, ex p. Lever and Connell* [1996] 1 Cr.App.R. 524 the Court of Appeal (Criminal Division) reviewed the principles which govern the forfeiture of a recognisance. The applicants provided sureties of £19,000 and £40,000 for the defendant who failed to attend his trial in the Crown Court. When, in breach of his bail, the accused failed to report to the police station one evening, the local police did not inform anyone, not even the police officer in charge of the case. Two days later one surety discovered that the accused had not been at home for two nights and telephoned the other surety and the police. At first instance the judge found that there was no culpability in either surety and that the police were negligent but nonetheless ordered forfeiture of £16,000 and £35,000 respectively. The Divisional Court then refused their application for judicial review. The Court of Appeal said:

> "The general principle is that the purpose of a recognisance is to bring the defendant to court for trial. The basis for estreatment is not as a matter of punishment of the surety, but because he has failed to fulfil the obligation which he undertook. The starting point on the failure to bring a defendant to court is the forfeiture of the full recognisance. The right to estreat is triggered by the non-attendance of the defendant at court. It is for the surety to establish to the satisfaction of the trial court that there are grounds upon which the court may remit for forfeiture part or, wholly exceptionally, the whole recognisance. The presence or absence of culpability is a factor but the absence of culpability, as found in this case by the judge, is not in itself a reason to reduce or set aside the obligation entered into by the surety to pay in the event of a failure to bring the defendant to court. The court may, in the exercise of a wide discretion, decide it would be fair and just to estreat some or all of the recognisance."

Any reduction in the amount of the recognisance should be confined to the really deserving cases and any reduction should be regarded as the exception rather than the rule.

This may be contrasted with the decision in *R. v. Southampton Justices, ex p. Green* [1976] Q.B. 11 where it was held that the magistrates had wrongly failed to consider the applicant's culpability. The statement in this case that the recognisance should be remitted in full if the surety used all due diligence and efforts to secure the appearance has been considered in later case law.

5–85   The court's approach was explained again in *R. v. Horseferry Stipendiary Magistrate, ex p. Pearson* [1976] 1 W.L.R. 511. The court should approach the question for forfeiture "on the footing that the surety has seriously entered into a serious obligation and ought to pay the amount which he or she has promised unless there are circumstances in the case, relating either to means or culpability, which make it fair and just to pay a smaller sum." In this case the surety made serious efforts to get something done when she feared that the accused would abscond which the court on appeal said had not been taken into account when the recognisance was forfeited.

In a later case it was repeated that it might be proper to remit the recognisance entirely where the surety acted with all due diligence and made every effort to secure the appearance of the accused: *R. v. Waltham Forest Justices, ex p. Parfrey* (1980) 2 Cr.App.R.(S.) 208.

The presumption has been said to be that the whole of the recognisance should be estreated in "normal cases" but the fact that a defendant had attended at all preliminary and committal hearings and had initially arrived at the Crown Court for his trial before absconding in the middle of the day meant that the case was not normal and the blameworthiness of the surety should have been assessed on that basis: *R. v. Crown Court at York, ex p. Coleman and How* (1988) 86 Cr.App.R. 151.

By contrast in another case the court said that the purpose of the surety is to force **5–86** the defendant to surrender to the court. If the defendant fails to do so, the recognisance should be paid and the surety cannot escape liability by showing he has no means nor that it was not his fault that the defendant did not attend: *R. v. Southampton Justices, ex p. Corker* (1976) 120 S.J. 214.

The case law indicates that each case should be dealt with on its merits and there is a wide discretion to remit the recognisance taking into account culpability and means.

Sureties should always be notified when a hearing date was fixed and if no date was fixed, they should be informed of the dates between which the case was likely to be listed. Ignorance of the date would not always be an answer to proceedings for forfeiture: *R. v. Reading Crown Court, ex p. Bello* (1991) 92 Cr.App.R. 303, CA (Civ. Div). An order for forfeiture was described as 'premature' when the question had been considered in advance of a fixed date for trial. The defendant had gone abroad in breach of his bail conditions. The matter should have been considered once it was known that he would not appear to stand trial: *R. v. Inner London Crown Court, ex p. Springall* (1987) 85 Cr.App.R. 214, DC

References in the authorities to consideration of means implies that the court should **5–87** consider the surety's ability to pay and the consequences to the surety of ordering payment in an amount which would inevitably lead to imprisonment for default. There may be cases where the culpability of the surety is so great that an amount may be estreated that he cannot afford thereby making a prison sentence likely: *R. v. Crown Court of Wood Green, ex p. Howe* (1991) 93 Cr.App.R. 213, DC

It is relevant for the court in deciding whether to exercise its power under section 120(4) to remit the whole or any part of a sum to consider the potential impact of making payment not just on the surety but others as well: *R. v. Leicestershire Sipendiary Magistrate, ex p. Kaur* (2000) 164 J.P. 127, DC.

When a surety is concerned that the defendant will abscond, he may notify the police in writing of that fact and that he wishes to be relieved of his obligation as a surety under section 7(3)(c). On receipt of such notice the police may then arrest the defendant. A surety is not automatically relieved of his duty by contacting the police to convey his concerns but the court should take into account the efforts made to secure attendance and means of the surety when any forfeiture is considered: *R. v. Crown Court at Ipswich, ex p. Reddington* [1981] Crim.L.R. 618. If a surety does wish to withdraw, the proper procedure appears to be that an application to vary bail should be made under section 3(8) but as such application can only be made by the prosecution or defence this seems to require that the defendant would need to be before the court when the application was made: *R. v. Crown Court at Wood Green, ex p. Howe* [1992] 3 All E.R. 366. When a surety was unrepresented the court should assist by explaining the relevant principles in ordinary language and giving the surety an opportunity to call evidence and advance arguments: *R. v. Uxbridge Justices, ex p. Heward-Mills* [1983] 1 W.L.R. 56, DC. Representation by the Criminal Defence Service or the Community Legal Service is not available to an unrepresented surety: *Access to Justice Act* 1999, s.12(2); *R. v. The Chief Clerk of Maidstone Crown Court, ex p. Clark* [1995] 2 Cr.App.R. 617, DC.

VII. REMANDS

(1) Introduction

A court may adjourn a case and remand the defendant in custody or bail. Under the **5–88**

Magistrates' Courts Act 1980, time limits are set on the period of remand. Before conviction when the defendant is remanded in custody the limits are as follows—

1. three days in custody to a Police Constable;
2. eight clear days in custody to prison;
3. 28 clear days in custody to prison where the next stage of the proceedings is fixed to occur within that time and the accused at the time of remand is before the court and has previously been remanded in custody by the court in the proceedings;
4. 28 clear days in custody to prison if the defendant is already serving a custodial sentence;
5. 28 clear days in custody to prison where the defendant consents to remands in future in custody in his absence for a maximum of three adjournments of eight clear days. The defendant must be produced in court on the fourth adjournment which will usually be 28 days later.

After conviction a defendant can be remanded into custody for a maximum of three weeks.

Where a defendant is granted bail before conviction the case can be adjourned for any period of time taking into account the interests of justice and the need to ensure a speedy trial. After conviction the time limit on adjournments on bail is four weeks.

(2) Adjournments and remands

Magistrates' Courts Act 1980, s.128

Remand in custody or on bail

5–89   **128.**—(1) Where a magistrates' court has power to remand any person, then, subject to section 4 of the *Bail Act* 1976 and to any other enactment modifying that power, the court may—

    (a) remand him in custody, that is to say, commit him to custody to be brought before the court, subject to subsection (3A) below, at the end of the period of remand or at such earlier time as the court may require; or

    (b) where it is inquiring into or trying an offence alleged to have been committed by that person or has convicted him of an offence, remand him on bail in accordance with the *Bail Act* 1976, that is to say, by directing him to appear as provided in subsection (4) below; or

    (c) except in a case falling within paragraph (b) above, remand him on bail by taking from him a recognizance (with or without sureties) conditioned as provided in that subsection;

and may, in a case falling within paragraph (c) above, instead of taking recognizances in accordance with that paragraph, fix the amount of the recognizances with a view to their being taken subsequently in accordance with section 119 above.

    (1A) Where—

    (a) on adjourning a case under section 5, 10(1), 17C, or 18(4) above the court proposes to remand or further remand a person in custody; and

    (b) he is before the court; and

    (d) he is legally represented in that court,

it shall be the duty of the court—

    (i) to explain the effect of subsections (3A) and (3B) below to him in ordinary language; and

    (ii) to inform him in ordinary language that, notwithstanding the procedure for a remand without his being brought before a court, he would be brought before a court for the hearing and determination of at least every fourth application for his remand, and of every application for his remand heard at a time when it appeared to the court that he had no legal representative acting for him in the case.

    (1B) For the purposes of subsection (1A) above a person is to be treated as legally represented in a court if, but only if, he has the assistance of a legal representative to represent him in the proceedings in that court.

    (1C) After explaining to an accused as provided by subsection (1A) above the court shall ask him whether he consents to hearing and determination of such applications in his absence.

(2) Where the court fixes the amount of a recognizance under subsection (1) above or section 8(3) of the *Bail Act* 1976 with a view to its being taken subsequently the court shall in the meantime commit the person so remanded to custody in accordance with paragraph (a) of the said subsection (1).

(3) Where a person is brought before the court after remand, the court may further remand him.

(3A) Subject to subsection (3B) below, where a person has been remanded in custody and the remand was not a remand under section 128A below for a period exceeding 8 clear days, the court may further remand him (otherwise than in the exercise of the power conferred by that section) on an adjournment under section 5, 10(1), 17C or 18(4) above without his being brought before it if it is satisfied—

(a) that he gave his consent, either in response to a question under subsection (1C) above or otherwise, to the hearing and determination in his absence of any application for his remand on an adjournment of the case under any of those provisions; and

(b) that he has not by virtue of this subsection been remanded without being brought before the court on more than two such applications immediately preceding the application which the court is hearing; and

(c) that he has not withdrawn his consent to their being so heard and determined.

(3B) The court may not exercise the power conferred by subsection (3A) above if it appears to the court, on an application for a further remand being made to it, that the person to whom the application relates has no legal representative acting for him in the case (whether present in court or not).

(3C) Where—

(a) a person has been remanded in custody on an adjournment of a case under section 5, 10(1), 17C or 18(4) above; and

(b) an application is subsequently made for his further remand on such an adjournment; and

(c) he is not brought before the court which hears and determines the application; and

(d) that court is not satisfied as mentioned in subsection (3A) above,

the court shall adjourn the case and remand him in custody for the period for which it stands adjourned.

(3D) An adjournment under subsection (3C) above shall be for the shortest period that appears to the court to make it possible for the accused to be brought before it.

(3E) Where—

(a) on an adjournment of a case under section 5, 10(1), 17C or 18(4) above a person has been remanded in custody without being brought before the court; and

(b) it subsequently appears—

(i) to the court which remanded him in custody; or

(ii) to an alternate magistrates' court to which he is remanded under section 130 below,

that he ought not to have been remanded in custody in his absence, the court shall require him to be brought before it at the earliest time that appears to the court to be possible.

(4) Where a person is remanded on bail under subsection (1) above the court may, where it remands him on bail in accordance with the *Bail Act* 1976 direct him to appear or, in any other case, direct that his recognizance be conditioned for his appearance—

(a) before that court at the end of the period of remand; or

(b) at every time and place to which during the course of the proceedings the hearing may be from time to time adjourned;

and, where it remands him on bail conditionally on his providing a surety during an inquiry into an offence alleged to have been committed by him, may direct that the recognizance of the surety be conditioned to secure that the person so bailed appears—

(d) at every time and place to which during the course of the proceedings the hearing may be from time to time adjourned and also before the Crown Court in the event of the person so bailed being committed for trial there.

(5) Where a person is directed to appear or a recognizance is conditioned for a person's

appearance in accordance with paragraph (b) or (c) of subsection (4) above, the fixing at any time of the time for him next to appear shall be deemed to be a remand; but nothing in this subsection or subsection (4) above shall deprive the court of power at any subsequent hearing to remand him afresh.

(6) Subject to the provisions of sections 128A and 129 below, a magistrates' court shall not remand a person for a period exceeding 8 clear days, except that—

    (a) if the court remands him on bail, it may remand him for a longer period if he and the other party consent;

    (b) where the court adjourns a trial under section 10(3) above or section 11 of the *Powers of Criminal Courts (Sentencing) Act* 2000, the court may remand him for the period of the adjournment;

    (c) where a person is charged with an offence triable either way, then, if it falls to the court to try the case summarily but the court is not at the time so constituted, and sitting in such a place, as will enable it to proceed with the trial, the court may remand him until the next occasion on which it will be practicable for the court to be so constituted, and to sit in such a place, as aforesaid, notwithstanding that the remand is for a period exceeding 8 clear days.

(7) A magistrates' court having power to remand a person in custody may, if the remand is for a period not exceeding 3 clear days, commit him to detention at a police station.

(8) Where a person is committed to detention at a police station under subsection (7) above—

    (a) he shall not be kept in such detention unless there is a need for him to be so detained for the purposes of inquiries into other offences;

    (b) if kept in such detention, he shall be brought back before the magistrates' court which committed him as soon as that need ceases;

    (c) he shall be treated as a person in police detention to whom the duties under section 39 of the *Police and Criminal Evidence Act* 1984 (responsibilities in relation to persons detained) relate;

    (d) his detention shall be subject to periodic review at the times set out in section 40 of that Act (review of police detention).

5–90   The direction to appear does not put an unconditional duty on a prison governor to produce any prisoner from custody who is on bail for other offences. A formal production order is required under section 29 of the *Criminal Justice Act* 1961 and a request to produce a prisoner at court must not be unreasonably refused: *R. v. Governor of Brixton Prison, ex p. Walsh* [1985] A.C. 154. It is usually the responsibility of the Crown Prosecution Service to arrange for such orders.

The computation of eight clear days is calculated by counting eight days intervening between the date of appearance and the day when the defendant will be brought before the court again.

When a defendant is remanded on conditional bail with a surety he will only be released once the surety is taken. If no surety is provided, the defendant must be produced from custody after eight days: *Criminal Procedure Rules* 2005, r.18.8 in Appendix G–74.

5–91   Section 10(3) of the *MCA* 1980 provides that after conviction the court may adjourn a case for inquiries or to determine the most suitable method of dealing with the case either for three weeks if the defendant is in custody or four weeks if he is on bail. Section 11 of the *PCC(S)A* 2000 allows for an adjournment for three weeks in custody or four weeks on bail for medical examination after conviction or when the court is satisfied that a defendant did the act or omission.

A defendant may be remanded in custody for a period exceeding eight clear days where he is legally represented and consents to remands in his absence. The safeguards are that the procedure and the defendant's rights must be clearly explained to him and his consent must be freely given whilst he has the benefit of legal representation and advice. The consent may be given to the maximum of the fourth adjournment after the first appearance and then on that occasion the defendant must be produced. The defendant may withdraw his consent at any time and the case will be re-listed.

Police detention for an adult is for a maximum of three days but for a child or young person it is 24 hours: *Children and Young Persons Act* 1969, s.23. Police detention to inquire into "other offences" is not to be given a restricted meaning but includes other offences that are related to those with which the defendant has already been charged: *Bailey and Smith* (1993) 97 Cr.App.R. 365.

Magistrates' Courts Act 1980, s.128A(2), (3)

Remands in custody for more than eight days
128A.—(2) A magistrates' court may remand the accused in custody for a period exceeding 8 **5–92**
clear days if—
    (a) it has previously remanded him in custody for the same offence; and
    (b) he is before the court,
but only if, after affording the parties an opportunity to make representations, it has set a date on which it expects that it will be possible for the next stage in the proceedings, other than a hearing relating to a further remand in custody or on bail, to take place, and only—
      (i) for a period ending not later than that date; or
      (ii) for a period of 28 clear days,
    whichever is the less.
  (3) Nothing in this section affects the right of the accused to apply for bail during the period of the remand.

This applies on a second appearance in custody when a remand can then be for up **5–93** to 28 days in custody if a specific event such as a committal or trial will occur on the next date. It does not apply to interim adjournment dates.

Magistrates' Courts Act 1980, s.129

Further remand
129.—(1) If a magistrates' court is satisfied that any person who has been remanded is unable **5–94** by reason of illness or accident to appear or be brought before the court at the expiration of the period for which he was remanded, the court may, in his absence, remand him for a further time; and section 128(6) above shall not apply.
  (2) Notwithstanding anything in section 128(1) above, the power of a court under subsection (1) above to remand a person on bail for a further time—
    (a) where he was granted bail in criminal proceedings, includes power to enlarge the recognizance of any surety for him to a later time;
    (b) where he was granted bail otherwise than in criminal proceedings, may be exercised by enlarging his recognizance and those of any sureties for him to a later time.
  (3) Where a person remanded on bail is bound to appear before a magistrates' court at any time and the court has no power to remand him under subsection (1) above, the court may in his absence—
    (a) where he was granted bail in criminal proceedings, appoint a later time as the time at which he is to appear and enlarge the recognizances of any sureties for him to that time;
    (b) where he was granted bail otherwise than in criminal proceedings, enlarge his recognizance and those of any sureties for him to a later time;
and the appointment of the time or the enlargement of his recognizance shall be deemed to be a further remand.
  (4) Where a magistrates' court commits a person for trial on bail and the recognizance of any surety for him has been conditioned in accordance with paragraph (a) of subsection (4) of section 128 above the court may, in the absence of the surety, enlarge his recognizance so that he is bound to secure that the person so committed for trial appears also before the Crown Court.

A remand in absence under this section applies equally to defendants in custody or **5–95** on bail where the defendant does not appear before the court because of illness or accident. The court must have been given solid grounds to found a reliable opinion relating to the illness or accident: *R. v. Liverpool City Justices, ex p. Grogan* [1991] 155 J.P. 450.

Magistrates' Courts Act 1980, s.130

Transfer of remand hearings

5–96   **130.**—(1) A magistrates' court adjourning a case under section 5, 10(1), 17C or 18(4) above, and remanding the accused in custody, may, if he has attained the age of 17, order that he be brought up for any subsequent remands before an alternate magistrates' court nearer to the prison where he is to be confined while on remand.

(2) The order shall require the accused to be brought before the alternate court at the end of the period of remand or at such earlier time as the alternate court may require.

(3) While the order is in force, the alternate court shall, to the exclusion of the court which made the order, have all the powers in relation to further remand (whether in custody or on bail) and [the grant of a right to representation funded by the Legal Services Commission as part of the Criminal Defence Service] which that court would have had but for the order.

(4) The alternate court may, on remanding the accused in custody, require him to be brought before the court which made the order at the end of the period of remand or at such earlier time as that court may require; and, if the alternate court does so, or the accused is released on bail, the order under subsection (1) above shall cease to be in force.

(4A) Where a magistrates' court is satisfied as mentioned in section 128(3A) above—

  (a) subsection (1) above shall have effect as if for the words "he be brought up for any subsequent remands before" there were substituted the words "applications for any subsequent remands be made to";

  (b) subsection (2) above shall have effect as if for the words "the accused to be brought before" there were substituted the words "an application for a further remand to be made to" and

  (c) subsection (4) above shall have effect as if for the words "him to be brought before" there were substituted the words "an application for a further remand to be made to".

(5) Schedule 5 to this Act shall have effect to supplement this section.

Magistrates' Courts Act 1980, s.131(1)–(2)

Remand of accused already in custody

5–97   **131.**—(1) When a magistrates' court remands an accused person in custody and he is already detained under a custodial sentence, the period for which he is remanded may be up to 28 clear days.

(2) But the court shall inquire as to the expected date of his release from that detention; and if it appears that it will be before 28 clear days have expired, he shall not be remanded in custody for more than 8 clear days or (if longer) a period ending with that date.

VIII. POLICE BAIL

5–98   The police may bail a defendant pending an attendance or return to the police station or an appearance at court. There are no statutory time limits.

Police and Criminal Evidence Act, s.38

Duties of custody officer after charge.

5–99   **38.**—(1) Where a person arrested for an offence otherwise than under a warrant endorsed for bail is charged with an offence, the custody officer shall, subject to section 25 of the *Criminal Justice and Public Order Act* 1994, order his release from police detention, either on bail or without bail, unless—

  (a)   if the person arrested is not an arrested juvenile—

    (i) his name or address cannot be ascertained or the custody officer has reasonable grounds for doubting whether a name or address furnished by him as his name or address is his real name or address;

    (ii) the custody officer has reasonable grounds for believing that the person arrested will fail to appear in court to answer to bail;

    (iii) in the case of a person arrested for an imprisonable offence, the custody officer has reasonable grounds for believing that the detention of the person arrested is necessary to prevent him from committing an offence;

(iiia) except in a case where (by virtue of subsection (9) of section 63B below) that section does not apply, the custody officer has reasonable grounds for believing that the detention of the person is necessary to enable a sample to be taken from him under that section;

(iv) in the case of a person arrested for an offence which is not an imprisonable offence, the custody officer has reasonable grounds for believing that the detention of the person arrested is necessary to prevent him from causing physical injury to any other person or from causing loss of or damage to property;

(v) the custody officer has reasonable grounds for believing that the detention of the person arrested is necessary to prevent him from interfering with the administration of justice or with the investigation of offences or of a particular offence; or

(vi) the custody officer has reasonable grounds for believing that the detention of the person arrested is necessary for his own protection;

(b) if he is an arrested juvenile—

(i) any of the requirements of paragraph (a) above is satisfied (but, in the case of paragraph (a)(iiia) above, only if the arrested juvenile has attained the minimum age); or

(ii) the custody officer has reasonable grounds for believing that he ought to be detained in his own interests.

(2) If the release of a person arrested is not required by subsection (1) above, the custody officer may authorise him to be kept in police detention but may not authorise a person to be kept in police detention by virtue of subsection (1)(a)(iiia) after the end of the period of six hours beginning when he was charged with the offence.

(2A) The custody officer, in taking the decisions required by subsection (1)(a) and (b) above (except (a)(i) and (vi) and (b)(ii)), shall have regard to the same considerations as those which a court is required to have regard to in taking the corresponding decisions under paragraph 2(1) of Part I of Schedule 1 to the *Bail Act* 1976 (disregarding paragraph 2(2) of that Part).

(3) Where a custody officer authorises a person who has been charged to be kept in police detention, he shall, as soon as practicable, make a written record of the grounds for the detention.

(4) Subject to subsection (5) below, the written record shall be made in the presence of the person charged who shall at that time be informed by the custody officer of the grounds for his detention.

(5) Subsection (4) above shall not apply where the person charged is, at the time when the written record is made—

(a) incapable of understanding what is said to him;

(b) violent or likely to become violent; or

(c) in urgent need of medical attention.

(6) Where a custody officer authorises an arrested juvenile to be kept in police detention under subsection (1) above, the custody officer shall, unless he certifies—

(a) that, by reason of such circumstances as are specified in the certificate, it is impracticable for him to do so; or

(b) in the case of an arrested juvenile who has attained the age of 12 years, that no secure accommodation is available and that keeping him in other local authority accommodation would not be adequate to protect the public from serious harm from him,

secure that the arrested juvenile is moved to local authority accommodation.

(6A) In this section—

"local authority accommodation" means accommodation provided by or on behalf of a local authority (within the meaning of the *Children Act* 1989);

"minimum age" means the age specified in section 63B(3) below;

"secure accommodation" means accommodation provided for the purpose of restricting liberty;

"sexual offence" and "violent offence" have the same meanings as in Part I of the *Criminal Justice Act* 1991 the *Powers of Criminal Courts (Sentencing) Act* 2000;

and any reference, in relation to an arrested juvenile charged with a violent or sexual offence, to protecting the public from serious harm from him shall be construed as a reference to protecting members of the public from death or serious personal injury, whether physical or psychological, occasioned by further such offences committed by him.

(6B) Where an arrested juvenile is moved to local authority accommodation under subsection (6) above, it shall be lawful for any person acting on behalf of the authority to detain him.

(7) A certificate made under subsection (6) abovein respect of an arrested juvenile shall be produced to the court before which he is first brought thereafter.

(7A) In this section "imprisonable offence" has the same meaning as in Schedule 1 to the *Bail Act* 1976.

(8) In this Part of this Act "local authority" has the same meaning as in the *Children and Young Persons Act* 1969.

[This section is reprinted as amended by the *Criminal Justice and Court Services Act* 2000, s.57(3)(b) and the *Criminal Justice Act* 2003, s.5(2)(b).]

Police and Criminal Evidence Act 1984, s.47

Bail after arrest

5–100   **47.**—(1) Subject to subsection (2) below, a release on bail of a person under this Part of this Act shall be a release on bail granted in accordance with sections 3, 3A, 5 and 5A of the *Bail Act* 1976 as they apply to bail granted by a constable.

(1A) The normal powers to impose conditions of bail shall be available to him where a custody officer releases a person on bail under section 38(1) above (including that subsection as applied by section 40(10) above) but not in any other cases.

In this subsection, "the normal powers to impose conditions of bail" has the meaning given in section 3(6) of the *Bail Act* 1976.

(2) Nothing in the *Bail Act* 1976 shall prevent the re-arrest without warrant of a person released on bail subject to a duty to attend at a police station if new evidence justifying a further arrest has come to light since his release.

(3) Subject to subsections (3A) and (4) below, in this Part of this Act references to "bail" are references to bail subject to a duty—

    (a) to appear before a magistrates' court at such time and such place; or

    (b) to attend at such police station at such time,

as the custody officer may appoint.

(3A) Where a custody officer grants bail to a person subject to a duty to appear before a magistrates' court, he shall appoint for the appearance—

    (a) a date which is not later than the first sitting of the court after the person is charged with the offence; or

    (b) where he is informed by the designated officer for the relevant local justice area that the appearance cannot be accommodated until a later date, that later date.

(4) Where a custody officer has granted bail to a person subject to a duty to appear at a police station, the custody officer may give notice in writing to that person that his attendance at the police station is not required.

(6) Where a person who has been granted bail and either has attended at the police station in accordance with the grant of bail or has been arrested under section 46A above is detained at a police station, any time during which he was in police detention prior to being granted bail shall be included as part of any period which falls to be calculated under this Part of this Act.

(7) Where a person who was released on bail subject to a duty to attend at a police station is re-arrested, the provisions of this Part of this Act shall apply to him as they apply to a person arrested for the first time; but this subsection does not apply to a person who is arrested under section 46A above or has attended a police station in accordance with the grant of bail (and who accordingly is deemed by section 34(7) above to have been arrested for an offence).

(8) In the *Magistrates' Courts Act* 1980—

    (a) the following section shall be substituted for section 43—

Bail on arrest

"**43.**—(1) Where a person has been granted bail under the *Police and Criminal Evidence Act* 1984 subject to a duty to appear before a magistrates' court, the court before which he is to appear may appoint a later time as the time at which he is to appear and may enlarge the recognizances of any sureties for him at that time.

(2) The recognizance of any surety for any person granted bail subject to a duty to attend at a police station may be enforced as if it were conditioned for his appearance before a magistrates' court for the petty sessions area in which the police station named in the recognizance is situated."

; and

(b) the following subsection shall be substituted for section 117(3)—

"(3) Where a warrant has been endorsed for bail under subsection (1) above—

(a) where the person arrested is to be released on bail on his entering into a recognizance without sureties, it shall not be necessary to take him to a police station, but if he is so taken, he shall be released from custody on his entering into the recognizance; and

(b) where he is to be released on his entering into a recognizance with sureties, he shall be taken to a police station on his arrest, and the custody officer there shall (subject to his approving any surety tendered in compliance with the endorsement) release him from custody as directed in the endorsement.".

Bail Act 1976, s.3A

Conditions of bail in case of police bail

3A.—(1) Section 3 of this Act applies, in relation to bail granted by a custody officer under **5–101** Part IV of the *Police and Criminal Evidence Act* 1984 in cases where the normal powers to impose conditions of bail are available to him, subject to the following modifications.

(2) Subsection (6) does not authorise the imposition of a requirement to reside in a bail hostel or any requirement under paragraph (d) or (e).

(3) Subsections (6ZAA), (6ZA), (6A) and (6F) shall be omitted.

(4) For subsection (8), substitute the following—

"(8) Where a custody officer has granted bail in criminal proceedings he or another custody officer serving at the same police station may, at the request of the person to whom it was granted, vary the conditions of bail; and in doing so he may impose conditions or more onerous conditions.".

(5) Where a constable grants bail to a person no conditions shall be imposed under subsections (4), (5), (6) or (7) of section 3 of this Act unless it appears to the constable that it is necessary to do so

(a) for the purposes of preventing that person from] failing to surrender to custody, or

(b) for the purposes of preventing that person from] committing an offence while on bail, or

(c) for the purposes of preventing that person from] interfering with witnesses or otherwise obstructing the course of justice, whether in relation to himself or any other person or

(d) for that person's own protection or, if he is a child or young person, for his own welfare or in his own interests.

(6) Subsection (5) above also applies on any request to a custody officer under subsection (8) of section 3 of this Act to vary the conditions of bail.

[The amendments of the *Criminal Justice Act* 2003, s.13 came into effect in April 2004.]

Bail Act 1976, s.5A

Supplementary provisions in cases of police bail.

5A.—(1) Section 5 of this Act applies, in relation to bail granted by a custody officer under **5–102** Part IV of the *Police and Criminal Evidence Act* 1984 in cases where the normal powers to impose conditions of bail are available to him, subject to the following modifications.

(1A) Subsections (2A) and (2B) shall be omitted.

(2) For subsection (3) substitute the following—

"(3) Where a custody officer, in relation to any person,—
    (a) imposes conditions in granting bail in criminal proceedings, or
    (b) varies any conditions of bail or imposes conditions in respect of bail in criminal
        proceedings,
the custody officer shall, with a view to enabling that person to consider requesting him or another custody officer, or making an application to a magistrates' court, to vary the conditions, give reasons for imposing or varying the conditions.".

(3) For subsection (4) substitute the following—

"(4) A custody officer who is by virtue of subsection (3) above required to give reasons for his decision shall include a note of those reasons in the custody record and shall give a copy of that note to the person in relation to whom the decision was taken.".

(4) Subsections (5) and (6) shall be omitted.

5–103   A custody officer who grants bail subject to conditions including a surety or security or varies the conditions of bail must give reasons and make a record of the decision, but there is no obligation to give reasons for the withholding of bail: *Bail Act* 1976, ss.5 and 5A.

IX. WARRANTS WITH AND WITHOUT BAIL

5–104   When a warrant of arrest is issued by the court, consideration must be given as to whether the warrant should be backed for bail or not. The decision will depend on the nature and gravity of the offence charged and the defendant's bail history.

Magistrates' Courts Act 1980, s.117

Warrant endorsed for bail

5–105   117.—(1) A justice of the peace on issuing a warrant for the arrest of any person may grant him bail by endorsing the warrant for bail, that is to say, by endorsing the warrant with a direction in accordance with subsection (2) below.

(2) A direction for bail endorsed on a warrant under subsection (1) above shall—
    (a) in the case of bail in criminal proceedings, state that the person arrested is to be
        released on bail subject to a duty to appear before such magistrates' court and at
        such time as may be specified in the endorsement;
    (b) ...(civil proceedings)
and the endorsement shall fix the amounts in which any sureties and, in a case falling within paragraph (b) above, that person is or are to be bound.

(3) Where a warrant has been endorsed for bail under subsection (1) above—
    (a) where the person arrested is to be released on bail on his entering into a
        recognizance without sureties, it shall not be necessary to take him to a police sta-
        tion, but if he is so taken, he shall be released from custody on his entering into
        the recognizance; and
    (b) where he is to be released on his entering into a recognizance with sureties, he
        shall be taken to a police station on his arrest, and the custody officer there shall
        (subject to his approving any surety tendered in compliance with the endorse-
        ment) release him from custody as directed in the endorsement.

X. CUSTODY TIME LIMITS

Introduction

5–106   The *Magistrates' Courts Act* 1980 and other enactments provide for limits on the periods of time for which a person may be remanded, either in custody or on bail.

Custody time limits also apply, which dictate the length of time over which a person may be remanded in custody during the progress of a criminal case. The limits are designed to ensure that where a defendant is in custody, the case will be expedited. If there is any delay the defendant may be released from custody for further adjournments. The custody time limit for cases tried summarily is 56 days from first appearance to trial and for cases going to the Crown Court, the limit is 70 days from first appearance to committal. Application may be made for the limits to be extended in specific circumstances. Time limits do not apply to defendants remanded on bail but all cases must be dealt with expeditiously in accordance with the *Criminal Procedure Rules* 2005.

Prosecution of Offences Act 1985, s.22

Power of Secretary of State to set time limits in relation to preliminary stages of criminal proceedings

22.—(1) The Secretary of State may by regulations make provision, with respect to any speci- **5–107** fied preliminary stage of proceedings for an offence, as to the maximum period—

  (a) to be allowed to the prosecution to complete that stage;

  (b) during which the accused may, while awaiting completion of that stage, be—
    (i) in the custody of a magistrates' court; or
    (ii) in the custody of the Crown Court;
  in relation to that offence.

(2) The regulations may, in particular—

  (a) be made so as to apply only in relation to proceedings instituted in specified areas, or proceedings of, or against persons of, specified classes or descriptions;

  (b) make different provision with respect to proceedings instituted in different areas, or different provision with respect to proceedings of, or against persons of, different classes or descriptions;

  (c) make such provision with respect to the procedure to be followed in criminal proceedings as the Secretary of State considers appropriate in consequence of any other provision of the regulations;

  (d) provide for the *Magistrates' Courts Act* 1980 and the *Bail Act* 1976 to apply in relation to cases to which custody or overall time limits apply subject to such modifica-
tions as may be specified (being modifications which the Secretary of State considers necessary in consequence of any provision made by the regulations); and

  (e) make such transitional provision in relation to proceedings instituted before the commencement of any provision of the regulations as the Secretary of State considers appropriate.

(3) The appropriate court may, at any time before the expiry of a time limit imposed by the regulations, extend, or further extend, that limit; but the court shall not do so unless it is satisfied—

  (a) that the need for the extension is due to—
    (i)   the illness or absence of the accused, a necessary witness, a judge or a mag-
istrate;
    (ii) a postponement which is occasioned by the ordering by the court of sepa-
rate trials in the case of two or more accused or two or more offences; or
    (iii) some other good and sufficient cause; and

  (b) that the prosecution has acted with all due diligence and expedition.

(4) Where, in relation to any proceedings for an offence, an overall time limit has expired before the completion of the stage of the proceedings to which the limit applies the appropriate court shall stay the proceedings.

(5) Where—

  (a) a person escapes from the custody of a magistrates' court or the Crown Court before the expiry of a custody time limit which applies in his case; or

  (b) a person who has been released on bail in consequence of the expiry of a custody time limit—
    (i) fails to surrender himself into the custody of the court at the appointed time; or
    (ii) is arrested by a constable on a ground mentioned in section 7(3)(b) of the *Bail Act* 1976 (breach, or likely breach, of conditions of bail);

the regulations shall, so far as they provide for any custody time limit in relation to the preliminary stage in question, be disregarded.

(6) Subsection (6A) below applies where—

    (a) a person escapes from the custody of a magistrates' court or the Crown Court; or

    (b) a person who has been released on bail fails to surrender himself into the custody of the court at the appointed time;

and is accordingly unlawfully at large for any period.

(6A) The following, namely—

    (a) the period for which the person is unlawfully at large; and

    (b) such additional period (if any) as the appropriate court may direct, having regard to the disruption of the prosecution occasioned by—

        (i) the person's escape or failure to surrender; and

        (ii) the length of the period mentioned in paragraph (a) above,

    shall be disregarded, so far as the offence in question is concerned, for the purposes of the overall time limit which applies in his case in relation to the stage which the proceedings have reached at the time of the escape or, as the case may be, at the appointed time.

(7) Where a magistrates' court decides to extend, or further extend, a custody or overall time limit or to give a direction under subsection (6A) above, the accused may appeal against the decision to the Crown Court.

(8) Where a magistrates' court refuses to extend, or further extend, a custody or overall time limit, or to give a direction under subsection (6A) above, the prosecution may appeal against the refusal to the Crown Court.

(9) An appeal under subsection (8) above may not be commenced after the expiry of the limit in question; but where such an appeal is commenced before the expiry of the limit the limit shall be deemed not to have expired before the determination or abandonment of the appeal.

(10) Where a person is convicted of an offence in any proceedings, the exercise, in relation to any preliminary stage of those proceedings, of the power conferred by subsection (3) above shall not be called into question in any appeal against that conviction.

(11) In this section—

"appropriate court" means—

    (a) where the accused has been committed for trial[, sent for trial under section 51 of the *Crime and Disorder Act* 1998] or indicted for the offence, the Crown Court; and

    (b) in any other case, the magistrates' court specified in the summons or warrant in question or, where the accused has already appeared or been brought before a magistrates' court, a magistrates' court for the same area;

"custody" includes local authority accommodation to which a person is remanded or committed by virtue of section 23 of the *Children and Young Persons Act* 1969, and references to a person being committed to custody shall be construed accordingly;

"custody of the Crown Court" includes custody to which a person is committed in pursuance of—

    (a) section 6 of the *Magistrates' Courts Act* 1980 (magistrates' court committing accused for trial); or

    (b) section 43A of that Act (magistrates' court dealing with a person brought before it following his arrest in pursuance of a warrant issued by the Crown Court); or

    (c) section 5(3)(a) of the *Criminal Justice Act* 1987 (custody after transfer order in fraud case); or

    (d) paragraph 2(1)(a) of Schedule 6 to the *Criminal Justice Act* 1991 (custody after transfer order in certain cases involving children).

"custody of a magistrates' court" means custody to which a person is committed in pursuance of section 128 of the *Magistrates' Courts Act* 1980 (remand);

"custody time limit" means a time limit imposed by regulations made under subsection (1)(b) above or, where any such limit has been extended by a court under subsection (3) above, the limit as so extended;

"preliminary stage", in relation to any proceedings, does not include any stage after the start of the trial (within the meaning given by subsections (11A) and (11B) below);

"overall time limit" means a time limit imposed by regulations made under subsection (1)(a) above or, where any such limit has been extended by a court under subsection (3) above, the limit as so extended; and

"specified" means specified in the regulations.

(11A) For the purposes of this section, the start of a trial on indictment shall be taken to occur when a jury is sworn to consider the issue of guilt or fitness to plead or, if the court accepts a plea of guilty before a jury is sworn, when that plea is accepted but this is subject to section 8 of the *Criminal Justice Act* 1987 and section 30 of the *Criminal Procedure and Investigations Act* 1996 (preparatory hearings).

(11ZA) For the purposes of this section, proceedings for an offence shall be taken to begin when the accused is charged with the offence or, as the case may be, an information is laid charging him with the offence.

(11B) For the purposes of this section, the start of a summary trial shall be taken to occur—

(a) when the court begins to hear evidence for the prosecution at the trial or to consider whether to exercise its power under section 37(3) of the *Mental Health Act* 1983 (power to make hospital order without convicting the accused), or

(b) if the court accepts a plea of guilty without proceeding as mentioned above, when that plea is accepted.

(12) For the purposes of the application of any custody time limit in relation to a person who is in the custody of a magistrates' court or the Crown Court—

(a) all periods during which he is in the custody of a magistrates' court in respect of the same offence shall be aggregated and treated as a single continuous period; and

(b) all periods during which he is in the custody of the Crown Court in respect of the same offence shall be aggregated and treated similarly.

(13) For the purposes of section 29(3) of the *Supreme Court Act* 1981 (High Court to have power to make prerogative orders in relation to jurisdiction of Crown Court in matters which do not relate to trial on indictment) the jurisdiction conferred on the Crown Court by this section shall be taken to be part of its jurisdiction in matters other than those relating to trial on indictment.

Prosecution of Offences (Custody Time Limits) (Amendment) Regulations 1989 (S.I. 1989 No. 767)

1.—(1) These *Regulations* may be cited as the *Prosecution of Offences (Custody Time   5–108 Limits) (Amendment) Regulations* 1989.

(2) In these *Regulations* "the principal regulations" means the *Prosecution of Offences (Custody Time Limits) Regulations* 1987 and references to a notice of transfer are references to a notice given under section 4 of the *Criminal Justice Act* 1987.

(3) These *Regulations* shall come into force on 1st June 1989, but—

(a) regulations 2 and 4(a) shall not apply in relation to proceedings for an offence instituted before that date except where—

(i) the accused is committed for trial in the Crown Court, or

(ii) notice of transfer is given in respect of the case, or

(iii) a bill of indictment is preferred against the accused under section 2(2)(b) of the *Administration of Justice (Miscellaneous Provisions) Act* 1933, on or after that date; and

(b) regulations 3 and 4(b) shall not apply in relation to proceedings for an offence instituted before that date.

Prosecution of Offences (Custody Time Limits) Regulations 1987, regs 4, 7

Custody time limits in magistrates' courts

4.—(1) The maximum period during which a person accused of an indictable offence other   5–109 than treason may be in the custody of a magistrates' court in relation to that offence while awaiting completion of any preliminary stage of the proceedings specified in the following provisions of this Regulation shall be as stated in those provisions.

(2) Except as provided in paragraph (3) below, in the case of an offence triable either way the maximum period of custody between the accused's first appearance and the start

of summary trial or, as the case may be, the time when the court decides whether or not to commit the accused to the Crown Court for trial shall be 70 days.

(3) In the case of an offence triable either way if, before the expiry of 56 days following the day of the accused's first appearance, the court decides to proceed to summary trial in pursuance of sections 19 to 24 of the 1980 Act the maximum period of custody between the accused's first appearance and the start of the summary trial shall be 56 days.

(4) In the case of an offence triable on indictment exclusively the maximum period of custody between the accused's first appearance and the time when the court decides whether or not to commit the accused to the Crown Court for trial, shall be 70 days.

(4A) In the case of a summary offence, the maximum period of custody beginning with the date of the accused's first appearance and ending with the date of the start of the summary trial shall be 56 days.

(5) The foregoing provisions of this regulation shall have effect as if any reference therein to the time when the court decides whether or not to commit the accused to the Crown Court for trial were a reference—

(a) where a court proceeds to inquire into an information as examining justices in pursuance of section 6(1) of the 1980 Act, to the time when it begins to hear evidence for the prosecution at the inquiry;

(b) where a notice has been given under section 4(1)(c) of the *Criminal Justice Act* 1987 (in these *Regulations* referred to as a "notice of transfer"), to the date on which notice of transfer was given.

Application for extension of custody time limit

5–110   **7.**—(1) An application to a court for the extension or further extension of a custody time limit under section 22(3) of the 1985 Act may be made orally or in writing.

(2) Subject to paragraphs (3) and (4) below the prosecution shall—

(a) not less than 5 days before making such an application in the Crown Court; and

(b) not less than 2 days before making such an application in a magistrates' court,

give notice in writing to the accused or his representative and to the proper officer of the court stating that it intends to make such an application.

(2A) In paragraph (2) above, "the proper officer of the court" means in relation to an application in the Crown Court the appropriate officer of the court and in relation to an application in a magistrates' court the clerk of the court.

(3) It shall not be necessary for the prosecution to comply with paragraph (2) above if the accused or his representative has informed the prosecution that he does not require such notice.

(4) If the court is satisfied that it is not practicable in all the circumstances for the prosecution to comply with paragraph (2) above, the court may direct that the prosecution need not comply with that paragraph or that the minimum period of notice required by that paragraph to be given shall be such lesser minimum period as the court may specify.

5–111   The period of custody begins at the close of the day during which the defendant was first remanded and expires at midnight on the relevant day. The relevant day is that prescribed by regulation 4 of the *Prosecution of Offences (Custody Time Limits) Regulations* 1987: *R. v. Governor of Canterbury Prison, ex p. Craig* [1991] 2 Q.B. 195; (1990) 91 Cr.App.R. 7. Once the limit has expired it is the duty of the court and not a prison governor to direct the release on bail of the defendant: *Olotu v. Home Office* [1997] 1 All E.R. 385.

The relevant limits are prescribed in rule 4 (*ante*) as 56 days in the case of summary or either way offences to be dealt with by way of summary trial and 70 days for either way or indictable offences that are to be committed to the Crown Court for trial. Application may be made to extend the time limits under section 22(3) and regulation 7. The requirement on the prosecution to give two days notice of an application has been held to be directory only and not mandatory, so the court retains the power to extend the time limit at any time before it expires: *R. v. Governor of Canterbury prison, ex p. Craig* [1991] 2 Q.B. 195; (1990) 91 Cr.App.R. 7.

Once a custody time limit has expired and the prosecution have failed to obtain an extension of time the court has no power to extend time and bail must be granted: *R. v. Sheffield Justices, ex p. Turner* [1991] 2 W.L.R. 987

Before the court will direct an extension of the time limit it must be satisfied on the **5–112** balance of probabilities that the two conditions of section 22(3) are met, namely that there is "good and sufficient cause" for an extension to the time limit and secondly that the prosecution have acted with all "due diligence and expedition". Guidance on the approach to be taken by the courts was given in *R. v. Crown Court at Manchester, ex p. MacDonald* [1999] 1 All E.R. 805. It is recognised that the there are an infinite number of matters that might amount to "good and sufficient cause". Lack of court time, listing difficulties because of the size and complexity of a case and the unavailability of a senior judge or any judge to hear the case have all been held to amount to "good and sufficient cause": *Re C* (2000) 164 J.P. 693; *R. (Eliot) v. Crown Court at Reading* [2002] 1 Cr.App.R. 3; *R. v. Central Criminal Court, ex p. Abu-Wardeh* [1997] 1 All E.R. 159; *R. v. Crown Court at Norwich, ex p. Cox* (1993) 97 Cr.App.R. 145; (1993) 157 J.P. 593. The seriousness of the offence and shortness of the extension sought do not qualify: *R. v. Governor of Winchester Prison, ex p. Roddie* [1991] 2 All E.R. 931.

In *R. (Bannister) v. Crown Court at Guildford* [2004] EWHC 221, the court took a more robust view and held that the chronic lack of resources which led to an inability to list an "utterly routine" case did not amount to "good and sufficient cause". The court said that positive judicial intervention at listing stage was to be encouraged to ensure that the time limits were observed. This approach was approved in the case of *R. (Miah) v. Snaresbrook Crown Court* [2006] EWHC 2873 where listing difficulties due to the normal pressure of work were held not to constitute "good and sufficient cause" for extending the time limits. There had to be some exceptional circumstances.

In assessing "good and sufficient cause" considerations relating to bail are not relevant and extending the limit for the protection of the public could not of itself amount to "good and sufficient cause": *R. v. Sheffield Crown Court, ex p. Headley* [2000] 2 Cr.App.R. 1; *R. (Eliot) v. Crown Court at Reading*. But see *R. v. Crown Court at Luton, ex p. Neaves* [1993] 157 J.P. 80 where it was held that an extension for the protection of an individual member of the public from violence was justified.

With regard to the second condition of "due diligence and expedition", the court will **5–113** require such diligence and expedition as would be expected from a competent prosecutor who is alert to his duty. It is an objective test: *R. v. Crown Court at Manchester, ex p. MacDonald (ante)*; *R. v. Governor of Winchester prison, ex p. Roddie (ante)*. When assessing whether due diligence has been used the limits set are to be seen not as a target but a maximum period of time and the prosecution must ensure that the evidence and papers are served on the defence within a reasonable time to permit them to be properly considered by the time of committal: *R. v. Crown Court at Norwich, ex p. Parker* (1993) 96 Cr.App.R. 68. The prosecution also had to expedite the case to allow for a contested rather than uncontested committal within the 70-day limit: *R. v. Leeds Crown Court, ex p. Briggs* [1998] 2 Cr.App.R. 424. Once the prosecution judge that a piece of evidence is likely to be important, it has a duty to ensure that the evidence reaches the defence swiftly. A case has to be advanced as to why there was a delay in delivering evidence: *R. v. Central Criminal Court, ex p. Behbehani* [1994] Crim.L.R. 352; *R. (Smith) v. Woolwich Crown Court* [2002] Crim.L.R. 915. In *R. (Thomas); R. (Stubbs) v. Central Criminal Court* [2006] EWHC 2138 the defendants were charged with attempted murder and firearms offences. The Crown Court extended the custody time limits for three months. The defence challenged this extension and referred to earlier delay by the prosecution which they submitted indicated that the prosecution had not acted with due diligence and expedition. It was held on appeal that when the court considers an application to extend custody time limits it must look at the circumstances that led to the need for an extension. The defence could not effectively use the same argument again in respect of delay in the past and seek to appeal an earlier decision. The court may take an overall view so that previous delay in the case could be relevant but only if it was the root cause of the reason for seeking a further extension. In this case the appeal was dismissed as the court found there were additional different reasons for the prosecution to seek extensions and the due diligence test was met.

In *R. (Gibson and Gibson) v. Winchester Crown Court* [2004] 1 W.L.R. 1623, it was held by the court that if "good and sufficient cause" were found, the fact that the prosecution had failed to act with due diligence may be irrelevant as the need for the extension may not be directly referable to their failure. The Court also commented that availability of resources could not be ignored but all relevant considerations must be taken into account when deciding on an extension.

When extending the time limits it is important that the defendant should understand without a doubt why his liberty is being restricted. The application must be clear and understandable and the defendant must be given an opportunity to object and make representations. The order of the court must be clear, detailed and properly recorded: *Re Ward, Ward and Bond* [1991] Crim.L.R. 558.

5–114   The procedure in such applications is informal and Article 6 is not engaged because it does not involve the trial of a criminal charge. Formal rules of evidence do not apply but the defendant must be allowed to question any areas of the application as he wishes: *Wildman v. DPP* [2001] Crim.L.R. 565. Where a defendant is charged with various offences at different times, each offence attracts its own custody time limit: *R. v. Wirral District Magistrates' Court, ex p. Meikle* [1990] 154 J.P. 1035. A new custody time limit then runs from the date of the new charge but it could amount to an abuse of process by the prosecution if the new charges were preferred solely for the purpose of defeating the custody time limits: *R. v. Waltham Forest Magistrates, ex p. Lee and Lee* (1993) 97 Cr.App.R. 287; *R. v. Wolverhampton Magistrates, ex p. Uppal* [1995] 159 J.P. 86.

The commencement of a new custody time limit with every new charge does not infringe the right to liberty under Article 5 ECHR. In *R. v. Crown Court at Leeds, ex p. Wardle* [2001] 2 Cr.App.R. 20, the defendant was charged originally with murder but the CPS substituted a charge of manslaughter at a later date. It was argued by the defence that new custody time limits did not attach to the new charge which was expressly or impliedly included in the original murder charge. It was also claimed that the detention was therefore in breach of Article 5 ECHR. It was held that a requirement on the magistrates' court to enquire into whether a new charge also constituted one of the potential offences for which a defendant might be convicted on the original charge would place an undue burden on the examining justices. Accordingly, each fresh and different offence charged did give rise to a new custody limit. No breach of Article 5 was found in view of the fact that the proceedings were both lawful and the consequences of the restriction imposed sufficiently accessible. Whilst there was always a risk that the custody time limit might be extended as a result of an arbitrary decision by the prosecution, that risk was subject to judicial control by the court.

More than one application can be made to extend time limits provided the application is made during the currency of the initial time limit or the time limit as extended by the court. This was confirmed in *R. (Haque) v. Central Criminal Court* [2003] EWHC 2457; [2003] 10 *Archbold News* 1, QBD. The court also said that the "root and principal cause" of the need for the extension must be looked at rather than whether the prosecution had contributed to that need.

CHAPTER 6

DISCLOSURE

I. OBLIGATIONS TO DISCLOSE EVIDENCE PRE-TRIAL

A. INTRODUCTION

Historically there has been no obligation on the defence to give the court or the pros- **6–1** ecution advance warning of any evidence that it may seek to adduce at the trial other than via a summons or complaint, which contains information about the alleged offence; this absence of obligation being a natural consequence of the rule that it is for the prosecution to prove the case against the accused. There has also been little legal requirement for the prosecution to give notice of its evidence pre-trial, although disclosure of witness statements to the defence has always been regarded as good practise. Since 1985 the obligation on the prosecutor has become more formalised and the law has reached a position where it imposes limited and varying obligations on both sides to reveal its case to the other before the trial.

The disclosure provisions contained in *Criminal Justice Act* 2003, Pt 5 are now in force subject to exceptions. The new regime alters the prosecutor's duty of primary disclosure (to become known as "initial duty"). There are new provisions concerned with the contents of defence statements and provision for the service of defence statements upon co-accused. Provisions in the *Criminal Justice Act* 2003 concerned with obligations on the defence to give notice of intention to call defence witnesses and to give the prosecution notification of the name and address of any expert who has been instructed by the defence whether or not that expert is to be relied upon have not been implemented. There are also new sanctions arising from failures on the part of the defence to comply with its obligation to disclose pre-trial.

It is also plain from the steer of both legislative and judicial policy that the obligations on the defence to disclose its case pre-trial will become ever more onerous and expansive. A major aim of the *Criminal Procedure Rules* 2005 is to encourage courts at every level to oblige both prosecution and defence to identify all issues of dispute and significance at a pre-trial stage. See *Jisl* [2004] EWCA Crim 696, especially paras 113–121.

B. OBLIGATIONS COMMON TO BOTH PARTIES

(1) Obligation to disclose evidence to be adduced in writing

6–2   The effect of the *CJA* 1967, s.9, is to require any party proposing to tender a *written statement* from a witness in evidence to serve to statement upon the other side at least seven days before the evidence is adduced. After the statement has been served the other party can prevent the evidence being adduced in written form by giving notice, within seven days of receipt of the statement, to the party that served the statement. The statement is only admissible if it complies with the requirements particularised in section 9 and therefore it is good practise for all witness statements to be drawn up in the approved form, so that the written document may be used in evidence if the need should arise. Provided no party objects, any statement which complies with the formalities of section 9 may be read in evidence even though less than seven days' notice has been given.

Criminal Justice Act 1967 s.9

Proof by written statement

6–3   **9.**—(1) In any criminal proceedings, other than committal proceedings, a written statement by any person shall, if such of the conditions mentioned in the next following subsection as are applicable are satisfied, be admissible as evidence to the like extent as oral evidence to the like effect by that person.

(2) The said conditions are—

  (a) the statement purports to be signed by the person who made it;

  (b) the statement contains a declaration by that person to the effect that it is true to the best of his knowledge and belief and that he made the statement knowing that, if it were tendered in evidence, he would be liable to prosecution if he wilfully stated in it anything which he knew to be false or did not believe to be true;

  (c) before the hearing at which the statement is tendered in evidence, a copy of the statement is served, by or on behalf of the party proposing to tender it, on each of the other parties to the proceedings; and

  (d) none of the other parties or their solicitors, within seven days from the service of the copy of the statement, serves a notice on the party so proposing objecting to the statement being tendered in evidence under this section:

Provided that the conditions mentioned in paragraphs (c) and (d) of this subsection shall not apply if the parties agree before or during the hearing that the statement shall be so tendered.

(3) The following provisions shall also have effect in relation to any written statement tendered in evidence under this section, that is to say—

  (a) if the statement is made by a person under the age of eighteen, it shall give his age;

  (b) if it is made by a person who cannot read it, it shall be read to him before he signs it and shall be accompanied by a declaration by the person who so read the statement to the effect that it was so read; and

  (c) if it refers to any other document as an exhibit, the copy served on any other party to the proceedings under paragraph (c) of the last foregoing subsection shall be accompanied by a copy of that document or by such information as may be necessary in order to enable the party on whom it is served to inspect that document or a copy thereof.

(4) Notwithstanding that a written statement made by any person may be admissible as evidence by virtue of this section—

  (a) the party by whom or on whose behalf a copy of the statement was served may call that person to give evidence; and

  (b) the court may, of its own motion or on the application of any party to the proceedings, require that person to attend before the court and give evidence.

(5) An application under paragraph (b) of the last foregoing subsection to a court other

than a magistrates' court may be made before the hearing and on any such application the powers of the court shall be exercisable by a puisne judge of the High Court, a Circuit judge or Recorder sitting alone.

(6) So much of any statement as is admitted in evidence by virtue of this section shall, unless the court otherwise directs, be read aloud at the hearing and where the court so directs an account shall be given orally of so much of any statement as is not read aloud.

(7) Any document or object referred to as an exhibit and identified in a written statement tendered in evidence under this section shall be treated as if it had been produced as an exhibit and identified in court by the maker of the statement.

(8) A document required by this section to be served on any person may be served—

(a) by delivering it to him or to his solicitor; or

(b) by addressing it to him and leaving it at his usual or last known place of abode or place of business or by addressing it to his solicitor and leaving it at his office; or

(c) by sending it in a registered letter or by the recorded delivery service or by first class post addressed to him at his usual or last known place of abode or place of business or addressed to his solicitor at his office; or

(d) in the case of a body corporate, by delivering it to the secretary or clerk of the body at its registered or principal office or sending it in a registered letter or by the recorded delivery service or by first class post addressed to the Secretary or clerk of that body at that office; and in paragraph (d) of this subsection references to the secretary, in relation to a limited liability partnership, are to any designated member of the limited liability partnership.

[Words added by *Limited Liability Partnerships Regulations* 2001 (S.I. 2001 No. 1090), Sched. 5, para. 4.]

(2) Obligation to disclose expert evidence

This obligation is created by rule 24 of the *Criminal Procedure Rules*.   **6–4**

Rule 24.1 requires a party to disclose any expert evidence which he proposes to adduce as soon as practicable after the plea is taken; rule 24.1(g)(ii) enables a party to examine the basis of any findings or opinions proposed to be adduced by way of expert evidence by another party. Rule 24.2 provides for a party to withhold any matter where he has reasonable grounds for suspecting that its disclosure might lead to intimidation or the course of justice being interfered with. In such a case the party is required to give to the other party notice in writing, which must include the grounds on which disclosure is being withheld. By rule 24.3 a party who fails to comply with rule 24.1 in respect of any evidence may not adduce that evidence without the leave of the court.

See *Criminal Procedure Rules* 2005, r.24 in the Appendix G–142 to G–145.   **6–5**

See also the disclosure obligations owed by experts at *post*, § 6–69.

Drafts of an expert's reports are privileged and are not to be disclosable by virtue of an obligation under the rules to give notice: *Jackson v. Marley Davenport Ltd* [2004] 1 W.L.R. 2926.

C. Obligations on the Defence

Other than the obligations to give advance notice of evidence to be adduced by written statements (*CJA* 1967, s.9, *ante*) and to disclose expert evidence, *ante*, there is no **6–6** obligation to disclose evidence pre-trial. Regardless, the defence has the option to provide the court with a defence statement after the prosecution has provided primary disclosure of unused material, see *post*, §§ 6–24 *et seq*.

D. Obligations on the Prosecution

(1) Summary offences

The *Advance Information Rules* 1985 only apply to offences which are triable either **6–7** way. There is no statutory or procedural requirement for advance disclosure of witness statements in summary proceedings: *R. v. Kingston upon Hull Justices, ex p. Mc-Cann* (1991) 155 J.P. 569. In the interest of ensuring a fair trial the prosecutor should consider disclosure of the evidence pre-trial. Whilst Article 6 of the European Convention on Human Rights does not require that prosecution witness statements be supplied to the accused before trial (*R. v. Stratford JJ., ex p. Imbert* [1999] 2 Cr.App.R. 276, DC), Article 6(1) guarantees that everyone charged with a criminal offence has the minimum right to have adequate time and facilities to prepare a defence; therefore if the defence is taken by surprise by evidence adduced during the trial an application for an adjournment, to prepare a response to the evidence, may be justified. The *Attorney General's Guidelines on Disclosure*, (updated April 2005), para. 57 instructs a prosecutor to provide to the defence all evidence on which the Crown propose to rely in a summary trial so as to allow the accused or their legal advisers sufficient time properly to consider the evidence before it is called.

Attorney General's Guidelines on Disclosure, para.57

Summary Trial

6–8   **57.** The prosecutor should in addition to complying with the obligations under the Act [CPIA], provide to the defence all evidence upon which the Crown proposes to rely is a summary trial. Such provision should allow the accused and their legal advisors sufficient time properly to consider the evidencebefore it is called.

(2) Offences triable either way

6–9   Pursuant to rule 21 of the *Criminal Procedure Rules* 2005, in all either way cases the defence are entitled to be provided with advance information of the prosecution case but this right only applies before the court determines mode of trial. If the parties agree to deal with mode of trial before the prosecution are able to provide advance disclosure then the parties may wish also to agree between themselves that the disclosure will be made voluntarily after mode of trial has been decided.

6–10   This rule applies to all proceeings for an offence triable either way and replaces the *Magistrates' Courts (Advance Information) Rules* 1985. However, rule 21 almost entirely reproduces rules 2–7 under the 1985 regime. Accordingly, it is submitted that authorities dealing with aspects of the 1985 regime remain valid under rule 21.

See *Criminal Procedure Rules* 2005 in Appendix G–134 to G–139.

6–11   The purpose of rule 21 is to enable the defendant and his or her advisers to decide on mode of trial or plea. It is not disclosure for the purposes of subsequent committal proceedings or summary trial. Magistrates have no power to direct that advance information be served. The court should adjourn the proceedings under rule 21.6 to allow the prosecution to comply with this rule.

Failure to provide the defendant with advance information is not of itself an abuse of process although continuing default might become an abuse of process: *R. v. Willesden Magistrates' Court, ex p. Clemmings* (1988) 152 J.P.N. 46. Nor does such a failure provide grounds for an information to be dismissed: *King v. Kucharz* (1989) 153 J.P. 336.

Rule 21.3 requires the prosecution to supply a written statement containing the facts and matters on which the prosecutor proposes to adduce evidence in the proceedings, or a summary of the facts and matters of which the prosecutor proposes to adduce evidence in the proceedings. A document includes a video for these purposes: *R. v. Calderdale Magistrates' Court, ex p. Donahue and Cutler* [2001] Crim.L.R. 141, DC. Where a summary of facts and matters upon which the prosecution intends to rely supplied in accordance with rule 4 contains a reference to DNA profiles that is not a reference to a document on which the prosecutor proposes to rely within the meaning of 21.3: *Croydon Magistrates' Court* [2001] Crim.L.R. 980, DC.

6–12   The prosecution, including local authorities, should reveal the identity of a complainant at an early stage before advance disclosure: *Daventry District Council v. Olins* [1990] C.O.D. 244, DC.

II. DISCLOSURE OF MATERIAL WHICH IS NOT RELIED UPON AS EVIDENCE (UNUSED MATERIAL)

A. General

With regard to offences into which a criminal investigation was commenced on or af-	**6–13**
ter April 1, 1997 the duties and responsibilities of parties with regard to disclosure are contained in Parts I and II of the *Criminal Procedure and Investigations Act* 1996. Part I created a staged approach to disclosure. Part II provides for the creation of a code of practice for regulating the conduct of the police in recording and retaining material obtained in the course of a criminal investigation and providing it to the prosecution who then decides on disclosure. The *CPIA* 1996 disclosure regime was significantly modified by the *Criminal Justice Act* 2003 and the changes were implemented on April 4, 2005 in relation to offences in respect of which a criminal investigation began on or after that date. The Attorney General has also issued guidelines on the disclosure of information which were last updated in April 2005. The introduction (paras 1–7) to the guidelines emphasises the overriding requirement of fair disclosure of unused material by a prosecutor. Paragraph 1 states that fair disclosure to an accused is an inseparable part of a fair trial. Paragraph 7 directs that the guidelines must be followed in proceedings in the magistrates' courts.

B. The European Convention

The right to fair trial means that the prosecution should disclose to the defence all	**6–14**
material evidence in their possession for and against the defendant. Only such measures restricting the right of the defence to disclosure which are strictly necessary are permissible: *Rowe and Davies v. UK* (2000) 30 E.H.R.R. 1; see especially paragraphs 60–62.

The approach of the European Court was endorsed by the House of Lords in *H. and C.* [2004] UKHL 3, see *post*, § 6–58.

C. Disclosure at Common Law

The Act does not alter the common law rules as to whether disclosure is in the public	**6–15**
interest, although it does regulate the procedure for making an application to the court for permission to withhold material for which public interest immunity is claimed: see *post*, § 6–55.

The Act does not abolish the common law obligations relating to the disclosure of information by the prosecution prior to committal for trial in the Crown Court. However, the provisions of the Act are such as to require that those obligations be radically recast. In *R. v. DPP, ex p. Lee* [1999] 2 Cr.App.R. 304, CA (Crim. Div.), the court considered the timing and extent of the prosecution's disclosure obligations. The disclosure provisions of the *Criminal Procedure and Investigations Act* 1996 commence when the court proceeds to summary trial or in the case of an offence triable on indictment upon committal for trial. Receiving disclosure at this stage ordinarily would not undermine the defendant's right to a fair trial. The prosecution should be aware of the need for advance disclosure of material which he or she recognises should be disclosed at that stage in the interests of justice and fairness. Four examples were considered: (a) prior convictions of a complainant or a deceased which might assist the defendant in a bail application; (b) material which might assist in applying for a stay of proceedings as an abuse of process; (c) material which might support a submission that the defendant should be committed on a lesser charge, or not at all, and (d) material which would allow preparation for trial in a significantly more effective manner than if disclosure were delayed, for example the names of witnesses the prosecution did not intend to call. It was clear that early disclosure in all cases would not normally exceed primary disclosure under section 3, being disclosure of material thought to undermine the prosecution's case. To the extent that a defendant revealed material normally disclosed in the defence statement, secondary disclosure, triggered in response to a defence statement, should be made in advance in respect of examples (a), (b) and (c), but disclosure of material of type (d) would depend on what the defendant revealed.

6–16   Paragraph 55 of the Attorney General's Guidelines on Disclosure advises prosecutors to make disclosure before initial disclosure if this is in the interests of justice and fairness. See Appendix C–18.

The prosecution's obligation of disclosure at common law is sufficient to require disclosure even where proceedings were instituted by summons for a speeding offence: *R. v. Stratford Magistrates' Court, ex p. Johnson* [2003] EWHC 353. The applicant argued the magistrate was incorrect in construing section 1 of the *Criminal Procedure and Investigations Act* 1996 as meaning that it did not apply to proceedings instituted by way of summons. The Divisional Court considered that it was unnecessary to determine the scope of section 1 of the 1996 Act because the prosecution's obligation of disclosure at common law was sufficient to require disclosure in the case.

D. Prosecution Initial Disclosure

Criminal Procedure and Investigations Act 1996, ss.1–2

Application of the CPIA to magistrates' court proceedings

6–17   **1.**—(1) This Part applies where—

     (a) a person is charged with a summary offence in respect of which a court proceeds to summary trial and in respect of which he pleads not guilty,

     (b) a person who has attained the age of 18 is charged with an offence which is triable either way, in respect of which a court proceeds to summary trial and in respect of which he pleads not guilty, or

     (c) a person under the age of 18 is charged with an indictable offence in respect of which a court proceeds to summary trial and in respect of which he pleads not guilty.

(3) This Part applies in relation to alleged offences into which no criminal investigation has begun before the appointed day.

(4) For the purposes of this section a criminal investigation is an investigation which police officers or other persons have a duty to conduct with a view to it being ascertained—

     (a) whether a person should be charged with an offence, or

     (b) whether a person charged with an offence is guilty of it.

(5) The reference in subsection (3) to the appointed day is to such day as is appointed for the purposes of this Part by the Secretary of State by order.

General interpretation

6–18   **2.**—(1) References to the accused are to the person mentioned in section 1(1) or (2).

(2) Where there is more than one accused in any proceedings this Part applies separately in relation to each of the accused.

(3) References to the prosecutor are to any person acting as prosecutor, whether an individual or a body.

(4) References to material are to material of all kinds, and in particular include references to—

     (a) information, and

     (b) objects of all descriptions.

(5) References to recording information are to putting it in a durable or retrievable form (such as writing or tape).

(6) This section applies for the purposes of this Part.

Initial Disclosure by Prosecutor CPIA 1996, ss.3–4

6–19   The prosecutor's duty of initial disclosure applies when the accused pleads not guilty and the court proceeds to summary trial. The disclosure obligations on the prosecution in section 3 only apply if the accused has pleaded not guilty: section 1. The defence is not entitled to disclosure where the accused has pleaded guilty or where the accused has been committed for sentence to the Crown Court following a plea in the magistrates' court. It is only in respect of summary trials that the prosecution is obliged to make initial disclosure. The prosecution's disclosure obligations do not apply to the pre-committal stage. As regards disclosure at this stage the common law rules on disclosure apply: section 21(3)(b), see *ante*.

Criminal Procedure and Investigations Act 1996, ss.3–4

Initial duty of prosecutor to disclose

3.—(1) The prosecutor must—　　　　　　　　　　　　　　　　　　**6–20**

  (a) disclose to the accused any prosecution material which has not previously been disclosed to the accused and which might reasonably be considered capable of undermining the case for the prosecution against the accused or of assisting the case for the accused, or

  (b) give to the accused a written statement that there is no material of a description mentioned in paragraph (a).

(2) For the purposes of this section prosecution material is material—

  (a) which is in the prosecutor's possession, and came into his possession in connection with the case for the prosecution against the accused, or

  (b) which, in pursuance of a code operative under Part II, he has inspected in connection with the case for the prosecution against the accused.

(3) Where material consists of information which has been recorded in any form the prosecutor discloses it for the purposes of this section—

  (a) by securing that a copy is made of it and that the copy is given to the accused, or

  (b) if in the prosecutor's opinion that is not practicable or not desirable, by allowing the accused to inspect it at a reasonable time and a reasonable place or by taking steps to secure that he is allowed to do so;

and a copy may be in such form as the prosecutor thinks fit and need not be in the same form as that in which the information has already been recorded.

(4) Where material consists of information which has not been recorded the prosecutor discloses it for the purposes of this section by securing that it is recorded in such form as he thinks fit and—

  (a) by securing that a copy is made of it and that the copy is given to the accused, or

  (b) if in the prosecutor's opinion that is not practicable or not desirable, by allowing the accused to inspect it at a reasonable time and a reasonable place or by taking steps to secure that he is allowed to do so.

(5) Where material does not consist of information the prosecutor discloses it for the purposes of this section by allowing the accused to inspect it at a reasonable time and a reasonable place or by taking steps to secure that he is allowed to do so.

(6) Material must not be disclosed under this section to the extent that the court, on an application by the prosecutor, concludes it is not in the public interest to disclose it and orders accordingly.

(7) Material must not be disclosed under this section to the extent that–

  (a) it has been intercepted in obedience to a warrant issued under section 2 of the *Interception of Communications Act* 1985, or

  (b) it indicates that such a warrant has been issued or that material has been intercepted in obedience to such a warrant.

(8) The prosecutor must act under this section during the period which, by virtue of section 12, is the relevant period for this section.

Initial duty to disclose: further provisions

4.—(1) This section applies where—　　　　　　　　　　　　　　**6–21**

  (a) the prosecutor acts under section 3, and

  (b) before so doing he was given a document in pursuance of provision included, by virtue of section 24(3), in a code operative under Part II.

(2) In such a case the prosecutor must give the document to the accused at the same time as the prosecutor acts under section 3.

The prosecution is obliged to disclose previously undisclosed material to the accused **6–22** in accordance with the test set out in section 3(1)(a), see *ante*. Disclosure pursuant to assisting an accused's case will depend on the extent to which the accused has disclosed their case, *e.g.* while being interviewed. If there is no such material then the defence must be given written notice to that effect.

6–23   A failure by the prosecution to make proper initial disclosure may result in a defence application to stay proceedings as an abuse of process.

In *DPP v. Wood and McGillicuddy* [2006] EWHC 32 it was held that the duty of disclosure under section 3 is satisfied without service of the non-sensitive schedule under section 4. The schedule could be served subsequently.

E. DEFENCE DISCLOSURE

6–24   In cases to be tried summarily, the accused is under no obligation to provide a defence statement or notice of alibi. Compulsory disclosure by the accused only arises where the case is to be tried on indictment and even then does not have to be undertaken until the case has been committed, sent or transferred for trial.

An accused, therefore, must choose whether to serve a defence statement or not. Section 6 of the *Criminal Procedure and Investigations Act* 1996 addresses the situation of such voluntary disclosure.

Criminal Procedure and Investigations Act 1996, ss.6–6E

Voluntary disclosure by accused
6–25   **6.**—(1) This section applies where—
    (a) this Part applies by virtue of section 1(1), and
    (b) the prosecutor complies with section 3 or purports to comply with it.
    (2) The accused—
    (a) may give a defence statement to the prosecutor, and
    (b) if he does so, must also give such a statement to the court.
    (3) [...]
    (4) If the accused gives a defence statement under this section he must give it during the period which, by virtue of section 12 is the relevant period for this section.

Contents of defence statement
6–26   **6A.**—(1) For the purposes of this Part a defence statement is a written statement—
    (a) setting out the nature of the accused's defence, including any particular defences on which he intends to rely,
    (b) indicating the matters of fact on which he takes issue with the prosecution,
    (c) setting out, in the case of each such matter, why he takes issue with the prosecution, and
    (d) indicating any point of law (including any point as to the admissibility of evidence or an abuse of process) which he wishes to take, and any authority on which he intends to rely for that purpose.
    (2) A defence statement that discloses an alibi must give particulars of it, including—
    (a) the name, address and date of birth of any witness the accused believes is able to give evidence in support of the alibi, or as many of those details as are known to the accused when the statement is given;
    (b) any information in the accused's possession which might be of material assistance in identifying or finding any such witness in whose case any of the details mentioned in paragraph (a) are not known to the accused when the statement is given.
    (3) For the purposes of this section evidence in support of an alibi is evidence tending to show that by reason of the presence of the accused at a particular place or in a particular area at a particular time he was not, or was unlikely to have been, at the place where the offence is alleged to have been committed at the time of its alleged commission.
    (4) The Secretary of State may by regulations make provision as to the details of the matters that, by virtue of subsection (1), are to be included in defence statements.

6–27   Section 6A(1) defines a defence statement and prescribes its necessary content. Accordingly if an accused elects to make a voluntary disclosure under section 6, their defence statement must comply with section 6A. Sections 6A(1)(a)–(d) requires the specification of the accused's defence and any other matters likely to be adverse to the prosecution case.

Sections 6B, 6C and 6D, *post*, were not implemented with the other amendments to the *CPIA* affected by the *Criminal Justice Act* 2003. No date for their implementation has been announced, but the sections are reproduced, *post*, in anticipation of this.

Updated disclosure by accused

6B.—(1) Where the accused has, before the beginning of the relevant period for this section, given a defence statement under section 5 or 6, he must during that period give to the court and the prosecutor either—   **6–28**

(a) a defence statement under this section (an "updated defence statement"), or

(b) a statement of the kind mentioned in subsection (4).

(2) The relevant period for this section is determined under section 12.

(3) An updated defence statement must comply with the requirements imposed by or under section 6A by reference to the state of affairs at the time when the statement is given.

(4) Instead of an updated defence statement, the accused may give a written statement stating that he has no changes to make to the defence statement which was given under section 5 or 6.

(5) Where there are other accused in the proceedings and the court so orders, the accused must also give either an updated defence statement or a statement of the kind mentioned in subsection (4), within such period as may be specified by the court, to each other accused so specified.

(6) The court may make an order under subsection (5) either of its own motion or on the application of any party.

Notification of intention to call defence witnesses

6C.—(1) The accused must give to the court and the prosecutor a notice indicating whether he intends to call any persons (other than himself) as witnesses at his trial and, if so—   **6–29**

(a) giving the name, address and date of birth of each such proposed witness, or as many of those details as are known to the accused when the notice is given;

(b) providing any information in the accused's possession which might be of material assistance in identifying or finding any such proposed witness in whose case any of the details mentioned in paragraph (a) are not known to the accused when the notice is given.

(2) Details do not have to be given under this section to the extent that they have already been given under section 6A(2).

(3) The accused must give a notice under this section during the period which, by virtue of section 12, is the relevant period for this section.

(4) If, following the giving of a notice under this section, the accused—

(a) decides to call a person (other than himself) who is not included in the notice as a proposed witness, or decides not to call a person who is so included, or

(b) discovers any information which, under subsection (1), he would have had to include in the notice if he had been aware of it when giving the notice,

he must give an appropriately amended notice to the court and the prosecutor.

Notification of names of experts instructed by accused

6D.—(1) If the accused instructs a person with a view to his providing any expert opinion for possible use as evidence at the trial of the accused, he must give to the court and the prosecutor a notice specifying the person's name and address.   **6–30**

(2) A notice does not have to be given under this section specifying the name and address of a person whose name and address have already been given under section 6C.

(3) A notice under this section must be given during the period which, by virtue of section 12, is the relevant period for this section.

Disclosure by accused: further provisions

6E.—(1) Where an accused's solicitor purports to give on behalf of the accused—   **6–31**

(a) a defence statement under section 5, 6 or 6B, or

(b) a statement of the kind mentioned in section 6B(4),

the statement shall, unless the contrary is proved, be deemed to be given with the authority of the accused.

(2) If it appears to the judge at a pre-trial hearing that an accused has failed to comply fully with section 5, 6B or 6C, so that there is a possibility of comment being made or inferences drawn under section 11(5), he shall warn the accused accordingly.

(3) In subsection (2) "pre-trial hearing" has the same meaning as in Part 4 (see section 39).

6–32   Section 6E states that where a defence statement is served, it is irrespective of whether or not it is signed by the accused, *i.e.* it is deemed to have the authority of the accused unless the contrary is proven. Sections 6E(4)–(6) concern trial only by jury and so are not reproduced here.

Implications of voluntary disclosure by accused

6–33   Although no adverse inference can be drawn against a defendant who fails to provide a statement, the prosecution have no obligation to provide beyond the scope of their initial duty of disclosure unless a defence statement is served. See, however, section 7A, *post*.

In contrast to proceedings in the Crown Court, there is no provision in the *Criminal Justice Act* 2003 to allow a magistrates' court to order cross-service of defence statements where there is more than one accused and where at least two of the accused have served defence statements on the court and prosecution but not to each other. However, where there are "cut-throat" defences, there is authority for the view that a cross-service may be ordered; see *Cairns* [2003] 1 Cr.App.R. 38.

6–34   Where the defendant, upon being confronted with a contradiction between the evidence and the defence statement, asserts that the latter contains a mistake, a judge ought to raise the matter with counsel: *Wheeler* [2001] 1 Cr.App.R. 10, CA. If a defendant volunteers a defence statement in a summary trial, there is the risk that an adverse inference may be drawn if the defence statement is inconsistent with the defence advanced at trial. Section 11 does not disallow or require leave for cross-examination of a defendant on differences between the defence at trial and the defence statement. It is unnecessary under section 11(3) to obtain leave to cross-examine the defendant on differences in the defence and the defence statement: *Tibbs* [2004] 2 Cr.App.R. 309, CA.

It is good practice for the defence statement to be signed by the defendant: *Wheeler, ante*. However, a judge has no power to issue a practice direction to the effect that the defendant must sign the defence statement (*R. v. Maidstone Crown Court, ex p. Sullivan* [2002] EWHC 967). Section 6E considered *ante*, deems that a defence statement is given with the authority of the defendant.

If the defence is one of alibi then the defence statement must contain the name and address of the proposed alibi witness or where that information is not available, any information which might be of assistance in locating the witness. See section 6A(2).

6–35   The Professional Conduct and Complaints Committee of the Bar Council has issued guidance as to the duties of counsel in relation to the preparation of defence statements. There is nothing unprofessional about counsel drafting a defence statement. Counsel has no obligation to do so if requested to do so for no fee; in publicly funded cases there is no provision for a fee to be payable for this task, unless counsel is assigned under the Representation Order which is most unlikely in a case to be tried summarily. The guidance reminds counsel of the importance of the need to have all the relevant evidence and statements from other material witnesses, as well as the importance of obtaining informed approval from the client before drafting the statement.

F. CONTINUING DUTY OF PROSECUTION DISCLOSURE

Criminal Procedure and Investigations Act 1996, ss.7A–8

Continuing duty of prosecutor to disclose

6–36   **7A.**—(1) This section applies at all times—

    (a) after the prosecutor has complied with section 3 or purported to comply with it, and

    (b) before the accused is acquitted or convicted or the prosecutor decides not to proceed with the case concerned.

(2) The prosecutor must keep under review the question whether at any given time (and, in particular, following the giving of a defence statement) there is prosecution material which—

    (a) might reasonably be considered capable of undermining the case for the prosecution against the accused or of assisting the case for the accused, and

    (b) has not been disclosed to the accused.

(3) If at any time there is any such material as is mentioned in subsection (2) the prosecutor must disclose it to the accused as soon as is reasonably practicable (or within the period mentioned in subsection (5)(a), where that applies).

(4) In applying subsection (2) by reference to any given time the state of affairs at that time (including the case for the prosecution as it stands at that time) must be taken into account.

(5) Where the accused gives a defence statement under section 5, 6 or 6B—

    (a) if as a result of that statement the prosecutor is required by this section to make any disclosure, or further disclosure, he must do so during the period which, by virtue of section 12, is the relevant period for this section;

    (b) if the prosecutor considers that he is not so required, he must during that period give to the accused a written statement to that effect.

(6) For the purposes of this section prosecution material is material—

    (a) which is in the prosecutor's possession and came into his possession in connection with the case for the prosecution against the accused, or

    (b) which, in pursuance of a code operative under Part 2, he has inspected in connection with the case for the prosecution against the accused.

(7) Subsections (3) to (5) of section 3 (method by which prosecutor discloses) apply for the purposes of this section as they apply for the purposes of that.

(8) Material must not be disclosed under this section to the extent that the court, on an application by the prosecutor, concludes it is not in the public interest to disclose it and orders accordingly.

(9) Material must not be disclosed under this section to the extent that it is material the disclosure of which is prohibited by section 17 of the *Regulation of Investigatory Powers Act* 2000 (c. 23).

This is an onerous continuing duty of disclosure; to keep under review at all times **6–37** whether there is any unused material which might reasonably be considered capable of undermining the prosecution case against the accused or assisting the case for the accused which has not previously been disclosed. Paragraph 18 and paragraphs 32 to 44 of the Attorney General's Guidelines on Disclosure (updated April 2005) provide mandatory guidance to prosecutors in carrying out this continuing duty. The scope of the duty is dependent upon the content of any defence statement but it applies irrespective of whether one has been served or not. This is particularly important as a defendant's application for specific disclosure under section 8, considered *post*, only arises if they have chosen to give a defence statement under section 6.

Application by accused for disclosure

    8.—(1) This section applies where the accused has given a defence statement under section 5, **6–38** 6 or 6B and the prosecutor has complied with section 7A(5) or has purported to comply with it or has failed to comply with it.

(2) If the accused has at any time reasonable cause to believe that there is prosecution material which is required by section 7A to be disclosed to him and has not been, he may apply to the court for an order requiring the prosecutor to disclose it to him.

(3) For the purposes of this section prosecution material is material—

    (a) which is in the prosecutor's possession and came into his possession in connection with the case for the prosecution against the accused.

    (b) which, in pursuance of a code operative under Part II, he has inspected in connection with the case for the prosecution against the accused, or

(c) which falls within subsection (4).

(4) Material falls within this subsection if in pursuance of a code operative under Part II the prosecutor must, if he asks for the material, be given a copy of it or be allowed to inspect it in connection with the case for the prosecution against the accused.

(5) Material must not be disclosed under this section to the extent that the court, on an application by the prosecutor, concludes it is not in the public interest to disclose it and orders accordingly.

(6) Material must not be disclosed under this section to the extent that[it is material the disclosure of which is prohibited by section 17 of the *Regulation of Investigatory Powers Act* 2000.

6–39   The meaning of subsections (3) and (4) were considered by Ouseley J. in *DPP v. Wood and McGillicudy* [2006] EWHC 32. The submission he considered in a drink-driving case was whether the manufacturer of "Intoximeters" who supplied these devices to the police and had continuing contractual obligations to maintain them had become part of the prosecution team for the purposes of these subsections. The court held that "prosecutor" meant the CPS (the prosecuting authority) alone, and that a contractual relationship between the police and a third party could never render material in the possession of that third party to be classed as "prosecution material".

The *Criminal Justice Act* 2003 inserted new subsections (1) and (2), *ante*, into section 8 of the *CPIA* 1996. The effect of this is to make defence applications under this section easier if a defence statement has been served; to have locus to make a section 8 application the defendant need only have made a defence statement and not also that its content relates to the terms of such an application.

Magistrates' Courts (Criminal Procedure and Investigations Act 1996) Disclosure Rules 1997, r.7

Disclosure: application by accused and order of court

6–40   **7.**—(1) This rule applies to an application by the accused under section 8(2).

(2) An application to which this rule applies shall be made by notice in writing to the [justices' chief executive for] the court and shall specify—

    (a) the material to which the application relates;

    (b) that the material has not been disclosed to the accused;

    (c) the reason why the material might be expected to assist the applicant's defence as disclosed by the defence statement given under section 6; and

    (d) the date of service of a copy of the notice on the prosecutor in accordance with paragraph (3) below.

(3) A copy of the notice referred to in paragraph (2) above shall be served on the prosecutor at the same time as it is sent to the [justices' chief executive for] the court.

(4) The prosecutor shall give notice in writing to the [justices' chief executive for] the court within 14 days of service of a notice under paragraph (3) above that—

    (a) he wishes to make representations to the court concerning the material to which the application relates; or

    (b) if he does not so wish, that he is willing to disclose that material;

and a notice under sub-paragraph (a) above shall specify the substance of the representations he wishes to make.

(5) Subject to paragraphs (6) and (7) below—

    (a) the designated officer for the court shall give notice in writing to the prosecutor and the applicant of the date and time when and the place where the hearing will take place;

    (b) the hearing shall be inter partes; and

    (c) the prosecutor and the applicant shall be entitled to make representations to the court.

(6) The court may determine the application without hearing representations from the applicant or the prosecutor unless—

    (a) the prosecutor has given notice under paragraph (4)(a) above and the court considers that the representations should be made at a hearing; or

(b) the court considers it necessary to hear representations from the applicant or the prosecutor in the interests of justice for the purposes of determining the application.

(7) Where the prosecutor applies to the court for leave to make representations in the absence of the accused, the court may for that purpose sit in the absence of the accused and any legal representative of his.

G. Aspects of the Prosecution's Duty of Disclosure

The decision as to whether disclosure should be made is for the prosecution. The fol- **6–41** lowing extract from the House of Lords case of *H. & C.* [2004] UKHL 3 should resound in the minds of prosecutors and courts alike:

> "35. If material does not weaken the prosecution case or strengthen that of the defendant, there is no requirement to disclose it. For this purpose the parties' respective cases should not be restrictively analysed. But they must be carefully analysed, to ascertain the specific facts the prosecution seek to establish and the specific grounds on which the charges are resisted.
>
> The trial process is not well served if the defence are permitted to make general and unspecified allegations and then seek far-reaching disclosure in the hope that material may turn up to make them good. Neutral material or material damaging to the defendant need not be disclosed and should not be brought to the attention of the court. Only in truly borderline cases should the prosecution seek a judicial ruling on the disclosability of material in its hands."

Commenting on *H. & C.* the Court of Appeal in *R. v. Nicholls* [2005] EWCA Crim 1797 said:

> "40. It is very important to recognise the effect of their Lordships' reasoning in H. It exemplifies, if we may respectfully say so, the classic common law blend of principle and pragmatism. Fairness requires the disclosure to the defence of relevant material. That is elementary. Sometimes other public interests militate against that requirement. That, too, is effectively elementary. Where there is a conflict in the criminal jurisdiction fairness to the defendant will come first, but if the material is neutral, or damaging to the defendant, fairness does not require its disclosure." (emphasis added).

It is a denial of natural justice for a prosecutor to fail to disclose witnesses' statements favourable to the defence or to call witnesses: *R. v. Leyland Justices, ex p. Hawthorn* [1979] 1 Q.B. 283. The defendant was convicted of driving without due care and attention contrary to the *Road Traffic Act* 1972, s.3. In issue at the trial was whether his car had been either partly or wholly over the centre line of the road. After the trial the police notified the defendant's solicitors of the existence of two further witnesses whose evidence might have been helpful to him. The police had not called these witnesses nor disclosed the existence of statements from these witnesses before. The conviction was quashed.

Where pivotal prosecution evidence comes from a witness with a known prison record it is incumbent upon the prosecution to acquire the prison records. Where disclosure is late, or does not occur, of material relating to a super grass, the test is: had disclosure occurred earlier, or at all, would the information have given rise to cross examination which would or might have materially affected the witnesses' credibility? See *McCartney, Hamlett* [2003] 6 *Archbold News* 2, CA. Non-disclosure of an important witness' previous convictions will not inevitably lead to a conviction being quashed. Convictions will be upheld where the Court of Appeal concludes that the jury would have convicted in any event: *Underwood* (2003) 147 S.J.L.B. 657, CA. Where materials are withheld from the court at first instance and the Court of Appeal, a violation of the right to a fair trial under Article 6 will have occurred: *Dowsett v. UK, The Times*, July 12, 2003, ECHR. Failure to disclose a previous witness statement that may have undermined a witness's credibility where the evidence determined a guilty verdict will render a conviction unsafe: *Kelly (deceased); Connolly (deceased)* [2003] EWCA Crim 2957.

In *Vasiliou* [2000] Crim.L.R. 845 the Court of Appeal held that the defendant's **6–42** conviction had been rendered unsafe because he could not challenge prosecution witnesses as to their character as the prosecution had not disclosed their previous convictions. Likewise in *Eccleston*, unreported, July 1, 2001, CA (Crim. Div.) the court said that where there has been a failure to disclose the convictions of a prosecution witness, the question was how relevant the missing information was likely to be to the defence, with that view varying according to whether the witness was the complainant or a third party witness whose evidence was not central to the issue. Whilst the courts have interpreted the scope of initial disclosure to include the disclosure of previous convictions of prosecution witnesses, Eccleston holds that a failure to disclose will not necessarily render the conviction unsafe.

In a Scottish case, *Holland v. H.M. Advocate*, May 11, 2005, the Privy Council held there may also be a duty of disclosure in relation to any outstanding charges against such witnesses.

In *Mills and Poole* [1998] A.C. 382, the House of Lords considered whether the prosecution has a duty to disclose the name and address of a witness who had given a statement but whom the prosecution had decided not to call because they regarded the witness as unreliable. The defence argued that the rule in *Bryant*, (1946) 31 Cr.App.R. 146, which distinguished between disclosing the statement of a credible witness to the defence and informing the defence about a witness considered to be untruthful, could no longer be sustained, as it conflicted with Court of Appeal decisions emphasising the importance of full prosecution disclosure. The House of Lords held that in some circumstances *Bryant* could result in an injustice and should not be retained unless there was strong argument to do so. The risk that disclosure could help the defence to tailor its evidence was outweighed by the risk of injustice and the rule did not conform with the principles of disclosure enunciated since 1990. Therefore, the rule should no longer be applied and the failure to disclose the statement represented a material irregularity in the course of the trial.

6–43   The identity of persons who might have witnessed an incident giving rise to criminal charges is material capable of undermining the prosecution case or supporting the defence case. Those who dial 999 to report such an incident fall into that category so the duty of disclosure extends to the telephone numbers of the makers of such calls. A general principle of non-disclosure of the identity of persons making 999 calls could not be justified there being no basis in the ordinary course of events for any expectation of confidentiality. However, it may be possible to argue otherwise in an individual case: *Heggart* [2001] 1 *Archbold News* 2, CA.

6–44   The prosecution may be obliged to disclose the statements of co-defendants: *Cairns* [2003] 1 Cr.App.R. 38. At trial the defendant had requested disclosure of the witness statements of her co-defendants but had been refused on the basis that the *Criminal Procedure and Investigations Act* 1996, s.5(5) limited such disclosure to the prosecution and to the court. The Court of Appeal (Crim. Div.) held that the statements of both co-defendants should have been disclosed because the prosecution was obliged to disclose a defence statement to a co-defendant if there was a chance that it would assist that co-defendant in his or her own defence.

6–45   The prosecution are not entitled to withhold information even if they consider that the defendant is unlikely to use the information during the trial: *Hilton* [2003] EWCA Crim 761. The defendant contended that the prosecution should have disclosed material that resulted from the search of a witness's house, who the prosecution argued the defendant had asked to obtain fake Rolex watches. The Crown argued that even if the material had been disclosed it was unlikely that he would have used it. The Court of Appeal (Crim. Div.) allowed the appeal on the basis that it was likely that the defendant would have used the undisclosed material in his defence.

H. TIME LIMITS

Criminal Procedure and Investigations Act 1996, ss.10, 12

Prosecutor's failure to observe time limits
6–46   **10.**—(1) This section applies if the prosecutor—

(a) purports to act under section 3 after the end of the period which, by virtue of section 12, is the relevant period for section 3, or

(b) purports to act under section 7A(5) after the end of the period which, by virtue of section 12, is the relevant period for section 7A.

(2) Subject to subsection (3) the failure to act during the period concerned does not on its own constitute grounds for staying the proceedings for abuse of process.

(3) Subsection (2) does not prevent the failure constituting such grounds if it involves such delay by the prosecutor that the accused is denied a fair trial.

Time limits

12.—(1) This section has effect for the purpose of determining the relevant period for sec- **6–47** tions 3, 5, 6, 6B, 6C and 7A(5).

(2) Subject to subsection (3), the relevant period is a period beginning and ending with such days as the Secretary of State prescribes by regulations for the purposes of the section concerned.

(3) The regulations may do one or more of the following—

(a) provide that the relevant period for any section shall if the court so orders be extended (or further extended) by so many days as the court specifies;

(b) provide that the court may only make such an order if an application is made by a prescribed person and if any other prescribed conditions are fulfilled;

(c) provide that an application may only be made if prescribed conditions are fulfilled;

(d) provide that the number of days by which a period may be extended shall be entirely at the court's discretion;

(e) provide that the number of days by which a period may be extended shall not exceed a prescribed number;

(f) provide that there shall be no limit on the number of applications that may be made to extend a period;

(g) provide that no more than a prescribed number of applications may be made to extend a period;

and references to the relevant period for a section shall be construed accordingly.

(4) Conditions mentioned in subsection (3) may be framed by reference to such factors as the Secretary of State thinks fit.

(5) Without prejudice to the generality of subsection (4), so far as the relevant period for section 3 or 7A(5) is concerned—

(a) conditions may be framed by reference to the nature or volume of the material concerned;

(b) the nature of material may be defined by reference to the prosecutor's belief that the question of non-disclosure on grounds of public interest may arise.

(6) In subsection (3) "prescribed" means prescribed byregulations under this section.

I. CODE OF PRACTICE

The *CPIA (Code of Practice) Order* 2005 implemented on April 4, 2005 a new **6–48** Code of Practice under section 23(1) of the *CPIA* 1996. The Code applies to alleged and suspected offences into which a criminal investigation commenced in England and Wales on or after April 4, 2005. The original *CPIA* Code applies to investigations which began between April 1, 1997 and April 3, 2005.

However, the two Codes are very similar, the majority of changes being due to the **6–49** modifications effected by the *Criminal Justice Act* 2003 into the *CPIA* 1996 which have been considered, *ante*. See also Appendix B. Section 23 of the *CPIA* 1996 prescribes what in general terms it should contain.

Criminal Procedure and Investigations Act 1996, s.26

Effect of code

26.—(1) A person other than a police officer who is charged with the duty of conducting an **6–50** investigation with a view to it being ascertained—

(a) whether a person should be charged with an offence, or

(b) whether a person charged with an offence is guilty of it,

shall in discharging that duty have regard to any relevant provision of a code which would apply if the investigation were conducted by police officers.

(2) A failure—

    (a) by a police officer to comply with any provision of a code for the time being in operation by virtue of an order under section 25, or

    (b) by a person to comply with subsection (1),

shall not in itself render him liable to any criminal or civil proceedings.

(3) In all criminal and civil proceedings a code in operation at any time by virtue of an order under section 25 shall be admissible in evidence.

(4) If it appears to a court or tribunal conducting criminal or civil proceedings that—

    (a) any provision of a code in operation at any time by virtue of an order under section 25, or

    (b) any failure mentioned in subsection (2)(a) or (b),

is relevant to any question arising in the proceedings, the provision or failure shall be taken into account in deciding the question.

6–51   The Code applies to police officers and other persons who under the *CPIA* 1996 are charged with the duty of conducting criminal investigations. It prescribes the duties and functions of investigators and specifies the procedures to be followed in recording information, retaining material, preparing material for the prosecutor and disclosure of material to the accused. It also instructs the police in relation to the handling of sensitive material.

J. ATTORNEY GENERAL'S GUIDELINES

6–52   In April 2005 the Attorney General issued revised guidelines on disclosure of information in criminal proceedings. They were adopted with immediate effect in relation to all cases submitted after that date to the prosecuting authorities in receipt of the guidelines. This reissue coincided with the implementation of the changes to the *CPIA* 1996 affected by the 2003 Act. The guidelines acknowledge that "fair disclosure to an accused is an inseparable part of a fair trial [under Article 6]" (para. 1). Whereas the Code issued under the *CPIA* 1996 is concerned with the responsibilities of investigators the Attorney General's guidelines are directed at lawyers, particularly prosecutors, as well as disclosure officers. Their scope is not confined to the regime governed by the *CPIA* 1996: there is guidance on the prosecutor's duty to disclose to the defence material significant information that might affect a bail decision (para. 34) and material relevant to sentence (para. 44). The guidelines also describe the circumstances in which an investigator, disclosure officer or prosecutor should take reasonable steps to obtain material which is in the possession of government departments, other Crown bodies and other agencies (paras 29–30). The 2005 Guidelines are available at *www.lslo.gov.uk* or see Appendix C.

In *DPP v. Wood and McGillicudy* (see *ante*, § 6–39) Ouseley J. held that a breach of the guidelines would not be sufficient to stay the prosecution for abuse of process; "it would still have to be shown that the consequence of any failure was that the very strict test for a stay had been satisfied." (para. 61)

K. CPS DISCLOSURE MANUAL

6–53   In April 2005 the Crown Prosecution Service issued a revised Disclosure Manual (www.cps.gov.uk/legal/section20/chapter__a.html). The manual is designed to assist CPS and police practitioners to perform their disclosure duties consistently and effectively. They are designed to provide a practical guide to disclosure principles and procedures, building on the framework of *CPIA* 1996, the Code and the Attorney General's guidelines. The Manual is a vast body of guidance to be read and followed by all police investigators and CPS prosecutors. It is divided into 37 chapters with 11 annexes.

L. THIRD PARTY DISCLOSURE

6–54   Where material is sought from a third party, upon whom there is no duty to disclose, the appropriate procedure is to obtain a summons under sections 97 and 97A of the *Magistrates' Courts Act* 1980 as amended by section 169 of the *Serious Organised Crime and Police Act* 2005. The effect of section 169 is to allow the court to issue a summons in more situations and earlier in the proceedings. The test now is one of interests of justice.

Rule 28 of the *Criminal Procedure Rules* deals with the procedure to be followed in connection with applications for the issuance of witness summonses. Rule 28.3 prescribes what the application for a summons must contain. In consequence of the *Criminal Procedure (Amendment) Rules* 2007, r.28 has been amended as of April 2, 2007. An important feature of the new rule is that before issuing a witness summons the court must be satisfied that it has taken proper account of the rights of any person the production of whose medical or other confidential records is being sought, and such a person—frequently the victim of the offence—must have had an opportunity to make representations. See Appendix G–160, *et seq.*

Documents in the possession of the Home Office are not in the possession of the prosecution for the purposes of the *Criminal Procedure and Investigations Act* 1996: *R. v. Stratford Magistrates' Court, ex p. Johnson* (see *ante*, § 6–16). In that case the DPP argued that the Home Office and ACPO were not part of the prosecution process so that a third party disclosure request was necessary. The Divisional Court held that the Home Office approval and conditions for use of an intoximeter device and the ACPO guidelines could not be said to be in the possession of the prosecution for the purposes of disclosure. See also *DPP v. Wood and McGillicudy* (see *ante*, § 6–39).

Paragraphs 47 to 54 of the Attorney General's guidelines address the situation of relevant unused material in the hands of a third party. An obligation is created by them upon an investigator and/or prosecutor to obtain such material for the benefit of the defence subject to PII. See, *e.g. McCartney and others* [2003] 6 *Archbold News* 2.

M. PROTECTED MATERIAL

(1) Public interest immunity

The common law rules as to public interest immunity survived the enactment of the **6–55** *Criminal Procedure and Investigations Act* 1996, s.21(1). Material must not be disclosed to the extent that the court, on an application by the prosecutor, concludes it is not in the public interest to disclose it and orders accordingly: *Criminal Procedure and Investigations Act* 1996, ss.7(5), 8(5), 9(8). The court is the final arbiter of whether the prosecution is entitled to avoid disclosure on the basis of PII. PII applications are a rarity in magistrates' court proceedings.

In *Davis, Johnson and Rowe* (1993) 97 Cr.App.R. 110, CA (Crim. Div.), the court set out guidance on the procedure which should be followed when the prosecution claims PII:

1. It is the prosecutor's duty to make disclosure voluntarily, and in accordance with **6–56** paragraph 2 of the Attorney General's guidelines.
2. If the prosecution wish to rely on public interest immunity or sensitivity to justify non-disclosure, then, whenever possible, which will be in most cases they must notify the defence that they are applying for a ruling from the court and indicate to the defence at least the category of material which they hold. The defence must then have the opportunity of making representations to the court.
3. Where disclosure of the category of material would be to reveal that which the prosecution contend it would not be in the public interest to reveal, a different procedure would apply. The prosecution should notify the defence of the application, but it need not specify the category of material and the application will be *ex parte*. If the court on hearing the application considers that the normal procedure should apply it will so order. Otherwise it will rule on the *ex parte* application.
4. In exceptional cases the prosecution might consider that to reveal even the fact

that an *ex parte* application has been made could "let the cat out of the bag" so as to stultify the application. If so then the prosecution should apply to the court *ex parte* without notice. If the court considered that notice should have been given, or that the normal *inter partes* hearing should have been adopted it can so order.

This procedure is now reproduced by magistrates' court rules, see *post*, §§ 6–62 —6–65.

6–57   The court emphasised that open justice requires maximum disclosure and the opportunity for the defendant to make representations on the basis of the fullest information. If the judge considers that the defendant should have had notice of the application, or of the nature of the material, or that the application should have been made *inter partes*, he or she should so direct.

6–58   The leading authority on PII is unquestionably *H. & C.* [2004] UKHL 3. The House held first that material subject to PII consideration was only that which was in the prosecutor's opinion relevant, *i.e.* material which either weakened the prosecution's case and/or strengthened the defence case. The defence cannot compel disclosure by making general and unspecified allegations and material neutral or damaging to the defence need not be disclosed (see para. 35). Second, where the prosecution seek on PII grounds to withhold relevant material from the defence, the House lay down a procedure to assist any court in determining disclosure.

When any issue of derogation from the golden rule of full disclosure comes before it, the court must address a series of questions:

(1) What is the material which the prosecution seek to withhold? This must be considered by the court in detail.

(2) Is the material such as may weaken the prosecution case or strengthen that of the defence? If No, disclosure should not be ordered. If Yes, full disclosure should (subject to (3), (4) and (5) below)be ordered.

(3) Is there a real risk of serious prejudice to an important public interest (and, if so, what) if full disclosure of the material is ordered? If No, full disclosure should be ordered.

(4) If the answer to (2) and (3) is Yes, can the defendant's interest be protected without disclosure or disclosure be ordered to an extent or in a way which will give adequate protection to the public interest in question and also afford adequate protection to the interests of the defence?

This question requires the court to consider, with specific reference to the material which the prosecution seek to withhold and the facts of the case and the defence as disclosed, whether the prosecution should formally admit what the defence seek to establish or whether disclosure short of full disclosure may be ordered. This may be done in appropriate cases by the preparation of summaries or extracts of evidence, or the provision of documents in an edited or anonymised form, provided the documents supplied are in each instance approved by the judge. In appropriate cases the appointment of special counsel may be a necessary step to ensure that the contentions of the prosecution are tested and the interests of the defendant protected (see para. 22, *ante*). In cases of exceptional difficulty the court may require the appointment of special counsel to ensure a correct answer to questions (2) and (3) as well as (4).

(5) Do the measures proposed in answer to (4) represent the minimum derogation necessary to protect the public interest in question? If No, the court should order such greater disclosure as will represent the minimum derogation from the golden rule of full disclosure.

(6) If limited disclosure is ordered pursuant to (4) or (5), may the effect be to render the trial process, viewed as a whole, unfair to the defendant? If Yes, then fuller disclosure should be ordered even if this leads or may lead the prosecution to discontinue the proceedings so as to avoid having to make disclosure.

(7) If the answer to (6) when first given is No, does that remain the correct answer as the trial unfolds, evidence is adduced and the defence advanced?

It is important that the answer to (6) should not be treated as a final, once-and-for-all, answer but as a provisional answer which the court must keep under review. [para. 36]

Under the heading "Conclusions" the House laid out general guidance to be followed by all courts. Two of these are reproduced below:

> "Throughout his or her consideration of any disclosure issue the trial judge must bear constantly in mind the overriding principles referred to in this opinion. In applying them, the judge should involve the defence to the maximum extent possible without disclosing that which the general interest requires to be protected but taking full account of the specific defence which is relied on. There will be very few cases indeed in which some measure of disclosure to the defence will not be possible, even if this is confined to the fact that an ex parte application is to be made. If even that information is withheld and if the material to be withheld is of significant help to the defendant, there must be a very serious question whether the prosecution should proceed, since special counsel, even if appointed, cannot then receive any instructions from the defence at all." [para. 37]

In relation to PII and proceedings in the magistrates' court, the House stated:

> "If PII applications are confined, as they should be, to material which undermines the prosecution case or strengthens that of the defence, the bench will not be alerted to material damaging to the defendant. If it is, the principles which should govern the court's decision whether to recuse itself are the same as in the case of any other tribunal of fact, but the court's duty of continuing review ordinarily militates in favour of continuing the proceedings before the court which determines the PII application. If a case raises complex and contentious PII issues, and the court has discretion to send the case to the crown court for trial, the magistrates' court should carefully consider whether those issues are best resolved in the crown court. The occasions on which it will be appropriate to appoint special counsel in the magistrates' court will be even rarer than in the crown court." [para. 44]

H. & C. has been followed in a number of subsequent authorities; see, *e.g. Ebcin* **6–59** [2005] EWCA 2006; *R. (DPP) v. Acton Youth Court* [2001] 1 W.L.R. 1828.

The Code of Practice on Disclosure gives categories of sensitive material. These categories are wider than the types of material which the courts might be prepared to protect via PII.

Criminal Procedure and Investigations Act 1996, ss.14, 16

Public interest: review for summary trials

14.—(1) This section applies where this Part applies by virtue of section 1(1),   **6–60**

(2) At any time—

    (a) after a court makes an order under section 3(6), 7(5), 8(5) or 9(8), and

    (b) before the accused is acquitted or convicted or the prosecutor decides not to proceed with the case concerned,

the accused may apply to the court for a review of the question whether it is still not in the public interest to disclose material affected by its order.

(3) In such a case the court must review that question, and if it concludes that it is in the public interest to disclose material to any extent—

    (a) it shall so order, and

    (b) it shall take such steps as are reasonable to inform the prosecutor of its order.

(4) Where the prosecutor is informed of an order made under subsection (3) he must act accordingly having regard to the provisions of this Part (unless he decides not to proceed with the case concerned).

Applications: opportunity to be heard

16. Where—   **6–61**

    (a) an application is made under section 3(6), 7(5), 8(5), 9(8), 14(2) or 15(4),

    (b) a person claiming to have an interest in the material applies to be heard by the court, and

    (c) he shows that he was involved (whether alone or with others and whether directly or indirectly) in the prosecutor's attention being brought to the material,

the court must not make an order under section 3(6), 7(5), 8(5), 9(8), 14(3) or 15(5) (as the case may be) unless the person applying under paragraph (b) has been given an opportunity to be heard.

Magistrates' Courts (Criminal Procedure and Investigations Act 1996) (Disclosure) Rules 1997, rr.2–5

Public interest: application by prosecutor

6–62   **2.**—(1) This rule applies to the making of an application by the prosecutor under section 3(6), 7(5), 8(5) or 9(8) where Part I applies by virtue of section 1(1) (summary trial).

(2) Notice of an application to which this rule applies shall be served on the designated officer for the magistrates' court trying the offence referred to in section 1(1) and shall specify the nature of the material to which the application relates.

(3) Subject to paragraphs (4) and (5) below, a copy of the notice of application shall be served on the accused by the prosecutor.

(4) Where the prosecutor has reason to believe that to reveal to the accused the nature of the material to which the application relates would have the effect of disclosing that which the prosecutor contends should not in the public interest be disclosed, paragraph (3) above shall not apply but the prosecutor shall notify the accused that an application to which this rule applies has been made.

(5) Where the prosecutor has reason to believe that to reveal to the accused the fact that an application is being made would have the effect of disclosing that which the prosecutor contends should not in the public interest be disclosed, paragraph (3) above shall not apply.

Public interest: hearing of application by prosecutor

6–63   **3.**—(1) This rule applies to the hearing of an application by the prosecutor under section 3(6), 7(5), 8(5) or 9(8) where Part I applies by virtue of section 1(1).

(2) Subject to paragraph (3) below and to rule 6(4), where a copy of the notice of application has been served on the accused in accordance with rule 2(3)—

(a) the designated officer for the court shall give notice to—
(i) the prosecutor;
(ii) the accused; and
(iii) any person claiming to have an interest in the material to which the application relates who has applied under section 16(b) to be heard by the court,
of the date and time when and the place where the hearing will take place and, unless the court orders otherwise, such notice shall be given in writing;
(b) the hearing shall be inter partes; and
(c) the prosecutor and the accused shall be entitled to make representations to the court.

(3) Where the prosecutor applies to the court for leave to make representations in the absence of the accused, the court may for that purpose sit in the absence of the accused and any legal representative of his.

(4) Subject to rule 6(4), where a copy of the notice of application has not been served on the accused in accordance with rule 2(3)—

(a) the hearing shall be ex parte;
(b) only the prosecutor shall be entitled to make representations to the court; and
(c) the accused shall not be given notice as specified in paragraph (2) above.

Public interest: non-disclosure order

6–64   **4.**—(1) This rule applies to an order under section 3(6), 7(5), 8(5) or 9(8).

(2) On making an order to which this rule applies, the court shall state its reasons for doing so.

(3) In a case where such an order is a made following—

(a) an application to which rule 2(4) applies, or
(b) an application notice of which has been served on the accused in accordance with rule 2(3) but the accused has not appeared or been represented at the hearing of that application,
the designated officer for the court shall notify the accused that an order has been made.

Note that rule 3(2)(a)(iii) contemplates the possibility of a third party, not the prosecutor, being able to make an *ex parte* PII application. In the court heard PII representation, it would follow the same *H. & C.* procedure as quoted, *ante*.

Review of non-disclosure order: application by accused

5.—(1) This rule applies to an application by the accused under section 14(2).   **6–65**

(2) An application to which this rule applies shall be made by notice in writing to the designated officer for the magistrates' court trying the offence referred to in section 1(1) and shall specify the reason why the accused believes the court should review the question mentioned in section 14(2).

(3) A copy of the notice referred to in paragraph (2) above shall be served on the prosecutor at the same time as it is sent to the designated officer for the court.

(4) On receipt of an application to which this rule applies the designated officer for the court shall take such steps as he thinks fit to ensure that the court determining the application has before it any document or other material which was available to the court which made the order mentioned in section 14(2).

(5) Subject to paragraphs (6) to (8) below and to rule 6(4), the hearing of an application to which this rule applies shall be inter partes and the accused and the prosecutor shall be entitled to make representations to the court.

(6) Where the court considers that there are no grounds on which it might conclude that it is in the public interest to disclose material to any extent it may determine the application without hearing representations from the accused, the prosecutor or any person claiming to have an interest in the material to which the application relates.

(7) Where after hearing the accused's representations the prosecutor applies to the court for leave to make representations in the absence of the accused, the court may for that purpose sit in the absence of the accused and any legal representative of his.

(8) Subject to rule 6(4), where the order to which the application relates was made following an application of which the accused was not notified under rule 2(3) or (4), the hearing shall be *ex parte* and only the prosecutor shall be entitled to make representations to the court.

(9) The designated officer for the court shall give notice in writing to—

(a) the prosecutor;

(b) except where a hearing takes place in accordance with paragraph (8) above, the accused; and

(c) any person claiming to have an interest in the material to which the application relates who has applied under section 16(b) to be heard by the court,

of the date and time when and the place where the hearing of an application to which this rule applies will take place and of any order which is made by the court following its determination of the application.

(2) Confidentiality

Criminal Procedure and Investigations Act 1996, s.17–18

Confidentiality of disclosed information

17.—(1) If the accused is given or allowed to inspect a document or other object under—   **6–66**

(a) section 3, 4, 7A, 14 or 15, or

(b) an order under section 8,

then, subject to subsections (2) to (4), he must not use or disclose it or any information recorded in it.

(2) The accused may use or disclose the object or information—

(a) in connection with the proceedings for whose purposes he was given the object or allowed to inspect it,

(b) with a view to the taking of further criminal proceedings (for instance, by way of appeal) with regard to the matter giving rise to the proceedings mentioned in paragraph (a), or

(c) in connection with the proceedings first mentioned in paragraph (b).

(3) The accused may use or disclose—

(a) the object to the extent that it has been displayed to the public in open court, or

(b) the information to the extent that it has been communicated to the public in open court;

but the preceding provisions of this subsection do not apply if the object is displayed or the information is communicated in proceedings to deal with a contempt of court under section 18.

(4) If—

    (a) the accused applies to the court for an order granting permission to use or disclose the object or information, and

    (b) the court makes such an order,

the accused may use or disclose the object or information for the purpose and to the extent specified by the court.

(5) An application under subsection (4) may be made and dealt with at any time, and in particular after the accused has been acquitted or convicted or the prosecutor has decided not to proceed with the case concerned: but this is subject to rules made by virtue of section 19(2).

(6) Where—

    (a) an application is made under subsection (4), and

    (b) the prosecutor or a person claiming to have an interest in the object or information applies to be heard by the court,

the court must not make an order granting permission unless the person applying under paragraph (b) has been given an opportunity to be heard.

(7) References in this section to the court are to—

    (a) a magistrates' court, where this Part applies by virtue of section 1(1);

    (b) the Crown Court, where this Part applies by virtue of section 1(2).

(8) Nothing in this section affects any other restriction or prohibition on the use or disclosure of an object or information, whether the restriction or prohibition arises under an enactment (whenever passed) or otherwise.

Confidentiality: contravention

6–67   **18.**—(1) It is a contempt of court for a person knowingly to use or disclose an object or information recorded in it if the use or disclosure is in contravention of section 17.

(2) The following courts have jurisdiction to deal with a person who is guilty of a contempt under this section—

    (a) a magistrates' court, where this Part applies by virtue of section 1(1),

    (b) the Crown Court, where this Part applies by virtue of section 1(2).

(3) A person who is guilty of a contempt under this section may be dealt with as follows—

    (a) a magistrates' court may commit him to custody for a specified period not exceeding six months or impose on him a fine not exceeding £5,000 or both;

    (b) the Crown Court may commit him to custody for a specified period not exceeding two years or impose a fine on him or both.

(4) If—

    (a) a person is guilty of a contempt under this section, and

    (b) the object concerned is in his possession,

the court finding him guilty may order that the object shall be forfeited and dealt with in such manner as the court may order.

(5) The power of the court under subsection (4) includes power to order the object to be destroyed or to be given to the prosecutor or to be placed in his custody for such period as the court may specify.

(6) If—

    (a) the court proposes to make an order under subsection (4), and

    (b) the person found guilty, or any other person claiming to have an interest in the object, applies to be heard by the court,

the court must not make the order unless the applicant has been given an opportunity to be heard.

(7) If—

    (a) a person is guilty of a contempt under this section and

    (b) a copy of the object concerned is in his possession,

the court finding him guilty may order that the copy shall be forfeited and dealt with in such manner as the court may order.

(8) Subsections (5) and (6) apply for the purposes of subsection (7) as they apply for the purposes of subsection (4), but as if references to the object were references to the copy.

(9) An object or information shall be inadmissible as evidence in civil proceedings if to adduce it would in the opinion of the court be likely to constitute a contempt under this section and "the court" here means the court before which the civil proceedings are being taken.

(10) The powers of a magistrates' court under this section may be exercised either of the court's own motion or by order on complaint.

(3) Sexual Offences (Protected Material) Act 1997

The *Sexual Offences (Protected Material) Act* 1997 makes provision for regulating **6–68** access by defendants and others to certain categories of information disclosed by the prosecution or the Criminal Cases Review Commission in connection with proceedings relating to certain sexual and other offences. Nothing in the Act applies to any proceedings for a sexual offence where the defendant was charged with the offence before the commencement of the Act. It comes into force on such day as the Secretary of State may appoint. At the time of writing the Act is still not in force and no date has been appointed for its commencement.

N. Expert Evidence

This subject is considered at § 10–105 in this work. However, in relation to disclosure **6–69** obligations owed by experts instructed by or on behalf of the CPS, in February 2006 an Annex K was added to the CPS Disclosure Manual which sets out comprehensive guidance to such experts as to their disclosure obligations. From this date any expert used by the CPS is required to certify that they had complied with this guidance. See also *Puaca* [2006] Crim.L.R. 341.

CHAPTER 7

PRE-TRIAL PROCEDURE

I. PRE-TRIAL HEARING

A. EARLY ADMINISTRATIVE HEARINGS

Some cases heard at the magistrates' court are concluded at the first listing but others **7–1** require more time for preparation and so will be adjourned. Cases are treated differently according to the plea to be tendered. When a not guilty plea is expected then preliminary steps will be taken at the first court appearance to prepare for trial. Pre-trial proceedings consist of considering legal representation, taking a plea and giving directions relating to trial issues and disclosure etc. For guilty pleas, the expectation is that the case will be dealt with on first appearance.

Sections 68 to 74 of the *Courts Act* 2003 provide a new statutory framework for rules **7–2** of procedure in the criminal courts. The rules are made by the Criminal Procedure Rule Committee and they apply in the magistrates' court, the Crown Court and the criminal division of the Court of Appeal. The purpose of the rules is to make sure that the criminal justice system is "accessible, fair and efficient" and the requirement on the committee is to make rules that are "simple and simply expressed".

The *Criminal Procedure Rules* 2005 (S.I. 2005 No. 384) came into force on April 4, 2005. They replace but also consolidate existing rules with additional provisions setting out the overriding objective and a new code for case management. The overriding objective is that criminal cases be dealt with justly and the rules indicate how this is to be achieved. For example dealing with a case justly includes acquitting the innocent and convicting the guilty, dealing with both parties fairly, recognising the defendant's rights and respecting the interests of witnesses and other third parties and keeping them informed of the progress of the case. In addition the case must be dealt with "efficiently and expeditiously". Appropriate information must be made available to the court on considering bail or sentence and the complexity, gravity and consequences of the case for the defendant and others as well as the needs of other cases must all be taken into account. The court has a general duty to further the overriding objective.

All participants in a case have a duty under the Rules to prepare and conduct the case in accordance with the overriding objective and to comply with not only the rules but also any relevant practice directions and specific court directions. In addition they have a duty to let the court know of any "significant failure" of compliance which might lead to the case not being dealt with justly. This duty extends to anyone involved in a case so could include witnesses and particularly expert witnesses whose unavailability can occasionally cause delay.

7–3   The rules also include principles relating to case management designed to secure that cases are dealt with "efficiently and expeditiously". The court and the parties have a duty to manage cases actively and the court may give directions to ensure that cases proceed swiftly. A new role of a Case Progression Officer is introduced and the court and all parties must each nominate an individual to take responsibility for progressing the case through the system. Wide powers of general case management are conferred on the court together with a system of forms and records to help monitor the process. The court also has power to require the parties to provide a certificate of readiness to ensure that trials proceed on the hearing date. Relevant parts of the rules are in Appendix G.

The Rule Committee will continue to review and codify existing rules addressing in future such topics as disclosure and expert evidence. Since the rules were first introduced, they have been amended three times: *Criminal Procedure (Amendment) Rules* 2006 (S.I. 2006 No. 353) (as from April 3, 2006); *Criminal Procedure (Amendment No. 2) Rules* 2006 (S.I. 2006 No. 2636) (as from November 6, 2006); and *Criminal Procedure (Amendment) Rules* 2007 (S.I. 2007 No. 699) (as from April 2, 2007).

Crime and Disorder Act 1998, s.50

Early administrative hearings

7–4   **50.**—(1) Where a person ("the accused") has been charged with an offence at a police station, the magistrates' court before whom he appears or is brought for the first time in relation to the charge may, *unless the accused falls to be dealt with under section 51 below*, consist of a single justice.

(2) At a hearing conducted by a single justice under this section the accused shall be asked whether he wishes to be granted a right to representation funded by the Legal Services Commission as part of the Criminal Defence Service.

(2A) Where the accused wishes to be granted such a right, the Legal Services Commission shall decide whether or not to grant him that right.

(3) At such a hearing the single justice—

(a) may exercise, subject to subsection (2) above, such of his powers as a single justice as he thinks fit; and

(b) on adjourning the hearing, may remand the accused in custody or on bail.

(4) This section applies in relation to a justices' clerk as it applies in relation to a single justice; but nothing in subsection (3)(b) above authorises such a clerk to remand the accused in custody or, without the consent of the prosecutor and the accused, to remand the accused on bail on conditions other than those (if any) previously imposed.

(4A) A hearing conducted by a single justice under this section may be—

(a) adjourned to enable the decision mentioned in subsection (2A) above to be taken, and

(b) subsequently resumed by a single justice.

[This section is printed as amended by the *Access to Justice Act* 1999, Sched. 15, and the *Criminal Defence Service (Representation Orders and Consequential Amendments) Regulations* 2006 (S.I. 2006 No. 2493). As from a day to be appointed, the words in italics in subsection (1) are to be repealed by the *Criminal Justice Act* 2003, Scheds 3 and 37.]

Police and Criminal Evidence Act 1984, s.47A

Early administrative hearings conducted by justices' clerks

7–5   **47A.** Where a person has been charged with an offence at a police station, any requirement imposed under this Part for the person to appear or be brought before a magistrates' court shall be taken to be satisfied if the person appears or is brought before a justices' clerk in order for the clerk to conduct a hearing under section 50 of the *Crime and Disorder Act* 1998 (early administrative hearings).

[This section was inserted by the *Crime and Disorder Act* 1998, Sched. 8. It is printed as amended by the *Courts Act* 2003, Sched. 8.]

Where a defendant is charged at a police station the custody officer may grant him **7–6** bail to appear at a magistrates' court: *Police and Criminal Evidence Act* 1984, s.47. The police and local court will have in place an arrangement for the listing of such cases and the intention is for them to be dealt with expeditiously and certainly within a matter of days: *Crime and Disorder Act* 1998, s.46. The prosecutor will attend at the police station the day before the cases are due to be heard to review the files and to assess whether there is likely to be a guilty or not guilty plea. If the offence is admitted on the police files, an early first hearing will take place at court in anticipation of a guilty plea. These cases may be prosecuted by a designated case worker (DCW) from the Crown Prosecution Service and must be heard before a bench of magistrates or a district judge. The DCW has limited rights of audience and cannot deal with contested trials or bail applications. In all other cases, the matter will be listed as an early administrative hearing. These cases can be dealt with by a magistrate sitting alone or by the justices' clerk or a member of the court staff to whom the justices' clerk has delegated the relevant powers. Usually the delegation will be to legal advisers. The powers of the justices' clerk in early administrative hearings are limited by section 50(4) and (4A).

Crime and Disorder Act 1998, s.49

Powers of magistrates' courts exercisable by single justice etc.

49.—(1) The following powers of a magistrates' court for any area may be exercised by a **7–7** single justice of the peace for that area, namely—

    (a) to extend bail or to impose or vary conditions of bail;

    (b) to mark an information as withdrawn;

    (c) to dismiss an information, or to discharge an accused in respect of an information, where no evidence is offered by the prosecution;

    (d) to make an order for the payment of defence costs out of central funds;

    (e) to request a pre-sentence report following a plea of guilty and, for that purpose, to give an indication of the seriousness of the offence;

    (f) to request a medical report and, for that purpose, to remand the accused in custody or on bail;

    (g) to remit an offender to another court for sentence;

    (h) where a person has been granted police bail to appear at a magistrates' court, to appoint an earlier time for his appearance;

        (i) to extend, with the consent of the accused, a custody time limit or an overall time limit;

    (j) [*Repealed*];

    (k) where an accused has been convicted of an offence, to order him to produce his driving licence;

    (l) to give a direction prohibiting the publication of matters disclosed or exempted from disclosure in court;

    (m) to give, vary or revoke directions for the conduct of a trial, including directions as to the following matters, namely—

        (i) the timetable for the proceedings;

        (ii) the attendance of the parties;

        (iii) the service of documents (including summaries of any legal arguments relied on by the parties);

        (iv) the manner in which evidence is to be given; and

    (n) to give, vary or revoke orders for separate or joint trials in the case of two or more accused or two or more informations.

(2) Criminal Procedure Rules may, subject to subsection (3) below, provide that any of the things which, by virtue of subsection (1) above, are authorised to be done by a single justice of the peace for any area may, subject to any specified restrictions or conditions, be done by a justices' clerk for that area.

(3) Criminal Procedure Rules which make such provision as is mentioned in subsection (2) above shall not authorise a justices' clerk—

  (a) without the consent of the prosecutor and the accused, to extend bail on conditions other than those (if any) previously imposed, or to impose or vary conditions of bail;

  (b) to give an indication of the seriousness of an offence for the purposes of a pre-sentence report;

  (c) to remand the accused in custody for the purposes of a medical report or, without the consent of the prosecutor and the accused, to remand the accused on bail for those purposes on conditions other than those (if any) previously imposed;

  (d) to give a direction prohibiting the publication of matters disclosed or exempted from disclosure in court; or

  (e) without the consent of the parties, to give, vary or revoke orders for separate or joint trials in the case of two or more accused or two or more informations.

(4) Before making any Criminal Procedure Rules which make such provision as is mentioned in subsection (2) above in relation to any area, the Criminal Procedure Rule Committee shall consult justices of the peace and justices' clerks for that area.

(5) In this section and section 50 below "justices' clerk" has the same meaning as in section 144 of the 1980 Act.

[This section is printed as amended by the *Access to Justice Act* 1999, Sched. 15, and the *Courts Act 2003 (Consequential Amendments) Order* 2004 (S.I. 2004 No. 2035).]

As to the powers of a single justice of peace which may be exercised by a justices' clerk (and the powers of a justices' clerk which may be exercised by an assistant clerk), see the *Justices' Clerks Rules* 2005 (S.I. 2005 No. 545).

B. PRE-TRIAL HEARING BY VIDEO LINK

Crime and Disorder Act 1998, Pt 3A

Introductory

7–8   **57A.**—(1) This Part—

  (a) applies to preliminary hearings and sentencing hearings in the course of proceedings for an offence; and

  (b) enables the court in the circumstances provided for in sections 57B, 57C and 57E to direct the use of a live link for securing the accused's attendance at a hearing to which this Part applies.

(2) The accused is to be treated as present in court when, by virtue of a live link direction under this Part, he attends a hearing through a live link.

(3) In this Part—

"custody"—

  (a) includes local authority accommodation to which a person is remanded or committed by virtue of section 23 of the *Children and Young Persons Act* 1969; but

  (b) does not include police detention;

"live link" means an arrangement by which a person (when not in the place where the hearing is being held) is able to see and hear, and to be seen and heard by, the court during a hearing (and for this purpose any impairment of eyesight or hearing is to be disregarded);

"police detention" has the meaning given by section 118(2) of the *Police and Criminal Evidence Act* 1984;

"preliminary hearing" means a hearing in the proceedings held before the start of the trial (within the meaning of subsection (11A) or (11B) of section 22 of the 1985 Act) including, in the case of proceedings in the Crown Court, a preparatory hearing held under—

  (a) section 7 of the *Criminal Justice Act* 1987 (cases of serious or complex fraud); or

  (b) section 29 of the *Criminal Procedure and Investigations Act* 1996 (other serious, complex or lengthy cases);

"sentencing hearing" means any hearing following conviction which is held for the purpose of—

    (a) proceedings relating to the giving or rescinding of a direction under section 57E;

    (b) proceedings (in a magistrates' court) relating to committal to the Crown Court for sentencing; or

    (c) sentencing the offender or determining how the court should deal with him in respect of the offence.

Use of live link at preliminary hearings where accused is in custody

57B.—(1) This section applies in relation to a preliminary hearing in a magistrates' court or **7–9** the Crown Court.

(2) Where it appears to the court before which the preliminary hearing is to take place that the accused is likely to be held in custody during the hearing, the court may give a live link direction under this section in relation to the attendance of the accused at the hearing.

(3) A live link direction under this section is a direction requiring the accused, if he is being held in custody during the hearing, to attend it through a live link from the place at which he is being held.

(4) If a hearing takes place in relation to the giving or rescinding of such a direction, the court may require or permit a person attending the hearing to do so through a live link.

(5) The court shall not give or rescind such a direction (whether at a hearing or otherwise) unless the parties to the proceedings have been given the opportunity to make representations.

(6) If in a case where it has power to do so a magistrates' court decides not to give a live link direction under this section, it must—

    (a) state in open court its reasons for not doing so; and

    (b) cause those reasons to be entered in the register of its proceedings.

Use of live link at preliminary hearings where accused is at police station

57C.—(1) This section applies in relation to a preliminary hearing in a magistrates' court. **7–10**

(2) Where subsection (3) or (4) applies to the accused, the court may give a live link direction in relation to his attendance at the preliminary hearing.

(3) This subsection applies to the accused if—

    (a) he is in police detention at a police station in connection with the offence; and

    (b) it appears to the court that he is likely to remain at that station in police detention until the beginning of the preliminary hearing.

(4) This subsection applies to the accused if he is at a police station in answer to live link bail in connection with the offence.

(5) A live link direction under this section is a direction requiring the accused to attend the preliminary hearing through a live link from the police station.

(6) But a direction given in relation to an accused to whom subsection (3) applies has no effect if he does not remain in police detention at the police station until the beginning of the preliminary hearing.

(7) A live link direction under this section may not be given unless the accused has given his consent to the court.

(8) A magistrates' court may rescind a live link direction under this section at any time before or during a hearing to which it relates.

(9) A magistrates' court may require or permit—

    (a) the accused to give or withhold consent under subsection (7) through a live link; and

    (b) any party to the proceedings who wishes to make representations in relation to the giving or rescission of a live link direction under this section to do so through a live link.

(10) Where a live link direction under this section is given in relation to an accused person who is answering to live link bail he is to be treated as having surrendered to the custody of the court (as from the time when the direction is given).

(11) In this section, "live link bail" means bail granted under Part 4 of the *Police and Criminal Evidence Act* 1984 subject to the duty mentioned in section 47(3)(b) of that Act.

Continued use of live link for sentencing hearing following a preliminary hearing

57D.—(1) Subsection (2) applies where— **7–11**

    (a) a live link direction under section 57B or 57C is in force;

    (b) the accused is attending a preliminary hearing through a live link by virtue of the direction;

    (c) the court convicts him of the offence in the course of that hearing (whether by virtue of a guilty plea or an indication of an intention to plead guilty); and

    (d) the court proposes to continue the hearing as a sentencing hearing in relation to the offence.

(2) The accused may continue to attend through the live link by virtue of the direction if—

    (a) the hearing is continued as a sentencing hearing in relation to the offence;

    (b) the accused consents to his continuing to attend through the live link; and

    (c) the court is satisfied that it is not contrary to the interests of justice for him to do so.

(3) But the accused may not give oral evidence through the live link during a continued hearing under subsection (2) unless—

    (a) he consents to give evidence in that way; and

    (b) the court is satisfied that it is not contrary to the interests of justice for him to give it in that way.

Use of live link in sentencing hearings

7–12   **57E.**—(1) This section applies where the accused is convicted of the offence.

(2) If it appears to the court by or before which the accused is convicted that it is likely that he will be held in custody during any sentencing hearing for the offence, the court may give a live link direction under this section in relation to that hearing.

(3) A live link direction under this section is a direction requiring the accused, if he is being held in custody during the hearing, to attend it through a live link from the place at which he is being held.

(4) Such a direction—

    (a) may be given by the court of its own motion or on an application by a party; and

    (b) may be given in relation to all subsequent sentencing hearings before the court or to such hearing or hearings as may be specified or described in the direction.

(5) The court may not give such a direction unless—

    (a) the offender has given his consent to the direction; and

    (b) the court is satisfied that it is not contrary to the interests of justice to give the direction.

(6) The court may rescind such a direction at any time before or during a hearing to which it relates if it appears to the court to be in the interests of justice to do so (but this does not affect the court's power to give a further live link direction in relation to the offender).

The court may exercise this power of its own motion or on an application by a party.

(7) The offender may not give oral evidence while attending a hearing through a live link by virtue of this section unless—

    (a) he consents to give evidence in that way; and

    (b) the court is satisfied that it is not contrary to the interests of justice for him to give it in that way.

(8) The court must—

    (a) state in open court its reasons for refusing an application for, or for the rescission of, a live link direction under this section; and

    (b) if it is a magistrates' court, cause those reasons to be entered in the register of its proceedings.

[This Part was substituted for the existing section 57 by the *Police and Justice Act* 2006, s.45. For the avoidance of doubt, there is no longer a section 57. The substitution of new sections 57A, 57B, 5D and 57E was effected as from January 15, 2007, by the *Police and Justice Act 2006 (Commencement No. 1, Transitional and Saving Provisions) Order* 2006 (S.I. 2006 No. 3364). The substitution of new section 57C was effected as from April 1, 2007, by the *Police and Justice Act 2006 (Commencement No. 2, Transitional and Saving Provisions) Order* 2007 (S.I. 2007 No. 709).]

7–13   Article 4 of S.I. 2006 No. 3364 makes transitional provision in connection with the substitution of those sections as follows: (i) any direction given under the pre-existing section 57 before January 15, 2007, is to continue to have effect; and if so, new section 57D has effect as if subsection 1(a) included a reference to the pre-existing section 57; and (ii) where a preliminary hearing in the magistrates' court or the Crown Court has commenced before January 15, 2007, the court may nevertheless give a direction under new section 57B on or after that date.

Section 45 of the *Police and Justice Act* 2006 has extended the use of live link under **7–14** section 57 of the 1998 Act beyond preliminary hearings where the accused is in custody in a prison or other institution. The new provisions in Part 3A of the 1998 Act make provision for directions to be given to secure the attendance of the accused at prelimi-nary hearings (including where the accused is in police custody) and sentencing hear-ings by live link. Section 57B applies to preliminary hearings where it appears to the court that the accused is likely to be in custody (which excludes police detention) at the time of the hearing, whereas section 57C applies to a preliminary hearings where the accused is either in police detention at a police station in connection with the offence and likely to remain there until the beginning of the hearing, or is at a police station in answer to "live link bail" in connection with the offence. Section 57D makes provision for continued use of a live link for a sentencing hearing following a preliminary hear-ing, whereas section 57E authorises the giving of a live link direction for a sentencing hearing where it appears likely that the accused will be in custody during any such hearing. It should be noted that directions under sections 57C, 57D and 57E may only be given with the consent of the accused. There is no such requirement in relation to a direction under section 57B.

C. Adjournments

Powers of adjournment are conferred on the court by sections 5, 6, 10, 17C, and 18 **7–15** of the *Magistrates' Courts Act* 1980, see *ante*, §§ 5–20 to 5–21 and 5–26 to 5–28.

Not all cases will be concluded at first hearing and requests for adjournment will be made to the court, which has a discretion whether to grant an adjournment or not. The party applying for the adjournment should explain the reasons why the case cannot proceed and the issues that need to be addressed with further time. Both parties may require an adjournment in the early stages of a case but the court must always consider the reasons for putting a case off and must make its decision taking into account the interests of justice. The court may require to know the history of the case and whether adjournments have been granted before and the reasons for them. These details should be available from the court file and will be recounted in open court by the legal adviser. The court should also make clear the expectations for progress at the next hearing.

Article 6(3)(b) of the ECHR requires that a defendant should have "adequate time and facilities" to prepare his defence. The time that is adequate will vary depending on the circumstances but some guidance can be extrapolated from various cases. Seventeen days and 10 days were both held to be a sufficient length of time to enable defence lawyers to prepare for trial: *X v. Austria* (1979) 15 D.R. 160 and *Perez Mahia v. Spain* (1987) 9 E.H.R.R. 91. The situation may well be different if there is a change of lawyers at a late stage and if instructions are only taken on the day of trial an adjourn-ment may be required: *Goddi v. Italy* (1984) 6 E.H.R.R. 457.

In considering adjournment requests, the court must continually balance the compet- **7–16** ing interests of time needed for preparation and the right to have a speedy trial.

In *R. v. Jisl and Tekin, The Times*, April 19, 2004, CA, the court confirmed the important role that the judge has to play in case management. It was said that with re-sources being limited it followed that the proper use of court time required judicial management and control. The court must be fair to all parties and potential problems as well as strategies for saving time needed to be fully canvassed in court. It was held that when a judge went through this process and then gave directions and set a timeta-ble, he would be supported on appeal. Criticism was more likely to be directed at those who chose to ignore the directions. However, the duty of the judge to manage the trial process and to be robust in doing so still has to be exercised with courtesy to counsel; discourtesy by a judge was held to affect confidence in the trial process, especially as far as the defendant was concerned and it led to the conviction being quashed: *R. v. Hare, R. v. Sullivan, The Times*, December 9, 2004, CA.

7–17   When dealing with applications for adjournments the court must also have regard to the Consolidated Criminal Practice Direction and the principles as to case management set out in Part 3 of the *Criminal Procedure Rules* 2005 (as to which, see Appendices F and G). These confirm and expand upon the principles previously identified in recent case law.

Under rule 3.2(1) the court has a duty to manage cases actively; and rule 3.2(2)(f) requires the court to discourage delay and avoid unnecessary hearings. Under rule 3.8 the court has to give directions to ensure that cases are concluded as soon as possible. This includes the duty to set a timetable and to give directions to expedite progress. Standard forms have been published to record such directions and a court may reserve a case to itself in order to monitor how effectively preparations for trial are proceeding.

In *R. (DPP) v. Chorley JJ.*, unreported, June 8, 2006, DC, it was said that the *Criminal Procedure Rules* 2005 had effected a "sea change" in the way that criminal cases were to be conducted, and that defendants could no longer expect to benefit by taking ambush points, failing to co-operate, and failing to identify what matters were in issue at an early stage; the duty of the court was to see that justice was done, and this might require the granting of an adjournment.

There are numerous reasons adjournments may be necessary and some principles can be identified from domestic cases. For a summary of the general principles, see *CPS v. Picton, post*, § 7–19.

At the first hearing a defendant may request an adjournment in order to obtain legal representation. The court may inquire into the action taken prior to the appearance but a defendant must be allowed a reasonable time to instruct solicitors and prepare his case. Where a summons was served and listed for hearing on the same day it was held to be a denial of natural justice to refuse an adjournment as the defendant's solicitors, instructed only on the day, did not have enough time to prepare the case: *R. v. Thames Magistrates' Court, ex p. Polemis* [1974] 1 W.L.R. 1371, DC.

7–18   A defendant who wished to seek his own expert evidence when the prosecution had already supplied an independent expert's report was held to have been refused an adjournment without sufficient reason: *R. v. Sunderland Justices, ex p. Dryden, The Times*, May 18, 1994, DC.

By the same token, a request for an adjournment by the prosecution must not be unreasonably refused. The court has a duty to ascertain the real reasons why the case cannot proceed and should be cautious to accept information at face value. The interests of victims and public confidence in the system of justice must be taken into account.

A complainant in a charge of indecent assault failed to attend at trial and the defence suggested she did not wish to pursue the charge. On appeal it was held that the refusal to adjourn was wrong. It was a serious charge and the witness had not been aware of the trial date: *R. v. Neath and Port Talbot Justices, ex p. DPP* [2000] 1 W.L.R. 1376, DC.

A complainant in an assault charge failed to attend at trial because she had been the victim of another unrelated serious attack just prior to the hearing. The prosecution requested an adjournment on the grounds that the witness was too ill to attend but did not disclose the full details of why this was so. On appeal the court held that the reason for failing to attend in this case was of secondary importance. Once it was accepted that a complainant through an unexpected event that was no fault of her own was not fit to attend, there was an extremely powerful argument for an adjournment and as there was no history of delay in the case, the argument for an adjournment became unanswerable: *DPP v. Birmingham Magistrates' Court*, unreported, July 29, 2003, DC ([2003] EWHC 2352).

Along a similar vein, it was held in *R. (Costello) v. North East Essex Magistrates*,

171 J.P. 153, QBD (Collins J.), that it would take a very strong case before it would be appropriate to refuse an application for an adjournment made on the basis that the defendant had gone through a severe trauma shortly before the date of the hearing; facing court proceedings was an ordeal of itself, and there would be a clear risk of prejudice to a defendant who was forced to give evidence when his mind might not be on the issues that mattered.

Recent case law indicates that rigorous scrutiny must be given to the reasons why the prosecution seek an adjournment and a full explanation must be sought if witnesses are not warned or otherwise fail to attend. Where the prosecution are the authors of their own misfortune by failing to prepare properly for trial adjournments should not be granted easily and where they are granted the court must be careful to give full and cogent reasons: *Essen v. DPP*, unreported, May 12, 2005, DC ([2005] EWHC 1077, Admin); *R. (Walden), R. (Stern) v. Highbury Corner Magistrates' Court* [2003] 4 *Archbold News* 2, QBD (Mitchell J.).

The fact that a court may direct that a case should proceed on the next occasion is not binding on a subsequent court. The court dealing with the adjourned case must consider the situation as it is on the day when the matter is presented before it.

In *Essen v. DPP* it was confirmed that the court must give reasons when adjourning a case. A conviction was quashed when the court having first refused an adjournment to the defence then allowed an adjournment to the prosecution on the failure to attend of witnesses who had not been warned. In the absence of any explanation from the court of the reasons why the interests of justice required an adjournment the decision to put the case over was not upheld. Requests for adjournment must be examined with rigorous scrutiny.

In *S. v. DPP*, 170 J.P. 707, DC, it was held that although magistrates had a wide discretion in relation to matters of case management, and whilst the efficient dispatch of court business had to be considered when exercising that discretion, an adjournment would have to be granted if the imperatives of justice so required; and such would be the case where the prosecution failed to disclose matters which ought to have been disclosed, unless there would be no prejudice caused to the defendant by proceeding.

Also in *R. (Watson) v. Dartford Magistrates' Court*, unreported, May 12, 2005, DC ([2005] EWHC 905, Admin) the court held that when an application for an adjournment had been refused then a second application could only be made to the court if there had been a change of circumstances. Magistrates erred in granting an adjournment to the prosecution when the unavailability of two of their witnesses was held by another bench to be insufficient reason to adjourn only a day before. No different reason was put forward by the prosecution and the court held that the defence were disadvantaged by the adjournment.

A court refused to grant an adjournment to the defence when it had previously been **7–19** observed that the case should proceed. Two essential defence witnesses failed to attend on the day fixed for trial. The refusal was held to be contrary to natural justice: *R. v. Bristol Magistrates' Court, ex p. Rowles* [1994] R.T.R. 40, DC.

There was a duty on the court to hear the case advanced for the defence in support of an adjournment despite the fact that there was a fixed expectation that the case would proceed: *R. v. Bradford Justices, ex p. Wilkinson*, 91 Cr.App.R. 390, DC.

The provisions of section 10 allow a court to adjourn a case for a re-trial before a different bench: *R. v. Ripon Liberty Justices, ex p. Bugg*, 155 J.P. 213, DC; *R. (Kendall) v. Selby Magistrates' Court*, unreported, November 13, 2003, DC ([2003] EWHC 2909, Admin).

In *CPS v. Picton*, 170 J.P. 567, DC, the court considered various of the authorities, *ante*, and summarised (at [9]) the following key points which, in its view, emerged:

"(a) A decision whether to adjourn is a decision within the discretion of the trial court. An appellate court will interfere only if very clear grounds for doing so are shown.

(b) Magistrates should pay great attention to the need for expedition in the prosecution of criminal proceedings; delays are scandalous; they bring the law into disrepute; summary justice should be speedy justice; an application for an adjournment should be rigorously scrutinised.

(c) Where an adjournment is sought by the prosecution, magistrates must consider both the interest of the defendant in getting the matter dealt with, and the interest of the public that criminal charges should be adjudicated upon, and the guilty convicted as well as the innocent acquitted. With a more serious charge the public interest that there be a trial will carry greater weight.

(d) Where an adjournment is sought by the accused, the magistrates must consider whether, if it is not granted, he will be able fully to present his defence and, if he will not be able to do so, the degree to which his ability to do so is compromised.

(e) In considering the competing interests of the parties the magistrates should examine the likely consequences of the proposed adjournment, in particular its likely length, and the need to decide the facts while recollections are fresh.

(f) The reason that the adjournment is required should be examined and, if it arises through the fault of the party asking for the adjournment, that is a factor against granting the adjournment, carrying weight in accordance with the gravity of the fault. If that party was not at fault, that may favour an adjournment. Likewise if the party opposing the adjournment has been at fault, that will favour an adjournment.

(g) The magistrates should take appropriate account of the history of the case, and whether there have been earlier adjournments and at whose request and why.

(h) Lastly, of course the factors to be considered cannot be comprehensively stated but depend upon the particular circumstances of each case, and they will often overlap. The court's duty is to do justice between the parties in the circumstances as they have arisen."

D. FAILURE TO APPEAR

(1) The accused

7–20   Statute provides for different courses of action when any party to the proceedings fails to attend at court.

Magistrates' Courts Act 1980, s.11

Non-appearance of accused: general provisions

7–21   **11.**—(1) Subject to the provisions of this Act, where at the time and place appointed for the trial or adjourned trial of an information the prosecutor appears but the accused does not, the court may proceed in his absence.

(2) Where a summons has been issued, the court shall not begin to try the information in the absence of the accused unless either it is proved to the satisfaction of the court, on oath or in such other manner as may be prescribed, that the summons was served on the accused within what appears to the court to be a reasonable time before the trial or adjourned trial or the accused has appeared on a previous occasion to answer to the information.

(3) A magistrates' court shall not in a person's absence sentence him to imprisonment or detention in a young offender institution or make a detention and training order or an order under para. 8(2)(a) or (b) of Schedule 12 to the *Criminal Justice Act* 2003 that a suspended sentence passed on him shall take effect.

(4) A magistrates' court shall not in a person's absence impose any disqualification on him, except on resumption of the hearing after an adjournment under section 10(3) above; and where a trial is adjourned in pursuance of this subsection the notice required by section 10(2) above shall include notice of the reason for the adjournment.

[This section is printed as amended by the *Criminal Justice Act* 1988, Sched. 8, the *Criminal Justice and Public Order Act* 1994, Sched. 10, the *Crime and Disorder Act* 1998, Sched. 8, the *Powers of Criminal Courts (Sentencing) Act* 2000, Sched. 9, the *Criminal Justice and Courts Services Act* 2000, Scheds 7 and 8, and the *Criminal Justice Act* 2003, Sched. 32.]

7–22   When a defendant fails to appear the court may proceed in his absence or it may adjourn the case or it may issue a warrant of arrest: *Magistrates' Courts Act* 1980, s.13, see *ante*, § 4–92. A defendant represented by his lawyer is deemed not to be absent

(*Magistrates' Courts Act* 1980, s.122) so the case may proceed as if he were there unless provisions of statute expressly require the presence of the accused as they do in sections 11(3) and (4). Disqualifications that may be imposed include disqualification from driving and also various disqualifications relating to the keeping of animals. A disqualification cannot be imposed in absence unless the case has been adjourned on at least one occasion to give the defendant the opportunity to attend and show cause why a disqualification should not be imposed. Should the defendant fail to attend on the adjourned hearing, the court may lawfully disqualify in absence but this may have repercussions if a defendant is later charged with driving whilst disqualified and claims that he was not aware of the conviction or disqualification order.

Article 6 of the ECHR guarantees the right to a fair trial which incorporates the principle of effective participation in the proceedings. It is in the interests of justice that a defendant be present at his trial: *Ekbetani v. Sweden* (1991) 13 E.H.R.R. 504, ECtHR. The right to be present at trial is not absolute and it has been recognised that there may be circumstances in which Article 6 will not be violated when a case proceeds in the absence of the accused. For example when the defendant absents himself by his own conduct by absconding or making himself so ill he is unfit to attend court. In such circumstances the court must balance the competing claims of giving the defence the opportunity to present their case and ensuring a trial is heard within a reasonable time.

It would be important to ensure that the defendant is not denied the right to representation in his absence and also the right to a re-hearing on the merits: *Ensslin v. Germany* (1978) 14 D.R. 64.

The defendant may also waive his right to be present at trial but this requires an unequivocal waiver. The state is obliged to show that adequate measures have been taken to trace the defendant and that he has been notified and is aware of the proceedings: *Colozza v. Italy* (1985) 7 E.H.R.R. 516, ECtHR. In *Stoickor v. Bulgaria*, (2007) 44 E.H.R.R. 14, ECtHR, it was said that where criminal proceedings had been held in absentia without any indication that the accused had waived his right to be present at the trial, it would be manifestly contrary to the provisions and principles of Article 6 if the accused was not then permitted to re-open the proceedings.

Domestic case law confirms that the approach to trials in absence must comply with **7–23** Article 6. The law was reviewed in great detail by the Court of Appeal and the House of Lords in *R. v. Hayward*; *R. v. Jones*; *R. v. Purvis* [2001] Q.B. 862 and *R. v. Jones* [2003] 1 A.C. 1. The House of Lords approved the Court of Appeal's judgement which identified a list of matters relevant to the court's exercise of its discretion to conduct a trial in the of absence of the defendant. It was recognised that the defendant has a general right to be present at his trial and to be legally represented. The defendant can waive these rights either wholly or in part. They may be waived wholly if the defendant deliberately or voluntarily absents himself from the court and they may be waived partially if he behaves in such a way during the proceedings as to obstruct their proper course. His rights may also be waived if he withdraws his instructions from those representing him at any time during the proceedings. The court retains the discretion to hear a trial in absence, which must be exercised with great care, and it is only in rare and exceptional cases that a trial should continue in the absence of a defendant, particularly when he is not represented. Fairness to the defence is of prime importance but fairness to the prosecution must not be disregarded. The court should have regard to all the circumstances including:

(1) The nature and circumstances of the defendant's behaviour in absenting him or herself from the trial or disrupting it, and in particular whether the behaviour was voluntary and so plainly waived the right to be present;

(2) Whether an adjournment would resolve the matter;

(3) The likely length of such an adjournment;

(4) Whether the defendant, though absent, wished to be represented or had waived his or her right to representation;

(5) Whether the defendant's representatives were able to receive instructions from him or her and the extent to which they could present the defence;

(6) The extent of the disadvantage to the defendant in not being able to present his or her account of events;

(7) The risk of the jury reaching an improper conclusion about the absence of the defendant;

(8) The general public interest that a trial should take place within a reasonable time;

(9) The effect of the delay on the memories of the witnesses;

(10) Where there was more than one defendant, and not all had absconded, the undesirability of having separate trials.

In reviewing and approving this judgement Lord Bingham in the House of Lords added in *Jones* that the overriding concern is that the trial, if conducted in absence was as fair as the circumstances could permit and led to a just outcome. Those objects were equally important whether the offence was serious or relatively minor. Also, it was generally desirable that the defendant be represented even if he had voluntarily absconded.

In *R. v. O'Hare* [2006] Crim.L.R. 950, CA, it was said that, in order for an accused to be taken to have waived his right to be present at his trial, it must be proved that he knew of, or was indifferent to, the consequences of being tried in his absence and without legal representation; and an incontrovertible means by which this would be proved would be where a court had given a direction to the accused when granting bail explaining the consequences of non-attendance at trial, and had then provided him with a written statement to the same effect. In *Re Boodhoo* [2007] 1 Cr.App.R. 32, CA, it was held that if a defendant voluntarily absented himself from the proceedings, a court would not be entitled to conclude that a solicitor's decision to withdraw from the case rather than to continue in the defendant's absence was "unreasonable" within the meaning of section 19A(3) of the *Prosecution of Offences Act* 1985 (*i.e.* so as to permit the court to make a wasted costs order against the solicitor) where it could not be inferred that the defendant had expected his legal representatives to continue to represent him in his absence and where the solicitor genuinely believed that it would not be in the defendant's best interests to continue to represent him.

7–24   See also *Consolidated Criminal Practice Directions* in Appendix F.

These cases related to proceedings in the Crown Court but the principles apply equally to trials in the magistrates' court. In summary proceedings the fact that there can be an appeal that is a complete rehearing and the power to re-open a case under section 142 of the *Magistrates' Courts Act* 1980 are also relevant. Minor offences, particularly road traffic cases are often dealt with in absence. The court needs to be satisfied that the defendant has been given notice of the hearing date which is proved by proper service of the summons or adjournment notice. The documents must be served in accordance with Part 4 of the *Criminal Procedure Rules* 2005, r.4.1, see Appendix G–14 *et seq*. When the case proceeds in absence the prosecution will either call witnesses or it may apply to proceed on the basis of written statements prepared in accordance with section 9 of the *Criminal Justice Act* 1967. The court will need to be satisfied that these statements have also been served on the defendant and then they can be read out as the prosecution case. The trial must be conducted in accordance with the usual procedure and rules of evidence and the prosecution retains the criminal burden of proof. This does not mean that the court can dismiss a charge against an absent defendant in reliance on a denial made of the offence recorded in the prosecution statement. In *DPP v. Gokceli*, 153 J.P. 109, DC, the defendant was summonsed for driving the wrong way down a one way street. When questioned by the officer he denied that he was the driver. The court dismissed the charge on the basis of this evidence. The court held that this was wrong and said that if doubts were raised whilst the prosecution evidence was only in written form then the case should be adjourned so the prosecution may call oral evidence and the defendant should be informed again of his right to be present to challenge the prosecution evidence.

Minor offences which are often heard in absence include television licence offences, vehicle excise licence offences and fare evasion offences on public transport.

The court may be invited to proceed in absence in cases involving more serious **7–25** charges and then the guidance of *Jones* should be referred to in detail.

In *Shirzadeh v. Maidstone Magistrates' Court*, unreported, August 21, 2003 ([2003] EWHC 2216, Admin), the Divisional Court considered the principles to be applied in dealing with cases in absence in the magistrates' court. The applicant had been convicted in his absence of a charge of indecent assault. He applied to have the conviction quashed. The court recognised that additional factors to those listed in the case of *Hayward etc.* (§ 7–23) applied in the magistrates' court. These were:

1. There was less risk from either a trained lay justice or a district judge (as opposed to a jury) drawing an impermissible inference from a defendant's absence;
2. The finder of fact (being the lay justices or district judge) could ask its own questions and test the evidence of prosecution witnesses;
3. A defendant had a right under section 142 of the *Magistrates' Courts Act* 1980 to have the case re-opened;
4. A defendant in summary proceedings had an automatic right of appeal to the Crown Court by way of a full re-hearing of the evidence.

Taking these further aspects into account, the court held that the justices had acted within their discretion in proceeding in the absence of the defendant. The *Practice Direction (Criminal Proceedings: Consolidated) Amendment No. 3* directs that the court must exercise the discretion to proceed in absence with the utmost care and caution, the overriding concern being to ensure that the trial is as fair as circumstances permit and leads to a just outcome. This case indicates that the discretion may be wider in the magistrates' court than in the Crown Court where a trial in absence of the defendant before a jury will only take place in rare and exceptional cases. The principles to be applied in deciding whether to proceed in absence were considered further in *R. (Neil Webb-Johnson) v. DPP*, unreported, December 8, 2006, QBD (Gibbs J.) ([2005] EWHC 3123). The court had proceeded in absence in the case of a defendant who was charged with harassment and unauthorised use of a computer. The case had been outstanding for 18 months and the defendant had a history of psychiatric problems. He had been an in-patient at hospital for two weeks suffering from anxiety, depression and personality disorder. He wrote to the court explaining he was unfit to stand trial. The court went ahead with the trial and he was convicted in his absence. On appeal it was held that the discretion to proceed in absence was to be used with the utmost caution. Where a defendant's absence was due to illness or incapacity the trial should only proceed in absence if the defendant was represented. In this case there was a history of incapacity and the defendant's claim to be unwell was not without credibility. His lawyer had withdrawn due to professional embarrassment and not a failure to instruct. In all the circumstances the principles of *Jones* could not be shown to have been fully considered and properly applied and so the appeal was allowed.

It has been held that arrest and detention by the police preventing a defendant from **7–26** attending his trial is not voluntary absence and the court was criticised for proceeding in absence in those circumstances: *R. (R.) v. Thames Youth Court*, 166 J.P. 613, QBD.

It is a well established principle that the court must be satisfied that the summons was served a reasonable time before the hearing in order to allow a proper opportunity to attend or that the defendant had previously appeared in answer to the summons and so is aware of the proceedings. It is incumbent on the court to be satisfied that not only has the notice of adjournment been sent but also that it has been received. Where a defendant complained that neither he nor his solicitor had received a notice of the adjourned hearing date, the trial in absence was held to be a nullity because of the court's failure to investigate fully the reason for the non-attendance: *R. v. Seisdon Justices, ex p. Dougan*, 76 Cr.App.R. 1, DC.

The reason why the defendant is absent is a crucial factor in the decision to proceed in absence. The court must inquire and check whether any explanation has been provided for the failure to appear. The court always has a duty to exercise its discretion judicially, giving a fair opportunity to the defendant to be present and to call witnesses and/or give evidence. Where the defendant's failure to attend results from a medical condition, in most cases a medical certificate or letter from a doctor would suffice. If the court suspects the grounds to be spurious or inadequate, it should ordinarily express its doubts, giving the defendant an opportunity to seek to resolve them. The court may call for better evidence, require further enquiries to be made or adopt any further fair expedient. A claim of illness with apparently responsible professional support should not be rejected without the court satisfying itself that it is proper to reject it and that no unfairness would result: *R. v. Bolton Magistrates' Court, ex p. Merna* [1991] Crim.L.R. 848, DC.

7–27   A defendant's right to a fair trial does not encompass the unlimited right to be present on their own terms. A defendant charged with harassment had his trial adjourned on several occasions because of his medical condition, proof of which was provided through certificates and other evidence. The court initially heard the case in absence but allowed a re-hearing. The court then refused an adjournment of the re-hearing applied for again on medical grounds.It was held on appeal that the court exercised its discretion properly and had been entitled to proceed in absence: *R. v. Ealing Magistrates' Court, ex p. Burgess*, 165 J.P. 82, DC.

A vital factor affecting the court's discretion to proceed in absence is the provision for the absent defendant to apply for a re-hearing. This may be done under section 14 of the *Magistrates' Courts Act* 1980 whereby proceedings can be declared invalid where the defendant did not know of them, see *ante*, §§ 4–95—4–97. The defendant may also appeal against a conviction and or sentence to the Crown Court, see *post*, §§ 11–6—11–27. The defendant may also apply for the case to be re-opened under section 142 of the *Magistrates' Courts Act* 1980 and the conviction can be deleted and the trial commenced again.

The court may also deal with a case in the absence of the defendant under the provisions of section 12 of the *Magistrates' Courts Act* 1980 which provides for written pleas of guilty to be submitted if certain conditions are fulfilled, see *post*, §§ 8–59—8–84.

(2) The prosecution

Magistrates' Courts Act 1980, s.15

Non-appearance of prosecutor

7–28   **15.**—(1) Where at the time and place appointed for the trial or adjourned trial of an information the accused appears or is brought before the court and the prosecutor does not appear, the court may dismiss the information or, if evidence has been received on a previous occasion, proceed in the absence of the prosecutor.

(2) Where, instead of dismissing the information or proceeding in the absence of the prosecutor, the court adjourns the trial, it shall not remand the accused in custody unless he has been brought from custody or cannot be remanded on bail by reason of his failure to find sureties.

7–29   A prosecutor is not absent if he is represented by counsel or solicitor: *Magistrates' Courts Act* 1980, s.122. The prosecutor may be absent if he is physically not present in court or if, although present he is not able to prosecute the case because he does not have the file.

It is apparent from case law that the appeal courts frown upon the use of the power in this section as a punitive measure. In *DPP v. Shuttleworth*, 166 J.P. 417, DC, a defendant indicated she would plead guilty but the prosecutor could not proceed with the case because he did not have the file. The court purported to dismiss the charge. It was held on appeal that there was a want of prosecution because the file was not available but the purpose of the hearing was for plea and not for trial. The choice for the court in view of the guilty plea was to adjourn the case or proceed without the information from the file. The dismissal of the case was a punitive measure against the CPS which was not a proper exercise of the courts discretion. Costs penalties were available for that and the court failed to have regard to public interests including those of the defendant and victim.

It is not reasonable to use this power to punish a prosecutor for late attendance **7–30** without taking into account all the circumstances. Where the CPS were told by the court that a trial was not in the court list and that the court was not sitting, the court acted unreasonably in dismissing the charge since the reason for the non-attendance was because the CPS had been misinformed. On discovering the mistake, a prosecutor contacted the court to say he was on his way. The court did not wait for him to arrive but dismissed the charge apparently as a means of punishing the prosecutor for perceived inefficiency which was held to be an improper exercise of its power: *R. v. Hendon Justices, ex p. DPP* [1994] Q.B. 167, DC; and see *R. (CPS) v. Portsmouth Crown Court* [2004] Crim.L.R. 224, DC.

Another device resorted to occasionally by the court is to direct a change of plea from guilty to not guilty so that a charge may be dismissed in the absence of the prosecutor.

The mere fact that a case could be dismissed for want of prosecution is not a good reason to allow a change of plea: *R. v. Uxbridge Justices, ex p. Smith* [1977] R.T.R. 93, DC. Allowing a change of plea in order to exercise the discretion to dismiss was held to be in breach of natural justice as the discretion should not be exercised in order to discipline the prosecution: *R. v. Sutton Justices, ex p. DPP*, 95 Cr.App.R. 180, DC.

(3) Non-appearance of both parties

Magistrates' Courts Act 1980, s.16

Non-appearance of both parties
   16. Subject to section 11(3) and (4) and to section 12 above, where at the time and place ap- **7–31** pointed for the trial or adjourned trial of an information neither the prosecutor nor the accused appears, the court may dismiss the information or, if evidence has been received on a previous occasion, proceed in their absence.

The circumstances in which the court would proceed in the absence of both the **7–32** prosecutor and defendant are very limited. It may not do so when the presence of the defendant is required for the imposition of custodial sentences and for disqualification in certain circumstances under section 11, see *ante*, § 7–21.

The prosecutor and defendant may not be present when a case is dealt with under section 12 which provides for cases to be heard in absence when a written plea of guilty has been received by the court.

(4) Death of the defendant

The court may receive information that the defendant has died. In such circum- **7–33** stances in the magistrates' court there is no legal requirement for strict proof of this fact. The court may require that a death certificate be produced or the case may be adjourned for the prosecution to investigate the veracity of the report. The prosecution will then make the appropriate application to withdraw the proceedings or offer no evidence with the court register being marked that the defendant is "deceased".

II. PLEA BEFORE VENUE AND MODE OF TRIAL (ALLOCATION)

A. INTRODUCTION

When a person is charged or summonsed to appear at the magistrates' court the **7–34** details of the charge will be recorded on the charge sheet or the summons. The classification of the offence must then be ascertained so that the defendant can be advised of the correct procedure that applies in his case. For summary only matters that can only be tried by the magistrates' court, it will be expected that a plea of guilty or not guilty will be entered at the earliest opportunity: *Magistrates' Courts Act* 1980, s.9. As an encouragement to promptness, an early plea of guilty attracts a discount on sentence: see the *Criminal Justice Act* 2003, s.144 (*post*, § 22–100), and the *Reduction in sentence* *for a guilty plea* guideline made by the Sentencing Guidelines Council. For indictable only matters that can only be tried at the Crown Court, the case will be sent for trial at the Crown Court at the first hearing unless there is good reason to adjourn: sections 51 and 51A of the *Crime and Disorder Act* 1998. In respect of offences that can be tried either way, *i.e.* either at the Crown Court or the magistrates' court a procedure is provided for decisions to be made relating to the "mode of trial" in order to determine at which court the case should be tried. This is found in sections 17A–22 of the *Magistrates' Courts Act* 1980.

As from a day to be appointed, the *Criminal Justice Act* 2003, s.41 and Sched. 3, will establish a new procedure of "allocation" of cases. A decision will still be made as to whether the case is more suitable for summary trial or trial on indictment and "allocation guidelines" will be issued under the Act. Various other amendments are also made to the procedure which are contained in detail in Sched. 3. This includes a power for the court to give an indication of sentence to a defendant before he decides whether to consent to summary trial. See Appendix H for draft guidelines on the allocation procedure issued by the Sentencing Guidelines Council.

7–35   So far as the existing procedure is concerned, sections 17A–C provide for the "plea before venue" procedure. A defendant facing an either way offence will be asked by the court at the earliest opportunity if he is prepared to give an indication of his plea. The indication will be that he will plead guilty or not guilty, or he has a right to give no indication of plea. If there is an indication of a guilty plea the court may then proceed as if he had been convicted of the offence and consider sentence. The court may also commit the defendant to the Crown Court for sentence if it is of the opinion that the powers of sentencing in the magistrates' court are not sufficient. If a not guilty plea is indicated or no indication of plea is given then the court must adopt the "mode of trial" procedure to decide where the case shall be tried. Sections 18–23 of the *MCA* 1980 set out the procedure to be followed. The prosecution is first invited to make representations as to where it considers it is most suitable for the matter to be tried. The defence will then be asked if it has any representations to make as to whether the magistrates' court or Crown Court would be a more suitable venue. Having heard the representations the court will then decide whether the charge is more suitable for summary trial or trial on indictment. In making this decision the court will take into account the powers of sentencing available in the magistrates' court and will consider whether, were there to be a conviction on the charge those powers would be sufficient. In making this decision the court is aided by the Mode of Trial Guidelines. If the court is of the opinion that on conviction of the offence a greater sentence might have to be imposed than it has power to inflict then the court will decline jurisdiction and direct that the case be dealt with at the Crown Court. The defendant is bound by this decision.

If the court is of the opinion that the case is suitable for summary trial because the powers of the magistrate' court would be sufficient then the defendant is asked whether he would consent to summary trial. If he does not consent to summary trial he will be tried at the Crown Court by judge and jury. He may then consent to summary trial or elect to be tried at the Crown Court by a jury. The right to jury trial cannot be denied to a defendant.

Section 17 defines the offences that are triable either way and they are listed in Schedule 1 to the Act. Under section 22, some offences that are triable either way according to the Schedule must be tried summarily if the value involved in the offence is small. The procedure for mode of trial may be adapted to cater for this.

Section 25 allows for a change of election so that a summary trial may be changed into a committal for trial or vice versa.

7–36   These provisions apply only to adults aged 18 and over. For the powers of the magistrates' court in relation to youth co-defendants see Ch.4. The mode of trial procedure in the youth court is dealt with in section 24 of the *Magistrates' Courts Act* 1980, see *post*, § 25–25.

B. PLEA BEFORE VENUE

(1) Intention as to plea in presence of accused

Magistrates' Courts Act 1980, s.17A

Initial procedure: accused to indicate intention as to plea

17A—(1) This section shall have effect where a person who has attained the age of 18 years **7–37** appears or is brought before a magistrates' court on an information charging him with an offence triable either way.

(2) Everything that the court is required to do under the following provisions of this section must be done with the accused present in court.

(3) The court shall cause the charge to be written down, if this has not already been done, and to be read to the accused.

(4) The court shall then explain to the accused in ordinary language that he may indicate whether (if the offence were to proceed to trial) he would plead guilty or not guilty, and that if he indicates that he would plead guilty—

    (a) the court must proceed as mentioned in subsection (6) below; and

    (b) *he may be committed for sentence to the Crown Court under section 3 of the* Powers of Criminal Courts (Sentencing) Act *2000 if the court is of such opinion as is mentioned in subsection (2) of that section* [he may (unless section 17D(2) below were to apply) be committed to the Crown Court under section 3 or (if applicable) 3A of the *Powers of Criminal Courts (Sentencing) Act* 2000 if the court is of such opinion as is mentioned in subsection (2) of the applicable section].

he may be committed for sentence to the Crown Court under [section 3 of the *Powers of Criminal Courts (Sentencing) Act* 2000] below if the court is of such opinion as is mentioned in subsection (2) of that section.

(5) The court shall then ask the accused whether (if the offence were to proceed to trial) he would plead guilty or not guilty.

(6) If the accused indicates that he would plead guilty the court shall proceed as if—

    (a) the proceedings constituted from the beginning the summary trial of the information; and

    (b) section 9(1) above was complied with and he pleaded guilty under it.

(7) If the accused indicates that he would plead not guilty section 18(1) below shall apply.

(8) If the accused in fact fails to indicate how he would plead, for the purposes of this section and section 18(1) below he shall be taken to indicate that he would plead not guilty.

(9) Subject to subsection (6) above, the following shall not for any purpose be taken to constitute the taking of a plea—

    (a) asking the accused under this section whether (if the offence were to proceed to trial) he would plead guilty or not guilty;

    (b) an indication by the accused under this section of how he would plead.

[(10) If in respect of the offence the court receives a notice under section 51B or 51C of the *Crime and Disorder Act* 1998 (which relate to serious or complex fraud cases and to certain cases involving children respectively), the preceding provisions of this section and the provisions of section 17B below shall not apply, and the court shall proceed in relation to the offence in accordance with section 51 or, as the case may be, section 51A of that Act.]

[This section was inserted by the *Criminal Procedure and Investigations Act* 1996. It is printed as amended by the *Powers of Criminal Courts (Sentencing) Act* 2000, Sched. 9. As from a day or days to be appointed, the words in italics in subsection (4)(b) will be substituted for those set out in square brackets and subsection 10 will be inserted: *Criminal Justice Act* 2003, Sched. 3.]

This section applies to a defendant who is 18 years of age or more. An offence triable **7–38** either way is one that is triable either at the Crown Court on indictment or summarily at the magistrates' court: *Interpretation Act* 1978, Sched. 1; section 17 of the *Magistrates' Courts Act* 1980 and Sched. 1 list offences which are triable either way. The legal adviser in court will explain the procedure for plea before venue to the defendant after identifying that the charge is triable either way. The charge should be read to the defen-

Part I

dant and then a recommended form of words has been suggested as follows—

"For this charge you may be tried either in the magistrates' court or by a jury in the Crown Court. First however this court must ask you whether, if the case proceeds to trial, you would plead guilty or not guilty. Before you answer that I want to explain what will happen then. If you say that you would plead guilty, the court will hear the prosecution case against you, listen to your mitigation and formally find you guilty. The court will then decide what sentence it thinks you should receive. Do you understand? (*If yes, say*) If the court believes that you deserve greater punishment than this court can give (or if you have to be sent to the Crown Court to be tried on a related charge) it will send you to the Crown Court to be sentenced. Otherwise you will be sentenced here. If you do not indicate a guilty plea the court will decide whether to send you to the Crown Court for trial Do you understand that or do you want anything to be explained further? (*Unless repeated or further explanation is required say*) Then if the charge against you was to go to trial, would you plead guilty or not guilty."

7–39   This pronouncement was devised by the Judicial Studies Board and approved in *R. v. Southampton Magistrates' Court, ex p. Sansome* [1999] 1 Cr.App.R. 112, DC. The form of words is not obligatory and many legal advisers will adopt their own favoured explanation which will include the right to give no indication of plea. This procedure was reviewed and explained in the case of *R. v. Warley Magistrates' Court, ex p. DPP* [1998] 2 Cr.App.R. 307, DC. The purpose of section 17A is to give the defendant the opportunity to enter a plea of guilty as soon as possible, to enable him to claim additional credit compared with a plea entered in the Crown Court and to ensure that cases which could properly be dealt with in the magistrates' court remained there. The court had the power to commit for sentence to the Crown Court but having received a plea of guilty and heard from the defence as well as the prosecution it could be fully informed before determining whether to commit for sentence. A plea of guilty before venue in the magistrates' court entitles the defendant who is committed for sentence to the Crown Court to a greater discount than if he had elected trial by jury but changed his plea to guilty only when he appeared at the Crown Court: *R. v. Rafferty* [1999] 1 Cr.App.R. 235, CA. For detailed commentary on committal for sentence see Sentencing, Pt IV in this work.

In order to secure the maximum benefit of an early plea the court will expect the plea before venue procedure to take place as soon as possible but the defendant is entitled to receive the relevant information from the prosecution that will affect his plea and the mode of trial decision. If a request for advanced disclosure under the provisions of the *Criminal Procedure Rules* 2005, Pt 21, which came into effect on April 4, 2005 has not been complied with, the court should adjourn the case unless it is satisfied that the failure to disclose does not prejudice the defendant: *R. v. Calderdale Magistrates' Courts, ex p. Donahue and Cutler* [2001] Crim.L.R. 141, DC. As to the duties of the prosecution to disclose advance information, see *ante*, §§ 6–7 *et seq.*

(2) Intention as to plea when the accused is absent

Magistrates' Courts Act 1980, ss.17B–17E

Intention as to plea: absence of accused

7–40   **17B.**—(1) This section shall have effect where—

(a) a person who has attained the age of 18 years appears or is brought before a magistrates' court on an information charging him with an offence triable either way.

(b) the accused is represented by a legal representative,

(c) the court considers that by reason of the accused's disorderly conduct before the court it is not practicable for proceedings under section 17A above to be conducted in his presence, and

(d) the court considers that it should proceed in the absence of the accused.

(2) In such a case—

(a) the court shall cause the charge to be written down, if this has not already been done, and to be read to the representative;

(b) the court shall ask the representative whether (if the offence were to proceed to trial) the accused would plead guilty or not guilty;

(c) if the representative indicates that the accused would plead guilty the court shall proceed as if the proceedings constituted from the beginning the summary trial of the information, and as if section 9(1) above was complied with and the accused pleaded guilty under it;

(d) if the representative indicates that the accused would plead not guilty section 18(1) below shall apply.

(3) If the representative in fact fails to indicate how the accused would plead, for the purposes of this section and section 18(1) below he shall be taken to indicate that the accused would plead not guilty.

(4) Subject to subsection (2)(c) above, the following shall not for any purpose be taken to constitute the taking of a plea—

(a) asking the representative under this section whether (if the offence were to proceed to trial) the accused would plead guilty or not guilty;

(b) an indication by the representative under this section of how the accused would plead.

[Section 17B was inserted by the *Criminal Procedure and Investigations Act* 1996.]

Intention as to plea adjournment

17C. A magistrates' court proceeding under section 17A or 17B above may adjourn the   **7–41** proceedings at any time, and on doing so on any occasion when the accused is present may remand the accused, and shall remand him if—

(a) on the occasion on which he first appeared, or was brought, before the court to answer to the information he was in custody or, having been released on bail, surrendered to the custody of the court; or

(b) he has been remanded at any time in the course of proceedings on the information;

and where the court remands the accused, the time fixed for the resumption of proceedings shall be that at which he is required to appear or be brought before the court in pursuance of the remand or would be required to be brought before the court but for section 128(3A) below.

[Section 17C was inserted by the *Criminal Procedure and Investigations Act* 1996.]

Maximum penalty under section 17A(6) or 17B(2)(c) for certain offences

[17D.—(1) If—   **7–42**

(a) the offence is a scheduled offence (as defined in section 22(1) below);

(b) the court proceeds in relation to the offence in accordance with section 17A(6) or 17B(2)(c) above; and

(c) the court convicts the accused of the offence,

the court shall consider whether, having regard to any representations made by him or by the prosecutor, the value involved (as defined in section 22(10) below) appears to the court to exceed the relevant sum (as specified for the purposes of section 22 below).

(2) If it appears to the court clear that the value involved does not exceed the relevant sum, or it appears to the court for any reason not clear whether the value involved does or does not exceed the relevant sum—

(a) subject to subsection (4) below, the court shall not have power to impose on the accused in respect of the offence a sentence in excess of the limits mentioned in section 33(1)(a) below; and

(b) sections 3 and 4 of the *Powers of Criminal Courts (Sentencing) Act* 2000 shall not apply as regards that offence.

(3) *Subsections (9) to (12) of section 22* below shall apply for the purposes of this section as they apply for the purposes of that section (reading the reference to subsection (1) in section 22(9) as a reference to subsection (1) of this section).

(4) Subsection (2)(a) above does not apply to an offence under section 12A of the *Theft Act* 1968 (aggravated vehicle-taking).]

[As from a day to be appointed, section 17D is to be inserted by the *Criminal Justice Act* 2003, Sched. 3.]

Functions under sections 17A to 17D capable of exercise by single justice

7–43   **[17E.**—(1) The functions of a magistrates' court under sections 17A to 17D above may be discharged by a single justice.

(2) Subsection (1) above shall not be taken as authorising—

     (a) the summary trial of an information (otherwise than in accordance with section 17A(6) or 17B(2)(c) above); or

     (b) the imposition of a sentence,

by a magistrates' court composed of fewer than two justices.]

[As from a day to be appointed, section 17E is to be inserted by the *Criminal Justice Act* 2003, Sched. 3.]

C. Mode Of Trial

General

Magistrates' Courts Act 1980, s.18

Initial procedure on information against adult for offence triable either way

7–44   **18.**—(1) Sections 19 to 23 below shall have effect where a person who has attained the age of 18 years appears or is brought before a magistrates' court on an information charging him with an offence triable either way and—

     (a) he indicates under section 17A above that (if the offence were to proceed to trial) he would plead not guilty, or

     (b) his representative indicates under section 17B above that (if the offence were to proceed to trial) he would plead not guilty.

(2) Without prejudice to section 11(1) above, everything that the court is required to do under sections 19 to 22 below must be done before any evidence is called and, subject to subsection (3) below and section 23 below, with the accused present in court.

(3) The court may proceed in the absence of the accused in accordance with such of the provisions of sections 19 to 22 below as are applicable in the circumstances if the court considers that by reason of his disorderly conduct before the court it is not practicable for the proceedings to be conducted in his presence; and subsections (3) to (5) of section 23 below, so far as applicable, shall have effect in relation to proceedings conducted in the absence of the accused by virtue of this subsection (references in those subsections to the person representing the accused being for this purpose read as references to the person, if any, representing him).

(4) A magistrates' court proceeding under sections 19 to 23 below may adjourn the proceedings at any time, and on doing so on any occasion when the accused is present may remand the accused, and shall remand him if—

     (a) on the occasion on which he first appeared, or was brought, before the court to answer to the information he was in custody or, having been released on bail, surrendered to the custody of the court; or

     (b) he has been remanded at any time in the course of proceedings on the information;

and where the court remands the accused, the time fixed for the resumption of the proceedings shall be that at which he is required to appear or be brought before the court in pursuance of the remand or would be required to be brought before the court but for section 128(3A) below.

(5) The functions of a magistrates' court under subsections 19 to 23 below may be discharged by a single justice, *but the foregoing provision shall not be taken to authorise the summary trial of an information by a magistrates' court composed of less than two justices* [but this subsection shall not be taken as authorising—

     (a) the summary trial of an information (otherwise than in accordance with section 20(7) below); or

     (b) the imposition of a sentence,

by a magistrates' court comprised of fewer than two justices.]

[This section is printed as amended by the *Criminal Justice Act* 1982, Sched. 9, the *Criminal Justice Act* 1991, Sched. 8, and the *Criminal Procedure and Investigations*

Act 1996, s.49. As from a day to be appointed, the words in italics in subsection (5) will be substituted by those set out in square brackets.]

The mode of trial procedure applies to defendants who are aged 18 or over. Whether **7–45** the right to elect jury trial under these provisions is engaged for a person who is under the age of 18 at the time when the offence was committed depends on the actual date when the defendant appears and the court decides to proceed to determine mode of trial. If a defendant has attained the age of 18 by the time the mode of trial decision falls to be made then he has the right to elect jury trial. It is irrelevant that the offence may have been committed or he may have been charged with the offence when he was under that age: *R. v. Islington North Juvenile Court, ex p. Daley* [1983] 1 A.C. 347, HL. The fact that a defendant reaches the age of 18 after the mode of trial has been decided in the youth court but before the trial has commenced does not confer the right to elect jury trial: *R. v. Nottingham Justices, ex p. Taylor* [1992] 1 Q.B. 557, DC. The taking of a plea in the youth court from a defendant who is under the age of 18 amounts to a decision as to the mode of trial: *R. v. West London Justices, ex p. Silely-Winditt*, 165 J.P. 112, DC.

These provisions are mandatory. Where the court proceeded to try an either way offence without adopting the procedure for determining mode of trial the defendant could not be said to have consented to summary trial and the proceedings were held to be a nullity: *R. v. Tottenham Justices, ex p. Arthurs Transport Services* [1981] Crim.L.R. 180, DC.

Once the decision has been made to try a case summarily and in the case of an adult there is consent to being so tried, it is too late to serve a notice of transfer: *R. v. Fareham Youth Court and Morey, ex p. CPS*, 163 J.P. 812, DC.

Magistrates' Courts Act 1980, s.19

Court to begin by considering which mode of trial appears more suitable

   19.—(1) *The court shall consider whether, having regard to the matters mentioned in* **7–46** *subsection (3) below and any representations made by the prosecutor or the accused, the offence appears to the court more suitable for summary trial or for trial on indictment.*

   (2) *Before so considering, the court—*

   (a) *[repealed]*

   (b) *shall afford first the prosecutor and then the accused an opportunity to make representations as to which mode of trial would be more suitable.*

   (3) *The matters to which the court is to have regard under subsection (1) above are the nature of the case; whether the circumstances make the offence one of serious character; whether the punishment which a magistrates' court would have power to inflict for it would be adequate; and any other circumstances which appear to the court to make it more suitable for the offence to be tried in one way rather than the other.*

   (4) *If the prosecution is being carried on by the Attorney General, the Solicitor General or the Director of Public Prosecutions and he applies for the offence to be tried on indictment, the preceding provisions of this section and sections 20 and 21 below shall not apply, and the court shall proceed to inquire into the information as examining justices.*

   (5) *The power of the Director of Public Prosecutions under subsection (4) above to apply for an offence to be tried on indictment shall not be exercised except with the consent of the Attorney General.*

Decision as to allocation

   [19.—(1) The court shall decide whether the offence appears to it more suitable for summary trial or for trial on indictment.

   (2) Before making a decision under this section, the court—

   (a) shall give the prosecution an opportunity to inform the court of the accused's previous convictions (if any); and

   (b) shall give the prosecution and the accused an opportunity to make representations as to whether summary trial or trial on indictment would be more suitable.

   (3) In making a decision under this section, the court shall consider—

   (a) whether the sentence which a magistrates' court would have power to impose for the offence would be adequate; and

     (b) any representations made by the prosecution or the accused under subsection
        (2)(b) above,
and shall have regard to any allocation guidelines (or revised allocation guidelines) issued as definitive guidelines under section 170 of the *Criminal Justice Act* 2003.

   (4) Where—

     (a) the accused is charged with two or more offences; and

     (b) it appears to the court that the charges for the offences could be joined in the
        same indictment or that the offences arise out of the same or connected circumstances,

subsection (3)(a) above shall have effect as if references to the sentence which a magistrates' court would have power to impose for the offence were a reference to the maximum aggregate sentence which a magistrates' court would have power to impose for all of the offences taken together.

   (5) In this section any reference to a previous conviction is a reference to—

     (a) a previous conviction by a court in the United Kingdom; or

     (b) *a previous finding of guilt in—*

        (i) *any proceedings under the* Army Act *1955, the* Air Force Act *1955 or the*
           Naval Discipline Act *1957 (whether before a court-martial or any other*
           court or person authorised under any of those Acts to award a punishment
           in respect of any offence); or

        (ii) *any proceedings before a Standing Civilian Court*

   [(b) a previous conviction of a service offence within the meaning of the *Armed Forces Act* 2006 ("conviction" here including anything that under section 376(1) and (2) of that Act is to be treated as a conviction)].

   (6) If, in respect of the offence, the court receives a notice under section 51B or 51C of the *Crime and Disorder Act* 1998 (which relate to serious or complex fraud cases and to certain cases involving children respectively), the preceding provisions of this section and sections 20, 20A and 21 below shall not apply, and the court shall proceed in relation to the offence in accordance with section 51(1) of that Act.]

[The italicised section is printed as amended by the *Prosecution of Offences Act* 1985, Sched. 1, and the *Criminal Procedure and Investigations Act* 1996, s.49. As from a day to be appointed, a new section 19 (set out in square brackets) will be substituted for the original section: *Criminal Justice Act* 2003, Sched. 3. As from a further day to be appointed, subsection (5)(b) in the substituted section will be amended by the *Armed Forces Act* 2006, Sched. 16 (the italicised text being replaced by that subsequently set out in square brackets).]

When the new scheme of allocation under the substituted section 19 is brought into force, the court will be required to have regard to allocation guidelines issued by the Sentencing Guidelines Council. Draft guidelines have been issued by the council, and are set out at Appendix H.

7–47   The mode of trial procedure allows for either the court or the defendant to decide that trial at the Crown Court would be most suitable. In the majority of cases the court will hear representations from the prosecution and the defence and then the court will decide on suitability. An exception to this procedure is where the prosecution can dictate that the case be tried at the Crown Court. Only if the prosecution is being conducted by one of the Chief Law Officers referred to in the section or the DPP with the consent of the Attorney General can the prosecution application for jury trial override any decision of the court or the defendant.

    The court must have regard to the matters mentioned in subsection (3). The decision is made on the basis of the facts of the case as outlined by the prosecution and the nature and seriousness of the offence must be made out. The court must consider whether its powers of sentencing would be sufficient in view of the information that it has received from the prosecution. Regard may also be had to other circumstances affecting the suitability of the case to be tried one way or the other. The question of plea or the strength of the evidence is not relevant in defence representations because at this stage the court is only concerned with trying to ensure that serious cases are dealt with by the Crown Court. The gravity of the offence will be assessed not on the basis of evidence but on the assertions made by the prosecution. The previous convictions or good character of the defendant are irrelevant to this decision and the court should neither hear nor take into account any information as to the defendant's previous record: *R. v. Colchester Justices, ex p. North East Essex Building Co Ltd* [1977] 1 W.L.R. 1109, DC. The defendant's criminal record only becomes relevant after conviction, not at mode of trial stage: *R. v. Hammersmith Juvenile Court, ex p. O*, (1988) 86 Cr.App.R. 343, DC.

The *Consolidated Criminal Practice Directions* (See Appendix F) contains the most **7–48** recent version of the National Mode of Trial Guidelines. The object of the guidelines is to provide guidance on the matters to be considered when determining mode of trial. They are not directive. The magistrates retain a duty to consider each case individually and on its own particular facts: *R. v. Derby Justices, ex p. DPP, The Times*, August 17, 1999, DC.

The guidelines indicate that offences triable either way should be tried summarily unless one of the stated special features is present and the magistrates' sentencing powers are inadequate. The magistrates' courts' powers of sentence are limited to a maximum fine of £5,000 or imprisonment of up to six months on a single offence or 12 months in total if there is more than one either-way offence. The factors identified are aggravating features that could make the offence more serious and so might attract a more severe sentence.

Cases in which the decision of the court on mode of trial have been reviewed involve instances of the court retaining jurisdiction for offences which should more properly have been dealt with at the Crown Court.

Jurisdiction was accepted in the magistrates' court for a defendant charged with a **7–49** VAT fraud case concerning nearly £200,000. It was held that if there was a conviction the Crown Court was likely to have imposed a heavier sentence. The decision on mode of trial was unreasonable and was quashed: *R. v. Northamptonshire Magistrates' Court, ex p. Commissioners of Customs and Excise* [1994] Crim.L.R. 598, DC. In another case of VAT fraud when jurisdiction was accepted the decision was quashed because it was held that the court had failed to apply its mind to the provisions of section 19(3). The court had not considered whether its powers of punishment were sufficient: *R. v. Flax Bourton Magistrates' Court, ex p. Commissioners of Customs and Excise*, 160 J.P. 481, DC. In another case the charge was one of possession of Class A drugs (114 ecstasy tablets) with intent to supply, an offence that would normally attract a prison sentence of between two to five years. It was held that the decision to retain summary jurisdiction was perverse. It was reiterated that close regard must be had to the guidelines in conjunction with section 19(3) when considering jurisdiction: *R. v. Horseferry Road Magistrates' Court, ex p. DPP* [1997] C.O.D. 89, DC. Interpretation of the guidelines was considered when it was held that an assault committed by banging the victim's head against a wall did not involve the "use of a weapon" within the meaning of the guidelines and so summary jurisdiction could be retained: *R. v. Derby Justices, ex p. DPP, The Times*, August 17, 1999, DC.

Any other circumstances may be taken into account when deciding on mode of trial. **7–50** The fact that it may be more "convenient and expeditious" to deal with serious offences summarily is not a relevant "other circumstance" and cannot amount to a reason for accepting jurisdiction. Summary trial is only appropriate where the sentencing powers of the court will be sufficient: *R. v. Coe*, 53 Cr.App.R. 66, CA.

The complexity and sensitivity of a case may be taken into account but this will generally contribute to the seriousness of the case in any event. Issues about disclosure cannot of themselves make a case more suitable for trial at the Crown Court. Where a defendant was charged with possession of a pitbull terrier in contravention of the *Dangerous Dogs Act* 1991 disclosure was sought from the prosecution of expert reports prepared for previous cases relating to the identification of dogs as pitbull terriers. The court declined jurisdiction on the basis that it had no power to order disclosure of the reports. It was held that the magistrates' court had power to order disclosure and summary jurisdiction could have been accepted: *R. v. Bromley Justices, ex p. Smith and Wilkins*; *R. v. Wells Street Stipendiary Magistrate, ex p. King* [1995] 2 Cr.App.R. 285, DC.

Once a court has made a decision on mode of trial it is not open to a subsequent court to change that decision, thereby acting as a court of appeal. Where a court declined summary jurisdiction, another bench cannot later hear representations and agree to summary trial: *R. v. Liverpool Justices, ex p. Crown Prosecution Service* (1990) 90 Cr.App.R. 261, DC. There is provision for the mode of trial to be changed but only after the trial or committal has begun, see section 25 *post*, at § 7–67 .

Magistrates' Courts Act 1980, s.20

Procedure where summary trial appears more suitable

7–51   **20.**—(1) *If, where the court has considered as required by section 19(1) above, it appears to the court that the offence is more suitable for summary trial, the following provisions of this section shall apply (unless excluded by section 23 below).*

(2) *The court shall explain to the accused in ordinary language—*

(a) *that it appears to the court more suitable for him to be tried summarily for the offence, and that he can either consent to be so tried or, if he wishes, be tried by a jury; and*

(b) *that if he is tried summarily and is convicted by the court, he may be committed for sentence to the Crown Court under section 3 of the* Powers of Criminal Courts (Sentencing) Act *2000 if the convicting court, is of such opinion as is mentioned in subsection (2) of that section.*

(3) *After explaining to the accused as provided by subsection (2) above the court shall ask him whether he consents to be tried summarily or wishes to be tried by a jury, and—*

(a) *if he consents to be tried summarily, shall proceed to the summary trial of the information;*

(b) *if he does not so consent, shall proceed to inquire into the information as examining justices.*

[*Procedure where summary trial appears more suitable*

20.—(1) If the court decides under section 19 above that the offence appears to it more suitable for summary trial, the following provisions of this section shall apply (unless they are excluded by section 23 below).

(2) The court shall explain to the accused in ordinary language—

(a) that it appears to the court more suitable for him to be tried summarily for the offence;

(b) that he can either consent to be so tried or, if he wishes, be tried on indictment; and

(c) in the case of a specified offence (within the meaning of section 224 of the *Criminal Justice Act* 2003), that if he is tried summarily and is convicted by the court, he may be committed for sentence to the Crown Court under section 3A of the *Powers of Criminal Courts (Sentencing) Act* 2000 if the committing court is of such opinion as is mentioned in subsection (2) of that section.

(3) The accused may then request an indication ("an indication of sentence") of whether a custodial sentence or non-custodial sentence would be more likely to be imposed if he were to be tried summarily for the offence and to plead guilty.

(4) If the accused requests an indication of sentence, the court may, but need not, give such an indication.

(5) If the accused requests and the court gives an indication of sentence, the court shall ask the accused whether he wishes, on the basis of the indication, to reconsider the indication of plea which was given, or is taken to have been given, under section 17A or 17B above.

(6) If the accused indicates that he wishes to reconsider the indication under section 17A or 17B above, the court shall ask the accused whether (if the offence were to proceed to trial) he would plead guilty or not guilty.

(7) If the accused indicates that he would plead guilty the court shall proceed as if—

(a) the proceedings constituted from that time the summary trial of the information; and

(b) section 9(1) above were complied with and he pleaded guilty under it.

(8) Subsection (9) below applies where—

   (a) the court does not give an indication of sentence (whether because the accused does not request one or because the court does not agree to give one);

   (b) the accused either—

      (i) does not indicate, in accordance with subsection (5) above, that he wishes; or

      (ii) indicates, in accordance with subsection (5) above, that he does not wish, to reconsider the indication of plea under section 17A or 17B above; or

   (c) the accused does not indicate, in accordance with subsection (6) above, that he would plead guilty.

(9) The court shall ask the accused whether he consents to be tried summarily or wishes to be tried on indictment and—

   (a) if he consents to be tried summarily, shall proceed to the summary trial of the information; and

   (b) if he does not so consent, shall proceed in relation to the offence in accordance with section 51(1) of the *Crime and Disorder Act* 1998.

Procedure where summary trial appears more suitable: supplementary

   20A.—(1) Where the case is dealt with in accordance with section 20(7) above, no court (whether a magistrates' court or not) may impose a custodial sentence for the offence unless such a sentence was indicated in the indication of sentence referred to in section 20 above.

   (2) Subsection (1) above is subject to sections 3A(4), 4(8) and 5(3) of the *Powers of Criminal Courts (Sentencing) Act* 2000.

   (3) Except as provided in subsection (1) above—

   (a) an indication of sentence shall not be binding on any court (whether a magistrates' court or not); and

   (b) no sentence may be challenged or be the subject of appeal in any court on the ground that it is not consistent with an indication of sentence.

   (4) Subject to section 20(7) above, the following shall not for any purpose be taken to constitute the taking of a plea—

   (a) asking the accused under section 20 above whether (if the offence were to proceed to trial) he would plead guilty or not guilty; or

   (b) an indication by the accused under that section of how he would plead.

   (5) Where the court gives an indication of sentence under section 20 above, it shall cause each such indication to be entered in the register.

   (6) In this section and in section 20 above, references to a custodial sentence are to a custodial sentence within the meaning of section 76 of the *Powers of Criminal Courts (Sentencing) Act* 2000, and references to a non-custodial sentence shall be construed accordingly.]

[The text set out in italics is the original text of section 20, printed as amended by the *Criminal Justice Act* 1991, Sched. 11, and the *Powers of Criminal Courts (Sentencing) Act* 2000, Sched. 9. As from a day to be appointed, the *Criminal Justice Act* 2003, Sched. 3, substitutes new sections 20 and 20A (the text set out in square brackets).]

Under the present section 20, after considering the representations of the prosecu- **7–52** tion and defence, the court may decide that the case is suitable for summary trial on the basis that if there were to be a conviction the powers of sentencing in the magistrates' court would be sufficient. The defendant must then be asked if he consents to summary trial. He is not bound to do so and there is a right to jury trial. The legal adviser will put the election to the defendant and will explain the procedure and his rights. The recommended form of words is as follows:

"It appears to this court more suitable for you to be tried here. You may now consent to be tried by this court, but if you wish, you may choose to be tried by a jury instead. If you are tried by this court and are found guilty, this court may still send you to the Crown Court for sentence if it is of the opinion that greater punishment should be inflicted for the offence than it has power to impose. Do you wish to be tried by this court or do you wish to be tried by a jury?"

This pronouncement was approved in *R. v. Southampton Magistrates' Court, ex p.*

Sansome [1999] 1 Cr.App.R. 112, DC. The defendant may then consent to be tried at the magistrates' court and the case will proceed as a summary trial, or he may elect trial at the Crown Court and a committal will then ensue.

7–53   The procedure of section 20 must be followed. A summary trial which led to the acquittal of a defendant who had not been put to his election was declared a nullity: *R. v. Cardiff Magistrates' Court, ex p. Cardiff City Council, The Times*, February 24, 1987, DC. The court has a discretion to allow a change of election but an application to have the election put again will only be granted if there is some doubt over whether the defendant understood or fully appreciated the procedure and the effect of his choice. In *R. v. Birmingham Justices, ex p. Hodgson* [1985] Q.B. 1131, DC, an unrepresented defendant consented to summary trial and in his plea of guilty disclosed a possible defence to the charge he faced. Later, he appeared represented and application was made to have the election put again. It was held that the election on mode of trial was final and binding only when the nature and significance of the choice being made was understood and the court was wrong to refuse to allow the election to be put again.

The fact that the court may feel itself able to deal adequately with the complexities of a case is no ground for refusing to vary an election. A defendant who was unrepresented and had not appreciated the importance and implications of his choice of summary trial was entitled to change his election: *R. v. Highbury Corner Metropolitan Stipendiary Magistrates, ex p. Weekes* [1985] Q.B. 1147, DC. The defendant must prove that he lacked the necessary comprehension but if the relevant evidence is not put before the court a proper determination cannot be made. It is incumbent upon the court to ensure that the defence put forward proper reasons which can be duly considered before refusing a request to change an election: *R. v. Forest Magistrates, ex p. Spicer*, 153 J.P. 81, DC.

7–54   That the defendant was unrepresented when the original election was made does not of itself compel the court to allow the election to be withdrawn: *R. v. Lambeth Stipendiary Magistrate, ex p. Wright* [1974] Crim.L.R. 444, DC. The court has an unfettered discretion whether to allow an application to change the election. If satisfied the defendant understood the difference between the two modes of trial, the court was entitled to refuse the application. The fact that a not guilty plea had been entered and the prosecution witnesses were ready to give evidence and the trial would be delayed further are not relevant to the understanding of the applicant: *R. v. Bourne Justices, ex p. Cope* [1989] C.O.D. 304, DC.

The defendant has a right to receive a summary of the prosecution case and/or copies of the statements of the proposed prosecution witnesses in advanced disclosure: *Criminal Procedure Rules* 2005, Pt 21, see Ch. 6 and Appendix G–134 *et seq.* Sight of these may be required so that the defendant can make an informed choice between summary trial and trial on indictment.

The right to consent to summary trial or to elect for trial at the Crown Court is given to each defendant individually. Where there are co-defendants, each person must be asked at which court they wish to be tried and different elections must be accepted. The fact that one defendant elects jury trial does not require that all defendants should go to the Crown Court: *R. v. Brentwood Justices, ex p. Nicholls* [1992] 1 A.C. 1, HL.

7–55   The decision on mode of trial should not be based on an indication given by defendants that they would elect jury trial. In *R. v. Ipswich Magistrates' Court, ex p. Callaghan*, 159 J.P. 748, DC, the legal adviser during the mode of trial procedure asked three defendants whether they were going to elect jury trial. Two defendants indicated that they would and so the court decided to direct Crown Court trial in respect of all three defendants. It was held on appeal that the preliminary inquiry by the legal adviser was incorrect and the court had to decide whether an offence was more suitable for summary or Crown Court trial. This decision cannot be based on a wish to avoid separate trials. Each defendant has an individual right of election which is exercised after the court has decided which mode of trial is more suitable. Once the court has indicated that a case is suitable for summary trial that decision cannot be changed at the request of the prosecutor for the purposes of ensuring that co-defendants, one of whom elected trial by jury, should all be committed to the Crown Court: *R. v. Wigan Magistrates' Court, ex p. Layland* [1995] Crim.L.R. 892, DC.

The defendant's right to jury trial does not oblige the prosecution to proceed on the most serious charges disclosed by the facts. Where alternative summary only charges were preferred by the prosecution and no evidence offered on either way offences it was held that no consent was required from the court for the prosecution to conduct the case that way and the defendant had not wrongfully been deprived of a right to elect trial at the Crown Court: *R. v. Canterbury and St Augustine Justices, ex p. Klisiak* [1982] Q.B. 398, DC. By the same token the prosecution may upgrade the offences. The addition or substitution of charges by the prosecution so that an offence becomes either way is not a ground for refusing the issue of a summons provided that such process could properly be issued in the light of the facts as presented by the prosecution: *R. v. Redbridge Justices and Fox, ex p. Whitehouse*, 94 Cr.App.R. 332, DC.

Under the *Criminal Justice Act* 2003, s.41 and Sched. 3, a new section 20 will be substituted and the defendant will be able to request the court to give an indication as to sentence before deciding whether to consent to summary trial. The court will have a discretion to indicate whether a custodial or non-custodial sentence would be more likely to be imposed if the defendant were to plead guilty. After hearing any such indication of sentence that the court may give the defendant may then re-consider his plea of not guilty. If no such indication of sentence is requested or the court does not agree to give one then the defendant will decide if he consents to summary trial.

Magistrates' Courts Act 1980, s.21

Procedure where trial on indictment appears more suitable

21. *If, where the court has considered as required by section 19(1) above, it appears to the*   **7–56**
court that the offence is more suitable for trial on indictment, the court shall tell the accused that the court has decided that it is more suitable for him to be tried for the offence by a jury, and shall proceed to inquire into the information as examining justices.

[Procedure where trial on indictment appears more suitable

21. If the court decides under section 19 above that the offence appears to it more suitable for trial on indictment, the court shall tell the accused that the court has decided that it is more suitable for him to be tried on indictment, and shall proceed in relation to the offence in accordance with section 51(1) of the *Crime and Disorder Act* 1998.]

[The text set out in italics is the original text of section 21. As from a day to be appointed, the *Criminal Justice Act* 2003, Sched. 3, will substitute a new section (the text set out in square brackets).]

Once the court has declined jurisdiction the defendant has no right to be put to his   **7–57**
election. The decision of the court overrides any wish he may have to consent to summary trial and committal to the Crown Court will take place. In some cases, a defendant will indicate a guilty plea to a serious charge which, had it been contested would have been considered more suitable to be tried at the Crown Court at the mode of trial stage. On an early guilty plea the court may not decline jurisdiction but the court may still send the defendant to the Crown Court for sentence if the magistrates' courts powers of sentencing are not sufficient. The defendant meanwhile will benefit at the Crown Court from a greater reduction in his sentence to give credit for his pleading guilty at the earliest opportunity.

If an earlier court has declined summary jurisdiction a later court cannot hear representations and agree to summary trial: *R. v. Liverpool Justices, ex p. Crown Prosecution Service*, 90 Cr.App.R. 261, DC.

Special procedure for criminal damage charges

Magistrates' Courts Act 1980, s.22

Certain offences triable either way to be tried summarily if value involved is small
   22.—(1) If the offence charged by the information is one of those mentioned in the first col-   **7–58**

umn of Schedule 2 to this Act (in this section referred to as "scheduled offences") then, the court shall, before proceeding in accordance with section 19 above, consider whether, having regard to any representations made by the prosecutor or the accused, the value involved (as defined in subsection (10) below) appears to the court to exceed the relevant sum.

For the purposes of this section the relevant sum is £5,000.

(2) If, where subsection (1) above applies, it appears to the court clear that, for the offence charged, the value involved does not exceed the relevant sum, the court shall proceed as if the offence were triable only summarily, and sections 19 to 21 above shall not apply.

(3) If, where subsection (1) above applies, it appears to the court clear that, for the offence charged, the value involved exceeds the relevant sum, the court shall thereupon proceed in accordance with section 19 above in the ordinary way without further regard to the provisions of this section.

(4) If, where subsection (1) above applies, it appears to the court for any reason not clear whether, for the offence charged, the value involved does or does not exceed the relevant sum, the provisions of subsections (5) and (6) below shall apply.

(5) The court shall cause the charge to be written down, if this has not already been done, and read to the accused, and shall explain to him in ordinary language—

    (a) that he can, if he wishes, consent to be tried summarily for the offence and that if he consents to be so tried, he will definitely be tried in that way; and

    (b) that if he is tried summarily and is convicted by the court, his liability to imprisonment or a fine will be limited as provided in section 33 below.

(6) After explaining to the accused as provided by subsection (5) above the court shall ask him whether he consents to be tried summarily and—

    (a) if he so consents, shall proceed in accordance with subsection (2) above as if that subsection applied;

    (b) if he does not so consent, shall proceed in accordance with subsection (3) above as if that subsection applied.

(7) [repealed]

(8) Where a person is convicted by a magistrates' court of a scheduled offence, it shall not be open to him to appeal to the Crown Court against the conviction on the ground that the convicting court's decision as to the value involved was mistaken.

(9) If, where subsection (1) above applies, the offence charged is one with which the accused is charged jointly with a person who has not attained the age of 18, the reference in that subsection to any representations made by the accused shall be read as including any representations made by the person under 18.

(10) In this section "the value involved", in relation to any scheduled offence, means the value indicated in the second column of Schedule 2 to this Act, measured as indicated in the third column of that Schedule; and in that Schedule "the material time" means the time of the alleged offence.

(11) Where—

    (a) the accused is charged on the same occasion with two or more scheduled offences and it appears to the court that they constitute or form part of a series of two or more offences of the same or a similar character; or

    (b) the offence charged consists in incitement to commit two or more scheduled offences,

this section shall have effect as if any reference in it to the value involved were a reference to the aggregate of the values involved.

(12) Subsection (8) of section 12A of the *Theft Act* 1968 (which determines when a vehicle is recovered) shall apply for the purposes of paragraph 3 of Schedule 2 to this Act as it applies for the purposes of that section.

[This section is printed as amended by the *Criminal Justice Act* 1988, s.38 and Sched. 16, the *Criminal Justice Act* 1991, Sched. 8, the *Aggravated Vehicle-Taking Act* 1992, s.2, and the *Criminal Justice and Public Order Act* 1994, s.46 and Sched. 11.]

7–59 The offences listed in Schedule 2 are—

    1. Offences under section 1 of the *Criminal Damage Act* 1971 (destroying or damaging property), excluding any offence committed by destroying or damaging property by fire.

    2. ...aiding, abetting, counselling or procuring the commission of any such offence; attempting or inciting such offence

3. Offences under section 12A of the *Theft Act* 1968 (aggravated vehicle taking) where no allegation is made under subsection (1)(b) other than of damage, whether to the vehicle or other property or both.

The Schedule also states that the value involved is the value of the property destroyed or if it is damaged the value of the damage done. It also gives details as to how the value is to be measured according to how much the property would have cost to buy or repair on the open market at the relevant time when the destruction or damage was caused.

The provisions of the Schedule which relate to the offence of criminal damage under section 1 of the *Criminal Damage Act* 1971 are to be treated as only applying to offences under subsection (1) of that section and do not cover offences under subsections (2) and (3) of criminal damage with intent to endanger life, *etc.* or arson: *R. v. Burt*, 161 J.P. 77, CA. The offence of aggravated vehicle taking may become summary only when the vehicle is taken without consent and driven and between the time the vehicle was taken and before it was recovered, damage was caused. If injury was also caused then the offence remains triable either way.

This section reduces offences of criminal damage and aggravated vehicle taking **7–60** where the value of the damage caused is small to offences that can only be tried summarily. The seriousness of the offence is reflected by the fact that the defendant is thereby deprived of the right to elect trial at the Crown Court unless a series of small value offences has been committed and the aggregate value takes them over the monetary threshold. The relevant amount was fixed at £5,000 by an amendment to this section under section 46 of the *Criminal Justice and Public Order Act* 1994.

Section 33 of the *Magistrates' Courts Act* 1980 provides that the maximum penalty for an offence of criminal damage tried summarily is three months' imprisonment or a fine not exceeding level 4 (£2,500). The maximum sentence for aggravated vehicle taking on summary trial is six months' imprisonment or a fine on level 5 (£5,000): *Magistrates' Courts Act* 1980, s.32.

When the defendant has been charged with a "scheduled offence" he may lose the right to elect trial at the Crown Court even though the offence is initially classified as triable either way. The procedure in sections 17A–21 of the *Magistrates' Courts Act* 1980 must be preceded by consideration of the value of the damage in question.

Section 18(1) provides that the mode of trial procedure (including section 22) has ef- **7–61** fect after a not guilty indication in plea before venue but there is no reference in section 17A as to when and if section 22 comes into operation. The situation was resolved in a case where a defendant was charged with aggravated vehicle taking and the value of the damage caused was below £5,000. The court treated the offence as either way from the outset and plea before venue was dealt with under section 17A. The defendant indicated a guilty plea and the court committed him to the Crown Court for sentence. It was held that section 22 specifically provides that if the value of the damage is below £5,000, the offence should be dealt with summarily. This imposes an absolute obligation on the court and takes precedence over the plea before venue procedure. The offence was not triable either way and the court was held to have no power to commit for sentence: *R. v. Kelly* [2001] R.T.R. 5, CA. The procedure provided for in section 22 of the *Magistrates' Courts Act* 1980 is taken to prevail over that in section 17A.

Section 22(10) defines "the value involved" by reference to Schedule 2 of the 1980 Act. Where the property is beyond repair, the value of the damage is measured as the amount that the property would probably have cost to buy in the open market at the material time, which is the time of the alleged offence. Where the property is capable of repair then the value is the amount that it would cost to repair the damage or the amount to replace the property on the open market, whichever is the less.

Schedule 2 is directed solely to the actual value of the damage caused to the property itself and is not concerned with any consequential damage. Where the actual damage to a GM maize crop was £750 but the consequential damage to research was put at over £5,000 it was held that under Schedule 2 if the property was beyond repair, the value of the damage was the market value at the material time so it was limited to £750: *R. v. Colchester Magistrates' Court, ex p. Abbott*, 165 J.P. 386, DC.

7–62   A different approach was taken in another case involving damage to an experimental crop of genetically modified maize. The court heard representations that the maize was grown as a development measure with significant investment costs and to treat it as ordinary maize was artificial. The crop was grown for research rather than for sale and was not marketed so it was not easy to assess the value of damage caused. In the circumstances, the value of the crop was uncertain and could well exceed £5,000. It was held that the value was not clear and so the court was entitled to take the view that the charge remained triable either way and the defendants had the right to choose the mode of trial: *R. (DPP) v. Prestatyn Magistrates' Court* [2002] Crim.L.R. 924, DC.

The court must consider whether, when the defendant is charged with two or more of the scheduled offences this constitutes or forms part of a series of offences of the same or similar character in which case the aggregate of the values is relevant to deciding whether the charges are triable either way or not: subsection 11.

If the offences are committed at different places and involve different types of property they may be too remote to form a series: *R. v. Braden*, 152 J.P. 92, DC. The offences do not have to arise out of the same circumstances but they must be of the same or similar character.

7–63   It is not necessary for the court to hear evidence as to the value of the property in question unless they wish to do so. Representations as to the value could comprise submissions, assertions of fact and the production of documents: *R. v. Canterbury and St Augustine Justices, ex p. Klisiak* [1982] Q.B. 398, DC. Where the case involved 30 defendants all of whom had driven into a bean field to destroy a crop valued at £5,8000, the prosecution calculated the individual defendant as having caused £100 of the total damage. It was held that the prosecution did not have to charge as a joint enterprise and their approach to calculating the damage was justifiable even if it resulted in the charge becoming summary only: *R. v. Salisbury Magistrates, ex p. Mastin* (1987) 84 Cr.App.R. 248. In *R. v. Brentwood Justices, ex p. Nicholls, ante,* the House of Lords said *(obiter)* that it was apparent that the procedure in section 22(4)–(6) refers to accused persons individually and not to accused persons collectively.

Procedure where accused is absent, but is represented in court

Magistrates' Courts Act 1980, s.23

Power of court, with consent of legally represented accused, to proceed in his absence

7–64   **23.**—(1) Where—

   (a) the accused is represented by a legal representative who in his absence signifies to the court the accused's consent to the proceedings for determining how he is to be tried for the offence being conducted in his absence; and

   (b) the court is satisfied that there is good reason for proceeding in the absence of the accused,

the following provisions of this section shall apply.

(2) Subject to the following provisions of this section, the court may proceed in the absence of the accused in accordance with such of the provisions of sections 19 to 22 above as are applicable in the circumstances.

(3) If, in a case where subsection (1) of section 22 above applies, it appears to the court as mentioned in subsection (4) of that section, subsections (5) and (6) of that section shall not apply and the court—

   (a) if the accused's consent to be tried summarily has been or is signified by the person representing him, shall proceed in accordance with subsection (2) of that section as if that subsection applied; or

   (b) if that consent has not been and is not so signified, shall proceed in accordance with subsection (3) of that section as if that subsection applied.

(4) *If, where the court has considered as required by section 19(1) above, it appears to the court that the offence is more suitable for summary trial then* [If the court decides under section 19 above that the offence appears to it more suitable for trial on indictment then]—

   (a) if the accused's consent to be tried summarily has been or is signified by the person representing him, section 20 above shall not apply, and the court shall proceed to the summary trial of the information; or

(b) if that consent has not been and is not so signified, section 20 above shall not apply and the court shall proceed *to inquire into the information as examining justices and may adjourn the hearing without remanding the accused* [in relation to the offence in accordance with section 51(1) of the *Crime and Disorder Act* 1998].

(5) *If, where the court has considered as required by section 19(1) above, it appears to the court that the offence is more suitable for trial on indictment, section 21 above shall not apply, and the court shall proceed to inquire into the information as examining justices and may adjourn the hearing without remanding the accused.*

[(5) If the court decides under section 19 above that the offence appears to it more suitable for trial on indictment, section 21 above shall not apply and the court shall proceed in relation to the offence in accordance with section 51(1) of the *Crime and Disorder Act* 1998.]

[This section is printed as amended by the *Courts and Legal Services Act* 1990, Sched. 18. As from a day or days to be appointed, the words in italics will be substituted by those set out in square brackets: *Criminal Justice Act* 2003, Sched. 3.]

Mode of trial can be dealt with in the absence of the defendant if he is represented **7–65** and his representative signifies the defendant's consent for the procedure of this section to be adopted.

Magistrates' Courts Act 1980, s.24

This section deals with mode of trial decisions for persons under the age of 18. For **7–66** the full text of this section, see *post*, Part V. The adult court only has jurisdiction in relation to mode of trial for young people under the age of 18 when they appear as co-defendants jointly charged with an adult: section 24(1)(b). The youth may be committed to the Crown Court when the court considers that it is in the interests of justice that all co-defendants be committed for trial. The court may also commit the youth for trial on any other indictable offence with which he is charged at the same time even though they are not joint charges with the adult: section 24(2).

Reverting and re-electing

Magistrates' Courts Act 1980, s.25

Power to change from summary trial to committal proceedings, and vice versa

25.—(1) Subsections (2) to (4) [(2D)] below shall have effect where a person who has attained **7–67** the age of 18 years appears or is brought before a magistrates' court on an information charging him with an offence triable either way.

(2) *Where the court has (otherwise than in pursuance of section 22(2) above) begun to try the information summarily, the court may, at any time before the conclusion of the evidence for the prosecution, discontinue the summary trial and proceed to inquire into the information as examining justices and, on doing so, shall adjourn the hearing.*

[(2) Where the court is required under section 20(9) above to proceed to the summary trial of the information, the prosecution may apply to the court for the offence to be tried on indictment instead.

(2A) An application under subsection (2) above—

(a) must be made before the summary trial begins; and

(b) must be dealt with by the court before any other application or issue in relation to the summary trial is dealt with.

(2B) The court may grant an application under subsection (2) above but only if it is satisfied that the sentence which a magistrates' court would have power to impose for the offence would be inadequate.

(2C) Where—

(a) the accused is charged on the same occasion with two or more offences; and

(b) it appears to the court that they constitute or form part of a series of two or more offences of the same or a similar character, subsection (2B) above shall have effect as if references to the sentence which a magistrates' court would have power to impose for the offence were a reference to the maximum aggregate sentence which a magistrates' court would have power to impose for all of the offences taken together.

(2D) Where the court grants an application under subsection (2) above, it shall proceed in relation to the offence in accordance with section 51(1) of the *Crime and Disorder Act* 1998.]

(3) *Where the court has begun to inquire into the information as examining justices, then, if at any time during the inquiry it appears to the court, having regard to any representations made in the presence of the accused by the prosecutor, or made by the accused, and to the nature of the case, that the offence is after all more suitable for summary trial, the court may, after doing as provided in subsection (4) below, ask the accused whether he consents to be tried summarily and, if he so consents, may subject to subsection (3A) below proceed to try the information summarily;*

(3A) *Where the prosecution is being carried on by the Attorney General or the Solicitor General, the court shall not exercise the power conferred by subsection (3) above without his consent and, where the prosecution is being carried on by the Director of Public Prosecutions, shall not exercise that power if the Attorney General directs that it should not be exercised.*

(4) *Before asking the accused under subsection (3) above whether he consents to be tried summarily, the court shall in ordinary language—*

    (a) *explain to him that it appears to the court more suitable for him to be tried summarily for the offence, but that this can only be done if he consents to be so tried; and*

    (b) *unless it has already done so, explain to him, as provided in section 20(2)(b) above, about the court's power to commit to the Crown Court for sentence.*

(5) *Where a person under the age of 18 years appears or is brought before a magistrates' court on an information charging him with an indictable offence other than homicide, and the court—*

    (a) *has begun to try the information summarily on the footing that the case does not fall within paragraph (a) or (b) of section 24(1) above and must therefore be tried summarily, as required by the said section 24(1); or*

    (b) *has begun to inquire into the case as examining justices on the footing that the case does so fall,*

subsection (6) or (7) below, as the case may be, shall have effect.

(6) *If, in a case falling within subsection (5)(a) above, it appears to the court at any time before the conclusion of the evidence for the prosecution that the case is after all one which under the said section 24(1) ought not to be tried summarily, the court may discontinue the summary trial and proceed to inquire into the information as examining justices and, on doing so, shall adjourn the hearing.*

(7) *If, in a case falling within subsection (5)(b) above, it appears to the court at any time during the inquiry that the case is after all one which under the said section 24(1) ought to be tried summarily, the court may proceed to try the information summarily.*

(8) *If the court adjourns the hearing under subsection (2) or (6) above it may (if it thinks fit) do so without remanding the accused.*

[This section is printed as amended by the *Prosecution of Offences Act* 1985, Scheds 1 and 2, the *Criminal Justice Act* 1991, Sched. 8, the *Criminal Procedure and Investigations Act* 1996, Sched. 1, and the *Criminal Justice Act* 2003, s.42. As from a day or days to be appointed, the *Criminal Justice Act* 2003, Sched. 3, will substitute for the italicised text, the text in square brackets.]

7–68   After the court has begun a summary trial or a committal it may change the procedure and switch from hearing a summary trial to inquiring into the offence as examining magistrates or it may discontinue a committal and with the defendant's consent, proceed to hear a summary trial of the charge. The decision will be made subject to the evidence that has been called, representations made and the nature of the case. These factors may mean that a less serious case becomes more serious or a case first believed to be serious enough to warrant committal is shown to be less serious. The intention is that the court should keep the mode of trial under continuous review

The power to change the proceedings can only be exercised when the court has begun the trial or committal. When exactly this happens has been the subject of several appeals and attempts to clarify the crucial moment.

The trial must actually have started and the court must have heard some evidence during the summary trial before changing to a committal: *R. v. Southend Justices, ex p. Wood*, 152 J.P. 97, DC. The fact that further indictable matters had been brought against the defendant and the court wished to commit on all charges did not affect the requirement to start to hear the evidence on the summary trial before changing to committal: *R. v. St Helen's Magistrates, ex p. Critchley*, 152 J.P. 102, DC. Neither did the fact that it was evident that jurisdiction should not have been accepted on a serious charge. Where the court indicated that summary trial was suitable for an offence of possessing cannabis with intent to supply and a later bench indicated that it would use the powers of section 25 to ensure that the case went to the Crown Court, the summary trial was held not to have begun when the court took a deposition from one prosecution witness and did not allow any cross examination. The summary trial had not begun and section 25 did not apply: *R. v. Birmingham Stipendiary Magistrate, ex p. Webb*, 95 Cr.App.R. 75, DC.

As to when the case has concluded after trial, it was held that when magistrates dis- **7–69** agree on a verdict and adjourn for a rehearing, the prosecution case had not been concluded: *R. v. Coventry Justices, ex p. Wilson* [1981] Crim.L.R. 787, DC.

The words "try" and "trial" are to be construed narrowly to mean the process of determining guilt or innocence. Although simply entering a not guilty plea does not start a trial, there may be circumstances where the trial process begins after the plea but before any evidence is called. Where the court had accepted jurisdiction in the case of a defendant who was later recommended for committal to the Crown Court for the purposes of a restriction order under the *Mental Health Act* 1983, it was held that the summary trial had started. Although no evidence had been called, the court had heard preliminary submissions regarding the trial process and issues of mental capability. The procedure under section 25 could be adopted and the case was properly committed to the Crown Court: *R. v. Horseferry Road Magistrates' Court, ex p. K* [1997] Q.B. 23, DC.

Section 25 does not apply to summary cases where a plea of guilty has been accepted. No trial then takes place. A defendant consented to summary trial and pleaded guilty to an offence of causing actual bodily harm. His co-defendant elected trial by jury. The court at the next hearing purported to discontinue the trial against the defendant and committed him for trial with his co-defendant. It was held that the power under section 25 was only exercisable during a trial when evidence was tendered to prove guilt. It did not apply after a guilty plea. The defendant could only have been committed to the Crown Court for sentence: *R. v. Dudley Justices, ex p. Gillard* [1986] A.C. 442, HL. This principle remains the same even where the basis of the guilty plea is disputed. It was held inappropriate for a court to direct a not guilty plea be entered and to decline jurisdiction to effect a committal to the Crown Court where the proper course would have been to conduct a Newton hearing and if need be commit for sentence: *R. v. Telford Magistrates' Court, ex p. Darlington*, 87 Cr.App.R. 194, DC.

Whilst the magistrates' court has a discretion to discontinue a summary trial and then **7–70** commit the defendant to trial in the Crown Court, it is unreasonable to use that procedure to circumvent the principle of individual right of election as expressed in the Brentwood Justices case (*ante*). Three defendants had been jointly charged with theft. Two of the defendants elected jury trial and the third defendant, who had been absent when the co-defendants elected trial, later consented to summary trial. After calling some evidence the prosecution asked the court to discontinue the summary trial pursuant to section 25(2) of the *Magistrates' Courts Act* 1980 and to commit the defendant to the Crown Court for trial with his co-defendants. This was held to be an inappropriate use of section 25: *R. v. West Norfolk Justices, ex p. McMullen*, 157 J.P. 461, DC; and see *R. v. Bradford Magistrates' Court, ex p. Grant*, 163 J.P. 717, DC.

In *R. (K.) v. Leeds Youth Court*, 165 J.P. 694, DC, it was held that the power under section 25(6) could be exercised where there had been a change of circumstances, which would include not only the emergence of new material in the course of the evidence, but also cases where, as the evidence unfolded, the manner in which it was presented by the witness or witnesses was, of itself, of a nature which justified the conclusion that the original decision as to mode of trial was no longer appropriate. In *R. (R.) v. Manchester City Youth Court*, 170 J.P. 217, QBD (Ouseley J.), it was held that the powers under subsections (5) and (7) could be exercised at any time once an inquiry had begun; they were not fettered by a previous decision of a different bench which a subsequent examination showed to be wrong.

III. SENDING CASES TO THE CROWN COURT

General

7–71   Indictable only offences cannot be dealt with at the magistrates' court. Such offences are sent to the Crown Court for trial under section 51 of the *Crime and Disorder Act* 1998. As from a day to be appointed, the *Criminal Justice Act* 2003, s.41 and Sched. 3, extends the regime of sending cases to the Crown Court under section 51 of the 1998 Act (by substituting new sections 51 to 51E) so that either way offences which might otherwise have been transferred or committed to the Crown Court will be sent to the Crown Court. The new regime has been brought into force to the very limited extent that a magistrates' court must send a child who has been charged with a "specified offence" (within the meaning of section 224 of the *Criminal Justice Act* 2003) to the Crown Court for trial if it appears that the criteria for imposing a sentence of detention for public protection or an extended sentence of detention would be met: see s.51A. The original text of section 51 (which remains in force until the new regime is brought into force) is set out, *post*, in italicised text; and the new provisions (including section 51A) are set out in the text which follows it.

Legislation

Crime and Disorder Act 1998, s.51

No committal proceedings for indictable-only offence

7–72   **51.**—(1) *Where an adult appears or is brought before a magistrates' court ("the court") charged with an offence triable only on indictment ("the indictable-only offence"), the court shall send him forthwith to the Crown Court for trial—*

        (a) *for that offence, and*

        (b) *for any either-way or summary offence with which he is charged which fulfils the requisite conditions (as set out in subsection (11) below).*

    (2) *Where an adult who has been sent for trial under subsection (1) above subsequently appears or is brought before a magistrates' court charged with an either-way or summary offence which fulfils the requisite conditions, the court may send him forthwith to the Crown Court for trial for the either-way or summary offence.*

    (3) *Where—*

        (a) *the court sends an adult for trial under subsection (1) above;*

        (b) *another adult appears or is brought before the court on the same or a subsequent occasion charged jointly with him with an either-way offence; and*

        (c) *that offence appears to the court to be related to the indictable-only offence,*

the court shall where it is the same occasion, and may where it is a subsequent occasion, send the other adult forthwith to the Crown Court for trial for the either-way offence.

    (4) *Where a court sends an adult for trial under subsection (3) above, it shall at the same time send him to the Crown Court for trial for any either-way or summary offence with which he is charged which fulfils the requisite conditions.*

    (5) *Where—*

        (a) *the court sends an adult for trial under subsection (1) or (3) above; and*

        (b) *a child or young person appears or is brought before the court on the same or a*

subsequent occasion charged jointly with the adult with an indictable offence for which the adult is sent for trial,
the court shall, if it considers it necessary in the interests of justice to do so, send the child or young person forthwith to the Crown Court for trial for the indictable offence.

(6) Where a court sends a child or young person for trial under subsection (5) above, it may at the same time send him to the Crown Court for trial for any either-way or summary offence with which he is charged which fulfils the requisite conditions.

(7) The court shall specify in a notice the offence or offences for which a person is sent for trial under this section and the place at which he is to be tried; and a copy of the notice shall be served on the accused and given to the Crown Court sitting at that place.

(8) In a case where there is more than one indictable-only offence and the court includes an either-way or a summary offence in the notice under subsection (7) above, the court shall specify in that notice the indictable-only offence to which the either-way offence or, as the case may be, the summary offence appears to the court to be related.

(9) The trial of the information charging any summary offence for which a person is sent for trial under this section shall be treated as if the court had adjourned it under section 10 of the 1980 Act and had not fixed the time and place for its resumption.

(10) In selecting the place of trial for the purpose of subsection (7) above, the court shall have regard to—

(a) the convenience of the defence, the prosecution and the witnesses;

(b) the desirability of expediting the trial; and

(c) any direction given by or on behalf of the Lord Chief Justice with the concurrence of the Lord Chancellor under section 75(1) of the Supreme Court Act 1981.

(11) An offence fulfils the requisite conditions if—

(a) if appears to the court to be related to the indictable-only offence; and

(b) in the case of a summary offence, it is punishable with imprisonment or involves obligatory or discretionary disqualification from driving.

(12) For the purposes of this section—

(a) "adult" means a person aged 18 or over, and references to an adult include references to a corporation;

(b) "either-way offence" means an offence which, if committed by an adult, is triable either on indictment or summarily;

(c) an either-way offence is related to an indictable-only offence if the charge for the either-way offence could be joined in the same indictment as the charge for the indictable-only offence;

(d) a summary offence is related to an indictable-only offence if it arises out of circumstances which are the same as or connected with those giving rise to the indictable-only offence.

[The Criminal Justice Act 2003, Sched. 3, substitutes new sections 51 to 51E (post) in place of this section. The substitution of new section 51A (except subs. (3)(a) to (c)) was effected as from April 4, 2005, by the Criminal Justice Act 2003 (Commencement No. 8 and Transitional and Saving Provisions Order 2005 (S.I. 2005 No. 950), as was the substitution of new sections 51D and 51E (but only insofar as they apply to cases sent under s.51A(3)(d)). In all other respects, the remaining sections and subsections are to be substituted as from a day or days to be appointed.]

Sending cases to the Crown Court: adults

[**51.**—(1) Where an adult appears or is brought before a magistrates' court ("the court") **7–73**
charged with an offence and any of the conditions mentioned in subsection (2) below is satisfied, the court shall send him forthwith to the Crown Court for trial for the offence.

(2) Those conditions are—

(a) that the offence is an offence triable only on indictment other than one in respect of which notice has been given under section 51B or 51C below;

(b) that the offence is an either-way offence and the court is required under section 20(9)(b), 21, 23(4)(b) or (5) or 25(2D) of the Magistrates' Courts Act 1980 to proceed in relation to the offence in accordance with subsection (1) above;

(c) that notice is given to the court under section 51B or 51C below in respect of the offence.

(3) Where the court sends an adult for trial under subsection (1) above, it shall at the same time send him to the Crown Court for trial for any either-way or summary offence with which he is charged and which—

    (a) (if it is an either-way offence) appears to the court to be related to the offence mentioned in subsection (1) above; or

    (b) (if it is a summary offence) appears to the court to be related to the offence mentioned in subsection (1) above or to the either-way offence, and which fulfils the requisite condition (as defined in subsection (11) below).

(4) Where an adult who has been sent for trial under subsection (1) above subsequently appears or is brought before a magistrates' court charged with an either-way or summary offence which—

    (a) appears to the court to be related to the offence mentioned in subsection (1) above; and

    (b) (in the case of a summary offence) fulfils the requisite condition,

the court may send him forthwith to the Crown Court for trial for the either-way or summary offence.

(5) Where—

    (a) the court sends an adult ("A") for trial under subsection (1) or (3) above;

    (b) another adult appears or is brought before the court on the same or a subsequent occasion charged jointly with A with an either-way offence; and

    (c) that offence appears to the court to be related to an offence for which A was sent for trial under subsection (1) or (3) above,

the court shall where it is the same occasion, and may where it is a subsequent occasion, send the other adult forthwith to the Crown Court for trial for the either-way offence.

(6) Where the court sends an adult for trial under subsection (5) above, it shall at the same time send him to the Crown Court for trial for any either-way or summary offence with which he is charged and which—

    (a) (if it is an either-way offence) appears to the court to be related to the offence for which he is sent for trial; and

    (b) (if it is a summary offence) appears to the court to be related to the offence for which he is sent for trial or to the either-way offence, and which fulfils the requisite condition.

(7) Where—

    (a) the court sends an adult ("A") for trial under subsection (1), (3) or (5) above; and

    (b) a child or young person appears or is brought before the court on the same or a subsequent occasion charged jointly with A with an indictable offence for which A is sent for trial under subsection (1), (3) or (5) above, or an indictable offence which appears to the court to be related to that offence,

the court shall, if it considers it necessary in the interests of justice to do so, send the child or young person forthwith to the Crown Court for trial for the indictable offence.

(8) Where the court sends a child or young person for trial under subsection (7) above, it may at the same time send him to the Crown Court for trial for any indictable or summary offence with which he is charged and which—

    (a) (if it is an indictable offence) appears to the court to be related to the offence for which he is sent for trial; and

    (b) (if it is a summary offence) appears to the court to be related to the offence for which he is sent for trial or to the indictable offence, and which fulfils the requisite condition.

(9) Subsections (7) and (8) above are subject to sections 24A and 24B of the *Magistrates' Courts Act* 1980 (which provide for certain cases involving children and young persons to be tried summarily).

(10) The trial of the information charging any summary offence for which a person is sent for trial under this section shall be treated as if the court had adjourned it under section 10 of the 1980 Act and had not fixed the time and place for its resumption.

(11) A summary offence fulfils the requisite condition if it is punishable with imprisonment or involves obligatory or discretionary disqualification from driving.

(12) In the case of an adult charged with an offence—

    (a) if the offence satisfies paragraph (c) of subsection (2) above, the offence shall be dealt with under subsection (1) above and not under any other provision of this section or section 51A below;

(b) subject to paragraph (a) above, if the offence is one in respect of which the court is required to, or would decide to, send the adult to the Crown Court under—
  (i) subsection (5) above; or
  (ii) subsection (6) of section 51A below,
the offence shall be dealt with under that subsection and not under any other provision of this section or section 51A below.

(13) The functions of a magistrates' court under this section, and its related functions under section 51D below, may be discharged by a single justice.]

[As noted, *ante*, this section is to be substituted as from a day to be appointed.]

Sending cases to the Crown Court: children and young persons

51A.—(1) This section is subject to sections 24A and 24B of the *Magistrates' Courts Act* **7–74** 1980 (which provide for certain offences involving children or young persons to be tried summarily).

(2) Where a child or young person appears or is brought before a magistrates' court ("the court") charged with an offence and any of the conditions mentioned in subsection (3) below is satisfied, the court shall send him forthwith to the Crown Court for trial for the offence.

(3) Those conditions are—
  [(a) that the offence falls within subsection (12) below;
  (b) that the offence is such as is mentioned in subsection (1) of section 91 of the *Powers of Criminal Courts (Sentencing) Act* 2000 (other than one mentioned in paragraph (d) below in relation to which it appears to the court as mentioned there) and the court considers that if he is found guilty of the offence it ought to be possible to sentence him in pursuance of subsection (3) of that section;
  (c) that notice is given to the court under section 51B or 51C below in respect of the offence;]
  (d) that the offence is a specified offence (within the meaning of section 224 of the *Criminal Justice Act* 2003) and it appears to the court that if he is found guilty of the offence the criteria for the imposition of a sentence under section 226(3) or 228(2) of that Act would be met.

(4) Where the court sends a child or young person for trial under subsection (2) above, it may at the same time send him to the Crown Court for trial for any indictable or summary offence with which he is charged and which—
  (a) (if it is an indictable offence) appears to the court to be related to the offence mentioned in subsection (2) above; or
  (b) (if it is a summary offence) appears to the court to be related to the offence mentioned in subsection (2) above or to the indictable offence, and which fulfils the requisite condition (as defined in subsection (9) below).

(5) Where a child or young person who has been sent for trial under subsection (2) above subsequently appears or is brought before a magistrates' court charged with an indictable or summary offence which—
  (a) appears to the court to be related to the offence mentioned in subsection (2) above; and
  (b) (in the case of a summary offence) fulfils the requisite condition,
the court may send him forthwith to the Crown Court for trial for the indictable or summary offence.

(6) Where—
  (a) the court sends a child or young person ("C") for trial under subsection (2) or (4) above; and
  (b) an adult appears or is brought before the court on the same or a subsequent occasion charged jointly with C with an either-way offence for which C is sent for trial under subsection (2) or (4) above, or an either-way offence which appears to the court to be related to that offence,
the court shall where it is the same occasion, and may where it is a subsequent occasion, send the adult forthwith to the Crown Court for trial for the either-way offence.

(7) Where the court sends an adult for trial under subsection (6) above, it shall at the same time send him to the Crown Court for trial for any either-way or summary offence with which he is charged and which—

    (a) (if it is an either-way offence) appears to the court to be related to the offence for which he was sent for trial; and

    (b) (if it is a summary offence) appears to the court to be related to the offence for which he was sent for trial or to the either-way offence, and which fulfils the requisite condition.

    (8) The trial of the information charging any summary offence for which a person is sent for trial under this section shall be treated as if the court had adjourned it under section 10 of the 1980 Act and had not fixed the time and place for its resumption.

    (9) A summary offence fulfils the requisite condition if it is punishable with imprisonment or involves obligatory or discretionary disqualification from driving.

    (10) In the case of a child or young person charged with an offence—

    (a) if the offence satisfies any of the conditions in subsection (3) above, the offence shall be dealt with under subsection (2) above and not under any other provision of this section or section 51 above;

    (b) subject to paragraph (a) above, if the offence is one in respect of which the requirements of subsection (7) of section 51 above for sending the child or young person to the Crown Court are satisfied, the offence shall be dealt with under that subsection and not under any other provision of this section or section 51 above.

    (11) The functions of a magistrates' court under this section, and its related functions under section 51D below, may be discharged by a single justice.

    (12) An offence falls within this subsection if—

    (a) it is an offence of homicide;

    (b) each of the requirements of section 51A(1) of the *Firearms Act* 1968 would be satisfied with respect to—

      (i) the offence; and

      (ii) the person charged with it,

    if he were convicted of the offence; or

    (c) section 29(3) of the *Violent Crime Reduction Act* 2006 (minimum sentences in certain cases of using someone to mind a weapon) would apply if he were convicted of the offence.

[This section is printed as amended by the *Violent Crime Reduction Act* 2006, Sched. 1. As noted *ante*, this section (other than the text set out in square brackets in subsection (3)) was brought into force as from April 4, 2005. The text set out in square brackets in subsection (3) is to be brought into force as from a day to be appointed.]

Notices in serious or complex fraud cases

7–75   **[51B.**—(1) A notice may be given by a designated authority under this section in respect of an indictable offence if the authority is of the opinion that the evidence of the offence charged—

    (a) is sufficient for the person charged to be put on trial for the offence; and

    (b) reveals a case of fraud of such seriousness or complexity that it is appropriate that the management of the case should without delay be taken over by the Crown Court.

    (2) That opinion must be certified by the designated authority in the notice.

    (3) The notice must also specify the proposed place of trial, and in selecting that place the designated authority must have regard to the same matters as are specified in paragraphs (a) to (c) of section 51D(4) below.

    (4) A notice under this section must be given to the magistrates' court at which the person charged appears or before which he is brought.

    (5) Such a notice must be given to the magistrates' court before any summary trial begins.

    (6) The effect of such a notice is that the functions of the magistrates' court cease in relation to the case, except—

    (a) for the purposes of section 51D below;

    (b) as provided by paragraph 2 of Schedule 3 to the *Access to Justice Act* 1999; and

    (c) as provided by section 52 below.

    (7) The functions of a designated authority under this section may be exercised by an officer of the authority acting on behalf of the authority.

(8) A decision to give a notice under this section shall not be subject to appeal or liable to be questioned in any court (whether a magistrates' court or not).

(9) In this section "designated authority" means—

    (a) the Director of Public Prosecutions;

    (b) the Director of the Serious Fraud Office;

    (c) the Commissioners for Her Majesty's Revenue and Customs;

    (d) …; or

    (e) the Secretary of State.]

[This section is printed as amended by the *Commissioners for Revenue and Customs Act* 2005, s.50. As noted above at § 7–72 under the italicised text of the original section 51, this section is to be substituted as from a day to be appointed.]

Notices in certain cases involving children

7–76

[**51C.**—(1) A notice may be given by the Director of Public Prosecutions under this section in respect of an offence falling within subsection (3) below if he is of the opinion—

    (a) that the evidence of the offence would be sufficient for the person charged to be put on trial for the offence;

    (b) that a child would be called as a witness at the trial; and

    (c) that, for the purpose of avoiding any prejudice to the welfare of the child, the case should be taken over and proceeded with without delay by the Crown Court.

(2) That opinion must be certified by the Director of Public Prosecutions in the notice.

(3) This subsection applies to an offence—

    (a) which involves an assault on, or injury or a threat of injury to, a person;

    (b) under section 1 of the *Children and Young Persons Act* 1933 (cruelty to persons under 16);

    (c) under the *Sexual Offences Act* 1956, the *Protection of Children Act* 1978 or the *Sexual Offences Act* 2003;

    (d) of kidnapping or false imprisonment, or an offence under section 1 or 2 of the *Child Abduction Act* 1984;

    (e) which consists of attempting or conspiring to commit, or of aiding, abetting, counselling, procuring or inciting the commission of, an offence falling within paragraph (a), (b), (c) or (d) above.

(4) Subsections (4), (5) and (6) of section 51B above apply for the purposes of this section as they apply for the purposes of that.

(5) The functions of the Director of Public Prosecutions under this section may be exercised by an officer acting on behalf of the Director.

(6) A decision to give a notice under this section shall not be subject to appeal or liable to be questioned in any court (whether a magistrates' court or not).

(7) In this section "child" means—

    (a) a person who is under the age of 17; or

    (b) any person of whom a video recording (as defined in section 63(1) of the *Youth Justice and Criminal Evidence Act* 1999) was made when he was under the age of 17 with a view to its admission as his evidence in chief in the trial referred to in subsection (1) above.]

[As noted, *ante*, this section is to be substituted as from a day to be appointed.]

Notice of offence and place of trial

7–77

51D.—(1) The court shall specify in a notice—

    (a) the offence or offences for which a person is sent for trial under section 51 or 51A above; and

    (b) the place at which he is to be tried (which, if a notice has been given under section 51B above, must be the place specified in that notice).

(2) A copy of the notice shall be served on the accused and given to the Crown Court sitting at that place.

(3) In a case where a person is sent for trial under section 51 or 51A above for more than one offence, the court shall specify in that notice, for each offence—

    (a) the subsection under which the person is so sent; and

    (b) if applicable, the offence to which that offence appears to the court to be related.

    (4) Where the court selects the place of trial for the purposes of subsection (1) above, it shall have regard to—

    (a) the convenience of the defence, the prosecution and the witnesses;

    (b) the desirability of expediting the trial; and

    (c) any direction given by or on behalf of the Lord Chief Justice with the concurrence of the Lord Chancellor under section 75(1) of the *Supreme Court Act* 1981.

[As noted, *ante*, this section is in force only to the extent that it applies where a case is sent under section 51A(3)(d). For all other purposes, it is to be brought into force as from a day or days to be appointed. Further, the words "Supreme Court" in subsection (4)(c) are to be replaced by the words "Senior Courts" as from a day to be appointed: *Constitutional Reform Act* 2005, Sched. 11.]

Interpretation of sections 50A to 51D

7–78   **51E.** For the purposes of sections 50A to 51D above—

    (a) "adult" means a person aged 18 or over, and references to an adult include a corporation;

    (b) "either-way offence" means an offence triable either way;

    (c) an either-way offence is related to an indictable offence if the charge for the either-way offence could be joined in the same indictment as the charge for the indictable offence;

    (d) a summary offence is related to an indictable offence if it arises out of circumstances which are the same as or connected with those giving rise to the indictable offence."

[As noted, *ante*, this section is in force only to the extent that it applies where a case is sent under section 51A(3)(d). For all other purposes, it is to be brought into force as from a day or days to be appointed.]

7–79   The word "charged" does not just mean offences charged at the police station or by the laying of an information but includes charges preferred at or after the first court appearance: *R. (Salubi) v. Bow Street Magistrates' Court* [2002] 2 Cr.App.R. 40, DC. Also in this case consideration was given to the question of whether the magistrates' court should deal with an abuse of process argument in section 51 proceedings. It was held that there may be rare cases where the magistrates could decide that a case was brought in bad faith or there was serious misconduct by the prosecution or police which warranted a stay of proceedings at this stage but that usually novel or complex points should be left to the Crown Court or High Court.

    Summary trial of an offence that is triable on indictment only is a nullity. The case must be dealt with at the Crown Court: *R. v. West* [1964] 1 Q.B. 15, CA.

VI. TRANSFER OF CASES TO THE CROWN COURT

7–80   Cases of serious fraud or offences involving children may be transferred to the Crown Court to prevent unnecessary delay.

(1) Transfer of serious fraud cases

Criminal Justice Act 1987, ss.4–5

Notices of transfer and designated authorities

7–81   **4.**—(1) *If—*

    (a) *a person has been charged with an indictable offence; and*

    (b) *in the opinion of an authority designated by subsection (2) below or of one of such an authority's officers acting on the authority's behalf the evidence of the offence charged—*

        (i) *would be sufficient for the person charged to be committed for trial; and*

      (ii) *reveals a case of fraud of such seriousness or complexity that it is appropri-
ate that the management of the case should without delay be taken over by
the Crown Court; and*

   (c) *before the magistrates' court in whose jurisdiction the offence has been charged
begins to inquire into the case as examining justices the authority or one of the
authority's officers acting on the authority's behalf gives the court a notice (in this
Act referred to as a "notice of transfer") certifying that opinion.*

*the functions of the magistrates' court shall cease in relation to the case, except as provided
by section 5(3), (7A) and (8) below and by paragraph 2 of Schedule 3 to the* Access to Justice
Act *1999.*

   (2) *The authorities mentioned in subsection (1) above (in this Act referred to as
"designated authorities") are—*

      (a) *the Director of Public Prosecutions;*

      (b) *the Director of the Serious Fraud Office;*

      (c) *the Commissioners of Revenue and Customs;*

      (d) *…; and*

      (e) *the Secretary of State.*

   (3) *A designated authority's decision to give notice of transfer shall not be subject to appeal or liable to be questioned in any court.*

   (4) *This section and sections 5 and 6 below shall not apply in any case in which section
51 of the* Crime and Disorder Act *1998 (no committal proceedings for indictable-only offences) applies.*

[This section is printed as amended by the *Criminal Justice Act* 1988, s.114, the
Legal Aid Act 1988, Sched. 5, the *Criminal Justice and Public Order Act* 1994,
Sched. 9, the *Crime and Disorder Act* 1998, Sched. 8, the *Access to Justice Act* 1999,
Sched. 4, and the *Commissioners for Revenue and Customs Act* 2005, s.50. As from a
day to be appointed, the whole section is to be repealed by the *Criminal Justice Act*
2003, Sched. 3, and replaced by the new scheme of sending for trial under sections 51
to 51E of the *Crime and Disorder Act* 1998 (*ante*, §§ 7–73 *et seq.*).]

Notices of transfer—procedure

   5.—(1) *A notice of transfer shall specify the proposed place of trial and in selecting that* **7–82**
*place the designated authority shall have regard to the considerations to which section 7 of
the* Magistrates' Courts Act *1980 requires a magistrates' court committing a person for trial to
have regard when selecting the place at which he is to be tried.*

   (2) *A notice of transfer shall specify the charge or charges to which it relates and include
or be accompanied by such additional matter as regulations under subsection (9) below may
require.*

   (3) *If a magistrates' court has remanded a person to whom a notice of transfer relates in
custody, it shall have power, subject to section 4 of the* Bail Act *1976 and regulations under
section 22 of the* Prosecution of Offences Act *1985—*

      (a) *to order that he shall be safely kept in custody until delivered in due course of law;
or*

      (b) *to release him on bail in accordance with the* Bail Act *1976, that is to say, by direct-
ing him to appear before the Crown Court for trial;*

*and where his release on bail is conditional on his providing one or more surety or sureties
and, in accordance with section 8(3) of the* Bail Act *1976, the court fixes the amount in
which the surety is to be bound with a view to his entering into his recognizance subsequently
in accordance with subsections (4) and (5) or (6) of that section, the court shall in the
meantime make an order such as is mentioned in paragraph (a) of this subsection.*

   (4) *If the conditions specified in subsection (5) below are satisfied, a court may exercise the
powers conferred by subsection (3) above in relation to a person charged without his being
brought before it in any case in which by virtue of section 128(3A) of the* Magistrates' Courts
Act *1980 it would have power further to remand him on an adjournment such as is
mentioned in that subsection.*

   (5) *The conditions mentioned in subsection (4) above are—*

      (a) *that the person in question has given his written consent to the powers conferred by
subsection (3) above being exercised without his being brought before the court;
and*

(b) *that the court is satisfied that, when he gave his consent, he knew that the notice of transfer had been issued.*

(6) *Where notice of transfer is given after a person to whom it relates has been remanded on bail to appear before a magistrates' court on an appointed day, the requirement that he shall so appear shall cease on the giving of the notice, unless the notice states that it is to continue.*

(7) *Where the requirement that a person to whom the notice of transfer relates shall appear before a magistrates' court ceases by virtue of subsection (6) above, it shall be his duty to appear before the Crown Court at the place specified by the notice of transfer as the proposed place of trial or at any place substituted for it by a direction under section 76 of the* Supreme Court Act *1981.*

(7A) *If the notice states that the requirement is to continue, when a person to whom the notice relates appears before the magistrates' court, the court shall have—*

(a) *the powers and duty conferred on a magistrates' court by subsection (3) above, but subject as there provided; and*

(b) *power to enlarge, in the surety's absence, a recognizance conditioned in accordance with section 128(4)(a) of the* Magistrates' Courts Act *1980 so that the surety is bound to secure that the person charged appears also before the Crown Court.*

(8) *For the purposes of the* Criminal Procedure (Attendance of Witnesses) Act *1965—*

(a) *any magistrates' court for the petty sessions area for which the court from which a case was transferred sits shall be treated as examining magistrates; and*

(b) *a person indicated in the notice of transfer as a proposed witness; shall be treated as a person who has been examined by the court.*

(9) *The Attorney General—*

(a) *shall by regulations make provision requiring the giving of a copy of a notice of transfer, together with copies of the documents containing the evidence (including oral evidence) on which any charge to which it relates is based—*

(i) *to any person to whom the notice of transfer relates; and*

(ii) *to the Crown Court sitting at the place specified by the notice of transfer as the proposed place of trial; and*

(b) *may by regulations make such further provision in relation to notices of transfer, including provision as to the duties of a designated authority in relation to such notices, as appears to him to be appropriate.*

(9A) *Regulations under subsection (9)(a) above may provide that there shall be no requirement for copies of documents to accompany the copy of the notice of transfer if they are referred to, in documents sent with the notice of transfer, as having already been supplied.*

(10) *The power to make regulations conferred by subsection (9) above shall be exercisable by statutory instrument subject to annulment in pursuance of a resolution of either House of Parliament.*

(11) *Any such regulations may make different provision with respect to different cases or classes of case.*

[This section is printed as amended by the *Criminal Justice Act* 1988, s.144, and the *Criminal Procedure and Investigations Act* 1996, s.45. As from a day to be appointed, the words "Supreme Court" in subsection (7) are to be replaced by the words "Senior Courts": *Constitutional Reform Act* 2005, Sched. 11. That amendment may never be effected, since the whole section is to be repealed by the *Criminal Justice Act* 2003, Sched. 3, as from a day to be appointed, and replaced by the new scheme of sending for trial under sections 51 to 51E of the *Crime and Disorder Act* 1998 (*ante*, §§ 7–73 *et seq.*).]

7–83   The *Criminal Justice Act 1987 (Notice of Transfer) Regulations* 1988 (S.I. 1988 No. 1691) (made under section 5(9) of the 1987 Act) prescribe standard forms (set out in the schedule to the regulations) in which the notice of transfer must be given; and require copies of the notice to be given to the defendant, the Crown Court and to any person who has custody of a person to whom the notice relates. The regulations have been amended by S.I. 1997 No. 737 and S.I. 2001 No. 444. As to procedural rules in connection with proceedings where a notice of transfer is given under section 4 of the 1987 Act, see Part 11 of the *Criminal Procedure Rules* 2005 in Appendix G–52 *et seq.*

(2) Transfer of certain cases involving children

Criminal Justice Act 1991, s.53

Notices of transfer in certain cases involving children

53.—(1) *If a person has been charged with an offence to which section 32(2) of the 1988*   **7–84**
Act applies (sexual offences and offences involving violence or cruelty) and the Director of
Public Prosecutions is of the opinion—

 (a) *that the evidence of the offence would be sufficient for the person charged to be*
   committed for trial;

 (b) *that a child who is alleged—*

   (i) *to be a person against whom the offence was committed; or*

   (ii) *to have witnessed the commission of the offence,*

  will be called as a witness at the trial; and

 (c) *that, for the purpose of avoiding any prejudice to the welfare of the child, the case*
   should be taken over and proceeded with without delay by the Crown Court,

a notice ("notice of transfer") certifying that opinion may be given by or on behalf of the
Director to the magistrates' court in whose jurisdiction the offence has been charged.

 (2) *A notice of transfer shall be given before the magistrates' court begins to inquire into*
the case as examining justices.

 (3) *On the giving of a notice of transfer the functions of the magistrates' court shall cease*
in relation to the case except as provided by paragraphs 2 and 3 of Schedule 6 to this Act or
by paragraph 2 of Schedule 3 to the Access to Justice Act 1999.

 (4) *The decision to give a notice of transfer shall not be subject to appeal or liable to be*
questioned in any court.

 (5) *Schedule 6 to this Act (which makes further provision in relation to notices of transfer)*
shall have effect.

 (6) *In this section "child" means a person who—*

 (a) *in the case of an offence falling within section 32(2)(a) or (b) of the 1988 Act,*
   is under fourteen years of age or, if he was under that age when any such
   video recording as is mentioned in section 32A(2) of that Act was made in re-
   spect of him, is under fifteen years of age;

 (b) *in the case of an offence falling within section 32(2)(c) of that Act, is under*
   seventeen years of age or, if he was under that age when any such video re-
   cording was made in respect of him, is under eighteen years of age.

 (7) *Any reference in subsection (6) above to an offence falling within paragraph (a), (b)*
or (c) of section 32(2) of that Act includes a reference to an offence which consists of at-
tempting or conspiring to commit, or of aiding, abetting, counselling, procuring or inciting
the commission of, an offence falling within that paragraph.

 (8) *This section shall not apply in any case in which section 51 of the Crime and Disorder*
Act 1998 (no committal proceedings for indictable-only offences) applies.

[This section is printed as amended by the *Criminal Justice and Public Order Act*
1994, Sched. 9, the *Crime and Disorder Act* 1998, Sched. 8, and the *Access to Justice*
Act 1999, Sched. 4. As from a day to be appointed, the whole section is to be repealed
by the *Criminal Justice Act* 2003, Sched. 3, and replaced by the new scheme of sending for trial under sections 51 to 51E of the *Crime and Disorder Act* 1998 (*ante*,
§§ 7–73 *et seq.*).]

As to procedural rules in connection with proceedings where a notice of transfer is   **7–85**
given under sections 53 of the 1991 Act, see Part 11 of the *Criminal Procedure Rules*
2005 in Appendix G–52 *et seq.*

There will be no need for committal proceedings and the case will be transferred   **7–86**
early on in the proceedings. The defendant may apply to the Crown Court for the
charge to be dismissed on the grounds that the evidence disclosed would not be sufficient for any jury to convict him on it.

V. COMMITTAL OF SUMMARY OFFENCES

Normally summary only offences will be tried by the magistrates' court and the ques-   **7–87** tion of mode of trial does not arise. The *Criminal Justice Act* 1988 does make provision for certain summary offences to be dealt with at the Crown Court but only if there is some evident connection between the either way offence that is being committed and the summary offence which justifies the offences being dealt with together. The powers are included in sections 40 and 41.

Criminal Justice Act 1988, s.40

Power to join in indictment count for common assault etc.

7–88   **40.**—(1) A count charging a person with a summary offence to which this section applies may be included in an indictment if the charge—

    (a) is founded on the same facts or evidence as a count charging an indictable offence; or

    (b) is part of a series of offences of the same or similar character as an indictable offence which is also charged,

but only if (in either case) the facts or evidence relating to the offence *were disclosed to a magistrates' court inquiring into the offence as examining justices or* are disclosed by material which, in pursuance of regulations made under paragraph 1 of Schedule 3 to the *Crime and Disorder Act* 1998 (procedure where person sent for trial under section 51 [or 51A]), has been served on the person charged.

(2) Where a count charging an offence to which this section applies is included in an indictment, the offence shall be tried in the same manner as if it were an indictable offence; but the Crown Court may only deal with the offender in respect of it in a manner in which a magistrates' court could have dealt with him.

(3) The offences to which this section applies are—

    (a) common assault;

    (aa) an offence under section 90(1) of the *Criminal Justice Act* 1991 (assaulting a prisoner custody officer);

    (ab) an offence under section 13(1) of the *Criminal Justice and Public Order Act* 1994 (assaulting a secure training centre custody officer);

    (b) an offence under section 12(1) of the *Theft Act* 1968 (taking motor vehicle or other conveyance without authority etc.);

    (c) an offence under section 103(1)(b) of the *Road Traffic Act* 1988 (driving a motor vehicle while disqualified);

    (d) an offence mentioned in the first column of Schedule 2 to the *Magistrates' Courts Act* 1980 (criminal damage etc.) which would otherwise be triable only summarily by virtue of section 22(2) of that Act; and

    (e) any summary offence specified under subsection (4) below.

(4) The Secretary of State may by order made by statutory instrument specify for the purposes of this section any summary offence which is punishable with imprisonment or involves obligatory or discretionary disqualification from driving.

(5) A statutory instrument containing an order under this section shall be subject to annulment in pursuance of a resolution of either House of Parliament.

[This section is printed as amended by the *Road Traffic (Consequential Provisions) Act* 1988, Sched. 3, the *Criminal Justice and Public Order Act* 1994, Sched. 9, the *Criminal Procedure and Investigations Act* 1996, Sched. 1, and the *Crime and Disorder Act* 1998, Sched. 8. As from a day to be appointed, the *Criminal Justice Act* 2003, Scheds 3 and 37, repeal the words in italics in subsection (1) and insert the words in square brackets. As from May 9, 2005, the *Criminal Justice Act 2003 (Commencement No. 9) Order* 2005 (S.I. 2005 No. 1267) brought the insertion of the words in square brackets into force for the limited purpose of cases sent for trial under section 51A(3)(d) of the *Crime and Disorder Act* 1998 (*ante*, § 7–74).]

7–89   Section 40 applies when the magistrates' court is dealing with a committal for trial under section 6 or sending a case for trial under section 51 of the *Crime and Disorder Act* 1998. The section does not extend to cases that involve children which are being transferred to the Crown Court under section 53 of the *Criminal Justice Act* 1991: *R. v. T and K* [2001] 1 Cr.App.R. 446, CA. The prosecution may prepare the indictment in advance and will list the offences to be tried at the Crown Court. Certain specific offences may be included in the indictment which would usually be tried summarily. The prerequisite is that the offence must be founded on the same facts or evidence as the indictable charge or be part of a series of offences of the same or similar character. The evidence supporting this connection must be disclosed to the court at the time of the committal or served on the defence where the case is sent. The Crown Court may then deal with the summary matter but its powers will be restricted to those of the magistrates' court. In *R. v. Cox* [2001] 5 *Archbold News* 2, CA, it was held that the words "founded on the same facts or evidence as a count charging an indictable offence" in section 40(1)(a) refer to the situation where there is a sufficient factual or evidential overlap to make it both just and convenient for the offences to be tried together; and that this would be the case where the evidence of the facts going to establish the summary offence would be admissible as part of the narrative leading up to the commission of the indictable offence.

The specific offences are listed in subsection (3) and include various types of assault, taking a conveyance without authority, driving whilst disqualified and summary only criminal damage. No other offence has been added under subsection (4). The offence of battery was held to be included in the term "common assault" under this section: *R. v. Lynsey* [1995] 2 Cr.App.R. 667, CA.

The offence of driving whilst disqualified was held to be founded on the same facts and evidence as an indictable offence of possessing an offensive weapon when the defendant was driving along with the weapon in his possession in the car: *R. v. Bird* [1996] R.T.R. 22, CA. The summary offence must be connected to an indictable offence of the same or similar character and not to another summary offence. Although taking a conveyance was similar to theft of vehicles, driving whilst disqualified was not and could not be said to be founded on the same facts: *R. v. Callaghan*, 94 Cr.App.R. 226, CA.

The way in which the Crown Court should deal with summary offences added to the   **7–90** indictment has been clarified to some extent particularly with regard to criminal damage offences where the interaction of section 22 and section 33 of the *Magistrates' Courts Act* 1980 and this section has given rise to difficulties. The principle that section 22 determined mode of trial procedure but did not change the classification of the offence as triable either way was first confirmed in *R. v . Fennell* [2000] 2 Cr.App.R. 310 at 318, CA.

The reasoning was examined further in a case where a defendant had an offence of criminal damage added on to the indictment and it was argued that the powers of the Crown Court were limited to those mentioned in section 33, *i.e.* three months imprisonment and/or a fine of £2,500. It was held that section 22 did not apply where the offence is added to the indictment under section 40 because the required determination of section 22 was not made. As the court had not categorised the offence as being one attracting the reduced penalties the Crown Court retained the sentencing powers of six months and/or a level 5 fine. The value of the damage would be relevant to sentence: *R. v. Alden* [2002] 2 Cr.App.R. 326, CA.

Criminal Justice Act 1988, s.41

Power of Crown Court to deal with summary offence where person committed for either way offence

    41.—(1) *Where a magistrates' court commits a person to the Crown Court for trial on*   **7–91** *indictment for an offence triable either way or a number of such offences, it may also commit him for trial for any summary offence with which he is charged and which—*

        (a) *is punishable with imprisonment or involves obligatory or discretionary disqualification from driving; and*

        (b) *arises out of circumstances which appear to the court to be the same as or connected with those giving rise to the offence, or one of the offences, triable either way,*

whether or not evidence relating to that summary offence appears on the depositions or written statements in the case; and the trial of the information charging the summary offence shall then be treated as if the magistrates' court had adjourned it under section 10 of the Magistrates' Courts Act *1980 and had not fixed the time and place for its resumption.*

(2) *Where a magistrates' court commits a person to the Crown Court for trial on indictment for a number of offences triable either way and exercises the power conferred by subsection (1) above in respect of a summary offence, the magistrates' court shall give the Crown Court and the person who is committed for trial a notice stating which of the offences triable either way appears to the court to arise out of circumstances which are the same as or connected with those giving rise to the summary offence.*

(3) *A magistrates' court's decision to exercise the power conferred by subsection (1) above shall not be subject to appeal or liable to be questioned in any court.*

(4) *The committal of a person under this section in respect of an offence to which section 40 above applies shall not preclude the exercise in relation to the offence of the power conferred by that section; but where he is tried on indictment for such an offence, the functions of the Crown Court under this section in relation to the offence shall cease.*

[(4A) *The committal of a person under this section in respect of an offence to which section 40 above applies shall not prevent him being found guilty of that offence under section 6(3) of the* Criminal Law Act *1967 (alternative verdicts on trial on indictment); but where he is convicted under that provision of such an offence, the functions of the Crown Court under this section in relation to the offence shall cease.]*

(5) *If he is convicted on the indictment, the Crown Court shall consider whether the conditions specified in subsection (1) above were satisfied.*

(6) *If it considers that they were satisfied, it shall state to him the substance of the summary offence and ask him whether he pleads guilty or not guilty.*

(7) *If he pleads guilty, the Crown Court shall convict him, but may deal with him in respect of that offence only in a manner in which a magistrates' court could have dealt with him.*

(8) *If he does not plead guilty, the Crown Court may try him for the offence, but may deal with him only in a manner in which a magistrates' court could have dealt with him.*

(9) *[Repealed]*

(10) *The Crown Court shall inform the designated officer for the magistrates' court of the outcome of any proceedings under this section.*

(11) *Where the Court of Appeal allows an appeal against conviction of an offence triable either way which arose out of circumstances which were the same as or connected with those giving rise to a summary offence of which the appellant was convicted under this section—*

    (a) *it shall set aside his conviction of the summary offence and give the designated officer for the magistrates' court notice that it has done so; and*

    (b) *it may direct that no further proceedings in relation to the offence are to be undertaken;*

and the proceedings before the Crown Court in relation to the offence shall thereafter be disregarded for all purposes.

(12) *A notice under subsection (11) above shall include particulars of any direction given under paragraph (b) of that subsection in relation to the offence.*

(13) *[Repealed]*.

[This section is re-printed as amended by the *Access to Justice Act* 1999, Scheds 13 and 15, and the *Courts Act* 2003, Scheds 8 and 10. As from a day or days to be appointed, the *Domestic Violence Crime and Victims Act* 2004, Sched. 10, inserts subsection (4A). The whole section is due to be repealed by the *Criminal Justice Act* 2003, Scheds 3 and 37, as from a day to be appointed.]

7–92   Section 41 provides for the magistrates' court which commits a person to the Crown Court for trial on an either way matter under section 6 of the *Magistrates' Courts Act* 1980 to also commit for trial certain summary offences with which he is charged. The summary offence must be punishable with imprisonment or carry a disqualification from driving. It must also arise out of the same circumstances as the indictable offence.

The summary offence must be charged from the outset rather than added to the indictment as under section 40 but evidence relating to it does not need to have been disclosed in the committal papers. The court will adjourn the summary offence 'sine die' (without a date being fixed) and await the outcome of the Crown Court proceedings. A notice must be served on the Crown Court and defence identifying the either way offence to which the summary offence is linked.

The section does not apply to cases sent under section 51 or 51A of the *Crime and*

Disorder Act 1998 or cases transferred under the *Criminal Justice Act* 1987 or the *Criminal Justice Act* 1991.

The Crown Court can only deal with a summary offence under this section when **7–93** there is a conviction on an indictable offence and a guilty plea to the summary offence. On conviction, the sentences available are those of the magistrates' court and the observations about section 22 and the categorisation of criminal damage offences apply equally under this section as they do under section 40. If the defendant is acquitted of the linked indictable offence or pleads not guilty to the summary offence the powers of the Crown Court cease. The Crown Court may then dismiss the case under section 41(9) or send the case back to the magistrates' court for trial.

In *R. v. Foote*, 94 Cr.App.R. 82, CA, a defendant was committed to the Crown Court for trial on a charge of reckless driving and was also committed under section 41 for on a charge of careless driving. At the Crown Court his plea of guilty to the lesser charge was accepted by the prosecution and the Crown Court proceeded to sentence him. It was held that the conviction and sentence at the Crown Court was a nullity. The case should have been remitted to the magistrates' court where it was deemed to have been adjourned and it should be dealt with there. The provisions of section 41 relating to the conviction of a summary charge on the indictment also applies to charges properly included on the indictment under section 40. Where a defendant pleaded guilty at the Crown Court to an offence of driving whilst disqualified which was a summary only offence which had been included on the indictment under section 40 with a charge of possessing an offensive weapon it was held that the Crown Court could impose a sentence even though the indictable offence was not proceeded with because there was a conviction on the indictment: *Bird, ante*.

VI. COMMITTAL OF EITHER WAY OFFENCES FOR TRIAL TO THE CROWN COURT

A. INTRODUCTION—CLASSIFICATION OF OFFENCES

(1) Introduction

Criminal offences are categorised into three types according to the seriousness of the **7–94** offence. The gravity of the offence is marked by the length of sentence that can be imposed. The powers of the magistrates' courts are limited to six months' imprisonment or a fine of £5,000 for as single offence. Where there are two or more either way offences the total sentencing powers of the court are increased to 12 months' imprisonment as a maximum. Less serious offences are classified as summary only. The most serious offences are triable on indictment only and must be dealt with at the Crown Court. In between are the either way offences which can be tried at the magistrates' court or the Crown Court. These are offences that cover a wide range of criminal conduct and aggravating features could affect the seriousness of the offence so that Crown Court trial is more suitable with the added sentencing powers of that court.

Summary offences must normally be dealt with in the magistrates' court (but see *Criminal Justice Act* 1988, ss.40 and 41). Either way offences may be tried either at the magistrates' court or the Crown Court. The mode of trial procedure is described *ante*: sections 17A–25. Where the case is to be dealt with at the Crown Court it must be committed under *Magistrates' Courts Act* 1980, ss.6(1) or 6(2). Indictable only charges cannot be dealt with at the magistrates' court and are sent to the Crown Court under section 51 of the *Crime and Disorder Act* 1998. By section 41 and Schedule 3 of the *Criminal Justice Act* 2003, committals will be abolished and all indictable only and either way cases that have been allocated for Crown Court trial will be sent to the Crown Court under the new scheme set out in sections 51 to 51E of the *Crime and Disorder Act* 1998 (*ante*, §§ 7–73 *et seq.*).]

A case can also be brought before the Crown Court by applying for a voluntary bill of indictment which is done directly to the Crown Court: *Administration of Justice (Miscellaneous Provisions) Act* 1933, s.2.

(2) General nature of committal proceedings

7–95   The court, when committing a case for trial is referred to in statute as 'examining justices'. Its role is to inquire into the charge and decide whether there is sufficient evidence to put the defendant on trial before a jury. If there is, the case is committed. If not, the case is discharged. The prosecution will prepare the committal documents which will consist of written statements from witnesses, depositions, documents and exhibits. Prior to the committal, a copy of all the papers must be served on the defence who will then review the evidence and decide whether to seek a committal without consideration of the evidence (section 6(2)) or request a contested committal on the basis that there is no case to answer that could be put before a jury: section 6(1).

Standard guidelines are applied locally for the preparation of committal bundles, usually six weeks for cases in custody and eight weeks for those on bail. The original papers will be served on the court to be forwarded to the Crown Court on committal.

When a case is either sent, transferred or committed to the Crown Court, the magistrates' court will set the date for the first Crown Court hearing. The *Practice Direction (Criminal Proceedings: Case Management)* [2005] 1 W.L.R. 1491 amended the *Practice Direction (Criminal Proceedings: Consolidation)* [2002] 1 W.L.R. 2870 in relation to the time scale for the fixing of hearings and also introduced prescribed forms to be used in the process of managing the progress of the case. For cases sent under section 51 of the *Crime and Disorder Act* 1998 the magistrates may if necessary fix an early preliminary hearing at the Crown Court within about 14 days. In every other case a plea and case management hearing should be set within 14 to 17 weeks of sending, or within 7 weeks of committal or transfer. This amended practice direction was issued to supplement the *Criminal Procedure Rules* 2005.

Magistrates' Courts Act 1980, s.4

General nature of committal proceedings

7–96   **4.**—(1) *The functions of examining justices may be discharged by a single justice.*

(2) *Examining justices shall sit in open court except where any enactment contains an express provision to the contrary and except where it appears to them as respects the whole or any part of committal proceedings that the ends of justice would not be served by their sitting in open court.*

(3) *Subject to subsection (4) below, evidence tendered before examining justices shall be tendered in the presence of the accused.*

(4) *Examining justices may allow evidence to be tendered before them in the absence of the accused if—*

   (a) *they consider that by reason of his disorderly conduct before them it is not practicable for the evidence to be tendered in his presence, or*

   (b) *he cannot be present for reasons of health but is represented by a legal representative and has consented to the evidence being tendered in his absence.*

[This section is printed as amended by the *Courts and Legal Services Act* 1990, Sched. 18, and the *Criminal Procedure and Investigations Act* 1996, Sched. 1. As from a day to be appointed, the whole section is to be repealed by the *Criminal Justice Act* 2003, Sched. 37.]

7–97   A committal can be heard by a single magistrate. The rule is for the committal to take place in open court. An exception to this is when a defendant is charged under the *Official Secrets Act* 1920. The presence of the accused at committal may be excused if he is behaving in a disorderly manner or if he is unwell and he may then be represented through his lawyer. This section relates only to the process of the committal when the evidence is considered by the court and not to the actual act of committal itself. The evidence must comply with the requirements of *Magistrates' Courts Act* 1980, ss.5A–5F.

(3) Evidence at committal proceedings

Magistrates' Courts Act 1980, ss.5A, 5B

Evidence which is admissible

5A.—(1) *Evidence falling within subsection (2) below, and only that evidence, shall be*   **7–98**
admissible by a magistrates' court inquiring into an offence as examining justices.

(2) *Evidence falls within this subsection if it—*

(a) *is tendered by or on behalf of the prosecutor, and*

(b) *falls within subsection (3) below.*

(3) *The following evidence falls within this subsection—*

(a) *written statements complying with section 5B below;*

(b) *the documents or other exhibits (if any) referred to in such statements;*

(c) *depositions complying with section 5C below;*

(d) *the documents or other exhibits (if any) referred to in such depositions;*

(e) *statements complying with section 5D below;*

(f) *documents falling within section 5E below.*

(4) *In this section "document" means anything in which information of any description is
recorded.*

[Sections 5A to 5F were inserted by the *Criminal Procedure and Investigations Act*
1996, Sched. 1. As from a day to be appointed, they are to be repealed by the *Criminal
Justice Act* 2003, Sched. 3, and replaced by the scheme of sending to the Crown Court
under sections 51 to 51E of the *Crime and Disorder Act* 1998 (*ante*, §§ 7–73 *et seq.*).]

Written statements

5B.—(1) *For the purposes of section 5A above a written statement complies with this sec-*   **7–99**
tion if—

(a) *the conditions falling within subsection (2) below are met, and*

(b) *such of the conditions falling within subsection (3) below as apply are met.*

(2) *The conditions falling within this subsection are that—*

(a) *the statement purports to be signed by the person who made it;*

(b) *the statement contains a declaration by that person to the effect that it is true to the
best of his knowledge and belief and that he made the statement knowing that, if it
were tendered in evidence, he would be liable to prosecution if he wilfully stated in
it anything which he knew to be false or did not believe to be true;*

(c) *before the statement is tendered in evidence a copy of the statement is given, by or
on behalf of the prosecutor, to each of the other parties to the proceedings.*

(3) *The conditions falling within this subsection are that—*

(a) *if the statement is made by a person under 18 years old, it gives his age;*

(b) *if it is made by a person who cannot read it, it is read to him before he signs it and
is accompanied by a declaration by the person who so read the statement to the effect that it was so read;*

(c) *if it refers to any other document as an exhibit, the copy given to any other party to
the proceedings under subsection (2)(c) above is accompanied by a copy of that document or by such information as may be necessary to enable the party to whom it is
given to inspect that document or a copy of it.*

(4) *So much of any statement as is admitted in evidence by virtue of this section shall, unless the court commits the accused for trial by virtue of section 6(2) below or the court
otherwise directs, be read aloud at the hearing; and where the court so directs an account
shall be given orally of so much of any statement as is not read aloud.*

(5) *Any document or other object referred to as an exhibit and identified in a statement
admitted in evidence by virtue of this section shall be treated as if it had been produced as an
exhibit and identified in court by the maker of the statement.*

(6) *In this section "document" means anything in which information of any description is
recorded.*

[Sections 5A to 5F were inserted by the *Criminal Procedure and Investigations Act*
1996, Sched. 1. As from a day to be appointed, they are to be repealed by the *Criminal*

Justice Act 2003, Sched. 3, and replaced by the scheme of sending to the Crown Court under sections 51 to 51E of the *Crime and Disorder Act* 1998 (*ante*, §§ 7–73 *et seq.*).]

7–100   Any statement must be that of the witness. If the witness does not speak English his statement must be recorded in the language in which it was made and signed by him and not written in English by an interpreter. The correct procedure is for the interpreter to provide a written translation of the statement which is then produced as an exhibit: *R. v. Raynor*, 165 J.P. 149, CA.

Magistrates' Courts Act 1980, s.5C

Depositions

7–101   **5C.**—(1) *For the purposes of section 5A above a deposition complies with this section if—*

    (a) *a copy of it is sent to the prosecutor under section 97A(9) below,*

    (b) *the condition falling within subsection (2) below is met, and*

    (c) *the condition falling within subsection (3) below is met, in a case where it applies.*

    (2) *The condition falling within this subsection is that before the magistrates' court begins to inquire into the offence concerned as examining justices a copy of the deposition is given, by or on behalf of the prosecutor, to each of the other parties to the proceedings.*

    (3) *The condition falling within this subsection is that, if the deposition refers to any other document as an exhibit, the copy given to any other party to the proceedings under subsection (2) above is accompanied by a copy of that document or by such information as may be necessary to enable the party to whom it is given to inspect that document or a copy of it.*

    (4) *So much of any deposition as is admitted in evidence by virtue of this section shall, unless the court commits the accused for trial by virtue of section 6(2) below or the court otherwise directs, be read aloud at the hearing; and where the court so directs an account shall be given orally of so much of any deposition as is not read aloud.*

    (5) *Any document or other object referred to as an exhibit and identified in a deposition admitted in evidence by virtue of this section shall be treated as if it had been produced as an exhibit and identified in court by the person whose evidence is taken as the deposition.*

    (6) *In this section "document" means anything in which information of any description is recorded.*

[Sections 5A to 5F were inserted by the *Criminal Procedure and Investigations Act* 1996, Sched. 1. As from a day to be appointed, they are to be repealed by the *Criminal Justice Act* 2003, Sched. 3, and replaced by the scheme of sending to the Crown Court under sections 51 to 51E of the *Crime and Disorder Act* 1998 (*ante*, §§ 7–73 *et seq.*).]

7–102   Depositions cover situations where a witness will not provide a statement voluntarily under sections 5B. The witness may be summonsed or brought before the court by warrant and then the evidence will be taken before the court in the form of a deposition: *Magistrates' Courts Act* 1980, s.97A.

Magistrates' Courts Act 1980, s.5D

Statements

7–103   **5D.**—(1) *For the purposes of section 5A above a statement complies with this section if the conditions falling within subsections (2) to (4) below are met.*

    (2) *The condition falling within this subsection is that, before the committal proceedings begin, the prosecutor notifies the magistrates' court and each of the other parties to the proceedings that he believes—*

    (a) *that the statement might by virtue of section 23 or 24 of the* Criminal Justice Act 1988 *(statements in certain documents) be admissible as evidence if the case came to trial, and*

    (b) *that the statement would not be admissible as evidence otherwise than by virtue of section 23 or 24 of that Act if the case came to trial.*

    (3) *The condition falling within this subsection is that—*

    (a) *the prosecutor's belief is based on information available to him at the time he makes the notification,*

    (b) *he has reasonable grounds for his belief, and*

    (c) *he gives the reasons for his belief when he makes the notification.*

(4) *The condition falling within this subsection is that when the court or a party is noti-fied as mentioned in subsection (2) above a copy of the statement is given, by or on behalf of the prosecutor, to the court or the party concerned.*

(5) *So much of any statement as is in writing and is admitted in evidence by virtue of this section shall, unless the court commits the accused for trial by virtue of section 6(2) below or the court otherwise directs, be read aloud at the hearing; and where the court so directs an account shall be given orally of so much of any statement as is not read aloud.*

[Sections 5A to 5F were inserted by the *Criminal Procedure and Investigations Act* 1996, Sched. 1. As from a day to be appointed, they are to be repealed by the *Criminal Justice Act* 2003, Sched. 3, and replaced by the scheme of sending to the Crown Court under sections 51 to 51E of the *Crime and Disorder Act* 1998 (*ante,* §§ 7–73 *et seq.*).]

These statements are those to which sections 23 and 24 of the *Criminal Justice Act* 1988 apply. But see *R. (CPS) v. City of London Magistrates' Court, The Times,* April 17, 2006, DC where it was noted that these sections have been repealed by the *Criminal Justice Act* 2003. In this case the court indicated that section 5D is now "otiose" as a result of the hearsay provisions of the *Criminal Justice Act* 2003. However, section 5D has yet to be repealed. It may be that the section can still apply but all reference to the repealed sections 23 and 24 should be read as applying to the hearsay sections of the *Criminal Justice Act* 2003 (see *post,* § 10–62).

7–104

Magistrates' Courts Act 1980, ss.5E, 5F

Other documents

5E.—(1) *The following documents fall within this section—*   **7–105**

    (a) *any document which by virtue of any enactment is evidence in proceedings before a magistrates' court inquiring into an offence as examining justices;*

    (b) *any document which by virtue of any enactment is admissible, or may be used, or is to be admitted or received, in or as evidence in such proceedings;*

    (c) *any document which by virtue of any enactment may be considered in such proceedings;*

    (d) *any document whose production constitutes proof in such proceedings by virtue of any enactment;*

    (e) *any document by the production of which evidence may be given in such proceedings by virtue of any enactment.*

(2) *In subsection (1) above—*

    (a) *references to evidence include references to prima facie evidence;*

    (b) *references to any enactment include references to any provision of this Act.*

(3) *So much of any document as is admitted in evidence by virtue of this section shall, un-less the court commits the accused for trial by virtue of section 6(2) below or the court otherwise directs, be read aloud at the hearing; and where the court so directs an account shall be given orally of so much of any document as is not read aloud.*

(4) *In this section "document" means anything in which information of any description is recorded.*

[Sections 5A to 5F were inserted by the *Criminal Procedure and Investigations Act* 1996, Sched. 1. As from a day to be appointed, they are repealed by the *Criminal Justice Act* 2003, Sched. 3, and replaced by the scheme of sending to the Crown Court under sections 51 to 51E of the *Crime and Disorder Act* 1998 (*ante,* §§ 7–73 *et seq.*).]

Proof by production of copy

5F.—(1) *Where a statement, deposition or document is admissible in evidence by virtue of*   **7–106**
section 5B, 5C, 5D or 5E above it may be proved by the production of—

    (a) *the statement, deposition or document, or*

    (b) *a copy of it or the material part of it.*

(2) *Subsection (1)(b) above applies whether or not the statement, deposition or document is still in existence.*

(3) *It is immaterial for the purposes of this section how many removes there are between a copy and the original.*

(4) *In this section "copy", in relation to a statement, deposition or document, means anything onto which information recorded in the statement, deposition or document has been copied, by whatever means and whether directly or indirectly."*

[Sections 5A to 5F were inserted by the *Criminal Procedure and Investigations Act* 1996, Sched. 1. As from a day to be appointed, they are repealed by the *Criminal Justice Act* 2003, Sched. 3, and replaced by the scheme of sending to the Crown Court under sections 51 to 51E of the *Crime and Disorder Act* 1998 (*ante*, §§ 7–73*et seq.*).]

(4) Decision to discharge or commit

Magistrates' Courts Act 1980, s.6

Discharge or committal for trial

7–107   **6.**—(1) *A magistrates' court inquiring into an offence as examining justices shall on consideration of the evidence—*

> (a) *commit the accused for trial if it is of opinion that there is sufficient evidence to put him on trial by jury for any indictable offence;*
> (b) *discharge him if it is not of that opinion and he is in custody for no other cause than the offence under inquiry;*

but the preceding provisions of this subsection have effect subject to the provisions of this and any other Act relating to the summary trial of indictable offences.

(2) *If a magistrates' court inquiring into an offence as examining justices is satisfied that all the evidence tendered by or on behalf of the prosecutor falls within section 5A(3) above, it may commit the accused for trial for the offence without consideration of the contents of any statements, depositions or other documents, and without consideration of any exhibits which are not documents, unless—*

> (a) *the accused or one of the accused has no legal representative acting for him in the case, or*
> (b) *a legal representative for the accused or one of the accused, as the case may be, has requested the court to consider a submission that there is insufficient evidence to put that accused on trial by jury for the offence;*

and subsection (1) above shall not apply to a committal for trial under this subsection.

(3) *Subject to section 4 of the* Bail Act *1976 and section 41 below, the court may commit a person for trial—*

> (a) *in custody, that is to say, by committing him to custody there to be safety kept until delivered in due course of law, or*
> (b) *on bail in accordance with the* Bail Act *1976, that is to say, by directing him to appear before the Crown Court for trial;*

and where his release on bail is conditional on his providing one or more surety or sureties and, in accordance with section 8(3) of the Bail Act *1976, the court fixes the amount in which the surety is to be bound with a view to his entering into his recognizance subsequently in accordance with subsections (4) and (5) or (6) of that section the court shall in the meantime commit the accused to custody in accordance with paragraph (a) of this subsection.*

(4) *Where the court has committed a person to custody in accordance with paragraph (a) of subsection (3) above, then, if that person is in custody for no other cause, the court may, at any time before his first appearance before the Crown Court, grant him bail in accordance with the* Bail Act *1976 subject to a duty to appear before the Crown Court for trial.*

(5) *Where a magistrates' court acting as examining justices commits any person for trial or determines to discharge him, the designated officer the court shall, on the day on which the committal proceedings are concluded or the next day, cause to be displayed in a part of the court house to which the public have access a notice—*

> (a) *in either case giving that person's name, address, and age (if known);*
> (b) *in a case where the court so commits him, stating the charge or charges on which he is committed and the court to which he is committed;*
> (c) *in a case where the court determines to discharge him, describing the offence charged and stating that it has so determined;*

but this subsection shall have effect subject to section 4 of the Sexual Offences (Amendment) Act *1976 (anonymity of complainant in rape etc. cases).*

(6) *A notice displayed in pursuance of subsection (5) above shall not contain the name or*

address of any person under the age of 18 years unless the justices in question have stated that in their opinion he would be mentioned in the notice apart from the preceding provisions of this subsection and should be mentioned in it for the purpose of avoiding injustice to him.

[This section is printed as amended by the *Criminal Justice Act* 1988, Sched. 15, the *Criminal Justice Act* 1991, Sched. 8, the *Criminal Procedure and Investigations Act* 1996, Sched. 1, and the *Courts Act* 2003, Sched. 8. As from a day to be appointed, the whole section is to be repealed by the *Criminal Justice Act* 2003, Sched. 3.]

Only an either way offence can be committed to the Crown Court for trial under this **7–108** section. The court does not sit as "examining justices" when it is dealing with a summary only matter. The committal of such an offence is a nullity: *Bannister v. Clarke* [1920] 3 K.B. 598, DC. But see the *Criminal Justice Act* 1988, ss.40 and 41, *ante* §§ 7–88 *et seq.*

There are two types of committal. Under subsection (2) the court need not consider the evidence contained in the prosecution statements, etc. if it is satisfied that all such documentation complies with the admissibility requirements of section 5A. Under subsection (2)(a) and (b), the court has to consider the evidence if the defendant is unrepresented or if he wishes to make a submission that there is not sufficient evidence in the prosecution case to put him on trial before a jury. The procedure in connection with the two different committals is set out in the *Criminal Procedure Rules* 2005, rr.10.2 and 10.3 (Appendix G–48 *et seq.*). A contested committal takes place on the basis of the written statements and no live witnesses will be called.

In the committal without consideration of the evidence the defence admits that there is sufficient evidence on the face of the statements for the case to go to trial. If no admission is forthcoming the evidence will be read out to the court and the committal will only take place if the court is of the opinion that there is sufficient evidence to put the defendant on trial. For a committal under section 6(2) to be valid, all that is necessary is that the magistrates' court is satisfied that all the evidence tendered by the prosecution falls within section 5A(3) of the 1980 Act and that no submission of no case is made; the mere fact that a statement essential to support the charge is omitted from the papers will not invalidate the committal: *R. v. Harding* [1998] Crim.L.R. 877, CA.

The function of committal proceedings is to ensure that no person should stand trial unless a prima facie case is made out. The onus of making out the case is on the prosecution: *R. v. Epping and Harlow Justices, ex p. Massaro* [1973] Q.B. 433, DC.

The test to be applied is whether there is any evidence that the crime alleged has been committed by the defendant and if there is, whether that evidence is such that a jury, properly directed could convict on it: *R. v. Galbraith* [1981] 1 W.L.R. 1039, CA.

The prosecution has a discretion as to which witnesses to rely on and need only bring **7–109** evidence of a prima facie case, not one beyond reasonable doubt. Failure to include the statement of any specific witness is not a breach of natural justice but the prosecution is subject to a duty to be fair and not to mislead the court: *Wilkinson v. DPP*, 162 J.P. 591, DC.

The court must be satisfied that the evidence tendered is admissible. Where the committal was based on transcripts of police interviews of co-defendants who implicated the defendant this was held to be inadmissible as it did not comply with section 5A. This was a procedural defect that could not be remedied and the committal was quashed: *R. v. Bedwellty Justices, ex p. Williams* [1997] A.C. 225, HL.

But it is not the role of the court to assess the weight of evidence and rule on its admissibility. Where the evidence is legally admissible the case should be committed as the discretion to reject the evidence rests with the trial judge: *R. v. Horsham Justices, ex p. Bukhari*, 74 Cr.App.R. 291, DC.

The court may commit on any indictable offence that is made out in the evidence. It **7–110** is not restricted to finding sufficient evidence for the offence formally charged. If the court contemplates committing on a lesser charge, it should allow legal representatives to address them and it is bad practice for the prosecution to invite the court to commit on charges made out after the substantive matter has been discharged: *R. v. Gloucester Magistrates' Court, ex p. Chung*, 153 J.P. 75, DC.

If the court is not of the opinion that there is sufficient evidence it will discharge the defendant. The prosecution may later charge the defendant again if more evidence comes to light and seek committal once more. There is no question of *autrefois acquit* arising as the case has not been tried on its merits. The court may entertain charges which have been discharged before but repeated use of the committal procedure may be vexatious or amount to an abuse of process: *R. v. Manchester City Justices, ex p. Snelson*, 66 Cr.App.R. 44, DC.

Section 4 allows for the committal proceedings to take place in the absence of the accused in certain circumstances. Section 6 provides for the court to commit the accused for trial and the *Criminal Procedure Rules* 2005 require that the charge be read to the accused. There is no reference to procedure in the absence of the defendant. It has been held that this does not preclude the court from committing a person in absence. Where the defendant was absent through ill health, but was represented the appeal court said that the provisions of section 4(4) of the *Magistrates' Courts Act* 1980 and section 122 (representation through lawyer) allowed the court to proceed in the absence of the accused as there were no statutory provisions to the contrary: *R. v. Liverpool Street Magistrates' Court, ex p. Quantrell* [1999] 2 Cr.App.R. 24, DC. See also *R. v. Bow Street Magistrates' Court, ex p. Government of Germany* [1998] Q.B. 556, DC.

7–111   In some committals there is a good deal of paperwork to be considered by the court. It is acceptable for the documents in the case to be lodged with the court in advance so that there may be an opportunity to read and digest the evidence. That this is done with out the defence consenting is immaterial. Copies of the statements have to be served on the court in any event under the *Criminal Procedure Rules* 2005, r.27.1 (Appendix G–158): *R. v. Colchester Stipendiary Magistrate, ex p. Beck* [1979] Q.B. 674, DC.

(5) Discharge or committal without consideration of evidence

7–112   See *Criminal Procedure Rules* 2005, r.10.2 in Appendix G–48.

7–113   See *Criminal Procedure Rules* 2005, r.10.3 in Appendix G–49.

(6) Reminder to defendant

7–114   On committal the defendant must be advised that live witnesses will not be called at the Crown Court trial unless he requests that they attend.

7–115   See *Criminal Procedure Rules* 2005, r.10.4 in Appendix G–50.

7–116   Where a defendant is charged with an offence involving a death the court has a duty to inform the coroner of the charge and proceedings. The coroner is responsible for an inquest: *Coroner's Act* 1988, s.17.

(7) Place of trial

Magistrates' Courts Act 1980, s.7

Place of trial on indictment

7–117   **7.** —*A magistrates' court committing a person for trial shall specify the place at which he is to be tried, and in selecting that place shall have regard to—*

(a) *the convenience of the defence, the prosecution and the witnesses,*

(b) *the expediting of the trial, and*

(c) *any direction given by or on behalf of the Lord Chief Justice with the concurrence of the Lord Chancellor under section 4(5) of the* Courts Act *1971.*

[As from a day to be appointed, this section is repealed by the *Criminal Justice Act* 2003, Scheds 3 and 37.]

7–118   The court will select the appropriate Crown Court according to its location and the directions in the *Consolidated Criminal Practice Directions* (see Appendix F) which allocate types of cases to different tiers of the Crown Court based on the seriousness of the offence. The case will be adjourned to a fixed date where a Plea and Case Management Hearing will take place. The Crown Court provides the appropriate dates. The Crown Court may change the venue once the case has been committed.

(8) Reporting restrictions

Magistrates' Courts Act 1980, s.8

Restrictions on reports of committal proceedings

8.—(1) *Except as provided by subsections (2), (3) and (8) below, it shall not be lawful to* **7–119** *publish in Great Britain a written report, or to include in a relevant programme for reception in Great Britain a report, of any committal proceedings in England and Wales containing any matter other than that permitted by subsection (4) below.*

(2) *Subject to subsection (2A) below a magistrates' court shall, on an application for the purpose made with reference to any committal proceedings by the accused or one of the accused, as the case may be, order that subsection (1) above shall not apply to reports of those proceedings.*

(2A) *Where in the case of two or more accused one of them objects to the making on an order under subsection (2) above, the court shall make the order if, and only if, it is satisfied, after hearing the representations of the accused, that it is in the interests of justice to do so.*

(2B) *An order under subsection (2) above shall not apply to reports of proceedings under subsection (2A) above, but any decisions of the court to make or not to make such an order may be contained in reports published or included in a relevant programme before the time authorised by subsection (3) below.*

(3) *It shall not be unlawful under this section to publish or include in a relevant programme a report of committal proceedings containing any matter other than that permitted by subsection (4) below—*

(a) *where the magistrates' court determines not to commit the accused, or determines to commit none of the accused, for trial, after it so determines;*

(b) *where the court commits the accused or any of the accused for trial, after the conclusion of his trial or, as the case may be, the trial of the last to be tried;*

and where at any time during the inquiry the court proceeds to try summarily the case of one or more of the accused under section 25(3) or (7) below, while committing the other accused or one or more of the other accused for trial, it shall not be unlawful under this section to publish or include in a relevant programme as part of a report of the summary trial, after the court determines to proceed as aforesaid, a report of so much of the committal proceedings containing any such matter as takes place before the determination.

(4) *The following matters may be contained in a report of committal proceedings published or included in a relevant programme without an order under subsection (2) above before the time authorised by subsection (3) above, that is to say—*

(a) *the identity of the court and the names of the examining justices;*

(b) *the names, addresses and occupations of the parties and witnesses and the ages of the accused and witnesses;*

(c) *the offence or offences, or a summary of them, with which the accused is or are charged;*

(d) *the names of the legal representatives engaged in the proceedings;*

(e) *any decision of the court to commit the accused or any of the accused for trial, and any decision of the court on the disposal of the case of any accused not committed;*

(f) *where the court commits the accused or any of the accused for trial, the charge or charges, or a summary of them, on which he is committed and the court to which he is committed;*

(g) *where the committal proceedings are adjourned, the date and place to which they are adjourned;*

(h) *any arrangements as to bail on committal or adjournment;*

(i) *whether a right to representation funded by the Legal Services Commission as part of the Criminal Defence Service was granted to the accused or any of the accused.*

(5) *If a report is published or included in a relevant programme in contravention of this section, the following persons, that is to say—*

    (a) *in the case of a publication of a written report as part of a newspaper or periodical, any proprietor, editor or publisher of the newspaper or periodical;*

    (b) *in the case of a publication of a written report otherwise than as part of a newspaper or periodical, the person who publishes it;*

    (c) *in the case of the inclusion of a report in a relevant programme, any body corporate which provides the service in which the programme is included and any person having functions in relation to the programme corresponding to those of an editor of a newspaper,*

shall be liable on summary conviction to a fine not exceeding level 5 on the standard scale.

    (6) *Proceedings for an offence under this section shall not, in England and Wales, be instituted otherwise than by or with the consent of the Attorney-General.*

    (7) *Subsection (1) above shall be in addition to, and not in derogation from, the provisions of any other enactment with respect to the publication of reports and proceedings of magistrates' and other courts.*

    (8) *For the purposes of this section committal proceedings shall, in relation to an information charging an indictable offence, be deemed to include any proceedings in the magistrates' court before the court proceeds to inquire into the information as examining justices; but where a magistrates' court which has begun to try an information summarily discontinues the summary trial in pursuance of section 25(2) or (6) below and proceeds to inquire into the information as examining justices, that circumstance shall not make it unlawful under this section for a report of any proceedings on the information which was published or included in a relevant programme before the court determined to proceed as aforesaid to have been so published or included in a relevant programme.*

    (9) *[Repealed]*

    (10) *In this section—*

        "publish", in relation to a report, means publish the report, either by itself or as part of a newspaper or periodical, for distribution to the public.

        "relevant programme" means a programme included in a programme service (within the meaning of the Broadcasting Act *1990).*

[This section is printed as amended by the *Contempt of Court Act* 1981, s.4, the *Criminal Justice (Amendment) Act* 1981, s.1, the *Criminal Justice Act* 1982, the *Broadcasting Act* 1990, Sched. 20, the *Courts and Legal Services Act* 1990, Sched. 18, and the *Access to Justice Act* 1999, Sched. 24. As from a day to be appointed, the whole section is to be repealed by the *Criminal Justice Act* 2003, Scheds 3 and 37.]

7–120 See the *Criminal Procedure Rules* 2005, r.10.1 in Appendix G–47.

7–121 Although committal proceedings must normally take place in open court (section 4) reporting restrictions automatically apply under section 8 and the effect of this must be explained to the defendant personally if he is present.

Application can be made for the restrictions to be lifted. If there is only one defendant the court shall lift the restrictions but if there are two or more defendants and not all of them wish to have the restrictions lifted then the court has to exercise its discretion in the interests of justice.

Subsection (4) lists the information that is not covered by the restrictions and basic details of this nature may be included in a report. Breach of the restrictions is a summary offence under subsection (5).

Before the court makes an order for the lifting of reporting restrictions at committal all the defendants must be present and be given an opportunity to make representations. The lifting of restrictions in a case of murder without hearing submissions from all the defendants was held to be in breach of natural justice: *R. v. Wirral District Magistrates' Court, ex p. Meikle* [1991] C.O.D. 2, DC.

Only where a very strong case is made out should the court lift restrictions when not all the accused wish to have them lifted. The interests of justice test was not met when one defendant wanted to lift the restrictions to publicise "sharp practice" by the police: *R v. Leeds Justices, ex p. Sykes,* (1983) 76 Cr.App.R. 129, DC.

7–122 Application can be made at any time in the proceedings and before the committal begins. Where a defendant faced several charges and there were several defendants, an application to lift the restrictions was dealt with at the preliminary stage. The case then led to several different sets of committal proceedings. The order made at the start of the initial committal was held to apply to all the committals in which the defendant was later involved. The appeal court did advise that the court should be precise about the extent and effect of the order: *Magistrates' Courts Act* 1980, s.8(8); *R. v. Bow Street Magistrates, ex p. Kray* [1969] 1 Q.B. 473, DC.

Section 4(2) of the *Contempt of Court Act* 1981 also applies to committals. The restrictions are imposed in different situations and for different purposes; that is where the publication of committal proceedings was prejudicial to the defendant's interests and where publication of proceedings, whether or not prejudicial to the defendant would be a contempt. A defendant applied for reporting restrictions to be lifted but later on in the committal the court made an order under section 4 of the *Contempt of Court Act* 1981 and re-imposed reporting restrictions. A journalist challenged this decision and the court held that the words "any other proceedings pending or imminent" in section 4(2) included potential proceedings in the Crown Court and so did apply: *R. v. Horsham Justices, ex p. Farquharson* [1982] Q.B. 762, DC and CA (Civ.Div).

(9) Committal of corporation

Magistrates' Courts Act 1980, Sched. 3, paras 1–3(1)

1.—(1) A magistrates' court may commit a corporation for trial by an order in writing **7–123** empowering the prosecutor to prefer a bill of indictment in respect of the offence named in the order.

(2) An order under this paragraph shall not prohibit the inclusion in the bill of indictment of counts that under section 2 of the *Administration of Justice (Miscellaneous Provisions) Act* 1933 may be included in the bill in substitution for, or in addition to, counts charging the offence named in the order.

2. A representative may on behalf of a corporation—
   (a) *make before examining justices such representations as could be made by an accused who is not a corporation;*
   (b) consent to the corporation being tried summarily;
   (c) enter a plea of guilty or not guilty on the trial by a magistrates' court of an information.

3.—(1) Where a representative appears, any requirement of this Act that anything shall be done in the presence of the accused, or shall be read or said to the accused, shall be construed as a requirement that that thing shall be done in the presence of the representative or read or said to the representative.

[The preceding paragraphs are printed as amended by the *Criminal Procedure and Investigations Act* 1996, Sched. 1. As from a day to be appointed, the words in italics in paragraph (2)(a) will be repealed by the *Criminal Justice Act* 2003, Scheds 3 and 37.]

The act of committal of a corporation is the oral determination by court, which will not be invalidated if the court subsequently uses the wrong form for the purposes of paragraph 1(1): *R. v. Nelson Group Services (Maintenance) Ltd* [1999] 1 W.L.R. 1526, CA.

VII. MISCELLANEOUS

(1) Separate trials of informations

A defendant appearing before the magistrates' court may be charged with several of- **7–124** fences arising from one incident or may face further charges concerning unrelated matters. The court must then decide whether to try the cases together or whether separate trials are required. Similarly there may be several co-accused charged with joint offences who may wish to be tried separately. The main issue for the court is to consider the interests of justice and whether a trial will be fair in compliance with Article 6 of the ECHR. Different charges being tried together may result in prejudice being caused to the defence.

In *Chief Constable of Norfolk v. Clayton* [1983] 2 A.C. 473, HL, the circumstances in which the court may hear and determine separate informations were reviewed. If in each case the facts are connected, then if the court thinks fit they can be heard together. Before embarking on a joint trial, the court should seek the consent of both the prosecution and the defence. If consent is not forthcoming the court should consider submissions and rule as they think fit in the interests of justice. The fact that the defence does not consent to joint trials is an important factor but does not deprive the court of its discretion to order joint trials. See also *R. v. Camberwell Green Stipendiary Magistrate, ex p. Martin* [2001] A.C.D. 8, DC.

When the prosecution and defence agree to separate trials, the court may still order joint trial but the court should be slow to reach such a conclusion: *R. v. Highbury Corner Magistrates' Court, ex p. McGinley*, 150 J.P. 257, DC. Where a defendant applies for a separate trial because an essential part of his defence consists of an attack on his co-defendant it remained a matter for the discretion of the court whether to allow separate trials: *R. v. Grondkowski* [1946] K.B. 369, CA. Separate representation may be granted which would protect the interests of the defendant.

7–125 Defendants jointly charged will appear in the dock together and may be jointly or separately represented. The practice of putting in the dock defendants who are not jointly charged and who have been arrested at different times and places is discouraged as it gives the impression of "group justice": *R. v. Mansfield Justices, ex p. Sharkey* [1985] Q.B. 613, DC.

It was held that under no circumstances may a court order that a summons and cross-summons should be heard together. Although in many cases joint trials were appropriate the court identified added difficulties with the conduct of such a case which made joint trial inappropriate: *R. v. Epsom Justices, ex p. Gibbons* [1984] Q.B. 574, DC.

If the informations are to be tried separately the question that then arises is whether the same bench should hear all the cases. It is a matter of discretion for the bench to decide whether it should try all the charges or whether they should be adjourned to different days before different benches. The court must apply its mind judicially to ensure there is no likelihood of bias. Where a court decided to proceed with hearing six sets of offences against a defendant no bias was apparent because the exercise of the discretion was plainly reviewed after hearing each batch of charges: *R. v. Sandwich Justices, ex p. Berry*, 74 Cr.App.R. 132, DC.

7–126 Joint trials either of co-defendants or of several charges may give rise to an appearance of bias. The test to be applied is whether a reasonable and fair-minded person, knowing all the facts, would have a reasonable suspicion that a fair trial would not be possible. That some unrelated charges are all included on the same charge sheet was held not to be improper and did not give rise to bias: *R. v. Weston-super-Mare Justices, ex p. Shaw* [1987] Q.B. 640, DC. But disclosing on the register sheets all charges pending against a defendant could give rise to the appearance of bias and was wrong in law as it did not comply with rule 66 of the *Magistrates' Courts Rules* 1981 (now see rule 6.1 of the *Criminal Procedure Rules* 2005 (Appendix G–29): *R. v. Liverpool City Justices, ex p. Topping*, 79 Cr.App.R. 170, DC.

Where a number of cases involving separate defendants have a common factual issue, the magistrates' court has a discretion to hear all the cases at the same time, without making the defendants co-defendants; to adopt such an approach, the court must separate out the evidence in each case, and permit no cross-examination of witnesses on factual issues where those issues related to one particular case: *Skinner v. DPP* [2005] R.T.R. 17, DC.

(2) Alternative charges

7–127 The magistrates' court has no inherent power to convict on a lesser offence rather than the one charged in a summary trial. The proper procedure is for the prosecution to charge offences in the alternative. This can be done either right from the start at charge or an alternative offence can be preferred during the course of the proceedings.

When an alternative charge is brought the defence has a right to an adjournment to consider it. It is a matter for the prosecution which charge to prefer. Where a defendant was charged with assault occasioning actual bodily harm the prosecution preferred an alternative charge of common assault. The defendant said this was an abuse of process because the prosecution wanted to deprive him of his right to jury trial. The motive for choosing a particular charge was held irrelevant in the absence of bad faith: *R. v. Sheffield Justices, ex p. DPP* [1993] Crim.L.R. 136, DC; *R. v. Canterbury and St Augustine Justices, ex p. Klisiak* [1982] Q.B. 398, DC.

In *R. (CPS) v. Blaydon Youth Court*, 168 J.P. 638, DC, at trial the defendant was charged with a racially aggravated offence under section 4A of the *Public Order Act* 1986 and also with the same offence but not aggravated. The prosecution said that the charges were in the alternative and a joint trial on both charges was held. The defendant neither objected nor consented at the time but the court took the view that the charges were duplicitous. At the Divisional Court it was held that the court was wrong and that there could be a joint trial of two informations. Where the charges arose from the same facts it would be inconvenient and expensive for them to be tried separately and it was not against the interests of justice for them to be tried together. The proper course if there was a conviction on the more serious offence would be to adjourn the remaining offence generally so it would remain as a charge if there were a successful appeal against conviction on the other offence. This case confirms that alternative verdicts are available in the magistrates'court provided alternative charges are brought.

(3) Prosecution not proceeding

After the defendant has been charged the prosecution may decide that it will not **7–128** proceed. The case may then be dealt with in one of three ways; withdrawal, no evidence offered, or discontinuance.

(4) Withdrawal of summons

The court has power to grant an application to withdraw a summons without an **7–129** adjudication being made. There is no requirement for the matter to be put and a plea to be entered: *R. v. Redbridge Justices, ex p. Sainty* [1981] R.T.R. 13, DC.

The withdrawal of a summons is not the equivalent to an acquittal and so will not act as a bar on the issue of a further summons in respect of the same charge where there has been no adjudication on the merits of the case: *R. v. Grays Justices, ex p. Low* [1990] 1 Q.B. 54, DC; *London Borough of Islington v. Michaelides* [2001] Crim.L.R. 843, DC.

(5) Offering no evidence

Once the accused has entered a plea of not guilty to the information, it is no longer **7–130** possible for the prosecution to ask for the matter to be withdrawn. The prosecution may offer no evidence and the case will be dismissed under section 9 of the *Magistrates' Courts Act* 1980. The charge cannot then be revived.

Where an accused has been lawfully acquitted by a magistrates' court of competent jurisdiction acting within its jurisdiction, he cannot be prosecuted again for the same offence, even if the acquittal resulted from the prosecution not offering any evidence: *R. v. Pressick* [1978] Crim.L.R. 377, CA; *R. v. Swansea Justices, ex p. Purvis*, 145 J.P. 252, DC. If the prosecution are of the view that the case is too weak to proceed, and that they would not resist a submission of no case to answer, they may nonetheless allow the proceedings to continue and to leave it to the judge to decide whether or not there is a case to answer; but it would be preferable for them to abandon the prosecution; and if the matter is allowed to proceed to a submission of no case to answer and it is ruled that there is a case to answer, it will be too late for the prosecution to abandon the case subsequently (although there is no obligation to cross-examine defence witnesses or to make a closing speech): *R. v. O.* [1999] 1 *Archbold News* 2, CA.

(6) Statutory discontinuance

Prosecution of Offences Act 1985, s.23

Discontinuance of proceedings in magistrates' courts

7–131   **23**—(1) Where the Director of Public Prosecutions has the conduct of proceedings for an offence, this section applies in relation to the preliminary stages of those proceedings.

(2) In this section, "preliminary stage" in relation to proceedings for an offence does not include—

    (a) *in the case of a summary offence, any stage of the proceedings after the court has begun to hear evidence for the prosecution at the trial;*

    [(a) any stage of the proceedings after the court has begun to hear evidence for the prosecution at a summary trial of the offence; or]

    (b) *in the case of an indictable offence, any stage of the proceedings after—*

        (i) *the accused has been committed for trial; or*

        (ii) *the court has begun to hear evidence for the prosecution at a summary trial of the offence;*

    [(b) any stage of the proceedings after the accused has been sent for trial for the offence.]

    (c) *in the case of any offence, any stage of the proceedings after the accused has been sent for trial under section 51 of the* Crime and Disorder Act *1998 (no committal proceedings for indictable-only and related offences).*

(3) Where, at any time during the preliminary stages of the proceedings, the Director gives notice under this section to the designated officer for the court that he does not want the proceedings to continue, they shall be discontinued with effect from the giving of that notice but may be revived by notice given by the accused under subsection (7) below.

(4) Where, in the case of a person charged with an offence after being taken into custody without a warrant, the Director gives him notice, at a time when no magistrates' court has been informed of the charge, that the proceedings against him are discontinued, they shall be discontinued with effect from the giving of that notice.

(5) The Director shall, in any notice given under subsection (3) above, give reasons for not wanting the proceedings to continue.

(6) On giving any notice under subsection (3) above the Director shall inform the accused of the notice and of the accused's right to require the proceedings to be continued; but the Director shall not be obliged to give the accused any indication of his reasons for not wanting the proceedings to continue.

(7) Where the Director has given notice under subsection (3) above, the accused shall, if he wants the proceedings to continue, give notice to that effect to the designated officer for the court within the prescribed period; and where notice is so given the proceedings shall continue as if no notice had been given by the Director under subsection (3) above.

(8) Where the designated officer for the court has been so notified by the accused he shall inform the Director.

(9) The discontinuance of any proceedings by virtue of this section shall not prevent the institution of fresh proceedings in respect of the same offence.

(10) In this section "prescribed" means prescribed by Criminal Procedure Rules.

[This section is printed as amended by the *Crime and Disorder Act* 1998, Sched. 8, and the *Courts Act* 2003, Sched. 8. The *Criminal Justice Act* 2003, Sched. 3, substitutes for the words set out in italics in subsection (2), the words which are set out in square brackets. That amendment was brought into force as from May 9, 2005, by the *Criminal Justice Act 2003 (Commencement No. 9) Order* 2005 (S.I. 2005 No. 1267), only for the purposes of cases sent to the Crown Court under section 51A(3)(d) of the 1998 Act. For all other purposes, the amendment is to be brought into force as from a day to be appointed.]

7–132   A notice of discontinuance may be served by the prosecution on the court and the defence during the preliminary stages of a case. The preliminary stages are defined in subsection (2). A case cannot be discontinued after a case has begun with prosecution evidence being heard in a summary trial or after an indictable case has been committed or sent to the Crown Court.

The defendant may require the proceedings to continue. He is also entitled to apply for costs after a discontinuance.

The prosecution may recharge the offence after a discontinuance.

This power does not affect the right of the prosecution to withdraw or offer no evidence in a case: *Cooke v. DPP and Brent Justices*, 156 J.P. 497, DC.

The *Commissioners for Revenue and Customs Act* 2005, s.36(3), and the *Serious Organised Crime and Police Act* 2005, s.38(5), apply section 23 of the 1985 Act (with necessary modifications) to proceedings conducted by the Director of the Revenue and Customs Prosecutions Office.

Part I

Part II

Summary Trial

<small>CHAPTER 8</small>

SUMMARY TRIAL

I. HEARING IN OPEN COURT

A. GENERAL PRINCIPLE

8–1   In general, criminal proceedings should be heard in open court: *Magistrates' Courts Act* 1980, s.121(4) and ECHR, Art. 6(1). It allows public scrutiny, guarantees a fair trial and maintains public confidence: *Pretto v. Italy*, 6 E.H.R.R. 182 at paragraph 21; *Stefanelli v. San Marino* (2001) 33 E.H.R.R. 16. The public and press must be admitted to the courtroom and evidence must be given publicly. If evidence is not given orally but by way of statement this is read aloud either fully or in summary. Matters of plea and sentence should be dealt with in open court, save exceptionally. It is no part of the justice system for anyone "to do deals in private" and any communication between a party and a court must be communicated to the other parties: *Bowers* [2006] EWCA Crim 1433. This was a case where counsel for two defendants had acted upon an indication of sentence given by a court official rather than the judge without bringing it to the notice of the court or the prosecution; the defendants could not rely upon such information and therefore could not complain when their sentences were longer than the indication suggested. A bail application should be heard in public unless there are sound reasons for not doing so: *Malik v. CCC*, unreported, June 27, 2006.

8–2   Access by the press is particularly important: *Axen v. Germany*, 6 E.H.R.R. 195 at paragraph 25. In *Att.-Gen. v. Leveller Magazine Ltd* [1979] A.C. 440 Lord Diplock stated:

> "If the way that the courts behave cannot be hidden from the public ear and eye this provides a safeguard against judicial arbitrariness or idiosyncrasy and maintains the public confidence in the administration of justice. The application of this principle of open justice has two aspects: as respects proceedings in the court itself it requires that they should be held in open court to which the press and public are admitted and that, in criminal cases at any rate, all evidence communicated to the court is communicated publicly. As respects the publication to a wider public of fair and accurate reports of proceedings that have taken place in court the principle requires that nothing should be done to discourage this.
>
> However, since the purpose of the general rule is to serve the ends of justice it may be necessary to depart from it where the nature or circumstances of the particular proceeding are such that the application of the general rule in its entirety would frustrate or render impracticable the administration of justice or would damage some other public interest for whose protection Parliament has made some statutory derogation from the rule. Apart from statutory exceptions, however, where a court in the exercise of its inherent power to control the conduct of the proceedings before it departs in any way from the general rule, the departure is justified to the extent and to no more than the extent that the court reasonably believes to be necessary in order to serve the ends of justice."

This has been confirmed in the case of *Hammond v. Secretary of State for the Home Department* [2006] 1 All E.R. 219, a case relating to the term of imprisonment following the imposition of a life sentence where it was decided that a discretion should be read into the legislation to allow an oral hearing. The case of *R. (A.) v. Central Criminal Court* [2006] EWCA Crim 4; [2006] 1 W.L.R. 1361, however, concerning appeals against orders restricting public access to criminal proceedings held that the absence of discretion to allow an oral hearing was not incompatible with Article 6 of the ECHR.

Where there is a case management hearing *K.* [2006] EWCA Crim 724 has decided that a Crown Court judge can deal with preliminary issues by way of written submissions and limit their contents. It is submitted that this can also happen in the magistrates' courts.

B. CLOSED COURT IN THE INTERESTS OF JUSTICE

8–3   A magistrates' court has the power to exclude the press and the public, but only when it is necessary for the administration of justice: *R. v. Malvern Justices, ex p. Evans*; *R. v. Evesham Justices, ex p. McDonogh* [1988] Q.B. 553; *Richards* 163 J.P. 246, CA, see Article 6(1) of the ECHR.

In *R. v. Denbigh Justices, ex p. Williams and Evans* [1974] Q.B. 759, DC, the court stated at 765 that:

> "The injunction to the presiding judge or magistrate is: do your best to enable the public to come in and see what is happening, having a proper common sense regard for the facilities available and the facility for keeping order, security and the like ... the presence of absence of the press is a vital factor in deciding whether a particular hearing was or was not in open court. I find it difficult to imagine a case which can be said to be held publicly if the press have been actively excluded. On the other hand, the fact that the press is present is not conclusive the other way ..."

This was confirmed in *Hammond v. Secretary of State for the Home Department* [2006] 1 All E.R. 219, a case relating to the term of imprisonment following the imposition of a life sentence where it was decided that a discretion should be read into the legislation to allow an oral hearing. The case of *R. (A.) v. Central Criminal Court* [2006] 1 W.L.R. 1361, however, concerning appeals against orders restricting public access to criminal proceedings, held that the absence of discretion to allow an oral hearing was not incompatible with Article 6 of the ECHR.

Where there is a case management hearing *Re K.* [2006] EWCA Crim 724; [2006] 2 All E.R. 552 has decided that a Crown Court judge can deal with preliminary issues by way of written submissions and limit their contents. It is submitted that this can also happen in the magistrates' courts.

In this case the court considered that persons of objectionable character or children **8–4** of "tender years" could be excluded if it was necessary for the proper conduct of the trial. In *X. v. Austria* (1963) App.No.1913/63 2 Digest 438, the public was excluded in a trial for sexual offences against children. In *McPherson v. McPherson* [1936] A.C. 177, PC, closure of the court was upheld where there was disorder or the anticipation of it.

Generally no distinction should be drawn between exclusion of the press and the public. There may be situations, however, where such a distinction may be necessary to ensure that justice can be done without a completely closed hearing. Where the court is satisfied that an important prosecution witness would refuse to give evidence unless the public were not permitted in court, it is entitled to close the court to the general public but with members of the press remaining: *Richards* (1999) 163 J.P. 246, CA; *Waterfield* (1974) 60 Cr.App.R. 296, CA.

Protection of public decency is not a sufficient reason to justify excluding the public from court: *Scott v. Scott* [1913] A.C. 417. In *Waterfield, ante*, the court considered that the public had no right to see exhibits, particularly if the exhibit is an obscene film, but it might want to know the type of films involved. If a judge excludes the general public when such films are shown, the press should normally be permitted to remain so that they can provide the public with information upon which to base opinions.

The risk of financial damage, or damage to reputation or goodwill, resulting from **8–5** the institution of proceedings concerning a person's business is not a valid reason for departing from the principle that proceedings should be heard in open court: *R. v. Dover Justices, ex p. Dover DC* [1992] Crim.L.R. 371, DC. The "necessity" principle does not justify a private sitting because of the embarrassing nature of the evidence, or to deny or prevent an opportunity to show interest: *R. v. Chancellor of Chichester Consistory Court, ex p. News Group Newspapers Ltd* [1992] C.O.D. 48, DC.

It may also be necessary to protect a witness's right to life under Article 2 ECHR: *R. v. Lord Saville of Newdigate, ex p. A.* [2000] 1 W.L.R. 1855. This case concerned the anonymity of soldiers giving evidence to the "Bloody Sunday" tribunal in Northern Ireland and their fear of reprisal. The court has to balance the conflicting interests of the defendant and any witness.

When a court considers excluding the public it should draw a distinction between matters which should never meet the public eye and matters where the concern is in relation to making matters known before the conclusion of the trial or related proceedings and the risk of prejudice arising therefrom. In the latter situation the risk of prejudice

Part II

can often be dealt with by an order under section 4(2) of the *Contempt of Court Act* 1981 or the postponing of a press report: *Crook*, 93 Cr.App.R. 17, CA.

Contempt of Court Act 1981 s.4(2)

8–6   **4.**—(2) In any such proceedings the court may, where it appears to be necessary for avoiding a substantial risk of prejudice to the administration of justice in those proceedings, or in any other proceedings pending or imminent, order that the publication of any report of the proceedings, or any part of the proceedings, be postponed for such period as the court thinks necessary for that purpose.

8–7   These powers should not be used where the court is concerned merely for the welfare of the defendant: *R. v. Newtownabbey Magistrates' Court, ex p. Belfast Telegraph Newspapers Ltd, The Times*, August 27, 1997, QBD. Restrictions under the *Contempt of Court Act* 1981 are only allowed where there is a substantial risk of prejudice to the administration of justice.

Even when it is claimed that the safety of the witness is at stake the court should consider whether he can be adequately protected by means which are less drastic than total exclusion of the public, *e.g.* the making of a statement or an order prohibiting the publication of a person's name under section 11 of the *Contempt of Court Act* 1981 or by using a letter to designate his name and the use of screens: *R. v. Reigate Justices, ex p. Argus Newspapers* (1983) 5 Cr.App.R.(S.) 181; *R. v. Lord Saville of Newdigate, ex p. A., ante.* The screening of an accused from a witness in a terrorist trial has been upheld: *X. v. U.K.* (1993) 15 E.H.R.R. CD 113. See *post*, § 9–26.

C. STATUTORY EXCEPTIONS

8–8   The general rule that a summary trial must be held in open court is subject to several statutory exceptions.

Children and Young Persons Act 1933, ss.36–37

Prohibition against children being present in court during the trial of other persons
8–9   **36.** No child (other than an infant in arms) shall be permitted to be present in court during the trial of any other person charged with an offence, or during any proceedings preliminary thereto, except during such time as his presence is required as a witness or otherwise for the purposes of justice or while the court consents to his presence; and any child present in court when under this section he is not to be permitted to be so shall be ordered to be removed ...

Power to clear court while child or young person is giving evidence in certain cases
8–10   **37.**—(1) Where, in any proceedings in relation to an offence against, or any conduct contrary to, decency or morality, a person who, in the opinion of the court, is a child or young person is called as a witness, the court may direct that all or any persons, not being members or officers of the court or parties to the case, their counsel or solicitors, or persons otherwise directly concerned in the case, be excluded from the court during the taking of the evidence of that witness:

Provided that nothing in this section shall authorise the exclusion of bona fide representatives of a newspaper or news agency.

(2) The powers conferred on a court by this section shall be in addition and without prejudice to any other powers of the court to hear proceedings in camera.

8–11   Children under fourteen years of age (other than babies) are generally excluded from court although application may be made to the court to allow such a child to be present. This sometimes happens when a defendant's child cannot be looked after elsewhere. It may also happen when a party of schoolchildren wish to visit the court. Each application will be dealt with on its merits and will, amongst other matters, depend upon the nature of the court proceedings. The court may also clear the court where a child is giving evidence.

Official Secrets Act 1920, s.8

Provisions as to trial and punishment of offences
8–12   **8.**—(4) In addition and without prejudice to any powers which a court may possess to order

the exclusion of the public from any proceedings if, in the course of proceedings before a court against any person for an offence under the principal Act or this Act or the proceedings on appeal, or in the course of the trial of a person for felony or misdemeanour under the principal Act or this Act, application is made by the prosecution, on the ground that the publication of any evidence to be given or of any statement to be made in the course of the proceedings would be prejudicial to the national safety, that all or any portion of the public shall be excluded during any part of the hearing, the court may make an order to that effect, but the passing of sentence shall in any case take place in public.

Although cases under this Act are finalised in the Crown Court there may be in- **8–13** stances where, *e.g.* on a bail application the prosecution will make use of this section.

Youth Justice and Criminal Evidence Act 1999, s.43

Procedure on applications under section 41

　　43.—(1) An application for leave shall be heard in private and in the absence of the **8–14** complainant.

　　In this section "leave" means leave under section 41.

　　(2) Where such an application has been determined, the court must state in open court (but in the absence of the jury, if there is one)—

　　　　(a) its reasons for giving, or refusing, leave, and

　　　　(b) if it gives leave, the extent to which evidence may be adduced or questions asked in pursuance of the leave,

and, if it is a magistrates' court, must cause those matters to be entered in the register of its proceedings.

　　(3) Rules of court may make provision—

　　　　(a) requiring applications for leave to specify, in relation to each item of evidence or question to which they relate, particulars of the grounds on which it is asserted that leave should be given by virtue of subsection (3) or (5) of section 41;

　　　　(b) enabling the court to request a party to the proceedings to provide the court with information which it considers would assist it in determining an application for leave;

　　　　(c) for the manner in which confidential or sensitive information is to be treated in connection with such an application, and in particular as to its being disclosed to, or withheld from, parties to the proceedings.

This section provides for a court to sit in private when hearing an application for leave to adduce evidence or to cross-examine on a complainant's sexual history.

An application under *Youth Justice and Criminal Evidence Act* 1999, s.46 may be **8–15** heard in camera.

The *Criminal Procedure Rules* 2005 provide for seven days' notice to be given **8–16** where an in camera sitting is sought for reasons of national security or for the protection of the identity of a witness or other person: rule 16.9. See Appendix G–81.

D. PUBLICITY

Contempt of Court Act 1981, ss.4, 11

Contemporary reports of proceedings

　　4.—(1) Subject to this section a person is not guilty of contempt of court under the strict li- **8–17** ability rule in respect of a fair and accurate report of legal proceedings held in public, published contemporaneously and in good faith.

　　(2) In any such proceedings the court may, where it appears to be necessary for avoiding a substantial risk of prejudice to the administration of justice in those proceedings, or in any other proceedings pending or imminent, order that the publication of any report of the proceedings, or any part of the proceedings, be postponed for such period as the court thinks necessary for that purpose.

　　(3) For the purposes of subsection (1) of this section a report of proceedings shall be treated as published contemporaneously—

　　　　(a) in the case of a report of which publication is postponed pursuant to an order

under subsection (2) of this section, if published as soon as practicable after that
order expires;

(b) in the case of a report of committal proceedings of which publication is permitted
by virtue only of subsection (3) of section 8 of the *Magistrates' Courts Act* 1980, if
published as soon as practicable after publication is so permitted.

Publication of matters exempted from disclosure in court

8–18   **11.** In any case where a court (having power to do so) allows a name or other matter to be
withheld from the public in proceedings before the court, the court may give such directions
prohibiting the publication of that name or matter in connection with the proceedings as appear
to the court to be necessary for the purpose for which it was so withheld.

The press plays an important part in keeping the public informed of court proceedings and it is important that reports are fair and accurate. Adverse publicity may give
rise to a breach of Article 6(1) of the European Convention on Human Rights and may
constitute grounds for a stay of the proceedings.

8–19   In *R. v. Bow Street Stipendiary Magistrate, ex p. DPP* (1992) 95 Cr.App.R. 9, DC
the defendants were police officers who had interviewed suspects who were later charged
and convicted of the Guildford and Woolwich pub bombings in 1974. The only evidence against those suspects was confession evidence obtained in an interview in the
presence of the defendant police officers. A subsequent police investigation revealed
discrepancies between the typed and handwritten notes of the interview made by the
defendant police officers. Those who had been convicted of the bombings successfully
appealed and were released in October 1989. In December 1990, the police officers
were charged with conspiring to pervert the course of justice and in a preliminary application argued abuse of process on the grounds that adverse media coverage of their
case was so prejudicial that a fair trial was not possible. The Stipendiary Magistrate upheld the application but on review the Divisional Court held that the publicity could not
affect the fairness of the trial and quashed the magistrate's decision. The publication of a
defendant's identity in a murder trial could not be prevented in order to protect the
privacy of the defendant's child who was not involved in the proceedings: *Re S. (a
child) (Identification: Restriction on Publication)* [2005] 1 A.C. 593.

The court may postpone the publication of reports under section 4 or restrict the
publication of reports under section 11 where it is necessary to avoid a substantial risk to
the prejudice of the administration of justice. Where there is likely to be a great deal of
legitimate public discussion and debate as a result of the reporting of proceedings, it is
unnecessary to postpone media reports until the conclusion of the trial of co-defendants
as there are two safeguards—the responsibility of the media to avoid inappropriate
comment and the trial process itself: In *Re Barot, The Times*, November 6, 2006. The
Practice Direction (Criminal Proceedings: Consolidation) [2002] 1 W.L.R. 2870,
paragraph I.3 directs that a permanent record of such orders is kept and that an order
is formulated in precise terms having regard to the decision in *R. v. Horsham Justices,
ex p. Farquharson* [1982] Q.B. 762. The order must be reduced into writing and must
state (a) its precise scope, (b) the time at which it shall cease to have effect, if appropriate,
and (c) the specific purpose of making the order. The court will give copies to the parties and display the order in a prominent position in the courthouse.

8–20   Representatives of the press may address the court before an order is made: *R. v.
Clerkenwell Magistrates' Court, ex p. Telegraph Plc* [1993] 2 All E.R. 183. In *ex p.
The Telegraph Group Plc* [2001] 1 W.L.R. 1983, it was stated that a court should take
a three stage approach. First, the court should consider whether reporting would give
rise to a "not insubstantial" risk of prejudice, secondly whether a section 4(2) order
would eliminate it or whether it could be overcome by less restrictive measures and
thirdly, whether the degree of risk contemplated would be tolerable as the "lesser of two
evils".

Before the application is heard the name or other matter must be withheld: *R. v.
Arundel Justices, ex p. Westminster Press Ltd* [1985] 2 All E.R. 390. In *Tower Bridge
Magistrates' Court, ex p. Osborne* [1988] Crim.L.R. 382, it was said that it is generally
necessary to hear such an application *in camera*.

The general right of publication in section 4(1) is subject to several statutory restrictions in relation to:

— Committal proceedings;
— Youths;
— Certain adult witnesses;
— Rape cases;
— Derogatory assertions made in mitigating statements;

For Youth Court, see Ch.25.

Magistrates' Courts Act 1980, s.8

Restrictions on reports of committal proceedings

8.—(1) Except as provided by subsections (2), (3) and (8) below, it shall not be lawful to pub- **8–21** lish in Great Britain a written report, or to include in a relevant programme for reception in Great Britain a report, of any committal proceedings in England and Wales containing any matter other than that permitted by subsection (4) below.

(2) Subject to subsection (2A) below a magistrates' court shall, on an application for the purpose made with reference to any committal proceedings by the accused or one of the accused, as the case may be, order that subsection (1) above shall not apply to reports of those proceedings.

(2A) Where in the case of two or more accused one of them objects to the making on an order under subsection (2) above, the court shall make the order if, and only if, it is satisfied, after hearing the representations of the accused, that it is in the interests of justice to do so.

(2B) An order under subsection (2) above shall not apply to reports of proceedings under subsection (2A) above, but any decisions of the court to make or not to make such an order may be contained in reports published or included in a relevant programme before the time authorised by subsection (3) below.

(3) It shall not be unlawful under this section to publish or include in a relevant programme a report of committal proceedings containing any matter other than that permitted by subsection (4) below--

(a) where the magistrates' court determines not to commit the accused, or determines to commit none of the accused, for trial, after it so determines;

(b) where the court commits the accused or any of the accused for trial, after the conclusion of his trial or, as the case may be, the trial of the last to be tried;

and where at any time during the inquiry the court proceeds to try summarily the case of one or more of the accused under section 25(3) or (7) below, while committing the other accused or one or more of the other accused for trial, it shall not be unlawful under this section to publish or include in a relevant programme as part of a report of the summary trial, after the court determines to proceed as aforesaid, a report of so much of the committal proceedings containing any such matter as takes place before the determination.

(4) The following matters may be contained in a report of committal proceedings published or included in a relevant programme without an order under subsection (2) above before the time authorised by subsection (3) above, that is to say--

(a) the identity of the court and the names of the examining justices;

(b) the names, addresses and occupations of the parties and witnesses and the ages of the accused and witnesses;

(c) the offence or offences, or a summary of them, with which the accused is or are charged;

(d) the names of the legal representatives engaged in the proceedings;

(e) any decision of the court to commit the accused or any of the accused for trial, and any decision of the court on the disposal of the case of any accused not committed;

(f) where the court commits the accused or any of the accused for trial, the charge or charges, or a summary of them, on which he is committed and the court to which he is committed;

(g) where the committal proceedings are adjourned, the date and place to which they are adjourned;

(h) any arrangements as to bail on committal or adjournment;

      (i) whether a right to representation funded by the Legal Services Commission as part of the Criminal Defence Service was granted to the accused or any of the accused.

(5) If a report is published or included in a relevant programme in contravention of this section, the following persons, that is to say—

      (a) in the case of a publication of a written report as part of a newspaper or periodical, any proprietor, editor or publisher of the newspaper or periodical;

      (b) in the case of a publication of a written report otherwise than as part of a newspaper or periodical, the person who publishes it;

      (c) in the case of the inclusion of a report in a relevant programme, any body corporate which provides the service in which the programme is included and any person having functions in relation to the programme corresponding to those of an editor of a newspaper,

shall be liable on summary conviction to a fine not exceeding level 5 on the standard scale.

(6) Proceedings for an offence under this section shall not, in England and Wales, be instituted otherwise than by or with the consent of the Attorney-General.

(7) Subsection (1) above shall be in addition to, and not in derogation from, the provisions of any other enactment with respect to the publication of reports and proceedings of magistrates' and other courts.

(8) For the purposes of this section committal proceedings shall, in relation to an information charging an indictable offence, be deemed to include any proceedings in the magistrates' court before the court proceeds to inquire into the information as examining justices; but where a magistrates' court which has begun to try an information summarily discontinues the summary trial in pursuance of section 25(2) or (6) below and proceeds to inquire into the information as examining justices, that circumstance shall not make it unlawful under this section for a report of any proceedings on the information which was published or included in a relevant programme before the court determined to proceed as aforesaid to have been so published or included in a relevant programme.

(10) In this section—

"publish", in relation to a report, means publish the report, either by itself or as part of a newspaper or periodical, for distribution to the public.

"relevant programme" means a programme included in a programme service (within the meaning of the *Broadcasting Act* 1990).

8–22   All defendants must be given an opportunity to make representations: *Wirral District Magistrates' Court, ex.p. Meikle* [1991] C.O.D. 2. Where there are conflicting representations the court must balance those views bearing in mind that section 8 states that committal proceedings should not be reported: *Leeds J.J., ex. P. Sykes*, 76 Cr.App.R 129.

The *Criminal Procedure Rules* 2005 provide for an explanation to be given to the defendant of the restrictions and his right to apply to have them removed: rule 10.1. See Appendix G–47.

Children and Young Persons Act 1933, s.39

Power to prohibit publication of certain matter in newspapers

8–23   **39.**—(1) In relation to any proceedings in any court [...], the court may direct that—

      (a) no newspaper report of the proceedings shall reveal the name, address or school, or include any particulars calculated to lead to the identification, of any child or young person concerned in the proceedings, either as being the person [by or against] or in respect of whom the proceedings are taken, or as being a witness therein:

      (b) no picture shall be published in any newspaper as being or including a picture of any child or young person so concerned in the proceedings as aforesaid;

except in so far (if at all) as may be permitted by the direction of the court.

(2) Any person who publishes any matter in contravention of any such direction shall on summary conviction be liable in respect of each offence to a fine not exceeding [level 5 on the standard scale].

[This section is reprinted as amended by the *Children and Young Persons Act* 1963, ss.57(1), 64 and Sched. 5, and the *Criminal Justice Act* 1982, ss.38, 46.]

This is a discretionary order which may be made in any court and is generally made **8–24** of the court's own motion. It is different from the general prohibition in the *Children and Young Persons Act* 1933, s.49 which applies to youth courts. In *R. v. Lee (Anthony William) (a minor)* [1993] 2 All E.R. 170 the term "any proceedings" was clarified as meaning any proceedings in the court making the order, not any proceedings anywhere, *e.g.* on appeal. In *Leicester Crown Court, ex.p. S.* [1992] 2 All E.R. 659, Watkins L.J. said that "reports of proceedings should not be restricted unless there were reasons to do so which outweigh the legitimate interests of the public in receiving fair and accurate reports of criminal proceedings and knowing the identity of those in the community who have been guilty of criminal conduct and who may present a danger or threat to the community in which they live. There must be a good reason for making an order under section 39 just as there must be one for lifting the restrictions on publicity under section 49." He went on to say that section 39 is a power designed for use whenever and wherever in some kind of judicial proceedings a curb needs to be imposed upon publicity in the interests of a child or young person and the broader public interest. An order under section 39 need not be made during the course of the proceedings to which it relates; it may be made at any time: *R. v. Harrow Crown Court, ex p. Perkins*; *R. v. Cardiff Crown Court, ex p. M. (a minor)* (1998) 162 J.P. 527, DC. In that case an order of Cardiff Crown Court under section 39 made on Monday July 7, in relation to proceedings concluded on Friday July 4, was upheld. The court accepted that normally a direction would be made when the case was first listed and in the absence of such a direction, publicity might make it inappropriate to make a direction at a later stage. The making of a direction is not an integral part of the trial process and there is no reason in law why a direction cannot be made in relation to proceedings which have been concluded at an earlier date. The amount of publicity would be a relevant factor in determining whether to make a direction or not.

When considering an application under section 39 in respect of a child or young person who is the defendant, considerable weight should be given to the actual age of the offender and to the potential damage to any young person of public identification as a criminal before becoming an adult: *R. v. Inner London Crown Court, ex p. B.* [1996] C.O.D. 17, DC. There must be good reason for making an order. It is not only in rare and exceptional cases that such an order would be made, or once made, would be lifted: *R. v. Leicester Crown Court, ex p. S. (a minor)* (1992) 94 Cr.App.R. 145, DC. In considering whether to lift an order the welfare of the child must be taken into account but the weight to be given to it changes where there has been a conviction, particularly in a serious case. It must be remembered that the public has a legitimate interest in knowing the outcome of proceedings in court and there is a potential deterrent effect in respect of the conduct of others in the disgrace accompanying the identification of those guilty of serious offences: *R. v. Central Criminal Court, ex p. S.* [1999] 1 F.L.R. 480, DC.

In relation to ASBOs each application under section 39 must be made on its merits. Factors and principles to be taken into account were identified in *R. (T.) v. St Albans Crown Court* [2002] EWHC 1129:

1) there must be a good reason for identifying a child/young person;
2) the age of the child/young person is relevant: the weight to be attached to age decreases as the age increases;
3) considerable weight should be given to the potential damage that may be caused to the child by identification, including the effect of the publicity on the prospects of rehabilitation;
4) any improvement in the behaviour of the child/young person since the proceedings began is relevant;
5) the deterrent effect of publicity is relevant;
6) there is a strong public interest in open justice and in the public knowing as much as possible about what goes on in court proceedings;

7) the public interest in open justice often takes on enhanced importance in ASBO proceedings because (a) that may increase the efficacy of the order and (b) the public generally want to know the identity of those whose conduct might damage the fabric of society;

8) the weight to be attributed to the different relevant factors may fluctuate depending on the stage in the proceedings.

Interim ASBOs were considered in *R. (Keating) v. Knowsley MBC* [2004] EWHC 1933; (2004) 168 J.P. 461 where it was said that the interim nature of the order must be considered.

In youth courts, section 41 of the *Serious Organised Crime and Police Act* 2005 disapplies section 49 in relation to ASBOs on conviction and to breaches of ASBOs generally.

8–25 A court has the discretion to hear anybody in support of, or in opposition to, the making of an order under section 39: *R. v. Central Criminal Court, ex p. Crook* [1995] 2 Cr.App.R. 212 where the judge heard representations on behalf of the press and the children in question. The onus is on the applicant to show why the restriction on publicity is necessary: *R. v. Central Criminal Court, ex p. W., B. and C.* [2001] 1 Cr.App.R. 2, DC.

Where the alleged victim is a ward of court, it is for the court in the criminal proceedings, not the wardship judge, to make any orders restraining reporting of the criminal trial. The guardian *ad litem* will provide the prosecution with the material necessary to make the application. In *R. (a minor) (Wardship: restriction on publication), Re* [1994] 2 F.L.R. 637, CA (Civ. Div.) the defendant applied for an order on the basis that he might feel inhibited in presenting his defence as he apprehended that it would lead to publicity harmful to his child and perhaps weaken his position in the wardship proceeding.

8–26 Although *R. v. Central Criminal Court, ex p. Crook*, ante, suggested a formal procedure for reducing orders under section 39 to writing by means of a *pro forma*, the normal practice in the magistrates' court is for the order to be written in precise terms in accordance with the section in the court register.

The order must be confined to the wording of the section; there is no scope for extending restrictions: *R. (Gazette Media Co Ltd) v. Teeside Crown Court* [2005] EWCA Crim 1983; [2006] Crim.L.R. 157. The right to private and family life under Article 8 co-exists with the right to freedom of expression under Article 10. Neither Article has precedence over the other. The correct approach is to focus on the comparative importance of the specific rights claimed in an individual case and the justifications for interfering or restricting each right should be taken into account.

Vague restrictions may cause a prosecution for contravening such an order under section 39(2) to founder: *Briffett and Bradshaw v. DPP* (2002) 166 J.P. 66, DC.

Permission may be given for the register to be inspected and the justices' clerk will always clarify matters for the press.

There is no power to prohibit the publication of the name of a defendant who is not a child or young person although this may be the unintentional result of such an order. Where this is likely the court may hear representations on the identification of particular details: *R. v. Southwark Crown Court, ex p. Godwin* [1992] Q.B. 190; (1992) 94 Cr.App.R. 34, CA.

In *R. v. Tyne Tees Television Ltd, The Times*, October 20, 1997 the Court of Appeal considered that where there has been an alleged breach of an order under section 39, the better course is to report the matter for consideration as to whether there should be a prosecution for the specific summary offence under section 39(2) rather than deal with the matter as an alleged contempt of court. The court declined to rule whether contempt proceedings would ever be appropriate in view of the specific statutory offence.

8–27 A court must balance competing Convention rights but it is appropriate to begin by acknowledging the force of the argument for unrestricted publicity of proceedings in a criminal trial. In the case of *Re (S.)* [2005] 1 A.C. 593 it was held not to be appropriate to restrict publicity of the identity of a victim or defendant on the grounds that it would lead to identification of his or her child where that child is not a witness or otherwise concerned in the proceedings. An appeal against the making of an order is by way of case stated or judicial review.

Youth Justice and Criminal Evidence Act 1999, s.44

Restrictions on reporting alleged offences involving persons under 18

44.—(1) This section applies (subject to subsection (3)) where a criminal investigation has **8–28** begun in respect of—

(a) an alleged offence against the law of—

    (i) England and Wales, or

    (ii) Northern Ireland; or

(b) an alleged civil offence (other than an offence falling within paragraph (a)) committed (whether or not in the United Kingdom) by a person subject to service law.

(2) No matter relating to any person involved in the offence shall while he is under the age of 18 be included in any publication if it is likely to lead members of the public to identify him as a person involved in the offence.

(3) The restrictions imposed by subsection (2) cease to apply once there are proceedings in a court (whether a court in England and Wales, a service court or a court in Northern Ireland) in respect of the offence.

(4) For the purposes of subsection (2) any reference to a person involved in the offence is to—

(a) a person by whom the offence is alleged to have been committed; or

(b) if this paragraph applies to the publication in question by virtue of subsection (5)—

    (i) a person against or in respect of whom the offence is alleged to have been committed, or

    (ii) a person who is alleged to have been a witness to the commission of the offence;

except that paragraph (b)(i) does not include a person in relation to whom section 1 of the *Sexual Offences (Amendment) Act* 1992 (anonymity of victims of certain sexual offences) applies in connection with the offence.

(5) Subsection (4)(b) applies to a publication if—

(a) where it is a relevant programme, it is transmitted, or

(b) in the case of any other publication, it is published,

on or after such date as may be specified in an order made by the Secretary of State.

(6) The matters relating to a person in relation to which the restrictions imposed by subsection (2) apply (if their inclusion in any publication is likely to have the result mentioned in that subsection) include in particular—

(a) his name,

(b) his address,

(c) the identity of any school or other educational establishment attended by him,

(d) the identity of any place of work, and

(e) any still or moving picture of him.

(7) Any appropriate criminal court may by order dispense, to any extent specified in the order, with the restrictions imposed by subsection (2) in relation to a person if it is satisfied that it is necessary in the interests of justice to do so.

(8) However, when deciding whether to make such an order dispensing (to any extent) with the restrictions imposed by subsection (2) in relation to a person, the court shall have regard to the welfare of that person.

(9) In subsection (7) "appropriate criminal court" means—

(a) in a case where this section applies by virtue of subsection (1)(a)(i) or (ii), any court in England and Wales or (as the case may be) in Northern Ireland which has any jurisdiction in, or in relation to, any criminal proceedings (but not a service court unless the offence is alleged to have been committed by a person subject to service law);

(b) in a case where this section applies by virtue of subsection (1)(b), any court falling within paragraph (a) or a service court.

(10) The power under subsection (7) of a magistrates' court in England and Wales may be exercised by a single justice.

(11) In the case of a decision of a magistrates' court in England and Wales, or a court of summary jurisdiction in Northern Ireland, to make or refuse to make an order under subsection (7), the following persons, namely—

(a) any person who was a party to the proceedings on the application for the order, and

(b) with the leave of the Crown Court, any other person,

may, in accordance with rules of court, appeal to the Crown Court against that decision or appear or be represented at the hearing of such an appeal.

(12) On such an appeal the Crown Court—

(a) may make such order as is necessary to give effect to its determination of the appeal; and

(b) may also make such incidental or consequential orders as appear to it to be just.

(13) In this section—

(a) "civil offence" means an act or omission which, if committed in England and Wales, would be an offence against the law of England and Wales;

(b) any reference to a criminal investigation, in relation to an alleged offence, is to an investigation conducted by police officers, or other persons charged with the duty of investigating offences, with a view to it being ascertained whether a person should be charged with the offence;

(c) any reference to a person subject to service law is to—

(i) a person subject to military law, air-force law or the *Naval Discipline Act* 1957, or

(ii) any other person to whom provisions of Part II of the *Army Act* 1955, Part II of the *Air Force Act* 1955 or Parts I and II of the *Naval Discipline Act* 1957 apply (whether with or without any modifications).

8–29   When this section comes into force then the reporting of a crime before proceedings commence where a person under the age of 18 is a victim or a potential witness or defendant is prohibited where it may lead to his identification. The court may lift the restriction if it satisfied that it is in the interests of justice to do so.

Youth Justice and Criminal Evidence Act 1999, s.45

Power to restrict reporting of criminal proceedings involving persons under 18

8–30   **45.**—(1) This section applies (subject to subsection (2)) in relation to—

(a) any criminal proceedings in any court (other than a service court) in England and Wales or Northern Ireland; and

(b) any proceedings (whether in the United Kingdom or elsewhere) in any service court.

(2) This section does not apply in relation to any proceedings to which section 49 of the *Children and Young Persons Act* 1933 applies.

(3) The court may direct that no matter relating to any person concerned in the proceedings shall while he is under the age of 18 be included in any publication if it is likely to lead members of the public to identify him as a person concerned in the proceedings.

(4) The court or an appellate court may by direction ("an excepting direction") dispense, to any extent specified in the excepting direction, with the restrictions imposed by a direction under subsection (3) if it is satisfied that it is necessary in the interests of justice to do so.

(5) The court or an appellate court may also by direction ("an excepting direction") dispense, to any extent specified in the excepting direction, with the restrictions imposed by a direction under subsection (3) if it is satisfied—

(a) that their effect is to impose a substantial and unreasonable restriction on the reporting of the proceedings, and

(b) that it is in the public interest to remove or relax that restriction;

but no excepting direction shall be given under this subsection by reason only of the fact that the proceedings have been determined in any way or have been abandoned.

(6) When deciding whether to make—

(a) a direction under subsection (3) in relation to a person, or

(b) an excepting direction under subsection (4) or (5) by virtue of which the restrictions imposed by a direction under subsection (3) would be dispensed with (to any extent) in relation to a person,

the court or (as the case may be) the appellate court shall have regard to the welfare of that person.

(7) For the purposes of subsection (3) any reference to a person concerned in the proceedings is to a person—

(a) against or in respect of whom the proceedings are taken, or

(b) who is a witness in the proceedings.

(8) The matters relating to a person in relation to which the restrictions imposed by a direction under subsection (3) apply (if their inclusion in any publication is likely to have the result mentioned in that subsection) include in particular—

(a) his name,

(b) his address,

(c) the identity of any school or other educational establishment attended by him,

(d) the identity of any place of work, and

(e) any still or moving picture of him.

(9) A direction under subsection (3) may be revoked by the court or an appellate court.

(10) An excepting direction—

(a) may be given at the time the direction under subsection (3) is given or subsequently; and

(b) may be varied or revoked by the court or an appellate court.

(11) In this section "appellate court", in relation to any proceedings in a court, means a court dealing with an appeal (including an appeal by way of case stated) arising out of the proceedings or with any further appeal.

When this section is in force the court will have power to restrict reporting in relation **8–31** to a witness or defendant under the age of 18. This section will supersede section 39 of the *Children and Young Persons Act* 1933, *ante*.

Youth Justice and Criminal Evidence Act 1999, s.46

Power to restrict reports about certain adult witness in criminal proceedings

46.—(1) This section applies where—   **8–32**

(a) in any criminal proceedings in any court (other than a service court) in England and Wales or Northern Ireland, or

(b) in any proceedings (whether in the United Kingdom or elsewhere) in any service court,

a party to the proceedings makes an application for the court to give a reporting direction in relation to a witness in the proceedings (other than the accused) who has attained the age of 18.

In this section "reporting direction" has the meaning given by subsection (6).

(2) If the court determines—

(a) that the witness is eligible for protection, and

(b) that giving a reporting direction in relation to the witness is likely to improve—

     (i)   the quality of evidence given by the witness, or

     (ii)   the level of co-operation given by the witness to any party to the proceedings in connection with that party's preparation of its case,

the court may give a reporting direction in relation to the witness.

(3) For the purposes of this section a witness is eligible for protection if the court is satisfied—

(a) that the quality of evidence given by the witness, or

(b) the level of co-operation given by the witness to any party to the proceedings in connection with that party's preparation of its case,

is likely to be diminished by reason of fear or distress on the part of the witness in connection with being identified by members of the public as a witness in the proceedings.

(4) In determining whether a witness is eligible for protection the court must take into account, in particular—

(a) the nature and alleged circumstances of the offence to which the proceedings relate;

(b) the age of the witness;

(c) such of the following matters as appear to the court to be relevant, namely—

   (i) the social and cultural background and ethnic origins of the witness,

   (ii) the domestic and employment circumstances of the witness, and

   (iii) any religious beliefs or political opinions of the witness;

(d) any behaviour towards the witness on the part of—

   (i) the accused,

   (ii) members of the family or associates of the accused, or

   (iii) any other person who is likely to be an accused or a witness in the proceedings.

(5) In determining that question the court must in addition consider any views expressed by the witness.

(6) For the purposes of this section a reporting direction in relation to a witness is a direction that no matter relating to the witness shall during the witness's lifetime be included in any publication if it is likely to lead members of the public to identify him as being a witness in the proceedings.

(7) The matters relating to a witness in relation to which the restrictions imposed by a reporting direction apply (if their inclusion in any publication is likely to have the result mentioned in subsection (6)) include in particular—

(a) the witness's name,

(b) the witness's address,

(c) the identity of any educational establishment attended by the witness,

(d) the identity of any place of work, and

(e) any still or moving picture of the witness.

(8) In determining whether to give a reporting direction the court shall consider—

(a) whether it would be in the interests of justice to do so, and

(b) the public interest in avoiding the imposition of a substantial and unreasonable restriction on the reporting of the proceedings.

(9) The court or an appellate court may by direction ("an excepting direction") dispense, to any extent specified in the excepting direction, with the restrictions imposed by a reporting direction if—

(a) it is satisfied that it is necessary in the interests of justice to do so, or

(b) it is satisfied—

   (i) that the effect of those restrictions is to impose a substantial and unreasonable restriction on the reporting of the proceedings, and

   (ii) that it is in the public interest to remove or relax that restriction;

   but no excepting direction shall be given under paragraph (b) by reason only of the fact that the proceedings have been determined in any way or have been abandoned.

(10) A reporting direction may be revoked by the court or an appellate court.

(11) An excepting direction—

(a) may be given at the time the reporting direction is given or subsequently; and

(b) may be varied or revoked by the court or an appellate court.

(12) In this section—

(a) "appellate court", in relation to any proceedings in a court, means a court dealing with an appeal (including an appeal by way of case stated) arising out of the proceedings or with any further appeal;

(b) references to the quality of a witness's evidence are to its quality in terms of completeness, coherence and accuracy (and for this purpose "coherence" refers to a witness's ability in giving evidence to give answers which address the questions put to the witness and can be understood both individually and collectively);

(c) references to the preparation of the case of a party to any proceedings include, where the party is the prosecution, the carrying out of investigations into any offence at any time charged in the proceedings.

8–33   This section came into force on October 7, 2004: *Youth Justice and Criminal Evidence Act 1999 (Commencement No. 10) (England and Wales) Order* 2004 (S.I. 2004 No. 2428). The court has the power to restrict reports about an adult witness' evidence if it believes that the witness is afraid or distressed about being identified and as a result the quality of the evidence that the witness would give or the witness' co-operation is likely to be diminished. The court will take into account the nature of the offence, the age, social, cultural background and ethnic origins, domestic and employment circumstances, religious or political beliefs of the witness and any behaviour of the defendant, his family and friends or other witnesses towards the witness. The court will also want to be satisfied that the order is likely to improve the quality of the evidence or the witness' co-operation. The court will take the witness' views into account.

The *Criminal Procedure Rules* 2005 provide for applications in respect of section 46: rules 16.1–16.8. See Appendix G–73—G–80.   **8–34**

Youth Justice and Criminal Evidence Act 1999, Sched. 7, para. 6

SCHEDULE 7

TRANSITIONAL PROVISIONS AND SAVINGS

6.—(1) Section 44 applies in relation to an alleged offence whether the criminal investiga-   **8–35** tion into it is begun before or after the coming into force of that section.

(2) The restrictions imposed by subsection (2) of section 44 do not apply to the inclusion of matter in a publication if—

   (a)   where the publication is a relevant programme, it is transmitted, or

   (b)   in the case of any other publication, it is published,

before the coming into force of that section.

(3) Nothing in section 45 or 46 applies in relation to proceedings instituted before the commencement date for that section.

(4) In sub-paragraph (3) the reference to the institution of proceedings shall be construed—

   (a)   in the case of proceedings in England in Wales (other than proceedings before a service court), in accordance with paragraph 1(2);

   (b)   in the case of proceedings in Northern Ireland (other than proceedings before a service court), in the accordance with sub-paragraph (5);

   (c)   in the case of proceedings before a service court (wherever held) in accordance with sub-paragraph (6).

(5) In the case of proceedings falling within sub-paragraph (4)(b)—

   (a)   proceedings other than proceedings on appeal are to be taken to be instituted—

      (i)   where a justice of the peace issues a summons under Article 20 of the *Magistrates' Courts (Northern Ireland) Order* 1981, when the complaint for the offence is made;

      (ii)   where a justice of the peace issues a warrant for the arrest of any person under that Article, when the complaint for the offence is made;

      (iii)   where a person is charged with the offence after being taken into custody without a warrant, when he is informed of the particulars of the charge;

      (iv)   where an indictment is presented under the authority of section 2(2)(c), (d), (e) or (f) of the *Grand Jury (Abolition) Act (Northern Ireland)* 1969, when the indictment is presented to the court;

and where the application of this paragraph would result in there being more than one time for the institution of the proceedings, they shall be taken to have been instituted at the earliest of those times; and

   (b)   proceedings on appeal are to be taken to be instituted at the time when the notice of appeal is given or (as the case may be) the reference under section 10 or 12 of the *Criminal Appeal Act* 1995 is made.

(6) In the case of proceedings falling within sub-paragraph (4)(c)—

   (a)   proceedings other than proceedings on appeal are to be taken to be instituted when the prosecuting authority prefers a charge in respect of the offence under section 83B(4) of the *Army Act* 1955, section 83B(4) of the *Air Force Act* 1955 or section 52I(4) of the *Naval Discipline Act* 1957; and

   (b)   proceedings on appeal are to be taken to be instituted when the application for leave to appeal is lodged in accordance with section 9 of the *Courts-Martial (Appeals) Act* 1968 or (as the case may be) the reference under section 34 of that Act is made.

Youth Justice and Criminal Evidence Act 1999, s.47

Restrictions on reporting directions under Chapter I or II

8–36　　　**47.**—(1) Except as provided by this section, no publication shall include a report of a matter falling within subsection (2).

(2) The matters falling within this subsection are—

(a) a direction under section 19 or 36 or an order discharging, or (in the case of a direction under section 19) varying, such a direction;

(b) proceedings—

(i) on an application for such a direction or order, or

(ii) where the court acts of its own motion to determine whether to give or make any such direction or order.

(3) The court dealing with a matter falling within subsection (2) may order that subsection (1) is not to apply, or is not to apply to a specified extent, to a report of that matter.

(4) Where—

(a) there is only one accused in the relevant proceedings, and

(b) he objects to the making of an order under subsection (3),

the court shall make the order if (and only if) satisfied after hearing the representations of the accused that it is in the interests of justice to do so; and if the order is made it shall not apply to the extent that a report deals with any such objections or representations.

(5) Where—

(a) there are two or more accused in the relevant proceedings, and

(b) one or more of them object to the making of an order under subsection (3),

the court shall make the order if (and only if) satisfied after hearing the representations of each of the accused that it is in the interests of justice to do so; and if the order is made it shall not apply to the extent that a report deals with any such objections or representations.

(6) Subsection (1) does not apply to the inclusion in a publication of a report of matters after the relevant proceedings are either—

(a) determined (by acquittal, conviction or otherwise), or

(b) abandoned,

in relation to the accused or (if there is more than one) in relation to each of the accused.

(7) In this section "the relevant proceedings" means the proceedings to which any such direction as is mentioned in subsection (2) relates or would relate.

(8) Nothing in this section affects any prohibition or restriction by virtue of any other enactment on the inclusion of matter in a publication.

8–37　　　The reporting of a direction in relation to special measures or prohibiting cross ex-amination of a particular witness or an order varying or discharging such a direction is prohibited unless the court directs otherwise. If the court is minded to allow publication it shall hear the objections or representations of any defendant and must only make the order if it is in the interests of justice and to the extent that the report deals with the objections or representations.

Youth Justice and Criminal Evidence Act 1999, s.49

Offences under Chapter IV

8–38　　　**49.**—(1) This section applies if a publication—

(a) includes any matter in contravention of section 44(2) or of a direction under sec-tion 45(3) or 46(2); or

(b) includes a report in contravention of section 47.

(2) Where the publication is a newspaper or periodical, any proprietor, any editor and any publisher of the newspaper or periodical is guilty of an offence.

(3) Where the publication is a relevant programme—

(a) any body corporate or Scottish partnership engaged in providing the programme service in which the programme is included, and

(b) any person having functions in relation to the programme corresponding to those of an editor of a newspaper, is guilty of an offence.

(4) In the case of any other publication, any person publishing it is guilty of an offence.

(5) A person guilty of an offence under this section is liable on summary conviction to a fine not exceeding level 5 on the standard scale.

(6) Proceedings for an offence under this section in respect of a publication falling within subsection (1)(b) may not be instituted—

    (a) in England and Wales otherwise than by or with the consent of the Attorney General, or

    (b) in Northern Ireland otherwise than by or with the consent of the Attorney General for Northern Ireland.

In *T. v. DPP*; *North East Press Ltd* [2003] EWHC Admin 2408; [2004] 168 J.P. **8–39** 194, the defendant had attained the age of 18 during the course of proceedings against him in the youth court. It was held that the restriction applies only for so long as the person concerned continues to be a child or young person.

Youth Justice and Criminal Evidence Act 1999, s.52

Decisions as to public interest for purposes of Chapter IV

52.—(1) Where for the purposes of any provision of this Chapter it falls to a court to **8–40** determine whether anything is (or, as the case may be, was) in the public interest, the court must have regard, in particular, to the matters referred to in subsection (2) (so far as relevant).

(2) Those matters are—

    (a) the interest in each of the following—

        (i) the open reporting of crime,

        (ii) the open reporting of matters relating to human health or safety, and

        (iii) the prevention and exposure of miscarriages of justice;

    (b) the welfare of any person in relation to whom the relevant restrictions imposed by or under this Chapter apply or would apply (or, as the case may be, applied); and

    (c) any views expressed—

        (i) by an appropriate person on behalf of a person within paragraph (b) who is under the age of 16 ("the protected person"), or

        (ii) by a person within that paragraph who has attained that age.

(3) In subsection (2) "an appropriate person", in relation to the protected person, has the same meaning as it has for the purposes of section 50.

Sexual Offences (Amendment) Act 1992, ss.1–4

Anonymity of victims of certain offences

1.—(1) Where an allegation has been made that an offence to which this Act applies has been **8–41** committed against a person, no matter relating to that person shall during that person's lifetime be included in any publication if it is likely to lead members of the public to identify that person as the person against whom the offence is alleged to have been committed.

(2) Where a person is accused of an offence to which this Act applies, no matter likely to lead members of the public to identify a person as the person against whom the offence is alleged to have been committed ("the complainant") shall during the complainant's lifetime be included in any publication.

(3) This section—

    (a) does not apply in relation to a person by virtue of subsection (1) at any time after a person has been accused of the offence, and

    (b) in its application in relation to a person by virtue of subsection (2), has effect subject to any direction given under section 3.

(3A) The matters relating to a person in relation to which the restrictions imposed by subsection (1) or (2) apply (if their inclusion in any publication is likely to have the result mentioned in that subsection) include in particular—

    (a) the person's name,

    (b) the person's address,

    (c) the identity of any school or other educational establishment attended by the person,

(d) the identity of any place of work, and

(e) any still or moving picture of the person.

(4) Nothing in this section prohibits the inclusion in a publication of matter consisting only of a report of criminal proceedings other than proceedings at, or intended to lead to, or on an appeal arising out of, a trial at which the accused is charged with the offence.

Offences to which this Act applies

8–42   **2.**—(1) This Act applies to the following offences against the law of England and Wales—

(aa) rape;

(ab) burglary with intent to rape;

(a) any offence under any of the provisions of the *Sexual Offences Act* 1956 mentioned in subsection (2);

(b) any offence under section 128 of the *Mental Health Act* 1959 (intercourse with mentally handicapped person by hospital staff etc.);

(c) any offence under section 1 of the *Indecency with Children Act* 1960 (indecent conduct towards young child);

(d) any offence under section 54 of the *Criminal Law Act* 1977 (incitement by man of his grand-daughter, daughter or sister under the age of 16 to commit incest with him);

(da) any offence under any of the provisions of Part 1 of the *Sexual Offences Act* 2003 except section 64, 65, 69 or 71;

(e) any attempt to commit any of the offences mentioned in paragraphs (aa) to (da);

(f) any conspiracy to commit any of those offences;

(g) any incitement of another to commit any of those offences;

(h) aiding, abetting, counselling or procuring the commission of any of the offences mentioned in paragraphs (aa) to (e) and (g).

(2) The provisions of the Act of 1956 are—

(a) section 2 (procurement of a woman by threats);

(b) section 3 (procurement of a woman by false pretences);

(c) section 4 (administering drugs to obtain intercourse with a woman);

(d) section 5 (intercourse with a girl under the age of 13);

(e) section 6 (intercourse with a girl between the ages of 13 and 16);

(f) section 7 (intercourse with a mentally handicapped person);

(g) section 9 (procurement of a mentally handicapped person);

(h) section 10 (incest by a man);

(i) section 11 (incest by a woman);

(j) section 12 (buggery);

(k) section 14 (indecent assault on a woman);

(l) section 15 (indecent assault on a man);

(m) section 16 (assault with intent to commit buggery);

(n) section 17 (abduction of woman by force).

(3) This Act applies to the following offences against the law of Northern Ireland—

(a) rape;

(b) burglary with intent to rape;

(c) any offence under any of the following provisions of the *Offences against the Person Act* 1861—

(i) section 52 (indecent assault on a female);

(ii) section 53 so far as it relates to abduction of a woman against her will;

(iii) section 61 (buggery);

(iv) section 62 (attempt to commit buggery, assault with intent to commit buggery or indecent assault on a male);

(d) any offence under any of the following provisions of the *Criminal Law Amendment Act* 1885—

(i) section 3 (procuring unlawful carnal knowledge of woman by threats, false pretences or administering drugs);

(ii) section 4 (unlawful carnal knowledge, or attempted unlawful carnal knowledge, of a girl under 14);

(iii) section 5 (unlawful carnal knowledge of a girl under 17);

(e) any offence under any of the following provisions of the *Punishment of Incest Act 1908*—
  (i)   section 1 (incest, attempted incest by males);
  (ii) section 2 (incest by females over 16);
(f) any offence under section 22 of the *Children and Young Persons Act (Northern Ireland)* 1968 (indecent conduct towards child);
(g) any offence under Article 9 of the Criminal Justice (Northern Ireland) Order 1980 (inciting girl under 16 to have incestuous sexual intercourse);
(h) any offence under any of the following provisions of the *Mental Health (Northern Ireland) Order* 1986—
  (i)   Article 122(1)(a) (unlawful sexual intercourse with a woman suffering from severe mental handicap);
  (ii) Article 122(1)(b) (procuring a woman suffering from severe mental handicap to have unlawful sexual intercourse);
  (iii) Article 123 (unlawful sexual intercourse by hospital staff, etc. with a person receiving treatment for mental disorder);
(ha) any offence under any of sections 15 to 21, 47 to 53, 57 to 59, 66, 67, 70 and 72 of the *Sexual Offences Act* 2003;
(i) any attempt to commit any of the offences mentioned in paragraphs (a) to (ha);
(j) any conspiracy to commit any of those offences;
(k) any incitement of another to commit any of those offences;
(l) aiding, abetting, counselling or procuring the commission of any of the offences mentioned in paragraphs (a) to (i) and (k).

(4) This Act applies to a service offence (wherever committed) if the corresponding civil offence is mentioned in subsection (1).

Power to displace section 1

3.—(1) If, before the commencement of a trial at which a person is charged with an offence **8–43** to which this Act applies, he or another person against whom the complainant may be expected to give evidence at the trial, applies to the judge for a direction under this subsection and satisfies the judge—
(a) that the direction is required for the purpose of inducing persons who are likely to be needed as witnesses at the trial to come forward; and
(b) that the conduct of the applicant's defence at the trial is likely to be substantially prejudiced if the direction is not given,
the judge shall direct that section 1 shall not, by virtue of the accusation alleging the offence in question, apply in relation to the complainant.

(2) If at a trial the judge is satisfied—
(a) that the effect of section 1 is to impose a substantial and unreasonable restriction upon the reporting of proceedings at the trial, and
(b) that it is in the public interest to remove or relax the restriction,
he shall direct that that section shall not apply to such matter as is specified in the direction.

(3) A direction shall not be given under subsection (2) by reason only of the outcome of the trial.

(4) If a person who has been convicted of an offence and has given notice of appeal against the conviction, or notice of an application for leave so to appeal, applies to the appellate court for a direction under this subsection and satisfies the court—
(a) that the direction is required for the purpose of obtaining evidence in support of the appeal; and
(b) that the applicant is likely to suffer substantial injustice if the direction is not given,
the court shall direct that section 1 shall not, by virtue of an accusation which alleges an offence to which this Act applies and is specified in the direction, apply in relation to a complainant so specified.

(5) A direction given under any provision of this section does not affect the operation of section 1 at any time before the direction is given.

(6) In subsections (1) and (2), "judge" means —
  (a) in the case of an offence which is to be tried summarily or for which the mode of trial has not been determined, any justice of the peace acting for the petty sessions area concerned; and

(b) in any other case, any judge of the Crown Court in England and Wales.

(6A) In its application to Northern Ireland, this section has effect as if—

(a) in subsections (1) and (2) for any reference to the judge there were substituted a reference to the court; and

(b) subsection (6) were omitted.

(7) If, after the commencement of a trial at which a person is charged with an offence to which this Act applies, a new trial of the person for that offence is ordered, the commencement of any previous trial shall be disregarded for the purposes of subsection (1).

Special rules for cases of incest or buggery

8–44   **4.**—(1) In this section—

"section 10 offence" means an offence under section 10 of the *Sexual Offences Act* 1956 (incest by a man) or an attempt to commit that offence;

"section 11 offence" means an offence under section 11 of that Act (incest by a woman) or an attempt to commit that offence;

"section 12 offence" means an offence under section 12 of that Act (buggery) or an attempt to commit that offence.

(2) Section 1 does not apply to a woman against whom a section 10 offence is alleged to have been committed if she is accused of having committed a section 11 offence against the man who is alleged to have committed the section 10 offence against her.

(3) Section 1 does not apply to a man against whom a section 11 offence is alleged to have been committed if he is accused of having committed a section 10 offence against the woman who is alleged to have committed the section 11 offence against him.

(4) Section 1 does not apply to a person against whom a section 12 offence is alleged to have been committed if that person is accused of having committed a section 12 offence against the person who is alleged to have committed the section 12 offence against him.

(5) Subsection (2) does not affect the operation of this Act in relation to anything done at any time before the woman is accused.

(6) Subsection (3) does not affect the operation of this Act in relation to anything done at any time before the man is accused.

(7) Subsection (4) does not affect the operation of this Act in relation to anything done at any time before the person mentioned first in that subsection is accused.

(8) In its application to Northern Ireland, this section has effect as if—

(a) subsection (1) were omitted;

(b) for references to a section 10 offence there were substituted references to an offence under section 1 of the *Punishment of Incest Act* 1908 (incest by a man) or an attempt to commit that offence;

(c) for references to a section 11 offence there were substituted references to an offence under section 2 of that Act (incest by a woman) or an attempt to commit that offence; and

(d) for references to a section 12 offence there were substituted references to an offence under section 61 of the *Offences against the Person Act* 1861 (buggery) or an attempt to commit that offence.

(9) For the purposes of this section, a service offence is a section 10 offence, a section 11 offence or a section 12 offence if the corresponding civil offence is a section 10 offence, a section 11 offence or a section 12 offence, as the case may be.

Sexual Offences (Amendment) Act 1992, s.6

Interpretation etc.

8–45   **6.**—(1) In this Act—

"complainant" has the meaning given in section 1(2);

"corresponding civil offence", in relation to a service offence, means the civil offence (within the meaning of the *Army Act* 1955, the *Air Force Act* 1955 or the *Naval Discipline Act* 1957) the commission of which constitutes the service offence;

"picture" includes a likeness however produced;

"publication" includes any speech, writing, relevant programme or other communication in whatever form, which is addressed to the public at large or any section of the public (and for this purpose every relevant programme shall be taken to be so addressed), but does not include an indictment or other document prepared for use in particular legal proceedings;

"relevant programme" means a programme included in a programme service, within the meaning of the *Broadcasting Act* 1990; and

"service offence" means an offence against section 70 of the *Army Act* 1955, section 70 of the *Air Force Act* 1955 or section 42 of the *Naval Discipline Act* 1957.

(2) For the purposes of this Act—

    (a) where it is alleged that an offence to which this Act applies has been committed, the fact that any person has consented to an act which, on any prosecution for that offence, would fall to be proved by the prosecution, does not prevent that person from being regarded as a person against whom the alleged offence was committed; and

    (b) where a person is accused of an offence of incest or buggery, the other party to the act in question shall be taken to be a person against whom the offence was committed even though he consented to that act.

(2A) For the purposes of this Act, where it is alleged or there is an accusation—

    (a) that an offence of conspiracy or incitement of another to commit an offence mentioned in section 2(1)(aa) to (d) or (3)(a) to (h) has been committed, or

    (b) that an offence of aiding, abetting, counselling or procuring the commission of an offence of incitement of another to commit an offence mentioned in section 2(1)(aa) to (d) or (3)(a) to (h) has been committed,

the person against whom the substantive offence is alleged to have been intended to be committed shall be regarded as the person against whom the conspiracy or incitement is alleged to have been committed.

In this subsection, "the substantive offence" means the offence to which the alleged conspiracy or incitement related.

(3) For the purposes of this Act, a person is accused of an offence, other than a service offence, if—

    (a) an information is laid, or (in Northern Ireland) a complaint is made, alleging that he has committed the offence,

    (b) he appears before a court charged with the offence,

    (c) a court before which he is appearing commits him for trial on a new charge alleging the offence, or

    (d) a bill of indictment charging him with the offence is preferred before a court in which he may lawfully be indicted for the offence,

and references in subsection (2A) and in section 3 to an accusation alleging an offence shall be construed accordingly.

(3A) For the purposes of this Act, a person is accused of a service offence if he is treated by section 75(4) of the *Army Act* 1955, section 75(4) of the *Air Force Act* 1955 or section 47A(4) of the *Naval Discipline Act* 1957 as charged with the offence, and references in section 3 to an accusation alleging an offence shall be construed accordingly.

(4) Nothing in this Act affects any prohibition or restriction imposed by virtue of any other enactment upon a publication or upon matter included in a relevant programme.

8–46   It has been held that legislation preventing the publication of information likely to lead members of the public to identify a child victim of alleged gross indecency is not disproportionate or in breach of the right of freedom of expression: *O'Riordan v. DPP The Times*, May 31, 2005; [2005] EWHC 1240.

Criminal Procedure and Investigations Act 1996, ss.58–61

Orders in respect of certain assertions

8–47   **58.**—(1) This section applies where a person has been convicted of an offence and a speech in mitigation is made by him or on his behalf before—

    (a) a court determining what sentence should be passed on him in respect of the offence, or

    (b) a magistrates' court determining whether he should be committed to the Crown Court for sentence.

(2) This section also applies where a sentence has been passed on a person in respect of an offence and a submission relating to the sentence is made by him or on his behalf before—

    (a) a court hearing an appeal against or reviewing the sentence, or

    (b) a court determining whether to grant leave to appeal against the sentence.

(3) Where it appears to the court that there is a real possibility that an order under subsection (8) will be made in relation to the assertion, the court may make an order under subsection (7) in relation to the assertion.

(4) Where there are substantial grounds for believing—

    (a) that an assertion forming part of the speech or submission is derogatory to a person's character (for instance, because it suggests that his conduct is or has been criminal, immoral or improper), and

    (b) that the assertion is false or that the facts asserted are irrelevant to the sentence,

the court may make an order under subsection (8) in relation to the assertion.

(5) An order under subsection (7) or (8) must not be made in relation to an assertion if it appears to the court that the assertion was previously made—

    (a) at the trial at which the person was convicted of the offence, or

    (b) during any other proceedings relating to the offence.

(6) Section 59 has effect where a court makes an order under subsection (7) or (8).

(7) An order under this subsection—

    (a) may be made at any time before the court has made a determination with regard to sentencing;

    (b) may be revoked at any time by the court;

    (c) subject to paragraph (b), shall cease to have effect when the court makes a determination with regard to sentencing.

(8) An order under this subsection—

    (a) may be made at any time before the court has made a determination with regard to sentencing, but only if it is made as soon as is reasonably practicable after the making of the determination;

    (b) may be revoked at any time by the court;

    (c) subject to paragraph (b), shall cease to have effect at the end of the period of 12 months beginning with the day on which it is made;

    (d) may be made whether or not an order has been made under subsection (7) with regard to the case concerned.

(9) For the purposes of subsection (7) and (8) the court makes a determination with regard to sentencing—

    (a) when it determines what sentence should be passed (where this section applies by virtue of subsection (1)(a),

    (b) when it determines whether the person should be committed to the Crown Court for sentence (where this section applies by virtue of subsection (1)(b));

    (c) when it determines what the sentence should be (where this section applies by virtue of subsection (2)(a));

    (d) when it determines whether to grant leave to appeal (where this section applies by virtue of subsection (2)(b).

Restriction on reporting of assertions

8–48   **59.**—(1) Where a court makes an order under section 58(7) or (8) in relation to any assertion, at any time when the order has effect the assertion must not—

    (a) be published in Great Britain in a written publication available to the public, or

    (b) be included in a relevant programme for reception in Great Britain.

(2) In this section—

    "relevant programme" means a programme included in a programme service, within the meaning of the *Broadcasting Act* 1990;

    "written publication" includes a film, a soundtrack and any other record in permanent form but does not include an indictment or other document prepared for use in particular legal proceedings.

(3) For the purposes of this section an assertion is published or included in a programme if the material published or included—

    (a) names the person about whom the assertion is made or, without naming him, contains enough to make it likely that members of the public will identify him as the person about whom it is made, and

    (b) reproduces the actual wording of the matter asserted or contains its substance.

Reporting of assertions: offences

60.—(1) If an assertion is published or included in a relevant programme in contravention of **8–49**
section 59, each of the following persons is guilty of an offence—

(a) in the case of publication in a newspaper or periodical, any proprietor, any editor
and any publisher of the newspaper or periodical;

(b) in the case of publication in any other form, the person publishing the assertion;

(c) in the case of an assertion included in a relevant programme, any body corporate
engaged in providing the service in which the programme is included and any
person having functions in relation to the programme corresponding to those of
an editor of a newspaper.

(2) A person guilty of an offence under this section is liable on summary conviction to a
fine of an amount not exceeding level 5 on the standard scale.

(3) Where a person is charged with an offence under this section it is a defence to prove
that at the time of the alleged offence—

(a) he was not aware, and neither suspected nor had reason to suspect, that an order
under section 58(7) or (8) had effect at that time, or

(b) he was not aware, and neither suspected nor had reason to suspect, that the publication or programme in question was of, or (as the case may be) included, the
assertion in question.

(4) Where an offence under this section committed by a body corporate is proved to
have been committed with the consent or connivance of, or to be attributable to any neglect on the part of—

(a) a director, manager, secretary or other similar officer of the body corporate, or

(b) a person purporting to act in any such capacity,

he as well as the body, corporate is guilty of the offence and liable to be proceeded against and
punished accordingly.

(5) In relation to a body corporate whose affairs are managed by its members "director"
in subsection (4) means a member of the body corporate.

(6) Subsections (2) and (3) of section 59 apply for the purposes of this section as they apply for the purposes of that.

Reporting of assertions: commencement and supplementary

61.—(1) Section 58 applies where the offence mentioned in subsection (1) or (2) of that sec-   **8–50**
tion is committed on or after the appointed day.

(2) The reference in subsection (1) to the appointed day is to such day as is appointed
for the purposes of this section by the Secretary of State by order.

(3) Nothing in section 58 or 59 affects any prohibition or restriction imposed by virtue
of any other enactment on a publication or on matter included in a programme.

(4) Nothing in section 58 or 59 affects section 3 of the *Law of Libel Amendment Act* 1888
(privilege of newspaper reports of court proceedings).

(5) Section 8 of the *Law of Libel Amendment Act* 1888 (order of judge required for prosecution for libel published in a newspaper) does not apply to a prosecution for an offence under
section 60.

(6) In section 159 of the *Criminal Justice Act* 1988 (appeal to Court of Appeal against
orders restricting reports etc.) in subsection (1) the following paragraph shall be inserted after
paragraph (a)—

"(aa) an order made by the Crown Court under section 58(7) or (8) of the *Criminal
Procedure and Investigations Act* 1996 of the *Criminal Procedure and Investigations Act* 1996 in a case where the Court has convicted a person on a trial on
indictment;".

When a plea in mitigation is made to the court the defendant or his representative   **8–51**
may try to minimise his offending behaviour by making remarks about the victim's
character suggesting that the victim's conduct has been immoral, improper or criminal.
If the court finds that there are substantial grounds for believing that the assertion is derogatory and that either it is false or irrelevant to the sentence, it can make a section 58
order. An interim order may be made as soon as the assertion has been made but only
if there is a real possibility that a final order will be made. A final order may be made
before sentence is passed or afterwards. If it is made after sentence it must be made as

soon as is reasonably practicable. The effect of such an order is to bar publication of the assertion which is the subject of the order. An order cannot be made if it appears that the assertion has previously been made at the trial or during any other proceedings in relation to the offence.

An interim order will cease when the defendant is sentenced. A final order continues until it is either revoked by the court or at the end of twelve months beginning on the day on which it is made.

For the purposes of section 61(1) where an offence is committed over a period of more than one day, or at some time during a period of more than one day, it must be taken to be committed on the last of the days in the period: *Criminal Procedure and Investigations Act* 1996, s.75(2), (3).

Reporting of magistrates' names

8–52   The names of district judges and magistrates do not routinely appear on court lists. An application may be made for the disclosure of such names to the legal adviser in court or after the hearing to the justices' clerk. Names but not addresses are usually given unless the clerk reasonably believes that the information is wanted for a purely mischievous purpose: *R. v. Felixstowe Justices, ex p. Leigh* [1987] Q.B. 582

Photographs

Criminal Justice Act 1925, s.41

Prohibition on taking photographs, &c., in court

8–53   **41.**—(1) No person shall—

    (a) take or attempt to take in any court any photograph, or with a view to publication make or attempt to make in any court any portrait or sketch, of any person, being a judge of the court or a juror or a witness in or a party to any proceedings before the court, whether civil or criminal; or

    (b) publish any photograph, portrait or sketch taken or made in contravention of the foregoing provisions of this section or any reproduction thereof;

and if any person acts in contravention of this section be shall, on summary conviction, be liable in respect of each offence to a fine not exceeding fifty pounds.

    (2) For the purposes of this section—

    (a) the expression "court" means any court of justice, including the court of a coroner:

    (b) the expression "Judge" includes […], registrar, magistrate, justice and coroner:

    (c) a photograph, portrait or sketch shall be deemed to be a photograph, portrait or sketch taken or made in court if it is taken or made in the court-room or in the building or in the precincts of the building in which the court is held, or if it is a photograph, portrait or sketch taken or made of the person while he is entering or leaving the court-room or any such building or precincts as aforesaid.

8–54   The issue here is one of identification of people. It is intended to ensure a fair trial. It is not a general prohibition on taking photographs of the court building. Neither does it prevent an artist who has sat in court and observed the proceedings from producing a sketch thereafter so long as the sketching does not take place within the prohibited areas. A person who has taken photographs by means of a mobile telephone can also be dealt with for criminal contempt of court: *D. (Vincent)* [2004] EWCA Crim 1271. The Court of Appeal stated it was concerned about the possibilities of intimidation. The taking of photographs in this way "has the potential to gravely prejudice the administration of criminal justice".

The precincts of the building could be taken to mean any area surrounding the courthouse a photograph of which would identify a person as being linked with that courthouse.

The filming of a defendant in the cell area of a magistrates' court for the purpose of having the film compared with a picture taken by CCTV of a person committing a robbery was held to be unlawful as being in breach of this prohibition: *Loveridge, Lee and Loveridge* [2001] 2 Cr.App.R. 29, CA.

Tape recordings

Contempt of Court Act 1981 s.9

Use of tape recorders

9.—(1) Subject to subsection (4) below, it is a contempt of court—　　　　**8–55**

(a) to use in court, or bring into court for use, any tape recorder or other instrument for recording sound, except with the leave of the court;

(b) to publish a recording of legal proceedings made by means of any such instrument, or any recording derived directly or indirectly from it, by playing it in the hearing of the public or any section of the public, or to dispose of it or any recording so derived, with a view to such publication;

(c) to use any such recording in contravention of any conditions of leave granted under paragraph (a).

(2) Leave under paragraph (a) of subsection (1) may be granted or refused at the discretion of the court, and if granted may be granted subject to such conditions as the court thinks proper with respect to the use of any recording made pursuant to the leave; and where leave has been granted the court may at the like discretion withdraw or amend it either generally or in relation to any particular part of the proceedings.

(3) Without prejudice to any other power to deal with an act of contempt under paragraph (a) of subsection (1), the court may order the instrument, or any recording made with it, or both, to be forfeited; and any object so forfeited shall (unless the court otherwise determines on application by a person appearing to be the owner) be sold or otherwise disposed of in such manner as the court may direct.

(4) This section does not apply to the making or use of sound recordings for purposes of official transcripts of proceedings.

The *Consolidated Criminal Practice Direction*, para. I.2 in Appendix F–4 gives　**8–56**
guidance on the exercise of the court's discretion stating the following factors may be of relevance:

— Reasonable need;

— Risk of briefing witnesses out of court;

— Distraction or disturbance by the use of the recorder.

Applications to sit in camera

The term "in camera" covers situations where the court sits in the absence of the　**8–57**
press and public. The court may exclude the press and the public during the application itself and will do so if it is intimated that the administration of justice could be prejudiced by the reasons for the application being stated in open court. Once it is clear that justice will not be prejudiced the court will open the courtroom again and will summarise what has occurred whilst "in camera". If the court decides to sit "in camera" for all or part of the hearing itself, it will open the court to announce that fact and give general reasons for so doing: *R. v. Tower Bridge J.J., ex.p. Osborne* (1989) 88 Cr.App.R. 28.

Generally a defendant and his advocate must not be excluded from a hearing "in camera" nor should restrictions be placed on an advocate as to what he may disclose to his client or his instructing solicitor if there is one: *Preston* (1994) 2 A.C. 130, HL.

Where the disclosure of certain matters might be against the public interest because it　**8–58**
might compromise state security or the proper functioning of a public service, the prosecutor will claim immunity from disclosure. Difficulties may arise where public interest immunity is sought by the prosecution and an application is made to hear arguments regarding disclosure in the absence of the defendant and his advocate. In most

cases the defence will be given notice of an application and may make representations. There will be a few highly sensitive cases, however, where the defendant and his advocate will be excluded. The court, in dealing with such an exceptional application, may consider the appointment of special independent counsel to take part in the proceedings but that is a course of last resort as it presents its own difficulties such as ethical problems with the taking of full instructions and the usual client/counsel relationship. The cardinal and overriding requirement is that of a fair: *H.*; *C.* [2004] UKHL 3; [2004] 2 W.L.R. 335 (see Public Interest Immunity, *post*, § 8–108).

II. LANGUAGE

A. GENERAL

8–59   Court proceedings are ordinarily conducted in English: see *Re Trepca Mines* [1960] 1 W.L.R. 24.

B. INTERPRETERS

8–60   Interpreters are used for witnesses and defendants where they do not understand English. In accordance with Article 6(3) ECHR, *ante*, where a defendant does not understand the English language or does not understand it sufficiently to follow court proceedings the evidence at trial should be translated to him. Similarly where the defendant is deaf, mute or both the court must ensure that proper means are taken to communicate to the defendant the case made against him and to enable him to make an answer to it. Sign language may be used or the evidence could be reduced to writing. The assistance of an interpreter is within the court's discretion and the court can itself assess whether a witness needs an interpreter. A court can determine the need by assessing the limits of the witness's comprehension and fluency when the evidence is given: *Sharma* [2006] 2 Cr.App.R. (S.) 63, CA. It has been held that where the indication of the need for an interpreter arose only during the defence case and that there had been no prejudice to the defendant the court's refusal to appoint an interpreter did not render the trial unfair: *Wei Hai Restaurant Ltd v. Kingston upon Hull City Council* (2002) 166 J.P. 185, DC.

Where the difficulty in interpretation was such as to make it impossible for a witness's evidence to be tested by cross-examination, the conviction was quashed: *Imrie*, 12 Cr.App.R. 282

It is important that the interpreter is someone who can be expected to interpret impartially: *Mitchell* [1970] Crim.L.R. 153, CA.

8–61   In *R. v. West London Youth Court, ex p. N.* [2000] 1 W.L.R. 2368, DC, the police interviewed the 11-year-old defendant who spoke only Bosnian Romany. A relative, acting as the appropriate adult, was used for the second limb of a double interpretation process consisting of interpretation from one language into a second language, and then from the second language into a third language. There were no competent or qualified interpreters from Bosnian Romany in the United Kingdom who could act as interpreters in the criminal proceedings and the designated interpreter did not have a high enough level of understanding to meet the needs of the case. The process of double translation was ruled unlawful by the magistrates' court. On review, the Divisional Court held that double interpretation was acceptable and a necessary method of interpretation during both interview and trial on the condition that it had been impossible to find an interpreter who spoke fluently both in English and in a language in which the defendant was fluent. Both interpreters have to be suitably qualified and wholly impartial. It is not sufficient to use an appropriate adult for one limb; they are not impartial as their function is to assist the person questioned. It is important to ensure a proper, mutual understanding between the defendant and the interpreter, between the two interpreters and their common language, and also to ensure that the second interpreter was fluent in the English language. The onus is on the court to ensure that the defendant is fully able to participate in the proceedings even where the defendant's lawyer is content to make do with an inadequate interpreter: *Cuscani v. UK* [2003] Crim.L.R. 50.

Evidence from a police officer as to what the defendant had said during an interview, **8–62** as related to the officer by an interpreter, is hearsay; the only valid witness is the interpreter: *Attard* (1959) 43 Cr.App.R. 90.

If the interpreter used at the police station is to be called as a prosecution witness, a separate interpreter should be used for the court.

Interpreters are paid fees by the court. The right to free interpretation is unqualified. A convicted person cannot therefore be ordered to pay the costs of an interpreter: *Luedicke, Belkacem and Koc v. Germany* (1979–80) 2 E.H.R.R. 149. The fees include travelling time but not travelling expenses. The latter may be claimed separately.

C. Courts in Wales and Monmouthshire

Welsh Language Act 1993, ss.22, 24

Use of Welsh in legal proceedings

22.—(1) In any legal proceedings in Wales the Welsh language may be spoken by any party, **8–63** witness or other person who desires to use it, subject in the case of proceedings in a court other than a magistrates' court to such prior notice as may be required by rules of court; and any necessary provision for interpretation shall be made accordingly.

(2) Any power to make rules of court includes power to make provision as to the use, in proceedings in or having a connection with Wales, of documents in the Welsh language.

Provision of interpreters

24. Lord Chancellor may make rules as to the provision and employment of interpreters of **8–64** the Welsh and English languages for the purposes of proceedings before courts in Wales.

(2) The interpreters shall be paid, out of the same fund as the expenses of the court are payable, such remuneration in respect of their services as the Lord Chancellor may determine.

(3) The Lord Chancellor's powers under this section shall be exercised with the consent of the Treasury.

The *Consolidated Criminal Practice Direction*, paras III.22 and 23 applies, see Ap- **8–65** pendix F. The purpose of the direction is to give effect to the *Welsh Language Act* 1993 which provides for equal status for Welsh and English in Wales. Legal representatives are under a duty to inform the court where Welsh will be used so that appropriate listing arrangements can be made.

III. REPRESENTATION OF THE DEFENDANT

A. Legal Representation

Magistrates' Courts Act 1980, s.122

Appearance by counsel or solicitor

122.—(1) A party to any proceedings before a magistrates' court may be represented by [a **8–66** legal representative].

(2) Subject to subsection (3) below, an absent party so represented shall be deemed not to be absent.

(3) Appearance of a party by [a legal representative] shall not satisfy any provision of any enactment or any condition of a recognizance expressly requiring his presence.

[This section is reprinted as amended by the *Courts and Legal Services Act* 1990, s.125(3), Sched. 18, para. 25(3)(b).]

As to rights of audience see *ante*, § 2–32.

Article 6(3) ECHR, *ante*, guarantees the right to legal representation. The provision of legal aid is subject to the means of the defendant and confined to cases where the interests of justice require it: see *post*, § 29–31.

A defendant is entitled to be represented by a lawyer of his choosing if it is reasonably practicable. It is not an absolute right although his choice should be respected: *Goddi v. Italy* (1984) 6 E.H.R.R. 457. The overriding consideration is the requirements of justice, for both prosecution and defence, in the circumstances of the case: *R. v. De Oliveira* [1997] Crim.L.R. 600, CA. It will depend not only on the defendant's choice but on the availability of the advocate, a suitably equipped court, witnesses as well as the time scale of the case. Where an advocate withdraws because of professional reasons or is dismissed by his client, the court has a discretion to grant an adjournment so that a new advocate can be instructed. It is not appropriate for the court to seek an explanation for the withdrawal or dismissal. The court is, however, entitled to take into account the likelihood that another advocate would suffer the same fate as the original, the interests of witnesses and of the public. Additional matters to consider are the stage that the trial has reached and the apparent ability of the defendant to conduct his or her own case: *Al-Zubeidi* [1999] Crim.L.R. 906, CA. The defendant is always at liberty to ask the court's permission to conduct his own defence: *Lyons* 68 Cr.App.R. 104, CA.

The wrongful denial of the defendant's right to legal representation is likely to result in the quashing of the conviction: *Kingston* (1948) 32 Cr.App.R. 183, CA; *Harris* [1985] Crim.L.R. 244, CA.

B. Right to Conduct Own Defence

8–67   A defendant has the right to conduct his own defence with or without the services of a solicitor: *Woodward* [1944] K.B. 118; *De Courcy*, 48 Cr.App.R. 323, CA. An unrepresented defendant cannot, however, rely on the disadvantages of lack of representation to support an argument that there was inequality of arms at trial to render the conviction unsafe: *Van Geyseghem v. Belgium* (2001) 35 E.H.R.R. 24; *Walton* [2001] 8 *Archbold News* 2, CA.

In magistrates' courts many defendants represent themselves and the legal adviser has a specific duty to assist by putting questions to witnesses on the defendant's behalf.

8–68   See *Criminal Procedure Rules* 2005, r.37.2(2) in Appendix G–162.

The more serious the charge, the more complex the case and the greater the potential for penalty, the more likely it is that representation will be needed to ensure a fair trial: *Hinds v. Att.-Gen. of Barbados* [2002] 2 W.L.R. 470, PC. A court may place reasonable restrictions on the right of a defendant to appear without a lawyer in a complex case: *Croissant v. Germany*, 16 E.H.R.R. 135; *Philis v. Greece* (1998) 25 E.H.R.R. 417. There are also restrictions on the right to cross examine witnesses: *Youth Justice and Criminal Evidence Act* 1999, s.36.

C. McKenzie Friends

8–69   Although a defendant may not be represented by someone who has no right of audience he may apply to the court to have with him a "friend" who will assist him by taking notes, prompting and quietly giving advice: *McKenzie v. McKenzie* (1970) 3 W.L.R. 472. The case of *R. v. Leicester City Justices, ex p. Barrow* [1991] 2 Q.B. 260 confirmed that the right does not go beyond assistance.

D. Representation of a Corporate Defendant

Magistrates' Courts Act 1980, Sched. 3, paras 2–3

8–70   2. A representative may on behalf of a corporation—

(a) make before examining justices such representations as could be made by an accused who is not a corporation;

(b) consent to the corporation being tried summarily;

(c) enter a plea of guilty or not guilty on the trial by a magistrates' court of an information.

3.—(1) Where a representative appears, any requirement of this Act that anything shall be done in the presence of the accused, or shall be read or said to the accused, shall be construed as a requirement that that thing shall be done in the presence of the representative or read or said to the representative.

(2) Where a representative does not appear, any such requirement, and any requirement that the consent of the accused shall be obtained for summary trial, shall not apply.

[This Schedule is reprinted as amended by *Criminal Procedure and Investigations Act* 1996, Sched. 1, para. 13.]

A company may be represented by an appointed lawyer, a director or the secretary. **8–71**
It is advisable for a solicitor to be appointed by the company's representative: *Birmingham and Gloucester Railway Co, TRe LCC and London Tramways Co*; *Manchester Corp* and *Ascanio Puck & Co and Paice* (1912) 76 J.P. 487. It is usual to request the completion of a form in the following words:

> X Co.
> *I appoint* .... *to represent the company in the above case*
>
> Signed A.B. Director/Secretary

This also applies to unincorporated bodies: *Companies Act* 1985, s.734.

IV. PLEA

A. GENERAL

The first stage in a summary trial is for the court through the legal adviser to read **8–72**
the information to the defendant and ask him whether he pleads guilty or not guilty.

Magistrates' Courts Act 1980, s.9

Procedure on trial
9.—(1) On the summary trial of an information, the court shall, if the accused appears, state **8–73**
to him the substance of the information and ask him whether he pleads guilty or not guilty.

(2) The court, after hearing the evidence and the parties, shall convict the accused or dismiss the information.

(3) If the accused pleads guilty, the court may convict him without hearing evidence.

See *Criminal Procedure Rules* 2005, r.37.2(1) in Appendix G–162. The expectation **8–74**
under the Rules is that cases are concluded as soon as possible.

The defendant, unless it is a company, should be asked personally to plead even **8–75**
where he is represented; *R. v. Wakefield Justices, ex.p. Butterworth* [1970] 1 All E.R.
1181. Where a defendant does not attend court but is represented, he is deemed to be present under *Magistrates' Courts Act* 1980, s.122. In those circumstances the court may allow the advocate to enter a plea of guilty on the defendant's behalf.

B. PLEA OF GUILTY

If the defendant pleads guilty to an information the court may convict the defendant **8–76**
without hearing any evidence. In the absence of a guilty plea, the court is under a duty to hear evidence and either convict the defendant or dismiss the information: *Magistrates' Courts Act* 1980, s.9(2). The prosecution will read out the facts in open court: The *Consolidated Criminal Practice Direction*, para. III.26, in Appendix F. Where the defendant is unrepresented the legal adviser will ensure that he understands the elements of the offence, especially if the facts suggest that he has a defence: *Griffiths*, 23 Cr.App.R. 153, CA; *R. v. Blandford Justices, ex p. G (an infant), ante.* A plea of guilty must be unequivocal: *R. v. Tottenham Justices, ex p. Rubens* [1970] 1 All E.R. 879.

Where the defendant unequivocally admits the essential ingredients of an offence but disputes various facts, the court should hear evidence on the facts disputed, make findings and proceed to sentence; it should not direct that pleas of not guilty are entered: *R. v. Telford Justices, ex p. Darlington* (1988) 87 Cr.App.R. 194. On the other hand, where a court receives facts in mitigation which are inconsistent with a guilty plea that plea must be considered equivocal and a plea of not guilty entered: *R. v. Durham Quarter Sessions, ex p. Virgo* [1952] 2 Q.B. 1. A court may allow a guilty plea to be withdrawn if it becomes apparent that a defendant did not appreciate the elements of the offence or where the prosecution facts do not add up to the offence charged; such a situation should be rare, for it is unlikely to arise where a defendant is represented and, where he is not, it is the duty of the court to make sure that the nature of the offence is made clear to him before a plea of guilty is accepted; in this case it was held incredible that the defendants did not understand the offence of dangerous driving thinking that instead they had been charged with nuisance: *Revitt v. DPP* [2006] 1.W.L.R. 3172.

8–77　　Pleas which are entered under duress may also be covered by the rule that the plea must be unequivocal: *R. v. Huntingdon Crown Court, ex p. Jordan* [1981] Q.B. 857. In that case, the defendant pleaded guilty to theft in the magistrates' court where she was jointly charged with her husband. She appealed against conviction to the Crown Court, on the ground that both the offence and the plea were made under the duress of her husband. The judge ruled that the defendant's plea had been unequivocal and that the court has no jurisdiction to entertain the appeal. On application for judicial review it was held that the Crown Court had jurisdiction to inquire into an allegedly equivocal plea and to remit the matter to the magistrates if satisfied that the plea was equivocal. That jurisdiction extended to cases where an apparently unequivocal plea was entered under duress and was in fact a nullity.

Where the defendant wishes to plead guilty but there is a substantial dispute between the prosecution and defence version of events, the court should conduct a *Newton* hearing: *Newton* (1982) 77 Cr.App.R. 13; *Williams* (1983) 5 Cr.App.R. 134. The procedure will follow that of a trial and the parties will be able to call witnesses. The court will then decide the facts upon which it proposes to sentence.

Criminal Justice Act 1925, s.33

Procedure on charge of offence against corporation

8–78　　**33.**—(1) [*repealed*]

(2) [*repealed*]

(3) On arrangement of a corporation, the corporation may enter in writing by its representative a plea of guilty or not guilty, and if either the corporation does not appear by a representative or, though it does so appear, fails to enter as aforesaid any plea, the court shall order a plea of not guilty to be entered and the trial shall proceed as though the corporation had duly entered a plea of not guilty.

(4) Provision may be made by rules under the *Indictments Act* 1915 with respect to the service on any corporation charged with an indictable offence of any documents requiring to be served in connection with the proceedings.

(5) [*repealed*]

(6) In this section the expression "representative" in relation to a corporation means a person duly appointed by the corporation to represent it for the purpose of doing any act or thing which the representative of a corporation is by this section authorized to do, but a person so appointed shall not, by virtue only of being so appointed, be qualified to act on behalf of the corporation before any court for any other purpose.

A representative for the purposes of this section need not be appointed under the seal of the corporation, and a statement in writing purporting to be signed by a managing director of the corporation, or by any person (by whatever name called) having, or being one of the persons having, the management of the affairs of the corporation, to the effect that the person named in the statement has been appointed as the representative of the corporation for the purposes of this section shall be admissible without further proof as prima facie evidence that that person has been so appointed.

Where a company via its representative (see *ante*) fails to appear the court will enter **8–79** a not guilty plea and will hear the evidence.

C. Plea of Guilty by Post

Magistrates' Courts Act 1980, s.12

Non-appearance of accused; plea of guilty

12.—(1) This section shall apply where—   **8–80**

(a) a summons has been issued requiring a person to appear before a magistrates' court, other than a youth court, to answer to an information for a summary offence, not being—

    (i) an offence for which the accused is liable to be sentenced to be imprisoned for a term exceeding 3 months; or

    (ii) an offence specified in an order made by the Secretary of State by statutory instrument; and

(b) the justices' chief executive for the court is notified by or on behalf of the prosecutor that the documents mentioned in subsection (3) below have been served upon the accused with the summons.

(2) The reference in subsection (1)(a) above to the issue of a summons requiring a person to appear before a magistrates' court other than a youth court includes a reference to the issue of a summons requiring a person who has attained the age of 16 at the time when it is issued to appear before a youth court.

(3) The documents referred to in subsection (1)(b) above are—

(a) a notice containing such statement of the effect of this section as may be prescribed;

(b) either of the following, namely—

    (i) a concise statement of such facts relating to the charge as will be placed before the court by the prosecutor if the accused pleads guilty without appearing before the court, or

    (ii) a copy of such written statement or statements complying with subsections (2)(a) and (b) and (3) of section 9 of the *Criminal Justice Act* 1967 (proof by written statement) as will be so placed in those circumstances; and

(c) if any information relating to the accused will or may, in those circumstances, be placed before the court by or on behalf of the prosecutor, a notice containing or describing that information.

(4) Where the justices' chief executive for the court receives a notification in writing purporting to be given by the accused or by a legal representative acting on his behalf that the accused desires to plead guilty without appearing before the court—

(a) the justices' chief executive for the court shall inform the prosecutor of the receipt of the notification; and

(b) the following provisions of this section shall apply:

(5) If at the time and place appointed for the trial or adjourned trial of the information—

(a) the accused does not appear; and

(b) it is proved to the satisfaction of the court, on oath or in such manner as may be prescribed, that the documents mentioned in subsection (3) above have been served upon the accused with the summons,

the court may, subject to section 11(3) and (4) above and subsections (6) to (8) below, proceed to hear and dispose of the case in the absence of the accused, whether or not the prosecutor is also absent, in like manner as if both parties had appeared and the accused had pleaded guilty.

(6) If at any time before the hearing the [justices' chief executive for] the court receives an indication in writing purporting to be given by or on behalf of the accused that he wishes to withdraw the notification—

(a) the [justices' chief executive for] the court shall inform the prosecutor of the withdrawal; and

(b) the court shall deal with the information as if the notification had not been given.

(7) Before accepting the plea of guilty and convicting the accused under subsection (5) above, the court shall cause the following to be read out before the court by the clerk of the court, namely—

(a) in a case where a statement of facts as mentioned in subsection (3)(b)(i) above was served on the accused with the summons, that statement;

(aa) in a case where a statement or statements as mentioned in subsection (3)(b)(ii) above was served on the accused with the summons and the court does not otherwise direct, that statement or those statements;

(b) any information contained in a notice so served, and any information described in such a notice and produced by or on behalf of the prosecutor;

(c) the notification under subsection (4) above; and

(d) any submission received with the notification which the accused wishes to be brought to the attention of the court with a view to mitigation of sentence.

(7A) Where the court gives a direction under subsection (7)(aa) above the court shall cause an account to be given orally before the court by the clerk of the court of so much of any statement as is not read aloud.

(7B) Whether or not a direction under paragraph (aa) of subsection (7) above is given in relation to any statement served as mentioned in that paragraph the court need not cause to be read out the declaration required by section 9(2)(b) of the *Criminal Justice Act* 1967.

(8) If the court proceeds under subsection (5) above to hear and dispose of the case in the absence of the accused, the court shall not permit—

(a) any other statement with respect to any facts relating to the offence charged; or

(b) any other information relating to the accused,

to be made or placed before the court by or on behalf of the prosecutor except on a resumption of the trial after an adjournment under section 10(3) above.

(9) If the court decides not to proceed under subsection (5) above to hear and dispose of the case in the absence of the accused, it shall adjourn or further adjourn the trial for the purpose of dealing with the information as if the notification under subsection (4) above had not been given.

(10) In relation to an adjournment on the occasion of the accused's conviction in his absence under subsection (5) above or to an adjournment required by subsection (9) above, the notice required by section 10(2) above shall include notice of the reason for the adjournment.

(11) No notice shall be required by section 10(2) above in relation to an adjournment—

(a) which is for not more than 4 weeks; and

(b) the purpose of which is to enable the court to proceed under subsection (5) above at a later time.

(12) No order shall be made under subsection (1) above unless a draft of the order has been laid before and approved by resolution of each House of Parliament.

(13) Any such document as is mentioned in subsection (3) above may be served in Scotland with a summons which is so served under the *Summary Jurisdiction (Process) Act* 1881.

Magistrates' Courts Act 1980, Sched. 3, para. 4

8–81   4.—(1) Notification or intimation for the purposes of subsections (2) and (3) of section 12 above may be given on behalf of a corporation by a director or the secretary of the corporation; and those subsections shall apply in relation to a notification or intimation purporting to be so given as they apply to a notification or intimation purporting to be given by an individual accused.

(2) In this paragraph "director", in relation to a corporation which is established by or under any enactment for the purpose of carrying on under national ownership any industry or part of an industry or undertaking and whose affairs are managed by the members thereof, means a member of that corporation.

8–82   The defendant may enter a plea of guilty by post if the conditions in section 12 of the *Magistrates' Courts Act* 1980 are met. Provided that the court receives the defendant's notification of a guilty plea by post before the hearing date, it does not matter that it was received after the return date specified in the summons: *R. v. Norham and Islandshire Justices, ex p. Sunter Bros Ltd* [1961] 1 W.L.R. 364. If there are several summonses it is essential that the defendant makes it clear to which one he is pleading guilty: *R. v. Burnham Bucks Justices, ex p. Ansorge* [1959] 1 W.L.R. 1041. If the offence is endorsable or disqualifiable the defendant must also send his driving licence and a statement of his date of birth and sex: *Road Traffic Offenders Act* 1988, s.8.

The defendant may withdraw a plea of guilty by post at any time before the hearing by giving the court written notice: *Magistrates' Courts Act* 1980, s.12(6). The court has jurisdiction at the hearing to allow a change of plea so that a defendant who has earlier pleaded guilty by post may contest the matter: *R. v. Bristol Justices, ex p. Sawyers* [1988] Crim.L.R. 754.

The notification of the guilty plea, the statement of facts served by the prosecution or the written statement under the *Criminal Justice Act* 1967, s.9 and any statements submitted in mitigation must be read out by the legal adviser in open court. Failure to do so will render the proceedings a nullity: *R. v. Oldham Justices, ex p. Morrissey* [1959] 1 W.L.R. 58; *R. v. Epping and Ongar Justices, ex p. Breach* [1987] R.T.R. 233. Such a defect cannot be remedied by section 142(2) of the *Magistrates' Courts Act* 1980 (see *post*) because the defendant has not been found guilty but has simply notified his or her intention to plead guilty. The prosecution may serve a fresh summons upon the original information: *R. v. Epping and Ongar Justices, ex p. Breachi, ante.*

The court has a residual discretion to decide that the case is not suitable to be dealt with by way of a plea of guilty by post. The court may adjourn the matter for the defendant to appear. The notice of adjournment sent to the defendant must specify the reason for the adjournment: *Mason* [1965] 2 All E.R. 308.

Magistrates' Courts Act 1980, s.12A

Application of section 12 where accused appears

12A.—(1) Where the clerk of the court has received such a notification as is mentioned in **8–83** subsection (4) of section 12 above but the accused nevertheless appears before the court at the time and place appointed for the trial or adjourned trial, the court may, if he consents, proceed under subsection (5) of that section as if he were absent.

(2) Where the clerk of the court has not received such a notification and the accused appears before the court at that time and place and informs the court that he desires to plead guilty, the court may, if he consents, proceed under section 12(5) above as if he were absent and the clerk had received such a notification.

(3) For the purposes of subsections (1) and (2) above, subsections (6) to (11) of section 12 above shall apply with the modifications mentioned in subsection (4) or, as the case may be, subsection (5) below.

(4) The modifications for the purposes of subsection (1) above are that—

(a) before accepting the plea of guilty and convicting the accused under subsection (5) of section 12 above, the court shall afford the accused an opportunity to make an oral submission with a view to mitigation of sentence; and

(b) where he makes such a submission, subsection (7)(d) of that section shall not apply.

(5) The modifications for the purposes of subsection (2) above are that—

(a) subsection (6) of section 12 above shall apply as if any reference to the notification under subsection (4) of that section were a reference to the consent under subsection (2) above;

(b) subsection (7)(c) and (d) of that section shall not apply; and

(c) before accepting the plea of guilty and convicting the accused under subsection (5) of that section, the court shall afford the accused an opportunity to make an oral submission with a view to mitigation of sentence.

Sometimes a defendant will appear in court despite having sent a written plea of **8–84** guilty by post. In those circumstances, the legal adviser will ask the defendant whether he wishes the guilty plea to stand and, if so, the written plea of guilty procedure will be followed save that the defendant will be offered an opportunity to address the court personally.

D. Plea of Not Guilty

Where the defendant pleads not guilty the court will proceed to trial. The case will **8–85** generally be adjourned to a date when the witnesses can attend and which, within a reasonable timescale, is convenient to the parties. Courts should make clear to all defendants that when they fail to attend a trial it is likely that the court will proceed in absence and possibly without legal representation: *O'Hare* [2006] EWCA Crim 471; [2006] Crim.L.R. 950 (CA (Crim. Div.)). Where a defendant is absent on the occasion of an adjournment the court must give him notice in writing of the trial date, place and time: *Criminal Procedure Rules* 2005, r.37.3. The court is under a duty, and the parties must assist, to manage the case so that it proceeds to trial on the date allocated. This will involve the early identification of the issues, the needs of witnesses, the making of appropriate orders and timetabling the case. The emphasis is on discouraging delay, avoiding unnecessary adjournments and ensuring that the evidence is presented at trial in the shortest and most clear way. The court and each party will nominate a case progression officer whose responsibility it is to progress the case, monitor any directions made and keep the court informed of progress. The responsibility must be exercised in a proactive rather than a reactive way, responding promptly to communications from other parties. The court may adjourn the case to a specific case management hearing where trial readiness is assessed and further directions may be given.

Where a court is asked to adjourn a trial it will have to balance the competing interests of the parties and will have regard to:

  (i) the need for expedition in criminal proceedings; summary justice has to be speedy;

 (ii) interests of justice and the interests of the public against the possible innocence of the defendant; the more serious the offence the greater weight should be given to the public interest;

(iii) whether the defence would be compromised if there were an adjournment;

(iv) the length of the trial and the need to examine facts before the witnesses' memories fade;

 (v) the history of the case and whether there have been other adjournments;

(vi) the particular circumstances of the case: *DPP v. Picton*, unreported, May 8, 2006.

E. FAILURE TO PLEAD

8–86   Where the defendant fails to plead to the information then the court will hear the evidence in accordance with section 9(2) of the *Magistrates' Courts Act* 1980 as if there had been a plea of not guilty.

F. CHANGE OF PLEA

8–87   A magistrates' court may in its discretion allow a defendant to change his plea from guilty to not guilty at any stage before sentence is passed: *S. (an infant) v. Recorder of Manchester* [1971] A.C. 481. The question is whether the original plea was unequivocal and entered with proper understanding of the charge.

There is no automatic rule that a defendant who was unrepresented when the plea was entered is entitled to change the plea upon subsequently obtaining legal representation in the period before sentencing: *R. v. South Tameside Magistrates' Court, ex p. Rowland* [1983] 3 All E.R. 689.

Where the defendant is represented and it becomes apparent that the advocate has advised the defendant to plead guilty under a mistaken view of the nature of the charge, the court should consider whether a change of plea should be allowed on the basis of equivocality: *P. Foster (Haulage) Ltd v. Roberts* [1978] 2 All E.R. 751.

8–88   Where a plea of guilty is withdrawn, evidence of that plea as a confession of fact is admissible at the trial. The court should, however, carefully balance the probative value of such evidence against its prejudicial nature and will not normally admit it: *Rimmer* [1972] 1 W.L.R. 268.

Where a defendant changes his plea from not guilty to guilty, it is improper for the court to inquire into the defendant's reasons or motives for the change of plea unless the new plea is equivocal: *R. v. Eccles Justices, ex p. Fitzpatrick* 89 Cr.App.R. 324.

The case of *R. v. Bow Street Magistrates' Court, ex p. Welcombe* (1992) 156 J.P. 609 is authority for saying that upon a change of plea, where the offence is triable either way the court should proceed to allow the defendant to consider whether to consent to summary trial. This case was heard before the plea before venue procedure was introduced. It is submitted that the same principles should now apply.

Once the court has pronounced sentence it is *functus officio* and the conviction re- **8–89** corded upon the plea of guilty can be challenged only by way of appeal to the Crown Court. Where it is clear that a mistake has arisen, however, the court may consider its powers under section 142(2) of the *Magistrates' Courts Act* 1980 (see *post*).

Similarly, if a plea of guilty is unequivocal the court should not make use of section 142 to allow it to be withdrawn in order to substitute a plea of not guilty: *R. v. Croydon Youth Court, ex p. DPP* [1997] 2 Cr.App.R. 411.

V. PRELIMINARY ISSUES

A. GENERAL

Rule 37.1 of the *Criminal Procedure Rules* 2005 sets out the order of evidence and **8–90** speeches in a summary trial: see Appendix G, G–223 to G–228. At the start of a trial certain preliminary matters may be dealt with, *e.g.* disqualification of magistrates, amendment of charge or summons, fitness to plead, pleas of autrefois acquit or convict, abuse of process and public interest immunity. Where a court is confronted by a failure to take a required step properly or at all, before a power is exercised (a procedural fail- ure, *i.e.* in this case the mode of trial procedure had not been followed), it should first consider whether it was the intention of the legislature that any act done following that procedural failure should be invalid. If that was not the intention of Parliament, then the court should go on to consider the interests of justice generally, in particular whether there was a real possibility that either the prosecution or defence might suffer prejudice on account of the procedural failure: *Thwaites* [2006] EWCA Crim 3235; (2006) 150 S.J.L.B. 1568.

The judiciary in magistrates' courts are arbiters of both law and fact and admissibility of evidence should not generally be decided as a separate issue. Sometimes, however, a court will deal with admissibility of evidence as a preliminary point: *ADC (an infant) v. Chief Constable of Greater Manchester* [1987] Crim.L.R. 497. In that case, once the question of admissibility is determined there is no need to repeat the evidence later: *F. (an infant) v. Chief Constable of Kent* [1982] Crim.L.R. 682.

A magistrates' court determines its own procedure within statutory restraints: *R. v. Epping and Ongar Justices, ex p. Manby* [1986] Crim.L.R.555.

B. FITNESS TO PLEAD

There is no procedure in the magistrates' courts for determining a person's fitness to **8–91** plead. The court may, if the offence is triable either way, commit him to the Crown Court to have the question of fitness determined by a jury.

The usual procedure is that, if the defendant is thought to be suffering from a mental disability, the court or the defence will request psychiatric reports. Many magistrates' courts have an on site facility to produce such reports. The prosecutor may then, in the light of such reports, not proceed with the charge. Alternatively, the court may hear ev- idence and, having satisfied itself that the defendant did the act or made an omission but without convicting him, make a hospital order under the *Mental Health Act* 1983, s.37(3). In the case of *R. v. Lincoln (Kesteven) Justices, ex p. O'Connor* [1983] 1 W.L.R. 335 it was held that in an exceptional case, where the defendant was legally represented the court could conclude that the offence had occurred without hearing evidence. See *post*, Mentally Disordered Offenders, Ch.28.).

C. AUTREFOIS ACQUIT AND AUTREFOIS CONVICT

8–92   A person cannot be tried for an offence if he or she has previously been acquitted or convicted of the same, or substantially the same, offence: *Connelly v. DPP* [1964] A.C. 1254. Punishable acts of importing and exporting the same drug prosecuted in different Schengen signatory states are to be considered the same acts: *Van Straaten v. Netherlands*, unreported, October 8, 2006, ECJ; see also *Gasparini (c-467/04)*, unreported, September 27, 2006, ECJ. It is not the legal classification but the nature of the acts which matters: *Van Esbroeck (C436/04)* [2006] E.C.R.I–2333. A person should not be tried for offences on an ascending scale of seriousness: *Beedie* [1998] Q.B. 356. In such circumstances the defendant may also plead *autrefois acquit* or *autrefois convict*.

Strictly speaking a plea of *autrefois acquit* or *autrefois convict* may only be raised in a trial on indictment, however, the principles giving rise to such pleas are the same in the magistrates' court: *DPP v. Porthouse* (1989) 89 Cr.App.R. 21. There is no special procedure in the magistrates' courts for pleading *autrefois acquit* or *autrefois convict*.

The defendant, however, has the burden of proving on the balance of probabilities that there has been a previous conviction or acquittal on the merits: *Coughlan and Young* (1976) 63 Cr.App.R. 33.

For a plea of *autrefois acquit* to succeed the defendant must have been put in genuine jeopardy at an earlier hearing: *Dabhade* [1993] 2 W.L.R. 129. There must have been a hearing on the merits: *Pressick* [1978] Crim.L.R. 377. A procedural irregularity resulting in an acquittal is not sufficient to put a defendant in jeopardy: *Williams v. DPP* (1991) 93 Cr.App.R. 319; [1991] 1 W.L.R. 1160; neither is the situation where a defendant has been charged and acquitted of an offence unknown to law: *DPP v. Porthouse (ante)*. Similarly, double jeopardy cannot apply where a person being prosecuted for offences under the *Terrorism Act* 2000 has previously appealed to the Special Immigration Appeals Commission against a certificate issued under the *Anti-terrorism, Crime and Security Act* 2001, since the latter proceedings are not criminal: *R. v. I.K.* [2007] EWCA Crim 971. The withdrawal of a summons does not equate with an acquittal: *R. v. Grays Justices, ex p. Low* [1990] 1 Q.B. 54.

8–93   Where a prosecutor has been properly asked to choose upon which information to proceed the plea of autrefois acquit cannot be raised. If a charge is summarily dismissed because the prosecution recognises the difficulties which exist in prosecuting that charge, and a new charge is substituted, a plea of *autrefois acquit* on the first charge cannot be made: *Broadbent v. High* [1985] R.T.R. 359. If there has been an acquittal of a lesser offence which contains the same ingredients of a greater offence the defendant cannot be convicted in a subsequent trial of the greater offence because the conviction would effectively reverse the acquittal for the lesser offence. A defendant could still be found guilty of the full offence, however, if he was acquitted of an attempt to commit that offence: *Velasquez* [1996] 1 Cr.App.R. 155.

A plea of *autrefois acquit* may not be raised when the prosecution chooses to offer no evidence on a lesser charge which contains the same ingredients of a more serious charge upon which the prosecution wishes to proceed: *DPP v. Khan* [1997] R.T.R. 82. In this case the defendant pleaded not guilty to charges of dangerous driving and driving without reasonable consideration for other road users. The prosecution offered no evidence on the without reasonable consideration and he was acquitted. The prosecution proceeded on the dangerous driving and the defendant was convicted. The Divisional Court, on an appeal from the Crown Court, held that the defendant had not been under a misapprehension that the prosecution intended to proceed with only the more serious charge and, at the time of acquittal on the lesser charge, the justices had not considered the merits of the charge. Where a court dismissed a charge of section 47 assault under section 27 of the *Magistrates' Courts Act* 1980 a defendant could claim autrefois acquit where he was later charged with section 20 assault and at the trial when the prosecution could not proceed it preferred a charge of section 47 assault as an alternative: *R. (A.) v. South Staffordshire Magistrates' Court* [2006] EWHC 1200; (2007) 171 J.P. 36.

Where the prosecution offers no evidence on an information charging an offence tri-   **8–94**
able either way, and no plea has been taken nor any decision reached as to the mode of
trial, a defendant is entitled to consent to summary trial, plead not guilty and have the
case dismissed. If fresh informations were then laid charging the same offences, it would
be open to the defendant to plead autrefois acquit: *R. v. Bradford Magistrates' Court,
ex p. Daniel, Independent,* June 16, 1997 (C.S.).

If the court acquits when acting outside its jurisdiction a plea of *autrefois acquit* cannot be made: *West* [1964] 1 Q.B. 15. In this case the magistrates had purported to
dismiss a charge which was triable on indictment only.

D. ABUSE OF PROCESS

The court will refuse to allow the prosecution to proceed where it considers that the   **8–95**
prosecution amounts to an abuse of the process of the court and is oppressive and
vexatious. The question is whether in the circumstances it is possible for the particular
defendant to have a fair trial.

In *R. v. Willesden Justices, ex p. Clemmings* (1988) 87 Cr.App.R. 280, Bingham
L.J. stated that there are two situations where abuse of process could lead to a magistrates' court's stopping a prosecution from going ahead. Either the prosecution has
manipulated or misused the process of the court so as to deprive the defendant of a
protection provided by law or taken unfair advantage of a technicality or on the balance
of probabilities that the defendant has been or would be prejudiced in the preparation
or conduct of his or her defence by delay on the part of the prosecution which was
unjustifiable. An abuse of process is something so unfair and wrong that the court
should not allow the prosecution to proceed: *Connelly v. DPP* (1964) A.C. 1254, HL;
DPP v. Humphreys (1977) A.C. 1, HL; *Hui Chi-Ming v. R.* (1992) 1 A.C. 34.

The power to stay a summary trial or committal proceedings on the ground of abuse
of process should be used sparingly: *R. v. Oxford City Justices, ex p. Smith* (1982) 75
Cr.App.R. 200; *R. v. Horsham Justices, ex p. Reeves* (1982) 75 Cr.App.R. 236; *R. v.
Telford Justices, ex p. Badhan* [1991] 2 Q.B. 78; *R. v. Barry Magistrates' Court, ex p.
Malpas* [1998] C.O.D. 90. In *Childs, The Times,* November 30, 2002, CA. It was said
that abuse of process arguments distort the trial process in cases where they are unwarranted; if such arguments are advanced without justification, courts should make it clear
that this is inappropriate conduct and should take appropriate steps where court time
has been wasted as a result.

In *R. v. Horseferry Road Magistrates' Court, ex p. Bennett* [1994] 1 A.C. 42, the   **8–96**
House of Lords confirmed that justices have the power to stay criminal proceedings for
abuse of process but held that such power should be strictly confined to matters directly
affecting the fairness of the trial of the particular defendant with whom they are dealing,
such as delay, or unfair manipulation of court procedures. The wider supervisory
responsibility for upholding the rule of law is vested in the High Court. Where a question arises as to the deliberate abuse of extradition procedures, the court should exercise
its discretion to grant an adjournment to facilitate an application to the High Court.
Even in cases concerning complaints directed to the fairness or propriety of the trial
process itself it is always open to a magistrates' court to decline jurisdiction and leave the
matter to be pursued in the High Court: *R. v. Belmarsh Magistrates' Court, ex p.
Watts* [1999] 2 Cr.App.R. 188, DC. In *R. v. Horseferry Magistrates' Court, ex p. DPP*
[1999] C.O.D. 441, DC the court suggested that in the sort of situation under
consideration an abuse of process application might be better addressed to the court of
trial than to the committal court. An application to the High Court by way of judicial
review would seek prohibition of the continuation of the proceedings rather than to
quash the decision to institute the proceedings.

In *R. v. Leeds Youth Court, ex p. P.(A.)* (2001) 165 J.P. 684, DC the court
considered the extent of the jurisdiction of magistrates in respect of an abuse of process.
The court held that whatever the exact limits might be, there is no jurisdiction to stay
proceedings on the basis of a failure by the prosecution to comply with the rules requir-

ing the giving of advance information. The proper remedy in such cases is to adjourn the proceedings to enable the information to be provided.

8–97   A private prosecution is not automatically an abuse of process where a defendant has already received a police caution: *Hayter v. L.* [1998] 1 W.L.R. 854. It could, however, be an abuse of process where a person had agreed to a caution on the assurance that he would not have to go before a criminal court: *Jones v. Whalley* [2006] 3 W.L.R. 179. An attempt to prefer fresh charges against a defendant based on similar charges already rejected in old-style committal proceedings is vexatious and frivolous and an abuse of process: *R. v. Horsham Justices, ex p. Reeves, ante.* Where a prosecuting party is under no independent duty to furnish evidence then a failure to do so does not amount to an abuse of process: *Aylesbury Vale DC v. Khan* [2005] EWCA 841.

The onus is on the accused to show on a balance of probabilities that a fair trial is no longer possible: *R. v. Telford Justices, ex p. Badhan, ante*; *R. v. Great Yarmouth Magistrates, ex p. Thomas* [1992] Crim.L.R. 116. That is true when deciding whether a fair trial can take place having regard to the intellectual capacity of a defendant and his ability to participate effectively in the proceedings; the test is not one of a real possibility that he would not: *R. (P.) v. West London Youth Court* [2005] EWHC 2583; [2006] 1 All E.R. 477. In *Tan v. Cameron* [1992] 2 A.C. 205, PC, however, the court considered that the question of whether the proceedings should be stayed is one that should be considered as a whole and nothing is to be gained by introducing shifting burdens of proof.

The court must determine an application to stay proceedings for an abuse of process on the material provided by the prosecution and defence. There is a right to call evidence: *R. v. Clerkenwell Magistrates' Court, ex p. Bell* [1991] Crim.L.R. 468.

Delay

8–98   In the *Att.-Gen.'s Reference (No. 2 of 2001)* [2003] UKHL 68; [2004] 2 A.C. 72, the House of Lords (Lords Hope and Rogers dissenting) stated that, in order for there to be a stay of proceedings on the grounds of delay, the court must be satisfied that either a fair hearing is no longer possible or it is for any compelling reason unfair to try the defendant.

Lord Bingham, delivering the judgement and referring to Article 6 of the ECHR, stated:

> "First, the right of a criminal defendant was to a hearing. The article required that hearing to have certain characteristics. If the hearing was shown not to have been fair, a conviction could be quashed and a retrial ordered if a fair trial could still be held. If the hearing was shown to have been by a tribunal lacking independence or impartiality or legal authority, a conviction could be quashed and a retrial ordered if a fair trial could still be held. If judgement had not been given publicly, judgement could be given publicly. But time, once spent, could not be recovered. If a breach of the reasonable time requirement was shown to have occurred it could not be cured. It would, however, be anomalous if breach of the reasonable time requirement had an effect more far-reaching than breach of the defendant's other article 6(1) rights when, as had to be assumed, the breach did not taint the basic fairness of the hearing at all, and even more anomalous that the right to a hearing should be vindicated by ordering that there should not be a hearing at all.
>
> Second, a rule of automatic termination of proceedings on breach of the reasonable time requirement could not sensibly be applied in civil proceedings. An unmeritorious defendant might no doubt be very happy to seize on such a breach to escape his liability, but termination of the proceedings would defeat the claimant's right to a hearing altogether and seeking to make good his loss in compensation from the state could well be a very unsatisfactory alternative.

8–99
> Third, a rule of automatic termination on proof of a breach of the reasonable time requirement had been shown to have the effect in practice of emasculating the right which the guarantee was designed to protect. It had to be recognised that the Convention was directed not to departures from the ideal but to infringements of basic human rights, and the thresh-

old of proving a breach of the reasonable time requirement was a high one, not easily crossed: see the privy Council decision in *Dyer v. Watson* [2002]3 W.L.R. 1488, 1508, paragraph 52). Judges should not be vexed with applications based on lapses of time which, even if they should not have occurred, aroused no serious concern. There was, however, a very real risk that if proof of a breach was held to require automatic termination of the proceedings the judicial response would be to set the threshold unacceptably high since, as Justice La Forest put it in *Rahey v. The Queen* (1987) 39 DLR 481, 516): 'Few judges relish the prospect of unleashing dangerous criminals on the public'.

Fourth, the Strasbourg jurisprudence gave no support to the contention that there should be no hearing of a criminal charge once a reasonable time has passed. It was of course true that the European Court of Human Rights examined cases retrospectively, and it could not quash convictions. But it was significant that, in its interpretation and application of the Convention it had never treated the holding of a hearing as a violation or a proper subject of compensation: see *Bunkate v. The Netherlands* (1995) 19 E.H.R.R. 477 at 484, paragraph 25). If, through the action or inaction of a public authority, a criminal charge was not determined at a hearing within a reasonable time, there was necessarily a breach of the defendant's Convention right under article 6(1). For such breach there had to be afforded such remedy as might be just (section 8(1) of the 1998 Act) and appropriate or, in Convention terms, effective, just and proportionate. The appropriate remedy would depend on the nature of the breach and all the circumstances, including particularly the stage of the proceedings at which the breach was established. If the breach was established before the hearing, the appropriate remedy might be a public acknowledgement of the breach, action to expedite the hearing to the greatest extent practicable and perhaps, if the defendant was in custody, his release on bail. It would not be appropriate to stay or dismiss the proceedings unless (a) there could no longer be a fair hearing or (b) it would otherwise be unfair to try the defendant. The public interest in the final determination of criminal charges required that such a charge should not be stayed or dismissed if any lesser remedy would be just and proportionate in all the circumstances. The prosecutor and the court would not act incompatibly with the defendant's Convention right in continuing to prosecute or entertain proceedings after a breach was established in a case where neither of conditions (a) or (b) was met, since the breach consisted in the delay which had accrued and not in the prospective hearing.

If the breach of the reasonable time requirement was established retrospectively, after there had been a hearing, the appropriate remedy might be a public acknowledgement of the breach, a reduction in the penalty imposed on a convicted defendant or the payment of compensation to an acquitted defendant. Unless (a) the hearing was unfair or (b) it was unfair to try the defendant at all, it would not be appropriate to quash any conviction. Again, in any case where, neither condition (a) nor (b) applied, the prosecutor and the court would not act incompatibly with the defendant's Convention right in prosecuting or entertaining the proceedings but only in failing to procure a hearing within a reasonable time.

There might well be cases where the delay was of such an order…as to make it unfair that the proceedings against a defendant should continue. Such cases would, however, be very exceptional and a stay would never be an appropriate remedy if any lesser remedy would adequately vindicate the defendant's Convention right."

The House of Lords confirmed that in considering whether a criminal charge has been determined within a reasonable time for the purposes of Article 6, the relevant time will normally start to run from the date when the defendant is charged by the police or served with a summons. Any period prior to a formal charge may be considered if the defendant has during that period been substantially affected by the conduct of the prosecution but time would not ordinarily run until after a suspect had been interviewed under caution. Arrest would not ordinarily mark the beginning of the period but an official indication that a person would be reported with a view to prosecution might do so. The interviewing of a person for the purposes of a regulatory inquiry would not meet the test: *Fayed v. UK* (1994) 18 E.H.R.R. 393.

In *Eastaway v. UK, The Times*, August 9, 2004, a civil matter, the European Court of Human Rights again confirmed that delay is a factor in the right to a fair trial. In *Henworth v. UK, The Times* November 22, 2004, where it was held that there had been a violation of Article 6 (1), it was stated that the reasonableness of the length of proceedings had to be assessed in the light of the circumstances of the case, its complex-

8–100

ity, the conduct of the parties and what is at stake for the defendant. The state is under a responsibility to proceed with due diligence. Applications to stay for abuse of process should be discouraged in cases of sexual assault where many years had passed by as it is sometimes very difficult for young children to speak out at that time: *Smolinski* [2004] EWCA Crim 1270. It is important to give a party an opportunity to explain his default: *DPP v. Ayres*, unreported, October 20, 2004.

In *Dyer v. Watson* [2002] 4 All E.R. 1, the Privy Council considered the effect of delay in criminal proceedings. It held that the threshold of proving that a trial has not occurred within a reasonable time is a high one. If the period which has elapsed is one which, on its face, gives rise to real concern, it is necessary to look into the detailed circumstances of the particular case and it must be possible to justify any lapse of time which appears to be excessive. Regard must be had to the complexity of the case, the conduct of the defendant and the manner in which the case has been dealt with by the prosecution and the courts. There is no general obligation on a prosecutor to act with all due expedition and diligence but a marked lack of expedition if unjustified would indicate a breach of the reasonable time requirement. A decision on delay is a judicial assessment dependant on judgement rather than on any conclusion as to facts based on evidence so the use of the phrases burden and standard of proof are potentially misleading. The correct approach is to bear in mind the following principles:

  (i) even where delay was unjustifiable, a permanent stay should be the exception rather than the rule;
  (ii) where there was no fault on the part of the complainant or the prosecution, it would be very rare for a stay to be granted;
  (iii) no stay should be granted in the absence of serious prejudice to the defence so that no fair trial could be held;
  (iv) when assessing possible serious prejudice, the judge should bear in mind his or her power to regulate the admissibility of evidence and that the trial process itself should ensure that all relevant factual issues arising from delay would be placed before the jury for their consideration in accordance with appropriate directions from the judge; and
  (v) if, having considered all those factors, a judge's assessment was that a fair trial would be possible, a stay should not be granted: *R. v. S* [2006] EWCA Crim 756.

In *Coghlan* [2006] EWCA Crim 1542 it was said that a court should exercise its discretion to stay proceedings only in exceptional circumstances; it is not to be used to punish the prosecution simply for delay; the issue is whether a fair trial can take place and magistrates must give reasons to indicate that they have considered factors such as the decline in witness memory or the death of witnesses: *Department of Work and Pensions v. Courts; Department of Work and Pensions v. Costello* [2006] EWHC 1156. Where charges had been preferred seven years after the incident and documents that were part of the material by which the victim's credibility could be assessed, had gone missing the trial should be stayed: *Ali v. CPS* [2007] EWCA Crim 691.

8–101   Where substantial delay has occurred which can be attributed in part to the inefficiency of the prosecutor and in part to the conduct of the defendant, the court must consider to what extent the delay is attributable to the prosecution. If it is substantial and the defendant has been or must have been prejudiced thereby this power must be exercised in the defendant's favour.

The fact that there is a six-month limitation period within which to bring most summary offences is an indication that such cases ought to be disposed of expeditiously. Although the information must be laid within the time limit the date of the summons may be outside that limit. The following cases must now, however, be read in the light of Lord Bingham's judgment in the *Att.-Gen.'s Reference (No. 2 of 2001), ante.*

The refusal of the issue of a summons when the information was laid on the last permissible day has been upheld: *R. v. Clerk to the Medway Justices, ex p. DHSS* [1986] Crim.L.R. 686, DC.

Where a summons is ambiguous as to which of two inconsistent offences may have been committed, it is an abuse of process for the prosecution not to give particulars of the offence to be proceeded with to the defence, before the expiry of the six month period: *R. v. Newcastle-Upon-Tyne Justices, ex p. Hindle* [1984] 1 All E.R. 770. A police officer saw the defendant after a road accident and formed the view he had been drinking. The defendant told the officer he had consumed alcohol since the accident. He was arrested, provided a specimen of blood which was above the limit. He was summoned for an offence under the *Road Traffic Act* 1972, s.6(1), pleaded not guilty and the matter was adjourned to a date outside the six month time limit. The defendant then received a summons for obstruction of a police officer. It was unclear whether the obstruction summons was on the basis that the defendant had lied to the officer about the drink (consistent with the section 6(1) summons) or because he had deliberately consumed alcohol to frustrate the excess alcohol summons (inconsistent with the section 6(1) summons). The prosecution refused to provide particulars. When the matters came before the court a defence submission that the obstruction summons was an abuse of process was rejected. On review it was held that since the obstruction summons was ambiguous and could have applied to inconsistent offences, and the prosecution had refused to give particulars, the summons was prejudicial and an abuse of process since it allowed the prosecution to postpone their decision on which offence to prosecute until after the expiry of the six-month period.

The inquiry into an offence does not begin merely by the hearing of submissions as **8–102** to abuse of process relating to the transfer of proceedings to another court. The inquiry into the offence begins only with the calling of witnesses, the opening of the prosecution case or some other pertinent step: *R. v. Worcester Magistrates' Court, ex p. Bell*, 157 J.P. 921, DC.

Manipulation or misuse of the process of court

In *R. v. Lincoln Magistrates' Court, ex p. Wickes Building Supplies Ltd, The* **8–103** *Times*, August 6, 1993, DC, it was held that the laying of a multiplicity of charges in respect of each Sunday trading breach under section 47 of the *Shops Act* 1950, when the lawfulness of that section was being challenged in the European Court of Justice, was not an abuse of process. It had been argued that the deliberate stacking up of informations by the prosecutor during a time when (a) the law was uncertain; (b) there was no possibility of conviction pending clarification of the law; and (c) the prosecuting local authority would not risk seeking a civil injunction, was oppressive and vexatious and amounted to a manipulation of the process that would make it unfair to try the accused.

In *R. v. Rotherham Justices, ex p. Brough* (1991) C.O.D. 89, DC, the prosecution had deliberately taken steps to ensure that a defendant who was charged with an offence that would be triable only on indictment in the case of an adult did not appear before the court until he had reached the age where the justices ceased to have a discretion whether or not to deal with it themselves. Although the court viewed the procedure as incorrect, it was held not to amount to an abuse of process because, on the facts the conduct of the prosecution showed at most a lack of judgment rather than misconduct or *mala fides*. There was no prejudice to the defendant because the delay involved had been minimal, the justices would probably have committed the case to the Crown Court anyway, and in the event of conviction the judge would undoubtedly take account of the defendant's age at the time of the offence and the circumstances of the committal. Where there is insufficient evidence to satisfy a local authority's public prosecution policy a prosecution will amount to an abuse of process: *Adaway* [2004] EWCA Crim 2831. Unlawful acts amounting to a deliberate violation of a suspected person's right to legal professional privilege can amount to an abuse of process: *R. v. Grant (Edward)* [2005] EWCA Crim 1089; [2005] 3 W.L.R. 437; [2006] Q.B. 60; [2005] C.M.L.R 955. The fact that the prosecution has expressed concerns about pre-trial reviews by reference to the conduct of criminal proceedings against an accused while those proceedings are still live does not amount to an abuse of process: *R. (Hussain) v. Peterborough*

Magistrates' Court [2007] EWHC 667, Admin. In this case a legal adviser, who had earlier been involved in a pre-trial hearing, had intervened in court shortly after the case had begun, stating that, on the authorities, there was no case to answer. When the prosecutor had found another authority the case had been adjourned. Subsequently the prosecutor had complained about the legal adviser's intervention and on the adjourned hearing a different legal adviser was in court. The complainant alleged that the legal adviser had been moved off the case as a result of the complaints and the way that the prosecution had gone about objecting was an abuse of process.

8–104 Where a summary trial is adjourned part-heard before the conclusion of the case for the prosecution and, at the adjourned hearing, the prosecution proposed to call a witness whom they had not intended to call at the original hearing but of whose existence they had always been aware, any objection based on an assertion that an unfair advantage had been taken should be dealt with by reference to section 78 of the *Police and Criminal Evidence Act* 1984, and not as an abuse of process.

It is an abuse of process for the prosecution, upon realising, after the magistrates had retired to consider sentence, that the charge was punishable only by way of fine, to invite the magistrates back into court, and then invite them to substitute a charge in respect of the same facts which carried the possibility of a custodial sentence: *R. v. Harlow Magistrates Court, ex p. O'Farrell* [2000] Crim.L.R. 589, DC.

Where one magistrates' court has refused to issue a summons in respect of an information alleging an offence, it is an abuse of process to apply for a summons to another magistrates' court in respect of an identical information without disclosing the fact of the first court's refusal to issue a summons: *Gleaves v. Insall*; *Bolton v. Insall*; *Gleaves v. Insall* [1999] 2 Cr.App.R. 466, DC.

8–105 The prosecution of a person who, in exchange for his co-operation, has received an undertaking, promise or representation from the police that he would not be charged with an offence, is capable of amounting to an abuse of process. It is not necessary for the applicant to show that the police had the power to make the decision not to prosecute; nor is it necessary for him to show that the case was one of bad faith: *R. v. Croydon JJ, ex p. Dean* 98 Cr.App.R. 76, DC.

In *R. v. Horseferry Road Magistrates' Court, ex p. DPP* (1999) C.O.D. 441, DC a prosecution had been instituted despite an assurance of no prosecution having been given by the police to the defendant's solicitor the court concluded that it would be unfair to try the defendant in such circumstances and stayed the proceedings. The Divisional Court disagreed; breach of an assurance not to prosecute cannot of itself amount to an abuse of process. The failure of a conditional offer of a fixed penalty to comply with statutory requirements did not make the subsequent proceedings an abuse of process as the court had not examined how the defendant was personally prejudiced and there was nothing to suggest that he could not have a fair trial: *DPP v. Holden* [2006] EWHC 658, Admin; [2007] R.T.R. 5. Non-disclosure of material held by a third party where the court exceeds its power to order that disclosure is not an abuse of process: *DPP v. Wood* [2006] EWHC 32; (2006) 170 J.P. 177. Missing documents cannot of themselves be grounds for abuse of process: *R. v. Martin* [2005] EWCA Crim 3212.

Save in special circumstances (the burden of proving which is on the prosecution) the prosecution is not allowed to bring a second set of proceedings arising from the same or substantially the same facts as proceedings that had already been concluded: *Phipps* [2005] EWCA Crim 33. Here the prosecutor had prosecuted dangerous driving when the sentence for an excess alcohol offence arising from the same accident had received adverse publicity due to leniency. This principle does not apply where the first set of proceedings were brought by foreign prosecutors in a foreign jurisdiction: *R. v. Cheong* [2006] EWCA Crim 524.

An abuse of process exists where a plaintiff in civil proceedings is in effective control of criminal proceedings against the same defendant to the extent that the prosecution is unable to exercise its duties independently: *R. v. Leominster Magistrates' Court, ex p. Aston Manor Brewery Co, The Times*, January 8, 1997, DC. An abuse of process will arise where illegal conduct on the part of the police or prosecutor is so grave as to threaten or undermine the rule of law. In *Grant* [2005] EWCA Crim 1089; [2005] 3 W.L.R. 437 it was held that deliberate interference by police with a detained suspect's right to the confidence of privileged communication with his solicitor by eavesdropping and taping a conversation justifies a stay of proceedings notwithstanding the absence of prejudice.

Machinations on the part of the prosecutor to prevent potential defence witnesses **8–106** from giving evidence would be highly likely to amount to an abuse of process: *Schlesinger* [1995] Crim.L.R. 137, CA.

In *R. (Ebrahim) v. Feltham Magistrates' Court*; *Mouat v. DPP* [2001] 2 Cr.App.R. 23, DC guidance was given as to the approach that should be followed when an application to stay proceedings as an abuse of process is founded on the non-availability of a video recording that would, allegedly, contain relevant material. The first issue in such cases is the nature and extent, in the particular circumstance of the case, of the duty, if any, of the investigating authority and/or of the prosecutor to obtain and/or retain the material in question. In this context, recourse should be had to the code of practice issued under section 25 of the *Criminal Procedure and Investigations Act* 1996 and the Attorney General's Guidance on Disclosure. If, in the circumstances, there was no duty to obtain and /or retain that material before the defence first sought its retention, then there can be no question of the subsequent trial being unfair on that ground. If there has been a breach of the obligation to obtain or retain the relevant material it will be necessary to decide whether the defence have shown, on a balance or probabilities, that owing to the absence of the relevant material the defendant would suffer serious prejudice to the extent that a fair trial could not take place and in ruling on that question the court should also bear in mind that the trial process itself is equipped to deal with the bulk of complaints on which applications for a stay are founded. A stay should also be granted if the behaviour of the prosecution has been so bad that it is not fair that the defendant should be tried, and in this regard a useful test is that there should be either an element of bad faith or at least some serious fault.

This was approved in *Sahdev* [2002] EWCA Crim 1064. Here the defendant had **8–107** been convicted of possession of a bladed article in a public place and two counts of racially aggravated common assault at Hammersmith Tube Station. The area was monitored by British Transport Police cameras. The incident may also have been filmed by other security cameras belonging to shops and unknown to the Police at the time. These cameras were not investigated and it was alleged that the defendant could not thus receive a fair trial. The Court of Appeal held that the failure of the Police to investigate the evidence from the other cameras was not unreasonable and therefore the appellant could receive a fair trial. Evidence arising from covert operations is normally dealt with under section 78 of *PACE* 1984 see *post*, § 10–140. Sometimes, however, an application is made to stay the proceedings on the grounds of abuse of process. The power to stay proceedings for abuse of process is wide enough to embrace an application challenging a decision to prosecute on the grounds it is arrived at under political pressure or influence or is motivated politically rather than by an objective review of proper prosecution considerations; the criminal process is more appropriate than judicial review in these circumstances: *Antoine v. Sharma* [2006] UKPC 57. In *Moon (Dianna Rose)* [2004] EWCA Crim 2872 it was held that, where a test purchase has caused a defendant to commit the offence rather than having merely provided the opportunity to do so in circumstances in which the defendant would have behaved in the same way if the opportunity had been offered by anyone else, it is unfair and an abuse of process.

Whilst serious failings on the part of the police or the prosecution may make it unfair to try a defendant in a particular case, that will be a rare occurrence in the absence of serious misbehaviour; if it is not such a case, then the only issue is whether it remains possible for the defendant to have a fair trial: *Sadler* (2002) 166 J.P. 481, CA. No abuse of process argument can be founded upon the assertion that findings in care proceedings are a final determination of criminal proceedings; they are not: *Levey* [2006] 1 W.L.R. 3092.

In the youth court there is an inherent jurisdiction to stay proceedings at any stage where the fairness of the trial is being called into question. It should only be exercised in exceptional circumstances on capacity issues and before evidence is called. The fact that a court of higher authority has held that a person was unfit to plead does not make it an abuse to try that person for further acts. The issue of the child's ability to participate effectively has to be decided afresh. Where medical evidence suggests that the child's condition had not changed since his appearance before that higher court, the decisions of that higher court would be relevant but not determinative or binding: *DPP v. P.* [2007] EWHC 946, Admin.

E. PUBLIC INTEREST IMMUNITY

8–108   This doctrine is normally encountered in the higher courts but may be argued in the magistrates' courts particularly in cases where informers are involved. It prevents material from being disclosed by the prosecution to the defence where the public interest in non-disclosure outweighs the public interest that, in the administration of justice, the courts should have the fullest possible access to all relevant material. Where disclosure is ordered the prosecution may often not proceed with the case.

The anonymity of informers has been upheld in several cases, *e.g.*: *Savage v. Chief Constable of Hampshire* [1997] 2 All E.R. 631. Those who allow premises to be used for police surveillance have been protected: *Johnson (K.)* 88 Cr.App.R. 131. Informations upon which search warrants have been issued as well as reports from the police to the DPP have also been protected through non-disclosure: *Taylor v. Anderton, The Times*, October 21, 1986. Information relating to the judicial process is covered as are documents relating to the welfare of children.

8–109   In *Rowe and Davis v. UK, The Times*, March 1, 2000, the ECHR stated that it is a fundamental aspect of the right to a fair trial that criminal proceedings should be adversarial and that there should be equality of arms between the prosecution and defence. The right to an adversarial trial means, in a criminal case, that the prosecution and defence must be given the opportunity to have knowledge of and comment on the observations filed and the evidence adduced by the other party. The court went on to state that courts have to weigh national security and the need to protect witnesses at risk of reprisals and keep secret police methods of investigation of crime against the interest of the accused.

In *H.; C. (ante)* the House of Lords confirmed that in cases where public interest immunity was argued, some derogation from the rule of full disclosure might be justified but it had to be the minimum necessary to protect the public interest in question. In giving the judgement Lord Bingham identified three classes of case:

"1. Most cases in which a public interest immunity issue arose.

The prosecution had to notify the defence that they were applying for a court ruling and had to indicate to the defence at least the category of material they held; namely, the broad ground on which immunity was claimed, and the defence had to have the opportunity to make representations to the court. Thus there was an inter partes hearing in open court with reference at least to the category of the material.

2. Cases where the prosecution contended that the public interest would be injured if disclosure were made even of the category of material.

The prosecution still had to notify the defence of the application, but the category of material need not be specified.

The defence would still have an opportunity to address the court on the procedure to be adopted, but the application would be made to the court in the absence of the defendant or his representatives.

If the court considered that the application fell into the first class it would order that procedure to be followed, otherwise it would rule it was a highly exceptional case.

3. Highly exceptional were cases where the public interest would be injured even by disclosure that an ex parte application was to be made.

In such cases the application would be without notice to the defence. But if the court considered that the case should be within class 1 or 2 it would so order."

He went on to say that the appointment of special counsel was a matter of last resort **8–110**
and gave guidance on the questions a court should ask:

"1. What was the material which the prosecution sought to withhold? That had to be
considered by the court in detail.

2. Was the material such as might weaken the prosecution case or strengthen that of the
defence? If "No", disclosure should not be ordered. If "Yes" full disclosure should, subject to
3,4 and 5, be ordered.

3. Was there a real risk of serious prejudice to an important public interest (and if so, what) if
full disclosure were ordered? If "No", full disclosure should be ordered.

4.If the answer to 2 and 3 was "Yes", could the defendant's interest be protected without
disclosure or disclosure be ordered to an extent or in a way which would give adequate
protection to the public interest in question and also afford adequate protection to the interest of the defence?

That question required the court to consider, with specific reference to the material which
the prosecutor sought to withhold, the facts of the case and the defence as disclosed, whether
the prosecution should formally admit what the defence sought to establish or whether
disclosure short of full disclosure might be ordered.

That might be done in appropriate cases by the preparation of summaries or extracts of evidence or the provision of documents in an edited or anonymised form, provided the documents supplied were in each instance approved by the judge.

In appropriate cases, the appointment of special counsel might be a necessary step to ensure
that the contentions of the prosecution were tested and the interests of the defendant
protected.

In cases of exceptional difficulty the court might require the appointment of special counsel
to ensure a correct answer to questions 2 and 3 as well as 4.

5.Did the measures proposed in answer to 4 represent the minimum derogation from the
golden rule of full disclosure

6.If limited disclosure was ordered under 4 or 5, might the effect be to render the trial process, viewed as a whole, unfair to the defendant?

If "Yes" then fuller disclosure should be ordered even if that led or might lead the prosecution to discontinue the proceedings so as to avoid having to make disclosure.

7.If the answer to 6 when first given as "No", did that remain the correct answer as the trial
unfolded, evidence was adduced and the defence advanced?

It was important that the answer to 6 should not be treated as a final, once—for-all answer,
but as a provisional answer which the court had to keep under review."

Lord Bingham gave specific guidance in relation to magistrates' courts:						**8–111**

"The relevant principles had been correctly applied in *R. (DPP) v. Acton Youth Court*
[2001] 1 W.L.R. 1828). If public interest immunity applications were confined, as they should
be, to material undermining the prosecution case or strengthening that of the defence, the
bench would not be alerted to material damaging to the defendant.

If it was, the principles governing the court's decision whether to recuse itself were the same
as in the case of any other tribunal of fact, but the court's duty of continuing review ordinarily
militated in favour of continuing proceedings before the court which determined the immunity application.

If a case raised complex and contentious immunity issues, and the court had discretion to
send the case to the crown court for trial, the magistrates court should carefully consider
whether those issues were best resolved at the crown court.

The occasions when it would be appropriate to appoint special counsel in the magistrates
court would be even rarer than in the crown court."

The *Criminal Procedure Rules* 2005, r.25 in Appendix G–145 makes provision for **8–112**
the service of notice, the form of hearing, interested persons and court order. It specifically provides for the service of notice on the accused unless the prosecutor has reason
to believe that notice would have the effect of disclosing that which might not be
disclosed in the public interest.

VI. THE PROSECUTION CASE

A. PROSECUTION OPENING SPEECH

8–113   The prosecutor's opening speech sets the parameters of the case. It succinctly outlines and sometimes analyses the facts upon which the prosecution relies. It must be borne in mind that the judiciary in the magistrates' courts do not need the same sort of explanations as a jury in the crown court. They will, however, appreciate the scene being set for the evidence to follow. The prosecutor is under no obligation to open its case and in many simple cases chooses not to do so.

Where a case has been adjourned part heard and the court has difficulty in remembering the evidence it may allow the prosecutor to open his case again on the adjourned hearing so that he may remind the court of the evidence given. In those circumstances, the defence advocate should also be allowed to address the court: *L. and B. v. DPP* [1998] 2 Cr.App.R. 69.

B. RULE REQUIRING PROSECUTION TO CALL ALL ITS EVIDENCE BEFORE THE CLOSE OF THE CASE

8–114   The general rule is that the prosecution must call all the evidence on which it intends to rely before the close of its case: *Pilcher*, 60 Cr.App.R. 1. The court has a discretion, however, in the interests of justice, to allow the prosecution to call evidence after it has closed its case and before the court considers its decision and this is not confined to technicalities: *Rice* (1963) 47 Cr.App.R. 79. The case of *Malcolm v. DPP* [2007] EWHC 363 has confirmed a series of cases where evidence was allowed. The case was one of drink driving where the prosecution had failed to provide evidence of a warning under section 7(7) of the *RTA* 1988 that a failure to provide a specimen might result in prosecution and where an officer was allowed to give further evidence of that fact. It strongly disapproves of the "classic and improper defence ambush of the prosecution". It states that:

(1) Even in a relatively straightforward trial in a magistrates' court, where there is not yet any requirement for a defence statement or a pre-trial review, it is the duty of the defence to make the real issues clear at the latest before the prosecution closed its case. That duty is implicit in r.3.3 of the Crim. P.R., which requires the parties actively to assist the exercise by the court of its case management powers, which require early identification of the real issues. In the instant case, to take the section 7(7) point in the final speech was a classic and improper defence ambush of the prosecution.

(2) What are special circumstances justifying permitting the prosecution to re-open its case will vary from time to time. Practitioners and the courts have to take into account the overall objective of criminal procedure, as set out in r.1.1 Crim.P.R., namely that criminal cases have to be dealt with justly which includes the acquittal of the innocent and the conviction of the guilty. That objective applies as much to motoring offences as to other criminal offences. There have been too many attempts to seek to avoid the conviction of those who had driven with excess alcohol by raising unmeritorious formal points.

In *Jolly v. DPP* [2000] Crim.L.R. 471, DC; [2000] All E.R. (D) 444 the prosecution was permitted to recall a witness after the close of the defence case in order to meet a point not previously raised as to the reliability of the computer used to measure the amount of alcohol on the defendant's breath. In *MacDonald v. Skelt* [1985] R.T.R. 321, on an application of no case to answer, the prosecutor was allowed to re-open the case to call evidence that the blood specimen taken from the defendant was the same as the specimen analysed. In *R. v. Gainsborough Justices, ex p. Green* 78 Cr.App.R. 9 two informations against the defendant had alleged various breaches of a community service order. The probation officer had called evidence to support one breach only. It transpired that the defendant had had a reasonable excuse for not attending (which the defendant formally admitted). Instead of acceding to a submission of no case to answer the magistrates allowed the officer to re-open the case and call evidence of the other alleged breaches. In *Francis* (1990) 154 J.P. 358 evidence of the defendant's identity was allowed as the failure to introduce it as part of the prosecution's case had arisen out of a misunderstanding over whether the name of the person who had been identified in a parade was in issue. In *James v. South Glamorgan County Council* (1994) 99 Cr.App.R. 321, a change of court location of which some witnesses had not been informed, meant that the magistrates were entitled to allow the prosecution to call evidence after it had closed its case.

In *Matthews v. Morris* [1981] Crim.L.R. 495 the Divisional Court held that the mag- **8–115** istrates were correct to have allowed the prosecution to reopen its case to tender a statement which by mistake had not been tendered as part of the prosecution case, but which had been served on the defendant under the *Criminal Justice Act* 1967, s.9. No injustice had been caused to the defendant by the admission of the evidence.

In *Doran* (1972) 56 Cr.App.R. 429 the judge allowed the prosecution to call two witnesses after the close of its case. The witnesses were members of the public who had been present at the trial and realised during the course of the defence case that they could give evidence.

If further evidence is to be called the court should ensure that proper notice of it has **8–116** been given to the defendant. The prosecution should serve the evidence by way of notice and the court should grant an adjournment if necessary: *Dartey* (1987) 84 Cr.App.R. 352.

C. Duty of Prosecution in Calling Witnesses

Once the prosecution has served witness statements it is those witnesses which it is **8–117** expected to call. The prosecution has a discretion whether to call witnesses to give evidence in chief or to tender them for cross-examination only.

Generally the prosecution ought to call or offer to call all the witnesses who give direct evidence of the primary facts of the case, unless for good reason, it regards the witnesses' evidence as unworthy of belief. In the case of *Oliva* (1965) 49 Cr.App.R. 298; [1965] 1 W.L.R. 1028, Lord Parker C.J. said at 309–310:

> "The prosecution does not, of course, put forward every witness as a witness of truth, but where the witness's evidence is capable of belief, then it is their duty, well recognised, that he should be called, even though the evidence that he is going to give is inconsistent with the case sought to be proved. Their discretion must be exercised in a manner which is calculated to further the interests of justice, and at the same time be fair to the defence. If the prosecution appear to be exercising that discretion improperly, it is open to the judge of trial to interfere and in his discretion in turn to invite the prosecution to call a particular witness, and, if they refuse, there is the ultimate sanction in the judge himself calling that witness."

In *R. v. Haringey Justices, ex p. DPP* [1996] 2 W.L.R. 114 the prosecution decided **8–118** not to call a police officer who had been suspended from duty. The defence wished the officer to be present. The court invited the prosecution to call the witness and when the prosecution declined to do so, dismissed the case. It was held that the court could not force the prosecution to call the witness but it could call the witness itself. See also *Baldwin* [1978] Crim.L.R. 104.

The prosecution must take all reasonable steps to secure the attendance of each of its witnesses at trial, including the making of an application for a summons or warrant— see *post*. If, however, despite such steps, it has proved impossible to have the witnesses present the court might in its discretion permit the trial to proceed, provided no injustice would be done: *Cavanagh and Shaw* (1972) 56 Cr.App.R. 407. In that case, the witness was out of the country and there was no information as to when he would be back. The court, in exercising its discretion, would consider the desire of the defence to call the witness if the prosecution did not, the extent to which the evidence would help the defence, the chances of securing the attendance of the witness in a reasonable time and whether delay would result in other witnesses not being available and the willingness of the prosecution to proceed.

In *R. v. Wellingborough Justices, ex p. Francois* (1994) 158 J.P. 813 the Divisional Court held that a prosecutor had acted improperly when she did not call two prosecution witnesses or tender them for cross-examination because she was due to prosecute another case in another court later that day. As a result it was open to the justices to invite the prosecution to tender the witness and, if it refused, to call the witnesses itself.

The prosecution has a discretion over the order in which it calls its witnesses. Any witness should remain outside the courtroom until called unless the witness is an expert who may need to hear the evidence because his opinion is based on the facts. This is a rule of practice not law: *R. v. Bexley Justices, ex p. King, ante; Moore v. Registrar of Lambeth County Court* [1969] 1 W.L.R. 141.

D. NO CASE TO ANSWER

8–119   At the close of the prosecution case, the court may dismiss the case of its own motion or on a submission that there is no evidence which the defendant need answer. The finding of a case to answer requires a determination of law separate from a finding of guilt; a decision to acquit after finding a case to answer is based on factual evidence and may not be perverse: *DPP v. Uddin* [2006] EWHC 1523.

In *Galbraith* 73 Cr.App.R. 124, CA the Court of Appeal set out the test to be applied in the Crown Court. Lord Lane C.J. stated at 127 that:

> "(1) If there is no evidence that the crime alleged has been committed by the defendant there is no difficulty—the judge will stop the case. (2) The difficulty arises where there is some evidence but it is of a tenuous character, for example, because of inherent weakness or vagueness or because it is inconsistent with other evidence. (a) Where the judge concludes that the prosecution evidence, taken at its highest, is such that a jury properly directed could not properly convict on it, it is his duty, on a submission being made, to stop the case. (b) Where however the prosecution evidence is such that its strength or weakness depends on the view to be taken of a witness's reliability, or other matters which are generally speaking within the province of the jury and where on one possible view of the facts there *is* evidence on which the jury could properly come to the conclusion that the defendant is guilty, then the judge should allow the matter to be tried by the jury."

This test is also used in the magistrates' courts. The court is entitled to dismiss a case of its own motion. If it proposes to do so, however, it should allow submissions to be made by the party it proposes to decide against: *DPP v. Cosier* [2000] C.O.D. 284. Questions of credibility do not normally arise in a finding that there is no case to answer: *Brooks v. DPP* [1994] 1 A.C. 568, PC; *R. v. Barking and Dagenham Justices, ex p. DPP* (1995) 159 J.P. 373.

8–120   In *R. v. Pydar Justices, ex p. Foster* (1996) 160 J.P. 87, evidence of the defendant's intoximeter reading had been handed to the prosecutor by the police officer in court and the case was then closed, but the defendant had submitted there was no case to answer because the reading had not been produced in evidence. His application for review was dismissed because an exhibit was available for the court to examine whenever it wished and, as the justices had jurisdiction over it, it was for the defence to lay the foundations for their submissions through cross-examination or by calling evidence. Defence counsel could not wait to point out the exhibit and then submit that there was no case to answer. Strong circumstantial evidence may be sufficient for the court to find a case to answer: *Danells* [2006] EWCA Crim 628.

A court can re-open a case despite acceding to a submission of no case to answer, where an error has been identified by the prosecution and agreed by the defence after the court has given its reasons: *Steward v. DPP, The Times*, September 25, 2003.

8–121   In *Gleeson* [2004] 1 Cr.App.R. 29, Auld L.J. stated that a criminal trial is not a game, its object is to ensure that the guilty are convicted and the innocent acquitted. It is contrary to defence counsel's professional duty and not in the legitimate interests of the defendant to take advantage of procedural errors made by the prosecution in delaying identifying those errors at issue in the case until the last possible moment. It is wrong to wait to make a submission of no case on an unanswerable legal challenge rather than point out a prosecution error earlier. Here the court allowed the indictment to be amended at that late stage.

There is no obligation on the court to give reasons for rejecting a submission of no case to answer: *Moran v. DPP* (2002) 166 J.P. 467; *Harrison v. Department of Social Security* [1997] C.O.D. 220.

VII. THE DEFENCE CASE

A. REPRESENTATION

A defendant may be represented or unrepresented. He or she may choose to give ev- **8–122** idence or to remain silent.

B. SEQUENCE OF THE DEFENCE EVIDENCE

At the conclusion of the prosecution's case, the defendant may address the court **8–123** regardless of whether or not he calls evidence: *Criminal Procedure Rules* 2005, r.37.1(2), *ante*. By making an opening speech however the defence is then deprived of the making a speech at the end of the case, unless leave of the court is obtained: r.37.1(4). If leave for a closing speech is given in these circumstances, then the prosecution must also be given the opportunity to address the court again: *Criminal Procedure Rules* 2005, r.37.1(5).

The defendant is not obliged to give evidence at trial or to call any witnesses. He may no longer make an unsworn statement from the dock.

Criminal Justice Act 1982, s.72

Abolition of right of accused to make unsworn statement

72.—(1) Subject to subsections (2) and (3) below, in any criminal proceedings the accused **8–124** shall not be entitled to make a statement without being sworn, and accordingly, if he gives evidence, he shall do so[(subject to sections 55 and 56 of the *Youth Justice and Criminal Evidence Act* 1999)] on oath and be liable to cross-examination; but this section shall not affect the right of the accused, if not represented by counsel or a solicitor, to address the court or jury otherwise than on oath on any matter on which, if he were so represented, counsel or a solicitor could address the court or jury on his behalf.

(2) Nothing in subsection (1) above shall prevent the accused making a statement without being sworn—

(a) if it is one which he is required by law to make personally; or

(b) if he makes it by way of mitigation before the court passes sentence upon him.

(3) Nothing in this section applies—

(a) to a trial; or

(b) to proceedings before a magistrates' court acting as examining justices,

which began before the commencement of this section.

In *R. v. Farnham Justices, ex p. Gibson* [1991] R.T.R. 309 the policy requiring a **8–125** defendant to give evidence from the dock, not from the witness box, was declared unlawful. At his trial for driving with excess breath-alcohol and for failing to stop after an accident, the defendant was compelled by the justices, as a matter of policy, to give his evidence from the dock, not from the witness box as the other witnesses had done. The defendant argued on review that the policy requiring him to give evidence from the dock was unlawful in the light of the *Criminal Evidence Act* 1898, s.1(g). It was held that the justices, in exceptional circumstances, could deny a person the right to give evidence from the witness box but that right could only be denied by reason of misconduct or some other specific consideration. By being compelled to give evidence from the dock, the defendant was adversely treated compared to the other witnesses and justice was not seen to be done.

If the defendant chooses to testify he must do so on oath and is liable to be cross-examined by both the advocate for the prosecution and for any co-defendants: *Hilton* [1972] 1 Q.B. 421; 55 Cr.App.R. 466.

Criminal Justice and Public Order Act 1994, s.35

Effect of accused's silence at trial

8–126   **35.**—(1) At the trial of any person for an offence, subsections (2) and (3) below apply unless—

(a) the accused's guilt is not in issue; or

(b) it appears to the court that the physical or mental condition of the accused makes it undesirable for him to give evidence;

but subsection (2) below does not apply if, at the conclusion of the evidence for the prosecution, his legal representative informs the court that the accused will give evidence or, where he is unrepresented, the court ascertains from him that he will give evidence.

(2) Where this subsection applies, the court shall, at the conclusion of the evidence for the prosecution, satisfy itself (in the case of proceedings on indictment, in the presence of the jury) that the accused is aware that the stage has been reached at which evidence can be given for the defence and that he can, if he wishes, give evidence and that, if he chooses not to give evidence, or having been sworn, without good cause refuses to answer any question, it will be permissible for the court or jury to draw such inferences as appear proper from his failure to give evidence or his refusal, without good cause, to answer any question.

(3) Where this subsection applies, the court or jury, in determining whether the accused is guilty of the offence charged, may draw such inferences as appear proper from the failure of the accused to give evidence or his refusal, without good cause, to answer any question.

(4) This section does not render the accused compellable to give evidence on his own behalf, and he shall accordingly not be guilty of contempt of court by reason of a failure to do so.

(5) For the purposes of this section a person who, having been sworn, refuses to answer any question shall be taken to do so without good cause unless—

(a) he is entitled to refuse to answer the question by virtue of any enactment, whenever passed or made, or on the ground of privilege; or

(b) the court in the exercise of its general discretion excuses him from answering it.

[...]

(7) This section applies—

(a) in relation to proceedings on indictment for an offence, only if the person charged with the offence is arraigned on or after the commencement of this section;

(b) in relation to proceedings in a magistrates' court, only if the time when the court begins to receive evidence in the proceedings falls after the commencement of this section.

8–127   The duty to warn the defendant about adverse inferences arises where the defendant is present. The *Practice Direction (Criminal Proceedings: Consolidation)*, para. IV.44, although applying to Crown Courts only, is generally used by magistrates' courts.

Where the defendant is represented, the representative should inform the court as to whether the defendant intends to give evidence. If the defendant intends to give evidence the case should proceed in the normal way. If the representative states that his client does not wish to give evidence, he should be asked whether he has advised his client of the provisions of the section. If he has, then the case should proceed.

Where the defendant is unrepresented the court has a duty under section 35(2) of the Act to "satisfy itself" that the defendant is aware of the provisions. The legal adviser will advise the unrepresented defendant in the terms of the practice direction.

Police and Criminal Evidence Act 1984, s.79

Time for taking accused's evidence

8–128   **79.** If at the trial of any person for an offence—

(a) the defence intends to call two or more witnesses to the facts of the case; and

(b) those witnesses include the accused,

the accused shall be called before the other witness or witnesses unless the court in its discretion otherwise directs.

Where there are co-defendants it is usual for the first charged or named on the court **8–129** list to give evidence first.

C. ROLE OF LEGAL REPRESENTATIVES

Barristers and solicitors are officers of the court and should not mislead it in any way. **8–130** They have a duty to draw the court's attention to the law and that includes guideline cases on sentencing: *Att.-Gen.'s Reference (No. 52 of 2003)* [2003] EWCA Crim 3731. The court, on the other hand, must not ask advocates questions which might compromise them in any way, *e.g.* a court should ask an advocate whether he has seen a list of previous convictions relating to his client not whether he has agreed them. It is the duty of a defence advocate to put his client's case to the court.

The following statement of principles which governs the conduct of defence counsel was made by the Chairman of the Bar following the rejection of complaints about defence counsel's conduct in *McFadden* (1976) 62 Cr.App.R. 187:

> "It is the duty of counsel when defending an accused on a criminal charge to present to the court, fearlessly and without regard to his personal interests, the defence of that accused. It is not his function to determine the truth or falsity of that defence, nor should he permit his personal opinion of that defence to influence his conduct of it. No counsel may refuse to defence because of his opinion of the character of the accused nor of the crime charged. That is a cardinal rule of the Bar ... Counsel also has a duty to the court and to the public. This duty includes the clear presentation of the issues and the avoidance of waste of time, repetition and prolixity. In the conduct of every case counsel must be mindful of this public responsibility."

The remarks made in *Att.-Gen.'s Reference (No. 52 of 2003)*, *ante*, also apply. It is **8–131** the duty of defence counsel to put the defendant's case whether or not he intends to call evidence in support of it; the fact that a defendant does not call evidence should be recorded by counsel in writing, along with a brief summary of the reasons for that decision and if possible endorsed by the defendant: *R. v. Ebanks* [2006] U.K.P.C. 16; *The Times*, March 31, 2006. Where a court proceeds in the absence of the defendant his counsel should conduct the case as though he were present and must be allowed to cross-examine witnesses: *Kepple* [2007] EWCA Crim 1339.

D. UNREPRESENTED DEFENDANT

The *Criminal Procedure Rules* 2005, r.37.2(2) in Appendix G–224 provide for the **8–132** court's assistance of an unrepresented defendant.

Although the rules refer to the court it is usual for the legal adviser, in accordance **8–133** with the *Consolidated Criminal Practice Direction*, para. V.55, in Appendix F, to assist an unrepresented defendant. The legal adviser will explain the nature of the charge, the consequences of not giving evidence (*Criminal Justice and Public Order Act* 1994, s.35, *ante*), and will assist the defendant in turning the statements he makes about his defence into questions which can be put to witnesses. The legal adviser is also under a duty to ensure that an unrepresented defendant understands evidential issues and that he is not prejudiced by conduct which might put his or her bad character in evidence. If such a course is anticipated by the nature of the questions asked by the defendant in person, the prosecution should ask for an adjournment so that the legal adviser may explain to the defendant the risk of pursuing such a line of questioning: *R. v. Weston-Super-Mare Justices, ex p. Townsend* (1968) 132 J.P. 526.

E. REBUTTAL OF EVIDENCE

At the conclusion of the defence case the prosecution may call rebuttal evidence. This **8–134** evidence should be confined to a matter which arises unexpectedly in the course of the defence case: *Whelan* (1881) 14 Cox C.C. 595; *Price v. Humphries* [1958] 2 Q.B. 353. In *Owen* [1952] 2 Q.B. 362 the prosecution was allowed to call evidence in order to rebut a matter which it could not have foreseen. Whether a matter is reasonably foreseeable is a matter for the court to determine in the circumstances of the case: *Mendy* (1977) 64 Cr.App.R. 4. The court has a discretion to allow evidence which is not strictly of a rebutting nature. This could also extend to calling evidence to rebut assertions made by a co-defendant.

F. Viewing the Scene of the Crime

8–135   The court may be invited to view the scene of an alleged offence. If the court agrees to view the scene, then both prosecution and defence should be present or be given the opportunity to be present. The view should take place before the conclusion of the evidence so that both parties have the opportunity of commenting on it: *Parry v. Boyle* (1986) 83 Cr.App.R. 310. The defendant, even when he is legally represented, should be allowed to be present. Failure to allow the defendant to attend a view is contrary to the fairness of the proceedings: *R. v. Ely Justices, ex p. Burgess* (1993) 157 J.P. 484.

If a magistrate attends the scene of an alleged offence unofficially during an adjournment it does not necessarily mean that an irregularity has occurred. If the parties allow the trial to continue with the knowledge that an unofficial view has occurred and no prejudice is alleged, then the conviction is unlikely to be quashed on that basis: *Telfer and Telfer v. DPP* (1996) 160 J.P. 512.

G. Closing Speech

8–136   The defence will address the court on both facts and law. The prosecution will have a right to reply to a legal argument. In those circumstances the defence will have a further opportunity to argue its case. It is general practice for the legal adviser to advise magistrates in open court so that the legal representatives know the exact basis of the advice. Where a legal adviser is called out to the retiring room to assist magistrates in the compilation of reasons the legal adviser should not say or do anything in relation to verdict until it is announced: *R. (Murchison) v. Southend Magistrates' Court* [2006] EWHC 569; (2006) 170 J.P. 230; *The Times*, January 24, 2006.

VIII. THE DECISION

8–137   Under section 9(2) of the *Magistrates' Courts Act* 1980, *ante*, the court has a statutory duty either to convict or acquit the defendant. A magistrates' court has no power to return a verdict of not guilty as charged in the information but guilty of a lesser offence: *Lawrence v. Ridsdale* [1968] 2 Q.B. 93. There are two statutory exceptions:

Road Traffic Offenders Act 1988, s.24(1)–(3)

Alternative verdicts: general

8–138   **24.**—(1) Where—

(a) a person charged with an offence under a provision of the *Road Traffic Act* 1988 specified in the first column of the Table below (where the general nature of the offences is also indicated) is found not guilty of that offence, but

(b) the allegations in the indictment or information (or in Scotland complaint) amount to or include an allegation of an offence under one or more of the provisions specified in the corresponding entry in the second column,

he may be convicted of that offence or of one or more of those offences.

(2) Where the offence with which a person is charged is an offence under section 3A of the *Road Traffic Act* 1988, subsection (1) above shall not authorise his conviction of any offence of attempting to drive.

(3) Where a person is charged with having committed an offence under section 4(1) or 5(1)(a) of the *Road Traffic Act* 1988 by driving a vehicle, he may be convicted of having committed an offence under the provision in question by attempting to drive.

Offence charged	Alternative
Section 1 (causing death by dangerous driving)	Section 2 (dangerous driving) Section 3 (careless, and inconsiderate, driving)
Section 2 (dangerous driving)	Section 3 (careless, and inconsiderate, driving)
Section 3A (causing death by careless driving when under influence of drink or drugs)	Section 3 (careless, and inconsiderate, driving)Section 4(1) (driving when unfit to drive through drink or drugs)Section 5(1)(a) (driving with excess alcohol in breath, blood or urine)Section 7(6) (failing to provide specimen)
Section 4(1) (driving or attempting to drive when unfit to drive through drink or drugs)	Section 4(2) (being in charge of a vehicle when unfit to drive through drink or drugs)
Section 5(1)(a) (driving or attempting to drive with excess alcohol in breath, blood or urine)	Section 5(1)(b) (being in charge of a vehicle with excess alcohol in breath, blood or urine)
Section 28 (dangerous cycling)	Section 29 (careless, and inconsiderate, cycling)

Theft Act 1968, s.12A(5)

Aggravated vehicle-taking

12A.—(5) If a person who is charged with an offence under this section is found not guilty of **8–139** that offence but it is proved that he committed a basic offence, he may be convicted of the basic offence.

Where an information charges an attempt but the evidence establishes the full of- **8–140** fence, the court may convict the defendant of the attempt: *Webley v. Buxton* [1977] Q.B. 481.

Magistrates are under a duty to reach a decision and a mandatory order will be granted against them if they do not: *R. v. Bridgend Justices, ex p. Randall* [1975] Crim.L.R. 287; *R. v. Bromley Justices, ex p. Haymills (Contractors) Ltd* [1984] Crim.L.R. 235. If the magistrates are unable to reach a decision on the issue of guilt then the prosecution has failed to prove its case and the proper decision is one of not guilty.

A bench of magistrates reaches its decisions by majority and that is the reason for securing an odd number of magistrates on the bench: *Barnsley v. Marsh* [1947] K.B. 672. There is no casting vote procedure. If magistrates are evenly numbered and equally divided, it will be necessary for the case to be adjourned for rehearing before a differently constituted court of three magistrates: *R. v. Redbridge Justices, ex p. Ram* [1992] Q.B. 384. Alternatively they may refuse to adjourn and may dismiss the information. The dismissal is a bar to a second information for the same offence: *Kinnis v. Graves* (1898) 67 L.J. Q.B. 583.

The court may use its local knowledge when deciding a question of fact, however, it should inform the prosecution and defence that it is going to do so, so that the parties may comment on the knowledge which the court claims to have: *Bowman v. DPP* [1991] R.T.R. 263; *Norbrook Laboratories (GB) Ltd v. Health & Safety Executive* [1998] E.H.L.R. 207. The fact that magistrates become aware of previous convictions after verdict has been decided but before it has been announced in court does not invalidate the decision : *R. (Murchison) v. Southend Magistrates' Court, ante*.

The court is not obliged to give detailed reasons for its decision: *R. v. Brent Justices, ex p. McGowan* (2002) 166 J.P. 29. It is unnecessary for reasons to be elaborate or in the form of a judgement reciting the charges, the evidence and the findings of fact. The essence of the exercise is to inform the defendant why he has been found guilty. This can be done in a few simple sentences: see *R. (H.) v. Thames Youth Court and the Crown Prosecution Service* [2002] EWHC 2046.

CHAPTER 9

WITNESSES

Part II

I. SECURING THE ATTENDANCE OF WITNESSES

Magistrates' Courts Act 1980, s.97

Summons to witness and warrant for his arrest

9-1   **97.**—[(1) Where a justice of the peace is satisfied that—

(a) any person in England or Wales is likely to be able to give material evidence, or produce any document or thing likely to be material evidence, at the summary trial of an information or hearing of a complaint by a magistrates' court, and

(b) it is in the interests of justice to issue a summons under this subsection to secure the attendance of that person to give evidence or produce the document or thing,

the justice shall issue a summons directed to that person requiring him to attend before the court at the time and place appointed in the summons to give evidence or to produce the document or thing.]

(2) If a justice of the peace is satisfied by evidence on oath of the matters mentioned in subsection (1) above, and also that it is probable that a summons under that subsection would not procure the attendance of the person in question, the justice may instead of issuing a summons issue a warrant to arrest that person and bring him before such a court as aforesaid at a time and place specified in the warrant; but a warrant shall not be issued under this subsection where the attendance is required for the hearing of a complaint.

(2A) A summons may also be issued under subsection (1) above if the justice is satisfied that the person in question is outside the British Islands but no warrant shall be issued under subsection (2) above unless the justice is satisfied by evidence on oath that the person in question is in England or Wales.

(2B) A justice may refuse to issue a summons under subsection (1) above in relation to the summary trial of an information if he is not satisfied that an application for the summons was made by a party to the case as soon as reasonably practicable after the accused pleaded not guilty.

(2C) In relation to the summary trial of an information, subsection (2) above shall have effect as if the reference to the matters mentioned in subsection (1) above included a reference to the matter mentioned in subsection (2B) above.

(3) On the failure of any person to attend before a magistrates' court in answer to a summons under this section, if—

(a) the court is satisfied by evidence on oath that he is likely to be able to give material evidence or produce any document or thing likely to be material evidence in the proceedings; and

(b) it is proved on oath, or in such other manner as may be prescribed, that he has been duly served with the summons, and that a reasonable sum has been paid or tendered to him for costs and expenses; and

(c) it appears to the court that there is no just excuse for the failure,

the court may issue a warrant to arrest him and bring him before the court at a time and place specified in the warrant.

(4) If any person attending or brought before a magistrates' court refuses without just excuse to be sworn or give evidence, or to produce any document or thing, the court may commit him to custody until the expiration of such period not exceeding one month as may be specified in the warrant or until he sooner gives evidence or produces the document or thing or impose on him a fine not exceeding £2,500 or both.

(5) A fine imposed under subsection (4) above shall be deemed, for the purposes of any enactment, to be a sum adjudged to be paid by a conviction.

[This section is printed as amended by the *Serious Organised Crime and Police Act* 2005, s.169(2).]

9-2   The court may issue a summons or a warrant to secure the attendance of a witness. The test for issuing a summons has been amended by the *Serious Organised Crime and Police Act* 2005. The court no longer has to be satisfied that a witness will not voluntarily attend court or produce a document or something else which is likely to be material evidence. The court may issue a summons if it is in the interests of justice and the court is satisfied with regard to the material evidence criteria. It is important that if the court is to serve the summons "conduct money", *i.e.* sufficient money to enable the witness to attend court is deposited with the court.

The *Criminal Procedure Rules* 2005, r.28.2 as amended by the *Criminal Procedure* **9–3** *(Amendment) Rules* 2007 in Appendix G–161 provide for a hearing to be in private unless the court otherwise directs. The applicant may make an application orally unless the court directs that it be in writing or it is an application usually known as third party disclosure, *i.e.* where the witness is asked to produce a document or thing (other than a banker's book) or where he is asked to give evidence about a confidential matter. The applicant must identify the witness; explain what evidence the proposed witness can give or produce, why the evidence is likely to be material and why it would be in the interests of justice to issue the summons. Where an application must be made in writing it must be in the proper form. Documents sought must be identified with sufficient certainty so as to leave no doubt in the mind of the person to whom the summons is addressed as to what to bring to court: *Tajik Aluminium Plant v. (1) Hydro Aluminium AS; (2) Abdukadir Ganievich Ermatov; (3) Alexander Shushko; (4) Avaz Nazarov; (5) Ashton Investments Ltd* [2005] EWCA Civ 1218.

The application must be served on the proposed witness, unless the court otherwise directs and, if the court directs, on the person to whom the proposed evidence relates and any other person the court directs. Service can be effected abroad although there is no sanction for non-compliance: *Crime (International Co-operation) Act* 2003, s.3. The court will not issue a summons where the application is required to be in writing unless anyone served has had fourteen days in which to make representation on the application or whether there should be a hearing before the summons is issued. The court must also be satisfied that it has been able to take adequate account of the duties and rights including confidentiality of the proposed witness and any other person to whom the evidence relates. Where a person objects to the production of a document on the ground that it is not likely to be material evidence or, if it were, the right of confidentiality would outweigh the issue of a summons, the court may require the document to be made available for the court to assess, with the help of the proposed witness or his representative or the person or his representative to whom the document relates.

It must be remembered that the provisions for disclosure are not directed to creating duties for third parties to follow; the duties are created in respect of material that the prosecution or police have and which the prosecution has inspected: *DPP v. Wood* [2006] EWHC 32. The Attorney General's Guidelines on Disclosure at Appendix C–17 direct the prosecution to take appropriate steps to obtain material in the hands of third parties which might reasonably be considered capable of undermining the prosecution case or assisting the defence. It is for the prosecution to determine what is deemed to be appropriate in the circumstances of each case; in an extreme case it might be so unfair to proceed in the absence of the third party material that the case should not proceed: *Alibhai* [2004] EWCA Crim 681. Where material comes into the hands of the prosecution then the third party must be consulted before disclosure takes place.

If a party refuses to supply the information the prosecution will consider applying for a witness summons. The applicant must then show that the likely evidence is material to the case: *R. v. Peterborough Magistrates' Court, ex p. Willis* (1987) 151 J.P. 785. It will be material if it is relevant to the case: *R. v. Reading J.J., ex. p. Berkshire County Council* [1996] 1 Cr.App.R.239, DC. In this case a summons was held to be improper where it had been issued to test whether files held by the Director of Social Services in respect of a fifteen year old boy who was a victim of an alleged assault by police officers might offer any relevant or important information. It is improper to use the witness summons procedure to obtain discovery or to require production of documents at a hearing when they are not likely to be material evidence but their presence in court is desired for cross-examination purposes (in this case many documents relating to the Lion Intoximeter device): *R v. Skegness Magistrates' Court ex p. Cardy* [1985] R.T.R. 49. The applicant must also show that the evidence is admissible. Where there is a suggestion that information about bad character, for example, is available then, it is submitted, the applicant must show through which gateway it will be adduced. If the material is not *prima facie* admissible the summons is likely to be set aside: *R. v. Cheltenham J.J., ex.p. Secretary of State for Trade* [1977] 1 W.L.R. 95, DC. That case involved transcripts and material obtained during an investigation which were to be used for the purposes of cross-examination only to contradict what witnesses might say. It was said that even if the documents were material, they should not be produced because the public interest in maintaining sources of information in respect of an inquiry of the kind carried out under section 165 of the *Companies Act* 1948 would outweigh the private disadvantage of non-disclosure. In *R. v. Derby Magistrates' Court, ex p. B.* [1996] A.C. 487 it was said that documents had to be admissible *per se* and a summons was not appropriate to obtain discovery of documents which might, or might not be, upon examination, admissible. Production of documents should not be ordered where they are likely merely to afford or assist a relevant line of inquiry or challenge: *H. (L.), Re* [1997] 1 Cr.App.R. 176. A court should not issue a witness summons to produce evidence where evidence had then to be given by expert witnesses as to its admissibility: *R. (Cunliffe) v. West London Magistrates' Court* [2006] EWHC 2081. In that case it was held that the summons for complete unedited settings of a breath test machine, engineers' reports, calibration/service sheets and the engineer's standing operating procedures had been wrongly issued.

A court must also be satisfied that the issue of a summons is in the public interest and this is where issues of confidentiality and Article 8 ECHR arise with respect to personal records, such as school, social service, income tax or medical records. It has been accepted that medical records are private and confidential: *Campbell v. MGN Ltd* [2004] 2 A.C. 457 at para. 145 and that includes psychiatric medical notes: *Ashworth Hospital Authority v. MGN* [2002] UKHL 29 at para. 63. In *R. (Axon) v. Secretary of State for Health* [2006] 2 W.L.R. 1130 it was said that the duty of confidence owed by a medical professional to a competent young person is a high one which should not be overridden except for a very powerful reason. In order to order disclosure, therefore, a court must be satisfied that it is proportionate and necessary to prevent crime or protect the rights and freedom of others, *i.e.* ensuring a fair trial. In *Re M., (a minor) (Disclosure of Material)* [1990] 2 F.L.R. 36 the court was of the opinion that social work reports prepared in circumstances concerning the welfare of children were subject to a special form of immunity and disclosure could only be justified in the circumstances of a particular case. Documents relating to family proceedings and filed with the court cannot be disclosed to anyone without the leave of the court: *Family Proceedings Rules* 1991, r.4.23.

A summons should not be refused where the preconditions are satisfied and where it is crucial to the applicant's case: *R. v. Bradford JJ. ex p. Wilkinson* [1990] 1 W.L.R. 692.

A court must carry out a balancing exercise, having regard to the weight of the public interest in non-disclosure and the importance of the documents to the defence. If the material might prove a person's innocence or avoid a miscarriage of justice, the balance should come down resoundingly in favour of disclosure: *Keane* [1994] 1 W.L.R. 746. A court must ensure that a defendant is not disadvantaged by a refusal to allow him to gather necessary evidence: *D.* [2006] EWCA Crim 2600. In that case the defendant had been charged with grievous bodily harm and sought to adduce evidence of the victim's bad character, including behaviour at school and college, a previous altercation between him and the defendant and an attack on a co-defendant. Evidence of the assault was allowed but not the disclosure of school records of pupils who had made complaints against the victim. On appeal it was held that, in view of the public interest in preserving the confidentiality of school records and Article 8 rights of those involved, the names of those involved, in so far as they were children, should not be disclosed but it was also held that the defendant had been disadvantaged as the evidence was relevant to the defendant's state of mind at the time and a simple admission by the prosecution that the defendant knew of the victim's reputation for bullying would have sufficed. It is the duty of the prosecution to co-operate in ensuring that a defendant has a fair trial.

It was said in *Rothon v. DPP* [2006] All E.R. (D) 367 that where evidence in an intoximeter case was accepted from an expert that the device was working correctly the magistrates should have ordered disclosure of the records relating to that device so that the defendant could cross-examine properly.

A summons may be withdrawn on application by the original applicant, the witness if he was not aware of the application and cannot give or produce material evidence or the person to whom the evidence relates if he was unaware of the application and the evidence is not likely to be material or even if it is, his rights or those of the witness outweigh the reasons for the issue of the summons: *Criminal Procedure Rules* 2005, r.28.7.

See *Criminal Procedure Rules* 2005, r.28.7 in Appendix G–166.   **9–4**

II. SWEARING OF A WITNESS

A. GENERAL

Unless a particular statute allows unsworn evidence, all evidence given before a mag-   **9–5** istrates' court will be given on oath: *Magistrates' Courts Act* 1980, s.98. A child's evidence will be given unsworn but witnesses aged 14 years or over must give evidence on oath: *Sharman* [1998] 1 Cr.App.R. 406; *Youth Justice and Criminal Evidence Act* 1999, s.55(2)(a).

B. FORM OF OATH

Oaths Act 1978, s.1

Manner of administration of oaths

1.—(1) Any oath may be administered and taken in England, Wales or Northern Ireland in   **9–6** the following form and manner—

The person taking the oath shall hold the New Testament, or, in the case of a Jew, the Old Testament, in his uplifted hand, and shall say or repeat after the officer administering the oath the words "I swear by Almighty God that ...", followed by the words of the oath prescribed by law.

(2) The officer shall (unless the person about to take the oath voluntarily objects thereto, or is physically incapable of so taking the oath) administer the oath in the form and manner aforesaid without question.

(3) In the case of a person who is neither a Christian nor a Jew, the oath shall be administered in any lawful manner.

(4) In this section "officer" means any person duly authorised to administer oaths.

Magistrates' courts have facilities to administer the oath in accordance with most   **9–7** religions and will ask a witness outside of court how he wishes to be sworn so that the oath taking in court proceeds in a proper manner.

The purpose of taking an oath is that it should be binding on a witness's conscience. The question whether a witness who is neither a Christian nor a Jew has been lawfully sworn depends on whether the oath appears to the court to be binding on the conscience of the witness and whether the witness himself considers his conscience bound. If a Muslim takes the oath using the New Testament he could still be lawfully sworn. The question of whether an oath is lawfully administered does not depend on what may be the considerable intricacies of the particular religion adhered to by the witness: *Kemble* [1990] 1 W.L.R. 1111.

It is not usual to ask whether someone objects to taking the oath. A witness is asked to choose between the oath and affirmation.

C. AFFIRMATION

Oaths Act 1978, ss.5–6

Making of solemn affirmations

5.—(1) Any person who objects to being sworn shall be permitted to make his solemn affir-   **9–8** mation instead of taking an oath.

(2) Subsection (1) above shall apply in relation to a person to whom it is not reasonably practicable without inconvenience or delay to administer an oath in the manner appropriate to his religious belief as it applies in relation to a person objecting to be sworn.

(3) A person who may be permitted under subsection (2) above to make his solemn affirmation may also be required to do so.

(4) A solemn affirmation shall be of the same force and effect as an oath.

Form of affirmation

9–9   **6.**—(1) Subject to subsection (2) below, every affirmation shall be as follows—

"I ... do solemnly, sincerely and truly declare and affirm,"

and then proceed with the words of the oath prescribed by law, omitting any words of imprecation or calling to witness.

(2) Every affirmation in writing shall commence—

"I ... do solemnly and sincerely affirm,"

and the form in lieu of jurat shall be "Affirmed at ... this ... day of ... 19..., Before me."

D. UNSWORN TESTIMONY

Youth Justice and Criminal Evidence Act 1999, ss.55–57

Determining whether witness to be sworn

9–10   **55.**—(1) Any question whether a witness in criminal proceedings may be sworn for the purpose of giving evidence on oath, whether raised—

(a) by a party to the proceedings, or

(b) by the court of its own motion,

shall be determined by the court in accordance with this section.

(2) The witness may not be sworn for that purpose unless—

(a) he has attained the age of 14, and

(b) he has a sufficient appreciation of the solemnity of the occasion and of the particular responsibility to tell the truth which is involved in taking an oath.

(3) The witness shall, if he is able to give intelligible testimony, be presumed to have a sufficient appreciation of those matters if no evidence tending to show the contrary is adduced (by any party).

(4) If any such evidence is adduced, it is for the party seeking to have the witness sworn to satisfy the court that, on a balance of probabilities, the witness has attained the age of 14 and has a sufficient appreciation of the matters mentioned in subsection (2)(b).

(5) Any proceedings held for the determination of the question mentioned in subsection (1) shall take place in the absence of the jury (if there is one).

(6) Expert evidence may be received on the question.

(7) Any questioning of the witness (where the court considers that necessary) shall be conducted by the court in the presence of the parties.

(8) For the purposes of this section a person is able to give intelligible testimony if he is able to—

(a) understand questions put to him as a witness, and

(b) give answers to them which can be understood.

Reception of unsworn evidence

9–11   **56.**—(1) Subsections (2) and (3) apply to a person (of any age) who—

(a) is competent to give evidence in criminal proceedings, but

(b) (by virtue of section 55(2)) is not permitted to be sworn for the purpose of giving evidence on oath in such proceedings.

(2) The evidence in criminal proceedings of a person to whom this subsection applies shall be given unsworn.

(3) A deposition of unsworn evidence given by a person to whom this subsection applies may be taken for the purposes of criminal proceedings as if that evidence had been given on oath.

(4) A court in criminal proceedings shall accordingly receive in evidence any evidence given unsworn in pursuance of subsection (2) or (3).

(5) Where a person ("the witness") who is competent to give evidence in criminal proceedings gives evidence in such proceedings unsworn, no conviction, verdict or finding in those proceedings shall be taken to be unsafe for the purposes of any of sections 2(1), 13(1) and 16(1) of the *Criminal Appeal Act* 1968 (grounds for allowing appeals) by reason only that it appears to the Court of Appeal that the witness was a person falling within section 55(2) (and should accordingly have given his evidence on oath).

Penalty for giving false unsworn evidence

9–12 **57.**—(1) This section applies where a person gives unsworn evidence in criminal proceedings in pursuance of section 56(2) or (3).

(2) If such a person wilfully gives false evidence in such circumstances that, had the evidence been given on oath, he would have been guilty of perjury, he shall be guilty of an offence and liable on summary conviction to—

   (a) imprisonment for a term not exceeding 6 months, or
   (b) a fine not exceeding £1,000,

or both.

(3) In relation to a person under the age of 14, subsection (2) shall have effect as if for the words following "on summary conviction" there were substituted "to a fine not exceeding £250".

9–13 A witness may not take the oath unless he is fourteen years old. He must also appreciate the solemnity of the occasion and the responsibility to tell the truth. This may be ascertained from the fact that he is able to give an intelligent explanation of what has happened. It is for the party calling the witness to satisfy the court of those matters on a balance of probabilities and, in certain circumstances, expert evidence may be received. If it is found that he is incapable of giving sworn evidence then his evidence will be taken unsworn.

III. COMPETENCE AND COMPELLABILITY

A. GENERAL

9–14 A witness is competent if he can lawfully give evidence and compellable if he can be lawfully required to give evidence.

Youth Justice and Criminal Evidence Act 1999, s.53

Competence of witnesses to give evidence

9–15 **53.**—(1) At every stage in criminal proceedings all persons are (whatever their age) competent to give evidence.

(2) Subsection (1) has effect subject to subsections (3) and (4).

(3) A person is not competent to give evidence in criminal proceedings if it appears to the court that he is not a person who is able to—

   (a) understand questions put to him as a witness, and
   (b) give answers to them which can be understood.

(4) A person charged in criminal proceedings is not competent to give evidence in the proceedings for the prosecution (whether he is the only person, or is one of two or more persons, charged in the proceedings).

(5) In subsection (4) the reference to a person charged in criminal proceedings does not include a person who is not, or is no longer, liable to be convicted of any offence in the proceedings (whether as a result of pleading guilty or for any other reason).

B. DETERMINING COMPETENCY

9–16 The general rule that all persons are competent to give evidence at every stage in criminal proceedings is subject to a test of competence contained in the *Youth Justice and Criminal Evidence Act* 1999, s.54.

Youth Justice and Criminal Evidence Act 1999, s.54

Determining competence of witnesses

9–17   **54.**—(1) Any question whether a witness in criminal proceedings is competent to give evidence in the proceedings, whether raised—

(a) by a party to the proceedings, or

(b) by the court of its own motion,

shall be determined by the court in accordance with this section.

(2) It is for the party calling the witness to satisfy the court that, on a balance of probabilities, the witness is competent to give evidence in the proceedings.

(3) In determining the question mentioned in subsection (1) the court shall treat the witness as having the benefit of any directions under section 19 which the court has given, or proposes to give, in relation to the witness.

(5) Expert evidence may be received on the question.

(6) Any questioning of the witness (where the court considers that necessary) shall be conducted by the court in the presence of the parties.

9–18   Any objection to a witness's competency must be made before he is sworn or gives evidence: *Hampshire* [1996] Q.B.1; [1995] 2 Cr.App.R. 319, CA. In *Yacoob* (1981) 72 Cr.App.R. 313, CA, the court said that the beginning of the trial was the appropriate time for determining competence and compellability of prosecution witnesses. If, prior to the hearing, an objection has been raised with the prosecution then the evidence to be given by that witness should not be referred to in the opening speech.

C. CHILDREN

9–19   All persons of whatever age are competent to give evidence: section 53(1), *ante*. The evidence of a child will be received unless it appears to the court that the child is incapable of giving intelligible testimony; that is evidence which is capable of being understood: *Hampshire* [1996] Q.B. 1. The procedure of determining intelligible testimony is the same for children as for adults: section 55. The issue of competence should be dealt with as early as possible, not as an act of "ratification" after the evidence has been given. It is not an issue to be resolved in response to an adversarial examination and cross-examination but is a matter for the court to decide having heard the child in person. The legal adviser will generally talk to the child about why he is there and whether he understands what telling the truth means. In *G. v. DPP* [1998] Q.B. 919 it was held that the test is within the competence of the court and there is no need for expert evidence unless there are special circumstances, *e.g.* the child is mentally handicapped. The fact that a child under ten years of age cannot be prosecuted for the offence of wilfully giving false evidence contrary to the *Youth Justice and Criminal Evidence Act* 1999, s.57 is not a reason for excluding the unsworn evidence of a competent child: *N.* (1992) 95 Cr.App.R. 256. It is essential that a very young child is interviewed as soon as possible after the event complained of and that the trial takes place very soon thereafter: *P.* [2006] EWCA Crim 3. The evidence of a child witness may be contaminated where the child says that his mother told him what to say: *C.* [2006] 1 W.L.R. 2994; [2006] 3 All E.R. 689.

The *Consolidated Criminal Practice Direction*, para. I.5, in Appendix F–7 applies to wards of court.

D. MENTALLY DISORDERED PERSONS

9–20   A witness who is prevented from giving rational testimony by reason of mental illness or drunkenness is not competent. Where a witness appears to be unable to give intelligible testimony by reason of mental illness or intoxication, the court should ascertain whether the witness is capable of understanding the questions put to him or to give answers which can be understood pursuant to the provisions of sections 54–57 of the *Youth Justice and Criminal Evidence Act* 1999. This may be done by calling expert evidence, see *Hill* (1851) 2 Den. 254; *Dunning* [1965] Crim.L.R. 372. The worth of the evidence will ultimately be a matter for the court. In cases of mental illness this will depend on degree. In *Hill, ante,* the circumstances were such that the proper course was to reject the evidence.

E. THE ACCUSED

Criminal Evidence Act 1898, s.1

Competency of witnesses in criminal cases

1.—(1) A person charged in criminal proceedings shall not be called as a witness in the **9–21** proceedings except upon his own application.

(2) Subject to section 101 of the *Criminal Justice Act* 2003 (admissibility of evidence of defendant's bad character), a person charged in criminal proceedings who is called as a witness in the proceedings may be asked any question in cross-examination notwithstanding that it would tend to criminate him as to any offence with which he is charged in the proceedings.

(3) [...]

(4) Every person charged in criminal proceedings who is called as a witness in the proceedings shall, unless otherwise ordered by the court, give his evidence from the witness box or other place from which the other witnesses give their evidence.

[This section is printed as amended by *Criminal Justice Act* 2003, Sched. 37.]

The defendant is not a compellable witness for the prosecution: *Rhodes* [1899] 1 **9–22** Q.B. 77 and a defendant cannot be compelled to give evidence against a co-defendant: *Payne* L.R. 1 C.C.R. 349; *Grant,* 30 Cr.App.R. 99; *Sharrock* (1948) 32 Cr.App.R. 124.

A defendant who has pleaded guilty is not a "person charged" within the meaning of section 1 of the 1898 Act because he is not concerned in any issue before the judge of fact. A defendant who has pleaded guilty is therefore competent and compellable to give evidence for a co-defendant: *Boal* [1965] 1 Q.B. 402. A plea of guilty by a co-defendant is not evidence against the defendant: *Smith* (1984) 148 J.P. 215.

A co-defendant who has been acquitted is not a "person charged" within the *Criminal Evidence Act* 1898, s.1, and is therefore compellable as a witness: *Conti* (1974) 58 Cr.App.R. 387, CA. Those concerned with the charge should not be called by the prosecution: *Pipe* (1967) 51 Cr.App.R. 17. The prosecution may, however, call an accomplice who is to be charged and tried separately: *Palmer* (1994) 99 Cr.App.R. 83.

The defendant is a competent witness for himself. He is not, however, a compellable witness for the defence: *Criminal Evidence Act* 1898, s.1(1). An acquitted person called by the defendant may be cross-examined by a co-defendant.

A defendant who gives evidence for a co-defendant is liable to be cross-examined on the issue of his own guilt: *Rowland* [1910] 1 K.B. 458. If a defendant refuses to answer questions incriminating other persons, the court is not bound to receive his or her evidence: *Minihane* 16 Cr.App.R. 38.

F. THE DEFENDANT'S SPOUSE

Police and Criminal Evidence Act 1984, s.80

Competence and compellability of the defendant's spouse

80.—(2) In any proceedings the wife or husband of a person charged in the proceedings **9–23** shall, subject to subsection (4) below, be compellable to give evidence on behalf of that person.

(2A) In any proceedings the wife or husband of a person charged in the proceedings shall, subject to subsection (4) below, be compellable—

    (a) to give evidence on behalf of any other person charged in the proceedings but only in respect of any specified offence with which that other person is charged; or

    (b) to give evidence for the prosecution but only in respect of any specified offence with which any person is charged in the proceedings.

(3) In relation to the wife or husband of a person charged in any proceedings, an offence is a specified offence for the purposes of subsection (2A) above if—

Part II

(a) it involves an assault on, or injury or a threat of injury to, the wife or husband or a person who was at the material time under the age of 16;

(b) it is a sexual offence alleged to have been committed in respect of a person who was at the material time under that age; or

(c) it consists of attempting or conspiring to commit, or of aiding, abetting, counselling, procuring or inciting the commission of, an offence falling within paragraph (a) or (b) above.

(4) No person who is charged in any proceedings shall be compellable by virtue of subsection (2) or (2A) above to give evidence in the proceedings.

(4A) References in this section to a person charged in any proceedings do not include a person who is not, or is no longer, liable to be convicted of any offence in the proceedings (whether as a result of pleading guilty or for any other reason).

(5) In any proceedings a person who has been but is no longer married to the accused shall be compellable to give evidence as if that person and the accused had never been married.

(6) Where in any proceedings the age of any person at any time is material for the purposes of subsection (3) above, his age at the material time shall for the purposes of that provision be deemed to be or to have been that which appears to the court to be or to have been his age at that time.

(7) In subsection (3)(b) above "sexual-offence" means an offence under the *Sexual Offences Act* 1956, the *Indecency with Children Act* 1960, the *Sexual Offences Act* 1967, section 54 of the *Criminal Law Act* 1977 or the *Protection of Children Act* 1978.

(8) [...]

(9) Section 1(d) of the *Criminal Evidence Act* 1898 (communications between husband and wife) and section 43(1) of the *Matrimonial Causes Act* 1965 (evidence as to marital intercourse) shall cease to have effect.

9–24   A spouse is competent to give evidence against a defendant but is only compellable in the terms of the statute.

Section 80 does not apply to the defendant's unmarried partner: *Pearce* [2002] 1 Cr.App.R. 39, CA. Although the compellability of a family member to give evidence against another might conflict with the right to family life under Article 8 of the European Convention on Human Rights the interference may be justified under Article 8(2) as necessary in a democratic society for the prevention of crime.

The position of a wife of a second polygamous marriage is no different from that of a woman who has not gone through a marriage ceremony at all or who has gone through a ceremony which was invalid: *Yacoob* (1981) 72 Cr.App.R. 313, CA; *Khan* (1987) 84 Cr.App.R. 44, CA.

The prosecution has a duty to disclose to the defence that a spouse has informed the prosecutor outside the court that he does not wish to give evidence against his spouse and that the statement given to the police is inaccurate: *R. v. Birmingham Justices, ex p. Shields, The Times*, August 3, 1994, CA. The prosecution must also inform the court so that the spouse can be warned that he need not give evidence. Once a spouse has started to give evidence he must complete it and may be treated as a hostile witness if he shows an unwillingness to continue: *Pitt* [1983] Q.B. 25.

The failure of a spouse to give evidence should not be subject to comment by the prosecution: section 80A of the *Police and Criminal Evidence Act* 1984.

G. OTHER WITNESSES

9–25   The sovereign is a competent but not compellable witness. Foreign heads of state, diplomatic and consular staff, members of the family of a diplomatic agent, members of the administrative and technical staff of a diplomatic mission and members of their families, persons connected with consular posts and members of staff of international organisations enjoy total or partial immunity from compellability to give evidence.

See *Diplomatic Privileges Act* 1964, s.1(1), Sched. 1, Arts 1, 30, 37, 38(2) and 39; *State Immunity Act* 1978, s.14; and the *International Organisations Act* 1968, s.5.

High Court judges and those of inferior courts are not compellable witnesses: *War-*

ren v. Warren [1997] 1 F.C.R. 237, CA. Magistrates and their legal advisers, however, are compellable: *Re McC (a minor)* [1985] A.C. 528.

IV. THE PROTECTION OF WITNESSES

A. GENERAL

Witnesses give their evidence in open court and with their identity disclosed. In **9–26** special circumstances a witness may be allowed to give evidence anonymously. The decision as to whether a witness may give evidence without being identified is a matter for the court's discretion: *Taylor* [1995] Crim.L.R. 253. The factors for the court to consider when exercising that discretion are:

1. Whether there are real grounds for fear of the consequences if evidence were given and the identity of the witness were revealed;
2. The evidence must be sufficiently relevant and important to make it unfair for the prosecution to proceed without that evidence;
3. The prosecution must satisfy the court that the creditworthiness of the witness has been fully investigated;
4. There must be no undue prejudice to the defendant; and
5. The court must balance the need for protection of the witness against the unfairness or the appearance of unfairness to the defendant.

In order to come to a decision the court ought to be told that a witness will refuse to give evidence unless the court exercises its discretion in favour of a particular measure: *R. (DPP) v. West London Youth Court* [2005] EWHC 2834. In that case the prosecution withdrew the case where an undercover officer was not allowed to give evidence behind a screen.

In *R. v. Watford Magistrates' Court, ex p. Lenman* [1993] Crim.L.R. 388 the **9–27** Divisional Court upheld the magistrates' decision to allow witnesses to give evidence anonymously because they were afraid of reprisals. If a court is satisfied that there is a real risk to the administration of justice because witnesses have reasonable grounds to fear for their safety if their identity is disclosed, it is entirely within its powers to take reasonable steps to protect and reassure the witnesses so that they will not be deterred from coming forward. The purpose is to secure justice.

The *Youth Justice and Criminal Evidence Act* 1999 has subsequently been enacted to provide for special measures to be taken for the protection of and assistance for vulnerable witnesses. These include screening witnesses from the defendant, giving evidence by live link, video-recorded evidence in chief, video-recorded examination and cross-examination, examination of a witness through an intermediary, protection from cross-examination by the defendant in person and restrictions on the type of questions asked.

In determining whether to order special measures and in considering the type of measure the court will balance the right of a defendant to have a normal hearing where the witness gives evidence openly in his presence and the need to protect the witness "in the interests, not only of the child witness but also of justice, to ensure that the witness will be able to give evidence and give evidence unaffected by the stress of appearing in court itself": *R. (DPP) v. Redbridge Youth Court; R. (L.) v. Bicester Youth Court* [2001] EWHC Admin 209. When used the court will direct itself that the special measures are there to assist witnesses in giving evidence and are in no way prejudicial to the defendant.

Where a defendant has learning difficulties the court may assist him in giving his evidence through either an interpreter, reading a defence statement and allowing leading questions: *R. v. H. (Special Measures)*, *The Times*, April 15, 2003.

B. SPECIAL MEASURES

Youth Justice and Criminal Evidence Act 1999, s.16

Witnesses eligible for assistance on grounds of age or incapacity

9–28   **16.**—(1) For the purposes of this Chapter a witness in criminal proceedings (other than the accused) is eligible for assistance by virtue of this section—

   (a) if under the age of 17 at the time of the hearing; or

   (b) if the court considers that the quality of evidence given by the witness is likely to be diminished by reason of any circumstances falling within subsection (2).

(2) The circumstances falling within this subsection are—

   (a) that the witness—

      (i) suffers from mental disorder within the meaning of the *Mental Health Act* 1983, or

      (ii) otherwise has a significant impairment of intelligence and social functioning;

   (b) that the witness has a physical disability or is suffering from a physical disorder.

(3) In subsection (1)(a) "the time of the hearing", in relation to a witness, means the time when it falls to the court to make a determination for the purposes of section 19(2) in relation to the witness.

(4) In determining whether a witness falls within subsection (1)(b) the court must consider any views expressed by the witness.

(5) In this Chapter references to the quality of a witness's evidence are to its quality in terms of completeness, coherence and accuracy; and for this purpose "coherence" refers to a witness's ability in giving evidence to give answers which address the questions put to the witness and can be understood both individually and collectively.

9–29   There is a strong presumption in favour of the use of special measures. A witness under the age of seventeen at the time of the hearing is automatically considered to be vulnerable.

Youth Justice and Criminal Evidence Act 1999, s.17

Witnesses eligible for assistance on grounds of fear or distress about testifying

9–30   **17.**—(1) For the purposes of this Chapter a witness in criminal proceedings (other than the accused) is eligible for assistance by virtue of this subsection if the court is satisfied that the quality of evidence given by the witness is likely to be diminished by reason of fear or distress on the part of the witness in connection with testifying in the proceedings.

(2) In determining whether a witness falls within subsection (1) the court must take into account, in particular—

   (a) the nature and alleged circumstances of the offence to which the proceedings relate;

   (b) the age of the witness;

   (c) such of the following matters as appear to the court to be relevant, namely—

      (i)   the social and cultural background and ethnic origins of the witness,

      (ii) the domestic and employment circumstances of the witness, and

      (iii) any religious beliefs or political opinions of the witness;

   (d) any behaviour towards the witness on the part of—

      (i)   the accused,

      (ii) members of the family or associates of the accused, or

      (iii) any other person who is likely to be an accused or a witness in the proceedings.

(3) In determining that question the court must in addition consider any views expressed by the witness.

(4) Where the complainant in respect of a sexual offence is a witness in proceedings relating to that offence (or to that offence and any other offences), the witness is eligible for assistance in relation to those proceedings by virtue of this subsection unless the witness has informed the court of the witness' wish not to be so eligible by virtue of this subsection.

9–31   Special measures directions may apply to certain witnesses but not to all witnesses in a case: *Brown* [2004] EWCA Crim 1620; [2004] Crim. L.R. 1034.

Youth Justice and Criminal Evidence Act 1999, s.18–21

Special measures available to eligible witnesses

18.—(1) For the purposes of this Chapter—

    (a) the provision which may be made by a special measures direction by virtue of each of sections 23 to 30 is a special measure available in relation to a witness eligible for assistance by virtue of section 16; and

    (b) the provision which may be made by such a direction by virtue of each of sections 23 to 28 is a special measure available in relation to a witness eligible for assistance by virtue of section 17;

but this subsection has effect subject to subsection (2).

(2) Where (apart from this subsection) a special measure would, in accordance with subsection (1)(a) or (b), be available in relation to a witness in any proceedings, it shall not be taken by a court to be available in relation to the witness unless—

    (a) the court has been notified by the Secretary of State that relevant arrangements may be made available in the area in which it appears to the court that the proceedings will take place, and

    (b) the notice has not been withdrawn.

(3) In subsection (2) "relevant arrangements" means arrangements for implementing the measure in question which cover the witness and the proceedings in question.

(4) The withdrawal of a notice under that subsection relating to a special measure shall not affect the availability of that measure in relation to a witness if a special measures direction providing for that measure to apply to the witness's evidence has been made by the court before the notice is withdrawn.

(5) The Secretary of State may by order make such amendments of this Chapter as he considers appropriate for altering the special measures which, in accordance with subsection (1)(a) or (b), are available in relation to a witness eligible for assistance by virtue of section 16 or (as the case may be) section 17, whether—

    (a) by modifying the provisions relating to any measure for the time being available in relation to such a witness,

    (b) by the addition—

        (i) (with or without modifications) of any measure which is for the time being available in relation to a witness eligible for assistance by virtue of the other of those sections, or

        (ii) of any new measure, or

    (c) by the removal of any measure.

Special measures direction relating to eligible witness

19.—(1) This section applies where in any criminal proceedings—

    (a) a party to the proceedings makes an application for the court to give a direction under this section in relation to a witness in the proceedings other than the accused, or

    (b) the court of its own motion raises the issue whether such a direction should be given.

(2) Where the court determines that the witness is eligible for assistance by virtue of section 16 or 17, the court must then—

    (a) determine whether any of the special measures available in relation to the witness (or any combination of them) would, in its opinion, be likely to improve the quality of evidence given by the witness; and

    (b) if so—

        (i) determine which of those measures (or combination of them) would, in its opinion, be likely to maximise so far as practicable the quality of such evidence; and

        (ii) give a direction under this section providing for the measure or measures so determined to apply to evidence given by the witness.

(3) In determining for the purposes of this Chapter whether any special measure or measures would or would not be likely to improve, or to maximise so far as practicable, the quality of evidence given by the witness, the court must consider all the circumstances of the case, including in particular—

    (a) any views expressed by the witness; and

9–32

9–33

(b) whether the measures or measures must tend to inhibit such evidence being effectively tested by a party to the proceedings.

(4) A special measures direction must specify particulars of the provision made by the direction in respect of each special measure which is to apply to the witness's evidence.

(5) In this Chapter "special measures direction" means a direction under this section.

(6) Nothing in this Chapter is to be regarded as affecting any power of a court to make an order or give leave of any description (in the exercise of its inherent jurisdiction or otherwise)—

(a) in relation to a witness who is not an eligible witness, or

(b) in relation to an eligible witness where (as, for example, in a case where a foreign language interpreter is to be provided) the order is made or the leave is given otherwise than by reason of the fact that the witness is an eligible witness.

Further provisions about directions: general

9–34   **20.**—(1) Subject to subsection (2) and section 21(8), a special measures direction has binding effect from the time it is made until the proceedings for the purposes of which it is made are either—

(a) determined (by acquittal, conviction or otherwise), or

(b) abandoned,

in relation to the accused or (if there is more than one) in relation to each of the accused.

(2) The court may discharge or vary (or further vary) a special measures direction if it appears to the court to be in the interests of justice to do so, and may do so either—

(a) on an application made by a party to the proceedings, if there has been a material change of circumstances since the relevant time, or

(b) of its own motion.

(3) In subsection (2) "the relevant time" means —

(a) the time when the direction was given, or

(b) if a previous application has been made under that subsection, the time when the application (or last application) was made.

(4) Nothing in section 24(2) and (3), 27(4) to (7) or 28(4) to (6) is to be regarded as affecting the power of the court to vary or discharge a special measures direction under subsection (2).

(5) The court must state in open court its reasons for—

(a) giving or varying,

(b) refusing an application for, or for the variation or discharge of, or

(c) discharging,

a special measures direction and, if it is a magistrates' court, must cause them to be entered in the register of its proceedings.

(6) Rules of court may make provision—

(a) for uncontested applications to be determined by the court without a hearing;

(b) for preventing the renewal of an unsuccessful application for a special measures direction except where there has been a material change of circumstances;

(c) for expert evidence to be given in connection with an application for, or for varying or discharging, such a direction;

(d) for the manner in which confidential or sensitive information is to be treated in connection with such an application and in particular as to its being disclosed to, or withheld from, a party to the proceedings.

Special provisions relating to child witnesses

9–35   **21.**—(1) For the purposes of this section—

(a) a witness in criminal proceedings is a "child witness" if he is an eligible witness by reason of section 16(1)(a) (whether or not he is an eligible witness by reason of any other provision of section 16 or 17);

(b) a child witness is "in need of special protection" if the offence (or any of the offences) to which the proceedings relate is—

(i) an offence falling within section 35(3)(a) (sexual offences etc.), or

(ii) an offence falling within section 35(3)(b), (c) or (d) (kidnapping, assaults etc.); and

(c) a "relevant recording", in relation to a child witness, is a video recording of an interview of the witness made with a view to its admission as evidence in chief of the witness.

(2) Where the court, in making a determination for the purposes of section 19(2), determines that a witness in criminal proceedings is a child witness, the court must—

(a) first have regard to subsections (3) to (7) below; and

(b) then have regard to section 19(2);

and for the purposes of section 19(2), as it then applies to the witness, any special measures required to be applied in relation to him by virtue of this section shall be treated as if they were measures determined by the court, pursuant to section 19(2)(a) and (b)(i), to be ones that (whether on their own or with any other special measures) would be likely to maximise, so far as practicable, the quality of his evidence.

(3) The primary rule in the case of a child witness is that the court must give a special measures direction in relation to the witness which complies with the following requirements—

(a) it must provide for any relevant recording to be admitted under section 27 (video recorded evidence in chief); and

(b) it must provide for any evidence given by the witness in the proceedings which is not given by means of a video recording (whether in chief or otherwise) to be given by means of a live link in accordance with section 24.

(4) The primary rule is subject to the following limitations—

(a) the requirement contained in subsection (3)(a) or (b) has effect subject to the availability (within the meaning of section 18(2)) of the special measure in question in relation to the witness;

(b) the requirement contained in subsection (3)(a) also has effect subject to section 27(2); and

(c) the rule does not apply to the extent that the court is satisfied that compliance with it would not be likely to maximise the quality of the witness's evidence so far as practicable (whether because the application to that evidence of one or more other special measures available in relation to the witness would have that result or for any other reason).

(5) However, subsection (4)(c) does not apply in relation to a child witness in need of special protection.

(6) Where a child witness is in need of special protection by virtue of subsection (1)(b)(i), any special measures direction given by the court which complies with the requirement contained in subsection (3)(a) must in addition provide for the special measure available under section 28 (video recorded cross-examination or re-examination) to apply in relation to—

(a) any cross-examination of the witness otherwise than by the accused in person, and

(b) any subsequent re-examination.

(7) The requirement contained in subsection (6) has effect subject to the following limitations—

(a) it has effect subject to the availability (within the meaning of section 18(2)) of that special measure in relation to the witness; and

(b) it does not apply if the witness has informed the court that he does not want that special measure to apply in relation to him.

(8) Where a special measures direction is given in relation to a child witness who is an eligible witness by reason only of section 16(1)(a), then—

(a) subject to subsection (9) below, and

(b) except where the witness has already begun to give evidence in the proceedings, the direction shall cease to have effect at the time when the witness attains the age of 17.

(9) Where a special measures direction is given in relation to a child witness who is an eligible witness by reason only of section 16(1)(a) and—

(a) the direction provides—

(i) for any relevant recording to be admitted under section 27 as evidence in chief of the witness, or

(ii) for the special measure available under section 28 to apply in relation to the witness, and

(b) if it provides for that special measure to so apply, the witness is still under the age of 17 when the video recording is made for the purposes of section 28, then, so far as it provides as mentioned in paragraph (a)(i) or (ii) above, the direction shall continue to have effect in accordance with section 20(1) even though the witness subsequently attains that age.

9–36 In the case of a child witness, the court will normally direct that a video-recorded interview will be admitted as the child's evidence in chief and any other evidence will be given by live link so long as facilities are available and the quality of the evidence would be improved. Cases are often transferred to adjacent courthouses where facilities exist. Safeguards in relation to video-recorded evidence in chief are contained in section 27(2). Where the child witness is in need of special protection under section 21(5) the quality of evidence test does not apply and it is almost automatic that a direction will be given to admit video-recorded evidence in chief and any other evidence by live link.

Youth Justice and Criminal Evidence Act 1999, ss.22–23

Extension of provisions of section 21 to certain witnesses over 17

9–37 22.—(1) For the purposes of this section—
  (a) a witness in criminal proceedings (other than the accused) is a "qualifying witness" if he—
    (i) is not an eligible witness at the time of the hearing (as defined by section 16(3)), but
    (ii) was under the age of 17 when a relevant recording was made;
  (b) a qualifying witness is "in need of special protection" if the offence (or any of the offences) to which the proceedings relate is—
    (i) an offence falling within section 35(3)(a) (sexual offences etc.), or
    (ii) an offence falling within section 35(3)(b), (c) or (d) (kidnapping, assaults etc.); and
  (c) a "relevant recording", in relation to a witness, is a video recording of an interview of the witness made with a view to its admission as evidence in chief of the witness.

(2) Subsections (2) to (7) of section 21 shall apply as follows in relation to a qualifying witness—
  (a) subsections (2) to (4), so far as relating to the giving of a direction complying with the requirement contained in subsection (3)(a), shall apply to a qualifying witness in respect of the relevant recording as they apply to a child witness (within the meaning of that section);
  (b) subsection (5), so far as relating to the giving of such a direction, shall apply to a qualifying witness in need of special protection as it applies to a child witness in need of special protection (within the meaning of that section); and
  (c) subsections (6) and (7) shall apply to a qualifying witness in need of special protection by virtue of subsection (1)(b)(i) above as they apply to such a child witness as is mentioned in subsection (6).

Screening witness from accused

9–38 23.—(1) A special measures direction may provide for the witness, while giving testimony or being sworn in court, to be prevented by means of a screen or other arrangement from seeing the accused.

(2) But the screen or other arrangement must not prevent the witness from being able to see, and to be seen by—
  (a) the judge or justices (or both) and the jury (if there is one);
  (b) legal representatives acting in the proceedings; and
  (c) any interpreter or other person appointed (in pursuance of the direction or otherwise) to assist the witness.

(3) Where two or more legal representatives are acting for a party to the proceedings, subsection (2)(b) is to be regarded as satisfied in relation to those representatives if the witness is able at all material times to see and be seen by at least one of them.

9–39 See *Criminal Procedure Rules* 2005, r.29 in Appendix G–168.

9–40 An application for a special measures direction may be made by the parties or the court may give a direction of its own motion. The court must be satisfied that either the witness is a child or the quality of evidence is likely to be impaired without a direction. In the latter case quality may be impaired on the grounds of mental or physical disability, impairment of intelligence, fear or distress.

An application must be made on a prescribed form sent to the court and copied to the other parties within fourteen days of a plea of not guilty or within twenty eight days of a defendant's first appearance if before the youth court. These time limits may be extended upon application with good reason: Time limits are discretionary not mandatory and it is for the court to determine whether any undue prejudice has been caused to a defendant by granting a late application: *Brown, ante.*

An unopposed application may be determined by a single justice. Where the application is opposed there must be a hearing of which all parties must receive notice as they have a right to attend and be heard. The court must give notice of its decision to the parties together with reasons

Upon a change of circumstances an application may be renewed, varied, or **9–41** discharged.

In *KL and LAK v. DPP* (2002) 166 J.P. 369, QBD, the precaution of bringing a **9–42** screen into court before an application was concluded was confirmed to be a sensible course of action and could not suggest that the magistrates had pre-judged the issue. Section 23 requires that the witness be prevented from seeing the accused. There is no requirement that the defendant should not be able to see the witness. This may prove difficult in practice because of courtroom layout. In *DJX* (1990) 91 Cr.App.R. 36, screens were placed between a child witness and the defendants. It was said that the necessity of trying to ensure that the children gave evidence without intimidation outweighed any possible prejudice to the defendants.

In *X.* (1990) 91 Cr.App.R. 36, CA where a screen was used and social workers had been permitted to sit alongside the child witnesses when they gave evidence, the Court of Appeal stated that to have anyone sitting alongside a witness was a course of conduct that had to be undertaken with considerable care and the court had to be astute to ensure that nothing improper occurred and no undue encouragement was given to the witness. The *Consolidation Criminal Practice Direction*, para. III.29 (see Appendix F) gives guidance on the use of a witness supporter. It states that the supporter should be independent, have no previous knowledge or personal involvement in the case and should be suitably trained. An usher should be available to assist.

Any special measures direction does not affect common law or statutory rules governing the admissibility of evidence: *R. (CPS) v. Brentford Youth Court* [2003] EWHC 2409; (2003) 167 J.P. 614.

Youth Justice and Criminal Evidence Act 1999, s.24

Evidence by live link

24.—(1) A special measures direction may provide for the witness to give evidence by means **9–43** of a live link.

(2) Where a direction provides for the witness to give evidence by means of a live link, the witness may not give evidence in any other way without the permission of the court.

(3) The court may give permission for the purposes of subsection (2) if it appears to the court to be in the interests of justice to do so, and may do so either—

  (a) on an application by a party to the proceedings, if there has been a material change of circumstances since the relevant time, or

  (b) of its own motion.

(4) In subsection (3) "the relevant time" means —

  (a) the time when the direction was given, or

  (b) if a previous application has been made under that subsection, the time when the application (or last application) was made.

(5) Where in proceedings before a magistrates' court—

  (a) evidence is to be given by means of a live link in accordance with a special measures direction, but

(b) suitable facilities for receiving such evidence are not available at any petty-sessional court-house in which that court can (apart from this subsection) lawfully sit,

the court may sit for the purposes of the whole or any part of those proceedings at a place where such facilities are available and which has been appointed for the purposes of this subsection by the justices acting for the petty sessions area for which the court acts.

(6) A place appointed under subsection (5) may be outside the petty sessions area for which it is appointed; but (if so) it is to be regarded as being in that area for the purpose of the jurisdiction of the justices acting for that area.

(7) In this section "petty-sessional court-house" has the same meaning as in the *Magistrates' Courts Act* 1980 and "petty sessions area" has the same meaning as in the *Justices of the Peace Act* 1997.

(8) In this Chapter "live link" means a live television link or other arrangement whereby a witness, while absent from the courtroom or other place where the proceedings are being held, is able to see and hear a person there and to be seen and heard by the persons specified in section 23(2)(a) to (c).

9–44   See *Criminal Procedure Rules* 2005, r.29.6 in Appendix G–173.

9–45   There is no power to make a special measures direction in relation to a defendant's evidence where he is in fear of his co-defendants: *R. (S.) v. Waltham Forest Youth Court* [2004] EWHC 715.

There is no power to order the video recording of the cross-examination or re-examination of a child witness who gives evidence over a live link: *Mullen* [2004] 2 Cr.App.R. 18; [2004] 2 Cr.App.R. 21.

Youth Justice and Criminal Evidence Act 1999, s.25

Evidence given in private

9–46   **25.**—(1) A special measures direction may provide for the exclusion from the court, during the giving of the witness's evidence, of persons of any description specified in the direction.

(2) The persons who may be so excluded do not include—

(a) the accused,

(b) legal representatives acting in the proceedings, or

(c) any interpreter or other person appointed (in pursuance of the direction or otherwise) to assist the witness.

(3) A special measures direction providing for representatives of news gathering or reporting organisations to be so excluded shall be expressed not to apply to one named person who—

(a) is a representative of such an organisation, and

(b) has been nominated for the purpose by one or more such organisations,

unless it appears to the court that no such nomination has been made.

(4) A special measures direction may only provide for the exclusion of persons under this section where—

(a) the proceedings relate to a sexual offence; or

(b) it appears to the court that there are reasonable grounds for believing that any person other than the accused has sought, or will seek, to intimidate the witness in connection with testifying in the proceedings.

(5) Any proceedings from which persons are excluded under this section (whether or not those persons include representatives of news gathering or reporting organisations) shall nevertheless be taken to be held in public for the purposes of any privilege or exemption from liability available in respect of fair, accurate and contemporaneous reports of legal proceedings held in public.

Criminal Justice Act 2003, Pt 8 (ss.51–53, 55–56)

PART 8

LIVE LINKS

Live links in criminal proceedings

9–47   **51.**—(1) A witness (other than the defendant) may, if the court so directs, give evidence through a live link in the following criminal proceedings.

(2) They are—
- (a) a summary trial,
- (b) an appeal to the Crown Court arising out of such a trial,
- (c) a trial on indictment,
- (d) an appeal to the criminal division of the Court of Appeal,
- (e) the hearing of a reference under section 9 or 11 of the *Criminal Appeal Act* 1995,
- (f) a hearing before a magistrates' court or the Crown Court which is held after the defendant has entered a plea of guilty, and
- (g) a hearing before the Court of Appeal under section 80 of this Act.

(3) A direction may be given under this section—
- (a) on an application by a party to the proceedings, or
- (b) of the court's own motion.

(4) But a direction may not be given under this section unless—
- (a) the court is satisfied that it is in the interests of the efficient or effective administration of justice for the person concerned to give evidence in the proceedings through a live link,
- (b) it has been notified by the Secretary of State that suitable facilities for receiving evidence through a live link are available in the area in which it appears to the court that the proceedings will take place, and
- (c) that notification has not been withdrawn.

(5) The withdrawal of such a notification is not to affect a direction given under this section before that withdrawal.

(6) In deciding whether to give a direction under this section the court must consider all the circumstances of the case.

(7) Those circumstances include in particular—
- (a) the availability of the witness,
- (b) the need for the witness to attend in person,
- (c) the importance of the witness's evidence to the proceedings,
- (d) the views of the witness,
- (e) the suitability of the facilities at the place where the witness would give evidence through a live link,
- (f) whether a direction might tend to inhibit any party to the proceedings from effectively testing the witness's evidence.

(8) The court must state in open court its reasons for refusing an application for a direction under this section and, if it is a magistrates' court, must cause them to be entered in the register of its proceedings.

Effect of, and rescission of, direction

52.—(1) Subsection (2) applies where the court gives a direction under section 51 for a **9–48** person to give evidence through a live link in particular proceedings.

(2) The person concerned may not give evidence in those proceedings after the direction is given otherwise than through a live link (but this is subject to the following provisions of this section).

(3) The court may rescind a direction under section 51 if it appears to the court to be in the interests of justice to do so.

(4) Where it does so, the person concerned shall cease to be able to give evidence in the proceedings through a live link, but this does not prevent the court from giving a further direction under section 51 in relation to him.

(5) A direction under section 51 may be rescinded under subsection (3)—
- (a) on an application by a party to the proceedings, or
- (b) of the court's own motion.

(6) But an application may not be made under subsection (5)(a) unless there has been a material change of circumstances since the direction was given.

(7) The court must state in open court its reasons—
- (a) for rescinding a direction under section 51, or
- (b) for refusing an application to rescind such a direction,

and, if it is a magistrates' court, must cause them to be entered in the register of its proceedings.

Magistrates' courts permitted to sit at other locations

53.—(1) This section applies where—					**9–49**

(a) a magistrates' court is minded to give a direction under section 51 for evidence to be given through a live link in proceedings before the court, and

(b) suitable facilities for receiving such evidence are not available at any petty-sessional court-house in which the court can (apart from subsection (2)) lawfully sit.

(2) The court may sit for the purposes of the whole or any part of the proceedings at any place at which such facilities are available and which has been appointed for the purposes of this section by the justices acting for the petty sessions area for which the court acts.

(3) A place appointed under subsection (2) may be outside the petty sessions area for which it is appointed; but (if so) it shall be deemed to be in that area for the purpose of the jurisdiction of the justices acting for that area.

Rules of court

9–50　　　**55.**—(1) [Criminal Procedure Rules] may make such provision as appears to the [Criminal Procedure Rule Committee] to be necessary or expedient for the purposes of this Part.

(2) [Criminal Procedure Rules] may in particular make provision—

(a) as to the procedure to be followed in connection with applications under section 51 or 52, and

(b) as to the arrangements or safeguards to be put in place in connection with the operation of live links.

(3) The provision which may be made by virtue of subsection (2)(a) includes provision—

(a) for uncontested applications to be determined by the court without a hearing,

(b) for preventing the renewal of an unsuccessful application under section 51 unless there has been a material change of circumstances,

(c) for the manner in which confidential or sensitive information is to be treated in connection with an application under section 51 or 52 and in particular as to its being disclosed to, or withheld from, a party to the proceedings.

(4) Nothing in this section is to be taken as affecting the generality of any enactment conferring power to make [Criminal Procedure Rules].

[This section is printed as amended by transitional provisions specified in the *Courts Act 2003 (Consequential Amendments) Order* (S.I. 2004 No. 2035), Art.2 and Sched. 1, para. 47.]

Interpretation of Part 8

9–51　　　**56.**—(1) In this Part—

"legal representative" means an authorised advocate or authorised litigator (as defined by section 119(1) of the *Courts and Legal Services Act* 1990),

"petty-sessional court-house" has the same meaning as in the *Magistrates'* Courts Act 1980,

"petty sessions area" has the same meaning as in the *Justices of the Peace Act* 1997,

"rules of court" means Magistrates' Courts Rules, Crown Court Rules or Criminal Appeal Rules,

"witness", in relation to any criminal proceedings, means a person called, or proposed to be called, to give evidence in the proceedings.

(2) In this Part "live link" means a live television link or other arrangement by which a witness, while at a place in the United Kingdom which is outside the building where the proceedings are being held, is able to see and hear a person at the place where the proceedings are being held and to be seen and heard by the following persons.

(3) They are—

(a) the defendant or defendants,

(b) the judge or justices (or both) and the jury (if there is one),

(c) legal representatives acting in the proceedings, and

(d) any interpreter or other person appointed by the court to assist the witness.

(4) The extent (if any) to which a person is unable to see or hear by reason of any impairment of eyesight or hearing is to be disregarded for the purposes of subsection (2).

(5) Nothing in this Part is to be regarded as affecting any power of a court—

(a) to make an order, give directions or give leave of any description in relation to any witness (including the defendant or defendants), or

    (b) to exclude evidence at its discretion (whether by preventing questions being put or otherwise).

[These sections are not yet in force.]

These measures are available to all vulnerable witnesses in summary trials. They **9–52** should be made in a timely manner as it is important that witnesses know from an early stage how they are going to give evidence. Special measures have been held to be compatible with the ECHR: *R. (D.) v. Camberwell Green Youth Court* [2005] UKHL 4; [2005] 1 W.L.R. 393; [2005] Crim.L.R. 497. The case considered six defendants who were all charged with offences of robbery or assault, and were all aged 16 or under. In applications for judicial review of the decisions to make special measures directions under the 1999 Act, it was submitted that as section 21(5) required the court to give a special measures direction in relation to the evidence of a child witness in need of special protection, the court was deprived of any power to consider whether the restriction on the rights of the defendant was necessary or in the interests of justice and thus the provision was incompatible with Article 6 of the European Convention on Human Rights.

The House of Lords held that it is not unjust for evidence to be given by live link and video where there is no reason to think that the child in question would be upset, traumatised, or intimidated by giving evidence in open court. The Convention does not guarantee a confrontation face to face. The court doubted, however, the decision in *R. (S.) v. Waltham Forest Youth Court, ante,* that there was no inherent power to allow a defendant to give evidence by live link. The situation of witnesses and defendants are different and it would be very rarely that a defendant would give evidence that way but he might, *e.g.* where he was very young and was too terrified to give evidence in the presence of a co-accused.

Since this case live links have been brought in for vulnerable defendants' evidence from January 15, 2007: *Police and Justice Act* 2006, s.47 (see *Police and Justice Act* 2006 (Commencement No. 1 Transitional and Savings Provisions) Order 2006 (S.I. 2006 No. 3364).

Police and Justice Act 2006, s.47

Evidence of vulnerable accused
    47— After section 33 of the *Youth Justice and Criminal Evidence Act* 1999 (c. 23) (inter- **9–53** pretation etc of Chapter 1 of Part 2) there is inserted—

    "**CHAPTER 1A** USE OF LIVE LINK FOR EVIDENCE OF CERTAIN ACCUSED PERSONS

Live link directions
    33A—(1) This section applies to any proceedings (whether in a magistrates' court or before **9–54** the Crown Court) against a person for an offence.

    (2) The court may, on the application of the accused, give a live link direction if it is satisfied—

        (a) that the conditions in subsection (4) or, as the case may be, subsection (5) are met in relation to the accused, and

        (b) that it is in the interests of justice for the accused to give evidence through a live link.

    (3) A live link direction is a direction that any oral evidence to be given before the court by the accused is to be given through a live link.

    (4) Where the accused is aged under 18 when the application is made, the conditions are that—

        (a) his ability to participate effectively in the proceedings as a witness giving oral evidence in court is compromised by his level of intellectual ability or social functioning, and

        (b) use of a live link would enable him to participate more effectively in the proceedings as a witness (whether by improving the quality of his evidence or otherwise).

(5) Where the accused has attained the age of 18 at that time, the conditions are that—

     (a) he suffers from a mental disorder (within the meaning of the *Mental Health Act* 1983) or otherwise has a significant impairment of intelligence and social function,

     (b) he is for that reason unable to participate effectively in the proceedings as a witness giving oral evidence in court, and

     (c) use of a live link would enable him to participate more effectively in the proceedings as a witness (whether by improving the quality of his evidence or otherwise).

(6) While a live link direction has effect the accused may not give oral evidence before the court in the proceedings otherwise than through a live link.

(7) The court may discharge a live link direction at any time before or during any hearing to which it applies if it appears to the court to be in the interests of justice to do so (but this does not affect the power to give a further live link direction in relation to the accused).

The court may exercise this power of its own motion or on an application by a party.

(8) The court must state in open court its reasons for—

     (a) giving or discharging a live link direction, or

     (b) refusing an application for or for the discharge of a live link direction,

and, if it is a magistrates' court, it must cause those reasons to be entered in the register of its proceedings.

Section 33A: meaning of "live link"

9–55   **33B**—(1) In section 33A "live link" means an arrangement by which the accused, while absent from the place where the proceedings are being held, is able—

     (a) to see and hear a person there, and

     (b) to be seen and heard by the persons mentioned in subsection (2),

and for this purpose any impairment of eyesight or hearing is to be disregarded.

(2) The persons are—

     (a) the judge or justices (or both) and the jury (if there is one),

     (b) where there are two or more accused in the proceedings, each of the other accused,

     (c) legal representatives acting in the proceedings, and

     (d) any interpreter or other person appointed by the court to assist the accused.

Saving

9–56   **33C**— Nothing in this Chapter affects—

     (a) any power of a court to make an order, give directions or give leave of any description in relation to any witness (including an accused), or

     (b) the operation of any rule of law relating to evidence in criminal proceedings."

V. METHODS OF GIVING ORAL TESTIMONY

A. VIDEO RECORDING

Youth Justice and Criminal Evidence Act 1999, s.27

Video recorded evidence in chief

9–57   **27.**—(1) A special measures direction may provide for a video recording of an interview of the witness to be admitted as evidence in chief of the witness.

(2) A special measures direction may, however, not provide for a video recording, or a part of such a recording, to be admitted under this section if the court is of the opinion, having regard to all the circumstances of the case, that in the interests of justice the recording, or that part of it, should not be so admitted.

(3) In considering for the purposes of subsection (2) whether any part of a recording should not be admitted under this section, the court must consider whether any prejudice to the accused which might result from that part being so admitted is outweighed by the desirability of showing the whole, or substantially the whole, of the recorded interview.

(4) Where a special measures direction provides for a recording to be admitted under this section, the court may nevertheless subsequently direct that it is not to be so admitted if—

    (a)　it appears to the court that—

        (i)　the witness will not be available for cross-examination (whether conducted in the ordinary way or in accordance with any such direction), and

        (ii)　the parties to the proceedings have not agreed that there is no need for the witness to be so available; or

    (b)　any rules of court requiring disclosure of the circumstances in which the recording was made have not been complied with to the satisfaction of the court.

  (5)　Where a recording is admitted under this section—

    (a)　the witness must be called by the party tendering it in evidence, unless—

        (i)　a special measures direction provides for the witness's evidence on cross-examination to be given otherwise than by testimony in court, or

        (ii)　the parties to the proceedings have agreed as mentioned in subsection (4)(a)(ii); and

    (b)　the witness may not give evidence in chief otherwise than by means of the recording—

        (i)　as to any matter which, in the opinion of the court, has been dealt with adequately in the witness's recorded testimony, or

        (ii)　without the permission of the court, as to any other matter which, in the opinion of the court, is dealt with in that testimony.

  (6)　Where in accordance with subsection (2) a special measures direction provides for part only of a recording to be admitted under this section, references in subsections (4) and (5) to the recording or to the witness's recorded testimony are references to the part of the recording or testimony which is to be so admitted.

  (7)　The court may give permission for the purposes of subsection (5)(b)(ii) if it appears to the court to be in the interests of justice to do so, and may do so either—

    (a)　on an application by a party to the proceedings, if there has been a material change of circumstances since the relevant time, or

    (b)　of its own motion.

  (8)　In subsection (7) "the relevant time" means —

    (a)　the time when the direction was given, or

    (b)　if a previous application has been made under that subsection, the time when the application (or last application) was made.

  (9)　The court may, in giving permission for the purposes of subsection (5)(b)(ii), direct that the evidence in question is to be given by the witness by means of a live link; and, if the court so directs, subsections (5) to (7) of section 24 shall apply in relation to that evidence as they apply in relation to evidence which is to be given in accordance with a special measures direction.

  (10)　A magistrates' court inquiring into an offence as examining justices under section 6 of the *Magistrates' Courts Act* 1980 may consider any video recording in relation to which it is proposed to apply for a special measures direction providing for it to be admitted at the trial in accordance with this section.

  (11)　Nothing in this section affects the admissibility of any video recording which would be admissible apart from this section.

    Video-recorded evidence in chief is currently available for child witnesses in cases of **9–58** violence or threats of violence, sexual offences, kidnapping, abduction and cruelty.

    See the Home Office *Achieving Best Evidence in Criminal Proceedings: Guidance for Vulnerable or Intimidated Witnesses including Children* (2002).

    In *R. (CPS, Harrow) v. Brentford Youth Court* [2003] EWHC 2409, Admin, the word "desirability" in section 27(3) was considered in the context of the inadmissibility of evidence. The legislative purpose of section 27(3) was said to be (i) to resolve in favour of video evidence its question of relative worth in relation to live evidence and (ii) to tackle the problem of the unusual case in which the evidence of a child or disabled person could not be given without referring to inadmissible matters. In that circumstance if the evidence could not be understood without the whole of it being played, and it was desirable that the whole should be played then the court should direct itself to ignore the inadmissible matters.

    In *G. v. DPP* [1997] 2 Cr.App.R. 78, DC the court held that failure to comply with **9–59** the earlier *Memorandum of Good Practice* was a matter to be taken into account by a court in deciding whether to exercise its discretion to refuse to admit the recording. The decision should not depend so much on the nature and extent of any breaches, as on whether the passages tainted by the breaches are confirmed by other untainted passages or are corroborated by independent evidence.

In *D. and S.* (2002) 166 J.P. 792, CA it was held that a failure to comply with the Home Office and Department of Health Memorandum of Good Practice did not *per se* render the complainant's video evidence inadmissible. The correct test for determining the admissibility of video-recorded evidence of a child is that provided in *Hanton* [2005] EWCA Crim 2009 of whether a reasonable jury properly directed can be sure that the witness has given a credible and accurate account on the video tape, notwithstanding any breaches of the relevant guidance for conducting interviews. It is possible for a court to consider other evidence that might corroborate the video evidence, but such consideration should be undertaken with considerable care: *K.* [2006] 2 Cr.App.R. 10.

Youth Justice and Criminal Evidence Act 1999, s.28

Video recorded cross-examination or re-examination

9–60   **28.**—(1) Where a special measures direction provides for a video recording to be admitted under section 27 as evidence in chief of the witness, the direction may also provide—

     (a) for any cross-examination of the witness, and any re-examination, to be recorded by means of a video recording; and

     (b) for such a recording to be admitted, so far as it relates to any such cross-examination or re-examination, as evidence of the witness under cross-examination or on re-examination, as the case may be.

(2) Such a recording must be made in the presence of such persons as rules of court or the direction may provide and in the absence of the accused, but in circumstances in which—

     (a) the judge or justices (or both) and legal representatives acting in the proceedings are able to see and hear the examination of the witness and to communicate with the persons in whose presence the recording is being made, and

     (b) the accused is able to see and hear any such examination and to communicate with any legal representative acting for him.

(3) Where two or more legal representatives are acting for a party to the proceedings, subsection (2)(a) and (b) are to be regarded as satisfied in relation to those representatives if at all material times they are satisfied in relation to at least one of them.

(4) Where a special measures direction provides for a recording to be admitted under this section, the court may nevertheless subsequently direct that it is not to be so admitted if any requirement of subsection (2) or rules of court or the direction has not been complied with to the satisfaction of the court.

(5) Where in pursuance of subsection (1) a recording has been made of any examination of the witness, the witness may not be subsequently cross-examined or re-examined in respect of any evidence given by the witness in the proceedings (whether in any recording admissible under section 27 or this section or otherwise than in such a recording) unless the court gives a further special measures direction making such provision as is mentioned in subsection (1)(a) and (b) in relation to any subsequent cross-examination, and re-examination, of the witness.

(6) The court may only give such a further direction if it appears to the court—

     (a) that the proposed cross-examination is sought by a party to the proceedings as a result of that party having become aware, since the time when the original recording was made in pursuance of subsection (1), of a matter which that party could not with reasonable diligence have ascertained by then, or

     (b) that for any other reason it is in the interests of justice to give the further direction.

(7) Nothing in this section shall be read as applying in relation to any cross-examination of the witness by the accused in person (in a case where the accused is to be able to conduct any such cross-examination).

[This section is not in force.]

Criminal Justice Act 2003, ss.137–138, 140

Evidence by video recording

137.—(1) This section applies where—   9–61

(a) a person is called as a witness in proceedings for an offence triable only on indictment, or for a prescribed offence triable either way,

(b) the person claims to have witnessed (whether visually or in any other way)—

   (i) events alleged by the prosecution to include conduct constituting the offence or part of the offence, or

   (ii) events closely connected with such events,

(c) he has previously given an account of the events in question (whether in response to questions asked or otherwise),

(d) the account was given at a time when those events were fresh in the person's memory (or would have been, assuming the truth of the claim mentioned in paragraph (b)),

(e) a video recording was made of the account,

(f) the court has made a direction that the recording should be admitted as evidence in chief of the witness, and the direction has not been rescinded, and

(g) the recording is played in the proceedings in accordance with the direction.

(2) If, or to the extent that, the witness in his oral evidence in the proceedings asserts the truth of the statements made by him in the recorded account, they shall be treated as if made by him in that evidence.

(3) A direction under subsection (1)(f)—

(a) may not be made in relation to a recorded account given by the defendant;

(b) may be made only if it appears to the court that—

   (i) the witness's recollection of the events in question is likely to have been significantly better when he gave the recorded account than it will be when he gives oral evidence in the proceedings, and

   (ii) it is in the interests of justice for the recording to be admitted, having regard in particular to the matters mentioned in subsection (4).

(4) Those matters are—

(a) the interval between the time of the events in question and the time when the recorded account was made;

(b) any other factors that might affect the reliability of what the witness said in that account;

(c) the quality of the recording;

(d) any views of the witness as to whether his evidence in chief should be given orally or by means of the recording.

(5) For the purposes of subsection (2) it does not matter if the statements in the recorded account were not made on oath.

(6) In this section "prescribed" means of a description specified in an order made by the Secretary of State.

[Section 137 is not yet in force.]

Video evidence: further provisions

138.—(1) Where a video recording is admitted under section 137, the witness may not give   9–62
evidence in chief otherwise than by means of the recording as to any matter which, in the opinion of the court, has been dealt with adequately in the recorded account.

(2) The reference in subsection (1)(f) of section 137 to the admission of a recording includes a reference to the admission of part of the recording; and references in that section and this one to the video recording or to the witness's recorded account shall, where appropriate, be read accordingly.

(3) In considering whether any part of a recording should be not admitted under section 137, the court must consider—

(a) whether admitting that part would carry a risk of prejudice to the defendant, and

(b) if so, whether the interests of justice nevertheless require it to be admitted in view of the desirability of showing the whole, or substantially the whole, of the recorded interview.

(4) A court may not make a direction under section 137(1)(f) in relation to any proceedings unless—

    (a) the Secretary of State has notified the court that arrangements can be made, in the area in which it appears to the court that the proceedings will take place, for implementing directions under that section, and

    (b) the notice has not been withdrawn.

(5) Nothing in section 137 affects the admissibility of any video recording which would be admissible apart from that section.

[Section 138 is not yet in force.]

Interpretation of Chapter 3

9–63   **140.** In this Chapter—

    "criminal proceedings" means criminal proceedings in relation to which the strict rules of evidence apply;

    "defendant", in relation to criminal proceedings, means a person charged with an offence in those proceedings;

    "document" means anything in which information of any description is recorded, but not including any recording of sounds or moving images;

    "oral evidence" includes evidence which, by reason of any disability, disorder or other impairment, a person called as a witness gives in writing or by signs or by way of any device;

    "video recording" means any recording, on any medium, from which a moving image may by any means be produced, and includes the accompanying sound-track.

B. Intermediary

Youth Justice and Criminal Evidence Act 1999, s.29

Examination of witness through intermediary

9–64   **29.**—(1) A special measures direction may provide for any examination of the witness (however and wherever conducted) to be conducted through an interpreter or other person approved by the court for the purposes of this section ("an intermediary").

(2) The function of an intermediary is to communicate—

    (a) to the witness, questions put to the witness, and

    (b) to any person asking such questions, the answers given by the witness in reply to them,

and to explain such questions or answers so far as necessary to enable them to be understood by the witness or person in question.

(3) Any examination of the witness in pursuance of subsection (1) must take place in the presence of such persons as rules of court or the direction may provide, but in circumstances in which—

    (a) the judge or justices (or both) and legal representatives acting in the proceedings are able to see and hear the examination of the witness and to communicate with the intermediary, and

    (b) (except in the case of a video recorded examination) the jury (if there is one) are able to see and hear the examination of the witness.

(4) Where two or more legal representatives are acting for a party to the proceedings, subsection (3)(a) is to be regarded as satisfied in relation to those representatives if at all material times it is satisfied in relation to at least one of them.

(5) A person may not act as an intermediary in a particular case except after making a declaration, in such form as may be prescribed by rules of court, that he will faithfully perform his function as intermediary.

(6) Subsection (1) does not apply to an interview of the witness which is recorded by means of a video recording with a view to its admission as evidence in chief of the witness; but a special measures direction may provide for such a recording to be admitted under section 27 if the interview was conducted through an intermediary and—

    (a) that person complied with subsection (5) before the interview began, and

    (b) the court's approval for the purposes of this section is given before the direction is given.

(7) Section 1 of the *Perjury Act* 1911 (perjury) shall apply in relation to a person acting as an intermediary as it applies in relation to a person lawfully sworn as an interpreter in a judicial proceeding; and for this purpose, where a person acts as an intermediary in any proceeding which is not a judicial proceeding for the purposes of that section, that proceeding shall be taken to be part of the judicial proceeding in which the witness's evidence is given.

9–65 Where provision is made for examination of a witness via a live link to be made through an intermediary the witness shall be accompanied at the link only by the intermediary and such others as may be acceptable to the court: *Criminal Procedure Rules* 2005, r.29.6(4). This is currently available in pilot areas only.

9–66 See *Criminal Procedure Rules* 2005, r.29.6 in Appendix G–173.

Youth Justice and Criminal Evidence Act 1999, ss.30–33

Aids to communication

9–67 **30.** A special measures direction may provide for the witness, while giving evidence (whether by testimony in court or otherwise), to be provided with such device as the court considers appropriate with a view to enabling questions or answers to be communicated to or by the witness despite any disability or disorder or other impairment which the witness has or suffers from.

Status of evidence given under Chapter I

9–68 **31.**—(1) Subsections (2) to (4) apply to a statement made by a witness in criminal proceedings which, in accordance with a special measures direction, is not made by the witness in direct oral testimony in court but forms part of the witness's evidence in those proceedings.

(2) The statement shall be treated as if made by the witness in direct oral testimony in court; and accordingly—

    (a) it is admissible evidence of any fact of which such testimony from the witness would be admissible;

    (b) it is not capable of corroborating any other evidence given by the witness.

(3) Subsection (2) applies to a statement admitted under section 27 or 28 which is not made by the witness on oath even though it would have been required to be made on oath if made by the witness in direct oral testimony in court.

(4) In estimating the weight (if any) to be attached to the statement, the court must have regard to all the circumstances from which an inference can reasonably be drawn (as to the accuracy of the statement or otherwise).

(5) Nothing in this Chapter (apart from subsection (3)) affects the operation of any rule of law relating to evidence in criminal proceedings.

(6) Where any statement made by a person on oath in any proceeding which is not a judicial proceeding for the purposes of section 1 of the *Perjury Act* 1911 (perjury) is received in evidence in pursuance of a special measures direction, that proceeding shall be taken for the purposes of that section to be part of the judicial proceeding in which the statement is so received in evidence.

(7) Where in any proceeding which is not a judicial proceeding for the purposes of that Act—

    (a) a person wilfully makes a false statement otherwise than on oath which is subsequently received in evidence in pursuance of a special measures direction, and

    (b) the statement is made in such circumstances that had it been given on oath in any such judicial proceeding that person would have been guilty of perjury,

he shall be guilty of an offence and liable to any punishment which might be imposed on conviction of an offence under section 57(2) (giving of false unsworn evidence in criminal proceedings).

(8) In this section "statement" includes any representation of fact, whether made in words or otherwise.

Warning to jury

9–69 **32.** Where on a trial on indictment evidence has been given in accordance with a special measures direction, the judge must give the jury such warning (if any) as the judge considers necessary to ensure that the fact that the direction was given in relation to the witness does not prejudice the accused.

Interpretation etc. of Chapter I

9–70 **33.**—(1) In this Chapter—

Part II

"eligible witness" means a witness eligible for assistance by virtue of section 16 or 17;

"live link" has the meaning given by section 24(8);

"quality", in relation to the evidence of a witness, shall be construed in accordance with section 16(5);

"special measures direction" means (in accordance with section 19(5)) a direction under section 19.

(2) In this Chapter references to the special measures available in relation to a witness shall be construed in accordance with section 18.

(3) In this Chapter references to a person being able to see or hear, or be seen or heard by, another person are to be read as not applying to the extent that either of them is unable to see or hear by reason of any impairment of eyesight or hearing.

(4) In the case of any proceedings in which there is more than one accused—

(a) any reference to the accused in sections 23 to 28 may be taken by a court, in connection with the giving of a special measures direction, as a reference to all or any of the accused, as the court may determine, and

(b) any such direction may be given on the basis of any such determination.

C. WITNESS OVERSEAS

9–71   Section 32 of the *Criminal Justice Act* 1988 allows witnesses who are overseas to give evidence by video link. It applies to certain offences only and because of this there is no provision for magistrates other than youth courts to hear evidence from witnesses overseas in this manner.

VI. WRITTEN EVIDENCE AT SUMMARY TRIAL

A. STATEMENTS

Criminal Justice Act 1967, s.9

Proof by written statement

9–72   **9.**—(1) In any criminal proceedings, other than committal proceedings, a written statement by any person shall, if such of the conditions mentioned in the next following subsection as are applicable are satisfied, be admissible as evidence to the like extent as oral evidence to the like effect by that person.

(2) The said conditions are—

(a) the statement purports to be signed by the person who made it;

(b) the statement contains a declaration by that person to the effect that it is true to the best of his knowledge and belief and that he made the statement knowing that, if it were tendered in evidence, he would be liable to prosecution if he wilfully stated in it anything which he knew to be false or did not believe to be true;

(c) before the hearing at which the statement is tendered in evidence, a copy of the statement is served, by or on behalf of the party proposing to tender it, on each of the other parties to the proceedings; and

(d) none of the other parties or their solicitors, within seven days from the service of the copy of the statement, serves a notice on the party so proposing objecting to the statement being tendered in evidence under this section:

Provided that the conditions mentioned in paragraphs (c) and (d) of this subsection shall not apply if the parties agree before or during the hearing that the statement shall be so tendered.

(3) The following provisions shall also have effect in relation to any written statement tendered in evidence under this section, that is to say—

(a) if the statement is made by a person under the age of eighteen, it shall give his age;

(b) if it is made by a person who cannot read it, it shall be read to him before he signs it and shall be accompanied by a declaration by the person who so read the statement to the effect that it was so read; and

(c) if it refers to any other document as an exhibit, the copy served on any other party to the proceedings under paragraph (c) of the last foregoing subsection shall be accompanied by a copy of that document or by such information as may be necessary in order to enable the party on whom it is served to inspect that document or a copy thereof.

(4) Notwithstanding that a written statement made by any person may be admissible as evidence by virtue of this section—

(a) the party by whom or on whose behalf a copy of the statement was served may call that person to give evidence; and

(b) the court may, of its own motion or on the application of any party to the proceedings, require that person to attend before the court and give evidence.

(5) An application under paragraph (b) of the last foregoing subsection to a court other than a magistrates' court may be made before the hearing and on any such application the powers of the court shall be exercisable by a puisne judge of the High Court, a Circuit judge or Recorder sitting alone.

(6) So much of any statement as is admitted in evidence by virtue of this section shall, unless the court otherwise directs, be read aloud at the hearing and where the court so directs an account shall be given orally of so much of any statement as is not read aloud.

(7) Any document or object referred to as an exhibit and identified in a written statement tendered in evidence under this section shall be treated as if it had been produced as an exhibit and identified in court by the maker of the statement.

(8) A document required by this section to be served on any person may be served—

(a) by delivering it to him or to his solicitor; or

(b) by addressing it to him and leaving it at his usual or last known place of abode or place of business or by addressing it to his solicitor and leaving it at his office; or

(c) by sending it in a registered letter or by the recorded delivery service or by first class post addressed to him at his usual or last known place of abode or place of business or addressed to his solicitor at his office; or

(d) in the case of a body corporate, by delivering it to the secretary or clerk of the body at its registered or principal office or sending it in a registered letter or by the recorded delivery service or by first class post addressed to the Secretary or clerk of that body at that office; and in paragraph (d) of this subsection references to the secretary, in relation to a limited liability partnership, are to any designated member of the limited liability partnership.

The principle that it is no longer acceptable for defence advocates to seek to take **9–73** advantage of prosecution errors by deliberately delaying identification of an issue of fact or law until the last possible moment applies equally where a statement has been served under section 9 even where it is a case before the youth court: *R. (P.) v. South and South East Hampshire Youth Court*, unreported, April 14, 2005. In this case the defence took a point on what was contained in the statement when it had not asked for the witness to attend and give evidence. The court used its discretion to adjourn the proceedings so that, in the interests of justice, the witness could be called. There must be strict compliance with the requirements of this section and the *Criminal Procedure Rules* 2005, r.27.1 otherwise the statement will be inadmissible: *Paterson v. DPP* [1990] Crim.L.R. 651. The Practice Direction provides a precedent of a notice for the prosecution to send to the defendant when it wants to tender a statement in evidence under section 9. A statement admitted in evidence pursuant to section 9 is not taken to be conclusive evidence. It will be treated as if the maker had given oral evidence and appropriate weight will be given to it. Where the evidence is crucial to the case it is desirable for the witness to be called in person: *Lister v. Quaife* (1982) 75 Cr.App.R. 313; [1983] 1 W.L.R. 48.

A statement may be edited where there is irrelevant, inadmissible or prejudicial material or several statements may be reduced to one statement: see *Consolidation Criminal Practice Direction* para. III.24 (see Appendix F).

An analyst's statement must be served under section 16 of the *Road Traffic Act* 1988 where different rules of service apply than to a section 9 statement, *i.e.* it must be served personally, by registered post or by recorded delivery and at least seven days before a hearing: *DPP v. Stephens* [2006] EWHC 1860. In relation the to the service of a statement under the *Road Traffic Offenders Act* 1988, s.20(8) the service was rejected

Part II

where the statement was of such poor quality that it could not be used: *Griffiths v. DPP* [2007] EWHC 619, Admin.

B. ADMISSION OF FACTS

Criminal Justice Act 1967, s.10

Proof by formal admission

9–74   **10.**—(1) Subject to the provisions of this section, any fact of which oral evidence may be given in any criminal proceedings may be admitted for the purpose of those proceedings by or on behalf of the prosecutor or defendant, and the admission by any party of any such fact under this section shall as against that party be conclusive evidence in those proceedings of the fact admitted.

(2) An admission under this section—

(a) may be made before or at the proceedings;

(b) if made otherwise than in court, shall be in writing;

(c) if made in writing by an individual, shall purport to be signed by the person making it and, if so made by a body corporate, shall purport to be signed by a director or manager, or the secretary or clerk, or some other similar officer of the body corporate;

(d) if made on behalf of a defendant who is an individual, shall be made by his counsel or solicitor;

(e) if made at any state before the trial by a defendant who is an individual, must be approved by his counsel or solicitor (whether at the time it was made or subsequently) before or at the proceedings in question.

(3) An admission under this section for the purpose of proceedings relating to any matter shall be treated as an admission for the purpose of any subsequent criminal proceedings relating to that matter (including any appeal or retrial).

(4) An admission under this section may with the leave of the court be withdrawn in the proceedings for the purpose of which it is made or any subsequent criminal proceedings relating to the same matter.

9–75   Where a fact is admitted orally in court by or on behalf of the prosecutor or defendant, the fact admitted will be written down and signed by or on behalf of the party making the admission: *Criminal Procedure Rules* 2005, 1.37.4. See Appendix G–225 A form is usually available at court for this purpose.

Leave to withdraw an admission is unlikely to be given under section 10(4) without cogent evidence that the admissions were made by reason of mistake or misunderstanding: *Kolton* [2000] Crim.L.R. 761.

VII. EXAMINATION IN CHIEF

A. GENERAL

9–76   After the witness has been sworn or has affirmed the party who calls the witness, either in person or through a legal representative, will ask him questions to adduce relevant and admissible evidence which is supportive of the party's case. No time limits are set for the examination or cross-examination of witnesses. Where counsel indulges in prolix and repetitious questioning however, the court is entitled and obliged to impose reasonable time limits to ensure fair and sensible trial management: *Butt* [2005] EWCA Crim 805.

B. IDENTIFICATION OF THE WITNESS

9–77   The witness will be asked to state his full name. A witness is only asked for his address in exceptional circumstances and if it is relevant to an issue at trial. He may be asked for his occupation and if he is, it is not considered objectionable: *D.S.* [1999] Crim.L.R. 911, CA.

C. LEADING QUESTIONS

Witnesses should not be asked leading questions in examination in chief unless they **9–78** relate to formal or introductory matters or facts which are not in dispute: *Robinson* (1897) 61 J.P. 520. A leading question is one which suggests the desired answer or assumes the existence of a disputed fact. If a person or object is to be identified in court a leading question may be used: *Watson* (1817) 2 Stark 116.

Whereas answers to leading questions are admissible, the weight of the evidence is reduced: *Wilson* 9 Cr.App.R. 124, CCA; *Moor v. Moor* [1954] 1 W.L.R. 927. In certain circumstances the court, in the interests of justice, may use its discretion to allow such questions. In *ex p. Bottomley* [1909] 2 K.B. 14, a magistrate died in the course of proceedings. When a witness was recalled before a new magistrate, a leading question was allowed to elicit whether a deposition represented the evidence already given.

Where a witness gives evidence of a fact and another witness is called in order to contradict him, the latter may be asked directly whether that fact ever took place: *Courteen v. Touse* (1807) 1 Camp. 43. Leading questions may also be asked when a witness has been classified as hostile: see *post*.

D. REFRESHING MEMORY

Criminal Justice Act 2003, s.139

Use of documents to refresh memory

139.—(1) A person giving oral evidence in criminal proceedings about any matter may, at **9–79** any stage in the course of doing so, refresh his memory of it from a document made or verified by him at an earlier time if—

    (a) he states in his oral evidence that the document records his recollection of the matter at that earlier time, and

    (b) his recollection of the matter is likely to have been significantly better at that time than it is at the time of his oral evidence.

(2) Where—

    (a) a person giving oral evidence in criminal proceedings about any matter has previously given an oral account, of which a sound recording was made, and he states in that evidence that the account represented his recollection of the matter at that time,

    (b) his recollection of the matter is likely to have been significantly better at the time of the previous account than it is at the time of his oral evidence, and

    (c) a transcript has been made of the sound recording,

he may, at any stage in the course of giving his evidence, refresh his memory of the matter from that transcript.

A witness may refresh his memory from a document made or checked earlier if he **9–80** states that it records his recollection at that time and at that time his recollection is likely to have been significantly better than the present. He may also, in similar circumstances, refer to a manuscript of a sound recording. The document is an aide-memoire and will not amount to corroboration: *Virgo* (1978) 67 Cr.App.R. 323, CA. The document does not have to have been made contemporaneously and it could have been written by someone else so long as it has been checked and verified by the witness. Under the previous law, a copy of a document might not be used where the original no longer existed and the witness had no independent recollection of the facts: *Harvey* (1869) 11 Cox 546. If a copy had been made or verified at the time it would have been admissible: *Burton v. Plummer* (1834) 2 A.&E. 341. It is submitted that the document may be inspected: *Senat v. Senat* [1965] P.172. The witness may be cross-examined on the document.

E. PREVIOUS CONSISTENT STATEMENTS

Such statements (sometimes called self serving statements) are now dealt with under **9–81** section 120 of the *Criminal Justice Act* 2003.

Criminal Justice Act 2003, s.120

Other previous statements of witnesses

9–82   **120.**—(1) This section applies where a person (the witness) is called to give evidence in criminal proceedings.

(2) If a previous statement by the witness is admitted as evidence to rebut a suggestion that his oral evidence has been fabricated, that statement is admissible as evidence of any matter stated of which oral evidence by the witness would be admissible.

(3) A statement made by the witness in a document—

    (a) which is used by him to refresh his memory while giving evidence,

    (b) on which he is cross-examined, and

    (c) which as a consequence is received in evidence in the proceedings,

is admissible as evidence of any matter stated of which oral evidence by him would be admissible.

(4) A previous statement by the witness is admissible as evidence of any matter stated of which oral evidence by him would be admissible, if—

    (a) any of the following three conditions is satisfied, and

    (b) while giving evidence the witness indicates that to the best of his belief he made the statement, and that to the best of his belief it states the truth.

(5) The first condition is that the statement identifies or describes a person, object or place.

(6) The second condition is that the statement was made by the witness when the matters stated were fresh in his memory but he does not remember them, and cannot reasonably be expected to remember them, well enough to give oral evidence of them in the proceedings.

(7) The third condition is that—

    (a) the witness claims to be a person against whom an offence has been committed,

    (b) the offence is one to which the proceedings relate,

    (c) the statement consists of a complaint made by the witness (whether to a person in authority or not) about conduct which would, if proved, constitute the offence or part of the offence,

    (d) the complaint was made as soon as could reasonably be expected after the alleged conduct,

    (e) the complaint was not made as a result of a threat or a promise, and

    (f) before the statement is adduced the witness gives oral evidence in connection with its subject matter.

(8) For the purposes of subsection (7) the fact that the complaint was elicited (for example, by a leading question) is irrelevant unless a threat or a promise was involved.

9–83   With the exception of section 120(7) these provisions apply to anyone who gives evidence including a defendant where oral evidence is given and a suggestion is made that the evidence has been fabricated. A previous statement can then be introduced to rebut that suggestion. It is admissible as evidence of the matter stated. The previous statement might have been given orally or in a document. It might be a witness statement, a statement under caution, an officer's notebook, letter or an oral complaint made to someone else. Where the previous statement is in a document that document will become evidence: see previous case law: *Owen v. Edwards* (1983) 77 Cr.App.R. 191, DC; *Sekhon* (1987) 85 Cr.App.R. 19, CA; *M.* [1999] 1.W.L.R. 307.

It has always been the view that evidence of identification was strengthened if it could be shown that soon after the commission of the offence the witness saw and recognized the defendant: *Fannon* (1922) 22 S.R. (NSW) 427; *Christie* [1914] A.C. 545. A photofit portrait may be introduced as it was in *Cook* [1987] Q.B. 417 and a police artist's impression in *Smith* [1976] Crim.L.R. 511. Section 120(5) extends identification to an object or place. This will include the identification of a motor vehicle and/or index number.

Recent complaints of victims extends beyond the former rule of recent complaints in sexual cases: section 120(7). They may be made as soon as they could reasonably be expected and that too is different from the previous qualification of first reasonable opportunity: see *Valentine* [1996] 2.Cr.App.R. 213 where the character of the complainant, the relationship to the person to whom the complaint was made and the relationship to the person the complainant had the opportunity to complain to but chose not to were taken into account.

The previous statement will not be an independent confirmation of the person's evidence: see *Wright* (1990) 90 Cr.App.R. 91; *Islam* [1999] 1 Cr.App.R. 22; *N.K.* [1999] Crim.L.R. 980.

F. UNFAVOURABLE AND HOSTILE WITNESSES

If a witness does not come up to proof he is regarded as unfavourable. In such a situation the party is only able to call another witness to prove what the unfavourable witness failed to establish: *Ewer v. Ambrose* (1825) 3 B. & C. 746. Where two equally credible witnesses contradict each other, in *Sumner and Leivesley v. John Brown & Co* (1909) 25 T.L.R. 745 it was said that the party calling them is not entitled to accredit one and discredit the other. In *Brent* [1973] Crim.L.R. 295 it was said that that case does not apply to criminal proceedings because the prosecution has a duty to call all relevant evidence. **9–84**

Criminal Procedure Act 1865, s.3

How far witness may be discredited by the party producing

3. A party producing a witness shall not be allowed to impeach his credit by general evidence of bad character; but he may, in case the witness shall in the opinion of the judge prove adverse, contradict him by other evidence, or, by leave of the judge, prove that he has made at other times a statement inconsistent with his present testimony; but before such last-mentioned proof can be given the circumstances of the supposed statement, sufficient to designate the particular occasion, must be mentioned to the witness, and he must be asked whether or not he has made such statement. **9–85**

A hostile witness is much more than an unfavourable witness. Hostility is defined as an unwillingness to tell the truth of what happened and is determined by the court's considering the witness's demeanour and answers, if any. It is the court's determination and it is within the court's discretion to allow a party to cross-examine its own witness: *Booth* (1982) 74 Cr.App.R. 123, CA; *Rice v. Howard* (1886) 26 Q.B.D. 681; *Honeyghon and Sayles* [1999] Crim.L.R. 221, CA. The court should also consider allowing the witness to refresh his memory from a witness statement: *Maw* [1994] Crim.L.R. 841, CA. **9–86**

The court must have regard to what is likely to happen if the witness is confronted with a previous statement, and to the possibility of serious prejudice and lack of credibility if a damaging statement is elicited. Where a witness is cross-examined on his previous inconsistent statement, the statement does not become evidence of the facts stated in it: *Dibble*, 1 Cr.App.R. 155; *R. v. Norton and Driver (No. 1)* [1987] Crim.L.R. 687. When a hostile witness admits making an unsworn statement but later states on oath, that the contents are untrue, the statement should not be exhibited and the effect is to render the evidence of the witness negligible: *Harris* [1927] 2 K.B. 587; 20 Cr.App.R. 144. Where a hostile witness admits that he has been threatened and the earlier statement was in fact true the court, if it believes the witness, may take that evidence into account. **9–87**

A hostile defence witness may be cross-examined on a previous inconsistent statement: *Booth* (1982) 74 Cr.App.R. 123. A witness may be treated as hostile at any stage of his evidence, including re-examination: *Powell* [1985] Crim.L.R. 592, CA. **9–88**

VIII. CROSS EXAMINATION

A. GENERAL

A sworn witness is liable to be cross-examined by the other party or anyone else hav- **9–89** ing a legitimate interest: *Bingham and Cooke* [1999] 1 W.L.R. 598. It is not necessary for the witness to have been examined-in-chief before being cross-examined. Sometimes a witness may be tendered as a witness simply for the purpose of being cross-examined.

A defendant has the right to cross-examine a co-defendant regardless of whether or not the co-defendant has given evidence against the defendant: *Hadwen* [1902] 1 K.B. 882; *Paul* [1920] 2 K.B. 183; *Hilton* [1972] 1 Q.B. 421; *Murdoch v. Taylor* [1965] A.C. 574.

The Crown need not call a witness on whom the Crown did not rely, merely so that the defendant could put the defence case in cross-examination: *Bradish & Hall* [2004] EWCA Crim 1340.

B. FORM OF QUESTIONING

9–90   Cross-examination should be conducted with restraint and with the courtesy and consideration which a witness is entitled to expect in a court of law: *Mechanical and General Inventions Co Ltd v. Austin* [1935] A.C. 346. Questions should be framed to elicit answers as to matters of fact: see *Randall v. The Queen* [2002] 1 W.L.R. 2237. Leading questions may be used: *Parkin v. Moon* (1836) 7 C. & P. 409.

Cross-examination is not confined to the issues that were raised in evidence in chief, however, questions must relate either to the issues in the case or to the credibility of the witness: *Treacey* [1944] 2 All E.R. 229. Questions may also be asked to elicit how evidence has been obtained: *Att.-Gen.'s Reference (No. 5 of 2002)* [2004] UKHL 40. In that case, questions were allowed to investigate whether intercept material relied on by the Crown had been obtained by tapping a private as opposed to a public telecommunications system.

A witness may not be asked about inadmissible evidence: *Thompson* [1912] 3 K.B. 19; *Treacy (ante); Rice* [1963] 1 Q.B. 857. A defendant may, however, be cross-examined by a co-defendant as to the contents of an inadmissible statement made by the defendant if he or she gives evidence which is inconsistent with the statement: *Rowson* 80 Cr.App.R. 218; *Lui Mei Lin v. R.* [1989] 2 W.L.R. 175.

9–91   If a party intends to call evidence to contradict that given by the witness, the party should put his version of events to the witness in cross-examination so that the witness may explain the contradiction: *Brown v. Dunn* (1869) 6 R. 67; *Hart* 23 Cr.App.R. 202.

The court does not have to accept the evidence of a witness just because it has not been challenged: *O'Connell v. Adams* [1973] R.T.R. 150. This was confirmed in *R. (Wilkinson) v. DPP* (2003) 167 J.P. 229, QBD, where Burton J. stated that it is the professional obligation of an advocate acting for the defence to put to prosecution witnesses conflicts between the defence case and the evidence given by the prosecution witness in question in order to give the prosecution witness an opportunity to comment on what is put: whether it is the possibility of a mistake or whether the prosecution witness is lying, whether his recollection is incorrect, whether he has been confused or whatever. The position in relation to the defence case is somewhat different. By the time the defence comes to give evidence, the prosecution evidence has been given, the defence is aware of what evidence has been given and is able, therefore, in chief, to ask witnesses whether or not they agree with the prosecution evidence and to comment on it. It is nonetheless the professional duty of the advocate acting for the defence to make it clear what evidence is rejected or disputed.

9–92   The court should disallow questions which are irrelevant or vexatious and keep cross-examination to the points in issue: *Kalia* 60 Cr.App.R. 200; *Simmonds* [1969] 1 Q.B. 685; *Maynard* 69 Cr.App.R. 309. It is the duty of the legal adviser to assist an unrepresented defendant in putting succinct questions to witnesses. Where the offence is of a sexual nature and the defendant is unrepresented, the court is under a duty to protect the complainant from intimidation or abuse by the manner of the defendant's questioning: *Brown* [1998] 2 Cr.App.R. 364.

For restrictions on cross-examination of such witnesses, see *post*, § 9–95.

Where more than one defendant is being tried and each is defended by different legal representatives, the rule is that in the absence of agreement between the representatives the court will call upon them to cross-examine in the order in which the names of the defendants appear on the court list.

C. The Duty of Legal Representatives

The duties of counsel in conducting cross-examination are contained in the Code of **9–93** Conduct for the Bar of England and Wales, pronouncements made to the profession by or on behalf of the Bar Council and judicial statements.

In *O'Neill* 34 Cr.App.R. 105 Lord Goddard C.J. stated:

> "In this case a violent attack was made on the police. It was suggested that they had done improper things ...The applicants had the opportunity of going into the box at the trial and explaining and supporting what they had instructed their counsel to say. They did not dare go into the box and therefore counsel, who knew they were not going into the box, ought not to have made these suggestions against the police ... It is ... entirely wrong to make such suggestions as were made in this case, namely that the police beat the prisoners until they made confessions, and then, when there is the chance for the prisoners to substantiate what has been said by going into the box, for counsel not to call them ..."

This was endorsed in *Callaghan* (1979) 69 Cr.App.R. 88, CA. The effect of such **9–94** comments is that the defendant may be forced to relinquish the right to refuse to give evidence: see *ante*.

Where a client requires police evidence to be challenged in the manner considered in *O'Neill* and *Callaghan* but refuses to give evidence because of his bad record, it is an advocate's duty to warn his client that the court will probably view the failure to give evidence adversely.

D. Restrictions on Cross Examination

Generally, the defendant is entitled to cross-examine in person any witness called by **9–95** the prosecution. This rule is subject to the common law and statutory exceptions.

In *Brown (Milton)* [1998] 2 Cr.App.R. 364, the Court of Appeal stated that a trial is **9–96** not fair if an unrepresented defendant gains an advantage he would not have otherwise have had by abusing the rules in relation to relevance and repetition when cross-examining. While it was vital that the judge did his utmost to ensure that such a defendant received a fair trial and was seen by the jury to have done so, the judge was also under a duty to protect the interests of other parties to the proceedings, particularly witnesses who were required to describe a traumatic incident which was alleged to have occurred. In those circumstances, it was preferable for the judge to meet with the defendant in the jury's absence to discuss the nature of the evidence the defendant wished to elicit from the complainant and from any defence witnesses.

In the magistrates' courts the duty to elicit the nature of the evidence lies with the legal adviser.

Youth Justice and Criminal Evidence Act 1999, s.34

Complainants in proceedings for sexual offences

34. No person charged with a sexual offence may in any criminal proceedings cross— exam- **9–97** ine in person a witness who is the complainant, either—

    (a) in connection with that offence, or

    (b) in connection with any other offence (of whatever nature) with which that person is charged in the proceedings.

There is no power to appoint counsel to cross-examine on a defendant's behalf **9–98** where the defendant is prohibited under section 34(a): *Smith* [2004] EWCA Crim 2414.

Youth Justice and Criminal Evidence Act 1999, ss.35–38

Child complainants and other child witnesses

35.—(1) No person charged with an offence to which this section applies may in any criminal **9–99** proceedings cross-examine in person a protected witness, either—

(a) in connection with that offence, or

(b) in connection with any other offence (of whatever nature) with which that person is charged in the proceedings.

(2) For the purposes of subsection (1) a "protected witness" is a witness who—

(a) either is the complainant or is alleged to have been a witness to the commission of the offence to which this section applies, and

(b) either is a child or falls to be cross-examined after giving evidence in chief (whether wholly or in part)—

(i) by means of a video recording made (for the purposes of section 27) at a time when the witness was a child, or

(ii) in any other way at any such time.

(3) The offences to which this section applies are—

(a) any offence under—

(i) the *Sexual Offences Act* 1956,

(ii) the *Indecency with Children Act* 1960,

(iii) the *Sexual Offences Act* 1967,

(iv) section 54 of the *Criminal Law Act* 1977, or

(v) the *Protection of Children Act* 1978;

(b) kidnapping, false imprisonment or an offence under section 1 or 2 of the *Child Abduction Act* 1984;

(c) any offence under section 1 of the *Children and Young Persons Act* 1933;

(d) any offence (not within any of the preceding paragraphs) which involves an assault on, or injury or a threat of injury to, any person.

(4) In this section "child" means—

(a) where the offence falls within subsection (3)(a), a person under the age of 17; or

(b) where the offence falls within subsection (3)(b), (c) or (d), a person under the age of 14.

(5) For the purposes of this section "witness" includes a witness who is charged with an offence in the proceedings.

Direction prohibiting accused from cross-examining particular witness

9–100   **36.**—(1) This section applies where, in a case where neither of sections 34 and 35 operates to prevent an accused in any criminal proceedings from cross— examining a witness in person—

(a) the prosecutor makes an application for the court to give a direction under this section in relation to the witness, or

(b) the court of its own motion raises the issue whether such a direction should be given.

(2) If it appears to the court—

(a) that the quality of evidence given by the witness on cross-examination—

(i) is likely to be diminished if the cross-examination (or further cross-examination) is conducted by the accused in person, and

(ii) would be likely to be improved if a direction were given under this section, and

(b) that it would not be contrary to the interests of justice to give such a direction,

the court may give a direction prohibiting the accused from cross-examining (or further cross-examining) the witness in person.

(3) In determining whether subsection (2)(a) applies in the case of a witness the court must have regard, in particular, to—

(a) any views expressed by the witness as to whether or not the witness is content to be cross-examined by the accused in person;

(b) the nature of the questions likely to be asked, having regard to the issues in the proceedings and the defence case advanced so far (if any);

(c) any behaviour on the part of the accused at any stage of the proceedings, both generally and in relation to the witness;

(d) any relationship (of whatever nature) between the witness and the accused;

(e) whether any person (other than the accused) is or has at any time been charged in the proceedings with a sexual offence or an offence to which section 35 applies, and (if so) whether section 34 or 35 operates or would have operated to prevent that person from cross-examining the witness in person;

(f) any direction under section 19 which the court has given, or proposes to give, in relation to the witness.

(4) For the purposes of this section—

(a) "witness", in relation to an accused, does not include any other person who is charged with an offence in the proceedings; and

(b) any reference to the quality of a witness's evidence shall be construed in accordance with section 16(5).

Further provisions about directions under 36

37.—(1) Subject to subsection (2), a direction has binding effect from the time it is made until **9–101** the witness to whom it applies is discharged.

In this section "direction" means a direction under section 36.

(2) The court may discharge a direction if it appears to the court to be in the interests of justice to do so, and may do so either—

(a) on an application made by a party to the proceedings, if there has been a material change of circumstances since the relevant time, or

(b) of its own motion.

(3) In subsection (2) "the relevant time" means—

(a) the time when the direction was given, or

(b) if a previous application has been made under that subsection, the time when the application (or last application) was made.

(4) The court must state in open court its reasons for—

(a) giving, or

(b) refusing an application for, or for the discharge of, or

(c) discharging,

a direction and, if it is a magistrates' court, must cause them to be entered in the register of its proceedings.

(5) Rules of court may make provision—

(a) for uncontested applications to be determined by the court without a hearing;

(b) for preventing the renewal of an unsuccessful application for a direction except where there has been a material change of circumstances;

(c) for expert evidence to be given in connection with an application for, or for discharging, a direction;

(d) for the manner in which confidential or sensitive information is to be treated in connection with such an application and in particular as to its being disclosed to, or withheld from, a party to the proceedings.

An application by the prosecutor for the court to give a direction under section 36 **9–102** must be sent to the court and every other party to the proceedings stating why, in his opinion, the evidence given by the witness is likely to be diminished if cross-examination is undertaken by the accused in person and why the evidence would be improved if a direction were given; *Criminal Procedure Rules*, r.31.4 as amended by the *Criminal Procedure (Amendment) Rules* 2007.

Defence representation for purposes of cross-examination

38.—(1) This section applies where an accused is prevented from cross-examining a witness **9–103** in person by virtue of section 34, 35 or 36.

(2) Where it appears to the court that this section applies, it must—

(a) invite the accused to arrange for a legal representative to act for him for the purpose of cross-examining the witness; and

(b) require the accused to notify the court, by the end of such period as it may specify, whether a legal representative is to act for him for that purpose.

(3) If by the end of the period mentioned in subsection (2)(b) either—

(a) the accused has notified the court that no legal representative is to act for him for the purpose of cross-examining the witness, or

(b) no notification has been received by the court and it appears to the court that no legal representative is to so act, the court must consider whether it is necessary in the interests of justice for the witness to be cross-examined by a legal representative appointed to represent the interests of the accused.

(4) If the court decides that it is necessary in the interests of justice for the witness to be so cross-examined, the court must appoint a qualified legal representative (chosen by the court) to cross-examine the witness in the interests of the accused.

(5) A person so appointed shall not be responsible to the accused.

(6) Rules of court may make provision—

    (a) as to the time when, and the manner in which, subsection (2) is to be complied with;

    (b) in connection with the appointment of a legal representative under subsection (4), and in particular for securing that a person so appointed is provided with evidence or other material relating to the proceedings.

(7) Rules of court made in pursuance of subsection (6)(b) may make provision for the application, with such modifications as are specified in the rules, of any of the provisions of—

    (a) Part I of the *Criminal Procedure and Investigations Act* 1996 (disclosure of material in connection with criminal proceedings), or

    (b) the *Sexual Offences (Protected Material) Act* 1997.

(8) For the purposes of this section—

    (a) any reference to cross-examination includes (in a case where a direction is given under section 36 after the accused has begun cross-examining the witness) a reference to further cross-examination; and

    (b) "qualified legal representative" means a legal representative who has a right of audience (within the meaning of the *Courts and Legal Services Act* 1990) in relation to the proceedings before the court.

9–104   The court may direct, in particular cases, that a defendant may not cross-examine a child or a complainant in proceedings for a sexual offence. It may also prevent cross-examination in person of any other witness if the quality of the evidence is likely to be diminished in those circumstances and that it would be improved if a direction were given and it is in the interests of justice.

The court will invite the defendant to be represented for the purposes of cross-examination and, in the event that the defendant chooses not to be, will arrange representation for him.

Youth Justice and Criminal Evidence Act 1999, ss.41–43

Restriction on evidence or questions about complainant's sexual history

9–105   **41.**—(1) If at a trial a person is charged with a sexual offence, then, except with the leave of the court—

    (a) no evidence may be adduced, and

    (b) no question may be asked in cross-examination,

by or on behalf of any accused at the trial, about any sexual behaviour of the complainant.

(2) The court may give leave in relation to any evidence or question only on an application made by or on behalf of an accused, and may not give such leave unless it is satisfied—

    (a) that subsection (3) or (5) applies, and

    (b) that a refusal of leave might have the result of rendering unsafe a conclusion of the jury or (as the case may be) the court on any relevant issue in the case.

(3) This subsection applies if the evidence or question relates to a relevant issue in the case and either—

    (a) that issue is not an issue of consent; or

    (b) it is an issue of consent and the sexual behaviour of the complainant to which the evidence or question relates is alleged to have taken place at or about the same time as the event which is the subject matter of the charge against the accused; or

    (c) it is an issue of consent and the sexual behaviour of the complainant to which the evidence or question relates is alleged to have been, in any respect, so similar—

        (i) to any sexual behaviour of the complainant which (according to evidence adduced or to be adduced by or on behalf of the accused) took place as part of the event which is the subject matter of the charge against the accused, or

    (ii) to any other sexual behaviour of the complainant which (according to such evidence) took place at or about the same time as that event,

that the similarity cannot reasonably be explained as a coincidence.

(4) For the purposes of subsection (3) no evidence or question shall be regarded as relating to a relevant issue in the case if it appears to the court to be reasonable to assume that the purpose (or main purpose) for which it would be adduced or asked is to establish or elicit material for impugning the credibility of the complainant as a witness.

(5) This subsection applies if the evidence or question—

    (a) relates to any evidence adduced by the prosecution about any sexual behaviour of the complainant; and

    (b) in the opinion of the court, would go no further than is necessary to enable the evidence adduced by the prosecution to be rebutted or explained by or on behalf of the accused.

(6) For the purposes of subsections (3) and (5) the evidence or question must relate to a specific instance (or specific instances) of alleged sexual behaviour on the part of the complainant (and accordingly nothing in those subsections is capable of applying in relation to the evidence or question to the extent that it does not so relate).

(7) Where this section applies in relation to a trial by virtue of the fact that one or more of a number of persons charged in the proceedings is or are charged with a sexual offence—

    (a) it shall cease to apply in relation to the trial if the prosecutor decides not to proceed with the case against that person or those persons in respect of that charge; but

    (b) it shall not cease to do so in the event of that person or those persons pleading guilty to, or being convicted of, that charge.

(8) Nothing in this section authorises any evidence to be adduced or any question to be asked which cannot be adduced or asked apart from this section.

Interpretation and application of section 41

    42.—(1) In section 41—   **9–106**

    (a) "relevant issue in the case" means any issue falling to be proved by the prosecution or defence in the trial of the accused;

    (b) "issue of consent" means any issue whether the complainant in fact consented to the conduct constituting the offence with which the accused is charged (and accordingly does not include any issue as to the belief of the accused that the complainant so consented);

    (c) "sexual behaviour" means any sexual behaviour or other sexual experience, whether or not involving any accused or other person, but excluding (except in section 41(3)(c)(i) and (5)(a)) anything alleged to have taken place as part of the event which is the subject matter of the charge against the accused; and

    (d) subject to any order made under subsection (2), "sexual offence" shall be construed in accordance with section 62.

(2) The Secretary of State may by order make such provision as he considers appropriate for adding or removing, for the purposes of section 41, any offence to or from the offences which are sexual offences for the purposes of this Act by virtue of section 62.

(3) Section 41 applies in relation to the following proceedings as it applies to a trial, namely—

    (a) proceedings before a magistrates' court inquiring into an offence as examining justices,

    (b) the hearing of an application under paragraph 5(1) of Schedule 6 to the *Criminal Justice Act* 1991 (application to dismiss charge following notice of transfer of case to Crown Court),

    (c) the hearing of an application under paragraph 2(1) of Schedule 3 to the *Crime and Disorder Act* 1998 (application to dismiss charge by person sent for trial under section 51 of that Act),

    (d) any hearing held, between conviction and sentencing, for the purpose of determining matters relevant to the court's decision as to how the accused is to be dealt with, and

    (e) the hearing of an appeal,

and references (in section 41 or this section) to with an offence accordingly include a person convicted of an offence.

Procedure on applications under section 41

9–107   **43.**—(1) An application for leave shall be heard in private and in the absence of the complainant.

In this section "leave" means leave under section 41.

(2) Where such an application has been determined, the court must state in open court (but in the absence of the jury, if there is one)—

    (a) its reasons for giving, or refusing, leave, and

    (b) if it gives leave, the extent to which evidence may be adduced or questions asked in pursuance of the leave,

and, if it is a magistrates' court, must cause those matters to be entered in the register of its proceedings.

(3) Rules of court may make provision—

    (a) requiring applications for leave to specify, in relation to each item of evidence or question to which they relate, particulars of the grounds on which it is asserted that leave should be given by virtue of subsection (3) or (5) of section 41;

    (b) enabling the court to request a party to the proceedings to provide the court with information which it considers would assist it in determining an application for leave;

    (c) for the manner in which confidential or sensitive information is to be treated in connection with such an application, and in particular as to its being disclosed to, or withheld from, parties to the proceedings.

9–108   The purpose of section 41 is to protect complainants from being subjected to unnecessary and embarrassing cross-examination. It is aimed not at preserving the sexual reputation of a complainant but at protecting her from having to relive previous experiences and ordeals except for those permitted by a judge's ruling: *Abdelrahman* [2005] EWCA Crim 1367. Section 41(2) does not require the court to give leave, it merely gives the court a discretion to grant leave: *Mokrecovas* [2002] 1 Cr.App.R. 20, CA. Questions relating to a complainant's failure to complain about alleged sexual assaults or about telling lies about those matters are not automatically excluded: *B.T.* [2002] 1 Cr.App.R. 254.

An application will be heard "in camera" with the reasons for any ruling being given in open court and entered in the court's register.

The section itself has been held to be incompatible with ECHR in that it renders inadmissible evidence which might be relevant to the charge concerned. The court will have to decide whether the evidence and the questioning in relation to it is so relevant that to exclude it would endanger a fair trial: *A. (No. 2)* [2002] 1 A.C. 45. In that case, which concerned the issue of consent, Lord Hope gave examples of what might fall within section 41(3)(a):

— Honest belief in consent;

— Bias on the part of the complainant against the accused or a motive to fabricate the evidence;

— An alternative explanation for the physical conditions on which the prosecution relies;

— The detail of the complainant's account (especially where the complainant is young) must have come from other sexual activity which provides an explanation for knowledge of that activity.

9–109   In *R.T.; M.H.* [2002] 1 W.L.R. 632, CA it was held that, for the purposes of section 41, a distinction is to be drawn between questions about sexual behaviour itself and questions concerning statements about such behaviour by the complainant, even if the questions concerned the credibility of the complainant they were not automatically barred by section 41. Where the issue at trial is consent, a defendant is allowed to cross-examine the complainant on what she said to him at the time even if it reveals that she is a virgin: *Soroya* [2006] All E.R. (D) 151. At a trial of a defendant charged with sexual offences it is permitted to question the victim about her previous sexual behaviour but only if the principal purpose is to strengthen the defence case and not if it is merely to impugn the victim's credibility: *Martin* [2004] EWCA Crim 916; [2004] 2 Cr.App.R. 22. Once the criteria for the admissibility of evidence are established, all the evidence relevant to the issues can be adduced: *F.* [2005] EWCA Crim 493; [2005] 1 W.L.R. 2848. It was said that although section 41(4) prevents the deployment of evidence "relating to a relevant issue in the case" where the purpose is to impugn the credibility of the complainant, in one sense, any evidence which directly challenged the evidence of the complainant or sought to demonstrate a malicious motive, involved an attack on credibility. It did not necessarily follow that, merely because cross-examination might impugn credibility, that that was its main purpose. A court must be careful not to impose such significant limits on the examination of a critical issue that a defendant is deprived of worthwhile support for his defence.

Other restrictions

A witness may not be cross-examined if he has not been sworn and has been called **9–110** merely to produce a document: *Sumners v. Moseley* (1834) 2 Cr. & M. 477. A witness who is called by mistake where matters are not within his knowledge is not liable to be cross-examined, provided that the mistake is discovered after the witness has been sworn but before examination in chief: *Wood v. Mackinson* (1840) 2 Mood. & R. 273. A witness called by the court may only be cross-examined with leave of the court. Leave should be given if the witness's evidence has been adverse to either party: *Coulson v. Disborough* [1894] 2 Q.B. 316; *Cliburn* (1898) 62 J.P. 232.

E. PREVIOUS INCONSISTENT STATEMENTS

Criminal Procedure Act 1865, ss.4–5

As to proof of contradictory statements of adverse witness

4. If a witness, upon cross-examination as to a former statement made by him relative to the **9–111** subject matter of the indictment or proceeding, and inconsistent with his present testimony, does not distinctly admit that he has made such statement, proof may be given that he did in fact make it; but before such proof can be given the circumstances of the supposed statement, sufficient to designate the particular occasion, must be mentioned to the witness, and he must be asked whether or not he has made such statement.

Cross-examinations as to previous statements in writing

5. A witness may be cross-examined as to previous statements made by him in writing, or **9–112** reduced into writing, relative to the subject matter of the indictment or proceeding, without such writing being shown to him; but if it is intended to contradict such witness by the writing, his attention must, before such contradictory proof can be given, be called to those parts of the writing which are to be used for the purpose of so contradicting him:

Provided always, that it shall be competent for the judge, at any time during the trial, to require the production of the writing for his inspection, and he may thereupon make such use of it for the purposes of the trial as he may think fit.

A witness may, when giving evidence, make a statement which contradicts what the **9–113** witness has said before thus undermining the witness in a material particular or credibility. It usually happens in cross-examination. The inconsistency should be put to the witness so that he has a chance of stating which facts are true. If the witness denies the statement evidence may be called to show that he did make the statement.

In *Derby Magistrates' Court, ex p. B.* [1996] A.C. 487, HL, it was said that section 4 applies to written as well as oral statements.

Criminal Justice Act 2003, s.119

119.—(1) If in criminal proceedings a person gives oral evidence and— **9–114**
    (a) he admits making a previous inconsistent statement, or
    (b) a previous inconsistent statement made by him is proved by virtue of section 3, 4 or 5 of the *Criminal Procedure Act* 1865,

the statement is admissible as evidence of any matter stated of which oral evidence by him would be admissible.

(2) If in criminal proceedings evidence of an inconsistent statement by any person is given under section 124(2)(c), the statement is admissible as evidence of any matter stated in it of which oral evidence by that person would be admissible.

9–115   Where a witness does not come up to proof a party may seek to introduce a previous statement as evidence. This is more likely to be done by the prosecution when trying to prove particular facts especially in domestic violence cases.

9–116   It is for the court to determine whether the statement relates to the subject matter of the proceedings: *Bashir* (1970) 54 Cr.App.R. 1.

In *Clarke and Hewins* [1999] *Archbold News* 2, CA, it was stated that when a witness is cross-examined on a previous statement, the questioning should be selective and done with precision; it is inappropriate to read long extracts from the statement and then merely to ask one or two short questions; such a method lengthens the proceedings, makes cross-examination difficult to follow and creates the risk that the witness's evidence will become confused with what was said on the previous occasion. The statement need not be shown to the witness but it must be available in court even if the advocate does not intend to use it: *Anderson* 21 Cr.App.R. 178. The witness's answers may not be contradicted by putting the document in evidence unless the witness has been shown the document and has been given the opportunity of explaining its contents.

9–117   A previous inconsistent statement may now prove the truth of what is stated i.e. what a witness has said earlier and what he says on oath are both capable of providing evidence of the truth of what happened. The court must evaluate the evidence: *Joyce* [2005] EWCA Crim 1785; see also *Read* [2005] EWCA Crim 3292. See *post*, § 10–78.

F. CROSS EXAMINATION AS TO CREDIBILITY

9–118   The credibility of a witness depends on: (a) his knowledge of the facts to which he testifies; (b) independence; (c) integrity; (d) veracity; and (e) being bound to speak the truth either on oath or by affirmation. Questions may be put to a witness in relation to any improper conduct of which he may be guilty in order to show that the witness should not be believed: *Edwards* 93 Cr.App.R. 48.

A witness can be compelled to answer questions about his credibility: *Cundell v. Pratt* (1827) M. & M. 108. The court has a discretion to direct that a witness should not answer where the court is of the opinion that an answer verifying the truth of the matter suggested would not in fact affect the credibility of the witness: *Sweet-Escott* 55 Cr.App.R. 316. In *Malik* [2000] 2 Cr.App.R. 8, CA, cross-examination of a police officer whose evidence in a previous case had been disbelieved resulting in an acquittal was allowed even though the misconduct alleged was of a different nature from that alleged in the earlier case. Cross-examination has been allowed as to credibility on a pre trial letter between a defendant's solicitors and CPS stating the defendant's willingness to plead guilty to a lesser offence: *Hayes* [2004] EWCA Crim 2844; [2005] 1 Cr.App.R. 33.

A witness may not be asked to draw an inference of fact which is discreditable to him: *Bernard* (1858) 1 F. & F. 240. A witness may not be asked questions about his religious beliefs for the purposes of discrediting him: *Darby v. Ouseley* (1856) 1 H. & N. 1.

9–119   Where particular allegations of misconduct are put to a witness, it is not open to the party calling the witness to call evidence of the good character of the witness for the purpose of rebutting the allegations. The character of the witness not being itself in issue, such evidence is excluded on the grounds of being collateral: *Hamilton, The Times*, July 25, 1998; *Beard* [1998] Crim.L.R. 585, CA.

Witnesses may be called to speak about a witness's general character, although not in relation to any particular offence of which he may be guilty: *Watson* (1817) 32 St. Tr. 1. Evidence is not admissible to contradict answers given on cross-examination as to credit: *Mendy* 64 Cr.App.R. 4, CA. The following instances are, however, exceptions and the list is not closed.

Bias

Facts showing that a witness is biased in relation to the party calling him may be **9–120** elicited in cross-examination and, if denied, independently proved. *Att.-Gen v. Hitchcock* (1847) 1 Ex. 91; *Denley* [1970] Crim.L.R. 583; *Phillips* 26 Cr.App.R. 17; *Mendy* 64 Cr.App.R. 4.

In *Busby* 75 Cr.App.R. 79, police officers were cross-examined to the effect that they had fabricated statements attributed to the defendant and indicative of his guilt and had threatened a potential defence witness to stop him from giving evidence. The judge ruled that the defence could not call that potential witness to give evidence that he had been threatened by the police officers because it would go solely to their credibility. The Court of Appeal held that the judge had been incorrect because, if the allegations were true, it showed that the police were prepared to go to improper lengths to secure a conviction, which would have supported the defence case that the statements attributed to the defendant had been fabricated.

In *Funderburk* 90 Cr.App.R. 466; [1990] 1 W.L.R. 587 it was said that the decision in *Busby* provided an exception to the general rule. In *Edwards* [1991] 1 W.L.R. 207, however, it was said that *Busby* related to the question of bias. Cross-examination is permissible to show that a witness was biased.

Medical issues

It is admissible to show that a witness suffers from a disease, defect or abnormality of **9–121** mind which affects the reliability of his evidence: *Toohey v. Metropolitan Police Commissioner* [1965] A.C. 595, HL.

Evidence is not admissible to contradict answers given by a witness to questions put in cross-examination which concern collateral matters, *i.e.* matters which go to credit but not the facts in issue: *Palmer v. Trower* (1852) 8 Exch 247.

G. CROSS EXAMINATION OF THE DEFENDANT

Criminal Evidence Act 1898, s.1

Competency of witnesses in criminal cases

1.—(1) A person charged in criminal proceedings shall not be called as a witness in the **9–122** proceedings except upon his own application.

(2) A person charged in criminal proceedings who is called as a witness in the proceedings may be asked any question in cross-examination notwithstanding that it would tend to criminate him as to any offence with which he is charged in the proceedings.

(3) A person charged in criminal proceedings who is called as a witness in the proceedings shall not be asked, and if asked shall not be required to answer, any question tending to show that he has committed or been convicted of or been charged with any offence other than one with which he is then charged, or is of bad character, unless—

    (i)　the proof that he has committed or been convicted of such other offence is admissible evidence to show that he is guilty of an offence with which he is then charged; or

    (ii)　he has personally or by his advocate asked questions of the witnesses for the prosecution with a view to establish his own good character, or has given evidence of his good character, or the nature or conduct of the defence is such as to involve imputations on the character of the prosecutor or the witnesses for the prosecution, or the deceased victim of the alleged crime; or

    (iii)　he has given evidence against any other person charged in the same proceedings.

(4) Every person charged in criminal proceedings who is called as a witness in the proceedings shall, unless otherwise ordered by the court, give his evidence from the witness box or other place from which the other witnesses give their evidence.

[This section is reprinted as amended by the *Youth Justice and Criminal Evidence Act* 1999, Sched. 4, para. 1.]

9–123   If the defendant admits his guilt in the witness box, the prosecution is still entitled to elicit evidence which incriminates co-defendants: *Paul and McFarlane* [1920] 2 K.B. 193; *O'Neill* [1969] Crim.L.R. 260, CA.

9–124   See *post*, §§ 10–127.

H. Re-examination

9–125   After cross-examination a witness may be re-examined by the party who called him. Unless the court gives leave, questions in re-examination are confined to matters arising out of cross-examination.

It is unclear whether a hostile witness may be re-examined after cross-examination: *Booth, ante*; *Wong* [1986] Crim.L.R. 683. In the latter case the prosecution was allowed to treat a witness as hostile and to examine him on previous inconsistent statements and following cross-examination by the defence, was allowed to re-examine the witness but only upon completely and genuinely new matters which had arisen from defence cross-examination where those matters were defined beforehand.

A witness may be treated as hostile during re-examination when he has shown hostility to the party calling him during cross-examination: *Powell* [1985] Crim.L.R. 592. In *Norton and Driver* [1987] Crim.L.R. 687 a prosecution witness said that he could not remember incidents relating to the offence charged, however, during cross-examination he gave evidence exculpating the defendants. The prosecution was permitted to treat him as hostile during re-examination.

IX. RECALL OF A WITNESS

9–126   Once a party has closed his case, further evidence other than rebuttal evidence may not be called: *Criminal Procedure Rules* 2005, r.37, see Appendix G–161. The court has a discretion to re-open a case at any time before final adjudication and this is not confined to technicalities. As a general rule and in the absence of special circumstances, magistrates should not allow evidence to be called once they have retired: *Webb v. Leadbetter* [1996] 2 All E.R. 114. In *MacDonald v. Skelt* [1985] R.T.R. 321 it had been argued that there was no case to answer as there was insufficient evidence to show that the blood specimen taken from the defendant and then analysed by the scientific officer were one and the same. The magistrates allowed the prosecutor to re-open its case and this was upheld. In that case it was said to be relevant that the defence had not taken any point about the sample during the prosecution evidence. The court should look carefully at the interests of justice and the risk of any prejudice to the defendant: *Jolly v. DPP* [2000] Crim.L.R. 471; *Cook v. DPP* [2001] Crim.L.R. 321. In *Malcolm v. DPP* (*ante*) it was said that what are special circumstances justifying permitting the prosecution to re-open its case varies from time to time. Courts must take the overall objective of criminal procedure in the *Criminal Procedure Rules* 2005, r.1.1 into account. The magistrates were upheld in allowing evidence to be called after they had retired and had partially announced their decision.

X. ILLNESS OR DEATH OF A WITNESS

9–127   If a witness becomes incapable of giving further evidence the court may allow the trial to continue on the basis of the evidence already given: *Stretton* 86 Cr.App.R. 7, CA. The evidence of such a witness remains admissible although little weight may attach to it: *Doolin* 1 Jebb CC 123. For statements see *post*, § 10–72.

XI. THE POWER OF THE COURT TO CALL WITNESSES

9–128   The court has a residuary discretion to call witnesses where either party has not called them. The discretion should be exercised sparingly and in the interests of justice and fairness: *Grafton* [1992] 3 W.L.R. 532.

This discretion may not usually be exercised after the defence has closed its case, nor after the magistrates have retired to deliberate: *Webb v. Leadbetter* [1966] 1 W.L.R. 245. Once the justices have retired to consider their verdict further evidence should only be called in exceptional circumstances: *French Dairies (Sevenoaks) Ltd v. Davis* [1973] Crim.L.R. 630; *Phelan v. Back* (1972) 56 Cr.App.R. 257.

In *Haringey Justices, exp. DPP* [1996] 2 W.L.R. 114, the defendant was charged with threatening behaviour and assaulting a police officer following an attack on two officers. One police officer was subsequently suspended following accusations concerning his honesty on an unrelated matter. The CPS, in accordance with its policy of not calling suspended officers if it could be avoided, gave notice that it would not be calling the suspended officer, and refused the defendant's request to tender him for cross examination. The justices dismissed the case on the grounds that it was an abuse of process, and the CPS sought judicial review of that decision. The application was granted on the basis that the prosecution has an unfettered discretion as to which witnesses to call. Where there were special reasons for not calling an important witness these should be disclosed to the defence and where the prosecution chose not to call a witness whose evidence was central to the case, and the justices were satisfied that the interests of justice required he be called, they should so rule. If the prosecution refused to call the witness the justices could do so.

It is highly undesirable for a judge or magistrate to cross-examine an unrepresented defendant in such a way as to appear to be siding with the prosecution: *Jahree v. State of Mauritius* [2005] 1 W.L.R. 1952; *The Times*, March 3, 2005.

The court's permission is required before the prosecution or defence may question a **9–129** witness called by the court.

The court has the power to recall a witness at any stage of the trial to put such questions as may be required in the interests of justice: *Sullivan* [1923] 1 K.B. 47.

The court may also question witnesses during the course of their examination by counsel, however, it should not actively interfere with counsel's examination: *Leggatt* [1970] 1 Q.B. 67; *Hulusi and Purvis* (1974) 58 Cr.App.R. 378. Questions should be for clarification purposes only.

XII. EXHIBITS

Where a witness produces an exhibit, the court will list the exhibit and identify it by **9–130** name and number, *e.g.* where Ann Smith produces an exhibit it becomes AS1.

At the conclusion of the case, the exhibits are generally not retained by the court but are returned to the producing party who then signs for them. The court may retain documentary exhibits.

XIII. WITNESS COACHING

Witness training for criminal trials is prohibited. That does not, however, preclude **9–131** pre-trial familiarisation which does not involve discussions about proposed or intended evidence: *Momodou* [2005] EWCA Crim 177; [2005] 2 All E.R. 571.

EVIDENCE

I. INTRODUCTION

Evidence is what the court will hear to determine the facts in issue. It may comprise **10–1** the testimony of witnesses either oral or by statement, documents, real evidence, *i.e.* exhibits and admissions. It may be direct evidence, *i.e.* what the witness saw or heard or it may be indirect in the form of hearsay (what the witness heard from someone else) or in the form of evidence of surrounding circumstances from which inferences may be drawn. The rules of evidence provide a framework for deciding whether evidence is admissible or not.

The role of the judiciary in magistrates' courts

In magistrates' courts, the judiciary decides both law and fact and will, therefore, **10–2** determine the admissibility of evidence. On questions of law, including the law of evidence, it is accepted that magistrates should accept the advice of the legal adviser. District judges (magistrates' courts) may also seek the advice of the legal adviser. Where the court decides that evidence is inadmissible it will put that evidence out of its mind when determining the facts in issue.

The judiciary should keep interventions to a minimum but may clarify evidence if an answer is ambiguous or inaudible and to curb repetition and irrelevance.

Facts in issue

10–3   The facts in issue are: (a) the facts which the prosecution bears the burden of proving or disproving in order to establish the guilt of the defendant; and (b) the facts which the defendant bears the burden of proving in order to succeed in his defence. Where the defendant has pleaded not guilty then "everything is in issue and the prosecution has to prove the whole of its case, including the identity of the accused, the nature of the act and the existence of any necessary knowledge or intent": *Sims* [1946] K.B. 531 at 539.

Relevance

10–4   Evidence is admissible only where it is relevant and this depends on the individual circumstances of each particular case. Evidence is relevant if it is logically probative of a matter which must be proved: *DPP v. Kilbourne* [1973] 1 All E.R. 440. It is also admissible if it relates to circumstantial facts which if proved make the facts in issue probable or not. In *Guney* [1998] 2 Cr.App.R.242, evidence that a large sum of cash was found in the same place as guns and drugs was held to be relevant in a case of possession of drugs with intent to supply. Where the offence is one of strict liability, evidence of motive, intention or knowledge is irrelevant and therefore inadmissible: *Sandhu* [1997] Crim.L.R. 288; *Byrne* [2002] 2 Cr.App.R. 311. In *Nethercott* [2002] 2 Cr.App.R. 7 the defence was that the defendant had acted under duress as a result of threats made by his co-defendant. Evidence of the fact that the co-defendant had subsequently attacked him with a knife was relevant to the defence because it made it more likely that the defendant, at the time of the offence, had genuinely feared for his safety.

Evidence relating to incidents outside the six-month limit contained in the *Magistrates' Courts Act* 1980, s.127 is admissible: *DPP v. Baker* [2004] EWHC 2782.

Formal admissions

10–5   Section 10 of the *Criminal Justice Act* 1967 provides for a party to admit certain facts and that formal admission becomes conclusive evidence of those facts.

Evidence of an acquittal could be admissible in a later trial where the acquittal is arguably attributable to some aspect of the evidence which is common to both trials or otherwise relevant to an issue in the later trial. This can be distinguished from the rule against double jeopardy: *Colman* [2004] EWCA Crim 3252.

II. BURDEN AND STANDARD OF PROOF

10–6   In criminal trials the legal burden of proving the guilt of the defendant is on the prosecution and remains so throughout the trial: *Woolmington v. DPP* [1935] A.C. 462; *Hunt* [1987] A.C. 352. The standard of proof is that of beyond reasonable doubt: *Ewing* 77 Cr.App.R. 47, CA. This does not mean proof beyond a shadow of a doubt. It is less than absolute certainty. In *Walters v. R.* [1969] 2 A.C. 26 at 30 the words referring to a jury "satisfied so they are sure" were approved.

On a breach of community order the prosecution is obliged to prove each element to the criminal standard including that the defendant is the person named in the order breached; an inference may be drawn from the court's having the name and address and the fact that the name is slightly unusual unless there is evidence to the contrary: *West Yorkshire Probation Board v. Boulter* [2005] EWHC 2342; [2006] 1 W.L.R. 232.

Where there is evidence available to satisfy a fact finder to the criminal standard of proof there is no set evidential procedure that requires the fact finder to give any weight to speculative possibilities as to how the offence might have occurred and such speculative possibilities can be safely dismissed weight of evidence: *Cox v. DPP*, unreported, October 25, 2005 (WL 2706862).

In *Edwards* [1975] Q.B. 27 the Court of Appeal held that there was an exception to the fundamental rule that the prosecution must prove every element of the offence charged. The exception was "limited to offences arising under enactments which prohibit the doing of an act save in specified circumstances or by persons of specified classes or with specified qualifications or with the licence or permission of specified authorities". The court rejected the view that only the evidential burden and not the legal burden shifted to the defendant. In that particular case, the onus was on the defendant to show that he had a licence when charged with the offence of selling liquor without a licence.

The legal burden lies on the defendant only where the defence is one of insanity and in the case of statutory exceptions: *Bratty v.Attorney General of Northern Ireland* [1963] A.C. 386. In those situations the standard of proof is on the balance of probabilities: *Carr-Briant* [1943] K.B. 607; 29 Cr.App.R. 76; *Islington London Borough v. Panico* [1973] 3 All E.R. 483. This means more probable than not.

Magistrates' Courts Act 1980, s.101

Onus of proving exceptions, etc

101. Where the defendant to an information or complaint relies for his defence on any **10–7** exception, exemption, proviso, excuse or qualification, whether or not it accompanies the description of the offence or matter of complaint in the enactment creating the offence or on which the complaint is founded, the burden of proving the exception, exemption, proviso, excuse or qualification shall be on him; and this notwithstanding that the information or complaint contains an allegation negativing the exception, exemption, proviso, excuse or qualification.

In the case of driving without a licence, *e.g.* it is for the driver to prove that he has a **10–8** current driving licence: *John v. Humphreys* [1955] 1 W.L.R. 325. The same applies to driving without insurance: *Williams v. Russell* (1933) 149 L.T. 190; *Philcox v. Carberry* [1960] Crim.L.R. 563.

In *Gatland v. Metropolitan Police Commissioner* [1968] 2 Q.B. 279, the defendant had been charged with leaving a skip on a road contrary to the *Highways Act* 1959, which provided that "if a person, without lawful authority or excuse, deposits anything whatsoever on a highway ... that person shall be guilty of an offence". It was held that the prosecution had to prove that the skip had been deposited on the highway but that the defendant had to prove lawful authority or excuse.

The House of Lords considered *Edwards* in *Hunt, ante*. It held that there is no rule **10–9** of law that the burden of proving a statutory defence lies on the defendant only where the statute specifically so provides. Such exceptions might be express or implied. The exception might be in the same clause that created the offence or in a subsequent proviso and that where a linguistic construction of the legislation did not indicate clearly on whom the burden of proof should be, the court might look to other considerations to determine the intention of Parliament. Each case turns on its own construction of the particular legislation, but a court should be slow to infer that Parliament intended to impose an onerous duty on the defendant to prove his innocence in a criminal case. In that case it was held that it was for the prosecution to prove that the compound in the defendant's possession contained morphine contrary to the *Misuse of Drugs Act* 1971. The defendant would have had difficulty in proving that there was either no morphine or that the level was within the permissible level as he had no ready access to scientific facilities for analysis.

The duty of a party to adduce sufficient evidence either by calling evidence or by cross-examination to put a matter in issue is called the evidential burden. This arises in cases of alibi, duress, provocation and self defence.

Article 6(2) of the European Convention on Human Rights (*ante*) does not prohibit **10–10** rules which transfer an evidential burden provided the overall burden of proving guilt remains with the prosecution: *Lingens v. Austria; Leitgens v. Austria* (1982) 4 E.H.R.R. 373 at para. 4; *Barbera, Messegue and Jabardo v. Spain* (1988) 11 E.H.R.R. 360; *Salabiaku v. France* (1988) 13 E.H.R.R. 379.

In *R. v. DPP, ex p. Kebilene* [2000] 2 A.C. 326, HL the court advised that in order to establish whether a statutory reverse burden provision is vulnerable to challenge under Article 6(2) it is necessary to determine its nature and whether it is an evidential burden requiring a defendant to adduce sufficient evidence to raise an issue or whether it is a persuasive burden requiring him to prove a fact essential to his guilt or innocence. A mandatory presumption of guilt would not necessarily be incompatible so long as it was confined within reasonable limits. In order to decide reasonableness in that context three questions should be asked:

1. What does the prosecution have to prove in order to transfer the onus to the defence?

2. Does the burden on the defendant relate to something which is likely to be difficult for him to prove or is it within his knowledge or to which he has ready access?

3. What is the nature of the threat faced by society which the provision is designed to combat?

10–11   In *Lambert* [2001] 3 W.L.R. 206 the House of Lords applied these principles to section 28(2) and (3) of the *Misuse of Drugs Act* 1971 which created "knowledge" defences to charges of possession. It was decided that the provisions could be read as imposing an evidential burden only. In this particular case, once the defendant raised the issue of knowledge, it was for the prosecution to prove the requisite knowledge beyond reasonable doubt.

In *R. (Grundy & Co Excavations Ltd) v. Halton Division Magistrates' Court* [2003] EWHC 272; 167 J.P. 387, it was held that, as the offence of felling trees without a licence under the *Forestry Act* 1967, was an absolute one and the onus of proving an exception, *i.e.* that a licence was either in existence or was unnecessary was on the defence, this derogated from the presumption of innocence in Article 6(2) but was justified as necessary and proportionate.

In *Johnstone* [2003] 1 W.L.R. 1736, an offence under the *Trade Marks Act* 1994, the legal burden was said to have passed to the defendant. Lord Nicholls stated that:

> "The extent and nature of the factual matters required to be proved by the accused, and their importance relative to the matters required to be proved by the prosecution, have to be taken into account. So also does the extent to which the burden on the accused relates to facts which, if they exist, are readily provable by him as matters within his own knowledge or to which he has ready access."

Again in *DPP v. Barker* [2004] EWHC 2502, a charge of driving whilst disqualified, it was said that where a defendant relies on the exemption in section 37(3) of the *Road Traffic Act* 1988 the burden is on the driver to show not only that he had been driving but also that he had a provisional licence and had complied with its conditions.

In *Att.-Gen.'s Reference (No. 4 of 2002); Sheldrake v. DPP* [2005] 1 A.C. 264 the House of Lords decided that the justifiability and fairness of provisions which imposed a burden of proof on a defendant in a criminal trial have to be judged in the particular context of each cases. In this case it was held that section 5(2) of the *Road Traffic Act* 1988 imposed a legal burden on the defendant to prove that there was no likelihood of his driving a vehicle while over the prescribed limit of alcohol and that this was not unreasonable as this was a matter which was so closely conditioned by his own knowledge and state of mind at the time as to make it more appropriate for him to prove on the balance of probabilities. The provisions of section 11(2) of the *Terrorism Act* 2000, however, were read down so as to impose an evidential burden as a legal burden, although clearly intended by Parliament, was not a proportionate and justifiable response to the activities threatened by a banned organisation.

The reasons given for this conclusion were that: (1) since an innocent person might fall within section 11(1) there would be a clear breach of the presumption of innocence and a real risk of unfair conviction. A defendant who tried and failed to establish a defence might be convicted on the basis of conduct which was non-criminal at the date of commission; (2) it might be impossible for a defendant to show that he had not taken part in the organisation's activities at any time while it was proscribed—there would be no records or documents he could produce and others were unlikely to testify on his behalf; (3) the subsection provides no flexibility and no room to exercise a discretion and if the defendant could not prove the matters in section 11(2) the court would have no choice but to convict; (4) the potential consequences for a defendant of failing to establish a defence were severe; (5) while security considerations had always to carry weight, they did not absolve member states from their duty to ensure that basic standards were observed; and (6) little significance could be attached to the requirement that the DPP had to give his consent to a prosecution.

Subsequently it has been held that the burden of proof on the defendant under section 2 of the *Asylum and Immigration (Treatment of Claimants etc) Act* 2004 is a legal burden on the balance of probabilities and compatible with ECHR as the defendant is likely to have the information required: *Navabi* [2005] EWCA Crim 2865. It has also been held that where a defendant seeks to rely on the statutory defence under section 31(1) of the *Immigration and Asylum Act* 1999 the evidential burden on proving refugee status is on the defendant whereas so far as the other matters in section 31(1) were concerned the legal burden is on the defendant on a balance of probabilities: *Makuwa* [2006] EWCA Crim 175; [2006] 2 Cr.App.R. 11. **10–12**

Whatever may be the justification for reverse burdens, a court will not assume a reverse burden unless it is driven by the clear words of a statute to that conclusion. Parliament must make it plain. Where section 444(1A) of the *Education Act* 1996 simply provides that the offence is created if the parent knows that his child is failing to attend regularly and fails without reasonable justification to cause him to do so, an evidential burden is created by that provision. If there is a failure to attend and if no material is laid before the court which could support a case that there was a reasonable justification, the court would be bound to convict; but once material is put before the court which could constitute a reasonable justification, then the court must consider it and may only convict if it is satisfied to the criminal standard that there was no reasonable justification. Reasonable justification does not mean that all possible avenues for ensuring regular schooling have been pursued. Reasonable justification relates to the failure to attend: *R. (P.) v. Liverpool City Magistrates' Court* [2006] EWHC 887, Admin; [2006] A.C.D. 73.

Where a defendant is charged with acquisition and possession of criminal property under section 329(a) and (c) of the *Proceeds of Crime Act* 2002 and raises the defence of having provided adequate payment for it there is an evidential burden on the defendant. It is then for the prosecution to prove that there is either no or inadequate consideration: *Hogan v. DPP (theft of scaffolding)*, *The Times*, February 28, 2007. In *Keogh* [2007] EWCA Crim 528 it was held that the reverse burden contained in the *Official Secrets Act* 1989, ss.2(3) and 3(4) was incompatible with the *Human Rights Act* as the *Official Secrets Act* could operate effectively without it.

There is no burden on the defence to show inconsistencies between two sets of photographs taken a few years apart and produced to the court to establish identification: *Zardad* [2007] EWCA Crim 279.

Where an application for bail is made during the currency of a custody time limit, section 25 of the *Criminal Justice and Public Order Act* 1994 should be read as placing a burden on the defendant. He has to rebut a presumption and if he fails he must be denied bail; section 25 must be construed as a guide to the proper operation of the *Bail Act* 1976. It operates to disapply the ordinary requirement that bail must be granted automatically to anyone whose custody time limit has expired: *R. (O.) v. Harrow Crown Court; Re O.* [2006] UKHL 42; [2006] 3 All E.R. 1157.

III. PRESUMPTIONS

10–13   A court may be required to make assumptions and those may relate to law or fact.

A. PRESUMPTIONS OF FACT

10–14   These are inferences which the court may or may not draw from the facts which are established, *e.g.* that a person is alive on a given day may be presumed from proof of his or her being alive on an antecedent day. If that fact is in issue, however, evidence will have to be called and the matter decided by the court

Other facts may be presumed from circumstantial evidence. So, for example where a defendant charged with handling stolen goods is found to be in possession of those goods without any explanation, this circumstantial evidence may give rise to a provisional conclusion that the defendant is the handler of those goods.

Lord Normand in *Teper v. R.* [1952] A.C. 480 at 489, PC, stated in relation to circumstantial evidence that:

> "It must always be narrowly examined, if only because evidence of this kind may be fabricated to cast suspicion on another.... It is also necessary before drawing the inference of the accused's guilt from circumstantial evidence to be sure that there are no other co-existing circumstances which would weaken or destroy the inference."

On the other hand it has been said that circumstantial evidence is often the best evidence. It is no derogation of evidence to say that it is circumstantial: *Taylor, Weaver and Donovan* 21 Cr.App.R. 20, CCA.

B. PRESUMPTIONS OF LAW

10–15   Presumptions of law may be rebuttable or irrebutable. Some presumptions do not depend upon proof of a basic fact, for example, the presumptions of innocence and sanity. Others depend upon proof of a basic fact

A presumption would be irrebuttable where on the proof or admission of a basic or primary fact, another fact could not be rebutted, *e.g.* if a court were satisfied that a child appearing before it were nine years of age then, under section 50 of the *Children and Young Persons Act* 1933, "it shall be conclusively presumed that no child under the age of 10 years can be guilty of an offence". See *Walters v. Lunt* [1951] 2 All E.R. 645.

Most presumptions of law, however, are rebuttable, *i.e.* evidence can be brought to show that the presumption is incorrect. If the defence relies on a rebuttable presumption, the prosecution must prove the presumed fact beyond reasonable doubt. If the prosecution relies on a rebuttable presumption, an evidential burden is placed on the defence to adduce evidence which might create a reasonable doubt. The prosecution is still required to prove the disputed fact beyond reasonable doubt: *Kay* (1887) 16 Cox C.C. 292.

10–16   It can be presumed that a police officer has been lawfully appointed: *Gordon* (1789) 1 Leach 515, that a solicitor has been admitted; *Berryman v. Wise* (1791) 4 Term. Rep. 366, that a limited company has been incorporated: *Langton* (1876) 2 Q.B.D. 296, or that a police officer requiring a breath test was in uniform: *Gage v. Jones* [1983] R.T.R. 508. A document can be presumed to have been made on the date it bears, and a signed deed to have been sealed and delivered: *Hall v. Bainbridge and Enderby* [1848] 12 Q.B. 699 (although a deed no longer needs to be sealed). Evidence of a ceremony of marriage presumes a valid marriage: *Mahadervan v. Mahadervan* [1964] P. 233. The procedure laid down for the preparation of kits used in the taking of blood samples from motorists stopped on suspicion of excess alcohol can be presumed to have been carried out correctly unless there is something in the matter before the court to suggest the contrary: *Carter v. DPP* [2006] EWHC 3328.

Presumptions of law must be drawn unless rebutted: presumptions of fact may be drawn. When presumptions conflict they cancel each other out and the issue is decided without reference to the presumptions: *Willshire* (1881) 6 Q.B.D. 366.

IV. DOCUMENTARY EVIDENCE

A. GENERAL

Statements contained in documents are subject to the general rules of the admissibil- **10–17** ity of evidence, particularly those relating to hearsay, opinion and privilege. Two issues arise: (a) how may the document be proved, and (b) what use may be made of its contents. It is only in relation to the second issue that the rule of hearsay arises. In that case the purpose for which the document is tendered must be identified; see *post*, § 10–75.

B. PUBLIC DOCUMENTS

Generally it is unnecessary to produce the original of any document made by a pub- **10–18** lic officer. Special provisions are made for the production of public documents such as Acts of Parliament, byelaws, judgments, treaties, previous convictions, court registers, marriage or death certificates etc. These can be regarded as exceptions to the hearsay rule and can prove the facts stated therein: *Sturla v. Freccia* (1880) 5 App. Cas. 623, HL; *Wilton & Co v. Phillips* [1903] T.L.R. 390.

Evidence Act 1845, ss.1, 3

Certain documents to be received in evidence without proof of seal or signature, &c. of person signing the same

1. Whenever by any Act now in force or hereafter to be in force any certificate, official or pub- **10–19** lic document, or document or proceeding of any corporation or joint stock or other company, or any certified copy of any document, bye law, entry in any register or other book, or of any other proceeding, shall be receivable in evidence of any particular in any court of justice, or before any legal tribunal, or either House of Parliament, or any committee of either House, or in any judicial proceeding, the same shall respectively be admitted in evidence, provided they respectively purport to be sealed or impressed with a stamp or sealed and signed, or signed alone, as required, or impressed with a stamp and signed, as directed by the respective Acts made or to be hereafter made, without any proof of the seal or stamp, where a seal or stamp is necessary, or of the signature or of the official character of the person appearing to have signed the same, and without any further proof thereof, in every case in which the original record could have been received in evidence.

Copies of private Acts, printed by Queen's printer, journals of Parliament, and proclamations, admissible as evidence

3. All copies of private and local and personal Acts of Parliament not public Acts, if purport- **10–20** ing to be printed by the Queen's printers, and all copies of the journals of either House of Parliament, and of royal proclamations, purporting to be printed by the printers to the crown or by the printers to either House of Parliament, or by any or either of them, shall be admitted as evidence thereof by all courts, judges, justices, and others without any proof being given that such copies were so printed.

Documentary Evidence Act 1882, s.2

Documents printed under superintendence of Stationery Office receivable in evidence

2. Where any enactment, whether passed before or after the passing of this Act, provides that **10–21** a copy of any Act of Parliament, proclamation, order, regulation, rule, warrant, circular, list, gazette, or document shall be conclusive evidence, or be evidence, or have any other effect, when purporting to be printed by the Government Printer, or the Queen's Printer, or a printer authorised by Her Majesty, or otherwise under Her Majesty's authority, whatever may be the precise expression used, such copy shall also be conclusive evidence, or evidence, or have the said effect (as the case may be) if it purports to be printed under the superintendence or authority of Her Majesty's Stationery Office.

Documentary Evidence Act 1868, ss.2, 3, 5 and 6

Mode of proving certain documents

2. Prima facie evidence of any proclamation, order, or regulation issued before or after the **10–22**

passing of this Act by Her Majesty, or by the Privy Council, also of any proclamation, order, or regulation issued before or after the passing of this Act by or under the authority of any such department of the Government or officer as is mentioned in the first column of the schedule hereto, may be given in all courts of justice, and in all legal proceedings whatsoever, in all or any of the modes herein-after mentioned; that is to say:

(1) By the production of a copy of the Gazette purporting to contain such proclamation, order, or regulation.

(2) By the production of a copy of such proclamation, order, or regulation, purporting to be printed by the Government printer, or, where the question arises in a court in any British colony or possession, of a copy purporting to be printed under the authority of the legislature of such British colony or possession.

(3) By the production, in the case of any proclamation, order or regulation issued by Her Majesty or by the Privy Council, of a copy or extract purporting to be certified to be true by the clerk of the Privy Council, or by any one of the lords or others of the Privy Council, and, in the case of any proclamation, order, or regulation issued by or under the authority of any of the said departments or officers, by the production of a copy or extract purporting to be certified to be true by the person or persons specified in the second column of the said schedule in connexion with such department or officer.

Any copy or extract made in pursuance of this Act may be in print or in writing, or partly in print and partly in writing.

No proof shall be required of the handwriting or official position of any person certifying, in pursuance of this Act, to the truth of any copy of or extract from any proclamation, order, or regulation.

Act to be in force in colonies

10–23   **3.** Subject to any law that may be from time to time made by the legislature of any British colony or possession, this Act shall be in force in every such colony and possession.

Definition of terms

10–24   **5.** The following words shall in this Act have the meaning herein-after assigned to them, unless there is something in the context repugnant to such construction; (that is to say),

"British colony and possession" shall for the purposes of this Act include the Channel Islands, the Isle of Man and all other Her Majesty's dominions.

"Legislature" shall signify any authority, other than the Imperial Parliament or Her Majesty in Council, competent to make laws for any colony or possession.

"Privy Council" shall include Her Majesty in Council and the lords and others of Her Majesty's Privy Council, or any of them, and any committee of the Privy Council that is not specially named in the schedule hereto.

"Government printer" shall mean and include the printer to Her Majesty, the Queen's Printer for Scotland, and any printer purporting to be the printer authorized to print the statutes, ordinances, acts of state, or other public acts of the legislature of any British colony or possession, or otherwise to be the Government printer of such colony or possession.

"Gazette" shall include the London Gazette, the Edinburgh Gazette, and the Belfast Gazette, or any of such Gazettes.

Act to be cumulative

10–25   **6.** The provisions of this Act shall be deemed to be in addition to, and not in derogation of, any powers of proving documents given by any existing statute, or existing at common law.

10–26   In *Clarke* [1969] 2 Q.B. 91 the Court of Appeal said that the word "order" in the 1868 Act should be given a wide meaning, covering "any executive act of government performed by the bringing into existence of a public document for the purposes of giving effect to an Act of Parliament". It held that the *Breath Test (Approval) (No. 1) Order* 1968, although not a statutory instrument, was an order within the meaning of the Act.

Evidence Act 1851, s.7

Foreign and colonial acts of state, judgments, etc.provable by certified copies, without proof of seal or signature or judicial character of person signing the same

10–27   **7.** All proclamations, treaties, and other acts of state of any foreign state or of any British colony, and all judgments, decrees, orders, and other judicial proceedings of any court of justice in any foreign state or in any British colony, and all affidavits, pleadings, and other legal documents filed or deposited in any such court, may be proved in any court of justice, or before any person having by law or by consent of parties authority to hear, receive, and examine evidence, either by examined copies or by copies authenticated as herein-after mentioned; that is to say, if the document sought to be proved be a proclamation, treaty, or other act of state, the authenticated copy to be admissible in evidence must purport to be sealed with the seal of the foreign state or British colony to which the original document belongs; and if the document sought to be proved be a judgment, decree, order, or other judicial proceeding of any foreign or colonial court, or an affidavit, pleading, or other legal document filed or deposited in any such court, the authenticated copy to be admissible in evidence must purport either to be sealed with the seal of the foreign or colonial court to which the original document belongs, or, in the event of such court having no seal, to be signed by the judge, or, if there be more than one judge, by any one of the judges of the said court, and such judge shall attach to his signature a statement in writing on the said copy that the court whereof he is a judge has no seal; but if any of the aforesaid authenticated copies shall purport to be sealed or signed as hereinbefore respectively directed, the same shall respectively be admitted in evidence in every case in which the original document could have been received in evidence, without any proof of the seal where a seal is necessary, or of the signature, or of the truth of the statement attached thereto, where such signature and statement are necessary, or of the judicial character of the person appearing to have made such signature and statement.

Authenticated or examined copies may be used to prove foreign law or judgments.

Births and Deaths Registration Act 1953, s.34

Entry in register as evidence of birth or death

34.—(1) The following provisions of this section shall have effect in relation to entries in registers under this Act or any enactment repealed by this Act.   **10–28**

(2) An entry or a certified copy of an entry of a birth or death in a register, or in a certified copy of a register, shall not be evidence of the birth or death unless the entry purports to be signed by some person professing to be the informant and to be such a person as might be required or permitted by law at the date of the entry to give to the registrar information concerning that birth or death:

Provided that this subsection shall not apply—

    (a) in relation to an entry of a birth which, not being an entry signed by a person professing to be a superintendent registrar, purports to have been made with the authority of the Registrar General; or

    (b) in relation to an entry of a death which purports to have been made upon a certificate from a coroner; or

    (c) in relation to an entry of a birth or death which purports to have been made in pursuance of the enactments with respect to the registration of births and deaths at sea;

    (d) in relation to the re-registration of a birth under section (5) of this Act.

(3) Where more than three months have intervened between the date of the birth of any child or the date when any living new-born child or still-born child was found exposed and the date of the registration of the birth of that child, the entry or a certified copy of the entry of the birth of the child in the register, or in a certified copy of the register, shall not be evidence of the birth unless—

    (a) if it appears that not more than twelve months have so intervened, the entry purports either to be signed by the superintendent registrar as well as by the registrar or to have been made with the authority of the Registrar General;

    (b) if more than twelve months have so intervened, the entry purports to have been made with the authority of the Registrar General:

Provided that this subsection shall not apply in any case where the original entry in the register was made before the first day of January, eighteen hundred and seventy-five.

(4) Where more than twelve months have intervened between the date of the death or of the finding of the dead body of any person and the date of the registration of that person's death, the entry or a certified copy of the entry of the death in the register, or in a certified copy of the register, shall not be evidence of the death unless the entry purports to have been made with the authority of the Registrar General:

Provided that this subsection shall not apply in any case where the original entry in the register was made before the first day of January, eighteen hundred and seventy-five.

(5) A certified copy of an entry in a register or in a certified copy of a register shall be deemed to be a true copy notwithstanding that it is made on a form different from that on which the original entry was made if any differences in the column headings under which the particulars appear in the original entry and the copy respectively are differences of form only and not of substance.

(6) The Registrar General shall cause any certified copy of an entry given in the General Register Office to be sealed or stamped with the seal of that Office; and, subject to the foregoing provisions of this section, any certified copy of an entry purporting to be sealed or stamped with the said seal shall be received as evidence of the birth or death to which it relates without any further or other proof of the entry, and no certified copy purporting to have been given in the said Office shall be of any force or effect unless it is sealed or stamped as aforesaid.

Local Government Act 1972, s.238

Evidence of byelaws

10–29   **238.** The production of a printed copy of a byelaw purporting to be made by a local authority, the Greater London Authority or a metropolitan county passenger transport authority upon which is endorsed a certificate purporting to be signed by the proper officer of the authority stating—

(a) that the byelaw was made by the authority;

(b) that the copy is a true copy of the byelaw;

(c) that on a specified date the byelaw was confirmed by the authority named in the certificate or, as the case may require, was sent to the Secretary of State and has not been disallowed;

(d) the date, if any, fixed by the confirming authority for the coming into operation of the byelaw;

shall be prima facie evidence of the facts stated in the certificate, and without proof of the handwriting or official position of any person purporting to sign the certificate.

Public Records Act 1958, s.9

Legal validity of public records and authenticated copies

10 30   **9.**—(1) The legal validity of any record shall not be affected by its removal under the provisions of this Act, or of the *Public Record Office Acts* 1838 to 1898, or by any provisions in those Acts with respect to its legal custody.

(2) A copy of or extract from a public record in the Public Record Office purporting to be examined and certified as true and authentic by the proper officer and to be sealed or stamped with the seal of the Public Record Office shall be admissible as evidence in any proceedings without any further or other proof thereof if the original record would have been admissible as evidence in those proceedings.

(3) An electronic copy of or extract from a public record in the Public Record Office which—

(a) purports to have been examined and certified as true and authentic by the proper officer; and

(b) appears on a website purporting to be one maintained by or on behalf of the Public Record Office,;

shall, when viewed on that website, be admissible as evidence in any proceedings without further or other proof if the original record would have been admissible as evidence in those proceedings.

(4) In this section any reference to the proper officer is a reference to the Keeper of Public Records or any other officer of the Public Record Office authorised in that behalf by the Keeper of Public Records, and, in the case of copies and extracts made before the commencement of this Act, the deputy keeper of the records or any assistant record keeper appointed under the *Public Record Office Act* 1838.

Police and Criminal Evidence Act 1984, ss.73–75

Proof of convictions and acquittals

10–31–32   **73.**—(1) Where in any proceedings the fact that a person has in the United Kingdom been convicted or acquitted of an offence otherwise than by a Service court is admissible in evidence, it may be proved by producing a certificate of conviction or, as the case may be, of acquittal relating to that offence, and proving that the person named in the certificate as having been convicted or acquitted of the offence is the person whose conviction or acquittal of the offence is to be proved.

(2) For the purposes of this section a certificate of conviction or of acquittal—

(a) shall, as regards a conviction or acquittal on indictment, consist of a certificate, signed by the proper officer of the court where the conviction or acquittal took place, giving the substance and effect (omitting the formal parts) of the indictment and of the conviction or acquittal; and

(b) shall, as regards a conviction or acquittal on a summary trial, consist of a copy of the conviction or of the dismissal of the information, signed by the of the court where the conviction or acquittal took place or by the proper officer of the court, if any, to which a memorandum of the conviction or acquittal was sent;

and a document purporting to be a duly signed certificate of conviction or acquittal under this section shall be taken to be such a certificate unless the contrary is proved.

(3) In subsection (2) above "proper officer" means—

(a) in relation to a magistrates' court in England and Wales, the justices' chief executive for the court; and

(b) in relation to any other court, the clerk of the court, his deputy or any other person having custody of the court record.

(4) The method of proving a conviction or acquittal authorised by this section shall be in addition to and not to the exclusion of any other authorised manner of proving a conviction or acquittal.

[This section is printed as amended by the *Access to Justice Act* 1999, s.90(1) and Sched. 13, para. 12.]

See *Criminal Procedure Rules* 2005, r.6.4 in Appendix G–32.

Conviction as evidence of commission of offence

74.—(1) In any proceedings the fact that a person other than the accused has been convicted **10–33** of an offence by or before any court in the United Kingdom or by a Service court outside the United Kingdom shall be admissible in evidence for the purpose of proving, where to do so is relevant to any issue in those proceedings, that that person committed that offence, whether or not any other evidence of his having committed that offence is given.

(2) In any proceedings in which by virtue of this section a person other than the accused is proved to have been convicted of an offence by or before any court in the United Kingdom or by a Service court outside the United Kingdom, he shall be taken to have committed that offence unless the contrary is proved.

(3) In any proceedings where evidence is admissible of the fact that the accused has committed an offence, in so far as that evidence is relevant to any matter in issue in the proceedings for a reason other than a tendency to show in the accused a disposition to commit the kind of offence with which he is charged, if the accused is proved to have been convicted of the offence—

(a) by or before any court in the United Kingdom; or

(b) by a Service court outside the United Kingdom,

he shall be taken to have committed that offence unless the contrary is proved.

(4) Nothing in this section shall prejudice—

(a) the admissibility in evidence of any conviction which would be admissible apart from this section; or

(b) the operation of any enactment whereby a conviction or a finding of fact in any proceedings is for the purposes of any other proceedings made conclusive evidence of any fact.

Provisions supplementary to section 74

75.—(1) Where evidence that a person has been convicted of an offence is admissible by **10–34** virtue of section 74 above, then without prejudice to the reception of any other admissible evidence for the purpose of identifying the facts on which the conviction was based—

(a) the contents of any document which is admissible as evidence of the conviction; and

(b) the contents of the information, complaint, indictment or charge-sheet on which the person in question was convicted,

shall be admissible in evidence for that purpose.

(2) Where in any proceedings the contents of any document are admissible in evidence by virtue of subsection (1) above, a copy of that document, or of the material part of it, purporting to be certified or otherwise authenticated by or on behalf of the court or authority having custody of that document shall be admissible in evidence and shall be taken to be a true copy of that document or part unless the contrary is shown.

(3) Nothing in any of the following—

(a) section 14 of the *Powers of Criminal Courts (Sentencing) Act* 2000 (under which a conviction leading to probation or discharge is to be disregarded except as mentioned in that section);

(b) section 247 of the *Criminal Procedure (Scotland) Act* 1995 (which makes similar provision in respect of convictions on indictment in Scotland); and

(c) section 8 of the *Probation Act (Northern Ireland)* 1950 (which corresponds to section 13 of the *Powers of Criminal Courts Act* 1973) or any legislation which is in force in Northern Ireland for the time being and corresponds to that section,

shall affect the operation of section 74 above; and for the purposes of that section any order made by a court of summary jurisdiction in Scotland under section 228 or section 246(3) of the said Act of 1995 shall be treated as a conviction.

(4) Nothing in section 74 above shall be construed as rendering admissible in any proceedings evidence of any conviction other than a subsisting one.

[This section is printed as amended by the *PCC(S)A* 2000, s.165(1) and Sched. 9, para. 98.]

10–35   There are other official documents which are not admissible or do not constitute *prima facie* evidence, *e.g.* circulars from government departments: *Peagram v. Peagram* [1926] 2 K.B. 165, a motor vehicle registration book is not evidence as to its contents: *Sealby* [1965] 1 All E.R. 701, and regimental records: *Andrews v. Cordiner* [1947] 1 All E.R. 777. These sections apply to UK convictions, however, foreign convictions can be proved under section 7 of the *Evidence Act* 1851: *Kordasinski* [2006] EWCA Crim 2984; *The Times*, November 16 2006.

C. PRIVATE DOCUMENTS

10–36   Usually the original must be produced but secondary evidence may be given where:

— the other party has the evidence and refuses to produce it after proper notice (a defendant is not generally required to produce evidence against himself): *Sanders* [1919] 1 K.B. 550; *Worsenham* (1701) 1 Ld. Raym. 705; *Stokes v. Grosvenor Hotel Co* [1897] 2 Q.B. 124;

— a third person has the document and refuses to produce it, *e.g.* because of privilege;

— the original is lost or destroyed: *Wayte* (1982) 76 Cr.App.R. 110;

— the original is not physically or conveniently removable or may not be lawfully moved: *Owner v. Bee Hive Spinning Co Ltd* [1914] 1 K.B. 105.

D. PROOF

(1) Legislation

Criminal Justice Act 1988, s.27

Proof of statements contained in documents

10–37   **27.** Where a statement contained in a document is admissible as evidence in criminal proceedings, it may be proved—

(a) by the production of that document; or

(b) (whether or not that document is still in existence) by the production of a copy of that document, or of the material part of it, authenticated in such manner as the court may approve; and it is immaterial for the purposes of this subsection how many removes there are between a copy and the original.

This section shall not apply to proceedings before a magistrates' court inquiring into an offence as examining justices.

[This section is reprinted as amended by the *Criminal Procedure and Investigations Act* 1996, s.47 and Sched. 1, para. 31.]

(2) Procedure

A witness who has attested a document may be called to prove it. A document which **10–38** is more that 20 years old and comes from proper custody, however, is presumed to have been duly executed. It is also presumed that: a document was made on the date which it bears: *Re Adamson* (1875) L.R. 3 P. & D. 253; a deed was duly sealed: *Re Sandilands* (1871) L.R. 6 C.P. 441; an alteration or erasure in a deed was made before execution, but that an alteration or erasure in a will was made after execution: *Doe d Tatum v. Catomore* [1851] 16 Q.B. 745. Where one deed is recited in another the proof of the deed is proof of the one recited.

Where the prosecution cannot prove the contents of an incriminating document, it **10–39** can prove the finding of the document and if the defendant gives evidence he may be asked if he was aware of the document and of its contents. If he answers in the affirmative he may be asked about the meaning of it: *Gillespie and Simpson* 51 Cr.App.R. 172, CA; *Cooper (WJ)* 82 Cr.App.R. 74, CA; *Cross* 91 Cr.App.R. 115, CA.

Statements which fall within the hearsay rule are admissible if they comply with the provisions of the *Criminal Justice Act* 2003, *post*.

(3) Handwriting

Handwriting may be proved by someone who has knowledge of the handwriting: **10–40** *McCartney and Hansen* (1928) 20 Cr.App.R. 179; *O'Brien* (1911) 7 Cr.App.R. 29.

(4) Bankers books

An entry in a banker's book may be proved by a copy produced by a witness in **10–41** person or by affidavit and examined as correct as being one of the ordinary books of the bank which is in that bank's custody or control and has been made in the usual course of business

(5) Absence of an entry in a record

The record must be produced by a person responsible for maintaining it who can **10–42** explain the significance of the entries and omissions: *Patel* 73 Cr.App.R. 117, CA; *Shone* 76 Cr.App.R. 72, CA.

(6) Microfilm

Police and Criminal Evidence Act 1984, s.71

Microfilm copies

71. In any proceedings the contents of a document may (whether or not the document is still **10–43** in existence) be proved by the production of an enlargement of a microfilm copy of that document or of the material part of it, authenticated in such manner as the court may approve.

Where the proceedings concerned are proceedings before a magistrates' court inquiring into an offence as examining justices this section shall have effect with the omission of the words "authenticated in such manner as the court may approve".

[This section is reprinted as amended by the *Criminal Procedure and Investigation Act* 1996, s.47, Sched. 1, para. 24.]

(7) Business and computer records

Information obtained from a computer, whether printed out or read from a display, **10–44** may be divided into three categories:

— where the computer was used to calculate or process information: *Wood* 76 Cr.App.R. 23; *Sophocleous v. Ringer* [1988] R.T.R. 52, DC;

— where the computer was programmed to record information: *Pettigrew* 71 Cr.App.R. 186; *Spiby* 91 Cr.App.R. 186, CA;

— where the information recorded and processed by the computer has been entered by a person, directly or indirectly. Information in this category is hearsay.

The court has a general discretion to refuse to admit such documents: section 25(1)(c).

(8) Medical records

10–45 Records are admissible to show that a witness suffers from some disease or defect or abnormality of mind that affects his reliability as a witness: *Toohey v. Metropolitan Police Commissioner* [1965] 1 All E.R. 506.

Police and Criminal Evidence Act, s.82(3)

Part VIII—interpretation.

10–46 82.—(3) Nothing in this Part of this Act shall prejudice any power of a court to exclude evidence (whether by preventing questions from being put or otherwise) at its discretion.

10–47 The admission of unlawfully obtained evidence does not violate the right to a fair trial. The use of the evidence is different, however, and the European Court of Human Rights will look to the strength of the evidence as a whole and the opportunities given to a defendant to challenge the evidence and cross-examine. It will only interfere where the UK court draws arbitrary or unfair conclusions from the evidence: *Schenk v. Switzerland* (1988) 13 E.H.R.R. 242; see also *Khan (Sultan) v. U.K.* (2001) 31 E.H.R.R. 242; *Edwards v. U.K.* (1993) 15 E.H.R.R. 417; *P.G. and J.H. v. U.K.* [2002] Crim.L.R. 308.

(9) Tape, video and DVD recordings

10–48 These are treated in the same way as other documents. So long as a tape recording is proved to be accurate and authentic it is admissible: *Ali (Maqsud)* [1966] 1 Q.B. 688; *Robson* (1972) 56 Cr.App.R. 450; see also Code of Practice, *ante*. Normally a summary is available to the court and the tape is made an exhibit. A video/DVD is generally shown in court.

(10) Photographs and sketches

10–49 A photograph or sketch is admissible provided it is verified on oath by a person able to speak to its accuracy, not necessarily the photographer: *Tolson* (1864) 4 F. & F. 103; *Mille v. Lamson, The Times*, October 29, 1892.

(11) Maps and plans

10–50 A map or a plan may be produced by its maker or authenticated by a witness producing it. A map or plan prepared for the trial and containing any references to occurrences which are the subject matter of the trial, but which did not exist when the map was prepared, is inadmissible if objection is made. In *Mitchell* (1852) 6 Cox C.C. 82, for example a skid mark which was visible on the road when the map was prepared is admissible whereas the position of a car which had been moved since the accident had occurred was not.

(12) Certificates and statutory declarations

10–51 Various matters are by statute provable by certificate.

Criminal Justice Act 1948, s.41

Evidence by certificate

10–52 41.—(1) In any criminal proceedings, a certificate purporting to be signed by a constable, or by a person having the prescribed qualifications, and certifying that a plan or drawing exhibited thereto is a plan or drawing made by him of the place or object specified in the certificate, and that the plan or drawing is correctly drawn to a scale so specified, shall be evidence of the relative position of the things shown on the plan or drawing.

(4) Nothing in this section shall be deemed to make a certificate admissible as evidence in proceedings for an offence except in a case where and to the extent to which oral evidence to the like effect would have been admissible in those proceedings.

(5) Nothing in this section shall be deemed to make a certificate admissible as evidence in proceedings for any offence—

    (a) unless a copy thereof has, not less than seven days before the hearing of trial, been served in the prescribed manner on the person charged with the offence; or

    (b) if that person, not later than three days before the hearing or trial or within such further time as the court may in special circumstances allow, serves notice in the prescribed from and manner on the prosecutor requiring the attendance at the trial of the person who signed the certificate

[(5A) Where the proceedings mentioned in subsection (1) above are proceedings before a magistrates' court inquiring into an offence as examining justices this section shall have effect with the omission of—

    (a) subsection (4), and

    (b) in subsection (5), paragraph (b) and the word "or" immediately preceding it.]

(6) In this section the expression "prescribed" means prescribed by rules made by the Secretary of State.

Evidence by Certificate Rules 1961 (S.I. 1962 No. 2319), rr.1–3

1. The prescribed qualifications for the purpose of subsection (1) of section forty-one of the **10–53** *Criminal Justice Act*, 1948 (which relates to the admissibility of certified plans and drawings in criminal proceedings), shall be—

    (a) registration as an architect under the Architects (Registration) Acts, 1931 to 1938, or

    (b) membership of any of the following bodies, that is to say, the Royal Institution of Chartered Surveyors, the Institution of Civil Engineers, the Institution of Municipal Engineers and the Land Agents Society.

2. A certificate under subsection (1) of section two hundred and forty-two of the *Road Traffic* **10–54** *Act*, 1960, shall be in the form numbered 1 in the Schedule hereto or in a form to the like effect and a notice under paragraph (b) of subsection (3) of that section or under paragraph (b) of subsection (5) of section forty-one of the *Criminal Justice Act*, 1948, shall be in the form numbered 2 in the Schedule hereto or in a form to the like effect.

3. Any certificate or other document required to be served by subsection (3) of the said sec- **10–55** tion two hundred and forty-two or by subsection (5) of the said section forty-one shall be served in the following manner, that is to say—

    (a) where the person to be served is a corporation, by addressing it to the corporation and leaving it at, or sending it by registered post or by the recorded delivery service to, the registered office of the corporation or, if there be no such office, its principal office or place at which it conducts its business;

    (b) in any other case, by delivering it personally to the person to be served or by addressing it to him and leaving it at, or sending it by registered post or by the recorded delivery service to, his last or usual place of abode or place of business.

Where one subsection of a section of a statute provides that a certificate as to a certain **10–56** matter "shall be admissible in evidence" as proof of its contents, and the following subsection provides that such certificate "shall not be received in evidence" unless certain steps have been taken, admissibility does not depend upon proof by the prosecution that such steps have been taken; it is for the defence to object to admissibility prior to the end of the trial. It is no ground of appeal against conviction that the requisite steps were not taken. If the defendant was unrepresented at trial, a failure to object should not be held against him on appeal. As to admissibility it would be otherwise where the statutory provision governing admissibility was to the effect that a certificate "is admissible only if" certain steps have been taken: *Att.-Gen. for the Cayman Islands v. Roberts* [2002] 1 W.L.R. 1842, PC; *McCormack v. DPP* [2002] R.T.R. 20, QBD.

V. PHYSICAL OBJECTS

10–57   Material objects are produced as exhibits by the person who found them.

The prosecution is not obliged to place every item of physical evidence before the court: *Hocking v. Ahlquist Brothers Ltd* [1944] K.B. 120. Where original exhibits are too large to be produced conveniently, photographs of them may be admitted: *R. v. Uxbridge Justices, ex p. Sofaer* (1987) 85 Cr.App.R. 367.

VI. JUDICIAL NOTICE

10–58   Courts may take judicial notice of matters which are so notorious, or clearly established, or susceptible of demonstration by reference to readily obtainable and authoritative source that evidence of their existence is unnecessary: *Mullen v. Hackney LBC* [1997] 1 W.L.R. 1103, CA (Civ. Div.).

The court in *Commonwealth Shipping Representative v. Peninsular and Oriental Branch Service* [1923] A.C. 191 at 212 said that:

> Judicial notice refers to facts, which a judge can be called upon to receive and to act upon, either from his general knowledge of them, or from inquiries to be made by himself for his own information from sources to which it is proper for which it is proper to refer.

Examples of such matters are: Rain falls: *Fay v. Prentice* (1845) 14 L.J.C. 298; butterfly knives are offensive weapons made or adapted for use for causing injury: *DPP v. Hynde* [1998] Crim.L.R. 72.

When a court takes judicial notice of a fact it finds that the fact exists although its existence has not been established by evidence. The court should be cautious in treating a factual conclusion as obvious even though the person in the street would unhesitatingly hold it to be so: *Carter v. Eastbourne BC* (2000) 164 J.P. 273, DC.

10–59   Although the court may, in arriving at its decision, use general information and a knowledge of the common affairs of life which people of ordinary intelligence possess, it may not act on its own private knowledge or belief regarding the facts of the particular case: *Sutton* (1816) 4 M & S 532; *Ingram v. Percival* [1969] 1 Q.B. 548, DC. In *Wetherall v. Harrison* [1976] Q.B. 773, DC, it was held that it was proper for a magistrate with specialised knowledge of the circumstances forming the background to a particular case to draw upon that knowledge in interpreting the evidence, but improper in effect to give evidence to himself and the other justices which is at variance with the evidence given, for it would offend the fundamental principle that evidence should be given in the presence of the parties and be subject to cross-examination. Magistrates are entitled to rely on knowledge of the area in concluding that residents are likely to be caused nuisance by practice of kerb-crawling: *Paul v. DPP* (1990) 90 Cr.App.R. 173, DC.

The judiciary in magistrates' courts must be circumspect in their use of local knowledge and inform the parties when reliance is being placed upon local knowledge. It must be within reasonable limits: *Keane v. Mount Vernon Colliery Co Ltd* [1933] A.C. 309 and should be of a general nature, not the type of knowledge that may be varied by the individual characteristics of a particular case: *Reynolds v. Llanelly Associated Tinplate Co Ltd* [1948] 1 All E.R. 140. Justices are encouraged to use their common sense and general local knowledge: *Hughes v. DPP* [2003] EWHC Admin 2470. In *Bowman v. DPP* [1990] Crim.L.R. 600, DC, the defendant was charged with driving in a public place having consumed excess alcohol contrary to the *Road Traffic Act* 1972, s.6. The issue was whether the car park was a public place. There was evidence that there were other cars in the car park and that there was no barrier present at the time. The magistrates, using their own local knowledge of the car park, found that the car park was a public place and convicted. On appeal it was held that the magistrates were entitled to find as they did on the basis of the evidence before them and their own local knowledge of the area. Where magistrates do use their own local knowledge they should make that known to the parties and give the parties an opportunity to comment.

In *Norbrook Laboratories (G.B.) Ltd v. Health and Safety Executive, The Times*, **10–60** February 23, 1998, DC, it was held that an appeal against a conviction under health and safety at work legislation would be allowed where magistrates had failed to inform the parties to the case that they were bringing their own local knowledge to bear in reaching a decision. Although it was perfectly legitimate for local knowledge to be relied upon by magistrates, both defence and prosecution should be informed so that they might be afforded an opportunity to comment upon the knowledge the magistrates claimed to have.

As lay magistrates are not legally qualified, they are in a unique position compared to judges. In *Wetherall v. Harrison* [1976] Q.B. 773, the question was whether the defendant had a reasonable excuse for failing to give a blood sample. The defendant said that he had had a fit but the prosecution alleged that it had not been genuine. One of the magistrates was a medical practitioner and gave his professional opinion to the other magistrates, who drew on their wartime experience of inoculations and the fear that they could create in certain cases. The Divisional Court held that magistrates lack the ability to exclude certain factors from their consideration. If a magistrate is a specialist, such as a doctor, it is not possible for him to approach the case as if he did not have that expertise and it would be a bad thing if that were required. One of the advantages of magistrates is the varied experience that they bring to the magistrates' courts. Although it would be wrong for the magistrate to give evidence personally, he can employ basic knowledge to the benefit of the other magistrates in considering and weighing the evidence.

Every statute passed since 1850 is a public Act to be judicially noted unless the contrary is expressly provided: *Interpretation Act* 1978, s.3, Sched. 2, para. 2. See *Pillai v. Mudanayaka* [1953] A.C. 514, PC.

Evidence Act 1845, s.2

Courts, &c. to take judicial notice of signature of equity or common law judges, &c.

2. All courts, judges, justices, masters in chancery, masters of courts, commissioners judicially **10–61** acting, and other judicial officers, shall henceforth take judicial notice of the signature of any of the equity or common law judges of the superior courts at the Royal Courts of Justice], provided such signature be attached or appended to any decree, order, certificate, or other judicial or official document.

VII. HEARSAY

A. GENERAL

Hearsay evidence is evidence given by a witness of what someone else said. The **10–62** previous rule against hearsay was defined as "an assertion other than one made by a person while giving oral evidence in the proceedings is inadmissible as evidence of any fact stated": *Sharp* [1988] 1 W.L.R. 7; *Kearley* [1992] 2 A.C. 228. The admissibility of evidence is a matter for regulation by national law. Article 6(3)(d) of the European Convention on Human Rights provides that everyone charged with a criminal offence is entitled to examine witnesses called against him but nothing in that article prevents reliance on hearsay evidence where there are counterbalancing factors which preserve the rights of the defence: *Kostovski v. Netherlands* (1989) 12 E.H.R.R. 434.

Hearsay evidence is now governed by the *Criminal Justice Act* 2003. The new provisions apply to all trials taking place after the commencement of the Act even where a preparatory hearing has taken place before: *H.* [2005] EWCA Crim 2083; [2006] 1 Cr.App.R. 4. They abolish the common law rules save for those expressly preserved and thus the majority view in *Kearley* (*ante*) regarding implied assertions has been set aside: *Singh* [2006] 1 W.L.R. 1564. In that case leave has been given to appeal to the House of Lords. The Act preserves the rules of public information, reputation, res gestae, confessions, admissions by agents, common enterprise and expert evidence: section 118. Leveson J. (as he then was) has said that "although the purpose of the hearsay provisions set out in the *Criminal Justice Act* 2003 was undeniably to relax the previously strict rules against the admission of hearsay, it is important to underline that care must be taken to analyse the precise provisions of the legislation and ensure that any route of admissibility is correctly identified": *Maher v. DPP* (2006) 170 J.P. 441.

B. Preservation of Common Law Rules

Criminal Justice Act 2003, s.118

Preservation of certain common law categories of admissibility

10–63   **118.**—(1) The following rules of law are preserved.

1. *Public information etc.*

   Any rule of law under which in criminal proceedings—

   (a) published works dealing with matters of a public nature (such as histories, scientific works, dictionaries and maps) are admissible as evidence of facts of a public nature stated in them,

   (b) public documents (such as public registers, and returns made under public authority with respect to matters of public interest) are admissible as evidence of facts stated in them,

   (c) records (such as the records of certain courts, treaties, Crown grants, pardons and commissions) are admissible as evidence of facts stated in them, or

   (d) evidence relating to a person's age or date or place of birth may be given by a person without personal knowledge of the matter.

2. *Reputation as to character*

   Any rule of law under which in criminal proceedings evidence of a person's reputation is admissible for the purpose of proving his good or bad character.

   Note

   The rule is preserved only so far as it allows the court to treat such evidence as proving the matter concerned.

3. *Reputation or family tradition*

   Any rule of law under which in criminal proceedings evidence of reputation or family tradition is admissible for the purpose of proving or disproving—

   (a) pedigree or the existence of a marriage,

   (b) the existence of any public or general right, or

   (c) the identity of any person or thing.

   Note

   The rule is preserved only so far as it allows the court to treat such evidence as proving or disproving the matter concerned.

4. *Res gestae*

   Any rule of law under which in criminal proceedings a statement is admissible as evidence of any matter stated if—

   (a) the statement was made by a person so emotionally overpowered by an event that the possibility of concoction or distortion can be disregarded,

   (b) the statement accompanied an act which can be properly evaluated as evidence only if considered in conjunction with the statement, or

   (c) the statement relates to a physical sensation or a mental state (such as intention or emotion).

5. *Confessions etc*

   Any rule of law relating to the admissibility of confessions or mixed statements in criminal proceedings.

6. *Admissions by agents etc*

   Any rule of law under which in criminal proceedings—

(a) an admission made by an agent of a defendant is admissible against the defendant as evidence of any matter stated, or

(b) a statement made by a person to whom a defendant refers a person for information is admissible against the defendant as evidence of any matter stated.

7. *Common enterprise*

Any rule of law under which in criminal proceedings a statement made by a party to a common enterprise is admissible against another party to the enterprise as evidence of any matter stated.

8. *Expert evidence*

Any rule of law under which in criminal proceedings an expert witness may draw on the body of expertise relevant to his field.

(2) With the exception of the rules preserved by this section, the common law rules governing the admissibility of hearsay evidence in criminal proceedings are abolished.

Where a statement is admissible under an exception to the rule against hearsay, it is admissible as evidence of the truth of its contents.   **10–64**

Confessions

As to the admissibility of confessions, see *post* § 10–132.   **10–65**

Statements falling within the res gestae principle

Statements or acts which are connected with the facts in issue and occur at the same time and are an integral part of what happened are admissible. In *Nye and Loan* 66 Cr.App.R. 252, CA, the statement of the victim of an assault which had taken place during an altercation after a road traffic accident, identifying one of the appellants as the assailant, was admitted. The statement had been made to a police officer shortly after the event. The Court of Appeal said it was difficult to imagine a more spontaneous identification.   **10–66**

The case of *Andrews* [1987] A.C. 281 set guidelines for the admissibility of *res gestae*.   **10–67**

"1. The primary question which the judge must ask himself is—can the possibility of concoction or distortion be disregarded?

2. To answer that question the judge must first consider the circumstances in which the particular statement was made, in order to satisfy himself that the event was so unusual or startling or dramatic as to dominate the thoughts of the victim, so that his utterance was an instinctive reaction to that event thus giving no real opportunity for reasoned reflection. In such a situation the judge would be entitled to conclude that the involvement or the pressure of the event would exclude the possibility of concoction or distortion, providing that the statement was made in conditions of approximate but not exact contemporaneity.

3. in order for the statement to be sufficiently 'spontaneous' it must be so closely associated with the event which has excited the statement, that it can be fairly stated that the mind of the declarant was still dominated by the event. Thus the judge must be satisfied that the event, which provided the trigger mechanism for the statement, was still operative. The fact that the statement was made in answer to a question is but one factor to consider under this heading.

4.Quite apart from the time factor, there may be special features in the case, which relate to the possibility of concoction or distortion … The judge must be satisfied that the circumstances were such that having regard to the special feature of malice there was no possibility of any concoction or distortion to the advantage of the maker or the disadvantage of the accused

5.As to the possibility of error in the facts narrated in the statement, if only the ordinary fallibility of human recollection is relied upon, this goes to the weight to be attached to and not to the admissibility of the statement … However … here there may be special features that may give rise to the possibility of error. In the instant case there was evidence that the deceased had drunk to excess.… Another example would be where the identification was made in circumstances of particular difficulty or where the declarant suffered from defective eyesight. In such circumstances the trial judge must consider whether he can exclude the possibility of error."

Statements of health or feelings are admissible as original evidence and are not exceptions to the hearsay rule: *Gilbey v. Great Western Ry Co* (1910) 102 L.T. 202.

Where a murder is undisputed, a defendant is entitled to adduce evidence that somebody else might have committed the murder, such as evidence that another person had been near the murder scene and appeared to have a motive: *Greenwood* [2005] 1 Cr.App.R. 7.

C. ADMISSIBILITY

Criminal Justice Act 2003, s.114

Admissibility of hearsay evidence

10–68   **114.**—(1) In criminal proceedings a statement not made in oral evidence in the proceedings is admissible as evidence of any matter stated if, but only if—

  (a) any provision of this Chapter or any other statutory provision makes it admissible,

  (b) any rule of law preserved by section 118 makes it admissible,

  (c) all parties to the proceedings agree to it being admissible, or

  (d) the court is satisfied that it is in the interests of justice for it to be admissible.

  (2) In deciding whether a statement not made in oral evidence should be admitted under subsection (1)(d), the court must have regard to the following factors (and to any others it considers relevant)—

  (a) how much probative value the statement has (assuming it to be true) in relation to a matter in issue in the proceedings, or how valuable it is for the understanding of other evidence in the case;

  (b) what other evidence has been, or can be, given on the matter or evidence mentioned in paragraph (a);

  (c) how important the matter or evidence mentioned in paragraph (a) is in the context of the case as a whole;

  (d) the circumstances in which the statement was made;

  (e) how reliable the maker of the statement appears to be;

  (f) how reliable the evidence of the making of the statement appears to be;

  (g) whether oral evidence of the matter stated can be given and, if not, why it cannot;

  (h) the amount of difficulty involved in challenging the statement;

  (i) the extent to which that difficulty would be likely to prejudice the party facing it.

  (3) Nothing in this Chapter affects the exclusion of evidence of a statement on grounds other than the fact that it is a statement not made in oral evidence in the proceedings.

10–69   Hearsay evidence, *i.e.* a statement not made in oral testimony will be admissible if:

  — it falls within statutory provisions;

  — the parties agree;

  — the court is satisfied, in the interests of justice, that it should be admitted.

In the latter case, the court will have regard to:

  — its probative value to matters in issue or its value to the understanding of other evidence;

  — what other evidence has or can be given on the matter;

  — the importance of the matter or the other evidence which needs to be understood;

  — the circumstances in which it was made;

  — the reliability of its maker;

  — the reliability of the making of the statement;

  — whether oral evidence can be given and, if not, why not;

  — difficulties in challenging the statement;

  — the extent that those difficulties would prejudice the defendant.

The statutory definition of statement includes pictorial, sketch or photofit representations. Evidence which is mechanically produced *e.g.* CCTV, computer printouts is not hearsay except where a person has input the data when it may be hearsay. In *Skinner* [2005] EWCA Crim 1439 printouts of screen images from a website were held to be admissible as real evidence and not hearsay.

The provisions apply to both trials and committal proceedings: *R. (CPS) v. City of London Magistrates' Court*, *The Times*, April 17, 2006.

The words "must have regard to" in section 114(2) do not impose an obligation to reach a conclusion on all nine of the factors identified before determining whether to admit hearsay evidence; the court is merely required to consider those factors and exercise judgment in the light of them: *Taylor*, *The Times*, February 7, 2006.

A court should not easily be persuaded that it is in the interests of justice to permit **10–70** evidence to be read. Under previous law, it was said that where a witness statement provides the sole or determinative evidence against the accused, permitting it to be read may well, depending on the circumstances, jeopardise the infringement of the defendant's Article 6(3)(d) right; even if it is not the only evidence, care must be taken that a fair trial is achieved: *Arnold* [2004] EWCA Crim 1293. A court must give weight and sufficient weight to the prejudicial effect that the inability to challenge evidence might have on the defence case: *McEwan v. DPP* [2007] EWHC 740, Admin. In this case the evidence admitted was that of a youth who had stated that he had seen the defendant scratch a car and his was the only eye-witness account. The witness had not attended court because of an illness and medical evidence indicated that the stress of attending court might be detrimental to his wellbeing. The magistrates had unduly focused on the probative value of the evidence and had failed properly to address the fact that this evidence was the crux of the prosecution case. The remaining evidence was circumstantial. The finding that the witness was not fit to attend court was not warranted on the medical evidence.

Where a court allows a witness statement to be read there is no absolute rule that, where that evidence was the decisive evidence, its admission would automatically lead to an infringement of the defendant's rights under *Human Rights Act* 1998. Where a defendant is shown to have kept a witness away by fear, he is the author of his inability to examine the witness and his Article 6 right is not infringed: *Sellick* [2005] EWCA Crim 651; [2005] 1 W.L.R. 3257.

The case of *Xhabri* [2005] EWCA Crim 3135; [2006] 1 All E.R. 776 has confirmed that the criteria for admitting hearsay evidence are compatible with Article 6 ECHR and went on to say that, to the extent that Article 6 might be infringed, the court has the power to exclude under section 126 and a duty to do so by virtue of the *Human Rights Act* 1998. As the hearsay provisions apply equally to prosecution and defence there is no inherent inequality of arms. Article 6(3)(d) does not give a defendant an absolute right to examine every witness whose testimony is adduced against him. It depends upon whether fairness of the trial requires him to examine every witness. In this case, the court was concerned with section 120 and double hearsay which derived directly or indirectly from the complainant who was available for cross-examination. The evidence of her communication to her mother, father, friend and a police officer was admissible under sections 120 and 121. The issue is whether the defendant is put under an unfair disadvantage through losing the right to cross-examine in the context of the proceedings as a whole: *Grant*, unreported, *Criminal Law Week*, January 23, 2006.

Competence is not a matter that engages the application of the test of admissibility under section 23 but notions close to it are capable of being relevant considerations as to admission of section 23 hearsay evidence under section 26 of the *Criminal Justice Act* 1988, section 78 of the *PACE Act* 1984 and Article 6(1): *Sed* [2004] 1 W.L.R. 3218.

A transcript of evidence in a previous trial was held potentially admissible under section 23(2)(a). It may have been admitted even where it was the only evidence and it was in the court's discretion to decide that and also whether the person was unfit to attend: *Lang* [2004] EWCA Crim 1701. References to telephone calls to a named person can be admissible under section 114(d) as part of the story of a commonsense series of events:

Isichei [2006] EWCA Crim 1815; (2006) 170 J.P. 753. If an application is made by one defendant to admit as hearsay evidence the out-of-court assertion of another defendant in cases involving cut-throat defences (not a confession), the question must be addressed under section 114(1)(d) (the interests of justice) and consideration must be given to the non-exhaustive list of factors contained in section 114(2), to any risk of manipulation by defendants acting together, and to all the circumstances of the offence: *X.*, unreported, January 30, 2007. It is incumbent upon a court to consider the criteria set down in section 114(2) in deciding whether to admit a document summarising the circumstances of a defendant's previous convictions, in particular the amount of difficulty involved in challenging the statement and the extent to which that difficulty would prejudice the defendant: *S.*, unreported, February 8, 2007.

Under the previous law, evidence in a statement could be introduced where another witness had given evidence on the same point; it was the weight of the evidence which was important: *M.* [2004] EWCA Crim 2283.

10–71   The party wishing to introduce hearsay evidence must give notice. See *Criminal Procedure Rules* 2005, r.34(2)–(8) in Appendix G–200—G–206.

Unavailability of witnesses

Criminal Justice Act 2003, s.116

10–72   **116.**—(1) In criminal proceedings a statement not made in oral evidence in the proceedings is admissible as evidence of any matter stated if—

     (a) oral evidence given in the proceedings by the person who made the statement would be admissible as evidence of that matter,

     (b) the person who made the statement (the relevant person) is identified to the court's satisfaction, and

     (c) any of the five conditions mentioned in subsection (2) is satisfied.

   (2) The conditions are—

     (a) that the relevant person is dead;

     (b) that the relevant person is unfit to be a witness because of his bodily or mental condition;

     (c) that the relevant person is outside the United Kingdom and it is not reasonably practicable to secure his attendance;

     (d) that the relevant person cannot be found although such steps as it is reasonably practicable to take to find him have been taken;

     (e) that through fear the relevant person does not give (or does not continue to give) oral evidence in the proceedings, either at all or in connection with the subject matter of the statement, and the court gives leave for the statement to be given in evidence.

   (3) For the purposes of subsection (2)(e) "fear" is to be widely construed and (for example) includes fear of the death or injury of another person or of financial loss.

   (4) Leave may be given under subsection (2)(e) only if the court considers that the statement ought to be admitted in the interests of justice, having regard—

     (a) to the statement's contents,

     (b) to any risk that its admission or exclusion will result in unfairness to any party to the proceedings (and in particular to how difficult it will be to challenge the statement if the relevant person does not give oral evidence),

     (c) in appropriate cases, to the fact that a direction under section 19 of the *Youth Justice and Criminal Evidence Act* 1999 (c. 23) (special measures for the giving of evidence by fearful witnesses etc) could be made in relation to the relevant person, and

     (d) to any other relevant circumstances.

   (5) A condition set out in any paragraph of subsection (2) which is in fact satisfied is to be treated as not satisfied if it is shown that the circumstances described in that paragraph are caused—

     (a) by the person in support of whose case it is sought to give the statement in evidence, or

     (b) by a person acting on his behalf,

In order to prevent the relevant person giving oral evidence in the proceedings (whether at all or in connection with the subject matter of the statement).

Where a person is dead; mentally or physically unfit; outside the UK and it is not **10–73** practicable for him to attend; unable to be found or afraid, then his statement may be admissible if his oral evidence would have been admissible and his identity is confirmed. In the case of fear, the court must also give leave: section 116(4). In considering sections 114 and 116 for evidence to be admissible it has to be logically probative of a fact in issue between the parties: *T.* [2007] 1 Cr.App.R. 4. In this case it was held to be wrong to submit a statement of another person who had admitted acts of sexual abuse against the victim.

Under the previous law statements of deceased persons could be used to prove tradi- **10–74** tions or custom or public rights where a witness would tell the court what he had heard from those who were now dead: *Antrobus* (1835) 3 A. & E. 788; *Bedfordshire* (1885) 4 E. & B. 535.

Declarations made by persons against their pecuniary or proprietary interests who are dead were admissible: *Rogers* [1995] 1 Cr.App.R. 374, CA.

A statement which it is the duty of a person to make in the ordinary course of his business or professional employment, was admissible after his decease provided it was made contemporaneously with the act to which it relates: *Mercer v. Denne* [1905] 2 Ch. 538; see also *McGuire* (1985) 81 Cr.App.R. 323, CA.

Death may be proved by a death certificate, physical or mental condition by a medical report. Where a witness, who is the sole witness of a crime, has made a statement to be used in a prosecution and has since died, there may be a strong public interest in the admission of the statement in evidence so that the prosecution can proceed. That cannot be allowed to override the requirement of a fair trial. Article 6(3)(d), relating to the right to examine witnesses, is one aspect of a fair trial but proceedings must be looked at as a whole: *Al-Khawaja* [2005] EWCA Crim 2697; [2006] 1 All E.R. 543 where a statement was admitted in a case of indecent assault. The prosecution has to establish beyond reasonable doubt that a witness is unfit because of his bodily or mental condition; the court has also to consider the importance of the statement, and the interests of justice and fairness to the defendant: *R. (Meredith) v. Harwich Magistrates' Court* [2006] EWHC 3336. In this road traffic case the witness had a long history of anxiety and panic attacks and the prospect of giving evidence had brought about a recurrence; her medical practitioner had certified that it would be better if she did not give evidence. It was held that the statement of the doctor was insufficient to prove the unfitness and as the evidence was so important the case ought to have been adjourned to explore other means of assisting the witness, *e.g.* video link.

In *Hurst* [1995] 1 Cr.App.R. 82, it was said that the words "reasonably practicable" involve a consideration of the normal steps which would be taken to secure the attendance of a witness; and the qualification of reasonableness includes other circumstances such as the costs and steps which may be available to secure the witness's attendance. Normal steps are the reasonable steps which a party would take, having regard to the means and resources available: *Maloney* [1994] Crim.L.R. 525. "Reasonably practicable" has to be judged on the basis of steps taken, or not taken, by the party seeking to secure the attendance of a witness. That is only the first stage. A court has also to consider whether to exercise its powers to exclude evidence under section 126 of the 2003 Act and section 78 of the *Police and Criminal Evidence Act* 1984. Whether it is fair to admit statements depends, in part, on what efforts should reasonably be made to secure the attendance of the witness or to arrange a procedure whereby the contents of the statements can be clarified and challenged. It is reasonable to make further enquiries as to why the witness has changed his mind and refused to give evidence via video-link: *C., K.* [2006] EWCA Crim 197.

In order to decide whether it is practicable for a witness to attend, a court must take into account the importance of the evidence, prejudice to the defence and the expense and inconvenience occasioned by the witness's attendance: *Castillo* [1996] 1 Cr.App.R.

438; *French* (1993) 97 Cr.App.R. 421; *Gonzales* (1993) 96 Cr.App.R. 399. In *Sawoniuk, ante,* elderly witnesses were brought from Poland because of the nature of the crime.

Previous cases on fear include *Belmarsh Magistrates' Court, ex p. Gilligan* [1998] 1 Cr.App.R. 14 where it was said that a statement by a witness himself that he was in fear was not admissible to prove that he was in fear and oral evidence of a police officer was necessary; *Greer* [1998] Crim.L.R. 572 where the statement of the witness alone was held to be sufficient; *Denton* [2001] 1 Cr.App.R. 16 where it was held that a judge should give valid reasons for allowing a statement. A broader approach appears to have been taken since the Act. It has been said that before admitting statements a court would be ill advised to seek to test the basis of a fear as it would undermine the very purpose that section 116 set out to achieve; fear is to be widely construed: *Davies* [2006] EWCA Crim 2643; (2006) 150 S.J.L.B. 1288. Where a witness is being subjected to subtle intimidation from a defendant, a court has to perform a balancing exercise between a subjective assessment of fear and an objective assessment of fairness in deciding whether a statement should be admitted under section 116: *Doherty* [2006] EWCA Crim 2716; (2007) 171 J.P. 79. In *H., A., The Times,* July 6, 2001, a kidnapping case, it was held that a witness's fear is to be assessed by reference to the time at which he is expected to give evidence. In that case, the witness's fear was held to be out of date as the indication was that he was afraid some weeks prior to the trial. A stringent approach should be taken particularly if the evidence was critical to the outcome of the case. A victim's state of mind has to be assessed against the history of the case: *Boulton* [2007] EWCA Crim 942. In this domestic violence case, threats against the victim and her financial resources were considered to be evidence in relation to her "fear".

Before granting an application a court should be informed of any, and if so, what efforts have been made to alleviate the fears, for example, witness protection or screens at court. In *Arnold* (2004) 148 S.J.L.B. 660, a case of grievous bodily harm, it was said that caution should be taken to ensure that attention is paid to the spirit and letter of Article 6 ECHR and a court should not be easily persuaded that it is in the interests of justice to permit evidence to be read. A party may wish to consider the point at which the application is made and make the exact nature of the application clear: *R. (CPS) v. Uxbridge Magistrates' Court & Gore* [2007] EWHC 205, Admin. The prosecutor was unsuccessful in an application to adjourn the trial on the grounds that the witness was not before the court. The prosecution then made an application to introduce the evidence of the victim under section 116 on the grounds that the witness was mentally unfit to give evidence on the basis that she had been "sectioned" under the *Mental Health Act* 1983 and was detained. The defence argued that this was a deliberate attempt to circumvent the court's decision to adjourn. The court refused to reconsider its earlier decision and was held to have been wrong in failing to address the application under section 116.

Business and other documents

Criminal Justice Act 2003, s.117

Business and other documents

10–75   117.—(1) In criminal proceedings a statement contained in a document is admissible as evidence of any matter stated if—

    (a) oral evidence given in the proceedings would be admissible as evidence of that matter,

    (b) the requirements of subsection (2) are satisfied, and

    (c) the requirements of subsection (5) are satisfied, in a case where subsection (4) requires them to be.

    (2) The requirements of this subsection are satisfied if—

    (a) the document or the part containing the statement was created or received by a person in the course of a trade, business, profession or other occupation, or as the holder of a paid or unpaid office,

    (b) the person who supplied the information contained in the statement (the relevant person) had or may reasonably be supposed to have had personal knowledge of the matters dealt with, and

    (c) each person (if any) through whom the information was supplied from the relevant person to the person mentioned in paragraph (a) received the information in the course of a trade, business, profession or other occupation, or as the holder of a paid or unpaid office.

(3) The persons mentioned in paragraphs (a) and (b) of subsection (2) may be the same person.

(4) The additional requirements of subsection (5) must be satisfied if the statement—   **10–76**

    (a) was prepared for the purposes of pending or contemplated criminal proceedings, or for a criminal investigation, but

    (b) was not obtained pursuant to a request under section 7 of the *Crime (International Co-operation) Act* 2003 or an order under paragraph 6 of Schedule 13 to the *Criminal Justice Act* 1988 (which relate to overseas evidence).

(5) The requirements of this subsection are satisfied if—

    (a) any of the five conditions mentioned in section 116(2) is satisfied (absence of relevant person etc), or

    (b) the relevant person cannot reasonably be expected to have any recollection of the matters dealt with in the statement (having regard to the length of time since he supplied the information and all other circumstances).

(6) A statement is not admissible under this section if the court makes a direction to that effect under subsection (7).

(7) The court may make a direction under this subsection if satisfied that the statement's reliability as evidence for the purpose for which it is tendered is doubtful in view of—

    (a) its contents,

    (b) the source of the information contained in it,

    (c) the way in which or the circumstances in which the information was supplied or received, or

    (d) the way in which or the circumstances in which the document concerned was created or received.

[This section replaces section 24 of the *Criminal Justice Act* 1988.]

Documents will include all business records, correspondence, diaries, logs and files   **10–77** both manual and computerised.

Documents will be admissible if:

— created or received in the course of a business *etc.*;

— the person supplying the information had personal knowledge;

— each person handling the information received it in the course of a business etc.;

— oral evidence of the fact would have been admissible;

— where the document was made for criminal proceedings or an investigation in UK the maker is dead, physically or mentally unfit, outside UK and impracticable for him to attend, unable to be found or afraid or he cannot be expected to have any recollection.

A label on a container identifying the name of the person whose blood it contained was admissible under the old law as it was said that a court could infer that it was prepared by a police officer in the normal course of his duties: *Khatibi v. DPP* (2004) 168 J.P. 361.

A computer printout recording successful and unsuccessful attempts to enter a website is admissible: *R. (O'Shea) v. Coventry Magistrates' Court* [2004] A.C.D. 50. Section 117 cannot be relied upon to justify the admission of a computerised police record providing short statements of the facts of the convictions and the methods used to commit those previous offences: *Humphris* (2005) 169 J.P. 441; see also *Burns (Bad character), post.* A police log noting the registration details of the defendant's vehicle left on the windscreen of the damaged vehicle was not admissible as a business document under section 117 but was admissible hearsay under section 114(2): *Maher v. DPP, ante.* Whilst the prosecution can adduce a mixed statement, the exculpatory parts being admissible as evidence of their truth, a defendant cannot introduce such a statement as part of his case: *Tine* [2006] EWCA Crim 1788.

In *Wellington v. DPP* [2007] EWCA Crim 1116 a PNC printout was admitted containing a list of aliases, one of which was the name which the defendant had given when stopped. It was said that it was an inescapable inference that the police officer supplying the information of aliases "had or could reasonably be supposed to have had personal knowledge" of the fact that the alias in question had been used. Although he could be expected to recall that aliases were used he could not be expected to recall details of those aliases.

The court may direct that the statement may not be introduced if it believes that its reliability is doubtful: section 117(7).

The rules of public information, reputation, *res gestae*, confessions, admissions by agents, common enterprise and expert evidence are preserved: section 118.

Criminal Justice Act 2003, ss.119–120

Inconsistent statements

10–78   **119.**—(1) If in criminal proceedings a person gives oral evidence and—
    (a) he admits making a previous inconsistent statement, or
    (b) a previous inconsistent statement made by him is proved by virtue of section 3, 4 or 5 the *Criminal Procedure Act* 1865,
the statement is admissible as evidence of any matter stated of which oral evidence by him would be admissible.

(2) If in criminal proceedings evidence of an inconsistent statement by any person is given under section 124(2)(c), the statement is admissible as evidence of any matter stated in it of which oral evidence by that person would be admissible.

10–79   The case of *N.* [2006] EWCA Crim 3309 clarifies the position of assertions under sections 115 and 119. The case involved inconsistent statements in an allegation of forcible rape where the victim's diary which had never been intended to be read by anyone nor to cause anyone to believe what was contained in it mentioned that sexual intercourse had been agreed for money. It had only come to light when it was read by the girl's mother. An assertion is defined as an act done with the purpose of making someone else believe or do something as a result. In the absence of a purpose to induce belief or action in someone else, the particular dangers against which the hearsay rule is designed to guard do not exist. The exclusionary hearsay rule should be confined to assertions, properly called; other facts, however, from which inferences my be drawn, are direct evidence and are admissible as such when relevant and are not subject to the limitations imposed upon the admissibility of hearsay. In this case if the diary was never intended to be read by anyone else it was not hearsay. It could, however, be admissible as direct evidence from which inferences could be drawn.

Other previous statements of witnesses

10–80   **120.**—(1) This section applies where a person (the witness) is called to give evidence in criminal proceedings.

(2) If a previous statement by the witness is admitted as evidence to rebut a suggestion that his oral evidence has been fabricated, that statement is admissible as evidence of any matter stated of which oral evidence by the witness would be admissible.

(3) A statement made by the witness in a document—
    (a) which is used by him to refresh his memory while giving evidence,
    (b) on which he is cross-examined, and
    (c) which as a consequence is received in evidence in the proceedings,
is admissible as evidence of any matter stated of which oral evidence by him would be admissible.

(4) A previous statement by the witness is admissible as evidence of any matter stated of which oral evidence by him would be admissible, if—
    (a) any of the following three conditions is satisfied, and
    (b) while giving evidence the witness indicates that to the best of his belief he made the statement, and that to the best of his belief it states the truth.

(5) The first condition is that the statement identifies or describes a person, object or place.

(6) The second condition is that the statement was made by the witness when the matters stated were fresh in his memory but he does not remember them, and cannot reasonably be expected to remember them, well enough to give oral evidence of them in the proceedings.

(7) The third condition is that—

    (a) the witness claims to be a person against whom an offence has been committed,

    (b) the offence is one to which the proceedings relate,

    (c) the statement consists of a complaint made by the witness (whether to a person in authority or not) about conduct which would, if proved, constitute the offence or part of the offence,

    (d) the complaint was made as soon as could reasonably be expected after the alleged conduct,

    (e) the complaint was not made as a result of a threat or a promise, and

    (f) before the statement is adduced the witness gives oral evidence in connection with its subject matter.

(8) For the purposes of subsection (7) the fact that the complaint was elicited (for example, by a leading question) is irrelevant unless a threat or a promise was involved.

This section allows the admission of more than one hearsay statement as to a complaint by a victim of crime. It provides its own criteria and does not merely codify the old law of recent complaint: *Openshaw* [2006] EWCA Crim 556; [2006] 2 Cr.App.R. 27. **10–81**

A statement will not be admissible to prove an earlier hearsay statement was made unless all parties agree, the statement would admissible under sections 117, 119 or 120, *ante*, or the court is satisfied that, taking into account the reliability of the statement, that its value is so high that the interests of justice require its admissibility: section 121.

Criminal Justice Act 2003, ss.124, 126, 127, 129

Credibility

124.—(1) This section applies if in criminal proceedings— **10–82**

    (a) a statement not made in oral evidence in the proceedings is admitted as evidence of a matter stated, and

    (b) the maker of the statement does not give oral evidence in connection with the subject matter of the statement.

(2) In such a case—

    (a) any evidence which (if he had given such evidence) would have been admissible as relevant to his credibility as a witness is so admissible in the proceedings;

    (b) evidence may with the court's leave be given of any matter which (if he had given such evidence) could have been put to him in cross-examination as relevant to his credibility as a witness but of which evidence could not have been adduced by the cross-examining party;

    (c) evidence tending to prove that he made (at whatever time) any other statement inconsistent with the statement admitted as evidence is admissible for the purpose of showing that he contradicted himself.

(3) If as a result of evidence admitted under this section an allegation is made against the maker of a statement, the court may permit a party to lead additional evidence of such description as the court may specify for the purposes of denying or answering the allegation.

(4) In the case of a statement in a document which is admitted as evidence under section 117 each person who, in order for the statement to be admissible, must have supplied or received the information concerned or created or received the document or part concerned is to be treated as the maker of the statement for the purposes of subsections (1) to (3) above.

Court's general discretion to exclude evidence

126.—(1) In criminal proceedings the court may refuse to admit a statement as evidence of a matter stated if— **10–83**

    (a) the statement was made otherwise than in oral evidence in the proceedings, and

    (b) the court is satisfied that the case for excluding the statement, taking account of the danger that to admit it would result in undue waste of time, substantially outweighs the case for admitting it, taking account of the value of the evidence.

  (2) Nothing in this Chapter prejudices—

    (a) any power of a court to exclude evidence under section 78 of the *Police and Criminal Evidence Act* 1984 (exclusion of unfair evidence), or

    (b) any other power of a court to exclude evidence at its discretion (whether by preventing questions from being put or otherwise).

Expert evidence: preparatory work

10–84   **127.**—(1) This section applies if—

    (a) a statement has been prepared for the purposes of criminal proceedings,

    (b) the person who prepared the statement had or may reasonably be supposed to have had personal knowledge of the matters stated,

    (c) notice is given under the appropriate rules that another person (the expert) will in evidence given in the proceedings orally or under section 9 of the *Criminal Justice Act* 1967 base an opinion or inference on the statement, and

    (d) the notice gives the name of the person who prepared the statement and the nature of the matters stated.

  (2) In evidence given in the proceedings the expert may base an opinion or inference on the statement.

  (3) If evidence based on the statement is given under subsection (2) the statement is to be treated as evidence of what it states.

  (4) This section does not apply if the court, on an application by a party to the proceedings, orders that it is not in the interests of justice that it should apply.

  (5) The matters to be considered by the court in deciding whether to make an order under subsection (4) include—

    (a) the expense of calling as a witness the person who prepared the statement;

    (b) whether relevant evidence could be given by that person which could not be given by the expert;

    (c) whether that person can reasonably be expected to remember the matters stated well enough to give oral evidence of them.

  (6) Subsections (1) to (5) apply to a statement prepared for the purposes of a criminal investigation as they apply to a statement prepared for the purposes of criminal proceedings, and in such a case references to the proceedings are to criminal proceedings arising from the investigation.

  (7) The appropriate rules are rules made—

    (a) under section 81 of the *Police and Criminal Evidence Act* 1984 (advance notice of expert evidence in Crown Court), or

    (b) under section 144 of the *Magistrates'* Courts Act 1980 by virtue of section 20(3) of the *Criminal Procedure and Investigations Act* 1996 (advance notice of expert evidence in magistrates' courts).

Representations other than by a person

10–85   **129.**—(1) Where a representation of any fact—

    (a) is made otherwise than by a person, but

    (b) depends for its accuracy on information supplied (directly or indirectly) by a person,

the representation is not admissible in criminal proceedings as evidence of the fact unless it is proved that the information was accurate.

  (2) Subsection (1) does not affect the operation of the presumption that a mechanical device has been properly set or calibrated.

10–86   The purpose of this section is to provide that, where a statement generated by a machine is based on information supplied by a human, the statement will be admissible only if it is proved that the information is accurate. Section 129(2) preserves the common law presumption that a mechanical device is in proper working order.

Criminal Justice Act 2003, s.133

Proof of statements in documents

133. Where a statement in a document is admissible as evidence in criminal proceedings, the statement may be proved by producing either— **10–87**

(a) the document, or

(b) (whether or not the document exists) a copy of the document or of the material part of it,

authenticated in whatever way the court may approve.

This section replaces section 27(9) of the *Criminal Justice Act* 1988. It is intended to cover all types of copying including the use of imaging technology. **10–88**

VIII. IDENTIFICATION EVIDENCE

A. GENERAL

The question whether identification is in dispute must be considered at the time of the investigation, not subsequently in the light of evidence given at trial: *Lambert* [2004] EWCA Crim 154. Identification, where a person disputes that he is the person who was previously convicted of an offence, according to *R. v. Derwentside Magistrates' Court ex p. Heaviside* [1996] R.T.R. 384 can be proved in two stages: **10–89**

(1) the production of the certificate of conviction; and

(2) proof to the criminal standard that the person to whom that relates is the accused.

That case went on to state that there was no defined method of proving the second part and gave three examples—admission, fingerprint or by witnesses. Those examples are not exhaustive; statements can also be used: *R. v. Derwentside Magistrates' Court ex p. Swift and R. v. Sunderland Justices ex p. Bate* [1997] R.T.R. 89; *DPP v. Mooney* [1997] R.T.R. 434.

It will normally be possible to establish a *prima facie* case on the basis of the consistency of details between the accused and the person named in the memorandum of conviction: *Pattison v. DPP* [2006] 2 All E.R. 317. The cases establish the following principles:

(a) the prosecution must prove to the criminal standard of proof that the person accused was a disqualified driver;

(b) any admissible means may prove that the driver was disqualified;

(c) it is an essential element of the prosecution case that the accused is proved to the criminal standard to be the person named in the certificate where that certificate is relied upon;

(d) the three clear ways in which identity can be proved are set out in *Heaviside*;

(e) there is no prescribed way in which identity must be proved;

(f) where there is no evidence contradicting a prima facie case, the evidence will be sufficient for the court to convict;

(g) failure by the accused to give any contradictory evidence in rebuttal will be a matter for the court to take into account.

The defendant's representative may be called to testify as to what happened in the courtroom and this is not considered to be breach of legal privilege: *R. (Howe) v. South Durham Magistrates' Court* [2005] R.T.R 4. In *West Yorkshire Probation Board v. Boulter, ante,* it was said that the court is entitled to draw an inference that it is the same person if the name, address and date of birth coincide. Whether an inference is sufficient will depend on the facts of the particular case; see also *Burns* [2006] 1 W.L.R. 1273.

Where the identity of the defendant is in issue the prosecution must call identification evidence. Code D of the Police Code of Practice issued under the *Police and Criminal Evidence Act* 1984 applies: see Appendix A.

The House of Lords held in *Forbes* [2001] 1 All E.R. 686 that in the case of a disputed identification, the police must hold an identification parade if the suspect consents unless one of the savings made by Code D applies or a parade would be futile because the witness makes it plain that he cannot identify the culprit or can only identify his clothing; or where the case is one of "pure recognition" of someone well known to the victim; or there exists "other exceptional circumstances". In *H.* (2003) 147 S.J.L.B. 237, a recognition case, the Court of Appeal held that Code D now requires an ID parade where a dispute as to identity might reasonably be expected. There is no need for an identification parade when the defendant and the victim are known to each other: In *Harris* (2003) 147 S.J. 237 it was held that an identification procedure should have been held where the witness had not seen the sixteen-year-old defendant for two years.

When a witness has failed to make a positive identification in an identification parade the witness may still be called as a witness to describe the offender and what had occurred on the identification parade: *George* [2003] Crim.L.R. 282.

10–90   Where a victim had identified the defendant in the street by twice being driven past him by the police, the second identification during which police officers had stood by the defendant did not breach the PACE Codes of Practice as it was one continuous identification: *B. v. DPP* [2006] EWHC 660.

There is no contamination of an identification where witnesses attending a police station for an identification parade had sat in the same waiting room as the defendant but had said that they had paid no attention to him: *Banks* [2005] EWCA Crim 1858. The issue can still be one of identification where a defendant had said that he was on the other side of the road from that where the offence occurred and an identification parade should be held: *M.*, unreported, October 13, 2005, CA.

10–91   In summary road traffic proceedings, it is permissible for the prosecution to seek and rely upon a dock identification of the defendant in circumstances where there has been no prior notification that identity is in issue. It is not a violation of the right to a fair trial for the court to expect, and in that sense require, an accused person to indicate prior to trial that identification is in issue: see *Karia v. DPP* (2002) 166 J.P. 753, QBD and *Barnes v. Chief Constable of Durham* [1997] 2 Cr.App.R. 505; *Holland v. HM Advocate* [2005] UKPC D1. A witness can identify the person in the dock where an out-of-court identification has taken place on a previous occasion: *Christie* [1914] A.C. 545. It can also take place where a defendant has refused to take part in an identification parade: *John* [1973] Crim.L.R. 113.

10–92   The *Att.-Gen.'s Reference (No. 2 of 2002)* [2003] 1 Cr.App.R. 21, CA, gave at least four circumstances where the court can conclude that the defendant is shown on a photographic image from the scene of the crime:

1. where the photographic image was sufficiently clear it could be compared to the defendant in the dock;
2. where the witness knew then defendant sufficiently well to recognise him as the offender depicted in the photograph image, he could give evidence of that;
3. where a witness did not know the defendant but had spent a substantial time viewing and analysing the photographic images from the scene and had therefore acquired special knowledge, he could give evidence of identification based upon a comparison between those images and a reasonably contemporary photograph of the defendant, provided the images and the photograph were available to the jury; or
4. a suitably qualified expert with facial mapping skills could give opinion evidence of identification from a comparison between images from the scene, whether expertly enhanced or not, and a reasonably contemporary photograph of the defendant, provided both were available to the court.

Where photographs have been shown to a victim of those whose names have been given to him as his assailants and he then identifies the same persons in a later identification parade, a court should direct itself of the potential dangers of such an identification, that the victim had identified those on the photographs rather than identifying them as assailants: *I.*, unreported, January 23, 2007.

When identity is in issue the court will follow the *Turnbull* guidelines: *Turnbull* **10–93**
[1977] Q.B. 244; (1976) 63 Cr.App.R. 132.

1. whenever the case against an accused depends wholly or substantially on the accuracy of one or more identifications of the accused which the defence alleges to
   be mistaken, there is a special need for caution before convicting the accused on
   those identifications;

2. the circumstances in which the identification by each witness came to be made
   should be examined closely. How long did the witness have the accused under
   observation? At what distance? In what light? Was the observation impeded in
   any way, for example, by passing traffic or a press of people? Had the witness
   ever seen the accused before? How often? If only occasionally, had he any
   special reason to remember? How long elapsed between the original observation
   and the subsequent identification to the police? Was there any material discrepancy between the description of the accused given to the police by the witness
   when first seen by him and the actual appearance of the defendant?

3. any special weaknesses in the identification evidence should be considered.

The guidelines are for all cases where identification is in dispute and are not limited
to "fleeting glance" cases: *B*. [2004] EWCA Crim 1481. Even where an eyewitness
recognises an accused the court should remind itself of the *Turnbull* direction: *Capron*
[2006] UKPC 34.

Where the identification of a defendant's companion is unchallenged the court need
not take into account the guidelines: *Bath* [1990] Crim.L.R. 716, CA.

The identification of a motor car is a different matter and need not be approached
with special caution: *Hampton, Brown* (2004) 148 S.J.L.B. 973.

Clothing may also be the subject of identification: *Hickin* [1996] Crim.L.R. 584, CA.

The court has discretion to exclude evidence of identification at a confrontation:
Lamb (1980) 71 Cr.App.R 198, CA. An identification by video (CCTV) recording has
been said to be analogous to a street identification: *Jones (M.A.)* (1994) 158 J.P. 293.
The use of unmasked images bearing little resemblance to the defendant in age and appearance, where a witness is unable to make an identification from images which masked
differently in appearance, in video identification procedures is unlawful: *Marcus* [2004]
EWCA Crim 3387. There are cases in which it is appropriate to admit facial mapping
evidence even when Code D has been breached by failure to hold an identification parade: *Tobin (William Donald)* [2004] EWCA Crim 1081.

Recognition may be more reliable than identification of a stranger but even then **10–94**
mistakes may be made by close friends and relatives.

All these matters relate to the quality of the evidence. Where the quality is poor, the
court should find that there is no case to answer: *Fergus (Ivan)* (1994) 98 Cr.App.R.
313, CA. Identification by more than one witness is a factor influencing the quality of
the evidence, *i.e.* one witness might support another: *Weeder* (1980) 71 Cr.App.R. 228,
CA; *Tyler* (1993) 96 Cr.App.R. 332, CA. Poor identification, however, is not improved
by mere repetition by different witnesses.

In *Bentley* [1991] Crim.L.R. 620, CA. Lord Lane C.V.J. reminded the court of the
expression "I could have sworn it was you" used by people who had thought that they
had seen someone in the street only to discover that they were wrong. Care must be
taken to ensure that identification by a name is from the witness's own knowledge. The
court is entitled to take into account that police officers are trained in observation:
Ramsden [1991] Crim.L.R. 295, CA; *Tyler, ante*; *Powell v. DPP* [1992] R.T.R. 270.
Previous convictions introduced under the bad character provisions can be taken into
account when considering whether the identification of a defendant is correct; they are
there to assist rather than bolster a poor identification: *Blake* [2006] EWCA Crim 871.

Fingerprints etc.

A person may be identified by fingerprints alone *Castleton* 3 Cr.App.R. 74, CCA. **10–95**

The prosecution must show that the fingerprints taken from the scene of the crime match those on the fingerprint form, and also identify the fingerprints on the form. Strict proof is required: *Chappell v. DPP* (1989) 89 Cr.App.R. 82, DC. Guidance was given in *Buckley* (1999) 163 J.P. 561. Rose L.J. stated that whether fingerprint evidence was admissible as a matter of law tending to prove guilt would depend on: (1) the experience and expertise of the witness; (2) the number of similar ridge characteristics (if there were fewer than eight admission would be unlikely); (3) whether there are dissimilar characteristics; (4) size of print relied on; and (5) quality and clarity of print.

Strict proof is also required for palm and ear prints. The weight to be attached to such evidence is a matter for the court: *Dallagher* [2003] 1 Cr.App.R. 12.

For voice identification, see *O'Doherty* [2002] Crim.L.R. 761.

DNA profiles

10–96   Where the perpetrator of a crime leaves a stain of blood or semen at the scene it may prove possible to extract sufficient sections of DNA to enable a comparison to be drawn with the same sections extracted for a sample of blood taken from the defendant. A DNA profile is not unique; it establishes probabilities. Specific guidance is found in *Doheny* [1997] 1 Cr.App.R. 369. There must be continuity of evidence: *Philips*, unreported, August 25, 2004; *R. (S.) v. Chief Constable of South Yorkshire* [2004] 1 W.L.R. 2194.

B. OPINION

(1) General

10–97   The general rule is that opinion evidence is excluded except as evidence of identity, feelings, physical condition, handwriting, impressions or expert evidence.

(2) Non-expert opinion

10–98   Evidence of the opinion of a witness who is not an expert may be admissible if the impression received by the witness is too vague to be otherwise described or if made as a way of conveying relevant facts perceived by him or her. A witness may give evidence of his opinion of the age of a person: *Cox* [1898] 1 Q.B. 179 (a "young woman"); *Wallworth v. Balmer* [1966] 1 W.L.R. 16 ("a child of about five"); *Davies* 46 Cr.App.R. 292; *Neal* [1962] Crim.L.R. 698.

(3) Expert opinion

10–99   Where a witness is qualified to express a credible opinion or belief on the subject then evidence of the witness's opinion is admissible: *Silverlock* [1894] 2 Q.B. 766. It is for the court to determine a witness's competence. If the court can form its own conclusions from the facts without help, then the opinion of an expert is unnecessary: *Turner* [1975] Q.B. 834; *Loughran* [1999] Crim.L.R. 404, CA.

An expert is now permitted to give his opinion on what has been called the "ultimate issue" that is the very issue to be determined by the court, for example on whether the defendant is suffering from diminished responsibility. The ultimate issue is, however, for the tribunal of fact to decide and the court is not bound to accept the expert's opinion: *Stockwell* (1993) 97 Cr.App.R. 260, CA. Caution needs to be exercised against the dangers of dogmatism - scientific knowledge can be dynamic and can be limited and incomplete: *Cannings* [2004] EWCA Crim 1.

In *Jeffries* [1997] Crim.L.R. 819, it was held that a police officer was able to give evidence as to the values and prices of drugs in order that the jury may interpret lists found at the defendant's premises but the officer could not express an opinion that the lists related to the sale of drugs because that would amount to a statement that the defendant was guilty of the offence charged.

Lip reading evidence from a video is a species of real evidence and is admissible; in each case it depends on factors such as the quality of the video and the skill of the interpreting witness and caution must be exercised because errors can occur: *Luttrell* [2004] 2 Cr.App.R. 31. There are strict limits of admissible expert evidence based upon memory research: *S.* [2006] EWCA Crim 1404, *Independent*, July 4, 2006; for a discussion of hypnotherapy and false memory syndrome see also: *C.*, unreported, February 3, 2006.

Before the court can assess the value of an opinion it must know the facts upon **10–100** which it is based. If the expert has been misinformed or has taken irrelevant facts into account, or has failed to consider relevant ones, the opinion is likely to be of little value. An expert witness should be asked to state the facts upon which the opinion is based: *J.P.* [1999] Crim.L.R. 401, CA; *Jackson* [1996] 2 Cr.App.R. 420, CA. Where there is a conflict of opinion between reputable expert witnesses, the expert evidence called by the Crown is not automatically neutralised; the findings are matters to be evaluated by the court: *Kai-Whitewind* [2005] 2 Cr.App.R. 31.

The witness need not have conducted any test or examination himself. The opinion may be given on the basis of facts proved in court: *Mason* 7 Cr.App.R. 67. The fact that a witness did not personally conduct a test or examination will go to the weight to be attached to the opinion.

Expert witnesses may refer not only to their own research, tests and experiments but also to works of authority, learned articles, research papers and other similar materials written by others and forming part of the general body of knowledge falling within their field of expertise: *Davie v. Magistrates of Edinburgh*, 1953 S.C. 34; *Seyfang v. J.D. Searle & Co* [1973] Q.B. 148; *H. v. Schering Chemicals Ltd* [1983] 1 W.L.R. 143.

Expert medical evidence as to the weight to be attached to a witness's evidence is now admissible even where no physical examination of the witness has been carried out if it demonstrates some form of abnormality relevant to the reliability of a defendant's confession or evidence: *Pinfold* [2004] 2 Cr.App.R. 5. Where the prosecution asserts that a guilty motive is to be inferred from a defendant's actions, medical evidence suggesting that those actions could instead have been caused by the effects of post traumatic stress disorder is admissible on appeal: *Huckerby* [2004] EWCA Crim 3251. The ability of a witness to remember facts is normally within the experience of the court. It would be extremely rare for an expert to have to give evidence on possible unreliability: *X.*, unreported, July 1, 2005. In that case an expert was said to be able to give evidence of childhood amnesia only where it was relevant and admissible and in a case where a witness described an incident of an early event in an unrealistic amount of detail.

This principle does not however extend to purely anecdotal evidence. In *Edwards* **10–101** [2001] All E.R. (D) 271; [2001] EWCA Crim 2185 the question was whether ecstasy tablets found in the defendant's possession were for personal consumption or supply. The prosecution and defence sought to call persons neither of whom had formal medical or toxicological training to give evidence based on their experience rather than on statistical surveys or reports as to the personal consumption rates of ecstasy tablet users. It was held that the trial judge had properly excluded their evidence as inadmissible hearsay.

An expert witness should give reasons for his conclusions: *Hipson* [1969] Crim.L.R. 85, CA.

In the shaken baby syndrome co-joined cases: *Harris (Lorraine)* [2005] EWCA Crim 1980; [2006] 1 Cr.App.R. 5 the Court of Appeal refused to give fresh guidance on expert evidence. It referred to the cases of *Bonython* [1984] 38 S.A.S.R. 45 and *Clarke* [1985] 2 Cr.App.R. 425 and went on to say that developments in scientific thinking should not be kept from the court simply because they remain at the stage of hypothesis. Courts were to be reminded of the obligations of an expert witness summarised in *Ikarian Reefer* [1993] 2 Lloyds Rep. 68:

    (1) expert evidence presented to the court should be and seen to be the independent product of the expert uninfluenced as to form or content by the exigencies of legislation;

(2) an expert witness should provide independent assistance to the court by way of objective unbiased opinion in relation to matters within his expertise . . . [he] should never assume the role of advocate;

(3) an expert witness should state the facts or assumptions on which his opinion is based. He should not omit to consider material facts which detract from his concluded opinion;

(4) an expert should make it clear when a particular question or issue falls outside his expertise;

(5) if an expert's opinion is not properly researched because he considers that insufficient data is available then this must be stated with an indication that the opinion is no more than a provisional one;

(6) if after exchange of reports, an expert witness changes his view on material matters, such change of view should be communicated to the other side without delay and when appropriate to the court.

Further guidance on specific factors to be included in an expert report was given in *Bowman* [2006] 2 Cr.App.R. 3:

(a) details of the expert's academic record and professional qualifications, range of experience and any limitations on expertise;

(b) the substance of the instructions received, questions upon which an opinion was sought, the materials provided and considered and the information or assumptions that were material to the opinions expressed;

(c) information about who carried out measurements and tests, the methodology, and whether they were supervised by the expert;

(d) where there was a range of opinion in the matters dealt with in the report, a summary of the range of opinion and the reasons for the opinion given. In that connection any material facts or matters that detracted from the expert's opinion and any points that should fairly be made against any opinions expressed should be set out;

(e) relevant extracts of literature or other material that might assist the court;

(f) a statement that the expert had complied with his duty to the court to provide independent assistance by way of objective unbiased opinion, and an acknowledgement that the expert would inform all parties and where appropriate the court if his opinion changed on any material issue;

(g) the same guidelines should be followed in any supplemental report.

This was emphasised in the case of *S.*, *Independent*, July 4, 2006, which repeated the current strict limits of admissible expert evidence based upon memory research.

Criminal Justice Act 1988, s.30

Expert reports

10–102   **30.**—(1) An expert report shall be admissible as evidence in criminal proceedings, whether or not the person making it attends to give oral evidence in those proceedings.

(2) If it is proposed that the person making the report shall not give oral evidence, the report shall only be admissible with the leave of the court.

(3) For the purpose of determining whether to give leave the court shall have regard—

(a) to the contents of the report;

(b) to the reasons why it is proposed that the person making the report shall not give oral evidence;

(c) to any risk, having regard in particular to whether it is likely to be possible to controvert statements in the report if the person making it does not attend to give oral evidence in the proceedings, that its admission or exclusion will result in unfairness to the accused or, if there is more than one, to any of them; and

(d) to any other circumstances that appear to the court to be relevant.

(4) An expert report, when admitted, shall be evidence of any fact or opinion of which the person making it could have given oral evidence.

(4A) Where the proceedings mentioned in subsection (1) above are proceedings before a magistrates' court inquiring into an offence as examining justices this section shall have effect with the omission of—

    (a) in subsection (1) the words "whether or not the person making it attends to give oral evidence in those proceedings", and

    (b) subsections (2) to (4).

    (5) In this section "expert report" means a written report by a person dealing wholly or mainly with matters on which he is (or would if living be) qualified to give expert evidence.

This section allows for the receipt of reports whether or not the expert gives oral evidence. Notice needs to be given of expert evidence.

Disclosure of expert opinion

See *Criminal Procedure Rules*, r.24 in Appendix G–142.   **10–103**

It is the duty of an expert instructed by the prosecution to act in the interests of   **10–104** justice: *Ward* (1993) 96 Cr.App.R. 1, CA. If an expert has carried out a test which casts doubt on his opinion, or if such a test has been carried out in his laboratory and is known to him, the expert is under a duty to disclose this to the solicitor instructing him, who in turn has a duty to disclose it to the defence.

Part II

C. EXPERT EVIDENCE / OPINION PREPARATORY WORK

Criminal Justice Act 2003, s.127

Expert evidence: preparatory work

127.—(1) This section applies if—   **10–105**

    (a) a statement has been prepared for the purposes of criminal proceedings,

    (b) the person who prepared the statement had or may reasonably be supposed to have had personal knowledge of the matters stated,

    (c) notice is given under the appropriate rules that another person (the expert) will in evidence given in the proceedings orally or under section 9 of the *Criminal Justice Act* 1967 (c. 80) base an opinion or inference on the statement, and

    (d) the notice gives the name of the person who prepared the statement and the nature of the matters stated.

    (2) In evidence given in the proceedings the expert may base an opinion or inference on the statement.

    (3) If evidence based on the statement is given under subsection (2) the statement is to be treated as evidence of what it states.

    (4) This section does not apply if the court, on an application by a party to the proceedings, orders that it is not in the interests of justice that it should apply.

    (5) The matters to be considered by the court in deciding whether to make an order under subsection (4) include—

    (a) the expense of calling as a witness the person who prepared the statement;

    (b) whether relevant evidence could be given by that person which could not be given by the expert;

    (c) whether that person can reasonably be expected to remember the matters stated well enough to give oral evidence of them.

    (6) Subsections (1) to (5) apply to a statement prepared for the purposes of a criminal investigation as they apply to a statement prepared for the purposes of criminal proceedings, and in such a case references to the proceedings are to criminal proceedings arising from the investigation.

    (7) The appropriate rules are rules made—

    (a) under section 81 of the *Police and Criminal Evidence Act* 1984 (advance notice of expert evidence in Crown Court), or

    (b) under section 144 of the *Magistrates' Courts Act* 1980 by virtue of section 20(3) of the *Criminal Procedure and Investigations Act* 1996 (advance notice of expert evidence in magistrates' courts).

IX. CHARACTER

A. GOOD CHARACTER

10–106   A defendant may call evidence of his good character, *i.e.* his general reputation: *Rowton* (1865) Le. & Ca. 520. Such evidence is relevant to a defendant's credibility and to whether it is likely that he committed the offence with which he is charged. The calling of such evidence may have implications—see *post*, bad character.

Where a defendant is of good character the court should direct itself on its relevance to credibility where the defendant gives evidence or has made pre trial statements and should direct itself on its relevance to propensity whether or not he gave evidence or made pre trial statements: *Vye* 97 Cr.App.R. 134. Ultimately it all goes to the issue of credibility, *i.e.* whether the court believes the defendant: *Mentor* [2004] EWCA Crim 3104.

A defendant may be treated by the court as of good character even where he has a previous conviction so long as that conviction is of a different nature: *Timson, Hales* [1993] Crim.L.R. 58 or spent; *Lawrence (Irvin)* [1995] Crim.L.R. 815; *Nye* 75 Cr.App.R. 247. A caution may, however, prevent a defendant from being considered as of good character: *Maillet* [2005] EWCA Crim 3159. The court can direct itself on the good character of one defendant despite possible prejudice to a co-accused: *Louden-Barratnew* [2004] EWCA Crim 1753; *Payton* (2006) 150 S.J.L.B. 741.

B. BAD CHARACTER

10–107   The *Criminal Justice Act* 2003 makes statutory provision for the evidence of bad character for both defendants and non-defendants although they are different in each case. The common law rules are abolished: *Bradley* [2005] 1 Cr.App.R. 24 made it clear that the provisions apply after December 15, 2004. The reasons for any rulings must be entered in the court register: section 110.

Criminal Justice Act 2003, s.98

"Bad character"

10–108   **98.** References in this Chapter to evidence of a person's "bad character" are to evidence of, or of a disposition towards, misconduct on his part, other than evidence which—
   (a) has to do with the alleged facts of the offence with which the defendant is charged, or
   (b) is evidence of misconduct in connection with the investigation or prosecution of that offence.

10–109   Misconduct means the commission of an offence or other reprehensible behaviour: *Criminal Justice Act* 2003, s.112. It is a very wide definition. Reprehensible is defined in the Oxford dictionary as blameworthy, deserving of censure or rebuke. Shouting at a partner and becoming aggressive when failing to take medication for paranoid schizophrenia, in the context of a case of murdering a friend, was held not to be reprehensible behaviour: *Osbourne* [2007] EWCA Crim 481. Evidence of previous convictions fall within this definition. Convictions when under the age of fourteen are admissible: *Criminal Justice Act* 2003, s.108(1). If the defendant is aged twenty one or over, however, evidence of a previous conviction when under the age of fourteen is not admissible unless that offence and the one being tried are triable only on indictment and the court is satisfied that it is in the interests of justice to admit it: section 108(2). Evidence suggesting that a person has committed an offence even where he has not been convicted or charged may also be admissible if relevant: *Criminal Justice Act* 2003, s.108(2). It is necessary to distinguish between the admissibility of evidence and how that evidence may be proved. Section 99(1) abolished the common law rule in *Hollington v. Hewthorn* so far as it might ever have applied and therefore foreign convictions can be proved under section 7 of the *Evidence Act* 1851 and are admissible pursuant to and subject to section 101: *Kordasinski, ante.* The safeguard of fairness contained in sections

101(3) and 103 meant that the entire Polish record, or large parts of it, could never have fairly been admitted. The prosecution must limit the details and it is open to a defendant to give evidence denying or challenging the underlying factual basis for the convictions.

The section also includes evidence of a disposition towards misconduct, *c.f.* the previous similar fact rule. A defendant cannot give evidence of use of and offer to supply drugs as bad character where the offer was part of the very circumstances in which the alleged crime occurred: *Machado* [2006] EWCA Crim 837; (2006) 170 J.P 400. Where there is a possibility that evidence may be contaminated, *i.e.* by deliberate collusion, improper pressure or inadvertence, evidence of bad character should not be admitted until the evidence of complainants and other witnesses has been heard. It is at that stage that consideration must be given to whether section 107 applies: *Card*, *The Times*, May 11, 2006.

Evidence is "to do with the alleged facts of the offence.   . .." where there is some nexus in time between the offence with which the defendant is charged and the evidence of misconduct which the prosecution seeks to adduce. There is a potential overlap between evidence that "has to do with" the alleged facts of the case and evidence that might be admitted through one of the section 101(1) gateways. The relevance and purpose for which the evidence is being used should be clear: *Tirnaveanu* [2007] EWCA Crim 1239.

The *Criminal Procedure Rules* 2005 make provision for notice of such evidence to be served before its introduction and sets time limits. The court has a discretion to extend that time limit under rule 35.8 and that is not limited to exceptional circumstances. Two of the key considerations are whether there is a good explanation of the failure to give notice within the time limit and whether the opposing party has suffered any prejudice: *R. (Robinson) v. Sutton Coldfield Magistrates' Court* [2006] EWHC 307, Admin; [2006] 2 Cr.App.R. 13. In the case of *Hassan* [2007] EWCA Crim 1287 although notice was late the matter of a previous conviction had been raised in interview and it was said that the defendant could plainly have been expected to know the position. Since there is discretion to allow bad character evidence to be adduced, despite notice not having been given, by permitting notice to be given orally or in a different form to that prescribed, and there is power to shorten time for it, it must be implicit in that power to shorten time that it can be shortened to any degree, and thus dispensed with: *Lawson* [2007] 1 Cr.App.R. 11.

In many instances especially where notice under the *Criminal Procedure Rules* has been waived the court will hear all the evidence before deciding to admit or exclude. If it decides to exclude then it must put all matters out of its mind.

Criminal Justice Act 2003, s.100

Non-defendant's bad character
100.—(1) In criminal proceedings evidence of the bad character of a person other than the **10–110** defendant is admissible if and only if—
    (a) it is important explanatory evidence,
    (b) it has substantial probative value in relation to a matter which—
       (i) is a matter in issue in the proceedings, and
       (ii) is of substantial importance in the context of the case as a whole, or
    (c) all parties to the proceedings agree to the evidence being admissible.
  (2) For the purposes of subsection (1)(a) evidence is important explanatory evidence if—
    (a) without it, the court or jury would find it impossible or difficult properly to understand other evidence in the case, and
    (b) its value for understanding the case as a whole is substantial.
  (3) In assessing the probative value of evidence for the purposes of subsection (1)(b) the court must have regard to the following factors (and to any others it considers relevant)—
    (a) the nature and number of the events, or other things, to which the evidence relates;

    (b) when those events or things are alleged to have happened or existed;

    (c) where—

        (i) the evidence is evidence of a person's misconduct, and

        (ii) it is suggested that the evidence has probative value by reason of similarity between that misconduct and other alleged misconduct,

    the nature and extent of the similarities and the dissimilarities between each of the alleged instances of misconduct;

    (d) where—

        (i) the evidence is evidence of a person's misconduct,

        (ii) it is suggested that that person is also responsible for the misconduct charged, and

        (iii) the identity of the person responsible for the misconduct charged is disputed,

    the extent to which the evidence shows or tends to show that the same person was responsible each time.

    (4) Except where subsection (1)(c) applies, evidence of the bad character of a person other than the defendant must not be given without leave of the court.

10–111   Prior to the *Criminal Justice Act* 2003, witnesses have been cross-examined on previous convictions or bad character. Prosecution witnesses were protected to the extent that a defendant might be liable to be cross-examined on his own bad character. The *Criminal Justice Act* 2003 ensures that, unless both parties agree, the leave of the court is sought before a witness is examined on his bad character. It sets out clear limitations on the introduction of such evidence through what is called gateways.

The questions to ask are:
1. What is the misconduct alleged?
    (a) Previous convictions? – if there are, go to 2.
    (b) Behaviour? What is it? Is it to do with the facts of the case?– If Yes, irrelevant. If No, consider whether reprehensible. If No, not admissible. If Yes, go to 2.
2. Is its submission agreed? If Yes, admissible. If No, go to 3.
3. Do any of the following apply?
    (i) Important explanatory evidence. If No, not admissible, if Yes, consider whether its value to the understanding of the case is substantial. If No, not admissible. If Yes, go to 4
    (ii) Substantial probative value in relation to a matter in issue in the proceedings and is of substantial importance in the context of the case as a whole What is the issue in the proceedings?
    Is it probative applying the enhanced relevance test, *i.e.* Nature, number of events or things to which the evidence relates – are they recent/old? Similar to other misconduct? Is the witness being blamed for the acts the subject of the charge?
    If No – not admissible, if Yes – consider whether of substantial importance as a whole?
    If No – not admissible, if Yes go to 4.
4. Should the evidence be admitted? – court's final discretion

---

    Previously, cross-examination of a police officer has been allowed where evidence in a previous case had been disbelieved resulting in an acquittal even where the misconduct alleged was of a different nature: *Malik* [2002] 2 Cr.App.R. 8, CA. It was held in *Edwards* 93 Cr.App.R. 48 that a police officer could be questioned about any relevant criminal offences or disciplinary charges found proved against him. Where a witness denies a previous conviction, it may be proved under the *Criminal Procedure Act* 1865, s.6.

10–112   Whilst propensity to commit offences with which a defendant is charged is included in matters in issue there is no analogue to section 103(1)(a) in section 100. In some circumstances previous convictions may have probative value to a matter in issue, *e.g.* to support an argument that a complainant had a propensity to act dishonestly: *S.* , unreported, April 28, 2006. The case of *D.* [2006] EWCA Crim 2600 (see § 9–3, *ante*) involved an application by defendants, charged with assault, to produce the school records of the victim to show his violent behaviour. It was held that, in view of the public interest in preserving the confidentiality of school records, the court was correct not to require disclosure of the names of those involved in the school incidents, at least in so far as they were children. The evidence was, however, relevant to the state of mind of the defendant as he entered the park where the assault took place and the reason for his carrying a weapon. It was suggested that a simple admission by the prosecution that the defendant knew of the victim's reputation and that an earlier incident had occurred between the two of them might have been the way forward.

See *Criminal Procedure Rules* 2005, r.35.2 in Appendix G–208.   **10–113**

Defendant's bad character

There is now an inclusionary approach to the admissibility of a defendant's bad **10–114** character. The parties may agree to its admission but beyond that it is admissible via what is called gateways unless certain circumstances prevail when the court has a discretion to exclude.

In *Hanson; Gilmore; Pickstone* [2005] EWCA Crim 824; [2005] 1 W.L.R. 3169, the Court of Appeal stated that bearing in mind that Parliament's purpose in the legislation, as divined from the terms of the Act, was to assist in the evidence-based conviction of the guilty, without putting those who were not guilty at risk of conviction by prejudice, it was to be hoped that prosecution application to adduce such evidence would not be made routinely, simply because a defendant had previous convictions, but would be based on the particular circumstances of each case.

The guidelines on summing up in *Hansen, ante*, were held not to be a blueprint: *Edwards*, unreported, June 29, 2005. That case set out a model direction applicable in crown courts. It underlines the fact that a defendant should not be convicted only because he is of bad character. The direction refers to evidence being admitted to help understand other evidence and to resolve an issue between the defence and prosecution, namely whether the defendant had a tendency or inclination to commit offences of the kind with which he was charged. It stressed that even if the court thought he had a propensity to commit offences of a particular type then it did not necessarily prove that he would commit further offences or that he had committed the offences with which he was charged or that if he had previous convictions for dishonesty that he was not telling the truth.

In *Bovell, Dowds* [2005] EWCA Crim 1091; [2005] 2 Cr.App.R. 27 the court stated that:

1) It is necessary for all parties to have the appropriate information in relation to convictions and other evidence of bad character, whether in relation to the defendant or to some other person, in good time. The rules relating to notice should be complied with.
2) There were concerns in respect of the retention of relevant material.
3) It is doubtful whether an allegation is capable of being evidence within section 100(1) and where it is withdrawn that doubt increases. A court should be discharged from delving into 'satellite' matters.
4) Where a defendant attacks another's character a court should not conduct an investigation into why a defendant has given the answer he has in order to assess the "adverse effect on the nature of the proceedings".

The Court of Appeal in *Renda* [2005] EWCA Crim 2826; [2006] 1 Cr.App.R. 24 said **10–115** that the circumstances in which it is likely to interfere with judicial discretion to admit evidence will be limited as rulings are likely to be fact specific and any observations might be counterproductive.

Several points were covered in *Weir* [2005] EWCA Crim 2866; [2006] 1 Cr.App.R. 19:

1) The opening words of section 104(2) indicate that a defendant's propensity to commit offences of the kind with which he is charged can be proved in ways other than by evidence that he has been convicted of an offence of the same description or the same category, *e.g.* by cautions or TICs.

2) The 2003 Act completely reverses the pre-existing general rule that evidence of bad character was inadmissible on the ground that its prejudicial effect was likely to outweigh its probative value. Evidence is now admissible if it satisfies the Act's criteria. "Enhanced relevance" in the explanatory notes to the Act refers to section 100 only where there is a higher test in respect of a non-defendant's bad character.

3) The exclusion of evidence under section 101(3) should be considered whenever it appears that the admission might have adverse effects on the fairness of the proceedings.

4) Section 100(1) does cover matters of credibility.

5) There are cases where previous conduct of a defendant is of probative value and relevant yet cannot come within the bad character provisions. Section 99(1) abolishing common law rules of bad character does not apply as in these cases the conduct does not amount to evidence of bad character and therefore the evidence might be admissible.

Where the prosecution seeks to adduce evidence of previous convictions in order to show propensity to commit sexual offences, it is important for the prosecution to determine whether it needs any more evidence than the actual previous conviction to achieve the purpose for which it wants the evidence to be admitted. That evidence would normally be a statement or oral evidence of the complainant relating to the previous conviction and such a statement is not to be demanded lightly. A statement by a police officer drawn from police records is insufficient: *Humphris, ante.*

Where there is a dispute between the prosecution and defence on the facts supporting the previous convictions it is not enough for the prosecution to rely on the police national computer. Evidence should be adduced from the complainant, although there is a need for caution, as the defendant might have been sentenced on a different basis to that advanced by the complainant. Care also has to be taken to avoid satellite issues arising: *Ainscough* (2006) 170 J.P. 517.

A distinction must be drawn between admissibility of bad character which depends on getting through one of the gateways and the use to which it is put once admitted. The use to which it can be put depends on its relevance rather than upon the gateway through which it is admitted: *Highton* [2005] EWCA Crim 1985; [2005] 1 W.L.R. 3472. Here evidence had been admitted as a result of an attack on another person's character and was used to show the propensity to commit offences of the kind with which the defendant was charged. A protection would be found in section 101(3) and in addition section 78 of the *Police and Criminal Evidence Act* 1984.

10–116   In *Edwards* [2005] EWCA Crim 3244; [2006] 1 W.L.R. 1524, the Court of Appeal ruled that (and with the author's amendments for magistrates' courts):

1) Often the first enquiry is whether it is necessary to go through the "bad character" gateways at all. In that regard, section 98 is not to be overlooked. It excludes from the definition of bad character such evidence which "has to do with the alleged facts of the offence" or evidence of "misconduct in connection with the investigation or prosecution of the offence". Whilst difficult questions can arise as to whether evidence of background or motive fall to be admitted under those exclusions in section 98 or require consideration under section 101(1)(c) it does not follow that merely because evidence fails to come within the section 101 gateway it will be inadmissible.

2) Applications to admit bad character evidence may well arise at an early stage, giving rise to real difficulty for the trial tribunal. Some applications, *e.g.* under

  section 101(1)(b) cannot be refused; others, for instance, brought under section 101(1)(e) may well be difficult to refuse. Parties should reflect at the time of the application, as to the use to which such evidence is likely to be put and to be in a position to assist the court in that regard.

3) Under the new regime, it is apparent that Parliament has intended that evidence of bad character will be put before the court more frequently than before. The role of the judiciary is to determine admissibility under the statutory gateways and any question of exclusion, *e.g.* under sections 101(3), 103(3) or section 78 of *Police and Criminal Evidence Act* 1984. Once evidence of bad character is admitted (and not excluded) questions of weight will follow.

4) Where evidence of bad character is admitted, the court should direct itself on the matters outlined in *Hanson* and *Highton* and may need to pull threads together on an issue where the ground may have shifted considerably since the evidence was admitted. By that stage, the evidence could be of very little weight.

5) Simply because an application to admit evidence of bad character is made by a co-defendant, a court is not bound to admit it. The gateway in section 101(1)(c) has to be gone through. Sections 101(1)(d) and (e) give rise to different considerations. In determining an application under section 101(1)(e), analysis with a fine tooth comb is unlikely to be helpful; it is the context of the case as a whole which matters. Section 112 makes that clear by its definition of what amounts to an important matter in issue.

6) As to the position of co-defendants; (1) the gateways under sections 101(1)(d), (f) and (g) are not open to them, as only prosecution evidence, as defined in section 112, is admissible (sections 103(6), 105(7) and 106(3); (ii) section 104(1) is not exhaustive of the scope of section 101(1)(e)—it limits evidence relevant to a defendant's propensity to be untruthful; (iii) whether a defendant's stance amounts to no more than a denial of participation or gives rise to an important matter in issue between a defendant and a co-defendant will inevitably turn on the facts of the individual case

7) Whilst there is considerable doubt as to whether the mere making of an allegation is capable of being evidence within section 100(1), it is so capable when considering the effect of section 109 in relation to an issue under section 101(1)(d). However, that is an area in which it is important to guard against "satellite litigation". It is appropriate to proceed with caution and with due regard to the court's discretion to exclude evidence.

8) It is to be borne in mind that "admissibility" and "use" give rise to different questions. The "feel" of the trial court is very important.

10–117   A defendant is entitled to adduce evidence of a co-defendant's propensity to show that his version of events is more believable than that of his co-accused, even if the evidence concerns facts relating to an offence for which that co-accused has not been convicted: *Rafiq* [2005] EWCA Crim 1423. Where two defendants deny a crime and one claims innocence and blames the other, evidence of that defendant's previous convictions does not go simply to truthfulness but to his propensity to commit a crime and therefore can be admitted: *De Vos*, unreported, June 23, 2006.

It has also been held that allegations of sexual abuse which would have supported counts in an indictment but for the case being stayed as an abuse of process can be admitted as bad character to establish propensity: *Smith (David)*, *The Times*, January 2, 2006.

Criminal Justice Act 2003, s.101–106

Defendant's bad character

10–118   **101.**—(1) In criminal proceedings evidence of the defendant's bad character is admissible if, but only if—

 (a) all parties to the proceedings agree to the evidence being admissible,

 (b) the evidence is adduced by the defendant himself or is given in answer to a question asked by him in cross-examination and intended to elicit it,

Part II

    (c) it is important explanatory evidence,

    (d) it is relevant to an important matter in issue between the defendant and the prosecution,

    (e) it has substantial probative value in relation to an important matter in issue between the defendant and a co-defendant,

    (f) it is evidence to correct a false impression given by the defendant, or

    (g) the defendant has made an attack on another person's character.

(2) Sections 102 to 106 contain provision supplementing subsection (1).

(3) The court must not admit evidence under subsection (1)(d) or (g) if, on an application by the defendant to exclude it, it appears to the court that the admission of the evidence wouldhave such an adverse effect on the fairness of the proceedings that the court ought not to admit it.

(4) On an application to exclude evidence under subsection (3) the court must have regard, in particular, to the length of time between the matters to which that evidence relates and the matters which form the subject of the offence charged.

10–119   Bad character evidence which satisfies the requirements of section 101(1) of the *Criminal Justice Act* 2003 is admissible notwithstanding that it might not have satisfied the pre-existing similar fact test for admissibility: *Weir* [2006] 1 W.L.R. 1885.

    Evidence can be admitted under section 9 despite its being more appropriate under section 101 gateways as showing a propensity to untruthfulness: *Malone* [2006] EWCA Crim 1860. The prosecution had, in presenting its case, sought to illustrate the behaviour and movements of the defendant after the victim was killed by putting in a document purporting to be a report from a private detective detailing the victim's lies to the defendant about her movements. The evidence was circumstantial. It was allowed under section 98(a) but could also have been admitted under section 101 had there been an application. The fact that no notice was served under the *Criminal Procedure Rules* was not an insuperable obstacle to admission.

The questions to ask are:
1. What is the misconduct alleged?
   (a) Previous convictions? If Yes, go to 2.
   (b) Behaviour? Is it to do with the facts of the case?– If Yes, the provisions do
       not apply. If No, consider whether reprehensible. If No, inadmissible. If Yes,
       go to 2.
2. Is its submission agreed? If Yes, admissible, If No, go to 3.
3. Do any of the following apply?
   (i) Defendant has given evidence of his own bad character If Yes – admissible, if
       No – not admissible
   (ii) Important explanatory evidence
       If No – not admissible, if Yes – consider whether its value for understanding
       the case is substantial.
       If Yes – admissible, if No – not admissible
   (iii) Relevant to an important matter in issue between prosecution and
       defendant.
       What is the important matter in issue – propensity to commit type of case or
       be untruthful?
       If Yes – admissible, if No – not admissible.
       Is it relevant ? – see s.103.
   (iv) Substantial probative value to an important matter in issue between
       defendant and co-defendant.
       What is the matter in issue – propensity to be untruthful?
       Does it have probative value? Would it undermine the co-defendant's
       defence?
       If No – not admissible, if Yes – consider whether admission would have such
       an adverse effect on the proceedings that it ought not to be admitted.
       If Yes – not admissible, if No – admissible.
   (v) Corrects a false impression given by the defendant.
       Has a false impression been given by the defendant?
       If No – not admissible, if Yes – consider whether this evidence would correct
       it.
       If Yes – admissible, if No – not admissible
   (vi) Attack on another person's character?
       What is the nature of the defendant's attack?
       Committed an offence/behaved or disposed to have behaved in a
       reprehensible way?
       Would admission have such an adverse effect on the proceedings that it
       ought not to be admitted?
       If Yes – not admissible, if No – admissible

Important explanatory evidence
102. For the purposes of section 101(1)(c) evidence is important explanatory evidence if—   **10–120**
   (a) without it, the court or jury would find it impossible or difficult properly to
       understand other evidence in the case, and
   (b) its value for understanding the case as a whole is substantial.

Explanatory evidence was defined in *Pettman*, unreported, May 2, 1985, CA where   **10–121**
Purchas L.J. said that it was "evidence of part of a continual background of history relevant to the offence charged….and without the totality of which the account….would be
incomplete or incomprehensible". Such evidence was given in the case of *Sawoniuk*,
ante, where, in a war crimes trial, evidence was given about the prevailing circumstances in occupied Poland during the Second World War.

Matter in issue between the defendant and the prosecution
103.—(1) For the purposes of section 101(1)(d) the matters in issue between the defendant   **10–122**
and the prosecution include—
   (a) the question whether the defendant has a propensity to commit offences of the
       kind with which he is charged, except where his having such a propensity makes
       it no more likely that he is guilty of the offence;
   (b) the question whether the defendant has a propensity to be untruthful, except
       where it is not suggested that the defendant's case is untruthful in any respect.
   (2) Where subsection (1)(a) applies, a defendant's propensity to commit offences of the

kind with which he is charged may (without prejudice to any other way of doing so) be established by evidence that he has been convicted of—

    (a) an offence of the same description as the one with which he is charged, or

    (b) an offence of the same category as the one with which he is charged.

(3) Subsection (2) does not apply in the case of a particular defendant if the court is satisfied, by reason of the length of time since the conviction or for any other reason, that it would be unjust for it to apply in his case.

(4) For the purposes of subsection (2)—

    (a) two offences are of the same description as each other if the statement of the offence in a written charge or indictment would, in each case, be in the same terms;

    (b) two offences are of the same category as each other if they belong to the same category of offences prescribed for the purposes of this section by an order made by the Secretary of State.

(5) A category prescribed by an order under subsection (4)(b) must consist of offences of the same type.

(6) Only prosecution evidence is admissible under section 101(1)(d).

10–123   A court must strike a balance between the prosecution's right to adduce evidence of propensity and the defendant's right not to have prejudicial evidence admitted. It was said in *Hanson, ante*, that where the prosecution seeks to adduce evidence of previous convictions to establish a defendant's propensity to commit offences of the kind with which he is charged there were essentially three questions to be considered:

    (i) Did the history of his convictions establish a propensity to commit offences of the kind charged?

    (ii) Did that propensity make it more likely that the defendant had committed the offence charged?

    (iii) Was it unjust to rely on the convictions of the same description or category; and, in any event, would the proceedings be unfair if they were admitted?

A defendant who is defending himself against the evidence of a person whose history of criminal behaviour or other misconduct is such as to be capable of showing him to be unscrupulous and/or otherwise unreliable should be enabled to present that history to the court for its evaluation of the evidence of the witness, to ascertain whether he is telling the truth or not. That may be shown by conduct ranging from large-scale drug or people trafficking via housebreaking to criminal violence. Whether in a particular case it has substantive probative value is a matter for the court: *Lawson* [2007] 1 Cr.App.R. 11.

A court can permit evidence of a former long term partner to be adduced under section 101(1)(d), to establish a propensity to commit an offence of the kind charged: *Williams* [2006] EWCA Crim 2052. This was a murder case where the evidence was of attempts to strangle.

10–124   In *Chopra* [2006] EWCA Crim 2133 evidence of each complainant of assault was allowed to be given as supportive evidence for each other. Guidance was given as to "important matter in issue" under section 101(1)(d).

    (1) The common law rules as to the admissibility of bad character evidence were abolished by the 2003 Act and the right way to deal with the new law was not first to ask what would have been the position under the old law. A sea-change in the law's starting point had been affected by the 2003 Act in a number of respects in relation to bad character generally. In particular, whereas previously, evidence of the defendant's propensity to offend in the manner now charged was prima facie admissible, following the 2003 Act it is prima facie admissible.

    (2) Evidence of several complainants was cross-admissible pursuant to section 101(1)(d) of the 2003 Act if, but only if, it was relevant to an important matter in issue between the defendant and the prosecution. Where propensity was advanced by way of multiple complaints, none of which had yet been proved, and whether they were proved or not was the question which the jury had to answer, that was a different case form that in which propensity was advanced through proof of a previous conviction. However, the 2003 Act governed all ev-

idence of bad character, not only conclusive or undisputable evidence. In a case of the kind in the instant case, the critical question was whether or not the evidence of one complainant was relevant as going, or being capable of going, to establish propensity to commit offences of the kind charged. Not all evidence of other misbehaviour would by any means do so. There had to be sufficient connection between the facts of the several allegations for it properly to be capable of saying that they might establish propensity to offend in the manner charged.

(3) In cases of multiple similar complaints the proposition which the jury had to consider was not that it was not possible to have independent similar false complaints, but rather that each similar complaint made each other similar complaint the more likely.

(4) When considering admissibility the judge would be required to assume that the evidence was truthful unless no jury could reasonably believe it. Whether it was in fact truthful was for the jury. Moreover, propensity to commit an offence was still propensity to do so even if it were a common offence or one which could readily be imagined by someone bent on making a false allegation. That did not mean that all evidence of other alleged offending was necessarily admissible under section 101(1)(d), but rather, there had in each case to be an examination of whether the evidence really did tend to establish the relevant propensity. There would have to be sufficient similarity to make it more likely that each allegation was true. The likelihood or unlikelihood of innocent coincidence would continue to be a relevant and sometimes critical test. However, there was a myriad of possible situations which might arise.

Section 103(2) does not permit all convictions to be introduced. The greater the **10–125** similarity between the offences, the more probative value the previous convictions would have; this need not be striking similarity but there must be some degree of similarity: *Tully*, unreported, March 16, 2006. Speeding convictions were not admitted to show propensity on a charge of causing death by dangerous driving: *Whitehead*, unreported, May 23, 2007.

Section 103(2) is not exhaustive of the types of conviction which might be relied upon to show evidence of propensity to commit offences of the kind charged. Nor is it necessarily sufficient in order to show such propensity that a conviction should be of the same description or category as that charged. The fewer the number of convictions, the weaker the evidence of propensity. A single previous conviction for an offence of the same description or category would often not show propensity but it might do so, where, *e.g.* it showed a tendency to unusual behaviour. If there is no or very little other evidence against a defendant it is unlikely to be just to admit previous convictions whatever they are. If there is a substantial gap between the date of commission and the date of conviction for the earlier offences, the date of commission is generally of more significance than the date of conviction for assessing admissibility. It is a matter for a court to decide whether it can determine propensity at the time of committing an offence by reference to offences committed thereafter: *Adenusi* [2006] EWCA Crim 1059; [2006] Crim.L.R. 929. Each individual conviction often ought to be examined but the sentence would not normally be probative. Where past events were disputed, the court has to take care not to permit the trial to be unreasonably diverted. Where previous convictions were admitted, the court should not conclude that the defendant is guilty or untruthful merely because he has previous convictions. If the convictions showed a propensity that does not mean that the defendant has committed the offence or been untruthful. It is for the court to decide propensity taking into account what the defendant says about the previous convictions. Where propensity is found the court is entitled to take that into account when determining guilt but it is only one relevant factor and its significance must be assessed in the light of all the other evidence in the case. This case takes a broad view of section 103(2) and appears not to find favourable the argument that offences should be of exactly the same description: section 103(4)(a). Previous convictions of dishonesty were excluded where they did not indicate "walk-in theft" and where there was a real possibility that they were being used to bolster a weak case (identification was by a police officer purporting to recognise the defendant from unclear CCTV): *DPP v. Chand* [2007] EWHC 90.

So far as propensity to commit the crime assessed from other misconduct is concerned previous case law has stated that there had to be a distinct link between what had gone before and the crime charged. In *Straffen* [1952] 2 Q.B. 911 there were similar features in the strangulation of a child to previous murders of which the defendant had been convicted; the evidence of the previous murders was admissible not to show that the defendant was a strangler but that he had strangled that particular child. Consider also *Smith (G.J.)* 11 Cr.App.R. 229—the "brides in the bath" case. In *West* [1996] 2 Cr.App.R. 374, evidence was admitted in the murder trial to show that Rosemary West was an energetic and committed participator, together with her husband, in acts of sexual violence and that she had derived sexual gratification from such acts. In a case of murder, evidence of bad character was held to be relevant and admissible to show a propensity to use knives in a violent manner: *Lamb* [2006] All E.R. (D) 333. Previous convictions for criminal offences involving street violence were admitted to show propensity on charges of grievous and actual bodily harm where the attack took place in a street: *Eastlake* [2007] EWCA Crim 603; (2007) 151 S.J.L.B. 258.

The example given in the Home Office White Papers *Justice for All*, regarding a propensity for untruthfulness concerned a doctor who had denied a charge of indecent assault against a patient. Previous trials arising out of similar complaints had resulted in acquittals. It is suggested that those previous complaints are of probative value and should therefore be admissible. In *Hanson, ante*, it was said that previous convictions, whether for dishonesty or otherwise, are likely to be capable of showing a propensity to be untruthful only where in the case being tried, truthfulness is an issue and, in the earlier cases, either there was a plea of not guilty and the defendant had given an account which had not been believed or the way in which the offence was committed showed a propensity for untruthfulness, *e.g.* by the making of false representation.

Matter in issue between the defendant and a co-defendant

10–126   104.—(1) Evidence which is relevant to the question whether the defendant has a propensity to be untruthful is admissible on that basis under section 101(1)(e) only if the nature or conduct of his defence is such as to undermine the co-defendant's defence.

(2) Only evidence—

    (a) which is to be (or has been) adduced by the co-defendant, or

    (b) which a witness is to be invited to give (or has given) in cross-examination by the co-defendant,

is admissible under section 101(1)(e).

10–127   For a "cut-throat" defence, *i.e.* where a defendant's defence is that the offence was committed by a co-defendant, see the case of *Lowery v. R.* [1974] A.C. 85 where two men were charged and blamed each other for the murder of a young girl. Evidence of a psychologist was allowed to show that one was immature and likely to be dominated by the other whereas the other was aggressive and had sadistic tendencies. Where two co-defendants run a cut-throat defence, evidence of a previous conviction of co-defendant X can be used in the defence of co-defendant Y to suggest less propensity to commit the crime than X; however, even if it amounts to similar fact evidence, it is not relevant to the criminal propensity of X himself: *Mertens* [2004] EWCA Crim 2252.

Once evidence is admissible under section 101(1)(e) there is no power to exclude on the basis of unfairness; evidence could only be excluded where there is a failure to comply with the requirements of the *Criminal Procedure Rules*: *Musone, The Times*, June 11, 2007.

Evidence to correct a false impression

10–128   105.—(1) For the purposes of section 101(1)(f)—

    (a) the defendant gives a false impression if he is responsible for the making of an express or implied assertion which is apt to give the court or jury a false or misleading impression about the defendant;

(b) evidence to correct such an impression is evidence which has probative value in correcting it.

(2) A defendant is treated as being responsible for the making of an assertion if—

(a) the assertion is made by the defendant in the proceedings (whether or not in evidence given by him),

(b) the assertion was made by the defendant—

(i) on being questioned under caution, before charge, about the offence with which he is charged, or

(ii) on being charged with the offence or officially informed that he might be prosecuted for it,

and evidence of the assertion is given in the proceedings,

(c) the assertion is made by a witness called by the defendant,

(d) the assertion is made by any witness in cross-examination in response to a question asked by the defendant that is intended to elicit it, or is likely to do so, or

(e) the assertion was made by any person out of court, and the defendant adduces evidence of it in the proceedings.

(3) A defendant who would otherwise be treated as responsible for the making of an assertion shall not be so treated if, or to the extent that, he withdraws it or disassociates himself from it.

(4) Where it appears to the court that a defendant, by means of his conduct (other than the giving of evidence) in the proceedings, is seeking to give the court or jury an impression about himself that is false or misleading, the court may if it appears just to do so treat the defendant as being responsible for the making of an assertion which is apt to give that impression.

(5) In subsection (4) "conduct" includes appearance or dress.

(6) Evidence is admissible under section 101(1)(f) only if it goes no further than is necessary to correct the false impression.

(7) Only prosecution evidence is admissible under section 101(1)(f).

Giving a false impression includes appearance or dress: section 105(5) could cover **10–129** someone who wears, *e.g.* the clothes of a priest. Evidence of an interview with police (in this case Dutch police) where admissions had been made to being involved with the supply of drugs can be admitted to correct a false impression where a defendant says he had never been involved in drug supply: *Spartley*, unreported, May 15, 2007.

See *Criminal Procedure Rules* 2005, r.35.4–9 in Appendix G–210—G–215.

Attack on another person's character

106.—(1) For the purposes of section 101(1)(g) a defendant makes an attack on another **10–130** person's character if—

(a) he adduces evidence attacking the other person's character,

(b) he (or any legal representative appointed under section 38(4) of the *Youth Justice and Criminal Evidence Act* 1999 to cross-examine a witness in his interests) asks questions in cross-examination that are intended to elicit such evidence, or are likely to do so, or

(c) evidence is given of an imputation about the other person made by the defendant—

(i) on being questioned under caution, before charge, about the offence with which he is charged, or

(ii) on being charged with the offence or officially informed that he might be prosecuted for it.

(2) In subsection (1) "evidence attacking the other person's character" means evidence to the effect that the other person—

(a) has committed an offence (whether a different offence from the one with which the defendant is charged or the same one), or

(b) has behaved, or is disposed to behave, in a reprehensible way;

and "imputation about the other person" means an assertion to that effect.

(3) Only prosecution evidence is admissible under section 101(1)(g).

There are many instances in previous case law of allegations put to prosecution wit- **10–131** nesses which were interpreted as an attack on another person's character: *Clark* [1955] 2 Q.B. 469 where it was put to police officers that they had made up a statement. In *Selvey v. DPP* [1970] A.C. 304, it was said that an allegation could be that the prosecution witness has previous convictions or a serious suggestion of immorality or a claim that the evidence has been fabricated.

Under the old law a defence of self defence on the basis that the victim had struck the first blow could not involve an imputation on the character of the victim: *Blackford* [2005] EWCA Crim 3515. Section 101(1)(g) is not confined to situations as arose under the old law where a defendant personally or through his advocate attacked the character of a prosecution witness, the prosecutor or a deceased victim. The 2003 Act extends to attacks made on the character of a non-witness although the court still has discretion under section 78 whether to admit or not. It would be unusual for evidence of a defendant's bad character to be admitted when the only basis of that application was an attack on the character of a non-witness who was also a non-victim. The fairness of the proceedings would normally be damaged in such circumstances. Whilst it is true that an attack by a defendant in interview might, by virtue of section 106(1)(c) satisfy the requirement in section 101(1)(g), it depends on whether, in fact, evidence is given at trial of such an attack. It is improper to seek to admit comments in interview which have no relevance to the issues in the trial: *Nelson* [2006] All E.R. (D) 290.

X. UNFAIRLY OR ILLEGALLY OBTAINED EVIDENCE

A. CONFESSIONS

Police and Criminal Evidence Act 1984, ss.76–76A

Confessions

10–132   **76.**—(1) In any proceedings a confession made by an accused person may be given in evidence against him in so far as it is relevant to any matter in issue in the proceedings and is not excluded by the court in pursuance of this section.

(2) If, in any proceedings where the prosecution proposes to give in evidence a confession made by an accused person, it is represented to the court that the confession was or may have been obtained—

    (a) by oppression of the person who made it; or

    (b) in consequence of anything said or done which was likely, in the circumstances existing at the time, to render unreliable any confession which might be made by him in consequence thereof.

the court shall not allow the confession to be given in evidence against him except in so far as the prosecution proves to the court beyond reasonable doubt that the confession (notwithstanding that it may be true) was not obtained as aforesaid.

(3) In any proceedings where the prosecution proposes to give in evidence a confession made by an accused person, the court may of its own motion require the prosecution, as a condition of allowing it to do so, to prove that the confession was not obtained as mentioned in subsection (2) above.

(4) The fact that a confession is wholly or partly excluded in pursuance of this section shall not affect the admissibility in evidence—

    (a) of any facts discovered as a result of the confession; or

    (b) where the confession is relevant as showing that the accused speaks, writes or expresses himself in a particular way, of so much of the confession as is necessary to show that he does so.

(5) Evidence that a fact to which this subsection applies was discovered as a result of a statement made by an accused person shall not be admissible unless evidence of how it was discovered is given by him or on his behalf.

(6) Subsection (5) above applies—

    (a) to any fact discovered as a result of a confession which is wholly excluded in pursuance of this section; and

    (b) to any fact discovered as a result of a confession which is partly so excluded, if the fact is discovered as a result of the excluded part of the confession.

(7) Nothing in Part VII of this Act shall prejudice the admissibility of a confession made by an accused person.

(8) In this section "oppression" includes torture, inhuman or degrading treatment, and the use or threat of violence (whether or not amounting to torture).

(9) Where the proceedings mentioned in subsection (1) above are proceedings before a magistrates' court inquiring into an offence as examining justices this section shall have effect with the omission of—

(a) in subsection (1) the words "and is not excluded by the court in pursuance of this section", and

(b) subsections (2) to (6) and (8).

Confessions may be given in evidence for co-accused

76A.—(1) In any proceedings a confession made by an accused person may be given in evidence for another person charged in the same proceedings (a co-accused) in so far as it is relevant to any matter in issue in the proceedings and is not excluded by the court in pursuance of this section.   **10–133**

(2) If, in any proceedings where a co-accused proposes to give in evidence a confession made by an accused person, it is represented to the court that the confession was or may have been obtained—

(a) by oppression of the person who made it; or

(b) in consequence of anything said or done which was likely, in the circumstances existing at the time, to render unreliable any confession which might be made by him in consequence thereof,

the court shall not allow the confession to be given in evidence for the co-accused except in so far as it is proved to the court on the balance of probabilities that the confession (notwithstanding that it may be true) was not so obtained.

The method by which evidence is obtained is irrelevant to its admissibility: *Kuruma*   **10–134**
v. R. [1955] A.C. 197. Confessions are the exception: section 76. There is also a general discretion to exclude evidence which may render the trial unfair: section 78. Where an objection to evidence is based on section 76, the court shall not admit the confession unless it is satisfied that it was not obtained by oppression or by words or conduct likely to render it unreliable: *Police and Criminal Evidence Act* 1984, s.76(2). The court must determine the question as soon as it is raised and, if it is necessary to hear evidence, to do so upon a *voire dire*: *R. v. Liverpool Juvenile Court, ex p. R.* [1988] Q.B. 1.

A confession is defined as any statement wholly or partly adverse to the person who made it, whether made to a person in authority or not and whether made in words or otherwise: section 82(1). A confession does not include a statement intended by the maker to be exculpatory or neutral and which appears to be so on its face, but which becomes damaging to him at trial, because, for example its contents could then be shown to be evasive or false or inconsistent with the maker's evidence on oath: *Hasan* [2005] 2 W.L.R. 709. It can be made to a police officer or to someone else, in court, at a police station or anywhere else. It may be in writing, spoken or in other circumstances. A prison officer who overhears incriminating remarks does not need to caution a defendant: *Ristic* (2004) 148 S.J.L.B. 942. Where a probation officer is involved in the preparation of a report caution should be exercised. The court must bear in mind the difference between an interview with a police officer with its protection and that with a probation officer who needs frank disclosure for the preparation of a report: *Elleray* [2003] 2 Cr.App.R. 11, CA.

A confession can include:

- A self incriminating telephone call from a defendant resulting from a cooperative conversation: *De Silva* [2003] Crim.L.R. 474.

- A confession made in court at a previous trial: *McGregor* [1968] 1 Q.B. 371.

- Conduct: *Parkes v. R.* 64 Cr.App.R. 25 where when asked why he had stabbed a girl and being threatened with being held until the police arrived, the defendant brought out a knife.

- In mitigation (via his solicitor): *Turner* (1975) 61 Cr.App.R. 67 but not at a pretrial review: *Hutchinson* (1986) 82 Cr.App.R. 51.

- An unsigned form under section 172(2) of the *Road Traffic Act* 1988 where there is sufficient evidence that the defendant completed it: *Mawdsley v. Chief Constable of Cheshire Constabulary; Yorke v. Same* [2004] 1 All E.R. 58.

Exculpatory statements have been held not included: *Sat-Bhambra* (1989) 88 Cr.App.R. 55. In *Pearce* (1979) 69 Cr.App.R. 365, Lord Widgery C.J. said "a denial does not become an admission because it is inconsistent with another denial".

When the case against a defendant in a joint trial depends on the prosecution's proving the guilt of a co-defendant (as the evidence against the co-defendant consists solely of his own out of court confession) then that confession will be admissible against the defendant but only in so far as it goes to prove the co-defendant's guilt: *Hayter* [2005] UKHL 6. Where a co-accused has pleaded guilty and does not stand trial with a defendant, the co-accused's confession cannot be used as evidence at that defendant's trial under this section: *Finch* [2007] EWCA Crim 36. In this case the confession was neither admitted under section 114(1)(d) as hearsay evidence as it was not in the interests of justice so to do.

In *Saunders v. UK* [1997] 23 E.H.R.R. 313, the admission of a transcript of interviews by the DTI inspectors violated Article 6(1) as at the time of interrogation *Saunders* was under a duty to answer, a duty enforceable by proceedings for contempt. Disciplinary interviews were admitted in *Welcher* [2007] EWCA Crim 480. The defendant was charged with conspiracy to corrupt and conspiracy to defraud in relation to bribes taken as an employee. Once the matter had come to light the defendant had been subject to disciplinary interviews within the workplace, admitted the matters and was dismissed for gross misconduct. During the trial he gave accounts consistent with the police interview but inconsistent with the disciplinary interview which were then admitted as evidence of the defendant's untruthfulness.

In *Fulling* [1987] Q.B. 426 it was held that "oppression" was to be given its ordinary dictionary meaning. In making a judgement about what is oppressive or likely to make a confession unreliable, the court may have regard to the character and experience of the suspect: *Seelig* 94 Cr.App.R. 17, CA. Maltreatment will amount to oppression: *Montgomery v. HM Advocate* [2003] 1 A.C. 641.

Hostile and aggressive questioning which puts pressure on a defendant will not necessarily render the confession unreliable. The length of the interviews and the nature of the questioning are the important considerations: *L.* [1994] Crim.L.R. 839, CA.

10–135 Raised police voices are not necessarily oppressive: *Heaton* [1993] Crim.L.R. 593, but where shouting amounts to bullying and intimidation it will be: *Paris* (1993) 97 Cr.App.R. 99. Breaches of the Code of Practice may not amount to oppression: *Parker* [1995] Crim.L.R. 233. It has been held, however, that a failure to caution renders the confession unreliable: *Doolan* [1988] Crim.L.R. 747, CA. In *Mullings* [2004] EWCA Crim 2875, it was said that where a line of questioning is to be pursued, a caution is required.

The denial of access to a solicitor led to inadmissibility in *McGovern* (1991) 92 Cr.App.R. 228, CA but not in *Alladice* (1988) 87 Cr.App.R. 380. The breach must be significant and substantial: *Keenan* (1990) 90 Cr.App.R. 1; *Absolam* (1989) 88 Cr.App.R. 332; *Canale* (1990) 91 Cr.App.R. 1. A repeated denial of legal advice had led to incorrect admissions in *Simmons* [2006] UKPC 19. Proper advice from a solicitor will rarely provide a basis for excluding a confession: *Wahab* [2003] 1 Cr.App.R. 15, CA, but interjections from a legal representative during interview have made a confession unreliable: *M,* [2000] 8 *Archbold News* 2, CA.

Under the PACE Code "interview", is defined as the questioning of a person regarding his involvement or suspected involvement in a criminal offence….which is required to be carried out under caution. One question may amount to an interview: *Miller* [1998] Crim.L.R. 209, CA. It is irrelevant if the questions are put by an officer not involved in the investigation, *e.g.* custody officer: *Absolam, ante.* Questions arising out of curiosity or to eliminate the person from further inquiries will amount to an interview: *Hunt* [1992] Crim.L.R. 582, CA.

The court may take into account the defendant's state of mind: *Walker* [1998] Crim.L.R. 211, CA. The disorder must be a significant deviation from the norm: *O'Brien* [2000] Crim.L.R. 676, CA; see also *Miller* (1986) 83 Cr.App.R. 192 and *Everett* [1988] Crim.L.R. 826. Psychiatric evidence should be produced.

Unreliable means "cannot be relied upon as being the truth": *Crampton* (1991) 92 Cr.App.R. 369, CA. Expert evidence concerning the phenomenon of false confessions and the circumstances in which research has shown that a vulnerable individual, after a prolonged period of questioning, might give a coerced compliant confession is admissible: *Blackburn* [2005] 2 Cr.App.R. 30. If the court concludes that what was said and done is likely to make any confession unreliable then it must not be admitted: *Kenny* [1994] Crim.L.R. 284, CA. Facts discovered as a result of an inadmissible confession can be introduced: section 76(4). A retrial of a defendant can be ordered even where confessions were made in the mistaken belief that he could not be convicted once he had been acquitted: *Dunlop* [2006] EWCA Crim 1354; [2007] 1 All E.R. 593.

Police and Criminal Evidence Act 1984, s.77

Confessions by mentally handicapped persons

10–136

77.—(1) Without prejudice to the general duty of the court at a trial on indictment to direct the jury on any matter on which it appears to the court appropriate to do so, where at such a trial—

  (a) the case against the accused depends wholly or substantially on a confession by him; and

  (b) the court is satisfied—

    (i) that he is mentally handicapped; and

    (ii) that the confession was not made in the presence of an independent person,

  the court shall warn the jury that there is special need for caution before convicting the accused in reliance on the confession, and shall explain that the need arises because of the circumstances mentioned in paragraphs (a) and (b) above.

(2) In any case where at the summary trial of a person for an offence it appears to the court that a warning under subsection (1) above would be required if the trial were on indictment, the court shall treat the case as one in which there is a special need for caution before convicting the accused on his confession.

(3) In this section—

  "independent person" does not include a police officer or a person employed for, or engaged on, police purposes;

  "mentally handicapped", in relation to a person, means that he is in a state of arrested or incomplete development of mind which includes significant impairment of intelligence and social functioning; and

  "police purposes" has the meaning assigned to it by section 101(2) of the *Police Act* 1996.

[This section is reprinted as amended by the *Summary Appeal Court (Navy) Rules* 2000, Sched. 3(III), para. 18(d).]

10–137

Special caution must be taken with confessions of defendants who are mentally handicapped as defined in the section. A solicitor can be an "independent person" even though he is not an "appropriate adult": *Lewis (M.)* [1996] Crim.L.R. 260, CA.

10–138

Section 128 of the *Criminal Justice Act* 2003, when in force, makes provision for confessions to be given in evidence for a co-accused.

Criminal Justice Act 2003, s.128

Confessions

10–139

128.—(1) In the *Police and Criminal Evidence Act* 1984 (c. 60) the following section is inserted after section 76—

Confessions may be given in evidence for co-accused

"**76A.**—(1) In any proceedings a confession made by an accused person may be given in evidence for another person charged in the same proceedings (a co-accused) in so far as it is relevant to any matter in issue in the proceedings and is not excluded by the court in pursuance of this section.

(2) If, in any proceedings where a co-accused proposes to give in evidence a confession made by an accused person, it is represented to the court that the confession was or may have been obtained—

    (a) by oppression of the person who made it; or

    (b) in consequence of anything said or done which was likely, in the circumstances existing at the time, to render unreliable any confession which might be made by him in consequence thereof,

the court shall not allow the confession to be given in evidence for the co-accused except in so far as it is proved to the court on the balance of probabilities that the confession (notwithstanding that it may be true) was not so obtained.

(3) Before allowing a confession made by an accused person to be given in evidence for a co-accused in any proceedings, the court may of its own motion require the fact that the confession was not obtained as mentioned in subsection (2) above to be proved in the proceedings on the balance of probabilities.

(4) The fact that a confession is wholly or partly excluded in pursuance of this section shall not affect the admissibility in evidence—

    (a) of any facts discovered as a result of the confession; or

    (b) where the confession is relevant as showing that the accused speaks, writes or expresses himself in a particular way, of so much of the confession as is necessary to show that he does so.

(5) Evidence that a fact to which this subsection applies was discovered as a result of a statement made by an accused person shall not be admissible unless evidence of how it was discovered is given by him or on his behalf.

(6) Subsection (5) above applies—

    (a) to any fact discovered as a result of a confession which is wholly excluded in pursuance of this section; and

    (b) to any fact discovered as a result of a confession which is partly so excluded, if the fact is discovered as a result of the excluded part of the confession.

(7) In this section "oppression" includes torture, inhuman or degrading treatment, and the use or threat of violence (whether or not amounting to torture)."

(2) Subject to subsection (1), nothing in this Chapter makes a confession by a defendant admissible if it would not be admissible under section 76 of the *Police and Criminal Evidence Act* 1984.

(3) In subsection (2) "confession" has the meaning given by section 82 of that Act.

B. Unfair Evidence

Police and Criminal Evidence Act 1984, s.78

Exclusion of unfair evidence

10–140   **78.**—(1) In any proceedings the court may refuse to allow evidence on which the prosecution proposes to rely to be given if it appears to the court that, having regard to all the circumstances, including the circumstances in which the evidence was obtained, the admission of the evidence would have such an adverse effect on the fairness of the proceedings that the court ought not to admit it.

(2) Nothing in this section shall prejudice any rule of law requiring a court to exclude evidence.

(3) This section shall not apply in the case of proceedings before a magistrates' court inquiring into an offences as examining justices.

10–141   This section allows the court to exclude admissible evidence where it feels it would be unfair to admit it. It may be used where other avenues have failed. It may, *e.g.* be used to exclude improperly obtained, identification or bad character evidence.

In *DPP v. Marshall* [1988] 3 All E.R. 683, it was held that magistrates were wrong to exclude the evidence of police officers who, when making test purchases in order to establish whether the defendant was selling liquor without a licence, had not announced they were police officers. In *Ealing LBC v. Woolworths Plc* [1995] Crim.L.R. 58, the evidence of an eleven-year-old boy, the son of a Trading Standards officer, was not excluded in a case involving the sale of an eighteen-year-old certificated video, in breach of the *Video Recordings Act* 1984.

In extradition proceedings, where the judge is concerned with the fairness of admit-   **10–142** ting evidence, he must have regard to the extradition context in which the issue arises; his decision is in, and solely for the purpose of, his determination on the issue of extradition and he should only exclude evidence where to admit it would outrage civilised values: *R. v. Bow Street Magistrates' Court, ex p. Proulx* [2001] 1 All E.R. 57; *Saifi* [2001] 4 All E.R. 168. The concept of the burden of proof has no part to play in the exercise of the discretion.

Before deciding whether it is unfair to exclude evidence the court must consider the full facts of any undercover operation including what evidence was gained as a result: *Christou and Wright* [1992] Q.B. 979. Where surveillance has been undertaken by a third party but the police know of it and are prepared to use any evidence in a criminal prosecution, it is not police surveillance. The degree of police involvement can be a factor in deciding admissibility under section 78: *Rosenberg* [2006] EWCA Crim 6.

Exclusion is not automatic where there has been a breach of the Act or the Codes of practice *Walsh* (1989) 91 Cr.App.R. 161. Case law has suggested that the breach should be significant and substantial before discretion is exercised: *Absalom* 88 Cr.App.R. 332. In *Stewart* [1995] Crim.L.R. 500, CA it was pointed out that it was the nature and not the number of breaches that was the important factor.

There is no requirement of bad faith on the part of police officers before evidence is excluded although case law in breath test cases suggests that evidence will not be excluded unless there is bad faith: *Matto v. Wolverhampton Crown Court* [1987] R.T.R. 337, DC; *Fox v. Chief Constable of Gwent* [1986] A.C. 281, HL. In other cases bad faith means that evidence is usually excluded: *Alladice* 87 Cr.App.R. 380, CA. Good faith, on the other hand, will not excuse serious breaches: *Samuel* [1988] Q.B. 615.

Although entrapment does not *per se* afford a defence to a criminal charge, proceedings may be stayed or evidence may be excluded under section 78: *Sang* [1980] A.C. 402. In *Smurthwaite; Gill* (1994) 98 Cr.App.R. 437, CA, it was said that the following factors but not an exhaustive list ought to be considered: was the officer acting as an agent provocateur in the sense that he was enticing the defendant to commit an offence he would not otherwise have committed? What was the nature of any entrapment? Does the evidence consist of admissions to a completed offence, or does it consist of the actual commission of the offence? How active or passive was the officer's role in obtaining the evidence? Was there an unassailable record of what occurred, or was it strongly corroborated? Had the undercover officer abused his role to ask questions which ought properly to have been asked as a police officer and in accordance with the codes? In *Loosely; Att.-Gen.'s Reference (No. 3 of 2000)* [2002] 1 Cr.App.R. 29, it was held that the appropriate remedy would be staying the prosecution as an abuse of process rather than excluding evidence; but the use of a covert operation may affect the admissibility of particular pieces of evidence and in such circumstances section 78 would apply. A court, being a public authority, cannot be acting illegally under ECHR if it admits evidence, which has been obtained by covert surveillance in breach of Article 8. The court's obligation is to decide whether or not its admissibility is unfair under section 78: *Button* [2005] EWCA Crim 516.

C. ADMISSIONS

An admission made in the course of judicial proceedings, whether at an earlier stage   **10–143** of proceedings for the same offence or in separate proceedings will come within the definition of "confession" in section 82(1) of the *Police and Criminal Evidence Act* 1984. The *Fraud Act*, s.13, similar to section 31 of the *Theft Act* 1968, protects a person from incriminating himself for the purposes of offences under the Act (and related offences) but a person is still obliged to co-operate with civil proceedings relating to property.

Fraud Act 2006, s.13

Evidence

10–144   **13.**—(1) A person is not to be excused from—

      (a) answering any question put to him in proceedings relating to property, or

      (b) complying with any order made in proceedings relating to property, on the ground that doing so may incriminate him or his spouse or civil partner of an offence under this Act or a related offence.

      (2) But, in proceedings for an offence under this Act or a related offence, a statement or admission made by the person in—

      (a) answering such a question, or

      (b) complying with such an order,

is not admissible in evidence against him or (unless they married or became civil partners after the making of the statement or admission) his spouse or civil partner.

      (3) "Proceedings relating to property" means any proceedings for—

      (a) the recovery or administration of any property,

      (b) the execution of a trust, or

      (c) an account of any property or dealings with property,

and "property" means money or other property whether real or personal (including things in action and other intangible property).

      (4) "Related offence" means—

      (a) conspiracy to defraud;

      (b) any other offence involving any form of fraudulent conduct or purpose.

10–145   Admissions by a person in a former trial or enquiry are excluded by certain statutes, *e.g.* the *Explosive Substances Act* 1883, s.6(2)

An admission made during the course of a trial is admissible in the event of a retrial: *McGregor* [1968] 1 Q.B. 372.

XI. ADVERSE INFERENCES

10–146   At common law, a statement made in the presence of the defendant, which accuses him of having committed a crime, upon an occasion which may be expected reasonably to call for some explanation or denial, is not evidence against him of the facts stated, save except in so far as he accepts the statement so as to make it in effect his own. Statute has, however, created restrictions.

Before admitting a prejudicial statement made in the defendant's presence to which he does not demure, the court must consider whether the defendant's reaction (or lack of reaction) to that statement is potentially relevant: *Osborne* [2005] EWCA Crim 2826. Where it is alleged that a defendant, by his conduct, acquiesces in and adopts a statement the three questions that arise are:

      1) Can the court conclude that the defendant adopted the statement in question?

      2) If so, is it of sufficient relevance to justify its introduction as evidence?

      3) If so, would the admission have such an adverse effect on the fairness of the proceedings that it should not be admitted?

In that case, a verbal exchange had taken place between a group of youths, one of whom was the defendant and an Asian male following which a fight ensued and the Asian youth died. Two days later, the defendant was asked, "What did you hit him for? I bet he ain't done nothing to you," whereupon one of the youths in the defendant's group said, "Of course we don't like Asian people. They stink. Why do they come over to our country?" The defendant said nothing. The evidence demonstrated that the defendant was hostile to the deceased and was admitted but that had no bearing on the issue of intent.

Criminal Justice and Public Order Act 1994, s.34

Effect of accused's failure to mention facts when questioned or charged.

10–147   **34.**—(1) Where, in any proceedings against a person for an offence, evidence is given that the accused—

  (a) at any time before he was charged with the offence, on being questioned under caution by a constable trying to discover whether or by whom the offence had been committed, failed to mention any fact relied on in his defence in those proceedings; or

  (b) on being charged with the offence or officially informed that he might be prosecuted for it, failed to mention any such fact,

being a fact which in the circumstances existing at the time the accused could reasonably have been expected to mention when so questioned, charged or informed, as the case may be, subsection (2) below applies.

 (2) Where this subsection applies—

  (a) a magistrates' court inquiring into the offence as examining justices;

  (b) a judge, in deciding whether to grant an application made by the accused under—

   (i) section 6 of the *Criminal Justice Act* 1987 (application for dismissal of charge of serious fraud in respect of which notice of transfer has been given under section 4 of that Act; or

   (ii) paragraph 5 of Schedule 6 to the *Criminal Justice Act* 1991 (application for dismissal of charge of violent or sexual offence involving child in respect of which notice of transfer has been given under section 53 of that Act);

  (c) the court, in determining whether there is a case to answer; and

  (d) the court or jury, in determining whether the accused is guilty of the offence charged,

may draw such inferences from the failure as appear proper.

 (2A) Where the accused was at an authorised place of detention at the time of the failure, subsections (1) and (2) above do not apply if he had not been allowed an opportunity to consult a solicitor prior to being questioned, charged or informed as mentioned in subsection (1) above.

 (3) Subject to any directions by the court, evidence tending to establish the failure may be given before or after evidence tending to establish the fact which the accused is alleged to have failed to mention.

 (4) This section applies in relation to questioning by persons (other than constables) charged with the duty of investigating offences or charging offenders as it applies in relation to questioning by constables; and in subsection (1) above "officially informed" means informed by a constable or any such person.

 (5) This section does not—

  (a) prejudice the admissibility in evidence of the silence or other reaction of the accused in the face of anything said in his presence relating to the conduct in respect of which he is charged, in so far as evidence thereof would be admissible apart from this section; or

  (b) preclude the drawing of any inference from any such silence or other reaction of the accused which could properly be drawn apart from this section.

 (6) This section does not apply in relation to a failure to mention a fact if the failure occurred before the commencement of this section.

[This section is reprinted as amended by the *Youth Justice and Criminal Evidence Act* 1999, s.58(2). Subsection 2A is not yet in force.]

 The European Court has confirmed that the right to silence is not an absolute right **10–148** but is at the heart of the notion of a fair trial. Caution must therefore be exercised before drawing adverse inferences. In *Averill v. UK* (2001) 31 E.H.R.R. 839, it was said that the extent to which adverse inferences may be drawn in this context should be limited. In *Argent* [1997] 2 Cr.App.R. 27, Lord Bingham defined the six conditions which had to be met before adverse inferences could be drawn:

 — proceedings for an offence must be in existence;

 — failure to answer must have occurred before charge;

 — failure to answer must have occurred during questioning under caution by a police officer or relevant person;

 — the questioning was intended to discover whether or by whom the offence was committed;

 — the failure had to be with regard to the mention of a fact which was then relied upon in the proceedings; and

— the fact concerned and the one which the defendant had failed to mention must have been one which he could reasonably have been expected to mention at the time of questioning, given the circumstances of the interview.

In *Brizzalari* [2004] EWCA Crim 310, the Court of Appeal discouraged prosecutors from too readily seeking to activate the provisions under section 34 unless the merits of the individual case required that that should be done. An adverse inference should not be drawn from a defendant's refusal to leave a police cell in order to be interviewed: *Johnson, Hind* [2005] EWCA Crim 971.

10–149   In *Condron and Condron* [1997] 1 Cr.App.R. 185, it was said that legal advice to remain silence cannot of itself prevent an adverse inference being drawn. The defendant and his solicitor may have to state the basis or the reason for the advice given. There may be good reason for such advice. The European Court of Human Rights found that there had been a violation of Article 6(1) on the ground that an adverse inference could have been drawn even if satisfied that it was for good reason. It therefore said that where silence cannot be attributed to a defendant's having no answer, or none that would stand up in cross-examination, no adverse inference should be drawn. The reason for the silence, if proffered, and its plausibility should be taken into account: *Condron v. UK* [2000] Crim.L.R. 679.

In *Roble* [1997] Crim.L.R. 449, CA it was suggested that good reasons might be that the interviewing officer had not disclosed the nature of the case or the offence or the evidence was so complex or old that an immediate response cannot be given; see also *Beard* [2002] Crim.L.R. 684, CA. In *Howell* [2003] EWCA Crim 1169, it was also said that the kind of circumstances which may most likely justify silence are ill health, in particular mental disability, confusion, shock, intoxication, inability to recollect events without documents to hand or speaking to others. There must always be soundly based reasons for silence.

The court may draw inferences upon a submission of no case to answer: section 34(2)(c) but section 38(3) states that a case to answer shall not be based solely on an adverse inference. In *Hart and McLean* [1998] 6 *Archbold News* 1, it was said that this could apply where the defence is putting a positive case which might include documentation.

10–150   In *Webber* [2004] 1 Cr.App.R. 40, it was held that a positive suggestion put to a witness by or on behalf of a defendant might amount to a fact relied on in his defence even if that suggestion was not adopted by the witness. The word "fact" should be given a wide meaning. It covers any fact in issue and which was put forward as part of the defence case. A defendant relies on a fact not only when he has given or adduced evidence of it but also when his advocate put a specific and positive case to prosecution witnesses.

A court should not draw inferences where it believes that the defendant genuinely and reasonably relied on the advice of his solicitor: *Beckles* [2005] 1 W.L.R. 2829. In *Hoare* [2005] 1 W.L.R. 1804 it was said that ultimately the question is whether "regardless of advice, genuinely given and genuinely accepted, an accused has remained silent not because of that advice but because he had no or no satisfactory explanation to give". These cases were highlighted in *Bresa* [2005] EWCA Crim 1414 which referred to the JSB specimen directions to a jury.

It is good practice for a defence case statement to be signed: *K.V.* (2005) 149 S.J.L.B. 301.

A defendant must waive privilege if he or his solicitor seeks to put forward the reason for the solicitor's advice: *Bowden* [1999] 2 Cr.App.R. 176. If a solicitor, following consultations with his client, chooses in the presence and hearing of his client to say something expressly for the record as to why his client is going to remain silent in interview, such a statement is admissible: *Fitzgerald* [1998] 4 *Archbold News* 2, CA. If a defendant asserts that his solicitor, in advising him to remain silent, had a conflict of interest because of his acting for a co-defendant, then privilege should be waived: *Hill* [2003] 5 *Archbold News* 2, CA. If adverse inferences are likely to be drawn a defendant should be given the opportunity to make representations.

Criminal Justice and Public Order Act 1994, s.35

Effect of accused's silence at trial

35.—(1) At the trial of any person for an offence, subsections (2) and (3) below apply unless—   **10–151**

    (a) the accused's guilt is not in issue; or

    (b) it appears to the court that the physical or mental condition of the accused makes it undesirable for him to give evidence;

but subsection (2) below does not apply if, at the conclusion of the evidence for the prosecution, his legal representative informs the court that the accused will give evidence or, where he is unrepresented, the court ascertains from him that he will give evidence.

(2) Where this subsection applies, the court shall, at the conclusion of the evidence for the prosecution, satisfy itself (in the case of proceedings on indictment, in the presence of the jury) that the accused is aware that the stage has been reached at which evidence can be given for the defence and that he can, if he wishes, give evidence and that, if he chooses not to give evidence, or having been sworn, without good cause refuses to answer any question, it will be permissible for the court or jury to draw such inferences as appear proper from his failure to give evidence or his refusal, without good cause, to answer any question.

(3) Where this subsection applies, the court or jury, in determining whether the accused is guilty of the offence charged, may draw such inferences as appear proper from the failure of the accused to give evidence or his refusal, without good cause, to answer any question.

(4) This section does not render the accused compellable to give evidence on his own behalf, and he shall accordingly not be guilty of contempt of court by reason of a failure to do so.

(5) For the purposes of this section a person who, having been sworn, refuses to answer any question shall be taken to do so without good cause unless—

    (a) he is entitled to refuse to answer the question by virtue of any enactment, whenever passed or made, or on the ground of privilege; or

    (b) the court in the exercise of its general discretion excuses him from answering it.

[repealed]

    (7) This section applies—

    (a) in relation to proceedings on indictment for an offence, only if the person charged with the offence is arraigned on or after the commencement of this section;

    (b) in relation to proceedings in a magistrates' court, only if the time when the court begins to receive evidence in the proceedings falls after the commencement of this section.

[This section is reprinted as amended by the *Crime and Disorder Act* 1998, Sched. 10, para. 1.]

Section 38(3) of the Act prohibits a conviction on an inference alone. In *Murray v.*   **10–152**
U.K. (1996) 22 E.H.R.R. 29, it was said that it would be incompatible with the rights of the defendant to base a conviction solely or mainly on his silence or on a refusal to answer questions or give evidence himself. A defendant does not need to give evidence where the prosecution case is weak. The principle in *Murray* was confirmed in *Beccles v. U.K.* (2002) 36 E.H.R.R. 162; see also *Milford* [2001] Crim.L.R. 330; *Chenia* [2003] 2 Cr.App.R. 6. A court is only entitled to draw adverse inferences from a failure to give evidence if the case against him is sufficiently strong: *Iqbal v. DPP* [2004] EWHC 2567. For a court to exercise its discretion under section 35 properly there has to be an evidential basis as to why it is undesirable for a defendant to give evidence. A statement by a legal representative that a defendant might not give evidence is not sufficient: *DPP v. Kavanagh* [2005] EWHC 820.

Criminal Justice and Public Order Act 1994, ss.36–37

Effect of accused's failure or refusal to account for objects, substances or marks

36.—(1) Where—   **10–153**

    (a) a person is arrested by a constable, and there is—

        (i) on his person; or

Part II

        (ii)   in or on his clothing or footwear; or

        (iii) otherwise in his possession; or

        (iv) in any place in which he is at the time of his arrest,

    any object, substance or mark, or there is any mark on any such object; and

   (b) that or another constable investigating the case reasonably believes that the presence of the object, substance or mark may be attributable to the participation of the person arrested in the commission of an offence specified by the constable; and

   (c) the constable informs the person arrested that he so believes, and requests him to account for the presence of the object, substance or mark; and

   (d) the person fails or refuses to do so,

then if, in any proceedings against the person for the offence so specified, evidence of those matters is given, subsection (2) below applies.

   (2) Where this subsection applies—

   (a) a magistrates' court inquiring into the offence as examining justices;

   (b) a judge, in deciding whether to grant an application made by the accused under—

        (i)   section 6 of the *Criminal Justice Act* 1987 (application for dismissal of charge of serious fraud in respect of which notice of transfer has been given under section 4 of that Act); or

        (ii) paragraph 5 of Schedule 6 to the *Criminal Justice Act* 1991 (application for dismissal of charge of violent or sexual offence involving child in respect of which notice of transfer has been given under section 53 of that Act);

   (c) the court, in determining whether there is a case to answer; and

   (d) the court or jury, in determining whether the accused is guilty of the offence charged,

may draw such inferences from the failure or refusal as appear proper.

   (3) Subsections (1) and (2) above apply to the condition of clothing or footwear as they apply to a substance or mark thereon.

   (4) Subsections (1) and (2) above do not apply unless the accused was told in ordinary language by the constable when making the request mentioned in subsection (1)(c) above what the effect of this section would be if he failed or refused to comply with the request.

   (4A) Where the accused was at an authorised place of detention at the time of the failure or refusal, subsections (1) and (2) above do not apply if he had not been allowed an opportunity to consult a solicitor prior to the request being made.

   (5) This section applies in relation to officers of customs and excise as it applies in relation to constables.

   (6) This section does not preclude the drawing of any inference from a failure or refusal of the accused to account for the presence of an object, substance or mark or from the condition of clothing or footwear which could properly be drawn apart from this section.

   (7) This section does not apply in relation to a failure or refusal which occurred before the commencement of this section.

Effect of accused's failure or refusal to account for presence at a particular place

10–154   **37.**—(1) Where—

   (a) a person arrested by a constable was found by him at a place at or about the time the offence for which he was arrested is alleged to have been committed; and

   (b) that or another constable investigating the offence reasonably believes that the presence of the person at that place and at that time may be attributable to his participation in the commission of the offence; and

   (c) the constable informs the person that he so believes, and requests him to account for that presence; and

   (d) the person fails or refuses to do so,

then if, in any proceedings against the person for the offence, evidence of those matters is given, subsection (2) below applies.

   (2) Where this subsection applies—

   (a) a magistrates' court inquiring into the offence as examining justices;.

   (b) a judge, in deciding whether to grant an application made by the accused under—

   (i)   section 6 of the *Criminal Justice Act* 1987 (application for dismissal of charge
         of serious fraud in respect of which notice of transfer has been given under sec-
         tion 4 of that Act); or
   (ii) paragraph 5 of Schedule 6 to the *Criminal Justice Act* 1991 (application for
         dismissal of charge of violent or sexual offence involving child in respect of
         which notice of transfer has been given under section 53 of that Act);
   (c)   the court, in determining whether there is a case to answer; and
   (d)   the court or jury, in determining whether the accused is guilty of the offence
         charged,
may draw such inferences from the failure or refusal as appear proper.

   (3) Subsections (1) and (2) do not apply unless the accused was told in ordinary language
by the constable when making the request mentioned in subsection (1)(c) above what the
effect of this section would be if he failed or refused to comply with the request.

   (3A) Where the accused was at an authorised place of detention at the time of the failure or refusal, subsections (1) and (2) do not apply if he had not been allowed an opportunity to consult a solicitor prior to the request being made.

   (4) This section applies in relation to officers of customs and excise as it applies in relation to constables.

   (5) This section does not preclude the drawing of any inference from a failure or refusal
of the accused to account for his presence at a place which could properly be drawn apart
from this section.

   (6) This section does not apply in relation to a failure or refusal which occurred before
the commencement of this section.

The above two sections are concerned with failures to provide explanations when   **10–155**
asked to do so after arrest. A court must be satisfied that a defendant has failed to account for the relevant matter before drawing proper inferences: *Compton* [2002] All
E.R. 149.

Criminal Procedure and Investigations Act 1996, s.11

Faults in disclosure by accused

   [**11.**—(1) This section applies in the three cases set out in subsections (2), (3) and (4).   **10–156**
   (2) The first case is where section 5 applies and the accused—
   (a)   fails to give an initial defence statement,
   (b)   gives an initial defence statement but does so after the end of the period which,
         by virtue of section 12, is the relevant period for section 5,
   (c)   is required by section 6B to give either an updated defence statement or a state-
         ment of the kind mentioned in subsection (4) of that section but fails to do so,
   (d)   gives an updated defence statement or a statement of the kind mentioned in sec-
         tion 6B(4) but does so after the end of the period which, by virtue of section 12,
         is the relevant period for section 6B,
   (e)   sets out inconsistent defences in his defence statement, or
   (f)   at his trial—
         (i)   puts forward a defence which was not mentioned in his defence statement
                or is different from any defence set out in that statement,
         (ii)   relies on a matter which, in breach of the requirements imposed by or
                under section 6A, was not mentioned in his defence statement,
         (iii) adduces evidence in support of an alibi without having given particulars of
                the alibi in his defence statement, or
         (iv)   calls a witness to give evidence in support of an alibi without having
                complied with section 6A(2)(a) or (b) as regards the witness in his defence
                statement.
   (3) The second case is where section 6 applies, the accused gives an initial defence statement, and the accused—
   (a)   gives the initial defence statement after the end of the period which, by virtue of
         section 12, is the relevant period for section 6, or
   (b)   does any of the things mentioned in paragraphs (c) to (f) of subsection (2).
   (5) Where this section applies—

    (a) the court or any other party may make such comment as appears appropriate;

    (b) the court or jury may draw such inferences as appear proper in deciding whether the accused is guilty of the offence concerned.

  (6) Where—

    (a) this section applies by virtue of subsection (2)(f)(ii) (including that provision as it applies by virtue of subsection (3)(b)), and

    (b) the matter which was not mentioned is a point of law (including any point as to the admissibility of evidence or an abuse of process) or an authority,

comment by another party under subsection (5)(a) may be made only with the leave of the court.

  (8) Where the accused puts forward a defence which is different from any defence set out in his defence statement, in doing anything under subsection (5) or in deciding whether to do anything under it the court shall have regard—

    (a) to the extent of the differences in the defences, and

    (b) to whether there is any justification for it.

  (9) Where the accused calls a witness whom he has failed to include, or to identify adequately, in a witness notice, in doing anything under subsection (5) or in deciding whether to do anything under it the court shall have regard to whether there is any justification for the failure.

  (10) A person shall not be convicted of an offence solely on an inference drawn under subsection (5).

  (12) In this section—

    (a) "initial defence statement" means a defence statement given under section 5 or 6;

    (b) "updated defence statement" means a defence statement given under section 6B;

    (c) a reference simply to an accused's "defence statement" is a reference—

      (i) where he has given only an initial defence statement, to that statement;

      (ii) where he has given both an initial and an updated defence statement, to the updated defence statement;

      (iii) where he has given both an initial defence statement and a statement of the kind mentioned in section 6B(4), to the initial defence statement;

    (d) a reference to evidence in support of an alibi shall be construed in accordance with section 6A(3);

    (e) "witness notice" means a notice given under section 6C.]

10–157   Where a defence statement is discretionary and one is served out of time or sets out inconsistent defences or at trial the defendant puts forward a new defence, relies on a matter which is not included in the statement or calls an alibi witness not mentioned in the defence statement, adverse inferences may be drawn by the court and there may be comments by the other party: section 11(5) of the *Criminal Procedure and Investigations Act* 1996, as amended.

XII. PRIVILEGE

A. General

10–158   A witness may refuse to produce documentary evidence or give oral testimony on the ground that the information sought is privileged. In respect of documents he is protected from giving oral evidence as to their content, or his knowledge or belief founded thereupon. Privilege prevents the production of evidence. It is not concerned with its admissibility, which depends upon its relevance: *R. v. Governor of Pentonville Prison, ex p. Osman* (1990) 90 Cr.App.R. 281, DC.

    Courts may order disclosure of confidential but not privileged information: *R. v. Manchester Crown Court, ex p. Rogers* [1999] 4 All E.R. 35. The case went on to say that privileged information is not confined to contentious business and it may only be waived by the person who owns it. This was confirmed in *R. v. Minshull Street Crown Court, ex p. Miller Gardner Solicitors* [2002] EWHC 3077.

B. Legal Professional Privilege

10–159   The right to consult legal advisers without fear of the communication's being revealed is a fundamental condition on which the administration of justice rests: *R. v. Derby Magistrates' Court, ex p. B.* [1996] A.C. 487, HL. This privilege covers confidential written or oral communications made between a professional legal adviser and his client or any person representing the client in connection with the giving of legal advice to the client and in connection with or contemplation of litigation: *Greenough v. Gaskell* (1833) 1 M. & K. 98. The second limb, know as litigation privilege, includes communications between the professional adviser, the client and any other person. An assertion, in defence of allegations of recent fabrication, *i.e* an alibi, that the defendant had remained silent at interview on legal advice, is not waiver of privilege and a solicitor's notes could not be ordered to be produced: *Wishart* [2005] EWCA Crim 1337.

The privilege is strictly confined to counsel and solicitors, their clerks, agents and interpreters between them and their clients: *R. v. Thames Magistrates' Courts, ex p. Bozkurt* [2002] R.T.R. 15, DC. Once a defendant or a defendant's solicitor gives evidence of the content or the reason for the advice given, privilege is waived: *Loizou* [2006] EWCA Crim 1719; (2006) 150 S.J.L.B. 1187.

In *R. (Howe) v. South Durham Magistrates' Court* [2005] R.T.R. 4, it was held **10–160** that it is not a breach of legal professional privilege for the defendant's solicitor to be summoned to give evidence at his trial for allegedly driving whilst disqualified where no other means or proving disqualification is available.

The privilege does not extend to communications which are made for the purposes of obtaining advice on the commission of a future crime or which are themselves part of a crime: *Cox and Railton* (1884) 14 Q.B.D. 153. Documents or information obtained in contravention of domestic or foreign law cannot be privileged: *Dubai Aluminium Co Ltd v. Al-Alwai* [1999] 1 W.L.R. 1964, QBD. There must be *prima facie* evidence that it was the client's intention to obtain advice in furtherance of his criminal purposes: *O'Rourke v. Darbishire* [1920] A.C. 581, HL. In deciding whether a document came into existence in furtherance of a crime the court may be entitled to look at the document itself: *R. v. Governor of Pentonville Prison, ex p. Osman, ante.*

A document does not become privileged simply by being handed to a lawyer. A solicitor who holds a document for or relating to his or her client can assert in respect of its seizure no greater authority than the client possesses: *R. v. Peterborough Justices, ex p. Hicks* [1977] 1 W.L.R. 1371, DC. If an unprivileged document in counsel's possession is called for in court, it must be produced: *Bursill v. Tanner* (1885) 16 Q.B.D. 1. Privilege does not attach to documents obtained by a client or his legal adviser for the purpose of litigation unless the document has been created for the purpose of litigation: *Ventouris v. Mountain* [1991] 1 W.L.R. 607, CA (Civ. Div.). Copies of non-privileged documents are privileged only if (a) the copy was made for the purpose of litigation; and (b) the original document is not and has not at any time been in the control of the party claiming privilege: *The Palermo* (1884) L.R. 9 P.D. 6; *Watson v. Cammel Laird & Co Ltd* [1959] 1 W.L.R. 702, CA. Copy documents sent to a lawyer for legal advice do not thereby become privileged where the original in the hands of the maker of the copy is not privileged: *Dubai Bank Ltd v. Galadari* [1990] Ch 98, CA (Civ. Div.).

Privilege does not extend to protect material in the hands of a solicitor from being **10–161** disclosed where there is independent and free-standing evidence of a plot to pervert the course of justice: *Hallinan, Blackburn, Gittings & Nott (a firm) v. Middlesex Crown Court* [2005] 1 W.L.R. 766.

If a prosecutor comes into possession of material in respect of which the defence can justifiably claim legal professional privilege (and that claim is either conceded or upheld) the defence may contend that the way in which the material came into the possession of the prosecutor needs to be investigated and/or the disclosure of that material has so prejudiced the conduct of the defence that the case should not proceed. The prosecutor's duty, in those circumstances, is to explain to the court, either by calling evidence or from uncontested statements of fact, how he came into possession of the material and what use he has made of it, failing which the court may infer that a) he has obtained it by improper means, and/or b) his use of it will unfairly prejudice the defendant. The defence may also wish to call evidence. The court will then be in a position, in any abuse argument, to decide what course of action to take: *R. (Customs and Excise Commissioners) v. Nottingham Magistrates' Court* [2004] EWHC 1922. Legal professional privilege is inapplicable once the material is in the hands of the prosecution: *Willis* [2004] EWCA Crim 3472, CA.

10–162　　Where the selection of documents copied or assembled by a solicitor betrays the trend of the advice given to his client, the documents so selected are privileged: *Lyell v. Kennedy (No. 3)* (1884) 27 Ch.D 1.

Translations of documents should be treated in the same way as copies: *Sumitomo Corporation v. Credit Lyonnais Rouse Ltd* [2002] 1 W.L.R. 479, CA (Civ. Div.).

A document or communication is always privileged once it becomes privileged: *Calcraft v. Guest* [1898] 1 Q.B. 759. Legal professional privilege must be upheld in the public interest, even where the witness no longer has any recognisable interest in preserving the confidentiality: *R. v. Derby Magistrates' Court, ex p. B.* [1996] A.C. 487, HL.

10–163　　Where the expert's opinion is to an extent based on privileged material, the opinion itself is also privileged. Consequently the defence can object if the prosecution seeks to elicit evidence from an expert who has been abandoned and not relied upon by the defence: see *Davies* (2002) 166 J.P. 243, CA. A person interviewed by a doctor at the instigation of his own lawyers for the purpose of his defence is entitled to assume that what he says to the doctor has the same status as communications with his lawyers. Both the interview and the opinion based upon it are privileged: *Davies, ante*. An expert's opinion on DNA is privileged where it is based upon a blood sample taken form the defendant and sent to the expert by his solicitors in contemplation of criminal proceedings because the blood sample itself is an item subject to the legal professional privilege within the meaning of the *Police and Criminal Evidence Act* 1984, s.10: *R.* [1995] 1 Cr.App.R. 183, CA.

C.　Privilege against Self-Incrimination

10–164　　A witness is entitled to claim the privilege against self-incrimination in respect of any piece of information or evidence on the basis of which the prosecution might wish to establish guilt or decide to prosecute under English law: *Den Norske Bank ASA v. Antonatos* [1999] Q.B. 271 at 287, CA (Civ. Div.).

Although it has been held that a witness must object personally on oath: *Downie v. Coe, The Times*, November 28, 1997, it is the legal adviser who will normally warn of self incrimination so that the court may rule on whether the witness has to answer the question or not. If the witness is wrongly compelled to answer and the defendant is convicted, the defendant cannot use the witness's compulsion to answer as a ground for appeal: *Kinglake* (1870) 11 Cox 499.

If the witness does not object, his replies once given will be admissible evidence in any proceedings brought against him: *Sloggett* (1865) Dears 656. If the witness objects but is compelled to answer the answers are not admissible in evidence in later proceedings: *Garbett* (1847) 1 Den 236.

There must be reasonable grounds for claiming the privilege and the danger must be real and appreciable: *Boyes* (1861) 1 B. & S. 311.

The privilege may be expressly removed by statute. Statutory exceptions include the *Criminal Evidence Act* 1898, s.1(e) and the *Theft Act* 1968, s.31. See *Khan v. Khan* [1982] 1 W.L.R. 513 in respect of the *Theft Act* 1968. The *Criminal Justice Act* 2003 allows its introduction.

10–165　　In *Saunders* [1996] 1 Cr.App.R. 463 the Court of Appeal rejected an argument that the trial judge should have excluded the transcript of interviews with DTI inspectors because the questioning under section 434 of the *Companies Act* 1985 was outside the safeguards of an interview under caution and the defendants were deprived of their protection against self-incrimination. Lord Taylor C.J. said that Parliament's intention was clear in section 434(5) and it could not be right for a judge to exercise his or her discretion to exclude evidence of interviews simply on the basis that Parliament ought not to countenance the possibility of self-incrimination. The European Court of Human Rights held that Saunders had been denied a fair trial because the use of statements obtained from him by the DTI inspectors amounted to an unjustifiable infringement of the right to silence and the right not to incriminate oneself: *Saunders v. UK* (1997) 23 E.H.R.R. 313. The court said that the question whether the use made by the prosecution of the statements obtained by the inspectors amounted to such an infringement must be examined in the light of all the circumstances in particular whether the applicant had been subject to compulsion to give principles of a fair procedure inherent in Article 6(1). See also *Heaney and McGovern v. Ireland* (2001) 33 E.H.R.R. 12. See *ante,* § 10–144 for the impact of section 13 of the *Fraud Act* 2006.

The privilege relates to any risk of prosecution under English law: *Den Norske Bank* **10–166** *ASA v. Antonatos, ante.* No privilege arises where matters are covered by a pardon: *Boyes* (1861) 1 B. & S. 311, by undertakings and immunities from prosecution given by the DPP, or where the risk relates to liability for debt in civil proceedings. The privilege does not extend to incrimination under foreign law however the court has a discretion to excuse a witness from giving evidence or producing documents which may so incriminate him: *Brannigan v. Davidson* [1997] A.C. 238, PC. A remote possibility of prosecution is not enough. The danger must be "real and appreciable, with reference to the ordinary operation of law and in the ordinary course of things": *Boyes, ante.* Provided that the risk of proceedings being taken against the witness is real and not remote or insubstantial, the witness does not have to show that proceedings are likely or could probably be taken against him: *Re Westinghouse Electric Corp* [1977] 3 All E.R. 703.

D. Confidential Communications

No legal privilege arises out of the relationship between doctor and patient: *Mc-* **10–167** *Donald* [1991] Crim.L.R. 122, CA. It does not arise between journalist and informer: *Att.-Gen. v. Mulholland and Foster* [1963] 2 Q.B. 477. See, however, the *Contempt of Court Act* 1981, s.10. The position of priest and penitent has not been authoritively decided but the tendency of judicial dicta is that while in strict law the privilege does not exist, a minister of religion should not be required to give evidence as to a confession made to him: *Griffin* (1853) 6 Cox 219; *Hay* (1896) 2 F. & F. 4.

The court has a discretion to excuse a witness from answering a question where to do so would involve a breach of confidence. In *Hunter v. Mann* [1974] Q.B. 767, 59 Cr.App.R 37, DC, Lord Widgery C.J. said (*obiter*):

> "If a doctor, giving evidence ... is asked a question which he finds embarrassing because it involves him talking about things which he would normally regard as confidential, he can seek the protection of the judge and ask the judge if it is necessary for him to answer. The judge, by virtue of the overriding discretion to control his court which all English judges have, can, if he thinks fit, tell the doctor that he need not answer the question. Whether or not the judge would take that line, of course, depends largely on the importance of the potential answer to the issues being tried."

Before compelling disclosure, the court should be satisfied that the potential answer is relevant and will serve a useful purpose in relation to the proceedings, and then weigh the conflicting interests to determine whether confidentiality should be overridden or respected: *Att.-Gen. v. Mulholland and Foster, ante.*

The *Police and Criminal Evidence Act* 1984 imposed restrictions on the extent to which access may be obtained to confidential information for the purposes of a criminal investigation: *PACE* 1984, ss.8–13.

XIII. CORROBORATION

Corroboration is evidence which supports a witness's testimony. Where one piece of **10–168** evidence confirms and supports another, corroboration takes place if both pieces of evidence are accepted by the tribunal of fact.

Part II

A definition of corroboration was found in *Baskerville* [1916] 2 K.B. 658. Lord Reid said at 667:

> "Evidence in corroboration must be independent testimony which affects the accused by connecting or tending to connect him with the crime. In other words, it must be evidence which implicates him, that is, which confirms in some material particular not only the evidence that the crime has been committed, but also that the prisoner committed it. The test applicable to determine the nature and extent of the corroboration is thus the same whether the case falls within the rule of practice at common law or within that class of offences for which corroboration is required by statute."

In general there is no requirement for corroboration. Some statutes, however, do require corroboration. In the magistrates' courts this applies to speeding offences: *Road Traffic Regulation Act* 1984, s.89(2). In certain cases it has been considered dangerous to convict on the evidence of a single person unless the court was convinced of the guilt of the defendant:

— evidence of a complaint in any allegation of a sexual offence;
— evidence of an accomplice when called by the prosecutor;
— evidence of children.

10–169   Legislation has abolished the requirement to warn juries of the danger in the above cases. Sections 32 and 33 of the *Criminal Justice and Public Order Act* 1994 abolished the rule requiring a corroboration warning to be given in relation to the evidence of accomplices and the evidence of complainants in sexual offences and the requirement for corroboration in offences under the *Sexual Offences Act* 1956 in trials on indictment.

In the magistrates' courts, the judiciary will exercise caution in convicting without corroboration in certain circumstances, *e.g.* where a witness is considered unreliable, is shown to have lied, to have made previous false complaints, is of bad character, is a co-defendant, bears the defendant a grudge or has an improper motive: *Makanjuola*; *Easton* [1995] 2 Cr.App.R. 469, CA; *Knowlden and Knowlden* (1983) 77 Cr.App.R. 94, CA; *Beck* (1982) 74 Cr.App.R. 221; *Witts and Witts* [1991] Crim.L.R 562, CA; *Chan Wai-Keung v. R* [1995] 2 Cr.App.R. 194.

XIV PROCEDURE FOR CHALLENGING ADMISSIBILITY

10–170   Since the judiciary in magistrates' courts are judges of both fact and law they must rule on the admissibility of evidence and decide the question of the defendant's guilt. If they rule evidence inadmissible they must ignore that evidence when deciding whether to convict or acquit the defendant.

The magistrates' court has an overall responsibility for ensuring that the defendant receives a fair trial according to law: *Sang, ante*. It should not wait for an objection to be taken to the admissibility of evidence but should itself stop questions likely to elicit such evidence: *Ellis* [1910] 2 K.B. 746; *Stirland v. DPP* [1944] A.C. 315.

The point at which the magistrates' court should rule upon a question of admissibility is a matter for its discretion: *F. (an infant) v. Chief Constable of Kent* [1982] Crim.L.R. 682. The Divisional Court held that a trial within a trial is not an appropriate procedure in the magistrates' court. This is because the purpose of a *voire dire* is to allow the judge to determine a question of law in the absence of the jury. Incidental matters, such as the admissibility of evidence, should be decided as separate issues from that of guilt.

10–171   In *R. v. Epping and Ongar Justices, ex p. Manby* [1986] Crim.L.R. 555, the defendant had been charged with driving an overweight vehicle. The prosecution relied upon a police officer's certificate that the defendant had admitted responsibility for the vehicle pursuant to the *Road Traffic Act* 1972, s.181. The defendant's solicitor wished to challenge the admissibility of the certificate but did not require the officer to be called to give evidence. The justices refused to hear evidence from the defendant on the point as a preliminary issue and proceeded with the prosecution case. No defence evidence was called. The application for review of the decision to refuse to decide the issue of admissibility as a preliminary issue was dismissed since, within statutory restraints, justices determine their own procedure. Since the defendant had not required the officer to be called, the justices were entitled to accept the prosecution evidence as providing a prima facie case on the point.

It has also been said, however, that the court should not rule on the admissibility of evidence until the evidence has been tendered and objection taken: *Sang* 69 Cr.App.R. 282; *Williams v. Mohamed* [1977] R.T.R. 12.

Where an application is made under section 78, a magistrates' court has a discretion either to deal with the application by way of a *voire dire* when it arises or to leave the decision until the end of the hearing when all the evidence has been heard. The aim should always be to secure a trial which is fair to both sides: *Vel v. Owen* [1987] Crim.L.R. 496, DC. In *Halawa v. Federation Against Copyright Theft* [1995] 1 Cr.App.R. 21, DC, the court said:

— A proper understanding of what is fair will lead in some cases to the conclusion that, if the defendant wishes to proceed by way of a *voire dire*, he or she should be allowed to do so because, unless there is good reason to take a different course, he or she should have the opportunity to secure the exclusion of unfair evidence before he or she decides whether to give evidence. If he or she is unfairly denied that opportunity, the right to silence is impaired.

— If the application is made as alternative to a submission under section 76 of the 1984 Act, it should be examined at the same time in accordance with the procedure set out in *R. v. Liverpool Juvenile Court, ex p. R* [1988] Q.B. 1.

— If the point is raised only under section 78 in most cases the better course will be for the whole of the prosecution case to be heard, including the disputed evidence, before any *voire dire* is held.

— In order to decide which course to take, the court may ask the defence the extent of the issues to be address by the defendant's evidence on the *voire dire*. If the issues are limited to the circumstances in which the evidence was obtained, there would in most cases be no apparent reason why the defendant should be heard as on a *voire dire*. If however the defendant intends to contradict some part of the prosecution's account of "all the circumstances" it would be open to the court to conclude that the proceedings on the *voire dire* might be protracted and would introduce issues which would have to be re-examined in the remaining stages of the trial if a *prima facie* case is held to be established, in which case the securing of a fair trial to both sides would not require a *voire dire*. For this purpose the court would be entitled to take account of the nature and extent of the cross-examination of the prosecution witnesses for an understanding of the extent of any dispute as to "all the circumstances".

Where the court is determining the admissibility of a confession under section 76 of the *Police and Criminal Evidence Act* 1984 then it has been held that admissibility should be determined by way of *voire dire*: *R. v. Liverpool Juvenile Court, ex p. R.* [1988] Q.B. 1. Section 76(2) of the same Act provides that if it is represented that the confession has or may have been obtained in either of the two ways set out in that subsection, the court shall not allow it to be given in evidence except insofar as the prosecution proves beyond reasonable doubt that it was not so obtained. Section 76(2) accordingly obliges a magistrates' court to hold a trial within a trial in such cases. This rule also applies to committal proceedings: *R. v. Oxford City Justices, ex p. Berry* [1988] Q.B. 507.

If an application to exclude evidence is made under section 78 of the *Police and Criminal Evidence Act* 1984 the court is not obliged to hold a trial within a trial: *Vel v. Owen* [1987] Crim.L.R. 496. The defendant has no right to have the admissibility of evidence determined under section 78 in advance of evidence being given because the court under section 78 has a discretion to exclude evidence if it would bear unfairly on the proceedings and there is no burden on the prosecution to disprove unfairness.

10–172

The court does not have the power to delegate the function of determining the admissibility of evidence to another bench: *R. v. Ormskirk Justices, ex p. Davies*

(1994) 158 J.P. 1145. After the court rules that evidence is inadmissible, it must then ignore that evidence when determining the issue of guilt. If a court hears of a defendant's convictions or pending charges, it may be necessary to adjourn the case to be heard by another bench. In *R. v. Liverpool Justices, ex p. Topping* (1983) 76 Cr.App.R. 170 the court said that the test in such circumstances is "would a reasonable and fair-minded person sitting in court and knowing all the relevant facts have a reasonable suspicion that a fair trial for the [defendant] was not possible?"

The court may reverse a previous decision as to inadmissibility provided that there is good reason to do so and that no injustice is caused. Such reversals should, however, be exceptional: *R. v. Faversham and Sittingbourne Justices ex p. Stickings* (1996) 160 J.P. 801.

There is no need for evidence to be repeated after the question of admissibility has been determined: *F. (an infant) v. Chief Constable of Kent, ante.*

CHALLENGING DECISIONS

I. RE-OPENING A CASE

Magistrates' Courts Act 1980, s.142

Power of magistrates' court to re-open cases to rectify mistakes etc.

142.—(1) A magistrates' court may vary or rescind a sentence or other order imposed or **11–1** made by it when dealing with an offender if it appears to the court to be in the interests of justice to do so, and it is hereby declared that this power extends to replacing a sentence or order which for any reason appears to be invalid by another which the court has power to impose or make.

(1A) The power conferred on a magistrates' court by subsection (1) above shall not be exercisable in relation to any sentence or order imposed or made by it when dealing with an offender if—

    (a) the Crown Court has determined an appeal against—

        (i) that sentence or order;

        (ii) the conviction in respect of which that sentence or order was imposed or made; or

        (iii) any other sentence or order imposed or made by the magistrates' court when dealing with the offender in respect of that conviction (including a sentence or order replaced by that sentence or order); or

    (b) the High Court has determined a case stated for the opinion of that court on any question arising in any proceeding leading to or resulting from the imposition or making of the sentence or order.

(2) Where a person is convicted by a magistrates' court and it subsequently appears to the court that it would be in the interests of justice that the case should be heard again by different justices, the court may so direct.

(2A) The power conferred on a magistrates' court by subsection (2) above shall not be exercisable in relation to a conviction if—

    (a) the Crown Court has determined an appeal against—

        (i) the conviction; or

        (ii) any sentence or order imposed or made by the magistrates' court when dealing with the offender in respect of the conviction; or

    (b) the High Court has determined a case stated for the opinion of that court on any question arising in any proceeding leading to or resulting from the conviction.

(3) Where a court gives a direction under subsection (2) above—

    (a) the conviction and any sentence or other order imposed or made in consequence thereof shall be of no effect; and

    (b) section 10(4) above shall apply as if the trial of the person in question had been adjourned.

[(4) ...repealed]

(5) Where a sentence or order is varied under subsection (1) above, the sentence or other order, as so varied, shall take effect from the beginning of the day on which it was originally imposed or made, unless the court otherwise directs.

11–2   The provisions are wide. They should be used to rectify obvious mistakes. In *R. v. Croydon Youth Court, ex p. DPP* [1997] 2 Cr.App.R. 411, it was said that it is wrong to employ section 142(2) as a method by which a defendant could obtain a rehearing in circumstances where he could not appeal to the Crown Court by reason of his unequivocal plea of guilty, nor was it in the interests of justice. The interests of justice were defined as including the interests of the courts and the public, that people who had pleaded guilty with the advice of counsel should continue to be regarded as guilty, and that there should be certainty and an end to litigation. In *Traves v. DPP* [2005] EWHC 1482 no special circumstances had been found to allow the prosecution to open its case when it had forgotten, in a charge of driving whilst disqualified, to produce the memorandum of conviction indicating the disqualification.

The power is not available where the prosecutor has withdrawn the charge: *Coles v. East Penwith Justices* (1998) 162 J.P. 687. The power extends only to cases where the defendant has been found guilty and not where he has been acquitted: *R. v. Gravesend Justices, ex p. Dexter* [1977] Crim.L.R. 298. This is true even where the acquittal follows the prosecutor's offering no evidence: *R. (O.) v. Stratford Youth Court* [2004] All E.R. 245.

Only in rare circumstances should it be used to review a sentence in order that consideration might be given to an increase where material facts had not been brought to the court's attention at the time of sentence, particularly if the increase might lead to custody: *R. (Holme) v. Liverpool Magistrates' Justices* [2004] EWHC 3131.

11–3   A hospital order under section 37(3) of the *Mental Health Act* 1983 where the court was satisfied that he "did the act" may be rescinded under section 142: *R. v. Thames Magistrates' Court, ex p. Ramadan* [1999] 1 Cr.App.R. 386, DC.

It can also be used to re-open such an order where the accused wished to challenge the finding: *R. (Bartram) v. Southend Magistrates' Court* [2004] EWHC 2691.

A court may review orders including the issue of a warrant for detention under section 136 of the *MCA* 1980 following non-payment of a fine: *R. v. Sheffield City J.J., ex p. Foster, The Times*, November 2, 1999, DC. A court may review an incorrect sentence and increase it: *Jane v. Broome, The Times*, November 2, 1987, DC. It may not increase a sentence for misbehaviour in the court: *Powell* (1985) 7 Cr.App.R.(S.) 247.

11–4   There is no time limit for making an application under this section. Mere delay in making an application is not a ground for refusing the application, however it is a factor for the court to take into account along with all other relevant circumstances: *R. v. Eal-*

ing Justices, ex p. Sahota (1998) 162 J.P. 73. This was confirmed in *R. (Dunlop) v. DPP* [2004] EWHC 225. In that case informations alleging offences of using a motor vehicle without insurance, driving without a licence and having no test certificate were laid in March 2001. The defendant did not appear in court in April 2001 to answer the summonses. In May 2001, he was sentenced in his absence. When he appeared voluntarily after a warrant had been issued for his arrest, he said that he had not received the summonses and had not owned a car or held a licence. He had first known about the convictions in March 2002. The magistrates' court refused to re-open under section 142 in view of the length of time which had elapsed. The appeal was allowed.

In *R. v. Gwent Magistrates' Court, ex p. Carey* (1996) 160 J.P. 613 on review of the magistrates' decision not to reopen the matter under section 142, the court said that the magistrates are entitled to emphasise the inconvenience to witnesses when defendants do not attend due to their own conduct. They should also weigh the strength of the prosecution case.

The court must exercise its discretion judicially. The late arrival at court of a defen- **11–5** dant was not a proper ground for refusing a rehearing: *R. v. Camberwell Green Magistrates' Court, ex p. Ibrahim* (1984) 148 J.P. 400.

II. APPEAL TO CROWN COURT

A. GENERAL

Magistrates' Courts Act 1980, s.108

Right of appeal to the Crown Court
   108.—(1) A person convicted by a magistrates' court may appeal to the Crown Court— **11–6**
      (a) if he pleaded guilty, against his sentence;
      (b) if he did not, against the conviction or sentence.
   (1A) [Section 14 of the *Powers of Criminal Courts (Sentencing) Act* 2000] (under which a conviction of an offence for which an order for conditional or absolute discharge is made is deemed not to be a conviction except for certain purposes) shall not prevent an appeal under this Act, whether against conviction or otherwise.
   (2) A person sentenced by a magistrates' court for an offence in respect of which an order for conditional discharge has been previously made may appeal to the Crown Court against the sentence.
   (3) In this section "sentence" includes any order made on conviction by a magistrates' court, not being—
      (b) an order for the payment of costs;
      (c) an order under section 2 of the *Protection of Animals Act* 1911 (which enables a court to order the destruction of an animal); or
      (d) an order made in pursuance of any enactment under which the court has no discretion as to the making of the order or its terms and also includes a declaration of relevance under the *Football Spectators Act* 1989.

[This section is reprinted as amended by the *Powers of Criminal Courts (Sentencing) Act* 2000, Sched. 9, para. 71.]

Where a defendant pleaded guilty he may only appeal against the sentence imposed. **11–7** Where a defendant pleaded not guilty he may appeal against both conviction and sentence. Appeals by young persons against conviction and/or sentence in the youth court are governed by these provisions, since youth courts are magistrates' courts: *Magistrates' Courts Act* 1980, ss.148, 152; *Children and Young Persons Act* 1933, ss.45, 46 and the *Powers of Criminal Courts (Sentencing) Act* 2000, s.137.

B. AGAINST CONVICTION

A plea of guilty in the magistrates' court usually means that the defendant cannot ap- **11–8** peal against conviction to the Crown Court: *Magistrates' Courts Act* 1980, s.108. In *R. v. Birmingham Crown Court, ex p. Sharma* [1988] Crim.L.R. 741 the defendant pleaded guilty by post to failing to stop at a traffic light and driving without insurance. He sought leave to appeal to the Crown Court out of time against conviction on the grounds that he had not intended to plead guilty to driving without insurance, and had in fact been insured. On review of the decision to refuse leave it was held that the defendant was not within any exception to the rule that a plea of guilty in the magistrates' court was final. It made no difference that he had pleaded guilty by post.

The Crown Court has no jurisdiction to entertain an application, set aside the conviction or remit the case to the magistrates simply because the defendant has subsequently regretted pleading guilty and thinks that he has an arguable defence: *R. v. Marylebone Justices, ex p. Westminster City Council* [1971] 1 W.L.R. 567; [1971] 1 All E.R. 1025.

The Crown Court has a limited jurisdiction to hear appeals against conviction where the defendant has pleaded guilty. This will arise when there has been an equivocal plea or where a plea has been made under duress: *R. v. Durham Quarter Sessions, ex p. Virgo*; *R. v. Huntingdon Crown Court, ex p. Jordan* 73 Cr.App.R. 194. For an appeal against conviction to proceed on the basis that a guilty plea was tendered following erroneous legal advice, that advice must go to the heart of the plea so that the plea of guilty was not a true acknowledgement of guilt: *Saik, The Times*, November 29, 2004.

11–9   If a defendant pleads guilty but is then committed to the Crown Court for sentence, the Crown Court has a general discretion to remit to the lower court whenever it considers it just to do so: *R. v. Inner London Crown Court, ex p. Sloper* (1979) 69 Cr.App.R. 1.

The duties of the Crown Court and the magistrates whose conviction following a guilty plea is being challenged were examined in *R. v. Plymouth Justices, ex p. Hart* [1986] Q.B. 950. If the Crown Court conducts a proper inquiry into whether the defendant's plea was equivocal and it has sufficient evidence before it to conclude that it was, the Crown Court's direction that a not guilty plea be entered and a summary trial be held is binding on the magistrates. The magistrates should assist the Crown Court in its inquiry into equivocality of the plea by supplying affidavits.

The Crown Court must make proper inquiry as to what happened in the magistrates' court before considering remitting the case: *R. v. Marylebone Justices, ex p. Westminster City Council, ante.* It is not under such a duty, however, unless something indicates that the magistrates should have considered permitting a change of plea: *R. v. Coventry Crown Court, ex p. Manson* (1978) 67 Cr.App.R. 315.

Where equivocality of plea is raised on appeal, the Crown Court should first decide if there is *prima facie* evidence of equivocality. If there is, it should request affidavit evidence from the Bench, the clerk or both. Only if it is then satisfied that the plea was equivocal should the case be remitted for a fresh plea to be taken: *R. v. Rochdale Justices, ex p. Allwork* (1981) 73 Cr.App.R. 319.

11–10   If the Crown Court finds the defendant not guilty of the offence charged, it may not convict the defendant of an attempt to commit the offence as that was not within the powers of the magistrates' court: *R. v. Manchester Crown Court, ex p. Hill* (1985) 149 J.P.N. 29.

There is no power to appeal against acquittal or dismissal unless provided for by statute: *London Keepers of the Peace and Justices* [1945] K.B. 528.

C. AGAINST SENTENCE

11–11   There is no appeal against the making of a costs order, the destruction of an animal or a non-discretionary order.

Where a defendant appeals against a sentence imposed by a magistrates' court, the Crown Court should not review the decision reached by the magistrates but should carry out a complete rehearing of the issues and form an independent view, on all the evidence, of the correct sentence: *R. v. Swindon Crown Court, ex p. Murray* (1998) 162 J.P. 36.

The Crown Court is not bound by findings of fact made by a magistrates' court in a way that could limit its sentencing powers. Where a defendant appeals against sentence to the Crown Court, the court is entitled to decide the appeal on a different factual basis from that accepted by the magistrates' court. Where the Crown Court rejects the view taken by the magistrates' court, the court should make the position plain to the appellant and give him an opportunity, under the *Newton* principle, to challenge the factual basis adopted by the court: *Bussey v. DPP* [1999] 1 Cr.App.R. 125.

The Crown Court has no power to order that the sentence, which was the subject of **11–12** the appeal, should be consecutive to a sentence passed after the justices had imposed the sentence in question: *R. v. Portsmouth Crown Court, ex p. Ballard* (1990) 154 J.P. 109.

In *R. v. Isleworth Crown Court, ex p. Irvin* [1992] R.T.R. 281, the court adjourned the matter for inquiries before sentencing in such a way that the defendant formed the opinion that he would not receive a custodial sentence if the reports were favourable. In such circumstances it was held that where the reports are favourable then the Crown Court may not impose or uphold a custodial sentence.

There is no right to appeal against committal to the Crown Court for sentencing: *R. v. London Sessions, ex p. Rogers* [1951] 2 K.B. 74.

D. Against Binding Over Order

Magistrates' Courts (Appeals from Binding Over Orders) Act 1956, s.1

Right of appeal to quarter sessions

1.—(1) Where, under the *Justices of the Peace Act* 1361, or otherwise, a person is ordered **11–13** by a magistrates' court (as defined in the *Magistrates' Courts Act* 1980) to enter into a recognisance with or without sureties to keep the peace or to be of good behaviour, he may appeal to [the Crown Court]

(2) In the case of an appeal under this section—

(a) the other party to the proceedings which were the occasion of the making of the order shall be the respondent to the appeal;

(b) [...] in relation to an appellant in custody for failure to comply with the order, so much of section [twenty-two of the *Criminal Justice Act* 1967], as relates to the release of convicted persons from custody pending an appeal to [the Crown Court] shall, with the necessary adaptations, apply as if the appeal were an appeal against a conviction.

(3) Nothing in this section shall apply in relation to any order an appeal from which lies to [the Crown Court] apart from the provisions of this section.

(4) This section shall not apply to any order made before the expiration of a period of one month beginning with the date of the passing of this Act.

An appeal against a binding over order is by way of rehearing. Unless the appellant **11–14** admits the facts upon which the order was based, sworn evidence must be adduced and will be open to cross-examination: *Shaw v. Hamilton* [1982] 1 W.L.R. 1308.

E. Constitution of Crown Court on Appeal

Supreme Court Act 1981, s.74

Appeals and committals for sentence

74.—(1) On any hearing by the Crown Court— **11–15**

(a) of any appeal;

the Crown Court shall consist of a judge of the High Court or a Circuit judge or a Recorder who, subject to the following provisions of this section, shall sit with not less than two nor more than four justices of the peace.

(2) *Crown Court Rules* may, with respect to hearings falling within subsection (1)—

(a) prescribe the number of justices of the peace constituting the court (within the limits mentioned in that subsection); and

(b) prescribe the qualifications to be possessed by any such justices of the peace; and the rules may make different provision for different descriptions of cases, different places of sitting or other different circumstances.

(3) *Crown Court Rules* may authorise or require a judge of the High Court, Circuit judge or Recorder, in such circumstances as are specified by the rules, to enter on, or at any stage to continue with, any proceedings with a court not comprising the justices required by subsections (1) and (2).

(4) The Lord Chancellor may from time to time, having regard to the number of justices, or the number of justices with any prescribed qualifications, available for service in the Crown Court, give directions providing that, in such descriptions of proceedings as may be specified by the Lord Chancellor, the provisions of subsections (1) and (2) shall not apply.

(5) Directions under subsection (4) may frame descriptions of proceedings by reference to the place of trial, or by reference to the time of trial, or in any other way.

(6) No decision of the Crown Court shall be questioned on the ground that the court was not constituted as required by or under subsections (1) and (2) unless objection was taken by or on behalf of a party to the proceedings not later than the time when the proceedings were entered on, or when the alleged irregularity began.

(7) *Crown Court Rules* may make provision as to the circumstances in which—

(a) a person concerned with a decision appealed against is to be disqualified from hearing the appeal;

(c) proceedings on the hearing of an appeal [...] are to be valid notwithstanding that any person taking part in them is disqualified.

[This section is reprinted as amended by the *Access to Justice Act* 1999, Sched. 15(V)(4), para. 1.]

11–16   On an appeal to the Crown Court a judge will sit with magistrates who have not adjudicated at the hearing in the magistrates' court: *Criminal Procedure Rules* 2005, rule 63.8. On the hearing of an appeal from a youth court, a judge will sit with two magistrates each of whom is a member of the youth panel and who are chosen so that the court includes a man and a woman: r.63.7. Dispensations relating to the required constitution of the appeal bench apply in special circumstances.

11–17   See Appendix G–307, r.63.8.

F. PROCEDURE

11–18   See *Criminal Procedure Rules* 2005, r.63.2–63.3 in Appendix G–300—G–302.

11–19   A notice of appeal to the Crown Court must be given in writing within 21 days of the adjudication. Forms are available in courthouses for this purpose. A magistrates' court will accept notice of appeal out of time and will forward it to the Crown Court while at the same time notifying the appellant that it is out of time. The Crown Court should give brief reasons to the appellant of any refusal of an extension: *Re Worth (application for judicial review)* (1979) 1 F.L.R. 159; (1979) 10 Fam. Law 54. Where an extension is given the appellant must give notice to any other party to the appeal. The Crown Court will give notice of the hearing to the parties and the magistrates' court: *Crown Court Rules* 1982, r.8. The appeal will be by way of a rehearing: *Supreme Court Act* 1981, s.79(3).

The court may deal with a procedural irregularity: *R. v. Teeside Magistrates' Court, ex p. Bujinowski* [1997] Crim.L.R. 51. In that case, it was held that, on appeal against conviction for failing to surrender to bail, the Crown Court had jurisdiction to determine the matter on the basis that the magistrates had acted in breach of the relevant practice direction.

11–20   Where a defendant appeals to the Crown Court against conviction, the justices' clerk is not under a duty to provide the defendant with any notes of evidence unless the defendant is legally aided. There is no rule at common law which entitles the defendant to a copy of the clerk's notes and the *Criminal Procedure Rules* 2005, r.63.3 do not require the clerk to send any notes of evidence to the Crown Court when a defendant appeals against conviction, unless it refers to section 37 of the *Mental Health Act* 1983, unlike rule 43.1, which requires such notes to be sent to a Crown Court if the defendant is committed to the Crown Court for sentence after conviction. It is desirable that there should be no difference in procedure as far as possible between appeals by legally-aided defendants and non-legally aided defendants and therefore, requests for copies of notes of evidence should be viewed sympathetically by justices' clerks: *R. v. Clerk to Highbury Justices, ex p. Hussein* [1986] 1 W.L.R. 1266.

Where a judge sitting with magistrates in the Crown Court fails to give reasons when dismissing an appeal from the magistrates' court, he may prepare a note of the reasons subsequently; there is no need for the justices to provide supporting affidavits or to sign the judge's note: *R. v. Snaresbrook Crown Court, ex p. Input Management Ltd* (1999) 163 J.P. 533. In order to reassure an appellant that there has been no after-the-event rationalisation, reasons for the ruling should be given contemporaneously. Reasons will enable a defendant to understand the findings and to consider whether there are grounds for a further appeal to the Divisional Court by way of case stated. The failure to provide reasons is not always fatal to the Crown Court's decision since the reasons may be obvious, the decision is simple or the subject matter of the appeal is unimportant: *R. v. Kingston Crown Court, ex p. Bell* (2000) 164 J.P. 633.

The magistrates whose decision is under appeal have a right to appear and to call ev- **11–21** idence: *R. v. Kent Justices, ex p. Metropolitan Police Commissioner* [1936] 1 K.B. 547. In these circumstances they do not make themselves a party to the appeal and so incur no liability for costs: *Davidson, Nanson and Marley* (1871) 35 J.P. 500. This practice is highly unusual in criminal matters.

G. POWERS OF CROWN COURT ON APPEAL

Supreme Court Act 1981, s.48

Appeals to Crown Court

48.—(1) The Crown Court may, in the course of hearing any appeal, correct any error or **11–22** mistake in the order or judgment incorporating the decision which is the subject of the appeal.

(2) On the termination of the hearing of an appeal the Crown Court—

    (a) may confirm, reverse or vary the decision appealed against any part of the decision appealed against, including a determination not to impose a separate penalty in respect of an offence; or

    (b) may remit the matter with its opinion thereon to the authority whose decision is appealed against; or

    (c) may make such other order in the matter as the court thinks just, and by such order exercise any power which the said authority might have exercised.

(3) Subsection (2) has effect subject to any enactment relating to any such appeal which expressly limits or restricts the powers of the court on the appeal.

(4) [Subject to section 11(6) of the *Criminal Appeal Act* 1995, if] the appeal is against a conviction or a sentence, the preceding provisions of this section shall be construed as including power to award any punishment, whether more or less severe than that awarded by the magistrates' court whose decision is appealed against, if that is a punishment which that magistrates' court might have awarded.

(5) This section applies whether or not the appeal is against the whole of the decision.

(6) In this section "sentence" includes any order made by a court when dealing with an offender, including—

    (a) a hospital order under Part III of the *Mental Health Act* 1983, with or without a restriction order, and an interim hospital order under that Act; and

    (b) a recommendation for deportation made when dealing with an offender.

(7) The fact that an appeal is pending against an interim hospital order under the said Act of 1983 shall not affect the power of the magistrates' court that made it to renew or terminate the order or to deal with the appellant on its termination; and where the Crown Court quashes such an order but does not pass any sentence or make any other order in its place the Court may direct the appellant to be kept in custody or released on bail pending his being dealt with by that magistrates' court.

(8) Where the Crown Court makes an interim hospital order by virtue of subsection (2)—

    (a) the power of renewing or terminating the order and of dealing with the appellant on its termination shall be exercisable by the magistrates' court whose decision is appealed against and not by the Crown Court; and

    (b) that magistrates' court shall be treated for the purposes of section 38(7) of the said Act of 1983 (absconding offenders) as the court that made the order.

[This section is reprinted as amended by the *Criminal Appeal Act* 1995, Sched. 2, para. 14 and the *Criminal Justice Act* 1988, s.156.]

11–23   The Crown Court has no power to amend an information on appeal: *R. v. Swansea Crown Court, ex p. Stacey* [1990] R.T.R. 183, *ante*. It may not hear an appeal against a magistrate's amendment of an information: *Fairgrieve v. Newman* (1986) 82 Cr.App.R. 60.

H. Abandonment of Appeal

Magistrates' Courts Act 1980, s.109

Abandonment of appeal

11–24   **109.**—(1) Where notice to abandon an appeal has been duly given by the appellant—

    (a) the court against whose decision the appeal was brought may issue process for enforcing that decision, subject to anything already suffered or done under it by the appellant; and

    (b) the said court may, on the application of the other party to the appeal, order the appellant to pay to that party such costs as appear to the court to be just and reasonable in respect of expenses properly incurred by that party in connection with the appeal before notice of the abandonment was given to that party.

(2) In this section "appeal" means an appeal from a magistrates' court to the Crown Court, and the reference to a notice to abandon an appeal is a reference to a notice shown to the satisfaction of the magistrates' court to have been given in accordance with Crown Court rules.

11–25   An appeal may be abandoned by giving notice in writing to the other party and to the magistrates' court no later than the third day before the date set for the hearing: *Criminal Procedure Rules* 2005, r.63.5 and 63.6. The magistrates' court's decision may then be enforced.

If the appellant fails to attend the Crown Court hearing but has not given notice of withdrawal then the Crown Court is entitled to hear the appeal in his absence as it is a rehearing: *R. v. Guildford Crown Court, ex p. Brewer* (1988) 87 Cr.App.R. 265.

Where a person appealing to the Crown Court is represented at the hearing by counsel there is no obligation upon him to be present in person: *R. v. Croydon Crown Court, ex p. Clair* [1986] 1 W.L.R. 746. Where neither party appears the court should dismiss the appeal.

I. Enforcement of Crown Court Orders on Appeal

Magistrates' Courts Act 1980, s.110

Enforcement of decision of the Crown Court

11–26   **110.** After the determination by the Crown Court of an appeal from a magistrates' court the decision appealed against as confirmed or varied by the Crown Court, or any decision of the Crown Court substituted for the decision appealed against, may, without prejudice to the powers of the Crown Court to enforce the decision, be enforced—

    (a) by the issue by the court by which the decision appealed against was given of any process that it could have issued if it had decided the case as the Crown Court decided it;

    (b) so far as the nature of any process already issued to enforce the decision appealed against permits, by that process;

and the decision of the Crown Court shall have effect as if it had been made by the magistrates' court against whose decision the appeal is brought.

[This section is reprinted as amended by the *Access to Justice Act* 1999, Sched. 4, para. 22.]

Any order made by the Crown Court on appeal may be enforced by the magistrates' **11–27** court.

III. APPEAL BY WAY OF CASE STATED

A. Application to State Case

Magistrates' Courts Act 1980, s.111

Statement of case by magistrates' court

111.—(1) Any person who was a party to any proceeding before a magistrates' court or is aggrieved by the conviction, order, determination or other proceeding of the court may question the proceeding on the ground that it is wrong in law or is in excess of jurisdiction by applying to the justices composing the court to state a case for the opinion of the High Court on the question of law or jurisdiction involved; but a person shall not make an application under this section in respect of a decision against which he has a right of appeal to the High Court or which by virtue of any enactment passed after 31st December 1879 is final.   **11–28**

(2) An application under subsection (1) above shall be made within 21 days after the day on which the decision of the magistrates' court was given.

(3) For the purpose of subsection (2) above, the day on which the decision of the magistrates' court is given shall, where the court has adjourned the trial of an information after conviction, be the day on which the court sentences or otherwise deals with the offender.

(4) On the making of an application under this section in respect of a decision any right of the applicant to appeal against the decision to the Crown Court shall cease.

(5) If the justices are of opinion that an application under this section is frivolous, they may refuse to state a case, and, if the applicant so requires, shall give him a certificate stating that the application has been refused; but the justices shall not refuse to state a case if the application is made by or under the direction of the Attorney General.

(6) Where justices refuse to state a case, the High Court may, on the application of the person who applied for the case to be stated, make an order of mandamus requiring the justices to state a case.

If a party is aggrieved by a magistrates' courts' finding of fact the proper course is to   **11–29** appeal to the Crown Court: *James v. Chief Constable of Kent, The Times*, June 7, 1986. If a person wishes to complain about the harshness of the sentence passed, the appeal should also be to the Crown Court, despite the risk that the Crown Court might take a decision to his disadvantage: *Tucker v. DPP* (1992) 13 Cr.App.R. 495; *Allen v. West Yorkshire Probation Service* [2001] EWCA Admin 2; 165 J.P. 313, DC, *The Times*, February 20, 2001.

Where the final determination is a decision on an application for costs the 21-day time limit starts to run from the date of the decision on costs: *Liverpool City Council v. Worthington, The Times*, June 16, 1998. The time limit cannot be varied by the High Court: *Michael v. Gowland* [1977] 1 W.L.R. 296; *R. v. Clerkenwell Magistrates' Court, ex p. DPP* [1984] Q.B. 821. Where an application which does not comply with the requirements of the *Criminal Procedure Rules 2005*, r.64, is laid within time, the Divisional Court will still accept jurisdiction even if the defect is remedied outside the 21-day time limit: *Parsons v. F.W. Woolworth and Co Ltd* [1980] 1 W.L.R. 1472; *R. v. Croydon Justices, ex p. Lefore Holdings Ltd* [1980] 1 W.L.R. 1465.

The case must be concluded before the magistrates' court may state a case: *Streames v. Copping* [1985] Q.B. 920; *Loade v. DPP* [1990] 1 Q.B. 1052. There is no jurisdiction to state a case in respect of interlocutory matters: *R. v. Greater Manchester Justices, ex p. Aldi GmbH and Co KG* (1995) 159 J.P. 717. This was confirmed in *Gillan v. DPP* [2007] EWHC 380 where it said that the proper course, depending on the circumstances, was judicial review. Neither mistakes of law in committal proceedings nor the decision of committal itself can be challenged by way of case stated: *Dewing v. Cummings* [1971] R.T.R. 1295.

11–30   If a magistrates' court considers that the application to state a case is frivolous it may refuse to state a case and must certify that fact to the applicant: *Magistrates' Courts Act* 1980, s.111(5). "Frivolous" in this context means that the magistrates' court considers the application to be futile, misconceived, hopeless or academic. Although it is not a conclusion which a court should often or easily reach, it is entitled to do so in appropriate circumstances, and reasons should be given: *Mildenhall Magistrates' Court, ex p. Forest Heath DC* (1997) 161 J.P. 401.

11–31   If a court refuses to state a case then the applicant may apply for judicial review and seek a mandatory order to compel the stating of a case: *R. v. Blackfriars Crown Court, ex p. Sunworld Ltd* [2000] 1 W.L.R. 2102; [2000] 2 All E.R. 837. In that case the court gave some guidance on the approach for the Divisional Court. The aggrieved party should immediately apply for permission to bring an application for judicial review. If the court has already given a reasoned judgment which contains all the necessary factual findings and has explained why it has refused to state a case in a manner which clearly raises the true point of law in question, the single judge should grant permission for judicial review which challenges the order in question. It may be possible then to proceed immediately to a substantive determination of the merits however this will depend on whether the interested parties are represented and prepared and on the availability of court time: *R. v. Thames Magistrates' Court, ex p. Levy, The Times,* July 17, 1997.

If the court refuses to state a case having been ordered to do so following judicial review the members of the court are liable to pay costs: *R. v. Huntingdon Magistrates' Court, ex p. Percy, The Times,* March 4, 1994.

Magistrates' Courts Act 1980, ss.112, 114

Effect of decision of High Court on case stated by magistrates' court

11–32   **112.** Any conviction, order, determination or other proceeding of a magistrates' court varied by the High Court on an appeal by case stated, and any judgment or order of the High Court on such an appeal, may be enforced as if it were a decision of the magistrates' court from which the appeal was brought.

Recognizances and fees on case stated

11–33   **114.** Justices to whom application has been made to state a case for the opinion of the High Court on any proceeding of a magistrates' court shall not be required to state the case until the applicant has entered into a recognizance, with or without sureties, before the magistrates' court, conditioned to prosecute the appeal without delay and to submit to the judgment of the High Court and pay such costs as that Court may award; and (except in any criminal matter) the clerk of a magistrates' court shall not be required to deliver the case to the applicant until the applicant has paid [the fees payable for the case and for the recognizances to the justices' chief executive for the court].

[This section is reprinted as amended by the *Access to Justice Act* 1999, Sched. 13, para. 113.]

11–34   A magistrates' court may make the stating of a case conditional on the applicant's entering into a recognisance in order to discourage the waste of resources and to ensure that the applicant fully intends to pursue his claim.

Constitution of High Court

11–35   An appeal by way of case stated is heard by the Divisional Court of the Queen's Bench Division. At least two judges of the division must sit on the appeal: *Supreme Court Act* 1981, s.66(3). If the opinion of a two-judge court is divided then the appeal fails: *Flanagan v. Shaw* [1920] 3 K.B. 96.

B. PROCEDURE

11–36   See *Criminal Procedure Rules* 2005, r.64.1–64.6 in Appendix G–309—G–314.

The above rules outline the exact procedure and timetables to be followed in an application to state a case. A case stated should be succinct. It is usual for the court to draft its own case but there is no reason why the court could not invite the parties to submit the first draft, indicating any areas of disagreement: *Vehicle Inspectorate v. George Jenkins Transport Ltd* [2003] EWHC 2879, Admin where the following guidelines were given: **11–37**

(1) where there are a number of informations raising the same question, the case does not need to set out the detail of each where nothing turned on the differences between them;

(2) the case should set out the facts found/accepted with any requests for documents and responses thereto;

(3) the submissions of both sides should be included;

(4) the court's conclusions on matters in issue and questions for consideration should be set out;

(5) a party may be asked to prepare a first draft but the final case should be in proper form.

The question stated for the High Court should be one the answer to which will resolve the issue in dispute: *Corcoran v. Anderton* (1980) 71 Cr.App.R. 104. It should be drafted as simply as possible and directed to the crucial issues upon which the case turns. Further observations were given in *Oladimeji v. DPP* [2006] EWHC 1199 by Keene L.J. who criticised the way the case was set out. The case had given a summary of the evidence and had not separated out the findings of fact from the evidence; there was no numbering of paragraphs and the questions were largely those of fact not law, *e.g.*: "Were we right to conclude that there was no evidence to support Dr X's conclusion that...?" Speaking of the *Criminal Procedure Rules* he said:

> "Those provisions derive from the fact that the function of this court . .is to determine whether the decision of the justices is 'wrong in law or is in excess of jurisdiction'...This court is consequently only concerned with the state of the evidence in so far as it is said that the findings of fact made by them demonstrate an error of law or jurisdiction...The justices should decline to pose questions for this court unless those questions are ones of law...The weight to be attached to particular pieces of evidence is a matter for the justices. Only if no reasonable Bench could have reached the finding in question will that finding produce an error of law or an *ultra vires* act. If a defendant believes that the justices have arrived at a finding for which there was evidence but at which he contends they should not have arrived (for example, because it was against the weight of the evidence) his remedy lies in an appeal to the Crown Court."

Where a document forms a material part of the case stated, it or a copy should be appended: *Gainster v. Marlow* [1984] Q.B. 218; *Kent County Council v. Multi Media Marketing (Canterbury) Ltd, The Times*, December 7, 1994.

Post, is a form of case stated.

Part II

11–38   **CASE STATED**

In the High Court of Justice
Queen's Bench Division

Between (insert name)   Appellant
                                              And
         (insert name)   Respondent

Case stated by Justices [District Judge (name)] for the ....Commission Area of
............., acting in and for the Petty Sessional Area of........., in respect of their (his)
adjudication as a magistrates' court sitting at................

Case

1. On the ......day of......20..., an information was laid by the appellant (or
    respondent) against the respondent (or appellant) that he/she (insert offence and
    statute)
2. We heard the said information on the.... ......(insert date) and found the
    following facts:- (here the findings but not the evidence should be set out in
    numbered paragraphs)
3. The following is a short statement of the evidence:- (this paragraph should only
    be inserted where the question asks whether there was evidence upon which the
    court could convict)
4. It was contended by the appellant that (here the argument should be summarised
    briefly)
5. It was contended by the respondent that (here the opposing argument should be
    summarised briefly)
6. We were referred to the following cases:-
7. We were (I was) of the opinion that (insert the grounds upon which the decision
    was made) and accordingly (insert either convicted or acquitted together with any
    sentence or order).

Question
8. The question for the opinion of the High Court is...........

Dated the ....day of..........20..

                                    (Insert signatures of the Justices/ one of them on
                       behalf of all/District Judge/ Justices' Clerk on behalf of the Justices)

                                               Magistrate
                                               District Judge
                                               Justices' Clerk.

The appellant may withdraw the appeal by way of case stated without having to
obtain the leave of the court: *Collett v. Broomsgrove DC* (1996) 160 J.P. 593.

Upon an application being made to a magistrates' court to state a case the applicant
loses the right to appeal to the Crown Court: *Magistrates' Courts Act* 1980, s.111(4).
This rule is still effective even if the application to state a case does not arrive within the
statutory twenty one days, provided that it was made within the prescribed time and
would have in the normal course of events arrived within the prescribed time: *P. and
M. Supplies (Essex) Ltd v. Hackney LBC* (1990) 154 J.P. 814.

APPEAL TO THE HIGH COURT BY WAY OF CASE STATED
(CRIMINAL PROCEDURE RULES, PART 64)

Recognizance to prosecute on appeal before the High Court on case stated and for bail pending appeal under s.114 Magistrates' Courts Act 1980

.............................Magistrates' Court (code)

Date:

Principal:

Address:

I acknowledge my obligation to pay the court the sum specified opposite my signature if I fail to comply with the conditions specified below.

Surety:

Address:

I acknowledge my obligation to pay the court the sum specified opposite my signature if the principal fails to comply with the conditions specified below.

Signature: .... £

CONDITIONS

The principal shall prosecute without delay the principal's appeal to the High Court from the following decision.

Signature: .... £

Magistrates' Court ....

Offence/order and date ....

Decision subject to appeal

and shall submit to the judgment of the High Court and pay such costs as may be awarded by the High Court (and, unless the decision appealed against is reversed, appear before the above Magistrates' Court within ten days after the judgment is given*). This recognizance shall then be void but otherwise shall remain in force.

*Delete if the principal is not to be released on bail.

[Note: Formerly form 121, Magistrates' Courts' (Forms) Rules 1981 (SI 1981/553), relating to rule 76 of the Magistrates' Courts Rules 1981 and section 111 of the Magistrates' Courts Act 1980].

C. POWERS OF HIGH COURT ON CASE STATED

Supreme Court Act 1981, s.28A

Proceedings on case stated by magistrates' court or Crown Court

28A.—(1) This section applies where a case is stated for the opinion of the High Court—   **11–39**

    (a) by a magistrates' court under section 111 of the *Magistrates' Courts Act* 1980; or

    (b) by the Crown Court under section 28(1) of this Act.

(2) The High Court may, if it thinks fit, cause the case to be sent back for amendment and, where it does so, the case shall be amended accordingly.

(3) The High Court shall hear and determine the question arising on the case (or the case as amended) and shall—

(a) reverse, affirm or amend the determination in respect of which the case has been stated; or

(b) remit the matter to the magistrates' court, or the Crown Court, with the opinion of the High Court,

and may make such other order in relation to the matter (including as to costs) as it thinks fit.

(4) Except as provided by the *Administration of Justice Act* 1960 (right of appeal to House of Lords in criminal cases), a decision of the High Court under this section is final.

[This section is reprinted as amended by the *Access to Justice Act* 1999, s.61.]

11–40   The appeal takes the form of legal argument and no evidence is called. On an appeal by way of case stated, the High Court cannot refuse to determine a pure point of law simply because that point of law was only first appreciated after the conviction of the defendant: *Whitehead v. Haines* [1965] 1 Q.B. 200, QBD. The High Court has the power to order a rehearing: *Griffith v. Jenkins* [1992] 2 A.C. 76; 95 Cr.App.R. 35.

IV. JUDICIAL REVIEW

A. GENERAL

11–41   The purpose of judicial review is to prevent magistrates' courts exceeding their jurisdiction and to compel them to exercise their correct jurisdiction. It is a review of the way in which the court's decision was made: *Chief Constable of North Wales v. Evans* [1982] 1 W.L.R. 1155, HL. It is the most appropriate procedure for challenging a magistrates' court decision, where the issue is the extent of that court's jurisdiction: *North Essex Justices, ex p. Lloyd* [2001] 2 Cr.App.R.(S.) 15.

The proceedings in the magistrates' court must be complete before the Administrative Court will consider a quashing order: *R. (Hoar-Stevens) v. Richmond Upon Thames Magistrates' Court* [2003] EWHC 2660. The case concerned the adequacy of disclosure of material to the defence. The court stated that it was of the utmost importance that the course of a criminal trial in the magistrates' court should not be punctuated by applications for adjournments to test a ruling in the Divisional Court, especially when in reality if the case proceeded, the ruling might turn out to be of little or no importance. That was so even where there was an important substantive point which arose during a trial. The proper course was to proceed to the end of the trial in the lower court and then to test the matter, almost certainly by way of case stated. Any decision, before trial, to refuse bail was amenable to judicial review but, following the abolition of the High Court's concurrent jurisdiction to determine bail applications, it is only in exceptional cases that a decision would be reviewed: *R. (Shergill) v. Harrow Crown Court* [2005] EWHC 648.

Where case stated is available it is the preferred procedure: *R. v. Oldbury Justices, ex p. Smith* (1995) 159 J.P. 316 but that is not to say that judicial review cannot be used: *R. v. Hereford Magistrates' Court, ex p. Rowlands* [1998] Q.B. 110. In *R. v. Morpeth Ward Justices, ex p. Ward* (1992) 95 Cr.App.R. 215, it was stated that where the identification of facts as found is critical to challenging the decision, the better course is to appeal by way of case stated. Applications for judicial review are made in accordance with the procedures set out in the *Supreme Court Act* 1981, ss.29 and 31 and Part 54 of the *Civil Procedure Rules* 1998.

B. PROCEDURE FOR BRINGING CLAIM

Supreme Court Act 1981, s.29

Orders of mandamus, prohibition and certiorari

11–42   **29.**—(1) Subject to subsection (3A), the High Court shall have jurisdiction to make orders of mandamus, prohibition and certiorari in those classes of cases in which it had power to do so immediately before the commencement of this Act.

(2) Every such order shall be final, subject to any right of appeal therefrom.

(3) In relation to the jurisdiction of the Crown Court, other than its jurisdiction in matters relating to trial on indictment, the High Court shall have all such jurisdiction to make orders of mandamus, prohibition or certiorari as the High Court possesses in relation to the jurisdiction of an inferior court.

(3A) The High Court shall have no jurisdiction to make orders of mandamus, prohibition or certiorari in relation to the jurisdiction of a court-martial in matters relating to—

(a) trial by court-martial for an offence, or

(b) appeals from a Standing Civilian Court;

and in this subsection "court-martial" means a court-martial under the *Army Act* 1955, the *Air Force Act* 1955 or the *Naval Discipline Act* 1957.

(4) The power of the High Court under any enactment to require justices of the peace or a judge or officer of a county court to do any act relating to the duties of their respective offices, or to require a magistrates' court to state a case for the opinion of the High Court, in any case where the High Court formerly had by virtue of any enactment jurisdiction to make a rule absolute, or an order, for any of those purposes, shall be exercisable by order of mandamus.

(5) In any enactment—

(a) references to a writ of mandamus, of prohibition or of certiorari shall be read as references to the corresponding order; and

(b) references to the issue or award of any such writ shall be read as references to the making of the corresponding order.

(6) In subsection (3) the reference to the Crown Court's jurisdiction in matters relating to trial on indictment does not include its jurisdiction relating to orders under section 17 of the *Access to Justice Act* 1999.

[This section is reprinted as amended by the *Access to Justice Act* 1999 and the **11–43** *Armed Forces Act* 2001, s.23(3).]

By virtue of the *Practice Direction (Administrative Court: Establishment)* [2000] 1 **11–44** W.L.R. 1654 the names of *mandamus*, prohibition and *certiorari* were changed to mandatory order, prohibiting order and quashing order respectively.

Supreme Court Act 1981, s.31

Application for judicial review

31.—(1) An application to the High Court for one or more of the following forms of relief, **11–45** namely—

(a) an order of mandamus, prohibition or certiorari;

(b) a declaration or injunction under subsection (2); or

(c) an injunction under section 30 restraining a person not entitled to do so from acting in an office to which that section applies,

shall be made in accordance with rules of court by a procedure to be known as an application for judicial review.

(2) A declaration may be made or an injunction granted under this subsection in any case where an application for judicial review, seeking that relief, has been made and the High Court considers that, having regard to—

(a) the nature of the matters in respect of which relief may be granted by orders of mandamus, prohibition or certiorari;

(b) the nature of the persons and bodies against whom relief may be granted by such orders; and

(c) all the circumstances of the case,

it would be just and convenient for the declaration to be made or the injunction to be granted, as the case may be.

(3) No application for judicial review shall be made unless the leave of the High Court has been obtained in accordance with rules of court; and the court shall not grant leave to make such an application unless it considers that the applicant has a sufficient interest in the matter to which the application relates.

(4) On an application for judicial review the High Court may award damages to the applicant if—

(a) he has joined with his application a claim for damages arising from any matter to which the application relates; and

(b) the court is satisfied that, if the claim had been made in an action begun by the applicant at the time of making his application, he would have been awarded damages.

(5) If, on an application for judicial review seeking an order of certiorari, the High Court quashes the decision to which the application relates, the High Court may remit the matter to the court, tribunal or authority concerned, with a direction to reconsider it and reach a decision in accordance with the findings of the High Court.

(6) Where the High Court considers that there has been undue delay in making an application for judicial review, the court may refuse to grant—

(a) leave for the making of the application; or

(b) any relief sought on the application,

if it considers that the granting of the relief sought would be likely to cause substantial hardship to, or substantially prejudice the rights of, any person or would be detrimental to good administration.

(7) Subsection (6) is without prejudice to any enactment or rule of court which has the effect of limiting the time within which an application for judicial review may be made.

11–46 See *Civil Procedure Rules* 1998, Pt 54, rr.1–3.

11–47 See *Civil Procedure Rules* 1998, Pt 54, rr.5–9.

11–48 Upon receipt of a claim form, a party must acknowledge it within the required timescale. Failure to do so may result in not being able to take part in the hearing which decides whether to give the applicant permission to proceed with the judicial review. As permission is often refused where sufficient information is given, a party on whom a claim form is served must act swiftly. In any event, the position with regard to costs at a full hearing needs to be borne in mind.

C. RESPONSE TO CLAIM

11–49 See *Civil Procedure Rules* 1998, Pt 54, r.14.

11–50 A magistrates' court which is in the position of having to respond to a claim may wish to instruct solicitors on its behalf.

D. LEAVE TO PROCEED

11–51 Pursuant to section 31(3) of the *Supreme Court Act* 1981 requires that an applicant for judicial review obtain leave from the High Court before bringing an application.

11–52 See *Civil Procedure Rules* 1998, Pt 54, rr.4, 10–13.

11–53 See *Civil Procedure Rules* 1998, Pt 54, r.15.

11–54 See *R. v. Blackfriars Crown Court, ex p. Sunworld Ltd* [2000] 1 W.L.R. 2102, *ante*.

E. HEARING

11–55 See *Civil Procedure Rules* 1998, Pt 54, rr.16–18.

11–56 An expedited hearing may be sought, in appropriate circumstances, by contacting the Head of the Administrative Court Office: *R. (DPP) v. Camberwell Youth Court* [2004] 168 J.P. 481.

F. STANDING

11–57 The High Court will not grant leave to bring a claim for judicial review unless it considers that the applicant has a sufficient interest in the matter to which the application relates.

G. GROUNDS FOR REVIEW

11–58 Lord Diplock in the case of *CCSU v. Minister for the Civil Service* [1985] A.C. 374 outlined the main grounds for review:

— illegality—has the decision maker understood the law

— procedural impropriety—failure to observe procedural rules, basic rules of natural justice or a failure to act with procedural fairness

— irrationality—"Wednesbury unreasonableness", *i.e.* a decision which is so outrageous in its defiance of logic or of accepted moral standards that no sensible person who had applied his mind to the question to be decided could have arrived at it: *Associated Picture Houses Ltd v. Wednesbury Corp* [1948] 1 K.B. 223.

The question of proportionality was left open but the *Human Rights Act* requires courts to take proportionality into account.

The Divisional Court may intervene if police procedures are shown to be manifestly **11–59** producing a result which induces a plea of guilty: *R. v. Bolton Magistrates' Court, ex p. Scally* [1991] 1 Q.B. 537; *R. v. Kingston-Upon-Thames Justices, ex p. Khana* [1986] R.T.R. 364. In the former case the defendants applied to have their convictions for drink driving quashed. They had been arrested on suspicion of drink driving and when blood tests had revealed excessive alcohol levels they had been obliged to plead guilty. That the swabs used were impregnated with alcohol was not known at the time by the prosecution authorities, the magistrates or the defendants. It was held that the prosecutor had unwittingly corrupted the process leading to conviction in a way which was detrimental to the defendants because it left them with no choice but to plead guilty and denied them a complete defence. The police had failed in their duty to exercise care when supplying blood-sampling kits. The prosecution case was tantamount to "fraud, collusion or perjury" and the convictions were quashed.

It is a denial of natural justice for a prosecutor to fail to disclose witnesses' statements favourable to the defence: *R. v. Leyland Justices, ex p. Hawthorn* [1979] Q.B. 283.

Mere procedural impropriety on the part of the bench or a plea of guilty resulting from poor advice from the defendant's solicitors does not confer jurisdiction on the Divisional Court to quash the resultant conviction: *R. v. Home Secretary, ex p. Al-Mehdawi* [1990] 1 A.C. 876.

The jurisdiction of the Divisional Court to quash convictions following a plea of guilty **11–60** is confined to cases where the plea was obtained by fraud, collusion or perjury on the part of the prosecution: *R. v. Burton-Upon-Trent Justices, ex p. Woolley* (1995) 159 J.P. 183; [1995] R.T.R. 139; [1996] R.T.R. 340.

H. REVIEW OF COMMITTAL PROCEEDINGS

These proceedings are now rare.   **11–61**

It is not the practice of the Divisional Court to review committal proceedings which have not been concluded: *R. v. Wells Street Stipendiary Magistrate, ex p. Seillon* 69 Cr.App.R. 77, DC; *R. v. Horsham Justices, ex p. Bukhari* (1982) 74 Cr.App.R. 291, DC.

Judicial review lies in respect of committal proceedings where there has been a procedural flaw: *R. v. Oxford City Justices, ex p. Berry* [1988] Q.B. 507; 85 Cr.App.R. 89, DC; *R. v. Horseferry Road Magistrates' Court, ex p. Doung, The Times*, March 22, 1996; *R. v. Wigan Justices, ex p. Sullivan* [1999] C.O.D. 21, DC. The remedy is discretionary, and is unlikely to be granted if the defendant's own conduct has contributed to the procedural failure or if an application to quash the indictment is an adequate alternative remedy.

Judicial review may be available to quash a committal on the ground of inadmissibility or insufficiency of the evidence: *Neill v. North Antrim Magistrates' Court* 97 Cr.App.R. 121, HL; *R. v. Bedwelty Justices, ex p. Williams* [1997] A.C. 225, HL. It is a misuse of judicial review to challenge a committal for trial on the basis of insufficiency of evidence except in the clearest cases: *R. v. Whitehaven Justices, ex p. Thompson* [1999] C.O.D. 15, DC.

I. REMEDIES

The most common remedy sought by way of judicial review is the quashing order **11–62** where the defendant seeks to have the conviction quashed.

11–63   See *Civil Procedure Rules* 1998, Pt 54, r.19.

11–64   Remedies in judicial review are discretionary. In deciding whether to grant a remedy the court will take into account a variety of factors including waiver, bad faith, the premature nature of the application, the absence of any injustice, and whether the decision would have been the same regardless of the error.

11–65   In *R. v. Hereford Magistrates' Court, ex p. Rowlands* [1997] 2 W.L.R. 854, CA, Lord Bingham C.J. confirmed the court's supervisory jurisdiction over magistrates' courts as a guarantee of the integrity of proceedings in those courts which ensures that high standards of procedural fairness and impartiality are maintained. He outlined the approach of the court:

> "First, leave to move should not be granted unless the applicant advances an apparently plausible complaint which, if made good, might arguably be held to vitiate the proceedings in the magistrates court. Immaterial and minor deviations from best practice would not have that effect, and the court should be respectful of discretionary decisions of magistrates' courts as of all other courts. This court should be generally slow to intervene, and should do so only where good (or arguably good) grounds for doing so are shown. Secondly, the decision whether or not to grant relief by way of judicial review is always, in the end, a discretionary one. Many factors may properly influence the exercise of discretion, and it would be both foolish and impossible to seek to anticipate them all. The need for an applicant to make full disclosure of all matters relevant to the exercise of discretion should require no emphasis. We do not, however, consider that the existence of a right of appeal to the Crown Court, particularly if unexercised, should ordinarily weigh against the grant of leave to move for judicial review, or the grant of substantive relief, in a proper case."

11–66   In *R. v. DPP, ex p. Kebilene* [1999] 3 W.L.R. 175 Lord Bingham C.J. went on to say at p.183:

> "Where the grant of leave to move judicial review would delay or obstruct the conduct of criminal proceedings which ought, in the public interest, to be resolved with all appropriate expedition, the court will always scrutinise the application with greatest care, both to satisfy itself that there are sound reasons for making the application and satisfy itself that there are no discretionary grounds (such as delay or the availability of alternative remedies or vexatious conduct by the applicant) which should lead it to refuse leave. The court would be very slow to intervene where the applicant's complaint is one that can be met by appropriate orders or directions in the criminal proceedings ..."

V. SUSPENDING DECISIONS PENDING OUTCOME

A. Bail

Magistrates' Courts Act 1980, s.113

Bail on appeal or case stated

11–67   **113.**—(1) Where a person has given notice of appeal to the Crown Court against the decision of a magistrates' court or has applied to a magistrates' court to state a case for the opinion of the High Court, then, if he is in custody, the magistrates' court may, subject to section 25 of the *Criminal Justice and Public Order Act* 1994 grant him bail.

(2) If a person is granted bail under subsection (1) above, the time and place at which he is to appear (except in the event of the determination in respect of which the case is stated being reversed by the High Court) shall be—

         (a) if he has given notice of appeal, the Crown Court at the time appointed for the hearing of the appeal;

         (b) if he has applied for the statement of a case, the magistrates' court at such time within 10 days after the judgment of the High Court has been given as may be specified by the magistrates' court;

and any recognizance that may be taken from him or from any surety for him shall be conditioned accordingly.

(3) Subsection (1) above shall not apply where the accused has been committed to the Crown Court for sentence under [sentence 37] [above or section 3 of the *Powers of Criminal Court (Sentencing) Act* 2000].

(4) Section 37(6) of the *Criminal Justice Act* 1948 (which relates to the currency of a sentence while a person is released on bail by the High Court) shall apply to a person released on bail by a magistrates' court under this section pending the hearing of a case stated as it applies to a person released on bail by the High Court under section 22 of the *Criminal Justice Act* 1967.

[This section is reprinted as amended by *Powers of Criminal Courts (Sentencing) Act* 2000, Sched. 9, para. 72.]

A magistrates' court has the power to grant bail where the defendant, being in custody, challenges its decision by way of appeal or case stated. It does not, however, have the power to grant bail where the challenge is by way of judicial review. **11–68**

B. Sentence

A sentence is in force and enforceable once it has been passed. The lodging of an appeal against conviction does not prevent the sentence from being enforced: *Greater Manchester Probation Service v. Bent* (1996) 160 J.P. 297. There is statutory provision for the suspension of a driving disqualification pending appeal—see *Road Traffic Offenders Act* 1988, s.39, (*post* § 17–198). **11–69**

Part II

Part III

Specific Offences

CHAPTER 12

GENERAL PRINCIPLES

I. ACTUS REUS

(1) General

The *actus reus* consists of the prohibited conduct which forms the basis of the rele- **12–1**
vant offence. In the majority of cases, this conduct must be voluntary. It is possible to
commit an offence through involuntary conduct, such as where the prohibited act
consists of a state of affairs, as was the case in *Winzar v. Chief Constable of Kent*, *The
Times*, March 28, 1983, where the relevant offence was "being found drunk on a
highway" contrary to the *Licensing Act* 1872, s.12. It was held that the defendant fell
within section 12 of the *Licensing Act* 1872 if he was on the highway and was "perceived
to be drunk", notwithstanding that his presence there was momentary and not of his
own volition.

There is no liability for a failure to do something, unless the law imposes some
specific duty upon the individual to act. Specific statutory duties are imposed in the
context of many regulatory offences, such as the *Companies Act* 1985, which imposes a
positive duty on a company to keep accounting records, or the *Water Resources Act*
1991 which makes it an offence to cause or knowingly permit any poisonous, noxious or
polluting matter or any solid waste matter to enter any controlled waters. Other statutes
make it a criminal offence to fail to disclose certain information. The *Terrorism Act*
2000, s.19 makes it an offence to fail to disclose a belief or suspicion that another person
has committed an offence connected with terrorism and sections 330, 331 and 332 of
the *Proceeds of Crime Act* 2002 create offences of failing to disclose possible money
laundering activities.

Liability for omissions may also stem from the existence of a special relationship between the victim and the accused, which creates a duty to act on the part of the accused.
There exist various situations where such a duty of care will arise.

(2) Duty arising from the assumption of care or control of children

12–2   The *Children and Young Persons Act* 1933, s.1 creates the offence of wilful neglect and imposes a duty on parents and those who are legally responsible for children to provide or obtain adequate food, clothing and medical care for the child.

(3) Duty arising from the assumption of care for another

12–3   A person who voluntarily assumes the care and responsibility for another person, that other being incapable of caring for himself, may incur a duty to discharge that undertaking. In *Stone (John Edward)* [1977] Q.B. 354, CA, the accused's sister came to live with him and his mistress. The sister was suffering from anorexia, and became unable to care for herself. The accused did not call for medical assistance and left her to die from atoxemia spreading from infected bed scores, prolonged immobilisation and lack of food. Both the accused and his mistress were convicted of manslaughter. The Court of Appeal upheld their convictions, holding that as they had taken the sister into their home, they had assumed a duty of care towards her and had been grossly negligent in the performance of that duty.

(4) Duty arising from contract

12–4   A duty to act may arise from the existence of a contract requiring some conduct from the defendant. In *Pittwood* [1902] 19 T.L.R. 37, the accused was employed to operate a level crossing on a railway. He failed to close the crossing gates when a train was signalled, causing a cart which was crossing when the train came through to be struck leading to the death of one of the carters. The accused was convicted of gross negligent manslaughter, his duty to act arising from the contract with his employers, which required him to discharge his duty as a level crossing operator appropriately.

(5) Duty arising from the fact that the accused creates the relevant danger

12–5   In *Miller* [1983] 2 A.C. 161, HL, Lord Diplock stated (at 176):

> "I see no rational ground for excluding from conduct capable of giving rise to criminal liability, conduct which consists of failing to take measures that lie within one's power to counteract a danger that one has oneself created, if at the time of such conduct one's state of mind is such as constitutes a necessary ingredient of the offence."

(6) Duty arising from the doctor patient/relationship

12–6   If a doctor or medical staff refuse to treat a patient who has withheld his consent to treatment, they will not be guilty of failing to discharge their duty to provide medical care for their patients: *Re C. (Adult: Refusal of Treatment)* [1994] 1 W.L.R. 290.

The doctor's duty towards his patient does not however require him to keep the patient alive at all costs. In *Airedale NHS Trust v. Bland* [1993] A.C. 789, HL, a patient in a persistent vegetative state was able to breathe normally, but was only sustained by the administration of food being fed through tubes. The House of Lords held that this treatment could be withdrawn, as a large body of informed and responsible medical opinion was of the view that existence in the persistent vegetative state was not a benefit to the patient. Hence the principle of the sanctity of life, which is not absolute, was not violated by ceasing to give medical treatment and care involving invasive manipulation of the patient's body, to which he had not consented and which conferred no benefit upon him. Lord Goff made a vital distinction between acts and omissions in this context, stating that:

> "...the law draws a crucial distinction between cases in which a doctor decides not to provide, or to continue to provide, for his patient treatment or care which could or might prolong his life, and those in which he decides, for example by administering a lethal drug, actively to bring his patient's life to an end. As I have already indicated, the former may be lawful, either

because the doctor is giving effect to his patient's wishes by withholding the treatment or care, or even in certain circumstances in which [on principles which I shall describe] the patient is incapacitated from stating whether or not he gives his consent. But it is not lawful for a doctor to administer a drug to his patient to bring about his death, even though that course is prompted by a humanitarian desire to end his suffering, however great that suffering may be…So to act is to cross the Rubicon which runs between on the one hand the care of the living patient and on the other hand euthanasia—actively causing his death to avoid or to end his suffering." (at 865)

Certain offences cannot be based on omissions. In *Ahmad* [1987] 84 Cr.App.R. 64, **12–7** CA, it was held that the words "does acts" in the *Protection from Eviction Act* 1977 mean that the offence may not be committed by omission. However, the offence of committing acts of gross indecency with a child may be committed by omission: in *Speck* (1977) 65 Cr.App.R. 161, an eight-year-old girl had placed her hand on the accused's trousers over his penis. The accused failed to move her hand, and was convicted of committing acts of gross indecency, his liability hinging on his failure to remove her hand. This would seem to be inconsistent with the view that references to acts exclude omissions, though Ashworth (*Principles of Criminal Law*, 4th edn, 2003) suggests that the case may also be viewed as involving an invitation on the part of the accused (constituted by his inactivity in failing to remove the girl's hand) which can be characterised as an act for the purposes of the offence.

II. CAUSATION

(1) General

Causation is relevant to the commission of result crimes (those crimes which require a **12–8** specific consequence to flow from the prohibited act, (*e.g.* theft)). These crimes are distinguished from what are termed "conduct" crimes, whose *actus reus* consists in the doing of the prohibited act, rather than in the consequences flowing from the commission of this act, (*e.g.* rape). For a defendant to be guilty of a result crime, a factual link must first be established between the defendant's conduct and the result he is alleged to have caused.

Once this factual link has been established, the prosecution must then prove that the defendant's conduct was a legal cause of the result alleged to be a consequence of the defendant's actions. For a factual cause to also be a legal cause it must be an "operating and substantial" cause of the consequence in issue: *Smith* [1959] 2 Q.B. 35, CA. The following principles are relevant to the determination of legal causation. They are largely distilled from principles developed in homicide cases, though it may be worth considering the rather different application of the rules of causation in relation to crimes of strict liability or negligence, where considerations of the defendant's culpability in bringing about the prescribed result are less potent. For example, in *Empress Car Co (Abertillery) Ltd v. National Rivers Authority* [1999] 2 A.C. 22, HL, the defendant company maintained a diesel tank in a yard. This tank was tampered with by an unknown person, causing the contents of the tank to pass into a nearby river. The House of Lords held that if a necessary additional condition of the actual escape was the act of a third party or a natural event, the justices should consider whether that act or event should be regarded as a matter of ordinary occurrence, which would not negative the effect of the defendant's act, or something extraordinary, leaving open a finding that the defendant did not cause the pollution. Only if the escape could be regarded as something extraordinary would the defendant company escape liability. The issue of culpability was treated as irrelevant to determination of the issue of causation. This approach is in stark contrast to consideration of causation in homicide cases, where the distinction between "but for" and legal causation is used to avoid the conviction of the "morally innocent". Such considerations may be less prevalent in the context of statutory offences, and a different approach may be taken. See also *Express Ltd v. Environment Agency (t/a Express Dairies Distribution)* [2005] 1 W.L.R. 223, where the licensee of a dairy depot had been transferring cream from a tanker to another vehicle and an accident had resulted in the spillage of 10 litres of cream, some of which had escaped into the controlled waters of a local brook. An analysis of the brook had found there was potential for harm. The licensee had pleaded guilty to an offence contrary to section 85(1) of the Act and the owner was charged under section 217(3) of the Act. The owner, the appellant, submitted that as there was no statutory duty to carry out a risk assessment in respect of activities carried out on its premises, therefore it had not defaulted, and that despite the obvious discolouration of the water in the brook, the cream had not caused any harm, therefore it could not be said to have polluted the brook. The QBD dismissed the appeal. Section 85(1) of the Act required every person not to cause or knowingly permit polluting matter to enter controlled waters, which put the owner under an obligation to act. The owner had failed to carry out a risk assessment, which might have prevented the pollution from occurring. That constituted a default, contrary to section 217(3) of the Act, which gave rise to the offence committed by the licensee. Where a landowner allowed an operation on his land that could give rise to a risk of pollution, then, in order not to fall foul of section 85(1) of the Act, the landowner was to carry out a risk assessment and respond to what that assessment revealed. The wording of section 85(1) of the Act did not expressly state nor imply that harm had to be caused in order for the release of a pollutant into a controlled waterway to be an offence contrary to that section. It was sufficient that the pollutant, in this case cream, stained or tainted the water.

(2) The defendant's act must be more than a minimal cause of the result

12–9   In *Cato* [1976] 62 Cr.App.R. 41, CA, Lord Widgery C.J., looking at the ingredients of the offence of manslaughter stated that:

> "As a matter of law, it was sufficient if the prosecution could establish that it (the defendant's act) was *a* cause, provided it was a cause outside the *de minimis* range, and effectively bearing upon the acceleration of the moment of the victim's death."

In *Notman* [1994] Crim.L.R. 518, CA, it was held that the expression "a substantial cause" was convenient to indicate that the cause must have been more than just de minimis and avoids the necessity to go into the details of legal causation and remoteness. This approach was also applied in the context of road traffic offences in *Hennigan* [1971] 3 All E.R. 133, CA, where the defendant's conviction for death caused by dangerous driving was upheld, the Court holding that there was nothing in section 1 of the *Road Traffic Act* 1960 which required the manner of the driving to be a substantial or major cause of death. So long as the dangerous driving was a cause and something more than *de minimis*, the statute would operate.

However, indirect causes of the proscribed result may constitute legal causation. In *McKechnie* [1992] 94 Cr.App.R. 51, CA, the defendants attacked the victim, causing serious head injuries. The victim also had a duodenal ulcer, which could not be operated on due to the head injuries inflicted by the defendants. The victim then died when this ulcer burst. The Court of Appeal upheld the manslaughter conviction, despite the fact that the injuries inflicted were not in themselves the cause of the victim's death. In *Miller* [1992] 95 Cr.App.R. 421 it was held that to establish that property has been obtained by deception it is not necessary to isolate the moment when the money or other property is handed over to see whether at that time the lies told operated to deceive the victim. If on the evidence as a whole it can legitimately be said that the various deceptions alleged in the indictment were the cause of the money being handed over it is, or may be, irrelevant that at the final moment the victim suspected or even believed that he or she had been swindled.

(3) The "eggshell skull" rule

12–10   In *Blaue* [1975] 1 W.L.R. 1411, CA, Lawton L.J. stated that:

"It has long been the policy of the law that those who use violence on other people must take their victims as they find them. This in our judgment means the whole man, not just the physical man."

Hence a defendant who stabbed a woman, who then refused to have a blood transfusion due to her faith, was properly convicted of manslaughter, despite the fact that a blood transfusion would have saved the victim's life.

(4) Novus actus interveniens

An intervening act will absolve the defendant from any kind of responsibility for the **12–11** result caused. The intervening act may be the act of a third party, and act of the victim or an unforeseeable natural event (sometimes called "act of God").

(5) Acts of third parties

Unforeseeable acts

The intervention of a third party may break the chain of causation if the intervention **12–12** is free, deliberate and informed: *Pagett* [1983] 76 Cr.App.R. 279, CA. In *Pagett*, the defendant shot at police officers who were attempting to arrest him. He had with him his girlfriend, and against her will used her body to shield him from any retaliation by the officers. The officers returned the appellant's fire and as a result the girl was killed. The Court upheld the defendant's manslaughter conviction, holding that the police's actions had not broken the chain of causation between the defendant's act and the victim's death because their action had been a reasonable act performed for the purpose of self-preservation, as well as in the execution of their legal duty to arrest the defendant.

(6) Medical intervention

Negligent medical treatment will only break the chain of causation where it was so in- **12–13** dependent of the defendant's acts and in itself so potent in causing death that they regarded the contribution made by the defendants acts as insignificant: *Cheshire* [1991] 93 Cr.App.R. 251, CA, (medical complications following from the treatment for gunshot wounds leading to the death of the victim.). In *Cheshire, ante*, Beldham L.J. concluded that:

> "…when the victim of a criminal attack is treated for wounds or injuries by doctors or other medical staff attempting to repair the harm done, it will only be in the most extraordinary and unusual case that such treatment can be said to be so independent of the acts of the accused that it could be regarded in law as the cause of the victim's death to the exclusion of the accused's acts." (at 257)

> "In a case in which the jury have to consider whether negligence in the treatment of injuries inflicted by the accused was the cause of death we think it is sufficient for the judge to tell the jury that they must be satisfied that the Crown have proved that the acts of the accused caused the death of the deceased adding that the accused's acts need not be the sole cause or even the main cause of death it being sufficient that his acts contributed significantly to that result. Even though negligence in the treatment of the victim was the immediate cause of his death, the jury should not regard it as excluding the responsibility of the accused unless the negligent treatment was so independent of his acts, and in itself so potent in causing death, that they regard the contribution made by his acts as insignificant." (at 258)

(7) Acts of the victim

The victim's own act can be said to break the chain of causation between the **12–14** defendant's act and the result caused. In *Roberts* (1972) 56 Cr.App.R. 95, CA, the victim had jumped from a moving car because the defendant had assaulted and threatened her. The appellant was convicted of assault occasioning actual bodily harm. Stephenson L.J. stated:

> "The test is: Was it the natural result of what the alleged assailant said and did, in the sense that it was something that could reasonably have been foreseen as the consequences of what

he was saying or doing? As it was put in one of the old cases, it had got to be shown to be his act, and if of course the victim does something so 'daft,' in the words of the appellant in this case, or so unexpected, not that this particular assailant did not actually foresee it but that no reasonable man could be expected to foresee it, then it is only in a very remote and unreal sense a consequence of his assault, it is really occasioned by a voluntary act on the part of the victim which could not reasonably be foreseen and which breaks the chain of causation between the assault and the harm or injury." (at 102)

In *Williams* [1992] 1 W.L.R. 380, CA, the victim had been killed when he jumped from a car driven by the defendants after they had threatened him. The Court of Appeal quashed the defendants' conviction for manslaughter, stating that the defendants would only be guilty if the victim's response was proportionate to the threat issued, in that it was within the ambit of reasonableness and not so daft as to amount to his own voluntary act which would constitute a *novus actus interveniens*. When considering whether the victim acted reasonably, the judge/jury must consider "any particular characteristics of the victim and the fact that in the agony of the moment he may act without thought or deliberation."

12–15   The question of what could reasonably be foreseen by the defendant provides an objective test: *Marjoram* [2000] Crim.L.R. 372, CA. The defendant, aged 16, was among a group of people who broke into the victim's hostel room, whereupon she fell or jumped into the street and was seriously injured. The defendant appealed against his conviction for grievous bodily harm, contending that in directing the jury on foreseeability, the judge had failed properly to direct the jury that they should consider it in terms of a person of the same age and sex as M involved in similar circumstances. The Court dismissed his appeal holding that the test of causation was objective. The 'reasonable man' would have foreseen the victim's conduct as a natural result of the defendant's actions.

(8) Unforeseeable natural events

12–16   In *Southern Water Authority v. Pegrum* [1989] Crim.L.R. 442, it was held that when deciding whether an intervening cause constitutes a defence, the question is whether the intervening cause was of so powerful a nature that the conduct of the defendant was not a cause at all, but was merely part of the surrounding circumstances.

III. MENS REA

A. GENERAL

12–17   Once the prosecution have established that the defendant committed the *actus reus* of the relevant offence, it must then be proved that the defendant did so with the relevant *mens rea*, *i.e.* that he had the guilty mind necessary for the commission of the offence. Different offences require different mental elements. A fault element may also be applied differently in relation to different offences, hence whilst the most commonly found mental elements can be here outlined for the sake of exposition, it is necessary to bear in mind that their application will vary.

B. SPECIFIC REQUIREMENTS AS TO STATE OF MIND

(1) "With intent to"

12–18   The leading cases on intention arise out of convictions for murder; however the relevant principles are of general application: *per* Lord Bridge in *Moloney* [1985] A.C. 905, HL. The relevant cases are *Moloney* (*ante*); *Hancock and Shankland* [1986] A.C. 455, HL; *Nedrick* 83 Cr.App.R. 267, CA, and *Woolin* [1999] 1 A.C. 82, HL.

In *Nedrick* (1986), *ante*, Lord Lane C.J. stated:

"When determining whether the defendant had the necessary intent, it may therefore be helpful for a jury to ask themselves two questions: [1] How probable was the consequence which resulted from the defendant's voluntary act? [2] Did he foresee that consequence?

If he did not appreciate that death or really serious harm was likely to result from his act, he cannot have intended to bring it about. If he did, but thought that the risk to which he was exposing the person killed was only slight, then it may be easy for the jury to conclude that he did not intend to bring about that result. On the other hand, if the jury are satisfied that at the material time the defendant recognised that death or serious harm would be virtually certain (barring some unforeseen intervention) to result from his voluntary act, then that is a fact from which they may find it easy to infer that he intended to kill or do serious bodily harm, even though he may not have had any desire to achieve that result." (at 270)

Woollin, ante, concerned the death of a three-month old baby, as a result of his be- **12–19** ing thrown against a wall. The House of Lords held that, where the charge is murder, in the rare cases where the simple direction is not enough, the jury should be directed that they are not entitled to infer the necessary intention, unless they feel sure that death or serious bodily harm was a virtual certainty (barring some unforeseen intervention) as a result of the defendant's actions, and the defendant appreciated that such was the case. The decision was one for the jury to reach upon a consideration of all the evidence. The use of the phrase "virtual certainty" was not confined to cases where the evidence of intent was limited to actions of the accused and the consequences of those actions. If the principles gleaned from these murder cases can be extrapolated to all offences, then it seems appropriate to conclude that, ordinarily, the issue of intention is one to be left to common sense.

(2) "Unlawfully"

This means without lawful justification or excuse such as self-defence.   **12–20**

(3) "Maliciously"

This mental requirement appears in the *Offences Against the Person Act* 1861. It is **12–21** established that malice in the sense of ill-will is not required, rather the word requires either actual intention to cause the relevant harm or foresight of the risk of causing that particular kind of harm: *Cunningham* [1957] 2 Q.B. 296, CCA. This decision was upheld in *Savage, Parmenter* [1992] 1 A.C. 699, HL.

(4) "Wilfully"

In *Sheppard* [1981] A.C. 394, HL, Lord Diplock stated that the proper direction to **12–22** be given to a jury on a charge of wilful neglect of a child under section 1 of the *Children and Young Persons Act* 1933 by failing to provide adequate medical aid is that the jury must be satisfied (1) that the child did in fact need medical aid at the time at which the parent is charged with failing to provide it, the *actus reus*; and (2) either that the parent was aware at that time that the child's health might be at risk if it was not provided with medical aid or that the parent's unawareness of this fact was due to his not caring whether his child's health was at risk or not.

(5) "Knowingly"

This requires the prosecution to prove that the defendant knew of all the material **12–23** circumstances of the offence. In *Dunne* (1998) 162 J.P. 399, CA, the offender was convicted of being knowingly concerned in the fraudulent evasion of a prohibition on the importation of goods contrary to section 170(2) of the *Customs and Excise Management Act* 1979 after being arrested on his arrival in the UK by customs officers who suspected that videos in his possession, which the defendant referred to as "blue movies", were obscene. He appealed against conviction, contending that a person could not "know" whether an article he was importing was such as would tend to deprave and corrupt within the meaning of the *Obscene Publications Act* 1959, s.1(1) until a jury had found that it was. The Court dismissed his appeal, holding that "knowingly", in the

Part III

offence of being knowingly concerned in the fraudulent evasion of a prohibition on the importation of an obscene article, was to be construed as emphasising the requirement of *mens rea*. Whilst a defendant who believed that the obscene videos he was importing were actually videos of sporting events should not be convicted, a defendant who was aware of the true nature of the goods would be liable to conviction if the jury determined that the material fell within the 1959 Act, s.1(1). As the defendant was aware of the nature of the videos and had conceded that they were obscene, there was no basis upon which the defendant could claim that his conviction was unsafe.

(6) "Recklessly"

12–24   Prior to the decision in *G*. [2003] 3 W.L.R. 1060, HL, the concept of recklessness in the criminal law was variable according to the substantive offence charged. The decisions in *Caldwell* [1982] A.C 341 (criminal damage) and *Lawrence* [1982] A.C. 510 (causing death by reckless driving) introduced the concept of objective recklessness, departing from the prior view expressed in *Cunningham* [1957] 2 Q.B. 396, CCA, that recklessness necessarily imparted some degree of subjective fault on the part of the defendant. In *G*. [2003] 3 W.L.R. 1060, two children, one aged 11 and the other 12, set fire to newspapers with a lighter and threw some of the papers under a large plastic wheelie-bin, which was in the yard behind a shop. They then left, and the resulting fire caused approximately £1 million worth of damage. It was accepted that neither boy appreciated that there was any risk of the fire spreading in the way that it did. They were convicted of arson, contrary to section 1 of the *Criminal Damage Act* 1971, the judge having ruled that he was bound to direct the jury in accordance with *Caldwell*, *ante*. The House of Lords quashed their convictions, and overruled the majority decision of the House of Lords in *Caldwell*. Lord Bingham first looked to the legislative background of the *Criminal Damage Act* 1971, and stated that:

> "[T]he starting point is to ascertain what Parliament meant by 'reckless' in 1971...section 1 as enacted followed, subject to an immaterial addition, the draft proposed by the Law Commission. It cannot be supposed that by 'reckless' Parliament meant anything different from the Law Commission. The Law Commission's meaning was made plain both in its report [Law Com No. 29] and in Working Paper No 23 which preceded it. These materials [not, it would seem, placed before the House in *R v. Caldwell*] reveal a very plain intention to replace the old-fashioned and misleading expression 'maliciously' by the more familiar expression 'reckless' but to give the latter expression the meaning which *R v. Cunningham* [1957] 2 All E.R. 412, [1957] 2 Q.B. 396 and Professor Kenny had given to the former. In treating this authority as irrelevant to the construction of 'reckless' the majority fell into understandable but clearly demonstrable error. No relevant change in the mens rea necessary for proof of the offence was intended, and in holding otherwise the majority misconstrued section 1 of the Act." (at para. 29)

12–25   He then went on to examine reasons justifying a departure from the decision established in *Caldwell*:

> "First, it is a salutary principle that conviction of serious crime should depend on proof not simply that the defendant caused [by act or omission] an injurious result to another but that his state of mind when so acting was culpable...But it is not clearly blameworthy to do something involving a risk of injury to another if [for reasons other than self-induced intoxication [see *DPP v. Majewski* [1976] 2 All E.R. 142, [1977] A.C. 443] one genuinely does not perceive the risk. Such a person may fairly be accused of stupidity or lack of imagination, but neither of those failings should expose him to conviction of serious crime or the risk of punishment." (at para. 32)
>
> "Secondly...the model direction formulated by Lord Diplock is capable of leading to obvious unfairness...It is neither moral nor just to convict a defendant [least of all a child] on the strength of what someone else would have apprehended if the defendant himself had no such apprehension. Nor, the defendant having been convicted, is the problem cured by imposition of a nominal penalty." (at para. 33)
>
> "Thirdly, I do not think the criticism of *Caldwell* expressed by academics, judges and practitioners should be ignored. A decision is not, of course, to be overruled or departed

from simply because it meets with disfavour in the learned journals. But a decision which attracts reasoned and outspoken criticism by the leading scholars of the day, respected as
authorities in the field, must command attention…" (at para. 34)

"Fourthly, the majority's interpretation of 'reckless' in s 1 of the 1971 Act was, as already
shown, a misinterpretation. If it were a misinterpretation that offended no principle and gave
rise to no injustice there would be strong grounds for adhering to the misinterpretation and
leaving Parliament to correct it if it chose. But this misinterpretation is offensive to principle
and is apt to cause injustice. That being so, the need to correct the misinterpretation is
compelling." (at para. 35)

The reasoning of Lord Bingham was accepted by the majority of the House, and the **12–26**
concept of recklessness is now restored to the situation before *Caldwell*. The defendant
will now be judged to have acted recklessly with respect to (1) a circumstance when he
was aware of a risk that it existed or would exist; (2) a result when he was aware of a risk
that it would occur; and it was, in the circumstances known to him, unreasonable to
take the risk. This is the definition recommended by the Law Commission in the Draft
Criminal Code of 1989 (Law Com. No.177).

(7) "Dishonesty"

See exposition in relation to the offence of theft at *post*, § 15–3.   **12–27**

(8) "Causes"

The general rule applicable to a statutory offence of causing another person to do a **12–28**
prohibited act is that the offence is only committed if the accused contemplated or
desired that the act would ensue and was done on his express or implied authority or as
a result of him exercising control or influence over the other person: *Att.-Gen of Hong
Kong v. Tse Hung-Lit* [1986] A.C. 876, PC.

Where a statute prohibits the causing of a particular result, the word "causes" is to be
given a common sense meaning, and does not imply either knowledge or negligence:
Alphacell v. Woodward [1972] A.C. 824, HL. In *Environmental Agency v. Empress
Car Co (Abertillery) Ltd* [1999] 2 A.C. 22, HL, it was held that on a prosecution for
causing pollution under section 85(1) of the *Water Resources Act* 1991 it was necessary
to identify what the defendant was alleged to have done to cause the pollution. The
prosecution need not prove that the defendant did something which was the immediate
cause of the pollution and when the prosecution had identified some act done by the
defendant the justices had to decide whether it caused the pollution. If a necessary additional condition of the actual escape was the act of a third party or a natural event, the
justices should consider whether that act or event should be regarded as a matter of
ordinary occurrence, which would not negative the effect of the defendant's act, or
something extraordinary, leaving open a finding that the defendant did not cause the
pollution; that the distinction between ordinary and extraordinary was one of fact and
degree to which the justices had to apply their common sense and knowledge of what
occurred in the locality but see *ante*, § 12–8, on causation.

(9) "Negligently"

An example of negligence being the relevant mental state for the commission of an **12–29**
offence can be found in section 3 of the *Road Traffic Act* 1988, which creates the offence of driving without due care and attention. Negligence imports an objective standard for behaviour, which does not vary according to the characteristics of the individual offender.

Certain statutes provide a defence of mistaken belief on reasonable grounds. Thus,
section 1 of the *Protection from Eviction Act* 1977 makes it an offence for any person
to unlawfully deprive a residential occupier of his occupation of the premises or any
part thereof, unless he proves that he believed, and had reasonable cause to believe, that
the residential occupier had ceased to reside in the premises. In *Phekoo* [1981] 1
W.L.R. 1117, CA, it was held that there must be a reasonable basis for the asserted belief

on behalf of a person charged with an offence under section 1 of the *Protection from Eviction Act* 1977 that the persons he attempts to evict are not residential occupiers of the premises in question. In *King* [1964] 1 Q.B. 285, CA, it was held that an honest belief on reasonable grounds as to the invalidity of a previous marriage, just as an honest belief on reasonable grounds that the spouse is dead, were good defences to a charge of bigamy.

The reasonableness of the defendant's belief will not always be relevant. Where the relevant statute does not indicate that a belief held by a defendant has to be reasonable, the court is to assume that Parliament did not intend to impart any requirement of reasonableness into the belief providing the basis for a defence. In *B. v. DPP* [2000] 2 W.L.R. 452, HL, the defendant, aged 15, had repeatedly asked a girl, aged 13, who was sitting next to him on a bus to perform oral sex with him. He was charged with inciting a girl under the age of 14 to commit an act of gross indecency with him, contrary to section 1(1) of the *Indecency with Children Act* 1960. It was accepted that he had honestly believed that the girl was over the age of 14, and the justices were asked to rule whether his state of mind could constitute a defence to the charge. The justices ruled that it could not, and he changed his plea to guilty. No finding was made as to whether he had had reasonable grounds for his belief. His conviction was quashed by the House of Lords: *mens rea* was an essential element of every criminal offence unless Parliament expressly or by necessary implication provided to the contrary and, on a true construction of section 1(1) of the Act of 1960 in its statutory context, Parliament had not so provided in respect of the age ingredient of the offence. It was therefore necessary for the prosecution to prove the absence of a genuine belief on the part of the defendant, for which he did not have to have had reasonable grounds, that the victim had been 14 or over. See also *K.* [2002] 1 A.C. 462 and *Kumar* [2005] 1 W.L.R. 1352; [2005] 1 Cr.App.R. 34; [2005] Crim.L.R. 470 (where it was held that on a charge under section 12 of the *Sexual Offences Act* 1956, the defendant was entitled to raise the defence that he had believed that the complainant had attained the age of 16).

(10) "Strict liability"

12–30   Offences of strict liability do not require any *mens rea* as to one or more elements of the *actus reus*. All offences of strict liability are statutory offences. Thus in *Pharmaceutical Society of Great Britain v. Storkwain Ltd* (1986) 83 Cr.App.R. 359, HL, where the appellants, retail chemists, supplied prescription-only drugs in accordance with a forged prescription and without fault on their part, they were afforded no defence to a charge under section 58(2)(a) of the *Medicines Act* 1968, which prohibits the selling of goods on the basis of a forged prescription 1968 Act, for the prosecution did not have to prove *mens rea*. However, in *Sweet v. Parsley* [1970] A.C. 32, HL, they held that for the purposes of the offence of being concerned in the management of premises used for the purpose of smoking cannabis resin contrary to section 5(b) of the *Dangerous Drugs Act* 1965, *mens rea* as to the circumstances of the offence was required. A defendant who was the tenant of a farm, and who sub-let rooms there for short periods was not guilty of the offence under section 5 where she was living elsewhere at the time of the alleged offence and where she visited the farm only occasionally.

It may be thus difficult to determine when the courts will uphold strict liability in respect of a particular statutory offence: the approach in *B. v. DPP, ante,* may be useful.

(11) "Transferred malice"

12–31   If a person by mistake, or, *e.g.* bad aim causes injury to a person or property other than the person or property which he intended to attack, he is guilty of a crime to the same degree as if he had achieved his object: *Latimer* [1886] 17 Q.B.D. 359. The harm caused must be of the same kind as the harm intended: *Pembliton* [1874] L.R. C.C.R. 119.

IV. ACCESSORIAL LIABILITY

(1) Legislation

Magistrates Courts Act 1980, s.44

Aiders and abettors

44.—(1) A person who aids, abets, counsels or procures the commission by another person of **12–32** a summary offence shall be guilty of the like offence and may be tried [whether or not he is charged as a principal] either by a court having jurisdiction to try that other person or by a court having by virtue of his own offence jurisdiction to try him.

(2) Any offence consisting in aiding, abetting, counselling or procuring the commission of an offence triable either way [other than an offence listed in Schedule 1 to this Act] shall by virtue of this subsection be triable either way.

The words "aids, abets, counsels or procures" should be given their ordinary meaning. The use of four words suggests that there is a difference between the words for if there were none, Parliament would be wasting time in using four words where two or three would do: *Att.-Gen.'s Reference (No. 1 of 1975)* [1975] Q.B. 773, CA.

(a) *Aiders and abettors*

The words "aiding and abetting" can include acts committed before the commission **12–33** of the *actus reus* of the offence. In *Blakely v. DPP* [1991] R.T.R. 405, DC, McCullough J. said, at 411, that there are many accessories before the fact of whose activity none of the words 'counselling, procuring and commanding' would seem to be apt; whilst the words aiding and abetting would seem more appropriate to describe such activity. In *National Coal Board v. Gamble* [1959] 1 Q.B. 11; 42 Cr.App.R. 240, DC, the defendant's conviction for aiding and abetting the driving of an overweight lorry was upheld; the servant had loaded coal onto the lorry of the principal knowing that this load had rendered the lorry overweight and that the driver intended to take it onto the highway and complete the sale of the coal, thus facilitating the commission of the offence.

To establish aiding and abetting, it must be proved that the defendant intended to encourage, and *wilfully* encouraged the crime committed. Mere continued voluntary presence at the scene of the commission of a crime does not of itself necessarily amount to encouragement; but the fact that a person was voluntarily and purposely present witnessing the commission of a crime, and offered no opposition to it, though he might reasonably be expected to prevent and had the power so to do, or at least to express his dissent, might in some circumstances afford cogent evidence upon which to justify finding that he wilfully encouraged, and so aided and abetted; but this is a question of fact: *Clarkson* 55 Cr.App.R. 445, Ct-MAC. Knowledge of the principal's offence, plus an ability to control his actions, coupled with a deliberate decision not to exercise such control may constitute aiding and abetting: *J.F. Alford Transport Ltd* [1997] 2 Cr.App.R. 326, CA. See also *Nedrick-Smith v. DPP* [2006] EWHC 3015, QBD at § 13–14.

A person may be an aider and abettor even though his age or sex renders him incapable of being a principal: *Eldershaw* [1828] 3 C. & P. 396. A person protected by the offence in question cannot be convicted for aiding and abetting the person who committed the offence against them: *Tyrell* [1894] 1 Q.B. 710, CCR (unlawful sexual intercourse with a girl under 16); *Whitehouse* [1977] Q.B. 868; 65 Cr.App.R. 33, CA (girl under 16 cannot aid and abet incest by her father).

(b) *Joint enterprise*

Where two of more persons embark on a joint enterprise, each is responsible for acts **12–34** done within the scope of that joint enterprise. This shared liability ends when a party to the joint enterprise goes beyond what was agreed as part of the common enterprise. It is for the tribunal of fact to decide whether what was done could be construed as being within the joint enterprise or whether it exceeded it: *Anderson and Morris* [1966] 1

Q.B. 110, CCA; *Lovesey and Peterson* [1970] 1 Q.B. 352, CA; *Powell, English* [1999] 1 A.C. 1, HL.

Where the principal does an act which was within the joint enterprise yet with an intent which was outside the contemplation of the other participants to the joint enterprise, the accessory will not escape all liability, and may be found guilty of the degree of offence appropriate to the intention with which he acted: *Gilmour* [2000] 2 Cr.App.R. 407 (an appellant who foresaw that the principals would carry out the act of throwing a petrol bomb into a house, but did not realise that in doing so they intended to kill or do grievous bodily harm to the occupants, would be guilty of manslaughter).

(c) *Counsellors and procurers*

12–35   The word "counsel" does not imply any causal connection with the offence; the essential elements are that there should be counselling, and the principal offence should be committed by the person counselled acting within the scope of his authority and not by accident: *Calhaem* [1985] Q.B. 808, CA.

As regards procurement, in *Att.-Gen.'s Reference (No. 1 of 1975)* [1975] Q.B. 773, CA, it was held that:

> "To procure means to produce by endeavour. You procure a thing by setting out to see that it happens and taking the appropriate steps to produce that happening. We think that there are plenty of instances in which a person may be said to procure the commission of a crime by another even though there is no sort of conspiracy between the two, even though there is no attempt at agreement or discussion as to the form which the offence should take." (at 779).

12–36   With procurement, there must be a causal link between what the accessory did and the commission of the offence. In *Att.-Gen.'s Reference (No.1 of 1975)* [1975] Q.B. 773, CA, the defendant had surreptitiously laced with spirits the drinks of a motorist whom she knew was about to drive home. This led to the motorist driving home while the alcohol concentration in his blood was above the prescribed limit contrary to section 6(1) of the *Road Traffic Act* 1972 and, following the motorist's conviction of this offence, the defendant was convicted as having procured the commission of the motorists' offence due to the fact that there was a causal link between the defendant's act and the offence by the motorist who would not have committed it otherwise.

(d) *Agents provocateurs*

12–37   Whilst the defendant who would not have committed an offence but for the activity of an agent provocateur will have no defence, the question here is whether the agent provocateur may himself be prosecuted. The following principles may be deduced from the relevant authorities: it is unlawful for a police officer to counsel or procure the commission of an offence which would otherwise not take place, but it may be proper for a police officer to take part in, or to encourage an informer to take part in, an offence which is already "laid on" solely for the purpose of apprehending the offenders: *Birtles* 53 Cr.App.R. 469, CA; *McCann* 56 Cr.App.R. 359, CA; *Clarke (D.G.)* 80 Cr.App.R. 344, CA.

(e) *Withdrawal*

12–38   A secondary party may be able to escape liability for aiding, abetting, counselling or procuring an offence if he makes an effective withdrawal before the offence is actually committed. In *Whitefield* 79 Cr.App.R. 36, CA it was held that if a person has counselled another to commit a crime, he may escape liability by withdrawal before the crime is committed, but it is not sufficient that he should merely repent or change his mind. If his participation is confined to advice or encouragement, he must at least communicate his change of mind to the other, and the communication must be such as will serve unequivocal notice upon the other party to the common unlawful cause that if he proceeds upon it he does so without the aid and assistance of those who withdraw.

In *Bryce* [2004] 2 Cr.App.R. 35, it was held that, in the absence of some overwhelming supervening event, only an act taken by D which amounted to the countermanding of his earlier assistance and a withdrawal from the common purpose would suffice to avoid liability. Repentance alone unsupported by action taken to demonstrate withdrawal would be insufficient. If D had the necessary mens rea at the time of the act of assistance the fact that his mind was innocent at the time when the crime was committed was no defence (paras 75–76).

In *Robinson* [2000] 5 *Archbold News* 2, CA, it was said that only exceptionally can a person withdraw from a crime he has initiated. To do so, he must communicate his withdrawal in order to give the principal[s] the opportunity to desist rather than complete the crime. This communication is even necessary in the context of spontaneous violence, where the accessory will only be excused from not giving such an opportunity to desist if it is not practicable or reasonable so to communicate, an example of such circumstances being found in *Mitchell and King* 163 J.P. 75, CA, where the accused had thrown down his weapon and moved away before the final and fatal blows were struck.

(f) *Acquittal of principal*

A secondary party may be convicted of an offence where the actual perpetrator of the **12–39** *actus reus* of the substantive offence is either acquitted or convicted of a lesser offence. The secondary party may be convicted of the offence for which the principal is acquitted where there is evidence against the secondary party that may not be admitted against the principal: *Humphreys and Turner* [1965] 3 All E.R. 689, or where there is insufficient evidence that the person charged as a principal was in fact involved in the offence: *Davis* [1977] Crim.L.R. 542, CA.

The secondary party may also be convicted where the principal has some defence that does not benefit the secondary party: *Bourne* 36 Cr.App.R. 125, CCA; *Cogan and Leek* [1976] 1 Q.B. 217, CA; *DPP v. K and B* [1997] 1 Cr.App.R. 36, DC. In *Pickford* [1995] 1 Cr.App.R. 420, CA, it was said, *obiter* that the decisions in *Bourne* and *Cogan and Leek* do not support the proposition that where the principal offender lacks all legal capacity to commit the crime in question another may nevertheless be guilty of aiding and abetting him. They were rather cases in which the person who had committed the acts said to constitute the principal offence was fully capable in law of committing that offence but had a complete defence on the facts.

(2) Mental element of accessories

There are two parts to the mental element: **12–40**

(i) The accessory must intend to aid, abet, counsel or procure: *Lynch v. DPP for Northern Ireland* [1975] A.C. 653, HL; *Powell, English* [1999] 1 A.C. 1, HL (where it was held that a secondary party is guilty of murder if he participates in a joint venture, realising (but without agreeing thereto) that in the course thereof the principal might use force with intent to kill or cause grievous bodily harm, and the principal does so. The secondary party has lent himself to the enterprise and by doing so, has given assistance and encouragement to the principal in carrying out an enterprise which the secondary party realises may involve murder).

This approach should be adopted in relation to all charges against defendants accused of aiding and abetting the commission of a crime, whatever the crime alleged. Where the defendant is alleged to have counselled or procured the commission of the relevant offence it seems that it is necessary to prove that the defendant intended that the offence or an offence of the same type should be committed: *Ferguson v. Weaving* [1951] 1 K.B. 814, at 819; *Att.-Gen.'s Reference (No 1 of 1975)* [1975] Q.B. 773, CA and *Blakely v. DPP* [1991] R.T.R. 405, DC.

(ii) The secondary party must also know of the essential matters that constitute the offence: *per* Lord Goddard C.J. in *Johnson v. Youden* [1950] 1 K.B. 544, at 546. This is so even where the principal's offence is one of strict liability. In *Smith v. Mellors* [1987] 84 Cr.App.R. 279, DC, both defendants were charged under section 6(1) of the *Road Traffic Act* 1972, for driving with excess alcohol (now section 5(1)(a) of the *RTA* 1988). As it could not be determined who was the driver and who was the passenger, it was held that there was no case to answer, as for the purposes of the strict liability offence under section 6(1), for the secondary party to be convicted, it would be necessary to prove that he knew that the principal was driving with excess alcohol. As it could not be determined who was the driver and who the passenger, the question of knowledge could not be addressed.

V. ASSISTING OFFENDERS

(1) Legislation

Criminal Law Act 1967, s.4

Penalties for assisting offenders

12–41   **4.**—(1) Where a person has committed a relevant offence, any other person who, knowing or believing him to be guilty of the offence or of some other relevant offence, does without lawful authority or reasonable excuse any act with intent to impede his apprehension or prosecution shall be guilty of an offence.

(1A) In this section and section 5 below 'relevant offence' means—

(a) an offence for which the sentence is fixed by law,

(b) an offence for which a person of 18 years or over (not previously convicted) may be sentenced to imprisonment for a term of five years (or might be so sentenced but for the restrictions imposed by section 33 of the Magistrates' Courts Act 1980).

(2) If on the trial of an indictment for [a relevant offence] the jury are satisfied that the offence charged (or some other offence of which the accused might on that charge be found guilty) was committed, but find the accused not guilty of it, they may find him guilty of any offence under subsection (1) above of which they are satisfied that he is guilty in relation to the offence charged (or that other offence).

(3) A person committing an offence under subsection (1) above with intent to impede another person's apprehension or prosecution shall on conviction on indictment be liable to imprisonment according to the gravity of the other person's offence, as follows—

(a) if that offence is one for which the sentence is fixed by law, he shall be liable to imprisonment for not more than ten years;

(b) if it is one for which a person [not previously convicted] may be sentenced to imprisonment for a term of fourteen years, he shall be liable to imprisonment for not more than seven years;

(c) if it is not one included above but is one for which a person [not previously convicted] may be sentenced to imprisonment for a term of ten years, he shall be liable to imprisonment for not more than five years;

(d) in any other case, he shall be liable to imprisonment for not more than three years.

(4) No proceedings shall be instituted for an offence under subsection (1) above except by or with the consent of the Director of Public Prosecutions:

[This section is printed as amended by the Serious Organised Crime and Police Act 2005, Sched. 7(3) para. 40(2)(6).]

(2) Proof of guilt

12–42   Proof of the other person's guilt is essential to proof of the commission of this offence. However, it is not necessary that the principal offender has been convicted of the relevant offence: *Donald and Donald* 83 Cr.App.R. 49, CA. There can be no charge of attempting to commit an offence under section 4 of the *CLA* 1967: *Criminal Attempts Act* 1981, s.1(4).

The policy of this section is that those who assist offenders do so at their peril, the punishment being directly related to the nature of the principal offence rather than the knowledge of the defendant. The defendant must however know or positively believe in the guilt of the person convicted, and mere suspicion as to guilt will be insufficient. The statute does not however require that the defendant knew of the particular offence that the assisted person had committed, though the defendant's state of mind may be a relevant factor in mitigation: *Morgan (M.M.)* [1972] 1 Q.B. 436, CA. The defendant does not have to be proved to have known the identity of the principal offender: *Brindley and Long* [1971] 2 Q.B. 300, CA.

VI. INCHOATE OFFENCES

A. STATUTORY CONSPIRACY

The *Criminal Law Act* 1977 replaced common law conspiracy with a statutory of- **12–43** fence, preserving only common law conspiracy to defraud, and conspiracy to do acts tending to corrupt public morals or outrage public decency. Conspiracy is triable only on indictment and is hence outside the scope of this work.

B. ATTEMPT

(1) Definition

Criminal Attempts Act 1981, ss.1–4

Attempting to commit an offence

1.—(1) If, with intent to commit an offence to which this section applies, a person does an act **12–44** which is more than merely preparatory to the commission of the offence, he is guilty of attempting to commit the offence.

(1A) Subject to section 8 of the *Computer Misuse Act* 1990 [relevance of external law], if this subsection applies to an act, what the person doing it had in view shall be treated as an offence to which this section applies.

(1B) Subsection (1A) above applies to an act if—

(a) it is done in England and Wales; and

(b) it would fall within subsection (1) above as more than merely preparatory to the commission of an offence under section 3 of the *Computer Misuse Act* 1990 but for the fact that the offence, if completed, would not be an offence triable in England and Wales.

(2) A person may be guilty of attempting to commit an offence to which this section applies even though the facts are such that the commission of the offence is impossible.

(3) In any case where—

(a) apart from this subsection a person's intention would not be regarded as having amounted to an intent to commit an offence; but

(b) if the facts of the case had been as he believed them to be, his intention would be so regarded,

then, for the purposes of subsection (1) above, he shall be regarded as having had an intent to commit that offence.

(4) This section applies to any offence which, if it were completed, would be triable in England and Wales as an indictable offence, other than—

(a) conspiracy [at common law or under section 1 of the *Criminal Law Act* 1977 or any other enactment];

(b) aiding, abetting, counselling, procuring or suborning the commission of an offence;

(c) offences under section 4(1) [assisting offenders] or 5(1) [accepting or agreeing to accept consideration for not disclosing information about an arrestable offence] of the *Criminal Law Act* 1967.

Extended jurisdiction in relation to certain attempts

1A.—(1) If this section applies to an act, what the person doing the act had in view shall be **12–45** treated as an offence to which section 1(1) above applies.

(2) This section applies to an act if—

    (a) it is done in England and Wales, and

    (b) it would fall within section 1(1) above as more than merely preparatory to the commission of a Group A offence but for the fact that that offence, if completed, would not be an offence triable in England and Wales.

(3) In this section "Group A offence" has the same meaning as in Part 1 of the *Criminal Justice Act* 1993.

(4) Subsection (1) above is subject to the provisions of section 6 of the Act of 1993 [relevance of external law].

(5) Where a person does any act to which this section applies, the offence which he commits shall for all purposes be treated as the offence of attempting to commit the relevant Group A offence.

Application of procedural and other provisions to offences under s.1

12–46   **2.**—(1) Any provision to which this section applies shall have effect with respect to an offence under section 1 above of attempting to commit an offence as it has effect with respect to the offence attempted.

(2) This section applies to provisions of any of the following descriptions made by or under any enactment (whenever passed)—

    (a) provisions whereby proceedings may not be instituted or carried on otherwise than by, or on behalf or with the consent of, any person (including any provisions which also make other exceptions to the prohibition);

    (b) provisions conferring power to institute proceedings;

    (c) provisions as to the venue of proceedings;

    (d) provisions whereby proceedings may not be instituted after the expiration of a time limit;

    (e) provisions conferring a power of arrest or search;

    (f) provisions conferring a power of seizure and detention of property;

    (g) provisions whereby a person may not be convicted [or committed for trial] on the uncorroborated evidence of one witness (including any provision requiring the evidence of not less than two credible witnesses);

    (h) provisions conferring a power of forfeiture, including any power to deal with anything liable to be forfeited;

    (i) provisions whereby, if an offence committed by a body corporate is proved to have been committed with the consent or connivance of another person, that person also is guilty of the offence.

Offences of attempt under other enactments

12–47   **3.**—(1) Subsections (2) to (5) below shall have effect, subject to subsection (6) below and to any inconsistent provision in any other enactment, for the purpose of determining whether a person is guilty of an attempt under a special statutory provision.

(2) For the purposes of this Act an attempt under a special statutory provision is an offence which—

    (a) is created by an enactment other than section 1 above, including an enactment passed after this Act; and

    (b) is expressed as an offence of attempting to commit another offence (in this section referred to as "the relevant full offence").

(3) A person is guilty of an attempt under a special statutory provision if, with intent to commit the relevant full offence, he does an act which is more than merely preparatory to the commission of that offence.

(4) A person may be guilty of an attempt under a special statutory provision even though the facts are such that the commission of the relevant full offence is impossible.

(5) In any case where—

    (a) apart from this subsection a person's intention would not be regarded as having amounted to an intent to commit the relevant full offence; but

    (b) if the facts of the case had been as he believed them to be, his intention would be so regarded,

then, for the purposes of subsection (3) above, he shall be regarded as having had an intent to commit that offence.

(6) Subsections (2) to (5) above shall not have effect in relation to an act done before the commencement of this Act.

(2) Allocation

Trial and penalties

4.—(1) A person guilty by virtue of section 1 above of attempting to commit an offence **12–48**
shall—

    (a) if the offence attempted is murder or any other offence the sentence for which is fixed by law, be liable on conviction on indictment to imprisonment for life; and

    (b) if the offence attempted is indictable but does not fall within paragraph (a) above, be liable on conviction on indictment to any penalty to which he would have been liable on conviction on indictment of that offence; and

    (c) if the offence attempted is triable either way, be liable on summary conviction to any penalty to which he would have been liable on summary conviction of that offence.

(2) In any case in which a court may proceed to summary trial of an information charging a person with an offence and an information charging him with an offence under section 1 above of attempting to commit it or an attempt under a special statutory provision, the court may, without his consent, try the informations together.

(3) Where, in proceedings against a person for an offence under section 1 above, there is evidence sufficient in law to support a finding that he did an act falling within subsection (1) of that section, the question whether or not his act fell within that subsection is a question of fact.

(4) Where, in proceedings against a person for an attempt under a special statutory provision, there is evidence sufficient in law to support a finding that he did an act falling within subsection (3) of section 3 above, the question whether or not his act fell within that subsection is a question of fact.

(5) Subsection (1) above shall have effect—

    (a) subject to section 37 of and Schedule 2 to the *Sexual Offences Act* 1956 [mode of trial of and penalties for attempts to commit certain offences under that Act]; and

    (b) notwithstanding anything—

        (i) in section 32(1) [no limit to fine on conviction on indictment] of the *Criminal Law Act* 1977; or

        (ii) in section 78(1) and (2) [maximum of six months' imprisonment on summary conviction unless express provision made to the contrary] of the *Powers of Criminal Courts (Sentencing) Act* 2000.

An offence which is triable only summarily may not be the subject of a criminal at- **12–49**
tempt under section 1 of the 1981 Act, however, provisions creating summary offences will sometimes create corresponding offences of attempt. Such offences are within the scope of section 3 of the 1981 Act which provides that attempts created by special statutory provision shall be governed by the same rules as those contained in subsections 1(1) to (3) of the 1981 Act.

(3) Elements of the offence

"More than merely preparatory"

The words should be given their natural and ordinary meaning: *Jones* 91 Cr.App.R. **12–50**
351, CA. In *Geddes* [1996] Crim.L.R. 894, CA, it was held that there was no clear delineation between acts amounting to an attempt and those which were merely preparatory and each case depends upon its facts. For an offence to be committed under section 1 the defendant must have moved from the stage of planning and preparation to implementing his intention. In *Qadir and Khan* [1998] Crim.L.R. 828, CA, the court stated that "attempt begins at the moment when the defendant embarks upon the crime proper, as opposed to taking steps rightly regarded as merely preparatory."

"With intent to commit an offence"

In *Mohan* (1974) 60 Cr.App.R. 272, CA, in relation to the necessary mental element **12–51** for criminal attempts at common law, James L.J. stated that:

> "The bounds are presently set requiring proof of specific intent, a decision to bring about, in so far as it lies within the accused's power, the commission of the offence which it is alleged the accused attempted to commit, no matter whether the accused desired that consequence of his act or not." (p.278)

This was approved in *Pearman* (1985) 80 Cr.App.R. 259, CA. Hence, it must ordinarily be proved that the defendant acted with a specific intent to commit the particular crime attempted, even if the necessary *mens rea* for the particular crime falls below this high threshold.

12–52   However, whilst intent is required as to the consequences of the prohibited act, the Court of Appeal has held that something less may be sufficient in terms of the circumstances surrounding the offence. In *Att.-Gen.'s Reference (No. 3 of 1992)* 98 Cr.App.R. 383, CA, the defendant had thrown a petrol bomb at the victim but it smashed into a wall. The Court of Appeal considered whether he could be convicted of attempting to commit aggravated criminal damage, contrary to section 1(2) of the *Criminal Damage Act* 1971. The Court of Appeal held that the substantive offence would be committed if the defendant had a specific intent to cause damage by fire to property and was mentally reckless whether the life of another would thus be endangered. Hence it was possible to convict of attempt if the prosecution proved that the respondents, in that state of mind, intended to damage property by throwing a bomb at it.

Attempting the impossible

12–53   Following the decision in *Shivpuri* [1987] A.C. 1, HL, a defendant may be guilty of an attempt, notwithstanding that the commission of the actual offence was impossible. In *Shivpuri*, applying the language of section 1 of the *Criminal Attempts Act* 1981 to the facts of the case (attempted drugs importation) Lord Bridge stated:

> "[T]he first question to be asked is whether the appellant intended to commit the offences of being knowingly concerned in dealing with and harbouring drugs of Class A or Class B with intent to evade the prohibition on their importation. Translated into more homely language the question may be rephrased, without in any way altering its legal significance, in the following terms: did the appellant intend to receive and store (harbour) and in due course pass on to third parties (deal with) packages of heroin or cannabis which he knew had been smuggled into England from India? The answer is plainly yes, he did. Next, did he in relation to each offence, do an act which was more than merely preparatory to the commission of the offence? (at 19)
>
> ... Here then is the nub of the matter. Does the 'act which is more than merely preparatory to the commission of the offence' in section 1 (1) of the Act of 1981 (the *actus reus* of the statutory offence of attempt) require any more than an act which is more than merely preparatory to the commission of the offence which the defendant intended to commit? Section 1 (2) must surely indicate a negative answer; if it were otherwise, whenever the facts were such that the commission of the actual offence was impossible, it would be impossible to prove an act more than merely preparatory to the commission of that offence and subsections (1) and (2) would contradict each other." (at 20)

12–54   A defendant who is not mistaken as to the facts, but who erroneously believes that his actions amount to a criminal office may not be convicted of a criminal attempt. Section 1(2) does not apply in relation to such cases.

(4) Jurisdiction

12–55   The general rule is that if the completed offence would be triable in England and Wales, and attempt to commit it will be so triable: see section 1(1) and (4) of the 1981 Act.

C. INCITEMENT

(1) General

Serious Crime Bill 2006–7

The Serious Crime Bill creates two new offences of assisting or encouraging crime **12–56** that will replace the current inchoate offence of incitement. Future editions of this work will deal fully with the offences created by the Serious Crime Bill 2006–7 should it come into force.

Incitement involves soliciting, encouraging or pressurising another person to commit an offence. It is primarily a common law offence, although there are also certain statutory offences of incitement. Where the offence incited is triable summarily only, incitement to commit that offence will be triable summarily only, and where the offence incited is triable either way, incitement to commit that offence will be triable either way: *Magistrates Courts Act* 1980, s.45 and Sched. 1, para. 35.

In *Invicta Plastics Ltd v. Clare* [1976] R.T.R. 251, DC, it was held that a company which advertised a device that could detect police radar traps was properly convicted at common law for inciting people to use unlicensed apparatus for wireless telegraphy in contravention of section 1(1) of the *Wireless Telegraphy Act* 1949. In *Race Relations Board v. Applin* [1973] 1 Q.B. 815, Lord Denning M.R. stated that "a person may incite another to do an act by threatening or by pressure, as well as persuasion."

Mens rea

The defendant must intend that the offence incited will be committed, though as **12–57** with attempts, it may sometimes be the case that recklessness as to the circumstances of the offence will suffice. It is not necessary for the person incited to have the necessary *mens rea* to commit the offence, nor is it necessary that he actually go on to commit the offence incited: *DPP v. Armstrong* [2000] Crim.L.R. 379.

In *Shaw (Obtaining by Deception: Incitement)* [1994] Crim.L.R. 365, CA, the appellant was charged with incitement to obtain property by deception by dishonestly inciting a fellow employee to obtain cheques from their employers by falsely accepting bogus invoices, supplied by the appellant, as real invoices for work done. He argued that he was not dishonest, as his intention was to expose the lax nature of the company's security arrangements. The Court of Appeal accepted that if true, this would be a valid defence. For a criticism of this decision, and the view that the appellant was guilty even if his evidence was believed, see the commentary at [1994] Crim.L.R. 365. However, it appears from the case transcript (p.7F) that the prosecution conducted its case on the basis that they were alleging (and had to prove) that the inciter was dishonest. *Archbold Crown* submits that this may have been unnecessary, but may go someway towards explaining the decision.

Miscellaneous statutory provisions

See the *Perjury Act* 1911, s.7(2), "inciting to commit perjury"; and the *Official* **12–58** *Secrets Act* 1920, s.7, "inciting, counselling or attempting to procure another to commit an offence against the *Official Secrets Acts* 1911 and 1920".

(2) Jurisdiction

The common law jurisdiction in respect of incitement is the same as that for **12–59** conspiracy.

(3) Extended jurisdiction

(a) *Fraud and related offences*

Part I of the *Criminal Justice Act* 1993 gives the courts in England and Wales juris- **12–60** diction to try certain cases of fraud and related offences where there is a significant foreign element in their perpetration and where the jurisdictional rules might prevent them from being so tried.

(b) *Sexual offences*

Sexual Offences (Conspiracy and Incitement) Act 1996, ss.2–3

Incitement to commit certain sexual acts outside the United Kingdom

12–61   **2.**—(1) This section applies where—

(a) any act done by a person in England and Wales would amount to the offence of incitement to commit a listed sexual offence but for the fact that what he had in view would not be an offence triable in England and Wales,

(b) the whole or part of what he had in view was intended to take place in a country or territory outside the United Kingdom, and

(c) what he had in view would involve the commission of an offence under the law in force in that country or territory.

(2) Where this section applies—

(a) what he had in view is to be treated as that listed sexual offence for the purposes of any charge of incitement brought in respect of that act, and

(b) any such charge is accordingly triable in England and Wales.

(3) Any act of incitement by means of a message [however communicated] is to be treated as done in England and Wales if the message is sent or received in England and Wales.

Sections 1 and 2: supplementary

12–62   **3.**—(1) Conduct punishable under the law in force in any country or territory is an offence under that law for the purposes of section 2 however it is described in that law.

(2) Subject to subsection (3), a condition in section 2(1)(c) is to be taken to be satisfied unless, not later than rules of court may provide, the defence serve on the prosecution a notice—

(a) stating that, on the facts as alleged with respect to what the accused had in view, the condition is not in their opinion satisfied,

(b) showing their grounds for that opinion, and

(c) requiring the prosecution to show that it is satisfied.

(3) [...]

(4) The court, if it thinks fit, may permit the defence to require the prosecution to show that the condition is satisfied without the prior service of a notice under subsection (2).

(5) In the Crown Court the question whether the condition is satisfied is to be decided by the judge alone.

(6) In any proceedings in respect of any offence triable by virtue of section 2 it is immaterial to guilt whether or not the accused was a British citizen at the time of any act or other event proof of which is required for conviction of the offence.

(7) [...]

(8) References to an offence of incitement to commit a listed sexual offence include an offence triable in England and Wales as such an incitement by virtue of section 2 [without prejudice to subsection (2) of that section].

(9) Subsection (8) applies to references in any enactment, instrument or document [except those in section 2 of this Act and in Part I of the *Criminal Law Act* 1977].

Sexual Offences (Conspiracy and Incitement) Act 1996, Sched.

Section 5   SCHEDULE

LISTED SEXUAL OFFENCES

England and Wales

12–63   1.—(1) In relation to England and Wales, the following are listed sexual offences:

(a) [*repealed by* Sexual Offences Act *2003, s.140 and Sched. 7*];

(b) an offence under any of sections 1 to 12, 14 and 15 to 26 of the *Sexual Offences Act* 2003.

(2) Sub-paragraph (1)(b) does not apply where the victim of the offence has attained the age of sixteen years.

2. [*Northern Ireland.*]

[The Schedule is printed as amended by the *Sexual Offences Act* 2003, s.139, and Sched. 6, para. 35.]

(c) *Particular offences*

Section 5(7) of the *Criminal Law Act* 1977 abolished the offence of incitement to **12–64** conspire. As regards incitements to attempt to commit a crime, it would seem that an incitement to attempt to commit an offence must necessarily be an incitement to commit that offence. Where a letter is sent soliciting and inciting the addressee to commit a crime, but it is not proved to have reached the intended recipient, the sender may be properly convicted of an attempt to incite the commission of the crime: *Banks* [1873] 12 Cox. 393; *Krause*, 66 J.P. 121; *Cope* 16 Cr.App.R. 77. It was also held in *Goldman* [2001] Crim.L.R. 822, CA, that a defendant attempted to incite the addressee of his letter to distribute indecent photographs of children even where he was responding to an offer made by the addressee to supply such photographs.

(d) *Inciting the impossible*

At common law, incitement to commit an offence could not be committed where it **12–65** was impossible to commit the offence alleged to have been incited. It is necessary to analyse the evidence in order to decide precisely what the defendant is alleged to have incited and whether it was possible to commit that offence: *Fitzmaurice* [1983] Q.B. 1083, CA.

VII. *GENERAL DEFENCES*

A. INTRODUCTION

Defences can be loosely categorised as those that involve a denial of the necessary **12–66** *mens rea*, and those that do not deny any of the components of the offence, but which claim that there was some reason for the defendant's conduct that will operate to justify or excuse his offending behaviour.

B. DEFENCES DENYING MENS REA

(1) Infancy

Crime and Disorder Act 1998, s.34

Abolition of rebuttable presumption that a child is doli incapax
34. The rebuttable presumption of criminal law that a child aged 10 or over is incapable of **12–67** committing an offence is hereby abolished.

Following enactment of this section (September 30, 1998) the law relating to the **12–68** culpability of juveniles can be summarised as follows:

Children aged under 10 are not responsible in criminal law.

Children aged 10–14 are no longer presumed to be incapable of criminal responsibility. The child's age may, however, be a relevant factor in determining the reasonableness of his actions (where such a factor is relevant.)

(2) Insanity and automatism

Insanity is dealt with in Ch.28.   **12–69**

Involuntary acts will not attract the sanction of the criminal law, hence a defendant who committed the prohibited act in a state of automatism will have a defence. The relationship between insanity and automatism has been considered in numerous cases:

12–70   In *Quick* [1973] Q.B. 910, CA, the accused was diabetic and raised the defence of automatism due to an imbalance of insulin, which he was taking on prescription. The Court of Appeal held that as the defendant's mental condition stemmed from the use of insulin, rather than his diabetes, his condition stemmed from an external factor, rather than a bodily disorder, hence the defence of automatism should have been available.

In *Bailey* 77 Cr.App.R. 76, CA, the defendant had assaulted his victim during a period of loss of consciousness caused by hypoglaecemia because of his failure to take sufficient food following his last dose of insulin. The Court of Appeal held that self-induced automatism, other than that due to intoxication from alcohol or drugs, may provide a defence to crimes of basic intent. The question in each case will be whether the prosecution have proved the necessary element of recklessness. For example in cases of assault, if the accused knows that his actions or inaction are likely to make him aggressive, unpredictable or uncontrolled with the result that he may cause some injury to others and he persists in the action or takes no remedial action when he knows it is required, it will then be open to the jury to find that he was reckless.

12–71   In *Hennessy* 89 Cr.App.R. 10, CA, the defendant was an insulin dependent diabetic and the offences with which he was charged were committed at a time when he had not taken insulin or eaten for several days and was in a hyperglycaemic state. The relevant question was whether the defendant's state was caused by disease or by some external factor. Hyperglycaemia caused by an inherent defect and not corrected by insulin was a disease and any malfunction of the mind thus caused might fall within the *M'Naghten Rules*. However, the stress, anxiety and depression suffered by the appellant could be the result of the operation of external factors; but not in themselves separately or together external factors of the kind capable in law of causing or contributing to a state of automatism. They constituted a state of mind which was prone to recur and lacked the feature of novelty or accident, hence the defence of automatism should not have been available to the defendant.

12–72   However, in *Roach* [2002] 3 *Archbold News* 1, CA; [2001] EWCA Crim 2698, it was held that the defence of automatism should have been left to the jury. The legal definition of automatism allows that if external factors (taking of prescription drugs and drink) are operative on an underlying condition ("mixed personality disorder") which would not otherwise produce a state of automatism, then the defence should be left to the jury.

12–73   In *Burgess* (1991) 93 Cr.App.R. 41, CA, the defendant was sleepwalking at the time of commission of the charged offence and alleged non-insane automatism as his defence. The Court of Appeal held that on the question of automatism the judge had to decide, first, whether a proper evidential foundation for the defence of automatism had been laid; and, secondly, whether the evidence showed the case to be one of insane automatism falling within the *M'Naghten Rules*, or one of non-insane automatism. The Court held that sleepwalking was an abnormality or disorder, albeit transitory, due to an internal factor, whether functional or organic. It was a disorder or abnormality which might recur, though the possibility of it recurring in the form of serious violence was unlikely. It therefore amounted to a disease of the mind and the trial judge was correct in ruling that the medical evidence adduced amounted to evidence of insanity within the *M'Naghten Rules*.

(3) Intoxication

Introduction

12–74   Different rules apply depending on whether the intoxication is voluntary or involuntary. The intoxication will be classed as voluntary where the defendant knowingly takes alcohol or other intoxicating drugs (except when he acts under medical supervision or direction.) A defendant who drinks a spiked drink will be treated as being involuntarily intoxicated. A defendant who forms the *mens rea* required for the crime will not be able to rely on his intoxication as a defence, be that intoxication voluntary or involuntary: *Kingston* (1994) 99 Cr.App.R. 286, HL.

As regards intoxicating drugs, in *Bailey* (1983) 77 Cr.App.R. 76, CA, the Court of Appeal stated that for crimes of basic intent, intoxication due to voluntary consumption of dangerous drugs could not amount to a defence as recklessness will suffice for the *mens rea* of the offence, and such recklessness can be found in the decision to consume dangerous drugs. However, in the context of non-dangerous drugs, such as insulin taken by a diabetic, such recklessness cannot be so easily found as whilst "It is common knowledge that those who take alcohol to excess or certain sorts of drugs may become aggressive or do dangerous or unpredictable things ... the same cannot be said without more of a man who fails to take food after an insulin injection. If he does appreciate the risk that such a failure may lead to aggressive, unpredictable and uncontrollable conduct and he nevertheless deliberately runs the risk or otherwise disregards it, this will amount to recklessness"; *per* Griffiths L.J. (at 80). In *Hardie* 80 Cr.App.R. 157, CA, the defendant, charged with an offence under the *Criminal Damage Act* 1971, had taken a number of valium tablets (prescribed for someone else). The Court of Appeal held that this did not necessarily amount to voluntary intoxication, Parker L.J stating that:

> "...if the effect of a drug is merely soporific or sedative the taking of it, even in some excessive quantity, cannot in the ordinary way raise a *conclusive* presumption against the admission of proof of intoxication for the purpose of disproving *mens rea* in ordinary crimes, such as would be the case with alcoholic intoxication or incapacity or automatism resulting from the self-administration of dangerous drugs." (at 160)

The relevant question was whether the taking of the drug itself was reckless, which **12–75** would provide the necessary *mens rea* of the offence.

Voluntary intoxication

Voluntary intoxication may negate the *mens rea* requirements of crimes of specific **12–76** intent. The exact meaning of this phrase, and whether the lines between crimes of specific and crimes of basic intent are clearly made out is not beyond dispute. Broadly speaking, crimes of specific intent are those for which only intention will suffice as the necessary mental element. The Court of Appeal considered the distinction between crimes of basic intent and crimes of specific intent in *Heard* [2007] EWCA Crim 125, CA, defining, *obiter*, crimes of specific intent as those which require proof of purpose, or consequence. In this case, the appellant was convicted of sexual assault contrary to section 3 of the *Sexual Offences Act* 2003. Counsel for the appellant argued that the appellant's voluntary intoxication prevented him from having an intention to touch the victim (the offence under section 3 requires an "intentional touching"). Referring to *DPP v. Majewski* (see *post*) the Court held that it had never been the case that voluntary intoxication could prevent a defendant forming an intention to touch, and that the *Sexual Offences Act* 2003 did not alter this position. Lord Justice Hughes, *obiter*, cast doubt on the notion that offences could be neatly separated into crimes of specific intent and crimes of basic intent, stating: "it should not be supposed that every offence can be categorised simply as either one of specific intent or of basic intent. So to categorise an offence may conceal the truth that different elements of it may require proof of different states of mind." (para. 30)

Lord Justice Hughes went on to discuss the distinction between specific and basic intent:

> "It is necessary to go back to *Majewski* in order to see the basis for the distinction there upheld between crimes of basic and of specific intent. It is to be found most clearly in the speech of Lord Simon, at pages 478B to 479B. Lord Simon's analysis had been foreshadowed in his speech in *DPP v Morgan* [1976] A.C. 182, 216 (dissenting in the result), which analysis was cited and approved in *Majewski* by Lord Elwyn-Jones (at 471). It was that crimes of specific

intent are those where the offence requires proof of purpose or consequence, which are not confined to, but amongst which are included, those where the purpose goes beyond the actus reus (sometimes referred to as cases of 'ulterior intent'). By that test, element (a) (the touching) in sexual assault contrary to section 3 of the *Sexual Offences Act* 2003 is an element requiring no more than basic intent. It follows that voluntary intoxication cannot be relied upon to negate that intent" (para. 31).

However, Lord Justice Hughes also recognised that the decision as to whether a crime was one of specific or basic intent, and thus whether voluntary intoxication may be relied upon to negative intention "involves a great deal of policy" and "common sense" (para. 32).

In *Sheehan and Moore* 60 Cr.App.R. 308, Geoffrey Lane L.J. stated:

> "in cases where drunkenness and its possible effect upon the defendant's *mens rea* is an issue, we think that the proper direction to a jury is, first, to warn them that the mere fact that the defendant's mind was affected by drink so that he acted in a way in which he would not have done had he been sober does not assist him at all, provided that the necessary intention was there. A drunken intent is nevertheless an intent.
>
> Secondly, and subject to this, the jury should merely be instructed to have regard to all the evidence, including that relating to drink, to draw such inferences as they think proper from the evidence, and on that basis to ask themselves whether they feel sure that at the material time the defendant had the requisite intent." (at 312)

In *Alden and Jones* [2001] 5 *Archbold News* 3, Ct-MAC, the court said that so far as the question of alcohol and specific intent was concerned, the crucial question where there is evidence of the consumption by the defendant of a substantial quantity of drink is whether there is an issue as to the defendant's formation of specific intent by reason of the alcohol which he has taken and that the necessary pre-requisite to a direction of the kind identified in *Sheehan v. Moore, ante,* is that there must be an issue as to the effect of drunkenness upon the defendant's state of mind.

12–77   Where the prosecution has to prove recklessness, *G.* [2004] 1 Cr.App.R. 21, HL, preserves the position whereby the voluntarily intoxicated defendant cannot rely on his intoxication to assert that he did not appreciate the consequences of his actions. Although the House of Lords overruled *Caldwell* as regards the definition of recklessness for the purposes of section 1 of the *Criminal Damage Act* 1971, holding that "a person acts recklessly within the meaning of section 1 of the 1971 Act with respect to (i) a circumstance when he is aware of a risk that it exists or will exist; (ii) a result when he is aware of a risk that it will occur; and it is, in the circumstances known to him, unreasonable to take the risk", the House held that it was not blameworthy to do something involving a risk of injury to another if (for reasons other than self-induced intoxication) one genuinely did not perceive the risk. The subjective view of recklessness is also adopted in cases involving malicious wounding and assault. In such cases, the fact that the accused was unaware of the relevant risk due to the effect of alcohol will not avail him, provided that the risk is one he would have been aware of had he been sober: *Aitken* 95 Cr.App.R. 304, Ct-MAC; *Richardson and Irwin* [1999] 1 Cr.App.R. 392, CA.

12–78   When the question of drunkenness arises, it is not a question of the capacity of the defendant to form the particular intent which is in issue; what is in issue is simply whether he did form such an intent: *Garlick* 72 Cr.App.R. 291, CA.

In *DPP v. Majewski* (1977) A.C. 443, HL, the appellant had been convicted of assaults occasioning actual bodily harm and assaults on police officers in the execution of their duty. His defence was that by reason of drugs voluntarily taken he did not know what he was doing. The House of Lords held that as regards crimes of basic intent, where the necessary mental element is recklessness, or in the context of assault, foresight that the accused actions would cause another person to have apprehension of immediate and unlawful violence, or would possibly have such a consequence, a voluntarily intoxicated defendant will not be able to assert that due to the intoxication he was senseless and therefore had neither recklessness nor intent as regards the *actus reus* of the offence. Lord Elwyn-Jones L.C. stated:

"If a man of his own volition takes a substance which causes him to cast off the restraints of reason and conscience, no wrong is done to him by holding him answerable criminally for any injury he may do while in that condition. His course of conduct in reducing himself by drugs and drink to that condition in my view supplies the evidence of *mens rea*, of guilty mind certainly sufficient for crimes of basic intent. It is a reckless course of conduct and recklessness is enough to constitute the necessary *mens rea* in assault cases ... The drunkenness is itself an intrinsic, an integral part of the crime, the other part being the evidence of the unlawful use of force against the victim. Together they add up to criminal recklessness. On this I adopt the conclusion of Stroud in (1920) 36 L.Q.R. at p. 273 ... By allowing himself to get drunk and thereby putting himself in such a condition as to be no longer amenable to the law's commands, a man shows such regardlessness as amounts to *mens rea* for the purpose of all ordinary crimes." (at 464–475)

And at 475:

"My noble and learned friends and I think it may be helpful if we give the following indication of the general lines on which in our view the jury should be directed as to the effect upon the criminal responsibility of the accused of drink or drugs or both, whenever death or physical injury to another person results from something done by the accused for which there is no legal justification and the offence with which the accused is charged is manslaughter or assault at common law or the statutory offence of unlawful wounding under section 20, or of assault occasioning actual bodily harm under section 47 of the *Offences against the Person Act* 1861.

In the case of these offences it is no excuse in law that, because of drink or drugs which the accused himself had taken knowingly and willingly, he had deprived himself of the ability to exercise self-control, to realise the possible consequences of what he was doing, or even to be conscious that he was doing it. As in the instant case, the jury may be properly instructed that they "can ignore the subject of drink or drugs as being in any way a defence" to charges of this character."

Thus for crimes where recklessness is the sufficient *mens rea*, voluntary intoxication **12–79** will not afford an defence. These crimes would seem to include (for the purposes of the magistrates' courts) common assault, assault occasioning actual bodily harm, assault on a police officer in the execution of his duty, malicious wounding against section 20 of the *Offences Against the Person Act* 1861, taking a conveyance without the owner's authority contrary to section 12(1) of the *Theft Act* 1968, arson or criminal damage contrary to section 1(1) of the *Criminal Damage Act* 1971 if recklessness is charged, arson or criminal damage contrary to section 1(2) of the *Criminal Damage Act* 1971 if recklessness is alleged.

DPP v. Majewski was approved in *G.*, *ante*.

(4) Consent

For some offences (common assault) it is necessary for the prosecution to prove **12–80** absence of consent. For other, more serious, offences, consent will be no defence in the absence of good reason. Properly conducted games and sports, lawful chastisement, reasonable surgical interference, dangerous exhibitions may constitute good reason: *Att.-Gen.'s Reference (No. 6 of 1980)* [1981] Q.B. 715; sado-masochistic pleasure does not constitute good reason: according to the majority of the HL in *Brown* [1994] 1 A.C. 212, upheld by the ECHR in *Laskey, Jaggard and Brown v. UK* 24 E.H.R.R. 39. *Brown* was distinguished in *Wilson* [1996] 2 Cr.App.R. 241, but followed in *Emmett*, *The Times*, October 15, 1999; [1999] 8 *Archbold News* 4, where "high-risk" sexual activity had resulted on one occasion in haemorrhages to the victim's eyes and bruising to her neck caused by asphyxiation, and on another in burns to her breast. The Court of Appeal upheld D's conviction.

More recently, in *Barnes* [2005] 1 W.L.R. 910; [2005] 1 Cr.App.R. 30, D appealed against his conviction under section 20 of the *Offences against the Person Act* 1861. The CA held that the prosecution of those who inflicted injury on another in the course of a sporting event was reserved for those situations where the conduct was sufficiently grave to be properly categorised as criminal. Where injuries were sustained in the course of contact sports, such as football, public policy limited the availability of the defence of consent to situations where there had been implicit consent to what had occurred. Whether conduct reached the required threshold to be criminal would depend on all the circumstances. The fact that the play had been within the rules and practice of the game and had not gone beyond it would be a firm indication that what had occurred was not criminal. However, in highly competitive sports, where conduct outside the rules could be expected to occur in the heat of the moment, such conduct might not reach the threshold level required for it to be criminal. That level was an objective one which would be determined by the type of sport, the level at which it was played, the nature of the act, the degree of force used, the extent of the risk of injury and D's state of mind.

Fraud does not necessarily vitiate consent: *Richardson* [1998] 2 Cr.App.R. 200 (victim did not know that dentist was suspended from practice: no assault), but see also *Cort* [2004] 1 Cr.App.R. 18, where D induced women waiting at bus stops to accept a lift by falsely pretending that the bus had broken down, the CA upheld convictions for kidnapping. In *Konzani* [2005] 2 Cr.App.R. 14 the CA held that, in the context of inflicting HIV by sexual intercourse (section 20 of the *Offences against the Person Act* 1861), there was a critical distinction between taking a risk as to the various potentially adverse and possibly problematic consequences of unprotected consensual sexual intercourse, and the giving of informed consent to the risk of infection with a fatal disease. For consent to the risk of contracting HIV to provide a defence, the consent had to be an informed consent. Where consent provided a defence to an offence against the person, it was generally the case that an honest belief in consent would also provide a defence. However, in the circumstances, the defendant's honest belief had to be concomitant with the consent which provided a defence. Unless the consent would provide a defence, an honest belief in it would not assist a defendant. In *Dica* [2005] EWCA Crim 2304 the CA held that it was bound by its own decision in the first appeal (*Dica* [2004] Q.B. 1257) but certified a question of public importance, namely, "in what circumstances, if any, may a defendant who knows or believes he is infected with a serious sexually transmitted infection and recklessly transmits it to another through consensual sexual activity be convicted of an offence of inflicting grievous bodily harm contrary to the *Offences against the Person Act* 1861, s.20." Leave to appeal to the HL was refused by both the CA and HL.

For theft, it is not necessary to prove that the victim did not consent: see § 15–6. For consent in relation to offences under the *Sexual Offences Act* 2003, see §§ 14–79 – 14–82.

(5) Mistake of fact

12–81   Since the decision in *Tolson* (1889) L.R. 23 Q.B.D. 168 it has been an accepted principle that mistake of fact, in the sense of a belief in circumstances which, if true would make the defendant's conduct innocent, is a defence to some, but not all criminal charges. The QBD (Crown Cases Reserved) in *Tolson* held that it was a good defence to a charge of bigamy that the accused believed on reasonable grounds, that the first spouse was dead.

Mistake negativing ingredient of offence

12–82   In *Williams (G.)* 78 Cr.App.R. 276, CA, the decision in *Morgan* [1976] A.C. 182, HL, was applied to a case of assault occasioning actual bodily harm. One of the elements of this offence is that the accused was acting unlawfully, *i.e.* not acting in self-defence, in the defence of others or for the prevention of crime. The prosecution must establish that the accused was aware of the unlawful nature of his actions. Hence if the accused establishes that he believed in facts which would, were they true, have rendered his conduct lawful, the prosecution have failed to prove their case. The reasonableness of the defendant's belief was only relevant to the question of determining whether he did in fact hold that belief. *Williams* was applied in the cases of *Jones (Terence)* 83 Cr.App.R. 375, CA and *Blackburn v. Bowering* (1994) 1 W.L.R. 1324, CA (Civ Div) Note the presumptions in the *Sexual Offences Act* 2003 with the effect that *Morgan* no longer applies to sexual offences: see *post*, § 14–79.

Mistake not negativing ingredient of offence

In *Tolson, ante*, where the defendant was charged with bigamy, her belief that her **12–83** first spouse was dead provided her with a defence as it was found to be based on reasonable grounds. *Tolson* was applied in *Albert v. Lavin* (1981) 72 Cr.App.R. 178, DC to a charge of assaulting a police constable in the execution of his duty. It was held that a mistaken belief that the victim was not a police constable would not avail the defendant if there were no reasonable grounds for such a belief. In *Phekoo* 73 Cr.App.R. 107, it was held that the offence under section 1(3) of the *Protection from Eviction Act* 1977 was not an absolute offence, and that it had to be proved that the defendant intended to harass someone he knew or believed to be a residential occupier, rather than a squatter. The defendant would be entitled to be acquitted if his belief that the person was not a residential occupier was based on reasonable grounds.

The distinction between mistakes which negative an element of the offence and those that do not has been blurred by the decision of the House of Lords in *B. (a minor) v. DPP* [2000] 2 A.C. 428. The defendant was charged with an offence contrary to section 1 of the *Indecency with Children Act* 1960, which provided that a person "who commits an act of gross indecency with or towards a child under the age of fourteen (subsequently amended to 16) is guilty of an offence." The House of Lords held that if the defendant honestly believed that the child was 14 or over, he would not be guilty of the offence. The reasonableness of that belief was not relevant.

Mistake is not an available defence as regards offences of strict liability, which carry no requirement of *mens rea*. In *Howells* [1977] Q.B. 614, 65 Cr.App.R. 86, CA, it was held that an honest and reasonable belief that a firearm was an antique, and therefore exempt from the *Firearms Act* 1968 was no defence. See also *Bradish* [1990] 1 Q.B. 981.

Mistake of law

An honest and reasonable belief that an action is not criminal is no defence, though it **12–84** may afford considerable mitigation: *Johnson v. Youden* [1950] 1 K.B. 544 at 546.

A mistake as to the civil law may have the effect of negativing *mens rea*. For example, section 2(1)(a) of the *Theft Act* 1968 provides that a person's conduct will not be regarded as dishonest if he appropriates the property in the belief that he has in law the right to deprive the other of it, on behalf of himself or of a third person. In *Smith* [1974] Q.B. 354; 58 Cr.App.R. 320, CA it was held that mistaken belief as to ownership of property is a defence to a charge of criminal damage. As regards alleged contravention of a statutory instrument, section 3(2) of the *Statutory Instruments Act* 1946 provides:

> "In any proceedings against any person for an offence consisting of a contravention of any such statutory instrument, it shall be a defence to prove that the instrument had not been issued by or under the authority of His Majesty's Stationery Office at the date of the alleged contravention unless it is proved that at that date reasonable steps had been taken for the purpose of bringing the purport of the instrument to the notice of the public, or of persons likely to be affected by it, or of the person charged."

C. DEFENCES CLAIMING CONDUCT WAS EXCUSABLE OR JUSTIFIED

(1) Duress

In *Lynch v. DPP for Northern Ireland* [1975] A.C. 653, HL, Lord Simon stated **12–85** that "Where so little is clear, this at least seems to be established: that the type of threat which affords a defence must be one of human physical harm (including, possibly, imprisonment), so that threat of injury to property is not enough" (at 686). The threat may relate to a person for whose safety the defendant would have reasonably regarded himself as responsible: *Wright* [2000] Crim.L.R. 510, CA. In *Howe* [1987] A.C. 417, HL, it was held that the relevant test whether a person when charged with a criminal offence was acting under duress is an objective, not subjective, one. This test could be stated as; was the threat was so grave as to cause a person of reasonable firmness, sharing the characteristics of the defendant, to act as he did?

The question of what are the relevant characteristics to which the court should have regard was considered in *Bowen* [1996] 2 Cr.App.R. 157, CA. Stewart-Smith L.J. stated that the following principles apply:

"(1) The mere fact that the accused is more pliable, vulnerable, timid or susceptible to threats than a normal person are not characteristics with which it is legitimate to invest the reasonable/ordinary person for the purpose of considering the objective test.

(2) The defendant may be in a category of persons who the jury may think less able to resist pressure than people not within that category. Obvious examples are age, where a young person may well not be so robust as a mature one; possibly sex, though many women would doubtless consider they had as much moral courage to resist pressure as men; pregnancy, where there is added fear for the unborn child; serious physical disability, which may inhibit self protection; recognised mental illness or psychiatric condition, such as post traumatic stress disorder leading to learned helplessness.

(3) Characteristics which may be relevant in considering provocation, because they relate to the nature of the provocation, itself will not necessarily be relevant in cases of duress. Thus homosexuality may be relevant to provocation if the provocative words or conduct are related to this characteristic; it cannot be relevant in duress, since there is no reason to think that homosexuals are less robust in resisting threats of the kind that are relevant in duress cases.

(4) Characteristics due to self-induced abuse, such as alcohol, drugs or glue-sniffing, cannot be relevant.

(5) Psychiatric evidence may be admissible to show that the accused is suffering from some mental illness, mental impairment or recognised psychiatric condition provided persons generally suffering from such condition may be more susceptible to pressure and threats and thus to assist the jury in deciding whether a reasonable person suffering from such a condition might have been impelled to act as the defendant did. It is not admissible simply to show that in the doctor's opinion an accused, who is not suffering from such illness or condition, is especially timid, suggestible or vulnerable to pressure and threats. Nor is medical opinion admissible to bolster or support the credibility of the accused." (at 166–167)

12–86   The threat must have been effective when the crime was committed, but it is not fatal to the defence if the threat is not of immediate injury in the event of non-compliance: *Hudson and Taylor* [1971] 2 Q.B. 202, CA; *Abdul-Hussain* [1999] Crim.L.R. 570, CA. The defendant must avail himself of an opportunity which was reasonably open to him to render the threat ineffective. If he does not, the threat will no longer operate as a defence.

12–87   In *Hasan* [2005] 2 A.C. 467 the HL allowed the Crown's appeal and restored D's conviction. The defence of duress was excluded when as a result of D's voluntary association with others he foresaw or ought reasonably to have foreseen the risk of being subjected to any compulsion by threats of violence. The decision of the CA in *Baker and Ward* [1999] 2 Cr.App.R. 355 was overruled: the law of duress did not require there to have been foresight of coercion to commit crimes of the kind with which D was charged. Policy pointed towards an objective test of what D, placed as he was and knowing what he did, ought reasonably to have foreseen. The policy of the law had to be to discourage association with known criminals, and it should be slow to excuse the criminal conduct of those who did so. (N.B. Lord Bingham, with whom three other Law Lords agreed, suggested that the defence is excluded when as a result of D's voluntary association with others engaged in criminal activity, he foresaw or ought reasonably to have foreseen the risk of being subjected to any compulsion by threats of violence; Lady Hale, dissenting on this point, concluded that the defence should only be excluded when D foresaw the risk of being subjected to compulsion to commit criminal offences.)

A secondary party is liable to conviction of the full offence, although the principal has the defence of duress: *Bourne* 36 Cr.App.R. 125, CA.

(2) Necessity/duress of circumstances

In *Shayler* [2001] 1 W.L.R. 2206, CA, Lord Woolf C.J. stated that "the distinction be-   **12–88** tween duress of circumstances and necessity has, correctly, been by and large ignored or blurred by the courts…the law has tended to treat duress of circumstances and necessity as one and the same." (at para. 55) He then approved the statement in *Archbold Crown* at § 17–124 that:

> "There has in recent years developed the expression 'duress of circumstances'. The use of the word 'duress' in this contest is misleading. Duress, whether in criminal law or civil law, suggests pressure being brought to bear by one person on another person to persuade that other person to do something which he is unwilling to do. 'Duress of circumstances' has nothing to do with one person being told to commit a crime 'or else': it relates to a situation where a person is driven to commit a crime by force of circumstances. Accordingly, duress of circumstances is more conveniently dealt with under the heading of 'necessity' … Indeed, it may be that duress, strictly so called, should itself be regarded as a form of the defence of necessity: see *per* Lord Hailsham L.C. in *Howe* and others…"

Stephen, *Digest of the Criminal Law*, p.9, stated that an act which would otherwise be a crime may in some cases be excused if the defendant can show that:

(a) it was done only to avoid consequences which could not otherwise be avoided and which if they had followed, would have inflicted upon him, or upon others whom he was bound to protect, inevitable and irreparable evil;

(b) that no more was done than was reasonably necessary for that purpose; and

(c) that the evil inflicted by it was not disproportionate to the evil avoided.

This statement was approved by Brooke L.J. in *A. (Children) (Conjoined Twins: Surgical Separation), Re* [2001] Fam. 147, HL, where he concluded that the separation of conjoined twins to save the life of one twin, whilst entailing death for the other would satisfy Stephen's three criteria, and was hence appropriate (at p.204). Each of the three judges in *Re A.* stressed the unique nature of the case, and, as *Archbold Crown* notes at § 17–128, it would seem that the defence would only succeed where the inevitable consequence of taking no action would have been the death of two individuals, whereas the consequence of the defendant taking action was to save the life of one of those individuals, albeit at the cost of accelerating the death of the other. As Ward L.J. stated (at p.204):

> "[I]t is important to restate the unique circumstances for which this case is authority. They are that it must be impossible to preserve the life of X without bringing about the death of Y, that Y by his or her very continued existence will inevitably bring about the death of X within a short period of time, and that X is capable of living an independent life but Y is incapable under any circumstances, including all forms of medical intervention, of viable independent existence. As I said at the beginning of this judgment, this is a very unique case."

In *Conway* (1989) Q.B. 290, the Court of Appeal concluded that: **12–89**

> "necessity can only be a defence to a charge of reckless driving where the facts establish 'duress of circumstances,' …i.e., where the defendant was constrained by circumstances to drive as he did to avoid death or serious bodily harm to himself or some other person… Whether 'duress of circumstances' is called 'duress' or 'necessity' does not matter" [at p.164]

Conway was applied in *Martin* (1989) 88 Cr.App.R. 343, CA where Simon Brown J.   **12–90** stated:

> "The principles may be summarised thus: first, English law does, in extreme circumstances, recognise a defence of necessity. Most commonly this defence arises as duress, that is, pressure on the accused's will from the wrongful threats or violence of another. Equally however it can arise from other objective dangers threatening the accused or others. Arising thus it is conveniently called 'duress of circumstances'.
> Second, the defence is available only if, from an objective standpoint, the accused can be said

Part III

to be acting reasonably and proportionately in order to avoid a threat of death or serious injury.

Third, assuming the defence to be open to the accused on his account of the facts, the issue should be left to the jury, who should be directed to determine these two questions: first, was the accused, or may he have been, impelled to act as he did because as a result of what he reasonably believed to be the situation he had good cause to fear that otherwise death or serious physical injury would result second, if so, would a sober person of reasonable firmness, sharing the characteristics of the accused, have responded to that situation by acting as the accused acted? If the answer to both those questions was Yes, then the jury would acquit the defence of necessity would have been established." [at pp.345–346]

In *DPP v. Bell* (1992) R.T.R. 335, DC, the defendant was charged with driving after consuming alcohol in excess of the prescribed limit. He had been out drinking with friends, and it had always been the plan that he would drive home. However, the Crown Court had found as a fact that the defendant was at the time of driving in terror of being caused serious personal injury. They had hence upheld the defendant's plea of duress and quashed the conviction imposed by the justices. The question for the opinion of the High Court was whether, given the defendant's intention to drive anyway, the Crown Court was correct to accept that the defence of duress of circumstance applied to the defendant's driving away from the car park on account of the threatened violence. The DC held that as the Crown Court had accepted that the defendant drove off in terror, the question of the relevance of the fact that the duress may not have been the sine qua non of the defendant's conduct was not a question forming part of the case stated.

12–91   The applicability of necessity as a defence to a charges under sections 1 and 4 of the *Official Secrets Act* 1989 was examined in *Shayler* [2001] 1 W.L.R. 2206, CA. The Court of Appeal held that the defence of necessity was available to such charges, though in the instant case there were a number of difficulties relating to the establishment of the defence. The Court therefore concluded that there was no necessity or duress as those words are ordinarily understood (the HL rejected a further appeal on other grounds). In *Jones* [2006] UKHL 16, the House of Lords held, unanimously, in the context of trials of protestors against the war on Iraq, that even if the Government had committed the international law crime of aggression in preparing to make war on Iraq, this did not justify the defendants otherwise unlawful conduct. (The HL dealt less specifically with the defence of necessity than had the CA at *Jones* [2005] Q.B. 259; [2004] 3 W.L.R. 1362; [2005] 1 Cr.App.R. 12).

(3) Self-defence/protection of private property

12–92   In *Beckford v. The Queen* [1988] A.C. 130, Lord Griffiths stated:

"The common law recognises that there are many circumstances in which one person may inflict violence upon another without committing a crime, as for instance, in sporting contests, surgical operations or in the most extreme example judicial execution. The common law has always recognised as one of these circumstances the right of a person to protect himself from attack and to act in the defence of others and if necessary to inflict violence on another in so doing. If no more force is used than is reasonable to repel the attack such force is not unlawful and no crime is committed. Furthermore a man about to be attacked does not have to wait for his assailant to strike the first blow or fire the first shot; circumstances may justify a pre-emptive strike." (at p.144)

He then referred to the speech of Lord Lane C.J. in *Williams (Gladstone)* (1984) 78 Cr.App.R. 276, which he stated as giving the correct definition of the English law of self-defence: Lord Lane said:

"In a case of self-defence, where self-defence or the prevention of crime is concerned, if the jury came to the conclusion that the defendant believed, or may have believed, that he was being attacked or that a crime was being committed, and that force was necessary to protect himself or to prevent the crime, then the prosecution have not proved their case. If however the defendant's alleged belief was mistaken and if the mistake was an unreasonable one, that may be a powerful reason for coming to the conclusion that the belief was not honestly held and should be rejected. Even if the jury come to the conclusion that the mistake was an unreasonable one, if the defendant may genuinely have been labouring under it, he is entitled to rely upon it." (at p.281)

An accused who misjudges the degree of force required and who uses force that is **12–93** seen as excessive will be deprived of the defence: *Palmer v. The Queen* [1971] A.C. 814. When deciding whether a defendant has used reasonable force in self defence it was not appropriate, save in exceptional circumstances which would make the evidence especially probative, to take into account whether he was suffering from some psychiatric condition. In *Canns* [2005] EWCA Crim 2264, the CA held that the judge had been right to direct that it was not for a defendant in his own mind to set the standard of reasonableness, but for the jury, considering all the circumstances but not the psychiatric condition, to set the standards of reasonableness in considering the individual case. An accused who mistakenly believes that he is being attacked may still be able to rely on the defence of self-defence. In *Williams* (1984) 78 Cr.App.R. 276, the Court held that the accused's mistake in believing that he was being attacked does not need to be a reasonable one. This subjective approach to mistake will not pertain where the defendant's mistake is due to his own voluntary intoxication: *O'Grady* [1987] Q.B. 995, CA. *O'Grady* was followed in *O'Connor* [1991] Crim.L.R. 135.

Where the accused's mistake is that he believed there were no circumstances warranting the use of force in self defence when in fact there were, the defence of self defence will be unavailable: *Dadson* (1850) 2 Den CC 35.

In *Clegg* [1995] 1 A.C. 482, it was held that that there was no distinction to be drawn between the use of excessive force in self-defence and the use of excessive force in the prevention of crime or in arresting an offender. In *Beckford, ante*, Lord Griffiths also held that the test of self-defence involves looking at the use of force to defence the accused or another.

It is a principle of common law that a person may use such force to defend his prop- **12–94** erty or the property of others from attack or the threat of imminent attack. The court should ask whether:

(i) the use of force was reasonable to defend property from actual or imminent damage which constituted or could constitute an unlawful or criminal act;

(ii) on the facts as the defendant considered them to be, whether objectively the force used was no more than reasonable in all the circumstances, given the beliefs.

See *DPP v. Bayer* [2004] 1 W.L.R. 2856, (sowing of genetically modified maize not unlawful so defence of defence of property not available to those charged with aggravated trespass contrary to section 68 of the *Criminal Justice and Public Order Act* 1994).

See also *Criminal Law Act* 1967, s.3(1):

A person may use such force as is reasonable in the circumstances in the prevention of crime, or in effecting or assisting in the lawful arrest of offenders or suspected offenders or of persons unlawfully at large.

(4) Marital coercion

Criminal Justice Act 1925, s.47

Abolition of presumption of coercion of married woman by husband
47. Any presumption of law that an offence committed by a wife in the presence of her **12–95** husband is committed under the coercion of the husband is hereby abolished, but on a charge against a wife for any offence other than treason or murder it shall be a good defence to prove that the offence was committed in the presence of, and under the coercion of, the husband.

Coercion was defined in *DPP for Northern Ireland v. Lynch* [1975] A.C. 653 as an **12–96** external force which cannot be resisted and which impels its subject to act otherwise than he would wish, *per* Lord Simon.

In *Shortland* [1996] 1 Cr.App.R. 116, CA it was held that to establish the defence of marital coercion under section 47 of the *Criminal Justice Act* 1925, a jury had to be satisfied, on the balance of probabilities, that the will of the defendant wife was so overborne by the wishes of her husband that she had been forced to participate unwillingly. That defence did not necessarily require proof of physical force or the threat of physical force. To succeed, the woman has to prove, on the balance of probabilities that her will was so overborne by the wishes of her husband that she had been forced to participate in the unlawful conduct unwillingly.

OFFENCES OF VIOLENCE

I. DANGEROUS OFFENDERS AND VIOLENT CRIME

Dangerous offenders

The *Criminal Justice Act* 2003, ss.225–228, provides for sentences of imprisonment **13–1** to be imposed for public protection and for extended sentences. Such sentences can be passed in respect of offenders aged 18 or over who are convicted of certain violent or sexual offences. The offences are specified in Schedule 15 of the Act and they are serious specified offences if they carry a maximum sentence of life imprisonment or a determinate sentence of at least 10 years (section 224). The specified offences in this chapter are assault occasioning actual bodily harm; malicious wounding or inflicting grievous bodily harm; racially or religiously aggravated assaults; assault with intent to resist arrest; abandonment of children under two; putting people in fear of violence and the racially or religiously aggravated offence of that nature. Child cruelty and making threats to kill are serious specified offences. See also Ch.23—Sentencing.

Violent crime

The *Violent Crime Reduction Act* 2006 received Royal Assent on November 8, **13–2** 2006. Part 1 of the Act establishes powers to address alcohol-related violence and disorder. Section 23 of the Act inserts new sections 147A and 147B into the *Licensing Act* 2003, creating the summary offence of "persistently selling alcohol to children", which carries a maximum fine of £10,000. Section 27 of the 2006 Act confers powers on constables in uniform to issue directions to individuals aged 16 and over to leave a particular locality and not return for 48 hours if it is thought the presence of that individual is likely to contribute to the occurrence of alcohol-related disorder in that locality and the direction is necessary to remove that likelihood. Failure to comply with such a direction is a summary offence. Section 27 is not in force at the time of writing.

Part 2 of the Act creates several new summary offences relating to the possession and sale of weapons. Section 32 creates a new summary offence committed where in the course of the sale of an air weapon to an individual not registered as a firearms dealer, the seller transfers possession of the weapon when both parties are not present in person. Section 34 inserts a new section 21A into the *Firearms Act* 1968, creating a summary offence of firing a missile from an air weapon beyond premises. Section 35 creates summary offences of selling, buying, or attempting to buy a cap-type primer designed for use in metallic ammunition for a firearm, or an empty cartridge case incorporating such a primer. Section 36 creates a summary offence prohibiting the manufacture, sale or importation of "realistic imitation firearms" (defined in section 38). Sections 32 and 34 were not in force at the time of writing and future editions of this work will deal fully with these offences when they come into force. Sections 35 and 36 came into force on April 6, 2007.

13–3   Section 40 inserts a new section 24A in the *Firearms Act* 1968, creating a summary offence of purchasing an imitation firearm when aged under 18, or selling an imitation firearm to persons under 18. Section 41 amends Schedule 6 to the *Firearms Act* 1968, creating an either-way offence of possessing an imitation firearm in a public place. Section 43 amends section 141A of the *Criminal Justice Act* 1988 (prohibition on the sale of knives, etc, to persons under 16) making it unlawful to sell such articles to those under 18. Section 44 amends sections 1–3 of the *Crossbows Act* 1987 to increase the age referred to in those sections from 17 to 18. None of these sections are in force at the time of writing, and future editions of this work will deal fully with these offences when they come into force.

Part 3 of the Act contains miscellaneous provisions relating to the *Football Disorder Act* 2000, the *Football Spectators Act* 1989 and the *Sexual Offences Act* 2003 which fall outside the scope of this chapter. Part 4 concerns commencement of the legislation.

Sentencing Guidelines

13–4   In September 2005, the Sentencing Advisory Panel issued a consultation paper on the sentencing of assault and other offences against the person. On June 27, 2007 the Sentencing Guidelines Council published a Consultation Guideline on sentencing offenders for assault and other offences against the person; see the Sentencing Guidelines Council's website for further details: http://www.sentencing-guidelines.gov.uk.

II. ASSAULT

A. ASSAULT AND BATTERY

(1) Definition

Criminal Justice Act 1988, s.39

Common assault and battery to be summary offences

13–5   **39.** Common assault and battery shall be summary offences and a person guilty of either of them shall be liable to a fine not exceeding level 5 on the standard scale, to imprisonment for a term not exceeding six months, or to both.

13–6   An assault occurs when the defendant intentionally or recklessly causes another to apprehend immediate unlawful violence: *Burstow* [1998] A.C. 147, HL. It is the causing of another to apprehend violence, regardless of whether any violence is used, which defines an assault. A battery is committed when a person intentionally or recklessly applies unlawful force to the complainant. A single information which includes both assault and battery is bad for duplicity and where the allegation is that the defendant intentionally or recklessly applied unlawful force to the complainant then the information should allege "assault by beating": *Norman* [1994] Crim.L.R. 518.

(2) Allocation

Common assault and battery are triable summarily. The *Crime and Disorder Act* **13–7**
1998 (see *post*) created an aggravated form of this offence, committed when an attack is
motivated by racial or religious hostility, which is triable either way.

(3) Elements of the offence

Section 11 of the *Domestic Violence, Crime and Victims Act* 2004 which came into   **13–8**
force on March 31, 2005 provides for common assault to be an alternative verdict to
more serious offences of assault in certain circumstances.

(4) Sentence

The maximum sentence for either offence is a fine not exceeding level 5 on the stan- **13–9**
dard scale, imprisonment for a term not exceeding six months, or both. After commencement of the relevant provisions, the maximum custodial sentence in a magistrates' court will be 12 months' imprisonment: *Criminal Justice Act* 2003, ss.181, 280–
282 (see Ch.23). For sentencing provisions relating to the aggravated form of the
offence, see *post*, § 13–27.

The *Magistrates' Court Sentencing Guidelines* (2004) state:

> Aggravating factors include on hospital/medical premises, group action, offender in position
> of authority, premeditated, injury, weapon, victim particularly vulnerable, victim serving the
> public, offence committed on bail, relevant previous convictions and any failure to respond to
> previous sentences.
>
> Mitigating factors include impulsive action, minor injury, provocation and single blow.
>
> **Guideline**: Is it serious enough for a community penalty?

Racial or religious aggravation cannot be used as an aggravating factor by the sen- **13–10**
tencer when sentencing for the basic offence of common assault. Where there is evidence that the offence was racially or religiously motivated, the aggravated form of the
offence should be charged. See *post*, § 13–24.

Violence between motorists will in the vast majority of cases lead to custodial sentences: *Fenton* (1994) 15. Cr.App.R.(S.) 682. In the course of a dispute with another
motorist, the offender pushed the other motorist in the chest. His sentence of fourteen
days' imprisonment was reduced to seven.

The trend in sentencing for violence between motorists has recognised the increase
in the number and severity of incidents. In *Sharpe* [2000] 1 Cr.App.R(S.) 1 it was stated
that custody in such cases is almost inevitable and that, where any significant injury was
caused, the period would be more likely to be measured in months than in weeks.

A similar principle applies within the context of sporting fixtures. Whilst some level of
physical contact is to be expected, nonetheless violence beyond that will often merit a
custodial sentence. In *Thelwell* [2004] EWCA Crim 208, during a football match, the
defendant punched another player in the mouth and then on the back of the neck
causing tenderness and pain. He then headbutted the same victim but without breaking
the victim's nose. He was convicted of two charges of common assault. Concurrent sentences of one month and three months respectively were upheld on appeal as "deserved
and correct".

B. ASSAULT OCCASIONING ACTUAL BODILY HARM

(1) Definition

Offences against the Person Act 1861, s.47

Assault occasioning bodily harm. Common assault
  47. Whosoever shall be convicted upon an indictment of any assault occasioning actual bodily **13–11**
harm shall be liable ... to imprisonment for not more than five years.

Part III

13–12   As regards the racially or religiously aggravated form of this offence created by the *Crime and Disorder Act* 1998, s.29, see *post*, § 13–24.

(2) Allocation

13–13   The offence is triable either way. For guidance as to mode of trial, see *Consolidated Criminal Practice Direction* (2002), Appendix F–54.

Due to the fact that the seriousness of this offence can differ depending on the circumstances, it is of particular importance that the magistrates hear the facts before making a decision as to whether to accept jurisdiction.

(3) Elements of the offence

13–14   There must be an assault or battery (see *ante*, § 13–7) which causes some bodily harm. The harm caused may be a direct or indirect consequence of the assault or battery. The harm caused must be something which the defendant could reasonably have foreseen as the consequence of what he was saying or doing towards the complainant: *Roberts* 56 Cr.App.R. 95, CA.

The *mens rea* is the same as for common assault and battery. The prosecution must prove that some hurt or injury calculated to interfere with the health or comfort of the victim was inflicted. The injury need not be permanent, but must be more than merely transient or trifling; *Donovan* [1934] 2 K.B. 498. Cutting off a person's hair without their consent is capable of constituting actual bodily harm: *DPP v. Smith* [2006] 2 All E.R. 16, QBD. The actual bodily harm may consist of psychiatric injury but emotional distress or panic are insufficient. If the prosecution allege that the actual bodily harm was psychiatric injury then it should be proved by expert evidence: *Chan-Fook* 99 Cr.App.R. 147, CA. Psychological injury not amounting to recognisable psychiatric illness does not fall within the ambit of bodily harm for the purposes of the 1861 Act: *D* [2006] EWCA Crim 1136, CA.

A defendant can be criminally liable for an offence of assault if they do not enter the premises where an assault takes place, do not strike a blow forming part of the assault and do not provide any active encouragement to those engaged in the assault: *Nedrick-Smith v. DPP* [2006] EWHC 3015, QBD.

In this case the appellant appealed against her conviction for assault occasioning actual bodily harm. She had driven three women to the victim's house and then watched the three women assault the victim. The appellant knew that there had been a recent incident between the victim and one of the women involved in the assault, that there remained ill-feeling between these women, and that the purpose of the visit was to sort this matter out.

The Divisional Court upheld her conviction, stating that the appellant was:

> "a party to driving a car to the premises of the victim with the object of sorting things out. She knew of the incident the week before. She foresaw that violence might take place and she aided the possible attack by driving the other girls there. Far from withdrawing when she saw that violence was taking place, she came up to the house and watched them, doing nothing to stop the violence. Those facts support both a finding that she was an aider and abetter and that she was a party to a joint enterprise". (*per* Lord Justice Waller, para. 15).

The *actus reus* of the offence may be established where someone, by act or word or a combination of the two, creates a danger and thereby exposes another to a reasonably foreseeable risk of injury that materialised: *DPP v. Santana-Bermudez* [2004] Crim.L.R. 471, DC.

In this case, a police officer was injured by a hypodermic needle when conducting a search of the defendant. The Divisional Court held that the *actus reus* of the offence could be established by the defendant's assurances before the search commenced that he was not carrying needles or sharps. Whilst this decision may be followed, it should not be regarded as authoritative as the respondent did not make representations at the hearing.

(4) Sentence

When tried summarily the maximum penalty for the offence is six months' imprison- **13–15**
ment, a fine not exceeding level five on the standard scale or both. After commencement of the relevant provisions, the maximum custodial sentence in a magistrates' court
will be 12 months' imprisonment: *Criminal Justice Act* 2003, ss.154 and 282.

The *Magistrates' Court Sentencing Guidelines* (2004) state:

> Aggravating factors include deliberate kicking or biting, extensive injuries (may be psychiat-
> ric) head butting, group action, offender in position of authority, on hospital/medical
> premises, premeditated, victim particularly vulnerable, victim serving public, weapon, offence
> committed on bail, relevant previous convictions and any failures to respond to previous sen-
> tences, abuse of trust (domestic setting).
> Mitigating factors include minor injury, provocation and single blow.
> **Guideline**: Is it so serious that only custody is appropriate? Are Magistrates' sentencing pow-
> ers appropriate?

It is usual for racially aggravated forms of the offence to be committed to the Crown
Court for sentence.

In *Porter* [2002] EWCA Crim 2124, the offender became involved in a scuffle in a **13–16**
public house, during which he threw a glass bottle at a barman's head, causing much
blood loss and the need for three stitches. Sentencing him to eight months' imprisonment, the judge emphasised the common nature of such offences, committed by men of
otherwise good character, and the obligation of the courts to discourage such behaviour.
See also *Audit* (1994) 15 Cr.App.R.(S.) 36.

A sentence of four months' imprisonment was appropriate for an offender who had
fractured someone's nose in the course of an altercation in a taxi queue: *Marples* (1998)
1 Cr.App.R.(S.) 335.

Custodial sentences will almost always be appropriate where the assault on a police
constable causes actual bodily harm: *Roughsedge (Att.-Gen.'s Reference (No. 7 of
1993))* [1994] R.T.R. 322. A sentence of nine months' imprisonment was appropriate
where the offender headbutted a police officer, chipping his tooth and splitting his lip:
Broyd [2002] 1 Cr.App.R.(S.) 47, CA. Persons in positions of authority may also expect
the protection of the courts, hence violence towards public transport employees will be
met by immediate prison sentences: *Tremlett* (1983) 5 Cr.App.R.(S.) 199, as will violence
towards traffic wardens: *Charlton* (1995) 16 Cr.App.R.(S.) 703. A sentence of nine
months' imprisonment was imposed on an offender convicted of assaulting a
schoolteacher: *Byrne* [2000] 1 Cr.App.R.(S.) 282. Heavier sentences will also be passed
when the victim of the assault is a hospital worker: *Eastwood* [2002] 2 Cr.App.R. (S.) 72
(offender who assaulted a nurse sentenced to 15 months' imprisonment, Mitchell J. saying that "if drunks assault staff in hospitals, leniency is the last thing they should expect.")

Equally, prisoners are entitled to the protection of the courts, and prison officers who
assault inmates can expect heavy sentences. In *Fryer* [2002] 2 Cr.App.R. (S). 122, three
prison officers who brutally assaulted an inmate were sentenced to either three or four
years' imprisonment. Newman J. described such conduct as going beyond a breach of
trust in respect of the individual prisoner concerned, being rather a breach of trust to
society generally.

C. WOUNDING OR INFLICTING GRIEVOUS BODILY HARM

(1) Definition

Offences against the Person Act 1861, s.20

Inflicting bodily injury, with or without weapon

20. Whosoever shall unlawfully and maliciously wound or inflict any grievous bodily harm **13–17**
upon any other person, either with or without any weapon or instrument, shall be guilty of an
offence, and being convicted thereof shall be liable to imprisonment for not more than five years

As to the racially aggravated version of this offence created by the *Crime and Disorder Act* 1998, s.20, see *post*, section 4.

(2) Allocation

13–18　　Both the basic and the religiously or racially aggravated form of the offence are triable either way.

For guidance as to mode of trial, see *post*, the *Consolidated Criminal Practice Direction* (2002), App. F, para. V.51.

(3) Elements of the offence

13–19　　For harm to amount to a "wound" the continuity of the skin must be broken: *Wood* 1 Mood. 278.

The prosecution does not have to prove the defendant intended or foresaw that his act would cause grievous bodily harm or wounding; it is sufficient that the defendant intended or foresaw that his act would cause physical harm to some person, albeit only of a minor character: *Savage* [1992] 1 A.C. 699, HL. See also *DPP v. W* [2006] EWHC 92, QBD, Admin. The word "maliciously" adds no meaning over and above the requirement for recklessness (in the subjective sense): *Mowatt* [1968] 1 Q.B. 421, CA.

13–20　　On the issue of whether consent is relevant where the victim is caused to contract HIV by the defendant see, *Dica* [2005] EWCA Crim 2304.

(4) Sentence

13–21　　When tried summarily the maximum penalty for both offences is six months' imprisonment, a fine not exceeding level six on the standard scale or both: *Magistrates' Court Act* 1980, s.32(1) and *Crime and Disorder Act* 1998, s.29(2). After commencement of the relevant provisions, the maximum custodial sentence in a magistrates' court will be 12 months' imprisonment: *Criminal Justice Act* 2003, ss.154 and 282.

As regards the basic offence, when dealt with summarily, the *Magistrates' Court Sentencing Guidelines* (2004) state:

> Aggravating factors include deliberate kicking/biting, extensive injuries, group action, offender in position of authority, on hospital/medical premises, premeditated, victim particularly vulnerable, victim serving public, weapon, offence committed on bail, relevant previous convictions and any failures to respond to previous sentences, abuse of trust (domestic setting).
>
> Mitigating factors include single blow, minor wound and provocation.
>
> **Guideline**: Is it so serious that only custody is appropriate? Are magistrates' sentencing powers appropriate?

13–22　　In *Rogers* (1993) 15 Cr.App.R.(S.) 393, the offender head-butted an opponent during a football match, causing a fracture. Given the defendant's good character and likely effect of a long custodial sentence, the original sentence of nine months' imprisonment was reduced on appeal to four months. See also *Moss* [2000] 1 Cr.App.R.(S.) 307 for injuries inflicted in the course of a rugby match and *Thelwell* (*ante*) for injuries inflicted in the course of a football match.

13–23　　In *Clare* [2002] 2 Cr.App.R.(S.) 97, Aikens J. issued guidelines on the correct sentencing approach when the attack involves a single blow leading to injury to the victim. The first relevant factor is the strength of the blow that has been imposed. The second relevant factor is the consequence to the victim. In *Clare*, the blow was described as obviously hard as the victim lost consciousness, with the consequence of two injuries and the need for at least one operation to treat the injuries. A sentence of eighteen months' imprisonment was imposed.

The use of a weapon is likely to necessitate a custodial sentence beyond the sentencing powers of the magistrates. In *Robertson* [1998] 1 Cr.App.R.(S.) 21, the offender attacked a man in a public house by thrusting a beer glass into his face. His sentence of two and a half years' imprisonment was reduced to two years on appeal. In *Simpson* [1998] 1 Cr.App.R.(S.) 197 an unprovoked attack with a chisel resulted in four years' imprisonment.

D. RACIALLY OR RELIGIOUSLY AGGRAVATED OFFENCES

(1) Definition

Crime and Disorder Act, 1998, s.29

Racially or religiously aggravated assaults

29.—(1) A person is guilty of an offence under this section if he commits—   **13–24**

   (a) an offence under section 20 of the *Offences Against the Person Act* 1861 (malicious wounding or grievous bodily harm);

   (b) an offence under section 47 of that Act (actual bodily harm); or

   (c) common assault, which is racially or religiously aggravated for the purposes of this section.

  (2) A person guilty of an offence falling within subsection (1)(a) or (b) above shall be liable

   (a) on summary conviction, to imprisonment for a term not exceeding six months or to a fine not exceeding the statutory maximum, or to both;

   (b) on conviction on indictment, to imprisonment for a term not exceeding seven years or to a fine, or to both.

  (3) A person guilty of an offence falling within subsection (1)(c) above shall be liable—

   (a) on summary conviction, to imprisonment for a term not exceeding six months or to a fine not exceeding the statutory maximum, or to both;

   (b) on conviction on indictment, to imprisonment for a term not exceeding two years or to a fine, or to both.

[The words "or religiously" were inserted by the *Anti-Terrorism, Crime and Security Act* 2001, s.39(5) and (6)(a). This amendment has no effect in relation to anything done before it came into effect, December 14, 2001: section 42.]

(2) Allocation

Offences contrary to section 29 are triable either way.   **13–25**

(3) Elements of the offence

For meaning of "racially or religiously aggravated" see *Crime and Disorder Act* **13–26** 1998, s.28. See *post*, § 22–70.

Whilst the legislation refers to a "racial group", this does not mean that a purely inclusive definition of those words should be adopted. The size of the group is immaterial and words or actions can be directed to large or small groups irrespective of origin: *DPP v. M.* [2004] 1 W.L.R. 2758, QBD. Hostility demonstrated to foreigners because they were foreign could be just as objectionable as hostility based on a more limited racial characteristic: *Rogers* [2006] 1 W.L.R. 962, CA. The word "immediately" in section 28(1)(a) of the Act qualifies both the words "before" and "after" in the section; hostility therefore has to be demonstrated immediately in either case. Hostility can be demonstrated even if the victim was absent, as long as it occurs in the immediate context of the substantive offence: *Parry v. DPP* [2005] A.C.D. 64, CA. Whether using the word "immigrant" is capable of demonstrating hostility based on the victim's membership (or perceived membership) of a racial group as defined by the *Crime and Disorder Act* 1998, s.28(4) is a question of fact: *Att.-Gen.'s Reference (No. 4 of 2004)* [2005] 1 W.L.R. 2810, CA. In this case, the CA held that it was for the jury to decide whether a defendant's use of the term "immigrant doctor" was an allegation of non-Britishness or part of a demonstration by the defendant of hostility to the victim within the terms of section 28(1)(a) because she perceived his non-Britishness to derive from his race, colour, nationality or ethnic or national origins.

(4) Sentence

13–27　　When tried summarily the maximum penalty for these offences is six months' imprisonment, a fine not exceeding the statutory maximum or both: section 29(2) and (3). After commencement of the relevant provisions, the maximum custodial sentence in a magistrates' court will be 12 months' imprisonment: *Criminal Justice Act* 2003, ss.154 and 282.

The *Magistrates' Court Sentencing Guidelines* (2004) provide a higher guideline for the racially aggravated form of assault, the guideline being "is the offence so serious that only custody is justified?" For assault occasioning actually bodily harm, the guideline is the same as for the basic form of the offence, though the court is directed to treat the level of racial aggravation as relevant when determining the seriousness of the offence.

Guidance as to the correct sentencing approach was given in *Saunders* [2000] 2 Cr.App.R.(S.) 71, where the Court of Appeal advised the sentencing court to first consider the appropriate sentence for the offence in the absence of racial aggravation, and then add a further term for the racial element, so the total term reflects the overall criminality. Even if the basic offence would not have crossed the custody threshold, the element of racial aggravation may well result in the custody threshold being passed. Relevant factors when determining sentence would be the nature of the hostile demonstration, whether by language, gestures or weapons; its length, whether isolated repeated or persistent; its location, whether public or private; the number both of those demonstrating and those demonstrated against; and the presence or absence of other features. A discount will be appropriate for, amongst other things, genuine remorse, a plea of guilty and previous good character.

13–28　　In *Kelly and Donnelly* [2001] 2 Cr.App.R.(S.) 73, factors seriously aggravating the racial element of the offence in terms of the offender's intention were identified as planning by the offender, the offence being part of a pattern of racist offending by the offender, membership of a group promoting racist activities and the deliberate setting up of the victim for the purpose of humiliating him or being offensive towards him.

Factors aggravating the offence in terms of its impact on the victim include the offence taking place at the victims home; the victim being particularly vulnerable or providing a service to the public; the timing and location of the offence being such as to maximise the harm or distress it caused; the expressions of racial hostility being repeated or prolonged; fear and distress being caused throughout a particular community and particular distress being caused to the victim or the victim's family.

In *Beglin* [2003] 1 Cr.App.R.(S.) 21 the approach in *Saunders* and *Kelly and Donnelly* of demarcating the sentence appropriate for the basic form of the offence and then indicating the addition for the racially aggravated element was affirmed. In the case of a racially aggravated common assault, a sentence of four months' imprisonment was held to be sufficient for the basic form of the offence, hence a sentence of twelve months' imprisonment in total was too long. A sentence of eight months' imprisonment was substituted, with four months being the appropriate sentence for both the basic part of the offence and the addition for the racial element.

In some cases, the racial aggravation will be so inherent and integral to the offence itself that it will not be possible to assess the overall criminality involved in a discrete way. In such cases, the court must assess the seriousness of the offence as a whole: *Fitzgerald* [2003] 1 Cr.App.R.(S.) 74, CA. In this case, the appellant swore and addressed deeply distressing racial abuse and obscenities to an officer during the course of arrest. A sentence of ten months' imprisonment was imposed, Burnton J. stating that the offender's history, which showed repeated offences against the police, did not aggravate the present offence, yet was significant as to its context and background, and provided grounds for distinguishing the case from authorities such as *Kelly and Donnelly* [2001] 2 Cr.App.R.(S.) 341.

Where an assault itself is not such as to justify a custodial sentence, and it is the racial aggravation that makes a custodial sentence appropriate, the correct sentencing approach is to treat the appropriate custodial sentence for the assault itself as a notional, or very short one, and then to decide the appropriate uplift for the element of racial aggravation: *Slater* [2005] EWCA Crim 2882, CA.

E. ASSAULT WITH INTENT TO RESIST OR PREVENT ARREST

(1) Definition

Offences against the Person Act 1861, s.38

Assault with intent to commit felony, or on peace officers &c.

38. Whosoever [...] shall assault any person with intent to resist or prevent the lawful ap- **13–29** prehension or detainer of himself or of any other person for any offence, shall be guilty of a misdemeanour, and being convicted thereof shall be liable, at the discretion of the court, to be imprisoned for any term not exceeding two years, [...]

[This section is printed as amended by the *Police Act* 1964, Sched. 10, Pt I; the *Criminal Law Act* 1967, Sched. 3 Pt III and the *Criminal Justice Act* 1948, s.1(2).]

(2) Allocation

This offence is triable either way.   **13–30**

(3) Elements of the offence

The prosecution must prove: **13–31**
  – an assault, see *ante*, §§ 13–5;
  – that the person assaulted had the right to apprehend or detain the defendant:
    see *Self* 95 Cr.App.R. 42;
  – an intention to resist or prevent the lawful apprehension or detainer of the defendant or another person.

(4) Sentence

When tried summarily the maximum penalty for this offence is six months' imprison- **13–32** ment, a fine not exceeding the statutory maximum, or both. After commencement of the relevant provisions, the maximum custodial sentence in a magistrates' court will be 12 months' imprisonment: *Criminal Justice Act* 2003, ss.154 and 282.

Sentencing considerations for this offence are largely similar to those for assault upon a police officer occasioning actual bodily harm: see section 2, *ante*.

F. ASSAULT ON CONSTABLE IN EXECUTION OF DUTY

(1) Definition

Police Act 1996, s.89(1), (3)–(6)

Assaults on constables

89.—(1) Any person who assaults a constable in the execution of his duty, or a person assist- **13–33** ing a constable in the execution of his duty, shall be guilty of an offence and liable on summary conviction to imprisonment for a term not exceeding six months or to a fine not exceeding level 5 on the standard scale, or to both.

(3) This section also applies to a constable who is a member of a police force maintained in Scotland or Northern Ireland when he is executing a warrant or otherwise acting in England or Wales, by virtue of any enactment conferring powers on him in England and Wales.

(4) In this section references to a person assisting a constable in the execution of his duty include references to any person who is neither a constable nor in the company of a constable but who—
  (a) is a member of an international joint investigation team that is led by a member of a police force; and

551

(b) is carrying out his functions as a member of that team.

(5) In this section 'international joint investigation team' means any investigation team formed in accordance with—

> (a) any framework decision on joint investigation teams adopted under Article 34 of the Treaty on European Union;
> (b) the Convention on Mutual Assistance in Criminal Matters between the Member States of the European Union, and the Protocol to that Convention, established in accordance with that Article of that Treaty; or
> (c) any international agreement to which the United Kingdom is a party and which is specified for the purposes of this section in an order made by the Secretary of State.

(6) A statutory instrument containing an order under subsection (5) shall be subject to annulment in pursuance of a resolution of either House of Parliament.

[This section is printed as amended by the *Serious Organised Crime and Police Act* 2005, Sched. 17(2), para. 1]

(2) Allocation

13–34   This offence is triable summarily: *Police Act* 1996, s.89(1).

(3) Elements of the offence

13–35   The prosecution must prove:

- an assault, see *ante*, § 13–5;
- of a constable;
- in the execution of his duty.

Charges under section 89 necessarily include the offence of common assault, however magistrates' courts do not have the power to convict for included offences. Therefore, where there is doubt concerning whether the constable was acting in execution of their duty it may be advisable to draft alternative charges: *Bentley v. Brudzinski* 75 Cr.App.R. 217, DC; *Kerr v. DPP* [1995] Crim.L.R. 394, or proceed with a charge of common assault: *C. v. DPP* [2003] EWHC 2780.

Where justices had found that a defendant had bitten the hand of a police officer, yet had rejected the prosecution case that the bite had been deliberate and intentional, it was open to them to convict the defendant of an assault on the basis of recklessness as when the defendant brought the policeman's hand to his mouth in the course of a struggle to avoid recapture, justices were entitled to find that there was a clearly foreseeable risk, taken by the defendant, of contact with the defendant's teeth as he shouted and struggled: *D. v. DPP* [2005] Crim.L.R. 962; [2005] EWHC 967, QBD.

The general powers, duties and responsibilities of police officers are governed by the *Police Act* 1996. Powers concerning the stopping and searching of persons or vehicles, the seizure of articles, entering premises with or without search warrants and the arrest and detention of persons are largely contained in the *Police and Criminal Evidence Act* 1984. See Ch.1.

Whether the detention of a citizen by a police officer short of arrest is unlawful is a question of fact which depends on the circumstances proceeding it and the degree of force used: *Bentley v. Brudzinski* 75 Cr.App.R. 217, DC; *Mepstead v. DPP* (1996) 160 J.P.N. 448, DC. Not every interference with a citizen's liberty will amount to a course of conduct sufficient to take the constable outside the execution of their duty: *Donnelly v. Jackman*, 54 Cr.App.R. 229, DC.

13–36   An officer will not be considered to be acting within the execution of their duty when they fail to adduce any evidence establishing that an arrest and subsequent search of the individual's property was lawful: *R. (Odewale) v. DPP* 2000 WL 33148750, DC. See also *Kynaston v. DPP* 87 Cr.App.R. 200, DC (attempting to arrest individuals when police officers knew a robbery had been committed, desired to arrest a known person and communicated that intention to those they were trying to arrest judged to be action within the scope of the officers' duty).

Where a person has been arrested whilst impeding the arrest of a third party, for the second arrest to be lawful, it must be shown that the first arrest was lawful: *Riley v. DPP* 91 Cr.App.R. 14, DC. A police officer may exceed their powers even though they are acting in good faith: *C. v. DPP* [2003] EWHC 2780, DC (failure to explain the reasons for restraining a 16-year-old girl to her boyfriend, coupled with a failure to allow the girl to explain her conduct sufficed to remove the officer's actions from the scope of his duty).

It is not necessary for the prosecution to prove that the defendant knew that the person assaulted was a police constable or in the execution of his duty, though a mistake of fact (a belief that the person was not a constable) may be a defence.

When the police received an emergency call giving them reason to believe that a child was at risk at a property, they were fully entitled, as an exercise of their discretion under section 17(1)(e) of the *Police and Criminal Evidence Act* 1984, to enter on to that property without a warrant to investigate. Their presence on the property concerned will therefore be lawful. The police will also not be acting outside the scope of their duty when they arrest an individual on the basis of abundant evidence indicating that there had been a breach of the peace, and that another breach was imminent. Where it was not practicable for an officer to inform a detainee of the reason for his arrest, the arrest should be maintained until it was possible to inform him of the reason. But any delay in informing the detainee of the reason for his arrest could not retrospectively render unlawful his correct and lawful arrest by the officer for breach of the peace: *Blench v. DPP* [2004] EWHC 2717, QBD.

Police officers may still be acting in the execution of their duty in arresting someone they believed to be committing an offence under section 5 of the *Public Order Act* 1996 even though the prosecution may fail to prove that the individual arrested had committed this offence; the issue is whether it was reasonable for the arresting officers to suspect that the individual's conduct would cause someone to feel alarm or distress: *Burrell v. CPS* [2005] EWHC 786, QBD.

Where police officers are contemplating a search within the meaning of section 2(2) of the *Police and Criminal Evidence Act* 1984, they are required to comply with section 2(3) of that Act. The strict requirements of the Act and the Codes have to be complied with prior to an intended search notwithstanding that the person apprehending the suspect was obviously a police officer and that that officer had genuine concerns about another officer's safety: *Bonner v. DPP* [2004] EWHC 2415.

A conviction for assaulting a police officer in the execution of his duty could not stand where the officer had exercised his powers unlawfully by arresting the defendant for a purported actual breach of the peace in the absence of any violent conduct: *Hawkes v. DPP*, *The Times*, November 29, 2005.

The test of whether an individual has revoked an implied license for police officers to enter their property is objective: *R. (Fullard) v. Woking Magistrates' Court* [2005] EWHC 2922, QBD. Furthermore, if implied permission to be on the premises is revoked, the person concerned has to be given a reasonable opportunity to leave: *ibid*.

(4) Sentence

The maximum penalties for this offence are six months' imprisonment, a fine not **13–37** exceeding level five on the standard scale or both: *Police Act* 1996, s.89(1) and (2).

The *Magistrates' Court Sentencing Guidelines* (2004) state:

Aggravating factors include any injuries caused, gross disregard for public authority, group action, premeditated, racial aggravation, religious aggravation, offence committed whilst on bail, relevant previous convictions and any failures to respond to previous sentences.

Mitigating factors include impulsive action and being unaware that the victim was a police officer.

Guideline: Is it so serious that only custody is appropriate?

Sentencing considerations for assault causing actual bodily harm when the victim is a police officer will also be relevant here: see section 2 above.

G. Resisting or Wilfully Obstructing Constable

(1) Definition

Police Act 1996, s.89(2)

Assaults on constables

13–38   89.—(2) Any person who resists or wilfully obstructs a constable in the execution of his duty, or a person assisting a constable in the execution of his duty, shall be guilty of an offence and liable on summary conviction to imprisonment for a term not exceeding one month or to a fine not exceeding level 3 on the standard scale, or to both.

(2) Allocation

13–39   This offence is triable summarily: *Police Act* 1996, s.89(2).

(3) Elements of the offence

13–40   Obstruction is defined as making it more difficult for a police officer to carry out his duty: *Hinchcliffe v. Sheldon* [1955] 1 W.L.R. 1207.

Consequently, resisting an unlawful arrest will not amount to obstruction: *Edwards v. DPP* (1993) 97 Cr.App.R 301. In *Redmond-Bate v. DPP* (1999) 163 J.P. 789, the appellant was one of a group of women preachers who had been arrested on the steps of a cathedral by a constable fearing a breach of the peace following the reaction of some members of the crowd who had gathered to listen. As the actions of the police officer in arresting the appellant were not reasonable, there being no reason to suspect a breach of the peace, the Court of Appeal held that the constable was acting unlawfully when he attempted to arrest her, and she could not be said to be obstructing him in the execution of his duty when she resisted arrest.

In *Green v. Moore* [1982] Q.B. 1044, it was held that it is an obstruction of a constable in the execution of his duty, to warn someone so that he may postpone the commission of a crime. Although the net result was the prevention of a crime, liability hinged on the defendant's *mens rea* and the question of whether the defendant's intention was to assist the potential criminals or to assist the police.

If a constable is acting unlawfully then he is not acting in the course of his duty and the person who obstructs a constable not acting in accordance with his duty cannot be guilty of an offence: *Edwards v. DPP* (1993) 97 Cr.App.R. 301.

Where a police officer has ample grounds to justify making an arrest, their conduct will not be rendered unlawful by them not formally using the word "arrest" until investigations into the conduct justifying the arrest are completed: *Fiak (Engin)* [2005] EWCA Crim 2381, CA.

Where a driver warned other drivers as to the presence of a speed trap set up by a police officer on a road, the actus reus of the offence under section 89(2) will only be established where it is proved that the drivers warned were, or were likely to be, exceeding the speed limit at the location of the speed trap: *DPP v. Glendinning*, *Daily Telegraph*, October 27, 2005, DC.

Running away to avoid apprehension after being approached by police officers is capable of amounting to an offence under section 89(2): *Sekfali v. DPP* (2006) 170 J.P. 393, QBD.

13–41   The obstruction must also be wilful. Hence making the police officers task more difficult by genuinely trying to offer assistance will not found a charge under this section: *Wilmott v. Atack* [1977] Q.B. 498.

A solicitor who attempts to interview witnesses for the purpose of preparing the defence of his client in criminal proceedings and in so doing acts against the instruction of a police officer, is not thereby guilty of obstructing the officer: *Connolly v. Dale* [1996] 1 Cr.App.R. 200.

(4) Sentence

The maximum penalties are one months' imprisonment, a fine not exceeding level **13–42** three on the standard scale, or both: *Police Act* 1996, s.89(2). After the commencement of the relevant provisions, the maximum custodial sentence in a magistrates' court will be 12 months' imprisonment: *Criminal Justice Act* 2003, ss.154 and 282 (see *post*, Ch.23).

The *Magistrates' Court Sentencing Guidelines* (2004) state:

> Aggravating factors include racial aggravation, group action, premeditated, offence committed on bail, relevant previous convictions and any failures to respond to previous sentences, religious aggravation.
>
> Mitigating factors include genuine misjudgement, impulsive action and minor obstruction.
>
> **Guideline**: Is discharge or fine appropriate?

H. Obstruction of Emergency Workers

(1) Definition

Emergency Workers (Obstruction) Act 2006, ss.1–4

Obstructing or hindering certain emergency workers responding to emergency circumstances

1.—(1) A person who without reasonable excuse obstructs or hinders another while that **13–43** other person is, in a capacity mentioned in subsection (2) below, responding to emergency circumstances, commits an offence.

(2) The capacity referred to in subsection (1) above is—

(a) that of a person employed by a fire and rescue authority in England and Wales;

(b) in relation to England and Wales, that of a person (other than a person falling within paragraph (a)) whose duties as an employee or as a servant of the Crown involve—

　(i) extinguishing fires; or

　(ii) protecting life and property in the event of a fire;

(c) that of a person employed by a relevant NHS body in the provision of ambulance services (including air ambulance services), or of a person providing such services pursuant to arrangements made by, or at the request of, a relevant NHS body;

(d) that of a person providing services for the transport of organs, blood, equipment or personnel pursuant to arrangements made by, or at the request of, a relevant NHS body;

(e) that of a member of Her Majesty's Coastguard;

(f) that of a member of the crew of a vessel operated by—

　(i) the Royal National Lifeboat Institution, or

　(ii) any other person or organisation operating a vessel for the purpose of providing a rescue service, or a person who musters the crew of such a vessel or attends to its launch or recovery.

(3) For the purposes of this section and section 2 of this Act, a person is responding to emergency circumstances if the person—

(a) is going anywhere for the purpose of dealing with emergency circumstances occurring there; or

(b) is dealing with emergency circumstances or preparing to do so.

(4) For the purposes of this Act, circumstances are "emergency" circumstances if they are present or imminent and—

(a) are causing or are likely to cause—

　(i) serious injury to or the serious illness (including mental illness) of a person;

　(ii) serious harm to the environment (including the life and health of plants and animals);

　(iii) serious harm to any building or other property; or

　(iv) a worsening of any such injury, illness or harm; or

(b) are likely to cause the death of a person.

(5) In subsection (2) above "relevant NHS body" means—

(a) in relation to England and Wales, an NHS foundation trust, National Health Service trust, Special Health Authority, Primary Care Trust or Local Health Board;

(b) in relation to Northern Ireland, a Health and Social Services trust or Health and Social Services Board.

Obstructing or hindering persons assisting emergency workers

13–44   **2.**—(1) A person who without reasonable excuse obstructs or hinders another in the circumstances described in subsection (2) below commits an offence.

(2) Those circumstances are where the person being obstructed or hindered is assisting another while that other person is, in a capacity mentioned in section 1(2) of this Act, responding to emergency circumstances.

Provisions supplementary to sections 1 and 2

13–45   **3.**—(1) A person may be convicted of the offence under section 1 or 2 of this Act notwithstanding that it is—

(a) effected by means other than physical means; or

(b) effected by action directed only at any vehicle, vessel, apparatus, equipment or other thing or any animal used or to be used by a person referred to in that section.

(2) For the purposes of section 1 or 2 of this Act, circumstances to which a person is responding are to be taken to be emergency circumstances if the person believes and has reasonable grounds for believing they are or may be emergency circumstances.

Penalties

13–46   **4.**—   A person guilty of an offence under this Act is liable on summary conviction to a fine not exceeding level 5 on the standard scale.

(2) Allocation

13–47   The offences are triable summarily: section 1(4).

(3) Elements of the offence

13–48   The *Emergency Workers (Obstruction) Act* 2006 creates two offences of obstructing or hindering certain emergency workers and obstructing those assisting certain emergency workers. The Act came into force on February 20, 2007. The Prosecution must prove that:

— The defendant, without reasonable excuse;

— Obstructed or hindered;

— A person acting in one of the capacities listed in the *Emergency Workers (Obstruction) Act* 2006, s.1(2); or a person assisting someone acting in such a capacity;

— While that person was responding to emergency circumstances (defined in the *Emergency Workers (Obstruction) Act* 2006, s.3(2)).

(4) Sentence

13–49   The maximum penalty for each offence is a fine not exceeding level 5 on the standard scale: section 3.

III. OFFENCES INVOLVING CHILDREN

A. ABANDONMENT OF CHILDREN UNDER TWO

(1) Definition

Offences Against the Person Act 1861, s.27

Exposing children whereby life is endangered

13–50   **27.** Whosoever shall unlawfully abandon or expose any child, being under the age of two years, whereby the life of such child shall be endangered, or the health of such child shall have been or shall be likely to be permanently injured, shall be guilty of a misdemeanor, and being convicted thereof shall be liable to imprisonment for a term not exceeding five years.

(2) Allocation

This offence is triable either way.   **13–51**

(3) Elements of the offence

The prosecution must prove that: **13–52**
- the defendant wilfully abandoned or exposed the child;
- that the child was then under two;
- that its life was thereby endangered or its health was likely to be permanently injured.

(4) Sentence

When tried summarily, the maximum penalty is six months' imprisonment, a fine **13–53** not exceeding the statutory maximum or both. After commencement of the relevant provisions, the maximum custodial sentence in a magistrates' court will be 12 months' imprisonment: *Criminal Justice Act* 2003, ss.154 and 282.

B. Child Cruelty

(1) Definition

Children and Young Persons Act 1933, s.1

Cruelty to persons under sixteen

1.—(1) If any person who has attained the age of sixteen years and has responsibility for any **13–54** child or young person under that age, wilfully assaults, ill-treats, neglects, abandons, or exposes him, or causes or procures him to be assaulted, ill-treated, neglected, abandoned, or exposed, in a manner likely to cause him unnecessary suffering or injury to health (including injury to or loss of sight, or hearing, or limb, or organ of the body, and any mental derangement), that person shall be guilty of a misdemeanour, and shall be liable—
- (a) on conviction on indictment, to a fine or alternatively, or in addition thereto, to imprisonment for any term not exceeding ten years;
- (b) on summary conviction, to a fine not exceeding £400 pounds, or alternatively,, or in addition thereto, to imprisonment for any term not exceeding six months.

(2) For the purposes of this section—
- (a) a parent or other person legally liable to maintain a child or young person, or the legal guardian of a child or young person, shall be deemed to have neglected him in a manner likely to cause injury to his health if he has failed to provide adequate food, clothing, medical aid or lodging for him, or if, having been unable otherwise to provide such food, clothing, medical aid or lodging, he has failed to take steps to procure it to be provided under the enactments applicable in that behalf;
- (b) where it is proved that the death of an infant under three years of age was caused by suffocation (not being suffocation caused by disease or the presence of any foreign body in the throat or air passages of the infant) while the infant was in bed with some other person who has attained the age of sixteen years, that other person shall, if he was, when he went to bed, under the influence of drink, be deemed to have neglected the infant in a manner likely to cause injury to its health.

(3) A person may be convicted of an offence under this section—
- (a) notwithstanding that actual suffering or injury to health, or the likelihood of actual suffering or injury to health, was obviated by the action of another person;
- (b) notwithstanding the death of the child or young person in question.

[This section is printed as amended by the *Children Act* 2004, Sched. 5.]

(2) Allocation

13–55   This offence is triable either way, when tried summarily, the *Children and Young Persons Act* 1933, s.14 has effect.

It is usual, unless one of the following factors is present, to try this offence summarily:
— neglect over a long period of time, even where the injury may not be substantial;
— injuries that exhibit a sadistic nature;
— where substantial injury is caused.

Children and Young Persons Act 1933, s.14

Mode of charging offences and limitation of time

13–56   **14.**—(1) Where a person is charged with committing any of the offences mentioned in the First Schedule to this Act in respect of two or more children or young persons, the same information or summons may charge the offence in respect of all or any of them, but the person charged shall not, if he is summarily convicted, be liable to a separate penalty in respect of each child or young person except upon separate information.

(2) The same information or summons may charge him with the offences of assault, ill-treatment, neglect, abandonment, or exposure, together or separately, and may charge him with committing all or any of those offences in a manner likely to cause unnecessary suffering or injury to health, alternatively or together, but when those offences are charged together the person charged shall not, if he is summarily convicted, be liable to a separate penalty for each.

(4) When any offence mentioned in the First Schedule to this Act charged against any person is a continuous offence, it shall not be necessary to specify in the information, summons, or indictment, the date of the acts constituting the offence.

(3) Elements of the offence

13–57   The prosecution must prove that:
– the defendant is 16 or over;
– he had responsibility for the child (under 16);
– he acts wilfully: see *Shepherd* [1981] A.C. 394;
– he assaults, ill-treats, neglects, etc. in a manner likely to cause unnecessary suffering or injury to health.

It is no mitigation that motivation of the defendant was a deluded belief that the child was possessed by spirits; such motivation did not reduce the culpability of such offences: *The Times*, March 17, 2006, CA

(4) Sentence

13–58   The maximum penalty is six months' imprisonment, a fine not exceeding the statutory maximum or both. After commencement of the relevant provisions, the maximum custodial sentence in a magistrates' court will be 12 months' imprisonment: *Criminal Justice Act* 2003, ss.154 and 282.

In *Weaver* [1998] 2 Cr.App.R.(S.) 56, a sentence of six years' imprisonment for neglect of a child by its mother which resulted in the death of the child was reduced to three years' imprisonment, and a sentence of three years' imprisonment for neglect of a child causing death by its father was reduced to two years' imprisonment. The mother pleaded guilty on the basis that she had failed to ensure that the child was adequately nourished, that she had failed to get medical attention when the child required it, that she had failed to keep the flat where they lived sufficiently clean, and that she had assaulted the child by slapping his thigh. The father pleaded guilty on the basis that he had failed to notice the child's declining condition and to ensure that something was done about it.

In *Harvey* [1987] 9 Cr.App.R.(S.) 524, a mother was convicted of four counts of cruelty to her children. The offender was frequently drunk and smoking cannabis; the family's living accommodation was not kept clean, pornographic material was left about, and the children were told about the appellant's sexual activities; the children were not kept clean and in some cases were denied affection. In one case the appellant failed to arrange medical attention when it was necessary. A sentence of nine months' imprisonment was upheld. A sentence of eight months' imprisonment was appropriate for a mother who has held an iron to the leg of her four-year-old son, despite the Court finding that the mother was an "inadequate young woman" (*per* Forbes, J.) who suffered considerable stress and isolation as a result of bringing up four small children: *Potova* [2004] 2 Cr.App.R.(S.) 32, CA.

In *Melanie O.* [2006] EWCA Crim 1158; [2007] 1 Cr.App.R. (S.) 15, CA, a sentence of fifteen months' imprisonment for neglect of three young children by allowing them to be outside unsupervised and inadequately clothed in cold weather was varied to six months. The Court of Appeal acknowledged that the appellant's addiction to crack cocaine was the root of the offences and stated that every alternative to custody had been explored before the original sentencing hearing. The Court further stated that the facts of the case involved only one incident, rather than a course of neglect, and there was no element of violence or injury to the children and no emotional or sexual abuse. The Court of Appeal described the case as on the cusp of the custody threshold, but found that the sentencing judge had no option but to pass a custodial sentence in view of the appellant's response to efforts by the probation service to consider alternatives to custody. However, a sentence of six months' imprisonment on each count concurrent would be appropriate.

The act of failing to seek medical assistance can amount to neglect for the purposes of **13–59** a charge under this section. In *S.* [1999] 1 Cr.App.R.(S.) 67, the offence was made out by the failure to seek medical help, and a sentence of four months imprisonment was imposed. In *Laut* [2002] 2 Cr.App.R.(S.) 7, the offender's child fell whilst holding the door of the washing machine closed on his mother's instructions. The offender had been warned on a previous occasion that such conduct was likely to result in injury to the child. The Court stated that its normal practice was not to impose a custodial sentence for a single, albeit wilful act of neglect. However, given the prior warning, the offender's conduct could be classed as a case of serious neglect and hence a sentence of imprisonment was justified. Her original sentence of four months' imprisonment was, however, reduced to 12 weeks.

The approach to sentencing for offences of child cruelty which involve violence to **13–60** young children was again considered by the Court of Appeal in two cases. In *Att.-Gen.'s Reference (No. 81 of 2004)* [2004] EWCA Crim 3315, the Court allowed an appeal against the imposition of a community rehabilitation order where the basis of the charge was the deliberate manhandling of a child aged 23 months. Although the offender had been suffering from post-traumatic stress following two serious assaults, "the only sentence that was appropriate ... was an immediate custodial sentence". A sentence of 18 months' imprisonment was substituted.

In *Faruk Ahmed* [2003] 1 Cr.App.R.(S.) 40, the position was set out as "Infants are entitled to care at the hands of those who, despite stresses and strains, can contain their temper and control unwelcome impulses. For an attack upon a child, custody will almost always be inevitable" (*per* Rafferty J. at para. 11 of his judgment).

C. CHILD ABDUCTION

(1) Definition

Child Abduction Act 1984, ss.1–2

Offence of abduction of child by parent, etc.

  1.—(1) Subject to subsections (5) and (8) below, a person connected with a child under the **13–61**

age of sixteen commits an offence if he takes or sends the child out of the United Kingdom without the appropriate consent.

(2) A person is connected with a child for the purposes of this section if—

    (a) he is a parent of the child; or

    (b) in the case of a child whose parents were not married to each other at the time of his birth, there are reasonable grounds for believing that he is the father of the child; or

    (c) he is a guardian of the child; or

    (ca) he is a special guardian of the child; or

    (d) he is a person in whose favour a residence order is in force with respect to the child; or

    (e) he has custody of the child.

(3) In this section 'the appropriate consent', in relation to a child, means—

    (a) the consent of each of the following—

        (i) the child's mother;

        (ii) the child's father, if he has parental responsibility for him;

        (iii) any guardian of the child;

        (iiia) any special guardian of the child;

        (iv) any person in whose favour a residence order is in force with respect to the child;

        (v) any person who has custody of the child; or

    (b) the leave of the court granted under or by virtue of any provision of Part II of the *Children Act* 1989; or

    (c) if any person has custody of the child, the leave of the court which awarded custody to him.

13–62   (4) A person does not commit an offence under this section by taking or sending a child out of the United Kingdom without obtaining the appropriate consent if—

    (a) he is a person in whose favour there is a residence order in force with respect to the child, and he takes or sends the child out of the United Kingdom for a period of less than one month; or

    (b) he is a special guardian of the child and he takes or sends the child out of the United Kingdom for a period of less than three months.

(4A) [...]

(5) A person does not commit an offence under this section by doing anything without the consent of another person whose consent is required under the foregoing provisions if—

    (a) he does it in the belief that the other person—

        (i) has consented; or

        (ii) would consent if he was aware of all the relevant circumstances; or

    (b) he has taken all reasonable steps to communicate with the other person but has been unable to communicate with him; or

    (c) the other person has unreasonably refused to consent.

(5A) Subsection (5)(c) above does not apply if—

    (a) the person who refused to consent is a person—

        (i) in whose favour there is a residence order in force with respect to the child;

        (ia) who is a special guardian of the child; or

        (ii) who has custody of the child; or

    (b) the person taking or sending the child out of the United Kingdom is, by so acting, in breach of an order made by a court in the United Kingdom.

(6) Where, in proceedings for an offence under this section, there is sufficient evidence to raise an issue as to the application of subsection (5) above, it shall be for the prosecution to prove that that subsection does not apply.

(7) For the purposes of this section—

    (a) "guardian of a child", "special guardian", "residence order" and "parental responsibility" have the same meaning as in the Children Act 1989; and

    (b) a person shall be treated as having custody of a child if there is in force an order of a court in the United Kingdom awarding him (whether solely or jointly with another person) custody, legal custody or care and control of the child.

(8) This section shall have effect subject to the provisions of the Schedule to this Act in relation to a child who is in the care of a local authority detained in a place of safety, remanded to a local authority accommodation or the subject of proceedings or an order relating to adoption.

[This section is printed as amended by the *Adoption and Children Act* 2002, Sched. 3.]

Offence of abduction of child by other persons

2.—(1) Subject to subsection (3) below, a person, other than one mentioned in subsection (2) **13–63** below. commits an offence if, without lawful authority or reasonable excuse, he takes or detains a child under the age of sixteen—

    (a) so as to remove him from the lawful control of any person having lawful control of the child; or

    (b) so as to keep him out of the lawful control of any person entitled to lawful control of the child.

[(2) The persons are—

    (a) where the father and mother of the child in question were married to each other at the time of his birth, the child's father and mother;

    (b) where the father and mother of the child in question were not married to each other at the time of his birth, the child's mother; and

    (c) any other person mentioned in section 1(2)(c) to (e) above.

(3) In proceedings against any person for an offence under this section, it shall be a defence for that person to prove—

    (a) where the father and mother of the child in question were not married to each other at the time of his birth—

        (i) that he is the child's father; or

        (ii) that, at the time of the alleged offence, he believed, on reasonable grounds, that he was the child's father; or

    (b) that, at the time of the alleged offence, he believed that the child had attained the age of sixteen.

(2) Allocation

The offence under section 1 is triable either way. The consent of the DPP is required **13–64** before a prosecution under section 1 of the Act can be brought: *Child Abduction Act* 1984, s.(4)(1).

The offence under section 2 is also triable either way, though there is no need to obtain the DPP's consent before a prosecution can proceed.

(3) Elements of the offence

The prosecution must prove that: **13–65**

    – the defendant caused the child to accompany him;

    – the child was thus removed from the control of his lawful guardian;

    – that the child is under 16;

    – the defendant intended to keep the child.

An offence under section 2(1)(a) of the *Child Abduction Act* 1984 requires that at the time when the child was taken or detained he was in the lawful control of someone: *Foster v. DPP* [2005] 1 W.L.R. 1400. A defendant who believes that a child is over 16 will have a defence to a charge under section 2 of the 1984 Act: *ibid.*

(4) Sentence

The maximum penalty is six months' imprisonment, a fine not exceeding level five **13–66** on the standard scale or both. After commencement of the relevant provisions, the maximum custodial sentence in a magistrates' court will be 12 months' imprisonment: *Criminal Justice Act* 2003, ss.154 and 282.

IV. HARASSMENT OFFENCES

A. HARASSMENT

(1) Definition

Protection from Harassment Act 1997, ss.1–2

Prohibition of harassment

13–67   **1.**—(1) A person must not pursue a course of conduct—

    (a) which amounts to harassment of another, and

    (b) which he knows or ought to know amounts to harassment of the other.

(1A) A person must not pursue a course of conduct—

    (a) which involves harassment of two or more persons, and

    (b) which he knows or ought to know involves harassment of those persons, and

    (c) by which he intends to persuade any person (whether or not one of those mentioned above)—

        (i) not to do something that he is entitled or required to do, or

        (ii) to do something that he is not under any obligation to do;

(2) For the purposes of this section, the person whose course of conduct is in question ought to know that it amounts to or involves harassment of another if a reasonable person in possession of the same information would think the course of conduct amounted to or involved harassment of the other.

(3) Subsection (1) or subsection (1A) does not apply to a course of conduct if the person who pursued it shows—

    (a) that it was pursued for the purpose of preventing or detecting crime,

    (b) that it was pursued under any enactment or rule of law or to comply with any condition or requirement imposed by any person under any enactment, or

    (c) that in the particular circumstances the pursuit of the course of conduct was reasonable.

Offence of harassment

13–68   **2.**—(1) A person who pursues a course of conduct in breach of section 1 or (1A) is guilty of an offence.

(2) A person guilty of an offence under this section is liable on summary conviction to imprisonment for a term not exceeding six months, or a fine not exceeding level 5 on the standard scale, or both.

[This section is printed as amended by the *Serious Organised Crime and Police Act* 2005, s.125.]

For the racially or religiously aggravated from of this offence, see *post*, § 13–76: *Crime and Disorder Act* 1998, s.32.

(2) Allocation

13–69   The basic form of the offence is triable summarily only: section 2(2). The racially or religiously aggravated form of the offence is triable either way.

(3) Elements of the offence

Protection from Harassment Act 1997, s.7

Interpretation of this group of sections

13–70   **7.**—(1) This section applies for the interpretation of sections 1 to 5

(2) References to harassing a person include alarming the person or causing the person distress.

(3) A "course of conduct" must involve—

    (a) in the case of conduct in relation to a single person (see section 1(1)), conduct on at least two occasions in relation to that person, or

(b) in the case of conduct in relation to two or more persons (see section 1(1A)), conduct on at least one occasion in relation to each of those persons.

(3A) A person's conduct on any occasion shall be taken, if aided, abetted, counselled or procured by another—

(a) to be conduct on that occasion of the other (as well as conduct of the person whose conduct it is); and

(b) to be conduct in relation to which the other's knowledge and purpose, and what he ought to have known, are the same as they were in relation to what was contemplated or reasonably foreseeable at the time of the aiding, abetting, counselling or procuring.

(4) "Conduct" includes speech.

(5) References to a person, in the context of the harassment of a person, are references to a person who is an individual.

[This section is printed as amended by the *Serious Organised Crime and Police Act* 2005, s.125(7)(b).]

Proof of two incidents can establish the offence, yet the fewer the occasions and the **13–71** wider they are spread the less likely they are to result in a finding of harassment: *Lau v. DPP* (2000) 1 F.L.R. 799. The stalking type of behaviour at which this Act was intended was "miles away" from a prosecution based on two incidents six months apart between two people who were partners and lived together: *Hills* [2001] 1 F.L.R. 580, CA.

Three threatening and abusive telephone calls made consecutively can amount to a course of conduct, even though the victim listened to all three messages together, and was hence only distressed on one occasion: *Kelly v. DPP* (2002) 166 J.P. 621.

In *Singh v. Bhakar and Bhakar* (2006) 150 S.J. 112, Nottingham County Court, the court found that conduct by the mother-in-law of a devout Sikh (who was living with her husband's family) which included forcing her to depart from Sikh practice, having to do excessive and pointless housework, controlling her contact with her family and isolating her generally was "more than enough" to amount to harassment within sections 1 and 7 of the *Protection from Harassment Act* 1997.

When addressing the question of lawful conduct as a defence to charges under section 2 of the 1997 Act, it has been established that conduct in contravention of an injunction designed to prevent it cannot be reasonable: *DPP v. Selvanayagam, The Times*, June 23, 1999, DC.

Where the course of conduct lasted two years and eight months, section 127 of the **13–72** *Magistrates' Courts Act* 1980 is not violated so long as at least one incident occurred within the six month limitation period. Evidence prior to the six-month limitation period could be admitted as "highly relevant" background evidence: *DPP v. Baker* (2005) 169 J.P.N. 78.

(4) Sentence

As regards the basic offence, the maximum penalty is six months' imprisonment, a **13–73** fine not exceeding level five on the standard scale or both: section 2(2). After commencement of the relevant provisions, the maximum custodial sentence in a magistrates' court will be 12 months' imprisonment: *Criminal Justice Act* 2003, ss.154 and 282. The *Magistrates' Court Sentencing Guidelines* (2004) provide that the same considerations apply as for an offence under section 4 of the 1997 Act, with the guideline starting point being a community penalty.

As regards the racially or religiously aggravated form of the offence, when tried summarily the maximum penalty is six months' imprisonment, a fine not exceeding the statutory maximum or both. After commencement of the relevant provisions, the maximum custodial sentence in a magistrates' court will be 12 months' imprisonment: *Criminal Justice Act* 2003, ss.154 and 282.

In *Wells* [2006] EWCA Crim 610, CA, a sentence of 12 months' imprisonment was held appropriate for an offence of racially aggravated harassment where the offender had sent four voicemail messages to a neighbour in which he described her, among other things, as a "Jewish cunt bitch". The victim was left feeling shaken and scared to live at her home address. The Court of Appeal stated that the offence was extremely unpleasant, and its effect on the victim should not be overlooked. However, given the appellant's early guilty plea and the comparatively short duration of the offence, a sentence of 15 months was too long, and a sentence of 12 months' imprisonment was appropriate. The court may also make a restraining order: under section 5 or section 32(7).

Protection from Harassment Act 1997 s.5

Restraining orders.

13–74　　**5.**—(1) A court sentencing or otherwise dealing with a person ("the defendant") convicted of an offence under section 2 or 4 may (as well as sentencing him or dealing with him in any other way) make an order under this section.

(2) The order may, for the purpose of protecting the victim or victims of the offence, or any other person mentioned in the order, from further conduct which

(a) amounts to harassment, or

(b) will cause a fear of violence,

prohibit the defendant from doing anything described in the order.

(3) The order may have effect for a specified period or until further order.

(4) The prosecutor, the defendant or any other person mentioned in the order may apply to the court which made the order for it to be varied or discharged by a further order.

(5) If without reasonable excuse the defendant does anything which he is prohibited from doing by an order under this section, he is guilty of an offence.

(6) A person guilty of an offence under this section is liable

(a) on conviction on indictment, to imprisonment for a term not exceeding five years, or a fine, or both, or

(b) on summary conviction, to imprisonment for a term not exceeding six months, or a fine not exceeding the statutory maximum, or both.

[This section is printed as amended by the *Serious Organised Crime and Police Act* (2005 c.15), Pt 4, s.125(6).]

B. PUTTING PEOPLE IN FEAR OF VIOLENCE

(1) Definition

Protection from Harassment Act 1997, s.4

Putting people in fear of violence

13–75　　**4.**—(1) A person whose course of conduct causes another to fear, on at least two occasions, that violence will be used against him is guilty of an offence if he knows or ought to know that his course of conduct will cause the other so to fear on each of those occasions.

(2) For the purposes of this section, the person whose course of conduct is in question ought to know that it will cause another to fear that violence will be used against him on any occasion if a reasonable person in possession of the same information would think the course of conduct would cause the other so to fear on that occasion.

(3) It is a defence for a person charged with an offence under this section to show that—

(a) his course of conduct was pursued for the purpose of preventing or detecting crime,

(b) his course of conduct was pursued under any enactment or rule of law or to comply with any condition or requirement imposed by any person under any enactment, or

(c) the pursuit of his course of conduct was reasonable for the protection of himself or another or for the protection of his or another's property.

(4) A person guilty of an offence under this section is liable—

(a) on conviction on indictment, to imprisonment for a term not exceeding five years, or a fine, or both, or

(b) on summary conviction, to imprisonment for a term not exceeding six months, or a fine not exceeding the statutory maximum, or both.

(5) If on the trial on indictment of a person charged with an offence under this section the jury find him not guilty of the offence charged, they may find him guilty of an offence under section 2

(6) The Crown Court has the same powers and duties in relation to a person who is by virtue of subsection (5) convicted before it of an offence under section 2 as a magistrates' court would have on convicting him of the offence.

Crime and Disorder Act 1998, s.32

Racially or religiously aggravated harassment etc.

32.—(1) A person is guilty of an offence under this section if he commits—   **13–76**

    (a) an offence under section 2 of the *Protection from Harassment Act* 1997 (offence of harassment); or

    (b) an offence under section 4 of that Act (putting people in fear of violence), which is racially or religiously aggravated for the purposes of this section.

(3) A person guilty of an offence falling within subsection (1)(a) above shall be liable—

    (a) on summary conviction, to imprisonment for a term not exceeding six months or to a fine not exceeding the statutory maximum, or to both;

    (b) on conviction on indictment, to imprisonment for a term not exceeding two years or to a fine, or to both.

(4) A person guilty of an offence falling within subsection (1)(b) above shall be liable—

    (a) on summary conviction, to imprisonment for a term not exceeding six months or to a fine not exceeding the statutory maximum, or to both;

    (b) on conviction on indictment, to imprisonment for a term not exceeding seven years or to a fine, or to both.

(2) Allocation

Both forms of the offence are triable either way: *Protection from Harassment Act* **13–77** 1997, s.4(4) and *Crime and Disorder Act* 1998, s.32(4).

In general, summary trial is appropriate except where one or more of the following factors is present:

— racial motivation,

— a course of conduct over a long period of time,

— where the victim was particularly vulnerable.

(3) Elements of the offence

The prosecution must prove: **13–78**

    – a course of conduct which causes another to fear, on at least two occasions, violence against him;

    – that the defendant knew or ought to have known that his course of conduct would have caused fear or each occasion.

See also *ante*, § 13–70 for interpretation provisions.

(4) Sentence

Note that section 12 of the *Domestic Violence, Crime and Victims Act* 2004 contains **13–79** a number of amendments to section 5 of the *Protection from Harassment Act* 1997 (restraining orders). In particular, when this provision is brought into force, the court will be able to impose a restraining order following an acquittal, where the court considers it necessary to do so to protect a person from harassment.

As regards the basic offence, when tried summarily the maximum penalty is six **13–80** months' imprisonment, a fine not exceeding the statutory maximum or both. The court may also impose a restraining order upon an offender convicted of an offence under section 4: *Protection from Harassment Act* 1997, s.5. After the commencement of the

Part III

relevant provisions, the maximum custodial sentence in a magistrates' court will be 12 months' imprisonment: *Criminal Justice Act* 2003, ss.154 and 282.

The *Magistrates' Court Sentencing Guidelines* (2004) state:

> Aggravating factors include disregard of warning, excessive persistence, interference with employment/business, invasion of victims home, involvement of others, threat to use weapons or substance (including realistic imitations), use of violence or grossly offensive material, where photographs or images of a personal nature are involved, offence committed on bail, relevant previous convictions and any failures to respond to previous sentences.
>
> Mitigating factors include initial provocation and short duration.
>
> **Guideline**: Is it so serious that only custody is appropriate?

13–81   As regards the racially or religiously aggravated form of the offence, when tried summarily the maximum penalty is six months' imprisonment, a fine not exceeding the statutory maximum or both. After commencement of the relevant provisions, the maximum custodial sentence in a magistrates' court will be 12 months' imprisonment: *Criminal Justice Act* 2003, ss.154 and 282.

The *Magistrates Courts' Sentencing Guidelines* provide the same guideline as for the basic form of the offence.

Where the offender has previously breached a court order or has been convicted for the same offence previously, it is usual for the magistrates to commit for sentence: *Liddle* [2000] 1 Cr.App.R.(S.) 131.

A restraining order may be granted in respect of a conviction under this section subject to the usual requirements for an order of this type. Breach of a restraining order without reasonable excuse is an offence punishable by imprisonment: section 5.

C. DIRECTIONS STOPPING HARASSMENT

(1) Definitions

Criminal Justice and Police Act 2001, s.42

Police directions stopping the harassment etc of

13–82   **42.**—(1) Subject to the following provisions of this section, a constable who is at the scene may give a direction under this section to any person if—

   (a) that person is present outside or in the vicinity of any premises that are used by any individual ("the resident") as his dwelling;

   (b) that constable believes, on reasonable grounds, that that person is present there for the purpose (by his presence or otherwise) of representing to the resident or another individual (whether or not one who uses the premises as his dwelling), or of persuading the resident or such another individual—

     (i) that he should not do something that he is entitled or required to do; or

     (ii) that he should do something that he is not under any obligation to do; and

   (c) that constable also believes, on reasonable grounds, that the presence of that person (either alone or together with that of any other persons who are also present)—

     (i) amounts to, or is likely to result in, the harassment of the resident; or

     (ii) is likely to cause alarm or distress to the resident.

   (2) A direction under this section is a direction requiring the person to whom it is given to do all such things as the constable giving it may specify as the things he considers necessary to prevent one or both of the following—

   (a) the harassment of the resident; or

   (b) the causing of any alarm or distress to the resident.

   (3) A direction under this section may be given orally; and where a constable is entitled to give a direction under this section to each of several persons outside, or in the vicinity of, any premises, he may give that direction to those persons by notifying them of his requirements either individually or all together.

   (4) The requirements that may be imposed by a direction under this section include—

   (a) a requirement to leave the vicinity of the premises in question, and

(b) a requirement to leave that vicinity and not to return to it within such period as
the constable may specify, not being longer than 3 months;
and (in either case) the requirement to leave the vicinity may be to do so immediately or after a
specified period of time.

(5) A direction under this section may make exceptions to any requirement imposed by
the direction, and may make any such exception subject to such conditions as the constable
giving the direction thinks fit; and those conditions may include—

(a) conditions as to the distance from the premises in question at which, or otherwise
as to the location where, persons who do not leave their vicinity must remain;
and

(b) conditions as to the number or identity of the persons who are authorised by the
exception to remain in the vicinity of those premises.

(6) The power of a constable to give a direction under this section shall not include—

(a) any power to give a direction at any time when there is a more senior-ranking
police officer at the scene; or

(b) any power to direct a person to refrain from conduct that is lawful under section
220 of the *Trade Union and Labour Relations (Consolidation) Act* 1992 (c. 52)
(right peacefully to picket a work place); but it shall include power to vary or withdraw
a direction previously given under this section.

(7) Any person who knowingly fails to comply with a requirement in a direction given
to him under this section (other than a requirement under subsection (4)(b)) shall be guilty
of an offence and liable, on summary conviction, to imprisonment for a term not exceeding three months or to a fine not exceeding level 4 on the standard scale, or to both.

(7A) Any person to whom a constable has given a direction including a requirement
under subsection (4)(b) commits an offence if he—

(a) returns to the vicinity of the premises in question within the period specified in
the direction beginning with the date on which the direction is given; and

(b) does so for the purpose described in subsection (1)(b).

(7B) A person guilty of an offence under subsection (7A) shall be liable, on summary
conviction, to imprisonment for a term not exceeding 51 weeks or to a fine not exceeding
level 4 on the standard scale, or to both.

(7C) In relation to an offence committed before the commencement of section 281(5) of
the *Criminal Justice Act* 2003 (alteration of penalties for summary offences), the reference in
subsection (7B) to 51 weeks is to be read as a reference to 6 months;

(9) In this section "dwelling" has the same meaning as in Part 1 of the *Public Order Act*
1986 (c. 64).

[This section is printed as amended by the *Serious Organised Crime and Police Act*
2005, Sched. 15.]

(2) Allocation

Both offences in this section are triable summarily only: section 42(7), 42(7B).   **13–83**

(3) Elements of the offence

There are two offences; failure to comply with a direction and returning to the vicin- **13–84**
ity to harass. In respect of each the prosecution must prove:

— A direction was issued by a constable
— The nature of the requirements of the direction
— That the direction was communicated to the individuals or a group
— That the defendant knowingly failed to comply with a requirement in the direc-
tion OR in the case of an offence under section 42 (4) (b) that the defendant
returned to the vicinity within the prohibited period in order to harass.

A direction cannot be made when there is peaceful picketing in furtherance of a
trade dispute.

(4) Sentence

For the offence of knowingly failing to comply with a direction the sentence is a **13–85**
period of imprisonment up to three months or a fine up to level 4.

For the offence of returning to the vicinity the sentence is a period of imprisonment up to 51 weeks or a fine up to level 4.

D. Harassment in the Home

(1) Definitions

Criminal Justice and Police Act 2001, s.42A

Offence of harassment etc. of a person in his home

13–86   **42A.**—(1) A person commits an offence if—

     (a) that person is present outside or in the vicinity of any premises that are used by any individual ("the resident") as his dwelling;

     (b) that person is present there for the purpose (by his presence or otherwise) of representing to the resident or another individual (whether or not one who uses the premises as his dwelling), or ofpersuading the resident or such another individual—

         (i) that he should not do something that he is entitled or required to do; or

         (ii) that he should do something that he is not under any obligation to do;

     (c) that person—

         (i) intends his presence to amount to the harassment of, or to cause alarm or distress to, the resident; or

         (ii) knows or ought to know that his presence is likely to result in the harassment of, or to cause alarm or distress to, the resident; and

     (d) the presence of that person—

         (i) amounts to the harassment of, or causes alarm or distress to, any person falling within subsection (2); or

         (ii) is likely to result in the harassment of, or to cause alarm or distress to, any such person.

(2) A person falls within this subsection if he is—

     (a) the resident,

     (b) a person in the resident's dwelling, or

     (c) a person in another dwelling in the vicinity of the resident's dwelling.

(3) The references in subsection (1)(c) and (d) to a person's presence are references to his presence either alone or together with that of any other persons who are also present.

(4) For the purposes of this section a person (A) ought to know that his presence is likely to result in the harassment of, or to cause alarm or distress to, a resident if a reasonable person in possession of the same information would think that A's presence was likely to have that effect.

(5) A person guilty of an offence under this section shall be liable, on summary conviction, to imprisonment for a term not exceeding 51 weeks or to a fine not exceeding level 4 on the standard scale, or to both.

(6) In relation to an offence committed before the commencement of section 281(5) of the *Criminal Justice Act* 2003 (alteration of penalties for summary offences), the reference in subsection (5) to 51 weeks is to be read as a reference to 6 months.

(7) In this section "dwelling" has the same meaning as in Part 1 of the *Public Order Act* 1986.

[This section is printed as inserted by the *Serious Organised Crime and Police Act* 2005, s.126.]

(2) Allocation

13–87   The offence is triable summarily: section 42A(5).

(3) Elements of the offence

13–88   The prosecution must prove that:

     — Premises are the dwelling of any individual (the resident)

- The defendant is outside or in the vicinity of the dwelling
- His purpose (by his presence or otherwise) is to represent to or persuade the resident or any individual not to do something he is entitled or required to do OR to do something he is not obliged to do
- AND
- The defendant intends his presence to amount to harassment alarm or distress to the resident AND
- The presence of the defendant amounts to or is likely to cause harassment alarm or distress to the resident or any person in the dwelling or any person in the vicinity of the resident's dwelling.

(4) Sentence

The maximum sentence is 51 weeks' imprisonment or a fine up to level 4: section **13–89**
42A(5).

E. Threats to Kill

(a) *Definition*

Offences Against the Person Act 1861, s.16

Threats to kill
16.—   A person who without lawful excuse makes to another a threat, intending that that **13–90**
other would fear it would be carried out, to kill that other or a third person shall be guilty of an offence and liable on conviction on indictment to imprisonment for a term not exceeding ten years.

(b) *Procedure*

This offence is triable either way.   **13–91**

(c) *Elements of the offence*

"Maliciously" means wilfully or intentionally and without lawful excuse. In *Solanke* **13–92**
[1970] 1 W.L.R. 1, CA, the appellant sent a letter threatening to murder his wife to his probation officer. The Court of Appeal upheld his conviction under section 16, holding that that so long as the sender of a letter acts intentionally with full knowledge of its contents and without lawful excuse, he does so "maliciously" and it is unnecessary to look for an ulterior evil motive. Implied threats can amount to a threat to kill: *Solanke, ibid.* Evidence of a previous assault is admissible as tending to prove that the accused intended his victim to take the threat seriously: *Williams* (1987) 84 Cr.App.R. 299, CA.

It is the person to whom the threat is made that must believe that the threat will be carried out, not the person to be killed. A threat to a pregnant woman to kill her unborn baby before its birth will not fall under section 16, as a foetus in utero is not a person distinct from its mother; there is thus no threat to kill a third person contrary to section 16: *Tait* [1990] 1 Q.B. 290, CA. However, it would seem that a threat to kill a child after its birth at a time when it was still a foetus was an offence under section 16: *Tait, ibid.*

The prosecution must prove that there was no lawful excuse. A lawful excuse could exist if a threat to kill was made for the prevention of crime or self-defence, provided that it was reasonable in the circumstances to make such a threat: *Cousins* [1982] Q.B. 526, CA.

(d) *Sentence*

As threatening to kill is a serious specified offence for the purposes of sections 225– **13–93**
229 of the *Criminal Justice Act* 2003, a court should consider whether to commit the offender to the Crown Court for sentence.

In *Hull* (1992) 13 Cr.App.R. (S.) 223 the Court of Appeal recognised the breadth of circumstances in which threats to kill may be made, and provided guidance on factors to take into consideration when sentencing. Lord Justice Bedlam stated:

> "threats to kill are made in many differing circumstances. It is the circumstances and the effect which the threat has, whether they are really intended to be carried out and the surrounding facts which determine the sentence which is appropriate in a given case. Sometimes threats are made by a person who is under emotional stress or a person suffering from depression. Sometimes it is clear that the threat is an idle threat, and is realised by the victim to be an idle threat. Sometimes the threat is accompanied by the flourish of a weapon which adds to the effect it had on the victim. Sometimes, after the threat, remorse is expressed. All these are circumstances which the court takes into account."

Choudhury [1997] 2 Cr.App.R. (S.) 300, CA gives an example of a less serious offence under section 16. The offender had been arrested for a public order offence, and after being released on bail, sat on a wall outside the police station. When the officers left the police station the appellant shouted at one of them "you're a dead man". The appellant then addressed the officer in Punjabi, which the officer understood, threatening to kill him and his family. The Court of Appeal held that this was not the most serious of its kind and a sentence of two years' imprisonment would be appropriate.

In *Williams* [2006] EWCA Crim 2565 the appellant had been drinking heavily all day and got into an argument with a passer-by. The passer-by threatened the appellant, who then lost his temper, and began searching for knives in his former partner's home to attack the victim. This frightened his former partner so much that she locked all the doors and windows of the house to prevent him leaving, and called the police. When the police arrested the appellant, he said "you better get my right name for that, I was going to stab him. Good job you showed up or I'd be banged up for murder." He later said he had been wound up by the passer-by and had no intention of carrying out the threats and he was acting in bravado. The Court of Appeal reduced his sentence of three years' imprisonment to two years, after finding that the passer-by played a significant part in bringing about the loss of self-control, and never took these threats seriously, however much they were to be deplored.

In *S.M.* [2003] EWCA Crim 2683, CA, a sentence of three years' imprisonment was held appropriate where a father claimed to be taking his child to school, yet took her on a long journey, during which he made phonecalls to the child's mother stating he would only return the child if the mother agreed to meet him, and made statements which the court found to be calculated to convince the mother that the threat to the child was real and imminent. The threat lasted from 10.40 when the child was taken to 14.50 when the appellant was arrested. The victim had no doubt that this was a real threat and had contacted the police. The Court of Appeal held that the fact that the threat was elliptical made it no less convincing, and upon arrest there was no display of remorse, the father offering a false exculpatory account for his actions.

SEXUAL OFFENCES

Part III

I. SEXUAL OFFENCES

Introduction—the old and new law

14–1   The *Sexual Offences Act* 2003 substantially reformed the law relating to sexual offences. It came into force on May 1, 2004 and created many new offences. The new offences are dealt with in *post*, §§ 14–78 *et seq*. Whilst the 2003 Act did not repeal all earlier legislation in this area, most of the old legislation was either repealed or amended. As the old offences may still be the subject of proceedings in the courts, they are dealt with in this chapter but readers are urged to bear in mind that many "old" offences were repealed on May 1, 2004 and therefore can only be used to prosecute offences committed before that date.

II. OFFENCES PRIOR TO THE INTRODUCTION OF THE SEXUAL OFFENCES ACT 2003

A. SEXUAL INTERCOURSE WITH A GIRL UNDER SIXTEEN

(1) Definition

Sexual Offences Act 1956, s.6

Intercourse with girl between thirteen and sixteen

6.—(1) It is an offence, subject to the exceptions mentioned in this section, for a man to have **14–2** unlawful sexual intercourse with a girl under the age of sixteen.

(2) Where a marriage is invalid under section two of the *Marriage Act* 1949, or section one of the *Age of Marriage Act* 1929 (the wife being a girl under the age of sixteen), the invalidity does not make the husband guilty of an offence under this section because he has sexual intercourse with her, if he believes her to be his wife and has reasonable cause for the belief.

(3) A man is not guilty of an offence under this section because he has unlawful sexual intercourse with a girl under the age of sixteen, if he is under the age of twenty-four and has not previously been charged with a like offence, and he believes her to be of the age of sixteen or over and has reasonable cause for the belief.

In this subsection, "a like offence" means an offence under this section or an attempt to commit one, or an offence under paragraph (1) of section five of the *Criminal Law Amendment Act* 1885 (the provision replaced for England and Wales by this Section).

[This section is printed as amended by the *CLA* 1967, s.10(1) and Sched. 2, para. 14. It was repealed by the *Sexual Offences Act* 2003, Sched. 7, on May 1, 2004.]

Section 6 applies to sexual intercourse with a girl aged 13 or over but under 16.

(2) Allocation

This offence is triable either way. The *Consolidated Criminal Practice Direction* (see **14–3** F–55–F–56) provides that cases of unlawful sexual intercourse should be tried summarily unless the court considers that one or more of the following features are present and that its sentencing powers are insufficient:

(a) Wide disparity of age;

(b) Breach of position of trust;

(c) The victim is particularly vulnerable.

(3) Sentence

When tried summarily, the maximum penalty for this offence is six months' imprison- **14–4** ment, a fine not exceeding the statutory maximum or both: *Sexual Offences Act* 1956, s.37 and Sched. 2; *Magistrates' Courts Act* 1980, s.32.

In *Taylor* 64 Cr.App.R 182, CA the Court laid down guidelines for sentencing people convicted of this offence. Lawton L.J. referred to the wide spectrum of guilt covered by the offence known as having unlawful sexual intercourse with a girl under the age of sixteen. He distinguished cases of "virtuous friendship" between two people of a similar age and the case where the man in a supervisory capacity sets out deliberately to seduce a girl under the age of 16 who is in his charge. In the first type of case it would be inappropriate to pass sentences of a punitive nature. As regards the second a sentence near the maximum allowed by law would be appropriate. In between there are many degrees of guilt. Lawton L.J. gave the example of a common type of offender being the youth who picks up a girl of loose morals at a dance, takes her out into the local park and, behind the bushes, has sexual intercourse with her. That is the kind of offence that would normally be dealt with by a fine.

In *Att.-Gen.'s Reference (No. 80 of 2000)* [2001] 2 Cr.App.R.(S.) 12, the Attorney General sought leave to refer a sentence of 100 hours' community service imposed for one offence of indecent assault and four offences of unlawful sexual intercourse on account of it being unduly lenient. The victim was 13 years old when they began a consensual sexual relationship. The sentence was held to be too lenient and a period of imprisonment of at least 12 months' should have been imposed.

In *Reeves* [2002] 1 Cr.App.R.(S.) 15 the Court of Appeal held that a sentence of two years' imprisonment imposed for indecently assaulting a 15-year old girl should be reduced to 18 months to provide the offender with a discount for his plea of guilty.

A case at the bottom end of the scale was *Cooke* (1979) 1 Cr.App.R.(S.) 325. The offender pleaded guilty to one act of unlawful sexual intercourse with a girl aged 14 years and 10 months who was sexually experienced and looked older than her true age. A sentence of six months' imprisonment was substituted for the original sentence of nine months' imprisonment. In *Wood* (1990) 12 Cr.App.R.(S.) 129, the offender admitted unlawful sexual intercourse with the 15-year-old daughter of the woman he had been living with for a number of years. He was sentenced to nine months' imprisonment. In *Wong* [2001] All E.R. (D.) 162 (May) the offender pleaded guilty on the basis that the girl instigated the offence and he admitted being reckless as to whether the girl was 15 or 16. He was sentenced to three months' imprisonment.

In *Cronshaw* [2004] EWCA Crim 2057, earlier authorities were reviewed and guidance given on sentencing a defendant who has been convicted of both unlawful sexual intercourse and indecent assault. Where the indecent assaults are no more than unlawful sexual intercourse, the maximum penalty that should be imposed is two years, *i.e.* the maximum penalty for unlawful sexual intercourse (and not 10 years, the maximum penalty for indecent assault).

See also *O'Grady* (1978) 66 Cr.App.R.(S.) 279 and *Harding* (1979) 1 Cr.App.R.(S.) 160.

B. GROSS INDECENCY

(1) Definition

Sexual Offences Act 1956, s.13

Indecency between men

14–5   13. It is an offence for a man to commit an act of gross indecency with another man otherwise than in the circumstances described below, whether in public or private, or to be a party to the commission by a man of an act of gross indecency with another man, or to procedure the commission by a man of an act of gross indecency with another man.

The circumstances referred to above are that the man is under the age of sixteen and the other man has attained that age.

[This section is printed as amended by the *Sexual Offences (Amendment) Act* 2000, s.2(2)(a) and (b) and was repealed by the *Sexual Offences Act* 2003, Sched. 7, para. 1 on May 1, 2004.]

14–6   Gross Indecency is no longer an offence when committed in private by two consenting persons over the age of sixteen: *Sexual Offences Act* 1967, ss.1 and 4(3). Sections 1 and 4 of the *Sexual Offences Act* 1967 are repealed by the *Sexual Offences Act* 2003, Sched. 7.

In *ADT v. UK* (2001) 31 E.H.R.R. 33, the European Court of Human Rights held unanimously that the very existence of legislation relating to gross indecency between two men was in breach of Article 8. It follows that charges should no longer be brought for buggery or gross indecency between consenting adults, even if those offences were committed prior to the implementation of the *Sexual Offences Act* 2003.

(2) Allocation

14–7   This offence is triable either way. Proceedings may not be instituted after the expiration of 12 months since the commission of the offence: *Sexual Offences Act* 1967, s.7. Where either man was under 16 years of age at the time of the offence, proceedings may not be instituted without the consent of the DPP: *SOA* 1967, s.8.

(3) Elements of the offence

There is no need for physical contact between the men, but both must participate.   **14–8**

(4) Sentence

When tried summarily, the maximum penalty for this offence is six months imprison-   **14–9**
ment, a fine not exceeding the statutory maximum or both: *SOA* 1956, Sched. 2.

The guideline judgment for this offence is *Morgan and Dockerty* (CSP B4–92001)
where Lawton L.J. stated that in general, first time offenders using public lavatories and
behaving in this sort of way in them do not get sent to prison. They are generally fined.
The offenders' sentences of three months and six weeks' imprisonment were varied to
fines of £100 and £50 respectively.

In *Clayton* (1981) 3 Cr.App.R.(S.) 67 the offenders were sentenced to four months'
imprisonment, recommended in one case for deportation. These sentences were
replaced with fines of £50 on appeal, Eastham J. describing the original sentences as
excessive, and stating that the appropriate penalty for men of hitherto good character
should be a financial penalty.

C. PERMITTING GIRLS TO USE PREMISES FOR UNLAWFUL SEXUAL INTERCOURSE

(1) Definition

Sexual Offences Act 1956, s.26

Permitting girl between thirteen and sixteen to use premises for intercourse
26. It is an offence for a person who is the owner or occupier of any premises, or who has, or   **14–10**
acts or assists in, the management or control of any premises, to induce or knowingly suffer a
girl under the age of sixteen, to resort to or be on those premises for the purposes of having
unlawful sexual intercourse with men or with a particular man.

[Repealed by the *Sexual Offences Act* 2003, Sched. 7, on May 1, 2004.]

(2) Allocation

This offence is triable either way.   **14–11**

(3) Sentence

When tried summarily, the maximum penalty for this offence is six months' imprison-   **14–12**
ment, a fine not exceeding the statutory maximum or both: *Sexual Offences Act* 1956,
s.37 and Sched. 2 and *Magistrates' Courts Act* 1980, s.32.

D. INDECENT ASSAULT

(1) Definition

Sexual Offences Act 1956, ss.14–15

Indecent assault on a woman
14.—(1) It is an offence, subject to the exception mentioned in subsection (3) of this section,   **14–13**
for a person to make an indecent assault on a woman.

(2) A girl under the age of sixteen cannot in law give any consent which would prevent
an act being an assault for the purposes of this section.

(3) Where a marriage is invalid under section two of the *Marriage Act* 1949, or section
one of the *Age of Marriage Act* 1929 (the wife being a girl under the age of sixteen), the invalidity does not make the husband guilty of any offence under this section by reason of her
incapacity to consent while under that age, if he believes her to be his wife and has reasonable
cause for the belief.

(4) A woman who is a defective cannot in law give any consent which would prevent an act being an assault for the purposes of this section, but a person is only to be treated as guilty of an indecent assault on a defective by reasons of that incapacity to consent, if that person knew or had reason to suspect her to be a defective.

Indecent assault on a man

14–14   **15.**—(1) It is an offence for a person to make an indecent assault on a man.

(2) A boy under the age of sixteen cannot in law give any consent which would Prevent an act being an assault for the purposes of this section.

(3) A man who is a defective cannot in law give any consent which would prevent an act being an assault for the purposes of this section, but a persons is only to be treated as guilty of an indecent assault on a defective by reason of that incapacity to consent, if that person knew or had reason to suspect him to be a defective

[Sections 14 and 15 were repealed by the *Sexual Offences Act* 2003, Sched. 7, on May 1, 2004.]

(2) Allocation

14–15   This offence is triable either way. The *Consolidated Criminal Practice Direction* (see F–55–F–56) provides that cases of unlawful sexual intercourse should be tried summarily unless the court considers that one or more of the following features is present and that its sentencing powers are insufficient:

     (a) Substantial disparity in age between victim and defendant, and the assault is more than trivial;

     (b) Violence or threats of violence;

     (c) Relationship of trust and responsibility between defendant and victim;

     (d) Several similar offences and the assault more than trivial;

     (e) The victim is particularly vulnerable

     (f) Serious nature of the assault.

Cases that have been held suitable for summary disposal include *Tanyildiz* [1998] 1 Cr.App.R.(S.) 362 and *Yazbek* [1998] 1 Cr.App.R.(S.) 406 (both concerning indecent assaults on underground trains).

(3) Elements of the offence

14–16   For a full analysis of the offences of indecent assault, see *Court* [1989] A.C. 28, HL (which will not apply to offences under the *Sexual Offences Act* 2003).

(4) Sentence

14–17   When tried summarily, an offence under sections 14 or 15 carries a maximum penalty of six months' imprisonment, a fine not exceeding the statutory maximum or both: *Sexual Offences Act* 1956, s.37 and Sched. 2.

The Magistrates' Association advises that if the victim is a young girl the case ought to go to the Crown Court if the indecency is serious. Any suggestion of attempted penetration or use of force also indicates that the matter should be sent to the Crown Court for sentence. If there is any suggestion that the defendant is not of full adult capacity, it may be appropriate for sentence at summary level. Where the victim is an adolescent girl who "consents", consideration should be given to sending the matter to the Crown Court for sentence where there are features such as digital interference or oral sex: *Pickup* (1992) 14 Cr.App.R.(S.) 271, CA. (It should be noted that oral sex would now constitute rape).

In *Tanyildz* (1998) 1 Cr.App.R.(S.) 362, the offender assaulted a woman on an underground train by pushing his erect penis against her on three occasions. He was sentenced to three months' imprisonment. See also *Townsend* (1994) 16 Cr.App.R.(S.) 553, CA, three months' imprisonment where the offender indecently assaulted female passenger on underground train.

The fact that the assault constitutes a breach of trust may result in a higher penalty. **14–18**
In *Att.-Gen.'s Reference (No. 25 of 1997) (Williams)* [1998] 1 Cr.App.R.(S.) 310, CA,
the offender was a shop keeper who indecently assaulted a 15-year-old girl working at
his shop on a work placement. His sentence of fines totalling £500 was varied to eight
months' imprisonment by the Court of Appeal, the Court stating that this was a campaign of sexual harassment towards a girl in relation to whom he was in a position of
trust. In *Owen* [2001] All E.R. (D) 96 (August) the offender pleaded guilty to indecently
assaulting three girls aged 12 or 14 who stayed overnight with his daughter at parties at
which he supplied alcohol. He was sentenced to four months' imprisonment in respect
of each offence, to be served consecutively; the Court emphasising that the offences
were sordid, and involved some deliberation as the offender had engineered the parties
and excessive drinking. He had also acted in breach of trust. See *Att.-Gen.'s Reference
(No. 70 of 2003)* [2004] EWCA Crim 163 for guidance on the circumstances in which
a community sentence may be merited for an indecent assault.

E. LIVING ON THE EARNINGS OF PROSTITUTION

(1) Definition

Sexual Offences Act 1956, s.30

Man living on earnings of prostitution
30.—(1) It is an offence for a man knowingly to live wholly or in part on the earnings of **14–19**
prostitution.
(2) For the purposes of this section a man who lives with or is habitually in the company
of a prostitute, or who exercises control, direction or influence over a prostitute's movements in a way which shows he is aiding, abetting or compelling her prostitution with others, shall be presumed to be knowingly living on the earnings of prostitutions, unless he
proves the contrary.

[Repealed by the *Sexual Offences Act* 2003, Sched. 7, on May 1, 2004.]

(2) Allocation

This offence is triable either way: *Sexual Offences Act* 1956, s.37(2).   **14–20**

(3) Elements of the offence

The presumptions raised in section 30(2) are raised on proof that   **14–21**
  – the accused was living with the prostitute;
  – he was habitually at the material time in her company;
  – he exercised control, direction or influence over her movements in a way which
    showed him to be aiding or abetting her prostitution.
It is then presumed that he is living on immoral earnings and that he is doing so
knowingly.

(4) Sentence

When tried summarily, the maximum penalty for this offence is six months' imprison- **14–22**
ment, a fine not exceeding the statutory maximum or both: *Sexual Offences Act* 1956,
s.37 and Sched. 2.
Sentencing guidance is given in *Farrugia* (1979) 69 Cr.App.R 108, Lawton L.J. seeing the presence or absence of coercion as a crucial factor in the sentencing decision. In
the absence of any evidence of coercion, whether physical or mental, or of corruption,
the old maximum of two years' imprisonment was described as adequate. Anything
exceeding two years should be reserved for a case where there is an element of coercion
or there is strong evidence of corruption. Where the offender is running a business of
encouraging prostitution, and the circumstances are such that he can be said to be living

wholly or in part on the earnings of prostitution, the Court should keep in mind the desirability of taking the profit out of such a way of life.

In *Powell* [2001] 1 Cr.App.R.(S.) 76 the offender's sentence of five years' imprisonment following his conviction for living on the earnings of prostitution was upheld. The victim had been ordered to work as a prostitute by the offender and she agreed because she was scared of him. It was held that five years' imprisonment was not inappropriate where coercion and corruption was evidenced.

Where the prostitute is carrying on her own business without coercion or corruption by the offender a more lenient approach will be taken: *Charlery* (1988) 10 Cr.App.R.(S.) 53, a sentence of four months' imprisonment plus a fine of was £1,500 imposed.

F. WOMAN EXERCISING CONTROL OVER PROSTITUTE

(1) Definition

Sexual Offences Act 1956, s.31

Woman exercising control over prostitute

14–23   31. It is an offence for a woman for purposes of gain to exercise control, direction or influence over a prostitute's movements in a way which shows she is aiding, abetting or compelling her prostitution.

[Repealed by the *Sexual Offences Act* 2003, Sched. 7, on May 1, 2004.]

(2) Allocation

14–24   This offence is triable either way: *Sexual Offences Act* 1956, s.37(2) and Sched. 2, para. 1.

(3) Sentence

14–25   When tried summarily, the maximum penalty for this offence is six months' imprisonment, a fine not exceeding the statutory maximum or both: *Sexual Offences Act* 1956, s.37 and Sched. 2.

G. SOLICITATION FOR IMMORAL PURPOSES

(1) Definition

Sexual Offences Act 1956, s.32

Solicitation by men

14–26   32. It is an offence for a man persistently to solicit or importune in a public place for immoral purposes.

[Repealed by the *Sexual Offences Act* 2003, Sched. 7, on May 1, 2004.]

(2) Allocation

14–27   This offence is triable either way.

(3) Elements of the offence

14–28   Two separate acts of importuning in the period constitute "persistently". An immoral purpose has to be some kind of sexual activity.

(4) Sentence

14–29   When tried summarily, the maximum penalty for this offence is six months' imprison-

ment, a fine not exceeding the statutory maximum or both: *Sexual Offences Act* 1956, s.37(3) and Sched. 2, para. 32 and *Magistrates' Courts Act* 1980, ss.32 34(3)(a).

H. KEEPING A BROTHEL

(1) Definition

Those offences contained in sections 33–36 of the 1956 Act were not repealed by the **14–30** 2003 Act. Section 36 was amended so as to make no distinction between male and female prostitution and section 33A was inserted.

Sexual Offences Act 1956, ss.33–36

Keeping a brothel
    33. It is an offence for a person to keep a brothel, or to manage, or act or assist in the **14–31** management of, a brothel.

Keeping a brothel used for prostitution
    33A.—(1) It is an offence for a person to keep, or to manage, or act or assist in the manage- **14–32** ment of, a brothel to which people resort for practices involving prostitution (whether or not also for other practices).
    (2) In this section "prostitution" has the meaning given by section 51(2) of the *Sexual Offences Act* 2003.

Landlord letting premises for use as brothel
    34. It is an offence for the lessor or landlord of any premises or his agent to let the whole or **14–33** part of the premises with the knowledge that it is to be used, in whole or in part, as a brothel, or, where the whole or part of the premises is used as a brothel, to be wilfully a party to that use continuing.

Tenant permitting premises to be used as brothel
    35.—(1) It is an offence for the tenant or occupier, or person in charge, of any premises **14–34** knowingly to permit the whole or part of the premises to be used as a brothel.
    (2) Where the tenant or occupier of any premises is convicted (whether under this section or, for an offence committed before the commencement of this Act, under section thirteen of the *Criminal Law Amendment Act* 1885) of knowingly permitting the whole or part of the premises to be used as a brothel, the First Schedule to this Act shall apply to enlarge the rights of the lessor or landlord with respect to the assignment or determination of the lease or other contract under which the premises are held by the person convicted.
    (3) Where the tenant or occupier of any premises is so convicted, or was so convicted under the said section thirteen before the commencement of this Act, and either—
    (a) the lessor or landlord, after having the conviction brought to his notice, fails or failed to exercise his statutory rights in relation to the lease or contract under which the premises are or were held by the person convicted; or
    (b) The lessor or landlord, after exercising his statutory rights so as to determine that lease or contract, grants or granted a new lease or enters or entered into a new contract of tenancy of the premises to, with or for the benefit of the same person, without having all reasonable provisions to prevent the recurrence of the offence inserted in the new lease or contract;
then, if subsequently an offence under this section is committed in respect of the premises during the subsistence of the lease or contract referred to in paragraph (a) of this subsection or (where paragraph (b) applies) during the subsistence of the new lease or contract, the lessor or landlord shall be deemed to be a party to that offence unless he shows that he took all reasonable steps to prevent the recurrence of the offence.
    References in this subsection to the statutory rights of a lessor or landlord refer to his rights under the First Schedule to this Act or under subsection (1) of section five of the *Criminal Law Amendment Act* 1912 (the provision replaced for England and Wales by that Schedule).

Tenant permitting premises to be used for prostitution
    36. It is an offence for the tenant or occupier of any premises knowingly to permit the whole **14–35**

or part of the premises to be used for the purposes of habitual prostitution (whether any prostitute involved is male or female).

[These sections are printed as amended by *Sexual Offences Act* 2003. Section 33A was added by the *Sexual Offences Act* 2003, s.55.]

(2) Allocation

14–36   These offences are triable summarily only: *Sexual Offences Act* 1956, s.37 and Sched. 2, except for the new offence created by section 33A, which is triable either way.

(3) Elements of the offence

14–37   A brothel is a place where people of opposite sexes are allowed to resort for sexual intercourse, whether the women are common prostitutes or not: *Winter v. Woolfe* [1931] 1 K.B. 549. A place which is used by one woman for the purposes of her own prostitution is not a brothel: *Stevens v. Christy* (1987) 85 Cr.App.R. 249.

It is not necessary to prove that normal sexual intercourse was offered on the premises to succeed in classifying a premises as a brothel, it will suffice to prove that more than one woman offered herself as a participant in physical acts of indecency for the gratification of men: *Kelly v. Purvis* [1983] Q.B. 663.

It is not necessary that a person charged with assisting the management of a brothel exercises control over the management of the brothel. That would be acting in the management of a brothel. The question of assisting in the management of a brothel is a question of fact: *Jones v. DPP* (1992) 96 Cr.App.R. 130.

(4) Sentence

14–38   For each section, the first commission of the offence carries a maximum penalty of three months' imprisonment, a fine not exceeding level three on the standard scale or both. For each section, for every offence committed after the first offence, the maximum penalty is six months' imprisonment, a fine not exceeding level four on the standard scale or both: *Sexual Offences Act* 1956, s.37 and Sched. 2.

Upon summary conviction the maximum sentence for the new section 33A offence is six months' imprisonment and/or a fine. After commencement of the relevant provisions, the maximum custodial sentence in a magistrates' court will be 12 months' imprisonment: *Criminal Justice Act* 2003, ss.154 and 282. In *Ramaj and Atesogullari* [2006] EWCA Crim 448, the appellants, a 22 year old and a 19 year old of previous good character were sentenced to 18 months' imprisonment (amongst other sentences) for keeping a brothel contrary to section 33A. The operation was amateurish and operable for only four days. The sentence was reduced to three months' imprisonment (*Rousseau* [2002] EWCA Crim 1252; [2003] 1 Cr.App.R.(S.) 15 and *Middleton* [2004] EWCA Crim 1487; [2005] 1 Cr.App.R.(S.) 42 were considered).

14–39   See section 7, *ante*, for the offence of soliciting for immoral purposes under *Sexual Offences Act* 1956, s.32.

I. Solicitation of a Woman for the Purposes of Prostitution

(1) Definition

Sexual Offences Act 1985, ss.1–2

Kerb-crawling

14–40   **1.**—(1) A man commits an offence if he solicits a woman (or different women) for the purpose of prostitution—

       (a) from a motor vehicle while it is in a street or public place; or

       (b) in a street or public place while in the immediate vicinity of a motor vehicle that he has just got out of or off, persistently or, in such manner or in such circumstances as to be likely to cause annoyance to the woman (or any of the women) solicited, or nuisance to other persons in the neighbourhood.

(2) A person guilty of an offence under this section shall be liable on summary conviction to a fine not exceeding level 3 on the standard scale

(3) In this section "motor vehicle" has the meaning as in the *Road Traffic Act* 1972.

Persistent soliciting of women for the purpose of prostitution

2.—(1) A man commits an offence if in a street or public place he persistently solicits a woman (or different women) for the purpose of prostitution.   **14–41**

(2) A person guilty of an offence under this section shall be liable on summary conviction to a fine not exceeding level 3 on the standard scale.

Sections 1 and 2 of the *Sexual Offences Act* 1985 were not repealed by the *Sexual*   **14–42** *Offences Act* 2003 but amended by Sched. 1, para. 4(1)–(4) so as to make no distinction as to gender. The offences of "soliciting for the purposes of prostitution" (which includes "kerb-crawling") now apply equally regardless of the gender of the person committing the act of soliciting or the gender of the person being solicited.

(2) Allocation

These offences are triable summarily: section 1(2) and 2(2).   **14–43**

(3) Elements of the offence

Sexual Offences Act 1985, s.4

Interpretation

4.—(1) References in this Act to a person soliciting another person for the purpose of prostitu-   **14–44** tion are references to his soliciting that person for the purpose of obtaining a person's services as a prostitute.

(4) For the purposes of this Act "street" includes any bridge, road, lane, footway, subway, square, court, alley or passage, whether a thoroughfare or not, which is for the time being open to the public; and the doorways and entrances of premises abutting on a street (as hereinbefore defined), and any ground adjoining and open to a street, shall be treated as forming part of the street.

[This is printed as amended by Schedule 7, paragraph 1 of the *Sexual Offences Act* 2003.]

(4) Sentence

Both offences carry a maximum penalty of a fine not exceeding level three on the   **14–45** standard scale: section 1(2) and 2(2).

J. Loitering or Soliciting for the Purpose of Prostitution

(1) Definition

Street Offences Act 1959, s.1

Loitering or soliciting for purposes of prostitution

1.—(1) It shall be an offence for a common prostitute whether male or female to loiter or   **14–46** solicit in a street or public place for the purpose of prostitution.

(2) A person guilty of an offence under this section shall be liable on summary conviction to a fine of an amount not exceeding level 2 on the standard scale, or, for an offence committed after a previous conviction, to a fine of an amount not exceeding level 3 on that scale.

(3) [...]

(4) For the purposes of this section "street" includes any bridge, road, lane, footway, subway, square, court, alley or passage, whether a thoroughfare or not, which is for the

time being open to the public; and the doorways and entrances of premises abutting on a street (as hereinbefore defined), and any ground adjoining and open to a street, shall be treated as forming part of the street.

[This section is printed as amended by the *Sexual Offences Act* 2003, Sched. 1, para. 2. Sub-paragraph (3) has been repealed subject to the transitory provisions specified in S.I. 2005 No. 3495 article 2(2) by the *Serious Organised Crime and Police Act* 2005, Sched. 17(2), para. 1.]

(2) Allocation

14–47   This offence is triable summarily: *Street Offences Act* 1959, s.1(2).

(3) Elements of the offence

14–48   Section 1(1) of the *Street Offences Act* 1959 was, prior to the *Sexual Offences Act* 2003, confined to women, hence solicitation consisted of any conduct by a woman that invites or importunes another to engage in an act of prostitution: *DPP v. Bull* [1995] Q.B. 88. Changes effected by the *Sexual Offences Act* 2003, Sched. 1, para. 4 mean that this section will now apply regardless of the gender of the prostitute.

The woman does not have to be present in the public place to which she is projecting her solicitous efforts, yet she must be physically present to solicit. An advertisement displaying her services will not suffice: *Weisz v. Monahan* [1962] 1 W.L.R. 262.

"Public place" is not defined in section 1 and is a question of fact for the magistrates.

(4) Sentence

14–49   The first offence under this section carries a maximum penalty of a fine not exceeding level two on the standard scale. Each offence thereafter carries a maximum penalty of a fine not exceeding level three on the standard scale: *Street Offences Act* 1959, s.1(2).

K. INDECENCY WITH CHILDREN

(1) Definition

Indecency with Children Act 1960, s.1

Indecent conduct towards young child

14–50   **1.**—(1) Any person who commits an act of gross indecency with or towards a child under the age of sixteen or who incites a child under that age to such an act with him or another, shall be liable on conviction on indictment to imprisonment for a term not exceeding ten years, or on summary conviction to imprisonment for a term not exceeding six months, to a fine not exceeding the prescribed sum, or to both.

(2) *[...]*

(3) References in the *Children and Young Persons Act* 1933 to the offences mentioned in the First Schedule to that Act shall include offences under this section.

(4) Offences under this section shall be deemed to be offences against the person for the purpose of section three of the *Visiting Forces Act* 1952 (which restricts the trial by United Kingdom courts of offenders connected with visiting forces).

[Subsection (1) is printed as amended by the *C(S)A* 1997, s.52 (substitutuion of "ten" for "two") and the *CJCSA* 2000, s.39 (substitution of "sixteen" for "fourteen"). The first of these amendments took effect on October 1, 1997, but does not apply to offences committed before that date: *Crime (Sentences) Act (Commencement No. 2 and Transitional Provisions) Order* 1997 (S.I. 1997 No. 2200). The second amendment took effect on January 11, 2001: *Criminal Justice and Court Services Act 2000 (Commencement No. 1) Order* 2000 (S.I. 2000 No. 3302). Subsection (2) was repealed by the *Police and Criminal Evidence Act* 1984, Sched 7. This section is repealed by the *Sexual Offences Act* 2003, Sched. 7, on May 1, 2004.]

(2) Allocation

This offence is triable either way: section 1(1).   **14–51**

(3) Elements of the offence

There must be an act, but allowing a child to continue an activity may constitute an   **14–52**
act.

(4) Sentence

When tried summarily, the maximum penalty for this offence is imprisonment for a   **14–53**
term not exceeding six months, a fine not exceeding £400 or both: section 1(1).

L. MISCELLANEOUS OFFENCES

(1) Outraging public decency: indecent exposure

(a) *Definition*

Vagrancy Act 1824, s.4

Persons committing certain offences to be deemed rogues and vagabonds
    4. Every person committing any of the offences herein-before mentioned, after having been   **14–54**
convicted as an idle and disorderly person; every person wandering abroad and lodging in any
barn or outhouse, or in any deserted or unoccupied building, or in the open air, or under a
tent, or in any cart or wagon, and not giving a good account of himself or herself; every person
wandering abroad, and endeavouring by the exposure of wounds or deformities to obtain or
gather alms; every person going about as a gatherer or collector of alms, or endeavouring to
procure charitable contributions of any nature or kind, under any false or fraudulent pretence;
every person being found in or upon any dwelling house, warehouse, coach-house, stable, or
outhouse, or in any inclosed yard, garden, or area, for any unlawful purpose; every suspected
person or reputed thief, frequenting any river, canal, or navigable stream, dock, or basin, or any
quay, wharf, or warehouse near or adjoining thereto, or any street, highway, or avenue leading
thereto, or any place of public resort, or any avenue leading thereto, or any street, with intent to
commit an arrestable offence; and every person apprehended as an idle and disorderly person,
and violently resisting any constable, or other peace officer so apprehending him or her, and being subsequently convicted of the offence for which he or she shall have been so apprehended;
shall be deemed a rogue and vagabond, within the true intent and meaning of this Act; and,
subject to section 70 of the *Criminal Justice Act* 1982, it shall be lawful for any justice of the
peace to commit such offender (being thereof convicted before him by the confession of such offender, or by the evidence on oath of one or more credible witness or witnesses,) to the house of
correction, for any time not exceeding three calendar months.

Town Police Clauses Act 1847, s.28

Penalty on persons committing any of the offences herein named
    28. Every person who in any street, to the obstruction, annoyance, or danger of the residents   **14–55**
or passengers, commits any of the following offences, shall be liable to a penalty not exceeding
level 3 on the standard scale for each offence, or, in the discretion of the justice before whom he
is convicted, may be committed to prison, there to remain for a period not exceeding fourteen
days, and any officer appointed by virtue of this or the special Act or any constable shall take into
custody, without warrant, and forthwith convey before a justice, any person who within his view
commits any such offence; (that is to say,)

(b) *Allocation*

Both offences are triable summarily.   **14–56**

(c) *Sentence*

The maximum penalty for the offence under the *Vagrancy Act* 1824 is three months'   **14–57** imprisonment, a fine not exceeding level three on the standard scale or both. On a second conviction and committal to the Crown Court, the maximum penalty is imprisonment for 12 months. After commencement of the relevant provisions, the following offences committed under section 4 of the *Vagrancy Act* 1824—

    (a) the offence of going about as a gatherer or collector of alms, or endeavouring to procure charitable contributions of any nature or kind, under any false or fraudulent pretence;

    (b) the offence of being found in or upon any dwelling house, warehouse, coach-house, stable, or outhouse, or in any inclosed yard, garden, or area, for any unlawful purpose; and

    (c) the offence of being apprehended as an idle and disorderly person, and violently resisting any constable, or other peace officer so apprehending him or her, and being subsequently convicted of the offence for which he or she shall have been so apprehended

will no longer be punishable with imprisonment: section 280(1) and Schedule 25 of the *Criminal Justice Act* 2003; and offences committed contrary to section 28 of the *Town Police Clauses Act* 1847, will no longer be punishable with imprisonment: section 280(1) and Schedule 25 of the *Criminal Justice Act* 2003.

The maximum penalty for an offence under the *Town Police Clauses Act* 1847 is imprisonment for a period not exceeding fourteen days and/or, a fine not exceeding level three on the standard scale.

(2) Abuse of a position of trust

(a) *Definition*

Sexual Offences (Amendment) Act 2000, s.3

Abuse of position of trust

14–58   **3.**—(1) Subject to subsections (2) and (3) below, it shall be an offence for a person aged 18 or over—

    (a) to have sexual intercourse (whether vaginal or anal) with a person under that age; or

    (b) to engage in any other sexual activity with or directed towards such a person, if (in either case) he is in a position of trust in relation to that person.

    (2) Where a person ("A") is charged with an offence under this section of having sexual intercourse with, or engaging in any other sexual activity with or directed towards, another person ("B"), it shall be a defence for A to prove that, at the time of the intercourse or activity—

    (a) he did not know, and could not reasonably have been expected to know, that B was under 18;

    (b) he did not know, and could not reasonably have been expected to know, that B was a person in relation to whom he was in a position of trust; or

    (c) he was lawfully married to B.

    (3) It shall not be an offence under this section for a person ("A") to have sexual intercourse with, or engage in any other sexual activity with or directed towards, another person ("B") if immediately before the commencement of this Act—

    (a) A was in a position of trust in relation to B; and

    (b) a sexual relationship existed between them.

    (4) A person guilty of an offence under this section shall be liable—

    (a) on summary conviction, to imprisonment for a term not exceeding six months, or to a fine not exceeding the statutory maximum, or to both;

    (b) on conviction on indictment, to imprisonment for a term not exceeding five years, or to a fine, or to both.

[Repealed by the *Sexual Offences Act* 2003, Sched. 7 on May 1, 2004.]

(b) *Allocation*

14–59   This offence is triable either way: section 3(4).

(c) *Elements of the offence*

Sexual Offences (Amendment) Act 2000, ss.3(5), 4

3.—(5) In this section, "sexual activity"—   **14–60**

    (a) does not include any activity which a reasonable person would regard as sexual only with knowledge of the intentions, motives or feelings of the parties; but

    (b) subject to that, means any activity which such a person would regard as sexual in all the circumstances.

Meaning of "position of trust"

4.—(1) For the purposes of section 3 above, a person aged 18 or over ("A") is in a position of **14–61**
trust in relation to a person under that age ("B") if any of the four conditions set out below, or any condition specified in an order made by the Secretary of State by statutory instrument, is fulfilled.

(2) The first condition is that A looks after persons under 18 who are detained in an institution by virtue of an order of a court or under an enactment, and B is so detained in that institution.

(3) The second condition is that A looks after persons under 18 who are resident in a home or other place in which—

    (a) accommodation and maintenance are provided by an authority under section 23(2) of the *Children Act* 1989 or Article 27(2) of the *Children (Northern Ireland) Order* 1995;

    (b) accommodation is provided by a voluntary organisation under section 59(1) of that Act or Article 75(1) of that *Order*; or

    (c) accommodation is provided by an authority under section 26(1) of the *Children (Scotland) Act* 1995,

and B is resident, and is so provided with accommodation and maintenance or accommodation, in that place.

(4) The third condition is that A looks after persons under 18 who are accommodated and cared for in an institution which is—

    (a) a hospital;

    (b) a residential care home, nursing home, mental nursing home or private hospital;

    (c) a community home, voluntary home, children's home or residential establishment; or

    (d) a home provided under section 82(5) of the *Children Act* 1989,

and B is accommodated and cared for in that institution.

(5) The fourth condition is that A looks after persons under 18 who are receiving full-time education at an educational institution, and B is receiving such education at that institution.

(6) No order shall be made under subsection (1) above unless a draft of the order has been laid before and approved by a resolution of each House of Parliament.

(7) A person looks after persons under 18 for the purposes of this section if he is regularly involved in caring for, training, supervising or being in sole charge of such persons.

(8) For the purposes of this section a person receives full-time education at an educational institution if—

    (a) he is registered or otherwise enrolled as a full-time pupil or student at the institution; or

    (b) he receives education at the institution under arrangements with another educational institution at which he is so registered or otherwise enrolled.

(9) In this section, except where the context otherwise requires—

"authority" means

    (a) in relation to Great Britain, a local authority; and

    (b) in relation to Northern Ireland, an authority within the meaning given by Article 2(2) of the *Children (Northern Ireland) Order* 1995;

"children's home" has—

    (a) in relation to England and Wales, the meaning which would be given by subsection (3) of section 63 of the *Children Act* 1989 if the reference in paragraph (a) of that subsection to more than three children were a reference to one or more children; and

   (b) in relation to Northern Ireland, the meaning which would be given by
        Article 90(1) of the *Children (Northern Ireland) Order* 1995 if, in Article
        91(2) of that *Order*, paragraphs (f) and (g) and the words after paragraph (h)
        were omitted;
"community home" has the meaning given by section 53(1) of the *Children Act* 1989;
"hospital" has—
   (a) in relation to England and Wales, the meaning given by section 128(1) of
        the *National Health Service Act* 1977;
   (b) in relation to Scotland, the meaning given by section 108(1) of the *National
        Health Service (Scotland) Act* 1978; and
   (c) in relation to Northern Ireland, the meaning given by Article 2(2) of the
        Health and Personal Social Services (Northern Ireland) Order 1972;
"mental nursing home" has, in relation to England and Wales, the meaning given by section 22(1) of the *Registered Homes Act* 1984;
"nursing home" —
   (a) in relation to England and Wales, has the meaning given by section 21(1)
        of the *Registered Homes Act* 1984;
   (b) in relation to Scotland, means a nursing home registered under section 1
        of the *Nursing Homes Registration (Scotland) Act* 1938; and
   (c) in relation to Northern Ireland, has the meaning given by Article 16(1) of
        the *Registered Homes (Northern Ireland) Order* 1992;
"private hospital" has—
   (a) in relation to Scotland, the meaning given by section 12(2) of the *Mental
        Health (Scotland) Act* 1984; and
   (b) in relation to Northern Ireland, the meaning given by Article 90(2) of the
        Mental Health (Northern Ireland) Order 1986;
"residential care home" —
   (a) in relation to England and Wales, has the meaning given by section 1(2)
        of the *Registered Homes Act* 1984;
   (b) in relation to Scotland, means an establishment in respect of which a
        person is registered under section 62 or 63 of the *Social Work (Scotland)
        Act* 1968; and
   (c) in relation to Northern Ireland, has the meaning given by Article 3(1) of
        the *Registered Homes (Northern Ireland) Order* 1992;
"residential establishment" has the meaning given by section 93(1) of the *Children
(Scotland) Act* 1995 as the meaning of that expression in relation to a place in Scotland;
"voluntary home" has—
   (a) in relation to England and Wales, the meaning given by section 60(3) of
        the *Children Act* 1989; and
   (b) in relation to Northern Ireland, the meaning given by Article 74(1) of the
        Children (Northern Ireland) Order 1995.

(d) *Sentence*

14–62   When tried summarily, the maximum penalty for this offence is six months' imprisonment, a fine not exceeding the statutory maximum or both: section 3(4).

(3) Indecent photographs of children

(a) *Definition*

14–63   The 1978 legislation was not repealed but was amended by the 2003 *Act*, s.45 so as to
extend the protection to children aged 16 and 17. A marriage defence is also included
at section 1A. The marriage defence applies provided the defendant and the subject
were married at the time of the offence charged. The photograph must show the
subject alone or with the defendant, but not any third party, and must be of the subject
aged 16 or over.
   In terms of consent, where the charge is one of taking a photo, the evidential burden
lies on the defendant to show that the subject consented or, the defendant reasonably

believed that to be so. It is then for the prosecution to rebut that. Where the charge is under s.1(1)(c) the prosecution must prove absence of consent.

Protection of Children Act 1978, ss.1–1B

Indecent photographs of children

1.—(1) [Subject to sections 1A and 1B] it is an offence for a person—   **14–64**

    (a) to take, or permit to be taken or to make, any indecent photograph or pseudo-photograph of a child; or

    (b) to distribute or show such indecent photographs or pseudo-photographs; or

    (c) to have in his possession such indecent photographs or pseudo- photographs, with a view to their being distributed or shown by himself or others; or

    (d) to publish or cause to be published any advertisement likely to be understood as conveying that the advertiser distributes or shows such indecent photographs or pseudo-photographs, or intends to do so.

(2) For purposes of this Act, a person is to be regarded as distributing an indecent photograph or pseudo-photographs if he parts with possession of it to, or exposes or offers it for acquisition by, another person.

(3) Proceedings for an offence under this Act shall not be instituted except by or with the consent of the Director of Public Prosecutions.

(4) Where a person is charged with an offence under subsection (1)(b) or (c), it shall be a defence for him to prove—

    (a) that he had a legitimate reason for distributing or showing the photographs or pseudo-photographs or (as the case may be) having them in his possession; or

    (b) that he had not himself seen the photographs or pseudo-photographs and did not know, nor had any cause to suspect, them to be indecent.

(5) References in the *Children and Young Persons Act* 1933 (except in sections 15 and 99) to the offences mentioned in Schedule 1 to that Act shall include an offence under subsection (1)(a) above.

Marriage and other relationships

1A.—(1) This section applies where, in proceedings for an offence under section 1(1)(a) of   **14–65** taking or making an indecent photograph of a child, or for an offence under section 1(1)(b) or (c) relating to an indecent photograph of a child, the defendant proves that the photograph was of the child aged 16 or over, and that at the time of the offence charged the child and he—

    (a) were married, or

    (b) lived together as partners in an enduring family relationship.

(2) Subsections (5) and (6) also apply where, in proceedings for an offence under section 1(1)(b) or (c) relating to an indecent photograph of a child, the defendant proves that the photograph was of the child aged 16 or over, and that at the time when he obtained it the child and he—

    (a) were married, or civil partners of each other, or

    (b) lived together as partners in an enduring family relationship.

(3) This section applies whether the photograph showed the child alone or with the defendant, but not if it showed any other person.

(4) In the case of an offence under section 1(1)(a), if sufficient evidence is adduced to raise an issue as to whether the child consented to the photograph being taken or made, or as to whether the defendant reasonably believed that the child so consented, the defendant is not guilty of the offence unless it is proved that the child did not so consent and that the defendant did not reasonably believe that the child so consented.

(5) In the case of an offence under section 1(1)(b), the defendant is not guilty of the offence unless it is proved that the showing or distributing was to a person other than the child.

(6) In the case of an offence under section 1(1)(c), if sufficient evidence is adduced to raise an issue both—

    (a) as to whether the child consented to the photograph being in the defendant's possession, or as to whether the defendant reasonably believed that the child so consented, and

    (b) as to whether the defendant had the photograph in his possession with a view to its being distributed or shown to anyone other than the child, the defendant is not guilty of the offence unless it is proved either that the child did not so consent and that the defendant did not reasonably believe that the child so consented, or that the defendant had the photograph in his possession with a view to its being distributed or shown to a person other than the child.

Exception for criminal proceedings, investigations etc.

14–66   **1B.**—(1) In proceedings for an offence under section 1(1)(a) of making an indecent photograph or pseudo-photograph of a child, the defendant is not guilty of the offence if he proves that—

(a) it was necessary for him to make the photograph or pseudo-photograph for the purposes of the prevention, detection or investigation of crime, or for the purposes of criminal proceedings, in any part of the world,

(b) at the time of the offence charged he was a member of the Security Service, and it was necessary for him to make the photograph or pseudo-photograph for the exercise of any of the functions of the Service, or

(c) at the time of the offence charged he was a member of GCHQ, and it was necessary for him to make the photograph or pseudo-photograph for the exercise of any of the functions of GCHQ.

(2) In this section "GCHQ" has the same meaning as in the *Intelligence Services Act* 1994.

[Sections 1, 1A and 1B are printed as amended and repealed in part by the *CJPOA* 1994, ss.84(2), 168(3), Sched. 11 and the *Civil Partnership Act* 2004, Sched. 27, para. 60, which came into force on December 5, 2005.]

(b) *Allocation*

14–67   This offence is triable either way: *Protection of Children Act* 1978, s.6(1)

The magistrates also have power to order searches of premises and powers of forfeiture:

Protection of Children Act 1978, ss.4, 5

Entry, search and seizure

14–68   **4.**—(1) The following applies where a justice of the peace is satisfied by information on oath, laid by or on behalf of the Director of Public Prosecutions or by a constable, that there is reasonable ground for suspecting that, in any premises in the petty sessions area for which he acts, there are indecent photographs of children and that such photographs—

(a) are or have been taken there; or

(b) are or have been shown there, or are kept there with a view to their being distributed or shown is an indecent photograph or pseudo-photograph of a child

(2) The justice may issue a warrant under his hand authorising any constable to enter (if need be by force) and search the premises, and to seize and remove any articles which he believes (with reasonable cause) to be or include indecent photographs or pseudo-photographs of children.

(3) Articles seized under the authority of the warrant, and not returned to the occupier of the premises, shall be brought before a justice of the peace acting in the local justice area in which the articles were seized.

(4) This section and section 5 below apply in relation to any stall or vehicle, as they apply in relation to premises, with the necessary modifications of references to premises and the substitution of references to use for references to occupation.

Forfeiture

14–69   **5.**—(1) The justice before whom any articles are brought in pursuance of section 4 above may issue a summons to the occupier of the premises to appear on a day specified in the summons before a magistrates' court acting in that local justice area to show cause why they should not be forfeited.

(2) If the court is satisfied that the articles are in fact indecent photographs or pseudo-photographs of children, the court shall order them to be forfeited; but if the person summoned does not appear, the court shall not make an order unless service of the summons is proved.

(3) In addition to the persons summoned, any other person being the owner of the articles brought before the court, or the persons who made them, or any other person through whose hands they had passed before being seized, shall be entitled to appear before the court on the day specified in the summons to show cause why they should not be forfeited.

(4) Where any of the articles are ordered to be forfeited under subsection (2), any person who appears, or was entitled to appear, to show cause against the making of the order may appeal to the Crown Court.

(5) If as respects any articles brought before it the court does not order forfeiture, the court may if it thinks fit order the person on whose information the warrant for their seizure was issued to pay such costs as the court thinks reasonable to any person who has appeared before it to show cause why the photographs or pseudo-photographs should not be forfeited; and costs ordered to be paid under this subsection shall be recoverable as a civil debt.

(6) Where indecent photographs or pseudo-photographs of children are seized under section 4 above, and a person is convicted under section 1(1) or section 160 of the *Criminal Justice Act* 1988 of offences in respect of those photographs or pseudo-photographs, the court shall order them to be forfeited.

(7) An order made under subsection (2) or (6) above (including an order made on appeal) shall not take effect until the expiration of the ordinary time within which an appeal may be instituted or, where such an appeal is duly instituted, until the appeal is finally decided or abandoned; and for this purpose—

(a) an application for a case to be stated or for leave to appeal shall be treated as the institution of an appeal; and

(b) where a decision on appeal is subject to a further appeal, the appeal is not finally decided until the expiration of the ordinary time within which a further appeal may be instituted or, where a further appeal is duly instituted, until the further appeal is finally decided or abandoned.

[These sections are printed as amended and repealed in part by the *CJA* 1988, s.170(1) and Sched. 15, paras. 61 and 62; the *CJPOA* 1994, s.168(1), (2) and Sched. 9, para. 23, and Sched. 10, para. 37; and the *Courts Act* 2003, Sched. 8, paras 199(3) and para. 200.]

(c) *Elements of the offence*

In deciding whether the photograph is indecent, the test to be applied is the recog- **14–70** nised standard of propriety: *Stamford* [1972] 2. Q.B. 391. In a case of "taking", the circumstances and motivation of the taker of the photograph may be relevant as to whether his taking was accidental or intentional; it would not be relevant for determining whether the photograph was indecent: *Graham-Kerr* (1989) 88 Cr.App.R. 302, CA and *Smethurst* [2002] 1 Cr.App.R. 6, CA. In determining whether the photograph is indecent the age of the child is of relevance: *Owen* (1988) 86 Cr.App.R. 291, CA.

Opening an email attachment of an indecent photograph may constitute "making" the photograph or pseudo-photograph if at the time it was opened, the individual did so intentionally and with the knowledge that what he was "making" was, or was likely to be an indecent image of a child. The same would apply to downloading an image from the internet to a computer screen. It is not necessary to prove in either scenario that the individual intended to save the image: *Bowden* [2000] 1 Cr.App.R. 438; *Atkins v. DPP* [2000] 2 Cr.App.R. 248, DC.

Responding to an advertisement offering to supply indecent photographs of children, by placing an order may amount to an offence of inciting the commission of an offence of distribution of indecent photographs of children, contrary to section 1(1)(b), or with an attempt if the order was never received. Likewise, the supplier would be guilty of an offence of distribution as distinct from an offence relating to the advertisement: *Goldman* [2001] Crim.L.R. 822, CA; see also, *R. (O.)* [2004] Crim.L.R. 948, DC.

Where indecent photographs of a child were stored in a shared folder, the offence of possessing indecent photographs of a child with a view to distributing them would be made out if the intention in storing them in a shared folder was in order for other users to have access to them: *Dooley* [2005] EWCA Crim 3093.

Part III

(d) Sentence

14–71 When tried summarily, the maximum penalty for this offence is imprisonment for a term not exceeding six months, a fine not exceeding the prescribed sum or both: *Protection of Children Act* 1978, s.6(3). After commencement of the relevant provisions, the maximum custodial sentence in a magistrates' court will be 12 months' imprisonment: *Criminal Justice Act* 2003, ss.154 and 282.

In *Toomer* [2001] 2 Cr.App.R.(S.) 8, the Court of Appeal issued guidance on sentencing under this section, Kennedy L.J. stating that:

"First, sentences up to statutory maximum should be imposed where there is a contested case, and there is evidence of commercial or large scale exploitation, and the amount of material is significant, especially if the offender has previous convictions.

Secondly, non-custodial disposals should normally be reserved for isolated offences where the amount of material is very small, and it is for personal use, or use within a very restricted circle, as for example by passing it to one other recipient, when there is no commercial element and the defendant has pleaded guilty and is a first offender. Thirdly, Where between those two extremes a particular case falls, will depend on the circumstances, and in particular on, first of all, the quality and nature of the material and the quantity thereof, and whether there is any element of exploitation or commercial gain.

Thirdly, whether the offence is simply one of making; that is to say, in most cases downloading and saving or also involves distribution and, if so, to what extent there has been distribution, whether it has been by e-mail to a single specified recipient, or whether the distribution has been significantly more widespread.

Fourthly, the character of the defendant is an important factor, and also the effect of the conviction upon the individual.

Finally, it is of great importance to consider whether there has been a plea of guilty coupled with co-operation from the outset in the investigation."

14–72 In *Jefferson* [2001] EWCA Crim 1278, the offender, 56, was a man of good character who admitted downloading indecent images of children. The images were for his own use and he said he did not know such action was a crime. His appeal against a sentence of three months' imprisonment was allowed, the Court stating that a fine would have been the appropriate penalty, however, as he had served four weeks of his prison sentence he was conditionally discharged. Aggravating factors will include the degree of obscenity involved in the image, the age and number of children involved, whether the children were of one or both sexes and the nature of the conduct to which they were subjected or in which they are depicted as taking part: *Allison* [2001] EWCA Crim 1971 (six months' imprisonment where offender pleaded guilty to distributing indecent photographs or pseudo indecent photographs of children).

(4) Possession of indecent photographs of children

(a) Definition

14–73 The *Criminal Justice Act* 1988, s.60 was amended by the *Sexual Offences Act* 2003, s.45. In much the same way that the new legislation amends the *POCA* 1978, *ante*, the *CJA* 1988 has also been amended to extend protection to those aged 16 and 17. A new section 160A is created, which provides an exception for marriage and other relationships. The existing defence in section 160(2) is retained.

Criminal Justice Act 1988, s.160

Possession of indecent photograph of child
14–74 **160.**—(1) It is an offence for a person to have any indecent photograph or pseudo-photograph of a child in his possession.

(2) Where a person is charged with an offence under subsection (1) above, it shall be a defence for him to prove—

(a) that he had a legitimate reason for having the photograph or pseudo-photograph in his possession; or

(b) that he had not himself seen the photograph or pseudo-photograph and did not know, nor had any cause to suspect, it to be indecent; or

(c) that the photograph or pseudo-photograph was sent to him without any prior request made by him or on his behalf and that he did not keep it for an unreasonable time.

(2A) A person shall be liable on conviction on indictment of an offence under this section to imprisonment for a term not exceeding five years or a fine, or both

(3) A person shall be liable on summary conviction of an offence under this section to imprisonment for a term not exceeding six months or a fine not exceeding level 5 on the standard scale, or both.

(4) Sections 1(3), 2(3), 3 and 7 of the *Protection of Children Act* 1978 shall have effect as if any reference in them to that Act included a reference to this section.

[This section is printed as amended and repealed in part by the *CJPOA* 1994, ss.84(4)(a) and (b), 86(1) and 168(3) and Sched. 11; and the *CJCSA* 2000, s.41(3) (insertion of subsection (2A)). The amendment effected by the 2000 Act came into force on January 11, 2001: *Criminal Justice and Court Services Act 2000 (Commencement No. 1) Order* 2000 (S.I. 2000 No. 3302). There is no transitional provision in the statute or the commencement order. The combined effect of section 3 of the *Human Rights Act* 1988 and Article 7 of the European Convention will, however, be such as to require that the increase in penalty should apply only to offences committed on or after the commencement date.]

(b) *Allocation*

This offence is triable either way: section 160(2A) and (3).   **14–75**

(c) *Elements of the offence*

The offence of possession is not committed unless the defendant knows he has the   **14–76** photographs in his possession: *Atkins v. DPP* [2000] 2 All E.R. 425, DC.

In the case of deleted computer images contained on the hard drive of a computer, if a person could not retrieve or gain access to an image without the use of specialist forensic techniques to which he did not have access, then he no longer had custody or control of them within the meaning of the section: *Porter* [2006] EWCA Crim 560.

(d) *Sentence*

When tried summarily, the maximum penalty for this offence is imprisonment for a   **14–77** term not exceeding six months, a fine not exceeding level five on the standard scale, or both: section 160(3). After commencement of the relevant provisions, the maximum custodial sentence in a magistrates' court will be 12 months' imprisonment: *Criminal Justice Act* 2003, ss.154 and 282. Custodial sentences of less than 12 months will consist of a custody plus order (see *post*, Ch.23). The leading authority on sentencing for offences relating to the possession of child pornography is *Oliver* [2003] 1 Cr.App.R. 28. In sentencing two factors need to be taken into consideration: the nature of the material and the extent of the offender's involvement with it. The material should be graded into categories:

(i) images depicting erotic posing with no sexual activity;

(ii) sexual activity between children or solo masturbation;

(iii) non-penetrative sexual activity involving an adult;

(iv) penetrative activity with an adult; and

(v) adism or bestiality.

Aggravating features include the proximity to the sexual abuse; commercial activity; wide scale distribution even for little or no profit; original films or photographs are more serious that downloads; to actually download an image rather than just view it on the internet is more serious. Offences involving pseudo-photographs will generally be less serious than those involving real people. In cases on the cusp of the custody threshold suitability for treatment should be considered. A fine would normally be appropriate where the offender was in possession of material solely for his own use and the material was no more than a small quantity of level (i) material. A community sentence may be appropriate in a case of possession of a large amount of level (i) material, and/or a small amount of level 2 material, provided it has not been distributed. Simple possession of a large amount of level (ii) or a small amount of level (iii) material will usually result in a sentence of up to six months' imprisonment. Showing or distributing a large amount of level (ii) or a small amount of level (iii) material, or possessing a small amount of level (iv) or (v) material may result in a sentence of up to 12 months' imprisonment.

In *G.* [2006] EWCA Crim 2439, the Court of Appeal considered *Oliver* (*ante*) in which it was said "some, but not much, weight should be attached to good character". The appellant in this case was a soldier who in mitigation asserted positive good character. The court held that it was impossible to believe that such an assertion was not relevant to mitigation and suspended an immediate sentence of nine months' imprisonment.

III. THE SEXUAL OFFENCES ACT 2003

A. INTRODUCTION

14–78   The *Sexual Offences Act* 2003 came into force on May 1, 2004.

The Act re-codifies many existing offences and creates a number of new ones. The case law that follows emanates from offences charged under the previous legislation but remains valid nonetheless. All of the offences created in the 2003 Act are either triable either way or only on indictment, save for the single exception of the new offence of sexual activity in a public lavatory, which is triable only in the magistrates' court (see *post*, § 14–258). One feature of the Act is that it creates some widely defined offences with considerable overlap, thus placing considerable reliance on prosecutorial discretion. In July 2004, the Crown Prosecution Service produced guidance as to which offence should be charged under the new Act, and on priority between charging options. Additional information as to relevant considerations of Prosecutors when charging can be found at www.cps.gov.uk/legal. Regarding sentence, there are no Magistrates' Association Guidelines. The Sentencing Guidelines Council published a consultation guideline in relation to offences under the *Sexual Offences Act* 2003 in June 2006, as yet there is no definitive set of guidelines. The consultation guideline is available from www.sentencing-guideline.gov.uk.

B. CONSENT—SS.74 TO 76

14–79   The legislation brings with it statutory provisions regarding consent contained in sections 74–76. The redefinition of consent is one of the most radical innovations in the 2003 Act. The decision in *DPP v. Morgan* [1976] A.C. 182 is replaced by the statutory definition. Under the new law the prosecution must prove that B did not consent and that A did not reasonably believe that B was consenting. An honest but unreasonable belief as to the consent of the complainant will no longer entitle the defendant to an acquittal. In determining whether the defendant's belief in consent is reasonable, the court will need to have regard to all the circumstances at the time in question, including any steps the defendant may have taken to establish that the complainant did consent to the sexual activity. The statute introduces both conclusive presumptions about consent (section 76) and "rebuttable" evidential presumptions about consent: section 75.

Sexual Offences Act 2003, ss.74–76

"Consent"

14–80   **74.** For the purposes of this Part, a person consents if he agrees by choice, and has the freedom and capacity to make that choice.

Evidential presumptions about consent

75.—(1) If in proceedings for an offence to which this section applies it is proved—   **14–81**

    (a) that the defendant did the relevant act,

    (b) that any of the circumstances specified in subsection (2) existed, and

    (c) that the defendant knew that those circumstances existed,

the complainant is to be taken not to have consented to the relevant act unless sufficient evidence is adduced to raise an issue as to whether he consented, and the defendant is to be taken not to have reasonably believed that the complainant consented unless sufficient evidence is adduced to raise an issue as to whether he reasonably believed it.

    (2) The circumstances are that—

    (a) any person was, at the time of the relevant act or immediately before it began, using violence against the complainant or causing the complainant to fear that immediate violence would be used against him;

    (b) any person was, at the time of the relevant act or immediately before it began, causing the complainant to fear that violence was being used, or that immediate violence would be used, against another person;

    (c) the complainant was, and the defendant was not, unlawfully detained at the time of the relevant act;

    (d) the complainant was asleep or otherwise unconscious at the time of the relevant act;

    (e) because of the complainant's physical disability, the complainant would not have been able at the time of the relevant act to communicate to the defendant whether the complainant consented;

    (f) any person had administered to or caused to be taken by the complainant, without the complainant's consent, a substance which, having regard to when it was administered or taken, was capable of causing or enabling the complainant to be stupefied or overpowered at the time of the relevant act.

    (3) In subsection (2)(a) and (b), the reference to the time immediately before the relevant act began is, in the case of an act which is one of a continuous series of sexual activities, a reference to the time immediately before the first sexual activity began.

Conclusive presumptions about consent

76.—(1) If in proceedings for an offence to which this section applies it is proved that the defendant did the relevant act and that any of the circumstances specified in subsection (2) existed, it is to be conclusively presumed—   **14–82**

    (a) that the complainant did not consent to the relevant act, and

    (b) that the defendant did not believe that the complainant consented to the relevant act.

    (2) The circumstances are that—

    (a) the defendant intentionally deceived the complainant as to the nature or purpose of the relevant act;

    (b) the defendant intentionally induced the complainant to consent to the relevant act by impersonating a person known personally to the complainant.

C. Sexual Activity

Sexual Offences Act 2003, s.78

"Sexual"

78. For the purposes of this Part (except section 71), penetration, touching or any other activity is sexual if a reasonable person would consider that—   **14–83**

    (a) whatever its circumstances or any person's purpose in relation to it, it is because of its nature sexual, or

    (b) because of its nature it may be sexual and because of its circumstances or the purpose of any person in relation to it (or both) it is sexual.

Part III

IV. OFFENCES UNDER THE SEXUAL OFFENCES ACT 2003

A. Aꜱꜱᴀᴜʟᴛ ʙʏ Pᴇɴᴇᴛʀᴀᴛɪᴏɴ

(1) Definition

Sexual Offences Act 2003, s.2

14–84   2.—(1) A person (A) commits an offence if–

      (a) he intentionally penetrates the vagina or anus of another person (B) with a part of his body or anything else:

      (b) the penetration is sexual;

      (c) B does not consent to the penetration, and

      (d) A does not reasonably believe that B consents.

    (2) Whether a belief is reasonable is to be determined having regard to all the circumstances, including any steps A has taken to ascertain whether B consents.

    (3) Sections 75 and 76 apply to an offence under this section.

(2) Allocation

14–85   This offence is triable only on indictment.

(3) Sentence

14–86   The maximum sentence is life imprisonment.

In two cases decided on October 25, 2004, *Att.-Gen.'s Reference (No. 104 of 2004)* [2004] EWCA Crim 2672 and *Minshull* [2004] EWCA Crim 2673, both concerning digital penetration, the Court of Appeal indicated that previous decisions regarding the level of sentence appropriate for indecent assault involving digital penetration could no longer be regarded as authoritative given the maximum sentence under section 2 of the *Sexual Offences Act* 2003 of life imprisonment. Sentences would be at a higher level than was previously appropriate for an offence of indecent assault.

In *Child* [2005] EWCA Crim 3310 the appellant pleaded guilty to assault by penetration. The appellant had spent the evening socialising with the complainant and her boyfriend at a mutual friends' home. Later that evening they all went to sleep on a mattress in an upstairs room. In the night the complainant awoke to find the appellant had two fingers in her vagina. He also licked her. The complainant immediately raised the alarm and the appellant was removed from the house. The Court of Appeal considered the *Att.-Gen's Reference (No. 104 of 2004)*, see *ante*. The appeal was allowed in that the sentence of three years' imprisonment was substituted for two-and-a-half-years' imprisonment.

B. Sᴇxᴜᴀʟ Aꜱꜱᴀᴜʟᴛ

(1) Definition

Sexual Offences Act 2003, s.3

Sexual assault

14–87   3.—(1) A person (A) commits an offence if—

      (a) he intentionally touches another person (B),

      (b) the touching is sexual,

      (c) B does not consent to the touching, and

      (d) A does not reasonably believe that B consents.

    (2) Whether a belief is reasonable is to be determined having regard to all the circumstances, including any steps A has taken to ascertain whether B consents.

    (3) Sections 75 and 76 apply to an offence under this section.

14–88   See *ante*, §§ 14–81–14–82, regarding sections 75 and 76. Section 79(8) of the Act provides that:

79(8) Touching includes touching—
(a) with any part of the body,
(b) with anything else,
(c) through anything,
and in particular includes touching amounting to penetration.

Where the victim is under 13, the offence is contained in section 7 and is identical save that there is no "reasonable belief in consent" defence.

In *H.* [2005] EWCA Crim 732, the Court ruled that where a man had grabbed at the trousers of a female complainant, shortly after asking her "Do you fancy a shag?", the touching was "sexual" for the purposes of section 79(8) and the behaviour amounted to a section 3 offence. The Court set out the correct approach where an activity may be sexual. There are two distinct questions which should be considered: first, whether the touching could, because of its nature, be sexual, and secondly, whether because of the circumstances or the purpose of any person in relation to it, it was sexual.

In *Heard* [2007] EWCA Crim 125 a man was charged with an offence contrary to section 3. He sought to rely on self-induced intoxication as defence, namely that he was unable to form the specific or purposive intent required to intentionally touch someone. The Court of Appeal held, that despite "intentional touching" being an element of the offence which has to be proved this was not a crime of specific intent, a defendant therefore could not rely on self-induced intoxication as a defence.

(2) Allocation

This offence is triable either way. See Appendix F–57 for mode of trial guidelines.   **14–90**

(3) Sentence

Upon summary conviction the maximum sentence is six months' imprisonment. After commencement of the relevant provisions, the maximum custodial sentence in a magistrates' court is 12 months' imprisonment: *Criminal Justice Act* 2003, ss.154 and 282.   **14–91**

Where the touching is brief and takes place over clothing, recent decisions of the Court of Appeal would suggest that the magistrates' court's sentencing powers are sufficient.

In *Gledhill* [2005] EWCA Crim 290 the appellant, aged 41, pleaded guilty to one count of sexual assault. He had approached the 17-year-old victim on the street twice and touched her upper leg and groin area over her trousers. He admitted the offence in interview. He had one similar previous conviction dating from 1981, but was otherwise of good character. The Court of Appeal took account of the strong mitigation available and the Pre-Sentence Report, which suggested that he would be susceptible to one-on-one treatment. The sentence of imprisonment was substituted with a three year Community Rehabilitation Order.

In *Elvidge* [2005] EWCA Crim 1194 the Court of Appeal allowed an appeal against a sentence of eight months' imprisonment for an offence under section 3. The appellant had placed his hand on the complainant's seat in a pub, so that when she returned to her seat and sat down his hand went between her legs and touched her genitals over her trousers. The appellant was found guilty after trial, but had no previous convictions for sexual offences. The appeal was allowed in that a sentence of three months' imprisonment was substituted.

In *Mazzon* [2005] EWCA Crim 1702 the 23-year-old victim was followed into her hotel, at night, by the appellant who pushed her against a wall and touched her breast whilst his penis was exposed—his fly was undone. The appellant was 40 years old and effectively of good character. The Court of Appeal was referred to *Jolil* [2003] EWCA Crim 3395 and *Hayworth* [2004] EWCA Crim 2243. The appeal was allowed in that six months' imprisonment was substituted for the original sentence.

In *Bamonadio* [2005] EWCA Crim 3355 a sentence of six months' imprisonment was upheld where the appellant had rubbed himself against a 16-year-old girl, tried to kiss her, and pulled down her top to touch her breasts whilst attempting to pull her into an alleyway.

In *Wain* [2005] EWCA Crim 3488, the Court of Appeal considered the sentence for an offence contrary to section 7 of the Act (complainant under 13). The appellant had, whilst lying on the floor in a drunken stupor, opened the front of his trousers and grabbed the hand of an 11-year-old girl pulling it towards his crotch. He pleaded guilty at the magistrates' court; he had no previous convictions for sexual offences. The court substituted a three year community order with supervision requirements in order to reduce the risk of re-offending, but noted that a custodial sentence of around six months could well have been appropriate.

In *DPP v. Clutterbuck* [2006] EWHC 3447 the DPP appealed by way of case stated against the decision of a magistrates' court to sentence the respondent to a community order of less than 12 months, the impact of which meant that the respondent would be subject to a shorter period of registration on the sex offenders register, and would not be able to complete the full sex offenders programme which it was contended by probation would require a 24-month period. The questions posed for the High Court were (i) in light of the DPP's representations regarding how the court should approach sentencing, whether the decision of the court to impose a community order of less than 12 months was correct in law; (ii) the court should reconsider the length of the community order to enable a sex offenders' programme to be completed. Dismissing the appeal it was held that, the magistrates' had not erred in law, they had taken into consideration the effect the community order would have on the respondents' liberty, his previous good character and the pre-sentence report. In all the circumstances the community order of 11 months was appropriate.

C. Causing a Person to Engage in Sexual Activity without Consent

(1) Definition

Sexual Offences Act 2003, s.4

Causing a person to engage in sexual activity without consent

14–92   **4.**—(1) A person (A) commits an offence if—

    (a) he intentionally causes another person (B) to engage in an activity,

    (b) the activity is sexual,

    (c) B does not consent to engaging in the activity, and

    (d) A does not reasonably believe that B consents.

(2) Whether a belief is reasonable is to be determined having regard to all the circumstances, including any steps A has taken to ascertain whether B consents.

(3) Sections 75 and 76 apply to an offence under this section.

14–93   Section 8 of the Act creates a separate offence where the complainant is a child under 13. The offence is identical to this one save that there is no "reasonable belief in consent" defence.

See *ante*, §§ 14–81–14–82, regarding sections 75 and 76.

(2) Allocation

14–94   This offence is triable either way. If however, one or more of the following factors is present, the offence *must* be tried on indictment:

    (a) penetration of B's anus or vagina;

    (b) penetration of B's mouth with a person's penis;

    (c) penetration of a person's anus or vagina with a part of B's body or by B with anything else;

    (d) penetration of a person's mouth with B's penis.

Note that an offence under section 8 of the act (child under 13) must always be tried on indictment regardless of the facts.

(3) Sentence

The maximum sentence is one of six months' imprisonment if tried summarily, **14–95**
and/or a fine. After commencement of the relevant provisions, the maximum custodial
sentence in a magistrates' court will be 12 months' imprisonment: *Criminal Justice Act*
2003, ss.154 and 282.

V. CHILD SEX OFFENCES UNDER THE SEXUAL OFFENCES ACT 2003

A. INTRODUCTION

Child sex offences are those in which the complainant is under the age of 16. There **14–96**
are now statutory provisions with respect to the relevance of the complainant's age.

Relevant age provisions

The prosecution is required to prove that the child is under 16. In cases where the **14–97**
defendant claims to have believed that the child was 16 or over, it will be for the prosecution to prove that he did not believe this or that his belief was not reasonably held.
This provision as to mistaken belief in age does not apply where the child is under 13.

General sentencing provisions

The maximum sentence where an offender aged 18 or over is convicted summarily **14–98**
of a child sex offence is six months' imprisonment or a fine not exceeding the statutory
maximum or both. After commencement of the relevant provisions, the maximum
custodial sentence in a magistrates' court will be 12 months' imprisonment: *Criminal
Justice Act* 2003, ss.154 and 282.

Section 13 of the Act also provides that any of the child sex offences in sections 9 to
12 can be committed by a person under the age of 18, in which case the maximum
sentence is reduced to five years' custody. Such offences would normally, of course, be
tried in the youth court but the power to commit such offence to the Crown Court as
grave crimes is preserved by the amendment to section 91 of PCC(S)A 2000 contained
in Schedule 6, paragraph 13(2) to the *Sexual Offences Act* 2003.

In *Corran* [2005] EWCA Crim 192 the Court of Appeal, presided over by the Vice-
President of the Criminal Division, Rose L.J., considered sentences in respect of sexual
offences committed against children. Although the judgment is principally concerned
with rape of a child under 13 (an indictable only offence not included in this chapter),
the Court gave guidance that the same considerations, *i.e.* the defendant's age in relation to the complainant's age, the nature of the relationship of those involved, their
character and maturity, remorse, the use of contraception, and the consequences for the
complainant, should be taken into account when sentencing for offences under ss.9 and
10 of the Act.

In *Ismail* [2005] EWCA Crim 397, the Court of Appeal held that for offences which
appear to have had a significant impact on the victim it is essential for sentencing judges
to have victim impact statements, especially where a sexual offence has been committed
against a young victim, so that that impact can be taken into account when determining
the appropriate sentence.

B. SEXUAL ACTIVITY WITH A CHILD

(1) Definition

Sexual Offences Act 2003, s.9

Sexual activity with a child
   9.—(1) A person aged 18 or over (A) commits an offence if—   **14–99**

Part III

(a) he intentionally touches another person (B),

(b) the touching is sexual, and

(c) either—

   (i) B is under 16 and A does not reasonably believe that B is 16 or over, or

   (ii) B is under 13.

Touching is defined in section 79(8).

[See *ante*, § 14–89.]

(2) Allocation

14–100 The offence is triable either way except in the following circumstances where it *must* be tried on indictment:

Where the defendant is over 18 years of age and one or more of the following occurred:

(a) penetration of B's anus or vagina;

(b) penetration of B's mouth with a person's penis;

(c) penetration of a person's anus or vagina with a part of B's body or by B with anything else;

(d) penetration of a person's mouth with B's penis.

(3) Elements of the offence

14–101 Touching is defined in section 79(8) of the Act (see *ante*, § 14–89).

(4) Sentence

14–102 The maximum sentence is 6 six months' imprisonment and/or a fine when tried summarily. After commencement of the relevant provisions, the maximum custodial sentence in a magistrates' court will be 12 months' imprisonment: *Criminal Justice Act* 2003, ss.154 and 282.

In *Couch* [2005] EWCA Crim 1309, the Court of Appeal substituted a sentence of four months' detention for an offence under this section in a case involving an 18-year-old appellant and a 14-year-old complainant. After a family gathering involving heavy drinking, the complainant had consented to sexual touching, oral sex and some penile penetration. The complainant had made it clear that she was consenting from the outset of the investigation. The appellant pleaded guilty. The Court of Appeal relied upon Rose L.J.'s comments in *Corran* [2005] EWCA Crim 192 to the effect that where everyone is young and everyone consents, a very short period of custody is likely to suffice for a teenager.

In *Att-Gen.'s Reference (No.59 of 2006), Re (Nelson Doe)* [2006] EWCA Crim 2096, a sentence of 51 weeks' imprisonment suspended for two years was held to be unduly lenient, despite early guilty pleas in a case where the defendant had developed a sexual relationship with a 14 year old. The aggravating features of a breach of a position of trust—he was considered a father figure to her and had a close relationship with her family and the recurring nature of the offence meant a sentence of 51 weeks' imprisonment could not be justified. Taking into account the double jeopardy rule the court imposed a sentence of 18 months' immediate imprisonment.

In *Held* [2006] EWCA Crim 2174 the Court of Appeal upheld a sentence of 12 months' imprisonment, following a guilty plea to three counts of sexual activity with a child. A 41-year-old woman of previous good character, had developed an inappropriate relationship with a 14-year-old girl, who was a friend of her daughters and whom she coached as a member of a football team. The sexual activity had included kissing her breasts, touching over clothing and partial digital penetration of her vagina. The Court of Appeal reiterated that when adults are placed in a position of trust in relation to children which they abuse, the punishment is likely to be significant.

C. CAUSING OR INCITING A CHILD TO ENGAGE IN SEXUAL ACTIVITY

(1) Definition

Sexual Offences Act 2003, s.10

Causing or inciting a child to engage in sexual activity
   10.—(1) A person aged 18 or over (A) commits an offence if—   **14–103**
     (a) he intentionally causes or incites another person (B) to engage in an activity,
     (b) the activity is sexual, and
     (c) either
        (i)   B is under 16 and A does not reasonably believe that B is 16 or over, or
        (ii) B is under 13.

(2) Allocation

The offence is triable either way except in the following circumstances where it *must* **14–104**
be tried on indictment:

Where the defendant is over 18 years of age and one or more of the following occurred:
   (a) penetration of B's anus or vagina;
   (b) penetration of B's mouth with a person's penis;
   (c) penetration of a person's anus or vagina with a part of B's body or by B with
      anything else;
   (d) penetration of a person's mouth with B's penis.

(3) Sentence

The maximum sentence is six months' imprisonment and/or a fine when tried **14–105**
summarily. After the commencement of the relevant provisions, the maximum custodial
sentence in a magistrates' court will be 12 months' imprisonment: *Criminal Justice Act*
2003, ss.154 and 282. See *Corran, ante* at § 14–98.

D. ENGAGING IN SEXUAL ACTIVITY IN THE PRESENCE OF A CHILD

(1) Definition

Sexual Offences Act 2003, s.11

Engaging in sexual activity in the presence of a child
   11.—(1) A person aged 18 or over (A) commits an offence if—   **14–106**
     (a) he intentionally engages in an activity,
     (b) the activity is sexual,
     (c) for the purpose of obtaining sexual gratification, he engages in it—
        (i)   when another person (B) is present or is in a place from which A can be
           observed, and
        (ii) knowing or believing that B is aware, or intending that B should be aware,
           that he is engaging in it,
     (d) either
        (i)   B is under 16 and A does not reasonably believe that B is 16 or over, or
        (ii) is under 13.

(2) Allocation

This offence is triable either way.   **14–107**

(3) Sentence

The maximum sentence is six months' imprisonment and/or a fine when tried **14–108**

Part III

summarily. After the commencement of the relevant provisions, the maximum custodial sentence in a magistrates' court will be 12 months' imprisonment: *Criminal Justice Act* 2003, ss.154 and 282.

In *W. & T.* [2005] EWCA Crim 2448 the Court of Appeal substituted sentences of six months' imprisonment for the 12-month sentences originally imposed. The appellants were a couple who pleaded guilty. The womans' nine-year-old daughter had taken photographs of the couple having sexual intercourse. The judge made a finding of fact that the photographs were posed. The appellants were of previous good character and were assessed as not posing a risk to children in general. It was noted that only an immediate custodial sentence was appropriate.

E. CAUSING A CHILD TO WATCH A SEXUAL ACT

(1) Definition

Sexual Offences Act 2003, s.12

Causing a child to watch a sexual act

14–109　　12.—(1) A person aged 18 or over (A) commits an offence if—

　　(a) for the purpose of obtaining sexual gratification, he intentionally causes another person (B) to watch a third person engaging in an activity, or to look at an image of any person engaging in an activity,

　　(b) the activity is sexual, and

　　(c) either

　　　　(i) B is under 16 and A does not reasonably believe that B is 16 or over, or

　　　　(ii) is under 13.

(2) Allocation

14–110　　This offence is triable either way.

(3) Elements of the offence

14–111　　It is an element of the offence that the defendant caused the child to watch the sexual act for the purpose of obtaining sexual gratification; the sexual gratification need not be immediate, it can be long-term, short-term, immediate or deferred: *Abdullahi* [2006] EWCA Crim 2060.

(4) Sentence

14–112　　The maximum sentence is six months' imprisonment and/or a fine when tried summarily. After commencement of the relevant provisions, the maximum custodial sentence in a magistrates' court will be 12 months' imprisonment: *Criminal Justice Act* 2003, ss.154 and 282.

In *Corran*, (*ante*), it was suggested that the age and character of the child and the defendant, the nature of the act, the number of incidents, the impact on the child, remorse, and future risk were all relevant considerations when sentencing for offences under sections 11 and 12.

F. ARRANGING OR FACILITATING A CHILD SEX OFFENCE

(1) Definition

Sexual Offences Act 2003, s.14

Arranging or facilitating commission of a child sex offence

14–113　　14.—(1) A person commits an offence if—

　　(a) he intentionally arranges or facilitates something that he intends to do, intends another person to do, or believes that another person will do, in any part of the world, and

    (b) doing it will involve the commission of an offence under any of sections 9 to 13.

(2) A person does not commit an offence under this section if—

    (a) he arranges or facilitates something that he believes another person will do, but that he does not intend to do or intend another person to do, and

    (b) any offence within subsection (1)(b) would be an offence against a child for whose protection he acts.

(3) For the purposes of subsection (2)facilitating, a person acts for the protection of a child if he acts for the purpose of—

    (a) protecting the child from sexually transmitted infection,

    (b) protecting the physical safety of the child,

    (c) preventing the child from becoming pregnant, or

    (d) promoting the child's emotional well-being by the giving of advice,

and not for the purpose of obtaining sexual gratification or for the purpose of causing or encouraging the activity constituting the offence within subsection (1)(b) or the child's participation in it.

(2) Defence

The defence to this offence is afforded to anyone who acts to protect the physical **14–114** safety or emotional wellbeing of a child. It covers anyone providing contraception, contraceptive or family planning advice, and advice or guidance in sexual matters, including doctors, nurses, family planning clinic staff, teachers, magazine or newspaper columnists, parents and other relatives or friends. The test is that the actions were designed to protect the child and were not perpetrated for the purpose of obtaining sexual gratification.

(3) Allocation

This offence is triable either way. **14–115**

(4) Sentence

The maximum sentence is six months' imprisonment if tried summarily. After com- **14–116** mencement of the relevant provisions, the maximum custodial sentence in a magistrates' court will be 12 months' imprisonment: *Criminal Justice Act* 2003, ss.154 and 282. An offence contrary to section 14 is a "lifestyle offence" within the *Proceeds of Crime Act* 2002, Sched. 2, in respect of which a financial reporting order may be made under the *Serious Organised Crime and Police Act* 2005, s.76.

In *Harrison* [2005] EWCA Crim 3458, the Court of Appeal considered the appropriate sentence for an offence contrary to section 14 of the Act. Amongst other offences, the appellant had pleaded guilty to inciting a 14-year-old girl to engage in masturbation whilst on the telephone with him. The basis of plea stated that there was never to be a meeting between the appellant and the victim. The appellant was a man of good character except for a caution in 2001 for masturbation in a public place. The court substituted a sentence of 18 months' imprisonment for the 27 months originally imposed, and ordered that it run concurrently to the sentences for offences involving indecent photographs of children imposed in respect of other counts.

G. MEETING A CHILD FOLLOWING SEXUAL GROOMING

(1) Definition

Sexual Offences Act 2003, s.15

Meeting a child following sexual grooming etc.

    15.—(1) A person aged 18 or over (A) commits an offence if— **14–117**

    (a) having met or communicated with another person (B) on at least two earlier occasions, he—

      (i) intentionally meets B, or

      (ii) travels with the intention of meeting B in any part of the world,

    (b) at the time, he intends to do anything to or in respect of B, during or after the meeting and in any part of the world, which if done will involve the commission by A of a relevant offence,

    (c) B is under 16, and

    (d) A does not reasonably believe that B is 16 or over.

  (2) In subsection (1)—

    (a) the reference to A having met or communicated with B is a reference to A having met B in any part of the world or having communicated with B by any means from, to or in any part of the world;

    (b) "relevant offence" means—

      (i) an offence under this Part,

      (ii) an offence within any of paragraphs 61 to 92 of Schedule 3, or

      (iii) anything done outside England and Wales and Northern Ireland which is not an offence within sub-paragraph (i) or (ii) but would be an offence within sub-paragraph (i) if done in England and Wales.

14–118   Note that this offence enables charges to be brought before any other substantive offence takes place.

(2) Allocation

14–119   This offence is triable either way.

(3) Sentence

14–120   The maximum sentence is six months' imprisonment if tried summarily. After commencement of the relevant provisions, the maximum custodial sentence in a magistrates' court will be 12 months' imprisonment: *Criminal Justice Act* 2003, ss.154 and 282.

H. ABUSE OF A POSITION OF TRUST

(1) Definition

14–121   The abuse of trust offences are identical to the child sex offences at section 9 to 12 inasmuch as they cover sexual activity of the same nature, but they are committed in circumstances where a breach of trust by the offender is an inherent element of the offence. The complainant must be under 18 for the offences above to be properly charged.

Sexual Offences Act 2003, ss.16–19

Abuse of position of trust: sexual activity with a child

14–122   **16.**—(1) A person aged 18 or over (A) commits an offence if—

    (a) he intentionally touches another person (B),

    (b) the touching is sexual,

    (c) A is in a position of trust in relation to B,

    (d) where subsection (2) applies, A knows or could reasonably be expected to know of the circumstances by virtue of which he is in a position of trust in relation to B, and

    (e) either—

      (i) B is under 18 and A does not reasonably believe that B is 18 or over, or

      (ii) B is under 13.

  (2) This subsection applies where A—

    (a) is in a position of trust in relation to B by virtue of circumstances within section 21(2), (3), (4) or (5), and

(b) is not in such a position of trust by virtue of other circumstances.

(3) Where in proceedings for an offence under this section it is proved that the other person was under 18, the defendant is to be taken not to have reasonably believed that that person was 18 or over unless sufficient evidence is adduced to raise an issue as to whether he reasonably believed it.

(4) Where in proceedings for an offence under this section—

(a) it is proved that the defendant was in a position of trust in relation to the other person by virtue of circumstances within section 21(2), (3), (4) or (5), and

(b) it is not proved that he was in such a position of trust by virtue of other circumstances,

it is to be taken that the defendant knew or could reasonably have been expected to know of the circumstances by virtue of which he was in such a position of trust unless sufficient evidence is adduced to raise an issue as to whether he knew or could reasonably have been expected to know of those circumstances.

Abuse of position of trust: causing or inciting a child to engage in sexual activity

17.—(1) A person aged 18 or over (A) commits an offence if— **14–123**

(a) he intentionally causes or incites another person (B) to engage in an activity,

(b) the activity is sexual,

(c) A is in a position of trust in relation to B,

(d) where subsection (2) applies, A knows or could reasonably be expected to know of the circumstances by virtue of which he is in a position of trust in relation to B, and

(e) either—

(i) B is under 18 and A does not reasonably believe that B is 18 or over, or

(ii) B is under 13.

(2) This subsection applies where A—

(a) is in a position of trust in relation to B by virtue of circumstances within section 21(2), (3), (4) or (5), and

(b) is not in such a position of trust by virtue of other circumstances.

(3) Where in proceedings for an offence under this section it is proved that the other person was under 18, the defendant is to be taken not to have reasonably believed that that person was 18 or over unless sufficient evidence is adduced to raise an issue as to whether he reasonably believed it.

(4) Where in proceedings for an offence under this section—

(a) it is proved that the defendant was in a position of trust in relation to the other person by virtue of circumstances within section 21(2), (3), (4) or (5), and

(b) it is not proved that he was in such a position of trust by virtue of other circumstances,

it is to be taken that the defendant knew or could reasonably have been expected to know of the circumstances by virtue of which he was in such a position of trust unless sufficient evidence is adduced to raise an issue as to whether he knew or could reasonably have been expected to know of those circumstances.

Abuse of position of trust: sexual activity in the presence of a child

18.—(1) A person aged 18 or over (A) commits an offence if— **14–124**

(a) he intentionally engages in an activity,

(b) the activity is sexual,

(c) for the purpose of obtaining sexual gratification, he engages in it—

(i) when another person (B) is present or is in a place from which A can be observed, and

(ii) knowing or believing that B is aware, or intending that B should be aware, that he is engaging in it,

(d) A is in a position of trust in relation to B,

(e) where subsection (2) applies, A knows or could reasonably be expected to know of the circumstances by virtue of which he is in a position of trust in relation to B, and

(f) either—

(i) B is under 18 and A does not reasonably believe that B is 18 or over, or

(ii) B is under 13.

(2) This subsection applies where A—

    (a) is in a position of trust in relation to B by virtue of circumstances within section 21(2), (3), (4) or (5), and

    (b) is not in such a position of trust by virtue of other circumstances.

(3) Where in proceedings for an offence under this section it is proved that the other person was under 18, the defendant is to be taken not to have reasonably believed that that person was 18 or over unless sufficient evidence is adduced to raise an issue as to whether he reasonably believed it.

(4) Where in proceedings for an offence under this section—

    (a) it is proved that the defendant was in a position of trust in relation to the other person by virtue of circumstances within section 21(2), (3), (4) or (5), and

    (b) it is not proved that he was in such a position of trust by virtue of other circumstances,

it is to be taken that the defendant knew or could reasonably have been expected to know of the circumstances by virtue of which he was in such a position of trust unless sufficient evidence is adduced to raise an issue as to whether he knew or could reasonably have been expected to know of those circumstances.

Abuse of position of trust: causing a child to watch a sexual act

14–125　　19.—(1) A person aged 18 or over (A) commits an offence if—

    (a) for the purpose of obtaining sexual gratification, he intentionally causes another person (B) to watch a third person engaging in an activity, or to look at an image of any person engaging in an activity,

    (b) the activity is sexual,

    (c) A is in a position of trust in relation to B,

    (d) where subsection (2) applies, A knows or could reasonably be expected to know of the circumstances by virtue of which he is in a position of trust in relation to B, and

    (e) either—

      (i) B is under 18 and A does not reasonably believe that B is 18 or over, or

      (ii) B is under 13.

(2) This subsection applies where A—

    (a) is in a position of trust in relation to B by virtue of circumstances within section 21(2), (3), (4) or (5), and

    (b) is not in such a position of trust by virtue of other circumstances.

(3) Where in proceedings for an offence under this section it is proved that the other person was under 18, the defendant is to be taken not to have reasonably believed that that person was 18 or over unless sufficient evidence is adduced to raise an issue as to whether he reasonably believed it.

(4) Where in proceedings for an offence under this section—

    (a) it is proved that the defendant was in a position of trust in relation to the other person by virtue of circumstances within section 21(2), (3), (4) or (5), and

    (b) it is not proved that he was in such a position of trust by virtue of other circumstances,

it is to be taken that the defendant knew or could reasonably have been expected to know of the circumstances by virtue of which he was in such a position of trust unless sufficient evidence is adduced to raise an issue as to whether he knew or could reasonably have been expected to know of those circumstances.

(2) Elements of the offence

Position of trust

Sexual Offences Act 2003, ss.21–22

Positions of trust

14–126　　21.—(1) For the purposes of sections 16 to 19, a person (A) is in a position of trust in relation to another person (B) if—

(a) any of the following subsections applies, or

(b) any condition specified in an order made by the Secretary of State is met.

(2) This subsection applies if A looks after persons under 18 who are detained in an institution by virtue of a court order or under an enactment, and B is so detained in that institution.

(3) This subsection applies if A looks after persons under 18 who are resident in a home or other place in which—

(a) accommodation and maintenance are provided by an authority under section 23(2) of the *Children Act* 1989 (c. 41) or Article 27(2) of the *Children (Northern Ireland) Order* 1995 (S.I. 1995 No. 755 (N.I. 2)), or

(b) accommodation is provided by a voluntary organisation under section 59(1) of that Act or Article 75(1) of that *Order*,

and B is resident, and is so provided with accommodation and maintenance or accommodation, in that place.

(4) This subsection applies if A looks after persons under 18 who are accommodated and cared for in one of the following institutions—

(a) a hospital,

(b) an independent clinic,

(c) a care home, residential care home or private hospital,

(d) a community home, voluntary home or children's home,

(e) a home provided under section 82(5) of the *Children Act* 1989, or

(f) a residential family centre,

and B is accommodated and cared for in that institution.

(5) This subsection applies if A looks after persons under 18 who are receiving education at an educational institution and B is receiving, and A is not receiving, education at that institution.

(6) This subsection applies if A is appointed to be the guardian of B under Article 159 or 160 of the *Children (Northern Ireland) Order* 1995 (S.I. 1995 No. 755 (N.I. 2)).

(7) This subsection applies if A is engaged in the provision of services under, or pursuant to anything done under—

(a) sections 8 to 10 of the *Employment and Training Act* 1973 (c. 50), or

(b) section 114 of the *Learning and Skills Act* 2000 (c. 21),

and, in that capacity, looks after B on an individual basis.

(8) This subsection applies if A regularly has unsupervised contact with B (whether face to face or by any other means)—

(a) in the exercise of functions of a local authority under section 20 or 21 of the *Children Act* 1989 (c. 41), or

(b) in the exercise of functions of an authority under Article 21 or 23 of the *Children (Northern Ireland) Order* 1995.

(9) This subsection applies if A, as a person who is to report to the court under section 7 of the *Children Act* 1989 or Article 4 of the *Children (Northern Ireland) Order* 1995 on matters relating to the welfare of B, regularly has unsupervised contact with B (whether face to face or by any other means).

(10) This subsection applies if A is a personal adviser appointed for B under—

(a) section 23B(2) of, or paragraph 19C of Schedule 2 to, the *Children Act* 1989, or

(b) Article 34A(10) or 34C(2) of the *Children (Northern Ireland) Order* 1995,

and, in that capacity, looks after B on an individual basis.

(11) This subsection applies if—

(a) B is subject to a care order, a supervision order or an education supervision order, and

(b) in the exercise of functions conferred by virtue of the order on an authorised person or the authority designated by the order, A looks after B on an individual basis.

(12) This subsection applies if A—

(a) is an officer of the Service appointed for B under section 41(1) of the *Children Act* 1989,

(b) is appointed a children's guardian of B under rule 6 or rule 18 of the *Adoption Rules* 1984 (S.I. 1984 No. 265), or

(c) is appointed to be the guardian ad litem of B under rule 9.5 of the *Family*

Proceedings Rules 1991 (S. I. 1991/1247) or under Article 60(1) of the *Children (Northern Ireland) Order* 1995,

and, in that capacity, regularly has unsupervised contact with B (whether face to face or by any other means).

(13) This subsection applies if—

    (a) B is subject to requirements imposed by or under an enactment on his release from detention for a criminal offence, or is subject to requirements imposed by a court order made in criminal proceedings, and

    (b) A looks after B on an individual basis in pursuance of the requirements.

Positions of trust: interpretation

14–127   **22.**—(1) The following provisions apply for the purposes of section 21.

(2) Subject to subsection (3), a person looks after persons under 18 if he is regularly involved in caring for, training, supervising or being in sole charge of such persons.

(3) A person (A) looks after another person (B) on an individual basis if—

    (a) A is regularly involved in caring for, training or supervising B, and

    (b) in the course of his involvement, A regularly has unsupervised contact with B (whether face to face or by any other means).

(4) A person receives education at an educational institution if—

    (a) he is registered or otherwise enrolled as a pupil or student at the institution, or

    (b) he receives education at the institution under arrangements with another educational institution at which he is so registered or otherwise enrolled.

(5) In section 21—

"authority" —

    (a) in relation to England and Wales, means a local authority;

    (b) in relation to Northern Ireland, has the meaning given by Article 2(2) of the *Children (Northern Ireland) Order* 1995 (S.I. 1995 No. 755 (N.I. 2));

"care home" means an establishment which is a care home for the purposes of the *Care Standards Act* 2000 (c. 14);

"care order" has—

    (a) in relation to England and Wales, the same meaning as in the *Children Act* 1989 (c. 41), and

    (b) in relation to Northern Ireland, the same meaning as in the *Children (Northern Ireland) Order* 1995;

"children's home" has—

    (a) in relation to England and Wales, the meaning given by section 1 of the *Care Standards Act* 2000, and

    (b) in relation to Northern Ireland, the meaning that would be given by Article 9 of the *Health and Personal Social Services (Quality, Improvement and Regulation) (Northern Ireland) Order* 2003 (S.I. 2003 No. 431 (N.I. 9)) ("the 2003 Order") if in paragraph (4) of that Article sub-paragraphs (d), (f) and (g) were omitted;

"community home" has the meaning given by section 53 of the *Children Act* 1989;

"education supervision order" has—

    (a) in relation to England and Wales, the meaning given by section 36 of the *Children Act* 1989, and

    (b) in relation to Northern Ireland, the meaning given by Article 49(1) of the *Children (Northern Ireland) Order* 1995;

"hospital" —

    (a) in relation to England and Wales, means a hospital within the meaning given by section 128(1) of the *National Health Service Act* 1977 (c. 49), or any other establishment which is a hospital within the meaning given by section 2(3) of the *Care Standards Act* 2000 (c. 14);

    (b) in relation to Northern Ireland, means a hospital within the meaning given by Article 2(2) of the *Health and Personal Social Services (Northern Ireland) Order* 1972 (S.I. 1972 No. 1265 (N.I. 14)), or any other establishment which is a hospital within the meaning given by Article 2(2) of the 2003 Order;

"independent clinic" has—

(a) in relation to England and Wales, the meaning given by section 2 of the *Care Standards Act* 2000;

(b) in relation to Northern Ireland, the meaning given by Article 2(2) of the 2003 Order;

"private hospital" has the meaning given by Article 90(2) of the *Mental Health (Northern Ireland) Order* 1986 (S.I. 1986 No. 595 (N.I. 4));

"residential care home" means an establishment which is a residential care home for the purposes of the 2003 Order;

"residential family centre" has the meaning given by section 22 of the *Health and Personal Social Services Act (Northern Ireland)* 2001 (c. 3);

"supervision order" has—

(a) in relation to England and Wales, the meaning given by section 31(11) of the *Children Act* 1989 (c. 41), and

(b) in relation to Northern Ireland, the meaning given by Article 49(1) of the *Children (Northern Ireland) Order* 1995 (S.I. 1995 No. 755 (N.I. 2));

"voluntary home" has—

(a) in relation to England and Wales, the meaning given by section 60(3) of the *Children Act* 1989, and

(b) in relation to Northern Ireland, the meaning given by Article 74(1) of the *Children (Northern Ireland) Order* 1995.

Consent

The offences are drafted so as to protect all children under 18, but they are primarily intended to be charged in relation to victims who are over the age of consent and where the sexual activity would not be an offence save for the abuse of trust. Any sexual activity involving a child under 16 is unlawful and one of the generic child sex offences or offences against a child under 13 should be charged. The breach of trust will be an aggravating factor for sentencing purposes. Sections 6–19 apply regardless of consent between the parties. Importantly, therefore, the normal age of consent at 16 will not apply to offences under these sections. **14–128**

(3) Defences

There are a number of specific defences to the offences within these sections. **14–129**

Where the complainant is over 16 at the time of the conduct and:

(i) the parties are lawfully married at the time of the offence (s.23); and

(ii) a lawful sexual relationship existed between the parties immediately before the position of trust arose (s.24);

no offence will have been committed. There is an evidential burden on the defendant to prove that either of these circumstances existed at the time of the offence.

The *Civil Partnership Act* 2004 extended the marriage exceptions in the *Sexual Offences Act* 2003 to include "civil partnerships" as defined.

The age of the complainant at the time of the offence

If the child is between 13 and 18 at the time of the offence the prosecution must prove that the defendant did not reasonably believe that the child was over 18. **14–130**

It will be taken that the defendant did not reasonably believe that the complainant was aged 18 or over, unless he can raise significant evidence to the contrary. This presumption does not apply where the defendant looks after the complainant in one of the following settings:

(a) the complainant is detained by virtue of a court order or enactment;

(b) the complainant is in a hospital, independent clinic, care home or residential family centre;

(c) the complainant is receiving education at an educational institution and the defendant is not receiving education at that institution;

and the defendant looks after the complainant in a caring or training role.

Knowledge of the position of trust

14–131　　If the defendant looks after the complainant in one of the scenarios (a) to (c) *ante*, there will be a presumption that the defendant knew or could reasonably have been expected to know of the position of trust unless he can raise significant evidence to the contrary.

(4) Sentence

14–132　　In respect of each offence the maximum sentence upon summary conviction is six months' imprisonment and/or a fine. After commencement of the relevant provisions, the maximum custodial sentence in a magistrates' court will be 12 months' imprisonment: *Criminal Justice Act* 2003, ss.154 and 282.

VI. FAMILIAL SEXUAL OFFENCES UNDER THE SEXUAL OFFENCES ACT 2003

A. Definition of a Family Relationship

14–133　　Subsections (3), (4) and (5) of section 27 set out the different circumstances in which a family relationship between the defendant and the complainant will exist.

Sexual Offences Act 2003, s.27

Family relationships

14–134　　27.—(1) The relation of one person (A) to another (B) is within this section if—

　　　(a) it is within any of subsections (2) to (4), or

　　　(b) it would be within one of those subsections but for section 67 of the *Adoption and Children Act* 2002 (c. 38) (status conferred by adoption).

　　(2) The relation of A to B is within this subsection if—

　　　(a) one of them is the other's parent, grandparent, brother, sister, half-brother, half-sister, aunt or uncle, or

　　　(b) A is or has been B's foster parent.

　　(3) The relation of A to B is within this subsection if A and B live or have lived in the same household, or A is or has been regularly involved in caring for, training, supervising or being in sole charge of B, and—

　　　(a) one of them is or has been the other's step-parent,

　　　(b) A and B are cousins,

　　　(c) one of them is or has been the other's stepbrother or stepsister, or

　　　(d) the parent or present or former foster parent of one of them is or has been the other's foster parent.

　　(4) The relation of A to B is within this subsection if—

　　　(a) A and B live in the same household, and

　　　(b) A is regularly involved in caring for, training, supervising or being in sole charge of B.

　　(5) For the purposes of this section—

　　　(a) "aunt" means the sister or half-sister of a person's parent, and "uncle" has a corresponding meaning;

　　　(b) "cousin" means the child of an aunt or uncle;

　　　(c) a person is a child's foster parent if—

　　　　(i) he is a person with whom the child has been placed under section 23(2)(a) or 59(1)(a) of the *Children Act* 1989 (c. 41) (fostering for local authority or voluntary organisation), or

　　　　(ii) he fosters the child privately, within the meaning given by section 66(1)(b) of that Act;

　　　(d) a person is another's partner (whether they are of different sexes or the same sex) if they live together as partners in an enduring family relationship;

(e) "step-parent" includes a parent's partner and "stepbrother" and "stepsister" include the child of a parent's partner.

B. RELEVANCE OF AGE

Where the complainant is under 13, the offences are ones of strict liability. If the complainant is between 13 and 18, the defendant will have the evidential burden of showing that he reasonably believed that the complainant was over 18. **14–135**

C. DEFENCES

(1) Marriage exception

The marriage defence applies where the complainant was aged 16 or over at the time of the alleged offence. **14–136**

The *Civil Partnership Act* 2004 extended the marriage exceptions in the *Sexual Offences Act* 2003 to include "civil partnerships" as defined.

(2) Knowledge of the family relationship

There is an evidential burden on the defendant to prove that he did not know and could not reasonably have been expected to know that a familial relationship existed. **14–137**

D. SEXUAL ACTIVITY WITH A FAMILY MEMBER

(1) Definition

Sexual Offences Act 2003, s.25

Sexual activity with a child family member
   25.—(1) A person (A) commits an offence if—   **14–138**
     (a) he intentionally touches another person (B),
     (b) the touching is sexual,
     (c) the relation of A to B is within section 27,
     (d) A knows or could reasonably be expected to know that his relation to B is of a description falling within that section
Touching is defined in section 79(8), see *ante*, § 14–89.

(2) Allocation

This offence is triable either way except in the following circumstances when it must be tried on indictment: Where the defendant is aged 18 or over and one or more of the following occurred: **14–139**
   (a) penetration of B's anus or vagina with a part of A's body or anything else;
   (b) penetration of B's mouth with A's penis;
   (c) penetration of A's anus or vagina with a part of B's body; or
   (d) penetration of A's mouth with B's penis.

Note that section 8 of the Act creates a separate offence where a child under 18 is the victim; this must always be tried as indictment regardless of the facts.

(3) Sentence

Upon summary conviction the maximum sentence is six months' imprisonment. After commencement of the relevant provisions, the maximum custodial sentence in a magistrates' court will be 12 months' imprisonment: *Criminal Justice Act* 2003, ss.154 and 282. **14–140**

In *Thomas* [2005] EWCA Crim 2343 the Court of Appeal held that categorising the seriousness of an offence contrary to section 25 according to the particular type of relationship between the parties, *i.e.* incest/sexual intercourse with a child in foster care, etc. was not entirely appropriate. The seriousness of the offence lay in the abuse of the relationship with a child. The court in sentencing should take into consideration the age of the parties (the younger the child and the greater the gap in ages the more serious the offence), the extent and nature of the sexual activity and the number of occasions upon which it occurred.

E. Inciting a Child Family Member to Engage in Sexual Activity

(1) Definition

Sexual Offences Act 2003, s.26

Inciting a child family member to engage in sexual activity

14–141   **26.**—(1) A person (A) commits an offence if—
   (a) he intentionally incites another person (B) to touch, or allow himself to be touched by, A,
   (b) the touching is sexual,
   (c) the relation of A to B is within section 27,
   (d) A knows or could reasonably be expected to know that his relation to B is of a description falling within that section,

(2) Allocation

14–142   This offence is triable either way. If however, one or more of the following factors is present, the offence *must* be tried on indictment:
   (a) penetration of B's anus or vagina;
   (b) penetration of B's mouth with a person's penis;
   (c) penetration of a person's anus or vagina with a part of B's body or by B with anything else;
   (d) penetration of a person's mouth with B's penis.

Note that section 8 of the act creates a separate offence where a child under 13 is the victim; this must always be tried on indictment regardless of the facts.

(3) Sentence

14–143   Upon summary conviction the maximum sentence is six months' imprisonment and/or a fine. After commencement of the relevant provisions, the maximum custodial sentence in a magistrates' court will be 12 months' imprisonment: *Criminal Justice Act* 2003, ss.154 and 282.

In *R.* [2005] EWCA Crim 1296 the Court held that there was nothing wrong in principle in passing a custodial sentence for this offence. The court reduced the sentence to one of six months' imprisonment plus a 12-month extended licence where the appellant had asked his 12-year-old step-daughter if he could perform a sexual act on her. It should be noted that this case was tried on indictment.

F. Sex with an Adult Relative

14–144   The act defines two offences, one of penetration and the other of another consenting to the complainant penetrating them.

(1) Definition

Sexual Offences Act 2003, ss.64(1)–(4), 65(1)–(4)

Sex with an adult relative: penetration

14–145   **64.**—(1) A person aged 16 or over (A) commits an offence if—

(a) he intentionally penetrates another person's vagina or anus with a part of his body or anything else, or penetrates another person's mouth with his penis,

(b) the penetration is sexual,

(c) the other person (B) is aged 18 or over,

(d) A is related to B in a way mentioned in subsection (2), and

(e) A knows or could reasonably be expected to know that he is related to B in that way.

(2) The ways that A may be related to B are as parent, grandparent, child, grandchild, brother, sister, half-brother, half-sister, uncle, aunt, nephew or niece.

(3) In subsection (2)—

(a) "uncle" means the brother of a person's parent, and "aunt" has a corresponding meaning;

(b) "nephew" means the child of a person's brother or sister, and "niece" has a corresponding meaning.

(4) Where in proceedings for an offence under this section it is proved that the defendant was related to the other person in any of those ways, it is to be taken that the defendant knew or could reasonably have been expected to know that he was related in that way unless sufficient evidence is adduced to raise an issue as to whether he knew or could reasonably have been expected to know that he was.

Sex with an adult relative: consenting to penetration

65.—(1) A person aged 16 or over (A) commits an offence if—   **14–146**

(a) another person (B) penetrates A's vagina or anus with a part of B's body or anything else, or penetrates A's mouth with B's penis,

(b) A consents to the penetration,

(c) the penetration is sexual,

(d) B is aged 18 or over,

(e) A is related to B in a way mentioned in subsection (2), and

(f) A knows or could reasonably be expected to know that he is related to B in that way.

(2) The ways that A may be related to B are as parent, grandparent, child, grandchild, brother, sister, half-brother, half-sister, uncle, aunt, nephew or niece.

(3) In subsection (2)—

(a) "uncle" means the brother of a person's parent, and "aunt" has a corresponding meaning;

(b) "nephew" means the child of a person's brother or sister, and "niece" has a corresponding meaning.

(4) Where in proceedings for an offence under this section it is proved that the defendant was related to the other person in any of those ways, it is to be taken that the defendant knew or could reasonably have been expected to know that he was related in that way unless sufficient evidence is adduced to raise an issue as to whether he knew or could reasonably have been expected to know that he was.

(2) Allocation

Both of these offences are triable either way.   **14–147**

(3) Sentence

Upon summary conviction the maximum sentence is six months' imprisonment **14–148** and/or a fine. After commencement of the relevant provisions, the maximum custodial sentence in a magistrates' court will be 12 months' imprisonment: *Criminal Justice Act* 2003, ss.154 and 282.

VII. OFFENCES AGAINST PERSONS WITH MENTAL DISORDERS UNDER THE SEXUAL OFFENCES ACT 2003

A. MENTAL DISORDER

The act changed significantly the previous legislation in this area which required the **14–149** victim to be deemed "defective" and prosecutions could only be brought with the consent of the DPP.

14–150   The meaning of "mental disorder" is contained in section 79(6) of the Act and mirrors section 1 of the *Mental Health Act* 1983 in its meaning.

Mental Health Act 1983, s.1

Application of Act: "mental disorder"

14–151   **1.**—(1) The provisions of this Act shall have effect with respect to the reception, care and treatment of mentally disordered patients, the management of their property and other related matters.

(2) In this Act—

"mental disorder" means mental illness, arrested or incomplete development of mind, psychopathic disorder and any other disorder or disability of mind and "mentally disordered" shall be construed accordingly;

"severe mental impairment" means a state of arrested or incomplete development of mind which includes severe impairment of intelligence and social functioning and is associated with abnormally aggressive or seriously irresponsible conduct on the part of the person concerned and "severely mentally impaired" shall be construed accordingly;

"mental impairment" means a state of arrested or incomplete development of mind (not amounting to severe mental impairment) which includes significant impairment of intelligence and social functioning and is associated with abnormally aggressive or seriously irresponsible conduct on the part of the person concerned and "mentally impaired" shall be construed accordingly;

"psychopathic disorder" means a persistent disorder or disability of mind (whether or not including significant impairment of intelligence) which results in abnormally aggressive or seriously irresponsible conduct on the part of the person concerned;

and other expressions shall have the meanings assigned to them in section 145 below.

(3) Nothing in subsection (2) above shall be construed as implying that a person may be dealt with under this Act as suffering from mental disorder, or from any form of mental disorder described in this section, by reason only of promiscuity or other immoral conduct, sexual deviancy or dependence on alcohol or drugs.

B. Sexual Activity with a Person with a Mental Disorder Impeding Choice and Causing or Inciting a Person with a Mental Disorder Impeding Choice to Engage in Sexual Activity

14–152   The offences in sections 30 to 32 relate to persons whose mental functioning is so impaired at the time of the sexual activity that they are deemed to be "unable to refuse" either because of, or for a reason relating to, their mental disorder. Examples of activity covered include where D causes X to have sex with him / D causes X to undress for him for sexual gratification / D causes X to have sex with D's friend.

Section 31 "inciting", is included to cover scenarios where the actual act(s) does not take place.

The definition of being "unable to refuse" is contained in subsection (2) of sections 30 to 33, and is only relevant to these offences. B is unable to refuse if—

(a) he lacks the capacity to choose whether to agree to the touching (whether because he lacks sufficient understanding of the nature or reasonably foreseeable consequences of what is being done, or for any other reason); or

(b) he is unable to communicate such a choice to A.

(1) Definition

Sexual Offences Act 2003, ss.30(1), 31(1)

Sexual activity with a person with a mental disorder impeding choice

14–153   **30.**—(1) A person (A) commits an offence if—

    (a) he intentionally touches another person (B),

    (b) the touching is sexual,

    (c) B is unable to refuse because of or for a reason related to a mental disorder, and

    (d) A knows or could reasonably be expected to know that B has a mental disorder and that because of it or for a reason related to it B is likely to be unable to refuse.

Causing or inciting a person, with a mental disorder impeding choice, to engage in sexual activity

31.—(1) A person (A) commits an offence if—   **14–154**

    (a) he intentionally causes or incites another person (B) to engage in an activity,

    (b) the activity is sexual,

    (c) B is unable to refuse because of or for a reason related to a mental disorder, and

    (d) A knows or could reasonably be expected to know that B has a mental disorder and that because of it or for a reason related to it B is likely to be unable to refuse.

(2) Allocation

This offence is triable either way. If however, one or more of the following factors is **14–155** present, the offence *must* be tried on indictment:

    (a) penetration of B's anus or vagina;

    (b) penetration of B's mouth with a person's penis;

    (c) penetration of a person's anus or vagina with a part of B's body or by B with anything else;

    (d) penetration of a person's mouth with B's penis.

(3) Elements of the offence

In *Hulme v. DPP* [2006] EWHC 1347 it was held that a woman suffering with cere- **14–156** bral palsy with a mental age well below her chronological 27 years, although she was able to speak she was not able to communicate her choice of whether to agree to sexual touching within the meaning of section 30(2) and was therefore "unable to refuse because of or for a reason related to a mental disorder" (s.30(1)(c)).

(4) Sentence

Upon summary conviction the maximum sentence is six months' imprisonment. Af- **14–157** ter commencement of the relevant provisions, the maximum custodial sentence in a magistrates' court will be 12 months' imprisonment: *Criminal Justice Act* 2003, ss.154 and 282.

In *D. (Donald David)* [2005] EWCA Crim 1459, the 74-year-old appellant had pleaded guilty to an offence under section 30. The complainant was his partner's grand-daughter, aged 25 but with a mental age of between four and eight years old. The appellant had previously been cautioned for indecently assaulting the complainant, and was charged after being found with his hand down her trousers and between her legs. He denied digital penetration in an accepted basis of plea. The Court of Appeal regarded the matter as a gross breach of trust, but found there were exceptional circumstances and reduced the custodial element of the sentence to six months but maintained the extended licence period of two years and nine months.

In *Jones* [2005] EWCA Crim 3414, CA the appellant was convicted of an offence under section 31. The complainant was a 19-year-old who suffered from Down's syndrome. He had the mental age of a five-year-old. The appellant was seen in the toilets of a public house with his hand on the complainant's shoulder and his penis exposed. A psychiatrist concluded that the complainant did not have the capacity to consent to sexual activity. The appellant was apprehended at the scene and badly beaten by the family. The Court of Appeal held that the general considerations set out in *Milberry and Others* [2003] 2 Cr.App.R.(S.) 31, in relation to the level of culpability of the offender and the level of risk posed by the offender to society also applied to sexual offences other than rape. Also that offences of this kind, depending on the facts, could be commensurable in terms of seriousness to offences against children. The appellant was treated as a man of good character. The appeal was allowed in that the sentence of three years imprisonment was reduced to 15 months' imprisonment.

In *Att.-Gen.'s Reference (No. 106 of 2005), Re (Hunter)* [2006] EWCA Crim 510 a two-year community rehabilitation order with a condition of residence at a probation hostel for six months was upheld on appeal. The defendant, a 45-year-old man, pleaded guilty to having unprotected sexual intercourse and oral sex with a 17-year-old girl with learning difficulties, whilst her mother had left her in his care. The complainant had indicated consent and did not appear to be either physically or psychologically affected. The conduct had stopped prior to it being discovered.

C. Engaging in Sexual Activity in the Presence of a Person with a Mental Disorder Impeding Choice

14–158   This offence occurs where the defendant engages in sexual activity with another in the presence of the complainant with a mental disorder for the purpose of sexual gratification. The defendant must know or believe that the complainant is aware of the activity or intends them to be aware of it.

This offence can also include situations where the defendant commits a sexual act that does not involve a third party, for example where he engages in self-masturbation. Offences under this section can be committed either in the physical presence of the complainant or in a place from which the defendant can be observed by the complainant, *e.g.* via a webcam.

(1) Definition

Sexual Offences Act 2003, s.32(1)

Engaging in sexual activity in the presence of a person with a mental disorder impeding choice

14–159   **32.**—(1) A person (A) commits an offence if—

    (a) he intentionally engages in an activity,

    (b) the activity is sexual,

    (c) for the purpose of obtaining sexual gratification, he engages in it—

        (i) when another person (B) is present or is in a place from which A can be observed, and

        (ii) knowing or believing that B is aware, or intending that B should be aware, that he is engaging in it,

    (d) B is unable to refuse because of or for a reason related to a mental disorder, and

    (e) A knows or could reasonably be expected to know that B has a mental disorder and that because of it or for a reason related to it B is likely to be unable to refuse.

(2) Allocation

14–160   This offence is triable either way.

(3) Sentence

14–161   Upon summary conviction the maximum sentence is six months' imprisonment. After commencement of the relevant provisions, the maximum custodial sentence in a magistrates' court will be 12 months' imprisonment: *Criminal Justice Act* 2003, ss.154 and 282.

D. Causing a Person with a Mental Disorder to Watch a Sexual Act

(1) Definition

Sexual Offences Act 2003, s.33(1)

Causing a person, with a mental disorder impeding choice, to watch a sexual act
33.—(1) A person (A) commits an offence if—   **14–162**
   (a) for the purpose of obtaining sexual gratification, he intentionally causes another person (B) to watch a third person engaging in an activity, or to look at an image of any person engaging in an activity,
   (b) the activity is sexual,
   (c) B is unable to refuse because of or for a reason related to a mental disorder, and
   (d) A knows or could reasonably be expected to know that B has a mental disorder and that because of it or for a reason related to it B is likely to be unable to refuse.

Sexual Offences Act 2003, s.79(5)

Part 1: general interpretation
79.—(5) References to an image of a person include references to an image of an imaginary   **14–163**
person.

Note that the defendant must know or be reasonably expected to know that the complainant has a mental disorder and is unable to consent.

(2) Allocation

This offence is triable either way.   **14–164**

(3) Sentence

Upon summary conviction the maximum sentence is six months' imprisonment. Af-   **14–165**
ter commencement of the relevant provisions, the maximum custodial sentence in a magistrates' court will be 12 months' imprisonment: *Criminal Justice Act* 2003, ss.154 and 282.

E. Procuring Sexual Activity with a Person with a Mental Disorder

The offences in sections 34 to 37 relate to persons who have a mental disorder where   **14–166**
their agreement to sexual activity is secured through inducement, threat (*e.g.* harm to complainant or someone complainant knows) or deception (*e.g.* complainant will get into trouble by not engaging in this activity).

(1) Definition

Sexual Offences Act 2003, s.34(1)

Inducement, threat or deception to procure sexual activity with a person with a mental disorder
34.—(1) A person (A) commits an offence if—   **14–167**
   (a) with the agreement of another person (B) he intentionally touches that person,
   (b) the touching is sexual,
   (c) A obtains B's agreement by means of an inducement offered or given, a threat made or a deception practised by A for that purpose,
   (d) B has a mental disorder, and
   (e) A knows or could reasonably be expected to know that B has a mental disorder.

(2) Allocation

This offence is triable either way. If however, one or more of the following factors is   **14–168**
present, the offence *must* be tried on indictment:

615

Part III

(a) penetration of B's anus or vagina;

(b) penetration of B's mouth with a person's penis;

(c) penetration of a person's anus or vagina with a part of B's body or by B with anything else;

(d) penetration of a person's mouth with B's penis.

(3) Sentence

14–169   Upon summary conviction the maximum sentence is six months' imprisonment. After commencement of the relevant provisions, the maximum custodial sentence in a magistrates' court will be 12 months' imprisonment: *Criminal Justice Act* 2003, ss.154 and 282.

F. ENGAGING IN SEXUAL ACTIVITY IN THE PRESENCE, PROCURED BY INDUCEMENT, THREAT OR DECEPTION, OF A PERSON WITH A MENTAL DISORDER

(1) Definition

Sexual Offences Act 2003, s.36(1)

Engaging in sexual activity in the presence, procured by inducement, threat or deception, of a person with a mental disorder

14–170   **36.**—(1) A person (A) commits an offence if—

     (a) he intentionally engages in an activity,

     (b) the activity is sexual,

     (c) for the purpose of obtaining sexual gratification, he engages in it—

         (i) when another person (B) is present or is in a place from which A can be observed, and

         (ii) knowing or believing that B is aware, or intending that B should be aware, that he is engaging in it,

     (d) B agrees to be present or in the place referred to in paragraph (c)(i) because of an inducement offered or given, a threat made or a deception practised by A for the purpose of obtaining that agreement,

     (e) B has a mental disorder, and

     (f) A knows or could reasonably be expected to know that B has a mental disorder.

(2) Allocation

14–171   This offence is triable either way.

(3) Sentence

14–172   Upon summary conviction the maximum sentence is six months' imprisonment. After commencement of the relevant provisions the maximum custodial sentence in a magistrates' court will be 12 months' imprisonment: *Criminal Justice Act* 2003, ss.154 and 282.

G. CAUSING A PERSON WITH A MENTAL DISORDER TO WATCH A SEXUAL ACT BY INDUCEMENT, THREAT OR DECEPTION

(1) Definition

Sexual Offences Act 2003, s.37(1)

Causing a person with a mental disorder to watch a sexual act by inducement, threat or deception

14–173   **37.**—(1) A person (A) commits an offence if—

   (a) for the purpose of obtaining sexual gratification, he intentionally causes another person (B) to watch a third person engaging in an activity, or to look at an image of any person engaging in an activity,

   (b) the activity is sexual,

   (c) B agrees to watch or look because of an inducement offered or given, a threat made or a deception practised by A for the purpose of obtaining that agreement,

   (d) B has a mental disorder, and

   (e) A knows or could reasonably be expected to know that B has a mental disorder.

(2) Allocation

This offence is triable either way.   **14–174**

(3) Sentence

Upon summary conviction the maximum sentence is six months' imprisonment. Af- **14–175** ter commencement of the relevant provisions, the maximum custodial sentence in a magistrates' court will be 12 months' imprisonment: *Criminal Justice Act* 2003, ss.154 and 282.

H. Care Workers

The act creates separate offences that can be committed by the mentally disordered **14–176** person's care worker. Section 42 defines what a care worker is for the purposes of the offences created in sections 38 to 41.

The offences in sections 38 to 41 relate to persons who have a mental disorder regardless of their ability to choose whether or not to take part in sexual activity, whose actions may be influenced by their familiarity with, or dependence upon, a care worker. Therefore, within this close relationship, the existence of a mental disorder is sufficient in establishing that aspect of the offence and further, it is no defence to say that the complainant consented to the act.

Each offence that falls under this section must be read with reference to the following definitions and defences.

(1) Care worker definition

Sexual Offences Act 2003, s.42

Care workers: interpretation

   42.—(1) For the purposes of sections 38 to 41, a person (A) is involved in the care of another **14–177** person (B) in a way that falls within this section if any of subsections (2) to (4) applies.

   (2) This subsection applies if—

      (a) B is accommodated and cared for in a care home, community home, voluntary home or children's home, and

      (b) A has functions to perform in the home in the course of employment which have brought him or are likely to bring him into regular face to face contact with B.

   (3) This subsection applies if B is a patient for whom services are provided—

      (a) by a National Health Service body or an independent medical agency, or

      (b) in an independent clinic or an independent hospital,

and A has functions to perform for the body or agency or in the clinic or hospital in the course of employment which have brought him or are likely to bring him into regular face to face contact with B.

   (4) This subsection applies if A—

      (a) is, whether or not in the course of employment, a provider of care, assistance or services to B in connection with B's mental disorder, and

      (b) as such, has had or is likely to have regular face to face contact with B.

   (5) In this section—

     "care home" means an establishment which is a care home for the purposes of the *Care Standards Act* 2000 (c. 14);

Part III

"children's home" has the meaning given by section 1 of that Act;

"community home" has the meaning given by section 53 of the *Children Act* 1989 (c. 41);

"employment" means any employment, whether paid or unpaid and whether under a contract of service or apprenticeship, under a contract for services, or otherwise than under a contract;

"independent clinic", "independent hospital" and "independent medical agency" have the meaning given by section 2 of the *Care Standards Act* 2000;

"National Health Service body" means—

(a) a Health Authority,

(b) a National Health Service trust,

(c) a Primary Care Trust, or

(d) a Special Health Authority;

"voluntary home" has the meaning given by section 60(3) of the *Children Act* 1989.

Defences to offences under this section

(2) Defence: awareness of condition

14–178   There is an evidential burden on the defendant to prove that he did not know and could not reasonably have been expected to know that the complainant had a mental disorder. If this evidential burden is discharged, it is then for the Prosecution to prove that he could reasonably be expected to know about the condition.

The relevant provisions contained in subsection (2) of the relevant sections providing for the offences.

Sexual Offences Act 2003, ss.38(2), 39(2), 40(2), 41(2)

14–179   (2) Where in proceedings for an offence under this section it is proved that the other person had a mental disorder, it is to be taken that the defendant knew or could reasonably have been expected to know that that person had a mental disorder unless sufficient evidence is adduced to raise an issue as to whether he knew or could reasonably have been expected to know it.

I. MARRIAGE EXCEPTION

Sexual Offences Act 2003, s.43

Sections 38 to 41: exception for spouses and civil partners

14–180   **43.**—(1) Conduct by a person (A) which would otherwise be an offence under any of sections 38 to 41 against another person (B) is not an offence under that section if at the time—

(a) B is 16 or over, and

(b) A and B are lawfully married or civil partners of each other.

(2) In proceedings for such an offence it is for the defendant to prove that A and B were married lawfully at the time, or civil partners of each other.

[This section is printed as amended by the *Civil Partnership Act* 2004, Sched. 27, para. 175.]

J. EXISTING SEXUAL RELATIONSHIP

14–181   The pre-existing sexual relationship defence provides that any lawful sexual relationship that existed *immediately before* the care relationship will not be criminalised as a result of the relationship of care.

Sexual Offences Act 2003, s.44

Sections 38 to 41: sexual relationships which pre-date care relationships

14–182   **44.**—(1) Conduct by a person (A) which would otherwise be an offence under any of sections 38 to 41 against another person (B) is not an offence under that section if, immediately before A became involved in B's care in a way that falls within section 42, a sexual relationship existed between A and B.

(2) Subsection (1) does not apply if at that time sexual intercourse between A and B would have been unlawful.

(3) In proceedings for an offence under any of sections 38 to 41 it is for the defendant to prove that such a relationship existed at that time.

K. CARE WORKERS—SEXUAL ACTIVITY WITH A PERSON WITH A MENTAL DISORDER

(1) Definition

Sexual Offences Act 2003, s.38(1)

Care workers: sexual activity with a person with a mental disorder

38.—(1) A person (A) commits an offence if—   **14–183**
  (a) he intentionally touches another person (B),
  (b) the touching is sexual,
  (c) B has a mental disorder,
  (d) A knows or could reasonably be expected to know that B has a mental disorder, and
  (e) A is involved in B's care in a way that falls within section 42.

(2) Allocation

This offence is triable either way. If however, one or more of the following factors is **14–184** present, the offence *must* be tried on indictment:
  (a) penetration of B's anus or vagina;
  (b) penetration of B's mouth with a person's penis;
  (c) penetration of a person's anus or vagina with a part of B's body or by B with anything else;
  (d) penetration of a person's mouth with B's penis.

(3) Sentence

Upon summary conviction the maximum sentence is six months' imprisonment. Af- **14–185** ter commencement of the relevant provisions, the maximum custodial sentence in a magistrates' court will be 12 months' imprisonment: *Criminal Justice Act* 2003, ss.154 and 282.

L. CARE WORKERS—CAUSING OR INCITING SEXUAL ACTIVITY

(1) Definition

Sexual Offences Act 2003, s.39(1)

Care workers: causing or inciting sexual activity

39.—(1) A person (A) commits an offence if—   **14–186**
  (a) he intentionally causes or incites another person (B) to engage in an activity,
  (b) the activity is sexual,
  (c) B has a mental disorder,
  (d) A knows or could reasonably be expected to know that B has a mental disorder, and
  (e) A is involved in B's care in a way that falls within section 42.

(2) Allocation

This offence is triable either way. If however, one or more of the following factors is **14–187** present, the offence *must* be tried on indictment:

    (a) penetration of B's anus or vagina;

    (b) penetration of B's mouth with a person's penis;

    (c) penetration of a person's anus or vagina with a part of B's body or by B with anything else;

    (d) penetration of a person's mouth with B's penis.

(3) Sentence

14–188   Upon summary conviction the maximum sentence is six months' imprisonment. After commencement of the relevant provisions, the maximum custodial sentence in a magistrates' court will be 12 months' imprisonment: *Criminal Justice Act* 2003, ss.154 and 282.

M. CARE WORKERS—SEXUAL ACTIVITY IN THE PRESENCE OF A PERSON WITH A MENTAL DISORDER

(1) Definition

Sexual Offences Act 2003, s.40(1)

Care workers: sexual activity in the presence of a person with a mental disorder

14–189   **40.**—(1) A person (A) commits an offence if—

    (a) he intentionally engages in an activity,

    (b) the activity is sexual,

    (c) for the purpose of obtaining sexual gratification, he engages in it—

        (i) when another person (B) is present or is in a place from which A can be observed, and

        (ii) knowing or believing that B is aware, or intending that B should be aware, that he is engaging in it,

    (d) B has a mental disorder,

    (e) A knows or could reasonably be expected to know that B has a mental disorder, and

    (f) A is involved in B's care in a way that falls within section 42.

(2) Allocation

14–190   This offence is triable either way.

(3) Sentence

14–191   Upon summary conviction the maximum sentence is six months' imprisonment. After commencement of the relevant provisions, the maximum custodial sentence in a magistrates' court will be 12 months' imprisonment: *Criminal Justice Act* 2003, ss.154 and 282.

N. CARE WORKERS—CAUSING A PERSON WITH A MENTAL DISORDER TO WATCH A SEXUAL ACT

(1) Definition

Sexual Offences Act 2003, s.41(1)

Care workers: causing a person with a mental disorder to watch a sexual act

14–192   **41.**—(1) A person (A) commits an offence if—

    (a) for the purpose of obtaining sexual gratification, he intentionally causes another person (B) to watch a third person engaging in an activity, or to look at an image of any person engaging in an activity,

    (b) the activity is sexual,

(c) B has a mental disorder,

(d) A knows or could reasonably be expected to know that B has a mental disorder, and

(e) A is involved in B's care in a way that falls within section 42.

(2) Allocation

This offence is triable either way.   **14–193**

(3) Sentence

Upon summary conviction the maximum sentence is six months' imprisonment. Af-   **14–194**
ter commencement of the relevant provisions, the maximum custodial sentence in a
magistrates' court will be 12 months' imprisonment: *Criminal Justice Act* 2003, ss.154
and 282.

VIII. PROSTITUTION / PORNOGRAPHY OFFENCES UNDER THE SEXUAL OFFENCES ACT 2003

A. Paying for the Sexual Services of a Child

(1) Definition

Sexual Offences Act 2003, s.47(1)–(2)

Paying for sexual services of a child

47.—(1) A person (A) commits an offence if—   **14–195**

(a) he intentionally obtains for himself the sexual services of another person (B),

(b) before obtaining those services, he has made or promised payment for those services to B or a third person, or knows that another person has made or promised such a payment, and

(c) either—

(i) B is under 18, and A does not reasonably believe that B is 18 or over, or

(ii) B is under 13.

(2) In this section, "payment" means any financial advantage, including the discharge of an obligation to pay or the provision of goods or services (including sexual services) gratuitously or at a discount.

(2) Allocation

This offence is triable either way. If however, one or more of the following factors is   **14–196**
present, the offence *must* be tried on indictment:

(a) penetration of B's anus or vagina;

(b) penetration of B's mouth with a person's penis;

(c) penetration of a person's anus or vagina with a part of B's body or by B with anything else;

(d) penetration of a person's mouth with B's penis.

(3) Elements of the offence

If the child is aged between 13 and 17 and the defendant raises the issue that they   **14–197**
believed that child was over 18, it is for the prosecution to prove that this belief was not
reasonably held.

Where a child is under 13, there is no issue as to the defendant's belief; this element
of the offence will have been committed.

(4) Sentence

Upon summary conviction the maximum sentence is six months' imprisonment. Af-   **14–198** ter commencement of the relevant provisions, the maximum custodial sentence in a magistrates' court will be 12 months' imprisonment: *Criminal Justice Act* 2003, ss.154 and 282.

B. Causing or Inciting Child Prostitution or Pornography

(1) Definition

Sexual Offences Act 2003, s.48(1)

Causing or inciting child prostitution or pornography

14–199   **48.**—(1) A person (A) commits an offence if—

  (a) he intentionally causesor incites another person (B) to become a prostitute, or to be involved in pornography, in any part of the world, and

  (b) either—

   (i) B is under 18, and A does not reasonably believe that B is 18 or over, or

   (ii) B is under 13.

(2) Allocation

14–200   This offence is triable either way.

(3) Elements of the offence

Sexual Offences Act 2003, s.51(1)

Sections 48 to 50: interpretation

14–201   **51.**—(1) For the purposes of sections 48 to 50, a person is involved in pornography if an indecent image of that person is recorded; and similar expressions, and "pornography", are to be interpreted accordingly.

Pornography is defined at section 51(1).

Sexual Offences Act 2003, s.51(2)

Sections 48 to 50: interpretation

14–202   **51.**—(2) In those sections "prostitute" means a person (A) who, on at least one occasion and whether or not compelled to do so, offers or provides sexual services to another person in return for payment or a promise of payment to A or a third person; and "prostitution" is to be interpreted accordingly.

Prostitute is defined at section 51(2).

14–203   If the child is aged between 13 and 17 and the defendant raises the issue that they believed that child was over 18, it is for the prosecution to prove that this belief was not reasonably held.

Where a child is under 13, there is no issue as to the defendant's belief; this element of the offence will have been committed.

(4) Sentence

14–204   Upon summary conviction the maximum sentence is six months' imprisonment. After commencement of the relevant provisions, the maximum custodial sentence in a magistrates' court will be 12 months' imprisonment: *Criminal Justice Act* 2003, ss.154 and 282.

C. CAUSING OR INCITING PROSTITUTION FOR GAIN

(1) Definition

Sexual Offences Act 2003, s.52(1)

Causing or inciting prostitution for gain
  52.—(1) A person commits an offence if—   **14–205**
    (a) he intentionally causes or incites another person to become a prostitute in any part of the world, and
    (b) he does so for or in the expectation of gain for himself or a third person.

(2) Allocation

This offence is triable either way.   **14–206**

(3) Elements of the offence

Gain is defined in section 54.   **14–207**

Sexual Offences Act 2003, s.54

Sections 52 and 53: interpretation
  54.—(1) In sections 52 and 53, "gain" means—   **14–208**
    (a) any financial advantage, including the discharge of an obligation to pay or the provision of goods or services (including sexual services) gratuitously or at a discount; or
    (b) the goodwill of any person which is or appears likely, in time, to bring financial advantage.
  (2) In those sections "prostitute" and "prostitution" have the meaning given by section 51(2).

(4) Sentence

Upon summary conviction the maximum sentence is six months' imprisonment. Af-   **14–209**
ter commencement of the relevant provisions, the maximum custodial sentence in a
magistrates' court will be 12 months' imprisonment: *Criminal Justice Act* 2003, ss.154
and 282. An offence contrary to section 52(1) is a "lifestyle offence" within the *Proceeds
of Crime Act* 2002, Sched. 2, in respect of which a financial reporting order may be
made under the *Serious Organised Crime and Police Act* 2005, s.76.

D. CONTROLLING A CHILD PROSTITUTE OR A CHILD INVOLVED IN PORNOGRAPHY

(1) Definition

Sexual Offences Act 2003, s.49(1)

Controlling a child prostitute or a child involved in pornography
  49.—(1) A person (A) commits an offence if—   **14–210**
    (a) he intentionally controls any of the activities of another person (B) relating to B's prostitution or involvement in pornography in any part of the world, and
    (b) either—
      (i) B is under 18, and A does not reasonably believe that B is 18 or over, or
      (ii) B is under 13.

(2) Allocation

This offence is triable either way.   **14–211**

(3) Elements of the offence

14–212   If the child is aged between 13 and 17 and the defendant raises the issue that they believed that child was over 18, it is for the prosecution to prove that this belief was not reasonably held.

Where a child is under 13, there is no issue as to the defendant's belief; this element of the offence will have been committed.

(4) Sentence

14–213   Upon summary conviction the maximum sentence is six months' imprisonment. After commencement of the relevant provisions, the maximum custodial sentence in a magistrates' court will be 12 months' imprisonment: *Criminal Justice Act* 2003, ss.154 and 282.

E. ARRANGING OR FACILITATING CHILD PROSTITUTION OR PORNOGRAPHY

(1) Definition

Sexual Offences Act 2003, s.50(1)

Arranging or facilitating child prostitution or pornography

14–214   **50.**—(1) A person (A) commits an offence if—

(a) he intentionally arranges or facilitates the prostitution or involvement in pornography in any part of the world of another person (B), and

(b) either—

(i) B is under 18, and A does not reasonably believe that B is 18 or over, or

(ii) B is under 13.

(2) Allocation

14–215   This offence is triable either way.

(2) Elements of the offence

14–216   If the child is aged between 13 and 17 and the defendant raises the issue that they believed that child was over 18, it is for the prosecution to prove that this belief was not reasonably held.

Where a child is under 13, there is no issue as to the defendant's belief; this element of the offence will have been committed.

(4) Sentence

14–217   Upon summary conviction the maximum sentence is six months' imprisonment. After commencement of the relevant provisions, the maximum custodial sentence in a magistrates' court will be 12 months' imprisonment: *Criminal Justice Act* 2003, ss.154 and 282.

F. CONTROLLING PROSTITUTION FOR A GAIN

(1) Definition

Sexual Offences Act 2003, ss.53(1)

Controlling prostitution for gain

14–218   **53.**—(1) A person commits an offence if—

(a) he intentionally controls any of the activities of another person relating to that person's prostitution in any part of the world, and

(b) he does so for or in the expectation of gain for himself or a third person.

Gain is defined in section 54, *ante*.   **14–219**

(2) Allocation

This offence is triable either way.   **14–220**

(3) Sentence

Upon summary conviction the maximum sentence is six months' imprisonment **14–221** and/or a fine. After commencement of the relevant provisions, the maximum custodial sentence in a magistrates' court will be 12 months' imprisonment: *Criminal Justice Act* 2003, ss.154 and 282. An offence contrary to section 53 is a "lifestyle offence" within the *Proceeds of Crime Act* 2002, Sched. 2, in respect of which a financial reporting order may be made under the *Serious Organised Crime and Police Act* 2005, s.76.

G. Trafficking into, within and out of the UK for Sexual Exploitation

(1) Definition

Sexual Offences Act 2003, ss.57(1), 58(1), 59(1)

Trafficking into the UK for sexual exploitation
    57.—(1) A person commits an offence if he intentionally arranges or facilitates the arrival in **14–222** the United Kingdom of another person (B) and eithe—
    (a) he intends to do anything to or in respect of B, after B's arrival but in any part of the world, which if done will involve the commission of a relevant offence, or
    (b) he believes that another person is likely to do something to or in respect of B, after B's arrival but in any part of the world, which if done will involve the commission of a relevant offence.

Trafficking within the UK for sexual exploitation
    58.—(1) A person commits an offence if he intentionally arranges or facilitates travel within **14–223** the United Kingdom by another person (B) and either—
    (a) he intends to do anything to or in respect of B, during or after the journey and in any part of the world, which if done will involve the commission of a relevant offence, or
    (b) he believes that another person is likely to do something to or in respect of B, during or after the journey and in any part of the world, which if done will involve the commission of a relevant offence.

Trafficking out of the UK for sexual exploitation
    59.—(1) A person commits an offence if he intentionally arranges or facilitates the departure **14–224** from the United Kingdom of another person (B) and either—
    (a) he intends to do anything to or in respect of B, after B's departure but in any part of the world, which if done will involve the commission of a relevant offence, or
    (b) he believes that another person is likely to do something to or in respect of B, after B's departure but in any part of the world, which if done will involve the commission of a relevant offence.

(2) Allocation

This offence is triable either way.   **14–225**

(3) Elements of the offence

The provisions as to what a relevant offence is are set out at section 60(1) of the Act. **14–226** Section 60 further considers issues of jurisdiction.

Part III

Sexual Offences Act 2003, s.60

Sections 57 to 59: interpretation and jurisdiction

14–227   **60.**—(1) In sections 57 to 59, "relevant offence" means—

    (a) an offence under this Part,

    (b) an offence under section 1(1)(a) of the *Protection of Children Act* 1978 (c. 37),

    (c) an offence listed in Schedule 1 to the *Criminal Justice (Children) (Northern Ireland) Order* 1998 (S.I. 1998 No. 1504 (N.I. 9)),

    (d) an offence under Article 3(1)(a) of the *Protection of Children (Northern Ireland) Order* 1978 (S.I. 1978 No. 1047 (N.I. 17)), or

    (e) anything done outside England and Wales and Northern Ireland which is not an offence within any of paragraphs (a) to (d) but would be if done in England and Wales or Northern Ireland.

(2) Sections 57 to 59 apply to anything done—

    (a) in the United Kingdom, or

    (b) outside the United Kingdom, by a body incorporated under the law of a part of the United Kingdom or by an individual to whom subsection (3) applies.

(3) This subsection applies to—

    (a) a British citizen,

    (b) a British overseas territories citizen,

    (c) a British National (Overseas),

    (d) a British Overseas citizen,

    (e) a person who is a British subject under the *British Nationality Act* 1981 (c. 61),

    (f) a British protected person within the meaning given by section 50(1) of that Act.

(4) Sentence

14–228   Upon summary conviction the maximum sentence is six months' imprisonment and/or a fine. After commencement of the relevant provisions, the maximum custodial sentence in a magistrates' court will be 12 months' imprisonment: *Criminal Justice Act* 2003, ss.154 and 282.

In *Maka* [2005] EWCA Crim 3365 the Court of Appeal approved a total sentence of 18 years' imprisonment for four offences under section 58(1) and one offence under section 57(1) committed by a man with no previous convictions where the victim was a 15-year-old Lithuanian girl.

In *Ramaj and Atesogullari* [2006] EWCA Crim 448 a sentence of ten years' imprisonment was reduced on appeal to five years' imprisonment. The appellant was 19 years old and of previous good character; he was the principal involved in bringing an 18-year-old girl into the UK from Lithuania. The complainant whilst naïve was not an unwilling participant, she was put to work in a brothel and worked there for two days (*Roci and Ismailaj* [2005] EWCA Crim 3404 and *Maka, ante,* were considered).

IX. MISCELLANEOUS OFFENCES UNDER THE SEXUAL OFFENCES ACT 2003

A. ADMINISTERING A SUBSTANCE WITH INTENT

(1) Definition

Sexual Offences Act 2003, s.61(1)

Administering a substance with intent

14–229   **61.**—(1) A person commits an offence if he intentionally administers a substance to, or causes a substance to be taken by, another person (B)—

    (a) knowing that B does not consent, and

    (b) with the intention of stupefying or overpowering B, so as to enable any person to engage in a sexual activity that involves B.

(2) Allocation

This offence is triable either way.   **14–230**

(3) Sentence

Upon summary conviction the maximum sentence is six months' imprisonment   **14–231**
and/or a fine. After commencement of the relevant provisions, the maximum custodial
sentence in a magistrates' court will be 12 months' imprisonment: *Criminal Justice Act*
2003, ss.154 and 282. Custodial sentences of less than 12 months will consist of a custody
plus order.

B. COMMITTING AN OFFENCE WITH INTENT TO COMMIT A SEXUAL OFFENCE

(1) Definition

Sexual Offences Act 2003, s.62(1)–(2)

Committing an offence with intent to commit a sexual offence
62.—(1) A person commits an offence under this section if he commits any offence with the   **14–232**
intention of committing a relevant sexual offence.
(2) In this section, "relevant sexual offence" means any offence under this Part (including an offence of aiding, abetting, counselling or procuring such an offence).
(3) A person guilty of an offence under this section is liable on conviction on indictment,
where the offence is committed by kidnapping or false imprisonment, to imprisonment for
life.
(4) Unless subsection (3) applies, a person guilty of an offence under this section is liable—
  (a) on summary conviction, to imprisonment for a term not exceeding 6 months or
      a fine not exceeding the statutory maximum or both;
  (b) on conviction on indictment, to imprisonment for a term not exceeding 10 years.

[In section 62(2) "this part" refers to Part I of the *Sexual Offences Act* 2003, *i.e.* the
part creating substantive offences, and therefore excludes notification and orders
covered in Part II.]

(2) Allocation

This offence is triable either way, except where the offence is committed by kidnap-   **14–233**
ping or false imprisonment, and then the offence is indictable only.

(3) Sentence

Upon summary conviction the maximum sentence is six months' imprisonment   **14–234**
and/or a fine. After commencement of the relevant provisions the maximum custodial
sentence in a magistrates' court will be 12 months' imprisonment: *Criminal Justice Act*
2003, ss.154 and 282.
The case of *Wisniewski* [2004] EWCA Crim 3361 sets out, in relation to battery with
intent, the factors that should be taken into account by sentencers. These are (a) the
method and degree of force used; (b) the nature and extent of the indecency
perpetrated or intended; (c) the degree of harm to the victim; (d) the nature and general circumstances of the attack including the time, the place and level of risk posed by
the offender; (e) good character, which affords only limited mitigation.

C. TRESPASS WITH INTENT TO COMMIT A SEXUAL OFFENCE

(1) Definition

Sexual Offences Act 2003, s.63

Trespass with intent to commit a sexual offence
63.—(1) A person commits an offence if—   **14–235**

(a) he is a trespasser on any premises,

(b) he intends to commit a relevant sexual offence on the premises, and

(c) he knows that, or is reckless as to whether, he is a trespasser.

(2) In this section—

"premises" includes a structure or part of a structure;

"relevant sexual offence" has the same meaning as in section 62;

"structure" includes a tent, vehicle or vessel or other temporary or movable structure.

(2) Allocation

14–236   This offence is triable either way.

(3) Sentence

14–237   Upon summary conviction the maximum sentence is six months' imprisonment and/or a fine. After commencement of the relevant provisions, the maximum custodial sentence in a magistrates' court will be 12 months' imprisonment: *Criminal Justice Act* 2003, ss.154 and 282.

D. EXPOSURE

(1) Definition

Sexual Offences Act 2003, s.66(1)

Exposure

14–238   **66.**—(1) A person commits an offence if—

(a) he intentionally exposes his genitals, and

(b) he intends that someone will see them and be caused alarm or distress.

(2) Allocation

14–239   This offence is triable either way.

(3) Sentence

14–240   Upon summary conviction the maximum sentence is six months' imprisonment and/or a fine. After the commencement of the relevant provisions, the maximum custodial sentence in a magistrates' court will be 12 months' imprisonment: *Criminal Justice Act* 2003, ss.154 and 282.

In *Mailer* [2006] EWCA Crim 665 the appellant a 26 year old with numerous previous convictions for like offences pleaded guilty to two offences of exposing his penis and masturbating on a bus whilst sitting next to a young woman. He was subject to a community rehabilitation order for similar offending at the time. The court upheld a sentence of six months' imprisonment with an order that the existing community sentence continue.

E. VOYEURISM

(1) Definition

Sexual Offences Act 2003, ss.67(1)–(4), 68

Voyeurism

14–241   **67.**—(1) A person commits an offence if—

(a) for the purpose of obtaining sexual gratification, he observes another person doing a private act, and

(b) he knows that the other person does not consent to being observed for his sexual gratification.

(2) A person commits an offence if—

    (a) he operates equipment with the intention of enabling another person to observe, for the purpose of obtaining sexual gratification, a third person (B) doing a private act, and

    (b) he knows that B does not consent to his operating equipment with that intention.

(3) A person commits an offence if—

    (a) he records another person (B) doing a private act,

    (b) he does so with the intention that he or a third person will, for the purpose of obtaining sexual gratification, look at an image of B doing the act, and

    (c) he knows that B does not consent to his recording the act with that intention.

(4) A person commits an offence if he instals equipment, or constructs or adapts a structure or part of a structure, with the intention of enabling himself or another person to commit an offence under subsection (1).

Voyeurism: interpretation

68.—(1) For the purposes of section 67, a person is doing a private act if the person is in a   **14–242**
place which, in the circumstances, would reasonably be expected to provide privacy, and—

    (a) the person's genitals, buttocks or breasts are exposed or covered only with underwear,

    (b) the person is using a lavatory, or

    (c) the person is doing a sexual act that is not of a kind ordinarily done in public.

(2) In section 67, "structure" includes a tent, vehicle or vessel or other temporary or movable structure.

(2) Allocation

This offence is triable either way.   **14–243**

(3) Sentence

Upon summary conviction the maximum sentence is six months' imprisonment   **14–244**
and/or a fine. After the commencement of the relevant provisions, the maximum custodial sentence in a magistrates' court will be 12 months' imprisonment: *Criminal Justice Act* 2003, ss.154 and 282.

In *I.P.* [2004] EWCA Crim 2646 the Court ruled that a custodial sentence was not justified on the facts of the case—the offender had recorded an adult stepdaughter in the shower, and he had not shown his video recording to anyone else. The appropriate sentence was held to be a community sentence.

P. (*ante*) was considered by the Court of Appeal in *Turner* [2006] EWCA Crim 63, when it substituted a sentence of nine months' imprisonment for an offence contrary to section 67(3). The appellant, who was a man of good character and worked as the manager of a gym, had recorded video images of women showering and using sun beds in the gym. He pleaded guilty to three offences and asked for a fourth to be taken into consideration. The court stated that in this case the abuse of a position of trust took it over the custody threshold, although it was made clear that this was not to be taken as a guideline for all cases involving an abuse of trust, and treatment in the community may in particular circumstances be appropriate.

In *McCann* [2006] EWCA Crim 1078 the appellant, a 28-year-old serving police officer of previous good character, obtained a surveillance camera and hid it in the bathroom of a neighbour whilst a guest at her home. The camera was discovered and attempts were made to retrieve it. There was no evidence that any footage had actually been obtained. The appellant was convicted and sentenced to six months' imprisonment. The Court of Appeal considered *I.P.* and *Turner* and held that whilst a breach of trust should not necessarily result in a custodial sentence, in this case the appellant was a serving police officer, there was a breach of trust and no guilty plea; the custody threshold had been passed. The appeal was allowed in that the sentence was reduced to 90 days' imprisonment.

F. INTERCOURSE WITH AN ANIMAL

(1) Definition

Sexual Offences Act 2003, s.69

Intercourse with an animal

14–245   **69.**—(1) A person commits an offence if—

     (a) he intentionally performs an act of penetration with his penis,

     (b) what is penetrated is the vagina or anus of a living animal, and

     (c) he knows that, or is reckless as to whether, that is what is penetrated.

     (2) A person (A) commits an offence if—

     (a) A intentionally causes, or allows, A's vagina or anus to be penetrated,

     (b) the penetration is by the penis of a living animal, and

     (c) A knows that, or is reckless as to whether, that is what A is being penetrated by.

(2) Allocation

14–246   This offence is triable either way.

(3) Sentence

14–247   Upon summary conviction the maximum sentence is six months' imprisonment and/or a fine. After commencement of the relevant provisions, the maximum custodial sentence in a magistrates' court will be 12 months' imprisonment: *Criminal Justice Act 2003*, ss.154 and 282.

G. SEXUAL PENETRATION OF A CORPSE

(1) Definition

Sexual Offences Act 2003, s.70(1)

Sexual penetration of a corpse

14–248   **70.**—(1) A person commits an offence if—

     (a) he intentionally performs an act of penetration with a part of his body or anything else,

     (b) what is penetrated is a part of the body of a dead person,

     (c) he knows that, or is reckless as to whether, that is what is penetrated, and

     (d) the penetration is sexual.

(2) Allocation

14–249   This offence is triable either way.

(3) Sentence

14–250   Upon summary conviction the maximum sentence is six months' imprisonment and/or a fine. After commencement of the relevant provisions, the maximum custodial sentence in a magistrates' court will be 12 months' imprisonment: *Criminal Justice Act 2003*, ss.154 and 282.

H. SEXUAL ACTIVITY IN A PUBLIC LAVATORY

(1) Definition

Sexual Offences Act 2003, s.71(1)–(2)

Sexual activity in a public lavatory

14–251   **71.**—(1) A person commits an offence if—

(a) he is in a lavatory to which the public or a section of the public has or is permitted to have access, whether on payment or otherwise,

(b) he intentionally engages in an activity, and,

(c) the activity is sexual.

(2) For the purposes of this section, an activity is sexual if a reasonable person would, in all the circumstances but regardless of any person's purpose, consider it to be sexual.

(2) Allocation

This offence is triable summarily only.   **14–252**

(3) Sentence

The maximum custodial sentence in a magistrates' court will be 51 weeks' imprison- **14–253** ment: *Criminal Justice Act* 2003, s.281(4)-(6) and or a fine. Custodial sentences of less than 51 weeks will consist of a custody plus order (but section 154 of the *Criminal Justice Act* 2003 has not yet been implemented).

Part III

CHAPTER 15

PROPERTY OFFENCES

Part III

633

I. OFFENCES UNDER THE THEFT ACTS 1968 AND 1978

A. THEFT

(1) Definition

Theft Act 1968, s.1

Basic definition of theft

15–1   **1.**—(1) A person is guilty of theft if he dishonestly appropriates property belonging to another with the intention of permanently depriving the other of it; and "thief" and "steal" shall be construed accordingly.

(2) It is immaterial whether the appropriation is made with a view to gain, or is made for the thief's own benefit.

(3) The five following sections of this Act shall have effect as regards the interpretation and operation of this section (and, except as otherwise provided by this Act, shall apply only for purposes of this section).

(2) Allocation

15–2   Theft is triable either way: *Magistrates' Courts Act* 1980, s.17(1) and Sched. 1. The *Consolidated Criminal Practice Direction*, Pt V.51.7 *(Mode of Trial)* states that theft should be tried summarily unless one of the aggravating features is present and sentencing powers are insufficient. See Appendix F–49.

(3) Elements of the offence

15–3   The prosecution must prove that the defendant:
— dishonestly;
— appropriated;
— property;
— belonging to another;
— With the intention of permanently depriving the other of that property.

Dishonestly

Theft Act 1968, s.2

"Dishonestly"

15–4   **2.**—(1) A person's appropriation of property belonging to another is not to be regarded as dishonest—
(a) if he appropriates the property in the belief that he has in law the right to deprive the other of it, on behalf of himself or of a third person; or
(b) if he appropriates the property in the belief that he would have the other's consent if the other knew of the appropriation and the circumstances of it; or

(c) (except where the property came to him as trustee or personal representative) if he appropriates the property in the belief that the person to whom the property belongs cannot be discovered by taking reasonable steps.

(2) A person's appropriation of property belonging to another may be dishonest notwithstanding that he is willing to pay for the property.

The test of dishonestly is that contained in *Feely* [1973] Q.B. 530 and *Ghosh* [1982] Q.B. 1053; 75 Cr.App.R. 154, CA. The relevant test is to consider the conduct of the defendant by the standards of reasonable and honest people. If the conduct is not found dishonest by these standards then the prosecution will fail. If the conduct is found to be dishonest, the next stage is to consider whether the defendant himself realised that his conduct was dishonest by those standards. If so, then the defendant will be held to have been acting dishonestly. The second question need only be considered when the defendant raises this issue: *Price* (1990) 90 Cr.App.R. 409.

Claim of right

Section 2(1) offers three occasions when the defendant's appropriation is not to be **15–5** considered as dishonest. To come within the terms of section 2(1)(a) the defendant must believe that in law he had the right to deprive the other of his property: *Bernard* 26 Cr.App.R. 137, CCA. It does not matter that there is no basis in law for such a belief: *Bernard, ante,* though belief in a moral right is no defence: *Harris v. Harrison* [1963] Crim.L.R. 497, DC.

Appropriates

Theft Act 1968, s.3

"Appropriates"

3.—(1) Any assumption by a person of the rights of an owner amounts to an appropriation, **15–6** and this includes, where he has come by the property (innocently or not) without stealing it, any later assumption of a right to it by keeping or dealing with it as owner.

(2) Where property or a right or interest in property is or purports to be transferred for value to a person acting in good faith, no later assumption by him of rights which he believed himself to be acquiring shall, by reason of any defect in the transferor's title, amount to theft of the property.

Appropriation will be established by the assumption of any of the owner's rights in **15–7** the goods in question. It is not necessary to show assumption of all of the owner's rights: *Morris* [1984] A.C. 320, HL. It is not necessary to show that the appropriation was without the consent of the owner: *Lawrence v. Metropolitan Police Commissioner* [1972] A.C. 626, HL; *DPP v. Gomez* [1993] A.C. 442, HL; *Hinks* [2001] 2 A.C. 241.

Gifts

Following the majority decision of the House of Lords in *Hinks* [2001] 2 A.C. 241, **15–8** HL, it is now established that where the defence to a charge of theft is that the property is question was given as a gift, the question of the belief in the owner's consent to the giving of the gift is only relevant to the question of dishonesty. Hence the acquisition of indefeasible title to property is capable of amounting to an appropriation of property belonging to another for the purposes of the offence of theft.

Property

Theft Act 1968, s.4

"Property"

4.—(1) "Property" includes money and all other property, real or personal, including things **15–9** in action and other intangible property.

(2) A person cannot steal land, or things forming part of land and severed from it by him or by his directions, except in the following cases, that is to say—

    (a) when he is a trustee or personal representative, or is authorised by power of attorney, or as liquidator of a company, or otherwise, to sell or dispose of land belonging to another, and he appropriates the land or anything forming part of it by dealing with it in breach of the confidence reposed in him; or

    (b) when he is not in possession of the land and appropriates anything forming part of the land by severing it or causing it to be severed, or after it has been severed; or

    (c) when, being in possession of the land under a tenancy, he appropriates the whole or part of any fixture or structure let to be used with the land.

For purposes of this subsection "land" does not include incorporeal hereditaments; "tenancy" means a tenancy for years or any less period and includes an agreement for such a tenancy, but a person who after the end of a tenancy remains in possession as statutory tenant or otherwise is to be treated as having possession under the tenancy, and "let" shall be construed accordingly.

(3) A person who picks mushrooms growing wild on any land, or who picks flowers, fruit or foliage from a plant growing wild on any land, does not (although not in possession of the land) steal what he picks, unless he does it for reward or for sale or other commercial purpose.

For purposes of this subsection "mushroom" includes any fungus, and "plant" includes any shrub or tree.

(4) Wild creatures, tamed or untamed, shall be regarded as property; but a person cannot steal a wild creature not tamed nor ordinarily kept in captivity, or the carcass of any such creature, unless either it has been reduced into possession by or on behalf of another person and possession of it has not since been lost or abandoned, or another person is in course of reducing it into possession.

Things or choses in action

15–10   A chose in action is a right over property which can only be claimed or enforced by action, rather than by taking physical possession. A debt owed by a bank to a customer is a chose in action and can hence be appropriated. In *Kohn* 69 Cr.App.R. 395, CA, the defendant drew cheques on the account of a company of which he was a director for the benefit of various third parties. However, the cheques were intended for the benefit of the defendant, who was charged with theft of the chose in action (being the debt owed by the bank to the company) and theft of the cheque (being the property of the company). Where the account was in credit, or within the agreed overdraft limit (where the bank had an obligation to honour the cheques drawn) it was held that the defendant had appropriated a chose in action. Where the account was beyond the agreed overdraft limit (where the bank had no such obligation to honour the cheques drawn) it was held that there could be no appropriation as there was no chose in action.

Intangible property

15–11   Confidential information *per se* will not be classed as property for the purposes of section 4(1): *Oxford v. Moss* 68 Cr.App.R. 183, DC. In *Att.-Gen. for Hong Kong v. Nai-Keung* (1987) 1 W.L.R. 1339, PC, export quotas which were transferable for value on a temporary or permanent basis were held to be property within the meaning of a provision identically worded to section 4(1) of the 1968 Act.

Belonging to another

Theft Act 1968, s.5

"Belonging to another"

15–12   5.—(1) Property shall be regarded as belonging to any person having possession or control of it, or having in it any proprietary right or interest (not being an equitable interest arising only from an agreement to transfer or grant an interest).

(2) Where property is subject to a trust, the persons to whom it belongs shall be regarded as including any person having a right to enforce the trust, and an intention to defeat the trust shall be regarded accordingly as an intention to deprive of the property any person having that right.

(3) Where a person receives property from or on account of another, and is under an obligation to the other to retain and deal with that property or its proceeds in a particular way, the property or proceeds shall be regarded (as against him) as belonging to the other.

(4) Where a person gets property by another's mistake, and is under an obligation to make restoration (in whole or in part) of the property or its proceeds or of the value thereof, then to the extent of that obligation the property or proceeds shall be regarded (as against him) as belonging to the person entitled to restoration, and an intention not to make restoration shall be regarded accordingly as an intention to deprive that person of the property or proceeds.

(5) Property of a corporation sole shall be regarded as belonging to the corporation notwithstanding a vacancy in the corporation.

15–13 Property will belong to any person who has possession or control of it, or any proprietary right or interest in it, other than an equitable proprietary interest arising from an agreement to transfer or grant an interest. Train tickets purchased from travellers and then sold on will be deemed to remain the property of the train company who issued the tickets, as they retain a proprietary interest in the tickets after their purchase by a customer. Buying and then selling on such tickets will constitute theft: *Marshall* [1998] 2 Cr.App.R. 282, CA.

A company partner, who has a proprietary interest in the shares of the company may steal such shares as the other partners also have a proprietary interest in the shares: *Bonner* (1970) 1 W.L.R. 838.

Things which have been abandoned are not capable of being stolen: *White* 7 Cr.App.R. 266, CCA.

As regards section 5(3) the "obligation" must be a legal one, as opposed to a social or moral one: *Gilks* 56 Cr.App.R. 734, CA; *Klineberg and Marsden* [1999] 1 Cr.App.R. 427, CA. The obligation must also be one of which the defendant was aware: *Wills* 92 Cr.App.R. 297, CA. As regards section 5(4) the obligation to make restoration of another's property acquired by mistake, must be a legal one: *Gilks* (*ante*).

With the intention of permanently depriving the other of it

Theft Act 1968, s.6

"With the intention of permanently depriving the other of it"

15–14 **6.**—(1) A person appropriating property belonging to another without meaning the other permanently to lose the thing itself is nevertheless to be regarded as having the intention of permanently depriving the other of it if his intention is to treat the thing as his own to dispose of regardless of the other's rights; and a borrowing or lending of it may amount to so treating it if, but only if, the borrowing or lending is for a period and in circumstances making it equivalent to an outright taking or disposal.

(2) Without prejudice to the generality of subsection (1) above, where a person, having possession or control (lawfully or not) of property belonging to another, parts with the property under a condition as to its return which he may not be able to perform, this (if done for purposes of his own and without the other's authority) amounts to treating the property as his own to dispose of regardless of the other's rights.

15–15 In *Fernandes* [1996] 1 Cr.App.R. 175, CA, the Court held that section 6 should not be given a restrictive interpretation, and that the critical notion is whether the "defendant intended to treat the thing as his own to dispose of regardless of the other's rights". The second limb of subsections (1) and (2) are to be construed as illustrations of this general principle.

A conditional appropriation will not suffice to establish the offence of theft: *Easom* [1971] 2 Q.B. 315, CA.

(4) Sentence

15–16   When tried summarily the maximum penalty for this offence is imprisonment for a term not exceeding six months or a fine not exceeding the statutory maximum, or both (*TA* 1968, s.1(7)). After commencement of the relevant provisions, the maximum custodial sentence in a magistrates' court will be 12 months' imprisonment: *Criminal Justice Act* 2003, ss.154 and 282.

The *Magistrates' Court Sentencing Guidelines on Theft* (2004) state:

> Aggravating factors include the high value of goods stolen, planned, sophisticated, adult involving children, organised team, related damage, vulnerable victim, offence committed on bail and previous convictions and failure to respond to previous sentences (if relevant.)
>
> Mitigating factors include impulsive action and the low value of the goods stolen.
>
> **Guideline**: Is it serious enough to warrant a community penalty?

15–17   The *Magistrates' Court Sentencing Guidelines on Theft in Breach of Trust* (2004) state that:

> Aggravating factors include casting suspicion on others, racial aggravation, committed over a period, high value, organised team, planned, senior employee, sophisticated, vulnerable victim, offence committed on bail, relevant previous convictions and any failures to respond to previous sentences.
>
> Mitigating factors include impulsive action, low value of goods taken, previous inconsistent attitude of employer, single item and unsupported junior.

Thieves who steal from shops should be committed to the Crown Court where there is evidence of careful planning and the incident involves removal of goods of some value: *Bailey* (1993) 15 Cr.App.R.(S.) 27. Custodial sentences are generally not thought appropriate for petty thefts, such as shoplifting. In *Bond* (1994) 15 Cr.App.R.(S.) 430, the offender pleaded guilty to theft of goods worth about £3.50 from a shop. The Court of Appeal substituted a probation order of 12 months' duration for the offender's original sentence of three months' imprisonment on the ground that the offence was not so serious that only a custodial sentence could be justified. Custodial sentences for pick-pocketing have been upheld by the Court of Appeal when the offender had a record of similar offending (*Mullins* [2000] 2 Cr.App.R. 372 (sentence of three years' imprisonment imposed for pick-pocketing when offender had 36 previous convictions.) However, isolated actions of pick-pocketing committed by one individual should not attract a heavy custodial sentence (*Masagh* (1990-91) 12 Cr.App.R.(S.) 568: sentence of eighteen months' imprisonment reduced to four months' imprisonment).

15–18   In *Flynn and Flynn* (1993) 14 Cr.App.R.(S.) 422 the offenders stole furniture from an elderly couple with a view to persuading them to buy replacements. Their original sentences of six months' and eight months' imprisonment respectively were reduced to three months and four months' imprisonment on appeal, the Court stating that an isolated theft of property worth about £30 (the estimated value of the couple's furniture) would not normally attract a custodial sentence, but this was not a straightforward case of petty dishonesty, as it involved an elderly couple being intimidated in their own home.

Theft from a public telephone box, where the offence is pre-planned and involves a degree of specialist knowledge will warrant a custodial sentence. In *Ulus Arslan* (1994) 15 Cr.App.R.(S.) 90, whilst on bail, the offender had drilled through the back of the cash box in the early hours of the morning and stolen £82. He was sentenced to four months' imprisonment.

Theft of mail and pick-pocketing may warrant a custodial sentence. In *Smith and Read* [1997] 1 Cr.App.R.(S.) 342 the offenders were convicted of attempted theft after having tried to steal from a woman's bag that she was carrying. They each received a sentence of 12 months' imprisonment. In *Muir* (1994) 15 Cr.App.R.(S.) 112, the offender stole a cheque from the mail of another tenant in his house. He then used the cheque to open an account with a false name, and withdrew money from this account. He was sentenced to six months' imprisonment.

Theft in breach of trust will warrant a more severe penalty, and the *Magistrates'* **15–19**
Court Sentencing Guidelines (2004) advise committal for sentence. In *Clark* [1998] 2
Cr.App.R.(S.) 95 the Court of Appeal suggested guidelines as to appropriate terms of
imprisonment. Where the amount stolen is less than £17,500 terms of imprisonment
from the very short up to 21 months' will be appropriate. Two to three years' imprisonment would be appropriate for sums between £17,500 and £100,000. Three to four
years' imprisonment would be appropriate for sums between £100,000 and £250,000.
Five to nine years' imprisonment for sums between £250,000 and £1 million and 10
years' imprisonment or more for sums of £1 million or more, with appropriate discounts
where guilty pleas were entered. Consecutive sentences might be justified where sums
were stolen on more than one occasion or directed at more than one victim.

In *Pottay* [2001] EWCA Crim 1411, a security guard at a car auction took a car
worth £7,000 and two other cars. He was of previous good character, except for the related theft of a tax disc, and he pleaded guilty. His sentence of 12 months' imprisonment concurrent for each theft was reduced to a total of six months' imprisonment. In
Hill [2001] EWCA Crim 2314, CA, the offender was filmed stealing small amounts of
money whilst she worked at the Post Office. She pleaded guilty to eighteen charges of
theft, the total amount stolen being £210. She was sentenced to three months' imprisonment, the aggravating factor of her theft being in breach of trust being balanced against
considerable mitigating circumstances including the recent end of her marriage. In
Ross-Goulding [1997] 2 Cr.App.R.(S.) 348, the offender was a care assistant employed
to look after a person suffering from multiple sclerosis. She stole £8,000 from the
patient's building society account by forging her signature, and was sentenced to 15
months' imprisonment. See also *Margaret McCormick* (1995) 16 Cr.App.R.(S.) 134 and
Lazaretti [2001] All E.R. (D) 244.

Note: these are all appeals from the Crown Court to the Court of Appeal. In *Goatley*
[2006] 1 Cr.App.R. (S.) 24 the CA, following *Clark* (*ante*), reduced sentences totaling
five years, with 12 months consecutive for a bail offence, for obtaining valuable items
from elderly people by pretexts, reduced to three-and-a-half years. The appellant
pleaded guilty to three counts of theft. He had approached a man aged 94 whose wife
owned a picture that had been in her family for many years and took possession of the
picture under a pretext. He later telephoned the owner, an elderly lady with poor
eyesight, to say that he was going to restore the picture. Eventually he returned with a
painting that was not the painting which he had taken. When challenged, he said that
the stolen painting was with a friend and he would require a payment of £750 for its
return. The other offences were of a similar nature and the appellant had previous
convictions for similar offences. The aggravating feature of the case was the manner in
which the goods were stolen and the effect that the thefts had on the victims.

B. Burglary

(1) Definition

Theft Act 1968, s.9

Burglary
9.—(1) A person is guilty of burglary if—   **15–20**

    (a) he enters any building or part of a building as a trespasser and with intent to
commit any such offence as is mentioned in subsection (2) below; or

    (b) having entered any building or part of a building as a trespasser he steals or at-
tempts to steal anything in the building or that part of it or inflicts or attempts to
inflict on any person therein any grievous bodily harm.

    (2) The offences referred to in subsection (1)(a) above are offences of stealing anything
in the building or part of a building in question, of inflicting on any person therein any
grievous bodily harm therein, and of doing unlawful damage to the building or anything
therein.

    (3) A person guilty of burglary shall on conviction on indictment be liable to imprison-
ment for a term not exceeding—

(a) where the offence was committed in respect of a building or part of a building which is a dwelling, fourteen years;

(b) in any other case, ten years.

(4) References in subsections (1) and (2) above to a building, and the reference in subsection (3) above to a building which is a dwelling, shall apply also to an inhabited vehicle or vessel, and shall apply to any such vehicle or vessel at times when the person having a habitation in it is not there as well as at times when he is.

[This section is printed as amended by the *Sexual Offences Act* 2003, Sched. 7.]

(2) Allocation

15–21 Burglary is triable either way: *MCA* 1980, s.17 and Sched.1, para.28. Burglary will be triable on indictment only if (i) the burglary comprises the commission of, or an intention to commit an offence which is triable only on indictment: *MCA* 1980, Sched. 1, para. 28(b) or (ii) if the burglary is in a dwelling house and any person in the dwelling was subjected to violence or the threat of violence, the offence is triable only on indictment: *MCA* 1980, Sched. 1, para. 28(c).

The *Consolidated Criminal Practice Direction* Pt V.51.65 and 6 [2002] 1 W.L.R. 2870 *(Mode of Trial)* gives separate guidelines for burglary of a dwelling house and burglary of a non-dwelling. See Appendix F–49 and F–50.

15–22 The *Powers of Criminal Courts (Sentencing) Act* 2000 provides that the court must impose a minimum custodial sentence of three years where an offender aged 18 or over is convicted of a third "domestic burglary" where all of the three domestic burglaries were committed on or after November 30, 1999 and where the circumstances of the offence or the offender do not state that it would be unjust in all the circumstances to impose such a penalty: *PCC(S)A* 2000, s.111. Section 111(4) provides that where a person is charged with a domestic burglary which would be triable either way, and the circumstances are such that, if he were convicted of the burglary, he could be sentenced for it under subsection (2) *ante*, the burglary shall be triable only on indictment. The Court will rely on the prosecution to provide appropriate information relating to the defendant's previous convictions to identify whether the charge is indictable only or not, and this must be clarified before mode of trial is considered.

(3) Elements of the offence

15–23 The prosecution must prove that:
— the defendant entered a building or part of a building;
— with the intention to steal anything in the building or part of the building in question OR with the intention to inflict on any person in the building grievous bodily harm OR of doing unlawful damage to the building or anything therein; OR
— the defendant had entered a building as a trespasser; and
  he then stole or attempted to steal anything in the building; OR
  he inflicted or attempted to inflict upon any person therein grievous bodily harm.

The building

15–24 The word "building" is to be treated as an ordinary word of the English language and its meaning is a question of fact not law: *Brutus v. Cozens* [1973] A.C. 854, HL.

Entry as a trespasser

15–25 The definition of trespass is that used in the law of tort; *i.e.* any intentional, reckless or negligent entry into a building which is in the possession of another person who does not consent to the entry. The defendant must intend, or be reckless as to the facts which make the entry a trespass: *Collins* [1973] Q.B. 100, CA.

The entry

In *Collins* (*ante*) Lord Edmund-Davies said the entry in question had to be "effective **15–26** and substantial." In *Brown (V.)* [1985] Crim.L.R. 212, CA, the Court held that a man who had both feet on the ground outside a shop "entered" it when he leant through a broken window with the upper half of his body.

(4) Sentence

The maximum sentence varies depending on whether the burglary is of a dwelling **15–27** or non-dwelling.

(a) Burglary of a dwelling

The maximum penalty for burglary of a building or part of a building which is a **15–28** dwelling is 14 years' imprisonment on indictment, six months or a fine not exceeding the statutory maximum or both summarily (*TA* 1968, s.9(4)). After commencement of the relevant provisions, the maximum custodial sentence in a magistrates' court will be 12 months' imprisonment: *Criminal Justice Act* 2003, ss.154 and 282.

The *Magistrates' Court Sentencing Guidelines* (2004) state:

> Aggravating factors include force being used or threatened, group enterprise, high value (in economic or sentimental terms) property stolen, more than minor trauma caused, professional planning/organisation/execution, racially aggravated, significant damage or vandalism, victim injured, victim present at time, vulnerable victim.
>
> Mitigating factors include first offence of its type and low value property such as electrical items or jewellery stolen and no significant damage or disturbance and no injury or violence, minor part played, theft from attached garage, vacant property.
>
> The Guidelines also state that if the offence is racially or religiously aggravated, or the offender is on bail, this offence is more serious. If the offender has previous convictions their relevance and any failure to respond to previous convictions may increase seriousness.
>
> **Guideline**: Are Magistrates' sentencing powers appropriate?

In *Brewster* [1998] 1 Cr.App.R.(S.) 181, CA, Lord Bingham C.J. stated that not all dwelling house burglars must necessarily receive a custodial sentence. Cases involving impulsive action and goods of little value may be suitable for sentence in the magistrates' court. However, such cases will be comparatively rare, and in general, magistrates should decline from passing sentence for this offence. A custodial sentence was held inappropriate in *Suker* (1990) 12 Cr.App.R.(S.) 290, CA, where the offender, aged 19 with one previous conviction for an offence of a different nature, pleaded guilty to burglary of a dwelling. A householder apprehended S, drunk and climbing through a bathroom window, and held him until the police arrived. S claimed that he was looking for money for a taxi home and would not have harmed anyone or taken any property. A conditional discharge was held to be a more appropriate sentence than detention in a young offenders' institution. In *Finney* [1998] 2 Cr.App.R.(S.) 239, CA, a custodial sentence was held to be inappropriate for an impulsive act committed under the influence of drink, and a sentence of nine months' imprisonment was substituted by probation for two years. In *Fogarty and Mahoney* (1992) 13 Cr.App.R.(S.) 328, the offenders had pleaded guilty to a single count of burglary. They had driven to a rural area and broken into an unoccupied house. They had not stolen anything and were of previous good character. They received sentences of twelve months' imprisonment. A sentence of 18 months' imprisonment was held appropriate for an opportunistic domestic burglary in *Joseph Ashton* [2000] All E.R. (D) 1961 where the offender, who pleaded guilty and had previous convictions, had gained access to a basement flat and was found in possession of property worth £600.

McInerney [2003] Crim.L.R. 209, CA offers guidance on the use of custody as a penalty for domestic burglaries. Cases in which a court would previously have been looking to starting points of up to 18 months' imprisonment may now be dealt with by the imposition of a community sentence. If and only if the court is satisfied that the offender has demonstrated by his or her behaviour that punishment in the community was not practicable should the court resort to a custodial sentence. Where a custodial sentence is necessary, it should be no longer than necessary. Aggravating and mitigating features would alter the appropriate starting point. High level aggravating features included the use or threat of force, injury or especially traumatic effect on the victim, professional planning, vandalism, racially aggravated offences or the deliberate targeting of a vulnerable victim. Medium level aggravating features included the theft of high value goods, burglars working as a group and the victim being at home during the commission of the offence. Mitigating features included the crime being a first offence, nothing or low value property being stolen, the fact that an offender played only a minor part in the offence, the impulsive nature of the crime, the fact that no property was damaged and the entering of an early guilty plea.

(b) Burglary of a non-dwelling

15–29   As regards burglary of a non-dwelling, when tried summarily, the maximum penalty is six months' imprisonment or a fine not exceeding the statutory maximum or both: *TA* 1968, s.9(4).

The *Magistrates' Court Sentencing Guidelines* (2004) state:

> Aggravating factors include forcible entry, group offence, harm to business, night time, occupants frightened, professional operation, repeat victimisation, school premises, soiling, ransacking, damage, racial aggravation, offence committed on bail, relevant previous convictions and any failures to respond to previous sentences.
>
> Mitigating factors include low value of goods stolen, nobody frightened, no damage or disturbance, no forcible entry.
>
> **Guideline**: Is it serious enough for a community penalty?

15–30   A custodial sentence was approved in *Dorries and Dorries* [1993] Crim.L.R. 408, CA where the offenders removed bricks from a wall to gain entry, and were found with a hammer, jemmy and radio scanner in their car. In *Anson* [1999] 1 Cr.App.R.(S.) 331, a sentence of two and a half years imprisonment was upheld for the burglary of a shop, where the offender had disconnected the alarm, forced several doors and stolen goods to the value of £11,913. The courts adopt a more lenient approach in the context of non-residential burglary; in *Carlton* [1993] Crim.L.R. 981, CA it was held that burglary of an unoccupied office late at night involving the theft of a fax machine might not justify a custodial sentence. In *Tetteh* [1993] Crim.L.R. 629, the offender had broken into a YMCA club. Nothing was taken, and the offence was seen as opportunistic and unplanned. The Court of Appeal held that this case warranted a community sentence.

C. REMOVAL OF ARTICLES FROM PLACES OPEN TO THE PUBLIC

(1) Definition

Theft Act 1968, s.11

Removal of articles from places open to the public

15–31   **11.**—(1) Subject to subsections (2) and (3) below, where the public have access to a building in order to view the building or part of it, or a collection or part of a collection housed in it, any person who without lawful authority removes from the building or its grounds the whole or part of any article displayed or kept for display to the public in the building or that part of it or in its grounds shall be guilty of an offence.

For this purpose "collection" includes a collection got together for a temporary purpose, but references in this section to a collection do not apply to a collection made or exhibited for the purpose of effecting sales or other commercial dealings.

(2) It is immaterial for purposes of subsection (1) above, that the public's access to a

building is limited to a particular period or particular occasion; but where anything removed from a building or its grounds is there otherwise than as forming part of, or being on loan for exhibition with, a collection intended for permanent exhibition to the public, the person removing it does not thereby commit an offence under this section unless he removes it on a day when the public have access to the building as mentioned in subsection (1) above.

(3) A person does not commit an offence under this section if he believes that he has lawful authority for the removal of the thing in question or that he would have it if the person entitled to give it knew of the removal and the circumstances of it.

(2) Allocation

Removal of an article from a place open to the public is triable either way: *MCA* 1980, s.17 and Sched. 1, para. 28.

15–32

(3) Elements of the offence

The prosecution must prove that:

15–33

— the defendant had access to a building to view it or any part of it, or to view a collection or part of a collection housed there; and
— he removed from the building or its grounds the whole or part of any article displayed or kept in the building for display to the public;
— without lawful authority.

The words "a collection intended for permanent exhibition to the public" mean simply a collection intended to be permanently available for exhibition to the public, for example, a local authority's settled practice of periodically displaying to the public at the gallery the pictures in their permanent collection: *Durkin* [1973] 1 Q.B. 786, CA.

(4) Statutory defence under s.11(3)

Where the defendant raises the issue of whether he believed he had lawful authority for the removal of the articles concerned, or that he would have had, had the person entitled to authorise the removal known of the removal and its attendant circumstances, the burden is on the prosecution to establish the defendant's bad faith.

15–34

(5) Sentence

The maximum penalty when tried on indictment is five years imprisonment (*TA* 1968, s.11(4)). When tried summarily, the maximum penalty is six months' imprisonment and/or a fine not exceeding the statutory maximum. After commencement of the relevant provisions, the maximum custodial sentence in a magistrates' court will be 12 months' imprisonment: *Criminal Justice Act* 2003, ss.154 and 282.

15–35

D. Taking a Conveyance Without Authority

(1) Definition

Theft Act 1968, s.12(1)–(4C)

Taking motor vehicle or other conveyance without authority

12.—(1) Subject to subsections (5) and (6) below, a person shall be guilty of an offence if, without having the consent of the owner or other lawful authority, he takes any conveyance for his own or another's use or, knowing that any conveyance has been taken without such authority, drives it or allows himself to be carried in or on it.

15–36

(2) A person guilty of an offence under subsection (1) above shall be liable on summary conviction to a fine not exceeding level 5 on the standard scale, to imprisonment for a term not exceeding six months, or to both.

(3) [...]

(4) If on the trial of an indictment for theft the jury are not satisfied that the accused

committed theft, but it is proved that the accused committed an offence under subsection (1) above, the jury may find him guilty of the offence under subsection (1).

and if he is found guilty of it, he shall be liable as he would have been liable under subsection (2) above on summary conviction.

(4A) Proceedings for an offence under subsection (1) above (but not proceedings of a kind falling within subsection (4) above) in relation to a mechanically propelled vehicle—

(a) shall not be commenced after the end of the period of three years beginning with the day on which the offence was committed; but

(b) subject to that, may be commenced at any time within the period of six months beginning with the relevant day.

(4B) In subsection (4A)(b) above "the relevant day" means—

(a) in the case of a prosecution for an offence under subsection (1) above by a public prosecutor, the day on which sufficient evidence to justify the proceedings came to the knowledge of any person responsible for deciding whether to commence any such prosecution;

(b) in the case of a prosecution for an offence under subsection (1) above which is commenced by a person other than a public prosecutor after the discontinuance of a prosecution falling within paragraph (a) above which relates to the same facts, the day on which sufficient evidence to justify the proceedings came to the knowledge of the person who has decided to commence the prosecution or (if later) the discontinuance of the other prosecution;

(c) in the case of any other prosecution for an offence under subsection (1) above, the day on which sufficient evidence to justify the proceedings came to the knowledge of the person who has decided to commence the prosecution.

(4C) For the purposes of subsection (4A)(b) above a certificate of a person responsible for deciding whether to commence a prosecution of a kind mentioned in subsection (4B)(a) above as to the date on which such evidence as is mentioned in the certificate came to the knowledge of any person responsible for deciding whether to commence any such prosecution shall be conclusive evidence of that fact.

[Subsections (4A) to (4C) apply only in relation to offences committed on or after their commencement (October 1, 2001): section 37(2).]

(2) Allocation

15–37   This offence is triable summarily. However, an offence under section 12 may be included in an indictment for another offence in the circumstances set out in the *Criminal Justice Act* 1988, s.40. See *ante*, § 7–88.

(3) Elements of the offence

15–38   The prosecution must prove that:

— the defendant took any conveyance for his own or another's use;

— without having the consent of the owner, or lawful authority;
       OR

— the defendant allowed himself to be carried in, or drove himself, any conveyance;

— which had, to the defendant's knowledge, been taken without the owner's consent or other lawful authority.

(4) Statutory defence

Theft Act 1968, s.12(5)–(7)

Taking motor vehicle or other conveyance without authority

15–39   **12.**—(5) Subsection (1) above shall not apply in relation to pedal cycles; but, subject to subsection (6) below, a person who, without having the consent of the owner or other lawful authority, takes a pedal cycle for his own or another's use, or rides a pedal cycle knowing it to have been taken without such authority, shall on summary conviction be liable to a fine not exceeding level 3 on the standard scale

(6) A person does not commit an offence under this section by anything done in the belief that he has lawful authority to do it or that he would have the owner's consent if the owner knew of his doing it and the circumstances of it.

(7) For purposes of this section—

(a) "conveyance" means any conveyance constructed or adapted for the carriage of a person or persons whether by land, water or air, except that it does not include a conveyance constructed or adapted for use only under the control of a person not carried in or on it, and "drive" shall be construed accordingly; and

(b) "owner", in relation to a conveyance which is the subject of a hiring agreement or hire-purchase agreement, means the person in possession of the conveyance under that agreement.

Where the defendant raises the issue of whether he believed he had lawful authority **15–40** for the taking of the conveyance the burden is on the prosecution to establish the defendant's bad faith.

(5) Sentence

The maximum penalty for taking a conveyance without authority is six months' **15–41** imprisonment and/or a fine not exceeding level 5 on the standard scale (section 12(2)). If the offence is committed or attempted in relation to a motor vehicle, there is discretionary disqualification (*Road Traffic Offenders Act* 1988, Sched. 2). After commencement of the relevant provisions, the maximum custodial sentence in a magistrates' court will be 12 months: *Criminal Justice Act* 2003, ss.181, 280–282 (see *post*, Ch.23).

The *Magistrates' Court Sentencing Guidelines* (2004) state:

Aggravating factors shall include group action, premeditated, related damage, professional hallmarks, vulnerable victim, offence committed on bail, relevant previous convictions and any failures to respond to previous sentences.

Mitigating factors shall include the presence of a misunderstanding with the owner, soon returned, vehicle belonging to family or friend.

Guideline: is it serious enough for a community penalty?

A custodial sentence may be imposed where the offence forms part of a series of of- **15–42** fences arising out of the same circumstances: in *Jeary* (1986) 8 Cr.App.R.(S.) 491 a sentence of four months' detention was deemed appropriate when the offender stole vehicles, drove them around a city at high speed, eventually colliding head on leaving one car damaged beyond repair. The offender later stated that the cars had been taken for "a bit of fun" and pleaded guilty to two counts of occasioning actual bodily harm, two counts of taking a conveyance, two counts of theft as well as asking two other offences to be taken into consideration. In the view of the Court, these were serious offences involving taking vehicles and deliberately destroying them, and custody was fully merited.

In *Ahmad (Asif)* (1992) 12 Cr.App.R.(S.) 212, CA, the offender pleaded guilty to taking a conveyance without authority, reckless driving and driving while disqualified. A sentence of 200 hours' community service and a compensation order was upheld.

E. Aggravated Vehicle Taking

(1) Definition

Theft Act 1968, s.12A(1)–(3)

Aggravated vehicle-taking

12A.—(1) Subject to subsection (3) below, a person is guilty of aggravated taking of a vehicle **15–43** if—

    (a) he commits an offence under section 12(1) above (in this section referred to as a "basic offence") in relation to a mechanically propelled vehicle; and

    (b) it is proved that, at any time after the vehicle was unlawfully taken (whether by him or another) and before it was recovered, the vehicle was driven, or injury or damage was caused, in one or more of the circumstances set out in paragraphs (a) to (d) of subsection (2) below.

(2) The circumstances referred to in subsection (1)(b) above are—

    (a) that the vehicle was driven dangerously on a road or other public place;

    (b) that, owing to the driving of the vehicle, an accident occurred by which injury was caused to any person;

    (c) that, owing to the driving of the vehicle, an accident occurred by which damage was caused to any property, other than the vehicle;

    (d) that damage was caused to the vehicle.

(3) A person is not guilty of an offence under this section if he proves that, as regards any such proven driving, injury or damage as is referred to in subsection (1)(b) above, either—

    (a) the driving, accident or damage referred to in subsection (2) above occurred before he committed the basic offence; or

    (b) he was neither in nor on nor in the immediate vicinity of the vehicle when that driving, accident or damage occurred.

(2) Allocation

15–44   This offence is triable either way. However, where the only allegation is of damage to the vehicle or other property or both and the total value of the damage alleged to have been caused is less than the relevant sum, *i.e.* £5,000, the offender has no right to elect trial on indictment: *MCA* 1980, ss.22 and 33 and Sched. 2.

If a person charged with the offence under section 12A is found not guilty of that offence, he may still be found guilty of the basic form of the offence: section 12A(5) of the *TA* 1968. This section applies to trial in the magistrates' court as much as to trial in the Crown Court: *R. (H.) v. Liverpool Youth Court* [2001] Crim.L.R. 487.

(3) Elements of the offence

15–45   The prosecution must prove that:

    — the defendant committed an offence under section 12(1) of the *Theft Act* 1968;

    — in relation to a mechanically propelled vehicle;

    — and injury or damage was caused at any time between the taking of the vehicle and its recovery;

    — when the vehicle was being driven dangerously on a road or other public place; OR

    — when an accident occurred which caused injury and was due to the driving of the vehicle; OR

    — when an accident occurred which caused damage to any property other than the vehicle and was due to the driving of the vehicle; OR

    — damage was caused to the vehicle.

Theft Act 1968, s.12A(7), (8)

Aggravated vehicle-taking

15–46   **12A.**—(7) For the purposes of this section a vehicle is driven dangerously if—

    (a) it is driven in a way which falls far below what would be expected of a competent and careful driver; and

    (b) it would be obvious to a competent and careful driver that driving the vehicle in that way would be dangerous.

(8) For the purposes of this section a vehicle is recovered when it is restored to its owner or to other lawful possession or custody; and in this subsection "owner" has the same meaning as in section 12 above.

(4) Statutory defence in s.12A(3)

A person will not be guilty of an offence under this section if he proves that, as **15–47** regards any such proven driving, injury or damage as is referred to in subsection (1)(b) either the driving, accident or damage referred to in subsection (2), *ante*, occurred before he committed the basic offence or he was neither in nor on nor in the immediate vicinity of the vehicle when that driving, accident or damage occurred.

(5) Sentence

The maximum penalty on summary conviction is a term of imprisonment not exceed- **15–48** ing six months or a fine not exceeding the statutory maximum or both. Section 33(1) of the *Magistrates' Courts Act* 1980 reducing the maximum sentence to three months for offences of criminal damage where the value is under £5,000 does not apply to the offence of aggravated vehicle taking: section 33(3) of the *Magistrates' Courts Act* 1980. After commencement of the relevant provisions, the maximum custodial sentence in a magistrates' court will be 12 months' imprisonment: *Criminal Justice Act* 2003, ss.154 and 282.

This section carries obligatory disqualification and endorsement (3 to 11 points): *Road Traffic Offenders Act* 1988, ss.28, 34, 44, 96 and 97 and Sched. 2, Pt. II. The fact that the defendant did not drive the vehicle during the commission of the offence is not a reason to avoid obligatory disqualification (*Road Traffic Offenders Act* 1988, s.34).

The *Magistrates' Court Sentencing Guidelines* (2004) state:

> Aggravating factors include trying to avoid detection or arrest, competitive driving, racing, showing off, disregard of warnings from passengers, group action, police chase, premeditated, serious injury/damage, serious risk, offence committed whilst on bail, relevant previous convictions or any failure to respond to previous sentences.
>
> Mitigating factors include no competitiveness/racing, passenger only, single incident of bad driving, speed not excessive and very minor injury/damage.
>
> **Guideline**: is it so serious that only custody is appropriate?

In *Bird* (1993) 14 Cr.App.R.(S.) 343, CA, Lord Taylor C.J. stated that the aggravating features of this offence will be primarily the overall culpability of the driving; how bad it was and for how long, and to a lesser extent, how much injury or damage, or both was caused. Drink would affect the culpability of the driving, but where it had played a large part it would usually be the subject of another charge. A guilty plea will be a mitigating feature if made with contrition, though the youth of the offender will be less significant in mitigation as the Act is aimed at young offenders.

See also *Timothy* (1995) 16 Cr.App.R.(S.) 1028 and *Frostick* [1998] 1 Cr.App.R.(S.) 257.

F. TAKING OR RIDING A PEDAL CYCLE WITHOUT AUTHORITY

(1) Definition

Theft Act 1968, s.12

Taking motor vehicle or other conveyance without authority

12.—(5) Subsection (1) above shall not apply in relation to pedal cycles; but, subject to subsec- **15–49** tion (6) below, a person who, without having the consent of the owner or other lawful authority, takes a pedal cycle for his own or another's use, or rides a pedal cycle knowing it to have been taken without such authority, shall on summary conviction be liable to a fine not exceeding level 3 on the standard scale

(6) A person does not commit an offence under this section by anything done in the belief that he has lawful authority to do it or that he would have the owner's consent if the owner knew of his doing it and the circumstances of it.

(2) Allocation

This offence is triable summarily only: section 12(6).   **15–50**

Part III

(3) Elements of the offence

15–51   The prosecution must prove that:
— the defendant took a pedal cycle for his own or another's use;
— without the consent of the owner or other lawful authority;
    OR
— the defendant rode a pedal cycle knowing it to have been taken without the consent of the owner or other lawful authority.

The owner of the pedal cycle does not need to be identified; if the offender admits that he did not have the owner's consent, the court is entitled to find that the prosecution had made out a case to answer as it is entitled to infer that the bicycle had an owner: *Sturrock v. DPP* (1996) R.T.R. 216.

(4) Sentence

15–52   The maximum penalty is a fine not exceeding level 3 on the standard scale: *Theft Act* 1968, s.12(5).

G. ABSTRACTING ELECTRICITY

(1) Definition

Theft Act 1968, s.13

Abstracting of electricity
15–53   **13.** A person who dishonestly uses without due authority, or dishonestly causes to be wasted or diverted, any electricity shall on conviction on indictment be liable to imprisonment for a term not exceeding five years.

(2) Allocation

15–54   Abstracting electricity is triable either way: *MCA* 1980, s.17 and Sched. 1, para. 28.

(3) Elements of the offence

15–55   The prosecution must prove that:
— the defendant dishonestly, or without due authority;
— used any electricity; OR
— caused any electricity to be wasted or diverted.

"Dishonesty" has the same meaning in this context as it does in the context of the offence of theft.

In *McCreadie and Tume* 96 Cr.App.R. 143, CA, it was held that the offence does not require tampering with the electricity meter. It is sufficient to prove that electricity was used without the authority of the electricity supplier by a person who had no intention of paying for it.

(4) Sentence

15–56   When tried summarily, the maximum sentence is six months' imprisonment, a fine not exceeding the statutory maximum or both: *Theft Act* 1968, s.13. After commencement of the relevant provisions, the maximum custodial sentence in a magistrates' court will be 12 months' imprisonment: *Criminal Justice Act* 2003, ss.154 and 282.

In *Hodkinson* (1980) 2 Cr.App.R.(S.) 331, CA, the offender had fitted a device to the electricity meter at his home, causing the meter to give a false reading. A sentence of one month's imprisonment and a fine of £750 was upheld, the necessity for deterrent sentences being emphasised.

See also *Western* (1987) 9 Cr.App.R.(S.) 6 and *Wright* (1981) 3 Cr.App.R.(S.) 242.

H. False Accounting

(1) Definition

Theft Act 1968, s.17(1)

False accounting

17.—(1) Where a person dishonestly, with a view to gain for himself or another or with **15–57**
intent to cause loss to another,—

(a) destroys, defaces, conceals or falsifies any account or any record or document
made or required for any accounting purpose; or

(b) in furnishing information for any purpose produces or makes use of any account, or any such record or document as aforesaid, which to his knowledge is or
may be misleading, false or deceptive in a material particular;

he shall, on conviction on indictment, be liable to imprisonment for a term not exceeding seven
years.

(2) Procedure

The offence is triable either way (*MCA* 1980, s.17 and Sched. 1, para. 28). For guid- **15–58**
ance as to when summary trial of fraud cases is appropriate, see *Consolidated Criminal
Practice Direction*, Pt V.51.7, Appendix F–51.

(3) Elements of the offence

The prosecution must prove that;   **15–59**
— the defendant dishonestly,
— with a view to gain for himself or another or with intent to cause loss to another,
— destroyed, defaced, concealed or falsified any account or any record or document made or required for any accounting purpose; OR
— in furnishing information for any purpose, produced or makes use of any account, or any such record or document as aforesaid, which to his knowledge
was or may have been misleading, false or deceptive in a material particular.

Theft Act 1968, s.17(2)

False accounting

17.—(2) For purposes of this section a person who makes or concurs in making in an account **15–60**
or other document an entry which is or may be misleading, false or deceptive in a material particular, or who omits or concurs in omitting a material particular from an account or other document, is to be treated as falsifying the account or document.

(4) Sentence

When tried summarily, the maximum penalty is six months' imprisonment, a fine **15–61**
not exceeding the statutory maximum or both.

In *Kefford* [2002] 2 Cr.App.R.(S.) 106, CA, Lord Woolf issued guidance for sentencing in the context of economic crimes, stating that when the offender was of previous
good character alternative sentences to imprisonment could be an appropriate
punishment. In view of the overcrowded prison system a sentence of imprisonment
should only be imposed when necessary and only for as long as necessary. A starting
point of 18 months following guilty pleas for theft and false accounting was held to be
excessive, and the sentence was reduced to four months, with 12 months being the appropriate starting point.

In *Spencer* [2002] EWCA Crim 2196, CA (Crim. Div.) a sentence of 18 months'
imprisonment concurrent on each of six counts of false accounting was reduced to a
sentence of six months' imprisonment. The appellant was of previous good character,
and evidence suggested she had been initially forced to make the fraudulent claims by a

violent partner. The Court of Appeal affirmed the propriety of taking into consideration the Lord Chief Justice's comments in *Kefford* (*ante*) about prison overcrowding.

15–62   See also *Smith* (1994) 15 Cr.App.R.(S.) 145.

I. False Statements by Officers of a Company or Association

(1) Definition

Theft Act 1968, s.19(1)

False statements by company directors, etc.

15–63   **19.**—(1) Where an officer of a body corporate or unincorporated association (or person purporting to act as such), with intent to deceive members or creditors of the body corporate or association about its affairs, publishes or concurs in publishing a written statement or account which to his knowledge is or may be misleading, false or deceptive in a material particular, he shall on conviction on indictment be liable to imprisonment for a term not exceeding seven years.

(2) Allocation

15–64   The offence is triable either way (*MCA* 1980, s.17 and Sched. 1, para. 28) For guidance as to when summary trial of fraud cases is appropriate, see Appendix F–51.

(3) Elements of the offence

15–65   The prosecution must prove that:
— the defendant was the officer of a body corporate or unincorporated association, or was purporting to act as such, and;
— with intent to deceive members or creditors of the body corporate or association about its affairs, he;
— published or concurred in publishing a written statement or account which;
— to his knowledge was or might have been misleading, false or deceptive in a material particular.

Theft Act 1968, s.19(2)–(3)

False statements by company directors, etc.

15–66   **19.**—(2) For purposes of this section a person who has entered into a security for the benefit of a body corporate or association is to be treated as a creditor of it.

(3) Where the affairs of a body corporate or association are managed by its members, this section shall apply to any statement which a member publishes or concurs in publishing in connection with his functions of management as if he were an officer of the body corporate or association.

(4) Sentence

15–67   When tried summarily, the maximum penalty is six months' imprisonment, a fine not exceeding the statutory maximum or both. After commencement of the relevant provisions, the maximum custodial sentence in a magistrates' court is 12 months' imprisonment: *Criminal Justice Act* 2003, ss.154 and 282.

For sentencing guidelines in fraud cases generally, see *ante*, § 15–63.

J. Suppression of Documents

(1) Definition

Theft Act 1968, s.20(1), (3)

Suppression, etc. of documents

15–68   **20.**—(1) A person who dishonestly, with a view to gain for himself or another or with intent to cause loss to another, destroys, defaces or conceals any valuable security, any will or other testamentary document or any original document of or belonging to, or filed or deposited in, any court of justice or any government department shall on conviction on indictment be liable to imprisonment for a term not exceeding seven years.

(3) For purposes of this section "valuable security" means any document creating, transferring, surrendering or releasing any right to, in or over property, or authorising the payment of money or delivery of any property, or evidencing the creation, transfer, surrender or release of any such right, or the payment of money or delivery of any property, or the satisfaction of any obligation.

[This section is printed as amended by the *Fraud Act* 2006.]

(2) Allocation

This offence is triable either way (*MCA* 1980, s.17 and Sched. 1, para. 28). For guidance as to when summary trial of fraud cases is appropriate, see Appendix F–51.   **15–69**

(3) Elements of the offence

The prosecution must prove that: **15–70**
— the defendant dishonestly,
— with a view to gain for himself or another OR with intent to cause loss to another,
— destroyed, defaced or concealed,
— any valuable security, any will or other testamentary document or any original document of or belonging to, or filed or deposited in any court of justice or any government department.

(4) Sentence

When tried summarily the maximum penalty for this offence is six months' imprisonment, a fine not exceeding statutory maximum or both. After commencement of the relevant provisions, the maximum custodial sentence in a magistrates' court will be 12 months' imprisonment: *Criminal Justice Act* 2003, ss.154 and 282.   **15–71–72**

K. HANDLING STOLEN GOODS

(1) Definition

Theft Act 1968, s.22

Handling stolen goods
22.—(1) A person handles stolen goods if (otherwise than in the course of the stealing) knowing or believing them to be stolen goods he dishonestly receives the goods, or dishonestly undertakes or assists in their retention, removal, disposal or realisation by or for the benefit of another person, or if he arranges to do so.   **15–73**

(2) A person guilty of handling stolen goods shall on conviction on indictment be liable to imprisonment for a term not exceeding fourteen years.

(2) Allocation

This offence is triable either way (*MCA* 1980, s.17 and Sched. 1, para. 28). The *Consolidated Criminal Practice Direction*, para. V.51.8 provides that cases of handling should be tried summarily unless the court considers that one or more of several features are present and that its sentencing powers are insufficient. See Appendix F–52.   **15–74**

(3) Elements of the offence

The prosecution must prove that: **15–75**

— the defendant dishonestly,
— received OR undertook or assisted in the retention, removal, disposal or realisation by or for the benefit of another person, OR arranged to so undertake or assist, of,
— goods which he knew or believed to be stolen,
— otherwise than in the course of stealing them.

Stolen goods

15–76   The term "goods" is defined in section 34(2)(b) of the 1968 Act as including money and every other description of property except land, and things severed from the land by stealing. The fact that the goods are stolen may be proved by the thief or by circumstantial evidence.

Handling

15–77   Handling is proved by establishing that the defendant either received the goods, or arranged to do so, or undertook or assisted in their retention, removal, disposal or realisation by or for the benefit of another person, or arranged to do so.

In *Frost* (1964) 48 Cr.App.R. 284, CCA it was held that for a defendant to be convicted of receiving, it must be established that he took possession or control of the property, either jointly or exclusively. The requirement that control is taken of the goods means that proof that the defendant physically handled the goods will not suffice.

Where a person is charged with undertaking or assisting etc, there is no need to prove possession or control. In *Bloxham* (1983) 1 A.C. 109, HL, the HL examined the ambit of the second limb of the offence established by section 22(1) and concluded that the second limb creates a second offence that can be committed in a number of ways, the activities envisaged by the section being retention, removal, disposal and realisation. Lord Bridge stated:

15–78   "The offence can be committed in relation to any one of these activities in one or other of two ways. First, the offender may himself undertake the activity *for the benefit of* another person. Secondly, the activity may be undertaken by another person and the offender may assist him. Of course, if the thief or an original receiver and his friend act together in, say, removing the stolen goods, the friend may be committing the offence in both ways. But this does not invalidate the analysis and if the analysis holds good, it must follow, I think, that the category of other persons contemplated by the subsection is subject to the same limitations in whichever way the offence is committed."

The words "or if he arranges to do so" apply to both limbs of section 22(1).

Dishonestly

15–79   The relevant test if that established by the case of *Ghosh*, see *ante*, § 15–4.

The defendant's knowledge or belief that the goods were stolen at the material time may be established by the direct evidence of the principal offender or circumstantially. This question is subjective, and it is not enough that the goods were handled in circumstances that would put the reasonable man on inquiry. Suspicion that the goods were stolen, even coupled with the fact that the defendant shut his eyes to the circumstances, is not enough, although those matters may be taken into account: *Moys* 79 Cr.App.R. 72, CA.

Proof of guilty knowledge by evidence of the possession of other stolen property by previous conviction

Theft Act 1968, s.27(3), (5)

Evidence and procedure on charge of theft or handling stolen goods

15–80   **27.**—(3) Where a person is being proceeded against for handling stolen goods (but not for any offence other than handling stolen goods), then at any stage of the proceedings, if evidence has been given of his having or arranging to have in his possession the goods the subject of the charge, or of his undertaking or assisting in, or arranging to undertake or assist in, their retention, removal, disposal or realisation, the following evidence shall be admissible for the purpose of proving that he knew or believed the goods to be stolen goods—

(a) evidence that he has had in his possession, or has undertaken or assisted in the retention, removal, disposal or realisation of, stolen goods from any theft taking place not earlier than twelve months before the offence charged; and

(b) (provided that seven days' notice in writing has been given to him of the intention to prove the conviction)

evidence that he has within the five years preceding the date of the offence charged been convicted of theft or of handling stolen goods.

(5) This section is to be construed in accordance with section 24 of this Act; and in subsection (3)(b) above the reference to handling stolen goods shall include any corresponding offence committed before the commencement of this Act.

(4) Sentence

When tried summarily the maximum penalty for this offence is six months' imprisonment, a fine not exceeding the statutory maximum or both. After commencement of the relevant provisions, the maximum custodial sentence in a magistrates' court will be 12 months' imprisonment: *Criminal Justice Act* 2003, ss.154 and 282. **15–81**

The *Magistrates' Court Sentencing Guidelines* (2004) amend the guidelines on handling stolen goods in line with Court of Appeal guidance. They state:

Aggravating factors include commission of the offence whilst on bail, high level of profit accruing to handler, high value (including sentimental) of goods, provision by handler of regular outlet for stolen goods, proximity of the handler to the primary offence, seriousness of the primary offence, sophistication, the particular facts e.g. the goods handled were the proceeds of a domestic burglary and threats of violence or abuse of power by handler in order to obtain goods.

Mitigating factors include: Immediate offer of restitution to victim, isolated offence committed by defendant of hitherto good character, little or no benefit accruing to handler and low monetary value of goods.

Guideline: Is it serious enough for a community penalty?

In *Webbe* [2002] 1 Cr.App.R.(S.) 22, the Court of Appeal considered guidelines for sentencing in cases of handling stolen goods proposed by the Sentencing Advisory Panel. The Court agreed with the panel's view that the handler's advance knowledge of the original offence was an important question; where the handler had knowledge of the original offence, the seriousness of the handling was inevitably linked to the seriousness of the original offence. The replacement value of the goods involved a helpful indication of the seriousness of the offence, although not the determining factor. Other factors identified as relevant considerations were the level of sophistication of the handler; the ultimate destination of the goods; the criminal origin of the goods; the impact on the victim; the level of profit made or expected by the handler and the precise role played by the handler. The Court also held that handling cases at or towards the lower end of the scale were characterised by the handler having no connection with the original offence; an absence of sophistication on the part of the handler; the less serious nature of the original offence; the relatively low value of goods and the absence of any significant profit. **15–82**

Aggravating factors include: closeness of the handler to the primary offence; particular seriousness in the primary offence; high value of goods to the loser, including sentimental value; the fact that the goods were the proceeds of a domestic burglary; sophistication in relation to the handling; a high level of profit made or expected by the handler; the provision by the handler of a regular outlet for the stolen goods. Threats of violence or abuse of power by the handler over others, for example an adult commissioning criminal activity by children or a drug dealer pressurising addicts to steal to pay for their habit and the commission of an offence while on bail are aggravating factors.

Mitigating factors include the low monetary value of goods; the fact that the offence was a one-off offence committed by an otherwise honest defendant; the fact that there was little no benefit to the defendant and the fact that voluntary restitution had been made. The Court also agreed that other mitigating factors included personal mitigation; ready co-operation with the police and a timely plea of guilty. Previous convictions were relevant. In *Wilson* (1980) 2 Cr.App.R.(S.) 196, the offender, a man of good character pleaded guilty to handling stolen caravans worth some £4,500. The Court of Appeal stated that imprisonment was the only way of dealing with these offences since the property was of considerable value. However, for a man in the appellant's position a short immediate sentence of imprisonment, perhaps coupled with a fine, was likely to have the deterrent effect desired. The offender was sentenced to two months' imprisonment. See also *Raper* [2003] EWCA Crim 1860.

L. RETAINING A WRONGFUL CREDIT

(1) Definition

Theft Act 1968, s.24A

Dishonestly retaining a wrongful credit

15–83   **24A.**—(1) A person is guilty of an offence if—

> (a) a wrongful credit has been made to an account kept by him or in respect of which he has any right or interest;
>
> (b) he knows or believes that the credit is wrongful; and
>
> (c) he dishonestly fails to take such steps as are reasonable in the circumstances to secure that the credit is cancelled.

(2) References to a credit are to a credit of an amount of money.

(2A) A credit to an account is wrongful to the extent that it derives from—

> (a) theft;
>
> (b) blackmail;
>
> (c) fraud (contrary to section 1 of the *Fraud Act* 2006); or
>
> (d) stolen goods.

(5) In determining whether a credit to an account is wrongful, it is immaterial (in particular) whether the account is overdrawn before or after the credit is made.

(6) A person guilty of an offence under this section shall be liable on conviction on indictment to imprisonment for a term not exceeding ten years.

(7) Subsection (8) below applies for purposes of provisions of this Act relating to stolen goods (including subsection (2A) above).

(8) References to stolen goods include money which is dishonestly withdrawn from an account to which a wrongful credit has been made, but only to the extent that the money derives from the credit.

(9) "Account" means an account kept with—

> (a) a bank;
>
> (b) a person carrying on a business which falls within subsection (10) below; or
>
> (c) an issuer of electronic money (as defined for the purposes of Part 2 of the *Financial Services and Markets Act* 2000).

(10) A business falls within this subsection if—

> (a) in the course of the business money received by way of deposit is lent to others; or
>
> (b) any other activity of the business is financed, wholly or to any material extent, out of the capital of or the interest on money received by way of deposit.

(11) References in subsection (10) above to a deposit must be read with—

> (a) section 22 of the *Financial Services and Markets Act* 2000;
>
> (b) any relevant order under that section; and
>
> (c) Schedule 2 to that Act;

but any restriction on the meaning of deposit which arises from the identity of the person making it is to be disregarded.

(12) For the purposes of subsection (10) above—

(a) all the activities which a person carries on by way of business shall be regarded as a single business carried on by him; and

(b) "money" includes money expressed in a currency other than sterling.

[This section is printed as amended by the *Fraud Act* 2006, Sched. 1, para. 7.]

(2) Allocation

This offence is triable either way (*MCA* 1980, s.17 and Sched. 1, para. 28).   **15–84**

(3) Elements of the offence

The prosecution must prove that: **15–85**

— a wrongful credit was made to an account kept by the defendant, or to an account in respect of which he had any right or interest, and

— the defendant knew or believed that the credit was wrongful, and

— he dishonestly,

— failed to take such steps as were reasonable in the circumstances to secure that the credit is cancelled.

Theft Act 1968, s.24A(2)–(9)

Dishonestly retaining a wrongful credit

24A.—(2) References to a credit are to a credit of an amount of money.   **15–86**

(3) A credit to an account is wrongful if it is the credit side of a money transfer obtained contrary to section 15A of this Act.

(4) A credit to an account is also wrongful to the extent that it derives from—

(a) theft;

(b) an offence under section 15A of this Act;

(c) blackmail; or

(d) stolen goods.

(5) In determining whether a credit to an account is wrongful, it is immaterial (in particular) whether the account is overdrawn before or after the credit is made.

(6) A person guilty of an offence under this section shall be liable on conviction on indictment to imprisonment for a term not exceeding ten years.

(7) Subsection (8) below applies for purposes of provisions of this Act relating to stolen goods (including subsection (4) above).

(8) References to stolen goods include money which is dishonestly withdrawn from an account to which a wrongful credit has been made, but only to the extent that the money derives from the credit.

(9) In this section "account" and "money" shall be construed in accordance with section 15B of this Act.

(4) Sentence

When tried summarily, the maximum penalty is six months' imprisonment, a fine **15–87** not exceeding the statutory maximum or both. After commencement of the relevant provisions, the maximum custodial sentence in a magistrates' court will be 12 months' imprisonment: *Criminal Justice Act* 2003, ss.154 and 282.

M. ADVERTISING REWARDS FOR RETURN OF GOODS STOLEN OR LOST

(1) Definition

Theft Act 1968, s.23

Advertising rewards for return of goods stolen or lost

23. Where any public advertisement of a reward for the return of any goods which have **15–88** been stolen or lost uses any words to the effect that no questions will be asked, or that the person producing the goods will be safe from apprehension or inquiry, or that any money paid for the purchase of the goods or advanced by way of loan on them will be repaid, the person advertising the reward and any person who prints or publishes the advertisement shall on summary conviction be liable to a fine not exceeding level 3 on the standard scale.

(2) Allocation

15–89   This offence is triable summarily only: *Theft Act* 1968, s.23.

(3) Elements of the offence

15–90   The prosecution must prove that:
— the defendant advertised a reward for the return of any goods stolen or lost, or printed or published such an advertisement, and
— the advertisement used words to the effect that no questions will be asked, or that the person producing the goods will be safe from apprehension or inquiry or that any money paid for the purchase of the goods or advanced by way of loan will be repaid.

15–91   The offence is one of strict liability; publishing an advert for the return of goods for a reward stating that no questions would be asked will establish the offence. *Mens rea* does not need to be proved: *Denham v. Scott* (1983) 77 Cr.App.R. 210.

(4) Sentence

15–92   The maximum penalty for this offence is a fine not exceeding level three on the standard scale: *Theft Act* 1968, s.23.

N. GOING EQUIPPED

(1) Definition

Theft Act 1968, s.25(1), (3)–(5)

Going equipped for stealing, etc.
15–93   **25.**—(1) A person shall be guilty of an offence if, when not at his place of abode, he has with him any article for use in the course of or in connection with any burglary, theft or cheat.

(2) [indictment only]

(3) Where a person is charged with an offence under this section, proof that he had with him any article made or adapted for use in committing a burglary, theft or cheat shall be evidence that he had it with him for such use.

(5) For purposes of this section an offence under section 12(1) of this Act of taking a conveyance shall be treated as theft.

[This section is printed as amended by the *Fraud Act* 2006, Sched. 1, para. 8.]

(2) Allocation

15–94   This offence is triable either way: *MCA* 1980, s.17 and Sched. 1, para. 28.

(3) Elements of the offence

15–95   The prosecution must prove that:
— the defendant was not at his place of abode and;
— he had with him any article for use in the course of or in connection with any burglary or theft.

(4) Sentence

15–96   When tried summarily, the maximum penalty for this offence is six months' imprison-

ment, a fine not exceeding the statutory maximum or both. After commencement of the relevant provisions, the maximum custodial sentence in a magistrates' court will be 12 months' imprisonment: *Criminal Justice Act* 2003, ss.154 and 282.

The *Magistrates' Court Sentencing Guidelines* (2004) state:

> Aggravating factors include premeditated, group action, sophisticated, specialised equipment, number of items, people put in fear, offence committed on bail, relevant previous convictions and any failure to respond to previous sentences.
>
> No mitigating factors are listed.
>
> **Guideline**: Is it serious enough for a community penalty? Consider forfeiture of equipment.

In *Ferry and Wynn* [1997] 2 Cr.App.R.(S.) 42 a sentence of 12 months' imprisonment for going equipped to steal from telephone boxes was upheld by the Court of Appeal. The offenders were in possession of a cordless drill and other tools, and a map indicating the location of other telephone boxes. A custodial sentence was held to be justified as the offences involved a sustained enterprise to break into telephone boxes in rural areas, and could not be compared with a single attack on a telephone box in an urban area.

O. Making Off Without Payment

(1) Definition

Theft Act 1978, s.3

Making off without payment

3.—(1) Subject to subsection (3) below, a person who, knowing that payment on the spot for **15–97** any goods supplied or service done is required or expected from him, dishonestly makes off without having paid as required or expected and with intent to avoid payment of the amount due shall be guilty of an offence.

(2) For purposes of this section "payment on the spot" includes payment at the time of collecting goods on which work has been done or in respect of which service has been provided.

(3) Subsection (1) above shall not apply where the supply of the goods or the doing of the service is contrary to law, or where the service done is such that payment is not legally enforceable.

[This section is printed as amended by the *Serious Organised Crime and Police Act* 2005, Sched. 17, para. 1.]

(2) Allocation

This offence is triable either way (*Theft Act* 1978, s.4(1)). For guidance as to when **15–98** the offence is appropriately tried summarily, see *ante*.

(3) Elements of the offence

The prosecution must prove that: **15–99**
— the defendant knew that payment on the spot for any goods supplied or service done was required or expected of him, and
— he dishonestly,
— made off without having paid as required or expected,
— with intent to avoid payment of the amount due.

"Making off" involves a departure from the spot where payment was required: *Brooks* 76 Cr.App.R. 66, CA. In *Allen* (1985) A.C. 1029, HL it was held that the following must be proved to secure a conviction under s.3(1) that the defendant in fact made off without making payment on the spot; (2) the following mental elements—(a) knowledge that payment on the spot was required or expected of him; and (b) dishonesty; and (c) intent to avoid payment of the amount due.

(4) Sentence

15–100   When tried summarily, the maximum penalty is six months' imprisonment, a fine not exceeding the statutory maximum or both. After commencement of the relevant provisions, the maximum custodial sentence in a magistrates' court will be 12 months' imprisonment: *Criminal Justice Act* 2003, ss.154 and 282.

For sentencing guidelines on offences of fraud generally, see *Magistrates' Court Sentencing Guidelines* (2004) pertaining to the *Theft Act* 1968, s.15.

When dealt with summarily, the *Magistrates' Court Sentencing Guidelines* (2004) state:

> Aggravating factors include deliberate plan, high value, two or more involved, racial aggravation, victim particularly vulnerable, offence committed on bail, relevant previous convictions and any failures to respond to previous sentences.
> Mitigating factors include impulsive action, low value.
> **Guideline**: is it serious enough for a community penalty?

15–101   In *Foster* (1994) 15 Cr.App.R.(S.) 340 a sentence of three months' imprisonment was upheld for making off without payment of taxi fares of between £37 and £63. The appellant had previous convictions for conspiracy to burgle and theft, and was subject to a suspended sentence of nine months at the time of the offences. That sentence was activated consecutively, meaning that the total sentence was one of 12 months' imprisonment.

II. OFFENCES UNDER THE FRAUD ACT 2006

A. GENERAL

(1) Definition

Fraud Act 2006, s.1

Fraud

15–102   **1**—(1) A person is guilty of fraud if he is in breach of any of the sections listed in subsection (2) (which provide for different ways of committing the offence).

(2) The sections are—

     (a) section 2 (fraud by false representation),

     (b) section 3 (fraud by failing to disclose information), and

     (c) section 4 (fraud by abuse of position).

(3) A person who is guilty of fraud is liable—

     (a) on summary conviction, to imprisonment for a term not exceeding 12 months or to a fine not exceeding the statutory maximum (or to both);

     (b) on conviction on indictment, to imprisonment for a term not exceeding 10 years or to a fine (or to both).

(4) Subsection (3)(a) applies in relation to Northern Ireland as if the reference to 12 months were a reference to 6 months.

This offence can be committed in any one of three different ways.

B. FRAUD BY FALSE REPRESENTATION

(1) Definition

Fraud Act 2006, s.2

Fraud by false representation

15–103   **2**—(1) A person is in breach of this section if he—

     (a) dishonestly makes a false representation, and

(b) intends, by making the representation—

    (i) to make a gain for himself or another, or

    (ii) to cause loss to another or to expose another to a risk of loss.

(2) A representation is false if—

    (a) it is untrue or misleading, and

    (b) the person making it knows that it is, or might be, untrue or misleading.

(3) "Representation" means any representation as to fact or law, including a representation as to the state of mind of—

    (a) the person making the representation, or

    (b) any other person.

(4) A representation may be express or implied.

(5) For the purposes of this section a representation may be regarded as made if it (or anything implying it) is submitted in any form to any system or device designed to receive, convey or respond to communications (with or without human intervention).

(2) Allocation

The offence is triable either way   **15–104**

(3) Elements of the offence

"Dishonestly" will presumably be defined as before: see *Feely* [1973] Q.B. 530 and **15–105** *Ghosh* [1982] Q.B. 1053 (at § 15–4.).

D must make the representation with the intention of making a gain or causing loss or risk of loss to another. The gain or loss does not actually have to take place. Gain and loss are defined in section 5, *post*.

Fraud Act 2006, s.5

"Gain" and "loss"

    5—(1) The references to gain and loss in sections 2 to 4 are to be read in accordance with this **15–106** section.

    (2) "Gain" and "loss"—

        (a) extend only to gain or loss in money or other property;

        (b) include any such gain or loss whether temporary or permanent;

and "property" means any property whether real or personal (including things in action and other intangible property).

    (3) "Gain" includes a gain by keeping what one has, as well as a gain by getting what one does not have.

    (4) "Loss" includes a loss by not getting what one might get, as well as a loss by parting with what one has.

"False": see section 2(2). The representation must be untrue or misleading, and D **15–107** must know that it is or might be untrue or misleading.

"Representation": see section 2(3). A representation is defined as false if it is untrue or misleading and the person making it knows that it is, or might be, untrue or misleading. It means any representation as to fact or law, including a representation as to a person's state of mind. It may be express or implied. It can be stated in words or communicated by conduct. There is no limitation on the way in which the representation must be expressed. So it could be written or spoken or posted on a website. A representation may also be implied by conduct. Misusing a credit card is clearly caught: by tendering the card, D is falsely representing that he has the authority to use it for that transaction, whether or not the person accepting the card for payment is deceived by the representation. The *Explanatory Notes* state that this offence would also be committed by someone who engages in "phishing": *i.e.* where a person disseminates an email to large groups of people falsely representing that the email has been sent by a legitimate financial institution. The email prompts the reader to provide information such as credit card and bank account numbers so that the "phisher" can gain access to others'

Part III

assets. The main purpose of section 2(5) is "to ensure that fraud can be committed where a person makes a representation to a machine and a response can be produced without any need for human involvement" (*e.g.* where a person enters a number into a "CHIP and PIN" machine). The Law Commission had concluded that, although it was not clear whether a representation could be made to a machine, such a provision was unnecessary (see para. 8.4 of their report). But section 2(5) is expressed in "fairly general terms", we are told, because it would be artificial to distinguish situations involving modern technology, where it is doubtful whether there has been a "representation", because the only recipient of the false statement is a machine or a piece of software, from other situations not involving modern technology where a false statement is submitted to a system for dealing with communications but is not in fact communicated to a human being, (*e.g.* postal or messenger systems).

(4) Sentence

15–108   On summary conviction, the maximum penalty for this offence is imprisonment for a term not exceeding 12 months or a fine not exceeding the statutory maximum (or both). But Schedule 2, paragraph 1 provides for 12 months to be 6 months pending the increase in sentencing powers in a magistrates' court (section 154 of the *Criminal Justice Act* 2003 has yet to be implemented).

C. FRAUD BY FAILING TO DISCLOSE INFORMATION

(1) Definition

Fraud Act 2006, s.3

Fraud by failing to disclose information
15–109   **3—**   A person is in breach of this section if he—
     (a) dishonestly fails to disclose to another person information which he is under a legal duty to disclose, and
     (b) intends, by failing to disclose the information—
        (i) to make a gain for himself or another, or
        (ii) to cause loss to another or to expose another to a risk of loss.

(2) Allocation

15–110   The offence is triable either way.

(3) Elements of the offence

15–111   "Dishonestly" will presumably be defined as before: see *Feeley* and *Ghosh* (at § 15–4).
    D must fail to disclose the information with the intention of making a gain or causing loss or risk of loss to another. The gain or loss does not actually have to take place. Gain and loss are defined in section 5 (see *ante*).
    A legal duty to disclose information may include duties under oral contracts as well as written contracts. According to the Law Commission's Report on Fraud (Law Com No. 276, Cm 5560, 2002):

> "7.28. Such a duty may derive from statute (such as the provisions governing company prospectuses), from the fact that the transaction in question is one of the utmost good faith (such as a contract of insurance), from the express or implied terms of a contract, from the custom of a particular trade or market, or from the existence of a fiduciary relationship between the parties (such as that of agent and principal).
> 7.29. For this purpose there is a legal duty to disclose information not only if the defendant's failure to disclose it gives the victim a cause of action for damages, but also if the law gives the victim a right to set aside any change in his or her legal position to which he or she may consent as a result of the non-disclosure. For example, a person in a fiduciary position has a duty to disclose material information when entering into a contract with his or her benefi-

ciary, in the sense that a failure to make such disclosure will entitle the beneficiary to rescind the contract and to reclaim any property transferred under it."

The *Explanatory Notes* to the Act suggest that the failure of a solicitor to share vital information with a client within the context of their work relationship, in order to perpetrate a fraud upon that client, would be covered by the section. Similarly, an offence could be committed under this section if a person intentionally failed to disclose information relating to his heart condition when making an application for life insurance.

(4) Sentence

On summary conviction, the maximum penalty for this offence is imprisonment for a term not exceeding 12 months or a fine not exceeding the statutory maximum (or both). But Schedule 2, paragraph 1 of the Act provides for 12 months to be 6 months pending the increase in sentencing powers in a magistrates' court (section 154 of the *Criminal Justice Act* 2003 has yet to be implemented).   **15–112**

D. Fraud by Abuse of Position

(1) Definition

Fraud Act 2006, s.4

Fraud by abuse of position

4—(1) A person is in breach of this section if he—   **15–113**
    (a) occupies a position in which he is expected to safeguard, or not to act against, the financial interests of another person,
    (b) dishonestly abuses that position, and
    (c) intends, by means of the abuse of that position—
        (i) to make a gain for himself or another, or
        (ii) to cause loss to another or to expose another to a risk of loss.

(2) A person may be regarded as having abused his position even though his conduct consisted of an omission rather than an act.

(2) Allocation

The offence is triable either way   **15–114**

(3) Elements of the offence

"Dishonestly" will presumably be defined as before: see *Feeley* and *Ghosh* (at § 15–4).   **15–115**

D must abuse his position with the intention of making a gain or causing loss or risk of loss to another. The gain or loss does not actually have to take place. Gain and loss are defined in section 5 (see *ante*).

D must abuse his position. The Law Commission (Law Com No. 276, Cm 5560, 2002) explained the meaning of "position" (and this is not further clarified in the statute):

"The necessary relationship will be present between trustee and beneficiary, director and company, professional person and client, agent and principal, employee and employer, or between partners. It may arise otherwise, for example within a family, or in the context of voluntary work, or in any context where the parties are not at arm's length. In nearly all cases where it arises, it will be recognised by the civil law as importing fiduciary duties, and any relationship that is so recognised will suffice. We see no reason, however, why the existence of such duties should be essential. This does not of course mean that it would be entirely a matter for the fact-finders whether the necessary relationship exists. The question whether the particular facts alleged can properly be described as giving rise to that relationship will be an issue capable of being ruled upon by the judge and, if the case goes to the jury, of being the subject of directions." (at para. 7.38)

15–116   The term "abuse" is not defined (or as the *Explanatory Notes* put it "not limited by a definition"!). Note that section 4(2) makes clear that the offence can be committed by omission as well as by positive action. The *Explanatory Notes* give the following examples. An employee who fails to take up the chance of a crucial contract in order that an associate or rival company can take it up instead at the expense of the employer, commits an offence under this section. An employee of a software company who uses his position to clone software products with the intention of selling the products on would commit an offence under this section. Or a person who is employed to care for an elderly or disabled person has access to that person's bank account and abuses his position by transferring funds to invest in a high-risk business venture of his own.

(4) Sentence

15–117   On summary conviction, the maximum penalty for this offence is imprisonment for a term not exceeding 12 months or a fine not exceeding the statutory maximum (or both). But Schedule 2, paragraph 1 of the Act provides for 12 months to be 6 months pending the increase in sentencing powers in a magistrates' court (section 154 of the *Criminal Justice Act* 2003 has yet to be implemented).

E. POSSESSION ETC. OF ARTICLES FOR USE IN FRAUD

(1) Definition

Fraud Act 2006, s.6

Possession etc. of articles for use in frauds

15–118   6—(1) A person is guilty of an offence if he has in his possession or under his control any article for use in the course of or in connection with any fraud.

(2) A person guilty of an offence under this section is liable—

(a) on summary conviction, to imprisonment for a term not exceeding 12 months or to a fine not exceeding the statutory maximum (or to both);

(b) on conviction on indictment, to imprisonment for a term not exceeding 5 years or to a fine (or to both).

(3) Subsection (2)(a) applies in relation to Northern Ireland as if the reference to 12 months were a reference to 6 months.

(2) Allocation

15–119   The offence is triable either way

(3) Elements of the offence

15–120   This broad preliminary offence is similar to section 25 of the *Theft Act* 1968 (without the need for absence from place of abode). The prosecution must prove that:

— D possessed or controlled the article(s). "Article" is defined in section 8:

Fraud Act 2006, s.8

"Article"

15–121   8—(1) For the purposes of—

(a) sections 6 and 7, and

(b) the provisions listed in subsection (2), so far as they relate to articles for use in the course of or in connection with fraud,

"article" includes any program or data held in electronic form.

(2) The provisions are—

(a) section 1(7)(b) of the *Police and Criminal Evidence Act* 1984 (c. 60),

(b) section 2(8)(b) of the *Armed Forces Act* 2001 (c. 19), and

(c) Article 3(7)(b) of the *Police and Criminal Evidence (Northern Ireland) Order*

1989 (S.I. 1989/1341 (N.I. 12)) (meaning of "prohibited articles" for the purposes of stop and search powers).

Although not expressly stated, it would appear that D must possess the article for the **15–122** purpose or with the intention of using it in the course of fraud. It is not necessary to prove that he intended to use it in a specific fraud, or that he intended to use it himself: *Ellames* (1974) 60 Cr.App.R. 7.

(4) Sentence

On summary conviction, the maximum penalty for this offence is imprisonment for a **15–123** term not exceeding 12 months or a fine not exceeding the statutory maximum (or both). But Schedule 2, paragraph 1 of the Act provides for 12 months to be 6 months pending the increase in sentencing powers in a magistrates' court (section 154 of the *Criminal Justice Act* 2003 has yet to be implemented).

F. Making or Supplying Articles for Use in Frauds

(1) Definition

Fraud Act 2006, s.7

Making or supplying articles for use in frauds

7—(1) A person is guilty of an offence if he makes, adapts, supplies or offers to supply any **15–124** article—

(a) knowing that it is designed or adapted for use in the course of or in connection with fraud, or

(b) intending it to be used to commit, or assist in the commission of, fraud.

(2) A person guilty of an offence under this section is liable—

(a) on summary conviction, to imprisonment for a term not exceeding 12 months or to a fine not exceeding the statutory maximum (or to both);

(b) on conviction on indictment, to imprisonment for a term not exceeding 10 years or to a fine (or to both).

(3) Subsection (2)(a) applies in relation to Northern Ireland as if the reference to 12 months were a reference to 6 months.

(2) Allocation

The offence is triable either way   **15–125**

(3) Elements of the offence

For this preliminary offence, the prosecution must prove that: **15–126**

— D makes, adapts, supplies of offers to supply any article. "Article" is defined in section 8 (*ante*) and includes any program or data held in electronic form. The *Explanatory Notes* give the example of someone who makes devices which when attached to electricity meters cause the meter to malfunction.

— D must intend or know that it will be used in connection with fraud. For knowledge, see *ante*, § 12–23.

(4) Sentence

On summary conviction, the maximum penalty for this offence is imprisonment for a **15–127** term not exceeding 12 months or a fine not exceeding the statutory maximum (or both). But Schedule 2, paragraph 1 of the Act provides for 12 months to be 6 months pending the increase in sentencing powers in a magistrates' court (section 154 of the *Criminal Justice Act* 2003 has yet to be implemented).

Part III

G. Participating in Fraudulent Business carried on by Sole Trader etc.

(1) Definition

Fraud Act 2006, s.9

Participating in fraudulent business carried on by sole trader etc.

15–128   **9**—(1) A person is guilty of an offence if he is knowingly a party to the carrying on of a business to which this section applies.

(2) This section applies to a business which is carried on—

     (a) by a person who is outside the reach of section 458 of the *Companies Act* 1985 (c. 6) or Article 451 of the *Companies (Northern Ireland) Order* 1986 (S.I. 1986/1032) (N.I. 6)) (offence of fraudulent trading), and

     (b) with intent to defraud creditors of any person or for any other fraudulent purpose.

(3) The following are within the reach of section 458 of the 1985 Act—

     (a) a company (within the meaning of that Act);

     (b) a person to whom that section applies (with or without adaptations or modifications) as if the person were a company;

     (c) a person exempted from the application of that section.

(4) The following are within the reach of Article 451 of the 1986 Order—

     (a) a company (within the meaning of that Order);

     (b) a person to whom that Article applies (with or without adaptations or modifications) as if the person were a company;

     (c) a person exempted from the application of that Article.

(5) "Fraudulent purpose" has the same meaning as in section 458 of the 1985 Act or Article 451 of the 1986 Order.

(6) A person guilty of an offence under this section is liable—

     (a) on summary conviction, to imprisonment for a term not exceeding 12 months or to a fine not exceeding the statutory maximum (or to both);

     (b) on conviction on indictment, to imprisonment for a term not exceeding 10 years or to a fine (or to both).

(7) Subsection (6)(a) applies in relation to Northern Ireland as if the reference to 12 months were a reference to 6 months.

(2) Allocation

15–129   The offence is triable either way.

(3) Elements of the offence

15–130   This offence is similar to that under the *Companies Act* 1985, s.458, but extends the offence to non-corporate traders. (Section 10 of the *Fraud Act* 2006 increases the maximum custodial sentence for fraudulent trading under the companies legislation to 10 years.) Under section 9, the prosecution must prove:

     — dishonesty, which will presumably be defined as before: see *Feeley* and *Ghosh* (at § 15–4);

     — an intention to defraud;

     — that D exercised some kind of controlling or managerial function within the company.

(4) Sentence

15–131   On summary conviction, the maximum penalty for this offence is imprisonment for a term not exceeding 12 months or a fine not exceeding the statutory maximum (or both). But Schedule 2, paragraph 1 of the Act provides for 12 months to be 6 months pending the increase in sentencing powers in a magistrates' court (section 154 of the *Criminal Justice Act* 2003 has yet to be implemented).

H. OBTAINING SERVICES DISHONESTLY

(1) Definition

Fraud Act 2006, s.11

Obtaining services dishonestly

11—(1) A person is guilty of an offence under this section if he obtains services for himself or **15–132**
another

    (a) by a dishonest act, and

    (b) in breach of subsection (2).

  (2) A person obtains services in breach of this subsection if—

    (a) they are made available on the basis that payment has been, is being or will be made for or in respect of them;

    (b) he obtains them without any payment having been made for or in respect of them or without payment having been made in full, and

    (c) when he obtains them, he knows—

        (i) that they are being made available on the basis described in paragraph (a), or

        (ii) that they might be,

    but intends that payment will not be made, or will not be made in full.

  (3) A person guilty of an offence under this section is liable—

    (a) on summary conviction, to imprisonment for a term not exceeding 12 months or to a fine not exceeding the statutory maximum (or to both);

    (b) on conviction on indictment, to imprisonment for a term not exceeding 5 years or to a fine (or to both).

  (4) Subsection (3)(a) applies in relation to Northern Ireland as if the reference to 12 months were a reference to 6 months.

(2) Allocation

The offence is triable either way.   **15–133**

(3) Elements of the offence

This offence replaces the offence under section 1 of the *Theft Act* 1978 (though there **15–134**
is no longer any need for a deception). The prosecution must prove that:

  — D dishonestly obtained services from another. The *Explanatory Notes* give the example of someone who attaches a decoder to her TV to enable access to satellite TV channels for which she has no intention of paying;

  — knowing that the services are to be paid for or knowing that they might have to be paid for;

  — with the intent to avoid payment in whole or in part.

(4) Sentence

On summary conviction, the maximum penalty for this offence is imprisonment for a **15–135**
term not exceeding 12 months or a fine not exceeding the statutory maximum (or both). But Schedule 2, paragraph 1 of the Act provides for 12 months to be 6 months pending the increase in sentencing powers in a magistrates' court (section 154 of the *Criminal Justice Act* 2003 has yet to be implemented).

III. OFFENCES OF FORGERY, PERSONATION AND CHEATING

A. FORGERY

(1) Definition

Forgery and Counterfeiting Act 1981, s.1

The offence of forgery

15–136   **1.** A person is guilty of forgery if he makes a false instrument, with the intention that he or another shall use it to induce somebody to accept it as genuine, and by reason of so accepting it to do or not to do some act to his own or any other person's prejudice.

(2) Allocation

15–137   This offence is triable either way: *Forgery and Counterfeiting Act* 1981, s.6.

(3) Elements of the offence

15–138   The prosecution must prove that:
— the defendant made a false instrument,
— with the intention that he or another should use it to induce somebody to accept it as genuine and to hence,
— do or not do some act to his own or another person's prejudice by reason of that acceptance.

The intention required for a charge under section 1 is (a) the intention that the false instrument will be used to induce somebody to accept it as genuine and (b) the intention to induce somebody by reason of so accepting it to do or not do some act to his own or another person's prejudice: *Campbell* 80 Cr.App.R. 47, CA.

Forgery and Counterfeiting Act 1981, ss.8–10

Meaning of "instrument"

15–139   **8.**—(1) Subject to subsection (2) below, in this Part of this Act "instrument" means—
  (a) any document, whether of a formal or informal character;
  (b) any stamp issued or sold by a postal operator;
  (c) any Inland Revenue stamp; and
  (d) any disc, tape, sound track or other device on or in which information is re-corded or stored by mechanical, electronic or other means.

(2) A currency note within the meaning of Part II of this Act is not an instrument for the purposes of this Part of this Act.

(3) A mark denoting payment of postage which a postal operator authorises to be used instead of an adhesive stamp is to be treated for the purposes of this Part of this Act as if it were a stamp issued by the postal operator concerned.

(3A) In this section "postal operator" has the same meaning as in the *Postal Services Act* 2000.

(4) In this Part of this Act "Inland Revenue stamp" means a stamp as defined in section 27 of the *Stamp Duties Management Act* 1891.

Meaning of "false" and "making"

15–140   **9.**—(1) An instrument is false for the purposes of this Part of this Act—
  (a) if it purports to have been made in the form in which it is made by a person who did not in fact make it in that form; or
  (b) if it purports to have been made in the form in which it is made on the authority of a person who did not in fact authorise its making in that form; or
  (c) if it purports to have been made in the terms in which it is made by a person who did not in fact make it in those terms; or
  (d) if it purports to have been made in the terms in which it is made on the authority of a person who did not in fact authorise its making in those terms; or

(e) if it purports to have been altered in any respect by a person who did not in fact alter it in that respect; or

(f) if it purports to have been altered in any respect on the authority of a person who did not in fact authorise the alteration in that respect; or

(g) if it purports to have been made or altered on a date on which, or at a place at which, or otherwise in circumstances in which, it was not in fact made or altered; or

(h) if it purports to have been made or altered by an existing person but he did not in fact exist.

(2) A person is to be treated for the purposes of this Part of this Act as making a false instrument if he alters an instrument so as to make it false in any respect (whether or not it is false in some other respect apart from that alteration).

Meaning of "prejudice" and "induce"

10.—(1) Subject to subsections (2) and (4) below, for the purposes of this Part of this Act an **15–141** act or omission intended to be induced is to a person's prejudice if, and only if, it is one which, if it occurs—

(a) will result—

    (i) in his temporary or permanent loss of property; or

    (ii) in his being deprived of an opportunity to earn remuneration or greater remuneration; or

    (iii) in his being deprived of an opportunity to gain a financial advantage otherwise than by way of remuneration; or

(b) will result in somebody being given an opportunity—

    (i) to earn remuneration or greater remuneration from him; or

    (ii) to gain a financial advantage from him otherwise than by way of remuneration; or

(c) will be the result of his having accepted a false instrument as genuine, or a copy of a false instrument as a copy of a genuine one, in connection with his performance of any duty.

(2) An act which a person has an enforceable duty to do and an omission to do an act which a person is not entitled to do shall be disregarded for the purposes of this Part of this Act.

(3) In this Part of this Act references to inducing somebody to accept a false instrument as genuine, or a copy of a false instrument as a copy of a genuine one, include references to inducing a machine to respond to the instrument or copy as if it were a genuine instrument or, as the case may be, a copy of a genuine one.

(4) Where subsection (3) above applies, the act or omission intended to be induced by the machine responding to the instrument or copy shall be treated as an act or omission to a person's prejudice.

(5) In this section "loss" includes not getting what one might get as well as parting with what one has.

Section 31 of the *Immigration and Asylum Act* 1999 provides a defence based on **15–142** 31(1) of the Refugee Convention for a defendant charged with an offence under this section.

Immigration and Asylum Act 1999, s.31

Defences based on Article 31(1) of the Refugee Convention.

31.—(1) It is a defence for a refugee charged with an offence to which this section applies to **15–143** show that, having come to the United Kingdom directly from a country where his life or freedom was threatened (within the meaning of the Refugee Convention), he—

(a) presented himself to the authorities in the United Kingdom without delay;

(b) showed good cause for his illegal entry or presence; and

(c) made a claim for asylum as soon as was reasonably practicable after his arrival in the United Kingdom.

(2) If, in coming from the country where his life or freedom was threatened, the refugee stopped in another country outside the United Kingdom, subsection (1) applies only if he shows that he could not reasonably have expected to be given protection under the Refugee Convention in that other country.

(3) In England and Wales and Northern Ireland the offences to which this section applies are any offence, and any attempt to commit an offence, under—

    (a) Part I of the *Forgery and Counterfeiting Act* 1981 (forgery and connected offences);

    (aa) section 25(1) or (5) of the *Identity Cards Act* 2006;

    (b) section 24A of the 1971 Act (deception); or

    (c) section 26(1)(d) of the 1971 Act (falsification of documents).

(4) In Scotland, the offences to which this section applies are those—

    (a) of fraud,

    (b) of uttering a forged document,

    (ba) under section 25(1) or (5) of the *Identity Cards Act* 2006;

    (c) under section 24A of the 1971 Act (deception), or

    (d) under section 26(1)(d) of the 1971 Act (falsification of documents), and any attempt to commit any of those offences.

(5) A refugee who has made a claim for asylum is not entitled to the defence provided by subsection (1) in relation to any offence committed by him after making that claim.

(6) "Refugee" has the same meaning as it has for the purposes of the Refugee Convention.

(7) If the Secretary of State has refused to grant a claim for asylum made by a person who claims that he has a defence under subsection (1), that person is to be taken not to be a refugee unless he shows that he is.

[This section is printed as amended by the *Identity Cards Act* 2006.]

15–144 Where a defendant raises a defence under section 31(1) of the *Immigration and Asylum Act* 1999 they must adduce sufficient evidence to support their claim to refugee status to raise the issue. The prosecution bears the burden of proving that the defendant is not in fact a refugee. Section 31(1) also imposes a legal burden of proof on the defendant to prove that they presented themselves to the authorities without delay, showed good cause for their illegal entry or presence, and made a claim for asylum as soon as was reasonably practicable. The existence of the reverse burden of proof in section 31(1) does not prevent a defendant receiving a fair trial: *Makuwa (Liliane)* [2006] EWCA Crim 175, CA.

(4) Sentence

15–145 When tried summarily, the maximum penalty for this offence is six months' imprisonment or a fine not exceeding the statutory maximum or both: *Forgery and Counterfeiting Act* 1981, s.6. After commencement of the relevant provisions, the maximum custodial sentence in a magistrates' court will be 12 months' imprisonment: *Criminal Justice Act* 2003, ss.154 and 282.

In *Lincoln* (1994) 15 Cr.App.R.(S.) 333, a husband forged his estranged wife's signature on a contract of sale of house and Land Registry transfer. The original sentence of twelve months' imprisonment for this offence was reduced to six months' imprisonment on appeal. It was held that forgery of documents of title to property must be visited by an immediate custodial sentence in all but the most exceptional circumstances yet in view of the mitigating circumstances, the sentence would be reduced to six months.

In *Dover* (1995) 16 Cr.App.R.(S.) 61, the offender pleaded guilty to two counts of forgery, one of procuring the execution of a valuable security by deception and one of theft. The offender had forged an estimate for the repair of the storm-damaged block of flats that he was responsible for managing, and then kept the difference between the actual cost of repair and the insurance companies' payment for himself. He was sentenced to five months' imprisonment, the court stating "having regard to the breach of trust involved in the offence of theft and the serious nature of the forgeries involving as they do fraud upon an insurance company, five months was, looked at in the round a very lenient sentence."

B. Copying a False Instrument

(1) Definition

Forgery and Counterfeiting Act 1981, s.2

The offence of copying a false instrument
2. It is an offence for a person to make a copy of an instrument which is, and which he knows **15–146**
or believes to be, a false instrument, with the intention that he or another shall use it to induce
somebody to accept it as a copy of a genuine instrument, and by reason of so accepting it to do
or not to do some act to his own or any other person's prejudice

(2) Allocation

This offence is triable either way: *Forgery and Counterfeiting Act* 1981, s.6.   **15–147**

(3) Elements of the offence

The prosecution must prove that: **15–148**
— the defendant made a copy of an instrument which,
— he knew or believed to be a false instrument, and
— he intended that he or another should use the copy to induce somebody to accept it as a copy of a genuine instrument, and
— to cause that other person to do or not do some act to his or another person's
prejudice by reason of so accepting the copy.

For the definition of "instrument", see section 8 of the 1981 Act (*ante*); of "false", section 9 (*ante*) and of "prejudice" or "induce" see section 10 (*ante*). Section 31 of the *Immigration and Asylum Act* 1999 provides a defence based on 31(1) of the Refugee
Convention for a defendant charged with an offence under this section, see *ante*, §§ 15–
142–15–144.

(4) Sentence

When tried summarily, the maximum penalty is six months' imprisonment, a fine **15–149**
not exceeding the statutory maximum or both: *Forgery and Counterfeiting Act* 1981,
s.6. After commencement of the relevant provisions, the maximum custodial sentence in
a magistrates' court will be 12 months' imprisonment: *Criminal Justice Act* 2003, ss.154
and 282.

C. Using a False Instrument, Using Copy of a False Instrument

(1) Definition

Forgery and Counterfeiting Act 1981, ss.3–4

The offence of using a false instrument
3. It is an offence for a person to use an instrument which is, and which he knows or believes **15–150**
to be, false, with the intention of inducing somebody to accept it as genuine, and by reason of so
accepting it to do or not to do some act to his own or any other person's prejudice.

The offence of using a copy of a false instrument
4. It is an offence for a person to use a copy of an instrument which is, and which he knows **15–151**
or believes to be, a false instrument, with the intention of inducing somebody to accept it as a
copy of a genuine instrument, and by reason of so accepting it to do or not to do some act to his
own or any other person's prejudice.

(2) Allocation

This offence is triable either way: *Forgery and Counterfeiting Act* 1981, s.6.   **15–152**

(3) Elements of the offence

15–153   The prosecution must prove that either:
— the defendant used an instrument that is, and that he knew or believed to be, false
— with the intention of inducing somebody to accept it as genuine, and
— to cause that person to do or not to do some act to his own or any other person's prejudice by reason of so accepting the instrument as genuine;

OR

— the defendant used a copy of an instrument that is, and that he knew or believed to be false,
— with the intention of inducing somebody to accept it as a copy of a genuine instrument and,
— to cause that person to do or not to do some act to his own or any other person's prejudice by reason of so accepting the instrument as a copy of a genuine instrument.

Section 31 of the *Immigration and Asylum Act* 1999 provides a defence based on 31(1) of the Refugee Convention for a defendant charged with an offence under this section, see *ante*, §§ 15–142–15–144.

(4) Sentence

15–154   When tried summarily, the maximum penalty is six months' imprisonment, a fine not exceeding the statutory maximum or both: *Forgery and Counterfeiting Act* 1981, s.6. After commencement of the relevant provision, the maximum custodial sentence in a magistrates' court will be 12 months' imprisonment: *Criminal Justice Act* 2003, ss.154 and 282.

In *Duffy* (1994) 15 Cr.App.R.(S.) 677, the offender pleaded guilty to forgery of a candidate's nomination form in connection with a local election and was sentenced to six months' imprisonment. It was held that the offence here was a technical one. As such, a custodial sentence was unwarranted; a substantial financial penalty would have been appropriate. As the defendant had served a month in custody, an absolute discharge was substituted.

In *Balasubramaniam* [2002] 2 Cr.App.R.(S.) 17, a sentence of twelve months' imprisonment for attempting to use a false passport to travel to Canada to visit the appellant's sick mother was reduced to six months. This was a case where there was a plea of guilty by a person of good character, but it was not an exceptional case where a sentence of less than six months could be justified. There were no aggravating features to justify a sentence in excess of six to nine months. This was not a case of using a false passport for financial gain or to subvert entry requirements or to seek employment in a country that would not otherwise grant admission. The facts placed the particular case at the bottom of the six months to nine months bracket.

In *Daljit Singh* [1999] 1 Cr.App.R.(S.) 490, the offender pleaded guilty before a magistrates' court to using a false passport in order to board a flight to Canada. The Court of Appeal upheld his sentence of eight months' imprisonment. Rose L.J. explaining that for reasons of deterrence "cases involving the use of false passports will almost always merit a significant period of custody."

D. CUSTODY OR CONTROL OF CERTAIN FALSE INSTRUMENTS AND MANUFACTURE, CUSTODY OR CONTROL OF EQUIPMENT OR MATERIALS WITH WHICH SUCH INSTRUMENTS MAY BE MADE

(1) Definition

Forgery and Counterfeiting Act 1981, s.5(1)–(4)

Offences relating to money orders, share certificates, passports, etc.

15–155   **5.**—(1) It is an offence for a person to have in his custody or under his control an instrument to which this section applies which is, and which he knows or believes to be, false, with the intention that he or another shall use it to induce somebody to accept it as genuine, and by reason of so accepting it to do or not to do some act to his own or any other person's prejudice.

(2) It is an offence for a person to have in his custody or under his control, without lawful authority or excuse, an instrument to which this section applies which is, and which he knows or believes to be, false.

(3) It is an offence for a person to make or to have in his custody or under his control a machine or implement, or paper or any other material, which to his knowledge is or has been specially designed or adapted for the making of an instrument to which this section applies, with the intention that he or another shall make an instrument to which this section applies which is false and that he or another shall use the instrument to induce somebody to accept it as genuine, and by reason of so accepting it to do or not to do some act to his own or any other person's prejudice.

(4) It is an offence for a person to make or to have in his custody or under his control any such machine, implement, paper or material, without lawful authority or excuse.

(2) Allocation

These offences are triable either way: *Forgery and Counterfeiting Act* 1981, s.6.   **15–156**

(3) Elements of the offence

The prosecution must prove that either: **15–157**
— the defendant had in his custody or under his control,
— an instrument of the kind listed in section 5(3) of the 1981 Act which
— he knows or believes to be false,
— with the intention that he or another shall induce somebody to accept it as genuine, and
— cause that person to do or not do some act to his own or another person's prejudice by reason of him accepting the instrument as genuine;
OR
— the defendant had in his custody or under his control;
— an instrument of the kind listed in section 5(3) of the 1981 Act which,
— is, and which he knows to be false,
— without lawful authority or excuse;
OR
— the defendant had in his custody or under his control,
— a machine or implement, or paper or any other material,
— which to his knowledge is or has been designed or adapted for the making of an instrument of the kind listed in section 5(3) of the 1981 Act,
— with the intention that he or another shall make an instrument of the kind listed in section 5(3) of the 1981 Act which is false, and
— that he or another shall use the instruments to induce somebody to accept it as genuine, and
— cause that person to do or not do some act to his own or another person's prejudice by reason of him accepting the instrument as genuine;
OR
— the defendant had in his custody or under his control,
— any such machine, implement, paper or material as described in section 5(3)
— without lawful authority or excuse.

Forgery and Counterfeiting Act 1981, s.5(5), (6)

Offences relating to money orders, share certificates, passports, etc.
5.—(5) The instruments to which this section applies are—   **15–158**
    (a) money orders;

      (b) postal orders;

      (c) United Kingdom postage stamps;

      (d) Inland Revenue stamps;

      (e) share certificates;

      (f) passports and documents which can be used instead of passports;

      (g) cheques;

      (h) travellers' cheques;

      (j) cheque cards;

      (k) credit cards;

      (l) certified copies relating to an entry in a register of births, adoptions, marriages or deaths and issued by the Registrar General, the Registrar General for Northern Ireland, a registration officer or a person lawfully authorised to register marriages; and

      (m) certificates relating to entries in such registers.

(6) In subsection (5)(e) above "share certificate" means an instrument entitling or evidencing the title of a person to a share or interest—

      (a) in any public stock, annuity, fund or debt of any government or state, including a state which forms part of another state; or

      (b) in any stock, fund or debt of a body (whether corporate or unincorporated) established in the United Kingdom or elsewhere.

15–159   Section 31 of the *Immigration and Asylum Act* 1999 provides a defence based on 31(1) of the Refugee Convention for a defendant charged with an offence under this section, see *ante*, §§ 15–142–15–144.

(4) Sentence

15–160   When tried summarily, the maximum penalty is six months' imprisonment, a fine not exceeding the statutory maximum or both: *Forgery and Counterfeiting Act* 1981, s.6. After commencement of the relevant provisions, the maximum custodial sentence in a magistrates' court will be 12 months' imprisonment: *Criminal Justice Act* 2003, ss.154 and 282.

In *Siliavski* [2000] 1 Cr.App.R.(S.) 23, the offender pleaded guilty to possessing forged passports after four forged Greek passports were found concealed in his trousers at Heathrow Airport. He was sentenced to 12 months' imprisonment and recommended for deportation. This sentence was reduced to six months on appeal, the Garland J. drawing a distinction between cases involving use of a false passport and cases involving mere carrying. This distinction was disapproved in *Cheema* [2002] 2 Cr.App.R.(S.) 79, CA. A sentence of three years' imprisonment was substituted for a sentence of four years imprisonment where the offender had been convicted of having custody or control of twelve false passports. Pill L.J. disapproved of lenient treatment in the context of carrying in of false passports and advocated the use of deterrent sentences to stop others "taking part as couriers in a lucrative but obnoxious trade."

E. COUNTERFEITING NOTES OR COINS

(1) Definition

Forgery and Counterfeiting Act 1981, s.14

Offences of counterfeiting notes and coins

15–161   **14.**—(1) It is an offence for a person to make a counterfeit of a currency note or of a protected coin, intending that he or another shall pass or tender it as genuine.

(2) It is an offence for a person to make a counterfeit of a currency note or of a protected coin without lawful authority or excuse.

(2) Allocation

15–162   These offences are triable either way: *Forgery and Counterfeiting Act* 1981, s.22.

(3) Elements of the offence

The prosecution must prove either that;   **15–163**
— the defendant made a counterfeit of a currency note or a protected coin,
— with the intention that he or another should pass or tender it as genuine;
OR
— the defendant made a counterfeit of a currency note or a protected coin,
— without lawful authority or excuse.

Forgery and Counterfeiting Act 1981, s.27

Meaning of "currency note" and "protected coin"

27.—(1) In this Part of this Act—   **15–164**
"currency note" means—
    (a) any note which—
        (i) has been lawfully issued in England and Wales, Scotland, Northern Ireland, any of the Channel Islands, the Isle of Man or the Republic of Ireland; and
        (ii) is or has been customarily used as money in the country where it was issued; and
        (iii) is payable on demand; or
    (b) any note which—
        (i) has been lawfully issued in some country other than those mentioned in paragraph (a)(i) above; and
        (ii) is customarily used as money in that country; and
"protected coin" means any coin which—
    (a) is customarily used as money in any country; or
    (b) is specified in an order made by the Treasury for the purposes of this Part of this Act.
(2) The power to make an order conferred on the Treasury by subsection (1) above shall be exercisable by statutory instrument.
(3) A statutory instrument containing such an order shall be laid before Parliament after being made.

The *Forgery and Counterfeiting (Protected Coins) Order* 1981 (S.I. 1981 No. 1505)   **15–165**
specifies the following coins for the purposes of Pt II of the Act:
    Sovereign;
    Half Sovereign;
    Krugerrand;
    Any coin denominated as a fraction of a Kruggerand;
    Maria-Theresa thaler bearing the date of 1780.
The *Forgery and Counterfeiting (Protected Coins) Order* (1999) (S.I. 1999 No. 2095) specifies any euro coin produced in accordance with Council Regulation No 975/98/EC by or at the instance of a member state which has adopted the single currency, for the purposes of Pt II of the 1981 Act.

Forgery and Counterfeiting Act 1981, s.28

Meaning of "counterfeit"

28.—(1) For the purposes of this Part of this Act a thing is a counterfeit of a currency note or   **15–166**
of a protected coin—
    (a) if it is not a currency note or a protected coin but resembles a currency note or protected coin (whether on one side only or on both) to such an extent that it is reasonably capable of passing for a currency note or protected coin of that description; or
    (b) if it is a currency note or protected coin which has been so altered that it is reasonably capable of passing for a currency note or protected coin of some other description.

(2) For the purposes of this Part of this Act—

    (a) a thing consisting of one side only of a currency note, with or without the addition of other material, is a counterfeit of such a note;

    (b) a thing consisting—

        (i) of parts of two or more currency notes; or

        (ii) of parts of a currency note, or of parts of two or more currency notes, with the addition of other material,

    is capable of being a counterfeit of a currency note.

(3) References in this Part of this Act to passing or tendering a counterfeit of a currency note or a protected coin are not to be construed as confined to passing or tendering it as legal tender.

(4) Sentence

15–167   When tried summarily, offences under both section 14(1) and (2) are punishable by a maximum sentence of six months' imprisonment, a fine not exceeding the statutory maximum or both. After commencement of the relevant provisions, the maximum custodial sentence in a magistrates' court will be 12 months' imprisonment: *Criminal Justice Act* 2003, ss.154 and 282.

In *Howard* (1986) 82 Cr.App.R. 262, CA it was said that where a defendant is convicted of passing counterfeit notes, the issue of which undermines the whole economy of the country, in nearly every case this requires a custodial sentence to punish the wrongdoer and deter him from committing the same sort of offence in the future and to act as a deterrent to others. The offender pleaded guilty to having custody of counterfeit currency (£20 notes) and tendering one such counterfeit note, and was sentenced to concurrent terms of two years' imprisonment. *Howard* was followed in *Luxford* [1996] 1 Cr.App.R.(S.) 186, CA, where the offender pleaded guilty to having custody of a counterfeit currency note and was sentenced to nine months' imprisonment. He appealed against sentence, submitting that the judge gave insufficient credit for a plea of guilty, good character and the pre-sentence report. The court held that whilst the sentence imposed was excessive, a custodial sentence would be an inevitable punishment for this offence. A sentence of four months' imprisonment was substituted. See also *Crick* (1981) 3 Cr.App.R.(S.) 275.

F. PASSING COUNTERFEIT NOTES AND COINS

(1) Definition

Forgery and Counterfeiting Act 1981, s.15

Offences of passing etc. counterfeit notes and coins

15–168   **15.**—(1) It is an offence for a person—

    (a) to pass or tender as genuine any thing which is, and which he knows or believes to be, a counterfeit of a currency note or of a protected coin; or

    (b) to deliver to another any thing which is, and which he knows or believes to be, such a counterfeit, intending that the person to whom it is delivered or another shall pass or tender it as genuine.

(2) It is an offence for a person to deliver to another, without lawful authority or excuse, any thing which is, and which he knows or believes to be, a counterfeit of a currency note or of a protected coin.

(2) Procedure

15–169   These offences are triable either way: *Forgery and Counterfeiting Act* 1981, s.22.

(3) Elements of the offence

15–170   The prosecution must prove that either:

- the defendant passed or tendered;
  OR
- delivered to another,
- any thing which is, and which he knows to be a counterfeit of a currency note or a protected coin,
- intending that the person to whom it is delivered shall pass or tender it as genuine;

OR

- the defendant delivered to another,
- without lawful authority or excuse,
- any thing which is, and which he knows to be a counterfeit of a currency note or a protected coin.

For the meaning of "currency note" "protected coin" and "counterfeit" see sections 27 and 28 of the 1981 Act (*ante*).

(4) Sentence

When tried summarily, offences under both sections 14(1) and (2) are punishable by **15–171** a maximum sentence of six months' imprisonment, a fine not exceeding the statutory maximum or both. After commencement of the relevant provisions, the maximum custodial sentence in a magistrates' court will be 12 months' imprisonment: *Criminal Justice Act* 2003, ss.154 and 282.

In *Derbyshire* (1992) 13 Cr.App.R.(S.) 126 the offender pleaded guilty to three counts of delivering counterfeit goods with intent, having bought nine forged notes which he then sold on to three other men. He was sentenced to twelve months' imprisonment. On appeal, it was held that the offences were at or near the bottom of the scale for offences of their type and the appropriate sentence was six months' imprisonment. In *Shah* (1987) 9 Cr.App.R.(S.) 167 the offender was convicted of tendering a counterfeit note. He had attempted to buy a record offering a forged £50 note. The offender claimed he had picked up the note without realising what it was, and there was no other evidence of dealing with counterfeit notes. The Court of Appeal upheld his sentence of twelve months' imprisonment, to be suspended for two years, with a supervision order, Steyn J. stating that in the absence of exceptional circumstances an immediate custodial sentence is necessary in all cases involving the tendering or passing of forged banknotes. A case lying towards the less serious end of the spectrum is *Dickens* (1993) 14 Cr.App.R.(S.) 76. The offender had tendered a counterfeit £20 note in a shop. He admitted that he knew the note was counterfeit, but claimed that he had received it innocently in change for a £50 note, and decided to pass it on. He was sentenced to 12 months' imprisonment. On appeal, the propriety of an immediate custodial sentence was approved, yet 12 months was manifestly excessive, and a sentence of six months was substituted.

In *Wake* (1992) 13 Cr.App.R.(S.) 422, the offender was convicted of two counts of passing a counterfeit note. The Court of Appeal held that although an immediate custodial sentence was entirely appropriate, a sentence of 12 months' imprisonment for this offence was manifestly excessive and a sentence of three months' imprisonment was appropriate. A sentence of four months' imprisonment was imposed where the offender had been in possession of 47 counterfeit £5 notes for 20 minutes after the driver of the car in which he was a passenger gave him them to conceal from the police: *Luxford* [1996] 1 Cr.App.R.(S.) 186, CA.

G. Custody or Control of Counterfeits

(1) Definition

Forgery and Counterfeiting Act 1981, s.16

Offences involving the custody or control of counterfeit notes and coins
  16.—(1) It is an offence for a person to have in his custody or under his control any thing **15–172**

which is; and which he knows or believes to be, a counterfeit of a currency note or of a protected coin, intending either to pass or tender it as genuine or to deliver it to another with the intention that he or another shall pass or tender it as genuine.

(2) It is an offence for a person to have in his custody or under his control, without lawful authority or excuse, any thing which is, and which he knows or believes to be, a counterfeit of a currency note or of a protected coin.

(3) It is immaterial for the purposes of subsections (1) and (2) above that a coin or note is not in a fit state to be passed or tendered or that the making or counterfeiting of a coin or note has not been finished or perfected.

(2) Allocation

15–173   These offences are triable either way: *Forgery and Counterfeiting Act* 1981, s.22.

(3) Elements of the offence

15–174   The prosecution must prove that:
— the defendant had in his custody or under his control,
— any thing which was and which he knew or believed to be,
— a counterfeit of a currency note or protected coin,
— intending either to pass or tender it as genuine or to deliver it to another with the intention that he or another shall pass or tender it as genuine;
OR
— the defendant had in his custody or under his control,
— any thing which was and which he knew or believed to be,
— a counterfeit of a currency note or protected coin.

For the meaning of "currency note" "protected coin" and "counterfeit" see *ante*, sections 27 and 28 of the 1981 Act: § 15–155 and § 15–157.

(4) Sentence

15–175   When tried summarily, offences under both section 14(1) and (2) are punishable by a maximum sentence of six months' imprisonment, a fine not exceeding the statutory maximum or both. After commencement of the relevant provisions, the maximum custodial sentence in a magistrates' court will be 12 months' imprisonment: *Criminal Justice Act* 2003, ss.154 and 282.

In *Torry* (1983) 5 Cr.App.R.(S.) 326, CA, the offender pleaded guilty to one count of handling stolen goods and one of having custody or control of a counterfeit currency note. Forty-six counterfeit £20 had been found at his house, and he received a sentence of eighteen months' imprisonment for possession of the counterfeit notes. This was substituted for a sentence of 12 months on appeal due to the mitigating circumstances of the offender. See also *Carter* (1983) 5 Cr.App.R.(S.) 256.

H. MAKING, CUSTODY OR CONTROL OF COUNTERFEITING MATERIALS AND IMPLEMENTS

(1) Definition

Forgery and Counterfeiting Act, s.17

Offences involving the making or custody or control of counterfeiting materials and implements
15–176   **17.**—(1) It is an offence for a person to make, or to have in his custody or under his control, any thing which he intends to use, or to permit any other person to use, for the purpose of making a counterfeit of a currency note or of a protected coin with the intention that it be passed or tendered as genuine.

(2) It is an offence for a person without lawful authority or excuse—

    (a) to make; or

    (b) to have in his custody or under his control,

any thing which, to his knowledge, is or has been specially designed or adapted for the making of a counterfeit of a currency note.

    (3) Subject to subsection (4) below, it is an offence for a person to make, or to have in his custody or under his control, any implement which, to his knowledge, is capable of imparting to any thing a resemblance—

    (a) to the whole or part of either side of a protected coin; or

    (b) to the whole or part of the reverse of the image on either side of a protected coin.

    (4) It shall be a defence for a person charged with an offence under subsection (3) above to show—

    (a) that he made the implement or, as the case may be, had it in his custody or under his control, with the written consent of the Treasury; or

    (b) that he had lawful authority otherwise than by virtue of paragraph (a) above, or a lawful excuse, for making it or having it in his custody or under his control.

(2) Allocation

These offences are triable either way: *Forgery and Counterfeiting Act* 1981, s.22. **15–177**

(3) Elements of the offence

The prosecution must prove that: **15–178**
  — the defendant made, or had in his custody or under his control,
  — any thing which he intends to use, or to permit any other person to use, for the purpose of making a counterfeit of a currency note or of a protected coin with,
  — with the intention that it be passed or tendered as genuine;

OR
  — the defendant made, or had in his custody or under his control,
  — any thing which, to his knowledge, had been specially designed or adapted for the making of a counterfeit of a currency note,
  — without lawful authority or excuse;

OR
  — the defendant made, or had in his custody or control,
  — any implement which, to his knowledge was capable of imparting to any thing a resemblance either to the whole or part of a protected coin, or to the whole or part of the reverse of the image on either side of a protected coin, and,
  — the defendant did not make the implement or, have it in his custody or under his control with the written consent of the Treasury; or with lawful authority otherwise than by virtue of permission of the Treasury, or lawful excuse.

For the meaning of "currency note" "protected coin" and "counterfeit" see *ante*, sections 27 and 28 of the 1981 Act: § 15–155 and § 15–157.

(4) Sentence

When tried summarily, offences under both section 17(1) and (2) are punishable by a **15–179** maximum sentence of six months' imprisonment, a fine not exceeding the statutory maximum or both. After commencement of the relevant provisions, the maximum custodial sentence in a magistrates' court will be 12 months' imprisonment: *Criminal Justice Act* 2003, ss.154 and 282.

I. Reproducing British Currency

(1) Definition

Forgery and Counterfeiting Act 1981 ss.18(1), 19(1)

The offence of reproducing British currency notes

    18.—(1) It is an offence for any person, unless the relevant authority has previously consented **15–180**

in writing, to reproduce on any substance whatsoever, and whether or not on the correct scale, any British currency note or any part of a British currency note.

Offences of making etc. imitation British coins

15–181   **19.**—(1) It is an offence for a person—

     (a) to make an imitation British coin in connection with a scheme intended to promote the sale of any product or the making of contracts for the supply of any service; or

     (b) to sell or distribute imitation British coins in connection with any such scheme, or to have imitation British coins in his custody or under his control with a view to such sale or distribution,

unless the Treasury have previously consented in writing to the sale or distribution of such imitation British coins in connection with that scheme.

(2) Allocation

15–182   These offences are triable either way: *Forgery and Counterfeiting Act* 1981, s.22

(3) Elements of the offence

15–183   The prosecution must prove that:

— the defendant produced, on any substance, or to any scale whatsoever,

— any British currency note or any part of a British currency note,

— without the written consent of the relevant consenting authority;

OR

— the defendant made an imitation British coin,

— in connection with a scheme intended to promote the sale of any product or the making of contracts for the supply of any service;

OR

— the defendant sold or distributed imitation British coins,

— in connection with a scheme intended to promote the sale of any product or the making of contracts for the supply of any service;

OR

— the defendant had imitation British coins in his custody or control,

— with a view to their sale or distribution,

— without the written consent of the Treasury to such sale or distribution of imitation British coins.

Forgery and Counterfeiting Act 1981, ss.18(2) and 19(2)

The offence of reproducing British currency notes

15–184   **18.**—(2) In this section—

"British currency note" means any note which—

     (a) has been lawfully issued in England and Wales, Scotland or Northern Ireland; and

     (b) is or has been customarily used as money in the country where it was issued; and

     (c) is payable on demand; and

"the relevant authority", in relation to a British currency note of any particular description, means the authority empowered by law to issue notes of that description.

Offences of making etc. imitation British coins

15–185   **19.**—(2) In this section—

"British coin" means any coin which is legal tender in any part of the United Kingdom; and

"imitation British coin" means any thing which resembles a British coin in shape, size and the substance of which it is made.

(4) Sentence

15–186   When tried summarily, offences under both section 14(1) and (2) are punishable by a maximum sentence of six months' imprisonment, a fine not exceeding the statutory maximum or both. After commencement of the relevant provisions, the maximum custodial sentence in a magistrates' court will be 12 months' imprisonment: *Criminal Justice Act* 2003, ss.154 and 282.

J. PROHIBITION OF IMPORTATION AND EXPORTATION ON COUNTERFEITS

(1) Definition

Forgery and Counterfeiting Act 1981, ss.20–21

Prohibition of importation of counterfeit notes and coins
20. The importation, landing or unloading of a counterfeit of a currency note or of a **15–187** protected coin without the consent of the Treasury is hereby prohibited.

Prohibition of exportation of counterfeit notes and coins
21.—(1) The exportation of a counterfeit of a currency note or of a protected coin without **15–188** the consent of the Treasury is hereby prohibited.

(2) A counterfeit of a currency note or of a protected coin which is removed to the Isle of Man from the United Kingdom shall be deemed to be exported from the United Kingdom—

(a) for the purposes of this section; and

(b) for the purposes of the customs and excise Acts, in their application to the prohibition imposed by this section.

(3) [Amends *Isle of Man Act* 1979, s.9(1)]

(2) Procedure

Sections 20 and 21 do not create offences, rather they impose prohibitions. The rele- **15–189** vant offences are those committed under the *Customs and Excise Management Act* 1979, ss.50 and 68. See *post*, §§ 19–17 and 19–25.

IV. MISCELLANEOUS OFFENCES

A. OFFENCES UNDER THE IDENTITY CARDS ACT 2006

Introduction

The *Identity Cards Act* 2006 received Royal Assent on March 30, 2006. Section 25, **15–190** which came into force on June 7, 2006, creates three offences relating to the possession of false identity documents. Subsection (1) creates the offence of possessing false identity documents, improperly obtained identification documents or identification documents belonging to someone else with the intention of using such documents to establish registrable facts about himself or others. Subsection (3) creates the offence of making, or possessing, apparatus designed or adapted to make false identity documents with the intention of making false identity documents in order to establish, ascertain or verify registrable facts about a person. Both of these offences are triable on indictment only. Subsection (5) creates the offence of possessing false identity documents or apparatus to make false identity documents without reasonable excuse, which is triable either way.

(1) Possession of false identity documents

(a) *Definition*

Identity Cards Act 2006, s.25(5)

Possession of false identity documents etc.
25.—(5) It is an offence for a person to have in his possession or under his control, without **15–191** reasonable excuse—

    (a) an identity document that is false;

    (b) an identity document that was improperly obtained;

    (c) an identity document that relates to someone else; or

    (d) any apparatus, article or material which, to his knowledge, is or has been specially designed or adapted for the making of false identity documents or to be used in the making of such documents.

(6) A person guilty of an offence under subsection (1) or (3) shall be liable on conviction on indictment to imprisonment for a term not exceeding 10 years or to a fine or both.

(7) A person guilty of an offence under subsection (5) shall be liable—

    (a) on conviction on indictment, to imprisonment for a term not exceeding two years or to a fine, or to both;

    (b) on summary conviction in England and Wales, to imprisonment for a term not exceeding twelve months or to a fine not exceeding the statutory maximum, or to both;

    (c) on summary conviction in Scotland or Northern Ireland, to imprisonment for a term not exceeding six months or to a fine not exceeding the statutory maximum, or to both;

but, in relation to an offence committed before the commencement of section 154(1) of the *Criminal Justice Act* 2003 (c. 44), the reference in paragraph (b) to twelve months is to be read as a reference to six months.

(8) For the purposes of this section—

    (a) an identity document is false only if it is false within the meaning of Part 1 of the *Forgery and Counterfeiting Act* 1981 (c. 45) (see section 9(1) of that Act); and

    (b) an identity document was improperly obtained if false information was provided, in or in connection with the application for its issue or an application for its modification, to the person who issued it or (as the case may be) to a person entitled to modify it;

and references to the making of a false identity document include references to the modification of an identity document so that it becomes false.

(9) Subsection (8)(a) does not apply in the application of this section to Scotland.

(10) In this section "identity document" has the meaning given by section 26.

(b) *Allocation*

15–192   The offence is triable either way: *Identity Cards Act* 2006, s.25(7), unless it is an offence under s.25(1) or (3) when it is indictable only.

(c) *Elements of the offence*

Identity Cards Act 2006, s.26

Identity documents for the purposes of s.25

15–193   **26.**—(1) In section 25 "identity document" means any document that is, or purports to be—

    (a) an ID card;

    (b) a designated document;

    (c) an immigration document;

    (d) a United Kingdom passport (within the meaning of the *Immigration Act* 1971 (c. 77));

    (e) a passport issued by or on behalf of the authorities of a country or territory outside the United Kingdom or by or on behalf of an international organisation;

    (f) a document that can be used (in some or all circumstances) instead of a passport;

    (g) a UK driving licence; or

    (h) a driving licence issued by or on behalf of the authorities of a country or territory outside the United Kingdom.

(2) In subsection (1) "immigration document" means—

    (a) a document used for confirming the right of a person under the Community Treaties in respect of entry or residence in the United Kingdom;

    (b) a document which is given in exercise of immigration functions and records information about leave granted to a person to enter or to remain in the United Kingdom; or

(c) a registration card (within the meaning of section 26A of the *Immigration Act* 1971); and in paragraph (b) "immigration functions" means functions under the Immigration Acts (within the meaning of the *Asylum and Immigration (Treatment of Claimants, etc.) Act* 2004 (c. 19)).

(3) In that subsection "UK driving licence" means—

(a) a licence to drive a motor vehicle granted under Part 3 of the *Road Traffic Act* 1988 (c. 52); or

(b) a licence to drive a motor vehicle granted under Part 2 of the *Road Traffic (Northern Ireland) Order* 1981 (S.I. 1981/154 (N.I. 1)).

(4) The Secretary of State may by order modify the list of documents in subsection (1).

(5) The Secretary of State must not make an order containing (with or without other provision) any provision that he is authorised to make by subsection (4) unless a draft of the order has been laid before Parliament and approved by a resolution of each House.

Section 31 of the *Immigration and Asylum Act* 1999 provides a defence based on **15–194** 31(1) of the Refugee Convention for a defendant charged with an offence under this section, see *ante*, §§ 15–142–15–144.

(d) *Sentence*

After commencement of the relevant provisions the maximum custodial sentence in a **15–195** magistrates' court will be 12 months' imprisonment: section 25(7). The maximum penalty for offences committed before the commencement of section 154(1) of the *Criminal Justice Act* 2003 is imprisonment for a term not exceeding six months or a fine not exceeding the statutory maximum or both: section 125(3)(a).

B. INTERFERENCE WITH VEHICLES

(1) Definition

Criminal Attempts Act 1981 s.9

Interference with vehicles

9.—(1) A person is guilty of the offence of vehicle interference if he interferes with a motor **15–196** vehicle or trailer or with anything carried in or on a motor vehicle or trailer with the intention that an offence specified in subsection (2) below shall be committed by himself or some other person.

(2) The offences mentioned in subsection (1) above are—

(a) theft of the motor vehicle or trailer or part of it;

(b) theft of anything carried in or on the motor vehicle or trailer; and

(c) an offence under section 12(1) of the *Theft Act* 1968 (taking and driving away without consent);

and, if it is shown that a person offender of an offence under this section intended that one of those offences should be committed, it is immaterial that it cannot be shown which it was.

[This section is printed as amended by the *CJA* 1982, s.46; the *Police and Criminal Evidence Act* 1984, Sched. 7 and the *Road Traffic (Consequential Provisions) Act* 1988, Sched. 3.]

(2) Allocation

The offence is triable summarily: *Criminal Attempts Act* 1981, s.9(3).   **15–197**

(3) Elements of the offence

The prosecution must prove that: **15–198**

— the defendant interfered. Interference is not defined within the Act. In *Reynolds and Warren v. Metropolitan Police* [1982] Crim.L.R. 831 it was held that more than looking into vehicles and touching them was necessary to establish interference.

— with a motor vehicle or trailer or with anything carried in or on a motor vehicle or trailer,

— with the intention that one of the following offences should be committed by himself or some other person; theft of the motor vehicle or trailer or part of it; theft of anything carried in or on the motor vehicle or trailer; taking or diving a vehicle away without consent (offence created by section 12(1) of the *Theft Act* 1968).

"Motor vehicle" and "trailer" have the meanings assigned to them by section 185(1) of the *Road Traffic Act* 1988 (s.9(5)).

(4) Sentence

15–199   The maximum penalty for this offence is imprisonment for a term not exceeding three months or a fine not exceeding level four on the standard scale or both: *Criminal Attempts Act* 1981, s.9(3). Section 280(2) and Schedule 26, paragraph 28 of the *Criminal Justice Act* 2003 increases the maximum term to 51 weeks (not yet in force).

The *Magistrates' Court Sentencing Guidelines* (2004) state:

> Aggravating factors include disabled passenger vehicle, emergency service vehicle, racial aggravation, group action, planned, related damage, offence committed on bail, relevant previous convictions and any failures to respond to previous sentences.
> Mitigating factors shall include impulsive action.
> **Guideline**: Is it serious enough for a community penalty?

C. DISHONESTLY OBTAINING ELECTRONIC COMMUNICATIONS SERVICES

(1) Definition

Communications Act 2003, s.125

Dishonestly obtaining electronic communications services

15–200   **125.**—(1) A person who—

     (a) dishonestly obtains an electronic communications service, and

     (b) does so with intent to avoid payment of a charge applicable to the provision of that service, is guilty of an offence.

(2) It is not an offence under this section to obtain a service mentioned in section 297(1) of the *Copyright, Designs and Patents Act* 1988 (c. 48) (dishonestly obtaining a broadcasting service provided from a place in the UK).

(3) A person guilty of an offence under this section shall be liable—

     (a) on summary conviction, to imprisonment for a term not exceeding six months or to a fine not exceeding the statutory maximum, or to both;

     (b) on conviction on indictment, to imprisonment for a term not exceeding five years or to a fine, or to both.

(2) Allocation

15–201   This offence is triable either way.

(3) Elements of the offence

15–202   The prosecution must prove that:

— The defendant dishonestly obtained,

— An electronic communications service,

— With the intention to permanently avoid payment of any charge applicable to the provision of that service.

It is not an offence to obtain a service mentioned in section 297(1) of the *Copyright, Designs and Patents Act* 1988 (section 125(2)).

(4) Sentence

15–203   When tried summarily, the maximum penalty for this offence is imprisonment for a term not exceeding six months or a fine not exceeding the statutory maximum or both: section 125(3)(a). After commencement of the relevant provisions the maximum custodial sentence in a magistrates' court will be 12 months' imprisonment: *Criminal Justice Act* 2003, ss.154 and 282.

In *Nadig* (1993) 14 Cr.App.R.(S.) 49, the offenders were seen using a telephone in a public telephone box to make an international call whilst one of the offenders was using a tone-dialling device. Their original sentences of two months' imprisonment, suspended, and a fine of 1,000 pounds each was varied to conditional discharge on appeal, the fact tat they were first time offenders and that this was an isolated offence being significant.

D. Possession or Supply of Apparatus to Dishonestly Obtain Electronic Communication Services

(1) Definition

Communications Act 2003, s.126

Possession or supply of apparatus etc. for contravening s. 125

126.—(1) A person is guilty of an offence if, with an intention falling within subsection (3), he has in his possession or under his control anything that may be used— **15–204**
- (a) for obtaining an electronic communications service; or
- (b) in connection with obtaining such a service.

(2) A person is guilty of an offence if—
- (a) he supplies or offers to supply anything which may be used as mentioned in subsection (1); and
- (b) he knows or believes that the intentions in relation to that thing of the person to whom it is supplied or offered fall within subsection (3).

(3) A person's intentions fall within this subsection if he intends—
- (a) to use the thing to obtain an electronic communications service dishonestly;
- (b) to use the thing for a purpose connected with the dishonest obtaining of such a service;
- (c) dishonestly to allow the thing to be used to obtain such a service; or
- (d) to allow the thing to be used for a purpose connected with the dishonest obtaining of such a service.

(4) An intention does not fall within subsection (3) if it relates exclusively to the obtaining of a service mentioned in section 297 (1) of the *Copyright, Designs and Patents Act* 1988 (c. 48).

(5) A person guilty of an offence under this section shall be liable—
- (a) on summary conviction, to imprisonment for a term not exceeding six months or to a fine not exceeding the statutory maximum, or to both; and
- (b) on conviction on indictment, to imprisonment for a term not exceeding five years or to a fine, or to both.

(6) In this section, references, in the case of a thing used for recording data, to the use of that thing include references to the use of data recorded by it.

(2) Allocation

These offences are triable either way.   **15–205**

(3) Elements of the offence

As regards the offence under section 126, (1) the prosecution must prove that: **15–206**
- — The defendant had in his possession or under his control,
- — anything that may be used for obtaining an electronic communications service, or
- — anything that may be used in connection with obtaining such a service.

As regards the offence under section 126, (2) the prosecution must prove that:

— The defendant supplied or offered to supply anything which may be used for obtaining an electronic communications service, or
— in connection with obtaining such a service AND
— The defendant knew or believed that the person to whom the article is supplied intended to use the article to obtain an electronic communications service dishonestly OR
— Intended to use the thing for a purpose connected with the dishonest obtaining of such a service OR
— Intended dishonestly to allow the thing to be used to obtain such a service; or
— Intended to allow the thing to be used for a purpose connected with the dishonest obtaining of such a service.

It is not an offence under section 126(3) to supply or offer to supply an article to someone whose intentions relate exclusively to the obtaining of a service mentioned in section 297(1) of the *Copyright, Designs and Patents Act* 1988: section 126(4).

(4) Sentence

15–207   When tried summarily, the maximum penalty for this offence is imprisonment for a term not exceeding six months or a fine not exceeding the statutory maximum or both: section 125(3)(a). After commencement of the relevant provisions the maximum custodial sentence in a magistrates' court will be 12 months' imprisonment: *Criminal Justice Act* 2003, ss.154 and 282.

In *Stephens* [2002] 2 Cr.App.R.(S) 67, the defendant had modified mobile telephones to enable calls to be made for free. His original sentence of 18 months' imprisonment was reduced to twelve months' imprisonment on appeal. Whilst the offence was held to definitely pass the custody threshold, an appropriate discount for the defendant's guilty plea had to be given.

E. RE-PROGRAMMING MOBILE TELEPHONES

(1) Definition

Mobile Telephones (Re-programming) Act 2002, s.1

Re-programming mobile telephone etc.
15–208   **1.**—(1) A person commits an offence if—
   (a) he changes a unique device identifier, or
   (b) he interferes with the operation of a unique device identifier, or
   (c) he offers or agrees to change, or interfere with the operation of, a unique device identifier, or
   (d) he offers or agrees to arrange for another person to change, or interfere with the operation of, a unique device identifier.
   (2) A unique device identifier is an electronic equipment identifier which is unique to a mobile wireless communications device.
   (3) But a person does not commit an offence under this section if—
   (a) he is the manufacturer of the device, or
   (b) he does the act mentioned in subsection (1) with the written consent of the manufacturer of the device.
   (4) A person guilty of an offence under this section is liable—
   (a) on summary conviction, to imprisonment for a term not exceeding 6 months or to a fine not exceeding the statutory maximum or to both, or
   (b) on conviction on indictment, to imprisonment for a term not exceeding 5 years or to a fine or to both.

[This section is printed as amended by the *Violent Crime Reduction Act* 2006, s.62.]

(2) Allocation

15–209   This offence is triable either way.

(3) Elements of the offence

The prosecution must prove that: **15–210**
— The defendant changed a unique device identifier OR
— Interfered with the operation of a unique device identifier OR
— Offered or agreed to change, or interfere with the operation of, a unique device identifier, OR
— Offered or agreed to arrange for another person to change, or interfere with the operation of, a unique device identifier.

The manufacturer of the device, or someone acting with the consent of the manufacturer of the device, will not commit an offence under this section if he modifies or changes the device's unique device identifier.

(4) Sentence

When tried summarily, the maximum penalty for this offence is imprisonment for a **15–211** term not exceeding six months or a fine not exceeding the statutory maximum or both: section 125(3)(a). After commencement of the relevant provisions the maximum custodial sentence in a magistrates' court will be 12 months' imprisonment: *Criminal Justice Act* 2003, ss.154 and 282.

F. POSSESSION OR SUPPLY OF ANYTHING FOR RE-PROGRAMMING MOBILE TELEPHONES

(1) Definition

Mobile Telephones (Re-programming) Act 2002, s.2

Possession or supply of anything for re-programming purposes
2.—(1) A person commits an offence if—   **15–212**
  (a) he has in his custody or under his control anything which may be used for the purpose of changing or interfering with the operation of a unique device identifier, and
  (b) he intends to use the thing unlawfully for that purpose or to allow it to be used unlawfully for that purpose.
(2) A person commits an offence if—
  (a) he supplies anything which may be used for the purpose of changing or interfering with the operation of a unique device identifier, and
  (b) he knows or believes that the person to whom the thing is supplied intends to use it unlawfully for that purpose or to allow it to be used unlawfully for that purpose.
(3) A person commits an offence if—
  (a) he offers to supply anything which may be used for the purpose of changing or interfering with the operation of a unique device identifier, and
  (b) he knows or believes that the person to whom the thing is offered intends if it is supplied to him to use it unlawfully for that purpose or to allow it to be used unlawfully for that purpose.
(4) A unique device identifier is an electronic equipment identifier which is unique to a mobile wireless communications device.
(5) A thing is used by a person unlawfully for a purpose if in using it for that purpose he commits an offence under section 1.
(6) A person guilty of an offence under this section is liable—
  (a) on summary conviction, to imprisonment for a term not exceeding 6 months or to a fine not exceeding the statutory maximum or to both, or
  (b) on conviction on indictment, to imprisonment for a term not exceeding 5 years or to a fine or to both.

(2) Allocation

This offence is triable either way.   **15–213**

Part III

(3) Elements of the offence

15–214   The prosecution must prove that:
— The defendant had in his custody or under his control anything which may be used for the purpose of changing or interfering with the operation of a unique device identifier AND
— They intended to use the thing unlawfully for that purpose or to allow it to be used unlawfully for that purpose OR
— The defendant supplied anything which may be used for the purpose of changing or interfering with the operation of a unique device identifier AND
— They knew or believed that the person to whom the thing was supplied intended to use it unlawfully for that purpose or to allow it to be used unlawfully for that purpose OR
— The defendant offered to supply anything which may be used for the purpose of changing or interfering with the operation of a unique device identifier AND
— They knew or believed that the person to whom the thing was offered intended if it was supplied to him, to use it unlawfully for that purpose or to allow it to be used unlawfully for that purpose.

(4) Sentence

15–215   When tried summarily, the maximum penalty for this offence is imprisonment for a term not exceeding six months or a fine not exceeding the statutory maximum or both: section 125(3)(a). After commencement of the relevant provisions the maximum custodial sentence in a magistrates' court will be 12 months' imprisonment: *Criminal Justice Act* 2003, ss.154 and 282.

G. FRAUDULENT RECEIPT OF PROGRAMMES

(1) Definition

Copyright Designs and Patents Act 1988, s. 297

Offence of fraudulently receiving programmes
15–216   **297.**—(1) A person who dishonestly receives a programme included in a broadcasting service provided from a place in the United Kingdom with intent to avoid payment of any charge applicable to the reception of the programme commits an offence and is liable on summary conviction to a fine not exceeding level 5 on the standard scale.

(2) Where an offence under this section committed by a body corporate is proved to have been committed with the consent or connivance of a director, manager, secretary or other similar officer of the body, or a person purporting to act in any such capacity, he as well as the body corporate is guilty of the offence and liable to be proceeded against and punished accordingly. In relation to a body corporate whose affairs are managed by its members "director" means a member of the body corporate.

[This section is printed as amended by S.I. 2003 No. 2498, reg.32 by S.I. 2003 No. 2498 (*Copyright and Related Rights Regulations*), Sched. 2, para. 1.]

(2) Allocation

15–217   This offence is triable summarily only (section 297(1)).

(3) Elements of the offence

15–218   The prosecution must prove that:
— the defendant dishonestly,
— received a programme included in a broadcasting service provided from a place in the UK,

— with intent to avoid payment of any charge applicable to the reception of the programme.

(4) Sentence

The maximum penalty for this offence is a fine not exceeding level 5 on the standard **15–219** scale: section 297(1).

H. HARASSMENT OF DEBTORS

(1) Definition

Administration of Justice Act 1970, s.40

Punishment for unlawful harassment of debtors

40.—(1) A person commits an offence if, with the object of coercing another person to pay **15–220** money claimed from the other as a debt due under a contract, he—

(a) harasses the other with demands for payment which, in respect of their frequency or the manner or occasion of making any such demand, or of any threat or publicity by which any demand is accompanied, are calculated to subject him or members of his family or household to alarm, distress or humiliation;

(b) falsely represents, in relation to the money claimed, that criminal proceedings lie for failure to pay it;

(c) falsely represents himself to be authorised in some official capacity to claim or enforce payment; or

(d) utters a document falsely represented by him to have some official character or purporting to have some official character which he knows it has not.

(2) A person may be guilty of an offence by virtue of subsection (1)(a) above if he concerts with others in the taking of such action as is described in that paragraph, notwithstanding that his own course of conduct does not by itself amount to harassment.

(3) Subsection (1)(a) above does not apply to anything done by a person which is reasonable (and otherwise permissible in law) for the purpose—

(a) of securing the discharge of an obligation due, or believed by him to be due, to himself or to persons for whom he acts, or protecting himself or them from future loss; or

(b) of the enforcement of any liability by legal process.

(4) A person guilty of an offence under this section shall be liable on summary conviction to a fine of not more than £100, and on a second or subsequent conviction to a fine of not more than £400.

(2) Allocation

This offence is triable summarily only (section 40(4)).   **15–221**

(3) Elements of the offence

The prosecution must prove that the defendant: **15–222**

— harassed one of his debtors with demands for payment which, in respect of their frequency or the manner or occasion of making any such demand, or of any threat or publicity by which any demand is accompanied, were calculated to subject him or members of his family or household to alarm, distress or humiliation or,

— falsely represented, in relation to the money claimed, that criminal proceedings lay for failure to pay it, or

— falsely represented himself to be authorised in some official capacity to claim or enforce payment; or

— uttered a document falsely represented by him to have some official character or purporting to have some official character which he knows it has not, with

— the object of coercing the debtor to pay money claimed from as a debt due under a contract.

687

15–223　　An agreement for the supply of electricity between a tariff customer and a public electricity supplier under the *Electricity Act* 1989 is not a contract, as the rights and liabilities under this arrangement are governed by statute: *Norweb Plc v. Dixon* [1995] 3 All E.R. 952.

　　The phrase "calculated to subject" in section 40(1) means "likely to subject" and not "intending to subject": *Norweb Plc v. Dixon* (*ante*).

(4) Sentence

15–224　　The maximum penalty for the first commission of this offence is a fine of not more than £100, and on a second or subsequent conviction, a fine of not more than £400: section 40(4).

V. CRIMINAL DAMAGE AND RELATED OFFENCES

A. CRIMINAL DAMAGE

(1) Definition

Criminal Damage Act 1971, s.1

Destroying or damaging property

15–225　　**1.**—(1) A person who without lawful excuse destroys or damages any property belonging to another intending to destroy or damage any such property or being reckless as to whether any such property would be destroyed or damaged shall be guilty of an offence.

　　(2) A person who without lawful excuse destroys or damages any property, whether belonging to himself or another—

　　　　(a)　intending to destroy or damage any property or being reckless as to whether any property would be destroyed or damaged; and

　　　　(b)　intending by the destruction or damage to endanger the life of another or being reckless as to whether the life of another would be thereby endangered;
shall be guilty of an offence.

　　(3) An offence committed under this section by destroying or damaging property by fire shall be charged as arson.

(2) Allocation

15–226　　For the special procedure for criminal damage charges, see *ante*, §§ 7–58–7–63. See also *Drayton* [2005] 169 J.P 593. Where the value of the damage done is under £5,000 and the offence is not one or arson, or one endangering life, the offence is triable summarily only. Otherwise it is triable summarily or on indictment.

(3) Elements of the offence

15–227　　The prosecution must prove:
　　— damage;
　　— recklessness: see *ante*, §§ 12–24—12–27;
　　— "Without lawful excuse": section 5(2) and (3) provide a defence.

Criminal Damage Act 1971, s.5

"Without lawful excuse"

15–228　　**5.**—(1) This section applies to any offence under section 1(1) above and any offence under section 2 or 3 above other than one involving a threat by the person charged to destroy or damage property in a way which he knows is likely to endanger the life of another or involving an intent by the person charged to use or cause or permit the use of something in his custody or under his control so to destroy or damage property.

　　(2) A person charged with an offence to which this section applies, shall, whether or not

he would be treated for the purposes of this Act as having a lawful excuse apart from this subsection, be treated for those purposes as having a lawful excuse—

(a) if at the time of the act or acts alleged to constitute the offence he believed that the person or persons whom he believed to be entitled to consent to the destruction of or damage to the property in question had so consented, or would have so consented to it if he or they had known of the destruction or damage and its circumstances; or

(b) if he destroyed or damaged or threatened to destroy or damage the property in question or, in the case of a charge of an offence under section 3 above, intended to use or cause or permit the use of something to destroy or damage it, in order to protect property belonging to himself or another or a right or interest in property which was or which he believed to be vested in himself or another, and at the time of the act or acts alleged to constitute the offence he believed—

(i) that the property, right or interest was in immediate need of protection; and

(ii) that the means of protection adopted or proposed to be adopted were or would be reasonable having regard to all the circumstances.

(3) For the purposes of this section it is immaterial whether a belief is justified or not if it is honestly held.

(4) For the purposes of subsection (2) above a right or interest in property includes any right or privilege in or over land, whether created by grant, licence or otherwise. This section shall not be construed as casting doubt on any defence recognised by law as a defence to criminal charges.

The fact that a person was intoxicated at the time does not preclude reliance on this defence: *Jaggard v. Dickinson* (1981) 72 Cr.App.R. 33. **15–229**

In *Booth v. CPS* [2006] EWHC 192, QBD the appellant appealed against his conviction for criminal damage pursuant to the *Criminal Damage Act* 1971, ss.1(1) and 4. The appellant, who had been drinking and smoking drugs but was not drunk or incapable, had run into the path of a motor vehicle without looking and had collided with it, damaging the vehicle. The magistrates found that the damage was an obviously foreseeable consequence of the appellant's actions and that he "would have appreciated" the risk. The appellant argued that the magistrates had applied an objective rather than a subjective test as to recklessness and that, if the appellant had appreciated any risk at the time of the incident, it would have been a risk of personal injury and not property damage. The appellant also argued that as he had crossed the road without checking for traffic he was clearly not aware of any risk of damage to vehicles, and he had genuinely had not intended or foreseen the risk of damage. Dismissing the appeal, the Court held that the magistrates had applied the correct test for recklessness. Their use of the words "would have appreciated" was not inconsistent with their finding that the appellant was in fact aware of the risks associated with running into the road, including the risk of property damage. Applying *G.* [2003] UKHL 50, the Court held that the appellant had been aware of such risks, and then put them out of his mind. Although the risk of personal injury would have been uppermost in the appellant's mind, the magistrates were entitled to conclude that the appellant had also appreciated that there was a risk to property inherent in the overall risk of a collision.

(4) Sentence

There are no sentencing guidelines for this offence. Otherwise, the maximum **15–230** sentence for criminal damage is six months' imprisonment. When the offence is summary only because the value of the damage is below £5,000, the maximum sentence is three months' imprisonment or a fine up to level 4: *Magistrates' Courts Act* 1980, s.33. After commencement of the relevant provisions, the maximum custodial sentence in a magistrates' court will be 12 months' imprisonment: *Criminal Justice Act* 2003, ss.154 and 282.

B. THREATS TO DESTROY OR DAMAGE PROPERTY

(1) Definition

Criminal Damage Act 1971, s.2

Threats to destroy or damage property

15–231   **2.** A person who without lawful excuse makes to another a threat, intending that that other would fear it would be carried out—

(a) to destroy or damage any property belonging to that other or a third person; or

(b) to destroy or damage his own property in a way which he knows is likely to endanger the life of that other or third person;

shall be guilty of an offence.

(2) Allocation

15–232   For the special procedure for criminal damage charges, see *ante*, §§ 7–58–7–63.

(3) Elements of the offence

15–233   See *ante*, § 15–225.

(4) Sentence

15–234   There are no sentencing guidelines for this offence. When tried summarily, the maximum sentence for criminal damage is six months' imprisonment. After commencement of the relevant provisions, the maximum custodial sentence in a magistrates' court will be 12 months' imprisonment: *Criminal Justice Act* 2003, ss.154 and 282.

C. POSSESSING ANYTHING WITH INTENT TO DESTROY OR DAMAGE PROPERTY

(1) Definition

Criminal Damage Act 1971, s.3

Possessing anything with intent to destroy or damage property.

15–235   **3.** A person who has anything in his custody or under his control intending without lawful excuse to use it or cause or permit another to use it—

(a) to destroy or damage any property belonging to some other person; or

(b) to destroy or damage his own or the user's property in a way which he knows is likely to endanger the life of some other person;

shall be guilty of an offence.

(2) Allocation

15–236   For the special procedure for criminal damage charges, see *ante*, §§ 7–58–7–63.

(3) Elements of the offence

15–237   See *ante*, § 15–225.

(4) Sentence

15–238   There are no sentencing guidelines for this offence. When tried summarily, the maximum sentence for criminal damage is six months' imprisonment. After commencement of the relevant provisions, the maximum custodial sentence in a magistrates' court will be 12 months' imprisonment: *Criminal Justice Act* 2003, ss.154 and 282.

D. RACIALLY OR RELIGIOUSLY AGGRAVATED CRIMINAL DAMAGE

(1) Definition

Crime and Disorder Act 1998, s.30

Racially or religiously aggravated criminal damage

30.—(1) A person is guilty of an offence under this section if he commits an offence under **15–239** section 1(1) of the *Criminal Damage Act* 1971 (destroying or damaging property belonging to another) which is [racially or religiously aggravated] for the purposes of this section.

(2) A person guilty of an offence under this section shall be liable—

    (a) on summary conviction, to imprisonment for a term not exceeding six months or to a fine not exceeding the statutory maximum, or to both;

    (b) on conviction on indictment, to imprisonment for a term not exceeding fourteen years or to a fine, or to both.

(3) For the purposes of this section, section 28(1)(a) above shall have effect as if the person to whom the property belongs or is treated as belonging for the purposes of that Act were the victim of the offence.

(2) Allocation

For the special procedure for criminal damage charges, see *ante*, §§ 7–50–7–55.   **15–240**

(3) Elements of the offence

On criminal damage, see *ante*, § 15–225; on other racially or religiously aggravated **15–241** offences, see *ante*, § 13–24.

(4) Sentence

A person guilty of an offence under this section shall be liable on summary convic- **15–242** tion, to imprisonment for a term not exceeding six months or to a fine not exceeding the statutory maximum, or to both: s.30(2). After commencement of the relevant provisions, the maximum custodial sentence in a magistrates' court will be 12 months' imprisonment: *Criminal Justice Act* 2003, ss.154 and 282.

There are no sentencing guidelines for this offence, but see *Saunders* [2000] 1 Cr.App.R. 458 and *Morrison* [2001] 1 Cr.App.R.(S.) 5 for general guidance.

E. COMPUTER MISUSE

Unauthorised access to computer material

(1) Definition

Computer Misuse Act 1990, s.1

Unauthorised access to computer material

1.—(1) A person is guilty of an offence if—   **15–243**

    (a) he causes a computer to perform any function with intent to secure access to any program or data held in any computer;

    (b) the access he intends to secure is unauthorised; and

    (c) he knows at the time when he causes the computer to perform the function that that is the case.

(2) The intent a person has to have to commit an offence under this section need not be directed at—

    (a) any particular program or data;

    (b) a program or data of any particular kind; or

    (c) a program or data held in any particular computer.

(3) A person guilty of an offence under this section shall be liable on summary conviction to imprisonment for a term not exceeding six months or to a fine not exceeding level 5 on the standard scale or to both.

(2) Allocation

15–244   This is a summary offence.

(3) Elements of the offence

15–245   The prosecution must prove:
— unauthorised access;
— intent to access a program or data;
— knowledge of lack of authorisation.

(4) Sentence

15–246   A person guilty of an offence under this section shall be liable on summary conviction to imprisonment for a term not exceeding six months or to a fine not exceeding level 5 on the standard scale or to both. After commencement of the relevant provisions, the maximum custodial sentence in a magistrates' court will be 12 months' imprisonment: *Criminal Justice Act* 2003, ss.154 and 282.

F. UNAUTHORISED ACCESS WITH INTENT TO COMMIT OR FACILITATE COMMISSION OF FURTHER OFFENCES

(1) Definition

Computer Misuse Act 1990, s.2

Unauthorised access with intent to commit or facilitate commission of further offences
15–247   **2.**—(1) A person is guilty of an offence under this section if he commits an offence under section 1 above ("the unauthorised access offence") with intent—
(a) to commit an offence to which this section applies; or
(b) to facilitate the commission of such an offence (whether by himself or by any other person);
and the offence he intends to commit or facilitate is referred to below in this section as the further offence.
(2) This section applies to offences—
(a) for which the sentence is fixed by law; or
(b) for which a person of twenty-one years of age or over (not previously convicted) may be sentenced to imprisonment for a term of five years (or, in England and Wales, might be so sentenced but for the restrictions imposed by section 33 of the *Magistrates' Courts Act* 1980).
(3) It is immaterial for the purposes of this section whether the further offence is to be committed on the same occasion as the unauthorised access offence or on any future occasion.
(4) A person may be guilty of an offence under this section even though the facts are such that the commission of the further offence is impossible.
(5) A person guilty of an offence under this section shall be liable—
(a) on summary conviction, to imprisonment for a term not exceeding six months or to a fine not exceeding the statutory maximum or to both; and
(b) on conviction on indictment, to imprisonment for a term not exceeding five years or to a fine or to both.

(2) Allocation

15–248   This offence is triable either way.

(3) Elements of the offence

See *ante*, § 15–243. There must also be an intent to commit an offence punishable   **15–249**
with a term of five years' imprisonment.

(4) Sentence

A person guilty of an offence under this section shall be liable on summary convic-   **15–250**
tion, to imprisonment for a term not exceeding six months or to a fine not exceeding
the statutory maximum or to both: section 2(5). After commencement of the relevant
provisions, the maximum custodial sentence in a magistrates' court will be 12 months'
imprisonment: *Criminal Justice Act* 2003, ss.154 and 282.

G. Unauthorised Modification of Computer Material

(1) Definition

Computer Misuse Act 1990, s.3

Unauthorised modification of computer material
   3.—(1) A person is guilty of an offence if—   **15–251**
   (a) he does any act which causes an unauthorised modification of the contents of any
       computer; and
   (b) at the time when he does the act he has the requisite intent and the requisite
       knowledge.
   (2) For the purposes of subsection (1)(b) above the requisite intent is an intent to cause a
modification of the contents of any computer and by so doing—
   (a) to impair the operation of any computer;
   (b) to prevent or hinder access to any program or data held in any computer; or
   (c) to impair the operation of any such program or the reliability of any such data.
   (3) The intent need not be directed at—
   (a) any particular computer;
   (b) any particular program or data or a program or data of any particular kind; or
   (c) any particular modification or a modification of any particular kind.
   (4) For the purposes of subsection (1)(b) above the requisite knowledge is knowledge
that any modification he intends to cause is unauthorised.
   (5) It is immaterial for the purposes of this section whether an unauthorised modification or any intended effect of it of a kind mentioned in subsection (2) above is, or is
intended to be, permanent or merely temporary.
   (6) For the purposes of the *Criminal Damage Act* 1971 a modification of the contents of a
computer shall not be regarded as damaging any computer or computer storage medium unless
its effect on that computer or computer storage medium impairs its physical condition.
   (7) A person guilty of an offence under this section shall be liable—
   (a) on summary conviction, to imprisonment for a term not exceeding six months or
       to a fine not exceeding the statutory maximum or to both; and
   (b) on conviction on indictment, to imprisonment for a term not exceeding five years
       or to a fine or to both.

(2) Allocation

This offence is triable either way.   **15–252**

(3) Elements of the offence

   — an act which causes unauthorised modification of the contents of any computer.   **15–253**
   — an intent to cause a modification: see *ante*, section 3(2).
   In *DPP v. Lennon* [2006] EWHC 1201, QBD, the DPP appealed against the decision of a district judge sitting in a youth court that the respondent had no case to
answer to a charge of causing an unauthorised modification to the contents of a

company's computer. After being dismissed from the company, the respondent had used a program that automatically sent continuous emails to the company's server, which led to the company's server receiving over 500,000 emails. The district judge had held that section 3 was intended to deal with the sending of malicious material such as viruses and Trojan horses rather than email and that as the company's server was configured to receive emails the company had accepted the modification of its computers by the addition of data in the form of emails. Allowing the appeal, the Court stated that it was clear that the emails had resulted in the modification of the data on the company's computers so that the key question was whether the company had consented to that modification. The owner of a computer able to receive emails would ordinarily be taken to have consented to the sending of emails to his computer. However, such implied consent was not without limits, and the consent did not cover emails that had been sent not for the purpose of communication with the owner but to interrupt the proper operation and use of his system. Further, the emails could not be considered on an email-by-email basis but as a whole. It was probable that the response from the company if asked whether it would receive an email from the respondent would differ from its response if asked whether it would receive 500,000 emails from him.

(4) Sentence

15–254   A person guilty of an offence under this section shall be liable on summary conviction, to imprisonment for a term not exceeding six months or to a fine not exceeding the statutory maximum or to both: section 3(7). On commencement of the relevant provisions, the maximum custodial sentence in a magistrates' court will be 12 months' imprisonment: *Criminal Justice Act* 2003, ss.154 and 282.

PUBLIC ORDER OFFENCES

Part III

I. OFFENCES UNDER THE PUBLIC ORDER ACT 1936

A. PROHIBITION OF UNIFORMS IN CONNECTION WITH POLITICAL OBJECTS

(1) Definition

Public Order Act 1936, s.1(1)

Prohibition of uniforms in connection with political objects

16–1   **1.**—(1) Subject as hereinafter provided, any person who in any public place or at any public meeting wears uniform signifying his association with any political organisation or with the promotion of any political object shall be guilty of an offence:

Provided that, if the chief officer of police is satisfied that the wearing of any such uniform as aforesaid on any ceremonial, anniversary, or other special occasion will not be likely to involve risk of public disorder, he may, with the consent of a Secretary of State, by order permit the wearing of such uniform on that occasion either absolutely or subject to such conditions as may be specified in the order.

(2) Allocation

16–2   This offence is triable summarily. Section 1(2) provides that proceedings may not be instituted without the consent of the Attorney General.

(3) Elements of the offence

16–3   The prosecution must prove that:

— the defendant wore a uniform signifying his association with any political organisation or promotion of any political object,

— in a public place or at a public meeting and,

— the chief officer of police had not, with the consent of the Secretary of State, made an order permitting the wearing of such a uniform.

Any item worn to show mutual association can amount to a "uniform" without proof of its previous use as such. In *O'Moran v. DPP* [1975] Q.B. 864, the Court of Appeal took the view that the wearer's association with a political organisation may be proved

696

either by showing that the uniform has in the past been associated with a political organisation or by proving that the conduct of the wearer on the occasion complained of indicates activity of a political character. The prosecution does not have to specify the particular political organisation.

The terms "meeting", "public meeting" and "public place" are defined in section 9 of the 1936 Act:

Public Order Act 1936, s.9(1)

Interpretation, &c.

9.—(1) In this Act the following expressions have the meanings hereby respectively assigned to them, that is to say—   **16–4**

"Meeting" means a meeting held for the purpose of the discussion of matters of public interest or for the purpose of the expression of views on such matters;

"Public meeting" includes any meeting in a public place and any meeting which the public or any section thereof are permitted to attend, whether on payment or otherwise.

"Public place" includes any highway, or in Scotland any road within the meaning of the *Roads (Scotland) Act* 1984 and any other premises or place to which at the material time the public have or are permitted to have access, whether on payment or otherwise.

In *Marsh v. Arscott* (1982) 75 Cr.App.R. 211, DC, McCullough J. stated that "it is   **16–5** important to have regard to the words 'at the material time' in the definition of 'public place'." The Court held that a shop car park could not amount to a public place at 11.30p.m. on a Saturday night when the shop was closed. Where the public do have access to a given place at the material time, it will be classed as a public place, despite the fact that entry can be refused to certain people: in *Lawrenson v. Oxford* [1982] Crim.L.R. 185, a public house with open doors inviting the public to enter was held to be a public place. A place will still be classed as a public place even where the public are denied access to certain parts, hence in *Cawley v. Frost* (1977) 64 Cr.App.R. 20, a football ground was classed as a public place, with Lord Widgery C.J. stating that "*Prima facie* the whole establishment should be considered and the court should not be deterred … merely by finding that access to certain portions of the establishment had been denied to the public." remises such as a front garden will not be classed as a public place, as people are only entitled to enter on an individual basis as visitors: *Edwards* (1978) 67 Cr.App.R. 228.

(4) Sentence

The maximum penalty is three months or a fine not exceeding level four on the stan-   **16–6** dard scale: *Public Order Act* 1936, s.7(2). Section 280(2) and Schedule 26, paragraph 8 of the *Criminal Justice Act* 2003 increases the maximum term to 51 weeks (not yet in force). On commencement of the relevant provisions, the maximum custodial sentence able to be imposed in a magistrates' court will be a custody plus order: *Criminal Justice Act* 2003, ss.181, 280–282 (see *post*, Ch.23).

B. PROHIBITION OF QUASI-MILITARY ORGANISATIONS

(1) Definition

Public Order Act 1936, s.2

2.—(1) If the members or adherents of any association of persons, whether incorporated or   **16–7** not, are—

(a) organised or trained or equipped for the purposes of enabling them to be employed in usurping the functions of the police or of the armed forces of the Crown; or

(b) organised and trained or organised and equipped either for the purpose of enabling them to be employed for the use or display of physical force in promoting any political object, or in such manner as to arouse reasonable apprehension that they are organised and either trained or equipped for that purpose;

then any person who takes part in the control or management of the association, or in so organising or training as aforesaid any members or adherents thereof, shall be guilty of an offence under this section.

Provided that in any proceedings against a person charged with the offence of taking part in the control or management of such an association as aforesaid it shall be a defence to that charge to prove that he neither consented to nor connived at the organisation, training, or equipment of members or adherents of the association in contravention of the provisions of this section.

(2) No prosecution shall be instituted under this section without the consent of the Attorney-General.

(3) [powers of the High Court]

(4) In any criminal or civil proceedings under this section proof of things done or of words written, spoken or published (whether or not in the presence of any party to the proceedings) by any person taking part in the control or management of an association or in organising, training or equipping members or adherents of an association shall be admissible as evidence of the purposes for which, or the manner in which, members or adherents of the association (whether those persons or others) were organised, or trained, or equipped.

(5) [powers of the High Court]

(6) Nothing in this section shall be construed as prohibiting the employment of a reasonable number of persons as stewards to assist in the preservation of order at any public meeting held upon private premises, or the making of arrangements for that purpose or the instruction of the persons to be so employed in their lawful duties as such stewards, or their being furnished with badges or other distinguishing signs.

(2) Allocation

16–8   This offence is triable either way: *Public Order Act* 1936, s.7(1). Section 2(2) of the 1936 Act establishes that no prosecution shall take place without the consent of the Attorney General.

(3) Elements of the offence

16–9   The prosecution need to prove that:

— the defendant has managed or controlled an association, or has organised or taken part in the organisation or training of an association whose members are,

— organised or trained or equipped for the purposes of enabling them to be employed in usurping the functions of the police or of the armed forces of the Crown,

    OR

— organised and trained or organised and equipped either for the purpose of enabling them to be employed for the use or display of physical force in promoting any political object,

    OR

— arouse reasonable apprehension that they are organised and either trained or equipped for that purpose.

The fact that there was no evidence of actual attacks or plans for attacks on opponents will not necessarily remove the grounds for "reasonable apprehension" that the association is organised and equipped for the purpose of enabling them to be employed for use or display of physical force in promoting a political object: *Jordan and Tyndall* [1963] Crim.L.R. 124, CCA.

(4) Specific defences

16–10   A specific defence to proceedings brought under this section is established in section 2 of the 1936 Act:

Public Order Act 1936, s.2(1)

Prohibition of quasimilitary organisations

16–11   2.—(1) ... Provided that in any proceedings against a person charged with the offence of taking part in the control or management of such an association as aforesaid it shall be a defence to that charge to prove that he neither consented to nor connived at the organisation, training, or equipment of members or adherents of the association in contravention of the provisions of this section.

Public Order Act 1936, s.2(6)

Prohibition of quasimilitary organisations

2.—(6) Nothing in this section shall be construed as prohibiting the employment of a reason- **16–12** able number of persons as stewards to assist in the preservation of order at any public meeting held upon private premises, or the making of arrangements for that purpose or the instruction of the persons to be so employed in their lawful duties as such stewards, or their being furnished with badges or other distinguishing signs.

(5) Sentence

When tried summarily, the maximum penalty for this offence is six months' imprison- **16–13** ment or a fine not exceeding the prescribed sum or both: *Public Order Act* 1936, s.7(1). On commencement of the relevant provisions, the maximum custodial sentence in a magistrates' court will be 12 months' imprisonment: *Criminal Justice Act* 2003, ss.154 and 282. Custodial sentences of less than 12 months will consist of a custody plus order (see *post*, Ch.23).

II. OFFENCES UNDER THE PUBLIC ORDER ACT 1986

A. VIOLENT DISORDER

(1) Definition

Public Order Act 1986, s.2

Violent disorder

2.—(1) Where 3 or more persons who are present together use or threaten unlawful violence **16–14** and the conduct of them (taken together) is such as would cause a person of reasonable firmness present at the scene to fear for his personal safety, each of the persons using or threatening unlawful violence is guilty of violent disorder.

(2) It is immaterial whether or not the 3 or more use or threaten unlawful violence simultaneously.

(3) No person of reasonable firmness need actually be, or be likely to be, present at the scene.

(4) Violent disorder may be committed in private as well as in public places.

(5) A person guilty of violent disorder is liable on conviction on indictment to imprison- ment for a term not exceeding 5 years or a fine or both, or on summary conviction to imprisonment for a term not exceeding 6 months or a fine not exceeding the statutory maximum or both.

(2) Allocation

Violent disorder is triable either way, though the *Practice Direction (Criminal* **16–15** *Proceedings: Consolidation)*, para. V.51.11 provides that "cases of violent disorder should normally be committed for trial".

(3) Elements of the offence

The prosecution need to prove that: **16–16**
— three or more persons who were present together,
— used or threatened unlawful violence and,
— the conduct of them taken together is such as would cause a person of reason- able firmness present at the scene to fear for his personal safety.

"3 or more persons"

As to the requirement that there be three of more persons present together using or threatening unlawful violence before there can be a conviction of anyone, see *Fleming* (1989) 153 J.P. 517 and *Worton* (1989) 154 J.P. 201. See also *Mahroof* (1988) 88 Cr.App.R. 317. If one of more of the named defendants is acquitted due to a lack of *mens rea*, the remaining defendants may be found guilty, even if there are only two of them: *Public Order Act* 1986, s.6(7).

"Use or threaten"

16–17   Being part of a group of people following a man for three-quarters of a mile along a footpath in the middle of the night is capable of amounting to violent disorder: *Brodie* [2000] Crim.L.R. 775, CA. The Court held that such conduct would involve a considerable implicit menace, amounting to a threat and that a person of reasonable firmness present during and throughout such action would have been put in fear for his or her personal safety. See also *I. v. DPP; M. v. DPP; H. v. DPP* [2001] 1 Cr.App.R. 251.

"Unlawful violence"

16–18   The defences of self-defence and reasonable defence of others are preserved by the use of the phrase "unlawful violence". Actions no more than necessary to restore the peace are also permissible: *Rothwell and Barton* [1993] Crim.L.R. 626, CA.

(4) Sentence

16–19   When tried summarily the maximum penalty is six months' imprisonment, a fine not exceeding the statutory maximum or both: section 2(5). On commencement of the relevant provisions, the maximum custodial sentence in a magistrates' court will be 12 months' imprisonment: *Criminal Justice Act* 2003 ss.154 and 282. Custodial sentences of less than 12 months will consist of a custody plus order (see *post*, Ch.23).

The *Magistrates' Court Sentencing Guidelines* (2004) state:

> Aggravating factors include racial aggravation, busy public place, fighting between rival groups, large group, people actually put in fear, planned, vulnerable victims, weapon, offence committed on bail, relevant previous convictions and failure to respond to previous sentences. Mitigating factors include impulsive action, nobody afraid and provocation. **Guideline**: is custody or committal for sentence appropriate?

It is not just the precise acts of individuals which matter but also the fact that in taking part in a violent disorder defendants have been part of the whole threatening and alarming activity. In sentencing for public order offences generally the court must have regard to the whole picture. Although what an individual had himself done was relevant, it was simply part of the whole to which he was contributing: *R. v. Fox and Hicks* [2006] 1 Cr.App.R.(S.) 17.

In *Tomlinson* (1993) 157 J.P. 695, it was held that the essence of the offence of violent disorder lies in the using of violence in circumstances where so many people were present as to cause or inspire fear in the general public. The offenders' participation in a demonstration against poll tax culminated in fighting and shouting that caused fear amongst the general public. D1 was sentenced to four months' imprisonment, and D2 and D3 were sentenced to six months' imprisonment and youth custody respectively.

16–20   In *Shanoor* (1998) 162 J.P. 731, the involvement of the offender in a brawl outside a nightclub was characterised as spontaneous, with no weapon being used and no injury caused. A sentence of six months' imprisonment imposed by the Crown Court was substituted by a short Community Service Order at the Court of Appeal. In *Pickard* (2000) the defendant was sentenced to eighteen months' detention in a young offenders' institution following a guilty plea to violent disorder. His co-defendants (all younger) received non-custodial sentences, however a distinction was drawn in his case due to his age and history of violent offending. As he had engaged in a racially motivated confrontation and had previously failed to respond to community sentences, custody was inevitable, however his sentence was reduced to twelve months on appeal.

B. Affray

(1) Definition

Public Order Act 1986 s.3

Affray

3.—(1) A person is guilty of affray if he uses or threatens unlawful violence towards another **16–21** and his conduct is such as would cause a person of reasonable firmness present at the scene to fear for his personal safety.

(2) Where 2 or more persons use or threaten the unlawful violence, it is the conduct of them taken together that must be considered for the purposes of subsection (1).

(3) For the purposes of this section a threat cannot be made by the use of words alone.

(4) No person of reasonable firmness need actually be, or be likely to be, present at the scene.

(5) Affray may be committed in private as well as in public places.

(6) [*Repealed*]

(7) A person guilty of affray is liable on conviction on indictment to imprisonment for a term not exceeding 3 years or a fine or both, or on summary conviction to imprisonment for a term not exceeding 6 months or a fine not exceeding the statutory maximum or both.

[This section is printed as amended by the *Serious Organised Crime and Police Act* 2005, ss.111 and 174(2).]

(2) Allocation

Affray is triable either way. The *Practice Direction (Criminal Proceedings: Consoli-* **16–22** *dation)*, para. V.51.11 provides that cases of affray should be tried summarily unless the court consider that one or more of the following features is present in the case and that their sentencing powers are insufficient:

(a) Organised violence or use of weapons;

(b) Significant injury or substantial damage;

(c) The offence has clear racial motivation;

(d) An attack upon police officers, ambulance staff, fire-fighters and the like.

(3) Elements of the offence

The prosecution must prove that: **16–23**

— the defendant has used or threatened unlawful violence towards another, or two or more persons, their conduct being considered together, have used or threatened unlawful violence, and,

— this conduct is such as would cause a person of reasonable firmness present at the scene to fear for his personal safety.

In *Thind* [1999] Crim.L.R. 842, CA, the Court stated that "for an affray to take place there needs to be: (a) the use or threat of violence by the defendant; (b) to another person; which (c) would cause a third person to fear for his or her own safety." What amounts to a threat depends on the facts of each case. In *I. v. DPP, M. v. DPP, H. v. DPP* [2002] 1 A.C. 285, HL, it was held that whilst the mere possession of petrol bombs which were neither brandished nor waved might constitute a threat of unlawful violence for the purposes of an affray under the 1986 Act, the offence required a threat to be directed towards another person present at the scene; where only police officers were present at the scene, no such threat would be made. Making a threat in an aggressive tone of voice is not enough: *Robinson* [1993] Crim.L.R. 581, CA.

The conduct is judged by the standard of the hypothetical person of reasonable firmness, this person does not necessarily have to be at the scene of the offence: *Davison* [1992] Crim.L.R. 31, CA. It is this hypothetical reasonable bystander that has to be put in fear of his safety, not the victim himself: *Sanchez* [1996] Crim.L.R. 572, CA.

The use of the word "unlawful" means that the defences of self defence, acting in the defence of others etc are all available: see *Rothwell and Barton*, § 16–18, *ante*.

(4) Sentence

16–24   When tried summarily, the maximum penalty is six months' imprisonment, a fine not exceeding the statutory maximum or both: s.3(7). On commencement of the relevant provisions, the maximum custodial sentence in a magistrates' court will be 12 months' imprisonment: *Criminal Justice Act* 2003, ss.154 and 282. Custodial sentences of less than 12 months will consist of a custody plus order (see *post*, Ch.23).

The *Magistrates' Court Sentencing Guidelines* (2004) state:

> Aggravating factors include racial aggravation, busy public place, group action, injuries caused, people actually put in fear, vulnerable victim, offence committed on bail, relevant previous convictions and any failures to respond to previous sentences. If the offence is football related, this will be treated as an aggravating factor.
>
> Mitigating factors include offender acting alone, provocation, did not start the trouble, stopped as soon as the police arrived. **Guideline**: is custody or committal for sentence appropriate?

In sentencing in cases of affray, and public order offences generally, the court should bear in mind that although what an individual had himself done was of relevance, it was simply part of the whole to which he was contributing: *R. v. Fox and Hicks* [2006] 1 Cr.App.R.(S.) 17.

An unprovoked attack in a public place with a racial motive will warrant a deterrent sentence: *M. (Paul Simon) (A Juvenile)* [1998] 2 Cr.App.R.(S.) 398. In *Fox* [1999] 1 Cr.App.R.(S.) 332, the Court of Appeal reduced a sentence of nine months' imprisonment to four months. The offender pleaded guilty to affray, having intervened during the arrest of a friend. A custodial sentence was held to be necessary, though one of four months was appropriate.

16–25   In *Charles & Jones* (1989) 11 Cr.App.R.(S.) 125, CA, the offenders, both of previous good character had a fight in a restaurant, following offensive remarks made by a party at another table. The fight involved chairs being broken and used as weapons and some members of the other party were slightly injured. The CA considered a sentence of three months' imprisonment appropriate. In *Grzybowski and Grzybowski* (1994) 15 Cr.App.R.(S.) 139, CA, a gang of youths went to the home of another late at night armed with a piece of wood. One offender broke a window and later put his fist through the window. The householder then squirted the second offender with ammonia, who then ran away. A sentence of 12 months' detention in a young offender institution and 18 months' imprisonment for the older offender was upheld by the CA, who emphasised that "the gravamen of this type of offence was its effect on law-abiding members of the public." See also *Holmes* [1999] 2 Cr.App.R.(S.) 100 and *Oliver* [1999] 1 Cr.App.R.(S.) 394.

In *Bradley* [2005] EWCA Crim 1461; [2006] 1 Cr.App.R.(S.) 42 the CA upheld twelve months' detention in a young offender institution imposed on each of three young men and women who took part in an episode of street fighting. The appellants, a man aged 21 and two women aged 19 and 18, each pleaded guilty to affray. None had any serious previous conviction. Following an exchange of words inside a club and outside a chip shop between two groups of young people, arguments and fights developed. The appellants and others armed themselves with various weapons, including bricks and wood. Two benches were thrown at the other youths. The court reminded itself that the maximum sentence for affray was three years. It had been said in *Caird* (1970) 54 Cr.App.R. 499, that any participation, irrespective of its precise form, in an unlawful or riotous assembly derived its gravity from becoming one of those who by weight of numbers pursued a common and unlawful purpose. The CCTV record of the incident showed an episode in which a number of young people of both sexes carried on for a prolonged period sporadic fights with each other on the pavements and road. The behaviour of most of them was fuelled by alcohol. Conduct of this sort was frightening for innocent people walking home at night and a considerable inconvenience to drivers of vehicles on the road. Quelling such incidents took police time and resources. In the court's judgment, the sentences were not excessive. A recent sentencing decision in the context of football violence is *Fox* [2005] EWCA Crim 1122; [2006] 1 Cr.App.R. (S.) 17 where the CA upheld a sentence of 12 months' imprisonment imposed on one appellant, but reduced the sentence on the other to eight months' imprisonment in recognition that he was the only one of the group with no previous convictions.

C. Fear or Provocation of Violence

(1) Definition

Public Order Act 1986, s.4

Fear or provocation of violence

4.—(1) A person is guilty of an offence if he—   **16–26**

    (a) uses towards another person threatening, abusive or insulting words or behaviour, or

    (b) distributes or displays to another person any writing, sign or ostensible representation which is threatening, abusive or insulting,

    (c) with intent to cause that person to believe that immediate unlawful violence will be used against him or another by any person, or to provoke the immediate use of unlawful violence by that person or another,

    (d) or whereby that person is likely to believe that such violence will be used or it is likely that such violence will be provoked.

(2) An offence under this section may be committed in a public or a private place, except that no offence is committed where the words or behaviour are used, or the writing, sign or ostensible representation is distributed or displayed, by a person inside a dwelling and the other person is also inside that or another dwelling.

(3) [*Repealed*]

(4) A person guilty of an offence under this section is liable on summary conviction to imprisonment for a term not exceeding 6 months or a fine not exceeding level 5 on the standard scale or both.

[This section is printed as amended by the *Serious Organised Crime and Police Act* 2005, ss.111 and 174(2).]

Crime and Disorder Act, s.28

Meaning of "racially or religiously aggravated"

28.—(1) An offence is racially or religiously aggravated for the purposes of sections 29 to 32   **16–27**
below if—

    (a) at the time of committing the offence, or immediately before or after doing so, the offender demonstrates towards the victim of the offence hostility based on the victim's membership (or presumed membership) of a racial or religious group; or

    (b) the offence is motivated (wholly or partly) by hostility towards members of a racial or religious group based on their membership of that group.

(2) In subsection (1)(a) above—

    "membership", in relation to a racial or religious group, includes association with members of that group;

    "presumed" means presumed by the offender.

(3) It is immaterial for the purposes of paragraph (a) or (b) of subsection (1) above whether or not the offender's hostility is also based, to any extent, on any other factor not mentioned in that paragraph.

(4) In this section "racial group" means a group of persons defined by reference to race, colour, nationality (including citizenship) or ethnic or national origins.

[(5) In this section "religious group" means a group of persons defined by reference to religious belief or lack of religious belief.]

The language of the statute should be given a broad and non-technical meaning: *White (Anthony)* [2001] 1 W.L.R. 1352, CA.

Crime and Disorder Act 1998, s.31

Racially or religiously aggravated public order offences

16–28   **31.**—(1) A person is guilty of an offence under this section if he commits—

    (a) an offence under section 4 of the *Public Order Act* 1986 (fear or provocation of violence);

    (b) an offence under section 4A of that Act (intentional harassment, alarm or distress); or

    (c) an offence under section 5 of that Act (harassment, alarm or distress),

[hich is racially [or religiously] aggravated for the purposes of this section.

(2) A constable may arrest without warrant anyone whom he reasonably suspects to be committing an offence falling within subsection (1)(a) or (b) above.

(3) A constable may arrest a person without warrant if—

    (a) he engages in conduct which a constable reasonably suspects to constitute an offence falling within subsection (1)(c) above;

    (b) he is warned by that constable to stop; and

    (c) he engages in further such conduct immediately or shortly after the warning.

The conduct mentioned in paragraph (a) above and the further conduct need not be of the same nature.

(4) A person guilty of an offence falling within subsection (1)(a) or (b) above shall be liable—

    (a) on summary conviction, to imprisonment for a term not exceeding six months or to a fine not exceeding the statutory maximum, or to both;

    (b) on conviction on indictment, to imprisonment for a term not exceeding two years or to a fine, or to both.

(5) A person guilty of an offence falling within subsection (1)(c) above shall be liable on summary conviction to a fine not exceeding level 4 on the standard scale.

(6) If, on the trial on indictment of a person charged with an offence falling within subsection (1)(a) or (b) above, the jury find him not guilty of the offence charged, they may find him guilty of the basic offence mentioned in that provision.

(7) For the purposes of subsection (1)(c) above, section 28(1)(a) above shall have effect as if the person likely to be caused harassment, alarm or distress were the victim of the offence.

16–29   The words "or religiously" were added as from December 14, 2001, with no retrospective effect: *Anti-Terrorism, Crime and Security Act* 2001, ss.39(5), (6), 42.

(2) Allocation

16–30   The basic form of this offence is triable summarily only: section 4(4).

The racially aggravated form of the offence is triable either way: *Crime and Disorder Act* 1998, s.31(4).

(3) Elements of the offence

16–31   As regards the basic form of the offence, the prosecution must prove that:

    — the defendant used threatening, abusive or insulting words or behaviour towards another person OR

    — the defendant distributed or displayed to another person any writing, sign or other visible representation which is threatening or abusive or insulting AND

    — the defendant intended to cause that person to believe that immediate unlawful violence would be used against him or another by any other person OR

    — the defendant intended to provoke the immediate use of unlawful violence by that person or another OR

    — the person is likely to believe that unlawful violence will be used or it is likely that such violence will be provoked.

As regards the racially or religiously aggravated form of this offence, the prosecution must prove:

— The defendant committed an offence under section 4 of the *Public Order Act 1986* and

— The offence was racially or religiously aggravated; *i.e.* that at the time of committing the offence or immediately before or after doing so the offender demonstrated towards the victim hostility based on the victim's membership (or perceived membership) of a racial or religious group OR the offence was motivated, wholly or partly, by hostility towards members of a racial group based on their membership of that racial group.

"Threatening, abusive or insulting"

"Insulting" is to be given its ordinary meaning and the question whether words or **16–32** behaviour are insulting is a question of fact: *Brutus v. Cozens* (1973) A.C. 854. See *post*, § 16–41.

"Likely to"

It is the state of mind of the victim which is crucial, rather than the statistical risk of **16–33** violence occurring within a short space of time: *DPP v. Ramos* [2000] Crim.L.R. 768, DC. In *Valentine v. DPP* (1997) COD 339, DC, it was held that the defendant's threats caused a woman to fear immediate unlawful violence the next time she went to work, but only because she may have gone to work the same evening that the threat was made.

"Uses towards"

The words "used towards" in section 4(1)(a) connote present physical presence, so **16–34** that the person against whom the words were used must perceive with his own senses the threatening words and behaviour: *Atkin v. DPP* (1989) 89 Cr.App.R. 199, DC. It was not necessary for the victim to give evidence in court to prove that he did perceive the words or behaviour: *Swanston v. DPP* 161 J.P. 203, DC.

"Immediate unlawful violence"

The word "immediate" does not mean "instantaneous," but only a relatively short **16–35** time interval may elapse between the act which is threatening, abusive or insulting and the unlawful violence. "Immediate" connotes proximity in time and proximity in causation; that it is likely that violence will result within a relatively short period of time and without any other intervening occurrence: *Horseferry Road Magistrates Court, ex p. Siadatan* [1991] 1 Q.B. 280, DC.

(4) Sentence

The maximum penalty for the basic form of the offence is six months' imprisonment, **16–36** a fine not exceeding level 5 on the standard scale or both: section 4(4). On commencement of the relevant provisions, the maximum custodial sentence in a magistrates' court will be 12 months' imprisonment: *Criminal Justice Act* 2003, ss.154 and 282. Custodial sentences of less than 12 months will consist of a custody plus order (see *post*, Ch.23).

The *Magistrates' Court Sentencing Guidelines* (2004) state:

Aggravating factors include group action, people put in fear, vulnerable victims, on hospital/medical premises, victim serving the public, offence committed on bail, relevant previous convictions and any failure to respond to previous sentences.

Mitigating factors include minor matter, short duration.

Guideline: is it serious enough for a community penalty?

When tried summarily, the maximum penalty for the aggravated form of the offence **16–37** is six months' imprisonment, a fine not exceeding the statutory maximum or both: *Crime and Disorder Act* 1998, s.31(4). The *Magistrates' Court Sentencing Guidelines* also provide a higher guideline for sentencing the aggravated form of the offence, stating: is the offence so serious that only custody is appropriate?

In *Saunders* [2000] 2 Cr.App.R.(S.) 71, CA, Rose L.J. issued guidance in relation to racially aggravated assaults and racially aggravated offences more generally. He stated that those who indulge in racially aggravated violence must expect to be punished severely, in order to discourage the repetition of that behaviour by them or others. Relevant factors for the purposes of determining the increase in sentence to reflect the racially or religiously aggravated element of the offence will include the nature of the hostile demonstration, whether by language, gestures or weapons; its length, whether isolated, repeated, or persistent; its location, whether public or private; the number both of those demonstrating and those demonstrated against; and the presence or absence of other features. A discount in the overall sentence will be appropriate in accordance with general sentencing principles for, among other things, genuine remorse, a plea of guilty and previous good character.

In *Miller* [1999] 2 Cr.App.R.(S.) 392, CA the offender was sentenced to 18 months' imprisonment for racially aggravated threatening words and behaviour and to travelling on a railway without a ticket. Although M pleaded guilty, the evidence against him was overwhelming and he had a record of many previous convictions, some of them serious. The sentence was recognised as severe, yet upheld as it needed to be, to reflect public concern about conduct which damaged good racial relations within the community.

D. Intentionally Causing Harassment, Alarm or Distress

(1) Definition

Public Order Act 1986, s.4A

Intentional harassment, alarm or distress

16–38   **4A.**—(1) A person is guilty of an offence if, with intent to cause a person harassment, alarm or distress, he—

     (a) uses threatening, abusive or insulting words or behaviour, or disorderly behaviour, or

     (b) displays any writing, sign or ostensible representation which is threatening, abusive or insulting,

thereby causing that or another person harassment, alarm or distress.

(2) An offence under this section may be committed in a public or a private place, except that no offence is committed where the words or behaviour are used, or the writing, sign or ostensible representation is displayed, by a person inside a dwelling and the person who is harassed, alarmed or distressed is also inside that or another dwelling.

(3) It is a defence for the accused to prove—

     (a) that he was inside a dwelling and had no reason to believe that the words or behaviour used, or the writing, sign or ostensible representation displayed, would be heard or seen by a person outside that or any other dwelling, or

     (b) that his conduct was reasonable.

16–39   For definition of the racially or religiously aggravated form of this offence see *Crime and Disorder Act* 1998, s.31 (§ 16–28, *ante*).

(2) Allocation

16–40   The basic form of this offence is triable summarily only: section 4A(5). The racially aggravated form of the offence is triable either way: *Crime and Disorder Act* 1998, s.31(4). The *Magistrates' Court Sentencing Guidelines* recommend committal for sentence.

(3) Elements of the offence

16–41   As regards the basic form of the offence the prosecution need to prove that:

     — the defendant used threatening, abusive or insulting words or behaviour or displayed any writing, sign or ostensible representation which was threatening, abusive or insulting,

— the defendant so behaved with the intention to cause a person harassment, alarm or distress, and,

— the defendant thereby caused that or another person alarm or distress.

As regards the racially aggravated form of the offence the prosecution need to prove that:

— the defendant committed an offence under section 4A of the *Public Order Act* 1986 and

— the offence was racially or religiously aggravated; *i.e.* that at the time of committing the offence or immediately before or after doing so the offender demonstrated towards the victim hostility based on the victim's membership (or perceived membership) of a racial or religious group

OR

— the offence was motivated, wholly or partly, by hostility towards members of a racial group based on their membership of that racial group.

An intention to cause harassment alarm or distress must be established: *DPP v. Weeks, Independent,* July 17, 2000. Harassment, alarm and distress are to be treated as ordinary words of the English language, the approach of the Court in *Brutus v. Cozens* (1973) A.C. 854, being adopted in this context.

"Distress" requires some degree of emotional disturbance or upset, which, while it need not be grave, should not be trivialised: *R. (R.) v. DPP* 170 J.P. 661. See also *DPP v. Orum,* 88 Cr.App.R. 261.

(4) Specific defence

Section 4A(3) establishes that the accused will have a defence if he can prove that he **16–42** had no reason to believe that there was any person within hearing or sight who was likely to be caused harassment, alarm or distress, or that he was inside a dwelling and had no reason to believe that the words or behaviour used, or the writing, sign or ostensible representation displayed, would be heard or seen by a person outside that or any other dwelling, or that his conduct was reasonable.

For the purposes of section 4A(3) a "dwelling" does not include a police cell: *R. v. Francis, The Times,* January 17, 2007.

(5) Sentence

The maximum penalty for the basic form of the offence is six months' imprisonment, **16–43** a fine not exceeding level five on the standard scale or both: section 4A(5). On commencement of the relevant provisions, the maximum custodial sentence in a magistrates' court will be 12 months' imprisonment: *Criminal Justice Act* 2003, ss.154 and 282. Custodial sentences of less than 12 months will consist of a custody plus order (see *post,* Ch.23).

The *Magistrates' Court Sentencing Guidelines* (2004) state:

Aggravating factors include football hooliganism, group action, victims specially targeted high degree of planning, night-time offence, weapon, offence committed on bail, relevant previous convictions and any failures to respond to previous sentences.

Mitigating factors include short duration of offence.

Guideline: is it serious enough for a community penalty?

When tried summarily, the maximum penalty for the aggravated form of the offence **16–44** is six months' imprisonment, a fine not exceeding the statutory maximum or both: *Crime and Disorder Act* 1998, s.31(4).

The *Magistrates' Court Sentencing Guidelines* (2004) provide a higher guideline **16–45** for the aggravated form of the offence, the guideline being whether the offence is so serious that only a custodial sentence is appropriate.

E. Harassment, Alarm or Distress

(1) Definition

Public Order Act 1986, s.5(1), (2)

Harassment, alarm or distress

16–46   **5.**—(1) A person is guilty of an offence if he—

     (a) uses threatening, abusive or insulting words or behaviour, or disorderly behaviour, or

     (b) displays any writing, sign or ostensible representation which is threatening, abusive or insulting,

within the hearing or sight of a person likely to be caused harassment, alarm or distress thereby.

(2) An offence under this section may be committed in a public or a private place, except that no offence is committed where the words or behaviour are used, or the writing, sign or ostensible representation is displayed, by a person inside a dwelling and the other person is also inside that or another dwelling.

16–47   For definition of the racially or religiously aggravated form of this offence see the *Crime and Disorder Act* 1998, s.31 (§ 16–28, *ante*).

(2) Allocation

16–48   Both the basic and the aggravated forms of this offence are triable summarily only.

(3) Elements of the offence

16–49   As regards the basic form of this offence, the prosecution need to prove that:

     — the defendant used threatening, abusive or insulting words or behaviour, or disorderly behaviour

     — OR

     — the defendant displayed any writing sign or ostensible representation which is threatening, abusive or insulting and

     — such conduct took place within the hearing or sight of a person likely to be caused harassment, alarm or distress thereby.

As regards the racially or religiously aggravated form of the offence, the prosecution must prove that:

     — the defendant committed an offence under section 4A of the *Public Order Act* 1986 and

     — the offence was racially or religiously aggravated; *i.e.* that at the time of committing the offence or immediately before or after doing so the offender demonstrated towards the victim hostility based on the victim's membership (or perceived membership) of a racial or religious group OR the offence was motivated, wholly or partly, by hostility towards members of a racial group based on their membership of that racial group.

"Threatening, abusive or insulting"

16–50   In *Vigon v. DPP* (1998) 162 J.P. 115 it was held that that installing a partially hidden video camera in a changing area, so that customers trying on swimwear would be filmed amounted to insulting behaviour, the wording of section 5 not being limited to "rowdy behaviour".

In *Hammond v. DPP* [2004] EWHC 69; (2004) 168 J.P. 601, where an evangelical preacher held up a sign saying "Stop immortality; stop homosexuality; stop lesbianism" and was convicted under section 5, the Divisional Court held that interference with D's rights under Articles 9 and 10 of the ECHR was justified by the pressing social need to show tolerance to others. It had not been perverse for the magistrates to hold that the words used on the sign were insulting and D had no defence of reasonable conduct.

"Harassment, alarm or distress"

Whether a person is likely to be caused harassment, alarm or distress is a matter of **16–51** fact to be determined by the magistrates; it is not necessary that the victim's alarm is due to fears for his own personal safety, he could be concerned about the safety of some third party: *Lodge v. DPP*, *The Times*, October 26, 1998.

"Distress" requires some degree of emotional disturbance or upset, which, while it need not be grave, should not be trivialised: *R. (R.) v. DPP*, 170 J.P. 661. See also *DPP v. Orum*, 88 Cr.App.R. 261.

"Within sight of a person"

In *Holloway v. DPP* (2005) 169 J.P. 14, D appealed by way of case stated against a **16–52** conviction for the offence of disorderly conduct contrary to the *POA* 1986, s.5. he had used a video recorder to film a group of school children. While doing this, he stood naked in view of the camera whilst the children were in the background some distance away. The D.J. found that anyone seeing D naked would be likely to be caused harassment, alarm or distress, and that D must have been aware of the likely effect of his naked state on others in a public place. The question for the court was whether a person who had not been seen but could have been seen by anybody had committed an offence under section 5. However, the Divisional Court allowed the appeal, stating that section 5 required the insulting words or behaviour to be "within the . . . sight of a person". Those words meant that some person must have actually seen the abusive or insulting words or behaviour. It was not enough that somebody merely might have seen or could possibly have seen that behaviour. If Parliament had intended that an offence under section 5 would have been committed if the offensive behaviour could have seen by somebody, even it not actually seen, then it would have inserted a provision to that effect in section 5. In contrast, a person could be convicted of an offence of affray under section 3 if a notional person would have seen the conduct complained of, but the legislature did not adopt such wording in section 5, indicating that the parliamentary intention was that the two provisions should be construed differently. Furthermore, the view that someone would have committed an offence under section 5(1) if they could have been seen by somebody entailed a rewriting of the section and there was no reason why it should be rewritten or construed in that way.

"Display"

In *Chappell v. DPP* (1988) 89 Cr.App.R. 82, it was held that dropping letters **16–53** through a letter box was not an offence under section 5 because the writing of words which were then concealed in an envelope was not a "display" within section 5(1)(b). Where the letter was opened in the absence of the sender it could not be said that the sender "uses ... words or behaviour ... within the hearing or sight of that person" within section 5(1)(a).

Mens rea

The accused must intend his words, behaviour, representation or sign to be threaten- **16–54** ing, abusive or insulting, or be aware that they may be threatening, abusive or insulting, or he must intend his behaviour to be, or be aware that it could be disorderly: *Public Order Act* 1986, s.6(4).

(4) Specific defence

Public Order Act 1986, s.5(3)

Harassment, alarm or distress

5.—(3) It is a defence for the accused to prove— **16–55**

    (a) that he had no reason to believe that there was any person within hearing or sight who was likely to be caused harassment, alarm or distress, or

    (b) that he was inside a dwelling and had no reason to believe that the words or behaviour used, or the writing, sign or other visible representation displayed, would be heard or seen by a person outside that or any other dwelling, or

    (c) that his conduct was reasonable.

16–56 The defence of reasonable conduct is to be proved objectively: *DPP v. Clarke* (1992) 94 Cr.App.R. 359; (1991) 156 J.P. 267. In *Percy v. DPP* (2002) 166 J.P. 93 the offender had defaced an American flag, and while outside an American airbase she put the flag on the road and trod upon it. The court was asked to consider whether the offender's protest fell within her right to freedom of expression under the *Human Rights Act* 1998. It was held that whilst it had been open to the district judge to find a pressing social need to prevent the denigration of objects of veneration and cultural importance, the next issue to consider was whether the restriction on the offender's freedom of expression through the imposition of a criminal penalty was proportionate. The fact that she could have demonstrated her message by some other means other than defacing the flag was a factor to be taken into account but was only one of a number of factors. Other relevant considerations included whether the accused's behaviour had gone beyond legitimate protest, whether the behaviour had not been part of an open expression on an issue of public interest but had been disproportionate and unreasonable, the knowledge of the accused of the likely effect of his or her conduct upon those who witnessed it and whether the use of a flag had no relevance to the conveying of the message of protest and had been used as a gratuitous and calculated insult.

In *Norwood v. DPP* [2003] EWHC 1564; *The Times*, July 30, 2003 a regional organiser of the British National Party appealed against his conviction for an offence of causing alarm or distress under the *Public Order Act* 1986, s.5(1)(b). He had visibly displayed a poster on the window of his flat bearing the words "Islam out of Britain" with graphic references to the attacks on the World Trade Centre on September 11, 2001. A passer-by complained to the police and the poster was subsequently removed. The trial judge found that the poster was abusive and insulting to Islam and to the followers of that religion. It was likely to cause harassment, alarm or distress and its display was not objectively reasonable within section 5(3)(c) of the 1986 Act. The Court dismissed the appeal. The judge had been right to conclude that the aggravated offence had been made out as N had displayed the poster with the necessary intention. On the face of it the poster was "clearly racially directed and racially insulting" towards those following the Muslim faith and not simply towards the faith itself. The poster was in such a position that it could be seen by, and cause offence to, people passing by N's window. It was not necessary to show that a Muslim had actually seen or been caused offence by the poster. Once the judge had found that N had the state of mind for the offence to be proved, he could not "sensibly" have found that N had acted "reasonably" to bring him within the defence set out in section 5(3) of the 1986 Act. As N's behaviour was not objectively reasonable, his Article 10 rights had not been infringed since it was right in such circumstances that his freedom of expression be curtailed in order to protect the public interest: *Percy v. DPP* (*ante*) applied.

(5) Sentence

16–57 The maximum penalty for the basic form of the offence is a fine not exceeding level three on the standard scale: *Public Order Act* 1986, s.5(6).

The *Magistrates' Court Sentencing Guidelines* (2004) state:

Aggravating factors include group action, vulnerable victim, offence committed on bail, relevant previous convictions and any failure to respond to previous sentences.
Mitigating factors include stopping as soon as police arrived and trivial incident.
Guideline: Is discharge or fine appropriate?

16–58 The maximum penalty for the aggravated form of the offence is a fine not exceeding level four on the standard scale: *Crime and Disorder Act* 1998, s.31(5). The *Magistrates' Court Sentencing Guidelines* (2004) provide a higher guideline for the aggravated form of the offence, being whether the offence is serious enough for a community sentence.

F. Control of Processions, Assemblies and Meetings

(1) Notice and conditions relating to public processions

(a) *Definition*

Public Order Act 1986, ss.11, 12

Advance notice of public processions

11.—(1) Written notice shall be given in accordance with this section of any proposal to hold **16–59** a public procession intended—

    (a) to demonstrate support for or opposition to the views or actions of any person or body of persons,

    (b) to publicise a cause or campaign, or

    (c) to mark or commemorate an event,

unless it is not reasonably practicable to give any advance notice of the procession.

(2) Subsection (1) does not apply where the procession is one commonly or customarily held in the police area (or areas) in which it is proposed to be held or is a funeral procession organised by a funeral director acting in the normal course of his business.

(3) The notice must specify the date when it is intended to hold the procession, the time when it is intended to start it, its proposed route, and the name and address of the person (or of one of the persons) proposing to organise it.

(4) Notice must be delivered to a police station—

    (a) in the police area in which it is proposed the procession will start, or

    (b) where it is proposed the procession will start in Scotland and cross into England, in the first police area in England on the proposed route.

(5) If delivered not less than 6 clear days before the date when the procession is intended to be held, the notice may be delivered by post by the recorded delivery service; but section 7 of the *Interpretation Act* 1978 (under which a document sent by post is deemed to have been served when posted and to have been delivered in the ordinary course of post) does not apply.

(6) If not delivered in accordance with subsection (5), the notice must be delivered by hand not less than 6 clear days before the date when the procession is intended to be held or, if that is not reasonably practicable, as soon as delivery is reasonably practicable.

(7) Where a public procession is held, each of the persons organising it is guilty of an offence if—

    (a) the requirements of this section as to notice have not been satisfied, or

    (b) the date when it is held, the time when it starts, or its route, differs from the date, time or route specified in the notice.

(8) It is a defence for the accused to prove that he did not know of, and neither suspected nor had reason to suspect, the failure to satisfy the requirements or (as the case may be) the difference of date, time or route.

(9) To the extent that an alleged offence turns on a difference of date, time or route, it is a defence for the accused to prove that the difference arose from circumstances beyond his control or from something done with the agreement of a police officer or by his direction.

(10) A person guilty of an offence under subsection (7) is liable on summary conviction to a fine not exceeding level 3 on the standard scale.

Imposing conditions on public processions

12.—(1) If the senior police officer, having regard to the time or place at which and the cir- **16–60** cumstances in which any public procession is being held or is intended to be held and to its route or proposed route, reasonably believes that—

    (a) it may result in serious public disorder, serious damage to property or serious disruption to the life of the community, or

    (b) the purpose of the persons organising it is the intimidation of others with a view to compelling them not to do an act they have a right to do, or to do an act they have a right not to do,

he may give directions imposing on the persons organising or taking part in the procession such

711

conditions as appear to him necessary to prevent such disorder, damage, disruption or intimidation,including conditions as to the route of the procession or prohibiting it from entering any public place specified in the directions.

(2) In subsection (1) "the senior police officer" means—

    (a) in relation to a procession being held, or to a procession intended to be held in a case where persons are assembling with a view to taking part in it, the most senior in rank of the police officers present at the scene, and

    (b) in relation to a procession intended to be held in a case where paragraph does not apply, the chief officer of police.

(3) A direction given by a chief officer of police by virtue of subsection (2) shall be given in writing.

(4) A person who organises a public procession and knowingly fails to comply with a condition imposed under this section is guilty of an offence, but it is a defence for him to prove that the failure arose from circumstances beyond his control.

(5) A person who takes part in a public procession and knowingly fails to comply with a condition imposed under this section is guilty of an offence, but it is a defence for him to prove that the failure arose from circumstances beyond his control.

(6) A person who incites another to commit an offence under subsection (5) is guilty of an offence.

(7) A constable in uniform may arrest without warrant anyone he reasonably suspects is committing an offence under subsection (4), (5) or (6).

(8) A person guilty of an offence under subsection (4) is liable on summary conviction to imprisonment for a term not exceeding 3 months or a fine not exceeding level 4 on the standard scale or both.

(9) A person guilty of an offence under subsection (5) is liable on summary conviction to a fine not exceeding level 3 on the standard scale.

(10) A person guilty of an offence under subsection (6) is liable on summary conviction to imprisonment for a term not exceeding 3 months or a fine not exceeding level 4 on the standard scale or both, notwithstanding section 45(3) of the *Magistrates' Courts Act* 1980 (inciter liable to same penalty as incited).

(11) In Scotland this section applies only in relation to a procession being held, and to a procession intended to be held in a case where persons are assembling with a view to taking part in it.

(b) *Allocation*

16–61   Both of these offences are triable summarily only.

(c) *Elements of the offence*

16–62   Regarding the offence of failing to give notice of a public procession, the prosecution must prove that:

    — the organiser of a public procession (it not being one to which section 11(2) of the 1986 Act applies) failed to give notice to a police station in the area in which the procession started

        OR

    — notice having been given to the relevant police station, the date when the procession was held, the time when it started, or its route, differed from the date, time or route specified in the notice.

Regarding the offence of failing to comply with conditions imposed on public processions, the prosecution must prove that:

    — an organiser of a public procession knowingly failed to comply with conditions imposed under section 12 of the *Public Order Act* 1986

        OR

    — a participant in a public procession knowingly failed to comply with conditions imposed under section 12 of the *Public Order Act* 1986

        OR

    — a person incited another to commit an offence under section 12(5) of the *Public Order Act* 1986.

(d) *Specific defence*

A defendant will have a defence to a charge under section 11 if he can prove that he **16–63** did not know of, and neither suspected nor had reason to suspect, the failure to satisfy the requirements or (as the case may be) the difference of date, time or route: *Public Order Act* 1986, s.11(8). Monthly campaigning cycle rides through central London could not be considered commonly and customarily held processions for the purposes of section 11(2) of the 1986 Act, because although they occurred at the same time each month and always began from the same starting point, they followed no fixed route: *R. (Kay) v. Commissioner of Police of the Metropolis, The Times*, June 13, 2007, CA.

A defendant will have a defence to a charge under section 12 if he can prove that the failure to comply with a condition imposed was due to circumstances beyond the defendant's control: *Public Order Act* 1986, s.12(5)

(e) *Sentence*

The maximum penalty for both these offences is a fine not exceeding level three on **16–64** the standard scale. Section 280(2) and Schedule 26, paragraph 37 of the *Criminal Justice Act* 2003 increases the maximum term in both section 12(8) and section 12(10) from three months to 51 weeks (not yet in force). On commencement of the relevant provisions, the maximum custodial sentence able to be imposed in a magistrates' court will be a custody plus order: *Criminal Justice Act* 2003, ss.181, 280–282 (see *post*, Ch.23).

(2) Contravention of prohibition on a public procession

(a) *Definition*

Public Order Act 1986, s.13

Prohibiting public processions

13.—(1) If at any time the chief officer of police reasonably believes that, because of particular **16–65** circumstances existing in any district or part of a district, the powers under section 12 will not be sufficient to prevent the holding of public processions in that district or part from resulting in serious public disorder, he shall apply to the council of the district for an order prohibiting for such period not exceeding 3 months as may be specified in the application the holding of all public processions (or of any class of public procession so specified) in the district or part concerned.

(2) On receiving such an application, a council may with the consent of the Secretary of State make an order either in the terms of the application or with such modifications as may be approved by the Secretary of State.

(3) Subsection (1) does not apply in the City of London or the metropolitan police district.

(4) If at any time the Commissioner of Police for the City of London or the Commissioner of Police of the Metropolis reasonably believes that, because of particular circumstances existing in his police area or part of it, the powers under section 12will not be sufficient to prevent the holding of public processions in that area or part from resulting in serious public disorder, he may with the consent of the Secretary of State make an order prohibiting for such period not exceeding 3 months as may be specified in the order the holding of all public processions (or of any class of public procession so specified) in the area or part concerned.

(5) An order made under this section may be revoked varied by a subsequent order made in the same way, that is, in accordance with subsections (1) and (2) or subsection (4), as the case may be.

(6) Any order under this section shall, if not made in writing, be recorded in writing as soon as practicable after being made.

(7) A person who organises a public procession the holding of which he knows is prohibited by virtue of an order under this section is guilty of an offence.

(8) A person who takes part in a public procession the holding of which he knows is prohibited by virtue of an order under this section is guilty of an offence.

(9) A person who incites another to commit an offence under subsection (8) is guilty of an offence.

(10) A constable in uniform may arrest without warrant anyone he reasonably suspects is committing an offence under subsection (7), (8) or (9).

(11) A person guilty of an offence under subsection (7) is liable on summary conviction to imprisonment for a term not exceeding 3 months or a fine not exceeding level 4 on the standard scale or both.

(12) A person guilty of an offence under subsection (8) is liable on summary conviction to a fine not exceeding level 3 on the standard scale.

(13) A person guilty of an offence under subsection (9) is liable on summary conviction to imprisonment for a term not exceeding 3 months or a fine not exceeding level 4 on the standard scale or both, notwithstanding section 45(3) of the *Magistrates' Courts Act* 1980.

(b) *Allocation*

16–66   An offence under this section is triable summarily only.

(c) *Elements of the offence*

16–67   The prosecution must prove that:
— a person organised a public procession the holding of which he knows to be prohibited under section 13 of the *Public Order Act* 1986,
    OR
— a person incited another to commit an offence under section 13(8) of the *Public Order Act* 1986.

(d) *Sentence*

16–68   The maximum penalty for the offence of organising, or inciting the commission of an offence by another is imprisonment for a term not exceeding three months, or a fine not exceeding level four on the standard scale or both. The maximum penalty for the offence of participating in the prohibited procession is a fine not exceeding level three on the standard scale. Section 280(2) and Schedule 26, paragraph 37 of the *Criminal Justice Act* 2003 increases the maximum term in both section 12(8) and section 12(10) from three months to 51 weeks (not yet in force). After commencement of the relevant provisions, the maximum custodial sentence able to be imposed in a magistrates' court will be a custody plus order: *Criminal Justice Act* 2003, ss.181, 280–282 (see *post*, Ch.23).

(3) Contravening prohibition on trespassory assemblies

(a) *Definition*

Public Order Act 1986, ss.14, 14A–14C

Imposing conditions on public assemblies

16–69   **14.**—(1) If the senior police officer, having regard to the time or place at which and the circumstances in which any public assembly is being held or is intended to be held, reasonably believes that—

    (a) it may result in serious public disorder, serious damage to property or serious disruption to the life of the community, or

    (b) the purpose of the persons organising it is the intimidation of others with a view to compelling them not to do an act they have a right to do, or to do an act they have a right not to do,

he may give directions imposing on the persons organising or taking part in the assembly such conditions as to the place at which the assembly may be (or continue to be) held, its maximum duration, or the maximum number of persons who may constitute it, as appear to him necessary to prevent such disorder, damage, disruption or intimidation.

(2) In subsection (1) "the senior police officer" means —

    (a) in relation to an assembly being held, the most senior in rank of the police offic-
ers present at the scene, and

    (b) in relation to an assembly intended to be held, the chief officer of police.

(3) A direction given by a chief officer of police by virtue of subsection (2)(b) shall be given in writing.

(4) A person who organises a public assembly and knowingly fails to comply with a condition imposed under this section is guilty of an offence, but it is a defence for him to prove that the failure arose from circumstances beyond his control.

(5) A person who takes part in a public assembly and knowingly fails to comply with a condition imposed under this section is guilty of an offence, but it is a defence for him to prove that the failure arose from circumstances beyond his control.

(6) A person who incites another to commit an offence under subsection (5) is guilty of an offence.

[...]

(8) A person guilty of an offence under subsection (4) is liable on summary conviction to imprisonment for a term not exceeding 3 months or a fine not exceeding level 4 on the standard scale or both.

(9) A person guilty of an offence under subsection (5) is liable on summary conviction to a fine not exceeding level 3 on the standard scale.

(10) A person guilty of an offence under subsection (6) is liable on summary conviction to imprisonment for a term not exceeding 3 months or a fine not exceeding level 4 on the standard scale or both, notwithstanding section 45(3) of the *Magistrates' Courts Act* 1980.

[This is printed as amended by the *Serious Organised Crime and Police Act* 2005, Sched. 17(2), para. 1.]

Prohibiting trespassory assemblies

    14A.—(1) If at any time the chief officer of police reasonably believes that an assembly is **16–70** intended to be held in any district at a place on land to which the public has no right of access or only a limited right of access and that the assembly—

    (a) is likely to be held without the permission of the occupier of the land or to conduct itself in such a way as to exceed the limits of any permission of his or the limits of the public's right of access, and

    (b) may result—

        (i) in serious disruption to the life of the community, or

        (ii) where the land, or a building or monument on it, is of historical, architectural, archaeological or scientific importance, in significant damage to the land, building or monument,

he may apply to the council of the district for an order prohibiting for a specified, period the holding of all trespassory assemblies in the district or a part of it, as specified.

(2) On receiving such an application, a council may—

    (a) in England and Wales, with the consent of the Secretary of State make an order either in the terms of the application or with such modifications as may be approved by the Secretary of State; or

    (b) in Scotland, make an order in the terms of the application.

(3) Subsection (1) does not apply in the City of London or the metropolitan police district.

(4) If at any time the Commissioner of Police for the City of London or the Commissioner of Police of the Metropolis reasonably believes that an assembly is intended to be held at a place on land to which the public has no right of access or only a limited right of access in his police area and that the assembly—

    (a) is likely to be held without the permission of the occupier of the land or to conduct itself in such a way as to exceed the limits of any permission of his or the limits of the public's right of access, and

    (b) may result—

        (i) in serious disruption to the life of the community, or

        (ii) where the land, or a building or monument on it, is of historical, architectural, archaeological or scientific importance, in significant damage to the land, building or monument,

715

he may with the consent of the Secretary of State make an order prohibiting for a specified period the holding of all trespassory assemblies in the area or a part of it, as specified.

(5) An order prohibiting the holding of trespassory assemblies operates to prohibit any assembly which—

    (a) is held on land to which the public has no right of access or only a limited right of access, and

    (b) takes place in the prohibited circumstances, that is to say, without the permission of the occupier of the land or so as to exceed the limits of any permission of his or the limits of the public's right of access.

(6) No order under this section shall prohibit the holding of assemblies for a period exceeding 4 days or in an area exceeding an area represented by a circle with a radius of 5 miles from a specified centre.

(7) An order made under this section may be revoked varied by a subsequent order made in the same way, that is, in accordance with subsection (1) and (2) or subsection (4), as the case may be.

(8) Any order under this section shall, if not made in writing, be recorded in writing as soon as practicable after being made.

(9) In this section and sections 14B and 14C—

    "assembly" means an assembly of 20 or more persons;

    "land" means land in the open air;

    "limited", in relation to a right of access by the public to land, means that their use of it is restricted to use for a particular purpose (as in the case of a highway or road) or is subject to other restrictions;

    "occupier" means—

        (a) in England and Wales, the person entitled to possession of the land by virtue of an estate or interest held by him; or

        (b) in Scotland, the person lawfully entitled to natural possession of the land, and in subsections (1) and (4) includes the person reasonably believed by the authority applying for or making the order to be the occupier;

    "public" includes a section of the public; and

    "specified" means specified in an order under this section.

[(9A) In relation to Scotland, the references in this section to the public's rights (or limited right) of access do not include any right which the public or any member of the public may have by way of access rights within the meaning of the *Land Reform (Scotland) Act* 2003 (asp 2).]

(10) In relation to Scotland, the references in subsection (1) above to a district and to the council of the district shall be construed—

    (a) as respects applications before 1st April 1996, as references to the area of a regional or islands authority and to the authority in question; and

    (b) as respects applications on and after that date, as references to a local government area and to the council for that area.

(11) In relation to Wales, the references in subsection (1) above to a district and to the council of the district shall be construed, as respects applications on and after 1st April 1996, as references to a county or county borough and to the council for that county or county borough.

Offences in connection with trespassory assemblies and arrest therefor

16–71   **14B.**—(1) A person who organises an assembly the holding of which he knows is prohibited by an order under section 14A is guilty of an offence.

(2) A person who takes part in an assembly which he knows is prohibited by an order under section 14A is guilty of an offence.

(3) In England and Wales, a person who incites another to commit an offence under subsection (2) is guilty of an offence.

(5) A person guilty of an offence under subsection (1) is liable on summary conviction to imprisonment for a term not exceeding 3 months or a fine not exceeding level 4 on the standard scale or both.

(6) A person guilty of an offence under subsection (2) is liable on summary conviction to a fine not exceeding level 3 on the standard scale.

(7) A person guilty of an offence under subsection (3) is liable on summary conviction to imprisonment for a term not exceeding 3 months or a fine not exceeding level 4 on the standard scale or both, notwithstanding section 45(3) of the *Magistrates' Courts Act* 1980.

(8) Subsection (3) above is without prejudice to the application of any principle of Scots Law as respects art and part guilt to such incitement as is mentioned in that subsection.

Stopping persons from proceeding to trespassory assemblies

14C.—(1) If a constable in uniform reasonably believes that a person is on his way to an as- **16–72** sembly within the area to which an order under section 14A applies which the constable reasonably believes is likely to be an assembly which is prohibited by that order, he may, subject to subsection (2) below—

(a) stop that person, and

(b) direct him not to proceed in the direction of the assembly.

(2) The power conferred by subsection (1) may only be exercised within the area to which the order applies.

(3) A person who fails to comply with a direction under subsection (1) which he knows has been given to him is guilty of an offence.

(5) A person guilty of an offence under subsection (3) is liable on summary conviction to a fine not exceeding level 3 on the standard scale.

[These sections are printed as amended by the *Serious Organised Crime and Police Act* 2005, Sched. 17(2), para. 1.]

(b) *Allocation*

The offences under this section are triable summarily only.   **16–73**

(c) *Elements of the offence*

The prosecution must prove that: **16–74**

— a person organised an assembly which he knew was prohibited by an order made under section 14A of the *Public Order Act* 1986,

OR

— a person participated in an assembly which he knew to be prohibited under section 14A of the *Public Order Act* 1986,

OR

— a person incited another to commit an offence under section 14B(2) of the *Public Order Act* 1986.

(d) *Defences*

In *Jones v. DPP* (1999) 2 A.C. 240, the HL (allowing the appeal by a majority) held **16–75** that there was a public right of peaceful assembly on a public highway and provided those activities are reasonable, they should not constitute a trespass, it being a question of fact and degree for the court of trial to in each case to decide whether the user was reasonable, this right being subject to the requirement that the activity in question does not amount to a public or private nuisance and does not obstruct the highway by unreasonably impeding the primary right of the general public to pass and repass. Although the matter was essentially one to be judged in the light of the particular case, a peaceful assembly which did not obstruct the highway did not necessarily constitute a trespassory assembly so as to constitute the circumstances for an offence within section 14B(2) of the 1986 Act, where an order under section 14A was in force, *per* Lord Hutton.

(e) *Sentence*

The maximum penalty for the offence of organising a trespassory assembly, or incit- **16–76** ing another to commit an offence under section 14B is imprisonment for a term not exceeding three months or a fine not exceeding level 4 on the standard scale or both.

The maximum penalty for the offence of participating in a trespassory assembly is a fine not exceeding level three on the standard scale. Section 280(2) and Schedule 26, paragraph 37 of the *Criminal Justice Act* 2003 increases the maximum term in sections 14(8), 14(10), 14B(5) and 14B(7) from three months to 51 weeks (not yet in force). After commencement of the relevant provisions, the maximum custodial sentence able to be imposed in a magistrates' court will be a custody plus order: *Criminal Justice Act* 2003, ss.181, 280–282 (see *post*, Ch.23).

(4) Interpretation

Public Order Act 1986, s.16

Interpretation.

16–77   **16.** In this Part—

"the City of London" means the City as defined for the purposes of the Acts relating to the City of London police;

"the metropolitan police district" means that district as defined in section 76 of the *London Government Act* 1963;

"public assembly" means an assembly of 2 or more persons in a public place which is wholly or partly open to the air;

"public place" means —

> (a) any highway, or in Scotland any road within the meaning of the *Roads (Scotland) Act* 1984, and
>
> (b) any place to which at the material time the public or any section of the public has access, on payment or otherwise, as of right or by virtue of express or implied permission;

"public procession" means a procession in a public place.

G. Acts Intended or Likely to stir up Racial Hatred

(1) Definition

Public Order Act 1986, s.18

Use of words or behaviour or display of written material

16–78   **18.**—(1) A person who uses threatening, abusive or insulting words or behaviour, or displays any written material which is threatening, abusive or insulting, is guilty of an offence if—

> (a) he intends thereby to stir up racial hatred, or
>
> (b) having regard to all the circumstances racial hatred is likely to be stirred up thereby.

(2) An offence under this section may be committed in a public or a private place, except that no offence is committed where the words or behaviour are used, or the written material is displayed, by a person inside a dwelling and are not heard or seen except by other persons in that or another dwelling.

(3) [*Repealed*]

(4) In proceedings for an offence under this section it is a defence for the accused to prove that he was inside a dwelling and had no reason to believe that the words or behaviour used, or the written material displayed, would be heard or seen by a person outside that or any other dwelling.

(5) A person who is not shown to have intended to stir up racial hatred is not guilty of an offence under this section if he did not intend his words or behaviour, or the written material, to be, and was not aware that it might be, threatening, abusive or insulting.

(6) This section does not apply to words or behaviour used, or written material displayed, solely for the purpose of being included in a programme included in a programme service.

[This section is printed as amended by the *Broadcasting Act* 1990, s.164(1), (2) and the *Serious Organised Crime and Police Act* 2005 ss.111 and 174(2).]

(2) Allocation

This offence is triable either way. No proceedings may be instituted without the **16–79** consent of the Attorney General: *Public Order Act* 1986, s.27(3).

(3) Elements of the offence

The prosecution must prove that: **16–80**
— the defendant used threatening, abusive or insulting words or behaviour, or displayed any written material which is threatening, abusive or insulting
  AND
— he intended to stir up racial hatred by so doing
  OR
— having regard to all the circumstances, racial hatred was likely to be stirred up by his actions.

Public Order Act 1986, ss.17, 26, 29

Meaning of "racial hatred"
17. In this Part "racial hatred" means hatred against a group of persons defined by reference **16–81** to colour, race, nationality (including citizenship) or ethnic or national origins.

Savings for reports of parliamentary or judicial proceedings
26.—(1) Nothing in this Part applies to a fair and accurate report of proceedings in Parlia- **16–82** ment or in the Scottish Parliament.
(2) Nothing in this Part applies to a fair and accurate report of proceedings publicly heard before a court or tribunal exercising judicial authority where the report is published contemporaneously with the proceedings or, if it is not reasonably practicable or would be unlawful to publish a report of them contemporaneously, as soon as publication is reason- ably practicable and lawful.

Interpretation
29. In this Part—   **16–83**
  "distribute", and related expressions, shall be construed in accordance with section 19(3) (written material) and section 21(2) (recordings);
  "dwelling" means any structure or part of a structure occupied as a person's home or other living accommodation (whether the occupation is separate or shared with others) but does not include any part not so occupied, and for this purpose "structure" includes a tent, caravan, vehicle, vessel or other temporary or movable structure;
  "programme" means any item which is included in a programme service
  "programme service" has the same meaning as in the *Broadcasting Act* 1990;
  "publish", and related expressions, in relation to written material, shall be construed in ac- cordance with section 19(3)
  "racial hatred" has the meaning given by section 17
  "recording" has the meaning given by section 21(2) and "play" and "show", and related expressions, in relation to a recording, shall be construed in accordance with that pro- vision;
  "written material" includes any sign or ostensible representation.

For the meaning of "threatening, abusive or insulting" see the materials on section 4A of the *Public Order Act* 1986 (§ 16–38, *ante*).

(4) Defences

Section 19(2) establishes a defence for a defendant who did not intend to stir up **16–84** racial hatred if he can prove that he was not aware of the content of the material and did not suspect, and had no reason to suspect that it was threatening, abusive or insulting. The burden of proof of establishing this defence lies on the accused.

The defence in section 26 of the *Public Order Act* 1986 relating to exceptions for reports of Parliamentary and judicial proceedings applies to section 19.

(5) Sentence

16–85   When tried summarily, the maximum penalty is six months' imprisonment, a fine not exceeding the statutory maximum or both. The court also has power under section 25 of the 1986 Act to order forfeiture when the offence consists of displaying written material. On commencement of the relevant provisions, the maximum custodial sentence in a magistrates' court will be 12 months' imprisonment: *Criminal Justice Act* 2003, ss.154 and 282. Custodial sentences of less than 12 months will consist of a custody plus order (see *post*, Ch.23).

Possession of threatening, abusive or insulting material with a view to publication led to a 12-month custodial sentence in *Gray* [1999] 1 Cr.App.R.(S.) 50, Judge Peter Crawford Q.C. emphasising the grave social damage done by offences and remarks of a racist nature.

H. PUBLISHING OR DISTRIBUTING WRITTEN MATERIAL STIRRING UP RACIAL HATRED

(1) Definition

Public Order Act 1986, s.19

Publishing or distributing written material

16–86   **19.**—(1) A person who publishes or distributes written material which is threatening, abusive or insulting is guilty of an offence if—

    (a) he intends thereby to stir up racial hatred, or

    (b) having regard to all the circumstances racial hatred is likely to be stirred up thereby.

(2) In proceedings for an offence under this section it is a defence for an accused who is not shown to have intended to stir up racial hatred to prove that he was not aware of the content of the material and did not suspect, and had no reason to suspect, that it was threatening, abusive or insulting.

(3) References in this Part to the publication or distribution of written material are to its publication or distribution to the public or a section of the public.

(2) Allocation

16–87   This offence is triable either way. No proceedings may be instituted without the consent of the Attorney General: *Public Order Act* 1986, s.27(3).

(3) Elements of the offence

16–88   The prosecution must prove that:

    — the defendant published or distributed written material which is threatening, abusive or insulting, and,

    — he intended to stir up racial hatred

       OR

    — having regard to all the circumstances, racial hatred was likely to be stirred up by such publication or distribution.

For the meaning of "Racial Hatred" see section 17 of the 1986 Act, *ante*. For the meaning of "threatening, abusive or insulting", see § 16–32 and *Brutus v. Cozens* (1973) A.C. 854, *ante*. For the meaning of "written material" see section 29 of the 1986 Act, *ante*.

(4) Defences

16–89   The defence established by section 26 of the 1986 Act applies to proceedings instituted under this section.

(5) Sentence

16–90   When tried summarily, the maximum penalty is six months' imprisonment, a fine not exceeding the statutory maximum, or both. On commencement of the relevant provisions, the maximum custodial sentence in a magistrates' court will be 12 months' imprisonment: *Criminal Justice Act* 2003, ss.154 and 282. Custodial sentences of less than 12 months will consist of a custody plus order (see *post*, Ch.23).

I. Public Performance, Distribution, Broadcasting and Possession of Materials Stirring up Racial Hatred

(1) Public performance of a play stirring up racial hatred

(a) *Definition*

Public Order Act 1986, s.20(1), (5), (6)

Public performance of play

20.—(1) If a public performance of a play is given which involves the use of threatening, abusive or insulting words or behaviour, any person who presents or directs the performance is guilty of an offence if—   **16–91**
  (a) he intends thereby to stir up racial hatred, or
  (b) having regard to all the circumstances (and, in particular, taking the performance as a whole) racial hatred is likely to be stirred up thereby.

  (5) In this section "play" and "public performance" have the same meaning as in the *Theatres Act* 1968.

  (6) The following provisions of the *Theatres Act* 1968 apply in relation to an offence under this section as they apply to an offence under section 2 of that Act—

section 9 (script as evidence of what was performed),
section 10(power to make copies of script),
section 15 (powers of entry and inspection).

(b) *Allocation*

This offence is triable either way. Proceedings may not be instituted without the   **16–92** consent of the Attorney General: *Public Order Act* 1986, s.27.

(c) *Elements of the offence*

The prosecution must prove that: **16–93**
  — the defendant was the director or presenter of a play involving the use of threatening, abusive or insulting words or behaviour and,
  — the play was performed for the public and,
  — the defendant intended thereby to stir up racial hatred
    OR
  — having regard to all the circumstances, racial hatred was likely to be stirred up by the performance of the play.

For the meaning of racial hatred, see section 17 of the 1986 Act, *ante*.

The words "play" and "public performance" have the same meaning as in the *Theatres Act* 1968.

(d) *Sentence*

When tried summarily, the maximum penalty is six months' imprisonment, a fine   **16–94** not exceeding the statutory maximum, or both. On commencement of the relevant provisions, the maximum custodial sentence in a magistrates' court will be 12 months' imprisonment: *Criminal Justice Act* 2003, ss.154 and 282. Custodial sentences of less than 12 months will consist of a custody plus order (see *post*, Ch.23).

Theatres Act 1968, s.18(1)

Interpretation
  18.—(1) In this Act—   **16–95**

"play" means—

    (a) any dramatic piece, whether involving improvisation or not, which is given wholly or in part by one or more persons actually present and performing and in which the whole or a major proportion of what is done by the person or persons performing, whether by way of speech, singing or action, involves the playing of a role; and

    (b) any ballet given wholly or in part by one or more persons actually present and performing, whether or not it falls within paragraph (a) of this definition;

"public performance" includes any performance in a public place within the meaning of the *Public Order Act* 1936 and any performance which the public or any section thereof are permitted to attend, whether on payment or otherwise;

(e) *Defences*

Public Order Act 1986, s.20(2)–(4)

Public performance of play

16–96   **20.**—(2) If a person presenting or directing the performance is not shown to have intended to stir up racial hatred, it is a defence for him to prove—

    (a) that he did not know and had no reason to suspect that the performance would involve the use of the offending words or behaviour, or

    (b) that he did not know and had no reason to suspect that the offending words or behaviour were threatening, abusive or insulting, or

    (c) that he did not know and had no reason to suspect that the circumstances in which the performance would be given would be such that racial hatred would be likely to be stirred up.

(3) This section does not apply to a performance given solely or primarily for one or more of the following purposes—

    (a) rehearsal,

    (b) making a recording of the performance, or

    (c) enabling the performance to be included in a programme service;

but if it is proved that the performance was attended by persons other than those directly connected with the giving of the performance or the doing in relation to it of the things mentioned in paragraph (b) or (c), the performance shall, unless the contrary is shown, be taken not to have been given solely or primarily for the purposes mentioned above.

(4) For the purposes of this section—

    (a) a person shall not be treated as presenting a performance of a play by reason only of his taking part in it as a performer,

    (b) a person taking part as a performer in a performance directed by another shall be treated as a person who directed the performance if without reasonable excuse he performs otherwise than in accordance with that person's direction, and

    (c) a person shall be taken to have directed a performance of a play given under his direction notwithstanding that he was not present during the performance;

and a person shall not be treated as aiding or abetting the commission of an offence under this section by reason only of his taking part in a performance as a performer.

(f) *Sentence*

16–97   When tried summarily, the maximum penalty for an offence under this section is six months' imprisonment, a fine not exceeding the statutory maximum or both: *POA* 1986, s.27(3). On commencement of the relevant provisions, the maximum custodial sentence in a magistrates' court will be 12 months' imprisonment: *Criminal Justice Act* 2003, ss.154 and 282. Custodial sentences of less than 12 months will consist of a custody plus order (see *post*, Ch.23).

(2) Distributing, showing or playing a recording stirring up racial hatred

(a) *Definition*

Public Order Act 1986, s.21

Distributing, showing or playing a recording

21.—(1) A person who distributes, or shows or plays, a recording of visual images or sounds **16–98** which are threatening, abusive or insulting is guilty of an offence if—

(a) he intends thereby to stir up racial hatred, or

(b) having regard to all the circumstances racial hatred is likely to be stirred up thereby.

(2) In this Part "recording" means any record from which visual images or sounds may, by any means, be reproduced; and references to the distribution, showing or playing of a recording are to its distribution, showing or playing to the public or a section of the public.

(3) In proceedings for an offence under this section it is a defence for an accused who is not shown to have intended to stir up racial hatred to prove that he was not aware of the content of the recording and did not suspect, and had no reason to suspect, that it was threatening, abusive or insulting.

(4) This section does not apply to the showing or playing of a recording solely for the purpose of enabling the recording to be included in a programme service.

(b) *Allocation*

This offence is triable either way. Proceedings may not be instituted without the **16–99** consent of the Attorney General: *POA* 1986, s.27(1).

(c) *Elements of the offence*

The prosecution must prove that: **16–100**

— the defendant distributed, showed or played a recording or visual images or sounds and,

— these visual images or sounds were threatening, abusive or insulting and,

— he so acted with the intention to stir up racial hatred

OR

— having regard to all the circumstances, racial hatred was likely to be stirred up by such actions.

For the meaning of "racial hatred" see section 18 of the 1986 Act, *ante*. For the meaning of "threatening, abusive or insulting", see *Brutus v. Cozens, ante*.

(d) *Defence*

A person who is not shown to have intended to stir up racial hatred will have a **16–101** defence if he can prove that he was not aware of the contents of the recording and he did not suspect, or have any reason to suspect that the recording was threatening, abusive or insulting: *POA* 1986, s.21(2).

The defence applying to fair and accurate reports of parliamentary or judicial proceedings is also available: *POA* 1986, s.26.

(e) *Sentence*

When tried summarily, the maximum penalty for this offence is six months' imprison- **16–102** ment, a fine not exceeding the statutory maximum, or both: *POA* 1986, s.27(3). On commencement of the relevant provisions, the maximum custodial sentence in a magistrates' court will be 12 months' imprisonment: *Criminal Justice Act* 2003, ss.154 and 282. Custodial sentences of less than 12 months will consist of a custody plus order (see *post*, Ch.23).

(3) Broadcasting a programme stirring up racial hatred

(a) *Definition*

Public Order Act 1986, s.22

Broadcasting or including programme in cable programme service

16–103   **22.**—(1) If a programme involving threatening, abusive or insulting visual images or sounds is included in a programme service, each of the persons mentioned in subsection (2) is guilty of an offence if—

    (a) he intends thereby to stir up racial hatred, or

    (b) having regard to all the circumstances racial hatred is likely to be stirred up thereby.

    (2) The persons are—

    (a) the person providing the programme service,

    (b) any person by whom the programme is produced or directed, and

    (c) any person by whom offending words or behaviour are used.

    (3) If the person providing the service, or a person by whom the programme was produced or directed, is not shown to have intended to stir up racial hatred, it is a defence for him to prove that—

    (a) he did not know and had not reason to suspect that the programme would involve the offending material, and

    (b) having regard to the circumstances in which the programme was included in a programme service, it was not reasonably practicable for him to secure the removal of the material.

    (4) It is a defence for a person by whom the programme was produced or directed who is not shown to have intended to stir up racial hatred to prove that he did not know and had not reason to suspect—

    (a) that the programme would be included in a programme service, or

    (b) that the circumstances in which the programme would be so included would be such that racial hatred would be likely to be stirred up.

    (5) It is a defence for a person by whom offending words or behaviour were used and who is not shown to have intended to stir up racial hatred to prove that he did not know and had no reason to suspect—

    (a) that a programme involving the use of the offending material would be included in a programme service, or

    (b) that the circumstances in which a programme involving the use of the offending material would be so included, or in which a programme so included would involve the use of the offending material, would be such that racial hatred would be likely to be stirred up.

    (6) A person who is not shown to have intended to stir up racial hatred is not guilty of an offence under this section if he did not know, and had no reason to suspect, that the offending material was threatening, abusive or insulting.

[This section is printed as amended by the *Broadcasting Act* 1990, s.164(3).]

(b) *Allocation*

16–104   This offence is triable either way. Proceedings may not be instituted without the consent of the Attorney General: *POA* 1986, s.27(1).

(c) *Elements of the offence*

16–105   The prosecution must prove that:

    — a programme involving threatening, abusive or insulting visual images or sounds was included in a programme service and

    — the defendant was either the person providing the programme service, a person by whom the programme is produced or directed or a person by whom offending words and behaviour are used and

— he intended to stir up racial hatred
  OR
— having regard to all the circumstances racial hatred is likely to be stirred up by
  such actions.

For the meaning of "racial hatred" see section 18 of the 1986 Act, *ante*. For the meaning of "threatening, abusive or insulting", see *Brutus v. Cozens, ante*.

(d) *Defence*

A person providing the service, or directing or producing the programme who is not **16–106** shown to have intended to stir up racial hatred will have a defence if it can be shown that he did not know and had no reason to suspect that the programme would involve the offending material and having regard to all the circumstances in which the programme was included in the programme service, it was not reasonably practicable for him to secure the removal of the programme from the programme service: *POA* 1986, s.22(3).

A person directing or producing the programme who is shown not to intend to stir up racial hatred will have a defence if it can be shown that he did not know and had no reason to suspect that the programme would be included in the programme service or that the circumstances of the programme's inclusion in the programme service would be such as to stir up racial hatred: *POA* 1986, s.22(4). A person who used offending words or behaviour in the programme who is not shown to have intended to stir up racial hatred will have a defence if he can prove he did not know and had no reason to suspect that the programme involving the offending conduct would be included in the service programme or that the circumstances involving the use of the programme in the service programme would involve the use of the offending material, or that the circumstances in which a programme so included would involve the use of the offending material would be such as to involve the stirring up of racial hatred: *POA* 1986, s.22(5).

A person who is not shown to have intended to stir up racial hatred will not be guilty of an offence if he did not know and had no reason to suspect that the offending material was abusive, threatening or insulting: section 22(6).

(e) *Sentence*

When tried summarily, the maximum penalty for this offence is six months' imprison- **16–107** ment, a fine not exceeding the statutory maximum, or both: *POA* 1986, s.27(3). On commencement of the relevant provisions, the maximum custodial sentence in a magistrates' court will be 12 months' imprisonment: *Criminal Justice Act* 2003, ss.154 and 282. Custodial sentences of less than 12 months will consist of a custody plus order (see *post*, Ch.23).

(4) Possession of racially inflammatory material

(a) *Definition*

Public Order Act 1986, s.23

Possession of racially inflammatory material

23.—(1) A person who has in his possession written material which is threatening, abusive or **16–108** insulting, or a recording of visual images or sounds which are threatening, abusive or insulting, with a view to—

  (a) in the case of written material, its being displayed, published, distributed, or
      included in a cable programme service, whether by himself or another, or
  (b) in the case of a recording, its being distributed, shown, played, or included in a
      cable programme service, whether by himself or another,

is guilty of an offence if he intends racial hatred to be stirred up thereby or, having regard to all the circumstances, racial hatred is likely to be stirred up thereby.

(2) For this purpose regard shall be had to such display, publication, distribution, showing, playing, or inclusion in a programme service as he has, or it may reasonably be inferred that he has, in view.

(3) In proceedings for an offence under this section it is a defence for an accused who is not shown to have intended to stir up racial hatred to prove that he was not aware of the content of the written material or recording and did not suspect, and had no reason to suspect, that it was threatening, abusive or insulting.

[This section is printed as amended by the *Broadcasting Act* 1990, s.164(4).]

(b) *Allocation*

16–109   This offence is triable either way and requires the consent of the Attorney General before proceedings can be instituted: *POA* 1986, s.27(1).

(c) *Elements of the offence*

16–110   For the meaning of "racial hatred" see section 18 of the 1986 Act, *ante*. For the meaning of "threatening, abusive or insulting", see *Brutus v. Cozens, ante*. "Written material" means any sign or other visible representation: *POA* 1986, s.29.

(d) *Defence*

16–111   A person who is not shown to have intended to stir up racial hatred will have a defence if he can prove that he was not aware of the content of the written material or recording, and did not suspect and had no reason to suspect that it was threatening, abusive or insulting: *POA* 1986, s.23(3).

(e) *Sentence*

16–112   When tried summarily this offence carries a maximum penalty of six months' imprisonment, a fine not exceeding the statutory maximum or both: *POA* 1986, s.27(3). On commencement of the relevant provisions, the maximum custodial sentence in a magistrates' court will be 12 months' imprisonment: *Criminal Justice Act* 2003, ss.154 and 282. Custodial sentences of less than 12 months will consist of a custody plus order (see *post*, Ch.23).

J. ACTS INTENDED TO STIR UP RELIGIOUS HATRED

16–113   As from a day to be appointed, the *Racial and Religious Hatred Act* 2006 inserts new sections 29A to 29N into the *Public Order Act* 1986.

(1) Definition

Public Order Act 1986, s.29B

Use of words or behaviour or display of written material
16–114   **29B.**—(1) A person who uses threatening words or behaviour, or displays any written material which is threatening, is guilty of an offence if he intends thereby to stir up religious hatred.

(2) An offence under this section may be committed in a public or a private place, except that no offence is committed where the words or behaviour are used, or the written material is displayed, by a person inside a dwelling and are not heard or seen except by other persons in that or another dwelling.

(3) A constable may arrest without warrant anyone he reasonably suspects is committing an offence under this section.

(4) In proceedings for an offence under this section it is a defence for the accused to prove that he was inside a dwelling and had no reason to believe that the words or behaviour used, or the written material displayed, would be heard or seen by a person outside that or any other dwelling.

(5) This section does not apply to words or behaviour used, or written material

displayed, solely for the purpose of being included in a programme service.

(2) Allocation

This offence is triable either way. No proceedings may be instituted without the consent of the Attorney General: *Public Order Act* 1986, s.29L(1). **16–115**

(3) Elements of the offence

The prosecution must prove that: **16–116**

    (a) the defendant used threatening words or behaviour, or displayed written material which was threatening,

AND

    (b) he intended to stir up religious hatred by doing so.

Public Order Act 1986, ss.29A, 29J, 29K, 29N

Meaning of "religious hatred"

29A. In this Part "religious hatred" means hatred against a group of persons defined by reference to religious belief or lack of religious belief. **16–117**

Protection of freedom of expression

29J. Nothing in this Part shall be read or given effect in a way which prohibits or restricts discussion, criticism or expressions of antipathy, dislike, ridicule, insult or abuse of particular religions or the beliefs or practices of their adherents, or of any other belief system or the beliefs or practices of its adherents, or proselytising or urging adherents of a different religion or belief system to cease practising their religion or belief system. **16–118**

Savings for reports of parliamentary or judicial proceedings

29K.—(1) Nothing in this Part applies to a fair and accurate report of proceedings in Parliament or in the Scottish Parliament. **16–119**

(2) Nothing in this Part applies to a fair and accurate report of proceedings publicly heard before a court or tribunal exercising judicial authority where the report is published contemporaneously with the proceedings or, if it is not reasonably practicable or would be unlawful to publish a report of them contemporaneously, as soon as publication is reasonably practicable and lawful.

Interpretation

29N. In this Part— **16–120**

    "distribute", and related expressions, shall be construed in accordance with section 29C(2) (written material) and section 29E(2) (recordings);

    "dwelling" means any structure or part of a structure occupied as a person's home or other living accommodation (whether the occupation is separate or shared with others) but does not include any part not so occupied, and for this purpose "structure" includes a tent, caravan, vehicle, vessel or other temporary or movable structure;

    "programme" means any item which is included in a programme service;

    "programme service" has the same meaning as in the *Broadcasting Act* 1990;

    "publish", and related expressions, in relation to written material, shall be construed in accordance with section 29C(2);

    "religious hatred" has the meaning given by section 29A;

    "recording" has the meaning given by section 29E(2), and "play" and "show", and related expressions, in relation to a recording, shall be construed in accordance with that provision;

    "written material" includes any sign or other visible representation.

(4) Sentence

When tried summarily, the maximum sentence is six months' imprisonment, a fine not exceeding the statutory maximum or both. The court also has power under section 29I of the 1986 Act to order forfeiture where the offence consists of displaying written **16–121**

Part III

material, publishing or distributing such material, distributing, showing or playing a recording or possessing inflamatory material. On commencement of the relevant provisions, the maximum custodial sentence in a magistrates' court will be 12 months' imprisonment: *Criminal Justice Act* 2003, ss.154 and 282. Custodial sentences of less than 12 months will consist of a custody plus order (see *post*, Ch.23).

K. PUBLISHING OR DISTRIBUTING WRITTEN MATERIAL STIRRING UP RELIGIOUS HATRED

(1) Definition

Public Order Act 1986, s.29C

Publishing or distributing written material

16–122   **29C.**—(1) A person who publishes or distributes written material which is threatening is guilty of an offence if he intends thereby to stir up religious hatred.

(2) References in this Part to the publication or distribution of written material are to its publication or distribution to the public or a section of the public.

(2) Allocation

16–123   This offence is triable either way. No proceedings may be instituted without the consent of the Attorney General: *Public Order Act* 1986, s.29L(1).

(3) Elements of the offence

16–124   The prosecution must prove that:

(c) the defendant published or distributed to the public or a section of the public written material,

AND

(d) he intended to stir up religious hatred by doing so.

(4) Sentence

16–125   When tried summarily, the maximum penalty is six months' imprisonment, a fine not exceeding the statutory maximum, or both. On commencement of the relevant provisions, the maximum custodial sentence in a magistrates' court will be 12 months' imprisonment: *Criminal Justice Act* 2003, ss.154 and 282. Custodial sentences of less than 12 months will consist of a custody plus order (see *post*, Ch.23).

L. PUBLIC PERFORMANCE, DISTRIBUTION, BROADCASTING AND POSSESSION OF MATERIALS STIRRING UP RELIGIOUS HATRED

(1) Public performance of a play stirring up religious hatred

(a) *Definition*

Public Order Act 1986, s.29D(1), (4), (5)

Public performance of play

16–126   **29D.**—(1) If a public performance of a play is given which involves the use of threatening words or behaviour, any person who presents or directs the performance is guilty of an offence if he intends thereby to stir up religious hatred.

(4) In this section "play" and "public performance" have the same meaning as in the *Theatres Act* 1968.

(5) The following provisions of the *Theatres Act* 1968 apply in relation to an offence under this section as they apply to an offence under section 2 of that Act—

section 9 (script as evidence of what was performed),

section 10 (power to make copies of script),
section 15 (powers of entry and inspection).

(b) *Allocation*

This offence is triable either way. No proceedings may be instituted without the **16–127** consent of the Attorney General: *Public Order Act* 1986, s.29L(1).

(c) *Elements of the offence*

The prosecution must prove that: **16–128**
- – the defendant was the presenter or director of a play involving the use of threatening words or behaviour and,
- – the play was performed for the public and,
- – the defendant intended thereby to stir up religious hatred.

The words "play" and "public performance" have the same meaning as in the *Theatres Act* 1968 (see § 16–95, *ante*).

(d) *Sentence*

When tried summarily, the maximum penalty is six months' imprisonment, a fine **16–129** not exceeding the statutory maximum, or both. On commencement of the relevant provisions, the maximum custodial sentence in the magistrates' court will be 12 months' imprisonment: *Criminal Justice Act* 2003, ss.154 and 282. Custodial sentences of less than 12 months will consist of a custody plus order (see *post*, Ch.23).

(e) *Defences*

Public Order Act 1986, s.29D(2), (3)

29D.—(2) This section does not apply to a performance given solely or primarily for one or **16–130** more of the following purposes—
  (a) rehearsal,
  (b) making a recording of the performance, or
  (c) enabling the performance to be included in a programme service;
but if it is proved that the performance was attended by persons other than those directly connected with the giving of the performance or the doing in relation to it of the things mentioned in paragraph (b) or (c), the performance shall, unless the contrary is shown, be taken not to have been given solely or primarily for the purpose mentioned above.
  (3) For the purposes of this section—
  (a) a person shall not be treated as presenting a performance of a play by reason only of his taking part in it as a performer,
  (b) a person taking part as a performer in a performance directed by another shall be treated as a person who directed the performance if without reasonable excuse he performs otherwise than in accordance with that person's direction, and
  (c) a person shall be taken to have directed a performance of a play given under his direction notwithstanding that he was not present during the performance;
and a person shall not be treated as aiding or abetting the commission of an offence under this section by reason only of his taking part in a performance as a performer.

(2) Distributing, showing or playing a recording stirring up religious hatred

(a) *Definition*

Public Order Act 1986, s.29E

Distributing, showing or playing a recording
  29E.—(1) A person who distributes, or shows or plays, a recording of visual images or sounds **16–131** which are threatening is guilty of an offence if he intends thereby to stir up religious hatred.

Part III

(2) In this Part "recording" means any record from which visual images or sounds may, by any means, be reproduced; and references to the distribution, showing or playing of a recording are to its distribution, showing or playing to the public or a section of the public.

(3) This section does not apply to the showing or playing of a recording solely for the purpose of enabling the recording to be included in a programme service.

(b) *Allocation*

16–132   This offence is triable either way. Proceedings may not be instituted without the consent of the Attorney General: *Public Order Act* 1986, s.29L(1).

(c) *Elements of the offence*

16–133   The prosecution must prove that:
— the defendant distributed, showed or played a recording of visual images or sounds and,
— these visual images or sounds were threatening and,
— he so acted with the intention to stir up religious hatred.

(d) *Sentence*

16–134   When tried summarily, the maximum penalty for this offence is six months' imprisonment, a fine not exceeding the statutory maximum, or both. On commencement of the relevant provisions, the maximum sentence in a magistrates' court will be 12 months' imprisonment: *Criminal Justice Act* 2003, ss.154 and 282. Custodial sentences of less than 12 months will consist of a custody plus order (see *post*, Ch.23).

(3) Broadcasting a programme stirring up religious hatred

(a) *Definition*

Public Order Act 1986, s.29F

Broadcasting or including programme in programme service
16–135   **29F.**—(1) If a programme involving threatening visual images or sounds is included in a programme service, each of the persons mentioned in subsection (2) is guilty of an offence if he intends thereby to stir up religious hatred.

(2) The persons are—
     (a) the person providing the programme service,
     (b) any person by whom the programme is produced or directed, and
     (c) any person by whom offending words or behaviour are used.

(b) *Allocation*

16–136   This offence is triable either way. Proceedings may not be instituted without the consent of the Attorney General: *Public Order Act* 1986, s.29L(1).

(c) *Elements of the offence*

16–137   The prosecution must prove that:
— a programme involving threatening visual images or sounds was included in a programme service and,
— the defendant was either the person providing the programme service, a person by whom the programme was produced or directed or a person by whom offending words or behaviour were used and,
— he intended to stir up religious hatred.

(d) *Sentence*

16–138   When tried summarily, the maximum penalty for this offence is six months' imprison-

ment, a fine not exceeding the statutory maximum, or both. On commencement of the relevant provisions, the maximum custodial sentence in a magistrates' court will be 12 months' imprisonment: *Criminal Justice Act* 2003, ss.154 and 282. Custodial sentences of less than 12 months will consist of a custody plus order (see *post*, Ch.23).

(4) Possession of religiously inflammatory material

(a) *Definition*

Public Order Act 1986, s.29G

Possession of inflammatory material

29G.—(1) A person who has in his possession written material which is threatening, or a re-   **16–139**
cording of visual images or sounds which are threatening, with a view to—
    (a) in the case of written material, its being displayed, published, distributed, or included in a programme service whether by himself or another, or
    (b) in the case of a recording, its being distributed, shown, played, or included in a programme service, whether by himself or another,
is guilty of an offence if he intends religious hatred to be stirred up thereby.

(2) For this purpose regard shall be had to such display, publication, distribution, showing, playing, or inclusion in a programme service as he has, or it may be reasonably be inferred that he has, in view.

(b) *Allocation*

This offence is triable either way. Proceedings may not be instituted without the   **16–140**
consent of the Attorney General: *Public Order Act* 1986, s.29L(1).

(c) *Elements of the offence*

The prosecution must prove that: **16–141**
— the defendant had in his possession written material or a recording of visual images or sounds which were threatening,
— in the case of written material, with a view to displaying, publishing, distributing or including it in a programme service,
— in the case of a recording, distributing, showing, playing or including it in a programme service and,
— he intends to stir up religious hatred.

(d) *Sentence*

When tried summarily, the maximum penalty for this offence is six months' imprison-   **16–142**
ment, a fine not exceeding the statutory maximum, or both. On commencement of the relevant provisions, the maximum custodial sentence in a magistrates' court will be 12 months' imprisonment: *Criminal Justice Act* 2003, ss.154 and 282. Custodial sentences of less than 12 months will consist of a custody plus order (see *post*, Ch.23).

M. Contamination of or Interference with Goods

(1) Definition

Public Order Act 1986, s.38(1)–(3)

Contamination of or interference with goods with intention of causing public alarm or anxiety, etc.

38.—(1) It is an offence for a person, with the intention—   **16–143**
    (a) of causing public alarm or anxiety, or
    (b) of causing injury to members of the public consuming or using the goods, or

    (c) of causing economic loss to any person by reason of the goods being shunned by members of the public, or

    (d) of causing economic loss to any person by reason of steps taken to avoid any such alarm or anxiety, injury or loss,

to contaminate or interfere with goods, or make it appear that goods have been contaminated or interfered with, or to place goods which have been contaminated or interfered with, or which appear to have been contaminated or interfered with, in a place where goods of that description are consumed, used, sold or otherwise supplied.

(2) It is also an offence for a person, with any such intention as is mentioned in paragraph (a), (c) or (d) of subsection (1), to threaten that he or another will do, or to claim that he or another has done, any of the acts mentioned in that subsection.

(3) It is an offence for a person to be in possession of any of the following articles with a view to the commission of an offence under subsection (1)—

    (a) materials to be used for contaminating or interfering with goods or making it appear that goods have been contaminated or interfered with, or

    (b) goods which have been contaminated or interfered with, or which appear to have been contaminated or interfered with.

(2) Allocation

16–144   These offences are triable either way: *POA* 1986, s.38(4).

(3) Elements of the offence

16–145   The prosecution must prove that:

— the defendant had the intention of causing public alarm or anxiety

    OR

    causing injury to members of the public consuming or using the goods OR causing economic loss to any person by reason of the goods being shunned by members of the public OR causing economic loss to any person by reason of steps taken to avoid such anxiety and,

— he contaminated or interfered with goods OR made it appear that goods had been contaminated OR placed goods which had been or appeared to be contaminated or interfered with in a place where goods of that description are sold, used or otherwise supplied,

    OR

— he threatened that he or another would do, or claimed that he or another had done, any of the acts mentioned above

    OR

— the defendant was in possession of materials to be used for the contamination of or interference with goods or materials used for making it appear that goods have been contaminated or interfered with or the defendant was in possession of goods which have been contaminated or interfered with, or which appear to have been contaminated or interfered with.

Public Order Act 1986, s.38(5), (6)

Contamination of or interference with goods with intention of causing public alarm or anxiety, etc.

16–146   **38.**—(5) In this section "goods" includes substances whether natural or manufactured and whether or not incorporated in or mixed with other goods.

(6) The reference in subsection (2) to a person claiming that certain acts have been committed does not include a person who in good faith reports or warns that such acts have been, or appear to have been, committed.

(4) Sentence

16–147   When tried summarily, the maximum penalty is six months' imprisonment, a fine not exceeding the statutory maximum or both. On commencement of the relevant provisions, the maximum custodial sentence in a magistrates' court will be 12 months' imprisonment: *Criminal Justice Act* 2003, ss.154 and 282. Custodial sentences of less than 12 months will consist of a custody plus order (see *post*, Ch.23).

III. OFFENCES IN CONNECTION WITH SPORTING ACTIVITY

A. Football Offences

(1) Definition

Football (Offences) Act 1991, ss.2–4

Throwing of missiles

2. It is an offence for a person at a designated football match to throw anything at or **16–148**
towards—

    (a) the playing area, or any area adjacent to the playing area to which spectators are not generally admitted, or

    (b) any area in which spectators or other persons are or may be present,

without lawful authority or lawful excuse (which shall be for him to prove).

Indecent or racialist chanting

3.—(1) It is an offence to engage or take part in chanting of an indecent or racialist nature at **16–149**
a designated football match.

    (2) For this purpose—

    (a) "chanting" means the repeated uttering of any words or sounds (whether alone or in concert with one or more others); and

    (b) "of a racialist nature" means consisting of or including matter which is threatening, abusive or insulting to a person by reason of his colour, race, nationality (including citizenship) or ethnic or national origins.

Going onto the playing area

4. It is an offence for a person at a designated football match to go onto the playing area, or **16–150**
any area adjacent to the playing area to which spectators are not generally admitted, without lawful authority or lawful excuse (which shall be for him to prove).

(2) Allocation

These offences are all triable summarily: *Football (Offences) Act* 1991, s.5(2).   **16–151**

(3) Elements of the offence

To establish the offence of throwing of missiles, the prosecution must prove that: **16–152**

    — the defendant was at a designated football match and,

    — he threw something at or towards the playing area, or any area adjacent to the playing area to which spectators are not normally admitted OR

    — he threw something at or towards any area in which spectators or other persons are or may be present without lawful authority or lawful excuse.

To establish the offence of indecent or racialist chanting, the prosecution must prove that:

    — the defendant was at a designated football match and,

    — he engaged in indecent or racialist chanting.

To establish the offence of going on to the playing area, the prosecution must prove that:

    — the defendant was at a designated football match and,

    — he went onto the playing area, or onto any area adjacent to the playing area to which spectators are not generally admitted, without lawful authority or lawful excuse.

Part III

Football (Offences) Act 1991, s.1

Designated football matches

16–153   1.—(1) In this Act a "designated football match" means an association football match designated, or of a description designated, for the purposes of this Act by order of the Secretary of State.

Any such order shall be made by statutory instrument which shall be subject to annulment in pursuance of a resolution of either House of Parliament.

(2) References in this Act to things done at a designated football match include anything done at the ground—

> (a) within the period beginning two hours before the start of the match or (if earlier) two hours before the time at which it is advertised to start and ending one hour after the end of the match; or
>
> (b) where the match is advertised to start at a particular time on a particular day but does not take place on that day, within the period beginning two hours before and ending one hour after the advertised starting time.

(4) Sentence

16–154   The maximum penalty for these offences is a fine not exceeding level three on the standard scale: *Football (Offences) Act* 1991, s.5(2).

B. OFFENCES UNDER THE FOOTBALL SPECTATORS ACT 1989

(1) Unauthorised attendance

(a) *Definition*

The Football Spectators Act 1989, s.2

Offences relating to unauthorised attendance at designated football matches

16–155   2.—(1) If a person who is not, in relation to the match, an authorised spectator enters or remains on premises as a spectator during a period relevant to a designated football match that person commits an offence and so does a person who attempts to commit an offence under this subsection of entering premises.

(2) Where a person is charged under subsection(1) above with an offence of entering or remaining on premises, and was at the time of the alleged offence not disqualified from being a member of the national football membership scheme, it shall be a defence to prove that he was allowed to enter the premises as a spectator by a person reasonably appearing to him to have lawful authority to do so.

(3) A person guilty of an offence under subsection (1) above shall be liable on summary conviction to imprisonment for a term not exceeding one month or a fine not exceeding level 3 on the standard scale or to both.

(4) A constable who reasonably suspects that a person has committed an offence under subsection (1) above may arrest him without a warrant.

(b) *Allocation*

16–156   This offence is triable summarily.

(c) *Elements of the offence*

16–157   The prosecution must prove that:

> — the defendant was not an authorised spectator and
> — he entered or remained on premises as a spectator during a designated football match OR
> — he attempted to do so.

The *Football Spectators (Prescription) Order* 2000 (S.I. 2000 No. 2126) designates matches for the purposes of this Act.

(d) *Defence*

Where a person was not disqualified from being a member of the national football **16–158** membership scheme at the time of the alleged offence he shall have a defence if he can prove that he was allowed to enter the premises as a spectator by a person reasonably appearing to him to have lawful authority to do so: *Football Spectators Act* 1989, s.2(3)

(e) *Sentence*

The maximum penalty is one months' imprisonment, a fine not exceeding the level 3 **16–159** on the standard scale, or both. Section 280(2) and Schedule 26, paragraph 41 of the *Criminal Justice Act* 2003 increases the maximum term to 51 weeks (not yet in force). On commencement of the relevant provisions, the maximum custodial sentence able to be imposed in a magistrates' court will be a custody plus order: *Criminal Justice Act* 2003, ss.181, 280–282 (see *post*, Ch.23).

(2) Admitting spectators to unlicensed premises

(a) *Definition*

Football Spectators Act 1989, s.9

Offence of admitting spectators to unlicensed premises

  9.—1) Subject to subsection (2) below, if persons are admitted as spectators to, or permitted **16–160** to remain as spectators on, any premises during a period relevant to a designated football match without a licence to admit spectators being in force, any responsible person commits an offence.

  (2) Where a person is charged with an offence under this section it shall be a defence to prove either that the spectators were admitted in an emergency or—

  (a) that the spectators were admitted without his consent; and
  (b) that he took all reasonable precautions and exercised all due diligence to avoid the commission of such an offence.

  (3) A person guilty of an offence under this section shall be liable—

  (a) on summary conviction, to a fine not exceeding the statutory maximum; or
  (b) on conviction on indictment, to a fine or to imprisonment for a term not exceeding two years, or to both.

(b) *Allocation*

This offence is triable summarily only.   **16–161**

(c) *Elements of the offence*

The prosecution has to prove that: **16–162**

  — persons were admitted as spectators, or allowed to remain as spectators to any premises during a period relevant to a designated football match and,
  — there was no license to admit spectators in force and,
  — the defendant was responsible.

The *Football Spectators (Prescription) Order* 2004 (S.I. 2004 No. 2409) (in force from October 11, 2004) designates matches for the purposes of this Act.

The *Football Spectators (Prescription) Order* 2004 (S.I. 2004 No. 2409) revokes the *Football Spectators (Prescription) Order* 2000 (S.I. 2000 No. 2126), with effect from October 11, 2004. Articles 3 and 4 describe the football matches in England and Wales and outside England and Wales which are regulated football matches for the purposes of Part II of the 1989 Act. In England and Wales, a regulated match is any match in which either team is a member of the Football League, the Premier League, the Football Conference or the League of Wales, or represents a country or territory. Outside England and Wales, a regulated match is one involving a national team representing England or Wales or a team representing a Football League, Premier League, Football

735

Conference or League of Wales club. Article 5 prescribes the Football Banning Orders Authority (established under the *Police Act* 1996, s.57) as the enforcing authority for the purposes of Part II of the 1989 Act, and the Chief Executive of the Football Association for the purposes of section 18(1) and (2) of that Act (person to whom a banning order and an order terminating a banning order must be copied).

The relevant licenses are issued by the Football Licensing Authority under the *Football Spectators (Seating) Order* 1994 (S.I. 1994 No. 1666). Section 10(13) of the 1989 Act also creates a summary offence of failing to observe any term or condition of a licence granted to admit spectators to any premises for the purpose of watching any designated football match played there. A defendant accused of such an offence will have a defence if he can prove that the contravention took place without his consent and that he took all precautions and exercised due diligence to avoid the commission of such an offence.

(d) *Defences*

16–163   The defendant will have a defence if he can establish that he admitted the spectators in an emergency that he took all reasonable precautions and exercised all due diligence to avoid the commission of such an offence: *Football Spectators Act* 1989, s.9(2).

(e) *Sentence*

16–164   When tried summarily, the offence under section 9 carries a maximum penalty of a fine not exceeding the statutory maximum.

C. BREACH OF BANNING ORDERS

(1) Definition

Football Spectators Act 1989, ss.14J, 19

Offences

16–165   **14J.**—(1) A person subject to a banning order who fails to comply with—
(a) any requirement imposed by the order, or
(b) any requirement imposed under section 19(2B) or (2C) below,
is guilty of an offence.

(2) A person guilty of an offence under this section is liable on summary conviction to imprisonment for a term not exceeding six months, or a fine not exceeding level 5 on the standard scale, or both.

Functions of enforcing authority and local police

16–166   **19.**—(1) The enforcing authority and the officer responsible for the police station at which he reports initially shall have the following functions as respects any person subject to a banning order.

(2) On a person reporting initially at the police station, the officer responsible for the station may make such requirements of that person as are determined by the enforcing authority to be necessary or expedient for giving effect to the banning order, so far as relating to regulated football matches outside England and Wales.

(2A) If, in connection with any regulated football match outside England and Wales, the enforcing authority is of the opinion that requiring any person subject to a banning order to report is necessary or expedient in order to reduce the likelihood of violence or disorder at or in connection with the match, the authority must give him a notice in writing under subsection (2B) below.

(2B) The notice must require that person—
(a) to report at a police station specified in the notice at the time, or between the times, specified in the notice,
(b) if the match is outside the United Kingdom and the order imposes a requirement as to the surrender by him of his passport, to surrender his passport at a police station specified in the notice at the time, or between the times, specified in the notice,

and may require him to comply with any additional requirements of the order in the manner specified in the notice.

(2C) In the case of any regulated football match, the enforcing authority may by notice in writing require any person subject to a banning order to comply with any additional requirements of the order in the manner specified in the notice.

(2D) The enforcing authority may establish criteria for determining whether any requirement under subsection (2B) or (2C) above ought to be imposed on any person or any class of person.

(2E) A notice under this section—

    (a) may not require the person subject to the order to report except in the control period in relation to a regulated football match outside England and Wales or an external tournament,

    (b) may not require him to surrender his passport except in the control period in relation to a regulated football match outside the United Kingdom or an external tournament which includes such matches.

(2F) Where a notice under this section requires the person subject to the order to surrender his passport, the passport must be returned to him as soon as reasonably practicable after the end of the control period in question.

(5) The enforcing authority, in exercising their functions under this section, shall have regard to any guidance issued by the Secretary of State under section 21 below.

(6) A person who, without reasonable excuse, fails to comply with any requirement imposed on him under subsection (2) above shall be guilty of an offence.

(7) A person guilty of an offence under subsection (6) above shall be liable on summary conviction to a fine not exceeding level 2 on the standard scale.

(2) Allocation

Breach of any requirement of a Banning Order imposed under section 19(2B) or **16–167** (2C) is a summary offence: section 14J.

Breach of any requirement of a Banning Order imposed under section 19(2) is a summary offence: section 19(6).

(3) Elements of the offence

Football Spectators Act 1989, s.14

Main definitions

    14.—(1) This section applies for the purposes of this Part.   **16–168**

(2) "Regulated football match" means an association football match (whether in England and Wales or elsewhere) which is a prescribed match or a match of a prescribed description.

(3) "External tournament" means a football competition which includes regulated football matches outside England and Wales.

(4) "Banning order" means an order made by the court under this Part which—

    (a) in relation to regulated football matches in England and Wales, prohibits the person who is subject to the order from entering any premises for the purpose of attending such matches, and

    (b) in relation to regulated football matches outside England and Wales, requires that person to report at a police station in accordance with this Part.

(5) "Control period", in relation to a regulated football match outside England and Wales, means the period—

    (a) beginning five days before the day of the match, and

    (b) ending when the match is finished or cancelled.

(6) "Control period", in relation to an external tournament, means any period described in an order made by the Secretary of State—

    (a) beginning five days before the day of the first football match outside England and Wales which is included in the tournament, and

    (b) ending when the last football match outside England and Wales which is included in the tournament is finished or cancelled, but, for the purposes of paragraph (a), any football match included in the qualifying or pre-qualifying stages of the tournament is to be left out of account.

(7) References to football matches are to football matches played or intended to be played.

(8) "Relevant offence" means an offence to which Schedule 1 to this Act applies.

(4) Sentence

16–169   The offence under section 14J carries a maximum penalty of imprisonment for a term not exceeding six months, or a fine not exceeding level 5 on the standard scale, or both.

On commencement of the relevant provisions, the maximum custodial sentence in a magistrates' court will be 12 months' imprisonment: *Criminal Justice Act* 2003, ss.154 and 282. Custodial sentences of less than 12 months will consist of a custody plus order (see *post*, Ch.23). The offence under section 19(6) carries a maximum penalty of a fine not exceeding level two on the standard scale.

D. TICKET TOUTS

(1) Definition

Criminal Justice and Public Order Act 1994, s.166(1)

Sale of tickets by unauthorised persons

16–170   **166.**—(1) It is an offence for an unauthorised person to sell, or offer or expose for sale, a ticket for a designated football match in any public place or place to which the public has access or, in the course of a trade or business, in any other place.

(2) Allocation

16–171   This offence is triable summarily: *Criminal Justice and Public Order Act* 1994, s.166(3).

(3) Elements of the offence

16–172   The prosecution must prove that:
— the defendant sold, or offered, or exposed for sale,
— a ticket for a designated football match,
— in any public place or place to which the public have access, or any other place in the course of trade or business.

Criminal Justice and Public Order Act 1994, s.166(2)

Sale of tickets by unauthorised persons

16–173   **166.**—(2) For this purpose—
(a) a person is "unauthorised" unless he is authorised in writing to sell tickets for the match by the home club or by the organisers of the match;
(b) a "ticket" means anything which purports to be a ticket; and
(c) a "designated football match" means a football match of a description, or a particular football match, for the time being designated for the purposes of Part I of the *Football Spectators Act* 1989 or which is a regulated football match for the purposes of Part II of that Act.

(4) Sentence

16–174   The maximum penalty is a fine not exceeding level five on the standard scale: *Criminal Justice and Public Order Act* 1994, s.166(5).

E. Offences in connection with Alcohol on Coaches and Trains

(1) Definition

Sporting Events (Control of Alcohol etc.) Act 1985, s.1(1)–(4)

Offences in connection with alcohol on coaches and trains

1.—(1) This section applies to a vehicle which—   **16–175**
    (a) is a public service vehicle or railway passenger vehicle, and
    (b) is being used for the principal purpose of carrying passengers for the whole or part of a journey to or from a designated sporting event.

(2) A person who knowingly causes or permits intoxicating liquor to be carried on a vehicle to which this section applies is guilty of an offence—
    (a) if the vehicle is a public service vehicle and he is the operator of the vehicle or the servant or agent of the operator, or
    (b) if the vehicle is a hired vehicle and he is the person to whom it is hired or the servant or agent of that person.

(3) A person who has intoxicating liquor in his possession while on a vehicle to which this section applies is guilty of an offence.

(4) A person who is drunk on a vehicle to which this section applies is guilty of an offence.

(2) Allocation

These offences are triable summarily only: *Sporting Events (Control of Alcohol etc.)*   **16–176**
Act 1985, s.8.

(3) Elements of the offence

The prosecution must prove that: **16–177**
    — the defendant was the operator, or servant or agent of the operator of a public service vehicle or the defendant was the person to whom, or a servant or agent of the person to whom a hired vehicle was hired and,
    — the vehicle was being used to carry passengers to of from a designated sporting event and
    — the defendant knowingly caused or permitted intoxicating liquor to be carried on to the vehicle OR
    — the defendant was a passenger on such a vehicle and he had intoxicating liquor in his possession during a journey to or from a designated sporting event OR
    — the defendant was a passenger on such a vehicle and he was drunk during a journey to or from a designated sporting event.

Sporting Events (Control of Alcohol etc.) Act 1985, s.9(3)

Interpretation

9.—(3) "Designated sporting event"—   **16–178**
    (a) means a sporting event or proposed sporting event for the time being designated, or of a class designated, by order made by the Secretary of State, and
    (b) includes a designated sporting event within the meaning of Part V of the *Criminal Justice (Scotland) Act* 1980;
and an order under this subsection may apply to events or proposed events outside Great Britain as well as those in England and Wales.

(4) Sentence

Sporting Events (Control of Alcohol etc.) Act 1985, s.8(a)–(c)

Penalties for offences

8. A person guilty of an offence under this Act shall be liable on summary conviction—   **16–179**

(a) in the case of an offence under section 1(2) to a fine not exceeding level 4 on the standard scale,

(b) in the case of an offence under section 1(3) ... to a fine not exceeding level 3 on the standard scale or to imprisonment for a term not exceeding three months or both,

(c) in the case of an offence under section 1(4) ... to a fine not exceeding level 2 on the standard scale.

Section 280(2) and Schedule 26, para. 36 of the *Criminal Justice Act* 2003 increases the maximum term in section 8(b) to 51 weeks. After commencement of the relevant proceedings, the maximum custodial sentence able to be imposed in a magistrates' court will be a custody plus order: *Criminal Justice Act* 2003, ss.181, 280–282 (see *post*, Ch.23).

F. OFFENCES CONNECTED WITH ALCOHOL, CONTAINERS ETC. AT SPORTS GROUNDS

(1) Definition

Sporting Events (Control of Alcohol etc.) Act 1985, s.2(1)

Offences in connection with alcohol, containers etc. at sports grounds

16–180   2.—(1) A person who has intoxicating liquor or an article to which this section applies in his possession—

(a) at any time during the period of a designated sporting event when he is in any area of a designated sports ground from which the event may be directly viewed, or

(b) while entering or trying to enter a designated sports ground at any time during the period of a designated sporting event at that ground,

is guilty of an offence.

(2) Allocation

16–181   This offence is triable summarily: *Sporting Events (Control of Alcohol etc.) Act* 1985, s.8.

(3) Elements of the offence

16–182   The prosecution must prove that:

— the defendant was, during the period of a designated sporting event, in any area of a designated sports ground from which this event could be viewed, OR

— the defendant was entering or trying to enter a designated sports ground at any time during the period of a designated sporting event at the ground AND

— he had in his possession intoxicating liquor OR

— he had in his possession a bottle, can or other portable container (including such an article when crushed or broken) which is for holding any drink, and is of a kind which, when empty, is normally discarded or returned to, or left to be recovered by, the supplier, or forms part of such an article. (Note: Bottles/articles used for holding any medicinal product do not fall under this section.)

Sporting Events (Control of Alcohol etc.) Act 1985, ss.2(3), 9(1)–(4)

16–183   2.—(3) This section applies to any article capable of causing injury to a person struck by it, being—

(a) a bottle, can or other portable container (including such an article when crushed or broken) which—

(i) is for holding any drink, and

(ii) is of a kind which, when empty, is normally discarded or returned to, or left to be recovered by, the supplier, or

(b) part of an article falling within paragraph (a) above;

but does not apply to anything that is for holding any medicinal product (within the meaning of the *Medicines Act* 1968).

Interpretation

9.—(1) The following provisions shall have effect for the interpretation of this Act.   **16–184**

(2) "Designated sports ground" means any place—

(a) used (wholly or partly) for sporting events where accommodation is provided for spectators, and

(b) for the time being designated, or of a class designated, by order made by the Secretary of State; and an order under this subsection may include provision for determining for the purposes of this Act the outer limit of any designated sports ground.

(3) "Designated sporting event" —

(a) means a sporting event or proposed sporting event for the time being designated, or of a class designated, by order made by the Secretary of State, and

(b) includes a designated sporting event within the meaning of Part V of the *Criminal Justice (Scotland) Act* 1980;

and an order under this subsection may apply to events or proposed events outside Great Britain as well as those in England and Wales.

(4) The period of a designated sporting event is the period beginning two hours before the start of the event or (if earlier) two hours before the time at which it is advertised to start and ending one hour after the end of the event, but—

(a) where an event advertised to start at a particular time on a particular day is postponed to a later day, the period includes the period in the day on which it is advertised to take place beginning two hours before and ending one hour after that time, and

(b) where an event advertised to start at a particular time on a particular day does not take place, the period is the period referred to in paragraph (a) above.

(4) Sentence

In the case of an offence under section 2(1) the maximum penalty is a fine not   **16–185** exceeding level three on the standard scale or to imprisonment for a term not exceeding three months or both: *Sporting Events (Control of Alcohol etc.) Act* 1985, s.8(b). Section 280(2) and Schedule 26, paragraph 36 of the *Criminal Justice Act* 2003 increases the maximum term in section 8(b) to 51 weeks (not yet in force). On commencement of the relevant provisions, the maximum custodial sentence able to be imposed in a magistrates' court will be a custody plus order: *Criminal Justice Act* 2003, ss.181, 280–282 (see *post*, Ch.23).

In the case of an offence under section 2(2) the maximum penalty is a fine not exceeding level two on the standard scale: *Sporting Events (Control of Alcohol etc.) Act* 1985, s.8(c).

IV. OFFENCES CONNECTED WITH OFFENSIVE WEAPONS

A. OFFENCES RELATING TO FIREARMS

The *Violent Crime Reduction Act* 2006 amends the *Firearms Act* 1968 in several   **16–186** particulars.

Part 2 of the Act creates several new summary offences relating to the possession and sale of weapons. Section 32 creates a new summary offence committed where in the course of the sale of an air weapon to an individual not registered as a firearms dealer, the seller transfers possession of the weapon when both parties are not present in person. Section 34 inserts a new section 21A into the *Firearms Act* 1968, creating a summary offence of firing a missile from an air weapon beyond premises. Section 35 creates summary offences of selling, buying, or attempting to buy a cap-type primer designed for use in metallic ammunition for a firearm, or an empty cartridge case incorporating such a primer. Section 36 creates a summary offence prohibiting the manufacture, sale or importation of "realistic imitation firearms" (defined in section 38). Sections 32 and 34 were not in force at the time of writing. Sections 35 and 36 came into force on April 6, 2007.

Section 40 inserts a new section 24A in the *Firearms Act* 1968, creating a summary offence of purchasing an imitation firearm when aged under 18, or selling an imitation firearm to persons under 18. Section 41 amends Schedule 6 of the *Firearms Act* 1968, creating an either-way offence of possessing an imitation firearm in a public place. Section 43 amends section 141A of the *Criminal Justice Act* 1988 (prohibition on the sale of knives, etc, to persons under 16) making it unlawful to sell such articles to those under 18. Section 44 amends sections 1–3 of the *Crossbows Act* 1987 to increase the age referred to in those sections from 17 to 18. None of these sections are in force at the time of writing, and future editions of this work will deal fully with these offences when they come into force.

The mode of trial, maximum sentences, and powers of courts with respect to offences created by the *Firearms Act* 1968 are set out in Schedule 6 to that Act.

[See *Violent Crime Reduction Act 2005 (Commencement No. 1) Order* 2007 (S.I. 2007 No. 74) and *VCRA (Commencement Order No. 2) Order* 2007 (S.I. 2007 No. 858).]

Firearms Act 1968, Sched. 6

SCHEDULE 6

PROSECUTION AND PUNISHMENT OF OFFENCES

PART I

TABLE OF PUNISHMENTS

Section of this Act creating offence	General nature of offence	Mode of prosecution	Punishment	Additional provisions
Section 1(1)	Possessing etc. firearm or ammunition without firearm certificate.	(a) Summary	6 months or a fine of £400; or both	
		(b) On indictment	(i) where the offence is committed in an aggravated form within the meaning of section 4(4) of this Act, 7 years, or a fine; or both,	Paragraph 1 of Part II of this Schedule applies.
			(ii) in any other case, 5 years or a fine; or both.	
Section 1(2)	Non-compliance with condition of firearm certificate.	Summary	6 months or a fine of level 5 on the standard scale; or both.	Paragraph 1 of Part II of this Schedule applies.

16–187

Section of this Act creating offence	General nature of offence	Mode of prosecution	Punishment	Additional provisions
Section 2(1)	Possessing, etc., shot gun without shot gun certificate.	(a) Summary	6 months or the statutory maximum or both.	Paragraph 1 of Part II of this Schedule applies.
		(b) On indictment	3 years 5 years or a fine; or both.	
Section 2(2)	Non-compliance with condition of shot gun certificate.	Summary	6 months or a fine of level 5 on the standard scale; or both.	Paragraph 1 of Part II of this Schedule applies.
Section 3(1)	Trading in firearms without being registered as firearms dealer.	(a) Summary	6 months or a fine of £400 or both.	
		(b) On indictment	5 years or a fine; or both.	
Section 3(2)	Selling firearms to person without a certificate.	(a) Summary	6 months or a fine of £400; or both.	
		(b) On indictment	5 years or a fine; or both.	
Section 3(3)	Repairing, testing etc. firearm for person without a certificate.	(a) Summary	6 months or a fine of £400; or both.	
		(b) On indictment	5 years or a fine; or both.	
Section 3(5)	Falsifying certificate, etc., with view to acquisition of firearm.	(a) Summary	6 months or a fine of £400; or both.	
		(b) On indictment	5 years or a fine; or both	
Section 3(6)	Pawnbroker taking firearm in pawn.	Summary	3 months or a fine of level 3 on the standard scale; or both.	Maximum penalty will be increased to 51 weeks by section 280(2) and Schedule 26, paragraph 20 of the *CJA* 2003.
Section 4(1) (3)	Shortening a shot gun; conversion of firearms.	(a) Summary	6 months or a fine of £400 or both.	
		(b) On indictment	7 years or a fine; or both.	

Part III

Section of this Act creating offence	General nature of offence	Mode of prosecution	Punishment	Additional provisions
Section 5(1)(a), (ab), (aba), (ac), (ad), (ae), (af) or (c)	Possessing or distributing prohibited weapons or ammunition.	On indictment	10 years or a fine, or both.	
Section 5(1)(b)	Possessing or distributing prohibited weapon designed for discharge of noxious liquid etc.	(a) Summary	6 months or a fine of the statutory maximum, or both.	
		(b) On indictment	10 years or a fine or both.	
Section 5(1A)(a)	Possessing or distributing firearm disguised as other object.	On indictment	10 years or a fine, or both.	
Section 5(1A)(b), (c), (d), (e), (f) or (g)	Possessing or distributing other prohibited weapons.	(a) Summary	6 months or a fine of the statutory maximum, or both.	
		(b) On indictment	10 years or a fine, or both.	
Section 5(5)	Non-compliance with condition of Secretary of State authority.	Summary	6 months or a fine of level 5 on the standard scale; or both.	
Section 5(6)	Non-compliance with requirements to surrender authority to possess, etc., prohibited weapon or ammunition.	Summary	A fine of level 3 on the standard scale.	
Section 6(3)	Contravention of order under s. 6 (or corresponding Northern Irish order) restricting removal of arms.	Summary	3 months or, for each firearm or parcel of ammunition in respect of which the offence is committed, a fine of level 3 on the standard scale or both.	Paragraph 2 of Part II of this Schedule applies. Maximum penalty will be increased to 51 weeks by section 280(2) and Schedule 26, paragraph 20 of the *CJA* 2003.

Section of this Act creating offence	General nature of offence	Mode of prosecution	Punishment	Additional provisions
Section 7(2)	Making false statement in order to obtain police permit.	Summary	6 months or a fine of level 5 on the standard scale; or both.	
Section 9(3)	Making false statement in order to obtain permit for auction of firearms, etc.	Summary	6 months or a fine not exceeding level 5 on the standard scale; or both.	
		(b) On indictment	3 years or a fine; or both.	
Section 13(2)	Making false statement in order to obtain permit for removal of signalling apparatus.	Summary	6 months or a fine of level 5 on the standard scale; or both.	
Section 16	Possession of firearm with intent to endanger life or injure property.	On indictment	life imprisonment or a fine; or, both.	
Section 16A	Possession of firearm with intent to cause fear of violence.	On indictment	10 years or a fine; or both.	
Section 17(1)	Use of firearms to resist arrest.	On indictment	life imprisonment or a fine; or, both.	Paragraphs 3 to 5 of Part II of this Schedule apply.
Section 17(2)	Possessing firearms while committing an offence specified in Schedule 1 or, in Scotland, an offence specified in Schedule 2.	On indictment	Life imprisonment or a fine; or, both.	Paragraphs 3 and 6 of Part II of this Schedule apply.
Section 18(1)	Carrying firearms or imitation firearms with intent commit indictable offence (or, in Scotland, an offence specified in Schedule 2) or to resist arrest.	On indictment	Life imprisonment; or a fine; or, both.	

Part III

Section of this Act creating offence	General nature of offence	Mode of prosecution	Punishment	Additional provisions
Section 19	Carrying firearm or imitation firearm in public place.	(a) Summary [except if the firearm is a firearm specified in section 5(1)(a), (ab), (aba), (ac), (ad), (ae) or (af) or section 5(1A)(a) of this Act.]	6 months or a fine of £400; or both.	
		(b) On indictment (but not in the case of an imitation firearm or if the firearm is an air weapon).	7 years or a fine; or both.	
Section 20(1)	Trespassing with firearm or imitation firearm in a building.	(a) Summary [except if the firearm is a firearm specified in section 5(1)(a), (ab), (aba), (ac), (ad), (ae) or (af) or section 5(1A)(a) of this Act.]	6 months or a fine of £400; or both.	
		(b) On indictment (but not in the case of an imitation firearm or if the firearm is an air weapon)	5 years or a fine; or both.	

Section of this Act creating offence	General nature of offence	Mode of prosecution	Punishment	Additional provisions
Section 20(2)	Trespassing with firearm or imitation firearm on land.	Summary	3 months or a fine of level 4 on the standard scale; or both.	Maximum penalty will be increased to 51 weeks by section 280(2) and Schedule 26, paragraph 20 of the *CJA* 2003.
Section 21(4)	Contravention of provisions denying firearms to ex-prisoners and the like.	(*a*) Summary	6 months or a fine of £400; or both.	
		(*b*) On indictment	5 years of a fine; or both.	
Section 21(5)	Supplying firearms to person denied them under section 21.	(*a*) Summary	6 months or a fine of £400; or both.	
		(*b*) On indictment	5 years or a fine; or both.	
Section 22(1)	Person under 17 acquiring firearm.	Summary	6 months or a fine of level 5 on the standard scale; or both.	
Section 22(1A)	Person under 18 using certificated firearm for unauthorised purpose.	Summary	3 months or a fine of level 5 on the standard scale; or both.	Maximum penalty will be increased to 51 weeks by section 280(2) and Schedule 26, paragraph 20 of the *CJA* 2003.
Section 22(2)	Person under 14 having firearms in his possession without lawful authority.	Summary	6 months or a fine of level 5 on the standard scale; or both.	
Section 22(3)	Person under 15 having with him a shot gun without adult supervision.	Summary	A fine of level 3 on the standard scale	Paragraph 8 of Part II of this Schedule applies.
Section 22(4)	Person under 17 having with him an air weapon or ammunition therefor.	Summary	A fine of level 3 on the standard scale	Paragraphs 7 and 8 of Part II of this Schedule apply.

Section of this Act creating offence	General nature of offence	Mode of prosecution	Punishment	Additional provisions
Section 23(1)	Persons under 17 making improper use of air weapon when under supervision; person supervising him permitting such use.	Summary	A fine of level 3 on the standard scale	Paragraphs 7 and 8 of Part II of this Schedule apply.
Section 23(4)	Person under 17 making improper use of air weapon on private premises.	Summary	A fine of level 3 on the standard scale.	Paragraphs 7 and 8 of Part II of this Schedule apply.
Section 24(1)	Selling or letting on hire a firearm to person under 17.	Summary	6 months or a fine of level 5 on the standard scale; or both.	
Section 24(2)	Supplying firearm or ammunition (being of a kind to which section 1 of this Act applies) to person under 14.	Summary	6 months or a fine of level 5 on the standard scale; or both.	
Section 24(3)	Making gift of shot gun to person under 15.	Summary	A fine of level 3 on the standard scale	Paragraphs 9 of Part II of this Schedule applies.
Section 24(4)	Supplying air weapon to person under 17.	Summary	A fine of level 3 on the standard scale	Paragraphs 7 and 8 of Part II of this Schedule apply.
Section 25	Supplying firearm to person drunk or insane.	Summary	3 months or a fine of level 3 on the standard scale; or both.	Maximum penalty will be increased to 51 weeks by section 280(2) and Schedule 26, paragraph 20 of the *CJA* 2003.
Section 26(5)Section 28A(7)	Making false statement in order to procure grant or renewal of a firearm or shot gun certificate.	Summary	6 months or a fine of level 5 on the standard scale; or both.	
Section 29(3)	Making false statement in order to procure variation of a firearm certificate.	Summary	6 months or a fine of level 5 on the standard scale; or both.	
Section 30(4)Section 30D(3)	Failing to surrender certificate on revocation.	Summary	A fine of level 3 on the standard scale.	

Section of this Act creating offence	General nature of offence	Mode of prosecution	Punishment	Additional provisions
Section 32B(5)	Failure to surrender expired European firearms pass.	Summary	A fine of level 3 on the standard scale.	
Section 32C(6)	Failure to produce European firearms pass or Article 7 authority for variation or cancellation etc.; failure to notify loss or theft of firearm identified in pass or to produce pass for endorsement.	Summary	3 months or a fine of level 5 on the standard scale; or both.	Maximum penalty will be increased to 51 weeks by section 280(2) and Schedule 26, paragraph 20 of the *CJA* 2003.
Section 38(8)	Failure to surrender certificate of registration or register of transactions on removal of firearms dealer's name from from register.	Summary	A fine of level 3 on the standard scale	
Section 39(1)	Making false statement in order to secure registration or entry in register of a place of business.	Summary	6 months or a fine of level 5 on the standard scale; or both.	
Section 39(2)	Registered firearms dealer having place of business not entered in the register.	Summary	6 months or a fine of level 5 on the standard scale; or both.	
Section 39(3)	Non-compliance with condition of registration.	Summary	6 months or a fine of level 5 on the standard scale; or both.	
Section 40(5)	Non-compliance by firearms dealer with provisions as to register of transactions; making false entry in register.	Summary	6 months or a fine of level 5 on the standard scale; or both.	

Part III

Section of this Act creating offence	General nature of offence	Mode of prosecution	Punishment	Additional provisions
Section 42A	Failure to report transaction authorised by visitor's shot gun permit.	Summary …	3 months or a fine of level 5 on the standard scale; or both.	Maximum penalty will be increased to 51 weeks by section 280(2) and Schedule 26, paragraph 20 of the *CJA* 2003.
Section 46.	Obstructing constable or civilian officer in exercise of search powers.	Summary	6 months or a fine of level 5 on the standard scale; or both.	
Section 47(2)	Failure to hand over firearm or ammunition on demand by constable.	Summary	3 months, or a fine of level 4 on the standard scale; or both.	Maximum penalty will be increased to 51 weeks by section 280(2) and Schedule 26, paragraph 20 of the *CJA* 2003.
Section 48(3)	Failure to comply with requirement of a constable that a person shall declare his name and address.	Summary	A fine of level 3 on the standard scale.	
Section 48(4)	Failure to produce firearms pass issued in another member State.	Summary	A fine of level 3 on the standard scale.	
Section 49(3)	Failure to give constable facilities for examination of firearms in transit, or to produce papers.	Summary	3 months or, for each firearm or parcel of ammunition in respect of which the offence is committed, a fine of level 3 on the standard scale; or both.	Paragraph 2 of Part II of this Schedule applies. Maximum penalty will be increased to 51 weeks by section 280(2) and Schedule 26, paragraph 20 of the *CJA* 2003.
Section 52(2)(c)	Failure to surrender firearm or shot gun certificate cancelled by court on conviction.	Summary	A fine of level 3 on the standard scale	

PART II

SUPPLEMENTARY PROVISIONS AS TO TRIAL AND PUNISHMENT OF OFFENCES.

16–188   2. In the case of an offence against section 6(3) or 49(3) of this Act, the court before which the offender is convicted may, if the offender is the owner of the firearms or ammunition, make such order as to the forfeiture of the firearms or ammunition as the court thinks fit.

3.—(1) Where in England or Wales a person who has attained the age of seventeen is charged before a magistrates' court with an offence triable either way listed in Schedule 1 to the *Magistrates' Courts Act* 1980 ("the listed offence") and is also charged before that court with an offence under section 17(1) or (2) of this Act, the following provisions of this paragraph shall apply.

(2) Subject to the following sub-paragraph the court shall proceed as if the listed offence were triable only on indictment and sections 18 to 23 of the said Act of 1980 (procedure for determining mode of trial of offences triable either way) shall not apply in relation to that offence.

(3) If the court determines not to commit the accused for trial in respect of the offence under section 17(1) or (2), or if proceedings before the court for that offence are otherwise discontinued, the preceding sub-paragraph shall cease to apply as from the time when this occurs and—

(a) if at that time the court has not yet begun to inquire into the listed offence as examining justices, the court shall, in the case of the listed offence, proceed in the ordinary way in accordance with the said sections 18 to 23; but

(b) if at that time the court has begun so to inquire into the listed offence, those sections shall continue not to apply and the court shall proceed with its inquiry into that offence as examining justices, but shall have power in accordance with section 25(3) and (4) of the said Act of 1980 to change to summary trial with the accused's consent.

4. Where a person commits an offence under section 17(1) of this Act in respect of the lawful arrest or detention of himself for any other offence committed by him, he shall be liable to the penalty provided by Part I of this Schedule in addition to any penalty to which he may be sentenced for the other offence.

5. If on the trial of a person for an offence under section 17(1) of this Act the jury are not satisfied that he is guilty of that offence but are satisfied that he is guilty of an offence under section 17(2), the jury may find him guilty of the offence under section 17(2) and he shall then be punishable accordingly.

6. The punishment to which a person is liable for an offence under section 17(2) of this Act shall be in addition to any punishment to which he may be liable for the offence first referred to in section 17(2).

7. The court by which a person is convicted of an offence under section 22(4), 23(1) or 23(4) of this Act may make such order as it thinks fit as to the forfeiture or disposal of the air weapons or ammunition in respect of which the offence was committed.

8. The court by which a person is convicted of an offence under section 22(3) or (4), 23(1) or (4) may make such order as it thinks fit as to the forfeiture or disposal of any firearm or ammunition found in his possession.

9. The court by which a person is convicted of an offence under section 24(3) of this Act may make such order as it thinks fit as to the forfeiture or disposal of the shot gun or ammunition in respect of which the offence was committed.

This Schedule is printed as amended by the *Anti-Social Behaviour Act* 2003, s.38 and by the *Violent Crime Reduction Act* 2006, s.30(4). The amendments of VCRA are printed in square brackets. They came into force on April 6, 2007—see the *Violent Crime Reduction Act (Commencement Order No. 2)* (S.I. 2007 No. 858).

Note that after the commencement of the relevant provisions, the maximum custodial sentence in a magistrates' court will be 12 months' imprisonment: *Criminal Justice Act* 2003, ss.154 and 282. Custodial sentences of less than 12 months will consist of a custody plus order (see *post*, Ch.23).

B. Failure to Possess or to Purchase a Firearm or Shotgun Certificate

(1) Definition

Firearms Act 1968, ss.1–2

Requirement of firearms certificate.

1.—(1) Subject to any exemption under this Act, it is an offence for a person—   **16–189**

    (a) to have in his possession, or to purchase or acquire, a firearm to which this section applies without holding a firearm certificate in force at the time, or otherwise than as authorised by such a certificate;

    (b) to have in his possession, or to purchase or acquire, any ammunition to which this section applies without holding a firearm certificate in force at the time, or otherwise than as authorised by such a certificate, or in quantities in excess of those so authorised.

(2) It is an offence for a person to fail to comply with a condition subject to which a firearm certificate is held by him.

(3) This section applies to every firearm except—

    (a) a shot gun within the meaning of this Act, that is to say a smooth-bore gun (not being an air gun) which—

      (i) has a barrel not less than 24 inches in length and does not have any barrel with a bore exceeding 2 inches in diameter;

      (ii) either has no magazine or has a non-detachable magazine incapable of holding more than two cartridges; and

      (iii) is not a revolver gun; and

    (b) an air weapon (that is to say, an air rifle, air gun or air pistol which does not fall within section 5(1) and which is not of a type declared by rules made by the Secretary of State under section 53 of this Act to be specially dangerous).

(3A) A gun which has been adapted to have such a magazine as is mentioned in subsection (3)(a)(ii) above shall not be regarded as falling within that provision unless the magazine bears a mark approved by the Secretary of State for denoting that fact and that mark has been made, and the adaptation has been certified in writing as having been carried out in a manner approved by him, either by one of the two companies mentioned in section 58(1) of this Act or by such other person as may be approved by him for that purpose.

(4) This section applies to any ammunition for a firearm, except the following articles, namely:—

    (a) cartridges containing five or more shot, none of which exceeds 36 inch in diameter;

    (b) ammunition for an air gun, air rifle or air pistol; and

    (c) blank cartridges not more than one inch in diameter measured immediately in front of the rim or cannelure of the base of the cartridge.

Requirement of certificate for possession of shot guns.

16–190   **2.**—(1) Subject to any exemption under this Act, it is an offence for a person to have in his possession, or to purchase or acquire, a short gun without holding a certificate under this Act authorising him to possess shot guns.

(2) It is an offence for a person to fail to comply with a condition subject to which a shot gun certificate is held by him.

(2) Allocation

16–191   These offences are triable either way.

(3) Elements of the offence

16–192   The prosecution must prove that the defendant:

    — possesses or purchases or acquires a firearm OR any ammunition OR shotgun,

    — without a certificate or other authority.

This is an absolute offence: see *Waller* [1991] Crim.L.R. 381 where the Court of Appeal upheld the conviction of a defendent in possession of his friend's bag which he did not realise contained a firearm: *Steele* [1993] Crim.L.R. 298. An honest and reasonable belief that a certificate was not required is no defence: *Howells* [1977] Q.B. 614.

"Firearm" or "shotgun" are defined in section 1(3) and 1(3A), *ante*.

(4) Sentence

16–193   On summary conviction, the sentence can be six months' imprisonment or a fine of the prescribed sum. On commencement of the relevant provisions, the maximum custodial sentence in a magistrates' court will be 12 months' imprisonment: *Criminal Justice Act* 2003, ss.154 and 282. Custodial sentences of less than 12 months will consist of a custody plus order (see *post*, Ch.23).

C. Failure to Comply with Condition of Firearm or Shotgun Certificate

(1) Definition

Firearms Act 1968, s.1(2)

Requirement of firearms certificate

1.—(2) It is an offence for a person to fail to comply with a condition subject to which a **16–194** firearm certificate is held by him.

(2) Procedure

This offence is summary only. **16–195**

(3) Sentence

Sentence is six months' imprisonment or a fine on level 5. **16–196**

D. Carrying a Firearm in a Public Place

(1) Definition

Firearms Act 1968, s.19

Carrying firearm in a public place.

19. A person commits an offence if, without lawful authority or reasonable excuse (the proof **16–197** whereof lies on him) he has with him in a public place

    (a) a loaded shot gun,

    (b) an air weapon (whether loaded or not),

    (c) any other firearm (whether loaded or not) together with ammunition suitable for use in that firearm, or

    (d) an imitation firearm.

(2) Allocation

This offence is triable either way, unless the firearm is an air weapon, in which case it **16–198** is triable summarily only: section 51 and Schedule 6.

(3) Elements of the offence

The prosecution must prove that the defendant: **16–199**

— has the firearm with him,

— in a public place,

— without lawful authority or reasonable excuse (the proof of this lies on the defendant).

"Shotgun" is defined in section 1(3), *ante*.

"Imitation firearm": in *Bentham* [2005] 1 W.L.R. 1057 D had been convicted of possessing an imitation firearm during the course of a robbery contrary to the *Firearms Act* 1968, s.17(2). He had put his fingers inside his jacket during a robbery so as to give the appearance of having a gun. In dismissing his appeal, the CA had found that it did not matter whether the item was made of plastic, wood, or simply anorak fabric stiffened by a finger, if in the opinion of the jury at the relevant time, it had the appearance of a

Part III

firearm. The HL unanimously allowed the appeal. The definition of "imitation firearm" in section 57(4) of the Act meant that the offence in section 17(2) of the Act required an accused to be carrying a "thing" that was separate and distinct from himself and therefore capable of being possessed. An unsevered hand or finger was part of oneself and therefore could not be "possessed". Parliament had not created an offence of falsely pretending to have a firearm and although a purposive construction could have a valuable role where the meaning of a statutory provision was doubtful, it could not be relied upon to create an offence that Parliament had not created. The CA had erred in attaching importance to the impression made on the victim when deciding the issue of possession.

For trespassing with a firearm, see § 16–296.

(4) Sentence

16–200   On summary conviction, the sentence can be six months or a fine of the prescribed sum. On commencement of the relevant provisions, the maximum custodial sentence in a magistrates' court will be 12 months' imprisonment: *Criminal Justice Act* 2003, ss.154 and 282. Custodial sentences of less than 12 months will consist of a custody plus order (see *post*, Ch.23).

For sentence guidance, see *Avis* [1998] 1 Cr.App.R. 420.

E. Possession of Offensive Weapons

(1) Definition

Prevention of Crime Act 1953, s.1

Prohibition of the carrying of offensive weapons without lawful authority or reasonable excuse

16–201   **1.**—(1) Any person who without lawful authority or reasonable excuse, the proof whereof shall lie on him, has with him in any public place any offensive weapon shall be guilty of an offence, and shall be liable—

> (a) on summary conviction, to imprisonment for a term not exceeding six months or a fine not exceeding the prescribed sum or both;
>
> (b) on conviction on indictment, to imprisonment for a term not exceeding two years or a fine, or both.

(2) Where any person is convicted of an offence under subsection (1) of this section the court may make an order for the forfeiture or disposal of any weapon in respect of which the offence was committed.

(3) [...]

(4) In this section "public place" includes any highway and any other premises or place to which at the material time the public have or are permitted to have access, whether on payment or otherwise; and "offensive weapon" means any article made or adapted for use for causing injury to the person, or intended by the person having it with him for such use by him.

(2) Allocation

16–202   This offence is triable either way.

(3) Elements of the offence

16–203   The prosecution must prove that:

> — the defendant had an offensive weapon,
> — in his possession,
> — in a public place,
> — without lawful authority or reasonable excuse.

"Has with him"

16–204   The words "has with him in a public place" mean "knowingly has with him in any public place" it being for the prosecution to prove knowledge: *Cugullere* 45 Cr.App.R. 108, CCA. Once a person has something knowingly, he continues to have it until he does something to rid himself of it: *McCalla* 87 Cr.App.R. 372, CA. In *Glidewell* 163 J.P. 557, CA, it was held that forgetfulness could be a reasonable excuse; the defendant being a taxi driver who had not placed the relevant items in his car and who had intended to clear them out. The words "has with him" also denote something more than mere possession of the article: *McCalla* (*ante*) and *Daubney* (2000) 164 J.P. 519, CA.

Where a person uses an article offensively in a public place, the offensive use of the article is not conclusive of the question whether he had it with him as an offensive weapon within s.1(1): *Jura* [1954] 1 Q.B. 503, CA; *Veasey* [1999] Crim.L.R. 158, CA, (motorist assaulting horsewoman with Krooklock not necessarily guilty under section 1(1)); *C. v. DPP* [2002] Crim.L.R. 322, QBD (dog lead not an offensive weapon where its use on police officers was immediately preceded by detaching the lead from the dog.)

"Public place"

The definition in section 1(4) is the same as that in the *Firearms Act* 1968, the *Public Order Act* 1936 and the *Criminal Law Act* 1967. In *Knox v. Anderton* (1983) 76 Cr.App.R. 156, QBD the Divisional Court held that the justices were entitled to find that premises where there are no barriers or notices restricting access, such as the upper landing of a block of flats which could be entered by members of the public without hindrance, were a public place. Where access to the landing of a block of flats is restricted and can only be gained through the use of a key, security code, tenants intercom or caretaker, the landing will not be classified as a public place, access being dependant on the consent of the occupiers of the flats: *Williams v. DPP* (1992) 95 Cr.App.R. 415.   **16–205**

"Offensive weapon"

In *Simpson (C.)* 78 Cr.App.R. 115, CA, the Court identified two categories of offensive weapon: **16–206**

    (a) those made for use for causing injury to the person, *i.e.* offensive *per se* those adapted for such a purpose;

    (b) those not so made or adapted, but carried with the intention of causing injury to the person.

In the first two categories, the prosecution do not have to establish that the defendant had the weapon with him for the purpose of inflicting injury.

"Offensive per se"

In *Simpson* (*ante*) Lord Lane C.J. gave as instances of weapons offensive *per se* a bayonet, a stiletto or a handgun. Weapons which are manufactured for an innocent purpose are not offensive *per se*: *Petrie* (1961) 45 Cr.App.R. 72, CA (razor). Where there is doubt as to whether a weapon is an offensive weapon *per se*, the deciders of fact must have their attention drawn to the statutory definition, but determining whether any weapon is an offensive weapon is a matter of fact: *Williamson* (1978) 67 Cr.App.R. 35, CA.   **16–207**

"Adapted for use"

Whether an article falls into this category is a question of fact for the justices. Examples of weapons adapted for use include a bottle deliberately broken to attack the victim: *Simpson* (*ante*) and a potato with a razor blade inserted into it: *Williamson* (*ante*).   **16–208**

"Intended for use for causing injury"

Intention to use the weapon to cause injury must be proved for such an article to be categorised as an offensive weapon. It is for the prosecution to prove the element of intention: *Petrie* (1961) 1 W.L.R. 358. In *Patterson v. Block* (1984) 81 L.S.Gaz 2458, DC, the Court held that justices were entitled to find the requisite intention where the defendant had with him a lock knife for the purposes of self defence.   **16–209**

"Without lawful authority or reasonable excuse"

16–210   The burden of establishing lawful authority or reasonable excuse rests on the defendant. In *Bryan v. Mott* (1975) 62 Cr.App.R. 71, the Divisional Court held that the reference to lawful authority applies to those people who from time to time carry an offensive weapon as a matter of duty, for example a soldier with his rifle and a police officer with his truncheon.

The application of the excuse of self defence was explained by Lord Widgery C.J. in *Evans v. Hughes* 56 Cr.App.R. 813, DC where he said:

> "It may be a reasonable excuse for the carrying of an offensive weapon that the carrier is in anticipation of imminent attack and is carrying it for his own personal defence, but what is abundantly clear to my mind is that this Act never intended to sanction the permanent or constant carriage of an offensive weapon merely because of some constant or enduring supposed or actual threat or danger to the carrier."

(4) Sentence

16–211   When tried summarily, the maximum penalty for this offence is a term of imprisonment not exceeding six months, a fine not exceeding the prescribed sum or both. On commencement of the relevant provisions, the maximum custodial sentence in a magistrates' court will be 12 months' imprisonment: *Criminal Justice Act* 2003, ss.154 and 282. Custodial sentences of less than 12 months will consist of a custody plus order (see *post*, Ch.23).

The *Magistrates' Court Sentencing Guidelines* (2004) state:

> Aggravating factors include location of offence, group action or joint possession, racial aggravation, people put in fear/weapon brandished, planned use, very dangerous weapon, offence committed on bail, relevant previous convictions and any failure to respond to previous sentences.
>
> Mitigating factors include acting out of genuine fear, no attempt to use, not premeditated.
>
> **Guideline**: Is it so serious that only custody is appropriate?

16–212   A sentence of six months' imprisonment was held appropriate where the offender was convicted of possessing an offensive weapon (vegetable knife) and held two previous convictions for the same offence: *Shorter* (1988) 10 Cr.App.R.(S.) 4. In *Simpson* (1992) 13 Cr.App.R.(S.) 665, the offender was found in possession of an unopened flick knife with a three inch blade. He was sentenced to nine months' imprisonment. *Simpson* was distinguished in *Norman* (1995) 16 Cr.App.R.(S.) 848.

F. Having a Bladed Article in a Public Place

(1) Definition

Criminal Justice Act 1988, s.139

Offence of having article with blade or point in public place

16–213   **139.**—(1) Subject to subsections (4) and (5) below, any person who has an article to which this section applies with him in a public place shall be guilty of an offence.

(2) Subject to subsection (3) below, this section applies to any article which has a blade or is sharply pointed except a folding pocketknife.

(3) This section applies to a folding pocketknife if the cutting edge of its blade exceeds 3 inches.

(4) It shall be a defence for a person charged with an offence under this section to prove that he had good reason or lawful authority for having the article with him in a public place.

(5) Without prejudice to the generality of subsection (4) above, it shall be a defence for a person charged with an offence under this section to prove that he had the article with him—

    (a) for use at work;

    (b) for religious reasons; or

(c) as part of any national costume.

(6) A person guilty of an offence under subsection (1) above shall be liable

(a) on summary conviction, to imprisonment for a term not exceeding six months, or a fine not exceeding the statutory maximum, or both;

(b) on conviction on indictment, to imprisonment for a term not exceeding four years, or a fine, or both.

(7) In this section "public place" includes any place to which at the material time the public have or are permitted access, whether on payment or otherwise.

(8) This section shall not have effect in relation to anything done before it comes into force.

[This section is printed as amended by the *Violent Crime Reduction Act* 2006, s.42.]

(2) Allocation

This offence is triable either way.   **16–214**

(3) Elements of the offence

The prosecution must prove that: **16–215**

— the defendant had in his possession, in a public place,

— a bladed article, or article that was sharply pointed (folding pocketknifes being an exception under this section).

For the meaning of "has with him" see § 16–204, *ante*.

A lock-knife will not be classified as a folding pocketknife because it is not immediately foldable at all times: *Deegan* [1998] 2 Cr.App.R. 121, CA. "Blade": see *Brooker v. DPP* (2005) 169 J.P. 368; (2005) 169 J.P.N. 497. B had with him in a public place a blade from a butter knife which was 10cm long and had no handle, sharp edge or point. He appealed by way of case stated from the magistrates' decision that the butter knife constituted a blade and came within the ambit of section 139 of the 1988 *Act*. QBD (Admin) held that whilst a sharp blade or pointed article was the paradigm case to which section 139 of the 1988 Act was directed, the words of the Act were unqualified, and there was no rule that only sharp blades were caught: *Davis* [1998] Crim.L.R. 564 considered (concerning a screwdriver). It would create a great mischief if the Act was construed so as to invite argument, in case after case, as to whether or not the object in question was sharp. Section 139 of the 1988 Act was not enacted to fill a lacuna in the 1953 Act. The new provision was intended to complement the old.

The meaning of the phrases "good reason" and "for use at work" is to be determined by the jury, or justices when the offence is tried summarily: *Manning* [1998] Crim.L.R. 198.

(4) Defence

It shall be a defence for the accused to prove that he had the article with him for use   **16–216**
at work, for religious reasons or as part of any national costume: *Criminal Justice Act* 1988, s.139(4) and (5).

(5) Sentence

When tried summarily, the maximum penalty for this offence is imprisonment for a   **16–217**
term not exceeding six months, a fine of the prescribed sum or both: section 139(6)(a). On commencement of the relevant provisions, the maximum custodial sentence in a magistrates' court will be 12 months' imprisonment: *Criminal Justice Act* 2003, ss.154 and 282. Custodial sentences of less than 12 months will consist of a custody plus order (see *post*, Ch.23).

Part III

G. Having an Article with a Blade or Point (or Offensive Weapon) on School Premises

(1) Definition

Criminal Justice Act 1988, s.139A

Offence of having article with blade or point (or offensive weapon) on school premises

16–218   **139A.**—(1) Any person who has an article to which section 139 of this Act applies with him on school premises shall be guilty of an offence.

(2) Any person who has an offensive weapon within the meaning of section 1 of the *Prevention of Crime Act* 1953 with him on school premises shall be guilty of an offence.

(3) It shall be a defence for a person charged with an offence under subsection (1) or (2) above to prove that he had good reason or lawful authority for having the article or weapon with him on the premises in question.

(4) Without prejudice to the generality of subsection (3) above, it shall be a defence for a person charged with an offence under subsection (1) or (2) above to prove that he had the article or weapon in question with him—

  (a) for use at work,
  (b) for educational purposes,
  (c) for religious reasons, or
  (d) as part of any national costume.

(5) A person guilty of an offence—

  (a) under subsection (1) above shall be liable—
      (i) on summary conviction to imprisonment for a term not exceeding six months, or a fine not exceeding the statutory maximum, or both;
      (ii) on conviction on indictment, to imprisonment for a term not exceeding four years, or a fine, or both;
  (b) under subsection (2) above shall be liable—
      (i) on summary conviction, to imprisonment for a term not exceeding six months, or a fine not exceeding the statutory maximum, or both;
      (ii) on conviction on indictment, to imprisonment for a term not exceeding four years, or a fine, or both.

(6) In this section and section 139B, "school premises" means land used for the purposes of a school excluding any land occupied solely as a dwelling by a person employed at the school; and "school" has the meaning given by section 4 of the *Education Act* 1996

(7) [*Northern Ireland*]

[This section is printed as amended by the *Violent Crime Reduction Act*, s.42.]

(2) Allocation

16–219   This offence is triable either way.

(3) Elements of the offence

16–220   The prosecution must prove:
  — the defendant had an article to which section 139 of the *CJA* 1988 applies with him on school premises OR
  — the defendant had an offensive weapon within the meaning of section 1 of the *Prevention of Crime Act 1953* with him on school premises.

For the meaning of "has with him" see § 16–204, *ante*. For the meaning of "for good reason" and "for use at work", see § 16–215, *ante*.

(4) Defence

16–221   The defendant will have a defence if he can prove that he was carrying the article in question on the relevant premises for use at work, for educational purposes, for religious reasons or as part of any national costume: *CJA* 1988, s.139A(4).

(5) Sentence

When tried summarily, the offences carry a maximum punishment of six months'   **16–222**
imprisonment, a fine not exceeding the statutory maximum or both: *CJA* 1988,
s.139A(5). On commencement of the relevant provisions, the maximum custodial
sentence in a magistrates' court will be 12 months' imprisonment: *Criminal Justice Act*
2003, ss.154 and 282. Custodial sentences of less than 12 months will consist of a custody
plus order (see *post*, Ch.23).

V. OFFENCES UNDER THE KNIVES ACT 1997

A. Unlawful Marketing of Knives

(1) Definition

Knives Act 1997, ss.1–2

Unlawful marketing of knives
   1.—(1) A person is guilty of an offence if he markets a knife in a way which—   **16–223**
    (a) indicates, or suggests, that it is suitable for combat; or
    (b) is otherwise likely to stimulate or encourage violent behaviour involving the use
       of the knife as a weapon.
   (2) "Suitable for combat" and "violent behaviour" are defined in section 10.
   (3) For the purposes of this Act, an indication or suggestion that a knife is suitable for
combat may, in particular, be given or made by a name or description—
    (a) applied to the knife;
    (b) on the knife or on any packaging in which it is contained; or
    (c) included in any advertisement which, expressly or by implication, relates to the
       knife.
   (4) For the purposes of this Act, a person markets a knife if—
    (a) he sells or hires it;
    (b) he offers, or exposes, it for sale or hire; or
    (c) he has it in his possession for the purpose of sale or hire.
   (5) A person who is guilty of an offence under this section is liable—
    (a) on summary conviction to imprisonment for a term not exceeding six months or
       to a fine not exceeding the statutory maximum, or to both;
    (b) on conviction on indictment to imprisonment for a term not exceeding two years
       or to a fine, or to both.

Publications
   2.—(1) A person is guilty of an offence if he publishes any written, pictorial or other material   **16–224**
in connection with the marketing of any knife and that material—
    (a) indicates, or suggests, that the knife is suitable for combat; or
    (b) is otherwise likely to stimulate or encourage violent behaviour involving the use
       of the knife as a weapon.
   (2) A person who is guilty of an offence under this section is liable—
    (a) on summary conviction to imprisonment for a term not exceeding six months or
       to a fine not exceeding the statutory maximum, or to both;
    (b) on conviction on indictment to imprisonment for a term not exceeding two years
       or to a fine, or to both.

(2) Allocation

These offences are triable either way.   **16–225**

(3) Elements of the offence

Regarding the offence of unlawful marketing of knives, the prosecution must estab-   **16–226**
lish that:

Part III

— the defendant sold or hired, offered or exposed for sale or hire or had in his possession for the purpose of sale or hire a knife and,

— the manner in which he so marketed the knife indicates, or suggests that it is suitable for combat OR,

— is otherwise likely to stimulate or encourage violent behaviour involving the use of the knife as a weapon.

Regarding the offence of unlawful publication of materials in connection with the marketing of knives, the prosecution must prove that:

— the defendant published any written, pictorial or other material in connection with the marketing of any knife and

— that material suggests that the knife is suitable for combat OR

— is likely to stimulate or encourage violent behaviour involving the use of the knife as a weapon.

Knives Act 1997, s.10

Interpretation

16–227   **10.** In this Act—

"the court" means—

   (a) in relation to England and Wales or Northern Ireland, the Crown Court or a magistrate's court;
   (b) in relation to Scotland, the sheriff;

"knife" means an instrument which has a blade or is sharply pointed;

"marketing" and related expressions are to be read with section 1(4);

"publication" includes a publication in electronic form and, in the case of a publication which is, or may be, produced from electronic data, any medium on which the data are stored;

"suitable for combat" means suitable for use as a weapon for inflicting injury on a person or causing a person to fear injury;

"violent behaviour" means an unlawful act inflicting injury on a person or causing a person to fear injury.

(4) Defences

Knives Act 1997, ss.3–4

Exempt trades

16–228   **3.**—(1) It is a defence for a person charged with an offence under section 1 to prove that—

   (a) the knife was marketed—
      (i)   for use by the armed forces of any country;
      (ii) as an antique or curio; or
      (iii) as falling within such other category (if any) as may be prescribed;
   (b) it was reasonable for the knife to be marketed in that way; and
   (c) there were no reasonable grounds for suspecting that a person into whose possession the knife might come in consequence of the way in which it was marketed would use it for an unlawful purpose.

(2) It is a defence for a person charged with an offence under section 2 to prove that

   (a) the material was published in connection with marketing a knife—
      (i)   for use by the armed forces of any country;
      (ii) as an antique or curio; or
      (iii) as falling within such other category (if any) as may be prescribed;
   (b) it was reasonable for the knife to be marketed in that way; and
   (c) there were no reasonable grounds for suspecting that a person into whose possession the knife might come in consequence of the publishing of the material would use it for an unlawful purpose.

(3) In this section "prescribed" means prescribed by regulations made by the Secretary of State.

Other defences

4.—(1) It is a defence for a person charged with an offence under section 1 to prove that he did not know or suspect, and had no reasonable grounds for suspecting, that the way in which the knife was marketed—

    (a) amounted to an indication or suggestion that the knife was suitable for combat; or

    (b) was likely to stimulate or encourage violent behaviour involving the use of the knife as a weapon.

(2) It is a defence for a person charged with an offence under section 2 to prove that he did not know or suspect, and had no reasonable grounds for suspecting, that the material—

    (a) amounted to an indication or suggestion that the knife was suitable for combat; or

    (b) was likely to stimulate or encourage violent behaviour involving the use of the knife as a weapon.

(3) It is a defence for a person charged with an offence under section 1 or 2 to prove that he took all reasonable precautions and exercised all due diligence to avoid committing the offence

16–229

(5) Sentence

When tried summarily, the maximum penalty is six months' imprisonment, a fine not exceeding the prescribed sum, or both: section 1(5)(a) and section 2(2)(a). On commencement of the relevant provisions, the maximum custodial sentence in a magistrates' court will be 12 months' imprisonment: *Criminal Justice Act* 2003, ss.154 and 282. Custodial sentences of less than 12 months will consist of a custody plus order (see *post*, Ch.23).

16–230

B. Sale of Knives to persons under 16

(1) Definition

Criminal Justice Act 1988, s.141A

Sale of knives and certain articles with blade or point to persons under sixteen

141A.—(1) Any person who sells to a person under the age of sixteen years an article to which this section applies shall be guilty of an offence and liable on summary conviction to imprisonment for a term not exceeding six months, or a fine not exceeding level 5 on the standard scale, or both.

(2) Subject to subsection (3) below, this section applies to—

    (a) any knife, knife blade or razor blade,

    (b) any axe, and

    (c) any other article which has a blade or which is sharply pointed and which is made or adapted for use for causing injury to the person.

(3) This section does not apply to any article described in—

    (a) section 1 of the *Restriction of Offensive Weapons Act* 1959.

    (b) an order made under section 141(2) of this Act, or

    (c) an order made by the Secretary of State under this section.

(4) It shall be a defence for a person charged with an offence under subsection (1) above to prove that he took all reasonable precautions and exercised all due diligence to avoid the commission of the offence.

(5) The power to make an order under this section shall be exercisable by statutory instrument which shall be subject to annulment in pursuance of a resolution of either House of Parliament.

16–231

(2) Allocation

This offence is triable summarily.

16–232

(3) Elements of the offence

The prosecution must prove that:

16–233

— the defendant sold a person under the age of 16,

— any knife, knife blade or razor blade, any axe or any other article which has a blade or which is sharply pointed and which is made or adapted for use for causing injury to the person.

Regarding what constitutes an article made or adapted to cause injury, see section above.

(4) Defence

16–234   It will be a defence for the accused to establish that he took all reasonable precautions and exercised all due diligence to avoid the commission of the offence.

(5) Sentence

16–235   The maximum penalty for this offence is imprisonment for a term not exceeding six months, a fine not exceeding the level five on the standard scale or both. On commencement of the relevant provisions, the maximum custodial sentence in a magistrates' court will be 12 months' imprisonment: *Criminal Justice Act* 2003, ss.154 and 282. Custodial sentences of less than 12 months will consist of a custody plus order (see *post*, Ch.23).

C. OFFENCES RELATING TO THE MANUFACTURE OF OFFENSIVE WEAPONS

(1) General

16–236   The following four offences are all triable summarily only. They concern the manufacture, sale or hire of dangerous weapons, the manufacture, sale and hire of offensive weapons, the sale and letting of a crossbow to a person under 17, and the purchase and hiring of a crossbow by a person under 17.

(2) Legislation

Restriction of Offensive Weapons Act 1959, s.1

Penalties for offences in connection with dangerous weapons

16–237   **1.**—(1) Any person who manufactures, sells or hires or offers for sale or hire, or exposes or has in his possession for the purpose of sale or hire or lends to gives to any other person—

    (a) any knife which has a blade which opens automatically by hand pressure applied to a button, spring or other device in or attached to the handle of the knife, sometimes known as a "flick knife" or "flick gun"; or

    (b) any knife which has a blade which is released from the handle or sheath thereof by the force of gravity or the application of centrifugal force and which, when released, is locked in place by means of a button, spring, lever, or other device, sometimes known as a "gravity knife",

shall be guilty of an offence and shall be liable on summary conviction in the case of a first offence to imprisonment for a term not exceeding three months or to a fine not exceeding fifty pounds or to both such imprisonment and fine, and in the case of a second or subsequent offence to imprisonment for a term not exceeding six months or to a fine not exceeding two hundred pounds or to both such imprisonment and fine.

    (2) The importation of any such knife as is described in the foregoing subsection is hereby prohibited.

Criminal Justice Act 1988, s.141(1)

Offensive weapons

16–238   **141.**—(1) Any person who manufactures, sells or hires or offers for sale or hire, exposes or has in his possession for the purpose of sale or hire, or lends or gives to any other person, a weapon to which this section applies shall be guilty of an offence and liable on summary conviction to imprisonment for a term not exceeding six months or to a fine not exceeding level 5 on the standard scale or both.

This section applies to weapons listed by the Secretary of State in an order, and must not include any weapon subject to the *Firearms Act* 1968, or crossbows. The order currently in force is the *Criminal Justice Act 1988 (Offensive Weapons) Order* 1988 (S.I. 1988 No. 2019). See also the *Criminal Justice Act 1988 (Offensive Weapons) Order* 2002 (S.I. 2002 No. 1668) which adds the disguised knife to the list of specified weapons outlined in the 1988 Order.

Crossbows Act 1987, ss.1–2

Sale and letting on hire

1. A person who sells or lets on hire a crossbow or a part of a crossbow to a person under the age of seventeen is guilty of an offence, unless he believes him to be seventeen years of age or older and has reasonable ground for the belief.   **16–239**

Purchase and hiring

2. A person under the age of seventeen who buys or hires a crossbow or a part of a crossbow is guilty of an offence.   **16–240**

(3) Sentence

A person guilty of an offence under section 1 of the *Restriction of Offensive Weapons Act* 1959 is liable, in the case of a first offence, to imprisonment up to three months or to a fine of up to £50, or both; in the case of a subsequent offence, the maximum is six months' imprisonment or a fine of £200, or both. The maximum penalty for an offence under section 141 of the *Criminal Justice Act* 1988 is six months' imprisonment or a fine not exceeding level 5 on the standard scale, or both.   **16–241**

A person guilty of an offence under section 1 of the *Crossbows Act* 1987 is liable to imprisonment for a term not exceeding six months, to a fine not exceeding level five on the standard scale, or to both. The court may also make a forfeiture order regarding any crossbow or part of a crossbow in respect of which the offence was committed: s.6(1) and (3). A person guilty of an offence under section 2 is liable to a fine not exceeding level three on the standard scale. The court may also make a forfeiture order regarding any crossbow or part of a crossbow in respect of which the offence was committed: s.6(2) and (3). Note that, on commencement of the relevant provisions, the maximum custodial sentence in a magistrates' court will be 12 months' imprisonment: *Criminal Justice Act* 2003, ss.154 and 282. Custodial sentences of less than 12 months will consist of a custody plus order (see *post*, Ch.23).

VI. OFFENCES AFFECTING THE ENJOYMENT OF PROPERTY

A. Unlawful Eviction and Harassment of Occupier

(1) Definition

Protection from Eviction Act 1977, s.1

Unlawful eviction and harassment of occupier

1.—(1) In this section "residential occupier", in relation to any premises, means a person occupying the premises as a residence, whether under a contract or by virtue of any enactment or rule of law giving him the right to remain in occupation or restricting the right of any other person to recover possession of the premises.   **16–242**

(2) If any person unlawfully deprives the residential occupier of any premises of his occupation of the premises or any part thereof, or attempts to do so, he shall be guilty of an offence unless he proves that he believed, and had reasonable cause to believe, that the residential occupier had ceased to reside in the premises.

(3) If any person with intent to cause the residential occupier of any premises—

   (a) to give up the occupation of the premises or any part thereof; or

   (b) to refrain from exercising any right or pursuing any remedy in respect of the premises or part thereof;

does acts likely to interfere with the peace or comfort of the residential occupier or members of his household, or persistently withdraws or withholds services reasonably required for the occupation of the premises as a residence, he shall be guilty of an offence.

(3A) Subject to subsection (3B) below, the landlord of a residential occupier or an agent of the landlord shall be guilty of an offence if—

   (a) he does acts likely to interfere with the peace or comfort of the residential occupier or members of his household, or

   (b) he persistently withdraws or withholds services reasonably required for the occupation of the premises in question as a residence,

and (in either case) he knows, or has reasonable cause to believe, that that conduct is likely to cause the residential occupier to give up the occupation of the whole or part of the premises or to refrain from exercising any right or pursuing any remedy in respect of the whole or part of the premises.

(3B) A person shall not be guilty of an offence under subsection (3A) above if he proves that he had reasonable grounds for doing the acts or withdrawing or withholding the services in question.

(3C) In subsection (3A) above "landlord", in relation to a residential occupier of any premises, means the person who, but for—

   (a) the residential occupier's right to remain in occupation of the premises, or

   (b) a restriction on the person's right to recover possession of the premises,

     would be entitled to occupation of the premises and any superior landlord under whom that person derives title.

(4) A person guilty of an offence under this section shall be liable—

   (a) on summary conviction, to a fine not exceeding £400 or to imprisonment for a term not exceeding 6 months or to both;

   (b) on conviction on indictment, to a fine or to imprisonment for a term not exceeding 2 years or to both.

(5) Nothing in this section shall be taken to prejudice any liability or remedy to which a person guilty of an offence thereunder may be subject in civil proceedings.

(6) Where an offence under this section committed by a body corporate is proved to have been committed with the consent or connivance of, or to be attributable to any neglect on the part of, any director, manager or secretary or other similar officer of the body corporate or any person who was purporting to act in any such capacity, he as well as the body corporate shall be guilty of that offence and shall be liable to be proceeded against and punished accordingly.

(2) Allocation

16–243   These offences are triable either way.

(3) Elements of the offence

16–244   This section creates three offences. As regards the offence of unlawfully depriving the residential occupier of his occupation of the premises, the prosecution must prove that:

   — the defendant unlawfully deprived, or attempted to unlawfully deprive, the residential occupier (defined in s.1(1)) of his occupation of the premises; and

   — he did not believe, or have reasonable cause to believe that the residential occupier had ceased to reside in the premises.

As regards the offence of doing acts likely to interfere with the peace or comfort of the residential occupier, the prosecution must prove that:

   — the defendant intended to cause the residential occupier of any premises to give up his occupation of the premises or to refrain from exercising any right or pursuing any remedy in respect of the premises or part thereof; and

   — he did acts likely to interfere with the peace or comfort of the residential occupier or members of his household; OR

   — he persistently withdrew or withheld services reasonably required for the occupation of the premises as a residence.

As regards the offence of the landlord or agent of the landlord doings acts likely to interfere with the peace or comfort of the residential occupier, or withholding services, the prosecution must prove that:

— the defendant was the landlord, or agent of the landlord of the premises in question; and

— he did acts likely to interfere with the peace or comfort of the residential occupier or members of his household or persistently withdrew or withheld services reasonably required for the occupation of the premises in question as a residence; and

— he knew, or had reasonable cause to believe that such conduct is likely to cause the residential occupier to give up the occupation of the whole or part of the premises or to refrain from exercising any right or remedy in respect of the whole or part of the premises.

Whether the defendant believes, or has reasonable cause to believe that the residential occupier had ceased to reside in the premises are questions of fact for the jury (or justices when the offence is tried summarily): *Davidson-Acres* [1980] Crim.L.R. 50, CA.   **16–245**

In *Yuthiwattana* 80 Cr.App.R. 55, CA, the Court held that section 1(2) of the 1977 Act is concerned with eviction. The necessary eviction does not need to be permanent, but cases which would more accurately be described as "locking out" cases, where a person was shut out of premises for a short period of time but was allowed to remain in occupation of the premises would more accurately fall under subsection (3).

The offence under subsection (3) requires the necessary intention to cause the owner or occupier to give up occupation of the premises or to refrain from exercising any right or pursuing any remedy in respect of the premises. In *AMK (Property Management) Ltd* [1985] Crim.L.R. 600, CA, an appeal was successful because the trial judge had failed to make it clear that intent to cause the occupiers to leave was different from the consequences of building works being carried out being that the occupiers would have to leave. In *Schon v. Camden London Borough Council* (1986) 84 L.G.R. 830, it was held that whilst an intention to persuade the occupier to leave for a limited period of time would not establish an intention to cause her to leave the premises. It would however establish the intent required under the second limb of section 1(3) as it would be an intention to cause the occupier to refrain from exercising her right to live in and be physically present at the premises.

For examples of acts found to be likely to interfere with the peace and comfort of the occupier see *Yuthiwattana, ante,* (failure to provide a front door key as well as entering the occupier's room without permission, removing his record player and records and shouting at him).   **16–246**

(4) Defences

Section 1(2) of the 1977 Act makes it a defence to any eviction offence for the accused to prove that he believed, and had reasonable cause to believe that the residential occupier had ceased to reside in the premises. Section 1(3)(B) also provides a defence to a charge under subsection (3)(B) if the accused can prove that had reasonable grounds for doing the acts or withdrawing or withholding the services in question.   **16–247**

(5) Sentence

When tried summarily, the maximum punishment is a fine not exceeding the prescribed sum, imprisonment for a term not exceeding six months or both: *Protection From Eviction Act* 1977, s.1(4). Note that, on commencement of the relevant provisions, the maximum custodial sentence in a magistrates' court will be 12 months' imprisonment: *Criminal Justice Act* 2003, ss.154 and 282. Custodial sentences of less than 12 months will consist of a custody plus order (see *post*, Ch.23).   **16–248**

In *Pittard* (1994) 15 Cr.App.R.(S.) 108 the accused was convicted of unlawful eviction and interference with the peace and comfort of a residential occupier. He had let a house to a lady as a sole occupier. While she was away, he broke into the house, moved in, changed the locks and upon her return indicated his intention to stay in the house. His original sentence of a £600 in respect of each count and an order to pay £2000 towards the cost of the prosecution was reduced to a fine of £100, the costs order being upheld.

B. Use or Threat of Violence for the Purposes of Securing Entry to Premises

(1) Definition

Criminal Law Act 1977, s.6(1), (1A), (2), (4)

Violence for securing entry

16–249   **6.**—(1) Subject to the following provisions of this section, any person who, without lawful authority, uses or threatens violence for the purpose of securing entry into any premises for himself or for any other person is guilty of an offence, provided that—

         (a) there is someone present on those premises at the time who is opposed to the entry which the violence is intended to secure; and

         (b) the person using or threatening the violence knows that that is the case.

(1A) Subsection (1) above does not apply to a person who is a displaced residential occupier or a protected intending occupier of the premises in question or who is acting on behalf of such an occupier; and if the accused adduces sufficient evidence that he was, or was acting on behalf of, such an occupier he shall be presumed to be, or to be acting on behalf of, such an occupier unless the contrary is proved by the prosecution.

(2) Subject to subsection (1A) above, The fact that a person has any interest in or right to possession or occupation of any premises shall not for the purposes of subsection (1) above constitute lawful authority for the use or threat of violence by him or anyone else for the purpose of securing his entry into those premises.

(4) It is immaterial for the purposes of this section—

         (a) whether the violence in question is directed against the person or against property; and

         (b) whether the entry which the violence is intended to secure is for the purpose of acquiring possession of the premises in question or for any other purpose.

(2) Allocation

16–250   This is offence is triable summarily only: section 6(5).

Violence for securing entry.

     6.—(5) A person guilty of an offence under this section shall be liable on summary conviction to imprisonment for a term not exceeding six months or to a fine not exceeding level 5 on the standard scale or to both.

(3) Elements of the offence

16–251   The prosecution must establish that:

     — the defendant, without lawful authority, used or threatened violence for the purpose of securing entry into any premises; and

     — there is someone present on those premises at the time who is opposed to the entry which the violence is intended to secure; and

     — the defendant knew that this was the case.

16–252   It is immaterial whether the violence in question is directed against the person or against property: section 6(4)(a). Likewise, it is immaterial whether the entry which the violence is intended to secure is for the purpose of acquiring possession of the premises in question or for any other purpose: section 6(4)(b).

Key terms are defined in sections 12 and 12A of the 1977 Act.

Criminal Law Act 1977, ss.12, 12A(1)–(7)

Supplementary positions

12.—(1) In this Part of this Act—   **16–253**

(a) "premises" means any building, any part of a building under separate occupation, any land ancillary to a building, the site comprising any building or buildings together with any land ancillary thereto, and (for the purposes only of sections 10 and 11 above) any other place; and

(b) "access" means, in relation to any premises, any part of any site or building within which those premises are situated which constitutes an ordinary means of access to those premises (whether or not that is its sole or primary use).

(2) References in this section to a building shall apply also to any structure other than a movable one, and to any movable structure, vehicle or vessel designed or adapted for use for residential purposes; and for the purposes of subsection (1) above—

(a) part of a building is under separate occupation if anyone is in occupation or entitled to occupation of that part as distinct from the whole; and

(b) land is ancillary to a building if it is adjacent to it and used (or intended for use) in connection with the occupation of that building or any part of it.

(3) Subject to subsection (4) below, any person who was occupying any premises as a residence immediately before being excluded from occupation by anyone who entered those premises, or any access to those premises, as a trespasser is a displaced residential occupier of the premises for the purposes of this Part of this Act so long as he continues to be excluded from occupation of the premises by the original trespasser or by any subsequent trespasser.

(4) A person who was himself occupying the premises in question as a trespasser immediately before being excluded from occupation shall not by virtue of subsection (3) above be a displaced residential occupier of the premises for the purposes of this Part of this Act.

(5) A person who by virtue of subsection (3) above is a displaced residential occupier of any premises shall be regarded for the purposes of this Part of this Act as a displaced residential occupier also of any access to those premises.

(6) Anyone who enters or is on or in occupation of any premises by virtue of—

(a) any title derived from a trespasser; or

(b) any licence or consent given by a trespasser or by a person deriving title from a trespasser,

shall himself be treated as a trespasser for the purposes of this Part of this Act (without prejudice to whether or not he would be a trespasser apart from this provision); and references in this Part of this Act to a person's entering or being on or occupying any premises as a trespasser shall be construed accordingly.

(7) Anyone who is on any premises as a trespasser shall not cease to be a trespasser for the purposes of this Part of this Act by virtue of being allowed time to leave the premises, nor shall anyone cease to be a displaced residential occupier of any premises by virtue of any such allowance of time to a trespasser.

(7A) Subsection (6) also applies to the Secretary of State if the tenancy or licence is granted by him under Part III of the *Housing Associations Act* 1985.

(8) No rule of law ousting the jurisdiction of magistrates' courts to try offences where a dispute of title to property is involved shall preclude magistrates' courts from trying offences under this Part of this Act.

Protected intending occupiers: supplementary provisions

12A.—(1) For the purposes of this Part of this Act an individual is a protected intending oc-   **16–254**
cupier of any premises at any time if at that time he falls within subsection (2), (4) or (6) below.

(2) An individual is a protected intending occupier of any premises if—

(a) he has in those premises a freehold interest or a leasehold interest with not less than two years still to run;

(b) he requires the premises for his own occupation as a residence;

(c) he is excluded from occupation of the premises by a person who entered them, or any access to them, as a trespasser; and

(d) he or a person acting on his behalf holds a written statement—

(i) which specifies his interest in the premises;

767

    (ii) which states that he requires the premises for occupation as a residence for himself; and

    (iii) with respect to which the requirements in subsection (3) below are fulfilled.

(3) The requirements referred to in subsection (2)(d)(iii) above are—

 (a) that the statement is signed by the person whose interest is specified in it in the presence of a justice of the peace or commissioner for oaths; and

 (b) that the justice of the peace or commissioner for oaths has subscribed his name as a witness to the signature.

(4) An individual is also a protected intending occupier of any premises if—

 (a) he has a tenancy of those premises (other than a tenancy falling within subsection (2)(a) above or (6)(a) below) or a licence to occupy those premises granted by a person with a freehold interest or a leasehold interest with not less than two years still to run in the premises;

 (b) he requires the premises for his own occupation as a residence;

 (c) he is excluded from occupation of the premises by a person who entered them, or any access to them, as a trespasser; and

 (d) he or a person acting on his behalf holds a written statement—

    (i) which states that he has been granted a tenancy of those premises or a licence to occupy those premises;

    (ii) which specifies the interest in the premises of the person who granted that tenancy or licence to occupy ("the landlord");

    (iii) which states that he requires the premises for occupation as a residence for himself; and

    (iv) with respect to which the requirements in subsection (5) below are fulfilled.

(5) The requirements referred to in subsection (4)(d)(iv) above are—

 (a) that the statement is signed by the landlord and by the tenant or licensee in the presence of a justice of the peace or commissioner for oaths;

 (b) that the justice of the peace or commissioner for oaths has subscribed his name as a witness to the signatures.

(6) An individual is also a protected intending occupier of any premises if—

 (a) he has a tenancy of those premises (other than a tenancy falling within subsection (2)(a) or (4)(a) above) or a licence to occupy those premises granted by an authority to which this subsection applies;

 (b) he requires the premises for his own occupation as a residence;

 (c) he is excluded from occupation of the premises by a person who entered the premises, or any access to them, as a trespasser; and

 (d) there has been issued to him by or on behalf of the authority referred to in paragraph (a) above a certificate stating that—

    (i) he has been granted a tenancy of those premises or a licence to occupy those premises as a residence by the authority; and

    (ii) the authority which granted that tenancy or licence to occupy is one to which this subsection applies, being of a description specified in the certificate.

(7) Subsection (6) above applies to the following authorities—

 (a) any body mentioned in section 14 of the *Rent Act* 1977 (landlord's interest belonging to local authority etc.);

 (b) the Housing Corporation;

 (c) Housing for Wales and;

 (d) a registered social landlord within the meaning of the *Housing Act* 1985

(4) Sentence

16–255 The maximum penalty for this offence is imprisonment for a term not exceeding six months, a fine not exceeding level five on the standard scale or both: *Criminal Law Act* 1977, s.6(5). Note that, on commencement of the relevant provisions, the maximum custodial sentence in a magistrates' court will be 12 months' imprisonment: *Criminal Justice Act* 2003, ss.154 and 282. Custodial sentences of less than 12 months will consist of a custody plus order (see *post*, Ch.23).

C. ADVERSE OCCUPATION OF RESIDENTIAL PREMISES

(1) Definition

Criminal Law Act 1977, s.7(1)–(5), (7)

Adverse occupation of residential premises

7.—(1) Subject to the following provisions of this section and to section 12A(9) below, any **16–256** person who is on any premises as a trespasser after having entered as such is guilty of an offence if he fails to leave those premises on being required to do so by or on behalf of—

(a) a displaced residential occupier of the premises; or

(b) an individual who is a protected intending occupier of the premises.

(2) In any proceedings for an offence under this section it shall be a defence for the accused to prove that he believed that the person requiring him to leave the premises was not a displaced residential occupier or protected intending occupier of the premises or a person acting on behalf of a displaced residential occupier or protected intending occupier.

(3) In any proceedings for an offence under this section it shall be a defence for the accused to prove—

(a) that the premises in question are or form part of premises used mainly for non-residential purposes; and

(b) that he was not on any part of the premises used wholly or mainly for residential purposes.

(4) Any reference in the preceding provisions of this section to any premises includes a reference to any access to them, whether or not any such access itself constitutes premises, within the meaning of this Part of this Act.

(5) A person guilty of an offence under this section shall be liable on summary conviction to imprisonment for a term not exceeding six months or to a fine not exceeding level 5 on the standard scale or to both.

(7) Section 12 below contains provisions which apply for determining when any person is to be regarded for the purposes of this Part of this Act as a displaced residential occupier of any premises or of any access to any premises and section 12A below contains provisions which apply for determining when any person is to be regarded for the purposes of this Part of this Act as a protected intending occupier of any premises or of any access to any premises.

(2) Allocation

This offence is triable summarily: section 7(5).   **16–257**

(3) Elements of the offence

The prosecution must prove that: **16–258**

— the defendant entered the premises as a trespasser; and

— he was asked to leave the premises by a displaced residential occupier of the premises or by an individual who is a protected intending occupier of the premises; and

— he refused to leave.

For the meaning of "displaced residential occupier" and "protected intending occupier" see sections 12 and 12A of the 1977 Act, *ante*.

(4) Sentence

The maximum penalty is imprisonment for a term not exceeding six months, or a **16–259** fine not exceeding level five on the standard scale or both: section 7(5).

D. TRESPASSING DURING THE CURRENCY OF AN INTERIM POSSESSION ORDER

(1) Definition

Criminal Justice and Public Order Act 1994, s.76

Interim possession orders: trespassing during currency of order

16–260   **76.**—(1) This section applies where an interim possession order has been made in respect of any premises and served in accordance with rules of court; and references to "the order" and "the premises" shall be construed accordingly.

(2) Subject to subsection (3), a person who is present on the premises as a trespasser at any time during the currency of the order commits an offence.

(3) No offence under subsection (2) is committed by a person if—

    (a) he leaves the premises within 24 hours of the time of service of the order and does not return; or

    (b) a copy of the order was not fixed to the premises in accordance with rules of court.

(4) A person who was in occupation of the premises at the time of service of the order but leaves them commits an offence if he re-enters the premises as a trespasser or attempts to do so after the expiry of the order but within the period of one year beginning with the day on which it was served.

(5) A person guilty of an offence under this section shall be liable on summary conviction to imprisonment for a term not exceeding six months or a fine not exceeding level 5 on the standard scale or both.

(6) A person who is in occupation of the premises at the time of service of the order shall be treated for the purposes of this section as being present as a trespasser.

(7) A constable in uniform may arrest without a warrant anyone who is, or whom he reasonably suspects to be, guilty of an offence under this section.

(8) In this section—

    "interim possession order" has the same meaning as in section 75 above and "rules of court" is to be construed accordingly; and

    "premises" has the same meaning as in that section that is to say the same meaning as in Part II of the *Criminal Law Act* 1977 (offences relating to entering and remaining on property).

(2) Allocation

16–261   This offence is triable summarily only: *CJPOA* 1994, s.76(5).

(3) Elements of the offence

16–262   Regarding the offence of trespass, the prosecution must prove that:

    — the defendant was present on the premises as a trespasser,

    — during the currency of an interim possession order.

Regarding the offence of re-entering premises as a trespasser, the prosecution must prove that:

    — the defendant was in occupation of the premises at the time of service of the interim possession order and,

    — he then left the premises, and re-entered as a trespasser or attempted to re-enter the premises,

    — after the expiry of the order, but within one year of the date on which the order was served.

16–263   "Interim possession order" has the same meaning as in section 75(4) of the 1994 Act namely "an interim possession order made under rules of court for the bringing of summary proceedings for possession of premises which are occupied by trespassers."

By section 75(4) of the 1994 Act "premises" has the same meaning as in Part II of the *Criminal Law Act* 1977 (offences relating to entering and remaining on property) and "statement" in relation to an interim possession order means any statement, in writing or oral and whether as to fact or belief, made in or for the purpose of the proceedings.

(4) Defence

The accused will have a defence if he can establish that he left the premises within 24 **16–264** hours of the time of service of the order and does not return, or a copy of the order was not fixed to the premises in accordance with the rules of court: section 76(3).

(5) Sentence

The maximum penalty is a term of imprisonment not exceeding six months, a fine **16–265** not exceeding level 5 on the standard scale or both: *CJPOA* 1994, s.76(5). Note that, after commencement of the relevant provisions, the maximum custodial sentence in a magistrates' court will be 12 months' imprisonment: *Criminal Justice Act* 2003, ss.154 and 282. Custodial sentences of less than 12 months will consist of a custody plus order (see *post*, Ch.23).

E. Interim Possession Orders: False or Misleading Statements

(1) Definition

Criminal Justice and Public Order Act 1994, s.75

Interim possession orders: false or misleading statements

75.—(1) A person commits an offence if, for the purpose of obtaining an interim possession **16–266** order, he—

    (a) makes a statement which he knows to be false or misleading in a material particular; or

    (b) recklessly makes a statement which is false or misleading in a material particular.

(2) A person commits an offence if, for the purpose of resisting the making of an interim possession order, he—

    (a) makes a statement which he knows to be false or misleading in a material particular; or

    (b) recklessly makes a statement which is false or misleading in a material particular.

(3) A person guilty of an offence under this section shall be liable—

    (a) on conviction on indictment, to imprisonment for a term not exceeding two years or a fine or both;

    (b) on summary conviction, to imprisonment for a term not exceeding six months or a fine not exceeding the statutory maximum or both.

(4) In this section—

"interim possession order" means an interim possession order (so entitled) made under rules of court for the bringing of summary proceedings for possession of premises which are occupied by trespassers;

"premises" has the same meaning as in Part II of the *Criminal Law Act* 1977 (offences relating to entering and remaining on property); and

"statement", in relation to an interim possession order, means any statement, in writing or oral and whether as to fact or belief, made in or for the purposes of the proceedings.

(2) Allocation

This offence is triable either way: *CJPOA* 1994, s.75(3).   **16–267**

(3) Elements of the offence

The prosecution must prove that: **16–268**

  — the defendant knowingly or recklessly made a false or misleading statement,

  — for the purpose of obtaining an interim possession order or,

  — for the purpose of resisting the making of an interim possession order.

Criminal Justice and Public Order Act, s.75(4)

See § 16–266, *ante*.   **16–269**

(4) Sentence

16–270   When tried summarily, the maximum penalty is imprisonment for a term not exceeding six months or a fine not exceeding the statutory maximum or both: *CJPOA* 1994, s.75(3). Note that, on commencement of the relevant provisions, the maximum custodial sentence in a magistrates' court will be 12 months' imprisonment: *Criminal Justice Act* 2003, ss.154 and 282. Custodial sentences of less than 12 months will consist of a custody plus order (see *post*, Ch.23).

F. AGGRAVATED TRESPASS

(1) Definition

Criminal Justice and Public Order Act 1994, s.68(1)–(3), (5)

Offence of aggravated trespass

16–271   **68.**—(1) A person commits the offence of aggravated trespass if he trespasses on land in the open air and, in relation to any lawful activity which persons are engaging in or are about to engage in on that or adjoining land in the open air, does there anything which is intended by him to have the effect—

(a) of intimidating those persons or any of them so as to deter them or any of them from engaging in that activity,

(b) of obstructing that activity, or

(c) of disrupting that activity.

(2) Activity on any occasion on the part of a person or persons on land is "lawful" for the purposes of this section if he or they may engage in the activity on the land on that occasion without committing an offence or trespassing on the land.

(3) A person guilty of an offence under this section is liable on summary conviction to imprisonment for a term not exceeding three months or a fine not exceeding level 4 on the standard scale, or both.

(5) In this section "land" does not include—

(a) the highways and roads excluded from the application of section 61 by paragraph (b) of the definition of land in subsection (9) of that section; or

(b) a road within the meaning of the *Roads (Northern Ireland) Order* 1993.

(2) Allocation

16–272   The offence is triable summarily: *CJPOA* 1994, s.68(3).

(3) Elements of the offence

16–273   The prosecution must prove that:

— the defendant trespasses on land in the open air and,

— does something which is intended to intimidate, obstruct or disrupt,

— the lawful activities of people on the land.

"Lawful activity"

16–274   By section 68(2) an activity is lawful if the persons engaged in it may do so without committing an offence or trespassing on the land. The persons engaged in the lawful activity must be physically present on the land: *Tilly v. DPP* [2002] Crim.L.R. 128. See *ante*, § 12–91 for comments on *Jones* [2005] Q.B. 259 and *Ayliffe v. DPP* [2005] 3 W.L.R. 628; [2005] Crim.L.R. 959.

Disruption

16–275   Where the charge is under section 68(1)(c) an intention to disrupt the lawful activity must be proved, yet actual disruption need not be established. In *Winder v. DPP* (1996) 160 J.P. 713 when trespassers ran towards a hunt without actually disrupting it, the requisite intention to disrupt was found to be present and a charge under section 68(1)(c) could proceed.

(4) Sentence

The maximum penalty is a term of imprisonment not exceeding three months or a **16–276** fine not exceeding level four on the standard scale or both: *CJPOA* 1994, s.68(3). Note that, on commencement of the relevant provisions, the maximum custodial sentence in a magistrates' court will be 12 months' imprisonment: *Criminal Justice Act* 2003, ss.154 and 282. Custodial sentences of less than 12 months will consist of a custody plus order (see *post*, Ch.23).

G. FAILURE TO LEAVE OR RE-ENTRY TO LAND AFTER POLICE DIRECTION TO LEAVE

(1) Definition

Criminal Justice and Public Order Act 1994, s.61(4)

Power to remove trespassers on land

61.—(4) If a person knowing that a direction under subsection (1) above has been given **16–277** which applies to him—

(a) fails to leave the land as soon as reasonably practicable, or

(b) having left again enters the land as a trespasser within the period of three months beginning with the day on which the direction was given,

he commits an offence and is liable on summary conviction to imprisonment for a term not exceeding three months or a fine not exceeding level 4 on the standard scale, or both.

(2) Allocation

This offence is triable summarily: *CJPOA* 1994 s.61(4).   **16–278**

(3) Elements of the offence

The prosecution must prove that: **16–279**

— the defendant knew that a police direction to leave had been given to him,

— he then failed to leave the land as soon as was practicable or,

— he left the land, and then re-entered as a trespasser within a period of three months from the date on which the direction to leave was given.

A direction to leave must be given before the offence under section 61 can be committed.

Criminal Justice and Public Order Act 1994, s.61(1)

Power to remove trespassers on land

61.—(1) If the senior police officer present at the scene reasonably believes that two or more **16–280** persons are trespassing on land and are present there with the common purpose of residing there for any period, that reasonable steps have been taken by or on behalf of the occupier to ask them to leave and—

(a) that any of those persons has caused damage to the land or to property on the land or used threatening, abusive or insulting words or behaviour towards the occupier, a member of his family or an employee or agent of his, or

(b) that those persons have between them six or more vehicles on the land,

he may direct those persons, or any of them, to leave the land and to remove any vehicles or other property they have with them on the land.

A direction under section 61 cannot be issued until the trespassers have failed to **16–281** comply with steps taken by the occupier to ask them to leave. *R. (Fuller) v. Chief Constable of Dorset* [2003] Q.B. 480 held that a section 61 direction was invalid when given at the same time as instructions to leave the premises. The purported section 61 notice was also held to be invalid as it required vacation in two days' time, a section 61 notice can only direct immediate vacation of a site.

Key terms are defined in section 61(9) of the 1994 Act.

Criminal Justice and Public Order Act 1994, s.61(9), (1)

Power to remove trespassers on land

16–282   **61.**—(9) In this section—

"common land" means common land as defined in section 22 of the *Commons Registration Act* 1965;

"commoner" means a person with rights of common as defined in section 22 of the *Commons Registration Act* 1965;

"land" does not include—

(a) buildings other than—

(i) agricultural buildings within the meaning of, in England and Wales, paragraphs 3 to 8 of Schedule 5 to the *Local Government Finance Act* 1988 or, in Scotland, section 7(2) of the *Valuation and Rating (Scotland) Act* 1956, or

(ii) scheduled monuments within the meaning of the *Ancient Monuments and Archaeological Areas Act* 1979;

(b) land forming part of—

(i) a highway unless it falls within the classifications in section 54 of the *Wildlife and Countryside Act* 1981 (footpath, bridleway or byway open to all traffic or road used as a public path) or is a cycle track under the *Highways Act* 1980 or the *Cycle Tracks Act* 1984; or

(ii) a road within the meaning of the *Roads (Scotland) Act* 1984 unless it falls within the definitions in section 151(2)(a)(ii) or (b) (footpaths and cycle tracks) of that Act or is a bridleway within the meaning of section 47 of the *Countryside (Scotland) Act* 1967;

"the local authority", in relation to common land, means any local authority which has powers in relation to the land under section 9 of the *Commons Registration Act* 1965;

"occupier" (and in subsection (8) "the other occupier") means—

(a) in England and Wales, the person entitled to possession of the land by virtue of an estate or interest held by him; and

(b) in Scotland, the person lawfully entitled to natural possession of the land;

"property", in relation to damage to property on land, means—

(a) in England and Wales, property within the meaning of section 10(1) of the *Criminal Damage Act* 1971; and

(b) in Scotland, either—

(i) heritable property other than land; or

(ii) corporeal movable property, and

"damage" includes the deposit of any substance capable of polluting the land;

"trespass" means, in the application of this section—

(a) in England and Wales, subject to the extensions effected by subsection (7) above, trespass as against the occupier of the land;

(b) in Scotland, entering, or as the case may be remaining on, land without lawful authority and without the occupier's consent; and

"trespassing" and "trespasser" shall be construed accordingly;

"vehicle" includes—

(a) any vehicle, whether or not it is in a fit state for use on roads, and includes any chassis or body, with or without wheels, appearing to have formed part of such a vehicle, and any load carried by, and anything attached to, such a vehicle; and

(b) a caravan as defined in section 29(1) of the *Caravan Sites and Control of Development Act* 1960;

and a person may be regarded for the purposes of this section as having a purpose of residing in a place notwithstanding that he has a home elsewhere.

Power to remove trespassers on land

16–283   **61.**—(1) If the senior police officer present at the scene reasonably believes that two or more persons are trespassing on land and are present there with the common purpose of residing there for any period, that reasonable steps have been taken by or on behalf of the occupier to ask them to leave and—

    (a) that any of those persons has caused damage to the land or to property on the land or used threatening, abusive or insulting words or behaviour towards the occupier, a member of his family or an employee or agent of his, or

    (b) that those persons have between them six or more vehicles on the land,

he may direct those persons, or any of them, to leave the land and to remove any vehicles or other property they have with them on the land.

(4) Defence

The accused will have a defence if he can show that he was not trespassing on the **16–284** land, or that he had a reasonable excuse for failing to leave the land as soon as reasonably practicable or, as the case may be, for again entering the land as a trespasser: *CJPOA* 1994, s.61(6).

(5) Sentence

The maximum penalty is imprisonment for a term not exceeding three months or a **16–285** fine not exceeding level 4 on the standard scale or both: section 61(4). Note that, on commencement of the relevant provisions, the maximum custodial sentence in a magistrates' court will be 12 months' imprisonment: *Criminal Justice Act* 2003, ss.154 and 282. Custodial sentences of less than 12 months will consist of a custody plus order (see *post*, Ch.23).

H. Failure to Leave Land or Re-Entry to Land: Raves

(1) Definition

Criminal Justice and Public Order Act 1994, s.63

Powers to remove persons attending or preparing for a rave

    63.—(1) This section applies to a gathering on land in the open air of 20 or more persons **16–286** (whether or not trespassers) at which amplified music is played during the night (with or without intermissions) and is such as, by reason of its loudness and duration and the time at which it is played, is likely to cause serious distress to the inhabitants of the locality; and for this purpose—

    (a) such a gathering continues during intermissions in the music and, where the gathering extends over several days, throughout the period during which amplified music is played at night (with or without intermissions); and

    (b) "music" includes sounds wholly or predominantly characterised by the emission of a succession of repetitive beats.

    (1A) This section also applies to a gathering if–

    (a) it is a gathering on land of 20 or more persons who are trespassing on the land; and

    (b) it would be a gathering of a kind mentioned in subsection (1) above if it took place on land in the open air.

    (2) If, as respects any land, a police officer of at least the rank of superintendent reasonably believes that—

    (a) two or more persons are making preparations for the holding there of a gathering to which this section applies,

    (b) ten or more persons are waiting for such a gathering to begin there, or

    (c) ten or more persons are attending such a gathering which is in progress,

he may give a direction that those persons and any other persons who come to prepare or wait for or to attend the gathering are to leave the land and remove any vehicles or other property which they have with them on the land.

    (3) A direction under subsection (2) above, if not communicated to the persons referred to in subsection (2) by the police officer giving the direction, may be communicated to them by any constable at the scene.

    (4) Persons shall be treated as having had a direction under subsection (2) above communicated to them if reasonable steps have been taken to bring it to their attention.

(5) A direction under subsection (2) above does not apply to an exempt person.

(6) If a person knowing that a direction has been given which applies to him—

    (a) fails to leave the land as soon as reasonably practicable, or

    (b) having left again enters the land within the period of 7 days beginning with the day on which the direction was given,

he commits an offence and is liable on summary conviction to imprisonment for a term not exceeding three months or a fine not exceeding level 4 on the standard scale, or both.

(7) In proceedings for an offence under this section it is a defence for the accused to show that he had a reasonable excuse for failing to leave the land as soon as reasonably practicable or, as the case may be, for again entering the land.

(8) A constable in uniform who reasonably suspects that a person is committing an offence under this section may arrest him without a warrant.

(9) This section does not apply—

    (a) in England and Wales, to a gathering licensed by an entertainment licence; or

    (b) [Scotland]

(10) In this section—

    "entertainment licence" means a licence granted by a local authority under—

        (a) Schedule 12 to the *London Government Act* 1963;

        (b) section 3 of the *Private Places of Entertainment (Licensing) Act* 1967; or

        (c) Schedule 1 to the *Local Government (Miscellaneous Provisions) Act* 1982;

    "exempt person", in relation to land (or any gathering on land), means the occupier, any member of his family and any employee or agent of his and any person whose home is situated on the land;

    "land in the open air" includes a place partly open to the air;

    "local authority" means—

        (a) in Greater London, a London borough council or the Common Council of the City of London;

        (b) in England outside Greater London, a district council or the council of the Isles of Scilly;

        (c) in Wales, a county council or county borough council; and

    "occupier", "trespasser" and "vehicle" have the same meaning as in section 61.

(11) Until 1st April 1996, in this section "local authority" means, in Wales, a district council.

(2) Allocation

16–287   This offence is triable summarily: *CJPOA* 1994, s.63(6).

(3) Elements of the offence

16–288   The prosecution must prove that:

    — the relevant gathering is one to which section 63(1) applies,

    — the defendant knew that a police direction to leave had been issued to him, and

    — he failed to leave the land as soon as was reasonably practicable or,

    — he left the land, and then re-entered as a trespasser within a period of seven days from the date on which the direction to leave was given.

A direction under section 63(2) may be communicated by any constable at the scene (section 63(3)) and persons shall be treated as having had a direction under subsection (2) above communicated to them if reasonable steps have been taken to bring it to their attention (section 63(4)).

Section 63(5) establishes that a direction given under subsection (2) will not apply to an "exempt person". Such a person is defined by section 63(10) as "the occupier, any member of his family and any employee or agent of his and any person whose home is situated on the land." By section 63(9) the section does not apply to a gathering licensed by an entertainment licence.

(4) Defence

16–289   A person will also have a defence if he can establish that he had a reasonable excuse for failing to leave the land as soon as reasonably practicable or, as the case may be, for again entering the land: section 63(7).

(5) Sentence

The maximum penalty is imprisonment for a term not exceeding three months or a **16–290** fine not exceeding level four on the standard scale or both: *CJPOA* 1994, s.63(6).

A forfeiture order may be imposed under section 66(1) of the 1994 Act where a person has been convicted of this offence and the court is satisfied that sound equipment which has been seized from him under section 64(4) or which was in his possession or under his control at the relevant time, has been used at the gathering.

I. UNAUTHORISED CAMPERS: FAILURE TO LEAVE OR RETURNING TO THE LAND

(1) Definition

Criminal Justice and Public Order Act 1994, s.77

Power of local authority to direct unauthorised campers to leave land

77.—(1) If it appears to a local authority that persons are for the time being residing in a ve- **16–291** hicle or vehicles within that authority's area—

(a) on any land forming part of a highway;

(b) on any other unoccupied land; or

(c) on any occupied land without the consent of the occupier,

the authority may give a direction that those persons and any others with them are to leave the land and remove the vehicle or vehicles and any other property they have with them on the land.

(2) Notice of a direction under subsection (1) must be served on the persons to whom the direction applies, but it shall be sufficient for this purpose for the direction to specify the land and (except where the direction applies to only one person) to be addressed to all occupants of the vehicles on the land, without naming them.

(3) If a person knowing that a direction under subsection (1) above has been given which applies to him—

(a) fails, as soon as practicable, to leave the land or remove from the land any vehicle or other property which is the subject of the direction, or

(b) having removed any such vehicle or property again enters the land with a vehicle within the period of three months beginning with the day on which the direction was given,

he commits an offence and is liable on summary conviction to a fine not exceeding level 3 on the standard scale.

(4) A direction under subsection (1) operates to require persons who re-enter the land within the said period with vehicles or other property to leave and remove the vehicles or other property as it operates in relation to the persons and vehicles or other property on the land when the direction was given.

(5) In proceedings for an offence under this section it is a defence for the accused to show that his failure to leave or to remove the vehicle or other property as soon as practicable or his re-entry with a vehicle was due to illness, mechanical breakdown or other immediate emergency.

(6) In this section—

"land" means land in the open air;

"local authority" means—

(a) in Greater London, a London borough or the Common Council of the City of London;

(b) in England outside Greater London, a county council, a district council or the Council of the Isles of Scilly;

(c) in Wales, a county council or a county borough council;

"occupier" means the person entitled to possession of the land by virtue of an estate or interest held by him;

"vehicle" includes—

(a) any vehicle, whether or not it is in a fit state for use on roads, and includes any body, with or without wheels, appearing to have formed part of such a vehicle, and any load carried by, and anything attached to, such a vehicle; and

(b) a caravan as defined in section 29(1) of the *Caravan Sites and Control of Development Act* 1960;

and a person may be regarded for the purposes of this section as residing on any land notwithstanding that he has a home elsewhere.

(7) Until 1st April 1996, in this section "local authority" means, in Wales, a county council or a district council.

(2) Allocation

16–292   This offence is triable summarily only: *CJPOA* 1994, s.77(3).

(3) Elements of the offence

16–293   The prosecution must prove that:

— the local council issued a direction to leave the land to the defendant and,

— the defendant failed to leave the land, or remove any vehicle from the land that formed the subject matter of the local council's direction as soon as was reasonably practicable, or

— the defendant had removed any relevant vehicle or property and then re-entered the land within a period of three months beginning at the date at which the direction was given.

A direction to leave the land must be given before the offence can be committed: *CJPOA* 1994, s.77(1).

(4) Defence

16–294   The accused will have a defence if he can establish that his failure to leave or to remove the vehicle or other property as soon as practicable or his re-entry with a vehicle was due to illness, mechanical breakdown or other immediate emergency: section 77(5).

(5) Sentence

16–295   The maximum penalty is a fine not exceeding level three on the standard scale: *CJPOA* 1994, s.77(3).

J. Trespassing with Firearm in Building or on Land

(1) Definition

Firearms Act 1968, s.20(1), (2)

Trespassing with firearm

16–296   **20.**—(1) A person commits an offence if, while he has a firearm or imitation firearm with him, he enters or is in any building or part of a building as a trespasser and without reasonable excuse (the proof whereof lies on him).

(2) A person commits an offence if, while he has a firearm with him, he enters or is on any land as a trespasser and without reasonable excuse (the proof whereof lies on him).

[This section is printed as amended by the *Firearms (Amendment) Act* 1994, s.2.]

(2) Allocation

16–297   The offence of trespassing with a firearm in a building is triable either way, unless the weapon concerned is an air weapon or an imitation firearm, in which case the offence is summary only. The mode of trial for trespassing on any land with a firearm is summary only.

(3) Elements of the offence

The prosecution must prove that: **16–298**
— the defendant entered any building, part of a building or land as a trespasser
   and without reasonable excuse and,
— was carrying a firearm or imitation firearm with him.

The term "firearm" is defined in section 57 of the *Firearms Act* 1968 as a lethal bar-
relled weapon of any description from which any shot, bullet or other missile can be
discharged, and includes:

(a) any prohibited weapon, whether it is such a lethal weapon as aforesaid or not;
    and

(b) any component part of such a lethal or prohibited weapon; and

(c) any accessory to any such weapon designed or adapted to diminish the noise or
    flash caused by firing the weapon.

The *Firearms Act* 1968, s.20(3) defines "land" as including land covered by water. **16–299**
The offender must be proved to have the firearm with him, which denotes more than
mere possession, and involves a very close physical link and a degree of immediate
control over the weapon by the man alleged to have the firearm with him: *Kelt* [1977] 3
All E.R. 1099, CA.

(4) Sentence

When tried summarily, the offence of trespassing in a building with a firearm is pun- **16–300**
ishable by a term of imprisonment not exceeding six months or a fine not exceeding the
prescribed sum or both. The offence of trespassing with a firearm on any land is punishable with a term of imprisonment not exceeding three months and a fine not exceeding level four on the standard scale. Note that, on commencement of the relevant provisions, the maximum custodial sentence in a magistrates' court will be 12 months'
imprisonment: *Criminal Justice Act* 2003, ss.154 and 282. Custodial sentences of less
than 12 months will consist of a custody plus order (see *post*, Ch.23).

K. Trespassing with Weapons of Offence

(1) Definition

Criminal Law Act 1977, s.8(1)

Trespassing with a weapon of offence
8.—(1) A person who is on any premises as a trespasser, after having entered as such, is guilty **16–301**
of an offence if, without lawful authority or reasonable excuse, he has with him on the premises
any weapon of offence.

(2) Allocation

This offence is triable summarily: *CLA* 1977, s.8(3).   **16–302**

(3) Elements of the offence

The prosecution must prove that: **16–303**
— the defendant entered and was present on any premises as a trespasser and
— without any lawful authority or reasonable excuse, he had with him on the
   premises any weapon of offence.

The term "premises" bears the same meaning as it does in *Criminal Law Act* 1977,
s.12.

Section 8(2) defines "weapon of offence" as any article made or adapted for causing
injury to or incapacitating a person, or intended by the person having it with him for
such use.

(4) Sentence

16–304   The maximum penalty for this offence is six months' imprisonment, a fine not exceeding level 5 on the standard scale or both: *CLA* 1977, s.8(3). Note that, on commencement of the relevant provisions, the maximum custodial sentence in a magistrates' court will be 12 months' imprisonment: *Criminal Justice Act* 2003, ss.154 and 282. Custodial sentences of less than 12 months will consist of a custody plus order (see *post*, Ch.23).

L. OBSTRUCTION OF COURT OFFICERS EXECUTING PROCESS AGAINST UNAUTHORISED OCCUPIERS

(1) Definition

Criminal Law Act 1977, s.10(1)–(3)

Obstruction of enforcement officers and court officers executing High Court or county court process

16–305   **10.**—(1) Without prejudice to section 8(2) of the *Sheriffs Act* 1887 but subject to the following provisions of this section, a person is guilty of an offence if he resists or intentionally obstructs any person who is in fact an officer of a court engaged in executing any process issued by the High Court or by any county court for the purpose of enforcing any judgment or order for the recovery of any premises or for the delivery of possession of any premises.

(2) Subsection (1) above does not apply unless the judgment or order in question was given or made in proceedings brought under any provisions of rules of court applicable only in circumstances where the person claiming possession of any premises alleges that the premises in question are occupied solely by a person or persons (not being a tenant or tenants holding over after the termination of the tenancy) who entered into or remained in occupation of the premises without the licence or consent of the person claiming possession or any predecessor in title of his.

(3) In any proceedings for an offence under this section it shall be a defence for the accused to prove that he believed that the person he was resisting or obstructing was not an officer of a court.

(2) Allocation

16–306   This offence is triable summarily: *CLA* 1977, s.10(4).

(3) Elements of the offence

16–307   The prosecution must prove that:
— the defendant resisted, or intentionally obstructed any officer of the court who,
— was executing any process for the purpose of enforcing any judgement or order for the recovery of premises or the delivery of possession of any premises.

An "officer of the court" is defined as any sheriff, under sheriff, deputy sheriff, bailiff or officer of a sheriff and any bailiff or other person who is an officer of a county court within the meaning of the *County Courts Act* 1959, s.10(6).

For the definition of "premises" see *Criminal Law Act* 1977, s.12.

(4) Defence

16–308   The accused will have a defence if he can prove that he believed that the person he was restricting or obstructing was not an officer of the court: section 10(3).

(5) Sentence

16–309   The maximum penalty for this offence is imprisonment for a term not exceeding six months, a fine not exceeding level five on the standard scale, or both: *CLA* 1977, s.10(4).

Note that, on commencement of the relevant provisions, the maximum custodial sentence in a magistrates' court will be 12 months' imprisonment: *Criminal Justice Act* 2003, ss.154 and 282. Custodial sentences of less than 12 months will consist of a custody plus order (see *post*, Ch.23).

M. PUBLIC ORDER AND CONDUCT IN PUBLIC PLACES

(1) Definition

Serious Organised Crime and Police Act 2005, s.128

Offence of trespassing on a designated site
128.—(1) A person commits an offence if he enters, or is on, any designated site in England **16–310** and Wales or Northern Ireland as a trespasser.

(2) A "designated site" means a site—

(a) specified or described (in any way) in an order made by the Secretary of State, and

(b) designated for the purposes of this section by the order.

(3) The Secretary of State may only designate a site for the purposes of this section—

(a) it is comprised in Crown land; or

(b) it is comprised in land belonging to Her Majesty in Her private capacity or to the immediate heir to the Throne in his private capacity; or

(c) it appears to the Secretary of State that it is appropriate to designate the site in the interests of national security.

(4) It is a defence for a person charged with an offence under this section to prove that he did not know, and had no reasonable cause to suspect, that the site in relation to which the offence is alleged to have been committed was a designated site.

(5) [...]

(6) [...]

(7) For the purposes of this section a person who is on any designated site as a trespasser does not cease to be a trespasser by virtue of being allowed time to leave the site.

(8) In this section—

(a) "site" means the whole or part of any building or buildings, or any land, or both;

(b) "Crown land" means land in which there is a Crown interest or a Duchy interest.

(9) For this purpose—

"Crown interest" means an interest belonging to Her Majesty in right of the Crown, and

"Duchy interest" means an interest belonging to Her Majesty in right of the Duchy of Lancaster or belonging to the Duchy of Cornwall.

(2) Allocation

No proceedings for an offence under this section may be instituted against any **16–311** person, except by or with the consent of the Attorney General.

(3) Sentence

A person guilty of an offence under section 128 is liable on summary conviction to **16–312** imprisonment for a term not exceeding 51 weeks, or to a fine not exceeding level 5 on the standard scale, or to both.

VII. MISCELLANEOUS OFFENCES

A. DRUNK AND DISORDERLY

(1) Definition

Criminal Justice Act 1967, s.91(1)

Drunkenness in a public place
91.—(1) Any person who in any public place is guilty, while drunk, of disorderly behaviour **16–313**

shall be liable on summary conviction to a fine not exceeding level 3 on the standard scale.

The words "may be arrested without warrant by any person" were removed from this section by Schedule 17(2) of the *Serious Organised Crime and Police Act* 2005 (from January 1, 2006).

(2) Allocation

16–314   This offence is triable summarily: s.91(1).

The words "may be arrested without warrant by any person" were removed from this section by Sched. 17(2) of the *Serious Organised Crime and Police Act* 2005 (from January 1, 2006).

(3) Elements of the offence

16–315   The prosecution must prove that:
— the defendant was found in a public place whilst drunk and,
— behaving in a disorderly fashion.

"Drunk"

16–316   "Drunk" means the taking of intoxicating liquor to an extent which affects steady self-control. It does not apply to a person who is disorderly as a result of sniffing glue: *Neale v. RMJE (a minor)* (1985) 80 Cr.App.R. 20.

"Disorderly"

16–317   The meaning of the word "disorderly" has not been the subject of any reported decision and should bear its natural and ordinary meaning. In *H.v. DPP* [2005] EWHC 2459 it was held that an offence under section 91(1) consisted not of being drunk but of being disorderly whilst drunk. It was the disorderly behaviour that entitled police to arrest an individual without a warrant. In the instant case H had committed no disorderly conduct until after his arrest which was unjustified, accordingly no offence under section 91(1) had occurred (but note the amendment to the Act from January 1, 2006 at § 16–313).

"Public Place"

16–318   "Public place" includes any highway and any other premises or place which at the material time the public have or are permitted to have access, whether on payment or otherwise: section 91(4). The common parts of a block of flats, access to which is controlled so as to restrict entry to residents, their visitors and tradesmen and others who were there in a private capacity, not as members of the general public, will not be a public place: *Williams v. DPP* (1992) 156 J.P. 804.

(4) Sentence

16–319   The maximum penalty is a fine not exceeding level three on standard scale: section 91(1).

The *Magistrates' Court Sentencing Guidelines* state:

Aggravating factors include offensive language or behaviour, with group, on hospital/medical premises, offence committed on bail, relevant previous convictions and any failure to respond to previous sentences.

Mitigating factors include being induced by others, no significant disturbance and not threatening.

Guideline: Is discharge or fine appropriate?

B. Bomb Hoaxes

(1) Definition

Criminal Law Act 1977, s.51

Bomb hoaxes

51.—(1) A person who—

    (a) places any article in any place whatever; or

    (b) dispatches any article by post, rail or any other means whatever of sending things from one place to another,

with the intention (in either case) of inducing in some other person a belief that it is likely to explode or ignite and thereby cause personal injury or damage to property is guilty of an offence.

    In this subsection "article" includes substance.

    (2) A person who communicates any information which he knows or believes to be false to another person with the intention of inducing in him or any other person a false belief that a bomb or other thing liable to explode or ignite is present in any place or location whatever is guilty of an offence.

    (3) For a person to be guilty of an offence under subsection (1) or (2) above it is not necessary for him to have any particular person in mind as the person in whom he intends to induce the belief mentioned in that subsection.

    (4) A person guilty of an offence under this section shall be liable—

    (a) on summary conviction, to imprisonment for a term not exceeding six months or to a fine not exceeding £1,000, or both;

    (b) on conviction on indictment, to imprisonment for a term not exceeding seven years.

16–320

(2) Allocation

This offence is triable either way.

16–321

(3) Elements of the offence

The prosecution must prove that:

— the defendant placed any article in any place, or dispatched any article by post, rail or other means of sending things from one place to another and

— he intended to induce a belief in some person that such thing is likely to explode or ignite, thereby causing personal injury or damage to property OR

— the defendant communicated any information that he knows or believes to be false to another person and

— he intended to induce in that, or any other person, a false belief that a bomb or other thing liable to explode or ignite is present in any place or location.

    The words "There is a bomb" said to the operator on a 999 call were sufficient to give rise to an offence under section 51(2), a person communicating the false information does not need to specify a "place or location": *Webb, The Times*, June 19, 1995, CA.

16–322

(4) Sentence

    When tried summarily, the maximum penalty for this offence is imprisonment for a term not exceeding six months, or a fine not exceeding £1000 or both: section 51(4)(a). Note that, on commencement of the relevant provisions, the maximum custodial sentence in a magistrates' court will be 12 months' imprisonment: *Criminal Justice Act* 2003, ss.154 and 282. Custodial sentences of less than 12 months will consist of a custody plus order (see *post*, Ch.23).

16–323

C. Use of Noxious Substance or things to cause Harm and Intimidate

(1) Definition

Anti-Terrorism, Crime and Security Act 2001, s.113

Use of noxious substances or things to cause harm and intimidate

16–324   **113.**—(1) A person who takes any action which—

(a) involves the use of a noxious substance or other noxious thing;

(b) has or is likely to have an effect falling within subsection (2); and

(c) is designed to influence the government or to intimidate the public or a section of the public,

is guilty of an offence.

(2) Action has an effect falling within this subsection if it—

(a) causes serious violence against a person anywhere in the world;

(b) causes serious damage to real or personal property anywhere in the world;

(c) endangers human life or creates a serious risk to the health or safety of the public or a section of the public; or

(d) induces in members of the public the fear that the action is likely to endanger their lives or create a serious risk to their health or safety;

but any effect on the person taking the action is to be disregarded.

(3) A person who—

(a) makes a threat that he or another will take any action which constitutes an offence under subsection (1); and

(b) intends thereby to induce in a person anywhere in the world the fear that the threat is likely to be carried out,

is guilty of an offence.

(4) A person guilty of an offence under this section is liable—

(a) on summary conviction, to imprisonment for a term not exceeding six months or a fine not exceeding the statutory maximum (or both); and

(b) on conviction on indictment, to imprisonment for a term not exceeding fourteen years or a fine (or both).

(5) In this section—

"the government" means the government of the United Kingdom, of a part of the United Kingdom or of a country other than the United Kingdom; and

"the public" includes the public of a country other than the United Kingdom.

(2) Allocation

16–325   This offence is triable either way.

(3) Elements of the offence

16–326   Substance includes any biological agent and any other natural or artificial substance (whatever its form, origin or method of production): section 115(1).

For a person to be guilty of this offence, it is not necessary for him to have any particular person in mind as the person in whom he intends to induce the belief in question: section 115(2).

(4) Sentence

16–327   When tried summarily, the maximum penalty for this offence is imprisonment for a term not exceeding six months, or a fine not exceeding £1000 or both: section 113(4). Note that, on commencement of the relevant provisions, the maximum custodial sentence in a magistrates' court will be 12 months' imprisonment: *Criminal Justice Act* 2003, ss.154 and 282. Custodial sentences of less than 12 months will consist of a custody plus order (see *post*, Ch.23).

D. Hoaxes involving Noxious Substances or things

(1) Definition

Anti-Terrorism, Crime and Security Act 2001, s.114

Hoaxes involving noxious substances or things

114.—(1) A person is guilty of an offence if he—   **16–328**

    (a) places any substance or other thing in any place; or

    (b) sends any substance or other thing from one place to another (by post, rail or any other means whatever);

with the intention of inducing in a person anywhere in the world a belief that it is likely to be (or contain) a noxious substance or other noxious thing and thereby endanger human life or create a serious risk to human health.

(2) A person is guilty of an offence if he communicates any information which he knows or believes to be false with the intention of inducing in a person anywhere in the world a belief that a noxious substance or other noxious thing is likely to be present (whether at the time the information is communicated or later) in any place and thereby endanger human life or create a serious risk to human health.

(3) A person guilty of an offence under this section is liable—

    (a) on summary conviction, to imprisonment for a term not exceeding six months or a fine not exceeding the statutory maximum (or both); and

    (b) on conviction on indictment, to imprisonment for a term not exceeding seven years or a fine (or both).

(2) Allocation

This offence is triable either way.   **16–329**

(3) Elements of the offence

Substance includes any biological agent and any other natural or artificial substance **16–330** (whatever its form, origin or method of production): see section 115(1).

For a person to be guilty of this offence, it is not necessary for him to have any particular person in mind as the person in whom he intends to induce the belief in question: section 115(2).

(4) Sentence

When tried summarily, the maximum penalty for this offence is imprisonment for a **16–331** term not exceeding six months, or a fine not exceeding £1000 or both: section 114(3). Note that, on commencement of the relevant provisions, the maximum custodial sentence in a magistrates' court will be 12 months' imprisonment: *Criminal Justice Act 2003*, ss.154 and 282. Custodial sentences of less than 12 months will consist of a custody plus order (see *post*, Ch.23).

E. Information about Acts of Terrorism

(1) Definition

Terrorism Act 2000, s.38B

Information about acts of terrorism

38B.—(1) This section applies where a person has information which he knows or believes **16–332** might be of material assistance—

    (a) in preventing the commission by another person of an act of terrorism, or

    (b) in securing the apprehension, prosecution or conviction of another person, in the United Kingdom, for an offence involving the commission, preparation or instigation of an act of terrorism.

(2) The person commits an offence if he does not disclose the information as soon as reasonably practicable in accordance with subsection (3).

(3) Disclosure is in accordance with this subsection if it is made—

(a) in England and Wales, to a constable,

(b) in Scotland, to a constable, or

(c) in Northern Ireland, to a constable or a member of Her Majesty's forces.

(4) It is a defence for a person charged with an offence under subsection (2) to prove that he had a reasonable excuse for not making the disclosure.

(5) A person guilty of an offence under this section shall be liable—

(a) on conviction on indictment, to imprisonment for a term not exceeding five years, or to a fine or to both, or

(b) on summary conviction, to imprisonment for a term not exceeding six months, or to a fine not exceeding the statutory maximum or to both.

(6) Proceedings for an offence under this section may be taken, and the offence may for the purposes of those proceedings be treated as having been committed, in any place where the person to be charged is or has at any time been since he first knew or believed that the information might be of material assistance as mentioned in subsection (1).

(2) Allocation

16–333   This offence is triable either way.

(3) Sentence

16–334   When tried summarily, the maximum penalty for this offence is imprisonment for a term not exceeding six months, or a fine not exceeding £1000 or both: section 38B(5). Note that, on commencement of the relevant provisions, the maximum custodial sentence in a magistrates' court will be 12 months' imprisonment: *Criminal Justice Act* 2003, ss.154 and 282. Custodial sentences of less than 12 months will consist of a custody plus order (see *post*, Ch.23).

F. INTIMIDATION OR ANNOYANCE BY VIOLENCE OR OTHERWISE

(1) Definition

Trade Union and Labour Relations (Consolidation) Act 1992, s.241

Intimidation or annoyance by violence or otherwise

16–335   **241.**—(1) A person commits an offence who, with a view to compelling another person to abstain from doing or to do any act which that person has a legal right to do or abstain from doing, wrongfully and without legal authority—

(a) uses violence to or intimidates that person or his wife or children, or injures his property,

(b) persistently follows that person about from place to place,

(c) hides any tools, clothes or other property owned or used by that person, or deprives him of or hinders him in the use thereof,

(d) watches or besets the house or other place where that person resides, works, carries on business or happens to be, or the approach to any such house or place, or

(e) follows that person with two or more other persons in a disorderly manner in or through any street or road.

(2) A person guilty of an offence under this section is liable on summary conviction to imprisonment for a term not exceeding six months or a fine not exceeding level 5 on the standard scale, or both.

(3) A constable may arrest without warrant anyone he reasonably suspects is committing an offence under this section.

(2) Allocation

16–336   This offence is triable summarily: section 241(2).

(3) Elements of the offence

The prosecution must prove that: **16–337**

— the defendant used violence towards, or intimidated, another person, that person's wife or that person's children or the defendant injured that person's property, or

— the defendant wrongfully and without legal authority, persistently followed another person about from place to place, or

— the defendant wrongfully and without legal authority, hid any tools, clothes or other property owned or used by another person or deprived him or hindered him in the use of such items, or

— the defendant wrongfully and without legal authority, watched or beset the house or other place where another person resides, works, carries on business or happens to be, or watched or beset the approach of any such house or place, or

— the defendant wrongfully and without legal authority, followed another person with two or more persons in a disorderly manner in or through any street or road, with

— a view to compelling that other person to abstain from doing or to do any act which that person has a legal right to do or abstain from doing.

Application to peaceful picketing:

Trade Union and Labour Relations (Consolidation) Act 1992, s.220

Peaceful picketing

220.—(1) It is lawful for a person in contemplation or furtherance of a trade dispute to attend—   **16–338**

    (a) at or near his own place of work, or

    (b) if he is an official of a trade union, at or near the place of work of a member of the union whom he is accompanying and whom he represents,

for the purpose only of peacefully obtaining or communicating information, or peacefully persuading any person to work or abstain from working.

    (2) If a person works or normally works—

    (a) otherwise than at any one place, or

    (b) at a place the location of which is such that attendance there for a purpose mentioned in subsection (1) is impracticable,

his place of work for the purposes of that subsection shall be any premises of his employer from which he works or from which his work is administered.

    (3) In the case of a worker not in employment where—

    (a) his last employment was terminated in connection with a trade dispute, or

    (b) the termination of his employment was one of the circumstances giving rise to a trade dispute,

in relation to that dispute his former place of work shall be treated for the purposes of subsection (1) as being his place of work.

    (4) A person who is an official of a trade union by virtue only of having been elected or appointed to be a representative of some of the members of the union shall be regarded for the purposes of subsection (1) as representing only those members; but otherwise an official of a union shall be regarded for those purposes as representing all its members.

Section 241 may also be applied to the actions of an anti-roads protester: *Todd v.*   **16–339**
DPP [1996] Crim.L.R. 344.

(4) Sentence

The maximum penalty is six months' imprisonment, a fine not exceeding level five   **16–340**
on the standard scale or both: section 241(2). Note that, on commencement of the relevant provisions, the maximum custodial sentence in a magistrates' court will be 12

months' imprisonment: *Criminal Justice Act* 2003, ss.154 and 282. Custodial sentences of less than 12 months will consist of a custody plus order (see *post*, Ch.23).

G. Public Nuisance

16–341   Public nuisance is an offence at common law, triable either way. When tried summarily, the statutory maxima apply as regards sentencing: see *Magistrates' Courts Act* 1980, s.17(1) and Sched. 1.

A person is guilty of a public nuisance when he (a) does an act not warranted by law, or (b) omits to discharge a legal duty, if the effect of the act or omission is to endanger the life, health, property, morals or comfort of the public, or to obstruct the public in the exercise or enjoyment of rights common to all Her Majesty's subjects: *Stephen's Digest of the Criminal Law* (9th edn, 1900), p.184, definition approved in *Shorrock* [1994] Q.B. 279.

The question of how widely spread a nuisance must be for it to qualify as a public nuisance was addressed in *Att.-Gen. v. PYA Quarries Ltd* [1957] 2 Q.B. 169, CA where it was held that the question whether the local community within the sphere of a neighbourhood comprised a sufficient number of persons to constitute a class of the public was a question of fact in every case.

16–342   The mens rea of the offence will be established if the prosecution can show that the defendant knew or ought to have known that as a result of his action, a public nuisance would be committed: *Shorrock* [1994] Q.B. 279, 98 Cr.App.R. 67, CA. In *Goldstein* [2004] 1 Cr.App.R. 27, the CA held that the common law offence of causing a public nuisance had survived the *Human Rights Act* 1998 and was not in breach of Articles 7, 8 or 10 of the European Convention on Human Rights since the common law was sufficiently clear to enable a person, with legal advice if necessary, to foresee the consequences that his action might entail and to regulate his behaviour accordingly.

H. Breach of the Peace and Powers to bind over

(1) General

Public Order Act 1986, s.40(4)

Amendments, repeals and savings

16–343   **40.**—(4) Nothing in this Act affects the common law powers in England and Wales to deal with or prevent a breach of the peace.

16–344   In *Howell* [1982] Q.B. 416 it was held that there is a breach of the peace whenever harm is actually done or is likely to be done to a person or in his presence to his property or a person is in fear of being so harmed through an assault, an affray, a riot, unlawful assembly or other disturbance.

(2) Binding over to keep the peace

16–345   The magistrates may bind over a person to keep the peace following a complaint (*MCA* 1980, s.115) or by the court's own motion under common law and statutory powers, notably the *Justices of the Peace Act* 1361.

When the court is acting of its own motion, it may make a binding over order at any time before the conclusion of criminal proceedings, on withdrawal of the case by the prosecution, on a decision by the prosecution to offer no evidence, on an adjournment, or upon acquittal of the defendant, where the magistrate considers that there might be a breach of the peace in the future.

The person bound over is required to enter into a recognizance in an amount which will be forfeited if he fails to keep the peace for a specified period.

If the person fails, or refuses to enter into a recognisance the magistrates' may order imprisonment. This may be for a maximum of six months or until the person complies with the order: *MCA* 1980, s.115(3). The *PCC(S)A* 2000, s.89 provides that imprison-ment cannot be imposed on a person under the age of 21. A person between 18 and 20 who refuses to consent to be bound over may be detained under section 108 of the *PCC(S)A* 2000. A person under the age of 18 may be detained at an attendance centre.

The *PCC(S)A* 2000, s.139(1) establishes the relevant penalties for non-compliance with the terms of the binding over order. The court may forfeit the whole or part of the recognisance in its discretion, allow payment, direct time for payment, direct payment by instalments or reduce or discharge the recognisance. It is not allowed to impose a prison term.

In the magistrates' court, a recognisance can only be declared to be forfeit following an order on complaint: *MCA* 1980, s.20, by virtue of whichever power the bind over was originally imposed.

In *R. (Laporte) v. Chief Constable of Gloucestershire Constabulary* [2004] EWCA Civ 1639 the question arose as to whether the police action [escorting the buses of anti-war protesters back to London] was justifiable as falling within the ambit of action rea-sonably taken to prevent a breach of the peace:

> ... If the action on the present facts were to be regarded as justified, this would constitute a significant extension of the previously established principles. It would be a development that is more of a leap and a bound than a measured pace forward.
>
> The Defendant contends that all that was involved was requiring the passengers to make the return journey earlier than they would have done otherwise. This description of what was involved in our judgment underestimates the impact of the police action on the passengers' individual rights to freedom of action. We do not consider it necessary to decide that it would never be justifiable for the police to take action of this nature. However, we are satisfied that such action should be very much a matter of last resort and we are not persuaded that there were no less intrusive possible alternative courses of action here.
>
> Thus, it is not suggested in the evidence that the drivers of the coaches, who were profes-sional drivers, had indicated that they were not prepared to obey a lawful order given by the police. They could, in our judgment, have been lawfully ordered not to proceed to the air-base and to leave the area. The coaches could have been followed if this was thought neces-sary to see whether the order was obeyed. The order could have been backed up by a warn-ing that, if it was not observed, the police would exercise the powers of arrest which would then be available. ... Like the Administrative Court, we regard the actions that did take place as disproportionate and not justifiable at common law ...
>
> In these circumstances ..., we propose to accede to the submissions of the interested police parties that we should not determine further the application of Article 5 to what happened. We leave this to be decided on the facts of the pending case concerning policing of May Day 2001 in which the issue, we understand, will have to be confronted. In our judgment the ap-peal can be dismissed on the evidence without any further examination of either domestic or ECHR law (paras 53–56).

See also Part IV on Sentencing.

(3) Demonstrations in vicinity of Parliament

(a) *Definition*

Sections 132–138 of the *Serious Organised Crime and Police Act* 2005 create new **16–346** offences in relation to demonstrations in the vicinity of Parliament.

Serious Organised Crime and Police Act 2005, ss.132, 134(7), 135(3)

Demonstrating without authorisation in designated area.
    132.—(1) Any person who—   **16–347**
        (a) organises a demonstration in a public place in the designated area, or
        (b) takes part in a demonstration in a public place in the designated area, or
        (c) carries on a demonstration by himself in a public place in the designated area, is guilty of an offence if, when the demonstration starts, authorisation for the dem-onstration has not been given under section 134(2).

(2) It is a defence for a person accused of an offence under subsection (1) to show that he reasonably believed that authorisation had been given.

(3) Subsection (1) does not apply if the demonstration is—

    (a) a public procession of which notice is required to be given under subsection (1) of section 11 of the *Public Order Act* 1986 (c. 64), or of which (by virtue of subsection (2) of that section) notice is not required to be given, or

    (b) a public procession for the purposes of section 12 or 13 of that Act.

(4) Subsection (1) also does not apply in relation to any conduct which is lawful under section 220 of the *Trade Union and Labour Relations (Consolidation) Act* 1992 (c. 52).

(5) If subsection (1) does not apply by virtue of subsection (3) or (4), nothing in sections 133 to 136 applies either.

(6) Section 14 of the *Public Order Act* 1986 (imposition of conditions on public assemblies) does not apply in relation to a public assembly which is also a demonstration in a public place in the designated area.

(7) In this section and in sections 133 to 136—

    (a) "the designated area" means the area specified in an order under section 138,

    (b) "public place" means any highway or any place to which at the material time the public or any section of the public has access, on payment or otherwise, as of right or by virtue of express or implied permission,

    (c) references to any person organising a demonstration include a person participating in its organisation,

    (d) references to any person organising a demonstration do not include a person carrying on a demonstration by himself,

    (e) references to any person or persons taking part in a demonstration (except in subsection (1) of this section) include a person carrying on a demonstration by himself.

Authorisation of demonstrations in designated area

16–348   **134.**—(7) Each person who takes part in or organises a demonstration in the designated area is guilty of an offence if —

    (a) he knowingly fails to comply with a condition imposed under subsection (3) which is applicable to him (except where it is varied under section 135), or

    (b) he knows or should have known that the demonstration is carried on otherwise than in accordance with the particulars set out in the authorisation by virtue of subsection (5).

Supplementary directions

16–349   **135.**—(3) A person taking part in or organising the demonstration who knowingly fails to comply with a condition which is applicable to him and which is imposed or varied by a direction under this section is guilty of an offence.

(b) *Allocation*

16–350   These offences are summary only. In *R. (Haw) v. Secretary of State for the Home Department* [2005] EWHC 2061; the QBD (Admin) held by a majority that the Act as enacted did not apply to a continuing demonstration that had commenced before section 132(1) of the Act came into force on July 1, 2005. The *Serious Organised Crime and Police Act 2005 (Commencement No. 1, Transitional and Transitory Provisions) Order* 2005 extended the application of section 132(1) so as to criminalise conduct that was not so under the Act. As such the alteration made by the Order was in fact an amendment and ultra vires. It could not be said that Parliament intended the Act to catch continuing demonstrations.

(c) *Sentence*

16–351   The penalties for offences under sections 132–135 are found in section 136: a person guilty of an offence under section 132(1)(a) is liable on summary conviction to imprisonment for a term not exceeding 51 weeks, to a fine not exceeding level 4 on the standard scale, or to both; a person guilty of an offence under section 132(1)(b) or (c) is liable on summary conviction to a fine not exceeding level 3 on the standard scale; a person guilty of an offence under sections 134(7) or 135(3) is liable on summary conviction—

(a) if the offence was in relation to his capacity as organiser of the demonstration, to imprisonment for a term not exceeding 51 weeks, to a fine not exceeding level 4 on the standard scale, or to both,

(b) otherwise, to a fine not exceeding level 3 on the standard scale.

A person who is guilty of the offence of inciting another to—

(a) do anything which would constitute an offence mentioned in subsection (1), (2) or (3), or

(b) fail to do anything where the failure would constitute such an offence, is liable on summary conviction to imprisonment for a term not exceeding 51 weeks, to a fine not exceeding level 4 on the standard scale, or to both, notwithstanding s.45(3) of the *Magistrates' Courts Act* 1980.

I. DEFINITIONS

A. GENERAL

Throughout road traffic law, there are a number of words or phrases that recur and **17–1** which have developed a specialist meaning. The key words that relate to offences covered by this work are set out, *post*, and the key principles that apply to the interpretation is described. For further information, reference should be made to *Wilkinson's Road Traffic Offences*, Ch.1.

B. ACCIDENT

17–2　　There is no statutory definition of this term in relation to road traffic offences. Although some judicial suggestions have been made, it is recognised that the word is one in common use and, when faced with the issue, a court should ask itself "Would an ordinary man in the circumstances of the case say there had been an accident?": *Chief Constable of West Midlands Police v. Billingham* [1979] R.T.R. 446.

It is clear that it can be the result of a deliberate act. In *Chief Constable of Staffordshire v. Lees* [1981] R.T.R. 506, a defendant deliberately drove at a gate and smashed it. This was a breath test case and the powers of the police constable depended on there having been an accident. The court considered that it would be wrong for those powers to be exercisable where something happened as a result of a careless act but not where there had been a deliberate act. In the civil case of *Charlton v. Fisher* [2001] EWCA Civ 112; [2001] R.T.R. 33, a car was deliberately driven into the rear of another stationary car and a person in that car was injured. In order to be able to claim successfully against the driver's insurance, the injured person had to show there had been an accident and the Court of Appeal considered that there had been.

It is also clear that there does not need to be any contact between vehicles. In the Scottish case of *Bremner v. Westwater* (1993) 1994 S.L.T. 707, the issue arose in the context of whether a notice of intended prosecution, see *post*, § 17–13, was needed. The defendant had driven erratically at night without lights. In overtaking another vehicle, he had caused an oncoming vehicle to brake sharply and drive onto the verge in order to avoid a collision and the overtaken vehicle also had to brake sharply. It was held that this could properly be described as an accident.

C. IN CHARGE OF

17–3　　There is no statutory definition of this phrase which is very much a question of fact and degree. The leading case is *DPP v. Watkins* [1989] 2 W.L.R. 966 which identified two classes of cases which could be identified—those cases where the defendant was the owner or otherwise in lawful possession of the vehicle or had recently driven it and those cases where none of those descriptions applied. In the first situation, there would usually be an assumption that he was in charge unless he had given the charge of the vehicle to another person. However, if the defendant adduces sufficient evidence to show that there was no likelihood of him driving the vehicle whilst unfit, the prosecution must also prove that there was a real risk of him driving: *Road Traffic Act* 1988, ss.4(3) or 5(2). The House of Lords has held that, whilst this imposes a legal burden on the defendant, that is not oppressive. Even if the presumption of innocence is infringed, the provision was directed to a legitimate objective, did not go beyond what was necessary and reasonable and was not arbitrary. Accordingly, the provision did not contravene the European Convention on Human Rights: *Sheldrake v. DPP* [2005] 1 A.C. 264; [2005] R.T.R. 2. It is for the prosecution to prove that the defendant was in charge. If that is done, the defence may seek to assert that there was no likelihood of driving whilst unfit through drink or drugs or over the prescribed limit. The way that the statute is drafted has led to misunderstanding of who needs to prove what and in what order. The issue came before the Divisional Court again in *CPS v. Bate* [2004] EWHC 2811. The court had found no case to answer having concluded that the prosecution had to prove that he was in charge of the vehicle where the defendant had put forward reasons why he was in the vehicle. It was patently clear that the defendant was in charge of the vehicle but that he may well have been able to satisfy the court that there was no likelihood of him driving whilst over the limit. It seemed to the Divisional Court that the justices had confused the question of whether the defendant was in charge and whether the statutory defence was open to him. The statutory defence required the defendant to prove (on the balance of probabilities) that there was no likelihood of driving whilst he remained unfit. The justices concluded that the intention of the driver not to drive was sufficient to determine that he was not in charge but, as the Divisional Court stated, it is the likelihood of driving not the intention of the defendant that provides the defence.

The two may be closely related but they are not the same and it is for the defendant to satisfy the court that the defence has been made out.

Where the defendant was not the owner or in lawful possession or had not recently driven the vehicle but was nonetheless sitting in the vehicle or otherwise involved in some way with it, the court will look to see if he was, in practice, voluntarily in control or in such a position that he might be expected to take control imminently—where the defendant was, what he was doing and what his intentions were would all be relevant.

In either class of case the court will need to consider where the defendant was in relation to the vehicle (and, if he was inside, where he was), what he was doing, whether he had a key that fitted the ignition, any evidence showing that the defendant intended to demonstrate his control of the vehicle (whether by driving or in some other way) and, finally, whether anyone else was in or near the vehicle and, if so, for what reason. An unusual application of this principle was seen in *DPP v. Janman* [2004] R.T.R. 31. A person was supervising a provisional licence holder. He had consumed sufficient alcohol to be over the limit and was prosecuted for being "in charge". Although there may be exceptional cases where a supervisor could demonstrate that there was no likelihood of driving the vehicle, that will be a very difficult task for the supervisor. It is of the essence of the role of a supervisor of a provisional licence holder that they must be prepared to intervene when necessary.

D. Drive/Driver

Almost inevitably, the plain meaning of these words has been stretched to ensure that **17–4** culpable behaviour is properly brought within the remit of the various offences. That has been less necessary where an alternative of being "in charge" of a vehicle has been available.

The essence of driving is having control over the movement of the vehicle. Key elements can be drawn from the decisions in *MacDonagh* [1974] R.T.R. 372 and *Burgoyne v. Phillips* [1983] R.T.R. 49. This is a question of fact, needing to accord with the ordinary meaning of "driving". It will involve substantial control over the movement and direction of the vehicle. It will probably require the presence of the driver inside the vehicle, at least to some extent so standing outside pushing the vehicle has not generally been found to be "driving". It may however be "using" or "attempting to drive". In *R. (Traves) v. DPP* [2005] EWHC 1482; (2005) 169 J.P. 421, the appellant was in the driver's seat of his own vehicle which was being towed by another vehicle. The justices accepted that he had been steering and using the brakes to slow the vehicle down for approximately three miles. The issue arose as to whether he was "driving". Upholding the justices' decision that this amounted to "driving", the Divisional Court cited with approval the statement in *Whitfield v. DPP* [1998] Crim.L.R. 349 that "The essence of driving is the use of the driver's controls in order to direct the movement, however that movement is produced". Here, movement was produced by the vehicle being towed but the defendant's involvement in both steering and in controlling the movement through the use of the brakes was sufficient.

Issues have also arisen as to when driving stops as there will be times when a person is clearly driving a vehicle even though it is not in motion. Key principles were summarised in *Edkins v. Knowles* [1973] Q.B. 748. There will be interludes in a journey when the vehicle will stop and the questions to be asked will be concerning the purpose and length of the stop and whether the driver left the vehicle. If the journey is continuing and the stop of short duration or because of traffic congestion, then the driving will continue. If the journey has ended then, allowing for a short while to switch the engine off etc. the driving is likely to have come to an end. This may be particularly significant in prosecutions for using a hand held mobile telephone whilst driving. Whilst the purpose of creating the offence is one of road safety, there is no limitation of the definition of "drive" for that offence. However, it can be expected that prosecution will not follow where, although the driving continues, none the less there is no possible adverse effect on road safety, such as when a car is stationary at the roadside or stuck in traffic with no prospect of moving immediately.

17–5   More than one person may be driving the same vehicle. In *Tyler v. Whatmore* [1976] R.T.R. 83, a passenger was leaning across the person in the driving seat with both hands on the wheel and obstructing the view of the person in the driving seat who continued to control the propulsion of the vehicle but could not steer it. Both were driving. However, a passenger who grabbed the steering wheel causing the car to leave the road was not driving: *Jones v. Pratt* [1983] R.T.R. 54.

E. MECHANICALLY PROPELLED VEHICLE

17–6   There are a variety of terms defined in the *Road Traffic Act* 1988 and elsewhere to cover vehicles used on roads. In section 185 of the 1988 Act, a motor vehicle is defined as a "mechanically propelled vehicle intended or adapted for use on roads". There are further definitions of "motor car", "invalid carriage", "motor cycle" etc. which all use the phrase mechanically propelled vehicle.

This is a term which has been judicially considered on many occasions, often turning on whether a vehicle which undoubtedly has been a mechanically propelled vehicle continues to come within that definition even though it is no longer able to be driven. In connection with offences under the *Vehicle Excise and Registration Act* 1994, liability is being extended to vehicles that not only are mechanically propelled vehicles but also to ones that have at some stage been a mechanically propelled vehicle: Schedule 5 to the *Finance Act* 2002.

The test to be applied is set out in *Binks v. Department of the Environment* [1975] R.T.R. 318 as "whether the vehicle has reached such a stage that it can be said that there is no reasonable prospect of the vehicle ever being made mobile again".

F. ROAD OR OTHER PUBLIC PLACE

17–7   There are a range of definitions of "road" for various purposes and it will be a question of fact and degree whether something is a road or other public place in the circumstances of any alleged offence.

In essence, a "road" is a highway and any other road to which the public has access: *Road Traffic Act* 1988, s.192(1). It is a definable way for passage between two points: *Oxford v. Austin* [1981] R.T.R. 416. It will have the physical character of a defined or definable route or way, with ascertained or ascertainable edges, leading from one point to another with the function of serving as a means of access enabling travellers to move from one point to another along that route: *Cutter v. Eagle Star Insurance Co Ltd* [1998] 4 All E.R. 417. A public road is a road repairable at public expense.

A road to which the public have access is one on which the public generally can be found without having to overcome a physical obstruction or to defy an express or implied prohibition: *Harrison v. Hill*, 1932 J.C. 13. Connotations of public expense in maintaining it should not be imported: *DPP v. Cargo Handling Ltd* [1992] R.T.R. 318.

17–8   The extent of the definition of "other public place" has often arisen in the context of car parks. Provided the public generally could be expected to use the area (even if only for purposes that not every member of the public would choose to avail themselves of) then it is likely to be a public place. Thus, courts have brought within the definition a hospital car park: *DPP v. Greenwood* [1997] C.O.D. 278, an "airside" road at Heathrow Airport: *DPP v. Neville* (1996) 160 J.P. 758, a lane leading from a cross-Channel ferry through the immigration terminal: *DPP v. Coulman* [1993] R.T.R. 230 and a caravan park: *DPP v. Vivier* [1991] 4 All E.R. 18.

G. USING, CAUSING AND PERMITTING

17–9   These terms are commonly used in relation to road traffic offences and their meaning has been developed in attempts to ensure that the purposes of the legislation are achieved.

Certain statutory provisions impose absolute liability on the user; for instance, if a vehicle is used and the use is not covered by insurance, the user is generally liable whether or not aware of the absence of insurance cover. The user will be the driver but will also often include a person whose vehicle was being used by another person for his purposes and under his control—often the employer/employee relationship. However, "use" is defined more restrictively where there are alternatives such as "causing" or "permitting" which could be used.

"Causing" unlawful use requires proof of knowledge of the facts making the use unlawful where there is an alternative offence of "using". Where that alternative is not provided, "causing", though it requires a positive act, will not necessarily require knowledge.

"Permitting" unlawful use is less precise than "causing" it. The extent to which **17–10** knowledge is required will vary depending on the offence. For instance, permitting use without insurance will require proof that the use was permitted but not that it was known that the use was uninsured.

For a further exploration of these terms, see *Wilkinson's Road Traffic Offences*, Ch.1.

H. VEHICLE

This can have a very wide meaning. In most instances for road traffic offences it is **17–11** used with some other limiting factors, such as "motor vehicle" or "mechanically propelled vehicle" but it will sometimes be used on its own. In those circumstances, the dictionary definition of "a thing used for transporting people or goods on land" becomes relevant.

A bicycle is a vehicle as are trams, trolley buses and horse-drawn carts. In some circumstances, it may include a pram or a pushchair. For instance, one of the occasions in which the obligation to stop after an accident arises is where damage is caused to a vehicle and it is likely that a pram would be a vehicle for those purposes at least.

II. BAD DRIVING

A. GENERAL

There are two main offences dealt with in magistrates' courts where the issue is **17–12** whether the standard of driving fell below an acceptable standard. These offences are dangerous driving: *Road Traffic Act* 1988, s.2 and driving without due care and attention or without reasonable consideration for other road users: *Road Traffic Act* 1988, s.3. As well as issues surrounding the assessment of a particular piece of driving, there will be difficult decisions needing to be made on sentencing since the consequences of bad driving do not always correlate with the badness of the driving. Further offences have been created and the provisions are expected to be in force during the later part of 2007. These provide for situations where death arises from driving without due care and attention or following driving by a person disqualified, unlicensed or uninsured. These are either way offences and the provisions are set out at the appropriate place in the text, *post*. In January 2007 the Sentencing Advisory Panel published a consultation paper on sentencing for both offences and it may be that the offences will not be brought into force until sentencing guidelines are published; this consultation paper can be found at www.sentencing-guidelines.gov.uk. In addition, the Crown Prosecution Service has issued a consultation paper on prosecution policy and practice relating to the prosecution of bad driving: this can be found at www.cps.gov.uk/news. Amongst other things, this explores the boundary between dangerous driving and driving without due care and attention.

B. WARNING OF PROSECUTION

In order to secure a conviction under either section 2 or 3, the prosecution must **17–13**

Part III

have complied with the requirements to give notice of intended prosecution: *Road Traffic Offenders Act* 1988, s.1. Unless an accident has occurred of which the driver was aware (*Road Traffic Offenders Act* 1988, s.2(1)), the driver must receive warning of prosecution within 14 days of the offence. This warning may be given at the time of the offence, by service of the summons (or copy of a charge sheet) within 14 days of the offence or by the prosecutor sending notice to the driver or the registered keeper of the vehicle within 14 days. Where the notice is by service of the summons, that must take place within the 14 days. Where the notification is by notice, it is only necessary for that to be sent within the 14 days. For further information, refer to *Wilkinson's Road Traffic Offences*, Ch.2.

C. DANGEROUS DRIVING

(1) Definition

Road Traffic Act 1988, s.2

Dangerous driving

17-14   **2.** A person who drives a mechanically propelled vehicle dangerously on a road or other public place is guilty of an offence.

(2) What must the prosecution prove?

17-15   The elements of this offence that the prosecution must prove are that:
— the defendant was the driver;
— the vehicle was being driven;
— the vehicle was a mechanically propelled vehicle;
— the vehicle was being driven dangerously; and
— the vehicle was being driven on a road or other public place.

17-16   A defendant who is acquitted of dangerous driving may be found guilty of driving without due care and attention or without reasonable consideration even though no charge has been preferred—see Alternative Verdict, *post*, at § 17-23.

For issues of identification, see *ante*, §§ 10-89 *et seq.* in this work. For issues surrounding the meaning of "drive", see *ante*, § 17-4. The phrase "mechanically propelled vehicle" is wider than "vehicle"; again this is more fully explored in § 17-6, *ante*. The phrase "road or other public place" has been subject to detailed consideration; this also is explored more fully in §§ 17-7 and 17-8, *ante*.

(3) Allocation

17-17   Dangerous driving is an either way offence and particular care needs to be taken. In the Crown Court, approximately 2,300 offenders are sentenced each year. About 60 per cent of those convicted receive a custodial sentence. About 75 per cent of those sentences are for one year or less and about 25 per cent are for six months or less and so within the power of a magistrates' court. In magistrates' courts, approximately 2,000 are sentenced each year. About 27 per cent of those convicted receive a custodial sentence and about 64 per cent are for four months or less.

The mode of trial guidelines in the *Consolidated Criminal Practice Direction*, para.V.51.17 (see Appendix F, F-58) state that cases of dangerous driving should be tried summarily unless the court considers that one or more of the following features is present in the case *and* that its sentencing powers are insufficient. These features are:
(a) alcohol or drugs contributing to the dangerous driving;
(b) grossly excessive speed;
(c) racing;
(d) prolonged course of dangerous driving;
(e) other related offences; and

(f) significant injury or damage sustained.

These guidelines will be replaced by the *National Allocation Guidelines* issued by the Sentencing Guidelines Council once the new allocation procedures are implemented and magistrates' courts sentencing powers increased to a maximum of 12 months for a single either way offence. These guidelines are less related to specific offences. They emphasise that the primary consideration is the adequacy of the sentencing powers of the court taking the prosecution version of events as the basis. There will be occasions where a difficult choice needs to be made regarding whether to charge this offence and/or one of the offences contained in the *Offences Against the Person Act* 1861 (see *ante*, Ch.13). This may arise from a situation where injury is caused as a result of dangerous driving or it may arise where the vehicle itself is used as the equivalent of a weapon for the purpose of causing injury.

(4) Meaning of "dangerous driving"

The definition is set out in statute in *Road Traffic Act* 1988, s.2A.   **17–18**

Road Traffic Act 1988, s.2A

Meaning of dangerous driving

2A.—(1) For the purposes of sections 1 and 2 above a person is to be regarded as driving   **17–19**
dangerously if (and, subject to subsection (2) below, only if)—

    (a) the way he drives falls far below what would be expected of a competent and careful driver, and

    (b) it would be obvious to a competent and careful driver that driving in that way would be dangerous.

(2) A person is also to be regarded as driving dangerously for the purposes of sections 1 and 2 above if it would be obvious to a competent and careful driver that driving the vehicle in its current state would be dangerous.

(3) In subsections (1) and (2) above "dangerous" refers to danger either of injury to any person or of serious damage to property; and in determining for the purposes of those subsections what would be expected of, or obvious to, a competent and careful driver in a particular case, regard shall be had not only to the circumstances of which he could be expected to be aware but also to any circumstances shown to have been within the knowledge of the accused.

(4) In determining for the purposes of subsection (2) above the state of a vehicle, regard may be had to anything attached to or carried on or in it and to the manner in which it is attached or carried.

There are, therefore, two routes by which the offence is committed, one related to   **17–20**
the way of driving (section 2A(1)) and one related to the decision to drive the vehicle at all: section 2A(2). The first (and more common) route test has two main parts both of which relate to a "competent and careful driver" and both of which must be proved.

The first part requires that the manner of driving falls "far below" that of a competent and careful driver: section 2A(1)(a). (For the lesser offence under section 3 of careless driving, the test is "below the standard of a reasonable, prudent and competent driver" though this will change on the implementation of section 30 of the *Road Safety Act* 2006 (*post*, § 17–30.) This is an objective test and the authorities indicate that the court should not add in an element that imports to the "competent and careful driver" of the test any of the characteristics of the defendant concerned or what the offender believed the situation to be: *Collins* [1997] R.T.R. 439. The condition of the driver (perhaps that he was intoxicated) is admissible but that condition is not sufficient in itself to prove the offence of dangerous driving: *Webster* [2006] R.T.R. 19.

The second part (section 2A(1)(b)) requires proof that it would have been obvious to a competent and careful driver that driving in the way the defendant drove would be dangerous. Again an objective test and again two main elements, what is meant by "obvious" and what is meant by "dangerous".

In relation to "obvious", a dictionary definition of "seen or realised at first glance,   **17–21** evident" has been used in relation to offences under section 2A(2) and would be equally applicable here. Would it be obvious to the careful and competent driver that driving in this way would be dangerous? In addition, section 2A(3) requires a court to take account not only of what would be obvious to the careful and competent driver but also what was actually known to the defendant. Therefore, if something was known to the driver that would not have been obvious, the standard of driving has to be assessed in the light of that additional knowledge.

In relation to "dangerous", section 2A(3) is defined as meaning danger of injury to any person or of serious damage to property. The injury may be to any person, including the driver, and there is no limitation on the nature of the injury. However, it is suggested that that injury should be physical injury (as proposed in the Road Traffic Law Review (the North Report) that led to the creation of this offence) but there is no requirement that injury should have occurred, just that there was a danger of such injury occurring. In relation to property, there is again no further definition but there is the qualification that the damage must be "serious". Again, it would appear to be quite acceptable for that property to be the mechanically propelled vehicle being driven by the defendant as well as any other property.

The second route by which the offence is committed is by driving a mechanically propelled vehicle when it was obvious that to do so in its current state would be dangerous: section 2A(2). The state of the vehicle includes anything attached to it or carried on it or in it and the manner in which it is attached or carried: section 2A(4). Again the determinant of what is obvious is the careful and competent driver. The test is whether there is evidence that it would be obvious (that is, capable of being seen or realised at first glance, evident) that it would be dangerous (that is, liable to cause injury or serious damage to property) to drive the vehicle in that state. In addition, anything of which the driver was actually aware should be taken into account even where that would not have been obvious to a careful and competent driver: section 2A(3).

17–22   A difficult issue was considered in *Marchant* [2004] 1 All E.R. 1187; [2004] R.T.R. 15. An agricultural vehicle had (as part of its construction) a grab with spikes attached to its front. It was authorised by the Secretary of State for use on public roads. The grab was in the recommended position for use on the roads. Whilst the vehicle was waiting to turn off the road, a motor cyclist ran into it and was killed. The driver was prosecuted for causing death by dangerous driving relying on section 2A(2). Allowing the driver's appeal against conviction, the Court of Appeal (Criminal Division) stated that, whilst there will be cases where it will be appropriate to prosecute those responsible for vehicles in a dangerous condition even where they had been authorised by the Secretary of State, that would be where the driver had manoeuvred the vehicle in a dangerous fashion. Where, as here, the danger was in the design, it is unlikely to be appropriate to prosecute the user at all.

Despite this route being limited in the statute to the defective state of the vehicle, it appears to have been extended to circumstances where it was the "defective" state of the driver that caused the danger. In *Marison* [1997] R.T.R. 457, the driver suffered from diabetes and was aware that there was a real risk that he would suffer a sudden hypoglycaemic attack which would cause him to lose control of the vehicle. He did suffer such an attack resulting in the car crashing into an oncoming vehicle and killing the driver. The Judge drew an analogy with section 2A(2) and this was supported by the Court of Appeal.

Alternative verdict

17–23   A court faced with an offence of dangerous driving and finding the defendant not guilty can instead find the defendant guilty of driving without due care and attention even though no charge has been preferred and even though it would not be possible to lay an information because too much time had elapsed from the date of the offence: *Road Traffic Offenders Act* 1988, s.24.

(5) Penalty

The maximum sentence at present is two years' imprisonment on indictment and/or **17–24** an unlimited fine; on summary trial, six months' imprisonment and/or a fine up to level 5. In relation to offences committed on or after commencement of *Criminal Justice Act* 2003, ss.181, 280–282 (see *post*, Ch.23), the maximum custodial sentence in a magistrates' court is a custody plus order. Proposals to increase the maximum period of imprisonment on indictment are under consideration by the Government. A significant issue is the gap between the maximum custodial sentence for this offence and for causing death by dangerous driving which is 14 years' imprisonment. The same standard of driving may result in death, in very serious injury or in no injury at all and it is these issues that must be grappled with by those having to pass sentence.

Mandatory disqualification and endorsement follows (including an obligation to be re-tested). In the absence of "special reasons", see *post*, at § 17–206, the minimum period of disqualification is 12 months. For more information on disqualification and endorsement generally, see *post*, §§ 17–180 *et seq*.

See also the power to deprive the offender of the vehicle contained in section 143(1), (6) and (7) of the *Powers of Criminal Courts (Sentencing) Act* 2000, see *post*, § 17–209.

(6) Sentence

There are commonly agreed aggravating and mitigating factors. Closely following **17–25** recent guidance from the Court of Appeal (Criminal Division) in relation to the related offence of causing death by dangerous driving, the *Magistrates' Court Sentencing Guidelines* (2004) (under review) state that aggravating factors include seeking to avoid detection or apprehension, engagement in competitive driving including racing or showing off, disregard of warnings, perhaps from passengers or others in vicinity, evidence of alcohol or drugs, excessive speed, prolonged, persistent bad driving, serious risk and using a hand held mobile telephone. Mitigating circumstances include driving in an emergency and speed that was not excessive.

In *Cooksley*; *Stride*; *Cook (Att.-Gen.'s Reference (No. 152 of 2002))* [2003] 2 Cr.App.R. 18, the Court of Appeal issued a new guideline judgment for sentencing for the offence of causing death by dangerous driving, incorporating the advice of the Sentencing Advisory Panel. The judgment in *Cooksley* was reviewed by the Court of Appeal in *Richardson* [2006] EWCA Crim 3186 following varying interpretations by different constitutions of the Court of Appeal of the impact of the increase in the maximum penalty for causing death by dangerous driving. The aggravating and mitigating factors set out in *Cooksley* (and likely to be equally relevant where death does not occur) were affirmed as continuing to be appropriate. In January 2007, the Sentencing Advisory Panel published the consultation paper referred to in *ante*, § 17–12 which includes an evaluation of the effect of both *Cooksley* and *Richardson*. Although considering offences with the additional element of causing death and with a much higher maximum penalty, nonetheless the occurrence of death or serious injury may not depend on the nature of the driving and so the principles that relate to the quality of driving are likely to be equally applicable. The court identified factors indicating a highly culpable standard of driving at the time of the offence. In addition to those included in the *Magistrates' Court Sentencing Guidelines* (2004), these included aggressive driving, driving while the driver's attention was distracted, *e.g.* by reading or using a mobile phone, driving when knowingly suffering from a medical condition, driving when knowingly deprived of adequate sleep or rest, driving a poorly maintained or dangerously loaded vehicle, especially when motivated by commercial concerns, other offences committed at the same time, previous convictions for motoring offences, particularly offences involving bad driving or the consumption of alcohol before driving, irresponsible behaviour at the time of the offence, *e.g.* failing to stop, claiming one of the victims was responsible for the crash, and where the offence was committed on bail. Additional mitigating factors included a good driving record and the fact the offender had been seriously injured as a result of the dangerous driving.

Part III

In the course of the judgment, the Court emphasised that, although the offence is one which does not require an intention to drive dangerously (or an intention to injure), since the driving has to fall "far below" the standard of driving that would be expected of a competent and careful driver and the driving must be such that it would be obvious to the same competent and careful driver that driving in that way would be dangerous, it will usually be obvious to the offender that the driving was dangerous and he therefore deserves to be punished accordingly.

17–26   The courts have demonstrated a readiness to protect people who are particularly vulnerable to the commission of this offence. In *Joseph* [2002] 1 Cr.App.R.(S.) 20, the defendant had deliberately driven at a traffic warden and driven off with him on the bonnet of the vehicle, trying to shake him off. The Court of Appeal endorsed the observations of the sentencing judge that it was the duty of the courts to give protection to traffic wardens and other public servants who were carrying out public duties, and emphasised the propriety of a deterrent custodial sentence. The defendant was sentenced to ten months' imprisonment. Leveson J. stated:

> "Parking attendants, in particular, are subject to vilification and abuse if not worse. It is a very real reflection on the hazards of the job that this particular parking attendant felt it appropriate to carry a tape recorder with him to record what happened when confronted by angry motorists. The fact that others have complained about this particular attendant does not take this appellant's position or the character of his driving any further. An immediate custodial sentence, in the form of a deterrent sentence, which inevitably pays less attention to the individual circumstances of the offender was both proper and, in our judgement, inevitable" (at p. 75–76)

17–27   For "road rage" cases of dangerous driving, where no accident or injury results and there was no consumption of alcohol, but there is evidence to suggest furious driving in temper with an intent of causing fear and possible injury, the appropriate sentencing bracket lies between six and 12 months: *Howells* [2003] 1 Cr.App.R.(S.) 61, CA.

See also *Arthur* [2001] 2 Cr.App.R.(S.) 67; *Smith* [2002] 2 Cr.App.R.(S.) 28. Some more recent cases have given examples of approaches to sentencing for this offence.

In *A.*, unreported, July 22, 2004, CA (Civ. Div.), the two defendants had been "sharing" the driving of a motor car—one had been steering, the other changing the gears— over a distance over 20 miles until the car left the road at a bend at 60 mph. The car rolled over causing serious injuries to the three other passengers. At the time of the offence, the defendant who had been steering was 17 years old and had no driving experience and the other defendant was 19 years old. Both defendants were of good character. Sentences on each of 18 months' detention (after a guilty plea) were held not to be manifestly excessive.

17–28   In contrast, in *Andrews* (2004) 148 S.J. 1031, the defendant had driven at high speeds, mounted a pavement, failed to stop at junctions and crossed traffic lights at red. In addition he was drunk. On this occasion, a sentence of 10 months' imprisonment (following a guilty plea) was held not to be excessive. Indeed, a custodial sentence was inevitable.

In *Bentley* [2004] EWCA Crim 2162, the defendant was 18 years old at the time of the offence and had passed both ordinary and an advanced driving test. He was of exemplary character and showed a great deal of remorse for the serious injuries that were caused to one of his passengers. He had pleaded guilty at the earliest possible opportunity. The Judge sentenced on the basis that the defendant had been showing off, there having been information from the passengers that he had been driving very fast and swerving the car all over the road from time to time. He had attempted to negotiate a bend at 50 mph when the fastest safe speed was 39 mph, the car rolled, struck a stone wall and then a tree. The injured passenger had been travelling in the boot area of the hatchback car. Sentence at the Crown Court was to 12 months' detention and disqualification for three years and until an extended re-test had been taken. The Court of Appeal noted the positive good character of the defendant, the fact that the offence was out of character and more a product of irresponsibility than of criminality. Nonetheless, the grave consequences that arose could not be ignored. Although the court considered 12 months to be severe in the light of the plea, the good character, the remorse and the absence of the worst features of dangerous driving, it was not manifestly excessive and was not reduced. These cases appear to indicate the high probability of a custodial sentence especially where serious injury results. This reflects the statement, *ante*, at § 17–25 that, since the driving has to fall "far below" the standard of driving that would be expected, it will usually be obvious that the driving was dangerous.

In *Tomkins* [2004] EWCA Crim 2792, the defendant had committed a series of offences that led to him being sentenced by different magistrates' courts on two occasions in April 2004. The offences included driving whilst disqualified, taking without consent and aggravated vehicle taking. Whilst on bail, he also committed an offence of dangerous driving. Police officers had noticed the defendant in the driver's seat of a stationary car. When they approached him, he pulled away and drove towards them striking one officer who needed hospital treatment but was not seriously injured. The defendant then drove into a road against a "No Entry" sign and collided with an oncoming car causing the driver foot, stomach and knee injuries. He was sentenced to 18 months' imprisonment to run consecutively to a total of 11 months' imprisonment imposed at the April hearings. On appeal, the defence argued that, with a two year maximum sentence, since this was not the worst example of dangerous driving and given the guilty plea and mitigating circumstances, an 18 month sentence was excessive. The Court of Appeal disagreed and upheld the sentence. Should Parliament not choose to increase the maximum sentence, it may be that serious consideration may need to be given to prosecuting this type of use of a motor vehicle under the appropriate offence of assault or causing grievous bodily harm. Examples of such an approach can be found in three recent cases. In *Bain* [2005] 2 Cr.App.R.(S.) 53, the defendant was aged 19. In the course of driving dangerously, serious injuries were caused to a passenger in the vehicle that he was driving. He was charged with dangerous driving and with causing grievous bodily harm (section 20). Dangerous driving attracts a maximum of two years' imprisonment, GBH a maximum of five years. The Court of Appeal held that there was nothing wrong in principle in charging such offences even though they arose from the same course of conduct. However, since the offences did arise out of the same course of conduct, concurrent sentences should have been imposed that reflected the totality of the offending conduct. In *Ballard* [2005] 2 Cr.App.R.(S.) 31, a 17 year old had been charged with gross negligence manslaughter following a course of bad driving in which a person had been killed. This had been done with the express purpose of making available greater powers of sentence than would have been available following conviction of causing death by dangerous driving. That approach (and the subsequent lengthy sentence imposed) was held to be correct.

The level of sentence was considered in *Goldring* [2005] EWCA Crim 2254. The appellant was aged 19 when the offence was committed. Having been disqualified 14 days before the incident (for driving without insurance), he was observed by a police officer sitting at the wheel of a stationary vehicle. The officer attempted to give him a notice but the appellant drove the car, made a U-turn and then drove at the police officer causing him to jump out of the way. No injury was caused and the appellant was arrested five days later at his home. At the Crown Court a sentence of 18 months had been imposed with a further three months consecutive for driving whilst disqualified. On appeal, it was argued that this was a very short lived piece of dangerous driving, no injury was caused and no member of the public was endangered. Since the maximum is two years' imprisonment, this was not serious enough to warrant such a long sentence. Reducing the sentence to 12 months, the Court of Appeal agreed that 18 months was too high. Once the sentencing powers in a magistrates' court have increased to 12 months for a single offence, this type of incident, therefore, is likely to fall within the sentencing powers of a magistrates' court though consideration continues to be given to increasing the maximum sentence for the offence.

A useful reminder of the circumstances in which maximum sentences should be

Part III

considered for offences (such as this one) where there is a relatively low maximum penalty can be found in *Butt* [2006] EWCA Crim 47. The driving consisted of driving on the wrong side of the road whilst trying to evade the police; the driver was the worse for both drink and drugs. Upholding a sentence of 18 months imprisonment (after a guilty plea), the Court of Appeal drew attention to existing guidance on the circumstances in which it is appropriate to use the maximum as a starting point. In *Ambler* [1976] Crim.L.R. 266, it had been emphasised that, whilst the maximum should be passed only for the worst kind of offence, judicial imagination should not be stretched to attempt to identify unlikely examples—"what they should consider is the worst type of offence which comes before the court and ask themselves whether the particular case they are dealing with comes within the broad band of that type. When the maximum sentence is low, the band may be wide" (*per* Lawton L.J.) Similarly, it may be appropriate to consider consecutive sentences where the driver both drove dangerously and drove with excess alcohol or disqualified. Although the general practice is to impose concurrent sentences where the offences arose from a single incident, nonetheless there is a well recognised practice that, in circumstances such as these, consecutive sentences may be imposed. In *Hardy* [2005] EWCA Crim 3097, the defendant was convicted of dangerous driving, driving whilst disqualified and failing to provide a specimen. Consecutive sentences totalling two years were imposed in the Crown Court. Upholding those sentences and the approach, the Court of Appeal stated that, whilst consecutive sentences would not generally be appropriate where the matters arose out of the same incident "it would be bizarre that this man would in fact have a licence to drive with excess alcohol and while disqualified without any added penalty." An approach that may have less offended general sentencing principle would have been to have treated the alcohol and disqualification as aggravating factors and increased the sentence accordingly; however, the low maximum penalty does not allow that to happen so readily and this is perhaps another example of the problems that arise when maximum sentences are allowed to remain at a level that is too low.

D. CARELESS OR INCONSIDERATE DRIVING

(1) Definition

Road Traffic Act 1988, ss.3, 3ZA

Careless, and inconsiderate, driving

17–29　　3. If a person drives a mechanically propelled vehicle on a road or other public place without due care and attention, or without reasonable consideration for other persons using the road or place, he is guilty of an offence.

Meaning of careless, or inconsiderate, driving

17–30　　3ZA.—(1) This section has effect for the purposes of sections 2B and 3 above and section 3A below.

(2) A person is to be regarded as driving without due care and attention if (and only if) the way he drives falls below what would be expected of a competent and careful driver.

(3) In determining for the purposes of subsection (2) above what would be expected of a careful and competent driver in a particular case, regard shall be had not only to the circumstances of which he could be expected to be aware but also to any circumstances shown to have been within the knowledge of the accused.

(4) A person is to be regarded as driving without reasonable consideration for other persons only if those persons are inconvenienced by his driving.

[This section is inserted by section 30 of the *Road Safety Act* 2006 and will come into force as from a day to be appointed.]

(2) What must the prosecution prove?

17–31　　The elements of this offence that the prosecution must prove are that:

— the defendant was the driver;
— the vehicle was being driven;
— the vehicle was a mechanically propelled vehicle;
— the vehicle was being driven on a road or other public place;
— the vehicle was being driven without due care and attention; *or*
— the vehicle was being driven without reasonable consideration for other persons using the road or place.

For issues of identification, see *ante*, §§ 10–89 *et seq.* in this work.

For issues surrounding the meaning of "drive", see *ante*, § 17–4.   **17–32**

The phrase "mechanically propelled vehicle" is wider than "vehicle"; again this is more fully explored in § 17–6, *ante*.

The phrase "road or other public place" has been subject to detailed consideration; this also is explored more fully in §§ 17–7 and 17–8, *ante*.

(3) Allocation

These offences are summary only.   **17–33**

(4) Standard of driving

Until recently, statute has not assisted in defining the standard of driving for the of- **17–34** fences contained in section 3. The standard widely accepted has been that of a reasonable, prudent and competent driver in all the circumstances of the case. The standard has an element that is to be judged objectively (the reasonable etc. driver) and one that is subjective (the circumstances of the case). The most commonly prosecuted part of this section is the allegation of driving without due care and attention which is more widely drawn than the other limb of section 3. However, section 30 of the *Road Safety Act* 2006 (when implemented) will insert a new section 3ZA into the 1988 Act which attempts to provide that definition. The standard will for the future be that of the "competent and careful" driver in circumstances of which the driver could be expected to be aware or was aware, even if he would not otherwise have been expected to be aware of them. "Reasonable and prudent" is thus replaced by "careful" which may not be too much of a change in practice. The widening of the circumstances to include those of which the driver is aware may be a little more significant. In addition, the Crown Prosecution Service has issued a consultation paper on prosecution policy and practice relating to the prosecution of bad driving: this can be found at www.cps.gov.uk/news. Amongst other things, this explores the type of driving that might constitute careless or inconsiderate driving.

Driving without reasonable consideration is almost always going to be capable of falling within the offence of driving without due care and attention since no reasonable, prudent and competent driver would drive without reasonable consideration for other road users. However, that does not work in reverse since, for the second limb, there must be other persons using the road or other public place whereas that is not necessary for the first limb. It may be that there are now fewer reasons why the second limb should be prosecuted at all.

The cause of the failure to drive at the acceptable standard is not, therefore, relevant to conviction (though it may be to sentence) but how the driver would be expected to conduct himself or herself is to be judged on the basis of the circumstances as they actually were or as the driver could have expected to be aware. There can be some fine judgements as to whether the reasonable driver of the test would have avoided getting into the situation altogether or whether, accepting that the situation occurred, the actions of the driver have to be tested against this standard. Thus, the fact that the driver is a learner driver or otherwise inexperienced does not affect the assessment of what the standard of driving should be whereas the standard may well vary with the time of day, type of road, or weather conditions. There is no need for anyone to be adversely affected. However, where the allegation is of driving without reasonable consideration, it will be necessary to prove that others have been inconvenienced by the driving: section 3ZA(4).

17–35   It is not unusual for any accident to be observed by no one other than the driver. In those circumstances, the court is entitled to draw inferences from the nature of the circumstances in which the accident occurred to justify finding the offence proved providing the facts are strong enough to enable the court to be satisfied beyond reasonable doubt that the standard of driving was below that required: *Scott v. Warren* [1974] R.T.R. 104. If an explanation (other than a fanciful one) is put forward by the defendant, it is for the prosecution to disprove it: *Spurge* [1961] 2 All E.R. 688.

The Highway Code can be used to assist in understanding what is expected in any given situation. Failure to observe the Code does not of itself prove the case but it will tend to show that the standard of driving was unacceptable.

Once it is proved that the driving fell below the acceptable standard, there are a limited number of defences that have been created—mechanical defect, sudden loss of visibility or sudden illness. The underlying principle is that the driver has been deprived of control of the vehicle by something of which he was not aware. If the driver, without fault, can show that he was deprived of control because of a mechanical defect of which he was unaware and which he could not have discovered by the exercise of reasonable prudence then he ought to be acquitted. Similarly, if he finds himself unexpectedly blinded by headlights or by the sun and an accident occurs before he can stop, that can be a defence. In such circumstances, the competent and careful driver will quickly reduce speed or stop his vehicle but there will be a very short time in which it is accepted that the defence would arise. Finally, sudden illness may again raise a defence providing it could not be anticipated and the reactions of the driver when he became aware of the illness were those of a competent and careful driver. Falling asleep is not sufficient since that could have been anticipated: *Henderson v. Jones* (1955) 119 J.P. 305.

(5) Penalty

17–36   The maximum penalty is a fine of level 4 (£2,500). It is an endorsable offence within the range of 3–9 penalty points and so disqualification may be imposed. The maximum penalty is increased to a fine of level 5 (£5,000) for offences committed on or after the commencement of section 23 of the *Road Safety Act* 2006.

(6) Sentence

17–37   The *Magistrates' Court Sentencing Guidelines* (2004) (under review) provide that aggravating factors include driving at excessive speed, high degree of carelessness, serious risk and using a hand held mobile telephone. Mitigating factors include minor risk, momentary lapse of concentration, negligible/parking damage, sudden change in weather conditions. The guidelines also provide that death, serious injury or damage is capable of counting as an aggravating factor.

The most likely penalty is a fine with penalty points. However, disqualification should be considered where there is a risk of further poor driving. This may be until a further test is passed which will be particularly appropriate where there are concerns about the overall driving ability of the defendant.

A court will have to face situations where the seriousness of the result of the bad driving is greatly out of proportion to how bad the driving was—a relatively minor lapse can result in death. For many years, courts have based sentence for this offence primarily on the degree of fault. In *Krawec* (1984) 6 Cr.App.R.(S.) 367, the appellant was convicted of driving without due care and attention on an indictment for causing death by reckless driving. Reducing the fine, Lord Lane C.J. stated that:

the unforeseen and unexpected results of the carelessness are not in themselves relevant to penalty. The primary considerations are the quality of the driving, the extent to which the appellant on the particular occasion fell below the standard of the reasonably competent

THOMSON
™
SWEET & MAXWELL

Thank you for purchasing **Archbold Magistrates' Courts Criminal Practice 2008.**

☑ Don't miss important updates

So that you have all the latest information, **Archbold Magistrates' Courts Criminal Practice** is published annually and supplemented once a year. Sign up today for a Standing Order to ensure you receive the new editions and updating supplements as soon as they publish. Setting up a Standing Order with Sweet & Maxwell is hassle-free, simply tick complete and return this FREEPOST card and we'll do the rest.

You may cancel your Standing Order at any time by writing to us at Sweet & Maxwell, PO Box 2000, Andover, SP10 9AF stating the Standing Order you wish to cancel.

Alternatively, if you have purchased your copy of **Archbold Magistrates' Courts Criminal Practice 2008** from a bookshop or other trade supplier, please ask your supplier to ensure that you are registered to receive your supplements and new editions.

☐ Yes, please enter my Standing Order for future annual editions of **Archbold Magistrates' Courts Criminal Practice**, to be invoiced on publication unless countermanded.

Name:

Organisation:

Address:

Postcode:

Telephone:

Email:

S&M account number: (if known)

All orders are accepted subject to the terms of this order form, our Terms of Trading (see our website) and relevant Service Terms (available with the product or on request).

By submitting this order form, I confirm that I accept these terms and am authorised to sign on behalf of the customer.

Signed: Date:

Print name:

Job title:

Thomson Legal & Regulatory Limited (Company No. 1679046. Registered Office 100 Avenue Road, London, NW3 3PF) trades as Sweet & Maxwell, GEE, GEE Publishing, Consult GEE, W Green, Thomson Round Hall, Westlaw UK, Lawtel and Incomes Data Services and is part of The Thomson Corporation.

www.sweetandmaxwell.thomson.com

STANDING ORDERS
SWEET & MAXWELL
FREEPOST
PO BOX 2000
ANDOVER
SP10 9AH
UNITED KINGDOM

driver; in other words, the degree of carelessness and culpability. The unforeseen consequences may sometimes be relevant to those considerations. In the present case the fact that the appellant failed to see the pedestrian until it was too late and therefore collided with him was plainly a relevant factor. We do not think that the fact that the unfortunate man died was relevant on this charge.

However, that approach has been steadily changing and the different approach was evident in *Johnson* [1998] 2 Cr.App.R.(S.) 453, where the CA held that the consequences of the driver's carelessness were relevant to determination of his culpability.

In *King* [2001] 2 Cr.App.R.(S.) 114, CA, the Court of Appeal again approached the situation where driving without due care and attention results in tragic consequences. The appellant was convicted of three offences of driving without due care and attention having been acquitted of three counts of causing death by dangerous driving. He was fined £2,250 and disqualified for a period of three years. Holding that this sentence was too high, the Court of Appeal substituted a fine of £1,500 and disqualification for two years. While culpability remained the primary consideration in sentencing for driving without due care and attention where death had resulted, the sentencing judge was entitled to bear in mind that he was dealing with an offence that had led to death. Mackay J. reviewed the authorities on sentencing in this difficult situation, and stated:

> "The sentencer must still, therefore, make it his primary task to assess culpability, but should **17–38**
> not close his eyes to the fact that death has resulted, especially multiple death, where, as here,
> that was all too readily foreseeable as the consequence of the admitted lack of care in this
> case."

However, the maximum penalty remains a fine and that should be capable of being **17–39** paid within one year. As a result of concerns that the range of offences was not sufficient to enable sentence to be properly imposed where death results from careless or inconsiderate driving, Parliament has created new offences which are likely to be available during 2007. Details of these offences are set out in the next sections but the above guidance will continue to apply to offences committed before commencement or where serious injury is caused but death does not result.

E. Causing Death by Careless, or Inconsiderate, Driving

(1) Definition

Road Traffic Act 1988, s.2B
(to be inserted by section 20 of the Road Safety Act 2006 when in force)

Causing death by careless, or inconsiderate, driving

2B. A person who causes the death of another person by driving a mechanically propelled **17–40** vehicle on a road or other public place without due care and attention, or without reasonable consideration for other persons using the road or place, is guilty of an offence.

(2) What must the prosecution prove?

The elements of this offence that the prosecution must prove are that: **17–41**
— the defendant was the driver;
— the vehicle was being driven;
— the vehicle was a mechanically propelled vehicle;
— the vehicle was being driven on a road or other public place;
— the vehicle was being driven without due care and attention; *or*
— the vehicle was being driven without reasonable consideration for other persons using the road or place
— the death of another person is caused by that driving.
For issues of identification, see *ante*, §§ 10–89 *et seq.* in this work.
For issues surrounding the meaning of "drive", see *ante*, § 17–4.

Part III

The phrase "mechanically propelled vehicle" is wider than "vehicle"; again, this is explored more fully in § 17–6, *ante*.

The phrase "road or other public place" has been subject to detailed consideration; this also is explored more fully in §§ 17–7 and 17–8, *ante*.

(3) Allocation

17–42   This offence is triable either way. It can be expected that most cases will be dealt with in the Crown Court in recognition of the fact that death has occurred.

(4) Standard of driving

17–43   The standard set out in section 3ZA to the 1988 Act (see *ante*) applies also to this offence. The additional factor is that the driving below the requisite standard must have caused the death of a person other than the driver. This will include a person inside the vehicle driven by the defendant.

(5) Penalty

17–44   The maximum penalty is imprisonment of 12 months (subject to implementation of *Criminal Justice Act* 2003, s.154) and/or a fine of level 5 (£5,000) on summary conviction and imprisonment of five years or a fine on indictment. It is an endorsable offence within the range of 3–11 points but one that attracts mandatory disqualification in the absence of special reasons.

(6) Sentence

17–45   In January 2007 the Sentencing Advisory Panel issued a consultation paper on the approach to sentencing for this offence. This explores the consequences arising from an offence with a very high level of harm and a very low level of culpability. The offence itself has attracted a wide range of both support and criticism. In a debate in the House of Lords, it was said that:

> ". . . it will mean that the families of those killed by careless drivers feel that the law is adequate to deal with the circumstances and that the justice system is on their side so that if, in all the circumstances, a court feels that custody is appropriate, it will be available. Of course, there will be instances—probably the majority—where custody is not considered to be the most appropriate penalty."

However, it is difficult to see how a court could do other than give serious consideration to a custodial sentence where Parliament has prescribed a maximum penalty of five years' imprisonment and the range of potential culpability is narrow. In most circumstances, it is likely that an offence will be sentenced in the Crown Court.

F. CAUSING DEATH BY DRIVING: UNLICENSED, DISQUALIFIED OR UNINSURED DRIVERS

(1) Definition

Road Traffic Act 1988, s.3ZB
(to be inserted by section 21 of the Road Safety Act 2006 when in force)

17–46   **3ZB.** A person is guilty of an offence under this section if he causes the death of another person by driving a motor vehicle on a road and, at the time when he is driving, the circumstances are such that he is committing an offence under—

    (a) section 87(1) of this Act (driving otherwise than in accordance with a licence),

    (b) section 103(1)(b) of this Act (driving while disqualified), or

    (c) section 143 of this Act (using motor vehicle while uninsured or unsecured against third party risks.)

(2) What must the prosecution prove?

17–47   The elements of this offence that the prosecution must prove are that:

— the defendant was the driver;
— the vehicle was being driven;
— the vehicle was a motor vehicle;
— the vehicle was being driven on a road;
— the driver was committing an offence under section 87(1) *or* section 103(1)(b) *or* section 143;
— the death of another person is caused by that driving.

For issues of identification, see *ante*, §§ 10–89 *et seq.* in this work. For issues surrounding the meaning of "drive", see *ante*, § 17–4.

The phrase "motor vehicle" is different from "mechanically propelled vehicle"; again, this is explored more fully in § 17–6, *ante*.

The meaning of "road" has been subject to detailed consideration; this also is explored more fully in §§ 17–7 and 17–8, *ante*.

Note the exclusion of "other public place" in respect of this offence.

(3) Allocation

This offence is triable either way. It can be expected that many cases will be dealt with **17–48** in the Crown Court in recognition of the fact that death has occurred.

(4) Standard of driving

The offence is committed where the driving causes death and the offender is not **17–49** properly licensed, is disqualified or is uninsured. There is unlikely to be an allegation of bad driving because that would have most likely resulted in a prosecution for a different offence.

(5) Penalty

The maximum penalty is imprisonment of up to 12 months (subject to implementa- **17–50** tion of *Criminal Justice Act* 2003, s.154) and/or a fine of level 5 (£5,000) on summary conviction and imprisonment of two years or a fine on indictment. It is an endorsable offence within the range of 3–11 points but one that attracts mandatory disqualification in the absence of special reasons.

(6) Sentence

This offence raises difficult issues where the level of harm far exceeds the level of **17–51** culpability since it must be assumed that the fault of the driver was that of being on the road at all rather than the way in which the vehicle was driven. In the Sentencing Guidelines Council Guideline, *Overarching Principles: Seriousness* it is emphasised that, where there is an imbalance between harm and culpability, first consideration is to be given to the level of culpability. Nonetheless, it is clear that courts must now take fully into account the level of harm, particularly where death has resulted. In January 2007 the Sentencing Advisory Panel issued a consultation paper on the approach to sentencing for this offence. It explores the issues arising from an offence where the driver's culpability is to do with the decision to drive rather than to the manner of the driving. In most circumstances, because of the complexities of this offence in terms of sentence, it is likely that an offence will be sentenced in the Crown Court.

G. FAILING TO STOP AFTER AN ACCIDENT, FAILING TO REPORT AN ACCIDENT

(1) Definition

Road Traffic Act 1988, s.170

Duty of driver to stop, report accident and give information or documents
   170.—(1) This section applies in a case where, owing to the presence of a mechanically **17–52** propelled vehicle on a road or other public place, an accident occurs by which—

     (a) personal injury is caused to a person other than the driver of that mechanically propelled vehicle, or

     (b) damage is caused—

        (i) to a vehicle other than that mechanically propelled vehicle or a trailer drawn by that mechanically propelled vehicle, or

        (ii) to an animal other than an animal in or on that mechanically propelled vehicle or a trailer drawn by that mechanically propelled vehicle, or

        (iii) to any other property constructed on, fixed to, growing in or otherwise forming part of the land on which the road or place in question is situated or land adjacent to such land.

(2) The driver of the mechanically propelled vehicle must stop and, if required to do so by any person having reasonable grounds for so requiring, give his name and address and also the name and address of the owner and the identification marks of the vehicle.

(3) If for any reason the driver of the mechanically propelled vehicle does not give his name and address under subsection (2) above, he must report the accident.

(4) A person who fails to comply with subsection (2) or (3) above is guilty of an offence.

(5) If, in a case where this section applies by virtue of subsection (1)(a) above, the driver of a motor vehicle does not at the time of the accident produce such a certificate of insurance or security, or other evidence, as is mentioned in section 165(2)(a) of this Act—

     (a) to a constable, or

     (b) to some person who, having reasonable grounds for so doing, has required him to produce it,

the driver must report the accident and produce such a certificate or other evidence.

This subsection does not apply to the driver of an invalid carriage.

(6) To comply with a duty under this section to report an accident or to produce such a certificate of insurance or security, or other evidence, as is mentioned in section 165(2)(a) of this Act, the driver—

     (a) must do so at a police station or to a constable, and

     (b) must do so as soon as is reasonably practicable and, in any case, within twenty-four hours of the occurrence of the accident.

(7) A person who fails to comply with a duty under subsection (5) above is guilty of an offence, but he shall not be convicted by reason only of a failure to produce a certificate or other evidence if, within seven days after the occurrence of the accident, the certificate or other evidence is produced at a police station that was specified by him at the time when the accident was reported.

(8) In this section "animal" means horse, cattle, ass, mule, sheep, pig, goat or dog.

(2) What must the prosecution prove?

17–53   The elements of this offence that the prosecution must prove are that:

— an accident occurs;

— the accident was due to the presence of a mechanically propelled vehicle on a road or other public place;

— personal injury or damage was caused; and

— that the driver of the mechanically propelled vehicle failed to fulfil the obligation placed on him to stop and report.

For the meaning of "accident", "mechanically propelled vehicle" and "road or other public place" see *ante*, §§ 17–2 *et seq.*

17–54   The obligation on the driver arises regardless of the responsibility for the accident. Once an accident has occurred as a result of the presence of a mechanically propelled vehicle on a road or other public place and there has been the qualifying injury or damage, then the obligation is on the driver of that vehicle to stop, to give the requisite details on request and, in certain circumstances, to report the accident to the police.

A driver can avoid this responsibility where he proves that he did not know that an accident had occurred. Once the prosecution has proved that an accident has occurred where the obligation arose to stop, in order to avoid responsibility the defendant must prove (on the balance of probabilities) that he was unaware of the accident: *Harding v. Price* [1948] 1 All E.R. 283. The more obvious the accident (noise of impact or damage to defendant's vehicle may be relevant) the more difficult it will be for the defendant to discharge the onus of proof.

(3) Allocation

These offences are summary only.   **17–55**

(4) Driver

The accident must arise from the presence of a mechanically propelled vehicle on a **17–56** road or other public place. The obligations arising under this section fall on the driver of that vehicle. This is a potentially wide definition and there is no requirement to prove that the driver of the vehicle in question caused the accident. However, there must be a direct causal connection between the vehicle and the accident occurring. In *Quelch v. Phipps* [1955] 2 All E.R. 302, an accident occurred when a passenger got off a bus which he thought was slowing down for traffic lights. In fact, those lights had changed to green by the time the bus would have halted and so the driver continued. The driver was unaware of the accident until informed by the conductor at the next stop. Having not exchanged the necessary particulars with the passenger, the driver should have reported the accident. Since the accident happened through the passenger getting out of a motor vehicle on a road, it occurred "owing to the presence of a motor vehicle on a road" and came within the meaning of the section. Since the driver knew of the accident, albeit after the event, he was under an obligation to report it. The obligation to stop and report is designed to ensure that those who suffer as a result of bad driving have enough information to pursue any claims for compensation. A stationary vehicle may lead to liability if parked badly and the bad parking was such as to lead to the accident whereas a properly parked vehicle is unlikely to lead to liability.

(5) Qualifying injury or damage

For the obligations to arise, there must have been injury or damage. If injury is the **17–57** basis, the injury must be to a person other than the driver of the mechanically propelled vehicle. So, if *A* and *B* are involved in an accident and *B* is injured but there is no other damage, the obligations to stop and report fall on *A* but not on *B*. This applies equally whether *B* is in the same vehicle as *A* or in a different vehicle.

If damage is the basis, then that damage may be to another vehicle (or trailer), to an animal in that other vehicle or trailer or to property on or close to the road. The types of animal are described in section 170(8) which limits them to any horse, cattle, ass, mule, sheep, pig, goat or dog.

The property has to be constructed on, fixed to, growing in or otherwise forming **17–58** part of the land in question. It therefore has to have some degree of permanence— something placed temporarily on the land will not be sufficient.

(6) Obligation imposed

Where the obligation exists, the driver must stop. He must also give certain details. If **17–59** he fails to give those details he must provide them to the police within the time specified in the section.

It is an absolute obligation to stop. This means to stop and to remain at the scene long enough to allow someone who has the right to do so to require the driver to provide the information that the section obliges him to give: *Lee v. Knapp* [1966] 3 All E.R. 961. This does not have to be an indefinite time, simply something sufficient in the circumstances prevailing at the time. There is no obligation on a driver to go and look for somebody who may be entitled to the information: *Mutton v. Bates (No. 1)* [1984] R.T.R. 256. The stopping must be at the scene. Driving on for 80 yards before stopping and returning has been held to be insufficient compliance: *McDermott v. DPP* [1997] R.T.R. 474.

Any person having reasonable grounds for so doing, may require the driver to give his name and address and also the name and address of the owner and the identification marks of the vehicle. The purpose of this is to ensure that anyone who may have a claim against the driver has sufficient information to pursue it. It may be acceptable, therefore, for the address to be one through which the driver can be reached even if not the place where he is currently residing: *DPP v. McCarthy* [1999] R.T.R. 323.

17–60   Where personal injury has occurred to another person, if the driver does not produce proof of insurance at the scene to the police or to another person having reasonable grounds for requiring it, he must report the accident and produce the proof: section 170(5). Alternatively, if the proof of insurance is not produced when the accident is reported, that proof must be produced at a police station which must be a station specified by the driver when he reported the accident.

If a driver does not give his name and address to anyone (for whatever reason) or produce the insurance certificate where that is required, he must report the accident to the police. He must do this by reporting it to a police station or to a constable as soon as reasonably practicable. Even where it is not reasonably practicable, that time must be within 24 hours of the accident. This obligation arises even where the police were present at the scene and even where, though present, the police did not request information. In *DPP v. Hay* [2006] R.T.R. 3, the defendant was the driver of a car which hit a wall rendering the driver unconscious. The police were quickly on the scene but unable to speak to the driver who remained unconscious. The driver argued successfully before justices that the obligation to stop and report did not arise where the police were on the scene throughout. However, the Divisional Court held that the statutory requirement was plain and there was no exception (express or implied) where the police attended the accident but did not speak to the driver for whatever reason. The case was returned with a direction to convict.

The reporting must be done personally since the requirement is to report "at" a police station or "to" a constable: *Wisdom v. Macdonald* [1983] R.T.R. 186.

(7) Penalties

17–61   The maximum penalty for an offence under this section is a fine of level 5 (£5000) and/or six months imprisonment. All offences are endorsable with a range of 5–10 points. Disqualification can be imposed.

See also the power to deprive the offender of the vehicle contained in subsections 143(1), (6) and (7) of the *Powers of Criminal Courts (Sentencing) Act* 2000 (see *post*, §§ 17–209 and 23–229 *et seq.*).

(8) Sentence

17–62   This section contains a range of offences with differing levels of seriousness. A court passing sentence will do so against the background of the purpose of the section and the reason why the defendant failed to fulfil his obligation.

The purpose of the offences stems from the recognition that causing an accident will, at the very least, lead to issues of compensating those who have suffered loss as a result and may lead to criminal proceedings. The motivation of the defendant may range from panic or fear for personal safety through to a deliberate attempt to avoid responsibility for a more serious offence, perhaps because the driver suspected that his alcohol level was such that he would be liable for compulsory disqualification.

A defendant may commit an offence in the following ways:

s.170(2)	Failing to stop (but still reporting the accident)
	Stopping but not giving details (but reporting the accident)
	Stopping but not giving details (and not reporting the accident)

	Stopping, giving details but not producing proof of insurance even though personal injury caused to another person
s.170(3)	Not reporting the accident at all
	Reporting the accident but later than permitted
s.170(7)	Failing to produce proof of insurance when required—if it was not produced at the scene of the accident, it should be produced when reporting the accident or within 7 days of reporting it

The *Magistrates' Court Sentencing Guidelines* (2004) (under review) draw atten- **17–63** tion to the possibility that there could be evidence of driving after drinking alcohol or that there had been a serious injury or damage both of which would make the offence more serious. However, a belief that his identity was known or a decision to leave because of fear for his safety would mitigate the seriousness. Other mitigating factors include the defendant having later reported the incident despite his initial failure to stop, negligible damage being caused and the fact that there was no-one at the scene and the defendant failed to report, or that the defendant stayed at the scene but failed to give, or left before giving, full particulars.

Given the purposes behind the offence, the most serious offences are where a driver both fails to stop and to report the accident, the least serious where sufficient information for practical purposes was given voluntarily although not complying with the requirements of the section.

Although the offences are imprisonable, it is suggested that this power should be used only rarely. Use may be appropriate where the Court considers that the defendant was deliberately trying to evade responsibility for a more serious offence for which he would have received a custodial sentence or where serious injury was caused which could have been better treated if the defendant had stopped.

Those committing these offences are most likely to receive a financial penalty. **17–64** Disqualification should be considered for the more serious offences though short periods are likely to be sufficient to emphasise the importance of the responsibility place on drivers. If the offence was accompanied by driving below an acceptable standard, there is likely to be a separate offence.

In terms of penalty points, the top end should be reserved for circumstances where there is a failure both to stop and to report.

III. ALCOHOL/DRUGS RELATED OFFENCES

This is a highly complex (and much litigated) area of the criminal law. This work sets **17–65** out the key areas and the key issues. For a more detailed examination, reference should be made to *Wilkinson's Road Traffic Offences*. There are two main offences (those under sections 4 and 5) and then other offences arising from the two stages for produc- ing evidence to assess the amount of alcohol or drugs involved.

A. Driving etc. whilst Unfit through Alcohol or Drugs

(1) Definition

Road Traffic Act 1988, s.4

Driving, or being in charge, when under influence of drink or drugs

4.—(1) A person who, when driving or attempting to drive a mechanically propelled vehicle **17–66** on a road or other public place, is unfit to drive through drink or drugs is guilty of an offence.

(2) Without prejudice to subsection (1) above, a person who, when in charge of a mechanically propelled vehicle which is on a road or other public place, is unfit to drive through drink or drugs is guilty of an offence.

(3) For the purposes of subsection (2) above, a person shall be deemed not to have been

Part III

in charge of a mechanically propelled vehicle if he proves that at the material time the circumstances were such that there was no likelihood of his driving it so long as he remained unfit to drive through drink or drugs.

(4) The court may, in determining whether there was such a likelihood as is mentioned in subsection (3) above, disregard any injury to him and any damage to the vehicle.

(5) For the purposes of this section, a person shall be taken to be unfit to drive if his ability to drive properly is for the time being impaired.

(2) Allocation

17–67   These offences are summary only.

(3) What must the prosecution prove?

17–68   The prosecution must prove that:
— the defendant
— drove *or* attempted to drive *or* was in charge of
— a mechanically propelled vehicle
— on a road or other public place
— whilst unfit through drink or drugs.

For issues of identification, see *ante*, §§ 10–89 *et seq.* in this work.

For issues surrounding the meaning of "drive", see *ante*, § 17–4.

The phrase "mechanically propelled vehicle" is wider than "vehicle"; again this is more fully explored in § 17–6, *ante*.

The phrase "road or other public place" has been subject to detailed consideration; this also is explored more fully in §§ 17–7 and 17–8, *ante*.

In order to prove an offence under this section, the prosecution must prove that the defendant was unfit to drive and that that was due to drink or to drugs. To that extent, it is more widely drawn than section 5 which is restricted to alcohol and sets a standard that is capable of precise measurement. Since evidence available to support a charge under section 5 is also admissible under section 4, it is likely that charges under section 4 are more likely to be used where the presence of *alcohol* is not the cause of the unfitness.

A person is unfit to drive if "his ability to drive properly is for the time being impaired": section 4(5). It is the ability to drive *properly* that is impaired not the ability to drive at all. This may be evidenced by the way the vehicle was being driven, or by involvement in an accident where there was nothing that would normally cause such an accident or it may be evidenced by the condition of the defendant. Where alcohol is alleged to be the cause of the unfitness, a certificate of analysis obtained under section 7 of the 1988 Act (see *post*, § 17–94) is admissible and must be taken into account: section 15(2) and (3) of the *Road Traffic Offenders Act* 1988.

17–69   Where drugs are alleged to be the cause of the unfitness, section 11 of the *Road Traffic Act* 1988 defines "drug" as meaning any intoxicant other than alcohol. According to the Oxford Concise Dictionary, "intoxicate" can have three variants—it can mean to cause someone to lose control of their faculties; it can also mean to poison or to excite or exhilarate—presumably it is the first variant that is intended! It is possible that the effect of alcohol could be increased when taken in conjunction with certain drugs and a conviction under section 4 would be appropriate in such circumstances where the combined effect impaired the defendant's ability to drive properly whereas the amount of alcohol on its own may have caused the level in the body to be below the legal limit. Under section 7 of the 1988 Act, the police may require a person to provide samples of breath, blood or urine for analysis in the course of an investigation concerning a possible offence under section 4. A breath test will not disclose useful information about drugs. Where a medical practitioner advises the police officer that the defendant's condition might be due to drugs (and there must be a clear oral statement to that effect by the medical practitioner), the police officer can require the defendant to provide a specimen of blood or urine even if a specimen of breath has already been provided: section 7(3)(c). A certificate of analysis must be taken into account (sections 15 and 16 of the *Road Traffic Offenders Act* 1988) but, in contrast to a certificate relating to alcohol, there is no statutory assumption that the proportion of drug in a specimen is not less than at the time the offence was committed. Since the Act does not provide a level that must be exceeded for an offence under section 4 (as it does for an offence under section 5), it will be for the court to assess whether the defendant was unfit and whether this was due to the presence of the drugs identified in the certificate.

If the defendant wishes to allege that the level in the analysis was caused by consumption of alcohol or drugs after the driving, etc. had ceased but before the sample was provided, then the onus is on the defendant to satisfy the court on the balance of probabilities not only that that happened but also that the amount was sufficient to render the reading invalid as proof that the defendant was unfit at the time of the offence or, in the case of alcohol (see *ante*) the prescribed limit, section 15(3) of the *Road Traffic Offenders Act* 1988.

(4) Penalties

The maximum penalty for *driving or attempting to drive* is a fine of level 5 (currently £5000) and/or six months' imprisonment. In relation to offences committed on or after commencement of *Criminal Justice Act* 2003, ss.181, 280–282 (see *post*, Ch.23) the maximum custodial sentence able to be imposed in a magistrates' court will be a custody plus order. There is a mandatory requirement to disqualify from driving (in the absence of special reasons) for one year (though see *post*, § 17–177 for the circumstances where that minimum is increased). On endorsement only, there will be penalty points of between 3 and 11.   **17–70**

The maximum penalty for *being in charge* is a fine of level 4 (currently £2500) and/or three months' imprisonment. In relation to offences committed on or after commencement of *Criminal Justice Act* 2003, ss.181, 280–282 (see *post*, Ch.23), the maximum custodial sentence able to be imposed in a magistrates' court will be a custody plus order. There is a discretionary requirement to disqualify from driving. On endorsement, there will be penalty points of 10.

See also the power to deprive the offender of the vehicle contained in section 143(1), (6) and (7) of the *Powers of Criminal Courts (Sentencing) Act* 2000 (see *post*, §§ 17–209 and 23–229).

(5) Sentence

The primary factor for the court in determining sentence will be the extent of the intoxication. Lower penalties are generally imposed for being in charge than for driving.   **17–71**

Normally, financial penalties are considered sufficient together with the disqualification which is mandatory in the case of driving offences and discretionary for in charge offences.

Aggravating features set out in the *Magistrates' Court Sentencing Guidelines* (2004) (under review) include the extent to which driving was actually shown to be impaired and the type of vehicle being driven; for instance, whether it was carrying passengers for reward or driving a large goods vehicle.

A community order should certainly be considered for the higher readings or for a second offence. Particularly appropriate requirements may be unpaid work and a curfew. Whilst imprisonment is possible, since this is not an offence of violence imprisonment should be used only rarely and only when an offender has demonstrated an intention to continue to drive in an intoxicated state.   **17–72**

Regarding the offences arising from being "in charge", given that it is open to the defendant to show that there was no likelihood that he/she would drive (which would be a defence), it is likely that the overall penalty will be similar to that for the driving offences albeit on a slightly lower scale. The higher maximum penalty for the driving offence reflects the potential for the most serious offences to be in that category.

B. DRIVING ETC. WITH EXCESS ALCOHOL IN THE BODY

(1) Definition

Road Traffic Act 1988, s.5

Driving or being in charge of a motor vehicle with alcohol concentration above prescribed limit

17–73   5.—(1) If a person—

(a) drives or attempts to drive a motor vehicle on a road or other public place, or

(b) is in charge of a motor vehicle on a road or other public place,

after consuming so much alcohol that the proportion of it in his breath, blood or urine exceeds the prescribed limit he is guilty of an offence.

(2) It is a defence for a person charged with an offence under subsection (1)(b) above to prove that at the time he is alleged to have committed the offence the circumstances were such that there was no likelihood of his driving the vehicle whilst the proportion of alcohol in his breath, blood or urine remained likely to exceed the prescribed limit.

(3) The court may, in determining whether there was such a likelihood as is mentioned in subsection (2) above, disregard any injury to him and any damage to the vehicle.

(2) Allocation

17–74   These offences are summary only.

(3) What must the prosecution prove?

17–75   The prosecution must prove that:
— the defendant
— drove *or* attempted to drive *or* was in charge of
— a mechanically propelled vehicle
— on a road or other public place
— after consuming so much alcohol
— that the proportion in his breath, blood or urine
— exceeded the prescribed limit.

17–76   For issues of identification, see *ante*, §§ 10–89 *et seq.* in this work.

For issues surrounding the meaning of "drive", see *ante*, § 17–4.

The phrase "mechanically propelled vehicle" is wider than "vehicle"; again this is more fully explored in § 17–6, *ante*. The phrase "road or other public place" has been subject to detailed consideration; this also is explored more fully in §§ 17–7 and 17–8, *ante*.

"Consuming" has been defined more widely than just "drinking"; entry into the body by other means can also be included: *DPP v. Johnson (David)* [1995] R.T.R. 9.

The proportion of alcohol can be assessed through an analysis of breath or of blood or of urine. This is provided for by section 7—see *post*, § 17–95.

17–77   The prescribed limit is set out in section 11(2) of the *Road Traffic Act* 1988.

In breath, the limit is 35 microgrammes of alcohol in 100 millilitres of breath.

In blood, the limit is 80 milligrammes of alcohol in 100 millilitres of blood.

In urine, the limit is 107 milligrammes of alcohol in 100 millilitres of urine.

This limit must be exceeded before a prosecution can be commenced, *e.g.* the analysis must be at least 81mg in blood, 80 is not sufficient. In practice, in relation to analysis based on breath, the police will normally allow for a margin of error. When machinery was introduced that enabled the proportion of alcohol in breath to be measured, the accompanying Home Office Circular (46/1983) provided for an allowance to be made where the analysis showed that the limit was exceeded by a small amount. This was in recognition both of the similar practice undertaken in laboratory analysis of blood or urine and of the relatively new technology incorporated in those early breath testing machines. The circular provided for prosecution based on an analysis of breath only where the reading was 40 microgrammes or more. The relevant part provides:

> "The reading produced by the calibration check test must fall within 3 micrograms of 35 (*i.e.* within the range 32–38 inclusive) to establish that the instrument is working correctly. To cater for those occasions where the machine may be reading high, albeit within this range, the police will not proceed against offenders with a result of less than 40 micrograms. This will ensure that any offender prosecuted will have a result in excess of the prescribed limit. This allowance is comparable to the allowance currently subtracted from specimens analysed in the laboratory."

This was subsequently incorporated into the Code of Practice for Crown Prosecutors which provides:

> "In most cases of drink/driving, there will be scientific and/or medical evidence to show that the driver has exceeded the prescribed limit. In such cases a charge under section 5 will be proper.
>
> Although the prescribed breath alcohol limit is 35 microgrammes, a driver will not be prosecuted under section 5 with a breath alcohol level of less than 40 microgrammes. This is in accordance with the guidelines contained in Home Office Circular 46/1983. That level will usually be taken as that recorded by an evidential breath testing machine or by analysis of a blood/urine sample. However, it may be the level as determined by back calculations."

The allowance in relation to blood or urine will already have been taken into account when the analysis is undertaken.

If a defendant wishes to allege that the analysis showed an excess as a result of alcohol consumed after the driving, etc. had ceased but before the sample was taken, then the defendant must prove (on the balance of probabilities) both that alcohol had been consumed in those circumstances and that the amount would have been sufficient to take the reading over the limit: *Road Traffic Offenders Act* 1988, s.15(3). Unless the effect of the alcohol would have been obvious, expert evidence must be adduced.

There have been continual attempts to evade conviction for these offences by a range of technical arguments calling into question the machines or the process used. Likewise, the appeal courts have continued to decline to accept the arguments put forward.

In *DPP v. Stephens* [2006] EWHC 1860 there were issues about the admissibility of a statement from the doctor and a certificate from an analyst neither of which had been served in accordance with the provisions of section 16 of the *Road Traffic Offenders Act* 1988. The doctor's statement had, however, been properly served as a section 9 statement. The defence successfully sought to exclude both documents because they had not been served properly under the section 16 provisions. The court refused the prosecution application for an adjournment to serve them properly. Allowing the prosecution appeal, the Divisional Court stated that the court had been wrong to exclude the doctor's statement which should have been admissible under section 9 which was not overridden by the section 16 provisions. Whilst the certificate was not admissible, the court was wrong to refuse the prosecution's application for an adjournment. Although an appeal court will only interfere with the exercise of discretion whether to grant an adjournment where it is plain that substantial unfairness will be caused to one of the parties, this was such a situation. The refusal to grant the adjournment was irrational and could not be upheld.

In *Sneyd v. DPP* [2007] R.T.R. 6, the defendant had been one of two drivers stopped whilst driving a car out of the car park of a public house. He confirmed he had been drinking and then provided a positive specimen. That process was challenged by an assertion that the driver should have been cautioned before being asked whether he had been drinking. The Divisional Court rejected that argument—it is not an offence to drink so there was no suspicion that an offence had been committed until after the specimen had been provided. The answer was however adequate to raise a sufficient suspicion to justify the requirement to provide a specimen of breath. Evidence of the subsequent reading of the machine undertaking the analysis of breath was given orally rather than by a printout and there was no evidence that the machine was properly calibrated. The defence argument that this was unacceptable was robustly rejected. There was ample authority that oral evidence could be given and since the evidence that the machine was working properly was sufficiently clear, it followed that the machine was properly calibrated. It was for the defence to raise the issue by cross-examination rather than to assert subsequently that there had been no evidence.

(4) Penalties

17–78　　The maximum penalty for *driving or attempting to drive* is a fine of level 5 (currently £5000) and/or six months' imprisonment. In relation to offences committed on or after commencement of *Criminal Justice Act* 2003, ss.181, 280–282 (see *post*, Ch.23), the maximum custodial sentence in a magistrates' court will be a custody plus order. There is a mandatory requirement to disqualify from driving (in the absence of special reasons, see *post*, § 17–194) for one year (though see *post*, § 17–177 for circumstances where that minimum is increased). On endorsement only, there will be penalty points of between 3 and 11.

The maximum penalty for *being in charge* is a fine of level 4 (currently £2500) and/or three months' imprisonment. In relation to offences committed on or after commencement of *Criminal Justice Act* 2003, ss.181, 280–282 (see *post*, Ch.23), the maximum custodial sentence in a magistrates' court will be a custody plus order. There is a discretionary requirement to disqualify from driving. On endorsement, there will be penalty points of 10.

See also the power to deprive the offender of the vehicle contained in subsections 143(1), (6) and (7) of the *Powers of Criminal Courts (Sentencing) Act* 2000 (see *post*, § 17–197).

(5) Sentence

17–79　　The *Magistrates' Court Sentencing Guidelines* (2004) (under review) provide that aggravating circumstances include the defendant's ability to drive being seriously impaired, causing injury, fear or damage, the occurrence of a police chase, evidence of the nature of the driving. The type of vehicle is also relevant as a possible aggravating factor, *e.g.* if the defendant was carrying passengers for reward or was driving a large goods vehicle. The fact that the defendant gave a high reading when breathalysed will also be an aggravating factor. Mitigating factors include driving in an emergency, moving a vehicle a very short distance and the fact that the level of intoxication was due to drinks being spiked.

In *Shoult* [1996] 2 Cr.App.R.(S.) 234, the Court of Appeal approved the guidelines as to penalties set out by the Magistrates' Association in the equivalent of the *Magistrates' Court Sentencing Guidelines* notwithstanding the fact that each case must be judged on its won merits. However, since 1996, there has been a greater recognition that prison should be reserved for violent offences and there has also been a considerable change in the range of requirements available under a community sentence order. A community order should certainly be considered for the higher readings or for a second offence. Particularly appropriate requirements may be unpaid work and a curfew. Whilst imprisonment is possible, since this is not an offence of violence imprisonment should be used only rarely and only when an offender has demonstrated an intention to continue to drive in an intoxicated state.

C. FAILURE TO SUPPLY A PRELIMINARY SPECIMEN OF BREATH

(1) Definitions

Road Traffic Act 1988, ss.6–6E

Power to administer preliminary tests
17–80　　**6.**—(1) If any of subsections (2) to (5) applies a constable may require a person to cooperate

with any one or more preliminary tests administered to the person by that constable or another constable.

(2) This subsection applies if a constable reasonably suspects that the person—

(a) is driving, is attempting to drive or is in charge of a motor vehicle on a road or other public place, and

(b) has alcohol or a drug in his body or is under the influence of a drug.

(3) This subsection applies if a constable reasonably suspects that the person—

(a) has been driving, attempting to drive or in charge of a motor vehicle on a road or other public place while having alcohol or a drug in his body or while unfit to drive because of a drug, and

(b) still has alcohol or a drug in his body or is still under the influence of a drug.

(4) This subsection applies if a constable reasonably suspects that the person—

(a) is or has been driving, attempting to drive or in charge of a motor vehicle on a road or other public place, and

(b) has committed a traffic offence while the vehicle was in motion.

(5) This subsection applies if—

(a) an accident occurs owing to the presence of a motor vehicle on a road or other public place, and

(b) a constable reasonably believes that the person was driving, attempting to drive or in charge of the vehicle at the time of the accident.

(6) A person commits an offence if without reasonable excuse he fails to cooperate with a preliminary test in pursuance of a requirement imposed under this section.

(7) A constable may administer a preliminary test by virtue of any of subsections (2) to (4) only if he is in uniform.

(8) In this section—

(a) a reference to a preliminary test is to any of the tests described in sections 6A to 6C, and

(b) "traffic offence" means an offence under—

(i) a provision of Part II of the *Public Passenger Vehicles Act* 1981,

(ii) a provision of the *Road Traffic Regulation Act* 1984,

(iii) a provision of the *Road Traffic Offenders Act* 1988 other than a provision of Part III, or

(iv) a provision of this Act other than a provision of Part V.

Preliminary breath test

6A.—(1) A preliminary breath test is a procedure whereby the person to whom the test is **17–81** administered provides a specimen of breath to be used for the purpose of obtaining, by means of a device of a type approved by the Secretary of State, an indication whether the proportion of alcohol in the person's breath or blood is likely to exceed the prescribed limit.

(2) A preliminary breath test administered in reliance on section 6(2) to (4) may be administered only at or near the place where the requirement to cooperate with the test is imposed.

(3) A preliminary breath test administered in reliance on section 6(5) may be administered—

(a) at or near the place where the requirement to cooperate with the test is imposed, or

(b) if the constable who imposes the requirement thinks it expedient, at a police station specified by him.

Preliminary impairment test

6B.—(1) A preliminary impairment test is a procedure whereby the constable administering **17–82** the test—

(a) observes the person to whom the test is administered in his performance of tasks specified by the constable, and

(b) makes such other observations of the person's physical state as the constable thinks expedient.

(2) The Secretary of State shall issue (and may from time to time revise) a code of practice about—

(a) the kind of task that may be specified for the purpose of a preliminary impairment test,

(b) the kind of observation of physical state that may be made in the course of a preliminary impairment test,

(c) the manner in which a preliminary impairment test should be administered, and

(d) the inferences that may be drawn from observations made in the course of a preliminary impairment test.

(3) In issuing or revising the code of practice the Secretary of State shall aim to ensure that a preliminary impairment test is designed to indicate—

(a) whether a person is unfit to drive, and

(b) if he is, whether or not his unfitness is likely to be due to drink or drugs.

(4) A preliminary impairment test may be administered—

(a) at or near the place where the requirement to cooperate with the test is imposed, or

(b) if the constable who imposes the requirement thinks it expedient, at a police station specified by him.

(5) A constable administering a preliminary impairment test shall have regard to the code of practice under this section.

(6) A constable may administer a preliminary impairment test only if he is approved for that purpose by the chief officer of the police force to which he belongs.

(7) A code of practice under this section may include provision about—

(a) the giving of approval under subsection (6), and

(b) in particular, the kind of training that a constable should have undergone, or the kind of qualification that a constable should possess, before being approved under that subsection.

Preliminary drug test

17–83   **6C.**—(1) A preliminary drug test is a procedure by which a specimen of sweat or saliva is—

(a) obtained, and

(b) used for the purpose of obtaining, by means of a device of a type approved by the Secretary of State, an indication whether the person to whom the test is administered has a drug in his body.

(2) A preliminary drug test may be administered—

(a) at or near the place where the requirement to cooperate with the test is imposed, or

(b) if the constable who imposes the requirement thinks it expedient, at a police station specified by him.

Arrest

17–84   **6D.**—(1) A constable may arrest a person without warrant if as a result of a preliminary breath test the constable reasonably suspects that the proportion of alcohol in the person's breath or blood exceeds the prescribed limit.

(1A) The fact that specimens of breath have been provided under section 7 of this Act by the person concerned does not prevent subsection (1) above having effect if the constable who imposed on him the requirement to provide the specimens has reasonable cause to believe that the device used to analyse the specimens has not produced a reliable indication of the proportion of alcohol in the breath of the person.

(2) A constable may arrest a person without warrant if—

(a) the person fails to cooperate with a preliminary test in pursuance of a requirement imposed under section 6, and

(b) the constable reasonably suspects that the person has alcohol or a drug in his body or is under the influence of a drug.

(2A) A person arrested under this section may, instead of being taken to a police station, be detained at or near the place where the preliminary test was, or would have been, administered, with a view to imposing on him there a requirement under section 7 of this Act.

(3) A person may not be arrested under this section while at a hospital as a patient.

Power of entry

17–85   **6E.**—(1) A constable may enter any place (using reasonable force if necessary) for the purpose of—

(a) imposing a requirement by virtue of section 6(5) following an accident in a case where the constable reasonably suspects that the accident involved injury of any person, or

(b) arresting a person under section 6D following an accident in a case where the constable reasonably suspects that the accident involved injury of any person.

(2) This section—

(a) does not extend to Scotland, and

(b) is without prejudice to any rule of law or enactment about the right of a constable in Scotland to enter any place.

(2) Allocation

These offences are triable summarily only.   **17–86**

(3) What must the prosecution prove?

The prosecution must prove that: **17–87**

— the defendant

— having been required to provide a breath specimen under this section

— failed to do so

— [without reasonable excuse]

For issues of identification, see § 10–89 in this work.

A person commits an offence by failing to provide this preliminary specimen of **17–88**
breath without reasonable excuse. The purpose of the test is to obtain an indication whether the proportion of alcohol is likely to exceed the prescribed limit.

The prosecution must prove that the test was lawfully required but was not provided. It is for the defendant to initiate the "reasonable excuse" but, once that is done, it is for the prosecution to negative that defence.

There are a number of elements that must exist before a requirement is lawfully made under this section.

1) The test must be required by a *constable in uniform* where the reason for the requirement is that:

— the constable has reasonable cause to *suspect* that

— a person who is driving/attempting to drive/in charge of

— a motor vehicle (*note: not a "mechanically propelled vehicle"*)

— on a road or other place

— either

— has alcohol in his body (section 6(2)) or

— has committed a traffic offence whilst the vehicle was in motion (section 6(4)).

Similarly where the constable in uniform has reasonable cause to suspect that the person *has been* driving/attempting to drive/in charge of a motor vehicle with adjustments to reflect the fact that the driving, etc. has ceased: section 6(3).

2) The test may be required by a *constable* where the reason for the requirement is that:

— an accident has occurred

— owing to the presence of a motor vehicle on a road or other public place

— and the constable has reasonable cause to *believe*

— that the person was driving/in charge at the time of the accident (section 6(5)).

The test must be taken at or near the place where the requirement is made save that, **17–89**
where the requirement arises from an accident as in 2, *ante*, the constable may require it to be taken at a police station if he thinks fit: section 6A(3). If a person is at a hospital as a patient, the requirement for a breath test may only be made after notice has been given to the medical practitioner in charge of the case. The medical practitioner may

object on the grounds that either requiring or taking the test would be prejudicial to the proper care and treatment of the patient; in those circumstances, the requirement may not be made. If a requirement is made, it must be for the taking of this preliminary breath test at the hospital: section 9(1). "Hospital" is defined in section 11(2).

17–90   A "constable" is any police officer of whatever rank. The purpose of the requirement that the constable be in uniform is to ensure that he is easily identifiable as a police constable. Accordingly, not wearing a helmet but otherwise being in uniform was sufficient: *Wallwork v. Giles* (1969) 114 S.J. 36.

In relation to most circumstances, the constable must have reasonable cause to "suspect" that the qualifying circumstances exist. In relation to the power following an accident, the constable must have reasonable cause to "believe" that a person was the driver etc. The distinction is a matter of degree. It is for the prosecution to prove that the officer had reasonable cause to suspect or believe.

One of the grounds for requiring a test is where there is suspicion that the person has committed a traffic offence whilst the vehicle was in motion. "Traffic offence" is defined in section 6(8) and covers a wide variety of offences.

17–91   The breath test must be taken by means of a device of a type approved by the Secretary of State. A number of Breath Test (Type Approval) Orders have been made, including the Preliminary Breath Test Device Approval 2005. Each device will operate in different ways. In the absence of bad faith, it is not necessary to comply fully with the manufacturer's instructions (see *DPP v. Carey* [1969] 3 All E.R. 1662)—the specimen must be sufficient to enable the test to be carried out and for the objective of the test to be achieved: section 11(3). The validity and reliability of various devices has been much litigated. For a full review of the issues and authorities, see Wilkinson, *Road Traffic Offences*, 22nd edn, para. 4.187ff. The Appeal Courts have become increasingly intolerant of arguments about the validity of devices.

Refusal to take a test is a failure to take the test for the purposes of an offence under section 6 (see section 11(2)). Refusal can be inferred from the actions of the person concerned, such as an attempt to abscond. If a person fails to take the test in a way that complies with section 11(3), he may be arrested if the constable has reasonable cause to suspect that the person has alcohol in his body: section 6D(2). If a person takes the test and the device indicates that the level of alcohol is higher than permitted then that person also will be arrested: section 6(5)(a). A person who is at hospital as a patient may not be arrested under section 6: section 6D(3).

The range of reasonable excuses for failing to provide this specimen of breath is limited and largely restricted to circumstances where the person is physically unable to provide sufficient breath in a way that allows the test to be completed. It is not sufficient to assert that no alcohol had been consumed or that the person had not been driving, etc.

In *DPP v. Swan* [2004] EWHC 2432 Admin, the defendant was seen driving, stopped and asked to supply a specimen of breath. He was rude and aggressive and sought to delay providing the specimen of breath. As a consequence, he was handcuffed and arrested before the roadside breathalyser device was made available. It was argued that the offence was not made out because the device had not been proffered to the defendant and this was accepted by the justices. Allowing the prosecutor's appeal, the Court confirmed that it was not necessary for the roadside device to be made available where the driver's conduct showed he was either not willing to provide a specimen or he imposed unacceptable terms on which such a specimen would be provided. In this case, the behaviour of the defendant and delaying tactics clearly amounted to a failure to provide the specimen.

(4) Penalty

17–92   The maximum penalty is a fine of up to level 3 (currently £1000). It is endorsable with 4 penalty points and disqualification is discretionary.

(5) Sentence

The *Magistrates' Court Sentencing Guidelines* (2004) (under review) recommend a **17–93** starting point at level A (50 per cent of weekly income). The penalty will reflect the fact that refusal to supply this sample does not of itself prevent the gathering of evidence to show whether the principal offence has been committed.

D. Failure to Supply a Specimen for Analysis

(1) Definition

The requirement to provide for analysis a specimen of breath, blood or urine is the **17–94** key element in the gaining of evidence to support charges of driving etc. whilst under the influence of alcohol. This includes the offence of causing death by careless driving under the influence of drugs or alcohol.

If the specimen is provided, it will show the level of alcohol; if the person fails to provide a specimen without reasonable excuse, an offence is committed under section 7(6) and the maximum penalty is the same as for the substantive offence of which the person would have been liable to have been convicted if the specimen had been provided and the level of alcohol shown to be above the limit.

Road Traffic Act 1988, ss.7–11

Provision of specimen for analysis

7.—(1) In the course of an investigation into whether a person has committed an offence **17–95** under section 3A, 4 or 5 of this Act a constable may, subject to the following provisions of this section and section 9 of this Act, require him—

    (a) to provide two specimens of breath for analysis by means of a device of a type approved by the Secretary of State, or

    (b) to provide a specimen of blood or urine for a laboratory test

  (2) A requirement under this section to provide specimens of breath can only be made—

    (a) at a police station,

    (b) at a hospital, or

    (c) at or near a place where a relevant breath test has been administered to the person concerned or would have been so administered but for his failure to co-operate with it.

  (2A) For the purposes of this section "a relevant breath test" is a procedure involving the provision by the person concerned of a specimen of breath to be used for the purpose of obtaining an indication whether the proportion of alcohol in his breath or blood is likely to exceed the prescribed limit.

  (2B) A requirement under this section to provide specimens of breath may not be made at or near a place mentioned in subsection (2)(c) above unless the constable making it—

    (a) is in uniform, or

    (b) has imposed a requirement on the person concerned to co-operate with a relevant breath test in circumstances in which section 6(5) of this Act applies.

  (2C) Where a constable has imposed a requirement on the person concerned to co-operate with a relevant breath test at any place, he is entitled to remain at or near that place in order to impose on him there a requirement under this section.

  (2D) If a requirement under subsection (1)(a) above has been made at a place other than at a police station, such a requirement may subsequently be made at a police station if (but only if)—

    (a) a device or a reliable device of the type mentioned in subsection (1)(a) above was not available at that place or it was for any other reason not practicable to use such a device there, or

    (b) the constable who made the previous requirement has reasonable cause to believe that the device used there has not produced a reliable indication of the proportion of alcohol in the breath of the person concerned.

  (3) A requirement under this section to provide a specimen of blood or urine can only be made at a police station or at a hospital; and it cannot be made at a police station unless—

(a) the constable making the requirement has reasonable cause to believe that for medical reasons a specimen of breath cannot be provided or should not be required, or

(b) specimens of breath have not been provided elsewhere and at the time the requirement is made a device or a reliable device of the type mentioned in subsection (1)(a) above is not available at the police station or it is then for any other reason not practicable to use such a device there, or

(bb) a device of the type mentioned in subsection (1)(a) above has been used (at the police station or elsewhere) but the constable who required the specimens of breath has reasonable cause to believe that the device has not produced a reliable indication of the proportion of alcohol in the breath of the person concerned, or

(bc) as a result of the administration of a preliminary drug test, the constable making the requirement has reasonable cause to believe that the person required to provide a specimen of blood or urine has a drug in his body, or

(c) the suspected offence is one under section 3A or 4 of this Act and the constable making the requirement has been advised by a medical practitioner that the condition of the person required to provide the specimen might be due to some drug;

but may then be made notwithstanding that the person required to provide the specimen has already provided or been required to provide two specimens of breath.

(4) If the provision of a specimen other than a specimen of breath may be required in pursuance of this section the question whether it is to be a specimen of blood or a specimen of urine and, in the case of a specimen of blood, the question who is to be asked to take it shall be decided (subject to subsection (4A)) by the constable making the requirement.

(4A) Where a constable decides for the purposes of subsection (4) to require the provision of a specimen of blood, there shall be no requirement to provide such a specimen if—

(a) the medical practitioner who is asked to take the specimen is of the opinion that, for medical reasons, it cannot or should not be taken; or

(b) the registered health care professional who is asked to take it is of that opinion and there is no contrary opinion from a medical practitioner;

and, where by virtue of this subsection there can be no requirement to provide a specimen of blood, the constable may require a specimen of urine instead.

(5) A specimen of urine shall be provided within one hour of the requirement for its provision being made and after the provision of a previous specimen of urine.

(6) A person who, without reasonable excuse, fails to provide a specimen when required to do so in pursuance of this section is guilty of an offence.

(7) A constable must, on requiring any person to provide a specimen in pursuance of this section, warn him that a failure to provide it may render him liable to prosecution.

Specimens of blood taken from persons incapable of consenting

17–96   **7A.**—(1) A constable may make a request to a medical practitioner for him to take a specimen of blood from a person ('the person concerned') irrespective of whether that person consents if—

(a) that person is a person from whom the constable would (in the absence of any incapacity of that person and of any objection under section 9) be entitled under section 7 to require the provision of a specimen of blood for a laboratory test;

(b) it appears to that constable that that person has been involved in an accident that constitutes or is comprised in the matter that is under investigation or the circumstances of that matter;

(c) it appears to that constable that that person is or may be incapable (whether or not he has purported to do so) of giving a valid consent to the taking of a specimen of blood; and

(d) it appears to that constable that that person's incapacity is attributable to medical reasons.

(2) A request under this section—

(a) shall not be made to a medical practitioner who for the time being has any responsibility (apart from the request) for the clinical care of the person concerned; and

(b) shall not be made to a medical practitioner other than a police medical practitioner unless—

(i) it is not reasonably practicable for the request to made to a police medical practitioner; or

(ii) it is not reasonably practicable for such a medical practitioner (assuming him to be willing to do so) to take the specimen.

(3) It shall be lawful for a medical practitioner to whom a request is made under this section, if he thinks fit—

(a) to take a specimen of blood from the person concerned irrespective of whether that person consents; and

(b) to provide the sample to a constable.

(4) If a specimen is taken in pursuance of a request under this section, the specimen shall not be subjected to a laboratory test unless the person from whom it was taken—

(a) has been informed that it was taken; and

(b) has been required by a constable to give his permission for a laboratory test of the specimen; and

(c) has given his permission.

(5) A constable must, on requiring a person to give his permission for the purposes of this section for a laboratory test of a specimen, warn that person that a failure to give the permission may render him liable to prosecution.

(6) A person who, without reasonable excuse, fails to give his permission for a laboratory test of a specimen of blood taken from him under this section is guilty of an offence.

(7) In this section 'police medical practitioner' means a medical practitioner who is engaged under any agreement to provide medical services for purposes connected with the activities of a police force.

Choice of specimens of breath

8.—(1) Subject to subsection (2) below, of any two specimens of breath provided by any person in pursuance of section 7 of this Act that with the lower proportion of alcohol in the breath shall be used and the other shall be disregarded.   **17–97**

(2) If the specimen with the lower proportion of alcohol contains no more than 50 microgrammes of alcohol in 100 millilitres of breath, the person who provided it may claim that it should be replaced by such specimen as may be required under section 7(4) of this Act and, if he then provides such a specimen, neither specimen of breath shall be used.

(2A) If the person who makes a claim under subsection (2) above was required to provide specimens of breath under section 7 of this Act at or near a place mentioned in subsection (2)(c) of that section, a constable may arrest him without warrant.

(3) The Secretary of State may by regulations substitute another proportion of alcohol in the breath for that specified in subsection (2) above.

Protection for hospital patients

9.—(1) While a person is at a hospital as a patient he shall not be required to co-operate with a preliminary test or to provide a specimen under section 7 of this Act unless the medical practitioner in immediate charge of his case has been notified of the proposal to make the requirement; and—   **17–98**

(a) if the requirement is then made, it shall be for co-operation with a test administered, or for the provision of a specimen, at the hospital, but

(b) if the medical practitioner objects on the ground specified in subsection (2) below, the requirement shall not be made.

(1A) While a person is at a hospital as a patient, no specimen of blood shall be taken from him under section 7A of this Act and he shall not be required to give his permission for a laboratory test of a specimen taken under that section unless the medical practitioner in immediate charge of his case—

(a) has been notified of the proposal to take the specimen or to make the requirement; and

(b) has not objected on the ground specified in subsection (2).

(2) The ground on which the medical practitioner may object is—

(a) in a case falling within subsection (1), that the requirement or the provision of the specimen or (if one is required) the warning required by section 7(7) of this Act would be prejudicial to the proper care and treatment of the patient; and

(b) in a case falling within subsection (1A), that the taking of the specimen, the requirement or the warning required by section 7A(5) of this Act would be so prejudicial.

Detention of persons affected by alcohol or a drug

17–99   **10.**—(1) Subject to subsections (2) and (3) below, a person required under section 7 or 7A to provide a specimen of breath, blood or urine may afterwards be detained at a police station (or, if the specimen was provided otherwise than at a police station, arrested and taken to and detained at a police station) if a constable has reasonable grounds for believing that, were that person then driving or attempting to drive a mechanically propelled vehicle on a road, he would commit an offence under section 4 or 5 of this Act.

(2) Subsection (1) above does not apply to the person if it ought reasonably to appear to the constable that there is no likelihood of his driving or attempting to drive a mechanically propelled vehicle whilst his ability to drive properly is impaired or whilst the proportion of alcohol in his breath, blood or urine exceeds the prescribed limit.

(2A) A person who is at a hospital as a patient shall not be arrested and taken from there to a police station in pursuance of this section if it would be prejudicial to his proper care and treatment as a patient.

(3) A constable must consult a medical practitioner on any question arising under this section whether a person's ability to drive properly is or might be impaired through drugs and must act on the medical practitioner's advice.

Interpretation

17–100   **11.**—(1) The following provisions apply for the interpretation of sections 3A to 10 of this Act.

(2) In those sections—

"drug" includes any intoxicant other than alcohol,

"fail" includes refuse,

"hospital" means an institution which provides medical or surgical treatment for in-patients or out-patients,

"the prescribed limit" means, as the case may require—

(a) 35 microgrammes of alcohol in 100 millilitres of breath,

(b) 80 milligrammes of alcohol in 100 millilitres of blood, or

(c) 107 milligrammes of alcohol in 100 millilitres of urine, or such other proportion as may be prescribed by regulations made by the Secretary of State.

"registered health care professional" means a person (other than a medical practitioner) who is—

(a) a registered nurse; or

(b) a registered member of a health care profession which is designated for the purposes of this paragraph by an order made by the Secretary of State.

(2A) A health care profession is any profession mentioned in section 60(2) of the *Health Act* 1999 (c. 8) other than the profession of practising medicine and the profession of nursing.

(2B) An order under subsection (2) shall be made by statutory instrument; and any such statutory instrument shall be subject to annulment in pursuance of a resolution of either House of Parliament.

(3) A person does not provide a specimen of breath for a preliminary test or for analysis unless the specimen—

(a) is sufficient to enable the test or the analysis to be carried out, and

(b) is provided in such a way as to enable the objective of the test or analysis to be satisfactorily achieved.

(4) A person provides a specimen of blood if and only if—

(a) he consents to the taking of such a specimen from him; and

(b) the specimen is taken from him by a medical practitioner or, if it is taken in a police station, either by a medical practitioner or by a registered health care professional.

(2) Allocation

17–101   These offences are triable summarily only.

(3) What must the prosecution prove?

17–102   The prosecution must prove that:

— the defendant
— failed to provide a specimen
— [without reasonable excuse]
— when required to do so pursuant to section 7.

For issues of identification, see § 10–89.

"Fail" includes "refuse": section 11(2). A specimen of breath must be sufficient to enable the analysis to be carried out and the objective of the analysis to be satisfactorily achieved: s.11(3). A novel point was raised in relation to the meaning of "breath" in *Zafar v. DPP* [2005] R.T.R. 18. The defendant provided specimens of breath at a police station that were found to contain alcohol in excess of the prescribed limit. On appeal against conviction to the Crown Court, he argued that he had consumed only one pint of lager but that he suffered from heartburn which caused an occasional reflux of the stomach contents to the mouth for which he took medicine. Expert evidence was given that demonstrated that the Intoximeter was designed to detect alcohol in deep lung air as opposed to alcohol in the mouth. It also asserted that this particular machine was very poor at detecting mouth alcohol. The Crown Court dismissed the appeal holding that the prosecution was not obliged to show that the reading related to deep lung air. The distinction between that and mouth alcohol was not required by the Act and that "breath" in the statute did not distinguish between the two meanings. The Divisional Court dismissed the further appeal. The main dictionary definition of breath was "air exhaled from anything" and there was nothing in the statute that suggested that any other definition should be used.

Once the possibility of a reasonable excuse is raised by the defence, it is for the prosecution to satisfy the court beyond reasonable doubt that there was no reasonable excuse. Although it is a question of fact whether a defendant has a reasonable excuse, nonetheless it is a question of law as to whether particular circumstances can be a reasonable excuse for failing to provide a specimen. The category has been very narrowly drawn and little can justify failing or refusing to provide a specimen unless it arises out of a physical or mental inability to provide a specimen or a substantial risk to health in its provision: *Lennard* [1973] R.T.R. 252. In *DPP v. Coulter* [2005] EWHC 1533, the defendant was prosecuted for failing to provide a specimen of breath. During the procedure, he had been asked whether he had eaten anything and replied that he might have had a tic-tac. The station procedure general booklet that was being followed said that, if anything had been eaten, there should be a 20 minute wait before the test. The officer conducting the procedure did not wait. It was argued that there should have been a 20 minute wait and the request for a test was therefore unlawful. Dismissing the appeal, the Divisional Court commented that there was no evidence of the effect that a tic-tac would have had on the reading and that there was no suggestion that the failure to provide the specimen had anything to do with the consumption of the tic-tac. The Court quoted with approval part of the judgment in *DPP v. Smith* [2000] R.T.R. 341 in which the Court (though dealing with a different point) had stated:

> "I have examined the forms MG DD/A and B and conclude that they are, in essence, no more than what I would describe as the "plain man's guide" to a simple understanding of the procedures provided by the Act of 1988 to ensure, in a practical way, that those called upon to operate the procedures do not omit a relevant step; that, at stages where there is a choice of steps, they appreciate that such a choice exists; and it also offers quite clearly some common sense guidance as to the way in which choices should be exercised when they fall to be made."

The Court in *Coulter* then concluded that:

> "If there is a failure to follow the guidance, it is possible, in certain circumstances, that that might affect the reliability of a specimen that was in fact provided. There are limited circumstances in which a challenge to the reliability of a specimen that is provided can arise. That, in my view, is not relevant here. No specimen was provided. There was a failure to provide a specimen."

It would seem that a challenge to the procedure can only follow the provision of a specimen not to justify a failure to provide one at all.

17–103

Part III

The majority of the circumstances have arisen in connection with specimens of blood. In relation to the provision of specimens of breath, most normal people could do what is required without effort. It will, therefore, require powerful evidence to justify finding a reasonable excuse and courts have been warned not to be gullible: *DPP v. Eddowes* [1991] R.T.R. 35. Most commonly, issues are likely to be raised in the context of the driver suffering from asthma. The statement of the Court of Appeal in *Lennard* that "No excuse can be adjudged a reasonable one unless a person from whom the specimen is required is physically or mentally unable to provide it or the provision of the specimen would entail a substantial risk to his health" has been re-iterated in the context of asthma sufferers in both *Eddowes* [1991] R.T.R. 35 and *DPP v. Curtis* [1993] R.T.R. 72. For a situation where a reasonable excuse was found, see *DPP v. Falzarano* [2001] R.T.R. 14 where evidence was given by her doctor that the driver was subject to panic attacks in stressful situations. A sufficient causative link was found on the facts between the condition and the failure to provide the specimen.

In relation to specimens of urine, the obligation is to provide two specimens, the second (which is to be used for analysis) within an hour of the first. A genuine physical inability to provide the second specimen can amount to a reasonable excuse but is likely to be followed by the police utilising the power to require a specimen of blood.

17–104 Inability to understand the statutory warning that a person is liable for prosecution for failing to provide a specimen for analysis may amount to a reasonable excuse where that is due to the person's limited command of English. Where it cannot be understood by the defendant because of self induced intoxication, then that cannot be a reasonable excuse.

There is no entitlement to delay the taking of a specimen to any significant extent in order to enable the suspect to receive legal advice: *Campbell v. DPP* [2004] R.T.R. 5; *Kennedy v. DPP* [2004] R.T.R. 6. Similarly, an attempt by the person arrested to impose conditions on his agreement to provide the specimen is unlikely to be successful. In *DPP v. Swan* [2004] EWHC 243 Admin, the defendant was seen driving, stopped and asked to supply a specimen of breath. He was rude and aggressive and sought to delay providing the specimen of breath. As a consequence, he was handcuffed and arrested before the roadside breathalyser device was made available. At the police station, he continued to be rude and abusive and wanted photographs of the injuries to his wrists caused by the handcuffs to be taken before he would supply the specimen, or, at least, a guarantee that they would be taken. The officer in charge refused to give that guarantee, the defendant continued to insist and the breath analysis machine timed out! The officer took the view that the defendant had refused to supply a specimen and charged him accordingly. Justices dismissed the charge on the basis that the request for photographs to be taken was not an "outrageous condition". The Divisional Court allowed the prosecutor's appeal. There was no threshold for outrageous conditions and, if a matter could not amount to a reasonable excuse for failing to supply a specimen, it was difficult to see how it could be relied on as a basis for saying there had not been a failure to provide the specimen. Whether there is a refusal is a question of fact and reference to the term "outrageous" is unhelpful in interpreting the effect of a condition placed on consent by the driver.

Another in the series of cases where the defendant has sought to obtain legal advice before providing a specimen and then seeks to justify the failure to provide a specimen by reference to the lack of that advice is *Causey v. DPP* (2005) 169 J.P. 331. The court set out a series of principles and emphasised that recourse to the appeal courts on this issue should only be in exceptional cases. The main principles are that there was no general duty on the police to delay taking a specimen pending advice and that specimens must be taken as close as possible to the time of the alleged offence, that it was a question of fact and degree, depending on the circumstances of the case, whether the custody officer had acted without delay and permitted the defendant to consult a solicitor without delay and that, if a custody officer knew that a solicitor was immediately available, the defendant should be allowed to consult before deciding whether or not to provide specimens. However, a solicitor could not have added anything of significance to the information already given to the defendant orally by the custody officer and in the form with which the defendant had been provided.

A further example of the tough line taken where a defendant seeks to put forward a reasonable excuse for failing to supply a specimen is *DPP v. Mukandiwa* [2006] R.T.R 24. The defendant put forward his reaction to the sight of blood as a reason to excuse his failure to provide a specimen. He asserted that the sight of blood could drive him into a trance in which he could become violent to himself and to others. This was accepted as a reasonable excuse by a district judge but the Divisional Court held that that was not a conclusion open to the judge on the facts. A distinction was to be drawn between the sight of blood and the taking of it. There was no reason why the defendant should have to see the blood when it was taken.

Another example of robustness from the appeal courts can be seen in *DPP v. Wood*; *DPP v. McGillicuddy* [2006] EWHC 32; (2006) 170 J.P. 17. The defence had successfully obtained the stay of proceedings as a result of issues regarding disclosure of information relating to the machines used to measure alcohol in breath. The Divisional Court held that those proceedings should not have been stayed. The lawfulness of type approval was not a matter which could be raised as a defence. Where the contention was that the device which was originally type-approved had been altered in such a way as to take it beyond its approval, and disclosure was sought to further that contention, the court would require more than the asserted fact of unapproved modification to justify disclosure. There would have to be some material which explained how the alteration could go to loss of type approval and how disclosure could advance that point. On the facts of the instant case there was no material sufficient to justify the disclosure orders that had been made. Further detail on this complex and much litigated area of the law can be found in *Wilkinson's Road Traffic Offences*, Ch.4.

(4) "Required pursuant to s.7"

There needs to be an investigation into whether a person has committed an offence **17–105** under section 3A (causing death by careless driving under the influence of drink or drugs), section 4 (driving etc. whilst unfit through drink or drugs) or section 5 (driving etc. with excess alcohol in the body). If there is, a constable may require that person to provide a specimen for analysis. That specimen may consist of two specimens of breath (which will be analysed by a device approved by the Secretary of State) or a specimen of blood or a specimen of urine: section 7(1). The constable requiring the specimen must warn that a failure to provide the specimen may lead to prosecution: section (7).

Specimens of *breath* can only be required at a police station: section 7(2). There is no obligation that requires the police to explain to a suspect why a breath test cannot be taken in these circumstances other than at a police station. The law does not allow such a test and that is sufficient. Previous conflicting authorities on this point were resolved by the decision in *Jones v. DPP* [2005] R.T.R. 15. Specimens of *blood* or *urine* can only be required at a police station or a hospital: section 7(3). Such a specimen can only be required at a police station in circumstances set out in section 7(3) but, if any of these circumstances exist, the request can be made even if the person has already provided (or been required to provide) two specimens of breath.

Once it is possible to require a specimen of blood or urine, it is for the constable to **17–106** choose which: section 7(4). Although that is a very wide discretion, it is a statutory discretion and will be reviewed by a Court in accordance with the *Wednesbury* principles. In *Joseph v. DPP* (2004) 168 J.P. 575, the Divisional Court made it clear that, in a section 8(2) case (that is, where the lower of the two specimens contained no more than 50 microgrammes of alcohol in 100 millilitres of breath), there is no ground on which a driver can expect to be asked to indicate whether a sample of blood or of urine is preferred. However, in this case, the defendant genuinely believed that it was against the tenets of his religion to give blood and this was known to the officer before he decided whether to require blood or urine. The officer considered that, in the absence of a medical reason, he could only ask for a specimen of blood in these circumstances.

The Court held that this was wrong. Without wishing to imply that the views of the defendant should be sought, where there is no reason for not choosing urine in preference to blood, if a valid reason is put forward why urine should be the choice, the officer must at least consider that reason. If the officer concludes without reason that it should be the method to which the defendant objects, that decision may be categorised as perverse or it may be concluded that the statutory procedure has not been properly completed.

A different situation arose in *Myles v. DPP* [2004] 2 All E.R. 902; [2005] R.T.R. 1. Here the result of the breath test was unsatisfactory and a police surgeon was called to take a specimen of blood. The defendant refused to give a specimen and was considered by the surgeon to be obstructive. Warned of the consequences of refusal, the defendant maintained that he required legal advice. He was charged with failing to provide the specimen and argued that the evidence of the request for a sample should be disregarded because he had been denied the right to the services of a solicitor. Reviewing domestic and commonwealth authorities, the Court concluded that there was no justification for delaying the completion of the procedures for taking the specimen. This was the clear line of authority.

It is also for the constable to choose who is to be asked to take a sample of blood which may be a medical practitioner or a registered health care professional (as defined in section 11(2)). The person must consent to the taking of blood: section 11(4). The medical practitioner or registered health care professional may form the opinion that the specimen of blood cannot or should not be taken. In those circumstances, the requirement may not be made: section 7(4A). This still leaves the option of breath or urine. If the opinion is that of a registered health care professional, it can be overridden by a medical practitioner: section 7(4A)(b). If the person subject to the requirement is in hospital as a patient, the medical practitioner in immediate charge of the case must be notified. If he objects on the ground that either giving the statutory warning or taking the specimen would be prejudicial to the proper care and treatment of the patient, then the requirement must not be made. If it is made, the specimen must be provided at the hospital and will then be of blood or urine: section 9.

17–107   As stated in § 17–100 *ante*, section 11(4) requires a person to consent to the taking of a specimen of blood. Section 7A, however, provides an additional procedure where a constable considers that the subject of the requirement is incapable (for medical reasons) of giving valid consent. This procedure arises where the subject has been involved in an accident that is part of the matter under investigation and is a person from whom a specimen would normally be requested (subject to the possibility of objection under section 9—prejudicial to the proper care and treatment of the patient). In such circumstances, a constable may request a medical practitioner to take a specimen from the subject. That medical practitioner will not be a medical practitioner who has current responsibility for the clinical care of the subject and will normally be a police medical practitioner (as defined in section 7A(7)) unless it is not reasonably practicable to ask a police medical practitioner or for such a medical practitioner to take the specimen: section 7A(2). A specimen taken in this way may not be sent for analysis until the subject has been told it has been taken and has given his permission for it to be sent for analysis. He must be warned that failure to give permission may render him liable for prosecution. It is an offence to fail to give permission without reasonable excuse.

Where specimens of breath are given, the one with the lower reading is to be used: section 8(1). If that reading is 50 microgrammes or below, the person providing it may claim that it be replaced by such a specimen as may be required under section 7(4) (blood or urine—at the choice of the constable). If that alternative specimen is provided, neither breath specimens may be used: section 8(2).

(5) Penalty (s.7 or s.7A)

17–108   The maximum penalty for *driving or attempting to drive* is a fine of level 5 (currently £5000) and/or six months' imprisonment. In relation to offences committed on or after commencement of *Criminal Justice Act* 2003, ss.181, 280–282 (see *post*, Ch.23), the maximum custodial sentence in a magistrates' court will be a custody plus order. There is a mandatory requirement to disqualify from driving (in the absence of special reasons) for one year (though see *post*, § 17–177 for the circumstances where that minimum is increased). On endorsement only, there will be penalty points of between 3 and 11.

The maximum penalty for *being in charge* is a fine of level 4 (currently £2500) and/or three months' imprisonment. In relation to offences committed on or after commencement of *Criminal Justice Act* 2003, ss.181, 280–282 (see *post*, Ch.23), the maximum custodial sentence in a magistrates' court will be a custody plus order: There is a discretionary requirement to disqualify from driving. On endorsement, there will be penalty points of 10.

(6) Sentence

The *Magistrates' Court Sentencing Guidelines* (2004) (under review) provide that **17–109** aggravating factors include the occurrence of a police chase, the causing of injury, fear or damage, the type of vehicle driven, any evidence of the nature of the driving and the defendant's ability to drive being seriously impaired. Mitigating factors include the defendant not being the driver of the vehicle.

See also the power to deprive the offender of the vehicle contained in section 143(1), (6) and (7) of the *Powers of Criminal Courts (Sentencing) Act* 2000 (see *post*, §§ 17–209 and 23–229).

IV. DISQUALIFICATION OFFENCES

A. DRIVING WHILST DISQUALIFIED; OBTAINING A LICENCE WHILST DISQUALIFIED

A person may be disqualified from driving in a number of different ways, see *post*, **17–110** § 17–191. Once disqualified *by a court*, it is an offence either to obtain a licence or to drive a vehicle. Where the disqualification is until a relevant test is passed (see *post*, § 17–195), the disqualified person can drive as a learner driver pending passing that test.

A person who is disqualified from holding a particular licence because of their age (section 102 of the *Road Traffic Act* 1988—*e.g.* under 16 for a moped, under 17 for a motor bicycle or car—but nonetheless drives a vehicle of the type in question, is liable to be prosecuted for the offence of driving without holding an appropriate licence: *Road Traffic Act* 1988, s.87, see *post*, § 17–140.

Road Traffic Act 1988, s.103

Obtaining licence, or driving, while disqualified
    103.—(1) A person is guilty of an offence if, while disqualified for holding or obtaining a **17–111** licence, he—
    (a) obtains a licence, or
    (b) drives a motor vehicle on a road.
    (2) A licence obtained by a person who is disqualified is of no effect (or, where the disqualification relates only to vehicles of a particular class, is of no effect in relation to vehicles of that class).'
    (3) A constable in uniform may arrest without warrant any person driving a motor vehicle on a road whom he has reasonable cause to suspect of being disqualified.
    (4) Subsections (1) and (3) above do not apply in relation to disqualification by virtue of section 101 of this Act.
    (5) Subsections (1)(b) and (3) above do not apply in relation to disqualification by virtue of section 102 of this Act.
    (6) In the application of subsections (1) and (3) above to a person whose disqualification is limited to the driving of motor vehicles of a particular class by virtue of—

Part III

(a) section 102, 117 or 117A of this Act, or

(b) subsection (9) of section 36 of the *Road Traffic Offenders Act* 1988 (disqualification until test is passed),

the references to disqualification for holding or obtaining a licence and driving motor vehicles are references to disqualification for holding or obtaining a licence to drive and driving motor vehicles of that class.

B. DISQUALIFICATION OF PERSONS UNDER AGE

Road Traffic Act 1988, s.101

Disqualification of persons under age

17–112   **101.**—(1) A person is disqualified for holding or obtaining a licence to drive a motor vehicle of a class specified in the following Table if he is under the age specified in relation to it in the second column of the Table.

TABLE

Class of motor vehicle	Age (in years)
1. Invalid carriage	16
2. Moped	16
3. Motor bicycle	17
4. Agricultural or forestry tractor	17
5. Small vehicle	17
6. Medium-sized goods vehicle	18
7. Other motor vehicle	21

In relation to certain classes of vehicles and in certain circumstances, different ages apply (see regulation 9 of the *Motor Vehicles (Driving Licence) Regulations* 1999 (S.I. 1999 No. 2864). These variants are shown in the Table, *post*, against the classes as numbered in the table, *ante*.

TABLE

Class of motor vehicle	Age (in years)
3. Certain large motor bicycles	21
4. Certain agricultural or forestry tractors	16
5. Small vehicles driven by certain people	16
6. Heavier medium-sized goods vehicle	21
7. Various other motor vehicles	18

C. DISQUALIFICATION TO PREVENT DUPLICATION OF LICENCES

(1) Definition

Road Traffic Act 1988, s.102

Disqualification to prevent duplication of licences

17–113   **102.** A person is disqualified for obtaining a licence authorising him to drive a motor vehicle of any class so long as he is the holder of another licence authorising him to drive a motor vehicle of that class, whether the licence is suspended or not.

832

(2) What must the prosecution prove?

Obtaining a licence whilst disqualified
— the defendant was disqualified (other than by age);　　　**17–114**
— the defendant obtained a licence.

Since it is possible to obtain licences in advance of the commencement date, this offence is committed where a licence is obtained that purports to give authority to drive covering a period while the person to whom it is issued is disqualified.

Driving while disqualified
The prosecution must prove that:　　　**17–115**
— the defendant was the driver;
— the defendant was disqualified (other than by age);
— the vehicle was being driven;
— the vehicle was a motor vehicle;
— the vehicle was being driven on a road.

For issues concerning identification, see §§ 10–89 *et seq.* in this work.

For "drive", "motor vehicle" and "road", see *ante*, §§ 17–4 *et seq.* Note that this is an offence committed on a road and not on a road or other public place.

The obligation is on the prosecution to prove that the defendant was disqualified. For **17–116** a number of years, imaginative attempts have been made to persuade courts that the prosecution has not satisfied its obligation to prove that the person before the court is the person disqualified from driving. In the case of *Ellis v. Jones* [1973] 2 All E.R. 893, this led the court to describe the defence submission as "... another example of submissions made by advocates for the defence in circumstances which are wholly inappropriate and which give rise to a great deal of waste of time and money". There has to be cogent evidence linking the person who drove the vehicle with the person who had been disqualified. There are many ways in which evidence can be brought to prove this link. In *R. v. Derwentside JJ, ex p. Heaviside* [1996] R.T.R. 384, three methods of proof were given—formal admission by the defendant, fingerprints, and then the evidence of the person in court when the defendant was disqualified. This is not an exhaustive list and the court will need to act on any cogent evidence. In *DPP v. Mooney* [1997] R.T.R. 434 the defendant had made admissions to the police (but not the formal admission listed, *ante*) and this was held sufficient to support the certificate of conviction recording the order of disqualification. In *Moran v. CPS* (2000) 164 J.P 562 an admission to the police and confirmation that that admission had been made by the defendant whilst giving evidence in court was held to be sufficient even without a certificate of conviction. In *Pattison v. DPP* [2006] R.T.R. 13; (2006) 170 J.P. 51, the Divisional Court, after an extensive review of the legal provisions and the authorities, concluded that:

> "The principle that emerges from the cases is that it will normally be possible to establish a prima facie case on the basis of consistency of details between the accused and the person named on the memorandum of conviction. If the accused calls no evidence to contradict that prima facie case, it will be open to the court to be satisfied that identity is proved."

The court set out a number of principles able to be extracted from the cases. It emphasised that it was for the prosecution to prove to the criminal standard that the accused was a disqualified driver but that it could do so by any admissible means including a non-formal admission. *Heaviside* identifies three clear ways but there are no prescribed ways. An example of another way is where there is a match between the personal details of the accused and those recorded on the certificate of conviction. Even where the personal details (such as the name) are not uncommon, a match will be sufficient for a prima facie case. In the absence of evidence contradicting this prima facie case, the evidence will be sufficient for the court to find identity proved. If the accused does not give evidence in rebuttal, that is a matter that the court can take into account.

If it is proper to do so (and provided a warning has been given), that can also give rise to an adverse inference (*Criminal Justice and Public Order Act* 1994, s.35(2)). Similarly, in *West Yorkshire Probation Board v. Boulter* (2005) 169 J.P. 601, a person subject to a community rehabilitation order was brought before a magistrates' court on a warrant for breaching the order. The proceedings were adjourned. The defendant did not attend subsequent hearings but was legally represented. Justices accepted defence submissions that the prosecution had failed to prove that the person summoned to appear was the person made subject to the order and that the coincidence of names, date of birth and address was insufficient to prove identity beyond reasonable doubt. The Divisional Court upheld the prosecution appeal:

> "When magistrates have evidence that the person before them has the same name, date of birth and address as the person previously convicted, it was open to them to draw an inference that he is the same person. Whether that inference is to be drawn in any particular case depends on all the facts of that case."

Where all three of those personal details coincided, it was to be expected that justices would draw such an inference unless there was some other factor which cast doubt on the inference.

In *R. (Howe) v. South Durham Magistrates' Court* [2005] R.T.R. 4, the prosecution had obtained a witness summons against the solicitor who had represented the defendant in the proceedings in which he had been disqualified asserting that he could give evidence of what transpired in court on that occasion without breaching legal professional privilege. A further complication was that this solicitor was also retained to act for the defendant in the current proceedings. The defendant appealed against the issuing of that summons but that appeal was dismissed. The solicitor was to be asked solely about issues of fact that did not require any breach of privilege, and, although the consequence of the summons would be to deprive the defendant of the services of the solicitor in the current proceedings, the right to a solicitor of one's own choice is not an absolute one.

The extent of the obligation on the prosecution was considered in *DPP v. Barker* [2004] 168 J.P. 617. The defendant had been disqualified for a fixed period and then until he passed an extended driving test. He was found driving after the fixed period was ended and the issue arose as to whether the prosecution need to prove the absence of "L" plates and a supervisor. The Court held that that burden fell on the defendant. This was wholly proportionate and followed the approach set out under earlier provisions in *Scott v. Jelfe* [1974] R.T.R. 256.

17–117 Once it is proved that the defendant was the driver of the motor vehicle on a road at a time when he was disqualified, then it is no defence that the defendant was unaware either of his disqualification or that the disqualification was still in force. This has meant a defendant being convicted even though his driving licence had been returned to him by the licensing authority by mistake: *Bowsher* [1973] R.T.R. 202. Similarly, a defendant was convicted even where he mistakenly believed he was not driving on a "road": *Miller* [1973] R.T.R. 479. Even where a disqualification is subsequently quashed on appeal, a person who drives whilst the disqualification is in force commits the offence under section 103: *R. v. Thames Magistrates' Court, ex p. Levy* [1997] T.L.R. 394. A court may suspend a disqualification pending appeal, but, in the absence of such an order, the disqualification applies regardless of the outcome of the appeal.

A person from outside Great Britain can be disqualified by a court and will commit an offence under section 103(1) by driving a motor vehicle on a road while disqualified even though a licence or permit issued by another state is held. Similarly, a person disqualified elsewhere is not necessarily disqualified from driving in this country though he may be committing the offence of driving otherwise than in accordance with a licence; it will depend on the effect of the disqualification as provided for in the law of the country in which it was imposed.

(3) Allocation

17–118 These offences are summary only.

834

(4) Penalties

For *driving while disqualified*, the maximum penalty is a fine at level 5 and/or six **17–119** months' imprisonment or both. In relation to offences committed on or after commencement of *Criminal Justice Act* 2003, ss.181, 280–282 (see *post*, Ch.23), the maximum custodial sentence in a magistrates' court will be a custody plus order. It is an endorsable offence requiring six penalty points. Disqualification is discretionary.

For *obtaining a licence while disqualified*, the maximum penalty is a fine of level 3. The offence is not endorsable.

(5) Sentence

Aggravating and mitigating factors for driving whilst disqualified are set out in the **17–120** *Magistrates' Court Sentencing Guidelines* (2004) (under review). They emphasise driving for remuneration, efforts being made to avoid detection, taking a long distance drive, planned, long term evasion, previous disqualified driving and recent disqualification as aggravating factors. Mitigating factors include driving in an emergency, the situation where the full period of disqualification had expired but the test had not been retaken and driving for a short distance. The *Road Safety Act* 2006 contains a new offence of causing death by driving where the driver was unlicensed, disqualified from driving or uninsured. This is described at § 17–46, *ante*.

There are different views on the appropriate level of sentence. There are many who consider that this offence is often a flagrant disregard for an order of the court and that imprisonment should be the starting point. Others point to the fact that people committing this offence have not committed a violent offence and, in the absence of any other offences, have not caused damage to other people or to property; accordingly, a non-custodial sentence should usually be appropriate.

Sentencing practice indicates that, during 2002, approximately 49 per cent of those convicted received a custodial sentence. Almost half of the adults sentenced to custody received a sentence of three months or less. However, from January 1, 2004, the revised *Magistrates' Court Sentencing Guidelines* (currently under review) changed the entry point for this offence from custody to a community sentence. Given the emphasis on a custodial sentence being reserved for dangerous, violent or seriously persistent offenders, it is likely that greater use will be made of community sentences, particularly those containing an element of punishment such as unpaid work and curfew orders. The latest information on sentencing shows that approximately 47 per cent receive a custodial sentence. In about one third of those cases, the sentence is suspended. Of those where imprisonment is ordered to be served immediately, about 40 per cent are for three months or less. A further 40 per cent receive a community order and about 12 per cent receive a fine, discharge or other sentence.

A manifestation of the concerns about the extent to which persons who are disqualified continue to drive has been seen in the growing use of the imposition of an anti-social behaviour order in addition to the sentence for the offence. The plethora of cases considering the circumstances of the making of such orders (and the approach to sentencing of those who breach them) is covered in more detail in § 23–273, *post*, but there have been some considerations particularly relevant to orders made following conviction for driving whilst disqualified. One of the issues has been the extent to which an ASBO should prohibit something which is already a criminal offence. This is particularly significant where the maximum penalty for the offence is less than for a breach of an ASBO—this is the case for driving whilst disqualified which carries a maximum of six months' imprisonment (51 weeks for offences committed on or after commencement of custody plus orders) compared with a maximum of five years for a breach of an ASBO. In *Hall* [2004] EWCA Crim 2671, the defendant had an appalling driving record and had committed other serious offences. The court concluded that the regularity of the defendant's offending demonstrated total disregard for the law and imposed an unlimited ASBO prohibiting the defendant from driving any mechanically propelled vehicle on a public road in the UK without being the holder of a valid driving licence and certificate of insurance. A primary purpose was to increase the sentencing powers of any court faced with dealing with a further offence. Whilst requiring the ASBO to be for a set period, the Court of Appeal considered that the order was not wrong in principle in these circumstances. It was precise and capable of being understood by the appellant.

A different view was taken by a differently constituted court in *Kirby* [2005] EWCA Crim 1228. Again, the defendant had a bad driving record. An ASBO was made for 10 years prohibiting him, *inter alia*, from driving a motor vehicle until the expiry of his period of disqualification. The Court of Appeal doubted whether it was right to impose an order simply in order to increase the maximum penalty available for further offending. There had to be a demonstrable necessity for such an order.

The approach in *Kirby* has been followed in two further cases, *Lawson* [2005] EWCA Crim 1840; [2005] Crim.L.R. 871 and *Williams* [2005] EWCA Crim 1796; (2005) 169 J.P. 588 and has been specifically endorsed by the Court of Appeal following a review of various cases in *Boness* (2005) 169 J.P. 621 (see further § 23–273, *post*). Before an order can be made, the court must be satisfied both that the offender had acted in an anti-social manner and that an order was necessary to protect persons in England and Wales from further anti-social acts from him.

V. REGULATORY OFFENCES

A. Using a Motor Vehicle without Insurance

(1) Definitions

17–121   The requirement for insurance to be obtained to cover some of the adverse consequences of the use of a motor vehicle reflects the need to ensure that the damage caused by a motor vehicle can be financially compensated. In addition, vehicle owners or users can choose to insure against damage to their own vehicle, however caused. Where damage is caused as a result of the use of a motor vehicle and the user is not insured, it may be possible for compensation to be obtained through the Motor Insurers Bureau (MIB): see *Wilkinson's Road Traffic Offences*, Ch.10.

Section 153 of the *Serious Organised Crime and Police Act* 2005 provides regulation making power to enable the Secretary of State to make provision for the disclosure of information relating to the insurance status of a vehicle. The *Disclosure of Vehicle Insurance Regulations* 2005 (S.I. 2005 No. 2833) provide for the Motor Insurers' Information Centre to supply information to the Police Information Technology Organisation. This may be used to assist a police officer in deciding whether to use the power under section 165 of the *Road Traffic Act* 1988 to require a person who is (or may have been) driving a vehicle to produce evidence that the use of the vehicle is insured. There is a further power under sections 165A and 165B to seize and retain a vehicle where the evidence is not produced.

Road Traffic Act 1988, ss.143–145, 147–150, 165A–165B

Users of motor vehicles to be insured or secured against third-party risks

17–122   **143.**—(1) Subject to the provisions of this Part of this Act—

    (a) a person must not use a motor vehicle on a road or other public place unless there is in force in relation to the use of the vehicle by that person such a policy of insurance or such a security in respect of third party risks as complies with the requirements of this Part of this Act, and

    (b) a person must not cause or permit any other person to use a motor vehicle on a road or other public place unless there is in force in relation to the use of the vehicle by that other person such a policy of insurance or such a security in respect of third party risks as complies with the requirements of this Part of this Act.

    (2) If a person acts in contravention of subsection (1) above he is guilty of an offence.

    (3) A person charged with using a motor vehicle in contravention of this section shall not be convicted if he proves—

(a) that the vehicle did not belong to him and was not in his possession under a contract of hiring or of loan,

(b) that he was using the vehicle in the course of his employment, and

(c) that he neither knew nor had reason to believe that there was not in force in relation to the vehicle such a policy of insurance or security as is mentioned in subsection (1) above.

(4) This Part of this Act does not apply to invalid carriages.

Exceptions from requirement of third-party insurance or security

144.—(1) Section 143 of this Act does not apply to a vehicle owned by a person who has **17–123** deposited and keeps deposited with the Accountant General of the Supreme Court the sum of £500, 000, at a time when the vehicle is being driven under the owner's control.

(1A) [...]

(1B) [...]

(2) Section 143 does not apply—

(a) to a vehicle owned—

   (i) by the council of a county or county district in England and Wales the Broads Authority, the Common Council of the City of London, the council of a London borough, a National Park authority, the Inner London Education Authority, the London Fire and Emergency Planning Authority, or a joint authority (other than a police authority) established by Part IV of the *Local Government Act* 1985,

   (ii) ... or

   (iii) by a joint board or committee in England or Wales, or joint committee in Scotland, which is so constituted as to include among its members representatives of any such council,

   at a time when the vehicle is being driven under the owner's control,

(b) to a vehicle owned by a police authority, at a time when it is being driven under the owner's control, or to a vehicle at a time when it is being driven for police purposes by or under the direction of a constable, or by a person employed by a police authority, or

(c) to a vehicle at a time when it is being driven on a journey to or from any place undertaken for salvage purposes pursuant to Part IX of the *Merchant Shipping Act* 1995,

(d) to the use of a vehicle for the purpose of its being provided in pursuance of a direction under section 166(2)(b) of the *Army Act* 1955 or under the corresponding provision of the *Air Force Act* 1955,

(da) to a vehicle owned by a health service body, as defined in section 60(7) of the *National Health Service and Community Care Act* 1990 by a Primary Care Trust established under section 16A of the *National Health Service Act* 1977, by a Local Health Board established under section 16BA of that Act or by the Commission for Health Improvement, at a time when the vehicle is being driven under the owner's control.

(db) to an ambulance owned by a National Health Service trust established under Part I of the *National Health Service and Community Care Act* 1990 or the *National Health Service (Scotland) Act* 1978, at a time when a vehicle is being driven under the owner's control

(e) to a vehicle which is made available by the Secretary of State to any person, body or local authority in pursuance of section 23 or 26 of the *National Health Service Act* 1977 at a time when it is being used in accordance with the terms on which it is so made available,

(f) to a vehicle which is made available by the Secretary of State to any local authority, education authority or voluntary organisation in Scotland in pursuance of section 15 or 16 of the *National Health Service (Scotland) Act* 1978 at a time when it is being used in accordance with the terms on which it is so made available.

Offence of keeping vehicle which does not meet insurance requirements (inserted by Road Safety Bill when enacted and in force)

144A.—(1) If a motor vehicle registered under the *Vehicle Excise and Registration Act* **17–124** 1994 does not meet the insurance requirements, the person in whose name the vehicle is registered is guilty of an offence.

Part III

(2) For the purposes of this section a vehicle meets the insurance requirements if—

  (a) it is covered by a such a policy of insurance or such a security in respect of third party risks as complies with the requirements of this Part of this Act, and

  (b) either of the following conditions is satisfied.

(3) The first condition is that the policy or security, or the certificate of insurance or security which relates to it, identifies the vehicle by its registration mark as a vehicle which is covered by the policy or security.

(4) The second condition is that the vehicle is covered by the policy or security because—

  (a) the policy or security covers any vehicle, or any vehicle of a particular description, the owner of which is a person named in the policy or security or in the certificate of insurance or security which relates to it, and

  (b) the vehicle is owned by that person.

(5) For the purposes of this section a vehicle is covered by a policy of insurance or security if the policy of insurance or security is in force in relation to the use of the vehicle.

Exceptions to section 144A offence

17–125   **144B.**—(1) A person ("the registered keeper") in whose name a vehicle which does not meet the insurance requirements is registered at any particular time ("the relevant time") does not commit an offence under section 144A of this Act at that time if any of the following conditions are satisfied.

(2) The first condition is that at the relevant time the vehicle is owned as described—

  (a) in subsection (1) of section 144 of this Act, or

  (b) in paragraph (a), (b), (da), (db), (dc) or (g) of subsection (2) of that section, (whether or not at the relevant time it is being driven as described in that provision).

(3) The second condition is that at the relevant time the vehicle is owned with the intention that it should be used as described in paragraph (c), (d), (e) or (f) of section 144(2) of this Act.

(4) The third condition is that the registered keeper—

  (a) is not at the relevant time the person keeping the vehicle, and

  (b) if previously he was the person keeping the vehicle, he has by the relevant time complied with any requirements under subsection (7)(a) below that he is required to have complied with by the relevant or any earlier time.

(5) The fourth condition is that—

  (a) the registered keeper is at the relevant time the person keeping the vehicle,

  (b) at the relevant time the vehicle is not used on a road or other public place, and

  (c) the registered keeper has by the relevant time complied with any requirements under subsection (7)(a) below that he is required to have complied with by the relevant or any earlier time.

(6) The fifth condition is that—

  (a) the vehicle has been stolen before the relevant time,

  (b) the vehicle has not been recovered by the relevant time, and

  (c) any requirements under subsection (7)(b) below that, in connection with the theft, are required to have been complied with by the relevant or any earlier time have been complied with by the relevant time.

(7) Regulations may make provision—

  (a) for the purposes of subsection (4)(b) and (5)(c) above, requiring a person in whose name a vehicle is registered to furnish such particulars and make such declarations as may be prescribed, and to do so at such times and in such manner as may be prescribed, and

  (b) for the purposes of subsection (6)(c) above, as to the persons to whom, the times at which and the manner in which the theft of a vehicle is to be notified.

(8) Regulations may make provision amending this section for the purpose of providing for further exceptions to section 144A of this Act (or varying or revoking any such further exceptions).

(9) A person accused of an offence under section 144A of this Act is not entitled to the benefit of an exception conferred by or under this section unless evidence is adduced that is sufficient to raise an issue with respect to that exception; but where evidence is so adduced it is for the prosecution to prove beyond reasonable doubt that the exception does not apply.

Requirements in respect of policies of insurance

145.—(1) In order to comply with the requirements of this Part of this Act, a policy of insur-   **17–126**
ance must satisfy the following conditions.

(2) The policy must be issued by an authorised insurer.

(3) Subject to subsection (4) below, the policy—

(a) must insure such person, persons or classes of persons as may be specified in the
policy in respect of any liability which may be incurred by him or them in respect
of the death of or bodily injury to any person or damage to property caused by,
or arising out of, the use of the vehicle on a road or other public place in Great
Britain, and

(aa) must, in the case of a vehicle normally based in the territory of another member
State, insure him or them in respect of any civil liability which may be incurred
by him or them as a result of an event related to the use of the vehicle in Great
Britain if,—

(i) according to the law of that territory, he or they would be required to be
insured in respect of a civil liability which would arise under that law as a
result of that event if the place where the vehicle was used when the event
occurred were in that territory, and

(ii) the cover required by that law would be higher than that required by
paragraph (a) above, and

(b) must, in the case of a vehicle normally based in Great Britain, insure him or
them in respect of any liability which may be incurred by him or them in respect
of the use of the vehicle and of any trailer, whether or not coupled, in the territory other than Great Britain and Gibraltar of each of the member States of the
Communities according to—

(i) the law on compulsory insurance against civil liability in respect of the use
of vehicles of the State in whose territory the event giving rise to the liability occurred; or

(ii) if it would give higher cover, the law which would be applicable under this
Part of this Act if the place where the vehicle was used when that event occurred were in Great Britain; and

(c) must also insure him or them in respect of any liability which may be incurred by
him or them under the provisions of this Part of this Act relating to payment for
emergency treatment.

(4) The policy shall not, by virtue of subsection (3)(a) above, be required—

(a) to cover liability in respect of the death, arising out of and in the course of his
employment, of a person in the employment of a person insured by the policy or
of bodily injury sustained by such a person arising out of and in the course of his
employment, or

(b) to provide insurance of more than £250,000 in respect of all such liabilities as
may be incurred in respect of damage to property caused by, or arising out of,
any one accident involving the vehicle, or

(c) to cover liability in respect of damage to the vehicle, or

(d) to cover liability in respect of damage to goods carried for hire or reward in or
on the vehicle or in or on any trailer (whether or not coupled) drawn by the vehicle, or

(e) to cover any liability of a person in respect of damage to property in his custody
or under his control, or

(f) to cover any contractual liability.

(4A) In the case of a person—

(a) carried in or upon a vehicle, or

(b) entering or getting on to, or alighting from, a vehicle,

the provisions of paragraph (a) of subsection (4) above do not apply unless cover in respect of
the liability referred to in that paragraph is in fact provided pursuant to a requirement of the
Employers' Liability (Compulsory Insurance) Act 1969.

(5) "Authorised insurer" has the same meaning as in section 95.

(6) If any person or body of persons ceases to be a member of the Motor Insurers'
Bureau, that person or body shall not by virtue of that cease to be treated as an authorised

insurer for the purposes of this Part of this Act or the *Road Traffic (NHS Charges) Act* 1999—

> (a) in relation to any policy issued by the insurer before ceasing to be such a member, or
>
> (b) in relation to any obligation (whether arising before or after the insurer ceased to be such a member) which the insurer may be called upon to meet under or in consequence of any such policy or under section 157 of this Act or section 1 of the Act of 1999 by virtue of making a payment in pursuance of such an obligation.

Issue and surrender of certificates of insurance and of security

17–127   **147.**—(1) A policy of insurance shall be of no effect for the purposes of this Part of this Act unless and until there is delivered by the insurer to the person by whom the policy is effected a certificate (in this Part of this Act referred to as a "certificate of insurance") in the prescribed form and containing such particulars of any conditions subject to which the policy is issued and of any other matters as may be prescribed.

(2) A security shall be of no effect for the purposes of this Part of this Act unless and until there is delivered by the person giving the security to the person to whom it is given a certificate (in this Part of this Act referred to as a "certificate of security") in the prescribed form and containing such particulars of any conditions subject to which the security is issued and of any other matters as may be prescribed.

(3) Different forms and different particulars may be prescribed for the purposes of subsection (1) or (2) above in relation to different cases or circumstances.

(4) Where a certificate has been delivered under this section and the policy or security to which it relates is cancelled by mutual consent or by virtue of any provision in the policy or security, the person to whom the certificate was delivered must, within seven days from the taking effect of the cancellation—

> (a) surrender the certificate to the person by whom the policy was issued or the security was given, or
>
> (b) if the certificate has been lost or destroyed, make a statutory declaration to that effect.

(5) A person who fails to comply with subsection (4) above is guilty of an offence.

Avoidance of certain exceptions to policies or securities

17–128   **148.**—(1) Where a certificate of insurance or certificate of security has been delivered under section 147 of this Act to the person by whom a policy has been effected or to whom a security has been given, so much of the policy or security as purports to restrict—

> (a) the insurance of the persons insured by the policy, or
>
> (b) the operation of the security,

(as the case may be) by reference to any of the matters mentioned in subsection (2) below shall, as respects such liabilities as are required to be covered by a policy under section 145 of this Act, be of no effect.

(2) Those matters are—

> (a) the age or physical or mental condition of persons driving the vehicle,
>
> (b) the condition of the vehicle,
>
> (c) the number of persons that the vehicle carries,
>
> (d) the weight or physical characteristics of the goods that the vehicle carries,
>
> (e) the time at which or the areas within which the vehicle is used,
>
> (f) the horsepower or cylinder capacity or value of the vehicle,
>
> (g) the carrying on the vehicle of any particular apparatus, or
>
> (h) the carrying on the vehicle of any particular means of identification other than any means of identification required to be carried by or under the *Vehicle Excise and Registration Act* 1994.

(3) Nothing in subsection (1) above requires an insurer or the giver of a security to pay any sum in respect of the liability of any person otherwise than in or towards the discharge of that liability.

(4) Any sum paid by an insurer or the giver of a security in or towards the discharge of any liability of any person which is covered by the policy or security by virtue only of subsection (1) above is recoverable by the insurer or giver of the security from that person.

(5) A condition in a policy or security issued or given for the purposes of this Part of this Act providing—

(a) that no liability shall arise under the policy or security, or

(b) that any liability so arising shall cease,

in the event of some specified thing being done or omitted to be done after the happening of the event giving rise to a claim under the policy or security, shall be of no effect in connection with such liabilities as are required to be covered by a policy under section 145 of this Act.

(6) Nothing in subsection (5) above shall be taken to render void any provision in a policy or security requiring the person insured or secured to pay to the insurer or the giver of the security any sums which the latter may have become liable to pay under the policy or security and which have been applied to the satisfaction of the claims of third parties.

(7) Notwithstanding anything in any enactment, a person issuing a policy of insurance under section 145 of this Act shall be liable to indemnify the persons or classes of persons specified in the policy in respect of any liability which the policy purports to cover in the case of those persons or classes of persons.

Avoidance of certain agreements as to liability towards passengers

149.—(1) This section applies where a person uses a motor vehicle in circumstances such that **17–129** under section 143 of this Act there is required to be in force in relation to his use of it such a policy of insurance or such a security in respect of third-party risks as complies with the requirements of this Part of this Act.

(2) If any other person is carried in or upon the vehicle while the user is so using it, any antecedent agreement or understanding between them (whether intended to be legally binding or not) shall be of no effect so far as it purports or might be held—

(a) to negative or restrict any such liability of the user in respect of persons carried in or upon the vehicle as is required by section 145 of this Act to be covered by a policy of insurance, or

(b) to impose any conditions with respect to the enforcement of any such liability of the user.

(3) The fact that a person so carried has willingly accepted as his the risk of negligence on the part of the user shall not be treated as negativing any such liability of the user.

(4) For the purposes of this section—

(a) references to a person being carried in or upon a vehicle include references to a person entering or getting on to, or alighting from, the vehicle, and

(b) the reference to an antecedent agreement is to one made at any time before the liability arose.

Insurance or security in respect of private use of vehicle to cover use under car-sharing arrangements

150.—(1) To the extent that a policy or security issued or given for the purposes of this Part **17–130** of this Act—

(a) restricts the insurance of the persons insured by the policy or the operation of the security (as the case may be) to use of the vehicle for specified purposes (for example, social, domestic and pleasure purposes) of a non-commercial character, or

(b) excludes from that insurance or the operation of the security (as the case may be)—

(i) use of the vehicle for hire or reward, or

(ii) business or commercial use of the vehicle, or

(iii) use of the vehicle for specified purposes of a business or commercial character,

then, for the purposes of that policy or security so far as it relates to such liabilities as are required to be covered by a policy under section 145 of this Act, the use of a vehicle on a journey in the course of which one or more passengers are carried at separate fares shall, if the conditions specified in subsection (2) below are satisfied, be treated as falling within that restriction or as not falling within that exclusion (as the case may be).

(2) The conditions referred to in subsection (1) above are—

(a) the vehicle is not adapted to carry more than eight passengers and is not a motor cycle,

(b) the fare or aggregate of the fares paid in respect of the journey does not exceed the amount of the running costs of the vehicle for the journey (which for the purposes of this paragraph shall be taken to include an appropriate amount in respect of depreciation and general wear), and

(c) the arrangements for the payment of fares by the passenger or passengers carried at separate fares were made before the journey began.

(3) Subsections (1) and (2) above apply however the restrictions or exclusions described in subsection (1) are framed or worded.

(4) In subsections (1) and (2) above "fare" and "separate fares" have the same meaning as in section 1(4) of the *Public Passenger Vehicles Act* 1981.

Power to seize vehicles driven without licence or insurance

17–131   165A.—(1) Subsection (5) applies if any of the following conditions is satisfied.

(2) The first condition is that—

(a) a constable in uniform requires, under section 164, a person to produce his licence and its counterpart for examination,

(b) the person fails to produce them, and

(c) the constable has reasonable grounds for believing that a motor vehicle is or was being driven by the person in contravention of section 87(1).

(3) The second condition is that—

(a) a constable in uniform requires, under section 165, a person to produce evidence that a motor vehicle is not or was not being driven in contravention of section 143,

(b) the person fails to produce such evidence, and

(c) the constable has reasonable grounds for believing that the vehicle is or was being so driven.

(4) The third condition is that—

(a) a constable in uniform requires, under section 163, a person driving a motor vehicle to stop the vehicle,

(b) the person fails to stop the vehicle, or to stop the vehicle long enough, for the constable to make such lawful enquiries as he considers appropriate, and

(c) the constable has reasonable grounds for believing that the vehicle is or was being driven in contravention of section 87(1) or 143.

(5) Where this subsection applies, the constable may—

(a) seize the vehicle in accordance with subsections (6) and (7) and remove it;

(b) enter, for the purpose of exercising a power falling within paragraph (a), any premises (other than a private dwelling house) on which he has reasonable grounds for believing the vehicle to be;

(c) use reasonable force, if necessary, in the exercise of any power conferred by paragraph (a) or (b).

(6) Before seizing the motor vehicle, the constable must warn the person by whom it appears that the vehicle is or was being driven in contravention of section 87(1) or 143 that he will seize it—

(a) in a section 87(1) case, if the person does not produce his licence and its counterpart immediately;

(b) in a section 143 case, if the person does not provide him immediately with evidence that the vehicle is not or was not being driven in contravention of that section.

But the constable is not required to give such a warning if the circumstances make it impracticable for him to do so.

(7) If the constable is unable to seize the vehicle immediately because the person driving the vehicle has failed to stop as requested or has driven off, he may seize it at any time within the period of 24 hours beginning with the time at which the condition in question is first satisfied.

(8) The powers conferred on a constable by this section are exercisable only at a time when regulations under section 165B are in force.

(9) In this section—

(a) a reference to a motor vehicle does not include an invalid carriage;

(b) a reference to evidence that a motor vehicle is not or was not being driven in contravention of section 143 is a reference to a document or other evidence within section 165(2)(a);

(c) "counterpart" and "licence" have the same meanings as in section 164;

(d) "private dwelling house" does not include any garage or other structure occupied with the dwelling house, or any land appurtenant to the dwelling house.

Retention etc. of vehicles seized under section 165A

165B.—(1) The Secretary of State may by regulations make provision as to—   **17–132**

(a) the removal and retention of motor vehicles seized under section 165A; and

(b) the release or disposal of such motor vehicles.

(2) Regulations under subsection (1) may, in particular, make provision—

(a) for the giving of notice of the seizure of a motor vehicle under section 165A to a
person who is the registered keeper, the owner or the driver of that vehicle;

(b) for the procedure by which a person who claims to be the registered keeper or
the owner of a motor vehicle seized under section 165A may seek to have it
released;

(c) for requiring the payment, by the registered keeper, owner or driver of the vehicle, of fees, charges or costs in relation to the removal and retention of such a
motor vehicle and to any application for its release;

(d) as to the circumstances in which a motor vehicle seized under section 165A may
be disposed of;

(e) as to the destination—

(i) of any fees or charges payable in accordance with the regulations;

(ii) of the proceeds (if any) arising from the disposal of a motor vehicle seized
under section 165A;

(f) for the delivery to a local authority, in circumstances prescribed by or determined
in accordance with the regulations, of any motor vehicle seized under section
165A.

(3) Regulations under subsection (1) must provide that a person who would otherwise
be liable to pay any fee or charge under the regulations is not liable to pay it if—

(a) he was not driving the motor vehicle at the time in question, and

(b) he did not know that the vehicle was being driven at that time, had not consented
to its being driven and could not, by the taking of reasonable steps, have
prevented it from being driven.

(4) Regulations under subsection (1) may make different provision for different cases.

(5) In this section—

"local authority"—

(a) in relation to England, means—

(i) a county council,

(ii) the council of a district comprised in an area for which there is no
county council,

(iii) a London borough council,

(iv) the Common Council of the City of London, or

(v) transport for London;

(b) in relation to Wales, means the council of a county or county borough;
and

(c) in relation to Scotland, means a council constituted under section 2 of the
Local Government etc. (Scotland) Act 1994;

"registered keeper", in relation to a motor vehicle, means the person in whose name the
vehicle is registered under the *Vehicle Excise and Registration Act* 1994.

(2) What must the prosecution prove?

For an offence contrary to section 143, the prosecution must prove that the defen-   **17–133**
dant used (or caused or permitted another person to use) a vehicle on a road or other
public place. Having done that, it is for the defence to prove (on the balance of probabilities) that the use was covered by insurance or a relevant security. A new offence will
be created through the insertion of section 144A to the 1988 Act by section 22 of the
Road Safety Act when in force. If a registered vehicle does not meet the insurance
requirements, the registered owner is guilty of an offence. A series of exceptions are set
out in section 144B which incorporates those set out in section 144 but also provides for

circumstances where the person shown as the registered owner is no longer the keeper of the vehicle and has complied with notification requirements or where the vehicle has been stolen and notification requirements have again been complied with.

For identification, see *ante*, §§ 10–89 *et seq*. For use and for causing or permitting use, see *ante*, §§ 17–9 and 17–10. For "vehicle", see *ante*, § 17–11 (note the exemption for invalid carriages: s.143(4)). For "road" or "other public place", see *ante*, §§ 17–7 and 17–8.

(3) Allocation

17–134   This offence is summary only. Proceedings for an offence must be commenced within six months of the offence coming to the knowledge of the prosecutor providing that is no more than three years from the date the offence was committed.

(4) Insurance

17–135   The obligation is to be insured against third party risks. The insurance in force may be limited so as to restrict the circumstances in which the vehicle is used; this may be by reference to the purposes for which the vehicle is being used or the person who is using it. It is not possible for the insurance to exclude certain things—see sections 145, 148 and 150.

Certain vehicles can be used without insurance, generally vehicles owned and being used for the purposes of specified national or local government functions: section 144. Crown vehicles are also exempt. The situations most commonly encountered are vehicles owned by a County Council at a time when the vehicle is being driven under the control of the owner (section 144(2)(a)) and vehicles owned by a police authority and driven under the control of the authority or any vehicle when it is being driven for police purposes by or under the direction of a constable or employee of a police authority: section 144(2)(b).

To satisfy the provisions of section 143, an insurance policy does not become effective until a certificate is delivered to the person taking out the cover. The certificate must be in the prescribed form. Those issuing the certificate must keep a record and, on request, must give details without charge to the Secretary of State or to any Chief Officer of Police. If a defendant who has lost his copy of the certificate is facing difficulties obtaining a duplicate, a formal police request will need to be complied with by the insurance company.

(5) Defence

17–136   A special defence is provided for those using in the course of their employment vehicles they do not own whilst unaware of the lack of cover: section 143(3).

It is for the defendant to prove (on the balance of probabilities) that:
— the vehicle did not belong to him;
— he was using the vehicle in the course of his employment;
— he did not know (and had no reason to believe) that the vehicle was not insured.

(6) Penalty

17–137   The maximum penalty for an offence contrary to section 143 is a fine up to a maximum of level 5 (£5000). It is an endorsable offence with a range of 6–8 penalty points. Disqualification is discretionary. The maximum penalty for an offence contrary to section 144A is a fine up to a maximum of level 3 (£1,000). It is not endorsable.

(7) Sentence

17–138   The offence can be committed in a very wide range of circumstances from the conscientious individual who (after years of proper insurance) overlooked the need to renew or believed on reasonable (but mistaken) grounds that the use was covered to the individual who deliberately chooses not to insure, probably because he perceives the cost of insurance to be so high and the risk of detection so low that it is a risk worth taking.

The dilemma for a court is that the financial penalty it could legitimately impose on the relatively feckless offender is probably substantially below the cost of insurance. However, this is a regulatory offence; the consequence for any victim can be great but it is not in itself an offence that is dangerous or violent.

The *Magistrates' Court Sentencing Guidelines* (2004) (under review) identify as aggravating factors deliberate driving without insurance, giving false details, the type of vehicle (use of a LGV, HGV, PCV, PSV or taxi or private hire vehicle warranting a higher penalty) and no reference to insurance ever having been held. Mitigating factors include an accidental oversight, a genuine mistake, responsibility for insurance resting with another (*e.g.* the parent, owner, lender, hirer) and the type of vehicle (smaller vehicles, *e.g.* moped, warranting less severe penalties). The starting point for consideration is whether discharge or a fine is appropriate. It is most likely to be a financial penalty. It should be noted that the user may have been offered a fixed penalty and that will have been in the sum of £200 (s.143) or £100 (s.144A).

In addition to a financial penalty, a court may impose a period of disqualification, **17–139** perhaps for a relatively short period depending on the circumstances. However, the recurring dilemma for courts is that the annual cost of insurance can outweigh any financial penalty that can realistically be paid within one year. In those circumstances, the court may wish to consider a community order containing a punishment element such as unpaid work or a curfew requirement.

B. Using a Vehicle without Holding a Driving Licence

(1) Definition

Road Traffic Act 1988, s.87

Drivers of motor vehicles to have driving licences

   87.—(1) It is an offence for a person to drive on a road a motor vehicle of any class otherwise **17–140** than in accordance with a licence authorising him to drive a motor vehicle of that class.

   (2) It is an offence for a person to cause or permit another person to drive on a road a motor vehicle of any class otherwise than in accordance with a licence authorising that other person to drive a motor vehicle of that class.

(2) Allocation

This offence is triable summarily only.   **17–141**

(3) What must the prosecution prove?

— the defendant   **17–142**
— drove
— on a road
— a motor vehicle

The *defence* must then show (on the balance of probabilities) that that driving was in accordance with a licence granted to the defendant.

For issues of identification, see §§ 10–89 *et seq.* in this work. For issues surrounding the meaning of "drive", see *ante*, § 17–4. The phrase "mechanically propelled vehicle" is wider than "vehicle"; see *ante*, § 17–6. The phrase "road or other public place" has been subject to detailed consideration; see *ante*, §§ 17–7 and 17–8.

The offence is committed by driving a motor vehicle whilst not holding a licence au- **17–143** thorising the use of that type of vehicle. Licences may be restricted by virtue of the type of vehicle able to be used or by the age of the person entitled to use a particular type of vehicle. A full licence will only be issued following the passing of an appropriate test (both theory and practical); in most circumstances, a provisional licence can be issued enabling a person to use a vehicle in controlled circumstances (usually involving supervision by a full licence holder aged over 21).

Different tests are administered for different vehicles; for instance, a person holding a full driving licence authorising the use of a motor car and small goods vehicles will need to pass a separate test before being authorised to drive medium sized goods vehicles or small buses.

All licences have an age restriction; a moped can be used by a person 16 or over, a motor car or motor bicycle by a person aged 17 or over, most HGV licences require the driver to be aged at least 21 (see *ante*, § 17–112, for further detail). Full licences are granted until the age of 70 (except where the presence of disease or disability requires a shorter period). Thereafter, they may be renewed for three year periods. If the licence is issued as a photocard, then that photocard must be surrendered at least every 10 years in order that a more recent photograph can be incorporated.

17–144   A person who drives a motor vehicle whilst under the age at which a licence could be granted (*e.g.* 15 year old driving a car) commits an offence under this section rather than that of driving whilst disqualified under section 103. Although a person below the set age is disqualified from holding or obtaining a licence (section 101), section 103(4) provides that they do not commit an offence under that section by driving, see *ante*, § 17–100.

The most complex conditions apply to provisional licence holders. In respect of motorcycles, there are limits on the size of the engine in the vehicle which can be used (generally "learner motor cycles") and "L" plates must be displayed. Passengers may not be carried. A person who fails to comply with those obligations commits an offence under this section. In respect of other vehicles, there is a general requirement that provisional licence holders be supervised by a "qualified driver" present in the vehicle. Generally, this will be a full licence holder for that class of vehicle who is over 21 years of age and has held that type of licence for at least three years. Whilst any "qualified driver" can supervise or teach a provisional licence holder, in relation to motor cars instruction for money or money's worth can only be given by a person registered or licensed under Pt V of the *Road Traffic Act* 1988.

There are further extensive provisions governing the entitlement of drivers from abroad—see *Wilkinson's Road Traffic Offences*, Ch.11.

(4) Sentence

17–145   The maximum penalty is a fine of level 3 (£1000). The *Magistrates' Court Sentencing Guidelines* (2004) (under review) provide that the starting point for this offence is guideline fine A (50 per cent of the defendant's weekly income).

It is endorsable (and thus disqualifiable) in some circumstances with a range of 3–6 penalty points.

The offence is endorsable where the driving did not accord with any licence that could have been granted to the driver. Thus, a full licence holder whose licence had expired but who would have been entitled to have it renewed and who drove a vehicle authorised by that licence would not be subject to endorsement or disqualification. However, a provisional licence holder who fails to display "L" plates or to be properly supervised would be liable to endorsement. Similarly, a person who drives a vehicle for which a licence could not have been issued (*e.g.* a 15 year old driving a car) is subject to endorsement. Some full licences give provisional entitlement for other classes of vehicle. A person driving a vehicle in circumstances which are only covered by the provisional entitlement who fails to comply with the conditions of the provisional licence will be liable to endorsement.

C. FORGERY OF DOCUMENTS

(1) Definition

17–146   With the increased emphasis on safety which affects both the testing of vehicles and the licensing of their users, there will be a risk that some will seek to avoid the law by fraudulent means. These sections provide a series of offences designed to penalise those who make misrepresentations (whether or not in documentary form) and those who create documents that are false.

Road Traffic Act 1988, ss.173–174, 176

Forgery of documents, etc

173.—(1) A person who, with intent to deceive—   **17–147**

 (a) forges, alters or uses a document or other thing to which this section applies, or

 (b) lends to, or allows to be used by, any other person a document or other thing to which this section applies, or

 (c) makes or has in his possession any document or other thing so closely resembling a document or other thing to which this section applies as to be calculated to deceive,

is guilty of an offence.

 (2) This section applies to the following documents and other things—

 (a) any licence under any Part of this Act or, in the case of a licence to drive, any counterpart of such a licence,

 (aa) any counterpart of a Community licence,

 (b) any test certificate, goods vehicle test certificate, plating certificate, certificate of conformity or Minister's approval certificate (within the meaning of Part II of this Act),

 (c) any certificate required as a condition of any exception prescribed under section 14 of this Act,

 (cc) any seal required by regulations made under section 41 of this Act with respect to speed limiters,.

 (d) any plate containing particulars required to be marked on a vehicle by regulations under section 41 of this Act or containing other particulars required to be marked on a goods vehicle by sections 54 to 58 of this Act or regulations under those sections,

 (dd) any document evidencing the appointment of an examiner under section 66A of this Act,

 (e) any records required to be kept by virtue of section 74 of this Act,

 (f) any document which, in pursuance of section 89(3) of this Act, is issued as evidence of the result of a test of competence to drive,

 (ff) any certificate provided for by regulations under section 97(3A) of this Act relating to the completion of a training course for motor cyclists,

 (g) any certificate under section 133A or any badge or certificate prescribed by regulations made by virtue of section 135 of this Act,

 (h) any certificate of insurance or certificate of security under Part VI of this Act,

 (j) any document produced as evidence of insurance in pursuance of Regulation 6 of the *Motor Vehicles (Compulsory Insurance) (No. 2) Regulations* 1973,

 (k) any document issued under regulations made by the Secretary of State in pursuance of his power under section 165(2)(a) of this Act to prescribe evidence which may be produced in lieu of a certificate of insurance or a certificate of security,

 (l) any international road haulage permit, and

 (m) a certificate of the kind referred to in section 34B(1) of the *Road Traffic Offenders Act* 1988, and

 (n) any document produced as evidence of the passing of an appropriate driving test within the meaning of section 36 of that Act.

 (3) In the application of this section to England and Wales "forges" means makes a false document or other thing in order that it may be used as genuine.

 (4) In this section "counterpart" and "Community licence" have the same meanings as in Part III of this Act.

False statements and withholding material information

174.—(1) A person who knowingly makes a false statement for the purpose— **17–148**

 (a) of obtaining the grant of a licence under any Part of this Act to himself or any other person, or

847

    (b) of preventing the grant of any such licence, or

    (c) of procuring the imposition of a condition or limitation in relation to any such licence, or

    (d) of securing the entry or retention of the name of any person in the register of approved instructors maintained under Part V of this Act, or

    (dd) of obtaining the grant to any person of a certificate under section 133A of this Act, or

    (e) of obtaining the grant of an international road haulage permit to himself or any other person,

is guilty of an offence.

(2) A person who, in supplying information or producing documents for the purposes either of sections 53 to 60 and 63 of this Act or of regulations made under sections 49 to 51, 61, 62 and 66(3) of this Act—

    (a) makes a statement which he knows to be false in a material particular or recklessly makes a statement which is false in a material particular, or

    (b) produces, provides, sends or otherwise makes use of a document which he knows to be false in a material particular or recklessly produces, provides, sends or otherwise makes use of a document which is false in a material particular,

is guilty of an offence.

(3) A person who—

    (a) knowingly produces false evidence for the purposes of regulations under section 66(1) of this Act, or

    (b) knowingly makes a false statement in a declaration required to be made by the regulations,

is guilty of an offence.

(4) A person who—

    (a) wilfully makes a false entry in any record required to be made or kept by regulations under section 74 of this Act, or

    (b) with intent to deceive, makes use of any such entry which he knows to be false,

is guilty of an offence.

(5) A person who makes a false statement or withholds any material information for the purpose of obtaining the issue—

    (a) of a certificate of insurance or certificate of security under Part VI of this Act, or

    (b) of any document issued under regulations made by the Secretary of State in pursuance of his power under section 165(2)(a) of this Act to prescribe evidence which may be produced in lieu of a certificate of insurance or a certificate of security,

is guilty of an offence.

Power to seize articles in respect of which offences under sections 173 to 175 may have been committed

17–149   **176.**—(1) If a constable has reasonable cause to believe that a document produced to him—

    (a) in pursuance of section 137 of this Act, or

    (b) in pursuance of any of the preceding provisions of this Part of this Act,

is a document in relation to which an offence has been committed under section 173, 174 or 175 of this Act or under section 115 of the *Road Traffic Regulation Act* 1984, he may seize the document.

(1A) Where a licence to drive or a counterpart of any such licence or of any Community licence may be seized by a constable under subsection (1) above, he may also seize the counterpart, the licence to drive or the Community licence (as the case may be) produced with it.

(2) When a document is seized under subsection (1) above, the person from whom it was taken shall, unless—

    (a) the document has been previously returned to him, or

    (b) he has been previously charged with an offence under any of those sections,

be summoned before a magistrates' court or, in Scotland, the sheriff to account for his possession of the document.

(3) The court or sheriff must make such order respecting the disposal of the document and award such costs as the justice of the case may require.

(3A) An order under subsection (3) above respecting the disposal of any such licence or Community licence to drive or a counterpart of any such licence or Community licence may include an order respecting the disposal of any document seized under subsection (1A) above.

(4) If a constable, an examiner appointed under section 66A of this Act has reasonable cause to believe that a document or plate carried on a motor vehicle or by the driver of the vehicle is a document or plate to which this subsection applies, he may seize it.

For the purposes of this subsection the power to seize includes power to detach from a vehicle.

(5) Subsection (4) above applies to a document or plate in relation to which an offence has been committed under sections 173, 174 or 175 of this Act in so far as they apply—

(a) to documents evidencing the appointment of examiners under section 66A of this Act, or

(b) to goods vehicle test certificates, plating certificates, certificates of conformity or Minister's approval certificates (within the meaning of Part II of this Act), or

(c) to plates containing plated particulars (within the meaning of that Part) or containing other particulars required to be marked on goods vehicles by sections 54 to 58 of this Act or regulations made under them, or

(d) to records required to be kept by virtue of section 74 of this Act, or

(e) to international road haulage permits.

(6) When a document or plate is seized under subsection (4) above, either the driver or owner of the vehicle shall, if the document or plate is still detained and neither of them has previously been charged with an offence in relation to the document or plate under section 173, 174 or 175 of this Act, be summoned before a magistrates' court or, in Scotland, the sheriff to account for his possession of, or the presence on the vehicle of, the document or plate.

(7) The court or sheriff must make such order respecting the disposal of the document or plate and award such costs as the justice of the case may require.

(8) In this section "counterpart" and "Community licence" have the same meanings as in Part III of this Act.

(2) Allocation

These offences are triable either way. General mode of trial considerations are listed **17–150** in the *Consolidated Criminal Practice Direction*. In relation to offences of fraud, there is a presumption towards summary trial (see para. V.51.7: Appendix F, F–49). Factors that might suggest trial on indictment include breach of trust by a person in a position of *substantial* authority or in whom a high degree of trust is placed, conducting (or disguising) the fraud in a sophisticated manner, organised gang and victim particularly vulnerable. These guidelines will be replaced by the National Allocation Guidelines issued by the Sentencing Guidelines Council once the new allocation procedures are implemented. These guidelines are less related to specific offences. They emphasise that the primary consideration is the adequacy of the sentencing powers of the court taking the prosecution version of events as the basis.

(3) What must the prosecution prove?

There are a range of elements: in each case there must be an intent to deceive and **17–151** the offences must be committed in relation to a document or similar to which the section applies—these are listed in section 173(2). Perhaps the most common subjects of the offence are test and insurance certificates but a wide range of other documents are included.

If the document is one to which the section applies and if there is an intent to deceive, an offence is committed either by creating a document intended to deceive or using such a document in one way or another.

(4) Creating a document or other thing

This can be by forgery, by altering or by creating something that so closely resembles **17–152** the real thing (without actually copying the real thing) as to be calculated to deceive.

"Forges" is defined in section 173(3) as meaning "making … in order that it may be used as genuine".

(5) Using a document etc.

17–153   This can be straightforward use but also includes lending a document or thing to another person (or at least allowing them to use it) or having in your possession a document so closely resembling the real things as to be calculated to deceive.

For an offence of "using" under section 173(1)(a), the use must be of one of the specified documents. If it is a forgery or an altered document, it may be that the prosecution would need to be under section 173(1)(c): see *Holloway v. Brown* [1978] R.T.R. 537. However, that strict interpretation may be less likely now.

(6) Making false statements or withholding material information

17–154   It is an offence to make false statements in order to secure one of four effects set out in section 175(1) or in the circumstances set out in section 175(2) or (3) or (5). The prosecution must prove that:
— the defendant
— knowingly (or, in relation to section 174(2), recklessly)
— made a false statement
— for one of the specified purposes.
For issues of identification, see *ante*, §§ 10–89 *et seq.*

(7) Issuing false documents

17–155   It is also an offence to issue a document of certain specified types in the knowledge that it is false in a material particular.

(8) Penalties

17–156   Forgery, etc. of documents (under section 173(1)) and making false statements (under section 174) are either way offences. At the Crown Court, they are punishable by up to two years imprisonment and/or an unlimited fine. In a magistrates' court, the maximum punishment is a fine of level 5, and, in respect of section 174, six months' imprisonment increasing to 12 months for offences committed on or after commencement of *Criminal Justice Act* 2003, s.154. The offences are not endorsable.

(9) Sentencing

17–157   These offences are punishable by imprisonment in the Crown Court only. In most instances, a financial penalty will result but, for the more serious offences, a community order would be appropriate particularly one containing a significant punishment element. Since these are not violent offences, a custodial sentence would only be appropriate where there has been a sophisticated and substantial organisation or a very substantial breach of trust.

D. Traffic Signs

(1) Definition

17–158   It is an offence to fail to comply with traffic signs properly placed. This section states the law generally and then deals specifically with the four signs that, on conviction, are endorsable.

Road Traffic Act 1988, s.36

Drivers to comply with traffic signs
17–159   **36.**—(1) Where a traffic sign, being a sign—

(a) of the prescribed size, colour and type, or

(b) of another character authorised by the Secretary of State under the provisions in that behalf of the *Road Traffic Regulation Act* 1984,

has been lawfully placed on or near a road, a person driving or propelling a vehicle who fails to comply with the indication given by the sign is guilty of an offence.

(2) A traffic sign shall not be treated for the purposes of this section as having been lawfully placed unless either—

(a) the indication given by the sign is an indication of a statutory prohibition, restriction or requirement, or

(b) it is expressly provided by or under any provision of the Traffic Acts that this section shall apply to the sign or to signs of a type of which the sign is one;

and, where the indication mentioned in paragraph (a) of this subsection is of the general nature only of the prohibition, restriction or requirement to which the sign relates, a person shall not be convicted of failure to comply with the indication unless he has failed to comply with the prohibition, restriction or requirement to which the sign relates.

(3) For the purposes of this section a traffic sign placed on or near a road shall be deemed—

(a) to be of the prescribed size, colour and type, or of another character authorised by the Secretary of State under the provisions in that behalf of the *Road Traffic Regulation Act* 1984, and

(b) (subject to subsection (2) above) to have been lawfully so placed,

unless the contrary is proved.

(4) Where a traffic survey of any description is being carried out on or in the vicinity of a road, this section applies to a traffic sign by which a direction is given—

(a) to stop a vehicle,

(b) to make it proceed in, or keep to, a particular line of traffic, or

(c) to proceed to a particular point on or near the road on which the vehicle is being driven or propelled,

being a direction given for the purposes of the survey (but not a direction requiring any person to provide any information for the purposes of the survey).

(5) Regulations made by the Secretary of State for the Environment, Transport and the Regions, the Secretary of State for Wales and the Secretary of State for Scotland acting jointly may specify any traffic sign for the purposes of column 5 of the entry in Schedule 2 to the *Road Traffic Offenders Act* 1988 relating to offences under this section (offences committed by failing to comply with certain signs involve discretionary disqualification).

(2) What the prosecution must prove

The prosecution must prove that: **17–160**

— the defendant

— drove or propelled

— a vehicle

— failed to comply with a sign.

Although a sign has to be lawfully placed and to be of a prescribed size etc., there is a presumption that that is the case unless the contrary is proved: section 36(3). Thus it is for the defence to prove (on the balance of probabilities) that a sign was not lawfully placed or was not of the prescribed size, colour, type or character (for more detail, see *Wilkinson*, Pt 2, B83). The Divisional Court gave detailed consideration to the signage indicating a speed limit in *Coombes v. DPP* [2007] R.T.R. 31. In this case, one of the signs at the start of a speed limit had become overgrown and was not visible. The court considered all the relevant obligations regarding the placing and maintenance of such signs. Although allowing the appeal against conviction on a single aspect, the court drew attention to the limits on the obligations of the authority responsible for the signs.

(3) Allocation

This offence is summary only.   **17–161**

(4) Sentencing

Contravention of most traffic signs is punishable by a fine only—up to level 3 (£1000). **17–162**

851

However, in respect of a small number of signs, it is endorsable with three penalty points and thus subject to discretionary disqualification. The relevant signs are traffic lights, pedestrian crossings, double white lines, stop signs.

E. SPEEDING

(1) Definition

Road Traffic Regulation Act 1984, ss.81, 82, 84–87, 89

General speed limit for restricted roads

17–163   **81.**—(1) It shall not be lawful for a person to drive a motor vehicle on a restricted road at a speed exceeding 30 miles per hour.

(2) The Ministers acting jointly may by order made by statutory instrument and approved by a resolution of each House of Parliament increase or reduce the rate of speed fixed by subsection (1) above, either as originally enacted or as varied under this subsection.

What roads are restricted roads

17–164   **82.**—(1) Subject to the provisions of this section and of section 84(3) of this Act, a road is a restricted road for the purposes of section 81 of this Act if—

(a) in England and Wales, there is provided on it a system of street lighting furnished by means of lamps placed not more than 200 yards apart;

(b) in Scotland, there is provided on it a system of carriageway lighting furnished by means of lamps placed not more than 185 metres apart and the road is of a classification or type specified for the purposes of this subsection in regulations made by the Secretary of State.

(2) The traffic authority for a road may direct—

(a) that the road which is a restricted road for the purposes of section 81 of this Act shall cease to be a restricted road for those purposes, or

(b) that the road which is not a restricted road for those purposes shall become a restricted road for those purposes.

(3) A special road is not a restricted road for the purposes of section 81 on or after the date declared by the traffic authority, by notice published in the prescribed manner, to be the date on which the special road, or the relevant part of the special road, is open for use as a special road.

Speed limits on roads other than restricted roads

17–165   **84.**—(1) An order made under this subsection as respects any road may prohibit—

(a) the driving of motor vehicles on that road at a speed exceeding that specified in the order,

(b) the driving of motor vehicles on that road at a speed exceeding that specified in the order during periods specified in the order, or

(c) the driving of motor vehicles on that road at a speed exceeding the speed for the time being indicated by traffic signs in accordance with the order.

(1A) An order made by virtue of subsection (1)(c) above may—

(a) make provision restricting the speeds that may be indicated by traffic signs or the periods during which the indications may be given, and

(b) provide for the indications to be given only in such circumstances as may be determined by or under the order;

but any such order must comply with regulations made under subsection (1B) below, except where the Secretary of State authorises otherwise in a particular case.

(1B) The Secretary of State may make regulations governing the provision which may be made by orders of local authorities under subsection (1)(c) above, and any such regulations may in particular—

(a) prescribe the circumstances in which speed limits may have effect by virtue of an order,

(b) prescribe the speed limits which may be specified in an order, and

(c) make transitional provision and different provision for different cases.

(2) The power to make an order under subsection (1) is exercisable by the traffic authority, who shall before exercising it in any case give public notice of their intention to do so.

(3) While an order made by virtue of subsection (1)(a) above is in force as respects a road, that road shall not be a restricted road for the purposes of section 81 of this Act.

(4) This section does not apply to any part of a special road which is open for use as a special road.

(5) Section 68(1)(c) of this Act shall apply to any order made under subsection (1) above.

(6) Any reference in a local Act to roads subject to a speed limit shall, unless the contrary intention appears, be treated as not including a reference to roads subject to a speed limit imposed only by virtue of subsection (1)(b) or (c) above.

Traffic signs for indicating speed restrictions

85.—(1) For the purpose of securing that adequate guidance is given to drivers of motor **17–166** vehicles as to whether any, and if so what, limit of speed is to be observed on any road, it shall be the duty of the Secretary of State, in the case of a road for which he is the traffic authority, to erect and maintain traffic signs in such positions as may be requisite for that purpose.

(2) In the case of any other road, it is the duty of the local traffic authority—

   (a) to erect and maintain traffic signs in such positions as may be requisite in order to give effect to general or other directions given by the Secretary of State for the purpose mentioned in subsection (1) above, and

   (b) to alter or remove traffic signs as may be requisite in order to give effect to such directions, either in consequence of the making of an order by the Secretary of State or otherwise.

(3) If a local traffic authority makes default in executing any works required for the performance of the duty imposed on them by subsection (2) above, the Secretary of State may himself execute the works; and the expense incurred by him in doing so shall be recoverable by him from the local traffic authority and, in England or Wales, shall be so recoverable summarily as a civil debt.

(4) Where no such system of street or carriageway lighting as is mentioned in section 82(1) is provided on a road, but a limit of speed is to be observed on the road, a person shall not be convicted of driving a motor vehicle on the road at a speed exceeding the limit unless the limit is indicated by means of such traffic signs as are mentioned in subsection (1) or subsection (2) above.

(5) In any proceedings for a contravention of section 81 of this Act, where the proceedings relate to driving on a road provided with such a system of street or carriageway lighting, evidence of the absence of traffic signs displayed in pursuance of this section to indicate that the road is not a restricted road for the purposes of that section shall be evidence that the road is a restricted road for those purposes.

(6) Where by regulations made under section 17(2) of this Act a limit of speed is to be observed, then, if it is to be observed—

   (a) on all special roads, or

   (b) on all special roads provided for the use of particular classes of traffic, or

   (c) on all special roads other than special roads of such description as may be specified in the regulations, or

   (d) as mentioned in paragraph (a), (b) or (c) above except for such lengths of special road as may be so specified,

this section shall not apply in relation to that limit (but without prejudice to its application in relation to any lower limit of maximum speed or, as the case may be, any higher limit of minimum speed, required by any such regulations to be observed on any specified length of any specified special road).

(7) The power to give general directions under subsection (2) above shall be exercisable by statutory instrument

Speed limits for particular classes of vehicles

86.—(1) It shall not be lawful for a person to drive a motor vehicle of any class on a road at a **17–167** speed greater than the speed specified in Schedule 6 to this Act as the maximum speed in relation to a vehicle of that class.

(2) Subject to subsections (4) and (5) below, the Secretary of State may by regulations vary, subject to such conditions as may be specified in the regulations, the provisions of that Schedule.

(3) Regulations under this section may make different provision as respects the same class of vehicles in different circumstances.

(5) The Secretary of State shall not have power under this section to vary the speed limit imposed by section 81 of this Act.

(6) The Secretary of State shall not have power under this section to impose a speed limit, as respects driving on roads which are not restricted roads for the purposes of section 81 of this Act, on a vehicle which—

(a) is constructed solely for the carriage of passengers and their effects;

(b) is not adapted to carry more than 8 passengers exclusive of the driver;

(c) is neither a heavy motor car nor an invalid carriage;

(d) is not drawing a trailer; and

(e) is fitted with pneumatic tyres on all its wheels.

Exemption of fire brigade, ambulance and police vehicles from speed limits

17–168   **87.**—(1) No statutory provision imposing a speed limit on motor vehicles shall apply to any vehicle on an occasion when—

(a) it is being used for fire and rescue authority purposes or for or in connection with the exercise of any function of a relevant authority as defined in section 6 of the *Fire (Scotland) Act 2005*, for ambulance purposes or for police or Serious Organised Crime Agency purposes,

(b) it is being used for other prescribed purposes in such circumstances as may be prescribed, or

(c) it is being used for training persons to drive vehicles for use for any of the purposes mentioned in paragraph (a) or (b) above,

if the observance of that provision would be likely to hinder the use of the vehicle for the purpose for which it is being used on that occasion.

(2) Subsection (1) above does not apply unless the vehicle is being driven by a person who—

(a) has satisfactorily completed a course of training in the driving of vehicles at high speed provided in accordance with regulations under this section, or

(b) is driving the vehicle as part of such a course.

(3) The Secretary of State may by regulations make provision about courses of training in the driving of vehicles at high speed.

(4) The regulations may include—

(a) provision about the nature of courses,

(b) provision for the approval by the Secretary of State of persons providing courses or giving instruction on courses and the withdrawal of approvals (including provision for appeals against refusal and withdrawal of approvals),

(c) provision specifying the maximum fees that a person may be required to pay for a course,

(d) provision for the training or assessment, or the supervision of the training or assessment, of persons providing courses or giving instruction on courses,

(e) provision for the evidencing of the successful completion of courses,

(f) provision authorising the Secretary of State to make available information about persons providing courses or giving instruction on courses, and

(g) provision treating courses of training in the driving of vehicles at high speed which have been completed before the coming into force of the regulations as if they had been provided in accordance with the regulations.

(5) The regulations may include provision for the charging of reasonable fees in respect of any function conferred or imposed on the Secretary of State by the regulations.

(6) The regulations may make different provision—

(a) for different classes of vehicle,

(b) for different descriptions of persons, or

(c) otherwise for different circumstances.

[As amended by section 19 of the *Road Safety Act* 2006 when in force.]

Speeding offences generally

17–169   **89.**—(1) A person who drives a motor vehicle on a road at a speed exceeding a limit imposed by or under any enactment to which this section applies shall be guilty of an offence.

(2) A person prosecuted for such an offence shall not be liable to be convicted solely on the evidence of one witness to the effect that, in the opinion of the witness, the person prosecuted was driving the vehicle at a speed exceeding a specified limit.

(3) The enactments to which this section applies are—

  (a) any enactment contained in this Act except section 17(2);

  (b) section 2 of the *Parks Regulation (Amendment) Act* 1926; and

  (c) any enactment not contained in this Act, but passed after 1st September 1960, whether before or after the passing of this Act.

(4) If a person who employs other persons to drive motor vehicles on roads publishes or issues any time-table or schedule, or gives any directions, under which any journey, or any stage or part of any journey, is to be completed within some specified time, and it is not practicable in the circumstances of the case for that journey (or that stage or part of it) to be completed in the specified time without the commission of such an offence as is mentioned in subsection (1) above, the publication or issue of the time-table or schedule, or the giving of the directions, may be produced as prima facie evidence that the employer procured or (as the case may be) incited the persons employed by him to drive the vehicles to commit such an offence.

(2) What must the prosecution prove?

— the defendant   **17–170**

— drove

— a motor vehicle

— on a road (note only "road" not "other public place")

— at a speed

— exceeding a limit imposed by or under an enactment to which this section applies.

(3) Allocation

This offence is summary only.   **17–171**

A prosecution must be initiated within six months.

(4) Warning of intended prosecution

By virtue of Schedule 1 to the *Road Traffic Offenders Act* 1988, the prosecution **17–172** must have complied with the requirements to give notice of intended prosecution: *Road Traffic Offenders Act* 1988, s.1. Unless an accident has occurred of which the driver was aware (*Road Traffic Offenders Act* 1988, s.2(1)), the driver must receive warning of prosecution within 14 days of the offence. This warning may be given at the time of the offence, by service of the summons (or copy of a charge sheet) within 14 days of the offence or by the prosecutor sending notice to the driver or the registered keeper of the vehicle within 14 days. Where the notice is by service of the summons, that must take place within the 14 days. Where the notification is by notice, it is only necessary for that to be sent within the 14 days. However, by virtue of section 2(3) of the Act, failure to comply with these requirements is not to be a bar to conviction where the name and address of the driver or the registered keeper could not have been ascertained by the exercise of reasonable diligence in time to comply with the requirements of the section. Similarly where the accused contributed to the failure by his own conduct—perhaps by leaving the scene or not registering the vehicle correctly.

For further information, refer to *Wilkinson's Road Traffic Offences*, Ch.2.

(5) Limits and exceptions

Limits can apply to roads or to different types of vehicle and care must be taken **17–173** regarding both factors. Many prosecutions are under section 89 of the *Road Traffic Regulation Act* 1984 (see *ante*, at § 17–169). In *R. (Harrison) v. Flintshire Magistrates' Court* (2004) 168 J.P. 653, an unusual situation arose which served to emphasise the pragmatic approach of the appeal courts to regulatory provisions. The defendant was prosecuted in the belief that a 30 mph limit applied to the road and the information alleged "... contrary to ss. 81(1) and 89(1)" of the 1984 Act. It was subsequently discovered that the national speed limit (60 mph) applied in which case the information should have alleged "... contrary to ss. 84 and 89(1)" of the 1984 Act. The recorded speed was 67 mph. The defendant was fined and disqualified. If it was known that the limit was 60 mph, it was unlikely that disqualification would have resulted. The Divisional Court declined to overturn the conviction but agreed that sentence should be reconsidered.

A further case explored the authority under which a County Council (as a traffic authority) can designate that a road is subject to a 30 mph limit. In *DPP v. Evans* [2004] EWHC 2785 Admin, the court had to examine section 82(2)(b) of the 1984 *Act* (see *ante*, § 17–156). This complements the well known provision in section 82(1) that a road is a restricted road for the purposes of section 81 if there is a system of lighting by lamps not more than 200 yards apart. A traffic authority, by section 82(2), may designate that such a road should not be a restricted road or that a road that is not so lit should become a restricted road. In such circumstances, signs need to be displayed of the limit in force: section 85(4). The defence argument that section 82(2) was not a power generally available to a traffic authority but narrow and restricted in application was rebuffed by the Divisional Court.

Although, by section 89(2), the evidence of one witness is not sufficient for the defendant to be convicted, a wide range of devices have been developed for producing supporting evidence ranging from the humble speedometer to sophisticated radar and camera devices.

The principal exemption is contained in section 87 (which is replaced by section 19 of the *Road Safety Act* 2006 when in force). It exempts certain vehicles driven by those who have completed a course of training in driving vehicles at high speed provided in accordance with regulations or who are driving the vehicle as part of such a course. The vehicle must be one being used for fire and rescue authority purposes, for ambulance purposes, for police purposes or for the purposes of the Serious Organised Crime Agency in circumstances where observance of the speed limit would be likely to hinder the use of the vehicle for the purpose for which it is being used on that occasion. It will be for the defence to prove (on the balance of probabilities) the purpose for which the vehicle was being used, the need to drive more quickly than the limit and the qualification of the driver. The vehicle does not have to be an ambulance or a fire engine, *etc.* but it must be being used for the purposes specified and adherence to the speed limit must hinder the use of the vehicle on that occasion. Thus, bringing a human organ from one part of the country to another for use in a transplant operation where speed is of the essence is likely to meet the criteria. The exemption is only from speed limits— there is still the obligation to drive with due care and attention, *etc.*

(6) Penalty

17–174 Exceeding the speed limit is generally subject to a maximum fine of level 3; the exception is where the speed limit exceeded is the overall maximum on a motorway when it becomes level 4 (currently £2,500). The level of financial penalty (and the number of penalty points) will generally vary by reference to the speed and the proportion by which it exceeded the limit. Thus, exceeding a 30 mph limit by 15 mph will be more serious than exceeding a 60 mph limit by the same amount. Also relevant as aggravating factors will be the type of vehicle (LGV, HGV, PCV or taxi/private hire vehicle), the location, time of day and visibility at the time of the offence, serious risk taken and the fact that the defendant was towing a caravan or trailer at the time of the offence. Mitigating factors include driving in an emergency. The starting point is generally a fine.

Many offences are dealt with by a fixed penalty and, in that case, three penalty points will be endorsed on the licence. If the offender is convicted by a court, there is a range of 3–6 points; again the point in the range will depend mainly on the proportion by which the actual speed exceeded the limit. When in force, the *Road Safety Act 2006*, s.17 changes this range to 2–6. If a fixed penalty would have been offered but for some reason it was not, the court is often inclined to stay with both the financial penalty and the number of penalty points.

Disqualification for relatively short periods will be appropriate where the risks were greater, and is usually considered seriously in any case once a speed limit is exceeded by 30 mph.

F. Being in Proper Control of a Vehicle

(1) General

For many years there has been an offence of failing to be in proper control of a **17–175** vehicle. More recently, this has been complemented by specific provisions relating to the use of a mobile telephone whilst driving. Section 26 of the *Road Safety Act* 2006 introduces a new section 41D to the *Road Traffic Act* 1988 which becomes the provision creating such offences.

Road Traffic Act 1988, s.41D

41D.—   A person who contravenes or fails to comply with a construction and use require-   **17–176**
ment—
- (a) as to not driving a motor vehicle in a position which does not give proper control or a full view of the road and traffic ahead, or not causing or permitting the driving of a motor vehicle by another person in such a position, or
- (b) as to not driving or supervising the driving of a motor vehicle while using a hand-held mobile telephone or other hand-held interactive communication device, or not causing or permitting the driving of a motor vehicle by another person using such a telephone or other device

is guilty of an offence.

(2) What must the prosecution prove?

In respect of the part relating to mobile telephones,   **17–177**
- — the defendant
- — drove (or was supervising the driving)
- — a motor vehicle
- — whilst using
- — a hand held mobile telephone

Where the telephone was not hand held, it is still possible that an offence will be committed under section 41D(a) if it can be shown that the driver was not in proper control of the vehicle. There is no exception provided for this offence but the definition of "driving" is wide (see *ante*, § 17–4). This could mean that the offence would be committed where the vehicle was stationary not just when it was in motion providing the defendant was still "driving" in the technical sense.

(3) Allocation

This offence is summary only.   **17–178**

(4) Penalty

The offence is a fixed penalty offence. If prosecuted, an offender will be liable to a   **17–179**
maximum penalty of Level 4 (currently £2,500) if committed in respect of a goods vehicle or a vehicle adapted to carry more than 8 eight passengers or to a maximum of Level 3 (currently £1,000) in any other case. Disqualification is discretionary; endorsement is mandatory with three points.

VI. EFFECT OF PENALTIES

A. General

Many road traffic offences lead, on conviction, to a requirement that details of the of-   **17–180** fender be endorsed onto the offender's driving record and/or to the possibility of disqualification from driving. In most cases, disqualification is at the discretion of the court but, in some cases, the court is obliged to disqualify the offender unless there are "special reasons" (see *post*) for not doing so. Similarly, where endorsement is required, it is always mandatory in the absence of "special reasons". There is also the consequential power to deprive an offender of the vehicle used in certain circumstances.

B. Endorsement

Road Traffic Offenders Act 1988, ss.44–48, 28(1)–(6), 30A

Orders for endorsement

17–181   **44.**—(1) Where a person is convicted of an offence involving obligatory endorsement, the court must order there to be endorsed on the counterpart of any licence held by him particulars of the conviction and also—

(a) if the court orders him to be disqualified, particulars of the disqualification, or

(b) if the court does not order him to be disqualified—

(i) particulars of the offence, including the date when it was committed, and

(ii) the penalty points to be attributed to the offence.

(2) Where the court does not order the person convicted to be disqualified, it need not make an order under subsection (1) above if for special reasons it thinks fit not to do so.

(3) In relation to Scotland, references in this section to the court include the district court.

(3A) Where a person who is not the holder of a licence is convicted of an offence involving obligatory endorsement, subsection (1) above applies as if the reference to the counterpart of any licence held by him were a reference to his driving record.

(4) This section is subject to section 48 of this Act.

[This section will be amended following the enactment of the Road Safety Bill.]

Endorsement of driving record in accordance with order

17–182   **44A.**—(1) Where the court orders the endorsement of a person's driving record with any particulars or penalty points it must send notice of the order to the Secretary of State.

(2) On receiving the notice, the Secretary of State must endorse those particulars or penalty points on the person's driving record.

(3) A notice sent by the court to the Secretary of State in pursuance of this section must be sent in such manner and to such address and contain such particulars as the Secretary of State may require.

Effect of endorsement

17–183   **45.**—(1) An order that any particulars or penalty points are to be endorsed on the counterpart of any licence held by the person convicted shall, whether he is at the time the holder of a licence or not, operate as an order that the counterpart of any licence he may then hold or may subsequently obtain is to be so endorsed until he becomes entitled under subsection (4) below to have a licence issued to him with its counterpart free from the particulars or penalty points.

(2) On the issue of a new licence to a person, any particulars or penalty points ordered to be endorsed on the counterpart of any licence held by him shall be entered on the counterpart of the licence unless he has become entitled under subsection (4) below to have a licence issued to him with its counterpart free from those particulars or penalty points.

(3) [...]

(4) A person the counterpart of whose licence has been ordered to be endorsed is entitled to have a new licence issued to him free from the endorsement if, after the end of the period for which the endorsement remains effective, issued to him with effect from the end of the period for which the endorsement remains effective a new licence with a counterpart free from the endorsement if he applies for a new licence in pursuance of section 97(1) of the *Road Traffic Act* 1988, surrenders any subsisting licence and its counterpart, pays the fee prescribed by regulations under Part III of that Act and satisfies the other requirements of section 97(1).

(5) An endorsement ordered on a person's conviction of an offence remains effective (subject to subsections (6) and (7) below)—

 (a) if an order is made for the disqualification of the offender, until four years have elapsed since the conviction, and

 (b) if no such order is made, until either—

  (i) four years have elapsed since the commission of the offence, or

  (ii) an order is made for the disqualification of the offender under section 35 of this Act.

(6) Where the offence was one under section 1 of that Act (causing death by dangerous driving and dangerous driving), the endorsement remains in any case effective until four years have elapsed since the conviction.

(7) Where the offence was one—

 (a) under section 3A, 4(1) or 5(1)(a) of that Act (driving offences connected with drink or drugs), or

 (b) under section 7(6) of that Act (failing to provide specimen) involving obligatory disqualification,

the endorsement remains effective until eleven years have elapsed since the conviction.

Combination of disqualification and endorsement with probation orders and orders for discharge

46.—(1) Notwithstanding anything in section 14(3) of the *Powers of Criminal Courts* **17–184** *(Sentencing) Act* 2000(conviction of offender discharged to be disregarded for the purposes of enactments relating to disqualification), a court in England and Wales which on convicting a person of an offence involving obligatory or discretionary disqualification makes—

 (a) a probation order, or

 (b) an order discharging him absolutely or conditionally,

may on that occasion also exercise any power conferred, and must also discharge any duty imposed, on the court by sections 34, 35, 36 or 44 of this Act.

(2) A conviction—

 (a) in respect of which a court in England and Wales has ordered a person to be disqualified, or

 (b) of which particulars have been endorsed on the counterpart of any licence held by him,

is to be taken into account, notwithstanding anything in section 14(1) of the *Powers of Criminal Courts (Sentencing) Act* 2000 (conviction of offender discharged to be disregarded for the purpose of subsequent proceedings), in determining his liability to punishment or disqualification for any offence involving obligatory or discretionary disqualification committed subsequently.

(3) Where—

 (a) a person is charged in Scotland with an offence involving obligatory or discretionary disqualification, and

 (b) the court makes an order in respect of the offence under section 228(probation) or 246(2) or (3) (absolute discharge) of the *Criminal Procedure (Scotland) Act* 1995,

then, for the purposes of sections 34, 35, 36, 44 and 45 of this Act, he shall be treated as if he had been convicted of an offence of the kind in question and section 247 of that Act shall not apply.

Supplementary provisions as to disqualifications and endorsements

47.—(1) In any case where a court exercises its power under section 34, 35 or 44 of this Act **17–185** not to order any disqualification or endorsement or to order disqualification for a shorter period than would otherwise be required, it must state the grounds for doing so in open court and, if it is a magistrates' court or, in Scotland, a court of summary jurisdiction, must cause them to be entered in the register (in Scotland, record) of its proceedings.

(2) Where a court orders the endorsement of the counterpart of any licence held by a person it may, and where a court orders the holder of a licence to be disqualified for a period of 56 days or more it must, send the licence, on its licence and its counterpart, on its their being produced to the court, to the Secretary of State; and if the court orders the endorsement but does not send the licence and its counterpart to the Secretary of State it must send him notice of the endorsement.

(2A) Subsection (2) above is subject to section 2(2) of and paragraph 7(2) of Schedule 1

Road Traffic (New Drivers) Act 1995 (obligation of court to send licence and its counterpart to the Secretary of State).

(3) Where on an appeal against an order for the endorsement of a licence or the disqualification of a person the appeal is allowed, the court by which the appeal is allowed must send notice of that fact to the Secretary of State.

(4) A notice sent by a court to the Secretary of State in pursuance of this section must be sent in such manner and to such address and contain such particulars as the Secretary of State may determine, and a licence and the counterpart of a licence so sent in pursuance of this section must be sent to such address as the Secretary of State may determine.

Exemption from disqualification and endorsement for certain construction and use offences

17–186   **48.**—(1) Where a person is convicted of an offence under section 40A of the *Road Traffic Act* 1988 (using vehicle in dangerous condition etc) the court must not—

  (a) order him to be disqualified, or
  (b) order any particulars or penalty points to be endorsed on the counterpart of any licence held by him,

if he proves that he did not know, and had no reasonable cause to suspect, that the use of the vehicle involved a danger of injury to any person.

(2) Where a person is convicted of an offence under section 41A of the *Road Traffic Act* 1988 (breach of requirement as to brakes, steering-gear or tyres) the court must not—

  (a) order him to be disqualified, or
  (b) order any particulars or penalty points to be endorsed on the counterpart of any licence held by him,

if he proves that he did not know, and had no reasonable cause to suspect, that the facts of the case were such that the offence would be committed.

(3) In relation to licences which came into force before 1st June 1990, the references in subsections (1) and (2) above to the counterpart of a licence shall be construed as references to the licence itself.

Penalty points to be attributed to an offence

17–187   **28.**—(1) Where a person is convicted of an offence involving obligatory endorsement, then, subject to the following provisions of this section, the number of penalty points to be attributed to the offence is—

  (a) the number shown in relation to the offence in the last column of Part I or Part II of Schedule 2 to this Act, or
  (b) where a range of numbers is shown, a number within that range.

(2) Where a person is convicted of an offence committed by aiding, abetting, counselling or procuring, or inciting to the commission of, an offence involving obligatory disqualification, then, subject to the following provisions of this section, the number of penalty points to be attributed to the offence is ten.

(3) Where both a range of numbers and a number followed by the words "(fixed penalty)" is shown in the last column of Part I of Schedule 2 to this Act in relation to an offence, that number is the number of penalty points to be attributed to the offence for the purposes of sections 57(5) and 77(5) of this Act; and, where only a range of numbers is shown there, the lowest number in the range is the number of penalty points to be attributed to the offence for those purposes.

(4) Where a person is convicted (whether on the same occasion or not) of two or more offences committed on the same occasion and involving obligatory endorsement, the total number of penalty points to be attributed to them is the number or highest number that would be attributed on a conviction of one of them (so that if the convictions are on different occasions the number of penalty points to be attributed to the offences on the later occasion or occasions shall be restricted accordingly).

(5) In a case where (apart from this subsection) subsection (4) above would apply to two or more offences, the court may if it thinks fit determine that that subsection shall not apply to the offences (or, where three or more offences are concerned, to any one or more of them).

(6) Where a court makes such a determination it shall state its reasons in open court and, if it is a magistrates' court, or in Scotland a court of summary jurisdiction, shall cause them to be entered in the register (in Scotland, record) of its proceedings.

Reduced penalty points for attendance on course

17–188   **30A.**—(1) This section applies where—

(a) a person is convicted of a specified offence by or before a court,

(b) penalty points are to be attributed to the offence and the court does not order him to be disqualified, and

(c) at least seven but no more than eleven penalty points are to be taken into account on the occasion of the conviction.

(2) In this section "specified offence" means—

(a) an offence under section 3 of the *Road Traffic Act* 1988 (careless, and inconsiderate, driving),

(b) an offence under section 36 of that Act (failing to comply with traffic signs),

(c) an offence under section 17(4) of the *Road Traffic Regulation Act* 1984 (use of special road contrary to scheme or regulations), or

(d) an offence under section 89(1) of that Act (exceeding speed limit).

(3) But the Secretary of State may by regulations amend subsection (2) above by adding other offences or removing offences.

(4) Where this section applies, the court may make an order that three of the penalty points attributed to the offence (or all of them if three or fewer are so attributed) shall not be taken into account under section 29(1)(b) of this Act on the occasion of any conviction of an offence after the end of the period of twelve months beginning with the date of the order if, by the relevant date, the offender completes an approved course specified in the order.

(5) In subsection (4) above—

"an approved course" means a course approved by the appropriate national authority for the purposes of this section in relation to the description of offence of which the offender is convicted, and "the relevant date" means such date, no later than ten months after the day on which the order is made, as is specified in the order.

(6) A court shall not make an order under this section in the case of an offender convicted of an offence if—

(a) the offender has, during the period of three years ending with the date on which the offence was committed, committed a specified offence and successfully completed an approved course pursuant to an order made under this section or section 34A of this Act on conviction of that offence, or

(b) the offence was committed during his probationary period.

(7) A court shall not make an order under this section in the case of an offender unless—

(a) the court is satisfied that a place on the course specified in the order will be available for the offender,

(b) the offender appears to the court to be of or over the age of 17,

(c) the court has informed the offender (orally or in writing and in ordinary language) of the effect of the order and of the amount of the fees which he is required to pay for the course and when he must pay them, and

(d) the offender has agreed that the order should be made.

[Introduced by section 34 of the *Road Safety Act* 2006 when in force.]

The offences involving obligatory endorsement are set out in the *Road Traffic Offenders Act* 1988, Sched. 2. Where endorsement is required, it will contain particulars of the conviction, any disqualification or, if no disqualification is imposed, particulars of the offence and the penalty points attributed to the offence. Codes have been allocated to all endorsable offences and to all sentences that could be imposed. **17–189**

The number of penalty points may be fixed by statute or a range may be given (for example, careless driving has a range of 3–9 points) which allows the court to reflect the varying levels of seriousness. When the number of points reaches a particular level (see *post*), the court must disqualify the offender in the absence of "mitigating circumstances" (see *post*).

The requirement is to endorse "any licence held by" the offender. The order must be made whether or not the offender actually holds a licence: see *Road Traffic Offenders Act* 1988, s.45. The licence referred to is one issued under Part III of the *Road Traffic Act* 1988 (*Road Traffic Act* 1988, s.108) and does not include, *e.g.* international driving permits, foreign driving licences or heavy goods vehicles licences. However, the details need to be notified to the Secretary of State and a record kept. An accumulation of points will still lead to disqualification even though no licence issued under Part III is ever held.

17–190   Where an offender is convicted of more than one offence committed on the same occasion, the court will generally attribute just the highest number of points to be allocated to any one of the offences: *Road Traffic Offenders Act* 1988, s.28(4). Thus, where an offender is convicted of careless driving and of using a vehicle without insurance and the court decides to impose four penalty points for the careless driving and seven penalty points for the no insurance, it will be the 7 points alone that will be endorsed on the licence. However, the court retains the discretion to endorse more than one set of points where it thinks fit (section 28(5)) but must then give its reasons for so doing (section 28(6)). If that was applied to the example, *ante*, the offender would then have 11 points endorsed. Where the court disqualifies the offender, no further penalty points are endorsed either for the offence on which the disqualification is ordered or any other offence of which he is convicted on the same occasion: *Martin v. DPP* [2000] R.T.R. 188. This is also the case where the disqualification is obligatory: *Road Traffic Offenders Act* 1988, s.44(1).

In considering what level of points to attribute where a range is prescribed, the court will be primarily concerned with the gravity of the offence—the more serious the offence within its class, the higher the number of points. However, this decision will also be taken within the context of the overall purpose of sentencing in criminal cases which will encompass the need to impose a punishment proportionate to the offence and the need to reduce the likelihood of the offender committing further offences. Since the court will always have the power to disqualify wherever it is required to endorse, there will be no need to increase the penalty points beyond what the offence justifies. However, a court may legitimately take the view that the goal of reducing crime justifies fixing the level of points in a way that leaves the offender in no doubt that a further conviction will lead to disqualification.

C. Disqualification

(1) Legislation

Road Traffic Offenders Act 1988, ss.34, 34A, 34D, 35–39, 42, 43, 26, 29,

Disqualification for certain offences

17–191   **34.**—(1) Where a person is convicted of an offence involving obligatory disqualification, the court must order him to be disqualified for such period not less than twelve months as the court thinks fit unless the court for special reasons thinks fit to order him to be disqualified for a shorter period or not to order him to be disqualified.

(1A) Where a person is convicted of an offence under section 12A of the *Theft Act* 1968 (aggravated vehicle-taking), the fact that he did not drive the vehicle in question at any particular time or at all shall not be regarded as a special reason for the purposes of subsection (1) above.

(2) Where a person is convicted of an offence involving discretionary disqualification, and either—

    (a) the penalty points to be taken into account on that occasion number fewer than twelve, or

    (b) the offence is not one involving obligatory endorsement,

the court may order him to be disqualified for such period as the court thinks fit.

(3) Where a person convicted of an offence under any of the following provisions of the *Road Traffic Act* 1988, that is—

    (aa) section 3A (causing death by careless driving when under the influence of drink or drugs),

    (a) section 4(1) (driving or attempting to drive while unfit),

    (b) section 5(1)(a) (driving or attempting to drive with excess alcohol),

    (c) section 7(6) (failing to provide a specimen) where that is an offence involving obligatory disqualification,

    (d)　section 7A(6) (failing to allow a specimen to be subjected to laboratory test) where that is an offence involving obligatory disqualification;
has within the ten years immediately preceding the commission of the offence been convicted of any such offence, subsection (1) above shall apply in relation to him as if the reference to twelve months were a reference to three years.

    (4)　Subject to subsection (3) above, subsection (1) above shall apply as if the reference to twelve months were a reference to two years—

        (a)　in relation to a person convicted of—

            (i)　manslaughter, or in Scotland culpable homicide, or

            (ii)　an offence under section 1 of the *Road Traffic Act* 1988 (causing death by dangerous driving), or

            (iii)　an offence under section 3A of that Act (causing death by careless driving while under the influence of drink or drugs), and

        (b)　in relation to a person on whom more than one disqualification for a fixed period of 56 days or more has been imposed within the three years immediately preceding the commission of the offence.

    (4A)　For the purposes of subsection (4)(b) above there shall be disregarded any disqualification imposed under section 26 of this Act or section 147 of the *Powers of Criminal Courts (Sentencing) Act* 2000 or section 223A or 436A of the *Criminal Procedure (Scotland) Act* 1975 (offences committed by using vehicles) and any disqualification imposed in respect of an offence of stealing a motor vehicle, an offence under section 12 or 25 of the *Theft Act* 1968, an offence under section 178 of the *Road Traffic Act* 1988, or an attempt to commit such an offence.

    (5)　The preceding provisions of this section shall apply in relation to a conviction of an offence committed by aiding, abetting, counselling or procuring, or inciting to the commission of, an offence involving obligatory disqualification as if the offence were an offence involving discretionary disqualification.

    (6)　This section is subject to section 48 of this Act.

[Sections 34A–34D are printed as amended or inserted by the *Road Safety Act* 2006 when in force.]

Reduced disqualification period for attendance on courses

    34A.—(1) This section applies where—　　　　　　　　　　　　**17–192**

        (a)　a person is convicted of a relevant drink offence or a specified offence by or before a court, and

        (b)　the court makes an order under section 34 of this Act disqualifying him for a period of not less than twelve months.

    (2)　In this section "relevant drink offence" means—

        (a)　an offence under paragraph (a) of subsection (1) of section 3A of the *Road Traffic Act* 1988 (causing death by careless driving when unfit to drive through drink) committed when unfit to drive through drink,

        (b)　an offence under paragraph (b) of that subsection (causing death by careless driving with excess alcohol),

        (c)　an offence under paragraph (c) of that subsection (failing to provide a specimen) where the specimen is required in connection with drink or consumption of alcohol,

        (d)　an offence under section 4 of that Act (driving or being in charge when under influence of drink) committed by reason of unfitness through drink,

        (e)　an offence under section 5(1) of that Act (driving or being in charge with excess alcohol),

        (f)　an offence under section 7(6) of that Act (failing to provide a specimen) committed in the course of an investigation into an offence within any of the preceding paragraphs, or

        (g)　an offence under section 7A(6) of that Act (failing to allow a specimen to be subjected to a laboratory test) in the course of an investigation into an offence within any of the preceding paragraphs.

    (3)　In this section "specified offence" means—

        (a)　an offence under section 3 of the *Road Traffic Act* 1988 (careless, and inconsiderate, driving),

863

    (b) an offence under section 36 of that Act (failing to comply with traffic signs),

    (c) an offence under section 17(4) of the *Road Traffic Regulation Act* 1984 (use of special road contrary to scheme or regulations), or

    (d) an offence under section 89(1) of that Act (exceeding speed limit).

(4) But the Secretary of State may by regulations amend subsection (3) above by adding other offences or removing offences.

(5) Where this section applies, the court may make an order that the period of disqualification imposed under section 34 of this Act ("the unreduced period") shall be reduced if, by the relevant date, the offender satisfactorily completes an approved course specified in the order.

(6) In subsection (5) above—

    "an approved course" means a course approved by the appropriate national authority for the purposes of this section in relation to the description of offence of which the offender is convicted, and

    "the relevant date" means such date, at least two months before the last day of the period of disqualification as reduced by the order, as is specified in the order.

(7) The reduction made in a period of disqualification by an order under this section is a period specified in the order of—

    (a) not less than three months, and

    (b) not more than one quarter of the unreduced period,

(and, accordingly, where the unreduced period is twelve months, the reduced period is nine months).

(8) A court shall not make an order under this section in the case of an offender convicted of a specified offence if—

    (a) the offender has, during the period of three years ending with the date on which the offence was committed, committed a specified offence and successfully completed an approved course pursuant to an order made under this section or section 30A of this Act on conviction of that offence, or

    (b) the specified offence was committed during his probationary period.

(9) A court shall not make an order under this section in the case of an offender unless—

    (a) the court is satisfied that a place on the course specified in the order will be available for the offender,

    (b) the offender appears to the court to be of or over the age of 17,

    (c) the court has informed the offender (orally or in writing and in ordinary language) of the effect of the order and of the amount of the fees which he is required to pay for the course and when he must pay them, and

    (d) the offender has agreed that the order should be made.

Reduced disqualification period: alcohol ignition interlock programme orders

17–193   **34D.**—(1) This section applies where—

    (a) a person is convicted of a relevant drink offence by or before a court,

    (b) he has committed another relevant drink offence at any time during the period of ten years ending with the date of the conviction,

    (c) the court makes an order under section 34 of this Act but does not make an order under section 34A of this Act, and

    (d) the period stated by the court as that for which, apart from this section, he would be disqualified ("the unreduced period") is not less than two years.

(2) In this section "relevant drink offence" means—

    (a) an offence under paragraph (a) of subsection (1) of section 3A of the *Road Traffic Act* 1988 (causing death by careless driving when unfit to drive through drink) committed when unfit to drive through drink,

    (b) an offence under paragraph (b) of that subsection (causing death by careless driving with excess alcohol),

    (c) an offence under paragraph (c) of that subsection (failing to provide a specimen) where the specimen is required in connection with drink or consumption of alcohol,

    (d) an offence under section 4 of that Act (driving or being in charge when under influence of drink) committed by reason of unfitness through drink,

(e) an offence under section 5(1) of that Act (driving or being in charge with excess alcohol),

(f) an offence under section 7(6) of that Act (failing to provide a specimen) committed in the course of an investigation into an offence within any of the preceding paragraphs, or

(g) an offence under section 7A(6) of that Act (failing to allow a specimen to be subjected to a laboratory test) in the course of an investigation into an offence within any of the preceding paragraphs.

(3) Where this section applies, the court may specify a lesser period of disqualification ("the reduced period") if it also makes an order (an "alcohol ignition interlock programme order") requiring the offender to comply with the alcohol ignition interlock conditions.

(4) The difference between the unreduced period and the reduced period shall be a period specified in the order of—

(a) not less than 12 months, and

(b) not more than one half of the unreduced period.

(5) If the offender contravenes the alcohol ignition interlock conditions, a further order under section 34 disqualifying him for the rest of the unreduced period is to be treated as having been made by the court immediately before the contravention.

(6) "The alcohol ignition interlock conditions" are that the offender—

(a) must participate fully in an approved alcohol ignition interlock programme specified in the order during such part of the unreduced period as is so specified, and

(b) during the part of that period following the reduced period, must not drive a motor vehicle unless it is fitted with an alcohol ignition interlock in good working order and must not drive a motor vehicle which is so fitted when not using the alcohol ignition interlock properly.

(7) A court shall not make an alcohol ignition interlock programme order in the case of an offender unless—

(a) the court is satisfied that a place on the approved alcohol ignition interlock programme specified in the order will be available for the offender,

(b) the offender appears to the court to be of or over the age of 17,

(c) the court has informed the offender (orally or in writing and in ordinary language) of the effect of the order and the amount of the fees which he is required to pay for the programme and when he must pay them, and

(d) the offender has agreed that the order should be made.

(8) For the purposes of this section an "approved alcohol ignition interlock programme" is a programme approved by the appropriate national authority and involving the provision of an alcohol ignition interlock for use by the offender, training in its use and other education and counselling relating to the consumption of alcohol and driving.

(9) For the purposes of this section "alcohol ignition interlock" means a device—

(a) of a type approved by the Secretary of State, and

(b) designed to be fitted to a motor vehicle with the purpose of preventing the driving of the vehicle by a person who does not, both before starting driving the vehicle and at regular intervals while driving it, provide specimens of breath in which the proportion of alcohol is likely not to exceed the limit specified in subsection (10) below.

(10) That limit is 9 microgrammes of alcohol in 100 millilitres of breath or such other proportion of alcohol to breath as the Secretary of State may by regulations prescribe.

(11) For the purposes of this section an offender uses an alcohol ignition interlock properly if (and only if) he is complying with all the instructions given to him about its use as part of the approved alcohol ignition interlock programme.

(12) Where an alcohol ignition interlock is fitted to a motor vehicle as part of an approved alcohol ignition interlock programme relating to an offender, a person commits an offence if—

(a) he interferes with the alcohol ignition interlock with intent to cause it not to function or not to function properly, or

(b) he is a person other than the offender and provides or attempts to provide a specimen of breath for the purposes of the alcohol ignition interlock with intent to enable the driving (or continued driving) of the vehicle by the offender.

Part III

Disqualification for repeated offences

17–194　　35.—(1) Where—

(a) a person is convicted of an offence to which this subsection applies, and

(b) the penalty points to be taken into account on that occasion number twelve or more,

the court must order him to be disqualified for not less than the minimum period unless the court is satisfied, having regard to all the circumstances, that there are grounds for mitigating the normal consequences of the conviction and thinks fit to order him to be disqualified for a shorter period or not to order him to be disqualified.

(1A) Subsection (1) above applies to—

(a) an offence involving discretionary disqualification and obligatory endorsement, and

(b) an offence involving obligatory disqualification in respect of which no order is made under section 34 of this Act.

(2) The minimum period referred to in subsection (1) above is—

(a) six months if no previous disqualification imposed on the offender is to be taken into account, and

(b) one year if one, and two years if more than one, such disqualification is to be taken into account;

and a previous disqualification imposed on an offender is to be taken into account if it was for a fixed period of 56 days or more and was imposed within the three years immediately preceding the commission of the latest offence in respect of which penalty points are taken into account under section 29 of this Act.

(3) Where an offender is convicted on the same occasion of more than one offence to which subsection (1) above applies—

(a) not more than one disqualification shall be imposed on him under subsection (1) above,

(b) in determining the period of the disqualification the court must take into account all the offences, and

(c) for the purposes of any appeal any disqualification imposed under subsection (1) above shall be treated as an order made on the conviction of each of the offences.

(4) No account is to be taken under subsection (1) above of any of the following circumstances—

(a) any circumstances that are alleged to make the offence or any of the offences not a serious one,

(b) hardship, other than exceptional hardship, or

(c) any circumstances which, within the three years immediately preceding the conviction, have been taken into account under that subsection in ordering the offender to be disqualified for a shorter period or not ordering him to be disqualified.

(5) References in this section to disqualification do not include a disqualification imposed under section 26 of this Act or section 147 of the *Powers of Criminal Courts (Sentencing) Act* 2000 or section 223A or 436A of the *Criminal Procedure (Scotland) Act* 1975 (offences committed by using vehicles) or a disqualification imposed in respect of an offence of stealing a motor vehicle, an offence under section 12 or 25 of the *Theft Act* 1968, an offence under section 178 of the *Road Traffic Act* 1988, or an attempt to commit such an offence.

(5A) The preceding provisions of this section shall apply in relation to a conviction of an offence committed by aiding, abetting, counselling, procuring, or inciting to the commission of, an offence involving obligatory disqualification as if the offence were an offence involving discretionary disqualification.

(6) In relation to Scotland, references in this section to the court include the district court.

(7) This section is subject to section 48 of this Act.

Disqualification until test is passed

17–195　　36.—(1) Where this subsection applies to a person the court must order him to be disqualified until he passes the appropriate driving test.

(2) Subsection (1) above applies to a person who is disqualified under section 34 of this Act on conviction of—

(a) manslaughter, or in Scotland culpable homicide, by the driver of a motor vehicle, or

(b) an offence under section 1 (causing death by dangerous driving) or section 2 (dangerous driving) of the *Road Traffic Act* 1988.

(3) Subsection (1) above also applies—

(a) to a person who is disqualified under section 34 or 35 of this Act for such period, in such circumstances or for such period and in such circumstances as the Secretary of State may by order specify, or

(b) to such other persons convicted of such offences involving obligatory endorsement as the Secretary of State may by order specify.

(4) Where a person to whom subsection (1) above does not apply is convicted of an offence involving obligatory endorsement, the court may order him to be disqualified until he passes the appropriate driving test (whether or not he has previously passed any test).

(5) In this section—

"appropriate driving test" means—

(a) an extended driving test, in such circumstances as the Secretary of State my prescribe, and

(b) otherwise, a test of competence to drive, which is not an extended driving test.

"extended driving test" means a test of competence to drive prescribed for the purposes of this section by regulations made by the Secretary of State, and

"test of competence to drive" means a test prescribed by virtue of section 89(3) of the *Road Traffic Act* 1988.

(6) In determining whether to make an order under subsection (4) above, the court shall have regard to the safety of road users.

(7) Where a person is disqualified until he passes the extended driving test—

(a) any earlier order under this section shall cease to have effect, and

(b) a court shall not make a further order under this section while he is so disqualified.

(8) Subject to subsection (9) below, a disqualification by virtue of an order under this section shall be deemed to have expired on production to the Secretary of State of evidence, in such form as may be prescribed by regulations made by the Secretary of State that the person disqualified has passed the test in question since the order was made.

(9) A disqualification shall be deemed to have expired only in relation to vehicles of such classes as may be prescribed in relation to the test passed by regulations made by the Secretary of State.

(10) Where there is issued to a person a licence on the counterpart of which are endorsed particulars of a disqualification under this section, there shall also be endorsed the particulars of any test of competence to drive that he has passed since the order of disqualification was made.

(11) For the purposes of an order under this section, a person shall be treated as having passed a test of competence to drive other than an extended driving test if he passes a corresponding test conducted—

(a) under the law of Northern Ireland, the Isle of Man, any of the Channel Islands, another EEA State, Gibraltar or a designated country or territory, or

(b) for the purposes of obtaining a British Forces licence (as defined by section 88(8) of the *Road Traffic Act* 1988);

and accordingly subsections (8) to (10) above shall apply in relation to such a test as they apply in relation to a test prescribed by virtue of section 89(3) of that Act.

(11A) For the purposes of subsection (11) above, "designated country or territory" means a country or territory designated by order under section 108(2) of the *Road Traffic Act* 1988 but a test conducted under the law of such a country or territory shall not be regarded as a corresponding test unless a person passing such a test would be entitled to an exchangeable licence as defined in section 108(1) of that Act.

(12) This section is subject to section 48 of this Act.

(13) The power to make an order under subsection (3) above shall be exercisable by statutory instrument; and no such order shall be made unless a draft of it has been laid before and approved by resolution of each House of Parliament.

(13A) Before making an order under subsection (3) above the Secretary of State must consult with such representative organisations as he thinks fit.

Effect of order of disqualification

37.—(1) Where the holder of a licence is disqualified by an order of a court, the licence shall **17–196** be treated as being revoked with effect from the beginning of the period of disqualification.

(1A) Where—
(a) the disqualification is for a fixed period shorter than 56 days in respect of an offence involving obligatory endorsement, or
(b) the order is made under section 26 of this Act,

subsection (1) above shall not prevent the licence from again having effect at the end of the period of disqualification.

(2) Where the holder of the licence appeals against the order and the disqualification is suspended under section 39 of this Act, the period of disqualification shall be treated for the purpose of subsection (1) above as beginning on the day on which the disqualification ceases to be suspended.

(3) Notwithstanding anything in Part III of the *Road Traffic Act* 1988, a person disqualified by an order of a court under section 36 of this Act is (unless he is also disqualified otherwise than by virtue of such an order) entitled to obtain and to hold a provisional licence and to drive a motor vehicle in accordance with the conditions subject to which the provisional licence is granted.

Appeal against disqualification

17–197   **38.**—(1) A person disqualified by an order of a magistrates' court under section 34 or 35 of this Act may appeal against the order in the same manner as against a conviction.

(2) A person disqualified by an order of a court in Scotland may appeal against the order in the same manner as against a sentence.

Suspension of disqualification pending appeal

17–198   **39.**—(1) Any court in England and Wales (whether a magistrates' court or another) which makes an order disqualifying a person may, if it thinks fit, suspend the disqualification pending an appeal against the order.

(2) The court by or before which a person disqualified by an order of a court in Scotland was convicted may, if it thinks fit, suspend the disqualification pending an appeal against the order.

(3) Where a court exercises its power under subsection (1) or (2) above, it must send notice of the suspension to the Secretary of State.

(4) The notice must be sent in such manner and to such address and must contain such particulars as the Secretary of State may determine.

Removal of disqualification

17–199   **42.**—(1) Subject to the provisions of this section, a person who by an order of a court is disqualified may apply to the court by which the order was made to remove the disqualification.

(2) On any such application the court may, as it thinks proper having regard to—
(a) the character of the person disqualified and his conduct subsequent to the order,
(b) the nature of the offence, and
(c) any other circumstances of the case,

either by order remove the disqualification as from such date as may be specified in the order or refuse the application.

(3) No application shall be made under subsection (1) above for the removal of a disqualification before the expiration of whichever is relevant of the following periods from the date of the order by which the disqualification was imposed, that is—
(a) two years, if the disqualification is for less than four years,
(b) one half of the period of disqualification, if it is for less than ten years but not less than four years,
(c) five years in any other case;

and in determining the expiration of the period after which under this subsection a person may apply for the removal of a disqualification, any time after the conviction during which the disqualification was suspended or he was not disqualified shall be disregarded.

(4) Where an application under subsection (1) above is refused, a further application under that subsection shall not be entertained if made within three months after the date of the refusal.

(5) If under this section a court orders a disqualification to be removed, the court—
(a) must cause particulars of the order to be endorsed on the counterpart of the licence, if any, previously held by the applicant, and
(b) may in any case order the applicant to pay the whole or any part of the costs of the application.

(5A) Subsection (5)(a) above shall apply only where the disqualification was imposed in respect of an offence involving obligatory endorsement; and in any other case the court must send notice of the order made under this section to the Secretary of State.

(5B) A notice under subsection (5A) above must be sent in such manner and to such address, and must contain such particulars, as the Secretary of State may determine.

(6) The preceding provisions of this section shall not apply where the disqualification was imposed by order under section 36(1) of this Act.

Rule for determining end of period of disqualification
43. In determining the expiration of the period for which a person is disqualified by an order of a court made in consequence of a conviction, any time after the conviction during which the disqualification was suspended or he was not disqualified shall be disregarded.   **17–200**

Interim disqualification
26.—(1) Where a magistrates' court—   **17–201**
   (a) commits an offender to the Crown Court under section 6 of the *Powers of Criminal Courts (Sentencing) Act* 2000 or any enactment mentioned in subsection (4) of that section applies, or
   (b) remits an offender to another magistrates' court under section 10 of that Act,
to be dealt with for an offence involving obligatory or discretionary disqualification, it may order him to be disqualified until he has been dealt with in respect of the offence.

(2) Where a court in England and Wales—
   (a) defers passing sentence on an offender under section 1 of that Act in respect of an offence involving obligatory or discretionary disqualification, or
   (b) adjourns after convicting an offender of such an offence but before dealing with him for the offence,
it may order the offender to be disqualified until he has been dealt with in respect of the offence.

(3) Where a court in Scotland—
   (a) adjourns a case under section 179 or section 380 of the *Criminal Procedure (Scotland) Act* 1975 (for inquiries to be made or to determine the most suitable method of dealing with the offender);
   (b) remands a person in custody or on bail under section 180 or section 381 of the *Criminal Procedure (Scotland) Act* 1975 (to enable a medical examination and report to be made);
   (c) defers sentence under section 219 or section 432 of the *Criminal Procedure (Scotland) Act* 1975;
   (d) remits a convicted person to the High Court for sentence under section 104 of the *Criminal Procedure (Scotland) Act* 1975,
in respect of an offence involving obligatory or discretionary disqualification, it may order the accused to be disqualified until he has been dealt with in respect of the offence.

(4) Subject to subsection (5) below, an order under this section shall cease to have effect at the end of the period of six months beginning with the day on which it is made, if it has not ceased to have effect before that time.

(5) In Scotland, where a person is disqualified under this section where section 219 or section 432 of the *Criminal Procedure (Scotland) Act* 1975 (deferred sentence) applies and the period of deferral exceeds 6 months, subsection (4) above shall not prevent the imposition under this section of any period of disqualification which does not exceed the period of deferral.

(6) Where a court orders a person to be disqualified under this section ("the first order"), no court shall make a further order under this section in respect of the same offence or any offence in respect of which an order could have been made under this section at the time the first order was made.

(7) Where a court makes an order under this section in respect of any person it must—
   (a) require him to produce to the court any licence held by him and its counterpart, and
   (b) retain the licence and counterpart until it deals with him or (as the case may be) cause them to be sent to the proper officer of the court which is to deal with him.
(7A) In subsection (7) above "proper officer" means—
   (a) in relation to a magistrates' court in England and Wales, the justices' chief executive for the court, and
   (b) in relation to any other court, the clerk of the court.

(8) If the holder of the licence has not caused it and its counterpart to be delivered, or has not posted them, in accordance with section 7 of this Act and does not produce the licence and counterpart as required under subsection (7) above, then he is guilty of an offence.

(9) Subsection (8) above does not apply to a person who—

     (a) satisfies the court that he has applied for a new licence and has not received it, or

     (b) surrenders to the court a current receipt for his licence and its counterpart issued under section 56 of this Act, and produces the licence and counterpart to the court immediately on their return.

(10) Where a court makes an order under this section in respect of any person, sections 44(1), 47(2) and 91A(5) of this Act and section 109(3) of the *Road Traffic Act* 1988 (Northern Ireland drivers' licences) shall not apply in relation to the order, but—

     (a) the court must send notice of the order to the Secretary of State, and

     (b) if the court which deals with the offender determines not to order him to be disqualified under section 34 or 35 of this Act, it must send notice of the determination to the Secretary of State.

(11) A notice sent by a court to the Secretary of State in pursuance of subsection (10) above must be sent in such manner and to such address and contain such particulars as the Secretary of State may determine.

(12) Where on any occasion a court deals with an offender—

     (a) for an offence in respect of which an order was made under this section, or

     (b) for two or more offences in respect of any of which such an order was made,

any period of disqualification which is on that occasion imposed under section 34 or 35 of this Act shall be treated as reduced by any period during which he was disqualified by reason only of an order made under this section in respect of any of those offences.

(13) Any reference in this or any other Act (including any Act passed after this Act) to the length of a period of disqualification shall, unless the context otherwise requires, be construed as a reference to its length before any reduction under this section.

(14) In relation to licences which came into force before 1st June 1990, the references in this section to counterparts of licences shall be disregarded.

Penalty points to be taken into account on conviction

17–202   **29.**—(1) Where a person is convicted of an offence involving obligatory endorsement, the penalty points to be taken into account on that occasion are (subject to subsection (2) below)—

     (a) any that are to be attributed to the offence or offences of which he is convicted, disregarding any offence in respect of which an order under section 34 of this Act is made, and

     (b) any that were on a previous occasion ordered to be endorsed on the counterpart of any licence held by him, unless the offender has since that occasion and before the conviction been disqualified under section 35 of this Act.

(2) If any of the offences was committed more than three years before another, the penalty points in respect of that offence shall not be added to those in respect of the other.

(3) In relation to licences which came into force before 1st June 1990, the reference in subsection (1) above to the counterpart of a licence shall be construed as a reference to the licence itself.

(2) Driving licences

17–203   Wherever a court is obliged to endorse details of a conviction on a licence, it may also disqualify the offender from holding or obtaining a licence. A period of disqualification (or the number of penalty points) should not be reduced solely as a result of the reduction in sentence given when a defendant enters a guilty plea. The Sentencing Guidelines Council Guideline *Reduction in Sentence for a Guilty Plea* states that the reduction should apply to the punitive elements of a sentence not to the rehabilitative elements. However, it also makes it clear that the principle applies to the sentence itself and not to the ancillary orders. In those circumstances, neither the length of the disqualification nor the number of penalty points will be affected by the guideline. It is an offence to drive a motor vehicle whilst disqualified by an order of a court, see *ante*, § 17–100.

A disqualification is generally for a prescribed period during which the offender may not lawfully drive any vehicle on a road. The period starts from the moment it is imposed. However, a disqualification may also (or instead) be until the offender has passed a relevant driving test. In those circumstances, the offender may drive as if a provisional licence holder pending the successful taking of the test (though if this order is combined with a disqualification for a fixed period, that period must first expire before the offender can commence to drive as a provisional licence holder): section 37(3) of the *Road Traffic Offenders Act* 1988.

Orders of disqualification may be mandatory or discretionary. Mandatory disqualification follows conviction of "an offence involving obligatory disqualification". In these circumstances, the minimum period of disqualification is 12 months: section 34(1) of the *Road Traffic Offenders Act* 1988. This minimum is extended to two years where the offender has had at least two disqualifications of at least 56 days imposed on him within the three years that preceded the *commission* of the offence currently before the court: section 34(4)(b). The minimum is extended to three years in relation to the obligatorily disqualifiable offences relating to alcohol/drug influenced driving where the offender has been convicted of one of those offences within the 10 years preceding the *commission* of the current offence: section 34(3). The only discretion to not impose this disqualification either at all or for a lesser period arises where the court finds "special reasons" (see *post*). Where the disqualification is for at least 12 months and arises from certain alcohol/drug influenced offences, the court may authorise the period to be reduced if the offender satisfactorily completes a suitable course. The court will specify the extent of the reduction—at least three months but no more than one quarter of the total period: *Road Traffic Offenders Act* 1988, s.34A.

A further circumstance where a court is obliged to disqualify is where the total number of penalty points to be taken into account amounts to at least 12. The court must disqualify for at least six months unless it finds "mitigating circumstances" (see *post*). This period of six months is increased to one year or two years if there are previous disqualifications of at least 56 days imposed in the three years prior to the *commission* of the current offence. The increase to one year follows one such disqualification; the increase to two years follows two or more previous disqualifications. Certain disqualifications do not count for these purposes: section 35(5).

Points on a licence are taken into account and added to those imposed for the current offence. The points on a licence must be in respect of an offence committed within three years (before or after) of the current offence: section 29(2). However, those points will be disregarded if there has been a disqualification under section 35 (totting-up) between the earlier imposition of the points and the commission of the current offence: section 29(1)(b). Other disqualifications (*e.g.* obligatory disqualifications under section 34) do not have the same effect.

A different, more stringent, power applies where offences are committed within the first two years after a person first passes a driving test. If six points are acquired for offences committed prior to the end of that two year period, the licence is automatically revoked: *Road Traffic (New Drivers) Act* 1995. This is not a disqualification. A person whose licence is revoked who drives subsequently will not be driving whilst disqualified but may be driving other than in accordance with a licence. They will be able to apply for a further provisional licence and must comply with the conditions until an appropriate test is passed. This requirement is triggered where six points are acquired but not by a court ordered disqualification. Where a young driver is likely to receive sufficient points to trigger this requirement, it is inappropriate for a court to order disqualification simply to avoid the effects of revocation. If a court is considering disqualification from driving because of the nature of the offence or because it is mandatory, it is suggested that it should also give consideration to disqualifying until a test is passed.

Discretionary disqualification can follow commission of an endorsable offence. It may also be imposed on commission of certain other offences that are not endorsable. In those circumstances, there is no minimum period.

Different procedures regarding the retention of the licence by the court apply depending on whether the period of the disqualification is 56 days or more: section 47

17–204

Part III

of the *Road Traffic Offenders Act* 1988. Where the period is less than 56 days (or is an interim disqualification under section 29), the licence automatically has effect again at the end of the period: section 37(1A). Otherwise, the licence will be retained by the court and sent to the Secretary of State; the driver will need to apply for its return before the end of the period of disqualification to ensure that it is in his possession when he is entitled to drive again. When a person is disqualified from driving and the licence sent by the Court to the Secretary of State, any vocational licence held also ceases to be effective. Confusions have arisen because vocational licences are not returned automatically since each case will be referred by the DVLA to the Traffic Commissioner for the area in which the defendant resides. In a News Sheet (07/2004), the Justices' Clerks' Society recommends as good practice that, where a Court is aware that a person being disqualified holds a vocational licence (that is, one to drive either a large goods vehicle or a passenger carrying vehicle), a warning should be given to the disqualified person that the return of the vocational licence will not be automatic but subject to the decision of the Traffic Commissioner.

As well as a disqualification for a fixed period (after which the offender can drive as before) the court may impose a disqualification until the offender passes a driving test. This driving test will normally be the usual test of competence to drive but, where the offender is also disqualified under section 35 (totting-up) the test will be an extended one: section 36(4), (5).

A period of disqualification may be reduced following attendance on certain specified courses when imposed for the types of offences set out in section 34A(1) of the *Road Traffic Offenders Act* 1988. This provision will be repealed and replaced by the *Road Safety Act* 2006 when in force and extends to a wider range of offences than previously. It continues to apply to "relevant drink offences". However, it also applies to "specified offences", a category that can be expanded by the Secretary of State by regulations. At present, offences included are those of careless or inconsiderate driving (section 3 of the *Road Traffic Act* 1988), failing to comply with traffic signs (section 36 of the *Road Traffic Offenders Act* 1988), use of special road contrary to scheme or regulations (*Road Traffic Regulation Act* 1984, s.17(4)), and speeding (*Road Traffic Regulation Act* 1984, s.89(1)). Whichever category of offence, the period of disqualification must be at least 12 months and must have been imposed under section 34 of the *Road Traffic Offenders Act* 1988 (that is the normal obligatory or discretionary disqualification provisions) not under the "totting-up" provisions. Amendments in the Road Safety Bill (when in force) provide for similar reductions in the number of penalty points imposed. The provisions allow for a reduction of at least three months and not more than one quarter. In practice, it seems that a three month reduction is the most common. The purpose of the reduction is to reward a driver who takes steps to improve their awareness in the expectation that this will enable them to drive in a way that is more likely to be safe. However, it is difficult to see circumstances in which a reduction of more than three months is likely to be justified. By section 34A(8), it is not possible to make an order providing for a reduction in disqualification where an offender has completed an approved course as a result of an offence committed in the three years prior to the current offence or whilst the driver was in the probationary period provided for new drivers. When in force, a new section 34D provides for those convicted of a second relevant drink offence receiving a disqualification of at least two years to be offered a reduced disqualification if they participate successfully in an "alcohol ignition interlock programme". This will allow for a reduction of at least 12 months in (but no more than half of) the period of disqualification.

Interim disqualification

17–205   A court which adjourns a case for sentence after conviction or which defers sentence or remits an offender to another court for sentence may impose an interim disqualification in respect of any endorsable offence. This disqualification may not last longer than six months. Any period will be attributed to a disqualification imposed as a sentence.

Obligatory disqualification or endorsement can only be avoided where a court finds "special reasons" for doing so. Special reasons may reduce a period of disqualification below the minimum set by statute but may not reduce the penalty points below the lower limit fixed—in relation to points, finding special reasons will enable the court to avoid endorsing any points at all. Disqualification under section 35 (totting-up) may only be avoided where a court finds "mitigating circumstances". Even where either is found to exist, the court retains its discretion and may still disqualify or endorse if it thinks fit. Both these terms have been subject to extensive case law. For a full examination of the authorities, see *Wilkinson's Road Traffic Offences*, Ch.21. This is one of the inevitable consequences of courts being subject to mandatory orders—whilst this promotes consistency and reinforces the seriousness of the offences, it also requires an elaborate system to be created to avoid injustice in the small number of unusual cases that inevitably arise.

Special reasons

A special reason must be "special to the facts that constitute the offence". It must be **17–206** one relevant to the offence and not the offender and it must be something that a court ought properly to take into account when passing sentence: *Crossen* [1939] 1 N.I. 106; *Whittal v. Kirby* [1946] 2 All E.R. 552. In *Wickens* (1958) 42 Cr.App.R. 236 the court set out four criteria which have to be satisfied before special reasons can be found to exist. The circumstance put forward must be a mitigating or extenuating circumstance; it must not amount in law to a defence to the charge; it must be something which is directly connected with the offence and it must be something which is proper for the court to take into accountwhen imposing sentence. Courts are generally difficult to persuade that special reasons exist.

Given that Parliament has prescribed these orders as part of the penalty for the offences, it seems that the reason has to be outside of the mischief at which the offence is aimed: see *Nicholson v. Brown* [1974] R.T.R. 177.

Thus special reasons have been found where the defendant was coping with a true **17–207** emergency (though the courts have been very careful about what constitutes such an emergency and examine closely alternative courses of action in the circumstances) or where the driving was for a very short distance. However, courts have been very cautious over accepting the shortness of the distance driven as sufficient by itself for alcohol or drug related offences. In *Chatters v. Burke* [1986] 3 All E.R. 168, seven relevant factors were set out. As well as the distance driven, the court will consider the manner in which it was driven, the state of the vehicle, whether the driver intended to drive further, the road and traffic conditions at the time and the reason for the car being driven. The most important factor will be the extent to which it was possible that danger would be caused through contact with either other road users or with pedestrians. The restrictive approach was again demonstrated in *R. (Khan) v. DPP* [2004] EWHC 2505 Admin. In the early hours of New Year's Day, the defendant arrived home at 2.30 am. His wife (who had driven home) went to bed but he waited up for his sons (aged 14 and 15) to return from a local party. Some time later (when he was already apprehensive because they were later than expected), he received news of a fatal road accident on a nearby road and was made aware that young Asian boys were involved and that they had come from the same party as that attended by his sons. In addition, three years before, the defendant had attended a fatal road traffic accident in which the 19 year old son of a very close friend had been killed. Fearing that his sons had been killed or injured, the defendant wanted to reach the scene as quickly as possible and drove his car one mile to the scene. There was no evidence of bad driving. He was found to be about 2.5 times over the limit. His wife had not drunk alcohol at all but he did not wait for her and get her to drive. It was found as a fact that he could have walked to the scene in less than 20 minutes. The Justices found that special reasons did not exist and this was upheld by the Divisional Court. Referring to *DPP v. Bristow* [1998] R.T.R. 100 (would a sober, reasonable and responsible friend have advised the appellant not to drive in the circumstances?) and *Taylor v. Rajan* [1974] R.T.R. 304 (was the emergency sufficiently acute to justify the driver taking his car out? Justices to exercise their discretion in favour of the driver only in clear and compelling circumstances), the Divisional Court noted that the defendant was well over the limit and that his wife was perfectly capable of driving if she had been woken. A further example of the restrictive approach to the "emergency" argument can be seen in *DPP v. Harrison* [2007] EWHC 556, Admin. The Divisional Court emphasised the significance of the distance driven (446 yards), the level of alcohol and the alternatives available to the driver and concluded that the justices' decision to find special reasons could not be upheld.

In the context of offences concerning driving after the consumption of alcohol, the unexpected presence of alcohol may be capable of providing a special reason. This most commonly occurs where it is alleged that a drink has been "laced". The increasingly restrictive approach to assessing the circumstances in which those reasons can be seen demonstrated in *DPP v. Sharma* [2005] R.T.R. 27, although the Divisional Court was not prepared to overturn the magistrates' court on the facts. The defendant went for a drink after work with friends. Unknown to her, a friend added vodka to each of the two drinks that she drank believing that she was travelling home by taxi. Unaware of the additional alcoholic content and not feeling any effect, the defendant drove home, was stopped, breathalysed and found to be over the limit. The justices found that she was unaware of the alcohol that had been added, that she did not display any signs of impairment, that there had been nothing unusual about the manner of her driving and that she would not have been over the limit without the added alcohol. The Divisional Court re-iterated the test set out by the Court of Appeal in *DPP v. O'Connor* [1992] R.T.R. 66 that it is for the motorist whose drink has been "laced" to establish that fact by admissible and relevant evidence and also the fact that he did not know or suspect that the drink had been "laced". Additionally, the driver must establish that he would not have exceeded the prescribed limit without the additional alcohol – expert evidence will often be required. In *Sharma*, the Divisional Court observed that the justices' finding that the defendant was unaware of the additional alcohol was surprising but could not be said to be one to which they were not entitled to come on the evidence that they had heard. A different situation was considered in *Robinson v. DPP* [2004] 168 J.P. 522. The defendant was a Rastafarian who contended that drinking alcohol was contrary to his faith. He stated that he had been to a funeral of a friend and had drunk the punch supplied which he did not expect to be alcoholic. In fact, it contained approximately 28 per cent alcohol. Justices accepted that the defendant had chosen to drink the punch believing it to contain no alcohol but disqualified on the grounds that he had made no inquiries about what it contained. This approach was endorsed by the Divisional Court. The purpose of the legislation is to ensure that people do not drive when they have consumed alcohol sufficient to exceed the prescribed limit. If a driver attends a function at which alcohol is available, he must be able to show that he has done all that could reasonably be expected of him if he is to demonstrate that special reasons exist for mitigating the disqualification required by law. Emphasising the rigour of these provisions and the importance of the public interest, the Court went on to say that, even if the defendant had been told that the punch was non-alcoholic and had no reason to suspect alcohol in his body, then the magistrates, even though finding special reasons to exist, would have been entitled to have imposed the normal statutory period of disqualification because the level was so high (83/100).

It is for the defendant to satisfy the court that the special reason exists.

Mitigating circumstances

17–208   The obligation to disqualify a person who collects at least 12 penalty points is capable of being avoided only if the court is satisfied, having regard to all the circumstances, that there are grounds for mitigating the normal consequences of the conviction: section 35(1). The narrowness of this is emphasised in section 35(4). This precludes a court from taking into account any of the circumstances that are said to make the offence not serious, of hardship unless it is exceptional and states that nothing may be used to support the finding if it has been taken into account in the three years preceding conviction of the current offence in order to avoid or reduce a disqualification to which a defendant would otherwise have been liable under section 35.

It is for the defendant to satisfy the court that the grounds exist. It is not open to the defendant to argue that any of the offences are not serious; disqualification in these circumstances is designed for situations where a driver repeatedly commits offences that do not in themselves warrant disqualification. The wording of section 34(4)(a) seems clearly to encompass not only the latest offence but also any others that are taken into account. If the defendant wishes to rely on hardship then the court will need to be satisfied that that hardship is exceptional. The hardship may be experienced by someone other than the defendant but it must be more than the ordinary hardship that is likely to be experienced when a person is disqualified from driving. This is a question of fact and degree and no precise guidance is possible save that courts are generally difficult to persuade. If mitigating circumstances are found and the court is prepared to allow them to influence the disqualification, that may lead to a reduction in the minimum period or no disqualification at all. In the absence of mitigating circumstances, a court has no alternative but to disqualify for the minimum period provided by statute in the circumstances of the case.

D. DEPRIVATION OF MOTOR VEHICLE

Powers of Criminal Courts (Sentencing) Act 2000, s.143

Powers to deprive offender of property used etc. for purposes of crime

143.—(1) Where a person is convicted of an offence and the court by or before which he is convicted is satisfied that any property which has been lawfully seized from him, or which was in his possession or under his control at the time when he was apprehended for the offence or when a summons in respect of it was issued—   **17–209**

(a) has been used for the purpose of committing, or facilitating the commission of, any offence, or

(b) was intended by him to be used for that purpose,

the court may (subject to subsection (5) below) make an order under this section in respect of that property.

(2) Where a person is convicted of an offence and the offence, or an offence which the court has taken into consideration in determining his sentence, consists of unlawful possession of property which—

(a) has been lawfully seized from him, or

(b) was in his possession or under his control at the time when he was apprehended for the offence of which he has been convicted or when a summons in respect of that offence was issued,

the court may (subject to subsection (5) below) make an order under this section in respect of that property.

(3) An order under this section shall operate to deprive the offender of his rights, if any, in the property to which it relates, and the property shall (if not already in their possession) be taken into the possession of the police.

(4) Any power conferred on a court by subsection (1) or (2) above may be exercised—

(a) whether or not the court also deals with the offender in any other way in respect of the offence of which he has been convicted; and

(b) without regard to any restrictions on forfeiture in any enactment contained in an Act passed before 29th July 1988.

(5) In considering whether to make an order under this section in respect of any property, a court shall have regard—

(a) to the value of the property; and

(b) to the likely financial and other effects on the offender of the making of the order (taken together with any other order that the court contemplates making).

(6) Where a person commits an offence to which this subsection applies by—

(a) driving, attempting to drive, or being in charge of a vehicle, or

(b) failing to comply with a requirement made under section 7 or 7A of the *Road Traffic Act* 1988 (failure to provide specimen for analysis or laboratory test (or to give permission for such a test) in the course of an investigation into whether the offender had committed an offence while driving, attempting to drive or being in charge of a vehicle, or

(c) failing, as the driver of a vehicle, to comply with subsection (2) or (3) of section 17 of the *Road Traffic Act* 1988 (duty to stop and give information or report accident),

the vehicle shall be regarded for the purposes of subsection (1) above (and section 144(1)(b) below) as used for the purpose of committing the offence (and for the purpose of committing any offence of aiding, abetting, counselling or procuring the commission of the offence).

(7) Subsection (6) above applies to—

(a) an offence under the *Road Traffic Act* 1988 which is punishable with imprisonment;

(b) an offence of manslaughter; and

(c) an offence under section 35 of the *Offences Against the Person Act* 1861 (wanton and furious driving).

(8) Facilitating the commission of an offence shall be taken for the purposes of subsection (1) above to include the taking of any steps after it has been committed for the purpose of disposing of any property to which it relates or of avoiding apprehension or detection.

17–210   An additional sanction available to a court for some road traffic offences is the power to deprive the offender of the vehicle used while committing the offence. The effect of the order must be proportionate to the offence (section 143(5)) but it is a sanction which may have considerable impact. A motor vehicle used in connection with offences described in this chapter would not automatically fall within the remit of this section since it would not have been used for the purposes set out in section 143(1) nor would it come within section 143(2) which requires the offence to be one of unlawful possession. However, that remit is extended by subsections (6) and (7) to include offences punishable under the *Road Traffic Act* 1988 by imprisonment which consist of driving, attempting to drive or being in charge of the vehicle, failure to provide a specimen for analysis and failing to stop and report an accident. See *post*, § 23–229.

OFFENCES INVOLVING DRUGS

Part III

I. OFFENCES UNDER THE MISUSE OF DRUGS ACT 1971

A. PROHIBITION ON IMPORTATION AND EXPORTATION OF CONTROLLED DRUGS

(1) Definition

Misuse of Drugs Act 1971, s.3

Restriction of importation and exportation of controlled drugs

3.—(1) Subject to subsection (2) below—   **18–1**

    (a) the importation of a controlled drug; and

    (b) the exportation of a controlled drug,

are hereby prohibited.

  (2) Subsection (1) above does not apply—

    (a) to the importation or exportation of a controlled drug which is for the time being excepted from paragraph (a) or, as the case may be, paragraph (b) of subsection (1) above by regulations under section 7 of this Act; or

    (b) to the importation or exportation of a controlled drug under and in accordance with the terms of a licence issued by the Secretary of State and in compliance with any conditions attached thereto.

Section 3 does not create an offence: the offence of evading the prohibitions imposed **18–2** thereby arises from the combined effect of *Customs and Excise Management Act* 1979, ss.3 and 170—see Ch.19, § 19–48.

B. RESTRICTION OF PRODUCTION AND SUPPLY OF CONTROLLED DRUGS

(1) Definition

Misuse of Drugs Act 1971, ss.4, 4A

Restriction of production and supply of controlled drugs

18–3   **4.**—(1) Subject to any regulations under section 7 of this Act for the time being in force, it shall not be lawful for a person—

    (a) to produce a controlled drug; or

    (b) to supply or offer to supply a controlled drug to another.

(2) Subject to section 28 of this Act, it is an offence for a person—

    (a) to produce a controlled drug in contravention of subsection (1) above; or

    (b) to be concerned in the production of such a drug in contravention of that subsection by another.

(3) Subject to section 28 of this Act, it is an offence for a person—

    (a) to supply or offer to supply a controlled drug to another in contravention of subsection (1) above; or

    (b) to be concerned in the supplying of such a drug to another in contravention of that subsection; or

    (c) to be concerned in the making to another in contravention of that subsection of an offer to supply such a drug.

Aggravation of offence of supply of controlled drug

18–4   **4A.**—(1) This section applies if—

    (a) a court is considering the seriousness of an offence under section 4(3) of this Act, and

    (b) at the time the offence was committed the offender had attained the age of 18.

(2) If either of the following conditions is met the court—

    (a) must treat the fact that the condition is met as an aggravating factor (that is to say, a factor that increases the seriousness of the offence), and

    (b) must state in open court that the offence is so aggravated.

(3) The first condition is that the offence was committed on or in the vicinity of school premises at a relevant time.

(4) The second condition is that in connection with the commission of the offence the offender used a courier who, at the time the offence was committed, was under the age of 18.

(5) In subsection (3), a relevant time is—

    (a) any time when the school premises are in use by persons under the age of 18;

    (b) one hour before the start and one hour after the end of any such time.

(6) For the purposes of subsection (4), a person uses a courier in connection with an offence under section 4(3) of this Act if he causes or permits another person (the courier)—

    (a) to deliver a controlled drug to a third person, or

    (b) to deliver a drug related consideration to himself or a third person.

(7) For the purposes of subsection (6), a drug related consideration is a consideration of any description which—

    (a) is obtained in connection with the supply of a controlled drug, or

    (b) is intended to be used in connection with obtaining a controlled drug.

(8) In this section—

    "school premises" means land used for the purposes of a school excluding any land occupied solely as a dwelling by a person employed at the school; and

    "school" has the same meaning—

        (a) in England and Wales, as in section 4 of the *Education Act* 1996;

        (b) in Scotland, as in section 135(1) of the *Education (Scotland) Act* 1980;

        (c) in Northern Ireland, as in Article 2(2) of the *Education and Libraries (Northern Ireland) Order* 1986.

Section 4A was inserted by the *Drugs Act* 2005, s.1(1) and came into force on January 1, 2006. It does not apply to offences committed before that date.

(2) Allocation

This offence is triable either way. The *Consolidated Criminal Practice Direction* **18–5**
(2002) provides that cases of supplying Class A drugs should be committed for trial;
cases of supplying Class B drugs should be committed for trial unless there is only
small-scale supply for no payment. No guidelines are given in relation to Class C drugs.

Section 25(4) of the 1971 Act also provides that a magistrates' court in England and
Wales may try an information for an offence under the 1971 Act if the information was
laid at any time within twelve months from the commission of the offence.

(3) Elements of the offence

Misuse of Drugs Act 1971, s.2 and Sched. 2

Controlled drugs and their classification for purposes of this Act.
   2.—(1) In this Act—   **18–6**
   (a) the expression "controlled drug" means any substance or product for the time
       being specified in Part I, II, or III of Schedule 2 to this Act; and
   (b) the expressions "Class A drug", "Class B drug" and "Class C drug" mean any of
       the substances and products for the time being specified respectively in Part I,
       Part II and Part III of that Schedule;
and the provisions of Part IV of that Schedule shall have effect with respect to the meanings of
expressions used in that Schedule.

   (2) Her Majesty may by Order in Council make such amendments in Schedule 2 to this
Act as may be requisite for the purpose of adding any substance or product to, or removing any substance or product from, any of Parts I to III of that Schedule, including
amendments for securing that no substance or product is for the time being specified in a
particular one of those Parts or for inserting any substance or product into any of those
Parts in which no substance or product is for the time being specified.

   (3) An Order in Council under this section may amend Part IV of Schedule 2 to this
Act, and may do so whether or not it amends any other Part of that Schedule.

   (4) An Order in Council under this section may be varied or revoked by a subsequent
Order in Council thereunder.

   (5) No recommendation shall be made to Her Majesty in Council to make an Order
under this section unless a draft of the Order has been laid before Parliament and approved by a resolution of each House of Parliament; and the Secretary of State shall not
lay a draft of such an Order before Parliament except after consultation with or on the recommendation of the Advisory Council.

Part III

SCHEDULE 2

Controlled Drugs

Part I

Class A Drugs

1. The following substances and products, namely: **18–7**
        Acetorphine.
        Alfentanil.
        Allylprodine.
        Alphacetylmethadol.
        Alphameprodine.
        Alphamethadol.
        Alphaprodine.
        Anileridine.
        Benzethidine.
        Benzylmorphine (3-benzylmorphine).
        Betacetylmethadol.
        Betameprodine.

Betamethadol.
Betaprodine.
Bezitramide.
Bufotenine.
Carfentanil.
Clonitazene.
Coca leaf.
Cocaine.
Desomorphine.
Dextromoramide.
Diamorphine.
Diampromide.
Diethylthiambutene.
Difenoxin (1-(3-cyano-3,3-diphenylpropyl)-4-phenylpiperidine-4-carboxylic acid).
Dihydrocodeinone O-carboxymethyloxime.
Dihydroetorphine.
Dihydromorphine.
Dimenoxadole.
Dimepheptanol.
Dimethylthiambutene.
Dioxaphetyl butyrate.
Diphenoxylate.
Dipipanone.
Drotebanol (3,4-dimethoxy-17-methylmorphinan- 6β 14-diol).
Ecgonine, and any derivative of ecgonine which is convertible to ecgonine or to
    cocaine.
Ethylmethylthiambutene.
Eticyclidine.
Etonitazene.
Etorphine.
Etoxeridine.
Etryptamine.
Fentanyl.
Fungus (of any kind) which contains psilocin or an ester of psilocin.
Furethidine.
Hydrocodone.
Hydromorphinol.
Hydromorphone.
Hydroxypethidine.
Isomethadone.
Ketobemidone.
Levomethorphan.
Levomoramide.
Levophenacylmorphan.
Levorphanol.
Lofentanil.
Lysergamide.
Lysergide and other N-alkyl derivatives of lysergamide.
Mescaline.
Metazocine.
Methadone.
Methadyl acetate.
Methylamphetamine
Methyldesorphine.
Methyldihydromorphine (6-methyldihydromorphine).
Metopon.

Morpheridine.

Morphine.

Morphine methobromide, morphine *N*-oxide and other pentavalent nitrogen morphine derivatives.

Myrophine.

Nicomorphine (3,6-dinicotinoylmorphine).

Noracymethadol.

Norlevorphanol.

Normethadone.

Normorphine.

Norpipanone.

Opium, whether raw, prepared or medicinal.

Oxycodone.

Oxymorphone.

Pethidine.

Phenadoxone.

Phenampromide.

Phenazocine.

Phencyclidine.

Phenomorphan.

Phenoperidine.

Piminodine.

Piritramide.

Poppy-straw and concentrate of poppy-straw.

Proheptazine.

Properidine (1-methyl-4-phenylpiperidine-4-carboxylic acid isopropyl ester).

Psilocin.

Racemethorphan.

Racemoramide.

Racemorphan.

Remifentanil.

Rolicyclidine.

Sufentanil.

Tenocylidine.

Thebacon.

Thebaine.

Tilidate.

Trimeperidine.

4-Bromo-2,5-dimethoxy-α-methylphenethylamine.

4-Cyano-2-dimethylamino-4,4-diphenylbutane.

4-Cyano-1-methyl-4-phenylpiperidine.

N,N-Diethyltryptamine.

N,N-Dimethyltryptamine.

2,5-Dimethoxy-α 4-dimethylphenethylamine.

N-Hydroxy-tenamphetamine

1-Methyl-4-phenylpiperidine-4-carboxylic acid.

2-Methyl-3-morpholino-1,1-diphenylpropane-carboxylic acid.

4-Methyl-aminorex

4-Phenylpiperidine-4-carboxylic acid ethyl ester.

(b)   any compound (not being a compound for the time being specified in sub-paragraph (a) above) structurally derived from tryptamine or from a ring-hydroxy tryptamine by substitution at the nitrogen atom of the sidechain with one or more alkyl substituents but no other substituent;

(ba) the following phenethylamine derivatives, namely:—

Allyl(α-methyl-3,4-methylenedioxyphenethyl)amine

2-Amino-1-(2,5-dimethoxy-4-methylphenyl)ethanol

2-Amino-1-(3,4-dimethoxyphenyl)ethanol
Benzyl(α-methyl-3,4-methylenedioxyphenethyl)amine
4-Bromo-β,2,5-trimethoxyphenethylamine
N-(4-*sec*-Butylthio-2,5-dimethoxyphenethyl)hydroxylamine
Cyclopropylmethyl(α-methyl-3,4-methylenedioxyphenethyl)amine
2-(4,7-Dimethoxy-2,3-dihydro-1*H*-indan-5-yl)ethylamine
2-(4,7-Dimethoxy-2,3-dihydro-1*H*-indan-5-yl)-1-methylethylamine
2-(2,5-Dimethoxy-4-methylphenyl)cyclopropylamine
2-(1,4-Dimethoxy-2-naphthyl)ethylamine
2-(1,4-Dimethoxy-2-naphthyl)-1-methylethylamine
N-(2,5-Dimethoxy-4-propylthiophenethyl)hydroxylamine
2-(1,4-Dimethoxy-5,6,7,8-tetrahydro-2-naphthyl)ethylamine
2-(1,4-Dimethoxy-5,6,7,8-tetrahydro-2-naphthyl)-1-methylethylamine
α,α-Dimethyl-3,4-methylenedioxyphenethylamine
α,α-Dimethyl-3,4-methylenedioxyphenethyl(methyl)amine
Dimethyl(α-methyl-3,4-methylenedioxyphenethyl)amine
N-(4-Ethylthio-2,5-dimethoxyphenethyl)hydroxylamine
4-Iodo-2,5-dimethoxy-α-methylphenethyl(dimethyl)amine
2-(1,4-Methano-5,8-dimethoxy-1,2,3,4-tetrahydro-6-naphthyl)ethylamine
2-(1,4-Methano-5,8-dimethoxy-1,2,3,4-tetrahydro-6-naphthyl)-1-methylethylamine
2-(5-Methoxy-2,2-dimethyl-2,3-dihydrobenzo[*b*]furan-6-yl)-1-methylethylamine
2-Methoxyethyl(α-methyl-3,4-methylenedioxyphenethyl)amine
2-(5-Methoxy-2-methyl-2,3-dihydrobenzo[*b*]furan-6-yl)-1-methylethylamine
β-Methoxy-3,4-methylenedioxyphenethylamine
1-(3,4-Methylenedioxybenzyl)butyl(ethyl)amine
1-(3,4-Methylenedioxybenzyl)butyl(methyl)amine
2-(α-Methyl-3,4-methylenedioxyphenethylamino)ethanol
α-Methyl-3,4-methylenedioxyphenethyl(prop-2-ynyl)amine
N-Methyl-N-(α-methyl-3,4-methylenedioxyphenethyl)hydroxylamine
O-Methyl-N-(α-methyl-3,4-methylenedioxyphenethyl)hydroxylamine
α-Methyl-4-(methylthio)phenethylamine
β,3,4,5-Tetramethoxyphenethylamine
β,2,5-Trimethoxy-4-methylphenethylamine;

(c) any compound (not being methoxyphenamine or a compound for the time being specified in sub-paragraph (a) above) structurally derived from phenethylamine, an N-alkylphenethylamine, α-methylphenethylamine, an N-alkyl-α-methyl-phenethylamine, α-ethylphenethylamine, or an N-alkyl-α-ethylphenethylamine by substitution in the ring to any extent with alkyl, alkoxy, alkylenedioxy or halide substituents, whether or not further substituted in the ring by one or more other univalent substituents.

(d) any compound (not being a compound for the time being specified in sub-paragraph (a) above structurally derived from fentanyl by modification in any of the following ways, that is to say,
  (i)   by replacement of the phenyl portion of the phenethyl group by any hetero-monocycle whether or not further substituted in the heterocycle;
  (ii) by substitution in the phenethyl group with alkyl, alkenyl, alkoxy, hydroxy, halogeno, haloalkyl, amino or nitro groups;
  (iii) by substitution in the piperidine ring with alkyl or alkenyl groups;
  (iv) by substitution in the aniline ring with alkyl, alkoxy, alkylenedioxy, halogeno or haloalkyl groups;
  (v)   by substitution at the 4-position of the piperidine ring with any alkoxycarbonyl or alkoxyalkyl or acyloxy group;
  (vi) by replacement of the N-propionyl group by another acyl group;

(e) any compound (not being a compound for the time being specified in sub-paragraph (a) above) structurally derived from pethidine by modification in any of the following ways, that is to say,
  (i)   by replacement of the 1-methyl group by an acyl, alkyl whether or not unsaturated, benzyl or phenethyl group, whether or not further substituted;

    (ii) by substitution in the piperidine ring with alkyl or alkenyl groups or with a propano bridge, whether or not further substituted;

    (iii) by substitution in the 4-phenyl ring with alkyl, alkoxy, aryloxy, halogeno or haloalkyl groups;

    (iv) by replacement of the 4-ethoxycarbonyl by any other alkoxycarbonyl or any alkoxyalkyl or acyloxy group;

    (v) by formation of an N-oxide or of a quaternary base.

2. Any stereoisomeric form of a substance for the time being specified in paragraph 1 above not being dextromethorphan or dextrorphan. **18–8**

3. Any ester or ether of a substance for the time being specified in paragraph 1 or 2 above not being a substance for the time being specified in Part II of this Schedule.

4. Any salt of a substance for the time being specified in any of paragraphs 1 to 3 above.

5. Any preparation or other product containing a substance or product for the time being specified in any of paragraphs 1 to 4 above.

6. Any preparation designed for administration by injection which includes a substance or product for the time being specified in any of paragraphs 1 to 3 of Part II of this Schedule.

Part II

Class B Drugs

1. The following substances and products, namely: **18–9**
    (a) Acetyldihydrocodeine.
          Amphetamine.
          Codeine.
          Dihydrocodeine.
          Ethylmorphine (3-ethylmorphine).
          Glutethimide.
          Lefetamine.
          Mecloqualone.
          Methaqualone.
          Methcathinone
          α-Methylphenethylhydroxylamine.
          Methylphenidate.
          Methylphenobarbitone.
          Nicocodine.
          Nicodicodine (6-nicotinoyldihydrocodeine).
          Norcodeine.
          Pentazocine.
          Phenmetrazine.
          Pholcodine.
          Propiram.
          Zipeprol
    (b) any 5,5 disubstituted barbituric acid.

2. Any stereoisomeric form of a substance for the time being specified in paragraph 1 of this Part of this Schedule. **18–10**

3. Any salt of a substance for the time being specified in paragraph 1 or 2 of this Part of this Schedule.

4. Any preparation or other product containing a substance or product for the time being specified in any of paragraphs 1 to 3 of this Part of this Schedule, not being a preparation falling within paragraph 6 of Part I of this Schedule.

Part III

Class C Drugs

1. **18–11**
    (a) The following substances, namely:

Alprazolam.
Aminorex.
Benzphetamine.
Bromazepam.
Brotizolam.
Buprenorphine
Camazepam.
Cannabinol.
Cannabinol derivatives.
Cannabis and cannabis resin.
Cathine.
Cathinone.
Chlordiazepoxide.
Chlorphentermine.
Clobazam.
Clonazepam.
Clorazepic acid.
Clotiazepam.
Cloxazolam.
Delorazepam.
Dextropropoxyphene.
Diazepam.
Diethylpropion.
Estazolam.
Ethchlorvynol.
Ethinamate.
Ethyl loflazepate.
Fencamfamin.
Fenethylline.
Fenproporex.
Fludiazepam.
Flunitrazepam.
Flurazepam.
Halazepam.
Haloxazolam.
4-Hydroxy-n-butyric acid.
Ketamine.
Ketazolam.
Ketazolam.
Loprazolam.
Lorazepam.
Lormetazepam.
Mazindol.
Medazepam.
Mefenorex.
Mephentermine.
Meprobamate.
Mesocarb.
Methyprylone.
Midazolam.
Nimetazepam.
Nitrazepam.
Nordazepam.
Oxazepam.
Oxazolam.
Pemoline

Phendimetrazine.
Phentermine.
Pinazepam.
Pipradrol.
Prazepam.
Pyrovalerone.
Temazepam.
Tetrazepam.
Triazolam.
N-Ethylamphetamine.
Zolpidem.

(b) 4-Androstene-3, 17-dione.
5-Androstene-3, 17-diol.
Atamestane.
Bolandiol.
Bolasterone.
Bolazine.
Boldenone.
Bolenol.
Bolmantalate.
Calusterone.
4-Chloromethandienone.
Clostebol.
Drostanolone.
Enestebol.
Epitiostanol.
Ethyloestrenol.
Fluoxymesterone.
Formebolone.
Furazabol.
Mebolazine.
Mepitiostane.
Mesabolone.
Mestanolone.
Mesterolone.
Methandienone.
Methandriol.
Methenolone.
Methyltestosterone.
Metribolone.
Mibolerone.
Nandrolone.
19-Nor-4-Androstene-3, 17-dione.
19-Nor-5-Androstene-13, 17-diol.
Norboletone.
Norclostebol.
Norethandrolone.
Ovandrotone.
Oxabolone.
Oxandrolone.
Oxymesterone.
Oxymetholone.
Prasterone.
Propetandrol.
Quinbolone.
Roxibolone.

Part III

Silandrone.

Stanolone.

Stanozolol.

Stenbolone.

Testosterone.

Thiomesterone.

Trenbolone.

(c) any compound (not being Trilostane or a compound for the time being specified in sub-paragraph (b) above) structurally derived from 17-hydroxyandrostan-3-one or from 17-hydroxyestran-3-one by modification in any of the following ways, that is to say,

   (i) by further substitution at position 17 by a methyl or ethyl group;

   (ii) by substitution to any extent at one or more of positions 1, 2, 4, 6, 7, 9, 11 or 16, but at no other position;

   (iii) by unsaturation in the carbocyclic ring system to any extent, provided that there are no more than two ethylenic bonds in any one carbocyclic ring;

   (iv) by fusion of ring A with a heterocyclic system;

(d) any substance which is an ester or ether (or, where more than one hydroxyl function is available, both an ester and an ether) of a substance specified in sub-paragraph (b) or described in sub-paragraph (c) above or of cannabinol or a cannabinol derivative;

(e) Chorionic Gonadotrophin (HCG).

Clenbuterol.

Non-human chorionic gonadotrophin.

Somatotropin.

Somatrem.

Somatropin.

18–12   2. Any stereoisomeric form of a substance for the time being specified in paragraph 1 of this Part of this Schedule not being phenylpropanolamine.

3. Any salt of a substance for the time being specified in paragraph 1 or 2 of this Part of this Schedule.

4. Any preparation or other product containing a substance for the time being specified in any of paragraphs 1 to 3 of this Part of this Schedule.

PART IV

Meaning of Certain Expressions Used in This Schedule

18–13   For the purposes of this Schedule the following expressions (which are not among those defined in section 37(1) of this Act) have the meanings hereby assigned to them respectively, that is to say—

"cannabinol derivatives" means the following substances, except where contained in cannabis or cannabis resin, namely tetrahydro derivatives of cannabinol and 3-alkyl homologues of cannabinol or of its tetrahydro derivatives;

"coca leaf" means the leaf of any plant of the genus *Erythroxylon* from whose leaves cocaine can be extracted either directly or by chemical transformation;

"concentrate of poppy-straw" means the material produced when poppy-straw has entered into a process for the concentration of its alkaloids;

"medicinal opium" means raw opium which has undergone the process necessary to adapt it for medicinal use in accordance with the requirements of the British Pharmacopoeia, whether it is in the form of powder or is granulated or is in any other form, and whether it is or is not mixed with neutral substances;

"opium poppy" means the plant of the species *Papaver somniferum* L;

"poppy straw" means all parts, except the seeds, of the opium poppy, after mowing;

"raw opium" includes powdered or granulated opium but does not include medicinal opium.

18–14   The prosecution must prove that the drug in question is controlled. Drugs are divided into three classes as listed in Schedule 2 to the Act. Proof that the drug is controlled is provided either by admission or an analyst's certificate. Such a scientific report should identify the drug and level of purity: *Jones (K.)*, 161 J.P. 597, CA.

"Supply" includes distributing (section 37(1)) but the term is not further elaborated by the statute. The word "supply" has to be given its ordinary everyday meaning: *Holmes v. Chief Constable of Merseyside* [1976] Crim.L.R. 125, DC. In *Maginnis* [1987] A.C. 303, HL, the majority opinion drew a distinction between a "custodier" who has the necessary intent to supply when he returns controlled drugs to a person who had deposited them with him and a "depositor" who places the drugs in the temporary possession of the "custodier" without an intention of enabling the "custodier" to use the drugs for his own purposes. Establishing intent to supply does not require the defendant's offer to supply be proved genuine: *Prior* [2004] EWCA Crim 1147. It is neither necessary for the prosecution to establish that the supply was commercial nor to identify the intended recipient: *Ibrahima* [2005] Crim.L.R. 887, CA.

There is no defence of medical necessity in relation to a charge of possessing cannabis with intent to supply: *Att.-Gen's Reference (No. 2 of 2004)* 2 Cr.App.R. 34, CA.

Misuse of Drugs Act 1971, s.28

Proof of lack of knowledge etc. to be a defence in proceedings for certain offences

28.—(1) This section applies to offences under any of the following provisions of this Act, that **18–15** is to say section 4(2) and (3), section 5(2) and (3), section 6(2) and section 9.

(2) Subject to subsection (3) below, in any proceedings for an offence to which this section applies it shall be a defence for the accused to prove that he neither knew of nor suspected nor had reason to suspect the existence of some fact alleged by the prosecution which it is necessary for the prosecution to prove if he is to be convicted of the offence charged.

(3) Where in any proceedings for an offence to which this section applies it is necessary, if the accused is to be convicted of the offence charged, for the prosecution to prove that some substance or product involved in the alleged offence was the controlled drug which the prosecution alleges it to have been, and it is proved that the substance or product in question was that controlled drug, the accused—

(a) shall not be acquitted of the offence charged by reason only of proving that he neither knew nor suspected nor had reason to suspect that the substance or product in question was the particular controlled drug alleged; but

(b) shall be acquitted thereof—

(i) if he proves that he neither believed nor suspected nor had reasons to suspect that the substance or product in question was a controlled drug; or

(ii) if he proves that he believed the substance or product in question to be a controlled drug, or a controlled drug of a description, such that, if it had in fact been that controlled drug or a controlled drug of that description, he would not at the material time have been committing any offence to which this section applies.

(4) Nothing in this section shall prejudice any defence which it is open to a person charged with an offence to which this section applies to raise apart from this section.

(4) Sentence

It is necessary to draw a distinction between the three different classifications of **18–16** drugs. When tried summarily, an offence under section 4(2) committed in relation to a Class A or B drug carries a maximum penalty of six months' imprisonment, a fine not exceeding the prescribed sum, or both. Commission involving a Class C drug carries a maximum penalty of three months' imprisonment, a fine not exceeding £2,500 or both. An offence under section 4(3), when tried summarily, carries the same maximum penalties as regards each classification of drug: *Misuse of Drugs Act* 1971, s.25 and Sched. 4. After commencement of the relevant provisions, the maximum custodial sentence able to be imposed in a magistrates' court will be 12 months' imprisonment: *Criminal Justice Act* 2003, ss.154 and 282.

When cases of production and supply of Class A drugs are dealt with summarily, the *Magistrates' Court Sentencing Guidelines* (2004) state:

> Aggravating factors include commercial production, large amount, deliberate adulteration, quantity, venue, *e.g.* prisons, educational establishments, sophisticated operation, supply to children, offence committed on bail, relevant previous convictions and any failure to respond to previous sentences.
> Mitigating factors include: small amount of drug involved.
> **Guideline**: Are the magistrates' sentencing powers sufficient?

18–17   However, in the guideline judgment of *Aramah* (1982) 4 Cr.App.R.(S.) 407, Lord Lane C.J. indicated that it would rarely be appropriate for offences involving Class A drugs to be tried summarily, stating:

> "Class A drugs and particularly heroin and morphine: It is common knowledge that these are the most dangerous of all the addictive drugs…Consequently, anything which the courts of this country can do by way of deterrent sentences on those found guilty of crimes involving those Class A drugs should be done."

When cases of production and supply of Class B drugs are dealt with summarily, the *Magistrates' Court Sentencing Guidelines* (2004) state:

> Aggravating factors include commercial production, large amount, venue, *e.g.* prison, educational establishments, deliberate adulteration, offence committed on bail, relevant previous convictions and failures to respond to previous sentences.
> Mitigating factors include no commercial motive, small amount.
> In all cases forfeiture of all drugs and equipment should be considered.

18–18   The CA decision in *Ronchetti* [1998] 2 Cr.App.R.(S.) 100 gives guidance concerning appropriate penalties for particular quantities of drugs. Lord Justice Rose stated:

> "…we have been invited by the Crown to give some indication for the guidance of judges of first instance, in relation to the sort of level of sentence which is appropriate for importations of the order of 100 kg. In conformity with, but by way of addendum to, *Aramah*, we would suggest that, following a trial, the importation of 100 kg by persons playing more than a subordinate role, should attract a sentence of seven to eight years. In our judgment, 10 years is the appropriate starting point, following a trial, for importations of 500 kg or more, by such persons. Larger importations will, as the authorities show, attract a higher starting point. That starting point should, in our judgment, rise according to the roles played, the weight involved, and all the other circumstances of the case, up to the statutory maximum of 14 years provided by Parliament. The fact that, in a particular case of massive importation, an even greater quantity of the drug might one day have to be dealt with by the courts, is not in itself, in our judgment, a reason for not imposing the maximum sentence where those at the top of an organisation are before the court."

There are offenders who are unemployed addicts, supplying in order to finance their own addiction, who hold no stock of drugs, who have made a few retail supplies of Class A drugs, for example, to undercover police officers. For some such offenders a drug treatment and testing order would be appropriate. In other such cases, generally for a first drug-supply offence, adults, following a trial should be short term prisoners and, following a plea of guilty at the first reasonable opportunity, should be sentenced to a term of the order of two-and-a-half years' imprisonment: *R. v. Afonso*; *R. v. Sajid*; *R. v. Andrews* [2005] 1 Cr.App.R.(S.) 99, CA. In *R. v. Evans* (2005) 149 S.J. 1222, the Court of Appeal made it clear that such sentences are appropriate for those with no criminal record. For those with minor convictions for dishonesty or simple possession of drugs, who have not previously served a custodial sentence, sentences between two and two-and-a-half years' imprisonment are appropriate. For those with more serious convictions for dishonesty, minor violence or simple possession of drugs, who have served custodial sentences, three to three-and-a-half years is appropriate. Those with more serious convictions, including drug-supply offences, do not fall into the category of offender identified in *Afonso*.

In *Wijs* [1998] 2 Cr.App.R. 436, a case concerning the importation and possession of amphetamine with intent to supply the Court of Appeal stated that following conviction for importing amphetamine after a contested trial a custodial sentence will almost invariably be called for, save in exceptional circumstances or where the quantity of the drug is so small as to be compatible only with personal consumption by the importer. The ordinary level of sentence on conviction following a contested trial (and on quantities calculated on the basis of 100 per cent pure amphetamine base) should be:

(1) Up to 500 grammes: up to two years' imprisonment;
(2) More than 500 grammes but less than 2.5 kilos: two–four years' imprisonment;
(3) More than 2.5 kilos but less than 10 kilos: four–seven years' imprisonment;
(4) More than 10 kilos but less than 15 kilos: seven–10 years' imprisonment;
(5) More than 15 kilos: upwards of 10 years' imprisonment, subject to the statutory maximum of 14 years' imprisonment.

As to cannabis, the Court of Appeal has held that the level of sentence for supply and importation remains unchanged since its reclassification as a Class C drug: *Lappalainen* [2005] EWCA Crim 1458 (affirming the decision in *Donovan* [2005] 1 Cr.App.R.(S.) 16, CA).

C. RESTRICTION OF POSSESSION OF CONTROLLED DRUGS

(1) Definition

Misuse of Drugs Act 1971, s.5

Restriction of possession of controlled drugs

18–19 5.—(1) Subject to any regulations under section 7 of this Act for the time being in force, it shall not be lawful for a person to have a controlled drug in his possession.

(2) Subject to section 28 of this Act and to subsection (4) below, it is an offence for a person to have a controlled drug in his possession in contravention of subsection (1) above.

(3) Subject to section 28 of this Act, it is an offence for a person to have a controlled drug in his possession, whether lawfully or not, with intent to supply it to another in contravention of section 4(1) of this Act.

(4) In any proceedings for an offence under subsection (2) above in which it is proved that the accused had a controlled drug in his possession, it shall be a defence for him to prove—

(a) that, knowing or suspecting it to be a controlled drug, he took possession of it for the purpose of preventing another from committing or continuing to commit an offence in connection with that drug and that as soon as possible after taking possession of it he took all such steps as were reasonably open to him to destroy the drug or to deliver it into the custody of a person lawfully entitled to take custody of it; or

(b) that, knowing or suspecting it to be a controlled drug, he took possession of it for the purpose of delivering it into the custody of a person lawfully entitled to take custody of it and that as soon as possible after taking possession of it he took all such steps as were reasonably open to him to deliver it into the custody of such a person.

(5) Subsection (4) above shall apply in the case of proceedings for an offence under section 19(1) of this Act consisting of an attempt to commit an offence under subsection (2) above as it applies in the case of proceedings for an offence under subsection (2), subject to the following modifications, that is to say—

(a) for the references to the accused having in his possession, and to his taking possession of, a controlled drug there shall be substituted respectively references to his attempting to get, and to his attempting to take, possession of such a drug; and

(b) in paragraphs (a) and (b) the words from "and that as soon as possible" onwards shall be omitted.

(6) Nothing in subsection (4) or (5) above shall prejudice any defence which it is open to a person charged with an offence under this section to raise apart from that subsection.

(2) Allocation

18–20 This offence is triable either way: section 25 and Schedule 4 to the Act.

Part III

The *Consolidated Criminal Practice Direction* (2002), para.V.51.15, states that cases of possession of Class A drugs should be committed for trial unless the amount is small and consistent with only personal use; cases of Class B drugs should be committed for trial when the quantity is substantial. See Appendix F, F–57. No guideline is given in relation to Class C drugs.

Section 25(4) of the 1971 Act also provides that a magistrates' court in England and Wales may try an information for an offence under the 1971 Act if the information was laid at any time within twelve months from the commission of the offence.

(3) Elements of the offence

18–21   The specific defence provided by section 28 of the 1971 Act is also available to a charge under this section (see above).

"Possession" is not defined by the statute, save that "things which a person has in his possession shall be taken to include anything subject to his control which is in the custody of another: section 13(3). Possession requires physical custody of the drug and the intention to possess it: *Warner v. MPC* [1969] 2 A.C. 256. A person does not have possession of something which has been put into his pocket or house without his knowledge. But a mistake as to the precise quality of the substance under the defendant's control does not itself prevent him from being in possession (*e.g.* possession of heroin believing it to be cannabis or aspirin): *Searl v. Randolph* [1972] Crim.L.R. 779, DC. If the drugs are contained inside a package or box then the defendant was in possession of the contents; but the defendant was not in possession if the contents were quite different in kind from what he believed them to be: *McNamara* 87 Cr.App.R. 246, CA. Provided physical custody and knowledge can be proved, the quantity of the drug is not relevant to the issue of possession: *Boyesen* [1982] A.C. 768, HL; *DPP v. Brooks* [1974] A.C. 862.

(4) Sentence

18–22   It is necessary to draw a distinction between the three different classifications of drugs. When tried summarily, the maximum penalty for an offence under section 5(2) as regards a Class A is six months' imprisonment, a fine not exceeding the prescribed sum, or both. As regards a Class B drug, the maximum penalty is three months' imprisonment, a fine of not more than £3,000 or both, and as regards a Class C drug, three months' imprisonment, a fine of not more than £2,500 or both: *Misuse of Drugs Act* 1971, s.25 and Sched. 4. After commencement of the relevant provisions, the maximum custodial sentence in a magistrates' court will be 12 months' imprisonment: *Criminal Justice Act* 2003, ss.154 and 282.

When cases of simple possession of Class A drugs are dealt with summarily, the *Magistrates' Court Sentencing Guidelines* (2004) state:

> Aggravating factors include there being an amount other than a very small quantity, the offence is committed whilst on bail, relevant previous convictions and failure to respond to previous sentences.
>
> Mitigating factors include there being a very small quantity of the drug.
>
> **Guideline**: Is it serious enough for a community penalty?

18–23   However, following the guideline judgement of *Aramah* (1982) 4 Cr.App.R.(S.) 407 offences involving Class A drugs will rarely be tried summarily.

In *Busby* [2000] 1 Cr.App.R.(S.) 279, the offender pleaded guilty to possessing a Class A substance (Ecstasy) and a Class B drug (amphetamine) in each case with intent to supply. He possessed fourteen Ecstasy tablets and four amphetamine tablets. He admitted that he intended to share the drugs with two friends. His sentence was reduced from nine months to six months' imprisonment by the Court of Appeal. The short custodial sentence was explained by the fact that imprisonment sends out a clear message to others who need to hear the consequences of this kind of offence. In *Att.-Gen.'s Reference (No. 20 of 2002)* [2003] 1 Cr.App.R.(S.) 58 the offender pleaded guilty to possessing Ecstasy with intent to supply. He was found with 24 tablets in his car, and 760 tablets in his bedroom. He admitted he had been selling drugs for a year. He was sentenced to a community punishment and rehabilitation order and ordered to pay £200 prosecution costs. On appeal, this sentence was held to be unduly lenient and given that the offender had already completed his community punishment, a sentence of two years imprisonment was substituted, emphasising the need for custodial sentences in such cases. In *Campbell* (1992) 13 Cr.App.R.(S.) 630, the appellant was convicted of possessing a Class A drug, having been found in possession of 106 capsules each containing amphetamine sulphate and a strip of card impregnated with LSD. He was sentenced to 12 months' imprisonment.

Possession of cannabis with intent to supply is an offence which almost inevitably attracts a custodial sentence, even following reclassification of cannabis as a Class C drug. A six-month custodial sentence was appropriate following conviction of possession of cannabis with intent to supply where the offender's involvement in supply was very limited and he was of previous good character: *Donovan* [2004] EWCA Crim 1237, CA, *per* Gloster J.

When cases of simple possession of Class B drugs are dealt with summarily, the *Magistrates Court Sentencing Guidelines* (2004) state: **18–24**

> Aggravating factors include large amount, offence committed on bail, relevant previous convictions and any failures to respond to previous sentences
> Mitigating factors include small amount of the drug.
> **Guideline**: Is discharge or fine appropriate?

The guideline fine is starting point B and in all cases forfeiture of all drugs and equipment should be considered.   **18–25**

The *Aramah* guidelines indicate that in cases of simple possession of small amounts of cannabis for personal use, a fine will often be the appropriate penalty, unless the history shows a "persistent flouting of the law", which may render a custodial sentence appropriate.

In *Gregory* (1993) 14 Cr.App.R.(S.) 403 the offender pleaded guilty to possessing a Class A drug with intent to supply, possessing a Class A drug, possessing a Class B drug, and permitting premises to be used for smoking opium. G was sentenced to six months' imprisonment for possessing heroin with intent to supply, three months for possessing a Class A drug, three months for possessing a Class B drug, all concurrent, and 15 months' consecutive for allowing premises to be used for smoking opium.

The Court of Appeal held that in relation to Class B drugs, it might be appropriate to   **18–26**
pass a non-custodial sentence in respect of an offence of this kind, but any criminal conduct which facilitated the use of a Class A drug must be regarded as serious, even without a commercial motive. It was submitted that G had not corrupted those who used his flat, or profited from them but he had provided the venue in which they could take Class A drugs in comparative safety. However, the sentence of 15 months was considered too long and a sentence of six months was substituted, consecutive to the other sentences.

In *Doyle* [1996] 1 Cr.App.R.(S.) 449, the offender pleaded guilty to possession of cannabis with intent to supply and simple possession of cannabis. On a search of his premises the police had found a pot containing five grams of cannabis and a further 380 grams hidden in his garden. He was sentenced to six months' imprisonment. In *Busuttill* [2001] EWCA Crim 627, the defendant pleaded guilty to possession of forty packages of cannabis resin with intent to supply, stating that he was storing them for an associate without payment. He was sentenced to six months' imprisonment.

Supplying drugs to a serving prisoner may result in a more severe penalty. In *Doyle* [1998] 1 Cr.App.R.(S.) 79, CA, the defendant smuggled cannabis to her boyfriend who was serving a prison sentence. She was sentenced to twelve months' imprisonment, the Court stating that in view of the pressing nature of the issue of drug culture in prisons, "six months is no longer the tariff for passing drugs to a prisoner."

D. RESTRICTION OF CULTIVATION OF THE CANNABIS PLANT

(1) Definition

Misuse of Drugs Act 1971, s.6

Restriction of cultivation of cannabis plant

18–27　　6.—(1) Subject to any regulations under section 7 of this Act for the time being in force, it shall not be lawful for a person to cultivate any plant of the genus Cannabis.

(2) Subject to section 28 of this Act, it is an offence to cultivate any such plant in contravention of subsection (1) above.

(2) Allocation

18–28　　This offence is triable either way. Section 25(4) of the 1971 Act provides that a magistrates' court in England and Wales may try an information for an offence under the 1971 Act if the information was laid at any time within twelve months from the commission of the offence.

(3) Elements of the offence

18–29　　The specific defence provided by section 28 of the 1971 Act is also available to a charge under this section, above.

Authorisation of activities otherwise unlawful under ss.3 to 6

Misuse of Drugs Act 1971, s.7

Authorisation of activities otherwise unlawful under foregoing provisions

18–30　　7.—(1) The Secretary of State may by regulations—

(a) except from section 3(1)(a) or (b), 4(1)(a) or (b) or 5(1) of this Act such controlled drugs as may be specified in the regulations; and

(b) make such other provision as he thinks fit for the purpose of making it lawful for persons to do things which under any of the following provisions of this Act, that is to say sections 4(1), 5(1) and 6(1), it would otherwise be unlawful for them to do.

(2) Without prejudice to the generality of paragraph (b) of subsection (1) above, regulations under that subsection authorising the doing of any such thing as is mentioned in that paragraph may in particular provide for the doing of that thing to be lawful—

(a) if it is done under and in accordance with the terms of a licence or other authority issued by the Secretary of State and in compliance with any conditions attached thereto; or

(b) if it is done in compliance with such conditions as may be prescribed.

(3) Subject to subsection (4) below, the Secretary of State shall so exercise his power to make regulations under subsection (1) above as to secure—

(a) that it is not unlawful under section 4(1) of this Act for a doctor, dentist, veterinary practitioner or veterinary surgeon, acting in his capacity as such, to prescribe, administer, manufacture, compound or supply a controlled drug, or for a pharmacist or a person lawfully conducting a retail pharmacy business, acting in either case in his capacity as such, to manufacture, compound or supply a controlled drug; and

(b) that it is not unlawful under section 5(1) of this Act for a doctor, dentist, veterinary practitioner, veterinary surgeon, pharmacist or person lawfully conducting a retail pharmacy business to have a controlled drug in his possession for the purpose of acting in his capacity as such.

(4) If in the case of any controlled drug the Secretary of State is of the opinion that it is in the public interest—

(a) for production, supply and possession of that drug to be either wholly unlawful or unlawful except for purposes of research or other special purposes; or

(b) for it to be unlawful for practitioners, pharmacists and persons lawfully conducting retail pharmacy businesses to do in relation to that drug any of the things mentioned in subsection (3) above except under a licence or other authority issued by the Secretary of State,

he may by order designate that drug as a drug to which this subsection applies; and while there is in force an order under this subsection designating a controlled drug as one to which this subsection applies, subsection (3) above shall not apply as regards that drug.

(5) Any order under subsection (4) above may be varied or revoked by a subsequent order thereunder.

(6) The power to make orders under subsection (4) above shall be exercisable by statutory instrument, which shall be subject to annulment in pursuance of a resolution of either House of Parliament.

(7) The Secretary of State shall not make any order under subsection (4) above except after consultation with or on the recommendation of the Advisory Council.

(8) References in this section to a person's "doing" things include references to his having things in his possession.

(9) In its application to Northern Ireland this section shall have effect as if for references to the Secretary of State there were substituted references to the Ministry of Home Affairs for Northern Ireland and as if for subsection (6) there were substituted—

"(6) Any order made under subsection (4) above by the Ministry of Home Affairs for Northern Ireland shall be subject to negative resolution within the meaning of section 41(6) of the *Interpretation Act (Northern Ireland)* 1954 as if it were a statutory instrument within the meaning of that Act."

Misuse of Drugs Regulations 2001 (S.I. 2001 No. 3998)

18–31

These regulations, made under section 7, make lawful acts that would otherwise be offences under the *Misuse of Drugs Act* 1971. They provide for certain exemptions from the provisions of the 1971 Act, and make provision in relation to prescriptions, records and the furnishing of information concerning controlled drugs and for the supervision of the destruction of such drugs.

Part III

(4) Sentence

18–32

When tried summarily, the maximum penalty for this offence is six months' imprisonment, a fine not exceeding the prescribed sum, or both: section 25 and Schedule 4. After commencement of the relevant provisions, the maximum sentence in a magistrates' court will be 12 months' imprisonment: *Criminal Justice Act* 2003, ss.154 and 282.

When dealt with summarily, the *Magistrates' Court Sentencing Guidelines* (2004) state:

Aggravating factors include commercial cultivation, large quantity, offence committed on bail, relevant previous convictions and any failure to respond to previous sentences.

Mitigating factors include not for personal use, not commercial, not responsible for planting, small-scale cultivation.

Guideline: Is discharge or fine appropriate?

The guideline fine is starting point B. In all cases forfeiture of all drugs and equipment should be considered.

18–33

When sentencing for an offence contrary to section 6, a court should recognise the distinction between cultivating cannabis for personal use and cultivating with intent to supply: *Herridge* [2005] EWCA Crim 1410, CA. In *Marsland* (1994) 15 Cr.App.R.(S.) 665 the offender pleaded guilty to producing cannabis. Police officers searching the appellant's premises were shown a room in which 22 mature cannabis plants were growing; the room had been adapted for the purpose. A further 55 cannabis plants in various stages of growth were found in other parts of the house. The appellant claimed that he was producing cannabis solely for his own use, and he was sentenced to nine months' imprisonment.

E. Offences Committed by Occupiers of Premises

(1) Definition

Misuse of Drugs Act 1971, s.8

Occupiers etc. of premises to be punishable for permitting certain activities to take place there

18–34   **8.** A person commits an offence if, being the occupier or concerned in the management of any premises, he knowingly permits or suffers any of the following activities to take place on those premises, that is to say—

> (a) producing or attempting to produce a controlled drug in contravention of section 4(1) of this Act;
>
> (b) supplying or attempting to supply a controlled drug to another in contravention of section 4(1) of this Act, or offering to supply a controlled drug to another in contravention of section 4(1);
>
> (c) preparing opium for smoking;
>
> (d) smoking cannabis, cannabis resin or prepared opium

(2) Allocation

18–35   This offence is triable either way.

Section 25(4) of the 1971 Act also provides that a magistrates' court in England and Wales may try an information for an offence under the 1971 Act if the information was laid at any time within twelve months from the commission of the offence.

(3) Elements of the offence

18–36   The word "occupier" includes those with the requisite degree of control to be able to exclude those who might otherwise use the premises for the forbidden purposes. "Permits" involves an unwillingness to prevent the activity which may be inferred from failure to take reasonable steps (judged objectively) to prevent it.

(4) Sentence

18–37   When tried summarily, and the offence concerns a Class A or B drug, the maximum penalty is six months' imprisonment, a fine not exceeding the prescribed sum, or both. When the offence concerns a Class C drug, the maximum penalty is three months' imprisonment, a fine not exceeding £2,500 or both: s.25 and Sched. 4. After commencement of the relevant provisions the maximum custodial sentence in a magistrates' court will be 12 months' imprisonment: *Criminal Justice Act* 2003, ss.154 and 282.

In *Coulson* [2001] 1 Cr.App.R.(S.) 121, a sentence of 30 months' imprisonment was upheld in the case of an offender who had allowed his premises to be used for supplying heroin. See also *Setchall* [2002] 1 Cr.App.R.(S.) 76.

F. Opium: Prohibited Activities

(1) Definition

Misuse of Drugs Act 1971, s.9

Prohibition of certain activities etc. relating to opium

18–38   **9.** Subject to section 28 of this Act, it is an offence for a person—

> (a) to smoke or otherwise use prepared opium; or
>
> (b) to frequent a place used for the purpose of opium smoking; or
>
> (c) to have in his possession—
>
>> (i) any pipes or other utensils made or adapted for use in connection with the smoking of opium, being pipes or utensils which have been used by him or with his

knowledge and permission in that connection or which he intends to use or permit others to use in that connection; or

  (ii) any utensils which have been used by him or with his knowledge and permission in connection with the preparation of opium for smoking.

(2) Allocation

This offence is triable either way.   **18–39**

(3) Elements of the offence

"Prepared opium" means opium prepared for smoking and includes dross and any **18–40** other residues remaining after opium has been smoked: *Misuse of Drugs Act* 1971, s.37(1).

(4) Sentence

When tried summarily, the maximum penalty for this offence is six months' imprison- **18–41** ment, a fine not exceeding the prescribed sum, or both: section 25 and Schedule 4. After commencement of the relevant provisions, the maximum custodial sentence in a magistrates' court will be 12 months' imprisonment: *Criminal Justice Act* 2003, ss.154 and 282.

G. INCITEMENT

Misuse of Drugs Act 1971, s.19

Attempts etc. to commit offences
    19. It is an offence for a person to attempt to commit an offence under any other provision of **18–42** this Act or to incite or attempt to incite another to commit such an offence.

By section 25(3) of, and Schedule 4 to the 1971 Act, the offence of incitement is tri- **18–43** able and punishable in the same way as the substantive offence cited.

H. PARTICIPATION IN OFFENCES OUTSIDE THE UNITED KINGDOM

(1) Definition

Misuse of Drugs Act 1971, s.20

*Assisting in or inducing commission outside United Kingdom of offence punishable under a
    corresponding law*
    20. A person commits an offence if in the United Kingdom he assists in or induces the com- **18–44** mission in any place outside the United Kingdom of an offence punishable under the provisions of a corresponding law in force in that place.

(2) Allocation

This offence is triable either way.   **18–45**
    Section 25(4) of the 1971 Act also provides that a magistrates' court in England and Wales may try an information for an offence under the 1971 Act if the information was laid at any time within twelve months from the commission of the offence.

(3) Elements of the offence

"Assisting" is to be construed as an ordinary English word: *Vickers* (1975) 1 W.L.R. **18–46** 811.
    "Corresponding law" is defined in section 36 of the 1971 Act:

Misuse of Drugs Act 1971, s.36

Meaning of "corresponding law", and evidence of certain matters by certificate
    36.—(1) In this Act the expression "corresponding law" means a law stated in a certificate **18–47**

purporting to be issued by or on behalf of the government of a country outside the United Kingdom to be a law providing for the control and regulation in that country of the production, supply, use, export and import of drugs and other substances in accordance with the provisions of the Single Convention on Narcotic Drugs signed at New York on 30th March 1961 or a law providing for the control and regulation in that country of the production, supply, use, export and import of dangerous or otherwise harmful drugs in pursuance of any treaty, convention or other agreement or arrangement to which the government of that country and Her Majesty's Government in the United Kingdom are for the time being parties.

(2) A statement in any such certificate as aforesaid to the effect that any facts constitute an offence against the law mentioned in the certificate shall be evidence, and in Scotland sufficient evidence, of the matters stated.

(4) Sentence

18–48   When tried summarily, the maximum penalty for this offence is six months' imprisonment, a fine not exceeding the prescribed sum, or both: section 25 and Schedule 4. After commencement of the relevant provisions, the maximum custodial sentence in a magistrates' court will be 12 months' imprisonment: *Criminal Justice Act* 2003, ss.154 and 282.

This is also a drug trafficking offence: *Drug Trafficking Act* 1994, s.1(3)(b). A minimum custodial sentence of seven years applies to the third Class A drug trafficking offence. A forfeiture order or a confiscation order may also be imposed for a drug trafficking offence.

I. POWER TO DIRECT SPECIAL PRECAUTIONS AT CERTAIN PREMISES

(1) Definition

Misuse of Drugs Act 1971, s.11

Power to direct special precautions for safe custody of controlled drugs to be taken at
certain premises

18–49   **11.**—(1) Without prejudice to any requirement imposed by regulations made in pursuance of section 10(2)(a) of this Act, the Secretary of State may by notice in writing served on the occupier of any premises on which controlled drugs are or are proposed to be kept give directions as to the taking of precautions or further precautions for the safe custody of any controlled drugs of a description specified in the notice which are kept on those premises.

(2) It is an offence to contravene any directions given under subsection (1) above.

(2) Allocation

18–50   This offence is triable either way.

Section 25(4) of the 1971 Act provides that a magistrates' court in England and Wales may try an information for an offence under the 1971 Act if the information was laid at any time within twelve months from the commission of the offence

(3) Sentence

18–51   When tried summarily, the maximum penalty is six months' imprisonment, a fine not exceeding the prescribed sum, or both. After commencement of the relevant provisions, the maximum custodial sentence in a magistrates' court will be 12 months' imprisonment: *Criminal Justice Act* 2003, ss.154 and 282.

J. DIRECTION RELATING TO PRESCRIBING BY PRACTITIONERS

(1) Definition

Misuse of Drugs Act 1971, s.12–13

Directions prohibiting prescribing, supply etc. of controlled drugs by practitioners etc. convicted of certain offences.

12.—(1) Where a person who is a practitioner or pharmacist has after the coming into operation of this subsection been convicted—   **18–52**

    (a) of an offence under this Act or under the *Dangerous Drugs Act* 1965 or any enactment repealed by that Act; or

    (b) of an offence under section 45, 56 or 304 of the *Customs and Excise Act* 1952 or under section 50, 68 or 170 of the *Customs and Excise Management Act* 1979 in connection with a prohibition of or restriction on importation or exportation of a controlled drug having effect by virtue of section 3 of this Act or which has effect by virtue of any provision contained in or repealed by the *Dangerous Drugs Act* 1965;

    (c) of an offence under section 12 or 13 of the *Criminal Justice (International Co-operation) Act* 1990;

the Secretary of State may give a direction under subsection (2) below in respect of that person.

    (2) A direction under this subsection in respect of a person shall—

    (a) if that person is a practitioner, be a direction prohibiting him from having in his possession, prescribing administering, manufacturing, compounding and supplying and from authorising the administration and supply of such controlled drugs as may be specified in the direction;

    (b) if that person is a pharmacist, be a direction prohibiting him from having in his possession, manufacturing, compounding and supplying and from supervising and controlling the manufacture, compounding and supply of such controlled drugs as may be specified in the direction.

    (3) The Secretary of State may at any time give a direction cancelling or suspending any direction given by him under subsection (2) above, or cancelling any direction of his under this subsection by which a direction so given is suspended.

    (4) The Secretary of State shall cause a copy of any direction given by him under this section to be served on the person to whom it applies, and shall cause notice of any such direction to be published in the London, Edinburgh and Belfast Gazettes.

    (5) A direction under this section shall take effect when a copy of it is served on the person to whom it applies.

    (6) It is an offence to contravene a direction given under subsection (2) above.

Directions prohibiting prescribing, supply etc. of controlled drugs by practitioners in other cases.

13.—(1) In the event of a contravention by a doctor of regulations made in pursuance of   **18–53** paragraph (h) or (i) of section 10(2) of this Act, or of the terms of a licence issued under regulations made in pursuance of the said paragraph (i), the Secretary of State may, subject to and in accordance with section 14 of this Act, give a direction in respect of the doctor concerned prohibiting him from prescribing, administering and supplying and from authorising the administration and supply of such controlled drugs as may be specified in the direction.

    (2) If the Secretary of State is of the opinion that a practitioner is or has after the coming into operation of this subsection been prescribing, administering or supplying or authorising the administration or supply of any controlled drugs in an irresponsible manner, the Secretary of State may, subject to and in accordance with section 14 or 15 of this Act, give a direction in respect of the practitioner concerned prohibiting him from prescribing, administering and supplying and from authorising the administration and supply of such controlled drugs as may be specified in the direction.

    (3) A contravention such as is mentioned in subsection (1) above does not as such constitute an offence, but it is an offence to contravene a direction given under subsection (1) or (2) above.

(2) Allocation

These offences are triable either way: Sched. 4 to the *Misuse of Drugs Act* 1971.   **18–54**

Part III

(3) Sentence

18–55   When tried summarily, if it is a Class A or B drugs involved the maximum sentence is six months' imprisonment or a fine at level 5 or both. If the drug is Class C the maximum period of imprisonment is three months and a fine of £2,500 or both: see Sched. 4. After commencement of the relevant provisions the maximum custodial sentence will be 12 months: see *CJA* 2003, ss.154 and 282.

K. Failure to Comply with Notice Requiring Information Relating to Prescribing Supply etc of Drugs

(1) Definition

Misuse of Drugs Act 1971, s.17

Power to obtain information from doctors, pharmacists etc. in certain circumstances

18–56   **17.**—(1) If it appears to the Secretary of State that there exists in any area in Great Britain a social problem caused by the extensive misuse of dangerous or otherwise harmful drugs in that area, he may by notice in writing served on any doctor or pharmacist practising in or in the vicinity of that area, or on any person carrying on a retail pharmacy business within the meaning of the *Medicines Act* 1968 at any premises situated in or in the vicinity of that area, require him to furnish to the Secretary of State, with respect to any such drugs specified in the notice and as regards any period so specified, such particulars as may be so specified relating to the quantities in which and the number and frequency of the occasions on which those drugs—

     (a) in the case of a doctor, were prescribed, administered or supplied by him;

     (b) in the case of a pharmacist, were supplied by him; or

     (c) in the case of a person carrying on a retail pharmacy business, were supplied in the course of that business at any premises so situated which may be specified in the notice.

(2) A notice under this section may require any such particulars to be furnished in such manner and within such time as may be specified in the notice and, if served on a pharmacist or person carrying on a retail pharmacy business, may require him to furnish the names and addresses of doctors on whose prescriptions any dangerous or otherwise harmful drugs to which the notice relates were supplied, but shall not require any person to furnish any particulars relating to the identity of any person for or to whom any such drug has been prescribed, administered or supplied.

(3) A person commits an offence if without reasonable excuse (proof of which shall lie on him) he fails to comply with any requirement to which he is subject by virtue of subsection (1) above.

(4) A person commits an offence if in purported compliance with a requirement imposed under this section he gives any information which he knows to be false in a material particular or recklessly gives any information which is so false.

(5) In its application to Northern Ireland this section shall have effect as if for the references to Great Britain and the Secretary of State there were substituted respectively references to Northern Ireland and the Ministry of Home Affairs for Northern Ireland.

(2) Allocation

18–57   The offence under section 17(3) is triable summarily; the offence under section 17(4) is triable either way: section 25 and Schedule 4.

(3) Sentence

18–58   The maximum penalty for the offence under section 17(3) is a fine not exceeding level three on the standard scale: section 25 and Schedule 4. When tried summarily, the maximum sentence for an offence committed under section 17(4) will be six months' imprisonment, a fine not exceeding the prescribed sum, or both. After the commencement of the relevant provisions, the maximum custodial sentence for an offence under section 17(3) will be a custody plus order and for an offence under section 17(4) will be 12 months' imprisonment: *Criminal Justice Act* 2003, ss.154, 181 and 280–282.

L. MISCELLANEOUS OFFENCES

Misuse of Drugs Act 1971, s.18

Miscellaneous offences

18.—(1) It is an offence for a person to contravene any regulations made under this Act **18–59**
other than regulations made in pursuance of section 10(2)(h) or (i).

(2) It is an offence for a person to contravene a condition or other term of a licence issued under section 3 of this Act or of a licence or other authority issued under regulations made under this Act, not being a licence issued under regulations made in pursuance of section 10(2)(i).

(3) A person commits an offence if, in purported compliance with any obligation to give information to which he is subject under or by virtue of regulations made under this Act, he gives any information which he knows to be false in a material particular or recklessly gives any information which is so false.

(4) A person commits an offence if, for the purpose of obtaining, whether for himself or another, the issue or renewal of a licence or other authority under this Act or under any regulations made under this Act, he—

    (a) makes any statement or gives any information which he knows to be false in a material particular or recklessly gives any information which is so false; or

    (b) produces or otherwise makes use of any book, record or other document which to his knowledge contains any statement or information which he knows to be false in a material particular.

II. MISCELLANEOUS OFFENCES

A. INTOXICATING SUBSTANCES

(1) Definition

Intoxicating Substances (Supply) Act 1985, s.1

Offence of supply of intoxicating substance

1.—(1) It is an offence for a person to supply or offer to supply a substance other than a con- **18–60**
trolled drug—

    (a) to a person under the age of eighteen whom he knows, or has reasonable cause to believe, to be under that age; or

    (b) to a person—

        (i) who is acting on behalf of a person under that age; and

        (ii) whom he knows, or has reasonable cause to believe, to be so acting,

    if he knows or has reasonable cause to believe that the substance is, or its fumes are, likely to be inhaled by the person under the age of eighteen for the purpose of causing intoxication.

(2) In proceedings against any person for an offence under subsection (1) above it is a defence for him to show that at the time he made the supply or offer he was under the age of eighteen and was acting otherwise than in the course or furtherance of a business.

(3) A person guilty of an offence under this section shall be liable on summary conviction to imprisonment for a term not exceeding six months or to a fine not exceeding level 5 on the standard scale, or to both.

(4) In this section "controlled drug" has the same meaning as in the *Misuse of Drugs Act* 1971.

(2) Allocation

This offence is triable summarily only: section 1(3).   **18–61**

(3) Sentence

The maximum penalty for this offence is six months' imprisonment of a fine not **18–62** exceeding level five on the standard scale or both: section 1(3). After the commencement of the relevant provisions, the maximum custodial sentence in a magistrates' court will be a custody plus order: *Criminal Justice Act* 2003, ss.181 and 280–282.

B. Manufacture or Supply of Scheduled Substances

(1) Definition

Criminal Justice (International Co-operation) Act 1990, s.12

Manufacture and supply of scheduled substances

18–63   **12.**—(1) It is an offence for a person—

     (a) to manufacture a scheduled substance; or

     (b) to supply such a substance to another person,

knowing or suspecting that the substance is to be used in or for the unlawful production of a controlled drug.

(1A) A person does not commit an offence under subsection (1) above if he manufactures or, as the case may be, supplies the scheduled substance with the express consent of a constable.

(2) A person guilty of an offence under subsection (1) above is liable—

     (a) on summary conviction, to imprisonment for a term not exceeding six months or a fine not exceeding the statutory maximum or both;

     (b) on conviction on indictment, to imprisonment for a term not exceeding fourteen years or a fine or both.

(3) In this section "a controlled drug" has the same meaning as in the *Misuse of Drugs Act* 1971 and "unlawful production of a controlled drug" means the production of such a drug which is unlawful by virtue of section 4(1)(a) of that Act.

(4) In this section and elsewhere in this Part of this Act "a scheduled substance" means a substance for the time being specified in Schedule 2 to this Act.

(5) Her Majesty may by Order in Council amend that Schedule (whether by addition, deletion or transfer from one Table to the other) but—

     (a) no such Order shall add any substance to the Schedule unless—

         (i) it appears to Her Majesty to be frequently used in or for the unlawful production of a controlled drug; or

         (ii) it has been added to the Annex to the Vienna Convention under Article 12 of that Convention; and

     (b) no such Order shall be made unless a draft of it has been laid before and approved by a resolution of each House of Parliament.

(2) Allocation

18–64   This offence is triable either way, though no proceedings may be instituted without the consent of the DPP or the Commissioners of Customs and Excise: *Criminal Justice (International Co-operation) Act* 1990, s.21(2)(a).

(3) Elements of the offence

18–65   Schedule 2 to the 1990 Act specifies what shall be classed as a "scheduled substance".

Criminal Justice (International Co-operation) Act 1990, Sched. 2

SCHEDULE 2

Substances Useful for Manufacturing Controlled Drugs

Table I

18–66   *N*-Acetylanthranilic Acid

ephedrine
ergometrine
ergotamine
isosafrole
lysergic Acid
3, 4-Methylene-Dioxyphenyl-2-Propanone
norephedrine
1-Phenyl-2-Propanone
piperonal
pseudoephedrine
safrole

The salts of the substances listed in this Table whenever the existence of such salts is possible.

TABLE II

acetic Anhydride
acetone
anthranilic Acid
ethyl Ether
hydrochloric Acid
methyl Ethyl Ketone (also referred to as 2-Butanone or M.E.K.)
phenylacetic Acid
piperidine
potassium Permanganate
sulphuric Acid
toluene

The salts of the substances listed in this Table except hydrochloric acid and sulphuric acid whenever the existence of such salts is possible.

(4) Sentence

When tried summarily, the maximum sentence is six months' imprisonment, a fine **18–67** not exceeding the statutory maximum or both: section 12(2). The offence is classed as a drug trafficking offence (*Drug Trafficking Act* 1994, s.1(3)(d)), hence a minimum custodial sentence of seven years must be imposed for the third commission of the third Class A drug trafficking offence. A forfeiture or confiscation order may also be imposed. After commencement of the relevant provisions, the maximum custodial sentence in a magistrates' court will be 12 months' imprisonment: *Criminal Justice Act* 2003, ss.154 and 282.

C. Failure to comply with Regulations made under Criminal Justice (International Co-operation) Act 1990

(1) Definition

Criminal Justice (International Co-operation) Act 1990, s.13

Regulations about scheduled substances
    13.—(1) The Secretary of State may by regulations make provision—   **18–68**
      (a) imposing requirements as to the documentation of transactions involving scheduled substances;
      (b) requiring the keeping of records and the furnishing of information with respect to such substances;
      (c) for the inspection of records kept pursuant to the regulations;

Part III

(d) for the labelling of consignments of scheduled substances.

(2) Regulations made by virtue of subsection (1)(b) may, in particular, require—

(a) the notification of the proposed exportation of substances specified in Table I in Schedule 2 to this Act to such countries as may be specified in the regulations; and

(b) the production, in such circumstances as may be so specified, of evidence that the required notification has been given;

and for the purposes of section 68 of the *Customs and Excise Management Act* 1979 (offences relating to exportation of prohibited or restricted goods) any such substance shall be deemed to be exported contrary to a restriction for the time being in force with respect to it under this Act if it is exported without the requisite notification having been given.

(3) Regulations under this section may make different provision in relation to the substances specified in Table I and Table II in Schedule 2 to this Act respectively and in relation to different cases or circumstances.

(4) The power to make regulations under this section shall be exercisable by statutory instrument subject to annulment in pursuance of a resolution of either House of Parliament.

(5) Any person who fails to comply with any requirement imposed by the regulations or, in purported compliance with any such requirement, furnishes information which he knows to be false in a material particular or recklessly furnishes information which is false in a material particular is guilty of an offence and liable—

(a) on summary conviction, to imprisonment for a term not exceeding six months or a fine not exceeding the statutory maximum or both;

(b) on conviction on indictment, to imprisonment for a term not exceeding two years or a fine or both.

(6) No information obtained pursuant to the regulations shall be disclosed except for the purposes of criminal proceedings or of proceedings under the provisions of relating to the confiscation of the proceeds of drug trafficking or corresponding provisions in force in Northern Ireland [or of proceedings under Part 2, 3 or 4 of the *Proceeds of Crime Act* 2002.

(2) Allocation

18–69   This offence is triable either way: section 13(5).

(3) Elements of the offence

18–70   The *Controlled Drugs (Substances Useful for Manufacture) Regulations* 1991 (S.I. 1991 No. 1285) have been made in accordance with section 13.

Controlled Drugs (Substances Useful for Manufacture) Regulations 1991, regs 1–7

1.—(1) These Regulations may be cited as the *Controlled Drugs (Substances Useful for Manufacture) Regulations* 1991 and shall come into force on 1st July 1991.

(2) These Regulations are made under section 2(2) of the 1972 Act and section 13 of the 1990 Act, subject to the following exceptions:

(a) regulations 3 to 6 are made under section 2(2) of the 1972 Act alone; and

(b) regulation 7 is made under section 13 of the 1990 Act alone.

2. In these Regulations:

'the 1972 Act' means the *European Communities Act* 1972;

'the 1979 Act' means the *Customs and Excise Management Act* 1979;

'the 1990 Act' means the *Criminal Justice (International Co-operation) Act* 1990;

'the Community Regulation' means Council Regulation (EEC) No. 3677/90, and 'operator' has the same meaning as in that Regulation.

3. Subject to regulations 4 and 6 below:

(a) the obligations imposed on operators by Articles 2(2) and (3), 4 and 5 of the Community Regulation and by virtue of regulation 5 below shall be treated as if they were requirements imposed on them by regulations made under section 13(1) of the 1990 Act;

4. In Article 4 of the Community Regulation:

  (a) the words "the competent authorities of the Member State" shall be taken as a reference to the Secretary of State;

5.—(1) An operator who is concerned in an export, import or transit operation involving a scheduled substance shall ensure that he has the documentation required by Article 2(1) of the Community Regulation.

  In this paragraph, "export", "import", "scheduled substance" and "transit" have the same meanings as in the Community Regulation.

  (2) The obligations imposed by Article 2(4) of the Community Regulation shall be complied with by the operator mentioned in paragraph (1) of this regulation, and in that Article the words "the competent authorities" shall be taken as a reference to the Secretary of State.

5A.—(1) An operator who is concerned in an export operation involving a scheduled substance in Category 1 of the Annex to the Community Regulation shall ensure that he has the authorisation required by Article 4 of that Regulation.

  (2) An operator who is concerned in an export operation involving a scheduled substance in Category 2 of the Annex to the Community Regulation shall ensure that he has such authorisation as is required by Article 5 of that Regulation.

  (3) An operator who is concerned in an export operation involving a scheduled substance in Category 3 of the Annex to the Community Regulation shall ensure that he has such authorisation, if any, as is required by Article 5a of that Regulation.

  (4) For the purposes of section 68 of the 1979 Act (offences relating to exportation of prohibited or restricted goods) any scheduled substance shall be deemed to be exported contrary to a restriction for the time being in force with respect to it under these Regulations if it is exported without the requisite authorisation having been obtained.

  (5) In this regulation, "export" (except where it occurs in paragraph (4) above) and "scheduled substance" have the same meanings as in the Community Regulation, and in Articles 4, 5 and 5a of the Community Regulation the words "the competent authorities" shall be taken as a reference to the Secretary of State.

5B. An operator who fails to comply with any of the requirements imposed by Article 2a of the Community Regulation is guilty of an offence and liable:

  (a) on summary conviction, to imprisonment for a term not exceeding 3 months or a fine not exceeding the statutory maximum or both;

  (b) on conviction on indictment, to imprisonment for a term not exceeding two years or a fine or both.

5C.—(1) An operator who fails to comply with any of the requirements imposed by virtue of regulation 5A above is guilty of an offence and liable to the same penalties as an operator who is guilty of an offence under regulation 5B above.

  (2) The powers conferred by subsection (1) of section 23 of the *Misuse of Drugs Act* 1971 shall be exercisable also for the purposes of the execution of Articles 4, 5 and 5a of the Community Regulation and subsection (3) of that section (excluding paragraph (a)) shall apply also to the offence under paragraph (1) above, taking references in those subsections to controlled drugs as references to scheduled substances within the meaning of the Community Regulation.

5D. Any reference in regulations 5B and 5C above to an operator who fails to comply with the requirements mentioned in those regulations shall include an operator who, in purported compliance with any such requirement:

  (a) furnishes information which he knows to be false in a material particular; or

  (b) recklessly furnishes information which is false in a material particular.

6. Where a person is convicted of an offence contrary to section 68 of the 1979 Act [as a result of the application of regulation 5A above,] or section 13(5) of the 1990 Act as a result of the application of regulation 3 above:

  (a) section 68(1) of the 1979 Act shall have effect as if after the words 'greater' there were added the words 'but not exceeding the statutory maximum';

  (b) section 68(3)(a) of the 1979 Act shall have effect as if after the words 'greater' there were added the words 'but not exceeding the statutory maximum', and for the words '6 months' there were substituted the words '3 months';

  (c) section 68(3)(b) of the 1979 Act shall have effect as if for the words '7 years' there were substituted the words '2 years';

Part III

(d) section 13(5)(a) of the 1990 Act shall have effect as if for the words '6 months' there were substituted the words '3 months'.

7. A person who produces or supplies a scheduled substance specified in Table 1 in Schedule 2 to the 1990 Act shall:

(a) make a record of each quantity of such scheduled substance produced or supplied by him, as the case may be; and

(b) preserve all records made under this regulation for a period of not less than two years from the end of the calendar year in which the production or supply, as the case may be, took place.

In this regulation, 'produce' and 'supply' have the same meanings as in the *Misuse of Drugs Act* 1971.

(4) Sentence

18–71   When tried summarily, the maximum penalty for this offence is six months' imprisonment, a fine not exceeding the statutory maximum or both: section 13(5). After commencement of the relevant provisions, the maximum custodial sentence able to be imposed in a magistrates' court will be 12 months' imprisonment: *Criminal Justice Act* 2003, ss.154 and 282.

D. SHIPS USED FOR ILLICIT TRAFFIC

(1) Definition

Criminal Justice (International Co-operation) Act 1990, s.19

Ships used for illicit traffic

18–72   **19.**—(1) This section applies to a British ship, a ship registered in a state other than the United Kingdom which is a party to the Vienna Convention (a 'Convention state') and a ship not registered in any country or territory.

(2) A person is guilty of an offence if on a ship to which this sections applies, wherever it may be, he—

(a) has a controlled drug in his possession; or

(b) is in any way knowingly concerned in the carrying or concealing of a controlled drug on the ship,

knowing or having reasonable grounds to suspect that the drug is intended to be imported or has been exported contrary to section 3(1) of the *Misuse of Drugs Act* 1971 or the law of any state other than the United Kingdom.

(3) A certificate purporting to be issued by or on behalf of the government of any state to the effect that the importation or export of a controlled drug is prohibited by the law of that state shall be evidence, and in Scotland sufficient evidence, of the matters stated.

(4) A person guilty of an offence under this section is liable—

(a) in a case where the controlled drug is a Class A drug—

(i) on summary conviction, to imprisonment for a term not exceeding six months or a fine not exceeding the statutory maximum or both;

(ii) on conviction on indictment, to imprisonment for life or a fine or both;

(b) in a case where the controlled drug is a Class B drug—

(i) on summary conviction, to imprisonment for a term not exceeding six months or a fine not exceeding the statutory maximum or both;

(ii) on conviction on indictment, to imprisonment for a term not exceeding fourteen years or a fine or both;

(c) in a case where the controlled drug is a Class C drug—

(i) on summary conviction, to imprisonment for a term not exceeding three months or a fine not exceeding the statutory maximum or both;

(ii) on conviction on indictment, to imprisonment for a term not exceeding five years or a fine or both.

(5) In this section 'a controlled drug' and the references to controlled drugs of a specified Class have the same meaning as in the said Act of 1971; and an offence under this section shall be included in the offences to which section 28 of that Act (defences) applies.

(2) Allocation

Each offence is triable either way, though the consent of the DPP or the Director of **18–73** Revenue and Customs Prosecutions: *Criminal Justice (International Co-operation) Act* 1990, s.21(2)(a). The consent of the Secretary of State of the powers conferred by Schedule 3 is required to institute proceedings when the offence is alleged to have been committed outside the landward limits of the territorial sea of the UK on a ship registered in a state which is party to the Vienna Convention. The *Territorial Waters Jurisdiction Act* 1878, s.3 does not apply to these proceedings: *Criminal Justice (International Co-operation) Act* 1990, s.21(3).

(3) Elements of the offence

Criminal Justice (International Co-operation) Act 1990, s.24

Interpretation of Part II

24.—(1) In this Part of this Act—   **18–74**

'British ship' means a ship registered in the United Kingdom or a colony;

'Convention state' has the meaning given in section 19(1) above;

'scheduled substance' has the meaning given in section 12(4) above;

'ship' includes any vessel used in navigation;

'the territorial sea of the United Kingdom' includes the territorial sea adjacent to any of the Channel Islands, the Isle of Man or any colony;

'the Vienna Convention' means the United Nations Convention against Illicit Traffic in Narcotic Drugs and Psychotropic Substances which was signed in Vienna on 20th December 1988.

(2) Any expression used in this Part of this Act which is also used in the *Drug Trafficking Act* 1994 has the same meaning as in that Act and, in section 22(1), "drug trafficking offences" includes drug trafficking offences within the meaning of the *Criminal Justice (Confiscation) (Northern Ireland) Order* 1990.

(3) In relation to Scotland, any expression used in this Part of this Act which is also used in the *Criminal Justice (Scotland) Act* 1987 has the same meaning as in that Act and 'drug trafficking offence' means an offence to which section 1 of that Act relates.

(4) If in any proceedings under this Part of this Act any question arises whether any country or territory is a state or is a party to the Vienna Convention, a certificate issued by or under the authority of the Secretary of State shall be conclusive evidence on that question.

The defence established by section 28 of the *Misuse of Drugs Act* 1971 applies to this section: section 19(5).

(4) Sentence

Where the offence committed involves a Class A drug, when tried summarily, the **18–75** maximum penalty is six months' imprisonment, a fine not exceeding the statutory maximum or both: section 19(4)(a).

Where the offence committed involves a Class B drug, when tried summarily, the maximum penalty is six months' imprisonment, a fine not exceeding the statutory maximum or both: section 19(4)(b).

Where the offence committed involves a Class C drug, when tried summarily, the maximum penalty is three months' imprisonment, a fine not exceeding the statutory maximum or both: section 19(4)(c). After commencement of the relevant provisions, the maximum custodial sentence in a magistrates' court will be 12 months' imprisonment: *Criminal Justice Act* 2003, ss.154 and 282.

E. Failure to Provide a Sample at a Police Station for Testing

(1) Definition

Police and Criminal Evidence Act 1984, ss.63B, 63C

Testing for presence of Class A drugs

18–76   **63B.**—(1) A sample of urine or a non-intimate sample may be taken from a person in police detention for the purpose of ascertaining whether he has any specified Class A drug in his body if

    (a) either the arrest condition or the charge condition is met;

    (b) both the age condition and the request condition are met; and

    (c) the notification condition is met in relation to the arrest condition, the charge condition or the age condition (as the case may be).

(1A) The arrest condition is that the person concerned has been arrested for an offence but has not been charged with that offence and either—

    (a) the offence is a trigger offence; or

    (b) a police officer of at least the rank of inspector has reasonable grounds for suspecting that the misuse by that person of a specified Class A drug caused or contributed to the offence and has authorised the sample to be taken.

(2) The charge condition is either—

    (a) that the person concerned has been charged with a trigger offence; or

    (b) that the person concerned has been charged with an offence and a police officer of at least the rank of inspector, who has reasonable grounds for suspecting that the misuse by that person of any specified Class A drug caused or contributed to the offence, has authorised the sample to be taken.

(3) The age condition is—

    (a) if the arrest condition is met, that the person concerned has attained the age of 18;

    (b) if the charge condition is met, that he has attained the age of 14.

(4) The request condition is that a police officer has requested the person concerned to give the sample.

(4A) The notification condition is that—

    (a) the relevant chief officer has been notified by the Secretary of State that appropriate arrangements have been made for the police area as a whole, or for the particular police station, in which the person is in police detention, and

    (b) the notice has not been withdrawn.

(4B) For the purposes of subsection (4A) above, appropriate arrangements are arrangements for the taking of samples under this section from whichever of the following is specified in the notification—

    (a) persons in respect of whom the arrest condition is met;

    (b) persons in respect of whom the charge condition is met;

    (c) persons who have not attained the age of 18.

(5) Before requesting the person concerned to give a sample, an officer must—

    (a) warn him that if, when so requested, he fails without good cause to do so he may be liable to prosecution, and

    (b) in a case within subsection (1A)(b) or (2)(b) above, inform him of the giving of the authorisation and of the grounds in question.

(5A) In the case of a person who has not attained the age of 17—

    (a) the making of the request under subsection (4) above;

    (b) the giving of the warning and (where applicable) the information under subsection (5) above; and

    (c) the taking of the sample,

may not take place except in the presence of an appropriate adult.

(5B) If a sample is taken under this section from a person in respect of whom the arrest condition is met no other sample may be taken from him under this section during the same continuous period of detention but—

    (a) if the charge condition is also met in respect of him at any time during that period, the sample must be treated as a sample taken by virtue of the fact that the charge condition is met;

(b) the fact that the sample is to be so treated must be recorded in the person's custody record.

(5C) Despite subsection (1)(a) above, a sample may be taken from a person under this section if—

(a) he was arrested for an offence (the first offence),

(b) the arrest condition is met but the charge condition is not met,

(c) before a sample is taken by virtue of subsection (1) above he would (but for his arrest as mentioned in paragraph (d) below) be required to be released from police detention,

(d) he continues to be in police detention by virtue of his having been arrested for an offence not falling within subsection (1A) above, and

(e) the sample is taken before the end of the period of 24 hours starting with the time when his detention by virtue of his arrest for the first offence began.

(5D) A sample must not be taken from a person under this section if he is detained in a police station unless he has been brought before the custody officer.

(6) A sample may be taken under this section only by a person prescribed by regulations made by the Secretary of State by statutory instrument.

No regulations shall be made under this subsection unless a draft has been laid before, and approved by resolution of, each House of Parliament.

(6A) The Secretary of State may by order made by statutory instrument amend—

(a) paragraph (a) of subsection (3) above, by substituting for the age for the time being specified a different age specified in the order, or different ages so specified for different police areas so specified;

(b) paragraph (b) of that subsection, by substituting for the age for the time being specified a different age specified in the order.

(6B) A statutory instrument containing an order under subsection (6A) above shall not be made unless a draft of the instrument has been laid before, and approved by a resolution of, each House of Parliament.

(7) Information obtained from a sample taken under this section may be disclosed—

(a) for the purpose of informing any decision about granting bail in criminal proceedings (within the meaning of the *Bail Act* 1976) to the person concerned;

(aa) for the purpose of informing any decision about the giving of a conditional caution under Part 3 of the *Criminal Justice Act* 2003 to the person concerned;

(b) where the person concerned is in police detention or is remanded in or committed to custody by an order of a court or has been granted such bail, for the purpose of informing any decision about his supervision;

(c) where the person concerned is convicted of an offence, for the purpose of informing any decision about the appropriate sentence to be passed by a court and any decision about his supervision or release;

(ca) for the purpose of an assessment which the person concerned is required to attend by virtue of section 9(2) or 10(2) of the *Drugs Act* 2005;

(cb) for the purpose of proceedings against the person concerned for an offence under section 12(3) or 14(3) of that Act;

(d) for the purpose of ensuring that appropriate advice and treatment is made available to the person concerned.

(8) A person who fails without good cause to give any sample which may be taken from him under this section shall be guilty of an offence.

(10) In this section—

"appropriate adult", in relation to a person who has not attained the age of 17, means—

(a) his parent or guardian or, if he is in the care of a local authority or voluntary organisation, a person representing that authority or organisation; or

(b) a social worker of a local authority social services department; or

(c) if no person falling within paragraph (a) or (b) is available, any responsible person aged 18 or over who is not a police officer or a person employed by the police;

"relevant chief officer" means—

      (a) in relation to a police area, the chief officer of police of the police force for that police area; or

      (b) in relation to a police station, the chief officer of police of the police force for the police area in which the police station is situated.

[This section is printed as amended by the *Drugs Act* 2005, section 7 and Schedule 2, paragraph 1.]

Testing for presence of Class A drugs: supplementary

18–77   **63C.**—(1) A person guilty of an offence under section 63B above shall be liable on summary conviction to imprisonment for a term not exceeding three months, or to a fine not exceeding level 4 on the standard scale, or to both.

(2) A police officer may give an authorisation under section 63B above orally or in writing but, if he gives it orally, he shall confirm it in writing as soon as is practicable.

(3) If a sample is taken under section 63B above by virtue of an authorisation, the authorisation and the grounds for the suspicion shall be recorded as soon as is practicable after the sample is taken.

(4) If the sample is taken from a person detained at a police station, the matters required to be recorded by subsection (3) above shall be recorded in his custody record.

(5) Subsections (11) and (12) of section 62 above apply for the purposes of section 63B above as they do for the purposes of that section; and section 63B above does not prejudice the generality of sections 62 and 63 above.

(6) In section 63B above—

    "Class A drug" and "misuse" have the same meanings as in the *Misuse of Drugs Act* 1971;

    "specified" (in relation to a Class A drug) and "trigger offence" have the same meanings as in Part III of the *Criminal Justice and Court Services Act* 2000.

(2) Allocation

18–78   This offence is triable summarily. It was introduced as an amendment to *PACE* 1984 by section 57 of the *Criminal Justice and Court Services Act* 2000.

(3) Elements of the offence

18–79   Following the amendments introduced by section 7 of the *Drugs Act* 2005, the conditions for testing are as follows:

1. The person has been arrested for an offence that is either a trigger offence or a police officer of at least the rank of inspector has reasonable grounds for suspecting that the misuse by that person of a specified Class A drug caused or contributed to the offence and has authorised the sample to be taken (the "arrest condition") OR that the person concerned has been charged with an offence that is either a trigger offence or a police officer of at least the rank of inspector, who has reasonable grounds for suspecting that the misuse by that person of any specified Class A drug caused or contributed to the offence, has authorised the sample to be taken (the "charge condition"); and

2. In the case of a person satisfying the arrest condition, they have reached the age of 18, and in the case of a person satisfying the charge condition, they have reached the age of 14; and

3. The police officer has requested the person to give the sample; and

4. The relevant chief officer has been notified by the Secretary of State that appropriate arrangements for the taking of samples have been made for the police area as a whole, or for the particular police station, in which the person is in police detention, and that notice has not been withdrawn.

The police officer must warn the detainee of the consequences of failing to give a sample, and where an inspector has authorised the sample, the police officer must provide information regarding this authorisation and its grounds: *Police and Criminal Evidence Act* 1984, s.63B(5).

In the case of individuals under 17, an appropriate adult must be present when the request for a sample is made, the warning about the consequences of failing to give a sample or the information required under subsection (5) is given and when the sample is taken: *Police and Criminal Evidence Act* 1984, s.63B(5A).

A sample may also be taken from a person if he was arrested for an offence that satisfies the arrest condition but not the charge condition and before a sample is taken he would, but for his arrest for an offence not falling within subsection (1A), be required to be released from police detention, if the sample is taken within 24 hours of his detention following arrest for the offence that satisfies the arrest conditions: *Police and Criminal Evidence Act* 1984, s.63B(5C).

(4) Sentence

Maximum penalty is three months' imprisonment, or to fine not exceeding level 4 on **18–80** the standard scale, or both. After commencement of the relevant provisions, the maximum custodial sentence by in a magistrates' court is a custody plus order: *Criminal Justice Act* 2003, ss.181 and 280–282.

III. ARREST REFERRAL SCHEMES

In addition to the sentencing options available for offenders convicted of drug-related **18–81** offences, arrest referral schemes employ drug workers to make contact with arrestees in police cells and/or magistrates' courts to assess and refer drug-using offenders to treatment services. These schemes offer a good opportunity to identify drug-using offenders and help them reduce their drug use. Involvement is voluntary and is not an alternative to prosecution or due process.

Home Office guidelines specify that all adult arrestees should be offered the opportunity to see an arrest referral worker as part of the custody suite booking-in procedure (Home Office Drugs Prevention Advisory Service (1999) *Drugs interventions in the Criminal Justice System: guidance manual*). Beyond such guidelines, the operation of local schemes has been left broadly to the service providers' discretion. There is therefore considerable variety in practices across areas, and schemes depend on what services are available locally.

The *Drugs Act* 2005 enables police officers to require an individual who has tested positive for Class A drugs at the police station to attend an initial assessment with a suitably qualified person to determine whether they are dependent on or have a propensity to misuse any specified Class A drug; whether they might benefit from further assessment or treatment or to provide advice on what types of treatment are available: *Drugs Act* 2005, s.9.

Section 12 of the *Drugs Act* 2005 makes it an offence to fail to attend this appointment, or fail to stay for the duration of the appointment. This offence is triable summarily and has a maximum penalty of 51 weeks' imprisonment or a fine not exceeding level 4 on the standard scale: *Drugs Act* 2005, s.12(4). The results of these tests may also be used to inform bail decisions.

Drugs Act 2005, ss.9, 11–12, 15–19

Initial assessment following testing for presence of Class A drugs

  9.—(1) This section applies if— **18–82**

    (a) a sample is taken under section 63B of *PACE* (testing for presence of Class A drug) from a person detained at a police station,

    (b) an analysis of the sample reveals that a specified Class A drug may be present in the person's body,

    (c) the age condition is met, and

    (d) the notification condition is met.

  (2) A police officer may, at any time before the person is released from detention at the police station, require him to attend an initial assessment and remain for its duration.

(3) An initial assessment is an appointment with a suitably qualified person (an "initial assessor")—

    (a) for the purpose of establishing whether the person is dependent upon or has a propensity to misuse any specified Class A drug,

    (b) if the initial assessor thinks that he has such a dependency or propensity, for the purpose of establishing whether he might benefit from further assessment, or from assistance or treatment (or both), in connection with the dependency or propensity, and

    (c) if the initial assessor thinks that he might benefit from such assistance or treatment (or both), for the purpose of providing him with advice, including an explanation of the types of assistance or treatment (or both) which are available.

(4) The age condition is met if the person has attained the age of 18 or such different age as the Secretary of State may by order made by statutory instrument specify for the purposes of this section.

(5) In relation to a person ("A") who has attained the age of 18, the notification condition is met if—

    (a) the relevant chief officer has been notified by the Secretary of State that arrangements for conducting initial assessments for persons who have attained the age of 18 have been made for persons from whom samples have been taken (under section 63B of *PACE*) at the police station in which A is detained, and

    (b) the notice has not been withdrawn.

(6) In relation to a person ("C") who is of an age which is less than 18, the notification condition is met if—

    (a) the relevant chief officer has been notified by the Secretary of State that arrangements for conducting initial assessments for persons of that age have been made for persons from whom samples have been taken (under section 63B of *PACE*) at the police station in which C is detained, and

    (b) the notice has not been withdrawn.

(7) In subsections (5) and (6), "relevant chief officer" means the chief officer of police of the police force for the police area in which the police station is situated.

Requirements under sections 9 and 10: supplemental

18–83   **11.**—(1) This section applies if a person is required to attend an initial assessment and remain for its duration by virtue of section 9(2).

(2) A police officer must—

    (a) inform the person of the time when, and the place at which, the initial assessment is to take place, and

    (b) explain that this information will be confirmed in writing.

(3) A police officer must warn the person that he may be liable to prosecution if he fails without good cause to attend the initial assessment and remain for its duration.

(4) If the person is also required to attend a follow-up assessment and remain for its duration by virtue of section 10(2), a police officer must also warn the person that he may be liable to prosecution if he fails without good cause to attend the follow-up assessment and remain for its duration.

(5) A police officer must give the person notice in writing which—

    (a) confirms that he is required to attend and remain for the duration of an initial assessment or both an initial assessment and a follow-up assessment (as the case may be),

    (b) confirms the information given in pursuance of subsection (2), and

    (c) repeats the warning given in pursuance of subsection (3) and any warning given in pursuance of subsection (4).

(6) The duties imposed by subsections (2) to (5) must be discharged before the person is released from detention at the police station.

(7) A record must be made, as part of the person's custody record, of—

    (a) the requirement imposed on him by virtue of section 9(2),

    (b) any requirement imposed on him by virtue of section 10(2),

    (c) the information and explanation given to him in pursuance of subsection (2) above,

    (d) the warning given to him in pursuance of subsection (3) above and any warning given to him in pursuance of subsection (4) above, and

(e) the notice given to him in pursuance of subsection (5) above.

(8) If a person is given a notice in pursuance of subsection (5), a police officer or a suitably qualified person may give the person a further notice in writing which—

    (a) informs the person of any change to the time when, or to the place at which, the initial assessment is to take place, and

    (b) repeats the warning given in pursuance of subsection (3) and any warning given in pursuance of subsection (4).

Attendance at initial assessment

12.—(1) This section applies if a person is required to attend an initial assessment and remain **18–84** for its duration by virtue of section 9(2).

(2) The initial assessor must inform a police officer or a police support officer if the person—

    (a) fails to attend the initial assessment at the specified time and place, or

    (b) attends the assessment at the specified time and place but fails to remain for its duration.

(3) A person is guilty of an offence if without good cause—

    (a) he fails to attend an initial assessment at the specified time and place, or

    (b) he attends the assessment at the specified time and place but fails to remain for its duration.

(4) A person who is guilty of an offence under subsection (3) is liable on summary conviction to imprisonment for a term not exceeding 51 weeks, or to a fine not exceeding level 4 on the standard scale, or to both.

(5) If a person fails to attend an initial assessment at the specified time and place, any requirement imposed on him by virtue of section 10(2) ceases to have effect.

(6) In this section—

    (a) the specified time, in relation to the person concerned, is the time specified in the notice given to him in pursuance of subsection (5) of section 11 or, if a further notice specifying a different time has been given to him in pursuance of subsection (8) of that section, the time specified in that notice, and

    (b) the specified place, in relation to the person concerned, is the place specified in the notice given to him in pursuance of subsection (5) of section 11 or, if a further notice specifying a different place has been given to him in pursuance of subsection (8) of that section, the place specified in that notice.

(7) In relation to an offence committed before the commencement of section 281(5) of the *Criminal Justice Act* 2003 (alteration of penalties for summary offences), the reference in subsection (4) to 51 weeks is to be read as a reference to 3 months.

Disclosure of information about assessments

15.—(1) An initial assessor may disclose information obtained as a result of an initial assess- **18–85** ment to any of the following—

    (a) a person who is involved in the conduct of the assessment;

    (b) a person who is or may be involved in the conduct of any follow-up assessment.

(2) A follow-up assessor may disclose information obtained as a result of a follow-up assessment to a person who is involved in the conduct of the assessment.

(3) Subject to subsections (1) and (2), information obtained as a result of an initial or a follow-up assessment may not be disclosed by any person without the written consent of the person to whom the assessment relates.

(4) Nothing in this section affects the operation of section 17(4).

Samples submitted for further analysis

16.—(1) A requirement imposed on a person by virtue of section 9(2) or 10(2) ceases to have **18–86** effect if at any time before he has fully complied with the requirement—

    (a) a police officer makes arrangements for a further analysis of the sample taken from him as mentioned in section 9(1)(a), and

    (b) the analysis does not reveal that a specified Class A drug was present in the person's body.

(2) If a requirement ceases to have effect by virtue of subsection (1), a police officer must so inform the person concerned.

(3) Nothing in subsection (1) affects the validity of anything done in connection with the requirement before it ceases to have effect.

(4) If a person fails to attend an assessment which he is required to attend by virtue of section 9(2) or fails to remain for the duration of such an assessment but, at any time after his failure, the requirement ceases to have effect by virtue of subsection (1) above—

(a) no proceedings for an offence under section 12(3) may be brought against him, and

(b) if any such proceedings were commenced before the requirement ceased to have effect, those proceedings must be discontinued.

(5) If a person fails to attend an assessment which he is required to attend by virtue of section 10(2) or fails to remain for the duration of such an assessment but, at any time after his failure, the requirement ceases to have effect by virtue of subsection (1) above—

(a) no proceedings for an offence under section 14(3) may be brought against him, and

(b) if any such proceedings were commenced before the requirement ceased to have effect, those proceedings must be discontinued.

Relationship with Bail Act 1976 etc.

18–87   **17.**—(1) A requirement imposed on a person by virtue of section 9(2) or 10(2) ceases to have effect if at any time before he has fully complied with the requirement—

(a) he is charged with the related offence, and

(b) a court imposes on him a condition of bail under section 3(6D) of the *Bail Act 1976* (duty to impose condition to undergo relevant assessment etc.).

(2) For the purposes of section 3(6D) of the 1976 Act, a relevant assessment (within the meaning of that Act) is to be treated as having been carried out if—

(a) a person attends an initial assessment and remains for its duration, and

(b) the initial assessor is satisfied that the initial assessment fulfilled the purposes of a relevant assessment.

(3) For the purposes of paragraph 6B(2)(b) of Schedule 1 to the 1976 Act (exceptions to right to bail for drug users in certain areas), a person is to be treated as having undergone a relevant assessment (within the meaning of that Act) if—

(a) the person attends an initial assessment and remains for its duration, and

(b) the initial assessor is satisfied that the initial assessment fulfilled the purposes of a relevant assessment.

(4) An initial assessor may disclose information relating to an initial assessment for the purpose of enabling a court considering an application for bail by the person concerned to determine whether subsection (2) or (3) applies.

(5) Nothing in subsection (1) affects—

(a) the validity of anything done in connection with the requirement before it ceases to have effect, or

(b) any liability which the person may have for an offence under section 12(3) or 14(3) committed before the requirement ceases to have effect.

(6) In subsection (1), "the related offence" is the offence in respect of which the condition specified in subsection (1A) or (2) of section 63B of *PACE* is satisfied in relation to the taking of the sample mentioned in section 9(1)(a) of this Act.

Orders under this Part and guidance

18–88   **18.**—(1) A statutory instrument containing an order under section 9(4) or 10(5) must not be made unless a draft of the instrument has been laid before, and approved by a resolution of, each House of Parliament.

(2) Any such order may—

(a) make different provision for different police areas;

(b) make such provision as the Secretary of State considers appropriate in connection with requiring persons who have not attained the age of 18 to attend and remain for the duration of an initial assessment or a follow-up assessment (as the case may be), including provision amending this Part.

(3) In exercising any functions conferred by this Part, a police officer and a suitably qualified person must have regard to any guidance issued by the Secretary of State for the purposes of this Part.

Interpretation

19.—(1) This section applies for the purposes of this Part.   **18–89**

(2) "Class A drug" and "misuse" have the same meanings as in the *Misuse of Drugs Act 1971*.

(3) "Specified", in relation to a Class A drug, has the same meaning as in Part 3 of the *Criminal Justice and Court Services Act* 2000.

(4) "Initial assessment" and "initial assessor" must be construed in accordance with section 9(3).

(5) "Follow-up assessment" and "follow-up assessor" must be construed in accordance with section 10(3).

(6) "Suitably qualified person" means a person who has such qualifications or experience as are from time to time specified by the Secretary of State for the purposes of this Part.

(7) "Police support officer" means a person who is employed by a police authority under section 15(1) of the *Police Act* 1996 and who is under the direction and control of the chief officer of police of the police force maintained by that authority.

(8) "PACE" means the *Police and Criminal Evidence Act* 1984.

Part III

REVENUE AND CUSTOMS OFFENCES

I. INTRODUCTION

A. CUSTOMS AND EXCISE MANAGEMENT ACT 1979

(1) Definitions

Customs and Excise Management Act 1979, s.1

Interpretation

1.—(1) In this Act, unless the context otherwise requires—   **19–1**

"aerodrome" means any area of land or water designed, equipped, set apart of commonly used for affording facilities for the landing and departure of aircraft;

"approved wharf" has the meaning given by section 20A below;

"armed forces" means the Royal Navy, the Royal Marines, the regular army and the regular air force, and any reserve or auxiliary force of any of those services which has been called out on permanent service, or embodied;

"assigned matter" means any matter in relation to which the Commissioners are for the time being required in pursuance of any enactment to perform any duties;

"boarding station" means a boarding station for the time being appointed under section 19 below;

"boundary" means the land boundary of Northern Ireland;

"British ship" means a British ship within the meaning of the *Merchant Shipping Act 1995*;

"claimant", in relation to proceedings for the condemnation of any thing as being forfeited, means a person claiming that the thing is not liable to forfeiture;

"coasting ship" has the meaning given by section 69 below;

"commander", in relation to an aircraft, includes any person having or taking the charge or command of the aircraft;

"the Commissioners" means the Commissioners for Her Majesty's Revenue and Customs;

"Community transit goods" —

(a) in relation to imported goods, means—

(i)   goods which have been imported under the internal or external

Community transit procedure for transit through the United Kingdom with a view to exportation where the importation was and the transit and exportation are to be part of one Community transit operation; or

(ii) goods which have, at the port or airport at which they were imported, been placed under the internal or external Community transit procedure for transit through the United Kingdom with a view to exportation where the transit and exportation are to be part of one Community transit operation;

(b) in relation to goods for exportation, means—

(i) goods which have been imported as mentioned in paragraph (a)(i) of this definition and are to be exported as part of the Community transit operation in the course of which they were imported; or

(ii) goods which have, under the internal or external Community transit procedure, transited the United Kingdom from the port or airport at which they were imported and are to be exported as part of the Community transit operation which commenced at that port or airport and for the purposes of paragraph (a)(i) above the Isle of Man shall be treated as if it were part of the United Kingdom;

"container" includes any bundle or package and any box, cask or other receptacle whatsoever;

"the customs and excise Acts" means the Customs and Excise Acts 1979 and any other enactment for the time being in force relating to customs or excise;

"the Customs and Excise Acts 1979" means—

this Act,

the *Customs and Excise Duties (General Reliefs) Act* 1979,

the *Alcoholic Liquor Duties Act* 1979,

the *Hydrocarbon Oil Duties Act* 1979, and

the *Tobacco Products Duty Act* 1979;

"customs and excise airport" has the meaning given by section 21(7) below;

"customs and excise station" has the meaning given by section 26 below;

"designation order" has the meaning given by section 100A(5);

"drawback goods" means goods in the case of which a claim for drawback has been or is to be made;

"dutiable goods", except in the expression "dutiable or restricted goods", means goods of a class or description subject to any duty of customs or excise, whether or not those goods are in fact chargeable with that duty, and whether or not that duty has been paid thereon;

"dutiable or restricted goods" has the meaning given by section 52 below;

"examination station" has the meaning given by section 22A below;

"excise duty point" has the meaning given by section 1 of the *Finance (No. 2) Act* 1992;

"excise licence trade" means, subject to subsection (5) below, a trade or business for the carrying on of which an excise licence is required;

"excise warehouse" means a place of security approved by the Commissioners under subsection (1) (whether or not it is also approved under subsection (2)) of section 92 below, and, except in that section, also includes a distiller's warehouse;

"exporter", in relation to goods for exportation or for use as stores, includes the shipper of the goods and any person performing in relation to an aircraft functions corresponding with those of a shipper;

"free zone" has the meaning given by section 100A(2);

"free zone goods" are goods which are within a free zone;

"goods" includes stores and baggage;

"holiday", in relation to any part of the United Kingdom, means any day that is a bank holiday in that part of the United Kingdom under the *Banking and Financial Dealings Act* 1971, Christmas Day, Good Friday and the day appointed for the purposes of customs and excise for the celebration of Her Majesty's birthday;

"hovercraft" means a hovercraft within the meaning of the *Hovercraft Act* 1968;

"importer", in relation to any goods at any time between their importation and the time when they are delivered out of charge, includes any owner or other person for the time being possessed of or beneficially interested in the goods and, in relation to goods imported by means of a pipe-line, includes the owner of the pipe-line;

"justice" and "justice of the peace" in Scotland includes a sheriff and in Northern Ireland, in relation to any powers and duties which can under any enactment for the time being in force be exercised and performed only by a resident magistrate, means a resident magistrate;

"land" and "landing", in relation to aircraft, include alighting on water;

"law officer of the Crown" means the Attorney General or for the purpose of criminal proceedings in Scotland, the Lord Advocate or, for the purpose of civil proceedings in Scotland, the appropriate Law Officer within the meaning of section 4A of the *Crown Suits (Scotland) Act* 1857 or in Northern Ireland the Attorney General for Northern Ireland;

"licence year", in relation to an excise licence issuable annually, means the period of 12 months ending on the date on which that licence expires in any year;

"master", in relation to a ship, includes any person having or taking the charge or command of the ship;

"night" means the period between 11 pm and 5 am;

"occupier", in relation to any bonded premises, includes any person who has given security to the Crown in respect of those premises;

"officer" means, subject to section 8(2) below, a person commissioned by the Commissioners;

"owner", in relation to an aircraft, includes the operator of the aircraft; "owner", in relation to a pipe-line, means (except in the case of a pipe-line vested in the Crown which in pursuance of arrangements in that behalf is operated by another) the person in whom the line is vested and, in the said excepted case, means the person operating the line;

"perfect entry" means an entry made in accordance with regulation 5 of the *Customs Controls on Importation of Goods Regulations* 1991 or warehousing regulations as the case may require;

"pipe-line" has the meaning given by section 65 of the *Pipe-lines Act* 1962 (that Act being taken, for the purposes of this definition, to extend to Northern Ireland);

"port" means a port appointed by the Commissioners under section 19 below;

"prescribed area" means such an area in Northern Ireland adjoining the boundary as the Commissioners may by regulations prescribe;

"prescribed sum", in relation to the penalty provided for an offence, has the meaning given by section 171(2) below;

"prohibited or restricted goods" means goods of a class or description of which the importation, exportation or carriage coastwise is for the time being prohibited or restricted under or by virtue of any enactment;

"proper", in relation to the person by, with or to whom, or the place at which, anything is to be done, means the person or place appointed or authorised in that behalf by the Commissioners;

"proprietor", in relation to any goods, includes any owner, importer, exporter, shipping or other person for the time being possessed of or beneficially interested in those goods;

"Queen's warehouse" means any place provided by the Crown or appointed by the Commissioners for the deposit of goods for security thereof and of the duties chargeable thereon;

"registered excise dealer and shipper" means a revenue trader approved and registered by the Commissioners under section 100G below;

"registered excise dealers and shippers regulations" means regulations under section 100G below;

"representative", in relation to any person from whom the Commissioners assess an amount as being excise duty due, means his personal representative, trustee in bankruptcy or interim or permanent trustee, any receiver or liquidator appointed in relation to him or any of his property or any other person acting in a representative capacity in relation to him;

"the revenue trade provisions of the customs and excise Acts" means—

(a)   the provisions of the customs and excise Acts relating to the protection, security, collection or management of the revenues derived from the duties of excise on goods produced or manufactured in the United Kingdom;

Part III

    (b)   the provisions of the customs and excise Acts relating to any activity or facility for the carrying on or provision of which an excise licence is required;

    (c)   the provisions of the *Betting and Gaming Duties Act* 1972 (so far as not included in paragraph (b) above);

    (d)   the provisions of Chapter II of Part I of the *Finance Act* 1993;

    (e)   the provisions of sections 10 to 15 of, and Schedule 1 to, the *Finance Act* 1997;

"revenue trader" means—

    (a)   any person carrying on a trade or business subject to any of the revenue trade provisions of the customs and excise Acts, or which consists of or includes—

        (i)   the buying, selling, importation, exportation, dealing in or handling of any goods of a class or description which is subject to a duty of excise (whether or not duty is chargeable on the goods);

        (ia)   the buying, selling, importation, exportation, dealing in or handling of tickets or chances on the taking of which lottery duty is or will be chargeable;

        (ib)   being (within the meaning of sections 10 to 15 of the *Finance Act* 1997 the provider of any premises for gaming;

        (ic)   the organisation, management or promotion of any gaming (within the meaning of the *Gaming Act* 1968 or the *Betting, Gaming, Lotteries and Amusements (Northern Ireland) Order* 1985), or

        (ii)   the financing or facilitation of any such transactions or activities as are mentioned in sub-paragraph (i), (ia), (ib) or (ic) above, whether or not that trade or business is an excise licence trade, and;

    (b)   any person who is a wholesaler or an occupier of an excise warehouse (so far as not included in paragraph (a) above), and includes a registered club;

"ship" and "vessel" include any boat or other vessel whatsoever (and, to the extent provided in section 2 below, any hovercraft);

"shipment" includes loading into an aircraft, and "shipped" and cognate expressions shall be construed accordingly;

"stores" means, subject to subsection (4) below, goods for use in a ship or aircraft and includes fuel and spare parts and other articles of equipment, whether or not for immediate fitting;

"tons register" means the tons of a ship's net tonnage as ascertained and registered according to the tonnage regulations of the *Merchant Shipping Act* 1995 or, in the case of a ship which is not registered under that Act, ascertained in like manner as if it were to be so registered;

"transit goods", except in the expression "Community transit goods", means imported goods entered on importation for transit or transhipment;

"transit or transhipment", in relation to the entry of goods, means transit through the United Kingdom or transhipment with a view to the re-exportation of the goods in question or transhipment of those goods for use as stores;

"transit shed" has the meaning given by section 25A below;

"United Kingdom waters" means any waters (including inland waters) within the seaward limits of the territorial sea of the United Kingdom;

"vehicle" includes a railway vehicle;

"victualling warehouse" means a place of security approved by the Commissioners under subsection (2) (whether or not it is also a place approved under subsection (1) of section 92 below).

"warehouse", except in the expressions "Queen's warehouse" and "distiller's warehouse", means a place of security approved by the Commissioners under subsection (1) or (2) or subsections (1) and (2) of section 92 below and, except in that section, also includes a distiller's warehouse; and "warehoused" and cognate expressions shall, subject to subsection (4) of that section and any regulations made by virtue of section 93(2)(da)(i) or (ee) or (4) below, be construed accordingly;

"warehousing regulations" means regulations under section 93 below.

  (2) This Act and the other Acts included in the Customs and Excise Acts 1979 shall be

construed as one Act but where a provision of this Act refers to this Act that reference is not to be construed as including a reference to any of the others.

(3) Any expression used in this Act or in any instrument made under this Act to which a meaning is given by any other Act included in the Customs and Excise Acts 1979 has, except where the context otherwise requires, the same meaning in this Act or any such instrument as in that Act; and for ease of reference the Table below indicates the expressions used in this Act to which a meaning is given by any other such Act—

> *Alcoholic Liquor Duties Act* 1979
> "beer"
> "brewer" and "registered brewer"
> "cider"
> "compounder"
> "distiller"
> "distiller's warehouse"
> "dutiable alcoholic liquor"
> "licensed", in relation to producers of wine or made-wine
> "made-wine"
> "producer of made-wine"
> "producer of wine"
> "proof"
> "rectifier"
> "registered club"
> "spirits"
> "wholesaler"
> "wine"
> *Hydrocarbon Oil Duties Act* 1979
> "rebate"
> "refinery"
> *Tobacco Products Duty Act* 1979
> "tobacco products"

(4) Goods for use in a ship or aircraft as merchandise for sale to persons carried in the ship or aircraft shall be treated for the purposes of the customs and excise Acts as stores if, and only if—

(a) the goods are to be sold by retail either—
    (i) in the course of a relevant journey, or
    (ii) for consumption on board;
    and
(b) the goods are not treated as exported by virtue of regulations under section 12 of the *Customs and Excise Duties (General Reliefs) Act* 1979 (goods for use in naval ships or establishments).

(4A) For the purposes of subsection (4) above a relevant journey is any journey beginning in the United Kingdom and having an immediate destination outside the member States.

(4B) In relation to goods treated as stores by virtue of subsection (4) above, any reference in the customs and excise Acts to the consumption of stores shall be construed as referring to the sale of the goods as mentioned in paragraph (a) of that subsection.

(5) A person who deals in or sells tobacco products in the course of a trade or business carried on by him shall be deemed for the purposes of this Act to be carrying on an excise licence trade (and to be a revenue trader) notwithstanding that no excise licence is required for carrying on that trade or business.

(6) In computing for the purposes of this Act any period expressed therein as a period of clear days no account shall be taken of the day of the event from which the period is computed or of any Sunday or holiday.

(7) The provisions of this Act in so far as they relate to customs duties apply, notwithstanding that any duties are imposed for the benefit of the Communities, as if the revenue from duties so imposed remained part of the revenues of the Crown.

[This section is printed as amended by the *Isle of Man Act* 1979, s.13 and Sched. 1; the *Betting and Gaming Duties Act* 1981, s.34(1) and Sched. 5, para. 5(a); the *Finance*

Part III

Act 1981, s.11(1) and Sched. 8, Pt I, para. 1(1), (2); the *Finance Act* 1984, s.8 and Sched. 4, Pt II, para. 1; the *Finance (No.2) Act* 1987, s.103(3); the *Territorial Sea Act* 1987, s.3(1), (4), Sched. 1, para. 4(1) and Sched. 2; the *Finance Act* 1991, s.11(1), (?); the *Customs Controls on Importation of Goods Regulations* 1991 (S.I. 1991 No. 2724), reg. 6(1) and (2); the *Finance (No.2) Act* 1992, s.3 and Sched. 2; the *Finance Act* 1993, s.30; and the *Merchant Shipping Act* 1995, Sched. 13. Immaterial definitions in subs.(1) have been omitted.]

Customs and Excise Management Act 1979, s.5

Time of importation, exportation, etc.

19–2   **5.**—(1) The provisions of this section shall have effect for the purposes of the customs and excise Acts.

(2) Subject to subsections (3) and (6) below, the time of importation of any goods shall be deemed to be—

(a) where the goods are brought by sea, the time when the ship carrying them comes within the limits of a port;

(b) where the goods are brought by air, the time when the aircraft carrying them lands in the United Kingdom or the time when the goods are unloaded in the United Kingdom, whichever is the earlier;

(c) where the goods are brought by land, the time when the goods are brought across the boundary into Northern Ireland.

(3) In the case of goods brought by sea of which entry is not required under regulation 5 of the *Customs Controls on Importation of Goods Regulations* 1991, the time of importation shall be deemed to be the time when the ship carrying them came within the limits of the port at which the goods are discharged.

(4) Subject to subsections (5) and (7) below, the time of exportation of any goods from the United Kingdom shall be deemed to be—

(a) where the goods are exported by sea or air, the time when the goods are shipped for exportation;

(b) where the goods are exported by land, the time when they are cleared by the proper officer at the last customs and excise station on their way to the boundary.

(5) In the case of goods of a class or description with respect to the exportation of which any prohibition or restriction is for the time being in force under or by virtue of any enactment which are exported by sea or air, the time of exportation shall be deemed to be the time when the exporting ship or aircraft departs from the last port or customs and excise airport at which it is cleared before departing for a destination outside the United Kingdom.

(6) Goods imported by means of a pipe-line shall be treated as imported at the time when they are brought within the limits of a port or brought across the boundary into Northern Ireland.

(7) Goods exported by means of a pipe-line shall be treated as exported at the time when they are charged into that pipe-line for exportation.

(8) A ship shall be deemed to have arrived at or departed from a port at the time when the ship comes within or, as the case may be, leaves the limits of that port.

[This section is printed as amended by the *Customs and Excise (Single Market etc.) Regulations* 1992 (S.I. 1992 No. 3095), reg.10(1), Sched. 1, para. 3.]

(2) Proceedings in the magistrates' court

19–3   No proceedings for an offence under this Act shall be instituted except by order of the Commissioners and proceedings shall be in the name of an officer: section 145. Any officer authorised for that purpose may conduct proceedings in the magistrates' court: section 155. Proceedings may not be commenced for an indictable offence after twenty years have elapsed since the day the offence was committed and for a summary offence after three years but, subject to that, a summary offence may be commenced within six months from the date upon which sufficient evidence to warrant the proceedings came to the knowledge of the prosecuting authority: section 146A. A certificate of the latter fact is sufficient. Proceedings may be commenced in any court having jurisdiction in the place where the person charged with the offence resides or is found, where anything was seized or detained in connection with the charge or where the offence was committed: section 148.

Where two or more persons are liable for an offence they may be proceeded against **19–4** jointly or severally and shall each be liable for the full amount of any pecuniary penalty although the court may mitigate that penalty: section 150.

Proceedings take place in the normal way save that:

— the court may not change from committal proceedings to a summary trial without the consent of the Commissioners or, where the proceedings were brought in the name of the Attorney-General, his consent;

— the prosecutor may appeal to the Crown Court: section 147.

II. OFFENCES IN CONNECTION WITH COMMISSIONERS, OFFICERS, ETC.

A. IMPERSONATING A CUSTOMS OFFICER

(1) Definition

Customs and Excise Management Act 1979, s.13

Unlawful assumption of character of officer, etc.

13. If, for the purpose of obtaining admission to any house or other place, or of doing or **19–5** procuring to be done any act which he would not be entitled to do or procure to be done of his own authority, or for any other unlawful purpose, any person falsely assumes the name, designation or character of a Commissioner or officer or of a person appointed by the Commissioners he may be detained and shall, in addition to any other punishment to which he may have rendered himself liable, be liable—

(a) on summary conviction, to a penalty of the prescribed sum, or to imprisonment for a term not exceeding 3 months, or to both; or

(b) on conviction on indictment, to a penalty of any amount, or to imprisonment for a term not exceeding 2 years, or to both.

[This section is printed as amended by the *PACE* 1984, s.114(1).]

(2) Allocation

This offence is triable either way.   **19–6**

(3) Elements of the offence

The prosecution must prove that the defendant either: **19–7**

— committed an act or gained admission to a house or other place;

— acted unlawfully or outside his authority; or

— was impersonating an officer at the time.

(4) Sentence

The maximum penalty is three months' imprisonment, a £5000 fine or both: *Customs* **19–8** *and Excise Management Act* 1979, s.171. When the *Criminal Justice Act* 2003 is in force the maximum custodial sentence will be a custody plus order: sections 181, 280–282 (see *post*, Ch.23.).

B. BRIBERY AND COLLUSION

(1) Definition

Customs and Excise Management Act 1979, s.15

Bribery and collusion

19–9   **15.**—(1) If any Commissioner or officer or any person appointed or authorised by the Commissioners to discharge any duty relating to an assigned matter—

(a) directly or indirectly asks for or takes in connection with any of his duties any payment or other reward whatsoever, whether pecuniary or other, or any promise or security for any such payment or reward, not being a payment or reward which he is lawfully entitled to claim or receive; or

(b) enters into or acquiesces in any agreement to do, abstain from doing, permit, conceal or connive at any act or thing whereby Her Majesty is or may be defrauded or which is otherwise unlawful, being an act or thing relating to an assigned matter,

he shall be guilty of an offence under this section.

(2) If any person—

(a) directly or indirectly offers or gives to any Commissioner or officer or to any person appointed or authorised by the Commissioners as aforesaid any payment or other reward whatsoever, whether pecuniary or other, or any promise or security for any such payment or reward; or

(b) proposes or enters into any agreement with any Commissioner, officer or person appointed or authorised as aforesaid,

in order to induce him to do, abstain from doing, permit, conceal or connive at any act or thing whereby Her Majesty is or may be defrauded or which is otherwise unlawful, being an act or thing relating to an assigned matter, or otherwise to take any course contrary to his duty, he shall be guilty of an offence under this section.

(3) Any person committing an offence under this section shall be liable on summary conviction to a penalty of level 5 on the standard scale and may be detained.

(2) Allocation

19–10   This offence is triable summarily.

(3) Elements of the offence

19–11   In the case of an officer (section 15(1)) the prosecution must prove:

— he has asked for or has taken money or other reward to which he is not entitled;

— he has agreed to perform an act or omission as a result; or

— the act or omission will deprive the government of excise duty or is otherwise unlawful.

In the case of any person (section 15(2)) the prosecution must prove:

— he has given or offered money or a reward directly or indirectly to a customs officer or has made an agreement or proposed to a customs officer;

— that offer, gift, agreement or proposal is intended to make the officer perform an act or omission or allow or conceal something; or

— the act *etc*. may or has deprived the government of excise duty.

(4) Sentence

19–12   The maximum penalty is a fine of £5000.

C. Obstruction

(1) Definition

Customs and Excise Management Act 1979, s.16

Obstruction of officers, etc.

19–13

16.—(1) Any person who—

    (a) obstructs, hinders, molests or assaults any person duly engaged in the performance of any duty or the exercise of any power imposed or conferred on him by or under any enactment relating to an assigned matter, or any person acting in his aid; or

    (b) does anything which impedes or is calculated to impede the carrying out of any search for any thing liable to forfeiture under any such enactment or the detention, seizure or removal of any such thing; or

    (c) rescues, damages or destroys any thing so liable to forfeiture or does anything calculated to prevent the procuring or giving of evidence as to whether or not any thing is so liable to forfeiture; or

    (d) prevents the detention of any person by a person duly engaged or acting as aforesaid or rescues any person so detained.

or who attempts to do any of the aforementioned things, shall be guilty of an offence under this section.

(2) A person guilty of an offence under this section shall be liable—

    (a) on summary conviction, to a penalty of the prescribed sum, or to imprisonment for a term not exceeding 3 months, or to both; or

    (b) on conviction on indictment, to a penalty of any amount, or to imprisonment for a term not exceeding 2 years, or to both.

(3) Any person committing an offence under this section and any person aiding or abetting the commission of such an offence may be detained.

[This section is printed as amended by the *PACE* 1984, s.114(1).]

(2) Allocation

This offence is triable either way.

19–14

(3) Elements of the offence

The prosecution must prove that the defendant has:

19–15

— obstructed or assaulted someone acting in the course of his duty or assisting someone who is so acting; or

— impeded a search, detention or forfeiture;

— rescued, damaged, destroyed an item liable to forfeiture or evidence; or

— prevented the detention of a person by an officer.

It should be noted that this is a much wider section than that of obstructing a police officer in the execution of his duty and includes both obstruction and assault.

In *George and Davies* [1981] Crim.L.R.185 the giving of a false name was held to be obstruction.

(4) Sentence

The maximum penalty is three months' imprisonment or a fine of £5000 or both. When the *Criminal Justice Act* 2003 is in force the maximum custodial sentence will be a custody plus order: sections 181, 280–282 (see *post*, Ch.23).

19–16

There is no Magistrates' Courts Sentencing Guideline for this offence but the guideline for assaulting a police officer is custody and the guideline for obstruction is a discharge or fine.

Part III

III. OFFENCES OF ILLEGAL IMPORTATION AND EXPORTATION

A. Illegal Importation

(1) Definition

Customs and Excise Management Act 1979, s.50

Penalty for improper importation of goods

19–17   **50.**—(1) Subsection (2) below applies to goods of the following descriptions,that is to say—
  (a) goods chargeable with a duty which has not been paid; and
  (b) goods the importation, landing or unloading of which is for the time being prohibited or restricted by or under any enactment.

(2) If any person with intent to defraud Her Majesty of any such duty or to evade any such prohibition or restriction as is mentioned in subsection (1) above—
  (a) unships or lands in any port or unloads from any aircraft in the United Kingdom or from any vehicle in Northern Ireland any goods to which this subsection applies, or assists or is otherwise concerned in such unshipping, landing or unloading; or
  (b) removes from their place of importation or from any approved wharf, examination station, transit shed or customs and excise station any goods to which this subsection applies or assists or is otherwise concerned in such removal,
he shall be guilty of an offence under this subsection and may be detained.

(3) If any person imports or is concerned in importing any goods contrary to any prohibition or restriction for the time being in force under or by virtue of any enactment with respect to those goods, whether or not the goods are unloaded, and does so with intent to evade the prohibition or restriction, he shall be guilty of an offence under this subsection and may be detained.

(4) Subject to subsection (5), (5A) or (5B) below, a person guilty of an offence under subsection (2) or (3) above shall be liable—
  (a) on summary conviction, to a penalty of the prescribed sum or of three times the value of the goods, whichever is the greater, or to imprisonment for a term not exceeding 6 months, or to both; or
  (b) on conviction on indictment, to a penalty of any amount, or to imprisonment for a term not exceeding 7 years, or to both.

(5) In the case of an offence under subsection (2) or (3) above in connection with a prohibition or restriction on importation having effect by virtue of section 3 of the *Misuse of Drugs Act* 1971, subsection (4) above shall have effect subject to the modifications specified in Schedule 1 to this Act.

(5A) In the case of an offence under subsection (2) or (3) above in connection with the prohibition contained in section 20 of the *Forgery and Counterfeiting Act* 1981, subsection (4)(b) above shall have effect as if for the words "2 years" there were substituted the words "10 years".

(5B) In the case of an offence under subsection (2) or (3) above in connection with the prohibition contained in regulation 2 of the *Import of Seal Skins Regulations* 1996, subsection (4) above shall have effect as if—
  (a) for paragraph (a) there were substituted the following—

  "(a) on summary conviction, to a fine not exceeding the statutory maximum or to imprisonment for a term not exceeding three months, or to both"

and
  (b) in paragraph (b) for the words "7 years" there were substituted the words "2 years".

(6) If any person—
  (a) imports or causes to be imported any goods concealed in a container holding goods of a different description; or
  (b) directly or indirectly imports or causes to be imported or entered any goods found, whether before or after delivery, not to correspond with the entry made thereof,

he shall be liable on summary conviction to a penalty of three times the value of the goods or level 3 on the standard scale, whichever is the greater.

(7) In any case where a person would, apart from this subsection, be guilty of—

(a) an offence under this section in connection with the importation of goods contrary to a prohibition or restriction; and

(b) a corresponding offence under the enactment or other instrument imposing the prohibition or restriction, being an offence for which a fine or other penalty is expressly provided by that enactment or other instrument,

he shall not be guilty of the offence mentioned in paragraph (a) of this subsection.

[This section is printed as amended by the *Forgery and Counterfeiting Act* 1981, s.23(1) (insertion of subs.(5A)); the *CJA* 1982, ss.37, 46; *PACE* 1984, s.114(1); the *Finance Act* 1988, s.12(1)(a), (6) (substitution of "7 years" for "2 years" in subs.(4)(b)); and the *Import of Seal Skins Regulations* 1996 (S.I. 1996 No. 2686).]

(2) Allocation

This offence is triable either way.   **19–18**

(3) Elements of the offence

The prosecution must prove that (section 50(2)):   **19–19**

— the goods are taxable or prohibited or restricted;

— the defendant has either landed or assisted in the landing of the goods or has removed or assisted in the removal of the goods from an approved area; or

— the defendant either does not intend to pay the duty or intends to evade the prohibition or restriction.

The prosecutor must prove that the defendant (section 50(3)):

— has imported prohibited or restricted goods; or

— intended to evade the prohibition or restriction.

According to section 154 once importation has been proved it is presumed to be unlawful unless, the defence can prove otherwise. For time of importation see section 5 above. An intention to evade is necessary: *Frailey v. Charlton* [1920] 1 K.B. 147. In *Smith (Donald)* [1973] Q.B. 924, CA it was held that there can be no goods which are merely "unloaded" or "landed" and not imported. In *Hurford-Jones* (1977) 65 Cr.App.R. 263, CA it was held that "evade" does not have the same connotation as fraud or dishonesty in the revenue laws.

(4) Sentence

The maximum penalty is a fine of £5000 or a penalty of three times the value of the   **19–20** goods, whichever is the greater or imprisonment for a term not exceeding six months, or both.

There are enhanced penalties under section 50(5) and Schedule 1 for certain types of goods. In the case of drugs, where the drug concerned is a Class A or B drug, on summary conviction, the penalty is six months' imprisonment, a fine of £5000 or three times the value of the goods, whichever is the greater. If the drug is a Class C drug, on summary conviction, the maximum penalty is three months' imprisonment, a fine not exceeding £500 or three times the value of the goods, whichever is the greater. When the *Criminal Justice Act* 2003 is in force the maximum custodial sentence will be 12 months' imprisonment: sections 154 and 282. Custodial sentences of less than 12 months will consist of a custody plus order (see *post*, Ch.23).

B. IMPROPER UNLOADING OF GOODS LOADED ETC. FOR EXPORTATION

(1) Definition

Customs and Excise Management Act 1979, s.67

Offences in relation to exportation of goods

19–21   67.—(1) If any goods which have been loaded or retained on board any ship or aircraft for exportation are not exported to and discharged at a place outside the United Kingdom but are unloaded in the United Kingdom, then, unless—

(a) the unloading was authorised by the proper officer; and

(b) except where that officer otherwise permits, any duty chargeable and unpaid on the goods is paid and any drawback or allowance paid in respect thereof is repaid,

the master of the ship or the commander of the aircraft and any person concerned in the unshipping, relanding, landing, unloading or carrying of the goods from the ship or aircraft without such authority, payment or repayment shall each be guilty of an offence under this section.

(2) The Commissioners may impose such conditions as they see fit with respect to any goods loaded or retained as mentioned in subsection (1) above which are permitted to be unloaded in the United Kingdom.

(3) If any person contravenes or fails to comply with, or is concerned in any contravention of or failure to comply with, any condition imposed under subsection (2) above he shall be guilty of an offence under this section.

(4) Where any goods loaded or retained as mentioned in subsection (1) above or brought to a customs and excise station for exportation by land are—

(a) goods from warehouse, other than goods which have been kept, without being warehoused, in a warehouse by virtue of section 92(4) below;

(b) transit goods;

(c) other goods chargeable with a duty which has not been paid;

(d) drawback goods,

then if any container in which the goods are held is without the authority of the proper officer opened, or any mark, letter or device on any such container or on any lot of the goods is without that authority cancelled, obliterated or altered, every person concerned in the opening, cancellation, obliteration or alteration shall be guilty of an offence under this section.

(5) Any goods in respect of which an offence under this section is committed shall be liable to forfeiture and any person guilty of an offence under this section shall be liable on summary conviction to a penalty of three times the value of the goods or level 3 on the standard scale, whichever is the greater.

(2) Allocation

19–22   This offence is triable summarily.

(3) Elements of the offence

19–23   The prosecution must prove that:
— the goods are intended for export;
— the goods have been loaded on a vessel or aircraft;
— the goods have been unloaded without authorisation; or
— the duty has not been paid.

(4) Sentence

19–24   The maximum penalty is forfeiture of goods and a fine of three times the value of the goods or a fine not exceeding level three, *i.e.* £1000, whichever is the greater.

C. Illegal Exportation

(1) Definition

Customs and Excise Management Act 1979, s.68

Offences in relation to exportation of prohibited or restricted goods
    68.—(1) If any goods are—   **19–25**
    (a) exported or shipped as stores; or
    (b) brought to any place in the United Kingdom for the purpose of being exported
        or shipped as stores,
and the exportation or shipment is or would be contrary to any prohibition or restriction for the time being in force with respect to those goods under or by virtue of any enactment, the goods shall be liable to forfeiture and the exporter or intending exporter of the goods and any agent of his concerned in the exportation or shipment or intended exportation or shipment shall each be liable on summary conviction to a penalty of three times the value of the goods or level 3 on the standard scale, whichever is the greater.

    (2) Any person knowingly concerned in the exportation or shipment as stores, or in the attempted exportation or shipment as stores, of any goods with intent to evade any such prohibition or restriction as is mentioned in subsection (1) above shall be guilty of an offence under this subsection and may be detained.

    (3) Subject to subsection (4) or (4A)below, a person guilty of an offence under subsection (2) above shall be liable—
    (a) on summary conviction, to a penalty of the prescribed sum or of three times the
        value of the goods, whichever is the greater, or to imprisonment for a term not
        exceeding 6 months, or to both; or
    (b) on conviction on indictment, to a penalty of any amount, or to imprisonment for
        a term not exceeding 7 years, or to both.

    (4) In the case of an offence under subsection (2) above in connection with a prohibition or restriction on exportation having effect by virtue of section 3 of the *Misuse of Drugs Act* 1971, subsection (3) above shall have effect subject to the modifications specified in Schedule 1 to this Act.

    (4A) In the case of an offence under subsection (2) above in connection with the prohibition contained in section 21 of the *Forgery and Counterfeiting Act* 1981, subsection (3)(b) above shall have effect as if for the words "2 years" there were substituted the words "10 years".

    (5) If by virtue of any such restriction as is mentioned in subsection (1) above any goods may be exported only when consigned to a particular place or person and any goods so consigned are delivered to some other place or person, the ship, aircraft or vehicle in which they were exported shall be liable to forfeiture unless it is proved to the satisfaction of the Commissioners that both the owner of the ship, aircraft or vehicle and the master of the ship, commander of the aircraft or person in charge of the vehicle—
    (a) took all reasonable steps to secure that the goods were delivered to the particular
        place to which or person to whom they were consigned; and
    (b) did not connive at or, except under duress, consent to the delivery of the goods
        to that other place or person.

    (6) In any case where a person would, apart from this subsection, be guilty of—
    (a) an offence under subsection (1) or (2) above; and
    (b) a corresponding offence under the enactment or instrument imposing the prohi-
        bition or restriction in question, being an offence for which a fine or other penalty
        is expressly provided by that enactment or other instrument,
he shall not be guilty of the offence mentioned in paragraph (a) of this subsection.

(2) Allocation

This offence is triable either way.   **19–26**

(3) Elements of the offence

The prosecution must prove: **19–27**
   — the goods are prohibited from being exported;

927

— the goods have either been brought to a place to be exported or have been exported; or

— the defendant knew of the plan to export the goods and intended to evade the prohibition.

There is a statutory defence. In *Garrett v. Arthur Churchill (Glass) Ltd* [1970] 1 Q.B. 92, it was said that the question whether a defendant was knowingly concerned in the exportation of goods with intent to evade the prohibition should be treated as one question. In *R. v. Uxbridge Justices, ex p. Sofaer* (1987) 85 Cr.App.R. 367, it was held that destruction of the goods will not necessarily prejudice the defendant or breach natural justice where secondary evidence in the form of photographs can be put before the court.

(4) Sentence

19–28   The maximum penalty is a fine of £5000, or three times the value of the goods, whichever is the greater, or imprisonment for a term not exceeding six months or both.

The enhanced penalties provided for drug exportation are the same as those provided under section 67, and are provided by Schedule 1 to the Act and subsections (4) and (4A) of section 68. When the *Criminal Justice Act* 2003 is in force the maximum custodial sentence will be 12 months' imprisonment: sections 154 and 282. Custodial sentences of less than 12 months will consist of a custody plus order (see *post*, Ch.23).

D. Control of Persons Entering or Leaving the UK

(1) Definition

Customs and Excise Management Act 1979, s.78

Customs and excise control of persons entering or leaving the United Kingdom

19–29   **78.**—(1) Any person entering the United Kingdom shall, at such place and in such manner as the Commissioners may direct, declare any thing contained in his baggage or carried with him which—

(a) he has obtained outside the United Kingdom; or

(b) being dutiable goods or chargeable goods, he has obtained in the United Kingdom without payment of duty or tax,

and in respect of which he is not entitled to exemption from duty and tax by virtue of any order under section 13 of the *Customs and Excise Duties (General Reliefs) Act* 1979 (personal reliefs).

In this subsection "chargeable goods" means goods on the importation of which value added tax is chargeable or goods obtained in the United Kingdom before 1st April 1973 which are chargeable goods within the meaning of the *Purchase Tax Act* 1963; and "tax" means value added tax or purchase tax.

(1A) Subsection (1) above does not apply to a person entering the United Kingdom from the Isle of Man as respects anything obtained by him in the Island unless it is chargeable there with duty or value added tax and he has obtained it without payment of the duty or tax.

(1B) Subsection (1) above does not apply to a person entering the United Kingdom from another member State, except—

(a) where he arrives at a customs and excise airport in an aircraft in which he began his journey in a place outside the member States; or

(b) as respects such of his baggage as—

(i)   is carried in the hold of the aircraft in which he arrives at a customs and excise airport, and

(ii) notwithstanding that it was transferred on one or more occasions from aircraft to aircraft at an airport in a member State, began its journey by air from a place outside the member States.

(2) Any person entering or leaving the United Kingdom shall answer such questions as the proper officer may put to him with respect to his baggage and any thing contained

therein or carried with him, and shall, if required by the proper officer, produce that baggage and any such thing for examination at such place as the Commissioners may direct.

(2A) Subject to subsection (1A) above, where the journey of a person arriving by air in the United Kingdom is continued or resumed by air to a destination in the United Kingdom which is not the place where he is regarded for the purposes of this section as entering the United Kingdom, subsections (1) and (2) above shall apply in relation to that person on his arrival at that destination as they apply in relation to a person entering the United Kingdom.

(3) Any person failing to declare any thing or to produce any baggage or thing as required by this section shall be liable on summary conviction to a penalty of three times the value of the thing not declared or of the baggage or thing not produced, as the case may be, or level 3 on the standard scale, whichever is the greater.

(4) Any thing chargeable with any duty or tax which is found concealed, or is not declared, and any thing which is being taken into or out of the United Kingdom contrary to any prohibition or restriction for the time being in force with respect thereto under or by virtue of any enactment, shall be liable to forfeiture.

[This section is printed as amended by the *Isle of Man Act* 1979, s.13, Sched. 1; the *CJA* 1982, ss.38, 46; the *Finance (No.2) Act* 1992, s.5; and the *Customs and Excise (Single Market etc.) Regulations* 1992 (S.I. 1992 No. 3095), reg.3(10).]

(2) Allocation

This offence is triable summarily: s.78(3).   **19–30**

(3) Elements of the offence

The prosecution must prove: **19–31**
  — the goods are dutiable;
  — they were bought outside the UK; or
  — they were not declared or produced.

It is an absolute offence: *R. v. Customs and Excise Commissioners, ex p. Claus* (1988) 86 Cr.App.R. 189. It applies only to persons entering or leaving the United Kingdom, and no reasonable grounds to suspect that the person entering or leaving is carrying a prohibited or restricted article or a dutiable article on which duty has not been paid need exist. This distinction is however, qualified by the *Finance Act (No.2)* 1992, s.4. A thing carried with him may be the shoes that he wears: *Lucien* [1995] Crim.L.R. 807, CA. The mere fact that a person comes to an airport to meet or collect someone in whose bags drugs are identified does not constitute reasonable objective grounds to suspect involvement in drug smuggling: *Perpont* [2004] EWCA Crim 2562.

(4) Sentence

The maximum penalty is a fine of three times the value of the goods or a fine not **19–32** exceeding level three, *i.e.* £1000, whichever is greater.

Finance Act 1992, s.4

Enforcement powers

4.—(1) Except in a case falling within subsection (2) below, the powers to which this section **19–33** applies shall not be exercisable in relation to any person or thing entering or leaving the United Kingdom so as to prevent, restrict or delay the movement of that person or thing between different member States.

(2) The cases in which a power to which this section applies may be exercised as mentioned in subsection (1) above are those where it appears to the person on whom the power is conferred that there are reasonable grounds for believing that the movement in question is not in fact between different member States or that it is necessary to exercise the power for purposes connected with—

  (a) securing the collection of any Community customs duty or giving effect to any Community legislation relating to any such duty;

Part III

(b) the enforcement of any prohibition or restriction for the time being in force by virtue of any Community legislation with respect to the movement of goods into or out of the member States; or

(c) the enforcement of any prohibition or restriction for the time being in force by virtue of any enactment with respect to the importation or exportation of goods into or out of the United Kingdom.

(3) Subject to subsection (4) below, this section applies to any power which is conferred on the Commissioners of Customs and Excise or any officer or constable under any of the following provisions of the *Customs and Excise Management Act* 1979, that is to say—

(a) section 21 (control of movement of aircraft into and out of the United Kingdom);

(b) section 26(power to regulate movement by land into and out of Northern Ireland);

(c) section 27 (officers' powers of boarding);

(d) section 28 (officers' powers of access);

(e) section 29 (officers' powers to detain ships);

(f) section 34 (power to prevent flight of aircraft);

(g) section 78 (questions as to baggage of person entering or leaving the United Kingdom);

(h) section 164 (powers of search).

(4) The Treasury may by order made by statutory instrument add any power conferred by any enactment contained in the customs and excise Acts to the powers to which this section applies; and a statutory instrument containing an order under this subsection shall be subject to annulment in pursuance of a resolution of either House of Parliament.

(5) In this section—

"Community customs duty" includes any agricultural levy of the Economic Community; and

"the customs and excise Acts" and "goods" have the same meanings as in the *Customs and Excise Management Act* 1979;

and for the purposes of this section a power shall be taken to be exercised otherwise than in relation to a person or thing entering or leaving the United Kingdom in any case where the power is exercisable irrespective of whether the person or thing in question is entering or leaving the United Kingdom.

(6) This section shall come into force on 1st January 1993.

19–34   Section 78 does not provide a basis for permitting customs officers to conduct rub-down, strip or intimate searches. This power is only exercisable by virtue of section 164 of the 1979 Act: *Lucien, ante.*

19–35   The *Channel Tunnel (Customs and Excise) Order* 1990 (S.I. 1990 No. 2167), Sched., para. 17B (inserted by the *Channel Tunnel (International Arrangements) Order* 1993 (S.I. 1993 No. 1813) Sched. 5, para. 27) as amended by the *Channel Tunnel (Miscellaneous Provisions) Order* 1994 (S.I. 1994 No. 1405) provides that for the purposes of section 78 of the 1979 Act:

(a) a person intending to travel to the United Kingdom through the tunnel who has entered a control zone in France or Belgium shall be treated as being a person entering the United Kingdom,

(b) a person who has travelled from the United Kingdom through the tunnel and is in such a control zone shall be treated as still being a person leaving the United Kingdom, and

(c) concealment shall be taken to include concealment in such a control zone.

E. Smuggling

(1) Definition

Customs and Excise Management Act 1979, s.85(1)

Penalty for interfering with revenue vessels, etc.

19–36   85.—(1) Any person who save for just and sufficient cause interferes in any way with any ship, aircraft, vehicle, buoy, anchor, chain, rope or mark which is being used for the purposes of any functions of the Commissioners under Parts III to VII of this Act shall be liable on summary conviction to a penalty of level 1 on the standard scale.

(2) Allocation

This offence is triable summarily.   **19–37**

(3) Elements of the offence

The prosecution must prove that the defendant: **19–38**
— interfered with a customs vessel/vehicle/aircraft *etc.*; and
— had no just cause.

(4) Sentence

The maximum penalty is a level one fine, *i.e.* £200.   **19–39**

F. Untrue Declarations

(1) Definition

Customs and Excise Management Act 1979, s.167

Untrue declarations, etc.
   167.—(1) If any person either knowingly or recklessly—   **19–40**
   (a) makes or signs, or causes to be made or signed, or delivers or causes to be delivered to the Commissioners or an officer, any declaration, notice, certificate or other document whatsoever; or
   (b) makes any statement in answer to any question put to him by an officer which he is required by or under any enactment to answer,
being a document or statement produced or made for any purpose of any assigned matter, which is untrue in any material particular, he shall be guilty of an offence under this subsection and may be detained; and any goods in relation to which the document or statement was made shall be liable to forfeiture.

   (2) Without prejudice to subsection (4) below, a person who commits an offence under subsection (1) above shall be liable—
   (a) on summary conviction, to a penalty of the prescribed sum, or to imprisonment for a term not exceeding 6 months, or to both; or
   (b) on conviction on indictment, to penalty of any amount, or to imprisonment for a term not exceeding 2 years, or to both.

   (3) If any person—
   (a) makes or signs, or causes to be made or signed, or delivers or causes to be delivered to the Commissioners or an officer, any declaration, notice, certificate or other document whatsoever; or
   (b) makes any statement in answer to any question put to him by an officer which he is required by or under any enactment to answer.
being a document or statement produced or made for any purpose of any assigned matter, which is untrue in any material particular, then, without prejudice to subsection (4) below, he shall be liable on summary conviction to a penalty of level 4 on the standard scale.

   (4) Where by reason of any such document or statement as is mentioned in subsection (1) or (3) above the full amount of any duty payable is not paid or any overpayment is made in respect of any drawback, allowance, rebate or repayment of duty, the amount of the duty unpaid or of the overpayment shall be recoverable as a debt due to the Crown or may be summarily recovered as a civil debt.

   (5) An amount of excise duty, or the amount of an overpayment in respect of any drawback, allowance, rebate or repayment of any excise duty, shall not be recoverable as mentioned in subsection (4) above unless the Commissioners have assessed the amount of the duty or of the overpayment as being excise duty due from the person mentioned in subsection (1) or (3) above and notified him or his representative accordingly.

[Subsections (1)–(3) are printed as amended by the *CJA* 1982, ss.38 and 46; and *PACE* 1984, s.114(1). Subsection (5) was inserted by the *Finance Act* 1997, s.50 and Sched. 6, para. 5.]

(2) Allocation

19–41   This offence is triable either way.

(3) Elements of the offence

19–42   The prosecution must prove that the defendant:
— made a certificate or statement which was untrue; or
— knew or was reckless as to whether it was untrue.

(4) Sentence

19–43   The maximum penalty is six months' imprisonment and/or a fine not exceeding £5000. The duty may also be reclaimed. When the *Criminal Justice Act* 2003 is in force the maximum custodial sentence will be 12 months' imprisonment: sections 154 and 282. Custodial sentences of less than 12 months will consist of a custody plus order (see *post*, Ch.23).

G. COUNTERFEITING DOCUMENTS

(1) Definition

Customs and Excise Management Act 1979, s.168

Counterfeiting documents, etc.
19–44   **168.**—(1) If any person—
(a) counterfeits or falsifies any document which is required by or under any enactment relating to an assigned matter or which is used in the transaction of any business relating to an assigned matter; or
(b) knowingly accepts, receives or uses any such document so counterfeited or falsified; or
(c) alters any such document after it is officially issued; or
(d) counterfeits any seal, signature, initials or other mark of, or used by, any officer for the verification of such a document or for the security of goods or for any other purpose relating to an assigned matter,
he shall be guilty of an offence under this section and may be detained.
(2) A person guilty of an offence under this section shall be liable—
(a) on summary conviction, to a penalty of the prescribed sum, or to imprisonment for a term not exceeding 6 months, or to both; or
(b) on conviction on indictment, to a penalty of any amount, or to imprisonment for a term not exceeding 2 years, or to both.

[This section is printed as amended by *PACE* 1984, s.114(1).]

(2) Allocation

19–45   This offence is triable either way: s.168(2).

(3) Elements of the offence

19–46   The prosecution must prove that the defendant either:
— forged or falsified a document;
— accepted or used such a document;
— altered an official document; or
— forged a seal etc.

(4) Sentence

When tried summarily, the maximum penalty is six months' imprisonment, a fine **19–47** not exceeding the prescribed sum, or both: section 168(2)(b). When the *Criminal Justice Act* 2003 is in force the maximum custodial sentence will be 12 months' imprisonment: sections 154 and 282. Custodial sentences of less than 12 months will consist of a custody plus order (see *post*, Ch.23).

H. FRAUDULENT EVASION OF DUTY

(1) Definition

Customs and Excise Management Act 1979, s.170

Penalty for fraudulent evasion of duty, etc.

170.—(1) Without prejudice to any other provision of the Customs and Excise Acts 1979, if **19–48** any person—

    (a) knowingly acquires possession of any of the following goods, that is to say—
        (i) goods which have been unlawfully removed from a warehouse or Queen's warehouse;
        (ii) goods which are chargeable with a duty which has not been paid;
        (iii) goods with respect to the importation or exportation of which any prohibition or restriction is for the time being in force under or by virtue of any enactment; or
    (b) is in any way knowingly concerned in carrying, removing, depositing, harbouring, keeping or concealing or in any manner dealing with any such goods,

and does so with intent to defraud Her Majesty of any duty payable on the goods or to evade any such prohibition or restriction with respect to the goods he shall be guilty of an offence under this section and may be detained.

    (2) Without prejudice to any other provision of the Customs and Excise Acts 1979, if any person is, in relation to any goods, in any way knowingly concerned in any fraudulent evasion or attempt at evasion—

    (a) of any duty chargeable on the goods;
    (b) of any prohibition or restriction for the time being in force with respect to the goods under or by virtue of any enactment; or
    (c) of any provision of the Customs and Excise Acts 1979 applicable to the goods,

he shall be guilty of an offence under this section and may be detained.

    (3) Subject to subsection (4), (4A) or (4B) below, a person guilty of an offence under this section shall be liable—

    (a) on summary conviction, to a penalty of the prescribed sum or of three times the value of the goods, whichever is the greater, or to imprisonment for a term not exceeding 6 months, or to both; or
    (b) on conviction on indictment, to a penalty of any amount, or to imprisonment for a term not exceeding 7 years, or to both.

    (4) In the case of an offence under this section in connection with prohibition or restriction on importation or exportation having effect by virtue of section 3 of the *Misuse of Drugs Act* 1971, subsection (3) above shall have effect subject to the modifications specified in Schedule 1 to this Act.

    (4A) In the case of an offence under this section in connection with the prohibitions contained in sections 20 and 21 of the *Forgery and Counterfeiting Act* 1981, subsection (3)(b) above shall have effect as if for the words "2 years" there were substituted the words "10 years".

    (4B) In the case of an offence under subsection (1) or (2) above in connection with the prohibition contained in regulation 2 of the *Import of Seal Skins Regulations* 1996, subsection (3) above shall have effect as if—

    (a) for paragraph (a) there were substituted the following—

    "(a) on summary conviction, to a fine not exceeding the statutory maximum or to imprisonment for a term not exceeding three months, or to both"

; and

933

(b) in paragraph (b) for the words '7 years' there were substituted the words '2 years'.

(5) In any case where a person would, apart from this subsection, be guilty of—

(a) an offence under this section in connection with a prohibition or restriction; and

(b) a corresponding offence under the enactment or other instrument imposing the prohibition or restriction, being an offence for which a fine or other penalty is expressly provided by that enactment or other instrument,

he shall not be guilty of the offence mentioned in paragraph (a) of this subsection.

(6) Where any person is guilty of an offence under this section, the goods in respect of which the offence was committed shall be liable to forfeiture.

[This section is printed as amended by the *Forgery and Counterfeiting Act* 1981, s.23(3) (insertion of subs.(4A); the *PACE Act* 1984, s.144(1); the *Finance Act* 1988, s.12(1)(a) (substitution of "7 years" for "2 years" in subs.3(b))); the *Finance (No.2) Act* 1992, s.3, Sched. 2, para. 7; and the *Import of Seal Skins Regulations* 1996 (S.I. 1996 No. 2686).]

(2) Allocation

19–49 This offence is triable either way.

(3) Elements of the offence

19–50 The prosecution must prove:

— the goods fall within the categories listed in section 170(1)(a);

— possession or knowledge of the removal, keeping or hiding of goods subject to a prohibition or restriction; or

— an intention not to pay the duty or to evade a prohibition or restriction.

The prosecution must prove that there has been an importation and must establish a link between the offence and the prohibited importation: *Watts and Stack* [1980] Crim.L.R. 38. Further, the prosecution must prove that the defendant knows that the goods are subject to a prohibition or restriction and that the operation he is concerned with is an operation designed to get around that prohibition or restriction but it does not have to prove that the defendant knows the precise category of goods involved: *Hussain* [1969] 2 Q.B. 567; *Shivpuri* [1987] A.C. 1; *Forbes* [2001] 4 All E.R. 97. In *Taaffe* [1984] A.C. 539 it was held that the accused was to be judged on the facts as he believed them to be; see also *Ellis* [1987] Crim.L.R. 44. In *Cohen* [1951] 1 K.B. 505, it was held that possession raises a presumption that goods are knowingly in the defendant's possession.

Recklessness is insufficient: *Panayi (No.2) and Karte* [1989] 1 W.L.R. 187.

Trans-shipment within Heathrow airport customs area from one aircraft coming from one country to another aircraft going to another country falls within the section: *Smith* [1973] 2 All E.R. 1161. Steps taken abroad leading to fraudulent evasion in this country can lead to a charge in this country: *Wall* [1974] 2 All E.R. 245. A person prepared to look after a parcel sent from abroad for a friend, knowing that the parcel was likely to contain drugs having been promised some for himself, can be charged with fraudulent evasion: *Att.-Gen.'s Reference (No. 1 of 1998)* (1999) 163 J.P. 390. If an undercover customs officer undertook the importation the organiser could still be convicted (in this case of an attempt): *Latif* [1996] 1 All E.R. 353. The offence is a continuing one: *Green* [1975] 3 All E.R. 1011; *Neal* 77 Cr.App.R. 283. In the latter case the provision of a barn for the concealment of goods was sufficient evidence of being "knowingly concerned". The offence may be committed at any time after the actual importation and at any place: *Ardalan* 56 Cr.App.R. It is no defence that the defendant has acted fraudulently only after the goods have been imported innocently: *Coughlan* [1997] 8 *Archbold News* 2, CA; see also *Ciaparra* 87 Cr.App.R 316, *Mitchell* [1992] Crim.L.R. 594 and *Williams* 55 Cr.App.R. 275. The burden of proof is on the defendant to show that the duty has been paid: s.154.

(4) Sentence

The maximum sentence is a fine of £5000 or three times the value of the goods **19–51** concerned, whichever is the greater, and/or imprisonment for a term not exceeding six months. See § 19–31, *ante*.

The *Magistrates' Court Sentencing Guidelines* (2004) state:

> Aggravating factors of the offence include being an organiser, more than one journey, commercial operation, sophisticated operation, imports two or more dutiable goods, offence committed on bail, relevant previous convictions and any failures to respond to previous sentences.
>
> Mitigating factors of the offence include supply to a restricted group, small quantity of goods.
>
> **Guideline**: Is it so serious that only custody is appropriate? Are the court's sentencing powers appropriate?

In *Dosanjh* [1999] 1 Cr.App.R. 371, the Court of Appeal laid down guidelines for **19–52** cases of evading import duty. Emphasising the need for deterrent sentences in this context, the Court said that cases involving less than £10,000 will frequently be dealt with by the magistrates' court. When the amount evaded is thousands of pounds, custody will generally be called for and on a plea of guilty, sentences of up to six months will generally be appropriate.

This guidance was modified in *Czyzewski* [2003] EWCA Crim 2139 in relation to duty evasion on alcohol and tobacco following proposals from the Sentencing Advisory Panel. Following a trial, for a defendant with no previous convictions and disregarding any personal mitigation, the following starting points are appropriate: (i) where the duty evaded is less than £1,000 and the level of personal profit is small, a moderate fine. If there is particularly strong mitigation and provided there has been no earlier warning, a conditional discharge may be appropriate; (ii) where the duty evaded by a first time offender is not more than £10,000 (approx. 65,000 cigarettes) or the defendant's offending is at a low level, either within an organisation or persistently as an individual, a community sentence, or curfew order enforced by tagging, or higher level of fine. The custody threshold is likely to be passed if any of the aggravating factors below are present; (iii) where the duty evaded is between £10,000 and £100,000, whether the defendant is operating individually or at a low level within an organisation, up to nine months, custody. Some of these cases can appropriately be dealt with by magistrates but others, particularly if marked by any of the aggravating features, should be dealt with by the Crown Court; and (iv) when the duty evaded is in excess of £100,000, the length of the custodial sentence will be determined principally by the degree of professionalism of the defendant and the presence or absence of other aggravating factors. Subject to this, the duty evaded will indicate starting points as follows: (i) £100,000–£500,000, nine months to three years; (ii) £500,000–£1 million, three to five years; (iii) in excess of £1 million five to seven years.

The aggravating features mentioned are if a defendant: (i) played an organisational role; (ii) made repeated importations, particularly in the face of a warning from the authorities; (iii) was a professional smuggler; (iv) used a legitimate business as a front; (v) abused a position of privilege; (vi) used children or vulnerable adults; (vii) dealt in goods with an additional health risk because of possible contamination; or (viii) disposed of goods to under-aged purchasers.

I. TAKING STEPS TO EVADE EXCISE DUTY

(1) Definition

Customs and Excise Management Act 1979, s.170B

Offence of taking preparatory steps for evasion of excise duty
170B. Offence of taking preparatory steps for evasion of excise duty.   **19–53**
(1) If any person is knowingly concerned in the taking of any steps with a view to the

fraudulent evasion, whether by himself or another, of any duty of excise on any goods, he shall be liable—

    (a) on summary conviction, to a penalty of the prescribed sum or of three times the amount of the duty, whichever is the greater, or to imprisonment for a term not exceeding six months or to both; and

    (b) on conviction on indictment, to a penalty of any amount or to imprisonment for a term not exceeding seven years or to both.

(2) Where any person is guilty of an offence under this section, the goods in respect of which the offence was committed shall be liable to forfeiture.

[This section was inserted by the *Finance (No.2) Act* 1992, s.3 and Sched. 2, para. 8.]

(2) Allocation

19–54   This offence is triable either way: section 170B(1).

(3) Elements of the offence

19–55   The prosecution must prove that:

    — steps have been taken to evade duty; and

    — the defendant knew what he was doing.

Under legislation relating to value added tax, taking steps has been held to include omissions: *McCarthy* [1981] S.T.C. 298, CA.

(4) Sentence

19–56   The maximum sentence is imprisonment for a term not exceeding six months or a £5000 fine or three times the value of the goods, or both. When the *Criminal Justice Act* 2003 is in force the maximum custodial sentence will be 12 months' imprisonment: sections 154 and 282. Custodial sentences of less than 12 months will consist of a custody plus order (see *post*, Ch.23).

Chapter 20

REGULATORY OFFENCES

937

I. AEROPLANES AND AIRPORTS

A. OFFENCES IN RELATION TO CERTAIN DANGEROUS ARTICLES

(1) Definition

Aviation Security Act 1982, s.4

Offences in relation to certain dangerous articles

20–1   **4.**—(1) It shall be an offence for any person without lawful authority or reasonable excuse (the proof of which shall lie on him) to have with him—

    (a) in any aircraft registered in the United Kingdom, whether at a time when the aircraft is in the United Kingdom or not, or

    (b) in any other aircraft at a time when it is in, or in flight over, the United Kingdom, or

    (c) in any part of an aerodrome in the United Kingdom, or

    (d) in any air navigation installation in the United Kingdom which does not form part of an aerodrome,

any article to which this section applies.

    (2) This section applies to the following articles, that is to say—

    (a) any firearm, or any article having the appearance of being a firearm, whether capable of being discharged or not;

    (b) any explosive, any article manufactured or adapted (whether in the form of a bomb, grenade or otherwise) so as to have the appearance of being an explosive, whether it is capable of producing a practical effect by explosion or not, or any article marked or labelled so as to indicate that it is or contains an explosive; and

    (c) any article (not falling within either of the preceding paragraphs) made or adapted for use for causing injury to or incapacitating a person or for destroying or damaging property, or intended by the person having it with him for such use, whether by him or by any other person.

    (3) For the purposes of this section a person who is for the time being in an aircraft, or in part of an aerodrome, shall be treated as having with him in the aircraft, or in that part of the aerodrome, as the case may be, an article to which this section applies if—

    (a) where he is in an aircraft, the article, or an article in which it is contained, is in the aircraft and has been caused (whether by him or by any other person) to be brought there as being, or as forming part of, his baggage on a flight in the aircraft or has been caused by him to be brought there as being, or as forming part of, any other property to be carried on such a flight, or

    (b) where he is in part of an aerodrome (otherwise than in an aircraft), the article, or an article in which it is contained, is in that or any other part of the aerodrome and has been caused (whether by him or by any other person) to be brought into the aerodrome as being, or as forming part of, his baggage on a flight from that aerodrome or has been caused by him to be brought there as being, or as forming part of, any other property to be carried on such a flight on which he is also to be carried.

notwithstanding that the circumstances may be such that (apart from this subsection) he would not be regarded as having the article with him in the aircraft or in a part of the aerodrome, as the case may be.

    (4) A person guilty of an offence under this section shall be liable—

    (a) on summary conviction, to a fine not exceeding the statutory maximum or to imprisonment for a term not exceeding three months or to both;

    (b) on conviction on indictment, to a fine or to imprisonment for a term not exceed-
ing five years or to both.

    (5) Nothing in subsection (3) above shall be construed as limiting the circumstances in
which a person would, apart from that subsection, be regarded as having an article with
him as mentioned in subsection (1) above.

(2) Allocation

This offence is triable either way: section (4).   **20–2**

(3) Sentence

When tried summarily, the maximum penalty for this offence is a fine not exceeding **20–3**
the statutory maximum, imprisonment for a term not exceeding three months or both.

Aviation Security Act 1982, s.8

Prosecution of offences and proceedings
    8.—(1) Proceedings for an offence under any of the preceding provisions of this Part of this **20–4**
Act (other than sections 4 and 7) shall not be instituted—

    (a) in England and Wales, except by, or with the consent of, the Attorney General;
and

    (b) in Northern Ireland, except by, or with the consent of, the Attorney General for
Northern Ireland.

    (2) As respects Scotland, for the purpose of conferring on the sheriff jurisdiction to
entertain proceedings for an offence under or by virtue of section 2, 3 or 6(2)(b) or (c) of
this Act, any such offence shall, without prejudice to any jurisdiction exercisable apart from
this subsection, be deemed to have been committed in any place in Scotland where the offender may for the time being be.

B. AIRPORT BYELAWS

Airports Act 1986, ss.63, 64

Airport byelaws
    63.—(1) Where an airport is either—   **20–5**

    (a) designated for the purposes of this section by an order made by the Secretary of
State, or

    (b) managed by the Secretary of State,
the airport operator (whether the Secretary of State or some other person) may make byelaws
for regulating the use and operation of the airport and the conduct of all persons while within
the airport.

    (2) Any such byelaws may, in particular, include byelaws—

    (a) for securing the safety of aircraft, vehicles and persons using the airport and
preventing danger to the public arising from the use and operation of the airport;

    (b) for controlling the operation of aircraft within, or directly above, the airport for
the purpose of limiting or mitigating the effect of noise, vibration and atmospheric
pollution caused by aircraft using the airport;

    (c) for preventing obstruction within the airport;

    (d) for regulating vehicular traffic anywhere within the airport, except on roads
within the airport to which the road traffic enactments apply, and in particular
(with that exception) for imposing speed limits on vehicles within the airport and
for restricting or regulating the parking of vehicles or their use for any purpose
or in any manner specified in the byelaws;

    (e) for prohibiting waiting by hackney carriages except at standings appointed by
such person as may be specified in the byelaws;

    (f) for prohibiting or restricting access to any part of the airport;

    (g) for preserving order within the airport and preventing damage to property
within it;

    (h) for regulating or restricting advertising within the airport;

Part III

(i) for requiring any person, if so requested by a constable or airport official, to leave the airport or any particular part of it, or to state his name and address and the purpose of his being within the airport;

(j) for securing the safe custody and redelivery of any property which, while not in proper custody, is found within the airport or in an aircraft within the airport, and in particular—

    (i) for requiring charges to be paid in respect of any such property before it is redelivered; and

    (ii) for authorising the disposal of any such property if it is not redelivered before the end of such period as may be specified in the byelaws;

(k) for restricting the area which is to be taken as constituting the airport for the purposes of the byelaws.

(3) In paragraph (d) of subsection (2) "the road traffic enactments" means the enactments (whether passed before or after this Act) relating to road traffic, including the lighting and parking of vehicles, and any order or other instrument having effect by virtue of any such enactment.

(4) In paragraph (i) of subsection (2) "airport official" means a person authorised by the airport operator; and any such official shall not exercise any power under a byelaw made by virtue of that paragraph without producing written evidence of his authority if required to do so.

(5) Byelaws made under this section by a person other than the Secretary of State shall not have effect until they are confirmed by the Secretary of State, and the provisions of Schedule 3 shall apply to any such byelaws.

(6) Before any byelaws are made by the Secretary of State under this section, he shall take such steps as appear to him to be appropriate for giving public notice of the proposed byelaws and for affording an opportunity for representations to be made with respect to them; and the Secretary of State shall have regard to any such representations and may then make the byelaws in the form proposed or in that form with such modifications as he thinks fit.

(7) Any byelaws made by the Secretary of State under this section shall be made by statutory instrument.

(8) Section 236(9) of the *Local Government Act* 1972 and section 202(13) of the *Local Government (Scotland) Act* 1973 (notice of byelaws made by one local authority to be given to another) and section 237 of the Act of 1972 and section 203 of the Act of 1973 (penalties) shall not apply to any byelaws made by a local authority under this section.

Byelaws: penalties and power to revoke in certain cases

20–6   **64.**—(1) Any person contravening any byelaws made under section 63 shall be liable on summary conviction to a fine not exceeding such amount as, subject to subsection (2) of this section, may be specified by the byelaws in relation to the contravention.

(2) The maximum fines that byelaws may specify by virtue of subsection (1) are fines of an amount at the fourth level on the standard scale or of a lower amount.

(3) Where any person other than the Secretary of State has made any byelaw in relation to any airport by virtue of section 63(2)(b), the Secretary of State may, after consulting that person, by order—

(a) revoke or vary that byelaw if the Secretary of State considers it appropriate to do so by reason of his having designated the airport for the purposes of section 78 of the 1982 Act (regulation of noise and vibration from aircraft); or

(b) revoke or vary that byelaw to the extent that it appears to the Secretary of State to be inconsistent with the safety of persons or vehicles using the airport, of aircraft or of the general public or to be inconsistent with any international obligation of the United Kingdom.

20–7   The following airports in England and Wales have been designated:

Biggin Hill, Birmingham, Blackpool, Bournemouth (Hurn), Bristol, Cardiff-Wales, Coventry, East Midlands, Exeter, Humberside, Leeds/Bradford, Liverpool, London-Gatwick, London-Heathrow, London-Stanstead, Luton, Manchester, Newcastle, Norwich, Southampton, Southend, Tees-side: *Airport Byelaws (Designation) Order* 1987, (S.I. 1987 No. 380) and Bainbridge, Carlisle, Gloucester/Cheltenham, Redhill and Swansea: *Airport Byelaws (Designation) (No. 2) Order* 1987 (S.I. 1987 No. 2246).

II. ANIMALS

A. ANIMAL WELFARE

The *Animal Welfare Act* 2006 consolidates and updates the law relating to the treat- **20–8**
ment of animals, other than those in the wild. The Act is designed to promote the
welfare of animals and duties of those responsible for animals and rights of protection
for animals are provided for.

Sections 1–3 define the categories of animal;

Sections 4–8 set out the offences of animal cruelty and animal fighting;

Sections 9–17 relate to the promotion of animal welfare supported by a system of
inspection, licensing and registration all governed by Codes of Practice;

Sections 18–21 give powers to remove animals in distress;

Sections 30–35 provide for powers of prosecution and penalties and orders on
conviction.

The Act is lengthy and detailed and the sections set out below are those most likely to
be referred to in the magistrates courts. These provisions came into force on April 6,
2007 under the *Animal Welfare Act (Commencement No. 1) Order* (S.I. 2007 No.
499).

(1) Definition

Animal Welfare Act 2006, s.4

Unnecessary suffering
    4.—(1) A person commits an offence if—   **20–9**
        (a) an act of his, or a failure of his to act, causes an animal to suffer,
        (b) he knew, or ought reasonably to have known, that the act, or failure to act, would
            have that effect or be likely to do so,
        (c) the animal is a protected animal, and
        (d) the suffering is unnecessary.
    (2) A person commits an offence if—
        (a) he is responsible for an animal,
        (b) an act, or failure to act, of another person causes the animal to suffer,
        (c) he permitted that to happen or failed to take such steps (whether by way of
            supervising the other person or otherwise) as were reasonable in all the circum-
            stances to prevent that happening, and
        (d) the suffering is unnecessary.
    (3) The considerations to which it is relevant to have regard when determining for the
purposes of this section whether suffering is unnecessary include—
        (a) whether the suffering could reasonably have been avoided or reduced;
        (b) whether the conduct which caused the suffering was in compliance with any rele-
            vant enactment or any relevant provisions of a licence or code of practice issued
            under an enactment;
        (c) whether the conduct which caused the suffering was for a legitimate purpose,
            such as—
            (i) the purpose of benefiting the animal, or
            (ii) the purpose of protecting a person, property or another animal;
        (d) whether the suffering was proportionate to the purpose of the conduct
            concerned;
        (e) whether the conduct concerned was in all the circumstances that of a reasonably
            competent and humane person.
    (4) Nothing in this section applies to the destruction of an animal in an appropriate and
humane manner.

Animal Welfare Act 2006, s.8

Fighting etc.
    8.—(1) A person commits an offence if he—   **20–10**

941

(a) causes an animal fight to take place, or attempts to do so;

(b) knowingly receives money for admission to an animal fight;

(c) knowingly publicises a proposed animal fight;

(d) provides information about an animal fight to another with the intention of enabling or encouraging attendance at the fight;

(e) makes or accepts a bet on the outcome of an animal fight or on the likelihood of anything occurring or not occurring in the course of an animal fight;

(f) takes part in an animal fight;

(g) has in his possession anything designed or adapted for use in connection with an animal fight with the intention of its being so used;

(h) keeps or trains an animal for use for in connection with an animal fight;

(i) keeps any premises for use for an animal fight.

(2) A person commits an offence if, without lawful authority or reasonable excuse, he is present at an animal fight.

[(3) *A person commits an offence if, without lawful authority or reasonable excuse, he—*

(a) *knowingly supplies a video recording of an animal fight,*

(b) *knowingly publishes a video recording of an animal fight,*

(c) *knowingly shows a video recording of an animal fight to another, or*

(d) *possesses a video recording of an animal fight, knowing it to be such a recording, with the intention of supplying it.*]

[(4) *Subsection (3) does not apply if the video recording is of an animal fight that took place—*

(a) *outside Great Britain, or*

(b) *before the commencement date.*]

[(5) *Subsection (3) does not apply—*

(a) *in the case of paragraph (a), to the supply of a video recording for inclusion in a programme service;*

(b) *in the case of paragraph (b) or (c), to the publication or showing of a video recording by means of its inclusion in a programme service;*

(c) *in the case of paragraph (d), by virtue of intention to supply for inclusion in a programme service.*]

[(6) *Provision extending the application of an offence under subsection (3), so far as relating to the provision of information society services, may be made under section 2(2) of the European Communities Act 1972 (c. 68) (powers to implement Community obligations by regulations) notwithstanding the limits imposed by paragraph 1(1)(d) of Schedule 2 to that Act on the penalties with which an offence may be punishable on summary conviction.*]

(7) In this section—

"animal fight" means an occasion on which a protected animal is placed with an animal, or with a human, for the purpose of fighting, wrestling or baiting;

"commencement date" means the date on which subsection (3) comes into force;

"information society services" has the meaning given in Article 2(a) of Directive 2000/31/EC of the European Parliament and of the Council of 8 June 2000 on certain legal aspects of information society services, in particular electronic commerce in the Internal Market (Directive on electronic commerce);

"programme service" has the same meaning as in the *Communications Act* 2003 (c. 21);

"video recording" means a recording, in any form, from which a moving image may by any means be reproduced and includes data stored on a computer disc or by other electronic means which is capable of conversion into a moving image.

(8) In this section—

(a) references to supplying or publishing a video recording are to supplying or publishing a video recording in any manner, including, in relation to a video recording in the form of data stored electronically, by means of transmitting such data;

(b) references to showing a video recording are to showing a moving image reproduced from a video recording by any means.

[The subsections printed in italics are not yet in force]

Animal Welfare Act 2006, s.9

Duty of person responsible for animal to ensure welfare

9.—(1) A person commits an offence if he does not take such steps as are reasonable in all the **20–11** circumstances to ensure that the needs of an animal for which he is responsible are met to the extent required by good practice.

(2) For the purposes of this Act, an animal's needs shall be taken to include—

    (a) its need for a suitable environment,

    (b) its need for a suitable diet,

    (c) its need to be able to exhibit normal behaviour patterns,

    (d) any need it has to be housed with, or apart from, other animals, and

    (e) its need to be protected from pain, suffering, injury and disease.

(3) The circumstances to which it is relevant to have regard when applying subsection (1) include, in particular—

    (a) any lawful purpose for which the animal is kept, and

    (b) any lawful activity undertaken in relation to the animal.

(4) Nothing in this section applies to the destruction of an animal in an appropriate and humane manner.

(2) Allocation

The offences are triable summarily: section 35.   **20–12**

The offences may be prosecuted by the local authority as well as the CPS; s.30. The time limit for prosecutions is three years from the date of commission of the offence and six months from the time when evidence sufficient to justify proceedings comes to the prosecutor's knowledge. Section 31.

(3) Elements of the offence

Animal Welfare Act 2006, s.1

Animals to which the Act applies

1.—(1) In this Act, except subsections (4) and (5), "animal" means a vertebrate other than **20–13** man.

(2) Nothing in this Act applies to an animal while it is in its foetal or embryonic form.

(3) The appropriate national authority may by regulations for all or any of the purposes of this Act—

    (a) extend the definition of "animal" so as to include invertebrates of any description;

    (b) make provision in lieu of subsection (2) as respects any invertebrates included in the definition of "animal";

    (c) amend subsection (2) to extend the application of this Act to an animal from such earlier stage of its development as may be specified in the regulations.

(4) The power under subsection (3)(a) or (c) may only be exercised if the appropriate national authority is satisfied, on the basis of scientific evidence, that animals of the kind concerned are capable of experiencing pain or suffering.

(5) In this section, "vertebrate" means any animal of the Sub-phylum Vertebrata of the Phylum Chordata and "invertebrate" means any animal not of that Sub-phylum.

Animal Welfare Act, s.2

"Protected animal"

2. An animal is a "protected animal" for the purposes of this Act if—   **20–14**

    (a) it is of a kind which is commonly domesticated in the British Islands,

    (b) it is under the control of man whether on a permanent or temporary basis, or

    (c) it is not living in a wild state.

Animal Welfare Act 2006, s.3

Responsibility for animals

3.—(1) In this Act, references to a person responsible for an animal are to a person responsible **20–15** for an animal whether on a permanent or temporary basis.

(2) In this Act, references to being responsible for an animal include being in charge of it.

(3) For the purposes of this Act, a person who owns an animal shall always be regarded as being a person who is responsible for it.

(4) For the purposes of this Act, a person shall be treated as responsible for any animal for which a person under the age of 16 years of whom he has actual care and control is responsible.

(4) Sentence

Animal Welfare Act 2006, s.32

Imprisonment or fine

20–16   **32.**—(1) A person guilty of an offence under any of sections 4, 5, 6(1) and (2), 7 and 8 shall be liable on summary conviction to—

(a) imprisonment for a term not exceeding 51 weeks, or

(b) a fine not exceeding £20,000,

or to both.

(2) A person guilty of an offence under section 9, 13(6) or 34(9) shall be liable on summary conviction to—

(a) imprisonment for a term not exceeding 51 weeks, or

(b) a fine not exceeding level 5 on the standard scale,

or to both.

(3) A person guilty of an offence under regulations under section 12 or 13 shall be liable on summary conviction to such penalty by way of imprisonment or fine as may be provided by regulations under that section.

(4) A person guilty of any other offence under this Act shall be liable on summary conviction to—

(a) imprisonment for a term not exceeding 51 weeks, or

(b) a fine not exceeding level 4 on the standard scale,

or to both.

(5) In relation to an offence committed before the commencement of section 281(5) of the *Criminal Justice Act* 2003 (c. 44), the reference in each of subsections (1)(a), (2)(a) and (4)(a) to 51 weeks is to be read as a reference to 6 months.

Animal Welfare Act 2006, s.33

Deprivation

20–17   **33.**—(1) If the person convicted of an offence under any of sections 4, 5, 6(1) and (2), 7, 8 and 9 is the owner of an animal in relation to which the offence was committed, the court by or before which he is convicted may, instead of or in addition to dealing with him in any other way, make an order depriving him of ownership of the animal and for its disposal.

(2) Where the owner of an animal is convicted of an offence under section 34(9) because ownership of the animal is in breach of a disqualification under section 34(2), the court by or before which he is convicted may, instead of or in addition to dealing with him in any other way, make an order depriving him of ownership of the animal and for its disposal.

(3) Where the animal in respect of which an order under subsection (1) or (2) is made has any dependent offspring, the order may include provision depriving the person to whom it relates of ownership of the offspring and for its disposal.

(4) Where a court makes an order under subsection (1) or (2), it may—

(a) appoint a person to carry out, or arrange for the carrying out of, the order;

(b) require any person who has possession of an animal to which the order applies to deliver it up to enable the order to be carried out;

(c) give directions with respect to the carrying out of the order;

(d) confer additional powers (including power to enter premises where an animal to which the order applies is being kept) for the purpose of, or in connection with, the carrying out of the order;

(e) order the offender to reimburse the expenses of carrying out the order.

(5) Directions under subsection (4)(c) may—

(a) specify the manner in which an animal is to be disposed of, or

(b) delegate the decision about the manner in which an animal is to be disposed of to a person appointed under subsection (4)(a).

(6) Where a court decides not to make an order under subsection (1) or (2) in relation to an offender, it shall—

(a) give its reasons for the decision in open court, and

(b) if it is a magistrates' court, cause them to be entered in the register of its proceedings.

(7) Subsection (6) does not apply where the court makes an order under section 34(1) in relation to the offender.

(8) In subsection (1), the reference to an animal in relation to which an offence was committed includes, in the case of an offence under section 8, an animal which took part in an animal fight in relation to which the offence was committed.

(9) In this section, references to disposing of an animal include destroying it.

Animal Welfare Act 2006, s.34

Disqualification

34.—(1) If a person is convicted of an offence to which this section applies, the court by or **20–18** before which he is convicted may, instead of or in addition to dealing with him in any other way, make an order disqualifying him under any one or more of subsections (2) to (4) for such period as it thinks fit.

(2) Disqualification under this subsection disqualifies a person—

(a) from owning animals,

(b) from keeping animals,

(c) from participating in the keeping of animals, and

(d) from being party to an arrangement under which he is entitled to control or influence the way in which animals are kept.

(3) Disqualification under this subsection disqualifies a person from dealing in animals.

(4) Disqualification under this subsection disqualifies a person—

(a) from transporting animals, and

(b) from arranging for the transport of animals.

(5) Disqualification under subsection (2), (3) or (4) may be imposed in relation to animals generally, or in relation to animals of one or more kinds.

(6) The court by which an order under subsection (1) is made may specify a period during which the offender may not make an application under section 43(1) for termination of the order.

(7) The court by which an order under subsection (1) is made may—

(a) suspend the operation of the order pending an appeal, or

(b) where it appears to the court that the offender owns or keeps an animal to which the order applies, suspend the operation of the order, and of any order made under section 35 in connection with the disqualification, for such period as it thinks necessary for enabling alternative arrangements to be made in respect of the animal.

(8) Where a court decides not to make an order under subsection (1) in relation to an offender, it shall—

(a) give its reasons for the decision in open court, and

(b) if it is a magistrates' court, cause them to be entered in the register of its proceedings.

(9) A person who breaches a disqualification imposed by an order under subsection (1) commits an offence.

(10) This section applies to an offence under any of sections 4, 5, 6(1) and (2), 7, 8, 9 and 13(6) and subsection (9).

B. DANGEROUS DOGS

(1) Legislation

Dogs Act 1871, s.2

Dangerous dogs may be destroyed

20–19   2. Any court of summary jurisdiction may take cognizance of a complaint that a dog is dangerous, and not kept under proper control, and if it appears to the court having cognizance of such complaint that such dog is dangerous, the court may make an order in a summary way directing the dog to be kept by the owner under proper control or destroyed

A complaint may be made by a police officer: *Smith v. Baker*, 125 J.P. 53.

20–20   The court has jurisdiction to hear a complaint under this section even if the conduct complained of occurred outside of the commission area. Jurisdiction is founded on the location of the animal at the time when the summons is applied for and the complaint relates to the dangerousness of the animal which should be kept under proper control no matter where it might be: *Shufflebottom v. Chief Constable of Greater Manchester* (2003) 167 J.P. 153.

The term "dangerous" is to be given its ordinary, every day meaning and the question of whether it is kept under 'proper control' is a question of fact for the court. The dog does not have to be dangerous only to human beings or livestock. The fact that it is dangerous to other dogs is sufficient: *Briscoe v. Shattock* (1998) 163 J.P. 201. But the fact that a dog killed two pet rabbits on one occasion was held not to make it dangerous because it was in the nature of dogs to hunt and kill other small animals: *Sansom v. Chief Constable of Kent* [1981] Crim.L.R. 617.

The court may order destruction of the animal and further powers are contained in section 1 of the *Dangerous Dogs Act* 1989, *post*.

Costs may be ordered under section 64 of the *Magistrates Courts Act* 1980.

Dangerous Dogs Act 1989, s.1

Additional powers of court on complaint about dangerous dog

20–21   1.—(1) Where a magistrates' court makes an order under section 2 of the *Dogs Act* 1871 directing a dog to be destroyed it may also—

(a) appoint a person to undertake its destruction and require any person having custody of the dog to deliver it up for that purpose; and

(b) if it thinks fit, make an order disqualifying the owner for having custody of a dog for such period as is specified in the order.

(2) An appeal shall lie to the Crown Court against any order under section 2 of that Act or under subsection (1) above; and, unless the owner of a dog which is ordered to be delivered up and destroyed gives notice to the court that made the order that he does not intend to appeal against it, the dog shall not be destroyed pursuant to the order—

(a) until the end of the period within which notice of appeal to the Crown Court against the order can be given; and

(b) if notice of appeal is given within that period, until the appeal is determined or withdrawn.

(3) Any person who fails to comply with an order under section 2 of the said Act of 1871 to keep a dog under proper control or to deliver a dog up for destruction as required by an order under subsection (1)(a) above is guilty of an offence and liable on summary conviction to a fine not exceeding level 3 on the standard scale and the court may, in addition, make an order disqualifying him for having custody of a dog for such period as is specified in the order.

(4) A person who is disqualified for having custody of a dog by virtue of an order made under subsection (1)(b) or (3) above may, at any time after the end of the period of one year beginning with the date of the order, apply to the court that made it (or any magistrates' court acting for the same petty sessions area as that court) for a direction terminating the disqualification.

(5) On an application under subsection (4) above the court may—

(a) having regard to the applicant's character, his conduct since the disqualification was imposed and any other circumstances of the case, grant or refuse the application; and

(b) order the applicant to pay all or any part of the costs of the application;

and where an application in respect of an order is refused no further application in respect of that order shall be entertained if made before the end of the period of one year beginning with the date of the refusal.

(6) Any person who has custody of a dog in contravention of an order made under subsection (1)(b) or (3) above is guilty of an offence and liable on summary conviction to a fine not exceeding level 5 on the standard scale.

(7) This section shall apply to Scotland subject to the following adaptations—

(a) in subsection (1) for the words "magistrates' court" there shall be substituted the words "court of summary jurisdiction";

(b) in subsection (2)—

(i) for the words "shall lie to the Crown Court" there shall be substituted the words "may be made to the High Court within a period of 7 days commencing with the date of the order";

(ii) for paragraph (a) there shall be substituted—

"(a) until the end of the said period of 7 days;and ";

(c) in subsection (4) the words "(or any magistrates' court acting for the same petty sessions area as that court)" shall be omitted.

(2) Definition

Dangerous Dogs Act 1991, s.1

Dogs bred for fighting

1.—(1) This section applies to—

(a) any dog of the type known as the pit bull terrier;

(b) any dog of the type known as the Japanese tosa; and

(c) any dog of any type designated for the purposes of this section by an order of the Secretary of State, being a type appearing to him to be bred for fighting or to have the characteristics of a type bred for that purpose.

(2) No person shall—

(a) breed, or breed from, a dog to which this section applies;

(b) sell or exchange such a dog or offer, advertise or expose such a dog for sale or exchange;

(c) make or offer to make a gift of such a dog or advertise or expose such a dog as a gift;

(d) allow such a dog of which he is the owner or of which he is for the time being in charge to be in a public place without being muzzled and kept on a lead; or

(e) abandon such a dog of which he is the owner or, being the owner or for the time being in charge of such a dog, allow it to stray.

(3) After such day as the Secretary of State may by order appoint for the purposes of this subsection no person shall have any dog to which this section applies in his possession or custody except—

(a) in pursuance of the power of seizure conferred by the subsequent provisions of this Act; or

(b) in accordance with an order for its destruction made under those provisions;

but the Secretary of State shall by order make a scheme for the payment to the owners of such dogs who arrange for them to be destroyed before that day of sums specified in or determined under the scheme in respect of those dogs and the cost of their destruction.

(4) Subsection (2)(b) and (c) above shall not make unlawful anything done with a view to the dog in question being removed from the United Kingdom before the day appointed under subsection (3) above.

(5) The Secretary of State may by order provide that the prohibition in subsection (3) above shall not apply in such cases and subject to compliance with such conditions as are

specified in the order and any such provision may take the form of a scheme of exemption containing such arrangements (including provision for the payment of charges or fees) as he thinks appropriate.

(6) A scheme under subsection (3) or (5) above may provide for specified functions under the scheme to be discharged by such persons or bodies as the Secretary of State thinks appropriate.

(7) Any person who contravenes this section is guilty of an offence and liable on summary conviction to imprisonment for a term not exceeding six months or a fine not exceeding level 5 on the standard scale or both except that a person who publishes an advertisement in contravention of subsection (2)(b) or (c)—

> (a) shall not on being convicted be liable to imprisonment if he shows that he published the advertisement to the order of someone else and did not himself devise it; and
>
> (b) shall not be convicted if, in addition, he shows that he did not know and had no reasonable cause to suspect that it related to a dog to which this section applies.

(8) An order under subsection (1)(c) above adding dogs of any type to those to which this section applies may provide that subsections (3) and (4) above shall apply in relation to those dogs with the substitution for the day appointed under subsection (3) of a later day specified in the order.

(9) The power to make orders under this section shall be exercisable by statutory instrument which, in the case of an order under subsection (1) or (5) or an order containing a scheme under subsection (3), shall be subject to annulment in pursuance of a resolution of either House of Parliament.

(3) Allocation

20–23   This offence is triable summarily.

(4) Elements of the offence

20–24   This section applies specifically to dogs bred for fighting. The appointed day referred to in section 1(3) was November 30, 1991 (S.I. 1991 No. 1742). The word "type" has wider and different meaning from the description 'breed'. It was held to include any dog which had a substantial amount or most of the physical characteristics of the breed of dog in question, *e.g.* a pitbull terrier: *Crown Court at Knightsbridge ex p. Dunne* [1993] 4 All E.R. 491. An offence is committed if the dog is in a car, when the car itself is in a public place: *Bates v. DPP* (1993) 157 J.P. 1004.

This is an absolute offence and it is no defence to a charge of allowing a dog to be off the lead and unmuzzled for the owner to say he was intoxicated at the time: *DPP v. Kellet* (1994) 158 J.P. 1138. Nor is it a defence for the owner to say that the dog was not muzzled or kept on a lead as a necessity to avoid serious harm to the dog itself: *Cichon v. DPP* [1994] Crim.L.R.

(5) Sentence

20–25   The sentence is a maximum of six months' imprisonment or a fine not exceeding level 5 or both. After commencement of the relevant provisions, the maximum custodial sentence in a magistrates' court will be 12 months' imprisonment: *Criminal Justice Act* 2003, ss.154 and 282. Custodial sentences of less than 12 months will consist of a custody plus order (see *post*, Ch.23).

The court also has power to make destruction and disqualification orders under sections 4 and 4A (see *post*).

(1) Definition

Dangerous Dogs Act 1991, s.3

Keeping dogs under proper control

20–26   **3.**—(1) If a dog is dangerously out of control in a public place—

(a) the owner; and

(b) if different, the person for the time being in charge of the dog,

is guilty of an offence, or, if the dog while so out of control injures any person, an aggravated offence, under this subsection.

(2) In proceedings for an offence under subsection (1) above against a person who is the owner of a dog but was not at the material time in charge of it, it shall be a defence for the accused to prove that the dog was at the material time in the charge of a person whom he reasonably believed to be a fit and proper person to be in charge of it.

(3) If the owner or, if different, the person for the time being in charge of a dog allows it to enter a place which is not a public place but where it is not permitted to be and while it is there—

(a) it injures any person; or

(b) there are grounds for reasonable apprehension that it will do so,

he is guilty of an offence, or, if the dog injures any person, an aggravated offence, under this subsection.

(4) A person guilty of an offence under subsection (1) or (3) above other than an aggravated offence is liable on summary conviction to imprisonment for a term not exceeding six months or a fine not exceeding level 5 on the standard scale or both; and a person guilty of an aggravated offence under either of those subsections is liable—

(a) on summary conviction, to imprisonment for a term not exceeding six months or a fine not exceeding the statutory maximum or both;

(b) on conviction on indictment, to imprisonment for a term not exceeding two years or a fine or both.

(5) It is hereby declared for the avoidance of doubt that an order under section 2 of the *Dogs Act* 1871 (order on complaint that dog is dangerous and not kept under proper control)—

(a) may be made whether or not the dog is shown to have injured any person; and

(b) may specify the measures to be taken for keeping the dog under proper control, whether by muzzling, keeping on a lead, excluding it from specified places or otherwise.

(6) If it appears to a court on a complaint under section 2 of the said Act of 1871 that the dog to which the complaint relates is a male and would be less dangerous if neutered the court may under that section make an order requiring it to be neutered.

(7) The reference in section 1(3) of the *Dangerous Dogs Act* 1989 (penalties) to failing to comply with an order under section 2 of the said Act of 1871 to keep a dog under proper control shall include a reference to failing to comply with any other order made under that section; but no order shall be made under that section by virtue of subsection (6) above where the matters complained of arose before the coming into force of that subsection.

(2) Allocation

This offence is triable summarily only unless it is an aggravated offence in which case **20–27** it is triable either way. An offence is aggravated under section 3(1) if, while the dog is out of control, it injures any person.

(3) Elements of the offence

This section applies to any kind of dog. A dog is defined as being dangerously out of **20–28** control "on any occasion on which there are grounds for reasonable apprehension that it will injure any person, whether or not it actually does so, but references to a dog injuring a person or there being grounds for reasonable apprehension that it will do so do not include references to any case in which the dog is being used for a lawful purpose by a constable or a person in the service of the Crown.": section 10(3) of the Act. This is an objective test.

A public place is "any street, road or other place, (whether or not enclosed) to which the public have or are permitted to have access whether for payment or otherwise and includes the common parts of a building containing two or more separate dwellings.": section 10(2) of the Act.

An offence may be committed in a public place if the dog is dangerously out of control. An offence may also be committed in a place which is not a public place and where the dog is not permitted to be but only if the dog injures any person or there is a reasonable apprehension that it will do so: section 3(3). This offence is aggravated if a person is injured.

(4) Defence

20–29   This is an absolute offence. It is no defence for the owner to say that they never realised that the dog would behave in a dangerous manner: *Bezzina* 158 J.P. 671.

    The offence may be committed by the owner of the dog or any person for the time being in charge of the dog. The defence under section 3(2) requires clear and plain evidence that the owner has placed the dog in the charge of another identifiable person: *Huddart* [1999] Crim.L.R. 568.

(5) Sentence

20–30   For a summary offence the sentence is a maximum term of imprisonment of six months or a fine not exceeding level 5 or both.

    On conviction on indictment the sentence is a maximum term of imprisonment of two years and a fine or both. The court also has power to make destruction and disqualification orders under sections 4 and 4A, *post*.

    When imposing sentence the courts should look at the consequences of the offence. The nature and extent of the obligations of dog owners had to be marked by a custodial sentence when there was a seriously aggravated offence. In a case where a pack of five dogs attacked and seriously injured a boy of seven in a public park, a sentence of three months' imprisonment was held to be appropriate for a defendant of good character who entered a plea of guilty: *Cox*, [2004] EWCA Crim 282. On commencement of the relevant provisions, the maximum custodial sentence in a magistrates' court will be 12 months' imprisonment: *Criminal Justice Act* 2003, ss.154 and 282. Custodial sentences of less than 12 months will consist of a custody plus order (see *post*, Ch.23).

(6) Other penalties

Dangerous Dogs Act 1991, ss.4, 4A, 4B

Destruction and disqualification orders

20–31   **4.**—(1) Where a person is convicted of an offence under section 1 or 3(1) or (3) above or of an offence under an order made under section 2 above the court—

    (a) may order the destruction of any dog in respect of which the offence was committed and, subject to subsection (1A) below, shall do so in the case of an offence under section 1 or an aggravated offence under section 3(1) or (3) above; and

    (b) may order the offender to be disqualified, for such period as the court thinks fit, for having custody of a dog.

    (1A) Nothing in subsection (1)(a) above shall require the court to order the destruction of a dog if the court is satisfied—

    (a) that the dog would not constitute a danger to public safety; and

    (b) where the dog was born before 30th November 1991 and is subject to the prohibition in section 1 (3) above, that there is a good reason why the dog has not been exempted from that prohibition.

    (2) Where a court makes an order under subsection (1)(a) above for the destruction of a dog owned by a person other than the offender, the owner may appeal to the Crown Court against the order.

    (3) A dog shall not be destroyed pursuant to an order under subsection (1)(a) above—

    (a) until the end of the period for giving notice of appeal against the conviction or against the order; and

    (b) if notice of appeal is given within that period, until the appeal is determined or withdrawn,

unless the offender and, in a case to which subsection (2) above applies, the owner of the dog give notice to the court that made the order that there is to be no appeal.

(4) Where a court makes an order under subsection (1)(a) above it may—

    (a) appoint a person to undertake the destruction of the dog and require any person having custody of it to deliver it up for that purpose; and

    (b) order the offender to pay such sum as the court may determine to be the reasonable expenses of destroying the dog and of keeping it pending its destruction.

(5) Any sum ordered to be paid under subsection (4)(b) above shall be treated for the purposes of enforcement as if it were a fine imposed on conviction.

(6) Any person who is disqualified for having custody of a dog by virtue of an order under subsection (1)(b) above may, at any time after the end of the period of one year beginning with the date of the order, apply to the court that made it (or a magistrates' court acting for the same petty sessions area as that court) for a direction terminating the disqualification.

(7) On an application under subsection (6) above the court may—

    (a) having regard to the applicant's character, his conduct since the disqualification was imposed and any other circumstances of the case, grant or refuse the application; and

    (b) order the applicant to pay all or any part of the costs of the application;

and where an application in respect of an order is refused no further application in respect of that order shall be entertained if made before the end of the period of one year beginning with the date of the refusal.

(8) Any person who—

    (a) has custody of a dog in contravention of an order under subsection (1)(b) above; or

    (b) fails to comply with a requirement imposed on him under subsection (4)(a) above,

is guilty of an offence and liable on summary conviction to a fine not exceeding level 5 on the standard scale.

(9) In the application of this section to Scotland—

    (a) in subsection (2) for the words "Crown Court against the order" there shall be substituted the words "High Court of Justiciary against the order within the period of seven days beginning with the date of the order";

    (b) for subsection (3)(a) there shall be substituted—

"(a) until the end of the period of seven days beginning with the date of the order";

    (c) for subsection (5) there shall be substituted—

"(5) section 221 of the *Criminal Procedure (Scotland) Act* 1995 shall apply in relation to the recovery of sums ordered to be paid under subsection (4)(b) above as it applies to fines ordered to be recovered by civil diligence in pursuance of Part XI of that Act."

; and

    (d) in subsection (6) the words "(or a magistrates' court acting for the same petty sessions area as that court)" shall be omitted.

Contingent destruction orders

4A.—(1) Where—

    (a) a person is convicted of an offence under section 1 above or an aggravated offence under section 3(1) or (3) above;

    (b) the court does not order the destruction of the dog under section 4(1)(a) above; and

    (c) in the case of an offence under section 1 above, the dog is subject to the prohibition in section 1(3) above.

the court shall order that, unless the dog is exempted from that prohibition within the requisite period, the dog shall be destroyed.

(2) Where an order is made under subsection (1) above in respect of a dog, and the dog is not exempted from the prohibition in section 1(3) above within the requisite period, the court may extend that period.

(3) Subject to subsection (2) above, the requisite period for the purposes of such an order is the period of two months beginning with the date of the order.

(4) Where a person is convicted of an offence under section 3(1) or (3) above, the court may order that, unless the owner of the dog keeps it under proper control, the dog shall be destroyed.

20–32

(5) An order under subsection (4) above—

(a) may specify the measures to be taken for keeping the dog under proper control, whether by muzzling, keeping on a lead, excluding it from specified places or otherwise; and

(b) if it appears to the court that the dog is a male and would be less dangerous if neutered, may require it to be neutered.

(6) Subsections (2) to (4) of section 4 above shall apply in relation to an order under subsection (1) or (4) above as they apply in relation to an order under subsection (1)(a) of that section.

Destruction orders otherwise than on a conviction

20–33   **4B.**—(1) Where a dog is seized under section 5(1) or (2) below and it appears to a justice of the peace, or in Scotland a justice of the peace or sheriff—

(a) that no person has been or is to be prosecuted for an offence under this Act or an order under section 2 above in respect of that dog (whether because the owner cannot be found or for any other reason); or

(b) that the dog cannot be released into the custody or possession of its owner without the owner contravening the prohibition in section 1(3) above,

he may order the destruction of the dog and, subject to subsection (2) below, shall do so if it is one to which section 1 above applies.

(2) Nothing in subsection (1)(b) above shall require the justice or sheriff to order the destruction of a dog if he is satisfied—

(a) that the dog would not constitute a danger to public safety; and

(b) where the dog was born before 30th November 1991 and is subject to the prohibition in section 1(3) above, that there is a good reason why the dog has not been exempted from that prohibition.

(3) Where in a case falling within subsection (1)(b) above the justice or sheriff does not order the destruction of the dog, he shall order that, unless the dog is exempted from the prohibition in section 1(3) above within the requisite period, the dog shall be destroyed.

(4) Subsections (2) to (4) of section 4 above shall apply in relation to an order under subsection (1)(b) or (3) above as they apply in relation to an order under subsection (1)(a) of that section.

(5) Subsections (2) and (3) of section 4A above shall apply in relation to an order under subsection (3) above as they apply in relation to an order under subsection (1) of that section, except that the reference to the court in subsection (2) of that section shall be construed as a reference to the justice or sheriff.

[These sections are printed as amended by the *Dangerous Dogs (Amendment) Act* 1997, s.1(4), s.2 and s.3(1).]

20–34   Before an order of destruction is made, the rules of natural justice require that the owner, if he has not already been notified, should be advised of the hearing and be given the opportunity to attend court and make representations: *Trafford Magistrates' Court ex p. Riley* (1996) 160 J.P. 418.

The power under section 4B may not be exercised where a prosecution has been discontinued but if there is a further new incident involving the dog then fresh proceedings may be instituted after seizure and this will not be an abuse of the courts powers: *Walton Street Justices ex p. Crothers* (1996) 160 J.P. 427.

In *Holland* [2003] 1 Cr.App.R.(S.) 60, CA, a disqualification order disqualifying the appellant for 10 years from keeping a dog, and an order for the destruction of the dog, was upheld in a case where a bull terrier attacked a child. It was held that whilst the destruction order was mandatory under section 4(1)(a) and section 4(1A) of the 1991 Act unless the judge was satisfied that the dog did not constitute a danger to public safety, the order disqualifying the appellant from having the custody of the dog was discretionary. The disqualification order had been made to protect the victim child from anxiety when she visited her grandparents who lived next to the owner of the bull terrier. The Court stated that in cases of this kind, a balance should be struck between the sensitivities of the victim on the one hand and restriction on the freedom of the custodian on the other. The disqualification order prohibited the appellant from keeping any dog at all. The statute made provision for a disqualified person to apply to a court for a direction terminating the disqualification and it would be open to the appellant to make such an application in due course, so the disqualification order was upheld.

Dangerous Dogs Act 1991, s.5

Seizure, entry of premises and evidence.

5.—(1) A constable or an officer of a local authority authorised by it to exercise the powers **20–35** conferred by this subsection may seize—
- (a) any dog which appears to him to be a dog to which section 1 above applies and which is in a public place—
    - (i) after the time when possession or custody of it has become unlawful by virtue of that section; or
    - (ii) before that time, without being muzzled and kept on a lead;
- (b) any dog in a public place which appears to him to be a dog to which an order under section 2 above applies and in respect of which an offence against the order has been or is being committed; and
- (c) any dog in a public place (whether or not one to which that section or such an order applies) which appears to him to be dangerously out of control.

(2) If a justice of the peace is satisfied by information on oath, or in Scotland a justice of the peace or sheriff is satisfied by evidence on oath, that there are reasonable grounds for believing—
- (a) that an offence under any provision of this Act or of an order under section 2 above is being or has been committed; or
- (b) that evidence of the commission of any such offence is to be found,

on any premises he may issue a warrant authorising a constable to enter those premises (using such force as is reasonably necessary) and to search them and seize any dog or other thing found there which is evidence of the commission of such an offence.

(3) A warrant issued under this section in Scotland shall be authority for opening lock-fast places and may authorise persons named in the warrant to accompany a constable who is executing it.

(5) If in any proceedings it is alleged by the prosecution that a dog is one to which section 1 or an order under section 2 above applies it shall be presumed that it is such a dog unless the contrary is shown by the accused by such evidence as the court considers sufficient; and the accused shall not be permitted to adduce such evidence unless he has given the prosecution notice of his intention to do so not later than the fourteenth day before that on which the evidence is to be adduced.

[This section is printed as amended by the *Dangerous Dogs (Amendment) Act* 1997, s.3(2).]

Dangerous Dogs Act 1991, s.6

Dogs owned by young persons

6. Where a dog is owned by a person who is less than sixteen years old any reference to its **20–36** owner in section 1(2)(d) or (e) or 3 above shall include a reference to the head of the household, if any, of which that person is a member or, in Scotland, to the person who has his actual care and control.

III. CONSUMER PROTECTION

A. PROHIBITION OF FALSE TRADE DESCRIPTIONS

(1) Definition

Trade Descriptions Act 1968, ss.1–6

Prohibition of false trade descriptions

1.—(1) Any person who, in the course of a trade or business,—   **20–37**

      (a) applies a false trade description to any goods; or

      (b) supplies or offers to supply any goods to which a false trade description is applied;

shall, subject to the provisions of this Act, be guilty of an offence.

    (2) Sections 2 to 6 of this Act shall have effect for the purposes of this section and for the interpretation of expressions used in this section, wherever they occur in this Act.

Trade description

20–38   **2.**—(1) A trade description is an indication, direct or indirect, and by whatever means given, of any of the following matters with respect to any goods or parts of goods, that is to say—

      (a) quantity, size or gauge;

      (b) method of manufacture, production, processing or reconditioning;

      (c) composition;

      (d) fitness for purpose, strength, performance, behaviour or accuracy;

      (e) any physical characteristics not included in the preceding paragraphs;

      (f) testing by any person and results thereof;

      (g) approval by any person or conformity with a type approved by any person;

      (h) place or date of manufacture, production, processing or reconditioning;

      (i) person by whom manufactured, produced, processed or reconditioned;

      (j) other history, including previous ownership or use.

    (2) The matters specified in subsection (1) of this section shall be taken—

      (a) in relation to any animal, to include sex, breed or cross, fertility and soundness;

      (b) in relation to any semen, to include the identity and characteristics of the animal from which it was taken and measure of dilution.

    (3) In this sections "quantity" includes length, width, height, area, volume, capacity, weight and number.

    (4) Notwithstanding anything in the preceding provisions of this section, the following shall be deemed not to be trade descriptions, that is to say, any description or mark applied in pursuance of—

      (b) section 2 of the *Agricultural Produce (Grading and Marking) Act* 1928 (as amended by the *Agricultural Produce (Grading and Marking) Amendment Act* 1931) or any corresponding enactment of the Parliament of Northern Ireland;

      (c) the *Plant Varieties and Seeds Act* 1964;

      (d) the *Agriculture and Horticulture Act* 1964 or any Community grading rules within the meaning of Part III of that Act;

      (e) the *Seeds Act (Northern Ireland) 1965*;

      (f) the *Horticulture Act (Northern Ireland)* 1966;

any statement made in respect of, or mark applied to, any material in pursuance of Part IV of the *Agriculture Act* 1970, any name or expression to which a meaning has been assigned under section 70 of that Act when applied to any material in the circumstances specified in that section any mark prescribed by a system of classification compiled under section 5 of the *Agriculture Act* 1967 and any designation, mark or description applied in pursuance of a scheme brought into force under section 6(1) or an order made under section 25(1) of the *Agriculture Act* 1970.

      (g) the *Consumer Protection Act* 1987;

      (h) the *Plant Varieties Act* 1997.

    (5) Notwithstanding anything in the preceding provisions of this section, (a) where provision is made under the *Food Act* 1984, the *Food and Drugs (Scotland) Act* 1956 the *Food Safety Act* 1990 or the *Food and Drugs Act (Northern Ireland)* 1958 or the *Consumer Protection Act* 1987 prohibiting the application of a description except to goods in the case of which the requirements specified in that provision are complied with, that description, when applied to such goods, shall be deemed not to be a trade description.

      (b) where by virtue of any provision made under Part V of the *Medicines Act* 1968 (or made under any provisions of the said Part V as applied by an order made under section 104 or section 105 of that Act) anything which, in accordance with this Act, constitutes the application of a trade description to goods is subject to any requirements or restrictions imposed by that provision, any particular description specified in that provision, when applied to goods in circumstances to which those requirements or restrictions are applicable, shall be deemed not to be a trade description

False trade description

20–39   **3.**—(1) A false trade description is a trade description which is false to a material degree.

(2) A trade description which, though not false, is misleading, that is to say, likely to be taken for such an indication of any of the matters specified in section 2 of this Act as would be false to a material degree, shall be deemed to be a false trade description.

(3) Anything which, though not a trade description, is likely to be taken for an indication of any of those matters and, as such an indication, would be false to a material degree, shall be deemed to be a false trade description.

(4) A false indication, or anything likely to be taken as an indication which would be false, that any goods comply with a standard specified or recognised by any person or implied by the approval of any person shall be deemed to be a false trade description, if there is no such person or no standard so specified, recognised or implied.

Applying a trade description to goods

4.—(1) A person applies a trade description to goods if he— **20–40**
    (a) affixes or annexes it to or in any manner marks it on or incorporates it with—
        (i) the goods themselves, or
        (ii) anything in, on or with which the goods are supplied; or
    (b) places the goods in, on or with anything which the trade description has been affixed or annexed to, marked on or incorporated with, or places any such thing with the goods; or
    (c) uses the trade description in any manner likely to be taken as referring to the goods.

(2) An oral statement may amount to the use of a trade description.

(3) Where goods are supplied in pursuance of a request in which a trade description is used and the circumstances are such as to make it reasonable to infer that the goods are supplied as goods corresponding to that trade description, the person supplying the goods shall be deemed to have applied that trade description to the goods.

Trade descriptions used in advertisements

5.—(1) The following provisions of this section shall have effect where in an advertisement a **20–41** trade description is used in relation to any class of goods.

(2) The trade description shall be taken as referring to all goods of the class, whether or not in existence at the time the advertisement is published—
    (a) for the purpose of determining whether an offence has been committed under paragraph (a) of section 1(1) of this Act; and
    (b) where goods of the class are supplied or offered to be supplied by a person publishing or displaying the advertisement, also for the purpose of determining whether an offence has been committed under paragraph (b) of the said section 1(1).

(3) In determining for the purposes of this section whether any goods are of a class to which a trade description used in an advertisement relates regard shall be had not only to the form and content of the advertisement but also to the time, place, manner and frequency of its publication and all other matters making it likely or unlikely that a person to whom the goods are supplied would think of the goods as belonging to the class in relation to which the trade description is used in the advertisement.

Offer to supply

6. A person exposing goods for supply or having goods in his possession for supply shall be **20–42** deemed to offer to supply them.

(2) Allocation

This offence is triable either way: *Trade Descriptions Act* 1968, s.18. **20–43**

(3) Elements of the offence

"In the course of a trade or business"

Professionals are not excluded from the scope of the Act; the term "trade or business" **20–44** applies to them as well: *Roberts v. Leonard* (1995) 159 J.P. 711. A person engaging in a hobby of repairing and selling cars in his spare time was held not to be subject to the act as his activities could not be termed a "trade or business" for the purposes of section 1: *Blakemore v. Bellamy* (1982) 147 J.P. 89.

There needs to be some degree of regularity in the transactions for them to form part of the normal practice of a business, however this does not necessarily mean that a one-off venture in the nature of trade carried out with a view to profit would not fall under the scope of section 1(1): *Davies v. Sumner* [1984] 3 All E.R. 831.

The Act does not apply to an expert who gives an opinion in respect of the condition of goods: *Wycombe Marsh Garages Ltd v. Fowler* [1972] 3 All E.R. 248.

Trade description

20–45   The particular words complained of must be looked at as a whole: *Evans v. British Doughnut Co Ltd* [1944] 1 K.B. 102. Where functional goods are supplied with instructions for their use the goods must be fit for use in accordance with those instructions as understood by the reasonable purchaser: *Janbo Trading Ltd. v. Dudley MBC* (1993) 157 J.P. 1056.

20–46   This is a strict liability offence and the prosecution do not have to prove dishonesty: *Alec Norman Garages Ltd v. Phillips* (1984) 148 J.P. 741.

False trade descriptions are sometimes used in the second-hand car market. The Act provides for the offence of applying a false description, which might be done by an unscrupulous trader and also the offence of supplying goods to which a false trade description has been applied, which might be an offence committed by the less than careful trader. Whether an advertising slogan used to encourage buyers amounts to a false trade description is a matter of fact in each case but there is no requirement to prove that the buyer has actually been deceived. Where a car was described as being in 'excellent condition throughout' it was no defence to say that the car was in as good a condition as could be expected for a car of its age and mileage and in an unrepaired state. It was held that a false trade description had been applied as there were 17 defects in the car: *Chidwick v. Beer* [1974] R.T.R. 415. To say a car is in "showroom condition throughout" cannot be described as mere puff but it was held to be a false trade description as the car had defects requiring repair. The term referred to the interior, exterior and mechanical condition of the car and not just it's appearance: *Hawkins v. Smith* [1978] Crim.L.R. 578.

When the mileage on a car is altered the false reading on the odometer is capable of amounting to a false trade description: *Hammerton Cars Ltd v. London Borough of Redbridge* [1976] 3 All E.R. 758. A trader who alters the reading himself cannot hide behind any disclaimer that may be attached to the vehicle but where the car is supplied or offered for supply a disclaimer may neutralise any trade description attached if it is "bold, precise and compelling": *Norman v. Bennett* [1974] R.T.R. 441, *Southwood* [1987] 3 All E.R. 556.

(4) Sentence

20–47   When tried summarily the maximum penalty for this offence is a fine not exceeding the statutory maximum: *Trade Descriptions Act* 1968, s.18.

Trade Descriptions Act 1968, s.20

Offences by corporations

20–48   **20.**—(1) Where an offence under this Act which has been committed by a body corporate is proved to have been committed with the consent and connivance of, or to be attributable to any neglect on the part of, any director, manager, secretary or other similar officer of the body corporate, or any person who was purporting to act in any such capacity, he as well as the body corporate shall be guilty of that offence and shall be liable to be proceeded against and punished accordingly.

(2) In this section "director", in relation to any body corporate established by or under any enactment for the purpose of carrying on under national ownership any industry or part of an industry or undertaking, being a body corporate whose affairs are managed by the members thereof, means a member of that body corporate.

20–49   There must be evidence of conduct that amounts to neglect. In *Lewin v. Bland*

(1984) 148 J.P. 69 the defendant was the managing director of a garage that dealt in cars and he instructed his service manager to complete a service book in respect of a second hand car that had been sold. The book was completed inaccurately by his employee and the director was prosecuted for applying a false trade description. It was held that there was no evidence of neglect and the defendant was entitled to expect that his employee would follow his instructions properly without the need to check his work. The conviction was quashed.

Trade Descriptions Act 1968, s.19

Time limit for prosecutions
19.—(1) No prosecution for an offence under this Act shall be commenced after the expiration of three years from the commission of the offence or one year from its discovery by the prosecutor, whichever is the earlier. **20–50**

(2) Notwithstanding anything in section 127(1) of the *Magistrates' Courts Act* 1980, a magistrates' court may try an information for an offence under this Act if the information was laid at any time within twelve months from the commission of the offence.

(3) Notwithstanding anything in section 23 of the *Summary Jurisdiction (Scotland) Act* 1954 (limitation of time for proceedings in statutory offences) summary proceedings in Scotland for an offence under this section may be commenced at any time within twelve months from the time when the offence was committed, and subsection (2) of the said section 23 shall apply for the purposes of this subsection as it applies for the purposes of that section.

(4) Subsections (2) and (3) of this section do not apply where—
   (a) the offence was committed by the making of an oral statement; or
   (b) the offence was one of supplying goods to which a false trade description is applied, and the trade description was applied by an oral statement; or
   (c) the offence was one where a false trade description is deemed to have been applied to goods by virtue of section 4(3) of this Act and the goods were supplied in pursuance of an oral request.

An offence is discovered when all the relevant facts necessary to found a charge are disclosed to the prosecution: *Newham London Borough v. Co-operative Retail Services Ltd* (1985) 149 J.P. 421. **20–51**

The time limit for these either way offences is three years, (section 19(1)).

(5) Defences

Trade Descriptions Act 1968, ss.24, 25

Defence of mistake, accident, etc.
24.—(1) In any proceedings for an offence under this Act it shall, subject to subsection (2) of this section, be a defence for the person charged to prove— **20–52**
   (a) that the commission of the offence was due to a mistake or to reliance on information supplied to him or to the act or default of another person, an accident or some other cause beyond his control; and
   (b) that he took all reasonable precautions and exercised all due diligence to avoid the commission of such an offence by himself or any person under his control.

(2) If in any case the defence provided by the last foregoing subsection involves the allegation that the commission of the offence was due to the act or default of another person or to reliance on information supplied by another person, the person charged shall not, without leave of the court, be entitled to rely on that defence unless, within a period ending seven clear days before the hearing, he has served on the prosecutor a notice in writing giving such information identifying or assisting in the identification of that other person as was then in his possession.

(3) In any proceedings for an offence under this Act of supplying or offering to supply goods to which a false trade description is applied it shall be a defence for the person charged to prove that he did not know, and could not with reasonable diligence have ascertained, that the goods did not conform to the description or that the description had been applied to the goods.

Innocent publication of advertisement

20–53   **25.** In proceedings for an offence under this Act committed by the publication of an advertisement it shall be a defence for the person charged to prove that he is a person whose business it is to publish or arrange for the publication of advertisements and that he received the advertisement for publication in the ordinary course of business and did not know and had no reason to suspect that its publication would amount to an offence under this Act.

20–54   The defence under section 24(1) is available to those charged with applying a false trade description and those charged with supplying or offering to supply goods to which a false trade description has been applied. The defendant must prove on a balance of probabilities that he has done all that could be reasonably expected of him to investigate the person whom he says was responsible for the default: *McGuire v. Sittingbourne Co-op Society Ltd* [1976] Crim.L.R. 268. Notice of the details of the third party must be served on the prosecution, section 24(2).

The defence under subsection (3) is only available to those charged with supplying or offering to supply goods with a false trade description. The test of "reasonable diligence" is whether, in view of all the circumstances and the defendant's position as a trader, he used all diligence to ascertain whether the goods conformed to their description. A car salesman should be put on inquiry by an abnormally low odometer reading for a vehicle and although he may not be under a duty to trace the entire history of the car he should have made some inquiries and carefully examined the vehicle: *Simmons v. Ravenhill* (1983) 148 J.P. 109.

B. CRIMINAL LIABILITY FOR MAKING OR DEALING WITH INFRINGING ARTICLES ETC.

(1) Definition

Copyright, Design and Patents Act 1988, s.107

Criminal liability for making or dealing with infringing articles, &c.

20–55   **107.**—(1) A person commits an offence who, without the licence of the copyright owner—

    (a) makes for sale or hire, or

    (b) imports into the United Kingdom otherwise than for his private and domestic use, or

    (c) possesses in the course of a business with a view to committing any act infringing the copyright, or

    (d) in the course of a business—

        (i) sells or lets for hire, or

        (ii) offers or exposes for sale or hire, or

        (iii) exhibits in public, or

        (iv) distributes, or

    (e) distributes otherwise than in the course of a business to such an extent as to affect prejudicially the owner of the copyright,

an article which is, and which he knows or has reason to believe is, an infringing copy of a copyright work.

(2) A person commits an offence who—

    (a) makes an article specifically designed or adapted for making copies of a particular copyright work, or

    (b) has such an article in his possession,

knowing or having reason to believe that it is to be used to make infringing copies for sale or hire or for use in the course of a business.

(2A) A person who infringes copyright in a work by communicating the work to the public—

    (a) in the course of a business, or

    (b) otherwise than in the course of a business to such an extent as to affect prejudicially the owner of the copyright,

commits an offence if he knows or has reason to believe that, by doing so, he is infringing copyright in that work.

(3) Where copyright is infringed (otherwise than by reception of a communication to the public)—

    (a) by the public performance of a literary, dramatic or musical work, or

    (b) by the playing or showing in public of a sound recording or film,

any person who caused the work to be so performed, played or shown is guilty of an offence if he knew or had reason to believe that copyright would be infringed.

(4) A person guilty of an offence under subsection (1)(a), (b), (d)(iv) or (e) is liable—

    (a) on summary conviction to imprisonment for a term not exceeding six months or a fine not exceeding the statutory maximum, or both;

    (b) on conviction on indictment to a fine or imprisonment for a term not exceeding ten years, or both.

(4A) A person guilty of an offence under subsection (2A) is liable—

    (a) on summary conviction to imprisonment for a term not exceeding three months or a fine not exceeding the statutory maximum, or both;

    (b) on conviction on indictment to a fine or imprisonment for a term not exceeding two years, or both.

(5) A person guilty of any other offence under this section is liable on summary conviction to imprisonment for a term not exceeding six months or a fine not exceeding level 5 on the standard scale, or both.

(6) Sections 104 to 106 (presumptions as to various matters connected with copyright) do not apply to proceedings for an offence under this section; but without prejudice to their application in proceedings for an order under section 108 below.

[This section is printed as amended by the *Copyright etc. and Trade Marks (Offences and Enforcement) Act* 2002, s.1.]

(2) Allocation

This offence is triable either way: *Copyright, Design and Patents Act* 1988, s.107(4).   **20–56**

Copyright, Designs and Patents Act 1988, s.110

Offence by body corporate: liability of officers

    110.—(1) Where an offence under section 107 committed by a body corporate is proved to   **20–57** have been committed with the consent or connivance of a director, manager, secretary or other similar officer of the body, or a person purporting to act in any such capacity, he as well as the body corporate is guilty of the offence and liable to be proceeded against and punished accordingly.

    (2) In relation to a body corporate whose affairs are managed by its members "director" means a member of the body corporate.

(3) Sentence

    When tried summarily, the maximum sentence for this offence is imprisonment for a   **20–58** period not exceeding six months, a fine not exceeding the statutory maximum or both: *Copyright, Design and Patents Act* 1988, s.107(4). As regards offences concerning publication rights, the maximum punishment on summary conviction is imprisonment for a term not exceeding three months, or a fine not exceeding level five on the standard scale or both: *Copyright and Related Rights Regulations* 1996, (S.I. 1996 No. 2967). On commencement of the relevant provisions, the maximum custodial sentence in a magistrates' court will be 12 months' imprisonment: *Criminal Justice Act* 2003, ss.154 and 282. Custodial sentences of less than 12 months will consist of a custody plus order (see *post*, Ch.23).

    In *Carter* (1992) 13 Cr.App.R.(S.) 576, CA, a suspended sentence of nine months'   **20–59** imprisonment imposed for making and hiring pirate video tapes was upheld by the Court of Appeal, Jowitt J. stating that "counterfeiting of video films is a serious offence. In effect to make and distribute pirate copies of films is to steal from the true owner of the copyright, the property for which he has to expend money in order to possess it. It is an offence really of dishonesty."

C. UNAUTHORISED USE OF TRADE MARK

(1) Definition

Trade Marks Act 1994, s.92

Unauthorised use of trade mark, &c. in relation to goods

20–60   **92.**—(1) A person commits an offence who with a view to gain for himself or another, or with intent to cause loss to another, and without the consent of the proprietor—

     (a) applies to goods or their packaging a sign identical to, or likely to be mistaken for, a registered trade mark, or

     (b) sells or lets for hire, offers or exposes for sale or hire or distributes goods which bear, or the packaging of which bears, such a sign, or

     (c) has in his possession, custody or control in the course of a business any such goods with a view to the doing of anything, by himself or another, which would be an offence under paragraph (b).

(2) A person commits an offence who with a view to gain for himself or another, or with intent to cause loss to another, and without the consent of the proprietor—

     (a) applies a sign identical to, or likely to be mistaken for, a registered trade mark to material intended to be used—

         (i) for labelling or packaging goods,

         (ii) as a business paper in relation to goods, or

         (iii) for advertising goods, or

     (b) uses in the course of a business material bearing such a sign for labelling or packaging goods, as a business paper in relation to goods, or for advertising goods, or

     (c) has in his possession, custody or control in the course of a business any such material with a view to the doing of anything, by himself or another, which would be an offence under paragraph (b).

(3) A person commits an offence who with a view to gain for himself or another, or with intent to cause loss to another, and without the consent of the proprietor—

     (a) makes an article specifically designed or adapted for making copies of a sign identical to, or likely to be mistaken for, a registered trade mark, or

     (b) has such an article in his possession, custody or control in the course of a business,

knowing or having reason to believe that it has been, or is to be, used to produce goods, or material for labelling or packaging goods, as a business paper in relation to goods, or for advertising goods.

(4) A person does not commit an offence under this section unless—

     (a) the goods are goods in respect of which the trade mark is registered, or

     (b) the trade mark has a reputation in the United Kingdom and the use of the sign takes or would take unfair advantage of, or is or would be detrimental to, the distinctive character or the repute of the trade mark.

(5) It is a defence for a person charged with an offence under this section to show that he believed on reasonable grounds that the use of the sign in the manner in which it was used, or was to be used, was not an infringement of the registered trade mark.

(6) A person guilty of an offence under this section is liable—

     (a) on summary conviction to imprisonment for a term not exceeding six months or a fine not exceeding the statutory maximum, or both;

     (b) on conviction on indictment to a fine or imprisonment for a term not exceeding ten years, or both.

(2) Allocation

20–61   This offence is triable either way: *Trade Marks Act* 1994, s.92(6).

Trade Marks Act 1994, s.101

Offences by partnerships and bodies corporate

20–62   **101.**—(1) Proceedings for an offence under this Act alleged to have been committed by a partnership shall be brought against the partnership in the name of the firm and not in that of the partners; but without prejudice to any liability of the partners under subsection (4) below.

(2) The following provisions apply for the purposes of such proceedings as in relation to a body corporate—

    (a) any rules of court relating to the service of documents,

    (b) in England and Wales or Northern Ireland, Schedule 3 to the *Magistrates' Courts Act* 1980 or Schedule 4 to the *Magistrates' Courts (Northern Ireland) Order* 1981 (procedure on charge of offence).

(3) A fine imposed on a partnership on its conviction in such proceedings shall be paid out of the partnership assets.

(4) Where a partnership is guilty of an offence under this Act, every partner, other than a partner who is proved to have been ignorant of or to have attempted to prevent the commission of the offence, is also guilty of the offence and liable to be proceeded against and punished accordingly.

(5) Where an offence under this Act committed by a body corporate is proved to have been committed with the consent or connivance of a director, manager, secretary or other similar officer of the body, or a person purporting to act in any such capacity, he as well as the body corporate is guilty of the offence and liable to be proceeded against and punished accordingly.

(3) Elements of the offence

In *Johnstone* [2003] 2 Cr.App.R 33, CA, the defendant was involved in activities re- **20–63** lating to bootleg recordings on CDs of performances of well known bands all of whom had registered their names as trade marks. He claimed that the use of the names of the bands on the CD covers was not an indication of "trade origin" under the terms of section 11 of the Act but simply described the performer whose music was on the CD. It was held by the House of Lords that the inclusion of the artists' names did not amount to an offence against section 92 as the names were not an indication of "trade origin". Whether it was such an indication was a question of fact in each case and the onus of proof was on the prosecution; the test was how the use of the sign would be perceived by the average consumer of the type of goods in question. The defendant was held to be not guilty of the offence.

(4) Defences

Section 92(5) of the 1994 Act provides that a person will have a defence to a charge **20–64** under the section if he can prove he believed on reasonable grounds that the use of the sign in the manner in which it was used, or was to be used, was not an infringement of the registered trade mark.

In *Torbay Council v. Singh* [1999] 2 Cr.App.R. 451, DC, the defendant sold children's clothes bearing the identical logo to that of the registered trade mark of the 'Teletubbies'. He was assured by his supplier that the goods were not counterfeit and did not infringe any trade mark. He pleaded not guilty on the basis of the defence afforded by section 92(5) and that he believed on reasonable grounds that his use of the sign in the manner in which it was used was not an infringement of the registered trade mark. As he was ignorant of the existence of the registered trade mark it was argued that there had been no infringement. The court on appeal held that the subsection did not speak of a reasonable belief in the absence of a registration. It spoke of a reasonable belief that the "manner" of use of the sign did not infringe "the registered trade mark" which presupposed an awareness by a defendant of the existence of the registration against which he could match his manner of use of the allegedly offending sign. The trader could not rely on his ignorance as a defence to a charge under section 92. This case was overruled by the *Johnstone* case (above) where the House of Lords said that it made no sense to confine the defence of section 92(5) to cases where the defendant is aware of the existence of the trade mark but to exclude those where he is not. It was held that the defence did apply when the defendant was unaware of the registration.

However, subsection 92(5) does afford a defence for the trader who honestly and rea- **20–65** sonably believes that his goods are genuine. In *Rhodes* [2002] EWCA Crim 1390, it was held that section 92(5) of the *Trade Marks Act* 1994 provides a broad general defence albeit subject to the limitation that a person will be deemed to know about any registered trade mark so that he could not, relying on that subsection, assert a defence that he was ignorant of it. The defendant with an honest and reasonable belief in the authenticity of the goods will be able to rely on the defence in section 92(5).

(5) Sentence

20–66   When tried summarily, the maximum penalty for this offence is imprisonment for a period not exceeding six months, a fine not exceeding the statutory maximum or both: *Trade Marks Act* 1994, s.92(6). After commencement of the relevant provisions, the maximum custodial sentence in a magistrates' court will be 12 months' imprisonment: *Criminal Justice Act* 2003, ss.154 and 282. Custodial sentences of less than 12 months will consist of a custody plus order (see *post*, Ch.23).

D. SELLING FOOD NOT OF THE NATURE, SUBSTANCE OR QUALITY DEMANDED

(1) Definition

Food Safety Act 1990, s.14

Selling food not of the nature or substance or quality demanded
20–67   **14.**—(1) Any person who sells to the purchaser's prejudice any food which is not of the nature or substance or quality demanded by the purchaser shall be guilty of an offence.

(2) In subsection (1) above the reference to sale shall be construed as a reference to sale for human consumption; and in proceedings under that subsection it shall not be a defence that the purchaser was not prejudiced because he bought for analysis or examination.

(2) Allocation

20–68   This offence is triable either way: *Food Safety Act* 1990, s.35.

The person may be a limited company: *ICR Haulage Ltd* [1944] K.B. 551.

Vicarious liability applies so that a servant who sells on behalf of his master may be convicted: *Goodfellow v. Johnson* [1966] 1 Q.B. 83, and a master can be liable for the sale by his servant who has authority to sell: *United Dairies (London) Ltd v. Beckenham Corp* [1963] 1 Q.B. 434.

Food Safety Act 1990, s.36

Offences by bodies corporate
20–69   **36.**—(1) Where an offence under this Act which has been committed by a body corporate is proved to have been committed with the consent or connivance of, or to be attributable to any neglect on the part of—

(a) any director, manager, secretary or other similar officer of the body corporate; or

(b) any person who was purporting to act in any such capacity,

he as well as the body corporate shall be deemed to be guilty of that offence and shall be liable to be proceeded against and punished accordingly.

(2) In subsection (1) above "director", in relation to any body corporate established by or under any enactment for the purpose of carrying on under national ownership any industry or part of an industry or undertaking, being a body corporate whose affairs are managed by its members, means a member of that body corporate.

(3) Elements of the offence

Food Safety Act 1990, s.1

Meaning of "food" and other basic expressions
20–70   **1.**—(1) In this Act "food" includes—

    (a) drink;

    (b) articles and substances of no nutritional value which are used for human consumption;

    (c) chewing gum and other products of a like nature and use; and

    (d) articles and substances used as ingredients in the preparation of food or anything falling within this subsection.

(2) In this Act "food" does not include—

    (a) live animals or birds, or live fish which are not used for human consumption while they are alive;

    (b) fodder or feeding stuffs for animals, birds or fish;

    (c) controlled drugs within the meaning of the *Misuse of Drugs Act* 1971; or

    (d) subject to such exceptions as may be specified in an order made by the Secretary of State—

        (i) medicinal products within the meaning of the *Medicines Act* 1968 in respect of which product licences within the meaning of that Act are for the time being in force; or

        (ii) other articles or substances in respect of which such licences are for the time being in force in pursuance of orders under section 104 or 105 of that Act (application of Act to other articles and substances).

(3) In this Act, unless the context otherwise requires—

"business" includes the undertaking of a canteen, club, school, hospital or institution, whether carried on for profit or not, and any undertaking or activity carried on by a public or local authority;

"commercial operation", in relation to any food or contact material, means any of the following, namely—

    (a) selling, possessing for sale and offering, exposing or advertising for sale;

    (b) consigning, delivering or serving by way of sale;

    (c) preparing for sale or presenting, labelling or wrapping for the purpose of sale;

    (d) storing or transporting for the purpose of sale;

    (e) importing and exporting; and, in relation to any food source, means deriving food from it for the purpose of sale or for purposes connected with sale;

"contact material" means any article or substance which is intended to come into contact with food;

"food business" means any business in the course of which commercial operations with respect to food or food sources are carried out;

"food premises" means any premises used for the purposes of a food business;

"food source" means any growing crop or live animal, bird or fish from which food is intended to be derived (whether by harvesting, slaughtering, milking, collecting eggs or otherwise);

"premises" includes any place, any vehicle, stall or moveable structure and, for such purposes as may be specified in an order made by the Secretary of State, any ship or aircraft of a description so specified.

(4) The reference in subsection (3) above to preparing for sale shall be construed, in relation to any contact material, as a reference to manufacturing or producing for the purpose of sale.

[This section is printed as amended by *Medicines for Human Use (Marketing Authorisations Etc.) Regulations* 1994 (SI 1994/3144) and the *Food Standards Act* 1999, Sched. 5, para.8.]

A sale will not be prejudicial to the purchaser where it is brought to his notice that **20–71** the article offered to him is not of the same nature or quality as the article he has asked for: *Sandys v. Jackson* (1905) 69 J.P. 171. The fact that the goods are sold below the market price is not *prima facie* evidence of their quality deficiency: *Heywood v. Whitehead* (1897) 76 L.T. 781.

In the absence of a prescribed minimum standard for the product in question, where there is sufficient evidence for the justices to decide what is a proper standard for that product and that the product in question was below it, the justices will be entitled to find that the retailers are guilty of selling an article which was not the article demanded: *Tonkin v. Victor Value and Piper Products* [1962] 1 W.L.R. 339, DC.

(4) Defences

Food Safety Act 1990, s.21

Defence of due diligence

20–72   **21.**—(1) In any proceedings for an offence under any of the preceding provisions of this Part (in this section referred to as "the relevant provision"), it shall, subject to subsection (5) below, be a defence for the person charged to prove that he took all reasonable precautions and exercised all due diligence to avoid the commission of the offence by himself or by a person under his control.

(2) Without prejudice to the generality of subsection (1) above, a person charged with an offence under section 8, 14 or 15 above who neither—

(a) prepared the food in respect of which the offence is alleged to have been committed; nor

(b) imported it into Great Britain,

shall be taken to have established the defence provided by thatsubsection if he satisfies the requirements of subsection (3) or (4) below.

(3) A person satisfies the requirements of this subsection if he proves—

(a) that the commission of the offence was due to an act or default of another person who was not under his control, or to reliance on information supplied by such a person;

(b) that he carried out all such checks of the food in question as were reasonable in all the circumstances, or that it was reasonable in all the circumstances for him to rely on checks carried out by the person who supplied the food to him; and

(c) that he did not know and had no reason to suspect at the time of the commission of the alleged offence that his act or omission would amount to an offence under the relevant provision.

(4) A person satisfies the requirements of this subsection if he proves—

(a) that the commission of the offence was due to an act or default of another person who was not under his control, or to reliance on information supplied by such a person;

(b) that the sale or intended sale of which the alleged offence consisted was not a sale or intended sale under his name or mark; and

(c) that he did not know, and could not reasonably have been expected to know, at the time of the commission of the alleged offence that his act or omission would amount to an offence under the relevant provision.

(5) If in any case the defence provided by subsection (1) above involves the allegation that the commission of the offence was due to an act or default of another person, or to reliance on information supplied by another person, the person charged shall not, without leave of the court, be entitled to rely on that defence unless—

(a) at least seven clear days before the hearing; and

(b) where he has previously appeared before a court in connection with the alleged offence, within one month of his first such appearance,

he has served on the prosecutor a notice in writing giving such information identifying or assisting in the identification of that other person as was then in his possession.

(6) In subsection (5) above any reference to appearing before a court shall be construed as including a reference to being brought before a court.

20–73   In *Carrick DC v. Taunton Vale Meat Traders' Ltd* (1994) 158 J.P. 347, DC, it was held that an error of judgement by a meat inspector is a valid defence to the charge of supplying meat unfit for human consumption under the *Food Safety Act* 1990. No further precautions were deemed necessary to determine the fitness of the meat for human use. The defendant had had the meat examined by a meat inspector, and was therefore not liable for the inspector's error of judgement.

(5) Sentence

20–74   When tried summarily, the maximum penalty for this offence is six months' imprison-

ment or a fine not exceeding £20,000 or both: *Food Safety Act* 1990, s.35 (see *post*, § 20–99). After commencement of the relevant provisions, the maximum custodial sentence in a magistrates' court will be 12 months' imprisonment: *Criminal Justice Act* 2003, ss.154 and 282. Custodial sentences of less than 12 months will consist of a custody plus order (see *post*, Ch.23).

E. FALSELY DESCRIBING OR PRESENTING FOOD

(1) Definition

Food Safety Act 1990 s.15

Falsely describing or presenting food

15.—(1) Any person who gives with any food sold by him, or displays with any food offered **20–75** or exposed by him for sale or in his possession for the purpose of sale, a label, whether or not attached to or printed on the wrapper or container, which—

    (a) falsely describes the food; or

    (b) is likely to mislead as to the nature or substance or quality of the food,

shall be guilty of an offence.

(2) Any person who publishes, or is a party to the publication of, an advertisement (not being such a label given or displayed by him as mentioned in subsection (1) above) which—

    (a) falsely describes any food; or

    (b) is likely to mislead as to the nature or substance or quality of any food,

shall be guilty of an offence.

(3) Any person who sells, or offers or exposes for sale, or has in his possession for the purpose of sale, any food the presentation of which is likely to mislead as to the nature or substance or quality of the food shall be guilty of an offence.

(4) In proceedings for an offence under subsection (1) or (2) above, the fact that a label or advertisement in respect of which the offence is alleged to have been committed contained an accurate statement of the composition of the food shall not preclude the court from finding that the offence was committed.

(5) In this section references to sale shall be construed as references to sale for human consumption.

(2) Allocation

The offences created under this section are triable either way: *Food Safety Act* 1990, **20–76** s.35. The section creates distinct offences and the summons must be clear as to which of the offences is being alleged: *Ward v. Barking and Dagenham LBC* [2000] E.H.L.R. 263, QBD.

(3) Defences

In addition to the defence available under section 21 of the 1990 Act, see *ante*, § 16– **20–77** 113, the defendant may be able to rely on the defence relating to publication in the course of business established by section 22.

Food Safety Act 1990, s.22

Defence of publication in the course of business

22. In proceedings for an offence under any of the preceding provisions of this Part consist- **20–78** ing of the advertisement for sale of any food, it shall be a defence for the person charged to prove—

    (a) that he is a person whose business it is to publish or arrange for the publication of advertisements; and

    (b) that he received the advertisement in the ordinary course of business and did not know and had no reason to suspect that its publication would amount to an offence under that provision.

(4) Sentence

When tried summarily, the maximum penalty for this offence is six months' imprison- **20–79** ment or a fine not exceeding the statutory maximum or both: *Food Safety Act* 1990, s.35, see *post*, § 20–99. After commencement of the relevant proceedings, the maximum custodial sentence in a magistrates' court will be 12 months' imprisonment: *Criminal Justice Act* 2003, ss.154 and 282. Custodial sentences of less than 12 months will consist of a custody plus order (see *post*, Ch.23).

F. FOOD SAFETY AND CONSUMER PROTECTION

(1) Regulations

Food Safety Act 1990, s.16

Food safety and consumer protection

20–80   **16.**—(1) The Secretary of State may by regulations make—

(a) provision for requiring, prohibiting or regulating the presence in food or food sources of any specified substance, or any substance of any specified class, and generally for regulating the composition of food;

(b) provision for securing that food is fit for human consumption and meets such microbiological standards (whether going to the fitness of the food or otherwise) as may be specified by or under the regulations;

(c) provision for requiring, prohibiting or regulating the use of any process or treatment in the preparation of food;

(d) provision for securing the observance of hygienic conditions and practices in connection with the carrying out of commercial operations with respect to food or food sources;

(e) provision for imposing requirements or prohibitions as to, or otherwise regulating, the labelling, marking, presenting or advertising of food, and the descriptions which may be applied to food; and

(f) such other provision with respect to food or food sources, including in particular provision for prohibiting or regulating the carrying out of commercial operations with respect to food or food sources, as appears to them to be necessary or expedient—

(i) for the purpose of securing that food complies with food safety requirements or in the interests of the public health; or

(ii) for the purpose of protecting or promoting the interests of consumers.

(2) The Secretary of State may also by regulations make provision—

(a) for securing the observance of hygienic conditions and practices in connection with the carrying out of commercial operations with respect to contact materials which are intended to come into contact with food intended for human consumption;

(b) for imposing requirements or prohibitions as to, or otherwise regulating, the labelling, marking or advertising of such materials, and the descriptions which may be applied to them; and

(c) otherwise for prohibiting or regulating the carrying out of commercial operations with respect to such materials.

(3) Without prejudice to the generality of subsection (1) above, regulations under that subsection may make any such provision as is mentioned in Schedule 1 to this Act.

(4) In making regulations under subsection (1) above, the Secretary of State shall have regard to the desirability of restricting, so far as practicable, the use of substances of no nutritional value as foods or as ingredients of foods.

(5) In subsection (1) above and Schedule 1 to this Act, unless the context otherwise requires—

(a) references to food shall be construed as references to food intended for sale for human consumption; and

(b) references to food sources shall be construed as references to food sources from which such food is intended to be derived.

(2) Elements of the offence

20–81   A multitude of regulations have been made applying to various specific foodstuffs.

The *Food Safety (General Food Hygiene) Regulations* 1995 (S.I. 1995 No. 1763) as amended apply to proprietors of food businesses. The regulations impose a duty on proprietors to ensure that the preparation, processing, manufacturing, packaging storing, transportation, distribution, handling and offering for sale or supply of food are carried out hygienically: regulation 4. Schedule 1 to the regulations sets out the rules of hygiene that must be complied with. Offences against section 16 should state separately each specific requirement that it is alleged has been breached.

In *Asda Food Stores Ltd v. Wandsworth Borough Council* [2007] EWHC 433, Admin, it was held that the *Food Safety etc. Regulations* create more than one offence in a single regulation and it was not duplicitous or over-charging to prosecute for two separate offences under regulation 4(2) when one offence related to failing to ensure adequate procedures were in place to control pests and the other related to failing to place food so as to minimize the risk of contamination. The regulations refer to different ways in which and different times at which the offences can be committed and the prosecution could charge and specify the offences separately even where they were committed under one regulation only.

(3) Sentence

When tried summarily, the maximum penalty for failure to comply with regulations **20–82** made under this section is six months' imprisonment or a fine not exceeding the statutory maximum or both: *Food Safety Act* 1990, s.35, see *post*, § 20–99. After commencement of the relevant provisions, the maximum custodial sentence in a magistrates' court will be 12 months' imprisonment: *Criminal Justice Act* 2003, ss.154 and 282. Custodial sentences of less than 12 months will consist of a custody plus order (see *post*, Ch.23).

Food Safety Act 1990, ss.20, 34

Offences due to fault of another person

20. Where the commission by any person of an offence under any of the preceding provi- **20–83** sions of this Part is due to an act or default of some other person, that other person shall be guilty of the offence; and a person may be charged with and convicted of the offence by virtue of this section whether or not proceedings are taken against the first-mentioned person.

Time limit for prosecutions

34. No prosecution for an offence under this Act which is punishable under section 35(2) **20–84** below shall be begun after the expiry of—
    (a) three years from the commission of the offence; or
    (b) one year from its discovery by the prosecutor,
whichever is the earlier.

In the case of a continuing offence discovery may occur on any day that the offence **20–85** continues to be committed: *R. v. Thames Metropolitan Stipendiary Magistrate ex p. London Borough of Hackney* (1994) 158 J.P. 305.

Food Safety Act 1990, s.35

Punishment of offences

35.—(1) A person guilty of an offence under section 33(1) above shall be liable on summary **20–86** conviction to a fine not exceeding level 5 on the standard scale or to imprisonment for a term not exceeding three months or to both.

(2) A person guilty of any other offence under this Act shall be liable—
    (a) on conviction on indictment, to a fine or to imprisonment for a term not exceeding two years or to both;
    (b) on summary conviction, to a fine not exceeding the relevant amount or to imprisonment for a term not exceeding six months or to both.

(3) In subsection (2) above "the relevant amount" means —
    (a) in the case of an offence under section 7, 8 or 14 above, £ 20,000;

  (b) in any other case, the statutory maximum.
 (4) If a person who is—
   (a) licensed under section 1 of the *Slaughterhouses Act* 1974 to keep a knacker's yard;
   (b) registered under section 4 of the *Slaughter of Animals (Scotland) Act* 1980 in respect of any premises for use as a slaughterhouse; or
   (c) licensed under section 6 of the *Slaughter of Animals (Scotland) Act* 1980 to use any premises as a knacker's yard,
is convicted of an offence under Part II of this Act, the court may, in addition to any other punishment, cancel his licence or registration.

Section 33(1) referred to in this section is the offence of obstructing officers acting under their powers in the Act. Section 7 is the offence of rendering food injurious to health and section 8 is the offence of selling food not in compliance with food safety requirements.

IV. HIGHWAYS

A. OFFENCES UNDER THE HIGHWAYS ACT 1980

Highways Act 1980, s.328

Meaning of "highway"

20–87 **328.**—(1) In this Act, except where the context otherwise requires, "highway" means the whole or a part of a highway other than a ferry or waterway.

 (2) Where a highway passes over a bridge or through a tunnel, that bridge or tunnel is to be taken for the purposes of this Act to be a part of the highway.

 (3) In this Act, "highway maintainable at the public expense" and any other expression defined by reference to a highway is to be construed in accordance with the foregoing provisions of this section.

Section 329 includes further lengthy provisions on interpretation.

Highways Act 1980, s.312

Restriction on institution of proceedings

20–88 **312.**—(1) Subject to subsection (3) below, proceedings for an offence under any provision of this Act to which this section applies or under byelaws made under any such provision shall not, without the written consent of the Attorney General, be taken by any person other than the person aggrieved, or a highway authority or council having an interest in the enforcement of the provision or byelaws in question.

 (2) This section applies to sections 167 and 177 above and to the provisions of this Act specified in Schedule 22 to this Act.

 (3) A constable may take proceedings—
   (a) for an offence under paragraph (b) of section 171(6) above; or
   (b) for an offence under paragraph (c) of that subsection consisting of failure to perform a duty imposed by section 171(5)(a) above; or
   (c) for an offence under section 174 above,
without the consent of the Attorney General.

The offences referred to in this section are as follows: section 171(6) is one of failing without reasonable excuse to comply with directions relating to placing traffic signs in connection with a deposit or excavation; section 171(5) imposes a duty of signposting, fencing and lighting of obstructions and excavations on the highway; section 174 details the precautions to be taken by persons executing works in the street. The police may prosecute these offences.

Highways Act 1980, Sched. 22

SCHEDULE 22

PROVISIONS OF THIS ACT TO WHICH SECTIONS 288, 294, 312, 338, 339 AND 341 OF THIS ACT APPLY

Provisions contained in Part IV

1. Section 36(6) and (7) and section 38.   **20–89**

Provisions contained in Part V

2. Section 66(2) to (8), sections 73 and 77 and section 96(4) and (5).

Provisions contained in Part IX

3. Sections 133, and 151 to 153, section 154(1), and 154(4) so far as relating to a notice under 154(1), sections 163 and 165, sections 171 to 174, 176, 178 and 179, section 180 other than subsection (2) and subsection (4) so far as relating to subsection (2), and section 185.

Provisions contained in Part X

4. Sections 186 to 188, 190 to 107, 200 and 201.

Provisions contained in Part XI

5. The private street works code, sections 226 and 228, section 230(1) to (6), and sections 231, 233, 236 and 237.

Provisions contained in Part XII

6. Section 239(6) and section 241.

Provisions contained in Part XIV

7. Sections 286, 295, 297, 303, 304, and 305.

Highways Act 1980, s.314

Offences by body corporate

314.—(1) Where an offence under any provision of this Act to which this section applies is **20–90** committed by a body corporate and it is proved to have been committed with the consent or connivance of, or to be attributable to any neglect on the part of, any director, manager, secretary or other similar officer of the body corporate or any person who was purporting to act in any such capacity, he as well as the body corporate is guilty of that offence and liable to be proceeded against and punished accordingly.

(2) Where the affairs of a body corporate are managed by its members, subsection (1) above applies in relation to the acts and defaults of a member in connection with his functions of management as if he were a director of the body corporate.

(3) This section applies to sections 139, 140, 167, 168, 177 and 181 above.

[This section is printed as amended by the *New Roads and Street Works Act* 1991, Sched. 8.]

The offences referred to in this section are: section 139 relates to the control of build- **20–91** ers' skips; section 140 covers the removal of builders' skips; section 167 provides for powers relating to retaining walls near streets; section 168 relates to building operations affecting public safety; and section 177 imposes a restriction on the construction of buildings over highways.

Highways Act 1980, s.319

Judges and justices not to be disqualified by liability to rates

319. The judge of any court or a justice of the peace is not disqualified for acting in cases **20–92** arising under this Act by reason only of his being as one of several ratepayers, or as one of any other class of persons, liable in common with the others to contribute to, or to be benefited by, any rate or fund out of which any expenses of a council are to be defrayed.

B. DAMAGE TO HIGHWAY

(1) Definition

Highways Act 1980, s.131

Penalty for damaging highway etc.

20–93   **131.**—(1) If a person, without lawful authority or excuse—

     (a) makes a ditch or excavation in a highway which consists of or comprises a carriageway, or

     (b) removes any soil or turf from any part of a highway, except for the purpose of improving the highway and with the consent of the highway authority for the highway, or

     (c) deposits anything whatsoever on a highway so as to damage the highway, or

     (d) lights any fire, or discharges any firearm or firework, within 50 feet from the centre of a highway which consists of or comprises a carriageway, and in consequence thereof the highway is damaged,

he is guilty of an offence.

(2) If a person without lawful authority or excuse pulls down or obliterates a traffic sign placed on or over a highway, or a milestone or direction post (not being a traffic sign) so placed, he is guilty of an offence; but it is a defence in any proceedings under this subsection to show that the traffic sign, milestone or post was not lawfully so placed.

(3) A person guilty of an offence under this section is liable to a fine not exceeding level three on the standard scale.

[This section is printed as amended by the *Criminal Justice Act* 1982, ss.35, 38 and 46.]

(2) Allocation

20–94   This offence is triable summarily: *Highways Act* 1980, s.310.

(3) Sentence

20–95   The maximum penalty for the offences under this section is a fine not exceeding level three on the standard scale.

C. WILFUL OBSTRUCTION

(1) Definition

Highways Act 1980, s.137

Penalty for wilful obstruction

20–96   **137.**—(1) If a person, without lawful authority or excuse, in any way wilfully obstructs the free passage along a highway he is guilty of an offence and liable to a fine not exceeding level 3 on the standard scale.

(2) [...]

[This section is printed as amended by the *Criminal Justice Act* 1982, ss.38 and 46 and partially repealed by the *Police and Criminal Evidence Act* 1984, Sched. 7.]

(2) Allocation

20–97   This offence is triable summarily: *Highways Act* 1980, s.310.

(3) Elements of the offence

20–98   Lawful authority is given by permits and licences granted to market and street traders and those collecting for charitable causes. A lawful excuse may be found if the activities engaged in are lawful in themselves and they may or may not be reasonable.

The test of whether a particular use of a highway by a vehicle, such as a van selling hot-dogs, constitutes an obstruction is whether the use is unreasonable having regard to all the circumstances including its duration, position and purpose and whether it causes an actual, rather than a potential obstruction: *Nagy v. Weston* [1965] 1 All E.R. 78. It is sufficient to constitute the offence that the accused, without lawful authority or excuse, by exercise of his free will does something or omits to do something, which causes an obstruction or the continuance of an obstruction: *Arrowsmith v. Jenkins* [1963] 2 Q.B. 561. In *Waltham Forest LBC v. Mills* [1980] R.T.R. 201, QBD, the defendant conducted a business of serving tea and snacks to the public from a mobile snack bar which he stationed on a part of the highway which had been designated as a layby. People who stopped to buy snacks parked their motorcycles and cars in the layby and, on some occasions when the layby entrance was blocked by motorcycles, on the side of the carriageway itself. It was held that this constituted an unreasonable obstruction of the highway and that selling refreshments on the highway was of itself an unreasonable user. In *Hertfordshire County Council v. Bolden* (1987) 151 J.P. 252, the defendant owned premises adjoining a public highway. He sometimes used part of the highway verge bordering his premises for the display and sale of garden produce. It was held that such activities could form unreasonable obstructions for the purpose of the offence under section 137, that such obstructions could not be said to be *de minimis* and hence outside the scope of section 137 and that the fact that they did not cause inconvenience to anyone did not mean that they were insufficient to constitute offences.

As regards peaceful picketing under section 134 of the *Industrial Relations Act* **20–99** 1971 (now the *Trade Union and Labour Relations Act (Consolidation) Act* 1992, s.220), in *Broome v. DPP* [1974] 1 All E.R. 314, it was held that section 134 made lawful the attendance of pickets only for the purposes specified therein and did not require the person whom it was sought to persuade to submit to any constraint or restriction of his right to personal freedom. Hence whilst a driver can be invited to stop and listen to the protest, he cannot be compelled to stop by a blockade on the highway. Where the highway is obstructed by a peaceful protest the question of whether the use of the highway is reasonable or not must be considered: *Hirst v. Chief Constable of West Yorkshire* (1987) 85 Cr.App.R. 143.

The onus is on the prosecution to prove that the defendant was obstructing the highway without lawful authority or excuse. A defendant does not acquire a license to perform an unlawful act through the fact that the police or other prosecuting authority have refrained from prosecuting in respect of the alleged obstruction for a number of years: *Redbridge London Borough v. Jacques* (1971) 1 All E.R. 260.

In *Westminster City Council v. Haw* (2002) EWHC 2073, it was held that the Art.10 **20–100** right to freedom of expression contained in the ECHR is not a trump card to authorise any protest, but rather is a significant consideration to take into account when considering the reasonableness of the obstruction of the highway. In this case the court held that there was a wilful obstruction as protest placards encroached onto the pavement but the defendant's activities were neither unlawful nor unreasonable.

(4) Sentence

The maximum penalty for this offence is a fine not exceeding level three on the stan- **20–101** dard scale.

D. BUILDERS' SKIPS

(1) Definition

Highways Act 1980, s.139

Control of builders' skips

139.—(1) A builders' skip shall not be deposited on a highway without the permission of the **20–102** highway authority for the highway.

(2) A permission under this section shall be a permission for a person to whom it is granted to deposit, or cause to be deposited, a skip on the highway specified in the permission, and a highway authority may grant such permission either unconditionally or subject to such conditions as may be specified in the permission including, in particular, conditions relating to—

(a) the siting of the skip;

(b) its dimensions;

(c) the manner in which it is to be coated with paint and other material for the purpose of making it immediately visible to oncoming traffic;

(d) the care and disposal of its contents;

(e) the manner in which it is to be lighted or guarded;

(f) its removal at the end of the period of permission.

(3) If a builder's skip is deposited on a highway without a permission granted under this section, the owner of the skip is, subject to subsection (6) below, guilty of an offence and liable to a fine not exceeding level 3 on the standard scale.

(4) Where a builder's skip has been deposited on a highway in accordance with a permission granted under this section, the owner of the skip shall secure—

(a) that the skip is properly lighted during the hours of darkness and, where regulations made by the Secretary of State under this section require it to be marked in accordance with the regulations (whether with reflecting or fluorescent material or otherwise), that it is so marked;

(b) that the skip is clearly and indelibly marked with the owner's name and with his telephone number or address;

(c) that the skip is removed as soon as practicable after it has been filled;

(d) that each of the conditions subject to which that permission was granted is complied with;

and, if he fails to do so, he is, subject to subsection (6) below, guilty of an offence and liable to a fine not exceeding level 3 on the standard scale.

(5) Where the commission by any person of an offence under this section is due to the act or default of some other person, that other person is guilty of the offence, and a person may be charged with and convicted of the offence by virtue of this subsection whether or not proceedings are taken against the first-mentioned person.

(6) In any proceedings for an offence under this section it is a defence, subject to subsection (7) below, for the person charged to prove that the commission of the offence was due to the act or default of another person and that he took all reasonable precautions and exercised all due diligence to avoid the commission of such an offence by himself or any person under his control.

(7) A person charged with an offence under this section is not, without leave of the court, entitled to rely on the defence provided by subsection (6) above unless, within a period ending 7 clear days before the hearing, he has served on the prosecutor a notice in writing giving such information identifying or assisting in the identification of that other person as was then in his possession.

(8) Where any person is charged with an offence under any other enactment for failing to secure that a builder's skip which has been deposited on a highway in accordance with a permission granted under this section was properly lighted during the hours of darkness, it is a defence for the person charged to prove that the commission of the offence was due to the act or default of another person and that he took all reasonable precautions and exercised all due diligence to avoid the commission of such an offence by himself or any person under his control.

(9) Where a person is charged with obstructing, or interrupting any user of, a highway by depositing a builder's skip on it, it is a defence for the person charged to prove that the skip was deposited on it in accordance with a permission granted under this section and either—

(a) that each of the requirements of subsection (4) above had been complied with; or

(b) that the commission of any offence under that subsection was due to the act or default of another person and that he took all reasonable precautions and exercised all due diligence to avoid the commission of such an offence by himself or any person under his control.

(10) Nothing in this section is to be taken as authorising the creation of a nuisance or of a danger to users of a highway or as imposing on a highway authority by whom a permis-

sion has been granted under this section any liability for any injury, damage or loss resulting from the presence on a highway of the skip to which the permission relates.

(11) In this section section 140 and section 140A below—

"builder's skip" means a container designed to be carried on a road vehicle and to be
placed on a highway or other land for the storage of builders' materials, or for the
removal and disposal of builders' rubble, waste, household and other rubbish or
earth; and

"owner", in relation to a builder's skip which is the subject of a hiring agreement, being an agreement for a hiring of not less than one month, or a hire purchase
agreement, means the person in possession of the skip under that agreement.

[This section is printed as amended by the *Criminal Justice Act* 1982, ss.38 and 46,
the *Transport Act* 1982, s.65 and the *New Roads and Street Works Act* 1991, Sched.
8.]

(2) Allocation

This offence is triable summarily: *Highways Act* 1980, s.310.   **20–103**

(3) Elements of the offence

Depositing means more than just placing, putting down or delivering the skip. The **20–104**
offence applies to incidents of leaving or allowing the skip to remain: *Craddock v.
Green* [1983] R.T.R. 479.

Permission granted by the local authority must be in writing and specific to the location: *York City Council v. Poller* [1976] R.T.R. 479 and *Highways Act* 1980, s.320.

For the purposes of subsection 4(a) the relevant regulations are the *Builders' Skips
(Markings) Regulations* 1984 (S.I. 1984 No. 1933).

It is a defence under subsection 6 to prove that the commission of the offence was
due to the act or default of a person other than the person charged and that due diligence was exercised to avoid the commission of the offence. The other person does not
have to be identified: *P.G.M. Building Co Ltd v. Kensington and Chelsea (Royal)
LBC* [1982] R.T.R. 107. See also *York City Council v. Poller* [1976] R.T.R. 37. Note
the requirements contained in subsection (7) concerning the requirement that a defendant seeking to rely on the defence established by subsection (6) must serve on the
prosecutor a notice in writing giving information identifying or assisting in the identification of that other person as was then in his possession within a period ending seven
clear days before the hearing,

(4) Sentence

The maximum penalty for the offences under this section is fine not exceeding level **20–105**
3 on the standard scale.

E. REMOVAL OF BUILDERS' SKIPS

(1) Definition

Highways Act 1980, s.140

Removal of builders' skips

140.—(1) The following provisions of this section have effect in relation to a builder's skip **20–106**
deposited on a highway notwithstanding that it was deposited on it in accordance with a permission granted under section 139 above.

(2) The highway authority for the highway or a constable in uniform may require the
owner of the skip to remove or reposition it or cause it to be removed or repositioned.

(3) A person required to remove or reposition, or cause to be removed or repositioned,
a skip under a requirement made by virtue of subsection (2) above shall comply with the
requirement as soon as practicable, and if he fails to do so he is guilty of an offence and liable to a fine not exceeding level 3 on the standard scale.

(4) The highway authority for the highway or a constable in uniform may themselves remove or reposition the skip or cause it to be removed or repositioned.

(5) Where a skip is removed under subsection (4) above, the highway authority or, as the case may be, the chief officer of police shall, where practicable, notify the owner of its removal, but if the owner cannot be traced, or if after a reasonable period of time after being so notified he has not recovered the skip, the highway authority or chief officer of police may dispose of the skip and its contents.

(6) Any expenses reasonably incurred by a highway authority or chief officer of police in the removal or repositioning of a skip under subsection (4) above or the disposal of a skip under subsection (5) above may be recovered from the owner of the skip in any court of competent jurisdiction or summarily as a civil debt.

(7) Any proceeds of the disposal of a skip under subsection (5) above shall be used in the first place to meet the expenses reasonably incurred in the removal and disposal of the skip and thereafter any surplus shall be given to the person entitled to it if he can be traced and if not may be retained by the highway authority or the chief officer of police, as the case may be; and any surplus so retained by a chief officer of police shall be paid into the police fund.

(8) References in this section to expenses incurred in the removal of a skip include references to expenses incurred in storing the skip until it is recovered by the owner or, as the case may be, disposed of.

(9) The owner of a skip is not guilty of an offence under section 139(4) above of failing to secure that a condition relating to the siting of the skip was complied with if the failure resulted from the repositioning of the skip under subsection (3) or (4) above.

[This section is printed as amended by the *Criminal Justice Act* 1982, ss.38 and 46.]

(2) Allocation

20–107   This offence is triable summarily: *Highways Act* 1980, s.310.

(3) Elements of the offence

20–108   A requirement that a skip be removed must be communicated to a potential offender by a constable in uniform going to that person and telling him of the requirement: *R. v. Worthing Justices ex p. Waste Management Ltd* (1988) 152 J.P. 362.

(4) Sentence

20–109   The maximum penalty for the offence under this section is a fine not exceeding level three on the standard scale.

V. IMMIGRATION

A. ILLEGAL ENTRY AND SIMILAR OFFENCES

(1) Definition

Immigration Act 1971, s.24

Illegal entry and similar offences

20–110   **24.**—(1) A person who is not a British citizen shall be guilty of an offence punishable on summary conviction with a fine of not more than level 5 on the standard scale or with imprisonment for not more than six months, or with both, in any of the following cases—

    (a) if contrary to this Act he knowingly enters the United Kingdom in breach of a deportation order or without leave;

    (b) if, having only a limited leave to enter or remain in the United Kingdom, he knowingly either—

        (i) remains beyond the time limited by the leave; or

        (ii) fails to observe a condition of the leave;

(c) if, having lawfully entered the United Kingdom without leave by virtue of section 8(1) above, he remains without leave beyond the time allowed by section 8(1);

(d) if, without reasonable excuse, he fails to comply with any requirement imposed on him under Schedule 2 to this Act to report to a medical officer of health or to attend, or submit to a test or examination, as required by such an officer;

(e) if, without reasonable excuse, he fails to observe any restriction imposed on him under Schedule 2 or 3 to this Act as to residence, as to his employment or occupation or as to reporting to the police, to an immigration officer or to the Secretary of State;

(f) if he leaves a train in the United Kingdom after being placed on board under Schedule 2 or 3 to this Act with a view to his removal from the United Kingdom;

(g) if he leaves or seeks to leave the United Kingdom through the tunnel system in contravention of a restriction imposed by or under an Order in Council under section 3(7) of this Act.

(1A) A person commits an offence under subsection (1)(b)(i) above on the day when he first knows that the time limited by his leave has expired and continues to commit it throughout any period during which he is in the United Kingdom thereafter; but a person shall not be prosecuted under that provision more than once in respect of the same limited leave.

(3) The extended time limit for prosecutions which is provided for by section 28 below shall apply to offences under subsection (1)(a) and (c) above.

(4) In proceedings for an offence against subsection (1)(a) above of entering the United Kingdom without leave,—

(a) any stamp purporting to have been imprinted on a passport or other travel document by an immigration officer on a particular date for the purpose of giving leave shall be presumed to have been duly so imprinted, unless the contrary is proved;

(b) proof that a person had leave to enter the United Kingdom shall lie on the defence if, but only if, he is shown to have entered within six months before the date when the proceedings were commenced.

(2) Allocation

This offence is triable summarily: *Immigration Act* 1971, s.24.   **20–111**

(3) Elements of the offence

Section 8 allows for seamen and aircraft crew who arrive in the UK to enter without   **20–112**
leave and remain in the country until their vessel leaves again.

The power to give or refuse leave to enter or remain in the UK is only exercisable in writing: section 4(1). To prosecute under section 24 there must be evidence of a written notice. A defective stamp in a passport which omitted to note that leave was limited did not amount to sufficient notice although verbal information had been given: *Lamptey v. Owen* [1982] Crim.L.R. 42.

These are continuing offences which may be prosecuted at any time whilst the limited leave or conditions on leave apply: *Manickavasagar v. Metropolitan Police Commissioner* [1987] Crim.L.R. 50.

Immigration Act 1971, s.28

Proceedings

28.—(1) Where the offence is one to which, under section 24 or 26 above, an extended time   **20–113**
limit for prosecutions is to apply, then—

(a) an information relating to the offence may in England and Wales be tried by a magistrates' court if it is laid within six months after the commission of the offence, or if it is laid within three years after the commission of the offence and not more than two months after the date certified by an officer of police above the rank of chief superintendent to be the date on which evidence sufficient to justify proceedings came to the notice of an officer of the police force to which he belongs; and

    (b) summary proceedings for the offence may in Scotland be commenced within six months after the commission of the offence, or within three years after the commission of the offence and not more than two months after the date on which evidence sufficient in the opinion of the Lord Advocate to justify proceedings came to his knowledge; and

    (c) a complaint charging the commission of the offence may in Northern Ireland be heard and determined by a magistrates' court if it is made within six months after the commission of the offence, or if it is made within three years after the commission of the offence and not more than two months after the date certified by an officer of police not below the rank of assistant chief constable to be the date on which evidence sufficient to justify the proceedings came to the notice of the police in Northern Ireland.

(2) For purposes of subsection (1)(b) above proceedings shall be deemed to be commenced on the date on which a warrant to apprehend or to cite the accused is granted, if such warrant is executed without undue delay; and a certificate of the Lord Advocate as to the date on which such evidence as is mentioned in subsection (1)(b) came to his knowledge shall be conclusive evidence.

(3) For the purposes of the trial of a person for an offence under this Part of this Act, the offence shall be deemed to have been committed either at the place at which it actually was committed or at any place at which he may be.

(4) Any powers exercisable under this Act in the case of any person may be exercised notwithstanding that proceedings for an offence under this Part of this Act have been taken against him.

20–114   The certificate of awareness of sufficient evidence may be signed after a not guilty plea is entered but before the trial begins. The court does not start to try the case until evidence is called: *Quazi v. DPP* (1988) 152 J.P. 385.

(4) Sentence

20–115   The maximum penalty for this offence is a fine of not more than level 5 on the standard scale, imprisonment for a period of not more than six months or both: *Immigration Act* 1971, s.24(1). After commencement of the relevant provisions, the maximum custodial sentence in a magistrates' court will be 12 months' imprisonment: *Criminal Justice Act* 2003, ss.154 and 282. Custodial sentences of less than 12 months will consist of a custody plus order (see *post*, Ch.23).

A recommendation for deportation can be made by a court on convicting a person where the defendant is over 18 and not a British citizen of an imprisonable offence—see Sentencing, Part IV in this work.

B. DECEPTION

(1) Definition

Immigration Act 1971, s.24A

Deception
20–116   24A.—(1) A person who is not a British citizen is guilty of an offence if, by means which include deception by him—

    (a) he obtains or seeks to obtain leave to enter or remain in the United Kingdom; or

    (b) he secures or seeks to secure the avoidance, postponement or revocation of enforcement action against him.

(2) "Enforcement action", in relation to a person, means—

    (a) the giving of directions for his removal from the United Kingdom ("directions") under Schedule 2 to this Act or section 10 of the *Immigration and Asylum Act* 1999;

    (b) the making of a deportation order against him under section 5 of this Act; or

    (c) his removal from the United Kingdom in consequence of directions or a deportation order.

(3) A person guilty of an offence under this section is liable—

    (a) on summary conviction, to imprisonment for a term not exceeding six months or to a fine not exceeding the statutory maximum, or to both; or

    (b) on conviction on indictment, to imprisonment for a term not exceeding two years or to a fine, or to both.

[This section was inserted by the *Asylum and Immigration Act* 1996, s.28.]

(2) Allocation

This offence is triable either way: section 24A(3). The extended time limit for prosecutions provided under section 28 applies to this section: section 24A(4). **20–117**

(3) Sentence

The maximum penalty for an offence under this section is imprisonment for a term not exceeding six months, a fine not exceeding the statutory maximum or both: section 24(3). After commencement of the relevant provisions, the maximum custodial sentence in a magistrates' court will be 12 months' imprisonment: *Criminal Justice Act* 2003, ss.154 and 282. Custodial sentences of less than 12 months will consist of a custody plus order (see *post*, Ch.23). A recommendation for deportation can be made by a court on convicting a person over 18 who is not a British citizen of an imprisonable offence—see Sentencing, Part IV in this work. **20–118**

C. Assisting Illegal Entry and Harbouring

(1) Definition

Immigration Act 1971, s.25

Assisting unlawful immigration to member State

    25.—(1) A person commits an offence if he— **20–119**

    (a) does an act which facilitates the commission of a breach of immigration law by an individual who is not a citizen of the European Union,

    (b) knows or has reasonable cause for believing that the act facilitates the commission of a breach of immigration law by the individual, and

    (c) knows or has reasonable cause for believing that the individual is not a citizen of the European Union.

    (2) In subsection (1) "immigration law" means a law which has effect in a member State and which controls, in respect of some or all persons who are not nationals of the State, entitlement to—

    (a) enter the State,

    (b) transit across the State, or

    (c) be in the State.

    (3) A document issued by the government of a member State certifying a matter of law in that State—

    (a) shall be admissible in proceedings for an offence under this section, and

    (b) shall be conclusive as to the matter certified.

    (4) Subsection (1) applies to anything done—

    (a) in the United Kingdom,

    (b) outside the United Kingdom by an individual to whom subsection (5) applies, or

    (c) outside the United Kingdom by a body incorporated under the law of a part of the United Kingdom.

    (5) This subsection applies to—

    (a) a British citizen,

    (b) a British overseas territories citizen,

    (c) a British National (Overseas),

    (d) a British Overseas citizen,

     (e) a person who is a British subject under the *British Nationality Act* 1981, and

     (f) a British protected person within the meaning of that Act.

  (6) A person guilty of an offence under this section shall be liable—

     (a) on conviction on indictment, to imprisonment for a term not exceeding 14 years, to a fine or to both, or

     (b) on summary conviction, to imprisonment for a term not exceeding six months, to a fine not exceeding the statutory maximum or to both.

20–120   [This section is printed as amended by the *Criminal Law Act* 1977, s.28, the *MCA* 1980, s.32(2), the *British Nationality Act* 1981, Sched. 4, the *Criminal Justice Act* 1982, ss.38 and 46, the *Asylum and Immigration Act* 1996, s.5 and the *Immigration and Asylum Act* 1999, s.29 and Scheds 14 and 16 and the *British Overseas Territories Act* 2002, s.2(3).]

(2) Allocation

20–121   This offence is triable either way: section 25(1). The extended time limit for prosecutions provided under section 28 applies to this section: section 25(4).

(3) Elements of the offence

20–122   The offence under section 25(1) can relate to the implementation of arrangements for facilitating entry which, on usual principles, would be completed by the carrying out of such arrangements, irrespective of whether or not entry has taken place. The charge can properly relate to a would-be or intending illegal entrant, as opposed to someone who had already become an illegal entrant by reason of passing through or attempting to pass through immigration control by concealment or deception: *Eyck* [2000] All E.R. 569, CA. In *Eyck* (*ante*) the Court held that it was a matter for the jury to decide whether it had been proved that passengers carried in a car driven by the defendant onto a UK-bound ferry intended to enter or seek to enter illegally and whether the defendant was knowingly concerned in carrying out arrangements for facilitating such illegal entry. If they so decided, a conviction under section 25 would be appropriate. The Court also held that an offence under section 25(1)(b) may relate to an intending asylum claimant.

20–123   It is a crime to assist illegal immigrants to leave their disembarkation port, even if they have already technically entered the United Kingdom. In *Amat Jit Singh* (1973) 1 All E.R. 122, CA, Lawton L.J. stated that section 25 defines the offences which can be committed by those who help illegal entrants. He continued:

> 'The help may come in two ways: the illegal entrant may be given help to get into the United Kingdom or he may be helped after he has arrived here. Section 25 (1) was intended to deal with the first kind of help; section 25 (2) with the second: but they are not mutually exclusive. The help to get in may be, and often is, continued without any break long after the illegal entry has been effected. There may be no dividing line between helping to effect entry and helping by way of harbouring…Now those who are minded to enter the United Kingdom illegally have no wish to be discovered as soon as they disembark. Effective arrangements for an illegal entry would be likely to include plans for getting the entrant away as quickly as possible from the point of disembarkation. Those who made or carried out such plans would be facilitating entry into the United Kingdom.'

20–124   Section 25(2) creates two separate offences of harbouring: the first involves knowledge that a person is an "illegal entrant" as defined in section 33 and the second, knowledge that the person was an "overstayer" as defined in section 24. The prosecution must state in the information the illegal status relied upon for alleging that the accused knew or believed that status to exist. If the prosecution intends to establish one or other of the offences it must lay separate informations, otherwise it will lay itself open to arguments of duplicity: *Rahman and Qadir v. DPP* [1993] Crim.L.R. 874.

(4) Sentence

20–125   On summary conviction the maximum sentence is six months' imprisonment and/or the maximum fine. After commencement of the relevant provisions, the maximum custodial sentence in a magistrates' court will be 12 months' imprisonment: *Criminal Justice Act* 2003, ss.154 and 282. Custodial sentences of less than 12 months will consist of a custody plus order (see *post*, Ch.23). In *Sackey* [2004] 2 Cr.App.R. 556 the court held that a period of imprisonment for three years on a guilty plea was the guideline so such cases will generally be committed to the Crown Court for sentence.

D. ILLEGAL ENTRY AND SIMILAR OFFENCES

(1) Definition

Asylum and Immigration (Treatment of Claimants) Act 2004, s.2

Entering United Kingdom without passport, &c.

2—(1) A person commits an offence if at a leave or asylum interview he does not have with him an immigration document which–   **20–126**

    (a) is in force, and

    (b) satisfactorily establishes his identity and nationality or citizenship.

(2) A person commits an offence if at a leave or asylum interview he does not have with him, in respect of any dependent child with whom he claims to be travelling or living, an immigration document which–

    (a) is in force, and

    (b) satisfactorily establishes the child's identity and nationality or citizenship.

(3) But a person does not commit an offence under subsection (1) or (2) if–

    (a) the interview referred to in that subsection takes place after the person has entered the United Kingdom, and

    (b) within the period of three days beginning with the date of the interview the person provides to an immigration officer or to the Secretary of State a document of the kind referred to in that subsection.

(4) It is a defence for a person charged with an offence under subsection (1)–

    (a) to prove that he is an EEA national,

    (b) to prove that he is a member of the family of an EEA national and that he is exercising a right under the Community Treaties in respect of entry to or residence in the United Kingdom,

    (c) to prove that he has a reasonable excuse for not being in possession of a document of the kind specified in subsection (1),

    (d) to produce a false immigration document and to prove that he used that document as an immigration document for all purposes in connection with his journey to the United Kingdom, or

    (e) to prove that he travelled to the United Kingdom without, at any stage since he set out on the journey, having possession of an immigration document.

(5) It is a defence for a person charged with an offence under subsection (2) in respect of a child–

    (a) to prove that the child is an EEA national,

    (b) to prove that the child is a member of the family of an EEA national and that the child is exercising a right under the Community Treaties in respect of entry to or residence in the United Kingdom,

    (c) to prove that the person has a reasonable excuse for not being in possession of a document of the kind specified in subsection (2),

    (d) to produce a false immigration document and to prove that it was used as an immigration document for all purposes in connection with the child's journey to the United Kingdom, or

    (e) to prove that he travelled to the United Kingdom with the child without, at any stage since he set out on the journey, having possession of an immigration document in respect of the child.

(6) Where the charge for an offence under subsection (1) or (2) relates to an interview which takes place after the defendant has entered the United Kingdom–

    (a) subsections (4)(c) and (5)(c) shall not apply, but

(b) it is a defence for the defendant to prove that he has a reasonable excuse for not providing a document in accordance with subsection (3).

(7) For the purposes of subsections (4) to (6)–

(a) the fact that a document was deliberately destroyed or disposed of is not a reasonable excuse for not being in possession of it or for not providing it in accordance with subsection (3), unless it is shown that the destruction or disposal was–

(i) for a reasonable cause, or

(ii) beyond the control of the person charged with the offence, and

(b) in paragraph (a)(i) "reasonable cause" does not include the purpose of–

(i) delaying the handling or resolution of a claim or application or the taking of a decision,

(ii) increasing the chances of success of a claim or application, or

(iii) complying with instructions or advice given by a person who offers advice about, or facilitates, immigration into the United Kingdom, unless in the circumstances of the case it is unreasonable to expect non-compliance with the instructions or advice.

(8) A person shall be presumed for the purposes of this section not to have a document with him if he fails to produce it to an immigration officer or official of the Secretary of State on request.

(9) A person guilty of an offence under this section shall be liable–

(a) on conviction on indictment, to imprisonment for a term not exceeding two years, to a fine or to both, or

(b) on summary conviction, to imprisonment for a term not exceeding twelve months, to a fine not exceeding the statutory maximum or to both.

(10) If a constable or immigration officer reasonably suspects that a person has committed an offence under this section he may arrest the person without warrant.

(11) An offence under this section shall be treated as–

(a) a relevant offence for the purposes of sections 28B and 28D of the *Immigration Act* 1971 (c. 77) (search, entry and arrest), and

(b) an offence under Part III of that Act (criminal proceedings) for the purposes of sections 28(4), 28E, 28G and 28H (search after arrest, &c.) of that Act.

(12) In this section–

"EEA national" means a national of a State which is a contracting party to the Agreement on the European Economic Area signed at Oporto on 2nd May 1992 (as it has effect from time to time),

"immigration document" means –

(a) a passport, and

(b) a document which relates to a national of a State other than the United Kingdom and which is designed to serve the same purpose as a passport, and

"leave or asylum interview" means an interview with an immigration officer or an official of the Secretary of State at which a person–

(a) seeks leave to enter or remain in the United Kingdom, or

(b) claims that to remove him from or require him to leave the United Kingdom would breach the United Kingdom's obligations under the Refugee Convention or would be unlawful under section 6 of the *Human Rights Act* 1998 (c. 42) as being incompatible with his Convention rights.

(13) For the purposes of this section–

(a) a document which purports to be, or is designed to look like, an immigration document, is a false immigration document, and

(b) an immigration document is a false immigration document if and in so far as it is used–

(i) outside the period for which it is expressed to be valid,

(ii) contrary to provision for its use made by the person issuing it, or

(iii) by or in respect of a person other than the person to or for whom it was issued.

(14) Section 11 of the *Immigration Act* 1971 (c. 77) shall have effect for the purpose of the construction of a reference in this section to entering the United Kingdom.

(15) In so far as this section extends to England and Wales, subsection (9)(b) shall, until

the commencement of section 154 of the *Criminal Justice Act* 2003 (c. 44) (increased limit on magistrates' power of imprisonment), have effect as if the reference to twelve months were a reference to six months.

(16) In so far as this section extends to Scotland, subsection (9)(b) shall have effect as if the reference to twelve months were a reference to six months.

(17) In so far as this section extends to Northern Ireland, subsection (9)(b) shall have effect as if the reference to twelve months were a reference to six months.

This section came into force on September 22, 2004.

(2) Allocation

This offence is triable either way: section 2(9).   **20–127**

(3) Elements of the offence

This offence was introduced to counter the effect of people arriving in the UK who **20–128** destroyed or otherwise disposed of forged travel documents prior to going through immigration procedures. A person at a leave or asylum interview commits an offence if he does not have a valid passport or other document serving the same purpose as a passport which establishes identity and nationality or citizenship. The offence may be committed at the port of entry on arrival or at a later interview when 3 days may be allowed to produce the relevant documents. The statute provides defences under subsection 4 which include having a reasonable excuse for not being in possession of such a document. Deliberate destruction or disposal of the document does not amount to a reasonable excuse in itself unless there was reasonable cause to destroy or dispose of the document or the destruction or disposal was beyond the control of the person charged. A reasonable excuse might arise if a person is travelling in a family group and someone else had custody of the passports or where individuals are intimidated or threatened to such an extent by a third party that it is reasonable to expect that instructions to destroy or dispose of the document would be followed. In *Navabi* [2005] EWCA Crim 2865 it was held that a request for asylum is not a reasonable excuse under section 2(4)(c) for not being in possession of the relevant document. There is a reverse burden of proof on the defendant but it is compatible with Article 6 ECHR.

In *Thet v. DPP* [2006] EWHC 2701 the complex provisions of section 2 of the *Asylum and Immigration (Treatment of Claimants) Act* 2004 were considered. The appellant was a Burmese national who arrived in the UK and passed through immigration control with a false passport which was later returned to an agent. He subsequently attended asylum screening interviews and was unable to produce any travel documents either false or genuine. He claimed that he was unable to obtain a passport in his country of origin because he had been a political prisoner. The statutory defence under section 2(3) and 2(6)(b) was put forward at trial but rejected on the basis that the provisions applied only to any false immigration documents that may have been used on the journey and not to any non-existent genuine passport. On appeal it was held that the Act could not be restrictively interpreted to apply only to any false documents used on the journey. It was said that the natural reading of the section allowed for the defendant to rely on the defence of reasonable excuse for the failure to produce a genuine passport as well as false documents. The court observed that the statute was ambiguous and poorly drafted and accepted that this interpretation could well undermine the purpose of the legislation but as the outcome did not lead to absurdity that was the only proper way in which the section could be interpreted.

This case could have a profound effect on prosecutions against persons arriving in this country without valid travel documents. If the inability to obtain a passport in their home country provides a defence for failing to produce a proper travel document the courts may find defendants disposing of false travel documents before passing through immigration and raising this defence at the earliest opportunity.

(4) Sentence

On summary conviction the maximum sentence is six months' imprisonment and/or **20–129** a fine at level 5. After commencement of the relevant provisions, the maximum custodial sentence in a magistrates' court will be 12 months' imprisonment: *Criminal Justice Act* 2003, ss.154 and 282. Custodial sentences of less than 12 months will consist of a custody plus order (see *post*, Ch.23).

On conviction on indictment the maximum sentence is two years or a fine or both. Guidelines following forged passport cases indicate the starting point for a guilty plea and no previous convictions would be four months' imprisonment. In *Wang* [2005] EWCA Crim. 293, a sentence of 10 months' imprisonment for an offence under this section was reduced to two months on appeal. See also *Ai* [2005] EWCA Crim 936 where it was held that a five-month sentence of imprisonment for an offence of failing to have immigration documents was appropriate taking into account mitigation but also considering the deterrent effect of the sentence.

VI. POLICE

A. POWER TO MAKE ORDERS IN RESPECT OF PROPERTY IN POSSESSION OF POLICE

Police (Property) Act 1897, s.1

Power to make orders with respect to property in possession of police

20–130   **1.**—(1) Where any property has come into the possession of the police in connexion with their investigation of a suspected offence, a court of summary jurisdiction may, on application, either by an officer of police or by a claimant of the property, make an order for the delivery of the property to the person appearing to the magistrate or court to be the owner thereof, or, if the owner cannot be ascertained, make such order with respect to the property as to the magistrate or court may seem meet.

(2) An order under this section shall not affect the right of any person to take within six months from the date of the order legal proceedings against any person in possession of property delivered by virtue of the order for the recovery of the property, but on the expiration of those six months the right shall cease.

20–131   The police come into possession of property when investigating offences but if the charge is dropped or the accused acquitted and there is a dispute over ownership, it may be necessary for an order to be applied for to allow the police to release the property. If no relevant order is made at the end of the proceedings, the police or a claimant may apply to the magistrates court' for an order under the *Police (Property) Act* 1897. The court will decide who appears to be the "owner" of the property.

An application is made by way of complaint for a summons and costs may be ordered under section 64 of the *Magistrates' Courts Act* 1980: *R. v. Uxbridge Justices ex p. Metropolitan Police Commissioner* [1981] Q.B. 829.

20–132   The court should not make use of this procedure when there are real difficulties in deciding ownership or if questions of legal ownership are in dispute and the word "owner" should be given its ordinary and popular meaning: *Raymond Lyons & Co v. Metropolitan Police Commissioner* [1975] Q.B. 321. The fact that proceedings are pending at the County Court for delivery of the property does not of itself make the issue complex and beyond the magistrates' jurisdiction: *R. v. Maidstone Magistrates' Court ex p. Knight* (2000) WL 1027029. The fact that the owner of the property may have come by it illegally is irrelevant. The question at issue is who has good or better possessory title: *Costello v. Chief Constable of Derbyshire* [2001] 3 All E.R. 150 and *Haley v. Chief Constable of Northumbria* (2002) 166 J.P. 719. The morality of the claim is also irrelevant and where a claimant was acquitted of soliciting murder, it was held that the nature of the charge was not a good reason for the magistrates declining to return the £10,000 that was paid to a police officer who posed as a hired assassin: *R. (Carter) v. Ipswich Magistrates' Court* [2002] EWHC 332.

20–133   The police may come into possession of property taken from the accused on arrest and the return of the property may be sought during the proceedings by the defendant under the *Magistrates' Courts Act* 1980.

Magistrates' Courts Act 1980, s.48

Return of property taken from accused.

48. Where a summons or warrant has been issued requiring any person to appear or be brought before a magistrates' court to answer to an information, or where any person has been arrested without a warrant for an offence, and property has been taken from him after the issue of the summons or warrant or, as the case may be, on or after his arrest without a warrant, the police shall report the taking of the property, with particulars of the property, to the magistrates' court which deals with the case; and, if the court, being of opinion that the whole or any part of the property can be returned to the accused consistently with the interests of justice and the safe custody of the accused, so directs, the property, or such part of it as the court directs, shall be returned to the accused or to such other person as he may require.   **20–134**

This provision relates only to a person who has been charged and who wishes to **20–135** reclaim his property: *Arnell v. Harris* [1945] K.B. 60. It only covers property taken from the person of the defendant so if the property was taken from his premises at the time of arrest, there is no power to order its return under this section, but if the court is of the opinion that the property seized should be returned as a necessary part of the defence case it has the discretion to refuse to proceed. *R. v. Southampton Magistrates' Court ex p. Newman* [1988] 3 All E.R. 669.

B. Impersonation of a Police Officer

(1) Definition

Police Act 1996, s.90

Impersonation, etc.

90.—(1) Any person who with intent to deceive impersonates a member of a police force or **20–136** special constable, or makes any statement or does any act calculated falsely to suggest that he is such a member or constable, shall be guilty of an offence and liable on summary conviction to imprisonment for a term not exceeding six months or to a fine not exceeding level 5 on the standard scale, or to both.

(2) Any person who, not being a constable, wears any article of police uniform in circumstances where it gives him an appearance so nearly resembling that of a member of a police force as to be calculated to deceive shall be guilty of an offence and liable on summary conviction to a fine not exceeding level 3 on the standard scale.

(3) Any person who, not being a member of a police force or special constable, has in his possession any article of police uniform shall, unless he proves that he obtained possession of that article lawfully and has possession of it for a lawful purpose, be guilty of an offence and liable on summary conviction to a fine not exceeding level 1 on the standard scale.

(4) In this section—

   (a) "article of police uniform" means any article of uniform or any distinctive badge or mark or document of identification usually issued to members of police forces or special constables, or anything having the appearance of such an article, badge, mark or document.

   (aa) "member of a police force" includes a member of the British Transport Police Force, and

   (b) "special constable" means a special constable appointed for a police area.

[This section is printed as amended by the *Anti-Terrorism, Crime and Security Act* 2001, Sched. 7.]

(2) Allocation

The offences in this section are triable summarily: section 90(1), (2), (3).   **20–137**

(3) Elements of the offence

20–138   It is an offence to wear a uniform which is likely to deceive persons into thinking that one is a police officer, even if that deception is not intended. In *Turner v. Shearer* [1973] 1 All E.R. 397, DC, the defendant was wearing secondhand articles of police uniform, and persons were misled into thinking that he was a police officer. The defendant did not intend to mislead anyone. The Divisional Court held that "calculated" meant "likely," not "intended" and the defendant was convicted.

(4) Sentence

20–139   The offence under subsection (1) carries a maximum penalty of six months imprisonment, a fine not exceeding the statutory maximum or both: section 90(1). The offence under subsection (2) carries a maximum penalty of a fine not exceeding level three on the standard scale: section 90(2). The offence under subsection (3) carries a maximum penalty of a fine not exceeding level one on the standard scale: section 90(3). After commencement of the relevant provisions, the maximum custodial sentence in a magistrates' court will be 12 months' imprisonment: *Criminal Justice Act* 2003, ss.154 and 282. Custodial sentences of less than 12 months will consist of a custody plus order (see *post*, Ch.23).

VII. PRISONS

A. HARBOURING AN ESCAPED PRISONER

(1) Definition

Criminal Justice Act 1961, s.22

20–140   **22.**—(1) [...]

(2) If any person knowingly harbours a person who has escaped from a prison or other institution to which the said section thirty-nine applies, or who, having been sentenced in any part of the United Kingdom or in any of the Channel Islands or the Isle of Man to imprisonment or detention, is otherwise unlawfully at large, or gives to any such person any assistance with intent to prevent, hinder or interfere with his being taken into custody, he shall be liable—

    (a) on summary conviction, to imprisonment for a term not exceeding six months or to a fine not exceeding one hundred pounds, or to both;

    (b) on conviction on indictment, to imprisonment for a term not exceeding ten years, or to a fine, or to both.

(3) In the following enactments (which make provision for the application of sections thirty-nine to forty-two of the *Prison Act* 1952) that is to say, subsection (3) of section one hundred and twenty-two of the *Army Act* 1955, subsection (3) of section one hundred and twenty-two of the *Air Force Act* 1955 and subsection (3) of section eighty-two of the *Naval Discipline Act* 1957, references to the said section thirty-nine shall be construed as including references to subsection (2) of this section.

(4) [...]

(2) Allocation

20–141   This offence is triable either way: section 22(2).

(3) Elements of the offence

20–142   In *Darch v. Weight* (1984) 79 Cr.App.R 40, CA it was held that "harbour" meant to shelter or provide refuge and that could be done irrespective of any interest in the premises concerned. Merely giving assistance to an escaped prisoner without actually sheltering him would not amount to "harbouring" him. The defendant was a lodger in a house into which the landlady admitted three escaped prisoners. Both she and the landlady were charged and convicted, though the landlady's conviction was later quashed by the Crown Court. On the defendant's appeal, the Divisional Court held that as the defendant had done no positive act to provide shelter, she was not guilty of "harbouring" under section 22(2) of the 1961 Act.

The yard of a police station is not a "prison or other institution" within the meaning of the *Prison Act* 1952, s.39: *Nicoll v. Catron* (1985) 81 Cr.App.R 339, DC.

The offence of escaping from custody and being unlawfully at large is a common law offence, triable on indictment only. In *Dhillon* [2005] EWCA Crim 2996 the essential ingredients of the offence of escape were considered in detail. For the offence to be made out the defendant must actually be in custody; he must know or be reckless as to his being in custody and the custody must be lawful. In this case the conviction was quashed on appeal. The defendant had been arrested as an illegal immigrant but had then been accompanied to hospital. In the apparent absence of any officers he later walked out of the hospital. It was held that he had not committed the offence of escape as there was no continuity of custody and no evidence that the defendant was aware of any constraint placed upon him.

(4) Sentence

When tried summarily, the maximum penalty for this offence is imprisonment for a **20–143** term not exceeding six months, a fine not exceeding the statutory maximum or both: *CJA* 1961, s.22(2)(a). On commencement of the relevant provisions, the maximum custodial sentence in a magistrates' court will be 12 months' imprisonment: *Criminal Justice Act* 2003, ss.154 and 282. Custodial sentences of less than 12 months will consist of a custody plus order (see *post*, Ch.23).

VIII. PUBLIC HEALTH

A. PROHIBITION ON UNLICENSED DISPOSAL OF WASTE

(1) Definition

Control of Pollution Act 1974, s.3

Prohibition of unlicensed disposal of waste
  3.—(1) Except in prescribed cases, a person shall not—   **20–144**
  (a) deposit controlled waste on any land or cause or knowingly permit controlled waste to be deposited on any land; or
  (b) use any plant or equipment, or cause or knowingly permit any plant or equipment to be used, for the purpose of disposing of controlled waste or of dealing in a prescribed manner with controlled waste,
unless the land on which the waste is deposited or, as the case may be, which forms the site of the plant or equipment is occupied by the holder of a licence issued in pursuance of section 5 of this Act (in this Part of this Act referred to as a "disposal licence") which authorises the deposit or use in question and the deposit or use is in accordance with the conditions, if any, specified in the licence.

  (2) Except in a case falling within the following subsection, a person who contravenes any of the provisions of the preceding subsection shall, subject to subsection (4) of this section, be guilty of an offence and liable on summary conviction to a fine of an amount not exceeding £400 or on conviction on indictment to imprisonment for a term not exceeding two years or a fine or both.

  (3) A person who contravenes paragraph (a) of subsection (1) of this section in a case where—
  (a) the waste in question is of a kind which is poisonous, noxious or polluting; and
  (b) its presence on the land is likely to give rise to an environmental hazard; and
  (c) it is deposited on the land in such circumstances or for such a period that whoever deposited it there may reasonably be assumed to have abandoned it there or

to have brought it there for the purpose of its being disposed of (whether by himself or others) as waste,

shall, subject to the following subsection, be guilty of an offence and liable on summary conviction to imprisonment for a term not exceeding six months or a fine not exceeding £400 or both or, on conviction on indictment, to imprisonment for a term not exceeding five years or a fine or both.

(4) It shall be a defence for a person charged with an offence under this section to prove—

(a) that he—

    (i) took care to inform himself, from persons who were in a position to provide the information, as to whether the deposit or use to which the charge relates would be in contravention of subsection (1) of this section, and

    (ii) did not know and had no reason to suppose that the information given to him was false or misleading and that the deposit or use might be in contravention of that subsection; or

(b) that he acted under instructions from his employer and neither knew nor had reason to suppose that the deposit or use was in contravention of the said subsection (1); or

(c) in the case of an offence of making, causing or permitting a deposit or use otherwise than in accordance with conditions specified in a disposal licence, that he took all such steps as were reasonably open to him to ensure that the conditions were complied with; or

(d) that the acts specified in the charge were done in an emergency in order to avoid danger to the public and that, as soon as reasonably practicable after they were done, particulars of them were furnished to the disposal authority in whose area the acts were done.

(5) In this section and subsections (5) and (6) of the following section 'land' includes land covered with waters where the land is above the low-water mark of ordinary spring tides and the waters are not inland waters (within the meaning of Chapter I of Part III of the *Water Act* 1989).

[This section will be repealed by the *Environmental Protection Act* 1990, Sched. 16, when it comes into force.]

(2) Allocation

20–145　　This offence is triable either way: section (3)(c).

(3) Elements of the offence

20–146　　The offence of depositing controlled waste is committed when waste is left on land from which it will later be removed, and does not occur only when the waste reaches its final place of deposit: *R. v. Metropolitan Stipendiary Magistrate ex p. London Waste Regulation Authority* [1993] 3 All E.R. 113, QBD. This finding was approved in *Smith (David Brian)* [1999] Env.L.R. 433, CA, the Court emphasising that the purpose of the 1974 Act was to protect the environment from the consequences of dumping waste and it would diminish its efficacy if the meaning of "deposit" under section 3(1) was restricted to "final deposit".

Controlled waste is defined in section 30(1) of the 1974 Act as 'household, industrial and commercial waste or any such waste.' Section 30(5) provides that

'(a) household waste consists of waste from a private dwelling or residential home or from premises forming part of a university or school or other educational establishment or forming part of a hospital or nursing home (b) industrial waste consists of waste from any factory within the meaning of the *Factories Act* 1961 and any premises occupied by a body corporate established by or under any enactment for the purpose of carrying on under national ownership any industry or part of an industry or any undertaking, excluding waste from any mine or quarry and (c) commercial waste consists of waste from premises used wholly or mainly for the purposes of a trade or business or the purposes of sport, recreation or entertainment excluding—

(i) household and industrial waste and (ii) waste from any mine or quarry and waste from premises used for agriculture within the meaning of the *Agriculture Act* 1947 or, in Scotland, the *Agriculture (Scotland) Act* 1948, and (iii) waste of any other description prescribed for the purposes of this sub-paragraph.'

(4) Defences

Section 3(4) provides a defence to a charge under this section. In *Durham CC v. Peter Connors Industrial Services Ltd* [1993] Env.L.R. 197, QBD, it was held that in order to establish a defence under section 3(4) it had to be shown that the defendant company charged with depositing waste had received information about each specific deposit to which a charge related and then a judgment on whether that deposit might contravene the section could be formed. The defendant company had operated a blanket system of checks whereby drivers were instructed to check, so far as possible, that there were no toxic materials in the waste deposited. There was no reason for the defendant to believe that the information from the drivers was false or misleading but it was not specific enough to provide a defence under section 3(4). **20–147**

(5) Sentence

This offence is triable either way with a maximum sentence on summary conviction **20–148** of a fine not exceeding £400. If the offence is aggravated under subsection (3), the maximum offence on summary conviction is a fine not exceeding £400 or six months' imprisonment. After commencement of the relevant provisions, the maximum custodial sentence in a magistrates' court will be 12 months' imprisonment: *Criminal Justice Act* 2003, ss.154 and 282. Custodial sentences of less than 12 months will consist of a custody plus order (see *post*, Ch.23).

B. Prohibition on Unauthorised or Harmful Deposit Treatment of Waste

(1) Definition

Environmental Protection Act 1990, s.33

Prohibition on unauthorised or harmful deposit, treatment or disposal etc. of waste
    33.—(1) Subject to subsection (2) and (3) below and, in relation to Scotland, to section 54 **20–149** below, a person shall not—
        (a) deposit controlled waste, or knowingly cause or knowingly permit controlled waste to be deposited in or on any land unless a waste management licence authorising the deposit is in force and the deposit is in accordance with the licence;
        (b) treat, keep or dispose of controlled waste, or knowingly cause or knowingly permit controlled waste to be treated, kept or disposed of—
            (i) in or on any land, or
            (ii) by means of any mobile plant,
        except under and in accordance with a waste management licence;
        (c) treat, keep or dispose of controlled waste in a manner likely to cause pollution of the environment or harm to human health.
    (2) Subsection (1) above does not apply in relation to household waste from a domestic property which is treated, kept or disposed of within the curtilage of the dwelling by or with the permission of the occupier of the dwelling.
    (3) Subsection (1)(a), (b) or (c) above do not apply in cases prescribed in regulations made by the Secretary of State and the regulations may make different exceptions for different areas.
    (4) The Secretary of State, in exercising his power under subsection (3) above, shall have regard in particular to the expediency of excluding from the controls imposed by waste management licences—
        (a) any deposits which are small enough or of such a temporary nature that they may be so excluded;

Part III

(b) any means of treatment or disposal which are innocuous enough to be so excluded;

(c) cases for which adequate controls are provided by another enactment than this section.

(5) Where controlled waste is carried in and deposited from a motor vehicle, the person who controls or is in a position to control the use of the vehicle shall, for the purposes of subsection (1)(a) above, be treated as knowingly causing the waste to be deposited whether or not he gave any instructions for this to be done.

(6) A person who contravenes subsection (1) above or any condition of a waste management licence commits an offence.

(7) It shall be a defence for a person charged with an offence under this section to prove—

(a) that he took all reasonable precautions and exercised all due diligence to avoid the commission of the offence; or

(b) that he acted under instructions from his employer and neither knew nor had reason to suppose that the acts done by him constituted a contravention of subsection (1) above; or

(c) that the acts alleged to constitute the contravention were done in an emergency in order to avoid danger to human health in a case where—

(i) he took all such steps as were reasonably practicable in the circumstances for minimising pollution of the environment and harm to human health; and

(ii) particulars of the acts were furnished to the waste regulation authority as soon as reasonably practicable after they were done.

(8) Except in a case falling within subsection (9) below, a person who commits an offence under this section shall be liable—

(a) on summary conviction, to imprisonment for a term not exceeding six months or a fine not exceeding £20,000 or both; and

(b) on conviction on indictment, to imprisonment for a term not exceeding two years or a fine or both.

(9) A person who commits an offence under this section in relation to special waste shall be liable—

(a) on summary conviction, to imprisonment for a term not exceeding six months or a fine not exceeding £20,000 or both;

(b) on conviction on indictment, to imprisonment for a term not exceeding five years or a fine or both.

[This section is printed as amended by the *Environment Act* 1995, Sched. 22.]

(2) Allocation

20–150   This offence is triable either way: section 33(8).

(3) Elements of the offence

20–151   The requirement as to knowledge relates to knowledge that the waste is being deposited, rather than knowledge that the deposit breaches the license conditions. In *Shanks & McEwan (Teesside) Ltd v. Environment Agency* [1999] Q.B. 333, QBD, it was held that it was sufficient for the prosecution to prove that the company had on the relevant day knowingly operated and held out the site for the reception and deposit of controlled waste, and that the deposit had not been in accordance with a condition of the licence.

The burden of proof that a defendant had deposited or accepted delivery of "special waste" will lie on the prosecution. However, the burden of proving that the deposit of waste was conducted with prior approval will lie on the defendant, the standard of proof being on the balance of probabilities: *Environment Agency v. ME Foley Contractors Ltd* [2002] EWHC 258; [2002] 1 W.L.R. 1754, QBD.

(4) Defence

20–152   Subsection (6) provides a defence of due diligence, acting under employer instructions or acting under conditions of emergency.

(5) Sentence

When tried summarily, the maximum penalty for this offence is imprisonment for a **20–153** term not exceeding six months, a fine not exceeding £20,000 or both. On commencement of the relevant provisions, the maximum custodial sentence in a magistrates' court will be 12 months' imprisonment: *Criminal Justice Act* 2003, ss.154 and 282. Custodial sentences of less than 12 months will consist of a custody plus order (see *post*, Ch.23).

C. Leaving Litter

(1) Definition

Environmental Protection Act 1990, s.87

Offence of leaving litter

87.—(1) If any person throws down, drops or otherwise deposits in, into or from any place to **20–154** which this section applies, and leaves, any thing whatsoever in such circumstances as to cause, or contribute to, or tend to lead to, the defacement by litter of any place to which this section applies, he shall, subject to subsection (2) below, be guilty of an offence.

(2) No offence is committed under this section where the depositing and leaving of the thing was—

   (a) authorised by law, or

   (b) done with the consent of the owner, occupier or other person or authority having control of the place in or into which that thing was deposited.

(3) This section applies to any public open place and, in so far as the place is not a public open place, also to the following places—

   (a) any relevant highway or relevant road and any trunk road which is a special road;

   (b) any place on relevant land of a principal litter authority;

   (c) any place on relevant Crown land;

   (d) any place on relevant land of any designated statutory undertaker;

   (e) any place on relevant land of any designated educational institution;

   (f) any place on relevant land within a litter control area of a local authority.

(4) In this section "public open place" means a place in the open air to which the public are entitled or permitted to have access without payment; and any covered place open to the air on at least one side and available for public use shall be treated as a public open place.

(5) A person who is guilty of an offence under this section shall be liable on summary conviction to a fine not exceeding level 4 on the standard scale.

(6) A local authority, with a view to promoting the abatement of litter, may take such steps as the authority think appropriate for making the effect of subsection (5) above known to the public in their area.

(7) In any proceedings in Scotland for an offence under this section it shall be lawful to convict the accused on the evidence of one witness.

(2) Allocation

This offence is triable summarily only: section 87(5).   **20–155**

(3) Elements of the offence

A telephone kiosk will not be regarded as a "public open space" or a covered place **20–156** available for public use as they are not open to air on at least one side, but instead have three fixed sides and one door which was usually closed except for access: *DPP v. Felix* [1998] Crim.L.R. 657. The court added that the phrase "otherwise deposits in" was extremely wide and that "deposits" meant no more than places or puts.

The word "litter" should be given its natural meaning of "miscellaneous rubbish left lying about". This will include commercial waste: *Westminster City Council v. Riding* (1996) Env.L.R. 95, QBD.

(4) Sentence

20–157   The maximum penalty for this offence is a fine not exceeding level four on the standard scale: section 87(5).

D. HEALTH AND SAFETY OFFENCES

(1) Health and Safety at Work Act 1974

20–158   Sections 2–7 of the Act impose general duties on employers to ensure the health and safety and welfare at work of their employees and other persons who may be affected by the employer's undertaking, *e.g.* sub-contractors: section 2. A similar duty is imposed on self-employed persons and their workforce who are not employees: section 3.

Persons concerned with premises have a duty relating to health and safety towards persons other than their employees who use premises as a place of work: section 4.

Manufacturers have a duty as regards articles and substances for use at work: section 6.

Employees also have a general duty to take reasonable care for their own health and safety and that of other people affected by their actions: section 7.

(2) Definition

Health and Safety at Work Act 1974, s.33

Offences

20–159   **33.**—(1) It is an offence for a person—

    (a) to fail to discharge a duty to which he is subject by virtue of sections 2 to 7;

    (b) to contravene section 8 or 9;

    (c) to contravene any health and safety regulations or any requirement or prohibition imposed under any such regulations (including any requirement or prohibition to which he is subject by virtue of the terms of or any condition or restriction attached to any licence, approval, exemption or other authority issued, given or granted under the regulations);

    (d) to contravene any requirement imposed by or under regulations under section 14 or intentionally to obstruct any person in the exercise of his powers under that section;

    (e) to contravene any requirement imposed by an inspector under section 20 or 25;

    (f) to prevent or attempt to prevent any other person from appearing before an inspector or from answering any question to which an inspector may by virtue of section 20(2) require an answer;

    (g) to contravene any requirement or prohibition imposed by an improvement notice or a prohibition notice (including any such notice as modified on appeal);

    (h) intentionally to obstruct an inspector in the exercise or performance of his powers or duties or to obstruct a customs officer in the exercise of his powers under section 25A;

    (i) to contravene any requirement imposed by a notice under section 27(1);

    (j) to use or disclose any information in contravention of section 27(4) or 28;

    (k) to make a statement which he knows to be false or recklessly to make a statement which is false where the statement is made—

        (i) in purported compliance with a requirement to furnish any information imposed by or under any of the relevant statutory provisions; or

        (ii) for the purpose of obtaining the issue of a document under any of the relevant statutory provisions to himself or another person;

    (l) intentionally to make a false entry in any register, book, notice or other document required by or under any of the relevant statutory provisions to be kept, served or given or, with intent to deceive, to make use of any such entry which he knows to be false;

    (m) with intent to deceive, to use a document issued or authorised to be issued under any of the relevant statutory provisions or required for any purpose thereunder or to make or have in his possession a document so closely resembling any such document as to be calculated to deceive;

(n) falsely to pretend to be an inspector;

(o) to fail to comply with an order made by a court under section 42.

(1A) Subject to any provision made by virtue of section 15(6)(d), a person guilty of an offence under subsection (1)(a) above consisting of failing to discharge a duty to which he is subject by virtue of sections 2 to 6 shall be liable—

(a) on summary conviction, to a fine not exceeding £20,000;

(b) on conviction on indictment, to a fine.

(2) A person guilty of an offence under paragraph (d), (f), (h) or (n) of subsection (1) above, or of an offence under paragraph (e) of that subsection consisting of contravening a requirement imposed by an inspector under section 20, shall be liable on summary conviction to a fine not exceeding level 5 on the standard scale

(2A) A person guilty of an offence under subsection (1)(g) or (o) above shall be liable—

(a) on summary conviction, to imprisonment for a term not exceeding six months, or a fine not exceeding £20,000, or both;

(b) on conviction on indictment, to imprisonment for a term not exceeding two years, or a fine, or both.

(3) Subject to any provision made by virtue of section 15(6)(d) or (e) or by virtue of paragraph 2(2) of Schedule 3, a person guilty of an offence under subsection (1) above not falling within subsection (1A), (2) or (2A) above, or of an offence under subsection (1)(e) above not falling within the preceding subsection, or of an offence under any of the existing statutory provisions, being an offence for which no other penalty is specified, shall be liable—

(a) on summary conviction, to a fine not exceeding £400;

(b) on conviction on indictment—

(i) if the offence is one to which this sub-paragraph applies, to imprisonment for a term not exceeding two years, or a fine, or both;

(ii) if the offence is not one to which the preceding sub-paragraph applies, to a fine.

(4) Subsection (3)(b)(i) above applies to the following offences—

(a) an offence consisting of contravening any of the relevant statutory provisions by doing otherwise than under the authority of a licence issued by the Executive something for the doing of which such a licence is necessary under the relevant statutory provisions;

(b) an offence consisting of contravening a term of or a condition or restriction attached to any such licence as is mentioned in the preceding paragraph;

(c) an offence consisting of acquiring or attempting to acquire, possessing or using an explosive article or substance (within the meaning of any of the relevant statutory provisions) in contravention of any of the relevant statutory provisions;

(d) [...]

(e) an offence under subsection (1)(j) above.

(3) Allocation

All of the offences created by section 33(1) are triable either way, except those created **20–160** by subssection 1(d), (e), (f), (h) and (n) which are triable summarily only.

Health and Safety at Work Act 1974, s.34(1)–(4), 36–38

Extension of time for bringing summary proceedings

34.—(1) Where—　　　　　　　　　　　　　　　　　　　　　　　　**20–161**

(a) a special report on any matter to which section 14 of this Act applies is made by virtue of subsection (2)(a) of that section; or

(b) a report is made by the person holding an inquiry into any such matter by virtue of subsection (2)(b) of that section; or

(c) a coroner's inquest is held touching the death of any person whose death may have been caused by an accident which happened while he was at work or by a disease which he contracted or probably contracted at work or by any accident,

Part III

act or omission which occurred in connection with the work of any person whatsoever; or

  (d) a public inquiry into any death that may have been so caused is held under the *Fatal Accidents and Sudden Deaths Inquiry (Scotland) Act* 1976,

and it appears from the report or, in a case falling within paragraph (c) or (d) above, from the proceedings at the inquest or inquiry, that any of the relevant statutory provisions was contravened at a time which is material in relation to the subject-matter of the report, inquest or inquiry, summary proceedings against any person liable to be proceeded against in respect of the contravention may be commenced at any time within three months of the making of the report or, in a case falling within paragraph (c) or (d) above, within three months of the conclusion of the inquest or inquiry.

(2) Where an offence under any of the relevant statutory provisions is committed by reason of a failure to do something at or within a time fixed by or under any of those provisions, the offence shall be deemed to continue until that thing is done.

(3) Summary proceedings for an offence to which this subsection applies may be commenced at any time within six months from the date on which there comes to the knowledge of a responsible enforcing authority evidence sufficient in the opinion of that authority to justify a prosecution for that offence; and for the purposes of this subsection—

  (a) a certificate of an enforcing authority stating that such evidence came to its knowledge on a specified date shall be conclusive evidence of that fact; and

  (b) a document purporting to be such a certificate and to be signed by or on behalf of the enforcing authority in question shall be presumed to be such a certificate unless the contrary is proved.

(4) The preceding subsection applies to any offence under any of the relevant statutory provisions which a person commits by virtue of any provision or requirement to which he is subject as the designer, manufacturer, importer or supplier of any thing; and in that subsection "responsible enforcing authority" means an enforcing authority within whose field of responsibility the offence in question lies, whether by virtue of section 35 or otherwise.

Offences due to fault of other person

20–162   **36.**—(1) Where the commission by any person of an offence under any of the relevant statutory provisions is due to the act or default of some other person, that other person shall be guilty of the offence, and a person may be charged with and convicted of the offence by virtue of this subsection whether or not proceedings are taken against the first-mentioned person.

(2) Where there would be or have been the commission of an offence under section 33 by the Crown but for the circumstance that that section does not bind the Crown, and that fact is due to the act or default of a person other than the Crown, that person shall be guilty of the offence which, but for that circumstance, the Crown would be committing or would have committed, and may be charged with and convicted of that offence accordingly.

(3) The preceding provisions of this section are subject to any provision made by virtue of section 15(6).

Offences by bodies corporate

20–163   **37.**—(1) Where an offence under any of the relevant statutory provisions committed by a body corporate is proved to have been committed with the consent or connivance of, or to have been attributable to any neglect on the part of, any director, manager, secretary or other similar officer of the body corporate or a person who was purporting to act in any such capacity, he as well as the body corporate shall be guilty of that offence and shall be liable to be proceeded against and punished accordingly.

(2) Where the affairs of a body corporate are managed by its members, the preceding subsection shall apply in relation to the acts and defaults of a member in connection with his functions of management as if he were a director of the body corporate.

Restriction on institution of proceedings in England and Wales

20–164   **38.** Proceedings for an offence under any of the relevant statutory provisions shall not, in England and Wales, be instituted except by an inspector or the Environment Agency or by or with the consent of the Director of Public Prosecutions.

(4) Sentence

20–165   When tried summarily, the maximum penalty for the offence created by subsection

33(1)(a) (failing to discharge a duty to which the defendant is subject by virtue of sections 2 to 6 of the 1974 Act) is a fine not exceeding £20,000: section 33(1A).

When tried summarily, the maximum penalty for an offence under subsection 33(1)(g) or (o) is imprisonment for a term not exceeding six months, or a fine not exceeding £20, 000 or both: section 33(2A). After commencement of the relevant provisions, the maximum custodial sentence in a magistrates' court will be 12 months' imprisonment: *Criminal Justice Act* 2003, ss.154 and 282. Custodial sentences of less than 12 months will consist of a custody plus order (see *post*, Ch.23).

The maximum penalty for an offence under subsections 33(1)(d), (e), (f), (h) or (n) is a fine not exceeding level five on the standard scale: section 33(2).

All other offences created by this section carry the maximum penalty of a fine: section 33(3).

For guidelines on the level of fine to be imposed and the factors to be taken into account when sentencing companies for offences in breach of health and safety legislation: see *Howe and Son (Engineers) Ltd* [1999] 2 All E.R. 249. The court must take into the account the seriousness of the offence and the means of the corporate offender. In *B. & Q.* [2005] EWCA Crim 2297 it was held that the totality of the criminality of the defendant company must be considered including the degree of repetition and management failures. Fines of £550,000 were upheld as not manifestly excessive. The court also said that such fines imposed on large companies should be paid immediately or within days. Also in *P. & O. Ferries (Irish Sea) Ltd* [2004] EWCA Crim. 3236 the court held that fines for breach of Health and Safety requirements had to be significant so as to penalise large companies. A reduced fine of £200,000 was substituted on appeal where the breach had led to a fatality.

IX.　PUBLIC TRANSPORT

Public transport includes trains, underground railways and buses. This section covers the railways but regulations apply to other forms of public transport. For the purposes of this section, the principles explained apply equally to similar offences committed on other modes of transport but they are covered by specific, separate regulations etc.　**20–166**

A. Obstruction of the Officers of any Railway Company, Trespassing upon any Railway

(1) Definition

Railway Regulation Act 1840, s.16

For punishment of persons obstructing the officers of any railway company, or trespassing upon any railway

16. If any person shall wilfully obstruct or impede any officer or agent of any railway company **20–167** in the execution of his duty upon any railway, or upon or in any of the stations or other works or premises connected therewith, or if any person shall wilfully trespass upon any railway, or any of the stations or other works or premises connected therewith, and shall refuse to quit the same upon request to him made by any officer or agent of the said company, every such person so offending, and all others aiding or assisting therein, shall, upon conviction by a magistrates' court, at the discretion of the court, forfeit to her Majesty any sum not exceeding level 1 on the standard scale level 3 on the standard scale and in default of payment thereof shall or may be imprisoned.

[This section is printed as amended by the *Summary Jurisdiction Act* 1848, s.4, the *Statute Law Revision (No.2) Act* 1888, the *Statute Law Revision Act* 1892, the *Magistrates' Courts Act* 1952, Sched. 6, the *British Railways Act* 1965, s.35(1), the *London Transport Act* 1965, s.34(1), the *British Railways Act* 1977, Sched. 1, the *CJA* 1982, s.46 and the *Police and Criminal Evidence Act* 1984, Sched. 6.]

(2) Allocation

This offence is triable summarily.　　　　　　　　　　　　　　　　　　　　　**20–168**

Part III

(3) Elements of the offence

20–169   The word "railway" extends to all railways constructed under the powers of any Act of Parliament and intended for the conveyance of passengers in or upon carriages drawn or impelled by the power of steam or by any other mechanical power; "company" includes the proprietors for the time being of any such railway: *Railway Regulation Act* 1840, s.21.

The ambit of section 16 was considered in *R. (Mair) v. Criminal Injuries Compensation Board* [2002] P.I.Q.R. P4, QBD. The applicant was a railway employee seeking to challenge the refusal of the CICB to award him compensation for post traumatic stress disorder suffered as a result of watching a young boy lose his arm beneath the wheels of a train. The applicant argued that his PTSD was attributable to "an offence of trespass on a railway." The application was dismissed, the court finding that there had been no offence committed at the time of the incident. The section makes it an offence to refuse to leave railway premises when required, but the injured boy had only been required to leave the train and there was no implicit request to leave the track or the platform. Hence a request to leave a train will not found a charge of trespass if the individual chooses to remain on the train platform. Stanley Burnton J. explained the working of section 16 by stating:

> 'It can be seen that there are two parts of that particular statutory provision. The first part is concerned with a person who wilfully obstructs or impedes any officer or agent of a railway company in the execution of his duties. It is not suggested that that provision applied in this case. The second part is concerned with wilful trespass on a railway, and the words are "or if any person shall trespass upon any railway, or any of the stations or any works or premises connected therewith, and shall refuse to quit the same upon request to him made by any officer or agent of the said company".
>
> Pausing there for a moment, the words clearly refer to premises or land or works, works in the sense of an electrical substation. They do not refer to a train as such, and it is not suggested that they do. That is the first point. The second point is that the provision requires a refusal on the part of the offender to quit the same upon a request. If there is no request and a refusal to comply with the request, there is no offence committed under that part of this statute.'

A railway company can exclude anyone not wishing to use the railway, or anyone unwilling to comply with conditions: *Perth General Station Committee v. Ross* (1897) A.C. 479.

(4) Sentence

20–170   The offence under section 16 of the 1840 Act carries a maximum penalty of one month's imprisonment or a fine not exceeding level three on the standard scale.

B. PENALTY FOR TRESPASSING ON RAILWAYS

(1) Definition

Regulation of Railways Act 1868, s.23

20–171   **23.** If any person shall be or pass upon any railway, except for the purpose of crossing the same at any authorized crossing, after having once received warning by the company which works such railway, or by any of their agents or servants, not to go or pass thereon, every person so offending shall forfeit and pay any sum not exceeding level 1 on the standard scale for every such offence.

[This section is printed as amended by the *Regulation of Railways Act* 1871, s.14, the *Criminal Law Act* 1977, s.31 and the *CJA* 1982, s.46.]

(2) Allocation

20–172   This offence is triable summarily.

(3) Sentence

This offence is punishable by a fine not exceeding level 1 on the standard scale.   **20–173**

C. PENALTY FOR AVOIDING PAYMENT OF FARE

(1) Definition

Regulation of Railways Act 1889, s.5

5.—(1) Every passenger by a railway shall, on request by an officer or servant of a railway   **20–174**
company, either produce, and if so requested deliver up, a ticket showing that his fare is paid, or
pay his fare from the place whence he started, or give the officer or servant his name and address; and in case of default shall be liable on summary conviction to a fine not exceeding level 2
on the standard scale

(2) If a passenger having failed either to produce, or if requested to deliver up, a ticket
showing that his fare is paid, or to pay his fare, refuses or fails on request by an officer or
servant of a railway company, to give his name and address, any officer of the company or
any constable may detain him until he can be conveniently brought before some justice or
otherwise discharged by due course of law.

(3) If any person—

(a) Travels or attempts to travel on a railway without having previously paid his fare,
and with intent to avoid payment thereof; or

(b) Having paid his fare for a certain distance, knowingly and wilfully proceeds by
train beyond that distance without previously paying the additional fare for the
additional distance, and with intent to avoid payment thereof; or

(c) Having failed to pay his fare, gives in reply to a request by an officer of a railway
company a false name or address,

he shall be liable on summary conviction to a fine not exceeding level 3 on the standard scale, or,
in the discretion of the court to imprisonment for a term not exceeding three months

(4) The liability of an offender to punishment under this section shall not prejudice the
recovery of any fare payable by him.

(5) In this section—

(a) "railway company" includes an operator of a train, and

(b) "operator", in relation to a train, means the person having the management of
that train for the time being.

[This section is printed as amended by the *Transport Act* 1962, ss.84(2) and 93(1),
the *British Railways Act* 1965, s.35(5), the *British Railways Act* 1971, s.18, the *British
Railways Act* 1977, Sched. 1, the *CJA* 1982, ss.35 and 46, the *Police and Criminal
Evidence Act* 1984, Sched. 7 and *(SI* 1994/857).]

(2) Allocation

This offence is triable summarily: section 5(2)(c).   **20–175**

(3) Elements of the offence

The "fare" means the fare by the train and the class of carriage in which the pas-   **20–176**
senger travels; a person who had purchased a workman's ticket, marked "not transferable," which had been issued by a railway company to another person, from that person,
and had travelled on the railway without having purchased a ticket from the railway
company, had travelled on the railway "without having previously paid his fare, and
with intent to avoid payment thereof" within the meaning of the statute: *Reynolds v.
Beasley* [1919] 1 K.B. 215. A person travelling in a first class carriage with a second class
ticket and fraudulently intending to avoid payment of a first class fare may be convicted
for "without having previously paid his fare": *Gillingham v. Walker* (1881) 45 J.P. 470.

Proof of intent to avoid payment is the necessary mental element of the offence, this
intent does not have to be to defraud: *Browning v. Floyd* (1946). A person is still travelling on a railway for the purpose of *Regulation of Railways Act* 1889, s.5, after he has

995

alighted from his train and before he passes the ticket barrier. If, therefore, he conceives an intention to avoid payment of his fare at that stage he is guilty of an offence against the section: *Bremme v. Dubury* [1964] All E.R. 193, DC.

The intention to avoid payment does not have to be permanent. Where a fare was underpaid and the defendant said he intended to pay the excess if he were later tracked down and requested to do so this did not provide a defence: *Corbyn v. Saunders* [1978] 2 All E.R. 697.

(4) Sentence

20–177   This offence is punishable by a fine not exceeding level 2 on the standard scale.

X. SCHOOL ATTENDANCE

A. Failing to Secure Regular Attendance at School

(1) Definition

Education Act 1996, s.444

Offence: failure to secure regular attendance at school of registered pupil

20–178   **444.**—(1) If a child of compulsory school age who is a registered pupil at a school fails to attend regularly at the school, his parent is guilty of an offence.

(1A) If in the circumstances mentioned in subsection (1) the parent knows that his child is failing to attend regularly at the school and fails without reasonable justification to cause him to do so, he is guilty of an offence.

(2) Subsections (3) to (6) below apply in proceedings for an offence under this section in respect of a child who is not a boarder at the school at which he is a registered pupil.

(3) The child shall not be taken to have failed to attend regularly at the school by reason of his absence from the school—

     (a) with leave,

     (b) at any time when he was prevented from attending by reason of sickness or any unavoidable cause, or

     (c) on any day exclusively set apart for religious observance by the religious body to which his parent belongs.

(4) The child shall not be taken to have failed to attend regularly at the school if the parent proves—

     (a) that the school at which the child is a registered pupil is not within walking distance of the child's home, and

     (b) that no suitable arrangements have been made by the local education authority for any of the following—

         (i) his transport to and from the school,

         (ii) boarding accommodation for him at or near the school, or

         (iii) enabling him to become a registered pupil at a school nearer to his home.

(5) In subsection (4) "walking distance"—

     (a) in relation to a child who is under the age of eight, means 3.218688 kilometres (two miles), and

     (b) in relation to a child who has attained the age of eight, means 4.828032 kilometres (three miles), in each case measured by the nearest available route.

(6) If it is proved that the child has no fixed abode, subsection (4) shall not apply, but the parent shall be acquitted if he proves—

     (a) that he is engaged in a trade or business of such a nature as to require him to travel from place to place,

     (b) that the child has attended at a school as a registered pupil as regularly as the nature of that trade or business permits, and

     (c) if the child has attained the age of six, that he has made at least 200 attendances during the period of 12 months ending with the date on which the proceedings were instituted.

(7) In proceedings for an offence under this section in respect of a child who is a boarder at the school at which he is a registered pupil, the child shall be taken to have failed to attend regularly at the school if he is absent from it without leave during any part of the school term at a time when he was not prevented from being present by reason of sickness or any unavoidable cause.

(8) A person guilty of an offence under subsection (1) is liable on summary conviction to a fine not exceeding level 3 on the standard scale.

(8A) A person guilty of an offence under subsection (1A) is liable on summary conviction—

(a) to a fine not exceeding level 4 on the standard scale, or

(b) to imprisonment for a term not exceeding three months,

or both.

(8B) If, on the trial of an offence under subsection (1A), the court finds the defendant not guilty of that offence but is satisfied that he is guilty of an offence under subsection (1), the court may find him guilty of that offence.

(9) In this section "leave", in relation to a school, means leave granted by any person authorised to do so by the governing body or proprietor of the school.

(2) Allocation

These offences are triable summarily only.   **20–179**

(3) Elements of the offence

Under the Act every local education authority has a duty to secure that education is **20–180** available at primary, secondary and higher level to meet the needs of the population of their area. The Act places a duty on parents to ensure attendance at school of their children. Subsection (1) creates the offence of failing to attend school regularly and subsection (1A) creates the aggravated offence of knowing that a pupil is failing to attend school and failing without reasonable justification to cause the child to attend school. The latter offence requires an element of knowledge and connivance which attracts a more severe sentence on conviction.

Compulsory school age is defined as lasting between the ages of 5 to 16 years of age: section 8. The presumption that a child is of compulsory school age is rebuttable by the parent; section 445. The definition of parent includes a person with parental responsibility or one who cares for the child: section 576.

Unavoidable cause in subsection 3(b) does not include the chronic illness of a parent **20–181** or other family duties: *Jenkins v. Howells* [1949] 2 K.B. 218. The test of "unavoidable cause" is higher than that of "reasonable cause": *Jarman v. Mid Glamorgan Education Authority* (1985) LS Gaz.R. 1249.

In *Telford and Wrekin Council v. Ashley* [2001] C.L.Y. 1986, MC, a single parent was convicted of failing to secure her son's attendance at school. Over a four-month period, the boy's attendance had been recorded at 14 per cent. There had been five home visits by the Education Welfare Officer, together with two pupil planning meetings and both parents had received oral and written warnings, including a final written warning, and the boy had been excluded from school twice. The mother asserted a defence of duress based on the physical and verbal abuse she had endured from her son following her attempts to make him attend school. The justices held that whilst the defence of duress was applicable to charges under section 444 of the Act, notwithstanding the special defence of "unavoidable cause" provided for in that section, it could not be established that verbal abuse, accompanied by "pushing and shoving away" of the parent by the child, constituted duress so as to afford a parent a defence to a charge under section 444 of the Act.

In *Bath and North East Somerset District Council v. Warman* [1999] E.L.R. 81, **20–182** [1999] Ed.C.R. 517, QBD, a mother was prosecuted for failing to secure her daughter's attendance at school. The daughter had left home in mid 1997, whilst she was aged 15, and gone to live with her long-term boyfriend. The mother did not discover where she was living until Christmas 1997. The mother had objected to the daughter leaving home but could not stop her. She did not contact the police or social services because she did not think that they would do anything and she did not in any event think that her daughter would be at risk. The Divisional Court held that the circumstances of the case did not give rise to an unavoidable cause for the child's absence from school, and the justices' decision to acquit the mother was wrong. The case was remitted with a direction to convict, with a recommendation that the appropriate penalty would be a conditional discharge, the court questioning the propriety of prosecuting the mother for a criminal offence.

In *R. (P.) v. Liverpool City Magistrates' Court* [2006] EWHC 887, Admin, section 444(1A) of the *Education Act* 1996 was considered. The defendant was found guilty under the section. Her defence was that her son was a big and self-willed boy and that she had done everything she could to ensure he went to school short of physically dragging him there. The magistrates decided that the offence was almost one of strict liability which placed a reverse burden of proof on the defendant. In addition they said that she should have inquired into alternative forms of education for her son. On appeal it was held that there was no reverse burden of proof but the court could only convict if satisfied beyond reasonable doubt that no reasonable justification existed. This did not impose on the parent a requirement to explore all other alternative avenues for schooling. The availability of other forms of education was held to have no relevance to any failure to attend at the school where a child was registered.

In subsection 4(a) the route is not prevented from being available because of fears for the child's safety walking along that route alone. The pupil may need to be accompanied to guard against perceived dangers but the route remains available: *Essex County Council v. Rogers* [1987] A.C. 66.

Under subsection 4(b)(iii), it is the arrangements that must be suitable and not the choice of school nearer to the pupil's home: *R. v. Dyfed County Council ex p. S.* [1995] 1 F.C.R. 113.

The *Education Act* 2005, s.116, inserts section 444ZA into this Act which applies section 444 to alternative educational provision. It came into force on September 1, 2005.

(4) Sentence

20–183   The maximum penalty for the offence established by subsection (1) is a fine not exceeding level 3 on the standard scale. The maximum penalty for the offence established by subsection 1A is a fine not exceeding level 4 on the standard scale, imprisonment for a term not exceeding three months or both. After commencement of the relevant provisions, the maximum custodial sentence in a magistrates' court will be 12 months' imprisonment: *Criminal Justice Act* 2003, ss.154 and 282. Custodial sentences of less than 12 months will consist of a custody plus order (see *post*, Ch.23).

The *Magistrates' Court Sentencing Guidelines* (2004) provide that in relation to the offence under section 444(1A), aggravating factors include the relevant conduct having a harmful effect on other children in the family, the presence of a lack of parental effort to ensure attendance, parental collusion and the use of threats to teachers, pupils and/or officials. Mitigating factors include the absence being due to the physical or mental health of child, the presence of a substantiated history of bullying, drugs etc. The starting point for consideration of sentence is whether the offence is serious enough to warrant a community penalty.

Parenting orders may also be made following the commission of an offence under this section: *Crime and Disorder Act* 1998, s.8.

Crime and Disorder Act 1998, s.8

Parenting orders

20–184   8.—(1) This section applies where, in any court proceedings—
        (a) a child safety order is made in respect of a child;
        (b) an anti-social behaviour order or sex offender order is made in respect of a child or young person;

(c) a child or young person is convicted of an offence; or

(d) a person is convicted of an offence under section 443 (failure to comply with school attendance order) or section 444 (failure to secure regular attendance at school of registered pupil) of the *Education Act* 1996.

(2) Subject to subsection (3) and section 9(1) below and to section 19(5) of, and paragraph 13(5) of Schedule 1 to, the *Powers of Criminal Courts (Sentencing) Act* 2000, if in the proceedings the court is satisfied that the relevant condition is fulfilled, it may make a parenting order in respect of a person who is a parent or guardian of the child or young person or, as the case may be, the person convicted of the offence under section 443 or 444 ("the parent").

(3) A court shall not make a parenting order unless it has been notified by the Secretary of State that arrangements for implementing such orders are available in the are in which it appears to the court that the parent resides or will reside and the notice has not been withdrawn.

(4) A parenting order is an order which requires the parent—

(a) to comply, for a period not exceeding twelve months, with such requirements as are specified in the order; and

(b) subject to subsection (5) below, to attend, for a concurrent period not exceeding three months and not more than once in any week, such counselling or guidance sessions as may be specified in directions given by the responsible officer;

and in this subsection "week" means a period of seven days beginning with a Sunday.

(5) A parenting order may, but need not, include such a requirement as is mentioned in subsection (4)(b) above in any case where such an order has been made in respect of the parent on a previous occasion.

(6) The relevant condition is that the parenting order would be desirable in the interests of preventing—

(a) in a case falling within paragraph (a) or (b) of subsection (1) above, any repetition of the kind of behaviour which led to the child safety order, anti-social behaviour order or sex offender order being made;

(b) in a case falling within paragraph (c) of that subsection, the commission of any further offence by the child or young person;

(c) in a case falling within paragraph (d) of that subsection, the commission of any further offence under section 443 or 444 of the *Education Act* 1996.

(7) The requirements that may be specified under subsection (4)(a) above are those which the court considers desirable in the interests of preventing any such repetition or, as the case may be, the commission of any such further offence.

(8) In this section and section 9 below "responsible officer", in relation to a parenting order, means one of the following who is specified in the order, namely—

(a) an officer of a local probation board;

(b) a social worker of a local authority social services department; and

(bb) a person nominated by a person appointed as chief education officer under section 532 of the *Education Act* 1996.

(c) a member of a youth offending team.

See also *Bath and North East Somerset District Council v. Warman* (*ante*), where **20–185** the court recommended a conditional discharge as an appropriate penalty in the circumstances of the offence, and Rose L.J. stated "one can well understand that it is of the highest importance that the parents of children should be persuaded to comply with the statutory obligation which bears upon them in the terms of the section of the Act to ensure that their children do go to school. But, for my part, I have some doubt as to whether, in the particular circumstances of this case, the prosecution of the mother for a criminal offence was a wholly desirable exercise."

XI. SOCIAL SECURITY

A. Dishonest Representations for Obtaining Benefit

(1) Definition

Social Security Administration Act 1992, s.111A

Dishonest representations for obtaining benefit etc.

20–186   **111A.**—(1) If a person dishonestly—

     (a) makes a false statement or representation; or

     (b) produces or furnishes, or causes or allows to be produced or furnished, any document or information which is false in a material particular;

with a view to obtaining any benefit or other payment or advantage under the relevant social security legislation (whether for himself or for some other person), he shall be guilty of an offence.

     (1A) A person shall be guilty of an offence if—

     (a) there has been a change of circumstances affecting any entitlement of his to any benefit or other payment or advantage under any provision of the relevant social security legislation;

     (b) the change is not a change that is excluded by regulations from the changes that are required to be notified;

     (c) he knows that the change affects an entitlement of his to such a benefit or other payment or advantage; and

     (d) he dishonestly fails to give a prompt notification of that change in the prescribed manner to the prescribed person.

     (1B) A person shall be guilty of an offence if—

     (a) there has been a change of circumstances affecting any entitlement of another person to any benefit or other payment or advantage under any provision of the relevant social security legislation;

     (b) the change is not a change that is excluded by regulations from the changes that are required to be notified;

     (c) he knows that the change affects an entitlement of that other person to such a benefit or other payment or advantage; and

     (d) he dishonestly causes or allows that other person to fail to give a prompt notification of that change in the prescribed manner to the prescribed person.

     (1C) This subsection applies where—

     (a) there has been a change of circumstances affecting any entitlement of a person ('the claimant') to any benefit or other payment or advantage under any provision of the relevant social security legislation;

     (b) the benefit, payment or advantage is one in respect of which there is another person ('the recipient') who for the time being has a right to receive payments to which the claimant has, or (but for the arrangements under which they are payable to the recipient) would have, an entitlement; and

     (c) the change is not a change that is excluded by regulations from the changes that are required to be notified.

     (1D) In a case where subsection (1C) above applies, the recipient is guilty of an offence if—

     (a) he knows that the change affects an entitlement of the claimant to a benefit or other payment or advantage under a provision of the relevant social security legislation;

     (b) the entitlement is one in respect of which he has a right to receive payments to which the claimant has, or (but for the arrangements under which they are payable to the recipient) would have, an entitlement; and

     (c) he dishonestly fails to give a prompt notification of that change in the prescribed manner to the prescribed person.

     (1E) In a case where that subsection applies, a person other than the recipient is guilty of an offence if—

     (a) he knows that the change affects an entitlement of the claimant to a benefit or other payment or advantage under a provision of the relevant social security legislation;

(b) the entitlement is one in respect of which the recipient has a right to receive payments to which the claimant has, or (but for the arrangements under which they are payable to the recipient) would have, an entitlement; and

(c) he dishonestly causes or allows the recipient to fail to give a prompt notification of that change in the prescribed manner to the prescribed person.

(1F) In any case where subsection (1C) above applies but the right of the recipient is confined to a right, by reason of his being a person to whom the claimant is required to make payments in respect of a dwelling, to receive payments of housing benefit—

(a) a person shall not be guilty of an offence under subsection (1D) or (1E) above unless the change is one relating to one or both of the following—

   (i) the claimant's occupation of that dwelling;

   (ii) the claimant's liability to make payments in respect of that dwelling;
   but

(b) subsections (1D)(a) and (1E)(a) above shall each have effect as if after "knows" there were inserted "or could reasonably be expected to know".

(1G) For the purposes of subsections (1A) to (1E) above a notification of a change is prompt if, and only if, it is given as soon as reasonably practicable after the change occurs.

(3) A person guilty of an offence under this section shall be liable—

(a) on summary conviction, to imprisonment for a term not exceeding six months, or to a fine not exceeding the statutory maximum, or to both; or

(b) on conviction on indictment, to imprisonment for a term not exceeding seven years, or to a fine, or to both.

(4) In the application of this section to Scotland, in subsections (1) to (1E) for "dishonestly" substitute "knowingly".

(2) Allocation

These offences are triable either way: *Social Security Administration Act* 1992, s.111A(3).   **20–187**

Social Security Administration Act 1992, s.116

Legal Proceedings

116.—(1) Any person authorised by the Secretary of State in that behalf may conduct any **20–188** proceedings under any provision of this Act other than section 114 or under any provision of the *Jobseekers Act* 1995 before a magistrates' court although not a barrister or solicitor.

(2) Notwithstanding anything in any Act—

(a) proceedings for an offence under this Act other than an offence relating to housing benefit or council tax benefit, or for an offence under the *Jobseekers Act* 1995, may be begun at any time within the period of 3 months from the date on which evidence, sufficient in the opinion of the Secretary of State to justify a prosecution for the offence, comes to his knowledge or within a period of 12 months from the commission of the offence, whichever period last expires; and

(b) proceedings for an offence under this Act relating to housing benefit or council tax benefit may be begun at any time within the period of 3 months from the date on which evidence, sufficient in the opinion of the appropriate authority to justify a prosecution for the offence, comes to the authority's knowledge or within a period of 12 months from the commission of the offence, whichever period last expires.

(2A) Subsection (2) above shall not be taken to impose any restriction on the time when proceedings may be begun for an offence under section 111A above.

(3) For the purposes of subsection (2) above—

(a) a certificate purporting to be signed by or on behalf of the Secretary of State as to the date on which such evidence as is mentioned in paragraph (a) of that subsection came to his knowledge shall be conclusive evidence of that date; and

(b) a certificate of the appropriate authority as to the date on which such evidence as is mentioned in paragraph (b) of that subsection came to the authority's knowledge shall be conclusive evidence of that date.

(4) In subsection (2) and (3) above "the appropriate authority" means, in relation to an offence which relates to housing benefit and concerns any dwelling—

    (b) if it relates to a rent rebate, the authority who are the appropriate housing authority by virtue of that subsection; and

    (c) if it relates to rent allowance, the authority who are the appropriate local authority by virtue of that subsection.

  (5) In subsection (2) and (3) above "the appropriate authority" means, in relation to an offence relating to council tax benefit, such authority as is prescribed in relation to the offence.

  (5A) In relation to proceedings for an offence under section 114 above, the references in subsections (2)(a) and (3)(a) to the Secretary of State shall have effect as references to the Inland Revenue.

  (7) In the application of this section to Scotland, the following provisions shall have effect in substitution for subsections (1) to (5A) above—

    (a) proceedings for an offence under this Act or the *Jobseekers Act* 1995 may, notwithstanding anything in section 136 of the *Criminal Procedure (Scotland) Act* 1995, be commenced at any time within the period of 3 months from the date on which evidence, sufficient in the opinion of the Lord Advocate to justify proceedings, comes to his knowledge, or within the period of 12 months from the commission of the offence, whichever period last expires;

    (aa) this subsection shall not be taken to impose any restriction on the time when proceedings may be commenced for an offence under section 111A above;

    (b) for the purposes of this subsection—

      (i) a certificate purporting to be signed by or on behalf of the Lord Advocate as to the date on which such evidence as is mentioned above came to his knowledge shall be conclusive evidence of that date; and

      (ii) subsection (3) of section 136 of the said *Act of* 1995 (date of commencement of proceedings) shall have effect as it has effect for the purposes of that section.

[This section is printed as amended by the *Local Government Finance Act* 1992, Sched. 9, the *Jobseekers Act* 1995, Sched. 2, the *Social Security Administration (Fraud) Act* 1997, Sched. 1, the *Social Security Contributions (Transfer of Functions etc.) Act* 1999, Sched. 1 and the *Welfare Reform and Pensions Act* 1999, Sched. 11.]

(3) Elements of the offence

20–189   This section does not apply to cases where the benefit or other payment or advantage is or relates to, or the failure to notify relates to tax credit: *Tax Credit Act* 1999, Sched. 2

    The prosecution must prove dishonesty.

    The right to free legal advice under *PACE* Code C 3.15 will not apply to interviews conducted at the offices of the Benefits Agency: *R. (Secretary of State for Social Security) v. South Central Division Magistrates, Daily Telegraph*, November 28, 2000, QBD.

(4) Sentence

20–190   When tried summarily, the maximum penalty for this offence is imprisonment for a term not exceeding six months, a fine not exceeding the statutory maximum or both. After commencement of the relevant provisions, the maximum custodial sentence in a magistrates' court will be 12 months' imprisonment: *Criminal Justice Act* 2003, ss.154 and 282. Custodial sentences of less than 12 months will consist of a custody plus order (see *post*, Ch.23).

    In *Heath* [2003] EWCA Crim 2607, the defendant was aged 36. She was a mother of four children and was in receipt of income support, housing benefit and council tax benefit. She then obtained work as a cleaner in a cinema at weekends. Initially that was on a part-time basis and did not affect her entitlement to benefits; however, she later began working full-time without informing, as she should have done, the Benefits Agency. She was subsequently charged with three offences of making false statements to obtain benefits, contrary to section 111A of the *Social Security Administration Act* 1992, to which she pleaded guilty. Her original sentence of 12 months', imprisonment was reduced on appeal. The Court substituted a sentence of five months' imprisonment, given the net loss to the taxpayer, the early plea, the fact that initially her claims were lawful, and that there was no evidence pointing to luxurious living, indeed the reverse and having regard to the fact that she had four children to support.

For additional guidance on sentencing see *Stewart* [1987] 2 All E.R. 383, CA, but **20–191** bearing in mind the warning issued by Mr Justice Mitchell in *Heath* (*ante*) that it has of course to be remembered that £10,000 in 1987 is not worth the same today. In *Stewart*, relevant factors to be taken into account when sentencing for this offence included (1) a guilty plea; (2) the amount involved and the length of time over which the defalcations were persisted in; (3) the circumstances in which the offence began; (4) the use to which the money so obtained was put; (5) previous character; (6) matters special to the offender; and (7) any voluntary payment of the amounts overpaid.

In *Graham, Whatley* [2005] 1 Cr.App.R. 115 it was held that where imprisonment was necessary for benefit fraud cases, 9 to 12 months would usually be sufficient in a contested case where the amount overpaid was less than £20,000. The aggravating and mitigating factors identified in Stewart continue to be approved.

B. False Representations for Obtaining Benefit

(1) Definition

Social Security Administration Act 1992, s.112

False representations for obtaining benefit etc.

112.—(1) If a person for the purpose of obtaining any benefit or other payment under the **20–192** relevant social security legislation whether for himself or some other person, or for any other purpose connected with that legislation—

    (a) makes a statement or representation which he knows to be false; or

    (b) produces or furnishes, or knowingly causes or knowingly allows to be produced or furnished, any document or information which he knows to be false in a material particular,

he shall be guilty of an offence.

(1A) A person shall be guilty of an offence if—

    (a) there has been a change of circumstances affecting any entitlement of his to any benefit or other payment or advantage under any provision of the relevant social security legislation;

    (b) the change is not a change that is excluded by regulations from the changes that are required to be notified;

    (c) he knows that the change affects an entitlement of his to such a benefit or other payment or advantage; and

    (d) he fails to give a prompt notification of that change in the prescribed manner to the prescribed person.

(1B) A person is guilty of an offence under this section if—

    (a) there has been a change of circumstances affecting any entitlement of another person to any benefit or other payment or advantage under any provision of the relevant social security legislation;

    (b) the change is not a change that is excluded by regulations from the changes that are required to be notified;

    (c) he knows that the change affects an entitlement of that other person to such a benefit or other payment or advantage; and

    (d) he causes or allows that other person to fail to give a prompt notification of that change in the prescribed manner to the prescribed person.

(1C) In a case where subsection (1C) of section 111A above applies, the recipient is guilty of an offence if—

    (a) he knows that the change affects an entitlement of the claimant to a benefit or other payment or advantage under a provision of the relevant social security legislation;

    (b) the entitlement is one in respect of which he has a right to receive payments to

Part III

which the claimant has, or (but for the arrangements under which they are payable to the recipient) would have, an entitlement; and

(c) he fails to give a prompt notification of that change in the prescribed manner to the prescribed person.

(1D) In a case where that subsection applies, a person other than the recipient is guilty of an offence if—

(a) he knows that the change affects an entitlement of the claimant to a benefit or other payment or advantage under a provision of the relevant social security legislation;

(b) the entitlement is one in respect of which the recipient has a right to receive payments to which the claimant has, or (but for the arrangements under which they are payable to the recipient) would have, an entitlement; and

(c) he causes or allows the recipient to fail to give a prompt notification of that change in the prescribed manner to the prescribed person.

(1E) Subsection (1F) of section 111A above applies in relation to subsections (1C) and (1D) above as it applies in relation to subsections (1D) and (1E) of that section.

(1F) For the purposes of subsections (1A) to (1D) above a notification of a change is prompt if, and only if, it is given as soon as reasonably practicable after the change occurs.

(2) A person guilty of an offence under this section shall be liable on summary conviction to a fine not exceeding level 5 on the standard scale, or to imprisonment for a term not exceeding 3 months, or to both.

[This section is printed as amended by the *Social Security Administration (Fraud) Act* 1997, s.14 and Sched. 1, the *Child Support, Pensions and Social Security Act* 2000, Sched. 6 and the *Social Security Fraud Act* 2001, s.16(3).]

(2) Allocation

20–193   This offence is triable summarily. For provisions relating to the institution of legal proceedings, see *ante*, section 116 of the 1992 Act.

(3) Elements of the offence

20–194   This section does not apply to cases where the benefit or other payment or advantage is or relates to, or the failure to notify relates to tax credit: *Tax Credit Act* 1999, Sched. 2.

It is not necessary to prove that the false statement was made with the intention to defraud the Department of Social Security. The offence is made out when it is proved that the defendant made a statement that he knew to be false: *DSS v. Bavi* (1996) C.O.D. 260, QBD.

An applicant for housing benefit will be required to declare whether he was the registered owner of a property other than his main home. In *Fairbank v. Lambeth Magistrates' Court* [2002] EWHC 785, QBD, the defendant's failure to do so constituted a false representation under the *Social Security Administration Act* 1992, section 112 notwithstanding his claim that he held the property on trust for another.

(4) Sentence

20–195   The maximum penalty for this offence is a fine not exceeding level five on the standard scale, imprisonment for a term not exceeding three months or both. After commencement of the relevant provisions, the maximum custodial sentence in a magistrates' court will be 12 months' imprisonment: *Criminal Justice Act* 2003, ss.154 and 282. Custodial sentences of less than 12 months will consist of a custody plus order (see *post*, Ch.23).

Sentencing guidelines can be found in the cases of *Heath* and *Stewart*, *ante*.

XII. STREET TRADING

A. Unlicensed Street Trading

(1) Definition

London Local Authorities Act 1990, s.38

38.—(1) A person who—   **20–196**

    (a) is not the holder of a street trading licence or a temporary licence and who engages in street trading in a borough; or

    (b) is the holder of a temporary licence and who engages in street trading in a borough on a day or in a place not specified in that temporary licence;

shall be guilty of an offence and shall be liable on summary conviction to a fine not exceeding level 3 on the standard scale.

(2) In any proceedings for an offence under this section or for an offence of aiding, abetting, counselling or procuring the commission of an offence under this section where it is shown that—

    (a) any article or thing was displayed (whether or not in or on any receptacle) in any street; or

    (b) any receptacle or equipment used in the provision of any service was available in any street in such circumstances that a service was being offered;

the article or thing shall be presumed to have been exposed or offered for sale and the receptacle or equipment shall be presumed to have been available for the provision of a service at such time and in such position as it was displayed or available by the person having care or control or appearing to have care and control thereof unless in either case, it is shown to the satisfaction of the court that the article or thing or receptacle or equipment was brought into that street for some purpose other than for the purpose of selling it or exposing or offering it for sale or using it in the course of the provision of the service in a street.

(3) Where an offence under this section committed by a body corporate is proved to have been committed with the consent or connivance of, or to be attributable to any neglect on the part of, any director, manager, secretary or other similar officer of the body corporate, or any person who was purporting to act in any such capacity, he, as well as the body corporate, shall be guilty of the offence and liable to the same maximum penalty as the body corporate.

(4) If an authorised officer or a constable has reasonable grounds for suspecting that a person has committed an offence under this section he may seize any article or thing being offered or exposed for sale or receptacle being used by that person which may be required to be used in evidence in any proceedings in respect of that offence or may be thesubject of forfeiture under subsection (5) below, provided that no article or thing which is of a perishable nature shall be seized under the provisions of this subsection.

(4A)

    (a) The following provisions of this subsection shall have effect where any article or thing (including any receptacle) is seized under subsection (4) above and references in those provisions to proceedings are to proceedings in respect of the alleged offence in relation to which the article or thing is seized.

    (b) Subject to paragraph (e) below, at the conclusion of the proceedings the article or thing shall be returned to the person from whom it was seized unless the court orders it to be forfeited under subsection (5) below.

    (c) Subject to paragraph (d) below, where a receptacle seized under subsection (4) above is a motor vehicle used for ice cream trading, the borough council or the Commissioner of Police of the Metropolis (as the case may be) shall, within three days of the receipt of an application in writing by the owner or registered keeper of the vehicle, permit him to remove it.

    (d) Paragraph (c) above shall not apply where—

        (i) the owner or registered keeper of the vehicle has been convicted of an offence under this Part of this Act; or

        (ii) the owner or registered keeper of the vehicle is being prosecuted for a previous alleged offence under this Part of this Act; or

        (iii) the vehicle has been used in the commission of such an offence or previous alleged offence;

if the offence or previous alleged offence was committed or is alleged to have been committed no more than three years before the seizure and (in the case of an alleged offence) the proceedings are continuing.

(e) If no proceedings are instituted before the expiration of a period of 28 days beginning with the date of seizure, or any proceedings instituted within that period are discontinued, at the expiration of that period or, as the case may be, on the discontinuance of the proceedings, the article or thing shall be returned to the person from whom it was seized unless it has not proved possible, after diligent enquiry, to identify that person and ascertain his address.

(f) Where the article or thing is not returned because it has not proved possible to identify the person from whom it was seized and ascertain his address the borough council (whether the article or thing was seized by a constable or by an authorised officer) may apply to a magistrates' court for an order as to the manner in which it should be dealt with.

(5) Subject to subsection (6) below the court by or before which a person is convicted of an offence under this section or for an offence of aiding, abetting, counselling or procuring the commission of an offence under this section may order anything produced to the court, and shown to the satisfaction of the court to relate to the offence, to be forfeited and dealt with in such manner as the court may order.

(6) The court shall not order anything to be forfeited under subsection (5) above where a person claiming to be the owner of or otherwise interested in it applies to be heard by the court, unless an opportunity has been given to him to show cause why the order should not be made and in considering whether to make such an order a court shall have regard—

    (i) to the value of the property; and

    (ii) to the likely financial and other effects on the offender of the making of the order (taken together with any other order that the court contemplates making).

(7) An authorised officer shall produce his authority if required to do so by the person having care or control of anything seized in pursuance of the powers in subsection (4) above.

(8)

  (a) This subsection shall have effect where—

    (i) an article, thing or receptacle is seized under subsection (4) above; and

    (ii)

      (A) not less than six months have passed since the date of the seizure and no information has been laid against any person for an offence under this section in respect of the acts or circumstances which occasioned the seizure; or

      (B) proceedings for such an offence have been brought and either the person charged has been acquitted (whether or not on appeal) and the time for appealing against or challenging the acquittal (where applicable) has expired without an appeal or challenge being brought, or the proceedings (including any appeal) have been withdrawn by, or have failed for want of prosecution by, the person by whom the original proceedings were brought.

  (b) When this subsection has effect a person who has or at the time of seizure had a legal interest in the article, thing or receptacle seized may recover compensation from the borough council or (where it is seized by a constable) the Commissioner of Police of the Metropolis by civil action in the County Court in respect of any loss suffered by him as a result of the seizure.

  (c) The court may not make an order for compensation under paragraph (b) above unless it is satisfied that seizure was not lawful under subsection (4) above.

[This section is printed as amended by the *London Local Authorities Act* 1994, s.6.]

(2) Allocation

20–197   This offence is triable summarily only: section 38(1).

(3) Elements of the offence

20–198   In *Onasanya v. Newham LBC* [2006] EWHC 1775 the defendant was convicted of street trading. He displayed a "For Sale" sign in his car and left the vehicle parked on the public highway when he went to a doctor's appointment. He also had another vehicle which displayed a "For Sale" sign but he said he had lent that to a friend whilst he was out of the country and had expected the car to be kept in a garage. On appeal the issue was considered as to whether displaying such a sign on a car and leaving it in the highway amounted to street trading without a licence. It was held that section 38(2) provided a statutory defence if the item (in this case a car) was brought into the street for some purpose other than street trading. The fact that there may be more than one purpose for the presence of the car on the street did not prevent the defence from applying. The question to be asked was why the car was on the street and in no other place at the material time. In the first case the car was on the street as the defendant attended his GP and in the second case the vehicle was left parked on the street for the convenience of the borrower who left it close to his home. The defendant was acquitted on both charges.

Unlicensed street trading can range from selling small items from a box or tray to selling food from barbecues or braziers or ice-cream or hot-dogs from vans. Such trading is allowed but only under the control of licences issued by local authorities.

Items used in illegal street trading can be seized in an effort to prevent further offending. Perishables cannot be seized but grills and cooking utensils, vans and carts can be removed and forfeiture proceedings be taken.

In the case of ice-cream vans, the owner or keeper of the vehicle that has been seized has a limited right to have the vehicle returned. If there is a history of offending in relation to the owner or the vehicle then forfeiture proceedings may follow. In such applications the owner of any goods subject to possible forfeiture must be given the opportunity to attend court to show cause why the items should not be forfeited.

The power to order forfeiture contained in subsection (5) only applies to goods produced to the court. Goods can be produced to the court either by being brought physically into the courtroom or by the making of arrangements for the court to view the goods. Alternatively, in appropriate circumstances, a written statement could be made under the *Criminal Justice Act* 1967, s.9: *R. (London Borough of Islington) v. Jordan* (2002) 167 J.P. 1, DC. Where there is a late objection to the non-production of the goods magistrates have power to adjourn the matter to some later date to allow the item to be produced or to arrange to view the goods at some convenient occasion on the same or a future date (*ibid.*).

(4) Sentence

The maximum penalty for this offence is a fine not exceeding level 3 on the standard scale: section 38(1). The court also has a power to forfeit the relevant goods under section 38(5). **20–199**

XIII. TELEVISION LICENCES

The *Communications Act* 2003 covers the provision and regulation of electronic communication networks and broadcasting. It also deals with the "licensing of TV reception" in Part 4. Television receivers must be authorised for installation or use by a licence. **20–200**

(1) Definition

Communications Act 2003, ss.363–365

Licence required for use of TV receiver

363.—(1) A television receiver must not be installed or used unless the installation and use of the receiver is authorised by a licence under this Part. **20–201**

(2) A person who installs or uses a television receiver in contravention of subsection (1) is guilty of an offence.

(3) A person with a television receiver in his possession or under his control who—

(a) intends to install or use it in contravention of subsection (1), or

(b) knows, or has reasonable grounds for believing, that another person intends to install or use it in contravention of that subsection,

is guilty of an offence.

(4) A person guilty of an offence under this section shall be liable, on summary conviction, to a fine not exceeding level 3 on the standard scale.

(5) Subsection (1) is not contravened by anything done in the course of the business of a dealer in television receivers solely for one or more of the following purposes—

(a) installing a television receiver on delivery;

(b) demonstrating, testing or repairing a television receiver.

(6) The Secretary of State may by regulations exempt from the requirement of a licence under subsection (1) the installation or use of television receivers—

(a) of such descriptions,

(b) by such persons,

(c) in such circumstances, and

(d) for such purposes,

as may be provided for in the regulations.

(7) Regulations under subsection (6) may make any exemption for which such regulations provide subject to compliance with such conditions as may be specified in the regulations.

TV licences

20–202   **364.**—(1) A licence for the purposes of section 363 ("a TV licence")—

(a) may be issued by the BBC subject to such restrictions and conditions as the BBC think fit; and

(b) must be issued subject to such restrictions and conditions as the Secretary of State may require by a direction to the BBC.

(2) The matters to which the restrictions and conditions subject to which a TV licence may be issued may relate include, in particular—

(a) the description of television receivers that may be installed and used under the licence;

(b) the persons authorised by the licence to install and use a television receiver;

(c) the places where the installation and use of the television receiver is authorised by the licence;

(d) the circumstances in which the installation and use of such a receiver is so authorised;

(e) the purposes for which the installation and use of such a receiver is so authorised;

(f) the use of such receiver in a manner that causes, or may cause, interference (within the meaning of the *Wireless Telegraphy Act* 1949) with wireless telegraphy.

(3) The restrictions and conditions subject to which a TV licence may be issued do not include—

(a) a provision conferring a power of entry to any premises; or

(b) a provision prohibited by a direction to the BBC by the Secretary of State.

(4) A TV licence shall continue in force, unless previously revoked by the BBC, for such period as may be specified in the licence.

(5) The BBC may revoke or modify a TV licence, or the restrictions or conditions of such a licence—

(a) by a notice to the holder of the licence; or

(b) by a general notice published in such manner as may be specified in the licence.

(6) It shall be the duty of the BBC to exercise their power under subsection (5) to revoke or modify a TV licence, or any of its restrictions or conditions, if they are directed to do so by the Secretary of State.

(7) A direction by the Secretary of State under this section may be given either generally in relation to all TV licences (or all TV licences of a particular description) or in relation to a particular licence.

(8) A notice under subsection (5)(a) must be given—

(a) in the manner specified in the licence; or

(b) if no manner of service is so specified, in the manner authorised by section 394.

(9) For the purposes of the application, in relation to the giving of such a notice, of—

(a) section 394; and

(b) section 7 of the *Interpretation Act* 1978 (service by post) in its application for the purposes of that section,

a person's proper address is any address where he is authorised by a TV licence to install or use a TV receiver or, if there is no such address, his last known address.

TV licence fees

365.—(1) A person to whom a TV licence is issued shall be liable to pay—　　　**20–203**

(a) on the issue of the licence (whether initially or by way of renewal), and

(b) in such other circumstances as regulations made by the Secretary of State may provide,

such sum (if any) as may be provided for by any such regulations.

(2) Sums which a person is liable to pay by virtue of regulations under subsection (1) must be paid to the BBC and are to be recoverable by them accordingly.

(3) The BBC are entitled, in such cases as they may determine, to make refunds of sums received by them by virtue of regulations under this section.

(4) Regulations under this section may include provision—

(a) for the means by which an entitlement to a concession must be established; and

(b) for the payment of sums by means of an instalment scheme set out in the regulations.

(5) The reference to a concession in subsection (4) is a reference to any concession under which a person is, on the satisfaction of specified requirements—

(a) exempted from the liability to pay a sum in respect of a TV licence; or

(b) required to pay only a reduced sum in respect of such a licence.

(6) The consent of the Treasury shall be required for the making of any regulations under this section by the Secretary of State.

(7) Subject to subsection (8), sums received by the BBC by virtue of any regulations under this section must be paid into the Consolidated Fund.

(8) The BBC may retain, out of the sums received by them by virtue of regulations under this section, any sums they require for making refunds of sums so received.

(2) Allocation

The offence is triable summarily only. The procedure where the offence is committed　**20–204** by a body corporate is contained in section 404 of the *Communications Act* 2003.

Communications Act 2003, s.404

Criminal liability of company directors etc.

404.—(1) Where an offence under any enactment to which this section applies is committed　**20–205** by a body corporate and is proved to have been committed with the consent or connivance of, or to be attributable to any neglect on the part of—

(a) a director, manager, secretary or other similar officer of the body corporate, or

(b) a person who was purporting to act in any such capacity,

he (as well as the body corporate) is guilty of that offence and shall be liable to be proceeded against and punished accordingly.

(2) Where an offence under any enactment to which this section applies—

(a) is committed by a Scottish firm, and

(b) is proved to have been committed with the consent or connivance of, or to be attributable to any neglect on the part of a partner of the firm,

he (as well as the firm) is guilty of that offence and shall be liable to be proceeded against and punished accordingly.

(3) In this section "director", in relation to a body corporate whose affairs are managed by its members, means a member of the body corporate.

(4) The enactments to which this section applies are every enactment contained in—

(a) this Act;

(b) the *Wireless Telegraphy Act* 1949;

(c) the *Marine, etc.,Broadcasting (Offences) Act* 1967;

(d) the *Wireless Telegraphy Act* 1967; or

(e) the *Telecommunications Act* 1984.

(5) Section 14(2) of the *Wireless Telegraphy Act* 1949 (which is superseded by this section) shall cease to have effect.

(3) Elements of the offence

20–206   This Act replaces the provisions of the *Wireless Telegraphy Act* 1949 in so far as it applied to licences for television sets. Relevant regulations came into force on April 1, 2004 in the *Communications (Television Licensing) Regulations* 2004 (S.I. 2004 No. 692). Interpretation of the various terms used in the statute are found in the Act itself.

Communications Act 2003, ss.367–368

Interpretation of provisions about dealer notification

20–207   **367.**—(1) Section 6 of the *Wireless Telegraphy Act* 1967 (interpretation of provisions requiring notification of sale and hire of television sets) shall be amended as follows.

(2) In subsection (1), for the definitions of "television dealer", "television programme" and "television set" there shall be substituted—

"television dealer" means a person of any description specified in regulations made by the Secretary of State setting out the descriptions of persons who are to be television dealers for the purposes of this Part;

"television set" means any apparatus of a description specified in regulations made by the Secretary of State setting out the descriptions of apparatus that are to be television sets for the purposes of this Part.

(3) After that subsection there shall be inserted—

(1A) Regulations under subsection (1) defining a television set may provide for references to such a set to include references to software used in association with apparatus.

Meanings of "television receiver" and "use"

20–208   **368.**—(1) In this Part "television receiver" means any apparatus of a description specified in regulations made by the Secretary of State setting out the descriptions of apparatus that are to be television receivers for the purposes of this Part.

(2) Regulations under this section defining a television receiver may provide for references to such a receiver to include references to software used in association with apparatus.

(3) References in this Part to using a television receiver are references to using it for receiving television programmes.

(4) The power to make regulations under this section defining a television receiver includes power to modify subsection (3).

20–209   The definition of a television receiver is found in regulation 9.

Communications (Television Licensing) Regulations 2004, reg.9

Meaning of "television receiver"

20–210   **9.**—(1) In Part 4 of the Act (licensing of TV reception), "television receiver" means any apparatus installed or used for the purpose of receiving (whether by means of wireless telegraphy or otherwise) any television programme service, whether or not it is installed or used for any other purpose.

(2) In this regulation, any reference to receiving a television programme service includes a reference to receiving by any means any programme included in that service, where that programme is received at the same time (or virtually the same time) as it is received by members of the public by virtue of its being broadcast or distributed as part of that service.

20–211   A television licence applies to the specified location recorded on the licence and authorises the person living there or anyone else living at the premises or visiting or working there to install and use either black and white or colour television sets at that address. The location may include not only premises but also a vehicle, vessel or caravan. The regulations set the amount of the fees and also provide for concessions in certain circumstances.

The offences are those of using or installing the receiver, or of intending to use or install it or knowing that someone else intends to use or install it. This dispenses with the need for the prosecution to prove that the television receiver was actually being used without a licence but still requires the intention to be proved.

(4) Defence

Section 363(5) exempts television dealers from having a licence where the receiver is being installed on delivery or the receiver is being demonstrated, tested or repaired.   **20–212**

(5) Powers to enforce

Communications Act 2003, s.366

Powers to enforce TV licensing

366.—(1) If a justice of the peace, a sheriff in Scotland or a lay magistrate in Northern   **20–213**
Ireland is satisfied by information on oath that there are reasonable grounds for believing—

    (a) that an offence under section 363 has been or is being committed,

    (b) that evidence of the commission of the offence is likely to be on premises specified in the information, or in a vehicle so specified, and

    (c) that one or more of the conditions set out in subsection (3) is satisfied,

he may grant a warrant under this section.

(2) A warrant under this section is a warrant authorising any one or more persons authorised for the purpose by the BBC or by OFCOM—

    (a) to enter the premises or vehicle at any time (either alone or in the company of one or more constables); and

    (b) to search the premises or vehicle and examine and test any television receiver found there.

(3) Those conditions are—

    (a) that there is no person entitled to grant entry to the premises or vehicle with whom it is practicable to communicate;

    (b) that there is no person entitled to grant access to the evidence with whom it is practicable to communicate;

    (c) that entry to the premises or vehicle will not be granted unless a warrant is produced;

    (d) that the purpose of the search may be frustrated or seriously prejudiced unless the search is carried out by a person who secures entry immediately upon arriving at the premises or vehicle.

(4) A person is not to enter premises or a vehicle in pursuance of a warrant under this section at any time more than one month after the day on which the warrant was granted.

(5) The powers conferred by a warrant under this section on a person authorised by OFCOM are exercisable in relation only to a contravention or suspected contravention of a condition of a TV licence relating to interference with wireless telegraphy.

(6) A person authorised by the BBC, or by OFCOM, to exercise a power conferred by a warrant under this section may (if necessary) use such force as may be reasonable in the exercise of that power.

(7) Where a person has the power by virtue of a warrant under this section to examine or test any television receiver found on any premises, or in any vehicle, it shall be the duty—

    (a) of a person who is on the premises or in the vehicle, and

    (b) in the case of a vehicle, of a person who has charge of it or is present when it is searched,

to give the person carrying out the examination or test all such assistance as that person may reasonably require for carrying it out.

(8) A person is guilty of an offence if he—

    (a) intentionally obstructs a person in the exercise of any power conferred on that person by virtue of a warrant under this section; or

(b) without reasonable excuse, fails to give any assistance that he is under a duty to give by virtue of subsection (7).

(9) A person guilty of an offence under subsection (8) shall be liable, on summary conviction, to a fine not exceeding level 5 on the standard scale.

(10) In this section—

"interference", in relation to wireless telegraphy, has the same meaning as in the *Wireless Telegraphy Act* 1949; and

"vehicle" includes vessel, aircraft or hovercraft.

(11) In the application of this section to Scotland, the reference in subsection (1) to information on oath shall have effect as a reference to evidence on oath.

(12) In the application of this section to Northern Ireland, the reference in subsection (1) to a lay magistrate shall have effect, in relation to times before the coming into force of sections 9 and 10 of the *Justice (Northern Ireland) Act* 2002, as a reference to a justice of the peace.

Warrants of entry and search of premises may be granted together with a power to test equipment found there. The conditions of the section must be met and it is an offence intentionally to obstruct or fail to assist any person executing the warrant.

(6) Sentence

20–214   The maximum penalty is a fine not exceeding level 3.

XIV. VIDEO RECORDINGS

A. SUPPLYING VIDEO RECORDINGS OF UNCLASSIFIED WORK

(1) Definition

Video Recordings Act 1984, s.9

Supplying video recording of unclassified work

20–215   **9.**—(1) A person who supplies or offers to supply a video recording containing a video work in respect of which no classification certificate has been issued is guilty of an offence unless—

(a) the supply is, or would if it took place be, an exempted supply, or

(b) the video work is an exempted work.

(2) It is a defence to a charge of committing an offence under this section to prove that the accused believed on reasonable grounds—

(a) that the video work concerned or, if the video recording contained more than one work to which the charge relates, each of those works was either an exempted work or a work in respect of which a classification certificate had been issued, or

(b) that the supply was, or would if it took place be, an exempted supply by virtue of section 3(4) or (5) of this Act.

(3) A person guilty of an offence under this section shall be liable—

(a) on conviction on indictment, to imprisonment for a term not exceeding two years or a fine or both,

(b) on summary conviction, to imprisonment for a term not exceeding six months or a fine not exceeding £20,000 or both.

[This section is printed as amended by the *Criminal Justice and Public Order Act* 1994, s.88.]

(2) Allocation

20–216   This offence is triable either way: section 9(3).

Video Recordings Act 1984, s.15

Time limit for prosecutions

20–217   **15.**—(1) No prosecution for an offence under this Act shall be brought after the expiry of the period of three years beginning with the date of the commission of the offence or one year beginning with the date of its discovery by the prosecutor, whichever is earlier.

(2) In Scotland, the reference in subsection (1) above to the date of discovery by the prosecutor shall be construed as a reference to the date on which evidence sufficient in the opinion of the Lord Advocate to warrant proceedings came to his knowledge.

(3) For the purposes of subsection (2) above—

(a) a certificate signed by the Lord Advocate or on his behalf and stating the date on which evidence came to his knowledge shall be conclusive evidence of that fact;

(b) a certificate purporting to be signed as mentioned in paragraph (a) above shall be presumed to be so signed unless the contrary is proved; and

(c) a prosecution shall be deemed to be brought on the date on which a warrant to apprehend or to cite the accused is granted provided that the warrant is executed without undue delay.

Video Recordings Act 1984, s.16

Offences by bodies corporate

16.—(1) Where an offence under this Act committed by a body corporate is proved to have **20–218** been committed with the consent or connivance of, or to be attributable to any neglect on the part of, any director, manager, secretary or other similar officer of the body corporate, or any person who was purporting to act in any such capacity, he as well as the body corporate shall be guilty of the offence and shall be liable to be proceeded against and punished accordingly.

(2) Where the affairs of a body corporate are managed by its members, subsection (1) above shall apply in relation to the acts and defaults of a member in connection with his functions of management as if he were a director of the body corporate.

(3) Defence

Video Recordings Act 1984, s.14A

14A. Without prejudice to any defence specified in the preceding provisions of this Act in re- **20–219** lation to a particular offence, it is a defence to a charge of committing any offence under this Act to prove—

(a) that the commission of the offence was due to the act or default of a person other than the accused, and

(b) that the accused took all reasonable precautions and exercised all due diligence to avoid the commission of the offence by any person under his control.

In *Bilon v. W.H. Smith Trading Limited* (2001) 165 J.P. 701, QBD, the defendant **20–220** had supplied a video recording in respect of which no classification certificate had been issued. The recording had been in the form of a CD Rom attached to the cover of a magazine which had been supplied to the defendant by a long standing supplier. The defendant relied on the statutory defence contained in the *Video Recordings Act* 1984, s.14A(b), contending that it had taken all reasonable precautions and had exercised all due diligence. The Court held that they were entitled to rely on the defence of due diligence, despite having taken no positive steps to avoid the commission of the offence. Under section 14A(b) of the 1984 Act, the retailer merely had to show that he had acted without negligence. The defendant had traded with the supplier for 20 years, the supplier was a reputable publisher, and had supplied the defendant with discs previously without any cause for concern. In all the circumstances, it had not been negligent for the defendant to rely on the supplier not to supply a disc and magazine without the defendant having first ensured that the disc had obtained the necessary classification certificate.

(4) Sentence

When tried summarily the maximum penalty for this offence is imprisonment for a **20–221** term not exceeding six months, a fine not exceeding the £20,000 or both: section 9(3)(b). After commencement of the relevant provisions, the maximum custodial sentence in a magistrates' court will be 12 months' imprisonment: *Criminal Justice Act 2003*, ss.154 and 282. Custodial sentences of less than 12 months will consist of a custody plus order (see *post*, Ch.23).

Video Recordings Act 1984, s.21

Forfeiture

20–222 **21.**—(1) Where a person is convicted of any offence under this Act, the court may order any video recording—

 (a) produced to the court, and

 (b) shown to the satisfaction of the court to relate to the offence,

to be forfeited.

(2) The court shall not order any video recording to be forfeited under subsection (1) above if a person claiming to be the owner of it or otherwise interested in it applies to be heard by the court, unless an opportunity has been given to him to show cause why the order should not be made.

(3) References in this section to a video recording include a reference to any spool, case or other thing on or in which the recording is kept.

(4) An order made under subsection (1) above in any proceedings in England and Wales or Northern Ireland shall not take effect until the expiration of the ordinary time within which an appeal may be instituted or, where such an appeal is duly instituted, until the appeal is finally decided or abandoned; and for this purpose—

 (a) an application for a case to be stated or for leave to appeal shall be treated as the institution of an appeal; and

 (b) where a decision on appeal is subject to a further appeal, the appeal is not finally decided until the expiration of the ordinary time within which a further appeal may be instituted or, where a further appeal is duly instituted, until the further appeal is finally decided or abandoned.

(5) *[Scotland]*

B. POSSESSION OF VIDEO RECORDINGS OF UNCLASSIFIED WORK FOR THE PURPOSES OF SUPPLY

(1) Definition

Video Recordings Act 1984, s.10

Possession of video recording of unclassified work for the purposes of supply

20–223 **10.**—(1) Where a video recording contains a video work in respect of which no classification certificate has been issued, a person who has the recording in his possession for the purpose of supplying it is guilty of an offence unless—

 (a) he has it in his possession for the purpose only of a supply which, if it took place, would be an exempted supply, or

 (b) the video work is an exempted work.

(2) It is a defence to a charge of committing an offence under this section to prove—

 (a) that the accused believed on reasonable grounds that the video work concerned or, if the video recording contained more than one work to which the charge relates, each of those works was either an exempted work or a work in respect of which a classification certificate had been issued,

 (b) that the accused had the video recording in his possession for the purpose only of a supply which he believed on reasonable grounds would, if it took place, be an exempted supply by virtue of section 3(4) or (5) of this Act, or

 (c) that the accused did not intend to supply the video recording until a classification certificate had been issued in respect of the video work concerned.

(3) A person guilty of an offence under this section shall be liable—

 (a) on conviction on indictment, to imprisonment for a term not exceeding two years or a fine or both,

 (b) on summary conviction, to imprisonment for a term not exceeding six months or a fine not exceeding £20,000 or both.

(2) Allocation

This offence is triable either way: section 10(3). The provisions as to time limits for **20–224**
proceedings and offences by corporations detailed above apply to charges under this
section.

(3) Defences

The defence established by section 14A of the 1984 Act (*ante*) is applicable to a **20–225**
charge under this section.

(4) Sentence

When tried summarily the maximum penalty for this offence is imprisonment for a **20–226**
term not exceeding six months, a fine not exceeding the £20,000 or both: section
9(3)(b). After commencement of the relevant provisions, the maximum custodial
sentence in a magistrates' court will be 12 months' imprisonment: *Criminal Justice Act
2003*, ss.154 and 282. Custodial sentences of less than 12 months will consist of a custody
plus order (see *post*, Ch.23). The provisions regarding forfeiture detailed above are applicable to a charge under this section.

C. Supplying a Video Recording of Classified Work in Breach of Classification

(1) Definition

Video Recordings Act 1984, s.11

Supplying video recording of classified work in breach of classification

11.—(1) Where a classification certificate issued in respect of a video work states that no video **20–227**
recording containing that work is to be supplied to any person who has not attained the age
specified in the certificate, a person who supplies or offers to supply a video recording containing that work to a person who has not attained the age so specified is guilty of an offence unless
the supply is, or would if it took place be, an exempted supply.

(2) It is a defence to a charge of committing an offence under this section to prove—

(a) that the accused neither knew nor had reasonable grounds to believe that the
classification certificate contained the statement concerned,

(b) that the accused neither knew nor had reasonable grounds to believe that the
person concerned had not attained that age, or

(c) that the accused believed on reasonable grounds that the supply was, or would if
it took place be, an exempted supply by virtue of section 3(4) or (5) of this Act.

(3) A person guilty of an offence under this section shall be liable, on summary conviction, to imprisonment for a term not exceeding six months or a fine not exceeding level 5
on the standard scale or both.

[This section is printed as amended by the *Criminal Justice and Public Order Act*
1994, s.88.]

(2) Allocation

This offence is triable summarily: section 11(3). The provisions as to time limits for **20–228**
proceedings and offences by corporations detailed above apply to charges under this
section.

(3) Elements of the offence

The offence consists of supplying a classified video to a person under the specified **20–229**
age. A Trading Standards Officer instructed his son, who was under 18 to go and buy a
video meant for over 18s for the purposes of an investigation.The defence claimed that
the boy's evidence should be inadmissible. The court held that in the absence of any ev-

Part III

idence that the witness was acting as an "agent provocateur"his evidence was admissible: *Ealing London Borough v. Woolworths Plc* [1995] Crim.L.R. 58.

(4) Defences

20–230　　The defence established by section 14A of the 1984 Act, *ante*, is applicable to a charge under this section.

(5) Sentence

20–231　　The maximum penalty for this offence is imprisonment for a term not exceeding six months, a fine of level five on the standard scale or both: section 11(3). After commencement of the relevant provisions, the maximum custodial sentence in a magistrates' court will be 12 months' imprisonment: *Criminal Justice Act* 2003, ss.154 and 282. Custodial sentences of less than 12 months will consist of a custody plus order (see *post*, Ch.23). The provisions regarding forfeiture detailed above are applicable to a charge under this section.

Chapter 21

CORRUPTION, OFFENCES AGAINST PUBLIC MORALS AND POLICY AND OFFENCES AGAINST PUBLIC JUSTICE

I. BRIBERY AND CORRUPTION

A. COMMON LAW

Where a person in the position of trustee to perform a public duty takes a bribe to **21–1** act corruptly in discharging that duty, it is an offence in both parties: *Whitaker* [1914] 3 K.B. 1283, CCA. This formulation of the offence is wide enough to embrace those involved in the administration of justice, such as a juror (*Young* (1801) 2 East 14 at 16), a justice (*Gurney* (1867) 10 Cox 550), or a coroner (*Harrison* (1800) 1 East P.C. 382).

The offer of a bribe is an attempt to bribe, and is also an offence: 3 Co.Inst. 147; *Vaughan* (1769) 4 Burr. 2494.

The purchase and sale of public offices is said to be regarded by the common law as bribery. In *Pollman* (1809) 2 Camp 229n, a conspiracy to obtain money by procuring from the Treasury the appointment of a person to an office in the customs was held to be a misdemeanour at common law.

For the purpose of any common law offence of bribery, it is immaterial if the functions of the person who receives or is offered a reward have no connection with the United Kingdom and are carried out in a country or territory outside the United Kingdom: *Anti-terrorism, Crime and Security Act* 2001, s.108(1).

Bribery is punishable by fine and or imprisonment, whether the bribe is accepted or **21–2** not: 3 Co.Inst. 147. For sentence in a case of bribery of a prison officer, see *Garner*, 10 Cr.App.R.(S.) 445, CA.

B. STATUTE

(1) Corruption of public officers

(a) *Definition*

Public Bodies Corrupt Practices Act 1889, s.1

Corruption in office a misdemeanor

1.—(1) Every person who shall by himself or by or in conjunction with any other person, cor- **21–3** ruptly solicit or receive, or agree to receive, for himself, or for any other person, any gift, loan, fee, reward, or advantage whatever as an inducement to, or reward for, or otherwise on account of any member, officer, or servant of a public body as in this Act defined, doing or forbearing to do anything in respect of any matter or transaction whatsoever, actual or proposed, in which the said public body is concerned, shall be guilty of a misdemeanour.

(2) Every person who shall by himself or by or in conjunction with any other person corruptly give, promise, or offer any gift, loan, fee, reward, or advantage whatsoever to any person, whether for the benefit of that person or of another person, as an inducement to or reward for or otherwise on account of any member, officer, or servant of any public body as in this Act defined, doing or forbearing to do anything in respect of any matter or transaction whatsoever, actual or proposed, in which such public body as aforesaid is concerned, shall be guilty of a misdemeanour.

21–4　　A prosecution for an offence under this Act may not be instituted without the consent of the Attorney-General: 1889 Act, s.4(1).

(b) *Allocation*

21–5　　This offence is triable either way: s.2(a) (*post*, § 21–13).

(c) *Elements of the offence*

21–6　　The prosecution must prove that:
— the defendant, by himself or with any other person,
— corruptly solicited or received, or agreed to receive,
— for himself or any other person,
— any gift, loan, fee, reward or advantage,
— as an inducement to, or reward for or otherwise on account of any member, officer or servant of a public body,
— doing or forbearing from doing anything in respect of any matter or transaction, actual or proposed, in which the said public body is concerned;
Or, the prosecution must prove that:
— the defendant, by himself or with any other person,
— corruptly gave, promised or offered,
— any gift, loan, fee, reward or advantage whatsoever to any person,
— as an inducement to or reward for or otherwise on account for any member, officer or servant of any public body,
— doing or forbearing to do anything in respect of any matter or transaction, actual or proposed, in which the said public body is concerned.

Public Bodies Corrupt Practices Act 1889, s.7

Interpretation
21–7　　7. In this Act—
The expression "public body" means any council of a county or county of a city or town, any council of a municipal borough, also any board, commissioners, select vestry, or other body which has power to act under and for the purposes of any Act relating to local government, or the public health, or to poor law or otherwise to administer money raised by rates in pursuance of any public general Act, and includes any body which exists in a country or territory outside the United Kingdom and is equivalent to any body described above:
The expression "public office" means any office or employment of a person as a member, officer, or servant of such public body:
The expression "person" includes a body of persons, corporate or unincorporate:
The expression "advantage" includes any office or dignity, and any forbearance to demand any money or money's worth or valuable thing, and includes any aid, vote, consent, or influence, or pretended aid, vote, consent, or influence, and also includes any promise or procurement of or agreement or endeavour to procure, or the holding out of any expectation of any gift, loan, fee, reward, or advantage, as before defined.

[This section is printed as amended by the *Anti-terrorism, Crime and Security Act 2001*, s.108(3).]

The definition of "public body" is extended by the *Prevention of Corruption Act* 1916, s.4(2) (*post*, § 21–21). It also includes the Civil Aviation Authority: see the *Civil Aviation Act* 1982, s.19(1). And the *Government of Wales Act* 2006, s.44, declares the National Assembly for Wales and the National Assembly of Wales Commission to be public bodies for the purposes of this Act, and of the 1889 and 1906 Acts (*post*, §§ 21–17 *et seq.*).

"Corruptly"

The word "corruptly" as used in the Act denotes that the person making the offer did **21–8** so deliberately and with the intention that the person to whom it was addressed should enter into a corrupt bargain: *Smith* [1960] 2 Q.B. 423, CA.

Where a person solicited money from a third party on the basis that it would be paid as a bribe to a public official, it was unnecessary, for the purpose of establishing an offence of corruptly soliciting the bribe, to prove that the public official was aware that an improper offer had been made or a bribe passed. All that was necessary was that the apparent purpose of the transaction was to affect the conduct of such a person corruptly. This was so even where the person soliciting the money had no intention of using it to bribe a public official, but intended to keep it for himself: *Jagdeo Singh v. The State* [2006] 1 W.L.R. 146, PC.

Prevention of Corruption Act 1916, s.2

Presumption of corruption in certain cases

2. Where in any proceedings against a person for an offence under the *Prevention of Cor-* **21–9** *ruption Act* 1906, or the *Public Bodies Corrupt Practices Act* 1889, it is proved that any money, gift, or other consideration has been paid or given to or received by a person in the employment of His Majesty or any Government Department or a public body by or from a person, or agent of a person, holding or seeking to obtain a contract from His Majesty or any Government Department or public body, the money, gift, or consideration shall be deemed to have been paid or given and received corruptly as such inducement or reward as is mentioned in such Act unless the contrary is proved.

This section has no application in relation to anything which would not be an offence apart from ss.108 and 109 of the *Anti-Terrorism, Crime and Security Act* 2001; s.110 of the 2001 Act. As to section 108, see *ante*, §§ 21–1, 21–7, and *post*, § 21–17, 21–21. Section 109 extends the ambit of section 1 of the 1889 Act and of section 1 of the 1906 Act (*post*, § 21–17) to acts done abroad.

In *Braithwaite*, 77 Cr.App.R. 34, CA, Lord Lane C.J. offered guidance as to the **21–10** operation of the presumption created by s.2:

> "when the matters in that section have been fulfilled, the burden of proof is lifted from the shoulders of the prosecution and descends upon the shoulders of the defence. It then becomes necessary for the defendant to show, on a balance of probabilities, that what was going on was not reception corruptly as inducement or reward. In an appropriate case it is the judge's duty to direct the jury first of all that they must decide whether they are satisfied so as to feel sure that the defendant received money or gift or consideration, and then to go on to direct them that if they are so satisfied, then under section 2 of the 1916 Act the burden of proof shifts" (at p.38).

In *Mills*, 68 Cr.App.R. 154, CA, it was held that the presumption can be rebutted **21–11** only by evidence of an innocent explanation, supported by evidence, established on the balance of probabilities.

"Reward"

The word "reward" can be given its natural meaning of a "*post facto*" gift for a past **21–12** favour without there having been any agreement beforehand; any payment will be covered provided it is related to something done or omitted by the recipient in respect of any matter or transaction in which the public body, of which he is a member, officer or servant, is concerned: *Andrews-Weatherfoil Ltd*, 56 Cr.App.R. 31, CA; *Parker (K. R.)*, 82 Cr.App.R. 69, CA.

(d) *Sentence*

Public Bodies Corrupt Practices Act 1889, s.2

Penalty for offences

21–13   **2.** Any person on conviction for offending as aforesaid shall, at the discretion of the court before which he is convicted,

    (a) be liable

        (i) on summary conviction, to imprisonment for a term not exceeding 6 [12] months or to a fine not exceeding the statutory maximum, or to both; and

        (ii) on conviction on indictment, to imprisonment for a term not exceeding 7 years or to a fine, or to both; and

    (b) in addition be liable to be ordered to pay to such body, and in such manner as the court directs, the amount or value of any gift, loan, fee, or reward received by him or any part thereof; and

    (c) be liable to be adjudged incapable of being elected or appointed to any public office for five years from the date of his conviction, and to forfeit any such office held by him at the time of his conviction; and

    (d) in the event of a second conviction for a like offence he shall, in addition to the foregoing penalties, be liable to be adjudged to be for ever incapable of holding any public office, and to be incapable for five years of being registered as an elector, or voting at an election either of members to serve in Parliament or of members of any public body, and the enactments for preventing the voting and registration of persons declared by reason of corrupt practices to be incapable of voting shall apply to a person adjudged in pursuance of this section to be incapable of voting; and

    (e) if such person is an officer or servant in the employ of any public body upon such conviction he shall, at the discretion of the court, be liable to forfeit his right and claim to any compensation or pension to which he would otherwise have been entitled.

[This section is printed as amended by the *Representation of the People Act* 1948, ss.52(7) and 80; and the *CJA* 1988, s.47. In para. (a)(i), "12" is substituted for "6", as from a day to be appointed, by the *CJA* 2003, s.282(2) and (3). The increase has no application to offences committed before the substitution takes effect: s.282(4).]

21–14   When tried summarily, the maximum penalty is six months' imprisonment, a fine not exceeding the statutory maximum, or both: s.2 of the 1889 Act, *ante*. As from the date of commencement of the *Criminal Justice Act* 2003, s.282(2) and (3), the maximum custodial sentence on summary conviction will be increased to 12 months; but only in respect of offences committed on or after that date: s.282(4). Once section 181 of the 2003 Act is brought into force, custodial sentences of less than 12 months will consist of a custody plus order (see *post*, Ch.23).

21–15   In *Bennet and Wilson* [1996] 1 Cr.App.R.(S.) 162, CA, the offenders were convicted respectively of receiving and giving a bribe on two occasions. The first offender was employed in a government department responsible for the procurement of publicity material, the second was managing director of a group of companies involved in supplying printing work to the department. Their original sentences of nine months' imprisonment each were substituted by sentences of four months' imprisonment, the court affirming the propriety of a custodial sentence in cases of corruption. A sentence of three months' imprisonment was imposed in *Ozdemir*, 7 Cr.App.R.(S.) 382, CA, where the appellant was convicted of corruption after being stopped whilst in the passenger seat of a car driven by his 14-year-old son. When the police officer indicated that the boy would be reported for driving without a licence, O offered him £50 for a free meal at O's restaurant not to do so. The Court of Appeal was influenced by the fact that the appellant was a man of good character, the bribe involved only a small sum and the offence he was seeking to avoid by offering the bribe related to his son, not directly to him.

21–16   In *Dearnley* [2001] 2 Cr.App.R.(S.) 42, CA, the appellants were convicted of corruption. The first appellant was employed by a metropolitan council with responsibility for property management. The second appellant's companies provided security services to the council over a period of several years. The second appellant supplied to the first appellant a car valued at £5,445. The first appellant secured a loan from the council to pay for the car, and used the money so obtained to clear debts. Their original sentences of 18 months' imprisonment were reduced to 10 months' imprisonment by the Court of Appeal, Rafferty J. stating that

> "it is seldom a surprise when corrupt individuals prove to be of hitherto good character. Were it otherwise they would, in general, not be in a position from which to behave in a fashion which strikes at the principle of fair competition. Public confidence in people such as these appellants is undermined, irrespective of the amounts pocketed by an individual, by virtue of the evil which is corruption. Custody is inevitable; it is rightly seen as a deterrent to those tempted to depart from their usual scrupulous standards."

(2) Corruption of agents

(a) *Definition*

Prevention of Corruption Act 1906, s.1

Punishment of corrupt of transactions with agents

1.—(1) If any agent corruptly accepts or obtains, or agrees to accept or attempts to obtain, **21–17** from any person, for himself or for any other person, any gift or consideration as an inducement or reward for doing or forbearing to do, or for having after the passing of this Act done or forborne to do, any act in relation to his principal's affairs or business, or for showing or forbearing to show favour or disfavour to any person in relation to his principal's affairs or business; or

If any person corruptly gives or agrees to given or offers any gift or consideration to any agent as an inducement or reward for doing or forbearing to do, or for having after the passing of this Act done or forborne to do, any act in relation to his principal's affairs or business, or for showing or forbearing to show favour or disfavour to any person in relation to his principal's affairs or business; or

If any person knowingly gives to any agent, or if any agent knowingly uses with intent to deceive his principal, any receipt, account, or other document in respect of which the principal is interested, and which contains any statement which is false or erroneous or defective in any material particular, and which to his knowledge is intended to mislead the principal:

he shall be guilty of a misdemeanour, and shall be liable—

    (a) on summary conviction, to imprisonment for a term not exceeding 6 [12] months or to a fine not exceeding the statutory maximum, or to both; and

    (b) on conviction on indictment, to imprisonment for a term not exceeding 7 years or to a fine, or to both.

(2) For the purposes of this Act the expression "consideration" includes valuable consideration of any kind; the expression "agent" includes any person employed by or acting for another; and the expression "principal" includes an employer

(3) A person serving under the Crown or under any corporation or any, borough, county, or district council, or any board of guardians, is an agent within the meaning of this Act.

(4) For the purposes of this Act it is immaterial if—

    (a) the principal's affairs or business have no connection with the United Kingdom and are conducted in a country or territory outside the United Kingdom;

    (b) the agent's functions have no connection with the United Kingdom and are carried out in a country or territory outside the United Kingdom

[This section is printed as amended by the *CJA* 1988, s.47; and the *Anti-terrorism, Crime and Security Act* 2001, s.108(4); and as repealed in part by the *Local Authorities, etc. (Miscellaneous Provisions) (No. 2) Order* 1974 (S.I. 1974 No. 595). In subs. (1)(a), "12" is substituted for "6", as from a day to be appointed, by the *CJA* 2003, s.282(2) and (3). The increase has no application to offences committed before the substitution takes effect: s.282(4).]

A prosecution for an offence under this Act shall not be instituted without the consent of the Attorney-General: s.2(1).

(b) *Allocation*

21–18   This offence is triable either way: s.1(1), *ante*.

(c) *Elements of the offence*

21–19   The prosecution must prove that:
— the defendant corruptly accepted or obtained, or agreed to accept or attempted to obtain,
— from any other person,
— for himself or for any other person,
— any gift or consideration as an inducement or reward,
— for doing or forbearing to do, or for having done or forborne to do, any act in relation to his principal's affairs or business or for showing or forbearing to show favour or disfavour to any person in relation to his principal's affairs or business;

OR

— the defendant corruptly gave or agreed to give or offered,
— any gift or consideration,
— to any agent,
— as an inducement or reward,
— for doing or forbearing to do, or for having done or forborne to do, any act in relation to his principal's affairs or business or for showing or forbearing to show favour or disfavour to any person in relation to his principal's affairs or business;

OR

— the defendant knowingly gave to any agent, or any agent knowingly uses with intent to deceive his principal,
— any receipt, account or other document in respect of which the principal is interested,
— which contains any statement which is false or erroneous or defective in any material particular,
— which is, to his knowledge intended to mislead the principal.

"agent"

21–20   Whether someone is "serving under the Crown" will not be determined by looking to whether he is employed by the Crown, but by looking at whether the duties he performs are on behalf of the Crown, it being necessary for the Crown to exercise its functions through some human agency: *Barrett*, 63 Cr.App.R.174, CA.

"public body"

Prevention of Corruption Act 1916, s.4(2), (3)

Short title and interpretation
21–21   **4.**—(2) In this Act and in the *Public Bodies Corrupt Practices Act* 1889, the expression "public body" includes, in addition to the bodies mentioned in the last-mentioned Act, local and public authorities of all descriptions (including authorities existing in a country or territory outside the United Kingdom) [and companies which in accordance with Part V of the *Local Government and Housing Act* 1989 are under the control of one or more local authorities].

(3) A person serving under any such public body is an agent within the meaning of the *Prevention of Corruption Act* 1906, and the expressions "agent" and "consideration" in this Act have the same meaning as in the *Prevention of Corruption Act* 1906, as amended by this Act.

[Subs. (2) is printed as amended by the *Anti-terrorism, Crime and Security Act* 2001, s.108(4); and as amended, as from a day to be appointed, by the *Local Government and Housing Act* 1989, s.194(1), and Sched. 11, para. 3.]

21–22   The expression "public body" in section 7 of the 1889 Act (*ante*, § 21–7) and sections

2 (*ante*, § 21–20) and 4(2) of the 1916 Act is not restricted to local authorities but refers to any body which has public or statutory duties to perform and which performs those duties and carries out its transactions for the benefit of the public and not for private profit: *DPP v. Holly and Manners* [1978] A.C. 43, HL. Since, however, section 2 distinguishes between the Crown or any government department, on the one hand, and "a public body" on the other, the reference to "public authorities of all descriptions" in the definition of "public body" could not be construed as including either the Crown or a government department: *Natji* [2002] 2 Cr.App.R. 20, CA.

"corruptly"

See generally, *ante*, §§ 21–8 *et seq.*   **21–23**

"consideration"

The word "consideration" has to be given its legal meaning which indicates that there   **21–24**
was a contract or bargain of some kind between the parties which has to be contrasted with the word "gift" which envisages no such contract between the parties and therefore no consideration: *Braithwaite*, 77 Cr.App.R. 34, CA.

"in relation to his principal's affairs"

These words should be widely construed, and it is not necessary that the corrupt   **21–25**
consideration should be received as an agent: *Morgan v. DPP* [1970] 3 All E.R. 1053, QBD.

Document intended to deceive principal

The first two paragraphs of s.1(1) refer to dishonest conduct by an employee with a   **21–26**
third party affecting the employer. Since the ordinary meaning of "receipt" and "account" in the third paragraph refers to documents *inter partes*, the words "or other document" on their true construction also refer to documents passing *inter partes*. They do not apply to an internal document which had never been intended to go to a third party and had not come from one: *Tweedie* [1984] Q.B. 729, CA.

(d) *Sentence*

When tried summarily, the maximum penalty for this offence is imprisonment for a   **21–27**
term not exceeding six months or a fine not exceeding the statutory maximum, or both: see section 1(1)(a), *ante*, § 21–17. After commencement of the relevant provisions, the maximum custodial sentence in a magistrates' court will be 12 months' imprisonment.

In *Wilcox*, 16 Cr.App.R.(S.) 197, CA, the offender pleaded guilty to conspiring to act   **21–28**
corruptly, having received £32,000 in respect of the renewal of contracts by the company for whom he worked with another company. He had not, however, used any improper influence to secure the renewal of the contract and had not solicited payment. His sentence of 12 months' imprisonment was reduced to one of six months, although the aggravating effect of the large amounts of money involved was affirmed.

(3) Abuses in respect of honours

(a) *Definition*

Honours (Prevention of Abuses) Act 1925, s.1

Punishment of abuses in connection with the grant of honours

1.—(1) If any person accepts or obtains or agrees to accept or attempts to obtain from any   **21–29**
person, for himself or for any other person, or for any purpose, any gift, money or valuable consideration as an inducement or reward for procuring or assisting or endeavouring to procure the grant of a dignity or title of honour to any person, or otherwise in connection with such a grant, he shall be guilty of a misdemeanour.

(2) If any person gives, or agrees or proposes to give, or offers to any person any gift, money or valuable consideration as an inducement or reward for procuring or assisting or

endeavouring to procure the grant of a dignity or title of honour to any person, or otherwise in connection with such a grant, he shall be guilty of a misdemeanour.

(3) Any person guilty of a misdemeanour under this Act shall be liable on conviction on indictment to imprisonment for a term not exceeding two years or to a fine of any amount, or to both such imprisonment and such fine, or on summary conviction to imprisonment for a term not exceeding *three* [12] months or to a fine not exceeding the prescribed sum, or to both such imprisonment and such fine, and where the person convicted (whether on indictment or summarily) received any such gift, money, or consideration as aforesaid which is capable of forfeiture, he shall in addition to any other punishment be liable to forfeit the same to Her Majesty.

(4) [*Repealed by* Administration of Justice (Miscellaneous Provisions) Act *1933, Sched. 3, and* Criminal Justice Act (Northern Ireland) *1945, Sched. 4.*]

[This section is printed as amended by the *CLA* 1977 s.32(1); and the *MCA* 1980, s.32(2) (substitution of reference to "the prescribed sum"). In subs. (3), "12" is substituted for "three", as from a day to be appointed, by the *CJA* 2003, s.282(2) and (3). The increase has no application to offences committed before the substitution takes effect: s.282(4).]

(b) *Allocation*

21–30   This offence is triable either way: s.1(3) (*ante*).

(c) *Elements of the offence*

21–31   The prosecution must prove that:
— the defendant accepted or obtained, or agreed to accept or obtain from any person,
— for himself or for any other person, or for any purpose,
— any gift, money or valuable consideration as an inducement or reward,
— for procuring or assisting or endeavouring to procure the grant of a dignity or title of honour to any person or otherwise in connection with such a grant;

OR

— the defendant gave, agreed, or proposed to give, or offered,
— to any person,
— any gift, money or valuable consideration as an inducement or reward,
— for procuring or assisting or endeavouring to procure the grant of a dignity or title of honour to any person or otherwise in connection with such a grant.

(d) *Sentence*

21–32   When tried summarily, the maximum penalty for this offence is three months' imprisonment, a fine not exceeding the statutory maximum or both: s.1(3), *ante*. As from the date of commencement of the *Criminal Justice Act* 2003, s.282(2) and (3), the maximum custodial sentence on summary conviction will be increased to 12 months; but only in respect of offences committed on or after that date: s.282(4). Once section 181 of the 2003 Act is brought into force, custodial sentences of less than 12 months will consist of a custody plus order (see *post*, Ch.23).

II. OFFENCES AGAINST PUBLIC MORALS AND POLICY

A. Bigamy

(1) Definition

Offences against the Person Act 1861, s.57

21–33   **57.** Whosoever, being married, shall marry any other person during the life of the former husband or wife, whether the second marriage shall have taken place in England or Ireland or elsewhere, shall be guilty of felony, and being convicted thereof shall be liable to be imprisoned for any term not exceeding seven years...

Provided, that nothing in this section contained shall extend to any second marriage contracted elsewhere than in England and Ireland by any other than a subject of Her Majesty, or to any person marrying a second time whose husband or wife shall have been continually absent from such person for the space of seven years then last past, and shall not have been known by such person to be living within that time, or shall extend to any person who, at the time of such second marriage, shall have been divorced from the bond of the first marriage, or to any person whose former marriage shall have been declared void by the sentence of any court of competent jurisdiction.

(2) Allocation

This offence is triable either way: *Magistrates' Courts Act* 1980, s.17(1), and Sched. **21–34**
1.

(3) Elements of the offence

The prosecution must prove that: **21–35**
— the defendant was married,
— when he "married" another person,
— during the life of the former husband or wife.

"Being married"

The time for determining whether a person was "married" within the meaning of **21–36** section 57 is the time of the alleged bigamous ceremony. Accordingly, although the marriage which is to be the foundation for a prosecution for bigamy must be a monogamous marriage, since a potentially polygamous marriage may in certain circumstances change its character and become monogamous (*e.g.* by a change in domicile to a country where monogamy is part of the law, or by a change in the law of the country where the marriage was celebrated), a charge of bigamy is well founded where such a change has occurred by the time of the alleged bigamous ceremony of marriage: *Sagoo* [1975] Q.B. 885, CA.

The first marriage must be strictly proved by the production of the certificate of the registrar of marriages: *Lindsay*, 66 J.P. 505. The words "or elsewhere" in the statute mean that the marriage can have taken place in any other part of the world. A British subject resident in England is liable to be convicted of bigamy although both marriages were solemnised in Scotland: *Topping* (1856) Dears. 647.

"Second marriage"

Where a person, already bound by an existing marriage, goes through with another **21–37** person a form of marriage known to and recognised by the law as capable of producing a valid marriage, for the purpose of a pretended and fictitious marriage, such person is guilty of bigamy, notwithstanding any special circumstances which, independently of the bigamous character of the marriage, may constitute a legal disability in the parties, or make the form of marriage resorted to inapplicable to their case. Hence, in *Allen* (1872) L.R. 1 C.C.R. 367, a defendant who went through a ceremony of marriage with his wife's niece, whilst his wife was still living was properly found guilty of bigamy, despite the fact that the second marriage would be void for reasons of consanguinity. The validity of the second marriage is immaterial: *Robinson*, 26 Cr.App.R. 129, CCA.

(4) Defences

To establish the defence of seven years' absence provided in the statute, the defen- **21–38** dant must not have known at any period during the seven years that the spouse was alive: *Cullen* (1840) 9 C & P. 681.

The defence of seven years' absence of the lawful husband or wife continues to be available in relation to a third or subsequent marriage: *Taylor* [1950] 2 All E.R. 170, CCA.

21–39　　An honest belief on reasonable grounds as to the invalidity of a previous marriage, will be a good defence to a charge of bigamy: *King* [1964] 1 Q.B. 285, CCA. An honest and reasonable belief at the time of the second marriage that the first marriage had been dissolved will also be a good defence: *Gould* [1968] 2 Q.B. 65, CA; as will an honest belief on reasonable grounds that the first spouse had died before the second marriage, even though the seven years of continued absence specified in the Act had not expired: *Tolson* (1889) 23 Q.B.D. 168, CCR.

(5) Sentence

21–40　　When tried summarily, the maximum penalty for this offence is six months' imprisonment, a fine not exceeding the prescribed sum or both: *Magistrates' Courts Act* 1980, s.32(1). As from the date of commencement of the *Criminal Justice Act* 2003, s.282(1), the maximum custodial sentence on summary conviction will be increased to 12 months; but only in respect of offences committed on or after that date: s.282(4). Once section 181 of the 2003 Act is brought into force, custodial sentences of less than 12 months will consist of a custody plus order (see *post*, Ch.23).

A custodial sentence should be passed where the innocent party has been deceived and has suffered some injury as a consequence: *Smith (James)*, 15 Cr.App.R.(S.) 407, CA (bracket was four to six months).

Marriage to evade immigration control will require the imposition of a deterrent sentence and hence a custodial sentence is inevitable: *Cairns* [1997] 1 Cr.App.R.(S.) 118 (nine months' imprisonment upheld in the case of a man who married for money to enable the woman to evade immigration control).

B. Obscene or Indecent Publications or Displays, etc.

(1) Outraging public decency

21–41　　For the offence of outraging public decency, see *ante*, § 14–54.

(2) Obscene publications

(a) *Definition*

Obscene Publications Act 1959, s.2

Prohibition of publication of obscene matter

21–42　　**2.**—(1) Subject as hereinafter provided, any person who, whether for gain or not, publishes an obscene article or who has an obscene article for publication for gain (whether gain to himself or gain to another) shall be liable—

　　(a) on summary conviction to a fine not exceeding the prescribed sum or to imprisonment for a term not exceeding *six* [12] months;

　　(b) on conviction on indictment to a fine or to imprisonment for a term not exceeding three years or both.

(3) A prosecution for an offence against this section shall not be commenced more than two years after the commission of the offence.

(3A) Proceedings for an offence under this section shall not be instituted except by or with the consent of the Director of Public Prosecutions in any case where the article in question is a moving picture film of a width of not less than sixteen millimetres and the relevant publication or the only other publication which followed or could reasonably have been expected to follow from the relevant publication took place or (as the case may be) was to take place in the course of a film exhibition; and in this subsection "the relevant publication" means—

　　(a) in the case of any proceedings under this section for publishing an obscene article, the publication in respect of which the defendant would be charged if the proceedings were brought; and

(b) in the case of any proceedings under this section for having an obscene article for publication for gain, the publication which, if the proceedings were brought, the defendant would be alleged to have had in contemplation.

(4) A person publishing an article shall not be proceeded against for an offence at com- **21–43**
mon law consisting of the publication of any matter contained or embodied in the article
where it is of the essence of the offence that the matter is obscene.

(4A) Without prejudice to subsection (4) above, a person shall not be proceeded against
for an offence at common law—

(a) in respect of a film exhibition or anything said or done in the course of a film exhibition, where it is of the essence of the common law offence that the exhibition
or, as the case may be, what was said or done was obscene, indecent, offensive,
disgusting or injurious to morality; or

(b) in respect of an agreement to give a film exhibition or to cause anything to be
said or done in the course of such an exhibition where the common law offence
consists of conspiring to corrupt public morals or to do any act contrary to public
morals or decency.

(5) A person shall not be convicted of an offence against this section if he proves that he
had not examined the article in respect of which he is charged and had no reasonable
cause to suspect that it was such that his publication of it would make him liable to be
convicted of an offence against this section.

(6) In any proceedings against a person under this section the question whether an
article is obscene shall be determined without regard to any publication by another person
unless it could reasonably have been expected that the publication by the other person
would follow from publication by the person charged.

(7) In this section "film exhibition" has the same meaning as in the *Cinemas Act* 1985.

[This section is printed as amended by the *Obscene Publications Act* 1964, s.1(1); the
CLA 1977, s.53; the *MCA* 1980, s.32(2) (substitution of reference to "the prescribed
sum"); and the *Cinemas Act* 1985, s.24(1), and Sched. 2, para. 6; and as repealed in
part by the *CLA* 1977, s.65(5), and Sched. 13. In subs. (1)(a), "12" is substituted for
"six", as from a day to be appointed, by the *CJA* 2003, s.282(2) and (3). The increase
has no application to offences committed before the substitution takes effect: s.282(4).]

For the application of this section to matter in sound or television programmes or
intended to be included therein, see Schedule 15 to the *Broadcasting Act* 1990.

For the definition of "film exhibition", see section 21 of the 1985 Act (as amended by
the *Broadcasting Act* 1990, s.203(1), and Sched. 20, para. 40).

Obscene Publications Act 1964, s.1

Obscene articles intended for publication for gain

1.—(1) [*Amends section 2(1) of the 1959 Act*, ante, *§ 21–42.*]   **21–44**

(2) For the purpose of any proceedings for an offence against the said section 2 a
person shall be deemed to have an article for publication for gain if with a view to such
publication he has the article in his ownership, possession or control.

(3) In proceedings brought against a person under the said section 2 for having an
obscene article for publication for gain the following provisions shall apply in place of
subsections (5) and (6) of that section, that is to say,—

(a) he shall not be convicted of that offence if he proves that he had not examined
the article and had no reasonable cause to suspect that it was such that his having
it would make him liable to be convicted of an offence against that section; and

(b) the question whether the article is obscene shall be determined by reference to
such publication for gain of the article as in the circumstances it may reasonably
be inferred he had in contemplation and to any further publication that could
reasonably be expected to follow from it, but not to any other publication.

(4) Where articles are seized under section 3 of the *Obscene Publications Act* 1959 **21–45**
(which provides for the seizure and forfeiture of obscene articles kept for publication for gain),
and a person is convicted under section 2 of that Act of having them for publication for gain, the
court on his conviction shall order the forfeiture of those articles:

Part III

Provided that an order made by virtue of this subsection (including an order so made on appeal) shall not take effect until the expiration of the ordinary time within which an appeal in the matter of the proceedings in which the order was made may be instituted or, where such an appeal is duly instituted, until the appeal is finally decided or abandoned; and for this purpose—

(a) an application for a case to be stated or for leave to appeal shall be treated as the institution of an appeal; and

(a) where a decision on appeal is subject to a further appeal, the appeal shall not be deemed to be finally decided until the expiration of the ordinary time within which a further appeal may be instituted or, where a further appeal is duly instituted, until the further appeal is finally decided or abandoned.

(5) References in section 3 of the *Obscene Publications Act* 1959 and this section to publication for gain shall apply to any publication with a view to gain, whether the gain is to accrue by way of consideration for the publication or in any other way.

For section 3 of the 1959 Act, see *post* § 21–61.

Obscene Publications Act 1964, s.2

Negatives, etc. for production of obscene articles

21–46   **2.**—(1) The *Obscene Publications Act* 1959 (as amended by this Act) shall apply in relation to anything which is intended to be used, either alone or as one of a set, for the reproduction or manufacture therefrom of articles containing or embodying matter to be read, looked at or listened to, as if it were an article containing or embodying that matter so far as that matter is to be derived from it or from the set.

(2) For the purposes of the *Obscene Publications Act* 1959 (as so amended) an article shall be deemed to be had or kept for publication if it is had or kept for the reproduction or manufacture therefrom of articles for publication; and the question whether an article so had or kept is obscene shall—

(a) for purposes of section 2 of the Act be determined in accordance with section 1(3)(b) above as if any reference there to publication of the article were a reference to publication of articles reproduced or manufactured from it; and

(b) for purposes of section 3 of the Act be determined on the assumption that articles reproduced or manufactured from it would be published in any manner likely having regard to the circumstances in which it was found, but in no other manner.

Section 3 of the 1959 Act relates to powers of search and seizure: see *post*, § 21–61.

(b) *Allocation*

21–47   This offence is triable either way: *Obscene Publications Act* 1959, s.2(1) (*ante* § 21–42).

(c) *Elements of the offence*

21–48   The prosecution must prove that:
— the defendant published, or had for publication for gain,
— an obscene article.

"Obscene"

Obscene Publications Act 1959, s.1(1)

Test of obscenity

21–49   **1.**—(1) For the purposes of this Act an article shall be deemed to be obscene if its effect or (where the article comprises two or more distinct items) the effect of any one of its items is, if taken as a whole, such as to tend to deprave and corrupt persons who are likely, having regard to all relevant circumstances, to read, see or hear the matter contained or embodied in it.

21–50   The test of obscenity is whether the effect of the article was such as to tend to deprave and corrupt persons who were likely to read it, so that obscenity depends on the article and not the author; it follows that intention and the defendant's honesty of purpose will be irrelevant: *Shaw v. DPP* [1962] A.C. 220, HL.. Obscenity and depravity are not confined to sex, and include material that advocates drug taking: *John Calder (Publications) Ltd v. Powell* [1965] 1 Q.B. 508, DC. It also includes material that tends to induce violence: *DPP v. A. and B.C. Chewing Gum Ltd* [1968] 1 Q.B. 159, DC.

The sole test of obscenity is that provided by the Act: *Anderson* [1972] 1 Q.B. 304, **21–51** CA. The test for obscenity in an article consisting of individual items is to be applied to the items individually; if the test shows one item to be obscene it is enough to make the whole article obscene: *ibid*. The quality of indecency was to be determined by looking at the article alleged to be indecent and nothing else. It was an objective test: *O'Carroll* [2003] EWCA Crim 2338.

The meaning of the words "deprave" and "corrupt" were articulated by Byrne J. in the "Lady Chatterley" case:

> "To deprave means to make morally bad, to pervert, to debase or to corrupt morally. To corrupt means to render morally unsound or rotten, to destroy the moral purity or chastity, to pervert or ruin good quality, to debase, to defile" (*Penguin Books Ltd* [1961] Crim. L.R. 176 at 177).

This definition was approved in *Calder and Boyars Ltd* [1969] 1 Q.B. 151, CA. The words "deprave and corrupt" refer primarily to the effect on the minds, including the emotions, of the persons who read or see the article: *DPP v. Whyte* [1972] A.C. 849, HL.

In *Calder and Boyars Ltd*, *ante*, the Court of Appeal stated that the jury should **21–52** have been directed to consider whether the effect of the book was to tend to deprave or corrupt a significant proportion of those persons likely to read it. However, in *DPP v. Whyte*, *ante*, Lord Pearson observed (at p. 865) that although such a direction had been suitable on the facts of the case, the phrase "significant proportion" cannot be safely transplanted to cases of a different character. The statutory definition of obscenity contains no requirement as to the number of persons or as to the proportion of its readers which the article will tend to corrupt or deprave. That definition—

> "... refers to 'persons', which means some persons, though I think in a suitable case, if the number of persons likely to be affected is so small as to be negligible - really negligible - the *de minimis* principle might be applied. But if a seller of pornographic books has a large number of customers who are not likely to be corrupted by such books, he does not thereby acquire a licence to expose for sale or sell such books to a small number of customers who are likely to be corrupted by them" (*ibid.*, at p. 866).

Lords Simon (at p.868), Cross (at p.869) and Salmon (at p.873) accepted the "significant proportion" test, Lord Cross saying that a significant proportion of a class means a part which is not numerically negligible but which may be much less than half (at p.870). Lord Wilberforce did not specifically consider this issue. The justices had found that the class of likely customers for the defendant's pornographic publications was middle-aged men whose morals were already in a state of depravity and corruption, and they had not been satisfied, therefore, that the publications would have a tendency to deprave and corrupt a significant proportion (see *ante*) of likely readers. The House of Lords held that the Act was not merely concerned with the once and for all corruption of the wholly innocent; it equally protected the less innocent from further corruption and the addict from feeding or increasing his addiction.

"Article"

Obscene Publications Act 1959, s.1(2)

1.—(2) In this Act "article" means any description of article containing or embodying matter **21–53** to be read or looked at or both, any sound record, and any film or other record of a picture or pictures.

"Publishes"

Obscene Publications Act 1959, s.1(3)–(6)

21–54   **1.**—(3) For the purposes of this Act a person publishes an article who—

       (a) distributes, circulates, sells, lets on hire, gives, or lends it, or who offers it for sale or for letting on hire; or

       (b) in the case of an article containing or embodying matter to be looked at or a record, shows, plays or projects it, or, where the matter is data stored electronically, transmits that data.

(4) For the purposes of this Act a person also publishes an article to the extent that any matter recorded on it is included by him in a programme included in a programme service.

(5) Where the inclusion of any matter in a programme so included would, if that matter were recorded matter, constitute the publication of an obscene article for the purposes of this Act by virtue of subsection (4) above, this Act shall have effect in relation to the inclusion of that matter in that programme as if it were recorded matter.

(6) In this section "programme" and "programme service" have the same meaning as in the *Broadcasting Act* 1990.

[Subs. (3) is printed as amended by the *CLA* 1977, s.53; and the *CJPOA* 1994, s.168(1), and Sched. 9, para. 3; and as repealed in part by the *Broadcasting Act* 1990, ss.162 and 203(3), and Sched. 21. Subss. (4) to (6) were inserted by the 1990 Act, s.162(1)(b).]

For the definitions of "programme" and "programme service", see sections 202(1) and 201 of the 1990 Act, respectively.

21–55   The forms of publication included in the definition in s.1(3)(a) fall into three distinct groups: in the first group, comprising the words "sells, lets on hire, gives, or lends", publication is to an individual; in the second group, comprising the words "distributes, circulates", publication is on a wider scale involving more than one person; in the third group, a mere offer for sale or letting on hire constitutes publication: *Barker*, 46 Cr.App.R. 227, CCA.

21–56   In *Barker*, the court went on to say that in a case falling within the first group, assuming that publication is proved, the first issue for the court is whether the effect of the article was such as to tend to deprave and corrupt the individual to whom it was published. The second issue is whether any other person or persons were likely to see the article. In this connection, the issue is not whether republication has or has not taken place, but whether it could reasonably have been expected. If the answer to the second issue is "yes", a third issue will arise, namely, whether the article is such as to tend to deprave and corrupt the person or persons to whom republication could reasonably have been expected. On the first issue, a jury should take into consideration both the article itself and the age or occupation of the person to whom it was published, if there is evidence on this. On the second issue, whether republication could reasonably have been expected, such age and occupation are relevant, but they are not the only relevant factors. On the third issue, considerations similar to those involved in the first are applicable. It was further held that the fact that the defendant was wholly unaware of the age or occupation of the person to whom the article had been published is irrelevant. A person who sells potentially obscene matter to an unknown applicant takes the risk that the latter is someone whom the article would tend to deprave and corrupt. On the other hand, if the unknown applicant is not of that type, the defendant's ignorance of the applicant's character cannot make the article obscene.

Uploading or downloading of a webpage will constitute publication: *Perrin* [2002] 4 *Archbold News* 2, CA.

(d) *Defence*

Obscene Publications Act 1959, s.4

Defence of public good

21–57   **4.**—(1) Subject to subsection (1A) of this section a person shall not be convicted of an offence against section two of this Act, and an order for forfeiture shall not be made under the foregoing section, if it is proved that publication of the article in question is justified as being for the public good on the ground that it is in the interests of science, literature, art or learning, or of other objects of general concern.

(1A) Subsection (1) of this section shall not apply where the article in question is a moving picture film or soundtrack, but—

    (a) a person shall not be convicted of an offence against section 2 of this Act in relation to any such film or soundtrack, and

    (b) an order for forfeiture of any such film or soundtrack shall not be made under section 3 of this Act,

if it is proved that publication of the film or soundtrack is justified as being for the public good on the ground that it is in the interests of drama, opera, ballet or any other art, or of literature or learning.

(2) It is hereby declared that the opinion of experts as to the literary, artistic, scientific or other merits of an article may be admitted in any proceedings under this Act either to establish or to negative the said ground.

(3) In this section "moving picture soundtrack" means any sound record designed for playing with a moving picture film, whether incorporated with the film or not.

[This section is printed as amended by the *CLA* 1977, s.53(6), (7).]

In *DPP v. Jordan* [1977] A.C. 699, HL, it was held that consideration of whether **21–58** the defendant has succeeded in establishing this defence only falls to be considered once it has been established that the article in question was obscene and that it was published by the defendant.

The "other objects" and the nature of the "general concern" referred to in subsection (1) fall within the same area as science, literature, art and learning already mentioned, so that expert evidence relating to the alleged beneficial effect of the material on the sexual behaviour and attitudes of some particular persons will not be admissible: *ibid*.

(e) *Sentence*

When tried summarily, the maximum penalty for this offence is six months' imprison- **21–59** ment, a fine not exceeding the statutory maximum or both: s.2(1) of the 1959 Act (*ante*, § 21–42). As from the date of commencement of the *Criminal Justice Act* 2003, s.282(2) and (3), the maximum custodial sentence on summary conviction will be increased to 12 months; but only in respect of offences committed on or after that date: s.282(4). Once section 181 of the 2003 Act is brought into force, custodial sentences of less than 12 months will consist of a custody plus order (see *post*, Ch.23).

See *Holloway*, 4 Cr.App.R.(S.) 128, CA; *Pace* [1998] 1 Cr.App.R.(S.) 121, CA; *Ibra-* **21–60** *him* [1998] 1 Cr.App.R.(S.) 157, CA; and *Tunnicliffe and Greenwood* [1999] 2 Cr.App.R.(S.) 88, CA (all cases involving "front men" in video shops). In the last of these, it was said that a prison sentence would not always be necessary. For a case involving the shopkeeper himself, see *Singh (Jasjit)* [1999] 2 Cr.App.R.(S.) 160, CA.

(f) *Search and seizure*

Obscene Publications Act 1959, s.3

Powers of search and seizure

    3.—(1) If a justice of the peace is satisfied by information on oath that there is reasonable **21–61** ground for suspecting that, in any premises ..., or on any stall or vehicle ..., being premises or a stall or vehicle specified in the information, obscene articles are, or are from time to time, kept for publication for gain, the justice may issue a warrant under his hand empowering any constable to enter (if need be by force) and search the premises, or to search the stall or vehicle ... and to seize and remove any articles found therein or thereon which the constable has reason to believe to be obscene articles and to be kept for publication for gain.

    (2) A warrant under the foregoing subsection shall, if any obscene articles are seized under the warrant, also empower the seizure and removal of any documents found in the premises or, as the case may be, on the stall or vehicle which relate to a trade or business carried on at the premises or from the stall or vehicle.

(3) Subject to subsection (3A) of this section any articles seized under subsection (1) of this section shall be brought before a justice of the peace acting in the local justice area in which the articles were seized, who may thereupon issue a summons to the occupier of the premises or, as the case may be, the user of the stall or vehicle to appear on a day specified in the summons before a magistrates' court acting in that local justice area to show cause why the articles or any of them should not be forfeited; and if the court is satisfied, as respects any of the articles, that at the time when they were seized they were obscene articles kept for publication for gain, the court shall order those articles to be forfeited:

Provided that if the person summoned does not appear, the court shall not make an order unless service of the summons is proved.

Provided also that this subsection does not apply in relation to any article seized under subsection (1) of this section which is returned to the occupier of the premises or, as the case may be, to the user of the stall or vehicle in or on which it was found.

(3A) Without prejudice to the duty of a court to make an order for the forfeiture of an article where section 1(4) of the *Obscene Publications Act* 1964 applies (orders made on conviction), in a case where by virtue of subsection (3A) of section 2 of this Act proceedings under the said section 2 for having an article for publication for gain could not be instituted except by or with the consent of the Director of Public Prosecutions, no order for the forfeiture of the article shall be made under this section unless the warrant under which the article was seized was issued on an information laid by or on behalf of the Director of Public Prosecutions

21–62   (4) In addition to the person summoned, any other person being the owner, author or maker of any of the articles brought before the court, or any other person through whose hands they had passed before being seized, shall be entitled to appear before the court on the day specified in the summons to show cause why they should not be forfeited.

(5) Where an order is made under this section for the forfeiture of any articles, any person who appeared, or was entitled to appear, to show cause against the making of the order may appeal to the Crown Court, and no such order shall take effect until the expiration of the period within which notice of appeal to the Crown Court may be given against the order, or, if before the expiration thereof notice of appeal is duly given or application is made for the statement of a case for the opinion of the High Court, until the final determination or abandonment of the proceedings on the appeal or case.

(6) If as respects any articles brought before it the court does not order forfeiture, the court may if it thinks fit order the person on whose information the warrant for the seizure of the articles was issued to pay such costs as the court thinks reasonable to any person who has appeared before the court to show cause why those articles should not be forfeited; and costs ordered to be paid under this subsection shall be enforceable as a civil debt.

(7) For the purposes of this section the question whether an article is obscene shall be determined on the assumption that copies of it would be published in any manner likely having regard to the circumstances in which it was found, but in no other manner.

(8) [*Repeal of* Obscene Publications Act *1857.*]

[This section is printed as amended, and repealed in part, by the *Courts Act* 1971, s.56(2), Sched. 8, para. 37, and Sched. 9, Pt I; the *CLA* 1977, ss.53(5) and 65(4), and Sched. 12; the *PACE Act* 1984, s.119(2), and Sched. 7, Pt I; and the *Courts Act* 2003, s.109(1), and Sched. 8, para. 106.]

(3) Sending injurious, indecent or obscene articles, etc., by post

(a) *Definition*

Postal Services Act 2000, s.85

Prohibition on sending certain articles by post
21–63   **85.**—(1) A person commits an offence if he sends by post a postal packet which encloses any creature, article or thing of any kind which is likely to injure other postal packets in course of their transmission by post or any person engaged in the business of a postal operator.

(2) Subsection (1) does not apply to postal packets which enclose anything permitted (whether generally or specifically) by the postal operator concerned.

(3) A person commits an offence if he sends by post a postal packet which encloses—

(a) any indecent or obscene print, painting, photograph, lithograph, engraving, cinematograph film or other record of a picture or pictures, book, card or written communication, or

(b) any other indecent or obscene article (whether or not of a similar kind to those mentioned in paragraph (a)).

(4) A person commits an offence if he sends by post a postal packet which has on the packet, or on the cover of the packet, any words, marks or designs which are of an indecent or obscene character.

(5) A person who commits an offence under this section shall be liable—

(a) on summary conviction, to a fine not exceeding the statutory maximum,

(b) on conviction on indictment, to a fine or to imprisonment for a term not exceeding twelve months or to both.

(b) *Allocation*

This offence is triable either way: s.85(5) (*ante*). **21–64**

(c) *Elements of the offence*

The prosecution must prove that: **21–65**

— the defendant sent by post,

— a packet which encloses any creature, article or thing of any kind,

— which is likely to injure other postal packets in the course of their transmission by post or any person engaged in the business of a postal operator;

OR

— the defendant sent by post,

— any indecent or obscene print, painting, photograph, lithograph, engraving, cinematograph film or other record of a picture or pictures, book, card or written communication or any other indecent or obscene article;

OR

— the defendant sent by post,

— any postal packet which has on the packet or the cover of the packet,

— any words, marks or designs which are of an indecent or obscene character.

The meaning of "obscene" in section 11 of the *Post Office Act* 1953, on which this **21–66** provision is closely modelled, was held to be the ordinary meaning of that word which includes "shocking, lewd and indecent": see *Anderson* [1972] 1 Q.B. 304, CA. The test is objective, and the character of the addressee and the effect on the recipient are immaterial: see *Straker* [1965] Crim.L.R. 229, CCA.

(d) *Sentence*

When tried summarily, the maximum penalty for this offence is a fine not exceeding **21–67** the statutory maximum: *Postal Services Act* 2000, s.85(5).

Where the offence involves neither direct corruption nor commercial exploitation of pornography, and offender is of previous good character, a custodial sentence need not be imposed: *Littleford*, 6 Cr.App.R.(S.) 272, CA.

(4) Printing, publishing, selling, etc., works harmful to children

(a) *Definition*

Children and Young Persons (Harmful Publications) Act 1955, s.2

Penalty for printing, publishing, selling, &c., works to which this Act applies

2.—(1) A person who prints, publishes, sells or lets on hire a work to which this Act applies, **21–68** or has any such work in his possession for the purpose of selling it or letting it on hire, shall be guilty of an offence and liable, on summary conviction, to imprisonment for a term not exceeding *four months* [51 weeks] or to a fine not exceeding level 3 on the standard scale or to both:

Part III

Provided that, in any proceedings taken under this subsection against a person in respect of selling or letting on hire a work or of having it in his possession for the purpose of selling it or letting it on hire, it shall be a defence for him to prove that he had not examined the contents of the work and had no reasonable cause to suspect that it was one to which this Act applies.

(2) A prosecution for an offence under this section shall not, in England or Wales, be instituted except by, or with the consent, of the Attorney General.

[This section is printed as amended by the *CJA* 1982, ss.38 and 46. "51 weeks" is substituted for "four months" as from a day to be appointed by the *CJA* 2003, s.280(2), and Sched. 26, para. 15; but not in relation to any offence committed before the amendment takes effect: *ibid*. s.280(3).]

As to the works to which the Act applies, see *post*, § 21–71.

(b) *Allocation*

21–69　　This offence is triable summarily: s.(2)(1) (*ante*).

(c) *Elements of the offence*

21–70　　The prosecution must prove that:
— the defendant printed, published, sold or let out on hire, or had in his possession,
— a work to which the Act applies (as to which, see *post*, § 21–71),
— for the purposes of selling it or letting it on hire.

Children and Young Persons (Harmful Publications) Act 1955, s.1

Works to which this Act applies

21–71　　1. This Act applies to any book, magazine or other like work which is of a kind likely to fall into the hands of children or young persons and consists wholly or mainly of stories told in pictures (with or without the addition of written matter), being stories portraying—
(a) the commission of crimes; or
(b) acts of violence or cruelty; or
(c) incidents of a repulsive or horrible nature;
in such a way that the work as a whole would tend to corrupt a child or young person into whose hands it might fall.

21–72　　Section 5(2) of the 1955 Act defines "child" and "young person" by reference to the definitions of those expressions in section 107(1) of the *Children and Young Persons Act* 1933, *viz*. a child is a person under the age of 14 years, and a young person is one who has attained the age of 14 years but is under the age of 18 years.

(d) *Defence*

21–73　　See the proviso to section 2(1) (*ante*).

(e) *Sentence*

21–74　　The maximum penalty for this offence is four months' imprisonment, or a fine not exceeding level 3, or both: s.2(1) (*ante*). As from the date of commencement of the *Criminal Justice Act* 2003, s.280(2) and Sched. 26, para. 15, the maximum custodial sentence on summary conviction will be increased to 51 weeks; but only in respect of offences committed on or after that date: s.280(3). Once section 181 of the 2003 Act is brought into force, custodial sentences of less than 12 months will consist of a custody plus order (see *post*, Ch.23).

(5) Obscene, etc., theatrical performances

(a) *Definition*

Theatres Act 1968, s.2

Prohibition of presentation of obscene performances of plays

2.—(1) For the purposes of this section a performance of a play shall be deemed to be   **21–75**
obscene if, taken as a whole, its effect was such as to tend to deprave and corrupt persons who
were likely, having regard to all relevant circumstances, to attend it.

(2) Subject to sections 3 and 7 of this Act, if an obscene performance of a play is given,
whether in public or private, any person who (whether for gain or not) presented or
directed that performance shall be liable—

    (a) on summary conviction, to a fine not exceeding the prescribed sum or to
imprisonment for a term not exceeding *six* [12] months;

    (b) on conviction on indictment, to a fine or to imprisonment for a term not exceed-
ing three years, or both.

(3) A prosecution on indictment for an offence under this section shall not be commenced more than two years after the commission of the offence.

(4) No person shall be proceeded against in respect of a performance of a play or
anything said or done in the course of such a performance—

    (a) for an offence at common law where it is of the essence of the offence that the
performance or, as the case may be, what was said or done was obscene, indecent,
offensive, disgusting or injurious to morality; or

    (b) [*repealed by* Indecent Displays (Control) Act *1981*]

    (c) [*repealed by* Civic Government (Scotland) Act *1982*]

and no person shall be proceeded against for an offence at common law of conspiring to corrupt
public morals, or to do any act contrary to public morals or decency, in respect of an agreement
to present or give a performance of a play, or to cause anything to be said or done in the course
of such a performance.

[This section is printed as amended by the *MCA* 1980, s.32(2). In subs. (2)(a), "12" is
substituted for "six", as from a day to be appointed, by the *CJA* 2003, s.282(2) and (3).
The increase has no application to offences committed before the substitution takes effect: s.282(4).]

Proceedings for an offence under this section may not be instituted except by or with
the consent of the Attorney-General: s.8.

(b) *Allocation*

This offence is triable either way: s.2(2) (*ante*).   **21–76**

(c) *Evidence, etc.*

Theatres Act 1968, ss.9, 10

Script as evidence of what was performed

9.—(1) Where a performance of a play was based on a script, then, in any proceedings for an   **21–77**
offence under section 2... or 6 of this Act alleged to have been committed in respect of that performance—

    (a) an actual script on which that performance was based shall be admissible as evi-
dence of what was performed and of the manner in which the performance or
any part of it was given; and

    (b) if such a script is given in evidence on behalf of any party to the proceedings
then, except in so far as the contrary is shown, whether by evidence given on
behalf of the same or any other party, the performance shall be taken to have
been given in accordance with that script.

(2) In this Act "script", in relation to a performance of a play, means the text of the play
(whether expressed in words or in musical or other notation) together with any stage or

Part III

other directions for its performance, whether contained in a single document or not.

[This section is printed as repealed in part by the *Public Order Act* 1986, s.40, and Sched. 3.]

Power to make copies of scripts

21–78   **10.**—(1) If a police officer of or above the rank of superintendent has reasonable grounds for suspecting—

(a) that an offence under section 2... or 6 of this Act has been committed by any person in respect of a performance of a play; or

(b) that a performance of a play is to be given and that an offence under the said section 2... or 6 is likely to be committed by any person in respect of that, performance,

he may make an order in writing under this section relating to that person and that performance.

(2) Every order made under this section shall be signed by the police officer by whom it is made, shall name the person to whom it relates, and shall describe the performance to which it relates in a manner sufficient to enable that performance to be identified.

(3) Where an order under this section has been made, any police officer, on production if so required of the order—

(a) may require the person named in the order to produce, if such a thing exists, an actual script on which the performance was or, as the case may be, will be based; and

(b) if such a script is produced to him, may require the person so named to afford him an opportunity of causing a copy thereof to be made.

(4) Any person who without reasonable excuse fails to comply with a requirement under subsection (3) above shall be liable on summary conviction to a fine not exceeding level 3 on the standard scale.

(5) Where, in the case of a performance of a play based on a script, a copy of an actual script on which that performance was based has been made by or on behalf of a police officer by virtue of an order under this section relating to that performance, section 9(1) of this Act shall apply in relation to that copy as it applies in relation to an actual script on which the performance was based.

[This section is printed as amended, and repealed in part, by the *CJA* 1982, ss.38 and 46; and the *Public Order Act* 1986, s.40, and Sched. 3.]

(d) *Liability of corporate officers*

Theatres Act 1968, s.16

Offences by bodies corporate

21–79   **16.** Where any offence under this Act committed by a body corporate is proved to have been committed with the consent or connivance of, or to be attributable to any neglect on the part of, any director, manager, secretary or other similar officer of the body corporate, or any person purporting to act in any such capacity, he as well as the body corporate shall be guilty of that offence and shall be liable to be proceeded against and punished accordingly.

(e) *Elements of the offence*

21–80   The prosecution must prove that:

— the defendant,

— presented or directed a performance of a play,

— the effect of which (taken as a whole) was such as to tend to deprave and corrupt persons who were likely, having regard to all relevant circumstances, to have attended it.

Theatres Act 1968, s.18

Interpretation

21–81   **18.**—(1) In this Act—

"licensing authority" means—...

(c) [*Scotland*];

"play" means—

(a) any dramatic piece, whether involving improvisation or not, which is given wholly or in part by one or more persons actually present and performing and in which the whole or a major proportion of what is done by the person or persons performing, whether by way of speech, singing or action, involves the playing of a role; and

(b) any ballet given wholly or in part by one or more persons actually present and performing, whether or not it falls within paragraph (a) of this definition;

"police officer" means a member, or in Scotland a constable, of a police force;

"premises" includes any place;

"public performance" includes any performance in a public place within the meaning of the *Public Order Act* 1936 and any performance which the public or any section thereof are permitted to attend, whether on payment or otherwise;

"script" has the meaning assigned by section 9(2) of this Act.

(2) For the purposes of this Act—

(a) a person shall not be treated as presenting a performance of a play by reason only of his taking part therein as a performer;

(b) a person taking part as a performer in a performance of a play directed by another person shall be treated as a person who directed the performance if without reasonable excuse he performs otherwise than in accordance with that person's direction; and

(c) a person shall be taken to have directed a performance of a play given under his direction notwithstanding that he was not present during the performance;

and a person shall not be treated as aiding or abetting the commission of an offence under section 2 or 6 of this Act in respect of a performance of a play by reason only of his taking part in that performance as a performer.

[This section is printed as repealed in part by the *Public Order Act* 1986, s.40, and Sched. 3; and the *Licensing Act* 2003, ss.198(1) and 199, Sched. 6, paras 43 and 47, and Sched. 7.]

(f) *Defence and exceptions*

Theatres Act 1968, ss.3, 7

Defence of public good

3.—(1) A person shall not be convicted of an offence under section 2 of this Act if it is proved **21–82** that the giving of the performance in question was justified as being for the public good on the ground that it was in the interest of drama, opera, ballet or any other art, or of literature or learning.

(2) It is hereby declared that the opinion of experts as to the artistic, literary or other merits of a performance of a play may be admitted in any proceedings for an offence under section 2 of this Act either to establish or negative the said ground.

As to this provision, see *ante*, §§ 21–57, 21–58.

Exceptions for performances given in certain circumstances

7.—(1) Nothing in sections 2 to 4 of this Act shall apply in relation to a performance of a play **21–83** given on a domestic occasion in a private dwelling.

(2) Nothing in sections 2 to 6 of this Act shall apply in relation to a performance of a play given solely or primarily for one or more of the following purposes, that is to say—

(a) rehearsal; or

(b) to enable—

(i) a record or cinematograph film to be made from or by means of the performance; or

(ii) the performance to be broadcast; or

(iii) the performance to be included in a programme service (within the meaning of the *Broadcasting Act* 1990) other than a sound or television broadcasting service;

but in any proceedings for an offence under section 2 or 6 of this Act alleged to have been committed in respect of a performance of a play or an offence at common law alleged to have been committed in England and Wales by the publication of defamatory matter in the course of a performance of a play, if it is proved that the performance was attended by persons other than persons directly connected with the giving of the performance or the doing in relation thereto of any of the things mentioned in paragraph (b) above, the performance shall be taken not to have been given solely or primarily for one or more of the said purposes unless the contrary is shown.

(3) In this section—

"broadcast" means broadcast by wireless telegraphy (within the meaning of the *Wireless Telegraphy Act* 1949), whether by way of sound broadcasting or television;

"cinematograph film" means any print, negative, tape or other article on which a performance of a play or any part of such a performance is recorded for the purposes of visual reproduction;

"record" means any record or similar contrivance for reproducing sound, including the sound-track of a cinematograph film.

[This section is printed as amended, and repealed in part, by the *Public Order Act* 1986, s.40, and Sched. 3; the *Cable and Broadcasting Act* 1984, s.57, Sched. 5, para. 21, and Sched. 6; and the *Broadcasting Act* 1990, s.203(1), and Sched. 20, para. 13.]

(g) *Sentence*

21–84   When tried summarily, the maximum penalty for this offence is imprisonment for a term not exceeding six months or a fine not exceeding the prescribed sum or both: s.2(2)(a) (*ante*, § 21–75). As from the date of commencement of the *Criminal Justice Act* 2003, s.282(2) and (3), the maximum custodial sentence on summary conviction will be increased to 12 months; but only in respect of offences committed on or after that date: s.282(4). Once section 181 of the 2003 Act is brought into force, custodial sentences of less than 12 months will consist of a custody plus order (see *post*, Ch.23).

(6) Theatrical performances intended, or likely, to provoke breach of the peace

(a) *Definition*

Theatres Act 1968, s.6

Provocation of breach of peace by means of public performance of a play

21–85   **6.**—(1) Subject to section 7 of this Act, if there is given a public performance of a play involving the use of threatening, abusive or insulting words or behaviour, any person who (whether for gain or not) presented or directed that performance shall be guilty of an offence under this section if—

(a) he did so with intent to provoke a breach of the peace; or

(b) the performance, taken as a whole, was likely to occasion a breach of the peace.

(2) A person guilty of an offence under this section shall be liable on summary conviction to a fine not exceeding level 5 on the standard scale or to imprisonment for a term not exceeding *six months* [51 weeks] or to both.

[This section is printed as amended by the *CLA* 1977, ss.15 and 30, and Sched. 1; and the *CJA* 1982, s.46; and as amended, as from a day to be appointed, by the *CJA* 2003, s.281(4) and (5) (substitution of "51 weeks" for "six months"); but this has no application in relation to an offence before the amendment comes into force: s.281(6).]

Proceedings for an offence under this section may not be instituted except by or with the consent of the Attorney-General: s.8.

(b) *Allocation*

21–86   This offence is triable summarily: s.6(2) (*ante*).

(c) *Elements of the offence*

The prosecution must prove: **21–87**
— the giving of a public performance of a play,
— involving the use of threatening, abusive or insulting words or behaviour,
— the defendant presented or directed the performance,
— he did so with intent to provoke a breach of the peace, or the performance, taken as a whole, was likely to occasion a breach of the peace.

As to the meaning of "play" and "public performance", see section 18 (*ante*, § 21–81). **21–88**
As to the script as evidence of what was performed, see section 9 (*ante*, § 21–77).

(d) *Defence*

As to certain performances being excepted from section 6, see section 7(2) (*ante*, **21–89**
§ 21–83).

(e) *Sentence*

The maximum penalty for this offence is a fine not exceeding level 5 on the standard **21–90**
scale, six months' imprisonment, or both: s.6(2) (*ante*, § 21–85). As from the date of commencement of the *Criminal Justice Act* 2003, s.281(4) and (5), the maximum custodial sentence on summary conviction will be increased to 12 months; but only in respect of offences committed on or after that date: s.281(6). Once section 181 of the 2003 Act is brought into force, custodial sentences of less than 12 months will consist of a custody plus order (see *post*, Ch.23).

(7) **Indecent displays**

(a) *Definition*

Indecent Displays (Control) Act 1981, s.1

Indecent displays
1.—(1) If any indecent matter is publicly displayed the person making the display and any **21–91**
person causing or permitting the display to be made shall be guilty of an offence.

(2) Any matter which is displayed in or so as to be visible from any public place shall, for the purposes of this section, be deemed to be publicly displayed.

(3) In subsection (2) above, "public place", in relation to the display of any matter, means any place to which the public have or are permitted to have access (whether on payment or otherwise) while that matter is displayed except—
(a) a place to which the public are permitted to have access only on payment which is or includes payment for that display; or
(b) a shop or any part of a shop to which the public can only gain access by passing beyond an adequate warning notice; but the exclusions contained in paragraphs (a) and (b) above shall only apply where persons under the age of 18 years are not permitted to enter while the display in question is continuing.

(4) Nothing in this section applies in relation to any matter—
(a) included by any person in a television broadcasting service or other television programme service (within the meaning of the *Broadcasting Act* 1990);
(b) included in the display of an art gallery or museum and visible only from within the gallery or museum; or
(c) displayed by or with the authority of, and visible only from within a building occupied by, the Crown or any local authority; or
(d) included in a performance of a play (within the meaning of paragraph 14(1) of Schedule 1 to the *Licensing Act* 2003) in England and Wales or of a play (within the meaning of the *Theatres Act* 1968) in Scotland; or
(e) included in an exhibition of a film, within the meaning of paragraph 15 of Schedule 1 to the *Licensing Act* 2003, in England and Wales, or a film exhibition, as defined in the *Cinemas Act* 1985 in Scotland—

      (i)   given in a place which as regards that exhibition is required to be licensed under section 1 of that Act or by virtue only of section 5, 7 or 8 of that Act is not required to be so licensed; or

      (ii)   which is an exhibition to which section 6 of that Act applies given by an exempted organisation as defined by subsection (6) of that section.

(5) In this section "matter" includes anything capable of being displayed, except that it does not include an actual human body or any part thereof; and in determining for the purpose of this section whether any displayed matter is indecent—

    (a)   there shall be disregarded any part of that matter which is not exposed to view; and

    (b)   account may be taken of the effect of juxtaposing one thing with another.

(6) A warning notice shall not be adequate for the purposes of this section unless it complies with the following requirements—

    (a)   The warning notice must contain the following words, and no others—

"WARNING

Persons passing beyond this notice will find material on display which they may consider indecent. No admittance to persons under 18 years of age."

    (b)   The word "WARNING" must appear as a heading.

    (c)   No pictures or other matter shall appear on the notice.

    (d)   The notice must be so situated that no one could reasonably gain access to the shop or part of the shop in question without being aware of the notice and it must be easily legible by any person gaining such access.

[This section is printed as amended by the *Broadcasting Act* 1990, s.203(1), and Sched. 20, para. 30; the *Cinemas Act* 1985, s.24(1), and Sched. 2, para. 13; and the *Licensing Act* 2003, s.198(1), and Sched. 6, para. 80.]

(b) *Allocation*

21–92   This offence is triable either way: *Indecent Displays (Control) Act* 1981, s.4(1).

(c) *Liability of corporate officers*

Indecent Displays (Control) Act 1981, s.3

Offences by corporations

21–93   **3.**—(1) Where a body corporate is guilty of an offence under this Act and it is proved that the offence occurred with the consent or connivance of, or was attributable to any neglect on the part of, any director, manager, secretary or other officer of the body, or any person who was purporting to act in any such capacity he, as well as the body corporate, shall be deemed to be guilty of that offence and shall be liable to be proceeded against and punished accordingly.

(2) Where the affairs of a body corporate are managed by its members, subsection (1) shall apply in relation to the acts and defaults of a member in connection with his functions of management as if he were a director of the body corporate.

(d) *Sentence*

21–94   When tried summarily, the maximum penalty is a fine not exceeding the statutory maximum: *Indecent Displays (Control) Act* 1981, s.4(1)(a). When tried on indictment, the offence carries two years' imprisonment, or a fine, or both: *ibid.*, s.4(1)(b).

(e) *Search and seizure*

Indecent Displays (Control) Act 1981, s.2

Powers of arrest, seizure and entry

21–95   **2.**—(1) [...]

(2) A constable may seize any article which he has reasonable grounds for believing to be or to contain indecent matter and to have been used in the commission of an offence under this Act.

(3) In England and Wales, a justice of the peace if satisfied on information on oath that there are reasonable grounds for suspecting that an offence under this Act has been or is being committed on any premises and, in Scotland, a sheriff or justice of the peace on being so satisfied on evidence on oath, may issue a warrant authorising any constable to enter the premises specified in the information or, as the case may be, evidence (if need be by force) ... seize any article which the constable has reasonable grounds for believing to be or to contain indecent matter and to have been used in the commission of an offence under this Act.

[Subs. (1) and the words omitted from subs. (3) were repealed by the *PACE Act* 1984, s.119(2), and Sched. 7, Pt 1.]

III. OFFENCES AGAINST PUBLIC JUSTICE

A. CONTEMPT OF COURT

(1) General

The *Contempt of Court Act* 1981 gave statutory powers to magistrates to deal with **21–96** contempt in the face of the court. In addition, magistrates have powers of enforcement in respect of fine defaulters under sections 75 to 96 of the *Magistrates' Courts Act* 1980, and to punish defaults in respect of other orders under section 63 of that Act, which provides that any person disobeying an order of a magistrates' court to do anything other than the payment of money may be fined up to a maximum of £50 a day for every day during which he is in default or a sum not exceeding £5,000, or the court may commit him to custody until he has remedied his default or for a period not exceeding two months.

(2) Definition

Contempt of Court Act 1981, s.12

Offences of contempt of magistrates' courts
    12.—(1) A magistrates' court has jurisdiction under this section to deal with any person **21–97** who—
> (a) wilfully insults the justice or justices, any witness before or officer of the court or any solicitor or counsel having business in the court, during his or their sitting or attendance in court or in going to or returning from the court; or
> (b) wilfully interrupts the proceedings of the court or otherwise misbehaves in court.

    (2) In any such case the court may order any officer of the court, or any constable, to take the offender into custody and detain him until the rising of the court; and the court may, if it thinks fit, commit the offender to custody for a specified period not exceeding one month or impose on him a fine not exceeding £2,500, or both.

    (2A) A fine imposed under subsection (2) above shall be deemed, for the purposes of any enactment, to be a sum adjudged to be paid by a conviction.

    (4) A magistrates' court may at any time revoke an order of committal made under subsection (2) and, if the offender is in custody, order his discharge.

    (5) Section 135 of the *Powers of Criminal Courts (Sentencing) Act* 2000 (limits on fines in respect of young persons) and the following provisions of the *Magistrates' Courts Act* 1980 apply in relation to an order under this section as they apply in relation to a sentence on conviction or finding of guilty of an offence; and those provisions of the *Magistrates' Courts Act* 1980 are sections 75 to 91 (enforcement); section 108 (appeal to Crown Court); section 136 (overnight detention in default of payment); and section 142(1) (power to rectify mistakes).

[This section is printed as amended, and repealed in part, by the *CJA* 1982, s.78, and Sched. 16; the *CJA* 1991, s.17(3), and Sched. 4, Pts I and V; the *CJA* 1993, s.65(3) and (4), and Sched. 3, para. 6(4); and the *PCC(S)A* 2000, s.165(1), and Sched. 9, para. 83.]

Magistrates' Courts Act 1980, s.97(4)

Summons to witness and warrant for his arrest

21–98   **97.**—(4) If any person attending or brought before a magistrates' court refuses without just excuse to be sworn or give evidence, or to produce any document or thing, the court may commit him to custody until the expiration of such period not exceeding one month as may be specified in the warrant or until he sooner gives evidence or produces the document or thing or impose on him a fine not exceeding £2,500 or both.

[Subs. (4) is printed as amended by the *Contempt of Court Act* 1981, s.14, and Sched. 2, Pt III, para. 7; and the *CJA* 1991, s.17(3)(a) and (e), and Sched. 4, Pts I and V, para. 2.]

(3) Allocation

21–99   These offences are triable summarily only.

The *Consolidated Criminal Practice Direction*, para. V.54 (contempt in the face of a magistrates' court) (*post*, Appendix F–63) sets out the relevant principles governing the exercise of magistrates' powers under these sections.

(4) Elements of the offence

21–100   For the offence under section 12 of the *Contempt of Court Act* 1981, the prosecution must prove that:

— the defendant wilfully insulted the justice or justices, or any witness before or officer of the court or any solicitor or counsel having business in the court,
— during his or their sitting or attendance in court or in going to or returning from the court.

OR

— that the defendant wilfully interrupted the proceedings of the court or otherwise misbehaved in court.

Regarding the offence under section 97(4) of the 1980 Act, the prosecution must prove that:

— the defendant was attending or brought before a magistrates' court, and
— refused without just excuse to be sworn or give evidence, or to produce any document or thing.

21–101   As regards contempt in the face of the court under section 12, a person "wilfully" interrupts the proceedings of the court if he commits the acts causing disruption deliberately with the intention that they should interrupt the proceedings of the court or if, knowing that there is a risk that his acts will interrupt the proceedings, he nevertheless goes on deliberately to do those acts: *Bodden v. Metropolitan Police Commr* [1990] 2 Q.B. 397, CA. Section 12(a) does not apply to the making of threats: *R. v. Havant JJ., ex p. Palmer*, 149 J.P. 609, DC, though threats may constitute "misbehaviour" under paragraph (b) (witness, after giving his evidence, threatening to "get" the defendant and his solicitor who were waiting outside court whilst the magistrates considered their decision).

21–102   In construing the words "otherwise misbehaves" regard has to be had to the fact that the 1981 Act is a criminal statute and that the other prohibitions in section 12 are qualified by the word "wilfully". There has to be some element of defiance in the alleged contemnor's conduct, *Re Hooker* [1990] C.O.D. 190, DC.

(5) Sentence

21–103   The maximum penalty for this offence under section 12 is imprisonment for a term not exceeding one month, or a fine not exceeding £2,500, or both. The court may also order that the defendant be detained until the rising of the court. The maximum penalty for the offence under section 97 is committal to custody until the defendant gives evidence, or produces the relevant document, or for a period not exceeding one month, or a fine not exceeding £2,500, or both.

B. Perjury and Offences Akin to Perjury

(1) Introduction

Perjury, contrary to section 1(1) of the *Perjury Act* 1911 is triable only on indictment. **21–104**
All other offences under the 1911 Act are triable either way, either by virtue of express provision in the 1911 Act (see ss.3 and 4) or by virtue of the *Magistrates' Courts Act* 1980, s.17(1), and Sched. 1, para. 14. This includes the offences contrary to section 89 of the *Criminal Justice Act* 1967 (*post*, § 21-105) and section 106 of the 1980 Act (*post*, § 21–106), which are effectively assimilated into the 1911 Act on account of subsection (2) in each section.

(2) False statements for the purposes of criminal proceedings

(a) *Definition*

Criminal Justice Act 1967, s.89

False written statements tendered in evidence

89.—(1) If any person in a written statement tendered in evidence in criminal proceedings **21–105**
by virtue of section 9 of this Act *or in proceedings before a court-martial by virtue of the said section 9 as extended by section 12 above or by section 99A of the* Army Act *1955 or section 99A of the* Air Force Act *1955* wilfully makes a statement material in those proceedings which he knows to be false or does not believe to be true, he shall be liable on conviction on indictment to imprisonment for a term not exceeding two years or a fine or both.

(2) The *Perjury Act* 1911 shall have effect as if this section were contained in that Act.

[This section is printed as amended, and repealed in part, by the *Armed Forces Act* 1976, s.22(5), and Sched. 9, para. 15; and the *MCA* 1980, s.154(3), and Sched. 9; and as amended, as from a day to be appointed, by the *Armed Forces Act* 2006, s.378(2), and Sched. 17 (omission of words from "or in proceedings" to "*Air Force Act* 1955").]

Magistrates' Courts Act 1980, s.106

False written statements tendered in evidence

106.—*(1) If any person in a written statement admitted in evidence in criminal proceed-* **21–106**
ings by virtue of section 5B above wilfully makes a statement material in those proceedings which he knows to be false or does not believe to be true, he shall be liable on conviction on indictment to imprisonment for a term not exceeding 2 years or a fine or both.

(2) The Perjury Act *1911 shall have effect as if this section were contained in that Act.*

[This section is printed as amended by the *CPIA* 1996, s.47, and Sched. 1, Pt I, paras 1 and 12. It is repealed, as from a day to be appointed, by the *CJA* 2003, ss.41 and 332, Sched. 3, para. 51(1) and (6)(c), and Sched. 37, Pt 4.]

(b) *Allocation*

These offences are triable either way: see *ante*, § 21–104. **21–107**

(c) *Elements of the offences*

The prosecution must prove that: **21–108**
— the defendant, in a written statement tendered in evidence in criminal proceedings or in proceedings before a court-martial, or in a written statement admitted in evidence in criminal proceedings,
— wilfully made a statement,

     — material in those proceedings,
     — which he knew to be false or did not believe to be true.

Wilfully

21–109   The prosecution are required to prove that the statement was made deliberately and not inadvertently or by mistake: *Millward* [1985] Q.B. 519, CA.

Materiality

21–110   The matter of materiality is an issue to be determined objectively by the judge. The defendant's belief on the materiality of the statement is irrelevant: *Millward, ante*.

Falsity

21–111   The defendant may be convicted where the statement that he believed to be false turns out to be true, as the sections only require the making of a statement which is known or believed to be untrue.

Perjury Act 1911, s.13

Corroboration

21–112   **13.** A person shall not be liable to be convicted of any offence against this Act, or of any offence declared by any other Act to be perjury or subornation of perjury, or to be punishable as perjury or subornation of perjury, solely upon the evidence of one witness as to the falsity of any statement alleged to be false.

(d) *Sentence*

21–113   As these offences are triable either way by virtue of section 17(1) of, and Schedule 1 to, the *MCA* 1980 (see *ante*, § 21–104), the maximum penalties on summary conviction are prescribed by section 32(1) of that Act (six months' imprisonment (amended to 12 months, as from a day to be appointed, by the *CJA* 2003, s.282(1), but not in relation to an offence committed before the amendment takes effect: s.282(4)) or a fine not exceeding the prescribed sum): see *post*, § 23–129.

(3) **False statements for the purposes of judicial proceedings abroad**

(a) *Definition*

Perjury Act 1911, s.1A

False unsworn statement under Evidence (Proceedings in Other Jurisdictions) Act 1975

21–114   **1A.** If any person, in giving any testimony (either orally or in writing) otherwise than on oath, where required to do so by an order under section 2 of the *Evidence (Proceedings in Other Jurisdictions) Act* 1975, makes a statement—
     (a) which he knows to be false in material particular, or
     (b) which is false in a material particular and which he does not believe to be true,
he shall be guilty of an offence and shall be liable on conviction on indictment to imprisonment for a term not exceeding two years or a fine or both.

[This section was inserted by the 1975 Act, s.8(1), and Sched.]

(b) *Allocation*

21–115   This offence is triable either way: see *ante*, § 21–104.

(c) *Elements of the offence*

21–116   The prosecution must prove that:

1044

— the defendant, in giving any testimony, otherwise than on oath,

— where required to do so under section 2 of the 1975 Act

— made a statement which

— he knew to be false in a material particular or

— which was false in a material particular and he did not believe it to be true.

As to falsity, and its proof, see *ante*, §§ 21–111, 21–112.

(d) *Sentence*

See *ante*, § 21–113.   **21–117**

(4) False statements on oath otherwise than in a judicial proceeding

(a) *Definition*

Perjury Act 1911, s.2

False statements on oath made otherwise than in a judicial proceedings   **21–118**
   2. If any person—
     (1) being required or authorised by law to make any statement on oath for any
        purpose, and being lawfully sworn (otherwise than in a judicial proceeding) wil-
        fully makes a statement which is material for that purpose and which he knows
        to be false or does not believe to be true; or
     (2) wilfully uses any false affidavit for the purposes of the *Bills of Sale Act* 1878, as
        amended by any subsequent enactment,
he shall be guilty of a misdemeanour, and, on conviction thereof on indictment, shall be liable to
imprisonment for a term not exceeding seven years, or to a fine or to both such imprisonment
and fine.

(b) *Allocation*

This offence is triable either way: see *ante*, § 21–104.   **21–119**

(c) *Elements of the offence*

The prosecution must prove (para. (1)) that: **21–120**
— the defendant was required or authorised by law to make any statement on oath
   for any purpose, and

— was lawfully sworn (otherwise than in a judicial proceeding), and

— wilfully made a statement which was material for that purpose, and

— which he knew to be false or did not believe was true.

For the meaning of "wilfully", see *ante* § 21–109.

For the meaning of "falsity" and proof thereof, see *ante* §§ 21–111, 21–112.

(d) *Sentence*

See *ante*, § 21–113.   **21–121**

(5) False statements with reference to marriage

(a) *Definition*

Perjury Act 1911, s.3

False statements, &c. with reference to marriage   **21–122**
   3.—(1) If any person—
     (a) for the purpose of procuring a marriage, or a certificate or licence for marriage,
        knowingly and wilfully makes a false oath, or makes or signs a false declaration,

notice or certificate required under any Act of Parliament for the time being in force relating to marriage; or

(b) knowingly and wilfully makes, or knowingly and wilfully causes to be made, for the purposes of being inserted in any register of marriage, a false statement as to any particular required by law to be known and registered relating to any marriage; or

(c) forbids the issue of any certificate or licence for marriage by falsely representing himself to be a person whose consent to the marriage is required by law knowing such representation to be false, or

(d) with respect to a declaration made under section 16(1A) or 27B(2) of the *Marriage Act* 1949—

    (i) enters a caveat under subsection (2) of the said section 16, or

    (ii) makes a statement mentioned in subsection (4) of the said section 27B,

which he knows to be false in a material particular,

he shall be guilty of a misdemeanour, and, on conviction thereof on indictment, shall be liable to imprisonment for a term not exceeding seven years, or to a fine or to both such imprisonment and fine and on summary conviction thereof shall be liable to a penalty not exceeding the prescribed sum.

(2) No prosecution for knowingly and wilfully making a false declaration for the purpose of procuring any marriage out of the district in which the parties or one of them dwell shall take place after the expiration of eighteen months from the solemnization of the marriage to which the declaration refers.

[This section is printed as amended by the *CJA* 1925, s.28; the *Marriage (Prohibited Degrees of Relationship) Act* 1986, s.4; and the *MCA* 1980, s.32(2).]

(b) *Allocation*

21–123   This offence is triable either way: s.3(1), *ante*.

(c) *Elements of the offence*

21–124   The prosecution must prove that:

— the defendant for the purpose of procuring a marriage, or a certificate or licence for marriage,

— knowingly and wilfully made a false oath, or made or signed a false declaration, notice or certificate, required under an Act of Parliament, or

— knowingly and wilfully made, or knowingly and wilfully caused to be made, for the purposes of being inserted in any register of marriage, a false statement as to any particular required by law to be known and registered relating to any marriage, or

— forbade the issue of any certificate or licence for marriage by falsely representing himself to be a person whose consent to the marriage was required by law knowing such representation to be false, or

— with respect to a declaration made under section 16(1A) or 27B(2) of the *Marriage Act* 1949,

    entered a caveat under section 16(2), or

    made a statement mentioned in section 27B(4),

— which he knew to be false in a material particular.

(d) *Sentence*

21–125   When tried summarily, the maximum penalty for this offence is a fine not exceeding the prescribed sum (*i.e.* £5,000: see s.32(9) of the *MCA* 1980, § 23–28).

(6) False statements in relation to births and deaths

(a) *Definition*

Perjury Act 1911, s.4

False statements, &c. as to births or deaths

    4.—(1) If any person—   **21–126**

(a) wilfully makes any false answer to any question put to him by any registrar of
births or deaths relating to the particulars required to be registered concerning
any birth or death, or, wilfully gives to any such registrar any false information
concerning any birth or death or the cause of any death; or

(b) wilfully makes any false certificate or declaration under or for the purposes of
any Act relating to the registration of births or deaths, or, knowing any such certificate or declaration to be false, uses the same as true or gives or sends the same
as true to any person; or

(c) wilfully makes, gives or uses any false statement or declaration as to a child born
alive as having been still-born, or as to the body of a deceased person or a still-
born child in any coffin, or falsely pretends that any child born alive was still-
born; or

(d) makes any false statement with intent to have the same inserted in any register of
births or deaths:

he shall be guilty of a misdemeanour and shall be liable—

    (i) on conviction thereof on indictment to imprisonment for a term not
exceeding seven years, or to a fine; and

    (ii) on summary conviction thereof, to a penalty not exceeding the prescribed
sum.

    (2) A prosecution on indictment for an offence against this section shall not be com-
menced more than three years after the commission of the offence.

[This section is printed as amended by the *MCA* 1980, s.32(2).]

(b) *Allocation*

This offence is triable either way: s.4(1) (*ante*).   **21–127**

(c) *Sentence*

When tried summarily, the maximum penalty for this offence is a fine not exceeding   **21–128**
the prescribed sum (as to which, see *ante*, § 21–125).

(7) False statutory declarations and other statements not on oath

(a) *Definition*

Perjury Act 1911, s.5

False statutory declarations and other false statements without oath

    5. If any person knowingly and wilfully makes (otherwise than on oath) a statement false in a   **21–129**
material particular, and the statement is made—

(a) in a statutory declaration; or

(b) in an abstract, account, balance sheet, book, certificate, declaration, entry,
estimate, inventory, notice, report, return, or other document which he is authorised or required to make, attest, or verify, by any public general Act of Parliament for the time being in force; or

(c) in any oral declaration or oral answer which he is required to make by, under, or
in pursuance of any public general Act of Parliament for the time being in force,

he shall be guilty of a misdemeanour and shall be liable on conviction thereof on indictment to
imprisonment, for any term not exceeding two years, or to a fine or to both such imprisonment
and fine.

(b) *Allocation*

21–130   This offence is triable either way: see *ante*, § 21–104.

(c) *Elements of the offence*

21–131   The prosecution must prove that:
— the defendant knowingly and wilfully made,
— otherwise than on oath,
— a statement false in a material particular, and
— the statement was made
    in a statutory declaration, or
    in an abstract, account balance sheet, book, certificate, declaration, entry, estimate, inventory, notice, report, return, or other document which he was authorised to make, attest or verify by any public general Act of Parliament for the time being in force, or
    in any oral declaration or oral answer which he was required to make by, under or in pursuance of any such Act of Parliament.

(d) *Sentence*

21–132   See *ante*, § 21–113.

(8) False declarations to obtain registration

(a) *Definition*

Perjury Act 1911, s.6

False declarations, &c. to obtain registration, &c. for carrying on a vocation
21–133   **6.** If any person—
(a) procures or attempts to procure himself to be registered on any register or roll kept under or in pursuance of any public general Act of Parliament for the time being in force of persons qualified by law to practise any vocation or calling; or
(b) procures or attempts to procure a certificate of the registration of any person on any such register or roll as aforesaid,
by wilfully making or producing or causing to be made or produced either verbally or in writing, any declaration, certificate, or representation which he knows to be false or fraudulent, he shall be guilty of a misdemeanour and shall be liable on conviction thereof on indictment to imprisonment for any term not exceeding twelve months, or to a fine, or to both such imprisonment and fine.

(b) *Allocation*

21–134   This offence is triable either way: see *ante*, § 21–104.

(c) *Elements of the offence*

21–135   The prosecution must prove that:
— the defendant procured, or attempted to procure himself to be registered on any register or roll kept under or in pursuance of any public general Act of Parliament for the time being in force of persons qualified by law to practice any vocation or calling, or
— procured or attempted to procure a certificate of the registration of any person on any such register or roll as aforesaid,
— by wilfully making or producing or causing to be made or produced either verbally or in writing, any declaration, certificate, or representation,
— which he knew to be false or fraudulent.

(d) Sentence

See ante, § 21–113.

C. Intimidation of Witnesses, Jurors and Others

(1) Definition

Criminal Justice and Public Order Act 1994, s.51

51.—(1) A person commits an offence if—

  (a) he does an act which intimidates, and is intended to intimidate, another person ("the victim"),

  (b) he does the act knowing or believing that the victim is assisting in the investigation of an offence or is a witness or potential witness or a juror or potential juror in proceedings for an offence, and

  (c) he does it intending thereby to cause the investigation or the course of justice to be obstructed, perverted or interfered with.

(2) A person commits an offence if—

  (a) he does an act which harms, and is intended to harm, another person or, intending to cause another person to fear harm, he threatens to do an act which would harm that other person,

  (b) he does or threatens to do the act knowing or believing that the person harmed or threatened to be harmed ("the victim)", or some other person, has assisted in an investigation into an offence or has given evidence or particular evidence in proceedings for an offence, or has acted as a juror or concurred in a particular verdict in proceedings for an offence, and

  (c) he does or threatens to do it because of that knowledge or belief.

(3) For the purposes of subsections (1) and (2) it is immaterial that the act is or would be done, or that the threat is made—

  (a) otherwise than in the presence of the victim, or

  (b) to a person other than the victim.

(4) The harm that may be done or threatened may be financial as well as physical (whether to the person or a person's property) and similarly as respects an intimidatory act which consists of threats.

(5) The intention required by subsection (1)(c) and the motive required by subsection (2)(c) above need not be the only or the predominating intention or motive with which the act is done or, in the case of subsection (2), threatened.

(6) A person guilty of an offence under this section shall be liable—

  (a) on conviction on indictment, to imprisonment for a term not exceeding five years or a fine or both;

  (b) on summary conviction, to imprisonment for a term not exceeding six [12] months or a fine not exceeding the statutory maximum or both.

(7) If, in proceedings against a person for an offence under subsection (1) above, it is proved that he did an act falling within paragraph (a) with the knowledge or belief required by paragraph (b), he shall be presumed, unless the contrary is proved, to have done the act with the intention required by paragraph (c) of that subsection.

(8) If, in proceedings against a person for an offence under subsection (2) above, it is proved that he did or threatened to do an act falling within paragraph (a) within the relevant period—

  (a) he did an act which harmed, and was intended to harm, another person, or

  (b) intending to cause another person fear of harm, he threatened to do an act which would harm that other person,

and that he did the act, or (as the case may be) threatened to do the act with the knowledge or belief required by paragraph (b), he shall be presumed, unless the contrary is proved, to have done the act or (as the case may be) threatened to do the act with the motive required by paragraph (c) of that subsection.

(9) In this section—

"investigation into an offence" means such an investigation by the police or other person charged with the duty of investigating offences or charging offenders;

"offence" includes an alleged or suspected offence;

"potential" in relation to a juror, means a person who has been summoned for jury service at the court at which proceedings for the offence are pending; *and*

["public prosecutor", "requisition" and "written charge" have the same meaning as in section 29 of the *Criminal Justice Act* 2003;]

"the relevant period" —

    (a) in relation to a witness or juror in any proceedings for an offence, means the period beginning with the institution of the proceedings and ending with the first anniversary of the conclusion of the trial or, if there is an appeal or a reference under section 9 or 11 of the *Criminal Appeal Act* 1995, of the conclusion of the appeal;

    (b) in relation to a person who has, or is believed by the accused to have, assisted in an investigation into an offence, but was not also a witness in proceedings for an offence, means the period of one year beginning with any act of his, or any act believed by the accused to be an act of his, assisting in the investigation; and

    (c) in relation to a person who both has, or is believed by the accused to have, assisted in the investigation into an offence and was a witness in proceedings for the offence, means the period beginning with any act of his, or any act believed by the accused to be an act of his, assisting in the investigation and ending with the anniversary mentioned in paragraph (a) above.

(10) For the purposes of the definition of the relevant period in subsection (9) above—

    (a) proceedings for an offence are instituted at the earliest of the following times—

        (i) when a justice of the peace issues a summons or warrant under section 1 of the *Magistrates' Courts Act* 1980 in respect of the offence;

        [(ia) when a public prosecutor issues a written charge and requisition in respect of the offence;]

        (ii) when a person is charged with the offence after being taken into custody without a warrant;

        (iii) when a bill of indictment is preferred by virtue of section 2(2)(b) of the *Administration of Justice (Miscellaneous Provisions) Act* 1933;

    (b) proceedings at a trial of an offence are concluded with the occurrence of any of the following, the discontinuance of the prosecution, the discharge of the jury without a finding otherwise than in circumstances where the proceedings are continued without a jury, the acquittal of the accused or the sentencing of or other dealing with the accused for the offence of which he was convicted; and

    (c) proceedings on an appeal are concluded on the determination of the appeal or the abandonment of the appeal.

(11) This section is in addition to, and not in derogation of, any offence subsisting at common law.

[This section is printed as amended by the *Criminal Appeal Act* 1995, s.29(1), and Sched. 2, para. 19; the *YJCEA* 1999, s.67(1), and Sched. 4, para. 22; and the *CJA* 2003, s.331, and Sched. 36, paras 62 and 64; and, as from a day or days to be appointed, by the *CJA* 2003 as follows: by s.282(2) and (3) (substitution of "12" for "six" in subs. (6), but not in relation to an offence committed before the date of commencement: s.282(4)); and by s.331, and Sched. 36, para. 11 (omission of italicised word and insertion of words in square brackets in subss. (9) and (10)).]

(2) Allocation

21–138 Offences under this section are triable either way: s.51(6) (*ante*).

(3) Elements of the offence

21–139 For an offence under section 51(1), the prosecution must prove that the defendant:

— did an act which intimidated another person (but see *Patrascu, post*),

— he did the act intending that it should intimidate the other person,

— he did the act knowing or believing that the person intimidated was assisting in the investigation of an offence or was a witness or potential witness or a juror or a potential juror in proceedings for an offence, and

— he did it intending thereby to cause the investigation or the course of justice to be obstructed, perverted or interfered with.

For an offence under section 51(2), the prosecution must prove that the defendant:

— did an act which harmed, and which was intended to harm another person or, intending to cause another person to fear harm, he threatened to do an act which would harm that other person,

— he did or threatened to do the act knowing or believing that the person harmed or threatened, or some other person, had assisted an investigation into an offence or had given evidence in proceedings for an offence, or had acted as a juror or concurred in a particular verdict in proceedings for an offence, and

— he did the act or threatened to do it because of that knowledge or belief.

Intimidation

A person may be guilty of an offence contrary to section 51(1) notwithstanding that **21–140** the victim is not actually intimidated; a person does an act which intimidates another person within section 51(1)(a) if he puts the victim in fear, which is the ordinary meaning of "intimidate"; but the person also does so if he seeks to deter the victim from some relevant action by threat or violence; a threat unaccompanied by violence may be sufficient, and the threat need not necessarily be a threat of violence; the act must be intended to intimidate and must involve pressure which amounts to improper pressure; but the intimidation does not necessarily have to be successful in the sense that the victim does not actually have to be deterred or put in fear; this apparent contradiction arises from different shades of meaning of the active and passive use of the verb; an act may amount to intimidation and thus intimidate, even though the victim is sufficiently steadfast not to be intimidated: *Patrascu* [2005] 1 Cr.App.R. 35, CA.

Investigation

There must be an investigation under way at the time of the alleged act; it is insuf- **21–141** ficient that the defendant believed this to be the case: *Singh (B.)* [1999] Crim.L.R. 681, CA.

Harm

See subsection (4). Financial harm aside, "harm" in section 51 refers to physical harm **21–142** and does not include physical assaults (such as spitting), which do not cause injury: *Normanton* [1998] Crim.L.R. 220, CA.

Intention and motive

See subsections (5), (7) and (8). The reverse burden provision in subsection (7) was **21–143** held not to breach the presumption of innocence under Article 6(2) of the European Convention on Human Rights: *Att.-Gen.'s Reference (No. 1 of 2004)*; *R. v. Edwards*; *R. v. Denton*; *R. v. Hendley*; *R. v. Crowley* [2004] 1 W.L.R. 2111, CA.

(4) Sentence

When tried summarily, the maximum penalty for either offence is imprisonment for **21–144** a term not exceeding six months, or a fine not exceeding the statutory maximum, or both (s.51(6)). After commencement of the relevant provisions, the maximum custodial sentence will be 12 months' imprisonment, but not in relation to an offence committed before their commencement (see *ante*, § 21–137).

The fact that Parliament thought it necessary to enact section 51 was ample reason for holding that an offence contrary to it, that involved an assault, contained an extra element of criminality, above and beyond the assault: *Watmore* [1998] 2 Cr.App.R.(S.) 46, CA.

Part IV

Sentencing

CHAPTER 22

GENERAL PRINCIPLES OF SENTENCING

I. THE PURPOSES OF SENTENCING

Sentencing can range from a relatively complex task to a relatively straightforward **22–1** one. At its most difficult, it is a complex balance in which conflicting goals have to be addressed. The main sentencing statutes currently in force are the *Criminal Justice Act* 2003 and the *Powers of Criminal Courts (Sentencing) Act* 2000 *(PCC(S)A* 2000). Much of the *Powers of Criminal Courts (Sentencing) Act* 2000 has been repealed and replaced by provisions in the *Criminal Justice Act* 2003, predominantly for offences committed on or after April 4, 2005. The most significant provisions yet to come into force replace custodial sentences of less than 12 months with the custody plus order. In addition, in December 2004 the Sentencing Guidelines Council published its first definitive guidelines. Two of these guidelines are designed to assist courts in implementing the provisions in the 2003 Act (one on the assessment of seriousness and the other on the new sentences themselves) and the other consolidates and clarifies the approach to the giving of a reduction in sentence on account of the entry of a guilty plea (as revised). The training for judges, magistrates and court staff included these guidelines and practitioners will need to be familiar with them. Relevant parts are included at the appropriate point in this work. The full text can be found at www.sentencing-guidelines.gov.uk.

Section 142 of the 2003 Act requires every court to have regard to five specified purposes—punishment, reduction of crime, reform and rehabilitation, protection of the public and the making of reparation to those affected by the offence. Sentencing of youths (those aged under 18 at the time of conviction) is excluded from this obligation: section 142(2)(a). For adults, reduction of crime is simply listed as one of the five; for youths, there is a clear obligation to treat the prevention of offending by young people as the primary goal (section 37 of the *Crime and Disorder Act* 1998) supported by the obligation to have regard to the welfare of the youth: *Children and Young Persons Act* 1933, section 44.

Criminal Justice Act 2003, s.142

Purposes of sentencing

22–2   **142.**—(1) Any court dealing with an offender in respect of his offence must have regard to the following purposes of sentencing—

(a) the punishment of offenders,

(b) the reduction of crime (including its reduction by deterrence),

(c) the reform and rehabilitation of offenders,

(d) the protection of the public, and

(e) the making of reparation by offenders to persons affected by their offences.

(2) Subsection (1) does not apply—

(a) in relation to an offender who is aged under 18 at the time of conviction,

(b) to an offence the sentence for which is fixed by law,

(c) to an offence the sentence for which falls to be imposed under section 51A(2) of the *Firearms Act* 1968 (minimum sentence for certain firearms offences), under subsection (2) of section 110 or 111 of the *Sentencing Act* (required custodial sentences) under section 29(4) or (6) of the *Violent Crime Reduction Act* 2006 (minimum sentences in certain cases of using someone to mind a weapon) or under any of sections 225 to 228 of this Act (dangerous offenders), or

(d) in relation to the making under Part 3 of the *Mental Health Act* 1983 of a hospital order (with or without a restriction order), an interim hospital order, a hospital direction or a limitation direction.

(3) In this Chapter "sentence", in relation to an offence, includes any order made by a court when dealing with the offender in respect of his offence; and "sentencing" is to be construed accordingly

22–3   The sentencing framework established by the 2003 Act follows the previous framework in the 2000 Act in having as its central concept the seriousness of the offence. The assessment of seriousness determines whether any of the sentencing thresholds has been crossed, indicating what type of sentence is likely to be most appropriate. It is also the key element in determining the length of a custodial sentence, the onerousness of requirements to be included in a community order and the amount of any fine imposed.

Section 148 of the 2003 Act provides that a court must not pass a community sentence on an offender unless it is of the opinion that the offence, or the combination of the offence and one or more offences associated with it, was *serious enough* to warrant such a sentence. Section 152 provides that the court must not pass a custodial sentence unless it is of the opinion that the offence, or the combination of the offence and one or more offences associated with it, was *so serious* that neither a fine alone nor a community sentence can be justified for the offence. Whilst this is the same basic criterion as the *PCC(S)A* 2000, it is articulated a little differently. In its draft guideline on custodial sentences of less than 12 months the Sentencing Guidelines Council suggests that, taking together this revised wording and the change in character of community orders and the potential increase in onerousness of a custody plus order, the custodial threshold is now higher than it was.

22–4   By section 143 of the 2003 Act, any assessment of seriousness requires the court to consider both the culpability of the offender and any harm that was caused, intended to be caused or might foreseeably have been caused. When a court is considering sentence, it will be looking to identify the factors that assist it in determining both culpability and harm. Having done that, the court will take into account mitigating factors personal to the offender and then, having determined sentence, apply any reduction on account of a guilty plea. It is well established that a court will take account of injury caused to the victim of a crime. A court is not, however, required to gather extensive detail about the level of that injury. In *R. (Holme) v. Liverpool Magistrates' Court* (2005) 169 J.P. 306, the defendant was convicted of dangerous driving at a magistrates' court after a trial. The Divisional Court concluded both that (even though no specific information was given) the effect of the accident should have been recognised by the court given the nature of the impact between the defendant's vehicle and the victim and that the sentence imposed was about right. The court affirmed the importance of a court being aware of the injuries to a victim in such cases and was concerned that the justices in this case appeared to consider it was not a relevant matter. It was stated:

> ". . . benches of magistrates, when sentencing, should not consider it necessary that they should either hear oral evidence or receive medical reports which go into great detail. But, that said, a balance has to be struck in cases such as this between the injuries of the victim being expanded on to some degree to enable a balanced view to be formed by the court, and extensive detail being canvassed in court in too great detail. It would be helpful for magistrates to say, when they do sentence in a case in which there have been injuries, something to the effect that they have taken them into account. That is what they are entitled to do. Should this course be adopted there would be no reason for misunderstanding to occur as appears in this case to have occurred." (At para. 53, per Newman J.)

The guideline from the Sentencing Guidelines Council on seriousness (*Overarching Principles: Seriousness*) identifies 4 levels of criminal culpability. The offender who is most culpable is the one who has the *intention* to cause harm. The more the offence is planned rather than spontaneous, the higher the culpability. When this is combined with the level of harm caused, intended or foreseeable it will show the seriousness of the offence. The next level of culpability is where the offender is *reckless* as to whether harm is caused. In this context, the Council describes recklessness as "where the offender appreciates at least some harm would be caused but proceeds giving no thought to the consequences even though the extent of the risk would be obvious to most people". The third level of culpability is where the offender has knowledge of the specific risks entailed by his actions even though he does not intend to cause the harm that results. Finally, the lower level of culpability arises where the offender is guilty of negligence. The Council recognises that there are cases where liability is strict and there needs to be no proof of culpability in order to secure a conviction; however, even in those circumstances, the extent to which the offender was culpable is likely to be a key factor in determining the approach to sentence. It is the culpability of the offender that is the *initial* factor in determining seriousness.

The guideline also describes (at paras 1.8–1.14) different types of harm that are likely **22–5** to be caused and the amount of harm will clearly also be a critical factor in assessing seriousness. Culpability will be greater where an offender deliberately causes more harm than is necessary in order to commit the offence—the burglar who vandalises the property as well as stealing what is there, the robber who uses unnecessary violence over and above what is needed to take the property from the victim. The guidelines also draw attention (para. 1.18) to those circumstances where far greater harm was caused than was intended or was within the control of the offender; in those circumstances, a court will be looking to assess the extent to which that level of harm could have been foreseen.

A court is sometimes asked to approach the assessment of the seriousness of an offence on the basis that offences of this type have become particularly prevalent and so normal sentencing practice should change. Again this is addressed by the Sentencing Guidelines Council in its guideline on seriousness. It states that, whilst seriousness should be assessed on the basis of the harm and culpability of the particular offence rather than as part of a "collective social harm", it is nonetheless legitimate for the overall approach to sentencing levels for particular offences to be directed by their cumulative effect. Where there are exceptional local circumstances which suggest that prevalence should influence sentencing levels, the Council asserts that, as the pivotal issue will be the harm being caused to the community, "It is essential that sentencers both have supporting evidence from an external source (for example the local Criminal Justice Board) to justify claims that a particular crime is prevalent in their area and are satisfied that there is a compelling need to treat the offence more seriously than elsewhere." It is emphasised that sentencing patterns should return to normal once the exceptional circumstances cease to exist. This was reinforced by the Court of Appeal in *Oosthuizen* [2006] 1 Cr.App.R.(S.) 73. In this case, a judge had been dealing with an offence of street robbery and formed the view that this was becoming a prevalent offence in the area and sentenced accordingly. The attention of the judge had not been drawn to the guideline. The Court of Appeal disapproved of the approach of the judge (and an earlier authority of the Court of Appeal) emphasising in strong terms the legal obligation to have regard to a guideline issued by the Sentencing Guidelines Council. The Court stated:

"15. … If, in any particular town or city, there are statistics available to the Crown Prosecution Service, the Local Criminal Justice Board or otherwise, which demonstrate a prevalence greater than that nationally of a particular type of offence, those statistics can and should be made available to the Court.

16. In the absence of such statistics or other evidence identifying particular prevalence in a particular area, a judge, however experienced in a particular area, should not make the assumption that prevalence of that offence is more marked in the area with which he is familiar than it is nationally. Such an assumption will be particularly hazardous when, as in the present case, there is either a guideline decision of this Court, or a guideline issued by the Sentencing Guidelines Council, or specific guidance in relation to particular offences, intended to be of national application. *Lobban*, as the Lord Chief Justice pointed out, was not, strictly speaking, a guideline case, but it did afford guidance which was intended to be of general application. It follows that the learned judge was not entitled to impose, for reasons of local deterrence, a sentence higher than would otherwise be appropriate for that particular kind of offence by reference to national guidance."

Guideline: Overarching Principles: Seriousness

F. PREVALENCE

22–6   **1.38** The seriousness of an individual case should be judged on its own dimensions of harm and culpability rather than as part of a collective social harm. It is legitimate for the overall approach to sentencing levels for particular offences to be guided by their cumulative effect. However, it would be wrong to further penalise individual offenders by increasing sentence length for committing an individual offence of that type.

1.39 There may be exceptional local circumstances that arise which may lead a court to decide that prevalence should influence sentencing levels. The pivotal issue in such cases will be the harm being caused to the community. It is essential that sentencers both have supporting evidence from an external source (for example the local Criminal Justice Board) to justify claims that a particular crime is prevalent in their area and are satisfied that there is a compelling need to treat the offence more seriously than elsewhere.

The key factor in determining whether sentencing levels should be enhanced in response to prevalence will be the level of harm being caused in the locality. Enhanced sentences should be exceptional and in response to exceptional circumstances. Sentencers must sentence within the sentencing guidelines once the prevalence has been addressed.

Criminal Justice Act 2003, s.143

Determining the seriousness of an offence

22–7   **143.**—(1) In considering the seriousness of any offence, the court must consider the offender's culpability in committing the offence and any harm which the offence caused, was intended to cause or might foreseeably have caused.

(2) In considering the seriousness of an offence ("the current offence") committed by an offender who has one or more previous convictions, the court must treat each previous

conviction as an aggravating factor if (in the case of that conviction) the court considers that it can reasonably be so treated having regard, in particular, to—

    (a) the nature of the offence to which the conviction relates and its relevance to the current offence, and

    (b) the time that has elapsed since the conviction.

    (3) In considering the seriousness of any offence committed while the offender was on bail, the court must treat the fact that it was committed in those circumstances as an aggravating factor.

    (4) Any reference in subsection (2) to a previous conviction is to be read as a reference to—

    (a) a previous conviction by a court in the United Kingdom, or

    (b) a previous finding of guilt in service disciplinary proceedings.

    (5) Subsection (2) and (4) do not prevent the court from treating a previous conviction by a court outside the United Kingdom as an aggravating factor in any case where the court considers it appropriate to do so.

A court must take into account two aspects directly relevant to the offence itself—the **22–8** culpability of the offender and the harm which was caused, intended or could have been caused. No guidance is given in the Act as to different types of harm or the people by whom the harm has been/could have been suffered. A person damaging property in a minor way as part of a campaign by activists against certain (lawful) activity may be playing a part in a chain of events that causes serious financial harm to the country as a whole by deterring inward investment. To incorporate that level of harm is likely to be seen as stretching the chain too far. However, those sentenced for importing illegal drugs will be sentenced on the basis of the harm those drugs will have the potential to do to people far removed in the chain of events from the importer. Perhaps the link then is generally the extent to which the harm is an inevitable consequence of the conduct.

A more radical requirement is set out in section 143(2). There has long been an issue about the significance of previous convictions given the obligation to ensure that a sentence is not greater than is commensurate with the seriousness of the offence. This provision seeks to circumvent that by causing a previous conviction to aggravate the seriousness of the current offence, presumably because it influences the decision as to culpability.

II. ESTABLISHMENT OF SENTENCING GUIDELINES COUNCIL

The *Criminal Justice Act* 2003 establishes a Sentencing Guidelines Council to issue **22–9** guidelines for any issue that affects sentencing decisions. The Council was established in March 2004 and is gradually developing a body of guidelines to which each magistrates' court will have regard when passing sentence.

As well as dealing with individual offences, the guidelines will deal with more general issues such as the extent of the reduction in sentence following a guilty plea and the significance of previous convictions. The Council will also publish information about sentencing. Whilst some of this will be statistical information about current practice, some will also be about research into the effectiveness of different sentences. In April 2005 (and subsequent revisions), the Council published a compendium of guideline judgments of the Court of Appeal designed to give readier access to important sentencing decisions pending the publication of its own guidelines. Information on the Council and any guidelines can be found at www.sentencing-guidelines.gov.uk.

Judicial consideration to the effect of a guideline was given in *Oosthuizen* [2006] 1 Cr.App.R.(S.) 73. In an earlier case, a constitution of the Court of Appeal had expressed doubt about a part of the Council guideline on Seriousness. However, this constitution (headed by the Vice President) drew attention to the legal obligation to have regard to any guideline whilst retaining the discretion to reach a different conclusion in relation to the case under consideration.

"Individual judges and indeed constitutions of this Court may, from time to time, disagree with some aspect of a guideline issued by the Sentencing Guidelines Council. But it is not open to them to disregard what the Council says. On the contrary, by virtue of the statutory duty imposed by [*Criminal Justice Act* 2003] section 172, they must have regard to guidelines so issued. It does not necessarily follow that in every case a guideline will be followed. As was pointed out by Lord Woolf CJ in *Last & Ors* [2005] EWCA Crim. 106, para. 16: 'The fact that every Court must have regard to the relevant guideline does not mean that it has to be followed.'"

Where a court departs from a guideline, it is obliged to give reasons for so doing: *Criminal Justice Act* 2003, s.174(2). Similar sentiments were expressed in *Bowering* [2006] 2 Cr.App.R.(S.) 10 and in *Gisbourne* [2005] EWCA Crim. 2491. Increasingly, courts are being referred not only to definitive guidelines but, where no such guidelines exist, to the advice of the Sentencing Advisory Panel. In certain circumstances, and with due recognition of the status of such documents (including the fact that the definitive guideline may be different), this is acceptable. In *R. (W.) v. Brent Youth Court* [2006] EWHC Admin 95; (2006) 170 J.P. 198, the DC stated that "In cases where there is no guidance from the Sentencing Guidelines Council it is permissible and helpful for the court to consider any relevant publication of the Sentencing Advisory Panel". In *R. (DPP) v. Camberwell Youth Court* [2005] 1 Cr.App.R. 6, Kennedy L.J. said "that, although the Sentencing Advisory Panel's advice has no legal force, as it has yet to be acted upon, it is helpful as an indication of a considered response to a sentencing problem. In short, providing that the court recognises that the advice does not carry legal force, it is legitimate and helpful to consider such a publication." However, a consultation guideline should be used only with extreme caution, at least where there is pre-existing Court of Appeal guidelines: *Lloyd* [2007] EWCA Crim 590.

Typically, an offence guideline will apply to a first time offender who has been convicted after pleading not guilty. It will describe three types of activity falling within the broad definition of the offence and then provide a starting point and a range. In order to assist in the consistent interpretation of these terms, the Sentencing Guidelines Council and Sentencing Advisory Panel have published definitions:

MEANING OF "RANGE", "STARTING POINT" AND "FIRST TIME OFFENDER" WITHIN SENTENCING GUIDELINES COUCIL GUIDELINES

A Council guideline is generally for a *first time offender* convicted after a trial. It commonly provides a *starting point* based on an assessment of the seriousness of the offence and a *range* within which sentence will normally fall for most cases.

A clear, consistent understanding of each of these terms is essential and the Council and the Sentencing Advisory Panel have agreed the following definitions.

They are set out in a format that follows the structured approach to a sentencing decision which identifies first those aspects that affect the assessment of the seriousness of the offence, then those aspects that form part of personal mitigation and, finally, any reduction for a guilty plea.

In practice, the boundaries between these stages will not always be as clear cut but the underlying principles will remain the same.

In accordance with section 174 of the *Criminal Justice Act* 2003, a court is obliged to "*state in open court, in ordinary language and in general terms, its reasons for deciding on the sentence passed*".

In particular, "*where guidelines indicate that a sentence of a particular kind, or within a particular range, would normally be appropriate and the sentence is of a different kind, or is outside that range*" the court must give its reasons for imposing a sentence of a different kind or outside the range.

Assessing the seriousness of the offence
   —1.

(a) A typical Council guideline will apply to an offence that can be committed in a variety of circumstances with different levels of seriousness. It will apply to a **first time offender** who has been convicted after a trial. Within the guidelines, a **first time offender** is a person who does not have a conviction which, by virtue of section 143(2) of the *Criminal Justice Act* 2003, must be treated as an aggravating factor.

(b) As an aid to consistency of approach, a guideline will describe a number of types of activity which would fall within the broad definition of the offence. These will be set out in a column generally headed "type/nature of activity".

(c) The expected approach is for a court to identify the description that most nearly matches the particular facts of the offence for which sentence is being imposed. This provides a **starting point** from which the sentencer can depart to reflect aggravating or mitigating factors affecting the seriousness of the offence (beyond those contained in the description itself) to reach a **provisional sentence**.

(d) The range is the bracket into which the **provisional sentence** will normally fall after having regard to factors which aggravate or mitigate the seriousness of the offence. The particular circumstances may, however, make it appropriate that the provisional sentence falls outside the range.

2. Where the offender has previous convictions which aggravate the seriousness of the current offence, that may take the **provisional sentence** beyond the **range** given particularly where there are significant other aggravating factors present.

Personal Mitigation

—(3) Once the **provisional sentence** has been identified (by reference to the factors affecting the seriousness of the offence), the court will take into account any relevant factors of personal mitigation. Again, this may take the provisional sentence outside the range.

Reduction for guilty plea

—4. Where there has been a guilty plea, any reduction attributable to that plea will be applied to the sentence at this stage. This reduction may take the sentence below the **range** provided.

III. FUNCTION OF THE PROSECUTION IN RELATION TO SENTENCE

There is a substantial difference in the range and the volume of the workload between the Crown Court and the magistrates' courts. Not every prosecutor in a magistrates' court is a solicitor or barrister; not only do lay presenters appear on behalf of the Crown Prosecution Service, but also other prosecutors can authorise suitable individuals to prosecute on their behalf. In addition, the volume of cases and the speed of throughput is much greater in a magistrates' court and the existing guidelines are published more systematically.   **22–10**

The Code for Crown Prosecutors makes specific provision for the role of the Crown Prosecutor in relation to sentence. It states:

"11. Prosecutors' Role In Sentencing
1. Crown Prosecutors should draw the court's attention to:
   - any aggravating or mitigating factors disclosed by the prosecution case;
   - any victim personal statement;
   - where appropriate, evidence of the impact of the offending on a community;
   - any statutory provisions or sentencing guidelines which may assist; any relevant statutory provisions relating to ancillary orders (such as anti-social behaviour orders).
2. Crown Prosecutors should challenge any assertion made by the defence in mitigation that is inaccurate, misleading or derogatory. If the defence persist in the assertion, and it appears relevant to the sentence, the court should be invited to hear evidence to determine the facts and sentence accordingly."

This part of the Code follows the line of authority set out *post*. The requirement to draw to the attention of the court any "sentencing guidelines which may assist" is likely to be influenced greatly in practice by differences between a magistrates' court and the Crown Court, not least the presence of the legal adviser to the magistrates and the exis-

Part IV

tence of both the guidelines published by the Sentencing Guidelines Council and the *Magistrates' Courts Sentencing Guidelines*. The compendium of existing guideline decisions referred to *ante* should also assist busy advocates to find a relevant authority: see www.sentencing-guidelines.gov.uk.

Case law tends to come from proceedings in the Crown Court and needs to be read in the light of these differences. The principles that can be deduced from the cases are as follows.

22–11   1. In *Att.-Gen.'s Reference (No. 7 of 1997) (Fearon)* [1998] 1 Cr.App.R.(S.) 268 it was clearly stated that the role of the prosecution as regards sentencing includes providing assistance and guidance. Judges should not be slow to invite assistance from prosecuting counsel in these matters and counsel should be ready to offer assistance if asked. The Court hoped that judges would not be affronted if prosecuting counsel did offer to give guidance on the relevant provisions and appropriate authorities.

2. This approach was developed further by Lord Woolf C.J. in *Att.-Gen.'s Reference (No. 52 of 2003) (Webb)* [2003] EWCA Crim. 3731. It was emphasised that prosecuting counsel had a duty to draw relevant guideline cases to the attention of the court and it would be wrong for a judge to suggest that counsel should not do his duty. Prosecuting counsel, it was said, should be meticulous in drawing relevant guidelines to the attention of the judge and in having copies available if required.

   Whilst this is a desirable situation also in the magistrates' court, it is legitimate to expect the legal adviser to the magistrates to fulfil that function in normal circumstances. However, prosecution and defence advocates should always be aware of the existence of relevant guidance and be prepared to draw it to the attention of the court should the court seem to be unaware of it.

   See also *Blight* [1999] Crim.L.R. 426 for the duty on counsel to be ready to assist the court and *Hartery* [1993] Crim.L.R. 230 emphasising the duty of counsel to inform themselves of the extent of the court's powers, to know what options are open to the judge, and to correct the judge if a mistake is made.

22–12   3. Prosecution Counsel should be able to present the court with sufficient information about the offence to enable the court to assess its seriousness. It is not part of the function to influence the court with regard to that assessment. However, if a defendant is not legally represented it is proper to inform the judge of any mitigating circumstances about which counsel is instructed.

4. Counsel should also be in a position to assist the Court, if requested, as to any statutory provisions relevant to the offence or the offender. Counsel should be prepared to bring to the attention of the court any matters referred to *ante* in which he feels the Court has erred and should also bring to the attention of the Court any appropriate compensation, forfeiture and restitution matters which arise on conviction.

5. Counsel should draw the attention of the Court to any assertion of material fact put forward in mitigation which prosecuting counsel believes to be untrue: if the defence persist in this assertion, prosecuting counsel should invite the Court to consider requiring the issue to be determined through a *Newton* hearing (see *post*, § 25–2): para. 11.8(e) of the *Code of Conduct of the Bar Written Standards* (7th Ed.).

22–13   6. For defence counsel, the same rules apply to mitigation as to any other court proceedings. Defence counsel should notify the prosecution of anything which counsel is instructed to submit in mitigation which casts aspersions on the conduct or character of a victim or witness in the case. The purpose of this is to give prosecuting counsel sufficient opportunity to consider whether or not to challenge these assertions.

7. Paragraph 708(g) of the Code of Conduct of the Bar provides that a barrister must not make statements or ask questions which are merely scandalous or

intended or calculated only to vilify insult or annoy either a witness or some other person. The barrister must also, if possible, avoid naming in open court a third party whose conduct would be impugned thereby (para. 708(h)).

These obligations were re-emphasised with some force by the Court of Appeal (Crim. Div.) in *Cain and others* [2006] EWCA Crim 3233. Giving the judgment of the court, Lord Phillips CJ stated: **22–14**

> "It is not satisfactory for a prosecuting advocate, having secured a conviction, to sit back and leave sentencing to the defence. Nor can an advocate, when appearing for the prosecution for the purpose of sentence on a plea of guilty, limit the assistance that he provides to the court to the outlining of the facts and details of the defendant's previous convictions.
>
> The advocate for the prosecution should always be ready to assist the court by drawing attention to any statutory provisions that govern the court's sentencing powers. It is the duty of the prosecuting advocate to ensure that the judge does not, through inadvertence, impose a sentence that is outside his powers. The advocate for the prosecution should also be in a position to offer to draw the judge's attention to any relevant sentencing guidelines or guideline decisions of this court."

This obligation applies also to the defence advocate. The Court recognised the judge's duty to pass a lawful sentence but noted that advocates may well have had more time to prepare a case than the judge. Lord Phillips stated:

> "It is of course the duty of a judge to impose a lawful sentence, but sentencing has become a complex matter and a judge will often not see the papers very long before the hearing and does not have the time for preparation that advocates should enjoy. In these circumstances a judge relies on the advocates to assist him with sentencing. It is unacceptable for advocates not to ascertain and be prepared to assist the judge with the legal restrictions on the sentence that he can impose on their clients."

Although the judgment states that it applies equally to a magistrates' court, whilst advocates need to be aware of the guidance and law as they apply to a magistrates' court and to be prepared to draw them to the attention of the court, as pointed out *ante* there will also be a legal adviser (justices' clerk or assistant justices' clerk) present who can be expected to fulfil that function in normal circumstances.

The *Criminal Proceedings and Investigations Act* 1996, ss.58 to 60 give the court power to restrict the reporting of false or irrelevant assertions made during a speech in mitigation. Where there are substantial grounds for concluding that an assertion is both derogatory and either false or irrelevant to sentence (section 58(4)), the court may make an order which makes it an offence to publish that assertion: sections 59 and 60. An order may be made before the court determines sentences (section 58(7)), in which case it ceases on sentence being passed, or it may be made as soon as reasonably practicable after sentence in which case, unless earlier revoked, it will cease to be effective after 12 months: section 58(8).

Criminal Procedure and Investigations Act 1996, ss.58–60

Orders in respect of certain assertions

58.—(1) This section applies where a person has been convicted of an offence and a speech in mitigation is made by him or on his behalf before— **22–15**

    (a) a court determining what sentence should be passed on him in respect of the offence, or

    (b) a magistrates' court determining whether he should be committed to the Crown Court for sentence.

(2) This section also applies where a sentence has been passed on a person in respect of an offence and a submission relating to the sentence is made by him or on his behalf before—

    (a) a court hearing an appeal against or reviewing the sentence, or

    (b) a court determining whether to grant leave to appeal against the sentence.

(3) Where it appears to the court that there is a real possibility that an order under subsection (8) will be made in relation to the assertion, the court may make an order under subsection (7) in relation to the assertion.

Part IV

(4) Where there are substantial grounds for believing—

    (a) that an assertion forming part of the speech or submission is derogatory to a person's character (for instance, because it suggests that his conduct is or has been criminal, immoral or improper), and

    (b) that the assertion is false or that the facts asserted are irrelevant to the sentence,

the court may make an order under subsection (8) in relation to the assertion.

(5) An order under subsection (7) or (8) must not be made in relation to an assertion if it appears to the court that the assertion was previously made—

    (a) at the trial at which the person was convicted of the offence, or

    (b) during any other proceedings relating to the offence.

(6) Section 59 has effect where a court makes an order under subsection (7) or (8).

(7) An order under this subsection—

    (a) may be made at any time before the court has made a determination with regard to sentencing;

    (b) may be revoked at any time by the court;

    (c) subject to paragraph (b), shall cease to have effect when the court makes a determination with regard to sentencing.

(8) An order under this subsection—

    (a) may be made after the court has made a determination with regard to sentencing, but only if it is made as soon as is reasonably practicable after the making of the determination;

    (b) may be revoked at any time by the court;

    (c) subject to paragraph (b), shall cease to have effect at the end of the period of 12 months beginning with the day on which it is made;

    (d) may be made whether or not an order has been made under subsection (7) with regard to the case concerned.

(9) For the purposes of subsection (7) and (8) the court makes a determination with regard to sentencing—

    (a) when it determines what sentence should be passed (where this section applies by virtue of subsection (1)(a);

    (b) when it determines whether the person should be committed to the Crown Court for sentence (where this section applies by virtue of subsection (1)(b));

    (c) when it determines what the sentence should be (where this section applies by virtue of subsection (2)(a));

    (d) when it determines whether to grant leave to appeal (where this section applies by virtue of subsection (2)(b).

Restriction on reporting of assertions

22–16   **59.**—(1) Where a court makes an order under section 58(7) or (8) in relation to any assertion, at any time when the order has effect the assertion must not—

    (a) be published in Great Britain in a written publication available to the public, or

    (b) be included in a relevant programme for reception in Great Britain.

(2) In this section—

    "relevant programme" means a programme included in a programme service, within the meaning of the *Broadcasting Act* 1990;

    "written publication" includes a film, a soundtrack and any other record in permanent form but does not include an indictment or other document prepared for use in particular legal proceedings.

(3) For the purposes of this section an assertion is published or included in a programme if the material published or included—

    (a) names the person about whom the assertion is made or, without naming him, contains enough to make it likely that members of the public will identify him as the person about whom it is made, and

    (b) reproduces the actual wording of the matter asserted or contains its substance.

Reporting of assertions: offences

22–17   **60.**—(1) If an assertion is published or included in a relevant programme in contravention of section 59, each of the following persons is guilty of an offence—

    (a) in the case of publication in a newspaper or periodical, any proprietor, any editor and any publisher of the newspaper or periodical;

(b) in the case of publication in any other form, the person publishing the assertion;

(c) in the case of an assertion included in a relevant programme, any body corporate engaged in providing the service in which the programme is included and any person having functions in relation to the programme corresponding to those of an editor of a newspaper.

(2) A person guilty of an offence under this section is liable on summary conviction to a fine of an amount not exceeding level 5 on the standard scale.

(3) Where a person is charged with an offence under this section it is a defence to prove that at the time of the alleged offence—

(a) he was not aware, and neither suspected nor had reason to suspect, that an order under section 58(7) or (8) had effect at that time, or

(b) he was not aware, and neither suspected nor had reason to suspect, that the publication or programme in question was of, or (as the case may be) included, the assertion in question.

(4) Where an offence under this section committed by a body corporate is proved to have been committed with the consent or connivance of, or to be attributable to any neglect on the part of—

(a) a director, manager, secretary or other similar officer of the body corporate, or

(b) a person purporting to act in any such capacity,

he as well as the body, corporate is guilty of the offence and liable to be proceeded against and punished accordingly.

(5) In relation to a body corporate whose affairs are managed by its members "director" in subsection (4) means a member of the body corporate.

(6) Subsection (2) and (3) of section 59 apply for the purposes of this section as they apply for the purposes of that.

IV. LEGAL REPRESENTATION

There is no obligation on a person to be legally represented (although there are **22–18** certain things that an unrepresented defendant cannot do). However, the court must not impose a custodial sentence on an offender who is not legally represented unless an opportunity to apply for legal representation at public expense has been given and not taken or, though taken, has been withdrawn on the ground of the conduct of the defendant: *PCC(S)A* 2000, s.83(1)–(3).

For magistrates' courts, this additional requirement applies where a defendant aged 21 or over on conviction who is liable to receive imprisonment has not previously been so sentenced and is not legally represented: section 83(1) and (2). For defendants aged 18–20 on conviction, it applies regardless of whether a custodial sentence has previously been imposed—the only criterion is lack of legal representation: section 83(2).

Powers of Criminal Court (Sentencing) Act 2000, s.83

Restriction on imposing custodial sentences on persons not legally represented

83.—(1) A magistrates' court on summary conviction, or the Crown Court on committal for **22–19** sentence or on conviction on indictment, shall not pass a sentence of imprisonment on a person who—

(a) is not legally represented in that court, and

(b) has not been previously sentenced to that punishment by a court in any part of the United Kingdom,

unless he is a person to whom subsection (3) below applies.

(2) A magistrates' court on summary conviction, or the Crown Court on committal for sentence or on conviction on indictment, shall not—

(a) pass a sentence of detention under section 90 or 91 below,

[(aa) pass a sentence of imprisonment on a person who, when convicted, was aged at least 18 but under 21,]

(b) pass a sentence of custody for life under section 93 or 94 below,

(c) pass a sentence of detention in a young offender institution, or

(d) make a detention and training order,

on or in respect of a person who is not legally represented in that court unless he is a person to whom subsection (3) below applies.

(3) This subsection applies to a person if either—

(a) he was granted a right to representation funded by the Legal Services Commission as part of the Criminal Defence Service but the right was withdrawn because of his conduct; or

(b) having been informed of his right to apply for such representation and having had the opportunity to do so, he refused or failed to apply.

(4) For the purposes of this section a person is to be treated as legally represented in a court if, but only if, he has the assistance of counsel or a solicitor to represent him in the proceedings in that court at some time after he is found guilty and before he is sentenced.

(5) For the purposes of subsection (1)(b) above a previous sentence of imprisonment which has been suspended and which has not taken effect under section 119 below or under section 19 of the *Treatment of Offenders Act (Northern Ireland)* 1968 shall be disregarded.

(6) In this section "sentence of imprisonment" does not include a committal for contempt of court or any kindred offence.

[Subsections (2): paras (b), (c) substituted, by subsequent para. (aa), by the *Criminal Justice and Court Services Act* 2000, s.74, Sched. 7, Pt II, paras 160, 178 from a date to be appointed: see the *Criminal Justice and Court Services Act* 2000, s.80(1).]

V. FUNCTION OF THE LEGAL ADVISER (COURT CLERK) IN RELATION TO SENTENCE

22–20   The *Consolidated Criminal Practice Direction*, V.55 (clerk retiring with justices, see Appendix F, F–68) makes it clear that the justices' clerk is responsible for the advice tendered to justices in the area either directly or through a legal adviser. Job titles will vary but the term "legal adviser" has generally superseded that of "court clerk". The term "assistant to a Justices' Clerk" seems to be becoming the normal legal term following the implementation of the provisions in the *Courts Act* 2003 creating a unified court administration for the Crown Court and magistrates' courts. Both Direction 55 and the Legal Adviser competences (published by the Justices' Clerks' Society) make it clear that sentencing advice should be given and that it is the responsibility of the legal adviser to do so whether or not that advice is requested. Advice on sentencing will be required:

— where the plea before venue procedure is adopted, and the court is unsure of its sentencing powers;

— when the court is considering the issue of mode of trial and it needs to decide whether the sentencing powers would be sufficient should the defendant be convicted; and

— when passing sentence.

Direction 55.3 provides that it is the responsibility of the legal adviser to provide the justices with any advice they require to properly perform their functions whether or not the justices have requested that advice on, amongst other matters, the range of penalties available, the relevant decisions of the superior courts or other guidelines, other issues relevant to the matter before the court and the appropriate decision making structure to be applied in any given case. Paragraph 7 confirms that any legal advice given to justices other than in open court should clearly be stated to be provisional, and the adviser should subsequently repeat the substance of the advice in open court and give the parties an opportunity to make any representations they wish on that provisional advice. This procedure will ensure that any party can challenge the advice given where necessary.

VI. PRE-SENTENCE REPORTS

A. PROBATION SERVICE NATIONAL STANDARDS

(1) Legislative framework

Many of the provisions previously in the *PCC(S)A* 2000 are repealed and replaced **22–21**
by the *Criminal Justice Act* 2003. New National Standards have been developed to
reflect the changes and are being further revised. The Probation Service is gradually
becoming part of the new National Offender Management Service and so responsibilities or methods of working may change during the currency of this edition.

Criminal Justice Act 2003, ss.156–158

Pre-sentence reports and other requirements
   156.—(1) In forming any such opinion as is mentioned in section 148(1), (2)(b) or (3)(b),   **22–22**
section 152(2) or section 153(2), a court must take into account all such information as is available
to it about the circumstances of the offence or (as the case may be) of the offence and the offence
or offences associated with it, including any aggravating or mitigating factors.
   (2) In forming any such opinion as is mentioned in section 148(2)(a) or (3)(a), the court
may take into account any information about the offender which is before it.
   (3) Subject to subsection (4), a court must obtain and consider a pre-sentence report
before—
   (a) in the case of a custodial sentence, forming any such opinion as is mentioned in
       section 152(2), section 153(2), section 225(1)(b), section 226(1)(b), section 227(1)(b)
       or section 228(1)(b)(i), or
   (b) in the case of a community sentence, forming any such opinion as is mentioned
       in section 148(1), (2)(b) or (3)(b) or any opinion as to the suitability for the of-
       fender of the particular requirement or requirements to be imposed by the com-
       munity order.
   (4) Subsection (3) does not apply if, in the circumstances of the case, the court is of the
opinion that it is unnecessary to obtain a pre-sentence report.
   (5) In a case where the offender is aged under 18, the court must not form the opinion
mentioned in subsection (4) unless—
   (a) there exists a previous pre-sentence report obtained in respect of the offender,
       and
   (b) the court has had regard to the information contained in that report, or, if there
       is more than one such report, the most recent report.
   (6) No custodial sentence or community sentence is invalidated by the failure of a court
to obtain and consider a pre-sentence report before forming an opinion referred to in
subsection (3), but any court on an appeal against such a sentence—
   (a) must, subject to subsection (7), obtain a pre-sentence report if none was obtained
       by the court below, and
   (b) must consider any such report obtained by it or by that court.
   (7) Subsection (6)(a) does not apply if the court is of the opinion—
   (a) that the court below was justified in forming an opinion that it was unnecessary
       to obtain a pre-sentence report, or
   (b) that, although the court below was not justified in forming that opinion, in the
       circumstances of the case at the time it is before the court, it is unnecessary to
       obtain a pre-sentence report.
   (8) In a case where the offender is aged under 18, the court must not form the opinion
mentioned in subsection (7) unless—
   (a) there exists a previous pre-sentence report obtained in respect of the offender,
       and
   (b) the court has had regard to the information contained in that report, or, if there
       is more than one such report, the most recent report.

Additional requirements in case of mentally disordered offender
   157.—(1) Subject to subsection (2), in any case where the offender is or appears to be   **22–23**

mentally disordered, the court must obtain and consider a medical report before passing a custodial sentence other than one fixed by law.

(2) Subsection (1) does not apply if, in the circumstances of the case, the court is of the opinion that it is unnecessary to obtain a medical report.

(3) Before passing a custodial sentence other than one fixed by law on an offender who is or appears to be mentally disordered, a court must consider—

(a) any information before it which relates to his mental condition (whether given in a medical report, a pre-sentence report or otherwise), and

(b) the likely effect of such a sentence on that condition and on any treatment which may be available for it.

(4) No custodial sentence which is passed in a case to which subsection (1) applies is invalidated by the failure of a court to comply with that subsection, but any court on an appeal against such a sentence—

(a) must obtain a medical report if none was obtained by the court below, and

(b) must consider any such report obtained by it or by that court.

(5) In this section "mentally disordered", in relation to any person, means suffering from a mental disorder within the meaning of the *Mental Health Act* 1983 (c. 20).

(6) In this section "medical report" means a report as to an offender's mental condition made or submitted orally or in writing by a registered medical practitioner who is approved for the purposes of section 12 of the *Mental Health Act* 1983 by the Secretary of State as having special experience in the diagnosis or treatment of mental disorder.

(7) Nothing in this section is to be taken to limit the generality of section 156.

Meaning of "pre-sentence report"

22–24   **158.**—(1) In this Part "pre-sentence report" means a report which—

(a) with a view to assisting the court in determining the most suitable method of dealing with an offender, is made or submitted by an appropriate officer, and

(b) contains information as to such matters, presented in such manner, as may be prescribed by rules made by the Secretary of State.

(2) In subsection (1) "an appropriate officer" means—

(a) where the offender is aged 18 or over, an officer of a local probation board, and

(b) where the offender is aged under 18, an officer of a local probation board, a social worker of a local authority social services department or a member of a youth offending team.

(2) Assessment before sentence

Pre-sentence reports

22–25   The preparation of such a report will be in accordance with the Probation Circular 12/2007, which is effective from June 1, 2007. Its provisions do not wholly align with the National Standards published in 2005 but these standards are being reviewed. Where there is a conflict, report writers are directed to prepare the report in accordance with the Circular rather than the Standards.

There are three types of reports—standard delivery, fast delivery and oral reports. All are "pre-sentence reports" for the purposes of section 158 (see *ante*, § 22–24). Whilst a court has to be given the information needed to reach a sentencing decision, probation court officers can assist by advising the court of the report type most likely to best meet the need of the court.

The Circular states that an oral report is most suitable in low seriousness cases or where a court needs current information of the offender's progress against a sentence plan that already exists. Both the standard and fast delivery reports provide a fuller assessment. The fast delivery report will be based on OGRS and on an OASys risk of harm screening; the standard delivery report will be based on an OASys assessment.

Probation court officers are reminded through the Circular both of the need to "engage proactively" with a court to identify those cases where no probation involvement is required and of the advantages of early identification (ideally pre-hearing) of those cases where a report may be required. Where a report proposes a Community Order or a Suspended Sentence Order, it should detail the proposed arrangements and the sentence plan objectives. Where a programme is part of the proposal, the report should confirm that the offender is eligible and suitable and that the programme is available. Where a drug rehabilitation requirement is proposed, the informed consent of the offender should be confirmed in the report.

The provisions of section 156 continue to require a court to obtain and consider a **22–26** pre-sentence report in specified circumstances: s.156(3). That obligation may be avoided where the court considers that it is "unnecessary" to obtain such a report: s.156(4). Where the offender is under 18 years, the court may only reach that conclusion if there is a pre-sentence report already in existence which the court has considered: s.156(5). This is a little more restrictive than the previous provisions since it does not exempt a court dealing with an indictable only offence.

Where an offender is mentally disordered, there is a presumption that, before impos-ing a custodial sentence, a magistrates' court will obtain a medical report: s.157. Such a report may again be written or oral and must be by a registered medical practitioner approved by the Secretary of State as having special experience in this area: s.157(6). See *post*, Ch.28.

Section 159 of the 2003 *Act* governs the disclosure of reports. The court must give a copy of the report to the offender or the offender's legal representative (s.159(2)(a)) and to the prosecutor (s.159(2)(c)) subject to the discretion of the court where that prosecu-tor is not of a description prescribed by order and the court considers that disclosure would be inappropriate (s.159(4)).

The *Pre-Sentence Report Disclosure (Description of Prosecutors) Order* 1998 (S.I. **22–27** 1998 No. 191) prescribes the following descriptions of prosecutors for the purposes of section 159(4): a Crown Prosecutor, any other person acting on behalf of the Crown Prosecution Service, a person acting on behalf of the Commissioners of Revenue and Customs, the Secretary of State for Social Security, or the Director of the Serious Fraud Office. For these prosecutors, the court does not have a discretion and must give the prosecutor a copy of the report. In relation to an offender who is under 18 years, the court must also give a copy to any parent or guardian present in court (s.159(2)(b)). However, where an offender is under 18 and the court considers that disclosure of anything in the report would be likely to create a risk of significant harm to the of-fender, then it can withhold a complete copy of the report from the offender and/or the parent or guardian. The expectation must be that it would be possible to provide a partial copy, though it is still necessary to provide a complete copy to the offender's legal representative. Where an offender under 18 years is a person for whom a local author-ity has parental responsibility and is either in the care of the local authority or provided with accommodation by the authority, a copy of the report is to be given to the author-ity not to the parent or guardian: s.159(6).

In an ideal world, the report will be delivered to the court and to the parties at least a **22–28** day ahead of the court hearing which will give all parties the opportunity to consider its contents. This can be done by electronic means but it is a process which must be under the control of the court—the report is to the court; the statutory obligation to ensure copies are given out is also placed on the court.

However, in reality, the report will almost always be delivered to a magistrates' court on the day of the hearing and there will be local arrangements to ensure that copies get to the appropriate parties.

A report is a key element in assisting a court to decide the appropriate sentence; it also enables the commencement of post sentence planning and so needs to be done thoroughly and effectively. At its heart is the assessment of the risk of the offender re-offending and an analysis of ways in which any risk can be reduced.

In a magistrates' court, the court that passes sentence will often consist of different people from those who ordered the pre-sentence report. It is highly desirable that the court ordering the report identifies clearly what it sees as the issues both in terms of the

Part IV

assessment of seriousness of the offences committed and in terms of the offender's personal circumstances. This approach has been endorsed by the Sentencing Guidelines Council in its guidance on the approach to the imposition of sentences under the 2003 Act (see *post*, § 22–46).

22–29   When proceeding to sentence after a PSR has been prepared, the normal sequence will be for the court to hear from the prosecutor setting out the circumstances of the offence and any previous criminal activity of the defendant, for the court to consider the pre-sentence report (though it may have taken an opportunity to read the report in advance of hearing from the prosecution) and then for the court to hear from the defendant or his legal representative.

After hearing from the prosecution and reading the report, the court may wish to consider certain issues in detail—for instance, the report may have suggested a community order with certain requirements which seem to the court to be highly commendable or the court may have taken a completely different view from the report writer on either sentence or the seriousness of certain events. It is quite legitimate to put the defence on notice before the court is addressed, perhaps by way of "The court has read the report and heard from the prosecution. On what we know so far we can see merit in following the proposal in the pre-sentence report—do you wish to persuade us otherwise?" Where there is agreement, that can readily be identified. Where there is disagreement, the defence knows clearly what the issues are for the court and this enables the defence advocate to address those issues directly rather than having to try to guess what the court is thinking.

(3) Pre-sentence reports

22–30   Regarding the facts of the offence given to the probation officer for the preparation of a PSR, the offender may sometimes give an account which differs from that given by the prosecution. Guidance as to the approach of the court was given in *Tolera* [1999] 1 Cr.App.R. 29. Whilst this part of the pre-sentence report would, of course, be read by the court, it was not ordinarily to form part of the factual basis for the passing of sentence. If a defendant wishes to rely on this part of the pre-sentence report for the purposes of sentence, the defence should make this clear, and the prosecution should be forewarned. The issue could then be resolved, if necessary by the calling of evidence.

Criminal Justice Act 2003, s.159

Disclosure of pre-sentence reports

22–31   **159.**—(1) This section applies where the court obtains a pre-sentence report, other than a report given orally in open court.

(2) Subject to subsections (3) and (4), the court must give a copy of the report—

     (a) to the offender or his counsel or solicitor,

     (b) if the offender is aged under 18, to any parent or guardian of his who is present in court, and

     (c) to the prosecutor, that is to say, the person having the conduct of the proceedings in respect of the offence.

(3) If the offender is aged under 18 and it appears to the court that the disclosure to the offender or to any parent or guardian of his of any information contained in the report would be likely to create a risk of significant harm to the offender, a complete copy of the report need not be given to the offender or, as the case may be, to that parent or guardian.

(4) If the prosecutor is not of a description prescribed by order made by the Secretary of State, a copy of the report need not be given to the prosecutor if the court considers that it would be inappropriate for him to be given it.

(5) No information obtained by virtue of subsection (2)(c) may be used or disclosed otherwise than for the purpose of—

     (a) determining whether representations as to matters contained in the report need to be made to the court, or

     (b) making such representations to the court.

(6) In relation to an offender aged under 18 for whom a local authority have parental responsibility and who—

(a) is in their care, or

(b) is provided with accommodation by them in the exercise of any social services functions,

references in this section to his parent or guardian are to be read as references to that authority.

(7) In this section and section 160—

"harm" has the same meaning as in section 31 of the *Children Act* 1989 (c. 41);

"local authority" and "parental responsibility" have the same meanings as in that Act;

"social services functions", in relation to a local authority, has the meaning given by section 1A of the *Local Authority Social Services Act* 1970 (c. 42).

VII. OTHER REPORTS

Other reports may be obtained or are required to be obtained in certain other **22–32** circumstances. Whenever a report is obtained which is not a PSR, the court is obliged to ensure that a copy of the report is given to the offender or to his legal representative. Where the offender is under 18 years, section 160 sets out the power of the court to control or restrict distribution of such a report. These provisions mirror those in relation to pre-sentence reports in section 159 (see *ante*).

Criminal Justice Act 2003, s.160

Other reports of local probation boards and members of youth offending teams

160.—(1) This section applies where—   **22–33**

(a) a report by an officer of a local probation board or a member of a youth offending team is made to any court (other than a youth court) with a view to assisting the court in determining the most suitable method of dealing with any person in respect of an offence, and

(b) the report is not a pre-sentence report.

(2) Subject to subsection (3), the court must give a copy of the report—

(a) to the offender or his counsel or solicitor, and

(b) if the offender is aged under 18, to any parent or guardian of his who is present in court.

(3) If the offender is aged under 18 and it appears to the court that the disclosure to the offender or to any parent or guardian of his of any information contained in the report would be likely to create a risk of significant harm to the offender, a complete copy of the report need not be given to the offender, or as the case may be, to that parent or guardian.

(4) In relation to an offender aged under 18 for whom a local authority have parental responsibility and who—

(a) is in their care, or

(b) is provided with accommodation by them in the exercise of any social services functions,

references in this section to his parent or guardian are to be read as references to that authority.

VIII. PRE-SENTENCE DRUG TESTING

Testing may take place whilst a person is in police detention (see *ante*, Ch.18) and **22–34** there is a further power (not yet in force) to require a person to provide samples to find out whether there are traces of certain illegal drugs present in the body. The offender must be aged 14 years or over and the court must be considering a community sentence or a suspended sentence.

Criminal Justice Act 2003, s.161

Pre-sentence drug testing

161.—(1) Where a person aged 14 or over is convicted of an offence and the court is consider- **22–35** ing passing a community sentence or a suspended sentence, it may make an order under subsection (2) for the purpose of ascertaining whether the offender has any specified Class A drug in his body.

(2) The order requires the offender to provide, in accordance with the order, samples of any description specified in the order.

(3) Where the offender has not attained the age of 17, the order must provide for the samples to be provided in the presence of an appropriate adult.

(4) If it is proved to the satisfaction of the court that the offender has, without reasonable excuse, failed to comply with the order it may impose on him a fine of an amount not exceeding level 4.

(5) In subsection (4) "level 4" means the amount which, in relation to a fine for a summary offence, is level 4 on the standard scale.

(6) The court may not make an order under subsection (2) unless it has been notified by the Secretary of State that the power to make such orders is exercisable by the court and the notice has not been withdrawn.

(7) The Secretary of State may by order amend subsection (1) by substituting for the age for the time being specified there a different age specified in the order.

(8) In this section—

"appropriate adult", in relation to a person under the age of 17, means—

     (a)   his parent or guardian or, if he is in the care of a local authority or voluntary organisation, a person representing that authority or organisation,

     (b)   a social worker of a local authority social services department, or

     (c)   if no person falling within paragraph (a) or (b) is available, any responsible person aged 18 or over who is not a police officer or a person employed by the police;

"specified Class A drug" has the same meaning as in Part 3 of the *Criminal Justice and Court Services Act* 2000 (c. 43).

See also sections 35, 36 of the *Mental Health Act* 1983 for the power to remand a mentally disordered offender to hospital for a report on his medical condition, see *post*, §§ 28–9—28–14.

IX. ADJOURNMENTS AFTER CONVICTION AND BEFORE SENTENCE

22–36   A court may need to adjourn the proceedings to allow for the preparation of reports. This power is contained in section 10(3) of the *Magistrates' Courts Act* 1980.

Magistrates' Courts Act 1980, s.10

Adjournment of trial

22–37   **10.**—(1) A magistrates' court may at any time, whether before or after beginning to try an information, adjourn the trial, and may do so, notwithstanding anything in this Act, when composed of a single justice.

(2) The court may when adjourning either fix the time and place at which the trial is to be resumed, or, unless it remands the accused, leave the time and place to be determined later by the court; but the trial shall not be resumed at that time and place unless the court is satisfied that the parties have had adequate notice thereof.

(3) A magistrates' court may, for the purpose of enabling inquiries to be made or of determining the most suitable method of dealing with the case, exercise its power to adjourn after convicting the accused and before sentencing him or otherwise dealing with him; but, if it does so, the adjournment shall not be for more than 4 weeks at a time unless the court remands the accused in custody and, where it so remands him, the adjournment shall not be for more than 3 weeks at a time.

(3A) A youth court shall not be required to adjourn any proceedings for an offence at any stage by reason only of the fact—

     (a) that the court commits the accused for trial for another offence; or

     (b) that the accused is charged with another offence.

(4) On adjourning the trial of an information the court may remand the accused and, where the accused has attained the age of 18 years, shall do so if the offence is triable either way and—

     (a) on the occasion on which the accused first appeared, or was brought, before the

court to answer to the information he was in custody or, having been released on
bail, surrendered to the custody of the court; or
   (b) the accused has been remanded at any time in the course of proceedings on the
information;
and, where the court remands the accused, the time fixed for the resumption of the trial shall be
that at which he is required to appear or be brought before the court in pursuance of the
remand or would be required to be brought before the court but for section 128(3A) below.

Where a magistrates' court adjourns for reports after conviction, what is said at the **22–38**
time can restrict the options of the court that passes sentence. Great care, therefore,
needs to be taken to ensure that justice is done. The defendant should invariably be told
clearly that he must not assume from the fact that the court has ordered an assessment
or investigation, that he is likely to receive any particular form of sentence or that a
custodial sentence is ruled out: *Chamberlain* (1995) 16 Cr.App.R.(S.) 473, CA. Guidance from the Sentencing Guidelines Council (*New Sentences: Criminal Justice Act
2003*) regarding the approach to sentence and to the ordering of a pre-sentence report
demonstrates that more precision is required from a court in terms of both the purposes
of sentencing in the case in question and the court's assessment of seriousness on the
basis of the information before it. This may reduce the difficulties previously experienced
because courts will be more precise about the issues relevant to sentence.

Guideline: New Sentences: Criminal Justice Act 2003

Section 1—Community Sentences & Deferred Sentences
    Part 1: Community Sentences

B. Imposing a Community Sentence—The Approach

(i) Requirements

(a) Information for Sentencers
   1.1.15 In many cases, a pre-sentence report will be pivotal in helping a sentencer decide **22–39**
whether to impose a custodial sentence or whether to impose a community sentence and, if
so, whether particular requirements, or combinations of requirements, are suitable for an individual offender. The court must always ensure (especially where there are multiple requirements) that the restriction on liberty placed on the offender is proportionate to the seriousness of the offence committed. The court must also consider the likely effect of one
requirement on another, and that they do not place conflicting demands upon the offender.
   1.1.16 The Council supports the approach proposed by the Panel at paragraph 78 of its
Advice that, having reached the provisional view that a community sentence is the most appropriate disposal, the sentencer should request a pre-sentence report, indicating which of
the three sentencing ranges is relevant and the purpose(s) of sentencing that the package of
requirements is required to fulfil. Usually the most helpful way for the court to do this would
be to produce a written note for the report writer, copied on the court file. If it is known that
the same tribunal and defence advocate will be present at the sentencing hearing and a
probation officer is present in court when the request for a report is made, it may not be necessary to commit details of the request to writing. However, events may change during the
period of an adjournment and it is good practice to ensure that there is a clear record of the
request for the court. These two factors will guide the Probation Service in determining the
nature and combination of requirements that may be appropriate and the onerousness and
intensity of those requirements. A similar procedure should apply when ordering a pre-
sentence report when a custodial sentence is being considered.

Where the court fails to warn the offender that all sentencing options remain open to **22–40**
the court, a legitimate expectation may be created in the mind of the offender that a
non-custodial sentence may be imposed by the sentencing court. In *R. v. Inner London
Crown Court, ex p. Mentesh* [2001] 1 Cr.App.R.(S.) 94, the offender submitted that the
magistrates' actions in adjourning sentence to permit preparation of a further report in
addition to the pre-sentence report had created a legitimate expectation that, if all went

well, he would receive a non-custodial sentence and that the expectation should have been honoured by the sentencing court. The questions were:

     a) whether, when the magistrates adjourned the case, they created an expectation on the part of the applicant that if all went well he would receive a non-custodial sentence,

     b) whether it was legitimate, if there were such an expectation, that it should have been honoured by the sentencing court, and

     c) whether anything had intervened to change the position.

22–41   Following *Gillam* (1980) 2 Cr.App.R.(S.) 267 and *Chamberlain* (*ante*), the Court held that this case was squarely within the situations envisaged by previous authorities as giving rise to a legitimate expectation of a non-custodial sentence and the appeal against sentence was allowed. In *R. v. Southampton Magistrates' Court, ex p. Sansome* [1999] 1 Cr.App.R.(S.) 112, CA, the offender was tried summarily, despite representations by the prosecutor that the case should be heard by the Crown Court. The matter was then adjourned for a pre-sentence report which recommended a probation order. After considering the pre-sentence report, the Court decided to commit the offender to the Crown Court for sentence. Upholding this order, Schiemann L.J. said that nothing in the case constituted the breaking of a promise by the court, hence the decision to commit to the Crown Court for sentence could not be interfered with. However, in circumstances in which a reasonable expectation of a non-custodial sentence is created in the mind of the offender, and a favourable report is received, then, should the magistrates' court commit the offender to the Crown Court for sentence, the Crown Court should not impose a custodial sentence: *Rennes* (1985) 7 Cr.App.R.(S.) 343, CA. See also *Gutteridge v. DPP* (1987) 9 Cr.App.R.(S.) 279, DC. A process has been established to enable a defendant to seek an indication of likely sentence: *Goodyear* [2005] 3 All E.R. 117. However, this procedure does not apply in a magistrates' court.

22–42   It is an improper exercise of power for a court to adjourn solely to enable an offender to be sentenced as an adult. The date of conviction is taken to be the date of the finding of guilt or plea of guilty, not the date sentence is passed: *Danga* [1992] Q.B. 476, CA. When approaching sentence for an individual who has crossed a significant threshold between the date of the commission of the offence and the date of sentence, the court should start from a sentence appropriate if sentencing had taken place at the date of the commission of the offence: *Ghafoor* [2003] 1 Cr.App.R.(S.) 84.

X. INDICATION OF SENTENCE

22–43   When brought into force, as part of the changes to the allocation procedure (see *ante*, Ch.7) a defendant may seek an indication of sentence before consenting to an either way offence being heard in a magistrates' court.

Magistrates' Courts Act 1980, ss.20 and 20A

Procedure where summary trial appears more suitable

22–44   **20.**—(1) If the court decides under section 19 above that the offence appears to it more suitable for summary trial, the following provisions of this section shall apply (unless they are excluded by section 23 below).

     (2) The court shall explain to the accused in ordinary language—

     (a) that it appears to the court more suitable for him to be tried summarily for the offence;

     (b) that he can either consent to be so tried or, if he wishes, be tried on indictment; and

     (c) in the case of a specified offence (within the meaning of section 224 of the *Criminal Justice Act* 2003), that if he is tried summarily and is convicted by the court, he may be committed for sentence to the Crown Court under section 3A of the *Powers of Criminal Courts (Sentencing) Act* 2000 if the committing court is of such opinion as is mentioned in subsection (2) of that section.

     (3) The accused may then request an indication ("an indication of sentence") of whether

a custodial sentence or non-custodial sentence would be more likely to be imposed if he were to be tried summarily for the offence and to plead guilty.

(4) If the accused requests an indication of sentence, the court may, but need not, give such an indication.

(5) If the accused requests and the court gives an indication of sentence, the court shall ask the accused whether he wishes, on the basis of the indication, to reconsider the indication of plea which was given, or is taken to have been given, under section 17A or 17B above.

(6) If the accused indicates that he wishes to reconsider the indication under section 17A or 17B above, the court shall ask the accused whether (if the offence were to proceed to trial) he would plead guilty or not guilty.

(7) If the accused indicates that he would plead guilty the court shall proceed as if—

(a) the proceedings constituted from that time the summary trial of the information; and

(b) section 9(1) above were complied with and he pleaded guilty under it.

(8) Subsection (9) below applies where—

(a) the court does not give an indication of sentence (whether because the accused does not request one or because the court does not agree to give one);

(b) the accused either—

(i) does not indicate, in accordance with subsection (5) above, that he wishes; or

(ii) indicates, in accordance with subsection (5) above, that he does not wish, to reconsider the indication of plea under section 17A or 17B above; or

(c) the accused does not indicate, in accordance with subsection (6) above, that he would plead guilty.

(9) The court shall ask the accused whether he consents to be tried summarily or wishes to be tried on indictment and—

(a) if he consents to be tried summarily, shall proceed to the summary trial of the information; and

(b) if he does not so consent, shall proceed in relation to the offence in accordance with section 51(1) of the *Crime and Disorder Act* 1998.

Procedure where summary trial appears more suitable: supplementary

20A.—(1) Where the case is dealt with in accordance with section 20(7) above, no court **22–45** (whether a magistrates' court or not) may impose a custodial sentence for the offence unless such a sentence was indicated in the indication of sentence referred to in section 20 above.

(2) Subsection (1) above is subject to sections 3A(4), 4(8) and 5(3) of the *Powers of Criminal Courts (Sentencing) Act* 2000.

(3) Except as provided in subsection (1) above—

(a) an indication of sentence shall not be binding on any court (whether a magistrates' court or not); and

(b) no sentence may be challenged or be the subject of appeal in any court on the ground that it is not consistent with an indication of sentence.

(4) Subject to section 20(7) above, the following shall not for any purpose be taken to constitute the taking of a plea—

(a) asking the accused under section 20 above whether (if the offence were to proceed to trial) he would plead guilty or not guilty; or

(b) an indication by the accused under that section of how he would plead.

(5) Where the court gives an indication of sentence under section 20 above, it shall cause each such indication to be entered in the register.

(6) In this section and in section 20 above, references to a custodial sentence are to a custodial sentence within the meaning of section 76 of the *Powers of Criminal Courts (Sentencing) Act* 2000, and references to a non-custodial sentence shall be construed accordingly.

[As substituted by the *Criminal Justice Act* 2003, Sched. 3, para. 6 when in force.]

The approach to this provision has been considered by the Sentencing Advisory Panel in its advice to the Sentencing Guidelines Council and the key elements have been set out by the Council in its draft National Allocation Guidelines: www.sentencing-guidelines.gov.uk.

4. Indication of Sentence

A. THE STATUTORY PROCEDURE

22–46   **4.1** If it is clear whether or not a custodial sentence is likely, it will normally be helpful for a court to give the indication requested unless there is a good reason for not doing so.

4.2 The key elements of the approach to giving a sentence indication are:

(i) A court should assess the type of sentence realistically possible in the light of the facts as presented by the prosecution, with the additional element of a guilty plea tendered at this stage in the proceedings, and subject to defence representations as to the accuracy of the factual outline of the case. Wherever possible, the key elements of the basis upon which the indication is given should be recorded in writing.

(ii) A court should proceed with caution where an offender is unrepresented. The offender should be advised of the availability of independent legal advice. The Justices' Clerk (or assistant to the Justices' Clerk) present in court has a duty to assist the unrepresented party, and this will include drawing to the attention of an unrepresented defendant that there is an entitlement to request an indication of sentence.

(iii) A court should not give an indication of sentence where there are alternative charges unless the prosecution has indicated that an agreement as to acceptable pleas has been established following discussions with the defence, and there is an appropriate factual basis upon which an indication could be given.

(iv) The prosecution must ensure that the court is fully informed of the facts of the case and any relevant background.

(v) The court is entitled to expect that the Justices' Clerk (or assistant to the Justices' Clerk) present in court, and the prosecution and defence advocates, will ensure that the court considers any relevant guidelines or other authorities affecting sentence.

(vi) The information presented to the court will not include personal mitigation except in so far as it has influenced the facts of the case presented to the court or it is actively agreed by the prosecution advocate.

(vii) Any indication given must be recorded in writing and entered onto the court register.

B. REDUCTION IN SENTENCE FOR A GUILTY PLEA

22–47   **4.14** In order to set the maximum type of sentence in cases where the offence is close to the threshold for a custodial sentence, a magistrates' court would have to consider whether the maximum reduction in sentence for a guilty plea would potentially be available where a guilty plea is forthcoming only after a sentence indication has been given.

4.15 The Guideline, Reduction in Sentence for a Guilty Plea, at paragraph 4.3 (as amended) states:

4.3 The level of reduction should reflect the stage at which the offender indicated a willingness to admit guilt to the offence for which he is eventually sentenced:

(i) the largest recommended reduction will not normally be given unless the offender indicated willingness to admit guilt at the **first reasonable opportunity**; when this occurs will vary from case to case (*see Annex 1 for illustrative examples*);

(ii) where the admission of guilt comes later than the **first reasonable opportunity,** the reduction for guilty plea will be less than one third.

(iii) where the plea of guilty comes very late, it is still appropriate to give some reduction;

(iv) if after pleading guilty there is a *Newton* hearing and the offender's version of the circumstances of the offence is rejected, this should be taken into account in determining the level of reduction;

(v) if the not guilty plea was entered and maintained for tactical reasons (such as to retain privileges whilst on remand), a late guilty plea should attract very little, if any, discount.

In considering further when the "first reasonable opportunity" occurs, Annex 2 of the Guideline (Annex 1 in the revised guideline) emphasises the purpose of giving the reduction which is in recognition of "the benefits that come from a guilty plea both for those directly involved in the case in question but also in enabling Courts more quickly to deal with other outstanding cases".

4.16 There may only be a relatively short time gap between the opportunity to give an indication prior to allocation and the opportunity after an indication of sentence. However, the court will have had to consider allocation and determine summary trial and will then have to consider its response to the request for an indication of sentence. In those circumstances, it would appear that delay had taken place that could have been avoided and this will influence the extent of the reduction.

Where a guilty plea is indicated after the court has given an indication of the likely sentence, the appropriate reduction in sentence for the guilty plea should be a maximum of one quarter.

The power is much more restricted than that available in the Crown Court as set out **22–48** in *Goodyear* [2006] 1 Cr.App.R.(S.) 6. However, the Council has accepted the advice of the Sentencing Advisory Panel that the principles of *Goodyear* can be applied within the context of the more limited, statutory, procedure provided for a magistrates' court. Whilst there is a discretion to refuse to give an indication of sentence, when it is clear whether or not a custodial sentence is likely a court is expected to give the indication except where it has a serious concern that it would be unable to do justice either to the defendant or to others. The court is entitled to ensure that it has been given enough information to decide whether or not a custodial sentence ought to be available for consideration by the court that imposes sentence and will normally be more cautious about giving an indication to one of a number of co-defendants than to a sole defendant. If there is no firm factual basis, it would be inappropriate for an indication to be given, even though it is probably not as necessary (or practicable) to reduce that basis to writing as it is in the Crown Court. Other circumstances where a refusal may be appropriate include situations where a defendant is considered already to be under inappropriate pressure to plead guilty (perhaps from a co-defendant) or where there is concern about whether the defendant appreciates that a plea of guilty should only be entered where the defendant is guilty of the offence charged or where there is concern that the court could not judge properly the differing levels of culpability or responsibility amongst co-defendants. It is unlikely that a court will give reasons for its decision following the reasoning set out in *Goodyear*.

XI. POWERS OF YOUTH COURT TO REMIT TO ADULT COURT, AND SENTENCING POWERS OF ADULT COURT DEALING WITH YOUTH

An adult court has limited sentencing powers in respect of young offenders convicted **22–49** in an adult court: see *post*, Ch.27. Where a youth appearing in a youth court becomes 18 years old before sentence is passed, the youth court has the additional option of remitting the case to the adult court for sentence and that court will have its usual range of sentencing options. However, see *Ghafoor, ante*, emphasising that the starting point for sentence should be that which would have been passed if the defendant had been sentenced on the date on which the offence was committed.

Powers of Criminal Courts (Sentencing) 2000, s.9

Power of youth court to remit offender who attains age of 18 to magistrates' court other than youth court for sentence

9.—(1) Where a person who appears or is brought before a youth court charged with an of- **22–50** fence subsequently attains the age of 18, the youth court may, at any time after conviction and before sentence, remit him for sentence to a magistrates' court (other than a youth court) acting for the same petty sessions area as the youth court.

(2) Where an offender is remitted under subsection (1) above, the youth court shall adjourn proceedings in relation to the offence, and—

    (a) section 128 of the *Magistrates' Courts Act* 1980 (remand in custody or on bail) and all other enactments, whenever passed, relating to remand or the granting of bail in criminal proceedings shall have effect, in relation to the youth court's power or duty to remand the offender on that adjournment, as if any reference to the court to or before which the person remanded is to be brought or appear after remand were a reference to the court to which he is being remitted; and

   (b) subject to subsection (3) below, the court to which the offender is remitted ("the other court") may deal with the case in any way in which it would have power to deal with it if all proceedings relating to the offence which took place before the youth court had taken place before the other court.

(3) Where an offender is remitted under subsection (1) above, section 8(6) above (duty of adult magistrates' court to remit young offenders to youth court for sentence) shall not apply to the court to which he is remitted.

(4) Where an offender is remitted under subsection (1) above he shall have no right of appeal against the order of remission (but without prejudice to any right of appeal against an order made in respect of the offence by the court to which he is remitted).

(5) In this section—

   (a) "enactment" includes an enactment contained in any order, regulation or other instrument having effect by virtue of an Act; and

   (b) "bail in criminal proceedings" has the same meaning as in the *Bail Act* 1976.

XII. POWERS TO REMIT A YOUTH WHO APPEARS IN THE ADULT COURT TO THE YOUTH COURT FOR SENTENCE

22–51   The presumption is that a youth convicted in the adult court will be remitted to a youth court (usually the one for the area in which the youth resides) for sentence. The only circumstance in which a youth can be sentenced in an adult magistrates' court is where the sentence to be passed comes within section 8(7) or (8), that is, a referral order, a fine (note lower maximum penalties for youths), an absolute or conditional discharge or an order binding over parents to take proper control of the youth. If one of these sentences is being used, ancillary orders (such as endorsement or disqualification from driving) can also be made.

Powers of Criminal Courts (Sentencing) Act 2000, s.8

Power and duty to remit young offenders to youth courts for sentence

22–52   **8.**—(1) Subsection (2) below applies where a child or young person (that is to say, any person aged under 18) is convicted by or before any court of an offence other than homicide.

(2) The court may and, if it is not a youth court, shall unless satisfied that it would be undesirable to do so, remit the case—

   (a) if the offender was committed for trial or sent to the Crown Court for trial under section 51 of the *Crime and Disorder Act* 1998, to a youth court acting for the place where he was committed for trial or sent to the Crown Court for trial;

   (b) in any other case, to a youth court acting either for the same place as the remitting court or for the place where the offender habitually resides;

but in relation to a magistrates' court other than a youth court this subsection has effect subject to subsection (6) below.

(3) Where a case is remitted under subsection (2) above, the offender shall be brought before a youth court accordingly, and that court may deal with him in any way in which it might have dealt with him if he had been tried and convicted by that court.

(4) A court by which an order remitting a case to a youth court is made under subsection (2) above—

   (a) may, subject to section 25 of the *Criminal Justice and Public Order Act* 1994 (restrictions on granting bail), give such directions as appear to be necessary with respect to the custody of the offender or for his release on bail until he can be brought before the youth court; and

   (b) shall cause to be transmitted to the justices' chief executive for the youth court a certificate setting out the nature of the offence and stating—

      (i) that the offender has been convicted of the offence; and

      (ii) that the case has been remitted for the purpose of being dealt with under the preceding provisions of this section.

(5) Where a case is remitted under subsection (2) above, the offender shall have no right of appeal against the order of remission, but shall have the same right of appeal against

any order of the court to which the case is remitted as if he had been convicted by that court.

(6) Without prejudice to the power to remit any case to a youth court which is conferred on a magistrates' court other than a youth court by subsection (1) and (2) above, where such a magistrates' court convicts a child or young person of an offence it must exercise that power unless the case falls within subsection (7) or (8) below.

(7) The case falls within this subsection if the court would, were it not so to remit the case, be required by section 16(2) below to refer the offender to a youth offender panel (in which event the court may, but need not, so remit the case).

(8) The case falls within this subsection if it does not fall within subsection (7) above but the court is of the opinion that the case is one which can properly be dealt with by means of—

(a) an order discharging the offender absolutely or conditionally, or

(b) an order for the payment of a fine, or

(c) an order (under section 150 below) requiring the offender's parent or guardian to enter into a recognizance to take proper care of him and exercise proper control over him, with or without any other order that the court has power to make when absolutely or conditionally discharging an offender.

(9) In subsection (8) above "care" and "control" shall be construed in accordance with section 150(11) below.

(10) A document purporting to be a copy of an order made by a court under this section shall, if it purports to be certified as a true copy by the justices' chief executive for the court, be evidence of the order.

XIII. APPROACH TO SENTENCE

A. Structure of Decision

The standard approach to sentencing on which magistrates have been trained for **22–53** many years commences with an assessment of the seriousness of the offences (which sets the ceiling above which the sentence imposed should never rise) and then considers circumstances relevant to the offender which may mitigate the level of penalty that the offence would otherwise deserve. The *Magistrates' Courts Sentencing Guidelines* (2004), pp.9/10, explain the structure of the guidelines by reference to that approach. Although these guidelines are being revised, it is not anticipated that there will be any significant change in this respect. New forms are likely to come into use during the currency of this work reflecting the adjustments in approach that follow from the implementation of the provisions of the *Criminal Justice Act* 2003 and the guidelines from the Sentencing Guidelines Council (see *ante*, § 22–46). The court will first assess the seriousness of the offence itself, ensuring that it takes into account all factors which make this particular offence more or less serious. This will include statutory aggravating factors such as racial or religious aggravation or the fact that the offence was committed whilst the offender was on bail. The existence of "recent and relevant" previous convictions make the offence more serious. In any case, they are likely to indicate that the offender was more culpable since they demonstrate that he was clearly aware that what was being done was wrong.

Having formed a view of the seriousness of the offence, personal mitigation is considered and the sentence may be reduced accordingly. The absence of relevant previous convictions may assist a defendant by showing good character. Sentence is then determined taking account of other relevant factors such as credit for entering a timely guilty plea and periods spent in custody on remand.

B. Factual Basis for Sentence

A defendant wishing to ask the court to pass sentence on a basis other than that **22–54** disclosed in the prosecution case has to make that quite clear. Where a plea of guilty is tendered on the basis of facts which the Crown could not accept, and the discrepancy

Part IV

between the two accounts is such that the choice between them will potentially have a significant effect on the level of sentence, then the court has to consider resolving the issue by hearing evidence—a *Newton* hearing (see *Newton* (1983) 77 Cr.App.R. 13). When faced with differing versions of the facts of the offence, the choices available to the court are:

    (a) to hear evidence and come to a conclusion or

    (b) to hear no evidence, though, in the event of a substantial conflict between the versions of events, the version of the defendant must "so far as possible be accepted."

If the court does hear evidence, the normal rules of procedure apply, the court should apply the criminal standard of proof and must announce that it has done so when passing sentence: *Kerrigan* (1993) 14 Cr.App.R.(S.) 179, CA.

22–55   The procedure to be adopted following a guilty plea in such circumstances was further examined by Lord Bingham C.J. in *Tolera* [1999] 1 Cr.App.R. 29:

> "a) where a defendant pleads guilty and gives an account of the offence which the *prosecution* does not challenge, but which the *court* feels unable to accept, the court should make it clear before sentence that it did not accept the defence account. Failing any other resolution, evidence can be called and the prosecution can explore matters which the court wishes to explore.
>
> b) regarding the facts of the offence given to the probation officer for the preparation of a pre-sentence report, an offender may sometimes give an account which differs from that which emerged in the prosecution case. Whilst this part of the pre-sentence report would, of course, be read by the court, it was not ordinarily to form part of the factual basis for the passing of sentence. If the defendant wished to rely on this part of the pre-sentence report for the purposes of sentence, the defence should make this clear, and the prosecution should be forewarned. The issue could then be resolved, if necessary, by the calling of evidence."

22–56   In *Tolera*, the Court held that there was an onus on the prosecution to rebut an allegation that the defendant had been subject to a degree of compulsion, falling short of duress, to act as a drug courier. *Tolera* was followed in *Artwell* [2001] EWCA Crim 1387, CA where the offender appealed against his sentence of six years' imprisonment imposed for being concerned in the supply of heroin. He contended that there had been a large discrepancy between his basis of plea and the prosecution's case that he was the main organiser. The judge had not held a *Newton* hearing on this matter and had not clarified why he did not accept the defence account of the facts. The Court of Appeal held that the judge should have clarified why he did not accept the defence account and, failing a resolution, should have a held a *Newton* hearing. The offender's sentence was reduced from six years' imprisonment to three. If there is a meaningful discrepancy between the way in which the Crown put the case and the way in which the defence asked the court to sentence, there should either be a *Newton* hearing or the court has to be faithful to the basis of the plea.

Following the holding of a *Newton* hearing, the accused may still be entitled to receive some credit for his guilty plea in the form of a reduction of sentence. In its guideline in relation to the reduction in sentence following a guilty plea (revised July 2007), the Sentencing Guidelines Council considered the approach where such a hearing had been necessary. The Council states that the purpose of the reduction is to generate the benefits that come from an early guilty plea, in particular, the saving for victims and witnesses of the anxiety and apprehension surrounding the possible need to give evidence and the saving in time and resources. The maximum reduction would only be given where there was a guilty plea at the first reasonable opportunity. Even where there has been such a plea, if it subsequently becomes necessary to adduce evidence because of a dispute of essential facts and the offender's version of events is not wholly accepted, then at least some of the benefits will be lost: *Guideline: 4.3(iv)*.

22–57   A *Newton* hearing will not be necessary:

    (i) where the difference in the two versions of the facts of the case is immaterial to the sentence. In *Hall* (1984) 6 Cr.App.R.(S.) 321, the Court of Appeal held that the additional facts which the defendant disputed would not have affected the sentence, and in such a case the judge should proceed only on the defendant's version of events.

(ii) where the defence version can be described as "manifestly false" or "wholly implausible": *Walton* (1987) 9 Cr.App.R.(S.) 107, *Att.-Gen.'s Ref Nos. 3 and 4 of 1996 (Alan Anthony Healy and Robert William Taylor)* [1997] 1 Cr.App.R.(S.) 29, CA.

(iii) where the matters put forward do not challenge the prosecutor's version of events, but rather challenge extraneous matters, such as the background of the offence. These matters are likely to be outside the knowledge of the prosecution: *Broderick* (1994) 15 Cr.App.R.(S.) 476, CA.

A helpful summary of the limitations on the *Newton* hearing procedure is set out in *Underwood* [2004] EWCA Crim. 2256. In particular, it emphasises that care needs to be taken where guilty pleas are accepted on lesser charges to those originally preferred, especially in case involving multiple defendants. A *Newton* hearing will be unnecessary where the impact of any dispute on the sentencing decision will be minimal.

Where a *Newton* hearing has taken place in a magistrates' court and the defendant has then been committed for sentence, the Crown Court may allow the findings of fact to be re-opened but is unlikely to do so unless there has been some significant development or matter which has occurred since the magistrates' court reached its conclusion: *Gillan v. DPP* [2007] EWHC Admin 380. Accordingly, it is important that the Crown Court is properly informed of the facts found by the magistrates' court: *Warley J.J. ex p. DPP* [1999] 1 W.L.R. 216.

C. GENERAL AGGRAVATING FACTORS

22–58 As described earlier (see *ante*, § 22–4), provisions in the *Criminal Justice Act* 2003 concern the determination of the seriousness of an offence. As stated there, the issues of culpability and harm are paramount. There are, however, other factors which, if present, will make the offence more serious. In particular, section 143(2) of the *Criminal Justice Act* 2003 provides for the presence of recent and relevant convictions to be a factor aggravating the seriousness of the offence and section 143(3) of the *Criminal Justice Act* 2003 provides that the fact that an offence was committed while the offender was on bail must be treated as an aggravating factor. Further general guidance has been given by the Sentencing Guidelines Council where violence occurs in a domestic context: see guideline *Overarching Principles: Domestic Violence*, December 2006, www.sentencing-guidelines.gov.uk and § 22–62, *post*.

Criminal Justice Act 2003, s.143

Determining the seriousness of an offence

22–59 **143.**—(1) In considering the seriousness of any offence, the court must consider the offender's culpability in committing the offence and any harm which the offence caused, was intended to cause or might forseeably have caused.

(2) In considering the seriousness of an offence ("the current offence") committed by an offender who has one or more previous convictions, the court must treat each previous conviction as an aggravating factor if (in the case of that conviction) the court considers that it can reasonably be so treated having regard, in particular, to—

    (a) the nature of the offence to which the conviction relates and its relevance to the current offence, and

    (b) the time that has elapsed since the conviction.

(3) In considering the seriousness of any offence committed while the offender was on bail, the court must treat the fact that it was committed in those circumstances as an aggravating factor.

(4) Any reference in subsection (2) to a previous conviction is to be read as a reference to—

    (a) a previous conviction by a court in the United Kingdom, or

    (b) a previous finding of guilt in service disciplinary proceedings.

Part IV

(5) Subsections (2) and (4) do not prevent the court from treating a previous conviction by a court outside the United Kingdom as an aggravating factor in any case where the court considers it appropriate to do so.

22–60   In its guideline on the assessment of seriousness published in December 2004, the Sentencing Guidelines Council collated the most important aggravating factors of general application. Following the two-prong approach to the assessment of seriousness (culpability and harm), those factors are separated into those that suggest higher culpability and those that suggest a more than usually serious degree of harm. Inevitably, some of those factors will be an essential element of some offences and, therefore, care needs to be taken to avoid "double counting".

22–61   The Sentencing Guidelines Council guideline *Overarching Principles: Domestic Violence* applies to all offences sentenced on or after December 18, 2006. As is pointed out in the Foreword to the guideline, there is no specific offence of domestic violence and the guideline needs to encompass a wide range of circumstances and conduct. There is a clear statement not only that offences committed in a domestic context are no less serious than offences committed in any other context but also that, because an offence is committed in a domestic context, it is likely to have aggravating factors present that make it more serious.

In a magistrates' court there will be a wide range of offences dealt with, some in specialist courts, some in the ordinary mix of business. Often fine judgements will need to be made about the nature of the sanction necessary to reduce the risk of future violence and to protect the victim.

The guideline sets out 4 issues of principle:

Guideline: Overarching Principles: Domestic Violence

E. FACTORS TO TAKE INTO CONSIDERATION

The following points of principle should be considered by a court when imposing sentence for any offence of violence committed in domestic context.

1. Offences committed in a domestic context should be regarded as being no less serious than offences committed in a non-domestic context.

2. Many offences of violence in a domestic context are dealt with in a magistrates' court as an offence of common assault or assault occasioning actual bodily harm because the injuries sustained are relatively minor. Offences involving serious violence will warrant a custodial sentence in the majority of cases.

3. Some offences will be specified offences for the purposes of the dangerous offender provisions. In such circumstances, consideration will need to be given to whether there is a significant risk of serious harm to members of the public, which include, of course, family members. If so, the court will be required to impose a life sentence, imprisonment for public protection or an extended sentence.

4. Where the custody threshold is only just crossed, so that if a custodial sentence is imposed it will be a short sentence, the court will wish to consider whether the better option is a suspended sentence order or a community order, including in either case a requirement to attend an accredited domestic violence programme. Such an option will only be appropriate where the court is satisfied that the offender genuinely intends to reform his or her behaviour and that there is a real prospect of rehabilitation being successful. Such a situation is unlikely to arise where there has been a pattern of abuse.

22–62   The guideline also sets out aggravating and mitigating factors most likely to occur and these are set out *post*. They recognise that the violence is likely to take place in the context of a relationship and that it may include an abuse of both trust and of power. Some victims will be particularly vulnerable and a court must be alert to this possibility. The guideline draws attention to the impact of domestic violence on children both through witnessing the violence and through being aware of it occurring even when it is not witnessed.

Whilst the guideline draws attention to the general sentencing principle that the good character of the defendant can be relevant to sentence, it points out the ability of an offender to have "two personae" which can make it possible for domestic violence to continue for long periods.

Guideline: Overarching Principles: Domestic Violence

C. Aggravating and Mitigating Factors

3.1 Since domestic violence takes place within the context of a current or past relationship, the history of the relationship will often be relevant in assessing the gravity of the offence. Therefore, a court is entitled to take into account anything occurring within the relationship as a whole, which may reveal relevant aggravating or mitigating factors.

3.2 The following aggravating and mitigating factors (which are not intended to be exhaustive) are of particular relevance to offences committed in a domestic context, and should be read alongside the general factors set out in the Council guideline *Overarching Principles: Seriousness*.

Aggravating Factors

(i) *Abuse of trust and abuse of power*

3.3 The guideline *Overarching Principles: Seriousness* identifies abuse of a position of trust and abuse of power as factors that indicate higher culpability. Within the nature of relationship required to meet the definition of domestic violence set out above, trust implies a mutual expectation of conduct that shows consideration, honesty, care and responsibility. In some such relationships, one of the parties will have the power to exert considerable control over the other.

3.4 In the context of domestic violence:

- an *abuse of trust*, whether through direct violence or emotional abuse, represents a violation of this understanding;

- an *abuse of power* in a relationship involves restricting another individual's autonomy which is sometimes a specific characteristic of domestic violence. This involves the exercise of control over an individual by means which may be psychological, physical, sexual, financial or emotional.

3.5 Where an abuse of trust or abuse of power is present, it will aggravate the seriousness of an offence. These factors are likely to exist in many offences of violence within a domestic context.

3.6 However, the breadth of the definition of domestic violence (set out in 1.1 above) encompasses offences committed by a former spouse or partner. Accordingly, there will be circumstances where the abuse of trust or abuse of power may be a very minor feature of an offence or may be deemed no longer to exist—for example, where the offender and victim have been separated for a long period of time.

(ii) *Victim is particularly vulnerable*

3.7 For cultural, religious, language, financial or any other reasons, some victims of domestic violence may be more vulnerable than others, not least because these issues may make it almost impossible for the victim to leave a violent relationship.

3.8 Where a perpetrator has exploited a victim's vulnerability (for instance, when the circumstances have been used by the perpetrator to prevent the victim from seeking and obtaining help), an offence will warrant a higher penalty.

3.9 Age, disability or the fact that the victim was pregnant or had recently given birth at the time of the offence may make a victim particularly vulnerable.

3.10 Any steps taken to prevent the victim reporting an incident or obtaining assistance will usually aggravate the offence.

(iii) *Impact on children*

3.11 Exposure of children to an offence (either directly or indirectly) is an aggravating factor.

3.12 Children are likely to be adversely affected by directly witnessing violence or other abuse and by being aware of it taking place while they are elsewhere in the home.

Part IV

(iv) *Using contact arrangements with a child to instigate an offence*

3.13 An offence will be aggravated where an offender exploits contact arrangements with a child in order to commit an offence.

(v) *A proven history of violence or threats by the offender in a domestic setting*

3.14 It is important that an assessment of the seriousness of an offence recognises the cumulative effect of a series of violent incidents or threats over a prolonged period, where such conduct has been proved or accepted.

3.15 Where an offender has previously been convicted of an offence involving domestic violence either against the same or a different partner, this is likely to be a statutory aggravating factor.

(vi) *A history of disobedience to court orders*

3.16 A breach of an order that has been imposed for the purpose of protecting a victim can cause significant harm or anxiety. Where an offender's history of disobedience has had this effect, it will be an aggravating factor.

3.17 Commission of the offence in breach of a non-molestation order imposed in civil proceedings, in breach of a sentence (such as a conditional discharge) imposed for similar offending, or while subject to an ancillary order, such as a restraining order, will aggravate the seriousness of the offence.

3.18 The appropriate response to breach of a civil order is dealt with in a separate guideline *Breach of a Protective Order*.

(vii) *Victim forced to leave home*

3.19 An offence will be aggravated if, as a consequence, the victim is forced to leave home.

Mitigating Factors

(i) *Positive good character*

3.20 As a general principle of sentencing, a court will take account of an offender's positive good character. However, it is recognised that one of the factors that can allow domestic violence to continue unnoticed for lengthy periods is the ability of the perpetrator to have two personae. In respect of an offence of violence in a domestic context, an offender's good character in relation to conduct outside the home should generally be of no relevance where there is a proven pattern of behaviour.

3.21 Positive good character is of greater relevance in the rare case where the court is satisfied that the offence was an isolated incident.

(ii) *Provocation*

3.22 It may be asserted that the offence, at least in part, has been provoked by the conduct of the victim. Such assertions need to be treated with great care, both in determining whether they have a factual basis and in considering whether in the circumstances the alleged conduct amounts to provocation sufficient to mitigate the seriousness of the offence.

3.23 For provocation to be a mitigating factor, it will usually involve actual or anticipated violence including psychological bullying. Provocation is likely to have more of an effect as mitigation if it has taken place over a significant period of time.

22–63   The guideline also addresses the issue of how a court should approach situations where a victim expresses a wish for a particular type of sentence, generally one more lenient than might otherwise be thought appropriate. The guideline states very clearly that victims should not be put in a situation where they can be seen to have responsibility for the choice of sentence. Nonetheless, it also recognises that there will be situations where a victim genuinely and reasonably wishes a relationship to continue. A court should proceed with considerable caution in such circumstances.

Guideline: Overarching Principles: Domestic Violence

D. Other factors influencing sentence

Wishes of the victim and effect of the sentence

4.1 As a matter of general principle, a sentence imposed for an offence of violence should be determined by the seriousness of the offence, not by the expressed wishes of the victim.

4.2 There are a number of reasons why it may be particularly important that this principle is observed in a case of domestic violence:

- it is undesirable that a victim should feel a responsibility for the sentence imposed;
- there is a risk that a plea for mercy made by a victim will be induced by threats made by, or by a fear of, the offender;
- the risk of such threats will be increased if it is generally believed that the severity of the sentence may be affected by the wishes of the victim.

4.3 Nonetheless, there may be circumstances in which the court can properly mitigate a sentence to give effect to the expressed wish of the victim that the relationship be permitted to continue. The court must, however, be confident that such a wish is genuine, and that giving effect to it will not expose the victim to a real risk of further violence. Critical conditions are likely to be the seriousness of the offence and the history of the relationship. It is vitally important that the court has up-to-date information in a pre-sentence report and victim personal statement.

4.4 Either the offender or the victim (or both) may ask the court to take into consideration the interests of any children and to impose a less severe sentence. The court will wish to have regard not only to the effect on the children if the relationship is disrupted but also to the likely effect on the children of any further incidents of domestic violence.

D. The Assessment of Culpability and Harm

Guideline: Overarching Principles: Seriousness

D. Assessment of Culpability and Harm

(i) Aggravating Factors

1.20 Sentencing guidelines for a particular offence will normally include a list of aggravating features which, if present in an individual instance of the offence, would indicate either a higher than usual level of culpability on the part of the offender, or a greater than usual degree of harm caused by the offence (or sometimes both). **22–64**

1.21 The lists below bring together the most important aggravating features with potential application to more than one offence or class of offences. They include some factors (such as the vulnerability of victims or abuse of trust) which are integral features of certain offences; in such cases, the presence of the aggravating factor is already reflected in the penalty for the offence and ***cannot be used as justification for increasing the sentence further***. The lists are not intended to be comprehensive and the aggravating factors are not listed in any particular order of priority. On occasions, two or more of the factors listed will describe the same feature of the offence and care needs to be taken to avoid "doublecounting". Those factors starred with an asterisk are statutory aggravating factors where the statutory provisions are in force. Those marked with a hash are yet to be brought into force but as factors in an individual case are still relevant and should be taken into account.

1.22 Factors indicating higher culpability:

- Offence committed whilst on bail for other offences
- Failure to respond to previous sentences
- Offence was racially or religiously aggravated
- Offence motivated by, or demonstrating, hostility to the victim based on his or her sexual orientation (or presumed sexual orientation)
- Offence motivated by, or demonstrating, hostility based on the victim's disability (or presumed disability)
- Previous conviction(s), particularly where a pattern of repeat offending is disclosed
- Planning of an offence
- An intention to commit more serious harm than actually resulted from the offence

Part IV

- Offenders operating in groups or gangs
- "Professional" offending
- Commission of the offence for financial gain (where this is not inherent in the offence itself)
- High level of profit from the offence
- An attempt to conceal or dispose of evidence
- Failure to respond to warnings or concerns expressed by others about the offender's behaviour
- Offence committed whilst on licence
- Offence motivated by hostility towards a minority group, or a member or members of it
- Deliberate targeting of vulnerable victim(s)
- Commission of an offence while under the influence of alcohol or drugs
- Use of a weapon to frighten or injure victim
- Deliberate and gratuitous violence or damage to property, over and above what is needed to carry out the offence
- Abuse of power
- Abuse of a position of trust

1.23 Factors indicating a more than usually serious degree of harm:

- Multiple victims
- An especially serious physical or psychological effect on the victim, even if unintended
- A sustained assault or repeated assaults on the same victim
- Victim is particularly vulnerable
- Location of the offence (for example, in an isolated place)
- Offence is committed against those working in the public sector or providing a service to the public
- Presence of others e.g. relatives, especially children or partner of the victim
- Additional degradation of the victim (*e.g.* taking photographs of a victim as part of a sexual offence)
- In property offences, high value (including sentimental value) of property to the victim, or substantial consequential loss (*e.g.* where the theft of equipment causes serious disruption to a victim's life or business)

Previous convictions

22–65   The significance of previous convictions in assessing sentence has been the subject of debate for many years. At one extreme, the argument is that, once a person has been punished and that punishment completed, then the significance of the offence should be at an end. At the other, is the argument now contained in the *Criminal Justice Act* 2003 that each previous conviction should aggravate the seriousness of the current offence. The existence of a previous conviction for the same offence prevents any argument that the defendant was unaware of the significance of what was being done.

In practice, courts have tended to treat the absence of previous convictions as mitigating factor rather than the existence as an aggravating factor but the statutory provisions now ensure that those convictions (where recent and relevant) influence the assessment of the seriousness of the offence. There will be some circumstances where statute prescribes a minimum sentence where there have been previous convictions—for magistrates' courts, this tends to be for road traffic offences where, for instance, disqualification generally follows the acquisition of 12 penalty points and higher periods of disqualification become the minimum where previous disqualifications have been imposed.

Offence committed whilst on bail

22–66   If the offence is committed whilst the offender was on bail for some other matter, the court has to treat that fact as a factor that aggravates the seriousness of the present offence: *Criminal Justice Act* 2003, s.143(3).

Religious or racial aggravation

22–67   The existence of an element of racial or religious aggravation may cause a particular offence to be committed in an aggravated fashion with a higher maximum penalty (for example, certain assaults or criminal damage). Even where that is not the case, the existence of racial or religious aggravation (as defined in section 28 of the *Crime and Disorder Act* 1998) will make the offence more serious. This approach is continued in section 145 of the *Criminal Justice Act* 2003 and extended by section 146, to aggravation related to disability or sexual orientation. See *post*, § 22–71.

A situation may arise where a defendant has been charged with both the standard of-   **22–68**
fence and the racially or religiously aggravated offence. If found guilty of the standard offence but acquitted of the aggravated offence, can the court in its approach to sentencing still take into account racial or religious aggravation as an aggravating factor? In *G. and T. v. DPP* (2004) 168 J.P. 313, a youth had been charged (with others) with racially aggravated common assault and racially aggravated affray. Prior to trial, the racially aggravated elements were withdrawn from both offences before it was realised that there was no such offence as racially aggravated affray! The defendant was convicted and the District Judge took account of racial aggravation as a statutory aggravating factor in relation to the affray conviction. Allowing the defendant's appeal, the Divisional Court recognised the unusual circumstances in this case. In other cases there may be a different result. Whilst it is for the court to determine on the material before it the seriousness of the offence, ".   .   .nevertheless, the court is circumscribed by the ambit of the offence which is charged and the ambit of the offence for which the defendant is convicted." In the circumstances of this case, the defendant had been led to suppose that it was not necessary to deal with issues of racial aggravation because of the decisions in relation to the charges and so it was not open to the court to introduce those issues when considering sentence.

It now appears clear that, where the prosecution has withdrawn a charge of which this form of statutory aggravation is an essential element, the court cannot then impose a sentence for the standard offence which takes account of such aggravation. It is likely to be different if the aggravated form of the offence had never been charged.

The House of Lords has given consideration to the meaning of "racial group" in the context of the aggravated form of certain offences. The term used was "bloody foreigners" and the defence sought to argue that this was too wide to be a "racial group" within the meaning of the legislation. The House of Lords did not accept the argument. The statute intended a broad non-technical approach and the essence was denial of equal respect and dignity to all people which was damaging not only to the victims but also to the community as a whole: *Rogers* [2007] UKHL 8.

Criminal Justice Act 2003, s.145

Increase in sentences for racial or religious aggravation

145.—(1) This section applies where a court is considering the seriousness of an offence other   **22–69**
than one under sections 29 to 32 of the *Crime and Disorder Act* 1998 (racially or religiously aggravated assaults, criminal damage, public order offences and harassment etc).

(2) If the offence was racially or religiously aggravated, the court—

   (a) must treat that fact as an aggravating factor, and

   (b) must state in open court that the offence was so aggravated.

(3) Section 28 of the *Crime and Disorder Act* 1998 (meaning of "racially or religiously aggravated") applies for the purposes of this section as it applies for the purposes of sections 29 to 32 of that Act.

Crime and Disorder Act 1998, s.28

Meaning of "racially aggravated"

28.—(1) An offence is racially aggravated for the purposes of sections 29 to 32 below if—   **22–70**

   (a) at the time of committing the offence, or immediately before or after doing so, the offender demonstrates towards the victim of the offence hostility based on the victim's membership (or presumed membership) of a racial or religious group; or

(b) the offence is motivated (wholly or partly) by hostility towards members of a racial group based on their membership of that group.

(2) In subsection (1)(a) above—

"membership", in relation to a racial group, includes association with members of that group;

"presumed" means presumed by the offender.

(3) It is immaterial for the purposes of paragraph (a) or (b) of subsection (1) above whether or not the offender's hostility is also based, to any extent, on any other factor not mentioned in that paragraph.

(4) In this section "racial group" means a group of persons defined by reference to race, colour, nationality (including citizenship) or ethnic or national origins.

(5) In this section "religious group" means a group of persons defined by reference to religious belief or lack of religious belief.

Aggravation related to disability or sexual orientation

22–71   A new, but similar, provision is introduced by the 2003 Act in relation to disability or sexual orientation. Disability is defined as "any physical or mental impairment". Where hostility on such a basis is found to exist, a court must treat it as an aggravating factor. It can arise in two circumstances.

(i) Where the offence was motivated by hostility based on sexual orientation or disability. The hostility need not be the whole motivation for the offence, it need be just a part of the motivation. The victim does not need to be a person of the sexual orientation or possessing the disability in question as long as the offence is at least partially motivated by hostility to persons who do. Thus an offence would be aggravated where it was committed against a person who is not disabled but is motivated by hostility against someone that that person is supporting who is disabled.

(ii) where the offender demonstrated hostility to the victim based on the sexual orientation or disability of the victim. This includes presumed, as well as actual, orientation or disability. This hostility may be demonstrated at the time the offence is committed or immediately after or before it is committed.

The court must state in open court that the offence has been committed in the circumstances covered by this provision.

Criminal Justice Act 2003, s.146

Increase in sentences for aggravation related to disability or sexual orientation

22–72   **146.**—(1) This section applies where the court is considering the seriousness of an offence committed in any of the circumstances mentioned in subsection (2).

(2) Those circumstances are—

(a) that, at the time of committing the offence, or immediately before or after doing so, the offender demonstrated towards the victim of the offence hostility based on—

(i) the sexual orientation (or presumed sexual orientation) of the victim, or

(ii) a disability (or presumed disability) of the victim, or

(b) that the offence is motivated (wholly or partly)—

(i) by hostility towards persons who are of a particular sexual orientation, or

(ii) by hostility towards persons who have a disability or a particular disability.

(3) The court—

(a) must treat the fact that the offence was committed in any of those circumstances as an aggravating factor, and

(b) must state in open court that the offence was committed in such circumstances.

(4) It is immaterial for the purposes of paragraph (a) or (b) of subsection (2) whether or not the offender's hostility is also based, to any extent, on any other factor not mentioned in that paragraph.

(5) In this section "disability" means any physical or mental impairment.

Antecedents

Courts rely heavily on information regarding previous convictions provided through **22–73** the prosecution. Drawn from national records, there are times when the information is not as current as it ought to be and courts need to be on their guard in case there are apparent disparities between information sources. The prosecution will tender a list of previous convictions at the conclusion of its presentation once a defendant has been found guilty. Alternatively, for road traffic offenders, this information may come from the defendant's driving licence or from a copy of the driving record.

In addition to offences of which an offender has been convicted by a court, conditional cautions are citable. However, since a conditional caution is not a previous conviction, it will not be capable of being a statutory aggravating factor so as to make the current offence more serious. Whilst Penalty Notices for Disorder and Fixed Penalties are not citable, they may nonetheless come to the attention of the court, particularly where they have resulted in the endorsement of a driving licence. The proposed revision to the Magistrates' Court Sentencing Guidelines (2004) suggests that, in each case, the existence of such sanctions should not be treated as making the current offence more serious but might influence sentence selection within the range of options available.

For the standards for the provision of information of antecedents, see the *Consolidated Criminal Practice Direction*, para. III.27 (see Appendix F).

An antecedents statement should not refer to the fact that the offender has been **22–74** acquitted on a previous occasion. Where an offender disputes a statement of fact contained in an antecedents statement, it must be proved by admissible evidence or omitted from the evidence placed before the court: *Sargeant* (1974) 60 Cr.App.R. 74, CA. Particular care must be taken where the defendant denies that the record of a particular conviction relates to him.

Rehabilitation of offenders

One aspect of the approach to the rehabilitation of offenders is that many sentences **22–75** will become "spent" after a specified period. This means that the conviction does not have to be declared except in certain prescribed circumstances. The time scales for youths are less than for adults. One exception relates to criminal proceedings before a magistrates' court. A court is entitled to take into account convictions that are spent under the *Rehabilitation of Offenders Act* 1974. However, a court does not have an unfettered discretion, it must be demonstrated that justice cannot be done without the admission of such evidence for spent convictions to be admitted: *R. v. Hastings Magistrates' Court, ex p. McSpirit* (1998) 162 J.P. 44. In practice, the normal approach will be to ignore spent convictions.

Rehabilitation of Offenders Act 1974, s.5

Rehabilitation periods for particular sentences

    5.—(1) The sentences excluded from rehabilitation under this Act are—   **22–76**
      (a) a sentence of imprisonment for life;
      (b) a sentence of imprisonment, youth custody or corrective training for a term exceeding thirty months;
      (c) a sentence of preventive detention;
      (d) a sentence of detention during Her Majesty's pleasure or for life under section 90 or 91 of the *Powers of Criminal Courts (Sentencing) Act* 2000 or under section 205(2) or (3) of the *Criminal Procedure (Scotland) Act* 1975,, or a sentence of detention for a term exceeding thirty months passed under section 91 of the said Act of 2000 (young offenders convicted of grave crimes) or under section 206 of the said Act of 1975 (detention of children convicted on indictment) or a corresponding court-martial punishment;
      (e) a sentence of custody for life; and
      (f) a sentence of imprisonment for public protection under section 225 of the *Crim-*

Part IV

inal Justice Act 2003, a sentence of detention for public protection under section 226 of that Act or an extended sentence under section 227 or 228 of that Act and any other sentence is a sentence subject to rehabilitation under this Act.

(1A) In subsection (1)(d) above "corresponding court-martial punishment" means a punishment awarded under section 71A(3) or (4) of the *Army Act* 1955, section 71A(3) or (4) of the *Air Force Act* 1955 or section 43A(3) or (4) of the *Naval Discipline Act* 1957.

(2) For the purposes of this Act—

    (a) the rehabilitation period applicable to a sentence specified in the first column of Table A below is the period specified in the second column of that Table in relation to that sentence, or, where the sentence was imposed on a person who was under eighteen years of age at the date of his conviction, half that period; and

    (b) the rehabilitation period applicable to a sentence specified in the first column of Table B below is the period specified in the second column of that Table in relation to that sentence;

reckoned in either case from the date of the conviction in respect of which the sentence was imposed.

TABLE A: REHABILITATION PERIODS SUBJECT TO REDUCTION BY HALF FOR PERSONS UNDER 18

22–77

Sentence	Rehabilitation period
A sentence of imprisonment or youth custody or corrective training for a term exceeding six months but not exceeding thirty months.[1]	Ten years
A sentence of cashiering, discharge with ignominy or dismissal with disgrace from Her Majesty's service.	Ten years
A sentence of imprisonment or youth custody for a term not exceeding six months.	Seven years
A sentence of dismissal from Her Majesty's service.	Seven years
Any sentence of detention in respect of a conviction in service disciplinary proceedings.	Five years
A fine or any other sentence subject to rehabilitation under this Act, not being a sentence to which Table B below or any of subsection (3) to (8) below applies.	Five years
[1]In relation to England and Wales: A sentence of imprisonment, detention in a young offender institution or youth custody or corrective training for a term exceeding six months but not exceeding thirty months. [2]In relation to England and Wales: A sentence of imprisonment, detention in a young offender institution or youth custody for a term not exceeding six months.	

TABLE B: REHABILITATION PERIODS FOR CERTAIN SENTENCES CONFINED TO YOUNG OFFENDERS

22–78

Sentence	Rehabilitation period
A sentence of Borstal training.	Seven years

Sentence	Rehabilitation period	
		22–78
A custodial order under section 71AA of the *Army Act* 1955 or the *Air Force Act* 1955, or under section 43AA of the *Naval Discipline Act* 1957, where the maximum period of detention specified in the order is more than six months.	Seven years	
A custodial order under Schedule 5A to the *Army Act* 1955 or the *Air Force Act* 1955, or under Schedule 4A to the *Naval Discipline Act* 1957, where the maximum period of detention specified in the order is more than six months.	Seven years	
A sentence of detention for a term exceeding six months but not exceeding thirty months passed under section 91 of the *Powers of Criminal Courts (Sentencing) Act* 2000 or under 206 of the *Criminal Procedure (Scotland) Act* 1975.	Five years	
A sentence of detention for a term not exceeding six months passed under either of those provisions.	Three years	
An order for detention in a detention centre made under section 4 of the *Criminal Justice Act* 1982, section 4 of the *Criminal Justice Act* 1961.	Three years	
A custodial order under any of the Schedules to the said Acts of 1955 and 1957 mentioned above, where the maximum period of detention specified in the order is six months or less.	Three years	
A custodial order under section 71AA of the said Acts of 1955, or section 43AA or the said act of 1957, where the maximum period of detention specified in the order is six months or less.	Three years	

(3) The rehabilitation period applicable— **22–79**
  (a) to an order discharging a person absolutely for an offence; and
  (b) to the discharge by a children's hearing under section 69(1)(b) and (12) of the
    Children (Scotland) Act 1995 of the referral of a child's case;
shall be six months from the date of conviction.

(4) Where in respect of a conviction a person was conditionally discharged, bound over to keep the peace or be of good behaviour, the rehabilitation period applicable to the sentence shall be one year from the date of conviction or a period beginning with that date and ending when the order for conditional discharge or (as the case may be) the recognizance or bond of caution to keep the peace or be of good behaviour ceases or ceased to have effect, whichever is the longer.

(4A) Where in respect of a conviction a probation order or a community order under section 177 of the *Criminal Justice Act* 2003 was made, the rehabilitation period applicable to the sentence shall be—
  (a) in the case of a person aged eighteen years or over at the date of his conviction, five
    years from the date of conviction;
  (b) in the case of a person aged under the age of eighteen years at the date of his convic-
    tion, two and a half years from the date of conviction or a period beginning with the
    date of conviction and ending when the order in question ceases or ceased to have ef-
    fect, whichever is the longer.

(4B) Where in respect of a conviction a referral order (within the meaning of the *Powers of Criminal Courts (Sentencing) Act* 2000) is made in respect of the person convicted, the rehabilitation period applicable to the sentence shall be—
  (a) if a youth offender contract takes effect under section 23 of that Act between him and

a youth offender panel, the period beginning with the date of conviction and ending on the date when (in accordance with section 24 of that Act) the contract ceases to have effect;

(b) if no such contract so takes effect, the period beginning with the date of conviction and having the same length as the period for which such a contract would (ignoring any order under paragraph 11 or 12 of Schedule 1 to that Act) have had effect had one so taken effect.

(4C) Where in respect of a conviction an order is made in respect of the person convicted under paragraph 11 or 12 of Schedule 1 to the *Powers of Criminal Courts (Sentencing) Act* 2000 (extension of period for which youth offender contract has effect), the rehabilitation period applicable to the sentence shall be—

(a) if a youth offender contract takes effect under section 23 of that Act between the offender and a youth offender panel, the period beginning with the date of conviction and ending on the date when (in accordance with section 24 of that Act) the contract ceases to have effect;

(b) if no such contract so takes effect, the period beginning with the date of conviction and having the same length as the period for which, in accordance with the order, such a contract would have had effect had one so taken effect.

(5) Where in respect of a conviction any of the following sentences was imposed, that is to say—

(a) an order under section 57 of the *Children and Young Persons Act* 1933 or section 61 of the *Children and Young Persons (Scotland) Act* 1937 committing the person convicted to the care of a fit person;

(b) a supervision order under any provision of either of those Acts or of the 5;

(c) an order under section 413 of the *Criminal Procedure (Scotland) Act* 1975 committing a child for the purpose of his undergoing residential training:

(d) an approved school order under section 61 of the said Act of 1937;

(e) a supervision order under section 63(1) of the *Powers of Criminal Courts (Sentencing) Act* 2000; or

(f) a supervision requirement under any provision of the *Children (Scotland) Act* 1995;

(g) a community supervision order under Schedule 5A to the *Army Act* 1955 or the *Air Force Act* 1955, or under Schedule 4A to the *Naval Discipline Act* 1957;

the rehabilitation period applicable to the sentence shall be one year from the date of conviction or a period beginning with that date and ending when the order or requirement ceases or ceased to have effect, whichever is the longer.

(6) Where in respect of a conviction any of the following orders was made, that is to say—

(a) an order under section 54 of the said Act of 1933 committing the person convicted to custody in a remand home;

(b) an approved school order under section 57 of the said Act of 1933; or

(c) an attendance centre order under section 60 of the *Powers of Criminal Courts (Sentencing) Act* 2000;

(d) a secure training order under section 1 of the *Criminal Justice and Public Order Act* 1994;

the rehabilitation period applicable to the sentence shall be a period beginning with the date of conviction and ending one year after the date on which the order ceases or ceased to have effect.

(6A) Where in respect of a conviction a detention and training order was made under section 100 of the *Powers of Criminal Courts (Sentencing) Act* 2000, the rehabilitation period applicable to the sentence shall be—

(a) in the case of a person aged fifteen years or over at the date of his conviction, five years if the order was, and three and a half years if the order was not, for a term exceeding six months;

(b) in the case of a person aged under fifteen years at the date of his conviction, a period beginning with that date and ending one year after the date on which the order ceases to have effect.

(7) Where in respect of a conviction a hospital order under Part III of the *Mental Health Act* 1983 or under Part VI of the *Mental Health (Scotland) Act* 1984 (with or without a restriction order) was made, the rehabilitation period applicable to the sentence shall be the period of five years from the date of conviction or a period beginning with that date and ending two years after the date on which the hospital order ceases or ceased to have effect, whichever is the longer.

(8) Where in respect of a conviction an order was made imposing on the person convicted any disqualification, disability, prohibition or other penalty, the rehabilitation period applicable to the sentence shall be a period beginning with the date of conviction and ending on the date on which the disqualification, disability, prohibition or penalty (as the case may be) ceases or ceased to have effect.

(9) For the purposes of this section—

(a) "sentence of imprisonment" includes a sentence of detention under section 207 or 415 of the *Criminal Procedure (Scotland) Act* 1975 and a sentence of penal servitude, and "term of imprisonment" shall be construed accordingly;

(b) consecutive terms of imprisonment or of detention under section 91 of the *Powers of Criminal Courts (Sentencing) Act* 2000 or section 206 of the said Act of 1975, and terms which are wholly or partly concurrent (being terms of imprisonment or detention imposed in respect of offences of which a person was convicted in the same proceedings) shall be treated as a single term;

(c) no account shall be taken of any subsequent variation, made by a court in dealing with a person in respect of a suspended sentence of imprisonment, of the term originally imposed; and

(d) a sentence imposed by a court outside Great Britain shall be treated as a sentence of that one of the descriptions mentioned in this section which most nearly corresponds to the sentence imposed.

(10) References in this section to the period during which a probation order, or a supervision order under the *Powers of Criminal Courts (Sentencing) Act* 2000, or a supervision requirement under the *Children (Scotland) Act* 1995, is or was in force include references to any period during which any order or requirement to which this subsection applies, being an order or requirement made or imposed directly or indirectly in substitution for the first-mentioned order or requirement, is or was in force.

This subsection applies—

(a) to any such order or requirement as is mentioned above in this subsection;

(b) to any order having effect under section 25(2) of the *Children and Young Persons Act* 1969 as if it were a training school order in Northern Ireland; and

(c) to any supervision order made under section 72(2) of the said Act of 1968 and having effect as a supervision order under the *Children and Young Persons Act (Northern Ireland)* 1950.

(11) The Secretary of State may by order—

(a) substitute different periods or terms for any of the periods or terms mentioned in subsection (1) to (8) above; and

(b) substitute a different age for the age mentioned in subsection (2)(a) above.

Rehabilitation of Offenders Act 1974, s.6

The rehabilitation period applicable to a conviction

6.—(1) Where only one sentence is imposed in respect of a conviction (not being a sentence **22–80** excluded from rehabilitation under this Act) the rehabilitation period applicable to the conviction is, subject to the following provisions of this section, the period applicable to the sentence in accordance with section 5 above.

(2) Where more than one sentence is imposed in respect of a conviction (whether or not in the same proceedings) and none of the sentences imposed is excluded from rehabilitation under this Act, then, subject to the following provisions of this section, if the periods applicable to those sentences in accordance with section 5 above differ, the rehabilitation period applicable to the conviction shall be the longer or the longest (as the case may be) of those periods.

(3) Without prejudice to subsection (2) above, where in respect of a conviction a person was conditionally discharged or a probation order was made and after the end of the rehabilitation period applicable to the conviction in accordance with subsection (1) or (2) above he is dealt with, in consequence of a breach of conditional discharge or a breach of the order, for the offence for which the order for conditional discharge or a breach of the order was made, then, if the rehabilitation period applicable to the conviction in accordance with subsection (2) above (taking into account any sentence imposed when he is so dealt with) ends later than the rehabilitation period previously applicable to the conviction, he shall be treated for the purposes of this Act as not having become a rehabilitated person in respect

of that conviction, and the conviction shall for those purposes be treated as not having become spent, in relation to any period falling before the end of the new rehabilitation period.

(4) Subject to subsection (5) below, where during the rehabilitation period applicable to a conviction—

    (a) the person convicted is convicted of a further offence; and

    (b) no sentence excluded from rehabilitation under this Act is imposed on him in respect of the later conviction;

if the rehabilitation period applicable in accordance with this section to either of the convictions would end earlier than the period so applicable in relation to the other, the rehabilitation period which would (apart from this subsection) end the earlier shall be extended so as to end at the same time as the other rehabilitation period.

(5) Where the rehabilitation period applicable to a conviction is the rehabilitation period applicable in accordance with section 5(8) above to an order imposing on a person any disqualification, disability, prohibition or other penalty, the rehabilitation period applicable to another conviction shall not by virtue of subsection (4) above be extended by reference to that period; but if any other sentence is imposed in respect of the first-mentioned conviction for which a rehabilitation period is prescribed by any other provision of section 5 above, the rehabilitation period applicable to another conviction shall, where appropriate, be extended under subsection (4) above by reference to the rehabilitation period applicable in accordance with that section to that sentence or, where more than one such sentence is imposed, by reference to the longer or longest of the periods so applicable to those sentences, as if the period in question were the rehabilitation period applicable to the first-mentioned conviction.

(6) For the purposes of subsection (4)(a) above there shall be disregarded—

    (a) any conviction in England and Wales of a summary offence or of a scheduled offence (within the meaning of section 22 of the *Magistrates' Courts Act* 1980) tried summarily in pursuance of subsection (2) of that section (summary trial where value involved is small);

    (b) any conviction in Scotland of an offence which is not excluded from the jurisdiction of inferior courts of summary jurisdiction by virtue of section 4 of the *Summary Jurisdiction (Scotland) Act* 1954 (certain crimes not to be tried in inferior courts of summary jurisdiction);

  (bb) any conviction in service disciplinary proceedings for an offence listed in the Schedule to this Act; and

    (c) any conviction by or before a court outside Great Britain of an offence in respect of conduct which, if it had taken place in any part of Great Britain, would not have constituted an offence under the law in force in that part of Great Britain.

E. Mitigation

(1) General

22–81   A court has a wide discretion concerning what it chooses to take into account as mitigation. Factors that mitigate the seriousness of an offence may relate to the offence itself or to the offender. In relation to the sentences for individual offences, they are set out in earlier chapters that relate to those offences.

There may be times when a court has some difficulty in accepting what is put forward either as a description of the circumstances of the offence or as the circumstances of the offender. If a significant issue is put forward by the defence which the prosecution or the court is not prepared to accept as accurate, this will normally need to be resolved by the hearing of evidence—a *Newton* hearing (see *ante*, § 22–54, for a general discussion of the approach where there is a dispute about the factual basis on which sentence is to be passed).

However, situations are not always so straightforward to identify and defence advocates will often be instructed to put forward versions of events or the conduct of the defendant that it would not be appropriate to spend large amounts of court time disputing.

The offender or his/her legal representative should be able to address the court in mitigation, notwithstanding that the offender has been convicted by a jury after having denied the charge led against him: *Jones*, unreported, August 6, 1979, CA. The same principle applies where a defendant is convicted after a trial in a magistrates' court. The judge is also under a duty of fairness to alert defence counsel to the possibility that he may impose a sentence which the defence counsel is not anticipating. This is to allow defence counsel to make submissions on this issue: *Scott* (1989) 11 Cr.App.R.(S.) 249.

(2) General mitigating circumstances

Factors that generally assist a court in determining the level of culpability or harm are set out in the guideline on seriousness issued by the Sentencing Guidelines Council in December 2004 at paragraphs 1.20–1.29. The statutory provisions are contained in section 166 of the *Criminal Justice Act* 2003. The most significant change from the previous provisions is in section 166(2) where it is made clear that, even where the initial assessment of seriousness takes a case over the custody threshold (and therefore so serious that a community sentence could not be justified), nonetheless personal mitigation may allow a court to impose a community sentence. Whilst this was the approach of many courts under the previous framework, it is helpful to have this clarification.   **22–82**

Criminal Justice Act 2003, s.166

Savings for powers to mitigate sentences and deal appropriately with mentally disordered offenders
166.—(1) Nothing in—   **22–83**
    (a) section 148 (imposing community sentences),
    (b) section 152, 153 or 157 (imposing custodial sentences),
    (c) section 156 (pre-sentence reports and other requirements),
    (d) section 164 (fixing of fines),
prevents a court from mitigating an offender's sentence by taking into account any such matters as, in the opinion of the court, are relevant in mitigation of sentence.
    (2) Section 152(2) does not prevent a court, after taking into account such matters, from passing a community sentence even though it is of the opinion that the offence, or the combination of the offence and one or more offences associated with it, was so serious that a community sentence could not normally be justified for the offence.
    (3) Nothing in the sections mentioned in subsection (1)(a) to (d) prevents a court—
    (a) from mitigating any penalty included in an offender's sentence by taking into account any other penalty included in that sentence, and
    (b) in the case of an offender who is convicted of one or more other offences, from mitigating his sentence by applying any rule of law as to the totality of sentences.
    (4) Subsections (2) and (3) are without prejudice to the generality of subsection (1).
    (5) Nothing in the sections mentioned in subsection (1)(a) to (d) is to be taken—
    (a) as requiring a court to pass a custodial sentence, or any particular custodial sentence, on a mentally disordered offender, or
    (b) as restricting any power (whether under the *Mental Health Act* 1983 or otherwise) which enables a court to deal with such an offender in the manner it considers to be most appropriate in all the circumstances.
    (6) In subsection (5) "mentally disordered", in relation to a person, means suffering from a mental disorder within the meaning of the *Mental Health Act* 1983.

Guideline: Overarching Principles: Seriousness

D. ASSESSMENT OF CULPABILITY AND HARM

(ii) Mitigating factors

1.24 Some factors may indicate that an offender's culpability is **unusually** low, or that the harm caused by an offence is less than usually serious.   **22–84**
1.25 Factors indicating significantly lower culpability:
• A greater degree of provocation than normally expected

- Mental illness or disability
- Youth or age, where it affects the responsibility of the individual defendant
- The fact that the offender played only a minor role in the offence

(iii) Personal mitigation

1.26 Section 166(1) Criminal Justice Act 2003 makes provision for a sentencer to take account of any matters that "in the opinion of the court, are relevant in mitigation of sentence".

1.27 When the court has formed an initial assessment of the seriousness of the offence, then it should consider any offender mitigation. The issue of remorse should be taken into account at this point along with other mitigating features such as admissions to the police in interview.

(iv) Reduction for a guilty plea

1.28 Sentencers will normally reduce the severity of a sentence to reflect an early guilty plea. This subject is covered by a separate guideline and provides a sliding scale reduction with a normal maximum one-third reduction being given to offenders who enter a guilty plea at the first reasonable opportunity.

1.29 Credit may also be given for ready co-operation with the authorities. This will depend on the particular circumstances of the individual case.

(3) Mitigation for assistance

22–85   An offender who materially assists the police, perhaps by disclosing information of value to an investigation of offences committed by others, or relating to the involvement of others in the offence for which he is charged, may expect some degree of discount from the court: *Sinfield* (1981) 3 Cr.App.R.(S.) 258, CA. The size of the discount depends on the individual facts of the case: *Rose and Sapiano* (1980) 2 Cr.App.R.(S.) 239, CA. There is no "tariff" for people who give evidence against co-defendants, each case must be approached on its own particular facts, weighing up the criminality of the admitted offences against the offender's assistance to and co-operation with the police, and taking into account the public interest in encouraging others to come forward. Whilst most cases of this type will be dealt with in the Crown Court, there will be occasions when they will appear for sentence in a magistrates' court, perhaps with the additional complication that a lesser (summary only) charge has been preferred as a part of the response to the assistance given. Additional powers have now been provided to enable the prosecuting and enforcement authorities to encourage the giving of assistance. These include immunity from prosecution, undertakings regarding the giving of evidence and the provision of reductions in sentence: *Serious Organised Crime and Police Act* 2005, ss.71. The powers relating to reduction in sentence may only be exercised by the Crown Court.

The discount should be calculated by deciding what would have been the appropriate sentence had the offence not been admitted by the defendant and been contested at trial. The judge should then make an appropriate reduction which adequately reflects the nature and importance of the information and assistance actually given: *Sehitoglu and Ozakan* [1998] 1 Cr.App.R.(S.) 89, CA.

22–86   In *King* (1985) 7 Cr.App.R.(S.) 227 it was held that the correct approach is for the court first to assess the gravity and number of the offences committed by the defendant, which should result in what might be called a starting figure. The amount by which that figure should be reduced would depend on a number of variable features including the quality and quantity of the material disclosed by the informer, its accuracy and his willingness to confront other criminals or give evidence against them and the degree to which the offender had put himself and his family at risk of reprisal. The amount of that mitigation would vary from about one half to two thirds, according to the circumstances. The sentence must be tailored to punish the defendant, but at the same time reward him for the help he has given and to demonstrate to offenders that it is worth their while to disclose the criminal activities of others for the benefit of the law-abiding public in general: *Sivan* (1988) 10 Cr.App.R.(S.) 282, CA.

22–87   Further guidance on how to assess the accuracy of the information offered, given the defendant's desire to preserve anonymity, was stated in *Sivan, ante*. Lord Lane C.J. stated that, in important cases, it might be desirable for the court to have a letter from a senior officer in the investigating agency, unconnected with the case, who has examined all the facts and is able to certify that the facts are as reported by the officers conducting the investigation. There should be a statement in writing from the officer in charge of the investigation setting out those facts which will be certified by the senior unconnected officer. It would also be advisable in the more important cases to have the officer in charge of the investigation available to give evidence if necessary, whether in court or in the judge's chambers as the situation may demand. The shorthand writer should also be present taking a note of what transpires in the judge's private room.

Credit should only be given if the information is offered early enough for it to be potentially useful: *Debbag and Izzet* (1991) 12 Cr.App.R.(S.) 733, CA. This aversion to encouraging a system of negotiation is particularly so where the information offered proves to be of no practical assistance to the authorities. See also *A. and B.* [1999] 1 Cr.App.R.(S.) 52, CA and *X.* (1994) 15 Cr.App.R.(S.) 750, CA.

In *X. (No. 2)* [1999] 2 Cr.App.R.(S.) 294, CA, guidance was given on the appropriate approach when the defendant disagrees with the police account of the assistance he has given to the investigation of the case. Hughes J. stated:

> "We consider that the proper principles to be followed in a case of this kind are as follows: **22–88**
> 1. It is convenient to remember that a document of this kind, although supplied by a police officer, is supplied at the request of the defendant.
> 2. Except to the extent that the defendant's contention that he has given assistance is supported by the police, it will not generally be likely that the sentencing judge will be able to make any adjustment in sentence. A defendant's unsupported assertion to that effect is not normally likely to be a reliable basis for mitigation.
> 3. It follows from that, that courts must rely very heavily upon the greatest possible care being taken, in compiling such a document for the information of the judge. The judge will have to rely upon it, without investigation, if police inquiries are not to be damaged or compromised and other suspects, guilty or innocent, are not to be affected.
> We have to express our regret that the document in the present case had not been prepared with sufficient care. Those who prepare such documents, and senior officers who verify them, must realise the importance of ensuring that they are complete and accurate.
>
> 4. Except in very unusual circumstances, it will not be necessary, nor will it be desirable for a   **22–89**
> document of this kind to contain the kind of details which would attract a public interest immunity application. We should observe that, as it seems to us, the document in the present case did not do so.
> 5. If very exceptionally such a document does contain information attracting a public interest immunity consideration, then the usual rules about the conduct of such an application will apply. In particular, the *Crown Court (Criminal Procedure and Investigations Act 1996) (Disclosure) Rules* 1997, will apply. It will of course be a case in which the defence can and should be told of the public interest immunity application.
> 6. Absent any consideration of public interest immunity, which we take to be the general position, a document of this kind should be shown to counsel for the defence, who will no doubt discuss its contents with the defendant. That is not, we emphasise, because it will be necessary to debate its contents, but it is so that there should be no room for any unfounded suspicion that the judge has been told something potentially adverse to the defendant without his knowing about it. On general principles, a defendant is entitled to see documents put before the trial judge on which he is to be sentenced. Expeditions to the judge's chambers should not be necessary in these cases. There should never normally be any question of evidence being given, nor of an issue being tried upon the question of the extent of the information provided. To that extent, we entirely agree with the learned judge.
>
> 7. If the defendant wishes to disagree with the contents of such a document, it is not ap-   **22–90**
> propriate for there to be cross-examination of the policeman, whether in court or in chambers. The policeman is not a Crown witness, he has simply supplied material for the judge, at the request of the defendant. It would no doubt be possible, in an appropriate case, for a defendant to ask for an adjournment to allow any opportunity for further consideration to be given to the preparation of the document. Otherwise, if the defendant does not accept what the document says, his remedy is not to rely upon it.

Quite apart from the position of the police officer as an officer reporting at the request of the defendant, cross-examination on the usefulness of the information would almost inevitably be contrary to the public interest. It would be likely to damage inquiries still in train, trials yet to come, suspects guilty or innocent and quite possibly the defendant in the instant case. In a limited number of cases, such a request for cross-examination might even have been set up deliberately for such purpose, although we do not, for a moment, say that would have been the position here.

8. No doubt, the learned judge should ordinarily disregard such a document, if asked by the defendant to do so. In such case, he will no doubt not then be minded to entertain any submission that the defendant has given valuable assistance to the police.

9. If the judge does take the document into consideration he will, no doubt, say no more than is in accordance with the present practice, namely that he has taken into consideration all the information about the defendant, with which he has been provided."

(4) Mitigation where the offender avoids apprehension for a substantial period of time

22–91   Where the offender avoids apprehension for a substantial period of time, the sentencer may make such allowance in mitigation as he feels proper: *Bird* (1987) 9 Cr.App.R.(S.) 77, CA.

However, this principle does not extend to cases involving sexual abuse within a family, which are very likely to remain undetected for substantial periods: *Tiso* (1990) 12 Cr.App.R.(S.) 122, CA.

(5) Mitigation where the offender committed the offence as a young person but convicted of them as an adult

22–92   In cases where an offender has committed offences as a youth but is not convicted of them for many years, the proper approach for the sentencing judge is to identify the sentence which would have been passed if the defendant had been sentenced within a reasonable period after committing the offences and to take that sentence as a starting point in determining the proper sentence to be imposed: *Fowler (Alan)* [2002] 2 Cr.App.R.(S.) 99. See also *Dashwood* (1995) 16 Cr.App.R.(S.) 733, CA.

Similarly, where an offence is committed by an offender under eighteen, who is convicted after attaining the age of eighteen the starting point for consideration of the appropriate sentence is the sentence that the offender would have been likely to receive if he had been sentenced at the date of the commission of the offence: *Ghafoor* [2003] 1 Cr.App.R.(S.) 84. See also *M.* (2002) J.P.N. 963, where an offender who attained the age of fifteen between the date of offence and date of conviction should normally receive the same sentence as he would at the earlier date. A sentence may also be discounted to reflect the youth of the offender, see *Pinnock* (1979) 1 Cr.App.R.(S.) 169.

(6) Mitigation due to personal characteristics of the offender

22–93   A sentencer may give credit for meritorious conduct that is unrelated to the offence for which he is to be sentenced: *Alexander* [1997] 2 Cr.App.R.(S.) 74; but great care needs to be paid to whether that is appropriate. Whilst such credit may be acceptable in relation to non violent offences, it may be less so where the offender has inflicted injury on another person. So, for instance, a person with a good record of public service who is convicted of assaults taking place in a domestic context may not merit any reduction in sentence whereas such a person convicted of theft may do; see Sentencing Guidelines Council guideline *Overarching Principles—Domestic Violence* para.3.20 and § 22–62, *ante*.

The hardship inflicted on the offender's family may be a mitigating factor in exceptional cases: *Summers* (1979) 1 Cr.App.R.(S.) 13. In *Whitehead* [1996] 1 Cr.App.R.(S.) 111, CA the case was described as "finely balanced as to whether a custodial sentence was required or not." The matter tipping the balance in favour of a non-custodial sentence was the position of the three children, aged nine, seven and five. As a result of both parents being sent to prison, they were deprived of the care of both father and mother. The factor relating to the children was decisive in coming to the conclusion that the imprisonment was inappropriate and a 50-hour community service order was imposed.

Ill-health should not affect the length of the sentence imposed, but in exceptional cases the court could reduce the sentence imposed as an act of mercy: *Moore* (1994) 15 Cr.App.R.(S.) 97. Asperger's syndrome, an abnormality of development related to autism, characterised by subtle abnormalities of social interaction, preoccupation with special interests and abnormalities of personality may persuade the court to take an exceptional course: *Gibson* [2001] EWCA 656. A short life expectancy may also persuade the court to reduce the sentence it would otherwise impose: *Lewis* [2001] EWCA Crim 935.

(7) Mitigation relating to the circumstances of the offence

The fact that the offence was committed under the influence of alcohol is not normally **22–94** a mitigating factor: *Bradley* (1980) 2 Cr.App.R.(S.) 12 nor is the fact that the offence was committed to provide money to support an addiction: *Lawrence* (1988) 10 Cr.App.R.(S.) 463, CA.

The use of an agent provocateur to facilitate commission of the offence will not be a mitigating factor unless the officer concerned has acted improperly: *Underhill* (1979) 1 Cr.App.R.(S.) 270, CA; *Springer* [1999] 1 Cr.App.R.(S.) 217, CA. Entrapment as a result of the conduct of journalists rather than police officers will also result in mitigation of sentence: *Tonnessen* [1998] 2 Cr.App.R.(S.) 328, CA.

(8) Mitigation relating to mentally disordered offenders

Section 166(5) of the *CJA* 2003 makes it clear that the court is not fettered in regard **22–95** to making appropriate orders regarding mentally disordered offenders by the criteria for other sentences. An offender is mentally disordered if suffering from a mental disorder within the meaning of the *Mental Health Act* 1983: s.1. See *post*, Ch.28.

(9) The totality principle

A defendant will often face more than one offence, sometimes arising out of the same **22–96** circumstances, sometimes arising out of different circumstances. Each offence must receive a sentence (even if it is "no separate penalty"). As well as looking at the appropriate sentence for each offence, the court must also consider the appropriate sentence for the totality of the offending before it. When the court has calculated the sentence appropriate for each offence, it should then consider the aggregate sentence and decide whether the total sentence is just and appropriate: *Hewitt* [1980] Crim.L.R. 116; *Jones* [1996] 1 Cr.App.R.(S.) 153.

The effect of this is confirmed in section 166(3)(b) of the *CJA* 2003. A particular difficulty can arise where an offence has a maximum penalty that has become too low in comparison with other equivalent offences. A generally recognised example is the maximum sentence for dangerous driving. A useful reminder of the circumstances in which maximum sentences should be considered for such offences can be found in *Butt* [2006] EWCA Crim 47. The driving consisted of driving on the wrong side of the road whilst trying to evade the police; the driver was the worse for both drink and drugs. Upholding a sentence of 18 months' imprisonment (after a guilty plea), the Court of Appeal drew attention to existing guidance on the circumstances in which it is appropriate to use the maximum as a starting point. Similarly, it may be appropriate to consider consecutive sentences where the driver both drove dangerously and drove with excess alcohol or was disqualified. Although the general practice is to impose concurrent sentences where the offences arose from a single incident, nonetheless there is a well recognised practice that, in circumstances such as these, consecutive sentences may be imposed. In *Hardy* [2006] 2 Cr.App.R.(S.) 4, the defendant was convicted of dangerous driving, driving whilst disqualified and failing to provide a specimen. Consecutive sen-

Part IV

tences totalling two years were imposed in the Crown Court. Upholding those sentences and the approach, the Court of Appeal stated that, whilst consecutive sentences would not generally be appropriate where the matters arose out of the same incident "it would be bizarre that this man would in fact have a licence to drive with excess alcohol and while disqualified without any added penalty." An approach that may have less offended general sentencing principle would have been to have treated the alcohol and disqualification as aggravating factors and increased the sentence accordingly; however, the low maximum penalty does not allow that to happen so readily and this is perhaps another example of the problems that arise when maximum sentences are allowed to remain at a level that is too low.

22–97   This principle applies to community penalties and financial orders as well as to custodial sentences. In magistrates' courts, the issue is more likely to arise in relation to financial penalties than to custodial or community sentences with the additional obligation to set the penalty in the light of the resources available to the defendant.

Generally, financial penalties are in addition to other financial penalties imposed whereas community penalties will each start from the day of imposition. Custodial penalties are either concurrent with each other or consecutive to others as specified by the court at the time of sentence.

F. Taking Offences into Consideration and Specimen Charges

22–98   When passing sentence for the principal offence, the court may take into consideration other offences admitted by the defendant but which have not been charged, and in respect of which there will not be a conviction. The practice of taking offences into consideration has no statutory foundation, and has been described as "a convention under which if a court is informed that there are outstanding charges against a prisoner who is before it for a particular offence the court can, if the prisoner admits the offences and asks that they should be taken into account, take them into account." Lord Goddard C.J. in *Batchelor* (1952) 36 Cr.App.R. 64.

However, an offence should not be taken into consideration if the public interest requires that it should be the subject of a separate trial: *McClean*, 6 Cr.App.R.(S.), CA .

A court should also not take into consideration an offence which it is not empowered to try, hence a magistrates' court could not take into consideration a charge triable only on indictment: *Simons* (1953) 37 Cr.App.R. 120, CA. Some puzzlement as to the principles behind this practice were expressed by the Court of Appeal (Criminal Division) in *Sinfield* [2005] EWCA Crim 3638. In *Miles* [2006] EWCA Crim. 256, the court considered the issue further. It was emphasised that the sentence is intended to reflect the overall criminality of the offender. Asking for offences to be taken into consideration may bring credit to an offender by virtue of assistance given in clearing up crimes that would not otherwise have been cleared up and by demonstrating a genuine determination to wipe the slate clean. In this case, the offender was committing burglary as a consequence of long term addiction to drugs, had drawn the additional offences to the notice of the police and had already successfully completed a detoxification programme whilst in prison awaiting sentence. On the other hand, such offences may demonstrate a pattern of criminal activity involving careful planning or may reveal offences committed on bail or a return to crime shortly after sentence for earlier crimes. In those circumstances, they may substantially increase the sentence imposed. The approach has been reviewed in a consultation paper published by the Sentencing Advisory Panel: www.sentencing-guidelines.gov.uk.

22–99   An offence should not be taken into consideration where the court is required to disqualify the offender from driving or to endorse his driving licence in the event of conviction, as such measures cannot be taken where the offence is taken into consideration.

In *DPP v. Anderson* (1978) 142 J.P. 391, it was held that if justice is to be done the practice of taking cases into consideration should not be followed except with the express and unequivocal assent of the offender. Hence he should be informed explicitly of each offence which the judge proposes to be taken into consideration and should explicitly admit that he committed them and should state his desire that they should be taken into consideration in determining the sentence passed upon him.

A similar practice has grown up in relation to specimen charges. The prosecution may select a small number of occasions where an offence has been committed knowing that similar offences have taken place on other occasions. Providing the defendant clearly accepts responsibility for all offences, the court can sentence on the basis of the whole course of conduct.

G. CREDIT FOR GUILTY PLEA

Criminal Justice Act 2003, s.144

Reduction in sentences for guilty pleas

144.—(1) In determining what sentence to pass on an offender who has pleaded guilty to an **22–100** offence in proceedings before that or another court, a court must take into account—

   (a) the stage in the proceedings for the offence at which the offender indicated his intention to plead guilty, and

   (b) the circumstances in which this indication was given.

(2) In the case of an offence the sentence for which falls to be imposed under subsection (2) of section 110 or 111 of the Sentencing Act, nothing in that subsection prevents the court, after taking into account any matter referred to in subsection (1) of this section, from imposing any sentence which is not less than 80 per cent of that specified in that subsection.

In December 2004, the Sentencing Guidelines Council published a definitive **22–101** guideline to which all courts must have regard in passing sentence on any offender sentenced on or after January 10, 2005. This has been reviewed and a revised guideline now applies to offenders sentenced since July 2007.

Guideline: Reduction in Sentence for a Guilty Plea

B. STATEMENT OF PURPOSE

2.1 When imposing a custodial sentence, statute requires that a court must impose the **22–102** shortest term that is commensurate with the seriousness of the offence(s). Similarly, when imposing a community order, the restrictions on liberty must be commensurate with the seriousness of the offence(s). Once that decision is made, a court is required to give consideration to the reduction for any guilty plea. As a result, the final sentence after the reduction for a guilty plea will be less than the seriousness of the offence requires.

2.2 A reduction in sentence is appropriate because a guilty plea avoids the need for a trial (thus enabling other cases to be disposed of more expeditiously), shortens the gap between charge and sentence, saves considerable cost, and, in the case of an early plea, saves victims and witnesses from the concern about having to give evidence. The reduction principle derives from the need for the effective administration of justice and not as an aspect of mitigation.

2.3 Where a sentencer is in doubt as to whether a custodial sentence is appropriate, the reduction attributable to a guilty plea will be relevant consideration. Where this is amongst the factors leading to the imposition of a non-custodial sentence, there will be no need to apply a further reduction on account of the guilty plea. A similar approach is appropriate where the reduction for a guilty plea is amongst the factors leading to the imposition of a financial penalty or discharge instead of a community order.

2.4 When deciding the most appropriate length of sentence, the sentencer should address separately the issue of remorse, together with any other mitigating features, before calculating the reduction for the guilty plea. Similarly, assistance to the prosecuting or enforcement authorities is a separate issue which may attract a reduction in sentence under other procedures though care will need to be taken to ensure that there is no "double counting".

2.5 The implications of other offences that an offender has asked to be taken into consideration should be reflected in the sentence before the reduction for guilty plea has been applied.

2.6 A reduction in sentence should only be applied to the **punitive elements** of a penalty.

The guilty plea reduction has no impact on sentencing decisions in relation to ancillary orders, including orders of disqualification from driving.

C. APPLICATION OF THE REDUCTION PRINCIPLE

Recommended Approach

3.1 The court decides sentence for the offence(s) taking into account aggravating and mitigating factors and any other offences that have been formally admitted (TICs)

↓

The court selects the amount of the reduction by reference to the sliding scale

↓

The court applies the reduction

↓

When pronouncing sentence the court should usually state what the sentence would have been if there had been no reduction as a result of the guilty plea.

D. DETERMINING THE LEVEL OF REDUCTION

4.1 The level of reduction should be a proportion of the total sentence imposed, with the proportion calculated by reference to the circumstances in which the guilty plea was indicated, in particular the stage in the proceedings. The greatest reduction will be given where the plea was indicated at the "first reasonable opportunity".

4.2 Save where section 144(2) of the 2003 Act applies, the level of the reduction will be gauged on a sliding scale ranging from a recommended one third (where the guilty plea was entered at the first reasonable opportunity in relation to the offence for which sentence is being imposed), reducing to a recommended one quarter (where a trial date has been set) and to a recommended one tenth (for a guilty plea entered at the 'door of the court' or after the trial has begun). *See diagram below.*

4.3 The level of reduction should reflect the stage at which the offender indicated a *willingness to admit guilt* to the offence for which he is eventually sentenced:

(i) the largest recommended reduction will not normally be given unless the offender indicated willingness to admit guilt at the **first reasonable opportunity**; when this occurs will vary from case to case (*see Annex 1 for illustrative examples*);

(ii) where the admission of guilt comes later than the first reasonable opportunity, the reduction for guilty plea will normally be less than one third;

(iii) where the plea of guilty comes very late, it is still appropriate to give some reduction;

(iv) if after pleading guilty there is a Newton hearing and the offender's version of the circumstances of the offence is rejected, this should be taken into account in determining the level of reduction;

(v) if the not guilty plea was entered and maintained for tactical reasons (such as to retain privileges whilst on remand), a late guilty plea should attract very little, if any, discount.

In each category, there is a presumption that the recommended reduction will be given unless there are good reasons for a lower amount.

First reasonable opportunity	After a trial date is set	Door of the court/ after trial has begun
======= | ===== ========= ======	===== ========= ======	===== ========= ====== ===== |
recommended 1/3	**recommended 1/4**	**recommended 1/10**

E. WITHHOLDING A REDUCTION

On the basis of dangerousness

5.1 Where a sentence for a "dangerous offender" is imposed under the provisions in the *Criminal Justice Act* 2003, whether the sentence requires the calculation of a minimum term or is an extended sentence, the approach will be the same as for any other determinate sentence (see also paragraph 7 below).

Where the prosecution case is overwhelming

5.2 The purpose of giving credit is to encourage those who are guilty to plead at the earliest opportunity. Any defendant is entitled to put the prosecution to proof and so every defendant who is guilty should be encouraged to indicate that guilt at the first reasonable opportunity.

5.3 Where the prosecution case is overwhelming, it may not be appropriate to give the full reduction that would otherwise be given. Whilst there is a presumption in favour of the full reduction being given where a plea has been indicated at the first reasonable opportunity, the fact that the prosecution case is overwhelming without relying on admissions from the defendant may be a reason justifying departure from the guideline.

5.4 Where a court is satisfied that a lower reduction should be given for this reason, a recommended reduction of 20% is likely to be appropriate where the guilty plea was indicated at the first reasonable opportunity.

5.5 A Court departing from a guideline must state the reasons for doing so.

Where the maximum penalty for the offence is thought to be too low

5.6 The sentencer is bound to sentence for the offence with which the offender has been charged, and to which he has pleaded guilty. The sentencer cannot remedy perceived defects (for example an inadequate charge or maximum penalty) by refusal of the appropriate discount.

Where jurisdictional issues arise

(i) Where two or more summary only offences are to be sentenced

5.7 When the total sentence for both or all of the offences is 6 months imprisonment, a court may determine to impose consecutive sentences which, even allowing for a reduction for a guilty plea where appropriate on each offence, would still result in the imposition of the maximum sentence available. In such circumstances, in order to achieve the purpose for which the reduction principle has been established, some modest allowance should normally be given against the total sentence for the entry of a guilty plea.

(ii) Where a maximum sentence might still be imposed

5.8 Despite a guilty plea being entered which would normally attract a reduction in sentence, a magistrates' court may impose a sentence of imprisonment of 6 months for a single either-way offence where, but for the plea, that offence would have been committed to the Crown Court for sentence.

5.9 Similarly, a detention and training order of 24 months may be imposed on an offender aged under 18 if the offence is one which would but for the plea have attracted a sentence of long-term detention in excess of 24 months under the *Powers of Criminal Courts (Sentencing) Act* 2000, section 91.

22–103   This guideline seeks to define clearly the purpose of the reduction, the means of calculating the amount of that reduction and the significance of other factors, such as the offender being caught in circumstances where the prosecution case was "overwhelming", on which differing views have developed. The primary purpose of the guideline is to ensure consistency of approach and, by making the existence of the reduction better known and understood, to better achieve Parliament's aim in providing for such a reduction, which, the guideline states, is to increase the number of guilty offenders who plead guilty at the first reasonable opportunity. Courts will be expecting to be referred to this guideline as the basis for consideration rather than to previously decided authority. One of the most contentious issues has been the extent to which a reduction should be given where the prosecution case is overwhelming. One argument has been that, since the purpose of the reduction principle is purely pragmatic and since many defendants will continue to plead not guilty even in the face of a strong prosecution case, no distinction should be made based on the strength of that case. The contrary position has been that it is unjust to give a full reduction where the defendant is faced with a very strong case, particularly where the strength of the case is independent of any admission from the defendant. In the 2004 guideline, the Sentencing Guidelines Council accepted the first argument. However, in the light of a small number of exceptional cases and continuing concern about this aspect of the guideline, the revised guideline has opened the way for greater discretion: see paras. 5.2–5.5. Although there is a presumption in favour of the full reduction where a plea has been entered at the first reasonable opportunity, departure from the guideline may be justified where the prosecution case is overwhelming without reliance on admissions from the defendant. In such circumstances, the recommended reduction of one third reduces to 20 per cent. No guidance is given on the circumstances in which the prosecution case can be said to be "overwhelming" and this is likely to be an area where different views are taken. The obligation to give reasons will be important in such circumstances.

A further important (and related) aspect for a magistrates' court is the approach where a court is sentencing an offender for two or more offences where the maximum sentence overall is six months imprisonment. This could be where there are several summary only offences (*e.g.* two or more offences of driving whilst disqualified) or one either way offence and one or more summary only offences (*e.g.* theft and assault on a police officer and/or an offence under section 4 of the *Public Order Act* 1986). In such circumstances, it would be permissible to impose consecutive sentences resulting in the maximum of six months whilst allowing for the reduction in each individual case. However, the guideline provides (para. 5.7) that there should still be some "modest allowance" against the total sentence in order to give some encouragement towards a guilty plea.

The guideline states that the reduction should apply to the punitive elements of a sentence not to the rehabilitative elements. However, it also makes it clear that the principle applies to the sentence itself and not to the ancillary orders. In those circumstances, for example, neither the length of the disqualification nor the number of penalty points will be affected by any reduction based solely on the reduction for a guilty plea in accordance with the guideline.

Having stated that the reduction is purely pragmatic (para. 2.2), the guideline emphasises that issues of personal mitigation and remorse should be dealt with separately and before calculating the reduction on account of the guilty plea.

The scale of the reduction should never exceed one third and this will apply to the punitive (rather than rehabilitative) elements of the sentence—for example, within a community sentence, it would reduce the period of a curfew or unpaid work requirement but not a drug rehabilitation requirement. That maximum of one third will only be available where the guilty plea is entered at the "first reasonable opportunity". The Guideline recognises the difficulty of defining this term in a way that can be consistently applied and elaborates on it in Annex 1 to the guideline.

Guideline: Reduction in Sentence for a Guilty Plea

ANNEX 1

First Reasonable Opportunity

22–104   1. The critical time for determining the reduction for a guilty plea is the first reasonable opportunity for the defendant to have indicated a willingness to plead guilty. This opportunity will vary with a wide range of factors and the Court will need to make a judgement on the particular facts of the case before it.

2. The key principle is that the purpose of giving a reduction is to recognise the benefits that come from a guilty plea not only for those directly involved in the case in question but also in enabling Courts more quickly to deal with other outstanding cases.

3. This Annex seeks to help Courts to adopt a consistent approach by giving examples of circumstances where a determination will have to be made:

  a) the first reasonable opportunity may be the first time that a defendant appears before the court and has the opportunity to plead guilty;

  b) but the court may consider that it would be reasonable to have expected an indication of willingness even earlier, perhaps whilst under interview;

  Note: *For a) and b) to apply, the Court will need to be satisfied that the defendant (and any legal adviser) would have had sufficient information about the allegations*

  c) where an offence triable either way is committed to the Crown Court for trial and the defendant pleads guilty at the first hearing in that Court, the reduction will be less than if there had been an indication of a guilty plea given to the magistrates' court (recommended reduction of one third) but more than if the plea had been entered after a trial date had been set (recommended reduction of one quarter), and is likely to be in the region of 30%;

  d) where an offence is triable only on indictment, it may well be that the first reasonable opportunity would have been during the police station stage; where that is not the case, the first reasonable opportunity is likely to be at the first hearing in the Crown Court;

  (e) where a defendant is convicted after pleading guilty to an alternative (lesser) charge to that to which he/she had originally pleaded not guilty, the extent of any reduction will be determined by the stage at which the defendant first formally indicated to the court willingness to plead guilty to the lesser charge, and the reason why that lesser charge was proceeded with in preference to the original charge.

If a guilty plea is entered later than the first reasonable opportunity, the degree of **22–105** reduction will reduce. This follows the principle behind the reduction that it is designed to spare both the anxiety of victims and witnesses caused by prolonged court proceedings in which they may have to give evidence and the potential waste of police, prosecution and court time. Accordingly, if a guilty plea is entered after the trial date is set but before trial is due to commence, the reduction is not to exceed one quarter. If the plea is entered at the "door of the court" or even after the trial has begun, a reduction should still be given but this should not exceed 10 per cent.

The Guideline makes clear that, even with the reduction applied to the full, there will be circumstances where a defendant who pleads guilty will still receive the maximum sentence available in a magistrates' court. This would be the case where, for example, in the absence of a guilty plea, the case would have been committed to the Crown Court for sentence: paras 5.8–5.9. The guilty plea may also justify a change in the type of sentence, perhaps from a custodial sentence to a non-custodial sentence or from a community sentence to a fine: para. 2.3.

The Guideline also emphasises the benefit of a court stating what the sentence would have been if there had been no reduction as a result of the guilty plea: para. 3.1.

Section 144 does not confer a statutory discount, the issue remains one in the discre- **22–106** tion of the court. Where a court takes a guilty plea into account, it is important that it states that it has done so, for the benefit of the defendant and a later appeal court: *Fearon* [1996] 2 Cr.App.R.(S.) 25, CA; *Aroride* [1999] 2 Cr.App.R.(S.) 406, CA.

H. EXPLANATIONS OF SENTENCE

Giving reasons for a decision is now widely accepted as important both for the benefit **22–107** of those directly involved in a case and for the wider understanding of the court process. Whilst there is no general statutory duty, there are a number of individual obligations to give information to support specific decisions. In addition, giving of reasons helps to fulfil obligations under the European Convention on Human Rights to ensure a fair trial. Reasons should enable an interested observer to understand the significant factors in a decision. The more the decision differs from what might be considered a normal sentence in the circumstances, the more extensive the reasons should be. A court will also need to be aware of the anxiety being experienced by the defendant and that what is said is tempered to the occasion.

The requirements were previously contained in a range of provisions (primarily in the *PCC(S)A* 2000) but are now brought together in section 174 of the *Criminal Justice Act* 2003.

Criminal Justice Act 2003, s.174

Duty to give reasons for, and explain effect of, sentence

  174.—(1) Subject to subsections (3) and (4), any court passing sentence on an offender— **22–108**

    (a) must state in open court, in ordinary language and in general terms, its reasons for deciding on the sentence passed, and

    (b) must explain to the offender in ordinary language—

      (i) the effect of the sentence,

      (ii) where the offender is required to comply with any order of the court forming part of the sentence, the effects of non-compliance with the order,

       (iii)   any power of the court, on the application of the offender or any other person, to vary or review any order of the court forming part of the sentence, and

       (iv)   where the sentence consists of or includes a fine, the effects of failure to pay the fine.

(2) In complying with subsection (1)(a), the court must—

    (a)   where guidelines indicate that a sentence of a particular kind, or within a particular range, would normally be appropriate for the offence and the sentence is of a different kind, or is outside that range, state the court's reasons for deciding on a sentence of a different kind or outside that range,

    (b)   where the sentence is a custodial sentence and the duty in subsection (2) of section 152 is not excluded by subsection (1)(a) or (b) or (3) of that section, state that it is of the opinion referred to in section 152(2) and why it is of that opinion,

    (c)   where the sentence is a community sentence and the case does not fall within section 151(2), state that it is of the opinion that section 148(1) applies and why it is of that opinion,

    (d)   where as a result of taking into account any matter referred to in section 144(1), the court imposes a punishment on the offender which is less severe than the punishment it would otherwise have imposed, state that fact, and

    (e)   in any case, mention any aggravating or mitigating factors which the court has regarded as being of particular importance.

(3) Subsection (1)(a) does not apply—

    (a)   to an offence the sentence for which is fixed by law (provision relating to sentencing for such an offence being made by section 270), or

    (b)   to an offence the sentence for which falls to be imposed under section 51A(2) of the *Firearms Act* 1968 (c 27) or under subsection (2) of section 110 or 111 of the Sentencing Act (required custodial sentences).

(4) The Secretary of State may by order—

    (a)   prescribe cases in which subsection (1)(a) or (b) does not apply, and

    (b)   prescribe cases in which the statement referred to in subsection (1)(a) or the explanation referred to in subsection (1)(b) may be made in the absence of the offender, or may be provided in written form.

(5) Where a magistrates' court passes a custodial sentence, it must cause any reason stated by virtue of subsection (2)(b) to be specified in the warrant of commitment and entered on the register.

(6) In this section—

    "guidelines" has the same meaning as in section 172;

    "the register" has the meaning given by section 163 of the Sentencing Act.

22–109   There is a general obligation to state in ordinary language the reasons for deciding on the sentence to be passed and to explain to the offender the effect of the sentence, including what might happen if he fails to comply with the order of the court: section 174(1). Where a relevant guideline has been issued by the Sentencing Guidelines Council and the sentence is outside the range suggested in that guideline, the reasons must also show why that decision has been made: section 174(2)(a).

More specific obligations require a court:

    — when passing a custodial sentence to state why the offence is so serious than nothing other than custody is justified;

    — when passing a community sentence, to state why the offence was serious enough to warrant such a sentence (unless it was based on some other rationale such as that contained in section 151(2) of the *Criminal Justice Act* 2003 when in force);

    — when reducing a sentence on account of the defendant's guilty plea, to state that that has been done;

    — always to draw attention to any aggravating or mitigating factors that were of particular importance in determining sentence.

When the court has taken other offences into consideration when passing sentence, it should expressly state that it has done so.

The *Magistrates' Courts Sentencing Guidelines*(2004), p.84 (currently under **22–110** review), state that reasons for findings and decisions should normally be given. Victims are likely to want to know the reasons for the decision, the public are entitled to know what is going on in the criminal justice system and to have confidence in it and ill-informed criticism in the media may be reduced if reasons have been given in public and recorded.

However, the primary purpose of explanations is to ensure that there is a clear **22–111** understanding of what the court has chosen to do, and why, which is for the benefit of those directly involved in the case as well as for the wider public. The extent to which this is needed will vary from case to case both with the complexity of the case itself and the extent to which the court is making a decision different from what might reasonably have been expected. Much of the detailed explanation of the consequences of the sentence (which is primarily for the benefit of the offender) is likely to be lost in the apprehension of the moment and it is hoped that clarification will come as to better ways in which such information can be conveyed which both reduces the burden on the court and increases the understanding of the offender of what is expected as a result of the sentence imposed.

The principle of giving clear explanations is carried through to the point of requesting a pre-sentence report by the definitive guideline issued by the Sentencing Guidelines Council in December 2004 (*New Sentences: Criminal Justice Act 2003*). Wherever a court requests a pre-sentence report (note the wide definition under the 2003 Act which includes reports now commonly known by other names, such as the SDR) it will be expected to give clear guidance on the objectives of sentencing it is seeking to achieve and on those factors that make the offence more or less serious: see *ante*, § 22–39.

If a case has to be adjourned, and a differently constituted court sits on the next occasion, the later court must know the reasons for the decision of the earlier court.

Part IV

SPECIFIC SENTENCES

Part IV

I. SPECIFIC ASPECTS OF SENTENCING

A. DEFERMENT OF SENTENCE

(1) Legislation

Powers of Criminal Courts (Sentencing) Act 2000, ss.1–1D

DEFERMENT OF SENTENCE

1.—(1) The Crown Court or a magistrates' court may defer passing sentence on an offender **23–1** for the purpose of enabling the court, or any other court to which it falls to deal with him, to have regard in dealing with him to—

(a) his conduct after conviction (including, where appropriate, the making by him of reparation for his offence); or

(b) any change in his circumstances;

but this is subject to subsections (3) and (4) below.

(2) Without prejudice to the generality of subsection (1) above, the matters to which the court to which it falls to deal with the offender may have regard by virtue of paragraph (a) of that subsection include the extent to which the offender has complied with any requirements imposed under subsection (3)(b) below.

(3) The power conferred by subsection (1) above shall be exercisable only if—

(a) the offender consents;

(b) the offender undertakes to comply with any requirements as to his conduct during the period of the deferment that the court considers it appropriate to impose; and

(c) the court is satisfied, having regard to the nature of the offence and the character and circumstances of the offender, that it would be in the interests of justice to exercise the power.

(4) Any deferment under this section shall be until such date as may be specified by the court, not being more than six months after the date on which the deferment is announced by the court; and, subject to section 1D(3) below, where the passing of sentence has been deferred under this section it shall not be further so deferred.

(5) Where a court has under this section deferred passing sentence on an offender, it shall forthwith give a copy of the order deferring the passing of sentence and setting out any requirements imposed under subsection (3)(b) above—

(a) to the offender,

(b) where an officer of a local probation board has been appointed to act as a supervisor in relation to him, to that board, and

(c) where a person has been appointed under section 1A(2)(b) below to act as a supervisor in relation to him, to that person.

(6) Notwithstanding any enactment, a court which under this section defers passing sentence on an offender shall not on the same occasion remand him.

(7) Where—

(a) a court which under this section has deferred passing sentence on an offender proposes to deal with him on the date originally specified by the court, or

(b) the offender does not appear on the day so specified,

the court may issue a summons requiring him to appear before the court at a time and place specified in the summons, or may issue a warrant to arrest him and bring him before the court at a time and place specified in the warrant.

(8) Nothing in this section or sections 1A to 1D below shall affect—

(a) the power of the Crown Court to bind over an offender to come up for judgment when called upon; or

(b) the power of any court to defer passing sentence for any purpose for which it may lawfully do so apart from this section.

Further provision about undertakings

23–2   **1A.**—(1) Without prejudice to the generality of paragraph (b) of section 1(3) above, the requirements that may be imposed by virtue of that paragraph include requirements as to the residence of the offender during the whole or any part of the period of deferment.

(2) Where an offender has undertaken to comply with any requirements imposed under section 1(3)(b) above the court may appoint—

(a) an officer of a local probation board, or

(b) any other person whom the court thinks appropriate,

to act as a supervisor in relation to him.

(3) A person shall not be appointed under subsection (2)(b) above without his consent.

(4) It shall be the duty of a supervisor appointed under subsection (2) above—

(a) to monitor the offender's compliance with the requirements; and

(b) to provide the court to which it falls to deal with the offender in respect of the offence in question with such information as the court may require relating to the offender's compliance with the requirements.

Breach of undertakings

23–3   **1B.**—(1) A court which under section 1 above has deferred passing sentence on an offender may deal with him before the end of the period of deferment if—

(a) he appears or is brought before the court under subsection (3) below; and

(b) the court is satisfied that he has failed to comply with one or more requirements imposed under section 1(3)(b) above in connection with the deferment.

(2) Subsection (3) below applies where—

(a) a court has under section 1 above deferred passing sentence on an offender;

(b) the offender undertook to comply with one or more requirements imposed under section 1(3)(b) above in connection with the deferment; and

(c) a person appointed under section 1A(2) above to act as a supervisor in relation to the offender has reported to the court that the offender has failed to comply with one or more of those requirements.

(3) Where this subsection applies, the court may issue—

(a) a summons requiring the offender to appear before the court at a time and place specified in the summons; or

(b) a warrant to arrest him and bring him before the court at a time and place specified in the warrant.

Conviction of offence during period of deferment

1C.—(1) A court which under section 1 above has deferred passing sentence on an offender **23–4** may deal with him before the end of the period of deferment if during that period he is convicted in Great Britain of any offence.

(2) Subsection (3) below applies where a court has under section 1 above deferred passing sentence on an offender in respect of one or more offences and during the period of deferment the offender is convicted in England and Wales of any offence ("the later offence").

(3) Where this subsection applies, then (without prejudice to subsection (1) above and whether or not the offender is sentenced for the later offence during the period of deferment), the court which passes sentence on him for the later offence may also, if this has not already been done, deal with him for the offence or offences for which passing of sentence has been deferred, except that—

(a) the power conferred by this subsection shall not be exercised by a magistrates' court if the court which deferred passing sentence was the Crown Court; and

(b) the Crown Court, in exercising that power in a case in which the court which deferred passing sentence was a magistrates' court, shall not pass any sentence which could not have been passed by a magistrates' court in exercising that power.

(4) Where a court which under section 1 above has deferred passing sentence on an offender proposes to deal with him by virtue of subsection (1) above before the end of the period of deferment, the court may issue—

(a) a summons requiring him to appear before the court at a time and place specified in the summons; or

(b) a warrant to arrest him and bring him before the court at a time and place specified in the warrant.

Deferment of sentence: supplementary

1D.—(1) In deferring the passing of sentence under section 1 above a magistrates' court shall **23–5** be regarded as exercising the power of adjourning the trial conferred by section 10(1) of the Magistrates' Courts Act 1980, and accordingly sections 11(1) and 13(1) to (3A) and (5) of that Act (non-appearance of the accused) apply (without prejudice to section 1(7) above) if the offender does not appear on the date specified under section 1(4) above.

(2) Where the passing of sentence on an offender has been deferred by a court ("the original court") under section 1 above, the power of that court under that section to deal with the offender at the end of the period of deferment and any power of that court under section 1B(1) or 1C(1) above, or of any court under section 1C(3) above, to deal with the offender—

(a) is power to deal with him, in respect of the offence for which passing of sentence has been deferred, in any way in which the original court could have dealt with him if it had not deferred passing sentence; and

(b) without prejudice to the generality of paragraph (a) above, in the case of a magistrates' court, includes the power conferred by section 3 below to commit him to the Crown Court for sentence.

(3) Where—

    (a) the passing of sentence on an offender in respect of one or more offences has been deferred under section 1 above, and

    (b) a magistrates' court deals with him in respect of the offence or any of the offences by committing him to the Crown Court under section 3 below,

the power of the Crown Court to deal with him includes the same power to defer passing sentence on him as if he had just been convicted of the offence or offences on indictment before the court.

(4) Subsection (5) below applies where—

    (a) the passing of sentence on an offender in respect of one or more offences has been deferred under section 1 above;

    (b) it falls to a magistrates' court to determine a relevant matter; and

    (c) a justice of the peace is satisfied—

        (i) that a person appointed under section 1A(2)(b) above to act as a supervisor in relation to the offender is likely to be able to give evidence that may assist the court in determining that matter; and

        (ii) that that person will not voluntarily attend as a witness.

(5) The justice may issue a summons directed to that person requiring him to attend before the court at the time and place appointed in the summons to give evidence.

(6) For the purposes of subsection (4) above a court determines a relevant matter if it—

    (a) deals with the offender in respect of the offence, or any of the offences, for which the passing of sentence has been deferred; or

    (b) determines, for the purposes of section 1B(1)(b) above, whether the offender has failed to comply with any requirements imposed under section 1(3)(b) above."

(2) Purpose and effect

23–6   These provisions provide the potential to give new life to a sentence that was considered all but finished with by filling some of the gaps that had created problems. Most notably, there is now formal provision for the court to require undertakings from the offender to be complied with during the period of deferment (section 1(3) and section 1A), a power to appoint a person to oversee the completion of those undertakings (section 1A(2)) and the option of bringing the offender back to court for sentence earlier than the end of the period of deferment if those undertakings are not being complied with (section 1B). In addition, the Sentencing Guidelines Council has included within its definitive guidelines, published in December 2004 (*New Sentences: Criminal Justice Act* 2003), guidance on circumstances when it might be appropriate to defer sentence. The Guideline draws attention to the wide range of sentencing options available under the new framework and concludes that a deferred sentence is likely to be used only in limited circumstances. The Guideline sets out the purpose and possible benefits.

Guideline: New Sentences: Criminal Justice Act 2003

Section 1—Community Sentences & Deferred Sentences
    Part 2: Deferred Sentences

B. USE OF DEFERRED SENTENCES

23–7   **1.2.6** ...A deferred sentence enables the court to review the conduct of the defendant before passing sentence, having first prescribed certain requirements. It also provides several opportunities for an offender to have some influence as to the sentence passed–

    a) it tests the commitment of the offender not to re-offend;

    b) it gives the offender an opportunity to do something where progress can be shown within a short period;

    c) it provides the offender with an opportunity to behave or refrain from behaving in a particular way that will be relevant to sentence.

(3) General

23–8   There are now 3 conditions that need to be satisfied before sentence can be deferred:

(i) the court must be satisfied that deferral is in the interests of justice (subsection 1(3)(c)). In reaching that conclusion the court must have regard both to the offence and to the character and circumstances of the offender.

(ii) the offender must consent (subsection 1(3)(a)).

(iii) the offender must undertake to comply with requirements imposed by the court (subsection 1(3)(b)).

The extent of the requirements are at the discretion of the court and may include a residence requirement: section 1A(1). Given that the purpose of deferment is to enable the offender to influence sentence, it is imperative that the offender and the court are absolutely clear about what is expected. Again this is underlined by the Sentencing Guidelines Council:

Guideline: New Sentences: Criminal Justice Act 2003

Section 1—Community Sentences & Deferred Sentences
  Part 2: Deferred Sentences

B. Use of Deferred Sentences

1.2.8 A court may impose any conditions during the period of deferment that it considers **23–9** appropriate. These could be specific requirements as set out in the provisions for community sentences, or requirements that are drawn more widely. These should be specific, measurable conditions so that the offender knows exactly what is required and the court can assess compliance; the restriction on liberty should be limited to ensure that the offender has a reasonable expectation of being able to comply whilst maintaining his or her social responsibilities.

1.2.9 Given the need for clarity in the mind of the offender and the possibility of sentence by another court, the court should give a clear indication (and make a written record) of the type of sentence it would be minded to impose if it had not decided to defer and ensure that the offender understands the consequences of failure to comply with the court's wishes during the deferral period.

> **When deferring sentence, the sentencer must make clear the consequence of not complying with any requirements and should indicate the type of sentence it would be minded to impose. Sentencers should impose specific, measurable conditions that do not involve a serious restriction on liberty.**

The court may appoint a supervisor to oversee the completion of the requirements it **23–10** has imposed. This may be an officer of a local probation board or any other appropriate person willing to undertake the role: section 1A(2, 3). The supervisor's role is to monitor compliance with the requirements and to inform the court, as requested, about that compliance: s.1A(4). If the requirements are not complied with, the supervisor will be expected to draw that to the attention of the court (section 1B(2)) which may issue a summons or a warrant to bring the offender before the court: section 1B(3). An offender brought before the court following such a summons or a warrant who has not complied with one or more of the requirements may be sentenced by the court even though the period of deferment has not ended: section 1B(1).

As before, there are strong suggestions that, in most circumstances, a court would expect to impose sentence at the earliest opportunity and that the decision to defer is likely to be relatively infrequent.

Guideline: New Sentences: Criminal Justice Act 2003

Section 1—Community Sentences & Deferred Sentences
  Part 2: Deferred Sentences

B. Use of Deferred Sentences

1.2.7 Given the new power to require undertakings and the ability to enforce those undertak- **23–11**

Part IV

ings before the end of the period of deferral, the decision to defer sentence should be predominantly for a small group of cases at either the custody threshold or the community sentence threshold where the sentencer feels that there would be particular value in giving the offender the opportunities listed because, if the offender complies with the requirements, a different sentence will be justified at the end of the deferment period. This could be a community sentence instead of a custodial sentence or a fine or discharge instead of a community sentence. It may, rarely, enable a custodial sentence to be suspended rather than imposed immediately.

> **The use of deferred sentences should be predominantly for a small group of cases close to a significant threshold where, should the defendant be prepared to adapt his behaviour in a way clearly specified by the sentencer, the court may be prepared to impose a lesser sentence.**

(4) Convictions during period of deferment

23–12   If the defendant is convicted anywhere in Great Britain (*i.e.* England, Wales and Scotland) of another offence committed during the period of deferral, the *court that has deferred sentence* may deal with the defendant before the end of the period of deferment: section 1C(1). In order to bring the defendant before the court, a summons or a warrant may be issued: section 1C(4).

If a defendant subject to a deferred sentence is convicted in England and Wales of an offence, then *the court dealing with the later offence* may be able to deal with the offence on which sentence was deferred even though it was not the court which deferred sentence: section 1C(2), (3). However, a magistrates' court may not sentence for an offence that is subject to a deferred sentence imposed by the Crown Court: section 1C(3)(a). A Crown Court sentencing for an offence on which a magistrates' court has deferred sentence is limited to the maximum sentence that a magistrates' court could have passed: section 1C(3)(b). This limit applies even though one of the options available to a magistrates' court at the end of the period of deferment is to commit the defendant to the Crown Court for sentence: section 1D(2)(b).

(5) Sentence after deferment

23–13   The approach to sentence at the end of the period of deferment was also considered in *George*, 79 Cr.App.R.26.
   (i) be clear about the purpose of the deferment and any requirement imposed by the deferring court
   (ii) decide whether the defendant has substantially conformed or attempted to conform with the expectations of the deferring court.
   (iii) if he has, then the defendant may legitimately expect that an immediate custodial sentence will not be imposed: *Smith* (1979) 1 Cr.App.R.(S.) 339.
   (iv) if he has not, then the court should state clearly how the defendant has failed to do what the court required.

B. ABSOLUTE AND CONDITIONAL DISCHARGE

(1) Legislation

Powers of Criminal Courts (Sentencing) Act 2000, s.12

Absolute and conditional discharge

23–14   **12.**—(1) Where a court by or before which a person is convicted of an offence (not being an offence the sentence for which is fixed by law or falls to be imposed under section 110(2) or 111(2) below, section 51A(2) of the *Firearms Act* 1968 or section 225, 226, 227 or 228 of the *Criminal Justice Act* 2003 or section 29(4) or (6) of the *Violent Crime Reduction Act* 2006) is of the opinion, having regard to the circumstances including the nature of the offence and the character of the offender, that it is inexpedient to inflict punishment, the court may make an order either—

(a) discharging him absolutely; or

(b) if the court thinks fit, discharging him subject to the condition that he commits no offence during such period, not exceeding three years from the date of the order, as may be specified in the order.

(2) Subsection (1)(b) above has effect subject to section 66(4) of the *Crime and Disorder Act* 1998 (effect of reprimands and warnings).

(3) An order discharging a person subject to such a condition as is mentioned in subsection (1)(b) above is in this Act referred to as an "order for conditional discharge"; and the period specified in any such order is in this Act referred to as "the period of conditional discharge".

(4) [*repealed*]

(5) If (by virtue of section 13 below) a person conditionally discharged under this section is sentenced for the offence in respect of which the order for conditional discharge was made, that order shall cease to have effect.

(6) On making an order for conditional discharge, the court may, if it thinks it expedient for the purpose of the offender's reformation, allow any person who consents to do so to give security for the good behaviour of the offender.

(7) Nothing in this section shall be construed as preventing a court, on discharging an offender absolutely or conditionally in respect of any offence, from making an order for costs against the offender or imposing any disqualification on him or from making in respect of the offence an order under section 130, 143 or 148 below (compensation orders, deprivation orders and restitution orders).

(2) Purpose and effect

An offender suffers no penalty for the offence providing (in the case of a conditional **23–15** discharge) that he commits no further offence during the period specified. If he does, the court that deals with him for the later offence may also sentence him for the offence subject to the discharge.

(3) General

When making an order of conditional discharge, the court must explain to the of- **23–16** fender, in ordinary language, that, if he commits another offence during the period of the conditional discharge, he will be liable to be sentenced for the original offence: *Criminal Justice Act* 2003, s.174(1). This task does not have to be undertaken by the court; an undertaking from the defendant's counsel that they will explain the effect of the order will suffice: *Wehner* [1977] 3 All E.R. 553.

A discharge may not be combined with a fine for the same offence: *Sanck* (1990) 12 Cr.App.R.(S.) 155. A conditional discharge may be combined with an ancillary order such as a compensation order, a restitution order, an order to pay the costs of the prosecution, or a order depriving the offender of his rights in property under section 143 of the 2000 Act, or a recommendation for deportation order. A court which makes an order of discharge may exercise any power arising out of the *Road Traffic Offenders Act* 1988, ss.34, 35, 36 or 44 and must comply with any mandatory requirement of those sections: section 46 of the 1988 Act.

Magistrates' courts should not make an order of discharge in respect of an offence committed during the currency of a suspended sentence of imprisonment imposed by the Crown Court, the offender should be committed to the Crown Court so that both elements can be dealt with together: *Moore* [1995] Q.B. 353.

Powers of Criminal Courts (Sentencing) Act 2000, ss.13–15

Commission of further offence by person conditionally discharged

13.—(1) If it appears to the Crown Court, where that court has jurisdiction in accordance **23–17** with subsection (2) below, or to a justice of the peace having jurisdiction in accordance with that subsection, that a person in whose case an order for conditional discharge has been made—

(a) has been convicted by a court in Great Britain of an offence committed during the period of conditional discharge, and

(b) has been dealt with in respect of that offence,

that court or justice may, subject to subsection (3) below, issue a summons requiring that person to appear at the place and time specified in it or a warrant for his arrest.

(2) Jurisdiction for the purposes of subsection (1) above may be exercised—

    (a) if the order for conditional discharge was made by the Crown Court, by that court;

    (b) if the order was made by a magistrates' court, by a justice of the peace.

(3) A justice of the peace shall not issue a summons under this section except on information and shall not issue a warrant under this section except on information in writing and on oath.

(4) A summons or warrant issued under this section shall direct the person to whom it relates to appear or to be brought before the court by which the order for conditional discharge was made.

(5) If a person in whose case an order for conditional discharge has been made by the Crown Court is convicted by a magistrates' court of an offence committed during the period of conditional discharge, the magistrates' court—

    (a) may commit him to custody or release him on bail until he can be brought or appear before the Crown Court; and

    (b) if it does so, shall send to the Crown Court a copy of the minute or memorandum of the conviction entered in the register, signed by the designated officer by whom the register is kept.

(6) Where it is proved to the satisfaction of the court by which an order for conditional discharge was made that the person in whose case the order was made has been convicted of an offence committed during the period of conditional discharge, the court may deal with him, for the offence for which the order was made, in any way in which it could deal with him if he had just been convicted by or before that court of that offence.

(7) If a person in whose case an order for conditional discharge has been made by a magistrates' court—

    (a) is convicted before the Crown Court of an offence committed during the period of conditional discharge, or

    (b) is dealt with by the Crown Court for any such offence in respect of which he was committed for sentence to the Crown Court,

the Crown Court may deal with him, for the offence for which the order was made, in any way in which the magistrates' court could deal with him if it had just convicted him of that offence.

(8) If a person in whose case an order for conditional discharge has been made by a magistrates' court is convicted by another magistrates' court of any offence committed during the period of conditional discharge, that other court may, with the consent of the court which made the order, deal with him, for the offence for which the order was made, in any way in which the court could deal with him if it had just convicted him of that offence.

(9) Where an order for conditional discharge has been made by a magistrates' court in the case of an offender under 18 years of age in respect of an offence triable only on indictment in the case of an adult, any powers exercisable under subsection (6), (7) or (8) above by that or any other court in respect of the offender after he attains the age of 18 shall be powers to do either or both of the following—

    (a) to impose a fine not exceeding £5,000 for the offence in respect of which the order was made;

    (b) to deal with the offender for that offence in any way in which a magistrates' court could deal with him if it had just convicted him of an offence punishable with imprisonment for a term not exceeding six months.

(10) The reference in subsection (6) above to a person's having been convicted of an offence committed during the period of conditional discharge is a reference to his having been so convicted by a court in Great Britain.

Effect of discharge

23–18   **14.**—(1) Subject to subsection (2) below, a conviction of an offence for which an order is made under section 12 above discharging the offender absolutely or conditionally shall be deemed not to be a conviction for any purpose other than the purposes of the proceedings in which the order is made and of any subsequent proceedings which may be taken against the offender under section 13 above.

(2) Where the offender was aged 18 or over at the time of his conviction of the offence

in question and is subsequently sentenced (under section 13 above) for that offence, subsection (1) above shall cease to apply to the conviction.

(3) Without prejudice to subsections (1) and (2) above, the conviction of an offender who is discharged absolutely or conditionally under section 12 above shall in any event be disregarded for the purposes of any enactment or instrument which—

(a) imposes any disqualification or disability upon convicted persons; or

(b) authorises or requires the imposition of any such disqualification or disability.

(4) Subsections (1) to (3) above shall not affect—

(a) any right of an offender discharged absolutely or conditionally under section 12 above to rely on his conviction in bar of any subsequent proceedings for the same offence;

(b) the restoration of any property in consequence of the conviction of any such offender; or

(c) the operation, in relation to any such offender, of any enactment or instrument in force on 1st July 1974 which is expressed to extend to persons dealt with under section 1(1) of the *Probation of Offenders Act* 1907 as well as to convicted persons.

(5) In subsections (3) and (4) above—

"enactment" includes an enactment contained in a local Act; and

"instrument" means an instrument having effect by virtue of an Act.

(6) Subsection (1) above has effect subject to section 50(1A) of the *Criminal Appeal Act* 1968 and section 108(1A) of the *Magistrates' Courts Act* 1980 (rights of appeal); and this subsection shall not be taken to prejudice any other enactment that excludes the effect of subsection (1) or (3) above for particular purposes.

(7) Without prejudice to paragraph 1(3) of Schedule 11 to this Act (references to provisions of this Act to be construed as including references to corresponding old enactments), in this section—

(a) any reference to an order made under section 12 above discharging an offender absolutely or conditionally includes a reference to an order which was made under any provision of Part I of the *Powers of Criminal Courts Act* 1973 (whether or not reproduced in this Act) discharging the offender absolutely or conditionally;

(b) any reference to an offender who is discharged absolutely or conditionally under section 12 includes a reference to an offender who was discharged absolutely or conditionally under any such provision.

Discharge: Supplementary

15.—(1) The Secretary of State may by order direct that subsection (1) of section 12 above **23–19** shall be amended by substituting, for the maximum period specified in that subsection as originally enacted or as previously amended under this subsection, such period as may be specified in the order.

(2) Where an order for conditional discharge has been made on appeal, for the purposes of section 13 above it shall be deemed—

(a) if it was made on an appeal brought from a magistrates' court, to have been made by that magistrates' court;

(b) if it was made on an appeal brought from the Crown Court or from the criminal division of the Court of Appeal, to have been made by the Crown Court.

(3) In proceedings before the Crown Court under section 13 above, any question whether any person in whose case an order for conditional discharge has been made has been convicted of an offence committed during the period of conditional discharge shall be determined by the court and not by the verdict of a jury.

C. FINANCIAL PENALTIES

(1) Purpose and effect

A financial penalty is the sanction most often imposed in magistrates' courts. There **23–20** are three main types—the fine itself, a compensation order (which can be a sentence in itself or an ancillary order) and an order to pay the costs of the prosecution. In addition, where a court imposes a fine, it must (in most circumstances) impose a surcharge of £15, commonly called a "victims' surcharge". A fine is primarily a punishment for the current offence and a deterrent to future offending and so is designed to make sufficient impact on the spending power of the defendant to cause a degree of hardship commensurate with the seriousness of the offence.

A compensation order is primarily concerned with reparation, making financial compensation for the harm or loss caused by the offence. Where there is not enough money to pay a fine and compensation, then it is the compensation that must take priority. Where both a fine and compensation are ordered, money paid by the defendant is allocated first to paying off the compensation and then to any fines.

An order for costs reimburses, or contributes to, the costs incurred by the prosecution in bringing the case to court. Such an order takes priority over a fine but not over compensation.

The "victims' surcharge" should be imposed in each case where a court imposes a fine for an offence committed on or after April 1, 2007. It should be announced as a separate ingredient in the sentence. Where there are insufficient means to pay both the fine and the surcharge, it is the fine that must be reduced: *Criminal Justice Act* 2003, s.164(4A). Where there are insufficient means to pay both the surcharge and any compensation order, it is the surcharge that must be reduced (and may be avoided altogether): *Criminal Justice Act* 2003, s.161A(3). A surcharge will take priority over any order for costs. The surcharge will be enforceable as a fine.

(2) Assessment of amount

23–21   Fines are in the lowest tier of sanctions and there is no threshold criteria that need to be passed before a financial penalty can be imposed. However, any amount imposed must be balanced by the resources available to the defendant. In most circumstances, a fine must be capable of being paid within one year, compensation within no more than three years. Even where an offence is serious enough to justify a community sentence, a court may still impose a financial penalty instead where appropriate. This principle is re-affirmed by the Sentencing Guidelines Council in its definitive guideline, published in December 2004, which confirms that the crossing of a sentencing threshold empowers a court to impose a particular sentence but does not require it to do so.

Occasionally a court will be faced with a situation where it has the power to impose a fine much larger than normal. In such circumstances, where the defendant is a public funded body, a court may take account of how the fine is to be paid. Whilst public bodies are not immune from criminal prosecution because they have no shareholders, "if a very substantial financial penalty will inhibit the proper performance by a statutory body of the public function that it has been set up to perform that is not something to be disregarded. In the present case there is nothing to suggest that the cost of any fine can simply be recouped from customers by raising charges": *Milford Haven Port Authority* [2000] 2 Cr.App.R.(S) 423 cited with approval in *Southampton University Hospital NHS Trust* [2006] EWCA Crim 2971. Since there were no substantial aggravating factors, the court was prepared to take this factor into account and to reduce the fine from £100,000 to £40,000.

The Sentencing Advisory Panel has published proposals for a new edition of the Magistrates' Court Sentencing Guidelines which are likely to become effective during the currency of this work. This sets out two possible approaches to the assessment of financial penalties on which views are sought.

Guideline: Overarching Principles: Seriousness

E. The Sentencing Thresholds

The Threshold for Community Sentences

23–22   **1.36** Sentencers should consider all of the disposals available (within or below the threshold passed) at the time of sentence before reaching the provisional decision to make a community sentence, so that, even where the threshold for a community sentence has been passed, a financial penalty or discharge may still be an appropriate penalty.

Balancing the seriousness of the offence with the financial resources available to the offender is often a difficult task. The amount of the fine will, therefore, be determined by reference to the gravity of the offence with the court also taking into account the whole of the circumstances of the case including the financial circumstances of the offender. In *Cleminson* (1985) 7 Cr.App.R.(S.) 128, the Court of Appeal said that the correct approach was to decide the appropriate sentence for the offence and the offender and then to consider the offender's resources. The *Magistrates' Court Sentencing Guidelines* (2004) approaches the task by setting three levels of fine which relate to the weekly income of the offender. This approach is currently under review and is likely to change during the currency of this work: see *ante*, § 23–21. The sentencer must ensure that the fine imposed is such that the offender can afford to pay: *Chelmsford Crown Court, ex p. Birchall* (1989) 11 Cr.App.R.(S.) 510, DC. The sentencer may have regard to the earning capacity of the defendant as well as current savings: *Little*, unreported, April 14, 1976. A fine should not be imposed on the assumption that someone else will pay: *Charalambous* (1984) 6 Cr.App.R.(S.) 389.

The normal process followed by a court will be:
— Is a fine appropriate?
— What level of fine reflects the seriousness of the offence?
— What are the financial resources available to the offender?
— What is a suitable balance between the two?

A court is obliged to inquire into the financial circumstances of the offender before **23–23** fixing the amount of a fine: *Criminal Justice Act* 2003, s.164. The onus is on the offender to disclose evidence of his financial situation; if he does not, the court is entitled to draw whatever inferences it sees fit, and may conclude that the offender is being evasive about his financial circumstances and has the means to pay: *Higgins* (1988) 10 Cr.App.R.(S.) 144. Failure to comply with an order to disclose financial circumstances (s.162(1)) is itself an offence: s.162(3). In certain limited circumstances (when the relevant provisions are in force), where there are insufficient financial resources to pay a fine that properly reflects the serious of the offence, a court may be able to impose a community sentence where a fine would otherwise be appropriate and the threshold criterion is not passed.

There is nothing wrong in principle with the fine being paid in instalments. Where a compensation order is being paid, the instalment period may quite properly be longer than one year, provided that it is not an undue burden and too severe a punishment for the offender, having regard to the nature of the offence and the offender. There is authority that a two year period will seldom be too long and in exceptional circumstances, a three year period might prove unassailable: *Olliver and Olliver* (1989) 11 Cr.App.R.(S.) 10, CA. However, a court will always need to ensure that there is a realistic prospect of the order being paid and will be conscious of the impact on the victim also where payments received from a court extend over a lengthy period. Schedule 5, Part 3 to the *Courts Act* 2003 requires a court (when allowing time for payment on imposition) to make an attachment of earnings order or a deduction from benefit order in respect of an "existing defaulter" (as defined) unless that is impracticable and, for others, to make such an order with the consent of the person on whom the financial penalty has been imposed.

Where an offender has spent time in custody on remand before a fine is imposed, **23–24** credit should be given for that time when the amount of the fine is determined: *Warden* [1996] 2 Cr.App.R.(S.) 269, CA.

A fine cannot be imposed at the same time as a discharge (*PCC(S)A* 2000, s.12(1)) unless the offender is being sentenced for two or more offences: *Sanck* (1990) 12 Cr.App.R.(S.) 155. It will only rarely be appropriate to combine a fine with a custodial sentence in a magistrates' court. One of the effects of a custodial sentence is to reduce the employability of the offender and it is unlikely to aid the objective of reducing crime

Part IV

by having an offender released from custody with a continuing obligation to pay fines to the court. This may be different where a defendant has substantial savings or where the order seeks to reclaim the proceeds of the crime.

The *Magistrates' Court Sentencing Guidelines* (2004) (under review) suggest appropriate fines for particular circumstances, but emphasise that the guidance should not be used as a tariff and every offender's means should be individually considered. These suggestions are noted in the appropriate chapters, *ante*, in this work or can be found in the guidelines themselves.

Criminal Justice Act 2003, ss.161A, 162, 164

Surcharges

Court's duty to order payment of surcharge

23–25   **161A.**—(1) A court when dealing with a person for one or more offences must also (subject to subsections (2) and (3)) order him to pay a surcharge.

(2) Subsection (1) does not apply in such cases as may be prescribed by an order made by the Secretary of State.

(3) Where a court dealing with an offender considers—

(a) that it would be appropriate to make a compensation order, but

(b) that he has insufficient means to pay both the surcharge and appropriate compensation,

the court must reduce the surcharge accordingly (if necessary to nil).

(4) For the purposes of this section a court does not "deal with" a person if it—

(a) discharges him absolutely, or

(b) makes an order under the *Mental Health Act* 1983 in respect of him.

By virtue of the *Criminal Justice Act 2003 (Surcharge) (No. 2) Order* 2007 (SI 2007/1079), the amount of the surcharge is £15. The requirement does not apply to cases where the court is not imposing a fine—see also *ante*, § 23–20 and section 164(4A), *post*.

Powers to order statement as to offender's financial circumstances

23–26   **162.**—(1) Where an individual has been convicted of an offence, the court may, before sentencing him, make a financial circumstances order with respect to him.

(2) Where a magistrates' court has been notified in accordance with section 12(4) of the *Magistrates' Courts Act* 1980 that an individual desires to plead guilty without appearing before the court, the court may make a financial circumstances order with respect to him.

(3) In this section "a financial circumstances order" means, in relation to any individual, an order requiring him to give to the court, within such period as may be specified in the order, such a statement of his financial circumstances as the court may require.

(4) An individual who without reasonable excuse fails to comply with a financial circumstances order is liable on summary conviction to a fine not exceeding level 3 on the standard scale.

(5) If an individual, in furnishing any statement in pursuance of a financial circumstances order—

(a) makes a statement which he knows to be false in a material particular,

(b) recklessly furnishes a statement which is false in a material particular, or

(c) knowingly fails to disclose any material fact,

he is liable on summary conviction to a fine not exceeding level 4 on the standard scale.

(6) Proceedings in respect of an offence under subsection (5) may, notwithstanding anything in section 127(1) of the *Magistrates' Courts Act* 1980 (limitation of time), be commenced at any time within two years from the date of the commission of the offence or within six months from its first discovery by the prosecutor, whichever period expires the earlier.

Fixing of fines

23–27   **164.**—(1) Before fixing the amount of any fine to be imposed on an offender who is an individual, a court must inquire into his financial circumstances.

(2) The amount of any fine fixed by a court must be such as, in the opinion of the court, reflects the seriousness of the offence.

(3) In fixing the amount of any fine to be imposed on an offender (whether an individual or other person), a court must take into account the circumstances of the case including, among other things, the financial circumstances of the offender so far as they are known, or appear, to the court.

(4) Subsection (3) applies whether taking into account the financial circumstances of the offender has the effect of increasing or reducing the amount of the fine.

(4A) In applying subsection (3), a court must not reduce the amount of a fine on account of any surcharge it orders the offender to pay under section 161A, except to the extent that he has insufficient means to pay both.

(5) Where—

    (a) an offender has been convicted in his absence in pursuance of section 11 or 12 of the *Magistrates' Courts Act* 1980 (non-appearance of accused), or

    (b) an offender—

        (i) has failed to furnish a statement of his financial circumstances in response to a request which is an official request for the purposes of section 20A of the *Criminal Justice Act* 1991 (offence of making false statement as to financial circumstances),

        (ii) has failed to comply with an order under section 162(1), or

        (iii) has otherwise failed to co-operate with the court in its inquiry into his financial circumstances,

and the court considers that it has insufficient information to make a proper determination of the financial circumstances of the offender, it may make such determination as it thinks fit.

Criminal Justice Act 1982, s.37

The standard scale of fines for summary offences

37.—(1) There shall be a standard scale of fines for summary offences, which shall be known **23–28** as "the standard scale".

(2) The standard scale is shown below—

Level on the scale	Amount of fine
1	£200
2	£500
3	£1,000
4	£2,500
5	£5,000.

(3) Where any enactment (whether contained in an Act passed before or after this Act) provides—

    (a) that a person convicted of a summary offence shall be liable on conviction to a fine or a maximum fine by reference to a specified level on the standard scale; or

    (b) confers power by subordinate instrument to make a person liable on conviction of a summary offence (whether or not created by the instrument) to a fine or maximum fine by reference to a specified level on the standard scale,

it is to be construed as referring to the standard scale for which this section provides as that standard scale has effect from time to time by virtue either of this section or of an order under section 143 of the *Magistrates' Courts Act* 1980.

Magistrates' Courts Act 1980, s.32

Penalties on summary conviction for offences triable either way

32.—(1) On summary conviction of any of the offences triable either way listed in Schedule 1 **23–29** to this Act a person shall be liable to imprisonment for a term not exceeding 6 months (increased to 12 months on the bringing into force of *Criminal Justice Act* 2003, s.282) or to a fine not exceeding the prescribed sum or both, except that—

    (a) a magistrates' court shall not have power to impose imprisonment for an offence so listed if the Crown Court would not have that power in the case of an adult convicted of it on indictment;

Part IV

(b) on summary conviction of an offence consisting in the incitement to commit an offence triable either way a person shall not be liable to any greater penalty than he would be liable to on summary conviction of the last-mentioned offence: and

(2) For any offence triable either way which is not listed in Schedule 1 to this Act, being an offence under a relevant enactment, the maximum fine which may be imposed on summary conviction shall be virtue of this subsection be the prescribed sum unless the offence is one for which by virtue of an enactment other than this subsection a larger fine may be imposed on summary conviction.

(3) Where, by virtue of any relevant enactment, a person summarily convicted of an offence triable either way would, apart from this section, be liable to a maximum fine of one amount in the case of a first conviction and of a different amount in the case of a second or subsequent conviction, subsection (2) above shall apply irrespective of whether the conviction is a first, second or subsequent one.

(4) Subsection (2) above shall not affect so much of any enactment as (in whatever words) makes a person liable on summary conviction to a fine not exceeding a specified amount for each day on which a continuing offence is continued after conviction or the occurrence of any other specified event.

(5) Subsection (2) above shall not apply on summary conviction of any of the following offences—

(a) offences under section 5(2) of the *Misuse of Drugs Act* 1971 (having possession of a controlled drug) where the controlled drug in relation to which the offence was committed was a Class B or Class C drug;

(b) offences under the following provisions of that Act, where the controlled drug in relation to which the offence was committed was a Class C drug, namely—

(i) section 4(2) (production, or being concerned in the production, of a controlled drug);

(ii) section 4(3) (supplying or offering a controlled drug or being concerned in the doing of either activity by another);

(iii) section 5(3) (having possession of a controlled drug with intent to supply it to another);

(iv) section 8 (being the occupier, or concerned in the management, of premises and permitting or suffering certain activities to take place there);

(v) section 12(6) (contravention of direction prohibiting practitioner etc. from possessing, supplying etc. controlled drugs); or

(vi) section 13(3) (contravention of direction prohibiting practitioner etc. from prescribing, supplying etc. controlled drugs).

(6) Where, as regards any offence triable either way, there is under any enactment (however framed or worded) a power by subordinate instrument to restrict the amount of the fine which on summary conviction can be imposed in respect of that offence—

(a) subsection (2) above shall not affect that power or override any restriction imposed in the exercise of that power; and

(b) the amount to which that fine may be restricted in the exercise of that power shall be any amount less than the maximum fine which could be imposed on summary conviction in respect of the offence apart from any restriction so imposed.

(8) In subsection (5) above "controlled drug", "Class B drug" and "Class C drug" have the same meaning as in the *Misuse of Drugs Act* 1971.

(9) In this section—

"fine" includes a pecuniary penalty but does not include a pecuniary forfeiture or pecuniary compensation;

"the prescribed sum" means £5,000 or such sum as is for the time being substituted in this definition by an order in force under section 143(1) below;

"relevant enactment" means an enactment contained in the *Criminal Law Act* 1977 or in any Act passed before, or in the same Session as, that Act.

Magistrates' Courts Act 1980, ss.36, 75, 82(1), (6)

Restriction on fines in respect of young persons

23–30   **36.**—(1) Where a person under 18 years of age is found guilty by a magistrates' court of an offence for which, apart from this section, the court would have power to impose a fine of an amount exceeding £1,000, the amount of any fine imposed by the court shall not exceed £1,000.

(2) In relation to a person under the age of 14 subsection (1) above shall have effect as if for the words "£1,000", in both the places where they occur, there were substituted the words "£250"

Power to dispense with immediate payment

75.—(1) A magistrates' court by whose conviction or order a sum is adjudged to be paid may, **23–31** instead of requiring immediate payment, allow time for payment, or order payment by instalments.

(2) Where a magistrates' court has allowed time for payment, the court may, on application by or on behalf of the person liable to make the payment, allow further time or order payment by instalments.

(2A) An order under this section that a lump sum required to be paid under a maintenance order shall be paid by instalments (a "maintenance instalments order") shall be treated for the purposes of sections 59, 59B and 60 above as a maintenance order.

(2B) Subsections (5) and (7) of section 59 above (including those subsections as they apply for the purposes of section 60 above) shall have effect in relation to a maintenance instalments order—

(a) as if in subsection (5), paragraph (c) and the word "and" immediately preceding it were omitted; and

(b) as if in subsection (7)—

(i) the reference to the maintenance order were a reference to the maintenance order in respect of which the maintenance instalments order in question is made;

(ii) for the words "the person who applied for the maintenance order" there were substituted "the debtor".

(2C) Section 60 above shall have effect in relation to a maintenance instalments order as if in subsection (7), paragraph (c) and the word "and" immediately preceding it were omitted.

(3) Where a court has ordered payment by instalments and default is made in the payment of any one instalment, proceedings may be taken as if the default had been made in the payment of all the instalments then unpaid.

Restriction on power to impose imprisonment for default

82.—(1) A magistrates' court shall not on the occasion of convicting an offender of an offence **23–32** issue a warrant of commitment for a default in paying any sum adjudged to be paid by the conviction unless—

(a) in the case of an offence punishable with imprisonment, he appears to the court to have sufficient means to pay the sum forthwith;

(b) it appears to the court that he is unlikely to remain long enough at a place of abode in the United Kingdom to enable payment of the sum to be enforced by other methods; or

(c) on the occasion of that conviction the court sentences him to immediate imprisonment, youth custody or detention in a detention centre for that or another offence or he is already serving a sentence of custody for life, or a term of imprisonment, youth custody, detention under section 9 of the *Criminal Justice Act* 1982 or detention in a detention centre.

(6) Where a magistrates' court issues a warrant of commitment on the ground that one of the conditions mentioned in subsection (1) ... above is satisfied, it shall state that fact, specifying the ground, in the warrant.

Magistrates' Courts Act 1980, ss.88, 89

Supervision pending payment

88.—(1) Where any person is adjudged to pay a sum by a summary conviction and the **23–33** convicting court does not commit him to prison forthwith in default of payment, the court may, either on the occasion of the conviction or on a subsequent occasion, order him to be placed under the supervision of such person as the court may from time to time appoint.

(2) An order placing a person under supervision in respect of any sum shall remain in force so long as he remains liable to pay the sum or any part of it unless the order ceases to have effect or is discharged under subsection (3) below.

(3) An order under this section shall cease to have effect on the making of a transfer of fine order under section 89 below with respect to the sum adjudged to be paid and may be discharged by the court that made it, without prejudice in either case to the making of a new order.

(4) Where a person under 21 years old has been adjudged to pay a sum by a summary conviction and the convicting court does not commit him to detention under section 108 of the *Powers of Criminal Courts (Sentencing) Act* 2000 forthwith in default of payment, the court shall not commit him to such detention in default of payment of the sum, or for want of sufficient distress to satisfy the sum, unless he has been placed under supervision in respect of the sum or the court is satisfied that it is undesirable or impracticable to place him under supervision.

(5) Where a court, being satisfied as aforesaid, commits a person under 21 years old to such detention without an order under this section having been made, the court shall state the grounds on which it is so satisfied in the warrant of commitment.

(6) Where an order placing a person under supervision with respect to a sum is in force, a magistrates' court shall not commit him to prison in default of payment of the sum, or for want of sufficient distress to satisfy the sum, unless the court has before committing him taken such steps as may be reasonably practicable to obtain from the person appointed for his supervision an oral or written report on the offender's conduct and means and has considered any report so obtained, in addition, in a case where an inquiry is required by section 82 above, to that inquiry.

Transfer of fine order

23–34   **89.**—(1) Where a magistrates' court has, or is treated by any enactment as having, adjudged a person by a conviction to pay a sum and it appears to the court that the person is residing in any petty sessions area other than that for which the court acted, the court may make a transfer of fine order, that is to say, an order making payment enforceable in the petty sessions area in which it appears to the court that he is residing; and that area shall be specified in the order.

(2) As from the date on which a transfer of fine order is made with respect to any sum, all functions under this Part of this Act relating to that sum which, if no such order had been made, would have been exercisable by the court which made the order, or the justices' chief executive for that court, shall be exercisable by a court acting for the petty sessions area specified in the order, or the justices' chief executive for that court, as the case may be, and not otherwise.

(2A) The functions of the court to which subsection (2) above relates shall be deemed to include the court's power to apply to the Secretary of State under any regulations made by him under section 24(1)(a) of the *Criminal Justice Act* 1991 (power to deduct fines etc. from income support).

(3) Where it appears to a court by which functions in relation to any sum are for the time being exercisable by virtue of a transfer of fine order that the person liable to pay the sum is residing in a petty sessions area other than that for which the court is acting, the court may make a further transfer of fine order with respect to that sum.

(4) In this section and sections 90 and 91 below, references to this Part of this Act do not include references to section 81(1) above.

D. Power to Order Periodical Payments

Magistrates' Courts Act 1980, s.75

Power to dispense with immediate payment

23–35   **75.**—(1) A magistrates' court by whose conviction or order a sum is adjudged to be paid may, instead of requiring immediate payment, allow time for payment, or order payment by instalments.

(2) Where a magistrates' court has allowed time for payment, the court may, on application by or on behalf of the person liable to make the payment, allow further time or order payment by instalments.

(3) Where a court has ordered payment by instalments and default is made in the payment of any one instalment, proceedings may be taken as if the default had been made in the payment of all the instalments then unpaid.

E. Power to Order Appearance Before the Court if Any Part of the Sum Remains Unpaid

Magistrates' Courts Act 1980, s.86

Power of magistrates' court to fix day for appearance of offender at means inquiry etc.

86.—(1) A magistrates' court which has exercised in relation to a sum adjudged to be paid by **23–36** a conviction either of the powers conferred by section 75(1) above shall have power, either then or later, to fix a day on which, if the relevant condition is satisfied, the offender must appear in person before the court for either or both of the following purposes, namely—

(a) to enable an inquiry into his means to be made under section 82 above;

(b) to enable a hearing required by subsection (5) of the said section 82 to be held.

(1A) Where the power which the court has exercised is the power to allow time for payment of a sum ("the adjudged sum"), the relevant condition is satisfied if any part of that sum remains unpaid on the day fixed by the court.

(1B) Where the power which the court has exercised is the power to order payment by instalments, the relevant condition is satisfied if an instalment which has fallen due remains unpaid on the day fixed by the court.

(2) Except as provided in subsection (3) below, the power to fix a day under this section shall be exercisable only in the presence of the offender.

(3) Where a day has been fixed under this section, the court may fix a later day in subsection for the day previously fixed, and may do so—

(a) when composed of a single justice; and

(b) whether the offender is present or not.

(4) Subject to subsection (5) below, if on the day fixed under this section—

(a) the relevant condition is satisfied; and

(b) the offender fails to appear in person before the court,

the court may issue a warrant to arrest him and bring him before the court; and subsection (3) of section 83 above shall apply in relation to a warrant issued under this section.

(5) Where under subsection (3) above a later day has in the absence of the offender been fixed in substitution for a day previously fixed under this section, the court shall not issue a warrant under this section unless it is proved to the satisfaction of the court, on oath or in such other manner as may be prescribed, that notice in writing of the substituted day was served on the offender not less than what appears to the court to be a reasonable time before that day.

II. COMMUNITY ORDERS

A. Community Sentences

(1) General

In relation to adults, a community sentence is a sentence which consists of a com- **23–37** munity order. A community order consists of one or more "requirements" as provided for by the Act. It is not clear why we need both "community sentence" and "community order" though it is probably simply a legacy from the previous legislation although the justification has disappeared.

A community order can consist of any number of the requirements set out in sections **23–38** 177 and 199–214 of the *Criminal Justice Act* 2003. An order may be supported by electronic monitoring: section 177(3) and (4) and section 215. Once the threshold is passed (section 148(1)), whilst a court is able to choose from any (or all!) of these requirements, it must ensure that the restriction on liberty is commensurate with the seriousness of the offence, that the requirements are suitable for the offender and that interlocking requirements are compatible with each other: sections 148(2) and 177(6). As far as practicable, the requirements should not interfere with the religious beliefs, employment or education of the offender: section 217. There are some requirements which can only be made where the court has been informed that a suitable programme etc. is

Part IV

available for the offender; and some where a court must await confirmation that there are suitable facilities in the area before such requirements can be imposed: section 218. Whenever a community order is made, the offender must keep in touch with the "responsible officer" (see *post*) in the way prescribed by that officer and must notify any change of address: section 220(1). Although not a "requirement", this obligation is enforceable as if it were a requirement (see *post*, § 23–47: section 220(2). It should be noted that it is also possible to make a "supervision requirement" as a requirement of the order (see *post*, § 23–90): section 213. By virtue of section 178 of the *Criminal Justice Act* 2003, there is an order making power enabling the Secretary of State to enable a court that makes a Community Order to provide for that order to be reviewed periodically. Such an order has been made to allow periodic reviews at the Liverpool Community Justice Centre and at the Salford Magistrates' Court both of which are piloting different approaches to community justice arising from consideration of the Red Hook project in the USA. This pilot has now been extended to cover 10 other pilot courts.

(2) Guidelines

23–39　　In addition to the statutory provisions, a definitive guideline issued by the Sentencing Guidelines Council in December 2004 (*Overarching Principles: Seriousness*) sets out the approach to matching the seriousness of the offence and the characteristics of the offender to the order made. In a further guideline (*New Sentences: Criminal Justice Act 2003*), paras. 1.1.9—1.1.14 emphasise the need for a rigorous approach to determining both the need for an order and the content of that order. It is noted that there is evidence that, where an offender has a low risk of re-offending, an inappropriate order can actually increase the chances of re-offending rather than reduce them. It is also noted that the consequences of breach of a community sentence may well be a custodial sentence and great care needs to be taken in ensuring that every requirement (and combination of requirements) properly matches the statutory obligation both to balance the restriction on liberty with the seriousness of the offence and to make the requirement(s) the most suitable for the offender: *Criminal Justice Act* 2003, section 148. The court must always have clearly in its mind the objectives of sentencing that it is seeking to achieve.

Guideline: New Sentences: Criminal Justice Act 2003

Section 1—Community Sentences & Deferred Sentences
　　　　　Part 1: Community Sentences

B. Imposing a Community Sentence—The Approach

23–40　　**1.1.9** On pages 8 and 9 of the Seriousness guideline the two thresholds for the imposition of a community sentence are considered. Sentencers must consider all of the disposals available (within or below the threshold passed) at the time of sentence, and reject them before reaching the provisional decision to make a community sentence, so that even where the threshold for a community sentence has been passed a financial penalty or discharge may still be an appropriate penalty. Where an offender has a low risk of reoffending, particular care needs to be taken in the light of evidence that indicates that there are circumstances where inappropriate intervention can increase the risk of re-offending rather than decrease it. In addition, recent improvements in enforcement of financial penalties make them a more viable sentence in a wider range of cases.

　　　　1.1.10 Where an offender is being sentenced for a non-imprisonable offence or offences, great care will be needed in assessing whether a community sentence is appropriate since failure to comply could result in a custodial sentence.

　　　　1.1.11 Having decided (in consultation with the Probation Service where appropriate) that a community sentence is justified, the court must decide which requirements should be included in the community order. The requirements or orders imposed will have the effect of restricting the offender's liberty, whilst providing punishment in the community, rehabilitation for the offender, and/or ensuring that the offender engages in reparative activities.

> **The key issues arising are:**
>   (i) **which requirements to impose;**
>   (ii) **how to make allowance for time spent on remand; and**
>   (iii) **how to deal with breaches.**

(i) Requirements

1.1.12 When deciding which requirements to include, the court must be satisfied on three matters–

   (i) that the **restriction on liberty is commensurate with the seriousness** of the offence(s);

   (ii) that the **requirements are the most suitable** for the offender; and

   (iii) that, where there are two or more requirements included, they are **compatible with each other**.

1.1.13 Sentencers should have the possibility of breach firmly in mind when passing sentence for the original offence. If a court is to reflect the seriousness of an offence, there is little value in setting requirements as part of a community sentence that are not demanding enough for an offender. On the other hand, there is equally little value in imposing requirements that would "set an offender up to fail" and almost inevitably lead to sanctions for a breach.

> **In community sentences, the guiding principles are proportionality and suitability. Once a court has decided that the offence has crossed the community sentence threshold and that a community sentence is justified, the <u>initial</u> factor in defining which requirements to include in a community sentence should be the seriousness of the offence committed.**

1.1.14 This means that "seriousness" is an important factor in deciding whether the Court chooses the low, medium or high range (see below) but, having taken that decision, selection of the content of the order within the range will be determined by a much wider range of factors.

> • **Sentencing ranges must remain flexible enough to take account of the suitability of the offender, his or her ability to comply with particular requirements and their availability in the local area.**
> • **The justification for imposing a community sentence in response to persistent petty offending is the persistence of the offending behaviour rather than the seriousness of the offences being committed. The requirements imposed should ensure that the restriction on liberty is proportionate to the seriousness of the offending, to reflect the fact that the offences, of themselves, are not sufficiently serious to merit a community sentence.**

Once made, an order will name the local justice area in which the offender will reside (section 216) and a copy of that order must be given to those persons set out in section 219.

Criminal Justice Act 2003, ss.147–8, 177, 216, 217, 219, 220

General restrictions on community sentences

Meaning of "community sentence" etc.
   147.—(1) In this Part "community sentence" means a sentence which consists of or includes— **23–41**
       (a) a community order (as defined by section 177), or
       (b) one or more youth community orders.

Restrictions on imposing community sentences
   148.—(1) A court must not pass a community sentence on an offender unless it is of the **23–42** opinion that the offence, or the combination of the offence and one or more offences associated with it, was serious enough to warrant such a sentence.

(2) Where a court passes a community sentence which consists of or includes a community order—

   (a) the particular requirement or requirements forming part of the community order must be such as, in the opinion of the court, is, or taken together are, the most suitable for the offender, and

   (b) the restrictions on liberty imposed by the order must be such as in the opinion of the court are commensurate with the seriousness of the offence, or the combination of the offence and one or more offences associated with it.

(3) Where a court passes a community sentence which consists of or includes one or more youth community orders—

   (a) the particular order or orders forming part of the sentence must be such as, in the opinion of the court, is, or taken together are, the most suitable for the offender, and

   (b) the restrictions on liberty imposed by the order or orders must be such as in the opinion of the court are commensurate with the seriousness of the offence, or the combination of the offence and one or more offences associated with it.

(4) Subsections (1) and (2)(b) have effect subject to section 151(2).

Chapter 2

Community Orders: Offenders Aged 16 or Over

Community orders

23–43   **177.**—(1) Where a person aged 16 or over (**note this provision does not come into force for those aged 16 or 17 until [at least] April 4, 2009**) is convicted of an offence, the court by or before which he is convicted may make an order (in this Part referred to as a "community order") imposing on him any one or more of the following requirements—

   (a) an unpaid work requirement (as defined by section 199),
   (b) an activity requirement (as defined by section 201),
   (c) a programme requirement (as defined by section 202),
   (d) a prohibited activity requirement (as defined by section 203),
   (e) a curfew requirement (as defined by section 204),
   (f) an exclusion requirement (as defined by section 205),
   (g) a residence requirement (as defined by section 206),
   (h) a mental health treatment requirement (as defined by section 207),
   (i) a drug rehabilitation requirement (as defined by section 209),
   (j) an alcohol treatment requirement (as defined by section 212),
   (k) a supervision requirement (as defined by section 213), and
   (l) in a case where the offender is aged under 25, an attendance centre requirement (as defined by section 214).

(2) Subsection (1) has effect subject to sections 150 and 218 and to the following provisions of Chapter 4 relating to particular requirements—

   (a) section 199(3) (unpaid work requirement),
   (b) section 201(3) and (4) (activity requirement),
   (c) section 202(4) and (5) (programme requirement),
   (d) section 203(2) (prohibited activity requirement),
   (e) section 207(3) (mental health treatment requirement),
   (f) section 209(2) (drug rehabilitation requirement), and
   (g) section 212(2) and (3) (alcohol treatment requirement).

(3) Where the court makes a community order imposing a curfew requirement or an exclusion requirement, the court must also impose an electronic monitoring requirement (as defined by section 215) unless—

   (a) it is prevented from doing so by section 215(2) or 218(4), or
   (b) in the particular circumstances of the case, it considers it inappropriate to do so.

(4) Where the court makes a community order imposing an unpaid work requirement, an activity requirement, a programme requirement, a prohibited activity requirement, a residence requirement, a mental health treatment requirement, a drug rehabilitation

requirement, an alcohol treatment requirement, a supervision requirement or an attendance centre requirement, the court may also impose an electronic monitoring requirement unless prevented from doing so by section 215(2) or 218(4).

(5) A community order must specify a date, not more than three years after the date of the order, by which all the requirements in it must have been complied with; and a community order which imposes two or more different requirements falling within subsection (1) may also specify an earlier date or dates in relation to compliance with any one or more of them.

(6) Before making a community order imposing two or more different requirements falling within subsection (1), the court must consider whether, in the circumstances of the case, the requirements are compatible with each other.

Provisions applying to relevant orders generally

Petty sessions area to be specified in relevant order
216.—(1) A community order or suspended sentence order must specify the petty sessions **23–44** area in which the offender resides or will reside.

(2) A custody plus order or an intermittent custody order must specify the petty sessions area in which the offender will reside—
- (a) in the case of a custody plus order, during the licence period as defined by section 181(3)(b), or
- (b) in the case of an intermittent custody order, during the licence periods as defined by section 183(3).

Requirement to avoid conflict with religious beliefs, etc
217.—(1) The court must ensure, as far as practicable, that any requirement imposed by a **23–45** relevant order is such as to avoid—
- (a) any conflict with the offender's religious beliefs or with the requirements of any other relevant order to which he may be subject; and
- (b) any interference with the times, if any, at which he normally works or attends school or any other educational establishment.

(2) The responsible officer in relation to an offender to whom a relevant order relates must ensure, as far as practicable, that any instruction given or requirement imposed by him in pursuance of the order is such as to avoid the conflict or interference mentioned in subsection (1).

(3) The Secretary of State may by order provide that subsection (1) or (2) is to have effect with such additional restrictions as may be specified in the order.

Provision of copies of relevant orders
219.—(1) The court by which any relevant order is made must forthwith provide copies of **23–46** the order—
- (a) to the offender,
- (b) if the offender is aged 18 or over, to an officer of a local probation board assigned to the court,
- (c) if the offender is aged 16 or 17, to an officer of a local probation board assigned to the court or to a member of a youth offending team assigned to the court, and
- (d) where the order specifies a petty sessions area for which the court making the order does not act, to the local probation board acting for that area.

(2) Where a relevant order imposes any requirement specified in the first column of Schedule 14, the court by which the order is made must also forthwith provide the person specified in relation to that requirement in the second column of that Schedule with a copy of so much of the order as relates to that requirement.

(3) Where a relevant order specifies a petty sessions area for which the court making the order does not act, the court making the order must provide to the magistrates' court acting for that area—
- (a) a copy of the order, and
- (b) such documents and information relating to the case as it considers likely to be of assistance to a court acting for that area in the exercise of its functions in relation to the order.

Duty of offender to keep in touch with responsible officer

23–47   **220.**—(1) An offender in respect of whom a community order or a suspended sentence order is in force—

    (a) must keep in touch with the responsible officer in accordance with such instructions as he may from time to time be given by that officer, and

    (b) must notify him of any change of address.

(2) The obligation imposed by subsection (1) is enforceable as if it were a requirement imposed by the order.

23–48   In considering whether the threshold has been crossed, the court may take into account both the offence itself and any other offence "associated with it".

23–49   The fact that the threshold has been crossed does not require the court to pass a community sentence. That decision simply sets an upper limit on the most severe type of sentence that can be imposed. Prior to deciding on the sentence to be imposed, the court will:

— first decide whether the threshold has been crossed (section 148(1)) and

— then decide which order is most suitable for the offender (section 148(2)(a)) whilst

— ensuring that the restrictions on liberty that result from the imposition of the order(s) are commensurate with the seriousness of the offence(s) (section 148(2)(b)).

23–50   Issued under the previous sentencing framework, the *Magistrates' Courts Sentencing Guidelines* (2004) (under review) provide that a community penalty has three principal elements: restriction of liberty, reparation and the prevention of re-offending.

It is in making a community sentence that the conflict is often most apparent between the needs of the offender in order to reduce the likelihood of re-offending and the need to maintain the balance between the seriousness of the offence and the severity of the sanction. This can be seen in the shift away from financial penalties towards a community sentence. It may also be a factor in the increased use of custody since a person who has offended again after (or during) such a sentence is more likely to receive a custodial sentence.

23–51   Prior to making a community sentence, a court will consider what information it has and what else is needed. Information about the offence will assist the court particularly in relation to the threshold of seriousness and the extent to which any order(s) need to restrict the liberty of the defendant. Information about the offender will particularly assist in relation to deciding the most suitable order for the offender.

23–52   Given the open ended nature of the sentence, there is clear scope for widely differing applications. The resolution of this has been the Guideline issued by the Sentencing Guidelines Council on December 16, 2004 after extensive consultation: *New Sentences: Criminal Justice Act 2003*. As well as providing the basis of training for the judiciary, justices' clerks and legal advisers, the approach adopted by the Council has been imported into the guidance issued to probation officers. The Guideline emphasises the primacy of the assessment of "seriousness" of the offence as the starting point for sentence. Setting the scene by emphasising the importance of clarity of thought in the process of deciding what requirements to include in order to ensure both that the order properly reflects that seriousness and also realistically attempts to achieve the goals that the court considers important, the Guideline establishes three levels of seriousness. These provide a framework within which a court can consistently deal with the need to reflect the seriousness of the offence whilst allowing the flexibility to meet the other statutory obligations of suitability and compatibility.

Guideline: New Sentences: Criminal Justice Act 2003

Section 1—Community Sentences & Deferred Sentences
    Part 1: Community Sentences

B. IMPOSING A COMMUNITY SENTENCE—THE APPROACH

(i) Requirements

(b) Ranges of Sentence Within the Community Sentence Band

1.1.18 To enable the court to benefit from the flexibility that community sentences provide **23–53** and also to meet its statutory obligations, any structure governing the use of community requirements must allow the courts to choose the most appropriate sentence for each individual offender.

1.1.19 Sentencers have a statutory obligation to pass sentences that are commensurate with the seriousness of an offence. However, within the range of sentence justified by the seriousness of the offence(s), courts will quite properly consider those factors that heighten the risk of the offender committing further offences or causing further harm with a view to lessening that risk. The extent to which requirements are imposed must be capable of being varied to ensure that the restriction on liberty is commensurate with the seriousness of the offence.

1.1.20 The Council recognises that it would be helpful for sentencers to have a framework to help them decide on the most appropriate use of the new community sentence. While there is no single guiding principle, the seriousness of the offence that has been committed is an important factor. Three sentencing ranges (low, medium and high) within the community sentence band can be identified. It is not possible to position particular types of offence at firm points within the three ranges because the seriousness level of an offence is largely dependent upon the culpability of the offender and this is uniquely variable. The difficulty is particularly acute in relation to the medium range where it is clear that requirements will need to be tailored across a relatively wide range of offending behaviour.

1.1.21 In general terms, the lowest range of community sentence would be for those offenders whose offence was relatively minor within the community sentence band and would include persistent petty offenders whose offences only merit a community sentence by virtue of failing to respond to the previous imposition of fines. Such offenders would merit a "light touch" approach, for example, normally a single requirement such as a short period of unpaid work, or a curfew, or a prohibited activity requirement or an exclusion requirement (where the circumstances of the case mean that this would be an appropriate disposal without electronic monitoring).

1.1.22 The top range would be for those offenders who have only just fallen short of a custodial sentence and for those who have passed the threshold but for whom a community sentence is deemed appropriate.

1.1.23 In all three ranges there must be sufficient flexibility to allow the sentence to be varied to take account of the suitability of particular requirements for the individual offender and whether a particular requirement or package of requirements might be more effective at reducing any identified risk of re-offending. It will fall to the sentencer to ensure that the sentence strikes the right balance between proportionality and suitability.

There should be three sentencing ranges (low, medium and high) within the community sentence band based upon seriousness.

It is not intended that an offender necessarily progress from one range to the next on each sentencing occasion. The decision as to the appropriate range each time is based upon the seriousness of the new offence(s).

The decision on the nature and severity of the requirements to be included in a community sentence should be guided by:

(i)   **the assessment of offence seriousness (LOW, MEDIUM OR HIGH);**

(ii)   **the purpose(s) of sentencing the court wishes to achieve;**

(iii)   **the risk of re-offending;**

(iv)   **the ability of the offender to comply, and**

(v)   **the availability of requirements in the local area.**

The resulting restriction on liberty must be a proportionate response to the offence that was committed.

1.1.24 Below we set out a non-exhaustive description of examples of requirements that might be appropriate in the three sentencing ranges. These examples focus on punishment in

Part IV

the community, although it is recognised that not all packages will necessarily need to include a punitive requirement. There will clearly be other requirements of a rehabilitative nature, such as a treatment requirement or an accredited programme, which may be appropriate depending on the specific needs of the offender and assessment of suitability. Given the intensity of such interventions, it is expected that these would normally only be appropriate at medium and high levels of seriousness, and where assessed as having a medium or high risk of re-offending. In addition, when passing sentence in any one of the three ranges, the court should consider whether a rehabilitative intervention such as a programme requirement, or a restorative justice intervention might be suitable as an additional or alternative part of the sentence.

Low

1.1.25 For offences only just crossing the community sentence threshold (such as persistent petty offending, some public order offences, some thefts from shops, or interference with a motor vehicle, where the seriousness of the offence or the nature of the offender's record means that a discharge or fine is inappropriate).

1.1.26 Suitable requirements might include:

- 40 to 80 hours of unpaid work or
- a curfew requirement within the lowest range (*e.g.* up to 12 hours per day for a few weeks) or
- an exclusion requirement (where the circumstances of the case mean that this would be an appropriate disposal without electronic monitoring) lasting a few months or
- a prohibited activity requirement or
- an attendance centre requirement (where available).

1.1.27 Since the restriction on liberty must be commensurate with the seriousness of the offence, particular care needs to be taken with this band to ensure that this obligation is complied with. In most cases, only one requirement will be appropriate and the length may be curtailed if additional requirements are necessary.

Medium

1.1.28 For offences that obviously fall within the community sentence band such as handling stolen goods worth less than £1000 acquired for resale or somewhat more valuable goods acquired for the handler's own use, some cases of burglary in commercial premises, some cases of taking a motor vehicle without consent, or some cases of obtaining property by deception.

1.1.29 Suitable requirements might include:

- a greater number (*e.g.* 80 to 150) of hours of unpaid work or
- an activity requirement in the middle range (20 to 30 days) or
- a curfew requirement within the middle range (*e.g.* up to 12 hours for 2–3 months) or
- an exclusion requirement lasting in the region of 6 months or
- a prohibited activity requirement.

1.1.30 Since the restriction on liberty must be commensurate with the seriousness of the offence, particular care needs to be taken with this band to ensure that this obligation is complied with.

High

1.1.31 For offences that only just fall below the custody threshold or where the custody threshold is crossed but a community sentence is more appropriate in all the circumstances, for example some cases displaying the features of a standard domestic burglary committed by a first-time offender.

1.1.32 More intensive sentences which combine two or more requirements may be appropriate at this level. Suitable requirements might include an unpaid work order of between 150 and 300 hours; an activity requirement up to the maximum 60 days; an exclusion order lasting in the region of 12 months; a curfew requirement of up to 12 hours a day for 4–6 months.

(3) Implementation of the order

Responsible officer

23–54   In terms of the implementation of the order, the key person is designated as the "responsible officer": *Criminal Justice Act* 2003, s.197. This person will vary with the nature of the requirement imposed. The duty imposed on that officer is also set out: *Criminal Justice Act* 2003, s.198.

Criminal Justice Act 2003, ss.197–198

Meaning of "the responsible officer"

197.—(1) For the purposes of this Part, "the responsible officer", in relation to an offender to whom a relevant order relates, means— **23–55**

    (a) in a case where the order—

        (i) imposes a curfew requirement or an exclusion requirement but no other requirement mentioned in section 177(1) or, as the case requires, section 182(1) or 190(1), and

        (ii) imposes an electronic monitoring requirement, the person who under section 215(3) is responsible for the electronic monitoring required by the order;

    (b) in a case where the offender is aged 18 or over and the only requirement imposed by the order is an attendance centre requirement, the officer in charge of the attendance centre in question;

    (c) in any other case, the qualifying officer who, as respects the offender, is for the time being responsible for discharging the functions conferred by this Part on the responsible officer.

(2) The following are qualifying officers for the purposes of subsection (1)(c)—

    (a) in a case where the offender is aged under 18 at the time when the relevant order is made, an officer of a local probation board appointed for or assigned to the petty sessions area for the time being specified in the order or a member of a youth offending team established by a local authority for the time being specified in the order;

    (b) in any other case, an officer of a local probation board appointed for or assigned to the petty sessions area for the time being specified in the order.

(3) The Secretary of State may by order—

    (a) amend subsections (1) and (2), and

    (b) make any other amendments of this Part that appear to him to be necessary or expedient in consequence of any amendment made by virtue of paragraph (a).

(4) An order under subsection (3) may, in particular, provide for the court to determine which of two or more descriptions of "responsible officer" is to apply in relation to any relevant order.

Duties of responsible officer

198.—(1) Where a relevant order has effect, it is the duty of the responsible officer— **23–56**

    (a) to make any arrangements that are necessary in connection with the requirements imposed by the order,

    (b) to promote the offender's compliance with those requirements, and

    (c) where appropriate, to take steps to enforce those requirements.

(2) In this section "responsible officer" does not include a person falling within section 197(1)(a).

A more restricted duty falls on those responsible for curfew or exclusion require- **23–57** ments or for electronic monitoring than on those responsible for other requirements. In essence, this is because those obligations will be contracted out whilst the other requirements are most likely to remain under the responsibility of the National Offender Management Service.

B. Electronic Monitoring Requirement

The availability of electronic monitoring has become a well used option that has **23–58** enabled a court to ensure that its order is being obeyed and, consequentially, to be more sparing in the use of custodial sentences. In relation to some of the requirements being imposed, the imposition of electronic monitoring is obligatory. In other circumstances, the court may have the power to make such an order. In its Guideline, *New Sentences:*

Criminal Justice Act 2003, the Sentencing Guidelines Council (at para. 1.1.33) empha-sises this "primary purpose of promoting and monitoring compliance with other requirements" imposed by the court and that this most arises in situations where "the punishment of the offender and/or the need to safeguard the public and prevent re-offending are the most important concerns".

Criminal Justice Act 2003, ss.177, 215

Community orders

23–59   **177.**—(3) Where the court makes a community order imposing a curfew requirement or an exclusion requirement, the court must also impose an electronic monitoring requirement (as defined by section 215) unless—

       (a) it is prevented from doing so by section 215(2) or 218(4), or

       (b) in the particular circumstances of the case, it considers it inappropriate to do so.

     (4) Where the court makes a community order imposing an unpaid work requirement, an activity requirement, a programme requirement, a prohibited activity requirement, a residence requirement, a mental health treatment requirement, a drug rehabilitation requirement, an alcohol treatment requirement, a supervision requirement or an atten-dance centre requirement, the court may also impose an electronic monitoring require-ment unless prevented from doing so by section 215(2) or 218(4).

Electronic monitoring requirement

23–60   **215.**—(1) In this Part "electronic monitoring requirement", in relation to a relevant order, means a requirement for securing the electronic monitoring of the offender's compliance with other requirements imposed by the order during a period specified in the order, or determined by the responsible officer in accordance with the relevant order.

     (2) Where—

       (a) it is proposed to include in a relevant order a requirement for securing electronic monitoring in accordance with this section, but

       (b) there is a person (other than the offender) without whose co-operation it will not be practicable to secure the monitoring,

the requirement may not be included in the order without that person's consent.

     (3) A relevant order which includes an electronic monitoring requirement must include provision for making a person responsible for the monitoring; and a person who is made so responsible must be of a description specified in an order made by the Secretary of State.

     (4) Where an electronic monitoring requirement is required to take effect during a pe-riod determined by the responsible officer in accordance with the relevant order, the responsible officer must, before the beginning of that period, notify—

       (a) the offender,

       (b) the person responsible for the monitoring, and

       (c) any person falling within subsection (2)(b),

of the time when the period is to begin.

C. Community Orders — Requirements

23–61   The heart of the new community order is the requirements. Each has its own limits and options. Many are similar to previous community sentences or to requirements that could be included within a community rehabilitation order but there are changes to name or description and sometimes to content. Some requirements can only be included where specifically recommended by a probation officer. Subject to that and to the qualifying criteria, most requirements are available for all adult offenders. The excep-tion is the Attendance Centre requirement which has an upper age limit. The rarely used power to allow a person to give security for the offender"s good behaviour (*PCC(S)A* 2000, s.41(8)) has not been continued.

D. Unpaid Work Requirement

(1) General

23–62   This is the equivalent of the Community Punishment Order. The most significant change is the increase in the maximum hours to 300.

The work will generally be for the benefit of the community though this may be to the community as a whole or to an individual or smaller group within the community. Although primarily designed as having a large element of punishment and of reparation to the community, it is quite common for the involvement of the offender to lead on to continuing beneficial contact with the community group initially involved.

The court will need to be satisfied that the offender is suitable to perform work. In reaching that conclusion, the court may hear from an "appropriate officer", that is an officer of a local probation board.

(2) Content

The court will specify the number of hours to be completed. In total, there has to be **23–63** not less than 40 hours nor more than 300 hours: section 199(2). Those hours will normally be completed within a maximum of 12 months (section 200(2)) though this period may be extended by the court (Sched. 8, para. 20—see further in Enforcement at §§ 24–122 and 24–151, *post*).

If the court is making several orders on the same occasion, it is possible to make the hours in each order consecutive to each other: section 199(5). The maximum may not exceed 300 hours. In practice, making concurrent orders is usually simpler both for the defendant and the public to understand and also for the management of the orders. This is permissible because of the power of the court in assessing both the seriousness of the offence and the extent of restriction on liberty to consider both the offence and other offences associated with it: section 148(1).

Criminal Justice Act 2003, ss.199–200

Unpaid work requirement

199.—(1) In this Part "unpaid work requirement", in relation to a relevant order, means a **23–64** requirement that the offender must perform unpaid work in accordance with section 200.

(2) The number of hours which a person may be required to work under an unpaid work requirement must be specified in the relevant order and must be in the aggregate—

    (a) not less than 40, and

    (b) not more than 300.

(3) A court may not impose an unpaid work requirement in respect of an offender unless after hearing (if the courts thinks necessary) an appropriate officer, the court is satisfied that the offender is a suitable person to perform work under such a requirement.

(4) In subsection (3) "an appropriate officer" means—

    (a) in the case of an offender aged 18 or over, an officer of a local probation board, and

    (b) in the case of an offender aged under 18, an officer of a local probation board, a social worker of a local authority social services department or a member of a youth offending team.

(5) Where the court makes relevant orders in respect of two or more offences of which the offender has been convicted on the same occasion and includes unpaid work requirements in each of them, the court may direct that the hours of work specified in any of those requirements is to be concurrent with or additional to those specified in any other of those orders, but so that the total number of hours which are not concurrent does not exceed the maximum specified in subsection (2)(b).

Obligations of person subject to unpaid work requirement

200.—(1) An offender in respect of whom an unpaid work requirement of a relevant order is **23–65** in force must perform for the number of hours specified in the order such work at such times as he may be instructed by the responsible officer.

(2) Subject to paragraph 20 of Schedule 8 and paragraph 18 of Schedule 12 (power to extend order), the work required to be performed under an unpaid work requirement of a community order or a suspended sentence order must be performed during a period of twelve months.

(3) Unless revoked, a community order imposing an unpaid work requirement remains in force until the offender has worked under it for the number of hours specified in it.

(4) Where an unpaid work requirement is imposed by a suspended sentence order, the supervision period as defined by section 189(1)(a) continues until the offender has worked under the order for the number of hours specified in the order, but does not continue beyond the end of the operational period as defined by section 189(1)(b)(ii).

E. Activity Requirement, Programme Requirement, Prohibited Activity Requirement

(1) General

23–66   These are the equivalent of the requirements as to activities which could previously be included in a Community Rehabilitation Order. The previous provision included both participating in and refraining from activities in a single order. Under the new framework, these are separated out. The Activity Requirement is in section 201, the programme Requirement in section 202 and the Prohibited Activity Requirement in section 203. In the case of an Activity or Prohibited Activity Requirement, a court must consult a probation officer before making the order. In the case of a Programme Requirement, a court may only include it within a community order if the programme is an "accredited programme" (s.202(2)), is recommended to the court by a probation officer as being suitable for the offender (s.202(4)(a)) and is available at a place to be specified by the court (s.202(4)(b)).

Criminal Justice Act 2003, ss.201–203

Activity requirement

23–67   **201.**—(1) In this Part "activity requirement", in relation to a relevant order, means a requirement that the offender must do either or both of the following—

    (a) present himself to a person or persons specified in the relevant order at a place or places so specified on such number of days as may be so specified;

    (b) participate in activities specified in the order on such number of days as may be so specified.

(2) The specified activities may consist of or include activities whose purpose is that of reparation, such as activities involving contact between offenders and persons affected by their offences.

(3) A court may not include an activity requirement in a relevant order unless—

    (a) it has consulted—

        (i) in the case of an offender aged 18 or over, an officer of a local probation board,

        (ii) in the case of an offender aged under 18, either an officer of a local probation board or a member of a youth offending team, and

    (b) it is satisfied that it is feasible to secure compliance with the requirement.

(4) A court may not include an activity requirement in a relevant order if compliance with that requirement would involve the co-operation of a person other than the offender and the offender's responsible officer, unless that other person consents to its inclusion.

(5) The aggregate of the number of days specified under subsection (1)(a) and (b) must not exceed 60.

(6) A requirement such as is mentioned in subsection (1)(a) operates to require the offender—

    (a) in accordance with instructions given by his responsible officer, to present himself at a place or places on the number of days specified in the order, and

    (b) while at any place, to comply with instructions given by, or under the authority of, the person in charge of that place.

(7) A place specified under subsection (1)(a) must be—

    (a) a community rehabilitation centre, or

    (b) a place that has been approved by the local probation board for the area in which the premises are situated as providing facilities suitable for persons subject to activity requirements.

(8) Where the place specified under subsection (1)(a) is a community rehabilitation cen-

tre, the reference in subsection (6)(a) to the offender presenting himself at the specified place includes a reference to him presenting himself elsewhere than at the centre for the purpose of participating in activities in accordance with instructions given by, or under the authority of, the person in charge of the centre.

(9) A requirement to participate in activities operates to require the offender—

(a) in accordance with instructions given by his responsible officer, to participate in activities on the number of days specified in the order, and

(b) while participating, to comply with instructions given by, or under the authority of, the person in charge of the activities.

(10) In this section "community rehabilitation centre" means premises—

(a) at which non-residential facilities are provided for use in connection with the rehabilitation of offenders, and

(b) which are for the time being approved by the Secretary of State as providing facilities suitable for persons subject to relevant orders.

Programme requirement

202.—(1) In this Part "programme requirement", in relation to a relevant order, means a **23–68** requirement that the offender must participate in an accredited programme specified in the order at a place so specified on such number of days as may be so specified.

(2) In this Part "accredited programme" means a programme that is for the time being accredited by the accreditation body.

(3) In this section—

(a) "programme" means a systematic set of activities, and

(b) "the accreditation body" means such body as the Secretary of State may designate for the purposes of this section by order.

(4) A court may not include a programme requirement in a relevant order unless—

(a) the accredited programme which the court proposes to specify in the order has been recommended to the court as being suitable for the offender—

(i) in the case of an offender aged 18 or over, by an officer of a local probation board, or

(ii) in the case of an offender aged under 18, either by an officer of a local probation board or by a member of a youth offending team, and

(b) the court is satisfied that the programme is (or, where the relevant order is a custody plus order or an intermittent custody order, will be) available at the place proposed to be specified.

(5) A court may not include a programme requirement in a relevant order if compliance with that requirement would involve the co-operation of a person other than the offender and the offender's responsible officer, unless that other person consents to its inclusion.

(6) A requirement to attend an accredited programme operates to require the offender—

(a) in accordance with instructions given by the responsible officer, to participate in the accredited programme at the place specified in the order on the number of days specified in the order, and

(b) while at that place, to comply with instructions given by, or under the authority of, the person in charge of the programme.

(7) A place specified in an order must be a place that has been approved by the local probation board for the area in which the premises are situated as providing facilities suitable for persons subject to programme requirements.

Prohibited activity requirement

203.—(1) In this Part "prohibited activity requirement", in relation to a relevant order, **23–69** means a requirement that the offender must refrain from participating in activities specified in the order—

(a) on a day or days so specified, or

(b) during a period so specified.

(2) A court may not include a prohibited activity requirement in a relevant order unless it has consulted—

(a) in the case of an offender aged 18 or over, an officer of a local probation board;

Part IV

(b) in the case of an offender aged under 18, either an officer of a local probation board or a member of a youth offending team.

(3) The requirements that may by virtue of this section be included in a relevant order include a requirement that the offender does not possess, use or carry a firearm within the meaning of the *Firearms Act* 1968.

F. CURFEW REQUIREMENT

(1) General

23–70   The Curfew Requirement under the new framework replaces both the curfew requirement previously capable of being included within a Community Rehabilitation Order and the Curfew Order itself.

23–71   A curfew order is designed to keep a person in a certain place at specified times. Although it may have an element that helps reduce the likelihood of the offender committing further offences, its primary purpose is to impose punishment by restricting the liberty of the offender.

Prior to imposing the requirement, the court must consider information about the place(s) where the offender will have to be and the attitude of those people who are likely to be affected by the fact that the offender is required to be there: s.204(6).

(2) Content

23–72   The obligation on the offender is to remain at a specified place for the periods specified in the order. Those periods must add up to no less than two hours and no more than 12 hours in any one day: section 204(2). The order must not continue for more than six months: section 204(3).

The hours and the place may vary from time to time: section 204(2). Compliance with the order will often be monitored electronically; in these circumstances, the consent of anyone other than the offender who is involved in the monitoring will need to be obtained: section 215(2) (see *ante*, § 23–60) although blanket contracts will have been made for this purpose.

Criminal Justice Act 2003, s.204

Curfew requirement
23–73   **204.**—(1) In this Part "curfew requirement", in relation to a relevant order, means a requirement that the offender must remain, for periods specified in the relevant order, at a place so specified.

(2) A relevant order imposing a curfew requirement may specify different places or different periods for different days, but may not specify periods which amount to less than two hours or more than twelve hours in any day.

(3) A community order or suspended sentence order which imposes a curfew requirement may not specify periods which fall outside the period of six months beginning with the day on which it is made.

(4) A custody plus order which imposes a curfew requirement may not specify a period which falls outside the period of six months beginning with the first day of the licence period as defined by section 181(3)(b).

(5) An intermittent custody order which imposes a curfew requirement must not specify a period if to do so would cause the aggregate number of days on which the offender is subject to the requirement for any part of the day to exceed 182.

(6) Before making a relevant order imposing a curfew requirement, the court must obtain and consider information about the place proposed to be specified in the order (including information as to the attitude of persons likely to be affected by the enforced presence there of the offender).

G. EXCLUSION REQUIREMENT

(1) General

23–74   The Exclusion Requirement replaces the requirement capable of being included within a Community Rehabilitation Order by virtue of Schedule 2, para. 8 to the *PCC(S)A* 2000. It prohibits the offender from entering a place specified for the period prescribed. That period may not exceed two years when the requirement is included within a community order: section 205(2). As with a curfew requirement, different places can be specified for different periods or days.

Criminal Justice Act 2003, s.205

Exclusion requirement

    205.—(1) In this Part "exclusion requirement", in relation to a relevant order, means a pro- **23–75** vision prohibiting the offender from entering a place specified in the order for a period so specified.

    (2) Where the relevant order is a community order, the period specified must not be more than two years.

    (3) An exclusion requirement—

        (a) may provide for the prohibition to operate only during the periods specified in the order, and

        (b) may specify different places for different periods or days.

    (4) In this section "place" includes an area.

H. Residence Requirement

(1) General

    The Residence Requirement replaces Schedule 2, para. 1 to the *PCC(S)A* 2000 and **23–76** is worded a little more specifically. As well as providing where the offender must reside (section 206(1)), the court may authorise residence elsewhere with the prior approval of the "responsible officer" (section 206(2)). This introduces welcome flexibility for circumstances where the accommodation in the order ceases to be available or suitable. The place of residence specified by the court may only be a hostel or other institution where that is on the recommendation of a probation officer (section 206(4)).

Criminal Justice Act 2003, s.206

Residence requirement

    206.—(1) In this Part, "residence requirement", in relation to a community order or a **23–77** suspended sentence order, means a requirement that, during a period specified in the relevant order, the offender must reside at a place specified in the order.

    (2) If the order so provides, a residence requirement does not prohibit the offender from residing, with the prior approval of the responsible officer, at a place other than that specified in the order.

    (3) Before making a community order or suspended sentence order containing a residence requirement, the court must consider the home surroundings of the offender.

    (4) A court may not specify a hostel or other institution as the place where an offender must reside, except on the recommendation of an officer of a local probation board.

I. Mental Health Treatment Requirement

(1) General

    The Mental Health Treatment Requirement replaces the requirements as to treat- **23–78** ment for mental conditions etc. which could be included in a Community Rehabilitation Order by virtue of Schedule 2, para. 5 to the PCC(S)A 2000. Where the offender is under treatment as a resident patient as a result of this requirement, the remit of the "responsible officer" is limited to that necessary for the purpose of any revocation or amendment of the order (section 207(4)).

Criminal Justice Act 2003, s.207–208

Mental health treatment requirement

    207.—(1) In this Part, "mental health treatment requirement", in relation to a community or- **23–79**

Part IV

der or suspended sentence order, means a requirement that the offender must submit, during a period or periods specified in the order, to treatment by or under the direction of a registered medical practitioner or a chartered psychologist (or both, for different periods) with a view to the improvement of the offender's mental condition.

(2) The treatment required must be such one of the following kinds of treatment as may be specified in the relevant order—

    (a) treatment as a resident patient in an independent hospital or care home within the meaning of the *Care Standards Act* 2000 or a hospital within the meaning of the *Mental Health Act* 1983, but not in hospital premises where high security psychiatric services within the meaning of that Act are provided;

    (b) treatment as a non-resident patient at such institution or place as may be specified in the order;

    (c) treatment by or under the direction of such registered medical practitioner or chartered psychologist (or both) as may be so specified;

but the nature of the treatment is not to be specified in the order except as mentioned in paragraph (a), (b) or (c).

(3) A court may not by virtue of this section include a mental health treatment requirement in a relevant order unless—

    (a) the court is satisfied, on the evidence of a registered medical practitioner approved for the purposes of section 12 of the *Mental Health Act* 1983, that the mental condition of the offender—

        (i) is such as requires and may be susceptible to treatment, but

        (ii) is not such as to warrant the making of a hospital order or guardianship order within the meaning of that Act;

    (b) the court is also satisfied that arrangements have been or can be made for the treatment intended to be specified in the order (including arrangements for the reception of the offender where he is to be required to submit to treatment as a resident patient); and

    (c) the offender has expressed his willingness to comply with such a requirement.

(4) While the offender is under treatment as a resident patient in pursuance of a mental health requirement of a relevant order, his responsible officer shall carry out the supervision of the offender to such extent only as may be necessary for the purpose of the revocation or amendment of the order.

(5) Subsections (2) and (3) of section 54 of the *Mental Health Act* 1983 have effect with respect to proof for the purposes of subsection (3)(a) of an offender's mental condition as they have effect with respect to proof of an offender's mental condition for the purposes of section 37(2)(a) of that Act.

(6) In this section and section 208, "chartered psychologist" means a person for the time being listed in the British Psychological Society's Register of Chartered Psychologists.

Mental health treatment at place other than that specified in order

23–80   **208.**—(1) Where the medical practitioner or chartered psychologist by whom or under whose direction an offender is being treated for his mental condition in pursuance of a mental health treatment requirement is of the opinion that part of the treatment can be better or more conveniently given in or at an institution or place which—

    (a) is not specified in the relevant order, and

    (b) is one in or at which the treatment of the offender will be given by or under the direction of a registered medical practitioner or chartered psychologist,

he may, with the consent of the offender, make arrangements for him to be treated accordingly.

(2) Such arrangements as are mentioned in subsection (1) may provide for the offender to receive part of his treatment as a resident patient in an institution or place notwithstanding that the institution or place is not one which could have been specified for that purpose in the relevant order.

(3) Where any such arrangements as are mentioned in subsection (1) are made for the treatment of an offender—

    (a) at the medical practitioner or chartered psychologist by whom the arrangements are made shall give notice in writing to the offender's responsible officer, specifying the institution or place in or at which the treatment is to be carried out; and

    (b) the treatment provided for by the arrangements shall be deemed to be treatment to which he is required to submit in pursuance of the relevant order.

J. Drug Rehabilitation Requirement

(1) General

The power under Schedule 2, para.6 to the *PCC(S)A* 2000 to include in a Com- **23–81**
munity Rehabilitation Order requirements as to treatment for drug or alcohol
dependency and the power to make a Drug Treatment and Testing Order are now
brought within two separate provisions, one relating to drugs (sections 209-211) and the
other to alcohol (section 212). The review provisions that have been such a feature of
the Drug Treatment and Testing Order are continued within the Drug Rehabilitation
Requirement but there is no equivalent provision in the Alcohol Treatment
Requirement.

The aim of a drug rehabilitation requirement is to provide a chance for an offender **23–82**
to break (or reduce) his drug addiction and thereby cease offending: section 209(1)(a).
An order will consist of treatment by a suitably qualified person (section 209(1)(a)), and
the provision of samples as and when required to ascertain the presence of drugs in the
body (section 209(1)(b)). The treatment may be residential or non-residential as specified in the order (section 209(4)). There is power to establish reviews of progress by the
court: section 210.

These must be established if the treatment and testing period exceeds 12 months:
section 210(1). The treatment and testing period must be made for not less than six
months: section 209(3). A court must first be satisfied both that the offender is either dependent on drugs or has a tendency to misuse them and that this dependency or
propensity both requires treatment and is susceptible to treatment.

It must then be satisfied that arrangements can be made for the treatment it is
intended to require. This type of requirement can only be included where an officer of
a local probation board recommends it as suitable for the offender: section 209(2). The
requirement may only be included if the offender expresses willingness to comply: section 209(2)(d).

(2) When to include this requirement

This is often an even more complex balancing exercise than usual since those most **23–83**
needing treatment will often have committed offences that are both serious and prolific.
A spate of judicial consideration led to the Court of Appeal (Criminal Division) reviewing the authorities and identifying some of the most relevant factors: *Att.-Gen.'s Reference (No. 64 of 2003) (Boujettif, Harrison)* [2004] 2 Cr.App.R.(S.) 22. Although
these were decided in the context of the making of a Drug Treatment and Testing Order (DTTO) under the previous legislation, the principles are likely to continue to be
applicable. The Court concluded that, although a DTTO may well be suitable where a
substantial number of offences have been committed, such an order is not likely to be
appropriate for an offender who has committed a substantial number of serious offences
which either involve minor violence or have had a particularly damaging effect on the
victim(s)—"excessive weight must not be given to the prospect of rehabilitation at the
expense of proper regard for the criminality of the offender": Rose V.P. at para. 14. It
was also noted that a DTTO is more likely to be effective early in a criminal career but
that there will be exceptional cases justifying such orders at other times. There must be
clear evidence that the offender is determined to be free from drugs. Further
consideration was given to the decision whether to make such an order in the context of
offences serious enough to be sentenced in the Crown Court in *Woods* [2005] EWCA
Crim 2065; [2006] 1 Cr.App.R. (S.) 83. The Court of Appeal summarised propositions
arising from a range of cases much of which will apply equally in a magistrates' court
and these are set out *post* as an extract from the judgment. Proposition 6 is likely to be
the most significant.

> 1) A drug treatment and testing order is designed for, amongst others, repeat offenders
> whose offending is driven by drug dependence. Such offenders will often be those who

would otherwise have to be sent to prison and it may well be not for a short period. Such an order is not a soft option. It imposes significant obligations on the offender and the court retains quite intensive supervision of his progress and the power to substitute imprisonment if he fails.

2) That the defendant has been a prolific offender does not necessarily mean that a drug treatment and testing order will not be the right order. On the other hand, there will plainly be cases in which the nature of the offence or the scale of offending is such that only a custodial sentence is justified.

3) A drug treatment and testing order is an expensive order. It is in the interests neither of the public nor the offender for such an order to be made where there are not reasonable prospects of it succeeding. That would only divert scarce resources from other more deserving cases and, in addition, increase the risk that the defendant will offend again, thus depriving the public of protection against him and making it likely that, if he is caught, he will spend in the end even longer in prison. Conversely, no one should expect 100 per cent success rate and some lapse is often a feature of an order which turns out substantially successful.

4) It follows that the judge has difficult balancing decisions to be made at two stages—
    (a) does the case warrant adjournment for a report on the possible availability of such an order,
    (b) if there is such a report and it is favourable, is a drug treatment and testing order the right disposal?

5) We think that we should underline that a judge is not under an obligation to adjourn for a report in every case in which it is represented to him that the cause of offending is drug dependence and that the defendant would welcome a drug treatment and testing order. To adjourn for a report if there is no prospect of such an order being made would be wasteful and additionally would unjustifiably raise false expectations in the defendant.

6) Experienced trial judges sitting in criminal cases now have considerable knowledge of drug treatment and testing orders because they supervise their working. At the stage of considering whether or not to seek a report, they know to look (inter alia) for possible signs that such an order might be effective. Generally they will have the assistance of the standard pre-sentence report. They are likely to look for indications that the defendant is likely to engage with the order, and that he has sufficient stability in his home life to have reasonable prospects of its succeeding. They are also right at that stage to consider the nature of his offending. The gravity of the offences or the personal characteristics of the defendant, such as repeated breaches of community orders, might demonstrate that a drug treatment and testing order will plainly be inappropriate. They should not, however, reject the possibility of a DTTO simply on the ground that the defendant is a repeat thief or burglar for whom otherwise a custodial sentence would be inevitable. That is precisely the kind of offender who may—we emphasise may—be suitable. The Vice President, Rose L.J., put it this way in Robinson—

'It is well known that a high proportion of criminal offences against people and property are committed in order to provide funds to feed the drug habit of the perpetrator. If there were fewer drug addicts, it is likely that there would be fewer criminal offences. Accordingly, in our judgment, judges should be alert to pass sentences which have a realistic prospect of reducing drug addiction whenever it is possible sensibly to do so.'

7) If a report is obtained, then the judge has a second, often a very difficult, decision to make. The decision is, it should be remembered, his and not that of the probation officer. It is the judge who has to weigh in the balance the public interest as well as the interests of the defendant. It is the judge who has to assess the criminality of the defendant as well as the desirability and prospects of rehabilitation. In *Attorney-General's Reference No 28 of 2001*, which was a case of street robberies, this court held that a drug treatment and testing order was in that case an unduly lenient sentence. Judge L.J. put it in a single sentence—

'It gave excessive weight to the issue of rehabilitation and wholly insufficient weight to the actual criminality of the offender.'

8) If at either stage the judge has properly addressed the issue before him and exercised his judgment, we think it will be in comparatively rare cases that it would be right for this court to say that he has arrived at a decision which has erred in principle."

(3) Review of the court

23–84   In *Robinson* [2002] 2 Cr.App.R.(S.) 95, guidance was issued as to the treatment of offenders who commit further offences whilst the subject of a drug treatment and testing order.

Although this guidance was issued in the context of the making of a Drug Treatment and Testing Order (DTTO) under the previous legislation, the principles are likely to continue to be applicable. However, the more restricted options following the breach of an order (see *post*, § 24–87) may affect some of the choices available to the court. The fact that an order is being made in relation to someone with a drug dependency suggests that a court needs to take care to ensure that the purpose of its order is achieved wherever possible. In its guideline, *New Sentences: Criminal Justice Act 2003*, the Sentencing Guidelines Council emphasised that the primary response to the breach of an order was the importance of a court seeking to ensure that an offender complied with an order that it had made. The review provisions enable a court to take a more active role in ensuring that compliance and this is likely to benefit all involved. The offender will benefit by being required to account for his/her conduct to the court that made the order, the "responsible officer" will benefit from having the authority of the court to reinforce the requirements imposed and the court will benefit from seeing directly the outcome of an order that it has made. By section 210, the court that includes a drug rehabilitation requirement within a Community Order may provide for review hearings. The treatment and testing period must be for at least six months; if it is for more than 12 months, the review process must be undertaken, if it is for 12 months or less, the court has a discretion. The reviews must be no more frequently held than monthly, initially (at least) at a court hearing which the offender attends and which receives a report in writing from the responsible officer on the offender's progress and on the results of the samples taken to test whether there have been drugs in the offender's body: section 210(1).

At such a hearing, the court may amend the drug rehabilitation requirement with the offender's agreement but may not reduce the treatment and testing period below the minimum of six months: section 211(1), (2). If the offender does not agree to the amendment, the court may revoke the community order and re-sentence the offender: section 211(3).

If the court considers the offender"s progress to be satisfactory, it can provide for future reviews to be without a hearing: section 211(6). That can be revoked should the progress cease to be satisfactory: section 211(7).

Criminal Justice Act 2003, s.209–211

Drug rehabilitation requirement

209.—(1) In this Part "drug rehabilitation requirement", in relation to a community order or suspended sentence order, means a requirement that during a period specified in the order ("the treatment and testing period") the offender—

    (a) must submit to treatment by or under the direction of a specified person having the necessary qualifications or experience with a view to the reduction or elimination of the offender's dependency on or propensity to misuse drugs, and

    (b) for the purpose of ascertaining whether he has any drug in his body during that period, must provide samples of such description as may be so determined, at such times or in such circumstances as may (subject to the provisions of the order) be determined by the responsible officer or by the person specified as the person by or under whose direction the treatment is to be provided.

(2) A court may not impose a drug rehabilitation requirement unless—

    (a) it is satisfied—

        (i) that the offender is dependent on, or has a propensity to misuse, drugs, and

        (ii) that his dependency or propensity is such as requires and may be susceptible to treatment,

    (b) it is also satisfied that arrangements have been or can be made for the treatment intended to be specified in the order (including arrangements for the reception of the offender where he is to be required to submit to treatment as a resident),

23–85

    (c) the requirement has been recommended to the court as being suitable or the offender—

        (i) in the case of an offender aged 18 or over, by an officer of a local probation board, or

        (ii) in the case of an offender aged under 18, either by an officer of a local probation board or by a member of a youth offending team, and

    (d) the offender expresses his willingness to comply with the requirement.

(3) The treatment and testing period must be at least six months.

(4) The required treatment for any particular period must be—

    (a) treatment as a resident in such institution or place as may be specified in the order, or

    (b) treatment as a non-resident in or at such institution or place, and at such intervals, as may be so specified;

but the nature of the treatment is not to be specified in the order except as mentioned in paragraph (a) or (b) above.

(5) The function of making a determination as to the provision of samples under provision included in the community order or suspended sentence order by virtue of subsection (1)(b) is to be exercised in accordance with guidance given from time to time by the Secretary of State.

(6) A community order or suspended sentence order imposing a drug rehabilitation requirement must provide that the results of tests carried out on any samples provided by the offender in pursuance of the requirement to a person other than the responsible officer are to be communicated to the responsible officer.

(7) In this section "drug" means a controlled drug as defined by section 2 of the *Misuse of Drugs Act* 1971.

Drug rehabilitation requirement: provision for review by court

23–86   **210.**—(1) A community order or suspended sentence order imposing a drug rehabilitation requirement may (and must if the treatment and testing period is more than 12 months)—

    (a) provide for the requirement to be reviewed periodically at intervals of not less than one month,

    (b) provide for each review of the requirement to be made, subject to section 211(6), at a hearing held for the purpose by the court responsible for the order (a "review hearing"),

    (c) require the offender to attend each review hearing,

    (d) provide for the responsible officer to make to the court responsible for the order, before each review, a report in writing on the offender's progress under the requirement, and

    (e) provide for each such report to include the test results communicated to the responsible officer under section 209(6) or otherwise and the views of the treatment provider as to the treatment and testing of the offender.

(2) In this section references to the court responsible for a community order or suspended sentence order imposing a drug rehabilitation requirement are references—

    (a) where a court is specified in the order in accordance with subsection (3), to that court;

    (b) in any other case, to the court by which the order is made.

(3) Where the area specified in a community order or suspended sentence order which is made by a magistrates' court and imposes a drug rehabilitation requirement is not the area for which the court acts, the court may, if it thinks fit, include in the order provision specifying for the purposes of subsection (2) a magistrates' court which acts for the area specified in the order.

(4) Where a community order or suspended sentence order imposing a drug rehabilitation requirement has been made on an appeal brought from the Crown Court or from the criminal division of the Court of Appeal, for the purposes of subsection (2)(b) it shall be taken to have been made by the Crown Court.

Periodic review of drug rehabilitation requirement

23–87   **211.**—(1) At a review hearing (within the meaning given by subsection (1) of section 210) the court may, after considering the responsible officer's report referred to in that subsection, amend the community order or suspended sentence order, so far as it relates to the drug rehabilitation requirement.

(2) The court—

(a) may not amend the drug rehabilitation requirement unless the offender expresses his willingness to comply with the requirement as amended,

(b) may not amend any provision of the order so as to reduce the period for which the drug rehabilitation requirement has effect below the minimum specified in section 209(3), and

(c) except with the consent of the offender, may not amend any requirement or provision of the order while an appeal against the order is pending.

(3) If the offender fails to express his willingness to comply with the drug rehabilitation requirement as proposed to be amended by the court, the court may—

(a) revoke the community order, or the suspended sentence order and the suspended sentence to which it relates, and

(b) deal with him, for the offence in respect of which the order was made, in any way in which he could have been dealt with for that offence by the court which made the order if the order had not been made.

(4) In dealing with the offender under subsection (3)(b), the court—

(a) shall take into account the extent to which the offender has complied with the requirements of the order, and

(b) may impose a custodial sentence (where the order was made in respect of an offence punishable with such a sentence) notwithstanding anything in section 152(2).

(5) Where the order is a community order made by a magistrates' court in the case of an offender under 18 years of age in respect of an offence triable only on indictment in the case of an adult, any powers exercisable under subsection (3)(b) in respect of the offender after he attains the age of 18 are powers to do either or both of the following—

(a) to impose a fine not exceeding £5,000 for the offence in respect of which the order was made;

(b) to deal with the offender for that offence in any way in which the court could deal with him if it had just convicted him of an offence punishable with imprisonment for a term not exceeding twelve months.

(6) If at a review hearing (as defined by section 210(1)(b)) the court, after considering the responsible officer's report, is of the opinion that the offender's progress under the requirement is satisfactory, the court may so amend the order as to provide for each subsequent review to be made by the court without a hearing.

(7) If at a review without a hearing the court, after considering the responsible officer's report, is of the opinion that the offender's progress under the requirement is no longer satisfactory, the court may require the offender to attend a hearing of the court at a specified time and place.

(8) At that hearing the court, after considering that report, may—

(a) exercise the powers conferred by this section as if the hearing were a review hearing, and

(b) so amend the order as to provide for each subsequent review to be made at a review hearing.

(9) In this section any reference to the court, in relation to a review without a hearing, is to be read—

(a) in the case of the Crown Court, as a reference to a judge of the court;

(b) in the case of a magistrates' court, as a reference to a justice of the peace. [...].

[Repealed by the *Courts Act 2003 (Consequential Provisions) Order* (S.I. 2005 No. 886).]

K. ALCOHOL TREATMENT REQUIREMENT

(1) General

The power under Schedule 2, para. 6 to the *PCC(S)A* 2000 to include in a Com- **23–88** munity Rehabilitation Order requirements as to treatment for alcohol dependency has now become a separate requirement that can be included within a community order. There is no equivalent provision in the Alcohol Treatment Requirement to the review provisions that have been such a feature of the Drug Treatment and Testing Order and are now included within the Drug Rehabilitation Requirement.

This requirement obliges an offender to submit to treatment by a suitably qualified person for the period set by the court: section 212(1). The minimum period is six months: section 212(4). A court may only impose the requirement if satisfied that the offender is dependent on alcohol, that the dependency both requires and is susceptible to treatment and that arrangements can be made for the treatment to be required.

Criminal Justice Act 2003, s.212

Alcohol treatment requirement

23–89   **212.**—(1) In this Part "alcohol treatment requirement", in relation to a community order or suspended sentence order, means a requirement that the offender must submit during a period specified in the order to treatment by or under the direction of a specified person having the necessary qualifications or experience with a view to the reduction or elimination of the offender's dependency on alcohol.

(2) A court may not impose an alcohol treatment requirement in respect of an offender unless it is satisfied—

     (a) that he is dependent on alcohol,

     (b) that his dependency is such as requires and may be susceptible to treatment, and

     (c) that arrangements have been or can be made for the treatment intended to be specified in the order (including arrangements for the reception of the offender where he is to be required to submit to treatment as a resident).

(3) A court may not impose an alcohol treatment requirement unless the offender expresses his willingness to comply with its requirements.

(4) The period for which the alcohol treatment requirement has effect must be not less than six months.

(5) The treatment required by an alcohol treatment requirement for any particular period must be—

     (a) treatment as a resident in such institution or place as may be specified in the order,

     (b) treatment as a non-resident in or at such institution or place, and at such intervals, as may be so specified, or

     (c) treatment by or under the direction of such person having the necessary qualification or experience as may be so specified;

but the nature of the treatment shall not be specified in the order except as mentioned in paragraph (a), (b) or (c) above.

L. Supervision Requirement

(1) General

23–90   The Supervision Requirement is an optional requirement which places an obligation on the offender to attend appointments with the "responsible officer", or another person designated by the responsible officer. This requirement will last for the duration of the Community Order. The purpose of this requirement is to promote the offender's rehabilitation (s.213(2)). In the absence of this requirement, the responsible officer will have the obligations set out by section 198 (see *ante*) to make the arrangements necessary to ensure compliance with the requirements of the order, but will not have the authority or the obligation to make appointments for the purpose of promoting the offender's rehabilitation. This recognises that there will be situations where a Community Order is primarily about punishment or where there is no further beneficial work that needs to be done outside that taking place within the context of another requirement and enables the task of the responsible officer to accurately reflect what is required.

Criminal Justice Act 2003, s.213

Supervision requirement

23–91   **213.**—(1) In this Part "supervision requirement", in relation to a relevant order, means a requirement that, during the relevant period, the offender must attend appointments with the responsible officer or another person determined by the responsible officer, at such time and place as may be determined by the officer.

(2) The purpose for which a supervision requirement may be imposed is that of promoting the offender's rehabilitation.

(3) In subsection (1) "the relevant period" means—

    (a) in relation to a community order, the period for which the community order remains in force,

    (b) in relation to a custody plus order, the licence period as defined by section 181(3)(b),

    (c) in relation to an intermittent custody order, the licence periods as defined by section 183(3), and

    (d) in relation to a suspended sentence order, the supervision period as defined by section 189(1)(a).

M. Attendance Centre Requirement

(1) General

An Attendance Centre Requirement enables the equivalent of an Attendance Centre Order to be included within a Community Order. It may also be made as a sentence in its own right in the youth court since, by virtue of the provisions of Schedule 32, para. 102 to the *Criminal Justice Act* 2003, section 60 of the PCC(S)A 2000 continues in force in relation to those aged 16 or under. Where an appropriate centre is available, a requirement may be made on an offender aged under 25. **23–92**

(2) Purpose and effect

This order is available for youths and adults. In relation to youths, see chapter 34 later earlier in this work. For adults, there are a small number of centres available. An order will require the offender to attend at the centre as required until the hours fixed by the court are completed. Attendance is designed both to be a punishment (by intruding into the offender's time, and by requiring them to be at a certain place for a certain period and to obey the requirements of the centre) and to offer an opportunity for a positive challenge to continuing criminality. A centre is generally run by the police or by the Youth Offending Team. **23–93**

(3) Content

The court has the power to require a minimum of 12 hours attendance and a maximum of 36 hours for this age range (18 years and above). The court will specify the centre to be attended and will fix the date and time of the offender's first attendance. Attendance on any one day must not exceed three hours; in practice, it tends to be two hours on each attendance. **23–94**

The court must be satisfied that the specified centre is reasonably accessible to the offender given his age, the means of transport available and any other relevant circumstance. As far as practicable, the court should also seek to ensure that attendance at the centre will not conflict with the defendant's religious beliefs, the requirements of any other community penalties to which the defendant may be subject or interfere with normal work or education.

Criminal Justice Act 2003, s.214

Requirements available only in case of offenders aged under 25

Attendance centre requirement

    214.—(1) In this Part "attendance centre requirement", in relation to a relevant order, means a requirement that the offender must attend at an attendance centre specified in the relevant order for such number of hours as may be so specified. **23–95**

(2) The aggregate number of hours for which the offender may be required to attend at an attendance centre must not be less than 12 or more than 36.

(3) The court may not impose an attendance centre requirement unless the court is satisfied that the attendance centre to be specified in it is reasonably accessible to the offender concerned, having regard to the means of access available to him and any other circumstances.

(4) The first time at which the offender is required to attend at the attendance centre is a time notified to the offender by the responsible officer.

(5) The subsequent hours are to be fixed by the officer in charge of the centre, having regard to the offender's circumstances.

(6) An offender may not be required under this section to attend at an attendance centre on more than one occasion on any day, or for more than three hours on any occasion.

N. OFFENDER RESIDENT IN SCOTLAND OR NORTHERN IRELAND

23–96   Given the different provisions that apply in some circumstances in Scotland and Northern Ireland, specific provision is made where a court wishes to make a Community Order in respect of an offender who resides in Scotland or Northern Ireland or in order to ensure that an order is enforceable.

Criminal Justice Act 2003, Sched. 9

Section 180   SCHEDULE 9

TRANSFER OF COMMUNITY ORDERS TO SCOTLAND OR NORTHERN IRELAND

PART 1

SCOTLAND

23–97   1.—(1) Where the court considering the making of a community order is satisfied that the offender resides in Scotland, or will reside there when the order comes into force, the court may not make a community order in respect of the offender unless it appears to the court—

    (a) in the case of an order imposing a requirement mentioned in sub-paragraph (2), that arrangements exist for persons to comply with such a requirement in the locality in Scotland in which the offender resides, or will be residing when the order comes into force, and that provision can be made for him to comply with the requirement under those arrangements, and

    (b) in any case, that suitable arrangements for his supervision can be made by the council constituted under section 2 of the *Local Government etc. (Scotland) Act* 1994 in whose area he resides, or will be residing when the order comes into force.

(2) The requirements referred to in sub-paragraph (1)(a) are—

    (a) an unpaid work requirement,

    (b) an activity requirement,

    (c) a programme requirement,

    (d) a mental health treatment requirement,

    (e) a drug rehabilitation requirement,

    (f) an alcohol treatment requirement, and

    (g) an electronic monitoring requirement.

(3) Where—

    (a) the appropriate court for the purposes of paragraph 16 of Schedule 8 (amendment by reason of change of residence) is satisfied that an offender in respect of whom a community order is in force proposes to reside or is residing in Scotland, and

    (b) it appears to the court that the conditions in sub-paragraph (1)(a) and (b) are satisfied,

the power of the court to amend the order under Part 4 of Schedule 8 includes power to amend it by requiring it to be complied with in Scotland and the offender to be supervised in accordance with the arrangements referred to in sub-paragraph (1)(b).

(4) For the purposes of sub-paragraph (3), any reference in sub-paragraph (1)(a) and (b) to the time when the order comes into force is to be treated as a reference to the time when the amendment comes into force.

(5) The court may not by virtue of sub-paragraph (1) or (3) require an attendance centre requirement to be complied with in Scotland.

(6) A community order made or amended in accordance with this paragraph must—

   (a) specify the locality in Scotland in which the offender resides or will be residing when the order or amendment comes into force;

   (b) specify as the corresponding order for the purposes of this Schedule an order that may be made by a court in Scotland;

   (c) specify as the appropriate court for the purposes of subsection (4) of section 228 of the *Criminal Procedure (Scotland) Act* 1995 a court of summary jurisdiction (which, in the case of an offender convicted on indictment, must be the sheriff court) having jurisdiction in the locality specified under paragraph (a);

and section 216 (*[local justice area]* to be specified) does not apply in relation to an order so made or amended.

[Substituted by the *Courts Act 2003 (Consequential Provisions) Order* (S.I. 2005 No. 886).]

2.—(1) Where a court is considering the making or amendment of a community order **23–98** by virtue of paragraph 1, Chapter 4 of Part 12 of this Act has effect subject to the following modifications.

(2) Any reference to the responsible officer has effect as a reference to the officer of a council constituted under section 2 of the *Local Government etc. (Scotland) Act* 1994 responsible for the offender's supervision or, as the case may be, discharging in relation to him the functions in respect of community service orders assigned by sections 239 to 245 of the *Criminal Procedure (Scotland) Act* 1995.

(3) The following provisions are omitted—

   (a) subsection (7) of section 201 (activity requirement),

   (b) subsection (7) of section 202 (programme requirement),

   (c) subsection (4) of section 206 (residence requirement), and

   (d) subsection (4) of section 218 (availability of arrangements in local area).

(4) In section 207 (mental health treatment requirement), for subsection (2)(a) there is substituted—

   "(a) treatment as a resident patient in a hospital within the meaning of the *Mental Health (Care and Treatment) (Scotland) Act* 2003, not being a State hospital within the meaning of that Act;".

(5) In section 215 (electronic monitoring requirement), in subsection (3), the words from "and" onwards are omitted.

PART 2

NORTHERN IRELAND

3.—(1) Where the court considering the making of a community order is satisfied that **23–99** the offender resides in Northern Ireland, or will reside there when the order comes into force, the court may not make a community order in respect of the offender unless it appears to the court—

   (a) in the case of an order imposing a requirement mentioned in sub-paragraph (2), that arrangements exist for persons to comply with such a requirement in the petty sessions district in Northern Ireland in which the offender resides, or will be residing when the order comes into force, and that provision can be made for him to comply with the requirement under those arrangements, and

   (b) in any case, that suitable arrangements for his supervision can be made by the Probation Board for Northern Ireland.

(2) The requirements referred to in sub-paragraph (1) are—

   (a) an unpaid work requirement,

(b)   an activity requirement,

(c)   a programme requirement,

(d)   a mental health treatment requirement,

(e)   a drug rehabilitation requirement,

(f)   an alcohol treatment requirement,

(g)   an attendance centre requirement, and

(h)   an electronic monitoring requirement.

(3) Where—

(a)   the appropriate court for the purposes of paragraph 16 of Schedule 8 (amendment by reason of change of residence) is satisfied that the offender to whom a community order relates proposes to reside or is residing in Northern Ireland, and

(b)   it appears to the court that the conditions in sub-paragraphs (1)(a) and (b) are satisfied,

the power of the court to amend the order under Part 4 of Schedule 8 includes power to amend it by requiring it to be complied with in Northern Ireland and the offender to be supervised in accordance with the arrangements referred to in sub-paragraph (1)(b).

(4) For the purposes of sub-paragraph (3), any reference in sub-paragraph (1)(a) and (b) to the time when the order comes into force is to be treated as a reference to the time when the amendment comes into force.

(5) A community order made or amended in accordance with this paragraph must specify the petty sessions district in Northern Ireland in which the offender resides or will be residing when the order or amendment comes into force; and section 216 ([local justice area] to be specified) does not apply in relation to an order so made or amended.

(6) A community order made or amended in accordance with this paragraph must also specify as the corresponding order for the purposes of this Schedule an order that may be made by a court in Northern Ireland.

[Substituted by the *Courts Act 2003 (Consequential Provisions) Order* (S.I. 2005 No. 886).]

23–100   4.—(1) Where a court is considering the making or amendment of a community order by virtue of paragraph 3, Chapter 4 of Part 12 of this Act has effect subject to the following modifications.

(2) Any reference to the responsible officer has effect as a reference to the probation officer responsible for the offender's supervision or, as the case may be, discharging in relation to the offender the functions conferred by Part 2 of the *Criminal Justice (Northern Ireland) Order* 1996 (S.I. 1996/No. 3160 (N.I. 24)).

(3) The following provisions are omitted—

(a)   subsection (7) of section 201 (activity requirement),

(b)   subsection (7) of section 202 (programme requirement),

(c)   subsection (4) of section 206 (residence requirement), and

(d)   subsection (4) of section 218 (availability of arrangements in local area).

(4) In section 207 (mental health treatment requirement), for subsection (2)(a) there is substituted—

"(a)   treatment (whether as an in-patient or an out-patient) at such hospital as may be specified in the order, being a hospital within the meaning of the *Health and Personal Social Services (Northern Ireland) Order* 1972, approved by the Department of Health, Social Services and Public Safety for the purposes of paragraph 4(3) of Schedule 1 to the *Criminal Justice (Northern Ireland) Order* 1996 (S.I. 1996/No. 3160 (N.I. 24));".

(5) In section 214 (attendance centre requirement), any reference to an attendance centre has effect as a reference to a day centre, as defined by paragraph 3(6) of Schedule 1 to the *Criminal Justice (Northern Ireland) Order* 1996 (S.I. 1996/No. 3160 (N.I. 24)).

(6) In section 215 (electronic monitoring requirement), in subsection (3), the words from "and" onwards are omitted.

PART 3

GENERAL PROVISIONS

5. In this Part of this Schedule—   **23–101**

"corresponding order" means the order specified under paragraph 1(6)(b) or 3(6);

"home court" means —

    (a) if the offender resides in Scotland, or will be residing there at the relevant time, the sheriff court having jurisdiction in the locality in which he resides or proposes to reside, and

    (b) if he resides in Northern Ireland, or will be residing there at the relevant time, the court of summary jurisdiction acting for the petty sessions district in which he resides or proposes to reside;

"the local authority officer concerned", in relation to an offender, means the officer of a council constituted under section 2 of the *Local Government etc. (Scotland) Act* 1994 responsible for his supervision or, as the case may be, discharging in relation to him the functions in respect of community service orders assigned by sections 239 to 245 of the *Criminal Procedure (Scotland) Act* 1995;

"the probation officer concerned", in relation to an offender, means the probation officer responsible for his supervision or, as the case may be, discharging in relation to him the functions conferred by Part 2 of the *Criminal Justice (Northern Ireland) Order* 1996;

"the relevant time" means the time when the order or the amendment to it comes into force.

6. Where a community order is made or amended in accordance with paragraph 1 or **23–102** 3, the court which makes or amends the order must provide the home court with a copy of the order as made or amended, together with such other documents and information relating to the case as it considers likely to be of assistance to that court; and paragraphs (b) to (d) of subsection (1) of section 219 (provision of copies of relevant orders) do not apply.

7. In section 220 (duty of offender to keep in touch with responsible officer) the refer- **23–103** ence to the responsible officer is to be read in accordance with paragraph 2(2) or 4(2).

8. Where a community order is made or amended in accordance with paragraph 1 or **23–104** 3, then, subject to the following provisions of this Part of this Schedule—

    (a) the order is to be treated as if it were a corresponding order made in the part of the United Kingdom in which the offender resides, or will be residing at the relevant time, and

    (b) the legislation relating to such orders which has effect in that part of the United Kingdom applies accordingly.

9. Before making or amending a community order in those circumstances the court **23–105** must explain to the offender in ordinary language—

    (a) the requirements of the legislation relating to corresponding orders which has effect in the part of the United Kingdom in which he resides or will be residing at the relevant time,

    (b) the powers of the home court under that legislation, as modified by this Part of this Schedule, and

    (c) its own powers under this Part of this Schedule.

10. The home court may exercise in relation to the community order any power which **23–106** it could exercise in relation to the corresponding order made by a court in the part of the United Kingdom in which the home court exercises jurisdiction, by virtue of the legislation relating to such orders which has effect in that part, except the following—

    (a) any power to discharge or revoke the order (other than a power to revoke the order where the offender has been convicted of a further offence and the court has imposed a custodial sentence),

    (b) any power to deal with the offender for the offence in respect of which the order was made,

    (c) in the case of a community order imposing an unpaid work requirement, any power to vary the order by substituting for the number of hours of work specified in it any greater number than the court which made the order could have specified, and

Part IV

(d) in the case of a community order imposing a curfew requirement, any power to vary the order by substituting for the period specified in it any longer period than the court which made the order could have specified.

23–107   11. If at any time while legislation relating to corresponding orders which has effect in Scotland or Northern Ireland applies by virtue of paragraph 7 to a community order made in England and Wales—

(a) it appears to the home court—
   (i) if that court is in Scotland, on information from the local authority officer concerned, or
   (ii) if that court is in Northern Ireland, upon a complaint being made to a justice of the peace acting for the petty sessions district for the time being specified in the order,

that the offender has failed to comply with any of the requirements of the order, or

(b) it appears to the home court—
   (i) if that court is in Scotland, on the application of the offender or of the local authority officer concerned, or
   (ii) if it is in Northern Ireland, on the application of the offender or of the probation officer concerned,

that it would be in the interests of justice for a power conferred by paragraph 13 or 14 of Schedule 8 to be exercised,

the home court may require the offender to appear before the court which made the order or the court which last amended the order in England and Wales.

23–108   12. Where an offender is required by virtue of paragraph 11 to appear before a court in England and Wales that court—

(a) may issue a warrant for his arrest, and
(b) may exercise any power which it could exercise in respect of the community order if the offender resided in England and Wales,

and any enactment relating to the exercise of such powers has effect accordingly, and with any reference to the responsible officer being read as a reference to the local authority officer or probation officer concerned.

23–109   13. Paragraph 12(b) does not enable the court to amend the community order unless—

(a) where the offender resides in Scotland, it appears to the court that the conditions in paragraph 1(1)(a) and (b) are satisfied in relation to any requirement to be imposed, or
(b) where the offender resides in Northern Ireland, it appears to the court that the conditions in paragraph 3(1)(a) and (b) are satisfied in relation to any requirement to be imposed.

23–110   14. The preceding paragraphs of this Schedule have effect in relation to the amendment of a community order by virtue of paragraph 12(b) as they have effect in relation to the amendment of such an order by virtue of paragraph 1(3) or 3(3).

23–111   15. Where an offender is required by virtue of paragraph (a) of paragraph 11 to appear before a court in England and Wales—

(a) the home court must send to that court a certificate certifying that the offender has failed to comply with such of the requirements of the order as may be specified in the certificate, together with such other particulars of the case as may be desirable, and
(b) a certificate purporting to be signed by the clerk of the home court is admissible as evidence of the failure before the court which made the order.

III. CUSTODIAL SENTENCES

A. Committal for Sentence

23–112   If a magistrates' court has convicted a person aged 18 or over of an offence triable either way, it may form the view that the defendant requires a sentence that only the Crown Court has the power to impose. In those circumstances, the magistrates' court may have the power to commit the defendant to the Crown Court for sentence. The decision will be accompanied by a decision on whether the defendant should be remanded in custody or on bail. There have been suggestions that, since the committal is for a sentence beyond the powers of the magistrates' court, that committal should be in custody in most circumstances. However, that approach confuses two distinct decisions—that on the appropriate sentence and that on what is necessary to ensure the defendant attends court, etc. The better approach is to start from the basis of the status of the defendant before committal. Generally speaking, a defendant on bail up to committal would remain on bail pending sentence in the Crown Court whereas a defendant in custody would remain in custody: *Rafferty* [1999] 1 Cr.App.R. 235.

The power to commit for sentence will change significantly on the introduction of the **23–113** new allocation procedure set out in Schedule 3 to the *Criminal Justice Act* 2003. The underlying principle of the changes is that the same court should determine guilt and impose sentence in most circumstances. Where these provisions apply, a magistrates' court will cease to have a general power to commit for sentence an offence in respect of whom it has accepted summary trial for an either way offence where the offender had not indicated a guilty plea prior to the allocation decision. Where an offender does indicate a guilty plea at that stage, the court retains the power to commit the case to the Crown Court for sentence where it considers the offence to be sufficiently serious. In any case, there will continue to be specific powers of committal, for instance, for dangerous offenders or those in breach of Crown Court imposed orders.

For the power of committal for sentence to be used, the offence must be an either **23–114** way offence, the defendant must be 18 years old or over, the defendant must have indicated an intention to plead guilty during the initial allocation procedure (see *ante*, Ch.7) and the court must have convicted on the basis of that indication: section 3(1). If those criteria are met and the court considers that the offence (or the combination of the offence and one or more offences associated with it) was so serious that the Crown Court should have the power to deal with the offender as if the offender had been convicted at the Crown Court, it may commit the offender for sentence: section 3(2). These powers apply equally to a corporation: section 3(5).

A defendant committed to the Crown Court for sentence in relation to an either way **23–115** offence will generally be susceptible to the whole range of sentencing powers available to the Court but other cases may in certain circumstances also be committed and then the Crown Court will be restricted to the powers available to a magistrates' court. Where a defendant is committed for sentence for an either way offence, the court may also commit for sentence any other offence that is imprisonable or endorsable of which the court has convicted the defendant: section 6.

An additional power to commit for sentence is provided in respect of offenders who may require a sentence of imprisonment for public protection or an extended sentence. This power is available where an offender aged 18 or over is convicted of a "specified offence". This is defined in section 224 as a "specified violent offence or a specified sexual offence"—these are set out in Schedule 15 to the Act and contain a wide variety of offences that commonly come before a magistrates' court. It is not limited to those circumstances where a defendant has indicated a guilty plea during the initial (allocation) procedure nor is it constrained by the giving of an indication of a non-custodial sentence following a request under section 19 of the *Magistrates' Courts Act* 1980 for an indication of sentence. In relation to adult offenders there is a presumption in favour of imposing one of the new sentences where the offender who is convicted of a "specified offence" has previously been convicted of a "relevant offence": section 229(1), (3) and (4). A "relevant offence" is a specified offence or its equivalent under provisions in Scotland or Northern Ireland (set out in Schedules 16 and 17) since the trigger of the presumption is an offence of the prescribed nature committed anywhere in the UK.

For example, an offender aged 18 or over convicted for assault occasioning actual bodily harm with a previous conviction for affray would raise the presumption set out in section 229(3). Detailed consideration has been given to the assessment of the criterion for use of one of these sentences for public protection. Such a sentence is mandatory where the court imposing sentence considers that "there is a significant risk to members of the public of serious harm occasioned by the commission by the offender of further specified offences". As noted *ante*, by virtue of section 229(3) of the Act, if the offender was aged 18 or over when the current offence was committed and has been convicted previously of a relevant offence in any part of the United Kingdom, there is an assumption that that risk exists. All the sentences for dangerous offenders may only be imposed in the Crown Court. However, the issue will need to be considered by a magistrates' court where an offender has been convicted of a specified offence in order to determine whether or not to commit the offender for sentence.

The Court of Appeal set out a number of principles in *Lang* [2006] 2 Cr.App.R. (S.) 3.

> "In our judgment, the following factors should be borne in mind when a sentencer is assessing significant risk—
>
> (i) The risk identified must be significant. This is a higher threshold than mere possibility of occurrence and in our view can be taken to mean (as in the Oxford Dictionary) 'noteworthy, of considerable amount or importance'.
>
> (ii) In assessing the risk of further offences being committed, the sentencer should take into account the nature and circumstances of the current offence; the offender's history of offending including not just the kind of offence but its circumstances and the sentence passed, details of which the prosecution must have available, and, whether the offending demonstrates any pattern; social and economic factors in relation to the offender including accommodation, employability, education, associates, relationships and drug or alcohol abuse; and the offender's thinking, attitude towards offending and supervision and emotional state. Information in relation to these matters will most readily, though not exclusively, come from antecedents and pre-sentence probation and medical reports. The Guide for sentences for public protection issued in June 2005 for the National Probation Service affords valuable guidance for probation officers. The guidance in relation to assessment of dangerousness in paragraph 5 is compatible with the terms of this judgment. The sentencer will be guided, but not bound by, the assessment of risk in such reports. A sentencer who contemplates differing from the assessment in such a report should give both counsel the opportunity of addressing the point.
>
> (iii) If the foreseen specified offence is serious, there will clearly be some cases, though not by any means all, in which there may be a significant risk of serious harm. For example, robbery is a serious offence. But it can be committed in a wide variety of ways many of which do not give rise to a significant risk of serious harm. Sentencers must therefore guard against assuming there is a significant risk of serious harm merely because the foreseen specified offence is serious.
>
> (iv) If the foreseen specified offence is not serious, there will be comparatively few cases in which a risk of serious harm will properly be regarded as significant. The huge variety of offences in Schedule 15, includes many which, in themselves, are not suggestive of serious harm. Repetitive violent or sexual offending at a relatively low level without serious harm does not of itself give rise to a significant risk of serious harm in the future. There may, in such cases, be some risk of future victims being more adversely affected than past victims but this, of itself, does not give rise to significant risk of serious harm.
>
> (v) In relation to the rebuttable assumption to which section 229(3) gives rise, the court is accorded a discretion if, in the light of information about the current offence, the offender and his previous offences, it would be unreasonable to conclude that there is a significant risk. The exercise of such a discretion is, historically, at the very heart of judicial sentencing and the language of the statute indicates that judges are expected, albeit starting from the assumption, to exercise their ability to reach a reasonable conclusion in the light of the information before them. It is to be noted that the assumption will be rebutted, if at all, as an exercise of judgment: the statute includes no reference to the burden or standard of proof. As we have indicated *ante*, it will usually be unreasonable to conclude that the assumption applies unless information about the offences, pattern of behaviour and offender show a significant risk of serious harm from further offences.
>
> (vi) It cannot have been Parliament's intention, in a statute dealing with the liberty of the subject, to require the imposition of indeterminate sentences for the commission of relatively minor offences. On the contrary, Parliament's repeatedly expressed intention is to protect the public from serious harm (compare the reasoning of the Court in relation to automatic life sentences in *Offen* [2001] 2 Cr.App.R. (S.) 10, paras 96 to 99."

A magistrates' court will be dealing with specified offences that are not serious offences and it seems that the risk criterion is set at quite a high level for such offences. Where there is a risk of further offences, unless those further offences would be "serious offences" within the terms of the Act, the Court of Appeal stated that it was likely to be rare for there to be a "significant risk of serious harm". Even where the existence of previous convictions for relevant offences brings the statutory assumption of risk into play, the Court of Appeal again set the test high:

> "The provisions for assessment of dangerousness in section 229 distinguish between offenders aged 18 or over with a previous conviction for a specified offence and those under 18 or with no such previous conviction. In both cases, information is identified which the court must or may take into account in assessing dangerousness but there is a rebuttable assumption of dangerousness in relation to adults with a previous specified offence conviction. In our judgment, when sections 229 and 224 are read together, unless the information about offences, pattern of behaviour and the offender (to which regard must be paid under section 229(3)) show a significant risk of serious harm (defined by section 224 as death or serious injury) from further offences, it will usually be unreasonable to conclude that the assumption applies."

Further consideration on this point has been given by the Court of Appeal (Criminal Division) in *Johnson and others* [2006] EWCA Crim 2486 some of which will be relevant to the decisions to be taken in a magistrates' court whether a specified offence should be committed to the Crown Court. The judgment points out at para. [10] that:

> "(i) Just as the absence of previous convictions does not preclude a finding of dangerousness, the existence of previous convictions for specified offences does not compel such a finding. There is a presumption that it does so, which may be rebutted.
>
> (ii) If a finding of dangerousness can be made against an offender without previous specified convictions, it also follows that previous offences, not in fact specified for the purposes of section 229, are not disqualified from consideration. Thus, for example, as indeed the statute recognises, a pattern of minor previous offences of gradually escalating seriousness may be significant. In other words, it is not right . . . that unless the previous offences were specified offences they were irrelevant.
>
> (iii) Where the facts of the instant offence, or indeed any specified offences for the purposes of section 229(3) are examined, it may emerge that no harm actually occurred. That may be advantageous to the offender, and some of the cases examined in *Lang* exemplify the point. Another such example is *Isa* [2006] CLR 356. On the other hand the absence of harm may be entirely fortuitous. A victim cowering away from an armed assailant may avoid direct physical injury or serious psychological harm. Faced with such a case, the sentencer considering dangerousness may wish to reflect, for example, on the likely response of the offender if his victim, instead of surrendering, resolutely defended himself. It does not automatically follow from the absence of actual harm caused by the offender to date, that the risk that he will cause serious harm in the future is negligible.
>
> ...*Shaffi* [2006] EWCA Crim 418 ... is not authority for the proposition that as a matter of law offences which did not result in harm to the victim should be treated as irrelevant....
>
> (iv) We considered arguments based on the inadequacy, suggestibility, or vulnerability of the offender, and how these and similar characteristics may bear on dangerousness. Such characteristics may serve to mitigate the offender's culpability. In the final analysis however they may also serve to produce or reinforce the conclusion that the offender is dangerous. In one of the instant cases it was suggested that the sentence was wrong because an inadequate offender had suffered what was described as an "aberrant moment". But, as experience shows, aberrant moments may be productive of catastrophe. The sentencer is right to be alert to such risks of aberrant moments in the future, and their consequences.
>
> (v) In *Lang*, Rose LJ suggested that the prosecution should be in a position to describe the facts of previous specified offences. This is plainly desirable, (see also *Isa*) but this is not always practicable. There is no reason why the prosecution's failure to comply with this good practice, even when it can and should, should either make an adjournment obligatory, or indeed preclude the imposition of the sentence, when appropriate. In any such case, counsel for the defendant should be in a position to explain the circumstances, on the basis of his instructions. If the Crown is not in a position to challenge those instructions, then the court may proceed on the information it has. Equally, there are some situations in

which the sentence imposed by the court dealing with earlier specified offences may enable the sentencer to draw inferences about its seriousness, or otherwise. In short, failure to comply with best practice on this point should be discouraged, but it does not normally preclude the imposition of the sentence."

Powers of Criminal Court (Sentencing) Act 2000, ss.3, 3A, 4–6

Committal for sentence on indication of guilty plea to serious offence triable either way

23–116   **3.**—(1) Subject to subsection (4) below, this section applies where—

    (a) a person aged 18 or over appears or is brought before a magistrates' court ("the court") on an information charging him with an offence triable either way ("the offence");

    (b) he or his representative indicates under section 17A or (as the case may be) 17B of the *Magistrates' Courts Act* 1980 (initial procedure: accused to indicate intention as to plea), but not section 20(7) of that Act, that he would plead guilty if the offence were to proceed to trial; and

    (c) proceeding as if section 9(1) of that Act were complied with and he pleaded guilty under it, the court convicts him of the offence.

(2) If the court is of the opinion that—

    (a) the offence; or

    (b) the combination of the offence and one or more offences associated with it, was so serious that the Crown Court should, in the court's opinion, have the power to deal with the offender in any way it could deal with him if he had been convicted on indictment, the court may commit him in custody or on bail to the Crown Court for sentence in accordance with section 5(1) below.

(3) Where the court commits a person under subsection (2) above, section 6 below (which enables a magistrates' court, where it commits a person under this section in respect of an offence, also to commit him to the Crown Court to be dealt with in respect of certain other offences) shall apply accordingly.

(4) This section does not apply in relation to an offence as regards which this section is excluded by section 17D of the *Magistrates' Courts Act* 1980 (certain offences where value involved is small).

(5) The preceding provisions of this section shall apply in relation to a corporation as if—

    (a) the corporation were an individual aged 18 or over; and

    (b) in subsection (2) above, the words "in custody or on bail" were omitted.

[As substituted by Sched. 3 to the *Criminal Justice Act* 2003.]

Committal for sentence of dangerous adult offenders

23–117   **3A.**—(1) This section applies where on the summary trial of a specified offence triable either way a person aged 18 or over is convicted of the offence.

(2) If, in relation to the offence, it appears to the court that the criteria for the imposition of a sentence under section 225(3) or 227(2) of the *Criminal Justice Act* 2003 would be met, the court must commit the offender in custody or on bail to the Crown Court for sentence in accordance with section 5(1) below.

(3) Where the court commits a person under subsection (2) above, section 6 below (which enables a magistrates' court, where it commits a person under this section in respect of an offence, also to commit him to the Crown Court to be dealt with in respect of certain other offences) shall apply accordingly.

(4) In reaching any decision under or taking any step contemplated by this section—

    (a) the court shall not be bound by any indication of sentence given in respect of the offence under section 20 of the *Magistrates' Courts Act* 1980 (procedure where summary trial appears more suitable); and

    (b) nothing the court does under this section may be challenged or be the subject of any appeal in any court on the ground that it is not consistent with an indication of sentence.

(5) Nothing in this section shall prevent the court from committing a specified offence to the Crown Court for sentence under section 3 above if the provisions of that section are satisfied.

(6) In this section, references to a specified offence are to a specified offence within the meaning of section 224 of the *Criminal Justice Act* 2003.

[As inserted by Sched. 3 to the *Criminal Justice Act* 2003.]

Committal for sentence on indication of guilty plea to offence triable either way

4.—(1) This section applies where—   **23–118**

   (a) a person aged 18 or over appears or is brought before a magistrates' court ("the court") on an information charging him with an offence triable either way ("the offence");

   (b) he or (where applicable) his representative indicates under section 17A, 17B or 20(7) of the *Magistrates' Courts Act* 1980 that he would plead guilty if the offence were to proceed to trial; and

   (c) proceeding as if section 9(1) of that Act were complied with and he pleaded guilty under it, the court convicts him of the offence.

(1A) But this section does not apply to an offence as regards which this section is excluded by section 17D of that Act (certain offences where value involved is small).

(2) If the court has committed the offender to the Crown Court for trial for one or more related offences, that is to say, one or more offences which, in its opinion, are related to the offence, it may commit him in custody or on bail to the Crown Court to be dealt with in respect of the offence in accordance with section 5(1) below.

(3) If the power conferred by subsection (2) above is not exercisable but the court is still to determine to, or to determine whether to, send the offender to the Crown Court for trial under section 51 or 51A of the *Crime and Disorder Act* 1998 for one or more related offences—

   (a) it shall adjourn the proceedings relating to the offence until after it has made those determinations; and

   (b) if it sends the offender to the Crown Court for trial for one or more related offences, it may then exercise that power.

(4) Where the court—

   (a) under subsection (2) above commits the offender to the Crown Court to be dealt with in respect of the offence, and

   (b) does not state that, in its opinion, it also has power so to commit him under section 3(2) or, as the case may be, section 3A(2) above,

section 5(1) below shall not apply unless he is convicted before the Crown Court of one or more of the related offences.

(5) Where section 5(1) below does not apply, the Crown Court may deal with the offender in respect of the offence in any way in which the magistrates' court could deal with him if it had just convicted him of the offence.

(6) Where the court commits a person under subsection (2) above, section 6 below (which enables a magistrates' court, where it commits a person under this section in respect of an offence, also to commit him to the Crown Court to be dealt with in respect of certain other offences) shall apply accordingly.

(7) For the purposes of this section one offence is related to another if, were they both to be prosecuted on indictment, the charges for them could be joined in the same indictment.

(8) In reaching any decision under or taking any step contemplated by this section—

   (a) the court shall not be bound by any indication of sentence given in respect of the offence under section 20 of the *Magistrates' Courts Act* 1980 (procedure where summary trial appears more suitable); and

   (b) nothing the court does under this section may be challenged or be the subject of any appeal in any court on the ground that it is not consistent with an indication of sentence.

[As amended by Sched. 3 to the *Criminal Justice Act* 2003.]

Power of Crown Court on committal for sentence under ss.3, 3A and 4

5.—(1) Where an offender is committed by a magistrates' court for sentence under section 3,   **23–119**
3A or 4 above, the Crown Court shall inquire into the circumstances of the case and may deal with the offender in any way in which it could deal with him if he had just been convicted of the offence on indictment before the court.

(2) In relation to committals under section 4 above, subsection (1) above has effect subject to section 4(4) and (5) above.

(3) Section 20A(1) of the *Magistrates' Courts Act* 1980 (which relates to the effect of an indication of sentence under section 20 of that Act) shall not apply in respect of any specified offence (within the meaning of section 224 of the *Criminal Justice Act* 2003)—

    (a) in respect of which the offender is committed under section 3A(2) above; or

    (b) in respect of which—

        (i) the offender is committed under section 4(2) above; and

        (ii) the court states under section 4(4) above that, in its opinion, it also has power to commit the offender under section 3A(2) above.

[As substituted by Sched. 3 to the *Criminal Justice Act* 2003.]

Committal for sentence in certain cases where offender committed in respect of another offence

23–120   **6.**—(1) This section applies where a magistrates' court ("the committing court") commits a person in custody or on bail to the Crown Court under any enactment mentioned in subsection (4) below to be sentenced or otherwise dealt with in respect of an offence ("the relevant offence").

(2) Where this section applies and the relevant offence is an indictable offence, the committing court may also commit the offender, in custody or on bail as the case may require, to the Crown Court to be dealt with in respect of any other offence whatsoever in respect of which the committing court has power to deal with him (being an offence of which he has been convicted by that or any other court).

(3) Where this section applies and the relevant offence is a summary offence, the committing court may commit the offender, in custody or on bail as the case may require, to the Crown Court to be dealt with in respect of—

    (a) any other offence of which the committing court has convicted him, being either—

        (i) an offence punishable with imprisonment; or

        (ii) an offence in respect of which the committing court has a power or duty to order him to be disqualified under section 34, 35 or 36 of the *Road Traffic Offenders Act* 1988 (disqualification for certain motoring offences); or

    (b) any suspended sentence in respect of which the committing court has under para. 11(1) of Sched. 12 to the Criminal Justice Act power to deal with him.

(4) The enactments referred to in subsection (1) above are—

    (a) the *Vagrancy Act* 1824 (incorrigible rogues);

    (b) sections 3 to 4A above (committal for sentence for offences triable either way);

    (c) section 13(5) below (conditionally discharged person convicted of further offence);

    (d) [...]

    (e) para. 11(2) of Sched. 12 to the Criminal Justice Act (committal to Crown Court where offender convicted during operational period of suspended sentence).

[As amended by Sched. 3 to the *Criminal Justice Act* 2003.]

Criminal Justice Act 2003, s.224, 227, 229

Meaning of "specified offence" etc.

23–121   **224.**—(1) An offence is a "specified offence" for the purposes of this Chapter if it is a specified violent offence or a specified sexual offence.

(2) An offence is a "serious offence" for the purposes of this Chapter if and only if—

    (a) it is a specified offence, and

    (b) it is, apart from section 225, punishable in the case of a person aged 18 or over by—

        (i) imprisonment for life [or, in the case of a person aged at least 18 but under 21, custody for life], or

        (ii) imprisonment [or, in the case of a person aged at least 18 but under 21, detention in a young offender institution,] for a determinate period of ten years or more.

(3) In this Chapter—

"relevant offence" has the meaning given by section 229(4);

"serious harm" means death or serious personal injury, whether physical or psychological;

"specified violent offence" means an offence specified in Part 1 of Schedule 15;

"specified sexual offence" means an offence specified in Part 2 of that Schedule.

[Words inserted by the *Criminal Justice Act 2003 (Sentencing) (Transitory Provisions) Order* (S.I. 2005 No. 643).]

Extended sentence for certain violent or sexual offences: persons 18 or over

227.—(1) This section applies where—   **23–122**

(a) a person aged 18 or over is convicted of a specified offence, other than a serious offence, committed after the commencement of this section, and

(b) the court considers that there is a significant risk to members of the public of serious harm occasioned by the commission by the offender of further specified offences.

(2) The court must impose on the offender an extended sentence of imprisonment [or, in the case of a person aged at least 18 but under 21, an extended sentence of detention in a young offender institution], that is to say, a sentence of imprisonment [or detention in a young offender institution] the term of which is equal to the aggregate of—

(a) the appropriate custodial term, and

(b) a further period ("the extension period") for which the offender is to be subject to a licence and which is of such length as the court considers necessary for the purpose of protecting members of the public from serious harm occasioned by the commission by him of further specified offences.

(3) In subsection (2) "the appropriate custodial term" means a term of imprisonment [or detention in a young offender institution] (not exceeding the maximum term permitted for the offence) which—

(a) is the term that would (apart from this section) be imposed in compliance with section 153(2), or

(b) where the term that would be so imposed is a term of less than 12 months, is a term of 12 months.

(4) The extension period must not exceed—

(a) five years in the case of a specified violent offence, and

(b) eight years in the case of a specified sexual offence.

(5) The term of an extended sentence of imprisonment [or detention in a young offender institution] passed under this section in respect of an offence must not exceed the maximum term permitted for the offence.

[Words inserted by the *Criminal Justice Act 2003 (Sentencing) (Transitory Provisions) Order* (S.I. 2005 No. 643).]

The assessment of dangerousness

229.—(1) This section applies where—   **23–123**

(a) a person has been convicted of a specified offence, and

(b) it falls to a court to assess under any of sections 225 to 228 whether there is a significant risk to members of the public of serious harm occasioned by the commission by him of further such offences.

(2) If at the time when that offence was committed the offender had not been convicted in any part of the United Kingdom of any relevant offence or was aged under 18, the court in making the assessment referred to in subsection (1)(b)—

(a) must take into account all such information as is available to it about the nature and circumstances of the offence,

(b) may take into account any information which is before it about any pattern of behaviour of which the offence forms part, and

(c) may take into account any information about the offender which is before it.

(3) If at the time when that offence was committed the offender was aged 18 or over and had been convicted in any part of the United Kingdom of one or more relevant offences, the court must assume that there is such a risk as is mentioned in subsection (1)(b) unless, after taking into account—

Part IV

(a) all such information as is available to it about the nature and circumstances of each of the offences,

(b) where appropriate, any information which is before it about any pattern of behaviour of which any of the offences forms part, and

(c) any information about the offender which is before it,

the court considers that it would be unreasonable to conclude that there is such a risk.

(4) In this Chapter "relevant offence" means—

(a) a specified offence,

(b) an offence specified in Schedule 16 (offences under the law of Scotland), or

(c) an offence specified in Schedule 17 (offences under the law of Northern Ireland).

23–124   Where a court adjourns a case after conviction, care needs to be taken to avoid restricting the power of the next court to commit for sentence by raising a legitimate expectation in the mind of the defendant that he will not be committed. In *Feltham Justices, ex p. Rees* [2001] 2 Cr.App.R.(S.) 1, DC Rose L.J. outlined the circumstances leading to a finding of a legitimate expectation which may fetter the power of the Court to commit for sentence. In that case, the critical factors leading to a finding that there was a legitimate expectation were that:

— the justices had been addressed as to the adequacy of their sentencing powers on behalf of the applicant,

— the justices had specifically invited the applicant's solicitor to mitigate before them,

— the solicitor had proceeded to mitigate before them,

— the justices had then adjourned, apparently to consider the impact of that sentence, and that adjournment lasted some ten minutes.

— when the justices returned to court, they said that "they" were unable to sentence him on that date as "they" would require more information in the form of a pre-sentence report.

23–125   The justices had stated that they were "leaving all options open" but, in the light of the events listed *ante*, something more specific was needed if anything other than sentencing in the magistrates' court was envisaged. If justices have in mind that one of the options which is open to them is to commit for sentence, they should specifically say so. Even more care now needs to be taken since courts will be following the guideline of the Sentencing Guidelines Council to state clearly the purposes of sentencing and its assessment of seriousness when adjourning for such a report. It is likely that courts will become more ready to commit for sentence prior to receiving such a report in future.

See also Bingham L.J. in *Nottingham Magistrates' Court, ex p. Davidson* [2000] 1 Cr.App.R.(S.) 167, CA and Potts J. in *Horseferry Road Magistrates' Court, ex p. Rugless* [2000] 1 Cr.App.R.(S.) 484, CA.

23–126   When the Court adjourns sentence after specifically indicating to the defendant that he will not be committed for sentence, unless there is a change in the relevant circumstances, the offender may not be committed for sentence: *Norwich Magistrates' Court, ex p. Elliot* [2000] 1 Cr.App.R.(S.) 152, CA, where Otton L.J. referred to the "seminal judgment" of Kennedy L.J. in *Warley Justices, ex p. DPP* [1999] 1 Cr.App.R.(S.) 156, QBD, where he summarised the position as regards triable either way offences, following a guilty plea by the defendant:

"If, after allowance has been made for the plea of guilty, it appears to the court that it will or may be possible for the court to sentence properly by deploying its statutory power—if necessary to the full—then, as it seems to me, the court should proceed to hear the case in the normal way, and, so long as a committal for sentence remains a possibility, care should be taken to ensure that nothing is said or done which might indicate to an accused that that option has been ruled out.

If a court, initially minded to commit at an early stage of the proceedings, is persuaded not to adopt that course at that stage it can keep the option open by saying that is what it is going to do, and then for example, arranging for the preparation of a pre-sentence report. But if it says that it is satisfied that the case is not one in which it will be necessary for it to commit to the Crown Court for sentence, and then adjourns for the pre-sentence report, when the matter comes back before a differently constituted bench that second bench is likely to consider that so far as committal for sentence is concerned its hands are tied."

The decision to commit for sentence must be based on the assessment of the adequacy of the magistrates' sentencing powers to deal with the offence, not whether the offence would have been triable on indictment had the "plea before venue" procedure not been adopted. In making this assessment, the appropriate allowance should be made for the guilty plea. Where this discount results in sentence being able to be imposed in the magistrates' court, it would be helpful if this could be stated: *Warley Magistrates' Court, ex p. DPP, ante.* The definitive guideline issued by the Sentencing Guidelines Council on reductions for a guilty plea covers the situation where a guilty plea has been entered and that fact alone enables a court to decide not to commit the case for sentence. In such circumstances, it is legitimate for the magistrates' court to impose the maximum sentence available to it since the effect of the guilty plea has been to allow that court to pass sentence rather than to commit for sentence. The fact that that has been done should be stated clearly by the court (Guideline: *Reduction in Sentence for a Guilty Plea*, para. 5.8). **23–127**

A magistrates' court may also commit for sentence if it considers that, although a financial penalty is appropriate, the limits on the level of financial penalties it can impose is too low to deal with the offence: *North Essex Justices, ex p. Lloyd* [2001] 2 Cr.App.R.(S.) 86.

Where the Court is dealing with an offender who has breached a community order made by a magistrates' court by revoking the order, the Court may not commit him to the Crown Court for sentence for the offence in relation to which the order was made: *Jordan* [1998] 2 Cr.App.R.(S.) 83, DC. The magistrates may still deal with an offender who has been unlawfully committed: *Norfolk JJ, ex p. DPP* [1950] 2 K.B. 558, DC. Where a magistrates' court has revoked an order made by the Crown Court, such an offender may be committed to the Crown Court for sentence and remanded in custody or on bail: Sched. 8(9)(b). **23–128**

B. SENTENCES OF IMPRISONMENT

(1) Purpose and effect

Committing a person to a custodial sentence is the most severe punishment available and is hedged around by a number of conditions that need to be fulfilled: **23–129**

— the offence (or combination of the offence and one or more other associated with it) must be so serious that no other sentence is justified (with a few exceptions),

— the defendant must be legally represented (or have not taken the opportunity to be),

— in most circumstances, a pre-sentence report will be required and

— the length of the sentence must be no more than is commensurate with the seriousness of the offence.

In its Guideline, *Overarching Principles: Seriousness*, published in December 2004, the Sentencing Guidelines Council considered the threshold that has to be passed. The Council emphasises that the purpose of the threshold test is "to reserve prison as a punishment for the most serious offences" (para. 1.32). There is also a firm reminder that the passing of the threshold is only one of the early steps in determining sentence. The test is based on the seriousness of the offence alone. Other factors then come into play which may justify a non-custodial sentence (para. 1.32). The Guideline sets out (at para. 1.33) a series of questions to be asked by the court when considering a custodial sentence.

When the relevant provisions are brought into force, new powers will be available. Where a magistrates' court is dealing with an either way offence that is punishable with imprisonment in a magistrates' court, the maximum custodial sentence will be 12 months for a single offence and 65 weeks for two or more such offences: *Magistrates' Courts Act* 1980, ss.32 and 133; *Criminal Justice Act* 2003, ss.154 and 282. Where a magistrates' court is dealing with a summary offence that is imprisonable, the maximum is 51 weeks. (However, see the power to impose detention for one day either as a sentence or in default of payment of a fine: section 135, *Magistrates' Courts Act* 1980 *ante*, at § 24–83).

Criminal Justice Act 2003, ss.152–153

General restrictions on imposing discretionary custodial sentences

23–130   **152.**—(1) This section applies where a person is convicted of an offence punishable with a custodial sentence other than one—

(a) fixed by law, or

(b) falling to be imposed under section 51A(2) of the *Firearms Act* 1968, under section 110(2) or 111(2) of the Sentencing Act, under section 29(4) or (6) of the *Violent Crime Reduction Act* 2006 or under any of sections 225 to 228 of this Act.

(2) The court must not pass a custodial sentence unless it is of the opinion that the offence, or the combination of the offence and one or more offences associated with it, was so serious that neither a fine alone nor a community sentence can be justified for the offence.

(3) Nothing in subsection (2) prevents the court from passing a custodial sentence on the offender if—

(a) he fails to express his willingness to comply with a requirement which is proposed by the court to be included in a community order and which requires an expression of such willingness, or

(b) he fails to comply with an order under section 161(2) (pre-sentence drug testing).

Length of discretionary custodial sentences: general provision

23–131   **153.**—(1) This section applies where a court passes a custodial sentence other than one fixed by law or falling to be imposed under section 225 or 226.

(2) Subject to section 51A(2) of the *Firearms Act* 1968, section 110(2) and 111(2) of the Sentencing Act, section 29(4) or (6) of the *Violent Crime Reduction Act* 2006 and sections 227(2) and 228(2) of this Act, the custodial sentence must be for the shortest term (not exceeding the permitted maximum) that in the opinion of the court is commensurate with the seriousness of the offence, or the combination of the offence and one or more offences associated with it.

Magistrates' Courts Act 1980, s.132

Minimum term

23–132   **132.** A magistrates' court shall not impose imprisonment for less than five days.

Criminal Justice Act 2003, ss.157–158

Additional requirements in case of mentally disordered offender

23–133   **157.**—(1) Subject to subsection (2), in any case where the offender is or appears to be mentally disordered, the court must obtain and consider a medical report before passing a custodial sentence other than one fixed by law.

(2) Subsection (1) does not apply if, in the circumstances of the case, the court is of the opinion that it is unnecessary to obtain a medical report.

(3) Before passing a custodial sentence other than one fixed by law on an offender who is or appears to be mentally disordered, a court must consider—

(a) any information before it which relates to his mental condition (whether given in a medical report, a pre-sentence report or otherwise), and

(b) the likely effect of such a sentence on that condition and on any treatment which may be available for it.

(4) No custodial sentence which is passed in a case to which subsection (1) applies is invalidated by the failure of a court to comply with that subsection, but any court on an appeal against such a sentence—

(a) must obtain a medical report if none was obtained by the court below, and

(b) must consider any such report obtained by it or by that court.

(5) In this section "mentally disordered", in relation to any person, means suffering from a mental disorder within the meaning of the *Mental Health Act* 1983.

(6) In this section "medical report" means a report as to an offender's mental condition made or submitted orally or in writing by a registered medical practitioner who is approved for the purposes of section 12 of the *Mental Health Act* 1983 by the Secretary of State as having special experience in the diagnosis or treatment of mental disorder.

(7) Nothing in this section is to be taken to limit the generality of section 156.

Meaning of "pre-sentence report"

158.—(1) In this Part "pre-sentence report" means a report which—　　**23–134**

(a) with a view to assisting the court in determining the most suitable method of dealing with an offender, is made or submitted by an appropriate officer, and

(b) contains information as to such matters, presented in such manner, as may be prescribed by rules made by the Secretary of State.

(2) In subsection (1) "an appropriate officer" means—

(a) where the offender is aged 18 or over, an officer of a local probation board, and

(b) where the offender is aged under 18, an officer of a local probation board, a social worker of a local authority or a member of a youth offending team.

(2) Guideline

Guideline: Overarching Principles: Seriousness

E. THE SENTENCING THRESHOLDS

1.30 Assessing the seriousness of an offence is only the first step in the process of determining　**23–135** the appropriate sentence in an individual case. Matching the offence to a type and level of sentence is a separate and complex exercise assisted by the application of the respective threshold tests for custodial and community sentences.

The Custody Threshold

1.32 In applying the threshold test, sentencers should note:

- the clear intention of the threshold test is to reserve prison as a punishment for the most serious offences;
- it is impossible to determine definitively which features of a particular offence make it serious enough to merit a custodial sentence;
- passing the custody threshold does not mean that a custodial sentence should be deemed inevitable, and custody can still be avoided in the light of personal mitigation or where there is a suitable intervention in the community which provides sufficient restriction (by way of punishment) while addressing the rehabilitation of the offender to prevent future crime. For example, a prolific offender who currently could expect a short custodial sentence (which, in advance of custody plus, would have no provision for supervision on release) might more appropriately receive a suitable community sentence.

1.33 The approach to the imposition of a custodial sentence under the new framework should be as follows:

(a) has the custody threshold been passed?

(b) if so, is it unavoidable that a custodial sentence be imposed?

(c) if so, can that sentence be suspended? (sentencers should be clear that they would have imposed a custodial sentence if the power to suspend had not been available)

(d) if not, can the sentence be served intermittently?

(e) if not, impose a sentence which takes immediate effect for the term commensurate with the seriousness of the offence.

Custody is primarily for those convicted of violent offences, serious sexual offences　**23–136** and, perhaps, for persistent petty offenders. Considerable judicial and Parliamentary scrutiny has been given to the circumstances in which a custodial sentence is justified. The starting point is the seriousness of the offence. In considering that, the Court must

Part IV

treat as an aggravating factor each recent and relevant previous conviction of the offender (*Criminal Justice Act* 2003, s.143(2)) and must treat it as an aggravating factor if the offence was committed while the offender was on bail (s.143(3)) or was racially or religiously aggravated (s.145).

An offence which is deliberate and premeditated or which involves an excessive response to provocation; an offence which inflicts personal injury or mental trauma, particularly if permanent, will usually be more serious than one which inflicts financial loss only: *Howells* [1999] 1 Cr.App.R. 98, CA.

Where offending has been fuelled by addiction to drink or drugs, the Court may be inclined to look more favourably on an offender who has already demonstrated (by taking practical steps to that end) a genuine, self-motivated determination to address his addiction: see *ante*, § 23–87 in relation to drug rehabilitation requirements.

Youth and immaturity, while affording no defence, will often justify a less rigorous penalty than would be appropriate for an adult.

23–137   Some leniency will often be given to an offender of previous good character, the more so if there is evidence of positive good character (such as solid employment record or faithful discharge of family duties) as opposed to a mere absence of previous convictions. It will sometimes be appropriate to take account of family responsibilities, or physical or mental disability. However, care will be need to be taken to ensure that it is appropriate to do so. Where the primary purpose of the sentence is to show society's disapproval of the conduct (such as offences of violence in a domestic context), previous good character may be less significant. Similarly where offences are serious but likely to be committed by first offenders (for example, serious fraud on an employer).

Particular care should be taken when considering whether to impose a custodial sentence on a woman or on anyone on whom other people are dependent for their physical care.

While the Court will never impose a custodial sentence unless satisfied that it is necessary to do so, there will be even greater reluctance to impose a custodial sentence on an offender who has never before served such a sentence: *Seed, Stark* [2007] EWCA Crim 254.

23–138   Where the Court is of the opinion that an offence, or the combination of an offence and one or more offences associated with it, is so serious that neither a fine alone or a community sentence can be justified and that such a sentence should be passed, the sentence imposed should be no longer than is necessary to meet the penal purpose which the Court has in mind: *Ollerenshaw* [1999] 1 Cr.App.R.(S.) 65, CA. In any case, it must be no longer than is commensurate with the seriousness of the offence: section 153(2).

The need for caution in the selection of a custodial sentence was emphasised in *Kefford* [2002] EWCA Crim 519 where Lord Woolf C.J. stated that those who are responsible for imposing sentences have to take into account the impact on the prison system of the number of prisoners the prison estate is being required to accommodate at the present time. Whilst, the Court did not intend to deter courts from sending to prison for the appropriate period those who commit offences involving violence or intimidation or other grave crimes, there were other categories of offence where a community punishment or a fine can sometimes be a more appropriate form of sentence than imprisonment. Lord Woolf gave the example of economic crimes, such as obtaining undue credit by fraud, which may not, especially in the case of an offender of hitherto good character, require a custodial sentence.

23–139   See generally on the assessment of the seriousness of an offence in "General Principles of Sentencing" at § 22–3, *ante*.

The maximum sentence of imprisonment provided should be reserved for the worst forms of that offence: *Byrne* (1975) 62 Cr.App.R. 159, CA. When the sentencer is considering whether an offence is one of the worst examples of its kind, he should have regard to cases that have been encountered in practice, rather than unlikely or imaginary examples: *Ambler* [1976] Crim.L.R. 266. The maximum penalty for an offence should not normally be imposed where there is substantial mitigation: *Cade* (1984) 6 Cr.App.R.(S.) 28, CA. Most imprisonable offences are triable either way and so a magistrates' court will often have the option of committing for sentence for the more serious offences. However, for those summary offences that are imprisonable, a court will give credit for any guilty plea and also bear in mind that the longest sentence available should be reserved for the worst type of offending.

(3) Custody Plus Orders

When sections 181 and 182 of the *Criminal Justice Act* 2003 are brought into force, any custodial sentence (with a few exceptions) of less than 12 months will be made under the provisions that are commonly known as custody plus orders. Created in response to concerns that short custodial sentences were perceived as hugely ineffective in reducing re-offending, the order provides for a period in custody followed by a period under supervision in the community subject to requirements set by the court when sentence is imposed. An order will have three elements, an overall term (between 28 and 51 weeks), a custodial period (between 2 and 13 weeks) and a licence period (at least 26 weeks with a maximum up to the difference between the overall term and the custodial period). Accordingly, the shortest sentence will be for 28 weeks. Beyond that, there is a wide variety in options open to the court ranging from two weeks in custody and 49 weeks on licence to 13 weeks in custody and 26–38 weeks on licence. The sentence must be expressed in weeks. Many of the requirements that are available to be included in a community order can also be included in the licence requirements imposed as part of a custody plus order but it is not possible to include a residence requirement nor one of the three treatment requirements (mental health, alcohol and drug rehabilitation). In addition to the conditions imposed by the court, standard conditions will be imposed by the National Offender Management Service on release and these are primarily concerned with issues of residence and reporting to the responsible officer. Where there is a conflict between court imposed requirements and standard conditions, it is the court imposed requirements that take precedence. Where an offender fails to comply with the requirements, the sanction is recall to custody with release determined by the Parole Board—there is no further court involvement. Release from custody will normally be at the end of the period set by the court but, where that period is at least six weeks, there is power given to the Secretary of State to release the offender early provided at least half the sentence (and at least four weeks) have been served: *Criminal Justice Act* 2003, s.246(2). Additionally, when section 282 of the 2003 Act is brought into force, where the offence before the court is an either way offence punishable by imprisonment in a magistrates' court, that court may impose a sentence of 12 months' imprisonment. Such a sentence will not be a custody plus order and the offender will be entitled to be released after the completion of half of the sentence. The remainder of the sentence will be served on licence in the community subject to requirements imposed by the National Offender Management Service when the offender is released: *Criminal Justice Act* 2003, s.250(4). A court may recommend that particular conditions should be imposed on release; the Secretary of State must have regard to such a recommendation but is not bound by it: *Criminal Justice Act* 2003, s.238.

23–140

Criminal Justice Act 2003, ss.181, 182, 250–252, 254, 238

Prison sentences of less than 12 months

181.—(1) Any power of a court to impose a sentence of imprisonment for a term of less than 12 months on an offender may be exercised only in accordance with the following provisions of this section unless the court makes an intermittent custody order (as defined by section 183).

(2) The term of the sentence—

(a) must be expressed in weeks,

(b) must be at least 28 weeks,

(c) must not be more than 51 weeks in respect of any one offence, and

(d) must not exceed the maximum term permitted for the offence.

23–141

(3) The court, when passing sentence, must—

(a) specify a period (in this Chapter referred to as "the custodial period") at the end of which the offender is to be released on a licence, and

(b) by order require the licence to be granted subject to conditions requiring the offender's compliance during the remainder of the term (in this Chapter referred to as "the licence period") or any part of it with one or more requirements falling within section 182(1) and specified in the order.

(4) In this Part "custody plus order" means an order under subsection (3)(b).

(5) The custodial period—

(a) must be at least 2 weeks, and

(b) in respect of any one offence, must not be more than 13 weeks.

(6) In determining the term of the sentence and the length of the custodial period, the court must ensure that the licence period is at least 26 weeks in length.

(7) Where a court imposes two or more terms of imprisonment in accordance with this section to be served consecutively

(a) the aggregate length of the terms of imprisonment must not be more than 65 weeks, and

(b) the aggregate length of the custodial periods must not be more than 26 weeks.

(8) A custody plus order which specifies two or more requirements may, in relation to any requirement, refer to compliance within such part of the licence period as is specified in the order.

(9) Subsection (3)(b) does not apply where the sentence is a suspended sentence.

Licence conditions

23–142   **182.**—(1) The requirements falling within this subsection are—

(a) an unpaid work requirement (as defined by section 199),

(b) an activity requirement (as defined by section 201),

(c) a programme requirement (as defined by section 202),

(d) a prohibited activity requirement (as defined by section 203),

(e) a curfew requirement (as defined by section 204),

(f) an exclusion requirement (as defined by section 205),

(g) a supervision requirement (as defined by section 213), and

(h) in a case where the offender is aged under 25, an attendance centre requirement (as defined by section 214).

(2) The power under section 181(3)(b) to determine the conditions of the licence has effect subject to section 218 and to the following provisions of Chapter 4 relating to particular requirements—

(a) section 199(3) (unpaid work requirement),

(b) section 201(3) and (4) (activity requirement),

(c) section 202(4) and (5) (programme requirement), and

(d) section 203(2) (prohibited activity requirement).

(3) Where the court makes a custody plus order requiring a licence to contain a curfew requirement or an exclusion requirement, the court must also require the licence to contain an electronic monitoring requirement (as defined by section 215) unless—

(a) the court is prevented from doing so by section 215(2) or 218(4), or

(b) in the particular circumstances of the case, it considers it inappropriate to do so.

(4) Where the court makes a custody plus order requiring a licence to contain an unpaid work requirement, an activity requirement, a programme requirement, a prohibited activity requirement, a supervision requirement or an attendance centre requirement, the court may also require the licence to contain an electronic monitoring requirement unless the court is prevented from doing so by section 215(2) or 218(4).

(5) Before making a custody plus order requiring a licence to contain two or more different requirements falling within subsection (1), the court must consider whether, in the circumstances of the case, the requirements are compatible with each other.

Licence conditions

23–143   **250.**—(1) In this section—

(a) "the standard conditions" means such conditions as may be prescribed for the purposes of this section as standard conditions, and

(b) "prescribed" means prescribed by the Secretary of State by order.

(2) Subject to subsection (6) and section 251, any licence under this Chapter in respect of a prisoner serving one or more sentences of imprisonment of less than twelve months and no sentence of twelve months or more—

(a) must include—

(i) the conditions required by the relevant court order, and

(ii) so far as not inconsistent with them, the standard conditions, and

(b) may also include—

(i) any condition which is authorised by section 62 of the *Criminal Justice and Court Services Act* 2000 (electronic monitoring) or section 64 of that Act (drug testing requirements) and which is compatible with the conditions required by the relevant court order, and

(ii) such other conditions of a kind prescribed for the purposes of this paragraph as the Secretary of State may for the time being consider to be necessary for the protection of the public and specify in the licence.

(3) For the purposes of subsection (2)(a)(i), any reference in the relevant court order to the licence period specified in the order is, in relation to a prohibited activity requirement, exclusion requirement, residence requirement or supervision requirement, to be taken to include a reference to any other period during which the prisoner is released on licence under section 246 or 248.

(4) Any licence under this Chapter in respect of a prisoner serving a sentence of imprisonment[or detention in a young offender institution] for a term of twelve months or more (including such a sentence imposed under section 227) or any sentence of detention under section 91 of the Sentencing Act or section 228 of this Act—

(a) must include the standard conditions, and

(b) may include—

(i) any condition authorised by section 62 or 64 of the *Criminal Justice and Court Services Act* 2000, and

(ii) such other conditions of a kind prescribed by the Secretary of State for the purposes of this paragraph as the Secretary of State may for the time being specify in the licence.

(5) A licence under section 246 must also include a curfew condition complying with section 253.

(6) Where—

(a) a licence under section 246 is granted to a prisoner serving one or more sentences of imprisonment of less than 12 months and no sentence of 12 months or more, and

(b) the relevant court order requires the licence to be granted subject to a condition requiring his compliance with a curfew requirement (as defined by section 204),

that condition is not to be included in the licence at any time while a curfew condition required by section 253 is in force.

(7) The preceding provisions of this section have effect subject to section 263(3) (concurrent terms), section 264(3) and (4) (consecutive terms) and section 264A(3) (consecutive terms: intermittent custody).

(8) In exercising his powers to prescribe standard conditions or the other conditions referred to in subsection (4)(b)(ii), the Secretary of State must have regard to the following purposes of the supervision of offenders while on licence under this Chapter—

(a) the protection of the public,

(b) the prevention of re-offending, and

(c) securing the successful re-integration of the prisoner into the community.

Licence conditions on re-release of prisoner serving sentence of less than 12 months

251.—(1) In relation to any licence under this Chapter which is granted to a prisoner serving **23–144** one or more sentences of imprisonment of less than twelve months and no sentence of twelve months or more on his release in pursuance of a decision of the Board under section 254 or 256, subsections (2) and (3) apply instead of section 250(2).

(2) The licence—

(a) must include the standard conditions;

(b) may include—

   (i) any condition authorised by section 62 or 64 of the *Criminal Justice and Court Services Act* 2000, and

   (ii) such other conditions of a kind prescribed by the Secretary of State for the purposes of section 250(4)(b)(ii) as the Secretary of State may for the time being specify in the licence.

  (3) In exercising his powers under subsection (2)(b)(ii), the Secretary of State must have regard to the terms of the relevant court order.

  (4) In this section "the standard conditions" has the same meaning as in section 250.

Duty to comply with licence conditions

23–145 **252.** A person subject to a licence under this Chapter must comply with such conditions as may for the time being be specified in the licence.

Recall of prisoners while on licence

23–146 **254.**—(1) The Secretary of State may, in the case of any prisoner who has been released on licence under this Chapter, revoke his licence and recall him to prison.

  (2) A person recalled to prison under subsection (1)—

   (a) may make representations in writing with respect to his recall, and

   (b) on his return to prison, must be informed of the reasons for his recall and of his right to make representations.

  (3) The Secretary of State must refer to the Board the case of a person recalled under subsection (1).

  (4) Where on a reference under subsection (3) relating to any person the Board recommends his immediate release on licence under this Chapter, the Secretary of State must give effect to the recommendation.

  (5) In the case of an intermittent custody prisoner who has not yet served in prison the number of custodial days specified in the intermittent custody order, any recommendation by the Board as to immediate release on licence is to be a recommendation as to his release on licence until the end of one of the licence periods specified by virtue of section 183(1)(b) in the intermittent custody order.

  (6) On the revocation of the licence of any person under this section, he shall be liable to be detained in pursuance of his sentence and, if at large, is to be treated as being unlawfully at large.

  (7) Nothing in subsections (2) to (6) applies in relation to a person recalled under section 255.

Power of court to recommend licence conditions for certain prisoners

23–147 **238.**—(1) A court which sentences an offender to a term of imprisonment or detention in a young offender institution of twelve months or more in respect of any offence may, when passing sentence, recommend to the Secretary of State particular conditions which in its view should be included in any licence granted to the offender under this Chapter on his release from prison.

  (2) In exercising his powers under section 250(4)(b) in respect of an offender, the Secretary of State must have regard to any recommendation under subsection (1).

  (3) A recommendation under subsection (1) is not to be treated for any purpose as part of the sentence passed on the offender.

  (4) This section does not apply in relation to a sentence of detention under section 91 of the Sentencing Act or section 228 of this Act.

Criminal Justice (Sentencing) (Licence Conditions) Order 2005 (S.I. 2005 No. 648)

Citation, commencement and interpretation

23–148 **1.**—(1) This Order may be cited as the Criminal Justice (Sentencing) (Licence Conditions) Order 2005 and shall come into force on 4th April 2005.

  (2) In this Order—

   "the Act" means the *Criminal Justice Act* 2003;

   "the 1991 Act" means the Criminal Justice Act 1991

Standard conditions of licence

23–149 **2.**—(1) The conditions set out in paragraph (2) are the standard conditions prescribed for the purposes of section 250 (1) of the Act.

(2) The prisoner must—

(a) keep in touch with the responsible officer as instructed by him

(b) receive visits from the responsible officer as instructed by him

(c) permanently reside at an address approved by the responsible officer and obtain the prior permission of the responsible officer for any stay of one or more nights at a different address;

(d) undertake work (including voluntary work) only with the approval of the responsible officer and obtain his prior approval in relation to any change in the nature of that work;

(e) not travel outside the United Kingdom, the Channel Islands or the Isle of Man without the prior permission of the responsible officer, except where he is deported or removed from the United Kingdom in accordance with the Immigration Act 1971 or the Immigration and Asylum Act 1999

(f) be of good behaviour, and not behave in a way which undermines the purposes of the release on licence, which are to protect the public, prevent re-offending and promote successful re-integration into the community;

(g) not commit any offence.

Other conditions of licence

3.—(1) Conditions of a kind set out in paragraph (2) are prescribed for the purposes of section 250(2)(b)(ii) and (4) (b) (ii) of the Act.   **23–150**

(2) The conditions are those which impose on a prisoner:

(a) a requirement that he reside at a certain place;

(b) a requirement relating to his making or maintaining contact with a person;

(c) a restriction relating to his making or maintaining contact with a person;

(d) a restriction on his participation in, or undertaking of, an activity;

(e) a requirement that he participate in, or co-operate with, a programme or set of activities designed to further one or more of the purposes referred to in section 250(8) of the Act;

(f) a requirement that he comply with a curfew arrangement;

(g) a restriction on his freedom of movement (which is not a requirement referred to in sub-paragraph (f));

(h) a requirement relating to his supervision in the community by a responsible officer.

(3) For the purpose of this article, "curfew arrangement" means an arrangement under which a prisoner is required to remain at a specified place for a specified period of time which is not an arrangement contained in a condition imposed by virtue of section 37A(1) of the 1991 Act or section 250(5) of the Act.

Revocation and saving

4.—(1) The Criminal Justice (Sentencing) (Licence Conditions) Order 2003 is hereby revoked. **23–151**

(2) The revocation of the instrument referred to in paragraph (1) does not affect the validity of conditions included in any licence granted under Chapter 6 of Part 12 of the Act before 4th April 2005 and in force on that date.

With such a wide range of options open to the court, there will be much reliance on **23–152**
the approach set out by the Sentencing Guidelines Council in its Guideline *Custodial sentences of Less than 12 months: Criminal Justice Act 2003*. At the time of going to print, only the draft guideline had been published. The detail *post* will need to be checked against the definitive guideline when published. It is emphasised that this sentence should not be used where a non-custodial sentence would have been imposed under the previous provisions; indeed, the combination of new community orders and this order suggests that the custodial threshold has been raised: Guideline, Section C. The Guideline emphasises that the provisions are designed to allow a court to fit a sentence more closely to the needs of the offence and the offender and so consistency of approach is what is sought. It compares the sentence with other sentences such as the Community Order and the suspended sentence order and sets out the approach to be followed once it has been decided that an immediate custodial sentence is necessary. The first step is to determine the overall term of the order (between 28 and 51 weeks)

Part IV

and then to determine the length of the custodial period. Finally, the overall impact of the order should be checked to ensure that it is proportionate to the seriousness of the offence. As with the Guideline relating to a Community Order, this Guideline sets out three indicative levels of order and possible requirements that could be included depending on whether the seriousness of the offence is towards the higher or lower end of the spectrum. Great care must be taken not to place requirements into the order that make it likely that the offender will fail to comply. Although it is possible to impose a sentence of 12 months rather than a custody plus order for an either way offence (thus providing for 6 months in custody (subject to early release) rather than a maximum of 13 weeks), the Guideline suggests that such a sentence is likely to be rare in a magistrates' court.

Draft Guideline: Custodial sentences of Less than 12 months: Criminal Justice Act 2003

C. IMPOSING A CUSTODY PLUS ORDER

23–153   **A custodial sentence must be imposed only when an offence is so serious that neither a fine nor a community sentence can be justified.**

25. Now that the new sentencing framework is complete, sentencers will need to approach the decision regarding the crossing of the custody threshold and the decision on the content of a custody plus order in the light of the significant changes that have been made.

Custody threshold

26. A custodial sentence should only be imposed where a court forms the view that the offence (or the combination of the offence and one or more offences associated with it) was so serious that neither a fine alone nor a community sentence can be justified. Since both community orders and custody plus orders are potentially more onerous and restrictive on liberty than equivalent sentences under the previous framework and legislation, this threshold is higher than previously.

27. Once the threshold has been passed, a court may still select a non-custodial sentence.

28. Taking account of all the circumstances of the offence and the offender, the court should first consider whether a fine alone can be justified even though the offence seriousness crosses the custody threshold. If so, a fine should be imposed.

29. If a fine alone cannot be justified, the court should consider whether a community order can be justified. Again, this will take account of all the circumstances of the offence and the offender and the potential punishment and rehabilitation offered by a community order. See paragraphs 33-38 below for more detail concerning these considerations.

30. Only after these options have been eliminated will the proper course be to make a custody plus order.

31. Where a court decides on a custody plus order, it must consider whether that sentence can be suspended, whether it can be served intermittently or whether it must be served in full immediately.

32. Where a court imposes a custodial sentence, it must be for the "shortest term" that "in the opinion of the court is commensurate with the seriousness of the offence, or the combination of the offence and one or more offences associated with it".

A custody plus order should not be imposed where a community order would have been imposed under the existing legislative provisions. This would be wholly inappropriate.

D. THE STRUCTURE OF A CUSTODY PLUS ORDER

23–154   **48.** When imposing a custody plus order, the primary aims are to impose a sentence that taken as a whole:

i) restricts liberty to a degree that is proportionate to the seriousness of the offence committed,

ii) meets the purposes of sentencing directed by the court and

iii) imposes requirements on the offender that are realistic and achievable.

49. The general principles that follow are designed to ensure both a consistent approach to the sentencing decision and that the overall terms of custody plus orders are consistent for similar offending behaviour and for offences of similar degrees of seriousness.

50. In summary, the approach to determining the content of a custody plus order will be as follows:

i) **Having decided to impose a custody plus order, a court must begin by determining the provisional overall term of the order (within the 28 to 51 week range); this must be for the shortest term commensurate with the seriousness of the offence.**

ii) **The next step is to determine the length of the custodial period (within the 2 to 13 week range), which should also be the shortest term commensurate with the seriousness of the offence.**

iii) **Once the overall term of the order and the length of the custodial period have been decided, a court must impose suitable licence requirements and decide whether these are to be complied with during part or all of the licence period.**

iv) **The court should review all elements of the custody plus order to ensure proportionality.**

51. The structure of an order must depend on the particular circumstances of each individual case. The following part of the Guideline is designed to ensure consistency of approach.

52. As with a community order, offences justifying a custody plus order can be divided into three categories of general seriousness, **Low, Medium and High**. Sentencing ranges are set out below for each category. These are starting points designed to enable consistency of approach. A court will always need to be alert to the obligation to ensure that the order matches the seriousness of the offence and adjustments to one or other element must be considered in the light of the impact of the order taken as a whole.

53. The requirements proposed for each of the ranges are based on those recommended for community orders in the guideline on New Sentences recognising the additional factor that the offender is also being sentenced to a period in custody. An activity requirement (which, in practice, is most likely to involve education or life management skills training) is added as an option in the Low range and all three ranges include the option of a rehabilitative programme requirement.

54. Examples of suitable activity and programme requirements are not given as the nature of the requirement and the period of time for which it should run will need to be determined on an individual basis according to availability and offender need.

When deciding on the content of a custody plus order, a court must bear in mind that breach of a requirement will lead to executive recall and the offender will not be returned to court.

55. As the sentence includes a custodial element, it may not be necessary for all licences to include a primarily punitive requirement.

56. A court must ensure that the sentence strikes the right balance between proportionality and suitability and that, where more than one licence requirement is imposed, the requirements are mutually compatible.

57. A requirement should not be imposed unless there is good reason for it and it is achievable during the licence period; the nature of the requirements and the length of the licence period will vary between offenders.

58. The extent to which a licence includes a balance of punitive, reparative and rehabilitative requirements must be guided by the offender profile in an individual case, as identified in the pre-sentence report.

59. A court must always consider whether primarily rehabilitative requirements, including a supervision requirement and/or a programme requirement, would be more effective in reducing re-offending than primarily punitive requirements.

60. When deciding which requirements to include, the court needs to be aware that the standard licence conditions, which will apply in every case except where they are incompatible with requirements imposed by a court, already include an element of supervision. Supervision is key to the successful monitoring of the licence period and it would be sensible for the courts to impose a supervision requirement in all cases.

The decision whether to impose additional or more onerous requirements should be guided by the seriousness of the offence, as set out below:

Part IV

Low level of seriousness	Medium level of seriousness	High level of seriousness
For offences just crossing the custody threshold	For offences that obviously fall within the custody plus category	For offences that only just fall below the 12 months threshold
i. An overall term of up to 28 weeks	**i.** An overall term of up to 29–40 weeks	**i.** An overall term of up to 41–51 weeks
ii. A custodial period of 2 weeks	**ii.** A custodial period of up to 3–9 weeks with a variable licence period	**ii.** A custodial period of up to 10–13 weeks and a variable licence period
iii. A maximum of two requirements, one of which will normally be a supervision requirement	**iii.** In general no more than two licence requirements, one of which will normally be a supervision requirement	**iii.** It may be appropriate to include two or more requirements at this level, one of which will normally be a supervision requirement
Suitable requirements in addition to a supervision requirement <u>might</u> include: • 40 to 60 hours of unpaid work • an activity requirement in the low range (up to 20 days) • a prohibited activity requirement • an attendance centre requirement (where available) • a programme requirement • a curfew requirement within the lowest range e.g. up to 12 hours a day for a few weeks • an exclusion requirement lasting in the region of a few weeks or until the end of the order, depending on the purpose of the exclusion	Suitable requirements in addition to a supervision requirement <u>might</u> include: • 60 to 80 hours of unpaid work • an activity requirement in the middle range (up to 30 days) • a prohibited activity requirement • a programme requirement • a curfew requirement within the middle range e.g. up to 12 hours a day for 2 to 3 months • an exclusion requirement lasting in the region of a few months or until the end of the order, depending on the purpose of the exclusion	Suitable requirements in addition to a supervision requirement <u>might</u> include: 80 to 100 hours of unpaid work an activity requirement up to the maximum 60 days a programme requirement a curfew requirement up to a maximum of up to 12 hours a day for 4 to 6 months an exclusion order lasting until the end of the custody plus order
	Within this range it may not be necessary both to fix a longer custodial period **and** increase the number or length of requirements. The increased onerousness of the order may also be satisfied by increasing the period of time for which the requirements are imposed rather than by imposing additional requirements.	Within this range it may not be necessary both to fix a longer custodial period **and** increase the number or length of requirements. The increased onerousness of the order may also be satisfied by increasing the period of time for which the requirements are imposed rather than by imposing additional requirements.

H. A CUSTODY PLUS ORDER OR A CUSTODIAL SENTENCE OF 12 MONTHS?

23–155   **A magistrates' court will rarely impose a sentence of 12 months but may consider**

such a sentence where the seriousness of the offence requires the more significant impact of a longer custodial period, rather than a longer licence period.

A 12 month custodial sentence should be imposed when a one third reduction for a guilty plea is applied to an 18 month custodial sentence.

78. Once the relevant provisions are implemented, a magistrates' court will have the power to impose a fixed term custodial sentence of 12 months. This is close in length to the maximum overall term of a custody plus order, and it is therefore important to be clear about the circumstances in which a court should decide upon one type of custodial sentence rather than the other.

79. Subject to the early release provisions, a 12 month sentence would result in the offender:

- being in custody for 6 months and
- being on licence for 6 months
- the terms of the licence being determined by the Governor and the Probation Service at the time of release

80. A custody plus order will:

- vary in length from 28 weeks to 51 weeks;
- consist of a custodial period ranging from 2 weeks to 13 weeks for a single offence; and
- consist of a licence period of between 26 weeks and 49 weeks
- have conditions of the licence set primarily by the court at the time that sentence is imposed

81. The custodial element of any sentence imposes the maximum restriction on liberty and an offender will spend a significantly longer period in custody if a 12 months sentence is imposed. Therefore, the Council considers that this sentence should be imposed for a single offence only where the court is satisfied that the seriousness of the offence requires 6 months in custody as the shortest period of punishment. This is most likely to be the case where the impact of the custodial period better fulfils the purposes of sentencing that the court had in mind when imposing sentence, or where the offender has pleaded guilty at the first reasonable opportunity to an offence that would have warranted a sentence of 18 months following a not guilty plea.

82. A sentence of 12 months or more triggers a statutory duty on local probation boards to take reasonable steps to find out whether a victim of a sexual or violent offence wishes to be informed and consulted about arrangements for the offender's release from custody. One consequence of imposing a custody plus order will be that this statutory obligation will not be triggered. The general sentencing principle that a sentence must be for the shortest period that is commensurate with the seriousness of an offence should be applied and the decision on sentence length should not be influenced by trigger points for ancillary provisions.

(4) Concurrent and consecutive sentences

Magistrates' Courts Act 1980, s.133

Consecutive terms of imprisonment

133.—(1) Subject to section 265 of the *Criminal Justice Act* 2003 a magistrates' court impos-　**23–156** ing imprisonment or youth custody on any person may order that the term of imprisonment or youth custody shall commence on the expiration of any other term of imprisonment or youth custody imposed by that or any other court; but where a magistrates' court imposes two or more terms of imprisonment or youth custody to run consecutively the aggregate of such terms shall not, subject to the provisions of this section, exceed 6 months [65 weeks].

(2) If two or more of the terms imposed by the court are imposed in respect of an offence triable either way which was tried summarily otherwise than in pursuance of section 22(2) above, the aggregate of the terms so imposed and any other terms imposed by the court may exceed 6 months but shall not, subject to the following provisions of this section, exceed 12 months.

(2A) In relation to the imposition of terms of detention in a young offender institution subsection (2) above shall have effect as if the reference to an offence triable either way were a reference to such an offence or an offence triable only on indictment.

(3) The limitations imposed by subsection 1 above shall not operate to reduce the aggregate of the terms that the court may impose in respect of any offences below the term which the court has power to impose in respect of any one of those offences.

(4) Where a person has been sentenced by a magistrates' court to imprisonment and a fine for the same offence, a period of imprisonment imposed for non-payment of the fine,

or for want of sufficient distress to satisfy the fine, shall not be subject to the limitations imposed by the preceding subsections.

(5) For the purposes of this section a term of imprisonment shall be deemed to be imposed in respect of an offence if it is imposed as a sentence or in default of payment of a sum adjudged to be paid by the conviction or for want of sufficient distress to satisfy such a sum.

Criminal Justice Act 2003, ss.263, 264

Concurrent terms

23–157　　263.—(1) This section applies where—

    (a) a person ("the offender") has been sentenced by any court to two or more terms of imprisonment which are wholly or partly concurrent, and

    (b) the sentences were passed on the same occasion or, where they were passed on different occasions, the person has not been released under this Chapter at any time during the period beginning with the first and ending with the last of those occasions.

(2) Where this section applies—

    (a) nothing in this Chapter requires the Secretary of State to release the offender in respect of any of the terms unless and until he is required to release him in respect of each of the others,

    (b) section 244 does not authorise the Secretary of State to release him on licence under that section in respect of any of the terms unless and until that section authorises the Secretary of State to do so in respect of each of the others,

on and after his release under this Chapter the offender is to be on licence for so long, and subject to such conditions, as is required by this Chapter in respect of any of the sentences.

(3) Where the sentences include one or more sentences of twelve months or more and one or more sentences of less than twelve months, the terms of the licence may be determined by the Secretary of State in accordance with section 250(4)(b), without regard to the requirements of any custody plus order or intermittent custody order.

(4) In this section "term of imprisonment" includes a determinate sentence of detention under section 91 of the Sentencing Act or under section 228 of this Act [or a sentence of detention in a young offender institution under section 96 of the Sentencing Act or section 227 of this Act]

Consecutive terms

23–158　　264.—(1) This section applies where—

    (a) a person ("the offender") has been sentenced to two or more terms of imprisonment which are to be served consecutively on each other, and

    (b) the sentences were passed on the same occasion or, where they were passed on different occasions, the person has not been released under this Chapter at any time during the period beginning with the first and ending with the last of those occasions, and

    (c) none of those terms is a term to which an intermittent custody order relates.

(2) Nothing in this Chapter requires the Secretary of State to release the offender on licence until he has served a period equal in length to the aggregate of the length of the custodial periods in relation to each of the terms of imprisonment.

(3) Where any of the terms of imprisonment is a term of twelve months or more, the offender is, on and after his release under this Chapter, to be on licence—

    (a) until he would, but for his release, have served a term equal in length to the aggregate length of the terms of imprisonment, and

    (b) subject to such conditions as are required by this Chapter in respect of each of those terms of imprisonment.

(4) Where each of the terms of imprisonment is a term of less than twelve months, the offender is, on and after his release under this Chapter, to be on licence until the relevant time, and subject to such conditions as are required by this Chapter in respect of any of the terms of imprisonment, and none of the terms is to be regarded for any purpose as continuing after the relevant time.

(5) In subsection (4) "the relevant time" means the time when the offender would, but for his release, have served a term equal in length to the aggregate of—

    (a) all the custodial periods in relation to the terms of imprisonment, and

    (b) the longest of the licence periods in relation to those terms.

  (6) In this section—

    (a) "custodial period"—

       (i) in relation to an extended sentence imposed under section 227 or 228, means the appropriate custodial term determined under that section,

      (ii) in relation to a term of twelve months or more, means one-half of the term, and

     (iii) in relation to a term of less than twelve months complying with section 181, means the custodial period as defined by subsection (3)(a) of that section;

    (b) "licence period", in relation to a term of less than twelve months complying with section 181, has the meaning given by subsection (3)(b) of that section.

  (7) This section applies to a determinate sentence of detention under section 91 of the Sentencing Act or under section 228 of this Act[or a sentence of detention in a young offender institution under section 96 of the Sentencing Act or section 227 of this Act] as it applies to a term of imprisonment of 12 months or more.

An offender who is convicted of more than one offence must be given separate sen- **23–159** tences on each. These sentences may run concurrently or consecutively, or there may be a mixture of concurrent and consecutive sentences. If the court fails to make clear whether the sentences are concurrent or consecutive, it is presumed that the sentences are concurrent. The introduction of the custody plus order will produce considerable complications for both concurrent and consecutive sentences. It will be possible, in both the Crown Court and a magistrates' court, for sentences of 12 months and a custody plus order to be imposed on the same occasion but the release regimes are quite different as are those responsible for setting the requirements to which the licencee will be subject. Where those two different types of sentence are imposed, section 263 of the *Criminal Justice Act* 2003 provides that release will occur only once the longest custodial term has been completed and that the terms of the licence will be determined by the Secretary of State without regard to those of the custody plus order: section 263(3). The licence period to be completed again appears to be the longest required. Where concurrent custody plus orders are imposed, this could be interpreted as suggesting, for example, that an offender who receives two 51 weeks custody plus orders, one of two weeks custodial period and 49 weeks licence period and one of 13 weeks custodial period and 26 weeks licence period could be required to serve a total of 62 weeks (13 in custody, 49 on licence). However, the power to exceed 51 weeks only applies to consecutive sentences. Accordingly, it must be taken that licence periods start to run from the day on which the offender would otherwise have been released and so there would never be concurrent custody plus orders of more than 51 weeks overall.

In relation to consecutive sentences, it will be possible to impose sentences in a magistrates' court totalling 65 weeks: *Magistrates' Courts Act* 1980, s.133 (as amended by *Criminal Justice Act* 2003, s.155 when in force). Entitlement to release will arise on the completion of the aggregate of the custodial periods—for sentences of 12 months, half of that sentence, for a custody plus order, the custodial period set by the court: *Criminal Justice Act* 2003, s.264(3). Where the sentences are all custody plus orders, the aggregate of the custodial periods must not exceed 26 weeks (section 181(7)) and the licence period to be served will be the longest of the licence periods set by the court which will commence at the end of the aggregate of the custodial terms: sections 264(4) and (5). Since the longest licence period following a 13 week custodial period will be 38 weeks and since 26 weeks in custody and 38 weeks on licence add up to just 64 weeks, it may be necessary for a court to sentence for at least three offences (and to apply some creativity!) to reach 65 weeks!

Where a prison sentence is passed on an offender already serving a prison sentence, the court must make it clear whether this sentence is to be served consecutively or concurrently with the existing sentence.

The restriction on maximum sentences only applies to terms of imprisonment imposed on the same occasion, and the court may order that the sentence of imprisonment is to commence on the expiration of a term imposed by another court even though the offender will serve longer than the statutory maximum: *Prime* (1983) 5 Cr.App.R.(S.) 127, CA. However, this is subject to the totality principle: *Watts* [2000] 1 Cr.App.R.(S.) 460, CA.

23–160   Consecutive sentences should not generally be imposed for offences which arise out of the same transaction: *Jones* (1980) 2 Cr.App.R.(S.) 152, CA; *Noble* [2003] 1 Cr.App.R.(S.) 65, CA. The fact that this is not an absolute principle was emphasised in *Noble*, where it was said that the principle may admit of exceptions in exceptional circumstances. Consecutive sentences may be inappropriate where the offences concerned form a series of similar offences against the same victim, and are committed over a short period of time: *Paddon*, March 3, 1971, CA (Crim. Div.); however, care must be taken to avoid undue lenience—it is not necessarily less serious, for example, to assault the same person three times over a week period than it is to assault three different people. An application of this principle can be seen in *Bain* [2005] 2 Cr. App. R.(S) 53. The defendant was aged 19. In the course of driving dangerously, serious injuries were caused to a passenger in the vehicle that he was driving. He was charged with dangerous driving and with causing grievous bodily harm (section 20). Dangerous driving attracts a maximum of two years' imprisonment, GBH a maximum of five years. The Court of Appeal held that there was nothing wrong in principle in charging such offences even though they arose from the same course of conduct. However, since the offences did arise out of the same course of conduct, concurrent sentences should have been imposed that reflected the totality of the offending conduct. Where the offences import different or additional aspects, it may be appropriate to consider consecutive sentences. So, for example, where the driver both drove dangerously and drove with excess alcohol or disqualified, although the general practice is to impose concurrent sentences where the offences arose from a single incident, nonetheless there is a well recognised practice that, in such circumstances consecutive sentences may be imposed. In *Hardy* [2006] 2 Cr.App.R. (S.) 4, the defendant was convicted of dangerous driving, driving whilst disqualified and failing to provide a specimen. Consecutive sentences totalling two years were imposed in the Crown Court. Upholding those sentences and the approach, the Court of Appeal stated that, whilst consecutive sentences would not generally be appropriate where the matters arose out of the same incident "it would be bizarre that this man would in fact have a licence to drive with excess alcohol and while disqualified without any added penalty." An approach that may have less offended general sentencing principle would have been to have treated the alcohol and disqualification as aggravating factors and increased the sentence accordingly; however, the low maximum penalty does not allow that to happen so readily and this is perhaps another example of the problems that arise when maximum sentences are allowed to remain at a level that is too low.

Consecutive sentences may be appropriate where the offender uses violence to escape: *Bunch*, November 6, 1971, or where violence is used to resist arrest: *Wellington* (1988) 10 Cr.App.R.(S.) 384.

(5) Time served prior to imposition of sentence

Criminal Justice Act 2003, ss.240–242

Crediting of periods of remand in custody: terms of imprisonment and detention

23–161   **240.**—(1) This section applies where—

    (a) a court sentences an offender to imprisonment for a term in respect of an offence committed after the commencement of this section, and

    (b) the offender has been remanded in custody (within the meaning given by section 242) in connection with the offence or a related offence, that is to say, any other offence the charge for which was founded on the same facts or evidence.

   (2) It is immaterial for that purpose whether the offender—

    (a) has also been remanded in custody in connection with other offences; or

(b) has also been detained in connection with other matters.

(3) Subject to subsection (4), the court must direct that the number of days for which the offender was remanded in custody in connection with the offence or a related offence is to count as time served by him as part of the sentence.

(4) Subsection (3) does not apply if and to the extent that—

(a) rules made by the Secretary of State so provide in the case of—

(i) a remand in custody which is wholly or partly concurrent with a sentence of imprisonment, or

(ii) sentences of imprisonment for consecutive terms or for terms which are wholly or partly concurrent, or

(b) it is in the opinion of the court just in all the circumstances not to give a direction under that subsection.

(5) Where the court gives a direction under subsection (3), it shall state in open court—

(a) the number of days for which the offender was remanded in custody, and

(b) the number of days in relation to which the direction is given.

(6) Where the court does not give a direction under subsection (3), or gives such a direction in relation to a number of days less than that for which the offender was remanded in custody, it shall state in open court—

(a) that its decision is in accordance with rules made under paragraph (a) of subsection (4), or

(b) that it is of the opinion mentioned in paragraph (b) of that subsection and what the circumstances are.

(7) For the purposes of this section a suspended sentence—

(a) is to be treated as a sentence of imprisonment when it takes effect under paragraph 8(2)(a) or (b) of Schedule 12, and

(b) is to be treated as being imposed by the order under which it takes effect.

(8) For the purposes of the reference in subsection (3) to the term of imprisonment to which a person has been sentenced (that is to say, the reference to his "sentence"), consecutive terms and terms which are wholly or partly concurrent are to be treated as a single term if—

(a) the sentences were passed on the same occasion, or

(b) where they were passed on different occasions, the person has not been released under this Chapter at any time during the period beginning with the first and ending with the last of those occasions.

(9) Where an offence is found to have been committed over a period of two or more days, or at some time during a period of two or more days, it shall be taken for the purposes of subsection (1) to have been committed on the last of those days.

(10) This section applies to a determinate sentence of detention under section 91 of the Sentencing Act or section 228 of this Act [or a sentence of detention in a young offender institution under] section 96 [of the Sentencing Act or]section 227 [of this Act] as it applies to an equivalent sentence of imprisonment.

[Inserted by the *Criminal Justice Act 2003 (Sentencing) (Transitory Provisions) Order* (S.I. 2005 No. 643).]

Effect of direction under section 240 on release on licence

241.—(1) In determining for the purposes of this Chapter or Chapter 3 (prison sentences of **23–162** less than twelve months) whether a person to whom a direction under section 240 relates—

(a) has served, or would (but for his release) have served, a particular proportion of his sentence, or

(b) has served a particular period,

the number of days specified in the direction are to be treated as having been served by him as part of that sentence or period.

(2) In determining for the purposes of section 183 (intermittent custody) whether any part of a sentence to which an intermittent custody order relates is a licence period, the number of custodial days, as defined by subsection (3) of that section, is to be taken to be reduced by the number of days specified in a direction under section 240.

Interpretation of sections 240 and 241

242.—(1) For the purposes of sections 240 and 241, the definition of "sentence of imprison- **23–163**

Part IV

ment" in section 305 applies as if for the words from the beginning of the definition to the end of paragraph (a) there were substituted—

     " 'sentence of imprisonment' does not include a committal—

         (a)   in default of payment of any sum of money, other than one adjudged to be paid on a conviction,";

and references in those sections to sentencing an offender to imprisonment, and to an offender's sentence, are to be read accordingly.

     (2) References in sections 240 and 241 to an offender's being remanded in custody are references to his being—

         (a)   remanded in or committed to custody by order of a court,

         (b)   remanded or committed to local authority accommodation under section 23 of the *Children and Young Persons Act* 1969 and kept in secure accommodation or detained in a secure training centre pursuant to arrangements under subsection (7A) of that section, or

         (c)   remanded, admitted or removed to hospital under section 35, 36, 38 or 48 of the *Mental Health Act* 1983.

     (3) In subsection (2), "secure accommodation" has the same meaning as in section 23 of the *Children and Young Persons Act* 1969.

Remand in Custody (Effect of Concurrent and Consecutive Sentences of Imprisonment) Rules 2005 (S.I. 2005 No. 2054)

23–164   **1.**—(1) These Rules may be cited as the *Remand in Custody (Effect of Concurrent and Consecutive Sentences of Imprisonment) Rules* 2005 and shall come into force on the day after the day on which they are made.

     (2) In these Rules "the 2003 Act" means the *Criminal Justice Act* 2003.

23–165   **2.** Section 240(3) of the 2003 Act does not apply in relation to a day for which an offender was remanded in custody—

         (a)   if on that day he was serving a sentence of imprisonment (and it was not a day on which he was on licence under Chapter 6 of Part 12 of the 2003 Act or Part 2 of the *Criminal Justice Act* 1991);or

         (b)   where the term of imprisonment referred to in subsection (1) of that section is ordered to be served consecutively on another term of imprisonment, if the length of that other term falls to be reduced by the same day by virtue of section 67 of the *Criminal Justice Act* 1967.

23–166   Where an offender has spent time in custody before being made subject to a community order, and is later sentenced to custody for the same offence, the sentence should be reduced to allow for the time spent in custody on remand before the order was made, since that will not be automatically credited to the time to be served under the sentence.

     Where an offender who is sentenced to imprisonment has previously been in custody on remand for that or a related offence, the court must direct that that time is to be counted as time served as part of the sentence: *Criminal Justice Act* 2003, s.240. It is of no consequence if the offender has also been remanded in custody for other offences. A court may decline to credit all the days to sentence in certain circumstances, one of which is where the court considers that it would be just to so decline: s.240(4). In such a circumstance, the court must declare in open court the number of days on remand, the number for which credit is being given and the circumstances that have led it to conclude that it is just to reduce the number of days that count: section 240(5), (6). The circumstances that count as a remand in custody are set out in section 242(2). They are court ordered remands and so do not include time when an offender was in police custody prior to charge or between charge and first appearance.

     Two exceptions are provided by *Criminal Justice Act* 2003, s.240(4). One is where, in the opinion of the court, it is just not to give such a direction. The other exception provides for rules to be made by the Secretary of State. The *Remand in Custody (Effect of Concurrent and Consecutive Sentences of Imprisonment) Rules* 2005 (SI. 2005 No. 2054) have been made. They aim to prevent a court from making a direction that would have the effect of causing the remand days to be counted twice and provide for two circumstances. The first circumstance is where an offender has been remanded in custody for two or more offences for which sentence is imposed on different days. The second instance is where sentence is imposed on one occasion for an offence committed prior to April 4, 2005 and for an offence committed on or after that date. In respect of the earlier offence, the time on remand would be deducted from the sentence automatically and so it would be inappropriate for a court to make a further direction. An accompanying circular (HOC 37/2005) points out that the day on which sentence is imposed will be regarded as a sentence day and will not be regarded as a remand day. Accordingly, it does not need to be included in any direction under these provisions. Proper exercise of this duty requires accurate and timely information being provided to the court, an obligation emphasised by the Court of Appeal in *Oosthuizen* [2006] 1 Cr.App.R. (S.) 73. The importance of stating the effect of a custodial sentence, and whether or not days on remand should count towards the sentence, was emphasised in *Barber* [2006] EWCA Crim 162. The court should state the position clearly and unambiguously and both the prosecution and defence legal representatives should be alert to bring the requirements of the provisions to the attention of the court if it appeared that they were being overlooked. The court should put defence legal representatives on notice if it was considering that some or all of the days should not count. In *Gordon* [2007] EWCA Crim 165, the Court of Appeal reviewed various issues arising from these provisions particularly where a court was dealing with offences committed before and after the date on which these provisions were commenced. Offences committed before April 4, 2005 continue to be governed by the previous provisions contained in section 67 of the *Criminal Justice Act* 1967. A reminder was given about the need to give reasons where a court decided not to direct that time spent on remand should count towards sentence or to direct that a lesser time should count: *Criminal Justice Act* 2003, s.240(6). It was also confirmed that it was possible to adjourn the sentencing hearing in part where further calculation was needed, the court having indicated the appropriate period to be taken into account. In February 2007, the Senior Presiding Judge notified courts of a revised procedure to ensure that the correct information on periods that count should be conveyed accurately to the court imposing sentence. As well as reproducing the agreed procedures and forms, the Senior Presiding Judge emphasised the duty on advocates to agree the number of days for which a prisoner had been remanded in custody and which, therefore, were available to be credited against sentence. If there was a dispute, that should be resolved by the advocates before the hearing but, if that was not possible, the court would have the ambit of the dispute clearly defined. In its draft Guideline: *Custodial sentences of less than 12 months: Criminal Justice Act 2003*, the Sentencing Guidelines Council considers particular issues that will relate to a custody plus order in which the custodial term will inevitably be short. It is quite possible that the time spent on remand will be the equivalent of periods to be served under the order and so to count it in full will result in immediate release. The Guideline nonetheless expects a court to continue to impose the custody plus order where that would otherwise have been the sentence since that properly reflects the seriousness of the offence.

Draft Guideline: Custodial sentences of less than 12 months

G. Time spent on remand

Where the court considers that the correct sentence is a custody plus order and, **23–167** **because of the period of time the offender has spent on remand in custody, he or she will be eligible for immediate release, the court should still impose the custody plus order to mark the seriousness of the offence, unless it considers that a community order is more appropriate in all the circumstances, having particular regard to the desirability of reducing the risk of re-offending.**

It is not appropriate to impose a community order instead of a custody plus order solely because of the period of time spent on remand. The sentence must reflect the true seriousness of the offending behaviour.

Where an offender has spent more time in custody on remand than the custodial period of the custody plus order, the court might wish to consider whether the length or severity of the licence period should be reduced.

74. By virtue of sections 240 to 242 of the *Criminal Justice Act* 2003, a defendant will normally receive credit against sentence for time spent in custody on remand as a result of a court order in connection with the offence concerned or any other offence the charge for which was founded on the same facts or evidence. This period will reduce the time spent in custody but will not affect the length of the licence period.

75. Save for a small number of situations where there is potential for duplication of reduction, a court must direct that the time on remand is to count as time served unless the court considers it just not to give that direction.

76. Given the relatively short period of custody that can be imposed as part of a custody plus order, there may be situations where the imposition of a custody plus order will result in the immediate release from custody of the offender. In those circumstances, a court may be tempted to consider whether it should impose a community order with its longer period of supervision. In the guideline New Sentences: *Criminal Justice Act* 2003, the Council considered the equivalent position in relation to sentences of 12 months and above and stated that, in such circumstances, the court should continue to impose a custodial sentence. The Council's view is that this should also be the position with a custody plus order. Such a sentence properly marks the seriousness of the offence.

77. Nothing in this proposal is intended to discourage sentencers from imposing a non-custodial sentence (for example a community order with a drug treatment requirement) where the court considers that, even though the offence has crossed the custody threshold, a community order is likely to be more effective in rehabilitating the offender and reducing the likelihood of re-offending.

C. Suspended Sentences Orders

(1) Purpose and effect

23–168   This is an order that a period of imprisonment imposed by the court will not need to be served by the defendant unless he commits another imprisonable offence during the "operational period".

23–169   Profound changes have been made to these provisions by the *Criminal Justice Act* 2003 not least the ability to link the imposition of a custodial sentence (albeit suspended) with requirements to be undertaken. As well as the statutory provisions, a definitive guideline was issued by the Sentencing Guidelines Council in December 2004 (*New Sentences: Criminal Justice Act 2003*) which sets out the approach to the various decisions that have to be made as part of the imposition of this sentence. In particular, the Council emphasises the importance of a court ensuring that it would have imposed a custodial sentence if there had been no power to suspend. The provisions in the Act were drafted to apply when "custody plus" was in force; for offences committed prior to commencement, transitional provisions enable the power to be used within the previous sentencing powers. Both sets of provisions are set out *ante* with those relating to custody plus orders in italics. These provisions enable a court which passes a prison sentence of up to 12 months to suspend it for between six months and two years. The approach, the issues, the extent of requirements and the approach to breach of an order are clearly set out in the guidelines. An additional power is that to establish reviews by the court of compliance with the requirements contained within the order (ss.191, 192).

An issue has been raised as to whether a court must impose a requirement when making a suspended sentence order or whether it is sufficient simply to suspend the sentence of imprisonment. *Criminal Justice Act* 2003, s.189 requires a court first to determine that it must impose a sentence of imprisonment. Having made that decision, the section empowers a court to impose one or more requirements and to suspend the sentence of imprisonment. It would appear that the power to suspend does not arise unless a requirement is imposed: *Lees-Wolfenden* [2006] EWCA Crim 3068.

Criminal Justice Act 2003, ss.189–190

Suspended sentences of imprisonment
23–170   **189.**—(1) A court which passes a sentence of imprisonment or, in the case of a person aged

at least 18 but under 21, detention in a young offender institution for a term of at least 14 days but not more than twelve months, or in the case of a magistrates' court, at least 14 days but not more than six months may—

   (a) order the offender to comply during a period specified for the purposes of this paragraph in the order (in this Chapter referred to as "the supervision period") with one or more requirements falling within section 190(1) and specified in the order, and

   (b) order that the sentence of imprisonment [or detention in a young offender institution] is not to take effect unless either—

      (i) during the supervision period the offender fails to comply with a requirement imposed under paragraph (a), or

      (ii) during a period specified in the order for the purposes of this sub-paragraph (in this Chapter referred to as "the operational period") the offender commits in the United Kingdom another offence (whether or not punishable with imprisonment),

   and (in either case) a court having power to do so subsequently orders under paragraph 8 of Schedule 12 that the original sentence is to take effect.

(2) Where two or more sentences imposed on the same occasion are to be served consecutively, the power conferred by subsection (1) is not exercisable in relation to any of them unless the aggregate of the terms of the sentences does not exceed twelve months, or in the case of a magistrates' court, six months.

(3) The supervision period and the operational period must each be a period of not less than six months and not more than two years beginning with the date of the order.

(4) The supervision period must not end later than the operational period.

(5) A court which passes a suspended sentence on any person for an offence may not impose a community sentence in his case in respect of that offence or any other offence of which he is convicted by or before the court or for which he is dealt with by the court.

(6) Subject to any provision to the contrary contained in the *Criminal Justice Act* 1967, the Sentencing Act or any other enactment passed or instrument made under any enactment after 31st December 1967, a suspended sentence which has not taken effect under paragraph 8 of Schedule 12 is to be treated as a sentence of imprisonment [or in the case of a person aged at least 18 but under 21, a sentence of detention in a young offender institution] for the purposes of all enactments and instruments made under enactments.

(7) In this Part—

   (a) "suspended sentence order" means an order under subsection (1),

   (b) "suspended sentence" means a sentence to which a suspended sentence order relates, and

   (c) "community requirement", in relation to a suspended sentence order, means a requirement imposed under subsection (1)(a).

[Words inserted by the Criminal Justice Act 2003 (Sentencing) (Transitory Provisions) Order (S.I. 2005 No. 643).]

Imposition of requirements by suspended sentence order

   190.—(1) The requirements falling within this subsection are—   **23–171**

   (a) an unpaid work requirement (as defined by section 199),

   (b) an activity requirement (as defined by section 201),

   (c) a programme requirement (as defined by section 202),

   (d) a prohibited activity requirement (as defined by section 203),

   (e) a curfew requirement (as defined by section 204),

   (f) an exclusion requirement (as defined by section 205),

   (g) a residence requirement (as defined by section 206),

   (h) a mental health treatment requirement (as defined by section 207),

   (i) a drug rehabilitation requirement (as defined by section 209),

   (j) an alcohol treatment requirement (as defined by section 212),

   (k) a supervision requirement (as defined by section 213), and

   (l) in a case where the offender is aged under 25, an attendance centre requirement (as defined by section 214).

(2) Section 189(1)(a) has effect subject to section 218 and to the following provisions of Chapter 4 relating to particular requirements—

(a) section 199(3) (unpaid work requirement),

(b) section 201(3) and (4) (activity requirement),

(c) section 202(4) and (5) (programme requirement),

(d) section 203(2) (prohibited activity requirement),

(e) section 207(3) (mental health treatment requirement),

(f) section 209(2) (drug rehabilitation requirement), and

(g) section 212(2) and (3) (alcohol treatment requirement).

(3) Where the court makes a suspended sentence order imposing a curfew requirement or an exclusion requirement, it must also impose an electronic monitoring requirement (as defined by section 215) unless—

(a) the court is prevented from doing so by section 215(2) or 218(4), or

(b) in the particular circumstances of the case, it considers it inappropriate to do so.

(4) Where the court makes a suspended sentence order imposing an unpaid work requirement, an activity requirement, a programme requirement, a prohibited activity requirement, a residence requirement, a mental health treatment requirement, a drug rehabilitation requirement, an alcohol treatment requirement, a supervision requirement or an attendance centre requirement, the court may also impose an electronic monitoring requirement unless the court is prevented from doing so by section 215(2) or 218(4).

(5) Before making a suspended sentence order imposing two or more different requirements falling within subsection (1), the court must consider whether, in the circumstances of the case, the requirements are compatible with each other.

(2) Guideline

Guideline: New Sentences: Criminal Justice Act 2003

Section 2—Custodial Sentences
     Part 2: Suspended Sentences

B. Imposing a Suspended Sentence

23–172   **2.2.6** A suspended sentence is a sentence of imprisonment. It is subject to the same criteria as a sentence of imprisonment which is to commence immediately. In particular, this requires a court to be satisfied that the custody threshold has been passed and that the length of the term is the shortest term commensurate with the seriousness of the offence.

2.2.7 A court which passes a prison sentence of less than 12 months may suspend it for between 6 months and 2 years (the operational period).[1] During that period, the court can impose one or more requirements for the offender to undertake in the community. The requirements are identical to those available for the new community sentence.

2.2.8 The period during which the offender undertakes community requirements is "the supervision period" when the offender will be under the supervision of a "responsible officer"; this period may be shorter than the operational period. The court may periodically review the progress of the offender in complying with the requirements and the reviews will be informed by a report from the responsible officer.

The power to suspend a sentence is expected to come into force earlier than the provisions implementing "custody plus" and transitional provisions are expected to enable any sentence of imprisonment of under 12 months to be suspended. This guideline therefore is written in the language of the expected transitional provisions.

23–173   **2.2.9** If the offender fails to comply with a requirement during the supervision period, or commits a further offence during the operational period, the suspended sentence can be activated in full or in part or the terms of the supervision made more onerous. There is a presumption that the suspended sentence will be activated either in full or in part.

(i) The decision to suspend

23–174   **2.2.10** There are many similarities between the suspended sentence and the community sentence. In both cases, requirements can be imposed during the supervision period and the court can respond to breach by sending the offender to custody. The crucial difference is that the suspended sentence is a prison sentence and is appropriate only for an offence that passes the custody threshold and for which imprisonment is the only option. A community sentence may also be imposed for an offence that passes the custody threshold where the court considers that to be appropriate.

2.2.11 The full decision making process for imposition of custodial sentences under the new framework (including the custody threshold test) is set out in paragraphs 1.31–1.33 of the Seriousness guideline. For the purposes of suspended sentences the relevant steps are:

(a) **has the custody threshold been passed?**

(b) **if so, is it unavoidable that a custodial sentence be imposed?**

(c) **if so, can that sentence be suspended? (sentencers should be clear that they would have imposed a custodial sentence if the power to suspend had not been available)**

(d) if not, can the sentence be served intermittently?

(e) if not, impose a sentence which takes immediate effect for the term commensurate with the seriousness of the offence.

(ii) Length of sentence

2.2.12 Before making the decision to suspend sentence, the court must already have decided   **23–175**
that a prison sentence is justified and should also have decided the length of sentence that would be the shortest term commensurate with the seriousness of the offence if it were to be imposed immediately. The decision to suspend the sentence should not lead to a longer term being imposed than if the sentence were to take effect immediately.

A prison sentence that is suspended should be for the same term that would have applied if the offender were being sentenced to immediate custody.

2.2.13 When assessing the length of the operational period of a suspended sentence, the court should have in mind the relatively short length of the sentence being suspended and the advantages to be gained by retaining the opportunity to extend the operational period at a later stage (see below).

The operational period of a suspended sentence should reflect the length of the   **23–176**
sentence being suspended. As an approximate guide, an operational period of up to 12 months might normally be appropriate for a suspended sentence of up to 6 months and an operational period of up to 18 months might normally be appropriate for a suspended sentence of up to 12 months.

(iii) Requirements

2.2.14 The court will set the requirements to be complied with during the supervision   **23–177**
period. Whilst the offence for which a suspended sentence is imposed is generally likely to be more serious than one for which a community sentence is imposed, the imposition of the custodial sentence is a clear punishment and deterrent. In order to ensure that the overall terms of the sentence are commensurate with the seriousness of the offence, it is likely that the requirements to be undertaken during the supervision period would be less onerous than if a community sentence had been imposed. These requirements will need to ensure that they properly address those factors that are most likely to reduce the risk of re-offending.

Because of the very clear deterrent threat involved in a suspended sentence, requirements imposed as part of that sentence should generally be less onerous than those imposed as part of a community sentence. A court wishing to impose onerous or intensive requirements on an offender should reconsider its decision to suspend sentence and consider whether a community sentence might be more appropriate.

---

(3) Review of suspended sentence order

It will be possible for a court to provide for a Suspended Sentence Order to be   **23–178**
reviewed periodically by the court. It will be for the court to determine the frequency

Part IV

and nature of the review (section 191(1)). At such a hearing, the court may amend the community requirements. There is also power to dispense with the attendance of the offender where progress is satisfactory (section 192(4)). This can apply just to the next hearing or to all future hearings. If the latter, that can be rescinded if the progress ceases to be satisfactory (section 192(5)).

If, at a review hearing, the court forms the view that the offender has failed to comply with the requirements without reasonable excuse, the hearing must be adjourned for the purpose of a hearing under Schedule 12 to enforce the order.

Criminal Justice Act 2003, ss.191–192

Power to provide for review of suspended sentence order

23–179   191.—(1) A suspended sentence order may—

      (a) provide for the order to be reviewed periodically at specified intervals,

      (b) provide for each review to be made, subject to section 192(4), at a hearing held for the purpose by the court responsible for the order (a "review hearing"),

      (c) require the offender to attend each review hearing, and

      (d) provide for the responsible officer to make to the court responsible for the order, before each review, a report on the offender's progress in complying with the community requirements of the order.

(2) Subsection (1) does not apply in the case of an order imposing a drug rehabilitation requirement (provision for such a requirement to be subject to review being made by section 210).

(3) In this section references to the court responsible for a suspended sentence order are references—

      (a) where a court is specified in the order in accordance with subsection (4), to that court;

      (b) in any other case, to the court by which the order is made.

(4) Where the area specified in a suspended sentence order made by a magistrates' court is not the area for which the court acts, the court may, if it thinks fit, include in the order provision specifying for the purpose of subsection (3) a magistrates' court which acts for the area specified in the order.

(5) Where a suspended sentence order has been made on an appeal brought from the Crown Court or from the criminal division of the Court of Appeal, it is to be taken for the purposes of subsection (3)(b) to have been made by the Crown Court.

Periodic reviews of suspended sentence order

23–180   192.—(1) At a review hearing (within the meaning of subsection (1) of section 191) the court may, after considering the responsible officer's report referred to in that subsection, amend the community requirements of the suspended sentence order, or any provision of the order which relates to those requirements.

(2) The court—

      (a) may not amend the community requirements of the order so as to impose a requirement of a different kind unless the offender expresses his willingness to comply with that requirement,

      (b) may not amend a mental health treatment requirement, a drug rehabilitation requirement or an alcohol treatment requirement unless the offender expresses his willingness to comply with the requirement as amended,

      (c) may amend the supervision period only if the period as amended complies with section 189(3) and (4),

      (d) may not amend the operational period of the suspended sentence, and

      (e) except with the consent of the offender, may not amend the order while an appeal against the order is pending.

(3) For the purposes of subsection (2)(a)—

      (a) a community requirement falling within any paragraph of section 190(1) is of the same kind as any other community requirement falling within that paragraph, and

      (b) an electronic monitoring requirement is a community requirement of the same kind as any requirement falling within section 190(1) to which it relates.

(4) If before a review hearing is held at any review the court, after considering the responsible officer's report, is of the opinion that the offender's progress in complying with the community requirements of the order is satisfactory, it may order that no review hearing is to be held at that review; and if before a review hearing is held at any review, or at a review hearing, the court, after considering that report, is of that opinion, it may amend the suspended sentence order so as to provide for each subsequent review to be held without a hearing.

(5) If at a review held without a hearing the court, after considering the responsible officer's report, is of the opinion that the offender's progress under the order is no longer satisfactory, the court may require the offender to attend a hearing of the court at a specified time and place.

(6) If at a review hearing the court is of the opinion that the offender has without reasonable excuse failed to comply with any of the community requirements of the order, the court may adjourn the hearing for the purpose of dealing with the case under paragraph 8 of Schedule 12.

(7) At a review hearing the court may amend the suspended sentence order so as to vary the intervals specified under section 191(1).

(8) In this section any reference to the court, in relation to a review without a hearing, is to be read—

(a) in the case of the Crown Court, as a reference to a judge of the court, and

(b) in the case of a magistrates' court, as a reference to a justice of the peace [...]

[Repealed by the *Courts Act 2003 (Consequential Provisions) Order* (S.I. 2005 No. 886).]

(4) Offender who resides in Scotland or Northern Ireland

Given the different provisions that apply in some circumstances in Scotland and Northern Ireland, specific provision is made where a court wishes to make a Suspended Sentence Order which contains requirements in respect of an offender who resides in either Scotland or Northern Ireland.   **23–181**

Criminal Justice Act 2003, ss.195, 194

Interpretation of Chapter

Interpretation of Chapter 3

195. In this Chapter—   **23–182**

"custodial period", in relation to a term of imprisonment imposed in accordance with section 181, has the meaning given by subsection (3)(a) of that section;

"licence period" —

(a) in relation to a term of imprisonment imposed in accordance with section 181, has the meaning given by subsection (3)(b) of that section, and

(b) in relation to a term of imprisonment to which an intermittent custody order relates, has the meaning given by section 183(3);

"the number of custodial days", in relation to a term of imprisonment to which an intermittent custody order relates, has the meaning given by section 183(3);

"operational period" and "supervision period", in relation to a suspended sentence, are to be read in accordance with section 189(1);

"sentence of imprisonment" does not include a committal for contempt of court or any kindred offence.

Transfer of suspended sentence orders to Scotland or Northern Ireland

194. Schedule 13 (transfer of suspended sentence orders to Scotland or Northern Ireland)   **23–183**
shall have effect.

Criminal Justice Act 2003, Sched. 13

Section 194   SCHEDULE 13

TRANSFER OF SUSPENDED SENTENCE ORDERS TO SCOTLAND OR NORTHERN
IRELAND

PART 1

SCOTLAND

23–184   1.—(1) Where the court considering the making of a suspended sentence order is satisfied that the offender resides in Scotland, or will reside there when the order comes into
force, the court may not make a suspended sentence order in respect of the offender unless it appears to the court—

    (a) in the case of an order imposing a requirement mentioned in subparagraph (2),
that arrangements exist for persons to comply with such a requirement in the locality in Scotland in which the offender resides, or will be residing when the order comes into force, and that provision can be made for him to comply with the
requirement under those arrangements, and

    (b) in any case, that suitable arrangements for his supervision can be made by the
local authority in whose area he resides, or will be residing when the order
comes into force.

(2) The requirements referred to in sub-paragraph (1)(a) are—

    (a) an unpaid work requirement,

    (b) an activity requirement,

    (c) a programme requirement,

    (d) a mental health treatment requirement,

    (e) a drug rehabilitation requirement,

    (f) an alcohol treatment requirement, and

    (g) an electronic monitoring requirement.

(3) Where—

    (a) the appropriate court for the purposes of paragraph 14 of Schedule 12 (amend-
ment by reason of change of residence) is satisfied that an offender in respect of
whom a suspended sentence order is in force proposes to reside or is residing in
Scotland, and

    (b) it appears to the court that the conditions in sub-paragraph (1)(a) and (b) are
satisfied,

the power of the court to amend the order under Part 3 of Schedule 12 includes power to
amend it by requiring it to be complied with in Scotland and the offender to be supervised
in accordance with the arrangements referred to in sub-paragraph (1)(b).

(4) For the purposes of sub-paragraph (3), any reference in sub-paragraph (1)(a) and
(b) to the time when the order comes into force is to be treated as a reference to the time
when the amendment comes into force.

(5) The court may not by virtue of sub-paragraph (1) or (3) require an attendance centre requirement to be complied with in Scotland.

(6) The court may not provide for an order made in accordance with this paragraph to
be subject to review under section 191 or 210; and where an order which is subject to
review under either of those sections is amended in accordance with this paragraph, the
order shall cease to be so subject.

23–185   2. A suspended sentence order made or amended in accordance with paragraph 1
must—

    (a) specify the local authority area in which the offender resides or will be residing
when the order or amendment comes into force, and

    (b) require the local authority for that area to appoint or assign an officer who will be
responsible for discharging in relation to him the functions conferred on
responsible officers by Part 12 of this Act;

and section 216 ([local justice area] to be specified) does not apply in relation to an order
so made or amended.

3.—(1) Where a court makes or amends a suspended sentence order in accordance with **23–186**
paragraph 1, the court must provide the relevant documents to—
    (a) the local authority for the area specified in the order, and
    (b) the sheriff court having jurisdiction in the locality in which the offender resides or
        proposes to reside;
and paragraphs (b) to (d) of subsection (1) of section 219 (provision of copies of relevant orders)
do not apply in relation to an order so made or amended.

(2) In this paragraph, "the relevant documents" means—
    (a) a copy of the order as made or amended, and
    (b) such other documents and information relating to the case as the court mak-
        ing or amending the order considers likely to be of assistance.

4.—(1) In relation to the making or amendment of a suspended sentence order in ac- **23–187**
cordance with paragraph 1, and (except for the purposes of paragraph 20) in relation to
an order so made or amended, Chapter 4 of Part 12 of this Act has effect subject to the following modifications.

(2) Any reference to the responsible officer has effect as a reference to the officer appointed or assigned under paragraph 2(b).

(3) The following provisions are omitted—
    (a) subsection (7) of section 201 (activity requirement),
    (b) subsection (7) of section 202 (programme requirement),
    (c) subsection (4) of section 206 (residence requirement),
    (d) subsection (4) of section 218 (availability of arrangements in local area).

(4) In section 207 (mental health treatment requirement), for subsection (2)(a) there is
substituted—

    "(a) treatment as a resident patient in a hospital within the meaning of the *Mental
        Health (Care and Treatment) (Scotland) Act* 2003, not being a state hospital within
        the meaning of that Act;".

(5) In section 215 (electronic monitoring requirement), in subsection (3), the words
from "and" onwards are omitted.

5. In this Part of this Schedule "local authority" means a council constituted under sec- **23–188**
tion 2 of the *Local Government etc. (Scotland) Act* 1994; and any reference to the area of
such an authority is a reference to the local government area within the meaning of that Act.

[Substituted by the *Courts Act 2003 (Consequential Provisions) Order* (S.I. 2005
No. 886).]

PART 2

NORTHERN IRELAND

6.—(1) Where the court considering the making of a suspended sentence order is satis- **23–189**
fied that the offender resides in Northern Ireland, or will reside there when the order
comes into force, the court may not make a suspended sentence order in respect of the offender unless it appears to the court—
    (a) in the case of an order imposing a requirement mentioned in subparagraph (2),
        that arrangements exist for persons to comply with such a requirement in the
        petty sessions district in Northern Ireland in which the offender resides, or will
        be residing when the order comes into force, and that provision can be made for
        him to comply with the requirement under those arrangements, and
    (b) in any case, that suitable arrangements for his supervision can be made by the
        Probation Board for Northern Ireland.

(2) The requirements referred to in sub-paragraph (1)(a) are—
    (a) an unpaid work requirement,
    (b) an activity requirement,
    (c) a programme requirement,
    (d) a mental health treatment requirement,
    (e) a drug rehabilitation requirement,

Part IV

    (f) an alcohol treatment requirement,

    (g) an attendance centre requirement, and

    (h) an electronic monitoring requirement.

(3) Where—

    (a) the appropriate court for the purposes of paragraph 14 of Schedule 12 (amendment by reason of change of residence) is satisfied that an offender in respect of whom a suspended sentence order is in force proposes to reside or is residing in Northern Ireland, and

    (b) it appears to the court that the conditions in sub-paragraphs (1)(a) and (b) are satisfied,

the power of the court to amend the order under Part 3 of Schedule 12 includes power to amend it by requiring it to be complied with in Northern Ireland and the offender to be supervised in accordance with the arrangements referred to in sub-paragraph (1)(b).

(4) For the purposes of sub-paragraph (3), any reference in sub-paragraph (1)(a) and (b) to the time when the order comes into force is to be treated as a reference to the time when the amendment comes into force.

(5) The court may not provide for an order made in accordance with this paragraph to be subject to review under section 191 or 210; and where an order which is subject to review under either of those sections is amended in accordance with this paragraph, the order shall cease to be so subject.

23–190   7. A suspended sentence order made or amended in accordance with paragraph 6 must—

    (a) specify the petty sessions district in Northern Ireland in which the offender resides or will be residing when the order or amendment comes into force, and

    (b) require the Probation Board for Northern Ireland to appoint or assign a probation officer who will be responsible for discharging in relation to him the functions conferred on responsible officers by Part 12 of this Act;

and section 216 ([local justice area] to be specified) does not apply in relation to an order so made or amended.

[Substituted by the *Courts Act 2003 (Consequential Provisions) Order* (S.I. 2005 No. 886)]

23–191   8.—(1) Where a court makes or amends a suspended sentence order in accordance with paragraph 6, the court must provide the relevant documents to—

    (a) the Probation Board for Northern Ireland, and

    (b) the court of summary jurisdiction acting for the petty sessions district in which the offender resides or proposes to reside;

and paragraphs (b) to (d) of subsection (1) of section 219 (provision of copies of relevant orders) do not apply in relation to an order so made or amended.

(2) In this paragraph, "the relevant documents" means—

    (a) a copy of the order as made or amended, and

    (b) such other documents and information relating to the case as the court making or amending the order considers likely to be of assistance.

23–192   9.—(1) In relation to the making or amendment of a suspended sentence order in accordance with paragraph 6, and (except for the purposes of paragraph 20) in relation to an order so made or amended, Chapter 4 of Part 12 of this Act has effect subject to the following modifications.

(2) Any reference to the responsible officer has effect as a reference to the probation officer appointed or assigned under paragraph 7(b).

(3) The following provisions are omitted—

    (a) subsection (7) of section 201 (activity requirement),

    (b) subsection (7) of section 202 (programme requirement),

    (c) subsection (4) of section 206 (residence requirement),

    (d) subsection (4) of section 218 (availability of arrangements in local area).

(4) In section 207 (mental health treatment requirement), for subsection (2)(a) there is substituted—

"(a) treatment (whether as an in-patient or an out-patient) at such hospital as may be specified in the order, being a hospital within the meaning of the Health and Personal Social Services (Northern Ireland) Order 1972, approved by the Department of Health, Social Services and Public Safety for the purposes of paragraph 4(3) of Schedule 1 to the Criminal Justice (Northern Ireland) Order 1996 (S.I. 1996/ 3160 (N.I. 24));".

(5) In section 214 (attendance centre requirement), any reference to an attendance centre has effect as a reference to a day centre, as defined by paragraph 3(6) of Schedule 1 to the Criminal Justice (Northern Ireland) Order 1996 (S.I. 1996/3160 (N.I. 24).

(6) In section 215 (electronic monitoring requirement), in subsection (3), the words from "and" onwards are omitted.

PART 3

GENERAL PROVISIONS: BREACH OR AMENDMENT

10. This Part of this Schedule applies at any time while a suspended sentence order **23–193** made or amended in accordance with paragraph 1 or 6 is in force in respect of an offender.

11. In this Part of this Schedule—   **23–194**
"home court" means —
    (a) if the offender resides in Scotland, or will be residing there at the relevant time, the sheriff court having jurisdiction in the locality in which the offender resides or proposes to reside, and
    (b) if he resides in Northern Ireland, or will be residing there at the relevant time, the court of summary jurisdiction acting for the petty sessions district in which he resides or proposes to reside;
"local authority" and "local authority area" are to be read in accordance with paragraph 5;
"original court" means the court in England and Wales which made or last amended the order;
"the relevant officer" means —
    (a) where the order specifies a local authority area in Scotland, the local authority officer appointed or assigned under paragraph 2(b), and
    (b) where the court specifies a petty sessions district in Northern Ireland, the probation officer appointed or assigned under paragraph 7(b);
"the relevant time" means the time when the order or the amendment to it comes into force.

12.—(1) Where this Part of this Schedule applies, Schedule 12 has effect subject to the **23–195** following modifications.

(2) Any reference to the responsible officer has effect as a reference to the relevant officer.

(3) Any reference to a magistrates' court acting in the local justice area concerned has effect as a reference to a magistrates' court acting in the same local justice area as the original court; and any reference to a justice of the peace acting in the local justice area concerned has effect as a reference to a justice of the peace acting in the same local justice area as that court.

(4) Any reference to the appropriate court has effect as a reference to the original court.

(5) In paragraphs 4 and 5, any reference to causing an information to be laid before a justice of the peace has effect—
    (a) if the home court is in Scotland, as a reference to providing information to the home court with a view to it issuing a citation, and
    (b) if the home court is in Northern Ireland, as a reference to making a complaint to a justice of the peace in Northern Ireland.

(5A) In paragraph 6(3)(b), the words "before a magistrates' court acting in the local justice area in which the offender resides or, if it is not known where he resides," are omitted.

(6) In paragraph 14—
    (a) if the home court is in Scotland—

Part IV

(i)   any reference to the [local justice area] concerned has effect as a reference to the local authority area specified in the order, and

(ii) any other reference to a [local justice area] has effect as a reference to a local authority area, and

(b) if the home court is in Northern Ireland—

(i)   any reference to the [local justice area] concerned has effect as a reference to the petty sessions district specified in the order, and

(ii) any other reference to a [local justice area] has effect as a reference to a petty sessions district.

(7) Paragraph 22 is omitted.

(8) No court in England and Wales may—

(a) exercise any power in relation to any failure by the offender to comply with any community requirement of the order unless the offender has been required in accordance with paragraph 14(1)(b) or (2)(a) of this Schedule to appear before that court;

(b) exercise any power under Part 3 of Schedule 12 unless the offender has been required in accordance with paragraph 15(2) or 16 of this Schedule to appear before that court.

[Substituted by the *Courts Act 2003 (Consequential Provisions) Order* 2005 (S.I. 2005 No. 886).]

23–196   13.—(1) Sub-paragraph (2) applies where it appears to the home court—

(a) if that court is in Scotland, on information from the relevant officer, or

(b) if that court is in Northern Ireland, upon a complaint being made by the relevant officer,

that the offender has failed without reasonable excuse to comply with any of the community requirements of the suspended sentence order.

(2) The home court may—

(a) if it is in Scotland—

(i)   issue a citation requiring the offender to appear before it at the time specified in the citation, or

(ii) issue a warrant for the offender's arrest;

(b) if it is in Northern Ireland–

(i)   issue a summons requiring the offender to appear before it at the time specified in the summons, or

(ii) issue a warrant for the offender's arrest.

23–197   14.—(1) The court before which an offender appears or is brought by virtue of paragraph 13 must—

(a) determine whether the offender has failed without reasonable excuse to comply with any of the community requirements of the suspended sentence order, or

(b) require the offender to appear before the original court.

(2) If the home court determines that the offender has failed without reasonable excuse to comply with any of the community requirements of the order—

(a) the home court must require the offender to appear before the original court, and

(b) when the offender appears before the original court, paragraph 8 of Schedule 12 applies as if it had already been proved to the satisfaction of the original court that the offender failed without reasonable excuse to comply with such of the community requirements of the order as may have been determined.

(3) An offender who is required by any of the following community requirements of a suspended sentence order—

(a) a mental health treatment requirement,

(b) a drug rehabilitation requirement, or

(c) an alcohol treatment requirement,

to submit to treatment for his mental condition, or his dependency on or propensity to misuse drugs or alcohol, is not to be treated for the purposes of sub-paragraph (2) as having failed to comply with that requirement on the ground only that he had refused to undergo any surgical, electrical or other treatment if, in the opinion of the court, his refusal was reasonable having regard to all the circumstances.

(4) The evidence of one witness shall, for the purposes of sub-paragraph (2), be sufficient.

(5) Where the home court is in Scotland and the order contains an electronic monitoring requirement, section 245H of the *Criminal Procedure (Scotland) Act* 1995 (documentary evidence) applies to proceedings under this paragraph as it applies to proceedings under section 245F of that Act (breach of restriction of liberty order).

(6) Where an offender is required by virtue of sub-paragraph (2) to appear before the original court—

(a) the home court must send to the original court a certificate certifying that the offender has failed without reasonable excuse to comply with the requirements of the order in the respect specified, and

(b) such a certificate signed by the clerk of the home court is admissible before the original court as conclusive evidence of the matters specified in it.

23–198   15.—(1) The home court may exercise any power under Part 3 of Schedule 12 (amendment of suspended sentence order) as if it were the original court, except that the home court may not exercise the power conferred by paragraph 15(4) of that Schedule.

(2) Where paragraph 15(4) of Schedule 12 applies the home court must require the offender to appear before the original court.

(3) Subject to sub-paragraph (4), where the home court proposes to exercise the power conferred by paragraph 15(1) of Schedule 12, otherwise than on the application of the offender, the court—

(a) if it is in Scotland—
   (i) must issue a citation requiring the offender to appear before it, and
   (ii) if he does not appear in answer to the citation, may issue a warrant for the offender's arrest;

(b) if it is in Northern Ireland—
   (i) must issue a summons requiring the offender to appear before it, and
   (ii) if he does not appear in answer to the summons, may issue a warrant for the offender's arrest;

and paragraph 20 of Schedule 12 does not apply to the home court.

(4) Sub-paragraph (3) does not apply to an order cancelling any community requirement of a suspended sentence order.

(5) Where the home court is considering amending a suspended sentence order, any reference in Chapter 4 of Part 12 of this Act to a local probation board has effect as a reference to a local authority in Scotland or, as the case may be, the Probation Board for Northern Ireland.

23–199   16. Where by virtue of paragraph 15 any application is made to the home court under Part 3 of Schedule 12, the home court may (instead of dealing with the application) require the offender to appear before the original court.

23–200   17. No court may amend or further amend a suspended sentence order unless it appears to the court that the conditions in paragraph 1(1)(a) and (b) or, as the case may be, paragraph 6(1)(a) and (b) are satisfied in relation to any requirement to be imposed; but this paragraph does not apply to any amendment by virtue of paragraph 20(2).

23–201   18. The preceding paragraphs of this Schedule have effect in relation to any amendment of a suspended order by any court as they have effect in relation to the amendment of such an order by virtue of paragraph 1(3) or 6(3).

23–202   19. On the making of an order amending a suspended sentence order—

(a) the court must provide copies of the amending order to the offender and the relevant officer, and

(b) in the case of an amending order which substitutes a new local authority area or petty sessions district, paragraphs 2 and 3 or, as the case may be, 7 and 8 have effect in relation to the order as they have effect in relation to an order made or amended in accordance with paragraph 1 or 6.

23–203   20.—(1) This paragraph applies where the home court is satisfied that the offender is residing or proposes to reside in England and Wales.

(2) Subject to sub-paragraphs (3) and (4), the home court may, and on the application of the relevant officer must, amend the suspended sentence order by requiring it to be complied with in England and Wales.

(3) The court may not amend under this paragraph a suspended sentence order which contains requirements which, in the opinion of the court, cannot be complied with the local justice area in which the offender is residing or proposes to reside unless, in accordance with paragraph 15 of Schedule 12 it either—

(a) cancels those requirements, or

(b) substitutes for those requirements other requirements which can be complied with if the offender resides in that area.

(4) The court may not amend under this paragraph any suspended sentence order imposing a programme requirement unless it appears to the court that the accredited programme specified in the requirement is available in the [...] [*petty sessions area*] [local justice area] in England and Wales in which the offender is residing or proposes to reside.

(5) The suspended sentence order as amended must specify the petty sessions area in which the offender resides or proposes to reside.

(6) On the making under this paragraph of an order amending a suspended sentence order, the home court must—

(a) provide copies of the amending order to the offender, the relevant officer and the local probation board [acting in the new local justice area], and

(b) provide the magistrates' court [acting in that area] with a copy of the amending order and such other documents and information relating to the case as the home court considers likely to be of assistance to a court [acting in that area] in the exercise of its functions in relation to the order.

(7) Where an order has been amended under this paragraph, the preceding paragraphs of this Schedule shall cease to apply to the order as amended.

[Substituted by the *Courts Act 2003 (Consequential Provisions) Order* 2005 (S.I. 2005 No. 886).]

PART 4

SUPPLEMENTARY

23–204   21. Subsections (1) and (3) of section 245C of the *Criminal Procedure (Scotland) Act* 1995 (provision of remote monitoring) have effect as if they included a reference to the electronic monitoring of the community requirements of a suspended sentence order made or amended in accordance with paragraph 1 of this Schedule.

23–205   22.—(1) Section 4 of the *Summary Jurisdiction (Process) Act* 1881 (which provides, among other things, for service in England and Wales of Scottish citations or warrants) applies to any citation or warrant issued under paragraph 13(2)(a) or 15(3)(a) as it applies to a citation or warrant granted under section 134 of the *Criminal Procedure (Scotland) Act* 1995.

(2) A summons issued by a court in Northern Ireland under paragraph 13(2)(b) or 15(3)(b) may, in such circumstances as may be prescribed by rules of court, be served in England and Wales or Scotland.

(5) Breach of suspended sentence order

23–206   A Suspended Sentence Order may be breached either by the commission of a further offence or by failure to comply with the requirements without reasonable excuse. Note that the further offence does not need to be punishable by imprisonment (Sched. 12, para. 8(1)(b) to the *Criminal Justice Act* 2003). There is a presumption in favour of implementing the suspended sentence either in full or with a reduced custodial term. Where a court considers that such implementation would be unjust (Sched. 12, para. 8(3)) in all the circumstances (including the extent of compliance so far and the facts of the later offence (Sched. 12, para. 8(4)), then the court may only amend the order in one of three ways—imposing more onerous requirements, extending the supervision period or extending the operational period. There is no power to alter the custodial term at this stage, nor to "take no action". Where the breach is of one of the requirements, the Sentencing Guidelines Council's Guideline emphasises that the primary purpose of enforcement is to ensure that the order of the court is complied with. A court has required the offender to undertake certain requirements and the court can legitimately expect the offender to fulfil the obligation imposed by the court. However, it would have been made clear to the offender when sentence was passed that a custodial sentence would follow non–compliance, and, in many circumstances, there is likely to be little alternative. This again emphasises the need for particular care in choosing between a Community Order and a Suspended Sentence Order.

D. RELEASE FROM CUSTODY

(1) Purpose and effect

A defendant will be released before the end of the period ordered by the court. **23–207** There are rules that govern the earliest date of release which can be a complex blend of periods spent in custody on remand, the length of the sentence ordered by the court, and the availability of home detention curfew. In terms of sentencing in a magistrates' court, the critical distinction is that a person sentenced to under 12 months is currently released unconditionally on completing one half of the sentence whereas a person sentenced to 12 months will be released on licence on serving one half of the sentence: *Criminal Justice Act* 2003, s.244. When the relevant provisions are in force, a person subject to a custody plus order will be released on completion of the custodial period. There is also a discretionary power to release earlier on licence: section 246.

A person released early in these ways may be recalled.

Criminal Justice Act 2003, ss.244–246, 248–253

Duty to release prisoners

244.—(1) As soon as a fixed-term prisoner, other than a prisoner to whom section 247 ap- **23–208** plies, has served the requisite custodial period, it is the duty of the Secretary of State to release him on licence under this section.

(2) Subsection (1) is subject to section 245.

(3) In this section "the requisite custodial period" means—

    (a) in relation to a person serving a sentence of imprisonment for a term of twelve months or more or any determinate sentence of detention under section 91 section 91 or 96 of the Sentencing Act, one-half of his sentence,

    (b) in relation to a person serving a sentence of imprisonment for a term of less than twelve months (other than one to which an intermittent custody order relates), the custodial period within the meaning of section 181,

    (c) in relation to a person serving a sentence of imprisonment to which an intermittent custody order relates, any part of the term [...] [*which is not a licence period as defined by*] [which for the purposes of] section 183(3) section 183 [(as read with [(as read with] section 263(2) or 264A(2) [in the case of concurrent or consecutive sentences) is not a licence period], and

    (d) in relation to a person serving two or more concurrent or consecutive sentences [none of which falls within paragraph (c)], the period determined under sections 263(2) and 264(2).

[Substituted and inserted by the *Domestic Violence, Crime and Victims Act* 2004.]

Restrictions on operation of section 244(1) in relation to intermittent custody prisoners

245.—(1) Where an intermittent custody prisoner returns to custody after being unlawfully **23–209** at large within the meaning of section 49 of the Prison Act 1952 at any time during the currency of his sentence, section 244(1) does not apply until—

    (a) the relevant time (as defined in subsection (2)), or

    (b) if earlier, the date on which he has served in prison the number of custodial days required by the intermittent custody order.

(2) In subsection (1)(a) "the relevant time" means—

    (a) in a case where, within the period of 72 hours beginning with the return to custody of the intermittent custody prisoner, the Secretary of State or the responsible officer has applied to the court for the amendment of the intermittent custody order under paragraph 6(1)(b) of Schedule 10, the date on which the application is withdrawn or determined, and

    (b) in any other case, the end of that 72-hour period.

(3) Section 244(1) does not apply in relation to an intermittent custody prisoner at any time after he has been recalled under section 254, unless after his recall the Board has directed his further release on licence.

Power to release prisoners on licence before required to do so

23–210   **246.**—(1) Subject to subsections (2) to (4), the Secretary of State may—

    (a) release on licence under this section a fixed-term prisoner, other than an intermittent custody prisoner, at any time during the period of 135 days ending with the day on which the prisoner will have served the requisite custodial period, and

    (b) release on licence under this section an intermittent custody prisoner when 135 or less of the required custodial days remain to be served.

(2) Subsection (1)(a) does not apply in relation to a prisoner unless—

    (a) the length of the requisite custodial period is at least 6 weeks,

    (b) he has served—

        (i) at least 4 weeks of his sentence, and

        (ii) at least one-half of the requisite custodial period.

(3) Subsection (1)(b) does not apply in relation to a prisoner unless—

    (a) the number of required custodial days is at least 42, and

    (b) the prisoner has served—

        (i) at least 28 of those days, and

        (ii) at least one-half of the total number of those days.

(4) Subsection (1) does not apply where—

    (a) the sentence is imposed under section 227 or 228,

    (b) the sentence is for an offence under section 1 of the *Prisoners (Return to Custody) Act* 1995,

    (c) the prisoner is subject to a hospital order, hospital direction or transfer direction under section 37, 45A or 47 of the *Mental Health Act* 1983,

    (d) the sentence was imposed by virtue of paragraph 9(1)(b) or (c) or 10(1)(b) or (c) of Schedule 8 in a case where the prisoner has failed to comply with a curfew requirement of a community order,

    (e) the prisoner is subject to the notification requirements of Part 2 of the *Sexual Offences Act* 2003,

    (f) the prisoner is liable to removal from the United Kingdom,

    (g) the prisoner has been released on licence under this section during the currency of the sentence, and has been recalled to prison under section 255(1)(a),

    (h) the prisoner has been released on licence under section 248 during the currency of the sentence, and has been recalled to prison under section 254, or

    (i) in the case of a prisoner to whom a direction under section 240 relates, the interval between the date on which the sentence was passed and the date on which the prisoner will have served the requisite custodial period is less than 14 days or, where the sentence is one of intermittent custody, the number of the required custodial days remaining to be served is less than 14.

(5) The Secretary of State may by order—

    (a) amend the number of days for the time being specified in subsection (1)(a) or (b), (3) or (4)(i),

    (b) amend the number of weeks for the time being specified in subsection (2)(a) or (b)(i), and

    (c) amend the fraction for the time being specified in subsection (2)(b)(ii) or (3)(b)(ii).

(6) In this section—

    "the required custodial days", in relation to an intermittent custody prisoner, means—

        (a) the number of custodial days specified under section 183, [or]

> (b) in the case of two or more sentences of intermittent custody [which are consecutive], the aggregate of the numbers so specified [, or]
>
> [(c) in the case of two or more sentences of intermittent custody which are wholly or partly concurrent, the aggregate of the numbers so specified less the number of days that are to be served concurrently;]
>
> "the requisite custodial period" in relation to a person serving any sentence other than a sentence of intermittent custody, has the meaning given by paragraph (a), (b) or (d) of section 244(3);
>
> "sentence of intermittent custody" means a sentence to which an intermittent custody order relates.

[Inserted by the *Domestic Violence, Crime and Victims Act* 2004.]

Power to release prisoners on compassionate grounds

248.—(1) The Secretary of State may at any time release a fixed-term prisoner on licence if he is satisfied that exceptional circumstances exist which justify the prisoner's release on compassionate grounds. **23–211**

(2) Before releasing under this section a prisoner to whom section 247 applies, the Secretary of State must consult the Board, unless the circumstances are such as to render such consultation impracticable.

Duration of licence

249.—(1) Subject to subsections (2) and (3), where a fixed-term prisoner is released on licence, the licence shall, subject to any revocation under section 254 or 255, remain in force for the remainder of his sentence. **23–212**

(2) Where an intermittent custody prisoner is released on licence under section 244, the licence shall, subject to any revocation under section 254, remain in force—

> (a) until the time when he is required to return to prison at the beginning of the next custodial period of the sentence, or
>
> (b) where it is granted at the end of the last custodial period, for the remainder of his sentence.

(3) Subsection (1) has effect subject to sections 263(2) (concurrent terms) and 264(3) and (4) (consecutive terms) [and subsection (2) has effect subject to] section 264A(3) [(consecutive terms: intermittent custody)].

(4) In subsection (2) "custodial period", in relation to a sentence to which an intermittent custody order relates, means any period which is not a licence period as defined by 183(3).

[Inserted by the *Domestic Violence, Crime and Victims Act* 2004].

Licence conditions

250.—(1) In this section— **23–213**

> (a) "the standard conditions" means such conditions as may be prescribed for the purposes of this section as standard conditions, and
>
> (b) "prescribed" means prescribed by the Secretary of State by order.

(2) Subject to subsection (6) and section 251, any licence under this Chapter in respect of a prisoner serving one or more sentences of imprisonment of less than twelve months and no sentence of twelve months or more—

> (a) must include—
>
>> (i) the conditions required by the relevant court order, and
>>
>> (ii) so far as not inconsistent with them, the standard conditions, and
>
> (b) may also include—
>
>> (i) any condition which is authorised by section 62 of the *Criminal Justice and Court Services Act* 2000 (electronic monitoring) or section 64 of that Act (drug testing requirements) and which is compatible with the conditions required by the relevant court order, and
>>
>> (ii) such other conditions of a kind prescribed for the purposes of this paragraph as the Secretary of State may for the time being consider to be necessary for the protection of the public and specify in the licence.

(3) For the purposes of subsection (2)(a)(i), any reference in the relevant court order to

the licence period specified in the order is, in relation to a prohibited activity requirement, exclusion requirement, residence requirement or supervision requirement, to be taken to include a reference to any other period during which the prisoner is released on licence under section 246 or 248.

(4) Any licence under this Chapter in respect of a prisoner serving a sentence of imprisonment [or detention in a young offender institution] for a term of twelve months or more (including such a sentence imposed under section 227) or any sentence of detention under section 91 of the Sentencing Act or section 228 of this Act—

    (a) must include the standard conditions, and

    (b) may include—

        (i) any condition authorised by section 62 or 64 of the *Criminal Justice and Court Services Act* 2000, and

        (ii) such other conditions of a kind prescribed by the Secretary of State for the purposes of this paragraph as the Secretary of State may for the time being specify in the licence.

(5) A licence under section 246 must also include a curfew condition complying with section 253.

(6) Where—

    (a) a licence under section 246 is granted to a prisoner serving one or more sentences of imprisonment of less than 12 months and no sentence of 12 months or more, and

    (b) the relevant court order requires the licence to be granted subject to a condition requiring his compliance with a curfew requirement (as defined by section 204),

that condition is not to be included in the licence at any time while a curfew condition required by section 253 is in force.

(7) The preceding provisions of this section have effect subject to section 263(3) (concurrent terms), section 264(3) and (4), (consecutive terms) and section 264A(3) (consecutive terms: intermittent custody).

(8) In exercising his powers to prescribe standard conditions or the other conditions referred to in subsection (4)(b)(ii), the Secretary of State must have regard to the following purposes of the supervision of offenders while on licence under this Chapter—

    (a) the protection of the public,

    (b) the prevention of re-offending, and

    (c) securing the successful re-integration of the prisoner into the community.

[Inserted by the *Criminal Justice Act 2003 (Sentencing) (Transitory Provisions) Order* 2005 (S.I. 2005 No. 643).]

Licence conditions on re-release of prisoner serving sentence of less than 12 months

23–214   **251.**—(1) In relation to any licence under this Chapter which is granted to a prisoner serving one or more sentences of imprisonment of less than twelve months and no sentence of twelve months or more on his release in pursuance of a decision of the Board under section 254 or 256, subsections (2) and (3) apply instead of section 250(2).

(2) The licence—

    (a) must include the standard conditions, and

    (b) may include—

        (i) any condition authorised by section 62 or 64 of the *Criminal Justice and Court Services Act* 2000, and

        (ii) such other conditions of a kind prescribed by the Secretary of State for the purposes of section 250(4)(b)(ii) as the Secretary of State may for the time being specify in the licence.

(3) In exercising his powers under subsection (2)(b)(ii), the Secretary of State must have regard to the terms of the relevant court order.

(4) In this section "the standard conditions" has the same meaning as in section 250.

Duty to comply with licence conditions

23–215   **252.** A person subject to a licence under this Chapter must comply with such conditions as may for the time being be specified in the licence.

Curfew condition to be included in licence under section 246

23–216   **253.**—(1) For the purposes of this Chapter, a curfew condition is a condition which—

(a) requires the released person to remain, for periods for the time being specified in the condition, at a place for the time being so specified (which may be premises approved by the Secretary of State under section 9 of the *Criminal Justice and Court Services Act* 2000), and

(b) includes requirements for securing the electronic monitoring of his whereabouts during the periods for the time being so specified.

(2) The curfew condition may specify different places or different periods for different days, but may not specify periods which amount to less than 9 hours in any one day (excluding for this purpose the first and last days of the period for which the condition is in force).

(3) The curfew condition is to remain in force until the date when the released person would (but for his release) fall to be released on licence under section 244.

(4) Subsection (3) does not apply in relation to a released person to whom an intermittent custody order relates; and in relation to such a person the curfew condition is to remain in force until the number of days during which it has been in force is equal to the number of the required custodial days, as defined in section 246(6), that remained to be served at the time when he was released under section 246.

(5) The curfew condition must include provision for making a person responsible for monitoring the released person's whereabouts during the periods for the time being specified in the condition; and a person who is made so responsible shall be of a description specified in an order made by the Secretary of State.

(6) Nothing in this section is to be taken to require the Secretary of State to ensure that arrangements are made for the electronic monitoring of released persons' whereabouts in any particular part of England and Wales.

E. INTERMITTENT CUSTODY

(1) Purpose and effect

A custodial sentence can disrupt employment, family ties or caring responsibilities in a way that makes it less likely that a defendant will avoid re-offending after release. A further option provides for that to be served intermittently. Following piloting of the provisions in a small number of courts, the Government decided not to implement these provisions or to continue the piloting that had been taking place. Since the intermittent custody order was based on the custody plus order the Government decided that it should not be made available to the courts pending a decision on when (if at all) to implement the custody plus order. When the order is brought into force and a court considers that a custodial sentence is necessary and all the necessary criteria have been fulfilled, it will be able to direct that that sentence will be served intermittently, that is, short periods in custody interspersed with short periods on licence, under supervision, in the community: *Criminal Justice Act* 2003, ss.183 to 186. The offender must consent. **23–217**

Where an order is made, the custodial periods will be served in short blocks of a few days at a time, with the licence period running between the blocks of custody. If an offender fails to comply with the terms of the community part of the sentence, he will be returned to custody.

In relation to consecutive sentences of Intermittent Custody, section 264A has been inserted into the *Criminal Justice Act* 2003 by the *Domestic Violence, Crime and Victims Act* 2004. Section 264A provides that, where there are consecutive or concurrent orders of Intermittent Custody, the custodial days are to be treated as served only when all the custodial days have been served in aggregate: s.264A(2). Similarly for the licence period: s.264A(3)–(6).

Criminal Justice Act 2003, ss.183–186, 264A

Intermittent custody

183.—(1) A court may, when passing a sentence of imprisonment for a term complying with subsection (4)— **23–218**

    (a) specify the number of days that the offender must serve in prison under the sentence before being released on licence for the remainder of the term, and

    (b) by order—

        (i) specify periods during which the offender is to be released temporarily on licence before he has served that number of days in prison, and

        (ii) require any licence to be granted subject to conditions requiring the offender's compliance during the licence periods with one or more requirements falling within section 182(1) and specified in the order.

(2) In this Part "intermittent custody order" means an order under subsection (1)(b).

(3) In this Chapter—

"licence period", in relation to a term of imprisonment to which an intermittent custody order relates, means any period during which the offender is released on licence by virtue of subsection (1)(a) or (b)(i);

"the number of custodial days", in relation to a term of imprisonment to which an intermittent custody order relates, means the number of days specified under subsection (1)(a).

(4) The term of the sentence—

    (a) must be expressed in weeks,

    (b) must be at least 28 weeks,

    (c) must not be more than 51 weeks in respect of any one offence, and

    (d) must not exceed the maximum term permitted for the offence.

(5) The number of custodial days—

    (a) must be at least 14, and

    (b) in respect of any one offence, must not be more than 90.

(6) A court may not exercise its powers under subsection (1) unless the offender has expressed his willingness to serve the custodial part of the proposed sentence intermittently, during the parts of the sentence that are not to be licence periods.

(7) Where a court exercises its powers under subsection (1) in respect of two or more terms of imprisonment that are to be served consecutively—

    (a) the aggregate length of the terms of imprisonment must not be more than 65 weeks, and

    (b) the aggregate of the numbers of custodial days must not be more than 180.

(8) The Secretary of State may by order require a court, in specifying licence periods under subsection (1)(b)(i), to specify only—

    (a) periods of a prescribed duration,

    (b) periods beginning or ending at prescribed times, or

    (c) periods including, or not including, specified parts of the week.

(9) An intermittent custody order which specifies two or more requirements may, in relation to any requirement, refer to compliance within such licence period or periods, or part of a licence period, as is specified in the order.

Restrictions on power to make intermittent custody order

23–219   **184.**—(1) A court may not make an intermittent custody order unless it has been notified by the Secretary of State that arrangements for implementing such orders are available in the area proposed to be specified in the intermittent custody order and the notice has not been withdrawn.

(2) The court may not make an intermittent custody order in respect of any offender unless—

    (a) it has consulted an officer of a local probation board,

    (b) it has received from the Secretary of State notification that suitable prison accommodation is available for the offender during the custodial periods, and

    (c) it appears to the court that the offender will have suitable accommodation available to him during the licence periods.

(3) In this section "custodial period", in relation to a sentence to which an intermittent custody order relates, means any part of the sentence that is not a licence period.

Intermittent custody: licence conditions

23–220   **185.**—(1) Section 183(1)(b) has effect subject to section 218 and to the following provisions of Chapter 4 limiting the power to require the licence to contain particular requirements—

(a) section 199(3) (unpaid work requirement),

(b) section 201(3) and (4) (activity requirement),

(c) section 202(4) and (5) (programme requirement), and

(d) section 203(2) (prohibited activity requirement).

(2) Subsections (3) to (5) of section 182 have effect in relation to an intermittent custody order as they have effect in relation to a custody plus order.

Further provisions relating to intermittent custody

186.—(1) Section 21 of the 1952 Act (expenses of conveyance to prison) does not apply in re-   **23–221**
lation to the conveyance to prison at the end of any licence period of an offender to whom an intermittent custody order relates.

(2) The Secretary of State may pay to any offender to whom an intermittent custody order relates the whole or part of any expenses incurred by the offender in travelling to and from prison during licence periods.

(3) In section 49 of the 1952 Act (persons unlawfully at large) after subsection (4) there is inserted—

"(4A) For the purposes of this section a person shall also be deemed to be unlawfully at large if, having been temporarily released in pursuance of an intermittent custody order made under section 183 of the *Criminal Justice Act* 2003, he remains at large at a time when, by reason of the expiry of the period for which he was temporarily released, he is liable to be detained in pursuance of his sentence."

(4) In section 23 of the *Criminal Justice Act* 1961 (prison rules), in subsection (3) for "The days" there is substituted "Subject to subsection (3A), the days" and after subsection (3) there is inserted—

"(3A) In relation to a prisoner to whom an intermittent custody order under section 183 of the *Criminal Justice Act* 2003relates, the only days to which subsection (3) applies are Christmas Day, Good Friday and any day which under the *Banking and Financial Dealings Act* 1971 is a bank holiday in England and Wales."

(5) In section 1 of the *Prisoners (Return to Custody) Act* 1995 (remaining at large after temporary release) after subsection (1) there is inserted—

"(1A) A person who has been temporarily released in pursuance of an intermittent custody order made under section 183 of the *Criminal Justice Act* 2003 is guilty of an offence if, without reasonable excuse, he remains unlawfully at large at any time after becoming so at large by virtue of the expiry of the period for which he was temporarily released."

(6) In this section "the 1952 Act" means the *Prison Act* 1952.

Consecutive terms: intermittent custody

264A—(1) This section applies where—   **23–222**

(a) a person ("the offender") has been sentenced to two or more terms of imprisonment which are to be served consecutively on each other,

(b) the sentences were passed on the same occasion or, where they were passed on different occasions, the person has not been released under this Chapter at any time during the period beginning with the first and ending with the last of those occasions, and

(c) each of the terms is a term to which an intermittent custody order relates.

(2) The offender is not to be treated as having served all the required custodial days in relation to any of the terms of imprisonment until he has served the aggregate of all the required custodial days in relation to each of them.

(3) After the number of days served by the offender in prison is equal to the aggregate of the required custodial days in relation to each of the terms of imprisonment, the offender is to be on licence until the relevant time and subject to such conditions as are required by this Chapter in respect of any of the terms of imprisonment, and none of the terms is to be regarded for any purpose as continuing after the relevant time.

(4) In subsection (3) "the relevant time" means the time when the offender would, but for his release, have served a term equal in length to the aggregate of—

(a) all the required custodial days in relation to the terms of imprisonment, and

(b) the longest of the total licence periods in relation to those terms.

Part IV

(5) In this section–

"total licence period", in relation to a term of imprisonment to which an intermittent custody order relates, means a period equal in length to the aggregate of all the licence periods as defined by section 183 in relation to that term;

"the required custodial days", in relation to such a term, means the number of days specified under that section.

[This section was inserted by the *Domestic Violence, Crime and Victims Act* 2004, Sched. 6, para. 7.]

F. COMPENSATION ORDERS

(1) Purpose and effect

23–223   A compensation order enables a court to require an offender to provide financial compensation for loss or harm caused by the offence. It is designed for use in simple, straightforward circumstances. It can either be a sentence in its own right or an ancillary order. If no order is made in circumstances where the court has the power to make such an order, then the court must give its reasons for not making the compensation order. This emphasises the importance of this part of the sentencing task which directly recognises the impact of the crime on any victim.

Powers of Criminal Courts (Sentencing) Act 2000, ss.130, 131

Compensation orders against convicted persons

23–224   **130.**—(1) A court by or before which a person is convicted of an offence, instead of or in addition to dealing with him in any other way, may, on application or otherwise, make an order (in this Act referred to as a "compensation order") requiring him—

(a) to pay compensation for any personal injury, loss or damage resulting from that offence or any other offence which is taken into consideration by the court in determining sentence; or

(b) to make payments for funeral expenses or bereavement in respect of a death resulting from any such offence, other than a death due to an accident arising out of the presence of a motor vehicle on a road;

but this is subject to the following provisions of this section and to section 131 below.

(2) Where the person is convicted of an offence the sentence for which is fixed by law or falls to be imposed under section 110(2) or 111(2) above, section 51A(2) of the *Firearms Act* 1968 or section 225, 226, 227 or 228 of the *Criminal Justice Act* 2003 or section 29(4) or (6) of the *Violent Crime Reduction Act* 2006, subsection (1) above shall have effect as if the words "instead of or" were omitted.

(3) A court shall give reasons, on passing sentence, if it does not make a compensation order in a case where this section empowers it to do so.

(4) Compensation under subsection (1) above shall be of such amount as the court considers appropriate, having regard to any evidence and to any representations that are made by or on behalf of the accused or the prosecutor.

(5) In the case of an offence under the *Theft Act* 1968, where the property in question is recovered, any damage to the property occurring while it was out of the owner's possession shall be treated for the purposes of subsection (1) above as having resulted from the offence, however and by whomever the damage was caused.

(6) A compensation order may only be made in respect of injury, loss or damage (other than loss suffered by a person's dependants in consequence of his death) which was due to an accident arising out of the presence of a motor vehicle on a road, if—

(a) it is in respect of damage which is treated by subsection (5) above as resulting from an offence under the *Theft Act* 1968; or

(b) it is in respect of injury, loss or damage as respects which—

(i) the offender is uninsured in relation to the use of the vehicle; and

(ii) compensation is not payable under any arrangements to which the Secretary of State is a party.

(7) Where a compensation order is made in respect of injury, loss or damage due to an

1198

accident arising out of the presence of a motor vehicle on a road, the amount to be paid may include an amount representing the whole or part of any loss of or reduction in preferential rates of insurance attributable to the accident.

(8) A vehicle the use of which is exempted from insurance by section 144 of the *Road Traffic Act* 1988 is not uninsured for the purposes of subsection (6) above.

(9) A compensation order in respect of funeral expenses may be made for the benefit of any one who incurred the expenses.

(10) A compensation order in respect of bereavement may be made only for the benefit of a person for whose benefit a claim for damages for bereavement could be made under section 1A of the *Fatal Accidents Act* 1976; and the amount of compensation in respect of bereavement shall not exceed the amount for the time being specified in section 1A(3) of that Act.

(11) In determining whether to make a compensation order against any person, and in determining the amount to be paid by any person under such an order, the court shall have regard to his means so far as they appear or are known to the court.

(12) Where the court considers—

(a) that it would be appropriate both to impose a fine and to make a compensation order, but

(b) that the offender has insufficient means to pay both an appropriate fine and appropriate compensation,

the court shall give preference to compensation (though it may impose a fine as well).

Limit on amount payable under compensation order of magistrates' court.

131.—(1) The compensation to be paid under a compensation order made by a magistrates' court in respect of any offence of which the court has convicted the offender shall not exceed £5,000.   **23–225**

(2) The compensation or total compensation to be paid under a compensation order or compensation orders made by a magistrates' court in respect of any offence or offence taken into consideration in determining sentence shall not exceed the difference (if any) between—

(a) the amount or total amount which under subsection (1) above is the maximum for the offence or offences of which the offender has been convicted; and

(b) the amount or total amounts (if any) which are in fact ordered to be paid in respect of that offence or those offences.

Where there are limited financial resources, compensation takes priority over a fine   **23–226** and the "victims' surcharge" (see *ante*, § 23–20). Similarly, where both compensation and confiscation are available sentences, compensation is the first priority. If it is possible to impose both penalties, that course may be followed. If not the court can reduce the amount of the confiscation order by virtue of section 71(1C) of the *Criminal Justice Act* 1988, or make no confiscation order, or make both confiscation and compensation orders and add a direction under section 72(7) of the 1988 Act: *Mitchell and Mitchell* [2001] 2 Cr.App.R.(S.) 29, CA.

A compensation order may not be made in respect of admitted offences which have not been charged or formally taken into consideration: *Hose* (1995) 16 Cr.App.R.(S.) 682, CA.

The thorny question (of whether to make a compensation order when imposing a custodial sentence) fell to be considered again in *Cooper* [2004] EWCA Crim 950. The defendant had had a serious argument with his wife and completely lost self control. He got into his motor vehicle (for which he was not insured) and drove it around a housing estate. During that drive he damaged five other vehicles (three deliberately) as well as some gates and fences. He was self-employed as a tree surgeon. Whilst upholding the sentence of 18 months' imprisonment (for dangerous driving) and the three year disqualification from driving, the Court of Appeal set aside the compensation order. Confirming that "the court must have regard to the means of the offender when making such orders, so far as those means are known to the court, and that the compensation should not be of such an amount that the offender has no prospect of paying it from his available resources within a reasonable time", the court stated that the defendant would "need to re-establish himself in his chosen trade as a tree surgeon. He will have no little difficulty doing that without the ability to drive and his disqualification will have some years to run at that stage."

The amount of the order will be such as the court considers appropriate having regard to any evidence and to any representations that are made by or on behalf of the accused or the prosecutor up to the maximum of £5000 for each offence of which the defendant is convicted. Where the defendant challenges the basis on which any compensation order is made and real issues are raised as to whether the claimants have suffered any, and if so what loss, evidence must be received to establish the defendant's liability to pay compensation: *Horsham Justices, ex p. Richards* [1985] 2 All E.R. 1114, DC.

A compensation order must not be made on the basis of pure speculation as to the offender's future prospects: *Ellis* (1994) 158 J.P. 386, though when considering the defendant's means the court may have regard to possible future income: *Ford* [1977] Crim.L.R. 114.

23–227   The existence of civil liability is not a precondition to the making of a compensation order: *Chappel* (1985) 80 Cr.App.R. 31, CA. Causation must be established before a compensation order is made, though the court does not need to apply the strict test of causation applied in the field of tort: *Derby* (1990) 12 Cr.App.R.(S.) 502, CA.

The *Magistrates' Courts Sentencing Guidelines* (2004) (under review), at pp.89–90, provide that in calculating the gross amount of compensation, courts should consider compensating the victim for two types of loss. The first, sometimes called "special damages", includes compensation for financial loss sustained as a result of the offence. The second type of loss, sometimes called "general damages", covers compensation for the pain and suffering of the injury itself and for any loss of facility. General guidance is given to assist in identifying starting points for damages for common personal injuries such as a graze, bruise or wrist fracture.

The guidelines add that the amount of compensation should be determined in the light of medical evidence, the victim's sex and age, and any other factors which appear to the court to be relevant in the particular case. If there is insufficient evidence, a court will expect to adjourn the proceedings in order that it can be obtained.

23–228   Once the court has made a preliminary calculation of the appropriate compensation, it will then consider the means of the offender before making an order. Ideally, orders should be capable of being paid within one year but periods of up to two or even three years have been accepted where there is a real likelihood of the order being paid.

IV. ANCILLARY ORDERS

A. DEPRIVATION AND CONFISCATION ORDERS

(1) Purpose and effect

23–229   These are part of a package of powers to enable the court to remove property from an offender where that property was used to assist the commission of the crime or is part of the proceeds of the crime. It is a potentially complex area of the law and this section briefly summarises the key points that a busy practitioner will need.

Where property was lawfully seized from a defendant or in his possession or under his control at the time he was apprehended, on conviction (or on the offence being taken into consideration), the court can order that he be deprived of any rights over that property if satisfied that the property had been used (or intended to be used) to assist the commission of any offence, not just the offence for which the defendant was apprehended or subsequently convicted.

Where the offence is punishable by imprisonment under the Road Traffic Acts and consists of driving (or attempting to drive or being in charge of) a motor vehicle or failing to provide a specimen for analysis or of failing to stop after and/or report an accident, then the vehicle being used is deemed to have been used for the purpose of committing the offence: section 143(6) and (7).

In deciding whether or not to make an order, the court must consider the value of the property and the likely effect on the offender of making the order—the higher the value, the more careful the court will need to be in deciding whether the order is appropriate.

Powers of Criminal Courts (Sentencing) Act 2000, ss.143–145

Powers to deprive offender of property used etc. for purposes of crime
143.—(1) Where a person is convicted of an offence and the court by or before which he is **23–230** convicted is satisfied that any property which has been lawfully seized from him, or which was in his possession or under his control at the time when he was apprehended for the offence or when a summons in respect of it was issued—

(a) has been used for the purpose of committing, or facilitating the commission of, any offence, or

(b) was intended by him to be used for that purpose,

the court may (subject to subsection (5) below) make an order under this section in respect of that property.

(2) Where a person is convicted of an offence and the offence, or an offence which the court has taken into consideration in determining his sentence, consists of unlawful possession of property which—

(a) has been lawfully seized from him, or

(b) was in his possession or under his control at the time when he was apprehended for the offence of which he has been convicted or when a summons in respect of that offence was issued,

the court may (subject to subsection (5) below) make an order under this section in respect of that property.

(3) An order under this section shall operate to deprive the offender of his rights, if any, in the property to which it relates, and the property shall (if not already in their possession) be taken into the possession of the police.

(4) Any power conferred on a court by subsection (1) or (2) above may be exercised—

(a) whether or not the court also deals with the offender in any other way in respect of the offence of which he has been convicted; and

(b) without regard to any restrictions on forfeiture in any enactment contained in an Act passed before 29th July 1988.

(5) In considering whether to make an order under this section in respect of any property, a court shall have regard—

(a) to the value of the property; and

(b) to the likely financial and other effects on the offender of the making of the order (taken together with any other order that the court contemplates making).

(6) Where a person commits an offence to which this subsection applies by—

(a) driving, attempting to drive, or being in charge of a vehicle, or

(b) failing to comply with a requirement made under section 7 or 7A of the *Road Traffic Act* 1988 (failure to provide specimen for analysis or laboratory test or to give permission for such a test in the course of an investigation into whether the offender had committed an offence while driving, attempting to drive or being in charge of a vehicle, or

(c) failing, as the driver of a vehicle, to comply with subsection (2) or (3) of section 170 of the *Road Traffic Act* 1988 (duty to stop and give information or report accident),

the vehicle shall be regarded for the purposes of subsection (1) above (and section 144(1)(b) below) as used for the purpose of committing the offence (and for the purpose of committing any offence of aiding, abetting, counselling or procuring the commission of the offence).

(7) Subsection (6) above applies to—

(a) an offence under the *Road Traffic Act* 1988 which is punishable with imprisonment;

(b) an offence of manslaughter; and

(c) an offence under section 35 of the *Offences Against the Person Act* 1861 (wanton and furious driving).

(8) Facilitating the commission of an offence shall be taken for the purposes of subsection (1) above to include the taking of any steps after it has been committed for the purpose of disposing of any property to which it relates or of avoiding apprehension or detection.

Property which is in possession of police by virtue of section 143

23–231　　　**144.**—(1) The *Police (Property) Act* 1897 shall apply, with the following modifications, to property which is in the possession of the police by virtue of section 143 above—

    (a) no application shall be made under section 1(1) of that Act by any claimant of the property after the end of six months from the date on which the order in respect of the property was made under section 143 above; and

    (b) no such application shall succeed unless the claimant satisfies the court either—

        (i) that he had not consented to the offender having possession of the property; or

        (ii) where an order is made under subsection (1) of section 143 above, that he did not know, and had no reason to suspect, that the property was likely to be used for the purpose mentioned in that subsection.

(2) In relation to property which is in the possession of the police by virtue of section 143 above, the power to make regulations under section 2 of the *Police (Property) Act* 1897 (disposal of property in cases where the owner of the property has not been ascertained and no order of a competent court has been made with respect to it) shall, subject to subsection (3) below, include power to make regulations for disposal (including disposal by vesting in the relevant authority) in cases where no application by a claimant of the property has been made within the period specified in subsection (1)(a) above or no such application has succeeded.

(3) The regulations may not provide for the vesting in the relevant authority of property in relation to which an order has been made under section 145 below (court order as to application of proceeds of forfeited property).

(4) Nothing in subsection (2A)(a) or (3) of section 2 of the *Police (Property) Act* 1897 limits the power to make regulations under that section by virtue of subsection (2) above.

(5) In this section "relevant authority" has the meaning given by section 2(2B) of the *Police (Property) Act* 1897.

Application of proceeds of forfeited property.

23–232　　　**145.**—(1) Where a court makes an order under section 143 above in a case where—

    (a) the offender has been convicted of an offence which has resulted in a person suffering personal injury, loss or damage, or

    (b) any such offence is taken into consideration by the court in determining sentence,

the court may also make an order that any proceeds which arise from the disposal of the property and which do not exceed a sum specified by the court shall be paid to that person.

(2) The court may make an order under this section only if it is satisfied that but for the inadequacy of the offender's means it would have made a compensation order under which the offender would have been required to pay compensation of an amount not less than the specified amount.

(3) An order under this section has no effect—

    (a) before the end of the period specified in section 144(1)(a) above; or

    (b) if a successful application under section 1(1) of the *Police (Property) Act* 1897 has been made.

The power does not extend to real property: *Khan (Sultan Ashraf)* [1984] 1 W.L.R. 1405, CA.

23–233　　　As noted *ante*, the power under section 143(1) is widely drawn and is not restricted to property used in the offences currently before the court and an order may be made in respect of property intended to be used by the offender to commit any offence. In *O'Farrell* [1988] Crim.L.R. 387, the court ordered the forfeiture of a large sum of money found on a person convicted of supplying illegal drugs. The defendant sought to argue that the order could not be made as there was no evidence that the money was the proceeds of the current offence and that it was intended for use to fund future offences but the Court of Appeal agreed that the order had been rightly made.

An order should not be made unless the court has information before it relating to the value of the property concerned and the effect on the offender of making the order:

Ball [2003] 2 Cr.App.R.(S.) 18, CA. A deprivation order made against one offender, where several offenders are responsible for a single offence may give rise to an objectionable disparity: *Burgess* [2001] 2 Cr.App.R.(S.) 5, CA.

A deprivation order may be made in addition to other sentences imposed in respect **23–234** of the same offence. The order should be seen as part of the overall penalty, and the other sentences imposed should be adjusted accordingly: *Joyce* [1991] R.T.R. 241, CA. In *Highbury Corner Stipendiary Magistrate, ex p. Di Matteo* [1992] 1 All E.R. 102, DC, Watkins L.J. said that a court considering whether to make an order under section 143 should have regard to the totality principle and to the two matters specifically set out in subsection (5)—the value of the property concerned and the likely financial and other effects on the offender of making the order—taken together with any other order that the court was considering making.

In *Priestly* [1996] 2 Cr.App.R.(S.) 144, CA, a sentence of four years' imprisonment for applying false trademarks to perfumes and clothing so as to resemble goods manufactured by famous manufacturers was reduced to three years, to take account of an order made under the *Powers of Criminal Courts Act* 1973, s.43 (now *PCC(S)A* 2000, s.143). The Court held that the sentencer had failed to take into account the effect of the order as part of the total sentence, as was required by *Joyce* (1989) 11 Cr.App.R.(S.) 253, CA, and the sentence of four years imprisonment should be reduced to one of three.

A deprivation order will only be suitable in cases where it will not be difficult to **23–235** implement. In *Troth* [1980] Crim.L.R. 249, a case concerning partnership property, it was held that difficulties would arise in the implementation of a deprivation order where the property was subject to encumbrances, and it might be appropriate to impose "an increased financial penalty...in lieu of making a forfeiture order."

The power to order forfeiture of particular objects is also provided by various statutes. See the *Misuse of Drugs Act* 1971, s.27; *Firearms Act* 1968, s.52; *Salmon and Freshwater Fisheries Act* 1975, Sched. 4, para. 5 (fish and fishing tackle); *Licensing Act* 1964, ss.161, 162 (intoxicating liquor); *Obscene Publications Act* 1959, s.3 (obscene articles); *Prevention of Crime Act* 1953, s.1 (offensive weapons) and *Wireless Telegraphy Act* 1949, s.14 (wireless telegraphy apparatus).

B. CONFISCATION ORDERS UNDER THE CRIMINAL JUSTICE ACT 1988

The provisions of the *Criminal Justice Act* 1988, (ss.71 to 102) are repealed with ef- **23–236** fect from March 24, 2003 by the *Proceeds of Crime Act* 2002. The repeal does not apply to offences committed before that date and so the provisions of the *Criminal Justice Act* 1988 will continue to apply. However, orders under the 2002 Act can only be made in the Crown Court.

Confiscation orders may be made by a magistrates' court in respect of a limited number of summary offences, which are listed in Sched. 4 to the 1988 Act.

C. RECOMMENDATION FOR DEPORTATION

(1) Purpose and effect

Subject to various limitations, a court which sentences a person aged 17 or over who **23–237** is not a British citizen may, where the offence is one that is punishable with imprisonment, recommend to the Home Secretary that the defendant be deported from the United Kingdom. This order is additional to any sentence passed and must be preceded by formal notice of the possibility of the order being made. That notice must be given at least seven days before the making of the order is considered: section 6(2).

There is a further restriction on the court that limits the exercise of the power in relation to citizens of the European Community exercising their right to free movement under the Treaty of Rome. Such citizens may only be recommended for deportation if the court considers that the continued presence of the defendant in the UK represents

Part IV

a "genuine and sufficiently serious threat to the requirements of public policy affecting one of the fundamental interests of society". In such a case, reasons must be given for that view: *Nazari* [1980] 1 W.L.R. 1366.

There are also exceptions provided in sections 7 and 8 protecting long standing residents and also seamen, aircrews and other special cases such as members of diplomatic missions. At the time of going to print, the UK Borders Bill was before Parliament. If enacted it would remove the benefits of a court recommendation where certain sentences are imposed (possibly custodial sentences of 12 months or more). However, in relation to offenders being sentenced in a magistrates' court, it appears that it will remain a matter at the discretion of the court.

23-238　　The Home Secretary will consider any recommendation but is not bound to order deportation.

Immigration Act 1971, ss.3(6), (8), 6, 7

General provisions for regulation and control

23-239　　**3.**—(6) Without prejudice to the operation of subsection (5) above, a person who is not a British citizen shall also be liable to deportation from the United Kingdom if, after he has attained the age of seventeen, he is convicted of an offence for which he is punishable with imprisonment and on his conviction is recommended for deportation by a court empowered by this Act to do so.

(8) When any question arises under this Act whether or not a person is a British citizen, or is entitled to any exemption under this Act, it shall lie on the person asserting it to prove that he is.

Recommendations by court for deportation

23-240　　**6.**—(1) Where under section 3(6) above a person convicted of an offence is liable to deportation on the recommendation of a court, he may be recommended for deportation by any court having power to sentence him for the offence unless the court commits him to be sentenced or further dealt with for that offence by another court...

(2) A court shall not recommend a person for deportation unless he has been given not less than seven days notice in writing stating that a person is not liable to deportation if he is a British citizen, describing the persons who are British citizens and stating (so far as material) the effect of section 3(8) above and section 7 below; but the powers of adjournment conferred by section 10(3) of the *Magistrates' Courts Act* 1980, section 179 or 380 of the *Criminal Procedure (Scotland) Act* 1975 or any corresponding enactment for the time being in force in Northern Ireland shall include power to adjourn, after convicting an offender, for the purpose of enabling a notice to be given to him under this subsection or, if a notice was so given to him less than seven days previously, for the purpose of enabling the necessary seven days to elapse.

(3) For purposes of section 3(6) above—

　　(a) a person shall be deemed to have attained the age of seventeen at the time of his conviction if, on consideration of any available evidence, he appears to have done so to the court making or considering a recommendation for deportation; and

　　(b) the question whether an offence is one for which a person is punishable with imprisonment shall be determined without regard to any enactment restricting the imprisonment of young offenders or persons who have not previously been sentenced to imprisonment;

and for purposes of deportation a person who on being charged with an offence is found to have committed it shall, notwithstanding any enactment to the contrary and notwithstanding that the court does not proceed to conviction, be regarded as a person convicted of the offence, and references to conviction shall be construed accordingly.

(4) Notwithstanding any rule of practice restricting the matters which ought to be taken into account in dealing with an offender who is sentenced to imprisonment, a recommendation for deportation may be made in respect of an offender who is sentenced to imprisonment for life.

(5) Where a court recommends or purports to recommend a person for deportation, the validity of the recommendation shall not be called in question except on an appeal against the recommendation or against the conviction on which it is made; but—

　　(a) the recommendation shall be treated as a sentence for the purpose of any enactment providing an appeal against sentence

(b) [Scotland]

(6) A deportation order shall not be made on the recommendation of a court so long as an appeal or further appeal is pending against the recommendation or against the conviction on which it was made; and for this purpose an appeal or further appeal shall be treated as pending (where one is competent but has not been brought) until the expiration of the time for bringing that appeal or, in Scotland, until the expiration of twenty-eight days from the date of the recommendation.

(7) [*Scotland*]

Exemption from deportation for certain existing residents

7.—(1) Notwithstanding anything in section 3(5) or (6) above but subject to the provisions of **23–241** this section, a Commonwealth citizen or citizen of the Republic of Ireland who was such a citizen at the coming into force of this Act and was then ordinarily resident in the United Kingdom—

(a) shall not be liable under section 3(5)(a) if at the time of the Secretary of State's decision he had at all times since the coming into force of this Act been ordinarily resident in the United Kingdom and Islands;

(b) shall not be liable to deportation under section 3(5)(a) or (b) or 10 of the *Immigration and Asylum Act* 1999 if at the time of the Secretary of State's decision he had for the last five years been ordinarily resident in the United Kingdom and Islands;

(c) shall not on conviction of an offence be recommended for deportation under section 3(6) if at the time of the conviction he had for the last five years been ordinarily resident in the United Kingdom and Islands.

(2) A person who has at any time become ordinarily resident in the United Kingdom or in any of the Islands shall not be treated for the purposes of this section as having ceased to be so by reason only of his having remained there in breach of the immigration laws.

(3) The "last five years" before the material time under subsection (1)(b) or (c) above is to be taken as a period amounting in total to five years exclusive of any time during which the person claiming exemption under this section was undergoing imprisonment or detention by virtue of a sentence passed for an offence on a conviction in the United Kingdom and Islands, and the period for which he was imprisoned or detained by virtue of the sentence amounted to six months or more.

(4) For purposes of subsection (3) above—

(a) "sentence" includes any order made on conviction of an offence; and

(b) two or more sentences for consecutive (or partly consecutive) terms shall be treated as a single sentence; and

(c) a person shall be deemed to be detained by virtue of a sentence—

(i) at any time when he is liable to imprisonment or detention by virtue of the sentence, but is unlawfully at large; and

(ii) (unless the sentence is passed after the material time) during any period of custody by which under any relevant enactment the term to be served under the sentence is reduced.

In paragraph (c)(ii) above "relative enactment" means section 240 of the *Criminal Justice Act* 2003 and any similar enactment which is for the time being or has (before or after the passing of this Act) been in force in any part of the United Kingdom and Islands.

(5) Nothing in this section shall be taken to exclude the operation of section 3(8) above in relation to an exemption under this section.

Immigration Act 1971, s.8(2), (3), (3A)

Exceptions for seamen, aircrews and other special cases

8.—(2) The Secretary of State may by order exempt any person or class of persons, either **23–242** unconditionally or subject to such conditions as may be imposed by or under the order, from all or any of the provisions of this Act relating to those who are not British citizens.

An order under this subsection, if made with respect to a class of persons, shall be made by statutory instrument, which shall be subject to annulment in pursuance of a resolution of either House of Parliament.

(3) Subject to subsection (3A) below, the provisions of this Act relating to those who are not British citizens shall not apply to any person so long as he is a member of a mission (within the meaning of the *Diplomatic Privileges Act* 1964), a person who is a member of the

family and forms part of the household of such a member, or a person otherwise entitled to the like immunity from jurisdiction as is conferred by that Act on a diplomatic agent.

(3A) For the purposes of subsection (3), a member of a mission other than a diplomatic agent (as defined by the 1964 Act) is not to count as a member of a mission unless—

(a) he was resident outside the United Kingdom, and was not in the United Kingdom, when he was offered a post as such a member; and

(b) he has not ceased to be such a member after having taken up the post.

23–243   A British citizen may not be deported. A "British citizen" is, broadly, a person who has a right of abode in the UK. Persons who have the right of abode in the United Kingdom are entirely free from United Kingdom immigration control. They do not need to obtain the permission of an immigration officer to enter the UK, and may live and work here without restriction. Under section 2 of the *Immigration Act* 1971 (which was amended by section 39 of the *British Nationality Act* 1981), all British citizens and certain Commonwealth citizens have the right of abode in the United Kingdom. This is in contrast to persons given leave to enter or remain in the United Kingdom for a specific purpose, who are expected to leave the country when their limited right to enter or remain expires or when their reasons for being here no longer apply. A recommendation for deportation cannot be made in the case of a Commonwealth citizen or a citizen of the Irish Republic who was resident in the UK when the 1971 Act came into force (*i.e.* 1 January 1973) and has been ordinarily resident in the UK for at least the five years immediately prior to the date of conviction.

EU nationals in the UK exercising their right of free movement under the Treaty of Rome may be deported only if the requirements of EU law are satisfied. The court must consider that the continued presence of the offender in the UK represents 'a genuine and sufficiently serious threat to the requirements of public policy affecting one of the fundamental interests of society': *Bouchereau* [1978] Q.B. 732, ECJ. This decision is primarily about likely future conduct rather than criminal history (though the one is often deduced from the other): *Kraus* (1982) 4 Cr.App.R.(S.) 113. Reasons must be given to the Home Secretary and to the offender.

Deportation can only take place if another country or territory agrees to accept the deportee. Where a person subject to deportation proceedings lodges a claim for asylum (at any stage in the process) there must be a stay in the removal.

Immigration Rules, paragraph 364 provides:

". . .in considering whether deportation is the right course on the merits, the public interest will be balanced against any compassionate circumstances of the case. . ."

23–244   In *R. v. Secretary of State for the HD, ex p. Santillo* [1981] Q.B. 778, CA, the Court held that the existence of previous criminal convictions is not of itself a basis for making a recommendation. However, if the court considers that the previous record, including the offence with which the court is directly concerned, renders it likely that the person before them will offend again, the court may take account of the previous convictions since the possibility of re-offending is a very important factor in deciding whether to recommend deportation and taking account of it is permitted by the Council Directive. The Court also held that the sentencer should give reasons if a recommendation is to be made and that the reasons should include 'some indication of the extent to which the current and previous criminal convictions of the accused have been taken into account and, in so far as this has been done, the light which in the view of the court, such conviction or convictions throw on the likely nature of the accused's personal conduct in the future.'

23–245   Where a sentencer is considering making a deportation order, he should alert the offender or his counsel, so that mitigation can be advanced in relation to the making of an order: *Omojudi* (1992) 13 Cr.App.R.(S.) 346, CA. There is a formal obligation (section 6(2)) to ensure that the person concerned has received written notice setting out that a British citizen is not liable to deportation with information on who is a British citizen. This notice must be given at least seven days before making a recommendation

When a court makes a recommendation for deportation, it should give its reasons for doing so in adequate detail: *Rodney* [1996] 2 Cr.App.R.(S.) 230, CA. General guidance as to the making of deportation orders was given in *Nazari* [1980] 1 W.L.R. 1366, CA, where Lawton L.J. said:

> "We now indicate some guidelines which Courts should keep in mind when considering whether to make an order recommending deportation. But we stress that these are guidelines, not rigid rules. There may well be considerations which take a particular case out of the guidelines; that is a matter which will depend on the evidence.
>
> First, the Court must consider ... whether the accused's continued presence in the United Kingdom is to its detriment. This country has no use for criminals of other nationalities, particularly if they have committed serious crimes or have long criminal records ... The more serious the crime and the longer the record the more obvious it is that there should be an order recommending deportation. On the other hand, a minor offence would not merit an order recommending deportation. In the Greater London area, for example, shoplifting is an offence which is frequently committed by visitors to this country. Normally an arrest for shoplifting followed by conviction, even if there were more than one offence being dealt with, would not merit a recommendation for deportation. But a series of shoplifting offences on different occasions may justify a recommendation for deportation. Even a first offence of shoplifting might merit a recommendation if the offender were a member of a gang carrying out a planned raid on a departmental store.
>
> Secondly, the Courts are not concerned with the political systems which operate in other countries ... The Court has no knowledge of those matters over and above that which is common knowledge; and that may he wrong. In our judgment it would be undesirable for this Court or any other Court to express views about regimes which exist outside the United Kingdom...It is for the Home Secretary to decide in each case whether an offender's return to his country of origin would have consequences which would make his compulsory return unduly harsh.
>
> The next ... is the effect that an order recommending deportation will have upon others who are not before the Court and who are innocent persons. This Court and all other Courts would have no wish to break up families or impose hardship on innocent people.
>
> We wish to state clearly and firmly that all a Court does when it makes a recommendation for deportation is to indicate to the Secretary of State that in the opinion of the Court it is to the detriment of this country that the accused should remain here ... No doubt he will take into account the personal circumstances of each person whose case he is considering, and that will include the political situation in the country to which he will have to go if an order of deportation is made. These are matters solely for the Secretary of State."

In deciding whether to make an order recommending deportation, the key issue for the sentencer is whether the continued presence of the defendant in the U.K. would be to the detriment of the community: *Cravioto* (1990) 12 Cr.App.R.(S.) 71, CA. Where the offender has dependants who are resident in the U.K., the detriment caused to them by his removal must be balanced against the potential detriment that will arise from his continued presence in the country: *Cravioto* (*ante*). Article 8 of the European Convention on Human Rights states:

23–246

Part IV

> 1. Everyone has the right to respect for his private and family life, his home and his correspondence.
>
> 2. There shall be no interference by a public authority with the exercise of this right except such as is in accordance with the law and is necessary in a democratic society in the interests of national security, public safety or the economic well-being of the country, for the prevention of disorder or crime, for the protection of health or morals, or for the protection of the rights and freedoms of others.

However, it appears that a court is not required to consider in detail the defendant's rights under Article 8 of the European Convention on Human Rights: *Carmona* [2006] EWCA Crim. 508.

In *Aziz* [2004] EWCA Crim 1700, it was emphasised that the making of a recommendation is not part of the punishment for the offence and does not justify reducing the sentence imposed. The defendant (or his legal representative) must be given the opportunity to address the court specifically on whether or not the recommendation should be made. In *R. (N., Kenya) v. Secretary of State for the Home Department*

[2004] EWCA Civ 1094, the responsibility for determining the balance between the public interest and the compassionate circumstances of the case was examined as between the Home Secretary and an adjudicator considering an appeal against the decision of the Home Secretary to deport the offender. It is unclear to what extent the court must take account of the impact of deportation on the family of the offender. Given that it is at this stage simply a recommendation, one school of thought suggests that this is not a relevant issue for the court which is concerned only whether the continued presence of the offender would be to the detriment of the United Kingdom. Another school of thought suggests that the European Convention on Human Rights requires courts to take that into account through a combination of the application of Article 6 and Article 8. At present, the balance seems to be towards the former view that this is an issue for the Home Secretary rather than the court but it is hoped that guidance will be issued to clarify the point by the Sentencing Guidelines Council. An indication of a shift in view can be seen in *Harris* [2004] EWCA Crim 1738, where the Court of Appeal quashed a recommendation made in respect of an offender sentenced to three years nine months imprisonment for supplying drugs on the grounds that he had been in the country for 8 years and had built up "very strong roots". However, in *Dennis* [2004] EWCA Crim 2146, the Court of Appeal upheld a recommendation in respect of an offender convicted of supplying drugs holding that "… whilst [the defendant] has not apparently offended hitherto, the charges of drug dealing are extremely serious. They are more than potentially detrimental to the interests of this country."

Where a person enters the UK illegally, a recommendation for deportation may be appropriate, but the sentencer is not obliged to make a recommendation for deportation in every case involving an infringement of the Act: *Akan* (1972) 56 Cr.App.R. 716, CA. In *Ahemed* [2006] 1 Cr.App.R. (S.) 78, the defendant had pleaded guilty to obtaining leave to enter the U.K. by submitting documents purporting to show that his marriage to a co-accused was subsisting. In fact, it was a bogus marriage designed to facilitate the obtaining of indefinite leave to enter or remain in the UK. The defendant asserted that he was of previous good character, that he had obtained an extension of leave to remain of only a few days and that the Secretary of State had ample powers to remove him under an administrative power. The Court agreed with the prosecution that entering into a wholly bogus marriage and then using it as a means to deceive the Home Office in order to further prospects of remaining indefinitely was sufficient to justify a finding that his continued presence was to the detriment of the UK. The defendant's behaviour went well beyond the commission of a "mere" immigration offence. In *Benabbas* [2006] 1 Cr.App.R.(S.) 94, the defendant, an Algerian national, had pleaded guilty to using a forged instrument which was a stolen French passport. He admitted that he had bought the passport in France. The Court reviewed the authorities (confirming the leading authority of *Nazari* [1980] 1 W.L.R. 1366) and considered in particular the contrasting approaches where a defendant's presence in the country was lawful and regular and that where it was (as in this case) illegal or irregular. It stated that, where a defendant's presence in this country was lawful and regular, the *Nazari* approach involved a relatively straightforward exercise of balancing the aggravation of the defendant's wrongdoing, present, past and potential, against the mitigation which he could pray in aid, which included the interests of his family. That balance might on occasions be a difficult one to find. However, the test and the elements in it were plain and personal to the defendant. The detriment had to be judged by reference to the public interest and the requirements of public policy. The court was in no position to embark on any assessment of what would happen to the defendant on return to his country of origin. Whether a recommendation was made or not, those matters were ultimately for the Secretary of State. Where a defendant's presence in the UK was illegal or irregular, the position could be more complicated. Where the illegality or irregularity was the entirely irrelevant to the offence for which the defendant was sentenced, the general principle was that such incidental illegality or irregularity in the status of the defendant was irrelevant because the defendant was to be sentenced for the offence of which he had been convicted and not for his incidental status under statute.

Even so the defendant's status, if indeed it was clear, was not entirely irrelevant. It was part of the defendant's personal conduct which, as a matter of public interest, could be taken into account as part of the balancing exercise. The sentencing judge was correct in *Benabbas* to say that the use of stolen and forged passports undermined the good order of society. Such a view was consistent with authority (see *Bouchereau* [1978] Q.B. 732). It was right to distinguish between the case of a person who entered the UK by fraudulent means and a case of a person who was in the country unlawfully and was convicted of an offence unconnected with his status and the circumstances in which he entered the country. Whilst in this case the defendant was not charged with use of his forged passport to gain entry, it was overwhelmingly likely that he did so use it, or at least that he presented himself at the EU citizen entry channel thereby representing that he was a holder of a passport issued by a Member State. Although the defendant had not been in trouble since arriving in the UK and he had since been in employment, his failure to disclose his true address was a serious matter. As a result of the suppression of his Algerian passport and of his true address, nothing at all was known about him beyond his employment. The judge was therefore right to say that the defendant's use of a forged passport undermined the good order of society and that his presence in the U.K. would be a detriment to this country under the *Nazari* principles.

The sentencer should not consider circumstances of a personal nature which make it **23–247** difficult for the offender to return to his country of origin when considering whether to make a recommendation for deportation: *Bali* [2001] 2 Cr.App.R.(S.) 104, CA.

D. COSTS

The court has the power to compensate a party for costs incurred in relation to the **23–248** prosecution: see *post*, Ch.30.

E. BINDING OVER

(1) Purpose and effect

A requirement to be bound over is an order designed to prevent future misconduct. **23–249** It is an ancient power deriving statutory authority from one of the oldest statutes still in force as well as being provided for in more recent legislation. As with many crime prevention powers, it is designed to be flexible and easy to use. No formal procedure is required under the 1361 Act (though anyone who a court is proposing to be bound over must have proper opportunity to resist such an order if they wish); the 1980 Act requires a formal commencement though this can be done orally.

The order requires the person against whom it is made to enter into a recognisance to guarantee future conduct. In essence, this is a promise to pay a specified sum of money if the terms of the order are breached. It is a useful power made on over 20,000 occasions each year in magistrates' courts. Its use has come before the European Court of Human Rights, primarily because it can be used even where a person is acquitted of any offence and because of the lack of clarity in defining the conduct that will cause a court to consider whether the recognisance should be forfeited: *Steel v. United Kingdom* [1998] E.H.R.R. 603. A recommendation by the Law Commission that the power be abolished (Binding Over, Law Com. No. 222 (Cm. 2439)) was not widely supported and the Home Office has consulted on ways in which the power can be used in ways that comply with obligations on fairness, certainty and proportionality (*Binding Over; A Power for the 21st Century*: HO 2002).

Pending action following that consultation, courts may be well advised to specify with **23–250** as much precision as possible the type of conduct that it requires that comes within the category of keeping the peace or being of good behaviour. If a court orders a person to enter into a recognisance and they decline to do so, then, if the order is being made under the 1361 Act, the court has no sanction and cannot require the recognisance to be entered into. If the order is being made under the 1980 Act, then the court has the power to commit to custody for up to six months in default of entering into the recognisance; however, it is likely that the exercise of this power would be held to be out of proportion to the nature of the order being made. Clearly, if a person misbehaves in a way that contravenes the criminal law they can in any case be prosecuted for that offence; a bind over is designed for lower levels of misconduct and may gradually be superseded by the Anti-Social Behaviour Order (see *post*, §§ 23–241 *et seq.*).

Justices of the Peace Act 1361

23–251   ...First, that in every county of England shall be assigned for the keeping of the peace, one lord, and with him three or four of the most worthy in the county, with some learned in the law, and they shall have power to restrain the offenders, rioters, and all other barators and to pursue, arrest, take, and chastise them according their trespass or offence; and to cause them to be imprisoned and duly punished according to the law and customs of the realm, and according to that which to them shall seem best to do by their discretions and good advisement; ... and to take of all them that they may find by indictment, or by suspicion, and put them in prison; and to take of all them that be [not] of good fame, where they shall be found, sufficient surety and mainprise of their good behaviour towards the King and his people, and the other duly to punish; to the intent that the people be not by such rioters or rebels troubled nor endamaged, nor the peace blemished, nor merchants nor other passing by the highways of the realm disturbed, nor [put in the peril which may happen] of such offenders: ...

Magistrates' Courts Act 1980, s.115

Binding over to keep the peace or be of good behaviour

23–252   **115.**—(1) The power of a magistrates' court on the complaint of any person to adjudge any other person to enter into a recognizance, with or without sureties, to keep the peace or to be of good behaviour towards the complainant shall be exercised by order on complaint.

(2) Where a complaint is made under this section, the power of the court to remand the defendant under subsection (5) of section 55 above shall not be subject to the restrictions imposed by subsection (6) of that section.

(3) If any person ordered by a magistrates' court under subsection (1) above to enter into a recognizance, with or without sureties, to keep the peace or to be of good behaviour fails to comply with the order, the court may commit him to custody for a period not exceeding 6 months or until he sooner complies with the order.

23–253   The use of the power to bind over to keep the peace does not depend on conviction: it may be used against any person where a future breach of the peace is apprehended including a witness who has given evidence: *Sheldon v. Broomfield JJ.* [1964] 2 Q.B. 573, DC. Previous authorities stated that it is not possible to include specific conditions in an order binding over a person to keep the peace: *Randall* (1986) 8 Cr.App.R.(S.) 433, CA. However, considerable concerns have been expressed about the uncertainty contained in being bound over to keep the peace and/or be of good behaviour. If a person is to be sanctioned for conduct, then it needs to be clear what conduct will lead to the sanction being invoked. In future, therefore, a court, although limited to conditions that come within the scope of "keeping the peace" or "being of good behaviour", may need to state more precisely what that entails.

Where a court is considering binding over a person who is not the defendant in the proceedings before them, clear warning should be given and an opportunity to make representations. Where it is proposed to bind someone over in a substantial sum, it will be a breach of the rules of natural justice for a court to bind a person over without inquiring into his means or giving him an opportunity to make representations on the size of the sum: *R. v. Central Criminal Court, ex p. Boulding* (1984) 79 Cr.App.R. 100, DC; *Atkinson* (1988) 10 Cr.App.R.(S.) 470, CA.

23–254   A person who refuses to be bound over to keep the peace may be committed to prison by the magistrates' court: *Magistrates' Courts Act* 1980, s.115(3). A person under 21 and over 18 who refuses to be bound over by a magistrates' court may be detained under the *PCC(S)A* 2000, s.108. An offender under the age of 18 who refuses to be bound over by the magistrates' court may be ordered to attend at an attendance centre: *PCC(S)A* 2000, s.60(1)(b).

In *Steel v. United Kingdom* (1999) 38 E.H.R.R. 603, the European Court of Human Rights determined that the committal to prison of two protesters who refused to be bound over to keep the peace fell within the scope of Article 5(1)(b) for non-compliance with the order of a court, and that whilst binding orders are in rather vague and general terms, they were specific enough for the purposes of Article 5(1)(b). However, use of this sanction to secure compliance with this type of order is likely to be seen as disproportionate and, in practice, the order is made with the consent, or at least acquiescence, of the subject of the order.

The court will need to be satisfied that there is a risk of future conduct which ought **23–255** to be prevented. This information can come from many sources. Although the proceedings are civil in character, since the outcome of failure to comply is a criminal sanction, the standard of proof should follow the line developed in relation to an anti-social behaviour order. In *R. (McCann) v. Manchester Crown Court* [2003] 1 A.C. 787, the House of Lords considered the standard of proof to be applied when the court was considering imposing an anti-social behaviour order. Given that the behaviour leading to the making of an anti-social behaviour order are likely to be similar to the circumstances leading to the application for a bind over order, it appears the standard of proof applicable to the making of each order should be the same. In *McCann* (*ante*), the House of Lords held that the proceedings for the making of an ASBO were civil under domestic law and since the proceedings did not involve the determination of a criminal charge and could not result in the imposition of an immediate penalty on the defendant, they therefore could not be classified as criminal. However, given the seriousness of the matter involved, the court should be satisfied to the criminal standard of proof that a defendant had acted in an anti-social manner before making such an order. Given the similarity between the ASBO and binding over orders, it is submitted that the same standard of proof should apply to the making of the binding over order, and the court should be satisfied to the criminal standard of proof that the defendant's conduct will cause a breach of the peace or is likely to do so if the order is not made.

Where a person who has been bound over has been proved to have broken the terms of the recognisance, the court has power to order the person to pay the amount of the recognisance, but there is no power to order a sentence of imprisonment or otherwise for the breach itself.

F. Anti-Social Behaviour Orders

(1) Purpose and effect

This is an order with a potentially very wide scope that may be made to control a **23–256** wide range of behaviour that is deemed to be anti-social. An order can be made as a result of a specific application (*Crime and Disorder Act* 1998, s.1) or by a court that has convicted a defendant of an offence (*ibid.* section 1C) in which case no application is needed though the prosecutor can apply: section 1C(3). Evidence can be led by either the prosecution or the defence and is not restricted to that which would be admissible in relation to the offence itself: section 1C(3A) and (3B) as inserted by the *Anti-Social Behaviour Act* 2003. The order will be additional to the sentence passed for the offence: section 1C(4).

The order will prohibit the offender from doing anything described in the order: section 1C(2). The order will last for the period specified in the order which must be at least two years: section 1(7) as applied by section 1C(9).

For some, making the order is sufficient but, for others, making an order without providing additional support is unlikely to be successful in achieving the aims of the order. One example of this is the new section 1G and 1H of the *Crime and Disorder Act* 1998, inserted by the *Drugs Act* 2005, s.20. This provides for an "intervention order" in addition to an ASBO where a court is satisfied that misuse of controlled drugs is affecting the behaviour of the person to be subject to the ASBO and that, if an intervention order is made, "appropriate activities" (as defined in s.1G(10)) will be available.

Part IV

Such an order may not exceed 6 months. Failure to comply with an intervention order is a summary offence punishable with a fine not exceeding level 4 (currently £2,500). Proceedings under section 1C may be adjourned. This power may be exercisable even though sentence has been passed for the offence itself and it is only the making of an ASBO that remains to be determined. The court may issue a warrant of arrest for failure to attend subsequent hearings.

The legislative provisions have been much amended; we have set out below those provisions that appear most relevant to criminal proceedings in a consolidated form.

23–257   A person who does not comply with the order commits an offence punishable by up to six months' imprisonment or the statutory maximum fine on summary conviction or to imprisonment for up to five years or an unlimited fine on conviction on indictment. The maximum period of imprisonment on summary conviction will increase to 12 months on the implementation of the *Criminal Justice Act* 2003, s.282.

Crime and Disorder Act 1998, ss.1, 1A, 1AA, 1AB, 1C, 1CA, 1D, 1E, 1G, 1H, 1I

Anti-social behaviour orders

23–258   **1.**—(1) An application for an order under this section may be made by a relevant authority if it appears to the authority that the following conditions are fulfilled with respect to any person aged 10 or over, namely—

  (a) that the person has acted, since the commencement date, in an anti-social manner, that is to say, in a manner that caused or was likely to cause harassment, alarm or distress to one or more persons not of the same household as himself; and

  (b) that such an order is necessary to protect relevant persons from further anti-social acts by him.

(1A) In this section and sections 1B, 1CA, 1E and 1F "relevant authority" means—

  (a) the council for a local government area;

  (aa) in relation to England, a county council;

  (b) the chief officer of police of any police force maintained for a police area;

  (c) the chief constable of the British Transport Police Force; or

  (d) any person registered under section 1 of the *Housing Act* 1996 (c.52) as a social landlord who provides or manages any houses or hostel in a local government area.

  (e) a housing action trust established by order in pursuance of section 62 of the *Housing Act* 1988.

(1B) In this section "relevant persons" means—

  (a) in relation to a relevant authority falling within paragraph (a) of subsection (1A), persons within the local government area of that council;

  (aa) in relation to a relevant authority falling within paragraph (aa) of subsection (1A), persons within the county of the county council;

  (b) in relation to a relevant authority falling within paragraph (b) of that subsection, persons within the police area;

  (c) in relation to a relevant authority falling within paragraph (c) of that subsection—

    (i) persons who are within or likely to be within a place specified in section 31(1)(a) to (f) of the *Railways and Transport Safety Act* 2003 in a local government area; or

    (ii) persons who are within or likely to be within such a place;

  (d) in relation to a relevant authority falling within paragraph (d) or (e) of that subsection—

    (i) persons who are residing in or who are otherwise on or likely to be on premises provided or managed by that authority; or

    (ii) persons who are in the vicinity of or likely to be in the vicinity of such premises.

(3) Such an application shall be made by complaint to the magistrates' court.

(4) If, on such an application, it is proved that the conditions mentioned in subsection (1) above are fulfilled, the magistrates' court may make an order under this section (an "anti-social behaviour order") which prohibits the defendant from doing anything described in the order.

(5) For the purpose of determining whether the condition mentioned in subsection (1)(a) above is fulfilled, the court shall disregard any act of the defendant which he shows was reasonable in the circumstances.

(6) The prohibitions that may be imposed by an anti-social behaviour order are those necessary for the purpose of protecting persons (whether relevant persons or persons elsewhere in England and Wales) from further anti-social acts by the defendant.

(7) An anti-social behaviour order shall have effect for a period (not less than two years) specified in the order or until further order.

(8) Subject to subsection (9) below, the applicant or the defendant may apply by complaint to the court which made an anti-social behaviour order for it to be varied or discharged by a further order.

(9) Except with the consent of both parties, no anti-social behaviour order shall be discharged before the end of the period of two years beginning with the date of service of the order.

(10) If without reasonable excuse a person does anything which he is prohibited from doing by an anti-social behaviour order, he is guilty of an offence and liable—

(a) on summary conviction, to imprisonment for a term not exceeding six months or to a fine not exceeding the statutory maximum, or to both; or

(b) on conviction on indictment, to imprisonment for a term not exceeding five years or to a fine, or to both.

(10A) The following may bring proceedings for an offence under subsection (10)—

(a) a council which is a relevant authority;

(b) the council for the local government area in which a person in respect of whom an anti-social behaviour order has been made resides or appears to reside.

(10B) If proceedings for an offence under subsection (10) are brought in a youth court section 47(2) of the *Children and Young Persons Act* 1933 has effect as if the persons entitled to be present at a sitting for the purposes of those proceedings include one person authorised to be present by a relevant authority.

(10C) In proceedings for an offence under subsection (10), a copy of the original anti-social behaviour order, certified as such by the proper officer of the court which made it, is admissible as evidence of its having been made and of its contents to the same extent that oral evidence of those things is admissible in those proceedings.

(10D) In relation to proceedings brought against a child or a young person for an offence under subsection (10)—

(a) section 49 of the *Children and Young Persons Act* 1933 (restrictions on reports of proceedings in which children and young persons are concerned) does not apply in respect of the child or young person against whom the proceedings are brought;

(b) section 45 of the *Youth Justice and Criminal Evidence Act* 1999 [section 39 of the *Children and Young Persons Act* 1933] (power to restrict reporting of criminal proceedings involving persons under 18) does so apply.

(10E) If, in relation to any such proceedings, the court does exercise its power to give a direction under section 45 of the *Youth Justice and Criminal Evidence Act* 1999 [section 39 of the *Children and Young Persons Act* 1933], it shall give its reasons for doing so.

(11) Where a person is convicted of an offence under subsection (10) above, it shall not be open to the court by or before which he is so convicted to make an order under subsection (1)(b) (conditional discharge) of section 12 of the *Powers of Criminal Courts (Sentencing) Act* 2000 in respect of the offence.

(12) In this section—

"British Transport Police Force" means the force of constables appointed under section 53 of the *British Transport Commission Act* 1949;

"child" and "young person" shall have the same meaning as in the *Children and Young Persons Act* 1933;

"the commencement date" means the date of the commencement of this section;

"local government area" means—

(a) in relation to England, a district or London borough, the City of London, the Isle of Wight and the Isles of Scilly;

(b) in relation to Wales, a county or county borough.

Power of Secretary of State to add to relevant authorities

1A.—(1) The Secretary of State may by order provide that the chief officer of a body of **23–259**

constables maintained otherwise than by a police authority is, in such cases and circumstances as may be prescribed by the order, to be a relevant authority for the purposes of section 1 above.

(2) The Secretary of State may by order—

    (a) provide that a person or body of any other description specified in the order is, in such cases and circumstances as may be prescribed by the order, to be a relevant authority for the purposes of such of sections 1 above and 1B, 1CA, 1E and 1F below as are specified in the order; and

    (b) prescribe the description of persons who are to be "relevant persons" in relation to that person or body.

Individual support orders

23–260   **1AA.**—(1) Where a court makes an anti-social behaviour order in respect of a defendant who is a child or young person when that order is made, it must consider whether the individual support conditions are fulfilled.

(2) If it is satisfied that those conditions are fulfilled, the court must make an order under this section ("an individual support order") which—

    (a) requires the defendant to comply, for a period not exceeding six months, with such requirements as are specified in the order; and

    (b) requires the defendant to comply with any directions given by the responsible officer with a view to the implementation of the requirements under paragraph (a) above.

(3) The individual support conditions are—

    (a) that an individual support order would be desirable in the interests of preventing any repetition of the kind of behaviour which led to the making of the anti-social behaviour order;

    (b) that the defendant is not already subject to an individual support order; and

    (c) that the court has been notified by the Secretary of State that arrangements for implementing individual support orders are available in the area in which it appears to it that the defendant resides or will reside and the notice has not been withdrawn.

(4) If the court is not satisfied that the individual support conditions are fulfilled, it shall state in open court that it is not so satisfied and why it is not.

(5) The requirements that may be specified under subsection (2)(a) above are those that the court considers desirable in the interests of preventing any repetition of the kind of behaviour which led to the making of the anti-social behaviour order.

(6) Requirements included in an individual support order, or directions given under such an order by a responsible officer, may require the defendant to do all or any of the following things—

    (a) to participate in activities specified in the requirements or directions at a time or times so specified;

    (b) to present himself to a person or persons so specified at a place or places and at a time or times so specified;

    (c) to comply with any arrangements for his education so specified.

(7) But requirements included in, or directions given under, such an order may not require the defendant to attend (whether at the same place or at different places) on more than two days in any week; and "week" here means a period of seven days beginning with a Sunday.

(8) Requirements included in, and directions given under, an individual support order shall, as far as practicable, be such as to avoid—

    (a) any conflict with the defendant's religious beliefs; and

    (b) any interference with the times, if any, at which he normally works or attends school or any other educational establishment.

(9) Before making an individual support order, the court shall obtain from a social worker of a local authority or a member of a youth offending team any information which it considers necessary in order—

    (a) to determine whether the individual support conditions are fulfilled, or

    (b) to determine what requirements should be imposed by an individual support order if made,

and shall consider that information.

(10) In this section and section 1AB below "responsible officer", in relation to an individual support order, means one of the following who is specified in the order, namely—

    (a) a social worker of a local authority;

    (b) a person nominated by a person appointed as chief education officer under section 532 of the *Education Act* 1996;

    (c) a member of a youth offending team.

Individual support orders: explanation, breach, amendment etc.

1AB.—(1) Before making an individual support order, the court shall explain to the defendant in ordinary language—   **23–261**

    (a) the effect of the order and of the requirements proposed to be included in it;

    (b) the consequences which may follow (under subsection (3) below) if he fails to comply with any of those requirements; and

    (c) that the court has power (under subsection (6) below) to review the order on the application either of the defendant or of the responsible officer.

(2) The power of the Secretary of State under section 174(4) of the *Criminal Justice Act* 2003 includes power by order to—

    (a) prescribe cases in which subsection (1) above does not apply; and

    (b) prescribe cases in which the explanation referred to in that subsection may be made in the absence of the defendant, or may be provided in written form.

(3) If the person in respect of whom an individual support order is made fails without reasonable excuse to comply with any requirement included in the order, he is guilty of an offence and liable on summary conviction to a fine not exceeding—

    (a) if he is aged 14 or over at the date of his conviction, £1,000;

    (b) if he is aged under 14 then, £250.

(4) No referral order under section 16(2) or (3) of the *Powers of Criminal Courts (Sentencing) Act* 2000 (referral of young offenders to youth offender panels) may be made in respect of an offence under subsection (3) above.

(5) If the anti-social behaviour order as a result of which an individual support order was made ceases to have effect, the individual support order (if it has not previously ceased to have effect) ceases to have effect when the anti-social behaviour order does.

(6) On an application made by complaint by—

    (a) the person subject to an individual support order, or

    (b) the responsible officer,

the court which made the individual support order may vary or discharge it by a further order.

(7) If the anti-social behaviour order as a result of which an individual support order was made is varied, the court varying the anti-social behaviour order may by a further order vary or discharge the individual support order.

Orders on conviction in criminal proceedings

1C.—(1) This section applies where a person (the "offender") is convicted of a relevant offence.   **23–262**

(2) If the court considers—

    (a) that the offender has acted, at any time since the commencement date, in an anti-social manner, that is to say in a manner that caused or was likely to cause harassment, alarm or distress to one or more persons not of the same household as himself, and

    (b) that an order under this section is necessary to protect persons in any place in England and Wales from further anti-social acts by him,

it may make an order which prohibits the offender from doing anything described in the order.

(3) The court may make an order under this section—

    (a) if the prosecutor asks it to do so, or

    (b) if the court thinks it is appropriate to do so.

(3A) For the purpose of deciding whether to make an order under this section the court may consider evidence led by the prosecution and the defence.

(3B) It is immaterial whether evidence led in pursuance of subsection (3A) would have been admissible in the proceedings in which the offender was convicted.

(4) An order under this section shall not be made except—

    (a) in addition to a sentence imposed in respect of the relevant offence; or

(b) in addition to an order discharging him conditionally

(4A) The court may adjourn any proceedings in relation to an order under this section even after sentencing the offender.

(4B) If the offender does not appear for any adjourned proceedings, the court may further adjourn the proceedings or may issue a warrant for his arrest.

(4C) But the court may not issue a warrant for the offender's arrest unless it is satisfied that he has had adequate notice of the time and place of the adjourned proceedings.

(5) An order under this section takes effect on the day on which it is made, but the court may provide in any such order that such requirements of the order as it may specify shall, during any period when the offender is detained in legal custody, be suspended until his release from that custody.

(6)–(8) [...]

(9) Subsections (7), (10), (10C), (10D), (10E) and (11) of section 1 apply for the purposes of the making and effect of orders made by virtue of this section as they apply for the purposes of the making and effect of anti-social behaviour orders.

(9A) The council for the local government area in which a person in respect of whom an anti-social behaviour order has been made resides or appears to reside may bring proceedings under section 1(10) (as applied by subsection (9) above) for breach of an order under subsection (2) above.

(9B) Subsection (9C) applies in relation to proceedings in which an order under subsection (2) is made against a child or young person who is convicted of an offence.

(9C) In so far as the proceedings relate to the making of the order—

(a) section 49 of the *Children and Young Persons Act* 1933 (restrictions on reports of proceedings in which children and young persons are concerned) does not apply in respect of the child or young person against whom the order is made;

(b) section 39 of that Act (power to prohibit publication of certain matter) does so apply.

(10) In this section—

"child" and "young person" have the same meaning as in the *Children and Young Persons Act* 1933;

"the commencement date" has the same meaning as in section 1 above;

"the court" in relation to an offender means—

(a) the court by or before which he is convicted of the relevant offence; or

(b) if he is committed to the Crown Court to be dealt with for that offence, the Crown Court; and

"relevant offence" means an offence committed after the coming into force of section 64 of the *Police Reform Act* 2002.

[This section is printed as amended by the *Serious Organised Crime and Police Act* 2005 (omission of subss. (6)–(8)).]

Variation and discharge of orders under section 1C

23–263   **1CA.**—(1) An offender subject to an order under section 1C may apply to the court which made it for it to be varied or discharged.

(2) If he does so, he must also send written notice of his application to the Director of Public Prosecutions.

(3) The Director of Public Prosecutions may apply to the court which made an order under section 1C for it to be varied or discharged.

(4) A relevant authority may also apply to the court which made an order under section 1C for it to be varied or discharged if it appears to it that—

(a) in the case of variation, the protection of relevant persons from anti-social acts by the person subject to the order would be more appropriately effected by a variation of the order;

(b) in the case of discharge, that it is no longer necessary to protect relevant persons from anti-social acts by him by means of such an order.

(5) If the Director of Public Prosecutions or a relevant authority applies for the variation or discharge of an order under section 1C, he or it must also send written notice of the application to the person subject to the order.

(6) In the case of an order under section 1C made by a magistrates' court, the refer-

ences in subsections (1), (3) and (4) to the court by which the order was made include a reference to any magistrates' court acting in the same local justice area as that court.

(7) No order under section 1C shall be discharged on an application under this section before the end of the period of two years beginning with the day on which the order takes effect, unless—

    (a) in the case of an application under subsection (1), the Director of Public Prosecutions consents, or

    (b) in the case of an application under subsection (3) or (4), the offender consents.

Interim Orders

    1D.—(1) This section applies where—   **23–264**

    (a) an application is made for an anti-social behaviour order;

    (b) an application is made for an order under section 1B;

    (c) a request is made by the prosecution for an order under section 1C; or

    (d) the court is minded to make an order under section 1C of its own motion.

(2) If, before determining the application or request, or before deciding whether to make an order under section 1C of its own motion, the court considers that it is just to make an order under this section pending the determination of that application or request or before making that decision, it may make such an order.

(3) An order under this section is an order which prohibits the defendant from doing anything described in the order.

(4) An order under this section—

    (a) shall be for a fixed period;

    (b) may be varied, renewed or discharged;

    (c) shall, if it has not previously ceased to have effect, cease to have effect on the determination of the application or request mentioned in subsection (1), or on the court's making a decision as to whether or not to make an order under section 1C of its own motion.

(5) In relation to cases to which this section applies by virtue of paragraph (a) or (b) of subsection (1), subsections (6), (8) and (10) to (12) of section 1 apply for the purposes of the making and effect of orders under this section as they apply for the purposes of the making and effect of anti-social behaviour orders.

(6) In relation to cases to which this section applies by virtue of paragraph (c) or (d) of subsection (1)—

    (a) subsections (6) and (10) to (12) of section 1 apply for the purposes of the making and effect of orders under this section as they apply for the purposes of the making and effect of anti-social behaviour orders; and

    (b) section 1CA applies for the purposes of the variation or discharge of an order under this section as it applies for the purposes of the variation or discharge of an order under section 1C.

Consultation requirements

    1E.—(1) This section applies to—   **23–265**

    (a) applications for an anti-social behaviour order; and

    (b) applications for an order under section 1B.

(2) Before making an application to which this section applies, the council for a local government area shall consult the chief officer of police of the police force maintained for the police area within which that local government area lies.

(3) Before making an application to which this section applies, a chief officer of police shall consult the council for the local government area in which the person in relation to whom the application is to be made resides or appears to reside.

(4) Before making an application to which this section applies, a relevant authority other than a council for a local government area or a chief officer of police shall consult—

    (a) the council for the local government area in which the person in relation to whom the application is to be made resides or appears to reside; and

    (b) the chief officer of police of the police force maintained for the police area within which that local government area lies.

Intervention orders

    1G.—(1) This section applies if, in relation to a person who has attained the age of 18, a rele- **23–266** vant authority—

(a) makes an application for an anti-social behaviour order or an order under section 1B above (the behaviour order),

(b) has obtained from an appropriately qualified person a report relating to the effect on the person's behaviour of the misuse of controlled drugs or of such other factors as the Secretary of State by order prescribes, and

(c) has engaged in consultation with such persons as the Secretary of State by order prescribes for the purpose of ascertaining that, if the report recommends that an order under this section is made, appropriate activities will be available.

(2) The relevant authority may make an application to the court which is considering the application for the behaviour order for an order under this section (an intervention order).

(3) If the court—

(a) makes the behaviour order, and

(b) is satisfied that the relevant conditions are met,

it may also make an intervention order.

(4) The relevant conditions are—

(a) that an intervention order is desirable in the interests of preventing a repetition of the behaviour which led to the behaviour order being made (trigger behaviour);

(b) that appropriate activities relating to the trigger behaviour or its cause are available for the defendant;

(c) that the defendant is not (at the time the intervention order is made) subject to another intervention order or to any other treatment relating to the trigger behaviour or its cause (whether on a voluntary basis or by virtue of a requirement imposed in pursuance of any enactment);

(d) that the court has been notified by the Secretary of State that arrangements for implementing intervention orders are available in the area in which it appears that the defendant resides or will reside and the notice has not been withdrawn.

(5) An intervention order is an order which—

(a) requires the defendant to comply, for a period not exceeding six months, with such requirements as are specified in the order, and

(b) requires the defendant to comply with any directions given by a person authorised to do so under the order with a view to the implementation of the requirements under paragraph (a) above.

(6) An intervention order or directions given under the order may require the defendant—

(a) to participate in the activities specified in the requirement or directions at a time or times so specified;

(b) to present himself to a person or persons so specified at a time or times so specified.

(7) Requirements included in, or directions given under, an intervention order must, as far as practicable, be such as to avoid—

(a) any conflict with the defendant's religious beliefs, and

(b) any interference with the times (if any) at which he normally works or attends an educational establishment.

(8) If the defendant fails to comply with a requirement included in or a direction given under an intervention order, the person responsible for the provision or supervision of appropriate activities under the order must inform the relevant authority of that fact.

(9) The person responsible for the provision or supervision of appropriate activities is a person of such description as is prescribed by order made by the Secretary of State.

(10) In this section—

"appropriate activities" means such activities, or activities of such a description, as are prescribed by order made by the Secretary of State for the purposes of this section;

"appropriately qualified person" means a person who has such qualifications or experience as the Secretary of State by order prescribes;

"controlled drug" has the same meaning as in the *Misuse of Drugs Act* 1971;

"relevant authority" means a relevant authority for the purposes of section 1 above.

(11) An order under this section made by the Secretary of State may make different provision for different purposes.

(12) This section and section 1H below apply to a person in respect of whom a behaviour order has been made subject to the following modifications—

    (a) in subsection (1) above paragraph (a) must be ignored;

    (b) in subsection (2) above, for "is considering the application for" substitute "made";

    (c) in subsection (3) above paragraph (a), the word "and" following it and the word "also" must be ignored.

Intervention orders: explanation, breach, amendment etc.

1H.—(1) Before making an intervention order the court must explain to the defendant in ordinary language—   **23–267**

    (a) the effect of the order and of the requirements proposed to be included in it,

    (b) the consequences which may follow (under subsection (3) below) if he fails to comply with any of those requirements, and

    (c) that the court has power (under subsection (5) below) to review the order on the application either of the defendant or of the relevant authority.

(2) The power of the Secretary of State under section 174(4) of the *Criminal Justice Act* 2003 includes power by order to—

    (a) prescribe cases in which subsection (1) does not apply, and

    (b) prescribe cases in which the explanation referred to in that subsection may be made in the absence of the defendant, or may be provided in written form.

(3) If a person in respect of whom an intervention order is made fails without reasonable excuse to comply with any requirement included in the order he is guilty of an offence and liable on summary conviction to a fine not exceeding level 4 on the standard scale.

(4) If the behaviour order as a result of which an intervention order is made ceases to have effect, the intervention order (if it has not previously ceased to have effect) ceases to have effect when the behaviour order does.

(5) On an application made by—

    (a) a person subject to an intervention order, or

    (b) the relevant authority,

the court which made the intervention order may vary or discharge it by a further order.

(6) An application under subsection (5) made to a magistrates' court must be made by complaint.

(7) If the behaviour order as a result of which an intervention order was made is varied, the court varying the behaviour order may by a further order vary or discharge the intervention order.

(8) Expressions used in this section and in section 1G have the same meaning in this section as in that section.

Special measures for witnesses

1I.—(1) This section applies to the following proceedings—   **23–268**

    (a) any proceedings in a magistrates' court on an application for an anti-social behaviour order,

    (b) any proceedings in a magistrates' court or the Crown Court so far as relating to the issue whether to make an order under section 1C, and

    (c) any proceedings in a magistrates' court so far as relating to the issue whether to make an order under section 1D.

(2) Chapter 1 of Part 2 of the *Youth Justice and Criminal Evidence Act* 1999 (special measures directions in the case of vulnerable and intimidated witnesses) shall apply in relation to any such proceedings as it applies in relation to criminal proceedings, but with—

    (a) the omission of the provisions of that Act mentioned in subsection (3) (which make provision appropriate only in the context of criminal proceedings), and

    (b) any other necessary modifications.

(3) The provisions are—

    (a) section 17(4),

    (b) section 21(1)(b) and (5) to (7),

    (c) section 22(1)(b) and (2)(b) and (c),

    (d) section 27(10), and

    (e) section 32.

Part IV

(4) Any rules of court made under or for the purposes of Chapter 1 of Part 2 of that Act shall apply in relation to proceedings to which this section applies—
    (a) to such extent as may be provided by rules of court, and
    (b) subject to such modifications as may be so provided.
(5) Section 47 of that Act (restrictions on reporting special measures directions etc.) applies, with any necessary modifications, in relation to—
    (a) a direction under section 19 of the Act as applied by this section, or
    (b) a direction discharging or varying such a direction,
and sections 49 and 51 of that Act (offences) apply accordingly.

(2) Fulfilment of criteria

23–269   The criteria that must be fulfilled before a court makes an order in respect of a person convicted of an offence is that:
    — the offender has acted in an anti-social manner at any time since the commencement of this provision (December 2, 2002) and
    — that an order is necessary to protect other people in England and Wales from further anti-social acts from him

23–270   An "anti-social manner" is a manner that causes (or is likely to cause) harassment, alarm or distress to one or more people who are not of the same household as the offender: section 1CA.

Once made, an order can be varied or discharged but no application for discharge may be made until two years have elapsed: section 1C(6) and (8). If an order is made in relation to a person who is to remain in custody, then the provisions of the order may be suspended until release: section 1C(5). Although it may not be appropriate to make an order where a defendant is sentenced to a long period in custody, that is unlikely to be an issue in a magistrates' court: see *post*, *P*. Changes to the *Prosecution of Offences Act* 1985 give to the DPP the power to take over proceedings for variation or discharge of an ASBO made under section 1C.

23–271   For consideration of the standard of proof to be applied when the court is considering making an ASBO: *R. (McCann) v. Manchester Crown Court* [2003] 1 A.C. 787, HL. More detailed consideration was given to the making of orders under this provision in *C. v. Sunderland Youth Court* [2004] 1 Cr.App.R.(S.) 76 and in *P.* [2004] 2 Cr.App.R.(S.) 63. In the *Sunderland* case, the Divisional Court was reviewing an order made in a youth court. It emphasised that courts must act fairly and take account of all relevant considerations. Whilst that will vary with each case, the basis for both the order itself and its scope must be absolutely clear and the terms of the order must be clearly and accurately explained to the defendant by the court. The written order must correctly reflect the order made by the court.

In *P.*, the Court of Appeal considered a range of issues arising from sentencing in the Crown Court including the making of an order under section 1C. Endorsing the comments in the *Sunderland* case, six key principles emerged:
    — the test for making the order is the necessity to protect the public from further anti-social acts by the offender
    — the terms of the order must be precise
    — the terms of the order must be capable of being understood by the offender
    — the findings of fact giving rise to the making of the order must be recorded
    — the order must be explained to the offender
    — the exact terms of the order must both be pronounced in open court and accurately reproduced in the written order.

23–272   The Court considered whether it could be said that an order was "necessary" where a person had been sentenced to a substantial period in custody which would be followed by a period on licence in the community. Whilst provisions in the order (such as geographical constraints) may effectively supplement licence conditions, generally it would not be possible for a court to be satisfied that such an order was necessary when it would only become operative after a substantial period in custody—here the Crown

Court had been dealing with a youth and the sentence was four years detention (reduced to three on appeal). This is less likely to be the case in a magistrates' court but may be the case in a youth court where the maximum period in custody can be 24 months.

As emphasised in *P.*, the nature of an ASBO is such that clarity about the terms of **23–273** the order is of high importance and the written order must correctly reflect the order made by the court. An ingenious attempt was made to circumvent the terms of an order when the written order was at variance with the terms announced by the court in *R. (Walkling) v. DPP* (2004) 168 J.P. 65. An order was made in a magistrates' court for two years. The defendant was present when the order was made. The written order recorded that the appellant was subject to the terms of the order until a specified date which was one day less than the two years. The defendant breached the order and sought to evade responsibility by arguing that the order was a nullity. That was given short shrift—the order was that pronounced by the court and the difference in the written order did not have any effect on the nature of the breach. The Court was also very concerned that parts of the order were both too vague and general and could not readily be understood by a person of the age and educational attainment of the offender. Attention was drawn to the Home Office guide "A Guide to Anti-Social Behaviour Orders and Acceptable Behaviour Courses" which, the Court considered, contains helpful instruction on the drafting of orders.

Since these decisions, the increase in complexity and volume of orders has led to a substantial increase in case law also. The Sentencing Advisory Panel is currently reviewing the approach to dealing with breaches of an order and a consultation paper has been published. Much of the background and some of the current authorities have been set out clearly and succinctly in "ASBO Guidance", a document compiled by a small working group working to the Senior Presiding Judge, Lord Justice Thomas. This has been made available to all judges and courts and is available in hard copy and electronically. It has been reviewed and endorsed by the Judicial Studies Board but is not in the public domain. It should be accessible to all courts but not, at present, more widely to practitioners. One of the more important recent judgments is that in *Boness*; *Bebbington* (2005) 169 J.P. 621. This reviews a wide range of authorities and situations and seeks to provide substantial clarification.

i) Whilst an order may be made indefinitely (it must be for at least two years), that is not advisable. Not every part of an order need be required to last for at least two years and so the original provisions can be removed or amended during the first two years without avoiding the order provided that there must be at least one prohibition that does last for at least two years: *Lonerghan v. Lewes Crown Court* (2005) 169 J.P. 324.

ii) Two statutory criteria are provided—that the offender has acted in an anti-social manner in the past and that an order is necessary to protect persons from further anti-social acts by the offender. Once a court has decided that an order is necessary, it must consider what prohibitions to include. Each order (and each prohibition within an order) must be targeted at the individual and at the type of anti-social behaviour that it is aimed to prevent. The court should consider carefully the need for an order or for a particular prohibition against the background of the case—it is not appropriate to utilise a standard order: *Boness* (2005) 169 J.P. 621.

iii) The order must be proportionate to the legitimate aim pursued and commensurate with the risk to be guarded against: *ibid*.

iv) The order must be clear so that the offender will know precisely what it is he is prohibited from doing: ibid. An example of a condition too widely drawn can be seen in *R. (W.) v. DPP* [2005] EWCA Civ 1333 where the Court considered one of the conditions of an order that restrained W (a youth) from "Committing any criminal offence". There is a long running issue as to the extent that it is appropriate or lawful for an ASBO to prohibit what is already a criminal offence (see *below*). This case confirmed that orders must be sufficiently certain for the subject to know what is prohibited—it was not possible for a person (certainly a youth) to know what was and what was not a criminal offence.

Part IV

v) Furthermore, it was accepted that, where an order is plainly invalid (as the order was in this case), it was open to a magistrates' court to consider submissions to that effect without the need for proceedings before the High Court to declare the order (or at least the critical part of it) to be invalid. Note that this aspect has been doubted by later authorities.

vi) The order must also be clear in a way that enables any breach to be identified and enforced.

vii) There is no requirement that the acts prohibited by an ASBO should, in themselves, give rise to harassment, alarm or distress (*McGrath* [2005] EWCA Crim. 353) though the order must be designed to prevent further such acts from taking place. If such parts of the order are breached but there is no harassment, alarm or distress caused, that may influence the approach to sentence (see *post*).

viii) The purpose of an ASBO is not to punish the offender; it is to prevent further anti-social acts. A court should not allow itself to be persuaded to reduce the sentence that it would otherwise impose because it is making an ASBO: *Lonerghan*.

ix) ix) A number of orders have sought to prohibit conduct that would also be a criminal offence in its own right. This is now generally disapproved of: *Boness* (at. paras. 31–39) subject to a small number of exceptions. An ASBO is designed to enable intervention before a criminal act is committed and it should be targeting the preparatory or preliminary acts rather than the crimes themselves. Thus, in relation to orders made to increase the maximum sentence available (for example, driving whilst disqualified which carries a maximum of 6 months imprisonment), such an order should not be made unless the court is satisfied that the normal range of penalties would be insufficient deterrence. Where the offence itself is punishable with imprisonment, the court doubted whether the availability of a longer period would be significant and such a requirement would, therefore, fail the test of necessity. It may be different where the maximum penalty is a non-custodial sentence. The part of the judgment in *P.* (see *ante*) that suggested that there is unlikely to be any harm in reminding offenders that certain matters constitute criminal conduct by including prohibitions in the ASBO was doubted. The test should not be whether the offender needs reminding but whether the prohibitions are necessary. The later case of *Lamb* (see *post*) considered how to approach sentencing for a breach where the acts of the offender not only breached the terms of the order but were themselves a criminal offence with a lower maximum penalty for that for beaching the ASBO.

A further summary of the process and criteria to be considered has been set out by the Court of Appeal (Criminal Division). In *Wadmore, Foreman* [2006] EWCA Crim. 686 the Court considered a range of decisions including that of the House of Lords in *McCann* [2003] 1 A.C. 787, and of the Court of Appeal in *Boness, Bebbington* [2005] EWCA Crim 2395. It identified ten principles (statutory references are to the *Crime and Disorder Act* 1998 as amended):

(1) Proceedings under s.1C are civil in nature, so that hearsay evidence is admissible, but a court must be satisfied to a criminal standard that the defendant has acted in the anti-social manner alleged.

(2) The test of "*necessity*" set out in s.1C(2)(b) requires the exercise of judgement or evaluation; it does not require proof beyond reasonable doubt that the order is "necessary".

(3) It was particularly important that the findings of fact giving rise to the making of the order are recorded by the Court.

(4) The terms of the order made must be precise and capable of being understood by the offender.

(5) The conditions in the order must be enforceable in the sense that the conditions should allow a breach to be readily identified and capable of being proved. Therefore the conditions should not impose generic prohibitions, but should identify and prohibit the particular type of anti-social behaviour that gives rise to the necessity of an ASBO.

(6) There is power under s.1C(5) to suspend the starting point of an ASBO until an offender has been released from a custodial sentence. However, where a custodial sentence in excess of a few months is passed and the offender is liable to be released on licence and is thus subject to recall, the circumstances will be limited in which there would be a demonstrable necessity to make a suspended ASBO, to take effect on release. There might be cases where geographical restraints could supplement licence conditions.

(7) Because the test for making an ASBO and prohibiting an offender from doing something is one of necessity, each separate order prohibiting a person from doing a specified thing must be necessary to protect persons from anti-social behaviour by the offender. Therefore, each order must be specifically fashioned to deal with the offender concerned. The court has to ask: "is this order necessary to protect persons in any place in England and Wales from further anti-social acts by him".

(8) Not all conditions set out in an ASBO have to run for the full term of the ASBO itself. The test must always be is what is necessary to deal with the particular anti-social behaviour of the offender and what is proportionate in the circumstances.

(9) The order is there to protect others from anti-social behaviour by the offender. Therefore the court should not impose an order which prohibits an offender from committing specified criminal offences if the sentence which could be passed following conviction for the offence should be a sufficient deterrent.

(10) It is unlawful to make an ASBO as if it were a further sentence or punishment. An ASBO must therefore not be used merely to increase the sentence of imprisonment that the offender is to receive.

Another example demonstrating the need for care in determining whether an order is necessary can be found in *Barnard* [2006] EWCA Crim 2041. The defendant had been sentenced to 15 months imprisonment for theft from a motor vehicle. He had 11 previous convictions many for dishonesty offences. There was ample evidence that he habitually committed crimes against vehicles parked on the streets of West London and caused considerable distress. The court also made an ASBO covering the whole of Greater London and prohibiting the carrying of a stone or rock or similar object for breaking glass. In revoking the order, the court stated that:

"On the question of whether an ASBO was necessary in the present case, ... the Crown agreed that the purpose of an ASBO is preventative and that the test is one of necessity. [Counsel] submitted that, in this case, there was a real need for an ASBO because it could enable the police to act before the offender actually committed his crimes. However, we found ourselves unable to accept that submission. We can envisage this offender loitering in the streets near some parked cars. If he is known to the police he will be watched, as he was in the instant case, with, in this case, the assistance of CCTV, and if he attacks a car he will be arrested. [Counsel's] submission was that the police would be able to stop and search him for stones and rocks and other items for breaking glass before he could use them. However, in our view an order to that effect is likely to be of very limited use. The description of this offence demonstrated that it was the work of a few seconds. We do not think that the power given by this ASBO would provide any useful addition to the police's existing powers to arrest and initiate a prosecution. Accordingly, we are persuaded that this is not a case in which an ASBO should have been imposed. One is not necessary for the protection of the public from further anti-social acts. We stress that we are most sympathetic to the task of the police in trying to monitor and prevent this type of prevalent crime. But we do think that ordinary policing methods are the way in which it must be done and not by the imposition of an ASBO which does no more than to seek to prohibit the commission of a crime. We would add that if we had been minded to uphold the ASBO in this case we would have cut it down in both time and place, heeding the advice in *Boness* that such orders must be proportionate in the circumstances."

(3) Breach proceedings

The issue of how to deal with the breach of an order has been much litigated. *Brax-* **23–274** *ton* [2004] EWCA Crim 1374 appears to have become a leading authority. It sets out the rationale for the making of an ASBO which then indicates what should be the approach to a breach of that order:

"It is undeniable that this [order] represents a serious infringement upon the liberty of the applicant, not only because it represents a restriction on the right of free movement, but also because breach constitutes a criminal offence punishable with a term of up to 5 years imprisonment, which is greater than the maximum penalty that could be imposed for offences which might otherwise be reflected within the terms of the order. It is, however, a response by Parliament to increasing concern about the impact on the public of anti-social behaviour in its many constituent forms. It follows that this concern must be reflected in the sentences which the court imposes for breach of the order."

The judgment quotes, with support, a statement in the Court of Appeal judgment in an earlier appeal by the defendant:

"… a sentence close to the maximum should really be reserved for cases in which the anti-social behaviour order had itself been the subject of persistent and prolonged breaches, or where the breaches … had consisted of conduct more serious than abusive, offensive and insulting language or conduct, in other words, in which the behaviour was truly intimidating."

23–275   In *Lamb* [2005] EWCA Crim 3000, the Court of Appeal was again dealing with a substantial sentence following breaches of an ASBO. The breaches tended to consist of travelling on the Metro or being in buildings owned by the company that operated that service in Tyneside.

The judgment states that:

"Given that none of these breaches had been occasioned by anti-social behaviour properly so described (as opposed to being on property that was the subject of a prohibition in an order), it is not entirely clear … from what specific conduct the public required protection. The justification for imposing punishment was, and can only have been, based upon the appellant's persistent and deliberate failures to comply with the order of the court. That justification is perfectly sufficient but it is important to provide a measure of context."

The Court recognised the difficulty faced by the courts when dealing with an offender who repeatedly breaches the order of a court without committing a crime or actually harassing or causing distress to any member of the public. In contrast with *Braxton*, the social impact of the conduct of the offender in *Lamb* was very much less; in fact, it did not impact on the public in any way. Where breaches do not involve harassment, alarm or distress, community penalties should be considered in order to help the offender to live within the terms of the ASBO. Where there is no available community penalty, custodial penalties to maintain the authority of the court could be kept as short as possible.

In *Lamb*, the court also considered the apparent differences in approach of earlier courts to situations where the breach of an ASBO consisted of the commission of a criminal offence with a lower maximum penalty. One line of authority seemed to suggest that the court should not impose a penalty greater than the maximum for the offence. However, the Court preferred the approach in *Braxton* and *Tripp* (*post*) that emphasised the purpose of orders and the approach to breach as potentially more serious than the offence alone.

"We are conscious that, in *Morrison* [2005] EWCA Crim 2237, this Court held that, if the breach of an ASBO is no more than the commission of an offence for which the maximum penalty is prescribed by statute, it is normally wrong in principle to pass a sentence for a breach calculated by reference to the maximum for breach of an ASBO. With respect, that appears to ignore the impact of antisocial behaviour on the wider public which was the purpose of the legislation in the first place; it also means that antisocial behaviour short of a criminal offence could be more heavily punished than antisocial behaviour that coincidentally was also a criminal offence. We thus prefer the contrary approach of this Court in *Tripp* [2005] EWCA Crim 2253 which itself reflects *Braxton*."

23–276   However, this needs to be read together with the authorities on what an ASBO should prohibit in the first place. It is a different issue from whether the order itself should prohibit acts which are a crime in themselves. The Court of Appeal (Criminal Division) again considered the approach to sentence for a breach of an anti-social behaviour order where that breach consisted of a criminal offence with a lower maximum penalty in *H., Stevens and Lovegrove* [2006] EWCA Crim 255. Endorsing the approach in *Lamb* [2005] EWCA Crim 3000, Sir Igor Judge, President, stated:

> "[An] Anti-social Behaviour Order requires specific statutory criteria to be established. In brief, the order is intended to provide protection against harassment, alarm or distress, caused by anti-social behaviour. It is obvious that when passing sentence for breach of an Anti-social Behaviour Order, the court is sentencing for the offence of being in breach of that order. Plainly, any sentence, in any court, must be proportionate or, to use the word with which all sentencers are familiar, 'commensurate'. Therefore, if the conduct which constitutes the breach of the Anti-social Behaviour Order is also a distinct criminal offence, and the maximum sentence for the offence is limited to, say, 6 months' imprisonment, that is a feature to be borne in mind by the sentencing court in the interests of proportionality. It cannot, however, be right that the court's power is thereupon limited to the 6 months maximum imprisonment for the distinct criminal offence. That would treat the breach as if it were a stand alone offence, which at the time when it was committed did not amount to a breach of the court order. In reality, the breach is a distinct offence on its own right, created by statute, punishable by up to 5 years' imprisonment. We therefore reject the submission that it was wrong in principle for the judge to have imposed a custodial sentence, where, for the instant offence of drunkenness, the maximum sentence would have been a fine…. For the avoidance of controversy, we must add that we are not suggesting, and should not be taken to suggest, that an ASBO should be imposed as a kind of device to circumvent maximum penalties which are believed to be too modest. That is a distinct point which does not arise here. The principle is covered by two decisions of this Court, *R. v. Kirby* [2005] EWCA Crim. 1228 and *R. v. Boness* [2005] EWCA Crim. 2395. As we repeat, that is a distinct principle which relates to the circumstances in which it is proper to make an ASBO, not to the consequences which may follow its breach."

An order can be breached only if its terms are not complied with "without reasonable excuse". In *Nicholson* [2006] EWCA Crim 1518 the Court of Appeal (Criminal Division) considered the extent to which ignorance, forgetfulness or misunderstanding of the terms of the order could be capable of being a reasonable excuse. The defendant had been made subject to an anti-social behaviour order which included a prohibition on being within 500 metres of a named building. She subsequently was part of a demonstration within that area. She asserted that she had a reasonable excuse because she had never heard the building in question referred to by the name given in the order and mistakenly believed she was entitled to attend the demonstration. The judge considered the offence to be one of strict liability and that the defence should be narrowly construed. Accordingly, ignorance, forgetfulness or misunderstanding of the terms of the order could not be a reasonable excuse. The Court reviewed the authorities and concluded that, in this case, the issue should have been left to the jury to consider. The Court recognised the danger that such a defence might be used to frustrate the effective application and enforcement of the law but considered that the issue would be highly fact sensitive and should, therefore, be suitable for determination by a jury.

The Court of Appeal dealt with a case at the other end of the spectrum of seriousness in *Anthony* [2005] EWCA Crim2055. The defendant had made a habit of abusing GP surgery and hospital staff, usually when she was the worse for drink. She had breached an ASBO on eight occasions including assaulting a doctor, spitting at a police officer and kicking a female security officer. Offences occurred the day following the making of the ASBO. The Court agreed that the four-year sentence was appropriate, less the maximum discount resulting from early guilty pleas.

Similarly, in *Thomas* [2004] EWCA Crim. 1173, a persistent shoplifter was held to have merited an 18-month sentence for flagrantly and consistently breaching an ASBO. This defendant had acquired 237 convictions for 451 offences, 263 of which were for shoplifting or theft.

EXCLUSION, ALTERATION AND ENFORCEMENT

I. ANCILLARY ORDERS

A. BANNING ORDERS UNDER FOOTBALL SPECTATORS ACT 1989

(1) Purpose and effect

Disorder at and around professional football matches had become a major source of **24–1** public disorder. As part of the response to that, courts were given powers under the 1989 Act to restrict the activities of those considered likely to cause trouble. This was refined and developed by the *Football (Disorder) Act* 2000, in particular Schedule 1 which makes a series of amendments to Part II of, and the Schedule to, the 1989 Act. The *Violent Crime Reduction Act* 2006 also amends the statute.

An order may be made either on conviction of a "relevant offence" or after a specific complaint seeking simply an order under these provisions. Where a person is convicted of a relevant offence (see section 14(8)—an offence to which Schedule 1 to the 1989 Act applies) and the court is satisfied that there are reasonable grounds for believing that making a banning order will help to prevent violence or disorder (defined in section 14C), then that order can be made in addition to the sentence for the offence: section 14A(4). The prosecution can appeal against the failure to make a banning order. Where it is a magistrates' court that does not make the order, that appeal is to the Crown Court: section 14A(5A). If the court adjourns proceedings, it may remand the offender: section 14A(4BA). If that remand is on bail, conditions may include a requirement not to leave England and Wales before the court appearance and, if a match or tournament outside the UK is involved, a requirement for the surrender of the offender's passport. These amendments made by the *Violent Crime Reduction Act* 2006, Sched. 3 came into force on April 6, 2007.

24–2   The main effects of the order are to require the subject of the order to report to a police station within five days, prohibit the subject from entering premises to attend regulated football matches (section 14(4)), make arrangements for the surrender of the subject's passport when certain matches outside the UK are imminent (section 14E(3)) and make whatever additional requirements are necessary. Minimum and maximum periods for the order are specified: section 14F. There are also obligations to notify the enforcing authority of circumstances including changes of name or address and the making of an appeal or an application for termination of the order: section 14E(2A, 2B). Notification must be within seven days of the occurrence of the event starting with the day on which that event occurred: section 14E(2C).

These amendments made by the *Violent Crime Reduction Act* 2006, came into force on April 6, 2007. See the *Violent Crime Reduction Act 2006 (Commencement No. 2) Order* 2007 (S.I. No. 858 2007).

A court may order that the subject attend a specified police station and be required to have his photograph taken to assist in the enforcement of an order under these provisions: section 35 of the *Public Order Act* 1986.

Football Spectators Act 1989, s.1

Scope and interpretation of this Part

24–3   **1.**—(1) This Part of this Act applies in relation to association football matches played in England and Wales which are designated football matches and the following provisions have effect for its interpretation.

(2) "Designated football match" means any such match of a description for the time being designated for the purposes of this Part by order made by the Secretary of State or a particular such match so designated.

(4) An order under subsection (2) above—

     (a) may designate descriptions of football matches wherever played or when played at descriptions of ground or in any area specified in the order.

(8) Each of the following periods is "relevant to" a designated football match, that is to say—

     (a) the period beginning—

         (i)   two hours before the start of the match, or

         (ii)   two hours before the time at which it is advertised to start, or

         (iii)   with the time at which spectators are first admitted to the premises,

     whichever is the earliest, and ending one hour after the end of the match;

     (b) where a match advertised to start at a particular time on a particular day is postponed to a later day, or does not take place, the period in the advertised day beginning two hours before and ending one hour after that time.

(9) A person is a "responsible person" in relation to any designated football match at any premises if he is a person concerned in the management of the premises or in the organisation of the match.

(10) The power to make an order under subsection (2) above is exercisable by statutory instrument which shall be subject to annulment in pursuance of a resolution of either House of Parliament.

(11) The imposition under this Part of this Act of restrictions on the persons who may attend as spectators at any designated football match does not affect any other right of any person to exclude persons from admission to the premises at which the match is played.

Football Spectators Act 1989, s.14

Main definitions

24–4   **14.**—(1) This section applies for the purposes of this Part.

(2) "Regulated football match" means an association football match (whether in England and Wales or elsewhere) which is a prescribed match or a match of a prescribed description.

(3) "External tournament" means a football competition which includes regulated football matches outside England and Wales.

(4) "Banning order" means an order made by the court under this Part which—

    (a) in relation to regulated football matches in England and Wales, prohibits the person who is subject to the order from entering any premises for the purpose of attending such matches, and

    (b) in relation to regulated football matches outside England and Wales, requires that person to report at a police station in accordance with this Part.

(5) "Control period", in relation to a regulated football match outside England and Wales, means the period—

    (a) beginning five days before the day of the match, and

    (b) ending when the match is finished or cancelled.

(6) "Control period", in relation to an external tournament, means any period described in an order made by the Secretary of State—

    (a) beginning five days before the day of the first football match outside England and Wales which is included in the tournament, and

    (b) ending when the last football match outside England and Wales which is included in the tournament is finished or cancelled,

    but, for the purposes of paragraph (a), any football match included in the qualifying or pre-qualifying stages of the tournament is to be left out of account.

(7) References to football matches are to football matches played or intended to be played.

(8) "Relevant offence" means an offence to which Schedule 1 to this Act applies.

See the *Football Spectators (Prescription) Order* 2004 (S.I. 2004 No. 2409) (as **24–5** amended by *S.I. 2006 No. 71*) for football matches in England and Wales and outside England and Wales that are regulated football matches for the purposes of Part II of the 1989 Act.

Football Spectators Act 1989, ss.14A–14C, 14E–14H, 14J

Banning orders made on conviction of an offence

14A.—(1) This section applies where a person (the "offender") is convicted of a relevant **24–6** offence.

(2) If the court is satisfied that there are reasonable grounds to believe that making a banning order would help to prevent violence or disorder at or in connection with any regulated football matches, it must make such an order in respect of the offender.

(3) If the court is not so satisfied, it must in open court state that fact and give its reasons.

(3A) For the purpose of deciding whether to make an order under this section the court may consider evidence led by the prosecution and the defence.

(3B) It is immaterial whether evidence led in pursuance of subsection (3A) would have been admissible in the proceedings in which the offender was convicted.

(4) A banning order may only be made under this section—

    (a) in addition to a sentence imposed in respect of the relevant offence, or

    (b) in addition to an order discharging him conditionally.

(4A) The court may adjourn any proceedings in relation to an order under this section even after sentencing the offender.

(4B) If the offender does not appear for any adjourned proceedings, the court may further adjourn the proceedings or may issue a warrant for his arrest.

(4BA) If the court adjourns or further adjourns any proceedings under subsection (4A) or (4B), the court may remand the offender.

(4BB) A person who, by virtue of subsection (4BA), is remanded on bail may be required by the conditions of his bail—

    (a) not to leave England and Wales before his appearance before the court, and

    (b) if the control period relates to a regulated football match outside the United Kingdom or to an external tournament which includes such matches, to surrender his passport to a police constable, if he has not already done so.

(4C) The court may not issue a warrant under subsection (4B) above for the offender's arrest unless it is satisfied that he has had adequate notice of the time and place of the adjourned proceedings.

(5) A banning order may be made as mentioned in subsection (4)(b) above in spite of anything in sections 12 and 14 of the *Powers of the Criminal Courts (Sentencing) Act* 2000 (which relate to orders discharging a person absolutely or conditionally and their effect).

(5A) The prosecution has a right of appeal against a failure by the court to make a banning order under this section—

    (a) where the failure is by a magistrates' court, to the Crown Court; and

    (b) where it is by the Crown Court, to the Court of Appeal.

(5B) An appeal under subsection (5A)(b) may be brought only if the Court of Appeal gives permission or the judge who decided not to make an order grants a certificate that his decision is fit for appeal.

(5C) An order made on appeal under this section (other than one directing that an application be re-heard by the court from which the appeal was brought) is to be treated for the purposes of this Part as if it were an order of the court from which the appeal was brought.

(6) In this section, "the court" in relation to an offender means—

    (a) the court by or before which he is convicted of the relevant offence, or

    (b) if he is committed to the Crown Court to be dealt with for that offence, the Crown Court.

Banning orders made on a complaint

24–7   **14B.**—(1) An application for a banning order in respect of any person may be made by—

    (a) the relevant chief officer, or

    (b) the Director of Public Prosecutions,

if it appears to him that the condition in subsection (2) is met.

(1A) In subsection (1) 'the relevant chief officer' means—

    (a) the chief officer of police of any police force maintained for a police area; or

    (b) the chief constable of the British Transport Police Force.

(2) That condition is that the respondent has at any time caused or contributed to any violence or disorder in the United Kingdom or elsewhere.

(3) The application is to be made by complaint to a magistrates' court.

(4) If—

    (a) it is proved on the application that the condition in subsection (2) above is met, and

    (b) the court is satisfied that there are reasonable grounds to believe that making a banning order would help to prevent violence or disorder at or in connection with any regulated football matches,

the court must make a banning order in respect of the respondent.

(5) If the magistrates' court adjourns proceedings on an application under this section, the court may remand the person in respect of whom the application is made.

(6) A person who, by virtue of subsection (5) above, is remanded on bail under section 128 of the *Magistrates' Courts Act* 1980 may be required by the conditions of his bail—

    (a) not to leave England and Wales before his appearance before the court, and

    (b) if the control period relates to a regulated football match outside the United Kingdom or to an external tournament which includes such matches, to surrender his passport to a police constable, if he has not already done so.

Banning orders: supplementary

24–8   **14C.**—(1) In this Part, "violence" means violence against persons or property and includes threatening violence and doing anything which endangers the life of any person.

(2) In this Part, "disorder" includes—

    (a) stirring up hatred against a group of persons defined by reference to colour, race, nationality (including citizenship) or ethnic or national origins, or against an individual as a member of such a group,

    (b) using threatening, abusive or insulting words or behaviour or disorderly behaviour,

    (c) displaying any writing or other thing which is threatening, abusive or insulting.

(3) In this Part, "violence" and "disorder" are not limited to violence or disorder in connection with football.

(4) The magistrates' court may take into account the following matters (among others), so far as they consider it appropriate to do so, in determining whether to make an order under section 14B above—

(a) any decision of a court or tribunal outside the United Kingdom,
(b) deportation or exclusion from a country outside the United Kingdom,
(c) removal or exclusion from premises used for playing football matches, whether in the United Kingdom or elsewhere,
(d) conduct recorded on video or by any other means.

(5) In determining whether to make such an order—

(a) the magistrates' court may not take into account anything done by the respondent before the beginning of the period of ten years ending with the application under section 14B(1) above, except circumstances ancillary to a conviction,
(b) before taking into account any conviction for a relevant offence, where a court made a statement under section 14A(3) above (or section 15(2A) below or section 30(3) of the *Public Order Act* 1986), the magistrates' court must consider the reasons given in the statement,

and in this subsection "circumstances ancillary to a conviction" has the same meaning as it has for the purposes of section 4 of the *Rehabilitation of Offenders Act* 1974 (effect of rehabilitation).

(6) Subsection (5) does not prejudice anything in the *Rehabilitation of Offenders Act* 1974.

Banning orders: general

14E.—(1) On making a banning order, a court must in ordinary language explain its effect **24–9** to the person subject to the order.

(2) A banning order must require the person subject to the order to report initially at a police station in England and Wales specified in the order within the period of five days beginning with the day on which the order is made.

(2A) A banning order must require the person subject to the order to give notification of the events mentioned in subsection (2B) to the enforcing authority.

(2B) The events are—

(a) a change of any of his names;
(b) the first use by him after the making of the order of a name for himself that was not disclosed by him at the time of the making of the order;
(c) a change of his home address;
(d) his acquisition of a temporary address;
(e) a change of his temporary address or his ceasing to have one;
(f) his becoming aware of the loss of his travel authorisation;
(g) receipt by him of a new travel authorisation;
(h) an appeal made by him in relation to the order;
(i) an application made by him under section 14H(2) for termination of the order;
(j) an appeal made by him under section 23(3) against the making of a declaration of relevance in respect of an offence of which he has been convicted.

(2C) A notification required by a banning order by virtue of subsection (2A) must be given before the end of the period of seven days beginning with the day on which the event in question occurs and—

(a) in the case of a change of a name or address or the acquisition of a temporary address, must specify the new name or address;
(b) in the case of a first use of a previously undisclosed name, must specify that name; and
(c) in the case of a receipt of a new travel authorisation, must give details of that travel authorisation.

(3) A banning order must impose a requirement as to the surrender in accordance with this Part, in connection with regulated football matches outside the United Kingdom, of the passport of the person subject to the order.

(5) In the case of a person detained in legal custody—

(a) the requirement under this section to report at a police station, and
(b) any requirement imposed under section 19 below,

is suspended until his release from custody.

(6) If—

(a) he is released from custody more than five days before the expiry of the period for which the order has effect, and

(b) he was precluded by his being in custody from reporting initially,

the order is to have effect as if it required him to report initially at the police station specified in the order within the period of five days beginning with the date of his release.

Period of banning orders

24–10   **14F.**—(1) Subject to the following provisions of this Part, a banning order has effect for a period beginning with the day on which the order is made.

(2) The period must not be longer than the maximum or shorter than the minimum.

(3) Where the order is made under section 14A above in addition to a sentence of imprisonment taking immediate effect, the maximum is ten years and the minimum is six years; and in this subsection "imprisonment" includes any form of detention.

(4) In any other case where the order is made under section 14A above, the maximum is five years and the minimum is three years.

(5) Where the order is made under section 14B above, the maximum is five years and the minimum is three years.

Additional requirements of orders

24–11   **14G.**—(1) A banning order may, if the court making the order thinks fit, impose additional requirements on the person subject to the order in relation to any regulated football matches.

(2) The court by which a banning order was made may, on an application made by—

(a) the person subject to the order, or

(b) the person who applied for the order or who was the prosecutor in relation to the order,

vary the order so as to impose, replace or omit any such requirements.

(3) In the case of a banning order made by a magistrates' court, the reference in subsection (2) above to the court by which it was made includes a reference to any magistrates' court acting for the same petty sessions area as that court.

Termination of orders

24–12   **14H.**—(1) If a banning order has had effect for at least two-thirds of the period determined under section 14F above, the person subject to the order may apply to the court by which it was made to terminate it.

(2) On the application, the court may by order terminate the banning order as from a specified date or refuse the application.

(3) In exercising its powers under subsection (2) above, the court must have regard to the person's character, his conduct since the banning order was made, the nature of the offence or conduct which led to it and any other circumstances which appear to it to be relevant.

(4) Where an application under subsection (1) above in respect of a banning order is refused, no further application in respect of the order may be made within the period of six months beginning with the day of the refusal.

(5) The court may order the applicant to pay all or any part of the costs of an application under this section.

(6) In the case of a banning order made by a magistrates' court, the reference in subsection (1) above to the court by which it was made includes a reference to any magistrates' court acting for the same petty sessions area as that court.

Offences

24–13   **14J.**—(1) A person subject to a banning order who fails to comply with—

(a) any requirement imposed by the order, or

(b) any requirement imposed under section 19(2B) or (2C) below,

is guilty of an offence.

(2) A person guilty of an offence under this section is liable on summary conviction to imprisonment for a term not exceeding six months, or a fine not exceeding level 5 on the standard scale, or both.

Football Spectators Act 1989, s.18

Information

18.—(1) Where a court makes a banning order, the justices' chief executive for the court (in **24–14** the case of a magistrates' court) or the appropriate officer (in the case of the Crown Court)—

(a) shall give a copy of it to the person to whom it relates;

(b) shall (as soon as reasonably practicable) send a copy of it to the enforcing authority and to any prescribed person;

(c) shall (as soon as reasonably practicable) send a copy of it to the police station (addressed to the officer responsible for the police station) at which the person subject to the order is to report initially; and

(d) in a case where the person subject to the order is detained in legal custody, shall (as soon as reasonably practicable) send a copy of it to the person in whose custody he is detained.

(2) Where a court terminates a banning order under section 14H above, the clerk of the court (in the case of a magistrates' court) or the appropriate officer (in the case of the Crown Court)—

(a) shall give a copy of the terminating order to the person to whom the banning order relates;

(b) shall (as soon as reasonably practicable) send a copy of it to the enforcing authority; and

(c) in a case where the person subject to the banning order is detained in legal custody, shall (as soon as reasonably practicable) send a copy of the terminating order to the person in whose custody he is detained.

(3) Where a person subject to a banning order is released from custody and, in the case of a person who has not reported initially to a police station, is released more than five days before the expiry of the banning order, the person in whose custody he is shall (as soon as reasonably practicable) give notice of his release to the enforcing authority.

Article 5 of S.I. 2000 No. 2126 prescribes the Football Banning Orders Authority as **24–15** the enforcing authority for the purposes of Part II of the 1989 Act, and the Chief Executive of the Football Association for the purposes of section 18(1) and (2) of that Act.

For banning orders arising out of offences outside England and Wales, see section 22 of the 1989 Act and a series of orders made thereunder.

Football Spectators Act 1989, s.22A

Other interpretation, etc.

22A.—(1) In this Part—   **24–16**

"British citizen" has the same meaning as in the *British Nationality Act* 1981,

"country" includes territory,

"enforcing authority" means a prescribed organisation established by the Secretary of State under section 57 of the *Police Act* 1996 (central police organisations),

"passport" means a United Kingdom passport within the meaning of the *Immigration Act* 1971,

"prescribed" means prescribed by an order made by the Secretary of State.

(2) The Secretary of State may, if he considers it necessary or expedient to do so in order to secure the effective enforcement of this Part, by order provide for section 14(5) and (6) above to have effect in relation to any, or any description of, regulated football match or external tournament as if, for any reference to the number of days (not exceeding ten) specified in the order.

(3) Any power of the Secretary of State to make an order under this Part is exercisable by statutory instrument.

(4) An instrument containing an order made by the Secretary of State under this Part shall be subject to annulment in pursuance of a resolution of either House of Parliament.

Football Spectators Act 1989, s.23

Further provision about, and appeals against, declarations of relevance

23.—(1) Subject to subsection (2) below, a court may not make a declaration of relevance as **24–17**

respects any offence unless it is satisfied that the prosecutor gave notice to the defendant, at least five days before the first day of the trial, that it was proposed to show that the offence related to football matches, to a particular football match or to particular football matches (as the case may be).

(2) A court may, in any particular case, make a declaration of relevance notwithstanding that notice to the defendant as required by subsection (1) above has not been given if he consents to waive the giving of full notice or the court is satisfied that the interests of justice do not require more notice to be given.

(3) A person convicted of an offence as respects which the court makes a declaration of relevance may appeal against the making of the declaration of relevance as if the declaration were included in any sentence passed on him for the offence, and accordingly—

(a) in section 10(3) of the *Criminal Appeal Act* 1968 (appeals against sentence by Crown Court), in paragraph (c), after the sub-paragraph (iv) inserted by section 15(7) above there shall be inserted

"or

    (v) a declaration of relevance under the *Football Spectators Act* 1989;";

(b) in section 50(1) of that Act (meaning of "sentence"), at the end there shall be inserted the words "and a declaration of relevance under the *Football Spectators Act* 1989"; and

(c) in section 108(3) of the *Magistrates' Courts Act* 1980 (right of appeal to the Crown Court), at the end there shall be inserted the words "and also includes a declaration of relevance under the *Football Spectators Act* 1989"

(4) A banning order made upon a person's conviction of a relevant offence shall be quashed if the making of a declaration of relevance as respects that offence is reversed on appeal.

(5) In this section 'declaration of relevance' means a declaration by a court for the purposes of Schedule 1 to this Act that an offence related to football matches, or that it related to one or more particular football matches.

Football Spectators Act 1989, Sched. 1

SCHEDULE 1

Offences

24–18 1. This Schedule applies to the following offences:

(a) any offence under section 14J(1) or 21C(2) of this Act,

(b) any offence under section 2 or 2A of the *Sporting Events (Control of Alcohol etc.) Act* 1985 (alcohol, containers and fireworks) committed by the accused at any football match to which this Schedule applies or while entering or trying to enter the ground,

(c) any offence under section 4A or 5 of the *Public Order Act* 1986 (harassment, alarm or distress) or any provision of Part III of that Act (racial hatred) committed during a period relevant to a football match to which this Schedule applies at any premises while the accused was at, or was entering or leaving or trying to enter or leave, the premises,

(d) any offence involving the use or threat of violence by the accused towards another person committed during a period relevant to a football match to which this Schedule applies at any premises while the accused was at, or was entering or leaving or trying to enter or leave, the premises,

(e) any offence involving the use or threat of violence towards property committed during a period relevant to a football match to which this Schedule applies at any premises while the accused was at, or was entering or leaving or trying to enter or leave, the premises,

(f) any offence involving the use, carrying or possession of an offensive weapon or a firearm committed during a period relevant to a football match to which this Schedule applies at any premises while the accused was at, or was entering or leaving or trying to enter or leave, the premises,

(g) any offence under section 12 of the *Licensing Act* 1872 (persons found drunk in public places, etc.) of being found drunk in a highway or other public place committed while the accused was on a journey to or from a football match to which this

Schedule applies being an offence as respects which the court makes a declaration that the offence related to football matches,

(h)　any offence under section 91(1) of the *Criminal Justice Act* 1967 (disorderly behaviour while drunk in a public place) committed in a highway or other public place while the accused was on a journey to or from a football match to which this Schedule applies being an offence as respects which the court makes a declaration that the offence related to football matches,

(j)　any offence under section 1 of the *Sporting Events (Control of Alcohol etc.) Act* 1985 (alcohol on coaches or trains to or from sporting events) committed while the accused was on a journey to or from a football match to which this Schedule applies being an offence as respects which the court makes a declaration that the offence related to football matches,

(k)　any offence under section 4A or 5 of the *Public Order Act* 1986 (harassment, alarm or distress) or any provision of Part III of that Act (racial hatred) committed while the accused was on a journey to or from a football match to which this Schedule applies being an offence as respects which the court makes a declaration that the offence related to football matches,

(l)　any offence under section 4 or 5 of the *Road Traffic Act* 1988 (driving etc. when under the influence of drink or drugs or with an alcohol concentration above the prescribed limit) committed while the accused was on a journey to or from a football match to which this Schedule applies being an offence as respects which the court makes a declaration that the offence related to football matches,

(m)　any offence involving the use or threat of violence by the accused towards another person committed while one or each of them was on a journey to or from a football match to which this Schedule applies being an offence as respects which the court makes a declaration that the offence related to football matches,

(n)　any offence involving the use or threat of violence towards property committed while the accused was on a journey to or from a football match to which this Schedule applies being an offence as respects which the court makes a declaration that the offence related to football matches,

(o)　any offence involving the use, carrying or possession of an offensive weapon or a firearm committed while the accused was on a journey to or from a football match to which this Schedule applies being an offence as respects which the court makes a declaration that the offence related to football matches,

(p)　any offence under the *Football (Offences) Act 1991*,

(q)　any offence under section 4A or 5 of the *Public Order Act* 1986 (harassment, alarm or distress) or any provision of Part III of that Act (racial hatred)—

(i)　which does not fall within paragraph (c) or (k) above,

(ii)　which was committed during a period relevant to a football match to which this Schedule applies, and

(iii)　as respects which the court makes a declaration that the offence related to that match or to that match and any other football match which took place during that period,

(r)　any offence involving the use or threat of violence by the accused towards another person—

(i)　which does not fall within paragraph (d) or (m) above,

(ii)　which was committed during a period relevant to a football match to which this Schedule applies, and

(iii)　as respects which the court makes a declaration that the offence related to that match or to that match and any other football match which took place during that period,

(s)　any offence involving the use or threat of violence towards property—

(i)　which does not fall within paragraph (e) or (n) above,

(ii)　which was committed during a period relevant to a football match to which this Schedule applies, and

(iii)　as respects which the court makes a declaration that the offence related to that match or to that match and any other football match which took place during that period,

(t)　any offence involving the use, carrying or possession of an offensive weapon or a firearm—

(i)   which does not fall within paragraph (f) or (o) above,

(ii) which was committed during a period relevant to a football match to which this Schedule applies, and

(iii) as respects which the court makes a declaration that the offence related to that match or to that match and any other football match which took place during that period,

(u) any offence under section 166 of the *Criminal Justice and Public Order Act* 1994 (sale of tickets by unauthorised persons) which relates to tickets for a football match.

24–19

2. Any reference to an offence in paragraph 1 above includes—

(a) a reference to any attempt, conspiracy or incitement to commit that offence, and

(b) a reference to aiding and abetting, counselling or procuring the commission of that offence.

24–20

3. For the purposes of paragraphs 1(g) to (o) above—

(a) a person may be regarded as having been on a journey to or from a football match to which this Schedule applies whether or not he attended or intended to attend the match, and

(b) a person's journey includes breaks (including overnight breaks).

4.—(1) In this Schedule, "football match" means a match which is a regulated football match for the purposes of Part II of this Act.

(2) For the purposes of this Schedule each of the following periods is 'relevant to' a football match to which this Schedule applies—

(a) in the case of a match which takes place on the day on which it is advertised to take place, the period—

(i)   beginning 24 hours before whichever is the earlier of the start of the match and the time at which it was advertised to start; and

(ii) ending 24 hours after it ends;

(b) in the case of a match which does not take place on the day on which it was advertised to take place, the period—

(i)   beginning 24 hours before the time at which it was advertised to start on that day; and

(ii) ending 24 hours after that time.

Public Order Act 1986, s.35

Photographs

24–21

35.—(1) The court by which a domestic football banning order is made may make an order which—

(a) requires a constable to take a photograph of the person to whom the domestic football banning order relates or to cause such a photograph to be taken, and

(b) requires that person to go to a specified police station not later than 7 clear days after the day on which the order under this section is made, and at a specified time of day or between specified times of day, in order to have his photograph taken.

(2) In subsection (1) "specified" means specified in the order made under this section and 'banning order' has the same meaning as in Part II of the *Football Spectators Act* 1989.

(3) No order may be made under this section unless an application to make it is made to the court by or on behalf of the person who is the prosecutor in respect of the offence leading to the banning order (or in the case of a banning order made under section 14B of the *Football Spectators Act* 1989, the complainant)

(4) If the person to whom the exclusion order relates fails to comply with an order under this section a constable may arrest him without warrant in order that his photograph may be taken.

24–22

In *Gough v. Chief Constable of the Derbyshire Constabulary* [2002] 3 W.L.R. 289, CA, it was held that in order to justify the restriction on freedom of movement imposed by the banning order, an order should only be made where there are strong grounds for concluding that the individual who is the subject of the order has a propensity for taking part in football hooliganism. The principle of proportionality requires that the restraints on the individual's freedom of movement should be imposed following individual consideration of the case, should not be based simply on the individual's criminal record, should be rationally connected to the objective of preventing English football hooliganism abroad and should be the minimum necessary to achieve that legitimate objective.

When considering the conditions in section 14B, the appropriate standard of proof must also be applied, this standard being practically indistinguishable from the criminal standard of proof, given the consequences that will follow if the conditions for the banning order are made out. This follows the approach adopted regarding an application for an anti-social behaviour order and recommended in relation to an application for a Bind Over, see *post*, §§ 24–53 and 24–60.

B. Disqualification from Driving when Vehicle used for Purposes of Crime

Powers of Criminal Courts (Sentencing) Act 2000, ss.146, 147

Driving disqualification for any offence

146.—(1) The court by or before which a person is convicted of an offence committed after **24–23** 31st December 1997 may, instead of or in addition to dealing with him in any other way, order him to be disqualified, for such period as it thinks fit, for holding or obtaining a driving licence.

(2) Where the person is convicted of an offence the sentence for which is fixed by law or falls to be imposed under section 110(2) or 111(2) above; section 51A(2) of the *Firearms Act* 1968, section 225– 228 of the *Criminal Justice Act* 2003 or section 29(4) or (6) of the *Violent Crime Reduction Act* 2006; subsection (1) above shall have effect as if the words "instead of or" were omitted.

(3) A court shall not make an order under subsection (1) above unless the court has been notified by the Secretary of State that the power to make such orders is exercisable by the court and the notice has not been withdrawn.

(4) A court which makes an order under this section disqualifying a person for holding or obtaining a driving licence shall require him to produce—

    (a) any such licence held by him together with its counterpart; or

    (b) in the case where he holds a Community licence (within the meaning of Part III of the *Road Traffic Act* 1988), his Community licence and its counterpart (if any).

(5) In this section—

"driving licence" means a licence to drive a motor vehicle granted under Part III of the *Road Traffic Act* 1988;

"counterpart" —

    (a) in relation to a driving licence, has the meaning given in relation to such a licence by section 108(1) of that Act; and

    (b) in relation to a Community licence, has the meaning given by section 99B of that Act.

Driving disqualification where vehicle used for purposes of crime

147.—(1) This section applies where a person—   **24–24**

    (a) is convicted before the Crown Court of an offence punishable on indictment with imprisonment for a term of two years or more; or

    (b) having been convicted by a magistrates' court of such an offence, is committed under section 3 above to the Crown Court for sentence.

(2) This section also applies where a person is convicted by or before any court of common assault or of any other offence involving an assault (including an offence of aiding, abetting, counselling or procuring, or inciting to the commission of, an offence).

(3) If, in a case to which this section applies by virtue of subsection (1) above, the Crown Court is satisfied that a motor vehicle was used (by the person convicted or by anyone else) for the purpose of committing, or facilitating the commission of, the offence in question, the court may order the person convicted to be disqualified, for such period as the court thinks fit, for holding or obtaining a driving licence.

(4) If, in a case to which this section applies by virtue of subsection (2) above, the court is

satisfied that the assault was committed by driving a motor vehicle, the court may order the person convicted to be disqualified, for such period as the court thinks fit, for holding or obtaining a driving licence.

(5) A court which makes an order under this section disqualifying a person for holding or obtaining a driving licence shall require him to produce—

(a) any such licence held by him together with its counterpart; or

(b) in the case where he holds a Community licence (within the meaning of Part III of the *Road Traffic Act* 1988), his Community licence and its counterpart (if any).

(6) Facilitating the commission of an offence shall be taken for the purposes of this section to include the taking of any steps after it has been committed for the purpose of disposing of any property to which it relates or of avoiding apprehension or detection.

(7) In this section "driving licence" and "counterpart" have the meanings given by section 146(5) above.

24–25   Section 146 is significantly wider than the power under section 147 in that it is available to both the Crown Court and magistrates' courts, it is not limited to any particular offence, and it is not necessary that the offence should be connected in any way with the use of a motor vehicle. The section 147 power is, therefore, only likely to be used for offences committed before the powers under section 146 became available.

Home Office guidance that accompanied the implementation of section 146 suggests that the power should be used where the offence is in some way linked to the use of a vehicle although that is not necessary under the terms of the section. Any order needs to be proportionate to the offence and it may be that any disqualification for an offence where no vehicle or driving is involved would fall on that ground. In *Cliff* [2005] R.T.R. 11, the defendant committed an offence of affray. In the sequence of events leading up to the offence, it was clear that he had driven a motor vehicle whilst under the influence of drink and/or drugs but there was no offence charged relating to that driving. The court imposed a sentence of 15 months' imprisonment and two years' disqualification under section 146. On appeal, it was argued that it was wrong in principle to impose the disqualification because there was no link between the offence and the driving. The Court of Appeal disagreed although it reduced the period of disqualification to nine months. It is not necessary for the offence to be connected to the use of a motor car and the section provides an additional punishment available to the court. However, the Court also said that such an order cannot be imposed arbitrarily and there must be "sufficient reason" for it. No guidance was given as to what might constitute a sufficient reason but the Court drew attention to the driving that had occurred and to the fact that it was under the heavy influence of drink, drugs or both.

An offender who receives a custodial sentence should not be disqualified from driving for such a term that he will be prevented from securing employment upon his release from prison: *Wright* (1979) 1 Cr.App.R.(S.) 82, CA. However, there is no absolute principle that an offender's period of disqualification should come to an end before he is released from prison: *Arif* (1985) 7 Cr.App.R.(S.) 92, CA. When the nature of custodial sentences changes with the implementation of the *Criminal Justice Act* 2003, short orders such as these need to be seen in the context of the purpose and effect of the licence conditions that are imposed to apply for the remainder of the sentence after release from custody.

C. DISQUALIFICATION OF COMPANY DIRECTORS

(1) Purpose and effect

24–26   Where a person is convicted of certain offences concerned with the management of a company, the court may disqualify that person for a maximum of five years from being a company director, from acting as a receiver of the property of a company or of being directly or indirectly involved in the promotion, formation or management of a company or of acting as an insolvency practitioner.

The power arises on conviction for the offences described in section 5(1) of the 1986

Act. If it is an either way offence, the disqualification can follow any conviction of a qualifying offence. If it is a summary only offence, disqualification can follow only where there have been at least three default orders or convictions in the five years preceding the date of conviction: section 5(2) and (3).

Company Directors Disqualification Act 1986, ss.1, 5

Disqualification orders: general.

1.—(1) In the circumstances specified below in this Act a court may, and under sections 6 and **24–27** 9A shall, make against a person a disqualification order, that is to say an order that for a period specified in the order—

  (a) he shall not be a director of a company, act as receiver of a company's property or in any way, whether directly or indirectly, be concerned or take part in the promotion, formation or management of a company unless (in each case) he has the leave of the court, and

  (b) he shall not act as an insolvency practitioner.

(2) In each section of this Act which gives to a court power or, as the case may be, imposes on it the duty to make a disqualification order there is specified the maximum (and, in section 6, the minimum) period of disqualification which may or (as the case may be) must be imposed by means of the order and, unless the court otherwise orders, the period of disqualification so imposed shall begin at the end of the period of 21 days beginning with the date of the order.

(3) Where a disqualification order is made against a person who is already subject to such an order or to a disqualification undertaking, the periods specified in those orders or, as the case may be, in the order and the undertaking shall run concurrently.

(4) A disqualification order may be made on grounds which are or include matters other than criminal convictions, notwithstanding that the person in respect of whom it is to be made may be criminally liable in respect of those matters.

Disqualification on summary conviction

5.—(1) An offence counting for the purposes of this section is one of which a person is **24–28** convicted (either on indictment or summarily) in consequence of a contravention of, or failure to comply with, any provision of the companies legislation requiring a return, account or other document to be filed with, delivered or sent, or notice of any matter to be given, to the registrar of companies (whether the contravention or failure is on the person's own part or on the part of any company).

(2) Where a person is convicted of a summary offence counting for those purposes, the court by which he is convicted (or, in England and Wales, any other magistrates' court acting for the same petty sessions area) may make a disqualification order against him if the circumstances specified in the next subsection are present.

(3) Those circumstances are that, during the 5 years ending with the date of the conviction, the person has had made against him, or has been convicted of, in total not less than 3 default orders and offences counting for the purposes of this section; and those offences may include that of which he is convicted as mentioned in subsection (2) and any other offence of which he is convicted on the same occasion.

(4) For the purposes of this section—

  (a) the definition of "summary offence" in Schedule 1 to the *Interpretation Act* 1978 applies for Scotland as for England and Wales, and

  (b) "default order" means the same as in section 3(3)(b).

(5) The maximum period of disqualification under this section is 5 years.

The "management" of a company has been held to apply to cases of obtaining by **24–29** deception and similar activities committed during the course of trading by the company: *Corbin* (1984) 6 Cr.App.R.(S.) 17, DC; *Austen* (1985) 7 Cr.App.R.(S.) 214, CA and *Georgiou*, 87 Cr.App.R. 207, CA.

A disqualification order should not be combined with a compensation order, if the effect of the order would be to deprive the offender of his means to earn money with which to pay compensation: *Holmes* (1992) 13 Cr.App.R.(S.) 29, CA.

D. EXCLUSION FROM LICENSED PREMISES

When in force, Schedule 5 to the *Violent Crime Reduction Act* 2006 repeals the

1980 Act. The protection that that Act aimed to provide will then be provided by the "drinking banning order"—an order that will be able to be made on application to a magistrates' court, in county court proceedings and on conviction in criminal proceedings when sections 1–14 of the Act are brought into force. See *post*, Section E for provisions relating to the making of an order upon conviction.

(1) Purpose and effect

24–30   This power enables a court to give additional protection to licensees and others in licensed premises where a defendant has shown an inclination to commit offences or otherwise misbehave in such areas.

In order for an order to be made, the defendant must be convicted of an offence committed on licensed premises during which he used, offered or threatened violence. In those circumstances, in addition to sentence, the court may prohibit the defendant from entering the premises on which the offence was committed or any other premises that the court specifies unless he obtains the express consent of the licensee, his servant or his agent before doing so. The court will specify the length of the order which must be at least three months but no more than two years.

Licensed Premises (Exclusion of Certain Persons) Act 1980, ss.1, 2, 4

Exclusion orders

24–31   **1.**—(1) Where a court by or before which a person is convicted of an offence committed on licensed premises is satisfied that in committing that offence he resorted to violence or offered or threatened to resort to violence, the court may, subject to subsection (2) below, make an order (in this Act referred to as an "exclusion order") prohibiting him from entering those premises or any other specified premises, without the express consent of the licensee of the premises or his servant or agent.

(2) An exclusion order may be made either—

> (a) in addition to any sentence which is imposed in respect of the offence of which the person is convicted; or
>
> (b) where the offence was committed in England and Wales, notwithstanding the provisions of section 12 and 14 of the *Powers of Criminal Courts (Sentencing) Act* 2000 (cases in which absolute and conditional discharges may be made, and their effect), in addition to an order discharging him absolutely or conditionally;
>
> (c) [Scotland]

but not otherwise.

(3) An exclusion order shall have effect for such period, not less than three months or more than two years, as is specified in the order, unless it is terminated under section 2(2) below.

Penalty for non-compliance with exclusion order

24–32   **2.**—(1) A person who enters any premises in breach of an exclusion order shall be guilty of an offence and shall be liable on summary conviction or, in Scotland, on conviction in a court of summary jurisdiction to a fine not exceeding level 4 on the standard scale or to imprisonment for a term not exceeding one month or both.

(2) The court by which a person is convicted of an offence under subsection (1) above shall consider whether or not the exclusion order should continue in force, and may, if it thinks fit, by order terminate the exclusion order or vary it by deleting the name of any specified premises, but an exclusion order shall not otherwise be affected by a person's conviction for such an offence.

Supplemental

24–33   **4.**—(1) In this Act—

> "licensed premises", in relation to England and Wales, means premises in respect of which there is in force a justices' on-licence (within the meaning of section 1 of the *Licensing Act* 1964) and, in relation to Scotland, means premises in respect of which a licence under the *Licensing (Scotland) Act* 1976, other than an off-sales licence or a licence under Part III of that Act (licences for seamen's canteens), is in force; and

"licensee" in relation to any licensed premises means the holder of the licence granted in respect of those premises; and

"specified premises", in relation to an exclusion order, means any licensed premises which the court may specify by name and address in the order.

(2) In the application of section 1 above to Scotland, the reference in subsection (1) of that section to a person's being convicted of an offence shall, in relation to proceedings in a court of summary jurisdiction in which the court, without proceeding to conviction, discharges him absolutely under section 383 of the *Criminal Procedure (Scotland) Act* 1975 or makes a probation order under section 384 of that Act, shall be construed as a reference to the court's being satisfied that he committed the offence.

(3) Where a court makes an exclusion order or an order terminating or varying an exclusion order, the proper officer of the court shall send a copy of the order to the licensee of the premises to which the order relates.

(4) For the purposes of subsection (3) above—

(a) the proper officer of a magistrates' court in England and Wales is the designated officer for the court;

(b) the proper officer of the Crown Court is the appropriate officer; and

(c) the proper officer of a court in Scotland is the clerk of the court.

E. DRINKING BANNING ORDERS

(1) Purpose and effect

This power included in the *Violent Crime Reduction Act* 2006 enables a court to **24–34** impose any prohibition on the subject of the order that is "necessary" for the purpose of "protecting other persons from criminal or disorderly conduct by the subject while he is under the influence of alcohol". This includes protecting property from unlawful loss or damage (section 14(2)) and so may be usable in relation to those who persistently steal from shops whilst under the influence of alcohol. The order must include any necessary prohibitions on the subject entering premises licensed for the sale of alcohol by retail and those holding a club premises certificate for a similar purpose: section 1(3). An order must have effect for at least two months but for no more than two years: section 2(1). Individual provisions may have effect for different periods but never for less than two months nor more than two years: section 2(2). An order may be permitted to cease earlier than the designated time if the subject completes an "approved course" specified in the order: sections 2(3), 12 and 13.

Where an order is being made on conviction, the court must first be satisfied both that the proposed subject has, after the commencement of section 3 of the Act, "engaged in criminal or disorderly conduct while under the influence of alcohol" and that an order is necessary to protect others from such conduct by the subject while under the influence of alcohol.

The court may consider evidence led by the prosecution or the defence; that evidence need not have been admissible in criminal proceedings: section 7(1) and (2). An order may be made as an ancillary order not as a sentence in its own right: section 7(3); however, the consideration of the banning order may be adjourned even after sentence has been imposed for the offence itself: section 7(4). An interim order may be made: section 9(2).

An order may be varied or discharged; however, an order may not be discharged on application unless either half of the length of the order has been completed or the DPP has consented to earlier discharge: section 8(6). If an order is breached without reasonable excuse, the maximum penalty will be a fine of level 4 (currently £2,500): section 11.

Violent Crime Reduction Act 2006, ss.1, 2, 6, 7, 8, 9, 10, 11, 14

Drinking banning orders

1—(1) A drinking banning order is an order that prohibits the individual against whom it is **24–35** made ("the subject") from doing the things described in the order.

(2) Such an order may impose any prohibition on the subject which is necessary for the

purpose of protecting other persons from criminal or disorderly conduct by the subject while he is under the influence of alcohol.

(3) The prohibitions imposed by such an order must include such prohibition as the court making it considers necessary, for that purpose, on the subject's entering—

(a) premises in respect of which there is a premises licence authorising the use of the premises for the sale of alcohol by retail; and

(b) premises in respect of which there is a club premises certificate authorising the use of the premises for the supply of alcohol to members or guests.

(4) A drinking banning order may not impose a prohibition on the subject that prevents him—

(a) from having access to a place where he resides;

(b) from attending at any place which he is required to attend for the purposes of any employment of his or of any contract of services to which he is a party;

(c) from attending at any place which he is expected to attend during the period for which the order has effect for the purposes of education or training or for the purpose of receiving medical treatment; or

(d) from attending at any place which he is required to attend by any obligation imposed on him by or under an enactment or by the order of a court or tribunal.

(5) Expressions used in subsection (3) and in the *Licensing Act* 2003 (c. 17) or in a Part of that Act have the same meanings in that subsection as in that Act or Part.

Duration of drinking banning orders

24–36   **2**—(1) A drinking banning order has effect for a period specified in the order ("the specified period"), which must be not less than two months and not more than two years.

(2) A drinking banning order may provide that different prohibitions contained in the order have effect for different periods; but, in each case, the period ("the prohibition period") must be not less than two months and not more than two years.

(3) A drinking banning order may include provision for—

(a) the order, or

(b) a prohibition contained in it,

to cease to have effect before the end of the specified period or the prohibition period if the subject satisfactorily completes the approved course specified in the order.

(4) Provision under subsection (3) must fix the time at which the order or the prohibition will cease to have effect if the subject satisfactorily completes the specified approved course as whichever is the later of—

(a) the time specified in the order in accordance with subsection (5); and

(b) the time when he does satisfactorily complete that course.

(5) The time specified for the purposes of subsection (4)(a) must be a time after the expiry of at least half the specified period or (as the case may be) the prohibition period.

(6) Provision under subsection (3) may be included in a drinking banning order only if—

(a) the court making the order is satisfied that a place on the specified approved course will be available for the subject; and

(b) the subject has agreed to the inclusion of the provision in question in the order.

(7) Before making provision under subsection (3), the court must inform the subject in ordinary language (whether in writing or otherwise) about—

(a) the effect of including the provision in the order;

(b) what, in general terms, attendance on the course will involve if he undertakes it;

(c) any fees he will be required to pay for the course if he undertakes it; and

(d) when he will have to pay any such fees.

(8) Where a court makes a drinking banning order which does not include provision under subsection (3), it must give its reasons for not including such provision in open court.

(9) The Secretary of State may by regulations amend subsection (5) so as to modify the earliest time (after the completion of the specified approved course) when by virtue of that subsection—

(a) a drinking banning order, or

(b) a prohibition contained in such an order,

may cease to have effect.

Orders on conviction in criminal proceedings

6—(1) This section applies where—   **24–37**

(a) an individual aged 16 or over is convicted of an offence (the "offender"); and

(b) at the time he committed the offence, he was under the influence of alcohol.

(2) The court must consider whether the conditions in section 3(2) are satisfied in relation to the offender.

(3) If the court decides that the conditions are satisfied in relation to the offender, it may make a drinking banning order against him.

(4) If the court—

(a) decides that the conditions are satisfied in relation to the offender, but

(b) does not make a drinking banning order,

it must give its reasons for not doing so in open court.

(5) If the court decides that the conditions are not satisfied in relation to the offender, it must state that fact in open court and give its reasons.

Supplementary provision about orders on conviction

7—(1) For the purpose of deciding whether to make a drinking banning order under section   **24–38**
6 the court may consider evidence led by the prosecution and evidence led by the defence.

(2) It is immaterial whether the evidence would have been admissible in the proceedings in which the offender was convicted.

(3) A drinking banning order under section 6 must not be made except—

(a) in addition to a sentence imposed in respect of the offence; or

(b) in addition to an order discharging the offender conditionally.

(4) The court may adjourn any proceedings in relation to a drinking banning order under section 6 even after sentencing the offender.

(5) If the offender does not appear for any adjourned proceedings, the court may further adjourn the proceedings or may issue a warrant for his arrest.

(6) But the court may not issue a warrant for the offender's arrest unless it is satisfied that he has had adequate notice of the time and place of the adjourned proceedings.

(7) A drinking banning order under section 6 takes effect on—

(a) the day on which it is made; or

(b) if on that day the offender is detained in legal custody, the day on which he is released from that custody.

(8) Subsection (9) applies in relation to proceedings in which a drinking banning order is made under section 6 against a young person.

(9) In so far as the proceedings relate to the making of the order—

(a) section 49 of the *Children and Young Persons Act* 1933 (c. 12) (restrictions on reports of proceedings in which children and young persons are concerned) does not apply in respect of the young person against whom the order is made; and

(b) section 39 of that Act (power to prohibit publication of certain matters) does so apply.

(10) In section 3(2)(fa) of the *Prosecution of Offences Act* 1985 (c. 23) (functions of the Director), after the first occurrence of "conviction of certain offences)" insert ", section 6 of the Violent Crime Reduction Act 2006 (orders on conviction in criminal proceedings)".

(11) In this section and section 6 "the court" in relation to an offender means—

(a) the court by or before which he is convicted of the offence; or

(b) if he is committed to the Crown Court to be dealt with for the offence, the Crown Court.

Variation or discharge of orders under s.6

8—(1) The following persons may apply to the court which made a drinking banning order   **24–39**
under section 6 for the order to be varied or discharged by a further order—

(a) the subject;

(b) the Director of Public Prosecutions; or

(c) a relevant authority.

(2) If the subject makes an application under subsection (1), he must also send notice of his application to the Director of Public Prosecutions.

(3) If the Director of Public Prosecutions or a relevant authority makes an application under subsection (1), he or it must also send notice of the application to the subject.

(4) In the case of an order under section 6 made by a magistrates' court, the reference in subsection (1) to the court which made the order includes a reference to a relevant local court.

(5) An order under section 6 may not be varied so as to extend the specified period to more than two years.

(6) No order under section 6 is to be discharged on an application under subsection (1)(a) unless—

> (a) it is discharged from a time after the end of the period that is half the duration of the specified period; or
>
> (b) the Director of Public Prosecutions has consented to its earlier discharge.

(7) In section 3 of the *Prosecution of Offences Act* 1985 (c. 23) (functions of the Director of Public Prosecutions), in subsection (2) after paragraph (fc) insert—

> "(fd) where it appears to him appropriate to do so, to have the conduct of applications under section 8(1)(b) of the *Violent Crime Reduction Act* 2006 for the variation or discharge of orders made under section 6 of that Act;
>
> (fe) where it appears to him appropriate to do so, to appear on any application under section 8(1)(a) of that Act by a person subject to an order under section 6 of that Act for the variation or discharge of the order."

Interim orders

24–40   9—(1) This section applies in each of the following cases—

> (a) where an application is made for a drinking banning order;
>
> (b) where the court is required under section 6 to consider whether the conditions for making a drinking banning order are satisfied.

(2) Before—

> (a) determining the application, or
>
> (b) considering whether the conditions are satisfied,

the court may make an order under this section ("an interim order") if it considers that it is just to do so.

(3) Where this section applies by virtue of subsection (1)(a), an application for an interim order against an individual—

> (a) may be made without notice being given to that individual; and
>
> (b) may be heard in the absence of that individual.

(4) The following permission is required for the making or hearing of an application in accordance with subsection (3)—

> (a) in the case of proceedings in the county court, the permission of the court; and
>
> (b) in the case of an application to a magistrates' court, the permission of the proper officer.

(5) Permission may only be given under subsection (4) if the court or proper officer is satisfied—

> (a) that it is necessary for the application to be made without notice being given to the individual in question; and
>
> (b) that it is not necessary for the application to be heard in the presence of the individual.

(6) An interim order—

> (a) may contain any provision that may be contained in a drinking banning order; but
>
> (b) has effect, unless renewed, only for such fixed period of not more than four weeks as may be specified in the order.

(7) An interim order—

> (a) may be renewed (on one or more occasions) for a period of not more than four weeks from the end of the period when it would otherwise cease to have effect;
>
> (b) must cease to have effect (if it has not previously done so) on the determination of the application mentioned in subsection (1)(a) or on the court's making its decision whether to make a drinking banning order under section 6.

(8) Section 5 applies in relation to an interim order made in a case falling within subsection (1)(a) as it applies in relation to a drinking banning order made under section 3 or 4, but with the omission of section 5(5) and (6).

(9) Section 8 applies in relation to an interim order made in a case falling within subsec-

tion (1)(b) as it applies in relation to a drinking banning order made under section 6, but with the omission of section 8(5) and (6).

Appeals

10—(1) An appeal lies to the Crown Court against the making by a magistrates' court of a **24–41** drinking banning order under section 3 or 6.

(2) On such an appeal the Crown Court—

    (a) may make such orders as may be necessary to give effect to its determination of the appeal;

    (b) may also make such incidental or consequential orders as appear to it to be just.

(3) An order of the Crown Court made on an appeal under this section (other than one directing that an application be re-heard by a magistrates' court) shall be treated for the purposes of sections 5 and 8 as an order of the magistrates' court from which the appeal was brought.

Breach of drinking banning orders

11—(1) If the subject of a drinking banning order or of an interim order does, without rea- **24–42** sonable excuse, anything that he is prohibited from doing by the order, he is guilty of an offence.

(2) A person guilty of an offence under subsection (1) shall be liable, on summary conviction, to a fine not exceeding level 4 on the standard scale.

(3) If a person is convicted of an offence under subsection (1), it is not open to the court by or before which he is convicted to make an order under subsection (1)(b) (conditional discharge) of section 12 of the *Powers of Criminal Courts (Sentencing) Act* 2000 (c. 6).

(4) A local authority may bring proceedings for an offence under subsection (1).

(5) The Secretary of State may by order provide that a person of a description specified in the order may bring proceedings for an offence under subsection (1) in such cases and such circumstances as may be prescribed by the order.

(6) In proceedings for an offence under subsection (1), a copy of the original drinking banning order or interim order, certified as such by the proper officer of the court which made it, is admissible as evidence—

    (a) of its having been made, and

    (b) of its contents,

to the same extent that oral evidence of those things is admissible in those proceedings.

(7) If proceedings for an offence under subsection (1) are brought in a youth court, section 47(2) of the *Children and Young Persons Act* 1933 (c. 12) has effect as if the persons entitled to be present for the purposes of those proceedings included one person authorised to be present by a relevant authority.

(8) In relation to proceedings brought against a young person for an offence under subsection (1)—

    (a) section 49 of the *Children and Young Persons Act* 1933 (restrictions on reports of proceedings in which children and young persons are concerned) does not apply in respect of the young person against whom the proceedings are brought; and

    (b) section 45 of the *Youth Justice and Criminal Evidence Act* 1999 (c. 23) (power to restrict reporting on criminal proceedings involving persons under 18) does so apply.

(9) If, in relation to any such proceedings, the court does exercise its power to give a direction under section 45 of the *Youth Justice and Criminal Evidence Act* 1999, it must give its reasons for doing so.

(10) Subject to paragraph 2(2) of Schedule 2 to the *Youth Justice and Criminal Evidence Act* 1999, until section 45 of that Act comes into force, the references to it in this section are to be read as references to section 39 of the *Children and Young Persons Act* 1933 (power to prohibit publication of certain matters).

Interpretation of Chapter 1

14—(1) In this Chapter—   **24–43**

    "appropriate persons", in relation to an application for a drinking banning order or an application referred to in section 4(6)(b) or (c), means such of the following as is not a party to the application—

        (a) the chief officer of police of the police force for the police area where the conduct to which the application relates occurred;

(b) the chief officer of police of the police force for the police area in which the individual to whose conduct the application relates normally resides;

(c) every local authority in whose area the place where that individual normally resides is situated; and

(d) the Chief Constable of the British Transport Police Force;

"approved course" means a course approved by the Secretary of State for the purposes of section 2;

"drinking banning order" means an order under section 3, 4 or 6;

"interim order" means an order under section 9;

"local authority" means —

(a) a county council in England;

(b) a district council in England;

(c) a London borough council;

(d) the Common Council of the City of London;

(e) the Council of the Isles of Scilly;

(f) a county council or a county borough council in Wales;

"proper officer" —

(a) in relation to a magistrates' court, means the justices' clerk; and

(b) in relation to any other court, means the clerk of the court;

"relevant authority" means —

(a) the chief officer of police of a police force for a police area;

(b) the Chief Constable of the British Transport Police Force;

(c) a local authority;

"relevant local court", in relation to a drinking banning order, means a magistrates' court acting for the local justice area in which the subject normally resides;

"specified period", in relation to a drinking banning order, means the period specified in the order for the purposes of section 2(1) as the period for which the order is to have effect;

"subject", in relation to an order, means the individual against whom it is made;

"young person" has the same meaning as in the *Children and Young Persons Act* 1933 (c. 12) (see section 107(1) of that Act).

(2) References in this Chapter to protecting persons from criminal or disorderly conduct include references to protecting their property from unlawful loss or damage.

(3) The Secretary of State may by order provide that a person of a description specified in the order is to be regarded as a relevant authority for such purposes of the provisions of this Chapter as are specified in the order.

(4) A power of the Secretary of State to make an order or regulations under this Chapter shall be exercisable by statutory instrument.

(5) Every such power includes power—

(a) to make different provision for different cases;

(b) to make provision subject to such exemptions and exceptions as the Secretary of State thinks fit; and

(c) to make such incidental, supplemental, consequential and transitional provision as he thinks fit.

(6) No regulations shall be made under section 2 unless a draft of the regulations has been laid before Parliament and approved by a resolution of each House.

(7) A statutory instrument containing—

(a) regulations under section 12 or 13, or

(b) an order under section 11 or this section,

shall be subject to annulment in pursuance of a resolution of either House of Parliament.

(8) The power under subsection (5) to make incidental, supplemental and consequential provision includes power to modify so much of this section as defines "appropriate persons".

F. POWER TO RECTIFY SENTENCE

24–44   If a party considers a sentence to be wrong, generally it may only seek to rectify that by utilising the appeal procedure, an option more readily open to the defence than to the prosecution. However, there will be circumstances where it is subsequently recognised that a mistake has been made and a power has been provided to magistrates' courts which avoids the necessity for an appeal to be made.

This power exists wherever a court considers it necessary in the interests of justice. A hearing convened to consider such a change should only take place when notice has been given to all relevant parties and the court should take steps to enable everyone with an interest to be heard before a decision is made. The change could be to replace a sentence or part of a sentence which is wrong in law (*e.g.* one year mandatory disqualification imposed where law requires a minimum of three years) or to change a sentence because of new information becoming available that makes the original sentence less just. Although this is a widely drawn power, it is one that needs to be used with care where it is proposed to make a major change to a sentence for reasons other than a mistake or omission. In *R. (Holme) v. Liverpool Magistrates' Court* (2005) 169 J.P. 306, the defendant was convicted of dangerous driving at a magistrates' court after a trial. A sentence of 50 hours community service was imposed together with disqualification for 12 months and until a test had been passed. Subsequently, information came to light which gave considerably more information about the effect of the offence on the victim than had been formally presented to the court when considering sentence. Approximately five months after sentence, the CPS sought (successfully) to persuade the court to re-open the case with a view to re-considering sentence. The DC allowed the defendant's appeal against that decision. The DC concluded both that (even though no specific information was given) the effect of the accident should have been recognised by the court given the nature of the impact between the defendant's vehicle and the victim and that the sentence imposed was about right. In that context, although the requirement to exercise the power within 28 days had been removed by Parliament, it is a power which, in such circumstances, needed to be exercised speedily. A similar power in the Crown Court for correcting sentence (or for commencing an appeal against an unduly lenient sentence) had to be exercised within 28 days. The DC emphasised that, not least because of the importance of finality, it would only be in very rare circumstances that it would be appropriate to resort to section 142 to consider an increase in sentence, particularly if that increase brought about the possibility of a custodial sentence as opposed to another form of disposal.

Magistrates' Courts Act 1980, s.142

Power of magistrates' court to re-open cases to rectify mistakes etc.

142.—(1) A magistrates' court may vary or rescind a sentence or other order imposed or **24–45** made by it when dealing with an offender if it appears to the court to be in the interests of justice to do so, and it is hereby declared that this power extends to replacing a sentence or order which for any reason appears to be invalid by another which the court has power to impose or make.

(1A) The power conferred on a magistrates' court by subsection (1) above shall not be exercisable in relation to any sentence or order imposed or made by it when dealing with an offender if—

    (a) the Crown Court has determined an appeal against—

        (i) that sentence or order;

        (ii) the conviction in respect of which that sentence or order was imposed or made; or

        (iii) any other sentence or order imposed or made by the magistrates' court when dealing with the offender in respect of that conviction (including a sentence or order replaced by that sentence or order); or

    (b) the High Court has determined a case stated for the opinion of that court on any question arising in any proceeding leading to or resulting from the imposition or making of the sentence or order.

(2) Where a person is convicted by a magistrates' court and it subsequently appears to the court that it would be in the interests of justice that the case should be heard again by different justices, the court may so direct.

(2A) The power conferred on a magistrates' court by subsection (2) above shall not be exercisable in relation to a conviction if—

    (a) the Crown Court has determined an appeal against—
        (i) the conviction; or
        (ii) any sentence or order imposed or made by the magistrates' court when dealing with the offender in respect of the conviction; or
    (b) the High Court has determined a case stated for the opinion of that court on any question arising in any proceeding leading to or resulting from the conviction.

(3) Where a court gives a direction under subsection (2) above—
    (a) the conviction and any sentence or other order imposed or made in consequence thereof shall be of no effect; and
    (b) section 10(4) above shall apply as if the trial of the person in question had been adjourned.

(5) Where a sentence or order is varied under subsection (1) above, the sentence or other order, as so varied, shall take effect from the beginning of the day on which it was originally imposed or made, unless the court otherwise directs.

II. POWER TO ENFORCE FINANCIAL PENALTIES

A. INTRODUCTION

24–46   The court has a variety of options when dealing with an offender who has failed to pay a sum adjudged to be payable upon conviction.

B. POWER TO REMIT THE FINE

24–47   A court has the power to remit a fine that has been ordered. The power under section 85 of the 1980 Act requires a change in the circumstances of the defaulter: section 85(1). For these purposes, the definition of a fine is tighter than elsewhere or in common use and care needs to be taken to ensure that the penalty is truly a "fine" for these purposes: section 85(4). The most commonly found exception is an "excise penalty", which is the equivalent of a fine for some offences mainly those arising from use of a vehicle without a vehicle excise licence.

The power under section 129 covers situations where the court has fixed the amount of a fine in the absence of information about means from the offender and, that information having subsequently been provided, the court considers that a lower fine (or no fine) would have been imposed if that had been known. In those circumstances, the court can remit some or all of the fine imposed.

Magistrates' Courts Act 1980, s.85

Power to remit fine

24–48   **85.**—(1) Where a fine has been imposed on conviction of an offender by a magistrates' court, the court may at any time remit the whole or any part of the fine, but only if it thinks it just to do so having regard to a change of circumstances which has occurred—
    (a) where the court is considering whether to issue a warrant of commitment after the issue of such a warrant in respect of the fine has been postponed under subsection (2) of section 77 above, since the relevant time as defined in subsection (4) of that section; and
    (b) in any other case, since the date of the conviction.

(2) Where the court remits the whole or part of the fine after a term of imprisonment has been fixed, it shall also reduce the term by an amount which bears the same proportion to the whole term as the amount remitted bears to the whole or, as the case may be, shall remit the whole term.

(2A) Where the court remits the whole or part of the fine after an order has been made under section 35(2)(a) or (b) of the *Crime (Sentences) Act* 1997, it shall also reduce the total number of hours or days to which the order relates by a number which bears the same proportion as the amount remitted bears to the whole sum or, as the case may be, shall revoke the order.

(3) In calculating any reduction required by subsection (2) or (2A) above any fraction of a day or hour shall be left out of account.

(4) Notwithstanding the definition of "fine" in section 150(1) below, references in this section to a fine do not include any other sum adjudged to be paid on conviction, whether as a pecuniary penalty, forfeiture, compensation or otherwise.

The magistrates may not remit the whole or any part of a fine imposed by the Crown **24–49** Court, without the consent of the Crown Court: *PCC(S)A*, s.140(5). Neither costs nor compensation can be remitted but, with the consent of the beneficiary of the order, can be written out of the court records. When in force, Schedule 32, paragraph 28 to the *Criminal Justice Act* 2003 amends section 85(2A) to the 1980 *Act* by replacing the reference to the *Crime (Sentences) Act* 1997 by one to section 300(2) of the *Criminal Justice Act* 2003.

Powers of Criminal Courts (Sentencing) Act, s.129

Remission of fines
    129.—(1) This section applies where a court has, in fixing the amount of a fine, determined **24–50** the offender's financial circumstances under section 128(5) above.
    (2) If, on subsequently inquiring into the offender's financial circumstances, the court is satisfied that had it had the results of that inquiry when sentencing the offender it would—
        (a) have fixed a smaller amount, or
        (b) not have fined him,
it may remit the whole or any part of the fine.
    (3) Where under this section the court remits the whole or part of a fine after a term of imprisonment has been fixed under section 139 below (powers of Crown Court in relation to fines) or section 82(5) of the *Magistrates' Courts Act* 1980 (magistrates' powers in relation to default), it shall reduce the term by the corresponding proportion.
    (4) In calculating any reduction required by subsection (3) above, any fraction of a day shall be ignored.

C. Imprisonment in Default of Payment

The power to commit to prison in default of payment of a fine is hedged around by **24–51** many safeguards—it is the final step to be used only where every other option has been shown to be inappropriate or unsuccessful. This section is not an exhaustive study of this complex area but is designed to assist the busy practitioner in identifying the key points in the enforcement process. It is subject to rapid change as provisions to improve enforcement in the *Courts Act* 2003 and the *Criminal Justice Act* 2003 are introduced, sometimes after being piloted in a limited number of areas.

The conditions in which the court may order imprisonment in default of payment are set out in section 82 of the 1980 Act. A court may impose imprisonment as an alternative to payment on the day of conviction only if the offender has the means to pay immediately or is unlikely to remain at a place of abode in the Untied Kingdom for long enough for the fine to be enforced by other means. The minimum period for committal to prison is five days at the point of imposition (though this can be reduced by part payment) and the maximum is on a sliding scale depending on the amount owed. However, shorter periods can be imposed that are not *imprisonment* but have the same effect—see *post*, sections 135 and 136.

If commitment was not ordered at the point of sentence, it can only subsequently be ordered if the defaulter is already in custody serving a sentence or following a means inquiry: section 82(3). If the offence was punishable by imprisonment and the offender appears to the court to have the resources to pay straightaway, then the court can commit the person to prison in default of payment. Otherwise, commitment can only follow a decision that the default is due to the offender's wilful refusal or culpable neglect *and* that the court has considered or tried every other means of securing payment and each is inappropriate or unsuccessful: section 82(4). Generally the alternatives include allowing payment by instalments, issuing a distress warrant to seize the goods of the defaulter, making a money payment supervision order to assist the offender to manage their financial affairs in a way that allows the fine to be paid and either an attachment of earnings order or deduction from a qualifying state benefit. Additional initiatives are being taken to provide viable alternatives which increase the likelihood of a fine being paid.

24–52   When a means inquiry is conducted, the offender should be examined in detail on income, capital or savings, expenditure, circumstances of original failure to pay sums as they come due, failure to pay in accordance with any terms subsequently set by the court, likelihood of paying in the future: *R. v. Newport Pagnell Justices ex p. Smith* (1988) 152 J.P. 475.

Wilful refusal or culpable neglect pursuant to section 82(3) must be demonstrated to the criminal standard of proof: *R. v South Tyneside Justices ex. p. Martin, Independent*, September 20, 1995. The terms "wilful refusal" and "culpable neglect" denote deliberate defiance or reckless disregard of a court order: *R. v. Luton Magistrates' Court ex p. Sullivan* [1992] 2 F.L.R. 196. The defaulter should be given proper opportunity to put his case, and all relevant factors must have been taken into account before the court concludes that the default is due to "wilful failure" or "culpable neglect": *R. v. York Magistrates' Court ex p. Grimes* (1997) 161 J.P. 550. The court has an absolute duty to consider all other means of dealing with the defaulter: *R. v. Exeter City Magistrates' Court ex p. Sugar* (1993) 157 J.P. 766. These other methods are listed in section 82(4A) of the 1980 Act, see *post*.

The implications of Article 8 of the European Convention on Human Rights must be considered when making a decision as to whether to order imprisonment in default of payment; it appears committal will not be an appropriate response where the case involves a single mother with a large number of children with a very limited income, doing her level best to balance one monetary obligation against another. Whilst there might be a case in which the pursuit of the aim to make a mother comply with her legal obligations overrode the rights of her children to have the benefit of her care at home, committal must be a remedy of final resort if all else has failed: *R. (Stokes) v. Gwent Magistrates' Court* (2001) 165 J.P. 766, *per* Brooke L.J. If the defaulter is employed, the fact that his earnings fluctuate from week to week does not preclude the making of an attachment of earnings order: *R. v. Stockport Justices ex p. Conlon* [1997] 2 All E.R. 204.

24–53   Where the offender is already serving a sentence of custody for life, or a term of imprisonment or detention under section 108 of the *PCC(S)A* 2000 or detention in a young offenders' institution, the magistrates' court may order imprisonment, or detention in the case of offenders aged 18–20, under section 82(3) of the *MCA* 1980. This is often a convenient way of ensuring that a person released from custody is able to start again without debts to the court.

However, some care will need to be taken before proceeding too readily to wiping out debts to the court. In *Clacton Justices ex p. Commissioners of Customs and Excise* (1988) 152 J.P. 129, DC it was held that in exercising their discretion whether to issue a warrant of commitment or a warrant of distress to enforce payment of a fine, it was essential for the justices to consider the defaulter's means and to ascertain whether the prosecution held any assets belonging to him. The defendant cannot be allowed to choose between payment of his fine and imprisonment. In the instant case, the Customs and Excise Commissioners held, unknown to the magistrates, a substantial sum of money belonging to the defaulter. Bingham L.J. stated that had the magistrates known this, it was difficult to suppose that they would have concluded otherwise than that a warrant of distress would, if necessary, lie.

In *R. v. Grimsby and Cleethorpes Justices ex p. Walters* [1997] 1 W.L.R. 89, it was held that that where an offender had just been sentenced to imprisonment for substantive offences, he was then "already serving a term of imprisonment" within the terms of the *Magistrates' Courts Act* 1980, s.82(3)(a), and it was open to justices to sentence him in the same judgment to a consecutive term for failure to pay fines and a compensation order. Any sentence will take effect immediately after it is pronounced.

Magistrates' Courts Act 1980, s.82(2)–(6)

24–54   82.—(2) A magistrates' court shall not in advance of the issue of a warrant of commitment fix a term of imprisonment which is to be served by an offender in the event of a default in paying a sum adjudged to be paid by a conviction, except where it has power to issue a warrant of commitment forthwith, but postpones issuing the warrant under section 77(2) above.

(3) Where on the occasion of the offender's conviction a magistrates' court does not issue a warrant of commitment for a default in paying any such sum as aforesaid or fix a term of imprisonment under the said section 77(2) which is to be served by him in the event of any such default, it shall not thereafter issue a warrant of commitment for any such default or for want of sufficient distress to satisfy such a sum unless—

(a) he is already serving a sentence of custody for life, or a term of imprisonment, youth custody, detention under section 9 of the *Criminal Justice Act* 1982 or detention in a detention centre; or

(b) the court has since the conviction inquired into his means in his presence on at least one occasion.

(4) Where a magistrates' court is required by subsection (3) above to inquire into a person's means, the court may not on the occasion of the inquiry or at any time thereafter issue a warrant of commitment for a default in paying any such sum unless—

(a) in the case of an offence punishable with imprisonment, the offender appears to the court to have sufficient means to pay the sum forthwith; or

(b) the court—

  (i) is satisfied that the default is due to the offender's wilful refusal or culpable neglect; and

  (ii) has considered or tried all other methods of enforcing payment of the sum and it appears to the court that they are inappropriate or unsuccessful.

(4A) The methods of enforcing payment mentioned in subsection (4)(b)(ii) above are—

(a) a warrant of distress under section 76 above;

(b) an application to the High Court or county court for enforcement under section 87 below;

(c) an order under section 88 below;

(d) an attachment of earnings order;

(4B) The cases in which the offender's default may be regarded for the purposes of subsection (4)(b)(i) as being attributable to his wilful refusal or culpable neglect include any case in which–

(a) he has refused, otherwise than on reasonable grounds, to consent to a work order proposed to be made under Schedule 6 to the *Courts Act* 2003 (discharge of fines by unpaid work), or

(b) he has without reasonable excuse failed to comply with such an order.

(5) After the occasion of an offender's conviction by a magistrates' court, the court shall not, unless—

(a) the court has previously fixed a term of imprisonment under section 77(2) above which is to be served by the offender in the event of a default in paying a sum adjudged to be paid by the conviction; or

(b) the offender is serving a sentence of custody for life, or a term of imprisonment, youth custody, detention under section 9 of the *Criminal Justice Act* 1982 or detention in a detention centre,

issue a warrant of commitment for a default in paying the sum or fix such a term except at a hearing at which the offender is present.

(5A) A magistrates' court may not issue a warrant of commitment under subsection (5) above at a hearing at which the offender is not present unless the justices' chief executive for the court has first served on the offender a notice in writing stating that the court intends to hold a hearing to consider whether to issue such a warrant and giving the reason why the court so intends.

(5B) Where after the occasion of an offender's conviction by a magistrates' court the court holds a hearing for the purpose of considering whether to issue a warrant of commitment for default in paying a sum adjudged to be paid by the conviction, it shall consider such information about the offender's means as is available to it unless it has previously—

(a) inquired into the offender's means; and

(b) postponed the issue of the warrant of commitment under section 77(2) above.

(5C) A notice under subsection (5A) above—

(a) shall state the time and place appointed for the hearing; and

1251

(b) shall inform the offender that, if he considers that there are grounds why the warrant should not be issued, he may make representations to the court in person or in writing,

but the court may exercise its powers in relation to the issue of a warrant whether or not he makes representations.

(5D) Except as mentioned in subsection (5E) below, the time stated in a notice under subsection (5A) above shall not be earlier than 21 days after the issue of the notice.

(5E) Where a magistrates' court exercises in relation to an offender the power conferred by section 77(2) above and at the same hearing issues a notice under subsection (5A) above in relation to him, the time stated in the notice may be a time on any day following the end of the period for which the issue of the warrant of commitment has been postponed.

(5F) A notice under subsection (5A) above to be served on any person shall be deemed to be served on that person if it is sent by registered post or the recorded delivery service addressed to him at his last known address, notwithstanding that the notice is returned as undelivered or is for any other reason not received by that person.

(6) Where a magistrates' court issues a warrant of commitment on the ground that one of the conditions mentioned in subsection (1) or (4) above is satisfied, it shall state that fact, specifying the ground, in the warrant.

D. POWER TO MAKE A MONEY PAYMENTS SUPERVISION ORDER

Magistrates' Courts Act 1980, s.88

Supervision pending payment

24–55   **88.**—(1) Where any person is adjudged to pay a sum by a summary conviction and the convicting court does not commit him to prison forthwith in default of payment, the court may, either on the occasion of the conviction or on a subsequent occasion, order him to be placed under the supervision of such person as the court may from time to time appoint.

(2) An order placing a person under supervision in respect of any sum shall remain in force so long as he remains liable to pay the sum or any part of it unless the order ceases to have effect or is discharged under subsection (3) below.

(3) An order under this section shall cease to have effect on the making of a transfer of fine order under section 89 below with respect to the sum adjudged to be paid and may be discharged by the court that made it, without prejudice in either case to the making of a new order.

(4) Where a person under 21 years old has been adjudged to pay a sum by a summary conviction and the convicting court does not commit him to detention under section 108 of the *Powers of Criminal Courts (Sentencing) Act* 2000 forthwith in default of payment, the court shall not commit him to such detention in default of payment of the sum, or for want of sufficient distress to satisfy the sum, unless he has been placed under supervision in respect of the sum or the court is satisfied that it is undesirable or impracticable to place him under supervision.

(5) Where a court, being satisfied as aforesaid, commits a person under 21 years old to such detention without an order under this section having been made, the court shall state the grounds on which it is so satisfied in the warrant of commitment.

(6) Where an order placing a person under supervision with respect to a sum is in force, a magistrates' court shall not commit him to prison in default of payment of the sum, or for want of sufficient distress to satisfy the sum, unless the court has before committing him taken such steps as may be reasonably practicable to obtain from the person appointed for his supervision an oral or written report on the offender's conduct and means and has considered any report so obtained, in addition, in a case where an inquiry is required by section 82 above, to that inquiry.

E. POWER TO ORDER A DISTRESS WARRANT

Magistrates' Courts Act 1980, ss.76–78

Enforcement of sums adjudged to be paid

24–56   **76.**—(1) Subject to the following provisions of this Part of this Act, and to section 132 below, where default is made in paying a sum adjudged to be paid by a conviction or order of a magis-

trates' court, the court may issue a warrant of distress for the purposes of levying the sum or issue a warrant committing the defaulter to prison.

(2) A warrant of commitment may be issued as aforesaid either—

(a) where it appears on the return to a warrant of distress that the money and goods
of the defaulter are insufficient to satisfy the sum with the costs and charges of
levying the sum; or

(b) instead of a warrant of distress.

(3) The period for which a person may be committed to prison under such a warrant as
aforesaid shall not, subject to the provisions of any enactment passed after 31st December
1879, exceed the period applicable to the case under Schedule 4 to this Act.

(4) Where proceedings are brought for the enforcement of a magistrates' court maintenance order under this section, the court may vary the order by exercising one of its powers under paragraphs (a) to (d) of section 59(3) above.

(5) Subsections (4), (5) and (7) of section 59 above shall apply for the purposes of
subsection (4) above as they apply for the purposes of that section.

(6) Subsections (4) and (5) above shall not have effect in relation to a maintenance order
which is not a qualifying maintenance order (within the meaning of section 59 above).

Postponement of issue of warrant

77.—(1) Where a magistrates' court has power to issue a warrant of distress under this Part **24–57**
of this Act, it may, if it thinks it expedient to do so, postpone the issue of the warrant until such
time and on such conditions, if any, as the court thinks just.

(2) Where a magistrates' court has power to issue a warrant of commitment under this
Part of this Act, it may, if it thinks it expedient to do so, fix a term of imprisonment or
detention under section 108 of the *Powers of Criminal Courts (Sentencing) Act* 2000
(detention of persons aged 18 to 20 for default) and postpone the issue of the warrant until such
time and on such conditions, if any, as the court thinks just.

(3) A magistrates' court shall have power at any time to do either or both of the following—

(a) to direct that the issue of the warrant of commitment shall be postponed until a
time different from that to which it was previously postponed;

(b) to vary any of the conditions on which its issue is postponed,

but only if it thinks it just to do so having regard to a change of circumstances since the relevant
time.

(4) In this section "the relevant time" means—

(a) where neither of the powers conferred by subsection (3) above has been
exercised previously, the date when the issue of the warrant was postponed
under subsection (2) above; and

(b) in any other case, the date of the exercise or latest exercise of either or both
of the powers.

(5) Without prejudice to the generality of subsection (3) above, if on an application by a
person in respect of whom issue of a warrant has been postponed it appears to a justice of
the peace acting for the petty sessions area in which the warrant has been or would have
been issued that since the relevant time there has been a change of circumstances which
would make it just for the court to exercise one or other or both of the powers conferred
by that subsection, he shall refer the application to the court.

(6) Where such an application is referred to the court—

(a) the clerk of the court shall fix a time and place for the application to be heard;
and

(b) the justices' chief executive for the court shall give the applicant notice of that
time and place.

(7) Where such a notice has been given but the applicant does not appear at the time
and place specified in the notice, the court may proceed with the consideration of the application in his absence.

(8) If a warrant of commitment in respect of the sum adjudged to be paid has been issued before the hearing of the application, the court shall have power to order that the
warrant shall cease to have effect and, if the applicant has been arrested in pursuance of it,
to order that he shall be released, but it shall only make an order under this subsection if it
is satisfied that the change of circumstances on which the applicant relies was not put
before the court when it was determining whether to issue the warrant.

Defect in distress warrant and irregularity in its execution

24–58
    78.—(1) A warrant of distress issued for the purpose of levying a sum adjudged to be paid by the conviction or order of a magistrates' court shall not, if it states that the sum has been so adjudged to be paid, be held void by reason of any defect in the warrant.

(2) A person acting under a warrant of distress shall not be deemed to be a trespasser from the beginning by reason only of any irregularity in the execution of the warrant.

(3) Nothing in this section shall prejudice the claim of any person for special damages in respect of any loss caused by a defect in the warrant or irregularity in its execution.

(4) If any person removes any goods marked in accordance with the rules as articles impounded in the execution of a warrant of distress, or defaces or removes any such mark, he shall be liable on summary conviction to a fine not exceeding level 1 on the standard scale.

(5) If any person charged with the execution of a warrant of distress wilfully retains from the proceeds of a sale of the goods on which distress is levied, or otherwise exacts, any greater costs and charges than those properly payable, or makes any improper charge, he shall be liable on summary conviction to a fine not exceeding level 1 on the standard scale.

F. Power to Make an Attendance Centre Order

24–59
    The court may order an attendance centre order where a centre is available to the court and the offender is under 21 years of age: *PCC(S)A* 2000, s.60.

G. Collection Orders

24–60
    At § 24–51, *ante*, reference was made to the many changes being introduced to improve the enforcement of financial penalties. Some of these provisions are contained in the *Courts Act* 2003, some in the *Criminal Justice Act* 2003.

The majority of the new provisions are contained in section 97 and Schedule 5 to the *Courts Act* 2003 which provides for "collection orders". Whenever compensation is imposed (Schedule 5, paragraph 7A) or the court concludes that the offender is an existing defaulter (paragraph 8), unless it would be impracticable or inappropriate to do so, the court must make an attachment of earnings order (AEO) or application for benefit deductions (ABD). In other cases, the court may make an AEO or ABD with the offender's consent (paragraph 9). In every case in which a fine or compensation order is imposed, the court must make a collection order unless this would be impracticable or inappropriate (paragraph 12). The collection order must state the amount of the sum due, whether the court considers the offender to be an existing defaulter, whether an AEO or ABD has been made and information about the effect of the order, if the court has not made an AEO or ABD, the payment terms and, if an AEO or ABD has been made, the reserve terms (that is, the payment terms that will apply if the AEO or ABD fails). Commonly, a reserve term provides for payment in full within 14 days. If an offender defaults on a collection order and is not already subject to an AEO or ABD, a fines officer must make an AEO or ABD. Where this would be impracticable or inappropriate, or where the offender is already subject to an AEO or ABD, a fines officer must either issue a "further steps" notice advising that the officer intends to take any of the enforcement action listed *post* or refer the case to a magistrates' court.

A fines officer is able to take enforcement action to the extent of the making of an AEO or ABD, the issuing of a distress warrant, the registering of the sum in the register of judgments and orders, the taking of enforcement proceedings in the High Court or county court or the making of a clamping order. A magistrates' court may order the sale of the vehicle if the sum remains unpaid one month after the vehicle was clamped.

Where a fines officer refers the case to a magistrates' court, the court may vary the payment terms or reserve terms or take any of the enforcement steps available to a fines officer. Additionally, where the court is satisfied that the default is due to wilful refusal or culpable neglect, it may increase the fine by up to 50 per cent (paragraph 42A) or discharge the collection order and exercise any of the court's standard fine enforcement powers.

The case may also be referred to a magistrates' court if an offender appeals against a "further steps" notice issued by a fines officer. Standard fine enforcement powers are normally available where a collection order is not made or a case is referred to a magistrates' court by a fines officer or an offender appeals against a 'further steps' notice issued by a fines officer. Section 97 and Schedule 6 to the Act provide the details of how fines may be discharged by unpaid work. The power is not dissimilar to the power under section 300 of the *Criminal Justice Act* 2003 to impose an unpaid work requirement or a curfew order instead of issuing a warrant of commitment to prison in default of payment. By the *Discharge of Fines by Unpaid Work (Prescribed Hourly Sum) Order* 2004 (S.I. 2004 No. 2196), an hour's work discharges £6 worth of financial penalty. This is exempted from the provisions setting the national minimum wage: *National Minimum Wage Act* 1998, s.45a as inserted by Schedule 8, paragraph 382 to the *Courts Act* 2003. Such an order may be made only where, in view of the payer's financial circumstances, no other available means of enforcing the sum is likely to be practicable or appropriate. If so and the payer is both suitable for unpaid work and consents to the order, then the order may be made: *Courts Act* 2003, Sched. 6, para. 2. An offender who unreasonably refuses to consent to such an order may be found guilty of wilful refusal or culpable neglect and therefore susceptible to committal in default (see *ante*, § 24–41). The amount of hours is calculated by dividing the amount due by the "prescribed hourly sum" and rounding up to the next whole number: Schedule 6, paragraph 3(3).

Courts Act 2003, Sched. 6

Section 97(2)   SCHEDULE 6

DISCHARGE OF FINES BY UNPAID WORK

Introductory

1.—(1) This schedule applies if a person aged 18 or over ("P") is liable to pay a sum **24–61** which is or is treated for the purposes of Part 3 of the 1980 Act as a sum adjudged to be paid by conviction of a magistrates' court.

(2) In this Schedule–
   "the prescribed hourly sum" means such sum as may be prescribed by regulations;
   "regulations" means regulations made under this schedule by the lord chancellor;
   "the relevant court" means –
      (a) the court imposing the liability to pay the relevant sum, or
      (b) if that liability has previously been imposed, the magistrates' court responsible for enforcing payment of the relevant sum;
   "the relevant sum" means the sum for which P is liable as mentioned in sub-paragraph (1), but excluding any pecuniary compensation, any pecuniary forfeiture or any sum due in respect of prosecution costs.

Cases where work order may be made

2.—(1) The relevant court may, on the application of a fines officer or of its own motion, **24–62** make an order under this Schedule (a "work order") where—
   (a) it appears to the court that in view of P's financial circumstances all the following methods of enforcing payment of the relevant sum are likely to be impracticable or inappropriate—
      (i)   a warrant of distress under section 76 of the 1980 Act,
      (ii) an application to the high court or county court for enforcement under section 87 of the 1980 Act,
      (iii) an order under section 88 of the 1980 Act,
      (iv) an attachment of earnings order,
      (v)   an application for deductions to be made by virtue of section 24 of the *Criminal Justice Act* 1991 (recovery of fines etc. By deductions from income support etc.), and
      (vi) a collection order under Schedule 5,

(b) it appears to the court that P is a suitable person to perform unpaid work under this Schedule, and

(c) P consents to the making of the order.

(2) A court which is considering the making of a work order may issue a summons requiring P to appear before the court.

(3) A magistrates' court which is considering the making of a work order may order P to give to the court, within a specified period, such a statement of his means as the court may require.

(4) Subsections (2) to (4) of section 84 of the 1980 Act (offences in respect of statement of means) apply to an order made under sub-paragraph (3) as they apply to an order made under subsection (1) of that section.

Provisions of order

24–63   3.—(1) A work order is an order requiring P to perform unpaid work for a specified number of hours, in accordance with instructions to be given by the fines officer, in order to discharge by virtue of this Schedule his liability for the relevant sum.

(2) The order must also—

(a) state the amount of the relevant sum,

(b) specify a fines office to which the order is allocated, and

(c) specify a person ("the supervisor") who is to act as supervisor in relation to P.

(3) The specified number of hours is to be determined by dividing the relevant sum by the prescribed hourly sum and, where the result is not a whole number, adjusting the result upwards to the next whole number.

(4) A work order must specify a date ("the specified date") not later than which the required hours of unpaid work must be performed.

(5) In the following provisions of this Schedule "the fines officer", in relation to P, means any fines officer working at the fines office specified in the work order.

Effect of order on enforcement of payment

24–64   4.—(1) Where a work order has been made in respect of the relevant sum, payment of that sum may not be enforced against P unless the order is revoked.

(2) On making a work order, the court must revoke any order relating to the enforcement of the payment of the relevant sum.

Appointment of, and duties of, supervisor

24–65   5.—(1) A person may not be appointed as the supervisor without his consent.

(2) It is the duty of the supervisor—

(a) to monitor P's compliance with the requirements of the work order, and

(b) to provide the court with such information as the court may require relating to P's compliance with those requirements.

Obligations of person subject to work order, and effect of compliance

24–66   6.—(1) Where a work order is in force, P must perform for the number of hours specified in the order such work, at such places and at such times as he may be instructed by the fines officer.

(2) The fines officer must ensure, as far as practicable, that any instructions given to P in pursuance of the work order are such as to avoid—

(a) any conflict with P's religious beliefs, and

(b) any interference with the times, if any, at which he normally works or attends school or any other educational establishment.

(3) If not later than the specified date P performs work in accordance with the instructions of the fines officer for the specified number of hours, his liability to pay the relevant sum is discharged.

Effect of payment

24–67   7.—(1) Where a work order has been made in respect of any sum—

(a) on payment of the whole of the sum to any person authorised to receive it, the work order ceases to have effect, and

(b) on payment of part of the sum to any such person, the number of hours specified in the order is to be taken to be reduced by a proportion corresponding to that which the part paid bears to the whole of the relevant sum.

(2) In calculating any reduction required by sub-paragraph (1)(b), any fraction of an hour is to be disregarded.

Revocation or variation of order

8.—(1) If, on the application of the fines officer, it appears to the relevant court that P is **24–68** failing or has failed to comply with a work order without reasonable excuse, the court must revoke the order.

(2) If, on the application of the fines officer, it appears to the relevant court—

(a) that P has failed to comply with a work order but has a reasonable excuse for the failure, or

(b) that, because of a change in circumstances since the order was made, P is unlikely to be able to comply with a work order,

the court may revoke the order or postpone the specified date.

(3) The relevant court may of its own motion revoke a work order if it appears to the court that, because of a change in circumstances since the order was made, P is unlikely to be able to comply with the order.

(4) A work order may be revoked under any of sub-paragraphs (1) to (3), or varied under sub-paragraph (2), before the specified date (as well as on or after that date).

(5) Regulations may provide for the fines officer to have the power to issue a summons for the purpose of ensuring that P attends the court to which an application has been made under sub-paragraph (1) or (2).

Allowing for work done

9.—(1) If it appears to the court revoking a work order under paragraph 8(1), (2) or (3) **24–69** that P has performed at least one hour of unpaid work in accordance with the instructions of the fines officer, the court must by order specify the number of hours of work that have been performed; and for this purpose any fraction of an hour is to be disregarded.

(2) Where the court has specified a number of hours under this paragraph, P's liability to pay the relevant sum is discharged to the extent of the prescribed hourly sum in respect of each hour.

Effect of revocation

10.—(1) Where a work order is revoked under paragraph 8(1), (2) or (3), immediate **24–70** payment of the relevant sum (subject to any reduction under paragraph 9(2)) may be enforced against P.

(2) Sub-paragraph (1) does not limit the court's power, on or after the revocation of the work order, to allow time for payment or to direct payment by instalments.

Order not directly enforceable

11. The obligations of P under a work order are not enforceable against him except by **24–71** virtue of paragraph 10(1).

Evidence of supervisor

12.—(1) This paragraph applies where— **24–72**

(a) it falls to a court to determine whether P has performed unpaid work in accordance with a work order, and

(b) the court is satisfied–

(i) that the supervisor is likely to be able to give evidence that may assist the court in determining that matter, and

(ii) that the supervisor will not voluntarily attend as a witness.

(2) The court may issue a summons directed to that person requiring him to attend before the court at the time and place appointed in the summons to give evidence.

Provision of information

13. Regulations may— **24–73**

(a) require a work order to contain prescribed information,

(b) require the court making a work order to give a copy of the order to such persons as may be prescribed, and

(c) require the court revoking or varying a work order to give notice of the revocation or variation to such persons as may be prescribed.

When in force, the *Criminal Justice Act* 2003 provisions enable a court to make a **24–74** "default order" which will require completion of an unpaid work requirement or a curfew requirement as an alternative to commitment to prison. This power is not limited by the same criteria as the power under the *Courts Act* 2003, can be accompanied by electronic monitoring and will be enforced in the same way as a Community Order. Schedule 31 to the *Criminal Justice Act* 2003 provides for matching the amount in default to the extent of the requirement and provides for the lower minimum of 20 hours under the unpaid work requirement compared with a minimum of 40 hours where the requirement is made following conviction. If the order is not complied with and the court decides to revoke the requirement and to re-sentence, the powers of re-sentence are the powers of enforcing the default rather than the powers of sentence for the offence for which the financial penalty was imposed: Schedule 31, paragraph 4(3).

Criminal Justice Act 2003, s.300 and Sched. 31

Power to impose unpaid work requirement or curfew requirement on fine defaulter

24–75   **300.**—(1) Subsection (2) applies in any case where, in respect of a person aged 16 or over, a magistrates' court—

   (a) has power under Part 3 of the *Magistrates'* Courts Act 1980 to issue a warrant of commitment for default in paying a sum adjudged to be paid by a conviction (other than a sum ordered to be paid under section 6 of the *Proceeds of Crime Act* 2002), or

   (b) would, but for section 89 of the *Sentencing Act* (restrictions on custodial sentences for persons under 18), have power to issue such a warrant for such default.

(2) The magistrates' court may, instead of issuing a warrant of commitment or, as the case may be, proceeding under section 81 of the *Magistrates'* Courts Act 1980 (enforcement of fines imposed on young offender), order the person in default to comply with—

   (a) an unpaid work requirement (as defined by section 199), or

   (b) a curfew requirement (as defined by section 204).

(3) In this part "default order" means an order under subsection (2).

(4) Subsections (3) and (4) of section 177 (which relate to electronic monitoring) have effect in relation to a default order as they have effect in relation to a community order.

(5) Where a magistrates' court has power to make a default order, it may, if it thinks it expedient to do so, postpone the making of the order until such time and on such conditions (if any) as it thinks just.

(6) Schedule 8 (breach, revocation or amendment of community order), Schedule 9 (transfer of community orders to Scotland or Northern Ireland) and Chapter 4 (further provisions about orders under Chapters 2 and 3) have effect in relation to default orders as they have effect in relation to community orders, but subject to the modifications contained in Schedule 31.

(7) Where a default order has been made for default in paying any sum—

   (a) on payment of the whole sum to any person authorised to receive it, the order shall cease to have effect, and

   (b) on payment of a part of the sum to any such person, the total number of hours or days to which the order relates is to be taken to be reduced by a proportion corresponding to that which the part paid bears to the whole sum.

(8) In calculating any reduction required by subsection (7)(b), any fraction of a day or hour is to be disregarded.

Section 300   SCHEDULE 31

DEFAULT ORDERS: MODIFICATION OF PROVISIONS RELATING TO COMMUNITY ORDERS

General

24–76   1. Any reference to the offender is, in relation to a default order, to be read as a reference to the person in default.

Unpaid work requirement

24–77   2.—(1) In its application to a default order, section 199 (unpaid work requirement) is modified as follows.

(2) In subsection (2), for paragraphs (a) and (b) there is substituted—

"(a) not less than 20 hours, and

(b) in the case of an amount in default which is specified in the first column of the following Table, not more than the number of hours set out opposite that amount in the second column.

TABLE

Amount	Number of Hours
An amount not exceeding £200	40 hours
An amount exceeding £200 but not exceeding £500	60 hours
An amount exceeding £500	100 hours"

(3) Subsection (5) is omitted.

Curfew requirement

3.—(1) In its application to a default order, section 204 (curfew requirement) is modi- **24–78** fied as follows.

(2) After subsection (2) there is inserted—

"(2A) In the case of an amount in default which is specified in the first column of the following Table, the number of days on which the person in default is subject to the curfew requirement must not exceed the number of days set out opposite that amount in the second column.

TABLE

Amount	Number of days
An amount not exceeding £200	20 days
An amount exceeding £200 but not exceeding £500	30 days
An amount exceeding £500 but not exceeding £1,000	60 days
An amount exceeding £1,000 but not exceeding £2,500	90 days
An amount exceeding £2,500	180 days"

Enforcement, revocation and amendment of default order

4.—(1) In its application to a default order, Schedule 8 (breach, revocation or amend- **24–79** ment of community orders) is modified as follows.

(2) Any reference to the offence in respect of which the community order was made is to be taken to be a reference to the default in respect of which the default order was made.

(3) Any power of the court to revoke the community order and deal with the offender for the offence is to be taken to be a power to revoke the default order and deal with him in any way in which the court which made the default order could deal with him for his default in paying the sum in question.

(4) In paragraph 4 the reference to the Crown Court is to be taken as a reference to a magistrates' court.

(5) The following provisions are omitted—

(a) paragraph 9(1)(c), (5) and (8),

(b) paragraph 12,

(c) paragraph 13(5),

(d) paragraph 15,

(e) paragraph 17(5),
(f) paragraph 21(4), and
(g) paragraph 23(2)(b).

Power to alter amount of money or number of hours or days

24–80   5. The secretary of state may by order amend paragraph 2 or 3 by substituting for any reference to an amount of money or a number of hours or days there specified a reference to such other amount or number as may be specified in the order.

Transfer of default orders to Scotland or Northern Ireland

24–81   6. In its application to a default order, Schedule 9 (transfer of community orders to scotland or northern ireland) is modified as follows.

24–82   7. After paragraph 8 there is inserted—

"8A Nothing in paragraph 8 affects the application of section 300(7) to a default order made or amended in accordance with paragraph 1 or 3."

24–83   8. In paragraph 10, after paragraph (b) there is inserted—

"(bb) any power to impose a fine on the offender."

24–84   When in force, section 301 of the *Criminal Justice Act* 2003 will enable a court to utilise driving disqualification for up to 12 months instead of issuing a warrant of commitment.

Criminal Justice Act 2003, s.301

Fine defaulters: driving disqualification

24–85   **301.**—(1) Subsection (2) applies in any case where a magistrates' court—
          (a) has power under Part 3 of the *Magistrates'* Courts Act 1980 to issue a warrant of commitment for default in paying a sum adjudged to be paid by a conviction (other than a sum ordered to be paid under section 6 of the *Proceeds of Crime Act* 2002), or
          (b) would, but for section 89 of the *Sentencing Act* (restrictions on custodial sentences for persons under 18), have power to issue such a warrant for such default.
          (2) The magistrates' court may, instead of issuing a warrant of commitment or, as the case may be, proceeding under section 81 of the *Magistrates'* Courts Act 1980 (enforcement of fines imposed on young offenders), order the person in default to be disqualified, for such period not exceeding twelve months as it thinks fit, for holding or obtaining a driving licence.
          (3) Where an order has been made under subsection (2) for default in paying any sum—
          (a) on payment of the whole sum to any person authorised to receive it, the order shall cease to have effect, and
          (b) on payment of part of the sum to any such person, the total number of weeks or months to which the order relates is to be taken to be reduced by a proportion corresponding to that which the part paid bears to the whole sum.
          (4) In calculating any reduction required by subsection (3)(b) any fraction of a week or month is to be disregarded.
          (5) The Secretary of State may by order amend subsection (2) by substituting, for the period there specified, such other period as may be specified in the order.
          (6) A court which makes an order under this section disqualifying a person for holding or obtaining a driving licence shall require him to produce—
          (a) any such licence held by him together with its counterpart; or
          (b) in the case where he holds a Community licence (within the meaning of Part 3 of the *Road Traffic Act* 1988), his Community licence and its counterpart (if any).
          (7) In this section—
          "driving licence" means a licence to drive a motor vehicle granted under Part 3 of the *Road Traffic Act* 1988;
          "counterpart" —

(a) in relation to a driving licence, has the meaning given in relation to such a licence by section 108(1) of that act; and

(b) in relation to a Community licence, has the meaning given by Section 99B of that Act.

By Schedule 8, paragraph 220 to the *Courts Act* 2003, a new subsection 4B will be **24–86** added to enable a court to find wilful refusal or culpable neglect where an offender has unreasonably refused to consent to a work order or has failed to comply with such an order without reasonable excuse.

Section 35 of the 1997 Act will be repealed and replaced by Schedule 37 to the *Criminal Justice Act* 2003 when section 300 of the *Criminal Justice Act* 2003 is brought into force.

H. POWER TO ORDER DETENTION

A widely used power (both as a sentence in its own right and as an order in respect of **24–87** unpaid fines) is the power to order detention within the precincts of the court (or at any police station) for a specified period not later than 8 p.m. on the day on which the order is made. This is not a period of imprisonment and so does not have to meet the criteria for a custodial sentence or for imprisonment in default of a fine. However, it is a sentence for an offence and, where used in response to default on payment of a fine, it removes liability to pay the fine. It can be used either after time has been allowed for payment of the fine or where immediate payment is required.

Magistrates' Courts Act 1980, s.135

Detention of offender for one day in court-house or police station
   135.—(1) A magistrates' court that has power to commit to prison a person convicted of an **24–88** offence, or would have that power but for section 82 or 88 above, may order him to be detained within the precincts of the court-house or at any police station until such hour, not later than 8 o'clock in the evening of the day on which the order is made, as the court may direct, and, if it does so, shall not, where it has power to commit him to prison, exercise that power.
   (2) A court shall not make such an order under this section as will deprive the offender of a reasonable opportunity of returning to his abode on the day of the order.
   (3) This section shall have effect in relation to a person aged 18 or over but less than 21 as if references in it to prison were references to detention under of the *Powers of Criminal Courts (Sentencing) Act* 2000 (detention of persons aged 17 to 20 for default).

I. POWER TO ORDER DETENTION OVERNIGHT

This power enables a defendant aged 18 or over to discharge responsibility for pay- **24–89** ment of a fine by serving a night in custody. As it is not imprisonment (since it is "detention"), the court does not have to be satisfied of all that it must if ordering imprisonment in default. The effect of the warrant (which can be issued in the absence of the defaulter) is to require the defaulter to be arrested and detained in a police station until the 8 a.m. that follows arrest. However, the police may release the defaulter between 4 a.m. and 8 a.m. in the circumstances set out in section 136(3).

Magistrates' Courts Act 1980, s.136

Committal to custody overnight at police station for non-payment of sum adjudged by conviction
   136.—(1) A magistrates' court that has power to commit to prison a person in default of pay- **24–90** ment of a sum adjudged to be paid by a summary conviction, or would have that power but for section 82 or 88 above, may issue a warrant for his detention in a police station, and, if it does so, shall not, where it has power to commit him to prison, exercise that power.
   (2) A warrant under this section—
      (a) shall authorise the person executing it,
to arrest the defaulter and take him to a police station, and

(b) shall require the officer in charge of the station to detain him there until 8 o'clock in the morning of the day following that on which he is arrested, or, if he is arrested between midnight and 8 o'clock in the morning, until 8 o'clock in the morning of the day on which he is arrested.

(3) Notwithstanding subsection (2)(b) above, the officer may release the defaulter at any time within 4 hours before 8 o'clock in the morning if the officer thinks it expedient to do so in order to enable him to go to his work or for any other reason appearing to the officer to be sufficient.

(4) This section shall have effect in relation to a person aged 18 or over but less than 21 as if references in it to prison were references to detention under section 108 of the *Powers of Criminal Courts (Sentencing) Act* 2000 (detention of persons aged 18 to 20 for default).

III. ENFORCEMENT OF COMMUNITY ORDERS

A. Legislative Framework

(1) General

24–91   As well as substantial changes being made to the nature of a community order, the enforcement provisions have also been changed with a reduced number of options being made available to the court. In addition to the statutory guidelines, a definitive guideline issued by the Sentencing Guidelines Council sets out the approach to dealing with those who fail to comply with the order of the court.

24–92   Decisions on enforcement of a community sentence are often complex and finely balanced. On the one hand, there is the need to reinforce the authority of the court which made the order and of the supervisor in the knowledge that the prospect of a more severe sentence can be a major incentive assisting the offender to comply with the order. On the other hand, there is a desire to see the order properly completed and the realisation of the benefits that it brings particularly where the life style of the offender makes it more difficult to adjust to the self discipline required to complete an order.

(2) Breach provisions

24–93   The breach provisions which applied to orders made under the *PCC(S)A* 2000 have been replaced by a single set of provisions set out in Schedule 8 to the *Criminal Justice Act* 2003. The most significant change is to narrow the range of options available once a breach is proved. The schedule requires a court either to re-sentence or to make the original order more onerous. There is no power to impose a financial penalty for the breach and allow the order to continue nor to impose no sanction for the breach.

24–94   Responsibility for determining whether to take action on a breach starts with the "responsible officer" (see *ante*, § 23–47 and section 197). The trigger is a failure, without reasonable excuse, to comply with any of the requirements of the community order. The responsible officer must either give the offender a warning or initiate court proceedings (Schedule 8, paragraphs 5 and 6). A warning may not be given if the offender has already been given a warning within the preceding 12 months in relation to failing to comply with the requirements of the order (Schedule 8, paragraph 5). This can be any requirements of the order and is not limited to the same requirements as those subject to the later action. In relation to orders where the responsible officer is an officer of a local probation board, the process of enforcement set out in statute is complemented by requirements in National Standards.

24–95   If court proceedings are started, this will be by the laying of an information before a Justice of the Peace if the order was made by a magistrates' court or before the Crown Court if that is where the order was made. However, a Crown Court may (in the Community Order) direct that any failure to comply in respect of an order made in the Crown Court is to be dealt with by a magistrates' court and, in those circumstances, the information will be laid before a Justice of the Peace: Schedule 8, paragraph 5(4). Where there are a number of failures that are to be brought before the court, the question can arise as to whether there should be separate informations for each failure or whether a single information covering all failures is lawful. In its News Sheet 09/2004 of June 8, 2004, the Justices' Clerks' Society concludes that a single information is generally sufficient. In the same way as an allegation of theft from a shop may encompass a range of items stolen from different places in the shop, so the failure to comply with the order may be evidenced in different ways. The essence is the failure to comply with the order rather than the individual events that demonstrate that. Where some instances are disputed, it will be open to the court to amend the information or to make appropriate findings. Issues may arise concerning whether the person before the court is the person subject to the Community Order. This is an issue similar to that where the prosecution has to prove that the defendant to a charge of driving whilst disqualified is a disqualified driver. In *West Yorkshire Probation Board v. Boulter* (2005) 169 J.P. 601, a person subject to a community rehabilitation order was brought before a magistrates' court on a warrant for breaching the order. The proceedings were adjourned. The defendant did not attend subsequent hearings but was legally represented. Justices accepted defence submissions that the prosecution had failed to prove that the person summoned to appear was the person made subject to the order and that the coincidence of names, date of birth and address was insufficient to prove identity beyond reasonable doubt. The DC upheld the prosecution appeal:

"When magistrates have evidence that the person before them has the same name, date of birth and address as the person previously convicted, it was open to them to draw an inference that he is the same person. Whether that inference is to be drawn in any particular case depends on all the facts of that case."

Where all three of those personal details coincided, it was to be expected that justices would draw such an inference unless there was some other factor which cast doubt on the inference.

See *ante*, § 17–116 and, in particular, the case of *Pattison v. DPP* [2005] EWHC 2938, Admin; (2006) J.P. 51, which has reviewed all the leading authorities (including *Boulter*) and set out some general principles of approach.

If the court is satisfied that the offender has failed to comply and that that failure is without reasonable excuse, Schedule 8, paragraph 9 provides the court with two options. *The first option* is to amend the terms of the Community Order, but this may only be by imposing more onerous requirements. They must be requirements that the court could include if it was making the Community Order at that point: Schedule 8, paragraph 9(1)(a). This entails the obligation to ensure both the suitability for the offender and the continued matching of the restriction on liberty to the seriousness of the offence. It is not limited to increasing the onerousness of requirements already part of the order (*e.g.*, increasing the hours of unpaid work) but could enable the inclusion of a new requirement (*e.g.*, a curfew order). The court can extend the duration of any requirements (*e.g.* more unpaid work, longer curfew) but may not extend the overall length of the order: Schedule 8, paragraph 9(3). Additional restrictions apply in relation to those requirements including treatment—the mental health requirement, the alcohol treatment requirement and the drug rehabilitation requirement. The right to reasonably refuse certain treatment within such an order is preserved: Schedule 8, paragraph 11(1). Similarly, amendments to such requirements must have the agreement of the offender: Schedule 8, paragraph 11(2).

How much more onerous will be for the court to decide in the light of the breach and all the circumstances. No minimum level is prescribed. The general approach to dealing with breaches has been considered by the Sentencing Guidelines Council in its guidance on *New Sentences: Criminal Justice Act 2003* (see *post*).

The second option is to re-sentence for the offence(s) in relation to which the Community Order was made: Schedule 8, paragraph 9(1)(b). Where that offence was not punishable by imprisonment, nonetheless the court may impose a custodial sentence (where the offender is aged 18 or over) if there has been wilful and persistent failure to comply with the requirements of the order: Schedule 8, paragraph 9(1)(c). A custodial

24–96

sentence may be imposed on re-sentencing for an imprisonable offence even though the custody threshold was not passed for that offence, again provided the failure to comply with the requirements of the order is wilful and persistent: Schedule 8, paragraph 9(4). From time to time, a magistrates' court will be required to deal with a failure to comply by an offender aged 18 or over who was under 18 when the order was imposed. Issues have arisen concerning how to re-sentence when the offence leading to the order would have been triable only on indictment if the offender had been an adult rather than a youth. By Sched. 8, para. 12, in such cases the court may re-sentence by imposing a fine of up to £5,000 and/or imposing imprisonment for up to the maximum available in the magistrates' court for an adult offender (in the *Criminal Justice Act* 2003 this is expressed as 51 weeks but is restricted to 6 months in the transitional provisions pending the introduction of custody plus). It appears that there is no power to commit an offender to the Crown Court for sentence for the original offence where the community order was made by a magistrates' court. In *Andrews* [2006] EWCA Crim 2228, the Court considered and upheld the lines of authority culminating in *River Jordan* [1998] 2 Cr.App.R.(S) 83 under the previous statutory provisions. Although in *Andrews* the Court speculated that the provisions in the 2003 Act were differently worded, it appeared to be referring to the later provisions that concerned revocation of the order rather than the provisions of paragraphs 9 and 10 of the Schedule. Where a magistrates' court is entitled to sentence an offender following breach of a Crown Court imposed community order, it may commit such an offender to the Crown Court for sentence: Schedule 8, paragraph 9(6).

If the offender is re-sentenced, the court must revoke the Community Order if it has not already expired: Schedule 8, paragraph 9(5).

24–97   Whichever route the court chooses to follow, it must take into account the extent to which the requirements of the Community Order have been complied with. Thus the offender who fails to comply with a requirement in a relatively minor way towards the end of the order (perhaps having to be brought to court because there was an earlier warning) will be dealt with less severely than an offender who has made no serious attempt to comply.

24–98   Dealing effectively with breaches of an order is an important task for a court. On the one hand, a court has identified requirements designed both to reflect the seriousness of the offence and the suitability of the offender and it is important that the court ensures that everything possible is done to enable the purposes of its order to be achieved. On the other hand, offenders cannot be seen to ignore the order of a court without a suitable sanction. In its guideline on *New Sentences: Criminal Justice Act 2003* the Sentencing Guidelines Council sets out the approach to be adopted. Emphasising that the *primary* objective is to ensure the completion of the requirements, courts are urged to be vigilant to ensure that there is a realistic prospect of the purposes of the order being achieved.

(3) New sentences under the Criminal Justice Act 2003

Guideline: New Sentences: Criminal Justice Act 2003

Section 1—Community Sentences & Deferred Sentences
    Part 1: Community Sentences

B. IMPOSING A COMMUNITY SENTENCE—THE APPROACH

(iii) Breaches

24–99   **1.1.44** When increasing the onerousness of requirements, the court must consider the impact on the offender's ability to comply and the possibility of precipitating a custodial sentence for further breach. For that reason, and particularly where the breach occurs towards the end of the sentence, the court should take account of compliance to date [and may consider that extending the supervision or operational periods will be more sensible;] in other cases it might choose to add punitive or rehabilitative requirements instead. In making these changes the court must be mindful of the legislative restrictions on the overall length of community sentences and on the supervision and operational periods allowed for each type of requirement.

1.1.45 The court dealing with breach of a community sentence should have as its primary objective ensuring that the requirements of the sentence are finished, and this is important if the court is to have regard to the statutory purposes of sentencing. A court that imposes a custodial sentence for breach without giving adequate consideration to alternatives is in danger of imposing a sentence that is not commensurate with the seriousness of the original offence and is solely a punishment for breach. This risks undermining the purposes it has identified as being important. Nonetheless, courts will need to be vigilant to ensure that there is a realistic prospect of the purposes of the order being achieved.

> **Having decided that a community sentence is commensurate with the seriousness of the offence, the primary objective when sentencing for breach of requirements is to ensure that those requirements are completed.**

1.1.46 A court sentencing for breach must take account of the extent to which the offender has complied with the requirements of the community order, the reasons for breach and the point at which the breach has occurred. Where a breach takes place towards the end of the operational period and the court is satisfied that the offender's appearance before the court is likely to be sufficient in itself to ensure future compliance, then given that it is not open to the court to make no order, an approach that the court might wish to adopt could be to re-sentence in a way that enables the original order to be completed properly—for example, a differently constructed community sentence that aims to secure compliance with the purposes of the original sentence.

It should be noted that the Sentencing Guidelines Council guideline at 1.1.44 suggests that it is possible to extend the "supervision and operational periods" when acting in response to breach of a community sentence. The Council has noted that it is not possible to extend the supervision period (which must always be for the length of the order) and there is no operational period. It appears that these words have been inadvertently carried forward from the part of the guideline relating to a Suspended Sentence Order.

1.1.47 If the court decides to increase the onerousness of an order, it must give careful **24–100** consideration, with advice from the Probation Service, to the offender's ability to comply. A custodial sentence should be the last resort, where all reasonable efforts to ensure that an offender completes a community sentence have failed.

> - **The Act allows for a custodial sentence to be imposed in response to breach of a community sentence. Custody should be the last resort, reserved for those cases of deliberate and repeated breach where all reasonable efforts to ensure that the offender complies have failed.**
> - **Before increasing the onerousness of requirements, sentencers should take account of the offender's ability to comply and should avoid precipitating further breach by overloading the offender with too many or conflicting requirements.**
> - **There may be cases where the court will need to consider re-sentencing to a differently constructed community sentence in order to secure compliance with the purposes of the original sentence, perhaps where there has already been partial compliance or where events since the sentence was imposed have shown that a different course of action is likely to be effective.**

B. Revocation on Application

There continues to be a power to revoke a Community Order. In a magistrates' **24–101** court, this may be exercised in relation to an order made by a magistrates' court or to one made by the Crown Court which includes a direction that any failure to comply is to be dealt with by a magistrates' court: Schedule 8, paragraph 13(1). Either the offender or the responsible officer may apply for revocation. The power arises only where the court considers that it is in the interests of justice either to revoke the order or for the offender to be re-sentenced. This must be based on circumstances arising since the making of the order (which include the good progress of the offender under the order): Schedule 8, paragraphs 13(1) and (3). If it is not the offender's application, then the court must summons the offender to appear. Should the offender fail to attend in response to the summons, the court may issue a warrant. There appears to be no power to issue a warrant until there has been a failure to appear in response to a summons. This is in contrast to the power when dealing with a breach of the order.

24–102   The court may either revoke the order or revoke it and re-sentence. If the court re-sentences, it must take account of the extent of compliance with the order: Schedule 8, paragraph 13(4). There is a right of appeal to the Crown Court against sentence passed in these circumstances: Schedule 8, paragraph 13(5). No application to revoke an order under Schedule 8, paragraph 13 can be made whilst appeal against the Community Order is pending: Schedule 8, paragraph 24.

C. REVOCATION FOLLOWING SUBSEQUENT CONVICTION

24–103   A further power to revoke or to revoke and re-sentence arises where an offender subject to a Community Order is convicted of an offence. This power can be exercised by a magistrates' court when the Community Order was made by a magistrates' court. Again, the criterion is that the court considers that the exercise of these powers is in the interests of justice based on circumstances since the Community Order was made. This ensures that a court does not need to allow two potentially inconsistent sentences to run alongside each other whilst also avoiding the need for a specific application to revoke the order following, for example, a custodial sentence: Schedule 8, paragraph 21. If the offender is convicted in a magistrates' court but is subject to a Community Order made by the Crown Court, the court may commit the offender on bail or in custody to be dealt with: Schedule 8, paragraph 22. The Crown Court may only deal with an offender under these provisions where committed (see *ante*) or where convicted at the Crown Court: Schedule 9, paragraph 23. Where conviction takes place in the magistrates' court and there is no committal, the Crown Court will only have the power to revoke if an application is made under Schedule 8 paragraph 14 or breach proceedings are initiated.

D. AMENDMENT

24–104   Different provisions are made for 5 different circumstances for amendment —change of residence, general requirements, treatment requirements, drug rehabilitation requirement and unpaid work requirement: Schedule 9, Part 4. If the application is not made by the offender, the court must issue a summons for the offender's attendance. If the offender does not attend, a warrant may be issued: Schedule 8, paragraph 25(1). This process is not necessary in relation to the limited changes specified in paragraph 25(2).

Criminal Justice Act 2003, s.179, Sched. 8

Breach, revocation or amendment of community order

24–105   **179.** Schedule 8 (which relates to failures to comply with the requirements of community orders and to the revocation or amendment of such orders) shall have effect.

Section 179   SCHEDULE 8

BREACH, REVOCATION OR AMENDMENT OF COMMUNITY ORDER

PART 1

PRELIMINARY

Interpretation

24–106   1. In this Schedule—

"the offender", in relation to a community order, means the person in respect of whom the order is made;

"the petty sessions area concerned", in relation to a community order, means the petty sessions area for the time being specified in the order;

"the responsible officer" has the meaning given by section 197.

2. In this Schedule—   **24–107**

(a) references to a drug rehabilitation requirement of a community order being subject to review are references to that requirement being subject to review in accordance with section 210(1)(b);

(b) references to the court responsible for a community order imposing a drug rehabilitation requirement which is subject to review are to be construed in accordance with section 210(2).

3. For the purposes of this Schedule—   **24–108**

(a) a requirement falling within any paragraph of section 177(1) is of the same kind as any other requirement falling within that paragraph, and

(b) an electronic monitoring requirement is a requirement of the same kind as any requirement falling within section 177(1) to which it relates.

Orders made on appeal

4. Where a community order has been made on appeal, it is to be taken for the purposes   **24–109**
of this Schedule to have been made by the Crown Court.

PART 2

BREACH OF REQUIREMENT OF ORDER

Duty to give warning

5.—(1) If the responsible officer is of the opinion that the offender has failed without   **24–110**
reasonable excuse to comply with any of the requirements of a community order, the officer must give him a warning under this paragraph unless—

(a) the offender has within the previous twelve months been given a warning under this paragraph in relation to a failure to comply with any of the requirements of the order, or

(b) the officer causes an information to be laid before a justice of the peace in respect of the failure.

(2) A warning under this paragraph must—

(a) describe the circumstances of the failure,

(b) state that the failure is unacceptable, and

(c) inform the offender that, if within the next twelve months he again fails to comply with any requirement of the order, he will be liable to be brought before a court.

(3) The responsible officer must, as soon as practicable after the warning has been given, record that fact.

(4) In relation to any community order which was made by the Crown Court and does not include a direction that any failure to comply with the requirements of the order is to be dealt with by a magistrates' court, the reference in sub-paragraph (1)(b) to a justice of the peace is to be read as a reference to the Crown Court.

Breach of order after warning

6.—(1) If—   **24–111**

(a) the responsible officer has given a warning under paragraph 5 to the offender in respect of a community order, and

(b) at any time within the twelve months beginning with the date on which the warning was given, the responsible officer is of the opinion that the offender has since that date failed without reasonable excuse to comply with any of the requirements of the order,

the officer must cause an information to be laid before a justice of the peace in respect of the failure in question.

(2) In relation to any community order which was made by the Crown Court and does

not include a direction that any failure to comply with the requirements of the order is to be dealt with by a magistrates' court, the reference in sub-paragraph (1) to a justice of the peace is to be read as a reference to the Crown Court.

Issue of summons or warrant by justice of the peace

24–112   7.—(1) This paragraph applies to—

     (a) a community order made by a magistrates' court, or

     (b) any community order which was made by the Crown Court and includes a direction that any failure to comply with the requirements of the order is to be dealt with by a magistrates' court.

(2) If at any time while a community order to which this paragraph applies is in force it appears on information to a justice of the peace that the offender has failed to comply with any of the requirements of the order, the justice may—

     (a) issue a summons requiring the offender to appear at the place and time specified in it, or

     (b) if the information is in writing and on oath, issue a warrant for his arrest.

(3) Any summons or warrant issued under this paragraph must direct the offender to appear or be brought—

     (a) in the case of a community order imposing a drug rehabilitation requirement which is subject to review, before the magistrates' court responsible for the order, or

     (b) in any other case, before a magistrates' court acting for the petty sessions area in which the offender resides or, if it is not known where he resides, before a magistrates' court acting for the petty sessions area concerned.

(4) Where a summons issued under sub-paragraph (2)(a) requires the offender to appear before a magistrates' court and the offender does not appear in answer to the summons, the magistrates' court may issue a warrant for the arrest of the offender.

Issue of summons or warrant by Crown Court

24–113   8.—(1) This paragraph applies to a community order made by the Crown Court which does not include a direction that any failure to comply with the requirements of the order is to be dealt with by a magistrates' court.

(2) If at any time while a community order to which this paragraph applies is in force it appears on information to the Crown Court that the offender has failed to comply with any of the requirements of the order, the Crown Court may—

     (a) issue a summons requiring the offender to appear at the place and time specified in it, or

     (b) if the information is in writing and on oath, issue a warrant for his arrest.

(3) Any summons or warrant issued under this paragraph must direct the offender to appear or be brought before the Crown Court.

(4) Where a summons issued under sub-paragraph (2)(a) requires the offender to appear before the Crown Court and the offender does not appear in answer to the summons, the Crown Court may issue a warrant for the arrest of the offender.

Powers of magistrates' court

24–114   9.—(1) If it is proved to the satisfaction of a magistrates' court before which an offender appears or is brought under paragraph 7 that he has failed without reasonable excuse to comply with any of the requirements of the community order, the court must deal with him in respect of the failure in any one of the following ways—

     (a) by amending the terms of the community order so as to impose more onerous requirements which the court could include if it were then making the order;

     (b) where the community order was made by a magistrates' court, by dealing with him, for the offence in respect of which the order was made, in any way in which the court could deal with him if he had just been convicted by it of the offence;

     (c) where—

       (i) the community order was made by a magistrates' court,

       (ii) the offence in respect of which the order was made was not an offence punishable by imprisonment,

       (iii) the offender is aged 18 or over, and

       (iv) the offender has wilfully and persistently failed to comply with the requirements of the order, by dealing with him, in respect of that offence, by imposing a sentence of imprisonment for a term not exceeding 51 weeks.

(2) In dealing with an offender under sub-paragraph (1), a magistrates' court must take into account the extent to which the offender has complied with the requirements of the community order.

(3) In dealing with an offender under sub-paragraph (1)(a), the court may extend the duration of particular requirements (subject to any limit imposed by Chapter 4 of Part 12 of this Act) but may not extend the period specified under section 177(5).

(4) In dealing with an offender under sub-paragraph (1)(b), the court may, in the case of an offender who has wilfully and persistently failed to comply with the requirements of the community order, impose a custodial sentence (where the order was made in respect of an offence punishable with such a sentence) notwithstanding anything in section 152(2).

(5) Where a magistrates' court deals with an offender under sub-paragraph (1)(b) or (c), it must revoke the community order if it is still in force.

(5A) Where a magistrates' court dealing with an offender under sub-paragraph (1)(a) would not otherwise have the power to amend the community order under paragraph 16 (amendment by reason of change of residence), that paragraph has effect as if the references to the appropriate court were references to the court dealing with the offender.

(6) Where a community order was made by the Crown Court and a magistrates' court would (apart from this sub-paragraph) be required to deal with the offender under sub-paragraph (1)(a), (b) or (c), it may instead commit him to custody or release him on bail until he can be brought or appear before the Crown Court.

(7) A magistrates' court which deals with an offender's case under subparagraph (6) must send to the Crown Court—

(a) a certificate signed by a justice of the peace certifying that the offender has failed to comply with the requirements of the community order in the respect specified in the certificate, and

(b) such other particulars of the case as may be desirable;

and a certificate purporting to be so signed is admissible as evidence of the failure before the Crown Court.

(8) A person sentenced under sub-paragraph (1)(b) or (c) for an offence may appeal to the Crown Court against the sentence.

Powers of Crown Court

10.—(1) Where under paragraph 8 or by virtue of paragraph 9(6) an offender appears or is brought before the Crown Court and it is proved to the satisfaction of that court that he has failed without reasonable excuse to comply with any of the requirements of the community order, the Crown Court must deal with him in respect of the failure in any one of the following ways— **24–115**

(a) by amending the terms of the community order so as to impose more onerous requirements which the Crown Court could impose if it were then making the order;

(b) by dealing with him, for the offence in respect of which the order was made, in any way in which he could have been dealt with for that offence by the court which made the order if the order had not been made;

(c) where—

(i) the offence in respect of which the order was made was not an offence punishable by imprisonment,

(ii) the offender is aged 18 or over,

(iii) the offender has wilfully and persistently failed to comply with the requirements of the order,

by dealing with him, in respect of that offence, by imposing a sentence of imprisonment for a term not exceeding 51 weeks.

(2) In dealing with an offender under sub-paragraph (1), the Crown Court must take into account the extent to which the offender has complied with the requirements of the community order.

(3) In dealing with an offender under sub-paragraph (1)(a), the court may extend the duration of particular requirements (subject to any limit imposed by Chapter 4 of Part 12 of this Act) but may not extend the period specified under section 177(5).

(4) In dealing with an offender under sub-paragraph (1)(b), the Crown Court may, in

the case of an offender who has wilfully and persistently failed to comply with the requirements of the community order, impose a custodial sentence (where the order was made in respect of an offence punishable with such a sentence) notwithstanding anything in section 152(2).

(5) Where the Crown Court deals with an offender under sub-paragraph (1)(b) or (c), it must revoke the community order if it is still in force.

(6) In proceedings before the Crown Court under this paragraph any question whether the offender has failed to comply with the requirements of the community order is to be determined by the court and not by the verdict of a jury.

Restriction of powers in paragraphs 9 and 10 where treatment required

24–116   11.—(1) An offender who is required by any of the following requirements of a community order—

(a)   a mental health treatment requirement,

(b)   a drug rehabilitation requirement, or

(c)   an alcohol treatment requirement,

to submit to treatment for his mental condition, or his dependency on or propensity to misuse drugs or alcohol, is not to be treated for the purposes of paragraph 9 or 10 as having failed to comply with that requirement on the ground only that he had refused to undergo any surgical, electrical or other treatment if, in the opinion of the court, his refusal was reasonable having regard to all the circumstances.

(2) A court may not under paragraph 9(1)(a) or 10(1)(a) amend a mental health treatment requirement, a drug rehabilitation requirement or an alcohol treatment requirement unless the offender expresses his willingness to comply with the requirement as amended.

Supplementary

24–117   12. Where a community order was made by a magistrates' court in the case of an offender under 18 years of age in respect of an offence triable only on indictment in the case of an adult, any powers exercisable under paragraph 9(1)(b) in respect of the offender after he attains the age of 18 are powers to do either or both of the following—

(a)   to impose a fine not exceeding £5,000 for the offence in respect of which the order was made;

(b)   to deal with the offender for that offence in any way in which a magistrates' court could deal with him if it had just convicted him of an offence punishable with imprisonment for a term not exceeding 51 weeks.

PART 3

REVOCATION OF ORDER

Revocation of order with or without re-sentencing: powers of magistrates' court

24–118   13.—(1) This paragraph applies where a community order, other than an order made by the Crown Court and falling within paragraph 14(1)(a), is in force and on the application of the offender or the responsible officer it appears to the appropriate magistrates' court that, having regard to circumstances which have arisen since the order was made, it would be in the interests of justice—

(a)   for the order to be revoked, or

(b)   for the offender to be dealt with in some other way for the offence in respect of which the order was made.

(2) The appropriate magistrates' court may—

(a)   revoke the order, or

(b)   both—

    (i)   revoke the order, and

    (ii)   deal with the offender, for the offence in respect of which the order was made, in any way in which it could deal with him if he had just been convicted by the court of the offence.

(3) The circumstances in which a community order may be revoked under subparagraph (2) include the offender's making good progress or his responding satisfactorily to supervision or treatment (as the case requires).

(4) In dealing with an offender under sub-paragraph (2)(b), a magistrates' court must take into account the extent to which the offender has complied with the requirements of the community order.

(5) A person sentenced under sub-paragraph (2)(b) for an offence may appeal to the Crown Court against the sentence.

(6) Where a magistrates' court proposes to exercise its powers under this paragraph otherwise than on the application of the offender, it must summon him to appear before the court and, if he does not appear in answer to the summons, may issue a warrant for his arrest.

(7) In this paragraph "the appropriate magistrates' court" means—

    (a) in the case of an order imposing a drug rehabilitation requirement which is subject to review, the magistrates' court responsible for the order, and

    (b) in the case of any other community order, a magistrates' court acting for the petty sessions area concerned.

Revocation of order with or without re-sentencing: powers of Crown Court

14.—(1) This paragraph applies where— **24–119**

    (a) there is in force a community order made by the Crown Court which does not include a direction that any failure to comply with the requirements of the order is to be dealt with by a magistrates' court, and

    (b) the offender or the responsible officer applies to the Crown Court for the order to be revoked or for the offender to be dealt with in some other way for the offence in respect of which the order was made.

(2) If it appears to the Crown Court to be in the interests of justice to do so, having regard to circumstances which have arisen since the order was made, the Crown Court may—

    (a) revoke the order, or

    (b) both—

        (i) revoke the order, and

        (ii) deal with the offender, for the offence in respect of which the order was made, in any way in which he could have been dealt with for that offence by the court which made the order if the order had not been made.

(3) The circumstances in which a community order may be revoked under subparagraph (2) include the offender's making good progress or his responding satisfactorily to supervision or treatment (as the case requires).

(4) In dealing with an offender under sub-paragraph (2)(b), the Crown Court must take into account the extent to which the offender has complied with the requirements of the order.

(5) Where the Crown Court proposes to exercise its powers under this paragraph otherwise than on the application of the offender, it must summon him to appear before the court and, if he does not appear in answer to the summons, may issue a warrant for his arrest.

Supplementary

15. Paragraph 12 applies for the purposes of paragraphs 13 and 14 as it applies for the **24–120** purposes of paragraph 9 above, but as if for the words "paragraph 9(1)(b)" there were substituted "paragraph 13(2)(b)(ii) or 14(2)(b)(ii)".

PART 4

AMENDMENT OF ORDER

Amendment by reason of change of residence

16.—(1) This paragraph applies where, at any time while a community order is in force **24–121** in respect of an offender, the appropriate court is satisfied that the offender proposes to change, or has changed, his residence from the petty sessions area concerned to another petty sessions area.

(2) Subject to sub-paragraphs (3) and (4), the appropriate court may, and on the application of the responsible officer must, amend the community order by substituting the other petty sessions area for the area specified in the order.

(3) The court may not under this paragraph amend a community order which contains requirements which, in the opinion of the court, cannot be complied with unless the offender continues to reside in the petty sessions area concerned unless, in accordance with paragraph 17, it either—

Part IV

    (a) cancels those requirements, or

    (b) substitutes for those requirements other requirements which can be complied with if the offender ceases to reside in that area.

(4) The court may not amend under this paragraph a community order imposing a programme requirement unless it appears to the court that the accredited programme specified in the requirement is available in the other petty sessions area.

(5) In this paragraph "the appropriate court" means—

    (a) in relation to any community order imposing a drug rehabilitation requirement which is subject to review, the court responsible for the order,

    (b) in relation to any community order which was made by the Crown Court and does not include any direction that any failure to comply with the requirements of the order is to be dealt with by a magistrates' court, the Crown Court, and

    (c) in relation to any other community order, a magistrates' court acting for the petty sessions area concerned.

Amendment of requirements of community order

24–122   17.—(1) The appropriate court may, on the application of the offender or the responsible officer, by order amend a community order—

    (a) by cancelling any of the requirements of the order, or

    (b) by replacing any of those requirements with a requirement of the same kind, which the court could include if it were then making the order.

(2) The court may not under this paragraph amend a mental health treatment requirement, a drug rehabilitation requirement or an alcohol treatment requirement unless the offender expresses his willingness to comply with the requirement as amended.

(3) If the offender fails to express his willingness to comply with a mental health treatment requirement, drug rehabilitation requirement or alcohol treatment requirement as proposed to be amended by the court under this paragraph, the court may—

    (a) revoke the community order, and

    (b) deal with him, for the offence in respect of which the order was made, in any way in which he could have been dealt with for that offence by the court which made the order if the order had not been made.

(4) In dealing with the offender under sub-paragraph (3)(b), the court—

    (a) must take into account the extent to which the offender has complied with the requirements of the order, and

    (b) may impose a custodial sentence (where the order was made in respect of an offence punishable with such a sentence) notwithstanding anything in section 152(2).

(5) Paragraph 12 applies for the purposes of this paragraph as it applies for the purposes of paragraph 9, but as if for the words "paragraph 9(1)(b)" there were substituted "paragraph 17(3)(b)".

(6) In this paragraph "the appropriate court" has the same meaning as in paragraph 16.

Amendment of treatment requirements of community order on report of practitioner

24–123   18.—(1) Where the medical practitioner or other person by whom or under whose direction an offender is, in pursuance of any requirement to which this subparagraph applies, being treated for his mental condition or his dependency on or propensity to misuse drugs or alcohol—

    (a) is of the opinion mentioned in sub-paragraph (3), or

    (b) is for any reason unwilling to continue to treat or direct the treatment of the offender,

he must make a report in writing to that effect to the responsible officer and that officer must apply under paragraph 17 to the appropriate court for the variation or cancellation of the requirement.

(2) The requirements to which sub-paragraph (1) applies are—

    (a) a mental health treatment requirement,

    (b) a drug rehabilitation requirement, and

    (c) an alcohol treatment requirement.

(3) The opinion referred to in sub-paragraph (1) is—

    (a) that the treatment of the offender should be continued beyond the period specified in that behalf in the order,

    (b) that the offender needs different treatment,

    (c) that the offender is not susceptible to treatment, or

    (d) that the offender does not require further treatment.

    (4) In this paragraph "the appropriate court" has the same meaning as in paragraph 16.

Amendment in relation to review of drug rehabilitation requirement

    19. Where the responsible officer is of the opinion that a community order imposing a **24–124** drug rehabilitation requirement which is subject to review should be so amended as to provide for each subsequent periodic review (required by section 211) to be made without a hearing instead of at a review hearing, or vice versa, he must apply under paragraph 17 to the court responsible for the order for the variation of the order.

Extension of unpaid work requirement

    20.—(1) Where—   **24–125**

    (a) a community order imposing an unpaid work requirement is in force in respect of any offender, and

    (b) on the application of the offender or the responsible officer, it appears to the appropriate court that it would be in the interests of justice to do so having regard to circumstances which have arisen since the order was made,

the court may, in relation to the order, extend the period of twelve months specified in section 200(2).

    (2) In this paragraph "the appropriate court" has the same meaning as in paragraph 16.

PART 5

POWERS OF COURT IN RELATION TO ORDER FOLLOWING SUBSEQUENT CONVICTION

Powers of magistrates' court following subsequent conviction

    21.—(1) This paragraph applies where—   **24–126**

    (a) an offender in respect of whom a community order made by a magistrates' court is in force is convicted of an offence by a magistrates' court, and

    (b) it appears to the court that it would be in the interests of justice to exercise its powers under this paragraph, having regard to circumstances which have arisen since the community order was made.

    (2) The magistrates' court may—

    (a) revoke the order, or

    (b) both—

        (i)   revoke the order, and

        (ii)   deal with the offender, for the offence in respect of which the order was made, in any way in which he could have been dealt with for that offence by the court which made the order if the order had not been made.

    (3) In dealing with an offender under sub-paragraph (2)(b), a magistrates' court must take into account the extent to which the offender has complied with the requirements of the community order.

    (4) A person sentenced under sub-paragraph (2)(b) for an offence may appeal to the Crown Court against the sentence.

    22.—(1) Where an offender in respect of whom a community order made by the Crown **24–127** Court is in force is convicted of an offence by a magistrates' court, the magistrates' court may commit the offender in custody or release him on bail until he can be brought before the Crown Court.

    (2) Where the magistrates' court deals with an offender's case under subparagraph (1), it must send to the Crown Court such particulars of the case as may be desirable.

Powers of Crown Court following subsequent conviction

    23.—(1) This paragraph applies where—   **24–128**

    (a) an offender in respect of whom a community order is in force—

Part IV

> (i)   is convicted of an offence by the Crown Court, or
>
> (ii) is brought or appears before the Crown Court by virtue of paragraph 22 or having been committed by the magistrates' court to the Crown Court for sentence, and

(b) it appears to the Crown Court that it would be in the interests of justice to exercise its powers under this paragraph, having regard to circumstances which have arisen since the community order was made.

(2) The Crown Court may—

(a) revoke the order, or

(b) both—

> (i)   revoke the order, and
>
> (ii) deal with the offender, for the offence in respect of which the order was made, in any way in which he could have been dealt with for that offence by the court which made the order if the order had not been made.

(3) In dealing with an offender under sub-paragraph (2)(b), the Crown Court must take into account the extent to which the offender has complied with the requirements of the community order.

PART 6

SUPPLEMENTARY

24–129   24.—(1) No order may be made under paragraph 16, and no application may be made under paragraph 13, 17 or 20, while an appeal against the community order is pending.

(2) Sub-paragraph (1) does not apply to an application under paragraph 17 which—

(a) relates to a mental health treatment requirement, a drug rehabilitation requirement or an alcohol treatment requirement, and

(b) is made by the responsible officer with the consent of the offender.

24–130   25.—(1) Subject to sub-paragraph (2), where a court proposes to exercise its powers under Part 4 or 5 of this Schedule, otherwise than on the application of the offender, the court—

(a) must summon him to appear before the court, and

(b) if he does not appear in answer to the summons, may issue a warrant for his arrest.

(2) This paragraph does not apply to an order cancelling a requirement of a community order or reducing the period of any requirement, or substituting a new petty sessions area or a new place for the one specified in the order.

24–131   26. Paragraphs 9(1)(a), 10(1)(a) and 17(1)(b) have effect subject to the provisions mentioned in subsection (2) of section 177, and to subsections (3) and (6) of that section.

24–132   27.—(1) On the making under this Schedule of an order revoking or amending a community order, the proper officer of the court must—

(a) provide copies of the revoking or amending order to the offender and the responsible officer,

(b) in the case of an amending order which substitutes a new petty sessions area, provide a copy of the amending order to—

> (i)   the local probation board acting for that area, and
>
> (ii) the magistrates' court acting for that area, and

(c) in the case of an amending order which imposes or amends a requirement specified in the first column of Schedule 14, provide a copy of so much of the amending order as relates to that requirement to the person specified in relation to that requirement in the second column of that Schedule.

(d) where the court acts for a petty sessions area other than the one specified in the order prior to the revocation or amendment, provide a copy of the revoking or amending order to a magistrates' court acting for the area so specified.

(2) Where under sub-paragraph (1)(b) the proper officer of the court provides a copy of an amending order to a magistrates' court acting for a different area, the officer must also provide to that court such documents and information relating to the case as it considers likely to be of assistance to a court acting for that area in the exercise of its functions in relation to the order.

(3) In this paragraph "proper officer" means—

    (a) in relation to a magistrates' court, the justices' chief executive for the court; and

    (b) in relation to the Crown Court, the appropriate officer.

IV. ENFORCEMENT OF SUSPENDED SENTENCE ORDER

(1) General

A suspended sentence order may be breached by a failure to comply with the require- **24–133** ments of the order without reasonable excuse or by the commission of a further offence (not necessarily an imprisonable offence) during the operational period. Where it is alleged that there has been a breach as a result of failure to comply with the requirements of the order, the procedure follows closely that for breach of a Community Order. The responsible officer must either warn or institute proceedings and no more than one warning can be given in a 12 month period. A Crown Court may, when making a suspended sentence order, direct that any failure to comply with the requirements should be dealt with in a magistrates' court. In the absence of such a direction, proceedings commence at the level of court at which the order had been made: Schedule 12, paragraphs 4–6.

Where the offender is convicted of a further offence committed during the operational period, the suspended sentence may be dealt with in the Crown Court regardless of which level of court made the order and in a magistrates' court if the order was imposed in a magistrates' court: Schedule 12, paragraph 11. If a magistrates' court convicts the offender of an offence committed during the operational period of a Crown Court imposed suspended sentence order, that court may commit the offender to the Crown Court on bail or in custody: Schedule 12, paragraph 11(2)(a). If it does not do so, it must notify the Crown Court that the offender has been convicted (Schedule 12, paragraph 11(2)(b)) and the Crown Court can initiate proceedings to deal with the issue: Schedule 12, paragraph 12. Similarly, if a magistrates' court which imposed a suspended sentence order discovers that the offender has been convicted of a further offence but the suspended sentence has not been dealt with, that court may issue process in order for it to deal with the suspended sentence: Schedule 12, paragraph 12.

If the failure to comply with a requirement is proved or if the offender is convicted of another offence committed during the operational period, the options open to the court are set out in Schedule 12, paragraph 8. As with the suspended sentence itself, the statutory wording reflects the introduction of custody plus and there will need to be transitional provisions pending implementation of that sentence. The choices for the court are to implement the suspended sentence in full, to implement it with a reduced term or to amend the order. Any amendment must impose more onerous requirements and/or extend the supervision period and/or extend the operational period. If the extensions are considered, they cannot take the orders beyond the maximum periods that could have been imposed when the order was made: Schedule 12, paragraph 8(2)(c). There is a presumption that the court will implement the suspended sentence either in full or with the reduced term unless the court considers that it would be unjust: Schedule 12, paragraph8(3). Reasons must be given for not implementing the suspended sentence. In its guideline, *New Sentences: Criminal Justice Act 2003*, the Sentencing Guidelines Council issued guidance on the approach to breaches.

(2) New sentences under the Criminal Justice Act 2003

Guideline: New Sentences: Criminal Justice Act 2003

Section 2—Custodial Sentences

    Part 2: Suspended Sentences

C. Breaches

2.2.15 The essence of a suspended sentence is to make it abundantly clear to an offender **24–134**

that failure to comply with the requirements of the order or commission of another offence will almost certainly result in a custodial sentence. Where an offender has breached any of the requirements without reasonable excuse for the first time, the responsible officer must either give a warning or initiate breach proceedings. Where there is a further breach within a twelve-month period, breach proceedings must be initiated.

2.2.16 Where proceedings are brought the court has several options, including extending the operational period. However, the presumption (which also applies where breach is by virtue of the commission of a further offence) is that the suspended prison sentence will be activated (either with its original custodial term or a lesser term) unless the court takes the view that this would, in all the circumstances, be unjust. In reaching that decision, the court may take into account both the extent to which the offender has complied with the requirements and the facts of the new offence.

2.2.17 Where a court considers that the sentence needs to be activated, it may activate it in full or with a reduced term. Again, the extent to which the requirements have been complied with will be very relevant to this decision.

2.2.18 If a court amends the order rather than activating the suspended prison sentence, it must either make the requirements more onerous, or extend the supervision or operational periods (provided that these remain within the limits defined by the Act). In such cases, the court must state its reasons for not activating the prison sentence, which could include the extent to which the offender has complied with requirements or the facts of the subsequent offence.

24–135   **2.2.19** If an offender near the end of an operational period (having complied with the requirements imposed) commits another offence, it may be more appropriate to amend the order rather than activate it.

2.2.20 If a new offence committed is of a less serious nature than the offence for which the suspended sentence was passed, it may justify activating the sentence with a reduced term or amending the terms of the order.

2.2.21 It is expected that any activated suspended sentence will be consecutive to the sentence imposed for the new offence.

24–136   **2.2.22** If the new offence is non-imprisonable, the sentencer should consider whether it is appropriate to activate the suspended sentence at all.

> Where the court decides to amend a suspended sentence order rather than activate the custodial sentence, it should give serious consideration to extending the supervision or operational periods (within statutory limits) rather than making the requirements more onerous.

(3) Legislation

Criminal Justice Act 2003, Sched. 12

Section 193   SCHEDULE 12

BREACH OR AMENDMENT OF SUSPENDED SENTENCE ORDER, AND EFFECT OF FURTHER CONVICTION

PART 1

PRELIMINARY

Interpretation

24–137   1. In this Schedule—
"the offender", in relation to a suspended sentence order, means the person in respect of whom the order is made;
"the petty sessions area concerned", in relation to a suspended sentence order, means the petty sessions area for the time being specified in the order;
"the responsible officer" has the meaning given by section 197.

24–138   2. In this Schedule—
(a) any reference to a suspended sentence order being subject to review is a refer-

ence to such an order being subject to review in accordance with section 191(1)(b) or to a drug rehabilitation requirement of such an order being subject to review in accordance with section 210(1)(b);

(b) any reference to the court responsible for a suspended sentence order which is subject to review is to be construed in accordance with section 191(3) or, as the case may be, 210(2).

Orders made on appeal

3. Where a suspended sentence order is made on appeal it is to be taken for the purposes of this Schedule to have been made by the Crown Court.   **24–139**

PART 2

BREACH OF COMMUNITY REQUIREMENT OR CONVICTION OF FURTHER OF-FENCE

Duty to give warning in relation to community requirement

4.—(1) If the responsible officer is of the opinion that the offender has failed without reasonable excuse to comply with any of the community requirements of a suspended sentence order, the officer must give him a warning under this paragraph unless—   **24–140**

(a) the offender has within the previous twelve months been given a warning under this paragraph in relation to a failure to comply with any of the community requirements of the order, or

(b) the officer causes an information to be laid before a justice of the peace in respect of the failure.

(2) A warning under this paragraph must—

(a) describe the circumstances of the failure,

(b) state that the failure is unacceptable, and

(c) inform the offender that if within the next twelve months he again fails to comply with any requirement of the order, he will be liable to be brought before a court.

(3) The responsible officer must, as soon as practicable after the warning has been given, record that fact.

(4) In relation to any suspended sentence order which is made by the Crown Court and does not include a direction that any failure to comply with the community requirements of the order is to be dealt with by a magistrates' court, the reference in sub-paragraph (1)(b) to a justice of the peace is to be read as a reference to the Crown Court.

Breach of order after warning

5.—(1) If—   **24–141**

(a) the responsible officer has given a warning under paragraph 4 to the offender in respect of a suspended sentence order, and

(b) at any time within the twelve months beginning with the date on which the warning was given, the responsible officer is of the opinion that the offender has since that date failed without reasonable excuse to comply with any of the community requirements of the order,

the officer must cause an information to be laid before a justice of the peace in respect of the failure in question.

(2) In relation to any suspended sentence order which is made by the Crown Court and does not include a direction that any failure to comply with the community requirements of the order is to be dealt with by a magistrates' court, the reference in sub-paragraph (1) to a justice of the peace is to be read as a reference to the Crown Court.

Issue of summons or warrant by justice of the peace

6.—(1) This paragraph applies to—   **24–142**

(a) a suspended sentence order made by a magistrates' court, or

(b) any suspended sentence order which was made by the Crown Court and includes a direction that any failure to comply with the community requirements of the order is to be dealt with by a magistrates' court.

(2) If at any time while a suspended sentence order to which this paragraph applies is in force it appears on information to a justice of the peace that the offender has failed to comply with any of the community requirements of the order, the justice may—

(a) issue a summons requiring the offender to appear at the place and time specified in it, or

(b) if the information is in writing and on oath, issue a warrant for his arrest.

(3) Any summons or warrant issued under this paragraph must direct the offender to appear or be brought—

(a) in the case of a suspended sentence order which is subject to review, before the court responsible for the order,

(b) in any other case, before a magistrates' court acting for the petty sessions area in which the offender resides or, if it is not known where he resides, before a magistrates' court acting for the petty sessions area concerned.

(4) Where a summons issued under sub-paragraph (2)(a) requires the offender to appear before a magistrates' court and the offender does not appear in answer to the summons, the magistrates' court may issue a warrant for the arrest of the offender.

Issue of summons or warrant by Crown Court

24–143   7.—(1) This paragraph applies to a suspended sentence order made by the Crown Court which does not include a direction that any failure to comply with the community requirements of the order is to be dealt with by a magistrates' court.

(2) If at any time while a suspended sentence order to which this paragraph applies is in force it appears on information to the Crown Court that the offender has failed to comply with any of the community requirements of the order, the Crown Court may—

(a) issue a summons requiring the offender to appear at the place and time specified in it, or

(b) if the information is in writing and on oath, issue a warrant for his arrest.

(3) Any summons or warrant issued under this paragraph must direct the offender to appear or be brought before the Crown Court.

(4) Where a summons issued under sub-paragraph (1)(a) requires the offender to appear before the Crown Court and the offender does not appear in answer to the summons, the Crown Court may issue a warrant for the arrest of the offender.

Powers of court on breach of community requirement or conviction of further offence

24–144   8.—(1) This paragraph applies where—

(a) it is proved to the satisfaction of a court before which an offender appears or is brought under paragraph 6 or 7 or by virtue of section 192(6) that he has failed without reasonable excuse to comply with any of the community requirements of the suspended sentence order, or

(b) an offender is convicted of an offence committed during the operational period of a suspended sentence (other than one which has already taken effect) and either—

(i)   he is so convicted by or before a court having power under paragraph 11 to deal with him in respect of the suspended sentence, or

(ii) he subsequently appears or is brought before such a court.

(2) The court must consider his case and deal with him in one of the following ways—

(a) the court may order that the suspended sentence is to take effect with its original term and custodial period unaltered,

(b) the court may order that the sentence is to take effect with either or both of the following modifications—

(i)   the substitution for the original term of a lesser term complying with section 181(2), and

(ii) the substitution for the original custodial period of a lesser custodial period complying with section 181(5) and (6),

(c) the court may amend the order by doing any one or more of the following—

(i)   imposing more onerous community requirements which the court could include if it were then making the order,

(ii) subject to subsections (3) and (4) of section 189, extending the supervision period, or

(iii) subject to subsection (3) of that section, extending the operational period.

(3) The court must make an order under sub-paragraph (2)(a) or (b) unless it is of the opinion that it would be unjust to do so in view of all the circumstances, including the matters mentioned in sub-paragraph (4); and where it is of that opinion the court must state its reasons.

(4) The matters referred to in sub-paragraph (3) are—

  (a) the extent to which the offender has complied with the community requirements of the suspended sentence order, and

  (b) in a case falling within sub-paragraph (1)(b), the facts of the subsequent offence.

(4A) Where a magistrates' court dealing with an offender under sub-paragraph (2)(c) would not otherwise have the power to amend the suspended sentence order under paragraph 14 (amendment by reason of change of residence), that paragraph has effect as if the references to the appropriate court were references to the court dealing with the offender.

(5) Where a court deals with an offender under sub-paragraph (2) in respect of a suspended sentence, the appropriate officer of the court must notify the appropriate officer of the court which passed the sentence of the method adopted.

(6) Where a suspended sentence order was made by the Crown Court and a magistrates' court would (apart from this sub-paragraph) be required to deal with the offender under sub-paragraph (2)(a), (b) or (c) it may instead commit him to custody or release him on bail until he can be brought or appear before the Crown Court.

(7) A magistrates' court which deals with an offender's case under subparagraph (6) must send to the Crown Court—

  (a) a certificate signed by a justice of the peace certifying that the offender has failed to comply with the community requirements of the suspended sentence order in the respect specified in the certificate, and

  (b) such other particulars of the case as may be desirable;

and a certificate purporting to be so signed is admissible as evidence of the failure before the Crown Court.

(8) In proceedings before the Crown Court under this paragraph any question whether the offender has failed to comply with the community requirements of the suspended sentence order and any question whether the offender has been convicted of an offence committed during the operational period of the suspended sentence is to be determined by the court and not by the verdict of a jury.

Further provisions as to order that suspended sentence is to take effect

9.—(1) When making an order under paragraph 8(2)(a) or (b) that a sentence is to take **24–145** effect (with or without any variation of the original term and custodial period), the court—

  (a) must also make a custody plus order, and

  (b) may order that the sentence is to take effect immediately or that the term of that sentence is to commence on the expiry of another term of imprisonment passed on the offender by that or another court.

(2) The power to make an order under sub-paragraph (1)(b) has effect subject to section 265 (restriction on consecutive sentences for released prisoners).

(3) For the purpose of any enactment conferring rights of appeal in criminal cases, any order made by the court under paragraph 8(2)(a) or (b) is to be treated as a sentence passed on the offender by that court for the offence for which the suspended sentence was passed.

Restriction of powers in paragraph 8 where treatment required

10.—(1) An offender who is required by any of the following community requirements **24–146** of a suspended sentence order—

  (a) a mental health treatment requirement,

  (b) a drug rehabilitation requirement, or

  (c) an alcohol treatment requirement,

to submit to treatment for his mental condition, or his dependency on or propensity to misuse drugs or alcohol, is not to be treated for the purposes of paragraph 8(1)(a) as having failed to comply with that requirement on the ground only that he had refused to undergo any surgical, electrical or other treatment if, in the opinion of the court, his refusal was reasonable having regard to all the circumstances.

(2) A court may not under paragraph 8(2)(c)(i) amend a mental health treatment requirement, a drug rehabilitation requirement or an alcohol treatment requirement unless the offender expresses his willingness to comply with the requirement as amended.

Court by which suspended sentence may be dealt with under paragraph 8(1)(b)

11.—(1) An offender may be dealt with under paragraph 8(1)(b) in respect of a **24–147**

Part IV

suspended sentence by the Crown Court or, where the sentence was passed by a magistrates' court, by any magistrates' court before which he appears or is brought.

(2) Where an offender is convicted by a magistrates' court of any offence and the court is satisfied that the offence was committed during the operational period of a suspended sentence passed by the Crown Court—

(a) the court may, if it thinks fit, commit him in custody or on bail to the Crown Court, and

(b) if it does not, must give written notice of the conviction to the appropriate officer of the Crown Court.

Procedure where court convicting of further offence does not deal with suspended sentence

24–148   12.—(1) If it appears to the Crown Court, where that court has jurisdiction in accordance with sub-paragraph (2), or to a justice of the peace having jurisdiction in accordance with that sub-paragraph—

(a) that an offender has been convicted in the United Kingdom of an offence committed during the operational period of a suspended sentence, and

(b) that he has not been dealt with in respect of the suspended sentence,

that court or justice may, subject to the following provisions of this paragraph, issue a summons requiring the offender to appear at the place and time specified in it, or a warrant for his arrest.

(2) Jurisdiction for the purposes of sub-paragraph (1) may be exercised—

(a) if the suspended sentence was passed by the Crown Court, by that court;

(b) if it was passed by a magistrates' court, by a justice acting for the petty sessions area for which that court acted.

(3) Where—

(a) an offender is convicted in Scotland or Northern Ireland of an offence, and

(b) the court is informed that the offence was committed during the operational period of a suspended sentence passed in England or Wales,

the court must give written notice of the conviction to the appropriate officer of the court by which the suspended sentence was passed.

(4) Unless he is acting in consequence of a notice under sub-paragraph (3), a justice of the peace may not issue a summons under this paragraph except on information and may not issue a warrant under this paragraph except on information in writing and on oath.

(5) A summons or warrant issued under this paragraph must direct the offender to appear or be brought before the court by which the suspended sentence was passed.

PART 3

AMENDMENT OF SUSPENDED SENTENCE ORDER

Cancellation of community requirements of suspended sentence order

24–149   13.—(1) Where at any time while a suspended sentence order is in force, it appears to the appropriate court on the application of the offender or the responsible officer that, having regard to the circumstances which have arisen since the order was made, it would be in the interests of justice to do so, the court may cancel the community requirements of the suspended sentence order.

(2) The circumstances in which the appropriate court may exercise its power under sub-paragraph (1) include the offender's making good progress or his responding satisfactorily to supervision.

(3) In this paragraph "the appropriate court" means—

(a) in the case of a suspended sentence order which is subject to review, the court responsible for the order,

(b) in the case of a suspended sentence order which was made by the Crown Court and does not include any direction that any failure to comply with the community requirements of the order is to be dealt with by a magistrates' court, the Crown Court, and

(c) in any other case, a magistrates' court acting for the petty sessions area concerned.

Amendment by reason of change of residence

24–150   14.—(1) This paragraph applies where, at any time while a suspended sentence order is in force, the appropriate court is satisfied that the offender proposes to change, or has changed, his residence from the petty sessions area concerned to another petty sessions area.

(2) Subject to sub-paragraphs (3) and (4), the appropriate court may, and on the application of the responsible officer must, amend the suspended sentence order by substituting the other petty sessions area for the area specified in the order.

(3) The court may not amend under this paragraph a suspended sentence order which contains requirements which, in the opinion of the court, cannot be complied with unless the offender resides in the petty sessions area concerned unless, in accordance with paragraph 15 it either—

(a) cancels those requirements, or

(b) substitutes for those requirements other requirements which can be complied with if the offender does not reside in that area.

(4) The court may not amend under this paragraph any suspended sentence order imposing a programme requirement unless it appears to the court that the accredited programme specified in the requirement is available in the other petty sessions area.

(5) In this paragraph "the appropriate court" has the same meaning as in paragraph 13.

Amendment of community requirements of suspended sentence order

24–151

15.—(1) At any time during the supervision period, the appropriate court may, on the application of the offender or the responsible officer, by order amend any community requirement of a suspended sentence order—

(a) by cancelling the requirement, or

(b) by replacing it with a requirement of the same kind, which the court could include if it were then making the order.

(2) For the purposes of sub-paragraph (1)—

(a) a requirement falling within any paragraph of section 190(1) is of the same kind as any other requirement falling within that paragraph, and

(b) an electronic monitoring requirement is a requirement of the same kind as any requirement falling within section 190(1) to which it relates.

(3) The court may not under this paragraph amend a mental health treatment requirement, a drug rehabilitation requirement or an alcohol treatment requirement unless the offender expresses his willingness to comply with the requirement as amended.

(4) If the offender fails to express his willingness to comply with a mental health treatment requirement, drug rehabilitation requirement or alcohol treatment requirement as proposed to be amended by the court under this paragraph, the court may—

(a) revoke the suspended sentence order and the suspended sentence to which it relates, and

(b) deal with him, for the offence in respect of which the suspended sentence was imposed, in any way in which it could deal with him if he had just been convicted by or before the court of the offence.

(5) In dealing with the offender under sub-paragraph (4)(b), the court must take into account the extent to which the offender has complied with the requirements of the order.

(6) In this paragraph "the appropriate court" has the same meaning as in paragraph 13.

Amendment of treatment requirements on report of practitioner

24–152

16.—(1) Where the medical practitioner or other person by whom or under whose direction an offender is, in pursuance of any requirement to which this subparagraph applies, being treated for his mental condition or his dependency on or propensity to misuse drugs or alcohol—

(a) is of the opinion mentioned in sub-paragraph (3), or

(b) is for any reason unwilling to continue to treat or direct the treatment of the offender,

he must make a report in writing to that effect to the responsible officer and that officer must apply under paragraph 15 to the appropriate court for the variation or cancellation of the requirement.

(2) The requirements to which sub-paragraph (1) applies are—

Part IV

(a) a mental health treatment requirement,

(b) a drug rehabilitation requirement, and

(c) an alcohol treatment requirement.

(3) The opinion referred to in sub-paragraph (1) is—

(a) that the treatment of the offender should be continued beyond the period specified in that behalf in the order,

(b) that the offender needs different treatment,

(c) that the offender is not susceptible to treatment, or

(d) that the offender does not require further treatment.

(4) In this paragraph "the appropriate court" has the same meaning as in paragraph 13.

Amendment in relation to review of drug rehabilitation requirement

24–153   17. Where the responsible officer is of the opinion that a suspended sentence order imposing a drug rehabilitation requirement which is subject to review should be so amended as to provide for each periodic review (required by section 211) to be made without a hearing instead of at a review hearing, or vice versa, he must apply under paragraph 15 to the court responsible for the order for the variation of the order.

Extension of unpaid work requirement

24–154   18.—(1) Where—

(a) a suspended sentence order imposing an unpaid work requirement is in force in respect of the offender, and

(b) on the application of the offender or the responsible officer, it appears to the appropriate court that it would be in the interests of justice to do so having regard to circumstances which have arisen since the order was made,

the court may, in relation to the order, extend the period of twelve months specified in section 200(2).

(2) In this paragraph "the appropriate court" has the same meaning as in paragraph 13.

Supplementary

24–155   19.—(1) No application may be made under paragraph 13, 15 or 18, and no order may be made under paragraph 14, while an appeal against the suspended sentence is pending.

(2) Sub-paragraph (1) does not apply to an application under paragraph 15 which—

(a) relates to a mental health treatment requirement, a drug rehabilitation requirement or an alcohol treatment requirement, and

(b) is made by the responsible officer with the consent of the offender.

24–156   20.—(1) Subject to sub-paragraph (2), where a court proposes to exercise its powers under paragraph 15, otherwise than on the application of the offender, the court—

(a) must summon him to appear before the court, and

(b) if he does not appear in answer to the summons, may issue a warrant for his arrest.

(2) This paragraph does not apply to an order cancelling any community requirement of a suspended sentence order.

24–157   21. Paragraphs 8(2)(c) and 15(1)(b) have effect subject to the provisions mentioned in subsection (2) of section 190, and to subsections (3) and (5) of that section.

24–158   22.—(1) On the making under this Schedule of an order amending a suspended sentence order, the proper officer of the court must—

(a) provide copies of the amending order to the offender and the responsible officer,

(b) in the case of an amending order which substitutes a new petty sessions area, provide a copy of the amending order to—

(i) the local probation board acting for that area, and

(ii) the magistrates' court acting for that area, and

(c) in the case of an amending order which imposes or amends a requirement specified in the first column of Schedule 14, provide a copy of so much of the amending order as relates to that requirement to the person specified in relation to that requirement in the second column of that Schedule.

(d) where the court acts for a petty sessions area other than the one specified in the order prior to the revocation or amendment, provide a copy of the revoking or amending order to a magistrates' court acting for the area so specified.

(2) Where under sub-paragraph (1)(b) the proper officer of the court provides a copy of an amending order to a magistrates' court acting for a different area, the officer must also provide to that court such documents and information relating to the case as it considers likely to be of assistance to a court acting for that area in the exercise of its functions in relation to the order.

(3) In this paragraph "proper officer" means—

(a) in relation to a magistrates' court, the justices' chief executive for the court; and

(b) in relation to the Crown Court, the appropriate officer.

V. BREACH OF REQUIREMENTS OF ATTENDANCE CENTRE ORDER

Powers of Criminal Courts (Sentencing) Act 2000, Sched. 5

SCHEDULE 5

BREACH, REVOCATION AND AMENDMENT OF ATTENDANCE CENTRE ORDERS

Breach of order or attendance centre rules

1.—(1) Where an attendance centre order is in force and it appears on information to a **24–159** justice acting for a relevant petty sessions area that the offender—

(a) has failed to attend in accordance with the order, or

(b) while attending has committed a breach of rules made under section 62(3) of this Act which cannot be adequately dealt with under those rules,

the justice may issue a summons requiring the offender to appear at the place and time specified in the summons before a magistrates' court acting for the area or, if the information is in writing and on oath, may issue a warrant for the offender's arrest requiring him to be brought before such a court.

(2) For the purposes of this paragraph a petty sessions area is a relevant petty sessions area in relation to an attendance centre order—

(a) if the attendance centre which the offender is required to attend by the order or by virtue of an order under paragraph 5(1)(b) below is situated in it; or

(b) if the order was made by a magistrates' court acting for it.

2.—(1) If it is proved to the satisfaction of the magistrates' court before which an of- **24–160** fender appears or is brought under paragraph 1 above that he has failed without reasonable excuse to attend as mentioned in sub-paragraph (1)(a) of that paragraph or has committed such a breach of rules as is mentioned in sub-paragraph (1)(b) of that paragraph, that court may deal with him in any one of the following ways—

(a) it may impose on him a fine not exceeding £1,000;

(b) where the attendance centre order was made by a magistrates' court, it may deal with him, for the offence in respect of which the order was made, in any way in which he could have been dealt with for that offence by the court which made the order if the order had not been made; or

(c) where the order was made by the Crown Court, it may commit him to custody or release him on bail until he can be brought or appear before the Crown Court.

(2) Any exercise by the court of its power under sub-paragraph (1)(a) above shall be without prejudice to the continuation of the order.

(3) A fine imposed under sub-paragraph (1)(a) above shall be deemed, for the purposes of any enactment, to be a sum adjudged to be paid by a conviction.

(4) Where a magistrates' court deals with an offender under sub-paragraph (1)(b) above, it shall revoke the attendance centre order if it is still in force.

(5) In dealing with an offender under sub-paragraph (1)(b) above, a magistrates' court—

    (a) shall take into account the extent to which the offender has complied with the requirements of the attendance centre order; and

    (b) in the case of an offender who has wilfully and persistently failed to comply with those requirements, may impose a custodial sentence notwithstanding anything in section 79(2) of this Act.

(6) A person sentenced under sub-paragraph (1)(b) above for an offence may appeal to the Crown Court against the sentence.

(7) A magistrates' court which deals with an offender's case under sub-paragraph (1)(c) above shall send to the Crown Court—

    (a) a certificate signed by a justice of the peace giving particulars of the offender's failure to attend or, as the case may be, the breach of the rules which he has committed; and

    (b) such other particulars of the case as may be desirable;

and a certificate purporting to be so signed shall be admissible as evidence of the failure or the breach before the Crown Court.

3. [Crown Court]

Revocation of order with or without re-sentencing

24–161   4.—(1) Where an attendance centre order is in force in respect of an offender, an appropriate court may, on an application made by the offender or by the officer in charge of the relevant attendance centre, revoke the order.

(2) In sub-paragraph (1) above "an appropriate court" means—

    (a) where the court which made the order was the Crown Court and there is included in the order a direction that the power to revoke the order is reserved to that court, the Crown Court;

    (b) in any other case, either of the following—

        (i) a magistrates' court acting for the petty sessions area in which the relevant attendance centre is situated;

        (ii) the court which made the order.

(3) Any power conferred by this paragraph—

    (a) on a magistrates' court to revoke an attendance centre order made by such a court, or

    (b) on the Crown Court to revoke an attendance centre order made by the Crown Court,

includes power to deal with the offender, for the offence in respect of which the order was made, in any way in which he could have been dealt with for that offence by the court which made the order if the order had not been made.

(4) A person sentenced by a magistrates' court under sub-paragraph (3) above for an offence may appeal to the Crown Court against the sentence.

(5) The proper officer of a court which makes an order under this paragraph revoking an attendance centre order shall—

    (a) deliver a copy of the revoking order to the offender or send a copy by registered post or the recorded delivery service addressed to the offender's last or usual place of abode; and

    (b) deliver or send a copy to the officer in charge of the relevant attendance centre.

(6) In this paragraph "the relevant attendance centre", in relation to an attendance centre order, means the attendance centre specified in the order or substituted for the attendance centre so specified by an order made by virtue of paragraph 5(1)(b) below.

(7) In this paragraph "proper officer" means—

    (a) in relation to a magistrates' court, the justices' chief executive for the court; and

    (b) in relation to the Crown Court, the appropriate officer.

Amendment of order

24–162   5.—(1) Where an attendance centre order is in force in respect of an offender, an appropriate magistrates' court may, on an application made by the offender or by the officer in charge of the relevant attendance centre, by order—

      (a) vary the day or hour specified in the order for the offender's first attendance at the relevant attendance centre; or

      (b) substitute for the relevant attendance centre an attendance centre which the court is satisfied is reasonably accessible to the offender, having regard to his age, the means of access available to him and any other circumstances.

(2) In sub-paragraph (1) above "an appropriate magistrates' court" means—

      (a) a magistrates' court acting for the petty sessions area in which the relevant attendance centre is situated; or

      (b) (except where the attendance centre order was made by the Crown Court) the magistrates' court which made the order.

(3) The justices' chief executive for a court which makes an order under this paragraph shall—

      (a) deliver a copy to the offender or send a copy by registered post or the recorded delivery service addressed to the offender's last or usual place of abode; and

      (b) deliver or send a copy—

         (i) if the order is made by virtue of sub-paragraph (1)(a) above, to the officer in charge of the relevant attendance centre; and

        (ii) if it is made by virtue of sub-paragraph (1)(b) above, to the officer in charge of the attendance centre which the order as amended will require the offender to attend.

(4) In this paragraph "the relevant attendance centre" has the meaning given by paragraph 4(6) above.

Part V

Youth Courts

Chapter 25

JURISDICTIONAL ISSUES

I. INTRODUCTION

The youth court is part of the magistrates' court system. It is a court of summary ju- **25–1** risdiction that hears charges against children and young defendants aged between 10 and 17 years inclusive. It is conclusively presumed that no child under the age of 10 years can be guilty of any offence. Children over this age are subject to the criminal law in the same way as defendants in the adult magistrates' court. Courtroom procedure closely mirrors that of the adult court. However, the procedure is modified to reflect the age group that the youth court deals with. The geography of the courtroom is made less formal. The use of ordinary straightforward language is encouraged. Emphasis is put on the necessity of the court communicating and engaging directly with the defendants and their families. In the youth court it is usual to speak and refer to defendants by their first names.

II. THE YOUTH JUSTICE SYSTEM AND THE YOUTH COURT

(1) Aims and considerations

Crime and Disorder Act 1998, s.37

Aim of the youth justice system

37.—(1) It shall be the principal aim of the youth justice system to prevent offending by chil- **25–2** dren and young persons.

(2) In addition to any other duty to which they are subject, it shall be the duty of all persons and bodies carrying out functions in relation to the youth justice system to have regard to that aim.

Children and Young Persons Act 1933, s.44

General considerations.

44.—(1) Every court in dealing with a child or young person who is brought before it, either **25–3** as an offender or otherwise, shall have regard to the welfare of the child or young person, and shall in a proper case take steps for removing him from undesirable surroundings, and for securing that proper provision is made for his education and training.

Crime and Disorder Act 1998, s.39

25–4   It is the duty of each local authority to establish for their area one or more Youth Offending Teams.

Youth Offending Teams (YOT) play a vital part in the work of the youth court. There are now 155 YOTs covering all of England and Wales. The duty of the YOT is to co-ordinate the provision of youth justice services for all those in the authority's area. It is customary for a representative from the YOT to attend each sitting of the youth Cocurt and the YOT plays a most important part in assisting in the work of the court. More particularly the YOT will assist the court in dealing with the following matters—

(a) investigating and confirming the personal circumstances and antecedents of defendants;

(b) the provision of bail support (with or without an ISSP programme);

(c) the preparation of appropriate written reports required by the court as part of the sentencing process;

(d) the administration of many of the non-custodial penalties imposed by the youth court;

(e) the prosecution of defendants who have breached community penalties.

Defence advocates will obtain much important information by conferring with the YOT prior to the hearing of their clients case.

Intellectual capacity of the defendant

25–5   In *R. (P.) v. West London Youth Court* (2005) EWHC 2583, QBD (Admin) the DC considered the application of a 15-year-old who sought judicial review of a decision by the Youth Court not to stay proceedings against him on the basis of abuse of process. It was contended on his behalf that his intellectual capacity was such that he could not effectively participate in the court proceedings he faced, and therefore could not have a fair trial. In dismissing the application for judicial review the court emphasised the specialist nature of the youth court jurisdiction and went on to set out a number of steps that could and should be taken by that court to ensure that a defendant with learning difficulties would be able to effectively participate in his trial.

(2) Preliminary issues

Children and Young Persons Act 1933, s.34A

Attendance at court of parent or guardian

25–6   **34A.**—(1) Where a child or young person is charged with an offence or is for any other reason brought before a court, the court—

(a) may in any case; and

(b) shall in the case of a child or a young person who is under the age of sixteen years,

require a person who is a parent or guardian of his to attend at the court during all the stages of the proceedings, unless and to the extent that the court is satisfied that it would be unreasonable to require such attendance, having regard to the circumstances of the case.

(2) In relation to a child or young person for whom a Local Authority have parental responsibility and who—

(a) is in their care; or

(b) is provided with accommodation by them in the exercise of any functions (in particular those under the *Children Act* 1989) which are social services functions within the meaning of the *Local Authority Social Services Act* 1970,

the reference in subsection (1) above to a person who is a parent or guardian of his shall be construed as a reference to that Authority, where he is allowed to live with such a person, as including such a reference.

In this subsection "local authority" and "parental responsibility" have the same meanings as in the *Children Act* 1989.

25–7   It is essential that parents or guardians of young defendants attend the youth court with them. Section 34A above makes such attendance mandatory where the youth is under 16 years of age unless the court is satisfied that it would be unreasonable to require such attendance in all the circumstances of the case. If a defendant appears without a parent, the court must enquire as to why they are unaccompanied, and consider taking steps to ensure attendance. The court may write to the parent or guardian requesting attendance. Alternatively a summons may be issued and, if this does not remedy the situation, a warrant obtained.

Having secured parental attendance the court will be anxious to allow parents to address the court and to contribute to the hearing generally. It is important that the court engages with both the defendant and his family.

(3) Press and publicity

Persons who may be present at the sitting of a youth court are—   **25–8**

(a) members and officers of the court;

(b) parties to the case together with their solicitors and counsel, and other persons directly concerned in that case;

(c) accredited representatives of news agencies;

(d) the court may especially authorise other persons to be present who have good cause to be there.

Accredited press representatives are therefore allowed to observe and report on court proceedings in the youth court and their presence in the courtroom cannot be objected to by the parties. However, the press is restricted in the details it may report. More particularly no report of any proceedings in a youth court should reveal the name, address or school, or include any particulars likely to lead to the identification of any child or young person concerned in those proceedings. This restriction includes details of young witnesses who are concerned in the court proceedings and the publication of pictures.

Children and Young Persons Act 1933, s.49

Restrictions on reports of proceedings in which children or young persons are concerned.

49.—(1) The following prohibitions apply (subject to subsection (5) below) in relation to any   **25–9** proceedings to which this section applies, that is to say—

(a) no report shall be published which reveals the name, address or school of any child or young person concerned in the proceedings or includes any particulars likely to lead to the identification of any child or young person concerned in the proceedings; and

(b) no picture shall be published or included in a programme service as being or including a picture of any child or young person concerned in the proceedings.

(2) The proceedings to which this section applies are—

(a) proceedings in a youth court;

(b) proceedings on appeal from a youth court (including proceedings by way of case stated);

(c) proceedings under section 15 or 16 of the *Children and Young Persons Act* 1969 (proceedings for varying or revoking supervision orders); and

(d) proceedings on appeal from a magistrates' court arising out of proceedings under section 15 or 16 of that Act (including proceedings by way of case stated).

(3) The reports to which this section applies are reports in a newspaper and reports included in a programme service; and similarly as respects pictures.

(4) For the purposes of this section a child or young person is "concerned" in any proceedings whether as being the person against or in respect of whom the proceedings are taken or as being a witness in the proceedings.

(4A) If a court is satisfied that it is in the public interest to do so, it may, in relation to a child or young person who has been convicted of an offence, by order dispense to any specified extent with the requirements of this section in relation to any proceedings before it to which this section applies by virtue of subsection (2)(a) or (b) above, being proceedings relating to—

   (a) the prosecution or conviction of the offender for the offence;

   (b) the manner in which he, or his parent or guardian, should be dealt with in respect of the offence;

   (c) the enforcement, amendment, variation, revocation or discharge of any order made in respect of the offence;

   (d) where an attendance centre order is made in respect of the offence, the enforcement of any rules made under section 16(3) of the *Criminal Justice Act* 1982; or

   (e) where a detention and training order is made, the enforcement of any requirements imposed under section 76(6)(b) of the *Crime and Disorder Act* 1998.

  (4B) A court shall not exercise its power under subsection (4A) above without—

   (a) affording the parties to the proceedings an opportunity to make representations; and

   (b) taking into account any representations which are duly made.

  (5) Subject to subsection (7) below, a court may, in relation to proceedings before it to which this section applies, by order dispense to any specified extent with the requirements of this section in relation to a child or young person who is concerned in the proceedings if it is satisfied—

   (a) that it is appropriate to do so for the purpose of avoiding injustice to the child or young person; or

   (b) that, as respects a child or young person to whom this paragraph applies who is unlawfully at large, it is necessary to dispense with those requirements for the purpose of apprehending him and bringing him before a court or returning him to the place in which he was in custody.

  (6) Paragraph (b) of subsection (5) above applies to any child or young person who is charged with or has been convicted of—

   (a) a violent offence,

   (b) a sexual offence, or

   (c) an offence punishable in the case of a person aged 21 or over with imprisonment for fourteen years or more.

  (7) The court shall not exercise its power under subsection (5)(b) above—

   (a) except in pursuance of an application by or on behalf of the Director of Public Prosecutions; and

   (b) unless notice of the application has been given by the Director of Public Prosecutions to any legal representative of the child or young person.

  (8) The court's power under subsection (5) above may be exercised by a single justice.

  (9) If a report or picture is published or included in a programme service in contravention of subsection (1) above, the following persons, that is to say—

   (a) in the case of publication of a written report or a picture as part of a newspaper, any proprietor, editor or publisher of the newspaper;

   (b) in the case of the inclusion of a report or picture in a programme service, any body corporate which provides the service and any person having functions in relation to the programme corresponding to those of an editor of a newspaper,

shall be liable on summary conviction to a fine not exceeding level 5 on the standard scale.

  (10) In any proceedings under section 15 or 16 of the *Children and Young Persons Act* 1969 (proceedings for varying or revoking supervision orders) before a magistrates' court other than a youth court or on appeal from such a court it shall be the duty of the magistrates' court or the appellate court to announce in the course of the proceedings that this section applies to the proceedings; and if the court fails to do so this section shall not apply to the proceedings.

  (11) In this section—

"legal representative" means an authorised advocate or authorised litigator, as defined by section 119(1) of the *Courts and Legal Services Act* 1990;

"programme" and "programme service" have the same meaning as in the *Broadcasting Act* 1990;

"sexual offence" has the same meaning as in section 31(1) of the *Criminal Justice Act* 1991;

"specified" means specified in an order under this section;

"violent offence" has the same meaning as in section 31(1) of the *Criminal Justice Act* 1991;

and a person who, having been granted bail, is liable to arrest (whether with or without a warrant) shall be treated as unlawfully at large.

25–10   The youth court may order the lifting of press restrictions to any extent that it specifies in certain specific circumstances:

(1) that it is appropriate to do so for the purpose of avoiding injustice to the child or young person subject to the application;

(2) in respect of a child or young person who has been convicted of an offence and the court is satisfied that it is in the public interest that details of their identity are given in the press;

(3) where a defendant has been charged with or convicted of a violent or sexual offence or an offence punishable with imprisonment for 14 years or more if he/she is unlawfully at large and the court is satisfied on the application of the DPP that it is necessary to identify him in the press for the purpose of apprehending him to bring him before a court or to return him to the place in which he was held in custody.

The youth court's power to dispense with reporting restrictions under section 49 should be exercised with the greatest care and caution. International law and practice emphasises the necessity of protecting the privacy of children and young persons involved in legal proceedings. In the case of *McKerry v. Teesdale and Wear Valley J.J.* [2000] Crim.L.R. 594, the Divisional Court stated that the need for the full and fair reporting of the administration of justice must be balanced against the welfare of the youth involved. It would be wholly wrong to invoke the power by way of additional punishment and it would only be "very rarely" that the statutory criteria for "naming and shaming" would be met.

(4) Legal representation

A majority of youths who appear before the youth court will be legally represented **25–11** either under the duty solicitor scheme or as a result of instructing their own lawyers. Representation orders are applied for in the youth court in the same way as in the adult magistrates' court. The applications are considered under the Widgery criteria and decided on the basis of the interests of justice. In considering such an application the age of the applicant must be taken into account. In *R. v. Scunthorpe Justices, ex p. S.*, *The Times*, March 5, 1998, DC it was held that a refusal to grant legal aid to a 16-year-old defendant who wished to challenge a police constable as to whether he had acted in the execution of his duty was said to be irrational, as the expertise required to cross examine police witnesses and find, select and proof defence witnesses is beyond that of a defendant aged 16 years.

(5) Reprimands and final warnings (section 65 of the Crime and Disorder Act 1998)

These have replaced police cautions for young people. They are not court orders **25–12** and cannot be ordered by the court. However, they are frequently cited when the court is told about a defendants antecedent history, in dealing with issues relating to bail and sentencing.

A reprimand will be given for first time offenders and for less serious offences. However, if the offence is sufficiently serious a final warning may be given instead of a reprimand. A final warning is given to offenders who have been reprimanded previously. Once a final warning is given the offender cannot receive a further reprimand or final warning except where the new offence has been committed more than two years since the previous warning and is not sufficiently serious to be charged.

When a final warning is given, the YOT will be notified and the young person should be assessed with a view to work being done with him to prevent offending.

Before the police can give a reprimand or final warning the offender must admit the offence.

Reprimands and final warnings may be relevant in making a bail decision for a **25–13** youth. They will also be relevant in assessing his/her antecedent history for the purpose of sentencing. It should be noted that a young person who re-offends and is convicted within two years of receiving a final warning cannot be given a conditional discharge

(*Crime and Disorder Act* 1998, s.66) unless there are exceptional circumstances relating to the offence itself or the offender. See *post*, §§ 27–16—27–17.

After a defendant has been charged the youth court is sometimes asked to adjourn proceedings against him/her to allow a reprimand or final warning to be administered. This situation was considered by the Divisional Court in *F. v. CPS* (2004) 168 J.P. 93. In that case the court was asked to judicially review the decision of the CPS not to discontinue a prosecution after a decision had been made by the police not to administer a final warning. The Divisional Court emphasised that final warnings are meant to be administered quickly and that it was clearly envisaged that they should be given before charge. It would only be in exceptional circumstances that the police should administer a final warning or reprimand when the defendant had already been charged and had appeared before a court.

III. AGE AND JURISDICTION

(1) Presumption and determination of age

25–14   The youth court's jurisdiction is founded upon the age of the defendant. Therefore the court is under a duty to establish that the defendant is aged between 10 and 17 years. Additionally, the powers of the youth court in respect of bail, remand, and sentencing vary widely between the different age groups within the court jurisdiction.

In the vast majority of cases coming before the youth court establishing the age of a defendant does not cause any problem, however if an issue as to age does arise it is dealt with by the following statutory procedure.

Children and Young Persons Act 1933, s.99(1)

Presumption and determination of age

25–15   **99.**—(1) Where a person, whether charged with an offence or not, is brought before any court otherwise than for the purpose of giving evidence, and it appears to the court that he is a child or young person, the court shall make due inquiry as to the age of that person, and for that purpose shall take such evidence as may be forthcoming at the hearing of the case, but an order or judgment of the court shall not be invalidated by any subsequent proof that the age of that person has not been correctly stated to the court, and the age presumed or declared by the court to be the age of the person so brought before it shall, for the purposes of this Act, be deemed to be the true age of that person, and, where it appears to the court that the person so brought before it has attained the age of eighteen years, that person shall for the purposes of this Act be deemed not to be a child or young person.

25–16   If the youth court is not satisfied that it has been given accurate information regarding a defendant's age, this section places a duty on the court to determine the age of the defendant. For the purposes of determining age the court can hear oral evidence and consider both domestic or foreign documentation. The court can also take into account the physical appearance of the defendant in the courtroom. The YOT, with its wide experience of dealing with young people, may also have a valuable part to play in such hearings. At the end of the hearing the court will deem the defendant to be of a certain age or within a certain age group. If new relevant evidence emerges at future hearings of the case, the court may re-open the question of age and alter its original decision. However, this must be based on new factors that have come to light.

(2) Crossing the age barrier

25–17   The situation sometimes arises that a defendant who has been charged with an offence when under the age of 18 years, attains that age before proceedings against him in the youth court have been concluded. This has important implications for the defendant. It is submitted that the most common situations are as follows:

    (1) If a young person is charged with an offence whilst he is 17 years of age but turns 18 years of age before his first appearance before the court, then the

youth court does not have jurisdiction to deal with him: *R. v. Uxbridge Youth Court, ex p. H.* (1998) 162 J.P. 327.

(2) If the young person has appeared before the youth court when under 18 years of age but attains 18 during the proceedings then the following rules apply:

If, before summary trial in the youth court or, after conviction in the youth court but before sentence, the youth court may remit the person to the adult magistrates' court for the same petty sessions area as the youth court.

Powers of Criminal Courts (Sentencing) Act 2000, s.9(1), (2)

9.—(1) Where a person who appears or is brought before a youth court charged with an of- **25–18** fence subsequently attains the age of 18, the youth court may, at any time after conviction and before sentence, remit him for sentence to a magistrates' court (other than a youth court).

(2) Where an offender is remitted under subsection (1) above, the youth court shall adjourn proceedings in relation to the offence, and—

(a) section 128 of the *Magistrates' Courts Act* 1980 (remand in custody or on bail) and all other enactments, whenever passed, relating to remand or the granting of bail in criminal proceedings shall have effect, in relation to the youth court's power or duty to remand the offender on that adjournment, as if any reference to the court to or before which the person remanded is to be brought or appear after remand were a reference to the court to which he is being remitted; and

(b) subject to subsection (3), the court to which the offender is remitted ("the other court") may deal with the case in any way in which it would have power to deal with it if all proceedings relating to the offence which took place before the youth court had taken place before the other court.

Section 9 of the *PCC(S)A* 2000 gives the youth court discretion whether or not to **25–19** remit to the magistrates' court. If the youth court decides to retain the case the enabling provision to do so is below.

Although section 9 does not, in terms, exclude indictable only offences from the power to remit to the adult court, it plainly makes no sense to remit a person to an adult court if that court has no power to sentence him. In the case of *R. (Denny) v. Acton Youth Court* [2004] EWHC 948, the youth court convicted an 18-year-old defendant of attempted robbery. The offence had been committed when the defendant was 17 years of age. The youth court sought to remit him to the adult court for sentence. It was held that a youth court should never remit under section 9 in relation to an offence which would be triable only on indictment in the case of an adult.

Children and Young Persons Act 1963, s.29

29.—(1) Where proceedings in respect of a young person are begun for an offence and he **25–20** attains the age of eighteen before the conclusion of the proceedings, the court may deal with the case and make any order which it could have made if he had not attained that age.

If, during the course of proceedings against a defendant who the court believes to be **25–21** under 18 years of age, it emerges that the defendant is in fact 18 or over the youth court has discretion to continue to deal with the defendant under the provision below.

Children and Young Persons Act 1933, s.48(1)

48.—(1) A youth court sitting for the purpose of hearing a charge against a person who is **25–22** believed to be a child or young person may, if it thinks fit to do so, proceed with the hearing and determination of the charge, notwithstanding that it is discovered that the person in question is not a child or young person.

If a defendant under 18 appears before the youth court charged with an offence **25–23** which is "either way" in the case of an adult (not being a grave crime) and he attains the age of 18 years before his plea is taken, he may apply to the youth court to be remitted to the adult court. Once a defendant has attained 18 years of age he has the right to elect trial by jury in respect of either way charges. However, it seems that if a defendant has entered his plea prior to his 18th birthday it is then "too late" for him to elect

Crown Court trial although his trial in the youth court will not commence until after his 18th birthday. It is submitted that this is the interpretation to be given to the judgment in *R. v. Islington North Juvenile Court, ex p. Daley* [1982] 2 All E.R. 974. During his leading judgment Lord Diplock stated:

> "it seems to me that reason and justice combine to indicate that the only appropriate date at which to determine whether an accused person has attained an age which entitles him to elect trial by jury for offences which under section 18 or section 22 are triable either way is the date of his appearance before the court on the occasion when the court makes its decision as to mode of trial".

If the defendant is charged with a "grave crime" under section 24 of the *Magistrates' Courts Act* 1980 and the youth court decides to retain jurisdiction before the defendant attains 18 years, the matter must remain for summary trial in the youth court. The defendant does not, on attaining 18 years acquire a right of trial before a jury: *R. v. Nottingham Justices, ex p. Taylor* [1991] 4 All E.R. 860. If the defendant attains 18 years before the mode of trial decision, then the youth court has no power to proceed, and the case should be remitted to the adult court in accordance with section 9 of the *PCC(S)A* 2000 (see *ante*).

No matter whether the original charges are summary, either way or indictable, the youth court has no jurisdiction to deal with any further fresh charges after the defendant has turned 18 years. This is irrespective of whether the fresh charges arise from the same circumstances: *R. v. Chelsea Justices, ex p. DPP* [1963] 3 All E.R. 657.

(3) Sentencing across the age barrier

25–24   In *Ghafoor* [2002] Crim.L.R. 739, the Court of Appeal considered the approach to be adopted where a court sentences a defendant who crosses a relevant age threshold between the date of the commission of an offence and the date of conviction. The judgments of the court made it clear that the starting point for sentencing a defendant in such circumstances is the sentence that the defendant would have been likely to receive if he had been sentenced on the date of the commission of the offence. The "starting point" principle is a powerful factor in deciding sentence although other factors might have to be considered. However, a court would have to have good reason for departing from the starting point sentence and passing a sentence higher than would have been passed at the date of the commission of the offence.

In *L.M.* [2003] 2 Cr.App.R.(S.) 26, a 14-year-old defendant who was not a "persistent offender" was convicted when 15 years old of an offence of inflicting grievous bodily harm. He was sentenced to a detention and training order. He could not have received a custodial sentence when 14 but was eligible for such a sentence once he became 15. It was held that it was wrong for a detention and training order to be imposed as applying *Ghafoor* (*ante*) the starting point for sentence should be the sentence which he would have been likely to receive if he had been sentenced at the date of the commission of the offence when only 14 years old. In *R.* (2006) 150 S.J.L.B. 1607 the Court dealt with an appeal by a fifteen-year-old female who received an 18 month DTO for the offence of wounding with intent. On the date of the offence she was fourteen years old and was not a persistent young offender (see *post*, § 27–99). In applying the case of *Ghafoor* the Court stated that the emphasis for young offenders should be rehabilitation not retribution and deterrence. The starting point for sentencing the appellant was how she would have been sentenced on the date of the offence, when she could not have received a DTO. The order was quashed and substituted by a supervision order.

If an order of conditional discharge was made in respect of a young person, the youth court may deal with a breach of that order even though the person is over 18 years of age: *Children and Young Persons Act* 1933, s.48(2).

If the order of conditional discharge was made by the youth court for an offence which is indictable only in the case of an adult, and the accused has attained 18 years when breached, the re-sentencing courts powers are set out in the *PCC(S)A* 2000, s.13(9):

    (a) to impose a fine not exceeding £5,000 for the offence in respect of which the order was made;

    (b) to deal with the offender for that offence in any way in which a magistrates' court could deal with him if it had just convicted him of an offence punishable with imprisonment for a term not exceeding six months.

If, during the duration of a supervision order, breach proceedings are brought, and the offender has attained 18 years, then the proceedings are brought in the adult court. If the breach proceedings are commenced in the youth court whilst the offender is under 18 years, then they remain in the youth court to be concluded there: *PCC(S)A* 2000, Sched. 7, para. 1.

IV. JURISDICTION, GRAVE CRIMES AND DANGEROUSNESS

Magistrates' Courts Act 1980, s.24(1)

24.—(1) Where a person under the age of 18 years appears or is brought before a magistrates' court on an information charging him with an indictable offence other than one falling within subsection (1B) below, he shall be tried summarily unless— **25–25**

    (a) the offence is such as is mentioned in subsection (1) or (2) of section 91 of the *Powers of Criminal Courts (Sentencing) Act* 2000 (under which a young person convicted on indictment of certain grave crimes may be sentenced to be detained for long periods) and the court considers that if he is found guilty of the offence it ought to be possible to sentence him in pursuance of subsection (3) of that section; or

    (b) he is charged jointly with a person who has attained the age of 18 and the court considers it necessary in the interests of justice to commit them both for trial;

and accordingly in a case falling within paragraph (a) or (b) of this subsection the court shall commit the accused for trial if either it is of the opinion that there is sufficient evidence to put him on trial or it has power under section 6(2) above so to commit him without consider of the evidence.

It should be noted that possession of prohibited weapons and ammunition, contrary **25–26** to section 5 of the *Firearms Act* 1968, as amended by section 287 of the *Criminal Justice Act* 2003, now requires a minimum 5-year sentence to be imposed if the offence was:

    (a) committed after January 22, 2004; and

    (b) at the time of the offence, the defendant was aged 16 years or over.

Section 39 of the *Anti-Social Behaviour Act* 2003 extended the list of prohibited weapons contained in section 5, by adding any air rifle, air gun or air pistol which uses or is designed or adapted for use with a self-contained gas cartridge system. A young person fitting these criteria must be committed to the Crown Court for trial and in the event of conviction, for a sentence of detention to be passed under section 91 of the *PCC(S)A* 2000.

The plea before venue procedure that takes place in the adult court does not apply **25–27** to young people who do not have a right to elect Crown Court trial. The youth court has jurisdiction to try either way and indictable offences other than offences of homicide. However, if the offence alleged is one of the grave crimes (see section 91 of the *PCC(S)A* 2000), section 24(1), *ante*, must be considered by the youth court.

In such cases the youth court must consider whether it should retain jurisdiction and try the case, or whether it should decline jurisdiction and, if there is a case to answer, commit the defendant to the Crown Court. In such cases the court must consider the seriousness of the allegation and decide whether its own powers of punishment are sufficient or whether the allegation is of such a serious nature that, if found guilty, it ought to be possible to sentence the defendant to detention under section 91 of the *PCC(S)A* 2000.

The decision the youth court makes as to whether to accept jurisdiction is a most **25–28**

Part V

important one which may have a profound effect on the outcome of the case for the defendant. If the youth court accepts jurisdiction, and the defendant pleads guilty or is convicted, the youth court has no power to commit him/her to the Crown Court for sentence. In such cases the defendant must, therefore, be sentenced in accordance with the powers of the youth court.

The youth court's powers to impose a custodial sentence are limited in the following ways:

(a) In the case of defendants aged 10 or 11 years of age, the youth court has no power at all to impose a custodial sentence.

(b) In the case of defendants aged from 12 to 14 years, the court has power to impose a detention and training order for a maximum of two years but only if it is of the opinion that the defendant is a persistent offender. If not, the youth court has no power to impose a custodial sentence (persistent offender—see detention and training order—§ 27–98, *post*).

(c) Defendants aged 15, 16 and 17 years can be sentenced to a detention and training order up to a maximum of two years: *PCC(S)A* 2000, s.103.

If, however, the youth court decline jurisdiction and commit the defendant to the Crown Court for trial, he/she may then be sentenced by the Crown Court under section 91, below.

V. PUNISHMENT OF CERTAIN GRAVE CRIMES—PCC(S)A 2000, S.91

(1) Sentencing

25–29   Where a young offender is convicted on indictment of certain grave crimes, he may be sentenced to long-term detention. This sentence is available:

(a) where a person of at least 10 but not more than 17 years is convicted on indictment of any offence punishable in the case of an adult with imprisonment of 14 years or more not being an offence the sentence for which is fixed by law; or an offence under section 14 (indecent assault on a woman) or section 15 (indecent assault on a man) of the *Sexual Offences Act* 1956.

(b) where a young person is convicted of an offence under section 1 of the *Road Traffic Act* 1988 (causing death by dangerous driving); or an offence under section 3A of the *Road Traffic Act* 1988 (causing death by careless driving while under the influence of drink or drugs).

Section 91 of the *PCC(S)A* 2000 is available to the Crown Court if a young person is convicted on indictment of a grave crime. Detention under section 91 can be imposed upon defendants aged 10 to 17 years.

(2) The application of section 24

25–30   The application of section 24 by the youth court has been the subject of much litigation, and scrutiny by the higher courts. There is a considerable body of case law. It is submitted that the following are the principles for the court to apply:

(1) The test that the youth court must apply is whether the court considers that if convicted it ought to be possible to sentence the defendant in pursuance of section 91 of the *PCC(S)A* 2000. There must be a real possibility of such a sentence, not a vague or theoretical one. If the court is of a view that such a sentence is a real possibility, the court has no further discretion and must decline jurisdiction: *R. (D. & N.) v. Sheffield Youth Court* (2003) 167 J.P. 159, QBD.

(2) The youth court will hear the facts of the prosecution case. The defendant's criminal record will be considered: *R. (Tullet) v. Medway Magistrates' Court* (2003) 167 J.P. 541 and 896. The court must also consider defence submissions both on the undisputed facts of the prosecution case and any other factors relat-

ing to the defendant, his character, and his personal circumstances. Contentious mitigation should be ignored.

(3) In *R. (W.) v. Southampton Youth Court*; *R. (K.) v. Wirral Borough Magistrates' Court* [2003] 1 Cr.App.R.(S.) 87, the Lord Chief Justice emphasised the importance of trials for young offenders taking into account the needs of defendants of that age group: "While the need to impose the appropriate sentence is important, so is the need to ensure that wherever possible the trial should take place in the appropriate setting. That is more satisfactorily achieved in a Youth Court than in a Crown Court." The youth court should start therefore with a strong presumption against sending young offenders to the Crown Court unless satisfied that it is clearly required, notwithstanding the fact that the forum will not be as appropriate as the youth court. The younger the defendant is, so the stronger the presumption that he/she should be tried in the youth court.

(4) A youth court dealing with a defendant charged with rape should never accept jurisdiction to deal with the case itself but should commit the case to the Crown Court for trial: *Billam* [1986] 1 All E.R. 985. In the case of *R (W., F., and B.) v. DPP*, DC, January 13, 2006 the decision of a youth court to decline jurisdiction in respect of a 12-year-old defendant charged with raping a 13 year old was upheld. However, the court stated that it was possible that there were circumstances in which it would appropriate for a youth court to accept jurisdiction in cases of rape.

(5) In deciding whether it ought to be possible to sentence a defendant to detention under section 91 the youth court must consider the sentencing powers of the Crown Court and the guidance given on the exercise of those powers. If there is no real possibility of such a sentence, committal is inappropriate. In assessing a likely sentence, the youth court should take into account the age of the defendant. Youths aged 15 to 17 years will receive a substantially shorter sentence of custody than adults convicted of a similar crime. Those aged between 10 and 12 years are unlikely to receive any custodial sentence unless the crime is extremely grave. The same applies to the 12 to 15 age group unless they are persistent young offenders. Only in exceptional circumstances will it be appropriate to pass a sentence of less than two years detention under section 91 on a defendant who would be eligible for a detention and training order were he not too young for such an order to be made. This issue was considered in *Manchester City Youth Court* [2002] 1 Cr.App.R.(S.) 573 and in *W. v. Thetford Youth Justices v. DPP* [2003] 1 Cr.App.R.(S.) 67. In his judgment Gage J. said:

"in respect of offenders under 15 a custodial sentence will ordinarily only be available in the form of a detention and training order. If the court is prohibited from making such an order in general an order under section 91 will not be appropriate. I remain of the opinion that where an offence or offences are likely to attract a sentence of less than two years custody the appropriate sentence will be a detention and training order. In the case of an offender under 15, who is not a persistent offender, or a child under 12, the most likely sentence will be non-custodial sentence. It follows that in most cases the appropriate place of trial will be the youth court. I remain of the view that the mere fact that a youth court, unable to make a short detention and training order, considers that the option to pass a short custodial sentence should be available, does not mean that it should decline jurisdiction. It seems to me that Parliament intended that generally a non-custodial sentence should be passed. Perhaps it would be better to say that cases involving offenders under 15 for whom a detention and training order is not available will only rarely attract a period of detention under section 91; the more rarely if the offender is under 12".

See also *R. v. Balham Youth Court, ex p. R. (Admin)*, unreported, September 13, 2002.

Part V

25–31　　In *C. v. Balham Youth Court* (2003) 167 J.P. 525, QBD the youth court declined jurisdiction in dealing with a 14-year-old charged with robbery. On appeal the court held that where an offender is not able to be made the subject of a custodial sentence in the youth court because of his age, he should only be committed to the Crown Court for trial if a sentence of two years of more could be expected or if there were exceptional circumstances. The court stated that there was a general principle that first time offenders aged 13 or 14 should not be detained in custody and it was only rarely that a youth under 15 should be give a custodial sentence of under two years.

In the case of *A.* (2005) CA (Crim. Div.) June 14, 2005 it was emphasised that youths aged 15–17 years will receive a substantially shorter sentence of custody than adults convicted of a similar crime.

25–32　　This approach has been firmly emphasised in two further cases. In *R. (M.W.) v. West London Youth Court* [2004] EWHC 1144, two 14-year-old defendants were charged with robbery of a mobile telephone. Both were of good character and appealed against the decision of the youth court to decline jurisdiction. Allowing their appeal, it was held that neither defendant faced the real possibility of a sentence of, or approaching, two years in length and that therefore, the youth court should have retained jurisdiction. Subsequently, in the case of *R. (H.A. and O.) v. Southampton Youth Court* [2004] EWHC 2912, Admin, the three 13-year-old defendants were charged with indecent assault on a male of the same age. The circumstances of the assault were such that the youth court declined jurisdiction. On appeal it was held that jurisdiction should have been retained. In the course of his judgment, Leveson J. sought to summarise the law in a way that could be put before the youth court whenever this issue arose as follows:

(a) The general policy of the legislator is that those who are under 18 years of age and in particular children of under 15 years of age should, wherever possible, be tried in the youth court. A trial in the Crown Court with the inevitably greater formality and greatly increased number of people involved (including a jury and the public) should be reserved for the most serious of cases.

(b) It is a further policy of the legislature that, generally speaking, first time offenders aged 12–14 and all offenders under 12 should not be detained in custody and decisions as to jurisdiction should have regard to the fact that the exceptional power to detain for grave offences should not be used to water down the general principle. Those under 15 will rarely attract a period of detention and, even more rarely, those who are under 12.

(c) In each case the Court should ask itself whether there is a real prospect, having regard to his/her age, that this defendant whose case they are considering might require a sentence of, or in excess of, two years or, alternatively, whether although the sentence might be less than two years, there is some unusual feature of the case which justifies declining jurisdiction, bearing in mind that the absence of the power to impose a detention and training order because the defendant is under 15 is not an unusual feature.

In deciding the issue of jurisdiction in relation to defendants of different age groups it is submitted that the following principles should be applied.

(3) Defendants aged 10 or 11 years of age

25–33　　Such defendants should only be committed to the Crown Court when charged with exceptionally serious offences of such gravity that in spite of his/her age a custodial sentence exceeding two years is a realistic possibility. Committal to the Crown Court in other circumstances will be rare. In *T.*, CA (Crim. Div.), November 9, 2004, a 10 year old pleaded guilty to robbery, false imprisonment, and inflicting grievous bodily harm. He was sentenced to three years' detention under section 91. On appeal it was emphasised that it was very rare for a Court to make such an order in respect of such a young defendant. However, in this particular case it was essential both in the public interest and in the long term interest of the appellant himself. An unusual feature of the case is that the pre-sentence report also recommended a section 91 order in view of the circumstances of the offence and the defendant's chaotic and traumatic childhood.

(4) Defendants aged 12, 13 and 14 years

(a) *Non-persistent offenders*

The youth court has no power to make detention and training orders in respect of **25–34** this age group unless it finds that the defendant is a persistent offender. For definition of "persistent offender" see *post*, § 27–98.

If this is not the case there is a very strong presumption that trial should take place in the youth court. If, however, the youth court finds that in all the circumstances of the case the sentencing court ought to have available to it power to impose a custodial sentence greater than two years then, in spite of the defendants age, it should commit to the Crown Court.

(b) *Persistent young offenders*

If the defendant is a persistent offender the youth court has power to impose a **25–35** detention and training order of up to two years. If, in spite of the defendant's young age, the youth court finds that there is a real possibility that a sentence in excess of two years will be imposed, and that therefore the sentencing court ought to have such powers available to it, the youth court should commit for trial.

(5) Defendants aged 15, 16 and 17 years

The youth court has power to make a detention and training order up to a maximum **25–36** of two years for this age group whether or not they are persistent offenders. In dealing with jurisdiction the youth court must ask itself whether the circumstances of the alleged crime are so serious that the sentencing court ought to have available to it powers of custody exceeding two years and that such a sentence is more than a vague or theoretical possibility.

Once a youth court has made a decision retaining jurisdiction, albeit in ignorance of a legal provision, the only power to review such decision is limited to the circumstances specified in section 25 of the *Magistrates' Courts Act* 1980: *Grimsby and Cleethorpes Magistrates' Court* [2004] EWHC 2240.

The preferred way to challenge the decision of a youth court to accept jurisdiction is by way of Judicial Review and not an application for a voluntary bill of indictment: *R. (DPP) the Camberwell Youth Court, The Times*, August 12, 2004, QB.

VI. DANGEROUS DEFENDANTS IN THE YOUTH COURT

A. DANGEROUS OFFENDERS AND GRAVE CRIMES

The *Criminal Justice Act* 2003 creates new powers of sentencing designed to protect **25–37** the public from dangerous offenders. The new sentences are not available to the youth court, whose powers of custodial sentence remain unchanged. However, the Act gives the youth court powers to send youths to the Crown Court for trial or to commit them for sentence to the Crown Court if they are charged or convicted of a "specified offence". Schedule 15 to the *Criminal Justice Act* 2003 sets out some 153 offences which are so specified. If a youth appears before the youth court and is charged or convicted of a specified offence "dangerousness" must be considered. Some of the "specified" offences are also offences that are mentioned under *PCC(S)A* 2000, s.91 (see *ante*, § 25–25). These offences are therefore both specified offences and grave crimes under Section 91. In such circumstances the youth court must consider both procedures.

B. PRE-TRIAL PROCEDURE

Criminal Justice Act 2003, Sched. 3, para. 18

25–38   18. For section 51 [of the *Crime and Disorder Act 1998*] (no committal proceedings for indictable-only offences) there is substituted—

Sending cases to the Crown Court: children and young persons
        51A.—(1) This section is subject to sections 24A and 24B of the Magistrates' Courts Act 1980 (which provide for certain offences involving children or young persons to be tried summarily).
        (2) Where a child or young person appears or is brought before a magistrates' court ("the court") charged with an offence and any of the conditions mentioned in subsection (3) below is satisfied, the court shall send him forthwith to the Crown Court for trial for the offence.
        (3) Those conditions are—
            (d) that the offence is a specified offence (within the meaning of section 224 of the Criminal Justice Act 2003) and it appears to the court that if he is found guilty of the offence the criteria for the imposition of a sentence under section 226(3) or 228(2) of that Act would be met.
        [Note, section 51A(3)(d) is the only part of this section that presently applies].

25–39   This section requires a child or young person to be sent from the youth court to the Crown Court for trial if he is charged with a specified offence and it appears to the youth court that if he were convicted of it the criteria for the imposition of an indeterminate sentence under section 226 of the 2003 Act or an extended sentence under section 228 of the 2003 Act would be met. The assessment of dangerousness is made under the provisions of section 229 of the *Criminal Justice Act* 2003, see *post*.

        In the case of *R. (DPP) v. South East Surrey Youth Court* (2005) EWHC 2929 QBD (Admin) the DPP applied for judicial review of a decision of the youth court declining to send a youth for trial at the Crown Court under the dangerousness procedure for an offence of assault occasioning actual bodily harm (a specified offence). The Court had committed the defendant for trial to the Crown Court in respect of a completely separate charge of robbery under the section 91 *PCCSA* procedure. On appeal the Court emphasised it was not open to the youth court to ignore the provisions of section 51A of the 2003 Act. However, in considering the applicability of section 51A the youth court should bear in mind the following factors:

        (1) The policy is that those who are under 18 should wherever possible be tried in a youth court which is designed for their specific needs.
        (2) The youth court should bear in mind the guidance given in the case of *Lang*— (see *post*) to non-serious specified offences.
        (3) In relation to defendants under 18 years of age there is a need to be particularly rigorous before concluding that there is a significant risk of serious harm by the commission of further specified offences. Such a conclusion is unlikely to be appropriate in the absence of a pre-sentence report following assessment by a youth offender team.
        (4) In most cases where a non-serious specified offence was charged, an assessment of dangerousness would not be appropriate until after conviction when, if the dangerous criteria were met, the defendant could then be committed to the Crown Court for sentence.

        In *B. v. Barking Youth Court* (2006) EWHC 2121, Admin, the sixteen-year-old defendant sought to judicially review the decision of the youth court to send him for trial to the Crown Court under the provisions of section 51A (see *ante*). The defendant was charged with robbery (a specified offence) in which passengers on the London Underground at night were threatened, and their property taken. On appeal the Court repeated the judgment in the *South East Surrey Youth Court* case (*ante*). It was clearly desirable that criminal process against young defendants be dealt with expeditiously and those advising such offenders should use their best endeavours to obtain reports on the dangerousness issue at an early stage. In this case no such reports had been obtained but the defence had not asked for an adjournment to do so. In all the circumstances the magistrates were entitled to conclude that the dangerousness criteria had been met. The appeal was dismissed.

C. Post-Conviction Procedure

Criminal Justice Act 2003, Sched. 3, para.23

23. After section 3 [of the *Powers of the Criminal Courts (Sentencing) Act* 2000] there is **25–40**
inserted—

Committal for sentence of dangerous young offenders

3C.—(1) This section applies where on the summary trial of a specified offence a person aged under 18 is convicted of the offence.

(2) If, in relation to the offence, it appears to the court that the criteria for the imposition of a sentence under section 226(3) or 228(2) of the Criminal Justice Act 2003 would be met, the court must commit the offender in custody or on bail to the Crown Court for sentence in accordance with section 5A(1) below.

(3) Where the court commits a person under subsection (2) above, section 6 below (which enables a magistrates' court, where it commits a person under this section in respect of an offence, also to commit him to the Crown Court to be dealt with in respect of certain other offences) shall apply accordingly.

(4) Nothing in this section shall prevent the court from committing a specified offence to the Crown Court for sentence under section 3B above if the provisions of that section are satisfied.

(5) In this section, references to a specified offence are to a specified offence within the meaning of section 224 of the Criminal Justice Act 2003.

This section above allows the youth court to commit to the Crown Court for sentence **25–41**
defendants who have been convicted of a specified offence if the dangerousness provisions apply. The cases of *R. (DPP) v. South East Surrey Youth Court* (see *ante*, § 25–39) and *Lang* (see *post*, § 25–44) both give helpful guidance on the approach to be taken in dealing with young defendants.

The assessment of dangerousness

Before deciding whether to send a youth to the Crown Court for trial or commit him **25–42**
for sentence after conviction under the above provisions the youth court must assess "dangerousness" if the charge or conviction is for a specified offence.

Criminal Justice Act 2003, s.229(1), (2)

The assessment of dangerousness

229—(1) This section applies where—   **25–43**
   (a) a person has been convicted of a specified offence, and
   (b) it falls to a court to assess under any of sections 225 to 228 whether there is a significant risk to members of the public of serious harm occasioned by the commission by him of further such offences.

(2) If at the time when that offence was committed the offender had not been convicted in any part of the United Kingdom of any relevant offence or was aged under 18, the court in making the assessment referred to in subsection (1)(b)—
   (a) must take into account all such information as is available to it about the nature and circumstances of the offence,
   (b) may take into account any information which is before it about any pattern of behaviour of which the offence forms part, and
   (c) may take into account any information about the offender which is before it.

This section sets out matters to be taken into account by the youth court in assessing **25–44** dangerousness. In *Lang* [2005] EWCA Crim 2864; (2006) Crim. L.R. 174 the Court of Appeal dealt with a number of cases relating to dangerousness and gave guidance as to the principles applicable to the new sentences for both adults and youths. In relation to those under 18 the court emphasised the importance of bearing in mind the capacity of young people to change and develop for the better. In respect of youths this approach was further developed in the case of *R. (DPP) v. South East Surrey Youth Court* (see *ante*, § 25–39). It seems that both youth and adult courts at all levels have found the "dangerousness" provisions complex and somewhat confusing. It is to be hoped that this will be ended by the full implementation of the provisions of the CJA 2003. The reader is referred to *D. (Hollie Louise)* (2005) EWCA Crim. 2292, which sets out the Court of Appeals approach to the sentencing of a 13-year-old girl convicted of a number of specified offences. The reader is also referred to the case of *Shaffi (Zulfiqar)* (2006) EWCA Crim 418. This case involves an adult appellant. However, the judgment of the court emphasises the need for a significant evidential basis before establishing that a victim had suffered serious psychological harm within the meaning of the Act.

See Specific Sentences, *ante*, §§ 23–115–23–123.

BAIL IN THE YOUTH COURT

I. INTRODUCTION

The youth court has power to remand a young person on bail, into local authority **26–1** accommodation (with or without a security requirement) or into custody. The powers vary greatly, dependant upon the age and gender of the defendant as shown on the flow charts (see *post*, §§ 26–29—26–31).

The initial decision to be made by the youth court is whether bail, conditional or unconditional, should be granted.

The *Bail Act* 1976 applies to all youths, the only difference being that the accused may be refused bail for his "own welfare" rather than his "own protection", as is the case with adult offenders: *Bail Act* 1976, Sched. 1. The presumption in favour of granting unconditional bail contained in section 4 of the *Bail Act* 1976 applies equally to youths. It is only if bail is refused that the complex provisions of section 23 of the *CYPA* 1969 have to be invoked.

In deciding whether to grant bail, with or without conditions, the court must take **26–2** into account its statutory duties to prevent offending and also consider the welfare of the defendant. The Youth Offending Team (YOT) plays a vital role in any application for bail. More especially, the YOT will provide the court with up to date information relating to:

(a) the defendant's antecedents;

(b) his record in complying with previous bail conditions and any community penalties including referral orders;

(c) his home situation, health and welfare;

(d) confirmation of his attendance at school, college or work.

In addition, the YOT will investigate the viability of appropriate bail conditions which may meet the concerns of the court especially by way of a Bail Support Programme or an Intensive Supervision and Surveillance Programme (ISSP), see *post*, § 26–7.

If a remand into custody is contemplated by the court, the YOT will, in the case of 15 and 16–year–old males, carry out the "vulnerability" assessment as required by section 23(5A) of the *CYPA* 1969, (see *post*, § 26–19).

A remand into local authority accommodation is a refusal of bail and custody time limits apply in the same way as to a remand into custody.

II. THE BAIL APPLICATION

When the defendant is charged with offences that are not imprisonable, bail may **26–3** only be refused in the circumstances specified in Schedule 1, Part II of the 1976 Act. These circumstances are:

(1) The defendant has previously refused to surrender to bail, and in view of that failure, the court believes that the defendant would fail to surrender if released on bail on this occasion: Sched. 1, Pt II, para. 2.

Part V

(2) The court is satisfied that the defendant should be kept in custody for his own welfare: Sched. 1, Pt II, para. 3.

(3) The defendant is in custody in pursuance of a sentence of a court or of any authority acting under any of the Service Acts: Sched. 1, Pt II, para. 4.

(4) The defendant has been arrested under the 1976 Act for failing to surrender to the custody of the court or for being in breach of conditions of bail or likely to be in breach of such conditions: Sched. 1, Pt II, para. 5.

26–4 When the defendant is charged with offences that are punishable with imprisonment in the case of an adult offender, bail may be refused only in the circumstances specified in Sched. 1, Pt 1 of the 1976 Act. These circumstances are:

(1) The court is satisfied that there are substantial grounds for believing that the defendant would fail to surrender to custody, commit an offence whilst on bail, or interfere with witnesses or otherwise obstruct the course of justice whether in relation to himself or another person: Sched. 1, Pt I, para. 2.

(2) The defendant is charged with or convicted of an indictable offence (whether or not triable either way) committed whilst on bail in criminal proceedings: Sched. 1, Pt I, para. 2A.

(3) The defendant is in custody in pursuance of a sentence of a court or of any authority acting under any of the Service Acts: Sched. 1, Pt 1, para. 3.

(4) The court is satisfied that it has not been practicable to obtain sufficient information for the purpose of taking the decisions required regarding bail due to lack of time since the proceedings started: Sched. 1, Pt I, para. 5.

(5) The defendant had been released on bail in or in connection with proceedings for an offence, and had been arrested under section 7 of the 1976 Act for failing to surrender to the custody of the court or being in breach of conditions of bail or likely to be in breach of such conditions: Sched. 1, Pt I, para. 6.

(6) Where the court is adjourned for enquiries or for a report to be prepared and it a ppears to the court impracticable to complete the inquiries or make the report unless the defendant is kept in custody: Sched. 1, Pt I, para. 7.

(1) Conditions on bail

26–5 Conditions may be imposed following a grant of bail in the circumstances described in paragraph 8 of Schedule 1, Part I of the 1976 Act. These circumstances are when the court believes the conditions imposed are necessary to prevent a failure to surrender to custody, the commission of an offence whilst on bail or the interference with witnesses or any other obstruction of justice. Conditions may also be imposed if they are necessary for the purpose of enabling further inquiries to be made or a report to be made to assist the court in dealing with the offence.

Where the defendant is aged 17 years, electronic tagging may be used to monitor his compliance with the relevant conditions: *Bail Act* 1976, s.3.

Where the defendant is aged between 12 and 16 years electronic tagging may be used in accordance with the conditions laid down in section 3AA of the 1976 Act.

Bail Act 1976, s.3AA(1)–(6), (11), (12)

Electronic monitoring of compliance with bail conditions

26–6   **3AA.**—(1) A court shall not impose on a child or young person a requirement under section 3(6ZAA) above (an "electronic monitoring requirement") unless each of the following conditions is satisfied.

(2) The first condition is that the child or young person has attained the age of twelve years.

(3) The second condition is that—

(a) the child or young person is charged with or has been convicted of a violent or sexual offence, or an offence punishable in the case of an adult with imprisonment for a term of fourteen years or more; or

(b) he is charged with or has been convicted of one or more imprisonable offences which, together with any other imprisonable offences of which he has been convicted in any proceedings—

    (i) amount, or

    (ii) would, if he were convicted of the offences with which he is charged, amount,

to a recent history of repeatedly committing imprisonable offences while remanded on bail or to local authority accommodation.

(4) The third condition is that the court—

    (a) has been notified by the Secretary of State that electronic monitoring arrangements are available in each local justice area which is a relevant area; and

    (b) is satisfied that the necessary provision can be made under those arrangements.

(5) The fourth condition is that a youth offending team has informed the court that in its opinion the imposition of such a requirement will be suitable in the case of the child or young person.

(6) Where a court imposes an electronic monitoring requirement, the requirement shall include provision for making a person responsible for the monitoring; and a person who is made so responsible shall be of a description specified in an order made by the Secretary of State.

(11) In this section "local authority accommodation" has the same meaning as in the *Children and Young Persons Act* 1969.

(12) For the purposes of this section a petty sessions area is a relevant area in relation to a proposed electronic monitoring requirement if the court considers that it will not be practicable to secure the electronic monitoring in question unless electronic monitoring arrangements are available in that area.

(2) Intensive Supervision and Surveillance Programme (ISSP)

This programme is intended for the most prolific and serious young offenders. **26–7** Complete guidance is set out in relation to Supervision Orders (see sentencing— §§ 27–55 *et seq.*, *post*). The principal aim, when used as part of a bail package or as part of the conditions relating to a remand into local authority accommodation, is to prevent the commission of further offences. This is achieved by addressing the needs of young offenders by placing a particular emphasis on education and training. The programme is available for 10- to 17-year-olds but eligibility requires that the defendant fulfils the necessary criteria (see *post*, § 27–61).

Electronic tagging is available but not voice verification. The YOT will carry out an assessment as to suitability and make proposals on the content of the ISSP. Advocates and courts should be aware that the ISSP programme is a limited resource. It is a non-statutory scheme funded by the Youth Justice Board and even if a defendant is deemed a suitable candidate there may not be an ISSP programme available within the defendant's local authority.

III. APPEAL AGAINST REFUSAL OF BAIL

(1) Remands available following a refusal of bail

Options available to the court are entirely dependant on the age and gender of the **26–8** defendant.

(a) *Defendants aged 10 or 11 years*

(i) Remand to a local authority under section 23 of the Children Act 1989

Following a refusal of bail, the defendant must be remanded to local authority ac- **26–9** commodation, with or without conditions, under section 23 of the *Children and Young Persons Act* 1969.

Part V

Children and Young Persons Act 1969, s.23

Remands and committals to local authority accommodation

26-10   **23.**—(1) Where—

> (a) a court remands a child or young person charged with or convicted of one or more offences or commits him for trial or sentence; and
>
> (b) he is not released on bail,

the remand or committal shall be to local authority accommodation; and in the following provisions of this section, any reference (however expressed) to a remand shall be construed as including a reference to a committal.

(2) A court remanding a person to local authority accommodation shall designate the local authority who are to receive him; and that authority shall be—

> (a) in the case of a person who is being looked after by a local authority, that authority; and
>
> (b) in any other case, the local authority in whose area it appears to the court that he resides or the offence or one of the offences was committed.

(3) Where a person is remanded to local authority accommodation, it shall be lawful for any person acting on behalf of the designated authority to detain him.

(4)–(6) [security requirements, see below]

(7) Subject to section 23AA below, a court remanding a person to local authority accommodation without imposing a security requirement may, after consultation with the designated authority, require that person to comply with

> (a) any such conditions as could be imposed under section 3(6) of the *Bail Act* 1976 if he were then being granted bail; and
>
> (b) any conditions imposed for the purpose of securing the electronic monitoring of his compliance with any other condition imposed under this subsection.

(7A) [security requirements, see below]

(7B) [security requirements, see below]

(8) Where a court imposes on a person any such conditions as are mentioned in subsection (7) above, it shall be its duty to explain to him in open court and in ordinary language why it is imposing those conditions; and a magistrates' court shall cause a reason stated by it under this subsection to be specified in the warrant of commitment and to be entered in the register.

(9) A court remanding a person to local authority accommodation without imposing a security requirement may, after consultation with the designated authority, impose on that authority requirements—

> (a) for securing compliance with any conditions imposed on that person under subsection (7) above; or
>
> (b) stipulating that he shall not be placed with a named person.

(10) Where a person is remanded to local authority accommodation, a relevant court—

> (a) may, on the application of the designated authority, impose on that person any such conditions as could be imposed under subsection (7) above if the court were then remanding him to such accommodation; and
>
> (b) where it does so, may impose on that authority any requirements for securing compliance with the conditions so imposed.

(11) Where a person is remanded to local authority accommodation, a relevant court may, on the application of the designated authority or that person, vary or revoke any conditions or requirements imposed under subsections (7), (9) or (10) above.

(12) In this section—

> "children's home" has the same meaning as in the *Care Standards Act* 2000;
>
> "court" and "magistrates' court" include a justice;
>
> "imprisonable offence" means an offence punishable in the case of an adult with imprisonment;
>
> "prescribed description" means a description prescribed by reference to age or sex or both by an order of the Secretary of State;
>
> "relevant court", in relation to a person remanded to local authority accommodation, means the court by which he was so remanded, or any magistrates' court having jurisdiction in the place where he is for the time being;
>
> "secure accommodation" means accommodation which is provided in a children's home in

respect of which a person is registered under Part II of the *Care Standards Act* 2000 for the purpose of restricting liberty, and is approved for that purpose by the Secretary of State or the National Assembly for Wales;

"sexual offence" and "violent offence" have the same meanings as in the *PCC(S)A* 2000;

"young person" means a person who has attained the age of fourteen years and is under the age of seventeen years.

but, for the purposes of the definition of "secure accommodation", "local authority accommodation" includes any accommodation falling within section 61(2) of the *Criminal Justice Act* 1991.

(13) In this section—

(a) any reference to a person who is being looked after by a local authority shall be construed in accordance with section 22 of the *Children Act* 1989;

(b) any reference to consultation shall be construed as a reference to such consultation (if any) as is reasonably practicable in all the circumstances of the case; and

(c) any reference, in relation to a person charged with or convicted of a violent or sexual offence, to protecting the public from serious harm from him shall be construed as a reference to protecting members of the public from death or serious personal injury, whether physical or psychological, occasioned by further such offences committed by him.

(14) This section has effect subject to—

(b) section 128(7) of that Act (remands to the custody of a constable for periods of not more than three days),

but section 128(7) shall have effect in relation to a child or young person as if for the reference to three clear days there were substituted a reference to twenty-four hours.

Electronic monitoring may not be used to monitor compliance with the local authority remand conditions.   **26–11**

(ii) Remand in secure accommodation under s.25 of the Children Act 1989

Power exists under the *Children Act* 1989 to make a Secure Accommodation order. **26–12** This power exists under the civil jurisdiction of the court. If the court indicate to the YOT that the availability of secure accommodation should be investigated and invite the YOT to make enquiries, the YOT *may* subsequently make an application for such an order on behalf of the local authority in which the defendant is ordinarily resident. It is entirely an issue for the local authority as to whether this application is made or not.

Children Act 1989, s.25

Use of accommodation for restricting liberty

25.—(1) Subject to the following provisions of this section, a child who is being looked after **26–13** by a local authority may not be placed, and, if placed, may not be kept, in accommodation provided for the purpose of restricting liberty ("secure accommodation") unless it appears—

(a) that—

(i) he has a history of absconding and is likely to abscond from any other description of accommodation; and

(ii) if he absconds, he is likely to suffer significant harm; or

(b) that if he is kept in any other description of accommodation he is likely to injure himself or other persons.

(2) [powers of Secretary of State]

(3) It shall be the duty of a court hearing an application under this section to determine whether any relevant criteria for keeping a child in secure accommodation are satisfied in his case.

(4) If a court determines that any such criteria are satisfied, it shall make an order authorising the child to be kept in secure accommodation and specifying the maximum period for which he may be so kept.

(5) On any adjournment of the hearing of an application under this section, a court may make an interim order permitting the child to be kept during the period of the adjournment in secure accommodation.

(6) No court shall exercise the powers conferred by this section in respect of a child who is not legally represented in that court unless, having been informed of his right to apply for representation funded by the Legal Services Commission as part of the Community Legal Service or Criminal Defence Service and having had the opportunity to do so, he refused or failed to apply.

(7) [powers of Secretary of State]

(8) The giving of an authorisation under this section shall not prejudice any power of any court in England and Wales or Scotland to give directions relating to the child to whom the authorisation relates.

(9) This section is subject to section 20(8).

26–14　　Regulation 4 of the *Children (Secure Accommodation) Regulations* 1991 provides that a child under 13 may only be placed in secure accommodation with the approval of the Secretary of State for Health. Regulation 5(2)(a) provides that 16- and 17-year-olds accommodated under section 20(5) of the *Children Act* 1989 (which allows the local authority to provide accommodation for any person aged 16 to 20 years if they consider that doing so would safeguard or promote his own welfare) may not be placed in secure accommodation. Children detained under any provision of the *Mental Health Act* 1983 may not be the subject of an order under section 25.

Proceedings for a secure accommodation order are not criminal proceedings within the meaning of Article 6 of the ECHR: *Re C. (A Child) (Secure Accommodation order: Representation)* (2001) 2 F.L.R 169. However, a child facing such an application is entitled to the minimum rights to a fair trial set out in Article 6(3) of the European Convention. The requirement that the defendant is legally represented may, in exceptional cases, be satisfied where the defendant's solicitor is only served with the application on the day of the hearing. However, the preferred course of action in such circumstances would be the making of an interim order under section 25(5) of the *Children Act* 1989, which would authorise further detention in secure accommodation, and allow the defence adequate time to prepare its case: *Re C. (ante)*, *per* Thorpe and Brooke L.JJ.

26–15　　A court may make a secure accommodation order under section 25 of the *Children Act* 1989 where the criteria for detention in secure accommodation in section 23 of the *Children and Young Persons Act* are not satisfied: *Re G. (A Child) (Secure Accommodation order)* (2001) 1 F.L.R. 884. However, where a child has been remanded to local authority accommodation under section 23 of the *Children and Young Persons Act* 1969, the court may only make an order for secure accommodation where the criteria in regulation 6(2) of the *Children (Secure Accommodation) Regulations* 1991 are satisfied: *Re W. and D. (Secure Accommodation)* [1995] 2 F.L.R. 807.

(b) *Defendants aged 12, 13 or 14 years, and girls aged 15 or 16*

(i) Remand in secure accommodation following refusal of bail

26–16　　The court has the same powers to remand to local authority accommodation following refusal of bail as it does in the context of defendants aged 10 or 11 years. The additional powers are:

— The court may, after consultation with the YOT, impose a security requirement requiring the local authority to place and keep the youth in secure accommodation. A security requirement is defined in section 23(4) of the 1969 Act as a requirement that the youth be placed in secure accommodation, which is described in section 23(12) of the 1969 Act as accommodation which is provided in a children's home in respect of which a person is registered under Part II of the *Care Standards Act* 2000 for the purpose of restricting liberty. The conditions relating to the imposition of a security requirement are contained in section 23 of the 1969 Act.

— The provisions of the *CYPA* 1969, s.23AA can be made as a requirement of a remand into local authority accomodation.

(ii) Electronic monitoring on remand to local authority accommodation

Children and Young Persons Act 1969, s.23AA(1)–(6)

Electronic monitoring of conditions of remand

23AA.—(1) A court shall not impose a condition on a person under section 23(7)(b) above **26–17** (an "electronic monitoring condition") unless each of the following requirements is fulfilled.

(2) The first requirement is that the person has attained the age of twelve years.

(3) The second requirement is that—

(a) the person is charged with or has been convicted of a violent or sexual offence, or an offence punishable in the case of an adult with imprisonment for a term of fourteen years or more; or

(b) he is charged with or has been convicted of one or more imprisonable offence which, together with any other imprisonable offences of which he has been convicted in any proceedings—

    (i) amount, or

    (ii) would, if he were convicted of the offences with which he is charged, amount,

to a recent history of repeatedly committing imprisonable offences while remanded on bail or to local authority accommodation.

(4) The third requirement is that the court—

(a) has been notified by the Secretary of State that electronic monitoring arrangements are available in each petty sessions area which is a relevant area; and

(b) is satisfied that the necessary provision can be made under those arrangements.

(5) The fourth requirement is that a youth offending team has informed the court that in its opinion the imposition of such a condition will be suitable in the person's case.

(6) Where a court imposes an electronic monitoring condition, the condition shall include provision for making a person responsible for the monitoring; and a person who is made so responsible shall be of a description specified in an order made by the Secretary of State.

Thus, the court must consider the following questions when considering the use of **26–18** electronic monitoring:

(1) Is the youth aged 12–16?

(2) Is the offence a violent or sexual offence? OR

(3) Does it carry a punishment of fourteen years or more in the case of an adult offender? OR

(4) Is the defendant charged with or convicted of one or more imprisonable offences which together with any other imprisonable offences which relate to the defendant amounts to or would amount to a recent history of repeatedly committing imprisonable offences whilst remanded on bail or remanded to local authority accommodation?

(iii) Security requirement

Children and Young Persons Act 1969, s.23(4)–(5A), (6), (7A)–(8)

23.—(4) Subject to subsections (5) and (5A) below, a court remanding a person to local **26–19** authority accommodation may, after consultation with the designated authority, require that authority to comply with a security requirement, that is to say, a requirement that the person in question be placed and kept in secure accommodation.

(5) A court shall not impose a security requirement except in respect of a child who has attained the age of twelve, or a young person, who (in either case) is of a prescribed description, and then only if—

(a) he is charged with or has been convicted of a violent or sexual offence, or an offence punishable in the case of an adult with imprisonment for a term of fourteen years or more; or

(b) he is charged with or has been convicted of one or more imprisonable offences which, together with any other imprisonable offences of which he has been convicted in any proceedings—

    (i)   amount, or

    (ii)   would, if he were convicted of the offences with which he is charged, amount,

to a recent history of repeatedly committing imprisonable offences while remanded on bail or to local authority accommodation,

and (in either case) the condition set out in subsection (5AA) below is satisfied.

(5AA) The condition mentioned in subsection (5) above is that the court is of the opinion, after considering all the options for the remand of the person, that only remanding him to local authority accommodation with a security requirement would be adequate—

    (a)   to protect the public from serious harm from him; or

    (b)   to prevent the commission by him of imprisonable offences.

(5A) A court shall not impose a security requirement in respect of a child or young person who is not legally represented in the court unless—

    (a)   he was granted a right to representation funded by the Legal Services Commission as part of the Criminal Defence Service but the right was withdrawn because of his conduct or because it appeared that his financial resources were such that he was not eligible to be granted such a right;

    (aa)   he applied for such representation and the application was refused because it appeared that his financial resources were such that he was not eligible to be granted a right to it; or

    (b)   having been informed of his right to apply for such representation and had the opportunity to do so, he refused or failed to apply.

(6) Where a court imposes a security requirement in respect of a person, it shall be its duty—

    (a)   to state in open court that it is of such opinion as is mentioned in subsection (5AA) above; and

    (b)   to explain to him in open court and in ordinary language why it is of that opinion;

and a magistrates' court shall cause a reason stated by it under paragraph (b) above to be specified in the warrant of commitment and to be entered in the register.

(7A) Where a person is remanded to local authority accommodation and a security requirement is imposed in respect of him—

    (a)   the designated local authority may, with the consent of the Secretary of State, arrange for the person to be detained, for the whole or any part of the period of the remand or committal, in a secure training centre; and

    (b)   his detention there pursuant to the arrangements shall be lawful.

(7B) Arrangements under subsection (7A) above may include provision for payments to be made by the authority to the Secretary of State.

(8) Where a court imposes on a person any such conditions as are mentioned in subsection (7) above, it shall be its duty to explain to him in open court and in ordinary language why it is imposing those conditions; and a Magistrates' Court shall cause a reason stated by it under this subsection to be specified in the warrant of commitment and to be entered in the register.

26–20   In *H. (Steven) (Remand: Violent Offences)* [1999] C.L.Y. 1027, the offender was refused bail pending committal for sentence for the offence of taking a vehicle without consent, aggravated by damage caused to another vehicle. The prosecution submitted that the offender should be remanded to a remand centre on account of his having committed a violent offence. The court held that for an offence to be violent it was not necessary that physical harm should have been caused to a person. A collision with a car with people in it, in the circumstances of the offence, could lead to injury to a person. Hence this was a violent offence and remand to a remand centre was appropriate.

Thus the relevant questions for the court when considering the imposition of a security requirement are:

    (1)   Is the youth aged 12–14, or a girl aged 15–16?

    (2)   Is the offence a violent or sexual offence? OR

    (3)   An offence punishable in the case of an adult with a term of imprisonment for fourteen years or more? OR

(4) Is the defendant charged with or convicted of 1 or more imprisonable offences which together with any other imprisonable offences which relate to the defendant amounts to or would amount to a recent history of repeatedly committing imprisonable offences while remanded on bail ore remanded to local authority accommodation? AND

(5) Is the court of the opinion that only remanding the defendant to local authority accommodation with a security requirement would be adequate to protect the public from serious harm from him or to prevent the commission by him of imprisonable offences? AND

(6) Is the defendant legally represented?

The court may only impose a security requirement following consultation with the **26–21** designated local authority, the length of consultation being that which is reasonably practicable in all the circumstances of the case: section 23(13)(b) of the 1969 Act. The court imposing the security requirement must also state in open court and explain to the youth in ordinary language why it is of the opinion that a security requirement is necessary.

(c) *Male defendants who are aged 15 or 16 years*

The options available to a court dealing with a male youth aged 15 or 16 are the **26–22** same as those available for dealing with defendants aged 12 to 14 and 15 and 16-year-old females. However, section 23 of the *Children and Young Persons Act* 1969 is modified in relation to male youths of 15 or 16 years. The effect of these modifications is that the defendant will be remanded to local authority accommodation unless the court considers him to be an offender to whom section 23(5), as modified, applies.

The modification of section 23 was effected by section 98(2)–(6) of the *Crime and Disorder Act* 1998, as amended by section 130 of the *Criminal Justice and Police Act* 2001. The modified statute reads:

Children and Young Persons Act 1969, s.23

Remands and committals to local authority accommodation
    23.—(1) Where—   **26–23**
    (a) a court remands a child or young person charged with or convicted of one or more offences or commits him for trial or sentence; and
    (b) he is not released on bail,
the remand or committal shall be to local authority accommodation; and in the following provisions of this section, any reference (however expressed) to a remand shall be construed as including a reference to a committal.

(2) A court remanding a person to local authority accommodation shall designate the local authority who are to receive him; and that authority shall be—
    (a) in the case of a person who is being looked after by a local authority, that authority; and
    (b) in any other case, the local authority in whose area it appears to the court that he resides or the offence or one of the offences was committed.

(3) Where a person is remanded to local authority accommodation, it shall be lawful for any person acting on behalf of the designated authority to detain him.

(4) Where a court, after consultation with a probation officer, a social worker of a local authority social services department or a member of a youth offending team, declares a person to be one to whom subsection (5) below applies—
    (a) it shall remand him to local authority accommodation and require him to be placed and kept in secure accommodation, if—
        (i) it also, after such consultation, declares him to be a person to whom subsection (5A) below applies; and
        (ii) it has been notified that secure accommodation is available for him;
    (b) it shall remand him to a remand centre, if paragraph (a) above does not apply and it has been notified that such a centre is available for the reception from the court of persons to whom subsection (5) below applies; and

(c) it shall remand him to a prison, if neither paragraph (a) nor paragraph (b) above applies.

(4A) A court shall not declare a person who is not legally represented in the court to be a person to whom subsection (5) below applies unless—

(a) he applied for legal aid and the application was refused on the ground that it did not appear his means were such that he required assistance; or

(b) having been informed of his right to apply for legal aid and had the opportunity to do so, he refused or failed to apply.

(5) This subsection applies to a person who—

(a) is charged with or has been convicted of a violent or sexual offence, or an offence punishable in the case of an adult with imprisonment for a term of fourteen years or more; or

(b) has a recent history of absconding while remanded to local authority accommodation, and is charged with or has been convicted of an imprisonable offence alleged or found to have been committed while he was so remanded,

if (in either case) the court is of the opinion that only remanding him to a remand centre or prison, or to local authority accommodation with a requirement that he be placed and kept in secure accommodation, would be adequate to protect the public from serious harm from him.

(5AA) The condition mentioned in subsection (5) above is that the court is of the opinion, after considering all the options for the remand of the person, that only remanding him to local authority accommodation with a security requirement would be adequate—

(a) to protect the public from serious harm from him; or

(b) to prevent the commission by him of imprisonable offences.

(5A) This subsection applies to a person if the court is of opinion that, by reason of his physical or emotional immaturity or a propensity of his to harm himself, it would be undesirable for him to be remanded to a remand centre or a prison.

(6) Where a court declares a person to be one to whom subsection (5) above applies, it shall be its duty—

(a) to state in open court that it is of such opinion as is mentioned in subsection (5AA) above; and

(b) to explain to him in open court and in ordinary language why it is of that opinion; and a Magistrates' Court shall cause a reason stated by it under paragraph (b) above to be specified in the warrant of commitment and to be entered in the register.

(7) Subject to section 23AA below, a court remanding a person to local authority accommodation without imposing a security requirement (that is to say a requirement imposed under subsection (4)(a) above that the person be placed and kept in secure accommodation) may, after consultation with the designated authority, require that person to comply with

(a) any such conditions as could be imposed under section 3(6) of the *Bail Act* 1976 if he were then being granted bail; and

(b) any conditions imposed for the purpose of securing the electronic monitoring of his compliance with any other condition imposed under this subsection.

(7A) Where a person is remanded to local authority accommodation and a security requirement is imposed in respect of him—

(a) the designated local authority may, with the consent of the Secretary of State, arrange for the person to be detained, for the whole or any part of the period of the remand or committal, in a secure training centre; and

(b) his detention there pursuant to the arrangements shall be lawful.

(7B) Arrangements under subsection (7A) above may include provision for payments to be made by the authority to the Secretary of State.

(8) Where a court imposes on a person any such conditions as are mentioned in subsection (7) above, it shall be its duty to explain to him in open court and in ordinary language why it is imposing those conditions; and a magistrates' court shall cause a reason stated by it under this subsection to be specified in the warrant of commitment and to be entered in the register.

(9) A court remanding a person to local authority accommodation without imposing a security requirement may after consultation with the designated authority impose on that authority requirements—

(a) for securing compliance with any conditions imposed on that person under subsection (7) above; or

(b) stipulating that he shall not be placed with a named person.

(9A) Where a person is remanded to local authority accommodation without the imposition of a security requirement, a relevant court may, on the application of the designated authority, declare him to be a person to whom subsection (5) above applies; and on its doing so, subsection (4) above shall apply.

[Subsections (10)–(14) unchanged by the modifications.]

Hence the relevant questions for the court when considering whether to remand the **26–24** defendant in local authority accommodation or custody are:

(1) Is the youth a male aged 15–16?

(2) Is the offence violent or sexual? OR

(3) Is the offence punishable in the case of an adult with imprisonment for a term of 14 years or more? OR

(4) Has the defendant been charged with or convicted of 1 or more imprisonable offences which together with any other imprisonable offences of which he has been convicted in any proceedings amount to or would if he were convicted of the offences with which he has been charged amount to a recent history of repeatedly committing imprisonable offences while remanded on bail or remanded to local authority accommodation? AND

(5) Is the court of the opinion that only remanding the defendant to the local authority accommodation with a security requirement would be adequate to protect the public from serious harm from him or prevent the commission by him of imprisonable offences?

In *R. v. Croydon Youth Court, ex p. Grinham (A Minor), The Times*, May 3, **26–25** 1995, the Court of Appeal held that under section 23(5) a court has to be satisfied that a young person whom it was considering remanding was liable to cause harm that could sensibly be described as serious, on account of the nature of the offence or offences that might be committed, and not merely the risk of repetition. It is not the case that following commission of an offence punishable in the case of an adult with imprisonment for a term of fourteen years or more, the court can conclude that only remanding the offender to a remand centre would be adequate to protect the public from serious harm from him. Leggatt L.J. cited the example of the offence of burglary of a dwelling, stating that such an offence is:

> "not necessarily calculated to cause serious harm if, *e.g.* the burglar is careful only to enter unoccupied houses in daylight and steal television sets. A series of such offences, if apprehended, could not be aggregated so as to render serious such harm as might be caused by them".

The issue of vulnerability was examined in *R. (S.R.) v. Nottingham Magistrates'* **26–26** *Court* (2002) 166 J.P.N. 209. An offender described as emotionally immature, with a limited range of coping strategies such as to render him at greater risk of self-harm should he be placed in a punitive and stressful environment such as a Young Offenders Institution, was found to be vulnerable for the purposes of section 5A of the 1969 Act by the Divisional Court. The court also held that a young person who had been told by justices that they regarded him as vulnerable for remand purposes, had a legitimate expectation that such a conclusion would subsist up until the time of sentencing unless he was told that his status might change or another compelling reason existed to alter his status.

In *R. (M.) v. Inner London Crown Court* (2006) EWHC 2497, Admin, the Court considered an appeal by way of judicial review against the decision of the Crown Court to remand in custody a sixteen-year-old male charged with attempted robbery. The judgment of the Court sets out a structured approach in dealing with the "labyrinthine" provisions of section 23.

(d) *Defendants aged 17 years*

A defendant of either gender aged 17 will be treated in the same way as an adult, **26–27** hence refusal of bail will lead to remand in custody. See *post*, Ch.5 on Bail.

Part V

IV. APPEAL AGAINST REFUSAL OF BAIL: YOUTHS

26–28   Youths have the same rights as adults to appeal against bail decisions. See *post*, Ch.5, § 5–39.

FLOWCHART FOR BAIL DECISION MAKING

```
         ┌─────────────────────────────────────────┐
         │ Representations from Prosecution & Defence │
         │ & Youth Offending Team                     │
         └─────────────────────────────────────────┘
                          │
                          ▼
                 ┌───────────────────────┐
                 │ Are there any fears ?  │
                 └───────────────────────┘
            ┌──────────────┘         └──────────────┐
            ▼                                        ▼
        ┌────────┐                              ┌────────┐
        │   NO   │                              │  YES   │
        └────────┘                              └────────┘
            │                                        │
            │                    ┌───────────────────────────────────────┐
            │                    │ Do    the    Conditions/Bail  Support  │
            │                    │ Package/Electronic Monitoring meet the  │
            │                    │ fears?                                  │
            │                    └───────────────────────────────────────┘
            │                    ┌──────────────┘         └──────────────┐
            │                    ▼                                        ▼
            │                ┌────────┐                              ┌────────┐
            │                │  YES   │                              │   NO   │
            │                └────────┘                              └────────┘
            │                    │                                        │
            │                    ▼                                        ▼
            │        ┌──────────────────────────┐        ┌──────────────────────────┐
            │        │ Court announces exceptions │        │ Court announces exceptions │
            │        │ and reasons for Conditional │       │ and reasons for Refusal of │
            │        │ Bail                        │       │ BAIL                       │
            │        └──────────────────────────┘        └──────────────────────────┘
            │                    │                                        │
            ▼                    ▼                                        ▼
  ┌────────────────┐  ┌──────────────────────────┐  ┌──────────────────────────┐
  │ Unconditional   │  │ Bail with Conditions that  │  │ Court consulst the YOT on │
  │ Bail            │  │ are Relevant & Enforceable │  │ options:                  │
  └────────────────┘  │ & Proportionate           │  │   • Remand to LAA         │
                      └──────────────────────────┘  │   • Remand to LAA &       │
                                                     │     Conds                 │
                                                     │   • Secure Remand         │
                                                     │   • Remand to Custody     │
                                                     └──────────────────────────┘
```

35

Part V

26–30

**DECISION MAKING PROCESS FOR SECURE REMAND OF 15-16 YR OLDS
BOYS UNDER SEC 23(5) CYPA 1969 (AS AMENDED) BY CJPOA 2001**

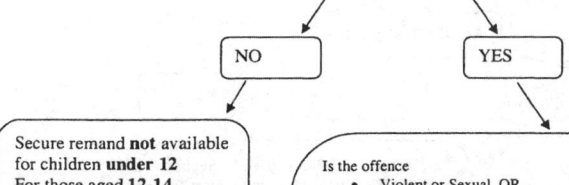

Is the Youth aged 15-16 ?
(BOY)

NO

YES

Secure remand **not** available
for children **under 12**
For those aged **12-14,**
specific rules apply- (see
other flowchart)

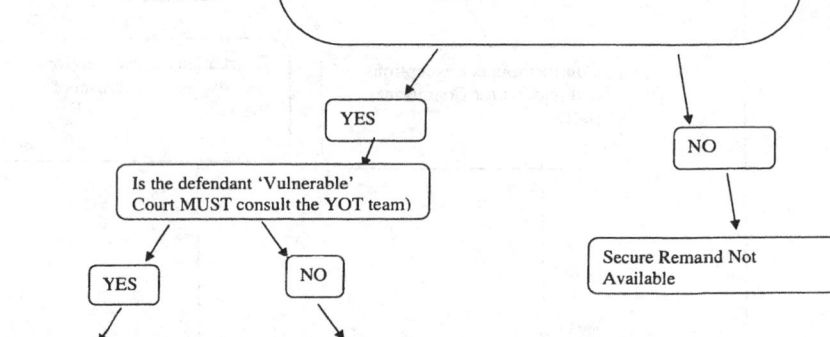

Is the offence
- Violent or Sexual OR
- Does it carry 14 years or more OR
- is the defendant charged with or convicted of 1 or more
  imprisonable offences which together with any other
  imprisonable offences which relate to the defendant amounts to
  or would amount to a **recent history of repeatedly committing
  imprisonable offences while remanded on bail or remanded
  to LAA**

AND :the court is of the opinion that only remanding to LAA with a
security requirement would be adequate –
- to protect the public from serious harm from him; OR
- to prevent the commission by him of imprisonable offences

MUST BE LEGALLY REPRESENTED

YES

NO

Is the defendant 'Vulnerable'
Court MUST consult the YOT team)

Secure Remand Not
Available

YES

NO

Secure Remand to LAA with
Security Requirement "Court
Ordered Secure Remand"

Remand in Custody to a
Remand Centre

**DECISION MAKING PROCESS FOR SECURE REMAND OF 12-14 YR OLDS
BOYS AND 12-16 YEAR OLD GIRLS UNDER SEC 23(5) CYPA 1969 (AS
AMENDED) BY SEC 130 CJPOA 2001**

26–31

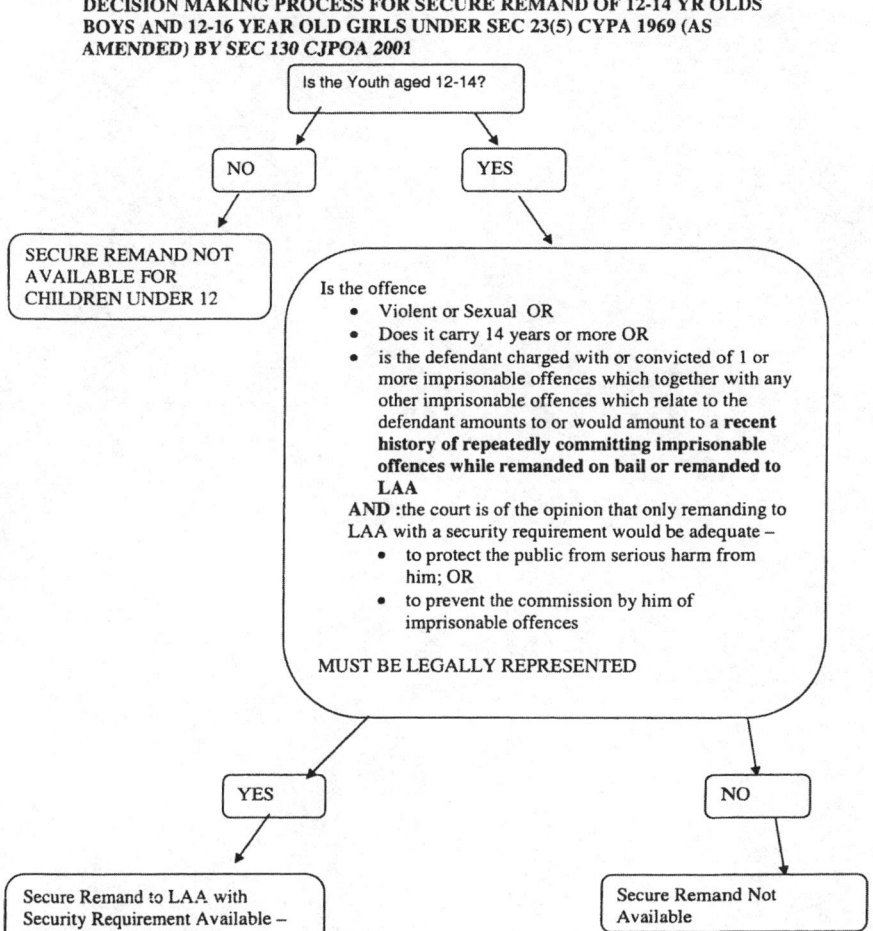

Is the Youth aged 12-14?

NO

YES

SECURE REMAND NOT
AVAILABLE FOR
CHILDREN UNDER 12

Is the offence
- Violent or Sexual OR
- Does it carry 14 years or more OR
- is the defendant charged with or convicted of 1 or
  more imprisonable offences which together with any
  other imprisonable offences which relate to the
  defendant amounts to or would amount to a **recent
  history of repeatedly committing imprisonable
  offences while remanded on bail or remanded to
  LAA**

AND :the court is of the opinion that only remanding to
LAA with a security requirement would be adequate –
- to protect the public from serious harm from
  him; OR
- to prevent the commission by him of
  imprisonable offences

MUST BE LEGALLY REPRESENTED

YES

NO

Secure Remand to LAA with
Security Requirement Available –
Sec 23(5) CYPA 1969 "Court
Ordered Secure Remand"

Secure Remand Not
Available

Part V

CHAPTER 27

SENTENCING IN THE YOUTH COURT

I. INTRODUCTION

The youth court is given wide and flexible powers of sentence. Sentencing young of- **27–1** fenders is a difficult duty, which involves balancing the seriousness of the offence and offending history, against the welfare needs of young offenders, many of whom have led highly disrupted lives. The availability of the various orders set out in this chapter partly depend on the age of the offender. In addition some of the orders can be combined with each other to produce a sentencing "package" specifically designed to meet the needs of individual offenders (see the sentence availability and combination charts, *post*).

The principal aim of the youth justice system is to prevent offending: *Crime and Disorder Act* 1998, s.37 (see *ante*, § 25–2). This is, therefore, the youth courts' principal aim in the sentencing process. The court must also have regard to the welfare principle: *Children and Young Persons Act* 1933, s.44 (see *ante*, § 25–3).

The aim of "preventing offending" may be given a wide interpretation. In *R. v. In-* **27–2** *ner London Crown Court, ex p. N. and S.* [2001] 1 Cr.App.R.(S.) 99 the Divisional Court stated (although the point had not been argued before them) that "in the light of section 37 of the Act (*CDA* 1998—see *ante*) in appropriate cases, the need to impose a deterrent sentence in relation to an offender under the age of 18 may take priority over section 44 of the *Children and Young Person Act* 1933, which requires the court to promote the welfare of the individual offender."

The welfare of young offenders remains a vitally important issue for the youth court to consider. However, the principal aim of the youth justice system is to "prevent offending." The welfare principal is therefore of relevance and importance to the sentencing court in so far as it is consistent with achieving the prevention of offending by the offender.

Part V

II. SENTENCING POWERS

27–3　　Like the adult magistrates' court, the youth court sentencing powers fall into the following categories:

    1. First Tier Penalties
        — absolute and conditional discharge
        — compensation order
        — fine
        — referral order
        — reparation order
    2. Community Penalties
        — attendance centre order
        — action plan order
        — supervision order
        — curfew order
        — community rehabilitation order
        — community punishment order
        — community punishment and rehabilitation order
        — drug treatment and testing order
    3. Custodial Sentence
        — The detention and training order
    4. Ancillary Orders
        — compensation
        — costs
        — anti-social behaviour order
        — parenting order
        — parental bindover

27–4　　Statutory restrictions on imposing community and custodial sentences apply to youths in the same way as they apply to adult offenders.

(1) Statutory restrictions

Criminal Justice Act 2003, s.148(1)–(3)

Restrictions on imposing community sentences

27–5　　　　**148.**—(1) A court must not pass a community sentence on an offender unless it is of the opinion that the offence, or the combination of the offence and one or more offences associated with it, was serious enough to warrant such a sentence.

(2) Where a court passes a community sentence which consists of or includes a community order—

    (a) the particular requirement or requirements forming part of the community order must be such as, in the opinion of the court, is, or taken together are, the most suitable for the offender, and

    (b) the restrictions on liberty imposed by the order must be such as in the opinion of the court are commensurate with the seriousness of the offence, or the combination of the offence and one or more offences associated with it.

(3) Where a court passes a community sentence which consists of or includes one or more youth community orders—

    (a) the particular order or orders forming part of the sentence must be such as, in the opinion of the court, is, or taken together are, the most suitable for the offender, and

    (b) the restrictions on liberty imposed by the order or orders must be such as in the opinion of the court are commensurate with the seriousness of the offence, or the combination of the offence and one or more offences associated with it.

[This act replaces the *Powers of Criminal Courts (Sentencing) Act* 2000, s.35(1)–(3).]

Criminal Justice Act 2003, s.152

General restrictions on imposing discretionary custodial sentences.

152.—(1) This section applies where a person is convicted of an offence punishable with a **27–6** custodial sentence other than one—

    (a) fixed by law; or

    (b) falling to be imposed under section 51A(2) of the *Firearms Act* 1968 (c. 27), under section 110(2) or 111(2) of the *Sentencing Act*, under section 29(4) or (6) of the *Violent Crime Reduction Act* 2006 or under any of sections 225 to 228 of this Act.

(2) The court must not pass a custodial sentence unless it is of the opinion that the offence, or the combination of the offence and one or more offences associated with it, was so serious that neither a fine alone nor a community sentence can be justified for the offence.

(3) Nothing in subsection (2) prevents the court from passing a custodial sentence on the offender if—

    (a) he fails to express his willingness to comply with a requirement which is proposed by the court to be included in a community order and which requires an expression of such willingness, or

    (b) he fails to comply with an order under section 161(2) (pre-sentence drug testing).

[This act replaces the *Powers of Criminal Courts (Sentencing) Act* 2000, s.79(1)–(3)(b).]

Powers of Criminal Courts (Sentencing) Act 2000, s.151(1)–(2)

Effect of previous convictions and of offending while on bail.

151.—(1) In considering the seriousness of any offence, the court may take into account any **27–7** previous convictions of the offender or any failure of his to respond to previous sentences.

(2) In considering the seriousness of any offence committed while the offender was on bail, the court shall treat the fact that it was committed in those circumstances as an aggravating factor.

In coming to its decision as to an appropriate sentence therefore, the youth court **27–8** must take, as its starting point the seriousness of the offence and/or offences associated with it, including any aggravating or mitigating factors. In assessing the seriousness of the offence the court must take into account the offender's criminal record.

Powers of Criminal Courts (Sentencing) Act 2000, s.152(1)–(2)

Reduction in sentences for guilty pleas.

152.—(1) In determining what sentence to pass on an offender who has pleaded guilty to an **27–9** offence in proceedings before that or another court, a court shall take into account—

    (a) the stage in the proceedings for the offence at which the offender indicated his intention to plead guilty; and

    (b) the circumstances in which this indication was given.

(2) If, as a result of taking into account any matter referred to in subsection (1) above the court imposes a punishment on the offender which is less severe than the punishment it would otherwise have imposed, it shall state in open court that it has done so.

If the offender has pleaded guilty he is entitled to be given credit for his plea and **27–10** that may be reflected in the sentence he receives.

In *Christopher Pitt* [2002] 1 Cr.App.R.(S.) 46 the Court of Appeal dealt with an appeal against an 18-months' detention and training order made against a 17-year-old defendant. The grounds of the appeal were that insufficient credit had been given to the appellant for his plea of guilty and also time he had spent in custody on remand. The Court of Appeal reduced the appellant's sentence to 12 months, that being the next "step down" from the 18-month sentence originally imposed.

(2) Procedure

The court will hear mitigation put forward by the defence. In the youth court, such **27–11** mitigation will inevitably refer to the contents of a pre-sentence report.

Written reports on defendants in the youth court are usually prepared by the YOT on the order of the court. Such reports play a vitally important role in the sentencing process. The court will indicate the type of penalty it has in mind on ordering the report. A report dealing with the offender's suitability for community penalties may be requested. Alternatively the court may indicate a specified penalty that it has in mind. If the court is considering a community penalty it must be satisfied that the offence or offences are serious enough to justify that type of penalty.

If the court considers that the offence or offences are so serious that a custodial sentence may be justified a full pre-sentence report will be ordered which must deal with the offender's suitability for such a order.

27–12 The contents of pre-sentence reports are governed by national standards. Such reports should include an analysis of the offence, an assessment of the offender, an assessment of his/her risk of re-offending and risk to the community, and a conclusion which may include a recommendation for the court's consideration. The court will expect the young offender, his parents, and his legal representative to be aware of the contents of any report that the YOT has prepared before the sentencing hearing begins.

This section will now go on to describe each of the various sentences the youth court has power to impose.

27–13

Sentencing Availability Matrix

Order/Age	10 to 11 years	12 to 13 years	14 years	15 years	16 to 17 years
Absolute Discharge	√	√	√	√	√
Referral Order	3 to 12 months	3 to 12 months	3 to 12 months	3 to 12 months	3 to 12 months
Conditional Discharge	Max. 3 year	Max. 3 year	Max. 3 year	Max. 3 year	Max. 3 year
Fine	Max. £250	Max. £250	Max. £1000	Max. £100	Max. £1000
Reparation Order	Max. 24 hours	Max. 24 hours	Max. 24 hours	Max. 24 hours	Max. 24 hours
Action Plan Order	3 months	3 months	3 months	3 months	3 months
Attendance Centre	Max. 12 hours	Max. 12 hours	Max. 24 hours	Max. 24 hours	Max. 36 hours
Supervision Order	Max. 3 year	Max. 3 year	Max. 3 year	Max. 3 year	Max. 3 year
Community Rehabilitation Order	×	×	×	×	6 months to 3 years
Community Punishment Order	×	×	×	×	40 to 240 hours
Community Rehabilitation & Punishment Order	×	×	×	×	1 to 3 years/40 to 100 hours
Curfew Order	3 months; 2 to 12 hours daily	3 months; 2 to 12 hours daily	3 months; 2 to 12 hours daily	3 months; 2 to 12 hours daily	6 months; 2 to 12 hours daily
Drug Treatment & Testing Order	×	×	×	×	6 months to 3 years
Detention & Training Order	×	4, 6, 8, 10, 12, 18, 24 months (if persistent)	4, 6, 8, 10, 12, 18, 24 months (if persistent)	4, 6, 8, 10, 12, 18, 24 months	4, 6, 8, 10, 12, 18, 24 months

27–14

Youth Court Sentence Compatibility Table

	A.D.	C.D.	Fine	Costs	Comp.	Refer Order	Parenting Order	Rep. Order	A.P.O.	Super.	ACO	CRO	CPO	CRO/CPO	Curfew	DTTO	DTO
A.D.			√		√		√										
C.D.			√	√			√										
Fine				√	√		√										
Costs	√	√	√		√	√	√	√	√	√	√	√	√	√	√	√	√
Comp	√	√	√	√		√	√	√	√	√	√	√	√	√	√	√	√
Refer. Order				√	√												
Parenting Order	√	√	√					√	√	√	√	√	√	√	√	√	√
Rep. Order				√	√		√										
Action Plan				√	√		√										
Super.				√	√		√								√		
ACO				√	√		√								√		
CRO				√	√		√								√		
CPO				√	√		√								√		
CRO/CPO				√	√		√								√		
Curfew				√	√		√		√	√	√	√	√	√			
DTTO				√	√		√		√	√	√	√	√	√			
DTO				√	√		√										

III. ABSOLUTE AND CONDITIONAL DISCHARGES

(1) Purpose and effect

Powers of Criminal Courts (Sentencing) Act 2000, s.12

Absolute and conditional discharge

12.—(1) Where a court by or before which a person is convicted of an offence (not being an **27–15**
offence the sentence for which is fixed by law or falls to be imposed under section 110(2) or
111(2) below, section 51A(2) of the *Firearms Act* 1968, section 225, 226, 227 or 228 of the
Criminal Justice Act 2003 or section 29(4) or (6) of the *Violent Crime Reduction Act* 2006) is
of the opinion, having regard to the circumstances including the nature of the offence and the
character of the offender, that it is inexpedient to inflict punishment, the court may make an order either—

    (a) discharging him absolutely; or

    (b) if the court thinks fit, discharging him subject to the condition that he commits
        no offence during such period, not exceeding 3 years from the date of the order
        as may be specified in the order.

(2) Subsection (1)(b) above has effect subject to section 66(4) of the *Crime and Disorder
Act* 1998 (effect of reprimands and warnings).

    (3)–(7) [*omitted*]

(2) Reprimands and warnings

Crime and Disorder Act 1998, ss.65, 66

Reprimands and warnings

65.—(1) Subsections (2) to (5) below apply where—   **27–16**

    (a) a constable has evidence that a child or young person (the offender) has commit-
        ted an offence;

    (b) the constable considers that the evidence is such that, if the offender were prose-
        cuted for the offence, there would be a realistic prospect of his being convicted;

    (c) the offender admits to the constable that he committed the offence;

    (d) the offender has not previously been convicted of an offence; and

    (e) the constable is satisfied that it would not be in the public interest for the offender
        to be prosecuted.

(2) Subject to subsection (4) below, the constable may reprimand the offender if the offender has not previously been reprimanded or warned.

(3) The constable may warn the offender if—

    (a) the offender has not previously been warned; or

    (b) where the offender has previously been warned, the offence was committed more
        than 2 years after the date of the previous warning and the constable considers
        the offence to be not so serious as to require a charge to be brought;
but no person may be warned under paragraph (b) above more than once.

(4) Where the offender has not been previously reprimanded, the constable shall warn
rather than reprimand the offender if he considers the offence to be so serious as to
require a warning.

(5) The constable shall—

    (a) give any reprimand or warning at a police station and, where the offender is
        under the age of 17, in the presence of an appropriate adult; and

    (b) explain to the offender and, where he is under that age, the appropriate adult in
        ordinary language—

        (i) in the case of a reprimand, the effect of subsection (5)(a) of section 66
          below; and

        (ii) in the case of a warning, the effect of subsections (1), (2), (4) and (5)(b) and
          (c) of that section, and any guidance issued under subsection (3) of that
          Section.

    (6)–(9) [*omitted*]

Part V

Effect of reprimands and warnings

27–17   **66.**—(1)–(3) [*omitted*]

(4) Where a person who has been warned under section 65 above is convicted of an offence committed within 2 years of the warning, the court by or before which he is so convicted—

    (a) shall not make an order under subsection (1) (b) (conditional discharge) of section 12 of the *Powers of Criminal Courts (Sentencing) Act* 2000 in respect of the offence unless it is of the opinion that there are exceptional circumstances relating to the offence or the offender which justify its doing so; and

    (b) where it does so, shall state in open court that it is of that opinion and why it is.

(5)–(6) [*omitted*]

27–18   The youth court may order the absolute discharge of an offender if, after assessing the seriousness of the case and taking into account personal mitigation, it is of the opinion that punishment is inappropriate.

If the youth court is of the view that immediate punishment is inappropriate providing the offender does not re-offend, it may discharge the offender on condition that he he/she does not re-offend for a period of a maximum of three years.

(3) Breach

27–19   If the offender does re-offend within the period of that conditional discharge he will be in breach of that order and will be liable to be sentenced for the original offence as well as being sentenced for the new offence that he has committed.

The use of orders of conditional discharge is restricted for young offenders. If the offender commits an offence within two years of receiving a warning under section 65, above, the youth court shall not make an order of conditional discharge unless it is of the opinion that there are exceptional circumstances which either relate to the offence or the offender which justify such an order. There is no definition in statute or case law as to what circumstances might be regarded as "exceptional" under this section.

(4) Conditional discharge orders

27–20   Conditional discharge orders used to be frequently imposed by the youth court, especially upon those falling to be sentenced by the court for the first time. However, this category of offender now usually falls to be dealt with by way of a referral order.

It should be noted that an order of absolute discharge may be made in respect of an offender who would otherwise be made the subject of a referral order under *PCC(S)A* 2000, s.16.

IV. REFERRAL ORDERS

(1) Purpose and effect

Powers of Criminal Courts (Sentencing) Act 2000, s.16

Duty and power to refer certain young offenders to youth offender panels

27–21   **16.**—(1) This section applies where a youth court or other magistrates' court is dealing with a person aged under 18 for an offence and—

    (a) neither the offence nor any connected offence is one for which the sentence is fixed by law;

    (b) the court is not in respect of the offence or any connected offence, proposing to impose a custodial sentence on the offender or make a hospital order in his case; and

    (c) the court is not proposing to discharge him absolutely in respect of the offence.

(2) If—

    (a) the compulsory referral conditions are satisfied in accordance with section 17 below; and

(b) referral is available to the court,

the court shall sentence the offender for the offence by ordering him to be referred to a youth offender panel.

(3) If—

(a) the discretionary referral conditions are satisfied in accordance with section 17 below; and

(b) referral is available to the court,

the court may sentence the offender for the offence by ordering him to be referred to a youth offender panel.

(4) For the purposes of this part an offence is connected with another if the offender falls to be dealt with for it at the same time as he is dealt with for the other offence (whether or not he is convicted of the offences at the same time or by or before the same court).

(5)–(7) [*omitted*]

Referral orders are a mandatory sentence for young offenders appearing before a **27–22** youth or magistrates' court for the first time. On making such an order, the defendant is referred to a youth offender panel.

The referral order must—

(a) specify the youth offending team responsible for implementing the order;

(b) require the offender to attend each meeting of a youth offender panel to be established by the team for the offender; and

(c) specify the period for which any youth offender contract taking effect between the offender and the panel is to have effect being a period of not less than 3 months nor more than 12 months.

The panel consists of a YOT officer and two community volunteers who are not members of a YOT. It is the defendant's responsibility to attend the panel. One of the main purposes of a referral order is for the panel to engage in a dialogue with the young offender and his parents or guardian. The panel is not a court and formalities are kept to a minimum. To this end, on making a referral order the youth court shall make an order requiring at least one parent or guardian to attend meetings with the YOT unless the court considers that it would be unreasonable to make such an order.

At the meetings members of the panel will speak to the defendant and his family. The aims of the panel are to stop further offending, help the offender right the wrong he did to his victim, and help the offender with any problems he might have. To this end they will discuss with him why he committed the crime in question. They will speak to him about other relevant aspects of his life. The victim may well be present at one or more of the meetings. The panel will then agree with the defendant a youth offender contract, which is a programme of behaviour aimed at preventing re-offending. It is for the sentencing court to specify the length of the contract which can be from 3 to 12 months duration. It is for the panel (and not the court) to agree the terms of the youth offender contract.

If the referral conditions set out in section 17(1), *post*, are satisfied the court must **27–23** make a referral order if the offence is an imprisonable one.

Powers of Criminal Courts (Sentencing) Act 2000, s.17(1)

The referral conditions

17.—(1) For the purposes of section 16(2) above the compulsory referral conditions are satis- **27–24** fied in relation to an offence if the offender—

(a) pleads guilty to the offence and to any connected offence;

(b) has never been convicted by or before a court in the United Kingdom of any offence other than the offence and any connected offence; and

(c) has never been bound over in criminal proceedings in England and Wales or Northern Ireland to keep the peace or be of good behaviour.

A referral order cannot be made unless the offender pleads guilty to the offence with **27–25** which he is charged. The order is clearly designed to encourage young people to admit their guilt by restricting the courts powers of sentence and allowing the conviction to become "spent" at an earlier stage.

Rehabilitation of Offenders Act 1974, s.5(4B)

27–26   **5.**—(4B) Where in respect of a conviction a referral order (within the meaning of the *Powers of Criminal Courts (Sentencing) Act* 2000 is made in respect of the person convicted, the rehabilitation period applicable to the sentence shall be—

  (a) if a youth offender contract takes effect under section 23 of that Act between him and a youth offender panel, the period beginning with the date of conviction and ending on the date when (in accordance with section 24 of that Act) the contract ceases to have effect;

  (b) if no such contract so takes effect, the period beginning with the date of conviction and having the same length as the period for which such a contract would (ignoring any order under paragraph 11 or 12 of Schedule 1 to that Act) have had any effect had one so taken effect.

(2) Referral orders and binding over

27–27   If a defendant has been convicted or bound over by or before a court in the UK he cannot be made the subject of a referral order. It should be noted that the existence of cautions, reprimands or final warnings do not prevent a referral order being made. The only circumstances in which the court may not make a referral order is if it considers the offence to be of such a nature that an absolute discharge is appropriate, or it considers the offence to be so serious that a custodial sentence is appropriate.

(3) Discretionary referral conditions

Powers of Criminal Courts (Sentencing) Act 2000, s.17(2)

The Discretionary Referral Conditions
27–28   **17.**—(2) For the purposes of section 16(3) above the discretionary referral conditions are satisfied in relation to an offence if—

  (a) the offender is being dealt with by the court for an offence and one or more connected offences whether or not any of them is an offence punishable with imprisonment;

  (b) although he pleaded guilty to at least one of the offences mentioned in paragraph (a) above he also pleaded not guilty to at least one of them;

  (c) he has never been convicted by or before a court in the United Kingdom of any offence other than the offences mentioned in paragraph (a) above; and

  (d) he has never been bound over in criminal proceedings in England and Wales or Northern Ireland to keep the peace or be of good behaviour.

27–29   If section 17(2) is satisfied, the court has a discretion whether or not to make a referral order.

This section now also applies if the offender has pleaded guilty to a non-imprisonable offence.

27–30   The distinction between imprisonable and non-imprisonable offences in relation to referral orders applies to those sentenced on and after August 18, 2003. If the court decides not to make a referral order in respect of a non-imprisonable offence it may impose any other sentence which it has the power to impose.

Where the first time offender is charged with a mix of imprisonable and non-imprisonable offences and in other respects qualifies for a referral order and the court make a referral order in respect of the imprisonable offences, it must also make a referral order in respect of the non-imprisonable offences.

On making a referral order the court must nominate the appropriate YOT responsible for the defendant. If the defendant is under 16 years of age the court must include a requirement that at least one of his parents attend the meetings with the youth offender panel.

On making a referral order the court can also make orders for compensation, forfeiture and deprivation and costs. The court may make a parenting order when making a referral order: *CJA* 2003, Sched. 34.

If the court is minded to make a parenting order with a referral order, it must first obtain and consider a report from the YOT, a local authority social worker, or a probation officer dealing with the need for such an order and what requirements might be included.

(4) Breach of referral order

The youth offender panel may refer an offender back to the youth court on the basis **27–31** that he/she has failed to comply with the referral order and the subsequent youth offender contract. The court must then cause the offender to appear before it by issuing a summons or, if the report is substantiated on oath, a warrant. If, at the subsequent hearing, the court is satisfied that the offender has breached the referral order, it may revoke that order and go on to deal with the offender in any other way he/she could have been dealt with for that offence by the court that made the order. In such circumstances the court will often be assisted by information from the YOT regarding the extent of the offender's compliance with the referral order and the circumstances of his referral back to the court. A written report from the YOT might also suggest an appropriate order to make on re-sentencing.

If on making a referral order a court requires that a parent/guardian attend panel meetings, and he/she fails to do so, the panel may:

(a) refer the parent/guardian to the youth court who may issue a summons to him/her to appear before that court; and

(b) may then make a parenting order if satisfied that the parent/guardian has failed without reasonable cause to comply with the requirement and that a parenting order would be desirable in the interests of preventing the commission of further offences by the offender.

(5) Further convictions during referral

Powers of Criminal Courts (Sentencing) Act 2000, Sched. 1, Pt II, paras 10–12

Extension of referral for further offences
10.—(1) Paragraphs 11 and 12 below apply where, at a time when an offender aged **27–32** under 18 is subject to referral, a youth court or other magistrates' court is dealing with him for an offence in relation to which paragraphs (a) to (c) of section 16(1) of this Act are applicable.

(2) But paragraphs 11 and 12 do not apply unless the offenders compliance period is less than 12 months.

Extension where further offences committed pre-referral
11. If— **27–33**
(a) the occasion on which the offender was referred back to the panel is the only other occasion on which it has fallen to a court in the United Kingdom to deal with the offender for any offence or offences, and
(b) the offender committed the offence mentioned in paragraph 10 above, and any connected offence, before he was referred to the panel,
the relevant court many sentence the offender for the offence by making an order extending his compliance period.

Extension where further offence committed after referral
12.—(1) If— **27–34**
(a) paragraph 11(a) above applies, but
(b) the offender committed the offence mentioned in paragraph 10 above or any connected offence, after he was referred to the panel,
the relevant court may sentence the offender for the offence by making an order extending his compliance period but only if the requirements of sub-paragraph (2) below are complied with.

(2) Those requirements are that the court must—

(a) be satisfied, on the basis of a report made to it by the relevant body that there are exceptional circumstances which indicate that, even though the offender has re-offended since being referred to the panel, extending his compliance period is likely to help prevent further re-offending by him; and

(b) state in open court that it is so satisfied and why it is.

(3) In sub paragraph (2) above "the relevant body" means the panel to which the offender has been referred, or if no contact has yet taken effect between the offender and the panel under section 23 of this Act, the specified team.

Paragraphs 10, 11 and 12 above deal with the situation where the offender has been further convicted during the course of his referral order. These paragraphs allow the original referral order to be extended in respect of the new offence. However, it should be noted that orders made under paragraphs 11 or 12 above must not extend the offender's referral order so as to cause it to exceed 12 months.

27–35   There are two scenarios. Under paragraph 11 above, the new offence is committed before the referral order was made. In such a case, the court has discretion to sentence the offender for the offence by making an order extending the compliance period, as long as it does not exceed 12 months in total. Under paragraph 12 above a new offence has been committed after the referral order was made. Under these circumstances the court may also extend the existing referral order up to the 12-month limit. However, before doing so the court must be satisfied with those matters set out in paragraph 12(2)(a) and (b), *ante*.

In either scenario, the youth court has discretion as to whether to extend the existing referral order. This will depend on the aggravating and mitigating factors that apply to the new offence. Additionally the court will wish to have a verbal or written report from the YOT indicating the offender's progress on the existing referral order. If the court considers that extending the referral order is inappropriate the offender will be sentenced in some other way for the new offence. This will have implications for the original referral order.

Powers of Criminal Courts (Sentencing) Act 2000 Sched. 1, Pt II, para. 14

Further convictions which lead to revocation of referral

27–36   14.—(1) This paragraph applies where, at a time when an offender is subject to referral, a court in England and Wales deals with him for an offence (whether committed before or after he was referred to the Panel) by making an order other than—

(a) an order under paragraph 11 or 12 above; or

(b) an order discharging him absolutely.

(2) In such a case the order of the court shall have the effect of revoking—

(a) the referral order (or orders); and

(b) any related order (or orders) under paragraph 11 or 12 above.

(3) Where any order is revoked by virtue of sub-paragraph (2) above, the court may, if it appears to the court that it would be in the interests of justice to do so, deal with the offender for the offence in respect of which the revoked order was made in any way which (assuming section 16 of this Act had not applied) he could have been dealt with for that offence by the court which made the order.

(4) When dealing with the offender under sub-paragraph (3) above, the court shall, where a contract has taken effect between the offender and the panel under section 23 of this Act, have regard to the extent of his compliance with the terms of the contract.

V. FINES AND OTHER FINANCIAL PENALTIES

A. FINES

27–37   The amount of a fine imposed by the youth court on a young offender must reflect the seriousness of the offence and the defendant's financial circumstances.

The maximum fine which may be imposed on a youth is dependent upon his age: *PCC(S)A* 2000, s.135, Pt III. The amounts are as follows:

(a) 10–13 years of age inclusive—the maximum fine is £250.

(b) 14–17 years of age inclusive—the maximum fine is £1,000.

Where the fine is imposed on a youth under the age of 16 years, the court is under a duty to order that the fine, compensation or costs awarded, be paid by the parent or guardian of the youth instead of by the youth himself, unless the court is satisfied that:

(a) the parent or guardian cannot be found;

(b) it would be unreasonable to make an order for payment having regard to the circumstances of the case.

Where the youth has attained the age of 16, the court duty to make an order against the parent or guardian is discretionary: *PCC(S)A* 2000, s.137, Pt III.

Before making an order against a parent or guardian the youth court must give such person the opportunity of being heard. If the parent or guardian has not attended, the court must require their attendance. If they fail to attend an order for payment may be made against them in their absence. When a fine or compensation is ordered to be paid by a parent or guardian, their means or financial circumstances must be taken into consideration. If, having imposed a financial penalty, the parent or guardian fails to pay, then enforcement powers will apply in the adult court.

Upon imposing a fine against a young offender the youth court may grant time to pay, fix periodical payments, or make a money payment supervision order. If there is default in payment, the court also has power:

(a) to make an attendance centre order (Attendance Centre—see *post*, §§ 27–45—27–48); or

(b) to order the parent or guardian (who must be given an opportunity to attend) to pay the fine, if the court is satisfied that the offender has had the means to pay the sum or any instalment of it on which he has defaulted and has refused or neglected to pay.

Where the offender is under the age of 18 years the youth court does not have power to fix a term of detention in default of payment of a fine.

B. COMPENSATION

Powers of Criminal Courts (Sentencing) Act 2000, s.137

Power to order parent or guardian to pay fine, costs, compensation or surcharge.

137.—(1) Where—

 (a) a child or young person (that is to say, any person aged under 18) is convicted of any offence for the commission of which a fine or costs may be imposed or a compensation order may be made, and

 (b) the court is of the opinion that the case would best be met by the imposition of a fine or costs or the making of such an order, whether with or without any other punishment, the court shall order that the fine, compensation or costs awarded be paid by the parent or guardian of the child or young person instead of by the child or young person himself, unless the court is satisfied—

  (i) that the parent or guardian cannot be found; or

  (ii) that it would be unreasonable to make an order for payment, having regard to the circumstances of the case.

(1A) Where but for this subsection a court would order a child or young person to pay a surcharge under section 161A of the *Criminal Justice Act* 2003, the court shall order that the surcharge be paid by the parent or guardian of the child or young person instead of by the child or young person himself, unless the court is satisfied—

 (a) that the parent or guardian cannot be found; or

 (b) that it would be unreasonable to make an order for payment, having regard to the circumstances of the case.

(2) Where but for this subsection a court would impose a fine on a child or young person under—

 (a) paragraph 4(1)(a) or 5(1)(a) of Schedule 3 to this Act (breach of curfew, probation, community service, combination or drug treatment and testing order),

27–38

(b) paragraph 2(1)(a) of Schedule 5 to this Act (breach of attendance centre order or attendance centre rules),

(c) paragraph 2(2)(a) of Schedule 7 to this Act (breach of supervision order),

(d) paragraph 2(2)(a) of Schedule 8 to this Act (breach of action plan order or reparation order),

(e) section 104(3)(b) above (breach of requirements of supervision under a detention and training order), or

(f) section 4(3)(b) of the *Criminal Justice and Public Order Act* 1994 (breach of requirements of supervision under a secure training order),

the court shall order that the fine be paid by the parent or guardian of the child or young person instead of by the child or young person himself, unless the court is satisfied—

(i) that the parent or guardian cannot be found; or

(ii) that it would be unreasonable to make an order for payment, having regard to the circumstances of the case.

(3) In the case of a young person aged 16 or over, [subsections (1) to (2)] above shall have effect as if, instead of imposing a duty, they conferred a power to make such an order as is mentioned in those subsections.

(4) Subject to subsection (5) below, no order shall be made under this section without giving the parent or guardian an opportunity of being heard.

(5) An order under this section may be made against a parent or guardian who, having been required to attend, has failed to do so.

(6) A parent or guardian may appeal to the Crown Court against an order under this section made by a magistrates' court.

(7) A parent or guardian may appeal to the Court of Appeal against an order under this section made by the Crown Court, as if he had been convicted on indictment and the order were a sentence passed on his conviction.

(8) In relation to a child or young person for whom a local authority have parental responsibility and who—

(a) is in their care, or

(b) is provided with accommodation by them in the exercise of any functions (in particular those under the *Children Act* 1989) which are social services functions within the meaning of the *Local Authority Social Services Act* 1970,

references in this section to his parent or guardian shall be construed as references to that authority.

(9) In subsection (8) above "local authority" and "parental responsibility" have the same meanings as in the *Children Act* 1989.

27–39   A compensation order may be made against a young offender as a penalty in itself or in addition to other penalties that the court has imposed.

Compensation is governed by section 137 of the *PCC(S)A* 2000. If the youth court decides that the victim of the offence has suffered a loss that deserved to be compensated and that the case would be appropriately dealt with by the imposition of a fine, costs or a compensation order with or without other punishment the court may make a compensation order. If the offender is under 16 the order for payment must be made against the parent or guardian. If over 16, such order may be made against the parent or guardian. The principles for payment and enforcement of a compensation order are similar to those as for a fine.

If a local authority has parental responsibility for a youth who is fined his parent or guardian shall be construed to be a reference to that Authority. Therefore an order for payment of a fine, costs or compensation may be made against such a local authority, unless the court is satisfied that it would be unreasonable to make an order for payment, having regard to the circumstances of the case.

C. Costs

27–40   Costs incurred by the prosecution can be awarded against the defendant and his parents/guardian may be ordered to pay in the same way as for a financial penalty. There is no maximum figure for costs. However, if a fine is imposed as well as costs, the amount of costs ordered by the court cannot exceed the amount of any fine imposed: section 18(5) of the *Prosecution of Offences Act* 1985, see *post*, § 30–22.

VI. REPARATION ORDER

(1) Purpose and effect

Powers of Criminal Courts (Sentencing) Act 2000, s.73

Reparation orders

73.—(1) Where a child or young person (that is to say any person aged under 18) is convicted   **27–41**
of an offence other than one for which the sentence is fixed by law, the court by or before which
he is convicted may make an order requiring him to make reparation specified in the order—

(a) to a person or person so specified; or

(b) to the community at large;

and any person so specified must be a person identified by the court as a victim of the offence or
a person otherwise affected by it.

(2)–(4) [*omitted*]

(5) Before making a reparation order, a court shall obtain and consider a written report
by an officer of a local probation board, a social worker of a local authority or a member of
a youth offending team indicating—

(a) the type of work that is suitable for the offender

and

(b) the attitude of the victim or victims to the requirements proposed to be included
in the order.

(6)–(8) [*omitted*]

Powers of Criminal Courts (Sentencing) Act 2000, s.74(1A)

74.—(1A) The Youth Court has power to make a Reparation order that must not require the   **27–42**
offender to work for more than 24 hours in aggregate or to require the offender to make reparation to any person without the consent of that person (*PCC(S)A* 2000 section 74(1)).

The requirements that the court specifies in a reparation order must be commensurate with the seriousness of the offence or offences that the court is dealing with:
PCC(S)A 2000, s.74(2).

The work to be done under the order will normally be undertaken under the supervision of the youth offending team, and must be completed within three months.

The requirements specified in a reparation order shall, as far as practicable, be such
as to avoid conflict with the offenders religious beliefs or with the requirements of any
community order to which he may be subject and should not cause any interference
with the times at which he attends work, school or any other educational establishment:
PCC(S)A 2000, s.74(3).

The legislation clearly envisages and stresses the importance of victim participation in   **27–43**
the reparation process. If the victim is unwilling to co-operate or cannot be found the
YOT will normally recommend a form of reparation to the community generally.

A reparation order is based on the concept of "restorative justice". Apart from reparation orders, a reparative element is often included as part of an action plan, supervision order, or community rehabilitation order, see *post*, §§ 27–55—27–63.

(2) Breach

Breach, revocation and amendment of reparation orders are dealt with under Sched.   **27–44**
8 of the *PCC(S)A (Sentencing) Act* 2000.

VII. ATTENDANCE CENTRE ORDERS

(1) Purpose and effect

Powers of Criminal Courts (Sentencing) Act 2000, s.60

60. The Youth Court has power to make an attendance centre order in the case of a youth   **27–45**

who has been found guilty of an offence that would be punishable with imprisonment in the case of an adult, or who has failed to comply with the requirements of a curfew order, a probation order, a supervision order, an action plan order or a reparation order.

27–46   An attendance centre order is a community penalty requiring the offender to attend a centre generally run by the police or by the YOT. The aggregate number of hours must not be less than 12 or exceed 36. However this is subject to restrictions relating to different age groups—

(a) A child under 14 years may be ordered to attend for less than 12 hours if the court is of the opinion having regard to his age or any other circumstances, that 12 hours would be excessive. He may not be ordered to attend for more than 12 hours.

(b) For a child under 16 years the court's powers start from a minimum of 12 hours to a maximum of 24 hours.

(c) For a young offender over 16, the court's powers start at 12 hours with a maximum of 36 hours.

27–47   Youths are usually required to attend the centre for two or three hours on alternate Saturdays and participate in a programme of activities. The order cannot be made until the court is satisfied that the specified centre is reasonably accessible to the offender and does not conflict with his religious beliefs, requirements of any other community penalties to which he may be subject and does not interfere with his normal work or education.

The order itself will name the centre and the court will fix the date and time of the offender's first attendance.

Although it is a community penalty, an attendance centre order does not require the preparation of a written report before it is imposed. This means that the court can proceed to sentence in this way with comparative rapidity. However, it may well be that more will need to be known about the circumstances of a young offender before a decision is reached as to the appropriate disposal.

Attendance at an attendance centre may also be a requirement of an action plan order made under *PCC(S)A* 2000, s.69, see *post*, § 27–51. Such a requirement is not an attendance centre order under section 60, *ante*, § 27–45, but is part of an action plan order.

(2) Breach of attendance centre order

27–48   Breach, revocation and amendment of attendance centre orders is dealt with under Schedule 5 to the *PCC(S)A* 2000.

Where an offender who is subject to an attendance centre order made by a youth court appears before either the youth court acting for the area where the attendance centre is situated, or before the youth court that made the attendance centre order, and the court is satisfied that he has failed without reasonable excuse to attend or has committed a breach of the attendance centre rules, that court may, without prejudice to the continuance of the order, impose a fine, or may revoke the attendance centre order and deal with the offender for the offence in respect of which the order was made in any manner in which he could have been dealt with for that offence.

An attendance centre order may be discharged or varied on an application made by the offender or the officer in charge of the attendance centre, the power to discharge includes the power to deal with the offender in any manner in which he could have been dealt with for the original offence.

VIII. ACTION PLAN ORDERS

(1) Purpose and effect

Powers of Criminal Courts (Sentencing) Act 2000, s.69(1)

27–49   69.—(1) Where a child or young person (that is to say, any person aged under 18) is convicted of an offence and the court by or before which he is convicted is of the opinion mentioned in subsection (3) below, the court may (subject to sections 148, 150 and 156 of the *Criminal Justice Act* 2003) make an order which—

    (a) requires the offender for a period of three months beginning with the date of the order, to comply with an action plan, that is to say, a series of requirements with respect to his actions and whereabouts during that period;

    (b) places the offender for that period under the supervision of the responsible officer;

    (c) requires the offender to comply with any directions given by the responsible officer with a view to the implementation of that plan;

and the requirements included in the order, and any directions given by the responsible officer, may include requirements authorised by section 70 below.

Powers of Criminal Courts (Sentencing) Act 2000, s.70(1)

70.—(1) Requirements included in an action plan order, or directions given by a responsible officer, may require the offender to do all or any of the following things namely—   **27–50**

    (a) to participate in activities specified in the requirements or directions at a time or times so specified;

    (b) to present himself to a person or persons specified in the requirements or directions at a place or places and at a time so specified;

    (c) subject to subsection (2) below, to attend at an attendance centre specified in the requirements or directions for a number of hours so specified;

    (d) to stay away from a place or places specified in the requirements or directions;

    (e) to comply with any arrangements for his education specified in the requirements or directions;

    (f) to make reparation specified in the requirements or directions to a person or persons so specified or to the community at large;

    (g) to attend any hearing fixed by the court under section 71 below.

Powers of Criminal Courts (Sentencing) Act 2000, s.69(6)

69.—(6) Before making an action plan order the court must obtain and consider—   **27–51**

    (a) a written report by an officer of a local probation board, a social worker of a local authority or a member of a youth offending team indicating—

        (i) the requirements proposed by that person to be included in the order;

        (ii) the benefit to the offender that the proposed requirements are designed to achieve; and

        (iii) the attitude of a parent or guardian of the offender to the proposed requirements; and

    (b) where the offender is under the age of 16 information about the offender's family circumstances and the likely effect of the order on those circumstances.

An action plan order is a community penalty placing the offender under supervision for a fixed period of three months duration. During that three months the offender will be subject to intense supervision and will be required to do all or any of the things specified in section 70(1) (see *ante*, § 27–50).   **27–52**

The purpose of an action plan is that supervision must be intensive, involving regular meetings with the YOT throughout its duration. The court must set out details of its requirements in its order and carefully explain to the offender his/her obligations. Typical requirements would be for an offender to attend school or training, see a drugs counsellor for advice and assistance, and to meet with his victim and make direct reparation to him or the community at large.

(2) Monitoring the action plan order

Powers of Criminal Courts (Sentencing) Act 2000, s.71

71.—(1) Immediately after making an action plan order a court may—   **27–53**

    (a) fix a hearing for a date not more than 21 days after the making of the order; and

(b) direct the responsible officer to make at that hearing a report as to the effectiveness of the order and the extent to which it has been implemented.

(2) At a hearing fixed under subsection (1) above, the court—

    (a) shall consider the responsible officer's report; and

    (b) may on the application of the responsible officer or the offender, amend the order—

        (i) by cancelling any provision included in it; or

        (ii) by inserting in it (either in addition to or in substitution for any of its provisions) and provision that the court could have originally included in it.

(3) Breach

27–54   The breach, revocation and amendment of action plan orders are dealt with in *Powers of Criminal Courts (Sentencing) Act* 2000, Sched. 8.

IX. SUPERVISION ORDERS

(1) Purpose and effect

Powers of Criminal Courts (Sentencing) Act 2000, s.63(1)

27–55   **63.**—(1) Where a child or young person (that is to say, any person aged under 18) is convicted of an offence, the court by or before which he is convicted may (subject to sections 148, 150 and 156 of the *Criminal Justice Act* 2003) make an order placing him under the supervision of—

    (a) a local authority designated by the order;

    (b) an officer of a local probation board; or

    (c) a member of a youth offending team.

27–56   A supervision order is a community penalty and is available for all youths and for all offences.

A pre-sentence report is required before such an order can be made. The order lasts for a maximum period of three years. There is no minimum period. The effect of the order is to place the offender under the supervision of the youth offending team or a probation officer. The supervising officer shall "advise, assist and befriend the offender". The emphasis of such orders is clearly on preventing offending by securing the rehabilitation of the offender. In order to assist in this process the court is given powers to impose a variety of conditions and requirements.

Powers of Criminal Courts (Sentencing) Act 2000, Sched. 6

27–57   1. A supervision order may require the offender to reside with an individual named in the order who agrees to the requirement, but a requirement imposed by a supervision order in pursuance or this paragraph shall be subject to any requirement of the order as is authorised by paragraph 2, 3, 6, 6A or 7 below.

27–58   2.—(1) Subject to paragraph (2) below, a supervision order may require the offender to comply with any directions given from time to time by the supervisor and requiring him to do all or any of the following things—

    (a) to live at a place or places specified in the directions for a period or periods so specified;

    (b) to present himself to a person or persons specified in the directions at a place or places on a day or days so specified;

    (c) to participate in activities specified in the directions on a day or days so specified.

(2) A supervision order shall not require compliance with directions given by virtue of sub-paragraph (1) above unless the court making it is satisfied that a scheme under section 66 of this Act (local authority schemes) is in force for the area where the offender resides or will reside; and no such directions may involve the use of facilities which are not for the time being specified in a scheme in force under that section for that area.

(3) A requirement imposed by a Supervision order in pursuance of sub-paragraph (1) above shall be subject to any requirement of the order as is authorised by paragraph 6 below (treatment for offender's mental condition).

(4) It shall be for the supervisor to decide—

    (a) whether and to what extent he exercises any power to give directions conferred on him by virtue of sub-paragraph (1) above; and

    (b) the form of any directions.

(5) The total number of days in respect of which an offender may be required to comply with directions given by virtue of paragraphs (a), (b), or (c), of sub-paragraph (1) above shall not exceed 180 or such lesser number, if any, as the order may specify for the purposes of this sub-paragraph.

(6) For the purpose of calculating the total number of days in respect of which such directions may be given the supervisor shall be entitled to disregard any day in respect of which directions were previously given in pursuance of the order and on which the directions were not complied with.

(7) Directions given by the supervisor by virtue of sub-paragraph (1)(b) or (c) above, shall as far as are practicable be such as to avoid—

    (a) any conflict with the offender's religious beliefs or with the requirements of any other youth community order or any community order to which he may be subject; and

    (b) any interference with the times, if any, at which he normally works or attends school or any other educational establishment.

3.—(1) This paragraph applies to a supervision order unless the order requires the of- **27–59** fender to comply with directions given by the supervisor under paragraph 2(1) above.

(2) Subject to the following provisions of this paragraph and paragraph 4 below, a supervision order to which this paragraph applies may require the offender—

    (a) to live at a place or places specified in the order for a period or periods so specified;

    (b) to present himself to a person or person(s) specified in the order at a place or places and on a day or day(s) so specified;

    (c) to participate in activities specified in the order on a day or day(s) so specified;

    (d) to make reparation specified in the order to a person or person(s) so specified or to the community at large;

    (f) to refrain from participating in activities specified in the order—

        (i) on a specified day or days during the period for which the supervision order is in force; or

        (ii) during the whole of that period or a specified portion of it;

    and in this paragraph "make reparation" means make reparation for the offence otherwise than by the payment of compensation.

(3) The total number of days in respect of which an offender may be subject to requirements imposed by virtue of paragraph (a), (b), (c), (d) of sub-paragraph (2) above shall not exceed 180.

(4) The court may not include requirements under sub-paragraph (2) above in a supervision order unless—

    (a) it has first consulted the supervisor as to—

        (i) the offender's circumstances; and

        (ii) the feasibility of securing compliance with the requirements,

    and is satisfied, having regard to the supervisor's report, that it is feasible to secure compliance with them;

    (b) having regard to the circumstances of the case it considers the requirement necessary for securing the good conduct of the offender or for preventing a repetition by him of the same offence or the commission of other offences; and

    (c) if the offender is aged under 16 it has obtained and considered information about his family circumstances and the likely effect of the requirements on those circumstances.

(5) The court shall not by virtue of sub-paragraph (2) above include in a supervision order—

    (a) any requirement that would involve the co-operation of a person other than the supervisor and the offender unless that other person consents to its inclusion;

    (b) any requirement to make reparation to any person unless that person—

        (i) is identified by the court as a victim of the offence or a person otherwise affected by it; and

Part V

(ii) consents to the inclusion of the requirement.

(c) any requirement requiring the offender to reside with a specified individual; or

(d) any such requirement as is mentioned in paragraph 6(2)(treatment for offender's mental condition).

(6) Requirements included in a supervision order by virtue of sub-paragraph (2)(b) or (c) above shall, as far as is practicable be such as to avoid—

(a) any conflict with the offender's religious beliefs or with the requirements of any other youth community order to which he may be subject; and

(b) any interference with the times, if any, at which he normally works or attends school or any other educational establishment;

and sub-paragraphs (7) below are without prejudice to this sub-paragraph.

(7) Subject to sub-paragraph (8) below a supervision order may not by virtue of sub-paragraph (2) above include—

(a) any requirement that would involve the offender in absence from home—

(i) for more than two consecutive nights, or

(ii) for more than two nights in any one week, or

(b) if the offender is of compulsory school age any requirement to participate in activities during normal school hours,

unless the court making the order is satisfied that the facilities whose use would be involved are for the time being specialised in a scheme in force under section 66 of this Act for the area in which the defendant resides or will reside.

(8)–(9) [*omitted*]

(2) Intensive Supervision and Surveillance Programme

27–60   Because of their flexibility supervision orders are used extensively in the youth court for offences of all degrees of gravity. A pre-sentence report is essential not just because it will deal with the offender's personal circumstances, but also because it will set out in detail the precise requirements that the youth offending team will ask the court to impose. These requirements can be complex and it is important that the offender understands precisely what is proposed for him before the hearing begins.

It should be noted that the requirements set out above of residence, specified activities, specified reparation, and presenting him/herself to a specified person can be imposed for a maximum of 90 days. A night restriction order may not be imposed in respect of more than 30 days in all.

An order made under section 3(2)(c)—(specified activities) may also involve participation in the Intensive Supervision and Surveillance Programme (ISSP).

ISSPs are a recently introduced programme which can be attached to a supervision order. The ISSP is not a separate court order and is not created by statute. The ISSP programme can be attached to a supervision order, a community rehabilitation order, as a condition of bail, and as a condition of release into the community half of a detention and training order. The ISSP programme is recognised as an effective way of sentencing young people who are prolific young offenders and who commit serious offences. It is financed by the Youth Justice Board and provided by the youth offending team. The programme involves extremely intense supervision, often backed up by a curfew order and electronic tagging. The maximum effect is to monitor an offender's activities on a 24 hour-per-day basis. For Bail ISSP, see *ante*, § 26–7.

27–61   The programme is available for all youths 10 to 17 years' inclusive. Having been piloted in various areas of England and Wales the ISSP is now available nationally. The programme is seen by the Youth Justice Board as offering the court an alternative to a short detention and training order. To qualify for the ISSP programme the offender must:

(a) be charged with or convicted of an imprisonable offence in the current proceedings;

(b) have been charged with an offence or warned four times in the previous 12 months and must also have been sentenced to a community penalty or custody at any time;

(c) be at risk of a custodial sentence relating to an offence which carries imprisonment of 14 years or more for an adult.

ISSP programmes are limited in availability depending on the resources of each YOT and the demand placed on those resources. Availability, and the offender's suitability for an ISSP programme will be dealt with in the context of a full Pre-Sentence Report ordered by the court.

The ISSP programme may offer the following facilities:

(1) A programme of education or other activities each week day at specified times and places.

(2) Five hours of contact time with the youth offending team each week day.

(3) Electronic surveillance either by electronic tagging or voice recognition or both.

(4) A tracker will be allocated. It is this person's job to track the whereabouts of offender's throughout the week and accompany them to appointments relating to work, education, or any other activities organised by the YOT.

(5) Weekend contact and supervision with the young person.

(6) A curfew order is often suggested by the YOT reinforced with electronic tagging. It should be noted that this must be done by way of a separate curfew order.

If the YOT proposes a supervision order coupled with an ISSP it will provide full **27–62** details to the court in a written report. The ISSP offers the opportunity for very intensive supervision and will therefore be tailored to the needs of the individual offender. If the court wishes to make such an order it must take the following steps:

(1) Make a supervision order for a period commensurate with the seriousness of the offence.

(2) Order a maximum of 180 days of specified activities in accordance with section 63.

(3) Attach to those specified activities the ISSP programme.

(4) If the court is making a community rehabilitation order the maximum number of days of specified activities is 90.

(3) Breach

Breach, revocation and amendment of supervision orders are dealt with under the **27–63** provisions of Schedule 7 to the *PCC(S)A* 2000.

X. COMMUNITY REHABILITATION ORDERS

(1) Purpose and effect

Powers of Criminal Courts (Sentencing) Act 2000, ss.41(1)–(6), 42

41.—(1) Where a person aged 16 or over is convicted of an offence and the court by or **27–64** before which he is convicted is of the opinion that his supervision is desirable in the interests of—

(a) securing his rehabilitation; or

(b) protecting the public from harm from him or preventing the commission by him of further offences,

the court may (subject to sections 34–36) make an order requiring him to be under supervision for a period specified in the order of not less than six months nor more than three years.

(2) An order under subsection (1) above in this Act is referred to as a "community rehabilitation order".

(3) A community rehabilitation order shall specify the petty sessions area in which the offender resides or will reside.

(4) If the offender is aged 18 or over at the time when the community rehabilitation order is made he shall, subject to paragraph 18 of Schedule 3 to this Act (offenders change of area), be required to be under the supervision of a probation officer appointed for or assigned to the petty sessions area specified in the order.

(5) If the offender is aged under 18 at that time, he shall, subject to paragraph 18 of Schedule 3, be required to be under the supervision of—

(a) a probation officer appointed for or assigned to the petty sessions area specified in the order; or

(b) a member of a Youth Offending Team established by a local authority specified in the order;

and if an order specifies a local authority for the purposes of paragraph (b) above, the authority specified must be the local authority within whose area it appears to the court that the offender resides or will reside.

(6) In this Act, "responsible officer", in relation to an offender who is subject to a probation order, means the probation officer or member of a Youth Offending Team responsible for his supervision.

27–65   **42.**—(1) Subject to subsection (3) below, a community rehabilitation order may in addition require the offender to comply during the whole or any part of the Probation period which such requirements as the court, having regard to the circumstances of the case, considers desirable in the interests of—

(a) securing the rehabilitation of the offender; or

(b) protecting the public from harm from him or preventing the commission by him of further offences.

(2) Without prejudice to the generality of subsection (1) above, the additional requirements which may be included in the rehabilitation order shall include the requirements which are authorised by Schedule 2 to this Act.

(3) Without prejudice to the power of the court under section 130 of this act to make a compensation order, the payment of sums by way of damages for injury or compensation for loss shall not be included among the additional requirements of a rehabilitation order.

(2) Procedure

27–66   A community rehabilitation order is a community penalty available to the youth court for offenders who are 16 years or over on the conviction. The order places an offender under the supervision of a probation officer or a member of a YOT. There is, therefore, some overlap between a community rehabilitation order and a supervision order under *PCC(S)A* 2000, s.63, see *ante*, § 27–55. However, the community rehabilitation order is particularly intended for the more mature offender who will benefit from the structured supervision that the community rehabilitation order provides.

27–67   Before making a community rehabilitation order (CRO), the youth court is required to obtain a pre-sentence report, unless it is of the opinion that it is unnecessary to obtain one. Where the offender is under 18 and the offence is not triable only on indictment the court may not draw such a conclusion unless it can establish that a pre-sentence report is unnecessary by referring to a previous report about the offender (*PCC(S)A* 2000, s.36(5) and (6)).

27–68   Schedule 2 to the *PCC(S)A* 2000 sets out the additional requirements which may be included in a CRO. The requirements are particularly designed for offenders needing intensive supervision and expert help for specific problems. The court may make requirement that the offender:

(1) Attends a community rehabilitation centre for not more than 60 days and complies with instructions given by the person in charge of the centre.

(2) Attends during the whole of the period of the CRO or a lesser time a registered medical practitioner and/or a chartered psychologist with a view to improvement of his/her mental condition.

(3) Attends during the whole of the rehabilitation period or a lesser time for treatment by or under the direction of a person having necessary qualifications or experience with a view to the reduction or elimination of the offender's dependency on drugs or alcohol.

(4) Remains, for period specified, at a place so specified for not less than two hours or more than 12 hours in any one day during a period which must not fall outside six months beginning with the day on which the order is made. This is not the same order as a curfew order made under section 37 of the Act. It is a requirement of a community rehabilitation order.

(5) Resides in an approved hostel or any other institution for the period set out in the order.

Any requirement in a CRO that involves the defendant receiving treatment of any nature requires the defendant's consent before it can be imposed.

(3) Breach of community rehabilitation order: Powers of Criminal Courts (Sentencing) Act 2000, s.43

Schedule 3 to this Act (which makes provision for dealing with failures to comply with **27–69** the requirements of certain community orders, for revoking such orders with or without the substitution of other sentences and for amending such orders) shall have effect so far as relating to community rehabilitation orders.

XI. CURFEW ORDERS

(1) Purpose and effect

Powers of Criminal Courts (Sentencing) Act 2000, ss.37(1)–(9), 38

Curfew orders.

37.—(1) Where a person aged under 16 is convicted of an offence, the court by or before **27–70** which he is convicted may (subject to sections 148, 150 and 156 of the Criminal Justice Act 2003) make an order requiring him to remain, for periods specified in the order, at a place so specified.

(2) An order under subsection (1) above is in this Act referred to as a "curfew order".

(3) A curfew order may specify different places or different periods for different days, but shall not specify—

    (a) periods which fall outside the period of six months beginning with the day on which it is made; or

    (b) periods which amount to less than two hours or more than twelve hours in any one day.

(5) The requirement in a curfew order shall, as far as practicable, be such as to avoid—

    (a) any conflict with the offender's religious beliefs or with the requirements of any other youth community order to which he may be subject; and

    (b) any interference with the times, if any, at which he normally works or attends school or any other educational establishment.

(6) A curfew order shall include provision for making a person responsible for monitoring the offender's whereabouts during the curfew periods specified in the order; and a person who is made so responsible shall be of a description specified in an order made by the Secretary of State.

(7) A court shall not make a curfew order unless the court has been notified by the Secretary of State that arrangements for monitoring the offender's whereabouts are available in the area in which the place proposed to be specified in the order is situated and the notice has not been withdrawn.

(8) Before making a curfew order, the court shall obtain and consider information about the place proposed to be specified in the order (including information as to the attitude of persons likely to be affected by the enforced presence there of the offender).

(9) Before making a curfew order in respect of an offender the court shall obtain and consider information about his family circumstances and the likely effect of such an order on those circumstances.

(11) The court by which a curfew order is made shall give a copy of the order to the offender and to the responsible officer.

(12) In this Act, "responsible officer", in relation to an offender subject to a curfew order, means the person who is responsible for monitoring the offender's whereabouts during the curfew periods specified in the order.

38.—(1) [Repealed]   **27–71**

(2) Procedure

A curfew order is a community penalty available for offenders of any age.   **27–72**

Part V

The length of the curfew imposed by the youth court may be between 2 and 12 hours per day. The court can specify between one and seven days per week.

If the offender is aged under 16, the maximum length of a curfew order is three months. If he/she is over 16 years of age, the maximum sentence is six months.

27–73   A pre-sentence report is not essential before making a curfew order. However, the court must obtain "information" regarding the following issues:

   (a) The address or addresses to which the offender will be ordered to remain.

   (b) Information as to the suitability of such addresses and the attitude of others who reside there as to the compulsory presence of the offender during the curfew hours.

   (c) Confirmation that the curfew order does not interfere with the offender's education, employment or religion.

   (d) In the case of an offender who is under 16 on conviction, information about his family circumstances and the effect of the proposed curfew order upon him.

27–74   It should be noted that a curfew order can be combined with other community penalties including an action plan order, a supervision order, a community punishment order and a community rehabilitation order.

A curfew order is considered to be an effective way of punishing young offenders, either in itself or in combination with other community penalties. The effectiveness of the order may be usefully reinforced by electronic tagging. It is a common misconception that curfew orders are only intended for offenders who commit crime at night. This is not so. The order is a restriction of liberty in itself. When used in combination with other community penalties it may be regarded as a way of reinforcing those penalties by stabilising and regulating the offender's lifestyle.

(3) Breach revocation and amendment of curfew orders

27–75   Schedule 3 to the *Powers of Criminal Courts (Sentencing) Act* 2000 relates to the breach and variation of curfew orders.

XII. COMMUNITY PUNISHMENT ORDERS

(1) Purpose and effect

Powers of Criminal Courts (Sentencing) Act 2000, s.46

Community punishment orders.

27–76   **46.**—(1) Where a person aged 16 or over is convicted of an offence punishable with imprisonment, the court by or before which he is convicted may (subject to sections 34 to 36 above) make an order requiring him to perform unpaid work in accordance with section 47 below.

(2) An order under subsection (1) above is in this Act referred to as a "community punishment order".

(3) The number of hours which a person may be required to work under a community punishment order shall be specified in the order and shall be in the aggregate—

   (a) not less than 40; and

   (b) not more than 240.

(4) A court shall not make a community punishment order in respect of an offender unless, after hearing (if the court thinks it necessary) an appropriate officer, the court is satisfied that the offender is a suitable person to perform work under such an order.

(5) In subsection (4) above "an appropriate officer" means—

   (a) in the case of an offender aged 18 or over, an officer of a local probation board or social worker of a local authority social services department; and

   (b) in the case of an offender aged under 18, an officer of a local probation board, a social worker of a local authority social services department or a member of a youth offending team.

(6) A court shall not make a community punishment order in respect of an offender un-

less it is satisfied that provision for him to perform work under such an order can be made under the arrangements for persons to perform work under such orders which exist in the petty sessions area in which he resides or will reside.

(7) Subsection (6) above has effect subject to paragraphs 3 and 4 of Schedule 4 to this Act (transfer of order to Scotland or Northern Ireland).

(8) Where a court makes community punishment orders in respect of two or more offences of which the offender has been convicted by or before the court, the court may direct that the hours of work specified in any of those orders shall be concurrent with or additional to those specified in any other of those orders, but so that the total number of hours which are not concurrent shall not exceed the maximum specified in subsection (3)(b) above.

(9) A community punishment order—

(a) shall specify the petty sessions area in which the offender resides or will reside; and

(b) where the offender is aged under 18 at the time the order is made, may also specify a local authority for the purposes of section 47(5)(b) below (cases where functions are to be discharged by member of a youth offending team);

and if the order specifies a local authority for those purposes; the authority specified must be the local authority within whose area it appears to the court that the offender resides or will reside.

(10) Before making a community punishment order, the court shall explain to the offender in ordinary language—

(a) the purpose and effect of the order (and in particular the requirements of the order as specified in section 47(1) to (3) below);

(b) the consequences which may follow (under Part II of Schedule 3 to this Act) if he fails to comply with any of those requirements; and

(c) that the court has power (under Parts III and IV of that Schedule) to review the order on the application either of the offender or of the responsible officer.

(11) The court by which a community punishment order is made shall forthwith give copies of the order to—

(a) if the offender is aged 18 or over, an officer of a local probation board assigned to the court, or

(b) if the offender is aged under 18, an officer of a local probation board or member of a youth offending team so assigned,

and he shall give a copy to the offender and to the responsible officer.

(12) The court by which such an order is made shall also, except where it itself acts for the petty sessions area specified in the order, send to the justices' chief executive for that area—

(a) a copy of the order; and

(b) such documents and information relating to the case as it considers likely to be of assistance to a court acting for that area in the exercise of its functions in relation to the order.

(13) In this section and Schedule 3 to this Act "responsible officer", in relation to an offender subject to a community punishment order, means the person mentioned in subsection (4) or (5)(b) of section 47 below who, as respects the order, is responsible for discharging the functions conferred by that section.

(2) Procedure

A community punishment order is a community penalty available to the youth court **27–77** for offenders who are aged 16 years or over. It requires the offender to do unpaid work for the community at the direction of the probation service or youth offending team.

The community punishment order requires the defendant to participate in a scheme of unpaid work at the direction of a community service officer for the number of hours set by the court. The minimum duration of the order is a period of 40 hours, and the maximum duration of the order is a period of 240 hours: section 46(3). The order is available to all offenders over the age of 16 who are convicted of an offence which would be punishable with imprisonment if tried in the adult court: section 46(1) Before making a community punishment order, the court must hear from an "appropriate officer" regarding the suitability of the offender for community service: section 46(4). Where the

Part V

offender is aged under 18 "an appropriate officer" means "a probation officer, a social worker of a local authority social services department or a member of a youth offending team": section 46(5)(b). The court is required to obtain a pre-sentence report, unless it is of the opinion that it is unnecessary to obtain one: *PCC(S)A* 2000, s.36(5). Where the offender is under 18 and the offence is not triable only on indictment the court may not draw such a conclusion unless it can establish that a pre-sentence report is unnecessary by referring to a previous report about the offender: section 36(6). The court must also be satisfied that arrangements can be made to provide work for the offender: section 46(6), and must explain the purpose and effect of the order, the consequences which may follow if the order is not complied with and that the court may review the order on application by the offender or responsible officer: section 46(10).

27–78　　The community punishment order has been considered appropriate where the offence is of a serious nature but bearing in mind the offender's age, and personal circumstances not so serious as to justify an immediate loss of liberty.

In *Mole* (1990) 12 Cr.App.R.(S.) 371, the young offender was convicted of burglary of a dwelling. The court of appeal concluded that community service was the appropriate penalty, having regard to the offender's minor role in the commission of the offence and his previous good character.

Community service was held to be the appropriate penalty for criminal damage in *Ferreira* (1988) 10 Cr.App.R.(S.) 343, where two youths had sprayed graffiti on train carriages at a London Underground depot, Farquharson J. stating that "This is the kind of offence for which, in the judgment of this court, a community service order is designed. They have done this wanton damage and therefore it behoves them to do some service to the public to put it right".

(3) Breach

27–79　　The breach, revocation and amendment of community punishment orders is dealt with under Schedule 3 to the *PCC(S)A* 2000.

XIII. COMMUNITY PUNISHMENT AND REHABILITATION ORDER

(1) Purpose and effect

Powers of Criminal Courts (Sentencing) Act 2000, s.51(1)–(3)

27–80　　51.—(1) Where a person aged 16 or over is convicted of an offence punishable with imprisonment and the court by or before which he is convicted is of the opinion mentioned in subsection (3) below, the court may (subject to sections 34–36 above) make an order requiring him both—

    (a) to be under supervision for a period specified in the order, being not less than 12 months nor more than 3 years; and

    (b) to perform unpaid work for a number of hours so specified being in the aggregate not less than 40 nor more than 100.

(2) An order under subsection (1) above is in this Act referred to as a "community punishment and rehabilitation order".

(3) The opinion referred to in subsection (1) above is that the making of a community punishment and Rehabilitation order is desirable in the interests of—

    (a) securing the rehabilitation of the offender; or

    (b) protecting the public from harm from him or preventing the commission by him of further offences.

(2) Procedure

27–81　　A community punishment and rehabilitation order is a community penalty which may place a high level of restriction on the offender's liberty. It is an order designed to combine community rehabilitation with community punishment. The offender will be ordered to perform unpaid work in the community at the same time as being under the supervision of a probation officer, or member of the YOT.

As part of the supervisory element of a community punishment and rehabilitation order the youth court may include additional requirements upon the offender under the *PCC(S)A* 2000, ss.41, 42, 46 and 47 and Sched. 2.

Before making a community punishment and rehabilitation order the youth court is **27–82** required to have before it a written report, usually from the YOT unless it is of the opinion that it is unnecessary to obtain one. Where the offender is under 18 and the offence is not triable only on indictment the court may not draw such a conclusion unless it can establish that a report is unnecessary by referring to a previous report about the offender: *PCC(S)A* 2000, section 36(5) and (6). The report should address the defendant's suitability for such an order and assess his suitability to perform community punishment.

(3) Breach

Breach, revocation and amendment of community punishment and rehabilitation **27–83** orders are dealt with in the *PCC(S)A* 2000, Sched. 3.

XIV. DRUG TREATMENT AND TESTING ORDERS

(1) Purpose and effect

Powers of Criminal Courts (Sentencing) Act 2000, ss.52–55

Drug treatment and testing orders.

52.—(1) Where a person aged 16 or over is convicted of an offence, the court by or before **27–84** which he is convicted may (subject to sections 34 to 36 above) make an order which—

    (a) has effect for a period specified in the order of not less than six months nor more than three years ("the treatment and testing period"); and

    (b) includes the requirements and provisions mentioned in sections 53 and 54 below;

but this section does not apply in relation to an offence committed before 30th September 1998.

(2) An order under subsection (1) above is in this Act referred to as a "drug treatment and testing order".

(3) A court shall not make a drug treatment and testing order in respect of an offender unless it is satisfied—

    (a) that he is dependent on or has a propensity to misuse drugs; and

    (b) that his dependency or propensity is such as requires and may be susceptible to treatment.

(4) For the purpose of ascertaining for the purposes of subsection (3) above whether the offender has any drug in his body, [(in a case where, at the time of conviction, he was aged under 18)] the court may by order require him to provide samples of such description as it may specify; but the court shall not make such an order unless the offender expresses his willingness to comply with its requirements.

(5) A court shall not make a drug treatment and testing order unless it has been notified by the Secretary of State that arrangements for implementing such orders are available in the area proposed to be specified in the order under section 54(1) below and the notice has not been withdrawn.

(6) Before making a drug treatment and testing order, the court shall explain to the offender in ordinary language—

    (a) the effect of the order and of the requirements proposed to be included in it;

    (b) the consequences which may follow (under Part II of Schedule 3 to this Act) if he fails to comply with any of those requirements;

    (c) that the order will be periodically reviewed at intervals as provided for in the order (by virtue of section 54(6) below); and

    (d) that the order may be reviewed (under Parts III and IV of Schedule 3) on the application either of the offender or of the responsible officer;

and "responsible officer" here has the meaning given by section 54(3) below.

(7) A court shall not make a drug treatment and testing order unless the offender expresses his willingness to comply with its requirements.

[This section is printed as amended as from a day to be appointed, by the *CJCSA* 2000, s.74 and Sched. 7, para. 170 (insertion of words in square brackets).]

The treatment and testing requirements.

27–85   **53.**—(1) A drug treatment and testing order shall include a requirement ("the treatment requirement") that the offender shall submit, during the whole of the treatment and testing period, to treatment by or under the direction of a specified person having the necessary qualifications or experience ("the treatment provider") with a view to the reduction or elimination of the offender's dependency on or propensity to misuse drugs.

(2) The required treatment for any particular period shall be—

     (a) treatment as a resident in such institution or place as may be specified in the order; or

     (b) treatment as a non-resident in or at such institution or place, and at such intervals, as may be so specified;

but the nature of the treatment shall not be specified in the order except as mentioned in paragraph (a) or (b) above.

(3) A court shall not make a drug treatment and testing order unless it is satisfied that arrangements have been or can be made for the treatment intended to be specified in the order (including arrangements for the reception of the offender where he is to be required to submit to treatment as a resident).

(4) A drug treatment and testing order shall include a requirement ("the testing requirement") that, for the purpose of ascertaining whether he has any drug in his body during the treatment and testing period, the offender shall during that period, at such times or in such circumstances as may (subject to the provisions of the order) be determined by the treatment provider, provide samples of such description as may be so determined.

(5) The testing requirement shall specify for each month the minimum number of occasions on which samples are to be provided.

Provisions of order as to supervision and periodic review.

27–86   **54.**—(1) A drug treatment and testing order shall include a provision specifying the petty sessions area in which it appears to the court making the order that the offender resides or will reside.

(2) A drug treatment and testing order shall provide that, for the treatment and testing period, the offender shall be under the supervision of an officer of a local probation board appointed for or assigned to the petty sessions area specified in the order.

(3) In this Act "responsible officer", in relation to an offender who is subject to a drug treatment and testing order, means the officer of a local probation board responsible for his supervision.

(4) A drug treatment and testing order shall—

     (a) require the offender to keep in touch with the responsible officer in accordance with such instructions as he may from time to time be given by that officer, and to notify him of any change of address; and

     (b) provide that the results of the tests carried out on the samples provided by the offender in pursuance of the testing requirement shall be communicated to the responsible officer.

(5) Supervision by the responsible officer shall be carried out to such extent only as may be necessary for the purpose of enabling him—

     (a) to report on the offender's progress to the court responsible for the order;

     (b) to report to that court any failure by the offender to comply with the requirements of the order; and

     (c) to determine whether the circumstances are such that he should apply to that court for the revocation or amendment of the order.

(6) A drug treatment and testing order shall—

     (a) provide for the order to be reviewed periodically at intervals of not less than one month;

     (b) provide for each review of the order to be made, subject to section 55(6) below, at a hearing held for the purpose by the court responsible for the order (a "review hearing");

     (c) require the offender to attend each review hearing;

(d) provide for the responsible officer to make to the court responsible for the order, before each review, a report in writing on the offender's progress under the order; and

(e) provide for each such report to include the test results communicated to the responsible officer under subsection (4)(b) above and the views of the treatment provider as to the treatment and testing of the offender.

(7) In this section references to the court responsible for a drug treatment and testing order are references to—

(a) where a court is specified in the order in accordance with subsection (8) below, that court;

(b) in any other case, the court by which the order is made.

(8) Where the area specified in a drug treatment and testing order made by a magistrate' court is not the area for which the court acts, the court may, if it thinks fit, include in the order provision specifying for the purposes of subsection (7) above a magistrates' court which acts for the area specified in the order.

(9) [*omitted*]

[This section is printed as amended by the *CJCSA* 2000, s.74, and Sched. 7, para. 4.]

Periodic reviews.

55.—(1) At a review hearing (within the meaning given by subsection (6) of section 54 above) **27–87** the court may, after considering the responsible officer's report referred to in that subsection, amend any requirement or provision of the drug treatment and testing order.

(2) The court—

(a) shall not amend the treatment or testing requirement unless the offender expresses his willingness to comply with the requirement as amended;

(b) shall not amend any provision of the order so as to reduce the treatment and testing period below the minimum specified in section 52(1) above, or to increase it above the maximum so specified; and

(c) except with the consent of the offender, shall not amend any requirement or provision of the order while an appeal against the order is pending.

(3) If the offender fails to express his willingness to comply with the treatment or testing requirement as proposed to be amended by the court, the court may—

(a) revoke the order; and

(b) deal with him, for the offence in respect of which the order was made, in any way in which it could deal with him if he had just been convicted by the court of the offence.

(4) In dealing with the offender under subsection (3)(b) above, the court—

(a) shall take into account the extent to which the offender has complied with the requirements of the order; and

(b) may impose a custodial sentence (where the order was made in respect of an offence punishable with such a sentence) notwithstanding anything in section 79(2) below.

(5) Where the order was made by a magistrates' court in the case of an offender under 18 years of age in respect of an offence triable only on indictment in the case of an adult, any powers exercisable under subsection (3)(b) above in respect of the offender after he attains the age of 18 shall be powers to do either or both of the following—

(a) to impose a fine not exceeding £5,000 for the offence in respect of which the order was made;

(b) to deal with the offender for that offence in any way in which the court could deal with him if it had just convicted him of an offence punishable with imprisonment for a term not exceeding six months.

(6) If at a review hearing the court, after considering the responsible officer's report, is of the opinion that the offender's progress under the order is satisfactory, the court may so amend the order as to provide for each subsequent review to be made by the court without a hearing.

(7) If at a review without a hearing the court, after considering the responsible officer's report, is of the opinion that the offender's progress under the order is no longer satisfactory, the court may require the offender to attend a hearing of the court at a specified time and place.

Part V

(8) At that hearing the court, after considering that report, may—

(a) exercise the powers conferred by this section as if the hearing were a review hearing; and

(b) so amend the order as to provide for each subsequent review to be made at a review hearing.

(9) In this section any reference to the court, in relation to a review without a hearing, shall be construed—

(a) in the case of the Crown Court, as a reference to a judge of the court;

(b) in the case of magistrates' court, as a reference to a justice of the peace acting for the commission area for which the court acts.

(2) Procedure

27–88   The court may make a drug treatment and testing order where the offender is dependant on, or has a propensity to misuse drugs, and where this dependency or propensity is such as requires and may be susceptible to treatment: section 52(3). This may be demonstrated by the offender's previous record, or by the current offences for sentence. A full pre-sentence report is required, and to enable the court to determine whether the criteria in section 52(3) are established, section 52(4) allows the court to require the defendant to provide samples, subject to the defendant's consent. The finding that the offender satisfies the conditions specified in section 52(3) must be announced with reasons to support such a conclusion. The offender must also express his willingness to comply with treatment: section 52(7) and the court may only impose a drug treatment and testing order when it has been notified that arrangements for implementing such orders are available in the area to be specified in the order: section 52(5).

The treatment requirement must state whether the treatment is residential or non-residential and the identity of the treatment provider: section 53(2). There must be a testing requirement with a specified frequency of drug testing and the court must set a minimum number of times a month samples should be provided for testing: section 53(4), (5). The court must also set a review period, with the reviews being not more than a month apart: section 54(6).

(3) Breach

27–89   The breach revocation and amendment of drug treatment and testing orders are dealt with under Schedule 3 to the *PCC(S)A* 2000.

XV. DETENTION AND TRAINING ORDER

(1) Purpose and effect

Powers of Criminal Courts (Sentencing) Act 2000, s.79(2)

27–90   **79.**—(2) The court shall not pass a custodial sentence on the offender unless it is of the opinion—

(a) that the offence or the combination of the offence and one or more offences associated with it, was so serious that only such a sentence can be justified for the offence; or

(b) where the offence is a violent or sexual offence, that only such a sentence would be adequate to protect the public from serious harm from him.

Powers of Criminal Courts (Sentencing) Act 2000, ss.100–103

Offenders under 18: detention and training orders

27–91   **100.**—(1) Subject to sections 90 and 91 above, sections 226 and 228 of the Criminal Justice Act 2003, and subsection (2) below, where—

(a) a child or young person (that is to say any person aged under 18) is convicted of an offence which is punishable with imprisonment in the case of a person aged 21 or over, and

(b) the court is of the opinion that subsection (2) of section 152 of the Criminal Justice Act 2003 applies or the case falls within subsection (3) of that section,

the sentence that the court is to pass is a detention and training order.

(2) A court shall not make a detention and training order—

(a) in the case of an offender under the age of 15 at the time of conviction unless it is of the opinion that he is a persistent offender;

(b) In the case of an offender under the age of 12 at that time unless—

(i) it is of the opinion that only a custodial sentence would be adequate to protect the public from further offending by him; and

(ii) the offence was committed on or after such date as the Secretary of State may by order appoint.

(3) A detention and training order is an order that the offender in respect of whom it is made shall be subject, for the term specified in the order, to a period of detention and training followed by a period of supervision.

Term of order, consecutive terms and taking account of remands

101.—(1) Subject to subsection (2) below, the term of a detention and training order made in **27–92** respect of an offence (whether by a magistrates' court or otherwise) shall be 4, 6, 8, 10, 12, 18 or 24 months.

(2) The term of a detention and training order may not exceed the maximum term of imprisonment that the Crown Court could (in the case of an offender aged 21 or over) impose for the offence.

(3) Subject to subsections (4) and (6) below, a court making a detention and training order may order that its term shall commence on the expiry of the term of any other detention and training order made by that or any other court.

(4) A court shall not make in respect of an offender a detention and training order the effect of which would be that he would be subject to detention and training orders for a term which exceeds 24 months.

(5) Where the term of the detention and training order to which an offender would otherwise be subject exceeds 24 months, the excess shall be treated as remitted.

(6) A court making a detention and training order shall not order that its term shall commence on the expiry of the term of a detention and training order under which the period of supervision has already begun under section 103(1).

(7) Where a detention and training order ("the new order") is made in respect of an offender who is subject to a detention and training order under which the period of supervision has begun ("the old order"), the old order shall be disregarded in determining—

(a) for the purpose of subsection (4) above whether the effect of the new order would be that the offender would be subject to detentionand training orders for a term which exceeds 24 months; and

(b) for the purposes of subsection (5) above whether the term of detention and training orders to which the offender would (apart from that subsection) be subject exceeds 24 months.

(8) In determining the term of the detention and training order for an offence, the court shall take into account any period for which the offender has been remanded in custody in connection with the offence, or any other offence, the charge for which was founded on the same facts or evidence.

(9) Where a court proposes to make a detention and training order in respect of an offender for two or more offences—

(a) subsection (8) above shall not apply; but

(b) in determining the total term of the detention and training orders it proposes to make in respect of the offender, the court shall take into account of the total period (if any) for which he has been remanded in custody in connection with any of those offences, or any other offence the charge for which was founded on the same facts or evidence.

(10) Once a period of remand has, under subsection (8) or (9) above been taken account of in relation to a detention and training order made in respect of an offender for any offence or offences, it shall not subsequently be taken into account (under either of those subsections) in relation to such an order made in respect of the offender for any other offence or offences.

(11) Any reference in subsection (8) or (9) above to an offender's being remanded in custody is a reference to his being—

    (a) held in police detention;

    (b) remanded in or committed to custody by order of the court;

    (c) remanded or committed to local authority accommodation under section 23 of the *Children and Young Person Act* 1969 and placed and kept in secure accommodation or detained in a secure training centre pursuant to arrangements under subsection (7A) of that section; or

    (d) remanded, admitted or removed to hospital under sections 35, 36, 38 or 48 of the *Mental Health Act* 1983.

(12) A person is in police detention for the purposes of subsection (11) above—

    (a) at any time when he is in police detention for the purposes of the *Police and Criminal Evidence Act* 1984; and

    (b) at any time when he is detained under section 41 of the *Terrorism Act* 2000;

and in that subsection "secure accommodation" has the same meaning as in section 23 of the *Children and Young Person Act* 1969.

(12A) Section 243 of the *Criminal Justice Act* 2003 (persons extradited to the United Kingdom) applies in relation to a person sentenced to a detention and training order as it applies in relation to a fixed-term prisoner, with the reference in subsection (2) of that section to section 240 being read as a reference to subsection (8) above.

(13) For the purpose of any reference in sections 102–105 below to the term of a detention and training order, consecutive terms of such orders and terms of such order which are wholly or partly concurrent shall be treated as a single term if—

    (a) the orders were made on the same occasion; or

    (b) where they were made on different occasions, the offender has not been released (by virtue of subsection (2), (3), (4) or (5) of section 102 below) at any time during the period beginning with the first and ending with the last of those occasions.

The period of detention and training

27–93   **102.**—(1) An offender shall serve the period of detention and training under a detention and training order in such secure accommodation as may be determined by the Secretary of State or by such other person as may be authorised by him for that purpose.

(2) Subject to subsections (3)–(5) below, the period of detention and training under a detention and training order shall be one half of the term of the order.

(3) The Secretary of State may at any time release the offender if he is satisfied that if exceptional circumstances exist which justify the offenders release on compassionate grounds.

(4) The Secretary of State may release the offender—

    (a) In the case of an order for a term of 8 months or more, but less than 18 months, one month before the half way point of the term of the order; and

    (b) in the case of an order for a term of 18 months or more, one month or two months before that point.

(5) If a youth court so orders on an application made by the Secretary of State for the purpose, the Secretary of State shall release the offender—

    (a) in the case of an order for a term of 8 months or more, but less than 18 months, one month after the half way point of the term of the order; and

    (b) in the case of an order for a term of 18 months or more, one month or two months after that point.

(6) An offender detained in pursuance of a detention and training order shall be deemed to be in legal custody.

The period of supervision

27–94   **103.**—(1) The period of supervision of an offender who is subject to a detention and training order—

    (a) shall begin with the offender's release whether at the half way point of the term of the order or otherwise; and

    (b) subject to subsection (2) below shall end when the term of the order ends.

(2) The Secretary of State may by order provide that the period of supervision shall end at such point during the term of a detention and training order as may be specified in the order under this subsection.

(3) During the period of supervision the offender shall be under the supervision of—

   (a) an officer of a local probation board;

   (b) a social worker of a local authority; or

   (c) a member of a youth offending team;

and the category of person to supervise the offender shall be determined from time to time by the Secretary of State.

(4) Where the supervision is to be provided by a probation officer, the probation officer shall be an officer appointed for or assigned to the petty sessions area within which the offender resides for the time being.

(5) Where the supervision is provided by—

   (a) a social worker of a local authority, or

   (b) a member of a youth offending team,

the social worker or member shall be a social worker of, or a member of a youth offending team established by, the local authority within whose area the offender resides for the time being.

(6)–(7) [*omitted*]

(2) Procedure

27–95 The detention and training order is the only custodial sentence for young offenders appearing in the youth court. The court's power to impose a custodial sentence is restricted.

A detention and training order may be imposed for fixed periods of 4, 6, 8, 10, 12, 18 or 24 months.

If the court having considered the facts of the case and the defendants antecedent history considers that a detention and training order may be appropriate it must first order the preparation of a full written pre-sentence report, unless there exists a previous report: *PCC(S)A* 2000, s.81. The report must specifically address custody as a sentencing option.

27–96 The offence itself must be one which is punishable with a minimum of four months' imprisonment in the adult court and is also so serious that only a custodial sentence of four months or over can be justified. Following the making of a detention and training order the offender is held in a custodial institution for one half of the duration of the order. He is then released into the community under the supervision of the YOT. Such supervision may included electronic tagging and an intensive supervision and surveillance programme. However, this is a matter purely for the YOT and does not involve an order of the court.

In determining the appropriate term of a detention and training order the court must take into account any period for which the offender has been remanded in custody. This includes time held in police detention, remanded to local authority accommodation and secure accommodation or remanded or admitted to hospital under the *Mental Health Act* 1983, ss.35, 36, 38 or 48. Although the court must take such periods of custody into account it is not required to discount the sentence on a one to one basis nor is the court required to fine tune the appropriate sentence by taking into account a few days spent in custody: *B.* [2000] Crim.L.R. 870, CA. In *R. v. Inner London Crown Court, ex p. N.S.* [2000] Crim.L.R. 871, CA, two offenders had each been sentenced to a detention and training order (DTO) of four months. Each appealed on the basis that the three days that they had both spent in custody on remand had not been taken into account in deciding the term of the DTO. The court held that it was neither appropriate or desirable that any precise reflection should be given, in the making of a DTO, of two or three days spent in custody. If a more substantial time of weeks or months had been spent on remand the proper approach would have been to reduce sentence to reflect that period.

27–97 In determining the length of a detention and training order the court must also take into account a plea of guilty in accordance with *PCC(S)A* 2000, section 152. In *Marley* [2002] 2 Cr.App.R.(S.) 21 a detention and training order of 24 months was reduced to 18 months on the ground that the appellant had pleaded guilty and it was inappropriate to impose the maximum sentence available. The provisions relating to detention and training orders were restricted as to their length. If the maximum sentence of 24 months was not to be imposed, the next permissible length below that level was 18 months.

In *Pye v. Leeds Youth Court* (2006) EWHC 2527, DC, October 3. 2006 a youth received a sentence of a four-month DTO for criminal damage to the value of £50. On appeal it was held that such a sentence was unlawful. The maximum sentence an adult could have received in such circumstances was three months' imprisonment. The *Powers of Criminal Courts (Sentencing) Act* 2000, s.101(2) applied. Youth was a mitigating factor not an aggravating one. The youth court had no power to impose a custodial sentence under these circumstances.

(3) Definition of "persistency"

27–98   Youths aged between 12 and 14 years cannot be given a detention and training order unless they are persistent offenders. In deciding whether a defendant is "persistent" it is appropriate to apply the currently understood meaning of that word. The court should assess whether the defendant's criminal behaviour demonstrates a sufficient degree of persistence. Previous findings of guilt and findings of guilt made after the commission of the offence in question will all count in assessing the defendant's criminal behaviour as will cautions, reprimands and final warnings: *Charlton* (2000) 164 J.P. 685. It is not necessary that a defendant should have committed a string of offences or that he has failed to comply with previous orders of the court: *B.* [2001] Crim.L.R. 50. However, in *J.D.* (2001) 165 J.P. 1, a 14 year old charged with affray was held not to be a persistent offender although he had a previous finding of guilt for handling stolen goods and a caution for a similar offence. The offence of affray was a different type of offence than those he had committed before. In *Smith* [2000] Crim.L.R. 613, a 14 year old who had pleaded guilty to robbery, offensive weapon and false imprisonment, all committed over a two-day period, was held to be a persistent offender although he had no previous convictions. In *G.* (2004), CA (Crim. Div.) a 14-year-old appellant appealed against an 18-month DTO on the grounds that he was not a "persistent offender". He had pleaded guilty to charges of possessing firearms, possessing ammunition, and possessing cannabis with intent to supply. He had received a conditional discharge for theft in 2002 and a six-month supervision order for aggravated vehicle taking in 2003. It was held that the instant offences were very serious, normally justifying an immediate custodial sentence. However, they had taken place at the very end of a supervision order and it was held that his criminal behaviour was not persistent. The sentence was quashed and a two-year supervision order substituted.

(4) Consecutive periods of detention

27–99   The youth court may impose consecutive detention and training orders for summary offences up to an aggregate of 24 months: *C. v. DPP* [2002] 1 Cr.App.R.(S.) 45. However, in *Norris* (2000) 164 J.P. 689 it was held that in passing a consecutive DTO upon an offender who was already serving such a sentence the aggregate of the two orders did not have to correspond with one of the periods set out in section 101 of the *PCC(S)A* 2000.

Where an offender is already serving a period of detention under section 91 of the *PCC(S)A* 2000 there is no power to impose a consecutive detention and training order for a further offence as the two sentencing regimes are incompatible.

(5) Offenders attaining 18 years during the course of proceedings

27–100   Where an offender attains 18 years of age during the course of proceedings the starting point for sentence is that which he would have been likely to receive had he been sentenced on the date of the commission of the offence: *Ghafoor* [2002] Crim.L.R. 739: see *ante*, § 25–24. In *Aldis v. DPP* [2002] 2 Cr.App.R.(S.) 88 it was held that an 18-year-old offender was correctly sentenced to a detention and training order as he had committed the offence when he was 17 years old. He appealed on the basis that, as an 18 year old at the time of sentence, he should have received a term of custody in a young offenders' institute.

(6) Imposition and duration of detention and training orders

There are a number of decisions giving guidance as to when a sentencing court **27–101** should impose a detention and training order and the appropriate length of such an order. The reader will note that several of the following cases involve convictions for the offence of robbery. This is currently a prevalent offence in the youth court jurisdiction. The reader is referred to the Sentencing Guidelines Council Sentencing Guidelines relating to the offence of robbery and more especially that part that deals with particular factors to be taken into account when dealing with young offenders. See www.sentencing-guidelines.gov.uk.

Att-Gen's References (Nos 4 and 7 of 2002) (Lobban and Sawyers) (Q) [2002] 2 Cr.App.R.(S.) 77, CA

In this case the Court of Appeal held that street robberies of mobile phones would be punished severely. Custodial sentences would be the only option available irrespective of the age of the offender or his previous good character, unless there are exceptional circumstances. The sentencing bracket would be 18 months to three years where no weapon is used.

L. [2003] All E.R. (D) 37 (APR)

In this case the 15-year-old defendants had both pleaded guilty to burglary and each were sentenced to a 12-month DTO. On appeal it was held that the circumstances of the burglary put it at the lower end of the scale. A custodial sentence could have been avoided as both defendants were young and had entered timely pleas. Each defendant had served the equivalent of a four-month sentence and the sentence of 12-months was reduced to four months accordingly.

F.A. [2003] 2 Cr.App.R.(S.)

In this case two applicants of good character had admitted a number of robberies of fellow pupils at their school. Each was sentenced to a DTO of 8 months. On appeal the court held that pupils at school who indulge in a campaign of intimidation and violence could expect to be dealt with severely. The sentences were upheld.

Hahn [2003] Cr.App.R.(S.) 106, CA

In this case it was held that as the appellant was 17 years at the date of conviction the power of the sentencing court was limited to a detention and training order. The power to order detention under section 91 of the *PCC(S)A* 2000 may be exercised only in cases where the offender was convicted of a "grave crime". Before imposing such a sentence the court must be of the opinion that none of the other methods in which the case might be dealt with was suitable. In this particular case it was held that a detention and training order was a suitable sentence and the appeal was allowed accordingly.

A. (2005) CA (Criminal Division) June 14, 2005

See *ante*, § 25–30. The defendant, who was 14 years old at the time of the offence and 15 years on sentence was the ringleader of a gang of six youths who robbed a young victim of his property including his mobile phone. No weapon was used. The defendant had several previous convictions for crimes of violence and dishonesty. It was held that although no weapon had been used, the robbery had involved an attack by six people. A starting point of four years custody was appropriate. However, the defendant's age had to be recognised and taken into account. Responsibility at 15 years of age was not that of an older man and a sentence of three years for a 15 year old was longer than a three year sentence for someone of a greater age. The sentence of three years detention was quashed and a two year detention and training order substituted.

T. (Att-Gen's Reference Numbers 102 and 103 of 2006), CA

The sixteen-year-old defendant together with an adult was convicted of robbery. The offence involved threats made to a young victim with a knife, forcing him to take the defendants to home, which they ransacked, and subsequently using gratuitous violence on the victim. The prosecution appealed against a sentence of a DTO for eighteen months. It was held that the aggravating features of the case meant that an adult would have received a prison sentence between five and six years. However, the Court had to bear in mind the appellant's age. Accordingly the sentence imposed was held to be too lenient and a sentence of four years' detention substituted under *PCCA* 2000, s.91 (see *ante*, § 25–18).

P. (Att-Gen's Reference Numbers 102 and 103 of 2006), CA

The defendant was seventeen years old and had pleaded guilty to two counts of assault leading to serious injury. Three days before sentence he had received a supervision order in the youth court in respect of another matter. The Court deferred sentence for six months in respect of the assault charges on the basis that the judge said she felt obliged to see whether the supervision order would be effective. On appeal it was held that the deferral was unduly lenient and was only applicable if a non-custodial sentence for the offences in question was a real possibility. This was not the case in view of the gravity of the offences. The judge should not have felt obliged to respect the supervision order. An extended sentence of $2^{1}/_{2}$ years' custody was substituted.

R. (2006) 150 S.J.L.B. 1607

See *ante*, § 25–24. The female defendant was fourteen years old at the time of the offence and pleaded guilty to wounding with intent. She had been persistently bullied at school by the victim and had taken two knives with her in order to keep herself safe. The victim found out about the knives and challenged the defendant, punching her in the fact several times. The defendant then produced one of the knives and stabbed the victim in the ribs causing a superficial wound. The defendant pleaded guilty to the offence and received an 18-month DTO. The custodial sentence was quashed in view of the defendant's age at the time of the offence (see *ante*, § 25–24). The Court stated that were it not for her age there would have been no alternative but to impose a custodial sentence. However, eighteen months would have been excessive and would have been reduced to six months on appeal.

(7) Breaches of supervision requirements in a detention and training order

Powers of Criminal Courts (Sentencing) Act 2000, s.103(1), (3)

27–102   103.—(1) The period of supervision of an offender who is subject to a detention and training order—

    (a) shall be given with the offender's release whether at the half way point of the term of the order or otherwise; and

    (b) subject to subsection (2) below, shall end when the term of the order ends.

(3) During the period of supervision the offender shall be under the supervision of—

    (a) an officer of a local probation board;

    (b) a social worker of a local authority; or

    (c) a member of a youth offending team;

and the category of person to supervise the offender shall be determined from time to time by the Secretary of State.

Powers of Criminal Courts (Sentencing) Act 2000, s.104(1), (3)

Breach of supervision requirements

27–103   104.—(1) Where a detention and training order is in force in respect of an offender and it appears on information to a justice of the peace that the offender has failed to comply with requirements under section 103(6)(b) above, the justice—

(a) may issue a summons requiring the offender to appear at the place and time specified in the summons; or

(b) if the information is in writing and on oath, may issue a warrant for the offender's arrest.

(3) If it is proved to the satisfaction of the youth court before which an offender appears or is brought under this section that he has failed to comply with requirements under section 103(6)(b) above, that court may—

(a) order the offender to be detained, in such secure accommodation as the Secretary of State may determine, for such period, not exceeding the shorter of three months or the remainder of the term of the detention and training order, as the court may specify; or

(b) impose on the offender a fine not exceeding level 3 on the standard scale.

(8) Committing an offence during the currency of a detention and training order

Powers of Criminal Courts (Sentencing) Act 2000, s.105(2), (3)

Offences during currency of order

105.—(2) Subject to section 8(6) above (duty of adult magistrates' court to remit young offenders to youth court for sentence), the court by or before which a person to whom this section applies is convicted of the new offence may, whether or not it passes any other sentence on him, order him to be detained in such secure accommodation as the Secretary of State may determine for the whole or any part of the period which—   **27–104**

(a) begins with the date of the court's order; and

(b) is equal in length to the period between the date on which the new offence was committed and the date mentioned in subsection (1) above.

(3) The period for which a person to whom this section applies is ordered under subsection (2) above to be detained in secure accommodation—

(a) shall, as the court may direct, either be served before and be followed by, or be served concurrently with, any sentence imposed for the new offence; and

(b) in either case, shall be disregarded in determining the appropriate length of that sentence.

The power to deal with a person for an offence committed during the currency of a   **27–105** detention and training order arises if that person after his release and before the date on which the term of the order ends, commits an offence punishable with imprisonment in the case of a person aged 21 or over, and before or after that date, he is convicted of that offence ("the new offence").

XVI. PARENTING ORDER

(1) Purpose and effect

Crime and Disorder Act 1998, ss.8–10

Parenting orders

8.—(1) This section applies where, in any court proceedings—   **27–106**

(a) a child safety order is made in respect of a child or the court determines on an application under section 12(6) below that a child has failed to comply with any requirement included in such an order;

(aa) a parental compensation order is made in relation to a child's behaviour;

(b) an anti-social behaviour order or sex offender order is made in respect of a child or young person;

(c) a child or young person is convicted of an offence; or

(d) a person is convicted of an offence under section 443 (failure to comply with school attendance order) or section 444 (failure to secure regular attendance at school of registered pupil) of the *Education Act* 1996.

(2) Subject to subsection (3) and section 9(1) below, if in the proceedings the court is satisfied that the relevant condition is fulfilled, it may make a parenting order in respect of a person who is a parent or guardian of the child or young person or, as the case may be, the person convicted of the offence under section 443 or 444 ("the parent").

(3) A court shall not make a parenting order unless it has been notified by the Secretary of State that arrangements for implementing such orders are available in the are in which it appears to the court that the parent resides or will reside and the notice has not been withdrawn.

(4) A parenting order is an order which requires the parent—

    (a) to comply, for a period not exceeding twelve months, with such requirements as are specified in the order; and

    (b) subject to subsection (5) below, to attend, for a concurrent period not exceeding three months, such counselling or guidance programme as may be specified in directions given by the responsible officer.

(5) A parenting order may, but need not, include such a requirement as is mentioned in subsection (4)(b) above in any case where a parenting order under this section or any other enactment has been made in respect of the parent on a previous occasion.

(6) The relevant condition is that the parenting order would be desirable in the interests of preventing—

    (a) in a case falling within paragraph (a), (aa) or (b) of subsection (1) above, any repetition of the kind of behaviour which led to the child safety order, parental compensation order, anti-social behaviour order or sex offender order being made;

    (b) in a case falling within paragraph (c) of that subsection, the commission of any further offence by the child or young person;

    (c) in a case falling within paragraph (d) of that subsection, the commission of any further offence under section 443 or 444 of the *Education Act* 1996.

(7) The requirements that may be specified under subsection (4)(a) above are those which the court considers desirable in the interests of preventing any such repetition or, as the case may be, the commission of any such further offence.

(7A) A counselling or guidance programme which a parent is required to attend by virtue of subsection (4)(b) above may be or include a residential course but only if the court is satisfied—

    (a) that the attendance of the parent at a residential course is likely to be more effective than his attendance at a non-residential course in preventing any such repetition or, as the case may be, the commission of any such further offence, and

    (b) that any interference with family life which is likely to result from the attendance of the parent at a residential course is proportionate in all the circumstances.

(8) In this section and section 9 below "responsible officer", in relation to a parenting order, means one of the following who is specified in the order, namely—

    (a) an officer of a local probation board;

    (b) a social worker of a local authority; and

    (bb) a person nominated by a person appointed as chief education officer under section 532 of the *Education Act* 1996.

    (c) a member of a youth offending team

Parenting orders: supplemental.

27–107   **9.**—(1) Where a person under the age of 16 is convicted of an offence, the court by or before which he is so convicted—

    (a) if it is satisfied that the relevant condition is fulfilled, shall make a parenting order; and

    (b) if it is not so satisfied, shall state in open court that it is not and why it is not.

(1A) The requirements of subsection (1) do not apply where the court makes a referral order in respect of the offence.

(1B) If an anti-social behaviour order is made in respect of a person under the age of 16 the court which makes the order—

    (a) must make a parenting order if it is satisfied that the relevant condition is fulfilled;

    (b) if it is not so satisfied, must state in open court that it is not and why it is not.

(2) Before making a parenting order—

(a) in a case falling within paragraph (a) of subsection (1) of section 8 above;

(b) in a case falling within paragraph (b) or (c) of that subsection, where the person concerned is under the age of 16; or

(c) in a case falling within paragraph (d) of that subsection, where the person to whom the offence related is under that age,

a court shall obtain and consider information about the person's family circumstances and the likely effect of the order on those circumstances.

(2A) In a case where a court proposes to make both a referral order in respect of a child or young person convicted of an offence and a parenting order, before making the parenting order the court shall obtain and consider a report by an appropriate officer—

(a) indicating the requirements proposed by that officer to be included in the parenting order;

(b) indicating the reasons why he considers those requirements would be desirable in the interests of preventing the commission of any further offence by the child or young person; and

(c) if the child or young person is aged under 16, containing the information required by subsection (2) above.

(2B) In subsection (2A) above "an appropriate officer" means—

(a) an officer of a local probation board;

(b) a social worker of a local authority; or

(c) a member of a youth offending team.

(3) Before making a parenting order, a court shall explain to the parent in ordinary language—

(a) the effect of the order and of the requirements proposed to be included in it;

(b) the consequences which may follow (under subsection (7) below) if he fails to comply with any of those requirements; and

(c) that the court has power (under subsection (5) below) to review the order on the application either of the parent or of the responsible officer.

(4) Requirements specified in, and directions given under, a parenting order shall, as far as practicable, be such as to avoid—

(a) any conflict with the parent's religious beliefs; and

(b) any interference with the times, if any, at which he normally works or attends an educational establishment.

(5) If while a parenting order is in force it appears to the court which made it, on the application of the responsible officer or the parent, that it is appropriate to make an order under this subsection, the court may make an order discharging the parenting order or varying it—

(a) by cancelling any provision included in it; or

(b) by inserting in it (either in addition to or in substitution for any of its provisions) any provision that could have been included in the order if the court had then had power to make it and were exercising the power.

(6) Where an application under subsection (5) above for the discharge of a parenting order is dismissed, no further application for its discharge shall be made under that subsection by any person except with the consent of the court which made the order.

(7) If while a parenting order is in force the parent without reasonable excuse fails to comply with any requirement included in the order, or specified in directions given by the responsible officer, he shall be liable on summary conviction to a fine not exceeding level 3 on the standard scale.

(7A) In this section "referral order" means an order under section 16(2) or (3) of the *Powers of Criminal Courts (Sentencing) Act* 2000 (referral of offender to youth offender panel).

Appeals against parenting orders.

10.—(1) An appeal shall lie—   **27–108**

(a) to the High court against the making of a parenting order by virtue of paragraph (a) of subsection (1) of section 8 above; and

(b) to the Crown Court against the making of a parenting order by virtue of paragraph (b) of that subsection.

(2) On an appeal under subsection (1) above the High court or the Crown Court—

    (a) may make such orders as may be necessary to give effect to its determination of the appeals; and

    (b) may also make such incidental or consequential orders as appear to it to be just.

(3) Any order of the High court or the Crown Court made on an appeal under subsection (1) above (other than one directing that an application be re-heard by a magistrates' court) shall, for the purposes of subsections (5) to (7) of section 9 above, be treated as if it were an order of the court from which the appeal was brought and not an order of the High Court or the Crown Court.

(4) A person in respect of whom a parenting order is made by virtue of section 8(1)(c) above shall have the same right of appeal against the making of the order as if—

    (a) the offence that led to the making of the order were an offence committed by him; and

    (b) the order were a sentence passed on him for the offence.

(5) A person in respect of whom a parenting order is made by virtue of section 8(1)(d) above shall have the same right of appeal against the making of the order as if the order were a sentence passed on him for the offence that led to the making of the order.

(6) The Lord Chancellor may by order make provision as to the circumstances in which appeals under subsection (1)(a) above may be made against decisions taken by courts on questions arising in connection with the transfer, or proposed transfer, of proceedings by virtue of any order under paragraph 2 of Schedule 11 (jurisdiction) to the *Children Act* 1989 ("the 1989 Act").

(7) Except to the extent provided for in any order made under subsection (6) above, no appeal may be made against any decision of a kind mentioned in that subsection.

(8) The Lord Chief Justice may nominate a judicial office holder (as defined in section 109(4) of the *Constitutional Reform Act* 2005) to exercise his functions under this section.

(2) Procedure

27–109   In summary, a parenting order may be imposed where:

    (a) a child safety order is made in respect of a child;

    (b) an anti-social behaviour order or a sex offender order is made in respect of a child or young person;

    (c) a child or young person is convicted of an offence;

    (d) a person is convicted of an offence under section 443 (failure to comply with school attendance order) or section 444 (failure to secure regular attendance at school of registered pupil) of the *Education Act* 1996;

    (e) a youth court may make a parenting order when making a referral order.

27–110   The parenting order consists of two elements; compliance with such requirements as are specified in the order and attendance at counselling or guidance sessions. These measures are designed to encourage parents to accept responsibility for their children's offending and to provide appropriate support and discipline to prevent further offending. The order may not be made unless the court has received notification from the Secretary of State that arrangements for implementing such orders are available in the area in which it appears to the court that the parent resides or will reside and the notice has not been withdrawn: *Crime and Disorder Act* 1998, s.8(3). The order may be imposed for a maximum of twelve months, and the requirement to attend counselling or guidance session may last for a maximum period of three months with attendance a maximum of one session a week: *Crime and Disorder Act* 1998, s.8(4).

27–111   The order is mandatory where the offender is under 16 and the court considers that the relevant condition (prevention of re-offending) is satisfied; where the court does not consider the relevant condition to be satisfied, it must state in open court why it has arrived at that conclusion: *Crime and Disorder Act* 1998, s.9(1). The order is discretionary in the case of offenders aged 16 or 17. The court does not have to obtain a pre-sentence report, but the court should obtain and consider information about the person's family circumstances and the likely effect of the order on those circumstances: *Crime and Disorder Act* 1998, s.9(2). Before making the order, the court must explain to the parent in ordinary language:

(1) The effect of the order and of the requirements proposed to be included in it.

(2) The consequences which may follow if he fails to comply with any of those requirements.

(3) That the court has power to review the order on the application either of the parent or of the responsible officer: *Crime and Disorder Act* 1998, s.9(4).

The requirements specified in the order must also be such as to avoid any conflict **27–112** with the parents religious beliefs, and any interference with the times at which he normally works or attends an educational establishment: *Crime and Disorder Act* 1998, s.9(5).

There is no longer a prohibition against a court making a parenting order at the same time as making a referral order. However, the obligation to make such an order, or to give reasons for not doing so, does not apply when a referral order is made: *Criminal Justice Act* 2003, s.324 and Sched. 34.

The court may vary or discharge the parenting order following an application made to the court by the responsible officer or the parent: section 9(5). If an application for variation or discharge is made and dismissed, a further such application may not proceed without the consent of the court which refused the original application: section 9(6). A person in respect of whom a parenting order is made by virtue of paras (c) or (d) of section 8 of the 1998 Act will have the same right of appeal against the making of the order as if the order were a sentence passed on him for the offence: *Crime and Disorder Act* 1998, s.10(4).

(3) Breach

Breach of a parenting order will result in the parent being liable upon summary **27–113** conviction to a fine not exceeding level three on the standard scale: section 9(7).

XVII. ANTI-SOCIAL BEHAVIOUR ORDERS

(1) Purpose and effect

An application for an ASBO against a child or young person as a free standing civil **27–114** order is heard in the adult magistrates' court. The youth court has no jurisdiction to hear an application for such an order. However, the youth court has jurisdiction to make an ASBO on conviction for a criminal offence.

Crime and Disorder Act 1998, s.1C

Orders on conviction in criminal proceedings

1C.—(1) This section applies where a person (the "offender") is convicted of a relevant **27–115** offence.

(2) If the court considers—

    (a) that the offender has acted, at any time since the commencement date, in an anti-social manner, that is to say in a manner that caused or was likely to cause harassment, alarm or distress to one or more persons not of the same household as himself, and

    (b) that an order under this section is necessary to protect persons in any place in England and Wales from further anti-social acts by him,

it may make an order which prohibits the offender from doing anything described in the order.

(3) The court may make an order under this section—

    (a) if the prosecutor asks it to do so, or

    (b) if the court thinks it is appropriate to do so.

(3A) For the purpose of deciding whether to make an order under this section the court may consider evidence led by the prosecution and the defence.

(3B) It is immaterial whether evidence led in pursuance of subsection (3A) would have been admissible in the proceedings in which the offender was convicted.

(4) An order under this section shall not be made except—

Part V

(a) in addition to a sentence imposed in respect of the relevant offence; or

(b) in addition to an order discharging him conditionally.

(4A) The court may adjourn any proceedings in relation to an order under this section even after sentencing the offender.

(4B) If the offender does not appear for any adjourned proceedings, the court may further adjourn the proceedings or may issue a warrant for his arrest.

(4C) But the court may not issue a warrant for the offender's arrest unless it is satisfied that he has had adequate notice of the time and place of the adjourned proceedings.

(5) An order under this section takes effect on the day on which it is made, but the court may provide in any such order that such requirements of the order as it may specify shall, during any period when the offender is detained in legal custody, be suspended until his release from that custody.

(9) Subsections (7), (10), (10C), (10D), (10E) and (11) of section 1 apply for the purposes of the making and effect of orders made by virtue of this section as they apply for the purposes of the making and effect of anti-social behaviour orders.

(9A) The council for the local government area in which a person in respect of whom an anti-social behaviour order has been made resides or appears to reside may bring proceedings under section 1(10) (as applied by subsection (9) above) for breach of an order under subsection (2) above.

(9B) Subsection (9C) applies in relation to proceedings in which an order under subsection (2) is made against a child or young person who is convicted of an offence.

(9C) In so far as the proceedings relate to the making of the order—

(a) section 49 of the Children and Young Persons Act 1933 (c. 12) (restrictions on reports of proceedings in which children and young persons are concerned) does not apply in respect of the child or young person against whom the order is made;

(b) section 39 of that Act (power to prohibit publication of certain matter) does so apply.

(10) In this section—

"child" and "young person" have the same meaning as in the *Children and Young Persons Act* 1933;

"the commencement date" has the same meaning as in section 1 above;

"the court" in relation to an offender means—

(a) the court by or before which he is convicted of the relevant offence; or

(b) if he is committed to the Crown Court to be dealt with for that offence, the Crown Court; and

"relevant offence" means an offence committed after the coming into force of section 64 of the *Police Reform Act* 2002.

(2) Procedure

27–116   The youth court may make an ASBO where an offender is convicted of an offence on or after December 2, 2002. The Court must consider that the offender has acted at any time since April 1, 1999 in a manner that was likely to cause harassment, alarm or distress to one or more persons not of the same household as himself. Having reached this conclusion the Court must then go on to consider whether an ASBO is necessary to protect persons in any place in England and Wales from further anti-social acts by the defendant. It must be proved to the criminal standard of proof that anti-social behaviour has been committed by the defendant, but the civil rules of evidence apply. The question of whether an order is necessary is a matter of judgment and evaluation by the Court.

The need for an order and the wording of appropriate prohibitions has been looked at extensively by the Court of Appeal in a number of decisions. The principles set out in those decisions apply equally to youths as they do to adults. In dealing with youths, however, the welfare provisions in section 44(1) of the *CYPA* 1933 must be taken into account (see *ante*, § 25–3). In *R. (A.) v. Leeds Magistrates' Court* (2004) EWHC 554, Admin, the Court held that welfare was a primary consideration but not the paramount consideration which was the interests of the public.

The youth court may make an ASBO under section 1C upon the application of any **27–117** agency concerned in the case that would be entitled to apply for such an order. In addition the youth court may make an order of its own volition.

In *Sheffield Magistrates' Court* [2004] EWHC 1830 the appellant youth appealed against an ASBO made against him. The applicant for the ASBO was the same local authority to whom he was in care pursuant to an order made under section 31 of the *Children Act* 1989. The Court was asked to consider whether the potential for conflict was such that a local authority could ever apply for an ASBO in respect of a child in its care. It was held that a local authority was not prevented from applying for an ASBO in such circumstances provided that measures were taken to prevent a breach of the rights of that child in connection with such an application.

Section 1C does not prescribe any particular procedure when consideration is given **27–118** as to whether an ASBO should be made on conviction. However, the youth court must act fairly and have regard to all relevant considerations. In *C. v. (1) Sunderland Youth Court (2) Northumbria Police and (3) CPS* [2004] 1 Cr.App.R.(S.) 76, DC a youth applied for judicial review of the youth court's decision to impose an ASBO under section 1(C) of the *CDA* 1998. The application was allowed, the court emphasising the importance of fairness, careful consideration of evidence, and clarity as to the reasons for its decision. It was also said to be vital that the terms of an ASBO were clearly and accurately explained to the offender by the court.

In the case of *P.*, *The Times*, February 19, 2004, CA a youth was sentenced to detention for four years. In addition an ASBO for two years was made, suspended until his release from custody. On appeal the ASBO was quashed because it was not possible for the court to determine that an ASBO was necessary to protect the public at a future date in view of the length of the sentence coupled with a 12-month period on licence. The court also confirmed the principles set out in *C. v. Sunderland Youth Court*— above.

In *Shane Tony* [2004] EWCA Crim 287, the Court of Appeal identified the following principles in relation to the making of an ASBO on conviction:

(a) The test for making an order is one of necessity to protect the public from further anti social acts by the offender.

(b) The terms of the order must be precise and capable of being understood by the offender.

(c) The findings of fact giving rise to the making of the order must be recorded.

(d) The order must be explained to the offender.

(e) The exact terms of the order must be pronounced in open court and the written order must accurately reflect the order pronounced.

(3) Breach of ASBO

The ASBO is a civil proceedings order with criminal penalties if breached. If without **27–119** reasonable excuse a person does anything which he is prohibited from doing by an ASBO, he shall be guilty of an offence which when tried summarily carries a penalty of imprisonment for a term not exceeding six months, a fine not exceeding the statutory maximum or both. Where a person is convicted of breach of ASBO the Court may not make an order of Conditional Discharge: section 1 of the *Crime and Disorder Act* 1998 (see *ante*, §§ 23–258 *et seq.*).

Breach proceedings against youths, whether in respect of a civil ASBO or an ASBO made on conviction are prosecuted in the youth court. The offence is not a "grave crime" or "scheduled" offence and there is therefore no power to send the matter to the Crown Court. On conviction in the youth court the referral order, community penalty and detention and training order apply in the same way as they do for other offences involving youths. The maximum sentence for breach of an ASBO in appropriate circumstances is a two-year DTO.

(4) Publicity in ASBO cases in the youth court

27–120   The restrictions on press and publicity in the youth court are set out under §§ 25–8–25–10, *ante*. However, in respect of ASBOs against youths different rules apply:

(i) As regard orders made on conviction in the youth court the restrictions on reporting set out in section 49 remain (see § 25–9, *ante*). However, section 1C(9C) of the 1998 Act provides that section 49 does not apply in relation to youths against whom an ASBO is made on conviction in so far as the proceedings relate to the making of the order. This means that, unless the Court exercises its discretion under section 39 of the 1933 Act, details of the child or young person may be published. However, details of the criminal offence which led to the order being made remain subject to automatic reporting restrictions.

(ii) Proceedings for breach of an ASBO in the youth court are not subject to section 49 and may be reported. However, it seems that the youth court may make an order prohibiting such reporting under the provisions of section 39 of the 1933 Act.

Part VI

Mentally Disordered Offenders

CHAPTER 28

MENTALLY DISORDERED OFFENDERS

I. INTRODUCTION

The Government presented a new Mental Health Bill to Parliament on November **28–1** 16, 2006. The Bill proposes a series of amendments to the *Mental Health Act* 1983, which would significantly affect the magistrates' courts' approach to mentally disordered offenders. First, the Bill proposes to change the current definition of "mental disorder" (*Mental Health Act* 1983, s.1) by replacing the existing four separate categories of mental disorder with a single streamlined definition of "mental disorder" as "any disorder or disability of the mind". The Bill continues to exclude dependence on alcohol and drugs from the definition of "mental disorder", yet removes the current exclusions for promiscuity, other immoral conduct and sexual deviancy. The Bill also introduces supervised community treatment orders, which would make compulsory community treatment available for offenders following their release from hospital. The Bill also replaces the current "treatability" test in the 1983 Act with a requirement that if patients are to be subject to detention for treatment or the new regime of supervised community treatment, appropriate treatment must be available.

The Bill has been criticised by mental health charities and service user groups, *e.g.* see the response of the Mental Health Alliance, available at www.mind.org.uk. The most recent amendments to the Bill were made on its third reading in the House of Lords, which proposed that the existing "treatability" test be retained; that the proposed definition of mental illness be reformulated so sexual orientation/identity, substance use and cultural/political/religious beliefs do not in themselves constitute mental illness and that the use of compulsory community treatment be restricted to those who have already been in hospital previously and deteriorated quickly when they returned home. At the time of writing, the Bill had just received its third reading in the House of Commons. Future editions of this work will deal fully with the amendments to the *Mental Health Act* 1983 affected by the 2006 Mental Health Bill, should it come into force.

II. DEFINITION OF "MENTAL DISORDER"

Mental Health Act 1983, s.1

Application of Act: "mental disorder"

28–2　　　**1.**—(1) The provisions of this Act shall have effect with respect to the reception, care and treatment of mentally disordered patients, the management of their property and other related matters.

(2) In this Act—

"mental disorder" means mental illness, arrested or incomplete development of mind, psychopathic disorder and any other disorder or disability of mind and 'mentally disordered' shall be construed accordingly;

"severe mental impairment" means a state of arrested or incomplete development of mind which includes severe impairment of intelligence and social functioning and is associated with abnormally aggressive or seriously irresponsible conduct on the part of the person concerned and 'severely mentally impaired' shall be construed accordingly;

"mental impairment" means a state of arrested or incomplete development of mind (not amounting to severe mental impairment) which includes significant impairment of intelligence and social functioning and is associated with abnormally aggressive or seriously irresponsible conduct on the part of the person concerned and "mentally impaired" shall be construed accordingly;

"psychopathic disorder" means a persistent disorder or disability of mind (whether or not including significant impairment of intelligence) which results in abnormally aggressive or seriously irresponsible conduct on the part of the person concerned;

and other expressions shall have the meanings assigned to them in section 145 below.

(3) Nothing in subsection (2) above shall be construed as implying that a person may be dealt with under this Act as suffering from mental disorder, or from any form of mental disorder described in this section, by reason only of promiscuity or other immoral conduct, sexual deviancy or dependence on alcohol or drugs.

28–3　　　The term "mental illness" is not further defined in the 1983 Act, though the Department of Social Security's Consultative Document on the *Mental Health Act 1959*: (DHSS (1976) *A Review of the Mental Heath Act 1959*: London: HMSO) suggested:

(a) more than temporary impairment of intellectual functions shown by a failure of memory, orientation, comprehension and learning capacity;

(b) more than temporary alteration of mood of such degree as to give rise to the patient having a delusional appraisal of his situation, his past or future or that of others or the lack of any appraisal;

(c) delusional beliefs persecutory, jealous or grandiose;

(d) abnormal perceptions associated with delusional misinterpretation of events;

(e) thinking so disordered as to prevent the patient making a reasonable appraisal of his situation or having reasonable communication with others.

However, there is no definitive definition of the term "mental illness", the lack of definition not being thought to cause any difficulties in practice (Department of Health and Social Security et al (1978) *Review of the Mental Health Act 1959*, Cmnd. 7320: London, HMSO).

III. DIVERSION FROM THE CRIMINAL JUSTICE SYSTEM

28–4　　　Two government policy documents encourage the diversion of mentally disordered offenders from the criminal justice system in appropriate cases. First, Home Office Circular 66/90 (*Provision for Mentally Disordered Offenders*) provides that government policy is to divert mentally disordered persons from the criminal justice system in cases where the public interest does not require their prosecution. Chief Officers of Police are therefore asked to ensure that, taking into account the public interest, consideration is always given to alternatives to prosecution, including taking no further action where appropriate and that effective arrangements are established with local health and social services authorities to ensure their speedy involvement when mentally disordered persons are taken into police custody. Where a prosecution is considered necessary, non-penal disposals should be used wherever appropriate and the police, courts and probation services should work with their local health and social services to make effective use of the provisions of the *Mental Health Act* 1983 and the services which exist to help the mentally disordered offender.

Secondly, further advice is contained in Home Office Circular 12/95 *Mentally Disordered Offenders—Inter-Agency Working*.

In deciding whether a prosecution should be commenced or continued prosecutors **28–5** should have regard to The Code for Crown Prosecutors (2004). The Code (at para. 5.10) provides some common public interest factors against prosecution, which include: if the prosecution is likely to have a bad effect on the victim's physical or mental health (always bearing in mind the seriousness of the offence) and whether the defendant is, or was at the time of the offence, suffering from significant mental or physical ill heath. The Code identifies the need for prosecutors to "balance the desirability of diverting a defendant who is suffering from significant mental or physical ill health with the need to safeguard the general public". The Code is reproduced in full in Appendix E.

IV. BAIL

(1) Bail from the police station

After charge at the police station, the general right to bail for persons accused of of- **28–6** fences in the magistrates' courts applies to the mentally disordered offender. The offender must be granted bail unless one of the conditions specified in section 38(1) of the *Police and Criminal Evidence Act* 1984 applies. Bail may be refused in specified circumstances, some of which may apply in the case of an accused who is suspected of suffering from mental disorder: see *ante*, §§ 4–49 *et seq*.

(2) Bail at the magistrates' court

The *Bail Act* 1976 applies to mentally disordered offenders as to any other offender. **28–7** Note the exceptions to right to bail where there are grounds for believing that the defendant may abscond, commit an offence or interfere with witnesses. The court may exercise its power to remand in custody for the defendant's own protection (*Bail Act* 1976, Sched. 1, Pt 1, para. 3).

Post conviction the court may exercise its power to impose a requirement that the offender makes himself available for the purpose of enabling enquiries or a report to be made to assist the court in dealing with him for the offence: *Bail Act* 1976, s.3(6)(d).

If a defendant is remanded in custody, the Home Secretary may direct that the defendant be transferred from prison to a hospital for the purpose of the preparation of medical reports on the accused's psychiatric condition: *Mental Health Act* 1983, s.48(2)(b). A transfer under section 48 may be ordered before or after conviction. It is an administrative alternative to a remand to hospital ordered by a court under section 35 or section 38, see *post*, §§ 28–8 and 28–27.

V. REMAND TO HOSPITAL FOR ASSESSMENT

Mental Health Act 1983, s.35

Remand to hospital for report on accused's mental condition.

35.—(1) Subject to the provisions of this section, the Crown Court or a magistrates' court **28–8** may remand an accused person to a hospital specified by the court for a report on his mental condition.

(2) For the purposes of this section an accused person is—

(a) in relation to the Crown Court, any person who is awaiting trial before the court for an offence punishable with imprisonment or who has been arraigned before the court for such an offence and has not yet been sentenced or otherwise dealt with for the offence on which he has been arraigned;

    (b) in relation to a magistrates' court, any person who has been convicted by the court of an offence punishable on summary conviction with imprisonment and any person charged with such an offence if the court is satisfied that he did the act or made the omission charged or he has consented to the exercise by the court of the powers conferred by this section.

(3) Subject to subsection (4) below, the powers conferred by this section may be exercised if—

    (a) the court is satisfied, on the written or oral evidence of a registered medical practitioner, that there is reason to suspect that the accused person is suffering from mental illness, psychopathic disorder, severe mental impairment or mental impairment; and

    (b) the court is of the opinion that it would be impracticable for a report on his mental condition to be made if he were remanded on bail;

but those powers shall not be exercised by the Crown Court in respect of a person who has been convicted before the court if the sentence for the offence of which he has been convicted is fixed by law.

(4) The court shall not remand an accused person to a hospital under this section unless satisfied, on the written or oral evidence of the registered medical practitioner who would be responsible for making the report or of some other person representing the managers of the hospital, that arrangements have been made for his admission to that hospital and for his admission to it within the period of seven days beginning with the date of the remand; and if the court is so satisfied it may, pending his admission, give directions for his conveyance to and detention in a place of safety.

(5) Where a court has remanded an accused person under this section it may further remand him if it appears to the court, on the written or oral evidence of the registered medical practitioner responsible for making the report, that a further remand is necessary for completing the assessment of the accused person's mental condition.

(6) The power of further remanding an accused person under this section may be exercised by the court without his being brought before the court if he is represented by counsel or a solicitor and his counsel or solicitor is given an opportunity of being heard.

(7) An accused person shall not be remanded or further remanded under this section for more than 28 days at a time or for more than 12 weeks in all; and the court may at any time terminate the remand if it appears to the court that it is appropriate to do so.

(8) An accused person remanded to hospital under this section shall be entitled to obtain at his own expense an independent report on his mental condition from a registered medical practitioner chosen by him and to apply to the court on the basis of it for his remand to be terminated under subsection (7) above.

(9) Where an accused person is remanded under this section—

    (a) a constable or any other person directed to do so by the court shall convey the accused person to the hospital specified by the court within the period mentioned in subsection (4) above; and

    (b) the managers of the hospital shall admit him within that period and thereafter detain him in accordance with the provisions of this section.

(10) If an accused person absconds from a hospital to which he has been remanded under this section, or while being conveyed to or from that hospital, he may be arrested without warrant by any constable and shall, after being arrested, be brought as soon as practicable before the court that remanded him; and the court may thereupon terminate the remand and deal with him in any way in which it could have dealt with him if he had not been remanded under this section.

28–9   Whilst the proceedings remain in the magistrates' court, this power to remand to hospital for assessment only arises if the defendant has been convicted of an offence which is punishable with imprisonment on summary conviction or if the defendant is charged with such an offence and the court have made a finding (without convicting) that the defendant did the act or made the omission charged, in accordance with section 37(3), see *post*, § 28–20.

VI. HOSPITAL ORDERS WITHOUT CONVICTION

(1) Mental Health Act 1983, s.37(3)

Where a person is tried summarily for an act or omission which would, upon convic- **28–10** tion, warrant a hospital order, the court may impose such an order once it is satisfied that the accused did the act or made the omission charged. The court must still have the reports of two registered medical practitioners testifying to the mental state of the accused, and a hospital bed must be available before this power becomes exercisable.

The order is available where the offender is charged with an offence triable either way and he elects trial by indictment: *R. v. Ramsgate Justices, ex p. Kazmarek* (1984) 80 Cr.App.R. 366. The order is also available where the offender was unable to consent to summary trial: *R. v. Lincolnshire (Kesteven) Justices, ex p. O'Connor* [1983] 1 W.L.R. 335, DC. Because section 37(3) gives the court the power to make a hospital order without convicting the accused, it has been held that it is not necessary that a trial be held: *R. v. Lincolnshire (Kesteven) Justices, ex p. O'Connor, ibid.*

To satisfy the court that the defendant did the act or made the omission charged, the prosecution need only prove the ingredients which comprise the *actus reus* of the offence: *Antoine* (2000) 2 All E.R. 208, HL. Whilst a finding under section 37(3) is not a conviction, a defendant against whom such an order is made has a right of appeal as if it were a conviction: section 45.

The consequence of consensual admission is little different from the consequence of a hospital order under section 37 of the *Mental Health Act* 1983, save that a patient detained under a hospital order may not apply for discharge until six months have elapsed.

(2) Fitness to plead

The question of fitness to plead is not relevant to proceedings in the magistrates' **28–11** court. The issue of fitness to plead arises only under the *Criminal Procedure (Insanity) Act* 1964 and the *Criminal Procedure (Insanity and Unfitness to Plead) Act* 1991, which apply only to proceedings in the Crown Court. The magistrates may commit an accused charged with an offence triable either way to the Crown Court, where the issue may be raised, though this power is not available if the accused is charged with an offence triable only summarily: *R. v. Metropolitan Stipendiary Magistrate Tower Bridge, ex p. Antifowosi* (1985) 144 J.P. 752.

(3) Insanity

Although the *Trial of Lunatics Act* 1883, s.2(1) provides that the special verdict of **28–12** not guilty by reason of insanity may only be returned by a jury, the defence is not limited to trials on indictment. The legal definition of insanity is that the accused was, at the time of commission of the act in question, labouring under a defect of reason, from disease of the mind as not to know the nature and the quality of the act he was doing, or if he did know it, he did not know it was wrong: *M'Naghten's case* (1843) 10 Cl. & Fin 200.

A disorder which impairs the accused's mental faculties of reason, memory and understanding so as to render him unaware of what he was doing, or unaware of the fact that what he was doing was wrong will be a "disease of the mind" causing a "defect of reason" within the M'Naghten Rules, whether the aetiology of the impairment was organic or functional and whether it was permanent or transient and intermittent: *Sullivan* (1984) A.C 156.

Insanity is a defence to any criminal charge as it operates as to render absent the **28–13** *mens rea* element of the crime. Insanity may therefore be raised against a charge tried summarily, though the court may not return the special verdict of "not guilty by reason of insanity": *Trial of Lunatics Act* 1883, *ante*. In *DPP v. Harper* [1997] 1 W.L.R. 1406, the respondent had been acquitted of driving a motor vehicle with an excess of alcohol in his blood, contrary to section 5(1)(a) of the *Road Traffic Act* 1988, on grounds of insanity. The prosecution appealed to the Divisional Court of the Queen's Bench Division, who granted the appeal holding that no defence of insanity is available in cases where the offence is one of strict liability. McCowan L.J. stated:

> "[I]nsanity can be a defence in the magistrates' court, but only if the offence charged is one in which *mens rea* is an element. Every man is assumed to be sane at the time of an alleged offence and, accordingly, the burden is on the accused to establish insanity at the time of the commission of the offence on the balance of probabilities. The defence is based on the absence of *mens rea*, but none is required for the offence of driving with an excess of alcohol. Hence, the defence of insanity has no relevance to such a charge, as it is an offence of strict liability." [at p.1409]

28–14		In addition to the inability to return the special verdict, the 1983 Act makes no provision for committal to the Crown Court by the magistrates for imposition of a restriction order under section 41 upon a person who has been acquitted of an offence by reason of insanity. The magistrates only have such a power to commit to the Crown Court for that purpose in the case of a person convicted of an imprisonable offence, whether indictable or summary only. This situation has been described as a "legislative lacuna": *R. v. Horseferry Road Magistrates' Court, ex p. K.* [1996] Cr.App.R. 574, DC.

VII. SENTENCING POWERS

A. PRE-SENTENCE REPORTS

28–15		Section 11 of the *Powers of Criminal Courts (Sentencing) Act* 2000 gives the court power to order a medical report on the offender's physical or mental condition when it considers such a report necessary for disposal of the case. The power arises when the offence is triable summarily, and punishable with imprisonment and the court is satisfied that the offender did the act or made the omission charged.

Powers of Criminal Courts (Sentencing) Act 2000, s.11

Remand by magistrates' court for medical examination

28–16		**11.**—(1) If, on the trial by a magistrates' court of an offence punishable on summary conviction with imprisonment, the court—

   (a) is satisfied that the accused did the act or made the omission charged, but

   (b) is of the opinion that an inquiry ought to be made into his physical or mental condition before the method of dealing with him is determined,

the court shall adjourn the case to enable a medical examination and report to be made, and shall remand him.

   (2) An adjournment under subsection (1) above shall not be for more than three weeks at a time where the court remands the accused in custody, nor for more than four weeks at a time where it remands him on bail.

   (3) Where on an adjournment under subsection (1) above the accused is remanded on bail, the court shall impose conditions under paragraph (d) of section 3(6) of the Bail Act 1976 and the requirements imposed as conditions under that paragraph shall be or shall include requirements that the accused—

   (a) undergo medical examination by a registered medical practitioner or, where the inquiry is into his mental condition and the court so directs, two such practitioners; and

   (b) for that purpose attend such an institution or place, or on such practitioner, as the court directs and, where the inquiry is into his mental condition, comply with any other directions which may be given to him for that purpose by any person specified by the court or by a person of any class so specified.

28–17		When exercising this power, the court must send a statement to the doctor where the offender is to be examined listing reasons for the request and any information before the court about the offender's mental and physical condition: *Criminal Procedure Rules* r.49.1: see Appendix G, G–273

In addition, the *Criminal Justice Act* 2003, s.157 (1) requires the Court, where the offender appears to be mentally disordered, to obtain and consider a medical report when passing a custodial sentence other than one fixed by law. However, this requirement does not apply if, in the circumstances of the case, the court is of the opinion that it is unnecessary to obtain a medical report.

Criminal Justice Act 2003, s.157

Additional requirements in case of mentally disordered offender

157.—(1) Subject to subsection (2), in any case where the offender is or appears to be mentally **28–18** disordered, the court must obtain and consider a medical report before passing a custodial sentence other than one fixed by law.

(2) Subsection (1) does not apply if, in the circumstances of the case, the court is of the opinion that it is unnecessary to obtain a medical report.

(3) Before passing a custodial sentence other than one fixed by law on an offender who is or appears to be mentally disordered, a court must consider–

(a) any information before it which relates to his mental condition (whether given in a medical report, a pre-sentence report or otherwise), and

(b) the likely effect of such a sentence on that condition and on any treatment which may be available for it.

(4) No custodial sentence which is passed in a case to which subsection (1) applies is invalidated by the failure of a court to comply with that subsection, but any court on an appeal against such a sentence—

(a) must obtain a medical report if none was obtained by the court below, and

(b) must consider any such report obtained by it or by that court.

(5) In this section "mentally disordered", in relation to any person, means suffering from a mental disorder within the meaning of the *Mental Health Act* 1983.

(6) In this section "medical report" means a report as to an offender's mental condition made or submitted orally or in writing by a registered medical practitioner who is approved for the purposes of section 12 of the *Mental Health Act* 1983 by the Secretary of State as having special experience in the diagnosis or treatment of mental disorder.

(7) Nothing in this section is to be taken to limit the generality of section 156.

See the *Criminal Procedure Rules* r.49.1: see Appendix G, G–273.　　　　　**28–19**

Where the court receives conflicting medical evidence in psychiatric reports, the court is entitled to prefer the evidence of one expert, and must resolve the issue in the light of the evidence and all the circumstances of the case: *Reid* [2005] EWCA Crim 392, CA.

B. Hospital/Guardianship Order

Mental Health Act 1983, s.37

Powers of courts to order hospital admission or guardianship

37.—(1) Where a person is convicted before the Crown Court of an offence punishable with **28–20** imprisonment other than an offence the sentence for which is fixed by law, or is convicted by a magistrates' court of an offence punishable on summary conviction with imprisonment, and the conditions mentioned in subsection (2) below are satisfied, the court may by order authorise his admission to and detention in such hospital as may be specified in the order or, as the case may be, place him under the guardianship of a local social services authority or of such other person approved by a local social services authority as may be so specified.

(1A) In the case of an offence the sentence for which would otherwise fall to be imposed—

(a) under section 51A(2) of the *Firearms Act* 1968,

(b) under section 110(2) or 111(2) of the *Powers of Criminal Courts (Sentencing) Act* 2000, or

(c) under any of sections 225 to 228 of the *Criminal Justice Act* 2003,

(d) under section 29(4) or (6) of the *Violent Crime Reduction Act* 2006 (minimum sentences in certain cases of using someone to mind a weapon) nothing in those provisions shall prevent a court from making an order under subsection (1) above for the admission of the offender to a hospital.

(1B) References in subsection (1A) above to a sentence falling to be imposed under any of the provisions mentioned in that subsection are to be read in accordance with section 305(4) of the *Criminal Justice Act* 2003.

(2) The conditions referred to in subsection (1) above are that—

    (a) the court is satisfied, on the written or oral evidence of two registered medical practitioners, that the offender is suffering from mental illness, psychopathic disorder, severe mental impairment or mental impairment and that either—

        (i) the mental disorder from which the offender is suffering is of a nature or degree which makes it appropriate for him to be detained in a hospital for medical treatment and, in the case of psychopathic disorder or mental impairment, that such treatment is likely to alleviate or prevent a deterioration of his condition; or

        (ii) in the case of an offender who has attained the age of 16 years, the mental disorder is of a nature or degree which warrants his reception into guardianship under this Act; and

    (b) the court is of the opinion, having regard to all the circumstances including the nature of the offence and the character and antecedents of the offender, and to the other available methods of dealing with him, that the most suitable method of disposing of the case is by means of an order under this section.

(3) Where a person is charged before a magistrates' court with any act or omission as an offence and the court would have power, on convicting him of that offence, to make an order under subsection (1) above in his case as being a person suffering from mental illness or severe mental impairment, then, if the court is satisfied that the accused did the act or made the omission charged, the court may, if it thinks fit, make such an order without convicting him.

(4) An order for the admission of an offender to a hospital (in this Act referred to as "a hospital order") shall not be made under this section unless the court is satisfied on the written or oral evidence of the registered medical practitioner who would be in charge of his treatment or of some other person representing the managers of the hospital that arrangements have been made for his admission to that hospital, and for his admission to it within the period of 28 days beginning with the date of the making of such an order; and the court may, pending his admission within that period, given such directions as it thinks fit for his conveyance to and detention in a place of safety.

(5) If within the said period of 28 days it appears to the Secretary of State that by reason of an emergency or other special circumstances it is not practicable for the patient to be received into the hospital specified in the order, he may give directions for the admission of the patient to such other hospital as appears to be appropriate instead of the hospital so specified; and where such directions are given—

    (a) the Secretary of State shall cause the person having the custody of the patient to be informed, and

    (b) the hospital order shall have effect as if the hospital specified in the directions were substituted for the hospital specified in the order.

(6) An order placing an offender under the guardianship of a local social services authority or of any other person (in this Act referred to as "a guardianship order") shall not be made under this section unless the court is satisfied that that authority or person is willing to receive the offender into guardianship.

(7) A hospital order or guardianship order shall specify the form or forms of mental disorder referred to in subsection (2)(a) above from which, upon the evidence taken into account under that subsection, the offender is found by the court to be suffering; and no such order shall be made unless the offender is described by each of the practitioners whose evidence is taken into account under that subsection as suffering from the same one of those forms of mental disorder, whether or not he is also described by either of them as suffering from another of them.

(8) Where an order is made under this section, the court shall not—

    (a) pass sentence of imprisonment or impose a fine or make a community order (within the meaning of Part 12 of the *Criminal Justice Act* 2003) in respect of the offence,

    (b) if the order under this section is a hospital order, make a referral order (within the meaning of the *Powers of Criminal Courts (Sentencing) Act* 2000) in respect of the offence, or

(c) make in respect of the offender a supervision order (within the meaning of that Act) or an order under section 150 of that Act (binding over of parent or guardian),

but the court may make any other order which it has power to make apart from this section; and for the purposes of this subsection "sentence of imprisonment" includes any sentence or order for detention.

[This section is printed as amended by the *Violent Crime Reduction Act* 2006.]

The court must be satisfied on the evidence of two registered medical practitioners **28–21** that the offender is suffering from a mental disorder, as defined in section 1 of the 1983 Act, of a nature or degree which makes it appropriate for him to be detained and treated in hospital for medical treatment and the court is of the opinion that this would be the most suitable method of disposal of the case. The court may make a hospital order without the offender's consent.

If the offender is aged over 14, and he has been convicted of a summary offence punishable with imprisonment, if the court considers that all the conditions for the making of a hospital order are satisfied and a restriction order (*Mental Health Act* 1983, s.41) is necessary for the effective punishment of the offender it should commit to the Crown Court for sentence: *Mental Health Act* 1983, s.43.

Where an offender is committed under section 43(1) and the magistrates' court by **28–22** which he is committed is satisfied on written or oral evidence that arrangements have been made for admission of the offender to hospital, the court may order the offender to be detained in hospital until the case is disposed of by the Crown Court: *Mental Health Act* 1983, s.44.

The hospital order has the "sole purpose" of ensuring "that the offender receives the **28–23** medical care and attention which he needs in the hope and expectation of course that the result will be to avoid the commission of further criminal acts": *Birch* (1989) 11 Cr.App.R.(S.) 202 The Court of Appeal also outlined the appropriate approach of a court when sentencing a mentally disordered offender:

> "First he should decide whether a period of compulsory detention is apposite. If the answer is that it is not, or may not be, the possibility of a probation order with a condition of outpatient treatment should be considered...
>
> Secondly the judge will ask himself whether the conditions contained in section 37(2)(a) for the making of a hospital order are satisfied. Here the judge acts on the evidence of the doctors. If he is left in doubt, he may wish to avail himself of the valuable provisions of sections 38 and 39.
>
> If the judge concludes that the conditions empowering him to make an order are satisfied, he will consider whether to make such an order, or whether "the most suitable method of disposing of the case (section 37(2)(b)) is to impose a sentence of imprisonment".

Where the psychiatric evidence given to a court is incomplete at the time of sentence **28–24** in that it fails to give a full picture of the defendant's mental state at the time of the offence, fresh evidence as to the mental state of the defendant may be submitted, and it may be appropriate to replace a sentence of imprisonment with a hospital order under section 37 of the *Mental Health Act* 1983: *Roden* [2006] EWCA Crim 1121, CA. In this case, the appellant appealed against concurrent sentences of six years' imprisonment imposed after he pleaded guilty to two counts of arson with intent to endanger life. A psychiatrist had given evidence that the appellant had no diagnosable mental disorder and was not mentally ill at the time of the offence. After sentencing, the appellant began to exhibit psychotic symptoms, and was transferred to a mental hospital. His Responsible Medical Officer concluded he was suffering from paranoid schizophrenia and had done so since before starting the fire.

The Court of Appeal held that the Responsible Medical Officer's evidence satisfied the requirements of the *Criminal Appeal Act* 1968, s.23(2), it was expedient in the interests of justice to receive it, and that the psychiatric evidence before the judge had been incomplete as it failed to give a full picture of the appellant's mental state at the time of the offence. The Court stated that the fresh evidence satisfied the criteria for making a hospital order under section 37(2) and had that evidence been before the judge, it would have been appropriate to make such an order. It was, therefore, appropriate to replace the appellant's sentence with a hospital order, together with a restriction order under section 41 of the *Mental Health Act* 1983.

28–25   The decision whether to make a hospital order lies within the court's discretion; there is no presumption that where an offender meets the conditions for a hospital order, a hospital order will be made. The offender's needs, specifically those relating to his psychiatric condition, are an important matter for the judge but they are not overriding: *Khelifi* [2006] 2 Cr.App.R. (S.) 100, CA. In this case, the appellant had been involved to a major extent in a serious and sophisticated fraud. There was evidence that he had been genuinely suffering from paranoid schizophrenia since 1994 and that he was at risk of self-harm if not treated. However, the Court of Appeal held that a sentence of imprisonment was not wrong in principle, though the appellant's circumstances and his basis of plea justified a reduction in the sentence from five years to three-and-a-half years' imprisonment.

This decision has been received with caution. For example, writing in *Criminal Law Week*, James Richardson states:

> "it should be remembered that prison is no place for the mentally ill, and that expectations about particular offenders being transferred promptly to hospital under s.37 are not always realised, and that delays may lead to a serious deterioration in the prisoner's mental health". (CLW/06/40/31)

28–26   See also *Criminal Procedure Rules* r.49.2: Appendix G, G–274.

C. INTERIM HOSPITAL ORDERS

Mental Health Act 1983, s.38

Interim hospital orders

28–27   **38.**—(1) Where a person is convicted before the Crown Court of an offence punishable with imprisonment (other than an offence the sentence for which is fixed by law) or is convicted by a magistrates' court of an offence punishable on summary conviction with imprisonment and the court before or by which he is convicted is satisfied, on the written or oral evidence of two registered medical practitioners—

> (a) that the offender is suffering from mental illness, psychopathic disorder, severe mental impairment or mental impairment; and
>
> (b) that there is reason to suppose that the mental disorder from which the offender is suffering is such that it may be appropriate for a hospital order to be made in his case,

the court may, before making a hospital order or dealing with him in some other way, make an order (in this Act referred to as "an interim hospital order") authorising his admission to such hospital as may be specified in the order and his detention there in accordance with this section.

(2) In the case of an offender who is subject to an interim hospital order the court may make a hospital order without his being brought before the court if he is represented by counsel or a solicitor and his counsel or solicitor is given an opportunity of being heard.

(3) At least one of the registered medical practitioners whose evidence is taken into account under subsection (1) above shall be employed at the hospital which is to be specified in the order.

(4) An interim hospital order shall not be made for the admission of an offender to a hospital unless the court is satisfied, on the written or oral evidence of the registered medical practitioner who would be in charge of his treatment or of some other person representing the managers of the hospital, that arrangements have been made for his admission to that hospital and for his admission to it within the period of 28 days beginning with the date of the order; and if the court is so satisfied the court may, pending his admission, given directions for his conveyance to and detention in a place of safety.

(5) An interim hospital order—

(a) shall be in force for such period, not exceeding 12 weeks, as the court may specify when making the order; but

(b) may be renewed for further periods of not more than 28 days at a time if it appears to the court, on the written or oral evidence of the responsible medical officer, that the continuation of the order is warranted;

but no such order shall continue in force for more than twelve months in all and the court shall terminate the order if it makes a hospital order in respect of the offender or decides after considering the written or oral evidence of the responsible medical officer to deal with the offender in some other way.

(6) The power of renewing an interim hospital order may be exercised without the offender being brought before the court if he is represented by counsel or a solicitor and his counsel or solicitor is given an opportunity of being heard.

(7) If an offender absconds from a hospital in which he is detained in pursuance of an interim hospital order, or while being conveyed to or from such a hospital, he may be arrested without warrant by a constable and shall, after being arrested, be brought as soon as practicable before the court that made the order; and the court may thereupon terminate the order and deal with him in any way in which it could have dealt with him if no such order had been made.

Where a court is unable to make an interim hospital order under section 37 (3) due **28–28** to the absence of any illness of such a nature or degree to warrant compulsory detention in hospital, the court is still able to make an guardianship order under section 37 (3) of the *Mental Health Act* 1983. A court cannot therefore order that a defendant suffering from a disorder that does not warrant hospital treatment must enter a formal plea, and be subject to normal criminal procedure; the guardianship order remains an option and must be considered: *R. (Bartram) v. Southend Magistrates' Court* [2004] EWHC 2691, QBD.

D. COMMUNITY ORDERS WITH A CONDITION OF MEDICAL TREATMENT

Criminal Justice Act 2003, s.207

Mental health treatment requirement

207—(1) In this Part, "mental health treatment requirement", in relation to a community or- **28–29** der or suspended sentence order, means a requirement that the offender must submit, during a period or periods specified in the order, to treatment by or under the direction of a registered medical practitioner or a chartered psychologist (or both, for different periods) with a view to the improvement of the offender's mental condition.

(2) The treatment required must be such one of the following kinds of treatment as may be specified in the relevant order—

(a) treatment as a resident patient in an independent hospital or care home within the meaning of the *Care Standards Act* 2000 or a hospital within the meaning of the *Mental Health Act* 1983, but not in hospital premises where high security psychiatric services within the meaning of that Act are provided;

(b) treatment as a non-resident patient at such institution or place as may be specified in the order;

(c) treatment by or under the direction of such registered medical practitioner or chartered psychologist (or both) as may be so specified;

but the nature of the treatment is not to be specified in the order except as mentioned in paragraph (a), (b) or (c).

(3) A court may not by virtue of this section include a mental health treatment requirement in a relevant order unless—

(a) the court is satisfied, on the evidence of a registered medical practitioner approved for the purposes of section 12 of the *Mental Health Act* 1983, that the mental condition of the offender—

(i) is such as requires and may be susceptible to treatment, but

(ii) is not such as to warrant the making of a hospital order or guardianship order within the meaning of that Act;

(b) the court is also satisfied that arrangements have been or can be made for the treatment intended to be specified in the order (including arrangements for the reception of the offender where he is to be required to submit to treatment as a resident patient); and

(c) the offender has expressed his willingness to comply with such a requirement.

(4) While the offender is under treatment as a resident patient in pursuance of a mental health requirement of a relevant order, his responsible officer shall carry out the supervision of the offender to such extent only as may be necessary for the purpose of the revocation or amendment of the order.

(5) Subsections (2) and (3) of section 54 of the *Mental Health Act* 1983 have effect with respect to proof for the purposes of subsection (3)(a) of an offender's mental condition as they have effect with respect to proof of an offender's mental condition for the purposes of section 37(2)(a) of that Act.

(6) In this section and section 208, 'chartered psychologist' means a person for the time being listed in the British Psychological Society's Register of Chartered Psychologists.

28–30　　Before making such an order, the court must be satisfied that arrangements have been or can be made for the treatment intended to be specified in the order (including arrangements for the reception of the offender where he is to be required to submit to treatment as a resident patient) and the offender has consented to the treatment: *Criminal Justice Act* 2003, s.207(3).

E. Imprisonment

28–31　　When considering passing a sentence of imprisonment, other than one fixed by law, on an offender who is or appears to be suffering from some form of mental disorder, the court must obtain and consider a medical report: *Criminal Justice Act* 2003, s.157 (see *ante*, § 28–18).

28–32　　The power to impose an extended sentence (either under the *Powers of Criminal Courts (Sentencing) Act* 2000 in respect of offences committed before April 4, 2005 or under the *Criminal Justice Act* 2003 for offences committed after April 4, 2005) should be considered, and may influence the magistrates in their decision whether or not to commit to the Crown Court for sentence.

28–33　　Where the court obtains a medical report to assist in determining whether an extended sentence would be appropriate, it is essential that for the guidance of the sentencing judge it addresses the risk of serious harm posed by the offender: *S*. [2006] 2 Cr.App.R. (S.) 35, CA.

F. Hospital Order with Restriction Order

28–34　　The magistrates' court has no power to attach to a hospital order an order restricting discharge from hospital: *Mental Health Act* 1883, s.41. If a restriction order may be necessary the magistrates court should exercise its power in cases triable either way to decline jurisdiction or commit to the Crown Court for sentence (on which, see *ante*, § 23–112.

Part VII

Legal Aid and Costs

Chapter 29

LEGAL REPRESENTATION

I. CRIMINAL DEFENCE REPRESENTATION ORDERS

A. GENERAL

The *Access to Justice Act* 1999 established a new framework for the public funding **29–1** of legal representation in the criminal courts. It created the Legal Services Commission to replace the Legal Aid Board, and the Criminal Defence Service, which secures access to legal advice, assistance and representation in criminal matters. The Community Legal Service, also created by the Act, deals with the public funding of civil matters. The Act has been supplemented by regulations. The *Criminal Defence Service Act* 2006 came into force on October 2, 2006 and amended the *Access to Justice Act* 1999 so that the Legal Services Commission now has responsibility for administering the legal aid system. The Commission has power to delegate some function to court officers. The interests of justice test applies and a means test has now been reintroduced. The new system is set out in the Regulations all of which came into force on October 2, 2006. The *Criminal Defence Service (General) (No. 2) (Amendment) Regulations* 2006 (S.I. 2006 No. 2490) amend the 2001 regulations of the same name to recognise the transfer of responsibility for granting legal aid from the court to the Legal Services Commission.

The *Criminal Defence Service (Representation Orders and Consequential Amendments) Regulations* 2006 (S.I. 2006 No. 2493) empower the Legal Services Commission to grant legal aid instead of the court.

The *Criminal Defence Service (Representation Orders: Appeals etc.) Regulations* (S.I. 2006 No. 2494) preserves the right of appeal against a refusal on the interests of justice grounds to the magistrates' court.

The *Criminal Defence Service (Financial Eligibilty) Regulations* 2006 (S.I. 2006 No. 2492) set out the criteria to be applied in the means test and imposes a duty to report any changes of circumstances which might affect eligibilty for legal aid. These regulations have been amended by the *Criminal Defence Service (Financial Eligibilty) (Amendment) Regulations* 2007 (S.I. 2007 No. 777), which came into force on April 2, 2007 and increased the financial eligibility limits and the cost of living allowances for all applications made on or after that date.

Financial eligibility

Applicants are automatically eligible for legal aid if: **29–2**
   • They are under 16; or

- They are under 18 and in full time education; or
- They are in receipt of a passporting benefit, *i.e.* income support, income based jobseekers allowance or guarantee credit under the *State Pension Credit Act* 2002;
- They earn less than a gross annual income of GBP 12,007 once allowances are taken into account for partners and dependants.

Applicants are ineligible if their gross annual income, taking into account allowances for partners and dependants exceeds GBP 21,487. The allowances to be made are listed in the Schedule to the *Criminal Defence Service (Financial Eligibility) Regulations* 2006 as amended. Applicants whose income falls between the two amounts are subject to a means assessment to calculate the disposable income and where that falls below GBP 3,270 then they are eligible for legal aid.

There is no discretion in respect of the means test and assessment. An arithmetical formula is applied and applicants either pass or fail the test. The income of a co-habiting partner is also taken into account but if that partner is in receipt of a passporting benefit then the applicant is automatically eligible. The income of a partner will be disregarded if the applicant is separated from the partner even though they may still share accommodation. The partner's income will also be disregarded where they are a complainant or witness in the case against the applicant. This also applies to same sex partnerships.

A general application form must be completed and a means form unless the applicant is automatically eligible.

Some cases must be referred to the Commission. This includes cases where the applicant or their partner is self-employed, a company director, a partner in a firm or where they have assets subject to a freezing order or an injunction.

The court staff have a discretion to refer any applications where there is:

- an aura of wealth, (*i.e.* no income but an expensive address);
- fraudulent claims on the application form;
- high profile applicant;
- no income declared;
- outgoings exceeding income.

Supporting evidence

29–3   The applicant must supply supporting documentary evidence of income with the application:

- Benefits—National Insurance number;
- Employment—Wage slips;
- Accommodation costs—Bank statements where the rent or mortgage payment exceeds GBP 500 per month;
- Child care costs—Bank statement where costs exceed GBP 500 per month;
- Self-employed—Business accounts or tax statements.

If the applicant is in custody and has no access to supporting evidence of income then he may make a statement of truth of income. Where the interests of justice test is passed but the means are still being assessed an early cover payment may be made to legal representatives provided the application is lodged with the court within two days of the defendant being charged or within five days in respect of an applicant in custody. A fixed fee may be payable where legal aid is refused provided the defendant is seen within 10 days of charge.

Appeals

29–4   Any appeal against a refusal on grounds of financial ineligibility must be made to the LSC. If the applicant fails the means test an application for hardship review can be made if there is an inability to pay. If further more detailed or accurate information of financial circumstances becomes available the application can be submitted again to the court. An appeal against a refusal on the interests of justice is still made to the court. See *post*, § 29–51.

The application forms and the means calculator are all available on-line at www.legalservices.gov.uk/docs/forms.

Legal aid is available to defendants to ensure that legal representation is provided. **29–5** Legal assistance is not automatic in criminal cases in the magistrates' court. The circumstances and impact of the charge will be taken into account in assessing whether it is in the interests of justice that representation should be paid for from public funds. Schedule 3, paragraph 5 to the *Access to Justice Act* 1999 lists the factors that are relevant. Once the interests of justice test is met the grant of legal aid is subject to means.

In the magistrates' court the application will be considered by a "proper officer of the court" who will usually be a trained member of staff to whom the power to grant legal representation orders has been delegated by the Legal Services Commission. The application must identify fully the reasons why it is in the interests of justice for an order to be granted in accordance with the provisions of Schedule 3 to the Act, otherwise the application may be refused. Information and evidence of means must also be provided. The form must also be signed and dated.

B. THE HUMAN RIGHTS ACT 1998

Under Article 6(3)(c) of the European Convention on Human Rights everyone **29–6** charged with a criminal offence has the right "to defend himself in person or through legal assistance of his own choosing or, if he does not have sufficient means to pay for legal assistance, to be given it free when the interests of justice require it."

In the magistrates' court, applications for legal representation will be granted if the interests of justice require it. The interests of justice tests are included in the *Access to Justice Act* 1999 and European case law also gives an indication of the factors to be taken into account when assessing the interests of justice. The complexity of the case is relevant; *Benham v. UK* [1996] 22 E.H.R.R. 293 as is the ability of the defendant to comprehend and present his case: *Hoang v. France* [1993] 16 E.H.R.R. 53. The likelihood of a custodial sentence is an important factor: *Benham v. UK, ante*.

The legal representation granted must be "practical and effective" and it is not suf- **29–7** ficient for a lawyer to be merely nominated by the state. The system for legal aid must ensure that advice and assistance is given: *Artico v. Italy* [1981] 3 E.H.R.R. 1.

The choice of lawyer is not absolute. Where legal aid is concerned, the wishes of the defendant will be given consideration but the state can override those wishes where necessary. Also the right to conduct a complex case unrepresented may be restricted: *Croissant v. Germany* [1993] 16 E.H.R.R. 135. Article 6 requires the hearing to be "fair" and if the conduct or incompetence of a legal representative assigned under a scheme affects the fairness of the trial, a court may be obliged to intervene: *Nangle* [2001] Crim.L.R. 506.

A defence application for an adjournment of criminal proceedings should normally be granted where the defendant has not had the opportunity to apply for legal representation. In such circumstances the right to legal representation (or to a proper opportunity to apply for it) will normally outweigh other considerations, such as the convenience of the other parties and the use of court resources: *Berry Trade Ltd v. Moussavi* [2002] 1 W.L.R. 1910.

C. THE LEGAL SERVICES COMMISSION

(1) Constitution of the Commission

Access to Justice Act 1999, ss.1–2

Legal Services Commission

29–8   **1.**—(1) There shall be a body known as the Legal Services Commission (in this Part referred to as "the Commission").

(2) The Commission shall have the functions relating to—

  (a) the Community Legal Service, and

  (b) the Criminal Defence Service,

which are conferred or imposed on it by the provisions of this Act or any other enactment.

(3) The Commission shall consist of—

  (a) not fewer than seven members, and

  (b) not more than twelve members;

but the Lord Chancellor may by order substitute for either or both of the numbers for the time being specified in paragraphs (a) and (b) such other number or numbers as he thinks appropriate.

(4) The members of the Commission shall be appointed by the Lord Chancellor; and the Lord Chancellor shall appoint one of the members to chair the Commission.

(5) In appointing persons to be members of the Commission the Lord Chancellor shall have regard to the desirability of securing that the Commission includes members who (between them) have experience in or knowledge of—

  (a) the provision of services which the Commission can fund as part of the Community Legal Service or Criminal Defence Service,

  (b) the work of the courts,

  (c) consumer affairs,

  (d) social conditions, and

  (e) management.

(6) Schedule 1 (which makes further provision about the Commission) has effect.

Power to replace Commission with two bodies

29–9   **2.**—(1) The Lord Chancellor may by order establish in place of the Commission two bodies—

  (a) one to have functions relating to the Community Legal Service, and

  (b) the other to have functions relating to the Criminal Defence Service.

(2) The order may make any consequential, incidental, supplementary or transitional provisions, and any savings, which appear to the Lord Chancellor to be appropriate.

(3) The order shall include amendments of—

  (a) any provisions of, or amended by, this Part which refer to the Commission, and

  (b) any other enactments which so refer,

to replace references to the Commission with references to either or both of the bodies established by the order.

(2) Powers of the Commission

Access to Justice Act 1999, s.3

Powers of Commission

29–10   **3.**—(1) Subject to the provisions of this Part, the Commission may do anything which it considers—

  (a) is necessary or appropriate for, or for facilitating, the discharge of its functions, or

  (b) is incidental or conducive to the discharge of its functions.

(2) In particular, the Commission shall have power—

  (a) to enter into any contract,

  (b) to make grants (with or without conditions),

  (c) to make loans,

  (d) to invest money,

    (e) to promote or assist in the promotion of publicity relating to its functions,

    (f) to undertake any inquiry or investigation which it may consider appropriate in relation to the discharge of any of its functions, and

    (g) to give the Lord Chancellor any advice which it may consider appropriate in relation to matters concerning any of its functions.

    (3) Subsections (1) and (2) do not confer on the Commission power to borrow money.

    (4) The Commission may make such arrangements as it considers appropriate for the discharge of its functions, including the delegation of any of its functions.

    (5) The Lord Chancellor may by order require the Commission—

    (a) to delegate any function specified in the order or to delegate any function so specified to a person (or person of a description) so specified,

    (b) not to delegate any function so specified or not to delegate any function so specified to a person (or person of a description) so specified, or

    (c) to make arrangements such as are specified in the order in relation to the delegation of any function so specified.

The Commission has made arrangements under section 3(4) of the *Access to Justice*   **29–11**
Act 1999. The Review Panel Arrangements, which are effective from April 1, 2000, provide for the creation of a Review Panel, the appointment from that Panel of Funding Review Committees and Cost Committees and the regulation of the proceedings of those committees. The Commission has also made the Criminal Defence Service Duty Solicitor Arrangements 2001, which govern the provision of advice and assistance by duty solicitors at police stations and magistrates' courts.

D. CRIMINAL DEFENCE SERVICE

(1) The role of the Criminal Defence Service

Access to Justice Act 1999, s.12

Criminal Defence Service

    12.—(1) The Commission shall establish, maintain and develop a service known as the Crim-   **29–12**
inal Defence Service for the purpose of securing that individuals involved in criminal investigations or criminal proceedings have access to such advice, assistance and representation as the interests of justice require.

    (2) In this Part "criminal proceedings" means—

    (a) proceedings before any court for dealing with an individual accused of an offence,

    (b) proceedings before any court for dealing with an individual convicted of an offence (including proceedings in respect of a sentence or order),

    (c) proceedings for dealing with an individual under section 9 of, or paragraph 6 of Schedule 1 to, the *Extradition Act* 1989,

    (d) proceedings for binding an individual over to keep the peace or to be of good behaviour under section 115 of the *Magistrates' Courts Act* 1980 and for dealing with an individual who fails to comply with an order under that section,

    (e) proceedings on an appeal brought by an individual under section 44A of the *Criminal Appeal Act* 1968,

    (f) proceedings for contempt committed, or alleged to have been committed, by an individual in the face of a court, and

    (g) such other proceedings concerning an individual, before any such court or other body, as may be prescribed.

    (3) The Commission shall fund services as part of the Criminal Defence Service in accordance with sections 13 to 15.

    (4) The Commission may accredit, or authorise others to accredit, persons or bodies providing services which may be funded by the Commission as part of the Criminal Defence Service; and any system of accreditation shall include provision for the monitoring of the services provided by accredited persons and bodies and for the withdrawal of accreditation from any providing services of unsatisfactory quality.

    (5) The Commission may charge—

(a) for accreditation,
(b) for monitoring the services provided by accredited persons and bodies, and
(c) for authorising accreditation by others;
and persons or bodies authorised to accredit may charge for accreditation, and for such monitoring, in accordance with the terms of their authorisation.

(6) The Lord Chancellor may by order require the Commission to discharge the functions in subsections (4) and (5) in accordance with the order.

29–13　　Additional criminal proceedings have been prescribed by the *Criminal Defence Service (General) Regulations (No. 2) 2001*. The Rules included here relate specifically to the magistrates' court. The *Criminal Defence Service (General) (No. 2) (Amendment) Regulations* 2005 (S.I. 2005 No.2784) extend the list of related proceedings, which although not strictly criminal are eligible for legal aid. It includes certain intervention orders under the *Crime and Disorder Act* 1998 as amended by the *Drugs Act* 2005; certain parenting orders under the *Anti-Social Behaviour Act* 2003; certain orders under the *Sexual Offences Act* 2003 and restraining orders following acquittal of offences under the *Protection from Harassment Act* 1997. The order came into force on October 31, 2005 except in respect of offences that are not yet themselves in force.

Criminal Defence Service (General) (No.2) Regulations 2001, reg.3(1)–(2)

Criminal proceedings
29–14　　**3.**—(1) For the purposes of this regulation, "the 1998 Act" means the *Crime and Disorder Act* 1998.

(2) The following proceedings are criminal proceedings for the purposes of section 12(2)(g) of the Act:

(a) civil proceedings in a magistrates' court arising from failure to pay a sum due or to obey an order of that court where such failure carries the risk of imprisonment;

(b) proceedings under [sections 1, 1D, 2, 2A and 4] of the 1998 Act relating to anti-social behaviour orders or sex offender orders;

(c) proceedings under section 8(1)(b) of the 1998 Act relating to parenting orders made where an anti-social behaviour order or a sex offender order is made in respect of a child;

(d) proceedings under section 8(1)(c) of the 1998 Act relating to parenting orders made on the conviction of a child;

(e) proceedings under section 9(5) of the 1998 Act to discharge or vary a parenting order made as mentioned in sub-paragraph (c) or (d);

(f) proceedings under section 10 of the 1998 Act to appeal against a parenting order made as mentioned in sub-paragraph (c) or (d);

(g) proceedings under sections 14B, 14D, 14G, 14H, 21B and 21D of the *Football Spectators Act* 1989 (banning orders and references to a court); and

(h) proceedings under section 137 of the *Financial Services and Markets Act* 2000 to appeal against a decision of the Financial Services and Markets Tribunal.

[This regulation is reprinted as amended by the *Criminal Defence Service (General) (No. 2) (Amendment No. 2) Regulations* 2002, reg.2(a) and the *Football (Disorder) Act* 2000, Sched. 1, paras 2, 21B, 21D, 4.]

29–15　　Case law under previous legislation clarified the meaning of "criminal proceedings". In *R. v. Recorder of Liverpool, ex. p. McCann, The Times*, May 4, 1994, DC the court held that an application for the removal of a driving disqualification under the *Road Traffic Offenders Act* 1988, s.42 qualified as "criminal proceedings" because they were proceedings "in respect of a sentence". In *R. v. Redbridge Magistrates' Court, ex. p. Guppy* (1995) 159 J.P. 622, it was held that proceedings for the enforcement of a compensation order were criminal proceedings in respect of sentence and so were eligible for legal aid. Applications under section 42(2) of the *Drug Trafficking Act* 1994 for the continued detention of cash seized under section 42(1), or for the forfeiture of that cash did not fall within the definition as the applicant was neither charged with nor convicted of an offence: *R. v. Crawley Justices, ex. p. Ohakwe, The Times*, May 26, 1994.

Under the regulations the "hybrid offences" of anti-social behaviour orders and parenting orders introduced by the *Crime and Disorder Act* 1998 qualify for legal representation. Football banning orders are also covered. A surety may be eligible for legal representation under the provision that defines some civil proceedings as criminal for the purposes of legal representation if there is a risk of imprisonment in default of payment of a sum of money: regulation 3(2)(a), *ante*.

(2) Funding of legal services in criminal proceedings

Access to Justice Act 1999, s.13

Advice and assistance

13.—(1) The Commission shall fund such advice and assistance as it considers appropriate— **29–16**
  (a) for individuals who are arrested and held in custody at a police station or other premises, and
  (b) in prescribed circumstances, for individuals who—
    (i)   are not within paragraph (a) but are involved in investigations which may lead to criminal proceedings,
    (ii) are before a court or other body in such proceedings, or
    (iii) have been the subject of such proceedings;
    and the assistance which the Commission may consider appropriate includes assistance in the form of advocacy.
  (2) The Commission may comply with the duty imposed by subsection (1) by—
  (a) entering into contracts with persons or bodies for the provision of advice or assistance by them,
  (b) making payments to persons or bodies in respect of the provision of advice or assistance by them,
  (c) making grants or loans to persons or bodies to enable them to provide, or facilitate the provision of, advice or assistance,
  (d) establishing and maintaining bodies to provide, or facilitate the provision of, advice or assistance,
  (e) making grants to individuals to enable them to obtain advice or assistance,
  (f) employing persons to provide advice or assistance, or
  (g) doing anything else which it considers appropriate for funding advice and assistance.
  (3) The Lord Chancellor may by order require the Commission to discharge the function in subsection (2) in accordance with the order.
  (4) The Commission may fund advice and assistance by different means—
  (a) in different areas in England and Wales, and
  (b) in relation to different descriptions of cases.

[This section is reprinted as amended by the *Criminal Defence Service (Advice and Assistance) Act* 2001, s.1(1), which provides that the amendment be retrospective in its effect.]

The Legal Services Commission is empowered to secure the services referred to in **29–17** section 12 through contracts with lawyers in private practice or by providing salaried defenders employed directly by the commission. This means that a suspect's choice of legal representation is limited to contracted or salaried defenders although the intention is to provide a choice in all but exceptional cases. This does not offend against the ECHR. The right to have a lawyer of one's own choosing under Article 6(3)(c) is not absolute, particularly where the representation is being publicly funded: *Croissant v. Germany* (see *ante*, § 29–7). As a general rule the defendant's choice of lawyer should be respected and there must be relevant and sufficient justification to appoint a lawyer against his wishes: *Goddi v. Italy* [1984] 6 E.H.R.R. 457. It might be argued that the scheme for control of legal firms supplying defence services by the Legal Services Commission ensures a high standard of service and so is justified. Private solicitors may only undertake publicly funded criminal defence work if they have a contract to provide such services with the Criminal Defence Service: *Criminal Defence Service (General) (No. 2) Regulations* 2001 (S.I. 2001 No. 1437), r.11. In 2001 the Legal Services Commission began a four-year trial of its own defender service comprised of six offices staffed by people employed directly by the Commission.

Criminal Defence Service (General) (No.2) Regulations 2001, regs.4–5

Advice and assistance—scope

29–18   **4.** The Commission shall fund such advice and assistance, including advocacy assistance, as it considers appropriate in relation to any individual who:

    (a) is the subject of an investigation which may lead to criminal proceedings;

    (b) is the subject of criminal proceedings;

    (c) requires advice and assistance regarding his appeal or potential appeal against the outcome of any criminal proceedings or an application to vary a sentence;

    (d) requires advice and assistance regarding his sentence;

    (e) requires advice and assistance regarding his application or potential application to the Criminal Cases Review Commission;

    (f) requires advice and assistance regarding his treatment or discipline in prison (other than in respect of actual or contemplated proceedings regarding personal injury, death or damage to property);

    (g) is the subject of proceedings before the Parole Board;

    (h) requires advice and assistance regarding representations to the Home Office in relation to a mandatory life sentence or other parole review;

    (i) is a witness in criminal proceedings and requires advice regarding self-incrimination;[…]

    (j) is a volunteer or

    (k) is detained under Schedule 7 to the *Terrorism Act* 2000.

[This regulation is reprinted as amended by the *Criminal Defence Service (General) (Amendment) (No. 2) Regulations* 2002, reg.6.]

29–19   A volunteer is any person who voluntarily attends at a police station or elsewhere to assist with an investigation without having been arrested. Pursuant to its obligations under this section the Legal Services Commission has established the Police Station Duty Solicitor Scheme and the Magistrates' Courts Duty Solicitor Scheme so that those who require advice and assistance at a police station or court have access to a duty solicitor who is accredited by the Commission. A Duty Solicitor will be available at most courts on a daily basis to provide advice for unrepresented defendants. In busy courts there may well be a "bail" duty solicitor and a "custody" duty solicitor.

Advice and assistance—financial eligibility

29–20   **5.**—(1) The following advice and assistance may be granted without reference to the financial resources of the individual:

    (a) all advice and assistance provided to an individual who is arrested and held in custody at a police station or other premises;

    (b) all advocacy assistance before a magistrates' court or the Crown Court;

    (c) all advice and assistance provided by a court duty solicitor in accordance with his contract with the Commission;

    (d) all advice and assistance provided to a volunteer during his period of voluntary attendance;

    (e) all advice and assistance provided to an individual being interviewed in connection with a serious service offence; and

    (f) all advice and assistance provided in respect of an individual who is the subject of an identification procedure carried out by means of video recordings in connection with that procedure, notwithstanding the individual's non-attendance at a police station at the time the procedure is carried out.

    (2) For the purposes of paragraph (1), a serious service offence is an offence under the

Army Act 1955, the *Air Force Act* 1955 or the *Naval Discipline Act* 1957 which cannot be dealt with summarily.

[This regulation is reprinted as amended by the *Arms Forces Discipline Act* 2000 and the *Criminal Defence Service (General) (No.2) (Amendment) Regulations* 2003, reg.4(2).]

E. REPRESENTATION

(1) General

Access to Justice Act 1999, s.14

Representation

14.—(1) Schedule 3 (which makes provision about the grant of a right to representation in criminal proceedings) has effect; and the Commission shall fund representation to which an individual has been granted a right in accordance with that Schedule.   **29–21**

(2) Subject to the following provisions, the Commission may comply with the duty imposed by subsection (1) by—

    (a) entering into contracts with persons or bodies for the provision of representation by them,

    (b) making payments to persons or bodies in respect of the provision of representation by them,

    (c) making grants or loans to persons or bodies to enable them to provide, or facilitate the provision of, representation,

    (d) establishing and maintaining bodies to provide, or facilitate the provision of, representation,

    (e) making grants to individuals to enable them to obtain representation,

    (f) employing persons to provide representation, or

    (g) doing anything else which it considers appropriate for funding representation.

(3) The Lord Chancellor—

    (a) shall by order make provision about the payments which may be made by the Commission in respect of any representation provided by non-contracted private practitioners, and

    (b) may by order make any other provision requiring the Commission to discharge the function in subsection (2) in accordance with the order.

(4) For the purposes of subsection (3)(a) representation is provided by a non-contracted private practitioner if it is provided, otherwise than pursuant to a contract entered into by the Commission, by a person or body which is neither—

    (a) a person or body in receipt of grants or loans made by the Commission as part of the Criminal Defence Service, nor

    (b) the Commission itself or a body established or maintained by the Commission.

(5) The provision which the Lord Chancellor is required to make by order under subsection (3)(a) includes provision for reviews of, or appeals against, determinations required for the purposes of the order.

(6) The Commission may fund representation by different means—

    (a) in different areas in England and Wales, and

    (b) in relation to different descriptions of cases.

(2) The right to representation

Access to Justice Act 1999, Sched. 3, para. 1(1)–(3)

1.—(1) A right to representation for the purposes of any kind of criminal proceedings before a court may be granted to an individual such as is mentioned in relation to that kind of proceedings in section 12(2).   **29–22**

(2) A right to representation for the purposes of criminal proceedings may also be granted to an individual to enable him to resist an appeal to the Crown Court otherwise than in an official capacity.

(3) In this Schedule "court" includes any body before which criminal proceedings take place.

29–23   The Criminal Defence Service must fund representation to an individual who has been granted a right of representation. Legal aid is not available to corporations.

(3) Application for representation order

Criminal Defence Service (General) (No.2) Regulations 2001, reg.6

Representation order

29–24   **6.**—(1) The date of any representation order is the date on which the application for the grant of such an order is received in accordance with these Regulations.

(2) Any application for the grant of a representation order in respect of proceedings in the Crown Court or the Court of Appeal which are mentioned in section 12(2)(a) to (f) of the Act and in regulation 3(2)(h), shall be made in accordance with regulations 9 and 10.

(3) Any application for the grant of a representation order in respect of the proceedings mentioned in regulation 3(2) (criminal proceedings for the purposes of section 12(2)(g) of the Act)[, except those mentioned in regulation 3(2)(h)]:

    (a) shall be made to the Commission; and

    (b) may be granted only by the Commission or a person acting on behalf of the Commission where such function has been delegated in accordance with section 3(4) of the Act.

(4) Where an application under paragraph (3) is refused, the Commission shall provide to the applicant:

    (a) written reasons for the refusal; and

    (b) details of the appeal process.

(5) Where the person who requires representation is aged less than 18, the application for the grant of a representation order may be made by his parent or guardian on his behalf.

(6) The appropriate officer of each court shall keep a record of every application to that court for a representation order, and of its outcome.

(7) The appropriate officer shall send to the Lord Chancellor such information from the record mentioned in paragraph (6) as the Lord Chancellor may request.

29–25   The LSC has delegated the function to grant legal aid to court staff: see *ante*, § 29–1.

Criminal Defence Service (General) (No.2) Regulations 2001, reg.7

General power to grant representation

29–26   **7.** The court, a judge of the court, or the registrar of criminal appeals may grant a representation order at any stage of criminal proceedings (other than criminal proceedings in a magistrates' court) in the circumstances set out in these Regulations whether or not an application has been made for such an order.

[This regulation is reprinted as amended by the *Criminal Defence Service (General) (No. 2) (Amendment) Regulations* 2002, reg.9.]

29–27   The LSC has not delegated its power to grant representation to the district judge or justices in court. All applications must be submitted in writing to court staff so the interests of justice and financial eligibility may be assessed.

Criminal Defence Service (General) (No.2) Regulations 2001, reg.18

29–28   **18.** Where an individual is committed or sent for trial by a lower court to a higher court, or appeals or applies for leave to appeal from a lower court to a higher court, the appropriate officer of the lower court shall send to the appropriate officer of the higher court the following documents:

    (a) a copy of any representation order previously made in respect of the same proceedings; and

    (b) a copy of any application for a representation order which has been refused.

A copy of the criminal defence representation order (CDRO) or a notice of refusal **29–29**
will be sent to the Crown Court with the committal documents.

Access to Justice Act 1999, Sched. 3, para. 5

5.—(1) Any question as to whether a right to representation should be granted shall be **29–30**
determined according to the interests of justice.

(2) In deciding what the interests of justice consist of in relation to any individual, the
following factors must be taken into account—

    (a) whether the individual would, if any matter arising in the proceedings is decided
against him, be likely to lose his liberty or livelihood or suffer serious damage to
his reputation,

    (b) whether the determination of any matter arising in the proceedings may involve
consideration of a substantial question of law,

    (c) whether the individual may be unable to understand the proceedings or to state
his own case,

    (d) whether the proceedings may involve the tracing, interviewing or expert cross-
examination of witnesses on behalf of the individual, and

    (e) whether it is in the interests of another person that the individual be represented.

(3) The Lord Chancellor may by order amend sub-paragraph (2) by adding new factors
or varying any factor.

(4) A right to representation shall always be granted in such circumstances as may be
prescribed.

A criminal defence representation order will be granted if it is in the interests of **29–31**
justice according to these criteria. The test in Schedule 3, paragraph 5 to the *Access to
Justice Act* 1999 is similar to that which governed the discretion to grant legal aid in the
now-repealed *Legal Aid Act* 1988, s.22(2). Cases concerning that section are of assistance in interpreting the test in the *Access to Justice Act* 1999.

When assessing whether a conviction might lead to deprivation of liberty, loss of
livelihood or damage to reputation, the authority asked to grant a representation order
should consider the nature of the facts alleged by the prosecution in the particular case
rather than the maximum penalty that might theoretically be imposed Although the offence may carry a maximum of five years' imprisonment, the court must make a subjective assessment of the likelihood of loss of liberty having regard to the circumstances of
the case: *R. v. Highgate Justices, ex. p. Lewis* [1977] Crim.L.R. 611.

In *R. v. Liverpool City Magistrates' Court, ex. p. McGhee* (1994) 158 J.P. 275, the
court considered that the imposition of a community punishment order could not be
regarded as depriving the accused of his liberty but it could still be a relevant factor
when deciding whether to grant a right of representation.

In *R. v. Chester Magistrates' Court, ex. p. Ball* (1999) 163 J.P. 757, DC, the refusal **29–32**
to grant legal aid was quashed where justices had considered only the likelihood of loss
of liberty in the event of conviction and had failed to have regard to whether a conviction was likely to lead to serious damage to the reputation of the defendant. In *R. v.
Brigg Justices, ex. p. Lynch* (1984) 148 J.P. 214, legal aid was justified because of the
serious consequences of a conviction to the reputation and livelihood of a solider who
had been charged with indecent exposure.

A defendant who intended to raise a special reason in order to avoid a disqualification from driving on conviction of driving with excess alcohol in his blood was eligible
for legal aid in the interests of justice. The suggestion was that his drink had been laced
and so the advice and assistance could extend to the instruction of an expert witness.
The case was likely to be complex and the obtaining of an expert witness and possible
cross-examination of another expert witness meant that the criteria were met: *R. v.
Gravesend Magistrates' Court, ex. p. Baker* (1997) 161 J.P. 765, DC.

In *R. v. Scunthorpe Justices, ex. p. S., The Times*, March 5, 1998, DC the refusal to
grant legal aid to a 16 year old charged with obstruction of a police officer in the execution of his duty was quashed as irrational where there was an issue as to whether the officer was acting in the execution of his duty. The expertise required for the purpose of

cross examining the officer and for tracing and taking evidence from defence witnesses and the need to trace and interview them was beyond that of a 16 year old and a conviction would have damaged a young man of good character on the threshold of his life. If the court is of the view that there is insufficient information about alleged defence witnesses, it should adjourn the matter rather than refuse the application. The inability to understand or follow proceedings may relate to the complexity of the case or individual factors affecting the applicant, such as his age, mental or physical health or language difficulties. In *R. (Matara) v. Brent Magistrates' Court*, 169 J.P. 576 DC it was held that a Criminal Defence Representation Order should have been granted to an applicant who needed an interpreter where his defence to a drink drive charge was that he had not understood what was said to him on arrest. The assistance of an interpreter did not address the question of whether without benefit of legal representation he would be able to state his case and have a fair trial. These issues may also be relevant as to whether it would be in the interests of another person such as the victim or witnesses for the defendant to be represented so that cross-examination in person by the defendant may be avoided where appropriate. It is generally not sufficient to simply tick or mark "yes" on the form. Full details in the application form indicating which of the criteria apply and the reasons why, should ensure that applications are dealt with expeditiously.

29–33　　Where an application for a representation order is made at the conclusion of proceedings in a magistrates' court, the interests of justice test should be applied on the basis of the facts as they appeared at the time when the solicitor was first consulted and not on the basis of hindsight. Where the defendant was charged with an imprisonable offence in relation to which there was a real and practical (not simply a theoretical) risk of imprisonment, an application made at the end of the proceedings should have been granted. It was not open to the appropriate officer to refuse the application on the ground that there was, in the end, no risk of imprisonment because the prosecution had substituted a charge of a non-imprisonable offence to which the defendant had pleaded guilty: *R. v. Horseferry Road Magistrates, ex. p. Punatar & Co* unreported, May 24, 2002, DC; [2002] EWHC 1196, Admin.

(4) Selection of the representative

Access to Justice Act 1999, s.15

Selection of representative

29–34　　**15.**—(1) An individual who has been granted a right to representation in accordance with Schedule 3 may select any representative or representatives willing to act for him; and, where he does so, the Commission is to comply with the duty imposed by section 14(1) by funding representation by the selected representative or representatives.

(2) Regulations may provide that in prescribed circumstances—

(a) the right conferred by subsection (1) is not to apply in cases of prescribed descriptions,

(b) an individual who has been provided with advice or assistance funded by the Commission under section 13 by a person whom he chose to provide it for him is to be taken to have selected that person as his representative pursuant to that right,

(c) that right is not to include a right to select a representative of a prescribed description,

(d) that right is to select only a representative of a prescribed description,

(e) that right is to select not more than a prescribed number of representatives to act at any one time, and

(f) that right is not to include a right to select a representative in place of a representative previously selected.

(3) Regulations under subsection (2)(b) may prescribe circumstances in which an individual is to be taken to have chosen a person to provide advice or assistance for him.

(4) Regulations under subsection (2) may not provide that only a person employed by

the Commission, or by a body established and maintained by the Commission, may be selected.

(5) Regulations may provide that in prescribed circumstances the Commission is not required to fund, or to continue to fund, representation for an individual by a particular representative (but such provision shall not prejudice any right of the individual to select another representative).

(6) The circumstances which may be prescribed by regulations under subsection (2) or (5) include that a determination has been made by a prescribed body or person.

The prescribed description is contained in r.11 and includes an employee in the **29–35** Criminal Defence Service or a lawyer who is franchised from the Legal Services Commission.

Criminal Defence Service (General) (No.2) Regulations 2001, reg.16A

16A.— Where an individual who is granted a right to representation is one of two or more **29–36** co-defendants whose cases are to be heard together, that individual must select the same representative as a co-defendant unless there is, or is likely to be, a conflict of interest.

Co-defendants should be represented by one solicitor unless there is a conflict of interest. That conflict must be clearly identified in the application where separate representation is sought.

(5) Employment by Legal Services Commission

Criminal Defence Service (General) (No.2) Regulations 2001, regs.11–12

11.—(1) The right conferred by section 15(1) of the Act, as regards representation in respect **29–37** of any proceedings to which this regulation applies, shall be exercisable only in relation to those representatives who are:
   (a) employed by the Commission to provide such representation; or
   (b) authorised to provide such representation under a crime franchise contract with the Commission which commences on or after 2nd April 2001 and specifies the rate of remuneration for such representation.

(2) This regulation applies to:
   (a) any criminal proceedings in a magistrates' court;
   (b) any proceedings in the Crown Court mentioned in regulation 3(2);
   (c) any appeal by way of case stated from a magistrates' court; and
   (d) any proceedings which are preliminary or incidental to proceedings mentioned in sub-paragraphs (a) to (c).

(3) This regulation does not apply to proceedings referred to in section 12(2)(f) of the Act (proceedings for contempt in the face of a court).

(6) Representation by an advocate

12.—(1) A representation order for the purposes of proceedings before a magistrates' court **29–38** may only include representation by an advocate in the case of:
   (a) any indictable offence, including an offence which is triable either way; or
   (b) proceedings under section 9 of, or paragraph 6 of Schedule 1 to, the *Extradition Act* 1989
where the court is of the opinion that, because of circumstances which make the proceedings unusually grave or difficult, representation by both a solicitor and an advocate would be desirable.

(2) A representation order for the purposes of proceedings before a magistrates' court may not include representation by an advocate other than as provided in paragraph (1).

Before the court can properly exercise its discretion to assign counsel in a case other **29–39** than a charge of murder, the applicant must show not only that the case is of unusual gravity or difficulty but also that circumstances lead to the conclusion that such representation is desirable in the particular proceedings—whether summary trial or committal proceedings. The proper approach is to recognise that in a large number of cases which might in themselves be grave or difficult it is nevertheless possible at an early stage for any competent solicitor to realise that no useful purpose would be likely to be served in the interests of his client in opposing, for example a simple committal for trial under section 6(2) of the *Magistrates' Courts Act* 1980. The mere multiplicity of simple, straightforward charges could not make it desirable for counsel to be instructed. The facts in relation to a single charge might be so complex that it is desirable that counsel should at least advise whether there were good grounds for opposing a committal under section 6(2). Assignment of counsel may be justified if a submission of no case to answer is to be made in a case of some gravity and weight: *R. v. Guildford Justices, ex. p. Scott* [1975] Crim.L.R. 286.

29–40   The principle of equality of arms under the ECHR, Article 6 does not require that a defendant should be represented by leading counsel merely because the prosecution were so represented. What is required is that the defendant be properly represented by an advocate who could ensure that the defendant's case was properly and adequately put before the court: *Lea (Att.-Gen's Reference (No. 82a of 2000)); Shatwell* [2002] 2 Cr.App.R. 24, CA. Rule 14, paragraph 14 of the regulations makes provision for representation by Queen's Counsel to be ordered in the magistrates court but only at the time when a murder charge is sent to the Crown Court or a case prosecuted by the SFO is transferred.

(7) Representation by advocate only

Criminal Defence Service (General) (No.2) Regulations 2001, reg.15

29–41   **15.** The court may grant a representation order for representation by an advocate alone:
    (a) in any proceedings referred to in section 12(2)(f) of the Act;
    (b) in respect of an appeal to the Court of Appeal or the Courts-Martial Appeal Court; or
    (c) in cases of urgency where it appears to the court that there is no time to instruct a solicitor:
        (i) in respect of an appeal to the Crown Court; or
        (ii) in proceedings in which a person is committed to or appears before the Crown Court for trial or sentence, or appears or is brought before that court to be dealt with.

29–42   A CDRO may be granted to a solicitor and it is open to them to brief counsel if they see fit but this rule restricts the circumstances in which an order can specify representation by a barrister.

Criminal Defence Service (General) (No.2) Regulations 2001, reg.22

29–43   **22.** Where a representation order has been made, the assisted person's solicitor or advocate whether acting under a representation order or otherwise shall not receive or be a party to the making of any payment for work done in connection with the proceedings in respect of which the representation order was made except such payments as may be made:
    (a) by the Lord Chancellor or the Commission; or
    (b) in respect of any expenses or fees incurred in:
        (i) preparing, obtaining or considering any report, opinion or further evidence, whether provided by an expert witness or otherwise; or
        (ii) obtaining any transcripts or recordings
    where an application for an authority to incur such fees or expenses has been refused by the Costs Committee.

(8) High cost cases

Criminal Defence Service (General) (No.2) Regulations 2001, reg.23

29–44   **23.**—(1) This regulation applies to very high cost cases where funded services are provided.
    (2) Any solicitor who has conduct of a case which is a very high cost case shall notify the Commission in writing accordingly as soon as is practicable.
    (3) Where a solicitor fails to comply with the provisions of this regulation without good

reason, and as a result there is a loss to public funds, the court or Costs Committee, as appropriate, may refuse payment of his costs up to the extent of such loss.

(4) No payment under paragraph (3) shall be refused unless the solicitor has been given a reasonable opportunity to show why it should not be refused.

Very high cost cases by definition will rarely be dealt with in the magistrates' court **29–45** but the original application for legal representation will be made there. The applicant or his solicitor should note the high cost of the case on the application at the earliest opportunity. The Court has a duty to check that the LSC have been notified and will advise that failure to notify may mean costs will not be recovered: *Practice Direction (Costs: Criminal Proceedings)* May, 2004.

(9) Expenditure, expert witnesses

Case law under the previous legislation clarified the situation relating to expert evi- **29–46** dence that could be commissioned at public expense. In *Silcott, Braithwaite and Raghip, The Times*, December 9, 1991, the Court of Appeal said that lawyers are under a duty not to involve the legal aid fund in unnecessary expenditure. It was not appropriate to continue to obtain reports until one favourable to the defence case was found. The fund would allow for one or at the most two expert's reports to be commissioned. "Expert shopping" was to be discouraged but in this case there were exceptional circumstances where the need for a further expert opinion could be demonstrated. Counsel should advise on evidence in support of an extension of the representation order to obtain expert's reports and the courts must rely on the proper professional standards being observed by all the lawyers concerned.

The court has no power to authorise the incurring of costs under a representation order for an expert witness, although it may express an opinion as to the desirability of the order being so extended: *Donnelly* [1998] Crim.L.R. 131, CA.

(10) Change of representative

Criminal Defence Service (General) (No.2) Regulations 2001, reg.16

16.—(1) Where a representation order has been granted an application may be made to the **29–47** court before which the proceedings are heard to select a representative in place of a representative previously selected, and any such application shall state the grounds on which it is made.

(2) The court may:
   (a) grant the application where:
      (i) the representative considers himself to be under a duty to withdraw from the case in accordance with his professional rules of conduct and, in such a case, the representative shall provide details of the nature of such duty;
      (ii) there is a breakdown in the relationship between the assisted person and the representative such that effective representation can no longer be provided and, in such a case, the representative shall provide details of the nature of such breakdown;
      (iii) through circumstances beyond his control, the representative is no longer able to represent the assisted person; or
      (iv) some other substantial compelling reason exists; or
   (b) refuse the application.

When legal advice and assistance is being publicly funded under a CDRO the court **29–48** has a duty to scrutinise the justification for changing solicitors which may result in a duplication of work and costs. A request for a change of representation should be in writing clearly explaining the reasons for the application. The court will require confirmation that the original solicitor is aware of and consents to the transfer. If there is no consent then representations should be heard.

(11) Withdrawal of representation order

Criminal Defence Service (General) (No.2) Regulations 2001, reg.17

17.—(1) Where any charge or proceedings against the assisted person are varied, the court **29–49**

before which the proceedings are heard or, in respect of any proceedings mentioned in regulation 3(2)(a) to (g), the Commission, must—

    (a) consider whether the interests of justice continue to require that he be represented in respect of the varied charge or proceedings; and

    (b) withdraw the representation order if the interests of justice do not so require.

(1A) The court before which the proceedings are heard or, in respect of any proceedings mentioned in regulation 3(2)(a) to (g), the Commission, must consider whether to withdraw the representation order in any of the following circumstances—

    (a) where the assisted person declines to accept the order in the terms which are offered;

    (b) otherwise at the request of the assisted person; or

    (c) where the representative named in the representation order declines to continue to represent the assisted person.

(2) Where representation is withdrawn, the appropriate officer or the Commission, as appropriate, shall provide written notification to the assisted person and to the solicitor (or, where there was no solicitor assigned, to the advocate), who shall inform any assigned advocate (or, where notification is given to the advocate, any other assigned advocate).

(3) On any subsequent application by the assisted person for a representation order in respect of the same proceedings,

    (a) he must declare the withdrawal of the previous representation order and the reason for it; and

    (b) where the representation order was withdrawn in the circumstances set out in paragraph (1) or paragraph (1A)(a) or (b) and a representation order is subsequently granted, the court or the Commission, as appropriate, must select the same representative, unless it considers that there are good reasons why it should select a different representative.

29–50   A CDRO may be withdrawn because of a breakdown in the relationship between the defendant and the solicitor. A fresh application for representation may then be made; but the same representative may be appointed.

(12) Appeal against refusal to grant representation

Criminal Defence Service (Representation Order: Appeals etc) Regulations 2006, reg.4

Appeals: magistrates' courts

29–51   4.—(1) In this regulation "court" means the magistrates' court in which the proceedings in respect of which the individual is seeking a representation order are being or are to be heard and includes a single justice.

(2) An individual may appeal to the court against a decision to refuse to grant a representation order made on the grounds that the interests of justice do not require such an order to be granted.

(3) The court must either—

    (a) uphold the decision, or

    (b) decide that it would be in the interests of justice for a representation order to be granted.

(4) Where the court makes a decision under paragraph (3)(b), the individual may apply to the representation authority for a representation order, and—

    (a) if the individual states in writing, verified by a statement of truth, that his financial resources have not changed materially since the date of his original application so as to make him financially ineligible for a representation order, the representation authority must grant the order, or

    (b) if his financial resources may have so changed, the representation authority—

        (i) must determine whether the individual is financially eligible to be granted a representation order in accordance with the Criminal Defence Service (Financial Eligibility) Regulations 2006; and

        (ii) if he is so eligible, must grant the order.

(5) An appeal does not lie against a decision to refuse to grant a representation order in

respect of proceedings in a magistrates' court made on the grounds that the individual is not financially eligible to be granted such an order.

COSTS

Part VII

I. INTRODUCTION

The *Prosecution of Offences Act* 1985, Pt II governs the award of costs in criminal **30–1** proceedings. It has been supplemented by the *Costs in Criminal Cases (General) Regulations* 1986 made under sections 19 and 20. The magistrates' court has power to make a defendant's costs order and a prosecution costs order for payment of costs from central or public funds. An order can also be made for the convicted defendant to pay the costs of the prosecution. The court may make a wasted costs order against either the prosecution or defence to cover any costs incurred by a party as a result of an unnecessary or improper act or omission by the other party to the proceedings. The court may also make an order for wasted costs against legal representatives. The *Courts Act* 2003 also adds a power for the court to award costs against third parties. The magistrates' court has no inherent jurisdiction to award the payment of costs in criminal cases. Any party making an application for costs must identify the statutory authority for the court to do so.

General

The *Prosecution of Offences Act* 1985 covers criminal proceedings only. It does not **30–2** extend to applications such as those under the *Police Property Act* 1897 for the release of property being held by the police: *R. v. Daventry Justices, ex p. Chief Constable of Northamptonshire Police* [2001] EWCA Admin 446. An application for access orders by Customs and Excise under the *Value Added Tax Act* 1994 was held not to be criminal proceedings as no person had been charged and a wasted costs order could not be made in the course of the application: *Customs and Excise Commissioners v. City of London Magistrates' Court* [2000] 4 All E.R. 763. There is power under section 64 of the *Magistrates' Courts Act* 1980 for the court to make an award of costs in civil cases where a complaint is made, which may be relevant in some applications.

Human Rights Act 1998

No absolute right to costs or expenses can be read into the European Convention on **30–3** Human Rights: *Lutz v. Germany* [1988] 10 E.H.R.R. 182. As a general principle, case law indicates that on acquittal costs should normally be awarded: *Sekanina v. Austria* [1993] 17 E.H.R.R. 221. If costs are refused to a defendant where the case has been dismissed or discontinued this could amount to a breach of Article 6 as a violation of the presumption of innocence where the reasons for the refusal amount in substance to a determination of guilt: *Minelli v. Switzerland* [1983] 5 E.H.R.R. 554. Where, however, a court refers to the state of suspicion against the defendant in support of its exercise of its discretion to refuse costs, there is no violation of the presumption of innocence: *Leutscher v. Netherlands* [1997] 24 E.H.R.R. 181. The possibility of the presumption of innocence being violated would appear to be more likely in relation to acquittals as compared to cases where the case is discontinued through a technicality: *Sekanina v. Austria, ante.*

II. COSTS, ORDERS AND ENFORCEMENT

A. Guides to the Award of Costs in Criminal Proceedings

30–4   On May 18, 2004, *Practice Direction (Costs: Criminal Proceedings)* [2004] 2 Cr.App.R. 26 was issued by the Lord Chief Justice. This replaced earlier Practice Notes and applies to magistrates' courts. A clear and detailed explanation of the power to award costs and the procedures is provided. It introduces directions on when costs should be awarded from Central Funds to an acquitted defendant and also gives guidance on the new power brought in by the *Courts Act* 2003 which allows the court to make an order for third party costs. In addition the role of the court in relation to costs is clarified. In Part VII of the directions it is stated:

> "the Judge has a much greater and more direct responsibility for costs in criminal proceedings than in civil and should keep the question of costs at the forefront of his mind at every stage of the case and ought to be prepared to take the initiative himself without any prompting from the parties."

The Justices' Clerks Society has published a Good Practice Guide for the Taxation of Costs which is directly relevant to the magistrates' courts and will be applied by the court or the appropriate officer when dealing with any claims for costs.

B. Defendant's Costs Orders

Prosecution of Offences Act 1985, s.16

Defence costs

30–5   **16.**—(1) Where—

    (a) an information laid before a justice of the peace for any area, charging any person with an offence, is not proceeded with;

    (b) a magistrates' court inquiring into an indictable offence as examining justices determines not to commit the accused for trial;

    (c) a magistrates' court dealing summarily with an offence dismisses the information;

that court or, in a case falling within paragraph (a) above, a magistrates' court for that area, may make an order in favour of the accused for a payment to be made out of central funds in respect of his costs (a "defendant's costs order").

    (2)–(5) deal with the powers of other courts to order costs.

    (6) A defendant's costs order shall, subject to the following provisions of this section, be for the payment out of central funds, to the person in whose favour the order is made, of such amount as the court considers reasonably sufficient to compensate him for any expenses properly incurred by him in the proceedings.

    (7) Where a court makes a defendant's costs order but is of the opinion that there are circumstances which make it inappropriate that the person in whose favour the order is made should recover the full amount mentioned in subsection (6) above, the court shall—

    (a) assess what amount would, in its opinion, be just and reasonable; and

    (b) specify that amount in the order.

    (9) Subject to subsection (7) above, the amount to be paid out of central funds in pursuance of a defendant's costs order shall—

    (a) be specified in the order, in any case where the court considers it appropriate for the amount to be so specified and the person in whose favour the order is made agrees the amount; and

(b) in any other case, be determined in accordance with regulations made by the Lord Chancellor for the purposes of this section.

(10) Subsection (6) above shall have effect, in relation to any case falling within subsection (1)(a) or (2)(a) above, as if for the words "in the proceedings" there were substituted the words "in or about the defence".

(11) Where a person ordered to be retried is acquitted at his retrial, the costs which may be ordered to be paid out of central funds under this section shall include—

(a) any costs which, at the original trial, could have been ordered to be so paid under this section if he had been acquitted; and

(b) if no order was made under this section in respect of his expenses on appeal, any sums for the payment of which such an order could have been made.

(12) [Refers to Crown Court powers.]

[This section is reprinted as amended by the *Criminal Justice and Public Order Act* 1994, Sched. 9, para. 25(a).]

At the end of a case in the magistrates' court where the defendant is found not guilty **30–6** of a charge tried summarily or is discharged on committal or the case is not proceeded with by the prosecution, he may apply for his costs to be paid out of central funds under this section. The application may be made in court immediately. The court may then, if the amount claimed is specified or can be readily assessed, make a defendant's costs order for the required amount to be paid out of central funds. The determined total figure must be expressed in the order: *Judd* [1971] 1 All E.R. 127. In *Galandauer v. Snaresbrook Crown Court* [2006] EWHC 1633 the appellant was partially successful in an appeal against sentence dealt with at the Crown Court but the judge only allowed him a reduced amount of costs. He appealed against that reduction which led to him being awarded about a quarter of what he had originally claimed. On appeal it was held that if the court intended that only a proportion of costs claimed should be paid then the reasons why the full amount was not considered justified must be clearly identified. There must be a rational basis for deciding that the amount ordered was just and reasonable. As this had not happened in this case the appeal challenging the reduction was upheld. If the amount is yet to be properly quantified or cannot be agreed then the court may order that the amount be "taxed" or assessed by an appropriate officer of the court under the regulations. Where a DCO is to be taxed, the claim must be submitted within three months: regulations (6) and (12) of the *Costs in Criminal Cases (General Regulations)*1986. There is no right of appeal to the Crown Court against the decision of the appropriate officer on costs: (section 108 of the *Magistrates' Courts Act* 1980) and any assessment of a claim can only be challenged by way of judicial review.

If an application for a costs order is not made immediately in court it may be made at a later date: *R. v. Bolton Justices, ex p. Wildish* (1983) 147 J.P. 309, DC; *R. v. Liverpool Magistrates' Court, ex p. Abiaka* [1999] (96) 14 L.S.G. 32, DC. The court must be satisfied that one of the circumstances listed in section 16, *ante*, apply. A case is not proceeded with when a notice of discontinuance is served by the prosecution and the court retains the jurisdiction to award costs to the defendant to cover the expense of preparation for the trial: *Denning v. DPP* [1991] 2 Q.B. 532. The reason why the case is not proceeded with is irrelevant. Where a case was unable to proceed because the information was found to have been laid out of time it was held that the court still had power to make an award of costs in favour of a defendant: *Patel v. Blakely* [1988] R.T.R. 65, DC.

A defendant's costs order may be made in favour of a parent or guardian of a child **30–7** or young person. The reference to "the accused" in section 16 covers a parent or guardian including a local authority looking after a child or young person: *R. v. Preston Crown Court, ex p. Lancashire CC*; *R. v. Burnley Crown Court, ex p. Same* [1999] 1 W.L.R. 142, DC.

The exception to the entitlement of a defendant's costs order, especially on acquittal is very narrow despite the court's discretion to make such an order: *South West Surrey Magistrates' Court, ex p. James* [2001] Crim.L.R. 690, DC. This is in accordance with

European case law. The *Practice Direction (Costs: Criminal Proceedings)* [2004] 2 Cr.App.R. 26 covers defence costs orders. In Part III it says that an order for defence costs should normally be made on acquittal unless there are positive reasons for not doing so. An example is given where a defendant's own conduct brings suspicion on him and misleads the prosecution into thinking that the case against him was stronger than it is. The directions also confirm that the court retains a discretion whether to order defence costs or not. It has been held that when an information is dismissed after a trial the fact that a prosecution was properly brought and was not malicious is irrelevant and does not constitute a good reason for a refusal to make a defendant's costs order: *R. v. Birmingham Juvenile Court, ex p. H.* (1992) 156 J.P. 445. In cases of discontinuance the conduct of the defendant must be carefully considered as it may provide a reason for refusal. The fact that the defendant has brought the prosecution on himself was held to amount to a reason for not making an order: *Spens, Independent*, March 18, 1992. But the suggestion that the defendant brought the prosecution on himself must be based on strong independent evidence in order to provide a positive reason to refuse costs: *Mooney v. Cardiff Magistrates' Court* (1999) 164 J.P. 220. Where a costs order was refused to a defendant whose case was dismissed in the absence of a prosecution witness, it was held that this could interfere with the presumption of innocence under Article 6 as it indicated a determination of guilt: *R. (Barrington) v. Preston Crown Court* [2001] EWHC Admin 599. See also *Hussain v. UK, The Times*, April 5, 2006 where it was held that a refusal of a costs order for the defendant where the judge commented that he had been acquitted only because of the failure of a key witness to give evidence was held to be incompatible with the presumption of innocence under Article 6.

30–8   The amount ordered to be taxed is for expenses "properly incurred" by the defendant. The court or the appropriate officer will consider whether the defendant has incurred costs and to what amount.

Under the *Prosecution of Offences Act* 1985, s.21(4A), the costs of a defendant who has the benefit of a criminal defence representation order shall not, for the purposes of a defendant's costs order, be taken to include any expenses incurred on his behalf by the Legal Services Commission or the Lord Chancellor. The costs are paid out of public funds in any event so he incurs no costs. A costs order may be appropriate in limited circumstances, for example, if the defendant was not legally aided until a late stage in the proceedings and paid for early representation personally.

Costs are incurred by a defendant when he is liable to his solicitors for the costs of his defence even if a third party, such as his employer or an insurance company has undertaken or is liable to pay any of the costs. Only if there is an express or implied agreement in binding form that in no circumstances would the solicitor seek to recover costs from the defendant could it be said that the defendant had incurred no costs: *Miller and Glennie* (1984) 78 Cr.App.R. 71, QBD.

30–9   Defence solicitors may be instructed privately with a contract to pay legal expenses but no money actually changing hands until the case is concluded. Difficulties might then arise as to whether costs were actually "incurred by the defendant". In the case of *R. (McCormick) v. Liverpool City Magistrates* [2001] 2 All E.R. 705, the precise meaning of "incurred" was considered in detail. One defendant had entered into a contract with his solicitor that he would not be expected to make any payment not within the ambit of public funds. Another defendant had instructed a solicitor privately but had not made any payment to him during the progression of the case. Both were refused DCOs as the court took the view that in these circumstances no legal costs had been incurred. It was held on appeal against the refusals that in the first case a liability had been incurred because the defendant may have been ordered to pay costs outside the ambit of public funds. In the second case the Act and Regulations were held only to require that costs be incurred and not actually paid by the defendant. In both cases it was held that the financial ability of the defendants to pay any costs incurred was not relevant and in the circumstances the refusals of the DCOs were quashed.

In *Jain, The Times*, December 10, 1987, CA, a defendant's costs order was made in favour of a named person other than the defendant, who had financed the proceedings. However, the judgment does not specify how the court dealt with the question of whether the Act allows costs awards in favour of persons other than the defendant.

A solicitor who represents himself in person in criminal proceedings incurs costs in **30–10** conducting his own case. He may claim for the fees chargeable by him had he been representing a defendant and not himself: *R. v. Stafford, Stone and Eccleshall Magistrates' Court, ex p. Robinson* [1988] 1 W.L.R. 369. A barrister who was represented by counsel in criminal proceedings was entitled to claim costs for his representation and also for the work he had done himself in preparing his own defence. The Code of Conduct prevented him from representing himself in a professional capacity: *Khan v. Lord Chancellor* [2003] 1 W.L.R. 2385.

A person in respect of whom a defendant's costs order is made may also be paid subsistence allowance and travelling expenses in relation to his attendances at court under regulation 23 of the *Costs on Criminal Cases (General) Regulations* 1986. The rates are fixed by the Lord Chancellor. No claim can be made for loss of earnings or loss of time.

There is no provision in criminal proceedings under the *Prosecution of Offences Act* 1985 or the Regulations to award interest on costs: *Westminster City Council v. Wingrove* [1991] 1 Q.B. 652.

Costs in Criminal Cases (General) Regulations 1986, regs.4–8, 12

PART III

COSTS OUT OF CENTRAL FUNDS

Application and definitions

4. This Part of these Regulations applies to costs payable out of central funds in pursuance of **30–11** an order made under or by virtue of Part II of the Act and in this Part of these Regulations—

"applicant" means the person in whose favour a costs order has been made;

"appropriate authority" has the meaning assigned to it by regulation 5;

"costs judge" means a costs judge of the Supreme Court;

"costs order" means an order made under or by virtue of Part II of the Act for the payment of costs out of central funds;

"disbursements" do not include any payment made out of central funds to a witness, interpreter or medical practitioner in accordance with Part V of these Regulations;

"presiding judge" means the judge who presided at the hearing in respect of which the costs are payable; and

The appropriate authority

5.—(1) Costs shall be determined by the appropriate authority in accordance with these **30–12** Regulations.

(2) Subject to paragraph (3), the appropriate authority shall be—

(a) the registrar of criminal appeals in the case of proceedings in the Court of Appeal,

(b) the master of the Crown Office in the case of proceedings in a Divisional Court of the Queen's Bench Division,

(c) an officer appointed by the Lord Chancellor in the case of proceedings in the Crown Court,

(d) the justices' clerk in the case of proceedings in a magistrates' court.

(3) The appropriate authority may appoint or authorise the appointment of determining officers to act on its behalf under these Regulations in accordance with directions given by it or on its behalf.

Claims for costs

6.—(1) Subject to regulation 12, no claim for costs shall be entertained unless it is submitted **30–13** within three months of the date on which the costs order was made.

Part VII

(2) Subject to paragraph (3), a claim for costs shall be submitted to the justices' chief executive for the court, in the case of proceedings in a magistrates' court, or to the appropriate authority, in the case of proceedings in any other court specified in regulation 5(2), in such form and manner as he or it may direct and shall be accompanied by receipts or other evidence of the applicant's payment of the costs claimed, and any receipts or other documents in support of any disbursements claimed.

(3) A claim shall—

    (a) summarise the items of work done by a solicitor;

    (b) state, where appropriate, the dates on which items of work were done, the time taken and the sums claimed,

    (c) specify any disbursements claimed, including counsel's fees, the circumstances in which they were incurred and the amounts claimed in respect of them, and

    (d) contain either full particulars, including the date and outcome, of any claim that regulation 44(7) of the *Legal Aid in Criminal and Care Proceedings (General) Regulations* 1989 should be applied in respect of any work comprised in the claim under these Regulations, or a certificate by the solicitor that he has not made, and will not make, any such claim.

(4) Where there are any special circumstances which should be drawn to the attention of the appropriate authority, the applicant shall specify them.

(5) The applicant shall supply such further particulars, information and documents as the appropriate authority may require.

Determination of costs

30–14   **7.**—(1) The appropriate authority shall consider the claim, any further particulars, information or documents submitted by the applicant under regulation 6 and shall allow such costs in respect of—

    (a) such work as appears to it to have been actually and reasonably done; and

    (b) such disbursements as appear to it to have been actually and reasonably incurred,

as it considers reasonably sufficient to compensate the applicant for any expenses properly incurred by him in the proceedings.

(2) In determining costs under paragraph (1) the appropriate authority shall taken into account all the relevant circumstances of the case including the nature, importance, complexity or difficulty of the work and the time involved.

(3) When determining costs for the purposes of this regulation, there shall be allowed a reasonable amount in respect of all costs reasonably incurred and any doubts which the appropriate authority may have as to whether the costs were reasonably incurred or were reasonable in amount shall be resolved against the applicant.

Payment of costs

30–15   **8.**—(1) When the appropriate authority has determined the costs payable to an applicant in accordance with these Regulations, the justices' chief executive for the court, in the case of proceedings in a magistrates' court, or the appropriate authority, in the case of proceedings in any other court specified in regulation 5(2), shall notify the applicant of the costs payable and authorise payment accordingly.

(2) Where the costs payable under paragraph (1) are varied as a result of a redetermination under regulation 9, an appeal to a costs judge under regulation 10, or an appeal to the High Court under regulation 11, then—

    (a) where the costs are increased, the appropriate authority shall authorise payment of the increase;

    (b) where the costs are decreased, the applicant shall repay the amount of such decrease; and

    (c) where the payment of the costs of an appeal is ordered under regulation 10(14) or 11(8), the appropriate authority shall authorise such payment to the applicant.

Time limits

30–16   **12.**—(1) Subject to paragraph (2), the time limit within which there must be made or instituted—

    (a) a claim for costs by an applicant under regulation 6, an application for a redetermination under regulation 9, or a request for an appropriate authority to give reasons for its decision on a redetermination under regulation 9;

   (b) an appeal to a costs judge under regulation 10 or an application for a certificate
        under regulation 11; or
   (c) an appeal to the High Court under regulation 11;
may, for good reason, be extended by the appropriate authority, the Senior Costs Judge or the
High Court, as the case may be.

   (2) Where an applicant without good reason has failed (or, if an extension were not
granted, would fail) to comply with a time limit, the appropriate authority, the Senior
Costs Judge or the High Court, as the case may be, may, in exceptional circumstances,
extend the time limit and shall consider whether it is reasonable in the circumstances to
reduce the costs; provided that the costs shall not be reduced unless the representative has
been allowed a reasonable opportunity to show cause orally or in writing why the costs
should not be reduced.

   (3) An applicant may appeal to the Senior Costs Judge against a decision made under
this regulation by an appropriate authority in respect of proceedings other than proceedings before a magistrates' court and such an appeal shall be instituted within 21 days of the
decision being given by giving notice in writing to the Senior Costs Judge specifying the
grounds of appeal.

[This regulation is printed as amended by the *Costs in Criminal Cases (General)*
(Amendments) Regulations 2005 (S.I. 2005 No. 2622), which came into force on
October 3, 2005).]

These regulations outline the procedure to be used when costs awarded under a **30–17**
defendant's costs order are assessed. In the magistrates' court the appropriate officer is
the justices' clerk who may delegate his powers to tax costs: regulation 5 The taxation
will be conducted in accordance with the regulations and Practice Notes. The Justices'
Clerks Society has also published a Good Practice Guide to the Taxation of Costs, which
gives detailed guidance on the proper approach to any assessment of claims and has
national application. A claim for costs must be submitted within three months of the order for costs being made by the court but the appropriate officer has a discretion to
extend that time limit (regulation 12). The case file will be provided to the court with a
written record of all the work done, including attendance notes for interviews, confer-
ences, telephone calls and correspondence together with a note of time spent on
research and preparation. An explanation will be required of the grade of lawyer
engaged and the hourly rate charged. There will also be an element of "care and
conduct" which is a percentage increase on the rate to reflect the gravity and complexity
of the case. The applicant will then multiply the hourly rate by the time spent to arrive
at a global figure to which VAT may be added. The appropriate officer may require
that all claims are evidenced in writing and the grade of lawyer chosen must be justified.
The figure assessed will include costs for the time spent on the case and for disbursements which are specific payments for identified items. The taxing officer will allow an
amount that he considers reasonable to compensate for the expenses incurred. A claimant may dispute the costs allowed and attempt to reach an agreement with the appropriate officer but the final decision of the appropriate officer can only be challenged
by way of judicial review as being "Wednesbury" unreasonable.

   In *R. v. Leeds Magistrates' Court, ex p. Castle* [1991] Crim.L.R. 770, the court
gave consideration to the test to be applied under section 16 and the Regulations. The
appellant had been disallowed the claim for representation by two counsel at a lengthy
committal. On appeal it was held that there was a two-stage test: first the determination
of whether work has been actually and reasonably done and second the consideration of
the sum reasonably sufficient to compensate for the expenses incurred. In this case the
appropriate officer had exercised his discretion reasonably.

   The officer must consider claims objectively and determine whether they were justifiable under regulation 7. The fact that solicitors submitted a claim does not automatically
prohibit the defendant from submitting his own claim for personal expenses incurred in
preparing his case: *R. v. Bedlington Magistrates' Court, ex p. Wilkinson* (2000) 164
J.P. 156.

   Claims may be disallowed if the grade and cost of the solicitor or counsel instructed is **30–18** considered to be too expensive. The test is not whether a more junior lawyer could have dealt with the case just as competently but whether it was reasonable in all the circumstances to instruct a more senior barrister: *R. v. Dudley Magistrates' Court, ex p. Power City Stores Ltd* (1990) 154 J.P. 654. For a defendant charged with common assault and battery the instruction of a solicitor of more than four years' standing was reasonable as was the agreement to incur costs using a flat hourly rate: *R. v. North Sefton Justices, ex p. Hale, The Times*, January 29, 2002, DC.

It may be reasonable to instruct solicitors who are not local and so may be more expensive, but the reasons for doing so must be advanced: *Wraith v. Sheffield Forgemasters* (1998) 1 All E.R. 82. Higher rates may be allowed for specialist lawyers if it is reasonable to incur such costs and the rate charged is justifiable in view of higher overheads *etc.*: *Jones v. Secretary of State for Wales* [1997] 2 All E.R. 507.

30–19   An application to extend the time limit within which a claim should be submitted may be made either before or after the limit of three months expires. The appropriate officer will then decide if there is good reason to extend the limit. An extension of time may also be granted if there are "exceptional circumstances" which led to the delay despite the fact that there was no good reason for it: *R. v. Clerk to the North Kent Justices, ex p. McGoldrick & Co* (1996) 160 J.P. 30. Under the amended regulation 12 the taxing officer may penalise the applicant for late applications by reducing the amount awarded but the applicant must be allowed to make representations about the proposed reduction of costs.

C. PROSECUTION COSTS

Prosecution of Offences Act 1985, s.17

Prosecution costs

30–20   **17.**—(1) Subject to subsection (2) below, the court may—

    (a) in any proceedings in respect of an indictable offence; and

    (b) in any proceedings before a Divisional Court of the Queen's Bench Division or the House of Lords in respect of a summary offence;

order the payment out of central funds of such amount as the court considers reasonably sufficient to compensate the prosecutor for any expenses properly incurred by him in the proceedings.

(2) No order under this section may be made in favour of—

    (a) a public authority; or

    (b) a person acting—

        (i)   on behalf of a public authority; or

        (ii) in his capacity as an official appointed by such an authority.

(3) Where a court makes an order under this section but is of the opinion that there are circumstances which make it inappropriate that the prosecution should recover the full amount mentioned in subsection (1) above, the court shall—

    (a) assess what amount would, in its opinion, be just and reasonable; and

    (b) specify that amount in the order.

(4) Subject to subsection (3) above, the amount to be paid out of central funds in pursuance of an order under this section shall—

    (a) be specified in the order, in any case where the court considers it appropriate for the amount to be so specified and the prosecutor agrees the amount; and

    (b) in any other case, be determined in accordance with regulations made by the Lord Chancellor for the purposes of this section.

(5) Where the conduct of proceedings to which subsection (1) above applies is taken over by the Crown Prosecution Service, that subsection shall have effect as if it referred to the prosecutor who had the conduct of the proceedings before the intervention of the Service and to expenses incurred by him up to the time of intervention.

(6) In this section "public authority" means—

    (a) a police force within the meaning of section 3 of this Act;

    (b) the Crown Prosecution Service or any other government department;

    (c) a local authority or other authority or body constituted for purposes of—
        (i) the public service or of local government; or
        (ii) carrying on under national ownership any industry or undertaking or part of an industry or undertaking; or
    (d) any other authority or body whose members are appointed by Her Majesty or by any Minister of the Crown or government department or whose revenues consist wholly or mainly of money provided by Parliament.

The Crown Prosecution Service and the police are already publicly funded so there is **30–21** no power to order their costs from central funds. This section refers to private prosecutions for either way offences and does not cover summary only cases. Costs may be awarded irrespective of the outcome of the case but the court has a discretion whether to order costs and to what amount. Expenses for a private prosecutor may include legal expenses, secretarial costs and travel expenses but a claim cannot be made for compensation for lost time: *R. v. Stockport Magistrates, ex p. Cooper* (1984) 148 J.P. 261.

D. AWARD OF COSTS AGAINST ACCUSED

Prosecution of Offences Act 1985, s.18

Award of costs against accused
  18.—(1) Where—   **30–22**
    (a) any person is convicted of an offence before a magistrates' court;
    (b) the Crown Court dismisses an appeal against such a conviction or against the sentence imposed on that conviction; or
    (c) any person is convicted of an offence before the Crown Court;
the court may make such order as to the costs to be paid by the accused to the prosecutor as it considers just and reasonable.
  (2) Relates to the Court of Appeal...
  (3) The amount to be paid by the accused in pursuance of an order under this section shall be specified in the order.
  (4) Where any person is convicted of an offence before a magistrates' court and—
    (a) under the conviction the court orders payment of any sum as a fine, penalty, forfeiture or compensation; and
    (b) the sum so ordered to be paid does not exceed £5;
the court shall not order the accused to pay any costs under this section unless in the particular circumstances of the case it considers it right to do so.
  (5) Where any person under the age of eighteen is convicted of an offence before a magistrates' court, the amount of any costs ordered to be paid by the accused under this section shall not exceed the amount of any fine imposed on him.
  (6) Relates to the Court of Appeal...

[This section is reprinted as amended by the *Criminal Justice and Public Order Act* 1994, Sched. 9, para. 26.]

The Crown Prosecution Service may make application to the court for costs of prose- **30–23** cuting the case to be paid by the convicted defendant. The court has a discretion whether to make the order and must specify the amount in accordance with section 18(3). This must be done in court as there is no provision for prosecution costs to be taxed. Where a fine is less than £5, the presumption is that no costs will be ordered and for a person under the age of 18, any costs awarded must not be greater than the amount of any fine imposed: sections 18(4) and (5).

The prosecution will state the amount of costs sought and may be required to submit full details if the amount claimed is high. On November 1, 2006 the Crown Prosecution Service issued revised guidelines on the amount of costs to be claimed against convicted defendants in the magistrates' court. Prosecutors will refer to these guideline rates based on the means of the defendant. The court will always retain a discretion in fixing the amount ordered to be paid.

Type of Proceedings	Below Average	Average	Above Average
	GBP	GBP	GBP
Early gulity plea (EFH)	43	60	70
Summary gulity plea	87	95	100
Summary trial	455	625	790
Either-way gulity plea	172	175	180
Either-way trial	500	670	840

Costs payable under such an order were held to be limited to such items as would be payable to the prosecution out of central funds were such an order possible. So counsels' fees, the DPP's costs and witness expenses could be claimed but the jury expenses and cost of security on a trial could not be included: *Maher* [1983] Q.B. 784.

30–24   Issues have arisen over whether the costs of the investigation can be included. It was held that the order for prosecution costs did not extend to cover the costs of the investigation, particularly when, as in the case, a different body carried out the investigation: *Seymour* (1987) 9 Cr.App.R.(S.) 395. In *Neville (Westminster City Council) v. Gardner Merchant Ltd* (1983) 82 L.G.R. 577 it was held that the court did have the discretion to include the cost of time spent by a salaried Environmental Health Officer in conducting the investigation and inspecting premises under the *Food Safety (General Food Hygiene) Regulations* 1995 (S.I. 1995 No. 1763). This was especially so if the investigation arose from a specific complaint rather than coming to light through a routine inspection.

More recently in *Associated Octel Ltd* [1997] 1 Cr.App.R. 435, CA, the court said that the costs incurred by the prosecuting authority (the Health and Safety Executive), in investigating a case for prosecution could be recovered under a prosecution costs order. In such a case it was advisable for the prosecution to serve notice on the defence of the full details of the claim so that the defence could consider the claim and make representations.

In cases where a defendant would have paid a fixed penalty if the option had been offered to him but the case ended up in court, it was held to be incumbent upon the court to either not award any costs or to give cogent reasons as to why costs would be awarded: *R. (Ritson) v. County Durham Magistrates' Court* (2002) 166 J.P. 218.

30–25   The prosecution will request a specific amount but the court has a discretion as to exactly how much it will order to be paid by the defence. In exercising this discretion there are several factors to take into account. The means of the defendant are relevant and it was suggested that an amount that could be paid off within 12 months would be reasonable: *R. v. Nottingham Justices, ex p. Fohmann* (1987) 84 Cr.App.R. 316, DC.

The court is obliged when fixing the amount to be paid to investigate the defendant's financial situation with adequate thoroughness and it was held not to be reasonable to make an order for costs that was five times the amount of the fines when the defendant had debts exceeding his savings: *R. v. Newham Justices, ex p. Samuels* [1991] C.O.D. 412, DC. Even if the financial situation is investigated with thoroughness the award made may be subject to quashing on appeal if it is considered that no reasonable court could have made such an order on the information obtained: *R. v. Croydon Justices, ex p. Summers* [1993] C.O.D. 202, DC. The court, however, declined to determine whether there ought to be some proportionality between fines and costs awards. In *BPS Advertising Ltd v. Barnet LBC* (2007) 171 J.P. 223, QBD it was said that costs awarded should not be grossly disproportionate to the fine imposed. In this case the defendants were fined the maximum for an offence under the *Town and Country Planning Act* 1990 with costs of almost seven times the amount of the fine. On appeal the costs were cut by two-thirds as they were considered to be over-inflated.

30–26   Where the defendant faces multiple charges it is not appropriate to multiply the costs by the number of summonses which related to offences all resulting from one incident.

The defendant was summonsed for 37 offences under the *Food Safety (General Food Hygiene) Regulations* 1995 (S.I. 1995 No. 1763) and separate costs orders were made in respect of each summons after written pleas of guilty were accepted. The costs ordered were held to be excessive: *R. v. Tottenham Justices, ex p. Joshi* (1982) 75 Cr.App.R. 72, DC. In a case of multiple offences it is acceptable to order a global figure of costs more truly reflecting the work done.

An award of costs should not be made with a view to punishing the defendant for the **30–27** way in which he chose to conduct his case but if his actions necessarily incur higher costs as for example by electing jury trial then this will inevitably be reflected in the amount ordered: *Hayden* (1964) 60 Cr.App.R. 304, CA. In *R. v. Northallerton Magistrates' Court, ex p. Dove* [2000] 1 Cr.App.R.(S.) 136, DC, the court held on appeal that where the costs ordered were almost five times the amount of the fine imposed that this was "grossly disproportionate". The court took the opportunity to issue guidelines for the assessment of prosecution costs to be paid by the defendant as follows:

1. The defendant's means and liability for any other financial order should be ascertained so that any order did not exceed a reasonable sum he was able to pay.
2. The sum should never be more than the costs incurred.
3. It was compensation for the prosecutor and not further punishment for the defendant.
4. The costs order should be proportionate to the fine and if the total amount is excessive, the costs should be reduced.
5. The onus was on the defendant to provide details of means and if he failed to do so, the court could deduce his financial circumstances from all available evidence.
6. The defendant must be given the opportunity to produce evidence of his means and should be put on notice of any unusual costs order intended.

A fine and costs against a company may be payable over a longer period of time than **30–28** would be regarded as reasonable for an individual defendant. In determining the appropriate amount for directors, the court should consider, on the one hand, the need to avoid the risk of double punishment which may arise where the directors of a small company were also its shareholders, and on the other, that it is important to mark the personal responsibility of the directors: *Rollco Screw and Rivet Co Ltd* [1999] 2 Cr.App.R. 436, CA.

The court has discretion to make a prosecution costs order whether the defendant pleads guilty or not guilty. On a guilty plea the costs should be greatly reduced because the expense of preparation and conduct of a trial is avoided. The stage at which the guilty plea is tendered will be relevant in assessing the amount of costs to be ordered. The court has a discretion to award costs on a written plea of guilty dealt with under section 12 of the *Magistrates' Courts Act* 1980. The application for costs should be notified to the defendant in the paperwork sent to him but it does not form part of the statement of facts so would not technically need to be read out by the legal adviser in court. It was held to be sufficient for the claim for costs to be drawn to the court's attention by the legal adviser: *R. v. Coventry Magistrates' Court, ex p. DPP* [1990] 3 All E.R. 277.

Where there are several defendants and only some of them have the ability to pay, it **30–29** is wrong to divide the total cost of the prosecution between those defendants. If it is not possible to say what part of the total costs is attributable to any defendant, the court should divide the total costs between the total number of defendants, and order those who do have sufficient means to pay their share only: *Ronson and Parnes* (1992) 13 Cr.App.R.(S.) 153, CA; *Harrison* [1993] 14 Cr.App.R.(S.) 419, CA.

In a case where corporate defendants were held to bear a greater responsibility for criminal conduct than the individual co-defendants it was held appropriate for the company to be ordered to pay a greater amount of costs: *R. v. Fresha Bakeries* [2003] 1 Cr.App.R.(S.) 44.

Part VII

E. Wasted Costs Awards

Prosecution of Offences Act 1985, s.19(1), (3)–(4)

Provision for orders as to costs in other circumstances

30–30   **19.**—(1) The Lord Chancellor may by regulations make provision empowering magistrates' courts, the Crown Court and the Court of Appeal, in any case where the court is satisfied that one party to criminal proceedings has incurred costs as a result of an unnecessary or improper act or omission by, or on behalf of, another party to the proceedings, to make an order as to the payment of those costs.

(2)–(5) [*contain the content of Regulations made under subsection (1) above*]

(3) The Lord Chancellor may by regulations make provision for the payment out of central fund, in such circumstances and in relation to such criminal proceedings as may be specified, of such sums as appear to the court to be reasonably necessary—

(a) to compensate any witness in the proceedings, and any other person who in the opinion of the court necessarily attends for the purposes of the proceedings otherwise than to give evidence, for the expense, trouble or loss of time properly incurred in or incidental to his attendance,

(b) to cover the proper expenses of an interpreter who is required because of the accused's lack of English;

(c) to compensate a duly qualified medical practitioner who—

(i) makes a report otherwise than in writing for the purposes of section 11 of the *powers of Criminal Courts(Sentencing) Act* 2000 (remand for medical examination); or

(ii) makes a written report to a court in pursuance of a request to which section 32(2) of the *Criminal Justice Act* 1967 (report by medical practitioner on medical condition of offender) applies;

for the expenses properly incurred in or incidental to his reporting to the court.

(d) to cover the proper fee or costs of a person appointed by the Crown Court under section 4A of the *Criminal Procedure (Insanity) Act* 1964 to put the case for the defence.

(e) To cover the proper fee or costs of a legal representative appointed under section 38(4) of the *Youth Justice and Criminal Evidence Act* 1999 (defence representation for purposes of cross-examination) and any expenses properly incurred in providing such a person with evidence or other material in connection with his appointment.

(3A) In subsection (3)(a) above "attendance" means attendance at the court or elsewhere.

(4) [Court of Appeal.]

[This section is reprinted as amended by the *Access to Justice Act* 1999, Sched. 4, para. 28.]

30–31   This section provides for an order to be made for wasted costs between parties and also for payments from public funds to witnesses. Pursuant to the power in section 19, the Lord Chancellor has made the *Costs in Criminal Cases (General) Regulations* 1986 which in Part V sets out the witnesses who are entitled to be paid allowances and the *Costs in Criminal Cases (General) Regulations* 1986— Rates of Allowances which fixes the amounts to be paid. The rates are amended periodically.

Costs in Criminal Cases (General) Regulations 1986, reg.3

Part II

Costs Unnecessarily or Improperly Incurred

Unnecessary or improper acts and omissions

30–32   **3.**—(1) Subject to the provisions of this regulation, where at any time during criminal proceedings—

(a) a magistrates' court,

(b) the Crown Court, or

(c) the Court of Appeal

is satisfied that costs have been incurred in respect of the proceedings by one of the parties as a result of an unnecessary or improper act or omission by, or on behalf of, another party to the proceedings, the court may, after hearing the parties, order that all or part of the costs so incurred by that party shall be paid to him by the other party.

(2) Before making an order under paragraph (1), the court shall take into account any other order as to costs (including any legal aid order) which has been made in respect of the proceedings.

(3) An order made under paragraph (1) shall specify the amount of costs to be paid in pursuance of the order.

(4) Where an order under paragraph (1) has been made, the court may take that order into account when making any other order as to costs in respect of the proceedings.

(5) No order under paragraph (1) shall be made by a magistrates' court which requires a person under the age of seventeen who has been convicted of an offence to pay an amount by way of costs which exceeds the amount of any fine imposed on him.

An order under section 19, in common with other orders under the Act, may only be **30–33** made in respect of criminal proceedings. For consideration of this term see section 16 *ante*, § 30–5. The power to award a wasted costs order acts not only as a compensation to any party who incurs extra costs but also as an encouragement to all parties involved in a criminal case to act with diligence and expedition. An application can be made at any time during the proceedings or at the conclusion of the case. The order is made between the parties.

The court must be satisfied that the costs were incurred as a result of "an unnecessary or improper act or omission." The word "improper" used in conjunction with "unnecessary" was held to encompass an act or omission resulting in costs which would not have been incurred in the proper conduct of the party's case: *DPP v. Denning* [1991] 2 Q.B. 532. *Per curiam* the court observed that "improper" did not connote "grave impropriety".

A causal connection must be shown to exist between the unnecessary or improper act **30–34** or omission and the incurring of the costs or expenses claimed under the order. Where the prosecution was ordered to pay wasted costs which covered the costs of a Crown Court case when no evidence was offered following committal, the court said that inquiries must be made into whether the prosecution's negligence was the cause of the defence costs: *R. v. Crown Court at Wood Green, ex p. DPP* [1993] 1 W.L.R. 723. In *A.* (2005) 149 S.J. 1350 a wasted costs order was made against the prosecution when they failed to disclose, within a reasonable time, information vital to the defence that affected the safety of the convictions.

Where the defendant has the benefit of a criminal defence representation order then for the purposes of section 19 of the *Prosecution of Offences Act* 1985 his costs shall be taken to include the cost of representation publicly funded for him: *Prosecution of Offences Act* 1985, s.21(4A)(b). A wasted costs order may not be appropriate against the prosecution in the case of a legally aided defendant as it simply means the transfer of public funds. Only in extraordinary cases or where the conduct of the police and the Crown Prosecution Service is open to criticism may it be appropriate to make an order. Otherwise the costs of the defence should be borne by the legal aid fund: *R. v. Oxford City Justices, ex p. Chief Constable Thames Valley Police*, The Times, April 24, 1987.

This section only allows for orders to be made between the parties. Orders cannot be **30–35** made against solicitors or counsel personally under section 19: *R. v. Crown Court at Isleworth, ex p. Montague & Co* [1990] C.O.D. 86, DC. As to costs awarded against representatives personally, see *post*.

F. ORDERS FOR COSTS AGAINST LEGAL REPRESENTATIVES

Prosecution of Offences Act 1985, s.19A

Costs against legal representatives

19A.—(1) In any criminal proceedings—   **30–36**

    (a) the Court of Appeal;

    (b) the Crown Court;

    (c) a magistrates' court,

may disallow, or (as the case may be) order the legal or other representative concerned to meet, the whole of any wasted costs or such part of them as may be determined in accordance with regulations.

(2) Regulations shall provide that a legal or other representative against whom action is taken by a magistrates' court under subsection (1) may appeal to the Crown Court and that a legal or other representative against whom action is taken by the Crown Court under subsection (1) may appeal to the Court of Appeal.

(3) In this section—

"legal or other representative" in relation to any proceedings, means a person who is exercising a right of audience, or right to conduct litigation, on behalf of any party to the proceedings;

"regulations" means regulations made by the Lord Chancellor; and

"wasted costs" means any costs incurred by a party—

    (a) as a result of any improper, unreasonable or negligent act or omission on the part of any representative or any employee of a representative; or

    (b) which, in the light of any such act or omission occurring after they were incurred, the court considers it is unreasonable to expect that party to pay.

Costs in Criminal Cases (General) Regulations 1986, regs.3A–3D

PART IIA

WASTED COSTS ORDERS

Application and definitions

30–37   **3A.** This Part of these Regulations applies to action taken by a court under section 19A of the Act and in this Part of these regulations—

"wasted costs order" means any action taken by a court under section 19A of the Act; and

"interested party" means the party benefiting from the wasted costs order and, where he was legally aided, or an order for the payment of costs out of central funds was made in his favour, shall include the authority responsible for determining costs payable in respect of work done under the legal aid order or out of central funds as the case may be.

General

30–38   **3B.**—(1) A wasted costs order may provide for the whole or any part of the wasted costs to be disallowed or ordered to be paid and the court shall specify the amount of such costs.

(2) Before making a wasted costs order the court shall allow the legal or other representative and any party to the proceedings to make representations.

(3) When making a wasted costs order the court may take into account any other order as to costs in respect of the proceedings and may take the wasted costs into account when making any other such order.

(4) Where a wasted costs order has been made the court shall notify any interested party of the order and the amount disallowed or ordered to be paid.

Appeals

30–39   **3C.**—(1) A legal or other representative against whom the wasted costs order is made may appeal—

    (a) in the case of an order made by a magistrates' court, to the Crown Court, and

    (b) in the case of an order made at first instance by the Crown Court, to the Court of Appeal.

(2) Subject to paragraph (4), an appeal shall be instituted within 21 days of the wasted costs order being made by the appellant's giving notice in writing to the court which made the order, stating the grounds of appeal.

(3) The appellant shall serve a copy of the notice of appeal and grounds, including any application for an extension of time in which to appeal, on any interested party.

(4) The time limit within which an appeal may be instituted may, for good reason, be extended before or after it expires—

(a) in the case of an appeal to the Crown Court, by a judge of that court;

(b) in the case of an appeal to the Court of Appeal, a judge of the High Court or Court of Appeal,

and in each case the court to which the appeal is made shall give notice of the extension to the appellant, the court which made the wasted costs order and any interested party.

(5) The court shall give notice of the hearing date to the appellant, the court which made the wasted costs order and any interested party and shall allow the interested party to make representations which may be made orally or in writing.

(6) The court may affirm, vary or revoke the order as it thinks fit and shall notify its decision to the appellant, any interested party and the court which made the order.

Recovery of sums due under a wasted costs order

3D. Where the person required to make a payment in respect of sums due under a wasted **30–40** costs order fails to do so, the payment may be recovered summarily as a sum adjudged to be paid as a civil debt by order of a magistrates' court by the party benefiting from the order, save that where he was legally aided or an order for the payment of costs out of central funds was made in his favour, the power to recover shall be exercisable by the Lord Chancellor.

Extra costs may arise when a lawyer is at fault in the conduct of a case before the **30–41** court. The court has power to order legal representatives to pay personally or be disallowed his own costs when wasted costs are incurred as a result of his actions or omissions. Wasted costs are defined in section 19A. This is a harsh measure and case law provides some guidance on how the Act and regulations should be applied.

In *Re A Barrister (Wasted Costs Order) (No. 1 of 1991)* [1993] Q.B. 293, the Court of Appeal gave the following guidance for the making of wasted costs orders against legal representatives.

1. There is a clear need for any court or judge intending to exercise the wasted costs jurisdiction to formulate carefully and concisely the complaint and the grounds upon which such an order may be sought. The measures are draconian and the grounds must be clear and particular.

2. Where necessary a transcript of the relevant part of the proceedings under discussion should be available. And in accordance with the Rules, a transcript of a wasted costs hearing must be made.

3. A defendant involved in a case where such proceedings are contemplated should be present, if after discussion, with counsel, it is thought that his interests may be affected and he should certainly be present and represented if the matter might affect the course of his trial. Regulation 3B(2) of the *Costs in Criminal Cases (General) (Amendment) Regulations* 1991 furthermore requires that before a wasted costs order is made "the court shall allow the legal or other representative and any party to the proceedings to make representations." There may be cases where it may be appropriate for counsel for the Crown to be present.

4. A three-stage test or approach is recommended when a wasted costs order is contemplated. (i) Has there been an improper, unreasonable or negligent act or omission? (ii) As a result, have any costs been incurred by a party? (iii) If these questions are answered in the affirmative, should the court exercise its discretion to disallow or order the representative to meet the whole or any party of the relevant costs, and if so what specific sum is involved?

5. It is inappropriate to propose any deal or settlement that the representative might forgo fees. The judge should formally state his complaint, in chambers, and invite the representative to make his or her own comments. After any other party has been heard the judge should give a formal ruling. Discursive conversations may be unfair and should certainly not take place.

6. The judge must specify the sum to be disallowed or ordered. Alternatively the

relevant available procedure should be substituted, should it be impossible to fix the sum.

30–42   In this case the wasted costs order was made against counsel whose unexplained and unrefuted remark led the judge to discharge the jury. Because the proper procedure was not followed the order was held invalid. The procedure in the magistrates' court will be slightly different as no full transcripts are taken so the hearing will be recorded only by way of the notes made by the legal adviser. The suggestion of dealing with the matter in chambers is not applicable to the magistrates' court although the court may be cleared in sensitive cases. The general principles enunciated should otherwise be followed. This guidance was approved in *Re Mintz (Wasted Costs Order), The Times,* July 16, 1999, CA, where an order was made against counsel who failed to reach prompt agreement about the removal of certain passages from interview transcripts. The judge did not indicate his complaint in chambers; counsel was not invited to make representations and the amount of costs was not specified. These irregularities led to the order being quashed. Failure to allow representations is in breach of regulation 3B and failure to specify the amount ordered is a fatal flaw. See also *Re Wiseman Lee (Solicitors) (Wasted Costs Order) (No. 5 of 2000), The Times,* April 5, 2001 and *Harry Jagdev & Co (Wasted Costs Order) (No.2 of 1999), The Times,* August 12, 1999.

30–43   Because of the procedural irregularities in these cases, the courts did not go into the question of whether the conduct complained of justified the making of such an order. Guidance on this issue is found in *Ridehalgh v. Horsefield* [1994] Ch. 205, CA. The court considered a number of applications and reviewed the level of conduct that could be said to give rise to wasted costs. It was stated that "improper, unreasonable and negligent" were words that bore their established meaning.

1. Improper included conduct that amounted to any significant breach of a substantial duty imposed by a relevant code of professional conduct and included conduct so regarded by the consensus of professional opinion.
2. Unreasonable described conduct which did not permit of a reasonable explanation.
3. Negligent was to be understood in a non-technical way to denote a failure to act with the competence reasonably to be expected of ordinary members of the profession.

30–44   It was further said that the conduct so characterised had to be established to be directly causative of any wasted costs. From the cases under consideration it was held that such an order was not appropriate for a solicitor pursuing a hopeless case. It was not improper, unreasonable or negligent to act for a defendant whose case was doomed to failure. Also late acceptance of a brief by counsel which led to delay in the case was held to be neither improper nor unnecessary as the "cab rank"principle applied and counsel was obliged to accept the case. In *Boodhoo* [2007] 1 Cr.App.R. 32 a wasted costs order was made against a solicitor who had withdrawn from representing a defendant who failed to attend for trial. The trial court wished to proceed in the defendant's absence but considered itself unable to do so as counsel said that the instructing solicitors would withdraw. The wasted costs order was made against the solicitor on the basis that his actions had led to the trial not proceeding. On appeal it was held that the behaviour of the solicitor was neither improper nor negligent. Nor did the appeal court consider that the decision to withdraw from the case was unreasonable. On the facts of the case it was held that the appellant was entitled to conclude that he could not properly represent the defendant at trial. The defendant had indicated he would not attend at his trial yet his defence rested on alibi evidence. In those circumstances it was held not to be unreasonable for the solicitor to conclude that he should withdraw.

This case demonstrates the importance of ensuring that the provisions of section 19(3) are not only applied but that a full explanation is given as to the finding of an improper, negligent or unreasonable act or ommission. The court said that the role of the independent, professional advocate in the administration of justice had to be borne in mind and it should not be undermined by illegitimate pressures. It appears that a wasted costs order should not be made simply as a mark of the court's displeasure when a certain course of action is taken but must be clearly justified because of impropriety, negligence or unreasonableness.

In *Re P. (A Barrister) (Wasted Costs Order)* [2002] 1 Cr.App.R. 207, CA it was held that a judge could decline to deal with an application for a wasted costs order arising from a case he has dealt with but the fact that the judge had expressed views in relation to the conduct of the barrister against whom the order was sought did not of itself amount to bias or the appearance of bias. The appeal court took the view that it was in the interest of both the public and the profession to retain the summary nature of the procedure which was quick, economical and effective so it was acceptable for the trial judge to deal with wasted costs and not adjourn the matter to another court. It was also held that the standard of proof was the normal civil standard unless the allegation was one of serious misconduct or crime. In this case the misconduct complained of was an inference by the defence that the defendant was of good character when in fact he had spent convictions. The jury was discharged as a result of hearing about the convictions and the wasted costs order was upheld.

G. AWARD OF COSTS AGAINST THIRD PARTIES

Courts Act 2003, s.93

Award of costs against third parties

93. After section 19A of the *Prosecution of Offences Act* 1985 insert—   **30–45**

Provision for award of costs against third parties

"**19B.**—(1) The Lord Chancellor may by regulations make provision empowering magistrates' courts, the Crown Court and the Court of Appeal to make a third party costs order if the condition in subsection (3) is satisfied.

(2) A "third party costs order" is an order as to the payment of costs incurred by a party to criminal proceedings by a person who is not a party to those proceedings ("the third party").

(3) The condition is that—

    (a) there has been serious misconduct (whether or not constituting a contempt of court) by the third party, and

    (b) the court considers it appropriate, having regard to that misconduct, to make a third party costs order against him.

(4) Regulations made under this section may, in particular—

    (a) specify types of misconduct in respect of which a third party costs order may not be made;

    (b) allow the making of a third party costs order at any time;

    (c) make provision for any other order as to costs which has been made in respect of the proceedings to be varied on, or taken account of in, the making of a third party costs order;

    (d) make provision for account to be taken of any third party costs order in the making of any other order as to costs in respect of the proceedings.

(5) Regulations made under this section in relation to magistrates' courts must provide that the third party may appeal to the Crown Court against a third party costs order made by a magistrates' court.

(6) Regulations made under this section in relation to the Crown Court must provide that the third party may appeal to the Court of Appeal against a third party costs order made by the Crown Court."

This section allows the Lord Chancellor to make regulations giving powers to the **30–46** courts, including magistrates' courts, to make an order for costs against a person who is not a party to the proceedings, known as a "third party costs order".

An order can only be made if the serious misconduct condition is met and the court considers such an order to be appropriate. The *Costs in Criminal Cases (General) (Amendment) Regulations* 2004 (S.I. 2004 No. 2408) came into force on October 18, 2004 and make provision for third party costs orders to be made in respect of any

Part VII

misconduct occurring after that date. The Regulations set out the procedure to be followed so that an order may be made at any time after the proceedings or also during the proceedings if the court decides there are good reasons for the order to be made then. There is a right of appeal to the Crown Court and the order is enforceable as a civil debt in the magistrates' court.

H. Enforcement

Magistrates' Courts Act 1980, s.76

Enforcement of sums adjudged to be paid

30–47   **76.**—(1) Subject to the following provi sions of this Part of this Act, and to section 132 below, where default is made in paying a sum adjudged to be paid by a conviction or order of a magistrates' court, the court may issue a warrant of distress for the purposes of levying the sum or issue a warrant committing the defaulter to prison.

(2) A warrant of commitment may be issued as aforesaid either—

    (a) where it appears on the return to a warrant of distress that the money and goods of the defaulter are insufficient to satisfy the sum with the costs and charges of levying the sum; or

    (b) instead of a warrant of distress.

(3) The period for which a person may be committed to prison under such a warrant as aforesaid shall not, subject to the provisions of any enactment passed after 31st December 1879, exceed the period applicable to the case under Schedule 4 to this Act.

(4)–(6) [apply to civil maintenance orders.]

[This section is reprinted as amended by the *Criminal Justice Act* 1982, section 78 and Sched. 16.]

30–48   Costs may be enforced in the same way as fines, see *ante*, Ch.24. A sum adjudged to be paid by a conviction or order includes costs, damages or compensation: section 150(3) of the *Magistrates' Courts Act* 1980. Any period of imprisonment ordered in default of payment cannot be less than five days: *Magistrates' Courts Act* 1980, s.132. Maximum periods of imprisonment in default are fixed according to the amount ordered to be paid. There is no power to remit costs, but nominal default orders may be made.

PACE CODES

POLICE AND CRIMINAL EVIDENCE ACT 1984

These Codes are issued under section 66 of the *Police and Criminal Evidence Act* 1984. There are presently eight Codes of Practice: Code A (stop and search); Code B (search and seizure); Code C (detention, treatment and questioning of persons); Code D (identification); Code E (tape recording of interviews); Code F (visual recording of interviews); Code G (arrest) and Code H (detention etc. under the *Terrorism Act* 2000). The most recent amendments have been effected as follows:

The *Police and Criminal Evidence Act 1984 (Codes of Practice) Order* 2005 (S.I 2005 No. 3503), which revised Codes A to F and added a new Code G, came into effect on January 1, 2006.

The *Police and Criminal Evidence Act 1984 (Code of Practice C and Code of Practice H) Order* 2006 (S.I. 2006 No. 1938), which revised Code C and added a new Code H as a consequence, came into effect on January 25, 2006.

The Police and Criminal Evidence Act 1984 (Codes of Practice) (Revisions to Code A) Order 2006 (S.I. 2006 No. 2165), which further revised Code A, came into effect on August 31, 2006. The Codes printed incorporate these amendments.

Code A

Code of Practice for the Exercise by: Police Officers of Statutory Powers of Stop and Search Police Officers and Police Staff of Requirements to Record Public Encounters

Commencement—Transitional Arrangements   **A–1**
This code applies to any search by a police officer and the requirement to record public encounters taking place after midnight on 31 December 2005.

General   **A–2**
This Code of Practice must be readily available at all police stations for consultation by police officers, police staff, detained persons and members of the public.

The notes for guidance included are not provisions of this Code, but are guidance to police officers and others about its application and interpretation. Provisions in the annexes to the Code are provisions of this Code.

This Code governs the exercise by police officers of statutory powers to search a person or a vehicle without first making an arrest. The main stop and search powers to which this Code applies are set out in Annex A, but that list should not be regarded as definitive. [See Note 1] In addition, it covers requirements on police officers and police staff to record encounters not governed by statutory powers. This Code does not apply to:

(a) the powers of stop and search under:
(i) *Aviation Security Act* 1982, section 27(2);
(ii) *Police and Criminal Evidence Act* 1984, section 6(1) (which relates specifically to powers of constables employed by statutory undertakers on the premises of the statutory undertakers).
(b) searches carried out for the purposes of examination under Schedule 7 to the *Terrorism Act* 2000 and to which the Code of Practice issued under paragraph

6 of Schedule 14 to the *Terrorism Act* 2000 applies.

1 PRINCIPLES GOVERNING STOP AND SEARCH

A–3   1.1 Powers to stop and search must be used fairly, responsibly, with respect for people being searched and without unlawful discrimination. The *Race Relations (Amendment) Act* 2000 makes it unlawful for police officers to discriminate on the grounds of race, colour, ethnic origin, nationality or national origins when using their powers.

1.2 The intrusion on the liberty of the person stopped or searched must be brief and detention for the purposes of a search must take place at or near the location of the stop.

1.3 If these fundamental principles are not observed the use of powers to stop and search may be drawn into question. Failure to use the powers in the proper manner reduces their effectiveness. Stop and search can play an important role in the detection and prevention of crime, and using the powers fairly makes them more effective.

1.4 The primary purpose of stop and search powers is to enable officers to allay or confirm suspicions about individuals without exercising their power of arrest. Officers may be required to justify the use or authorisation of such powers, in relation both to individual searches and the overall pattern of their activity in this regard, to their supervisory officers or in court. Any misuse of the powers is likely to be harmful to policing and lead to mistrust of the police. Officers must also be able to explain their actions to the member of the public searched. The misuse of these powers can lead to disciplinary action.

1.5 An officer must not search a person, even with his or her consent, where no power to search is applicable. Even where a person is prepared to submit to a search voluntarily, the person must not be searched unless the necessary legal power exists, and the search must be in accordance with the relevant power and the provisions of this Code. The only exception, where an officer does not require a specific power, applies to searches of persons entering sports grounds or other premises carried out with their consent given as a condition of entry.

2 EXPLANATION OF POWERS TO STOP AND SEARCH

A–4   2.1 This code applies to powers of stop and search as follows:

    (a) powers which require reasonable grounds for suspicion, before they may be exercised: that articles unlawfully obtained or possessed are being carried, or under section 43 of the *Terrorism Act* 2000 that a person is a terrorist;

    (b) authorised under section 60 of the *Criminal Justice and Public Order Act* 1994, based upon a reasonable belief that incidents involving serious violence may take place or that people are carrying dangerous instruments or offensive weapons within any locality in the police area;

    (c) authorised under section 44(1) and (2) of the *Terrorism Act* 2000 based upon a consideration that the exercise of one or both powers is expedient for the prevention of acts of terrorism;

    (d) powers to search a person who has not been arrested in the exercise of a power to search premises (see Code B paragraph 2.4).

Searches requiring reasonable grounds for suspicion

A–5   2.2 Reasonable grounds for suspicion depend on the circumstances in each case. There must be an objective basis for that suspicion based on facts, information, and/or intelligence which are relevant to the likelihood of finding an article of a certain kind or, in the case of searches under section 43 of the *Terrorism Act* 2000, to the likelihood that the person is a terrorist. Reasonable suspicion can never be supported on the basis of personal factors alone without reliable supporting intelligence or information or some specific behaviour by the person concerned. For example, a person's race, age, appearance, or the fact that the person is known to have a previous conviction, cannot be used alone or in combination with each other as the reason for searching that person. Reasonable suspicion cannot be based on generalisations or stereotypical images of certain groups or categories of people as more likely to be involved in criminal activity. A person's religion cannot be considered as reasonable grounds for suspicion and should never be considered as a reason to stop or stop and search an individual.

2.3 Reasonable suspicion can sometimes exist without specific information or intelligence and on the basis of some level of generalisation stemming from the behaviour of a person. For example, if an officer encounters someone on the street at night who is obviously trying to hide something, the officer may (depending on the other surrounding circumstances) base such suspicion on the fact that this kind of behaviour is often linked to stolen or prohibited articles being carried. Similarly, for the purposes of section 43 of the *Terrorism Act* 2000, suspicion that a person is a terrorist may arise from the person's behaviour at or near a location which has been identified as a potential target for terrorists.

2.4 However, reasonable suspicion should normally be linked to accurate and current intelligence or information, such as information describing an article being carried, a suspected offender, or a person who has been seen carrying a type of article known to have been stolen recently from premises in the area. Searches based on accurate and current intelligence or information are more likely to be effective. Targeting searches in a particular area at specified crime problems increases their effectiveness and minimises inconvenience to law-abiding members of the public. It also helps in justifying the use of searches both to those who are searched and to the public. This does not however prevent stop and search powers being exercised in other locations where such powers may be exercised and reasonable suspicion exists.

2.5 Searches are more likely to be effective, legitimate, and secure public confidence when reasonable suspicion is based on a range of factors. The overall use of these powers is more likely to be effective when up to date and accurate intelligence or information is communicated to officers and they are well-informed about local crime patterns.

2.6 Where there is reliable information or intelligence that members of a group or gang habitually carry knives unlawfully or weapons or controlled drugs, and wear a distinctive item of clothing or other means of identification to indicate their membership of the group or gang, that distinctive item of clothing or other means of identification may provide reasonable grounds to stop and search a person. [See *Note 9*]

2.7 A police officer may have reasonable grounds to suspect that a person is in innocent possession of a stolen or prohibited article or other item for which he or she is empowered to search. In that case the officer may stop and search the person even though there would be no power of arrest.

2.8 Under section 43(1) of the *Terrorism Act* 2000 a constable may stop and search a person whom the officer reasonably suspects to be a terrorist to discover whether the person is in possession of anything which may constitute evidence that the person is a terrorist. These searches may only be carried out by an officer of the same sex as the person searched.

2.9 An officer who has reasonable grounds for suspicion may detain the person concerned in order to carry out a search. Before carrying out a search the officer may ask questions about the person's behaviour or presence in circumstances which gave rise to the suspicion. As a result of questioning the detained person, the reasonable grounds for suspicion necessary to detain that person may be confirmed or, because of a satisfactory explanation, be eliminated. [See *Notes 2* and *3*] Questioning may also reveal reasonable grounds to suspect the possession of a different kind of unlawful article from that originally suspected. Reasonable grounds for suspicion however cannot be provided retrospectively by such questioning during a person's detention or by refusal to answer any questions put.

2.10 If, as a result of questioning before a search, or other circumstances which come to the attention of the officer, there cease to be reasonable grounds for suspecting that an article is being carried of a kind for which there is a power to stop and search, no search may take place. [See *Note 3*] In the absence of any other lawful power to detain, the person is free to leave at will and must be so informed.

2.11 There is no power to stop or detain a person in order to find grounds for a search. Police officers have many encounters with members of the public which do not involve detaining people against their will. If reasonable grounds for suspicion emerge during such an encounter, the officer may search the person, even though no grounds existed when the encounter began. If an officer is detaining someone for the purpose of a search, he or she should inform the person as soon as detention begins.

Searches authorised under section 60 of the Criminal Justice and Public Order Act 1994

2.12 Authority for a constable in uniform to stop and search under section 60 of the *Crim-*   **A–6**
inal Justice and Public Order Act 1994 may be given if the authorising officer reasonably believes:
> (a) that incidents involving serious violence may take place in any locality in the officer's police area, and it is expedient to use these powers to prevent their occurrence, or

(b) that persons are carrying dangerous instruments or offensive weapons without good reason in any locality in the officer's police area.

2.13 An authorisation under section 60 may only be given by an officer of the rank of inspector or above, in writing, specifying the grounds on which it was given, the locality in which the powers may be exercised and the period of time for which they are in force. The period authorised shall be no longer than appears reasonably necessary to prevent, or seek to prevent incidents of serious violence, or to deal with the problem of carrying dangerous instruments or offensive weapons. It may not exceed 24 hours. [See *Notes 10–13*]

2.14 If an inspector gives an authorisation, he or she must, as soon as practicable, inform an officer of or above the rank of superintendent. This officer may direct that the authorisation shall be extended for a further 24 hours, if violence or the carrying of dangerous instruments or offensive weapons has occurred, or is suspected to have occurred, and the continued use of the powers is considered necessary to prevent or deal with further such activity. That direction must also be given in writing at the time or as soon as practicable afterwards. [See *Note 12*]

Powers to require removal of face coverings

A–7   2.15 Section 60AA of the *Criminal Justice and Public Order Act* 1994 also provides a power to demand the removal of disguises. The officer exercising the power must reasonably believe that someone is wearing an item wholly or mainly for the purpose of concealing identity. There is also a power to seize such items where the officer believes that a person intends to wear them for this purpose. There is no power to stop and search for disguises. An officer may seize any such item which is discovered when exercising a power of search for something else, or which is being carried, and which the officer reasonably believes is intended to be used for concealing anyone's identity. This power can only be used if an authorisation under section 60 or an authorisation under section 60AA is in force.

2.16 Authority for a constable in uniform to require the removal of disguises and to seize them under section 60AA may be given if the authorising officer reasonably believes that activities may take place in any locality in the officer's police area that are likely to involve the commission of offences and it is expedient to use these powers to prevent or control these activities.

2.17 An authorisation under section 60AA may only be given by an officer of the rank of inspector or above, in writing, specifying the grounds on which it was given, the locality in which the powers may be exercised and the period of time for which they are in force. The period authorised shall be no longer than appears reasonably necessary to prevent, or seek to prevent the commission of offences. It may not exceed 24 hours. [See *Notes 10–13*]

2.18 If an inspector gives an authorisation, he or she must, as soon as practicable, inform an officer of or above the rank of superintendent. This officer may direct that the authorisation shall be extended for a further 24 hours, if crimes have been committed, or is suspected to have been committed, and the continued use of the powers is considered necessary to prevent or deal with further such activity. This direction must also be given in writing at the time or as soon as practicable afterwards. [See *Note 12*]

Searches authorised under section 44 of the Terrorism Act 2000

A–8   2.19 An officer of the rank of assistant chief constable (or equivalent) or above, may give authority for the following powers of stop and search under section 44 of the *Terrorism Act* 2000 to be exercised in the whole or part of his or her police area if the officer considers it is expedient for the prevention of acts of terrorism:

(a) under section 44(1) of the *Terrorism Act* 2000, to give a constable in uniform power to stop and search any vehicle, its driver, any passenger in the vehicle and anything in or on the vehicle or carried by the driver or any passenger; and

(b) under section 44(2) of the *Terrorism Act* 2000, to give a constable in uniform power to stop and search any pedestrian and anything carried by the pedestrian.

An authorisation under section 44(1) may be combined with one under section 44(2).

2.20 If an authorisation is given orally at first, it must be confirmed in writing by the officer who gave it as soon as reasonably practicable.

2.21 When giving an authorisation, the officer must specify the geographical area in which the power may be used, and the time and date that the authorisation ends (up to a maximum of 28 days from the time the authorisation was given). [See *Notes 12* and *13*]

2.22 The officer giving an authorisation under section 44(1) or (2) must cause the Secretary of State to be informed, as soon as reasonably practicable that such an authorisation has been given. An authorisation which is not confirmed by the Secretary of State within 48 hours of its having been given, shall have effect up until the end of that 48 hour period or the end of the period specified in the authorisation (whichever is the earlier). [See *Note 14*]

2.23 Following notification of the authorisation, the Secretary of State may:

   (i) cancel the authorisation with immediate effect or with effect from such other time as he or she may direct;

   (ii) confirm it but for a shorter period than that specified in the authorisation; or

   (iii) confirm the authorisation as given.

2.24 When an authorisation under section 44 is given, a constable in uniform may exercise the powers:

   (a) only for the purpose of searching for articles of a kind which could be used in connection with terrorism (see paragraph 2.25);

   (b) whether or not there are any grounds for suspecting the presence of such articles.

2.24A When a Community Support Officer on duty and in uniform has been conferred powers under section 44 of the *Terrorism Act* 2000 by a Chief Officer of their force, the exercise of this power must comply with the requirements of this Code of Practice, including the recording requirements.

2.25 The selection of persons stopped under section 44 of *Terrorism Act* 2000 should reflect an objective assessment of the threat posed by the various terrorist groups active in Great Britain. The powers must not be used to stop and search for reasons unconnected with terrorism. Officers must take particular care not to discriminate against members of minority ethnic groups in the exercise of these powers. There may be circumstances, however, where it is appropriate for officers to take account of a person's ethnic origin in selecting persons to be stopped in response to a specific terrorist threat (for example, some international terrorist groups are associated with particular ethnic identities). [See *Notes 12* and *13*]

2.26 The powers under sections 43 and 44 of the *Terrorism Act* 2000 allow a constable to search only for articles which could be used for terrorist purposes. However, this would not prevent a search being carried out under other powers if, in the course of exercising these powers, the officer formed reasonable grounds for suspicion.

Powers to search in the exercise of a power to search premises

2.27 The following powers to search premises also authorise the search of a person, not **A–9** under arrest, who is found on the premises during the course of the search:

   (a) section 139B of the *Criminal Justice Act* 1988 under which a constable may enter school premises and search the premises and any person on those premises for any bladed or pointed article or offensive weapon; and

   (b) under a warrant issued under section 23(3) of the *Misuse of Drugs Act* 1971 to search premises for drugs or documents but only if the warrant specifically authorises the search of persons found on the premises.

2.28 Before the power under section 139B of the *Criminal Justice Act* 1988 may be exercised, the constable must have reasonable grounds to believe that an offence under section 139A of the *Criminal Justice Act* 1988 (having a bladed or pointed article or offensive weapon on school premises) has been or is being committed. A warrant to search premises and persons found therein may be issued under section 23(3) of the *Misuse of Drugs Act* 1971 if there are reasonable grounds to suspect that controlled drugs or certain documents are in the possession of a person on the premises.

2.29 The powers in paragraph 2.27(a) or (b) do not require prior specific grounds to suspect that the person to be searched is in possession of an item for which there is an existing power to search. However, it is still necessary to ensure that the selection and treatment of those searched under these powers is based upon objective factors connected with the search of the premises, and not upon personal prejudice.

3 CONDUCT OF SEARCHES

3.1 All stops and searches must be carried out with courtesy, consideration and respect for **A–10** the person concerned. This has a significant impact on public confidence in the police. Every reasonable effort must be made to minimise the embarrassment that a person being searched may experience. [See *Note 4*]

3.2 The co-operation of the person to be searched must be sought in every case, even if the person initially objects to the search. A forcible search may be made only if it has been established that the person is unwilling to co-operate or resists. Reasonable force may be used as a last resort if necessary to conduct a search or to detain a person or vehicle for the purposes of a search.

3.3 The length of time for which a person or vehicle may be detained must be reasonable and kept to a minimum. Where the exercise of the power requires reasonable suspicion, the thoroughness and extent of a search must depend on what is suspected of being carried, and by whom. If the suspicion relates to a particular article which is seen to be slipped into a person's pocket, then, in the absence of other grounds for suspicion or an opportunity for the article to be moved elsewhere, the search must be confined to that pocket. In the case of a small article which can readily be concealed, such as a drug, and which might be concealed anywhere on the person, a more extensive search may be necessary. In the case of searches mentioned in paragraph 2.1(b), (c), and (d), which do not require reasonable grounds for suspicion, officers may make any reasonable search to look for items for which they are empowered to search. [See *Note 5*]

3.4 The search must be carried out at or near the place where the person or vehicle was first detained. [See *Note 6*]

3.5 There is no power to require a person to remove any clothing in public other than an outer coat jacket or gloves except under section 45(3) of the *Terrorism Act* 2000 (which empowers a constable conducting a search under section 44(1) or 44(2) of that Act to require a person to remove headgear and footwear in public) and under section 60AA of the *Criminal Justice and Public Order Act* 1994 (which empowers a constable to require a person to remove any item worn to conceal identity). [See *Notes 4* and *6*] A search in public of a person's clothing which has not been removed must be restricted to superficial examination of outer garments. This does not, however, prevent an officer from placing his or her hand inside the pockets of the outer clothing, or feeling round the inside of collars, socks and shoes if this is reasonably necessary in the circumstances to look for the object of the search or to remove and examine any item reasonably suspected to be the object of the search. For the same reasons, subject to the restrictions on the removal of headgear, a person's hair may also be searched in public (see paragraphs 3.1 and 3.3).

3.6 Where on reasonable grounds it is considered necessary to conduct a more thorough search (e.g. by requiring a person to take off a T-shirt), this must be done out of public view, for example, in a police van unless paragraph 3.7 applies, or police station if there is one nearby. [See *Note 6*] Any search involving the removal of more than an outer coat, jacket, gloves, headgear or footwear, or any other item concealing identity, may only be made by an officer of the same sex as the person searched and may not be made in the presence of anyone of the opposite sex unless the person being searched specifically requests it. [See *Notes 4.7* and *8*]

3.7 Searches involving exposure of intimate parts of the body must not be conducted as a routine extension of a less thorough search, simply because nothing is found in the course of the initial search. Searches involving exposure of intimate parts of the body may be carried out only at a nearby police station or other nearby location which is out of public view (but not a police vehicle). These searches must be conducted in accordance with paragraph 11 of Annex A to Code C except that an intimate search mentioned in paragraph 11(f) of Annex A to Code C may not be authorised or carried out under any stop and search powers. The other provisions of Code C do not apply to the conduct and recording of searches of persons detained at police stations in the exercise of stop and search powers. [See *Note 7*]

Steps to be taken prior to a search

A–11   3.8 Before any search of a detained person or attended vehicle takes place the officer must take reasonable steps to give the person to be searched or in charge of the vehicle the following information:

    (a) that they are being detained for the purposes of a search;

    (b) the officer's name (except in the case of enquiries linked to the investigation of terrorism, or otherwise where the officer reasonably believes that giving his or her name might put him or her in danger, in which case a warrant or other identification number shall be given) and the name of the police station to which the officer is attached;

(c) the legal search power which is being exercised; and

(d) a clear explanation of:

    (i) the purpose of the search in terms of the article for which there is a power to search; and

    (ii) in the case of powers requiring reasonable suspicion (see paragraph 2.1(a)), the grounds for that suspicion; or

    (iii) in the case of powers which do not require reasonable suspicion (see paragraph 2.1(b), and (c)), the nature of the power and of any necessary authorisation and the fact that it has been given.

3.9 Officers not in uniform must show their warrant cards. Stops and searches under the powers mentioned in paragraphs 2.1(b), and (c) may be undertaken only by a constable in uniform.

3.10 Before the search takes place the officer must inform the person (or the owner or person in charge of the vehicle that is to be searched) of his or her entitlement to a copy of the record of the search, including his entitlement to a record of the search if an application is made within 12 months, if it is wholly impracticable to make a record at the time. If a record is not made at the time the person should also be told how a copy can be obtained (see section 4). The person should also be given information about police powers to stop and search and the individual's rights in these circumstances.

3.11 If the person to be searched, or in charge of a vehicle to be searched, does not appear to understand what is being said, or there is any doubt about the person's ability to understand English, the officer must take reasonable steps to bring information regarding the person's rights and any relevant provisions of this Code to his or her attention. If the person is deaf or cannot understand English and is accompanied by someone, then the officer must try to establish whether that person can interpret or otherwise help the officer to give the required information.

4 Recording requirements

4.1 An officer who has carried out a search in the exercise of any power to which this **A–12** Code applies, must make a record of it at the time, unless there are exceptional circumstances which would make this wholly impracticable (e.g. in situations involving public disorder or when the officer's presence is urgently required elsewhere). If a record is not made at the time, the officer must do so as soon as practicable afterwards. There may be situations in which it is not practicable to obtain the information necessary to complete a record, but the officer should make every reasonable effort to do so. [See *Note 21*]

4.2 Except in the circumstances set out in paragraph 4.2A, a copy of a record made at the time must be given immediately to the person who has been searched. In all cases the officer must ask for the name, address and date of birth of the person searched, but there is no obligation on a person to provide these details and no power of detention if the person is unwilling to do so.

4.2A A receipt of the record rather than a copy of the record may be given immediately to the person who has been searched provided it is produced by electronic means, it states how the full record can be accessed and the officer providing the receipt operates from one of the designated areas set out in Annex D to this Code. When providing such a receipt, the officer must inform the person that the receipt is in place of a full written record, that the full record is available in electronic or in hard copy format and how the full record can be accessed. The person may request a copy in either format but not both. The full record must comply with paragraph 4.3 of this Code. [See *Note 22.*]

4.3 The following information must always be included in the record of a search even if the person does not wish to provide any personal details:

    (i) the name of the person searched, or (if it is withheld) a description;

    (ii) a note of the person's self-defined ethnic background; *[See Note 18]*

    (iii) when a vehicle is searched, its registration number; *[See Note 16]*

    (iv) the date, time, and place that the person or vehicle was first detained;

    (v) the date, time and place the person or vehicle was searched (if different from (iv));

    (vi) the purpose of the search;

(vii) the grounds for making it, or in the case of those searches mentioned in paragraph 2.1(b) and (c), the nature of the power and of any necessary authorisation and the fact that it has been given; *[See Note 17]*

(viii) its outcome (e.g. arrest or no further action);

(ix) a note of any injury or damage to property resulting from it;

(x) subject to paragraph 3.8(b), the identity of the officer making the search. *[See Note 15]*

4.4 Nothing in paragraph 4.3 (x) or 4.10A requires the names of police officers to be shown on the search record or any other record required to be made under this code in the case of enquiries linked to the investigation of terrorism or otherwise where an officer reasonably believes that recording names might endanger the officers. In such cases the record must show the officer's warrant or other identification number and duty station.

4.5 A record is required for each person and each vehicle searched. However, if a person is in a vehicle and both are searched, and the object and grounds of the search are the same, only one record need be completed. If more than one person in a vehicle is searched, separate records for each search of a person must be made. If only a vehicle is searched, the name of the driver and his or her self-defined ethnic background must be recorded, unless the vehicle is unattended.

4.6 The record of the grounds for making a search must, briefly but informatively, explain the reason for suspecting the person concerned, by reference to the person's behaviour and/or other circumstances.

4.7 Where officers detain an individual with a view to performing a search, but the search is not carried out due to the grounds for suspicion being eliminated as a result of questioning the person detained, a record must still be made in accordance with the procedure outlined in paragraph 4.12.

4.8 After searching an unattended vehicle, or anything in or on it, an officer must leave a notice in it (or on it, if things on it have been searched without opening it) recording the fact that it has been searched.

4.9 The notice must include the name of the police station to which the officer concerned is attached and state where a copy of the record of the search may be obtained and where any application for compensation should be directed.

4.10 The vehicle must if practicable be left secure.

4.10A When an officer makes a record of the stop electronically and is unable to produce a copy of the form at the time, the officer must explain how the person can obtain a full copy of the record of the stop or search and give the person a receipt which contains:

● a unique reference number and guidance on how to obtain a full copy of the stop or search;

● the name of the officer who carried out the stop or search (unless paragraph 4.4 applies); and

● the power used to stop and search them. [See *Note 21*]

Recording of encounters not governed by Statutory Powers

A–13   4.11 Not used.

4.12 When an officer requests a person in a public place to account for themselves, i.e. their actions, behaviour, presence in an area or possession of anything, a record of the encounter must be completed at the time, and except in the circumstances set out in paragraph 4.13A, a copy given to the person who has been questioned. The record must identify the name of the officer who has made the stop and conducted the encounter. This does not apply under the exceptional circumstances outlined in paragraph 4.1 of this code.

4.13 This requirement does not apply to general conversations such as when giving directions to a place, or when seeking witnesses. It also does not include occasions on which an officer is seeking general information or questioning people to establish background to incidents which have required officers to intervene to keep the peace or resolve a dispute.

4.13A A receipt of the record rather than a copy of the record may be given immediately to the person who has been searched provided it is produced by electronic means, it states how the full record can be accessed and the officer providing the receipt operates from one of the designated areas set out in Annex D to this Code. When providing such a receipt, the officer must inform the person that the receipt is in place of a full written record, that the full record is available in electronic or in hard copy format and how the full record can be accessed. The person may request a copy in either format but not both. The full record must comply with paragraph 4.17 of this Code. [See *Note 22*.]

4.14 A separate record need not be completed when:

> — stopping a person in a vehicle when an HORT/1 form, a Vehicle Defect Rectification Scheme Notice, or a Fixed Penalty Notice is issued. It also does not apply when a specimen of breath is required under section 6 of the *Road Traffic Act* 1988.

> — stopping a person when a Penalty Notice is issued for an offence.

4.15 Officers must inform the person of their entitlement to a copy of a record of the encounter.

4.16 The provisions of paragraph 4.4 of this code apply equally when the encounters described in 4.12 and 4.13 are recorded.

4.17 The following information must be included in the record:

(i) the date, time and place of the encounter;

(ii) if the person is in a vehicle, the registration number;

(iii) the reason why the officer questioned that person; [See *Note 17*]

(iv) a note of the person's self-defined ethnic background; [See *Note 18*]

(v) the outcome of the encounter.

4.18 There is no power to require the person questioned to provide personal details. If a person refuses to give their self-defined ethnic background, a form must still be completed, which includes a description of the person's ethnic background. [See *Note 18*]

4.19 A record of an encounter must always be made when the criteria set out in 4.12 have been met. If the criteria are not met but the person requests a record, the officer should provide a copy of the form but record on it that the encounter did not meet the criteria. The officer can refuse to issue the form if he or she reasonably believes that the purpose of the request is deliberately aimed at frustrating or delaying legitimate police activity. [See *Note 20*]

4.20 All references to officers in this section include police staff designated as Community Support Officers under section 38 of the *Police Reform Act* 2002.

Notes for Guidance

Officers exercising stop and search powers

1 *This code does not affect the ability of an officer to speak to or question a person in the* **A–14** *ordinary course of the officer's duties without detaining the person or exercising any element of compulsion. It is not the purpose of the code to prohibit such encounters between the police and the community with the co-operation of the person concerned and neither does it affect the principle that all citizens have a duty to help police officers to prevent crime and discover offenders. This is a civic rather than a legal duty; but when a police officer is trying to discover whether, or by whom, an offence has been committed he or she may question any person from whom useful information might be obtained, subject to the restrictions imposed by Code C. A person's unwillingness to reply does not alter this entitlement, but in the absence of a power to arrest, or to detain in order to search, the person is free to leave at will and cannot be compelled to remain with the officer.*

2 *In some circumstances preparatory questioning may be unnecessary, but in general a brief conversation or exchange will be desirable not only as a means of avoiding unsuccessful searches, but to explain the grounds for the stop/search, to gain co-operation and reduce any tension there might be surrounding the stop/search.*

3 *Where a person is lawfully detained for the purpose of a search, but no search in the event takes place, the detention will not thereby have been rendered unlawful.*

4 *Many people customarily cover their heads or faces for religious reasons—for example, Muslim women, Sikh men, Sikh or Hindu women, or Rastarfarian men or women. A police officer cannot order the removal of a head or face covering except where there is reason to believe that the item is being worn by the individual wholly or mainly for the purpose of disguising identity, not simply because it disguises identity. Where there may be religious sensitivities about ordering the removal of such an item, the officer should permit the item to be removed out of public view. Where practicable, the item should be removed in the presence of an officer of the same sex as the person and out of sight of anyone of the opposite sex.*

5 *A search of a person in public should be completed as soon as possible.*

6 *A person may be detained under a stop and search power at a place other than where the person was first detained, only if that place, be it a police station or elsewhere, is nearby. Such a place should be located within a reasonable travelling distance using whatever mode of travel (on foot or by car) is appropriate. This applies to all searches under stop and search powers, whether or not they involve the removal of clothing or exposure of intimate parts of the body (see paragraphs 3.6 and 3.7) or take place in or out of public view. It means, for example, that a search under the stop and search power in section 23 of the Misuse of Drugs Act 1971 which involves the compulsory removal of more than a person's outer coat, jacket or gloves cannot be carried out unless a place which is both nearby the place they were first detained and out of public view, is available. If a search involves exposure of intimate parts of the body and a police station is not nearby, particular care must be taken to ensure that the location is suitable in that it enables the search to be conducted in accordance with the requirements of paragraph 11 of Annex A to Code C.*

7 *A search in the street itself should be regarded as being in public for the purposes of paragraphs 3.6 and 3.7 above, even though it may be empty at the time a search begins. Although there is no power to require a person to do so, there is nothing to prevent an officer from asking a person voluntarily to remove more than an outer coat, jacket or gloves (and headgear or footwear under section 45(3) of the Terrorism Act 2000) in public.*

8 *Where there may be religious sensitivities about asking someone to remove headgear using a power under section 45(3) of the Terrorism Act 2000, the police officer should offer to carry out the search out of public view (for example, in a police van or police station if there is one nearby).*

9 *Other means of identification might include jewellery, insignias, tattoos or other features which are known to identify members of the particular gang or group.*

Authorising officers

A–15   10 *The powers under section 60 are separate from and additional to the normal stop and search powers which require reasonable grounds to suspect an individual of carrying an offensive weapon (or other article). Their overall purpose is to prevent serious violence and the widespread carrying of weapons which might lead to persons being seriously injured by disarming potential offenders in circumstances where other powers would not be sufficient. They should not therefore be used to replace or circumvent the normal powers for dealing with routine crime problems. The purpose of the powers under section 60AA is to prevent those involved in intimidatory or violent protests using face coverings to disguise identity.*

11 *Authorisations under section 60 require a reasonable belief on the part of the authorising officer. This must have an objective basis, for example: intelligence or relevant information such as a history of antagonism and violence between particular groups; previous incidents of violence at, or connected with, particular events or locations; a significant increase in knifepoint robberies in a limited area; reports that individuals are regularly carrying weapons in a particular locality; or in the case of section 60AA previous incidents of crimes being committed while wearing face coverings to conceal identity.*

12 *It is for the authorising officer to determine the period of time during which the powers mentioned in paragraph 2.1 (b) and (c) may be exercised. The officer should set the minimum period he or she considers necessary to deal with the risk of violence, the carrying of knives or offensive weapons, or terrorism. A direction to extend the period authorised under the powers mentioned in paragraph 2.1(b) may be given only once. Thereafter further use of the powers requires a new authorisation. There is no provision to extend an authorisation of the powers mentioned in paragraph 2.1(c): further use of the powers requires a new authorisation.*

13 *It is for the authorising officer to determine the geographical area in which the use of the powers is to be authorised. In doing so the officer may wish to take into account factors such as the nature and venue of the anticipated incident, the number of people who may be in the immediate area of any possible incident, their access to surrounding areas and the anticipated level of violence. The officer should not set a geographical area which is wider than that he or she believes necessary for the purpose of preventing anticipated violence, the carrying of knives or offensive weapons, acts of terrorism, or, in the case of section 60AA, the prevention of commission of offences. It is particularly important to ensure that constables exercising such powers are fully aware of where they may be used. If the area specified is smaller than the whole force area, the officer giving the authorisation should specify either the streets which form the boundary of the area or a divisional boundary within the force area. If the power is to be used in response to a threat or incident that straddles police force areas, an officer from each of the forces concerned will need to give an authorisation.*

14 *An officer who has authorised the use of powers under section 44 of the Terrorism Act 2000 must take immediate steps to send a copy of the authorisation to the National Joint Unit, Metropolitan Police Special Branch, who will forward it to the Secretary of State. The Secretary of State should be informed of the reasons for the authorisation. The National Joint Unit will inform the force concerned, within 48 hours of the authorisation being made, whether the Secretary of State has confirmed or cancelled or altered the authorisation.*

Recording

15 *Where a stop and search is conducted by more than one officer the identity of all the of-* **A–16**
ficers engaged in the search must be recorded on the record. Nothing prevents an officer who is present but not directly involved in searching from completing the record during the course of the encounter.

16 *Where a vehicle has not been allocated a registration number (e.g. a rally car or a trials motorbike) that part of the requirement under 4.3(iii) does not apply.*

17 *It is important for monitoring purposes to specify whether the authority for exercising a stop and search power was given under section 60 of the Criminal Justice and Public Order Act 1994 or under section 44(1) or 44(2) of the Terrorism Act 2000.*

18 *Officers should record the self-defined ethnicity of every person stopped according to the categories used in the 2001 census question listed in Annex B. Respondents should be asked to select one of the five main categories representing broad ethnic groups and then a more specific cultural background from within this group. The ethnic classification should be coded for recording purposes using the coding system in Annex B. An additional "Not stated" box is available but should not be offered to respondents explicitly. Officers should be aware and explain to members of the public, especially where concerns are raised, that this information is required to obtain a true picture of stop and search activity and to help improve ethnic monitoring, tackle discriminatory practice, and promote effective use of the powers. If the person gives what appears to the officer to be an "incorrect" answer (e.g. a person who appears to be white states that they are black), the officer should record the response that has been given. Officers should also record their own perception of the ethnic background of every person stopped and this must be done by using the PNC/Phoenix classification system. If the "Not stated" category is used the reason for this must be recorded on the form.*

19 *Arrangements for public scrutiny of records should take account of the right to confidentiality of those stopped and searched. Anonymised forms and/or statistics generated from records should be the focus of the examinations by members of the public.*

20 *Where an officer engages in conversation which is not pertinent to the actions or whereabouts of the individual (e.g. does not relate to why the person is there, what they are doing or where they have been or are going) then issuing a form would not meet the criteria set out in paragraph 4.12. Situations designed to impede police activity may arise, for example, in public order situations where individuals engage in dialogue with the officer but the officer does not initiate or engage in contact about the person's individual circumstances.*

21 *In situations where it is not practicable to provide a written record or a full copy of an electronic record or an electronic receipt (in accordance with paragraphs 42A and 4.13A above) of the stop or stop and search at that time, the officer should consider providing the person with details of the station to which the person may attend for a record. This may take the form of a simple business card, adding the date of the stop or stop and search.*

22 *The ability to provide an electronic receipt for a stop or stop and search is limited to officers from those British Transport Police (BTP) designated areas set out in Annex D to this Code and to a limited pilot period. The operational nature of BTP policing means that officers from these locations may provide electronic receipts in the course of their duties throughout England and Wales.*

ANNEX D

Use of an Electronic Receipt as an Interim Record of a Stop or Stop and Search

The use of an electronic receipt in accordance with paragraph 4.2A or paragraph 4.13A of this **A–17**
Code may be used by the following persons:

Constables of the British Transport Police (BTP) operating from any of the following BTP locations:

    (a) Hammersmith;

(b) Wembley; and
(c) West Ham,

in the exercise of their statutory powers throughout England and Wales.

5 MONITORING AND SUPERVISING THE USE OF STOP AND SEARCH POWERS

A–18   5.1 Supervising officers must monitor the use of stop and search powers and should consider in particular whether there is any evidence that they are being exercised on the basis of stereotyped images or inappropriate generalisations. Supervising officers should satisfy themselves that the practice of officers under their supervision in stopping, searching and recording is fully in accordance with this Code. Supervisors must also examine whether the records reveal any trends or patterns which give cause for concern, and if so take appropriate action to address this.

5.2 Senior officers with area or force-wide responsibilities must also monitor the broader use of stop and search powers and, where necessary, take action at the relevant level.

5.3 Supervision and monitoring must be supported by the compilation of comprehensive statistical records of stops and searches at force, area and local level. Any apparently disproportionate use of the powers by particular officers or groups of officers or in relation to specific sections of the community should be identified and investigated.

5.4 In order to promote public confidence in the use of the powers, forces in consultation with police authorities must make arrangements for the records to be scrutinised by representatives of the community, and to explain the use of the powers at a local level. [See *Note 19*]

Notes for Guidance

Officers exercising stop and search powers

A–19   1 *This code does not affect the ability of an officer to speak to or question a person in the ordinary course of the officer's duties without detaining the person or exercising any element of compulsion. It is not the purpose of the code to prohibit such encounters between the police and the community with the co-operation of the person concerned and neither does it affect the principle that all citizens have a duty to help police officers to prevent crime and discover offenders. This is a civic rather than a legal duty; but when a police officer is trying to discover whether, or by whom, an offence has been committed he or she may question any person from whom useful information might be obtained, subject to the restrictions imposed by Code C. A person's unwillingness to reply does not alter this entitlement, but in the absence of a power to arrest, or to detain in order to search, the person is free to leave at will and cannot be compelled to remain with the officer.*

2 *In some circumstances preparatory questioning may be unnecessary, but in general a brief conversation or exchange will be desirable not only as a means of avoiding unsuccessful searches, but to explain the grounds for the stop/search, to gain co-operation and reduce any tension there might be surrounding the stop/search.*

3 *Where a person is lawfully detained for the purpose of a search, but no search in the event takes place, the detention will not thereby have been rendered unlawful.*

4 *Many people customarily cover their heads or faces for religious reasons—for example, Muslim women, Sikh men, Sikh or Hindu women, or Rastarfarian men or women. A police officer cannot order the removal of a head or face covering except where there is reason to believe that the item is being worn by the individual wholly or mainly for the purpose of disguising identity, not simply because it disguises identity. Where there may be religious sensitivities about ordering the removal of such an item, the officer should permit the item to be removed out of public view. Where practicable, the item should be removed in the presence of an officer of the same sex as the person and out of sight of anyone of the opposite sex.*

5 *A search of a person in public should be completed as soon as possible.*

6 *A person may be detained under a stop and search power at a place other than where the person was first detained, only if that place, be it a police station or elsewhere, is nearby. Such a place should be located within a reasonable travelling distance using whatever mode of travel (on foot or by car) is appropriate. This applies to all searches under stop and search powers, whether or not they involve the removal of clothing or exposure of intimate parts of the body (see paragraphs 3.6 and 3.7) or take place in or out of public view. It means, for example, that a search under the stop and search power in section 23 of the Misuse of Drugs Act 1971 which*

involves the compulsory removal of more than a person's outer coat, jacket or gloves cannot be carried out unless a place which is both nearby the place they were first detained and out of public view, is available. If a search involves exposure of intimate parts of the body and a police station is not nearby, particular care must be taken to ensure that the location is suitable in that it enables the search to be conducted in accordance with the requirements of paragraph 11 of Annex A to Code C.

7 *A search in the street itself should be regarded as being in public for the purposes of paragraphs 3.6 and 3.7 above, even though it may be empty at the time a search begins. Although there is no power to require a person to do so, there is nothing to prevent an officer from asking a person voluntarily to remove more than an outer coat, jacket or gloves (and headgear or footwear under section 45(3) of the Terrorism Act 2000) in public.*

8 *Where there may be religious sensitivities about asking someone to remove headgear using a power under section 45(3) of the Terrorism Act 2000, the police officer should offer to carry out the search out of public view (for example, in a police van or police station if there is one nearby).*

9 *Other means of identification might include jewellery, insignias, tattoos or other features which are known to identify members of the particular gang or group.*

Authorising officers

10 *The powers under section 60 are separate from and additional to the normal stop and* **A–20** *search powers which require reasonable grounds to suspect an individual of carrying an offensive weapon (or other article). Their overall purpose is to prevent serious violence and the widespread carrying of weapons which might lead to persons being seriously injured by disarming potential offenders in circumstances where other powers would not be sufficient. They should not therefore be used to replace or circumvent the normal powers for dealing with routine crime problems. The purpose of the powers under section 60AA is to prevent those involved in intimidatory or violent protests using face coverings to disguise identity.*

11 *Authorisations under section 60 require a reasonable belief on the part of the authorising officer. This must have an objective basis, for example: intelligence or relevant information such as a history of antagonism and violence between particular groups; previous incidents of violence at, or connected with, particular events or locations; a significant increase in knife-point robberies in a limited area; reports that individuals are regularly carrying weapons in a particular locality; or in the case of section 60AA previous incidents of crimes being committed while wearing face coverings to conceal identity.*

12 *It is for the authorising officer to determine the period of time during which the powers mentioned in paragraph 2.1 (b) and (c) may be exercised. The officer should set the minimum period he or she considers necessary to deal with the risk of violence, the carrying of knives or offensive weapons, or terrorism. A direction to extend the period authorised under the powers mentioned in paragraph 2.1(b) may be given only once. Thereafter further use of the powers requires a new authorisation. There is no provision to extend an authorisation of the powers mentioned in paragraph 2.1(c): further use of the powers requires a new authorisation.*

13 *It is for the authorising officer to determine the geographical area in which the use of the powers is to be authorised. In doing so the officer may wish to take into account factors such as the nature and venue of the anticipated incident, the number of people who may be in the immediate area of any possible incident, their access to surrounding areas and the anticipated level of violence. The officer should not set a geographical area which is wider than that he or she believes necessary for the purpose of preventing anticipated violence, the carrying of knives or offensive weapons, acts of terrorism, or, in the case of section 60AA, the prevention of commission of offences. It is particularly important to ensure that constables exercising such powers are fully aware of where they may be used. If the area specified is smaller than the whole force area, the officer giving the authorisation should specify either the streets which form the boundary of the area or a divisional boundary within the force area. If the power is to be used in response to a threat or incident that straddles police force areas, an officer from each of the forces concerned will need to give an authorisation.*

14 *An officer who has authorised the use of powers under section 44 of the Terrorism Act 2000 must take immediate steps to send a copy of the authorisation to the National Joint Unit, Metropolitan Police Special Branch, who will forward it to the Secretary of State. The Secretary of State should be informed of the reasons for the authorisation. The National Joint Unit will inform the force concerned, within 48 hours of the authorisation being made, whether the Secretary of State has confirmed or cancelled or altered the authorisation.*

Recording

A–21　15 *Where a stop and search is conducted by more than one officer the identity of all the officers engaged in the search must be recorded on the record. Nothing prevents an officer who is present but not directly involved in searching from completing the record during the course of the encounter.*

16 *Where a vehicle has not been allocated a registration number (e.g. a rally car or a trials motorbike) that part of the requirement under 4.3(iii) does not apply.*

17 *It is important for monitoring purposes to specify whether the authority for exercising a stop and search power was given under section 60 of the Criminal Justice and Public Order Act 1994 or under section 44(1) or 44(2) of the Terrorism Act 2000.*

18 *Officers should record the self-defined ethnicity of every person stopped according to the categories used in the 2001 census question listed in Annex B. Respondents should be asked to select one of the five main categories representing broad ethnic groups and then a more specific cultural background from within this group. The ethnic classification should be coded for recording purposes using the coding system in Annex B. An additional "Not stated" box is available but should not be offered to respondents explicitly. Officers should be aware and explain to members of the public, especially where concerns are raised, that this information is required to obtain a true picture of stop and search activity and to help improve ethnic monitoring, tackle discriminatory practice, and promote effective use of the powers. If the person gives what appears to the officer to be an "incorrect" answer (e.g. a person who appears to be white states that they are black), the officer should record the response that has been given. Officers should also record their own perception of the ethnic background of every person stopped and this must be done by using the PNC/Phoenix classification system. If the "Not stated" category is used the reason for this must be recorded on the form.*

19 *Arrangements for public scrutiny of records should take account of the right to confidentiality of those stopped and searched. Anonymised forms and/or statistics generated from records should be the focus of the examinations by members of the public.*

20 *Where an officer engages in conversation which is not pertinent to the actions or whereabouts of the individual (e.g. does not relate to why the person is there, what they are doing or where they have been or are going) then issuing a form would not meet the criteria set out in paragraph 4.12. Situations designed to impede police activity may arise, for example, in public order situations where individuals engage in dialogue with the officer but the officer does not initiate or engage in contact about the person's individual circumstances.*

21 *In situations where it is not practicable to provide a written record of the stop or stop and search at that time, the officer should consider providing the person with details of the station to which the person may attend for a record. This may take the form of a simple business card, adding the date of the stop or stop and search.*

ANNEX A

Summary of Main Stop and Search Powers

A–22　THIS TABLE RELATES TO STOP AND SEARCH POWERS ONLY. INDIVIDUAL STATUTES BELOW MAY CONTAIN OTHER POLICE POWERS OF ENTRY SEARCH AND SEIZURE.

Power	Object of Search	Extent of Search	Where Exercisable
Unlawful articles general			
1. *Public Stores Act* 1875, s.6	HM Stores stolen or unlawfully obtained	Persons vehicles and vessels	Anywhere where the constabulary powers are exercisable

Power	Object of Search	Extent of Search	Where Exercisable
2. *Firearms Act* 1968, s.47	Firearms	Persons and vehicles	A public place or anywhere in the case of reasonable suspicion of offences of carrying firearms with criminal intent or trespassing with firearms
3. *Misuse of Drugs Act* 1971, s.23	Controlled drugs	Persons and vehicles	Anywhere
4. *Customs and Excise Management Act* 1979, s.163	Goods (a) on which duty has not been paid (b) being unlawfully removed. Imported or exported (c) otherwise liable to forfeiture to HM Customs and Excise	Vehicles and vessels only	Anywhere
5. *Aviation Security Act* 1982, s.27(1)	Stolen or unlawfully obtained goods	Airport employees and vehicles carrying airport employees or aircraft or any vehicle in a cargo area whether or not carrying an employee	Any designated airport
6. *Police and Criminal Evidence Act* 1984, s.1	Stolen goods articles for use in certain Theft Act offences offensive weapons including bladed or sharply-pointed articles (except folding pocket knives with a bladed cutting edge not exceeding 3 inches) prohibited possession of a category 4 (display grade) firework any person under 18 in possession of an adult firework in a public place	Persons and vehicles	Where there is public access
	Criminal Damage Articles made adapted or intended for use in destroying or damaging property	Persons and vehicles	Where there is public access

Power	Object of Search	Extent of Search	Where Exercisable
Police and Criminal Evidence Act 1984, s.6(3) (by a constable of the United Kingdom Atomic Energy Authority Constabulary in respect of property owned or controlled by British Nuclear Fuels plc	HM Stores (in the form of goods and chattels belonging to British Nuclear Fuels plc)	Persons vehicles and vessels	Anywhere where the constabulary powers are exercisable
7. *Sporting events (Control of Alcohol ETC.) Act* 1985, s.7	Intoxicating liquor	Persons coaches and trains	Designated sports grounds or coaches and trains travelling to or from a designated sporting event
8. *Crossbows Act* 1987, s.4	Crossbows or parts of crossbows except crossbows with a draw weight of less than 1.4 kilograms:	Persons and vehicles	Anywhere except dwellings
9. *Criminal Justice Act* 1988, s.139B	Offensive weapons bladed or sharply pointed article	Persons	School premises
Evidence of game and wildlife offences			
10. *Peaching Prevention Act* 1662, s.2	Game or poaching equipment	Persons and vehicles	A public place
11. *Deer Act* 1991, s.12	Evidence of offences under the Act	Persons and vehicles	Anywhere except dwellings
12. *Conservation of Seals Act* 1970, s.4	Seals or housing equipment	Vehicles only	Anywhere
13. *Badgers Act* 1992, s.11	Evidence of offences under the Act	Persons and vehicles	Anywhere
14. *Wildlife and Countryside Act* 1981, s.19	Evidence of wildlife offences	Persons and vehicles	Anywhere except dwellings
Other			
15. *Terrorism Act* 2000, s.43	*Evidence of habit/ to arrest under section 14 of the Act*	Persons	Anywhere
16. *Terrorism Act* 2000, s.44(1)	Articles which could be used for a purpose connected with the commission preparation or instigation of acts of terrorism	<u>Vehicles driver and passengers</u>	Anywhere within the area of local by authorised under subsection (1)

Power	Object of Search	Extent of Search	Where Exercisable
17. *Terrorism Act* 2000, s 44 (2)	*Articles which could be used for a purpose connected with the commission preparation or instigation of acts of terrorism*	Pedestrians	Anywhere within the area of locality authorised
18. Paragraphs 7 and 8 of Schedule 7 to the *Terrorism Act* 2000	*Anything relevant to determining if a person being examined falls within paragraph 2(1)(a) to (c) of Schedule 5*	Persons vehicles, vessels etc	Ports and airports
19. Section 63 *Criminal Justice and Public Order Act* 1994 as amended by s.8 of the *Knives Act* 1997	Offensive weapons or dangerous instruments to prevent incidents of serious violence of to deal with the carrying of such items	Persons and vehicles	Anywhere within a locality authorised under subsection (1)

ANNEX B

Self-Defined Ethnic Classification Categories

White	*W*	**A–23**
A. *White—British*	*W1*	
B. *White—Irish*	*W2*	
C. *Any other White background*	*W9*	
Mixed	*M*	
D. *White and Black Caribbean*	*M1*	
E. *White and Black African*	*M2*	
F. *White and Asian*	*M3*	
G. *Any other Mixed Background*	*M9*	
Asian / Asian—British	*A*	
H. *Asian—Indian*	*A1*	
I. *Asian—Pakistani*	*A2*	
J. *Asian—Bangladeshi*	*A3*	
K. *Any other Asian background*	*A9*	
Black / Black—British	*B*	
L. *Black—Caribbean*	*B1*	
M. *Black African*	*B2*	
N. *Any other Black background*	*B9*	
Other	*O*	
O. *Chinese*	*O1*	
P. *Any other*	*O9*	
Not Stated	**NS**	

Appendices

ANNEX C

Summary of Powers of Community Support Officers to Search and Seize

A–24   The following is a summary of the search and seizure powers that may be exercused by a community support officer (CSO) who has been designated with the relevant powers in accordance with Part 4 of the *Police Reform Act* 2002.

When exercising any of these powers a CSO must have regard to any relevant provisions of this Code including section 3 governing the conduct of searches and the steps to be taken prior to a search.

1. *Power to stop and search not requiring consent*

Designation	Power conferred	Object of Search	Extent of Search	Where Exercisable
Police Reform Act 2002, Schedule 4, paragraph 15	(a) *Terrorism Act* 2000, s.44(1)(a) and (d) and 45(2)	Items intended to be used in connection with terrorism	(a) Vehicles or anything caused in or on the vehicle and anything carried by driver or passenger	Anywhere within area of local by authorised and in the company and under the supervision of a constable
	(b) *Terrorism Act* 2000, s.44(2 (b) and 45(2)		(b) Anything carried by a pedestrian	

2. *Powers to search requiring the consent of the person and seizure*

A CSO may detain a person using reasonable force where necessary as set out in Part 1 of Schedule 4 to the *Police Reform Act* 2002 If the person has been lawfully detained, the CSO may search the person provided that person gives consent to such a search in relation to the following

Designation	Powers conferred	Object of Search	Extent of Search	Where Exercisable
Police Reform Act 2002, Schedule 4 paragraph 7A	(a) *Criminal Justice and Police Act* 2001, s.12(2)	(a) Alcohol or a contarer for alcohol	(a) Persons	(a) Designated public place
	(b) *Confiscation of Alcohol (Young Persons) Act* 1997, s.1	(b) Alcohol	(b) Persons under 18 years old	(b) Public place
	(c) *Children and Young Persons Act* 1933, s.7(3)	(c) Tobacco or cigarette papers	(c) Persons under 16 years old found smoking	(c) Public place

3. *Powers to search not requiring the consent of the person and seizure*

A CSO may detain a person using reasonable force where necessary as set out in Part 1 of

Schedule 4 to the *Police Reform Act* 2002 If the person has been lawfully detained the CSO may search the person without the need for that person's consent in relation to the following:

Designation	Power conferred	Object of Search	Extent of Search	Where Exercisable
Police Reform Act 2002, Schedule 4 paragraph 2A	*Police and Criminal Evidence Act* 1984, s.32	(a) Objects that might be used to cause physical injury to the person of the CSO (b) Items that might be used to assist escape	Persons made subject to a requirement to wait	Any place where the requirement to wait has been made

4. *Powers to seize without consent*

This power applies when drugs are found in the course of any search mentioned above.

Designation	Power conferred	Object of Seizure	Where Exercisable
Police Reform Act 2002, Schedule 4 paragraph 7B	*Police Reform Act* 2002, Schedule 4, paragraph 7B	Controlled drugs in a person's possession	Any place where the person is in possession of the drug

POLICE AND CRIMINAL EVIDENCE ACT 1984

Code B

Code of Practice for Searches of Premises by Police Officers and the Seizure of Property found by Police Officers on Persons or Premises

Commencement—Transitional Arrangements   A–25

This Code applies to applications for warrants made after midnight 31 December 2005 and to searches and seizures taking place after midnight on 31 December 2005.

1 INTRODUCTION

1.1 This Code of Practice deals with police powers to: A–26
- search premises
- seize and retain property found on premises and persons

1.1A These powers may be used to find:
- property and material relating to a crime
- wanted persons
- children who abscond from local authority accommodation where they have been remanded or committed by a court

1.2 A justice of the peace may issue a search warrant granting powers of entry. search and seizure. e.g. warrants to search for stolen property, drugs, firearms and evidence of serious offences. Police also have powers without a search warrant. The main ones provided by the *Police and Criminal Evidence Act* 1984 (PACE) include powers to search premises:
- to make an arrest
- after an arrest

1.3 The right to privacy and respect for personal property are key principles of the *Human Rights Act* 1998. Powers of entry, search and seizure should be fully and clearly justified before use because they may significantly interfere with the occupier's privacy. Officers should consider if the necessary objectives can be met by less intrusive means.

1.4 In all cases, police should:

- exercise their powers courteously and with respect for persons and property
- only use reasonable force when this is considered necessary and proportionate to the circumstances

1.5 If the provisions of *PACE* and this Code are not observed, evidence obtained from a search may be open to question.

2 GENERAL

A–27   2.1 This Code must be readily available at all police stations for consultation by:

- police officers
- police staff
- detained persons
- members of the public

2.2 The *Notes for Guidance* included are not provisions of this Code.

2.3 This Code applies to searches of premises:

(a) by police for the purposes of an investigation into an alleged offence, with the occupier's consent, other than:
- routine scene of crime searches
- calls to a fire or burglary made by or on behalf of an occupier or searches following the activation of fire or burglar alarms or discovery of insecure premises;
- searches when *paragraph 5.4* applies
- bomb threat calls

(b) under powers conferred on police officers by *PACE*, sections 17, 18 and 32;

(c) undertaken in pursuance of search warrants issued to and executed by constables in accordance with PACE, sections 15 and 16. [See *Note 2A*]

(d) subject to *paragraph 2.6*, under any other power given to police to enter premises with or without a search warrant for any purpose connected with the investigation into an alleged or suspected offence. [See *Note 2B*]

For the purposes of this Code, 'premises' as defined in PACE, section 23, includes any place, vehicle, vessel, aircraft, hovercraft, tent or movable structure and any offshore installation as defined in the *Mineral Workings (Offshore Installations) Act* 1971, section 1. [See *Note 2D*]

2.4 A person who has not been arrested but is searched during a search of premises should be searched in accordance with Code A. [See *Note 2C*]

2.5 This Code does not apply to the exercise of a statutory power to enter premises or to inspect goods, equipment or procedures if the exercise of that power is not dependent on the existence of grounds for suspecting that an offence may have been committed and the person exercising the power has no reasonable grounds for such suspicion.

2.6 This Code does not affect any directions of a search warrant or order, lawfully executed in England or Wales that any item or evidence seized under that warrant or order be handed over to a police force, court, tribunal, or other authority outside England or Wales. For example, warrants and orders issued in Scotland or Northern Ireland, see *Note 2B(f)* and search warrants issued under the *Criminal Justice (International Co-operation) Act* 1990, section 7.

2.7 When this Code requires the prior authority or agreement of an officer of at least inspector or superintendent rank, that authority may be given by a sergeant or chief inspector authorised to perform the functions of the higher rank under *PACE*, section 107.

2.8 Written records required under this Code not made in the search record shall, unless otherwise specified, be made:

- in the recording officer's pocket book ('pocket book' includes any official report book issued to police officers) or
- on forms provided for the purpose

2.9 Nothing in this Code requires the identity of officers, or anyone accompanying them during a search of premises, to be recorded or disclosed:

(a) in the case of enquires linked to the investigation of terrorism; or

(b) if officers reasonably believe recording or disclosing their names might put them in danger.

In these cases officers should use warrant or other identification numbers and the name of their police station. Police staff should use any identification number provided to them by the police force. [See *Note 2E*]

2.10 The 'officer in charge of the search' means the officer assigned specific duties and responsibilities under this Code. Whenever there is a search of premises to which this Code applies one officer must act as the officer in charge of the search. [See *Note 2F*]

2.11 In this Code:

(a) 'designated person' means a person other than a police officer, designated under the *Police Reform Act* 2002, Part 4 who has specified powers and duties of police officers conferred or imposed on them. [See *Note 2G*]

(b) any reference to a police officer includes a designated person acting in the exercise or performance of the powers and duties conferred or imposed on them by their designation.

(c) a person authorised to accompany police officers or designated persons in the execution of a warrant has the same powers as a constable in the execution of the warrant and the search and seizure of anything related to the warrant. These powers must be exercised in the company and under the supervision of a police officer. [See *Note 3C*]

2.12 If a power conferred on a designated person:

(a) allows reasonable force to be used when exercised by a police officer, a designated person exercising that power has the same entitlement to use force;

(b) includes power to use force to enter any premises, that power is not exercisable by that designated person except:

    (i) in the company and under the supervision of a police officer; or

    (ii) for the purpose of:

        ● saving life or limb; or

        ● preventing serious damage to property.

2.13 Designated persons must have regard to any relevant provisions of the Codes of Practice.

Notes for guidance

2A *PACE, sections 15 and 16 apply to all search warrants issued to and executed by constables* **A–28**
under any enactment, e.g. search warrants issued by a:

(a) *justice of the peace under the:*

    ● *Theft Act 1968, section 26—stolen property;*

    ● *Misuse of Drugs Act 1971, section 23—controlled drugs;*

    ● *PACE, section 8—evidence of an indictable offence;*

    ● *Terrorism Act 2000, Schedule 5, paragraph 1;*

(b) *judge of the High Court, a Circuit judge, a Recorder or a District Judge under:*

    ● *PACE, Schedule 1;*

    ● *Terrorism Act 2000, Schedule 5, paragraph 11.*

2B *Examples of the other powers in paragraph 2.3(d) include:*

(a) *Road Traffic Act 1988, section 6E(1) giving police power to enter premises under section 6E(1) to:*

    ● *require a person to provide a specimen of breath; or*

    ● *arrest a person following*

    — *a positive breath test;*

    — *failure to provide a specimen of breath;*

(b) *Transport and Works Act 1992, section 30(4) giving police powers to enter premises mirroring the powers in (a) in relation to specified persons working on transport systems to which the Act applies;*

(c) *Criminal Justice Act 1988, section 139B giving police power to enter and search school premises for offensive weapons, bladed or pointed articles;*

(d) *Terrorism Act 2000,, Schedule 5, paragraphs 3 and 15 empowering a superintendent in urgent cases to give written authority for police to enter and search premises for the purposes of a terrorist investigation;*

(e) *Explosives Act 1875, section 73(b) empowering a superintendent to give written authority for police to enter premises, examine and search them for explosives;*

(f) *search warrants and production orders or the equivalent issued in Scotland or Northern Ireland endorsed under the Summary Jurisdiction (Process) Act 1881 or the Petty Sessions (Ireland) Act 1851 respectively for execution in England and Wales.*

2C *The Criminal Justice Act 1988, section 139B provides that a constable who has reasonable grounds to believe an offence under the Criminal Justice Act 1988, section 139A has or is being committed may enter school premises and search the premises and any persons on the premises for any bladed or pointed article or offensive weapon. Persons may be searched under a warrant issued under the Misuse of Drugs Act 1971, section 23(3) to search premises for drugs or documents only if the warrant specifically authorises the search of persons on the premises.*

2D *The Immigration Act 1971, Part III and Schedule 2 gives immigration officers powers to enter and search premises, seize and retain property, with and without a search warrant. These are similar to the powers available to police under search warrants issued by a justice of the peace and without a warrant under PACE, sections 17, 18, 19 and 32 except they only apply to specified offences under the Immigration Act 1971 and immigration control powers. For certain types of investigations and enquiries these powers avoid the need for the Immigration Service to rely on police officers becoming directly involved. When exercising these powers, immigration officers are required by the Immigration and Asylum Act 1999, section 145 to have regard to this Code's corresponding provisions. When immigration officers are dealing with persons or property at police stations, police officers should give appropriate assistance to help them discharge their specific duties and responsibilities.*

2E *The purpose of paragraph 2.9(b) is to protect those involved in serious organised crime investigations or arrests of particularly violent suspects when there is reliable information that those arrested or their associates may threaten or cause harm to the officers or anyone accompanying them during a search of premises. In cases of doubt, an officer of inspector rank or above should be consulted.*

2F *For the purposes of paragraph 210, the officer in charge of the search should normally be the most senior officer present, Some exceptions are:*

(a) *a supervising officer who attends or assists at the scene of a premises search may appoint an officer of lower rank as officer in charge of the search if that officer is:*
  - *more conversant with the facts;*
  - *a more appropriate officer to be in charge of the search;*

(b) *when all officers in a premises search are the same rank. The supervising officer if available must make sure one of them is appointed officer in charge of the search, otherwise the officers themselves must nominate one of their number as the officer in charge;*

(c) *a senior officer assisting in a specialist role. This officer need not be regarded as having a general supervisory role over the conduct of the search or be appointed or expected to act as the officer in charge of the search.*

Except in (c), nothing in this Note diminishes the role and responsibilities of a supervisory officer who is present at the search or knows of a search taking place.

2G *An officer of the rank of inspector or above may direct a designated investigating officer not to wear a uniform for the purposes of a specific operation.*

3 Search warrants and production orders

(a) Before making an application

A–29   3.1 When information appears to justify an application, the officer must take reasonable steps to check the information is accurate, recent and not provided maliciously or irresponsibly. An application may not be made on the basis of information from an anonymous source if corroboration has not been sought. [See *Note 3A*]

3.2 The officer shall ascertain as specifically as possible the nature of the articles concerned and their location.

3.3 The officer shall make reasonable enquiries to:
  (i) establish if:
    - anything is known about the likely occupier of the premises and the nature of the premises themselves;

- the premises have been searched previously and how recently;

(ii) obtain any other relevant information.

3.4 An application:

(a) to a justice of the peace for a search warrant or to a judge of the High Court, a Circuit judge, a Recorder or a District Judge for a search warrant or production order under *PACE*, Schedule 1

must be supported by a signed written authority from an officer of inspector rank or above.

Note: If the case is an urgent application to a justice of the peace and an inspector or above is not readily available, the next most senior officer on duty can give the written authority.

(b) to a circuit judge under the *Terrorism Act* 2000, Schedule 5 for:

- a production order;
- search warrant; or
- an order requiring an explanation of material seized or produced under such a warrant or production order

must be supported by a signed written authority from an officer of superintendent rank or above.

3.5 Except in a case of urgency, if there is reason to believe a search might have an adverse effect on relations between the police and the community, the officer in charge shall consult the local police/community liaison officer:

- before the search; or
- in urgent cases, as soon as practicable after the search.

(b) Making an application

3.6 A search warrant application must be supported in writing, specifying:

(a) the enactment under which the application is made, see *Note 2A*;

(b)

(i) whether the warrant is to authorise entry and search of:
- one set of premises; or
- if the application is under *PACE* section 8, or Schedule 1, paragraph 12, more than one set of specified premises or all premises occupied or controlled by a specified person, and

(ii) the premises to be searched;

(c) the object of the search, see *Note 3B*;

(d) the grounds for the application, including, when the purpose of the proposed search is to find evidence of an alleged offence, an indication of how the evidence relates to the investigation;

(da) where the application is under *PACE* section 8, or Schedule 1, paragraph 12 for a single warrant to enter and search:

(i) more than one set of specified premises, the officer must specify each set of premises which it is desired to enter and search;

(ii) all premises occupied or controlled by a specified person, the officer must specify:
- as many sets of premises which it is desired to enter and search as it is reasonably practicable to specify;
- the person who is in occupation or control of those premises and any others which it is desired to search;
- why it is necessary to search more premises than those which can be specified;
- why it is not reasonably practicable to specify all the premises which it is desired to enter and search;

(db) whether an application under *PACE*, section 8 is for a warrant authorising entry and search on more than one occasion, and if so, the officer must state the grounds for this and whether the desired number of entries authorised is unlimited or a specified maximum.

(e) there are no reasonable grounds to believe the material to be sought, when making application to a:

(i) justice of the peace or a judge of the High Court, a Circuit judge, a Recorder or a District Judge, consists of or includes items subject to legal privilege;

(ii) justice of the peace, consists of or includes excluded material or special procedure material;

Note: this does not affect the additional powers of seizure in the *Criminal Justice and Police Act* 2001, Part 2 covered in paragraph 7.7, see *Note 3B*;

(f) if applicable, a request for the warrant to authorise a person or persons to accompany the officer who executes the warrant, see *Note 3C*.

3.7 A search warrant application under *PACE*, Schedule 1, paragraph 12(a), shall if appropriate indicate why it is believed service of notice of an application for a production order may seriously prejudice the investigation. Applications for search warrants under the *Terrorism Act* 2000, Schedule 5, paragraph 11 must indicate why a production order would not be appropriate.

3.8 If a search warrant application is refused, a further application may not be made for those premises unless supported by additional grounds.

Notes for guidance

A–30   3A *The identity of an informant need not be disclosed when making an application, but the officer should be prepared to answer any questions the magistrate or judge may have about:*

   • *the accuracy of previous information from that source*

   • *any other related matters*

3B *The information supporting a search warrant application should be as specific as possible, particularly in relation to the articles or persons being sought and where in the premises it is suspected they may be found. The meaning of 'items subject to legal privilege', 'excluded material' and 'special procedure material' are defined by PACE, sections 10, 11 and 14 respectively.*

3C *Under PACE, section 16(2), a search warrant may authorise persons other than police officers to accompany the constable who executes the warrant. This includes, e.g. any suitably qualified or skilled person or an expert in a particular field whose presence is needed to help accurately identify the material sought or to advise where certain evidence is most likely to be found and how it should be dealt with. It does not give them any right to force entry, but it gives them the right to be on the premises during the search and to search for or seize property without the occupier's permission.*

4 ENTRY WITHOUT WARRANT—PARTICULAR POWERS

(a) Making an arrest etc

A–31   4.1 The conditions under which an officer may enter and search premises without a warrant are set out in *PACE*, section 17. It should be noted that this section does not create or confer any powers of arrest. See other powers in *Note 2B(a)*.

(b) Search of premises where arrest takes place or the arrested person was immediately before arrest

4.2 When a person has been arrested for an indictable offence, a police officer has power under *PACE*, section 32 to search the premises where the person was arrested or where the person was immediately before being arrested.

(c) Search of premises occupied or controlled by the arrested person

4.3 The specific powers to search premises occupied or controlled by a person arrested for an indictable offence are set out in *PACE*, section 18. They may not be exercised, except if section 18(5) applies, unless an officer of inspector rank or above has given written authority. That authority should only be given when the authorising officer is satisfied the necessary grounds exist. If possible the authorising officer should record the authority on the Notice of Powers and Rights and, subject to *paragraph 2.9*, sign the Notice. The record of the grounds for the search and the nature of the evidence sought as required by section 18(7) of the Act should be made in:

   • the custody record if there is one, otherwise

   • the officer's pocket book, or

   • the search record

5 Search with consent

5.1 Subject to *paragraph 5.4*, if it is proposed to search premises with the consent of a person **A–32** entitled to grant entry the consent must, if practicable, be given in writing on the Notice of Powers and Rights before the search. The officer must make any necessary enquiries to be satisfied the person is in a position to give such consent. [See *Notes 5A* and *5B*]

5.2 Before seeking consent the officer in charge of the search shall state the purpose of the proposed search and its extent. This information must be as specific as possible, particularly regarding the articles or persons being sought and the parts of the premises to be searched. The person concerned must be clearly informed they are not obliged to consent and anything seized may be produced in evidence. If at the time the person is not suspected of an offence, the officer shall say this when stating the purpose of the search.

5.3 An officer cannot enter and search or continue to search premises under *paragraph 5.1* if consent is given under duress or withdrawn before the search is completed.

5.4 It is unnecessary to seek consent under *paragraphs 5.1* and *5.2* if this would cause disproportionate inconvenience to the person concerned. [See *Note 5C*]

Notes for guidance

5A *In a lodging house or similar accommodation, every reasonable effort should be made to* **A–33** *obtain the consent of the tenant, lodger or occupier. A search should not be made solely on the basis of the landlord's consent unless the tenant, lodger or occupier is unavailable and the matter is urgent.*

5B *If the intention is to search premises under the authority of a warrant or a power of entry and search without warrant, and the occupier of the premises co-operates in accordance with paragraph 6.4, there is no need to obtain written consent.*

5C *Paragraph 5.4 is intended to apply when it is reasonable to assume innocent occupiers would agree to, and expect, police to take the proposed action, e.g. if:*

- *a suspect has fled the scene of a crime or to evade arrest and it is necessary quickly to check surrounding gardens and readily accessible places to see if the suspect is hiding*
- *police have arrested someone in the night after a pursuit and it is necessary to make a brief check of gardens along the pursuit route to see if stolen or incriminating articles have been discarded*

6 Searching premises—general considerations

(a) Time of searches

6.1 Searches made under warrant must be made within three calendar months of the date **A–34** of the warrant's issue.

6.2 Searches must be made at a reasonable hour unless this might frustrate the purpose of the search.

6.3 When the extent or complexity of a search mean it is likely to take a long time, the officer in charge of the search may consider using the seize and sift powers referred to in *section 7*.

6.3A A warrant under PACE, section 8 may authorise entry to and search of premises on more than one occasion if, on the application, the justice of the peace is satisfied that it is necessary to authorise multiple entries in order to achieve the purpose for which the warrant is issued. No premises may be entered or searched on any subsequent occasions without the prior written authority of an officer of the rank of inspector who is not involved in the investigation. All other warrants authorise entry on one occasion only.

6.3B Where a warrant under *PACE* section 8, or Schedule 1, paragraph 12 authorises entry to and search of all premises occupied or controlled by a specified person, no premises which are not specified in the warrant may be entered and searched without the prior written authority of an officer of the rank of inspector who is not involved in the investigation.

(b) Entry other than with consent

6.4 The officer in charge of the search shall first try to communicate with the occupier, or any other person entitled to grant access to the premises, explain the authority under which entry is sought and ask the occupier to allow entry, unless:

    (i) the search premises are unoccupied;

    (ii) the occupier and any other person entitled to grant access are absent;

    (iii) there are reasonable grounds for believing that alerting the occupier or any other person entitled to grant access would frustrate the object of the search or endanger officers or other people.

6.5 Unless *sub-paragraph 6.4(iii)* applies, if the premises are occupied the officer, subject to *paragraph 2.9*, shall, before the search begins:

    (i) identify him or herself, show their warrant card (if not in uniform) and state the purpose of and grounds for the search;

    (ii) identify and introduce any person accompanying the officer on the search (such persons should carry identification for production on request) and briefly describe that person's role in the process.

6.6 Reasonable and proportionate force may be used if necessary to enter premises if the officer in charge of the search is satisfied the premises are those specified in any warrant, or in exercise of the powers described in *paragraphs 4.1* to *4.3*, and if:

    (i) the occupier or any other person entitled to grant access has refused entry;

    (ii) it is impossible to communicate with the occupier or any other person entitled to grant access; or

    (iii) any of the provisions of *paragraph 6.4* apply.

(c) Notice of Powers and Rights

6.7 If an officer conducts a search to which this Code applies the officer shall, unless it is impracticable to do so, provide the occupier with a copy of a Notice in a standard format:

    (i) specifying if the search is made under warrant, with consent, or in the exercise of the powers described in *paragraphs 4.1* to *4.3*. Note: the notice format shall provide for authority or consent to be indicated, see *paragraphs 4.3* and *5.1*;

    (ii) summarising the extent of the powers of search and seizure conferred by *PACE*;

    (iii) explaining the rights of the occupier, and the owner of the property seized;

    (iv) explaining compensation may be payable in appropriate cases for damages caused entering and searching premises, and giving the address to send a compensation application, see *Note 6A*;

    (v) stating this Code is available at any police station.

6.8 If the occupier is:

    • present, copies of the Notice and warrant shall, if practicable, be given to them before the search begins, unless the officer in charge of the search reasonably believes this would frustrate the object of the search or endanger officers or other people

    • not present, copies of the Notice and warrant shall be left in a prominent place on the premises or appropriate part of the premises and endorsed, subject to *paragraph 2.9* with the name of the officer in charge of the search, the date and time of the search

The warrant shall be endorsed to show this has been done.

(d) Conduct of searches

6.9 Premises may be searched only to the extent necessary to achieve the object of the search, having regard to the size and nature of whatever is sought.

6.9A A search may not continue under:

    • a warrant's authority once all the things specified in that warrant have been found

    • any other power once the object of that search has been achieved

6.9B No search may continue once the officer in charge of the search is satisfied whatever is being sought is not on the premises. [See *Note 6B*] This does not prevent a further search of the same premises if additional grounds come to light supporting a further application for a search warrant or exercise or further exercise of another power. For example, when, as a result of new information, it is believed articles previously not found or additional articles are on the premises.

6.10 Searches must be conducted with due consideration for the property and privacy of the occupier and with no more disturbance than necessary. Reasonable force may be used only when necessary and proportionate because the co-operation of the occupier cannot be obtained or is insufficient for the purpose. [See *Note 6C*]

6.11 A friend, neighbour or other person must be allowed to witness the search if the occupier wishes unless the officer in charge of the search has reasonable grounds for believing the presence of the person asked for would seriously hinder the investigation or endanger officers or other people. A search need not be unreasonably delayed for this purpose. A record of the action taken should be made on the premises search record including the grounds for refusing the occupier's request.

6.12 A person is not required to be cautioned prior to being asked questions that are solely necessary for the purpose of furthering the proper and effective conduct of a search, see Code C, *paragraph 10.1(c)*. For example, questions to discover the occupier of specified premises, to find a key to open a locked drawer or cupboard or to otherwise seek co-operation during the search or to determine if a particular item is liable to be seized.

6.12A If questioning goes beyond what is necessary for the purpose of the exemption in Code C, the exchange is likely to constitute an interview as defined by Code C, *paragraph 11.1A* and would require the associated safeguards included in Code C, *section 10*.

(e) Leaving premises

6.13 If premises have been entered by force, before leaving the officer in charge of the search must make sure they are secure by:

- arranging for the occupier or their agent to be present,
- any other appropriate means.

(f) Searches under PACE Schedule 1 or the Terrorism Act 2000, Schedule 5

6.14 An officer shall be appointed as the officer in charge of the search, see *paragraph 2.10*, in respect of any search made under a warrant issued under *PACE* 1984, Schedule 1 or the *Terrorism Act* 2000. Schedule 5. They are responsible for making sure the search is conducted with discretion and in a manner that causes the least possible disruption to any business or other activities carried out on the premises.

6.15 Once the officer in charge of the search is satisfied material may not be taken from the premises without their knowledge, they shall ask for the documents or other records concerned. The officer in charge of the search may also ask to see the index to files held on the premises, and the officers conducting the search may inspect any files which, according to the index, appear to contain the material sought. A more extensive search of the premises may be made only if:

- the person responsible for them refuses to:
  — produce the material sought, or
  — allow access to the index
- it appears the index is:
  — inaccurate, or
  — incomplete
- for any other reason the officer in charge of the search has reasonable grounds for believing such a search is necessary in order to find the material sought.

Notes for guidance

6A *Whether compensation is appropriate depends on the circumstances in each case.* **A–35**
Compensation for damage caused when effecting entry is unlikely to be appropriate if the search was lawful, and the force used can be shown to be reasonable, proportionate and necessary to effect entry. If the wrong premises are searched by mistake everything possible should be done at the earliest opportunity to allay any sense of grievance and there should normally be a strong presumption in favour of paying compensation.

6B *It is important that, when possible, all those involved in a search are fully briefed about any powers to be exercised and the extent and limits within which it should be conducted.*

6C *In all cases the number of officers and other persons involved in executing the warrant should be determined by what is reasonable and necessary according to the particular circumstances.*

7 SEIZURE AND RETENTION OF PROPERTY

(a) Seizure

A–36   7.1 Subject to *paragraph 7.2*, an officer who is searching any person or premises under any statutory power or with the consent of the occupier may seize anything:

      (a) covered by a warrant;

      (b) the officer has reasonable grounds for believing is evidence of an offence or has been obtained in consequence of the commission of an offence but only if seizure is necessary to prevent the items being concealed, lost, disposed of, altered, damaged, destroyed or tampered with;

      (c) covered by the powers in the *Criminal Justice and Police Act* 2001, Part 2 allowing an officer to seize property from persons or premises and retain it for sifting or examination elsewhere.

[See *Note 7B*]

7.2 No item may be seized which an officer has reasonable grounds for believing to be subject to legal privilege, as defined in *PACE*, section 10, other than under the *Criminal Justice and Police Act* 2001, Part 2.

7.3 Officers must be aware of the provisions in the *Criminal Justice and Police Act* 2001, section 59, allowing for applications to a judicial authority for the return of property seized and the subsequent duty to secure in section 60, see *paragraph 7.12(iii)*.

7.4 An officer may decide it is not appropriate to seize property because of an explanation from the person holding it but may nevertheless have reasonable grounds for believing it was obtained in consequence of an offence by some person. In these circumstances, the officer should identify the property to the holder, inform the holder of their suspicions and explain the holder may be liable to civil or criminal proceedings if they dispose of, after or destroy the property.

7.5 An officer may arrange to photograph, image or copy, any document or other article they have the power to seize in accordance with *paragraph 7.1*. This is subject to specific restrictions on the examination, imaging or copying of certain property seized under the *Criminal Justice and Police Act* 2001, Part 2. An officer must have regard to their statutory obligation to retain an original document or other article only when a photograph or copy is not sufficient.

7.6 If an officer considers information stored in any electronic form and accessible from the premises could be used in evidence, they may require the information to be produced in a form:

      ● which can be taken away and in which it is visible and legible; or

      ● from which it can readily be produced in a visible and legible form.

(b) Criminal Justice and Police Act 2001: Specific procedures for seize and sift powers

7.7 The *Criminal Justice and Police Act* 2001. Part 2 gives officers limited powers to seize property from premises or persons so they can sift or examine it elsewhere. Officers must be careful they only exercise these powers when it is essential and they do not remove any more material than necessary. The removal of large volumes of material, much of which may not ultimately be retainable, may have serious implications for the owners, particularly when they are involved in business or activities such as journalism or the provision of medical services. Officers must carefully consider if removing copies or images of relevant material or data would be a satisfactory alternative to removing originals. When originals are taken, officers must be prepared to facilitate the provision of copies or images for the owners when reasonably practicable. [See *Note 7C*]

7.8 Property seized under the *Criminal Justice and Police Act* 2001, sections 50 or 51 must be kept securely and separately from any material seized under other powers. An examination under section 53 to determine which elements may be retained must be carried out at the earliest practicable time, having due regard to the desirability of allowing the person from whom the property was seized, or a person with an interest in the property, an opportunity of being present or represented at the examination.

7.8A All reasonable steps should be taken to accommodate an interested person's request to be present, provided the request is reasonable and subject to the need to prevent harm to, interference with, or unreasonable delay to the investigatory process. If an examination proceeds in the absence of an interested person who asked to attend or their representative, the officer who exercised the relevant seizure power must give that person a written notice of why the examination was carried out in those circumstances. If it is necessary for security reasons or to maintain confidentiality officers may exclude interested persons from decryption or other processes which facilitate the examination but do not form part of it. [See *Note 7D*]

7.9 It is the responsibility of the officer in charge of the investigation to make sure property is returned in accordance with sections 53 to 55. Material which there is no power to retain must be:

> • separated from the rest of the seized property;
> • returned as soon as reasonably practicable after examination of all the seized property.

7.9A Delay is only warranted if very clear and compelling reasons exist, e.g. the:

> • unavailability of the person to whom the material is to be returned;
> • need to agree a convenient time to return a large volume of material.

7.9B Legally privileged, excluded or special procedure material which cannot be retained must be returned:

> • as soon as reasonably practicable;
> • without waiting for the whole examination.

7.9C As set out in section 58, material must be returned to the person from whom it was seized, except when it is clear some other person has a better right to it. [See *Note 7E*]

7.10 When an officer involved in the investigation has reasonable grounds to believe a person with a relevant interest in property seized under section 50 or 51 intends to make an application under section 59 for the return of any legally privileged, special procedure or excluded material, the officer in charge of the investigation should be informed as soon as practicable and the material seized should be kept secure in accordance with section 61. [See *Note 7C*]

7.11 The officer in charge of the investigation is responsible for making sure property is properly secured. Securing involves making sure the property is not examined, copied, imaged or put to any other use except at the request, or with the consent, of the applicant or in accordance with the directions of the appropriate judicial authority. Any request, consent or directions must be recorded in writing and signed by both the initiator and the officer in charge of the investigation. [See *Notes 7F* and *7G*]

7.12 When an officer exercises a power of seizure conferred by sections 50 or 51 they shall provide the occupier of the premises or the person from whom the property is being seized with a written notice:

> (i) specifying what has been seized under the powers conferred by that section;
> (ii) specifying the grounds for those powers;
> (iii) setting out the effect of sections 59 to 61 covering the grounds for a person with a relevant interest in seized property to apply to a judicial authority for its return and the duty of officers to secure property in certain circumstances when an application is made;
> (iv) specifying the name and address of the person to whom:
>> • notice of an application to the appropriate judicial authority in respect of any of the seized property must be given;
>> • an application may be made to allow attendance at the initial examination of the property.

7.13 If the occupier is not present but there is someone in charge of the premises, the notice shall be given to them. If no suitable person is available, so the notice will easily be found it should either be:

> • left in a prominent place on the premises;
> • attached to the exterior of the premises.

(c) Retention

7.14 Subject to *paragraph 7.15*, anything seized in accordance with the above provisions may be retained only for as long as is necessary. It may be retained, among other purposes:

> (i) for use as evidence at a trial for an offence;
> (ii) to facilitate the use in any investigation or proceedings of anything to which it is inextricably linked, see *Note 7H*;

Appendices

(iii) for forensic examination or other investigation in connection with an offence;

(iv) in order to establish its lawful owner when there are reasonable grounds for believing it has been stolen or obtained by the commission of an offence.

7.15 Property shall not be retained under *paragraph 7.14(i), (ii)* or *(iii)* if a copy or image would be sufficient.

(d) Rights of owners etc

7.16 If property is retained, the person who had custody or control of it immediately before seizure must on request be provided with a list or description of the property within a reasonable time.

7.17 That person or their representative must be allowed supervised access to the property to examine it or have it photographed or copied, or must be provided with a photograph or copy, in either case within a reasonable time of any request and at their own expense, unless the officer in charge of an investigation has reasonable grounds for believing this would:

(i) prejudice the investigation of any offence or criminal proceedings; or

(ii) lead to the commission of an offence by providing access to unlawful material such as pornography.

A record of the grounds shall be made when access is denied.

Notes for guidance

7A *Any person claiming property seized by the police may apply to a magistrates' court under the Police (Property) Act 1897 for its possession and should, if appropriate, be advised of this procedure.*

7B *The powers of seizure conferred by PACE, sections 18(2) and 19(3) extend to the seizure of the whole premises when it is physically possible to seize and retain the premises in their totality and practical considerations make seizure desirable For example, police may remove premises such as tents, vehicles or caravans to a police station for the purpose of preserving evidence.*

7C *Officers should consider reaching agreement with owners and/or other interested parties on the procedures for examining a specific set of property, rather than awaiting the judicial authority's determination. Agreement can sometimes give a quicker and more satisfactory route for all concerned and minimise costs and legal complexities.*

7D *What constitutes a relevant interest in specific material may depend on the nature of that material and the circumstances in which it is seized. Anyone with a reasonable claim to ownership of the material and anyone entrusted with its safe keeping by the owner should be considered.*

7E *Requirements to secure and return property apply equally to all copies, images or other material created because of seizure of the original property.*

7F *The mechanics of securing property vary according to the circumstances; "bagging up", i.e. placing material in sealed bags or containers and strict subsequent control of access is the appropriate procedure in many cases.*

7G *When material is seized under the powers of seizure conferred by PACE, the duty to retain it under the Code of Practice issued under the Criminal Procedure and Investigations Act 1996 is subject to the provisions on retention of seized material in PACE, section 22.*

7H *Paragraph 7.14 (ii) applies if inextricably linked material is seized under the Criminal Justice and Police Act 2001, sections 50 or 51. Inextricably linked material is material it is not reasonably practicable to separate from other linked material without prejudicing the use of that other material in any investigation or proceedings. For example, it may not be possible to separate items of data held on computer disk without damaging their evidential integrity. Inextricably linked material must not be examined, imaged, copied or used for any purpose other than for proving the source and/or integrity of the linked material.*

8 Action after searches

A–37   8.1 If premises are searched in circumstances where this Code applies, unless the exceptions in *paragraph 2.3(a)* apply, on arrival at a police station the officer in charge of the search shall make or have made a record of the search, to include:

(i) the address of the searched premises;

  (ii) the date, time and duration of the search;

  (iii) the authority used for the search:

    ● if the search was made in exercise of a statutory power to search premises without warrant, the power which was used for the search;

    ● if the search was made under a warrant or with written consent:

    — a copy of the warrant and the written authority to apply for it, see paragraph 3.4; or

    — the written consent;

    shall be appended to the record or the record shall show the location of the copy warrant or consent.

  (iv) subject to *paragraph 2.9*, the names of:

    ● the officer(s) in charge of the search;

    ● all other officers and any authorised persons who conducted the search;

  (v) the names of any people on the premises if they are known;

  (vi) any grounds for refusing the occupier's request to have someone present during the search, see *paragraph 6.11*;

  (vii) a list of any articles seized or the location of a list and, if not covered by a warrant, the grounds for their seizure;

  (viii) whether force was used, and the reason;

  (ix) details of any damage caused during the search, and the circumstances;

  (x) if applicable, the reason it was not practicable:

    (a) to give the occupier a copy of the Notice of Powers and Rights, see *paragraph 6.7*;

    (b) before the search to give the occupier a copy of the Notice, see *paragraph 6.8*;

  (xi) when the occupier was not present, the place where copies of the Notice of Powers and Rights and search warrant were left on the premises, see *paragraph 6.8*.

8.2 On each occasion when premises are searched under warrant, the warrant authorising the search on that occasion shall be endorsed to show:

  (i) if any articles specified in the warrant were found and the address where found;

  (ii) if any other articles were seized;

  (iii) the date and time it was executed and if present, the name of the occupier or if the occupier is not present the name of the person in charge of the premises;

  (iv) subject to paragraph 2.9. the names of the officers who executed it and any authorised persons who accompanied them;

  (v) if a copy, together with a copy of the Notice of Powers and Rights was:

    ● handed to the occupier; or

    ● endorsed as required by paragraph 6.8: and left on the premises and where.

8.3 Any warrant shall be returned within three calendar months of its issue or sooner on completion of the search(es) authorised by that warrant, if it was issued by a:

    ● justice of the peace, to the designated officer for the local justice area in which the justice was acting when issuing the warrant; or

    ● judge, to the appropriate officer of the court concerned.

9 SEARCH REGISTERS

9.1 A search register will be maintained at each sub-divisional or equivalent police station. **A–38** All search records required under *paragraph 8.1* shall be made, copied, or referred to in the register. [See *Note 9A*]

Note for guidance

9A *Paragraph 9.1 also applies to search records made by immigration officers. In these* **A–39** *cases, a search register must also be maintained at an immigration office. [See also Note 2D]*

POLICE AND CRIMINAL EVIDENCE ACT 1984

Code C

Code of Practice for the Detention, Treatment and Questioning of Persons by Police Officers

A–40   **Commencement—Transitional Arrangements**

This Code applies to people in police detention after midnight on 24 July 2006, notwithstanding that their period of detention may have commenced before that time.

1 GENERAL

A–41   1.1 All persons in custody must be dealt with expeditiously, and released as soon as the need for detention no longer applies.

1.1A A custody officer must perform the functions in this Code as soon as practicable. A custody officer will not be in breach of this Code if delay is justifiable and reasonable steps are taken to prevent unnecessary delay. The custody record shall show when a delay has occurred and the reason. [See *Note 1H*]

1.2 This Code of Practice must be readily available at all police stations for consultation by:
- police officers
- police staff
- detained persons
- members of the public.

1.3 The provisions of this Code:
- include the *Annexes*
- do not include the *Notes for Guidance*.

1.4 If an officer has any suspicion, or is told in good faith, that a person of any age may be mentally disordered or otherwise mentally vulnerable, in the absence of clear evidence to dispel that suspicion, the person shall be treated as such for the purposes of this Code. [*See Note 1G*]

1.5 If anyone appears to be under 17, they shall be treated as a juvenile for the purposes of this Code in the absence of clear evidence that they are older.

1.6 If a person appears to be blind, seriously visually impaired, deaf, unable to read or speak or has difficulty orally because of a speech impediment, they shall be treated as such for the purposes of this Code in the absence of clear evidence to the contrary.

A–42   1.7 'The appropriate adult' means, in the case of a:
    (a) juvenile:
        (i) the parent, guardian or, if the juvenile is in local authority or voluntary organisation care, or is otherwise being looked after under the *Children Act* 1989, a person representing that authority or organisation;
        (ii) a social worker of a local authority social services department;
        (iii) failing these, some other responsible adult aged 18 or over who is not a police officer or employed by the police.
    (b) person who is mentally disordered or mentally vulnerable: [See *Note 1D*]
        (i) a relative, guardian or other person responsible for their care or custody;
        (ii) someone experienced in dealing with mentally disordered or mentally vulnerable people but who is not a police officer or employed by the police;
        (iii) failing these, some other responsible adult aged 18 or over who is not a police officer or employed by the police.

1.8 If this Code requires a person be given certain information, they do not have to be given it if at the time they are incapable of understanding what is said, are violent or may become violent or in urgent need of medical attention, but they must be given it as soon as practicable.

1.9 References to a custody officer include any:—

- police officer; or
- designated staff custody officer acting in the exercise or performance of the powers and duties conferred or imposed on them by their designation

performing the functions of a custody officer. See *Note 1J*.

1.9A When this Code requires the prior authority or agreement of an officer of at least inspector or superintendent rank, that authority may be given by a sergeant or chief inspector authorised to perform the functions of the higher rank under the *Police and Criminal Evidence Act* 1984 (PACE), section 107.

1.10 Subject to *paragraph 1.12*, this Code applies to people in custody at police stations in England and Wales, whether or not they have been arrested, and to those removed to a police station as a place of safety under the *Mental Health Act* 1983, sections 135 and 136. *Section 15* applies solely to people in police detention, e.g. those brought to a police station under arrest or arrested at a police station for an offence after going there voluntarily.

1.11 People detained under the *Terrorism Act* 2000, Schedule 8 and section 41 and other provisions of that Act are not subject to any part of this Code. Such persons are subject to the Code of Practice for detention, treatment and questioning of persons by police officers detained under that Act.

1.12 This Code's provisions do not apply to people in custody:

   (i) arrested on warrants issued in Scotland by officers under the *Criminal Justice and Public Order Act* 1994, section 136(2), or arrested or detained without warrant by officers from a police force in Scotland under section 137(2). In these cases, police powers and duties and the person's rights and entitlements whilst at a police station in England or Wales are the same as those in Scotland;

   (ii) arrested under the *Immigration and Asylum Act* 1999. section 142(3) in order to have their fingerprints taken;

   (iii) whose detention is authorised by an immigration officer under the Immigration Act 1971;

   (iv) who are convicted or remanded prisoners held in police cells on behalf of the *Prison Service under the Imprisonment (Temporary Provisions) Act* 1980;

   (v) not used;

   (vi) detained for searches under stop and search powers except as required by Code A.

The provisions on conditions of detention and treatment in *sections 8* and *9* must be considered as the minimum standards of treatment for such detainees.

1.13 In this Code:

   (a) 'designated person' means a person other than a police officer, designated under the *Police Reform Act* 2002. Part 4 who has specified powers and duties of police officers conferred or imposed on them;

   (b) reference to a police officer includes a designated person acting in the exercise or performance of the powers and duties conferred or imposed on them by their designation.

1.14 Designated persons are entitled to use reasonable force as follows:

   (a) when exercising a power conferred on them which allows a police officer exercising that power to use reasonable force, a designated person has the same entitlement to use force; and

   (b) at other times when carrying out duties conferred or imposed on them that also entitle them to use reasonable force, for example:

- when at a police station carrying out the duty to keep detainees for whom they are responsible under control and to assist any other police officer or designated person to keep any detainee under control and to prevent their escape.
- when securing, or assisting any other police officer or designated person in securing, the detention of a person at a police station.
- when escorting, or assisting any other police officer or designated person in escorting, a detainee within a police station.
- for the purpose of saving life or limb; or
- preventing serious damage to property.

1.15 Nothing in this Code prevents the custody officer, or other officer given custody of

A–43

the detainee from allowing police staff who are not designated persons to carry out individual procedures or tasks at the police station if the law allows. However, the officer remains responsible for making sure the procedures and tasks are carried out correctly in accordance with the Codes of Practice. Any such person must be:

    (a) a person employed by a police authority maintaining a police force and under the control and direction of the Chief Officer of that force;

    (b) employed by a person with whom a police authority has a contract for the provision of services relating to persons arrested or otherwise in custody.

1.16 Designated persons and other police staff must have regard to any relevant provisions of the Codes of Practice.

1.17 References to pocket books include any official report book issued to police officers or other police staff.

Notes for guidance

A–44   1A *Although certain sections of this Code apply specifically to people in custody at police stations, those there voluntarily to assist with an investigation should be treated with no less consideration, e.g. offered refreshments at appropriate times, and enjoy an absolute right to obtain legal advice or communicate with anyone outside the police station.*

    1B *A person, including a parent or guardian, should not be an appropriate adult if they:*

        • *are*

        — *suspected of involvement in the offence*

        — *the victim*

        — *a witness*

        — *involved in the investigation*

        • *received admissions prior to attending to act as the appropriate adult.*

    Note: If a juvenile's parent is estranged from the juvenile, they should not be asked to act as the appropriate adult if the juvenile expressly and specifically objects to their presence.

    1C *If a juvenile admits an offence to, or in the presence of, a social worker or member of a youth offending team other than during the time that person is acting as the juvenile's appropriate adult, another appropriate adult should be appointed in the interest of fairness.*

    1D *In the case of people who are mentally disordered or otherwise mentally vulnerable, it may be more satisfactory if the appropriate adult is someone experienced or trained in their care rather than a relative lacking such qualifications. But if the detainee prefers a relative to a better qualified stranger or objects to a particular person their wishes should, if practicable, be respected.*

    1E *A detainee should always be given an opportunity, when an appropriate adult is called to the police station, to consult privately with a solicitor in the appropriate adult's absence if they want. An appropriate adult is not subject to legal privilege.*

    1F *A solicitor or independent custody visitor (formerly a lay visitor) present at the police station in that capacity may not be the appropriate adult.*

    1G *'Mentally vulnerable' applies to any detainee who, because of their mental state or capacity, may not understand the significance of what is said, of questions or of their replies. 'Mental disorder' is defined in the Mental Health Act 1983, section 1(2) as 'mental illness, arrested or incomplete development of mind, psychopathic disorder and any other disorder or disability of mind'. When the custody officer has any doubt about the mental state or capacity of a detainee, that detainee should be treated as mentally vulnerable and an appropriate adult called.*

    1H *Paragraph 1.1A is intended to cover delays which may occur in processing detainees e.g. if:*

        • *a large number of suspects are brought into the station simultaneously to be placed in custody;*

        • *interview rooms are all being used;*

        • *there are difficulties contacting an appropriate adult, solicitor or interpreter.*

    1I *The custody officer must remind the appropriate adult and detainee about the right to legal advice and record any reasons for waiving it in accordance with section 6.*

    1J *The designation of police staff custody officers applies only in police areas where an order commencing the provisions of the Police Reform Act 2002, section 38 and Schedule 4A, for designating police staff custody officers is in effect.*

    1K *This Code does not affect the principle that all citizens have a duty to help police officers to prevent crime and discover offenders. This is a civic rather than a legal duty, but when a police officer is trying to discover whether, or by whom an offence has been committed he is entitled to question any person from whom he thinks useful information can be obtained, subject to the restrictions imposed by this Code. A person's declaration that he is unwilling to reply does not alter this entitlement.*

2 CUSTODY RECORDS

2.1A When a person is brought to a police station: **A–45**
- under arrest;
- is arrested at the police station having attended there voluntarily; or
- attends a police station to answer bail

they should be brought before the custody officer as soon as practicable after their arrival at the station or, if appropriate, following arrest after attending the police station voluntarily. This applies to designated and non-designated police stations. A person is deemed to be "at a police station" for these purposes if they are within the boundary of any building or enclosed yard which forms part of that police station.

2.1 A separate custody record must be opened as soon as practicable for each person brought to a police station under arrest or arrested at the station having gone there voluntarily or attending a police station in answer to street bail. All information recorded under this Code must be recorded as soon as practicable in the custody record unless otherwise specified. Any audio or video recording made in the custody area is not part of the custody record.

2.2 If any action requires the authority of an officer of a specified rank, subject to *paragraph 2.6A*, their name and rank must be noted in the custody record.

2.3 The custody officer is responsible for the custody record's accuracy and completeness and for making sure the record or copy of the record accompanies a detainee if they are transferred to another police station. The record shall show the:
- time and reason for transfer;
- time a person is released from detention.

2.4 A solicitor or appropriate adult must be permitted to consult a detainee's custody record as soon as practicable after their arrival at the station and at any other time whilst the person is detained. Arrangements for this access must be agreed with the custody officer and may not unreasonably interfere with the custody officer's duties.

2.4A When a detainee leaves police detention or is taken before a court they, their legal representative or appropriate adult shall be given, on request, a copy of the custody record as soon as practicable. This entitlement lasts for 12 months after release.

2.5 The detainee, appropriate adult or legal representative shall be permitted to inspect the original custody record after the detainee has left police detention provided they give reasonable notice of their request. Any such inspection shall be noted in the custody record.

2.6 Subject to *paragraph 2.6A*, all entries in custody records must be timed and signed by the maker. Records entered on computer shall be timed and contain the operator's identification.

2.6A Nothing in this Code requires the identify of officers or other police staff to be recorded or disclosed:
- (a) not used;
- (b) if the officer or police staff reasonably believe recording or disclosing their name might put them in danger.

In these cases, they shall use their warrant or other identification numbers and the name of their police station. [See *Note 2A*]

2.7 The fact and time of any detainee's refusal to sign a custody record, when asked in accordance with this Code, must be recorded.

Note for guidance

2A *The purpose of paragraph 2.6A(b) is to protect those involved in serious organised crime* **A–46**
investigations or arrests of particularly violent suspects when there is reliable information that those arrested or their associates may threaten or cause harm to those involved. In cases of doubt, an officer of inspector rank or above should be consulted.

3 INITIAL ACTION

(a) Detained persons—normal procedure

A–47   3.1 When a person is brought to a police station under arrest or arrested at the station having gone there voluntarily, the custody officer must make sure the person is told clearly about the following continuing rights which may be exercised at any stage during the period in custody:

(i) the right to have someone informed of their arrest as in *section 5*;

(ii) the right to consult privately with a solicitor and that free independent legal advice is available;

(iii) the right to consult these Codes of Practice. [See *Note 3D*]

3.2 The detainee must also be given:

- a written notice setting out:
— the above three rights;
— the arrangements for obtaining legal advice;
— the right to a copy of the custody record as in *paragraph 2.4A*;
— the caution in the terms prescribed in *section 10*.
- an additional written notice briefly setting out their entitlements while in custody, see *Notes 3A* and *3B*.

Note: The detainee shall be asked to sign the custody record to acknowledge receipt of these notices. Any refusal must be recorded on the custody record.

3.3 A citizen of an independent Commonwealth country or a national of a foreign country, including the Republic of Ireland, must be informed as soon as practicable about their rights of communication with their High Commission, Embassy or Consulate. See *section 7*

3.4 The custody officer shall:

- record the offence(s) that the detainee has been arrested for and the reason(s) for the arrest on the custody record. See paragraph 10.3 and Code G paragraphs 2.2 and 4.3.
- note on the custody record any comment the detainee makes in relation to the arresting officer's account but shall not invite comment. If the arresting officer is not physically present when the detainee is brought to a police station, the arresting officer's account must be made available to the custody officer remotely or by a third party on the arresting officer's behalf. If the custody officer authorises a person's detention the detainee must be informed of the grounds as soon as practicable and before they are questioned about any offence;
- note any comment the detainee makes in respect of the decision to detain them but shall not invite comment;
- not put specific questions to the detainee regarding their involvement in any offence, nor in respect of any comments they may make in response to the arresting officer's account or the decision to place them in detention. Such an exchange is likely to constitute an interview as in *paragraph 11.1A* and require the associated safeguards in *section 11*.

See *paragraph 11.13* in respect of unsolicited comments.

3.5 The custody officer shall:

(a) ask the detainee, whether at this time, they:

(i) would like legal advice, see *paragraph 6.5*;

(ii) want someone informed of their detention, see *section 5*;

(b) ask the detainee to sign the custody record to confirm their decisions in respect of (*a*);

(c) determine whether the detainee:

(i) is, or might be, in need of medical treatment or attention, see *section 9*;

(ii) requires:

- an appropriate adult;
- help to check documentation;
- an interpreter;

(d) record the decision in respect of (*c*).

3.6 When determining these needs the custody officer is responsible for initiating an assessment to consider whether the detainee is likely to present specific risks to custody staff or themselves. Such assessments should always include a check on the Police National Computer, to be carried out as soon as practicable, to identify any risks highlighted in relation to the detainee. Although such assessments are primarily the custody officer's responsibility, it may be necessary for them to consult and involve others, e.g. the arresting officer or an appropriate health care professional, see *paragraph 9.13*. Reasons for delaying the initiation or completion of the assessment must be recorded.

3.7 Chief Officers should ensure that arrangements for proper and effective risk assessments required by *paragraph 3.6* are implemented in respect of all detainees at police stations in their area.

3.8 Risk assessments must follow a structured process which clearly defines the categories of risk to be considered and the results must be incorporated in the detainee's custody record. The custody officer is responsible for making sure those responsible for the detainee's custody are appropriately briefed about the risks. If no specific risks are identified by the assessment, that should be noted in the custody record. See *Note 3E* and *paragraph 9.14*

3.9 The custody officer is responsible for implementing the response to any specific risk assessment, e.g.:

- reducing opportunities for self harm;
- calling a health care professional;
- increasing levels of monitoring or observation.

3.10 Risk assessment is an ongoing process and assessments must always be subject to review if circumstances change.

3.11 If video cameras are installed in the custody area, notices shall be prominently displayed showing cameras are in use. Any request to have video cameras switched off shall be refused.

(b) Detained persons—special groups

3.12 If the detainee appears deaf or there is doubt about their hearing or speaking ability **A–48** or ability to understand English, and the custody officer cannot establish effective communication, the custody officer must, as soon as practicable, call an interpreter for assistance in the action under *paragraphs 3.1–3.5*. See *section 13*

3.13 If the detainee is a juvenile, the custody officer must, if it is practicable, ascertain the identity of a person responsible for their welfare. That person:

- may be:
  — the parent or guardian;
  — if the juvenile is in local authority or voluntary organisation care, or is otherwise being looked after under the *Children Act* 1989, a person appointed by that authority or organisation to have responsibility for the juvenile's welfare;
  — any other person who has, for the time being, assumed responsibility for the juvenile's welfare.
- must be informed as soon as practicable that the juvenile has been arrested, why they have been arrested and where they are detained. This right is in addition to the juvenile's right in *section 5* not to be held incommunicado. [See *Note 3C*]

3.14 If a juvenile is known to be subject to a court order under which a person or organisation is given any degree of statutory responsibility to supervise or otherwise monitor them, reasonable steps must also be taken to notify that person or organisation (the 'responsible officer'). The responsible officer will normally be a member of a Youth Offending Team, except for a curfew order which involves electronic monitoring when the contractor providing the monitoring will normally be the responsible officer.

3.15 If the detainee is a juvenile, mentally disordered or otherwise mentally vulnerable, the custody officer must, as soon as practicable:

- inform the appropriate adult, who in the case of a juvenile may or may not be a person responsible for their welfare, as in *paragraph 3.13*, of:
  — the grounds for their detention;
  — their whereabouts.
- ask the adult to come to the police station to see the detainee.

Appendices

3.16 It is imperative that a mentally disordered or otherwise mentally vulnerable person, detained under the *Mental Health Act* 1983, section 136, be assessed as soon as possible. If that assessment is to take place at the police station, an approved social worker and a registered medical practitioner shall be called to the station as soon as possible in order to interview and examine the detainee. Once the detainee has been interviewed, examined and suitable arrangements made for their treatment or care, they can no longer be detained under section 136. A detainee must be immediately discharged from detention under section 136 if a registered medical practitioner, having examined them, concludes they are not mentally disordered within the meaning of the Act.

3.17 If the appropriate adult is:
- already at the police station, the provisions of *paragraphs 3.1 to 3.5* must be complied with in the appropriate adult's presence;
- not at the station when these provisions are complied with, they must be complied with again in the presence of the appropriate adult when they arrive.

3.18 The detainee shall be advised that:
- the duties of the appropriate adult include giving advice and assistance;
- they can consult privately with the appropriate adult at any time.

3.19 If the detainee, or appropriate adult on the detainee's behalf, asks for a solicitor to be called to give legal advice, the provisions of *section 6* apply.

3.20 If the detainee is blind, seriously visually impaired or unable to read, the custody officer shall make sure their solicitor, relative, appropriate adult or some other person likely to take an interest in them and not involved in the investigation is available to help check any documentation. When this Code requires written consent or signing the person assisting may be asked to sign instead, if the detainee prefers. This paragraph does not require an appropriate adult to be called solely to assist in checking and signing documentation for a person who is not a juvenile, or mentally disordered or otherwise mentally vulnerable (see *paragraph 3.15*).

(c) Persons attending a police station voluntarily

A–49   3.21 Anybody attending a police station voluntarily to assist with an investigation may leave at will unless arrested. See *Note 1K*. If it is decided they shall not be allowed to leave, they must be informed at once that they are under arrest and brought before the custody officer, who is responsible for making sure they are notified of their rights in the same way as other detainees. If they are not arrested but are cautioned as in *section 10*, the person who gives the caution must, at the same time, inform them they are not under arrest, they are not obliged to remain at the station but if they remain at the station they may obtain free and independent legal advice if they want. They shall be told the right to legal advice includes the right to speak with a solicitor on the telephone and be asked if they want to do so.

3.22 If a person attending the police station voluntarily asks about their entitlement to legal advice, they shall be given a copy of the notice explaining the arrangements for obtaining legal advice. See *paragraph 3.2*

(d) Documentation

3.23 The grounds for a person's detention shall be recorded, in the person's presence if practicable.

3.24 Action taken under *paragraphs 3.12 to 3.20* shall be recorded.

(e) Persons answering street ball

3.25 When a person is answering street bail, the custody officer should link any documentation held in relation to arrest with the custody record. Any further action shall be recorded on the custody record in accordance with *paragraphs 3.23* and *3.24* above.

Notes for guidance

A–50   3A *The notice of entitlements should:*
- *list the entitlements in this Code, including:*
  - *— visits and contact with outside parties, including special provisions for Commonwealth citizens and foreign nationals;*
  - *— reasonable standards of physical comfort;*
  - *— adequate food and drink;*

— *access to toilets and washing facilities, clothing, medical attention, and
exercise when practicable.*

● *mention the*:

— *provisions relating to the conduct of interviews*;

— *circumstances in which an appropriate adult should be available to assist the
detainee and their statutory rights to make representation whenever the period of their detention is reviewed.*

3B *In addition to notices in English, translations should be available in Welsh, the main
minority ethnic languages and the principal European languages, whenever they are likely to
be helpful. Audio versions of the notice should also be made available.*

3C *If the juvenile is in local authority or voluntary organisation care but living with their
parents or other adults responsible for their welfare, although there is no legal obligation to
inform them, they should normally be contacted, as well as the authority or organisation unless
suspected of involvement in the offence concerned. Even if the juvenile is not living with their
parents, consideration should be given to informing them.*

3D *The right to consult the Codes of Practice does not entitle the person concerned to delay
unreasonably any necessary investigative or administrative action whilst they do so. Examples
of action which need not be delayed unreasonably include:*

● *procedures requiring the provision of breath, blood or urine specimens under
the Road Traffic Act 1988 or the Transport and Works Act 1992;*

● *searching detainees at the police station;*

● *taking fingerprints, footwear impressions or non-intimate samples without
consent for evidential purposes.*

3E *Home Office Circular 32/2000 provides more detailed guidance on risk assessments and
identifies key risk areas which should always be considered.*

4 DETAINEE'S PROPERTY

(a) Action

4.1 The custody officer is responsible for:

    (a) ascertaining what property a detainee:

      (i) has with them when they come to the police station, whether on:

        ● arrest or re-detention on answering to bail;

        ● commitment to prison custody on the order or sentence of a court;

        ● lodgement at the police station with a view to their production in court
from prison custody;

        ● transfer from detention at another station or hospital;

        ● detention under the *Mental Health Act* 1983, section 135 or 136;

        ● remand into police custody on the authority of a court

      (ii) might have acquired for an unlawful or harmful purpose while in custody;

    (b) the safekeeping of any property taken from a detainee which remains at the police
station.

The custody officer may search the detainee or authorise their being searched to the extent
they consider necessary, provided a search of intimate parts of the body or involving the removal of more than outer clothing is only made as in *Annex A*. A search may only be carried
out by an officer of the same sex as the detainee. [See *Note 4A*]

4.2 Detainees may retain clothing and personal effects at their own risk unless the custody
officer considers they may use them to cause harm to themselves or others, interfere with evidence, damage property, effect an escape or they are needed as evidence. In this event the
custody officer may withhold such articles as they consider necessary and must tell the
detainee why.

4.3 Personal effects are those items a detainee may lawfully need, use or refer to while in
detention but do not include cash and other items of value.

(b) Documentation

4.4 It is a matter for the custody officer to determine whether a record should be made of
the property a detained person has with him or had taken from him on arrest. Any record

A–51

made is not required to be kept as part of the custody record but the custody record but the custody record should be noted as to where such a record exists. Whenever a record is made the detainee shall be allowed to check and sign the record of property as correct. Any refusal to sign shall be recorded.

4.5 If a detainee is not allowed to keep any article of clothing or personal effects, the reason must be recorded.

Notes for guidance

A–52   4A *PACE, Section 54(i) and paragraph 4.1 require a detainee to be searched when it is clear the custody officer will have continuing duties in relation to that detainee or when that detainee's behaviour or offence makes an inventory appropriate. They do not require every detainee to be searched, e.g. if it is clear a person will only be detained for a short period and is not to be placed in a cell, the custody officer may decide not to search them. In such a case the custody record will be endorsed 'not searched', paragraph 4.4 will not apply, and the detainee will be invited to sign the entry. If the detainee refuses, the custody officer will be obliged to ascertain what property they have in accordance with paragraph 4.1.*

4B *Paragraph 4.4 does not require the custody officer to record on the custody record property in the detainee's possession on arrest if, by virtue of its nature, quantity or size, it is not practicable to remove it to the police station.*

4C *Paragraph 4.4 does not require items of clothing worn by the person be recorded unless withheld by the custody officer as in paragraph 4.2.*

5 RIGHT NOT TO BE HELD INCOMMUNICADO

(a) Action

A–53   5.1 Any person arrested and held in custody at a police station or other premises may, on request, have one person known to them or likely to take an interest in their welfare informed at public expense of their whereabouts as soon as practicable. If the person cannot be contacted the detainee may choose up to two alternatives. If they cannot be contacted, the person in charge of detention or the investigation has discretion to allow further attempts until the information has been conveyed. [See *Notes 5C* and *5D*]

5.2 The exercise of the above right in respect of each person nominated may be delayed only in accordance with *Annex B*.

5.3 The above right may be exercised each time a detainee is taken to another police station.

5.4 The detainee may receive visits at the custody officer's discretion. [See *Note 5B*]

5.5 If a friend, relative or person with an interest in the detainee's welfare enquires about their whereabouts, this information shall be given if the suspect agrees and *Annex B* does not apply. [See *Note 5D*]

5.6 The detainee shall be given writing materials, on request, and allowed to telephone one person for a reasonable time, see *Notes 5A* and *5E*. Either or both these privileges may be denied or delayed if an officer of inspector rank or above considers sending a letter or making a telephone call may result in any of the consequences in:

>   (a) *Annex B paragraphs 1* and *2* and the person is detained in connection with an indictable offence; or
>
>   (b) *Not used*

Nothing in this paragraph permits the restriction or denial of the rights in *paragraphs 5.1* and *6.1*.

5.7 Before any letter or message is sent, or telephone call made, the detainee shall be informed that what they say in any letter, call or message (other than in a communication to a solicitor) may be read or listened to and may be given in evidence. A telephone call may be terminated if it is being abused. The costs can be at public expense at the custody officer's discretion.

5.7A Any delay or denial of the rights in this section should be proportionate and should last no longer than necessary.

(b) Documentation

5.8 A record must be kept of any:

(a) request made under this section and the action taken;

(b) letters, messages or telephone calls made or received or visit received;

(c) refusal by the detainee to have information about them given to an outside enquirer. The detainee must be asked to countersign the record accordingly and any refusal recorded.

Notes for guidance

5A *A person may request an interpreter to interpret a telephone call or translate a letter.*   **A–54**

5B *At the custody officer's discretion. visits should be allowed when possible, subject to having sufficient personnel to supervise a visit and any possible hindrance to the investigation.*

5C *If the detainee does not know anyone to contact for advice or support or cannot contact a friend or relative, the custody officer should bear in mind any local voluntary bodies or other organisations who might be able to help. Paragraph 6.1 applies if legal advice is required.*

5D *In some circumstances it may not be appropriate to use the telephone to disclose information under paragraphs 5.1 and 5.5.*

5E *The telephone call at paragraph 5.6 is in addition to any communication under paragraphs 5.1 and 6.1.*

6 Right to legal advice

(a) Action

6.1 Unless *Annex B* applies, all detainees must be informed that they may at any time consult **A–55** and communicate privately with a solicitor, whether in person, in writing or by telephone, and that free independent legal advice is available from the duty solicitor. [See *paragraph 3.1. Note 6B* and *Note 6J*]

6.2 Not used

6.3 A poster advertising the right to legal advice must be prominently displayed in the charging area of every police station. [See *Note 6H*]

6.4 No police officer should, at any time, do or say anything with the intention of dissuading a detainee from obtaining legal advice.

6.5 The exercise of the right of access to legal advice may be delayed only as in *Annex B*. Whenever legal advice is requested, and unless *Annex B* applies, the custody officer must act without delay to secure the provision of such advice. If, on being informed or reminded of this right, the detainee declines to speak to a solicitor in person, the officer should point out that the right includes the right to speak with a solicitor on the telephone. If the detainee continues to waive this right the officer should ask them why and any reasons should be recorded on the custody record or the interview record as appropriate. Reminders of the right to legal advice must be given as in *paragraphs 3.5. 11.2. 15.4, 16.4, 2B of Annex A, 3 of Annex K* and *16.5* and Code D, *paragraphs 3.17(ii)* and *6.3.* Once it is clear a detainee does not want to speak to a solicitor in person or by telephone they should cease to be asked their reasons. [See *Note 6K*]

6.5A In the case of a juvenile, an appropriate adult should consider whether legal advice from a solicitor is required. If the juvenile indicates that they do not want legal advice, the appropriate adult has the right to ask for a solicitor to attend if this would be in the best interests of the person. However, the detained person cannot be forced to see the solicitor if he is adamant that he does not wish to do so.

6.6 A detainee who wants legal advice may not be interviewed or continue to be interviewed until they have received such advice unless:

(a) *Annex B* applies, when the restriction on drawing adverse inferences from silence in *Annex C* will apply because the detainee is not allowed an opportunity to consult a solicitor; or

(b) an officer of superintendent rank or above has reasonable grounds for believing that:

(i) the consequent delay might:

● lead to interference with, or harm to, evidence connected with an offence;

● lead to interference with, or physical harm to, other people;

● lead to serious loss of, or damage to, property;

- lead to alerting other people suspected of having committed an offence but not yet arrested for it;
- hinder the recovery of property obtained in consequence of the commission of an offence.

(ii) when a solicitor, including a duty solicitor, has been contacted and has agreed to attend, awaiting their arrival would cause unreasonable delay to the process of investigation.

Note: In these cases the restriction on drawing adverse inferences from silence in *Annex C* will apply because the detainee is not allowed an opportunity to consult a solicitor;

(c) the solicitor the detainee has nominated or selected from a list:

(i) cannot be contacted;

(ii) has previously indicated they do not wish to be contacted; or

(iii) having been contacted, has declined to attend; and

the detainee has been advised of the Duty Solicitor Scheme but has declined to ask for the duty solicitor.

In these circumstances the interview may be started or continued without further delay provided an officer of inspector rank or above has agreed to the interview proceeding.

Note: The restriction on drawing adverse inferences from silence in *Annex C* will not apply because the detainee is allowed an opportunity to consult the duty solicitor;

(d) the detainee changes their mind, about wanting legal advice.

In these circumstances the interview may be started or continued without delay provided that:

(i) the detainee agrees to do so, in writing or on the interview record made in accordance with Code E or F; and

(ii) an officer of inspector rank or above has inquired about the detainee's reasons for their change of mind and gives authority for the interview to proceed.

Confirmation of the detainee's agreement, their change of mind, the reasons for it if given and, subject to *paragraph 2.6A*, the name of the authorising officer shall be recorded in the written interview record or the interview record made in accordance with Code E or F. [See *Note 61*]

Note: In these circumstances the restriction on drawing adverse inferences from silence in *Annex C* will not apply because the detainee is allowed an opportunity to consult a solicitor if they wish.

A–56   6.7 If *paragraph 6.6(b)(i)* applies, once sufficient information has been obtained to avert the risk, questioning must cease until the detainee has received legal advice unless *paragraph 6.6(a)*, *(b)(ii)*, *(c)* or *(d)* applies.

6.8 A detainee who has been permitted to consult a solicitor shall be entitled on request to have the solicitor present when they are interviewed unless one of the exceptions in *paragraph 6.6* applies.

6.9 The solicitor may only be required to leave the interview if their conduct is such that the interviewer is unable properly to put questions to the suspect. [See *Notes 6D and 6E*]

6.10 If the interviewer considers a solicitor is acting in such a way, they will stop the interview and consult an officer not below superintendent rank, if one is readily available, and otherwise an officer not below inspector rank not connected with the investigation. After speaking to the solicitor, the officer consulted will decide if the interview should continue in the presence of that solicitor. If they decide it should not, the suspect will be given the opportunity to consult another solicitor before the interview continues and that solicitor given an opportunity to be present at the interview. [See *Note 6E*]

6.11 The removal of a solicitor from an interview is a serious step and, if it occurs, the officer of superintendent rank or above who took the decision will consider if the incident should be reported to the Law Society. If the decision to remove the solicitor has been taken by an officer below superintendent rank, the facts must be reported to an officer of superintendent rank or above who will similarly consider whether a report to the Law Society would be appropriate. When the solicitor concerned is a duty solicitor, the report should be both to the Law Society and to the Legal Services Commission.

6.12 'Solicitor' in this Code means:

- a solicitor who holds a current practising certificate
- an accredited or probationary representative included on the register of representatives maintained by the Legal Services Commission.

6.12A An accredited or probationary representative sent to provide advice by, and on behalf of, a solicitor shall be admitted to the police station for this purpose unless an officer of inspector rank or above considers such a visit will hinder the investigation and directs otherwise. Hindering the investigation does not include giving proper legal advice to a detainee as in *Note 6D*. Once admitted to the police station, *paragraphs 6.6* to *6.10* apply.

6.13 In exercising their discretion under *paragraph 6.12A*, the officer should take into account in particular:

- whether:
— the identity and status of an accredited or probationary representative have been satisfactorily established;
— they are of suitable character to provide legal advice, e.g. a person with a criminal record is unlikely to be suitable unless the conviction was for a minor offence and not recent.
- any other matters in any written letter of authorisation provided by the solicitor on whose behalf the person is attending the police station. [See *Note 6F*]

6.14 If the inspector refuses access to an accredited or probationary representative or a decision is taken that such a person should not be permitted to remain at an interview, the inspector must notify the solicitor on whose behalf the representative was acting and give them an opportunity to make alternative arrangements. The detainee must be informed and the custody record noted.

6.15 If a solicitor arrives at the station to see a particular person, that person must, unless *Annex B* applies, be so informed whether or not they are being interviewed and asked if they would like to see the solicitor. This applies even if the detainee has declined legal advice or, having requested it, subsequently agreed to be interviewed without receiving advice. The solicitor's attendance and the detainee's decision must be noted in the custody record.

(b) Documentation

6.16 Any request for legal advice and the action taken shall be recorded.

6.17 A record shall be made in the interview record if a detainee asks for legal advice and an interview is begun either in the absence of a solicitor or their representative, or they have been required to leave an interview.

Notes for guidance

6A *In considering if paragraph 6.6(b) applies, the officer should, if practicable, ask the so-* **A–57** *licitor for an estimate of how long it will take to come to the station and relate this to the time detention is permitted, the time of day (i.e. whether the rest period under paragraph 12.2 is imminent) and the requirements of other investigations. If the solicitor is on their way or is to set off immediately, it will not normally be appropriate to begin an interview before they arrive. If it appears necessary to begin an interview before the solicitor's arrival, they should be given an indication of how long the police would be able to wait before 6.6(b) applies so there is an opportunity to make arrangements for someone else to provide legal advice.*

6B *A detainee who asks for legal advice should be given an opportunity to consult a specific solicitor or another solicitor from that solicitor's firm or the duty solicitor. If advice is not available by these means, or they do not want to consult the duty solicitor, the detainee should be given an opportunity to choose a solicitor from a list of those willing to provide legal advice. If this solicitor is unavailable, they may choose up to two alternatives. If these attempts are unsuccessful, the custody officer has discretion to allow further attempts until a solicitor has been contacted and agrees to provide legal advice. Apart from carrying out these duties, an officer must not advise the suspect about any particular firm of solicitors.*

6C *Not Used*

6D *A detainee has a right to free legal advice and to be represented by a solicitor. The solicitor's only role in the police station is to protect and advance the legal rights of their client. On occasions this may require the solicitor to give advice which has the effect of the client avoiding giving evidence which strengthens a prosecution case. The solicitor may intervene in order to seek clarification, challenge an improper question to their client or the manner in which it is put, advise their client not to reply to particular questions, or if they wish to give their client further legal advice. Paragraph 6.9 only applies if the solicitor's approach or conduct prevents or unreasonably obstructs proper questions being put to the suspect or the suspect's response being recorded. Examples of unacceptable conduct include answering questions on a suspect's behalf or providing written replies for the suspect to quote.*

6E *An officer who takes the decision to exclude a solicitor must be in a position to satisfy the court the decision was properly made. In order to do this they may need to witness what is happening.*

6F *If an officer of at least inspector rank considers a particular solicitor or firm of solicitors is persistently sending probationary representatives who are unsuited to provide legal advice, they should inform an officer of at least superintendent rank, who may wish to take the matter up with the Law Society.*

A–58   6G *Subject to the constraints of Annex B, a solicitor may advise more than one client in an investigation if they wish. Any question of a conflict of interest is for the solicitor under their professional code of conduct. If however, waiting for a solicitor to give advice to one client may lead to unreasonable delay to the interview with another, the provisions of paragraph 6.6(b) may apply.*

6H *In addition to a poster in English, a poster or posters containing translations into Welsh, the main minority ethnic languages and the principal European languages should be displayed wherever they are likely to be helpful and it is practicable to do so.*

6I *Paragraph 6.6(d) requires the authorisation of an officer of inspector rank or above to the continuation of an interview when a detainee who wanted legal advice changes their mind. It is permissible for such authorisation to be given over the telephone, if the authorising officer is able to satisfy themselves about the reason for the detainee's change of mind and is satisfied it is proper to continue the interview in those circumstances.*

6J *Whenever a detainee exercises their right to legal advice by consulting or communicating with a solicitor, they must be allowed to do so in private. This right to consult or communicate in private is fundamental. If the requirement for privacy is compromised because what is said or written by the detainee or solicitor for the purpose of giving and receiving legal advice is overheard, listened to, or read by others without the informed consent of the detainee, the right will effectively have been denied. When a detainee chooses to speak to a solicitor on the telephone, they should be allowed to do so in private unless this is impractical because of the design and layout of the custody area or the location of telephones. However, the normal expectation should be that facilities will be available, unless they are being used, at all police stations to enable detainees to speak in private to a solicitor either face to face or over the telephone.*

6K *A detainee is not obliged to give reasons for declining legal advice and should not be pressed to do so.*

7 CITIZENS OF INDEPENDENT COMMONWEALTH COUNTRIES OR FOREIGN NATIONALS

(a) Action

A–59   7.1 Any citizen of an independent Commonwealth country or a national of a foreign country, including the Republic of Ireland, may communicate at any time with the appropriate High Commission. Embassy or Consulate. The detainee must be informed as soon as practicable of:

- this right;
- their right, upon request, to have their High Commission, Embassy or Consulate told of their whereabouts and the grounds for their detention. Such a request should be acted upon as soon as practicable.

7.2 If a detainee is a citizen of a country with which a bilateral consular convention or agreement is in force requiring notification of arrest, the appropriate High Commission, Embassy or Consulate shall be informed as soon as practicable, subject to *paragraph 7.4*. The countries to which this applies as at 1st April 2003 are listed in *Annex F*.

7.3 Consular officers may visit one of their nationals in police detention to talk to them and, if required, to arrange for legal advice. Such visits shall take place out of the hearing of a police officer.

7.4 Notwithstanding the provisions of consular conventions. if the detainee is a political refugee whether for reasons of race, nationality, political opinion or religion, or is seeking political asylum, consular officers shall not be informed of the arrest of one of their nationals or given access or information about them except at the detainee's express request.

(b) Documentation

7.5 A record shall be made when a detainee is informed of their rights under this section and of any communications with a High Commission, Embassy or Consulate.

Note for guidance

7A *The exercise of the rights in this section may not be interfered with even though Annex B* **A–60** *applies.*

8 Conditions of detention

(a) Action

8.1 So far as it is practicable, not more than one detainee should be detained in each cell. **A–61**

8.2 Cells in use must be adequately heated, cleaned and ventilated. They must be adequately lit. subject to such dimming as is compatible with safety and security to allow people detained overnight to sleep. No additional restraints shall be used within a locked cell unless absolutely necessary and then only restraint equipment, approved for use in that force by the Chief Officer, which is reasonable and necessary in the circumstances having regard to the detainee's demeanour and with a view to ensuring their safety and the safety of others. If a detainee is deaf, mentally disordered or otherwise mentally vulnerable, particular care must be taken when deciding whether to use any form of approved restraints.

8.3 Blankets, mattresses, pillows and other bedding supplied shall be of a reasonable standard and in a clean and sanitary condition. [See *Note 8A*]

8.4 Access to toilet and washing facilities must be provided.

8.5 If it is necessary to remove a detainee's clothes for the purposes of investigation, for hygiene, health reasons or cleaning, replacement clothing of a reasonable standard of comfort and cleanliness shall be provided. A detainee may not be interviewed unless adequate clothing has been offered.

8.6 At least two light meals and one main meal should be offered in any 24 hour period. See *Note 8B*. Drinks should be provided at meal times and upon reasonable request between meals. Whenever necessary, advice shall be sought from the appropriate health care professional, see *Note 9A*, on medical and dietary matters. As far as practicable, meals provided shall offer a varied diet and meet any specific dietary needs or religious beliefs the detainee may have. The detainee may, at the custody officer's discretion, have meals supplied by their family or friends at their expense. [See *Note 8A*]

8.7 Brief outdoor exercise shall be offered daily if practicable.

8.8 A juvenile shall not be placed in a police cell unless no other secure accommodation is available and the custody officer considers it is not practicable to supervise them if they are not placed in a cell or that a cell provides more comfortable accommodation than other secure accommodation in the station. A juvenile may not be placed in a cell with a detained adult.

(b) Documentation

8.9 A record must be kept of replacement clothing and meals offered.

8.10 If a juvenile is placed in a cell, the reason must be recorded.

8.11 The use of any restraints on a detainee whilst in a cell, the reasons for it and, if appropriate, the arrangements for enhanced supervision of the detainee whilst so restrained, shall be recorded. See *paragraph 3.9*

Notes for guidance

8A *The provisions in paragraph 8.3 and 8.6 respectively are of particular importance in* **A–62** *the case of a person detained under the Terrorism Act 2000, immigration detainees and others likely to be detained for an extended period. In deciding whether to allow meals to be supplied by family or friends, the custody officer is entitled to take account of the risk of items being con-*

cealed in any food or package and the officer's duties and responsibilities under food handling legislation.

8B *Meals should, so far as practicable, be offered at recognised meal times, or at other times that take account of when the detainee last had a meal.*

9 CARE AND TREATMENT OF DETAINED PERSONS

(a) General

A–63   9.1 Nothing in this section prevents the police from calling the police surgeon or, if appropriate, some other health care professional, to examine a detainee for the purposes of obtaining evidence relating to any offence in which the detainee is suspected of being involved. [See *Note 9A*]

9.2 If a complaint is made by, or on behalf of, a detainee about their treatment since their arrest, or it comes to notice that a detainee may have been treated improperly, a report must be made as soon as practicable to an officer of inspector rank or above not connected with the investigation. If the matter concerns a possible assault or the possibility of the unnecessary or unreasonable use of force, an appropriate health care professional must also be called as soon as practicable.

9.3 Detainees should be visited at least every hour. If no reasonably foreseeable risk was identified in a risk assessment, see *paragraphs 3.6–3.10*, there is no need to wake a sleeping detainee. Those suspected of being intoxicated through drink or drugs or having swallowed drugs, see *Note 9CA*, or whose level of consciousness causes concern must, subject to any clinical directions given by the appropriate health care professional, see *paragraph 9.13*:

- be visited and roused at least every half hour
- have their condition assessed as in *Annex H*
- and clinical treatment arranged if appropriate

[See *Notes 9B, 9C* and *9H*]

9.4 When arrangements are made to secure clinical attention for a detainee, the custody officer must make sure all relevant information which might assist in the treatment of the detainee's condition is made available to the responsible health care professional. This applies whether or not the health care professional asks for such information. Any officer or police staff with relevant information must inform the custody officer as soon as practicable.

(b) Clinical treatment and attention

A–64   9.5 The custody officer must make sure a detainee receives appropriate clinical attention as soon as reasonably practicable if the person:

- (a) appears to be suffering from physical illness; or
- (b) is injured; or
- (c) appears to be suffering from a mental disorder;
- (d) appears to need clinical attention.

9.5A This applies even if the detainee makes no request for clinical attention and whether or not they have already received clinical attention elsewhere. If the need for attention appears urgent, e.g. when indicated as in *Annex H*, the nearest available health care professional or an ambulance must be called immediately.

9.5B The custody officer must also consider the need for clinical attention as set out in Note for Guidance 9C in relation to those suffering the effects of alcohol or drugs.

9.6 *Paragraph 9.5* is not meant to prevent or delay the transfer to a hospital if necessary of a person detained under the *Mental Health Act* 1983, section 136. See *Note 9D*. When an assessment under that Act takes place at a police station, see *paragraph 3.16*, the custody officer must consider whether an appropriate health care professional should be called to conduct an initial clinical check on the detainee. This applies particularly when there is likely to be any significant delay in the arrival of a suitably qualified medical practitioner.

9.7 If it appears to the custody officer, or they are told, that a person brought to a station under arrest may be suffering from an infectious disease or condition, the custody officer must take reasonable steps to safeguard the health of the detainee and others at the station. In deciding what action to take, advice must be sought from an appropriate health care professional. See *Note 9E*. The custody officer has discretion to isolate the person and their property until clinical directions have been obtained.

9.8 If a detainee requests a clinical examination, an appropriate health care professional **A–65** must be called as soon as practicable to assess the detainee's clinical needs. If a safe and appropriate care plan cannot be provided, the police surgeon's advice must be sought. The detainee may also be examined by a medical practitioner of their choice at their expense.

9.9 If a detainee is required to take or apply any medication in compliance with clinical directions prescribed before their detention, the custody officer must consult the appropriate health care professional before the use of the medication. Subject to the restrictions in *paragraph 9.10*, the custody officer is responsible for the safekeeping of any medication and for making sure the detainee is given the opportunity to take or apply prescribed or approved medication. Any such consultation and its outcome shall be noted in the custody record.

9.10 No police officer may administer or supervise the self-administration of medically prescribed controlled drugs of the types and forms listed in the *Misuse of Drugs Regulations* 2001, Schedule 2 or 3. A detainee may only self-administer such drugs under the personal supervision of the registered medical practitioner authorising their use. Drugs listed in Schedule 4 or 5 may be distributed by the custody officer for self-administration if they have consulted the registered medical practitioner authorising their use, this may be done by telephone, and both parties are satisfied self-administration will not expose the detainee, police officers or anyone else to the risk of harm or injury.

9.11 When appropriate health care professionals administer drugs or other medications, or supervise their self-administration, it must be within current medicines legislation and the scope of practice as determined by their relevant professional body.

9.12 If a detainee has in their possession, or claims to need, medication relating to a heart condition, diabetes, epilepsy or a condition of comparable potential seriousness then, even though *paragraph 9.5* may not apply, the advice of the appropriate health care professional must be obtained.

9.13 Whenever the appropriate health care professional is called in accordance with this section to examine or treat a detainee, the custody officer shall ask for their opinion about:

- any risks or problems which police need to take into account when making decisions about the detainee's continued detention;
- when to carry out an interview if applicable; and
- the need for safeguards.

9.14 When clinical directions are given by the appropriate health care professional, whether orally or in writing, and the custody officer has any doubts or is in any way uncertain about any aspect of the directions, the custody officer shall ask for clarification. It is particularly important that directions concerning the frequency of visits are clear, precise and capable of being implemented. [See *Note 9F*]

(c) Documentation

9.15 A record must be made in the custody record of: **A–66**

(a) the arrangements made for an examination by an appropriate health care professional under *paragraph 9.2* and of any complaint reported under that paragraph together with any relevant remarks by the custody officer;

(b) any arrangements made in accordance with *paragraph 9.5*;

(c) any request for a clinical examination under *paragraph 9.8* and any arrangements made in response;

(d) the injury, ailment, condition or other reason which made it necessary to make the arrangements in *(a)* to *(c)*, see *Note 9G*;

(e) any clinical directions and advice, including any further clarifications, given to police by a health care professional concerning the care and treatment of the detainee in connection with any of the arrangements made in *(a)* to *(c)*, see *Note 9F*;

(f) if applicable, the responses received when attempting to rouse a person using the procedure in *Annex H, see Note 9H*.

9.16 If a health care professional does not record their clinical findings in the custody record, the record must show where they are recorded. See *Note 9G*. However, information which is necessary to custody staff to ensure the effective ongoing care and well being of the

Appendices

detainee must be recorded openly in the custody record, see *paragraph 3.8* and *Annex G, paragraph 7*.

9.17 Subject to the requirements of *Section 4*, the custody record shall include:

- a record of all medication a detainee has in their possession on arrival at the police station;

- a note of any such medication they claim to need but do not have with them.

Notes for guidance

A–67   9A *A 'health care professional' means a clinically qualified person working within the scope of practice as determined by their relevant professional body. Whether a health care professional is 'appropriate' depends on the circumstances of the duties they carry out at the time.*

9B *Whenever possible juveniles and mentally vulnerable detainees should be visited more frequently.*

9C *A detainee who appears drunk or behaves abnormally may be suffering from illness, the effects of drugs or may have sustained injury, particularly a head injury which is not apparent. A detainee needing or dependent on certain drugs, including alcohol, may experience harmful effects within a short time of being deprived of their supply. In these circumstances, when there is any doubt, police should always act urgently to call an appropriate health care professional or an ambulance. Paragraph 9.5 does not apply to minor ailments or injuries which do not need attention. However, all such ailments or injuries must be recorded in the custody record and any doubt must be resolved in favour of calling the appropriate health care professional.*

9CA *Paragraph 9.3 would apply to a person in police custody by order of a magistrates' court under the Criminal Justice Act 1988, section 152 (as amended by the Drugs Act 2005, section 8) to facilitate the recovery of evidence after being charged with drug possession or drug trafficking and suspected of having swallowed drugs. In the case of the healthcare needs of a person who has swallowed drugs, the custody officer subject to any clinical directions, should consider the necessity for rousing every half hour. This does not negate the need for regular visiting of the suspect in the cell.*

9D *Whenever practicable, arrangements should be made for persons detained for assessment under the Mental Health Act 1983, section 136 to be taken to a hospital. There is no power under that Act to transfer a person detained under section 136 from one place of safety to another place of safety for assessment.*

9E *It is important to respect a person's right to privacy and information about their health must be kept confidential and only disclosed with their consent or in accordance with clinical advice when it is necessary to protect the detainee's health or that of others who come into contact with them.*

9F *The custody officer should always seek to clarify directions that the detainee requires constant observation or supervision and should ask the appropriate health care professional to explain precisely what action needs to be taken to implement such directions.*

9G *Paragraphs 9.15 and 9.16 do not require any information about the cause of any injury, ailment or condition to be recorded on the custody record if it appears capable of providing evidence of an offence.*

9H *The purpose of recording a person's responses when attempting to rouse them using the procedure in Annex H is to enable any change in the individual's consciousness level to be noted and clinical treatment arranged if appropriate.*

10 Cautions

(a) When a caution must be given

A–68   10.1 A person whom there are grounds to suspect of an offence, see *Note 10A*, must be cautioned before any questions about an offence, or further questions if the answers provide the grounds for suspicion, are put to them if either the suspect's answers or silence, (i.e. failure or refusal to answer or answer satisfactorily) may be given in evidence to a court in a prosecution. A person need not be cautioned if questions are for other necessary purposes, e.g.:

   (a) solely to establish their identity or ownership of any vehicle;

   (b) to obtain information in accordance with any relevant statutory requirement, see *paragraph 10.9*;

   (c) in furtherance of the proper and effective conduct of a search, e.g. to determine the need to search in the exercise of powers of stop and search or to seek co-operation while carrying out a search;

(d) to seek verification of a written record as in *paragraph 11.13*;

(e) Not used.

10.2 Whenever a person not under arrest is initially cautioned, or reminded they are under caution, that person must at the same time be told they are not under arrest and are free to leave if they want to. [See *Note 10C*]

10.3 A person who is arrested, or further arrested, must be informed at the time, or as soon as practicable thereafter, that they are under arrest and the grounds for their arrest, see *paragraph 3.4*, *Note 10B* and *Code G, paragraphs 2.2* and *4.3*.

10.4 As per *Code G, section 3*, a person who is arrested, or further arrested, must also be cautioned unless:

(a) it is impracticable to do so by reason of their condition or behaviour at the time;

(b) they have already been cautioned immediately prior to arrest as in *paragraph 10.1*.

(b) Terms of the cautions

10.5 The caution which must be given on:

(a) arrest;

(b) all other occasions before a person is charged or informed they may be prosecuted, see *section 16*.

should, unless the restriction on drawing adverse inferences from silence applies, see *Annex C*, be in the following terms:

"You do not have to say anything. But it may harm your defence if you do not mention when questioned something which you later rely on in Court. Anything you do say may be given in evidence."

[See *Note 10G*]

10.6 *Annex C, paragraph 2* sets out the alternative terms of the caution to be used when the **A–69** restriction on drawing adverse inferences from silence applies.

10.7 Minor deviations from the words of any caution given in accordance with this Code do not constitute a breach of this Code, provided the sense of the relevant caution is preserved. [See *Note 10D*]

10.8 After any break in questioning under caution, the person being questioned must be made aware they remain under caution. If there is any doubt the relevant caution should be given again in full when the interview resumes. [See *Note 10E*]

10.9 When, despite being cautioned, a person fails to co-operate or to answer particular questions which may affect their immediate treatment, the person should be informed of any relevant consequences and that those consequences are not affected by the caution. Examples are when a person's refusal to provide:

● their name and address when charged may make them liable to detention;

● particulars and information in accordance with a statutory requirement, e.g. under the *Road Traffic Act* 1988, may amount to an offence or may make the person liable to a further arrest.

(c) Special warnings under the Criminal Justice and Public Order Act 1994, sections 36 and 37

10.10 When a suspect interviewed at a police station or authorised place of detention after **A–70** arrest fails or refuses to answer certain questions, or to answer satisfactorily, after due warning, see *Note 10F*, a court or jury may draw such inferences as appear proper under the *Criminal Justice and Public Order Act* 1994, sections 36 and 37. Such inferences may only be drawn when:

(a) the restriction on drawing adverse inferences from silence, see *Annex C*, does not apply; and

(b) the suspect is arrested by a constable and fails or refuses to account for any objects, marks or substances, or marks on such objects found:

● on their person;

● in or on their clothing or footwear;

● otherwise in their possession; or

　　　　● in the place they were arrested;

(c) the arrested suspect was found by a constable at a place at or about the time the offence for which that officer has arrested them is alleged to have been committed, and the suspect fails or refuses to account for their presence there.

When the restriction on drawing adverse inferences from silence applies, the suspect may still be asked to account for any of the matters in *(b)* or *(c)* but the special warning described in *paragraph 10.11* will not apply and must not be given.

10.11 For an inference to be drawn when a suspect fails or refuses to answer a question about one of these matters or to answer it satisfactorily, the suspect must first be told in ordinary language:

(a) what offence is being investigated;

(b) what fact they are being asked to account for;

(c) this fact may be due to them taking part in the commission of the offence;

(d) a court may draw a proper inference if they fail or refuse to account for this fact;

(e) a record is being made of the interview and it may be given in evidence if they are brought to trial.

(d) Juveniles and persons who are mentally disordered or otherwise mentally vulnerable

10.12 If a juvenile or a person who is mentally disordered or otherwise mentally vulnerable is cautioned in the absence of the appropriate adult, the caution must be repeated in the adult's presence.

(e) Documentation

10.13 A record shall be made when a caution is given under this section, either in the interviewer's pocket book or in the interview record.

Notes for guidance

A–71　10A *There must be some reasonable, objective grounds for the suspicion, based on known facts or information which are relevant to the likelihood the offence has been committed and the person to be questioned committed it.*

10B *An arrested person must be given sufficient information to enable them to understand that they have been deprived of their liberty and the reason they have been arrested, e.g. when a person is arrested on suspicion of committing an offence they must be informed of the suspected offence's nature, when and where it was committed. The suspect must also be informed of the reason or reasons why the arrest is considered necessary. Vague or technical language should be avoided.*

10C *The restriction on drawing inferences from silence, see Annex C, paragraph 1, does not apply to a person who has not been detained and who therefore cannot be prevented from seeking legal advice if they want, see paragraph 3.21.*

10D *If it appears a person does not understand the caution, the person giving it should explain it in their own words.*

10E *It may be necessary to show to the court that nothing occurred during an interview break or between interviews which influenced the suspect's recorded evidence. After a break in an interview or at the beginning of a subsequent interview, the interviewing officer should summarise the reason for the break and confirm this with the suspect.*

10F *The Criminal Justice and Public Order Act 1994, sections 36 and 37 apply only to suspects who have been arrested by a constable or Customs and Excise officer and are given the relevant warning by the police or customs officer who made the arrest or who is investigating the offence. They do not apply to any interviews with suspects who have not been arrested.*

10G *Nothing in this Code requires a caution to be given or repeated when informing a person not under arrest they may be prosecuted for an offence. However, a court will not be able to draw any inferences under the Criminal Justice and Public Order Act 1994, section 34, if the person was not cautioned.*

11 Interviews—general

(a) Action

11.1A An interview is the questioning of a person regarding their involvement or suspected **A–72** involvement in a criminal offence or offences which, under *paragraph 10.1*, must be carried out under caution. Whenever a person is interviewed they must be informed of the nature of the offence, or further offence. Procedures under the *Road Traffic Act* 1988, section 7 or the *Transport and Works Act* 1992, section 31 do not constitute interviewing for the purpose of this Code.

11.1 Following a decision to arrest a suspect, they must not be interviewed about the relevant offence except at a police station or other authorised place of detention, unless the consequent delay would be likely to:

    (a) lead to:
- interference with, or harm to, evidence connected with an offence;
- interference with, or physical harm to, other people; or
- serious loss of, or damage to, property;

    (b) lead to alerting other people suspected of committing an offence but not yet arrested for it; or

    (c) hinder the recovery of property obtained in consequence of the commission of an offence.

Interviewing in any of these circumstances shall cease once the relevant risk has been averted or the necessary questions have been averted or the necessary questions have been put in order to attempt to avert that risk.

11.2 Immediately prior to the commencement or re-commencement of any interview at a police station or other authorised place of detention, the interviewer should remind the suspect of their entitlement to free legal advice and that the interview can be delayed for legal advice to be obtained, unless one of the exceptions in *paragraph 6.6* applies. It is the interviewer's responsibility to make sure all reminders are recorded in the interview record.

11.3 Not Used

11.4 At the beginning of an interview the interviewer, after cautioning the suspect, see *section 10*, shall put to them any significant statement or silence which occurred in the presence and hearing of a police officer or other police staff before the start of the interview and which have not been put to the suspect in the course of a previous interview. See *Note 11A*. The interviewer shall ask the suspect whether they confirm or deny that earlier statement or silence and if they want to add anything.

11.4A A significant statement is one which appears capable of being used in evidence against the suspect, in particular a direct admission of guilt. A significant silence is a failure or refusal to answer a question or answer satisfactorily when under caution, which might, allowing for the restriction on drawing adverse inferences from silence, see *Annex C*, give rise to an inference under the *Criminal Justice and Public Order Act* 1994, Part III.

11.5 No interviewer may try to obtain answers or elicit a statement by the use of oppression. Except as in *paragraph 109*, no interviewer shall indicate, except to answer a direct question, what action will be taken by the police if the person being questioned answers questions makes a statement or refuses to do either. If the person asks directly what action will be taken if they answer questions, make a statement or refuse to do either, the interviewer may inform them what action the police propose to take provided that action is itself proper and warranted.

11.6 The interview or further interview of a person about an offence with which that person has not been charged or for which they have not been informed they may be prosecuted, must cease when:

    (a) the officer in charge of the investigation is satisfied all the questions they consider relevant to obtaining accurate and reliable information about the offence have been put to the suspect, this includes allowing the suspect an opportunity to give an innocent explanation and asking questions to test if the explanation is accurate and reliable, e.g. to clear up ambiguities or clarify what the suspect said;

    (b) the officer in charge of the investigation has taken account of any other available evidence; and

    (c) the officer in charge of the investigation, or in the case of a detained suspect, the custody officer, see paragraph 16.1, reasonably believes there is sufficient evidence to provide a realistic prospect of conviction for that offence. [See *Note 11B*]

This paragraph does not prevent officers in revenue cases or acting under the confiscation provisions of the *Criminal Justice Act* 1988 or the *Drug Trafficking Act* 1994 from inviting suspects to complete a formal question and answer record after the interview is concluded.

(b) Interview records

A–73
(a) An accurate record must be made of each interview, whether or not the interview takes place at a police station;

(b) The record must state the place of interview, the time it begins and ends, any interview breaks and, subject to *paragraph 2.6A*, the names of all those present: and must be made on the forms provided for this purpose or in the interviewer's pocket book or in accordance with the Codes of Practice E or F;

(b) Any written record must be made and completed during the interview, unless this would not be practicable or would interfere with the conduct of the interview, and must constitute either a verbatim record of what has been said or, failing this, an account of the interview which adequately and accurately summarises it.

11.8 If a written record is not made during the interview it must be made as soon as practicable after its completion.

11.9 Written interview records must be timed and signed by the maker.

11.10 If a written record is not completed during the interview the reason must be recorded in the interview record.

11.11 Unless it is impracticable, the person interviewed shall be given the opportunity to read the interview record and to sign it as correct or to indicate how they consider it inaccurate. If the person interviewed cannot read or refuses to read the record or sign it, the senior interviewer present shall read it to them and ask whether they would like to sign it as correct or make their mark or to indicate how they consider it inaccurate. The interviewer shall certify on the interview record itself what has occurred. [See *Note 11E*]

11.12 If the appropriate adult or the person's solicitor is present during the interview, they should also be given an opportunity to read and sign the interview record or any written statement taken down during the interview.

11.13 A written record shall be made of any comments made by a suspect, including unsolicited comments, which are outside the context of an interview but which might be relevant to the offence. Any such record must be timed and signed by the maker. When practicable the suspect shall be given the opportunity to read that record and to sign it as correct or to indicate how they consider it inaccurate. [See *Note 11E*]

11.14 Any refusal by a person to sign an interview record when asked in accordance with this Code must itself be recorded.

(c) Juveniles and mentally disordered or otherwise mentally vulnerable people

A–74
11.15 A juvenile or person who is mentally disordered or otherwise mentally vulnerable must not be interviewed regarding their involvement or suspected involvement in a criminal offence or offences, or asked to provide or sign a written statement under caution or record of interview, in the absence of the appropriate adult unless *paragraphs 11.1, 11.18 to 11.20* apply. [See *Note 11C*]

11.16 Juveniles may only be interviewed at their place of education in exceptional circumstances and only when the principal or their nominee agrees. Every effort should be made to notify the parent(s) or other person responsible for the juvenile's welfare and the appropriate adult, if this is a different person, that the police want to interview the juvenile and reasonable time should be allowed to enable the appropriate adult to be present at the interview, if awaiting the appropriate adult would cause unreasonable delay, and unless the juvenile is suspected of an offence against the educational establishment, the principal or their nominee can act as the appropriate adult for the purposes of the interview.

11.17 If an appropriate adult is present at an interview, they shall be informed:

● they are not expected to act simply as an observer; and

● the purpose of their presence is to:

— advise the person being interviewed;

— observe whether the interview is being conducted properly and fairly;

— facilitate communication with the person being interviewed.

(d) Vulnerable suspects—urgent interviews at police stations

11.18. The following persons may not be interviewed unless an officer of superintendent rank or above considers delay will lead to the consequences in *paragraph 11.1(a)* to *(c)*, and is satisfied the interview would not significantly harm the persons physical or mental state (see Annex G):

(a) a juvenile or person who is mentally disordered or otherwise mentally vulnerable if at the time of the interview the appropriate adult is not present;

(b) anyone other than in (a) who at the time of the interview appears unable to:

- appreciate the significance of questions and their answers; or
- understand what is happening because of the effects of drink, drugs or any illness, ailment or condition;

(c) a person who has difficulty understanding English or has a hearing disability, if at the time of the interview an interpreter is not present.

11.19   These interviews may not continue once sufficient information has been obtained to avert the consequences in *paragraph 11.1(a)* to *(c)*.

11.20.   A record shall be made of the grounds for any decision to interview a person under *paragraph 11.18*.

Notes for guidance

11A *Paragraph 11.4 does not prevent the interviewer from putting significant statements* **A–75** *and silences to a suspect again at a later stage or a further interview.*

11B *The Criminal Procedure and Investigations Act 1996 Code of Practice, paragraph 3.4 states 'In conducting an investigation, the investigator should pursue all reasonable lines of enquiry, whether these point towards or away from the suspect. What is reasonable will depend on the particular circumstances.' Interviewers should keep this in mind when deciding what questions to ask in an interview.*

11C *Although juveniles or people who are mentally disordered or otherwise mentally vulnerable are often capable of providing reliable evidence, they may, without knowing or wishing to do so, be particularly prone in certain circumstances to provide information that may be unreliable, misleading or self-incriminating. Special care should always be taken when questioning such a person, and the appropriate adult should be involved if there is any doubt about a person's age, mental state or capacity. Because of the risk of unreliable evidence it is also important to obtain corroboration of any facts admitted whenever possible.*

11D *Juveniles should not be arrested at their place of education unless this is unavoidable. When a juvenile is arrested at their place of education, the principal or their nominee must be informed.*

11E *Significant statements described in paragraph 11.4 will always be relevant to the offence and must be recorded. When a suspect agrees to read records of interviews and other comments and sign them as correct, they should be asked to endorse the record with, e.g. 'I agree that this is a correct record of what was said' and add their signature. If the suspect does not agree with the record, the interviewer should record the details of any disagreement and ask the suspect to read these details and sign them to the effect that they accurately reflect their disagreement. Any refusal to sign should be recorded.*

12   Interviews in police stations

(a) Action

12.1   If a police officer wants to interview or conduct enquiries which require the presence **A–76** of a detainee, the custody officer is responsible for deciding whether to deliver the detainee into the officer's custody.

12.2   Except as below, in any period of 24 hours a detainee must be allowed a continuous period of at least 8 hours for rest, free from questioning, travel or any interruption in connection with the investigation concerned. This period should normally be at night or other appropriate time which takes account of when the detainee last slept or rested. If a detainee is arrested at a police station after going there voluntarily, the period of 24 hours runs from the time of their arrest and not the time of arrival at the police station. The period may not be interrupted or delayed, except:

(a) when there are reasonable grounds for believing not delaying or interrupting the period would:

(i) involve a risk of harm to people or serious loss of, or damage to, property;

(ii) delay unnecessarily the person's release from custody;

(iii) otherwise prejudice the outcome of the investigation;

(b) at the request of the detainee, their appropriate adult or legal representative;

(c) when a delay or interruption is necessary in order to:

(i) comply with the legal obligations and duties arising under section 15;

(ii) to take action required under section 9 or in accordance with medical advice.

If the period is interrupted in accordance with *(a)*, a fresh period must be allowed. Interruptions under *(b)* and *(c)*, do not require a fresh period to be allowed.

12.3 Before a detainee is interviewed the custody officer, in consultation with the officer in charge of the investigation and appropriate health care professionals as necessary shall assess whether the detainee is fit enough to be interviewed. This means determining and considering the risks to the detainee's physical and mental state if the interview took place and determining what safeguards are needed to allow the interview to take place. See *Annex G*. The custody officer shall not allow a detainee to be interviewed if the custody officer considers it would cause significant harm to the detainee's physical or mental state. Vulnerable suspects listed at *paragraph 11.18* shall be treated as always being at some risk during an interview and these persons may not be interviewed except in accordance with *paragraphs 11.18* to *11.20*.

12.4 As far as practicable interviews shall take place in interview rooms which are adequately heated, lit and ventilated.

12.5 A suspect whose detention without charge has been authorised under *PACE*, because the detention is necessary for an interview to obtain evidence of the offence for which they have been arrested, may choose not to answer questions but police do not require the suspect's consent or agreement to interview them for this purpose. If a suspect takes steps to prevent themselves being questioned or further questioned, e.g. by refusing to leave their cell to go to a suitable interview room or by trying to leave the interview room, they shall be advised their consent or agreement to interview is not required. The suspect shall be cautioned as in *section 10*, and informed if they fail or refuse to co-operate, the interview may take place in the cell and that their failure or refusal to co-operate may be given in evidence. The suspect shall then be invited to co-operate and go into the interview room.

12.6 People being questioned or making statements shall not be required to stand.

A–77   12.7 Before the interview commences each interviewer shall, subject to *paragraph 2.6A*, identify themselves and any other persons present to the interviewee.

12.8 Breaks from interviewing should be made at recognised meal times or at other times that take account of when an interviewee last had a meal. Short refreshment breaks shall be provided at approximately two hour intervals, subject to the interviewer's discretion to delay a break if there are reasonable grounds for believing it would:

(i) involve a:

• risk of harm to people;

• serious loss of, or damage to, property;

(ii) unnecessarily delay the detainee's release;

(iii) otherwise prejudice the outcome of the investigation.

[See *Note 12B*]

12.9 If during the interview a complaint is made by or on behalf of the interviewee concerning the provisions of this Code, the interviewer should:

(i) record it in the interview record;

(ii) inform the custody officer, who is then responsible for dealing with it as in *section 9*.

(b) Documentation

A–78   12.10 A record must be made of the:

• time a detainee is not in the custody of the custody officer, and why

• reason for any refusal to deliver the detainee out of that custody

12.11 A record shall be made of:

(a) the reasons it was not practicable to use an interview room; and

(b) any action taken as in *paragraph 12.5*.

The record shall be made on the custody record or in the interview record for action taken whilst an interview record is being kept, with a brief reference to this effect in the custody record.

12.12 Any decision to delay a break in an interview must be recorded, with reasons, in the interview record.

12.13 All written statements made at police stations under caution shall be written on forms provided for the purpose.

12.14 All written statements made under caution shall be taken in accordance with *Annex D*. Before a person makes a written statement under caution at a police station they shall be reminded about the right to legal advice. [See *Note 12A*]

Notes for guidance

12A *It is not normally necessary to ask for a written statement if the interview was recorded* **A–79** *in writing and the record signed in accordance with paragraph 11.11 or audibly or visually recorded in accordance with Code E or F. Statements under caution should normally be taken in these circumstances only at the person's express wish. A person may however be asked if they want to make such a statement.*

12B *Meal breaks should normally last at least 15 minutes and shorter breaks after two hours should last at least 15 minutes. If the interviewer delays a break in accordance with paragraph 12.8 and prolongs the interview, a longer break should be provided. If there is a short interview, and another short interview is contemplated, the length of the break may be reduced if there are reasonable grounds to believe this is necessary to avoid any of the consequences in paragraph 12.8(i) to (iii).*

13 INTERPRETERS

(a) General

13.1 Chief officers are responsible for making sure appropriate arrangements are in place **A–80** for provision of suitably qualified interpreters for people who:
- are deaf;
- do not understand English.

Whenever possible, interpreters should be drawn from the National Register of Public Service Interpreters (NRPSI) or the Council for the Advancement of Communication with Deaf People (CADCP) Directory of British Sign Language/English Interpreters.

(b) Foreign languages

13.2 Unless *paragraphs 11.1, 11.18 to 11.20* apply, a person must not be interviewed in the absence of a person capable of interpreting if:
- (a) they have difficulty understanding English;
- (b) the interviewer cannot speak the person's own language;
- (c) the person wants an interpreter present.

13.3 The interviewer shall make sure the interpreter makes a note of the interview at the time in the person's language for use in the event of the interpreter being called to give evidence, and certifies its accuracy. The interviewer should allow sufficient time for the interpreter to note each question and answer after each is put, given and interpreted. The person should be allowed to read the record or have it read to them and sign it as correct or indicate the respects in which they consider it inaccurate. If the interview is audibly recorded or visually recorded, the arrangements in Code E or F apply.

13.4 In the case of a person making a statement to a police officer or other police staff other than in English:
- (a) the interpreter shall record the statement in the language it is made;
- (b) the person shall be invited to sign it;
- (c) an official English translation shall be made in due course.

(c) Deaf people and people with speech difficulties

13.5 If a person appears to be deaf or there is doubt about their hearing or speaking abil- **A–81** ity, they must not be interviewed in the absence of an interpreter unless they agree in writing to being interviewed without one or *paragraphs 11.1, 11.18 to 11.20* apply.

13.6 An interpreter should also be called if a juvenile is interviewed and the parent or

Appendices

guardian present as the appropriate adult appears to be deaf or there is doubt about their hearing or speaking ability, unless they agree in writing to the interview proceeding without one or *paragraphs 11.1, 11.18 to 11.20* apply.

13.7 The interviewer shall make sure the interpreter is allowed to read the interview record and certify its accuracy in the event of the interpreter being called to give evidence. If the interview is audibly recorded or visually recorded, the arrangements in Code E or F apply.

(d) Additional rules for detained persons

13.8 All reasonable attempts should be made to make the detainee understand that interpreters will be provided at public expense.

13.9 If *paragraph 6.1* applies and the detainee cannot communicate with the solicitor because of language, hearing or speech difficulties, an interpreter must be called. The interpreter may not be a police officer or any other police staff when interpretation is needed for the purposes of obtaining legal advice. In all other cases a police officer or other police staff may only interpret if the detainee and the appropriate adult, if applicable, give their agreement in writing or if the interview is audibly recorded or visually recorded as in Code E or F.

13.10 When the custody officer cannot establish effective communication with a person charged with an offence who appears deaf or there is doubt about their ability to hear, speak or to understand English, arrangements must be made as soon as practicable for an interpreter to explain the offence and any other information given by the custody officer.

(e) Documentation

13.11 Action taken to call an interpreter under this section and any agreement to be interviewed in the absence of an interpreter must be recorded.

14 QUESTIONING—SPECIAL RESTRICTIONS

A–82　　14.1 If a person is arrested by one police force on behalf of another and the lawful period of detention in respect of that offence has not yet commenced in accordance with *PACE*, section 41 no questions may be put to them about the offence while they are in transit between the forces except to clarify any voluntary statement they make.

14.2 If a person is in police detention at a hospital they may not be questioned without the agreement of a responsible doctor. [See *Note 14A*]

Note for guidance

A–83　　14A *If questioning takes place at a hospital under paragraph 14.2, or on the way to or from a hospital, the period of questioning concerned counts towards the total period of detention permitted.*

15 REVIEWS AND EXTENSIONS OF DETENTION

(a) Persons detained under PACE

A–84　　15.1 The review officer is responsible under *PACE*, section 40 for periodically determining if a person's detention, before or after charge, continues to be necessary. This requirement continues throughout the detention period and except as in *paragraph 15.10*, the review officer must be present at the police station holding the detainee. [See *Notes 15A* and *15B*]

15.2 Under *PACE*, section 42, an officer of superintendent rank or above who is responsible for the station holding the detainee may give authority any time after the second review to extend the maximum period the person may be detained without charge by up to 12 hours. Further detention without charge may be authorised only by a magistrates' court in accordance with *PACE*, sections 43 and 44. [See *Notes 15C, 15D* and *15E*]

15.2A Section 42(1) of PACE as amended extends the maximum period of detention for indictable offences from 24 hours to 36 hours. Detaining a juvenile or mentally vulnerable person for longer than 24 hours will be dependent on the circumstances of the case and with regard to the person's:

  (a) special vulnerability;
  (b) the legal obligation to provide an opportunity for representations to be made prior to a decision about extending detention;

(c) the need to consult and consider the views of any appropriate adult; and

(d) any alternatives to police custody.

15.3 Before deciding whether to authorise continued detention the officer responsible under *paragraphs 15.1* or *15.2* shall give an opportunity to make representations about the detention to:

(a) the detainee, unless in the case of a review as in *paragraph 15.1*, the detainee is asleep;

(b) the detainee's solicitor if available at the time; and

(c) the appropriate adult if available at the time.

15.3A Other people having an interest in the detainee's welfare may also make representations at the authorising officer's discretion.

15.3B Subject to *paragraph 15.10*, the representations may be made orally in person or by telephone or in writing. The authorising officer may, however, refuse to hear oral representations from the detainee if the officer considers them unfit to make representations because of their condition or behaviour. [See *Note 15C*]

15.3C The decision on whether the review takes place in person or by telephone or by video conferencing [see Note 15G] is a matter for the review officer. In determining the form the review may take, the review officer must always take full account of the needs of the person in custody. The benefits of carrying out a review in person should always be considered, based on the individual circumstances of each case with specific additional consideration if the person is:

(a) a juvenile (and the age of the juvenile); or

(b) mentally vulnerable; or

(c) has been subject to medical attention for other than routine minor ailments; or

(d) there are presentational or community issues around the person's detention.

15.4 Before conducting a review or determining whether to extend the maximum period **A–85** of detention without charge, the officer responsible must make sure the detainee is reminded of their entitlement to free legal advice, see *paragraph 6.5*, unless in the case of a review the person is asleep.

15.5 If, after considering any representations, the officer decides to keep the detainee in detention or extend the maximum period they may be detained without charge, any comment made by the detainee shall be recorded. If applicable, the officer responsible under *paragraph 15.1* or *15.2* shall be informed of the comment as soon as practicable. See also *paragraphs 11.4* and *11.13*

15.6 No officer shall put specific questions to the detainee:

● regarding their involvement in any offence; or

● in respect of any comments they may make:

— when given the opportunity to make representations; or

— in response to a decision to keep them in detention or extend the maximum period of detention.

Such an exchange could constitute an interview as in *paragraph 11.1A* and would be subject to the associated safeguards in *section 11* and, in respect of a person who has been charged, *paragraph 16.5*. See also *paragraph 11.13*

15.7 A detainee who is asleep at a review, see *paragraph 15.1*. and whose continued detention is authorised must be informed about the decision and reason as soon as practicable after waking.

15.8 Not used   **A–86**

(b) Telephone review of detention

15.9 *PACE*, section 40A provides that the officer responsible under section 40 for reviewing the detention of a person who has not been charged, need not attend the police station holding the detainee and may carry out the review by telephone.

15.9A *PACE*, section 45A(2) provides that the officer responsible under section 40 for reviewing the detention of a person who has not been charged, need not attend the police station holding the detainee and may carry out the review by video conferencing facilities. [See *Note 15G*]

15.9B A telephone review is not permitted where facilities for review by video conferencing exist and it is practicable to use them.

15.9C The review officer can decide at any stage that a telephone review or review by video conferencing should be terminated and that the review will be conducted in person. The reasons for doing so should be noted in the custody record.

[See *Note 15F*]

15.10 When a telephone review is carried out, an officer at the station holding the detainee shall be required by the review officer to fulfil that officer's obligations under *PACE* section 40 or this Code by:

(a) making any record connected with the review in the detainee's custody record;

(b) if applicable, making a record in (*a*) in the presence of the detainee; and

(c) giving the detainee information about the review.

15.11 When a telephone review is carried out, the requirement in *paragraph 15.3* will be satisfied:

(a) if facilities exist for the immediate transmission of written representations to the review officer, e.g. fax or email message, by giving the detainee an opportunity to make representations:

(i) orally by telephone; or

(ii) in writing using those facilities; and

(b) in all other cases, by giving the detainee an opportunity to make their representations orally by telephone.

(c) Documentation

15.12 It is the officer's responsibility to make sure all reminders given under *paragraph 15.4* are noted in the custody record.

15.13 The grounds for, and extent of, any delay in conducting a review shall be recorded.

15.14 When a telephone review is carried out, a record shall be made of:

(a) the reason the review officer did not attend the station holding the detainee;

(b) the place the review officer was;

(c) the method representations, oral or written, were made to the review officer, see *paragraph 15.11*.

15.15 Any written representations shall be retained.

15.16 A record shall be made as soon as practicable about the outcome of each review or determination whether to extend the maximum detention period without charge or an application for a warrant of further detention or its extension. If *paragraph 15.7* applies, a record shall also be made of when the person was informed and by whom. If an authorisation is given under *PACE*, section 42, the record shall state the number of hours and minutes by which the detention period is extended or further extended. If a warrant for further detention, or extension, is granted under section 43 or 44, the record shall state the detention period authorised by the warrant and the date and time it was granted.

Notes for guidance

15A *Review officer for the purposes of*:

• *PACE, sections 40 and 40A means, in the case of a person arrested but not charged, an officer of at least inspector rank not directly involved in the investigation and, if a person has been arrested and charged, the custody officer;*

15B *The detention of persons in police custody not subject to the statutory review requirement in paragraph 15.1 should still be reviewed periodically as a matter of good practice. Such reviews can be carried out by an officer of the rank of sergeant or above. The purpose of such reviews is to check the particular power under which a detainee is held continues to apply, any associated conditions are complied with and to make sure appropriate action is taken to deal with any changes. This includes the detainee's prompt release when the power no longer applies, or their transfer if the power requires the detainee be taken elsewhere as soon as the necessary arrangements are made. Examples include persons:*

(a) *arrested on warrant because they failed to answer bail to appear at court;*

(b) *arrested under the Bail Act 1976, section 7(3) for breaching a condition of bail granted after charge;*

(c) *in police custody for specific purposes and periods under the Crime (Sentences) Act 1997, Schedule 1;*

(d) *convicted, or remand prisoners, held in police stations on behalf of the Prison Service under the Imprisonment (Temporary Provisions) Act 1980, section 6;*

(e) *being detained to prevent them causing a breach of the peace;*

(f) *detained at police stations on behalf of the Immigration Service;*

(g) *detained by order of a magistrates' court under the Criminal Justice Act 1988, section 152 (as amended by the Drugs Act 2005, section 8) to facilitate the recovery of evidence after being charged with drug possession or drug trafficking and suspected of having swallowed drugs.*

The detention of persons remanded into police detention by order of a court under the Magistrates' Courts Act 1980, section 128 is subject to a statutory requirement to review that detention. This is to make sure the detainee is taken back to court no later than the end of the period authorised by the court or when the need for their detention by police ceases, whichever is the sooner.

15C *In the case of a review of detention, but not an extension, the detainee need not be woken for the review. However, if the detainee is likely to be asleep, e.g. during a period of rest allowed as in paragraph 12.2, at the latest time a review or authorisation to extend detention may take place, the officer should, if the legal obligations and time constraints permit, bring forward the procedure to allow the detainee to make representations. A detainee not asleep during the review must be present when the grounds for their continued detention are recorded and must at the same time be informed of those grounds unless the review officer considers the person is incapable of understanding what is said, violent or likely to become violent or in urgent need of medical attention.*

15D *An application to a Magistrates' Court under PACE, sections 43 or 44 for a warrant of further detention or its extension should be made between 10am and 9pm, and if possible during normal court hours. It will not usually be practicable to arrange for a court to sit specially outside the hours of 10am to 9pm. If it appears a special sitting may be needed outside normal court hours but between 10am and 9pm, the clerk to the justices should be given notice and informed of this possibility, while the court is sitting if possible.*

15E *In paragraph 15.2, the officer responsible for the station holding the detainee includes a superintendent or above who, in accordance with their force operational policy or police regulations, is given that responsibility on a temporary basis whilst the appointed long-term holder is off duty or otherwise unavailable.*

15F *The provisions of PACE, section 40A allowing telephone reviews do not apply to reviews of detention after charge by the custody officer or to reviews under the Terrorism Act 2000, Schedule 8, Part II in terrorism cases. When video conferencing is not required, they allow the use of a telephone to carry out a review of detention before charge. The procedure under PACE, section 42 must be done in person.*

15G *The use of video conferencing facilities for decisions about detention under section 45A of PACE is subject to the introduction of regulations by the Secretary of State.*

16 CHARGING DETAINED PERSONS

(a) Action

16.1 When the officer in charge of the investigation reasonably believes there is sufficient **A–88** evidence to provide a realistic prospect of conviction for the offence (*see paragraph 11.6*), they shall without delay, and subject to the following qualification, inform the custody officer who will be responsible for considering whether the detainee should be charged. *See Notes 11B and 16A.* When a person is detained in respect of more than one offence it is permissible to delay informing the custody officer until the above conditions are satisfied in respect of all the offences, but *see paragraph 11.6.* If the detainee is a juvenile, mentally disordered or otherwise mentally vulnerable, any resulting action shall be taken in the presence of the appropriate adult if they are present at the time. [See *Notes 16B and 16C*]

16.1A Where guidance issued by the Director of Public Prosecutions under section 37A is in force the custody officer must comply with that Guidance in deciding how to act in dealing with the detainee. [See *Notes 16AA and 16AB*]

16.1B Where in compliance with the DPP's Guidance the custody officer decides that the case should be immediately referred to the CPS to make the charging decision, consultation should take place with a Crown Prosecutor as soon as is reasonably practicable. Where the Crown Prosecutor is unable to make the charging decision on the information available at that time, the detainee may be released without charge and on bail (with conditions if necessary) under section 37(7)(a). In such circumstances, the detainee should be informed that they are being released to enable the Director of Public Prosecutions to make a decision under section 37B.

16.2 When a detainee is charged with or informed they may be prosecuted for an offence, see *Note 16B*, they shall, unless the restriction on drawing adverse inferences from silence applies, see *Annex C*, be cautioned as follows:

'*You do not have to say anything. But it may harm your defence if you do not mention now something which you later rely on in court. Anything you do say may be given in evidence.*'

Annex C. paragraph 2 sets out the alternative terms of the caution to be used when the restriction on drawing adverse inferences from silence applies.

16.3 When a detainee is charged they shall be given a written notice showing particulars of the offence and, subject to *paragraph 2.6A*, the officer's name and the case reference number. As far as possible the particulars of the charge shall be stated in simple terms, but they shall also show the precise offence in law with which the detainee is charged. The notice shall begin:

'*You are charged with the offence(s) shown below.*' Followed by the caution.

If the detainee is a juvenile, mentally disordered or otherwise mentally vulnerable, the notice should be given to the appropriate adult.

16.4 If, after a detainee has been charged with or informed they may be prosecuted for an offence, an officer wants to tell them about any written statement or interview with another person relating to such an offence, the detainee shall either be handed a true copy of the written statement or the content of the interview record brought to their attention. Nothing shall be done to invite any reply or comment except to:

    (a) caution the detainee. '*You do not have to say anything but anything you do say may be given in evidence.*'; and

    (b) remind the detainee about their right to legal advice.

16.4A If the detainee:

        ● cannot read, the document may be read to them

        ● is a juvenile, mentally disordered or otherwise mentally vulnerable, the appropriate adult shall also be given a copy, or the interview record shall be brought to their attention

A–89   16.5 A detainee may not be interviewed about an offence after they have been charged with, or informed they may be prosecuted for it, unless the interview is necessary:

        ● to prevent or minimise harm or loss to some other person, or the public

        ● to clear up an ambiguity in a previous answer or statement

        ● in the interests of justice for the detainee to have put to them, and have an opportunity to comment on, information concerning the offence which has come to light since they were charged or informed they might be prosecuted

Before any such interview, the interviewer shall:

    (a) caution the detainee. '*You do not have to say anything, but anything you do say may be given in evidence.*';

    (b) remind the detainee about their right to legal advice.

[See *Note 16B*]

16.6 The provisions of *paragraphs 16.2* to *16.5* must be complied with in the appropriate adult's presence if they are already at the police station. If they are not at the police station then these provisions must be complied with again in their presence when they arrive unless the detainee has been released.

[See *Note 16C*]

16.7 When a juvenile is charged with an offence and the custody officer authorises their continued detention after charge, the custody officer must try to make arrangements for the juvenile to be taken into the care of a local authority to be detained pending appearance in court unless the custody officer certifies it is impracticable to do so or, in the case of a juvenile of at least 12 years old, no secure accommodation is available and there is a risk to the public of serious harm from that juvenile, in accordance with PACE, section 38(6). [See *Note 16D*]

(b) Documentation

16.8 A record shall be made of anything a detainee says when charged.

16.9 Any questions put in an interview after charge and answers given relating to the offence shall be recorded in full during the interview on forms for that purpose and the record signed by the detainee or, if they refuse, by the interviewer and any third parties present. If the questions are audibly recorded or visually recorded the arrangements in Code E or F apply.

16.10 If it is not practicable to make arrangements for a juvenile's transfer into local authority care as in *paragraph 16.7*, the custody officer must record the reasons and complete a certificate to be produced before the court with the juvenile. [See *Note 16D*]

Notes for guidance

16A *The custody officer must take into account alternatives to prosecution under the Crime* **A–90** *and Disorder Act 1998, reprimands and warning applicable to persons under 18, and in national guidance on the cautioning of offenders, for persons aged 18 and over.*

16AA *When a person is arrested under the provisions of the Criminal Justice Act 2003 which allow a person to be re-tried after being acquitted of a serious offence which is a qualifying offence specified in Schedule 5 to that Act and not precluded from further prosecution by virtue of section 75(3) of that Act the detention provisions of PACE are modified and make an officer of the rank of superintendent or above who has not been directly involved in the investigation responsible for determining whether the evidence is sufficient to charge.*

16AB *Where Guidance issued by the Director of Public Prosecutions under section 37B is in force, a custody officer who determines in accordance with that Guidance that there is sufficient evidence to charge the detainee, may detain that person for no longer than is reasonably necessary to decide how that person is to be dealt with under PACE, section 37(7)(a) to (d), including, where appropriate, consultation with the Duty Prosecutor. The period is subject to the maximum period of detention before charge determined by PACE, sections 41 to 44. Where in accordance with the Guidance the case is referred to the CPS for decision, the custody officer should ensure that an officer involved in the investigation sends to the CPS such information as is specified in the Guidance.*

16B *The giving of a warning or the service of the Notice of Intended Prosecution required by the Road Traffic Offenders Act 1988, section 1 does not amount to informing a detainee they may be prosecuted for an offence and so does not preclude further questioning in relation to that offence.*

16C *There is no power under PACE to detain a person and delay action under paragraphs 16.2 to 16.5 solely to await the arrival of the appropriate adult. After charge, bail cannot be refused, or release on bail delayed, simply because an appropriate adult is not available, unless the absence of that adult provides the custody officer with the necessary grounds to authorise detention after charge under PACE, section 38.*

16D *Except as in paragraph 16.7. neither a juvenile's behaviour nor the nature of the offence provides grounds for the custody officer to decide it is impracticable to arrange the juvenile's transfer to local authority care. Similarly, the lack of secure local authority accommodation does not make it impracticable to transfer the juvenile. The availability of secure accommodation is only a factor in relation to a juvenile aged 12 or over when the local authority accommodation would not be adequate to protect the public from serious harm from them. The obligation to transfer a juvenile to local authority accommodation applies as much to a juvenile charged during the daytime as to a juvenile to be held overnight, subject to a requirement to bring the juvenile before a court under PACE, section 46.*

17 TESTING PERSONS FOR THE PRESENCE OF SPECIFIED CLASS A DRUGS

(a) Action

17.1 This section of Code C applies only in selected police stations in police areas where **A–91** the provisions for drug testing under section 63B of PACE (as amended by section 5 of the *Criminal Justice Act* 2003 and section 7 of the *Drugs Act* 2005) are in force and in respect of which the Secretary of State has given a notification to the relevant chief officer of police that arrangements for the taking of samples have been made. Such a notification will cover either a police area as a whole or particular stations within a police area. The notification indicates whether the testing applies to those arrested or charged or under the age of 18 as the case may be and testing can only take place in respect of the persons so indicated in the notification. Testing cannot be carried out unless the relevant notification has been given and has not been withdrawn. [See *Note 17F*]

17.2 A sample of urine or a non-intimate sample may be taken from a person in police detention for the purpose of ascertaining whether he has any specified Class A drug in his body only where they have been brought before the custody officer and:

    (a) either the arrest condition, see *paragraph 17.3*, or the charge condition see *paragraph 17.4*, is met;

    (b) the age condition see *paragraph 17.5*, is met;

    (c) the notification condition is met in relation to the arrest condition, the charge condition, or the age condition, as the case may be. (Testing on charge and/or arrest must be specifically provided for in the notification for the power to apply. In addition, the fact that testing of under 18s is authorised must be expressly provided for in the notification before the power to test such persons applies.). See *paragraph 17.1*; and

    (d) a police officer has requested the person concerned to give the sample (the request condition).

17.3 The arrest condition is met where the detainee:

    (a) has been arrested for a trigger offence, see *Note 17E*, but not charged with that offence; or

    (b) has been arrested for any other offence but not charged with that offence and a police officer of inspector rank or above, who has reasonable grounds for suspecting that their misuse of any specified Class A drug caused or contributed to the offence, has authorised the sample to be taken.

17.4 The charge condition is met where the detainee:

    (a) has been charged with a trigger offence, or

    (b) has been charged with any other offence and a police officer of inspector rank or above. who has reasonable grounds for suspecting that the detainee's misuse of any specified Class A drug caused or contributed to the offence, has authorised the sample to be taken.

17.5 The age condition is met where:

    (a) in the case of a detainee who has been arrested but not charged as in *paragraph 17.3*, they are aged 18 or over;

    (b) in the case of a detainee who has been charged as in *paragraph 17.4*, they are aged 14 or over.

17.6 Before requesting a sample from the person concerned, an officer must:

    (a) inform them that the purpose of taking the sample is for drug testing under PACE. This is to ascertain whether they have a specified Class A drug present in their body;

    (b) warn them that if. when so requested, they fail without good cause to provide a sample they may be liable to prosecution;

    (c) where the taking of the sample has been authorised by an inspector or above in accordance with *paragraph 17.3(b) or 17.4(b)* above, inform them that the authorisation has been given and the grounds for giving it;

    (d) remind them of the following rights, which may be exercised at any stage during the period in custody:

        (i) the right to have someone informed of their arrest [see *section 5*];

        (ii) the right to consult privately with a solicitor and that free independent legal advice is available [see section 6]; and

        (iii) the right to consult these Codes of Practice [see section 3].

17.7 In the case of a person who has not attained the age of 17:

    (a) the making of the request for a sample under *paragraph 17.2(d)* above;

    (b) the giving of the warning and the information under *paragraph 17.6* above; and

    (c) the taking of the sample,

may not take place except in the presence of an appropriate adult. [See *Note 17G*]

17.8 Authorisation by an officer of the rank of inspector or above within *paragraph 17.3(b) or 17.4(b)* may be given orally or in writing but, if it is given orally, it must be confirmed in writing as soon as practicable.

17.9 If a sample is taken from a detainee who has been arrested for an offence but not charged with that offence as in *paragraph 17.3*, no further sample may be taken during the same continuous period of detention. If during that same period the charge condition is also met in respect of that detainee, the sample which has been taken shall be treated as being taken by virtue of the charge condition, see *paragraph 17.4*, being met.

17.10 A detainee from whom a sample may be taken may be detained for up to six hours from the time of charge if the custody officer reasonably believes the detention is necessary to enable a sample to be taken. Where the arrest condition is met, a detainee whom the custody officer has decided to release on bail without charge may continue to be detained, but not beyond 24 hours from the relevant time (as defined in section 41(2) of PACE). to enable a sample to be taken.

17.11 A detainee in respect of whom the arrest condition is met, but not the charge condition. see *paragraphs 17.3* and *17.4*, and whose release would be required before a sample can be taken had they not continued to be detained as a result of being arrested for a further offence which does not satisfy the arrest condition, may have a sample taken at any time within 24 hours after the arrest for the offence that satisfies the arrest condition.

(b) Documentation

17.12 The following must be recorded in the custody record: **A–92**

    (a) if a sample is taken following authorisation by an officer of the rank of inspector or above, the authorisation and the grounds for suspicion;

    (b) the giving of a warning of the consequences of failure to provide a sample;

    (c) the time at which the sample was given; and

    (d) the time of charge or, where the arrest condition is being relied upon, the time of arrest and, where applicable, the fact that a sample taken after arrest but before charge is to be treated as being taken by virtue of the charge condition, where that is met in the same period of continuous detention. See *paragraph 17.9*

(c) General

17.13 A sample may only be taken by a prescribed person. [See *Note 17C*]   **A–93**

17.14 Force may not be used to take any sample for the purpose of drug testing.

17.15 The terms "Class A drug" and "misuse" have the same meanings as in the *Misuse of Drugs Act* 1971. "Specified" (in relation to a Class A drug) and "trigger offence" have the same meanings as in Part III of the *Criminal Justice and Court Services Act* 2000.

17.16 Any sample taken:

    (a) may not be used for any purpose other than to ascertain whether the person concerned has a specified Class A drug present in his body; and

    (b) must be retained until the person concerned has made their first appearance before the court.

(d) Assessment of misuse of drugs

17.17 Under the provisions of Part 3 of the *Drugs Act* 2005, where a detainee has tested positive for a specified Class A drug under section 63B of PACE a police officer may, at any time before the person's release from the police station, impose a requirement for them to attend an initial assessment of their drug misuse by a suitably qualified person and to remain for its duration. The requirement may only be imposed on a person if:

    (a) they have reached the age of 18

    (b) notification has been given by the Secretary of State to the relevant chief officer of police that arrangements for conducting initial assessments have been made for those from whom samples for testing have been taken at the police station where the detainee is in custody.

17.18 When imposing a requirement to attend an initial assessment the police officer must:

    (a) inform the person of the time and place at which the initial assessment is to take place;

    (b) explain that this information will be confirmed in writing; and

    (c) warn the person that he may be liable to prosecution if he fails without good cause to attend the initial assessment and remain for it's duration.

17.19 Where a police officer has imposed a requirement to attend an initial assessment in accordance with *paragraph 17.17*, he must, before the person is released from detention, give the person notice in writing which:

    (a) confirms that he is required to attend and remain for the duration of an initial assessment; and

    (b) confirms the information and repeats the warning referred to in *paragraph 17.18*.

17.20 The following must be recorded in the custody record:

    (a) that the requirement to attend an initial assessment has been imposed; and

    (b) the information, explanation, warning and notice given in accordance with *paragraphs 17.17* and *17.19*.

17.21 Where a notice is given in accordance with *paragraph 17.19*, a police officer can give the person a further notice in writing which informs the person of any change to the time or place at which the initial assessment is to take place and which repeats the warning referred to in *paragraph 17.18(c)*.

17.22 Part 3 of the *Drugs Act* 2005 also requires police officers to have regard to any guidance issued by the Secretary of State in respect of the assessment provisions.

Notes for guidance

A–94   17A *When warning a person who is asked to provide a urine or non-intimate sample in accordance with paragraph 17.6(b), the following form of words may be used:*

"You do not have to provide a sample, but I must warn you that if you fail or refuse without good cause to do so, you will commit an offence for which you may be imprisoned, or fined, or both".

17B *A sample has to be sufficient and suitable. A sufficient sample is sufficient in quantity and quality to enable drug-testing analysis to take place. A suitable sample is one which by its nature, is suitable for a particular form of drug analysis.*

17C *A prescribed person in paragraph 17.13 is one who is prescribed in regulations made by the Secretary of State under section 63B(6) of the Police and Criminal Evidence Act 1984. [The regulations are currently contained in regulation SI 2001 No. 2645, the Police and Criminal Evidence Act 1984 (Drug Testing Persons in Police Detention) (Prescribed Persons) Regulations 2001.]*

17D *The retention of the sample in paragraph 17.16(b) allows for the sample to be sent for confirmatory testing and analysis if the detainee disputes the test. But such samples, and the information derived from them, may not be subsequently used in the investigation of any offence or in evidence against the persons from whom they were taken.*

17E *Trigger offences are:*

    1. *Offences under the following provisions of the Theft Act 1968:*

section 1	*(theft)*
section 8	*(robbery)*
section 9	*(burglary)*
section 10	*(aggravated burglary)*
section 12	*(taking a motor vehicle or other conveyance without authority)*
section 12A	*(aggravated vehicle-taking)*
section 15	*(obtaining property by deception)*
section 22	*(handling stolen goods)*
section 25	*(going equipped for stealing etc.)*

    2. Offences under the following provisions of the Misuse of Drugs Act 1971, if committed in respect of a specified Class A drug:

section 4	*(restriction on production and supply of controlled drugs)*
section 5(2)	*(possession of a controlled drug)*
section 5(3)	*(possession of a controlled drug with intent to supply)*

    3. *An offence under section 1(1) of the Criminal Attempts Act 1981 if committed in respect of an offence under any of the following provisions of the Theft Act 1968:*

section 1	*(theft)*
section 8	*(robbery)*
section 9	*(burglary)*
section 15	*(obtaining property by deception)*
section 22	*(handling stolen goods)*

4. *Offences under the following provisions of the Vagrancy Act 1824:*

| *section 3* | *(begging)* |
| *section 4* | *(persistent begging)* |

17F *The power to take samples is subject to notification by the Secretary of State that appropriate arrangements for the taking of samples have been made for the police area as a whole or for the particular police station concerned for whichever of the following is specified in the notification:*

    (a) *persons in respect of whom the arrest condition is met;*

    (b) *persons in respect of whom the charge condition is met;*

    (c) *persons who have not attained the age of 18.*

Note: Notification is treated as having been given for the purposes of the charge condition in relation to a police area, if testing (on charge) under section 63B(2) of PACE was in force immediately before section 7 of the Drugs Act 2005 was brought into force; and for the purposes of the age condition, in relation to a police area or police station, if immediately before that day, notification that arrangements had been made for the taking of samples from persons under the age of 18 (those aged 14–17) had been given and had not been withdrawn.

17G *Appropriate adult in paragraph 17.7 means the person's:*

    (a) *parent or guardian or, if they are in the care of a local authority or voluntary organisation, a person representing that authority or organisation; or*

    (b) *a social worker of, in England, a local authority or, in Wales, a local authority social services department; or*

    (c) *if no person falling within (a) or (b) above is available, any responsible person aged 18 or over who is not a police officer or a person employed by the police.*

ANNEX A

Intimate and Strip Searches

A *Intimate search*

1. An intimate search consists of the physical examination of a person's body orifices other   **A–95**
than the mouth. The intrusive nature of such searches means the actual and potential risks
associated with intimate searches must never be underestimated.

(a) Action

2. Body orifices other than the mouth may be searched only: **A–96**

    (a) if authorised by an officer of inspector rank or above who has reasonable grounds
for believing that the person may have concealed on themselves:

        (i) anything which they could and might use to cause physical injury to themselves
or others at the station; or

        (ii) a Class A drug which they intended to supply to another or to export;
        and the officer has reasonable grounds for believing that an intimate
search is the only means of removing those items.; and

    (b) if the search is under *paragraph 2(a)(ii)* (a drug offence search), the detainee's appropriate consent has been given in writing.

2A. Before the search begins, a police officer, designated detention officer or staff custody
officer, must tell the detainee:

Appendices

    (a) that the authority to carry out the search has been given;

    (b) the grounds for giving the authorisation and for believing that the article cannot be removed without an intimate search.

2B. Before a detainee is asked to give appropriate consent to a search under *paragraph 2(a)(ii)* (a drug offence search) they must be warned that if they refuse without good cause their refusal may harm their case if it comes to trial, see Note A6. This warning may be given by a police officer or member of police staff. A detainee who is not legally represented must be reminded of their entitlement to have free legal advice, see *Code C, paragraph 6.5*, and the reminder noted in the custody record.

3. An intimate search may only be carried out by a registered medical practitioner or registered nurse, unless an officer of at least inspector rank considers this is not practicable and the search is to take place under *paragraph 2(a)(i)*, in which case a police officer may carry out the search. [See *Notes A1* to *A5*]

3A. Any proposal for a search under *paragraph 2(a)(i)* to be carried out by someone other than a registered medical practitioner or registered nurse must only be considered as a last resort and when the authorising officer is satisfied the risks associated with allowing the item to remain with the detainee outweigh the risks associated with removing it. [See *Notes A1* to *A5*]

4. An intimate search under:

        • *paragraph 2(a)(i)* may take place only at a hospital, surgery, other medical premises or police station

        • *paragraph 2(a)(ii)* may take place only at a hospital, surgery or other medical premises and must be carried out by a registered medical practitioner or a registered nurse

5. An intimate search at a police station of a juvenile or mentally disordered or otherwise mentally vulnerable person may take place only in the presence of an appropriate adult of the same sex, unless the detainee specifically requests a particular adult of the opposite sex who is readily available. In the case of a juvenile the search may take place in the absence of the appropriate adult only if the juvenile signifies in the presence of the appropriate adult they do not want the adult present during the search and the adult agrees. A record shall be made of the juvenile's decision and signed by the appropriate adult.

6. When an intimate search under *paragraph 2(a)(i)* is carried out by a police officer, the officer must be of the same sex as the detainee. A minimum of two people, other than the detainee, must be present during the search. Subject to *paragraph 5*, no person of the opposite sex who is not a medical practitioner or nurse shall be present, nor shall anyone whose presence is unnecessary. The search shall be conducted with proper regard to the sensitivity and vulnerability of the detainee.

(b) Documentation

7. In the case of an intimate search, the following shall be recorded as soon as practicable, in the detainee's custody record:

    (a) for searches under *paragraphs 2(a)(i) and (ii);*

        • the authorisation to carry out the search;

        • the grounds for giving the authorisation;

        • the grounds for believing the article could not be removed without an intimate search;

        • which parts of the detainee's body were searched;

        • who carried out the search;

        • who was present;

        • the result.

    (b) for searches under paragraph 2(a)(ii):

        • the giving of the warning required by paragraph 2B;

        • the fact that the appropriate consent was given or (as the case may be) refused, and if refused, the reason given for the refusal (if any).

8. If an intimate search is carried out by a police officer, the reason why it was impracticable for a registered medical practitioner or registered nurse to conduct it must be recorded.

B *Strip search*

9. A strip search is a search involving the removal of more than outer clothing. In this

Code, outer clothing includes shoes and socks.

(a) Action

10. A strip search may take place only if it is considered necessary to remove an article **A–99**
which a detainee would not be allowed to keep, and the officer reasonably considers the
detainee might have concealed such an article. Strip searches shall not be routinely carried
out if there is no reason to consider that articles are concealed.

The conduct of strip searches

11. When strip searches are conducted:
    (a) a police officer carrying out a strip search must be the same sex as the detainee;
    (b) the search shall take place in an area where the detainee cannot be seen by
        anyone who does not need to be present, nor by a member of the opposite sex
        except an appropriate adult who has been specifically requested by the detainee;
    (c) except in cases of urgency, where there is risk of serious harm to the detainee or
        to others, whenever a strip search involves exposure of intimate body parts, there
        must be at least two people present other than the detainee, and if the search is of
        a juvenile or mentally disordered or otherwise mentally vulnerable person, one of
        the people must be the appropriate adult. Except in urgent cases as above, a
        search of a juvenile may take place in the absence of the appropriate adult only if
        the juvenile signifies in the presence of the appropriate adult that they do not
        want the adult to be present during the search and the adult agrees. A record
        shall be made of the juvenile's decision and signed by the appropriate adult. The
        presence of more than two people, other than an appropriate adult, shall be
        permitted only in the most exceptional circumstances;
    (d) the search shall be conducted with proper regard to the sensitivity and vulner-
        ability of the detainee in these circumstances and every reasonable effort shall be
        made to secure the detainee's co-operation and minimise embarrassment. Detain-
        ees who are searched shall not normally be required to remove all their clothes at
        the same time, e.g. a person should be allowed to remove clothing above the waist
        and redress before removing further clothing;
    (e) if necessary to assist the search, the detainee may be required to hold their arms
        in the air or to stand with their legs apart and bend forward so a visual examina-
        tion may be made of the genital and anal areas provided no physical contact is
        made with any body orifice;
    (f) if articles are found, the detainee shall be asked to hand them over. If articles are
        found within any body orifice other than the mouth, and the detainee refuses to
        hand them over, their removal would constitute an intimate search, which must
        be carried out as in *Part A*;
    (g) a strip search shall be conducted as quickly as possible, and the detainee allowed to
        dress as soon as the procedure is complete.

(b) Documentation

12. A record shall be made on the custody record of a strip search including the reason it **A–100**
was considered necessary, those present and any result.

Notes for guidance

A1 *Before authorising any intimate search, the authorising officer must make every reason-* **A–101**
*able effort to persuade the detainee to hand the article over without a search. If the detainee
agrees, a registered medical practitioner or registered nurse should whenever possible be asked
to assess the risks involved and, if necessary, attend to assist the detainee.*

A2 *If the detainee does not agree to hand the article over without a search, the authorising
officer must carefully review all the relevant factors before authorising an intimate search. In
particular, the officer must consider whether the grounds for believing an article may be concealed are reasonable.*

A3 *If authority is given for a search under paragraph 2(a)(i), a registered medical
practitioner or registered nurse shall be consulted whenever possible. The presumption should be
that the search will be conducted by the registered medical practitioner or registered nurse and*

Appendices

the authorising officer must make every reasonable effort to persuade the detainee to allow the medical practitioner or nurse to conduct the search.

A4 *A constable should only be authorised to carry out a search as a last resort and when all other approaches have failed. In these circumstances, the authorising officer must be satisfied the detainee might use the article for one or more of the purposes in paragraph 2(a)(i) and the physical injury likely to be caused is sufficiently severe to justify authorising a constable to carry out the search.*

A5 *If an officer has any doubts whether to authorise an intimate search by a constable, the officer should seek advice from an officer of superintendent rank or above.*

A6 *In warning a detainee who is asked to consent to an intimate drug offence search, as in paragraph 2B, the following form of words may be used:*

"You do not have to allow yourself to be searched, but I must warn you that if you refuse without good cause, your refusal may harm your case if it comes to trial."

ANNEX B

Delay in Notifying Arrest or Allowing Access to Legal Advice

A *Persons detained under PACE*

A–102   1. The exercise of the rights in *Section 5* or *Section 6*, or both, may be delayed if the person is in police detention, as in *PACE,* section 118(2), in connection with an indictable offence, has not yet been charged with an offence and an officer of superintendent rank or above, or inspector rank or above only for the rights in Section 5, has reasonable grounds for believing their exercise will:

    (i) lead to:
- interference with, or harm to, evidence connected with an indictable offence; or
- interference with, or physical harm to, other people; or

    (ii) lead to alerting other people suspected of having committed an indictable offence but not yet arrested for it; or

    (iii) hinder the recovery of property obtained in consequence of the commission of such an offence.

2. These rights may also be delayed if the officer has reasonable grounds to believe that:

    (i) the person detained for an indictable offence has benefited from their criminal conduct (decided in accordance with Part 2 of the *Proceeds of Crime Act* 2002); and

    (ii) the recovery of the value of the property constituting that benefit will be hindered by the exercise of either right.

3. Authority to delay a detainee's right to consult privately with a solicitor may be given only if the authorising officer has reasonable grounds to believe the solicitor the detainee wants to consult will, inadvertently or otherwise, pass on a message from the detainee or act in some other way which will have any of the consequences specified under *paragraphs 1 or 2*. In these circumstances the detainee must be allowed to choose another solicitor. [See *Note B3*]

4. If the detainee wishes to see a solicitor, access to that solicitor may not be delayed on the grounds they might advise the detainee not to answer questions or the solicitor was initially asked to attend the police station by someone else. In the latter case the detainee must be told the solicitor has come to the police station at another person's request, and must be asked to sign the custody record to signify whether they want to see the solicitor.

5. The fact the grounds for delaying notification of arrest may be satisfied does not automatically mean the grounds for delaying access to legal advice will also be satisfied.

6. These rights may be delayed only for as long as grounds exist and in no case beyond 36 hours after the relevant time as in *PACE,* section 41. If the grounds cease to apply within this time, the detainee must, as soon as practicable, be asked if they want to exercise either right, the custody record must be noted accordingly, and action taken in accordance with the relevant section of the Code.

7. A detained person must be permitted to consult a solicitor for a reasonable time before

any court hearing.

B *Not used*

C *Documentation*

13. The grounds for action under this Annex shall be recorded and the detainee informed of them as soon as practicable.

14. Any reply given by a detainee under *paragraphs 6* or *11* must be recorded and the detainee asked to endorse the record in relation to whether they want to receive legal advice at this point.

D *Cautions and special warnings*

When a suspect detained at a police station is interviewed during any period for which access to legal advice has been delayed under this Annex, the court or jury may not draw adverse inferences from their silence.

Notes for guidance

B1 *Even if Annex B applies in the case of a juvenile, or a person who is mentally disordered* *or otherwise mentally vulnerable, action to inform the appropriate adult and the person responsible for a juvenile's welfare if that is a different person, must nevertheless be taken as in paragraph 3.13 and 3.15.*

B2 *In the case of Commonwealth citizens and foreign nationals, see Note 7A.*

B3 *A decision to delay access to a specific solicitor is likely to be a rare occurrence and only when it can be shown the suspect is capable of misleading that particular solicitor and there is more than a substantial risk that the suspect will succeed in causing information to be conveyed which will lead to one or more of the specified consequences.*

ANNEX C

Restriction on Drawing Adverse Inferences from Silence and Terms of the Caution when the Restriction Applies

(a) The restriction on drawing adverse inferences from silence

1. The *Criminal Justice and Public Order Act* 1994, sections 34, 36 and 37 as amended by the *Youth Justice and Criminal Evidence Act* 1999. section 58 describe the conditions under which adverse inferences may be drawn from a person's failure or refusal to say anything about their involvement in the offence when interviewed, after being charged or informed they may be prosecuted. These provisions are subject to an overriding restriction on the ability of a court or jury to draw adverse inferences from a person's silence. This restriction applies:

   (a) to any detainee at a police station, see *Note 10C* who, before being interviewed, see *section 11* or being charged or informed they may be prosecuted, see *section 16*, has:

       (i) asked for legal advice, see *section 6, paragraph 6.1;*

       (ii) not been allowed an opportunity to consult a solicitor, including the duty solicitor, as in this Code; and

       (iii) not changed their mind about wanting legal advice, see *section 6, paragraph 6.6(d).*

   Note the condition in (ii) will:

       — apply when a detainee who asked for legal advice is interviewed before speaking to a solicitor as in *section 6, paragraph 6.6(a)* or *(b).*

— not apply if the detained person declines to ask for the duty solicitor, see *section 6, paragraphs 6.6(c) and (d)*.

(b) to any person charged with, or informed they may be prosecuted for, an offence who:

    (i) has had brought to their notice a written statement made by another person or the contents of an interview with another person which relates to that offence, see *section 16, paragraph 16.4;*

    (ii) is interviewed about that offence see *section 16, paragraph 16.5;*

    (iii) maks a written statement about that offence, see *Annex D paragraphs 4* and *9.*

(b) Terms of the caution when the restriction applies

2. When a requirement to caution arises at a time when the restriction on drawing adverse inferences from silence applies, the caution shall be:

'You do not have to say anything, but anything you do say may be given in evidence.'

3. Whenever the restriction either begins to apply or ceases to apply after a caution has already been given, the person shall be re-cautioned in the appropriate terms. The changed position on drawing inferences and that the previous caution no longer applies shall also be explained to the detainee in ordinary language. [See *Note C2*]

    Notes for guidance

    C1 The restriction on drawing inferences from silence does not apply to a person who has not been detained and who therefore cannot be prevented from seeking legal advice if they want to, see paragraphs 10.2 and 3.15.

    C2 The following is suggested as a framework to help explain changes in the position on drawing adverse inferences if the restriction on drawing adverse inferences from silence:

    (a) begins to apply:

'The caution you were previously given no longer applies. This is because after that caution:

    (i) you asked to speak to a solicitor but have not yet been allowed an opportunity to speak to a solicitor. See paragraph 1(a); or

    (ii) you have been charged with/informed you may be prosecuted. See paragraph 1(b).

'This means that from now on, adverse inferences cannot be drawn at court and your defence will not be harmed just because you choose to say nothing. Please listen carefully to the caution I am about to give you because it will apply from now on. You will see that it does not say anything about your defence being harmed.'

    (b) ceases to apply before or at the time the person is charged or informed they may be prosecuted, see paragraph 1(a):

'The caution you were previously given no longer applies. This is because after that caution you have been allowed an opportunity to speak to a solicitor. Please listen carefully to the caution I am about to give you because it will apply from now on. It explains how your defence at court may be affected if you choose to say nothing.'

ANNEX D

Written Statements under Caution

A–106

(a) Written by a person under caution

1. A person shall always be invited to write down what they want to say.

2. A person who has not been charged with, or informed they may be prosecuted for, any offence to which the statement they want to write relates, shall:

    (a) unless the statement is made at a time when the restriction on drawing adverse inferences from silence applies, see Annex C, be asked to write out and sign the following before writing what they want to say:

'I make this statement of my own free will. I understand that I do not have to say anything

but that it may harm my defence if I do not mention when questioned something which I later rely on in court. This statement may be given in evidence.';

      (b) if the statement is made at a time when the restriction on drawing adverse inferences from silence applies, be asked to write out and sign the following before writing what they want to say:

'I make this statement of my own free will. I understand that I do not have to say anything. This statement may be given in evidence.'

3. When a person, on the occasion of being charged with or informed they may be prosecuted for any offence, asks to make a statement which relates to any such offence and wants to write it they shall:

      (a) unless the restriction on drawing adverse inferences from silence. see *Annex C*, applied when they were so charged or informed they may be prosecuted, be asked to write out and sign the following before writing what they want to say:

'I make this statement of my own free will. I understand that I do not have to say anything but that it may harm my defence if I do not mention when questioned something which I later rely on in court. This statement may be given in evidence.';

      (b) if the restriction on drawing adverse inferences from silence applied when they were so charged or informed they may be prosecuted, be asked to write out and sign the following before writing what they want to say:

'I make this statement of my own free will. I understand that I do not have to say anything. This statement may be given in evidence.'

4. When a person, who has already been charged with or informed they may be prosecuted for any offence, asks to make a statement which relates to any such offence and wants to write it they shall be asked to write out and sign the following before writing what they want to say:

'I make this statement of my own free will. I understand that I do not have to say anything. This statement may be given in evidence.'

5. Any person writing their own statement shall be allowed to do so without any prompting except a police officer or other police staff may indicate to them which matters are material or question any ambiguity in the statement.

(b) Written by a police officer or other police staff

6. If a person says they would like someone to write the statement for them, a police officer, or other police staff shall write the statement. **A–107**

7. If the person has not been charged with, or informed they may be prosecuted for, any offence to which the statement they want to make relates they shall, before starting, be asked to sign, or make their mark, to the following:

      (a) unless the statement is made at a time when the restriction on drawing adverse inferences from silence applies, see *Annex C*:

'I,...................., wish to make a statement. I want someone to write down what I say. I understand that I do not have to say anything but that it may harm my defence if I do not mention when questioned something which I later rely on in court. This statement may be given in evidence.';

      (b) if the statement is made at a time when the restriction on drawing adverse inferences from silence applies:

'I,...................., wish to make a statement. I want someone to write down what I say. I understand that I do not have to say anything. This statement may be given in evidence.'

8. If, on the occasion of being charged with or informed they may be prosecuted for any offence, the person asks to make a statement which relates to any such offence they shall before starting be asked to sign, or make their mark to, the following:

      (a) unless the restriction on drawing adverse inferences from silence applied, see *Annex C*. when they were so charged or informed they may be prosecuted.

'I,...................., wish to make a statement. I want someone to write down what I say. I understand that I do not have to say anything but that it may harm my defence if I do not mention when questioned something which I later rely on in court. This statement may be given in evidence.';

(b) if the restriction on drawing adverse inferences from silence applied when they were so charged or informed they may be prosecuted:

'I,....................., wish to make a statement. I want someone to write down what I say. I understand that I do not have to say anything. This statement may be given in evidence.'

9. If, having already been charged with or informed they may be prosecuted for any offence, a person asks to make a statement which relates to any such offence they shall before starting, be asked to sign, or make their mark to:

'I,....................., wish to make a statement. I want someone to write down what I say. I understand that I do not have to say anything. This statement may be given in evidence.'

10. The person writing the statement must take down the exact words spoken by the person making it and must not edit or paraphrase it. Any questions that are necessary. e.g. to make it more intelligible, and the answers given must be recorded at the same time on the statement form.

11. When the writing of a statement is finished the person making it shall be asked to read it and to make any corrections, alterations or additions they want. When they have finished reading they shall be asked to write and sign or make their mark on the following certificate at the end of the statement:

'I have read the above statement, and I have been able to correct, alter or add anything I wish. This statement is true. I have made it of my own free will.'

12. If the person making the statement cannot read, or refuses to read it, or to write the above mentioned certificate at the end of it or to sign it, the person taking the statement shall read it to them and ask them if they would like to correct, alter or add anything and to put their signature or make their mark at the end. The person taking the statement shall certify on the statement itself what has occurred.

ANNEX E

Summary of Provisions Relating to Mentally Disordered and Otherwise Mentally Vulnerable People

A–108 1. If an officer has any suspicion, or is told in good faith, that a person of any age may be mentally disordered or otherwise mentally vulnerable, or mentally incapable of understanding the significance of questions or their replies that person shall be treated as mentally disordered or otherwise mentally vulnerable for the purposes of this Code. See *paragraph 1.4*

2. In the case of a person who is mentally disordered or otherwise mentally vulnerable, 'the appropriate adult' means:

(a) a relative, guardian or other person responsible for their care or custody;

(b) someone experienced in dealing with mentally disordered or mentally vulnerable people but who is not a police officer or employed by the police;

(c) failing these, some other responsible adult aged 18 or over who is not a police officer or employed by the police.

See *paragraph 1.7(b) and Note 1D*

3. If the custody officer authorises the detention of a person who is mentally vulnerable or appears to be suffering from a mental disorder, the custody officer must as soon as practicable inform the appropriate adult of the grounds for detention and the person's whereabouts, and ask the adult to come to the police station to see them. If the appropriate adult:

● is already at the station when information is given as in *paragraphs 3.1* to *3.5* the information must be given in their presence

● is not at the station when the provisions of *paragraph 3.1* to *3.5* are complied with these provisions must be complied with again in their presence once they arrive.

See *paragraphs 3.15* to *3.17*

4. If the appropriate adult, having been informed of the right to legal advice, considers legal advice should be taken, the provisions of *section 6* apply as if the mentally disordered or otherwise mentally vulnerable person had requested access to legal advice. See *paragraph 3.19* and *Note E1.*

5. The custody officer must make sure a person receives appropriate clinical attention as soon as reasonably practicable if the person appears to be suffering from a mental disorder or in urgent cases immediately call the nearest health care professional or an ambulance. It is not intended these provisions delay the transfer of a detainee to a place of safety under the *Mental Health Act* 1983. section 136 if that is applicable. If an assessment under that Act is to take place at a police station, the custody officer must consider whether an appropriate health care professional should be called to conduct an initial clinical check on the detainee. See *paragraph 9.5* and *9.6*

6. It is imperative a mentally disordered or otherwise mentally vulnerable person detained under the *Mental Health Act* 1983, section 136 be assessed as soon as possible. If that assessment is to take place at the police station, an approved social worker and registered medical practitioner shall be called to the station as soon as possible in order to interview and examine the detainee. Once the detainee has been interviewed, examined and suitable arrangements been made for their treatment or care, they can no longer be detained under section 136. A detainee should be immediately discharged from detention if a registered medical practitioner having examined them, concludes they are not mentally disordered within the meaning of the Act. See *paragraph 3.16*

7. If a mentally disordered or otherwise mentally vulnerable person is cautioned in the absence of the appropriate adult, the caution must be repeated in the appropriate adult's presence. See *paragraph 10.12*

8. A mentally disordered or otherwise mentally vulnerable person must not be interviewed or asked to provide or sign a written statement in the absence of the appropriate adult unless the provisions of *paragraphs 11.1* or *11.18* to *11.20* apply. Questioning in these circumstances may not continue in the absence of the appropriate adult once sufficient information to avert the risk has been obtained. A record shall be made of the grounds for any decision to begin an interview in these circumstances. See *paragraphs 11.1, 11.15* and *11.18* to *11.20*

9. If the appropriate adult is present at an interview, they shall be informed they are not expected to act simply as an observer and the purposes of their presence are to:

- advise the interviewee
- observe whether or not the interview is being conducted properly and fairly
- facilitate communication with the interviewee

See *paragraph 11.17*

10. If the detention of a mentally disordered or otherwise mentally vulnerable person is **A–109** reviewed by a review officer or a superintendent, the appropriate adult must, if available at the time, be given an opportunity to make representations to the officer about the need for continuing detention. See *paragraph 15.3*

11. If the custody officer charges a mentally disordered or otherwise mentally vulnerable person with an offence or takes such other action as is appropriate when there is sufficient evidence for a prosecution this must be done in the presence of the appropriate adult. The written notice embodying any charge must be given to the appropriate adult. See *paragraphs 16.1* to *16.4A*

12. An intimate or strip search of a mentally disordered or otherwise mentally vulnerable person may take place only in the presence of the appropriate adult of the same sex, unless the detainee specifically requests the presence of a particular adult of the opposite sex. A strip search may take place in the absence of an appropriate adult only in cases of urgency when there is a risk of serious harm to the detainee or others. See *Annex A, paragraphs 5* and *11(c)*

13. Particular care must be taken when deciding whether to use any form of approved restraints on a mentally disordered or otherwise mentally vulnerable person in a locked cell. See *paragraph 8.2*

Notes for guidance

E1 *The purpose of the provision at paragraph 3.19 is to protect the rights of a mentally* **A–110** *disordered or otherwise mentally vulnerable detained person who does not understand the significance of what is said to them. If the detained person wants to exercise the right to legal advice, the appropriate action should be taken and not delayed until the appropriate adult arrives. A mentally disordered or otherwise mentally vulnerable detained person should always be given an opportunity, when an appropriate adult is called to the police station, to consult privately with a solicitor in the absence of the appropriate adult if they want.*

E2 *Although people who are mentally disordered or otherwise mentally vulnerable are often capable of providing reliable evidence, they may, without knowing or wanting to do so, be particularly prone in certain circumstances to provide information that may be unreliable, misleading or self-incriminating. Special care should always be taken when questioning such a person, and the appropriate adult should be involved if there is any doubt about a person's mental state or capacity. Because of the risk of unreliable evidence, it is important to obtain corroboration of any facts admitted whenever possible.*

E3 *Because of the risks referred to in Note E2, which the presence of the appropriate adult is intended to minimise, officers of superintendent rank or above should exercise their discretion to authorise the commencement of an interview in the appropriate adult's absence only in exceptional cases, if it is necessary to avert an immediate risk of serious harm. See paragraphs 11.1, 11.18 to 11.20*

ANNEX F

Countries with which Bilateral Consular Conventions or Agreements Requiring Notification of the Arrest and Detention of their Nationals are in Force as at 1 April 2003

A–111

Armenia	Kazakhstan
Austria	Macedonia
Azerbaijan	Mexico
Belarus	Moldova
Belgium	Mongolia
Bosnia-Herzegovina	Norway
Bulgaria	Poland
China•	Romania
Croatia	Russia
Cuba	Slovak Republic
Czech Republic	Slovenia
Denmark	Spain
Egypt	Sweden
France	Tajikistan
Georgia	Turkmenistan
German Federal Republic	Ukraine
Greece	USA
Hungary	Uzbekistan
Italy	Yugoslavia
Japan	

• Police are required to inform Chinese officials of arrest/detention in the Manchester consular district only. This comprises Derbyshire, Durham, Greater Manchester, Lancashire, Merseyside, North South and West Yorkshire, and Tyne and Wear.

ANNEX G

Fitness to be Interviewed

A–112   1. This Annex contains general guidance to help police officers and health care professionals assess whether a detainee might be at risk in an interview.

2. A detainee may be at risk in an interview if it is considered that:

   (a) conducting the interview could significantly harm the detainee's physical or mental state;

   (b) anything the detainee says in the interview about their involvement or suspected involvement in the offence about which they are being interviewed **might** be considered unreliable in subsequent court proceedings because of their physical or mental state.

3. In assessing whether the detainee should be interviewed, the following must be considered:

    (a) how the detainee's physical or mental state might affect their ability to understand the nature and purpose of the interview, to comprehend what is being asked and to appreciate the significance of any answers given and make rational decisions about whether they want to say anything;

    (b) the extent to which the detainee's replies may be affected by their physical or mental condition rather than representing a rational and accurate explanation of their involvement in the offence;

    (c) how the nature of the interview, which could include particularly probing questions, might affect the detainee.

4. It is essential health care professionals who are consulted consider the functional ability **A–113** of the detainee rather than simply relying on a medical diagnosis, e.g. it is possible for a person with severe mental illness to be fit for interview.

5. Health care professionals should advise on the need for an appropriate adult to be present, whether reassessment of the person's fitness for interview may be necessary if the interview lasts beyond a specified time, and whether a further specialist opinion may be required.

6. When health care professionals identify risks they should be asked to quantify the risks. They should inform the custody officer:

    • whether the person's condition:
    — is likely to improve
    — will require or be amenable to treatment; and
    • indicate how long it may take for such improvement to take effect

7. The role of the health care professional is to consider the risks and advise the custody officer of the outcome of that consideration. The health care professional's determination and any advice or recommendations should be made in writing and form part of the custody record.

8. Once the health care professional has provided that information, it is a matter for the custody officer to decide whether or not to allow the interview to go ahead and if the interview is to proceed, to determine what safeguards are needed. Nothing prevents safeguards being provided in addition to those required under the Code. An example might be to have an appropriate health care professional present during the interview, in addition to an appropriate adult, in order constantly to monitor the person's condition and how it is being affected by the interview.

ANNEX H

Detained Person: Observation List

1. If any detainee fails to meet any of the following criteria, an appropriate health care **A–114** professional or an ambulance must be called.

2. When assessing the level of rousability, consider:

    Rousability—can they be woken?
    • go into the cell
    • call their name
    • shake gently
    Response to questions—can they give appropriate answers to questions such as:
    • What's your name?
    • Where do you live?
    • Where do you think you are?
    Response to commands—can they respond appropriately to commands such as:
    • Open your eyes!
    • Lift one arm, now the other arm!

3. Remember to take into account the possibility or presence of other illnesses, injury, or mental condition, a person who is drowsy and smells of alcohol may also have the following:

- Diabetes
- Epilepsy
- Head injury
- Drug intoxication or overdose
- Stroke

ANNEX I

Not Used

A–115

ANNEX J

A–116 **Not Used**

ANNEX K

X-Rays and Ultrasound Scans

A–117

(a) Action

1. *PACE*, section 55A allows a person who has been arrested and is in police detention to have an X-ray taken of them or an ultrasound scan to be carried out on them (or both) if:

    (a) authorised by an officer of inspector rank or above who has reasonable grounds for believing that the detainee:

        (i) may have swallowed a Class A drug; and

        (ii) was in possession of that Class A drug with the intention of supplying it to another or to export; and

    (b) the detainee's appropriate consent has been given in writing.

2. Before an x-ray is taken or an ultrasound scan carried out, a police officer, designated detention officer or staff custody officer must tell the detainee:

    (a) that the authority has been given; and

    (b) the grounds for giving the authorisation.

3. Before a detainee is asked to give appropriate consent to an x ray or an ultrasound scan, they must be warned that if they refuse without good cause their refusal may harm their case if it comes to trial, see Notes K1 and K2. This warning may be given by a police officer or member of police staff. A detainee who is not legally represented must be reminded of their entitlement to have free legal advice, see *Code C, paragraph 6.5.* and the reminder noted in the custody record.

4. An x-ray may be taken, or an ultrasound scan may be carried out, only by a registered medical practitioner or registered nurse, and only at a hospital, surgery or other medical premises.

(b) Documentation

5. The following shall be recorded as soon as practicable in the detainee's custody record:

    (a) the authorisation to take the x-ray or carry out the ultrasound scan (or both);

    (b) the grounds for giving the authorisation;

    (c) the giving of the warning required by paragraph 3; and

    (d) the fact that the appropriate consent was given or (as the case may be) refused, and if refused, the reason given for the refusal (if any); and

    (e) if an x-ray is taken or an ultrasound scan carried out:
- where it was taken or carried out
- who took it or carried it out
- who was present
- the result

Paragraphs 1.4–1.7 of this Code apply and an appropriate adult should be present when consent is sought to any procedure under this Annex

Notes for guidance

K1 *If authority is given for an x-ray to be taken or an ultrasound scan to be carried out (or both), consideration should be given to asking a registered medical practitioner or registered nurse to explain to the detainee what is involved and to allay any concerns the detainee might have about the effect which taking an x-ray or carrying out an ultrasound scan might have on them. If appropriate consent is not given, evidence of the explanation may. If the case comes to trial, be relevant to determining whether the detainee had a good cause for refusing.*   **A–118**

K2 *In warning a detainee who is asked to consent to an X-ray being taken or an ultrasound scan being carried cut (or both), as in paragraph 3, the following form of words may be used:*

"You do not have to allow an x-ray of you to be taken or an ultrasound scan to be carried out on you, but I must warn you that if you refuse without good cause, your refusal may harm your case if it comes to trial."

Police and Criminal Evidence Act 1984

Code D

Code of Practice for the Identification of Persons by Police Officers

Commencement—Transitional Arrangements   **A–119**

This code has effect in relation to any identification procedure carried out after midnight on 31 December 2005

1 Introduction

1.1 This Code of Practice concerns the principal methods used by police to identify people in connection with the investigation of offences and the keeping of accurate and reliable criminal records.   **A–120**

1.2 Identification by witnesses arises, e.g., if the offender is seen committing the crime and a witness is given an opportunity to identify the suspect in a video identification, identification parade or similar procedure. The procedures are designed to:
- test the witness' ability to identify the person they saw on a previous occasion
- provide safeguards against mistaken identification.

While this Code concentrates on visual identification procedures, it does not preclude the police making use of aural identification procedures such as a "voice identification parade", where they judge that appropriate.

1.3 Identification by fingerprints applies when a person's fingerprints are taken to:
- compare with fingerprints found at the scene of a crime
- check and prove convictions
- help to ascertain a person's identity.

1.3A Identification using footwear impressions applies when a person's footwear impressions are taken to compare with impressions found at the scene of a crime.

1.4 Identification by body samples and impressions includes taking samples such as blood or hair to generate a DNA profile for comparison with material obtained from the scene of a crime, or a victim.

1.5 Taking photographs of arrested people applies to recording and checking identity and locating and tracing persons who: **A–121**

1485

- are wanted for offences
- fail to answer their bail.

1.6 Another method of identification involves searching and examining detained suspects to find, e.g., marks such as tattoos or scars which may help establish their identity or whether they have been involved in committing an offence.

1.7 The provisions of the *Police and Criminal Evidence Act* 1984 (PACE) and this Code are designed to make sure fingerprints, samples, impressions and photographs are taken, used and retained, and identification procedures carried out, only when justified and necessary for preventing, detecting or investigating crime. If these provisions are not observed, the application of the relevant procedures in particular cases may be open to question.

<h2 style="text-align:center">2 General</h2>

A–122   2.1 This Code must be readily available at all police stations for consultation by:
- police officers and police staff
- detained persons
- members of the public

2.2 The provisions of this Code:
- include the *Annexes*
- do not include the *Notes for guidance*.

2.3 Code C, paragraph 1.4, regarding a person who may be mentally disordered or otherwise mentally vulnerable and the *Notes for guidance* applicable to those provisions apply to this Code.

2.4 Code C, paragraph 1.5, regarding a person who appears to be under the age of 17 applies to this Code.

2.5 Code C, paragraph 1.6, regarding a person who appears blind, seriously visually impaired, deaf, unable to read or speak or has difficulty orally because of a speech impediment applies to this Code.

A–123   2.6 In this Code:
- 'appropriate adult' means the same as in Code C, paragraph 1.7
- 'solicitor' means the same as in Code C, paragraph 6.12

and the *Notes for guidance* applicable to those provisions apply to this Code.

2.7 References to custody officers include those performing the functions of custody officer, see *paragraph 1.9* of Code C.

2.8 When a record of any action requiring the authority of an officer of a specified rank is made under this Code, subject to *paragraph 2.18*, the officer's name and rank must be recorded.

2.9 When this Code requires the prior authority or agreement of an officer of at least inspector or superintendent rank, that authority may be given by a sergeant or chief inspector who has been authorised to perform the functions of the higher rank under PACE, section 107.

2.10 Subject to *paragraph 2.18*, all records must be timed and signed by the maker.

A–124   2.11 Records must be made in the custody record, unless otherwise specified. References to 'pocket book' include any official report book issued to police officers or police staff.

2.12 If any procedure in this Code requires a person's consent, the consent of a:
- mentally disordered or otherwise mentally vulnerable person is only valid if given in the presence of the appropriate adult
- juvenile, is only valid if their parent's or guardian's consent is also obtained unless the juvenile is under 14, when their parent's or guardian's consent is sufficient in its own right. If the only obstacle to an identification procedure in *section 3* is that a juvenile's parent or guardian refuses consent or reasonable efforts to obtain it have failed, the identification officer may apply the provisions of *paragraph 3.21*. [See Note 2A]

2.13 If a person is blind, seriously visually impaired or unable to read, the custody officer or identification officer shall make sure their solicitor, relative, appropriate adult or some other person likely to take an interest in them and not involved in the investigation is available to help check any documentation. When this Code requires written consent or signing, the person assisting may be asked to sign instead, if the detainee prefers. This paragraph does not require an appropriate adult to be called solely to assist in checking and signing documentation for a person who is not a juvenile, or mentally disordered or otherwise mentally vulnerable. See Note 2B and Code C *paragraph 3.15*.

2.14 If any procedure in this Code requires information to be given to or sought from a suspect, it must be given or sought in the appropriate adult's presence if the suspect is mentally disordered, otherwise mentally vulnerable or a juvenile. If the appropriate adult is not present when the information is first given or sought, the procedure must be repeated in the presence of the appropriate adult when they arrive. If the suspect appears deaf or there is doubt about their hearing or speaking ability or ability to understand English, and effective communication cannot be established, the information must be given or sought through an interpreter.

2.15 Any procedure in this Code involving the participation of a suspect who is mentally disordered, otherwise mentally vulnerable or a juvenile must take place in the presence of the appropriate adult. See *Code C paragraph 1.4*.

2.15A Any procedure in this Code involving the participation of a witness who is or appears to be mentally disordered, otherwise mentally vulnerable or a juvenile should take place in the presence of a pre-trial support person. However, the support-person must not be allowed to prompt any identification of a suspect by a witness. [See *Note 2AB*]

2.16 References to:

- 'taking a photograph', include the use of any process to produce a single, still or moving, visual image
- 'photographing a person', should be construed accordingly
- 'photographs', 'films', 'negatives' and 'copies' include relevant visual images recorded, stored, or reproduced through any medium
- 'destruction' includes the deletion of computer data relating to such images or making access to that data impossible.

2.17 Except as described, nothing in this Code affects the powers and procedures:

(i) for requiring and taking samples of breath, blood and urine in relation to driving offences, etc, when under the influence of drink, drugs or excess alcohol under the:

- *Road Traffic Act* 1988, sections 4 to 11
- *Road Traffic Offenders Act* 1988, sections 15 and 16
- *Transport and Works Act* 1992, sections 26 to 38

(ii) under the *Immigration Act* 1971, Schedule 2, paragraph 18, for taking photographs and fingerprints from persons detained under that Act. Schedule 2, paragraph 16 (Administrative Controls as to Control on Entry etc.): for taking fingerprints in accordance with the *Immigration and Asylum Act* 1999: sections 141 and 142(3), or other methods for collecting information about a person's external physical characteristics provided for by regulations made under that Act, section 144;

(iii) under the *Terrorism Act* 2000, Schedule 8, for taking photographs, fingerprints, skin impressions, body samples or impressions from people:

- arrested under that Act, section 41
- detained for the purposes of examination under that Act. Schedule 7, and to whom the Code of Practice issued under that Act. Schedule 14, paragraph 6, applies ('the terrorism provisions')

[See *Note 2C*]

(iv) for taking photographs, fingerprints, skin impressions, body samples or impressions from people who have been:

- arrested on warrants issued in Scotland, by officers exercising powers under the *Criminal Justice and Public Order Act* 1994, section 136(2)
- arrested or detained without warrant by officers from a police force in Scotland exercising their powers of arrest or detention under the *Criminal Justice an Public Order Act* 1994, section 137(2). (Cross Border powers of arrest etc.)

Note: In these cases, police powers and duties and the person's rights and entitlements whilst at a police station in England and Wales are the same as if the person had been arrested in Scotland by a Scottish police officer.

2.18 Nothing in this Code requires the identity of officers or police staff to be recorded or disclosed:

(a) in the case of enquires linked to the investigation of terrorism;

(b) if the officers or police staff reasonably believe recording or disclosing their names might put them in danger.

In these cases, they shall use warrant or other identification numbers and the name of their police station. [See *Note 2D*]

A–125   2.19 In this Code:

(a) 'designated person' means a person other than a police officer, designated under the *Police Reform Act* 2002, Part 4, who has specified powers and duties of police officers conferred or imposed on them;

(b) any reference to a police officer includes a designated person acting in the exercise or performance of the powers and duties conferred or imposed on them by their designation.

2.20 If a power conferred on a designated person:

(a) allows reasonable force to be used when exercised by a police officer, a designated person exercising that power has the same entitlement to use force;

(b) includes power to use force to enter any premises, that power is not exercisable by that designated person except:

(i) in the company, and under the supervision, of a police officer; or

(ii) for the purpose of:

- saving life or limb; or
- preventing serious damage to property.

2.21 Nothing in this Code prevents the custody officer, or other officer given custody of the detainee, from allowing police staff who are not designated persons to carry out individual procedures or tasks at the police station if the law allows. However, the officer remains responsible for making sure the procedures and tasks are carried out correctly in accordance with the Codes of Practice. Any such person must be:

(a) a person employed by a police authority maintaining a police force and under the control and direction of the Chief Officer of that force;

(b) employed by a person with whom a police authority has a contract for the provision of services relating to persons arrested or otherwise in custody.

2.22 Designated persons and other police staff must have regard to any relevant provisions of the Codes of Practice.

Notes for guidance

A–126   2A *For the purposes of paragraph 2.12, the consent required from a parent or guardian may, for a juvenile in the care of a local authority or voluntary organisation, be given by that authority or organisation. In the case of a juvenile, nothing in paragraph 2.12 requires the parent, guardian or representative of a local authority or voluntary organisation to be present to give their consent, unless they are acting as the appropriate adult under paragraphs 2.14 or 2.15. However, it is important that a parent or guardian not present is fully informed before being asked to consent. They must be given the same information about the procedure and the juvenile's suspected involvement in the offence as the juvenile and appropriate adult. The parent or guardian must also be allowed to speak to the juvenile and the appropriate adult if they wish. Provided the consent is fully informed and is not withdrawn, it may be obtained at any time before the procedure takes place.*

2AB *The Youth Justice and Criminal Evidence Act 1999 guidance "Achieving Best Evidence in Criminal Proceedings" indicates that a pre-trial support person should accompany a vulnerable witness during any identification procedure. It states that this support person should not be (or not be likely to be) a witness in the investigation.*

2B *People who are seriously visually impaired or unable to read may be unwilling to sign police documents. The alternative, i.e. their representative signing on their behalf, seeks to protect the interests of both police and suspects.*

2C *Photographs, fingerprints, samples and impressions may be taken from a person detained under the terrorism provisions to help determine whether they are, or have been, involved in terrorism, as well as when there are reasonable grounds for suspecting their involvement in a particular offence.*

2D *The purpose of paragraph 2.18(b) is to protect those involved in serious organised crime investigations or arrests of particularly violent suspects when there is reliable information that those arrested or their associates may threaten or cause harm to the officers. In cases of doubt, an officer of inspector rank or above should be consulted.*

3 Identification by witnesses

3.1 A record shall be made of the suspect's description as first given by a potential witness.   **A–127** This record must:

    (a) be made and kept in a form which enables details of that description to be accurately produced from it, in a visible and legible form, which can be given to the suspect or the suspects solicitor in accordance with this Code; and

    (b) unless otherwise specified, be made before the witness takes part in any identification procedures under *paragraphs 3.5 to 3.10, 3.21 or 3.23*.

A copy of the record shall where practicable, be given to the suspect or their solicitor before any procedures under *paragraphs 3.5 to 3.10, 3.21 or 3.23* are carried out. [See *Note 3E*]

(a) Cases when the suspect's identity is not known

3.2 In cases when the suspect's identity is not known, a witness may be taken to a particular neighbourhood or place to see whether they can identify the person they saw. Although the number, age, sex, race general description and style of clothing of other people present at the location and the way in which any identification is made cannot be controlled, the principles applicable to the formal procedures under *paragraphs 3.5 to 3.10* shall be followed as far as practicable. For example:

    (a) where this practicable to do so, a record should be made of the witness description of the suspect, as in paragraph 3.1(a), before asking the witness to make an identification;

    (b) care must be taken not to direct the witness' attention to any individual unless, taking into account all the circumstances, this cannot be avoided. However, this does not prevent a witness being asked to look carefully at the people around at the time or to look towards a group or in a particular direction, if this appears necessary to make sure that the witness does not overlook a possible suspect simply because the witness is looking in the opposite direction and also to enable the witness to make comparisons between any suspect and others who are in the area; [See *Note 3F*]

    (c) where there is more than one witness, every effort should be made to keep them separate and witnesses should be taken to see whether they can identify a person independently;

    (d) once there is sufficient information to justify the arrest of a particular individual for suspected involvement in the offence, e.g., after a witness makes a positive identification, the provisions set out from paragraph 3.4 onwards shall apply for any other witnesses in relation to that individual. Subject to *paragraphs 3.12* and *3.13*, it is not necessary for the witness who makes such a positive identification to take part in a further procedure;

    (e) the officer or police staff accompanying the witness must record, in their pocket book, the action taken as soon as, and in as much detail, as possible. The record should include: the date, time and place of the relevant occasion the witness claims to have previously seen the suspect: where any identification was made: how it was made and the conditions at the time (e.g., the distance the witness was from the suspect, the weather and light): If the witness attention was drawn to the suspect: the reason for this: and anything said by the witness or the suspect about the identification or the conduct of the procedure.

3.3 A witness must not be shown photographs, computerised or artist's composite likenesses or similar likenesses or pictures (including 'E-fit' images) if the identity of the suspect is known to the police and the suspect is available to take part in a video identification, an identification parade or a group identification if the suspect's identity is not known, the showing of such images to a witness to obtain identification evidence must be done in accordance with *Annex E*.

(b) Cases when the suspect is known and available

3.4 If the suspect's identity is known to the police and they are available, the identification   **A–128** procedures set out in paragraphs 3.5 to 3.10 may be used. References in this section to a suspect being 'known' mean there is sufficient information known to the police to justify the arrest of a particular person for suspected involvement in the offence. A suspect being 'available' means they are immediately available or will be within a reasonably short time and willing to take an effective part in at least one of the following which it is practicable to arrange:

- video identification;
- identification parade; or
- group identification.

Video identification

3.5 Change to: A 'video identification' is when the witness is shown moving images of a known suspect, together with similar images of others who resemble the suspect. Moving images must be used unless:

- the suspect is known but not available (see *paragraph 3.21* of this Code); or
- in accordance with *paragraph 2A of Annex A* of this Code, the identification officer does not consider that replication of a physical feature can be achieved or that it is not possible to conceal the location of the feature on the image of the suspect.

The identification officer may then decide to make use of video identification but using still images.

3.6 Video identifications must be carried out in accordance with *Annex A*.

Identification parade

3.7 An 'identification parade' is when the witness sees the suspect in a line of others who resemble the suspect.

3.8 Identification parades must be carried out in accordance with *Annex B*.

Group identification

3.9 A 'group identification' is when the witness sees the suspect in an informal group of people.

3.10 Group identifications must be carried out in accordance with *Annex C*.

Arranging identification procedures

3.11 Except for the provisions in *paragraph 3.19*, the arrangements for, and conduct of, the identification procedures in paragraphs 3.5 to 3.10 and circumstances in which an identification procedure must be held shall be the responsibility of an officer not below inspector rank who is not involved with the investigation, 'the identification officer'. Unless otherwise specified, the identification officer may allow another officer or police staff, see *paragraph 2.21* to make arrangements for, and conduct, any of these identification procedures. In delegating these procedures, the identification officer must be able to supervise effectively and either intervene or be contacted for advice. No officer or any other person involved with the investigation of the case against the suspect, beyond the extent required by these procedures, may take any part in these procedures or act as the identification officer. This does not prevent the identification officer from consulting the officer in charge of the investigation to determine which procedure to use When an identification procedure is required. In the interest of fairness to suspects and witnesses, it must be held as soon as practicable.

Circumstances in which an identification procedure must be held

A–129　3.12 Whenever:

(i) a witness has identified a suspect or purported to have identified them prior to any identification procedure set out in paragraphs 3.5 to 3.10 having been held; or

(ii) there is a witness available, who expresses an ability to identify the suspect, or where there is a reasonable chance of the witness being able to do so, and they have not been given an opportunity to identify the suspect in any of the procedures set out in paragraphs 3.5 to 3.10

and the suspect disputes being the person the witness claims to have seen, an identification procedure shall be held unless it is not practicable or it would serve no useful purpose in proving or disproving whether the suspect was involved in committing the offence. For example, when it is not disputed that the suspect is already well known to the witness who claims to have seen them commit the crime.

3.13 Such a procedure may also be held if the officer in charge of the investigation considers it would be useful.

Selecting an identification procedure

3.14 If because of paragraph 3.12 an identification procedure is to be held, the suspect shall initially be offered a video identification unless:

    a) a video identification is not practicable; or

    b) an identification parade is both practicable and more suitable than a video identification; or

    c) paragraph 3.16 applies.

The identification officer and the officer in charge of the investigation shall consult each other to determine which option is to be offered. An identification parade may not be practicable because of factors relating to the witnesses, such as their number, state of health, availability and travelling requirements. A video identification would normally be more suitable if it could be arranged and completed sooner than an identification parade.

3.15 A suspect who refuses the identification procedure first offered shall be asked to state their reason for refusing and may get advice from their solicitor and or if present, their appropriate adult. The suspect, solicitor and/or appropriate adult shall be allowed to make representations about why another procedure should be used. A record should be made of the reasons for refusal and any representations made. After considering any reasons given, and representations made, the identification officer shall if appropriate, arrange for the suspect to be offered an alternative which the officer considers suitable and practicable. If the officer decides it is not suitable and practicable to offer an alternative identification procedure, the reasons for that decision shall be recorded.

3.16 A group identification may initially be offered if the officer in charge of the investigation considers it is more suitable than a video identification or an identification parade and the identification officer considers it practicable to arrange.

Notice to suspect

3.17 Unless *paragraph 3.20* applies, before a video identification, an identification parade or **A–130** group identification is arranged, the following shall be explained to the suspect:

    (i) the purposes of the video identification, identification parade or group identification;

    (ii) their entitlement to free legal advice: see Code C, paragraph 6.5;

    (iii) the procedures for holding it, including their right to have a solicitor or friend present;

    (iv) that they do not have to consent to or co-operate in a video identification, identification parade or group identification;

    (v) that if they do not consent to, and co-operate in, a video identification, identification parade or group identification, their refusal may be given in evidence in any subsequent trial and police may proceed covertly without their consent or make other arrangements to test whether a witness can identify them, see *paragraph 3.21*;

    (vi) whether, for the purposes of the video identification procedure, images of them have previously been obtained, see *paragraph 3.20* and if so, that they may co-operate in providing further, suitable images to be used instead;

    (vii) if appropriate, the special arrangements for juveniles;

    (viii) if appropriate, the special arrangements for mentally disordered or otherwise mentally vulnerable people;

    (ix) that if they significantly alter their appearance between being offered an identification procedure and any attempt to hold an identification procedure, this may be given in evidence if the case comes to trial, and the identification officer may then consider other forms of identification, see *paragraph 3.21* and *Note 3C*;

    (x) that a moving image or photograph may be taken of them when they attend for any identification procedure;

    (xi) whether, before their identity became known, the witness was shown photographs, a computerised or artist's composite likeness or similar likeness or image by the police, see *Note 3B*;

Appendices

(xii) that if they change their appearance before an identification parade, it may not be practicable to arrange one on the day or subsequently and, because of the appearance change, the identification officer may consider alternative methods of identification, see *Note 3C*;

(xiii) that they or their solicitor will be provided with details of the description of the suspect as first given by any witnesses who are to attend the video identification, identification parade group identification or confrontation see *paragraph 3.1*.

3.18 This information must also be recorded in a written notice handed to the suspect. The suspect must be given a reasonable opportunity to read the notice, after which, they should be asked to sign a second copy to indicate if they are willing to co-operate with the making of a video or take part in the identification parade or group identification. The signed copy shall be retained by the identification officer.

3.19 The duties of the identification officer under *paragraphs 3.17* and *3.18* may be performed by the custody officer or other officer not involved in the investigation if:

(a) it is proposed to release the suspect in order that an identification procedure can be arranged and carried out and an inspector is not available to act as the identification officer, see *paragraph 3.11*, before the suspect leaves the station; or

(b) it is proposed to keep the suspect in police detention whilst the procedure is arranged and carried out and waiting for an inspector to act as the identification officer, see *paragraph 3.11*, would cause unreasonable delay to the investigation.

The officer concerned shall inform the identification officer of the action taken and give them the signed copy of the notice. [See *Note 3C*]

3.20 If the identification officer and officer in charge of the investigation suspect, on reasonable grounds that if the suspect was given the information and notice as in *paragraphs 3.17* and *3.18* they would then take steps to avoid being seen by a witness in any identification procedure, the identification officer may arrange for images of the suspect suitable for use in a video identification procedure to be obtained before giving the information and notice. If suspect's images are obtained in these circumstances, the suspect may, for the purposes of a video identification procedure, co-operate in providing new images which if suitable, would be used instead, see *paragraph 3.17(vi)*.

(c) Cases when the suspect is known but not available

A–131   3.21 When a known suspect is not available or has ceased to be available, see *paragraph 3.4*, the identification officer may make arrangements for a video identification (see Annex A). If necessary, the identification officer may follow the video identification procedures but using still images. Any suitable moving or still images may be used and these may be obtained covertly if necessary. Alternatively, the identification officer may make arrangements for a group identification. See *Note 3D*. These provisions may also be applied to juveniles where the consent of their parent or guardian is either refused or reasonable efforts to obtain that consent have failed (see *paragraph 2.12*).

3.22 Any covert activity should be strictly limited to that necessary to test the ability of the witness to identify the suspect.

3.23 The identification officer may arrange for the suspect to be confronted by the witness if none of the options referred to in paragraphs 3.5 to 3.10 or 3.21 are practicable. A "confrontation" is when the suspect is directly confronted by the witness. A confrontation does not require the suspect's consent. Confrontations must be carried out in accordance with Annex D.

3.24 Requirements for information to be given to, or sought from, a suspect or for the suspect to be given an opportunity to view images before they are shown to a witness, do not apply if the suspect's lack of co-operation prevents the necessary action.

(d) Documentation

A–132   3.25 A record shall be made of the video identification, identification parade, group identification or confrontation on forms provided for the purpose.

3.26 If the identification officer considers it is not practicable to hold a video identification or identification parade requested by the suspect, the reasons shall be recorced and explained to the suspect.

3.27 A record shall be made of a person's failure or refusal to co-operate in a video identification, identification parade or group identification and, if applicable, of the grounds for obtaining images in accordance with *paragraph 3.20*.

(e) Showing films and photographs of incidents and information released to the media

3.28 Nothing in this Code inhibits showing films or photographs to the public through the **A–133** national or local media, or to police officers for the purposes of recognition and tracing suspects. However, when such material is shown to potential witnesses, including police officers, see *Note 3A*, to obtain identification evidence, it shall be shown on an individual basis to avoid any possibility of collusion, and, as far as possible, the showing shall follow the principles for video identification if the suspect is known, see *Annex A*, or identification by photographs if the suspect is not known, see *Annex E*.

3.29 When a broadcast or publication is made, see *paragraph 3.28*, a copy of the relevant material released to the media for the purposes of recognising or tracing the suspect, shall be kept. The suspect or their solicitor shall be allowed to view such material before any procedures under *paragraphs 3.5* to *3.10, 3.21* or *3.23* are carried out, provided it is practicable and would not unreasonably delay the investigation. Each witness involved in the procedure shall be asked, after they have taken part, whether they have seen any broadcast or published films or photographs relating to the offence or any description of the suspect and their replies shall be recorded. This paragraph does not affect any separate requirement under the *Criminal Procedure and Investigations Act* 1996 to retain material in connection with criminal investigations.

(f) Destruction and retention of photographs taken or used in identification procedures

3.30 PACE, section 64A, see *paragraph 5.12*, provides powers to take photographs of suspects and allows these photographs to be used or disclosed only for purposes related to the prevention or detection of crime, the investigation of offences or the conduct of prosecutions by, or on behalf of, police or other law enforcement and prosecuting authorities inside and outside the United Kingdom or the enforcement of a sentence. After being so used or disclosed, they may be retained but can only be used or disclosed for the same purposes.

3.31 Subject to *paragraph 3.33*, the photographs (and all negatives and copies), of suspects not taken in accordance with the provisions in *paragraph 5.12* which are taken for the purposes of, or in connection with, the identification procedures in *paragraphs 35* to *3.10, 3.21* or *3.23* must be destroyed unless the suspect:

    (a) is charged with, or informed they may be prosecuted for a recordable offence;

    (b) is prosecuted for a recordable offence;

    (c) is cautioned for a recordable offence or given a warning or reprimand in accordance with the *Crime and Disorder Act* 1998 for a recordable offence; or

    (d) gives informed consent, in writing, for the photograph or images to be retained for purposes described in *paragraph 3.30*.

3.32 When *paragraph 3.31* requires the destruction of any photograph, the person must be given an opportunity to witness the destruction or to have a certificate confirming the destruction if they request one within five days of being informed that the destruction is required.

3.33 Nothing in *paragraph 3.31* affects any separate requirement under the *Criminal Procedure and Investigations Act* 1996 to retain material in connection with criminal investigations.

Notes for guidance

3A *Except for the provisions of Annex E. paragraph 1, a police officer who is a witness for* **A–134** *the purposes of this part of the Code is subject to the same principles and procedures as a civilian witness.*

3B *When a witness attending an identification procedure has previously been shown photographs, or been shown or provided with computerised or artist's composite likenesses, or similar likenesses or pictures, it is the officer in charge of the investigation's responsibility to make the identification officer aware of this.*

3C *The purpose of paragraph 3.19 is to avoid or reduce delay in arranging identification procedures by enabling the required information and warnings, see sub-paragraphs 3.17(ix) and 3.17(xii), to be given at the earliest opportunity.*

3D *Paragraph 3.21 would apply when a known suspect deliberately makes themself 'un-*

Appendices

available' in order to delay or frustrate arrangements for obtaining identification evidence. It also applies when a suspect refuses or fails to take part in a video identification, an identification parade or a group identification, or refuses or fails to take part in the only practicable options from that list. It enables any suitable images of the suspect, moving or still, which are available or can be obtained, to be used in an identification procedure. Examples include images from custody and other CCTV systems and from visually recorded interview records, see Code F Note for Guidance 2D.

3E *When it is proposed to show photographs to a witness in accordance with Annex E, it is the responsibility of the officer in charge of the investigation to confirm to the officer responsible for supervising and directing the showing, that the first description of the suspect given by that witness has been recorded. If this description has not been recorded, the procedure under Annex E must be postponed. See Annex E paragraph 2.*

3F *The admissibility and value of identification evidence obtained when carrying out the procedure under paragraph 3.2 may be compromised if:*

> (a) *before a person is identified, the witness' attention is specifically drawn to that person; or*

> (b) *the suspect's identity becomes known before the procedure.*

4 Identification by fingerprints and footwear impressions

(A) Taking fingerprints in connection with a criminal investigation

(a) *General*

A–135   4.1 References to 'fingerprints' means any record, produced by any method, of the skin pattern and other physical characteristics or features of a person's:

> (i) fingers; or
> (ii) palms.

(b) *Action*

4.2 A person's fingerprints may be taken in connection with the investigation of an offence only with their consent or if *paragraph 4.3* applies. If the person is at a police station consent must be in writing.

4.3 *PACE*, section 61(3), provides powers to take fingerprints without consent from any person over the age of ten years:

> (a) under section 61(3), from a person detained at a police station in consequence of being arrested for a recordable offence, see Note 4A, if they have not had their fingerprints taken in the course of the investigation of the offence unless those previously taken fingerprints are not a complete set or some or all of those fingerprints are not of sufficient quality to allow satisfactory analysis, comparison or matching.

> (b) under section 61(4), from a person detained at a police station who has been charged with a recordable offence, see Note 4A. or informed they will be reported for such an offence if they have not had their fingerprints taken in the course of the investigation of the offence unless those previously taken fingerprints are not a complete set or some or all of those fingerprints are not of sufficient quality to allow satisfactory analysis, comparison or matching.

> (c) under section 61(4A), from a person who has been bailed to appear at a court or police station if the person:

>> (i) has answered to bail for a person whose fingerprints were taken previously and there are reasonable grounds for believing they are not the same person; or

>> (ii) who has answered to bail claims to be a different person from a person whose fingerprints were previously taken;

> and in either case, the court or an officer of inspector rank or above, authorises the fingerprints to be taken at the court or police station.

> (d) under section 61(6), from a person who has been:

>> (i) convicted of a recordable offence;

>> (ii) given a caution in respect of a recordable offence which, at the time of the caution, the person admitted; or

    (iii) warned or reprimanded under the *Crime and Disorder Act* 1998, section 65, for a recordable offence.

4.4 *PACE*, section 27, provides power to:

    (a) require the person as in *paragraph 4.3(d)* to attend a police station to have their fingerprints taken if the:

        (i) person has not been in police detention for the offence and has not had their fingerprints taken in the course of the investigation of that offence; or

        (ii) fingerprints that were taken from the person in the course of the investigation of that offence, do not constitute a complete set or some, or all, of the fingerprints are not of sufficient quality to allow satisfactory analysis, comparison or matching; and

    (b) arrest, without warrant, a person who fails to comply with the requirement.

Note: The requirement must be made within one month of the date the person is convicted, cautioned, warned or reprimanded and the person must be given a period of at least 7 days within which to attend. This 7 day period need not fall during the month allowed for making the requirement.

4.5 A person's fingerprints may be taken, as above, electronically.

4.6 Reasonable force may be used, if necessary, to take a person's fingerprints without their consent under the powers as in *paragraphs 4.3* and *4.4*.

4.7 Before any fingerprints are taken with, or without, consent as above, the person must be informed:

    (a) of the reason their fingerprints are to be taken;

    (b) of the grounds on which the relevant authority has been given if the power mentioned in *paragraph 4.3(c) applies*;

    (c) that their fingerprints may be retained and may be subject of a speculative search against other fingerprints, see *Note 4B*, unless destruction of the fingerprints is required in accordance with *Annex F, Part (a)*; and

    (d) that if their fingerprints are required to be destroyed. they may witness their destruction as provided for in *Annex F, Part (a)*.

(c) *Documentation*

4.8 A record must be made as soon as possible, of the reason for taking a person's fingerprints without consent. If force is used, a record shall be made of the circumstances and those present.

4.9 A record shall be made when a person has been informed under the terms of *paragraph 4.7(c)*, of the possibility that their fingerprints may be subject of a speculative search.

(B) Taking fingerprints in connection with immigration enquiries

Action

4.10 A person's fingerprints may be taken for the purposes of Immigration Service **A–136** enquiries in accordance with powers and procedures other than under *PACE* and for which the Immigration Service (not the police) are responsible, only with the person's consent in writing or if *paragraph 4.11* applies.

4.11 Powers to take fingerprints for these purposes without consent are given to police and immigration officers under the:

    (a) *Immigration Act* 1971, Schedule 2, paragraph 18(2), when it is reasonably necessary for the purposes of identifying a person detained under the *Immigration Act* 1971, Schedule 2, paragraph 16 (Detention of person liable to examination or removal);

    (b) *Immigration and Asylum Act* 1999, section 141(7)(a), from a person who fails to produce, on arrival, a valid passport with a photograph or some other document satisfactorily establishing their identity and nationality if an immigration officer does not consider the person has a reasonable excuse for the failure;

    (c) *Immigration and Asylum Act* 1999, section 141(7)(b), from a person who has been refused entry to the UK but has been temporarily admitted if an immigration officer reasonably suspects the person might break a condition imposed on them relating to residence or reporting to a police or immigration officer, and their decision is confirmed by a chief immigration officer;

(d) *Immigration and Asylum Act* 1999, section 141(7)(c), when directions are given to remove a person:
- as an illegal entrant
- liable to removal under the *Immigration and Asylum Act* 1999, section 10
- who is the subject of a deportation order from the UK

(e) *Immigration and Asylum Act* 1999, section 141(7)(d), from a person arrested under UK immigration laws under the *Immigration Act* 1971, Schedule 2, paragraph 17;

(f) *Immigration and Asylum Act* 1999, section 141(7)(e), from a person who has made a claim:
- for asylum
- under Article 3 of the European Convention on Human Rights; or

(g) *Immigration and Asylum Act* 1999, section 141(7)(f), from a person who is a dependant of someone who falls into (b) to (f) above.

4.12 The *Immigration and Asylum Act* 1999, section 142(3), gives a police and immigration officer power to arrest, without warrant, a person who fails to comply with a requirement imposed by the Secretary of State to attend a specified place for fingerprinting.

4.13 Before any fingerprints are taken, with or without consent, the person must be informed:

(a) of the reason their fingerprints are to be taken;

(b) the fingerprints, and all copies of them, will be destroyed in accordance with *Annex F, Part B*.

4.14 Reasonable force may be used, if necessary, to take a person's fingerprints without their consent under powers as in *paragraph 4.11*.

4.15 *paragraphs 4.1* and *4.8* apply.

(C) Taking footwear impressions in connection with a criminal investigation

(a) *Action*

A–137 4.16 Impressions of a person's footwear may be taken in connection with the investigation of an offence only with their consent or if *paragraph 4.17* applies. If the person is at a police station consent must be in writing.

4.17 *PACE*, section 61A, provides power for a police officer to take footwear impressions without consent from any person over the age of ten years who is detained at a police station:

(a) in consequence of being arrested for a recordable offence, see *Note 4A*: or if the detainee has been charged with a recordable offence, or informed they will be reported for such an offence; and

(b) the detainee has not had an impression of their footwear taken in the course of the investigation of the offence unless the previously taken impression is not complete or is not of sufficient quality to allow satisfactory analysis, comparison or matching (whether in the case in question or generally)

4.18 Reasonable force may be used, if necessary, to take a footwear impression from a detainee without consent under the power in *paragraph 417*.

4.19 Before any footwear impression is taken with, or without, consent as above, the person must be informed:

(a) of the reason the impression is to be taken;

(b) that the impression may be retained and may be subject of a speculative search against other impressions, see *Note 4B*, unless destruction of the impression is required in accordance with *Annex F, Part (a)*; and

(c) that if their footwear impressions are required to be destroyed, they may witness their destruction as provided for in *Annex F, Part (a)*.

(b) *Documentation*

4.20 A record must be made as soon as possible, of the reason for taking a person's footwear impressions without consent. If force is used, a record shall be made of the circumstances and those present.

4.21 A record shall be made when a person has been informed under the terms of *paragraph 4.19(b)*, of the possibility that their footwear impressions may be subject of a speculative search.

Notes for guidance

4A *References to 'recordable offences' in this Code relate to those offences for which convictions, cautions, reprimands and warnings may be recorded in national police records. See PACE, section 27(4). The recordable offences current at the time when this Code was prepared, are any offences which carry a sentence of imprisonment on conviction (irrespective of the period, or the age of the offender or actual sentence passed) as well as the non-imprisonable offences under the Vagrancy Act 1824, sections 3 and 4 (begging and persistent begging), the Street Offences Act 1959, section 1 (loitering or soliciting for purposes of prostitution). the Road Traffic Act 1988, section 25 (tampering with motor vehicles), the Criminal Justice and Public Order Act 1994, section 167 (touting for hire car services) and others listed in the National Police Records (Recordable Offences) Regulations 2000 as amended.* **A–138**

4B *Fingerprints, footwear impressions or a DNA sample (and the information derived from it) taken from a person arrested on suspicion of being involved in a recordable offence, or charged with such an offence, or informed they will be reported for such an offence, may be subject of a speculative search. This means the fingerprints, footwear impressions or DNA sample may be checked against other fingerprints, footwear impressions and DNA records held by, or on behalf of, the police and other law enforcement authorities in, or outside, the UK, or held in connection with, or as a result of an investigation of an offence inside or outside the UK. Fingerprints, footwear impressions and samples taken from a person suspected of committing a recordable offence but not arrested, charged or informed they will be reported for it, may be subject to a speculative search only if the person consents in writing. The following is an example of a basic form of words:*

"I consent to my fingerprints, footwear impressions and DNA sample and information derived from it being retained and used only for purposes related to the prevention and detection of a crime, the investigation of an offence or the conduct of a prosecution either nationally or internationally.

I understand that my fingerprints, footwear impressions or DNA sample may be checked against other fingerprint, footwear impressions and DNA records held by or on behalf of relevant law enforcement authorities, either nationally or internationally.

I understand that once I have given my consent for my fingerprints, footwear impressions or DNA sample to be retained and used I cannot withdraw this consent."

See Annex F regarding the retention and use of fingerprints and footwear impressions taken with consent for elimination purposes.

Appendices

5 EXAMINATIONS TO ESTABLISH IDENTITY AND THE TAKING OF PHOTOGRAPHS

(A) Detainees at police stations

(a) *Searching or examination of detainees at police stations*

5.1 *PACE, section 54A (1)*, allows a detainee at a police station to be searched or examined or both, to establish: **A–139**

    (a) whether they have any marks, features or injuries that would tend to identify them as a person involved in the commission of an offence and to photograph any identifying marks, see *paragraph 5.5*; or

    (b) their identity, see *Note 5A.*

A person detained at a police station to be searched under a stop and search power, see Code A, is not a detainee for the purposes of these powers.

5.2 A search and/or examination to find marks under section 54A(1) (a) may be carried out without the detainee's consent, see *paragraph 2.12*, only if authorised by an officer of at least inspector rank when consent has been withheld or it is not practicable to obtain consent. [See *Note 5D*]

5.3 A search or examination to establish a suspect's identify under section 54A (1) (b) may be carried out without the detainee's consent, see *paragraph 2.12*, only if authorised by an officer of at least inspector rank when the detainee has refused to identify themselves or the authorising officer has reasonable grounds for suspecting the person is not who they claim to be.

5.4 Any marks that assist in establishing the detainee's identity, or their identification as a person involved in the commission of an offence, are identifying marks. Such marks may be photographed with the detainee's consent, see *paragraph 2.12*: or without their consent if it is withheld or it is not practicable to obtain it. [See *Note 5D*]

5.5 A detainee may only be searched, examined and photographed under section 54A, by a police officer of the same sex.

5.6 Any photographs of identifying marks, taken under section 54A, may be used or disclosed only for purposes related to the prevention or detection of crime, the investigation of offences or the conduct of prosecutions by, or on behalf of, police or other law enforcement and prosecuting authorities inside, and outside, the UK. After being so used or disclosed, the photograph may be retained but must not be used or disclosed except for these purposes. [See *Note 5B*]

5.7 The powers, as in *paragraph 5.1*, do not affect any separate requirement under the *Criminal Procedure and Investigations Act* 1996 to retain material in connection with criminal investigations.

A–140   5.8 Authority for the search and/or examination for the purposes of *paragraphs 5.2* and *5.3* may be given orally or in writing. If given orally, the authorising officer must confirm it in writing as soon as practicable. A separate authority is required for each purpose which applies.

5.9 If it is established a person is unwilling to co-operate sufficiently to enable a search and/or examination to take place or a suitable photograph to be taken, an officer may use reasonable force to:

(a) search and/or examine a detainee without their consent; and

(b) photograph any identifying marks without their consent.

5.10 The thoroughness and extent of any search or examination carried out in accordance with the powers in section 54A must be no more than the officer considers necessary to achieve the required purpose. Any search or examination which involves the removal of more than the person's outer clothing shall be conducted in accordance with Code C, Annex A, paragraph 11.

5.11 An intimate search may not be carried out under the powers in section 54A.

(b) *Photographing detainees at police stations and other persons elsewhere than at a police station*

5.12 Under *PACE*, section 64A, an officer may photograph:

(a) any person whilst they are detained at a police station; and

(b) any person who is elsewhere than at a police station and who has been:

(i) arrested by a constable for an offence;

(ii) taken into custody by a constable after being arrested for an offence by a person other than a constable;

(iii) made subject to a requirement to wait with a community support officer under *paragraph 2(3) or (3B)* of Schedule 4 to the Police Reform Act 2002;

(iv) given a penalty notice by a constable in uniform under Chapter 1 of Part 1 of the *Criminal Justice and Police Act* 2001, a penalty notice by a constable under section 444A of the *Education Act* 1996, or a fixed penalty notice by a constable in uniform under section 54 of the *Road Traffic Offenders Act* 1988;

(v) given a notice in relation to a relevant fixed penalty offence (within the meaning of paragraph 1 of Schedule 4 to the *Police Reform Act* 2002) by a community support officer by virtue of a designation applying that paragraph to him; or

(vi) given a notice in relation to a relevant fixed penalty offence (within the meaning of paragraph 1 of Schedule 5 to the *Police Reform Act* 2002) by an accredited person by virtue of accreditation specifying that that paragraph applies to him.

5.12A Photographs taken under *PACE*, section 64A:

(a) may be taken with the person's consent, or without their consent if consent is withheld or it is not practicable to obtain their consent, see *Note 5E*; and

(b) may be used or disclosed only for purposes related to the prevention or detection of crime, the investigation of offences or the conduct of prosecutions by, or on behalf of, police or other law enforcement and prosecuting authorities inside and outside the United Kingdom or the enforcement of any sentence or order made by a court when dealing with an offence. After being so used or disclosed, they may be retained but can only be used or disclosed for the same purposes, see *Note 5B*.

5.13 The officer proposing to take a detainee's photograph may for this purpose, require the person to remove any item or substance worn on, or over, all, or any part of, their head or face. If they do not comply with such a requirement, the officer may remove the item or substance.

5.14 If it is established the detainee is unwilling to co-operate sufficiently to enable a suitable photograph to be taken and it is not reasonably practicable to take the photograph covertly, an officer may use reasonable force, see *Note 5F*.

    (a) to take their photograph without their consent; and

    (b) for the purpose of taking the photograph, remove any item or substance worn on, or over, all, or any part of, the person's head or face which they have failed to remove when asked.

5.15 For the purposes of this Code, a photograph may be obtained without the person's consent by making a copy of an image of them taken at any time on a camera system installed anywhere in the police station.

(c) *Information to be given*

5.16 When a person is searched, examined or photographed under the provisions as in *paragraph 5.1* and *5.12*, or their photograph obtained as in *paragraph 5.15*, they must be informed of the: **A–141**

    (a) purpose of the search, examination or photograph;

    (b) grounds on which the relevant authority, if applicable, has been given; and

    (c) purposes for which the photograph may be used, disclosed or retained.

This information must be given before the search or examination commences or the photograph is taken, except if the photograph is:

    (i) to be taken covertly:

    (ii) obtained as in *paragraph 5.15*, in which case the person must be informed as soon as practicable after the photograph is taken or obtained.

(d) *Documentation*

5.17 A record must be made when a detainee is searched, examined, or a photograph of the person, or any identifying marks found on them, are taken. The record must include the:

    (a) identify, subject to paragraph 2.18, of the officer carrying out the search, examination or taking the photograph;

    (b) purpose of the search, examination or photograph and the outcome;

    (c) detainee's consent to the search, examination or photograph, or the reason the person was searched, examined or photographed without consent;

    (d) giving of any authority as in *paragraphs 5.2* and *5.3*, the grounds for giving it and the authorising officer.

5.18 If force is used when searching, examining or taking a photograph in accordance with this section, a record shall be made of the circumstances and those present.

(B) Persons at police stations not detained

5.19 When there are reasonable grounds for suspecting the involvement of a person in a criminal offence, but that person is at a police station **voluntarily** and not detained, the provisions of *paragraphs 5.1* to *5.18* should apply, subject to the modifications in the following paragraphs.   **A–142**

5.20 References to the 'person being detained' and to the powers mentioned in *paragraph 5.1* which apply only to detainees at police stations shall be omitted.

5.21 Force may not be used to:

    (a) search and/or examine the person to:

        (i) discover whether they have any marks that would tend to identify them as a person involved in the commission of an offence; or

        (ii) establish their identity, see *Note 5A*;

    (b) take photographs of any identifying marks, see *paragraph 5.4*; or

Appendices

    (c) take a photograph of the person.

5.22 Subject to *paragraph 5.24*, the photographs of persons or of their identifying marks which are not taken in accordance with the provisions mentioned in *paragraphs 5.1* or *5.12*, must be destroyed (together with any negatives and copies) unless the person:

    (a) is charged with, or informed they may be prosecuted for, a recordable offence;

    (b) is prosecuted for a recordable offence;

    (c) is cautioned for a recordable offence or given a warning or reprimand in accordance with the Crime and Disorder Act 1998 for a recordable offence; or

    (d) gives informed consent, in writing, for the photograph or image to be retained as in *paragraph 5.6*.

5.23 When *paragraph 5.22* requires the destruction of any photograph, the person must be given an opportunity to witness the destruction or to have a certificate confirming the destruction provided they so request the certificate within five days of being informed the destruction is required.

5.24 Nothing in *paragraph 5.22* affects any separate requirement under the Criminal procedure and Investigations Act 1996 to retain material in connection with criminal investigations.

Notes for guidance

A–143   5A *The conditions under which fingerprints may be taken to assist in establishing a person's identity, are described in Section 4.*

5B *Examples of purposes related to the prevention or detection of crime, the investigation of offences or the conduct of prosecutions include:*

    (a) *checking the photograph against other photographs held in records or in connection with, or as a result of an investigation of an offence to establish whether the person is liable to arrest for other offences;*

    (b) *when the person is arrested at the same time as other people, or at a time when it is likely that other people will be arrested, using the photograph to help establish who was arrested, at what time and where;*

    (c) *when the real identity of the person is not known and cannot be readily ascertained or there are reasonable grounds for doubting a name and other personal details given by the person, are their real name and personal details. In these circumstances, using or disclosing the photograph to help to establish or verify their real identity or determine whether they are liable to arrest for some other offence, e.g. by checking it against other photographs held in records or in connection with, or as a result of, an investigation of an offence;*

    (d) *when it appears any identification procedure in section 3 may need to be arranged for which the person's photograph would assist;*

    (e) *when the person's release without charge may be required, and if the release is:*

        (i) *on bail to appear at a police station, using the photograph to help verify the person's identity when they answer their bail and if the person does not answer their bail, to assist in arresting them; or*

        (ii) *without bail, using the photograph to help verify their identity or assist in locating them for the purposes of serving them with a summons to appear at court in criminal proceedings;*

    (f) *when the person has answered to bail at a police station and there are reasonable grounds for doubting they are the person who was previously granted bail, using the photograph to help establish or verify their identity;*

    (g) *when the person arrested on a warrant claims to be a different person from the person named on the warrant and a photograph would help to confirm or disprove their claim;*

    (h) *when the person has been charged with, reported for, or convicted of, a recordable offence and their photograph is not already on record as a result of (a) to (f) or their photograph is on record but their appearance has changed since it was taken and the person has not yet been released or brought before a court.*

5C *There is no power to arrest a person convicted of a recordable offence solely to take their photograph. The power to take photographs in this section applies only where the person is in custody as a result of the exercise of another power, e.g. arrest for fingerprinting under PACE, section 27.*

5D *Examples of when it would not be practicable to obtain a detainee's consent, see paragraph 2.12, to a search, examination or the taking of a photograph of an identifying mark include*:

(a) *when the person is drunk or otherwise unfit to give consent;*

(b) *when there are reasonable grounds to suspect that if the person became aware a search or examination was to take place or an identifying mark was to be photographed, they would take steps to prevent this happening. e.g. by violently resisting, covering or concealing the mark etc and it would not otherwise be possible to carry out the search or examination or to photograph any identifying mark;*

(c) *in the case of a juvenile, if the parent or guardian cannot be contacted in sufficient time to allow the search or examination to be carried out or the photograph to be taken.*

5E *Examples of when it would not be practicable to obtain the person's consent, see paragraph 2.12, to a photograph being taken include*:

(a) *when the person is drunk or otherwise unfit to give consent;*

(b) *when there are reasonable grounds to suspect that if the person became aware a photograph, suitable to be used or disclosed for the use and disclosure described in paragraph 5.6. was to be taken, they would take steps to prevent it being taken, e.g. by violently resisting, covering or distorting their face etc, and it would not otherwise be possible to take a suitable photograph;*

(c) *when, in order to obtain a suitable photograph, it is necessary to take it covertly: and*

(d) *in the case of a juvenile, if the parent or guardian cannot be contacted in sufficient time to allow the photograph to be taken.*

5F *The use of reasonable force to take the photograph of a suspect elsewhere than at a police station must be carefully considered. In order to obtain a suspect's consent and co-operation to remove an item of religious headwear to take their photograph, a constable should consider whether in the circumstances of the situation the removal of the headwear and the taking of the photograph should be by an officer of the same sex as the person. It would be appropriate for these actions to be conducted out of public view.*

6 Identification by body samples and impressions

(A) General

6.1 References to: A–144

(a) an 'intimate sample' mean a dental impression or sample of blood, semen or any other tissue fluid, urine, or pubic hair, or a swab taken from any part of a person's genitals or from a person's body orifice other than the mouth;

(b) a 'non-intimate sample' means:

  (i) a sample of hair, other than pubic hair, which includes hair plucked with the root, see Note 6A;

  (ii) a sample taken from a nail or from under a nail;

  (iii) a swab taken from any part of a person's body other than a part from which a swab taken would be an intimate sample;

  (iv) saliva;

  (v) a skin impression which means any record, other than a fingerprint, which is a record, in any form and produced by any method, of the skin pattern and other physical characteristics or features of the whole, or any part of, a person's foot or of any other part of their body.

(B) Action

(a) *Intimate samples*

6.2 *PACE*, section 62. provides that intimate samples may be taken under: A–145

(a) section 62(1), from a person in police detention only:

        (i) if a police officer of inspector rank or above has reasonable grounds to believe such an impression or sample will tend to confirm or disprove the suspect's involvement in a recordable offence, see Note 4A, and gives authorisation for a sample to be taken; and

        (ii) with the suspect's written consent;

    (b) section 62(1A). from a person not in police detention but from whom two or more non-intimate samples have been taken in the course of an investigation of an offence and the samples, though suitable, have proved insufficient if:

        (i) a police officer of inspector rank or above authorises it to be taken; and

        (ii) the person concerned gives their written consent. See Notes 6B and 6C

6.3 Before a suspect is asked to provide an intimate sample, they must be warned that if they refuse without good cause, their refusal may harm their case if it comes to trial, see *Note 6D*. If the suspect is in police detention and not legally represented, they must also be reminded of their entitlement to have free legal advice, see Code C. *paragraph 6.5*, and the reminder noted in the custody record. If *paragraph 6.2(b)* applies and the person is attending a station voluntarily, their entitlement to free legal advice as in Code C, *paragraph 3.21* shall be explained to them.

6.4 Dental impressions may only be taken by a registered dentist. Other intimate samples, except for samples of urine, may only be taken by a registered medical practitioner or registered nurse or registered paramedic.

    (b) *Non-intimate samples*

A–146   6.5 A non-intimate sample may be taken from a detainee only with their written consent or if *paragraph 6.6* applies.

    (a) under section 63, a non-intimate sample may not be taken from a person without consent and the consent must be in writing;

    (aa) A non-intimate sample may be taken from a person without the appropriate consent in the following circumstances:

        (i) under section 63(2A) where the person is in police detention as a consequence of his arrest for a recordable offence and he has not had a non-intimate sample of the same type and from the same part of the body taken in the course of the investigation of the offence by the police or he has had such a sample taken but it proved insufficient.

        (ii) Under section 63(3) (a) where he is being held in custody by the police on the authority of a court and an officer of at least the rank of inspector authorises it to be taken.

    (b) under section 63(3A), from a person charged with a recordable offence or informed they will be reported for such an offence; and

        (i) that person has not had a non-intimate sample taken from them in the course of the investigation; or

        (ii) if they have had a sample taken, it proved unsuitable or insufficient for the same form of analysis, see *Note 6B*; or

    (c) under section 63(3B), from a person convicted of a recordable offence after the date on which that provision came into effect. *PACE,* section 63A, describes the circumstances in which a police officer may require a person convicted of a recordable offence to attend a police station for a non-intimate sample to be taken.

6.7 Reasonable force may be used, if necessary, to take a non-intimate sample from a person without their consent under the powers mentioned in *paragraph 6.6.*

6.8 Before any intimate sample is taken with consent or non-intimate sample is taken with, or without, consent, the person must be informed:

    (a) of the reason for taking the sample;

    (b) of the grounds on which the relevant authority has been given;

    (c) that the sample or information derived from the sample may be retained and subject of a speculative search, see *Note 6E*, unless their destruction is required as in *Annex F*, Part A.

6.9 When clothing needs to be removed in circumstances likely to cause embarrassment to the person, no person of the opposite sex who is not a registered medical practitioner or registered health care professional shall be present, (unless in the case of a juvenile, mentally disordered or mentally vulnerable person, that person specifically requests the presence of an appropriate adult of the opposite sex who is readily available) nor shall anyone whose presence is unnecessary. However, in the case of a juvenile, this is subject to the overriding proviso that such a removal of clothing may take place in the absence of the appropriate adult only if the juvenile signifies, in their presence, that they prefer the adult's absence and they agree.

(c) *Documentation*

6.10 A record of the reasons for taking a sample or impression and, if applicable, of its destruction must be made as soon as practicable. If force is used, a record shall be made of the circumstances and those present. If written consent is given to the taking of a sample or impression, the fact must be recorded in writing.

6.11 A record must be made of a warning given as required by *paragraph 6.3*.

6.12 A record shall be made of the fact that a person has been informed as in *paragraph 6.8(c)* that samples may be subject of a speculative search.

Notes for guidance

6A *When hair samples are taken for the purpose of DNA analysis (rather than for other* **A–147** *purposes such as making a visual match). the suspect should be permitted a reasonable choice as to what part of the body the hairs are taken from. When hairs are plucked, they should be plucked individually, unless the suspect prefers otherwise and no more should be plucked than the person taking them reasonably considers necessary for a sufficient sample.*

    (a) *An insufficient sample is one which is not sufficient either in quantity or quality to provide information for a particular form of analysis, such as DNA analysis. A sample may also be insufficient if enough information cannot be obtained from it by analysis because of loss, destruction, damage or contamination of the sample or as a result of an earlier, unsuccessful attempt at analysis.*

    (b) *An unsuitable sample is one which, by its nature, is not suitable for a particular form of analysis.*

6C *Nothing in paragraph 6.2 prevents intimate samples being taken for elimination purposes with the consent of the person concerned but the provisions of paragraph 2.12 relating to the role of the appropriate adult, should be applied. Paragraph 6.2(b) does not, however, apply where the non-intimate samples were previously taken under the Terrorism Act 2000. Schedule 8, paragraph 10.*

6D *In warning a person who is asked to provide an intimate sample as in paragraph 6.3, the following form of words may be used:*

    "You do not have to provide this sample/allow this swab or impression to be taken, but I must warn you that if you refuse without good cause, your refusal may harm your case if it comes to trial."

6E *Fingerprints or a DNA sample and the information derived from it taken from a person arrested on suspicion of being involved in a recordable offence, or charged with such an offence, or informed they will be reported for such an offence, may be subject of a speculative search. This means they may be checked against other fingerprints and DNA records held by, or on behalf of, the police and other law enforcement authorities in or outside the UK or held in connection with, or as a result of, an investigation of an offence inside or outside the UK. Fingerprints and samples taken from any other person. e.g. a person suspected of committing a recordable offence but who has not been arrested, charged or informed they will be reported for it, may be subject to a speculative search only if the person consents in writing to their fingerprints being subject of such a search. The following is an example of a basic form of words:*

    "I consent to my fingerprints/DNA sample and information derived from it being retained and used only for purposes related to the prevention and detection of a crime, the investigation of an offence or the conduct of a prosecution either nationally or internationally.

    I understand that this sample may be checked against other fingerprint/DNA records held by or on behalf of relevant law enforcement authorities, either nationally or internationally.

    I understand that once I have given my consent for the sample to be retained and used I cannot withdraw this consent."

See Annex F regarding the retention and use of fingerprints and samples taken with consent for elimination purposes.

6F *Samples of urine and non-intimate samples taken in accordance with sections 63B and 63C of PACE may not be used for identification purposes in accordance with this Code. See Code C note for guidance 17D.*

ANNEX A

Video Identification

A–148

(a) General

1. The arrangements for obtaining and ensuring the availability of a suitable set of images to be used in a video identification must be the responsibility of an identification officer, who has no direct involvement with the case.

2. The set of images must include the suspect and at least eight other people who, so far as possible, resemble the suspect in age, general appearance and position in life. Only one suspect shall appear in any set unless there are two suspects of roughly similar appearance, in which case they may be shown together with at least twelve other people.

2A. If the suspect has an unusual physical feature. e.g., a facial scar, tattoo or distinctive hairstyle or hair colour which does not appear on the images of the other people that are available to be used, steps may be taken to:

    (a) conceal the location of the feature on the images of the suspect and the other people; or

    (b) replicate that feature on the images of the other people.

For these purposes, the feature may be concealed or replicated electronically or by any other method which it is practicable to use to ensure that the images of the suspect and other people resemble each other. The identification officer has discretion to choose whether to conceal or replicate the feature and the method to be used. If an unusual physical feature has been described by the witness, the identification officer should, if practicable, have that feature replicated. If it has not been described, concealment may be more appropriate.

2B. If the identification officer decides that a feature should be concealed or replicated, the reason for the decision and whether the feature was concealed or replicated in the images shown to any witness shall be recorded.

2C. If the witness requests to view an image where an unusual physical feature has been concealed or replicated without the feature being concealed or replicated, the witness may be allowed to do so.

3. The images used to conduct a video identification shall, as far as possible, show the suspect and other people in the same positions or carrying out the same sequence of movements. They shall also show the suspect and other people under identical conditions unless the identification officer reasonably believes:

    (a) because of the suspect's failure or refusal to co-operate or other reasons, it is not practicable for the conditions to be identical: and

    (b) any difference in the conditions would not direct a witness' attention to any individual image.

4. The reasons identical conditions are not practicable shall be recorded on forms provided for the purpose.

5. provision must be made for each person shown to be identified by number.

6. If police officers are shown, any numerals or other identifying badges must be concealed. If a prison inmate is shown, either as a suspect or not, then either all, or none of, the people shown should be in prison clothing.

A–149   7. The suspect or their solicitor, friend, or appropriate adult must be given a reasonable opportunity to see the complete set of images before it is shown to any witness. If the suspect has a reasonable objection to the set of images or any of the participants, the suspect shall be asked to state the reasons for the objection. Steps shall, if practicable, be taken to remove the grounds for objection. If this is not practicable, the suspect and/or their representative shall be told why their objections cannot be met and the objection, the reason given for it and why it cannot be met shall be recorded on forms provided for the purpose.

8. Before the images are shown in accordance with *paragraph 7*, the suspect or their solicitor shall be provided with details of the first description of the suspect by any witnesses who are to attend the video identification. When a broadcast or publication is made, as in *paragraph 3.28*, the suspect or their solicitor must also be allowed to view any material released to the media by the police for the purpose of recognising or tracing the suspect, provided it is practicable and would not unreasonably delay the investigation.

9. The suspect's solicitor, if practicable, shall be given reasonable notification of the time and place the video identification is to be conducted so a representative may attend on behalf of the suspect. If a solicitor has not been instructed, this information shall be given to the suspect. The suspect may not be present when the images are shown to the witness(es). In the absence of the suspect's representative, the viewing itself shall be recorded on video. No unauthorised people may be present.

(b) Conducting the video identification

10. The identification officer is responsible for making the appropriate arrangements to **A–150** make sure, before they see the set of images, witnesses are not able to communicate with each other about the case, see any of the images which are to be shown, see, or be reminded of, any photograph or description of the suspect or be given any other indication as to the suspect's identity, or overhear a witness who has already seen the material. There must be no discussion with the witness about the composition of the set of images and they must not be told whether a previous witness has made any identification.

11. Only one witness may see the set of images at a time. Immediately before the images are shown, the witness shall be told that the person they saw on a specified earlier occasion may, or may not, appear in the images they are shown and that if they cannot make a positive identification, they should say so. The witness shall be advised that at any point, they may ask to see a particular part of the set of images or to have a particular image frozen for them to study. Furthermore, it should be pointed out to the witness that there is no limit on how many times they can view the whole set of images or any part of them. However, they should be asked not to make any decision as to whether the person they saw is on the set of images until they have seen the whole set at least twice.

12. Once the witness has seen the whole set of images at least twice and has indicated that they do not want to view the images, or any part of them, again, the witness shall be asked to say whether the individual they saw in person on a specified earlier occasion has been shown and, if so, to identify them by number of the image. The witness will then be shown that image to confirm the identification, see *paragraph 17*.

13. Care must be taken not to direct the witness attention to any one individual image or give any indication of the suspect's identity. Where a witness has previously made an identification by photographs, or a computerised or artist's composite or similar likeness, the witness must not be reminded of such a photograph or composite likeness once a suspect is available for identification by other means in accordance with this Code. Nor must the witness be reminded of any description of the suspect.

14. After the procedure, each witness shall be asked whether they have seen any broadcast or published films or photographs, or any descriptions of suspects relating to the offence and their reply shall be recorded.

(c) Image security and destruction

15. Arrangements shall be made for all relevant material containing sets of images used for specific identification procedures to be kept securely and their movements accounted for. In particular, no-one involved in the investigation shall be permitted to view the material prior to it being shown to any witness.

16. As appropriate, *paragraph 3.30 or 3.31* applies to the destruction or retention of relevant sets of images.

(d) Documentation

17. A record must be made of all those participating in, or seeing, the set of images whose names are known to the police.

18. A record of the conduct of the video identification must be made on forms provided

for the purpose. This shall include anything said by the witness about any identifications or the conduct of the procedure and any reasons it was not practicable to comply with any of the provisions of this Code governing the conduct of video identifications.

ANNEX B

Identification Parades

A–151

(a) General

1. A suspect must be given a reasonable opportunity to have a solicitor or friend present, and the suspect shall be asked to indicate on a second copy of the notice whether or not they wish to do so.

2. An identification parade may take place either in a normal room or one equipped with a screen permitting witnesses to see members of the identification parade without being seen. The procedures for the composition and conduct of the identification parade are the same in both cases, subject to *paragraph 8* (except that an identification parade involving a screen may take place only when the suspect's solicitor, friend or appropriate adult is present or the identification parade is recorded on video).

3. Before the identification parade takes place, the suspect or their solicitor shall be provided with details of the first description of the suspect by any witnesses who are attending the identification parade. When a broadcast or publication is made as in *paragraph 3.28*, the suspect or their solicitor should also be allowed to view any material released to the media by the police for the purpose of recognising or tracing the suspect, provided it is practicable to do so and would not unreasonably delay the investigation.

(b) Identification parades involving prison inmates

4. If a prison inmate is required for identification, and there are no security problems about the person leaving the establishment, they may be asked to participate in an identification parade or video identification.

5. An identification parade may be held in a Prison Department establishment but shall be conducted, as far as practicable under normal identification parade rules. Members of the public shall make up the identification parade unless there are serious security, or control, objections to their admission to the establishment. In such cases, or if a group or video identification is arranged within the establishment, other inmates may participate. If an inmate is the suspect, they are not required to wear prison clothing for the identification parade unless the other people taking part are other inmates in similar clothing, or are members of the public who are prepared to wear prison clothing for the occasion.

(c) Conduct of the identification parade

A–152

6. Immediately before the identification parade, the suspect must be reminded of the procedures governing its conduct and cautioned in the terms of Code C, paragraphs 10.5 or 10.6, as appropriate.

7. All unauthorised people must be excluded from the place where the identification parade is held.

8. Once the identification parade has been formed, everything afterwards, in respect of it, shall take place in the presence and hearing of the suspect and any interpreter, solicitor, friend or appropriate adult who is present (unless the identification parade involves a screen, in which case everything said to, or by, any witness at the place where the identification parade is held, must be sad in the hearing and presence of the suspect's solicitor, friend or appropriate adult or be recorded on video).

9. The identification parade shall consist of at least eight people (in addition to the suspect) who, so far as possible, resemble the suspect in age, height, general appearance and position in life. Only one suspect shall be included in an identification parade unless there are two suspects of roughly similar appearance, in which case they may be paraded together with at least twelve other people. In no circumstances shall more than two suspects be included in one identification parade and where there are separate identification parades, they shall be made up of different people.

10. If the suspect has an unusual physical feature, e.g., a facial scar, tattoo or distinctive hairstyle or hair colour which cannot be replicated on other members of the identification parade, steps may be taken to conceal the location of that feature on the suspect and the other members of the identification parade if the suspect and their solicitor, or appropriate adult, agree. For example, by use of a plaster or a hat, so that all members of the identification parade resemble each other in general appearance.

11. When all members of a similar group are possible suspects, separate identification parades shall be held for each unless there are two suspects of similar appearance when they may appear on the same identification parade with at least twelve other members of the group who are not suspects. When police officers in uniform form an identification parade any numerals or other identifying badges shall be concealed.

12. When the suspect is brought to the place where the identification parade is to be held, they shall be asked if they have any objection to the arrangements for the identification parade or to any of the other participants in it and to state the reasons for the objection. The suspect may obtain advice from their solicitor or friend, if present, before the identification parade proceeds. If the suspect has a reasonable objection to the arrangements or any of the participants, steps shall, if practicable, be taken to remove the grounds for objection. When it is not practicable to do so, the suspect shall be told why their objections cannot be met and the objection, the reason given for it and why it cannot be met, shall be recorded on forms provided for the purpose.

13. The suspect may select their own position in the line, but may not otherwise interfere with the order of the people forming the line. When there is more than one witness, the suspect must be told, after each witness has left the room, that they can, if they wish, change position in the line. Each position in the line must be clearly numbered, whether by means of a number laid on the floor in front of each identification parade member or by other means.

14. Appropriate arrangements must be made to make sure, before witnesses attend the **A–153** identification parade, they are not able to:

    (i) communicate with each other about the case or overhear a witness who has already seen the identification parade;

    (ii) see any member of the identification parade:

    (iii) see, or be reminded of, any photograph or description of the suspect or be given any other indication as to the suspects identity, or

    (iv) see the suspect before or after the identification parade.

15. The person conducting a witness to an identification parade must not discuss with them the composition of the identification parade and, in particular, must not disclose whether a previous witness has made any identification.

16. Witnesses shall be brought in one at a time. Immediately before the witness inspects the identification parade, they shall be told the person they saw on a specified earlier occasion may, or may not, be present and if they cannot make a positive identification, they should say so. The witness must also be told they should not make any decision about whether the person they saw is on the identification parade until they have looked at each member at least twice.

17. When the officer or police staff (see paragraph 3.11) conducting the identification procedure is satisfied the witness has properly looked at each member of the identification parade, they shall ask the witness whether the person they saw on a specified earlier occasion is on the identification parade and, if so, to indicate the number of the person concerned, see *paragraph 28*.

18. If the witness wishes to hear any identification parade member speak, adopt any specified posture or move, they shall first be asked whether they can identify any person(s) on the identification parade on the basis of appearance only. When the request is to hear members of the identification parade speak, the witness shall be reminded that the participants in the identification parade have been chosen on the basis of physical appearance only. Members of the identification parade may then be asked to comply with the witness' request to hear them speak, see them move or adopt any specified posture.

19. If the witness requests that the person they have indicated remove anything used for **A–154** the purposes of *paragraph 10* to conceal the location of an unusual physical feature, that person may be asked to remove it.

20. If the witness makes an identification after the identification parade has ended, the

suspect and, if present, their solicitor, interpreter or friend shall be informed. When this occurs, consideration should be given to allowing the witness a second opportunity to identify the suspect.

21. After the procedure, each witness shall be asked whether they have seen any broadcast or published films or photographs or any descriptions of suspects relating to the offence and their reply shall be recorded.

22. When the last witness has left, the suspect shall be asked whether they wish to make any comments on the conduct of the identification parade.

(d) Documentation

23. A video recording must normally be taken of the identification parade. If that is impracticable, a colour photograph must be taken. A copy of the video recording or photograph shall be supplied, on request, to the suspect or their solicitor within a reasonable time.

24. As appropriate, *paragraph 3.30* or *3.31*, should apply to any photograph or video taken as in *paragraph 23*.

25. If any person is asked to leave an identification parade because they are interfering with its conduct, the circumstances shall be recorded.

26. A record must be made of all those present at an identification parade whose names are known to the police.

27. A record must be made of all those present at an identification parade whose names are known to the police.

28. A record of the conduct of any identification parade must be made on forms provided for the purpose. This shall include anything said by the witness or the suspect about any identifications or the conduct of the procedure, and any reasons it was not practicable to comply with any of this Code's provisions.

ANNEX C

Group Identification

A–155

(a) General

1. The purpose of this Annex is to make sure, as far as possible, group identifications follow the principles and procedures for identification parades so the conditions are fair to the suspect in the way they test the witness' ability to make an identification.

2. Group identifications may take place either with the suspect's consent and co-operation or covertly without their consent.

3. The location of the group identification is a matter for the identification officer, although the officer may take into account any representations made by the suspect, appropriate adult, their solicitor or friend.

4. The place where the group identification is held should be one where other people are either passing by or waiting around informally, in groups such that the suspect is able to join them and be capable of being seen by the witness at the same time as others in the group. For example people leaving an escalator, pedestrians walking through a shopping centre, passengers on railway and bus stations, waiting in queues or groups or where people are standing or sitting in groups in other public places.

5. If the group identification is to be held covertly, the choice of locations will be limited by the places where the suspect can be found and the number of other people present at that time. In these cases, suitable locations might be along regular routes travelled by the suspect, including buses or trains or public places frequented by the suspect.

A–156   6. Although the number, age, sex, race and general description and style of clothing of other people present at the location cannot be controlled by the identification officer, in selecting the location the officer must consider the general appearance and numbers of people likely to be present. In particular, the officer must reasonably expect that over the period the witness observes the group, they will be able to see, from time to time, a number of others whose appearance is broadly similar to that of the suspect.

7. A group identification need not be held if the identification officer believes, because of the unusual appearance of the suspect, none of the locations it would be practicable to use satisfy the requirements of *paragraph 6* necessary to make the identification fair.

8. Immediately after a group identification procedure has taken place (with or without the suspect's consent), a colour photograph or video should be taken of the general scene, if practicable, to give a general impression of the scene and the number of people present. Alternatively, if it is practicable, the group identification may be video recorded.

9. If it is not practicable to take the photograph or video in accordance with *paragraph 8*, a photograph or film of the scene should be taken later at a time determined by the identification officer if the officer considers it practicable to do so.

10. An identification carried out in accordance with this Code remains a group identification even though, at the time of being seen by the witness, the suspect was on their own rather than in a group.

11. Before the group identification takes place, the suspect or their solicitor shall be provided with details of the first description of the suspect by any witnesses who are to attend the identification. When a broadcast or publication is made, as in *paragraph 3.28*, the suspect or their solicitor should also be allowed to view any material released by the police to the media for the purposes of recognising or tracing the suspect, provided that it is practicable and would not unreasonably delay the investigation.

12. After the procedure, each witness shall be asked whether they have seen any broadcast or published films or photographs or any descriptions of suspects relating to the offence and their reply recorded.

(b) Identification with the consent of the suspect

13. A suspect must be given a reasonable opportunity to have a solicitor or friend present. **A–157**
They shall be asked to indicate on a second copy of the notice whether or not they wish to do so

14. The witness, the person carrying out the procedure and the suspect's solicitor, appropriate adult, friend or any interpreter for the witness, may be concealed from the sight of the individuals in the group they are observing, if the person carrying out the procedure considers this assists the conduct of the identification.

15. The person conducting a witness to a group identification must not discuss with them the forthcoming group identification and, in particular, must not disclose whether a previous witness has made any identification.

16. Anything said to, or by, the witness during the procedure about the identification should be said in the presence and hearing of those present at the procedure.

17. Appropriate arrangements must be made to make sure, before witness attend the group identification, they are not able to:

(i) communicate with each other about the case or overhear a witness who has already been given an opportunity to see the suspect in the group;

(ii) see the suspect; or

(iii) see, or be reminded of, any photographs or description of the suspect or be given any other indication of the suspect's identity.

18. Witnesses shall be brought one at a time to the place where they are to observe the group. Immediately before the witness is asked to look at the group, the person conducting the procedure shall tell them that the person they saw may, or may not, be in the group and that if they cannot make a positive indentification, they should say so. The witness shall be asked to observe the group in which the suspect is to appear. The way in which the witness should do this will depend on whether the group is moving or stationary.

Moving group

19. When the group in which the suspect is to appear is moving, e.g. leaving an escalator, **A–158**
the provisions of *paragraphs 20 to 24* should be followed.

20. If two or more suspects consent to a group identification, each should be the subject of separate identification procedures. These may be conducted consecutively on the same occasion.

21. The person conducting the procedure shall tell the witness to observe the group and ask them to point out any person they think they saw on the specified earlier occasion.

22. Once the witness has been informed as in *paragraph 21* the suspect should be allowed to take whatever position in the group they wish.

23. When the witness points out a person as in *paragraph 21* they shall, if practicable, be asked to take a closer look at the person to confirm the identification. If this is not practicable, or they cannot confirm the identification, they shall be asked how sure they are that the person they have indicated is the relevant person.

24. The witness should continue to observe the group for the period which the person conducting the procedure reasonably believes is necessary in the circumstances for them to be able to make comparisons between the suspect and other individuals of broadly similar appearance to the suspect as in *paragraph 6*.

Stationary groups

A–159   25. When the group in which the suspect is to appear is stationary, e.g. people waiting in a queue, the provisions of *paragraphs 26 to 29* should be followed.

26. If two or more suspects consent to a group identification, each should be subject to separate identification procedures unless they are of broadly similar appearance when they may appear in the same group. When separate group identifications are held, the groups must be made up of different people.

27. The suspect may take whatever position in the group they wish. If there is more than one witness, the suspect must be told, out of the sight and hearing of any witness, that they can, if they wish, change their position in the group.

28. The witness shall be asked to pass along, or amongst, the group and to look at each person in the group at least twice, taking as much care and time as possible according to the circumstances, before making an identification. Once the witness has done this, they shall be asked whether the person they saw on the specified earlier occasion is in the group and to indicate any such person by whatever means the person conducting the procedure considers appropriate in the circumstances. If this is not practicable, the witness shall be asked to point out any person they think they saw on the earlier occasion.

29. When the witness makes an indication as in *paragraph 28*, arrangements shall be made, if practicable, for the witness to take a closer look at the person to confirm the identification. If this is not practicable, or the witness is unable to confirm the identification, they shall be asked how sure they are that the person they have indicated is the relevant person.

All cases

A–160   30. If the suspect unreasonably delays joining the group, or having joined the group, deliberately conceals themselves from the sight of the witness, this may be treated as a refusal to co-operate in a group identification.

31. If the witness identifies a person other than the suspect, that person should be informed what has happened and asked if they are prepared to give their name and address. There is no obligation upon any member of the public to give these details. There shall be no duty to record any details of any other member of the public present in the group or at the place where the procedure is conducted.

32. When the group identification has been completed, the suspect shall be asked whether they wish to make any comments on the conduct of the procedure.

33. If the suspect has not been previously informed, they shall be told of any identifications made by the witnesses.

(c) Identification without the suspect's consent

A–161   34. Group identification held covertly without the suspect's consent should, as far as practicable, follow the rules for conduct of group identification by consent.

35. A suspect has no right to have a solicitor, appropriate adult or friend present as the identification will take place without the knowledge of the suspect.

36. Any number of suspects may be identified at the same time.

(d) Identification in police stations

37. Group identifications should only take place in police stations for reasons of safety, security or because it is not practicable to hold them elsewhere.

38. The group identification may take place either in a room equipped with a screen

permitting witnesses to see members of the group without being seen, or anywhere else in the police station that the identification officer considers appropriate.

39. Any of the additional safeguards applicable to identification parades should be followed if the identification officer considers it is practicable to do so in the circumstances.

(e) Identification involving prison inmates

40. A group identification involving a prison inmate may only be arranged in the prison **A–162** or at a police station.

41. When a group identification takes place involving a prison inmate, whether in a prison or in a police station, the arrangements should follow those in *paragraphs 37* to *39*. If a group identification takes place within a prison, other inmates may participate. If an inmate is the suspect, they do not have to wear prison clothing for the group identification unless the other participants are wearing the same clothing.

(f) Documentation

42. When a photograph or video is taken as in *paragraph 8* or *9*, a copy of the photograph or video shall be supplied on request to the suspect or their solicitor within a reasonable time.

43. *Paragraph 3.30* or *3.31*, as appropriate, shall apply when the photograph or film taken in accordance with *paragraph 8* or *9* includes the suspect.

44. A record of the conduct of any group identification must be made on forms provided for the purpose. This shall include anything said by the witness or suspect about any identifications or the conduct of the procedure and any reasons why it was not practicable to comply with any of the provisions of this Code governing the conduct of group identification.

ANNEX D

Confrontation by a Witness

1. Before the confrontation takes place, the witness must be told that the person they saw **A–163** may, or may not, be the person they are to confront and that if they are not that person, then the witness should say so.

2. Before the confrontation takes place the suspect or their solicitor shall be provided with details of the first description of the suspect given by any witness who is to attend. When a broadcast or publication is made, as in *paragraph 3.28*, the suspect or their solicitor should also be allowed to view any material released to the media for the purposes of recognising or tracing the suspect, provided it is practicable to do so and would not unreasonably delay the investigation.

3. Force may not be used to make the suspect's face visible to the witness.

4. Confrontation must take place in the presence of the suspect's solicitor, interpreter or friend unless this would cause unreasonable delay.

5. The suspect shall be confronted indepenoently by each witness, who shall be asked "Is this the person?". If the witness identifies the person but is unable to confirm the identification, they shall be asked how sure they are that the person is the one they saw on the earlier occasion.

6. The confrontation should normally take place in the police station, either in a normal room or one equipped with a screen permitting a witness to see the suspect without being seen. In both cases, the procedures are the same except that a room equipped with a screen may be used only when the suspect's solicitor, friend or appropriate adult is present or the confrontation is recorded on video.

7. After the procedure, each witness shall be asked whether they have seen any broadcast or published films or photographs or any descriptions of suspects relating to the offence and their reply shall be recorded.

ANNEX E

Showing Photographs

A–164

(a) Action

1. An officer of sergeant rank or above shall be responsible for supervising and directing the showing of photographs. The actual showing may be done by another officer or police staff, see *paragraph 3.11*.

2. The supervising officer must confirm the first description of the suspect given by the witness has been recorded before they are shown the photographs. If the supervising officer is unable to confirm the description has been recorded they shall postpone showing the photographs.

3. Only one witness shall be shown photographs at any one time. Each witness shall be given as much privacy as practicable and shall not be allowed to communicate with any other witness in the case.

4. The witness shall be shown not less than twelve photographs at a time, which shall, as far as possible, all be of a similar type.

5. When the witness is shown the photographs, they shall be told the photograph of the person they saw may, or may not, be amongst them and if they cannot make a positive identification, they should say so. The witness shall also be told they should not make a decision until they have viewed at least twelve photographs. The witness shall not be prompted or guided in any way but shall be left to make any selection without help.

6. If a witness makes a positive identification from photographs, unless the person identified is otherwise eliminated from enquiries or is not available, other witnesses shall not be shown photographs. But both they, and the witness who has made the identification, shall be asked to attend a video identification, an identification parade or group identification unless there is no dispute about the suspect's identification.

A–165   7. If the witness makes a selection but is unable to confirm the identification, the person showing the photographs shall ask them how sure they are that the photograph they have indicated is the person they saw on the specified earlier occasion.

8. When the use of a computerised or artist's composite or similar likeness has led to there being a known suspect who can be asked to participate in a video identification, appear on an identification parade or participate in a group identification, that likeness shall not be shown to other potential witnesses.

9. When a witness attending a video identification, an identification parade or group identification has previously been shown photographs or computerised or artist's composite or similar likeness (and it is the responsibility of the officer in charge of the investigation to make the identification officer aware that this is the case), the suspect and their solicitor must be informed of this fact before the identification procedure takes place.

10. None of the photographs shown shall be destroyed, whether or not an identification is made, since they may be required for production in court. The photographs shall be numbered and a separate photograph taken of the frame or part of the album from which the witness made an identification as an aid to reconstituting it.

(b) Documentation

A–166   11. Whether or not an identification is made, a record shall be kept of the showing of photographs on forms provided for the purpose. This shall include anything said by the witness about any identification or the conduct of the procedure, any reasons it was not practicable to comply with any of the provisions of this Code governing the showing of photographs and the name and rank of the supervising officer

12. The supervising officer shall inspect and sign the record as soon as practicable.

ANNEX F

Fingerprints, Footwear Impressions and Samples—Destruction and Speculative Searches

A–167

(a) Fingerprints, footwear impressions and samples taken in connection with a criminal investigation

1. When fingerprints, footwear impressions or DNA samples are taken from a person in connection with an investigation and the person is not suspected of having committed the offence, see **Note F1**, they must be destroyed as soon as they have fulfilled the purpose for which they were taken unless:

    (a) they were taken for the purpose of an investigation of an offence for which a person has been convicted; and

    (b) fingerprints, footwear impressions or samples were also taken from the convicted person for the purposes of that investigation.

However, subject to paragraph 2, the fingerprints, footwear impressions and samples, and the information derived from samples, may not be used in the investigation of any offence or in evidence against the person who is, or would be, entitled to the destruction of the fingerprints, footwear impressions and samples, see **Note F2**.

2. The requirement to destroy fingerprints, footwear impressions and DNA samples, and information derived from samples, and restrictions on their retention and use in paragraph 1 do not apply if the person gives their written consent for their fingerprints, footwear impressions or sample to be retained and used after they have fulfilled the purpose for which they were taken, see **Note F1**.

3. When a person's fingerprints, footwear impressions or sample are to be destroyed:

    (a) any copies of the fingerprints and footwear impressions must also be destroyed;

    (b) the person may witness the destruction of their fingerprints, footwear impressions or copies if they ask to do so within five days of being informed destruction is required;

    (c) access to relevant computer fingerprint data shall be made impossible as soon as it is practicable to do so and the person shall be given a certificate to this effect within three months of asking; and

    (d) neither the fingerprints, footwear impressions, the sample, or any information derived from the sample, may be used in the investigation of any offence or in evidence against the person who is, or would be, entitled to its destruction.

4. Fingerprints, footwear impressions or samples, and the information derived from samples, taken in connection with the investigation of an offence which are not required to be destroyed, may be retained after they have fulfilled the purposes for which they were taken but may be used only for purposes related to the prevention or detection of crime, the investigation of an offence or the conduct of a prosecution in, as well as outside, the UK and may also be subject to a speculative search. This includes checking them against other fingerprints, footwear impressions and DNA records held by, or on behalf of, the police and other law enforcement authorities in, as well as outside, the UK.

(b) Fingerprints taken in connection with immigration Service enquiries

5. Fingerprints taken for immigration Service enquiries in accordance with powers and procedures other than under PACE and for which the immigration Service, not the police, are responsible, must be destroyed as follows: **A–168**

    (a) fingerprints and all copies must be destroyed as soon as practicable if the person from whom they were taken proves they are a British or Commonwealth citizen who has the right of abode in the UK under the immigration Act 1971. section 2(1)(b);

    (b) fingerprints taken under the power as in *paragraph 4.11(g)* from a dependant of a person in *4.11 (b)* to *(f)* must be destroyed when that person's fingerprints are to be destroyed;

    (c) fingerprints taken from a person under any power as in *paragraph 4.11* or with the person's consent which have not already been destroyed as above, must be destroyed within ten years of being taken or within such period specified by the Secretary of State under the immigration and *Asylum Act* 1999, section 143(5).

Notes for guidance

F1 Fingerprints, footwear impressions and samples given voluntarily for the purpose of   **A–169** elimination play an important part in many police investigations. It is, therefore, important to make sure innocent volunteers are not deterred from participating and their consent to their fingerprints, footwear impressions and DNA being used for the purpose of a specific investigation is fully informed and voluntary. If the police or volunteer seek to have the fingerprints, footwear impressions or samples retained for use after the specific investigation ends, it is important the volunteer's consent to this is also fully informed and voluntary.

Examples of consent for:

- DNA/fingerprints/footwear impressions - to be used only for the purpose of a specific investigation;
- DNA/fingerprints/footwear impressions - to be used in the specific investigation and retained by the police for future use.

To minimise the risk of confusion, each consent should be physically separate and the volunteer should be asked to sign each consent.

(a) **DNA**:

 (i) DNA sample taken for the purposes of elimination or as part of an intelligence-led screening and to be used only for the purposes of that investigation and destroyed afterwards:

"I consent to my DNA/mouth swab being taken for forensic analysis. I understand that the sample will be destroyed at the end of the case and that my profile will only be compared to the crime stain profile from this enquiry. I have been advised that the person taking the sample may be required to give evidence and/or provide a written statement to the police in relation to the taking of it."

 (ii) DNA sample to be retained on the National DNA database and used in the future:

"I consent to my DNA sample and information derived from it being retained and used only for purposes related to the prevention and detection of a crime, the investigation of an offence or the conduct of a prosecution either nationally or internationally."

"I understand that this sample may be checked against other DNA records held by, or on behalf of, relevant law enforcement authorities, either nationally or internationally."

"I understand that once I have given my consent for the sample to be retained and used I cannot withdraw this consent."

(b) **Fingerprints:**

 (i) Fingerprints taken for the purposes of elimination or as part of an intelligence-led screening and to be used only for the purposes of that investigation and destroyed afterwards:

"I consent to my fingerprints being taken for elimination purposes. I understand that the fingerprints will be destroyed at the end of the case and that my fingerprints will only be compared to the fingerprints from this enquiry. I have been advised that the person taking the fingerprints may be required to give evidence and/or provide a written statement to the police in relation to the taking of it."

 (ii) **Fingerprints to be retained for future use:**

"I consent to my fingerprints being retained and used only for purposes related to the prevention and detection of a crime, the investigation of an offence or the conduct of a prosecution either nationally or internationally."

"I understand that my fingerprints may be checked against other records held by, or on behalf of, relevant law enforcement authorities, either nationally or internationally."

"I understand that once I have given my consent for my fingerprints to be retained and used I cannot withdraw this consent."

(c) **Footwear impressions:**

 (i) Footwear impressions taken for the purposes of elimination or as part of an intelligence-led screening and to be used only for the purposes of that investigation and destroyed afterwards:

"I consent to my footwear impressions being taken for elimination purposes. I understand that the footwear impressions will be destroyed at the end of the case and that my footwear impressions will only be compared to the footwear impressions from this enquiry. I have been advised that the person taking the footwear impressions may be required to give evidence and or provide a written statement to the police in relation to the taking of it."

 (ii) **Footwear impressions to be retained for future use:**

"I consent to my footwear impressions being retained and used only for purposes related to the prevention and detection of a crime, the investigation of an offence or the conduct of a prosecution, either nationally or internationally."

"I understand that my footwear impressions may be checked against other records held by or on behalf of relevant law enforcement authorities, either nationally or internationally."

"I understand that once I have given my consent for my footwear impressions to be retained and used I cannot withdraw this consent."

F2 The provisions for the retention of fingerprints, footwear impressions and samples in **A–170** paragraph 1 allow for all fingerprints, footwear impressions and samples in a case to be available for any subsequent miscarriage of justice investigation.

Police and Criminal Evidence Act 1984 (Pace)

Code E

Code of Practice on Audio Recording Interviews with Suspects

Commencement—Transitional Arrangements   **A–171**
This code applies to interviews carried out after midnight on 31 December 2005, notwithstanding that the interview may have commenced before that time.

1 General

1.1 This Code of Practice must be readily available for consultation by: **A–172**
  • police officers
  • police staff
  • detained persons
  • members of the public.

1.2 The *Notes for Guidance* included are not provisions of this Code.

1.3 Nothing in this Code shall detract from the requirements of Code C. the Code of practice for the detention, treatment and questioning of persons by police officers.

1.4 This Code does not apply to those people listed in Code C. *paragraph 1.12.*

1.5 The term:
  • 'appropriate adult' has the same meaning as in Code C. *paragraph 1.7*
  • 'solicitor' has the same meaning as in Code C. *paragraph 6.12.*

1.6 In this Code: **A–173**
  (aa) 'recording media' means any removable, physical audio recording medium (such as magnetic type, optical disc or solid state memory) which can be played and copied.
  (a) 'designated person' means a person other than a police officer, designated under the Police Reform Act 2002, Part 4 who has specified powers and duties of police officers conferred or imposed on them.
  (b) any reference to a police officer includes a designated person acting in the exercise or performance of the powers and duties conferred or imposed on them by their designation.

1.7 If a power conferred on a designated person:
  (a) allows reasonable force to be used when exercised by a police officer, a designated person exercising that power has the same entitlement to use force;
  (b) includes power to use force to enter any premises, that power is not exercisable by that designated person except:
    (i) in the company, and under the supervision, of a police officer; or
    (ii) for the purpose of:
      • saving life or limb; or
      • preventing serious damage to property.

1.8 Nothing in this Code prevents the custody officer, or other officer given custody of the **A–174** detainee, from allowing police staff who are not designated persons to carry out individual procedures or tasks at the police station if the law allows. However, the officer remains responsible for making sure the procedures and tasks are carried out correctly in accordance with these Codes. Any such police staff must be:

    (a) a person employed by a police authority maintaining a police force and under the control and direction of the Chief Officer of that force; or

    (b) employed by a person with whom a police authority has a contract for the provision of services relating to persons arrested or otherwise in custody.

1.9 Designated persons and other police staff must have regard to any relevant provisions of the Codes of Practice.

1.10 References to pocket book include any official report book issued to police officer or police staff.

1.11 References to a custody officer include those performing the functions of a custody officer as in *paragraph 1.9* of Code C.

2 Recording and sealing master recordings

A–175   2.1 Recording of interviews shall be carried out openly to instil confidence in its reliability as an impartial and accurate record of the interview.

2.2 One recording, the master recording, will be sealed in the suspect's presence. A second recording will be used as a working copy. The master recording is either of the two recordings used in a twin deck/drive machine or the only recording in a single deck/drive machine. The working copy is either the second/third recording used in a twin/triple deck/drive machine or a copy of the master recording made by a single deck/drive machine. [See *Notes 2A* and *2B*]

2.3 Nothing in this Code requires the identity of officers or police staff conducting interviews to be recorded or disclosed:

    (a) in the case of enquires linked to the investigation of terrorism; or

    (b) if the interviewer reasonably believes recording or disclosing their name might put them in danger.

In these cases interviewers should use warrant or other identification numbers and the name of their police station. [See Note 2C]

Notes for guidance

A–176   2A *The purpose of sealing the master recording in the suspect's presence is to show the recording's integrity is preserved. If a single deck/drive machine is used the working copy of the master recording must be made in the suspect's presence and without the master recording leaving their sight. The working copy shall be used for making further copies if needed.*

2B *Not used.*

2C *The purpose of paragraph 2.3(b) is to protect those involved in serious organised crime investigations or arrests of particularly violent suspects when there is reliable information that those arrested or their associates may threaten or cause harm to those involved. In cases of doubt, an officer of inspector rank or above should be consulted.*

3 Interviews to be audio recorded

A–177   3.1 Subject to *paragraphs 3.3* and *3.4*, audio recording shall be used at police stations for any interview:

    (a) with a person cautioned under Code C. *section 10* in respect of any indictable offence, including an offence triable either way: see *Note 3A*

    (b) which takes place as a result of an interviewer exceptionally putting further questions to a suspect about an offence described in *paragraph 3.1(a)* after they have been charged with, or told they may be prosecuted for, that offence, see Code C. *paragraph 16.5*

    (c) when an interviewer wants to tell a person, after they have been charged with, or informed they may be prosecuted for an offence described in *paragraph 3.1(a)*, about any written statement or interview with another person, see Code C, *paragraph 16.4*.

3.2 The *Terrorism Act* 2000 makes separate provision for a Code of Practice for the audio recording of interviews of those arrested under Section 41 or detained under Schedule 7 of the Act. The provisions of this Code do not apply to such interviews.

3.3 The custody officer may authorise the interviewer not to audio record the interview when it is:

(a) not reasonably practicable because of equipment failure or the unavailability of a suitable interview room or recorder and the authorising officer considers, on reasonable grounds, that the interview should not be delayed; or

(b) clear from the outset there will not be a prosecution.

Note: In these cases the interview should be recorded in writing in accordance with Code C. *section 11*. In all cases the custody officer shall record the specific reasons for not audio recording. [See *Note 3B*]

3.4 If a person refuses to go into or remain in a suitable interview room, see Code C *paragraph 12.5*, and the custody officer considers, on reasonable grounds, that the interview should not be delayed the interview may, at the custody officer's discretion, be conducted in a cell using portable recording equipment or, if none is available, recorded in writing as in Code C, *section 11*. The reasons for this shall be recorded.

3.5 The whole of each interview shall be audio recorded, including the taking and reading back of any statement.

Notes for guidance

3A *Nothing in this Code is intended to preclude audio recording at police discretion of* **A–178**
interviews at police stations with people cautioned in respect of offences not covered by paragraph 3.1. or responses made by persons after they have been charged with, or told they may be prosecuted for, an offence, provided this Code is complied with.

3B *A decision not to audio record an interview for any reason may be the subject of comment in court. The authorising officer should be prepared to justify that decision.*

4 THE INTERVIEW

(a) General

4.1 The provisions of Code C: **A–179**

- *sections 10 and 11*, and the applicable *Notes for Guidance* apply to the conduct of interviews to which this Code applies
- *paragraphs 11.7 to 11.14* apply only when a written record is needed.

4.2 Code C, *paragraphs 10.10. 10 11* and Annex C describe the restriction on drawing adverse inferences from a suspect's failure or refusal to say anything about their involvement in the offence when interviewed or after being charged or informed they may be prosecuted, and how it affects the terms of the caution and determines if and by whom a special warning under sections 36 and 37 can be given.

(b) Commencement of interviews

4.3 When the suspect is brought into the interview room the interviewer shall, without delay but in the suspect's sight, load the recorder with new recording media and set it to record. The recording media must be unwrapped or opened in the suspect's presence.

4.4 The interviewer should tell the suspect about the recording process. The interviewer shall:

(a) say the interview is being audibly recorded

(b) subject to *paragraph 2.3*, give their name and rank and that of any other interviewer present

(c) ask the suspect and any other party present, e.g. a solicitor, to identify themselves

(d) state the date, time of commencement and place of the interview

(e) state the suspect will be given a notice about what will happen to the copies of the recording.

See *Note 4A*

4.5 The interviewer shall:

● caution the suspect, see Code C, *section 10*

● remind the suspect of their entitlement to free legal advice, see Code C, *paragraph 11.2*.

4.6 The interviewer shall put to the suspect any significant statement or silence: see Code C, *paragraph 11.4*.

(c) Interviews with deaf persons

A–180   4.7 If the suspect is deaf or is suspected of having impaired hearing, the interviewer shall make a written note of the interview in accordance with Code C, at the same time as audio recording it in accordance with this Code. [See *Notes 4B* and *4C*]

(d) Objections and complaints by the suspect

4.8 If the suspect objects to the interview being audibly recorded at the outset. during the interview or during a break, the interviewer shall explain that the interview is being audibly recorded and that this Code requires the suspect's objections to be recorded on the audio recording. When any objections have been audibly recorded or the suspect has refused to have their objections recorded, the interviewer shall say they are turning off the recorder. give their reasons and turn it off. The interviewer shall then make a written record of the interview as in Code C, *section 11*. If, however, the interviewer reasonably considers they may proceed to question the suspect with the audio recording still on, the interviewer may do so. This procedure also applies in cases where the suspect has previously objected to the interview being visually recorded, see *Code F 4.8*, and the investigating officer has decided to audibly record the interview. [See *Note 4D*]

4.9 If in the course of an interview a complaint is made by or on behalf of the person being questioned concerning the provisions of this Code or Code C, the interviewer shall act as in Code C, *paragraph 12.9*. [See *Notes 4E* and *4F*]

4.10 If the suspect indicates they want to tell the interviewer about matters not directly connected with the offence and they are unwilling for these matters to be audio recorded, the suspect should be given the opportunity to tell the interviewer at the end of the formal interview.

(e) Changing recording media

4.11 When the recorder shows the recording media only has a short time left, the interviewer shall tell the suspect the recording media are coming to an end and round off that part of the interview. If the interviewer leaves the room for a second set of recording media, the suspect shall not be left unattended. The interviewer will remove the recording media from the recorder and insert the new recording media which shall be unwrapped or opened in the suspect's presence. The recorder should be set to record or the new media. To avoid confusion between the recording media, the interviewer shall mark the media with an identification number immediately after they are removed from the recorder.

(f) Taking a break during interview

A–181   4.12 When a break is taken, the fact that a break is to be taken, the reason for it and the time shall be recorded on the audio recording.

4.12A When the break is taken and the interview room vacated by the suspect. the recording media shall be removed from the recorder and the procedures for the conclusion of an interview followed, see *paragraph 4.18*.

4.13 When a break is a short one and both the suspect and an interviewer remain in the interview room, the recording may be stopped. There is no need to remove the recording media and when the interview recommences the recording should continue on the same recording media. The time the interview recommences shall be recorded on the audio recording.

4.14 After any break in the interview the interviewer must, before resuming the interview, remind the person being questioned that they remain under caution or, if there is any doubt, give the caution in full again. [See *Note 4G*]

(g) Failure of recording equipment

4.15 If there is an equipment failure which can be rectified quickly, e.g. by inserting new recording media, the interviewer shall follow the appropriate procedures as in *paragraph*

4.11. When the recording is resumed the interviewer shall explain what happened and record the time the interview recommences. If, however, it will not be possible to continue recording on that recorder and no replacement recorder is readily available, the interview may continue without being audibly recorded. If this happens, the interviewer shall seek the custody officer's authority as in *paragraph 3.3*. [See *Note 4H*]

(h) Removing recording media from the recorder

4.16 When recording media is removed from the recorder during the interview, they shall be retained and the procedures in *paragraph 4.18* followed.

(i) Conclusion of interview

4.17 At the conclusion of the interview, the suspect shall be offered the opportunity to clarify anything he or she has said and asked if there is anything they want to add.

4.18 At the conclusion of the interview, including the taking and reading back of any written statement, the time shall be recorded and the recording shall be stopped. The interviewer shall seal the master recording with a master recording label and treat it as an exhibit in accordance with force standing orders. The interviewer shall sign the label and ask the suspect and any third party present during the interview to sign it. If the suspect or third party refuse to sign the lable an officer of at least inspector rank, or if not available the custody officer, shall be called into the interview room and asked, subject to *paragraph 2.3*, to sign it.

4.19 The suspect shall be handed a notice which explains:

    • how the audio recording will be used

    • the arrangements for access to it

    • that if the person is charged or informed they will be prosecuted, a copy of the audio recording will be supplied as soon as practicable or as otherwise agreed between the suspect and the police.

Notes for guidance

4A *For the purpose of voice identification the interviewer should ask the suspect and any* **A–182** *other people present to identify themselves.*

4B *This provision is to give a person who is deaf or has impaired hearing equivalent rights of access to the full interview record as far as this is possible using audio recording.*

4C *The provisions of Code C, section 13 on interpreters for deal persons or for interviews with suspects who have difficulty understanding English continue to apply. However, in an audibly recorded interview the requirement on the interviewer to make sure the interpreter makes a separate note of the interview applies only to paragraph 4.7 (interviews with deaf persons).*

4D *The interviewer should remember that a decision to continue recording against the wishes of the suspect may be the subject of comment in court.*

4E *If the custody officer is called to deal with the complaint, the recorder should, if possible, be left on until the custody officer has entered the room and spoken to the person being interviewed. Continuation or termination of the interview should be at the interviewer's discretion pending action by an inspector under Code C, paragraph 9.2.*

4F *If the complaint is about a matter not connected with this Code or Code C, the decision* **A–183** *to continue is at the interviewer's discretion. When the interviewer decides to continue the interview, they shall tell the suspect the complaint will be brought to the custody officer's attention at the conclusion of the interview. When the interview is concluded the interviewer must, as soon as practicable, inform the custody officer about the existence and nature of the complaint made.*

4G *The interviewer should remember that it may be necessary to show to the court that nothing occurred during a break or between interviews which influenced the suspect's recorded evidence. After a break or at the beginning of a subsequent interview, the interviewer should consider summarising on the record the reason for the break and confirming this with the suspect.*

4H *Where the interview is being recorded and the media or the recording equipment fails the officer conducting the interview should stop the interview immediately. Where part of the interview is unaffected by the error and is still accessible on the media, that media shall be copied and sealed in the suspect's presence and the interview recommenced using new equipment/ media as required. Where the content of the interview has been lost in its entirety the media should be sealed in the suspect's presence and the interview begun again. If the recording equipment cannot be fixed or no replacement is immediately available the interview should be recorded in accordance with Code C, section 11.*

5 After the interview

A–184　　5.1 The interviewer shall make a note in their pocket book that the interview has taken place, was audibly recorded, its time, duration and date and the master recording's identification number.

5.2 If no proceedings follow in respect of the person whose interview was recorded, the recording media must be kept securely as in *paragraph 6.1* and *Note 6A*.

Note for guidance

A–185　　5A *Any written record of an audibly recorded interview should be made in accordance with national guidelines approved by the Secretary of State.*

6 Media security

A–186　　6.1 The officer in charge of each police station at which interviews with suspects are recorded shall make arrangements for master recordings to be kept securely and their movements accounted for on the same basis as material which may be used for evidential purposes, in accordance with force standing orders. [See *Note 6A*]

6.2 A police officer has no authority to break the seal on a master recording required for criminal trial or appeal proceedings. If it is necessary to gain access to the master recording, the police officer shall arrange for its seal to be broken in the presence of a representative of the Crown Prosecution Service. The defendant or their legal adviser should be informed and given a reasonable opportunity to be present. If the defendant or their legal representative is present they shall be invited to reseal and sign the master recording. If either refuses or neither is present this should be done by the representative of the Crown Prosecution Service. [See *Notes 6B* and *6C*]

6.3 If no criminal proceedings result or the criminal trial and, if applicable, appeal proceedings to which the interview relates have been concluded, the chief officer of police is responsible for establishing arrangements for breaking the seal on the master recording, if necessary.

6.4 When the master recording seal is broken, a record must be made of the procedure followed, including the date, time, place and persons present.

Notes for guidance

A–187　　6A *This section is concerned with the security of the master recording sealed at the conclusion of the interview. Care must be taken of working copies of recordings because their loss or destruction may lead to the need to access master recordings.*

6B *If the recording has been delivered to the crown court for their keeping after committal for trial the crown prosecutor will apply to the chief clerk of the crown court centre for the release of the recording for unsealing by the crown prosecutor.*

6C *Reference to the Crown Prosecution Service or to the crown prosecutor in this part of the Code should be taken to include any other body or person with a statutory responsibility for prosecution for whom the police conduct any audibly recorded interviews.*

Police and Criminal Evidence Act 1984 (Pace)

Code F

Code of Practice on Visual Recording with Sound of Interviews with Suspects

A–188　　　　　　**Commencement—Transitional Arrangements**

The contents of this code should be considered if an interviewing officer decides to make a visual recording with sound of an interview with a suspect after midnight on 31 December 2005.

There is no statutory requirement to visually record interviews

1 General

1.1 This code of practice must be readily available for consultation by police officers and **A–189**
other police staff, detained persons and members of the public.

1.2 The notes for guidance included are not provisions of this code. They form guidance
to police officers and others about its application and interpretation.

1.3 Nothing in this code shall be taken as detracting in any way from the requirements of
the Code of Practice for the Detention, Treatment and Questioning of Persons by Police Officers (Code C). [See *Note 1A*].

1.4 The interviews to which this Code applies are set out in paragraphs 3.1–3.3.

1.5 In this code, the term "appropriate adult", "solicitor" and "interview" have the same
meaning as those set out in Code C. The corresponding provisions and Notes for Guidance
in Code C applicable to those terms shall also apply where appropriate.

1.6 Any reference in this code to visual recording shall be taken to mean visual recording
with sound.

1.7 References to "pocket book" in this Code include any official report book issued to police officers.

Note for Guidance

1A *As in paragraph 19 of Code C, references to custody officers include those carrying out
the functions of a custody officer.*

2 Recording and sealing of master tapes

2.1 The visual recording of interviews shall be carried out openly to instil confidence in its **A–190**
reliability as an impartial and accurate record of the interview. [See *Note 2A*].

2.2 The camera(s) shall be placed in the interview room so as to ensure coverage of as
much of the room as is practicably possible whilst the interviews are taking place.

2.3 The certified recording medium will be of a high quality, new and previously unused.
When the certified recording medium is placed in the recorder and switched on to record,
the correct date and time, in hours, minutes and seconds, will be superimposed automatically, second by second, during the whole recording. [See *Note 2B*].

2.4 One copy of the certified recording medium, referred to in this code as the master
copy, will be sealed before it leaves the presence of the suspect. A second copy will be used as
a working copy. [See *Note 2C and 2D*].

2.5 Nothing in this code requires the identity of an officer to be recorded or disclosed if:

    (a) the interview or record relates to a person detained under the *Terrorism Act*
        2000; or

    (b) otherwise where the officer reasonably believes that recording or disclosing their name
        might put them in danger.

In these cases, the officer will have their back to the camera and shall use their warrant or
other identification number and the name of the police station to which they are attached.
Such instances and the reasons for them shall be recorded in the custody record. [See *Note
2E*]

Notes for Guidance

2A *Interviewing officers will wish to arrange that, as far as possible, visual recording ar-* **A–191**
*rangements are unobtrusive. It must be clear to the suspect, however, that there is no op-
portunity to interfere with the recording equipment or the recording media.*

2B *In this context, the certified recording media will be of either a VHS or digital CD
format and should be capable of having an image of the date and time superimposed upon
them as they record the interview.*

2C *The purpose of sealing the master copy before it leaves the presence of the suspect is to
establish their confidence that the integrity of the copy is preserved.*

2D *The recording of the interview may be used for identification procedures in accordance
with paragraph 3.21 or Annex E of Code D.*

2E The purpose of the paragraph 2.5 is to protect police officers and others involved in the investigation of serious organised crime or the arrest of particularly violent suspects when there is reliable information that those arrested or their associates may threaten or cause harm to the officers, their families or their personal property.

3 INTERVIEWS TO BE VISUALLY RECORDED

A–192   3.1 Subject to paragraph 3.2 below, if an interviewing officer decides to make a visual recording these are the areas where it might be appropriate:

(a) with a suspect in respect of an indictable offence (including an offence triable either way) [see *Notes 3A and 3B*];

(b) which takes place as a result of an interviewer exceptionally putting further questions to a suspect about an offence described in sub-paragraph (a) above after they have been charged with, or informed they may be prosecuted for, that offence [see *Note 3C*];

(c) in which an interviewer wishes to bring to the notice of a person, after that person has been charged with, or informed they may be prosecuted for an offence described in sub-paragraph (a) above, any written statement made by another person, or the content of an interview with another person [see *Note 3D*]

(d) with, or in the presence of, a deaf or deaf/blind or speech impaired person who uses sign language to communicate;

(e) with, or in the presence of anyone who requires an "appropriate adult"; or

(f) in any case where the suspect or their representative requests that the interview be recorded visually.

A–193   3.2 The *Terrorism Act* 2000 makes separate provision for a code of practice for the video recording of interviews in a police station of those detained under Schedule 7 or section 41 of the Act. The provisions of this code do not therefore apply to such interviews [see *Note 3E*].

3.3 The custody officer may authorise the interviewing officer not to record the interview visually:

(a) where it is not reasonably practicable to do so because of failure of the equipment, or the non-availability of a suitable interview room, or recorder, and the authorising officer considers on reasonable grounds that the interview should not be delayed until the failure has been rectified or a suitable room or recorder becomes available. In such cases the custody officer may authorise the interviewing officer to audio record the interview in accordance with the guidance set out in Code E;

(b) where it is clear from the outset that no prosecution will ensue; or

(c) where it is not practicable to do so because at the time the person resists being taken to a suitable interview room or other location which would enable the interview to be recorded, or otherwise fails or refuses to go into such a room or location, and the authorising officer considers on reasonable grounds that the interview should not be delayed until these conditions cease to apply.

In all cases the custody officer shall make a note in the custody records of the reasons for not taking a visual record. [See *Note 3F*].

3.4 When a person who is voluntarily attending the police station is required to be cautioned in accordance with Code C prior to being interviewed, the subsequent interview shall be recorded, unless the custody officer gives authority in accordance with the provisions of paragraph 3.3 above for the interview not to be so recorded.

3.5 The whole of each interview shall be recorded visually, including the taking and reading back of any statement.

3.6 A visible illuminated sign or indicator will light and remain on at all times when the recording equipment is activated or capable of recording or transmitting any signal or information.

Notes for Guidance

A–194   *3A Nothing in the code is intended to preclude visual recording at police discretion of interviews at police stations with people cautioned in respect of offences not covered by paragraph 3.1, or responses made by interviewees after they have been charged with, or informed they may be prosecuted for, an offence, provided that this code is complied with.*

3B *Attention is drawn to the provisions set out in Code C about the matters to be considered when deciding whether a detained person is fit to be interviewed.*

3C *Code C sets out the circumstances in which a suspect may be questioned about an offence after being charged with it.*

3D *Code C sets out the procedures to be followed when a person's attention is drawn after charge, to a statement made by another person. One method of bringing the content of an interview with another person to the notice of a suspect may be to play him a recording of that interview.*

3E *When it only becomes clear during the course of an interview which is being visually recorded that the interviewee may have committed an offence to which paragraph 3.2 applies, the interviewing officer should turn off the recording equipment and the interview should continue in accordance with the provisions of the Terrorism Act 2000.*

3F *A decision not to record an interview visually for any reason may be the subject of comment in court. The authorising officer should therefore be prepared to justify their decision in each case.*

4 THE INTERVIEW

(a) General

4.1 The provisions of Code C in relation to cautions and interviews and the Notes for **A–195** Guidance applicable to those provisions shall apply to the conduct of interviews to which this Code applies.

4.2 Particular attention is drawn to those parts of Code C that describe the restrictions on drawing adverse inferences from a suspect's failure or refusal to say anything about their involvement in the offence when interviewed, or after being charged or informed they may be prosecuted and how those restrictions affect the terms of the caution and determine whether a special warning under Sections 36 and 37 of the *Criminal Justice and Public Order Act* 1994 can be given.

(b) Commencement of interviews

4.3 When the suspect is brought into the interview room the interviewer shall without **A–196** delay, but in sight of the suspect, load the recording equipment and set it to record. The recording media must be unwrapped or otherwise opened in the presence of the suspect. [See *Note 4A*]

4.4 The interviewer shall then tell the suspect formally about the visual recording. The interviewer shall:

    (a) explain the interview is being visually recorded;

    (b) subject to paragraph 2.5, give his or her name and rank, and that of any other interviewer present;

    (c) ask the suspect and any other party present (e.g. his solicitor) to identify themselves;

    (d) state the date, time of commencement and place of the interview; and

    (e) state that the suspect will be given a notice about what will happen to the recording.

4.5 The interviewer shall then caution the suspect, which should follow that set out in Code C, and remind the suspect of their entitlement to free and independent legal advice and that they can speak to a solicitor on the telephone.

4.6 The interviewer shall then put to the suspect any significant statement or silence (i.e. failure or refusal to answer a question or to answer it satisfactorily) which occurred before the start of the interview, and shall ask the suspect whether they wish to confirm or deny that earlier statement or silence or whether they wish to add anything. The definition of a "significant" statement or silence is the same as that set out in Code C.

(c) Interviews with the deaf

4.7 If the suspect is deaf or there is doubt about their hearing ability, the provisions of **A–197** Code C on interpreters for the deaf or for interviews with suspects who have difficulty in understanding English continue to apply.

(d) Objections and complaints by the suspect

A–198 4.8 If the suspect raises objections to the interview being visually recorded either at the outset or during the interview or during a break in the interview, the interviewer shall explain the fact that the interview is being visually recorded and that the provisions of this code require that the suspect's objections shall be recorded on the visual recording. When any objections have been visually recorded or the suspect has refused to have their objections recorded, the interviewer shall say that they are turning off the recording equipment, give their reasons and turn it off. If a separate audio recording is being maintained, the officer shall ask the person to record the reasons for refusing to agree to visual recording of the interview. Paragraph 4.8 of Code E will apply if the person objects to audio recording of the interview. The officer shall then make a written record of the interview. If the interviewer reasonably considers they may proceed to question the suspect with the visual recording still on, the interviewer may do so. [See *Note 4G*]

4.9 If in the course of an interview a complaint is made by the person being questioned. or on their behalf, concerning the provisions of this code or of Code C, then the interviewer shall act in accordance with Code C, record it in the interview record and inform the custody officer. [See *Notes 4B and 4C*].

4.10 If the suspect indicates that they wish to tell the interviewer about matters not directly connected with the offence of which they are suspected and that they are unwilling for these matters to be recorded, the suspect shall be given the opportunity to tell the interviewer about these matters after the conclusion of the formal interview.

(e) Changing the recording media

A–199 4.11 In instances where the recording medium is not of sufficient length to record all of the interview with the suspect, further certified recording medium will be used. When the re-cording equipment indicates that the recording medium has only a short time left to run. the interviewer shall advise the suspect and round off that part of the interview. If the interviewer wishes to continue the interview but does not already have further certified recording media with him, they shall obtain a set. The suspect should not be left unattended in the interview room. The interviewer will remove the recording media from the recording equipment and insert the new ones which have been unwrapped or otherwise opened in the suspect's presence. The recording equipment shall then be set to record. Care must be taken, particularly when a number of sets of recording media have been used, to ensure that there is no confusion between them. This could be achieved by marking the sets of recording media with consecutive identification numbers.

(f) Taking a break during the interview

A–200 4.12 When a break is to be taken during the course of an interview and the interview room is to be vacated by the suspect, the fact that a break is to be taken, the reason for it and the time shall be recorded. The recording equipment must be turned off and the recording media removed. The procedures for the conclusion of an interview set out in paragraph 4.19, below, should be followed.

4.13 When a break is to be a short one, and both the suspect and a police officer are to remain in the interview room, the fact that a break is to be taken, the reasons for it and the time shall be recorded on the recording media. The recording equipment may be turned off, but there is no need to remove the recording media. When the interview is recommenced the recording shall continue on the same recording media and the time at which the interview recommences shall be recorded.

4.14 When there is a break in questioning under caution, the interviewing officer must ensure that the person being questioned is aware that they remain under caution. If there is any doubt, the caution must be given again in full when the interview resumes. [See *Notes 4D and 4E*].

(g) Failure of recording equipment

A–201 4.15 If there is a failure of equipment which can be rectified quickly, the appropriate procedures set out in paragraph 4.12 shall be followed. When the recording is resumed the interviewer shall explain what has happened and record the time the interview recommences.

If, however, it is not possible to continue recording on that particular recorder and no alternative equipment is readily available, the interview may continue without being recorded visually. In such circumstances, the procedures set out in paragraph 3.3 of this code for seeking the authority of the custody officer will be followed. [See *Note 4F*]

(h) Removing used recording media from recording equipment

4.16 Where used recording media are removed from the recording equipment during **A–202** the course of an interview, they shall be retained and the procedures set out in paragraph 4.18 below followed.

(i) Conclusion of interview

4.17 Before the conclusion of the interview, the suspect shall be offered the opportunity to **A–203** clarify anything he or she has said and asked if there is anything that they wish to add.

4.18 At the conclusion of the interview, including the taking and reading back of any written statement, the time shall be recorded and the recording equipment switched off. The master tape or CD shall be removed from the recording equipment, sealed with a master copy label and treated as an exhibit in accordance with the force standing orders. The interviewer shall sign the label and also ask the suspect and any appropriate adults or other third party present during the interview to sign it. If the suspect or third party refuses to sign the label, an officer of at least the rank of inspector, or if one is not available, the custody officer, shall be called into the interview room and asked to sign it.

4.19 The suspect shall be handed a notice which explains the use which will be made of the recording and the arrangements for access to it. The notice will also advise the suspect that a copy of the tape shall be supplied as soon as practicable if the person is charged or informed that he will be prosecuted.

Notes for Guidance
4A *The interviewer should attempt to estimate the likely length of the interview and ensure* **A–204** *that an appropriate quantity of certified recording media and labels with which to seal the master copies are available in the interview room.*

4B *Where the custody officer is called immediately to deal with the complaint, wherever possible the recording equipment should be left to run until the custody officer has entered the interview room and spoken to the person being interviewed. Continuation or termination of the interview should be at the discretion of the interviewing officer pending action by an inspector as set out in Code C.*

4C *Where the complaint is about a matter not connected with this code of practice or Code C, the decision to continue with the interview is at the discretion of the interviewing officer. Where the interviewing officer decides to continue with the interview, the person being interviewed shall be told that the complaint will be brought to the attention of the custody officer at the conclusion of the interview. When the interview is concluded, the interviewing officer must, as soon as practicable, inform the custody officer of the existence and nature of the complaint made.*

4D *In considering whether to caution again after a break, the officer should bear in mind that he may have to satisfy a court that the person understood that he was still under caution when the interview resumed.*

4E *The officer should bear in mind that it may be necessary to satisfy the court that nothing occurred during a break in an interview or between interviews which influenced the suspect's recorded evidence. On the re-commencement of an interview, the officer should consider summarising on the tape or CD the reason for the break and confirming this with the suspect.*

4F *If any part of the recording media breaks or is otherwise damaged during the interview, it should be sealed as a master copy in the presence of the suspect and the interview resumed where it left off. The undamaged part should be copied and the original sealed as a master tape in the suspect's presence, if necessary after the interview. If equipment for copying is not readily available, both parts should be sealed in the suspect's presence and the interview begun again.*

4G *The interviewer should be aware that a decision to continue recording against the wishes of the suspect may be the subject of comment in court.*

5 After the Interview

5.1 The interviewer shall make a note in his or her pocket book of the fact that the **A–205** interview has taken place and has been recorded, its time, duration and date and the identification number of the master copy of the recording media.

5.2 Where no proceedings follow in respect of the person whose interview was recorded, the recording media must nevertheless be kept securely in accordance with paragraph 6.1 and Note 6A.

Note for Guidance
5A *Any written record of a recorded interview shall be made in accordance with national guidelines approved by the Secretary of State, and with regard to the advice contained in the Manual of Guidance for the preparation, processing and submission of files.*

6 Master Copy Security

(a) General
A–206   6.1 The officer in charge of the police station at which interviews with suspects are recorded shall make arrangements for the master copies to be kept securely and their movements accounted for on the same basis as other material which may be used for evidential purposes, in accordance with force standing orders. [See *Note 6A*]

(b) Breaking master copy seal for criminal proceedings
A–207   6.2 A police officer has no authority to break the seal on a master copy which is required for criminal trial or appeal proceedings. If it is necessary to gain access to the master copy, the police officer shall arrange for its seal to be broken in the presence of a representative of the Crown Prosecution Service. The defendant or their legal adviser shall be informed and given a reasonable opportunity to be present. If the defendant or their legal representative is present they shall be invited to reseal and sign the master copy. If either refuses or neither is present, this shall be done by the representative of the Crown Prosecution Service. [See *Notes 6B and 6C*]

(c) Breaking master copy seal: other cases
A–208   6.3 The chief officer of police is responsible for establishing arrangements for breaking the seal of the master copy where no criminal proceedings result, or the criminal proceedings, to which the interview relates, have been concluded and it becomes necessary to break the seal. These arrangements should be those which the chief officer considers are reasonably necessary to demonstrate to the person interviewed and any other party who may wish to use or refer to the interview record that the master copy has not been tampered with and that the interview record remains accurate. [See *Note 6D*]

6.4 Subject to paragraph 6.6. a representative of each party must be given a reasonable opportunity to be present when the seal is broken, the master copy copied and resealed.

6.5 If one or more of the parties is not present when the master copy seal is broken because they cannot be contacted or refuse to attend or paragraph 6.6 applies, arrangements should be made for an independent person such as a custody visitor, to be present. Alternatively, or as an additional safeguard, arrangement should be made for a film or photographs to be taken of the procedure.

6.6 Paragraph 6.5 does not require a person to be given an opportunity to be present when:

    (a) it is necessary to break the master copy seal for the proper and effective further investigation of the original offence or the investigation of some other offence; and

    (b) the officer in charge of the investigation has reasonable grounds to suspect that allowing an opportunity might prejudice any such an investigation or criminal proceedings which may be brought as a result or endanger any person. [See *Note 6E*]

(d) Documentation
A–209   6.7 When the master copy seal is broken, copied and re-sealed, a record must be made of the procedure followed, including the date time and place and persons present.

Notes for Guidance

6A *This section is concerned with the security of the master copy which will have been* **A–210**
sealed at the conclusion of the interview. Care should, however, be taken of working copies
since their loss or destruction may lead unnecessarily to the need to have access to master copies.

6B *If the master copy has been delivered to the Crown Court for their keeping after commit-*
tal for trial the Crown Prosecutor will apply to the Chief Clerk of the Crown Court Centre for
its release for unsealing by the Crown Prosecutor.

6C *Reference to the Crown Prosecution Service or to the Crown Prosecutor in this part of*
the code shall be taken to include any other body or person with a statutory responsibility for
prosecution for whom the police conduct any recorded interviews.

6D *The most common reasons for needing access to master copies that are not required for*
criminal proceedings arise from civil actions and complaints against police and civil actions be-
tween individuals arising out of allegations of crime investigated by police.

6E *Paragraph 6.6 could apply, for example, when one or more of the outcomes or likely*
outcomes of the investigation might be: (i) the prosecution of one or more of the original
suspects, (ii) the prosecution of someone previously not suspected, including someone who was
originally a witness: and (iii) any original suspect being treated as a prosecution witness and
when premature disclosure of any police action, particularly through contact with any parties
involved, could lead to a real risk of compromising the investigation and endangering witnesses.

POLICE AND CRIMINAL EVIDENCE ACT 1984 (PACE)

Code G

Code of Practice for the Statutory Power of Arrest by Police Officers

Commencement A–211

This Code applies to any arrest made by a police officer after midnight on 31 December 2005

1. INTRODUCTION

1.1 This Code of Practice deals with statutory power of police to arrest persons suspected **A–212**
of involvement in a criminal offence.

1.2 The right to liberty is a key principle of the Human Rights Act 1998. The exercise of
the power of arrest represents an obvious and significant interference with that right.

1.3 The use of the power must be fully justified and officers exercising the power should
consider if the necessary objectives can be met by other, less intrusive means Arrest must
never be used simply because it can be used. Absence of justification for exercising the powers
of arrest may lead to challenges should the case proceed to court. When the power of arrest
is exercised it is essential that it is exercised in a nondiscriminatory and proportionate manner.

1.4 Section 24 of the *Police and Criminal Evidence Act* 1984 (as substituted by section 110 of
the *Serious Organised Crime and Police Act* 2005) provides the statutory power of arrest. If the
provisions of the Act and this Code are not observed, both the arrest and the conduct of any
subsequent investigation may be open to question.

1.5 This code of practice must be readily available at all police stations for consultation by
police officers and police staff, detained persons and members of the public.

1.6 The notes for guidance are not provisions of this code.

2 ELEMENTS OF ARREST UNDER SECTION 24 PACE

2.1 A lawful arrest requires two elements: **A–213**
A person's involvement or suspected involvement or attempted involvement in the commis-
sion of a criminal offence;
AND
Reasonable grounds for believing that the person's arrest is necessary.

2.2 Arresting officers are required to inform the person arrested that they have been arrested, even if this fact is obvious, and of the relevant circumstances of the arrest in relation to

both elements and to inform the custody officer of these on arrival at the police station. See Code C paragraph 3.4.

Involvement in the commission of an offence'

2.3 A constable may arrest without warrant in relation to any offence, except for the single exception listed in Note for Guidance 1. A constable may arrest anyone:

- who is about to commit an offence or is in the act of committing an offence
- whom the officer has reasonable grounds for suspecting is about to commit an offence or to be committing an offence
- whom the officer has reasonable grounds to suspect of being guilty of an offence which he or she has reasonable grounds for suspecting has been committed
- anyone who is guilty of an offence which has been committed or anyone whom the officer has reasonable grounds for suspecting to be guilty of that offence.

Necessity criteria

A–214 2.4 The power of arrest is only exercisable if the constable has reasonable grounds for believing that it is necessary to arrest the person. The criteria for what may constitute necessity are set out in paragraph 2.9. It remains an operational decision at the discretion of the arresting officer as to:

- what action he or she may take at the point of contact with the individual;
- the necessity criterion or criteria (if any) which applies to the individual; and
- whether to arrest, report for summons, grant street bail, issue a fixed penalty notice or take any other action that is open to the officer.

2.5 In applying the criteria, the arresting officer has to be satisfied that at least one of the reasons supporting the need for arrest is satisfied.

2.6 Extending the power of arrest to all offences provides a constable with the ability to use that power to deal with any situation. However applying the necessity criteria requires the constable to examine and justify the reason or reasons why a person needs to be taken to a police station for the custody officer to decide whether the person should be placed in police detention.

2.7 The criteria below are set out in section 24 of PACE as substituted by section 110 of the Serious Organised Crime and Police Act 2005. The criteria are exhaustive. However, the circumstances that may satisfy those criteria remain a matter for the operational discretion of individual officers. Some examples are given below of what those circumstances may be.

2.8 In considering the individual circumstances, the constable must take into account the situation of the victim, the nature of the offence, the circumstances of the suspect and the needs of the investigative process.

A–215 2.9 The criteria are that the arrest is necessary:

(a) to enable the name of the person in question to be ascertained (in the case where the constable does not know, and cannot readily ascertain, the person's name, or has reasonable grounds for doubting whether a name given by the person as his name is his real name)

(b) correspondingly as regards the person's address

an address is a satisfactory address for service of summons if the person will be at it for a sufficiently long period for it to be possible to serve him or her with a summons; or, that some other person at that address specified by the person will accept service of the summons on their behalf.

(c) to prevent the person in question —

(i) causing physical injury to himself or any other person;

(ii) suffering physical injury ;

(iii) causing loss or damage to property;

(iv) committing an offence against public decency (only applies where members of the public going about their normal business cannot reasonably be expected to avoid the person in question); or

(v) causing an unlawful obstruction of the highway;

(d) to protect a child or other vulnerable person from the person in question

(e) to allow the prompt and effective investigation of the offence or of the conduct of the person in question.

This may include cases such as:

  (i) Where there are reasonable grounds to believe that the person:
- has made false statements;
- has made statements which cannot be readily verified;
- has presented false evidence;
- may steal or destroy evidence;
- may make contact with co-suspects or conspirators;
- may intimidate or threaten or make contact with witnesses;
- where it is necessary to obtain evidence by questioning; or

  (ii) when considering arrest in connection with an indictable offence, there is a need to:
- enter and search any premises occupied or controlled by a person;
- search the person;
- prevent contact with others;
- take fingerprints, footwear impressions, samples or photographs of the suspect;

  (iii) ensuring compliance with statutory drug testing requirements.

(f) to prevent any prosecution for the offence from being hindered by the disappearance of the person in question.

This may arise if there are reasonable grounds for believing that
- if the person is not arrested he or she will fail to attend court
- street bail after arrest would be insufficient to deter the suspect from trying to evade prosecution

3 Information to be given on Arrest

(a) Cautions — when a caution must be given (taken from Code C section 10)

3.1 A person whom there are grounds to suspect of an offence (see Note 2) must be cautioned before any questions about an offence, or further questions if the answers provide the grounds for suspicion, are put to them if either the suspect's answers or silence, (i.e. failure or refusal to answer or answer satisfactorily) may be given in evidence to a court in a prosecution. A person need not be cautioned if questions are for other necessary purposes e.g.:   **A–216**

(a) solely to establish their identity or ownership of any vehicle;

(b) to obtain information in accordance with any relevant statutory requirement;

(c) in furtherance of the proper and effective conduct of a search, e.g. to determine the need to search in the exercise of powers of stop and search or to seek co-operation while carrying out a search;

(d) to seek verification of a written record as in *Code C paragraph 11.13*;

(e) when examining a person in accordance with the *Terrorism Act* 2000. Schedule 7 and the Code of Practice for Examining Officers issued under that Act. Schedule 14, paragraph 6.

3.2 Whenever a person not under arrest is initially cautioned, or reminded they are under caution, that person must at the same time be told they are not under arrest and are free to leave if they want to.

3.3 A person who is arrested, or further arrested, must be informed at the time, or as soon as practicable thereafter, that they are under arrest and the grounds for their arrest, see *Note 3*.

3.4 A person who is arrested, or further arrested, must also be cautioned unless:

(a) it is impracticable to do so by reason of their condition or behaviour at the time

(b) they have already been cautioned immediately prior to arrest as in *paragraph 3.1*

(c) Terms of the caution (Taken from Code C section 10)

3.5 The caution, which must be given on arrest, should be in the following terms:

"You do not have to say anything. But it may harm your defence if you do not mention when questioned something which you later rely on in Court. Anything you do say may be given in evidence."

See *Note 5*

3.6 Minor deviations from the words of any caution given in accordance with this Code do not constitute a breach of this Code. provided the sense of the relevant caution is preserved. See *Note 6*

3.7 When, despite being cautioned, a person fails to co-operate or to answer particular questions which may affect their immediate treatment, the person should be informed of any relevant consequences and that those consequences are not affected by the caution. Examples are when a person's refusal to provide:

- their name and address when charged may make them liable to detention;
- particulars and information in accordance with a statutory requirement, e.g. under the *Road Traffic Act* 1988. may amount to an offence or may make the person liable to a further arrest.

4 RECORDS OF ARREST

(a) General

A–217   4.1 The arresting officer is required to record in his pocket book or by other methods used for recording information:

- the nature and circumstances of the offence leading to the arrest
- the reason or reasons why arrest was necessary
- the giving of the caution
- anything said by the person at the time of arrest

4.2 Such a record should be made at the time of the arrest unless impracticable to do. If not made at that time, the record should then be completed as soon as possible thereafter.

4.3 On arrival at the police station, the custody officer shall open the custody record (see paragraph 1.1A and section 2 of Code C). The information given by the arresting officer on the circumstances and reason or reasons for arrest shall be recorded as part of the custody record. Alternatively, a copy of the record made by the officer in accordance with paragraph 4.1 above shall be attached as part of the custody record. See *paragraph 2.2* and *Code C paragraphs 3.4 and 10.3*.

4.4 The custody record will serve as a record of the arrest. Copies of the custody record will be provided in accordance with paragraphs 2.4 and 2.4A of Code C and access for inspection of the original record in accordance with paragraph 2.5 of Code C.

(b) Interviews and arrests

4.5 Records of interview, significant statements or silences will be treated in the same way as set out in sections 10 and 11 of Code C and in Code E (tape recording of interviews).

Notes for guidance

A–218   1 *The powers of arrest for offences under sections 4(1) and 5(1) of the Criminal Law Act 1967 require that the offences to which they relate must carry a sentence fixed by law or one in which a first time offender aged 18 or over could be sentenced to 5 years or more imprisonment*

2 *There must be some reasonable, objective grounds for the suspicion, based on known facts or information which are relevant to the likelihood the offence has been committed and the person to be questioned committed it.*

3 *An arrested person must be given sufficient information to enable them to understand they have been deprived of their liberty and the reason they have been arrested, e.g. when a person is arrested on suspicion of committing an offence they must be informed of the suspected offence's nature, when and where it was committed. The suspect must also be informed of the reason or reasons why arrest is considered necessary. Vague or technical language should be avoided.*

4 *Nothing in this Code requires a caution to be given or repeated when informing a person not under arrest they may be prosecuted for an offence. However, a court will not be able to*

draw any inferences under the Criminal Justice and Public Order Act 1994, section 34. if the person was not cautioned.

5 *If it appears a person does not understand the caution, the people giving it should explain it in their own words.*

6 *The powers available to an officer as the result of an arrest — for example, entry and search of premises, holding a person incommunicado, setting up road blocks—are only available in respect of indictable offences and are subject to the specific requirements on authorisation as set out in the 1984 Act and relevant PACE Code of Practice.*

POLICE AND CRIMINAL EVIDENCE ACT 1984 (PACE)

Code H

Code of Practice in Connection with the Detention, Treatment and Questioning by Police Officers of Persons under section 41 of, and Schedule 8 to, the Terrorism Act 2000

Commencement—Transitional Arrangements   A–219

This Code applies to people in police detention following their arrest under section 41 of the Terrorism Act 2000, after midnight (on 24 July 2006), notwithstanding that they may have been arrested before that time.

[This Code is not reproduced here.]

Appendices

CODE OF PRACTICE ON DISCLOSURE

Introduction

Pursuant to sections 23 and 25 of the 1996 Act, the Secretary of State prepared and published codes of practice governing the action the police must take in recording and retaining material obtained in the course of a criminal investigation and regulating its supply to the prosecutor for a decision on disclosure.

The first code came into force on the day appointed for the purpose of Part I of the 1996 Act, namely April 1, 1997 (S.I. 1997 No. 1033). It was revised with effect from April 4, 2005: *Criminal Procedure and Investigations Act 1996 (Code of Practice) Order* 2005 (S.I. 2005 No. 985).

Code of practice under Part II

Preamble

This code of practice is issued under Part II of the *Criminal Procedure and Investiga-* **B–1**
tions Act 1996 ('the Act'). It sets out the manner in which police officers are to record, retain and reveal to the prosecutor material obtained in a criminal investigation and which may be relevant to the investigation, and related matters.

Introduction

1.1 This code of practice applies in respect of criminal investigations conducted by police **B–2**
officers which begin on or after the day on which this code comes into effect. Persons other than police officers who are charged with the duty of conducting an investigation as defined in the Act are to have regard to the relevant provisions of the code, and should take these into account in applying their own operating procedures.

1.2 This code does not apply to persons who are not charged with the duty of conducting an investigation as defined in the Act.

1.3 Nothing in this code applies to material intercepted in obedience to a warrant issued under section 2 of the *Interception of Communications Act* 1985 or section 5 of the *Regulation of Investigatory Powers Act* 2000, or to any copy of that material as defined in section 10 of the 1985 Act or section 15 of the 2000 Act.

1.4 This code extends only to England and Wales.

Definitions

2.1 In this code: **B–3**

— a *criminal investigation* is an investigation conducted by police officers with a view to it being ascertained whether a person should be charged with an offence, or whether a person charged with an offence is guilty of it. This will include:

— investigations into crimes that have been committed;

— investigations whose purpose is to ascertain whether a crime has been committed, with a view to the possible institution of criminal proceedings; and

— investigations which begin in the belief that a crime may be committed, for example when the police keep premises or individuals under observation for a period of time, with a view to the possible institution of criminal proceedings;

— charging a person with an offence includes prosecution by way of summons;

— an *investigator* is any police officer involved in the conduct of a criminal investigation. All investigators have a responsibility for carrying out the duties imposed on them under this code, including in particular recording information, and retaining records of information and other material;

— the *officer in charge of an investigation* is any police officer involved in the conduct of a criminal investigation. All investigators have a responsibility for carrying out the duties imposed on them under this code, including in particular recording information, and retaining records of information and other material;

— the *disclosure officer* is the person responsible for examining material retained by the police during the investigation; revealing material to the prosecutor during the investigation and any criminal proceedings resulting from it, and certifying that he has done this; and disclosing material to the accused at the request of the prosecutor;

— the *prosecutor* is the authority responsible for the conduct, on behalf of the Crown, of criminal proceedings resulting from a specific criminal investigation;

— *material* is material of any kind, including information and objects, which is obtained in the course of a criminal investigation and which may be relevant to the investigation. This includes not only material coming into the possession of the investigator (such as documents seized in the course of searching premises) but also material generated by him (such as interview records);

— material may be *relevant to the investigation* if it appears to an investigator, or to the officer in charge of an investigation, or to the disclosure officer, that it has some bearing on any offence under investigation or any person being investigated, or on the surrounding circumstances of the case, unless it is incapable of having any impact on the case;

— *sensitive material* is material, the disclosure of which, the disclosure officer believes, would give rise to a real risk of serious prejudice to an important public interest;

— references to *prosecution disclosure* are to the duty of the prosecutor under sections 3 and 7A of the Act to disclose material which is in his possession or which he has inspected in pursuance of this code, and which might reasonably be considered capable of undermining the case against the accused, or of assisting the case for the accused;

— references to the disclosure of material to a person accused of an offence include references to the disclosure of material to his legal representative;

— references to police officers and to the chief officer of police include those employed in a police force as defined in section 3(3) of the *Prosecution of Offences Act* 1985.

As to the meaning of "criminal investigation", see *DPP v. Metten*, unreported, January 22, 1999, DC (§ 12–72 in the main work).

General responsibilities

B–4   3.1 The functions of the investigator, the officer in charge of an investigation and the disclosure officer are separate. Whether they are undertaken by one, two or more persons will depend on the complexity of the case and the administrative arrangements within each police force. Where they are undertaken by more than one person, close consultation between them is essential to the effective performance of the duties imposed by this code.

3.2 In any criminal investigation, one or more deputy disclosure officers may be appointed to assist the disclosure officer, and a deputy disclosure officer may perform any function of a disclosure officer as defined in paragraph 2.1.

3.3 The chief officer of police for each police force is responsible for putting in place arrangements to ensure that in every investigation the identity of the officer in charge of an investigation and the disclosure officer is recorded. The chief officer of police for each police force shall ensure that disclosure officers and deputy disclosure officers have sufficient skills and authority, commensurate with the complexity of the investigation, to discharge their functions effectively. An individual must not be appointed as disclosure officer, or continue in that role, if that is likely to result in a conflict of interest, for instance, if the disclosure officer is the victim of the alleged crime which is the subject of the investigation. The advice of a more senior officer must always be sought if there is doubt as to whether a conflict of interest precludes an individual acting as disclosure officer. If thereafter the doubt remains, the advice of a prosecutor should be sought.

3.4 The officer in charge of an investigation may delegate tasks to another investigator, to civilians employed by the police force, or to other persons participating in the investigation under arrangements for joint investigations, but he remains responsible for ensuring that these have been carried out and for accounting for any general policies followed in the investigation. In particular, it is an essential part of his duties to ensure that all material which may be relevant to an investigation is retained, and either made available to the disclosure officer or (in exceptional circumstances) revealed directly to the prosecutor.

3.5 In conducting an investigation, the investigator should pursue all reasonable lines of inquiry, whether these point towards or away from the suspect. What is reasonable in each case will depend on the particular circumstances. For example, where material is held on computer, it is a matter for the investigator to decide which material on the computer it is reasonable to inquire into, and in what manner.

3.6 If the officer in charge of an investigation believes that other persons may be in possession of material that may be relevant to the investigation, and if this has not been obtained under paragraph 3.5 above, he should ask the disclosure officer to inform them of the existence of the investigation and to invite them to retain the material in case they receive a request for its disclosure. The disclosure officer should inform the prosecutor that they may have such material. However, the officer in charge of an investigation is not required to make speculative enquiries of other persons; there must be some reason to believe that they may have relevant material. That reason may come from information provided to the police by the accused or from other inquiries made or from some other source.

3.7 If, during a criminal investigation, the officer in charge of an investigation or disclosure officer for any reason no longer has responsibility for the functions falling to him, either his supervisor or the police officer in charge of criminal investigations for the police force concerned must assign someone else to assume that responsibility. That person's identity must be recorded, as with those initially responsible for these functions in each investigation.

As to the meaning of "criminal investigation", see *DPP v. Metten*, unreported, January 22, 1999, DC (§ 12–72 in the main work).

Recording of information

4.1 If material which may be relevant to the investigation consists of information which is **B–5** not recorded in any form, the officer in charge of an investigation must ensure that it is recorded in a durable or retrievable form (whether in writing, on video or audio tape, or on computer disk).

4.2 Where it is not practicable to retain the initial record of information because it forms part of a larger record which is to be destroyed, its contents should be transferred as a true record to a durable and more easily-stored form before that happens.

4.3 Negative information is often relevant to an investigation. If it may be relevant it must be recorded. An example might be a number of people present in a particular place at a particular time who state that they saw nothing unusual.

4.4 Where information which may be relevant is obtained, it must be recorded at the time it is obtained or as soon as practicable after that time. This includes, for example, information obtained in house-to-house enquiries, although the requirement to record information promptly does not require an investigator to take a statement from a potential witness where it would not otherwise be taken.

Retention of material

(a) Duty to retain material

5.1 The investigator must retain material obtained in a criminal investigation which may **B–6** be relevant to the investigation. Material may be photographed, video-recorded, captured digitally or otherwise retained in the form of a copy rather than the original at any time, if the original is perishable; the original was supplied to the investigator rather than generated by him and is to be returned to its owner; or the retention of a copy rather than the original is reasonable in all the circumstances.

5.2 Where material has been seized in the exercise of the powers of seizure conferred by the *Police and Criminal Evidence Act* 1984, the duty to retain it under this code is subject to the provisions on the retention of seized material in section 22 of that Act.

5.3 If the officer in charge of an investigation becomes aware as a result of developments in the case that material previously examined but not retained (because it was not thought to be relevant) may now be relevant to the investigation, he should, wherever practicable, take steps to obtain it or ensure that it is retained for further inspection or for production in court if required.

5.4 The duty to retain material includes in particular the duty to retain material falling into the following categories, where it may be relevant to the investigation:

— crime reports (including crime report forms, relevant parts of incident report books or police officer's notebooks);

— custody records;

— records which are derived from tapes of telephone messages (for example, 999 calls) containing descriptions of an alleged offence or offender;

— final versions of witness statements (and draft versions where their content differs from the final version), including any exhibits mentioned (unless these have been returned to their owner on the understanding that they will be produced in court if required);

— interview records (written records, or audio or video tapes, of interviews with actual or potential witnesses or suspects);

— communications between the police and experts such as forensic scientists, reports of work carried out by experts, and schedules of scientific material prepared by the expert for the investigator, for the purposes of criminal proceedings;

— records of the first description of a suspect by each potential witness who purports to identify or describe the suspect, whether or not the description differs from that of subsequent descriptions by that or other witnesses;

— any material casting doubt on the reliability of a witness.

5.5 The duty to retain material, where it may be relevant to the investigation, also includes in particular the duty to retain material which may satisfy the test for prosecution disclosure in the Act, such as:

— information provided by an accused person which indicates an explanation for the offence with which he has been charged;

— any material casting doubt on the reliability of a confession;

— any material casting doubt on the reliability of a prosecution witness.

5.6 The duty to retain material falling into these categories does not extend to items which are purely ancillary to such material and possess no independent significance (for example, duplicate copies of records or reports).

(b) Length of time for which material is to be retained

5.7 All material which may be relevant to the investigation must be retained until a decision is taken whether to institute proceedings against a person for an offence.

5.8 If a criminal investigation results in proceedings being instituted, all material which may be relevant must be retained at least until the accused is acquitted or convicted or the prosecutor decides not to proceed with the case.

5.9 Where the accused is convicted, all material which may be relevant must be retained at least until:

— the convicted person is released from custody, or discharged from hospital, in cases where the court imposes a custodial sentence or a hospital order;

— six months from the date of conviction, in all other cases.

If the court imposes a custodial sentence or hospital order and the convicted person is released from custody or discharged from hospital earlier than six months from the date of conviction, all material which may be relevant must be retained at least until six months from the date of conviction.

5.10 If an appeal against conviction is in progress when the release or discharge occurs, or at the end of the period of six months specified in paragraph 5.9, all material which may be relevant must be retained until the appeal is determined. Similarly, if the Criminal Cases Review Commission is considering an application at that point in time, all material which may be relevant must be retained at least until the Commission decides not to refer the case to the Court.

Preparation of material for prosecutor

(a) Introduction

6.1 The officer in charge of the investigation, the disclosure officer or an investigator may **B–7** seek advice from the prosecutor about whether any particular item of material may be relevant to the investigation.

6.2 Material which may be relevant to an investigation, which has been retained in accordance with this code, and which the disclosure officer believes will not form part of the prosecution case, must be listed on a schedule.

6.3 Material which the disclosure officer does not believe is sensitive must be listed on a schedule of non-sensitive material. The schedule must include a statement that the disclosure officer does not believe the material is sensitive.

6.4 Any material which is believed to be sensitive must be either listed on a schedule of sensitive material or, in exceptional circumstances, revealed to the prosecutor separately. If there is no sensitive material, the disclosure officer must record this fact on a schedule of sensitive material.

6.5 Paragraphs 6.6 to 6.11 below apply to both sensitive and non-sensitive material. Paragraphs 6.12 to 6.14 apply to sensitive material only.

(b) Circumstances in which a schedule is to be prepared

6.6 The disclosure officer must ensure that a schedule is prepared in the following circumstances:
— the accused is charged with an offence which is triable only on indictment;
— the accused is charged with an offence which is triable either way, and it is considered either that the case is likely to be tried on indictment or that the accused is likely to plead not guilty at a summary trial;
— the accused is charged with a summary offence, and it is considered that he is likely to plead not guilty.

6.7 In respect of either way and summary offences, a schedule may not be needed if a person has admitted the offence, or if a police officer witnessed the offence and that person has not denied it.

6.8 If it is believed that the accused is likely to plead guilty at a summary trial, it is not necessary to prepare a schedule in advance. If, contrary to this belief, the accused pleads not guilty at a summary trial, or the offence is to be tried on indictment, the disclosure officer must ensure that a schedule is prepared as soon as is reasonably practicable after that happens.

(c) Way in which material is to be listed on schedule

6.9 The disclosure officer should ensure that each item of material is listed separately on the schedule, and is numbered consecutively. The description of each item should make clear the nature of the item and should contain sufficient detail to enable the prosecutor to decide whether he needs to inspect the material before deciding whether or not it should be disclosed.

6.10 In some enquiries it may not be practicable to list each item of material separately. For example, there may be many items of a similar or repetitive nature. These may be listed in a block and described by quantity and generic title.

6.11 Even if some material is listed in a block, the disclosure officer must ensure that any items among that material which might satisfy the test for prosecution disclosure are listed and described individually.

(d) Treatment of sensitive material

6.12 Subject to paragraph 6.13 below, the disclosure officer must list on a sensitive schedule any material, the disclosure of which he believes would give rise to a real risk of serious prejudice to an important public interest, and the reason for that belief. The schedule must include a statement that the disclosure officer believes the material is sensitive. Depending on the circumstances, examples of such material may include the following among others:

— material relating to national security;

— material received from the intelligence and security agencies;

— material relating to intelligence from foreign sources which reveals sensitive intelligence gathering methods;

— material given in confidence;

— material relating to the identity or activities of informants, or undercover police officers, or witnesses, or other persons supplying information to the police who may be in danger if their identities are revealed;

— material revealing the location of any premises or other place used for police surveillance, or the identity of any person allowing a police officer to use them for surveillance;

— material revealing, either directly or indirectly, techniques and methods relied upon by a police officer in the course of a criminal investigation, for example covert surveillance techniques, or other methods of detecting crime;

— material whose disclosure might facilitate the commission of other offences or hinder the prevention and detection of crime;

— material upon the strength of which search warrants were obtained;

— material containing details of persons taking part in identification parades;

— material supplied to an investigator during a criminal investigation which has been generated by an official of a body concerned with the regulation or supervision of bodies corporate or of persons engaged in financial activities, or which has been generated by a person retained by such a body;

— material supplied to an investigator during a criminal investigation which relates to a child or young person and which has been generated by a local authority social services department, an Area Child Protection Committee or other party contacted by an investigator during the investigation;

— material relating to the private life of a witness.

6.13 In exceptional circumstances, where an investigator considers that material is so sensitive that its revelation to the prosecutor by means of an entry on the sensitive schedule is inappropriate, the existence of the material must be revealed to the prosecutor separately. This will apply only where compromising the material would be likely to lead directly to the loss of life, or directly threaten national security.

6.14 In such circumstances, the responsibility for informing the prosecutor lies with the investigator who knows the detail of the sensitive material. The investigator should act as soon as is reasonably practicable after the file containing the prosecution case is sent to the prosecutor. The investigator must also ensure that the prosecutor is able to inspect the material so that he can assess whether it is disclosable and, if so, whether it needs to be brought before a court for a ruling on disclosure.

Revelation of material to prosecutor

B–8 7.1 The disclosure officer must give the schedules to the prosecutor. Wherever practicable this should be at the same time as he gives him the file containing the material for the prosecution case (or as soon as is reasonably practicable after the decision on mode of trial or the plea, in cases to which paragraph 6.8 applies).

7.2 The disclosure officer should draw the attention of the prosecutor to any material an investigator has retained (including material to which paragraph 6.13 applies) which may satisfy the test for prosecution disclosure in the Act, and should explain why he has come to that view.

7.3 At the same time as complying with the duties in paragraphs 7.1 and 7.2, the disclosure officer must give the prosecutor a copy of any material which falls into the following categories (unless such material has already been given to the prosecutor as part of the file containing the material for the prosecution case):

— information provided by an accused person which indicates an explanation for the offence with which he has been charged;

— any material casting doubt on the reliability of a confession;

— any material casting doubt on the reliability of a prosecution witness;

— any other material which the investigator believes may satisfy the test for prosecution disclosure in the Act.

— any other material which the investigator believes may fall within the test for primary prosecution disclosure in the Act.

7.4 If the prosecutor asks to inspect material which has not already been copied to him, the disclosure officer must allow him to inspect it. If the prosecutor asks for a copy of material which has not already been copied to him, the disclosure officer must give him a copy. However, this does not apply where the disclosure officer believes, having consulted the officer in charge of the investigation, that the material is too sensitive to be copied and can only be inspected.

7.5 If material consists of information which is recorded other than in writing, whether it should be given to the prosecutor in its original form as a whole, or by way of relevant extracts recorded in the same form, or in the form of a transcript, is a matter for agreement between the disclosure officer and the prosecutor.

Subsequent action by disclosure officer

8.1 At the time a schedule of non-sensitive material is prepared, the disclosure officer may **B–9** not know exactly what material will form the case against the accused, and the prosecutor may not have given advice about the likely relevance of particular items of material. Once these matters have been determined, the disclosure officer must give the prosecutor, where necessary, an amended schedule listing any additional material:

— which may be relevant to the investigation,

— which does not form part of the case against the accused,

— which is not already listed on the schedule, and

— which he believes is not sensitive,

unless he is informed in writing by the prosecutor that the prosecutor intends to disclose the material to the defence.

8.2 Section 7A of the Act imposes a continuing duty on the prosecutor, for the duration of criminal proceedings against the accused, to disclose material which satisfies the test for disclosure (subject to public interest considerations). To enable him to do this, any new material coming to light should be treated in the same way as the earlier material.

8.3 In particular, after a defence statement has been given, the disclosure officer must look again at the material which has been retained and must draw the attention of the prosecutor to any material which might reasonably be considered capable of undermining the case for the prosecution against the accused or of assisting the case for the accused; and he must reveal it to him in accordance with paragraphs 7.4 and 7.5 above.

Certification by disclosure officer

9.1 The disclosure officer must certify to the prosecutor that to the best of his knowledge **B–10** and belief, all relevant material which has been retained and made available to him has been revealed to the prosecutor in accordance with this code. He must sign and date the certificate. It will be necessary to certify not only at the time when the schedule and accompanying material is submitted to the prosecutor, and when relevant material which has been retained is reconsidered after the accused has given a defence statement, but also whenever a schedule is otherwise given or material is otherwise revealed to the prosecutor.

Disclosure of material to accused

10.1 If material has not already been copied to the prosecutor, and he requests its **B–11** disclosure to the accused on the ground that:

— it satisfies the test for prosecution disclosure, or

— it satisfies the test for prosecution disclosure, or

the disclosure officer must disclose it to the accused.

10.2 If material has been copied to the prosecutor, and it is to be disclosed, whether it is disclosed by the prosecutor or the disclosure officer is a matter of agreement between the two of them.

10.3 The disclosure officer must disclose material to the accused either by giving him a copy or by allowing him to inspect it. If the accused person asks for a copy of any material which he has been allowed to inspect, the disclosure officer must give it to him, unless in the opinion of the disclosure officer that is either not practicable (for example because the material consists of an object which cannot be copied, or because the volume of material is so great), or not desirable (for example because the material is a statement by a child witness in relation to a sexual offence).

10.4 If material which the accused has been allowed to inspect consists of information which is recorded other than in writing, whether it should be given to the accused in its original form or in the form of a transcript is matter for the discretion of the disclosure officer. If the material is transcribed, the disclosure officer must ensure that the transcript is certified to the accused as a true record of the material which has been transcribed.

10.5 If a court concludes that an item of sensitive material satisfies the prosecution disclosure test and that the interests of the defence outweigh the public interest in withholding disclosure, it will be necessary to disclose the material if the case is to proceed. This does not mean that sensitive documents must always be disclosed in their original form: for example, the court may agree that sensitive details still requiring protection should be blocked out, or that documents may be summarised, or that the prosecutor may make an admission about the substance of the material under section 10 of the *Criminal Justice Act* 1967.

ATTORNEY-GENERAL'S GUIDELINES ON DISCLOSURE

Disclosure

Introduction

On November 29, 2000, the Attorney-General issued guidelines on disclosure of in- **C–1** formation in criminal proceedings. They are to be adopted with immediate effect in relation to all cases submitted in future to the prosecuting authorities in receipt of the guidelines. They are also to be adopted as regards cases already submitted to which the *Criminal Procedure and Investigations Act* 1996 applies, so far as they relate to stages in the proceedings that have not yet been reached. The guidelines were updated in April 2005. They were published with a foreword and commentary which are not reproduced here. The guidelines themselves are reproduced in full.

Disclosure of Unused Material in Criminal Proceedings

Introduction

1. Every accused person has a right to a fair trial, a right long embodied in our law and **C–2** guaranteed under Article 6 of the European Convention on Human Rights (ECHR). A fair trial is the proper object and expectation of all participants in the trial process. Fair disclosure to an accused is an inseparable part of a fair trial.

2. What must be clear is that a fair trial consists of an examination not just of all the evidence the parties wish to rely on but also all other relevant subject matter. A fair trial should not require consideration of irrelevant material and should not involve spurious applications or arguments which serve to divert the trial process from examining the real issues before the court.

3. The scheme set out in the *Criminal Procedure and Investigations Act* 1996 (as amended by the *Criminal Justice Act* 2003) (the Act) is designed to ensure that there is fair disclosure of material which may be relevant to an investigation and which does not form part of the prosecution case. Disclosure under the Act should assist the accused in the timely preparation and presentation of their case and assist the court to focus on all the relevant issues in the trial. Disclosure which does not meet these objectives risks preventing a fair trial taking place.

4. This means that the disclosure regime set out in the Act must be scrupulously followed. These Guidelines build upon the existing law to help to ensure that the legislation is operated more effectively, consistently and fairly.

5. Disclosure must not be an open ended trawl of unused material. A critical element to **C–3** fair and proper disclosure is that the defence play their role to ensure that the prosecution are directed to material which might reasonably be considered capable of undermining the prosecution case or assisting the case for the accused. This process is key to ensuring prosecutors make informed determinations about disclosure of unused material.

6. Fairness does recognise that there are other interests that need to be protected, including those of victims and witnesses who might otherwise be exposed to harm. The scheme of the Act protects those interests. It should also ensure that material is not disclosed which overburdens the participants in the trial process, diverts attention from the relevant issues, leads to unjustifiable delay, and is wasteful of resources.

7. Whilst it is acknowledged that these Guidelines have been drafted with a focus on Crown Court proceedings the spirit of the Guidelines must be followed where they apply to proceedings in the magistrates' court.

General Principles

8. Disclosure refers to providing the defence with copies of, or access to, any material **C–4**

which might reasonably be considered capable of undermining the case for the prosecution against the accused, or of assisting the case for the accused, and which has not previously been disclosed.

9. Prosecutors will only be expected to anticipate what material might weaken their case or strengthen the defence in the light of information available at the time of the disclosure decision, and this may include information revealed during questioning.

10. Generally, material which can reasonably be considered capable of undermining the prosecution case against the accused or assisting the defence case will include anything that tends to show a fact inconsistent with the elements of the case that must be proved by the prosecution. Material can fulfil the disclosure test:

(a) by the use to be made of it in cross-examination; or

(b) by its capacity to support submissions that could lead to:

   (i) the exclusion of evidence; or

   (ii) a stay of proceedings; or

   (iii) a court or tribunal finding that any public authority had acted incompatibly with the accused 's rights under the ECHR, or

(c) by its capacity to suggest an explanation or partial explanation of the accused's actions.

C–5   11. In deciding whether material may fall to be disclosed under *paragraph 10*, especially *(b)(ii)*, prosecutors must consider whether disclosure is required in order for a proper application to be made. The purpose of this paragraph is not to allow enquiries to support speculative arguments or for the manufacture of defences.

12. Examples of material that might reasonably be considered capable of undermining the prosecution case or of assisting the case for the accused are:

   (i) Any material casting doubt upon the accuracy of any prosecution evidence.

   (ii) Any material which may point to another person, whether charged or not (including a co-accused) having involvement in the commission of the offence.

   (iii) Any material which may cast doubt upon the reliability of a confession.

   (iv) Any material that might go to the credibility of a prosecution witness.

   (v) Any material that might support a defence that is either raised by the defence or apparent from the prosecution papers.

   (vi) Any material which may have a bearing on the admissibility of any prosecution evidence.

13. It should also be borne in mind that while items of material viewed in isolation may not be reasonably considered to be capable of undermining the prosecution case or assisting the accused, several items together can have that effect.

14. Material relating to the accused's mental or physical health, intellectual capacity, or to any ill treatment which the accused may have suffered when in the investigator's custody is likely to fall within the test for disclosure set out in *paragraph 8* above.

Defence Statements

C–6   15. A defence statement must comply with the requirements of section 6A of the Act. A comprehensive defence statement assists the participants in the trial to ensure that it is fair. The trial process is not well served if the defence make general and unspecified allegations and then seek far-reaching disclosure in the hope that material may turn up to make them good. The more detail a defence statement contains the more likely it is that the prosecutor will make an informed decision about whether any remaining undisclosed material might reasonably be considered capable of undermining the prosecution case or of assisting the case for the accused, or whether to advise the investigator to undertake further enquiries. It also helps in the management of the trial by narrowing down and focussing on the issues in dispute. It may result in the prosecution discontinuing the case. Defence practitioners should be aware of these considerations when advising their clients.

16. Whenever a defence solicitor provides a defence statement on behalf of the accused it will be deemed to be given with the authority of the solicitor's client.

Continuing Duty of Prosecutor to Disclose

C–7   17. Section 7A of the Act imposes a continuing duty upon the prosecutor to keep under review at all times the question of whether there is any unused material which might reasonably be considered capable of undermining the prosecution case against the accused or assisting the case for the accused and which has not previously been disclosed. This duty arises after the prosecutor has complied with the duty of initial disclosure or purported to comply with it and before the accused is acquitted or convicted or the prosecutor decides not to proceed with the case. If such material is identified, then the prosecutor must disclose it to the accused as soon as is reasonably practicable.

18. As part of their continuing duty of disclosure, prosecutors should be open, alert and promptly responsive to requests for disclosure of material supported by a comprehensive defence statement. Conversely, if no defence statement has been served or if the prosecutor considers that the defence statement is lacking specificity or otherwise does not meet the requirements of section 6A of the Act, a letter should be sent to the defence indicating this. If the position is not resolved satisfactorily, the prosecutor should consider raising the issue at a hearing for directions to enable the court to give a warning or appropriate directions.

19. When defence practitioners are dissatisfied with disclosure decisions by the prosecution and consider that they are entitled to further disclosure, applications to the court should be made pursuant to section 8 of the Act and in accordance with the procedures set out in the Criminal Procedure Rules. Applications for further disclosure should not be made as ad hoc applications but dealt with under the proper procedures.

Applications for Non-disclosure in the Public Interest

20. Before making an application to the court to withhold material which would **C–8** otherwise fall to be disclosed, on the basis that to disclose would give rise to a real risk of serious prejudice to an important public interest, prosecutors should aim to disclose as much of the material as they properly can (for example, by giving the defence redacted or edited copies or summaries). Neutral material or material damaging to the defendant need not be disclosed and must not be brought to the attention of the court. It is only in truly borderline cases that the prosecution should seek a judicial ruling on the disclosability of material in its possession.

21. Prior to or at the hearing, the court must be provided with full and accurate information. Prior to the hearing the prosecutor and the prosecution advocate must examine all material, which is the subject matter of the application and make any necessary enquiries of the investigator. The prosecutor (or representative) and/or investigator should attend such applications.

22. The principles set out at paragraph 36 of *R v H & C* should be rigorously applied firstly by the prosecutor and then by the court considering the material. It is essential that these principles are scrupulously attended to to ensure that the procedure for examination of material in the absence of the accused is compliant with Article 6 of ECHR.

Responsibilities

Investigators and Disclosure Officers

23. Investigators and disclosure officers must be fair and objective and must work **C–9** together with prosecutors to ensure that disclosure obligations are met. A failure to take action leading to inadequate disclosure may result in a wrongful conviction. It may alternatively lead to a successful abuse of process argument, an acquittal against the weight of the evidence or the appellate courts may find that a conviction is unsafe and quash it.

24. Officers appointed as disclosure officers must have the requisite experience, skills, competence and resources to undertake their vital role. In discharging their obligations under the Act, code, common law and any operational instructions, investigators should always err on the side of recording and retaining material where they have any doubt as to whether it may be relevant.

25. An individual must not be appointed as disclosure officer, or continue in that role, if that is likely to result in a conflict of interest, for instance, if the disclosure officer is the victim of the alleged crime which is the subject of investigation. The advice of a more senior investigator must always be sought if there is doubt as to whether a conflict of interest precludes an individual acting as the disclosure officer. If thereafter a doubt remains, the advice of a prosecutor should be sought.

26. There may be a number of disclosure officers, especially in large and complex cases. **C–10** However, there must be a lead disclosure officer who is the focus for enquiries and whose

responsibility it is to ensure that the investigator's disclosure obligations are complied with. Disclosure officers, or their deputies, must inspect, view or listen to all relevant material that has been retained by the investigator, and the disclosure officer must provide a personal declaration to the effect that this task has been undertaken.

27. Generally this will mean that such material must be examined in detail by the disclosure officer or the deputy, but exceptionally the extent and manner of inspecting, viewing or listening will depend on the nature of material and its form. For example, it might be reasonable to examine digital material by using software search tools, or to establish the contents of large volumes of material by dip sampling. If such material is not examined in detail, it must nonetheless be described on the disclosure schedules accurately and as clearly as possible. The extent and manner of its examination must also be described together with justification for such action.

28. Investigators must retain material that may be relevant to the investigation. However, it may become apparent to the investigator that some material obtained in the course of an investigation because it was considered potentially relevant, is in fact incapable of impact. It need not then be retained or dealt with in accordance with these Guidelines, although the investigator should err on the side of caution in coming to this conclusion and seek the advice of the prosecutor as appropriate.

C–11   29. In meeting the obligations in *paragraph 6.9* and *8.1* of the Code, it is crucial that descriptions by disclosure officers in non-sensitive schedules are detailed, clear and accurate. The descriptions may require a summary of the contents of the retained material to assist the prosecutor to make an informed decision on disclosure. Sensitive schedules must contain sufficient information to enable the prosecutor to make an informed decision as to whether or not the material itself should be viewed, to the extent possible without compromising the confidentiality of the information.

30. Disclosure officers must specifically draw material to the attention of the prosecutor for consideration where they have any doubt as to whether it might reasonably be considered capable of undermining the prosecution case or of assisting the case for the accused.

31. Disclosure officers must seek the advice and assistance of prosecutors when in doubt as to their responsibility as early as possible. They must deal expeditiously with requests by the prosecutor for further information on material, which may lead to disclosure.

Prosecutors

C–12   32. Prosecutors must do all that they can to facilitate proper disclosure, as part of their general and personal professional responsibility to act fairly and impartially, in the interests of justice and in accordance with the law. Prosecutors must also be alert to the need to provide advice to, and where necessary probe actions taken by, disclosure officers to ensure that disclosure obligations are met.

33. Prosecutors must review schedules prepared by disclosure officers thoroughly and must be alert to the possibility that relevant material may exist which has not been revealed to them or material included which should not have been. If no schedules have been provided, or there are apparent omissions from the schedules, or documents or other items are inadequately described or are unclear, the prosecutor must at once take action to obtain properly completed schedules. Likewise schedules should be returned for amendment if irrelevant items are included. If prosecutors remain dissatisfied with the quality or content of the schedules they must raise the matter with a senior investigator, and if necessary, persist, with a view to resolving the matter satisfactorily.

34. Where prosecutors have reason to believe that the disclosure officer has not discharged the obligation in *paragraph 26* to inspect, view or listen to relevant material, they must at once raise the matter with the disclosure officer and, if it is believed that the officer has not inspected, viewed or listened to the material, request that it be done.

C–13   35. When prosecutors or disclosure officers believe that material might reasonably be considered capable of undermining the prosecution case or assisting the case for the accused, prosecutors must always inspect, view or listen to the material and satisfy themselves that the prosecution can properly be continued having regard to the disclosability of the material reviewed. Their judgement as to what other material to inspect, view or listen to will depend on the circumstances of each case.

36. Prosecutors should copy the defence statement to the disclosure officer and investiga-

tor as soon as reasonably practicable and prosecutors should advise the investigator if, in their view, reasonable and relevant lines of further enquiry should be pursued.

37. Prosecutors cannot comment upon, or invite inferences to be drawn from, failures in defence disclosure otherwise than in accordance with section 11 of the Act. Prosecutors may cross-examine the accused on differences between the defence case put at trial and that set out in his or her defence statement. In doing so, it may be appropriate to apply to the judge under section 6E of the Act for copies of the statement to be given to a jury, edited if necessary to remove inadmissible material. Prosecutors should examine the defence statement to see whether it points to other lines of enquiry. If the defence statement does point to other reasonable lines of inquiry further investigation is required and evidence obtained as a result of these enquiries may be used as part of the prosecution case or to rebut the defence.

38. Once initial disclosure is completed and a defence statement has been served requests **C–14** for disclosure should ordinarily only be answered if the request is in accordance with and relevant to the defence statement. If it is not, then a further or amended defence statement should be sought and obtained before considering the request for further disclosure.

39. Prosecutors must ensure that they record in writing all actions and decisions they make in discharging their disclosure responsibilities, and this information is to be made available to the prosecution advocate if requested or if relevant to an issue.

40. If the material does not fulfil the disclosure test there is no requirement to disclose it. For this purpose, the parties' respective cases should not be restrictively analysed but must be carefully analysed to ascertain the specific facts the prosecution seek to establish and the specific grounds on which the charges are resisted. Neutral material or material damaging to the defendant need not be disclosed and must not be brought to the attention of the court. Only in truly borderline cases should the prosecution seek a judicial ruling on the disclosability of material in its hands.

41. If prosecutors are satisfied that a fair trial cannot take place where material which satisfies the disclosure test cannot be disclosed, and that this cannot or will not be remedied including by, for example, making formal admissions, amending the charges or presenting the case in a different way so as to ensure fairness or in other ways, they must not continue with the case.

Prosecution Advocates

42. Prosecution advocates should ensure that all material that ought to be disclosed **C–15** under the Act is disclosed to the defence. However, prosecution advocates cannot be expected to disclose material if they are not aware of its existence. As far as is possible, prosecution advocates must place themselves in a fully informed position to enable them to make decisions on disclosure.

43. Upon receipt of instructions, prosecution advocates should consider as a priority all the information provided regarding disclosure of material. Prosecution advocates should consider, in every case, whether they can be satisfied that they are in possession of all relevant documentation and that they have been instructed fully regarding disclosure matters. Decisions already made regarding disclosure should be reviewed. If as a result, the advocate considers that further information or action is required, written advice should be promptly provided setting out the aspects that need clarification or action. Prosecution advocates must advise on disclosure in accordance with the Act. If necessary and where appropriate a conference should be held to determine what is required.

44. The prosecution advocate must keep decisions regarding disclosure under review until the conclusion of the trial. The prosecution advocate must in every case specifically consider whether he or she can satisfactorily discharge the duty of continuing review on the basis of the material supplied already, or whether it is necessary to inspect further material or to reconsider material already inspected. Prosecution advocates must not abrogate their responsibility under the Act by disclosing material which could not be considered capable of undermining the prosecution case or of assisting the case for the accused.

45. Prior to the commencement of a trial, the prosecuting advocate should always make decisions on disclosure in consultation with those instructing him or her and the disclosure officer. After a trial has started, it is recognised that in practice consultation on disclosure issues may not be practicable; it continues to be desirable, however, whenever this can be achieved without affecting unduly the conduct of the trial.

46. There is no basis in law or practice for disclosure on a "counsel to counsel" basis.

Involvement of Other Agencies

Material held by Government departments or other Crown bodies

C–16   47. Where it appears to an investigator, disclosure officer or prosecutor that a Government department or other Crown body has material that may be relevant to an issue in the case, reasonable steps should be taken to identify and consider such material. Although what is reasonable will vary from case to case, the prosecution should inform the department or other body of the nature of its case and of relevant issues in the case in respect of which the department or body might possess material, and ask whether it has any such material.

48. It should be remembered that investigators, disclosure officers and prosecutors cannot be regarded to be in constructive possession of material held by Government departments or Crown bodies simply by virtue of their status as Government departments or Crown bodies.

49. Departments in England and Wales should have identified personnel as established Enquiry Points to deal with issues concerning the disclosure of information in criminal proceedings.

50. Where, after reasonable steps have been taken to secure access to such material, access is denied the investigator, disclosure officer or prosecutor should consider what if any further steps might be taken to obtain the material or inform the defence.

Material held by Other Agencies

C–17   51. There may be cases where the investigator, disclosure officer or prosecutor believes that a third party (for example, a local authority, a social services department, a hospital, a doctor, a school, a provider of forensic services) has material or information which might be relevant to the prosecution case. In such cases, if the material or information might reasonably be considered capable of undermining the prosecution case or of assisting the case for the accused prosecutors should take what steps they regard as appropriate in the particular case to obtain it.

52. If the investigator, disclosure officer or prosecutor seeks access to the material or information but the third party declines or refuses to allow access to it, the matter should not be left. If despite any reasons offered by the third party it is still believed that it is reasonable to seek production of the material or information, and the requirements of section 2 of the *Criminal Procedure (Attendance of Witnesses) Act* 1965 or as appropriate section 97 of the *Magistrates' Courts Act* 1980 are satisfied, then the prosecutor or investigator should apply for a witness summons causing a representative of the third party to produce the material to the Court.

53. Relevant information which comes to the knowledge of investigators or prosecutors as a result of liaison with third parties should be recorded by the investigator or prosecutor in a durable or retrievable form (for example potentially relevant information revealed in discussions at a child protection conference attended by police officers).

54. Where information comes into the possession of the prosecution in the circumstances set out in *paragraphs 51–53* above, consultation with the other agency should take place before disclosure is made: there may be public interest reasons which justify withholding disclosure and which would require the issue of disclosure of the information to be placed before the court.

Other Disclosure

Disclosure Prior to Initial Disclosure

C–18   55. Investigators must always be alive to the potential need to reveal and prosecutors to the potential need to disclose material, in the interests of justice and fairness in the particular circumstances of any case, after the commencement of proceedings but before their duty arises under the Act. For instance, disclosure ought to be made of significant information that might affect a bail decision or that might enable the defence to contest the committal proceedings.

56. Where the need for such disclosure is not apparent to the prosecutor, any disclosure will depend on what the accused chooses to reveal about the defence. Clearly, such disclosure will not exceed that which is obtainable after the statutory duties of disclosure

arise.

Summary Trial

57. The prosecutor should, in addition to complying with the obligations under the Act, **C–19** provide to the defence all evidence upon which the Crown proposes to rely in a summary trial. Such provision should allow the accused and their legal advisers sufficient time properly to consider the evidence before it is called.

Material Relevant to Sentence

58. In all cases the prosecutor must consider disclosing in the interests of justice any ma- **C–20** terial, which is relevant to sentence (e.g. information which might mitigate the seriousness of the offence or assist the accused to lay blame in part upon a co-accused or another person).

Post-conviction

59. The interests of justice will also mean that where material comes to light after the **C–21** conclusion of the proceedings, which might cast doubt upon the safety of the conviction, there is a duty to consider disclosure. Any such material should be brought immediately to the attention of line management.

60. Disclosure of any material that is made outside the ambit of Act will attract confidentiality by virtue of *Taylor v SFO* [1998].

Applicability of these Guidelines

61. Although the relevant obligations in relation to unused material and disclosure **C–22** imposed on the prosecutor and the accused are determined by the date on which the investigation began, these Guidelines should be adopted with immediate effect in relation to all cases submitted to the prosecuting authorities in receipt of these Guidelines save where they specifically refer to the statutory or Code provisions of the Criminal Justice Act 2003 that do not yet apply to the particular case.

Appendices

ATTORNEY-GENERAL'S GUIDELINES ON THE ACCEPTANCE OF PLEAS AND THE PROSECUTOR'S ROLE IN THE SENTENCING EXERCISE

ACCEPTANCE OF PLEAS

Introduction

On December 7, 2000, the Attorney General issued guidelines on the acceptance of **D–1** pleas. This appears to have been prompted by the comments of the Court of Appeal in *Att.-Gen.'s Reference (No. 44 of 2000) (R. v. Peverett)* [2001] 1 Cr.App.R. 27. These guidelines were revised on October 21, 2005 and replace those originally issued. On June 8, 2007 the Attorney General issued a further amendment, which is included here.

Attorney-General's Guidelines on the Acceptance of Pleas and the Prosecutor's Role in the Sentencing Exercise

A. Foreword

A:1. Prosecutors have an important role in protecting the victim's interests in the criminal **D–2** justice process, not least in the acceptance of pleas and the sentencing exercise. The basis of plea, particularly in a case that is not contested, is the vehicle through which the victim's voice is heard. Factual inaccuracies in pleas in mitigation cause distress and offence to victims, the families of victims and witnesses. This can take many forms but may be most acutely felt when the victim is dead and the family hears inaccurate assertions about the victim's character or lifestyle. Prosecution advocates are reminded that they are required to adhere to the standards set out in the Victim's Charter, which places the needs of the victim at the heart of the criminal justice process, and that they will be subject to a similar obligation in respect of the Code of Practice for Victims of Crime when it comes into force.

A:2. The principle of fairness is central to the administration of justice. The implementation of *Human Rights Act* 1998 [*sic*] in October 2000 incorporated into domestic law the principle of fairness to the accused articulated in the European Convention on Human Rights. Accuracy and reasonableness of plea plays an important part in ensuring fairness both to the accused and to the victim.

A:3. The Attorney General's Guidelines on the Acceptance of Pleas issued on December 7, 2000 highlighted the importance of transparency in the conduct of justice. The basis of plea agreed by the parties in a criminal trial is central to the sentencing process. An illogical or unsupported basis of plea can lead to the passing of an unduly lenient sentence and has a consequential effect where consideration arises as to whether to refer the sentence to the Court of Appeal under section 36 of the *Criminal Justice Act* 1988.

A:4. These Guidelines, which expand upon and now replace the Guidelines issued on the 7 December 2000 [*sic*], give guidance on how prosecutors should meet these objectives of protection of victims' interests and of securing fairness and transparency in the process. They take into account the guidance issued by the Court of Appeal (Criminal) Division [*sic*] in *R. v. Beswick* [1996] 1 Cr.App.R. 343, *R. v. Tolera* [1999] 1 Cr.App.R. 25 and *R. v. Underwood* [2005] 1 Cr.App.R 13. They complement the Bar Council Guidance on Written Standards for the Conduct of Professional Work issued with the 7th edition of the Code of Conduct for the Bar of England and Wales and the Law Society's Professional Conduct Rules. When considering the acceptance of a guilty plea prosecution advocates are also reminded of the need to apply "The Farquharson Guidelines on The Role and Responsibilities of the Prosecution Advocate".

A:5. The Guidelines should be followed by all prosecutors and those persons designated under section 7 of the *Prosecution of Offences Act* 1985 (designated caseworkers) and apply to prosecutions conducted in England and Wales.

B. General Principles

D–3   **B:**1. Justice in this jurisdiction, save in the most exceptional circumstances, is conducted in public. This includes the acceptance of pleas by the prosecution and sentencing.

B:2. The Code for Crown Prosecutors governs the prosecutor's decision-making prior to the commencement of the trial hearing and sets out the circumstances in which pleas to a reduced number of charges, or less serious charges, can be accepted.

B:3. When a case is listed for trial and the prosecution form the view that the appropriate course is to accept a plea before the proceedings commence or continue, or to offer no evidence on the indictment or any part of it, the prosecution should whenever practicable speak to the victim or the victim's family, so that the position can be explained. The views of the victim or the family may assist in informing the prosecutor's decision as to whether it is the [*sic*] public interest, as defined by the Code for Crown Prosecutors, to accept or reject the plea. The victim or victim's family should then be kept informed and decisions explained once they are made at court.

B:4. The appropriate disposal of a criminal case after conviction is as much a part of the criminal justice process as the trial of guilt or innocence. The prosecution advocate represents the public interest, and should be ready to assist the court to reach its decision as to the appropriate sentence. This will include drawing the court's attention to:

— any victim personal statement or other information available to the prosecution advocate as to the impact of the offence on the victim;

— where appropriate, to any evidence of the impact of the offending on a community;

— any statutory provisions relevant to the offender and the offences under consideration;

— any relevant sentencing guidelines and guideline cases; and

— the aggravating and mitigating factors of the offence under consideration;

The prosecution advocate may also offer assistance to the court by making submissions, in the light of all these factors, as to the appropriate sentencing range.

In all cases, it is the prosecution advocate's duty to apply for appropriate ancillary orders, such as anti-social behaviour orders and confiscation orders. When considering which ancillary orders to apply for, prosecution advocates must always have regard to the victim's needs, including the question of his or her future protection.

C. The Basis of Plea

D–4   **C:**1. The basis of a guilty plea must not be agreed on a misleading or untrue set of facts and must take proper account of the victim's interests. An illogical or insupportable basis of plea will inevitably result in the imposition of an inappropriate sentence and is capable of damaging public confidence in the criminal justice system.

C:2. When the defendant indicates an acceptable plea, the defence advocate should reduce the basis of the plea to writing. This should be done in all cases save for those in which the issue is simple or where the defendant has indicated that the guilty plea has been or will be tendered on the basis of the prosecution case.

C:3. The written basis of plea must be considered with great care, taking account of the position of any other relevant defendant where appropriate. The prosecution should not lend itself to any agreement whereby a case is presented to the sentencing judge on a misleading or untrue set of facts or on a basis that is detrimental to the victim's interests. There will be cases where a defendant seeks to mitigate on the basis of assertions of fact which are outside the scope of the prosecution's knowledge. A typical example concerns the defendant's state of mind. If a defendant wishes to be sentenced on this basis, the prosecution advocate should invite the judge not to accept the defendant's version unless he or she gives evidence on oath to be tested in cross-examination.

C:4. The prosecution advocate should show the prosecuting authority any written record relating to the plea and agree with them the basis on which the case will be opened to the court.

C:5. It is the responsibility of the prosecution advocate thereafter to ensure that the defence advocate is aware of the basis on which the plea is accepted by the prosecution and the way in which the prosecution case will be opened to the court.

C:6. In all cases before the Crown Court, and in cases before the magistrates' court where the issues are complex or there is scope for misunderstanding, the prosecution must commit to writing the aggravating and mitigating factors that will form the opening of the prosecution case as well as any statutory limitations on sentencing. The prosecution will address, where relevant, the factors outlined at B4 including the matters set out in the next sub-paragraph.

The matters to be dealt with are:

- the aggravating and mitigating factors of the offence (not personal mitigation);
- any statutory provisions relevant to the offender and the offence under consideration so that the judge is made aware of any statutory limitations on sentencing;
- any relevant sentencing guidelines and guideline cases;
- identifying any victim personal statement or other information available to the prosecution advocate as to the impact of the offence on the victim;
- where appropriate, any evidence of the impact of the offending on a community;
- an indication, where applicable, of an intention to apply for any ancillary orders, such as anti-social behaviour orders and confiscation orders, and so far as possible, indicating the nature of the order to be sought.

C:7. When the prosecution advocate has agreed the written basis of plea submitted by the defence advocate, he or she should endorse the document accordingly. If the prosecution advocate takes issue with all or part of the written basis of plea, he or she should set out in writing what is accepted and what is rejected or not accepted. Where there is a dispute about a particular fact which the defence advocate believes to be effectively immaterial to the sentencing decision, the difference should be recorded so that the judge can make up his or her own mind. The signed original document should be made available to the trial judge and thereafter lodged with the court papers, as it will form part of the record of the hearing.

C:8. Where a defendant declines to admit an offence that he or she previously indicated should be taken into consideration, the prosecution advocate should indicate to the defence advocate and the court that, subject to further review, the offence may now form the basis of a new prosecution.

C:9. Where the basis of plea cannot be agreed and the discrepancy between the two accounts is such as to have a potentially significant effect on the level of sentence, it is the duty of the defence advocate so to inform the court before the sentencing process begins. There remains an overriding duty on the prosecution advocate to ensure that the sentencing judge is made aware of the discrepancy and of the consideration which must be given to the holding of a *Newton* hearing to resolve the issue. The court should be told where a derogatory reference to a victim, witness or third party is not accepted, even though there may be no effect on sentence.

C:10. Whenever an agreement as to the basis of plea is made between the prosecution and defence, any such agreement will be subject to the approval of the trial judge, who may of his or her own motion disregard the agreement and direct that a *Newton* hearing should be held to determine the proper basis on which sentence should be passed.

D.   Sentence Indications

D:1. Only in the Crown Court may sentence indications be sought. Advocates there are **D–5** reminded that indications as to sentence should not be sought from the trial judge unless issues between the prosecution and defence have been addressed and resolved. Therefore, in difficult or complicated cases, no less than seven days notice in writing of an intention to seek an indication should normally be given to the prosecution and the court. When deciding whether the circumstances of a case require such notice to be given, defence advocates are reminded that prosecutors should not agree a basis of plea unless and until the necessary consultation has taken place first with the victim and/or the victim's family and second, in the case of an independent prosecution advocate, with the prosecuting authority.

D:2. If there is no final agreement about the plea to the indictment, or the basis of plea, and the defence nevertheless proceeds to seek an indication of sentence, which the judge appears minded to give, the prosecution advocate should remind him or her of the guidance given in *R. v. Goodyear (Karl)* [2005] EWCA 888 [*sic*] that normally speaking an indication of sentence should not be given until the basis of the plea has been agreed or the judge has concluded that he or she can properly deal with the case without the need for a trial of the issue.

D:3. If an indication is sought, the prosecution advocate should normally enquire whether the judge is in possession of or has access to all the evidence relied on by the prosecution, including any victim personal statement, as well as any information about relevant previous convictions recorded against the defendant.

D:4. Before the judge gives the indication, the prosecution advocate should draw the judge's attention to any minimum or mandatory statutory sentencing requirements. Where the prosecution advocate would be expected to offer the judge assistance with relevant guideline cases or the views of the Sentencing Guidelines Council, he or she should invite the judge to allow them to do so. Where it applies, the prosecution advocate should remind the judge that the position [*sic*] of the Attorney General to refer any sentencing decision as unduly lenient is unaffected. In any event, the prosecution advocate should not say anything which may create the impression that the sentence indication has the support or approval of the Crown.

E. Pleas in Mitigation

D–6   **E:**1. The prosecution advocate must challenge any assertion by the defence in mitigation which is derogatory to a person's character (for instance, because it suggests that his or her conduct is or has been criminal, immoral or improper) and which is either false or irrelevant to proper sentencing considerations. If the defence advocate persists in that assertion, the prosecution advocate should invite the court to consider holding a *Newton* hearing to determine the issue.

E:2. The defence advocate must not submit in mitigation anything that is derogatory to a person's character without giving advance notice in writing so as to afford the prosecution advocate the opportunity to consider their position under paragraph E:1. When the prosecution advocate is so notified they must take all reasonable steps to establish whether the assertions are true. Reasonable steps will include seeking the views of the victim. This will involve seeking the views of the victim's family if the victim is deceased, and the victim's parents or legal guardian where the victim is a child. Reasonable steps may also include seeking the views of the police or other law enforcement authority, as appropriate. An assertion which is derogatory to a person's character will rarely amount to mitigation unless it has a causal connection to the circumstances of the offence or is otherwise relevant to proper sentencing considerations.

E:3. Where notice has not been given in accordance with paragraph E:2, the prosecution advocate must not acquiesce in permitting mitigation which is derogatory to a person's character. In such circumstances, the prosecution advocate should draw the attention of the court to the failure to give advance notice and seek time, and if necessary, an adjournment to investigate the assertion in the same way as if proper notice had been given. Where, in the opinion of the prosecution advocate, there are substantial grounds for believing that such an assertion is false or irrelevant to sentence, he or she should inform the court of their opinion and invite the court to consider making an order under section 58(8) of the *Criminal Procedure and Investigations Act* 1996, preventing publication of the assertion.

E:4. Where the prosecution advocate considers that the assertion is, if true, relevant to sentence, or the court has so indicated, he or she should seek time, and if necessary an adjournment, to establish whether the assertion is true. If the matter cannot be resolved to the satisfaction of the parties, the prosecution advocate should invite the court to consider holding a *Newton* hearing to determine the issue.

CODE FOR CROWN PROSECUTORS

CROWN PROSECUTORS

Introduction

The Crown Prosecution Service is the principal public prosecuting authority for **E–1** England and Wales and is headed by the Director of Public Prosecutions. The Attorney General is accountable to Parliament for the Service.

The Crown Prosecution Service is a national organisation consisting of 42 Areas. Each Area is headed by a Chief Crown Prosecutor and corresponds to a single police force area, with one for London. It was set up in 1986 to prosecute cases investigated by the police.

Although the Crown Prosecution Service works closely with the police, it is independent of them. The independence of Crown Prosecutors is of fundamental constitutional importance. Casework decisions taken with fairness, impartiality and integrity help deliver justice for victims, witnesses, defendants and the public.

The Crown Prosecution Service co-operates with the investigating and prosecuting agencies of other jurisdictions.

The Director of Public Prosecutions is responsible for issuing a Code for Crown Prosecutors under section 10 of the *Prosecution of Offences Act* 1985, giving guidance on the general principles to be applied when making decisions about prosecutions. For the purpose of this Code, 'Crown Prosecutor' includes members of staff in the Crown Prosecution Service who are designated by the Director of Public Prosecutions under section 7A of the Act and are exercising powers under that section.

Five editions of this Code have been issued. The most recent edition reproduced here was issued in 2004 and replaces all earlier versions.

Code for Crown Prosecutors

1. INTRODUCTION

1.1 The decision to prosecute an individual is a serious step. Fair and effective prosecution **E–2** is essential to the maintenance of law and order. Even in a small case a prosecution has serious implications for all involved – victims, witnesses and defendants. The Crown Prosecution Service applies the Code for Crown Prosecutors so that it can make fair and consistent decisions about prosecutions.

1.2 The Code helps the Crown Prosecution Service to play its part in making sure that justice is done. It contains information that is important to police officers and others who work in the criminal justice system and to the general public. Police officers should apply the provisions of this Code whenever they are responsible for deciding whether to charge a person with an offence.

1.3 The Code is also designed to make sure that everyone knows the principles that the Crown Prosecution Service applies when carrying out its work. By applying the same principles, everyone involved in the system is helping to treat victims, witnesses and defendants fairly, while prosecuting cases effectively.

2. GENERAL PRINCIPLES

2.1 Each case is unique and must be considered on its own facts and merits. However, **E–3**

1553

there are general principles that apply to the way in which Crown Prosecutors must approach every case.

2.2 Crown Prosecutors must be fair, independent and objective. They must not let any personal views about ethnic or national origin, disability, sex, religious beliefs, political views or the sexual orientation of the suspect, victim or witness influence their decisions. They must not be affected by improper or undue pressure from any source.

2.3 It is the duty of Crown Prosecutors to make sure that the right person is prosecuted for the right offence. In doing so, Crown Prosecutors must always act in the interests of justice and not solely for the purpose of obtaining a conviction.

2.4 Crown Prosecutors should provide guidance and advice to investigators throughout the investigative and prosecuting process. This may include lines of inquiry, evidential requirements and assistance in any pre-charge procedures. Crown Prosecutors will be proactive in identifying and, where possible, rectifying evidential deficiencies and in bringing to an early conclusion those cases that cannot be strengthened by further investigation.

2.5 It is the duty of Crown Prosecutors to review, advise on and prosecute cases, ensuring that the law is properly applied, that all relevant evidence is put before the court and that obligations of disclosure are complied with, in accordance with the principles set out in this Code.

2.6 The Crown Prosecution Service is a public authority for the purposes of the Human Rights Act 1998. Crown Prosecutors must apply the principles of the European Convention on Human Rights in accordance with the Act.

3. THE DECISION TO PROSECUTE

E–4   3.1 In most cases, Crown Prosecutors are responsible for deciding whether a person should be charged with a criminal offence, and if so, what that offence should be. Crown Prosecutors make these decisions in accordance with this Code and the Director's Guidance on Charging. In those cases where the police determine the charge, which are usually more minor and routine cases, they apply the same provisions.

3.2 Crown Prosecutors make charging decisions in accordance with the Full Code Test (see *section 5* below), other than in those limited circumstances where the Threshold Test applies (see *section 6* below).

3.3 The Threshold Test applies where the case is one in which it is proposed to keep the suspect in custody after charge, but the evidence required to apply the Full Code Test is not yet available.

3.4 Where a Crown Prosecutor makes a charging decision in accordance with the Threshold Test, the case must be reviewed in accordance with the Full Code Test as soon as reasonably practicable, taking into account the progress of the investigation.

4. REVIEW

E–5   4.1 Each case the Crown Prosecution Service receives from the police is reviewed to make sure that it is right to proceed with a prosecution. Unless the Threshold Test applies, the Crown Prosecution Service will only start or continue with a prosecution when the case has passed both stages of the Full Code Test.

4.2 Review is a continuing process and Crown Prosecutors must take account of any change in circumstances. Wherever possible, they should talk to the police first if they are thinking about changing the charges or stopping the case. Crown Prosecutors should also tell the police if they believe that some additional evidence may strengthen the case. This gives the police the chance to provide more information that may affect the decision.

4.3 The Crown Prosecution Service and the police work closely together, but the final responsibility for the decision whether or not a charge or a case should go ahead rests with the Crown Prosecution Service.

5. THE FULL CODE TEST

E–6   5.1 The Full Code Test has two stages. The first stage is consideration of the evidence. If the case does not pass the evidential stage it must not go ahead no matter how important or serious it may be. If the case does pass the evidential stage, Crown Prosecutors must proceed to the second stage and decide if a prosecution is needed in the public interest. The evidential and public interest stages are explained below.

The Evidential Stage

5.2 Crown Prosecutors must be satisfied that there is enough evidence to provide a 'realistic prospect of conviction' against each defendant on each charge. They must consider what the defence case may be, and how that is likely to affect the prosecution case.

5.3 A realistic prospect of conviction is an objective test. It means that a jury or bench of magistrates or judge hearing a case alone, properly directed in accordance with the law, is more likely than not to convict the defendant of the charge alleged. This is a separate test from the one that the criminal courts themselves must apply. A court should only convict if satisfied so that it is sure of a defendant's guilt.

5.4 When deciding whether there is enough evidence to prosecute, Crown Prosecutors must consider whether the evidence can be used and is reliable. There will be many cases in which the evidence does not give any cause for concern. But there will also be cases in which the evidence may not be as strong as it first appears. Crown Prosecutors must ask themselves the following questions:

Can the evidence be used in court?

(a) Is it likely that the evidence will be excluded by the court? There are certain legal rules which might mean that evidence which seems relevant cannot be given at a trial. For example, is it likely that the evidence will be excluded because of the way in which it was gathered? If so, is there enough other evidence for a realistic prospect of conviction?

Is the evidence reliable?

(b) Is there evidence which might support or detract from the reliability of a confession? Is the reliability affected by factors such as the defendant's age, intelligence or level of understanding?

(c) What explanation has the defendant given? Is a court likely to find it credible in the light of the evidence as a whole? Does it support an innocent explanation?

(d) If the identity of the defendant is likely to be questioned, is the evidence about this strong enough?

(e) Is the witness's background likely to weaken the prosecution case? For example, does the witness have any motive that may affect his or her attitude to the case, or a relevant previous conviction?

(f) Are there concerns over the accuracy or credibility of a witness? Are these concerns based on evidence or simply information with nothing to support it? Is there further evidence which the police should be asked to seek out which may support or detract from the account of the witness?

5.5 Crown Prosecutors should not ignore evidence because they are not sure that it can be used or is reliable. But they should look closely at it when deciding if there is a realistic prospect of conviction.

The Public Interest Stage

5.6 In 1951, Lord Shawcross, who was Attorney General, made the classic statement on **E–7** public interest, which has been supported by Attorneys General ever since: "It has never been the rule in this country – I hope it never will be – that suspected criminal offences must automatically be the subject of prosecution". (House of Commons Debates, volume 483, column 681, 29 January 1951.)

5.7 The public interest must be considered in each case where there is enough evidence to provide a realistic prospect of conviction. Although there may be public interest factors against prosecution in a particular case, often the prosecution should go ahead and those factors should be put to the court for consideration when sentence is being passed. A prosecution will usually take place unless there are public interest factors tending against prosecution which clearly outweigh those tending in favour, or it appears more appropriate in all the circumstances of the case to divert the person from prosecution (see *section 8* below).

5.8 Crown Prosecutors must balance factors for and against prosecution carefully and fairly. Public interest factors that can affect the decision to prosecute usually depend on the seriousness of the offence or the circumstances of the suspect. Some factors may increase the need to prosecute but others may suggest that another course of action would be better.

The following lists of some common public interest factors, both for and against prosecution, are not exhaustive. The factors that apply will depend on the facts in each case.

Some common public interest factors in favour of prosecution

5.9 The more serious the offence, the more likely it is that a prosecution will be needed in the public interest. A prosecution is likely to be needed if:

(a) a conviction is likely to result in a significant sentence;

(b) a conviction is likely to result in a confiscation or any other order;

(c) a weapon was used or violence was threatened during the commission of the offence;

(d) the offence was committed against a person serving the public (for example, a police or prison officer, or a nurse);

(e) the defendant was in a position of authority or trust;

(f) the evidence shows that the defendant was a ringleader or an organiser of the offence;

(g) there is evidence that the offence was premeditated;

(h) there is evidence that the offence was carried out by a group;

(i) the victim of the offence was vulnerable, has been put in considerable fear, or suffered personal attack, damage or disturbance;

(j) the offence was committed in the presence of, or in close proximity to, a child;

(k) the offence was motivated by any form of discrimination against the victim's ethnic or national origin, disability, sex, religious beliefs, political views or sexual orientation, or the suspect demonstrated hostility towards the victim based on any of those characteristics;

(l) there is a marked difference between the actual or mental ages of the defendant and the victim, or if there is any element of corruption;

(m) the defendant's previous convictions or cautions are relevant to the present offence;

(n) the defendant is alleged to have committed the offence while under an order of the court;

(o) there are grounds for believing that the offence is likely to be continued or repeated, for example, by a history of recurring conduct;

(p) the offence, although not serious in itself, is widespread in the area where it was committed; or

(q) a prosecution would have a significant positive impact on maintaining community confidence.

Some common public interest factors against prosecution

5.10 A prosecution is less likely to be needed if:

(a) the court is likely to impose a nominal penalty;

(b) the defendant has already been made the subject of a sentence and any further conviction would be unlikely to result in the imposition of an additional sentence or order, unless the nature of the particular offence requires a prosecution or the defendant withdraws consent to have an offence taken into consideration during sentencing;

(c) the offence was committed as a result of a genuine mistake or misunderstanding (these factors must be balanced against the seriousness of the offence);

(d) the loss or harm can be described as minor and was the result of a single incident, particularly if it was caused by a misjudgment;

(e) there has been a long delay between the offence taking place and the date of the trial, unless:

　　• the offence is serious;

- the delay has been caused in part by the defendant;
- the offence has only recently come to light; or
- the complexity of the offence has meant that there has been a long investigation;

(f) a prosecution is likely to have a bad effect on the victim's physical or mental health, always bearing in mind the seriousness of the offence;

(g) the defendant is elderly or is, or was at the time of the offence, suffering from significant mental or physical ill health, unless the offence is serious or there is real possibility that it may be repeated. The Crown Prosecution Service, where necessary, applies Home Office guidelines about how to deal with mentally disordered offenders. Crown Prosecutors must balance the desirability of diverting a defendant who is suffering from significant mental or physical ill health with the need to safeguard the general public;

(h) the defendant has put right the loss or harm that was caused (but defendants must not avoid prosecution or diversion solely because they pay compensation); or

(i) details may be made public that could harm sources of information, international relations or national security;

5.11 Deciding on the public interest is not simply a matter of adding up the number of factors on each side. Crown Prosecutors must decide how important each factor is in the circumstances of each case and go on to make an overall assessment.

The relationship between the victim and the public interest

5.12 The Crown Prosecution Service does not act for victims or the families of victims in the same way as solicitors act for their clients. Crown Prosecutors act on behalf of the public and not just in the interests of any particular individual. However, when considering the public interest, Crown Prosecutors should always take into account the consequences for the victim of whether or not to prosecute, and any views expressed by the victim or the victim's family.

5.13 It is important that a victim is told about a decision which makes a significant difference to the case in which they are involved. Crown Prosecutors should ensure that they follow any agreed procedures.

6. The Threshold Test

6.1 The Threshold Test requires Crown Prosecutors to decide whether there is at least a **E–8** reasonable suspicion that the suspect has committed an offence, and if there is, whether it is in the public interest to charge that suspect.

6.2 The Threshold Test is applied to those cases in which it would not be appropriate to release a suspect on bail after charge, but the evidence to apply the Full Code Test is not yet available.

6.3 There are statutory limits that restrict the time a suspect may remain in police custody before a decision has to be made whether to charge or release the suspect. There will be cases where the suspect in custody presents a substantial bail risk if released, but much of the evidence may not be available at the time the charging decision has to be made. Crown Prosecutors will apply the Threshold Test to such cases for a limited period.

6.4 The evidential decision in each case will require consideration of a number of factors including:

- the evidence available at the time;
- the likelihood and nature of further evidence being obtained;
- the reasonableness for believing that evidence will become available;
- the time it will take to gather that evidence and the steps being taken to do so;
- the impact the expected evidence will have on the case;
- the charges that the evidence will support.

6.5 The public interest means the same as under the Full Code Test, but will be based on the information available at the time of charge which will often be limited.

6.6 A decision to charge and withhold bail must be kept under review. The evidence gathered must be regularly assessed to ensure the charge is still appropriate and that continued objection to bail is justified. The Full Code Test must be applied as soon as reasonably practicable.

7. SELECTION OF CHARGES

E–9   7.1 Crown Prosecutors should select charges which:

    (a) reflect the seriousness and extent of the offending;

    (b) give the court adequate powers to sentence and impose appropriate post-conviction orders; and

    (c) enable the case to be presented in a clear and simple way.

This means that Crown Prosecutors may not always choose or continue with the most serious charge where there is a choice.

7.2 Crown Prosecutors should never go ahead with more charges than are necessary just to encourage a defendant to plead guilty to a few. In the same way, they should never go ahead with a more serious charge just to encourage a defendant to plead guilty to a less serious one.

7.3 Crown Prosecutors should not change the charge simply because of the decision made by the court or the defendant about where the case will be heard.

8. DIVERSION FROM PROSECUTION

Adults

E–10   8.1 When deciding whether a case should be prosecuted in the courts, Crown Prosecutors should consider the alternatives to prosecution. Where appropriate, the availability of suitable rehabilitative, reparative or restorative justice processes can be considered.

8.2 Alternatives to prosecution for adult suspects include a simple caution and a conditional caution.

Simple Caution

8.3 A simple caution should only be given if the public interest justifies it and in accordance with Home Office guidelines. Where it is felt that such a caution is appropriate, Crown Prosecutors must inform the police so they can caution the suspect. If the caution is not administered, because the suspect refuses to accept it, a Crown Prosecutor may review the case again.

Conditional Caution

8.4 A conditional caution may be appropriate where a Crown Prosecutor considers that while the public interest justifies a prosecution, the interests of the suspect, victim and community may be better served by the suspect complying with suitable conditions aimed at rehabilitation or reparation. These may include restorative processes.

8.5 Crown Prosecutors must be satisfied that there is sufficient evidence for a realistic prospect of conviction and that the public interest would justify a prosecution should the offer of a conditional caution be refused or the offender fail to comply with the agreed conditions of the caution.

8.6 In reaching their decision, Crown Prosecutors should follow the Conditional Cautions Code of Practice and any guidance on conditional cautioning issued or approved by the Director of Public Prosecutions.

8.7 Where Crown Prosecutors consider a conditional caution to be appropriate, they must inform the police, or other authority responsible for administering the conditional caution, as well as providing an indication of the appropriate conditions so that the conditional caution can be administered.

Youths

8.8 Crown Prosecutors must consider the interests of a youth when deciding whether it is in the public interest to prosecute. However Crown Prosecutors should not avoid prosecuting simply because of the defendant's age. The seriousness of the offence or the youth's past behaviour is very important.

8.9 Cases involving youths are usually only referred to the Crown Prosecution Service for prosecution if the youth has already received a reprimand and final warning, unless the offence is so serious that neither of these were appropriate or the youth does not admit committing the offence. Reprimands and final warnings are intended to prevent re-offending and the fact that a further offence has occurred indicates that attempts to divert the youth from the court system have not been effective. So the public interest will usually require a prosecution in such cases, unless there are clear public interest factors against prosecution.

9. Mode of Trial

9.1 The Crown Prosecution Service applies the current guidelines for magistrates who **E–11** have to decide whether cases should be tried in the Crown Court when the offence gives the option and the defendant does not indicate a guilty plea. Crown Prosecutors should recommend Crown Court trial when they are satisfied that the guidelines require them to do so.

9.2 Speed must never be the only reason for asking for a case to stay in the magistrates' **E–12** courts. But Crown Prosecutors should consider the effect of any likely delay if they send a case to the Crown Court, and any possible stress on victims and witnesses if the case is delayed.

10. Accepting Guilty Pleas

10.1 Defendants may want to plead guilty to some, but not all, of the charges. Alternatively, **E–13** they may want to plead guilty to a different, possibly less serious, charge because they are admitting only part of the crime. Crown Prosecutors should only accept the defendant's plea if they think the court is able to pass a sentence that matches the seriousness of the offending, particularly where there are aggravating features. Crown Prosecutors must never accept a guilty plea just because it is convenient.

10.2 In considering whether the pleas offered are acceptable, Crown Prosecutors should ensure that the interests of the victim and, where possible, any views expressed by the victim or victim's family, are taken into account when deciding whether it is in the public interest to accept the plea. However, the decision rests with the Crown Prosecutor.

10.3 It must be made clear to the court on what basis any plea is advanced and accepted. In cases where a defendant pleads guilty to the charges but on the basis of facts that are different from the prosecution case, and where this may significantly affect sentence, the court should be invited to hear evidence to determine what happened, and then sentence on that basis.

10.4 Where a defendant has previously indicated that he or she will ask the court to take an offence into consideration when sentencing, but then declines to admit that offence at court, Crown Prosecutors will consider whether a prosecution is required for that offence. Crown Prosecutors should explain to the defence advocate and the court that the prosecution of that offence may be subject to further review.

10.5 Particular care must be taken when considering pleas which would enable the defendant to avoid the imposition of a mandatory minimum sentence. When pleas are offered, Crown Prosecutors must bear in mind the fact that ancillary orders can be made with some offences but not with others.

11. Prosecutors' Role in Sentencing

11.1 Crown Prosecutors should draw the court's attention to: **E–14**
- any aggravating or mitigating factors disclosed by the prosecution case;
- any victim personal statement;
- where appropriate, evidence of the impact of the offending on a community;
- any statutory provisions or sentencing guidelines which may assist;
- any relevant statutory provisions relating to ancillary orders (such as anti-social behaviour orders).

11.2 The Crown Prosecutor should challenge any assertion made by the defence in mitigation that is inaccurate, misleading or derogatory. If the defence persist in the assertion, and

Appendices

it appears relevant to the sentence, the court should be invited to hear evidence to determine the facts and sentence accordingly.

12. RE-STARTING A PROSECUTION

12.1 People should be able to rely on decisions taken by the Crown Prosecution Service. Normally, if the Crown Prosecution Service tells a suspect or defendant that there will not be a prosecution, or that the prosecution has been stopped, that is the end of the matter and the case will not start again. But occasionally there are special reasons why the Crown Prosecution Service will re-start the prosecution, particularly if the case is serious.

10.2 These reasons include:

(a) rare cases where a new look at the original decision shows that it was clearly wrong and should not be allowed to stand;

(b) cases which are stopped so that more evidence which is likely to become available in the fairly near future can be collected and prepared. In these cases, the Crown Prosecutor will tell the defendant that the prosecution may well start again; and

(c) cases which are stopped because of a lack of evidence but where more significant evidence is discovered later.

12.3 There may also be exceptional cases in which, following an acquittal of a serious offence, the Crown Prosecutor may, with the written consent of the Director of Public Prosecutions, apply to the Court of Appeal for an order quashing the acquittal and requiring the defendant to be retried, in accordance with Part 10 of the Criminal Justice Act 2003.

E–15   The Code is a public document. It is available on the CPS Website: www.cps.gov.uk
Further copies may be obtained from:
Crown Prosecution Service
Communications Branch
50 Ludgate Hill
London
EC4M 7EX
Telephone: 020 7273 8442
Fax: 020 7329 8030
Email: publicity.branch[@000c]ps.gsi.gov.uk

© Crown Copyright 2004

CONSOLIDATED CRIMINAL PRACTICE DIRECTION

This is a consolidation first issued in 2002, of existing practice directions, statements **F–1** and notes as they affect proceedings in criminal courts except for costs. It is not a comprehensive statement of practice and procedure. The sections which apply to the Crown Court only and the Annexes which relate mainly to forms are not included in this appendix. The Practice Direction is printed as most recently amended with effect from April 2, 2007 by the *Criminal Practice Direction Amendment No. 15* (treatment of vulnerable defendants; binding over orders and conditional discharges; settling the indictment; management of cases to be heard in the Crown Court; and forms for use in criminal proceedings).

This Practice Direction is divided into the following Parts:

NOTE: Throughout this document words connoting the masculine include the feminine.

Part I: Directions Of General Application

PART I: DIRECTIONS OF GENERAL APPLICATION

PART I: DIRECTIONS OF GENERAL APPLICATION

I.1. Court Dress

F–3   **I.1.1** In magistrates' courts, advocates appear without robes or wigs. In all other courts, Queen's Counsel wear a short wig and a silk (or stuff) gown over a court coat with bands, junior counsel wear a short wig and stuff gown with bands, and solicitors and other advocates authorised under the *Courts and Legal Services Act* 1990 wear a black stuff gown with bands.

I.2. Unofficial Tape Recording of Proceedings

F–4   **I.2.1** Section 9 of the *Contempt of Court Act* 1981 contains provisions governing the unofficial use of tape recorders in court. Section 9(1) provides that it is a contempt of court (a) to use in court, or bring into court for use, any tape recorder or other instrument for recording sound, except with the leave of the Court; (b) to publish a recording of legal proceedings made by means of any such instrument, or any recording derived directly or indirectly from it, by playing it in the hearing of the public or any section of the public, or to dispose of it or any recording so derived, with a view to such publication; (c) to use any such recording in contravention of any conditions of leave granted under paragraph (a). These provisions do not apply to the making or use of sound recordings for purposes of official transcripts of the proceedings, upon which the *Act* imposes no restriction whatever.

I.2.2 The discretion given to the Court to grant, withhold or withdraw leave to use tape recorders or to impose conditions as to the use of the recording is unlimited, but the following factors may be relevant to its exercise: (a) the existence of any reasonable need on the part of the applicant for leave, whether a litigant or a person connected with the press or broadcasting, for the recording to be made; (b) the risk that the recording could be used for the purpose of briefing witnesses out of court; (c) any possibility that the use of the recorder would disturb the proceedings or distract or worry any witnesses or other participants.

I.2.3 Consideration should always be given whether conditions as to the use of a recording made pursuant to leave should be imposed. The identity and role of the applicant for leave and the nature of the subject matter of the proceedings may be relevant to this.

I.2.4 The particular restriction imposed by section 9(1)(b) applies in every case, but may not be present to the mind of every applicant to whom leave is given. It may therefore be desirable on occasion for this provision to be drawn to the attention of those to whom leave is given.

I.2.5 The transcript of a permitted recording is intended for the use of the person given leave to make it and is not intended to be used as, or to compete with, the official transcript mentioned in section 9(4).

I.3. Restrictions on Reporting Proceedings

I.3.1 Under section 4(2) of the *Contempt of Court Act* 1981 a court may, where it appears **F–5** necessary for avoiding a substantial risk of prejudice to the administration of justice in the proceedings before it or in any others pending or imminent, order that publication of any report of the proceedings or part thereof be postponed for such time as the court thinks necessary for that purpose. Section 11 of the *Act* provides that a court may prohibit the publication of any name or other matter in connection with the proceedings before it which it has allowed to be withheld from the public.

I.3.2 When considering whether to make such an order there is nothing which precludes the court from hearing a representative of the press. Indeed it is likely that the court will wish to do so.

I.3.3 It is necessary to keep a permanent record of such orders for later reference. For this purpose all orders made under section 4(2) must be formulated in precise terms having regard to the decision in *R v Horsham Justices ex parte Farquharson* [1982] QB 762; 76 Cr App R 87, and orders under both sections must be committed to writing either by the judge personally or by the clerk of the court under the judge's directions. An order must state (a) its precise scope, (b) the time at which it shall cease to have effect, if appropriate, and (c) the specific purpose of making the order. Courts will normally give notice to the press in some form that an order has been made under either section of the *Act* and the court staff should be prepared to answer any enquiry about a specific case, but it is, and will remain, the responsibility of those reporting cases, and their editors, to ensure that no breach of any orders occurs and the onus rests on them to make enquiry in any case of doubt.

I.4. Availability of Judgments given in the Court of Appeal and the High Court

I.4.1 Reference should be made to paragraph 9 of Practice Direction (Court of Appeal- **F–6** (Civil Division)) [1999]1 WLR 1027; [1999] 2 All ER 490.

I.5. Wards of Court

I.5.1 Where a child has been interviewed by the police in connection with contemplated **F–7** criminal proceedings and the child subsequently becomes a ward of court, no leave of the wardship court is required for the child to be called as a witness in those proceedings. Where, however, the police desire to interview a child who is already a ward of court, application must, other than in the exceptional cases referred to in *paragraph I.5.3*, be made to the wardship court, on summons and on notice to all parties, for leave for the police to do so. Where, however, a party may become the subject of a criminal investigation and it is considered necessary for the ward to be interviewed without that party knowing that the police are making inquiries, the application for leave may be made ex parte to a judge without notice to that party. Notice, should, where practicable, be given to the reporting officer.

I.5.2 Where leave is given the order should, unless some special reason requires the contrary, give leave for any number of interviews which may be required by the prosecution or the police. If it is desired to conduct any interview beyond what has been permitted by the order, a further application should be made.

I.5.3 The exceptional cases are those where the police need to deal with complaints or alleged offences concerning wards and it is appropriate, if not essential, for action to be taken straight away without the prior leave of the wardship court. Typical examples may be: (a) serious offences against the ward, such as rape, where medical examination and the collection of scientific evidence ought to be carried out promptly; (b) where the ward is suspected by the police of having committed a criminal act and the police wish to interview him about it; (c) where the police wish to interview the ward as a potential witness. The list is not exhaustive; there will inevitably be other instances where immediate action is appropriate. In such cases the police should notify the parent or foster parent with whom the ward is living or other "appropriate adult" within the Code of Practice for the Detention, Treatment and Questioning of Persons by Police Officers, so that that adult has the opportunity of being present when the police interview the child. Additionally, if practicable, the reporting officer (if one has been appointed) should be notified and invited to attend the police interview or to nominate a third party to attend on his behalf. A record of the interview or a copy of any statement made by the ward should be supplied to the reporting officer. Where the ward

1563

Appendices

has been interviewed without the reporting officer's knowledge, he should be informed at the earliest opportunity. So too, if it be the case that the police wish to conduct further interviews. The wardship court should be appraised of the situation at the earliest possible opportunity thereafter by the reporting officer, the parent, foster parent (through the local authority) or other responsible adult.

I.5.4 No evidence or documents in the wardship proceedings or information about the proceedings should be disclosed in the criminal proceedings without leave of the wardship court.

I.6. Spent Convictions

F–8 **I.6.1** The effect of section 4(1) of the *Rehabilitation of Offenders Act* 1974 is that a person who has become a rehabilitated person for the purpose of the *Act* in respect of a conviction (known as a "spent" conviction) shall be treated for all purposes in law as a person who has not committed or been charged with or prosecuted for or convicted of or sentenced for the offence or offences which were the subject of that conviction.

I.6.2 Section 4(1) of the 1974 Act does not apply, however, to evidence given in criminal proceedings: section 7(2)(a). Convictions are often disclosed in such criminal proceedings. When the Bill was before the House of Commons on 28 June 1974 the hope was expressed that the Lord Chief Justice would issue a Practice Direction for the guidance of the Crown Court with a view to reducing disclosure of spent convictions to a minimum and securing uniformity of approach. The direction is set out in the following paragraphs. The same approach should be adopted in all courts of criminal jurisdiction.

I.6.3 During the trial of a criminal charge, reference to previous convictions (and therefore to spent convictions) can arise in a number of ways. The most common is when the character of the accused or a witness is sought to be attacked by reference to his criminal record, but there are, of course, cases where previous convictions are relevant and admissible as, for instance, to prove system.

I.6.4 It is not possible to give general directions which will govern all these different situations, but it is recommended that both court and advocates should give effect to the general intention of Parliament by never referring to a spent conviction when such reference can reasonably be avoided.

I.6.5 After a verdict of guilty the court must be provided with a statement of the defendant's record for the purposes of sentence. The record supplied should contain all previous convictions, but those which are spent should, so far as practicable, be marked as such.

I.6.6 No one should refer in open court to a spent conviction without the authority of the judge, which authority should not be given unless the interests of justice so require.

I.6.7 When passing sentence the judge should make no reference to a spent conviction unless it is necessary to do so for the purpose of explaining the sentence to be passed.

I.7. Explanations for the Imposition of Custodial Sentences

F–9 **I.7.1** The practical effect of custodial sentences imposed by the courts is almost entirely governed by statutory provisions. Those statutory provisions, changed by Parliament from time to time, are not widely understood by the general public. It is desirable that when sentence is passed the practical effect of the sentence should be understood by the defendant, any victim and any member of the public who is present in court or reads a full report of the proceedings.

I.7.2 Whenever a custodial sentence is imposed on an offender the court should explain the practical effect of the sentence in addition to complying with existing statutory requirements. This will be no more than an explanation; the sentence will be that pronounced by the court.

I.7.3 Sentencers should give the explanation in terms of their own choosing, taking care to ensure that the explanation is clear and accurate. No form of words is prescribed. Annexed to this Practice Direction are short statements which may, adapted as necessary, be of value as models (see Annex C). These statements are based on the statutory provisions in force on 1 January 1998 and will, of course, require modification if those provisions are materially amended.

I.7.4 Sentencers will continue to give such explanation as they judge necessary of ancillary orders relating to matters such as disqualification, compensation, confiscation, costs and so on.

1.7.5 The power of the Secretary of State to release a prisoner early under supervision is not part of the sentence. The judge is therefore not required in his sentencing remarks to provide an explanation of this power. However, in explaining the effect of custodial sentences the judge should not say anything which conflicts with the existence of this power.

I.8. Words to be Used when Passing Sentence

I.8.1 Where a court passes on a defendant more than one term of imprisonment the **F–10** court should state in the presence of the defendant whether the terms are to be concurrent or consecutive. Should this not be done the court clerk should ask the court, before the defendant leaves court, to do so.

I.8.2 If a prisoner is, at the time of sentence, already serving two or more consecutive terms of imprisonment and the court intends to increase the total period of imprisonment, it should use the expression "consecutive to the total period of imprisonment to which you are already subject" rather than "at the expiration of the term of imprisonment you are now serving", lest the prisoner be not then serving the last of the terms to which he is already subject.

I.9. Substitution of Suspended Sentences for Immediate Custodial Sentences

I.9.1 Where an appellate court substitutes a suspended sentence of imprisonment for **F–11** one having immediate effect, the court should have in mind any period the appellant has spent in custody. If the court is of the opinion that it would be fair to do so, an approximate adjustment to the term of the suspended sentence should be made. Whether or not the court makes such adjustment, it should state that it had that period in mind. The court should further indicate that the operational period of suspension runs from the date the court passes the suspended sentence.

I.10. References to the European Court of Justice

I.10.1 These are the subject of Practice Direction: References to the European Court of **F–12** Justice by the Court of Appeal and the High Court under Article 177 of the EC Treaty [1999] 1 WLR 260; [1999] 1 Cr App R 452, to which reference should be made.

I.11. Devolution Issues

I.11.1 These are the subject of Practice Direction: (Supreme Court)(Devolution 11 Is- **F–13** sues) [1999] 1WLR 1592; [1999] 3 All ER 466; [1999] 2 Cr App R 486, to which reference should be made.

I.12. Preparation of Judgments: Neutral Citation

I.12.1 Since 11 January 2001 every judgment of the Court of Appeal, and of the **F–14** Administrative Court, and since 14 January 2002 every judgment of the High Court, has been prepared and issued as approved with single spacing, paragraph numbering (in the margins) and no page numbers. In courts with more than one judge the paragraph numbering continues sequentially through each judgment and does not start again at the beginning of each judgment. Indented paragraphs are not numbered. A unique reference number is given to each judgment. For judgments of the Court of Appeal this number is given by the official shorthand writers. For judgments of the High Court it is provided by the Mechanical Recording Department at the Royal Courts of Justice. Such a number will also be furnished, on request to the Mechanical Recording Department, Royal Courts of Justice, Strand, London WC2A 2LL (Tel: 020 7947 7771), to High Court judgments delivered outside London.

I.12.2 Each Court of Appeal judgment starts with the year, followed by EW (for England and Wales), then CA (for Court of Appeal), followed by Civ or Crim and finally the sequential number. For example *Smith v Jones* [2001] EWCA Civ 10.

I.12.3 In the High Court, represented by HC, the number comes before the divisional abbreviation and, unlike Court of Appeal judgments, the latter is bracketed: (Ch), (Pat), (QB), (Admin), (Comm), (Admlty), (TCC) or (Fam) as appropriate. For example, [2002] EWHC 123 (Fam) or [2002] EWHC 124 (QB) or [2002] EWHC 125 (Ch).

I.12.4 This "neutral citation", as it is called, is the official number attributed to the judgment and must always be used at least once when the judgment is cited in a later judgment. Once the judgment is reported this neutral citation appears in front of the familiar citation from the law reports series. Thus: *Smith v Jones* [2001] EWCA (Civ) 10; [2001] QB 124; [2001] 2 All ER 364, etc.

I.12.5 Paragraph numbers are referred to in square brackets. When citing a paragraph from a High Court judgment it is unnecessary to include the descriptive word in brackets: (Admin), (QB) or whatever. When citing a paragraph from a Court of Appeal judgment, however, Civ or Crim is included. If it is desired to cite more than one paragraph of a judgment each numbered paragraph should be enclosed with a square bracket. Thus paragraph 59 in *Green v White* [2002] EWHC 124 (QB) would be cited: *Green v White* [2002] EWHC 124 at [59]; paragraphs 30–35 in *Smith v Jones* would be *Smith v Jones* [2001] EWCA Civ 10 at [30]–[35]; similarly, where a number of paragraphs are cited: *Smith v Jones* [2001] EWCA Civ 10 at [30], [35] and [40–43].

I.12.6 If a judgment is cited more than once in a later judgment it is helpful if only one abbreviation is used, e.g. *Smith v Jones* or Smith's case, but preferably not both (in the same judgment.)

I.13 Bail: Failure to Surrender to Suurender and Trials in Absence

F–15   **I.13.1** The following directions take effect immediately.

I.13.2 The failure of the defendants to comply with the terms of their bail by not surrendering can undermine the administration of justice. It can disrupt proceedings. The resulting delays impact on victims, witnesses and other court users and also waste costs. A defendant's failure to surrender affects not only the case with which he is concerned, but also the courts' ability to administer justice more generally by damaging the confidence of victims, witnesses and the public in the effectiveness of the court system and the judiciary. It is, therefore most important that defendants who are granted bail appreciate the significance of the obligation to surrender to custody in accordance with the terms of their bail and that courts take appropriate action if they fail to do so.

I.13.3 There are at least three courses of action for the courts to consider taking:—

[A] imposing penalties for the failure to surrender;

[B] revoking bail or imposing more stringent bail conditions; and

[C] conducting trials in the absence of the defendant.

Penalties for Failure to Surrender

F–16   **I.13.4** A defendant who commits a section 6(1) or section 6(2) *Bail Act* 1976 offence commits an offence that stands apart from the proceedings in respect of which bail was granted. The seriousness of the offence can be reflected by an appropriate penalty being imposed for the *Bail Act* offence.

I.13.5 The common practice at present of courts automatically deferring disposal of a section 6(1) or section 6(2) *Bail Act* 1976 offence (failure to surrender) until the conclusion of the proceedings in respect of which bail was granted should no longer be followed. Instead, courts should now deal with defendants as soon as is practicable. In deciding what is practicable, the Court must take into account when the proceedings in respect of which bail was granted are expected to conclude, the seriousness of the offence for which the defendant is already being prosecuted, the type of penalty that might be imposed for the breach of bail and the original offence as well as any other relevant circumstances. If there is no good reason for postponing dealing with the breach until after the trial, the breach should be dealt with as soon as practicable. If the disposal of the breach of bail is deferred, then it is still necessary to consider imposing a separate penalty at the trial and the sentence for the breach of the bail should usually be custodial and consecutive to any other custodial sentence (as to which see I.13.13). In addition, bail should usually be revoked in the meantime (see I.13.14 to 16). In the case of offences which cannot, or are unlikely to, result in a custodial sentence, trial in the absence of the defendant may be a pragmatic sensible response to the situation (see I.13.17 to I.13.19). This is not a penalty for the *Bail Act* offence and a penalty may also be imposed for the *Bail Act* offence.

Initiating Proceedings—Bail granted by a police officer

I.13.6 When a person has been granted bail by a police officer to attend court and subsequently fails to surrender to custody, the decision whether to initiate proceedings for a section 6(1) or section 6(2) offence will be for the police/prosecutor.

I.13.7 The offence in this form is a summary offence and should be initiated as soon as practicable after the offence arises in view of the six month time limit running from the failure to surrender. It should be dealt with on the first appearance after arrest, unless an adjournment is necessary, as it will be relevant in considering whether to grant bail again.

Initiating Proceedings—Bail granted by a court

I.13.8 When a person has been granted bail by a court and subsequently fails to surrender to custody, on arrest that person should normally be brought as soon as appropriate before the court at which the proceedings in respect of which bail was granted are to be heard. (The six months time limit does not apply where bail was granted by the court). Should the defendant commit another offence outside the jurisdiction of the bail court, the *Bail Act* offence should, where practicable, be dealt with by the new court at the same time as the new offence. If impracticable, the defendant may, if this is appropriate, be released formally on bail by the new court so that the warrant may be executed for his attendance before the first court in respect of the substantive and *Bail Act* offences.

I.13.9 Given that bail was granted by a court, it is more appropriate that the court itself should initiate the proceedings by its own motion. The court will be invited to take proceedings by the prosecutor, if the prosecutor considers proceedings are appropriate.

Conduct of Proceedings

I.13.10 Proceedings under section 6 *Bail Act* 1976 may be conducted either as a summary offence or as a criminal contempt of court. Where the court is invited to take proceedings by the prosecutor, the prosecutor will conduct the proceedings and, if the matter is contested, call the evidence. Where the court initiates proceedings without such an invitation the same role can be played by the prosecutor at the request of the court, where this is practicable.

I.13.11 The burden of proof is on the defendant to prove that he had reasonable cause for his failure to surrender to custody (s6 (3) *Bail Act* 1976).

Proceedings to be progressed to disposal as soon as is practicable

I.13.12 If the court decides to proceed, the section 6 *Bail Act* offence should be concluded as soon as practicable.

Sentencing for a Bail Act offence

I.13.13 In principle, a custodial sentence for the offence of failing to surrender should be ordered to be served consecutively to any other sentence imposed at the same time for another offence unless there are circumstances that make this inappropriate (see White & McKinnon).

Relationship between the Bail Act Offence and Further Remands on Bail or in Custody.

I.13.14 When a defendant has been convicted of a *Bail Act* offence, the court should **F–17** review the remand status of the defendant, including the conditions of that bail, in respect of the main proceedings for which bail had been granted.

I.13.15 Failure by the defendant to surrender or a conviction for failing to surrender to bail in connection with the main proceedings will be significant factors weighing against the re-granting of bail or, in the case of offences which do not normally give rise to a custodial sentence, in favour of trial in the absence of the offender.

I.13.16 Whether or not an immediate custodial sentence has been imposed for the *Bail Act* offence, the court may, having reviewed the defendant's remand status, also remand the defendant in custody in the main proceedings.

Trials in Absence

I.13.17 A defendant has a right, in general, to be present and to be represented at his **F–18** trial. However, a defendant may choose not to exercise those rights by voluntarily absenting himself and failing to instruct his lawyers adequately so that they can represent him and, in the case of proceedings before the Magistrates' court, there is an express statutory power to hear trials in the defendant's absence (s11 of the *Magistrates' Courts Act* 1980). In such circumstances, the court has discretion whether the trial should take place in his/her absence.

I.13.18 The court must exercise its discretion to proceed in the absence of the defendant with the utmost care and caution. The overriding concern must be to ensure that such a trial is as fair as circumstances permit and leads to a just outcome.

I.13.19 Due regard should be had to the judgment of Lord Bingham in *R -v- Jones* [2003] AC 1, [2002] 2 AER 113 in which Lord Bingham identified circumstances to be taken into account before proceeding, which include: the conduct of the defendant, the disadvantage to the defendant, public interest, the effect of any delay and whether the attendance of the defendant could be secured at a later hearing. Other relevant considerations are the seriousness of the offence and likely outcome if the defendant is found guilty. If the defendant is only likely to be fined for a summary offence this can be relevant since the costs that a defendant might otherwise be ordered to pay as a result of an adjournment could be disproportionate. In the case of summary proceedings the fact that there can be an appeal that is a complete rehearing is also relevant, as is the power to re-open the case under s142 of the *Magistrates' Court Act* 1980.

PART III: FURTHER DIRECTIONS APPLYING IN THE CROWN COURT AND MAGISTRATES' COURTS

PART III: FURTHER DIRECTIONS APPLYING IN THE CROWN COURT AND MAGISTRATES' COURTS

III.21.1 Classification of Crown Court Business and Allocation to Crown Court Centres

Classification

F–19   **III.21.2**   For the purposes of trial in the Crown Court offences are classified as follows: Class 1: (a) Misprision of treason and treason felony; (b) Murder; (c) Genocide; (d) Torture, hostage-taking and offences under the *War Crimes Act* 1991; (e) An offence under the Official Secrets Acts; (f) Soliciting, incitement, attempt or conspiracy to commit any of the above offences. Class 2: (a) Manslaughter; (b) Infanticide; (c) Child destruction; (d) Abortion (section 58 of the *Offences against the Person Act* 1861); (e) Rape; (f) Sexual intercourse with a girl under 13; (g) Incest with girl under 13; (h) Sedition; (i) An offence under section 1 of the *Geneva Conventions Act* 1957; (j) Mutiny; (k) Piracy; (l) Soliciting, incitement, attempt or conspiracy to commit any of the above offences. Class 3: (a) All offences triable only on indictment other than those in Classes 1, 2 and 4; (b) Soliciting, incitement, attempt or conspiracy to commit any of the above offences. Class 4: (a) Wounding or causing grievous bodily harm with intent (section 18 of the *Offences against the Person Act* 1861); (b) Robbery or assault with intent to rob (section 8 of the *Theft Act* 1968); (c) Soliciting, incitement or attempt to commit any of the above offences; (d) Conspiracy at common law, or conspiracy to commit any offence other than those included in Classes 1, 2 and 3; (e) All offences which are triable either way.

Cases committed, transferred or sent for trial

F–20   **III.21.3**   Save as provided in paragraph III.21.4, for certain offences in Class 2 and offences in Class 3(a), the magistrates' court, upon either committing a person for trial under section 6 of the *Magistrates' Courts Act* 1980, transferring a person under either section 4 of the *Criminal Justice Act* 1987 or section 53 of the *Criminal Justice Act* 1991 or sending a person under section 51 of the *Crime and Disorder Act* 1998, shall, if the offence or any of the offences is included in Classes 1 or 2, specify the most convenient location of the Crown Court where a High Court Judge, or, where the case is included in Class 1, where a Circuit Judge duly approved for that purpose by the Lord Chief Justice regularly sits. These courts will be identified by the Presiding Judges on each Circuit. Where an offence is in Class 4 the magistrates' court shall specify the most convenient location of the Crown Court.

III.21.4   Where a Presiding Judge has directed that cases of rape, sexual intercourse with a girl under 13, incest with a girl under 13 or soliciting, incitement, attempt or conspiracy to commit any of these offences (all of which are within Class 2) or Class 3 offences, may be committed, transferred or sent from a specified magistrates' court or courts to a specified location of the Crown Court at which a High Court Judge does not regularly sit, the magistrates' court shall specify that location.

III.21.5   In selecting the most convenient location of the Crown Court the justices shall have regard to the considerations referred to in section 7 of the *Magistrates' Courts Act* 1980 and section 51(10) of the *Crime and Disorder Act* 1998 and the location or locations of the Crown Court designated by a Presiding Judge as the location to which cases should normally be committed from their petty sessions area.

III.21.6   Where on one occasion a person is committed in respect of a number of offences all the committals shall be to the same location of the Crown Court and that location shall be the one where a High Court Judge regularly sits if such a location is appropriate for any of the offences.

Committals for sentence or to be dealt with

III.21.7 Where a community rehabilitation order, an order for conditional discharge or **F–21** a community punishment order has been made, or suspended sentence has been passed, and the offender is committed to be dealt with for the original offence or in respect of the suspended sentence, he shall be committed in accordance with paragraphs III.21.8–III.21.11.

III.21.8 If the order was made or the sentence was passed by the Crown Court he shall be committed to the location of the Crown Court where the order was made or suspended sentence was passed unless it is inconvenient or impracticable to do so.

III.21.9 If he is not so committed and the order was made by a High Court Judge he shall be committed to the most convenient location of the Crown Court where a High Court Judge regularly sits.

III.21.10 In all other cases where a person is committed for sentence or to be dealt with he shall be committed to the most convenient location of the Crown Court.

III.21.11 In selecting the most convenient location of the Crown Court the justices shall have regard to the locations of the Crown Court designated by a Presiding Judge as the locations to which cases should normally be committed from their petty sessions area.

Notice of transfer in cases of serious or complex fraud

III.21.12 Where a notice of transfer is served under section 4 of the *Criminal Justice Act* **F–22** 1987 (cases of serious or complex fraud) the proposed place of trial to be specified in the notice shall be one of the following Crown Court centres:

(a) Midland Circuit: Birmingham (also sitting at West Midlands trial centre), Leicester, Northampton, Nottingham, Wolverhampton (also sitting at West Midlands trial centre);

(b) North Eastern: Bradford, Leeds, Newcastle, Sheffield, Teesside;

(c) Northern: Liverpool, Manchester;

(d) South Eastern: Central Criminal Court, Chelmsford, Harrow, Kingston, Knightsbridge, Luton, Maidstone, Middlesex Guildhall, Norwich, Oxford, Reading, Snaresbrook, Southwark, Wood Green;

(e) Wales and Chester: Cardiff, Chester, Mold, Swansea, Warrington;

(f) Western: Bristol, Plymouth, Portsmouth, Truro, Winchester.

Notice of transfer in child witness cases

III.21.13 Where a notice of transfer is served under section 53 of the *Criminal Justice* **F–23** *Act* 1991 (child witness cases) the proposed place of trial to be specified in accordance with paragraph 1(1) of Schedule 6 to the *Act* shall be a Crown Court centre which is equipped with live television link facilities. The following Crown Court centres are so equipped: Birmingham, Bradford, Bristol, Caernarfon, Cardiff, Carlisle, Central Criminal Court, Chelmsford, Croydon, Exeter, Gloucester, Grimsby, Guildford, Harrow, Hull, Leeds, Leicester, Lewes, Lincoln, Liverpool, Maidstone, Manchester, Mold, Newcastle, Northampton, Norwich, Nottingham, Plymouth, Portsmouth, Preston, Reading, Sheffield, Southwark, St Albans, Stafford, Swansea, Teesside, Truro, Winchester, Wolverhampton.

III.22 Applications for Evidence to be given in Welsh

III.22.1 If a defendant in a court in England asks to give or call evidence in the Welsh **F–24** language the case should not be transferred to Wales. In ordinary circumstances interpreters can be provided on request.

III.23 Use of the Welsh Language in Courts in Wales

III.23.1 The purpose of this direction is to reflect the principle of the *Welsh Language* **F–25** *Act* 1993 that in the administration of justice in Wales the English and Welsh languages should be treated on a basis of equality.

General

III.23.2 It is the responsibility of the legal representatives in every case in which the **F–26** Welsh language may be used by any witness or party or in any document which may be placed before the court to inform the court of that fact so that appropriate arrangements can be made for the listing of the case.

III.23.3 If the possible use of the Welsh language is known at the time of committal, transfer or appeal to the Crown Court, the court should be informed immediately after committal or transfer or when the notice of appeal is lodged. Otherwise the court should be informed as soon as possible use of the Welsh language becomes known.

III.23.4 If costs are incurred as a result of failure to comply with these directions, a wasted costs order may be made against the defaulting party and/or his legal representatives.

III.23.5 The law does not permit the selection of jurors in a manner which enables the court to discover whether a juror does or does not speak Welsh or to secure a jury whose members are bilingual to try a case in which the Welsh language may be used.

Plea and directions hearings

F–27 **III.23.6** An advocate in a case in which the Welsh language may be used must raise that matter at the plea and directions hearing and endorse details of it on the judge's questionnaire so that appropriate directions may be given for the 28 progress of the case.

Listing

F–28 **III.23.7** The listing officer, in consultation with the resident judge, should ensure that a case in which the Welsh language may be used is listed (a) wherever practicable before a Welsh speaking judge, and (b) in a court in Wales with simultaneous translation facilities.

Interpreters

F–29 **III.23.8** Whenever an interpreter is needed to translate evidence from English into Welsh or from Welsh into English, the court manager in whose court the case is to be heard shall ensure that the attendance is secured of an interpreter whose name is included in the list of approved court interpreters.

Jurors

F–30 **III.23.9** The jury bailiff when addressing the jurors at the start of their period of jury service shall inform them that each juror may take an oath or affirm in Welsh or English as he wishes.

III.23.10 After the jury has been selected to try a case, and before it is sworn, the court officer swearing in the jury shall inform the jurors in open court that each juror may take an oath or affirm in Welsh or English as he wishes.

Witnesses

F–31 **III.23.11** When each witness is called the court officer administering the oath or affirmation shall inform the witness that he may be sworn or affirm Welsh or English as he wishes.

Opening/closing of courts

F–32 **III.23.12** Unless it is not reasonably practicable to do so, the opening and closing of the court should be performed in Welsh and English.

Role of liaison judge

F–33 **III.23.13** If any question or problem arises concerning the implementation of *paragraphs III.23.1–III.23.12*, contact should in the first place be made with the liaison judge for Welsh language matters on circuit.

III.24 Evidence by Written Statement

F–34 **III.24.1** Where the prosecution proposes to tender written statements in evidence either under sections 5A and 5B of the *Magistrates' Courts Act* 1980 or section 9 of the *Criminal Justice Act* 1967 it will frequently be not only proper, but also necessary for the orderly presentation of the evidence, for certain statements to be edited. This will occur either because a witness has made more than one statement whose contents should conveniently be reduced into a single, comprehensive statement or where a statement contains inadmissible, prejudicial or irrelevant material. Editing of statements should in all circumstances be done by a Crown Prosecutor (or by a legal representative, if any, of the prosecutor if the case is not being conducted by the Crown Prosecution Service) and not by a police officer.

Composite statements

III.24.2 A composite statement giving the combined effect of two or more earlier state- **F–35** ments or settled by a person referred to in *paragraph III.24.1* must be prepared in compliance with the requirements of sections 5A and 5B of the 1980 Act or section 9 of the 1967 *Act* as appropriate and must then be signed by the witness.

Editing single statements

III.24.3 There are two acceptable methods of editing single statements. **F–36**

(a) By marking *copies* of the statement in a way which indicates the passages on which the prosecution will not rely. This merely indicates that the prosecution will not seek to adduce the evidence so marked. The *original signed statement* to be tendered to the court is not marked in any way. The marking on the copy statement is done by lightly striking out the passages to be edited so that what appears beneath can still be read, or by bracketing, or by a combination of both. It is not permissible to produce a photocopy with the deleted material obliterated, since this would be contrary to the requirement that the defence and the court should be served with copies of the signed original statement. Whenever the striking out/bracketing method is used, it will assist if the following words appear at the foot of the frontispiece or index to any bundle of copy statements to be tendered:

'The prosecution does not propose to adduce evidence of those passages of the attached copy statements which have been struck out 30 and/or bracketed (nor will it seek to do so at the trial unless a notice of further evidence is served).'

(b) By obtaining a fresh statement, signed by the witness, which omits the offending material, applying the procedure in *paragraph III.24.2*.

III.24.4 In most cases where a single statement is to be edited, the striking out/bracketing method will be the more appropriate, but the taking of a fresh statement is preferable in the following circumstances:

(a) When a police (or other investigating) officer's statement contains details of interviews with more suspects than are eventually charged, a fresh statement should be prepared and signed omitting all details of interview with those not charged except, insofar as it is relevant, for the bald fact that a certain named person was interviewed at a particular time, date and place.

(b) When a suspect is interviewed about more offences than are eventually made the subject of committal charges, a fresh statement should be prepared and signed omitting all questions and answers about the uncharged offences unless either they might appropriately be taken into consideration or evidence about those offences is admissible on the charges preferred, such as evidence of system. It may, however, be desirable to replace the omitted questions and answers with a phrase such as: "After referring to some other matters, I then said … ", so as to make it clear that part of the interview has been omitted.

(c) A fresh statement should normally be prepared and signed if the only part of the original on which the prosecution is relying is only a small proportion of the whole, although it remains desirable to use the alternative method if there is reason to believe that the defence might itself wish to rely, in mitigation or for any other purpose, on at least some of those parts which the prosecution does not propose to adduce.

(d) When the passages contain material which the prosecution is entitled to withhold from disclosure to the defence.

III.24.5 Prosecutors should also be aware that, where statements are to be tendered under section 9 of the 1967 *Act* in the course of *summary* proceedings, there will be a need to prepare fresh statements excluding inadmissible or prejudicial material rather than using the striking out or bracketing method.

III.24.6 None of the above principles applies, in respect of committal proceedings, to documents which are exhibited (including statements under caution and signed contemporaneous notes). Nor do they apply to oral statements of a defendant which are recorded in the witness statements of interviewing police officers, except in the circumstances referred to in *paragraph III.24.4(b)*. All this material should remain in its original state in the committal bundles, any editing being left to prosecuting counsel at the Crown Court (after discussion with defence counsel and, if appropriate, the trial judge).

1571

III.24.7 Whenever a fresh statement is taken from a witness, a copy of the earlier, unedited statement(s) of that witness will be given to the defence in accordance with the Attorney General's guidelines on the disclosure of unused material (*Practice Note* [1982] 1 All ER 734) unless there are grounds under *paragraph 6* of the guidelines for withholding such disclosure.

III.25 Bail During Trial

F–37   **III.25.1** *Paragraphs III.25.2 to III.25.5* are to be read subject to the *Bail Act* 1976, especially section 4.

III.25.2 Once a trial has begun the further grant of bail, whether during the short adjournment or overnight, is in the discretion of the trial judge. It may be a proper exercise of this discretion to refuse bail during the short adjournment if the accused cannot otherwise be segregated from witnesses and jurors.

III.25.3 An accused who was on bail while on remand should not be refused overnight bail during the trial unless in the opinion of the judge there are positive reasons to justify this refusal. Such reasons are likely to be:

(a) that a point has been reached where there is a real danger that the accused will abscond, either because the case is going badly for him, or for any other reason;

(b) that there is a real danger that he may interfere with witnesses or jurors.

III.25.4 There is no universal rule of practice that bail shall not be renewed when the summing-up has begun. Each case must be decided in the light of its own circumstances and having regard to the judge's assessment from time to time of the risks involved.

III.25.5 Once the jury has returned a verdict a further renewal of bail should be decided in the light of the gravity of the offence and the likely sentence to be passed in all the circumstances of the case.

III.26 Facts to be Stated on Pleas of Guilty

F–38   **III.26.1** To enable the press and the public to know the circumstances of an offence of which an accused has been convicted and for which he is to be sentenced, in relation to each offence to which an accused has pleaded guilty the prosecution shall state those facts in open court before sentence is imposed.

III.27 Antecedents

Standard for the provision of information of antecedents in the Crown Court and magistrates' courts

F–39   **III.27.1** In the Crown Court the police will provide brief details of the circumstances of the last three similar convictions and/or of convictions likely to be of interest to the court, the latter being judged on a case by case basis. This information should be provided separately and attached to the antecedents as set out below.

III.27.2 Where the current alleged offence could constitute a breach of an existing community order, e.g. community rehabilitation order, and it is known that that order is still in force then, to enable the court to consider the possibility of revoking that order, details of the circumstances of the offence leading to the community order should be included in the antecedents as set out below.

Preparation of antecedents and standard formats to be used

F–40   **III.27.3** In magistrates' courts and the Crown Court:

Personal details and summary of convictions and cautions—Police National Computer ["PNC"] Court/Defence/Probation Summary Sheet;

Previous convictions—PNC Court/Defence/Probation printout, supplemented by Form MG16 if the police force holds convictions not shown on PNC;

Recorded cautions—PNC Court/Defence/Probation printout, supplemented by Form MG17 if the police force holds cautions not shown on PNC.

and, in addition, in the Crown Court:

Circumstances of the last three similar convictions;

Circumstances of offence leading to a community order still in force;

Form MG(c). The detail should be brief and include the date of the offence.

Provision of antecedents to the court and parties

Crown Court

III.27.4 The Crown Court antecedents will be prepared by the police immediately fol- **F–41**
lowing committal proceedings, including committals for sentence, transfers under section 4
of the *Criminal Justice Act* 1987 or section 53 of the *Criminal Justice Act* 1991 or upon
receipt of a notice of appeal, excluding non-imprisonable motoring offences.

III.27.5 Seven copies of the antecedents will be prepared in respect of each defendant.
Two copies are to be provided to the Crown Prosecution Service ["CPS"] direct, the remaining five to be sent to the Crown Court. The court will send one copy to the defence and one
to the Probation Service. The remaining copies are for the court's use. Where following
conviction a custodial order is made one copy is to be attached to the order sent to the
prison.

III.27.6 The antecedents must be provided, as above, within 21 days of committal or
transfer in each case. Any points arising from them are to be raised with the police by the
defence solicitor as soon as possible and, where there is time, at least seven days before the
hearing date so that the matter can be resolved prior to that hearing.

III.27.7 Seven days before the hearing date the police will check the record of
convictions. Details of any additional convictions will be provided using the standard format
above. These will be provided as above and attached to the documents already supplied.
Details of any additional outstanding cases will also be provided at this stage.

Magistrates' courts

III.27.8 The magistrates' court antecedents will be prepared by the police and submitted
to the CPS with the case file.

III.27.9 Five copies of the antecedents will be prepared in respect of each defendant and
provided to the CPS who will be responsible for distributing them to others at the sentencing
hearing. Normally two copies will be provided to the court, one to the defence and one to
the Probation Service when appropriate. Where following conviction a custodial order is
made, one of the court's copies is to be attached to the order sent to the prison.

III.27.10 In instances where antecedents have been provided to the court some time
before the hearing the police will, if requested to do so by the CPS, check the record of
convictions. Details of any additional convictions will be provided using the standard format
above. These will be provided as above and attached to the documents already supplied.
Details of any additional outstanding cases will also be provided at this stage.

III.27.11 The above arrangements whereby the police provide the antecedents to the
CPS for passing on to others will apply unless there is a local agreement between the CPS
and the court that alters that arrangement.

III.28 Personal Statements of Victims

III.28.1 This section draws attention to a scheme, which started on 1 October 2001, to **F–42**
give victims a more formal opportunity to say how a crime has affected them. It may help to
identify whether they have a particular need for information, support and protection. It will
also enable the court to take the statement into account when determining sentence.

III.28.2 When a police officer takes a statement from a victim the victim will be told
about the scheme and given the chance to make a victim personal statement. A victim
personal statement may be made or updated at any time prior to the disposal of the case.
The decision about whether or not to make a victim personal statement is entirely for the
victim. If the court is presented with a victim personal statement the following approach
should be adopted:

    (a) The victim personal statement and any evidence in support should be considered
        and taken into account by the court prior to passing sentence.

    (b) Evidence of the effects of an offence on the victim contained in the victim personal
        statement or other statement, must be in proper form, that is a witness statement
        made under section 9 of the *Criminal Justice Act* 1967 or an expert's report, and
        served upon the defendant's solicitor or the defendant, if he is not represented, prior
        to sentence. Except where inferences can properly be drawn from the nature of or cir-
        cumstances surrounding the offence, a sentencer must not make assumptions unsup-
        ported by evidence about the effects of an offence on the victim.

    (c) The court must pass what it judges to be the appropriate sentence having regard to the

Appendices

circumstances of the offence and of the offender, taking into account, so far as the court considers it appropriate, the consequences to the victim. The opinions of the victim or the victim's close relatives as to what the sentence should be are therefore not relevant, unlike the consequence of the offence on them. Victims should be advised of this. If, despite the advice, opinions as to sentence are included in the statement, the court should pay no attention to them.

(d) The court should consider whether it is desirable in its sentencing remarks to refer to the evidence provided on behalf of the victim.

III.29 Support for Witnesses giving Evidence by Live Television Link

F–43   **III.29.1** This section of the Practice Direction is made pursuant to Rule 7 of the *Crown Court (Special Measures Directions and Directions Prohibiting Cross-examination) Rules* 2002 and Rule 7 of the *Magistrates' Courts (Special Measures Directions) Rules* 2002 and supersedes previous guidance given by the Senior Presiding Judges, Lord Justice Tasker Watkins in 1991 and Lord Justice Auld in 1998.

III.29.2 An increased degree of flexibility is now appropriate as to who can act as supporter of a witness giving evidence by live television link. Where a special measures direction is made enabling a vulnerable, intimidated or child witness to give evidence by means of a live television link, the trial judge will make a direction as to the identity of the witness supporter. Where practical, the direction will be made before the trial commences. In giving the direction, the trial judge will balance all relevant interests—see *paragraph 1.11* of the guidance "*Achieving Best Evidence*". The witness supporter should be completely independent of the witness and his or her family and have no previous knowledge of or personal involvement in the case. The supporter should also be suitably trained so as to understand the obligations of, and comply with, the National Standards relating to witness supporters. Providing these criteria are met, the witness supporter need not be an usher or court official. Thus, for example, the functions of the witness supporter may be performed by a representative of the Witness Service.

III.29.3 Where the witness supporter is someone other than the court usher, the usher should continue to be available both to assist the witness and the witness supporter, and to ensure that the judge's requirements are properly complied with in the CCTV room.

III.30.1 Treatment of Vulnerable Defendants

F–44   **(III.30.1)** This direction applies to proceedings in the Crown Court and in magistrates' courts on the trial, sentencing or (in the Crown Court) appeal of (a) children and young persons under 18 or (b) adults who suffer from a mental disorder within the meaning of the *Mental Health Act* 1983 or who have any other significant impairment of intelligence and social function. In this direction such defendants are referred to collectively as "vulnerable defendants". The purpose of this direction is to extend to proceedings in relation to such persons in the adult courts procedures analogous to those in use in youth courts.

(III.30.2) The steps which should be taken to comply with paragraphs III.30.3 to III.30.17 should be judged, in any given case, taking account of the age, maturity and development (intellectual, social and emotional) of the defendant concerned and all other circumstances of the case.

The overriding principle

(III.30.3) A defendant may be young and immature or may have a mental disorder within the meaning of the *Mental Health Act* 1983 or some other significant impairment of intelligence and social function such as to inhibit his understanding of and participation in the proceedings. The purpose of criminal proceedings is to determine guilt, if that is in issue, and decide on the appropriate sentence if the defendant pleads guilty or is convicted. All possible steps should be taken to assist a vulnerable defendant to understand and participate in those proceedings. The ordinary trial process should, so far as necessary, be adapted to meet those ends. Regard should be had to the welfare of a young defendant as required by section 44 of the *Children and Young Persons Act* 1933, and generally to Parts 1 and 3 of the Criminal Procedure Rules (the overriding objective and the court's powers of case management).

Before the trial, sentencing or appeal

(III.30.4) If a vulnerable defendant, especially one who is young, is to be tried jointly with one who is not, the court should consider at the plea and case management hearing, or at a case management hearing in a magistrates' court, whether the vulnerable defendant should be tried on his own and should so order unless of the opinion that a joint trial would be in accordance with Part 1 of the Criminal Procedure Rules (the overriding objective) and in the interests of justice. If a vulnerable defendant is tried jointly with one who is not, the court should consider whether any of the modifications set out in this direction should apply in the circumstances of the joint trial and so far as practicable make orders to give effect to any such modifications.

(**III.30.5**) At the plea and case management hearing, or at a case management hearing in a magistrates' court, the court should consider and so far as practicable give directions on the matters covered in paragraphs III.30.9 to III.30.17.

(**III.30.6**) It may be appropriate to arrange that a vulnerable defendant should visit, out of court hours and before the trial, sentencing or appeal hearing, the courtroom in which that hearing is to take place so that he can familiarise himself with it.

(**III.30.7**) If any case against a vulnerable defendant has attracted or may attract widespread public or media interest, the assistance of the police should be enlisted to try and ensure that the defendant is not, when attending the court, exposed to intimidation, vilification or abuse. Section 41 of the *Criminal Justice Act* 1925 prohibits the taking of photographs of defendants and witnesses (among others) in the court building or in its precincts, or when entering or leaving those precincts. A direction informing media representatives that the prohibition will be enforced may be appropriate.

(**III.30.8**) The court should be ready at this stage, if it has not already done so, where relevant to make a reporting restriction under section 39 of the *Children and Young Persons Act* 1933 or, on an appeal to the Crown Court from a youth court, to remind media representatives of the application of section 49 of that Act. Any such order, once made, should be reduced to writing and copies should on request be made available to anyone affected or potentially affected by it.

The trial, sentencing or appeal hearing

(**III.30.9**) Subject to the need for appropriate security arrangements the proceedings should, if practicable, be held in a courtroom in which all the participants are on the same or almost the same level.

(**III.30.10**) A vulnerable defendant, especially if he is young, should normally, if he wishes, be free to sit with members of his family or others in a like relationship, and with some other suitable supporting adult such as a social worker, and in a place which permits easy, informal communication with his legal representatives. The court should ensure that a suitable supporting adult is available throughout the course of the proceedings.

(**III.30.11**) At the beginning of the proceedings the court should ensure that what is to take place has been explained to a vulnerable defendant in terms he can understand, and at trial in the Crown Court it should ensure in particular that the role of the jury has been explained. It should remind those representing the vulnerable defendant and the supporting adult of their responsibility to explain each step as it takes place, and at trial to explain the possible consequences of a guilty verdict. Throughout the trial the court should continue to ensure, by any appropriate means, that the defendant understands what is happening and what has been said by those on the bench, the advocates and witnesses.

(**III.30.12**) A trial should be conducted according to a timetable which takes full account of a vulnerable defendant's ability to concentrate. Frequent and regular breaks will often be appropriate. The court should ensure, so far as practicable, that the trial is conducted in simple, clear language that the defendant can understand and that cross-examination is conducted by questions that are short and clear.

(**III.30.13**) A vulnerable defendant who wishes to give evidence by live link in accordance with section 33A of the *Youth Justice and Criminal Evidence Act* 1999 may apply for a direction to that effect. Before making such a direction the court must be satisfied that it is in the interests of justice to do so, and that the use of a live link would enable the defendant to participate more effectively as a witness in the proceedings. The direction will need to deal with the practical arrangements to be made, including the room from which the defendant will give evidence, the identity of the person or persons who will accompany him, and how it will be arranged for him to be seen and heard by the court.

(**III.30.14**) In the Crown Court robes and wigs should not be worn unless the court for good reason orders that they should. It may be appropriate for the court to be robed for sentencing in a grave case even though it has sat without robes for trial. It is generally desirable that those responsible for the security of a vulnerable defendant who is in custody, especially if he is young, should not be in uniform, and that there should be no recognisable police presence in the courtroom save for good reason.

(III.30.15) The court should be prepared to restrict attendance by members of the public in the court room to a small number, perhaps limited to those with an immediate and direct interest in the outcome. The court should rule on any challenged claim to attend.

(III.30.16) Facilities for reporting the proceedings (subject to any restrictions under section 39 or 49 of the *Children and Young Persons Act* 1933) must be provided. But the court may restrict the number of reporters attending in the courtroom to such number as is judged practicable and desirable. In ruling on any challenged claim to attend in the court room for the purpose of reporting the court should be mindful of the public's general right to be informed about the administration of justice.

(III.30.17) Where it has been decided to limit access to the courtroom, whether by reporters or generally, arrangements should be made for the proceedings to be relayed, audibly and if possible visually, to another room in the same court complex to which the media and the public have access if it appears that there will be a need for such additional facilities. Those making use of such a facility should be reminded that it is to be treated as an extension of the court room and that they are required to conduct themselves accordingly.

(III.30.18) Where the court is called upon to exercise its discretion in relation to any procedural matter falling within the scope of this practice direction but not the subject of specific reference, such discretion should be exercised having regard to the principles in paragraph III.30.3.

III.31.1 Binding Over Orders and Conditional Discharges

(III.31.1) This direction takes into account the judgments of the European Court of Human Rights in *Steel v United Kingdom* (1999) 28 EHRR 603, [1998] Crim. L.R. 893 and in *Hashman and Harrup v United Kingdom* (2000) 30 EHRR 241, [2000] Crim. L.R. 185. Its purpose is to give practical guidance, in the light of those two judgments, on the practice of imposing binding over orders. The direction applies to orders made under the court's common law powers, under the *Justices of the Peace Act* 1361, under section 1(7) of the *Justices of the Peace Act* 1968 and under section 115 of the *Magistrates' Courts Act* 1980. This direction also gives guidance concerning the court's power to bind over parents or guardians under section 150 of the *Powers of Criminal Courts (Sentencing) Act* 2000 and the Crown Court's power to bind over to come up for judgment. The court's power to impose a conditional discharge under section 12 of the *Powers of Criminal Courts (Sentencing) Act* 2000 is also covered by this direction.

Binding over to keep the peace

(III.31.2) Before imposing a binding over order, the court must be satisfied that a breach of the peace involving violence or an imminent threat of violence has occurred or that there is a real risk of violence in the future. Such violence may be perpetrated by the individual who will be subject to the order or by a third party as a natural consequence of the individual's conduct.

(III.31.3) In light of the judgment in *Hashman and Harrup*, courts should no longer bind an individual over "to be of good behaviour". Rather than binding an individual over to "keep the peace" in general terms, the court should identify the specific conduct or activity from which the individual must refrain.

Written order

(III.31.4) When making an order binding an individual over to refrain from specified types of conduct or activities, the details of that conduct or those activities should be specified by the court in a written order served on all relevant parties. The court should state its reasons for the making of the order, its length and the amount of the recognisance. The length of the order should be proportionate to the harm sought to be avoided and should not generally exceed 12 months.

Evidence

(III.31.5) Sections 51 to 57 of the *Magistrates' Courts Act* 1980 set out the jurisdiction of the magistrates' court to hear an application made on complaint and the procedure which is to be followed. This includes a requirement under section 53 to hear evidence and the parties before making any order. This practice should be applied to all cases in the magistrates' court and the Crown Court where the court is considering imposing a binding over order. The court should give the individual who would be subject to the order and the prosecutor the opportunity to make representations, both as to the making of the order and as to its terms. The court should also hear any admissible evidence the parties wish to call and which has not already been heard in the proceedings. Particularly careful consideration may be required where the individual who would be subject to the order is a witness in the proceedings.

(III.31.6) Where there is an admission which is sufficient to found the making of a binding over order and/or the individual consents to the making of the order, the court should nevertheless hear sufficient representations and, if appropriate, evidence, to satisfy itself that an order is appropriate in all the circumstances and to be clear about the terms of the order.

(III.31.7) Where there is an allegation of breach of a binding over order and this is contested, the court should hear representations and evidence, including oral evidence, from the parties before making a finding.

Burden of proof

(III.31.8) The court should be satisfied beyond reasonable doubt of the matters complained of before a binding over order may be imposed. Where the procedure has been commenced on complaint, the burden of proof rests on the complainant. In all other circumstances, the burden of proof rests upon the prosecution.

(III.31.9) Where there is an allegation of breach of a binding over order, the court should be satisfied beyond reasonable doubt that a breach has occurred before making any order for forfeiture of a recognisance. The burden of proof shall rest on the prosecution.

Recognisance

(III.31.10) The court must be satisfied on the merits of the case that an order for binding over is appropriate and should announce that decision before considering the amount of the recognisance. The individual who is made subject to the binding over order should be told he has a right of appeal from the decision.

(III.31.11) When fixing the amount of the recognisance, courts should have regard to the individual's financial resources and should hear representations from the individual or his legal representatives regarding finances.

Refusal to enter into a recognisance

(III.31.12) If there is any possibility that an individual will refuse to enter a recognisance, the court should consider whether there are any appropriate alternatives to a binding over order (for example, continuing with a prosecution). Where there are no appropriate alternatives and the individual continues to refuse to enter into the recognisance, the magistrates' court may use its power under section 115(3) of the *Magistrates' Courts Act* 1980, and the Crown Court may use its common law power, to commit the individual to custody.

(III.31.13) Before the court exercises a power to commit the individual to custody, the individual should be given the opportunity to see a duty solicitor or another legal representative and be represented in proceedings if the individual so wishes. Public funding should generally be granted to cover representation.

(III.31.14) In the event that the individual does not take the opportunity to seek legal advice, the court shall give the individual a final opportunity to comply with the request and shall explain the consequences of a failure to do so.

Antecedents

(III.31.15) Courts are reminded of the provisions of section 7(5) of the *Rehabilitation of Offenders Act* 1974 which excludes from a person's antecedents any order of the court "with respect to any person otherwise than on a conviction".

Binding over to come up for judgment

(III.31.16) If the Crown Court is considering binding over an individual to come up for judgment, the court should specify any conditions with which the individual is to comply in the meantime and not specify that the individual is to be of good behaviour.

Binding over of parent or guardian

(III.31.17) Where a court is considering binding over a parent or guardian under section 150 of the *Powers of Criminal Courts (Sentencing) Act* 2000 to enter into a recognisance to take proper care of and exercise proper control over a child or young person, the court should specify the actions which the parent or guardian is to take.

Security for good behaviour

1577

(III.31.18) Where a court is imposing a conditional discharge under section 12 of the *Powers of Criminal Courts (Sentencing) Act* 2000, it has the power, under section 12(6) to make an order that a person who consents to do so give security for the good behaviour of the offender. When making such an order, the court should specify the type of conduct from which the offender is to refrain.

PART V: FURTHER DIRECTIONS APPLYING IN THE MAGISTRATES' COURTS

PART V: FURTHER DIRECTIONS APPLYING IN THE MAGISTRATES' COURTS

V.51 Mode of Trial

F–46   **V.51.1** The purpose of these guidelines is to help magistrates decide whether or not to commit defendants charged with "either way" offences for trial in the Crown Court. Their object is to provide guidance not direction. They are not intended to impinge on a magistrate's duty to consider each case individually and on its own particular facts. These guidelines apply to all defendants aged 18 and above.

General mode of trial considerations

F–47   **V.51.2** Section 19 of the *Magistrates' Courts Act* 1980 requires magistrates to have regard to the following matters in deciding whether an offence is more suitable for summary trial or trial on indictment:

(a) the nature of the case;

(b) whether the circumstances make the offence one of a serious character;

(c) whether the punishment which a magistrates' court would have power to inflict for it would be adequate;

(d) any other circumstances which appear to the court to make it more suitable for the offence to be tried in one way rather than the other;

(e) any representations made by the prosecution or the defence.

   V.51.3 Certain general observations can be made:

(f) the court should never make its decision on the grounds of convenience or expedition;

(g) the court should assume for the purpose of deciding mode of trial that the prosecution version of the facts is correct;

(h) the fact that the offences are alleged to be specimens is a relevant consideration (although, it has to be borne in mind that difficulties can arise in sentencing in relation to specimen counts see *R v Clark* [1996] 2 Cr App R (S) 351 and *R v Canavan and others* [1998] 1 Cr App R (S) 243); the fact that the defendant will be asking for other offences to be taken into consideration, if convicted, is not;

(i) where cases involve complex questions of fact or difficult questions of law, including difficult issues of disclosure of sensitive material, the court should consider committal for trial;

(j) where two or more defendants are jointly charged with an offence each has an individual right to elect his mode of trial;

(k) in general, except where otherwise stated, either way offences should be tried summarily unless the court considers that the particular case has one or more of the features set out in paragraphs 0 to 0 and that its sentencing powers are insufficient;

(l) the court should also consider its power to commit an offender for sentence under sections 3 and 4 of the *Powers of Criminal Courts (Sentencing) Act* 2000, if information emerges during the course of the hearing which leads it to conclude that the offence is so serious, or the offender such a risk to the public, that its powers to sentence him are inadequate. This means that committal for sentence is no longer determined by reference to the character and antecedents of the offender.

Features relevant to individual offences

F–48   **V.51.4** Where reference is made in these guidelines to property or damage of "high value" it means a figure equal to at least twice the amount of the limit (currently £5,000)

1578

imposed by statute on a magistrates' court when making a compensation order.

Burglary: Dwelling-house

V.51.5 Cases should be tried summarily unless the court considers that one or more of **F–49** the following features is present in the case *and* that its sentencing powers are insufficient. Magistrates should take account of their powers under sections 3 and 4 of the *Powers of Criminal Courts (Sentencing) Act* 2000 to commit for sentence, see paragraph 0(g).

   (m) Entry in the daytime when the occupier (or another) is present;

   (n) Entry at night of a house which is normally occupied, whether or not the occupier (or another) is present;

   (o) The offence is alleged to be one of a series of similar offences;

   (p) When soiling, ransacking, damage or vandalism occurs;

   (q) The offence has professional hallmarks;

   (r) The unrecovered property is of high value: see paragraph 0 for definition of high value;

   (s) The offence is racially motivated.

Note: Attention is drawn to paragraph 28(c) of Schedule 1 to the *Magistrates' Courts Act* 1980 by which offences of burglary in a dwelling cannot be tried summarily if any person in the dwelling was subjected to violence or the threat of violence.

Burglary: Non-dwelling

V.51.6 Cases should be tried summarily unless the court considers that one or more of **F–50** the following features is present in the case *and* that its sentencing powers are insufficient. Magistrates should take account of their powers under sections 3 and 4 of the *Powers of Criminal Courts (Sentencing) Act* 2000 to commit for sentence, see paragraph 0(g).

   (t) Entry of a pharmacy or doctor's surgery;

   (u) Fear is caused or violence is done to anyone lawfully on the premises (e.g. night-watchman, security guard);

   (v) The offence has professional hallmarks;

   (w) Vandalism on a substantial scale;

   (x) The unrecovered property is of high value: see paragraph 0 for definition of high value;

   (y) The offence is racially motivated.

Theft and fraud

V.51.7 Cases should be tried summarily unless the court considers that one or more of **F–51** the following features is present in the case *and* that its sentencing powers are insufficient. Magistrates should take account of their powers under sections 3 and 4 of the *Powers of Criminal Courts (Sentencing) Act* 2000 to commit for sentence, see paragraph 0(g).

   (z) Breach of trust by a person in a position of substantial authority, or in whom a high degree of trust is placed;

   (aa) Theft or fraud which has been committed or disguised in a sophisticated manner;

   (bb) Theft or fraud committed by an organised gang;

   (cc) The victim is particularly vulnerable to theft or fraud, e.g. the elderly or infirm;

   (dd) The unrecovered property is of high value: see paragraph 0 for definition of high value.

Handling

V.51.8 Cases should be tried summarily unless the court considers that one or more of **F–52** the following features is present in the case *and* that its sentencing powers are insufficient. Magistrates should take account of their powers under sections 3 and 4 of the *Powers of Criminal Courts (Sentencing) Act* 2000 to commit for sentence, see paragraph 0(g).

   (ee) Dishonest handling of stolen property by a receiver who has commissioned the theft;

   (ff) The offence has professional hallmarks;

   (gg) The property is of high value: see paragraph 0 for definition of high value.

Appendices

Social security frauds

F–53   **V.51.9** Cases should be tried summarily unless the court considers that one or more of the following features is present in the case *and* that its sentencing powers are insufficient. Magistrates should take account of their powers under sections 3 and 4 of the *Powers of Criminal Courts (Sentencing) Act* 2000 to commit for sentence, see paragraph 0(g).

   (hh) Organised fraud on a large scale;

   (ii) The frauds are substantial and carried out over a long period of time.

Violence (sections 20 and 47 of the Offences against the Person Act 1861)

F–54   **V.51.10** Cases should be tried summarily unless the court considers that one or more of the following features is present in the case *and* that its sentencing powers are insufficient. Magistrates should take account of their powers under sections 3 and 4 of the *Powers of Criminal Courts (Sentencing) Act* 2000 to commit for sentence, see paragraph 0(g).

   (jj) The use of a weapon of a kind likely to cause serious injury;

   (kk) A weapon is used and serious injury is caused;

   (ll) More than minor injury is caused by kicking or head-butting;

   (mm) Serious violence is caused to those whose work has to be done in contact with the public or are likely to face violence in the course of their work;

   (nn) Violence to vulnerable people, e.g. the elderly and infirm;

   (oo) The offence has clear racial motivation.

              Note: the same considerations apply to cases of domestic violence.

Public Order Act Offences

F–55   **V.51.11** Cases should be tried summarily unless the court considers that one or more of the following features is present in the case *and* that its sentencing powers are insufficient. Magistrates should take account of their powers under sections 3 and 4 of the *Powers of Criminal Courts (Sentencing) Act* 2000 to commit for sentence, see paragraph 0(g).

   (pp) Cases of *violent disorder* should generally be committed for trial;

   (qq) *Affray*;

        (i) Organised violence or use of weapons;

        (ii) Significant injury or substantial damage;

        (iii) The offence has clear racial motivation;

        (iv) An attack on police officers, ambulance staff, fire-fighters and the like.

Violence to and neglect of children

F–56   **V.51.12** Cases should be tried summarily unless the court considers that one or more of the following features is present in the case *and* that its sentencing powers are insufficient. Magistrates should take account of their powers under sections 3 and 4 of the *Powers of Criminal Courts (Sentencing) Act* 2000 to commit for sentence, see paragraph 0(g):

   (rr) Substantial injury;

   (ss) Repeated violence or serious neglect, even if the physical harm is slight;

   (tt) Sadistic violence, e.g. deliberate burning or scalding.

Indecent assault

F–57   **V.51.13** Cases should be tried summarily unless the court considers that one or more of the following features is present in the case *and* that its sentencing powers are insufficient. Magistrates should take account of their powers under sections 3 and 4 of the *Powers of Criminal Courts (Sentencing) Act* 2000 to commit for sentence, see paragraph 0(g).

   (uu) Substantial disparity in age between victim and defendant, and a more serious assault;

   (vv) Violence or threats of violence;

   (ww) Relationship of trust or responsibility between defendant and victim;

   (xx) Several more serious similar offences;

   (yy) The victim is particularly vulnerable;

   (zz) Serious nature of the assault.

Unlawful sexual intercourse
    V.51.14 Cases should be tried summarily unless the court considers that one or more of   **F–58**
the following features is present in the case *and* that its sentencing powers are insufficient.
Magistrates should take account of their powers under sections 3 and 4 of the *Powers of Criminal Courts (Sentencing) Act* 2000 to commit for sentence, see paragraph 0(g).

    (aaa) Wide disparity of age;

    (bbb) Breach of position of trust;

    (ccc) The victim is particularly vulnerable.

Note: Unlawful sexual intercourse with a girl *under 13* is triable only on indictment.

Drugs
    V.51.15 Class A: **F–59**
    (ddd) Supply; possession with intent to supply:
        These cases should be committed for trial.
    (eee) Possession:
        Should be committed for trial unless the amount is consistent only with personal
        use.
    V.51.16 Class B:
    (fff) Supply; possession with intent to supply:
        Should be committed for trial unless there is only small scale supply for no payment.
    (ggg) Possession:
        Should be committed for trial when the quantity is substantial and not consistent
        only with personal use.

Dangerous driving and aggravated vehicle taking
    V.51.17 Cases should be tried summarily unless the court considers that one or more of   **F–60**
the following features is present in the case *and* that its sentencing powers are insufficient.
Magistrates should take account of their powers under sections 3 and 4 of the *Powers of Criminal Courts (Sentencing) Act* 2000 to commit for sentence, see paragraph 0(g).

    (hhh) Alcohol or drugs contributing to the dangerous driving;

    (iii) Grossly excessive speed;

    (jjj) Racing;

    (kkk) Prolonged course of dangerous driving;

    (lll) Other related offences;

  (mmm) Significant injury or damage sustained.

Criminal damage
    V.51.18 Cases should be tried summarily unless the court considers that one or more of   **F–61**
the following features is present in the case *and* that its sentencing powers are insufficient.
Magistrates should take account of their powers under sections 3 and 4 of the *Powers of Criminal Courts (Sentencing) Act* 2000 to commit for sentence, see paragraph 0(g).

    (nnn) Deliberate fire-raising;

    (ooo) Committed by a group;

    (ppp) Damage of a high value;

    (qqq) The offence has clear racial motivation.

Note: Offences set out in Schedule 2 to the *Magistrates' Courts Act* 1980 (which includes offences of criminal damage which do not amount to arson) *must* be tried summarily if the value
of the property damaged or destroyed is £5,000 or less.

V.52 Committal for Sentence and Appeals to Crown Court
    V.52.2 Any case notes should be sent to the Crown Court when there is an appeal,   **F–62**
thereby making them available to the judge if the judge requires them in order to decide
before the hearing questions of listing or representation or the like. They will also be available to the court during the hearing if it becomes necessary or desirable for the court to see
what happened in the lower court. On a committal for sentence or an appeal, any reasons

given by the magistrates for their decision should be included with the notes.

V.53 Bail before Committal for Trial

F–63   **V.53.1**   Rules 19 and 20 of the *Crown Court Rules* 1982: SI 1982/1109 apply to these applications.

V.53.2   Before the Crown Court can deal with an application it must be satisfied that the magistrates' court has issued a certificate under section 5(6A) of the *Bail Act* 1976 that it heard full argument on the application for bail before it refused the application. A copy of the certificate will be issued to the applicant and not sent directly to the Crown Court. It will therefore be necessary for the applicant's solicitors to attach a copy of the certificate to the bail application form. If the certificate is not enclosed with the application form it will be difficult to avoid some delay in listing.

Venue

F–64   **V.53.3**   Applications should be made to the court to which the defendant will be or would have been committed for trial. In the event of an application in a purely summary case, it should be made to the Crown Court centre which normally receives class 4 work. The hearing will be listed as a chambers matter unless a judge has directed otherwise.

V.54 Contempt in the Face of the Magistrates' Court

General

F–65   **V.54.1**   Section 12 of the *Contempt of Court Act* 1981 gives magistrates' courts the power to detain until the court rises, someone, whether a defendant or another person present in court, who wilfully insults anyone specified in section 12 or who interrupts proceedings. In any such case, the court may order any officer of the court, or any constable, to take the offender into custody and detain him until the rising of the court; and the court may, if it thinks fit, commit the offender to custody for a specified period not exceeding one month or impose a fine not exceeding level 4 on the standard scale or both. This power can be used to stop disruption of their proceedings. Detention is until the person can be conveniently dealt with without disruption of the proceedings. Prior to the court using the power the offender should be warned to desist or face the prospect of being detained.

V.54.2   Magistrates' courts also have the power to commit to custody any person attending or brought before a magistrates' court who refuses without just cause to be sworn or to give evidence under section 97(4) of the *Magistrates' Courts Act* 1980, until the expiration of such period not exceeding one month as may be specified in the warrant or until he sooner gives evidence or produces the document or thing, or impose on him a fine not exceeding £2,500, or both.

V.54.3   In the exercise of any of these powers, as soon as is practical, and in any event prior to an offender being proceeded against, an offender should be told of the conduct which it is alleged to constitute his offending in clear terms. When making an order under section 12 the justices should state their findings of fact as to the contempt.

V.54.4   Exceptional situations require exceptional treatment. While this direction deals with the generality of situations, there will be a minority of situations where the application of the direction will not be consistent with achieving justice in the special circumstances of the particular case. Where this is the situation, the compliance with the direction should be modified so far as is necessary so as to accord with the interests of justice.

V.54.5   The power to bind persons over to be of good behaviour in respect of their conduct in court should cease to be exercised.

Contempt consisting of wilfully insulting anyone specified in section 12 or interrupting proceedings

F–66   **V.54.6**   In the case of someone who wilfully insults anyone specified in section 12 or interrupts proceedings, if an offender expresses a willingness to apologise for his misconduct, he should be brought back before the court at the earliest convenient moment in order to make the apology and to give undertakings to the court to refrain from further misbehaviour.

V.54.7   In the majority of cases, an apology and a promise as to future conduct should be sufficient for justices to order an offender's release. However, there are likely to be certain cases where the nature and seriousness of the misconduct requires the justices to consider using their powers under section 12(2) of the *Contempt of Court* 1981 Act either to fine or to order the offender's committal to custody.

Where an offender is detained for contempt of court
V.54.8 Anyone detained under either of these provisions in paragraphs V.54.1 or V.54.2   **F–67**
should be seen by the duty solicitor or another legal representative and be represented in
proceedings if they so wish. Public funding should generally be granted to cover
representation. The offender must be afforded adequate time and facilities in order to
prepare his case. The matter should be resolved the same day if at all possible.
V.54.9 The offender should be brought back before the court before the justices conclude
their daily business. The justices should ensure that he understands the nature of the
proceedings, including his opportunity to apologise or give evidence and the alternative of
them exercising their powers.
V.54.10 Having heard from the offender's solicitor, the justices should decide whether to
take further action.

Sentencing of an offender who admits being in contempt
V.54.11 If an offence of contempt is admitted the justices should consider whether they   **F–68**
are able to proceed on the day or whether to adjourn to allow further reflection. The matter
should be dealt with on the same day if at all possible. If the justices are of the view to adjourn they should generally grant the offender bail unless one or more of the exceptions to
the right to bail in the *Bail Act* 1976 are made out.
V.54.12 When they come to sentence the offender where the offence has been admitted,
the justices should first ask the offender if he has any objection to them dealing with the
matter. If there is any objection to the justices dealing with the matter a differently constituted panel should hear the proceedings. If the offender's conduct was directed to the justices, it will not be appropriate for the same bench to deal with the matter.
V.54.13 The justices should consider whether an order for the offender's discharge is appropriate, taking into account any time spent on remand, whether the offence was admitted
and the seriousness of the contempt. Any period of committal should be for the shortest time
commensurate with the interests of preserving good order in the administration of justice.

Trial of the issue where the contempt is not admitted
V.54.14 Where the contempt is not admitted the justices' powers are limited to making   **F–69**
arrangements for a trial to take place. They should not at this stage make findings against
the offender.
V.54.15 In the case of a contested contempt the trial should take place at the earliest opportunity and should be before a bench of justices other than those before whom the alleged
contempt took place. If a trial of the issue can take place on the day such arrangements
should be made taking into account the offender's rights under Article 6 of the European
Convention for the Protection of Human Rights and Fundamental Freedoms (Rome, 4
November 1950; TS 71 (1953); Cmd 8969). If the trial cannot take place that day the justices
should again bail the offender unless there are grounds under the *Bail Act* 1976 to remand
him in custody.
V.54.16 The offender is entitled to call and examine witnesses where evidence is relevant.
If the offender is found by the court to have committed contempt the court should again
consider first whether an order for his discharge from custody is sufficient to bring proceedings to an end. The justices should also allow the offender a further opportunity to apologise
for his contempt or to make representations. If the justices are of the view that they must
exercise their powers to commit to custody under section12(2) of the 1981 *Act*, they must
take into account any time spent on remand and the nature and seriousness of the contempt.
Any period of committal should be for the shortest period of time commensurate with the
interests of preserving good order in the administration of justice.

V.55 Clerk Retiring with Justices
V.55.1 A justices' clerk is responsible for: **F–70**
    (a) the legal advice tendered to the justices within the area;
    (b) the performance of any of the functions set out below by any member of his staff
        acting as legal adviser;
    (c) ensuring that competent advice is available to justices when the justices' clerk is not
        personally present in court; and

Appendices

(d) the effective delivery of case management and the reduction of unnecessary delay.

V.55.2 Where a person other than the justices' clerk (a "legal adviser"), who is authorised to do so, performs any of the functions referred to in this direction he will have the same responsibilities as the justices' clerk. The legal adviser may consult the justices' clerk or other person authorised by the justices' clerk for that purpose before tendering advice to the bench. If the justices' clerk or that person gives any advice directly to the bench, he should give the parties or their advocates an opportunity of repeating any relevant submissions prior to the advice being given.

V.55.3 It shall be the responsibility of the legal adviser to provide the justices with any advice they require properly to perform their functions, whether or not the justices have requested that advice, on:

(a) questions of law (including European Court of Human Rights jurisprudence and those matters set out in section 2(1) of the *Human Rights Act* 1998);

(b) questions of mixed law and fact;

(c) matters of practice and procedure;

(d) the range of penalties available;

(e) any relevant decisions of the superior courts or other guidelines;

(f) other issues relevant to the matter before the court; and

(g) the appropriate decision-making structure to be applied in any given case.

In addition to advising the justices it shall be the legal adviser's responsibility to assist the court, where appropriate, as to the formulation of reasons and the recording of those reasons.

V.55.4 A justices' clerk or legal adviser must not play any part in making findings of fact, but may assist the bench by reminding them of the evidence, using any notes of the proceedings for this purpose.

V.55.5 A justices' clerk or legal adviser may ask questions of witnesses and the parties in order to clarify the evidence and any issues in the case. A legal adviser has a duty to ensure that every case is conducted fairly.

V.55.6 When advising the justices the justices' clerk or legal adviser, whether or not previously in court, should:

(a) ensure that he is aware of the relevant facts; and

(b) provide the parties with the information necessary to enable the parties to make any representations they wish as to the advice before it is given.

V.55.7 At any time justices are entitled to receive advice to assist them in discharging their responsibilities. If they are in any doubt as to the evidence which has been given, they should seek the aid of their legal adviser, referring to his notes as appropriate. This should ordinarily be done in open court. Where the justices request their adviser to join them in the retiring room, this request should be made in the presence of the parties in court. Any legal advice given to the justices other than in open court should be clearly stated to be provisional and the adviser should subsequently repeat the substance of the advice in open court and give the parties an opportunity to make any representations they wish on that provisional advice. The legal adviser should then state in open court whether the provisional advice is confirmed or if it is varied the nature of the variation.

V.55.8 The performance of a legal adviser may be appraised by a person authorised by the magistrates' courts committee to do so. For that purpose the appraiser may be present in the justices' retiring room. The content of the appraisal is confidential, but the fact that an appraisal has taken place, and the presence of the appraiser in the retiring room, should be briefly explained in open court.

V.55.9 The legal adviser is under a duty to assist unrepresented parties to present their case, but must do so without appearing to become an advocate for the party concerned.

V.55.10 The role of legal advisers in fine default proceedings or any other proceedings for the enforcement of financial orders, obligations or penalties is to assist the court. They must not act in an adversarial or partisan manner. With the agreement of the justices a legal adviser may ask questions of the defaulter to elicit information which the justices will require to make an adjudication, for example to facilitate his explanation for the default. A legal adviser may also advise the justices in the normal way as to the options open to them in dealing with the case. It would be inappropriate for the legal adviser to set out to establish wilful refusal or neglect or any other type of culpable behaviour, to offer an opinion on the facts, or to urge a particular course of action upon the justices. The duty of impartiality is the paramount consideration for the legal adviser at all times, and this takes precedence over any role he may have as a collecting officer. The appointment of other staff to "prosecute" the case for the collecting officer is not essential to ensure compliance with the law, including the *Human Rights Act* 1998. Whether to make such appointments is a matter for the justices' chief executive.

The Lord Chief Justice of England and Wales
8 July 2002
as amended 29 July 2004

APPENDIX G

CRIMINAL PROCEDURE RULES 2005

The *Criminal Procedure Rules* 2005 were first issued by the Rule Committee and **G–1**
came into force on April 4, 2005: *Criminal Procedure Rules* 2005 (S.I. 2005 No. 384).
They have been amended as follows:

  (i) The *Criminal Procedure (Amendment) Rules* 2006 (S.I. 2006 No. 353), which
       came into force on April 3, 2006.
 (ii) The *Criminal Procedure (Amendment No. 2) Rules* (S.I. 2006 No. 2636),
       which came into force on November 6, 2006.
(iii) The *Criminal Procedure (Amendment) Rules* 2007 (S.I. 2007 No. 699), which
       came into force on April 2, 2007.

The Rules are printed with all the amendments incorporated.

PART 1

THE OVERRIDING OBJECTIVE

The overriding objective
   1.1—(1) The overriding objective of this new code is that criminal cases be dealt with justly.
   (2) Dealing with a criminal case justly includes—
       (a) acquitting the innocent and convicting the guilty;
       (b) dealing with the prosecution and the defence fairly;
       (c) recognising the rights of a defendant, particularly those under Article 6 of the
            European Convention on Human Rights;
       (d) respecting the interests of witnesses, victims and jurors and keeping them
            informed of the progress of the case;
       (e) dealing with the case efficiently and expeditiously;
       (f) ensuring that appropriate information is available to the court when bail and
            sentence are considered; and
       (g) dealing with the case in ways that take into account—
             (i)   the gravity of the offence alleged,
             (ii) the complexity of what is in issue,
             (iii) the severity of the consequences for the defendant and others affected, and
             (iv) the needs of other cases.

The duty of the participants in a criminal case
   1.2—(1) Each participant, in the conduct of each case, must—
       (a) prepare and conduct the case in accordance with the overriding objective;
       (b) comply with these Rules, practice directions and directions made by the court;
            and
       (c) at once inform the court and all parties of any significant failure (whether or not
            that participant is responsible for that failure) to take any procedural step
            required by these Rules, any practice direction or any direction of the court. A
            failure is significant if it might hinder the court in furthering the overriding
            objective.
   (2) Anyone involved in any way with a criminal case is a participant in its conduct for
the purposes of this rule.

The application by the court of the overriding objective
   1.3—(1) The court must further the overriding objective in particular when—
       (a) exercising any power given to it by legislation (including these Rules);
       (b) applying any practice direction; or

(c) interpreting any rule or practice direction.

PART 2

UNDERSTANDING AND APPLYING THE RULES

When the Rules apply

G–2   **2.1**—(1) In general, the Criminal Procedure Rules apply—

(a) in all criminal cases in magistrates' courts and in the Crown Court; and

(b) in all cases in the criminal division of the Court of Appeal.

(2) If a rule applies only in one or two of those courts, the rule makes that clear.

(3) The Rules apply on and after 4th April, 2005, but do not affect any right or duty existing under the rules of court revoked by the coming into force of these Rules.

(4) The rules in Part 33 apply in all cases in which the defendant is charged on or after 6 November 2006 and in other cases if the court so orders.

(5) The rules in Part 14 apply in cases in which one of the events listed in sub-paragraphs (a) to (d) of rule 14.1(1) takes place on or after 2nd April 2007. In other cases the rules of court replaced by those rules apply.

(6) The rules in Part 28 apply in cases in which an application under rule 28.3 is made on or after 2nd April 2007. In other cases the rules replaced by those rules apply.

Definitions

2.2—(1) In these Rules, unless the context makes it clear that something different is meant:

"court" means a tribunal with jurisdiction over criminal cases. It includes a judge, recorder, District Judge (Magistrates' Court's), lay justice and, when exercising their judicial powers, the Registrar of Criminal Appeals, a justices' clerk or assistant clerk;

"court officer" means the appropriate member of the staff of a court; and

"Practice Direction" means the Lord Chief Justice's Consolidated Criminal Practice Direction, as amended.

(2) Definitions of some other expressions are in the rules in which they apply.

References to Acts of Parliament and to Statutory Instruments

2.3—(1) In these Rules, where a rule refers to an Act of Parliament or to subordinate legislation by title and year, subsequent references to that Act or to that legislation in the rule are shortened: so, for example, after a reference to the *Criminal Procedure and Investigations Act* 1996 that Act is called "the 1996 Act"; and after a reference to the *Criminal Procedure and Investigations Act 1996 (Defence Disclosure Time Limits) Regulations* 1997 those Regulations are called "the 1997 Regulations".

The glossary

2.4—(1) The glossary at the end of the Rules is a guide to the meaning of certain legal expressions used in them.

PART 3

CASE MANAGEMENT

The scope of this Part

G–3   **3.1** This Part applies to the management of each case in a magistrates' court and in the Crown Court (including an appeal to the Crown Court) until the conclusion of that case.

The duty of the court

G–4   **3.2**—(1) The court must further the overriding objective by actively managing the case.

(2) Active case management includes—

(a) the early identification of the real issues;

(b) the early identification of the needs of witnesses;

(c) achieving certainty as to what must be done, by whom, and when, in particular by the early setting of a timetable for the progress of the case;

(d) monitoring the progress of the case and compliance with directions;

(e) ensuring that evidence, whether disputed or not, is presented in the shortest and clearest way;

(f) discouraging delay, dealing with as many aspects of the case as possible on the same occasion, and avoiding unnecessary hearings;

(g) encouraging the participants to co-operate in the progression of the case; and

(h) making use of technology.

(3) The court must actively manage the case by giving any direction appropriate to the needs of that case as early as possible.

The duty of the parties

3.3 Each party must— **G–5**

(a) actively assist the court in fulfilling its duty under rule 3.2, without or if necessary with a direction; and

(b) apply for a direction if needed to further the overriding objective.

Case progression officers and their duties

3.4—(1) At the beginning of the case each party must, unless the court otherwise directs— **G–6**

(a) nominate an individual responsible for progressing that case; and

(b) tell other parties and the court who he is and how to contact him.

(2) In fulfilling its duty under rule 3.2, the court must where appropriate—

(a) nominate a court officer responsible for progressing the case; and

(b) make sure the parties know who he is and how to contact him.

(3) In this Part a person nominated under this rule is called a case progression officer.

(4) A case progression officer must—

(a) monitor compliance with directions;

(b) make sure that the court is kept informed of events that may affect the progress of that case;

(c) make sure that he can be contacted promptly about the case during ordinary business hours;

(d) act promptly and reasonably in response to communications about the case; and

(e) if he will be unavailable, appoint a substitute to fulfil his duties and inform the other case progression officers.

The court's case management powers

3.5—(1) In fulfilling its duty under rule 3.2 the court may give any direction and take any **G–7** step actively to manage a case unless that direction or step would be inconsistent with legislation, including these Rules.

(2) In particular, the court may—

(a) nominate a judge, magistrate, justices' clerk or assistant to a justices' clerk to manage the case;

(b) give a direction on its own initiative or on application by a party;

(c) ask or allow a party to propose a direction;

(d) for the purpose of giving directions, receive applications and representations by letter, by telephone or by any other means of electronic communication, and conduct a hearing by such means;

(e) give a direction without a hearing;

(f) fix, postpone, bring forward, extend or cancel a hearing;

(g) shorten or extend (even after it has expired) a time limit fixed by a direction;

(h) require that issues in the case should be determined separately, and decide in what order they will be determined; and

(i) specify the consequences of failing to comply with a direction.

(3) A magistrates' court may give a direction that will apply in the Crown Court if the case is to continue there.

(4) The Crown Court may give a direction that will apply in a magistrates' court if the case is to continue there.

(5) Any power to give a direction under this Part includes a power to vary or revoke that direction.

Application to vary a direction

G–8   **3.6**—(1) A party may apply to vary a direction if—
(a) the court gave it without a hearing;
(b) the court gave it at a hearing in his absence; or
(c) circumstances have changed.

(2) A party who applies to vary a direction must—
(a) apply as soon as practicable after he becomes aware of the grounds for doing so; and
(b) give as much notice to the other parties as the nature and urgency of his application permits.

Agreement to vary a time limit fixed by a direction

G–9   **3.7**—(1) The parties may agree to vary a time limit fixed by a direction, but only if—
(a) the variation will not—
(i) affect the date of any hearing that has been fixed, or
(ii) significantly affect the progress of the case in any other way;
(b) the court has not prohibited variation by agreement; and
(c) the court's case progression officer is promptly informed.

(2) The court's case progression officer must refer the agreement to the court if he doubts the condition in paragraph (1)(a) is satisfied.

Case preparation and progression

G–10   **3.8**—(1) At every hearing, if a case cannot be concluded there and then the court must give directions so that it can be concluded at the next hearing or as soon as possible after that.

(2) At every hearing the court must, where relevant—
(a) if the defendant is absent, decide whether to proceed nonetheless;
(b) take the defendant's plea (unless already done) or if no plea can be taken then find out whether the defendant is likely to plead guilty or not guilty;
(c) set, follow or revise a timetable for the progress of the case, which may include a timetable for any hearing including the trial or (in the Crown Court) the appeal;
(d) in giving directions, ensure continuity in relation to the court and to the parties' representatives where that is appropriate and practicable; and
(e) where a direction has not been complied with, find out why, identify who was responsible, and take appropriate action.

Readiness for trial or appeal

G–11   **3.9**—(1) This rule applies to a party's preparation for trial or (in the Crown Court) appeal, and in this rule and rule 3.10 trial includes any hearing at which evidence will be introduced.

(2) In fulfilling his duty under rule 3.3, each party must—
(a) comply with directions given by the court;
(b) take every reasonable step to make sure his witnesses will attend when they are needed;
(c) make appropriate arrangements to present any written or other material; and
(d) promptly inform the court and the other parties of anything that may—
(i) affect the date or duration of the trial or appeal, or
(ii) significantly affect the progress of the case in any other way.

(3) The court may require a party to give a certificate of readiness.

Conduct of a trial or an appeal

G–12   **3.10** In order to manage the trial or (in the Crown Court) appeal, the court may require a party to identify—
(a) which witnesses he intends to give oral evidence;
(b) the order in which he intends those witnesses to give their evidence;
(c) whether he requires an order compelling the attendance of a witness;
(d) what arrangements, if any, he proposes to facilitate the giving of evidence by a witness;
(e) what arrangements, if any, he proposes to facilitate the participation of any other person, including the defendant;

(f) what written evidence he intends to introduce;

(g) what other material, if any, he intends to make available to the court in the presentation of the case;

(h) whether he intends to raise any point of law that could affect the conduct of the trial or appeal; and

(i) what timetable he proposes and expects to follow.

Case management forms and records

3.11—(1) The case management forms set out in the Practice Direction must be used, and **G–13** where there is no form then no specific formality is required.

(2) The court must make available to the parties a record of directions given.

Criminal Procedure Rules

Parts 10.4 and 27.2: *reminders of right to object to written evidence being read at trial*

Part 12.2: *time for first appearance of accused sent for trial*

Part 13: *dismissal of charges sent or transferred to the Crown Court*t

Part 14: *the indictment*

Part 15: *preparatory hearings in serious fraud and other complex or lengthy cases*

Parts 21–26: *the rules that deal with disclosure*

Parts 27–36: *the rules that deal with evidence*

Part 37: *summary trial*

Part 38: *trial of children and young persons*

Part 39: *trial on indictment*

Regulations

Prosecution of Offences (Custody Time Limits) Regulations 1987

Criminal Justice Act 1987 (Notice of Transfer) Regulations 1988

Criminal Justice Act 1991 (Notice of Transfer) Regulations 1992

Criminal Procedure and Investigations Act 1996 (Defence Disclosure Time Limits) Regulations 1997

Crime and Disorder Act 1998 (Service of Prosecution Evidence) Regulations 2005

Provisions of Acts of Parliament

Sections 5, 10 and 18, *Magistrates' Courts Act 1980: powers to adjourn hearings*

Sections 128 and 129, *Magistrates' Courts Act 1980: remand in custody by magistrates' courts*

Part 1, *Criminal Procedure and Investigations Act 1996: disclosure*

Schedule 2, *Criminal Procedure and Investigations Act 1996: use of witness statements at trial*

Section 2, *Administration of Justice (Miscellaneous Provisions) Act 1933: procedural conditions for trial in the Crown Court*

Section 6, *Magistrates' Courts Act 1980: committal for trial*

Section 4, *Criminal Justice Act 1987:* section 53, *Criminal Justice Act 1991:* section 51 and (so far as it is in force) section 51A,, *Crime and Disorder Act 1998: other procedures by which a case reaches the Crown Court*

Section 7, *Criminal Justice Act 1987;* Parts III and IV, *Criminal Procedure and Investigations Act 1996 : pre-trial and preparatory hearings in the Crown Court*

Section 9, *Criminal Justice Act 1967: proof by written witness statement]*

PART 4

SERVICE OF DOCUMENTS

When this Part applies

4.1—(1) The rules in this Part apply to the service of every document in a case to which these **G–14** Rules apply, subject to any special rules in other legislation (including other Parts of these Rules) or in the Practice Direction.

Methods of service

G–15   **4.2**—(1) A document may be served by any of the methods described in rules 4.3 to 4.6 (subject to rule 4.7), or in rule 4.8.

Service by handing over a document

G–16   **4.3**—(1) A document may be served on—
 (a) an individual by handing it to him or her;
 (b) a corporation by handing it to a person holding a senior position in that corporation;
 (c) an individual or corporation who is legally represented in the case by handing it to that representative;
 (d) the prosecution by handing it to the prosecutor or to the prosecution representative;
 (e) the court officer by handing it to a court officer with authority to accept it at the relevant court office; and
 (f) the Registrar of Criminal Appeals by handing it to a court officer with authority to accept it at the Criminal Appeal Office.
 (2) If an individual is 17 or under, a copy of a document served under paragraph (1)(a) must be handed to his or her parent, or another appropriate adult, unless no such person is readily available.

Service by leaving or posting a document

G–17   **4.4**—(1) A document may be served by leaving it at the appropriate address for service under this rule or by sending it to that address by first class post or by the equivalent of first class post.
 (2) The address for service under this rule on—
 (a) an individual is an address where it is reasonably believed that he or she will receive it;
 (b) a corporation is its principal office in England and Wales, and if there is no readily identifiable principal office then any place in England and Wales where it carries on its activities or business;
 (c) an individual or corporation who is legally represented in the case is that representative's office;
 (d) the prosecution is the prosecutor's office;
 (e) the court officer is the relevant court office; and
 (f) the Registrar of Criminal Appeals is the Criminal Appeal Office, Royal Courts of Justice, Strand, London WC2A 2LL.

Service through a document exchange

G–18   **4.5**—(1) A document may be served by document exchange (DX) where—
 (a) the writing paper of the person to be served gives a DX box number; and
 (b) that person has not refused to accept service by DX.

Service by fax, e-mail or other electronic means

G–19   **4.6**—(1) A document may be served by fax, e-mail or other electronic means where—
 (a) the person to be served has given a fax, e-mail or other electronic address; and
 (b) that person has not refused to accept service by that means.
 (2) Where a document is served under this rule the person serving it need not provide a paper copy as well.

Documents that must be served only by handing them over, leaving or posting them

G–20   **4.7**—(1) The documents listed in this rule may be served—
 (a) on an individual only under rule 4.3(1)(a) or rule 4.4(1) and (2)(a); and
 (b) on a corporation only under rule 4.3(1)(b) or rule 4.4(1) and (2)(b).
 (2) Those documents are—
 (a) a summons, requisition or witness summons;
 (b) notice of an order under section 25 of the *Road Traffic Offenders Act* 1988;
 (c) a notice of registration under section 71(6) of that Act;
 (d) a notice of discontinuance under section 23(4) of the *Prosecution of Offences Act* 1985;

(e) notice under rule 37.3(1) of the date, time and place to which the trial of an information has been adjourned, where it was adjourned in the defendant's absence;

(f) a notice of fine or forfeited recognizance required by rule 52.1(1);

(g) notice under section 86 of the *Magistrates' Courts Act* 1980 of a revised date to attend a means inquiry;

(h) notice of a hearing to review the postponement of the issue of a warrant of commitment under section 77(6) of the *Magistrates' Courts Act* 1980;

(i) a copy of the minute of a magistrates' court order required by rule 52.7(1);

(j) an invitation to make observations or attend a hearing under rule 53.1(2) on the review of a compensation order under section 133 of the *Powers of Criminal Courts (Sentencing) Act* 2000;

(k) any notice or document served under Part 19.

Service by person in custody
4.8—(1) A person in custody may serve a document by handing it to the custodian addressed **G–21**
to the person to be served.

(2) The custodian must—

(a) endorse it with the time and date of receipt;

(b) record its receipt; and

(c) forward it promptly to the addressee.

Service by another method
4.9—(1) The court may allow service of a document by a method other than those described **G–22**
in rules 4.3 to 4.6 and in rule 4.8.

(2) An order allowing service by another method must specify—

(a) the method to be used; and

(b) the date on which the document will be served.

Date of service
4.10—(1) A document served under rule 4.3 or rule 4.8 is served on the day it is handed **G–23**
over.

(2) Unless something different is shown, a document served on a person by any other method is served—

(a) in the case of a document left at an address, on the next business day after the day on which it was left;

(b) in the case of a document sent by first class post or by the equivalent of first class post, on the second business day after the day on which it was posted or despatched;

(c) in the case of a document served by document exchange, on the second business day after the day on which it was left at the addressee's DX or at a correspondent DX;

(d) in the case of a document transmitted by fax, e-mail or other electronic means, on the next business day after it was transmitted; and

(e) in any case, on the day on which the addressee responds to it if that is earlier.

(3) Unless something different is shown, a document produced by a court computer system is to be taken as having been sent by first class post or by the equivalent of first class post to the addressee on the business day after the day on which it was produced.

(4) In this Part "business day" means any day except Saturday, Sunday, Christmas Day, Boxing Day, Good Friday, Easter Monday or a bank holiday.

(5) Where a document is served on or by the court officer, "business day" does not include a day on which the court office is closed.

Proof of service
4.11 The person who serves a document may prove that by signing a certificate explaining **G–24**
how and when it was served.

Court's power to give directions about service
4.12—(1) The court may specify the time as well as the date by which a document must be— **G–25**

(a) served under rule 4.3 or rule 4.8; or

(b) transmitted by fax, e-mail or other electronic means if it is served under rule 4.6.

(2) The court may treat a document as served if the addressee responds to it even if it was not served in accordance with the rules in this Part.

PART 5

FORMS

Forms

G–26   **5.1** The forms set out in the Practice Direction shall be used as appropriate in connection with the rules to which they apply.

Magistrates' court forms in Welsh

G–27   **5.2**—(1) Subject to the provisions of this rule, the Welsh language forms set out in the Practice Direction or forms to the like effect may be used in connection with proceedings in magistrates' courts in Wales.

(2) Both a Welsh form and an English form may be used in the same document.

(3) When only a Welsh form set out in the Practice Direction accompanying this rule, or only the corresponding English form, is used in connection with proceedings in magistrates' courts in Wales, there shall be added the following words in Welsh and English:

> "Darperir y ddogfen hon yn Gymraeg/Saesneg os bydd arnoch ei heisiau. Dylech wneud cais yn ddi-oed i (Glerc Llys yr Ynadon) (rhodder yma'r cyfeiriad) .. ..

This document will be provided in Welsh/English if you require it. You should apply immediately to (the Justices' Clerk to the Magistrates' Court) (address) .. ..
If a person other than a justices' clerk is responsible for sending or giving the document, insert that person's name."

(4) The justices' clerk or other person responsible for the service of a form bearing the additional words set out in paragraph (3) above shall, if any person upon whom the form is served so requests, provide him with the corresponding English or Welsh form.

(5) In this rule any reference to serving a document shall include the sending, giving or other delivery of it.

(6) In the case of a discrepancy between an English and Welsh text the English text shall prevail.

Signature of magistrates' court forms by justices' clerk

G–28   **5.3**—(1) Subject to paragraph (2) below, where any form prescribed by these Rules contains provision for signature by a justice of the peace only, the form shall have effect as if it contained provision in the alternative for signature by the justices' clerk.

(2) This rule shall not apply to any form of information, complaint, statutory declaration or warrant, other than a warrant of commitment or of distress.

(3) In this rule where a signature is required on a form or warrant other than an arrest, remand or commitment warrant, an electronic signature incorporated into the document will satisfy this requirement.

PART 6

COURT RECORDS

Magistrates' court register

G–29   **6.1**—(1) A magistrates' court officer shall keep a register in which there shall be entered—

(a) a minute or memorandum of every adjudication of the court; and

(b) a minute or memorandum of every other proceeding or thing required by these Rules or any other enactment to be so entered.

(2) The register may be stored in electronic form on the court computer system and entries in the register shall include, where relevant, the following particulars—

(a) the name of the informant, complainant or applicant;

(b) the name and date of birth (if known) of the defendant or respondent;
(c) the nature of offence, matter of complaint or details of the application;
(d) the date of offence or matter of complaint;
(e) the plea or consent to order; and
(f) the minute of adjudication.

(3) Particulars of any entry relating to a decision about bail or the reasons for any such decisions or the particulars of any certificate granted under section 5(6A) of the *Bail Act* 1976 may be made in a book separate from that in which the entry recording the decision itself is made, but any such separate book shall be regarded as forming part of the register.

(4) Where, by virtue of section 128(3A) of the *Magistrates' Courts Act* 1980, an accused gives his consent to the hearing and determination in his absence of any application for his remand on an adjournment of the case under sections 5, 10(1) or 18(4) of that Act, the court shall cause the consent of the accused, and the date on which it was notified to the court, to be entered in the register.

(5) Where any consent mentioned in paragraph (4) is withdrawn, the court shall cause the withdrawal of the consent and the date on which it was notified to the court to be entered in the register.

(6) On the summary trial of an information the accused's plea shall be entered in the register.

(7) Where a court tries any person summarily in any case in which he may be tried summarily only with his consent, the court shall cause his consent to be entered in the register and, if the consent is signified by a person representing him in his absence, the court shall cause that fact also to be entered in the register.

(8) Where a person is charged before a magistrates' court with an offence triable either way the court shall cause the entry in the register to show whether he was present when the proceedings for determining the mode of trial were conducted and, if they were conducted in his absence, whether they were so conducted by virtue of section 18(3) of the 1980 Act (disorderly conduct on his part) or by virtue of section 23(1) of that Act (consent signified by person representing him).

(9) In any case to which section 22 of the 1980 Act (certain offences triable either way to be tried summarily if value involved is small) applies, the court shall cause its decision as to the value involved or, as the case may be, the fact that it is unable to reach such a decision to be entered in the register.

(10) Where a court has power under section 53(3) of the 1980 Act to make an order with the consent of the defendant without hearing evidence, the court shall cause any consent of the defendant to the making of the order to be entered in the register.

(11) In the case of conviction or dismissal, the register shall clearly show the nature of the offence of which the accused is convicted or, as the case may be, the nature of the offence charged in the information that is dismissed.

(12) An entry of a conviction in the register shall state the date of the offence.

(13) Where a court is required under section 130(3) of the *Powers of Criminal Courts (Sentencing) Act* 2000 to give reasons for not making a compensation order the court shall cause the reasons given to be entered in the register.

(14) Where a court passes a custodial sentence, the court shall cause a statement of whether it obtained and considered a pre-sentence report before passing sentence to be entered in the register.

(15) Every register shall be open to inspection during reasonable hours by any justice of the peace, or any person authorised in that behalf by a justice of the peace or the Lord Chancellor.

(16) A record of summary conviction or order made on complaint required for an appeal or other legal purpose may be in the form of certified extract from the court register.

(17) Such part of the register as relates to proceedings in a youth court may be recorded separately and stored in electronic form on the court computer system.

Registration of endorsement of licence under section 57 of the Road Traffic Offenders Act 1988

6.2 A magistrates' court officer or justices' clerk who, as a fixed penalty clerk within the meaning of section 69(4) of the *Road Traffic Offenders Act* 1988, endorses a driving licence under section 57(3) or (4) of that Act (endorsement of licences without hearing) shall register the particulars of the endorsement in a book separate from the register kept under rule 6.1 but any

G–30

Appendices

such book shall be regarded as forming part of the register.

Registration of certificate issued under section 70 of the Road Traffic Offenders Act 1988

G–31   **6.3** A magistrates' court officer shall register receipt of a registration certificate issued under section 70 of the *Road Traffic Offenders Act* 1988 (sum payable in default of fixed penalty to be enforced as a fine) in a book separate from the register kept under rule 6.1 but any such book shall be regarded as forming part of the register.

Proof of proceedings in magistrates' courts

G–32   **6.4** The register of a magistrates' court, or an extract from the register certified by the magistrates' court officer as a true extract, shall be admissible in any legal proceedings as evidence of the proceedings of the court entered in the register.

PART 7

COMMENCING PROCEEDINGS IN MAGISTRATES' COURTS

Information and complaint

G–33   **7.1**—(1) An information may be laid or complaint made by the prosecutor or complainant in person or by his counsel or solicitor or other person authorised in that behalf.

(2) Subject to any provision of the *Magistrates' Courts Act* 1980 and any other enactment, an information or complaint need not be in writing or on oath.

Statement of offence

G–34   **7.2**—(1) Every written charge issued by a public prosecutor and every information, summons or warrant laid in or issued by a magistrates' court shall be sufficient if it—

(a) describes the offence with which the accused is charged, or of which he is convicted, in ordinary language avoiding as far as possible the use of technical terms; and

(b) gives such particulars as may be necessary to provide reasonable information about the nature of the charge.

(2) It shall not be necessary for any of those documents to—

(a) state all the elements of the offence; or

(b) negative any matter upon which the accused may rely.

(3) If the offence charged is one created by or under any Act, the description of the offence shall contain a reference to the section of the Act, or, as the case may be, the rule, order, regulation, bylaw or other instrument creating the offence.

Information or written charge to be for one offence only

G–35   **7.3**—(1) Subject to any Act passed after 2nd October 1848, a magistrates' court shall not proceed to the trial of an information or written charge that charges more than one offence.

(2) Nothing in this rule shall prohibit two or more informations or written charges being set out in one document.

(3) If, notwithstanding paragraph (1), it appears to the court at any stage in the trial of an information or written charge that the information or written charge charges more than one offence, the court shall call upon the prosecutor to elect on which offence he desires the court to proceed, whereupon the offence or offences on which the prosecutor does not wish to proceed shall be struck out of the information or written charge; and the court shall then proceed to try that information or written charge afresh.

(4) If a prosecutor who is called upon to make an election under paragraph (3) fails to do so, the court shall dismiss the information or written charge.

(5) Where, after an offence has or offences have been struck out of the information or written charge under paragraph (3), the accused requests an adjournment and it appears to the court that he has been unfairly prejudiced, it shall adjourn the trial.

Duty of court officer receiving statutory declaration under section 14(1) of the Magistrates' Courts Act 1980

G–36   **7.4** Where a magistrates' court officer receives a statutory declaration which complies with section 14(1) of the *Magistrates' Courts Act* 1980 (accused did not know of proceedings), he shall—

(a) note the receipt of the declaration in the register; and

(b) inform the prosecutor and, if the prosecutor is not a constable, the chief officer of police of the receipt of the declaration.

Notice of order under section 25 of the Road Traffic Offenders Act 1988

7.5—(1) Where a magistrates' court makes an order under section 25 of the *Road Traffic* **G–37** *Offenders Act* 1988 that an offender shall inform the court of his date of birth or sex or both and the offender is not present in court, the court officer shall serve notice in writing of the order on the offender.

Statutory declaration under section 72 and 73 of the Road Traffic Offenders Act 1988

7.6 Where a magistrates' court officer receives a statutory declaration under section 72 and **G–38** 73 of the *Road Traffic Offenders Act* 1988 (fixed penalty notice or notice fixed to vehicle invalid) he shall send a copy of it to the appropriate chief officer of police.

Form of summons or requisition

7.7—(1) A summons or requisition must state the name of the justice or public prosecutor **G–39** responsible for issuing it.

(2) A summons or requisition requiring a person to appear before a magistrates' court to answer to an information, written charge or complaint shall state shortly the matter of the information, written charge or complaint and shall state the time and place at which the defendant is required by the summons or requisition to appear.

(3) A single summons or requisition may be issued against a person in respect of several informations, written charges or complaints; but the summons or requisition shall state the matter of each information, written charge or complaint separately and shall have effect as several summonses or requisitions, each issued in respect of one information, written charge or complaint.

(4) In this rule where a signature is required, an electronic signature incorporated into the document shall satisfy this requirement.

Summons or warrant to secure attendance of a parent or guardian at a youth court

7.8 Where a child or young person is charged with an offence, or is for any other reason **G–40** brought before a court, a summons or warrant may be issued by a court to enforce the attendance of a parent or guardian under section 34A of the *Children and Young Persons Act* 1933, in the same manner as if an information were laid upon which a summons or warrant could be issued against a defendant under the *Magistrates' Courts Act* 1980 and a summons to the child or young person may include a summons to the parent or guardian to enforce his attendance for the said purpose.

Magistrates' court officer to have copies of documents sent to accused under section 12(1) of the Magistrates' Courts Act 1980

7.9 Where the prosecutor notifies a magistrates' court officer that the documents mentioned **G–41** in section 12(1)(a) and 12(1)(b) of the *Magistrates' Courts Act* 1980 have been served upon the accused, the prosecutor shall send to the court officer a copy of the document mentioned in section 12(1)(b).

PART 8

OBJECTING TO THE DISCONTINUANCE OF PROCEEDINGS IN A MAGISTRATES' COURT

Time for objecting

8.1 The period within which an accused person may give notice under section 23(7) of the **G–42** *Prosecution of Offences Act* 1985 that he wants proceedings against him to continue is 35 days from the date when the proceedings were discontinued under that section.

Form of notice

8.2 Notice under section 23(3), (4) or (7) of the *Prosecution of Offences Act* 1985 shall be **G–43** given in writing and shall contain sufficient particulars to identify the particular offence to which it relates.

Duty of Director of Public Prosecutions

G–44   **8.3** On giving notice under section 23(3) or (4) of the *Prosecution of Offences Act* 1985 the Director of Public Prosecutions shall inform any person who is detaining the accused person for the offence in relation to which the notice is given that he has given such notice and of the effect of the notice.

Duty of magistrates' court

G–45   **8.4** On being given notice under section 23(3) of the *Prosecution of Offences Act* 1985 in relation to an offence for which the accused person has been granted bail by a court, a magistrates' court officer shall inform—

(a) any sureties of the accused; and

(b) any persons responsible for securing the accused's compliance with any conditions of bail

that he has been given such notice and of the effect of the notice.

PART 9

PRE-TRIAL HEARINGS IN MAGISTRATES' COURTS

G–46   **1.** *[Note. There are currently no rules in this Part.]*

PART 10

COMMITTAL FOR TRIAL

Restrictions on reports of committal proceedings

G–47   **10.1**—(1) Except in a case where evidence is, with the consent of the accused, to be tendered in his absence under section 4(4)(b) of the *Magistrates'* Courts Act 1980 (absence caused by ill health), a magistrates' court acting as examining justices shall before admitting any evidence explain to the accused the restrictions on reports of committal proceedings imposed by section 8 of that Act and inform him of his right to apply to the court for an order removing those restrictions.

(2) Where a magistrates' court has made an order under section 8(2) of the 1980 Act removing restrictions on the reports of committal proceedings, such order shall be entered in the register.

(3) Where the court adjourns any such proceedings to another day, the court shall, at the beginning of any adjourned hearing, state that the order has been made.

Committal for trial without consideration of the evidence

G–48   **10.2**—(1) This rule applies to committal proceedings where the accused has a solicitor acting for him in the case and where the court has been informed that all the evidence falls within section 5A(2) of the *Magistrates'* Courts Act 1980.

(2) A magistrates' court inquiring into an offence in committal proceedings to which this rule applies shall cause the charge to be written down, if this has not already been done, and read to the accused and shall then ascertain whether he wishes to submit that there is insufficient evidence to put him on trial by jury for the offence with which he is charged.

(3) If the court is satisfied that the accused or, as the case may be, each of the accused does not wish to make such a submission as is referred to in paragraph (2) it shall, after receiving any written evidence falling within section 5A(3) of the 1980 Act, determine whether or not to commit the accused for trial without consideration of the evidence, and where it determines not to so commit the accused it shall proceed in accordance with rule 10.3.

Consideration of evidence at committal proceedings

G–49   **10.3**—(1) This rule does not apply to committal proceedings where under section 6(2) of the *Magistrates'* Courts Act of 1980 a magistrates' court commits a person for trial without consideration of the evidence.

(2) A magistrates' court inquiring into an offence as examining justices, having ascertained—

    (a) that the accused has no legal representative acting for him in the case; or

    (b) that the accused's legal representative has requested the court to consider a submission that there is insufficient evidence to put the accused on trial by jury for the offence with which he is charged, as the case may be,

shall permit the prosecutor to make an opening address to the court, if he so wishes, before any evidence is tendered.

(3) After such opening address, if any, the court shall cause evidence to be tendered in accordance with sections 5B(4), 5C(4), 5D(5) and 5E(3) of the 1980 Act, that is to say by being read out aloud, except where the court otherwise directs or to the extent that it directs that an oral account be given of any of the evidence.

(4) The court may view any exhibits produced before the court and may take possession of them.

(5) After the evidence has been tendered the court shall hear any submission which the accused may wish to make as to whether there is sufficient evidence to put him on trial by jury for any indictable offence.

(6) The court shall permit the prosecutor to make a submission—

    (a) in reply to any submission made by the accused in pursuance of paragraph (5); or

    (b) where the accused has not made any such submission but the court is nevertheless minded not to commit him for trial.

(7) After hearing any submission made in pursuance of paragraph (5) or (6) the court shall, unless it decides not to commit the accused for trial, cause the charge to be written down, if this has not already been done, and, if the accused is not represented by counsel or a solicitor, shall read the charge to him and explain it in ordinary language.

Court's reminder to a defendant of right to object to evidence being read at trial without further proof

10.4 A magistrates' court which commits a person for trial shall forthwith remind him of his **G–50** right to object, by written notification to the prosecutor and the Crown Court within 14 days of being committed unless that court in its discretion permits such an objection to be made outside that period, to a statement or deposition being read as evidence at the trial without oral evidence being given by the person who made the statement or deposition, and without the opportunity to cross-examine that person.

Material to be sent to court of trial

10.5—(1) As soon as practicable after the committal of any person for trial, and in any case **G–51** within 4 days from the date of his committal (not counting Saturdays, Sundays, Good Friday, Christmas Day or Bank Holidays), the magistrates' court officer shall, subject to the provisions of section 7 of the *Prosecution of Offences Act* 1985 (which relates to the sending of documents and things to the Director of Public Prosecutions), send to the Crown Court officer—

    (a) the information, if it is in writing;

    (b) (i) the evidence tendered in accordance with section 5A of the *Magistrates' Courts Act* 1980 and, where any of that evidence consists of a copy of a deposition or documentary exhibit which is in the possession of the court, any such deposition or documentary exhibit, and

      (ii) a certificate to the effect that that evidence was so tendered;

    (c) any notification by the prosecutor under section 5D(2) of the 1980 Act regarding the admissibility of a statement under section 23 or 24 of the *Criminal Justice Act* 1988 (first hand hearsay; business documents);

    (d) a copy of the record made in pursuance of section 5 of the *Bail Act* 1976 relating to the grant or withholding of bail in respect of the accused on the occasion of the committal;

    (e) any recognizance entered into by any person as surety for the accused together with a statement of any enlargement thereof under section 129(4) of the 1980 Act;

    (f) a list of the exhibits produced in evidence before the justices or treated as so produced;

    (g) such of the exhibits referred to in paragraph (1)(f) as have been retained by the justices;

(h) the names and addresses of any interpreters engaged for the defendant for the purposes of the committal proceedings, together with any telephone numbers at which they can be readily contacted, and details of the languages or dialects in connection with which they have been so engaged;

(i) if the committal was under section 6(2) of the 1980 Act (committal for trial without consideration of the evidence), a statement to that effect;

(j) if the magistrates' court has made an order under section 8(2) of the 1980 Act (removal of restrictions on reports of committal proceedings), a statement to that effect;

(k) the certificate of the examining justices as to the costs of the prosecution under the *Costs in Criminal Cases (General) Regulations* 1986;

(l) if any person under the age of 18 is concerned in the committal proceedings, a statement whether the magistrates' court has given a direction under section 39 of the *Children and Young Persons Act* 1933 (prohibition of publication of certain matter in newspapers);

(m) a copy of any representation order previously made in the case;

(n) a copy of any application for a representation order previously made in the case which has been refused; and

(o) any documents relating to an appeal by the prosecution against the granting of bail.

(2) The period of 4 days specified in paragraph (1) may be extended in relation to any committal for so long as the Crown Court officer directs, having regard to the length of any document mentioned in that paragraph or any other relevant circumstances.

PART 11

TRANSFER FOR TRIAL OF SERIOUS FRAUD CASES OR CASES INVOLVING CHILDREN

Interpretation of this Part

G–52   **11.1**—(1) In this Part:

"notice of transfer" means a notice referred to in section 4(1) of the *Criminal Justice Act* 1987 or section 53(1) of the *Criminal Justice Act* 1991 .

(2) Where this Part requires a document to be given or sent, or a notice to be communicated in writing, it may, with the consent of the addressee, be sent by electronic communication.

(3) Electronic communication means a communication transmitted (whether from one person to another, from one device to another or from a person to a device or vice versa)—

(a) by means of an electronic communications network (within the meaning of the *Communications Act* 2003); or

(b) by other means but while in an electronic form.

Transfer on bail

G–53   **11.2**—(1) Where a person in respect of whom notice of transfer has been given—

(a) is granted bail under section 5(3) or (7A) of the *Criminal Justice Act* 1987 by the magistrates' court to which notice of transfer was given; or

(b) is granted bail under paragraph 2(1) or (7) of Schedule 6 to the *Criminal Justice Act* 1991 by the magistrates' court to which notice of transfer was given,

the magistrates' court officer shall give notice thereof in writing to the governor of the prison or remand centre to which the said person would have been committed by that court if he had been committed in custody for trial.

(2) Where notice of transfer is given under section 4(1) of the 1987 Act in respect of a corporation the magistrates' court officer shall give notice thereof to the governor of the prison to which would be committed a male over 21 committed by that court in custody for trial.

Notice where person removed to hospital

G–54   **11.3** Where a transfer direction has been given by the Secretary of State under section 47 or 48 of the *Mental Health Act* 1983 in respect of a person remanded in custody by a magistrates' court and, before the direction ceases to have effect, notice of transfer is given in respect of that person, the magistrates' court officer shall give notice thereof in writing—

    (a) to the governor of the prison to which that person would have been committed by that court if he had been committed in custody for trial; and

    (b) to the managers of the hospital where he is detained.

Variation of arrangements for bail

11.4—(1) A person who intends to make an application to a magistrates' court under section **G–55** 3(8) of the *Bail Act* 1976 as that subsection has effect under section 3(8A) of that Act shall give notice thereof in writing to the magistrates' court officer, and to the designated authority or the defendant, as the case may be, and to any sureties concerned.

(2) Where, on an application referred to in paragraph (1), a magistrates' court varies or imposes any conditions of bail, the magistrates' court officer shall send to the Crown Court officer a copy of the record made in pursuance of section 5 of the 1976 Act relating to such variation or imposition of conditions.

Documents etc to be sent to Crown Court

11.5 As soon as practicable after a magistrates' court to which notice of transfer has been **G–56** given has discharged the functions reserved to it under section 4(1) of the *Criminal Justice Act* 1987 or section 53(3) of the *Criminal Justice Act* 1991, the magistrates' court officer shall send to the Crown Court officer—

    (a) a list of the names, addresses and occupations of the witnesses;

    (b) a copy of the record made in pursuance of section 5 of the *Bail Act* 1976 relating to the grant of withholding of bail in respect of the accused;

    (c) any recognizance entered into by any person as surety for the accused together with a statement of any enlargement thereof;

    (d) a copy of any representation order previously made in the case; and

    (e) a copy of any application for a representation order previously made in the case which has been refused.

PART 12

SENDING FOR TRIAL

Documents to be sent to the Crown Court

12.1—(1) As soon as practicable after any person is sent for trial (pursuant to section 51 of **G–57** the *Crime and Disorder Act* 1998, and in any event within 4 days from the date on which he is sent (not counting Saturdays, Sundays, Good Friday, Christmas Day or Bank Holidays), the magistrates' court officer shall, subject to section 7 of the *Prosecution of Offences Act* 1985 (which relates to the sending of documents and things to the Director of Public Prosecutions), send to the Crown Court officer

    (a) the information, if it is in writing;

    (b) the notice required by section 51(7) of the 1998 Act;

    (c) a copy of the record made in pursuance of section 5 of the *Bail Act* 1976 relating to the granting or withholding of bail in respect of the accused on the occasion of the sending;

    (d) any recognizance entered into by any person as surety for the accused together with any enlargement thereof under section 129(4) of the Magistrates' Courts Act 1980;

    (e) the names and addresses of any interpreters engaged for the defendant for the purposes of the appearance in the magistrates' court, together with any telephone numbers at which they can be readily contacted, and details of the languages or dialects in connection with which they have been so engaged;

    (f) if any person under the age of 18 is concerned in the proceedings, a statement whether the magistrates' court has given a direction under section 39 of the *Children and Young Persons Act* 1933 (prohibition of publication of certain matter in newspapers);

    (g) a copy of any representation order previously made in the case;

    (h) a copy of any application for a representation order previously made in the case which has been refused; and

Appendices

(i) any documents relating to an appeal by the prosecution against the granting of bail.

(2) The period of 4 days specified in paragraph (1) may be extended in relation to any sending for trial for so long as the Crown Court officer directs, having regard to any relevant circumstances.

Time for first appearance of accused sent for trial

G–58   **12.2—** A Crown Court officer to whom notice has been given under section 51(7) of the *Crime and Disorder Act* 1998, shall list the first Crown Court appearance of the person to whom the notice relates in accordance with any directions given by the magistrates' court.

PART 13

DISMISSAL OF CHARGES TRANSFERRED OR SENT TO THE CROWN COURT

Interpretation of this Part

G–59   **13.1** In this Part:

"notice of transfer" means a notice referred to in section 4(1) of the *Criminal Justice Act* 1987 or section 53(1) of the *Criminal Justice Act* 1991; and

"the prosecution" means the authority by or on behalf of whom notice of transfer was given under the 1987 or 1991 Acts, or the authority by or on behalf of whom documents were served under paragraph 1 of Schedule 3 to the *Crime and Disorder Act* 1998.

Written notice of oral application for dismissal

G–60   **13.2—**(1) Where notice of transfer has been given under the *Criminal Justice Act* 1987 or the *Criminal Justice Act* 1991, or a person has been sent for trial under the *Crime and Disorder Act* 1998, and the person concerned proposes to apply orally—

(a) under section 6(1) of the 1987 *Act*;

(b) under paragraph 5(1) of Schedule 6 to the 1991 *Act*; or

(c) under paragraph 2(1) of Schedule 3 to the 1998 *Act*

for any charge in the case to be dismissed, he shall give notice of his intention in writing to the Crown Court officer at the place specified by the notice of transfer under the 1987 or 1991 Acts or the notice given under section 51(7) of the 1998 *Act* as the proposed place of trial. Notice of intention to make an application under the 1987 or 1991 Acts shall be in the form set out in the Practice Direction.

(2) Notice of intention to make an application shall be given—

(a) in the case of an application to dismiss charges transferred under the 1987 Act, not later than 28 days after the day on which notice of transfer was given;

(b) in the case of an application to dismiss charges transferred under the 1991 Act, not later than 14 days after the day on which notice of transfer was given; and

(c) in the case of an application to dismiss charges sent under the 1998 Act, not later than 14 days after the day on which the documents were served under paragraph 1 of Schedule 3 to that Act,

and a copy of the notice shall be given at the same time to the prosecution and to any person to whom the notice of transfer relates or with whom the applicant for dismissal is jointly charged.

(3) The time for giving notice may be extended, either before or after it expires, by the Crown Court, on an application made in accordance with paragraph (4).

(4) An application for an extension of time for giving notice shall be made in writing to the Crown Court officer, and a copy thereof shall be given at the same time to the prosecution and to any other person to whom the notice of transfer relates or with whom the applicant for dismissal is jointly charged. Such an application made in proceedings under the 1987 or 1991 Acts shall be in the form set out in the Practice Direction.

(5) The Crown Court officer shall give notice in the form set out in the Practice Direction of the judge's decision on an application under paragraph (3)—

(a) to the applicant for dismissal;

(b) to the prosecution; and

(c) to any other person to whom the notice of transfer relates or with whom the applicant for dismissal is jointly charged.

(6) A notice of intention to make an application under section 6(1) of the 1987 *Act*,

paragraph 5(1) of Schedule 6 to the 1991 *Act* or paragraph 2(1) of Schedule 3 to the 1998 *Act* shall be accompanied by a copy of any material on which the applicant relies and shall—

    (a) specify the charge or charges to which it relates;

    (b) state whether the leave of the judge is sought under section 6(3) of the 1987 *Act*, paragraph 5(4) of Schedule 6 to the 1991 *Act* or paragraph 2(4) of Schedule 3 to the 1998 *Act* to adduce oral evidence on the application, indicating what witnesses it is proposed to call at the hearing; and

    (c) in the case of a transfer under the 1991 Act, confirm in relation to each such witness that he is not a child to whom paragraph 5(5) of Schedule 6 to that Act applies.

(7) Where leave is sought from the judge for oral evidence to be given on an application, notice of his decision, indicating what witnesses are to be called if leave is granted, shall be given in writing by the Crown Court officer to the applicant for dismissal, the prosecution and to any other person to whom the notice of transfer relates or with whom the applicant for dismissal is jointly charged. Notice of a decision in proceedings under the 1987 or 1991 Acts shall be in the form set out in the Practice Direction.

(8) Where an application for dismissal under section 6(1) of the 1987 *Act*, paragraph 5(1) of Schedule 6 to the 1991 *Act* or paragraph 2(1) of Schedule 3 to the 1998 *Act* is to be made orally, the Crown Court officer shall list the application for hearing before a judge of the Crown Court and the prosecution shall be given the opportunity to be represented at the hearing.

Written application for dismissal

13.3—(1) Application may be made for dismissal under section 6(1) of the *Criminal Justice Act* 1987, paragraph 5(1) of Schedule 6 to the *Criminal Justice Act* 1991 or paragraph 2(1) of Schedule 3 to the *Crime and Disorder Act* 1998 without an oral hearing. Such an application shall be in writing, and in proceedings under the 1987 or 1991 Acts shall be in the form set out in the Practice Direction.   **G–61**

(2) The application shall be sent to the Crown Court officer and shall be accompanied by a copy of any statement or other document, and identify any article, on which the applicant for dismissal relies.

(3) A copy of the application and of any accompanying documents shall be given at the same time to the prosecution and to any other person to whom the notice of transfer relates or with whom the applicant for dismissal is jointly charged.

(4) A written application for dismissal shall be made—

    (a) not later than 28 days after the day on which notice of transfer was given under the 1987 Act;

    (b) not later than 14 days after the day on which notice of transfer was given under the 1991 Act; or

    (c) not later than 14 days after the day on which documents required by paragraph 1 of Schedule 3 to the 1998 Act were served

unless the time for making the application is extended, either before or after it expires, by the Crown Court; and rule 13.2(4) and (5) shall apply for the purposes of this paragraph as if references therein to giving notice of intention to make an oral application were references to making a written application under this rule.

Prosecution reply

13.4—(1) Not later than seven days from the date of service of notice of intention to apply orally for the dismissal of any charge contained in a notice of transfer or based on documents served under paragraph 1 of Schedule 3 to the *Crime and Disorder Act* 1998, the prosecution may apply to the Crown Court under section 6(3) of the *Criminal Justice Act* 1987, paragraph 5(4) of Schedule 6 to the *Criminal Justice Act* 1991 or paragraph 2(4) of Schedule 3 to the 1998 *Act* for leave to adduce oral evidence at the hearing of the application, indicating what witnesses it is proposed to call.   **G–62**

(2) Not later than seven days from the date of receiving a copy of an application for dismissal under rule 13.3, the prosecution may apply to the Crown Court for an oral hearing of the application.

(3) An application under paragraph (1) or (2) shall be served on the Crown Court officer in writing and, in the case of an application under paragraph (2), shall state whether the leave of the judge is sought to adduce oral evidence and, if so, shall indicate what witnesses it is proposed to call. Where leave is sought to adduce oral evidence under

paragraph 5(4) of Schedule 6 to the 1991 Act, the application should confirm in relation to each such witness that he is not a child to whom paragraph 5(5) of that Schedule applies. Such an application in proceedings under the 1987 or 1991 Acts shall be in the form set out in the Practice Direction.

(4) Notice of the judge's determination upon an application under paragraph (1) or (2), indicating what witnesses (if any) are to be called shall be served in writing by the Crown Court officer on the prosecution, on the applicant for dismissal and on any other party to whom the notice of transfer relates or with whom the applicant for dismissal is jointly charged. Such a notice in proceedings under the 1987 or 1991 Acts shall be in the form set out in the Practice Direction.

(5) Where, having received the material specified in rule 13.2 or, as the case may be, rule 13.3, the prosecution proposes to adduce in reply thereto any written comments or any further evidence, the prosecution shall serve any such comments, copies of the statements or other documents outlining the evidence of any proposed witnesses, copies of any further documents and, in the case of an application to dismiss charges transferred under the 1991 Act, copies of any video recordings which it is proposed to tender in evidence, on the Crown Court officer not later than 14 days from the date of receiving the said material, and shall at the same time serve copies thereof on the applicant for dismissal and any other person to whom the notice of transfer relates or with whom the applicant is jointly charged. In the case of a defendant acting in person, copies of video recordings need not be served but shall be made available for viewing by him.

(6) The time for—

    (a) making an application under paragraph (1) or (2) above; or

    (b) serving any material on the Crown Court officer under paragraph (5) above

may be extended, either before or after it expires, by the Crown Court, on an application made in accordance with paragraph (7) below.

(7) An application for an extension of time under paragraph (6) above shall be made in writing and shall be served on the Crown Court officer, and a copy thereof shall be served at the same time on to the applicant for dismissal and on any other person to whom the notice of transfer relates or with whom the applicant for dismissal is jointly charged. Such an application in proceedings under the 1987 or 1991 Acts shall be in the form set out in the Practice Direction.

Determination of applications for dismissal—procedural matters

G–63   **13.5**—(1) A judge may grant leave for a witness to give oral evidence on an application for dismissal notwithstanding that notice of intention to call the witness has not been given in accordance with the foregoing provisions of this Part.

(2) Where an application for dismissal is determined otherwise than at an oral hearing, the Crown Court officer shall as soon as practicable, send to all the parties to the case written notice of the outcome of the application. Such a notice in proceedings under the 1987 and 1991 Acts shall be in the form set out in the Practice Direction.

G–64   **13.6** *[Revoked]*

PART 14

THE INDICTMENT

Signature and service of indictment

G–65   **14.1**—(1) The prosecutor must serve a draft indictment on the Crown Court officer not more than 28 days after—

    (a) service on the defendant and on the Crown Court officer of copies of the documents containing the evidence on which the charge or charges are based, in a case where the defendant is sent for trial;

    (b) a High Court judge gives permission to serve a draft indictment;

    (c) the Court of Appeal orders a retrial; or

    (d) The Crown Court may extend the time limit, even after it has expired.

(2) The Crown Court may extend the time limit, even after it has expired.

(3) Unless the Crown Court otherwise directs, the court officer must—

    (a) sign and date the draft, which then becomes an indictment; and

(b) serve a copy of the indictment on all parties.

Form and content of indictment

14.2—(1) An indictment must be in one of the forms set out in the Practice Direction and **G–66** must contain, in a paragraph called a "count"—

(a) a statement of the offence charged that—

  (i) describes the offence in ordinary language, and

  (ii) identifies any legislation that creates it; and

(b) such particulars of the conduct constituting the commission of the offence as to make clear what the prosecutor alleges against the defendant.

(2) More than one incident of the commission of the offence may be included in a count if those incidents taken together amount to a course of conduct having regard to the time, place or purpose of commission.

(3) An indictment may contain more than one count if all the offences charged—

(a) are founded on the same facts; or

(b) form or are a part of a series of offences of the same or a similar character.

(4) The counts must be numbered consecutively.

(5) An indictment may contain—

(a) any count charging substantially the same offence as one—

  (i) specified in the notice of the offence or offences for which the defendant was sent for trial,

  (ii) on which the defendant was committed for trial, or

  (iii) specified in the notice of transfer given by the prosecutor; and

(b) any other count based on the prosecution evidence already served which the Crown Court may try.

PART 15

PREPARATORY HEARINGS IN CASES OF SERIOUS FRAUD AND OTHER COMPLEX, SERIOUS OR LENGTHY CASES IN THE CROWN COURT

Application for a preparatory hearing

15.1—(1) A party who wants the court to order a preparatory hearing under section 7(2) of **G–67** the *Criminal Justice Act* 1987 or under section 29(4) of the *Criminal Procedure and Investigations Act* 1996 must—

(a) apply in the form set out in the Practice Direction;

(b) include a short explanation of the reasons for applying; and

(c) serve the application on the court officer and all other parties.

(2) A prosecutor who wants the court to order that—

(a) the trial will be conducted without a jury under section 43 or section 44 of the *Criminal Justice Act* 2003; or

(b) the trial of some of the counts included in the indictment will be conducted without a jury under section 17 of the *Domestic Violence, Crime and Victims Act* 2004,

must apply under this rule for a preparatory hearing, whether or not the defendant has applied for one.

Time for applying for a preparatory hearing

15.2—(1) A party who applies under rule 15.1 must do so not more than 28 days after — **G–68**

(a) the committal of the defendant;

(b) the consent to the preferment of a bill of indictment in relation to the case;

(c) the service of a notice of transfer; or

(d) where a person is sent for trial, the service of copies of the documents containing the evidence on which the charge or charges are based.

(2) A prosecutor who applies under rule 15.1 because he wants the court to order a trial without a jury under section 44 of the *Criminal Justice Act* 2003 (jury tampering) must do so as soon as reasonably practicable where the reasons do not arise until after that time limit has expired.

(3) The court may extend the time limit, even after it has expired.

Representations concerning an application

G–69   **15.3**—(1) A party who wants to make written representations concerning an application made under rule 15.1 must—

(a) do so within 7 days of receiving a copy of that application; and

(b) serve those representations on the court officer and all other parties.

(2) A defendant who wants to oppose an application for an order that the trial will be conducted without a jury under section 43 or section 44 of the *Criminal Justice Act* 2003 must serve written representations under this rule, including a short explanation of the reasons for opposing that application.

Determination of application

G–70   **15.4**—(1) Where an application has been made under rule 15.1(2), the court must hold a preparatory hearing.

(2) Other applications made under rule 15.1 should normally be determined without a hearing.

(3) The court officer must serve on the parties in the case, in the form set out in the Practice Direction—

(a) notice of the determination of an application made under rule 15.1; and

(b) an order for a preparatory hearing made by the court of its own initiative, including one that the court is required to make.

Orders for disclosure by prosecution or defence

G–71   **15.5**—(1) Any disclosure order under section 9 of the *Criminal Justice Act* 1987, or section 31 of the *Criminal Procedure and Investigations Act* 1996, must identify any documents that are required to be prepared and served by the prosecutor under that order.

(2) A disclosure order under either of those sections does not require a defendant to disclose who will give evidence, except to the extent that disclosure is required—

(a) by section 6A(2) of the 1996 Act (disclosure of alibi); or

(b) by Part 24 of these Rules (disclosure of expert evidence).

(3) The court officer must serve notice of the order, in the relevant form set out in the Practice Direction, on the parties.

G–72   **15.6** [*Revoked*]

PART 16

RESTRICTIONS ON REPORTING AND PUBLIC ACCESS

Application for a reporting direction under section 46(6) of the Youth Justice and Criminal Evidence Act 1999

G–73   **16.1**—(1) An application for a reporting direction made by a party to any criminal proceedings, in relation to a witness in those proceedings, must be made in the form set out in the Practice Direction or orally under rule 16.3.

(2) If an application for a reporting direction is made in writing, the applicant shall send that application to the court officer and copies shall be sent at the same time to every other party to those proceedings.

Opposing an application for a reporting direction under section 46(6) of the Youth Justice and Criminal Evidence Act 1999

G–74   **16.2**—(1) If an application for a reporting direction is made in writing, any party to the proceedings who wishes to oppose that application must notify the applicant and the court officer in writing of his opposition and give reasons for it.

(2) A person opposing an application must state in the written notification whether he disputes that the—

(a) witness is eligible for protection under section 46 of the *Youth Justice and Criminal Evidence Act* 1999; or

(b) granting of protection would be likely to improve the quality of the evidence given by the witness or the level of co-operation given by the witness to any party to the proceedings in connection with that party's preparation of its case.

(3) The notification under paragraph (1) must be given within five business days of the date the application was served on him unless an extension of time is granted under rule 16.6.

Urgent action on an application under section 46(6) of the Youth Justice and Criminal Evidence Act 1999

16.3—(1) The court may give a reporting direction under section 46 of the *Youth Justice and Criminal Evidence Act* 1999 in relation to a witness in those proceedings, notwithstanding that the five business days specified in rule 16.2(3) have not expired if—   **G–75**

(a) an application is made to it for the purposes of this rule; and

(b) it is satisfied that, due to exceptional circumstances, it is appropriate to do so.

(2) Any party to the proceedings may make the application under paragraph (1) whether or not an application has already been made under rule 16.1.

(3) An application under paragraph (1) may be made orally or in writing.

(4) If an application is made orally, the court may hear and take into account representations made to it by any person who in the court's view has a legitimate interest in the application before it.

(5) The application must specify the exceptional circumstances on which the applicant relies.

Excepting direction under section 46(9) of the Youth Justice and Criminal Evidence Act 1999

16.4—(1) An application for an excepting direction under section 46(9) of the *Youth Justice and Criminal Evidence Act* 1999 (a direction dispensing with restrictions imposed by a reporting direction) may be made by—   **G–76**

(a) any party to those proceedings; or

(b) any person who, although not a party to the proceedings, is directly affected by a reporting direction given in relation to a witness in those proceedings.

(2) If an application for an excepting direction is made, the applicant must state why—

(a) the effect of a reporting direction imposed places a substantial and unreasonable restriction on the reporting of the proceedings; and

(b) it is in the public interest to remove or relax those restrictions.

(3) An application for an excepting direction may be made in writing, pursuant to paragraph (4), at any time after the commencement of the proceedings in the court or orally at a hearing of an application for a reporting direction.

(4) If the application for an excepting direction is made in writing it must be in the form set out in the Practice Direction and the applicant shall send that application to the court officer and copies shall be sent at the same time to every party to those proceedings.

(5) Any person served with a copy of an application for an excepting direction who wishes to oppose it, must notify the applicant and the court officer in writing of his opposition and give reasons for it.

(6) The notification under paragraph (5) must be given within five business days of the date the application was served on him unless an extension of time is granted under rule 16.6.

Variation or revocation of a reporting or excepting direction under section 46 of the Youth Justice and Criminal Evidence Act 1999

16.5—(1) An application for the court to—   **G–77**

(a) revoke a reporting direction; or

(b) vary or revoke an excepting direction,

may be made to the court at any time after the commencement of the proceedings in the court.

(2) An application under paragraph (1) may be made by a party to the proceedings in which the direction was issued, or by a person who, although not a party to those proceedings, is in the opinion of the court directly affected by the direction.

(3) An application under paragraph (1) must be made in writing and the applicant shall send that application to the officer of the court in which the proceedings commenced, and at the same time copies of the application shall be sent to every party or, as the case may be, every party to the proceedings.

(4) The applicant must set out in his application the reasons why he seeks to have the direction varied or, as the case may be, revoked.

(5) Any person served with a copy of an application who wishes to oppose it, must notify the applicant and the court officer in writing of his opposition and give reasons for it.

(6) The notification under paragraph (5) must be given within five business days of the date the application was served on him unless an extension of time is granted under rule 16.6.

Application for an extension of time in proceedings under section 46 of the Youth Justice and Criminal Evidence Act 1999

G–78   **16.6**—(1) An application may be made in writing to extend the period of time for notification under rule 16.2(3), rule 16.4(6) or rule 16.5(6) before that period has expired.

(2) An application must be accompanied by a statement setting out the reasons why the applicant is unable to give notification within that period.

(3) An application must be sent to the court officer and a copy of the application must be sent at the same time to the applicant.

Decision of the court on an application under section 46 of the Youth Justice and Criminal Evidence Act 1999

G–79   **16.7**—(1) The court may—

> (a) determine any application made under rules 16.1 and rules 16.3 to 16.6 without a hearing; or
> (b) direct a hearing of any application.

(2) The court officer shall notify all the parties of the court's decision as soon as reasonably practicable.

(3) If a hearing of an application is to take place, the court officer shall notify each party to the proceedings of the time and place of the hearing.

(4) A court may hear and take into account representations made to it by any person who in the court's view has a legitimate interest in the application before it.

Proceedings sent or transferred to the Crown Court with direction under section 46 of the Youth Justice and Criminal Evidence Act 1999 in force

G–80   **16.8** Where proceedings in which reporting directions or excepting directions have been ordered are sent or transferred from a magistrates' court to the Crown Court, the magistrates' court officer shall forward copies of all relevant directions to the Crown Court officer at the place to which the proceedings are sent or transferred.

Hearings in camera and applications under section 46 of the Youth Justice and Criminal Evidence Act 1999

G–81   **16.9** If in any proceedings, a prosecutor or defendant has served notice under rule 16.10 of his intention to apply for an order that all or part of a trial be held in camera, any application under this Part relating to a witness in those proceedings need not identify the witness by name and date of birth.

Application to hold a Crown Court trial in camera

G–82   **16.10**—(1) Where a prosecutor or a defendant intends to apply for an order that all or part of a trial be held in camera for reasons of national security or for the protection of the identity of a witness or any other person, he shall not less than 7 days before the date on which the trial is expected to begin serve a notice in writing to that effect on the Crown Court officer and the prosecutor or the defendant as the case may be.

(2) On receiving such notice, the court officer shall forthwith cause a copy thereof to be displayed in a prominent place within the precincts of the Court.

(3) An application by a prosecutor or a defendant who has served such a notice for an order that all or part of a trial be heard in camera shall, unless the Court orders otherwise, be made in camera, after the defendant has been arraigned but before the jury has been sworn and, if such an order is made, the trial shall be adjourned until whichever of the following shall be appropriate—

> (a) 24 hours after the making of the order, where no application for leave to appeal from the order is made; or

(b) after the determination of an application for leave to appeal, where the application is dismissed; or

(c) after the determination of the appeal, where leave to appeal is granted.

Crown Court hearings in chambers

16.11—(1) The criminal jurisdiction of the Crown Court specified in the following paragraph **G–83** may be exercised by a judge of the Crown Court sitting in chambers.

(2) The said jurisdiction is—

(a) hearing applications for bail;

(b) issuing a summons or warrant;

(c) hearing any application relating to procedural matters preliminary or incidental to criminal proceedings in the Crown Court, including applications relating to legal aid;

(d) jurisdiction under rules 12.2 (listing first appearance of accused sent for trial), 28.3 (application for witness summons), 63.2(5) (extending time for appeal against decision of magistrates' court), and 64.7 (application to state case for consideration of High Court);

(e) hearing an application under section 41(2) of the *Youth Justice and Criminal Evidence Act* 1999 (evidence of complainant's previous sexual history);

(f) hearing applications under section 22(3) of the *Prosecution of Offences Act* 1985 (extension or further extension of custody time limit imposed by regulations made under section 22(1) of that Act);

(g) hearing an appeal brought by an accused under section 22(7) of the 1985 Act against a decision of a magistrates' court to extend, or further extend, such a time limit, or brought by the prosecution under section 22(8) of the same Act against a decision of a magistrates' court to refuse to extend, or further extend, such a time limit;

(h) hearing appeals under section 1 of the *Bail (Amendment) Act* 1993 (against grant of bail by magistrates' court); and

(i) hearing appeals under section 16 of the *Criminal Justice Act* 2003 (against condition of bail imposed by magistrates' court).

PART 17

EXTRADITION

Refusal to make an order of committal

17.1—(1) Where a magistrates' court refuses to make an order of committal in relation to a **G–84** person in respect of the offence or, as the case may be, any of the offences to which the authority to proceed relates and the state, country or colony seeking the surrender of that person immediately informs the court that it intends to make an application to the court to state a case for the opinion of the High Court, if the magistrates' court makes an order in accordance with section 10(2) of the *Extradition Act* 1989 releasing that person on bail, the court officer shall forthwith send a copy of that order to the Administrative Court Office.

(2) Where a magistrates' court refuses to make an order of committal in relation to a person in respect of the offence or, as the case may be, any of the offences to which the authority to proceed relates and the state, country or colony seeking his surrender wishes to apply to the court to state a case for the opinion of the High Court under section 10(1) of the 1989 Act, such application must be made to the magistrates' court within the period of 21 days following the day on which the court refuses to make the order of committal unless the court grants a longer period within which the application is to be made.

(3) Such an application shall be made in writing and shall identify the question or questions of law on which the opinion of the High Court is sought.

(4) Within 21 days after receipt of an application to state a case under section 10(1) of the 1989 Act, the magistrates' court officer shall send a draft case to the solicitor for the state, country or colony and to the person whose surrender is sought or his solicitor and shall allow each party 21 days within which to make representations thereon; within 21 days after the latest day on which such representations may be made the court of committal shall, after considering any such representations and making such adjustments, if any,

to the draft case as it thinks fit, state and sign the case which the court officer shall forth-with send to the solicitor for the state, country or colony.

Notice of waiver

G–85   **17.2**—(1) A notice given under section 14 of, or paragraph 9 of Schedule 1 to, the *Extradition Act* 1989 (notice of waiver under the simplified procedure) shall be in the form set out in the Practice Direction or a form to the like effect.

(2) Such a notice shall be signed in the presence of the Senior District Judge (Chief Magistrate) or another District Judge (Magistrates' Courts) designated by him for the purposes of the Act, a justice of the peace or a justices' clerk.

(3) Any such notice given by a person in custody shall be delivered to the Governor of the prison in whose custody he is.

(4) If a person on bail gives such notice he shall deliver it to, or send it by post in a registered letter or by recorded delivery service addressed to, the Under Secretary of State, Home Office, London SW1H 9AT.

Notice of consent

G–86   **17.3**—(1) A person arrested in pursuance of a warrant under section 8 of or paragraph 5 of Schedule 1 to the *Extradition Act* 1989 may at any time consent to his return; and where such consent is given in accordance with the following provisions of this rule, the Senior District Judge (Chief Magistrate) or another District Judge (Magistrates' Courts) designated by him for the purposes of the Act may order the committal for return of that person in accordance with section 14(2) of that Act or, as the case may be, paragraph 9(2) of Schedule 1 to the Act.

(2) A notice of consent for the purposes of this rule shall be given in the form set out in the Practice Direction and shall be signed in the presence of the Senior District Judge (Chief Magistrate) or another District Judge (Magistrates' Courts) designated by him for the purposes of the 1989 Act.

Notice of consent (parties to 1995 Convention)

G–87   **17.4**—(1) This rule applies as between the United Kingdom and states other than the Republic of Ireland that are parties to the Convention drawn up on the basis of Article 31 of the Treaty on European Union on Simplified Extradition Procedures between the Member States of the European Union, in relation to which section 14A of the *Extradition Act* 1989 applies by virtue of section 34A and Schedule 1A of that Act.

(2) Notice of consent for the purposes of section 14A(3) of the 1989 Act shall be given in the form set out in the Practice Direction and shall be signed in the presence of the Senior District Judge (Chief Magistrate) or another District Judge (Magistrates' Courts) designated by him for the purposes of that Act.

(3) A Senior District Judge (Chief Magistrate) or another District Judge (Magistrates' Courts) designated by him for the purposes of the Act may order the committal for return of a person if he gives consent under section 14A of the 1989 Act in accordance with paragraph (2) above before he is committed under section 9 of that Act.

Consent to early removal to Republic of Ireland

G–88   **17.5**—(1) A notice given under section 3(1)(a) of the *Backing of Warrants (Republic of Ireland) Act* 1965 (consent to surrender earlier than is otherwise permitted) shall be signed in the presence of a justice of the peace or a justices' clerk.

(2) Any such notice given by a person in custody shall be delivered to the Governor of the prison in whose custody he is.

(3) If a person on bail gives such notice, he shall deliver it to, or send it by post in a registered letter or by recorded delivery service addressed to, the police officer in charge of the police station specified in his recognizance.

(4) Any such notice shall be attached to the warrant ordering the surrender of that person.

Bail pending removal to Republic of Ireland

G–89   **17.6**—(1) The person taking the recognizance of a person remanded on bail under section 2(1) or 4(3) of the *Backing of Warrants (Republic of Ireland) Act* 1965 shall furnish a copy of the recognizance to the police officer in charge of the police station specified in the recognizance.

(2) The court officer for a magistrates' court which ordered a person to be surrendered and remanded him on bail shall deliver to, or send by post in a registered letter or by recorded delivery service addressed to, the police officer in charge of the police station specified in the recognizance the warrant ordering the person to be surrendered.

(3) The court officer for a magistrates' court which refused to order a person to be delivered under section 2 of the 1965 Act but made an order in accordance with section 2A(2) of that Act releasing that person on bail, upon the chief officer of police immediately informing the court that he intended to make an application to the court to state a case for the opinion of the High Court, shall forthwith send a copy of that order to the Administrative Court Office.

Delivery of warrant issued in Republic of Ireland

17.7—(1) The court officer for a magistrates' court which ordered a person to be surrendered **G–90** under section 2(1) of the *Backing of Warrants (Republic of Ireland) Act* 1965 shall deliver to, or send by post in a registered letter or by recorded delivery service addressed to—

(a) if he is remanded in custody under section 5(1)(a) of the 1965 Act, the prison Governor to whose custody he is committed;

(b) if he is remanded on bail under section 5(1)(b) of the 1965 Act, the police officer in charge of the police station specified in the recognizance; or

(c) if he is committed to the custody of a constable pending the taking from him of a recognizance under section 5(1) of the 1965 Act, the police officer in charge of the police station specified in the warrant of commitment,

the warrant of arrest issued by a judicial authority in the Republic of Ireland and endorsed in accordance with section 1 of the 1965 Act.

(2) The Governor or police officer to whom the said warrant of arrest is delivered or sent shall arrange for it to be given to the member of the police force of the Republic into whose custody the person is delivered when the person is so delivered.

Verification of warrant etc. issued in Republic of Ireland

17.8—(1) A document purporting to be a warrant issued by a judicial authority in the Re- **G–91** public of Ireland shall, for the purposes of section 7(a) of the *Backing of Warrants (Republic of Ireland) Act* 1965, be verified by a certificate purporting to be signed by a judicial authority, a clerk of a court or a member of the police force of the Republic and certifying that the document is a warrant and is issued by a judge or justice of a court or a peace commissioner.

(2) A document purporting to be a copy of a summons issued by a judicial authority in the Republic shall, for the purposes of section 7(a) of the 1965 Act, be verified by a certificate purporting to be signed by a judicial authority, a clerk of a court or a member of the police force of the Republic and certifying that the document is a true copy of such a summons.

(3) A deposition purporting to have been made in the Republic, or affidavit or written statement purporting to have been sworn therein, shall, for the purposes of section 7(c) of the 1965 Act, be verified by a certificate purporting to be signed by the person before whom it was sworn and certifying that it was so sworn.

Application to state a case where court declines to order removal to Republic of Ireland

17.9—(1) Where a magistrates' court refuses to make an order in relation to a person under **G–92** section 2 of the *Backing of Warrants (Republic of Ireland) Act* 1965, any application to the court under section 2A(1) of that Act to state a case for the opinion of the High Court on any question of law arising in the proceedings must be made to the court by the chief officer of police within the period of 21 days following the day on which the order was refused, unless the court grants a longer period within which the application is to be made.

(2) Such an application shall be made in writing and shall identify the question or questions of law on which the opinion of the High Court is sought.

Draft case where court declines to order removal to Republic of Ireland

17.10 Within 21 days after receipt of an application to state a case under section 2A(1) of the **G–93** *Backing of Warrants (Republic of Ireland) Act* 1965, the magistrates' court officer shall send a draft case to the applicant or his solicitor and to the person to whom the warrant relates or his solicitor and shall allow each party 21 days within which to make representations thereon; within 21 days after the latest day on which such representations may be made the court shall, after considering such representations and making such adjustments, if any, to the draft case as it thinks fit, state and sign the case which the court officer shall forthwith send to the applicant or his solicitor.

Forms for proceedings for removal to Republic of Ireland
G–94   **17.11** Where a requirement is imposed by the *Backing of Warrants (Republic of Ireland) Act* 1965 for the use of a form, and an appropriate form is contained in the Practice Direction, that form shall be used.

PART 18

WARRANTS

Scope of this Part and interpretation
G–95   **18.1**—(1) This Part applies to any warrant issued by a justice of the peace.
(2) Where a rule applies to some of those warrants and not others, it says so.
(3) In this Part, the "relevant person" is the person against whom the warrant is issued.

Warrants must be signed
G–96   **18.2** Every warrant under the *Magistrates' Courts Act* 1980 must be signed by the justice issuing it, unless rule 5.3 permits the justices' clerk to sign it.

Warrants issued when the court office is closed
G–97   **18.3**—(1) If a warrant is issued when the court office is closed, the applicant must —
        (a) serve on the court officer any information on which that warrant is issued; and
        (b) do so within 72 hours of that warrant being issued.
(2) In this rule, the court office is the office for the local justice area in which the justice is acting when he issues the warrant.

Commitment to custody must be by warrant
G–98   **18.4**—(1) A justice of the peace must issue a warrant of commitment when committing a person to—
        (a) a prison;
        (b) a young offender institution;
        (c) a remand centre;
        (d) detention at a police station under section 128(7) of the *Magistrates' Courts* 1980 Act; or
        (e) customs detention under section 152 of the *Criminal Justice Act* 1988.

Terms of a warrant of arrest
G–99   **18.5** A warrant of arrest must require the persons to whom it is directed to arrest the relevant person.

Terms of a warrant of commitment or detention: general rules
G–100   **18.6**—(1) A warrant of commitment or detention must require—
        (a) the persons to whom it is directed to—
            (i)   arrest the relevant person, if he is at large,
            (ii) take him to the prison or place specified in the warrant, and
            (iii) deliver him with the warrant to the governor or keeper of that prison or place; and
        (b) the governor or keeper to keep the relevant person in custody at that prison or place—
            (i)   for as long as the warrant requires, or
            (ii) until he is delivered, in accordance with the law, to the court or other proper place or person.

(2) Where the justice issuing a warrant of commitment or detention is aware that the relevant person is already detained in a prison or other place of detention, the warrant must be delivered to the governor or keeper of that prison or place.

Terms of a warrant committing a person to customs detention
18.7—(1) A warrant committing a person to customs detention under section 152 of the **G–101** 1988 Act must—
   (a) be directed to the officers of Her Majesty's Revenue and Customs; and
   (b) require those officers to keep the person committed in their custody, unless in the meantime he be otherwise delivered, in accordance with the law, to the court or other proper place or person, for a period (not exceeding 192 hours) specified in the warrant.
(2) Rules 18.6(1), 18.10 and 18.12 do not apply where this rule applies.

Form of warrant where male aged 15 or 16 is committed
18.8—(1) This rule applies where a male aged 15 or 16 years is remanded or committed to **G–102** —
   (a) local authority accommodation, with a requirement that he be placed and kept in secure accommodation;
   (b) a remand centre; or
   (c) a prison.
(2) The court must include in the warrant of commitment a statement of any declaration that is required in connection with that remand or committal.

Information to be included in a warrant
18.9— A warrant of arrest, commitment or detention must contain the following informa- **G–103** tion—
   (a) the name or a description of the relevant person; and
   (b) either—
      (i) a statement of the offence with which the relevant person is charged,
      (ii) a statement of the offence of which the person to be committed or detained was convicted; or
      (iii) any other ground on which the warrant is issued.

Persons who may execute a warrant
18.10— A warrant of arrest, commitment or detention may be executed by— **G–104**
   (a) the persons to whom it is directed; or
   (b) by any of the following persons, whether or not it was directed to them—
      (i) a constable for any police area in England and Wales, acting in his own police area, and
      (ii) any person authorised under section 125A (civilian enforcement officers) or section 125B (approved enforcement agencies) of the *Magistrates' Courts Act* 1980.

Making an arrest under a warrant
18.11—(1) The person executing a warrant of arrest, commitment or detention must, when **G–105** arresting the relevant person—
   (a) either—
      (i) show the warrant (if he has it with him) to the relevant person, or
      (ii) tell the relevant person where the warrant is and what arrangements can be made to let that person inspect it;
   (b) explain, in ordinary language, the charge and the reason for the arrest; and
   (c) (unless he is a constable in uniform) show documentary proof of his identity.
(2) If the person executing the warrant is one of the persons referred to in rule 18.10(b)(ii) (civilian enforcement officers or approved enforcement agencies), he must also show the relevant person a written statement under section 125A(4) or section 125B(4) of the *Magistrates' Courts Act* 1980, as appropriate.

Place of detention

G–106   **18.12**—(1) This rule applies to any warrant of commitment or detention.

(2) The person executing the warrant is required to take the relevant person to the prison or place of detention specified in the warrant.

(3) But where it is not immediately practicable to do so, or where there is some other good reason, the relevant person may be taken to any prison or place where he may be lawfully detained until such time when he can be taken to the prison or place specified in the warrant.

(4) If (and for as long as) the relevant person is detained in a place other than the one specified in the warrant, the warrant will have effect as if it specified the place where he is in fact being detained.

(5) The court must be kept informed of the prison or place where the relevant person is in fact being detained.

(6) The governor or keeper of the prison or place, to which the relevant person is delivered, must give a receipt on delivery.

Duration of detention where bail is granted subject to pre-release conditions

G–107   **18.13**—(1) This rule applies where a magistrates' court—

(a) grants bail to a person subject to conditions which must be met prior to release on bail; and

(b) commits that person to custody until those conditions are satisfied.

(2) The warrant of commitment must require the governor or keeper of the prison or place of detention to bring the relevant person to court either before or at the end of a period of 8 clear days from the date the warrant was issued, unless section 128(3A) or section 128A of the *Magistrates' Courts Act* 1980 applies to permit a longer period.

Validity of warrants that contain errors

G–108   **18.14**—   A warrant of commitment or detention will not be invalidated on the ground that it contains an error, provided that the warrant—

(a) is issued in relation to a valid—

(i) conviction, or

(ii) order requiring the relevant person to do, or to abstain from doing, something; and

(b) it states that it is issued in relation to that conviction or order.

Circumstances in which a warrant will cease to have effect

G–109   **18.15**—(1) A warrant issued under any of the provisions listed in paragraph (2) will cease to have effect when—

(a) the sum in respect of which the warrant is issued (together with the costs and charges of commitment, if any) is paid to the person who is executing the warrant;

(b) that sum is offered to, but refused by, the person who is executing the warrant; or

(c) a receipt for that sum given by—

(i) the court officer for the court which issued the warrant, or

(ii) the charging or billing authority,

is produced to the person who is executing the warrant.

(2) Those provisions are—

(a) section 76 (warrant to enforce fines and other sums);

(b) section 83(1) and (2) (warrant to secure attendance of offender for purposes of section 82);

(c) section 86(4) (warrant to arrest offender following failure to appear on day fixed for means inquiry);

(d) section 136 (committal to custody overnight at police station) of the Magistrates' Courts Act 1980.

(3) No person may execute, or continue to execute, a warrant that ceases to have effect under this rule.

Warrant endorsed for bail (record to be kept)

G–110   **18.16**—   A person executing a warrant of arrest that is endorsed for bail under section 117 of the Magistrates' Courts Act 1980 must—

   (a) make a record stating—
      (i) the name of the person arrested,
      (ii) the charge and the reason for the arrest,
      (iii) the fact that the person is to be released on bail,
      (iv) the date, time and place at which the person is required to appear before the court, and
      (v) any other details which he considers to be relevant; and
   (b) after making the record—
      (i) sign the record,
      (ii) invite the person arrested to sign the record and, if they refuse, make a note of that refusal on the record,
      (iii) make a copy of the record and give it to the person arrested, and
      (iv) send the original record to the court officer for the court which issued the warrant.

PART 19

BAIL IN MAGISTRATES' COURTS AND THE CROWN COURT

Application to a magistrates' court to vary conditions of police bail

19.1—(1) An application under section 43B(1) of the *Magistrates' Courts Act* of 1980 or section 47(1E) of the *Police and Criminal Evidence Act* 1984 shall— **G–111**
   (a) be made in writing;
   (b) contain a statement of the grounds upon which it is made;
   (c) where the applicant has been bailed following charge, specify the offence with which he was charged and in any other case, specify the offence under investigation.
   (d) specify, or be accompanied by a copy of the note of, the reasons given by the custody officer for imposing or varying the conditions of bail; and
   (e) specify the name and address of any surety provided by the applicant before his release on bail to secure his surrender to custody.
  (2) Any such application shall be sent to the court officer for—
   (a) the magistrates' court appointed by the custody officer as the court before which the applicant has a duty to appear; or
   (b) if no such court has been appointed, a magistrates' court acting for the local justice area in which the police station at which the applicant was granted bail or at which the conditions of his bail were varied, as the case may be, is situated.
  (3) The court officer to whom an application is sent under paragraph (2) above shall serve notice in writing of the date, time and place fixed for the hearing of the application on—
   (a) the applicant;
   (b) the prosecutor, or if the applicant has not been charged, the chief officer of police or other investigator, together with a copy of the application; and
   (c) any surety in connection with bail in criminal proceedings granted to, or the conditions of which were varied by a custody officer in relation to, the applicant.
  (4) The time fixed for the hearing shall be not later than 72 hours after receipt of the application. In reckoning for the purposes of this paragraph any period of 72 hours, no account shall be taken of Christmas Day, Boxing Day, Good Friday, any bank holiday, or any Saturday or Sunday.
  (5) [Revoked]
  (6) If the magistrates' court hearing an application under section 43B(1) of the 1980 Act or section 47(1E) of the *Police and Criminal Evidence Act* 1984 discharges or enlarges any recognizance entered into by any surety or increases or reduces the amount in which that person is bound, the court officer shall forthwith give notice thereof to the applicant and to any such surety.
  (7) In this rule, "the applicant" means the person making an application under section 43B(1) of the 1980 Act or section 47(1E) of the *Police and Criminal Evidence Act* 1984.

Application to a magistrates' court to reconsider grant of police bail

19.2—(1) The appropriate court for the purposes of section 5B of the *Bail Act* 1976 in relation to the decision of a constable to grant bail shall be— **G–112**

    (a) the magistrates' court appointed by the custody officer as the court before which the person to whom bail was granted has a duty to appear; or

    (b) if no such court has been appointed, a magistrates' court acting for the local justice area in which the police station at which bail was granted is situated.

(2) An application under section 5B(1) of the 1976 Act shall—

    (a) be made in writing;

    (b) contain a statement of the grounds on which it is made;

    (c) specify the offence which the proceedings in which bail was granted were connected with, or for;

    (d) specify the decision to be reconsidered (including any conditions of bail which have been imposed and why they have been imposed);

    (e) specify the name and address of any surety provided by the person to whom the application relates to secure his surrender to custody; and

    (f) contain notice of the powers available to the court under section 5B of the 1976 Act.

(3) The court officer to whom an application is sent under paragraph (2) above shall serve notice in writing of the date, time and place fixed for the hearing of the application on—

    (a) the prosecutor who made the application;

    (b) the person to whom bail was granted together with a copy of the application; and

    (c) any surety specified in the application.

(4) The time fixed for the hearing shall be not later than 72 hours after receipt of the application. In reckoning for the purpose of this paragraph any period of 72 hours, no account shall be taken of Christmas Day, Good Friday, any bank holiday or any Sunday.

(5) [*Revoked*]

(6) At the hearing of an application under section 5B of the 1976 Act the court shall consider any representations made by the person affected (whether in writing or orally) before taking any decision under that section with respect to him; and, where the person affected does not appear before the court, the court shall not take such a decision unless it is proved to the satisfaction of the court, on oath or in the manner set out by rule 4.2(1), that the notice required to be given under paragraph (3) of this rule was served on him before the hearing.

(7) Where the court proceeds in the absence of the person affected in accordance with paragraph (6)—

    (a) if the decision of the court is to vary the conditions of bail or impose conditions in respect of bail which has been granted unconditionally, the court officer shall notify the person affected;

    (b) if the decision of the court is to withhold bail, the order of the court under section 5B(5)(b) of the 1976 Act (surrender to custody) shall be signed by the justice issuing it or state his name and be authenticated by the signature of the clerk of the court.

(8) [*Revoked*]

Notice of change of time for appearance before magistrates' court

G–113   **19.3** Where—

    (a) a person has been granted bail under the *Police and Criminal Evidence Act* 1984 subject to a duty to appear before a magistrates' court and the court before which he is to appear appoints a later time at which he is to appear; or

    (b) a magistrates' court further remands a person on bail under section 129 of the *Magistrates' Courts Act* 1980 in his absence,

it shall give him and his sureties, if any, notice thereof.

Directions by a magistrates' court as to security, etc

G–114   **19.4** Where a magistrates' court, under section 3(5) or (6) of the *Bail Act* 1976, imposes any requirement to be complied with before a person's release on bail, the court may give directions as to the manner in which and the person or persons before whom the requirement may be complied with.

Requirements to be complied with before release on bail granted by a magistrates' court

G–115   **19.5**—(1) Where a magistrates' court has fixed the amount in which a person (including any surety) is to be bound by a recognizance, the recognizance may be entered into—

(a) in the case of a surety where the accused is in a prison or other place of detention, before the governor or keeper of the prison or place as well as before the persons mentioned in section 8(4)(a) of the *Bail Act* 1976;

(b) in any other case, before a justice of the peace, a justices' clerk, a magistrates' court officer, a police officer who either is of the rank of inspector or above or is in charge of a police station or, if the person to be bound is in a prison or other place of detention, before the governor or keeper of the prison or place; or

(c) where a person other than a police officer is authorised under section 125A or 125B of the *Magistrates' Courts Act* 1980 to execute a warrant of arrest providing for a recognizance to be entered into by the person arrested (but not by any other person), before the person executing the warrant.

(2) The court officer for a magistrates' court which has fixed the amount in which a person (including any surety) is to be bound by a recognizance or, under section 3(5), (6) or (6A) of the 1976 Act imposed any requirement to be complied with before a person's release on bail or any condition of bail shall issue a certificate showing the amount and conditions, if any, of the recognizance, or as the case may be, containing a statement of the requirement or condition of bail; and a person authorised to take the recognizance or do anything in relation to the compliance with such requirement or condition of bail shall not be required to take or do it without production of such a certificate as aforesaid.

(3) If any person proposed as a surety for a person committed to custody by a magistrates' court produces to the governor or keeper of the prison or other place of detention in which the person so committed is detained a certificate to the effect that he is acceptable as a surety, signed by any of the justices composing the court or the clerk of the court and signed in the margin by the person proposed as surety, the governor or keeper shall take the recognizance of the person so proposed.

(4) Where the recognizance of any person committed to custody by a magistrates' court or of any surety of such a person is taken by any person other than the court which committed the first-mentioned person to custody, the person taking the recognizance shall send it to the court officer for that court:

Provided that, in the case of a surety, if the person committed has been committed to the Crown Court for trial or under any of the enactments mentioned in rule 43.1(1), the person taking the recognizance shall send it to the Crown Court officer.

Notice to governor of prison, etc, where release from custody is ordered by a magistrates' court

19.6 Where a magistrates' court has, with a view to the release on bail of a person in custody, **G–116** fixed the amount in which he or any surety of such a person shall be bound or, under section 3(5), (6) or (6A) of the *Bail Act* 1976, imposed any requirement to be complied with before his release or any condition of bail—

(a) the magistrates' court officer shall give notice thereof to the governor or keeper of the prison or place where that person is detained by sending him such a certificate as is mentioned in rule 19.5(2); and

(b) any person authorised to take the recognizance of a surety or do anything in relation to the compliance with such requirement shall, on taking or doing it, send notice thereof by post to the said governor or keeper and, in the case of a recognizance of a surety, shall give a copy of the notice to the surety.

Release when notice received by governor of prison that recognizances have been taken or requirements complied with

19.7 Where a magistrates' court has, with a view to the release on bail of a person in custody, **G–117** fixed the amount in which he or any surety of such a person shall be bound or, under section 3(5) or (6) of the *Bail Act* 1976, imposed any requirement to be complied with before his release and given notice thereof in accordance with this Part to the governor or keeper of the prison or place where that person is detained, the governor or keeper shall, when satisfied that the recognizances of all sureties required have been taken and that all such requirements have been complied with, and unless he is in custody for some other cause, release him.

Notice from a magistrates' court of enlargement of recognizances

19.8—(1) If a magistrates' court before which any person is bound by a recognizance to ap- **G–118** pear enlarges the recognizance to a later time under section 129 of the *Magistrates' Courts Act* 1980 in his absence, it shall give him and his sureties, if any, notice thereof.

Appendices

(2) If a magistrates' court, under section 129(4) of the 1980 Act, enlarges the recognizance of a surety for a person committed for trial on bail, it shall give the surety notice thereof.

Further remand of minors by a youth court

G–119   **19.9** Where a child or young person has been remanded, and the period of remand is extended in his absence in accordance with section 48 of the Children and Young Persons Act 1933, notice shall be given to him and his sureties (if any) of the date at which he will be required to appear before the court.

Notes of argument in magistrates' court bail hearings

G–120   **19.10** Where a magistrates' court hears full argument as to bail, the clerk of the court shall take a note of that argument.

Bail records to be entered in register of magistrates' court

G–121   **19.11** Any record required by section 5 of the *Bail Act* 1976 to be made by a magistrates' court (together with any note of reasons required by section 5(4) to be included and the particulars set out in any certificate granted under section 5(6A)) shall be made by way of an entry in the register.

Notification of bail decision by magistrate after arrest while on bail

G–122   **19.12** Where a person who has been released on bail and is under a duty to surrender into the custody of a court is brought under section 7(4)(a) of the *Bail Act* 1976 before a justice of the peace, the justice shall cause a copy of the record made in pursuance of section 5 of that Act relating to his decision under section 7(5) of that Act in respect of that person to be sent to the court officer for that court:

Provided that this rule shall not apply where the court is a magistrates' court acting for the same local justice area as that for which the justice acts.

Transfer of remand hearings

G–123   **19.13**—(1) Where a magistrates' court, under section 130(1) of the *Magistrates' Courts Act* 1980, orders that an accused who has been remanded in custody be brought up for any subsequent remands before an alternate magistrates' court, the court officer for the first-mentioned court shall, as soon as practicable after the making of the order and in any case within 2 days thereafter (not counting Sundays, Good Friday, Christmas Day or bank holidays), send to the court officer for the alternate court—

    (a) a statement indicating the offence or offences charged;

    (b) a copy of the record made by the first-mentioned court in pursuance of section 5 of the *Bail Act* 1976 relating to the withholding of bail in respect of the accused when he was last remanded in custody;

    (c) a copy of any representation order previously made in the same case;

    (d) a copy of any application for a representation order;

    (e) if the first-mentioned court has made an order under section 8(2) of the 1980 Act (removal of restrictions on reports of committal proceedings), a statement to that effect.

    (f) a statement indicating whether or not the accused has a solicitor acting for him in the case and has consented to the hearing and determination in his absence of any application for his remand on an adjournment of the case under sections 5, 10(1) and 18(4) of the 1980 Act together with a statement indicating whether or not that consent has been withdrawn;

    (g) a statement indicating the occasions, if any, on which the accused has been remanded under section 128(3A) of the 1980 Act without being brought before the first-mentioned court; and

    (h) if the first-mentioned court remands the accused under section 128A of the 1980 Act on the occasion upon which it makes the order under section 130(1) of that Act, a statement indicating the date set under section 128A(2) of that Act.

(2) Where the first-mentioned court is satisfied as mentioned in section 128(3A) of the 1980 Act, paragraph (1) shall have effect as if for the words "an accused who has been remanded in custody be brought up for any subsequent remands before" there were

substituted the words "applications for any subsequent remands of the accused be made to".

(3) The court officer for an alternate magistrates' court before which an accused who has been remanded in custody is brought up for any subsequent remands in pursuance of an order made as aforesaid shall, as soon as practicable after the order ceases to be in force and in any case within 2 days thereafter (not counting Sundays, Good Friday, Christmas Day or bank holidays), send to the court officer for the magistrates' court which made the order—

(a) a copy of the record made by the alternate court in pursuance of section 5 of the 1976 Act relating to the grant or withholding of bail in respect of the accused when he was last remanded in custody or on bail;

(b) a copy of any representation order made by the alternate court;

(c) a copy of any application for a representation order made to the alternate court;

(d) if the alternate court has made an order under section 8(2) of the 1980 Act (removal of restrictions on reports of committal proceedings), a statement to that effect;

(e) a statement indicating whether or not the accused has a solicitor acting for him in the case and has consented to the hearing and determination in his absence of any application for his remand on an adjournment of the case under sections 5, 10(1) and 18(4) of the 1980 Act together with a statement indicating whether or not that consent has been withdrawn; and

(f) a statement indicating the occasions, if any, on which the accused has been remanded by the alternate court under section 128(3A) of the 1980 Act without being brought before that court.

(4) Where the alternate court is satisfied as mentioned in section 128(3A) of the 1980 Act paragraph (2) above shall have effect as if for the words "an accused who has been remanded in custody is brought up for any subsequent remands" there shall be substituted the words "applications for the further remand of the accused are to be made".

Notice of further remand in certain cases

19.14 Where a transfer direction has been given by the Secretary of State under section 47 of **G–124** the *Mental Health Act* 1983 in respect of a person remanded in custody by a magistrates' court and the direction has not ceased to have effect, the court officer shall give notice in writing to the managers of the hospital where he is detained of any further remand under section 128 of the *Magistrates' Courts Act* 1980.

Cessation of transfer direction

19.15 Where a magistrates' court directs, under section 52(5) of the *Mental Health Act* **G–125** 1983, that a transfer direction given by the Secretary of State under section 48 of that Act in respect of a person remanded in custody by a magistrates' court shall cease to have effect, the court officer shall give notice in writing of the court's direction to the managers of the hospital specified in the Secretary of State's direction and, where the period of remand has not expired or the person has been committed to the Crown Court for trial or to be otherwise dealt with, to the Governor of the prison to which persons of the sex of that person are committed by the court if remanded in custody or committed in custody for trial.

Lodging an appeal against a grant of bail by a magistrates' court

19.16—(1) Where the prosecution wishes to exercise the right of appeal, under section 1 of **G–126** the *Bail (Amendment) Act* 1993, to a judge of the Crown Court against a decision to grant bail, the oral notice of appeal must be given to the justices' clerk and to the person concerned, at the conclusion of the proceedings in which such bail was granted and before the release of the person concerned.

(2) When oral notice of appeal is given, the justices' clerk shall announce in open court the time at which such notice was given.

(3) A record of the prosecution's decision to appeal and the time the oral notice of appeal was given shall be made in the register and shall contain the particulars set out.

(4) Where an oral notice of appeal has been given the court shall remand the person concerned in custody by a warrant of commitment.

(5) On receipt of the written notice of appeal required by section 1(5) of the 1993 Act, the court shall remand the person concerned in custody by a warrant of commitment, until the appeal is determined or otherwise disposed of.

Appendices

(6) A record of the receipt of the written notice of appeal shall be made in the same manner as that of the oral notice of appeal under paragraph (3).

(7) If, having given oral notice of appeal, the prosecution fails to serve a written notice of appeal within the two hour period referred to in section 1(5) of the 1993 Act the justices' clerk shall, as soon as practicable, by way of written notice (served by a court officer) to the persons in whose custody the person concerned is, direct the release of the person concerned on bail as granted by the magistrates' court and subject to any conditions which it imposed.

(8) If the prosecution serves notice of abandonment of appeal on a court officer, the justices' clerk shall, forthwith, by way of written notice (served by the court officer) to the governor of the prison where the person concerned is being held, or the person responsible for any other establishment where such a person is being held, direct his release on bail as granted by the magistrates' court and subject to any conditions which it imposed.

(9) A court officer shall record the prosecution's failure to serve a written notice of appeal, or its service of a notice of abandonments.

(10) Where a written notice of appeal has been served on a magistrates' court officer, he shall provide as soon as practicable to a Crown Court officer a copy of that written notice, together with—

(a) the notes of argument made by the court officer for the court under rule 19.10; and

(b) a note of the date, or dates, when the person concerned is next due to appear in the magistrates' court, whether he is released on bail or remanded in custody by the Crown Court.

(11) References in this rule to "the person concerned" are references to such a person within the meaning of section 1 of the 1993 Act.

Notice to governor of prison of committal on bail

G–127   **19.19**—(1) Where the accused is committed or sent for trial on bail, a magistrates' court officer shall give notice thereof in writing to the governor of the prison to which persons of the sex of the person committed or sent are committed or sent by that court if committed or sent in custody for trial and also, if the person committed or sent is under 21, to the governor of the remand centre to which he would have been committed or sent if the court had refused him bail.

(2) Where a corporation is committed or sent for trial, a magistrates' court officer shall give notice thereof to the governor of the prison to which would be committed or sent a man committed or sent by that court in custody for trial.

Notices on committal of person subject to transfer direction

G–128   **19.20** Where a transfer direction has been given by the Secretary of State under section 48 of the *Mental Health Act* 1983 in respect of a person remanded in custody by a magistrates' court and, before the direction ceases to have effect, that person is committed or sent for trial, a magistrates' court officer shall give notice—

(a) to the governor of the prison to which persons of the sex of that person are committed or sent by that court if committed or sent in custody for trial; and

(b) to the managers of the hospital where he is detained.

Variation of arrangements for bail on committal to Crown Court

G–129   **19.21** Where a magistrates' court has committed or sent a person on bail to the Crown Court for trial or under any of the enactments mentioned in rule 43.1(1) and subsequently varies any conditions of the bail or imposes any conditions in respect of the bail, the magistrates' court officer shall send to the Crown Court officer a copy of the record made in pursuance of section 5 of the *Bail Act* 1976 relating to such variation or imposition of conditions.

Conditions attached to bail granted by the Crown Court

G–130   **19.22**—(1) Where the Crown Court grants bail, the recognizance of any surety required as a condition of bail may be entered into before an officer of the Crown Court or, where the person who has been granted bail is in a prison or other place of detention, before the governor or keeper of the prison or place as well as before the persons specified in section 8(4) of the *Bail Act* 1976.

(2) Where the Crown Court under section 3(5) or (6) of the 1976 Act imposes a require-

ment to be complied with before a person's release on bail, the Court may give directions as to the manner in which and the person or persons before whom the requirement may be complied with.

(4) A person who, in pursuance of an order made by the Crown Court for the grant of bail, proposes to enter into a recognizance or give security must, unless the Crown Court otherwise directs, give notice to the prosecutor at least 24 hours before he enters into the recognizance or gives security as aforesaid.

(5) Where, in pursuance of an order of the Crown Court, a recognizance is entered into or any requirement imposed under section 3(5) or (6) of the 1976 Act is complied with (being a requirement to be complied with before a person's release on bail) before any person, it shall be his duty to cause the recognizance or, as the case may be, a statement of the requirement to be transmitted forthwith to the court officer; and a copy of the recognizance or statement shall at the same time be sent to the governor or keeper of the prison or other place of detention in which the person named in the order is detained, unless the recognizance was entered into or the requirement was complied with before such governor or keeper.

(6) Where, in pursuance of section 3(5) of the 1976 Act, security has been given in respect of a person granted bail with a duty to surrender to the custody of the Crown Court and either—

    (a) that person surrenders to the custody of the Court; or

    (b) that person having failed to surrender to the custody of the Court, the Court decides not to order the forfeiture of the security,

the court officer shall as soon as practicable give notice of the surrender to custody or, as the case may be, of the decision not to forfeit the security to the person before whom the security was given.

Estreat of recognizances in respect of person bailed to appear before the Crown Court

19.23—(1) Where a recognizance has been entered into in respect of a person granted bail **G–131** to appear before the Crown Court and it appears to the Court that a default has been made in performing the conditions of the recognizance, other than by failing to appear before the Court in accordance with any such condition, the Court may order the recognizance to be estreated.

(2) Where the Crown Court is to consider making an order under paragraph (1) for a recognizance to be estreated, the court officer shall give notice to that effect to the person by whom the recognizance was entered into indicating the time and place at which the matter will be considered; and no such order shall be made before the expiry of 7 days after the notice required by this paragraph has been given.

Forfeiture of recognizances in respect of person bailed to appear before the Crown Court

19.24—(1) Where a recognizance is conditioned for the appearance of an accused before the **G–132** Crown Court and the accused fails to appear in accordance with the condition, the Court shall declare the recognizance to be forfeited.

(2) Where the Crown Court declares a recognizance to be forfeited under paragraph (1), the court officer shall issue a summons to the person by whom the recognizance was entered into requiring him to appear before the Court at a time and place specified in the summons to show cause why the Court should not order the recognizance to be estreated.

(3) At the time specified in the summons the Court may proceed in the absence of the person by whom the recognizance was entered into if it is satisfied that he has been served with the summons.

PART 20

CUSTODY TIME LIMITS

Appeal to the Crown Court against a decision of a magistrates' court in respect of a custody time limit

    20.1—(1) This rule applies—   **G–133**

        (a) to any appeal brought by an accused, under section 22(7) of the *Prosecution of Offences Act* 1985, against a decision of a magistrates' court to extend, or further extend, a custody time limit imposed by regulations made under section 22(1) of the 1985 Act; and

   (b) to any appeal brought by the prosecution, under section 22(8) of the 1985 Act, against a decision of a magistrates' court to refuse to extend, or further extend, such a time limit.

(2) An appeal to which this rule applies shall be commenced by the appellant's giving notice in writing of appeal—

   (a) to the court officer for the magistrates' court which took the decision;

   (b) if the appeal is brought by the accused, to the prosecutor and, if the prosecution is to be carried on by the Crown Prosecution Service, to the appropriate Crown Prosecutor;

   (c) if the appeal is brought by the prosecution, to the accused; and

   (d) to the Crown Court officer.

(3) The notice of an appeal to which this rule applies shall state the date on which the custody time limit applicable to the case is due to expire and, if the appeal is brought by the accused under section 22(7) of the 1985 Act, the date on which the custody time limit would have expired had the court decided not to extend or further extend that time limit.

(4) On receiving notice of an appeal to which this rule applies, the Crown Court officer shall enter the appeal and give notice of the time and place of the hearing to—

   (a) the appellant;

   (b) the other party to the appeal; and

   (c) the court officer for the magistrates' court which took the decision.

(5) Without prejudice to the power of the Crown Court to give leave for an appeal to be abandoned, an appellant may abandon an appeal to which this rule applies by giving notice in writing to any person to whom notice of the appeal was required to be given by paragraph (2) of this rule not later than the third day preceding the day fixed for the hearing of the appeal:

Provided that, for the purpose of determining whether notice was properly given in accordance with this paragraph, there shall be disregarded any Saturday and Sunday and any day which is specified to be a bank holiday in England and Wales under section 1(1) of the *Banking and Financial Dealings Act* 1971.

PART 21

ADVANCE INFORMATION

Scope of procedure for furnishing advance information

G–134   **21.1** This Part applies in respect of proceedings against any person ("the accused") for an offence triable either way.

Notice to accused regarding advance information

G–135   **21.2** As soon as practicable after a person has been charged with an offence in proceedings in respect of which this Part applies or a summons has been served on a person in connection with such an offence, the prosecutor shall provide him with a notice in writing explaining the effect of rule 21.3 and setting out the address at which a request under that section may be made.

Request for advance information

G–136   **21.3**—(1) If, in any proceedings in respect of which this Part applies, either before the magistrates' court considers whether the offence appears to be more suitable for summary trial or trial on indictment or, where the accused has not attained the age of 18 years when he appears or is brought before a magistrates' court, before he is asked whether he pleads guilty or not guilty, the accused or a person representing the accused requests the prosecutor to furnish him with advance information, the prosecutor shall, subject to rule 21.4, furnish him as soon as practicable with either—

   (a) a copy of those parts of every written statement which contain information as to the facts and matters of which the prosecutor proposes to adduce evidence in the proceedings; or

   (b) a summary of the facts and matters of which the prosecutor proposes to adduce evidence in the proceedings.

(2) In paragraph (1) above, "written statement" means a statement made by a person on whose evidence the prosecutor proposes to rely in the proceedings and, where such a person has made more than one written statement one of which contains information as to all the facts and matters in relation to which the prosecutor proposes to rely on the evidence of that person, only that statement is a written statement for purposes of paragraph (1) above.

(3) Where in any part of a written statement or in a summary furnished under paragraph (1) above reference is made to a document on which the prosecutor proposes to rely, the prosecutor shall, subject to rule 21.4, when furnishing the part of the written statement or the summary, also furnish either a copy of the document or such information as may be necessary to enable the person making the request under paragraph (1) above to inspect the document or a copy thereof.

Refusal of request for advance information

21.4—(1) If the prosecutor is of the opinion that the disclosure of any particular fact or matter in compliance with the requirements imposed by rule 21.3 might lead to any person on whose evidence he proposes to rely in the proceedings being intimidated, to an attempt to intimidate him being made or otherwise to the course of justice being interfered with, he shall not be obliged to comply with those requirements in relation to that fact or matter.   **G–137**

(2) Where, in accordance with paragraph (1) above, the prosecutor considers that he is not obliged to comply with the requirements imposed by rule 21.3 in relation to any particular fact or matter, he shall give notice in writing to the person who made the request under that section to the effect that certain advance information is being withheld by virtue of that paragraph.

Duty of court regarding advance information

21.5—(1) Subject to paragraph (2), where an accused appears or is brought before a magistrates' court in proceedings in respect of which this Part applies, the court shall, before it considers whether the offence appears to be more suitable for summary trial or trial on indictment, satisfy itself that the accused is aware of the requirements which may be imposed on the prosecutor under rule 21.3.   **G–138**

(2) Where the accused has not attained the age of 18 years when he appears or is brought before a magistrates' court in proceedings in respect of which this rule applies, the court shall, before the accused is asked whether he pleads guilty or not guilty, satisfy itself that the accused is aware of the requirements which may be imposed on the prosecutor under rule 21.3.

Adjournment pending furnishing of advance information

21.6—(1) If, in any proceedings in respect of which this Part applies, the court is satisfied that, a request under rule 21.3 having been made to the prosecutor by or on behalf of the accused, a requirement imposed on the prosecutor by that section has not been complied with, the court shall adjourn the proceedings pending compliance with the requirement unless the court is satisfied that the conduct of the case for the accused will not be substantially prejudiced by non-compliance with the requirement.   **G–139**

(2) Where, in the circumstances set out in paragraph (1) above, the court decides not to adjourn the proceedings, a record of that decision and of the reasons why the court was satisfied that the conduct of the case for the accused would not be substantially prejudiced by non-compliance with the requirement shall be entered in the register kept under rule 6.1.

PART 22

DISCLOSURE BY THE PROSECUTION

1. *[Note. There are currently no rules in this Part. As to the duty of the prosecution to make initial disclosure see sections 3 and 4 of the Criminal Procedure and Investigations Act 1996. As to the continuing duty of disclosure see section 7A of the same Act.]*   **G–140**

PART 23

DISCLOSURE BY THE DEFENCE

1. *[Note. There are currently no rules in this Part. As to the duty of the accused to make*   **G–141**

disclosure see sections 5 to 6E of the Criminal Procedure and Investigations Act 1996, and as to timing see the Criminal Procedure and Investigations Act 1996 (Defence Disclosure Time Limits) Regulations 1997.]

PART 24

DISCLOSURE OF EXPERT EVIDENCE

Requirement to disclose expert evidence

G-142   **24.1**—(1) Following—

(a) a plea of not guilty by any person to an alleged offence in respect of which a magistrates' court proceeds to summary trial;

(b) the committal for trial of any person;

(c) the transfer to the Crown Court of any proceedings for the trial of a person by virtue of a notice of transfer given under section 4 of the *Criminal Justice Act 1987*;

(d) the transfer to the Crown Court of any proceedings for the trial of a person by virtue of a notice of transfer served on a magistrates' court under section 53 of the *Criminal Justice Act 1991*;

(e) the sending of any person for trial under section 51 of the *Crime and Disorder Act 1998*;

(f) the preferring of a bill of indictment charging a person with an offence under the authority of section 2(2)(b) of the Administration of Justice (Miscellaneous Provisions) Act 1933; or

(g) the making of an order for the retrial of any person,

if any party to the proceedings proposes to adduce expert evidence (whether of fact or opinion) in the proceedings (otherwise than in relation to sentence) he shall as soon as practicable, unless in relation to the evidence in question he has already done so or the evidence is the subject of an application for leave to adduce such evidence in accordance with section 41 of the *Youth Justice and Criminal Evidence Act* 1999—

(i) furnish the other party or parties and the court with a statement in writing of any finding or opinion which he proposes to adduce by way of such evidence and notify the expert of this disclosure, and

(ii) where a request in writing is made to him in that behalf by any other party, provide that party also with a copy of (or if it appears to the party proposing to adduce the evidence to be more practicable, a reasonable opportunity to examine) the record of any observation, test, calculation or other procedure on which such finding or opinion is based and any document or other thing or substance in respect of which any such procedure has been carried out.

(2) A party may by notice in writing waive his right to be furnished with any of the matters mentioned in paragraph (1) and, in particular, may agree that the statement mentioned in paragraph (1)(a) may be furnished to him orally and not in writing.

(3) In paragraph (1), "document" means anything in which information of any description is recorded.

Withholding evidence

G-143   **24.2**—(1) If a party has reasonable grounds for believing that the disclosure of any evidence in compliance with the requirements imposed by rule 24.1 might lead to the intimidation, or attempted intimidation, of any person on whose evidence he intends to rely in the proceedings, or otherwise to the course of justice being interfered with, he shall not be obliged to comply with those requirements in relation to that evidence.

(2) Where, in accordance with paragraph (1), a party considers that he is not obliged to comply with the requirements imposed by rule 24.1 with regard to any evidence in relation to any other party, he shall give notice in writing to that party to the effect that the evidence is being withheld and the grounds for doing so.

Effect of failure to disclose

G-144   **24.3** A party who seeks to adduce expert evidence in any proceedings and who fails to comply with rule 24.1 shall not adduce that evidence in those proceedings without the leave of the court.

PART 25

APPLICATIONS FOR PUBLIC INTEREST IMMUNITY AND SPECIFIC
DISCLOSURE

Public interest: application by prosecutor

25.1—(1) This rule applies to the making of an application by the prosecutor under section   **G–145**
3(6), 7A(8) or 8(5) of the *Criminal Procedure and Investigations Act* 1996.

(2) Notice of such an application shall be served on the court officer and shall specify
the nature of the material to which the application relates.

(3) Subject to paragraphs (4) and (5) below, a copy of the notice of application shall be
served on the accused by the prosecutor.

(4) Where the prosecutor has reason to believe that to reveal to the accused the nature
of the material to which the application relates would have the effect of disclosing that
which the prosecutor contends should not in the public interest be disclosed, paragraph (3)
above shall not apply but the prosecutor shall notify the accused that an application to
which this rule applies has been made.

(5) Where the prosecutor has reason to believe that to reveal to the accused the fact that
an application is being made would have the effect of disclosing that which the prosecutor
contends should not in the public interest be disclosed, paragraph (3) above shall not
apply.

(6) Where an application is made in the Crown Court to which paragraph (5) above applies, notice of the application may be served on the trial judge or, if the application is
made before the start of the trial, on the judge, if any, who has been designated to conduct
the trial instead of on the court officer.

Public interest: hearing of application by prosecutor

25.2—(1) This rule applies to the hearing of an application by the prosecutor under section   **G–146**
3(6), 7A(8) or 8(5) of the *Criminal Procedure and Investigations Act* 1996.

(2) Where notice of such an application is served on the Crown Court officer, the officer
shall on receiving it refer it—

(a) if the trial has started, to the trial judge; or

(b) if the application is received before the start of the trial either—

    (i) to the judge who has been designated to conduct the trial, or

    (ii) if no judge has been designated for that purpose, to such judge as may be
designated for the purposes of hearing the application.

(3) Where such an application is made and a copy of the notice of application has been
served on the accused in accordance with rule 25.1(3), then subject to paragraphs (4) and
(5) below—

(a) the court officer shall on receiving notice of the application give notice to—

    (i) the prosecutor,

    (ii) the accused, and

    (iii) any person claiming to have an interest in the material to which the ap-
plication relates who has applied under section 16(b) of the 1996 Act to be
heard by the court,

    of the date and time when and the place where the hearing will take place and, unless
the court orders otherwise, such notice shall be given in writing;

(b) the hearing shall be inter partes; and

(c) the prosecutor and the accused shall be entitled to make representations to the
court.

(4) Where the prosecutor applies to the court for leave to make representations in the
absence of the accused, the court may for that purpose sit in the absence of the accused
and any legal representative of his.

(5) Subject to rule 25.5(4) (interested party entitled to make representations), where a
copy of the notice of application has not been served on the accused in accordance with
rule 25.1(3)—

(a) the hearing shall be ex parte;

(b) only the prosecutor shall be entitled to make representations to the court;

(c) the accused shall not be given notice as specified in paragraph (3)(a)(ii) of this rule; and

(d) where notice of the application has been served in the Crown Court in pursuance of rule 25.1(6), the judge on whom it is served shall take such steps as he considers appropriate to ensure that notice is given as required by paragraph (3)(a)(i) and (iii) of this rule.

Public interest: non-disclosure order

G–147   **25.3**—(1) This rule applies to an order under section 3(6), 7A(8) or 8(5) of the *Criminal Procedure and Investigations Act* 1996.

(2) On making an order to which this rule applies, the court shall state its reasons for doing so. Where such an order is made in the Crown Court, a record shall be made of the statement of the court's reasons.

(3) In a case where such an order is made following—

(a) an application to which rule 25.1(4) (nature of material not to be revealed) applies; or

(b) an application notice of which has been served on the accused in accordance with rule 25.1(3) but the accused has not appeared or been represented at the hearing of that application,

the court officer shall notify the accused that an order has been made. No notification shall be given in a case where an order is made following an application to which rule 25.1(5) (fact of application not to be revealed) applies.

Review of non-disclosure order: application by accused

G–148   **25.4**—(1) This rule applies to an application by the accused under section 14(2) or section 15(4) of the *Criminal Procedure and Investigations Act* 1996.

(2) Such an application shall be made by notice in writing to the court officer for the court that made the order under section 3(6), 7A(8) or 8(5) of the 1996 Act and shall specify the reason why the accused believes the court should review the question whether it is still not in the public interest to disclose the material affected by the order.

(3) A copy of the notice referred to in paragraph (2) shall be served on the prosecutor at the same time as it is sent to the court officer.

(4) Where such an application is made in a magistrates' court, the court officer shall take such steps as he thinks fit to ensure that the court has before it any document or other material which was available to the court which made the order mentioned in section 14(2) of the 1996 Act.

(5) Where such an application is made in the Crown Court, the court officer shall refer it—

(a) if the trial has started, to the trial judge; or

(b) if the application is received before the start of the trial either—

(i) to the judge who has been designated to conduct the trial, or

(ii) if no judge has been designated for that purpose, to the judge who made the order to which the application relates.

(6) The judge to whom such an application has been referred under paragraph (5) shall consider whether the application may be determined without a hearing and, subject to paragraph (7), may so determine it if he thinks fit.

(7) No application to which this rule applies shall be determined by the Crown Court without a hearing if it appears to the judge that there are grounds on which the court might conclude that it is in the public interest to disclose material to any extent.

(8) Where a magistrates' court considers that there are no grounds on which it might conclude that it is in the public interest to disclose material to any extent it may determine an application to which this rule applies without hearing representations from the accused, the prosecutor or any person claiming to have an interest in the material to which the application relates.

(9) Subject to paragraphs (10) and (11) of this rule and to rule 25.5(4) (interested party entitled to make representations), the hearing of an application to which this rule applies shall be inter partes and the accused and the prosecutor shall be entitled to make representations to the court.

(10) Where after hearing the accused's representations the prosecutor applies to the court for leave to make representations in the absence of the accused, the court may for that purpose sit in the absence of the accused and any legal representative of his.

(11) Subject to rule 25.5(4), where the order to which the application relates was made following an application of which the accused was not notified under rule 25.1(3) or (4), the hearing shall be ex parte and only the prosecutor shall be entitled to make representations to the court.

(12) The court officer shall give notice in writing to—

(a) the prosecutor;

(b) except where a hearing takes place in accordance with paragraph (11), the accused; and

(c) any person claiming to have an interest in the material to which the application relates who has applied under section 16(b) of the 1996 Act to be heard by the court,

of the date and time when and the place where the hearing of an application to which this rule applies will take place and of any order which is made by the court following its determination of the application.

(13) Where such an application is determined without a hearing in pursuance of paragraph (6), the court officer shall give notice in writing in accordance with paragraph (12) of any order which is made by the judge following his determination of the application.

Public interest applications: interested persons

25.5—(1) Where the prosecutor has reason to believe that a person who was involved   **G–149** (whether alone or with others and whether directly or indirectly) in the prosecutor's attention being brought to any material to which an application under section 3(6), 7A(8), 8(5), 14(2) or 15(4) of the *Criminal Procedure and Investigations Act* 1996 relates may claim to have an interest in that material, the prosecutor shall—

(a) in the case of an application under section 3(6), 7A(8) or 8(5) of the 1996 Act, at the same time as notice of the application is served under rule 25.1(2) or (6); or

(b) in the case of an application under section 14(2) or 15(4) of the 1996 Act, when he receives a copy of the notice referred to in rule 25.4(2),

give notice in writing to—

(i) the person concerned of the application, and

(ii) the court officer or, as the case may require, the judge of his belief and the grounds for it.

(2) An application under section 16(b) of the 1996 Act shall be made by notice in writing to the court officer or, as the case may require, the judge as soon as is reasonably practicable after receipt of notice under paragraph (1)(i) above or, if no such notice is received, after the person concerned becomes aware of the application referred to in that sub-paragraph and shall specify the nature of the applicant's interest in the material and his involvement in bringing the material to the prosecutor's attention.

(3) A copy of the notice referred to in paragraph (2) shall be served on the prosecutor at the same time as it is sent to the court officer or the judge as the case may require.

(4) At the hearing of an application under section 3(6), 7A(8), 8(5), 14(2) or 15(4) of the 1996 Act a person who has made an application under section 16(b) in accordance with paragraph (2) of this rule shall be entitled to make representations to the court.

Disclosure: application by accused and order of court

25.6—(1) This rule applies to an application by the accused under section 8(2) of the *Crimi-*   **G–150** *nal Procedure and Investigations Act* 1996.

(2) Such an application shall be made by notice in writing to the court officer and shall specify—

(a) the material to which the application relates;

(b) that the material has not been disclosed to the accused;

(c) the reason why the material might be expected to assist the applicant's defence as disclosed by the defence statement given under section 5 or 6 of the 1996 Act; and

(d) the date of service of a copy of the notice on the prosecutor in accordance with paragraph (3).

(3) A copy of the notice referred to in paragraph (2) shall be served on the prosecutor at the same time as it is sent to the court officer.

(4) Where such an application is made in the Crown Court, the court officer shall refer it—

    (a) if the trial has started, to the trial judge, or

    (b) if the application is received before the start of the trial—

        (i) to the judge who has been designated to conduct the trial, or

        (ii) if no judge has been designated for that purpose, to such judge as may be designated for the purposes of determining the application.

(5) A prosecutor receiving notice under paragraph (3) of an application to which this rule applies shall give notice in writing to the court officer within 14 days of service of the notice that—

    (a) he wishes to make representations to the court concerning the material to which the application relates; or

    (b) if he does not so wish, that he is willing to disclose that material,

and a notice under paragraph 5(a) shall specify the substance of the representations he wishes to make.

(6) A court may determine an application to which this rule applies without hearing representations from the applicant or the prosecutor unless—

    (a) the prosecutor has given notice under paragraph (5)(a) and the court considers that the representations should be made at a hearing; or

    (b) the court considers it necessary to hear representations from the applicant or the prosecutor in the interests of justice for the purposes of determining the application.

(7) Subject to paragraph (8), where a hearing is held in pursuance of this rule—

    (a) the court officer shall give notice in writing to the prosecutor and the applicant of the date and time when and the place where the hearing will take place;

    (b) the hearing shall be inter partes; and

    (c) the prosecutor and the applicant shall be entitled to make representations to the court.

(8) Where the prosecutor applies to the court for leave to make representations in the absence of the accused, the court may for that purpose sit in the absence of the accused and any legal representative of his.

(9) A copy of any order under section 8(2) of the 1996 Act shall be served on the prosecutor and the applicant.

Disclosure: application for extension of time limit and order of the court

G–151   **25.7**—(1) This rule applies to an application under regulation 3(2) of the *Criminal Procedure and Investigations Act 1996 (Defence Disclosure Time Limits) Regulations* 1997, including that regulation as applied by regulation 4(2).

(2) An application to which this rule applies shall be made by notice in writing to the court officer and shall, in addition to the matters referred to in regulation 3(3)(a) to (c) of the 1997 Regulations, specify the date of service of a copy of the notice on the prosecutor in accordance with paragraph (3) of this rule.

(3) A copy of the notice referred to in paragraph (2) of this rule shall be served on the prosecutor at the same time as it is sent to the court officer.

(4) The prosecutor may make representations to the court concerning the application and if he wishes to do so he shall do so in writing within 14 days of service of a notice under paragraph (3) of this rule.

(5) On receipt of representations under paragraph (4) above, or on the expiration of the period specified in that paragraph if no such representations are received within that period, the court shall consider the application and may, if it wishes, do so at a hearing.

(6) Where a hearing is held in pursuance of this rule—

    (a) the court officer shall give notice in writing to the prosecutor and the applicant of the date and time when and the place where the hearing will take place;

    (b) the hearing shall be inter partes; and

    (c) the prosecutor and the applicant shall be entitled to make representations to the court.

(7) A copy of any order under regulation 3(1) or 4(1) of the 1997 Regulations shall be

served on the prosecutor and the applicant.

Public interest and disclosure applications: general

25.8—(1) Any hearing held under this Part may be adjourned from time to time.   **G–152**

(2) Any hearing referred to in paragraph (1) other than one held under rule 25.7 may be held in private.

(3) Where a Crown Court hearing, or any part thereof, is held in private under paragraph (2), the court may specify conditions subject to which the record of its statement of reasons made in pursuance of rule 25.3(2) is to be kept.

(4) Where an application or order to which any provision of this rule applies is made after the start of a trial in the Crown Court, the trial judge may direct that any provision of this rule requiring notice of the application or order to be given to any person shall not have effect and may give such direction as to the giving of notice in relation to that application or order as he thinks fit.

PART 26

CONFIDENTIAL MATERIAL

Application for permission to use or disclose object or information

26.1—(1) This rule applies to an application under section 17(4) of the *Criminal Procedure*   **G–153**
and Investigations Act 1996.

(2) Such an application shall be made by notice in writing to the court officer for the court which conducted or is conducting the proceedings for whose purposes the applicant was given, or allowed to inspect, the object to which the application relates.

(3) The notice of application shall—

(a) specify the object which the applicant seeks to use or disclose and the proceedings for whose purposes he was given, or allowed to inspect, it;

(b) where the applicant seeks to use or disclose any information recorded in the object specified in pursuance of paragraph (3)(a), specify that information;

(c) specify the reason why the applicant seeks permission to use or disclose the object specified in pursuance of paragraph (3)(a) or any information specified in pursuance of paragraph (3)(b);

(d) describe any proceedings in connection with which the applicant seeks to use or disclose the object or information referred to in paragraph (3)(c); and

(e) specify the name and address of any person to whom the applicant seeks to disclose the object or information referred to in paragraph (3)(c).

(4) Where the court officer receives an application to which this rule applies, the court officer or the clerk of the magistrates' court shall fix a date and time for the hearing of the application.

(5) The court officer shall give the applicant and the prosecutor at least 28 days' notice of the date fixed in pursuance of paragraph (4) and shall at the same time send to the prosecutor a copy of the notice given to him in pursuance of paragraph (2).

(6) Where the prosecutor has reason to believe that a person may claim to have an interest in the object specified in a notice of application in pursuance of paragraph (3)(a), or in any information so specified in pursuance of paragraph (3)(b), he shall, as soon as reasonably practicable after receipt of a copy of that notice under paragraph (5), send a copy of the notice to that person and inform him of the date fixed in pursuance of paragraph (4).

Prosecutor or interested party wishing to be heard

26.2—(1) This rule applies to an application under section 17(6)(b) of the *Criminal Proce-*   **G–154**
dure and Investigations Act 1996.

(2) An application to which this rule applies shall be made by notice in writing to the court officer of the court referred to in rule 26.1(2) not less than 7 days before the date fixed in pursuance of rule 26.1(4).

(3) The applicant shall at the same time send to the person whose application under section 17(4) of the 1996 Act is concerned a copy of the notice given in pursuance of paragraph (2).

Decision on application for use or disclosure

G–155   **26.3**—(1) Where no application to which rule 26.2 applies is made in accordance with paragraph (2) of that rule, the court shall consider whether the application under section 17(4) of the *Criminal Procedure and Investigations Act* 1996 may be determined without hearing representations from the accused, the prosecutor or any person claiming to have an interest in the object or information to which the application relates, and may so determine it if the court thinks fit.

(2) Where an application to which rule 26.1 applies is determined without hearing any such representations the court officer shall give notice in writing to the person who made the application and to the prosecutor of any order made under section 17(4) of the 1996 Act or, as the case may be, that no such order has been made.

Unauthorised use or disclosure

G–156   **26.4**—(1) This rule applies to proceedings to deal with a contempt of court under section 18 of the *Criminal Procedure and Investigations Act* 1996.

(2) In such proceedings before a magistrates' court the *Magistrates' Courts Act* 1980 shall have effect subject to the modifications contained in paragraphs (3) to (7) (being provisions equivalent to those in Schedule 3 to the *Contempt of Court Act* 1981 subject to modifications which the Lord Chancellor considered appropriate after consultation with the rule committee for magistrates' courts).

(3) Where proceedings to which this rule applies are taken of the court's own motion the provisions of the 1980 Act listed in paragraph (4) shall apply as if a complaint had been made against the person against whom the proceedings are taken and subject to the modifications specified in paragraphs (5) and (6).

(4) The provisions referred to in paragraph (3) are—

    (a) section 51 (issue of summons);

    (b) section 53(1) and (2) (procedure on hearing);

    (c) section 54 (adjournment);

    (d) section 55 (non-appearance of defendant);

    (e) section 97(1) (summons to witness);

    (f) section 101 (onus of proving exceptions etc);

    (g) section 121(1) and (3)(a) (constitution and place of sitting of court); and

    (h) section 123 (defect in process).

(5) In—

    (a) section 55(1) for the words "the complainant appears but the defendant does not" there shall be substituted the words "the defendant does not appear"; and

    (b) section 55(2) the words "if the complaint has been substantiated on oath, and" shall be omitted.

(6) In section 123(1) and (2) the words "adduced on behalf of the prosecutor or complainant" shall be omitted.

(7) Where proceedings to which this rule applies are taken by way of complaint for an order—

    (a) section 127 of the 1980 Act (limitation of time) shall not apply to the complaint;

    (b) the complaint may be made by the prosecutor or by any other person claiming to have an interest in the object, or in any information recorded in an object, the use or disclosure of which is alleged to contravene section 17 of the 1996 Act; and

    (c) the complaint shall be made to the magistrates' court officer for the magistrates' court which conducted or is conducting the proceedings for whose purposes the object mentioned in paragraph (7)(b) was given or inspected.

(8) An application to the Crown Court for an order of committal or for the imposition of a fine in proceedings to which this rule applies may be made by the prosecutor or by any other person claiming to have an interest in the object, or in any information recorded in an object, the use or disclosure of which is alleged to contravene section 17 of the 1996 Act. Such an application shall be made in accordance with paragraphs (9) to (20).

(9) An application such as is referred to in paragraph (8) shall be made by notice in writing to the court officer at the same place as that in which the Crown Court sat or is sitting to conduct the proceedings for whose purposes the object mentioned in paragraph (2) was given or inspected.

(10) The notice referred to in paragraph (9) shall set out the name and a description of

the applicant, the name, description and address of the person sought to be committed or fined and the grounds on which his committal or the imposition of a fine is sought and shall be supported by an affidavit verifying the facts.

(11) Subject to paragraph (12), the notice referred to in paragraph (9), accompanied by a copy of the affidavit in support of the application, shall be served personally on the person sought to be committed or fined.

(12) The court may dispense with service of the notice under this rule if it is of the opinion that it is necessary to do so in order to protect the applicant or for another purpose identified by the court.

(13) Nothing in the foregoing provisions of this rule shall be taken as affecting the power of the Crown Court to make an order of committal or impose a fine of its own motion against a person guilty of a contempt under section 18 of the 1996 Act.

(14) Subject to paragraph (15), proceedings to which this rule applies shall be heard in open court.

(15) Proceedings to which this rule applies may be heard in private where—

(a) the object, the use or disclosure of which is alleged to contravene section 17 of the 1996 Act, is; or

(b) the information, the use or disclosure of which is alleged to contravene that section, is recorded in,

an object which is, or forms part of, material in respect of which an application was made under section 3(6), 7A(8) or 8(5) of the 1996 Act, whether or not the court made an order that the material be not disclosed:

Provided that where the court hears the proceedings in private it shall nevertheless, if it commits any person to custody or imposes a fine on him in pursuance of section 18(3) of the 1996 Act, state in open court the name of that person, the period specified in the order of committal or, as the case may be, the amount of the fine imposed, or both such period and such amount where both are ordered.

(16) Except with the leave of the court hearing an application for an order of committal or for the imposition of a fine no grounds shall be relied upon at the hearing except the grounds set out in the notice referred to in paragraph (9).

(17) If on the hearing of the application the person sought to be committed or fined expresses a wish to give oral evidence on his own behalf, he shall be entitled to do so.

(18) The court by whom an order of committal is made may by order direct that the execution of the order of committal shall be suspended for such period or on such terms or conditions as it may specify.

(19) Where execution of an order of committal is suspended by an order under paragraph (18), the applicant for the order of committal must, unless the court otherwise directs, serve on the person against whom it was made a notice informing him of the making and terms of the order under that paragraph.

(20) The court may, on the application of any person committed to custody for a contempt under section 18 of the 1996 Act, discharge him.

Forfeiture of object used or disclosed without authority

26.5—(1) Where the Crown Court finds a person guilty of contempt under section 18 of the **G–157** *Criminal Procedure and Investigations Act* 1996 and proposes to make an order under section 18(4) or (7), the court may adjourn the proceedings.

(2) Where the court adjourns the proceedings under paragraph (1), the court officer shall give notice to the person found guilty and to the prosecutor—

(a) that the court proposes to make such an order and that, if an application is made in accordance with paragraph (5), it will before doing so hear any representations made by the person found guilty, or by any person in respect of whom the prosecutor gives notice to the court under paragraph (3); and

(b) of the time and date of the adjourned hearing.

(3) Where the prosecutor has reason to believe that a person may claim to have an interest in the object which has been used or disclosed in contravention of section 17 of the 1996 Act he shall, on receipt of notice under paragraph (2), give notice of that person's name and address to the court office for the court which made the finding of guilt.

(4) Where the court officer receives a notice under paragraph (3), he shall, within 7 days of the finding of guilt, notify the person specified in that notice—

(a) that the court has made a finding of guilt under section 18 of the 1996 Act, that it proposes to make an order under section 18(4) or, as the case may be, 18(7) and that, if an application is made in accordance with paragraph (5), it will before doing so hear any representations made by him; and

(b) of the time and date of the adjourned hearing.

(5) An application under section 18(6) of the 1996 Act shall be made by notice in writing to the court officer not less than 24 hours before the time set for the adjourned hearing.

PART 27

WITNESS STATEMENTS

Witness statements in magistrates' courts

G–158   27.1—(1) Written statements to be tendered in evidence in accordance with section 5B of the *Magistrates'* Courts Act 1980 or section 9 of the *Criminal Justice Act* 1967 shall be in the form set out in the Practice Direction.

(2) When a copy of any of the following evidence, namely—

(a) evidence tendered in accordance with section 5A of the 1980 Act (committal for trial); or

(b) a written statement tendered in evidence under section 9 of the 1967 Act (proceedings other than committal for trial),

is given to or served on any party to the proceedings a copy of the evidence in question shall be given to the court officer as soon as practicable thereafter, and where a copy of any such statement as is referred to in sub-paragraph (b) is given or served by or on behalf of the prosecutor, the accused shall be given notice by or on behalf of the prosecutor of his right to object to the statement being tendered in evidence.

(3) Where—

(a) a statement or deposition to be tendered in evidence in accordance with section 5A of the 1980 Act; or

(b) a written statement to be tendered in evidence under section 9 of the 1967 Act,

refers to any document or object as an exhibit, that document or object shall wherever possible be identified by means of a label or other mark of identification signed by the maker of the statement or deposition, and before a magistrates' court treats any document or object referred to as an exhibit in such a statement or deposition as an exhibit produced and identified in court by the maker of the statement or deposition, the court shall be satisfied that the document or object is sufficiently described in the statement or deposition for it to be identified.

(4) If it appears to a magistrates' court that any part of any evidence tendered in accordance with section 5A of the 1980 Act or a written statement tendered in evidence under section 9 of the 1967 Act is inadmissible there shall be written against that part—

(a) in the case of any evidence tendered in accordance with section 5A of the 1980 Act, but subject to paragraph (5) of this rule, the words "Treated as inadmissible" together with the signature and name of the examining justice or, where there is more than one examining justice, the signature and name of one of the examining justices by whom the evidence is so treated;

(b) in the case of a written statement tendered in evidence under section 9 of the 1967 Act the words "Ruled inadmissible" together with the signature and name of one of the justices who ruled the statement to be inadmissible.

(5) Where the nature of the evidence referred to in paragraph (4)(a) is such that it is not possible to write on it, the words set out in that sub-paragraph shall instead be written on a label or other mark of identification which clearly identifies the part of the evidence to which the words relate and contains the signature and name of an examining justice in accordance with that sub-paragraph.

(6) Where, before a magistrates' court—

(a) a statement or deposition is tendered in evidence in accordance with section 5A of the 1980 Act; or

(b) a written statement is tendered in accordance with section 9 of the 1967 Act,

the name of the maker of the statement or deposition shall be read aloud unless the court otherwise directs.

(7) Where—

(a) under section 5B(4), 5C(4), 5D(5) or 5E(3) of the 1980 Act; or

(b) under section 9(6) of the 1967 Act,

in any proceedings before a magistrates' court any part of the evidence has to be read out aloud, or an account has to be given orally of so much of any evidence as is not read out aloud, the evidence shall be read or the account given by or on behalf of the party which has tendered the evidence.

(8) Statements and depositions tendered in evidence in accordance with section 5A of the 1980 Act before a magistrates' court acting as examining justices shall be authenticated by a certificate signed by one of the examining justices.

(9) Where, before a magistrates' court—

(a) evidence is tendered as indicated in paragraph (2)(a) of this rule, retained by the court, and not sent to the Crown Court under rule 10.5; or

(b) a written statement is tendered in evidence as indicated in paragraph (2)(b) of this rule and not sent to the Crown Court under rule 43.1 or 43.2,

all such evidence shall, subject to any direction of the court in respect of non-documentary exhibits falling within paragraph (9)(a), be preserved for a period of three years by the magistrates' court officer for the magistrates' court.

Right to object to evidence being read in Crown Court trial

27.2—(1) The prosecutor shall, when he serves on any other party a copy of the evidence to **G–159** be tendered in committal proceedings, notify that party that if he is committed for trial he has the right to object, by written notification to the prosecutor and the Crown Court within 14 days of being so committed unless the court in its discretion permits such an objection to be made outside that period, to a statement or deposition being read as evidence at the trial without oral evidence being given by the person who made the statement or deposition and without the opportunity to cross-examine that person.

(2) The prosecutor shall, on notifying a party as indicated in paragraph (1), send a copy of such notification to the magistrates' court officer.

(3) Any objection under paragraph 1(3)(c) or paragraph 2(3)(c) of Schedule 2 to the *Criminal Procedure and Investigations Act* 1996 to the reading out at the trial of a statement or deposition without further evidence shall be made in writing to the prosecutor and the Crown Court within 14 days of the accused being committed for trial unless the court at its discretion permits such an objection to be made outside that period.

PART 28

WITNESS SUMMONSES, WARRANTS AND ORDERS

When this Part applies

28.1—(1) This Part applies in magistrates' courts and in the Crown Court where— **G–160**

(a) a party wants the court to issue a witness summons, warrant or order under—

(i)   section 97 of the *Magistrates' Courts Act* 1980,

(ii) section 2 of the *Criminal Procedure (Attendance of Witnesses) Act* 1965, or

(iii) section 7 of the *Bankers' Books Evidence Act* 1879;

(b) the court considers the issue of such a summons, warrant or order on its own initiative as if a party had applied; or

(c) one of those listed in rule 28.7 wants the court to withdraw such a summons, warrant or order.

(2) A reference to a 'witness' in this Part is a reference to a person to whom such a summons, warrant or order is directed.

Issue etc. of summons, warrant or order with or without a hearing

28.2—(1) The court may issue or withdraw a witness summons, warrant or order with or **G–161** without a hearing.

(2) A hearing under this Part must be in private unless the court otherwise directs.

Application for summons, warrant or order: general rules

28.3—(1) A party who wants the court to issue a witness summons, warrant or order must **G–162** apply as soon as practicable after becoming aware of the grounds for doing so.

(2) The party applying must—

    (a) identify the proposed witness;
    (b) explain—
        (i)   what evidence the proposed witness can give or produce,
        (ii) why it is likely to be material evidence, and
        (iii) why it would be in the interests of justice to issue a summons, order or
            warrant as appropriate.
  (3) The application may be made orally unless—
    (a) rule 28.5 applies; or
    (b) the court otherwise directs.

Written application: form and service

G–163   **28.4**—(1) An application in writing under rule 28.3 must be in the form set out in the Practice Direction, containing the same declaration of truth as a witness statement.
  (2) The party applying must serve the application—
    (a) in every case, on the court officer and as directed by the court; and
    (b) as required by rule 28.5, if that rule applies.

Application for summons to produce a document, etc.: special rules

G–164   **28.5**—(1) This rule applies to an application under rule 28.3 for a witness summons requiring the proposed witness—
    (a) to produce in evidence a document or thing; or
    (b) to give evidence about information apparently held in confidence,
that relates to another person.
  (2) The application must be in writing in the form required by rule 28.4.
  (3) The party applying must serve the application—
    (a) on the proposed witness, unless the court otherwise directs; and
    (b) on one or more of the following, if the court so directs—
        (i)   a person to whom the proposed evidence relates,
        (ii) another party.
  (4) The court must not issue a witness summons where this rule applies unless—
    (a) everyone served with the application has had at least 14 days in which to make representations, including representations about whether there should be a hearing of the application before the summons is issued; and
    (b) the court is satisfied that it has been able to take adequate account of the duties and rights, including rights of confidentiality, of the proposed witness and of any person to whom the proposed evidence relates.
  (5) This rule does not apply to an application for an order to produce in evidence a copy of an entry in a banker's book.

Application for summons to produce a document, etc.: court's assessment of relevance and confidentiality

G–165   **28.6**—(1) This rule applies where a person served with an application for a witness summons requiring the proposed witness to produce in evidence a document or thing objects to its production on the ground that—
    (a) it is not likely to be material evidence; or
    (b) even if it is likely to be material evidence, the duties or rights, including rights of confidentiality, of the proposed witness or of any person to whom the document or thing relates outweigh the reasons for issuing a summons.
  (2) The court may require the proposed witness to make the document or thing available for the objection to be assessed.
  (3) The court may invite—
    (a) the proposed witness or any representative of the proposed witness; or
    (b) a person to whom the document or thing relates or any representative of such a person,
to help the court assess the objection.

Application to withdraw a summons, warrant or order

G–166   **28.7**—(1) The court may withdraw a witness summons, warrant or order if one of the following applies for it to be withdrawn—

(a) the party who applied for it, on the ground that it no longer is needed;

(b) the witness, on the grounds that—

   (i) he was not aware of any application for it, and

   (ii) he cannot give or produce evidence likely to be material evidence, or

   (iii) even if he can, his duties or rights, including rights of confidentiality, or those of any person to whom the evidence relates outweigh the reasons for the issue of the summons, warrant or order; or

(c) any person to whom the proposed evidence relates, on the grounds that—

   (i) he was not aware of any application for it, and

   (ii) that evidence is not likely to be material evidence, or

   (iii) even if it is, his duties or rights, including rights of confidentiality, or those of the witness outweigh the reasons for the issue of the summons, warrant or order.

(2) A person applying under the rule must—

(a) apply in writing as soon as practicable after becoming aware of the grounds for doing so, explaining why he wants the summons, warrant or order to be withdrawn; and

(b) serve the application on the court officer and as appropriate on—

   (i) the witness,

   (ii) the party who applied for the summons, warrant or order, and

   (iii) any other person who he knows was served with the application for the summons, warrant or order.

(3) Rule 28.6 applies to an application under this rule that concerns a document or thing to be produced in evidence.

Court's power to vary requirements under this Part

28.8—(1) The court may—   **G–167**

(a) shorten or extend (even after it has expired) a time limit under this Part; and

(b) where a rule or direction requires an application under this Part to be in writing, allow that application to be made orally instead.

(2) Someone who wants the court to allow an application to be made orally under paragraph (1)(b) of this rule must—

(a) give as much notice as the urgency of his application permits to those on whom he would otherwise have served an application in writing; and

(b) in doing so explain the reasons for the application and for wanting the court to consider it orally.

PART 29

SPECIAL MEASURES DIRECTIONS

Application for special measures directions

29.1—(1) An application by a party in criminal proceedings for a magistrates' court or the **G–168** Crown Court to give a special measures direction under section 19 of the *Youth Justice and Criminal Evidence Act* 1999 must be made in writing in the form set out in the Practice Direction.

(2) If the application is for a special measures direction—

(a) enabling a witness to give evidence by means of a live link, the information sought in Part B of that form must be provided;

(b) providing for any examination of a witness to be conducted through an intermediary, the information sought in Part C of that form must be provided; or

(c) enabling a video recording of an interview of a witness to be admitted as evidence in chief of the witness, the information sought in Part D of that form must be provided.

(3) The application under paragraph (1) above must be sent to the court officer and at the same time a copy thereof must be sent by the applicant to every other party to the proceedings.

(4) The court officer must receive the application—

Appendices

(a) in the case of an application to a youth court, within 28 days of the date on which the defendant first appears or is brought before the court in connection with the offence;

(b) in the case of an application to a magistrates' court, within 14 days of the defendant indicating his intention to plead not guilty to any charge brought against him and in relation to which a special measures direction may be sought; and

(c) in the case of an application to the Crown Court, within 28 days of

   (i) the committal of the defendant, or

   (ii) the consent to the preferment of a bill of indictment in relation to the case, or

   (iii) the service of a notice of transfer under section 53 of the *Criminal Justice Act* 1991, or

   (iv) where a person is sent for trial under section 51 of the *Crime and Disorder Act* 1998, the service of copies of the documents containing the evidence on which the charge or charges are based under paragraph 1 of Schedule 3 to that Act, or

   (v) the service of a Notice of Appeal from a decision of a youth court or a magistrates' court.

(5) A party to whom an application is sent in accordance with paragraph (3) may oppose the application for a special measures direction in respect of any, or any particular, measure available in relation to the witness, whether or not the question whether the witness is eligible for assistance by virtue of section 16 or 17 of the 1999 Act is in issue.

(6) A party who wishes to oppose the application must, within 14 days of the date the application was served on him, notify the applicant and the court officer, as the case may be, in writing of his opposition and give reasons for it.

(7) Paragraphs (5) and (6) do not apply in respect of an application for a special measures direction enabling a child witness in need of special protection to give evidence by means of a live link if the opposition is that the special measures direction is not likely to maximise the quality of the witness's evidence.

(8) In order to comply with paragraph (6)—

   (a) a party must in the written notification state whether he—

      (i) disputes that the witness is eligible for assistance by virtue of section 16 or 17 of the 1999 Act,

      (ii) disputes that any of the special measures available would be likely to improve the quality of evidence given by the witness or that such measures (or a combination of them) would be likely to maximise the quality of that evidence, and

      (iii) opposes the granting of a special measures direction; and

   (b) where the application relates to the admission of a video recording, a party who receives a recording must provide the information required by rule 29.7(7) below.

(9) Except where notice is received in accordance with paragraph (6), the court (including, in the case of an application to a magistrates' court, a single justice of the peace) may—

   (a) determine the application in favour of the applicant without a hearing; or

   (b) direct a hearing.

(10) Where a party to the proceedings notifies the court in accordance with paragraph (6) of his opposition to the application, the justices' clerk or the Crown Court must direct a hearing of the application.

(11) Where a hearing of the application is to take place in accordance with paragraph (9) or (10) above, the court officer shall notify each party to the proceedings of the time and place of the hearing.

(12) A party notified in accordance with paragraph (11) may be present at the hearing and be heard.

(13) The court officer must, within 3 days of the decision of the court in relation to an application under paragraph (1) being made, notify all the parties of the decision, and if the application was made for a direction enabling a video recording of an interview of a witness to be admitted as evidence in chief of that witness, the notification must state whether the whole or specified parts only of the video recording or recordings disclosed are to be admitted in evidence.

(14) In this Part:

"an intermediary" has the same meaning as in section 29 of the 1999 Act ; and
"child witness in need of protection" shall be construed in accordance with section
21(1) of the 1999 Act.

Application for an extension of time

29.2—(1) An application may be made in writing for the period of 14 days or, as the case **G–169**
may be, 28 days specified in rule 29.1(4) to be extended.

(2) The application may be made either before or after that period has expired.

(3) The application must be accompanied by a statement setting out the reasons why
the applicant is or was unable to make the application within that period and a copy of the
application and the statement must be sent to every other party to the proceedings.

(4) An application for an extension of time under this rule shall be determined by a
single justice of the peace or a judge of the Crown Court without a hearing unless the
justice or the judge otherwise directs.

(5) The court officer shall notify all the parties of the court's decision.

Late applications

29.3—(1) Notwithstanding the requirements of rule 29.1—   **G–170**

(a) an application may be made for a special measures direction orally at the trial; or

(b) a magistrates' court or the Crown Court may of its own motion raise the issue
whether a special measures direction should be given.

(2) Where an application is made in accordance with paragraph (1)(a)—

(a) the applicant must state the reasons for the late application; and

(b) the court must be satisfied that the applicant was unable to make the application
in accordance with rule 29.1.

(3) The court shall determine before making a special measures direction—

(a) whether to allow other parties to the proceedings to make representations on the
question;

(b) the time allowed for making such representations (if any); and

(c) whether the question should be determined following a hearing at which the
parties to the proceedings may be heard.

(4) Paragraphs (2) and (3) do not apply in respect of an application made orally at the
trial for a special measures direction—

(a) enabling a child witness in need of special protection to give evidence by means
of a live link; or

(b) enabling a video recording of such a child to be admitted as evidence in chief of
the witness,

if the opposition is that the special measures direction will not maximise the quality of the
witness's evidence.

Discharge or variation of a special measures direction

29.4—(1) An application to a magistrates' court or the Crown Court to discharge or vary a **G–171**
special measures direction under section 20(2) of the *Youth Justice and Criminal Evidence Act*
1999 must be in writing and each material change of circumstances which the applicant alleges
has occurred since the direction was made must be set out.

(2) An application under paragraph (1) must be sent to the court officer as soon as reasonably practicable after the change of circumstances occurs.

(3) The applicant must also send copies of the application to each party to the proceedings at the same time as the application is sent to the court officer.

(4) A party to whom an application is sent in accordance with paragraph (3) may oppose the application on the ground that it discloses no material change of circumstances.

(5) Rule 29.1(6) to (13) shall apply to an application to discharge or vary a special
measures direction as it applies to an application for a direction.

Renewal application following a material change of circumstances

29.5—(1) Where an application for a special measures direction has been refused by a magis- **G–172**
trates' court or the Crown Court, the application may only be renewed ("renewal application")
where there has been a material change of circumstances since the court refused the application.

(2) The applicant must—

    (a) identify in the renewal application each material change of circumstances which is alleged to have occurred; and

    (b) send the renewal application to the court officer as soon as reasonably practicable after the change occurs.

(3) The applicant must also send copies of the renewal application to each of the parties to the proceedings at the same time as the application is sent to the court officer.

(4) A party to whom the renewal application is sent in accordance with paragraph (3) above may oppose the application on the ground that it discloses no material change of circumstances.

(5) Rules 29.1(6) to (13), 29.6 and 29.7 apply to a renewal application as they apply to the application which was refused.

Application for special measures direction for witness to give evidence by means of a live television link

G–173   **29.6**—(1) Where the application for a special measures direction is made, in accordance with rule 29.1(2)(a), for a witness to give evidence by means of a live link, the following provisions of this rule shall also apply.

(2) A party who seeks to oppose an application for a child witness to give evidence by means of a live link must, in order to comply with rule 29.1(5), state why in his view the giving of a special measures direction would not be likely to maximise the quality of the witness's evidence.

(3) However, paragraph (2) does not apply in relation to a child witness in need of special protection.

(4) Where a special measures direction is made enabling a witness to give evidence by means of a live link, the witness shall be accompanied at the live link only by persons acceptable to the court.

(5) If the special measures directions combine provisions for a witness to give evidence by means of a live link with provision for the examination of the witness to be conducted through an intermediary, the witness shall be accompanied at the live link only by—

    (a) the intermediary; and

    (b) such other persons as may be acceptable to the court.

Video recording of testimony from witnesses

G–174   **29.7**—(1) Where an application is made to a magistrates' court or the Crown Court for a special measures direction enabling a video recording of an interview of a witness to be admitted as evidence in chief of the witness, the following provisions of this rule shall also apply.

(2) The application made in accordance with rule 29.1(1) must be accompanied by the video recording which it is proposed to tender in evidence and must include—

    (a) the name of the defendant and the offence to be charged;

    (b) the name and date of birth of the witness in respect of whom the application is made;

    (c) the date on which the video recording was made;

    (d) a statement as to whether, and if so at what point in the video recording, an oath was administered to, or a solemn declaration made by, the witness;

    (e) a statement that, in the opinion of the applicant, either—

        (i) the witness is available for cross-examination, or

        (ii) the witness is not available for cross-examination and the parties have agreed that there is no need for the witness to be so available;

    (f) a statement of the circumstances in which the video recording was made which complies with paragraph (4) of this rule; and

    (g) the date on which the video recording was disclosed to the other party or parties.

(3) Where it is proposed to tender part only of a video recording of an interview with the witness, the application must specify that part and be accompanied by a video recording of the entire interview, including those parts which it is not proposed to tender in evidence, and by a statement of the circumstances in which the video recording of the entire interview was made which complies with paragraph (4) of this rule.

(4) The statement of the circumstances in which the video recording was made referred to in paragraphs (2)(f) and (3) of this rule shall include the following information, except in so far as it is contained in the recording itself—

(a) the times at which the recording commenced and finished, including details of interruptions;

(b) the location at which the recording was made and the usual function of the premises;

(c) in relation to each person present at any point during, or immediately before, the recording—

    (i) their name, age and occupation,

    (ii) the time for which each person was present, and

    (iii) the relationship, if any, of each person to the witness and to the defendant;

(d) in relation to the equipment used for the recording—

    (i) a description of the equipment,

    (ii) the number of cameras used,

    (iii) whether the cameras were fixed or mobile,

    (iv) the number and location of the microphones,

    (v) the video format used; and

    (vi) whether it offered single or multiple recording facilities and, if so, which were used; and

(e) the location of the mastertape if the video recording is a copy and details of when and by whom the copy was made.

(5) If the special measures directions enabling a video recording of an interview of a witness to be admitted as evidence in chief of the witness with provision for the examination of the witness to be conducted through an intermediary, the information to be provided under paragraph (4)(c) shall be the same as that for other persons present at the recording but with the addition of details of the declaration made by the intermediary under rule 29.9.

(6) If the special measures directions enabling a video recording of an interview of a witness to be admitted as evidence in chief of the witness with provision for the witness, in accordance with section 30 of the *Youth Justice and Criminal Evidence Act* 1999, to be provided with a device as an aid to communication during the video recording of the interview the information to be included under paragraph (4)(d) shall include also details of any such device used for the purposes of recording.

(7) A party who receives a recording under paragraph (2) must within 14 days of its receipt, notify the applicant and the court officer, in writing—

(a) whether he objects to the admission under section 27 of the 1999 Act of any part of the video recording or recordings disclosed, giving his reasons why it would not be in the interests of justice for the recording or any part of it to be admitted;

(b) whether he would agree to the admission of part of the video recording or recordings and, if so, which part or parts; and

(c) whether he wishes to be represented at any hearing of the application.

(8) A party who seeks to oppose an application for a special measures direction enabling a video recording of an interview of a child witness to be admitted as evidence in chief of the witness must, in order to comply with rule 29.1(6), state why in his view the giving of a special measures direction would not be likely to maximise the quality of the witness's evidence.

(9) However, paragraph (8) does not apply if the witness is a child witness in need of special protection.

(10) Notwithstanding the provisions of rule 29.1 and this rule, any video recording which the defendant proposes to tender in evidence need not be sent to the prosecution until the close of the prosecution case at the trial.

(11) The court may determine an application by the defendant to tender in evidence a video recording even though the recording has not, in accordance with paragraph (10), been served upon the prosecution.

(12) Where a video recording which is the subject of a special measures direction is sent to the prosecution after the direction has been made, the prosecutor may apply to the court for the direction to be varied or discharged.

(13) An application under paragraph (12) may be made orally to the court.

(14) A prosecutor who makes an application under paragraph (12) must state—

(a) why he objects to the admission under section 27 of the 1999 Act of any part of the video recording or recordings disclosed, giving his reasons why it would not be in the interests of justice for the recording or any part of it to be admitted; and

(b) whether he would agree to the admission of part of the video recording or recordings and, if so, which part or parts.

(15) The court must, before determining the application—

(a) direct a hearing of the application; and

(b) allow all the parties to the proceedings to be present and be heard on the application.

(16) The court officer must notify all parties to the proceedings of the decision of the court as soon as may be reasonable after the decision is given.

(17) Any decision varying a special measures direction must state whether the whole or specified parts of the video recording or recordings subject to the application are to be admitted in evidence.

Expert evidence in connection with special measures directions

G–175   **29.8** Any party to proceedings in a magistrates' court or the Crown Court who proposes to adduce expert evidence (whether of fact or opinion) in connection with an application or re-newal application for, or for varying or discharging, a special measures direction must, not less than 14 days before the date set for the trial to begin—

(a) furnish the other party or parties and the court with a statement in writing of any finding or opinion which he proposes to adduce by way of such evidence and notify the expert of this disclosure; and

(b) where a request is made to him in that behalf by any other party to those proceed-ings, provide that party also with a copy of (or if it appears to the party propos-ing to adduce the evidence to be more practicable, a reasonable opportunity to examine) the record of any observation, test, calculation or other procedure on which such finding or opinion is based and notify the expert of this disclosure; and any document or other thing or substance in respect of which any such pro-cedure has been carried out.

Intermediaries

G–176   **29.9** The declaration required to be made by an intermediary in accordance with section 29(5) of the *Youth Justice and Criminal Evidence Act* 1999 shall be in the following form:

"I solemnly, sincerely and truly declare that I will well and faithfully communicate ques-tions and answers and make true explanation of all matters and things as shall be required of me according to the best of my skill and understanding."

PART 30

USE OF LIVE TELEVISION LINK OTHER THAN FOR VULNERABLE WITNESSES

Evidence by live television link in the Crown Court where witness is outside the United Kingdom

G–177   **30.1**—(1) Any party may apply for leave under section 32(1) of the *Criminal Justice Act* 1988 for evidence to be given through a live television link by a witness who is outside the United Kingdom.

(2) An application under paragraph (1), and any matter relating thereto which, by virtue of the following provisions of this rule, falls to be determined by the Crown Court, may be dealt with in chambers by any judge of the Crown Court.

(3) An application under paragraph (1) shall be made by giving notice in writing, which shall be in the form set out in the Practice Direction.

(4) An application under paragraph (1) shall be made within 28 days after the date of the committal of the defendant or, as the case may be, of the giving of a notice of transfer under section 4(1)(c) of the *Criminal Justice Act* 1987, or of the service of copies of the docu-ments containing the evidence on which the charge or charges are based under paragraph 1 of Schedule 3 to the *Crime and Disorder Act* 1998, or of the preferring of a bill of indictment in relation to the case.

(5) The period of 28 days in paragraph (4) may be extended by the Crown Court, either before or after it expires, on an application made in writing, specifying the grounds of the application. The court officer shall notify all the parties of the decision of the Crown Court.

(6) The notice under paragraph (3) or any application under paragraph (5) shall be sent to the court officer and at the same time a copy thereof shall be sent by the applicant to every other party to the proceedings.

(7) A party who receives a copy of a notice under paragraph (3) shall, within 28 days of the date of the notice, notify the applicant and the court officer, in writing—

    (a) whether or not he opposes the application, giving his reasons for any such opposition; and

    (b) whether or not he wishes to be represented at any hearing of the application.

(8) After the expiry of the period referred to in paragraph (7), the Crown Court shall determine whether an application under paragraph (1) is to be dealt with—

    (a) without a hearing; or

    (b) at a hearing at which the applicant and such other party or parties as the court may direct may be represented;

    (c) and the court officer shall notify the applicant and, where necessary, the other party or parties, of the time and place of any such hearing.

(9) The court officer shall notify all the parties of the decision of the Crown Court in relation to an application under paragraph (1) and, where leave is granted, the notification shall state—

    (a) the country in which the witness will give evidence;

    (b) if known, the place where the witness will give evidence;

    (c) where the witness is to give evidence on behalf of the prosecutor, or where disclosure is required by section 5(7) of the *Criminal Procedure and Investigations Act* 1996 (alibi) or by rules under section 81 of the *Police and Criminal Evidence Act* 1984 (expert evidence), the name of the witness;

    (d) the location of the Crown Court at which the trial should take place; and

    (e) any conditions specified by the Crown Court in accordance with paragraph (10).

(10) The Crown Court dealing with an application under paragraph (1) may specify that as a condition of the grant of leave the witness should give the evidence in the presence of a specified person who is able and willing to answer under oath or affirmation any questions the trial judge may put as to the circumstances in which the evidence is given, including questions about any persons who are present when the evidence is given and any matters which may affect the giving of the evidence.

PART 31

RESTRICTION ON CROSS-EXAMINATION BY A DEFENDANT ACTING IN PERSON

Restrictions on cross-examination of witness

31.1—(1) This rule and rules 31.2 and 31.3 apply where an accused is prevented from cross-examining a witness in person by virtue of section 34, 35 or 36 of the *Youth Justice and Criminal Evidence Act* 1999.

G–178

(2) The court shall explain to the accused as early in the proceedings as is reasonably practicable that he—

    (a) is prevented from cross-examining a witness in person; and

    (b) should arrange for a legal representative to act for him for the purpose of cross-examining the witness.

(3) The accused shall notify the court officer within 7 days of the court giving its explanation, or within such other period as the court may in any particular case allow, of the action, if any, he has taken.

(4) Where he has arranged for a legal representative to act for him, the notification shall include details of the name and address of the representative.

(5) The notification shall be in writing.

(6) The court officer shall notify all other parties to the proceedings of the name and address of the person, if any, appointed to act for the accused.

(7) Where the court gives its explanation under paragraph (2) to the accused either within 7 days of the day set for the commencement of any hearing at which a witness in respect of whom a prohibition under section 34, 35 or 36 of the 1999 Act applies may be cross-examined or after such a hearing has commenced, the period of 7 days shall be reduced in accordance with any directions issued by the court.

(8) Where at the end of the period of 7 days or such other period as the court has allowed, the court has received no notification from the accused it may grant the accused an extension of time, whether on its own motion or on the application of the accused.

(9) Before granting an extension of time, the court may hold a hearing at which all parties to the proceedings may attend and be heard.

(10) Any extension of time shall be of such period as the court considers appropriate in the circumstances of the case.

(11) The decision of the court as to whether to grant the accused an extension of time shall be notified to all parties to the proceedings by the court officer.

Appointment of legal representative

G–179   31.2—(1) Where the court decides, in accordance with section 38(4) of the *Youth Justice and Criminal Evidence Act* 1999, to appoint a qualified legal representative, the court officer shall notify all parties to the proceedings of the name and address of the representative.

(2) An appointment made by the court under section 38(4) of the 1999 Act shall, except to such extent as the court may in any particular case determine, terminate at the conclusion of the cross-examination of the witness or witnesses in respect of whom a prohibition under section 34, 35 or 36 of the 1999 Act applies.

Appointment arranged by the accused

G–180   31.3—(1) The accused may arrange for the qualified legal representative, appointed by the court under section 38(4) of the *Youth Justice and Criminal Evidence Act* 1999, to be appointed to act for him for the purpose of cross-examining any witness in respect of whom a prohibition under section 34, 35 or 36 of the 1999 Act applies.

(2) Where such an appointment is made—

(a) both the accused and the qualified legal representative appointed shall notify the court of the appointment; and

(b) the qualified legal representative shall, from the time of his appointment, act for the accused as though the arrangement had been made under section 38(2)(a) of the 1999 Act and shall cease to be the representative of the court under section 38(4).

(3) Where the court receives notification of the appointment either from the qualified legal representative or from the accused but not from both, the court shall investigate whether the appointment has been made, and if it concludes that the appointment has not been made, paragraph (2)(b) shall not apply.

(4) An accused may, notwithstanding an appointment by the court under section 38(4) of the 1999 Act, arrange for a legal representative to act for him for the purpose of cross-examining any witness in respect of whom a prohibition under section 34, 35 or 36 of the 1999 Act applies.

(5) Where the accused arranges for, or informs the court of his intention to arrange for, a legal representative to act for him, he shall notify the court, within such period as the court may allow, of the name and address of any person appointed to act for him.

(6) Where the court is notified within the time allowed that such an appointment has been made, any qualified legal representative appointed by the court in accordance with section 38(4) of the 1999 Act shall be discharged.

(7) The court officer shall, as soon as reasonably practicable after the court receives notification of an appointment under this rule or, where paragraph (3) applies, after the court is satisfied that the appointment has been made, notify all the parties to the proceedings—

(a) that the appointment has been made;

(b) where paragraph (4) applies, of the name and address of the person appointed; and

(c) that the person appointed by the court under section 38(4) of the 1999 Act has been discharged or has ceased to act for the court.

Prohibition on cross-examination of witness

31.4—(1) An application by the prosecutor for the court to give a direction under section 36 **G–181** of the *Youth Justice and Criminal Evidence Act* 1999 in relation to any witness must be sent to the court officer and at the same time a copy thereof must be sent by the applicant to every other party to the proceedings.

(2) In his application the prosecutor must state why, in his opinion—

    (a) the evidence given by the witness is likely to be diminished if cross-examination is undertaken by the accused in person;

    (b) the evidence would be improved if a direction were given under section 36(2) of the 1999 Act; and

    (c) it would not be contrary to the interests of justice to give such a direction.

(3) On receipt of the application the court officer must refer it—

    (a) if the trial has started, to the court of trial; or

    (b) if the trial has not started when the application is received—

        (i) to the judge or court designated to conduct the trial, or

        (ii) if no judge or court has been designated for that purpose, to such judge or court designated for the purposes of hearing that application.

(4) Where a copy of the application is received by a party to the proceedings more than 14 days before the date set for the trial to begin, that party may make observations in writing on the application to the court officer, but any such observations must be made within 14 days of the receipt of the application and be copied to the other parties to the proceedings.

(5) A party to whom an application is sent in accordance with paragraph (1) who wishes to oppose the application must give his reasons for doing so to the court officer and the other parties to the proceedings.

(6) Those reasons must be notified—

    (a) within 14 days of the date the application was served on him, if that date is more than 14 days before the date set for the trial to begin;

    (b) if the trial has begun, in accordance with any directions issued by the court; or

    (c) if neither paragraph (6)(a) nor (b) applies, before the date set for the trial to begin.

(7) Where the application made in accordance with paragraph (1) is made before the date set for the trial to begin and—

    (a) is not contested by any party to the proceedings, the court may determine the application without a hearing;

    (b) is contested by a party to the proceedings, the court must direct a hearing of the application.

(8) Where the application is made after the trial has begun—

    (a) the application may be made orally; and

    (b) the court may give such directions as it considers appropriate to deal with the application.

(9) Where a hearing of the application is to take place, the court officer shall notify each party to the proceedings of the time and place of the hearing.

(10) A party notified in accordance with paragraph (9) may be present at the hearing and be heard.

(11) The court officer must, as soon as possible after the determination of an application made in accordance with paragraph (1), give notice of the decision and the reasons for it to all the parties to the proceedings.

(12) A person making an oral application under paragraph (8)(a) must—

    (a) give reasons why the application was not made before the trial commenced; and

    (b) provide the court with the information set out in paragraph (2).

PART 32

INTERNATIONAL CO-OPERATION

Notice required to accompany process served outside the United Kingdom and translations

32.1—(1) The notice which by virtue of section 3(4)(b) of the *Crime (International Co-* **G–182** *operation) Act* 2003 (general requirements for service of process) must accompany any process served outside the United Kingdom must give the information specified in paragraphs (2) and (4) below.

(2) The notice must—

(a) state that the person required by the process to appear as a party or attend as a witness can obtain information about his rights in connection therewith from the relevant authority; and

(b) give the particulars specified in paragraph (4) about that authority.

(3) The relevant authority where the process is served—

(a) at the request of the prosecuting authority, is that authority; or

(b) at the request of the defendant or the prosecutor in the case of a private prosecution, is the court by which the process is served.

(4) The particulars referred to in paragraph (2) are—

(a) the name and address of the relevant authority, together with its telephone and fax numbers and e-mail address; and

(b) the name of a person at the relevant authority who can provide the information referred to in paragraph (2)(a), together with his telephone and fax numbers and e-mail address.

(5) The justices' clerk or Crown Court officer must send, together with any process served outside the United Kingdom—

(a) any translation which is provided under section 3(3)(b) of the 2003 Act; and

(b) any translation of the information required to be given by this rule which is provided to him.

(6) In this rule "process" has the same meaning as in section 51(3) of the 2003 Act.

Proof of service outside the United Kingdom

G–183   **32.2**—(1) A statement in a certificate given by or on behalf of the Secretary of State—

(a) that process has been served on any person under section 4(1) of the *Crime (International Co-operation) Act* 2003 (service of process otherwise than by post);

(b) of the manner in which service was effected; and

(c) of the date on which process was served;

shall be admissible as evidence of any facts so stated.

(2) In this rule "process" has the same meaning as in section 51(3) of the 2003 Act.

Supply of copy of notice of request for assistance abroad

G–184   **32.3** Where a request for assistance under section 7 of the *Crime (International Co-operation) Act* 2003 is made by a justice of the peace or a judge exercising the jurisdiction of the Crown Court and is sent in accordance with section 8(1) of the 2003 Act, the justices' clerk or the Crown Court officer shall send a copy of the letter of request to the Secretary of State as soon as practicable after the request has been made.

Persons entitled to appear and take part in proceedings before a nominated court and exclusion of public

G–185   **32.4** A court nominated under section 15(1) of the *Crime (International Co-operation) Act* 2003 (nominating a court to receive evidence) may—

(a) determine who may appear or take part in the proceedings under Schedule 1 to the 2003 Act before the court and whether a party to the proceedings is entitled to be legally represented; and

(b) direct that the public be excluded from those proceedings if it thinks it necessary to do so in the interests of justice.

Record of proceedings to receive evidence before a nominated court

G–186   **32.5**—(1) Where a court is nominated under section 15(1) of the *Crime (International Co-operation) Act* 2003 the justices' clerk or Crown Court officer shall enter in an overseas record—

(a) details of the request in respect of which the notice under section 15(1) of the 2003 Act was given;

(b) the date on which, and place at which, the proceedings under Schedule 1 to the 2003 Act in respect of that request took place;

(c) the name of any witness who gave evidence at the proceedings in question;

    (d) the name of any person who took part in the proceedings as a legal representative or an interpreter;

    (e) whether a witness was required to give evidence on oath or (by virtue of section 5 of the *Oaths Act* 1978) after making a solemn affirmation; and

    (f) whether the opportunity to cross-examine any witness was refused.

(2) When the court gives the evidence received by it under paragraph 6(1) of Schedule 1 to the 2003 Act to the court or authority that made the request or to the territorial authority for forwarding to the court or authority that made the request, the justices' clerk or Crown Court officer shall send to the court, authority or territorial authority (as the case may be) a copy of an extract of so much of the overseas record as relates to the proceedings in respect of that request.

Interpreter for the purposes of proceedings involving a television or telephone link

G–187

    32.6—(1) This rule applies where a court is nominated under section 30(3) (hearing witnesses in the UK through television links) or section 31(4) (hearing witnesses in the UK by telephone) of the *Crime (International Co-operation) Act* 2003.

(2) Where it appears to the justices' clerk or the Crown Court officer that the witness to be heard in the proceedings under Part 1 or 2 of Schedule 2 to the 2003 Act ("the relevant proceedings") is likely to give evidence in a language other than English, he shall make arrangements for an interpreter to be present at the proceedings to translate what is said into English.

(3) Where it appears to the justices' clerk or the Crown Court officer that the witness to be heard in the relevant proceedings is likely to give evidence in a language other than that in which the proceedings of the court referred to in section 30(1) or, as the case may be, 31(1) of the 2003 Act ("the external court") will be conducted, he shall make arrangements for an interpreter to be present at the relevant proceedings to translate what is said into the language in which the proceedings of the external court will be conducted.

(4) Where the evidence in the relevant proceedings is either given in a language other than English or is not translated into English by an interpreter, the court shall adjourn the proceedings until such time as an interpreter can be present to provide a translation into English.

(5) Where a court in Wales understands Welsh—

    (a) paragraph (2) does not apply where it appears to the justices' clerk or Crown Court officer that the witness in question is likely to give evidence in Welsh;

    (b) paragraph (4) does not apply where the evidence is given in Welsh; and

    (c) any translation which is provided pursuant to paragraph (2) or (4) may be into Welsh instead of English.

Record of television link hearing before a nominated court

G–188

    32.7—(1) This rule applies where a court is nominated under section 30(3) of the *Crime (International Co-operation) Act* 2003.

(2) The justices' clerk or Crown Court officer shall enter in an overseas record—

    (a) details of the request in respect of which the notice under section 30(3) of the 2003 Act was given;

    (b) the date on which, and place at which, the proceedings under Part 1 of Schedule 2 to that Act in respect of that request took place;

    (c) the technical conditions, such as the type of equipment used, under which the proceedings took place;

    (d) the name of the witness who gave evidence;

    (e) the name of any person who took part in the proceedings as a legal representative or an interpreter; and

    (f) the language in which the evidence was given.

(3) As soon as practicable after the proceedings under Part 1 of Schedule 2 to the 2003 Act took place, the justices' clerk or Crown Court officer shall send to the external authority that made the request a copy of an extract of so much of the overseas record as relates to the proceedings in respect of that request.

Record of telephone link hearing before a nominated court

G–189

    32.8—(1) This rule applies where a court is nominated under section 31(4) of the *Crime (International Co-operation) Act* 2003.

Appendices

(2) The justices' clerk or Crown Court officer shall enter in an overseas record—

    (a) details of the request in respect of which the notice under section 31(4) of the 2003 Act was given;

    (b) the date, time and place at which the proceedings under Part 2 of Schedule 2 to the 2003 Act took place;

    (c) the name of the witness who gave evidence;

    (d) the name of any interpreter who acted at the proceedings; and

    (e) the language in which the evidence was given.

Overseas record

G–190   **32.9**—(1) The overseas records of a magistrates' court shall be part of the register (within the meaning of section 150(1) of the *Magistrates'* Courts Act 1980) and shall be kept in a separate book.

(2) The overseas records of any court shall not be open to inspection by any person except—

    (a) as authorised by the Secretary of State; or

    (b) with the leave of the court.

PART 33

EXPERT EVIDENCE

Reference to expert

G–191   **33.1.** A reference to an 'expert' in this Part is a reference to a person who is required to give or prepare expert evidence for the purpose of criminal proceedings, including evidence required to determine fitness to plead or for the purpose of sentencing.

Expert's duty to the court

G–192   **33.2**—(1) An expert must help the court to achieve the overriding objective by giving objective, unbiased opinion on matters within his expertise.

(2) This duty overrides any obligation to the person from whom he receives instructions or by whom he is paid.

(3) This duty includes an obligation to inform all parties and the court if the expert's opinion changes from that contained in a report served as evidence or given in a statement under Part 24 or Part 29.

Content of expert's report

G–193   **33.3**—(1) An expert's report must—

    (a) give details of the expert's qualifications, relevant experience and accreditation;

    (b) give details of any literature or other information which the expert has relied on in making the report;

    (c) contain a statement setting out the substance of all facts given to the expert which are material to the opinions expressed in the report or upon which those opinions are based;

    (d) make clear which of the facts stated in the report are within the expert's own knowledge;

    (e) say who carried out any examination, measurement, test or experiment which the expert has used for the report and—

        (i) give the qualifications, relevant experience and accreditation of that person,

        (ii) say whether or not the examination, measurement, test or experiment was carried out under the expert's supervision, and

        (iii) summarise the findings on which the expert relies;

    (f) where there is a range of opinion on the matters dealt with in the report—

        (i) summarise the range of opinion, and

        (ii) give reasons for his own opinion;

    (g) if the expert is not able to give his opinion without qualification, state the qualification;

    (h) contain a summary of the conclusions reached;

    (i) contain a statement that the expert understands his duty to the court, and has complied and will continue to comply with that duty; and

    (j) contain the same declaration of truth as a witness statement.

(2) Only sub-paragraphs (i) and (j) of rule 33.3(1) apply to a summary by an expert of his conclusions served in advance of that expert's report.

Expert to be informed of service of report

33.4 A party who serves on another party or on the court a report by an expert must, at once, inform that expert of that fact.   **G–194**

Pre-hearing discussion of expert evidence

33.5—(1) This rule applies where more than one party wants to introduce expert evidence.   **G–195**

(2) The court may direct the experts to—

    (a) discuss the expert issues in the proceedings; and

    (b) prepare a statement for the court of the matters on which they agree and disagree, giving their reasons.

(3) Except for that statement, the content of that discussion must not be referred to without the court's permission.

Failure to comply with directions

33.6 A party may not introduce expert evidence without the court's permission if the expert has not complied with a direction under rule 33.5.   **G–196**

Court's power to direct that evidence is to be given by a single joint expert

33.7—(1) Where more than one defendant wants to introduce expert evidence on an issue at trial, the court may direct that the evidence on that issue is to be given by one expert only.   **G–197**

(2) Where the co-defendants cannot agree who should be the expert, the court may—

    (a) select the expert from a list prepared or identified by them; or

    (b) direct that the expert be selected in such other manner as the court may direct.

Instructions to a single joint expert

33.8—(1) Where the court gives a direction under rule 33.7 for a single joint expert to be used, each of the co-defendants may give instructions to the expert.   **G–198**

(2) When a co-defendant gives instructions to the expert he must, at the same time, send a copy of the instructions to the other co-defendant(s).

(3) The court may give directions about—

    (a) the payment of the expert's fees and expenses; and

    (b) any examination, measurement, test or experiment which the expert wishes to carry out.

(4) The court may, before an expert is instructed, limit the amount that can be paid by way of fees and expenses to the expert.

(5) Unless the court otherwise directs, the instructing co-defendants are jointly and severally liable for the payment of the expert's fees and expenses.

PART 34

HEARSAY EVIDENCE

When this Part applies

34.1 This Part applies in a magistrates' court and in the Crown Court where a party wants to introduce evidence on one or more of the grounds set out in section 114(1)(d), section 116, section 117 and section 121 of the *Criminal Justice Act* 2003, and in this Part that evidence is called "hearsay evidence".   **G–199**

Notice of hearsay evidence

34.2 The party who wants to introduce hearsay evidence must give notice in the form set out in the Practice Direction to the court officer and all other parties.   **G–200**

When the prosecutor must give notice of hearsay evidence

G–201   **34.3** The prosecutor must give notice of hearsay evidence—

    (a) in a magistrates' court, at the same time as he complies or purports to comply with section 3 of the *Criminal Procedure and Investigations Act* 1996 (disclosure by prosecutor); or

    (b) in the Crown Court, not more than 14 days after—

        (i) the committal of the defendant, or

        (ii) the consent to the preferment of a bill of indictment in relation to the case, or

        (iii) the service of a notice of transfer under section 4 of the *Criminal Justice Act* 1987 (serious fraud cases) or under section 53 of the *Criminal Justice Act* 1991 (certain cases involving children), or

        (iv) where a person is sent for trial under section 51 of the *Crime and Disorder Act* 1998 (indictable-only offences sent for trial), the service of copies of the documents containing the evidence on which the charge or charges are based under paragraph 1 of Schedule 3 to the 1998 Act.

When a defendant must give notice of hearsay evidence

G–202   **34.4** A defendant must give notice of hearsay evidence not more than 14 days after the prosecutor has complied with or purported to comply with section 3 of the *Criminal Procedure and Investigations Act* 1996 (disclosure by prosecutor).

Opposing the introduction of hearsay evidence

G–203   **34.5** A party who receives a notice of hearsay evidence may oppose it by giving notice within 14 days in the form set out in the Practice Direction to the court officer and all other parties.

G–204   **34.6** [*Revoked*]

Court's power to vary requirements under this Part

G–205   **34.7** The court may—

    (a) dispense with the requirement to give notice of hearsay evidence;

    (b) allow notice to be given in a different form, or orally; or

    (c) shorten a time limit or extend it (even after it has expired).

Waiving the requirement to give a notice of hearsay evidence

G–206   **34.8** A party entitled to receive a notice of hearsay evidence may waive his entitlement by so informing the court and the party who would have given the notice.

PART 35

EVIDENCE OF BAD CHARACTER

When this Part applies

G–207   **35.1** This Part applies in a magistrates' court and in the Crown Court when a party wants to introduce evidence of bad character as defined in section 98 of the *Criminal Justice Act* 2003.

Introducing evidence of non-defendant's bad character

G–208   **35.2** A party who wants to introduce evidence of a non-defendant's bad character or who wants to cross-examine a witness with a view to eliciting that evidence, under section 100 of the *Criminal Justice Act* 2003 must apply in the form set out in the Practice Direction and the application must be received by the court officer and all other parties to the proceedings—

    (a) not more than 14 days after the prosecutor has—

        (i) complied or purported to comply with section 3 of the *Criminal Procedure and Investigations Act* 1996 (initial disclosure by the prosecutor), or

        (ii) disclosed the previous convictions of that non-defendant; or

    (b) as soon as reasonably practicable, where the application concerns a non-defendant who is to be invited to give (or has given) evidence for a defendant.

Opposing introduction of evidence of non-defendant's bad character

G–209   **35.3** A party who receives a copy of an application under rule 35.2 may oppose that application by giving notice in writing to the court officer and all other parties to the proceedings not more than 14 days after receiving that application.

Prosecutor introducing evidence of defendant's bad character

35.4—(1) A prosecutor who wants to introduce evidence of a defendant's bad character or **G–210** who wants to cross-examine a witness with a view to eliciting that evidence, under section 101 of the *Criminal Justice Act* 2003 must give notice in the form set out in the Practice Direction to the court officer and all other parties to the proceedings.

(2) Notice under paragraph (1) must be given—

    (a) in a case to be tried in a magistrates' court, at the same time as the prosecutor complies or purports to comply with section 3 of the *Criminal Procedure and Investigations Act* 1996; and

    (b) in a case to be tried in the Crown Court, not more than 14 days after—

        (i) the committal of the defendant, or

        (ii) the consent to the preferment of a bill of indictment in relation to the case, or

        (iii) the service of notice of transfer under section 4(1) of the *Criminal Justice Act* 1987 (notices of transfer) or under section 53(1) of the *Criminal Justice Act* 1991 (notices of transfer in certain cases involving children), or

        (iv) where a person is sent for trial under section 51 of the *Crime and Disorder Act* 1998 (sending cases to the Crown Court) the service of copies of the documents containing the evidence on which the charge or charges are based under paragraph 1 of Schedule 3 to that Act.

Co-defendant introducing evidence of defendant's bad character

35.5 A co-defendant who wants to introduce evidence of a defendant's bad character or who **G–211** wants to cross-examine a witness with a view to eliciting that evidence under section 101 of the *Criminal Justice Act* 2003 must give notice in the form set out in the Practice Direction to the court officer and all other parties to the proceedings not more than 14 days after the prosecutor has complied or purported to comply with section 3 of the *Criminal Procedure and Investigations Act* 1996.

Defendant applying to exclude evidence of his own bad character

35.6 A defendant's application to exclude bad character evidence must be in the form set out **G–212** in the Practice Direction and received by the court officer and all other parties to the proceedings not more than 7 days after receiving a notice given under rules 35.4 or 35.5.

    35.7 [*Revoked*]   **G–213**

Court's power to vary requirements under this Part

    35.8 The court may—   **G–214**

    (a) allow a notice or application required under this rule to be given in a different form, or orally; or

    (b) shorten a time-limit under this rule or extend it even after it has expired.

Defendant waiving right to receive notice

35.9 A defendant entitled to receive a notice under this Part may waive his entitlement by so **G–215** informing the court and the party who would have given the notice.

PART 36

EVIDENCE ABOUT A COMPLAINANT'S SEXUAL BEHAVIOUR

When this Part applies

    36.1— This Part applies in magistrates' courts and in the Crown Court where a defendant **G–216** wants to—

    (a) introduce evidence; or

    (b) cross-examine a witness

about a complainant's sexual behaviour despite the prohibition insection 41 of the *Youth Justice and Criminal Evidence Act* 1999.

Appendices

Application for permission to introduce evidence or cross-examine

G–217   **36.2—**   The defendant must apply for permission to do so—

    (a) in writing; and

    (b) not more than 28 days after the prosecutor has complied or purported to comply with section 3 of the *Criminal Procedure and Investigations Act* 1996 (disclosure by prosecutor).

Content of application

G–218   **36.3—**   The application must—

    (a) identify the issue to which the defendant says the complainant's sexual behaviour is relevant;

    (b) give particulars of—

        (i) any evidence that the defendant wants to introduce, and

        (ii) any questions that the defendant wants to ask;

    (c) identify the exception to the prohibition in section 41 of the *Youth Justice and Criminal Evidence Act* 1999 on which the defendant relies; and

    (d) give the name and date of birth of any witness whose evidence about the complainant's sexual behaviour the defendant wants to introduce.

Service of application

G–219   **36.4—**   The defendant must serve the application on the court officer and all other parties.

Reply to application

G–220   **36.5—**   A party who wants to make representations about an application under rule 36.2 must—

    (a) do so in writing not more than 14 days after receiving it; and

    (b) serve those representations on the court officer and all other parties.

Application for special measures

G–221   **36.6—**   If the court allows an application under rule 36.2 then—

    (a) a party may apply not more than 14 days later for a special measures direction or for the variation of an existing special measures direction; and

    (b) the court may shorten the time for opposing that application.

Court's power to vary requirements under this Part

G–222   **36.7—**   The court may shorten or extend (even after it has expired) a time limit under this Part.

PART 37

SUMMARY TRIAL

Order of evidence and speeches: information

G–223   **37.1—**(1) On the summary trial of an information, where the accused does not plead guilty, the prosecutor shall call the evidence for the prosecution, and before doing so may address the court.

(2) At the conclusion of the evidence for the prosecution, the accused may address the court, whether or not he afterwards calls evidence.

(3) At the conclusion of the evidence, if any, for the defence, the prosecutor may call evidence to rebut that evidence.

(4) At the conclusion of the evidence for the defence and the evidence, if any, in rebuttal, the accused may address the court if he has not already done so.

(5) Either party may, with the leave of the court, address the court a second time, but where the court grants leave to one party it shall not refuse leave to the other.

(6) Where both parties address the court twice the prosecutor shall address the court for the second time before the accused does so.

Procedure on information where accused is not legally represented

G–224   **37.2—**(1) The court shall explain to an accused who is not legally represented the substance of the charge in simple language.

(2) If an accused who is not legally represented, instead of asking a witness in support of the charge questions by way of cross-examination, makes assertions, the court shall then put to the witness such questions as it thinks necessary on behalf of the accused and may for this purpose question the accused in order to bring out or clear up any point arising out of such assertions.

Adjournment of trial of information

37.3—(1) Where in the absence of the accused a magistrates' court adjourns the trial of an in-   **G–225**
formation, the court officer shall give to the accused notice in writing of the time and place at which the trial is to be resumed.

Formal admissions

37.4 Where under section 10 of the *Criminal Justice Act* 1967 a fact is admitted orally in   **G–226**
court by or on behalf of the prosecutor or defendant for the purposes of the summary trial of an offence the court shall cause the admission to be written down and signed by or on behalf of the party making the admission.

Notice of intention to cite previous convictions

37.5 Service on any person of a notice of intention to cite previous convictions under section   **G–227**
104 of the *Magistrates' Courts Act* 1980 or section 13 of the *Road Traffic Offenders Act* 1988 may be effected by delivering it to him or by sending it by post in a registered letter or by recorded delivery service, or by first class post addressed to him at his last known or usual place of abode.

Preservation of depositions where offence triable either way is dealt with summarily

37.6 The magistrates' court officer for the magistrates' court by which any person charged   **G–228**
with an offence triable either way has been tried summarily shall preserve for a period of three years such depositions as have been taken.

Order of evidence and speeches: complaint

37.7—(1) On the hearing of a complaint, except where the court determines under section   **G–229**
53(3) of the *Magistrates' Courts Act* 1980 to make the order with the consent of the defendant without hearing evidence, the complainant shall call his evidence, and before doing so may address the court.

(2) At the conclusion of the evidence for the complainant the defendant may address the court, whether or not he afterwards calls evidence.

(3) At the conclusion of the evidence, if any, for the defence, the complainant may call evidence to rebut that evidence.

(4) At the conclusion of the evidence for the defence and the evidence, if any, in rebuttal, the defendant may address the court if he has not already done so.

(5) Either party may, with the leave of the court, address the court a second time, but where the court grants leave to one party it shall not refuse leave to the other.

(6) Where the defendant obtains leave to address the court for a second time his second address shall be made before the second address, if any, of the complainant.

PART 38

TRIAL OF CHILDREN AND YOUNG PERSONS

Application of this Part

38.1—(1) This Part applies, subject to paragraph (3) of this rule, where proceedings to which   **G–230**
paragraph (2) applies are brought in a magistrates' court in respect of a child or young person ("the relevant minor").

(2) This paragraph applies to proceedings in which the relevant minor is charged with an offence, and, where he appears or is brought before the court, to proceedings under—

    (a) Paragraphs 1, 2, 5 and 6 of Schedule 7 to the *Powers of Criminal Courts (Sentencing) Act* 2000 (breach, revocation and amendment of supervision orders);

    (b) Part II, III or IV of Schedule 3 to the 2000 Act (breach, revocation and amendment of certain community orders);

(c) Paragraphs 4, 5, 6 and 7 of Schedule 5 to the 2000 Act (breach, revocation and amendment of attendance centre orders); and

(d) Schedule 8 to the 2000 Act (breach, revocation and amendment of action plan orders and reparation orders).

(3) Where the court is inquiring into an offence as examining justices, only rules 38.2, 38.3 and 38.5(3) apply, and where the proceedings are of a kind mentioned in paragraph (2)(a), (b) or (c) rule 38.4 does not apply.

Assistance in conducting case

G–231   **38.2**—(1) Except where the relevant minor is legally represented, the magistrates' court shall allow his parent or guardian to assist him in conducting his case.

(2) Where the parent or guardian cannot be found or cannot in the opinion of the court reasonably be required to attend, the court may allow any relative or other responsible person to take the place of the parent or guardian for the purposes of this Part.

Duty of court to explain nature of proceedings etc

G–232   **38.3**—(1) The magistrates' court shall explain to the relevant minor the nature of the proceedings and, where he is charged with an offence, the substance of the charge.

(2) The explanation shall be given in simple language suitable to his age and understanding.

Duty of court to take plea to charge

G–233   **38.4** Where the relevant minor is charged with an offence the magistrates' court shall, after giving the explanation required by rule 38.3, ask him whether he pleads guilty or not guilty to the charge.

Evidence in support of charge

G–234   **38.5**—(1) Where—

(a) the relevant minor is charged with an offence and does not plead guilty, or

(b) the proceedings are of a kind mentioned in rule 38.1(2)(a), (b) or (c),

the magistrates' court shall hear the witnesses in support of the charge or, as the case may be, the application.

(2) Except where—

(a) the proceedings are of a kind mentioned in rule 38.1(2)(a), (b) or (c), and

(b) the relevant minor is the applicant,

each witness may at the close of his evidence-in-chief be cross-examined by or on behalf of the relevant minor.

(3) If in any case where the relevant minor is not legally represented or assisted as provided by rule 38.2, the relevant minor, instead of asking questions by way of cross-examination, makes assertions, the court shall then put to the witness such questions as it thinks necessary on behalf of the relevant minor and may for this purpose question the relevant minor in order to bring out or clear up any point arising out of any such assertions.

Evidence in reply

G–235   **38.6** If it appears to the magistrates' court after hearing the evidence in support of the charge or application that a prima facie case is made out, the relevant minor shall, if he is not the applicant and is not legally represented, be told that he may give evidence or address the court, and the evidence of any witnesses shall be heard.

PART 39

TRIAL ON INDICTMENT

Time limits for beginning of trials

G–236   **39.1**—   The periods set out for the purposes of section 77(2)(a) and (b) of the *Supreme Court Act* 1981 shall be 14 days and 8 weeks respectively and accordingly the trial of a person committed by a magistrates' court—

(a) shall not begin until the expiration of 14 days beginning with the date of his committal, except with his consent and the consent of the prosecution; and

(b) shall, unless the Crown Court has otherwise ordered, begin not later than the expiration of 8 weeks beginning with the date of his committal.

Appeal against refusal to excuse from jury service or to defer attendance

39.2—(1) A person summoned under the *Juries Act* 1974 for jury service may appeal in ac-   **G–237**
cordance with the provisions of this rule against any refusal of the appropriate court officer to excuse him under section 9(2), or to defer his attendance under section 9A(1), of that Act.

(2) Subject to paragraph (3), an appeal under this rule shall be heard by the Crown Court.

(3) Where the appellant is summoned under the 1974 Act to attend before the High Court in Greater London the appeal shall be heard by a judge of the High Court and where the appellant is summoned under that Act to attend before the High Court outside Greater London or before a county court and the appeal has not been decided by the Crown Court before the day on which the appellant is required by the summons to attend, the appeal shall be heard by the court before which he is summoned to attend.

(4) An appeal under this rule shall be commenced by the appellant's giving notice of appeal to the appropriate court officer of the Crown Court or the High Court in Greater London, as the case may be, and such notice shall be in writing and shall specify the matters upon which the appellant relies as providing good reason why he should be excused from attending in pursuance of the summons or why his attendance should be deferred.

(5) The court shall not dismiss an appeal under this rule unless the appellant has been given an opportunity of making representations.

(6) Where an appeal under this rule is decided in the absence of the appellant, the appropriate court officer of the Crown Court or the High Court in Greater London, as the case may be, shall notify him of the decision without delay.

Appendices

PART 40

TAINTED ACQUITTALS

Time of certification

40.1 Where a person is convicted of an offence as referred to in section 54(1)(b) of the *Crim-*   **G–238**
inal Procedure and Investigations Act 1996 and it appears to the court before which the conviction has taken place that the provisions of section 54(2) are satisfied, the court shall make the certification referred to in section 54(2) at any time following conviction but no later than—

(a) immediately after the court sentences or otherwise deals with that person in respect of the offence; or

(b) where the court, being a magistrates' court, commits that person to the Crown Court, or remits him to another magistrates' court, to be dealt with in respect of the offence, immediately after he is so committed or remitted, as the case may be; or

(c) where that person is a child or young person and the court, being the Crown Court, remits him to a youth court to be dealt with in respect of the offence, immediately after he is so remitted.

Form of certification in the Crown Court

40.2 A certification referred to in section 54(2) of the *Criminal Procedure and Investiga-*   **G–239**
tions Act 1996 by the Crown Court shall be drawn up in the form set out in the Practice Direction.

Service of a copy of the certification

40.3—(1) Where a magistrates' court or the Crown Court makes a certification as referred to   **G–240**
in section 54(2) of the *Criminal Procedure and Investigations Act* 1996, the court officer shall, as soon as practicable after the drawing up of the form, serve a copy on the acquitted person referred to in the certification, on the prosecutor in the proceedings which led to the acquittal, and, where the acquittal has taken place before a court other than, or at a different place to, the court where the certification has been made, on—

(a) the clerk of the magistrates' court before which the acquittal has taken place; or

(b) the Crown Court officer at the place where the acquittal has taken place.

Entry in register or records in relation to the conviction which occasioned certification

G–241   **40.4** A clerk of a magistrates' court or an officer of a Crown Court which has made a certification under section 54(2) of the *Criminal Procedure and Investigations Act* 1996 shall enter in the register or records, in relation to the conviction which occasioned the certification, a note of the fact that certification has been made, the date of certification, the name of the acquitted person referred to in the certification, a description of the offence of which the acquitted person has been acquitted, the date of the acquittal, and the name of the court before which the acquittal has taken place.

Entry in the register or records in relation to the acquittal

G–242   **40.5** The court officer of the court before which an acquittal has taken place shall, as soon as practicable after receipt of a copy of a form recording a certification under section 54(2) of the *Criminal Procedure and Investigations Act* 1996 relating to the acquittal, enter in the register or records a note that the certification has been made, the date of the certification, the name of the court which has made the certification, the name of the person whose conviction occasioned the making of the certification, and a description of the offence of which that person has been convicted. Where the certification has been made by the same court as the court before which the acquittal has occurred, sitting at the same place, the entry shall be made as soon as practicable after the making of the certification. In the case of an acquittal before a magistrates' court the entry in the register shall be signed by the clerk of the court.

Display of copy certification form

G–243   **40.6**—(1) Where a court makes a certification as referred to in section 54(2) of the *Criminal Procedure and Investigations Act* 1996, the court officer shall, as soon as practicable after the drawing up of the form, display a copy of that form at a prominent place within court premises to which place the public has access.

(2) Where an acquittal has taken place before a court other than, or at a different place to, the court which has made the certification under section 54(2) of the 1996 Act in relation to the acquittal, the court officer at the court where the acquittal has taken place shall, as soon as practicable after receipt of a copy of the form recording the certification, display a copy of it at a prominent place within court premises to which place the public has access.

(3) The copy of the form referred to in paragraph (1), or the copy referred to in paragraph (2), shall continue to be displayed as referred to, respectively, in those paragraphs at least until the expiry of 28 days from, in the case of paragraph (1), the day on which the certification was made, or, in the case of paragraph (2), the day on which the copy form was received at the court.

Entry in the register or records in relation to decision of High Court

G–244   **40.7**—(1) The court officer at the court where an acquittal has taken place shall, on receipt from the Administrative Court Office of notice of an order made under section 54(3) of the *Criminal Procedure and Investigations Act* 1996 quashing the acquittal, or of a decision not to make such an order, enter in the register or records, in relation to the acquittal, a note of the fact that the acquittal has been quashed by the said order, or that a decision has been made not to make such an order, as the case may be.

(2) The court officer of the court which has made a certification under section 54(2) of the 1996 Act shall, on receipt from the Administrative Court Office of notice of an order made under section 54(3) of that Act quashing the acquittal referred to in the certification, or of a decision not to make such an order, enter in the register or records, in relation to the conviction which occasioned the certification, a note that the acquittal has been quashed by the said order, or that a decision has been made not to make such an order, as the case may be.

(3) The entries in the register of a magistrates' court referred to, respectively, in paragraphs (1) and (2) above shall be signed by the magistrates' court officer.

Display of copy of notice received from High Court

G–245   **40.8**—(1) Where the court officer of a court which has made a certification under section 54(2) of the *Criminal Procedure and Investigations Act* 1996 or before which an acquittal has occurred to which such a certification refers, receives from the Administrative Court Office notice of an order quashing the acquittal concerned, or notice of a decision not to make such an order, he shall, as soon as practicable after receiving the notice, display a copy of it at a prominent place within court premises to which place the public has access.

(2) The copy notice referred to in paragraph (1) shall continue to be displayed as referred to in that paragraph at least until the expiry of 28 days from the day on which the notice was received at the court.

PART 41

RETRIAL FOLLOWING ACQUITTAL FOR SERIOUS OFFENCE

Interpretation

41.1 In this Part: **G–246**

"business day" means any day other than a Saturday, Sunday, Christmas Day, Good Friday or a bank holiday under the Banking and Financial Dealings Act 1971, in England and Wales; and

"section 76 application" means an application made by a prosecutor under section 76(1) or (2) of the *Criminal Justice Act* 2003.

Notice of a section 76 application

41.2—(1) A prosecutor who wants to make a section 76 application must serve notice of that **G–247** application in the form set out in the Practice Direction on the Registrar and the acquitted person.

(2) That notice shall, where practicable, be accompanied by—

(a) relevant witness statements which are relied upon as forming new and compelling evidence of guilt of the acquitted person as well as any relevant witness statements from the original trial;

(b) any unused statements which might reasonably be considered capable of undermining the section 76 application or of assisting an acquitted person's application to oppose that application under rule 41.3;

(c) a copy of the indictment and paper exhibits from the original trial;

(d) copies of the transcript of the summing up and any other relevant transcripts from the original trial; and

(e) any other documents relied upon to support the section 76 application.

(3) The prosecutor must, as soon as practicable after service of that notice on the acquitted person, file with the Registrar a witness statement or certificate of service which exhibits a copy of that notice.

Response of the acquitted person

41.3—(1) An acquitted person who wants to oppose a section 76 application must serve a re- **G–248** sponse in the form set out in the Practice Direction on the Registrar and the prosecutor which—

(a) indicates if he is also seeking an order under section 80(6) of the *Criminal Justice Act* 2003 for—

(i) the production of any document, exhibit or other thing, or

(ii) a witness to attend for examination and to be examined before the Court of Appeal; and

(b) exhibits any relevant documents.

(2) The acquitted person must serve that response not more than 28 days after receiving notice under rule 41.2.

(3) The Court of Appeal may extend the period for service under paragraph (2), either before or after that period expires.

Examination of witnesses or evidence by the Court of Appeal

41.4—(1) Prior to the hearing of a section 76 application, a party may apply to the Court of **G–249** Appeal for an order under section 80(6) of the *Criminal Justice Act* 2003 for—

(a) the production of any document, exhibit or other thing; or

(b) a witness to attend for examination and to be examined before the Court of Appeal.

(2) An application under paragraph (1) must be in the form set out in the Practice Direction and must be sent to the Registrar and a copy sent to each party to the section 76 application.

(3) An application must set out the reasons why the order was not sought from the Court when—

    (a) the notice was served on the Registrar under rule 41.2, if the application is made by the prosecutor; or

    (b) the response was served on the Registrar under rule 41.3, if the application is made by the acquitted person.

(4) An application must be made at least 14 days before the day of the hearing of the section 76 application.

(5) If the Court of Appeal makes an order under section 80(6) of the 2003 Act on its own motion or on application from the prosecutor, it must serve notice and reasons for that order on all parties to the section 76 application.

Bail or custody hearings in the Crown Court

G–250   **41.5**—(1) Rules 19.18, 19.22 and 19.23 shall apply where a person is to appear or be brought before the Crown Court pursuant to sections 88 or 89 of the *Criminal Justice Act* 2003 (with the modification as set out in paragraph (2)), as if they were applications under rule 19.18(1).

(2) Substitute the following for Rule 19.18:

"Where a person is to appear or be brought before the Crown Court pursuant to sections 88 or 89 of the *Criminal Justice Act* 2003, the prosecutor must serve notice of the need for such a hearing on the court officer."

(3) Where a person is to appear or be brought before the Crown Court pursuant to sections 88 or 89 of the 2003 Act the Crown Court may order that the person shall be released from custody on entering into a recognizance, with or without sureties, or giving other security before—

    (a) the Crown Court officer; or

    (b) any other person authorised by virtue of section 119(1) of the *Magistrates' Courts Act* 1980 to take a recognizance where a magistrates' court having power to take the recognizance has, instead of taking it, fixed the amount in which the principal and his sureties, if any, are to be bound.

(4) The court officer shall forward to the Registrar a copy of any record made in pursuance of section 5(1) of the *Bail Act* 1976.

Further provisions regarding bail and custody in the Crown Court

G–251   **41.6**—(1) The prosecutor may only apply to extend or further extend the relevant period before it expires and that application must be served on the Crown Court officer and the acquitted person.

(2) A prosecutor's application for a summons or a warrant under section 89(3)(a) or (b) of the *Criminal Justice Act* 2003 must be served on the court officer and the acquitted person.

Bail or custody orders in the Court of Appeal

G–252   **41.7**—   Rules 68.8 and 68.9 shall apply to bail or custody orders made in the Court of Appeal under section 90 of the *Criminal Justice Act* 2003 as if they were orders made pursuant to an application under rule 68.7.

Application for restrictions on publication

G–253   **41.8**—(1) An application by the Director of Public Prosecutions, under section 82 of the *Criminal Justice Act* 2003, for restrictions on publication must be in the form set out in the Practice Direction and be served on the Registrar and the acquitted person.

(2) If notice of a section 76 application has not been given and the Director of Public Prosecution has indicated that there are reasons why the acquitted person should not be notified of the application for restrictions on publication, the Court of Appeal may order that service on the acquitted person is not to be effected until notice of a section 76 application is served on that person.

(3) If the Court of Appeal makes an order for restrictions on publication of its own motion or on application of the Director of Public Prosecutions, the Registrar must serve notice and reasons for that order on all parties, unless paragraph (2) applies.

Variation or revocation of restrictions on publication

41.9—(1) A party who wants to vary or revoke an order for restrictions on publication, under **G–254**
section 82(7) of the *Criminal Justice Act* 2003, may apply to the Court of Appeal in writing at
any time after that order was made.

(2) A copy of the application to vary or revoke shall be sent to all parties to the section
76 application unless paragraph (3) applies.

(3) If the application to vary or revoke is made by the Director of Public Prosecutions
and—

    (a) the notice of a section 76 application has not been given under rule 41.2; and

    (b) the Director of Public Prosecutions has indicted that there are reasons why the
acquitted person should not be notified of an application for restrictions on publication,

the Court of Appeal may order that service on the acquitted person is not to be effected until notice of a section 76 application is served on that person.

(4) If the Court of Appeal varies or revokes an order for restrictions on publication of its
own motion or on application, it must serve notice and reasons for that order on all parties, unless paragraph (3) applies.

Powers exercisable by a single judge of the Court of Appeal

41.10—(1) The following powers under the *Criminal Justice Act* 2003 and under this Part **G–255**
may be exercised by a single judge in the same manner as they may be exercised by the Court of
Appeal and subject to the same provisions, namely to—

    (a) order the production of any document, exhibit or thing under section 80(6)(a) of
the 2003 Act;

    (b) order any witness who would be a compellable witness in proceedings pursuant
to an order or declaration made on the application to attend for examination
and be examined before the Court of Appeal under section 80(6)(b) of the 2003
Act;

    (c) extend the time for service under rule 41.3(2); and

    (d) delay the requirement of service on the acquitted person of an application for
restrictions on publication under rules 41.8(2) and 41.9(3).

(2) A single judge may, for the purposes of exercising any of the powers specified in
paragraph (1), sit in such place as he appoints and may sit otherwise than in open court.

(3) Where a single judge exercises one of the powers set out in paragraph (1), the Registrar must serve notice of the single judge's decision on all parties to the section 76
application.

Powers exercisable by the Registrar

41.11—(1) The Registrar may require the Crown Court at the place of original trial to **G–256**
provide the Court of Appeal with any assistance or information which it may require for the
purposes of exercising its jurisdiction under Part 10 of the *Criminal Justice Act* 2003 or this
Part.

(2) The following powers may be exercised by the Registrar in the same manner as the
Court of Appeal and subject to the same provisions—

    (a) order the production of any document, exhibit or thing under section 80(6)(a) of
the 2003 Act;

    (b) order any witness who would be a compellable witness in proceedings pursuant
to an order or declaration made on the application to attend for examination
and be examined before the Court of Appeal under section 80(6)(b) of the 2003
Act; and

    (c) extend the time for service under rule 41.3(2).

(3) Where the Registrar exercises one of the powers set out in paragraph (2) the Registrar must serve notice of that decision on all parties to the section 76 application.

(4) Where the Registrar has refused an application to exercise any of the powers
referred to in paragraph (2), the party making the application may have it determined by
a single judge by serving a renewal in the form set out in the Practice Direction within 14
days of the day on which notice of the Registrar's decision is served on the party making
the application, unless that period is extended by the Court of Appeal.

Determination by full court

G–257   **41.12**—(1) Where a single judge has refused an application to exercise any of the powers referred to in rule 41.10, the applicant may have that application determined by the Court of Appeal by serving a notice of renewal in the form set out in the Practice Direction.

(2) A notice under paragraph (1) must be served on the Registrar within 14 days of the day on which notice of the single judge's decision is served on the party making the application, unless that period is extended by the Court of Appeal.

(3) If a notice under paragraph (1) is not served on the Registrar within the period specified in paragraph (2) or such extended period as the Court of Appeal has allowed, the application shall be treating as having been refused by the Court of Appeal.

Notice of the determination of the application

G–258   **41.13**—(1) The Court of Appeal may give its determination of the section 76 application at the conclusion of the hearing.

(2) If determination is reserved, the Registrar shall as soon as practicable, serve notice of the determination on the parties to the section 76 application.

(3) If the Court of Appeal orders under section 77 of the *Criminal Justice Act* 2003 that a retrial take place, the Registrar must as soon as practicable, serve notice on the Crown Court officer at the appropriate place of retrial.

Notice of application to set aside order for retrial

G–259   **41.14**—(1) If an acquitted person has not been arraigned before the end of 2 months after the date of an order under section 77 of the *Criminal Justice Act* 2003 he may apply in the form set out in the Practice Direction to the Court of Appeal to set aside the order.

(2) An application under paragraph (1) must be served on the Registrar and the prosecutor.

Leave to arraign

G–260   **41.15**—(1) If the acquitted person has not been arraigned before the end of 2 months after the date of an order under section 77 of the *Criminal Justice Act* 2003, the prosecutor may apply in the form set out in the Practice Direction to the Court of Appeal for leave to arraign.

(2) An application under paragraph (1) must be served on the Registrar and the acquitted person.

Leave to arraign

G–261   **41.16**—(1) A section 76 application may be abandoned by the prosecutor before the hearing of that application by serving a notice in the form set out in the Practice Direction on the Registrar and the acquitted person.

(2) The Registrar must, as soon as practicable, after receiving a notice under paragraph (1) send a copy of it endorsed with the date of receipt to the prosecutor and acquitted person.

G–262   **41.17** [Revoked]

PART 42

REMITTAL FROM ONE MAGISTRATES' COURT TO ANOTHER FOR SENTENCE

Remittal for sentence

G–263   **42.1**—(1) Where a magistrates' court remits an offender to some other magistrates' court under section 10 of the *Powers of Criminal Courts (Sentencing) Act* 2000 after convicting him of an offence, the court officer for the convicting court shall send to the court officer for the other court—

(a) a copy signed by the court officer for the convicting court of the minute or memorandum of the conviction and remittal entered in the register;

(b) a copy of any note of the evidence given at the trial of the offender, any written statement tendered in evidence and any deposition;

(c) such documents and articles produced in evidence before the convicting court as have been retained by that court;

(d) any report relating to the offender considered by the convicting court;

(e) if the offender is remitted on bail, a copy of the record made by the convicting court in pursuance of section 5 of the *Bail Act* 1976 relating to such bail and also any recognizance entered into by any person as his surety;

(f) if the convicting court makes an order under section 148 of the 2000 Act (restitution orders), a copy signed by the court officer for the convicting court of the minute or memorandum of the order entered in the register;

(g) a copy of any representation order previously made in the same case; and

(h) a copy of any application for a representation order.

(2) Where a magistrates' court remits an offender to some other magistrates' court as aforesaid and the other court remits him back to the convicting court under section 10(5) of the 2000 Act, the court officer for the other court shall send to the court officer for the convicting court—

(a) a copy signed by the court officer for the other court of the minute or memorandum of the remittal back entered in the register;

(b) if the offender is remitted back on bail, a copy of the record made by the other court in pursuance of section 5 of the *Bail Act* 1976 relating to such bail and also any recognizance entered into by any person as his surety; and

(c) all documents and articles sent in pursuance of paragraph (1) of this rule.

(3) In this rule "the offender", "the convicting court" and "the other court" have the same meanings as in section 10 of the 2000 Act.

PART 43

COMMITTAL TO THE CROWN COURT FOR SENTENCE

Committals for sentence, etc

43.1—(1) Where a magistrates' court commits an offender to the Crown Court under the **G–264** Vagrancy Act 1824, sections 3, 6, 116(3)(b) or 120(2)(a) of the *Powers of Criminal Courts (Sentencing) Act* 2000 or section 6 of the *Bail Act* 1976 after convicting him of an offence, the magistrates' court officer shall send to the Crown Court officer—

(a) a copy signed by the magistrates' court officer of the minute or memorandum of the conviction entered in the register;

(b) copy of any note of the evidence given at the trial of the offender, any written statement tendered in evidence and any deposition;

(c) such documents and articles produced in evidence before the court as have been retained by the court;

(d) any report relating to the offender considered by the court;

(e) if the offender is committed on bail, a copy of the record made in pursuance of section 5 of the 1976 Act relating to such bail and also any recognizance entered into by any person as his surety;

(f) if the court imposes under section 26 of the *Road Traffic Offenders Act* 1988 an interim disqualification for holding or obtaining a licence under Part III of the *Road Traffic Act* 1988, a statement of the date of birth and sex of the offender;

(g) if the court makes an order under section 148 of the 2000 Act (restitution orders), a copy signed by the clerk of the convicting court of the minute or memorandum of the order entered in the register; and

(h) any documents relating to an appeal by the prosecution against the granting of bail.

(2) Where a magistrates' court commits an offender to the Crown Court under the *Vagrancy Act* 1824 or sections 3, 6 or 120(2) of the 2000 Act and the magistrates' court on that occasion imposes, under section 26 of the *Road Traffic Offenders Act* 1988, an interim disqualification for holding or obtaining a licence under Part III of the *Road Traffic Act* 1988, the magistrates' court officer shall give notice of the interim disqualification to the Crown Court officer.

(3) Where a magistrates' court commits a person on bail to the Crown Court under any of the enactments mentioned in paragraph (2) of this rule or under section 6 of the *Bail Act* 1976 the magistrates' court officer shall give notice thereof in writing to the governor of the prison to which persons of the sex of the person committed are committed by that court if com-

mitted in custody for trial and also, if the person committed is under the age of 21, to the governor of the remand centre to which he would have been committed if the court had refused him bail.

Committal to Crown Court for order restricting discharge, etc

G–265   **43.2** Where a magistrates' court commits an offender to the Crown Court either—

(a) under section 43 of the *Mental Health Act* 1983 with a view to the making of a hospital order with an order restricting his discharge; or

(b) under section 3 of the *Powers of Criminal Courts (Sentencing) Act* 2000, as modified by section 43(4) of the 1983 Act, with a view to the passing of a more severe sentence than the magistrates' court has power to inflict if such an order is not made,

The magistrates' court officer shall send to the Crown Court officer—

(i) the copies, documents and articles specified in rule 43.1,

(ii) any written evidence about the offender given by a medical practitioner under section 37 of the 1983 Act or a copy of a note of any oral evidence so given,

(iii) the name and address of the hospital the managers of which have agreed to admit the offender if a hospital order is made, and

(iv) if the offender has been admitted to a hospital under section 37 of the 1983 Act, the name and address of that hospital.

PART 44

SENTENCING CHILDREN AND YOUNG PERSONS

Procedure after finding against minor in a magistrates' court

G–266   **44.1**—(1) This rule applies where—

(a) the relevant minor (as defined in rule 38.1) is found guilty by a magistrates' court of an offence, whether after a plea of guilty or otherwise; or

(b) in proceedings of a kind mentioned in rule 38.1(2)(a), (b) or (c) the court is satisfied that the case for the applicant—

(i) if the relevant minor is not the applicant, has been made out, or

(ii) if he is the applicant, has not been made out.

(2) Where this rule applies—

(a) the relevant minor and his parent or guardian, if present, shall be given an opportunity of making a statement;

(b) the court shall take into consideration all available information as to the general conduct, home surroundings, school record and medical history of the relevant minor and, in particular, shall take into consideration such information as aforesaid which is provided in pursuance of section 9 of the *Children and Young Persons Act* 1969;

(c) if such information as aforesaid is not fully available, the court shall consider the desirability of adjourning the proceedings for such inquiry as may be necessary;

(d) any written report of a probation officer, local authority, local education authority, educational establishment or registered medical practitioner may be received and considered by the court without being read aloud; and

(e) if the court considers it necessary in the interests of the relevant minor, it may require him or his parent or guardian, if present, to withdraw from the court.

(3) The court shall arrange for copies of any written report before the court to be made available to—

(a) the legal representative, if any, of the relevant minor;

(b) any parent or guardian of the relevant minor who is present at the hearing; and

(c) the relevant minor, except where the court otherwise directs on the ground that it appears to it impracticable to disclose the report having regard to his age and understanding or undesirable to do so having regard to potential serious harm which might thereby be suffered by him.

(4) In any case in which the relevant minor is not legally represented and where a report which has not been made available to him in accordance with a direction under paragraph (3)(c) has been considered without being read aloud in pursuance of paragraph

(2)(d) or where he or his parent or guardian has been required to withdraw from the court in pursuance of paragraph (2)(e), then—

    (a) the relevant minor shall be told the substance of any part of the information given to the court bearing on his character or conduct which the court considers to be material to the manner in which the case should be dealt with unless it appears to it impracticable so to do having regard to his age and understanding; and

    (b) the parent or guardian of the relevant minor, if present, shall be told the substance of any part of such information which the court considers to be material as aforesaid and which has reference to his character or conduct or to the character, conduct, home surroundings or health of the relevant minors, and if such a person, having been told the substance of any part of such information, desires to produce further evidence with reference thereto, the court, if it thinks the further evidence would be material, shall adjourn the proceedings for the production thereof and shall, if necessary in the case of a report, require the attendance at the adjourned hearing of the person who made the report.

Duty of magistrates' court to explain manner in which it proposes to deal with case and effect of order

44.2—(1) Before finally disposing of the case or before remitting the case to another court in **G–267** pursuance of section 8 of the *Powers of Criminal Courts (Sentencing) Act* 2000, the magistrates' court shall inform the relevant minor and his parent or guardian, if present, or any person assisting him in his case, of the manner in which it proposes to deal with the case and allow any of those persons so informed to make representations; but the relevant minor shall not be informed as aforesaid if the court considers it undesirable so to do.

(2) On making any order, the court shall explain to the relevant minor the general nature and effect of the order unless, in the case of an order requiring his parent or guardian to enter into a recognizance, it appears to it undesirable so to do.

PART 45

DEFERRED SENTENCE

Further conviction in magistrates' court after sentence deferred

45.1 Where under section 1 of the *Powers of Criminal Courts (Sentencing) Act* 2000 a **G–268** court has deferred passing sentence on an offender and before the expiration of the period of deferment he is convicted of any offence by a magistrates' court, the court officer for the convicting court shall, if the court which deferred passing sentence on the earlier occasion was another magistrates' court or the Crown Court, give notice of the conviction to the court officer for that court.

PART 46

CUSTODIAL SENTENCES

1. *[Note. There are currently no rules in this Part.]* **G–269**

PART 47

SUSPENDED SENTENCES OF IMPRISONMENT

Entries in magistrates' court register in respect of suspended sentences

47.1—(1) Where under section 119 of the *Powers of Criminal Courts (Sentencing) Act* **G–270** 2000 a magistrates' court deals with a person in respect of a suspended sentence otherwise than by making an order under section 119(1)(a), the court shall cause to be entered in the register its reasons for its opinion that it would be unjust to make such an order.

(2) Where an offender is dealt with under section 119 of the 2000 Act in respect of a suspended sentence passed by a magistrates' court, the court officer shall note this in the register, or where the suspended sentence was not passed by that court, shall notify the court officer for the court by which it was passed who shall note it in the register.

Suspended sentence supervision orders

G–271   **47.2**—(1) Where a magistrates' court makes an order under section 119(1)(a) or (b) of the *Powers of Criminal Courts (Sentencing) Act* 2000 in respect of a person who is subject to a suspended sentence supervision order, the court officer shall note this in the register, or where that order was not made by that court, shall—

(a) if the order was made by another magistrates' court, notify the court officer for that court who shall note the court register accordingly; or

(b) if the order was made by the Crown Court, notify the Crown Court officer.

(2) Where a magistrates' court discharges a suspended sentence supervision order under section 124(1) of the 2000 Act, the court officer shall note this in the register, or where that order was not made by that court, shall—

(a) if the order was made by another magistrates' court, notify the court officer for that court who shall note the court register accordingly; or

(b) if the order was made by the Crown Court, notify the Crown Court officer.

(3) Where a magistrates' court fines a person under section 123 of the 2000 Act for breach of the requirements of a suspended sentence supervision order which was not made by that court, the court officer shall—

(a) if the order was made by another magistrates' court, notify the court officer for that court; or

(b) if the order was made by the Crown Court, notify the Crown Court officer.

PART 48

COMMUNITY PENALTIES

Curfew order or requirement with electronic monitoring requirement

G–272   **48.1**—(1) This rule applies where the Crown Court makes—

(a) a curfew order with an electronic monitoring requirement under section 35 of the *Crime (Sentences) Act* 1997 or under sections 37 and 36B of the *Powers of Criminal Courts (Sentencing) Act* 2000; or

(b) a community rehabilitation order with curfew and electronic monitoring requirements under section 41 of and paragraph 7 of Schedule 2 to the 2000 Act.

(2) The court officer shall serve notice of the order on the person in respect of whom it is made by way of pages 1 and 2 of the form set out in the Practice Direction.

(3) The court officer shall serve notice of the order on the person responsible for electronically monitoring compliance with it by way of the form set out in the Practice Direction.

(4) Where any community order additional to the curfew order has been made in respect of the offender, the court officer shall serve a copy of the notice required by paragraph (3) on the local probation board or Youth Offending Team responsible for the offender.

PART 49

HOSPITAL AND GUARDIANSHIP ORDERS

Remand by magistrates' court for medical inquiries

G–273   **49.1** On exercising the powers conferred by section 11 of the *Powers of Criminal Courts (Sentencing) Act* 2000 a magistrates' court shall—

(a) where the accused is remanded in custody, send to the institution or place to which he is committed; or

(b) where the accused is remanded on bail, send to the institution or place at which, or the person by whom, he is to be examined,

a statement of the reasons why the court is of opinion that an inquiry ought to be made into his physical or mental condition and of any information before the court about his physical or mental condition.

Hospital or guardianship order imposed by a magistrates' court

G–274   **49.2**—(1) The magistrates' court by which a hospital order is made under section 37 of the *Mental Health Act* 1983 shall send to the hospital named in the order such information in the possession of the court as it considers likely to be of assistance in dealing with the patient to whom the order relates, and in particular such information about the mental condition, character and antecedents of the patient and the nature of the offence.

(2) The magistrates' court by which a guardianship order is made under section 37 of the 1983 Act shall send to the local health authority named therein as guardian or, as the case may be, the local health authority for the area in which the person so named resides, such information in the possession of the court as it considers likely to be of assistance in dealing with the patient to whom the order relates and in particular such information about the mental condition, character and antecedents of the patient and the nature of the offence.

(3) The magistrates' court by which an offender is ordered to be admitted to hospital under section 44 of the 1983 Act shall send to the hospital such information in the possession of the court as it considers likely to assist in the treatment of the offender until his case is dealt with by the Crown Court.

PART 50

SUPPLEMENTARY ORDERS MADE ON CONVICTION

Sexual offences prevention orders made by a magistrates' court on conviction

50.1—(1) A sexual offences prevention order made by a magistrates' court under section 104 **G–275**
of the *Sexual Offences Act* 2003 shall be in the form set out in the Practice Direction.

(2) An interim sexual offences prevention order made by a magistrates' court under section 109 of the 2003 Act shall be in the form set out in the Practice Direction.

(3) As soon as reasonably practicable after a sexual offences prevention order or an interim sexual offences prevention order has been made, the court officer shall serve a copy of that order on the defendant. Any copy of an order required to be sent under this rule to the defendant shall be either given to him in person or sent by post to his last known address and, if so given or sent, shall be deemed to have been received by him, unless the defendant proves that it was not received by him.

Parenting orders made by a magistrates' court on conviction

50.2—(1) A parenting order made by a magistrates' court under section 8 of the *Crime and* **G–276**
Disorder Act 1998 shall be in the form set out in the Practice Direction.

(2) A parenting order made by a magistrates' court under paragraph 9D of Schedule 1 to the *Powers of Criminal Courts (Sentencing) Act* 2000 shall be in the form set out in the Practice Direction.

Variation of certain orders by a magistrates' court

50.3—(1) An application to a magistrates' court for variation or discharge of any of the fol- **G–277**
lowing orders shall be by complaint:

    (a) A parenting order made under section 9(5) of the *Crime and Disorder Act* 1998;

    (b) A parenting order made under paragraph 9D of Schedule 1 to the *Powers of Criminal Courts (Sentencing) Act* 2000;

    (c) a reparation order, under paragraph 5 of Schedule 8 to the *Powers of Criminal Courts (Sentencing) Act* 2000; or

    (d) an action plan order, under that paragraph.

(2) An application under paragraph (1)(b) above shall be made to the magistrates' court which made the order, and shall specify the reason why the applicant for variation or discharge believes the court should vary or discharge the order, as the case may be.

Anti-social behaviour orders made by the Crown Court on conviction

50.4 An order made by the Crown Court under section 1C of the *Crime and Disorder Act* **G–278**
1998 on conviction in criminal proceedings shall be in the form set out in the Practice Direction.

PART 51

FINES

1. *[Note. There are currently no rules in this Part.]* **G–279**

PART 52

ENFORCEMENT OF FINES

Notice to defendant of fine or forfeited recognizance

G–280   **52.1**—(1) Where under section 140(1) of the *Powers of Criminal Courts (Sentencing) Act* 2000 or section 67(2) of the *Criminal Justice Act* 1988 a magistrates' court is required to enforce payment of a fine imposed or recognizance forfeited by the Crown Court or where a magistrates' court allows time for payment of a sum adjudged to be paid by a summary conviction, or directs that the sum be paid by instalments, or where the offender is absent when a sum is adjudged to be paid by a summary conviction, the magistrates' court officer shall serve on the offender notice in writing stating the amount of the sum and, if it is to be paid by instalments, the amount of the instalments, the date on which the sum, or each of the instalments, is to be paid and the places and times at which payment may be made; and a warrant of distress or commitment shall not be issued until the preceding provisions of this rule have been complied with.

Payment of fine to be made to magistrates' court officer

G–281   **52.2**—(1) A person adjudged by the conviction of a magistrates' court to pay any sum shall, unless the court otherwise directs, pay that sum, or any instalment of that sum, to the court officer.

(2) Where payment of any sum or instalment of any sum adjudged to be paid by the conviction or order of a magistrates' court is made to any person other than the court officer, that person, unless he is the person to whom the court has directed payment to be made or, in the case of a child, is the person with whom the child has his home, shall, as soon as may be, account for and, if the court officer so requires, pay over the sum or instalment to the court officer.

(3) Where payment of any sum adjudged to be paid by the conviction or order of a magistrates' court, or any instalment of such a sum, is directed to be made to the court officer for another court, the court officer for the court that adjudged the sum to be paid shall pay over any sums received by him on account of the said sum or instalment to the court officer for that other court.

Duty of magistrates' court officer to give receipt

G–282   **52.3** The court officer for a magistrates' court shall give or send a receipt to any person who makes a payment to him in pursuance of a conviction or order of a magistrates' court and who asks for a receipt.

Application to magistrates' court for further time

G–283   **52.4** An application under section 75(2) of the *Magistrates'* Courts Act 1980 (further time to pay) may, unless the court requires the applicant to attend, be made in writing.

G–284   **52.5** [*Revoked*]

Review of terms of postponement of warrant of commitment by magistrates' court

G–285   **52.6** An application under section 77(5) of the *Magistrates' Courts Act* 1980 may be made in writing or in person.

Notice to defendant before enforcing magistrates' court order

G–286   **52.7**—(1) A warrant of commitment shall not be issued for disobedience to an order of a magistrates' court unless the defendant has been previously served with a copy of the minute of the order, or the order was made in his presence and the warrant is issued on that occasion:

Provided that this paragraph shall not apply to an order to pay money.

Execution of magistrates' court distress warrant

G–287   **52.8**—(1) A warrant of distress issued for the purpose of levying a sum adjudged to be paid by a summary conviction or order—

    (a) shall name or otherwise describe the person against whom the distress is to be levied;

    (b) shall be directed to the constables of the police area in which the warrant is issued or to the civilian enforcement officers for the area in which they are employed, or to a person named in the warrant and shall, subject to, and in accordance with, the provisions of this rule, require them to levy the said sum by distress and sale of the goods belonging to the said person; and

(c) may where it is directed to the constables of a police area, instead of being executed by any of those constables, be executed by any person under the direction of a constable.

(2) The warrant shall authorise the person charged with the execution of it to take as well any money as any goods of the person against whom the distress is levied; and any money so taken shall be treated as if it were the proceeds of the sale of goods taken under the warrant.

(3) The warrant shall require the person charged with the execution to pay the sum to be levied to the court officer for the court that issued the warrant.

(4) A warrant to which this rule applies may be executed by the persons to whom it was directed or by any of the following persons, whether or not the warrant was directed to them—

(a) A constable for any police area in England and Wales, acting in his own police area;

(b) where the warrant is one to which section 125A of the *Magistrates' Courts Act* 1980 applies, a civilian enforcement officer within the meaning of section 125A of the 1980 Act; and

(c) where the warrant is one to which section 125A of the 1980 Act applies, any of the individuals described in section 125B(1) of the 1980 Act;

and in this rule any reference to the person charged with the execution of a warrant includes any of the above persons who is for the time being authorised to execute the warrant, whether or not they have the warrant in their possession at the time.

(5) A person executing a warrant of distress shall—

(a) either—

(i) if he has the warrant with him, show it to the person against whom the distress is levied, or

(ii) otherwise, state where the warrant is and what arrangements may be made to allow the person against whom distress is levied to inspect it;

(b) explain, in ordinary language, the sum for which distress is levied and the reason for the distress;

(c) where the person executing the warrant is one of the persons referred to in paragraph (4)(b) or (c) above, show the person against whom distress is levied a written statement under section 125A(4) or 125B(4) as appropriate; and

(d) in any case, show documentary proof of his identity.

(6) There shall not be taken under the warrant the clothing or bedding of any person or his family or the tools, books, vehicles or other equipment which he personally needs to use in his employment, business or vocation, provided that in this paragraph the word "person" shall not include a corporation.

(7) The distress levied under any such warrant as aforesaid shall be sold within such period beginning not earlier than the 6th day after the making of the distress as may be specified in the warrant, or if no period is specified in the warrant, within a period beginning on the 6th day and ending on the 14th day after the making of the distress:

Provided that with the consent in writing of the person against whom the distress is levied the distress may be sold before the beginning of the said period.

(8) The clerk of the court which issued the warrant may, on the application of the person charged with the execution of it, extend the period within which the distress must be sold by any number of days not exceeding 60; but following the grant of such an application there shall be no further variation or extension of that period.

(9) The said distress shall be sold by public auction or in such other manner as the person against whom the distress is levied may in writing allow.

(10) Notwithstanding anything in the preceding provisions of this rule, the said distress shall not be sold if the sum for which the warrant was issued and the charges of taking and keeping the distress have been paid.

(11) Subject to any direction to the contrary in the warrant, where the distress is levied on household goods, the goods shall not, without the consent in writing of the person against whom the distress is levied, be removed from the house until the day of sale; and so much of the goods shall be impounded as is in the opinion of the person executing the

warrant sufficient to satisfy the distress, by affixing to the articles impounded a conspicuous mark.

(12) The person charged with the execution of any such warrant as aforesaid shall cause the distress to be sold, and may deduct out of the amount realised by the sale all costs and charges incurred in effecting the sale; and he shall return to the owner the balance, if any, after retaining the amount of the sum for which the warrant was issued and the proper costs and charges of the execution of the warrant.

(13) The person charged with the execution of any such warrant as aforesaid shall as soon as practicable send to the court officer for the court that issued it a written account of the costs and charges incurred in executing it; and the court officer shall allow the person against whom the distress was levied to inspect the account within one month after the levy of the distress at any reasonable time to be appointed by the court.

(14) If any person pays or tenders to the person charged with the execution of any such warrant as aforesaid the sum mentioned in the warrant, or produces a receipt for that sum given by the court officer for the court that issued the warrant, and also pays the amount of the costs and charges of the distress up to the time of the payment or tender or the production of the receipt, the person as aforesaid shall not execute the warrant, or shall cease to execute it, as the case may be.

Payment after imprisonment imposed by magistrates' court

G–288   **52.9**—(1) The persons authorised for the purposes of section 79(2) of the *Magistrates' Courts Act* 1980 to receive a part payment are—

    (a) unless there has been issued a warrant of distress or commitment, the court officer for the court enforcing payment of the sum, or any person appointed under section 88 of that Act to supervise the offender;

    (b) where the issue of a warrant of commitment has been suspended on conditions which provide for payment to be made to the court officer for another magistrates' court, that court officer;

    (c) any constable holding a warrant of distress or commitment or, where the warrant is directed to some other person, that person; and

    (d) the governor or keeper of the prison or place in which the defaulter is detained, or other person having lawful custody of the defaulter:

Provided that—

      (i) the said governor or keeper shall not be required to accept any sum tendered in part payment under the said section 79(2) of the 1980 Act except on a week-day between 9 o'clock in the morning and 5 o'clock in the afternoon, and

      (ii) no person shall be required to receive in part payment under the said subsection (2) an amount which, or so much of an amount as, will not procure a reduction of the period for which the defaulter is committed or ordered to be detained.

(2) Where a person having custody of a defaulter receives payment of any sum he shall note receipt of the sum on the warrant of commitment.

(3) Where the magistrates' court officer for a court other than the court enforcing payment of the sums receives payment of any sum he shall inform the magistrates' court officer for the other court.

(4) Where a person appointed under section 88 of the 1980 Act to supervise an offender receives payment of any sum, he shall send it forthwith to the magistrates' court officer for the court which appointed him.

Order for supervision made by magistrates' court

G–289   **52.10**—(1) Unless an order under section 88(1) of the *Magistrates' Courts Act* 1980 is made in the offender's presence, the court officer for the court making the order shall deliver to the offender, or serve on him by post, notice in writing of the order.

(2) It shall be the duty of any person for the time being appointed under the said section to advise and befriend the offender with a view to inducing him to pay the sum adjudged to be paid and thereby avoid committal to custody and to give any information required by a magistrates' court about the offender's conduct and means.

Transfer of magistrates' court fine order

G–290   **52.11**—(1) The court officer for a magistrates' court which has made a transfer of fine order under section 89 or 90 or section 90 as applied by section 91 of the *Magistrates' Courts Act* 1980 shall send to the clerk of the court having jurisdiction under the order a copy of the order.

(2) Where a magistrates' court has made a transfer of fine order in respect of a sum adjudged to be paid by a court in Scotland or in Northern Ireland the court officer shall send a copy of the order to the clerk of the Scottish court or to the clerk of the Northern Irish court, as the case may be.

(3) Where a court officer receives a copy of a transfer of fine order (whether made in England and Wales, or in Scotland or in Northern Ireland) specifying his court as the court by which payment of the sum in question is to be enforceable, he shall thereupon, if possible, deliver or send by post to the offender notice in writing.

(4) Where under a transfer of fine order a sum adjudged to be paid by a Scottish court or by a Northern Irish court is enforceable by a magistrates' court—

(a) if the sum is paid, the court officer shall send it to the clerk of the Scottish court or to the clerk of the Northern Irish court, as the case may be; or

(b) if the sum is not paid, the court officer shall inform the clerk of the Scottish court or the clerk of the Northern Irish court, as the case may be, of the manner in which the adjudication has been satisfied or that the sum, or any balance thereof, appears to be irrecoverable.

Directions by magistrates' court that money found on defaulter shall not be applied in satisfaction of debt

52.12 Where the defaulter is committed to, or ordered to be detained in, a prison or other place of detention, any direction given under section 80(2) of the *Magistrates' Courts Act* 1980 shall be endorsed on the warrant of commitment. **G–291**

Particulars of fine enforcement to be entered in magistrates' court register

52.13—(1) Where the court on the occasion of convicting an offender of an offence issues a warrant of commitment for a default in paying a sum adjudged to be paid by the conviction or, having power to issue such a warrant, fixes a term of imprisonment under section 77(2) of the *Magistrates' Courts Act* 1980, the reasons for the court's action shall be entered in the register, or any separate record kept for the purpose of recording particulars of fine enforcement. **G–292**

(2) There shall be entered in the register, or any such record, particulars of any—

(a) means inquiry under section 82 of the 1980 Act;

(b) hearing under subsection (5) of the said section 82;

(c) allowance of further time for the payment of a sum adjudged to be paid by a conviction;

(d) direction that such a sum shall be paid by instalments including any direction varying the number of instalments payable, the amount of any instalments payable and the date on which any instalment becomes payable;

(e) distress for the enforcement of such a sum;

(f) attachment of earnings order for the enforcement of such a sum;

(g) decision of the Secretary of State to make deductions from income support under section 24 of the *Criminal Justice Act* 1991;

(h) order under the 1980 Act placing a person under supervision pending payment of such a sum;

(i) order under section 85(1) of the 1980 Act remitting the whole or any part of a fine;

(j) order under section 120(4) of the 1980 Act remitting the whole or any part of any sum enforceable under that section (forfeiture of recognizance);

(k) authority granted under section 87(3) of the 1980 Act authorising the taking of proceedings in the High Court or county court for the recovery of any sum adjudged to be paid by a conviction;

(l) transfer of fine order made by the court;

(m) order transferring a fine to the court;

(n) order under section 140(1) of the *Powers of Criminal Courts (Sentencing) Act* 2000 specifying the court for the purpose of enforcing a fine imposed or a recognizance forfeited by the Crown Court; and

(o) any fine imposed or recognizance forfeited by a coroner which has to be treated as imposed or forfeited by the court;

(p) reference by a justice of the peace of an application under section 77(5) of the 1980 Act for a review of the terms on which a warrant of commitment is postponed; or

(q) order under section 77(3) of the 1980 Act varying the time for which or the conditions subject to which a warrant of commitment is postponed.

Attendance Centre Order imposed by magistrates' court in default of payment of a financial penalty

G–293   **52.14**—(1) Where any person is ordered, under section 60 of the *Powers of Criminal Courts (Sentencing) Act* 2000, to attend at an attendance centre in default of payment of a sum of money, payment may thereafter be made—

(a) of the whole of the said sum, to the court officer for the magistrates' court which made the order, or

(b) of the whole or, subject to paragraph (2), any part of the said sum, to the officer in charge of the attendance centre specified in the order ("the officer in charge").

(2) The officer in charge may not accept a part payment that would not secure the reduction by one or more complete hours of the period of attendance specified in the order.

(3) On receiving a payment under paragraph (1) the court officer shall forthwith notify the officer in charge.

(4) The officer in charge shall pay any money received by him under paragraph (1) above to the court officer and shall note the receipt of the money in the register maintained at the attendance centre.

PART 53

COMPENSATION ORDERS

Review of compensation order made by a magistrates' court

G–294   **53.1**—(1) An application under section 133 of the *Powers of Criminal Courts (Sentencing) Act* 2000 for the review of a compensation order shall be by complaint.

(2) The court officer for the magistrates' court to which the complaint is made shall send a letter to the person for whose benefit the compensation order was made, inviting him to make observations and to attend any hearing of the complaint and advising him of his right to be heard.

PART 54

CONDITIONAL DISCHARGE

Further offence committed after offender conditionally discharged by a magistrates' court

G–295   **54.1**—(1) Where a magistrates' court deals with a person under section 13 of the *Powers of Criminal Courts (Sentencing) Act* 2000 in relation to an order for conditional discharge which was not made by that court the court officer shall give notice of the result of the proceedings to the court officer for the court by which the order was made.

(2) The court officer for a magistrates' court receiving a notice under this rule shall note the decision of the other court in the register.

PART 55

ROAD TRAFFIC PENALTIES

Endorsement of driving licence by magistrates' court

G–296   **55.1**—(1) Where a magistrates' court convicts a person of an offence and, under section 44 of the *Road Traffic Offenders Act* 1988 orders that particulars of the conviction, and, if the court orders him to be disqualified, particulars of the disqualification, shall be endorsed on any licence held by him, the particulars to be endorsed shall include—

(a) the name of the local justice area for which the court is acting;

(b) the date of the conviction and the date on which sentence was passed (if different);

(c) particulars of the offence including the date on which it was committed; and

(d) particulars of the sentence of the court (including the period of disqualification, if any).

(2) Where a magistrates' court orders that the licence of an offender be endorsed as mentioned in paragraph (1) or imposes an interim disqualification as mentioned in rule 43.1(1)(f) and the court officer knows or is informed of the date of birth and sex of the offender, the court officer shall send the information to the licensing authority which granted the licence.

Application to magistrates' court for removal of disqualification

55.2—(1) n application under section 42 of the *Road Traffic Offenders Act* 1988 or **G–297** paragraph 7 of Schedule 4 to the Road Traffic (Consequential Provisions) Act 1988 for an order removing a disqualification or disqualifications for holding or obtaining a licence shall be by complaint.

(2) The justice to whom the complaint is made shall issue a summons directed to the chief officer of police requiring him to appear before a magistrates' court to show cause why an order should not be made on the complaint.

(3) Where a magistrates' court makes an order under either of the provisions mentioned in paragraph (1) the court shall cause notice of the making of the order and a copy of the particulars of the order endorsed on the licence, if any, previously held by the applicant for the order to be sent to the licensing authority to which notice of the applicant's disqualification was sent.

Application to magistrates' court for review of course organiser's refusal to issue certificate of satisfactory completion of driving course

55.3—(1) An application to the supervising court under section 34B(6) or (7) of the *Road* **G–298** *Traffic Offenders Act* 1988 shall be served on the court officer within 28 days after the date specified in an order under section 34A(2) of the1988 Act, where that date falls on or after 24th May 1993.

(2) An application under section 34B(6) of the 1988 Act shall be accompanied by the notice under section 34B(5) of the 1988 Act.

(3) Where such an application is served on the court officer—

(a) he shall fix a date and time for the hearing of the application; and

(b) he shall—

(i) serve a copy of the application on the course organiser, and

(ii) serve notice of the hearing on the applicant and course organiser.

(4) If the course organiser fails to appear or be represented at the hearing of the application without reasonable excuse, the court may proceed to decide the application in his absence.

(5) In this rule, "course organiser" and "supervising court" have the meanings assigned to them in England and Wales by section 34C of the 1988 Act.

55.4 [*Revoked*] **G–299**

PART 63

APPEAL TO THE CROWN COURT AGAINST CONVICTION OR SENTENCE

Application of this Part

63.1 This Part shall apply to any appeal under section 108(1) of the *Magistrates' Courts Act* **G–300** 1980 (conviction and sentence), section 45(1) of the *Mental Health Act* 1983 (hospital or guardianship order in the absence of conviction) and paragraph 11 of Schedule 3 to the *Powers of Criminal Courts (Sentencing) Act* 2000 (re-sentencing on failure to comply with supervision order).

Notice of appeal

63.2—(1) An appeal shall be commenced by the appellant's giving notice of appeal in accor- **G–301** dance with the following provisions of this rule.

(2) The notice required by the preceding paragraph shall be in writing and shall be given to a court officer for the magistrates' court and to any other party to the appeal.

(3) Notice of appeal shall be given not later than 21 days after the day on which the decision appealed against is given and, for this purpose, where the court has adjourned the trial of an information after conviction, that day shall be the day on which the court sentences or otherwise deals with the offender:

Provided that, where a court exercises its power to defer sentence under section 1(1) of the *Powers of Criminal Courts (Sentencing) Act* 2000, that day shall, for the purposes of an appeal against conviction, be the day on which the court exercises that power.

(4) A notice of appeal shall state the grounds of appeal.

(5) The time for giving notice of appeal may be extended, either before or after it expires, by the Crown Court, on an application made in accordance with paragraph (6).

(6) An application for an extension of time shall be made in writing, specifying the grounds of the application and sent to a Crown Court officer.

(7) Where the Crown Court extends the time for giving notice of appeal, the Crown Court officer shall give notice of the extension to—

    (a) the appellant; and

    (b) the magistrates' court officer,

and the appellant shall give notice of the extension to any other party to the appeal.

Documents to be sent to Crown Court

G–302   **63.3**—(1) The magistrates' court officer shall as soon as practicable send to the Crown Court officer any notice of appeal to the Crown Court given to the magistrates' court officer.

(2) The magistrates' court officer shall send to the Crown Court officer, with the notice of appeal, a copy of the extract of the magistrates' court register relating to that decision and of the last known or usual place of abode of the parties to the appeal.

(3) Where any person, having given notice of appeal to the Crown Court, has been granted bail for the purposes of the appeal the magistrates' court officer for the court from whose decision the appeal is brought shall before the day fixed for the hearing of the appeal send to the Crown Court officer a copy of the record made in pursuance of section 5 of the *Bail Act* 1976.

(4) Where a notice of appeal is given in respect of a hospital order or guardianship order made under section 37 of the *Mental Health Act* 1983 (powers of courts to order hospital admission or guardianship), a magistrates' court officer for the court from which the appeal is brought shall send with the notice to the Crown Court officer any written evidence considered by the court under section 37(2) of the 1983 Act.

(5) Where a notice of appeal is given in respect of an appeal against conviction by a magistrates' court the magistrates' court officer shall send with the notice to the Crown Court officer any admission of facts made for the purposes of the summary trial under section 10 of the *Criminal Justice Act* 1967 (proof by formal admission).

(6) Where a notice of appeal is given in respect of an appeal against sentence by a magistrates' court, and where that sentence was a custodial sentence, the magistrates' court officer shall send with the notice to the Crown Court officer a statement of whether the magistrates' court obtained and considered a pre-sentence report before passing such sentence.

Entry of appeal and notice of hearing

G–303   **63.4** On receiving notice of appeal, the Crown Court officer shall enter the appeal and give notice of the time and place of the hearing to—

    (a) the appellant;

    (b) any other party to the appeal; and

    (c) the magistrates' court officer.

Abandonment of appeal — notice

G–304   **63.5**—(1) Without prejudice to the power of the Crown Court to give leave for an appeal to be abandoned, an appellant may abandon an appeal by giving notice in writing, in accordance with the following provisions of this rule, not later than the third day before the day fixed for hearing the appeal.

(2) The notice required by the preceding paragraph shall be given—

    (a) to the magistrates' court officer;

    (b) to the Crown Court officer; and

    (c) to any other party to the appeal.

(3) For the purposes of determining whether notice of abandonment was given in time there shall be disregarded any Saturday, Sunday and any day which is specified to be a bank holiday in England and Wales under section 1(1) of the *Banking and Financial Dealings Act* 1971.

Abandonment of appeal — bail

63.6 Where notice to abandon an appeal has been given by the appellant, any recognizance **G–305** conditioned for the appearance of the appellant at the hearing of the appeal shall have effect as if conditioned for the appearance of the appellant before the court from whose decision the appeal was brought at a time and place to be notified to the appellant by the court officer for that court.

Number and qualification of justices — appeals from youth courts

63.7 Subject to the provisions of rule 63.8 and to any directions under section 74(4) of the **G–306** *Supreme Court Act* 1981 (directions disapplying the set out number and qualifications of justices), on the hearing of an appeal from a youth court the Crown Court shall consist of a judge sitting with two justices each of whom is a member of a youth court panel and who are chosen so that the Court shall include a man and a woman.

Number and qualification of justices — dispensation for special circumstances

63.8—(1) The Crown Court may enter on any appeal notwithstanding that the Court is not **G–307** constituted as required by section 74(1) of the *Supreme Court Act* 1981 or rule 63.7 if it appears to the judge that the Court could not be constituted without unreasonable delay and the Court includes one justice who is a member of a youth court panel.

(2) The Crown Court may at any stage continue with any proceedings with a Court from which any one or more of the justices initially comprising the Court has withdrawn, or is absent for any reason.

Disqualifications

63.9 A justice of the peace shall not sit in the Crown Court on the hearing of an appeal in a **G–308** matter on which he adjudicated.

PART 64

APPEAL TO THE HIGH COURT BY WAY OF CASE STATED

Application to a magistrates' court to state a case

64.1—(1) An application under section 111(1) of the *Magistrates*' Courts Act 1980 shall be **G–309** made in writing and signed by or on behalf of the applicant and shall identify the question or questions of law or jurisdiction on which the opinion of the High Court is sought.

(2) Where one of the questions on which the opinion of the High Court is sought is whether there was evidence on which the magistrates' court could come to its decision, the particular finding of fact made by the magistrates' court which it is claimed cannot be supported by the evidence before the magistrates' court shall be specified in such application.

(3) Any such application shall be sent to a court officer for the magistrates' court whose decision is questioned.

Consideration of a draft case by a magistrates' court

64.2—(1) Within 21 days after receipt of an application made in accordance with rule 64.1, a **G–310** court officer for the magistrates' court whose decision is questioned shall, unless the justices refuse to state a case under section 111(5) of the *Magistrates' Courts Act* 1980, send a draft case in which are stated the matters required under rule 64.6 (content of case stated) to the applicant or his legal representative and shall send a copy thereof to the respondent or his legal representative.

(2) Within 21 days after receipt of the draft case under paragraph (1), each party may make representations thereon. Any such representations shall be in writing and signed by or on behalf of the party making them and shall be sent to the magistrates' court officer.

(3) Where the justices refuse to state a case under section 111(5) of the 1980 Act and they are required by a mandatory order of the High Court under section 111(6) to do so, this rule shall apply as if in paragraph (1)—

(a) for the words "receipt of an application made in accordance with rule 64.1" there were substituted the words "the date on which a mandatory order under section 111(6) of the 1980 Act is made"; and

(b) the words "unless the justices refuse to state a case under section 111(5) of the 1980 Act" were omitted.

Preparation and submission of final case to a magistrates' court

G–311

64.3—(1) Within 21 days after the latest day on which representations may be made under rule 64.2, the justices whose decision is questioned shall make such adjustments, if any, to the draft case prepared for the purposes of that rule as they think fit, after considering any such representations, and shall state and sign the case.

(2) A case may be stated on behalf of the justices whose decision is questioned by any 2 or more of them and may, if the justices so direct, be signed on their behalf by the justices' clerk.

(3) Forthwith after the case has been stated and signed a court officer for the court shall send it to the applicant or his legal representative, together with any statement required by rule 64.4.

Extension of time limits by a magistrates' court

G–312

64.4—(1) If a magistrates' court officer is unable to send to the applicant a draft case under rule 64.2(1) within the time required by that paragraph, he shall do so as soon as practicable thereafter and the provisions of that rule shall apply accordingly; but in that event a court officer shall attach to the draft case, and to the final case when it is sent to the applicant or his legal representative under rule 64.3(3), a statement of the delay and the reasons for it.

(2) If a magistrates' court officer receives an application in writing from or on behalf of the applicant or the respondent for an extension of the time within which representations on the draft case may be made under rule 64.2(2), together with reasons in writing for it, the justices' clerk may, by notice in writing sent to the applicant, or respondent as the case may be, by the magistrates' court officer, extend the time and the provisions of that paragraph and of rule 64.3 shall apply accordingly; but in that event the court officer shall attach to the final case, when it is sent to the applicant or his legal representative under rule 64.3(3), a statement of the extension and the reasons for it.

(3) If the justices are unable to state a case within the time required by rule 64.3(1), they shall do so as soon as practicable thereafter and the provisions of that rule shall apply accordingly; but in that event a court officer shall attach to the final case, when it is sent to the applicant or his legal representative under rule 64.3(3), a statement of the delay and the reasons for it.

G–313   **64.5** *[Revoked]*

Content of case stated by a magistrates' courts

G–314

64.6—(1) A case stated by the magistrates' court shall state the facts found by the court and the question or questions of law or jurisdiction on which the opinion of the High Court is sought.

(2) Where one of the questions on which the opinion of the High Court is sought is whether there was evidence on which the magistrates' court could come to its decision, the particular finding of fact which it is claimed cannot be supported by the evidence before the magistrates' court shall be specified in the case.

(3) Unless one of the questions on which the opinion of the High Court is sought is whether there was evidence on which the magistrates' court could come to its decision, the case shall not contain a statement of evidence.

Application to the Crown Court to state a case

G–315

64.7—(1) An application under section 28 of the *Supreme Court Act* 1981 to the Crown Court to state a case for the opinion of the High Court shall be made in writing to a court officer within 21 days after the date of the decision in respect of which the application is made.

(2) The application shall state the ground on which the decision of the Crown Court is questioned.

(3) After making the application, the applicant shall forthwith send a copy of it to the parties to the proceedings in the Crown Court.

(4) On receipt of the application, the Crown Court officer shall forthwith send it to the judge who presided at the proceedings in which the decision was made.

(5) On receipt of the application, the judge shall inform the Crown Court officer as to whether or not he has decided to state a case and that officer shall give notice in writing to the applicant of the judge's decision.

(6) If the judge considers that the application is frivolous, he may refuse to state a case and shall in that case, if the applicant so requires, cause a certificate stating the reasons for the refusal to be given to him.

(7) If the judge decides to state a case, the procedure to be followed shall, unless the judge in a particular case otherwise directs, be the procedure set out in paragraphs (8) to (12) of this rule.

(8) The applicant shall, within 21 days of receiving the notice referred to in paragraph (5), draft a case and send a copy of it to the Crown Court officer and to the parties to the proceedings in the Crown Court.

(9) Each party to the proceedings in the Crown Court shall, within 21 days of receiving a copy of the draft case under paragraph (8), either—

   (a) give notice in writing to the applicant and the Crown Court officer that he does not intend to take part in the proceedings before the High Court;

   (b) indicate in writing on the copy of the draft case that he agrees with it and send the copy to a court officer; or

   (c) draft an alternative case and send it, together with the copy of the applicant's case, to the Crown Court officer.

(10) The judge shall consider the applicant's draft case and any alternative draft case sent to the Crown Court officer under paragraph (9)(c).

(11) If the Crown Court so orders, the applicant shall, before the case is stated and delivered to him, enter before the Crown Court officer into a recognizance, with or without sureties and in such sum as the Crown Court considers proper, having regard to the means of the applicant, conditioned to prosecute the appeal without delay.

(12) The judge shall state and sign a case within 14 days after either—

   (a) the receipt of all the documents required to be sent to a court officer under paragraph (9); or

   (b) the expiration of the period of 21 days referred to in that paragraph,

whichever is the sooner.

(13) A case stated by the Crown Court shall state the facts found by the Crown Court, the submissions of the parties (including any authorities relied on by the parties during the course of those submissions), the decision of the Crown Court in respect of which the application is made and the question on which the opinion of the High Court is sought.

(14) Any time limit referred to in this rule may be extended either before or after it expires by the Crown Court.

(15) If the judge decides not to state a case but the stating of a case is subsequently required by a mandatory order of the High Court, paragraphs (7) to (14) shall apply to the stating of the case save that—

   (a) in paragraph (7) the words "If the judge decides to state a case" shall be omitted; and

   (b) in paragraph (8) for the words "receiving the notice referred to in paragraph (5)" there shall be substituted the words "the day on which the mandatory order was made".

PART 65

APPEAL TO THE COURT OF APPEAL AGAINST RULING IN PREPARATORY HEARING

Notice of appeal

   65.1—(1) An application to the judge of the Crown Court for leave to appeal under section **G–316** 9(11) of the *Criminal Justice Act* 1987 or section 35(1) of the *Criminal Procedure and Investigations Act* 1996 shall be made orally within two days of the making of the order or ruling to which it relates.

(2) Unless the application is made on the occasion of the order or ruling to which it re-

lates, the appellant shall serve notice in writing thereof, specifying the grounds of the application, on the Crown Court officer and on all parties to the hearing directly affected by the order or ruling in question.

(3) The appellant shall no later than the day referred to in paragraph (4) serve notice of appeal from an order or ruling under section 9(11) of the 1987 Act or section 31(3) of the 1996 Act or, as the case may be, of an application to the Court of Appeal for leave to appeal from such a ruling on—

(a) the Registrar;

(b) the Crown Court officer; and

(c) all parties to the preparatory hearing directly affected by the said order or ruling.

(4) The day referred to is—

(a) the day which occurs seven days after the making of the order or ruling; or

(b) where an application is made to the judge of the Crown Court for leave to appeal under section 31(3) of the 1996 Act as in paragraph (1), the day which occurs 7 days after such application is determined or withdrawn.

(5) The time for giving notice under paragraph (3) may be extended, before or after it expires, by the Court of Appeal.

(6) A notice of appeal or of an application for leave to appeal, or an application to the Court of Appeal for an extension of time as referred to in paragraph (5), shall be in the form set out in the Practice Direction.

(7) If notice in writing of an application for leave to appeal was, under paragraph (2), served on the Crown Court, a copy thereof shall accompany the notice of appeal or, as the case may be, of an application for leave to appeal required under paragraph (3) to be served on the Registrar.

(8) Notice of appeal or of an application for leave to appeal may be given either in respect of the whole or any part of the order to which it relates and shall—

(a) specify any question of law in respect of which the appeal is brought and, where appropriate, such facts of the case as are necessary for its proper consideration;

(b) summarise the arguments intended to be put to the Court of Appeal; and

(c) specify any authorities intended to be cited.

(9) Where the judge of the Crown Court has given leave to appeal the notice of appeal shall state that fact and specify the grounds on which leave is given.

(10) Notice of appeal or of an application for leave to appeal shall be accompanied by any documents or other things (or copies thereof) necessary for the proper determination of the appeal or application.

Respondent's notice

G–317   **65.2**—(1) Upon receiving notice of appeal or of an application for leave to appeal, the respondent if he desires to oppose the appeal, shall, within seven days of receipt of the notice, serve a notice in the form set out in the Practice Direction on the Registrar—

(a) stating the date on which the appellant's notice was received by the respondent;

(b) summarising his response to the arguments of the appellant; and

(c) specifying the authorities which he intends to cite,

and shall at the same time serve a copy thereof on the appellant and any other party to the proceedings directly affected by the order or ruling and on the Crown Court officer.

(2) The time for giving notice under this rule may be extended, either before or after it expires, by the Court of Appeal.

Persons in custody

G–318   **65.3**—(1) A person in custody shall be entitled to be present on the hearing of an appeal, or an application for leave to appeal, under section 9(11) of the *Criminal Justice Act* 1987 or section 35(1) of the *Criminal Procedure and Investigations Act* 1996, to which he is a party.

(2) Except as provided by paragraph (1) above, a person in custody shall not be entitled to be present on the hearing of an appeal, or an application for leave to appeal, under section 9(11) of the 1987 Act or section 35(1) of the 1996 Act except—

(a) on an application to the Crown Court for leave to appeal, with the leave of the judge; or

(b) on an appeal, or an application to the Court of Appeal for leave to appeal, with the leave of that Court.

(3) An application for leave to be present under paragraph (2) shall be made—
    (a) where paragraph (2)(a) applies, orally to the judge;
    (b) where paragraph (2)(b) applies, by serving notice in the form set out in the Practice Direction on the Registrar, or orally to the Court.

Supply of documentary and other exhibits
65.4— Rule 68.11 (supply of documentary and other exhibits) shall apply in relation to an **G–319** appellant and a respondent under section 9(11) of the *Criminal Justice Act* 1987 or section 35(1) of the *Criminal Procedure and Investigations Act* 1996 as it applies in relation to an appellant and a respondent under Part I of the *Criminal Appeal Act* 1968.

Abandonment of proceedings
65.5— Rule 68.22 (abandonment of proceedings) shall apply for the purposes of an appeal **G–320** or an application for leave to appeal by an appellant under section 9(11) of the *Criminal Justice Act* 1987 or section 35(1) of the *Criminal Procedure and Investigations Act* 1996 as it applies to an appeal or application for leave under Part I of the *Criminal Appeal Act* 1968, except that—
    (a) notice thereof shall be served on the Registrar in the alternative form set out in the Practice Direction; and
    (b) the requirement under rule 68.22(3) for the Registrar to send a copy of a notice of abandonment of proceedings to the Secretary of State shall be omitted.

Powers exercisable by single judge
65.6—(1) The following powers may be exercised by a judge of the court in the same man- **G–321** ner as they may be exercised by the court and subject to the same provisions, namely—
    (a) to give leave to appeal under section 9(11) of the *Criminal Justice Act* 1987 or section 35(1) of the *Criminal Procedure and Investigations Act* 1996;
    (b) to extend, under rule 65.1, the time within which notice of appeal or of an application for leave to appeal must be given;
    (c) to extend the time within which a notice under rule 65.2 of opposition to an appeal or application for leave to appeal must be given by the respondent; and
    (d) to give leave, in pursuance of rule 65.3, for a person in custody to be present at any proceedings.
(2) A judge of the court shall, for the purpose of exercising any of the powers specified above, sit in such place as he appoints, and may sit otherwise than in open court.

Determination by full court
65.7—(1) Where a judge of the court has refused an application on the part of an applicant **G–322** to exercise in his favour any of the powers referred to in rule 65.6, the applicant may have the application determined by the court by serving a notice in the form set out in the Practice Direction on the Registrar within 7 days, or such longer period as a judge of the court may fix, from the date on which notice of the refusal was served on him by the Registrar.
(2) The notice shall be signed by, or on behalf of, the applicant.
(3) If the notice is not signed by the applicant and the applicant is in custody, the Registrar shall, as soon as practicable after receiving the notice, send a copy of it to the applicant.
(4) If such a notice is not served on the Registrar within the said 7 days or such longer period as a judge of the court may fix, the application shall be treated as having been refused by the court.

Notice of determination of court
65.8—(1) The Registrar shall, as soon as practicable, serve notice of any determination by the **G–323** Court of Appeal or by any judge of the court under rule 65.6 on—
    (a) the applicant;
    (b) the respondent; and
    (c) and any other party who is directly affected by the ruling to which the appeal or application relates,
and notice of a determination by a single judge under rule 65.6 shall be served in the form set out in the Practice Direction.

Appendices

(2) The Registrar shall, as soon as practicable, serve notice on the Crown Court officer at the place of trial of the order of the Court of Appeal disposing of an appeal or application for leave to appeal.

G–324   **65.9** [*Revoked*]

The Registrar

G–325   **65.10**—(1) The Registrar may require the Crown Court at the place of trial to furnish the Court of Appeal with any assistance or information which it may require for the purpose of exercising its jurisdiction.

(2) Subject to paragraphs (3) and (4) the Registrar shall give as long notice in advance as reasonably possible of the date of hearing of any appeal or application

(a) to the appellant; and

(b) to the respondent and any other party directly affected by the order or ruling to which the appeal or application relates.

(3) Paragraph (2) shall not apply to proceedings before a judge of the court under rule 65.6.

(4) Where a party to whom notice is required to be given by this rule is at the material time in custody, notice shall instead be given to the person having custody of him.

Appeal against order following discharge of jury because of jury tampering

G–326   **65.11**—   The rules in this Part apply with the necessary modifications to an appeal under section 47 of the Criminal Justice Act 2003.

PART 68

APPEAL TO THE COURT OF APPEAL AGAINST CONVICTION SENTENCE OR SENTENCE REVIEW DECISION

G–327   **68.1** [*Revoked*]

Certificate of trial judge

G–328   **68.2**—(1) The certificate of the judge of the court of trial under section 1(2), 12 or 15(2) of the *Criminal Appeal Act* 1968 that a case is a fit case for appeal shall be in the form set out in the Practice Direction.

(2) The certificate shall be forwarded forthwith to the Registrar, whether or not the person to whom the certificate relates has applied for a certificate.

(3) A copy of the certificate shall be forwarded forthwith to the person to whom the certificate relates or to his legal representative.

Notice of appeal and application for extension of time

G–329   **68.3**—(1) Notice of appeal or of an application for leave to appeal under Part I of the *Criminal Appeal Act* 1968 or notice of appeal under section 13 (appeal in cases of contempt of court) of the *Administration of Justice Act* 1960 (as required by section 18A of the 1968 Act) against an order or decision of the Crown Court shall be given by completing Part 1 of the form set out in the Practice Direction, and so much of Part 2 thereof as relates to the notice and serving it on a Crown court officer.

(1A) Notice of an application for leave to appeal under paragraph 14 of Schedule 22 to the *Criminal Justice Act* 2003 shall be given by completing the form set out in the Practice Direction and serving it on the Registrar.

(1B) Notice of an application for leave to appeal under section 74(8) of the *Serious Organised Crime and Police Act* 2005 shall be given by completing the form set out in the Practice Direction and serving it on a Crown Court officer.

(1C) A document to be served on a Crown Court officer under this Part must be served on a court officer at the Crown Court centre at which the conviction, verdict, finding, decision or sentence appealed against was given or passed.

(2) A notice of appeal or of an application for leave to appeal shall be accompanied by a notice in the form set out in the Practice Direction containing the grounds of the appeal or application.

(3) A notice of the grounds of appeal or application in the form set out in the Practice Direction shall include notice—

(a) of any application to be made to the court for a declaration of incompatibility under section 4 of the *Human Rights Act* 1998; or

(b) of any issue for the court to decide which may lead to the court making such a declaration.

(4) Where the grounds of appeal or application include notice in accordance with paragraph (3)(b) above, a copy of the notice shall be served on the prosecutor by the appellant.

(5) If the appellant has been convicted of more than one offence, the notice of appeal or of an application for leave, referred to in paragraph (2), shall specify the convictions or sentences against which the appellant is appealing or applying for leave to appeal.

(6) The grounds of an appeal or application, referred to in paragraph (2), may, with the consent of the court, be varied or amplified within such time as the court may allow.

(7) Notice of an application to extend the time within which notice of appeal or of an application for leave to appeal may be given under—

(a) Part I of the 1968 Act;

(b) article 3 of the *Criminal Justice Act 2003 (Mandatory Life Sentences: Appeals in Transitional Cases) Order* 2005; or

(c) article 5 of the *Serious Organised Crime and Police Act 2005 (Appeals under section 74) Order* 2006,

by completing so much of the form, referred to in paragraph (2), as relates to the application and by giving notice of appeal or of an application for leave to appeal in accordance with the foregoing provisions of this rule.

(8) Notice of an application to extend the time within which notice of appeal or of an application for leave to appeal may be given under—

(a) Part I of the 1968 Act;

(b) article 3 of the 2005 Order; or

(c) article 5 of the 2006 Order,

shall specify the grounds of the application.

(9) An appellant who is appealing or applying for leave to appeal against conviction shall specify in the form, referred to in paragraph (2), any exhibit produced at the trial which he wishes to be kept in custody for the purposes of his appeal.

(10) The forms to which this rule relates, shall be signed by, or on behalf of, the appellant.

(11) If a form is not signed by the appellant and the appellant is in custody, the Registrar shall, as soon as practicable after receiving the form from the Crown Court, send a copy of it to the appellant.

(12) Where an appellant does not require leave to appeal, a notice of application for leave to appeal shall be treated as a notice of appeal; and where an appellant requires leave to appeal but serves only a notice of appeal, the notice of appeal shall be treated as an application for leave to appeal.

Appeal following reference by Criminal Cases Review Commission

68.4—(1) In this rule: "the Commission" means the Criminal Cases Review Commission, and **G–330** "reference" means the reference of a conviction, verdict, finding or sentence to the Court of Appeal by the Commission under section 9 of the *Criminal Appeal Act* 1995.

(2) The Registrar must serve on the appellant written notice of receipt of a reference.

(3) The appellant must give notice of appeal under rule 68.3 by serving it on the Registrar within—

(a) 28 days of the date of the notice served under paragraph (2), in the case of an appeal against sentence; or

(b) 56 days of the date of that notice, in the case of an appeal against conviction, verdict of not guilty by reason of insanity, finding that the appellant was under a disability, or finding that the appellant did the act or made the omission charged.

(4) The court may extend the time for giving notice of appeal, either before or after it expires.

(5) The grounds of appeal accompanying a notice of appeal must include—

(a) where a ground of appeal is said to relate to a reason given by the Commission for making the reference, an explanation of how it is related; and

(b) where a ground of appeal is said not to be so related, notice of application for leave to appeal on that ground.

(6) If a notice of appeal is not received within the time specified in paragraph (3), or within such longer period as the court allows under paragraph (4), the reasons given by the Commission for making the reference shall stand as the grounds of appeal.

(7) On receiving a notice of appeal the Registrar must serve a copy on the prosecutor and on any other party to the appeal.

Exercise of court's powers to give leave to appeal, etc: general rules

G–331   **68.5**—(1) This rule and rule 68.6 apply when the Registrar or a single judge exercises a power conferred by one of the following provisions—

  (a) section 31 of the *Criminal Appeal Act* 1968, article 8 of the *Criminal Justice Act 2003 (Mandatory Life Sentences: Appeals in Transitional Cases) Order* 2005 or article 11 of the *Serious Organised Crime and Police Act 2005 (Appeals under section 74) Order* 2006 (powers exercisable by a single judge);

  (b) section 31A of the 1968 Act, article 9 of the 2005 Order or article 12 of the 2006 Order (powers exercisable by the Registrar);

  (c) section 31B of the 1968 Act, article 10 of the 2005 Order or article 13 of the 2006 Order (procedural directions by a single judge or the Registrar); or

  (d) section 31C of the 1968 Act, article 11 of the 2005 Order or article 14 of the 2006 Order (appeals against procedural directions).

(2) An application to the Registrar, a single judge or the court for the exercise of any of the powers referred to in paragraph (1) should be in the relevant form set out in the Practice Direction or in the form required by the Registrar.

(3) An application by an appellant must be signed by him or on his behalf. If it is not signed by him and he is in custody, the Registrar must send him a copy as soon as practicable after receiving it.

(4) If an appellant makes an application for the exercise of any of the powers under the 1968 Act or the 2006 Order and he makes it when he gives notice of appeal or notice of an application for leave to appeal, the application must be served on the Crown Court officer. In all other cases, the application must be served on the Registrar.

(5) Neither a single judge nor the Registrar need sit in court to exercise any of the powers referred to in paragraph (1) of this rule.

Further applications to a judge or to the court: additional rules

G–332   **68.6**—(1) Where—

  (a) an appellant renews an application for the exercise of a power conferred by section 31 of the *Criminal Appeal Act* 1968, article 8 of the *Criminal Justice Act 2003 (Mandatory Life Sentences: Appeals in Transitional Cases) Order* 2005 or article 11 of the *Serious Organised Crime and Police Act 2005 (Appeals under section 74) Order* 2006 (powers exercisable by a single judge); or

  (b) an appellant renews an application for the exercise of a power conferred by section 31A of the 1968 Act, article 9 of the 2005 Order or article 12 of the 2006 Order (powers exercisable by the Registrar); or

  (c) an appellant or a respondent applies for procedural directions under section 31C of the 1968 Act, article 11 of the 2005 Order or article 14 of the 2006 Order (appeals against procedural directions),

then he must do so within 14 days. That period begins when the Registrar serves on him notice of the decision that prompts his further application. That period may be extended before or after it expires by the Registrar, by a single judge or by the court. The general rule is that an application for an extension of that period will be considered at the same time as the further application itself.

(2) Where—

  (a) an appellant may renew to the court an application for the exercise of a power conferred by section 31 of the 1968 Act, article 8 of the 2005 Order or article 11 of the 2006 Order; but

  (b) he does not do so within the period fixed by this rule or extended under it,

then his application shall be treated as having been refused by the court.

Application for bail pending appeal

G–333   **68.7**—(1) Notice of an application by the appellant to be granted bail pending the determination of his appeal or pending his retrial shall be in the form set out in the Practice Direction and, unless notice of appeal or of an application for leave to appeal has previously been given, shall be accompanied by such a notice and shall be served on the Registrar; save that where notice of such an application is given together with a notice of appeal or notice of application for leave to appeal, it shall be served on the Crown Court officer.

(2) An application as aforesaid may be made to the court orally.

(3) Notice in writing of intention to make an application relating to bail to the court shall, unless the court or a judge thereof otherwise directs, at least 24 hours before it is made be served on the prosecutor and on the Director of Public Prosecutions, if the prosecution was carried on by him or, if the application is to be made by the prosecutor or a constable under section 3(8) of the *Bail Act* 1976, on the appellant.

Bail with condition of surety

68.8—(1) Where the court grants bail to the appellant or, in an appeal brought by a specified **G–334** prosecutor under section 74(8) of the *Serious Organised Crime and Police Act* 2005, to the offender, the recognizance of any surety required as a condition of bail may be entered into before the Registrar or, where the person who has been granted bail is in a prison or other place of detention, before the governor or keeper of the prison or place as well as before the persons specified in section 8(4) of the *Bail Act* 1976.

(2) The recognizance of a surety shall be in the form set out in the Practice Direction, there being an alternative form for use in relation to an appellant granted bail pending his retrial or on the issue of a writ of venire de novo.

(3) Where, under section 3(5) or (6) of the 1976 Act, the court imposes a requirement to be complied with before a person's release on bail, the court may give directions as to the manner in which and the person or persons before whom the requirement may be complied with.

(4) A person who, in pursuance of an order for the grant of bail made by the court, proposes to enter into a recognizance as a surety or give security shall, unless the court or a judge thereof otherwise directs, give notice to the prosecutor at least 24 hours before he enters into the recognizance or gives security as aforesaid.

(5) Where the court has fixed the amount in which a surety is to be bound by a recognizance or, under section 3(5) or (6) of the 1976 Act, has imposed any requirement to be complied with before the appellant's or offender's release on bail, the Registrar shall issue a certificate in the form set out in the Practice Direction showing the amount and conditions, if any, of the recognizance or, as the case may be, containing a statement of the requirement; and a person authorised to take the recognizance or do anything in relation to the compliance with such requirement shall not be required to take or do it without production of such a certificate as aforesaid..

(6) Where, in pursuance of an order for the grant of bail made by the court, a recognizance is entered into or requirement complied with before any person, it shall be the duty of that person to cause the recognizance or, as the case may be, a statement that the requirement has been complied with, to be transmitted forthwith to the Registrar; and a copy of such recognizance or statement shall at the same time be sent to the governor or keeper of the prison or other place of detention in which the appellant is detained, unless the recognizance was entered into or the requirement complied with before such governor or keeper.

(7) A person taking a recognizance in pursuance of such an order shall give a copy thereof to the person entering into the recognizance.

(8) Where the court has fixed the amount in which a surety is to be bound by a recognizance or, under section 3(5) or (6) of the 1976 Act, has imposed any requirement to be complied with before the appellant's or offender's release on bail, the governor or keeper of the prison or other place of detention in which the appellant or offender is detained shall, on receipt of a certificate in the appropriate form stating that the recognizances of all sureties required have been taken and that all such requirements have been complied with or on being otherwise so satisfied, release the appellant or offender.

(9) Where the court has granted bail pending retrial or on ordering the issue of a writ of venire de novo, the Registrar shall forward to the Crown Court officer a copy of any record made in pursuance of section 5 of the 1976 Act relating to such bail and also all recognizances and statements sent to the Registrar under paragraph (6) of this rule.

(10) Any record required by section 5 of the 1976 Act shall be made by including in the file relating to the case in question—

    (a) where bail is granted, a copy of the form issued under paragraph (5) of this rule and a statement of the day on which, and the time and place at which, the appellant or offender is notified to surrender to custody; and

(b) in any other case, a copy of the notice served under rule 68.29(1) (notice of determination of court).

Forfeiture of recognizances in respect of person bailed to appear

G–335   **68.9**—(1) Where a recognizance has been entered into in respect of an appellant or, in an appeal brought by a specified prosecutor under section 74(8) of the *Serious Organised Crime and Police Act* 2005, in respect of an offender, and it appears to the court that a default has been made in performing the conditions of the recognizance, the court may order the recognizance to be forfeited and such an order may—

(a) allow time for the payment of the amount due under the recognizance;

(b) direct payment of that amount by instalments of such amounts and on such dates respectively as may be specified in the order; or

(c) discharge the recognizance or reduce the amount due thereunder.

(2) Where the court is to consider making an order under paragraph (1) for a recognizance to be forfeited, the Registrar shall give notice to that effect to the person by whom the recognizance was entered into indicating the time and place at which the matter will be considered; and no such order shall be made before the expiry of seven days after the notice required by this paragraph has been given.

Custody of exhibits

G–336   **68.10**—(1) On a conviction on indictment or on a coroner's inquisition a court officer of the court of trial shall, subject to any directions of the judge of the court of trial, make arrangements for any exhibit at the trial which in his opinion may be required for the purposes of an appeal against conviction to be kept in the custody of the court, or given into the custody of the person producing it at the trial or any other person for retention, until the expiration of 35 days from the date of conviction.

(2) Where an appellant has given notice of appeal, or of an application for leave to appeal, against conviction, the Registrar shall inform a court officer of the notice and give directions concerning the continued retention in custody of any exhibit which appears necessary for the proper determination of the appeal or application.

(3) Where the court orders an appellant to be retired, it shall make arrangements pending his retrial for the continued retention in custody of exhibits.

(4) Any arrangements under this rule may include arrangements for the inspection of an exhibit by an interested party.

Supply of documentary and other exhibits

G–337   **68.11**—(1) Unless the court otherwise directs, the Registrar shall, on request, supply to the appellant or respondent copies of documents or other things required for the appeal and in such case may make charges in accordance with scales and rates fixed for the time being by the Treasury.

(2) Unless the court otherwise directs, the Registrar shall, on request, make arrangements for the appellant or respondent to inspect any document or other thing required for the appeal.

(3) This rule shall not apply to the supply of the transcripts of any proceedings or part thereof.

Record of proceedings

G–338   **68.12**—(1) Except as provided by this rule, the whole of any proceedings in respect of which an appeal lies (with or without leave) to the court shall be recorded by means of shorthand notes or, with the permission of the Lord Chancellor, by mechanical means.

(2) Where such proceedings are recorded by means of shorthand notes, it shall not be necessary to record—

(a) of trial otherwise directs; or

(b) any other part of such proceedings which the judge of the court of trial directs need not be recorded.

(3) Where it is not practicable for such proceedings to be recorded by means of shorthand notes or by mechanical means, the judge of the court of trial shall direct how and to what extent the proceedings shall be recorded.

(4) The permission of the Lord Chancellor may contain conditions concerning the custody, and supply of transcripts, of a recording made by mechanical means.

Transcripts

68.13—(1) A transcript of the record of any proceedings or part thereof in respect of which **G–339** an appeal lies, with or without leave, to the court and which are recorded in accordance with the provisions of rule 68.12—

    (a) shall, on request be supplied to the Registrar; and

    (b) shall, on request, be supplied to any other person on payment of such charge as may be fixed for the time being by the Treasury, unless the court otherwise directs.

(2) Without prejudice to the provisions of paragraph (1) of this rule, the Registrar may, on request, supply to any interested party a transcript of the record of any proceedings or part thereof which is in his possession for the purposes of the appeal or application in question and in such case may make charges in accordance with scales and rates fixed for the time being by the Treasury:

Provided that in the case of an interested party who has been granted a right to representation by the Criminal Defence Service under Schedule 3 to the *Access to Justice Act* 1999 for the purpose of the appeal or any proceedings preliminary or incidental thereto such a transcript shall be supplied free.

Verification of record of proceedings

68.14—(1) An official shorthand writer who takes shorthand notes of any proceedings or **G–340** part thereof in respect of which an appeal lies (with or without leave) to the court shall—

    (a) at the beginning of the notes state the name of the parties to the proceedings;

    (b) in the case of shorthand notes of part of any proceedings, state the part concerned;

    (c) record his name in the notes; and

    (d) retain the shorthand notes for not less than five years.

(2) Verification of a transcript of the shorthand notes taken by an official shorthand writer of any proceedings or part thereof in respect of which an appeal lies (with or without leave) to the court shall be by a certificate by the person making the transcript that—

    (a) he has made a correct and complete transcript of the notes to the best of his skill and ability; and

    (b) the notes were either taken by him and were to the best of his skill and ability a complete and correct account of those proceedings or part thereof or were taken by another official shorthand writer.

(3) Verification of a transcript of the record of the proceedings or part thereof if recorded by mechanical means shall be by—

    (a) a certificate by the person making the transcript that he has made a correct and complete transcript of the recording to the best of his skill and ability; and

    (b) a certificate by a person responsible for the recording or a successor that the recording records so much of the proceedings as is specified in the certificate.

(4) Verification of a transcript of the record of the proceedings or part thereof if recorded in any other way shall be by—

    (a) a certificate by the person who made the record that he recorded the proceedings or part thereof to the best of his ability; and

    (b) a certificate by the person making the transcript that he has made a correct and complete transcript of the record to the best of his skill and ability.

Application for a witness order and for evidence to be received

68.15—(1) Notice of an application by the appellant, or, in an appeal brought by a specified **G–341** prosecutor under section 74(8) of the *Serious Organised Crime and Police Act* 2005, by the appellant or the offender—

    (a) that a witness who would have been a compellable witness at the trial be ordered to attend for examination by the court; or

    (b) that the evidence of a witness be received by the court;

shall be in the form set out in the Practice Direction and shall be served on the Registrar; save that where a notice of an application under sub-paragraph (a) or (b) is given together with a notice of appeal or notice of application for leave to appeal, it shall be served on the Crown Court officer.

(2) An application as aforesaid may be made to the court orally.

Examination of witnesses by the court

G–342   **68.16**—(1) An order of the court to a person to attend for examination as a witness shall be in the form set out in the Practice Direction and shall specify the time and place of attendance.

(2) The examination of a witness shall be conducted by the taking of a deposition and, unless the court directs otherwise, shall take place in public.

Vulnerable witness giving video recorded testimony

G–343   **68.17**—(1) A party to an appeal who applies for leave to call a witness may also apply for leave under section 32A of the *Criminal Justice Act* 1988 to tender in evidence a video recording of testimony from a witness where—

  (a) the offence charged is one to which section 32(2) of the 1988 Act applies;
  (b) in the case of an offence falling within section 32(2)(a) or (b) of the 1988 Act, the proposed witness is under the age of 14 or, if he was under 14 when the video recording was made, is under the age of 15;
  (c) in the case of an offence falling within section 32(2)(c) of the 1988 Act, the proposed witness is under the age of 17 or, if he was under 17 when the video recording was made, is under the age of 18; and
  (d) the video recording is of an interview conducted between an adult and a person coming within sub-paragraph (b) or (c) above (not being the accused or one of the accused) which relates to any matter in issue in the proceedings;

and references in this rule to an offence include references to attempting or conspiring to commit, or aiding, abetting, counselling, procuring or inciting the commission of, that offence.

(2) An application under paragraph (1) shall be made by serving a notice in writing on the Registrar. The application shall be accompanied by the video recording which it is proposed to tender in evidence and shall include the following, namely—

  (a) the name of the appellant or, in an appeal brought by a specified prosecutor under section 74(8) of the *Serious Organised Crime and Police Act* 2005, the name of the offender, and the offence or offences charged;
  (b) the name and date of birth of the witness in respect of whom the application is made;
  (c) the date on which the video recording was made;
  (d) a statement that in the opinion of the applicant the witness is willing and able to attend the appeal for cross-examination; and
  (e) a statement of the circumstances in which the video recording was made which complies with paragraph (4).

(3) Where it is proposed to tender part only of a video recording of an interview with the witness, an application under paragraph (1) must specify that part and be accompanied by a video recording of the entire interview, including those parts which it is not proposed to tender in evidence, and by a statement of the circumstances in which the video recording of the entire interview was made which complies with paragraph (4).

(4) The statement of the circumstances in which the video recording was made referred to in paragraphs (2)(e) and (3) shall include the following information, except in so far as it is contained in the recording itself, namely—

  (a) the times at which the recording commenced and finished, including details of any interruptions;
  (b) the location at which the recording was made and the usual function of the premises;
  (c) the name, age and occupation of any person present at any point during the recording, the time for which he was present, his relationship (if any) to the witness and to the appellant;
  (d) a description of the equipment used including the number of cameras used and whether they were fixed or mobile, the number and location of microphones, the video format used and whether there were single or multiple recording facilities; and

(e) the location of the mastertape if the video recording is a copy and details of when and by whom the copy was made.

(5) An application under paragraph (1) shall be made at the same time as the application for leave to call the witness or at any time thereafter, but no less than 14 days before the date fixed for the hearing of the appeal except with the leave of the court.

(6) The Registrar shall, as soon as practicable after receiving an application under paragraph (1), send a copy of the notice to the other parties to the appeal. Copies of any video recording required by paragraph (2) or (3) to accompany the notice shall be provided by the applicant and sent by the Registrar to any party to the appeal not already served with a copy. In the case of an appellant acting in person, a copy shall be made available for viewing by him.

(7) An application under paragraph (1) shall be determined without a hearing, unless the Court otherwise directs, and the Registrar shall notify the applicant and the other parties of the time and place of any hearing.

(8) Without prejudice to rule 68.29, the Registrar shall notify all the parties of the decision of the Court in relation to an application under paragraph (1) and, where leave is granted, the notification shall state whether the whole or specified parts only of the video recording or recordings disclosed are to be admitted in evidence.

Vulnerable witness giving video recorded testimony

68.18—(1) A party to an appeal who applies for leave to call a witness may also apply for **G–344** leave under section 32(1)(b) of the *Criminal Justice Act* 1988 for the evidence of that witness to be given through a live television link where—

    (a) the offence charged is one to which section 32(2) of the 1988 Act applies; and

    (b) the evidence is to be given by a witness who is either—

        (i) in the case of an offence falling within section 32(2)(a) or (b) of the 1988 Act, under the age of 14,

        (ii) in the case of an offence falling within section 32(2)(c) of the 1988 Act, under the age of 17, or

        (iii) a person who is to be cross-examined following the admission under section 32A of the 1988 Act of a video recording of testimony from him,

    and references in this rule to an offence include references to attempting or conspiring to commit, or aiding, abetting, counselling, procuring or inciting the commission of, that offence.

(2) An application under paragraph (1) shall be made by serving a notice in writing on the Registrar which shall state—

    (a) the grounds of the application;

    (b) the date of birth of the witness;

    (c) the name of the witness; and

    (d) the name, occupation and relationship (if any) to the witness of any person proposed to accompany the witness and the grounds for believing that person should accompany the witness.

(3) An application under paragraph (1) shall be made at the same time as the application for leave to call the witness or at any time thereafter, but no less than 14 days before the date fixed for the hearing of the appeal except with the leave of the court.

(4) The Registrar shall, as soon as practicable after receiving an application under paragraph (1), send a copy of the notice to the other parties to the appeal.

(5) An application under paragraph (1) shall be determined without a hearing, unless the Court otherwise directs, and the Registrar shall notify the applicant and the other parties of the time and place of any hearing.

(6) Without prejudice to rule 68.29, the Registrar shall notify all the parties and the person who is to accompany the witness (if known) of the decision of the court in relation to an application under paragraph (1). Where leave is granted, the notification shall state the name of the witness, and, if known, the name, occupation and relationship (if any) to the witness of the person who is to accompany the witness.

(7) A witness giving evidence through a television link pursuant to leave granted in accordance with this rule shall be accompanied by a person acceptable to the Court and, unless the Court otherwise directs, by no other person.

Appendices

Evidence through live television link where witness is outside the United Kingdom

G–345
    68.19—(1) A party to an appeal who applies for leave to call a witness may also apply for leave under section 32(1) of the *Criminal Justice Act* 1988 for the evidence of that witness to be given through a live television link where the witness is outside the United Kingdom.

    (2) An application under paragraph (1) shall be made by serving a notice in writing on the Registrar which shall state—

        (a) the grounds of the application;

        (b) the name of the witness;

        (c) the country and place where it is proposed the witness will be when giving evidence; and

        (d) the name and occupation of any person who it is proposed should be available for the purpose specified in paragraph (3).

    (3) The purpose referred to in paragraph (2)(d) is that of answering any questions the court may put, before or after the evidence of the witness is given, as to the circumstances in which the evidence is given, including questions about any persons who are present when the evidence is given and any matters which may affect the giving of the evidence.

    (4) An application under paragraph (1) shall be made at the same time as the application for leave to call the witness or at any time thereafter, but no less than 14 days before the date fixed for the hearing of the appeal except with the leave of the court.

    (5) The Registrar shall, as soon as practicable after receiving an application under paragraph (1), send a copy of the notice to the other parties to the appeal.

    (6) An application under paragraph (1) shall be determined without a hearing, unless the court otherwise directs, and the Registrar shall notify the applicant and the other parties of the time and place of any such hearing.

    (7) Without prejudice to rule 68.29, the Registrar shall notify all the parties of the decision of the court in relation to an application under paragraph (1), and, where leave is granted, the notification shall state the name of the witness and, where applicable, the name and occupation of any person specified by the court for the purpose set out in paragraph (3).

Procedure for the admission of hearsay evidence

G–346
    68.20—(1) Part 34 applies where a party wants to introduce hearsay evidence in an appeal or application for leave to appeal, except for rules 34.2, 34.3 and 34.4 (relating to the notice of hearsay evidence).

    (2) An appellant who wants to introduce hearsay evidence to support a ground of appeal contained in his notice under rule 68.3(2)—

        (a) must give notice in the form set out in the Practice Direction to the Crown Court officer with his notice of application for leave to appeal under rule 68.3(1); but

        (b) need not give a separate notice of application under rule 68.15(1) for that same evidence to be received by the court.

    (3) A party who wants to introduce hearsay evidence in any other circumstances must give notice in the form set out in the Practice Direction to the Registrar and all other parties not more than 28 days after—

        (a) leave to appeal is given; or

        (b) notice of appeal is given, if leave is not required.

Procedure for the admission of evidence of bad character

G–347
    68.21—   Part 35 applies to the introduction of evidence of bad character in proceedings before the Court of Appeal, except for rule 35.1 and with the following modifications—

        (a) a reference to a defendant should be read as a reference to an appellant or, where the appeal is brought by a specified prosecutor under section 74(8) of the *Serious Organised Crime and Police Act* 2005, as a reference to an offender, and "non-defendant" and "co-defendant" read accordingly;

        (b) a reference to a court officer should be read as a reference to the Registrar; and

        (c) an application under rule 35.2 (non-defendant's bad character) must be received, and a notice under rule 35.4 or 35.5 (defendant's bad character) must be given, not more than 28 days after—

            (i) leave to appeal is given, or

            (ii) notice of appeal is given, if leave is not required.

Abandonment of proceedings

68.22—(1) An appeal or an application for leave to appeal under Part I of the *Criminal Appeal Act* 1968, underparagraph 14 of Schedule 22 to the *Criminal Justice Act* 2003 or under section 74(8) of the *Serious Organised Crime and Police Act* 2005 may be abandoned before the hearing of the appeal or application by serving on the Registrar notice thereof in the form set out in the Practice Direction. **G–348**

(2) The notice shall be signed by, or on behalf of, the appellant.

(3) The Registrar shall, as soon as practicable after receiving a notice under this rule, send a copy of it, endorsed with the date of receipt, to the appellant, to the Secretary of State and to a court officer of the Crown Court.

(4) Where an appeal or an application for leave to appeal is abandoned, the appeal or application shall be treated as having been dismissed or refused by the court.

The Registrar

68.23—(1) The Registrar may require the Crown Court to furnish the court with any assistance or information which it may require for the purpose of exercising its jurisdiction. **G–349**

(2) The Registrar shall give as long notice in advance as reasonably possible of the date on which the court will hear any appeal or application by an appellant to—

(a) the appellant;

(b) any person having custody of the appellant; and

(c) any other interested party whom the court requires to be represented at the hearing.

(3) This paragraph shall not apply to proceedings before a single judge of the court under section 31 of the *Criminal Appeal Act* 1968.

Sittings in vacation

68.24— The Lord Chief Justice shall determine the days on which the court shall, if necessary, sit during vacations; and the court shall sit on such days in accordance with arrangements made by the Lord Chief Justice after consultation with the Master of the Rolls. **G–350**

Opinion of court on point referred by Criminal Cases Review Commission

68.25— Where the Criminal Cases Review Commission refers a point to the court under section 14(3) of the *Criminal Appeal Act* 1995 the court may consider the point in private if appropriate. **G–351**

Application to the Court of Appeal for leave to be present

68.26—(1) Notice of an application by the appellant to be given leave by the court to be present at proceedings for which such leave is required shall be in the form set out in the Practice Direction and shall be served on the Registrar; save that where a notice of such an application is given together with a notice of appeal or notice of application for leave to appeal, it shall be served on a Crown Court officer. **G–352**

(2) An application as aforesaid may be made to the court orally.

Declaration of incompatibility

68.27—(1) The court shall not consider making a declaration of incompatibility under section 4 of the *Human Rights Act* 1998 unless it has given written notice to the Crown. **G–353**

(2) Where notice has been given to the Crown, a Minister, or other person entitled under the 1998 Act to be joined as a party, shall be so joined on giving written notice to the court.

(3) A notice given under paragraph (1) above shall be given to—

(a) the person named in the list published under section 17(1) of the *Crown Proceedings Act* 1947; or

(b) in the case of doubt as to whether any and if so which of those departments is appropriate, the Treasury Solicitor

(4) A notice given under paragraph (1) above, shall provide an outline of the issues in the case and specify—

(a) the prosecutor and appellant;

(b) the date, judge and court of the trial in the proceedings from which the appeal lies; and

(c) the provision of primary legislation and the Convention right under question.

(5) Any consideration of whether a declaration of incompatibility should be made, shall be adjourned for —

    (a) 21 days from the date of the notice given under paragraph (1) above; or

    (b) such other period (specified in the notice), as the court shall allow in order that the relevant Minister or other person, may seek to be joined and prepare his case.

(6) Unless the court otherwise directs, the Minister or other person entitled under the 1998 Act to be joined as a party shall, if he is to be joined, give written notice to the court and every other party.

(7) Where a Minister of the Crown has nominated a person to be joined as a party by virtue of section 5(2)(a) of the 1998 Act, a notice under paragraph (6) above shall be accompanied by a written nomination signed by or on behalf of the Minister.

Dismissal of appeal against hospital order

G–354   **68.28**— If the court dismisses an appeal or an application for leave to appeal by an appellant who is subject to a hospital order under the *Mental Health Act* 1983 or an order under section 5(1) of the *Criminal Procedure (Insanity) Act* 1964 (power to deal with persons not guilty by reason of insanity or unfit to plead etc.) or the court affirms the order and the appellant has been released on bail pending his appeal, the court shall give such directions as it thinks fit for his conveyance to the hospital from which he was released on bail and for his detention, if necessary, in a place of safety as defined in section 55 of the 1983 Act pending his admission to the said hospital.

Notice of determination of court

G–355   **68.29**—(1) The Registrar shall, as soon as practicable, serve notice of any determination by the court or by any judge of the court under section 31 of the Criminal Appeal Act 1968, under article 8 of the *Criminal Justice Act 2003 (Mandatory Life Sentences: Appeals in Transitional Cases) Order* 2005 or under article 11 of the *Serious Organised Crime and Police Act 2005 (Appeals under section 74) Order* 2006 (powers exercisable by a single judge) on any appeal or application by an appellant on—

    (a) the appellant;

    (b) the Secretary of State;

    (c) any person having custody of the appellant;

    (d) in the case of an appellant detained under the *Mental Health Act* 1983 the responsible authority;

    (e) in the case of a declaration of incompatibility under section 4 of the *Human Rights Act* 1998, the declaration shall be served on—

        (i) all of the parties to the proceedings, and

        (ii) where a Minister of the Crown has not been joined as a party, the Crown (in accordance with rule 68.27(3) above); and

    (f) in the case of an appeal under section 74(8)of the *Serious Organised Crime and Police Act* 2005, on the specified prosecutor and on the offender.

(2) The Registrar shall, as soon as practicable serve notice of the order of the court disposing of an appeal or application for leave to appeal on a court officer of the Crown Court.

(3) In this rule the expression "responsible authority" means—

    (a) in relation to a patient liable to be detained under the 1983 Act in a hospital or mental nursing home, the managers of the hospital or home as defined in section 145(1) of that Act; and

    (b) in relation to a patient subject to guardianship, the responsible local health authority as defined in section 34(3) of the 1983 Act.

Enforcement of fines

G–356   **68.30**—(1) Where the court imposes a fine on an appellant, or, in an appeal brought by a specified prosecutor under section 74(8) of the *Serious Organised Crime and Police Act* 2005, on the offender, the court shall make an order fixing a term of imprisonment, not exceeding 12 months, which the appellant is to undergo if the fine is not duly paid or recovered.

(2) Such an order may—

(a) allow time for the payment of the fine; or

(b) direct payment of the fine by instalments of such amounts and on such dates respectively as may be specified in the order.

Notice of application after order for retrial

68.31— Notice of an application under section 8(1) of the *Criminal Appeal Act* 1968 for **G–357** leave to arraign, and notice of an application under section 8(1A) of that Act to set aside an order for retrial shall be in the form set out in the Practice Direction and shall be served on the prosecutor or the person ordered to be retried as the case may be, and on the Registrar.

Appendices

APPENDIX H

NATIONAL ALLOCATION GUIDELINES 2006

DRAFT GUIDELINES

Foreword

The Sentencing Guidelines Council was created in 2004 in order to frame guidelines **H–1** to assist courts as they deal with criminal cases across the whole of England and Wales.

The Council receives advice from the Sentencing Advisory Panel which consults widely before tendering that advice. The Council then produces a draft guideline on which it seeks the views of a limited group as provided by the Criminal Justice Act 2003. The Panel's advice to the Council in relation to allocation guidelines is being published simultaneously.

This draft guideline covers the legislative and other factors that should influence the decision whether an either-way offence is retained for trial in a magistrates' court or sent to the Crown Court to be dealt with (the allocation decision). It is within the remit of the Sentencing Guidelines Council to produce guidelines to support that decision and it is important that new guidelines be ready for use when legislative provisions changing the allocation procedure are brought into force.

The new allocation procedure has the added dimension of a sentence indication being given by a magistrates' court once it has decided that a case could be retained. This option is only available after the main part of the allocation decision has been made, but it is a key feature of the new procedures and guidance to courts is critical if consistency of approach is to be achieved. In *R. v. Goodyear*, the Court of Appeal (Criminal Division) considered sentence indications in reference to proceedings in the Crown Court and established a procedure for that Court. Although the procedure and approach of the Crown Court are very different from that in a magistrates' court, most of the principles identified in *Goodyear* can be applied to the statutory sentence indication procedure that follows an allocation decision.

The Panel's advice (and discussion paper that formed the basis of consultation seminars) contains further background details. All documents can be found at *www.sentencing-guidelines.gov.uk* or can be obtained from the Council's Secretariat at 85 Buckingham Gate, London SW1E 6PD.

When the consultation period is concluded (the closing date for responses is 10 April 2006), the Council will consider any responses received and then issue definitive guidelines to which every court must have regard in accordance with section 172 of the 2003 Act.

NATIONAL ALLOCATION GUIDELINES 2006

1. STATEMENT OF PURPOSE

1.1 In accordance with section 19 of the *Magistrates' Courts Act* 1980, where a defendant **H–2** has not indicated an intention to plead guilty, a magistrates' court must decide whether an offence triable either-way should be sent to the Crown Court for trial.

1.2 **The objectives of the allocation procedure are:**
   — to ensure (subject to exceptions) that the court that determines guilt also imposes sentence
   — where the determination is that trial on indictment is appropriate, the case reaches the Crown Court as soon as possible.

1.3 **The purpose of these guidelines is to provide guidance to those making that decision, applying the legislative criteria in the context of the sentencing framework as provided by the Criminal Justice Act 2003.**

1.4 These guidelines apply:

— to offenders aged 18 and over **and**

— in those cases where a youth is charged together with an adult and the plea before venue procedure applies.

2. STATUTORY CONSIDERATIONS

H–3 2.1 When deciding whether an offence is more suitable for summary trial or trial on indictment, section 19 of the *Magistrates' Courts Act* 1980 (as amended) requires that:

— before making a decision the court will be informed of the accused's previous convictions (if any) and shall consider any representations from the prosecution and defence as to whether summary trial or trial on indictment would be more suitable.

— in making a decision under this section, the court shall consider whether the sentence which a magistrates' court would have power to impose for the offence would be adequate

— the court shall have regard to any allocation guidelines (or revised allocation guidelines) issued as definitive guidelines under section 170 of the *Criminal Justice Act* 2003.

3. PROCEDURE AND PRINCIPLES

H–4 3.1 The court should invite representations from the prosecution and the defence as to the most appropriate venue for trial of the case. The existence of previous convictions recorded against an offender should be brought to the attention of the court at this time.

— **The primary test is the adequacy of the sentencing powers of the court.**

— **A court will start with a general presumption towards trial in a magistrates' court.**

— **The features set out in the following guidelines will need to be considered in order to determine whether the sentencing powers of a magistrates' court are sufficient to deal with the case justly.**

— **In deciding whether the powers of a magistrates' court would be adequate, a court is required to have regard to the approach to the assessment of seriousness set out in the Council Guideline Overarching Principles: Seriousness**

Principles for consideration

3.2 The principles set out below are relevant considerations in relation to the decision of the court as to whether an offence or offences would merit a custodial sentence of 12 months or more. The increased sentencing powers of a magistrates' court mean that more cases can now be dealt with at this level. Accordingly, it is expected that a magistrates' court will retain cases of greater seriousness than has historically been the case.

3.3 *Adequacy of sentencing powers to be based on an assumption that the prosecution version of the facts is correct*

The issue for the court is the extent of its sentencing powers for the offence(s) charged following conviction based on the prosecution case at its highest.

3.3.1 Given that the allocation decision is only required where a guilty plea indication is not given, the court should allocate either-way cases according to the seriousness of the alleged offence, looking at the case at its worst from the point of view of the defendant. The reduction for a guilty plea principle should not influence the court in making an allocation decision.

3.3.2 The assessment of seriousness will be based upon representations from the prosecution and defence on the nature and circumstances of the offence. These will include factors that aggravate (legislative, general or offence specific aggravating factors) or mitigate the seriousness of the offence, but will not extend to matters of personal mitigation.

3.3.3 The court will have regard to definitive guidelines issued by the Sentencing

Guidelines Council relating both to principles of sentencing and to specific offences, and to relevant judgments of the Court of Appeal (Criminal Division).

3.3.4 In order to properly assess the seriousness of the offending conduct, courts should make efforts to consider together as many outstanding cases as possible where an allocation decision is yet to be made, unless this would result in significant delay or injustice to the prosecution or defence. Where appropriate, consideration may need to be given to transferring a case to another magistrates' court for this purpose, after consultation with that other court.

3.3.5 In assessing the seriousness of the current offence(s), the court must consider the existence and relevance of any previous convictions, taking into consideration the nature of the offence(s) to which the conviction(s) relate(s), the relevance of them to the current offence, and the time that has elapsed since the conviction(s).

3.3.6 Where a defendant has already been convicted of other matters but not yet sentenced, those convictions will be relevant to the assessment of seriousness of the offence(s) currently before the court.

3.3.7 The existence of a suspended sentence order will be relevant to the allocation decision as it will be a recorded conviction. The question of whether the defendant is liable to have the order implemented will be considered following conviction and so is not relevant to the allocation decision.

3.3.8 Where an offence is a specified offence, the issue of whether the offender should be made subject to a sentence for public protection under sections 224-236 of the *Criminal Justice Act* 2003 will be considered following conviction.

3.4 *Charges and range of conduct to be considered*

3.4.1 The prosecuting authority should ensure that the charge(s) in a particular case present the court with sufficient information to know the extent of the criminality of the defendant. Where, for example, a defendant is alleged to have acted criminally over a long period, the charges need to be constructed with care as a court is not entitled to make assumptions about the extent of criminality where offences are neither admitted nor proved.

3.4.2 The possibility that, after conviction, an offender may ask for other matters to be taken into consideration will not be relevant to the seriousness of the offence before the court when considering allocation. A court could refuse to take additional offences into account when sentencing if they would render the powers of the court inadequate to deal with the case in an appropriate way.

3.5 *The need for a separate tribunal to determine fact*

3.5.1 The procedures in a magistrates' court are generally likely to be adequate for all cases where sentencing is within the powers of that court. Accordingly, it will rarely be appropriate for a magistrates' court to decline summary trial for an offence within its sentencing range for reasons unconnected with the adequacy of sentence.

3.5.2 However, there may be a few rare and exceptional cases (for example where unusually complex disclosure issues regarding public interest immunity or sensitivity are to be decided) where it will be especially important to have the separation between Judge and jury that is possible in the Crown Court.

3.6 *Presumption in favour of summary trial*

3.6.1 As many cases as possible should be dealt with in a magistrates' court. However, since there is no general power to commit for sentence after a determination for summary trial, where any uncertainty remains in relation to the adequacy of the sentencing powers available it should be resolved in favour of the case being dealt with in the Crown Court.

As many cases as possible should be dealt with in a magistrates' court. However, since there is no general power to commit for sentence after a determination for summary trial, where any uncertainty remains in relation to the adequacy of the sentencing powers available it should be resolved in favour of the case being dealt with in the Crown Court.

3.6.2 The court is entitled to expect the Justices' Clerk (or assistant to the Justices' Clerk) present in court, and the prosecution and defence advocates, to bring relevant guidelines and authorities to the attention of the court.

3.7 *Linked cases*

3.7.1 As a general rule, it is preferable for all issues to be dealt with in a single trial.

3.7.2 Where several defendants are contesting charges that are linked, the presumption is that a single trial will be in the interests of justice for the purpose of considering allocation.

3.7.3 Where one or more of the defendants is a youth, any presumption in favour of sending the youth to the Crown Court to be tried jointly with an adult who is being sent must be balanced with the general presumption that young offenders should be dealt with in a youth court. In determining which is the appropriate court, examples of factors that should be considered when deciding whether to separate the youth and adult defendants include:

— the young age of the offender, particularly where the age gap between the adult and youth offender is substantial

— the immaturity and intellect of the youth

— the relative culpability of the youth compared with the adult and whether or not the role played by the youth was minor

— lack of previous convictions on the part of the youth compared with the adult offender

— whether the trial of the adult and youth can be severed without inconvenience to witnesses or injustice to the case as a whole

3.8 *Any representations by the prosecution or defence*

3.8.1 The assessment of offence seriousness for the purposes of the allocation decision is based on the prosecution case at its highest (see 3.1 above). Defence representations should normally be directed to identifying inaccuracies in the factual outline of the case, assessing the adequacy of the court's sentencing powers and determining the relevance of an offender's previous convictions.

4. INDICATION OF SENTENCE

A. The Statutory Procedure

H–5   The relevant statutory provisions are reproduced at Annex 1.

4.1 If it is clear whether or not a custodial sentence is likely, it will normally be helpful for a court to give the indication requested unless there is a good reason for not doing so.

4.2 The key elements of the approach to giving a sentence indication are:

(i) **A court should assess the type of sentence realistically possible in the light of the facts as presented by the prosecution, with the additional element of a guilty plea tendered at this stage in the proceedings, and subject to defence representations as to the accuracy of the factual outline of the case. Wherever possible, the key elements of the basis upon which the indication is given should be recorded in writing.**

(ii) **A court should proceed with caution where an offender is unrepresented. The offender should be advised of the availability of independent legal advice. The Justices' Clerk (or assistant to the Justices' Clerk) present in court has a duty to assist the unrepresented party, and this will include drawing to the attention of an unrepresented defendant that there is an entitlement to request an indication of sentence.**

(iii) **A court should not give an indication of sentence where there are alternative charges unless the prosecution has indicated that an agreement as to acceptable pleas has been established following discussions with the defence, and there is an appropriate factual basis upon which an indication could be given.**

(iv) **The prosecution must ensure that the court is fully informed of the facts of the case and any relevant background.**

(v) **The court is entitled to expect that the Justices' Clerk (or assistant to the Justices' Clerk) present in court, and the prosecution and defence advocates, will ensure that the court considers any relevant guidelines or other authorities affecting sentence.**

(vi) **The information presented to the court will not include personal mitigation except in so far as it has influenced the facts of the case presented to the court or it is actively agreed by the prosecution advocate.**

(vii) **Any indication given must be recorded in writing and entered onto the court register.**

B. Reduction in Sentence for a Guilty Plea

4.14 In order to set the maximum type of sentence in cases where the offence is close to the threshold for a custodial sentence, a magistrates' court would have to consider whether the maximum reduction in sentence for a guilty plea would potentially be available where a guilty plea is forthcoming only after a sentence indication has been given.

4.15 The Guideline, Reduction in Sentence for a Guilty Plea, at paragraph 4.3 states:

(i) "The maximum reduction will be given only where the offender indicated willingness to admit guilt at the **first reasonable opportunity.** When this occurs will vary from case to case.

(ii) Where the admission of guilt comes later than the first reasonable opportunity, the reduction for guilty plea will be less than one third."

In considering further when the "first reasonable opportunity" occurs, Annex 2 of the Guideline emphasises the purpose of giving the reduction which is in recognition of "the benefits that come from a guilty plea both for those directly involved in the case in question but also in enabling Courts more quickly to deal with other outstanding cases".

4.16 There may only be a relatively short time gap between the opportunity to give an indication prior to allocation and the opportunity after an indication of sentence. However, the court will have had to consider allocation and determine summary trial and will then have to consider its response to the request for an indication of sentence. In those circumstances, it would appear that delay had taken place that could have been avoided and this will influence the extent of the reduction.

Where a guilty plea is indicated after the court has given an indication of the likely sentence, the appropriate reduction in sentence for the guilty plea should be a maximum of one quarter.

Annex 1

Sections 20 and 20A Magistrates' Courts Act 1980

Procedure where summary trial appears more suitable

20.—(1) If the court decides under section 19 above that the offence appears to it more suit- **H–6**
able for summary trial, the following provisions of this section shall apply (unless they are excluded by section 23 below).

(2) The court shall explain to the accused in ordinary language—

(a) that it appears to the court more suitable for him to be tried summarily for the offence;

(b) that he can either consent to be so tried or, if he wishes, be tried on indictment; and

(c) in the case of a specified offence (within the meaning of section 224 of the *Criminal Justice Act* 2003), that if he is tried summarily and is convicted by the court, he may be committed for sentence to the Crown Court under section 3A of the *Powers of Criminal Courts (Sentencing) Act* 2000 if the committing court is of such opinion as is mentioned in subsection (2) of that section.

(3) The accused may then request an indication ("an indication of sentence") of whether a custodial sentence or non-custodial sentence would be more likely to be imposed if he were to be tried summarily for the offence and to plead guilty.

(4) If the accused requests an indication of sentence, the court may, but need not, give such an indication.

(5) If the accused requests and the court gives an indication of sentence, the court shall ask the accused whether he wishes, on the basis of the indication, to reconsider the indication of plea which was given, or is taken to have been given, under section 17A or 17B above.

(6) If the accused indicates that he wishes to reconsider the indication under section 17A or 17B above, the court shall ask the accused whether (if the offence were to proceed to trial) he would plead guilty or not guilty.

(7) If the accused indicates that he would plead guilty the court shall proceed as if—

(a) the proceedings constituted from that time the summary trial of the information; and

(b) section 9(1) above were complied with and he pleaded guilty under it.

(8) Subsection (9) below applies where—

(a) the court does not give an indication of sentence (whether because the accused does not request one or because the court does not agree to give one);

(b) the accused either—

　　(i) does not indicate, in accordance with subsection (5) above, that he wishes; or

　　(ii) indicates, in accordance with subsection (5) above, that he does not wish, to reconsider the indication of plea under section 17A or 17B above; or

(c) the accused does not indicate, in accordance with subsection (6) above, that he would plead guilty.

(9) The court shall ask the accused whether he consents to be tried summarily or wishes to be tried on indictment and—

(a) if he consents to be tried summarily, shall proceed to the summary trial of the information; and

(b) if he does not so consent, shall proceed in relation to the offence in accordance with section 51(1) of the *Crime and Disorder Act* 1998.

[As substituted by the *Criminal Justice Act* 2003, Schedule 3, para. 6.]

Procedure where summary trial appears more suitable: supplementary

H–7　　**20A.**—(1) Where the case is dealt with in accordance with section 20(7) above, no court (whether a magistrates' court or not) may impose a custodial sentence for the offence unless such a sentence was indicated in the indication of sentence referred to in section 20 above.

(2) Subsection (1) above is subject to sections 3A(4), 4(8) and 5(3) of the *Powers of Criminal Courts (Sentencing) Act* 2000.

(3) Except as provided in subsection (1) above—

(a) an indication of sentence shall not be binding on any court (whether a magistrates' court or not); and

(b) no sentence may be challenged or be the subject of appeal in any court on the ground that it is not consistent with an indication of sentence.

(4) Subject to section 20(7) above, the following shall not for any purpose be taken to constitute the taking of a plea—

(a) asking the accused under section 20 above whether (if the offence were to proceed to trial) he would plead guilty or not guilty; or

(b) an indication by the accused under that section of how he would plead.

(5) Where the court gives an indication of sentence under section 20 above, it shall cause each such indication to be entered in the register.

(6) In this section and in section 20 above, references to a custodial sentence are to a custodial sentence within the meaning of section 76of the *Powers of Criminal Courts (Sentencing) Act* 2000, and references to a non-custodial sentence shall be construed accordingly.

INDEX

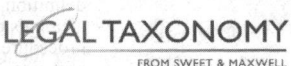

LEGAL TAXONOMY
FROM SWEET & MAXWELL

This index has been prepared using Sweet and Maxwell's Legal Taxonomy. Main index entries conform to keywords provided by the Legal Taxonomy except where references to specific documents or non-standard terms (denoted by quotation marks) have been included. These keywords provide a means of identifying similar concepts in other Sweet & Maxwell publications and online services to which keywords from the Legal Taxonomy have been applied. Readers may find some minor differences between terms used in the text and those which appear in the index. Suggestions to *taxonomy@sweetandmaxwell.co.uk*

(All references are to paragraph number)

INDEX

2008

	January				
M		7	**14**	**21**	**28**
T	1	8	15	22	29
W	2	9	16	23	30
T	3	10	17	24	31
F	4	11	18	25	
S	5	12	19	26	
S	6	13	20	27	

	February				
M		4	11	18	25
T		5	12	19	26
W		6	13	20	27
T		7	14	21	28
F	1	8	15	22	29
S	2	9	16	23	
S	3	10	17	24	

	March				
M		3	10	17	**24**	31
T		4	11	18	25
W		5	12	19	26
T		6	13	20	27
F		7	14	**21**	28
S	1	8	15	22	29
S	2	9	16	23	30

	April				
M		7	14	21	28
T	1	8	15	22	29
W	2	9	16	23	30
T	3	10	17	24	
F	4	11	18	25	
S	5	12	19	26	
S	6	13	20	27	

	May				
M		**5**	12	19	**26**
T		6	13	20	27
W		7	14	21	28
T	1	8	15	22	29
F	2	9	16	23	30
S	3	10	17	24	31
S	4	11	18	25	

	June				
M		2	9	16	23	30
T		3	10	17	24
W		4	11	18	25
T		5	12	19	26
F		6	13	20	27
S		7	14	21	28
S	1	8	15	22	29

	July				
M		7	14	21	28
T	1	8	15	22	29
W	2	9	16	23	30
T	3	10	17	24	31
F	4	11	18	25	
S	5	12	19	26	
S	6	13	20	27	

	August				
M		4	11	18	**25**
T		5	12	19	26
W		6	13	20	27
T		7	14	21	28
F	1	8	15	22	29
S	2	9	16	23	30
S	3	10	17	24	31

	September				
M	1	8	15	22	29
T	2	9	16	23	30
W	3	10	17	24	
T	4	11	18	25	
F	5	12	19	26	
S	6	13	20	27	
S	7	14	21	28	

	October				
M		6	13	20	27
T		7	14	21	28
W	1	8	15	22	29
T	2	9	16	23	30
F	3	10	17	24	31
S	4	11	18	25	
S	5	12	19	26	

	November				
M		3	10	17	24
T		4	11	18	25
W		5	12	19	26
T		6	13	20	27
F		7	14	21	28
S	1	8	15	22	29
S	2	9	16	23	30

	December				
M	1	8	15	22	29
T	2	9	16	23	30
W	3	10	17	24	31
T	4	11	18	**25**	
F	5	12	19	**26**	
S	6	13	20	27	
S	7	14	21	28	